Auditing and Reporting

2009–10

Extant at 30 April 2009

Auditing and Reporting 2009–10

Extant at 30 April 2009

General Editor
John Selwood

CCH
a Wolters Kluwer business

Wolters Kluwer (UK) Limited
145 London Road
Kingston upon Thames
Surrey KT2 6SR
Tel: 0844 561 8166
Fax: 020 8547 2638
Email: customerservices@cch.co.uk
www.cch.co.uk

Disclaimer
This publication is sold with the understanding that neither the publisher nor the authors, with regard to this publication, are engaged in rendering legal or professional services. The material contained in this publication neither purports, nor is intended to be, advice on any particular matter.

Although this publication incorporates a considerable degree of standardisation, subjective judgment by the user, based on individual circumstances, is indispensable. This publication is an 'aid' and cannot be expected to replace such judgment.

Neither the publisher nor the authors can accept any responsibility or liability to any person, whether a purchaser of this publication or not, in respect of anything done or omitted to be done by any such person in reliance, whether sole or partial, upon the whole or any part of the contents of this publication.

Telephone Helpline Disclaimer Notice
Where purchasers of this publication also have access to any Telephone Helpline Service operated by Wolters Kluwer (UK), then Wolters Kluwer's total liability to contract, tort (including negligence, or breach of statutory duty) misrepresentation, restitution or otherwise with respect to any claim arising out of its acts or alleged omissions in the provision of the Helpline Service shall be limited to the yearly subscription fee paid by the Claimant.

© 2009 Wolters Kluwer (UK) Limited

© Auditing Practices Board material reproduced with the permission of the CCAB Limited.

ISBN 978-1-84798-147-9

All rights reserved. No part of this publication may be reproduced or transmitted in any form or by any means or stored in any retrieval system of any nature without prior written permission, except for permitted fair dealing under the Copyright, Designs and Patents Act 1988 or in accordance with the terms of a licence issued by the Copyright Licensing Agency in respect of photocopying and/or reprographic reproduction. Application for permission for other use of copyright material, including permission to reproduce extracts in other published works, shall be made to the publisher. Full acknowledgement of author, publisher and source must be given.

No responsibility for loss occasioned to any person acting or refraining from action as a result of any material in this publication can be accepted by the author or publisher.

British Library Cataloguing-in-Publication Data

A catalogue record for this book is available from the British Library.

Typeset by YHT Ltd, London
Printed and bound in Italy by Legoprint-Lavis (TN)

Contents

		Page
Preface		
Part One	**The Auditing Practices Board**	1
	The scope and authority of APB pronouncements (revised)	3
Part Two	**APB Ethical Standards**	11
ES1	Integrity, objectivity and independence	13
ES1 (Revised)	Integrity, objectivity and independence	26
ES2	Financial, business, employment and personal relationships	40
ES2 (Revised)	Financial, business, employment and personal relationships	54
ES3	Long association with the audit engagement	69
ES3 (Revised)	Long association with the audit engagement	74
ES4	Fees, remuneration and evaluation policies, litigation, gifts and hospitality	80
ES4 (Revised)	Fees, remuneration and evaluation policies, litigation, gifts and hospitality	89
ES5	Non-audit services provided to audit clients	98
ES5 (Revised)	Non-audit services provided to audited entities	120
	Provisions available to small entities (PASE)	144
	Glossary of terms	152
	Provisions available to small entities (PASE) (Revised)	155
	Glossary of terms (Revised)	163
	Ethical Standard for Reporting Accountants	166
	Revised draft ethical standards for auditors	217
Part Three	**International Standard on Quality Control (UK & Ireland)**	237
ISQC1	Quality Control for Firms that Perform Audits and Reviews of Historical Financial Information, and other Assurance and Related Services Engagements	239
Part Four	**International Standards on Auditing (UK & Ireland)**	261
200	Objective and General Principles Governing an Audit of Financial Statements	263
210	Terms of Audit Engagements	271

220	Quality Control for Audits of Historical Financial Information	282
230	Audit Documentation (Revised)	293
240	The Auditor's Responsibility to Consider Fraud in an Audit of Financial Statements	305
250	Section A – Consideration of Laws and Regulations in an Audit of Financial Statements Section B – The Auditors' Right and Duty to Report to Regulators in the Financial Sector	341
260	Communication of Audit Matters With Those Charged With Governance	380
300	Planning an audit of financial statements	401
315	Obtaining an Understanding of the Entity and Its Environment and Assessing the Risks of Material Misstatement	412
320	Audit Materiality	449
330	The Auditor's Procedures in response to Assessed Risks	454
402	Audit Considerations Relating to Entities Using Service Organizations	472
500	Audit Evidence	491
501	Audit Evidence – Additional Considerations for Specific Items	501
505	External Confirmations	513
510	Initial Engagements – Opening Balances and Continuing Engagements – Opening Balances	522
520	Analytical Procedures	527
530	Audit Sampling and Other Means of Testing	535
540	Audit of Accounting Estimates	550
545	Auditing Fair Value Measurements and Disclosures	556
550	Related Parties	574
560	Subsequent Events	594
570	Going Concern	601
580	Management Representations	625
600	Using the Work of Another Auditor (Revised)	635
610	Considering the Work of Internal Audit	643
620	Using the Work of an Expert	648
700	The Auditor's Report on Financial Statements	653
700 (Revised)	The Auditor's Report on Financial Statements	673
710	Comparatives	699
720 (Revised)	Section A – Other information in documents containing audited financial statements Section B – The auditor's statutory reporting responsibility in relation to directors' reports	713
	APB Glossary of Terms	729

Part Five	**Standards for Investment Reporting (SIRs)**	751
	Introduction	753
1000	Investment Reporting Standards Applicable to all Engagements in Connection with an Investment Circular	754
2000	Investment Reporting Standards Applicable to Public Reporting Engagements on Historical Financial Information	781
3000	Investment Reporting Standards Applicable to Public Reporting Engagements on Profit Forecasts	816
4000	Investment Reporting Standards Applicable to Public Reporting Engagements on Pro Forma Financial Information	849
5000	Investment Reporting Standards applicable to public reporting engagements on financial information reconciliations under the Listing Rules	872
Part Six	**APB Practice Notes**	899
9	Reports by auditors under company legislation in the Republic of Ireland	901
10	Audit of financial statements of public sector bodies in the United Kingdom	938
10(I)	*Audit of Central Government Financial Statements in the Republic of Ireland (revised)	
11	The audit of charities in the United Kingdom (revised)	1043
12	Money laundering – Interim guidance for auditors in the United Kingdom (revised)	1135
14	The audit of registered social landlords in the United Kingdom (revised)	1157
15	The audit of occupational pension schemes in the United Kingdom (revised)	1230
15(I)	*Interim guidelines for auditors of occupational pension schemes in the Republic of Ireland	
16	Bank reports for audit purposes in the United Kingdom (revised)	1359
19	The audit of banks and building societies in the United Kingdom (revised)	1386
19(I)	*The audit of banks in the Republic of Ireland (Revised)	
20	The audit of insurers in the United Kingdom (revised)	1456
21	The audit of investment businesses in the United Kingdom (revised)	1557

22	The auditors' consideration of FRS 17 'Retirement benefits' – defined benefit schemes	1648
23	Auditing derivative financial instruments	1671
24	The audit of friendly societies in the United Kingdom (revised)	1701
25	Attendance at stocktaking	1786
26	Guidance on smaller entity audit documentation	1794
27	The audit of credit unions in the United Kingdom	1834
27(I)	*The audit of credit unions in the Republic of Ireland	

Part Seven **APB Bulletins** 1889

2000/3	Departure from Statements of Recommended Practice for the preparation of financial statements: guidance for auditors	1891
2001/1	The electronic publication of auditors' reports	1895
2001/3	E-business: identifying financial statement risks	1910
2002/2	The United Kingdom Directors' Remuneration Report Regulations 2002	1919
2002/3	Guidance for reporting accountants of stakeholder pension schemes in the United Kingdom	1925
2003/1	Corporate governance: requirements of public sector auditors (central government)	1938
2003/2	Corporate governance: requirements of public sector auditors (National Health Service Bodies)	1958
2004/2	Corporate governance: requirements of public sector auditors (local government bodies)	1975
2005/3	Guidance for Auditors on First-time Application of IFRSs in the United Kingdom and the Republic of Ireland	1988
2006/1	Auditor's Reports on Financial Statements in the Republic of Ireland	2027
2006/4	Regulatory and legislative background to the application of standards for investment reporting in the Republic of Ireland	2103
2006/5	The combined code on corporate governance: requirements of auditors under the listing rules of the Financial Services Authority and the Irish Stock Exchange	2128
2006/6	Auditor's reports on Financial Statements in the United Kingdom	2154
2007/1	Example reports by auditors under company legislation in Great Britain	2230
2007/2	The duty of auditors in the Republic of Ireland to report to the Director of Corporate Enforcement	2254

AUDIT 01/05	Chartered accountants' reports on the compilation of historical financial information of unincorporated entities	2973
AUDIT 02/05	Guidance on the implications of the Freedom of Information Act 2000	2983
AAF 01/06	Assurance reports on internal controls of service organisations made available to third parties	3000
AAF 02/06	Identifying and managing certain risks arising from the inclusion of reports from auditors and accountants in prospectuses (and certain other investment circulars)	3040
AAF 03/06	The ICAEW assurance service on unaudited financial statements	3052
AAF 04/06	Assurance Engagements: Management of Risk and Liability	3080
AAF 01/07	Independent Accountants Report on Packaging Waste	3088
AAF 02/07	A framework for assurance reports on third party operations	3106
AAF 01/08	Access to information by successor auditors	3136
AAF 01/09	Technical release: paid cheques	3158
	Audit regulations and guidance 2008	3163

* *These documents are not reproduced in this book, but copies may be obtained from the Auditing Practices Board*

Preface

Auditing and Reporting presents the current framework of standards and other pronouncements relevant to the conduct of audit practice in the United Kingdom and the Republic of Ireland. The majority of the pronouncements are issued by the Auditing Practices Board (APB) of the Financial Reporting Council (FRC). In addition, the technical releases issued by the Audit & Assurance Faculty of the Institute of Chartered Accountants in England & Wales (ICAEW) are given.

The APB's framework of standards comprises the:

- APB's Ethical Standards;
- International Standard on Quality Control (UK & Ireland); and
- International Standards on Auditing (UK & Ireland).

The framework of standards applies in the UK and Ireland to audits of accounting periods that commenced on or after 15 December 2004. The framework is largely based upon standards issued by the International Audit and Assurance Standards Board (IAASB). Relatively few revisions have been made to these standards since the majority of the framework was issued in 2004. A full explanation on the form of pronouncements issued by the APB is given below.

The IAASB's 'clarity project' is now complete and the APB have announced that the ISAs (UK and Ireland) will be changed for periods commencing 15 December 2009 onwards, although they will not be applicable to short accounting periods. This volume includes the existing ISAs (UK & Ireland) and a separate volume has been produced that contains the new Exposure Drafts. There are 13 revised Standards, 20 redrafted Standards and one new Standard, giving rise to significant change in the requirements.

As in past years the contents listed are comprehensive but to limit the size of the volume, the text has been restricted to documents deemed to be relevant to generalists and students. Accordingly, texts of statements relating to certain specialised audits have been omitted.

Where practicable, attention is drawn by way of editorial note to amendments to existing statements, arising from legislation, regulation and subsequent pronouncements. However, a number of statements which have not been superseded may no longer reflect current legislation, presentation and practice. Readers are therefore, cautioned to have regard to changes since publication and the need to ensure that all relevant sources of guidance are consulted.

APB Pronouncements

The APB issues pronouncements in the form of

- *Quality control standards* for firms that perform audits of financial statements, reports in connection with investment circulars and other assurance engagements;
- A framework of fundamental principles which the APB expects to guide the conduct of auditors;
- *Engagement standards* for audits of financial statements, reports in connection with investment circulars and other assurance engagements; and

- Guidance for auditors of financial statements, reporting accountants acting in connection with an investment circular and auditors involved in other assurance engagements.

The Engagement Statements include:
- *APB Ethical Standards*: These standards are concerned with the integrity, objectivity and independence of auditors.
- *International Standards on Auditing (UK and Ireland)*: These standards apply to all audits of financial statements and contain 'bold letter' paragraphs that set out the basic principles and essential procedures with which auditors must comply. The remainder of the text is termed 'grey letter' guidance and the APB have stated that auditors must consider this guidance in their application of the basic principles and essential procedures.

The guidance for auditors includes:
- *Practice Notes*: these contain guidance intended to assist auditors in applying Auditing Standards in particular circumstances or industries
- *Bulletins*: are intended to provide auditors with up-to-date guidance on new or emerging issues

The Companies Act 2006 first applies to company accounts for periods commencing 6 April 2008 onwards and the APB have issued further Bulletins that include relevant guidance.

ICAEW guidance on auditing and reporting

The ICAEW now primarily constitutes technical releases issued by the Audit and Assurance Faculty of the Institute.

John Selwood
May 2009

Part One

The Auditing Practices Board

The Auditing Practices Board – scope and authority of pronouncements (revised)

Contents

	Paragraph
Introduction	1 - 3
Nature and Scope of APB Pronouncements	4 - 7
Standards and Guidance for Audits of Financial Statements	8 - 11
Standards and Guidance for Reporting Accountants Acting in Connection With an Investment Circular	12 - 13
Standards and Guidance for Auditors Involved in Other Assurance Engagements	14
Authority of APB Pronouncements	15 - 20
Development of APB Pronouncements	21 - 25

Appendix 1 : Structure of APB Pronouncements at 15 December 2004

Appendix 2 : The Auditors' Code

> This statement, which describes the scope and authority of the Auditing Practices Board's (APB's) pronouncements, replaces a previous document of the same title which was issued in April 2003. The revised statement reflects the position of the APB (and of the Auditing Practices Board Limited) at the date of issue.

Introduction

1. The objectives of the Auditing Practices Board Limited, which is a constituent body of the Financial Reporting Council[1], are to:

    - Establish Auditing Standards which set out the basic principles and essential procedures with which external auditors in the United Kingdom and the Republic of Ireland are required to comply;
    - Issue guidance on the application of Auditing Standards in particular circumstances and industries and timely guidance on new and emerging issues;
    - Establish Standards and related guidance for accountants providing assurance services where they relate to activities that are reported in the public domain, and are therefore within the "public interest";
    - Establish Ethical Standards in relation to the independence, objectivity and integrity of external auditors and those providing assurance services;
    - Participate in the development of statutes, regulations and standards which affect the conduct of auditing and assurance services, both domestically and internationally; and
    - Contribute to efforts to advance public understanding of the roles and responsibilities of external auditors and the providers of assurance services including the sponsorship of research.

2. The Auditing Practices Board Limited discharges its responsibilities through a Board ('the APB'), comprising individuals who are eligible for appointment as company auditors and those who are not so eligible. Those who are eligible for appointment as company auditors may not exceed 40% of the APB by number.

3. The Nomination Committee of the Financial Reporting Council appoints members of the Board.

Nature and Scope of APB Pronouncements

4. APB pronouncements include:

    - 'Quality control standards' for firms that perform audits of financial statements, reports in connection with investment circulars and other assurance engagements;
    - A framework of fundamental principles which the APB expects to guide the conduct of auditors (see Appendix 2);
    - 'Engagement standards' for audits of financial statements, reports in connection with investment circulars and other assurance engagements; and
    - Guidance for auditors of financial statements, reporting accountants acting in connection with an investment circular and auditors involved in other assurance engagements.

    The structure of APB pronouncements is shown in Appendix 1.

5. Auditors and reporting accountants should not claim compliance with APB standards unless they have complied fully with all of those standards relevant to an engagement.

---

[1] Information about the Financial Reporting Council (FRC) and its structure, including its subsidiary bodies, can be found on the FRC's website (www.frc.org.uk/about).

APB quality control and engagement standards contain basic principles and essential procedures (identified in bold type lettering[2]) together with related guidance in the form of explanatory and other material, including appendices. The basic principles and essential procedures are to be understood and applied in the context of the explanatory and other material that provide guidance for their application. It is therefore necessary to consider the whole text of a Standard to understand and apply the basic principles and essential procedures.

In order to support the international harmonisation of auditing standards APB has decided to adopt the International Standard on Quality Control 1 (ISQC 1) and International Standards on Auditing (ISAs) issued by the International Audit and Assurance Standards Board[3] (IAASB). Where necessary APB has augmented such international standards by additional standards and guidance to maintain the requirements and clarity of previous UK and Irish auditing standards. This additional material is clearly differentiated from the original text of the international standards by the use of grey shading.

The ISAs (UK and Ireland) and ISQC 1 (UK and Ireland) require compliance with the APB's Ethical Standards and relevant ethical pronouncements relating to the work of auditors issued by the auditor's relevant professional body. This contrasts with the ISAs and ISQC 1 as issued by the IAASB, which require compliance ordinarily with Parts A and B of the IFAC Code of Ethics for Professional Accountants (the IFAC Code[4]) together with national requirements that are more restrictive.

When preparing them, the APB sought to ensure that the Ethical Standards adhered to the principles of the IFAC Code[5]. The APB is not aware of any significant instances where the relevant parts of the IFAC Code are more restrictive than the Ethical Standards[6].

Standards and Guidance for Audits of Financial Statements

The Auditors' Code, which is set out as Appendix 2, provides a framework of fundamental principles which encapsulate the concepts that govern the conduct of audits and underlie the APB's ethical and auditing standards.

APB engagement standards, which comprise APB Ethical Standards and International Standards on Auditing (UK and Ireland), apply to auditors carrying out:

[2] *In addition to the use of bold type lettering, the level of authority of the text in these paragraphs is identified by use of the expression "the auditor should ...". In some of the explanatory and other material the expression the "the auditor would ..." is used; the use of the word "would" in these paragraphs does not give them the same level of authority as the use of the word "should" in bold text.*

[3] *IAASB is a committee of the International Federation of Accountants (IFAC). The IAASB's constitution and due process is described in its 'Preface to the international standards on Quality Control, Auditing, Assurance and Related Services'.*

[4] *The IFAC Code is included in the IFAC 'Handbook of International Auditing, Assurance, and Ethics Pronouncements' and can be downloaded free of charge from the publications section of the IAASB website (www.ifac.org/IAASB).*

[5] *The Ethical Standards have also been designed to implement the requirements of the EC Recommendation on 'Statutory auditors' independence in the EU: a set of fundamental principles' in the UK and Ireland.*

[6] *Should auditors wish to state that an audit has been conducted in compliance with ISAs as issued by IAASB they will need to ensure that they have complied with the relevant parts of the IFAC Code.*

- Statutory audits of companies in accordance with the Companies Acts[7];
- Audits of financial statements of entities in accordance with other UK or Irish legislation, e.g. building societies, credit unions, friendly societies, pension funds, charities and registered social landlords;
- Public sector audits in the UK, including those carried out either on behalf of the national audit agencies or under contract to those agencies. (The standards governing the conduct and reporting of the audit of financial statements are a matter for the national audit agencies to determine. However, the heads of the national audit agencies[8] in the UK have chosen to adopt the APB's engagement standards and quality control standards for audits as the basis of their approach to the audit of financial statements);
- Other audits performed by audit firms registered with the members of the Consultative Committee of Accountancy Bodies (CCAB)[9] unless the nature of the engagement requires the use of other recognised auditing standards; and
- Other audits where audit firms not registered with members of the CCAB elect, or are required by contract, to perform the work in accordance with UK or Irish auditing standards.

12   The APB also issues guidance to auditors of financial statements in the form of Practice Notes and Bulletins. Practice Notes and Bulletins are persuasive rather than prescriptive and are indicative of good practice. Practice Notes assist auditors in applying APB engagement standards to particular circumstances and industries and Bulletins provide timely guidance on new or emerging issues. Auditors should be aware of and consider Practice Notes applicable to the engagement. Auditors who do not consider and apply the guidance included in a relevant Practice Note should be prepared to explain how the basic principles and essential procedures in APB standards have been complied with.

13   The APB also issues consultative documents, briefing papers and research studies to stimulate public debate and comment.

Standards and Guidance for Reporting Accountants Acting in Connection With an Investment Circular

14   APB engagement standards apply to reporting accountants when carrying out engagements involving investment circulars intended to be issued in connection with a securities transaction governed wholly or in part by the laws and regulations of the United Kingdom or the Republic of Ireland. They comprise APB Ethical Standards (when developed) and Statements of Investment Circular Reporting Standards (SIRs).

15   SIRs and Bulletins adopt the same style and format and have the same status as equivalent APB pronouncements applying to auditors of financial statements.

---

[7] *Companies Act 1985 in the UK and the Companies Acts 1963 - 2003 in the Republic of Ireland*

[8] *National audit agencies in the UK are the National Audit Office (for the Comptroller and Auditor General) the Welsh Audit Office (for the Auditor General for Wales), the Audit Commission, Audit Scotland (for the Auditor General for Scotland and the Accounts Commission) and the Northern Ireland Audit Office (for the Comptroller and Auditor General (Northern Ireland)).*

[9] *Members of CCAB are The Institute of Chartered Accountants in England & Wales, The Institute of Chartered Accountants of Scotland, The Institute of Chartered Accountants in Ireland, The Association of Chartered Certified Accountants, The Chartered Institute of Management Accountants and The Chartered Institute of Public Finance and Accountancy.*

Guidance for Auditors Involved in Other Assurance Engagements

16 The APB also issues standards and guidance for accountants on assurance engagements closely related to an audit of the financial statements. To date most of its pronouncements have taken the form of Bulletins (e.g. the auditors' statement on summary financial statements). However, the APB intends to issue standards for other assurance engagements as practice evolves and when the APB believes that this is in the public interest.

Authority of APB Pronouncements

17 In order to be eligible for appointment in Great Britain as auditors of companies, or of any of the other entities which require their auditors to be eligible for appointment as auditors under section 25 of the Companies Act 1989, persons must be registered with a Recognised Supervisory Body (RSB)[10] recognised under that Act and must be eligible for appointment under the rules of that RSB. The Companies Act 1989 requires RSBs to have rules and practices as to the technical standards to be applied in company audit work and as to the manner in which these standards are to be applied in practice[11]. Each RSB is also required to have arrangements in place for the effective monitoring and enforcement of compliance with these standards.

18 In the Republic of Ireland legislative requirements concerning qualifications for appointment as auditor and recognition of bodies[12] of accountants are contained in the Companies Act 1990. This Act requires bodies of accountants to have satisfactory rules and practices as to technical and other standards. The Act also empowers the Minister for Enterprise, Trade and Employment to revoke or suspend recognition or authorisation of a body of accountants or individual auditor[13].

19 The members of the CCAB have undertaken to adopt APB standards and guidance developed by the APB within three months of promulgation by the APB of such standards and guidance. In the Republic of Ireland, accountancy bodies which are not members of the CCAB but which are also recognised bodies for the supervision of auditors may choose to require their members to comply with APB standards.

20 Apparent failures by auditors to comply with APB standards are liable to be investigated by the relevant accountancy body. Auditors who do not comply with auditing standards when performing company or other audits make themselves liable

---

[10] *The Institute of Chartered Accountants in England & Wales, The Institute of Chartered Accountants of Scotland, The Institute of Chartered Accountants in Ireland, the Association of Authorised Public Accountants and The Association of Chartered Certified Accountants are Recognised Supervisory Bodies for the purpose of regulating auditors in the UK.*

[11] *In Northern Ireland, equivalent requirements are contained in Part III of the Companies (Northern Ireland) Order 1990.*

[12] *The Institute of Chartered Accountants in Ireland, the Institute of Certified Public Accountants in Ireland, the Institute of Incorporated Public Accountants, The Association of Chartered Certified Accountants, The Institute of Chartered Accountants in England and Wales and The Institute of Chartered Accountants in Scotland are "Recognised Bodies" in the Republic of Ireland.*

[13] *In the Republic of Ireland the Companies (Auditing and Accounting) Act 2003, has made provision for the establishment of The Irish Auditing and Accounting Supervisory Authority (IAASA), a new statutory supervisory body. The functions of IAASA will include a role in cooperating and working in partnership with the auditing profession and other interested parties in developing standards in relation to the independence of auditors and in developing auditing standards and practice notes.*

to regulatory action which may include the withdrawal of registration and hence of eligibility to perform company audits.

21 All relevant APB pronouncements and in particular auditing standards are likely to be taken into account when the adequacy of the work of auditors is being considered in a court of law or in other contested situations.

22 The nature of APB standards and associated guidance requires professional accountants to exercise professional judgment in applying them. In exceptional circumstances, auditors and reporting accountants may judge it necessary to depart from a basic principle or essential procedure of a standard to achieve more effectively the objective of the engagement. When such a situation arises, the auditor or reporting accountant documents the reasons for the departure.

Development of APB Pronouncements

23 Before publishing or amending its standards or Practice Notes the APB publishes an exposure draft on its website and sends a copy of the exposure draft to the members of the CCAB and to other parties.

24 The APB's aim is to allow three months for representations to be made on draft standards and Practice Notes. Where the draft standards are based on international standards the APB intends to co-ordinate its exposure process with that of IAASB.

25 Where exposure drafts would cause changes to be made to other previously issued publications, any such consequential changes will also be exposed for comment and published simultaneously. Representations received on exposure drafts will be given full and proper consideration by the APB, and will be available for public inspection.

26 Bulletins and other publications may be developed without the full process of consultation and exposure used for APB standards and Practice Notes. However, in the development of such documents, and before publication, the APB will decide the means by which it will obtain external views on them.

27 Each year the APB considers its priorities and consults on its proposed work programme with interested parties.

Scope and Authority of Pronouncements 9

Appendix 1

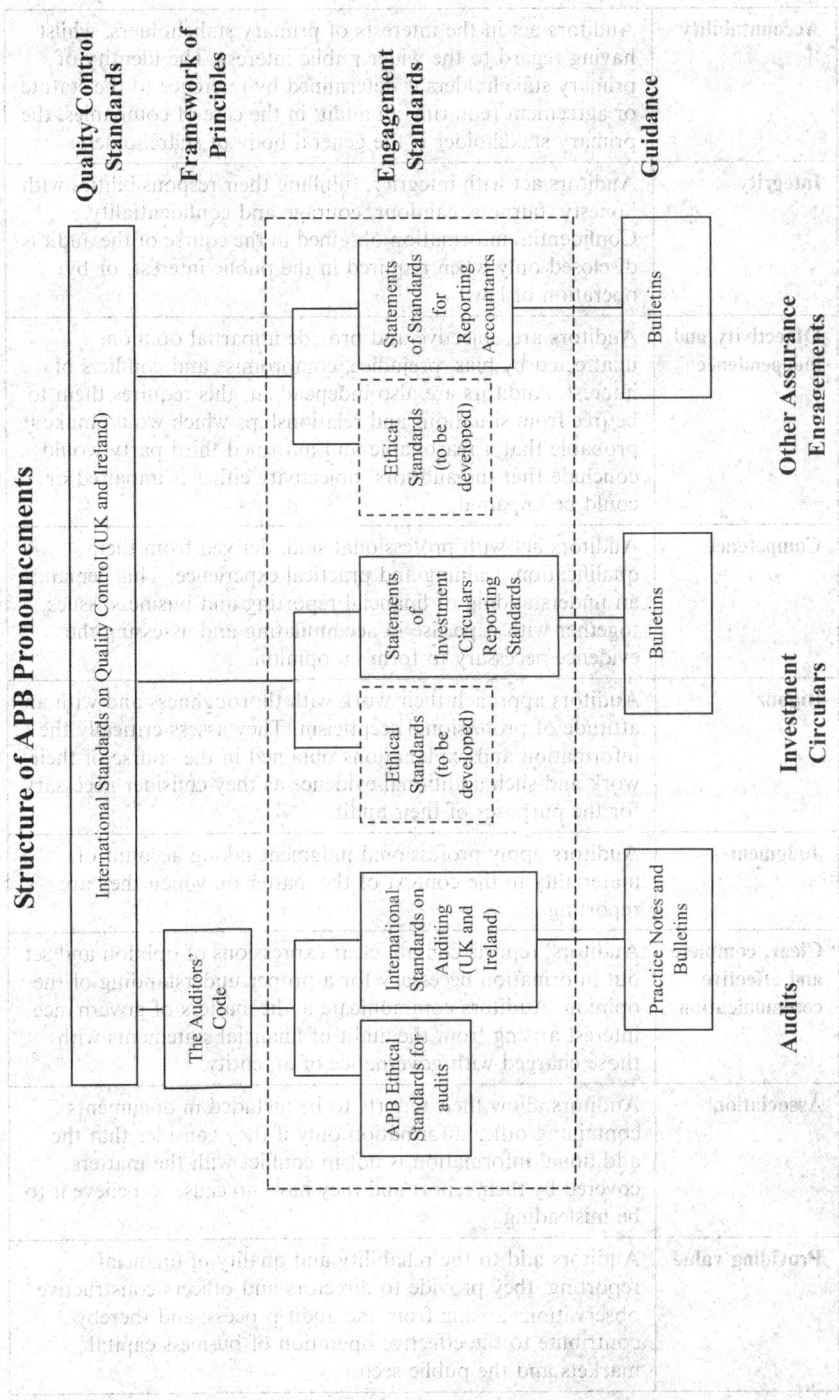

Appendix 2 – The Auditors' Code

Accountability	Auditors act in the interests of primary stakeholders, whilst having regard to the wider public interest. The identity of primary stakeholders is determined by reference to the statute or agreement requiring an audit: in the case of companies, the primary stakeholder is the general body of shareholders.
Integrity	Auditors act with integrity, fulfilling their responsibilities with honesty, fairness, candour, courage and confidentiality. Confidential information obtained in the course of the audit is disclosed only when required in the public interest, or by operation of law.
Objectivity and independence	Auditors are objective and provide impartial opinions unaffected by bias, prejudice, compromise and conflicts of interest. Auditors are also independent, this requires them to be free from situations and relationships which would make it probable that a reasonable and informed third party would conclude that the auditors' objectivity either is impaired or could be impaired.
Competence	Auditors act with professional skill, derived from their qualification, training and practical experience. This demands an understanding of financial reporting and business issues, together with expertise in accumulating and assessing the evidence necessary to form an opinion.
Rigour	Auditors approach their work with thoroughness and with an attitude of professional scepticism. They assess critically the information and explanations obtained in the course of their work and such additional evidence as they consider necessary for the purposes of their audit.
Judgment	Auditors apply professional judgment taking account of materiality in the context of the matter on which they are reporting.
Clear, complete and effective communication	Auditors' reports contain clear expressions of opinion and set out information necessary for a proper understanding of the opinion. Auditors communicate audit matters of governance interest arising from the audit of financial statements with those charged with governance of an entity.
Association	Auditors allow their reports to be included in documents containing other information only if they consider that the additional information is not in conflict with the matters covered by their report and they have no cause to believe it to be misleading.
Providing value	Auditors add to the reliability and quality of financial reporting; they provide to directors and officers constructive observations arising from the audit process; and thereby contribute to the effective operation of business capital markets and the public sector.

Part Two

APB Ethical Standards

Part Two

APB Ethical Standards

ES1
Integrity, objectivity and independence

(Re-issued December 2004)

Contents

	Paragraphs
Introduction	1 - 14
Compliance with ethical standards	15 - 26
Identification and assessment of threats	27 - 35
Identification and assessment of safeguards	36 - 40
Review by an independent partner	41 - 42
Overall conclusion	43 - 45
Other auditors involved in the audit of group financial statements	46 - 48
Communication with those charged with governance	49 - 53
Documentation	54 - 56
Effective date	57 - 59

Preface

APB Ethical Standards apply in the audit of financial statements. They should be read in the context of the Auditing Practices Board's Statement "The Auditing Practices Board – Scope and Authority of Pronouncements (Revised)" which sets out the application and authority of APB Ethical Standards.

The terms used in APB Ethical Standards are explained in the Glossary.

APB Ethical Standards apply to audits of financial statements in both the private and the public sectors. However, auditors in the public sector are subject to more complex ethical requirements than their private sector counterparts. This includes, for example, compliance with legislation such as the Prevention of Corruption Act 1916, concerning gifts and hospitality, and with Cabinet Office guidance.

Introduction

1   The financial statements of an entity may have a number of different users. For example, they may be used by suppliers and customers, joint venture partners, bankers and other suppliers of finance, taxation and regulatory authorities, employees, trades unions and environmental groups. In the case of a listed company, the financial statements are an important source of information to the capital markets. But the primary purpose of the financial statements of an entity is to provide its owners – the shareholders (or those in an equivalent position) – with information on the state of affairs of the entity and its performance and to assist them in assessing the stewardship exercised by the directors (or those in an equivalent position) over the business that has been entrusted to them.

2   The financial statements of an entity are the responsibility of its board of directors and are prepared by them, or by others on their behalf, for the shareholders or, in some circumstances, for other third parties.

3   The primary objective of an audit of the financial statements is for the auditors to provide independent assurance to the shareholders that the directors have prepared the financial statements properly. The auditors issue a report that includes their opinion as to whether or not the financial statements give a true and fair view in accordance with the relevant financial reporting framework.[1] Thus the auditors assist the shareholders to exercise their proprietary powers as shareholders in the Annual General Meeting.

4   Public confidence in the operation of the capital markets and in the conduct of public interest entities depends, in part, upon the credibility of the opinions and reports issued by the auditors in connection with the audit of the financial statements. Such credibility depends on beliefs concerning the integrity, objectivity and independence of the auditors and the quality of audit work they perform. APB establishes quality control, auditing and ethical standards to provide a framework for audit practice. The Auditors' Code underlies APB's standards and sets out the fundamental principles, which APB expects should guide the conduct of auditors.

5   APB Ethical Standards are concerned with the integrity, objectivity and independence of auditors. Ethical guidance on other matters, together with statements of

---

[1] *In the case of certain bodies in the public sector, the auditors express an opinion as to whether the financial statements 'present fairly' the financial position.*

fundamental ethical principles governing the work of all professional accountants, are issued by professional accountancy bodies.

Auditors should conduct the audit of the financial statements of an entity with integrity, objectivity and independence.   6

Integrity

Integrity is a prerequisite for all those who act in the public interest. It is essential that auditors act, and are seen to act, with integrity, which requires not only honesty but a broad range of related qualities such as fairness, candour, courage, intellectual honesty and confidentiality.   7

It is important that the directors and management of an audit client can rely on the auditors to treat the information obtained during an audit as confidential, unless they have authorised its disclosure, unless it is already known to third parties or unless the auditors have a legal right or duty to disclose it. Without this, there is a danger that the directors and management will fail to disclose such information to the auditors and that the effectiveness of the audit will thereby be impaired.   8

Objectivity

Objectivity is a state of mind that excludes bias, prejudice and compromise and that gives fair and impartial consideration to all matters that are relevant to the task in hand, disregarding those that are not. Objectivity requires that the auditors' judgment is not affected by conflicts of interests. Like integrity, objectivity is a fundamental ethical principle.   9

The need for auditors to be objective arises from the fact that many of the important issues involved in the preparation of financial statements do not relate to questions of fact but rather to questions of judgment. For example, there are choices to be made by the board of directors in deciding on the accounting policies to be adopted by the entity: the directors have to select the ones that they consider most appropriate and this decision can have a material impact on the financial statements. Furthermore, many items included in the financial statements cannot be measured with absolute precision and certainty. In many cases, estimates have to be made and the directors may have to choose one value from a range of possible outcomes. When exercising discretion in these areas, the directors have regard to the applicable financial reporting framework. If the directors, whether deliberately or inadvertently, make a biased judgment or an otherwise inappropriate decision, the financial statements may be misstated or misleading.   10

It is against this background that the auditors are required to express an opinion on the financial statements. Their audit involves considering the process followed and the choices made by the directors in preparing the financial statements and concluding whether the result gives a true and fair view in accordance with the relevant financial reporting framework. The auditors' objectivity requires that they express an impartial opinion in the light of all the available audit evidence and their professional judgment. Objectivity also requires that the auditors adopt a rigorous and robust approach and that they are prepared to disagree, where necessary, with the directors' judgments.   11

Independence

12   Independence is freedom from situations and relationships which make it probable that a reasonable and informed third party would conclude that objectivity either is impaired or could be impaired. Independence is related to and underpins objectivity. However, whereas objectivity is a personal behavioural characteristic concerning the auditors' state of mind, independence relates to the circumstances surrounding the audit, including the financial, employment, business and personal relationships between the auditors and their client.

13   The need for independence arises because, in most cases, users of the financial statements and other third parties do not have all the information necessary for judging whether the auditors are, in fact, objective. Although the auditors themselves may be satisfied that their objectivity is not impaired by a particular situation, a third party may reach a different conclusion. For example, if a third party were aware that the auditors had certain financial, employment, business or personal relationships with the audit client, that individual might reasonably conclude that the auditors could be subject to undue influence from the directors or would not be impartial or unbiased. Public confidence in the auditors' objectivity could therefore suffer as a result of this perception, irrespective of whether there is any actual impairment.

14   Accordingly, in evaluating the likely consequences of such situations and relationships, the test to be applied is not whether the auditors consider that their objectivity is impaired but whether it is probable that a reasonable and informed third party would conclude that the auditors' objectivity either is impaired or is likely to be impaired. There are inherent threats to the level of independence (both actual and perceived) that auditors can achieve as a result of the influence that the board of directors and management have over the appointment and remuneration of the auditors. The auditors consider the application of safeguards where there are threats to their independence (both actual and perceived.

Compliance with Ethical Standards

15   **The audit firm should establish policies and procedures, appropriately documented and communicated, designed to ensure that, in relation to each audit engagement, the audit firm, and all those who are in a position to influence the conduct and outcome of the audit, act with integrity, objectivity and independence.**

16   For the purposes of APB Ethical Standards, a person in a position to influence the conduct and outcome of the audit is:

(a) any person who is directly involved in the audit ('the engagement team'), including:
   (i) the audit partners, audit managers and audit staff ('the audit team');
   (ii) professional personnel from other disciplines involved in the audit (for example, lawyers, actuaries, taxation specialists, IT specialists, treasury management specialists);[2]
   (iii) those who provide quality control or direct oversight of the audit;
(b) any person, who forms part of the chain of command for the audit within the audit firm;
(c) any person within the audit firm who, due to any other circumstances, may be in a position to exert such influence.

---

[2] *Where external consultants are involved in the audit, ISA (UK and Ireland) 620 'Using the work of an Expert'* states that the auditor should evaluate the objectivity of the expert.

Compliance with the requirements regarding the auditors' integrity, objectivity and independence is a responsibility of both the audit firm and of individual partners and professional staff. The audit firm establishes policies and procedures, appropriate to the size and nature of the audit firm, to promote and monitor compliance with those requirements by any person who is in a position to influence the conduct and outcome of the audit.[3]

The leadership of the audit firm should take responsibility for establishing a control environment within the firm that places adherence to ethical principles and compliance with APB Ethical Standards above commercial considerations.

The leadership of the audit firm influences the internal culture of the firm by its actions and by its example ('the tone at the top'). Achieving a robust control environment requires that the leadership gives clear, consistent and frequent messages, backed up by appropriate actions, which emphasise the importance of compliance with APB Ethical Standards.

In order to promote a strong control environment, the audit firm establishes policies and procedures that include:

(a) requirements for partners and staff to report where applicable:
  - family and other personal relationships involving an audit client of the firm;
  - financial interests in an audit client of the firm;
  - decisions to join an audit client.
(b) monitoring of compliance with the firm's policies and procedures relating to integrity, objectivity and independence. Such monitoring procedures include, on a test basis, periodic review of the audit engagement partners' documentation of their consideration of the auditors' objectivity and independence, addressing, for example:
  - financial interests in audit clients;
  - economic dependence on audit clients;
  - the performance of non-audit services;
  - audit partner rotation;
(c) prompt communication of possible or actual breaches of the firm's policies and procedures to the relevant audit engagement partners;
(d) evaluation by audit engagement partners of the implications of any identified possible or actual breaches of the firm's policies and procedures that are reported to them;
(e) reporting by audit engagement partners of particular circumstances or relationships as required by APB Ethical Standards;
(f) prohibiting members of the audit team from making, or assuming responsibility for, management decisions for the audit client;
(g) operation of an enforcement mechanism to promote compliance with policies and procedures;
(h) empowerment of staff to communicate to senior levels within the firm any issue of objectivity or independence that concerns them; this includes establishing clear communication channels open to staff, encouraging staff to use these channels and ensuring that staff who use these channels are not subject to disciplinary proceedings as a result.

---

[3] *Monitoring of compliance with ethical requirements will often be performed as part of a broader quality control process. ISQC (UK & Ireland) 1* 'Quality Control for firms that perform audits and reviews of historical financial information and other assurance and related services engagements' *establishes the basic principles and essential procedures in relation to a firm's responsibilities for its system of quality control for audits.*

21   Save where the circumstances contemplated in paragraph 23 apply, the audit firm should designate a partner in the firm ('the ethics partner') as having responsibility for:

(a) the adequacy of the firm's policies and procedures relating to integrity, objectivity and independence, their compliance with APB Ethical Standards, and the effectiveness of their communication to partners and staff within the firm; and
(b) providing related guidance to individual partners.

22   In assessing the effectiveness of the firm's communication of its policies and procedures relating to integrity, objectivity and independence, ethics partners consider whether they are properly covered in induction programmes, professional training and continuing professional development for all partners and staff. Ethics partners also provide guidance on matters referred to them and on matters which they otherwise become aware of, where a difficult and objective judgment needs to be made or a consistent position reached.

23   In audit firms with three or less partners who are 'responsible individuals'[4], it may not be practicable for an ethics partner to be designated. In these circumstances all partners will regularly discuss ethical issues amongst themselves, so ensuring that they act in a consistent manner and observe the principles set out in APB Ethical Standards. In the case of a sole practitioner, advice on matters where a difficult and objective judgment needs to be made is obtained through the ethics helpline of their professional body, or through discussion with a practitioner from another firm. In all cases, it is important that such discussions are documented.

24   To be able to discharge his or her responsibilities, the ethics partner is an individual possessing seniority, relevant experience and authority within the firm and is provided with sufficient staff support and other resources, commensurate with the size of the firm. Alternative arrangements are established to allow for:

- the provision of guidance on those audits where the ethics partner is the audit engagement partner; and
- situations where the ethics partner is unavailable, for example due to illness or holidays.

25   Whenever a possible or actual breach of an APB Ethical Standard, or of policies and procedures established pursuant to the requirements of an APB Ethical Standard, is identified, the audit engagement partner, in the first instance, and the ethics partner, where appropriate, assesses the implications of the breach, determines whether there are safeguards that can be put in place or other actions that can be taken to address any potential adverse consequences and considers whether there is a need to resign from the audit engagement.

26   An inadvertent violation of this Standard does not necessarily call into question the audit firm's ability to give an audit opinion, provided that:

(a) the audit firm has established policies and procedures that require all partners and staff to report any breach promptly to the audit engagement partner or to the ethics partner, as appropriate;
(b) the audit engagement partner or ethics partner promptly notifies the relevant partner or member of staff that any matter which has given rise to a breach is to be addressed as soon as possible and ensures that such action is taken;

---

[4] A 'responsible individual' is a partner or employee of the audit firm who is responsible for audit work and designated as such under the audit regulations of a Recognised Supervisory Body.

(c) safeguards, where appropriate, are applied, (for example, having another partner review the work done by the relevant partner or member of staff or removing him or her from the engagement team); and
(d) the actions taken and the rationale for them are documented.

Identification and assessment of threats

Auditors identify and assess the circumstances, which could adversely affect the auditors' objectivity ('threats'), including any perceived loss of independence, and apply procedures ('safeguards'), which will either: 27

(a) eliminate the threat (for example, by eliminating the circumstances, such as removing an individual from the engagement team or disposing of a financial interest in the audit client); or
(b) reduce the threat to an acceptable level, that is a level at which it is not probable that a reasonable and informed third party would conclude that the auditors' objectivity is impaired or is likely to be impaired (for example, by having the audit work reviewed by another partner or by another audit firm).

When considering safeguards, where the audit engagement partner chooses to reduce rather than to eliminate a threat to objectivity and independence, he or she recognises that this judgment may not be shared by users of the financial statements and that he or she may be required to justify the decision.

Threats to objectivity and independence

The principal types of threats to the auditors' objectivity and independence are: 28

- *self-interest threat*
  A self-interest threat arises when auditors have financial or other interests which might cause them to be reluctant to take actions that would be adverse to the interests of the audit firm or any individual in a position to influence the conduct or outcome of the audit (for example, where they have an investment in the client, are seeking to provide additional services to the client or need to recover long-outstanding fees from the client).
- *self-review threat*
  A self-review threat arises when the results of a non-audit service performed by the auditors or by others within the audit firm are reflected in the amounts included or disclosed in the financial statements (for example, where the audit firm has been involved in maintaining the accounting records, or undertaking valuations that are incorporated in the financial statements). In the course of the audit, the auditors may need to re-evaluate the work performed in the non-audit service. As, by virtue of providing the non-audit service, the audit firm is associated with aspects of the preparation of the financial statements, it may be (or may be perceived to be) unable to take an impartial view of relevant aspects of those financial statements.
- *management threat*
  A management threat arises when the audit firm undertakes work that involves making judgments and taking decisions, which are the responsibility of management (for example, where it has been involved in the design, selection and implementation of financial information technology systems). In such work, the audit firm may become closely aligned with the views and interests of management and the auditors' objectivity and independence may be impaired, or may be perceived to be, impaired.

- ***advocacy threat***
  An advocacy threat arises when the audit firm undertakes work that involves acting as an advocate for an audit client and supporting a position taken by management in an adversarial context (for example, by acting as a legal advocate for the client in litigation). In order to act in an advocacy role, the audit firm has to adopt a position closely aligned to that of management. This creates both actual and perceived threats to the auditors' objectivity and independence.
- ***familiarity (or trust) threat***
  A familiarity (or trust) threat arises when the auditors are predisposed to accept or are insufficiently questioning of the client's point of view (for example, where they develop close personal relationships with client personnel through long association with the client).
- ***intimidation threat***
  An intimidation threat arises when the auditors' conduct is influenced by fear or threats (for example, where they encounter an aggressive and dominating individual).

These categories may not be entirely distinct: certain circumstances may give rise to more than one type of threat. For example, where an audit firm wishes to retain the fee income from a large audit client, but encounters an aggressive and dominating individual, there may be a self-interest threat as well as an intimidation threat.

29 Threats to the auditors' objectivity, including a perceived loss of independence, may arise where the audit firm is appointed to a non-audit service engagement for a non-audit client, but where an audit client makes this decision. In such cases, even if the non-audit client pays the fee for the non-audit service engagement, the auditors consider the implication of the threats (especially the self-interest threat) that arise from the appointment.

30 **The audit firm should establish policies and procedures to require persons in a position to influence the conduct and outcome of the audit to be constantly alert to circumstances that might reasonably be considered threats to their objectivity or the perceived loss of independence and, where such circumstances are identified, to report them to the audit engagement partner or to the ethics partner, as appropriate.**

31 Such policies and procedures require that threats to the auditors' objectivity and independence are communicated to the appropriate person, having regard to the nature of the threats and to the part of the firm and the identity of any person involved. The consideration of all threats and the action taken is documented. If the audit engagement partner is personally involved, or if he or she is unsure about the action to be taken, the matter is resolved through consultation with the ethics partner.

32 **The audit firm should establish policies and procedures to require the audit engagement partner to identify and assess the significance of threats to the auditors' objectivity, including any perceived loss of independence:**

   (a) **when considering whether to accept or retain an audit engagement;[5]**
   (b) **when planning the audit;**

---

[5] *Consideration of whether to accept or retain an audit engagement does not arise with those bodies in the public sector where responsibility for the audit is assigned by legislation.*

(c) when forming an opinion on the financial statements;[6]
(d) when considering whether to accept or retain an engagement to provide non-audit services to an audit client; and
(e) when potential threats are reported to him or her.

An initial assessment of the threats to objectivity and independence is required when the audit engagement partner is considering whether to accept or retain an audit engagement. That assessment is reviewed and updated at the planning stage of each audit. At the end of the audit process, when forming an opinion on the financial statements but before issuing the report, the audit engagement partner draws an overall conclusion as to whether any threats to objectivity and independence have been properly addressed in accordance with APB Ethical Standards. If, at any time, the auditors are invited to accept an engagement to provide non-audit services to an audit client, the audit engagement partner considers the impact this may have on the auditors' objectivity and independence. 33

When identifying and assessing threats to their objectivity and independence, auditors take into account their current relationships with the audit client (including non-audit service engagements), those that existed prior to the current audit engagement and any known to be in prospect following the current audit engagement. This is because those prior and subsequent relationships may be perceived as likely to influence the auditors in the performance of the audit or as otherwise impairing the auditors' objectivity and independence. 34

Where the audit client or a third party calls into question the objectivity and independence of the audit firm in relation to a particular client, the ethics partner carries out such investigations as may be appropriate. 35

Identification and assessment of safeguards

If the audit engagement partner identifies threats to the auditors' objectivity, including any perceived loss of independence, he or she should identify and assess the effectiveness of the available safeguards and apply such safeguards as are sufficient to eliminate the threats or reduce them to an acceptable level. 36

The nature and extent of safeguards to be applied depend on the significance of the threats. Where a threat is clearly insignificant, no safeguards are needed. 37

Other APB Ethical Standards address specific circumstances which can create threats to the auditors' objectivity or loss of independence. They give examples of safeguards that can, in some circumstances, eliminate the threat or reduce it to an acceptable level. In circumstances where this is not possible, either the auditors do not accept or withdraw from the audit engagement. 38

The audit engagement partner should not accept or should not continue an audit engagement if he or she concludes that any threats to the auditors' objectivity and independence cannot be reduced to an acceptable level. 39

Where a reasonable and informed third party would regard ceasing to act as the auditor as detrimental to the shareholders (or equivalent) of the audit client, then resignation may not be immediate. However, the audit firm discloses full details of 40

---

[6] *In the case of listed companies, the auditors also assess whether there is any threat to their objectivity and independence when discharging their responsibilities in relation to preliminary announcements and when reporting on interim results.*

the position to those charged with governance of the audit client, and establishes appropriate safeguards.

Review by an independent partner

41   In the case of listed companies the independent partner[7] should:

(a) consider the audit firm's compliance with APB Ethical Standards in relation to the audit engagement;

(b) form an independent opinion as to the appropriateness and adequacy of the safeguards applied; and

(c) consider the adequacy of the documentation of the audit engagement partner's consideration of the auditors' objectivity and independence.

42   The audit firm's policies and procedures will also set out the circumstances in which an independent review is performed for other audit engagements. These policies will take into consideration the nature of the entity's business, its size, the number of its employees and the range of its stakeholders.

Overall conclusion

43   At the end of the audit process, when forming an opinion but before issuing the report on the financial statements, the audit engagement partner should reach an overall conclusion that any threats to objectivity and independence have been properly addressed in accordance with APB Ethical Standards. If the audit engagement partner cannot make such a conclusion, he or she should not report and the audit firm should resign as auditors.

44   If the audit engagement partner remains unable to conclude that any threat to objectivity and independence has been properly addressed in accordance with APB Ethical Standards, or if there is a disagreement between the audit engagement partner and the independent partner, he or she consults the ethics partner.

45   In concluding on compliance with the requirements for objectivity and independence, the audit engagement partner is entitled to rely on the completeness and accuracy of the data developed by the audit firm's systems relating to independence (for example, in relation to the reporting of financial interests by staff), unless informed otherwise by the firm.

Other auditors involved in the audit of group financial statements

46   The group audit engagement partner should be satisfied that other auditors (whether a network firm or another audit firm) involved in the audit of the group financial statements, who are not subject to APB Ethical Standards, are objective and document the rationale for that conclusion.

47   The group audit engagement partner obtains written confirmation from the other auditors that they have a sufficient understanding of and have complied with the

---

[7] *ISA (UK and Ireland) 220* 'Quality control for audits of historical financial information', *requires the audit engagement partner to appoint an engagement quality control reviewer for all audits of listed entities...The engagement quality control review involves consideration of...the engagement team's evaluation of the independence of the firm...'*

IFAC Code of Ethics for Professional Accountants, including the independence requirements[8].

In the case of a listed company, the group audit engagement partner establishes that the company has communicated its policy on the engagement of external auditors to supply non-audit services to its affiliates and obtains confirmation that the other auditors will comply with this policy.

Communication with those charged with governance

The audit engagement partner should ensure that those charged with governance of the audit client are appropriately informed on a timely basis of all significant facts and matters that bear upon the auditors' objectivity and independence.

The audit committee, where one exists, is usually responsible for oversight of the relationship between the auditors and the entity and of the conduct of the audit process. It therefore has a particular interest in being informed about the auditors' ability to express an objective opinion on the financial statements. Where there is no audit committee, this role is undertaken by the board of directors.[9, 10]

The aim of these communications is to ensure full and fair disclosure by the auditors to those charged with governance of the audit client on matters in which they have an interest. These will generally include the key elements of the audit engagement partner's consideration of objectivity and independence, such as:

- the principal threats, if any, to objectivity and independence identified by the auditors, including consideration of all relationships between the audit client, its affiliates and directors and the audit firm;
- any safeguards adopted and the reasons why they are considered to be effective;
- any independent partner review;
- the overall assessment of threats and safeguards;
- information about the general policies and processes within the audit firm for maintaining objectivity and independence.

In the case of listed companies, the auditors, as a minimum:

(a) disclose in writing:
    (i) details of all relationships between the auditors and the client, its directors and senior management and its affiliates, including all services provided by the audit firm and its network to the client, its directors and senior management and its affiliates, that the auditors consider may reasonably be thought to bear on their objectivity and independence;
    (ii) the related safeguards that are in place; and
    (iii) the total amount of fees that the auditors and their network firms have charged to the client and its affiliates for the provision of services during the reporting period, analysed into appropriate categories, for example,

---

[8] Section 8 of the International Federation of Accountants (IFAC) Code of Ethics for Professional Accountants (the IFAC Code) establishes a conceptual framework for independence requirements for assurance engagements that is the international standard on which national standards should be based. No Member Body of IFAC is allowed to apply less stringent standards than those stated in that section. In addition, members of the IFAC Forum of Firms have agreed to apply ethical standards, which are at least as rigorous as those of the IFAC Code.

[9] Where there is no audit committee, references to communication with the audit committee are to be construed as including communication with the board of directors.

[10] Some bodies in the public sector have audit committees but others have different governance models.

statutory audit services, further audit services, tax advisory services and other non-audit services.[11] For each category, the amounts of any future services which have been contracted or where a written proposal has been submitted, are separately disclosed;

(b) confirm in writing that they comply with APB Ethical Standards and that, in their professional judgment, they are independent and their objectivity is not compromised, or otherwise declare that they have concerns that their objectivity and independence may be compromised (including instances where the group audit engagement partner does not consider the other auditors to be objective); and explaining the actions which necessarily follow from this; and

(c) seek to discuss these matters with the audit committee.

53 The most appropriate time for final confirmation of such matters is usually at the conclusion of the audit. However, communications between the auditors and those charged with the governance of the audit client will also be needed at the planning stage and whenever significant judgments are made about threats to objectivity and independence and the appropriateness of safeguards put in place, for example, when accepting an engagement to provide non-audit services.

Documentation

54 **The audit engagement partner should ensure that his or her consideration of the auditors' objectivity and independence is appropriately documented on a timely basis.**

55 The requirement to document these issues contributes to the clarity and rigour of the audit engagement partner's thinking and the quality of his or her judgments. In addition, such documentation provides evidence that the audit engagement partner's consideration of the auditors' objectivity and independence was properly performed and, for listed companies, provides the basis for review by the independent partner.

56 Matters to be documented[12] include all key elements of the process and any significant judgments concerning:

- threats identified and the process used in identifying them;
- safeguards adopted and the reasons why they are considered to be effective;
- review by an independent partner;
- overall assessment of threats and safeguards; and
- communication with those charged with governance.

Effective date

57 Effective for audits of financial statements for periods commencing on or after 15 December 2004.

58 Firms may complete audit engagements relating to periods commencing prior to 15 December 2004 in accordance with existing ethical guidance from the relevant

---

[11] *When considering how to present this analysis of fees, the auditors take account of any applicable legislation and whether the types of non-audit services provided differ substantially.*

[12] *The necessary working papers can be combined with those prepared pursuant to paragraph 12 of ISA (UK and Ireland) 220 'Quality control for audits of historical financial information', which states that: 'The engagement partner should ... document conclusions on independence and any relevant discussions with the firm that support these conclusions.'*

professional body, putting in place any necessary changes in the subsequent engagement period.

Firms may implement revisions to their policies and procedures as required under paragraphs 15 and 21 during the year commencing 15 December 2004. **59**

ES1 (Revised)*
Integrity, objectivity and independence

(Revised April 2008)

Contents

	Paragraph
Introduction	1 – 14
Compliance with ethical standards	15 – 26
Identification and assessment of threats	27 – 37
Identification and assessment of safeguards	38 – 45
Engagement quality control review	46 – 47
Overall conclusion	48 – 50
Other auditors involved in the audit of group financial statements	51 – 53
Network firms not involved in the audit	54 – 55
Communication with those charged with governance	56 – 63
Documentation	64 – 66
Effective date	67 – 69

---

* Revisions to this Standard became effective for audits of financial statements for periods commencing on or after 6 April 2008. The Standard effective before this date is available from the APB website.

Preface

APB Ethical Standards apply in the audit of financial statements. They are read in the context of the Auditing Practices Board's Statement "The Auditing Practices Board – Scope and Authority of Pronouncements (Revised)" which sets out the application and authority of APB Ethical Standards.

The terms used in APB Ethical Standards are explained in the Glossary.

APB Ethical Standards apply to audits of financial statements in both the private and the public sectors. However, auditors in the public sector are subject to more complex ethical requirements than their private sector counterparts. This includes, for example, compliance with legislation such as the Prevention of Corruption Act 1916, concerning gifts and hospitality, and with Cabinet Office guidance.

Introduction

1. The financial statements of an entity may have a number of different users. For example, they may be used by suppliers and customers, joint venture partners, bankers and other suppliers of finance, taxation and regulatory authorities, employees, trades unions and environmental groups. In the case of a listed company, the financial statements are an important source of information to the capital markets. But the primary purpose of the financial statements of an entity is to provide its owners – the shareholders (or those in an equivalent position) – with information on the state of affairs of the entity and its performance and to assist them in assessing the stewardship exercised by the directors (or those in an equivalent position) over the business that has been entrusted to them.

2. The financial statements of an entity are the responsibility of its board of directors and are prepared by them, or by others on their behalf, for the shareholders or, in some circumstances, for other third parties.

3. The primary objective of an audit of the financial statements is for the auditor to provide independent assurance to the shareholders that the directors have prepared the financial statements properly. The auditor issues a report that includes an opinion as to whether or not the financial statements give a true and fair view[1]. Thus the auditor assists the shareholders to exercise their proprietary powers as shareholders in the Annual General Meeting.

4. Public confidence in the operation of the capital markets and in the conduct of public interest entities depends, in part, upon the credibility of the opinions and reports issued by the auditor in connection with the audit of the financial statements. Such credibility depends on beliefs concerning the integrity, objectivity and independence of the auditor and the quality of audit work performed. APB establishes quality control, auditing and ethical standards to provide a framework for audit practice. The Auditors' Code underlies APB's standards and sets out the fundamental principles, which APB expects to guide the conduct of auditors.

5. APB Ethical Standards are concerned with the integrity, objectivity and independence of auditors. Ethical guidance on other matters, together with statements of

---

[1] In the case of certain bodies in the public sector, the auditor expresses an opinion as to whether the financial statements 'present fairly' the financial position.

fundamental ethical principles governing the work of all professional accountants, are issued by professional accountancy bodies.

6   **Auditors shall conduct the audit of the financial statements of an entity with integrity, objectivity and independence.**

Integrity

7   Integrity is a prerequisite for all those who act in the public interest. It is essential that auditors act, and are seen to act, with integrity, which requires not only honesty but a broad range of related qualities such as fairness, candour, courage, intellectual honesty and confidentiality.

8   It is important that the directors and management of an audited entity can rely on the auditor to treat the information obtained during an audit as confidential[2], unless they have authorised its disclosure, unless it is already known to third parties or unless the auditor has a legal right or duty to disclose it. Without this, there is a danger that the directors and management will fail to disclose such information to the auditor and that the effectiveness of the audit will thereby be impaired.

Objectivity

9   Objectivity is a state of mind that excludes bias, prejudice and compromise and that gives fair and impartial consideration to all matters that are relevant to the task in hand, disregarding those that are not. Objectivity requires that the auditor's judgment is not affected by conflicts of interest. Like integrity, objectivity is a fundamental ethical principle.

10 The need for auditors to be objective arises from the fact that many of the important issues involved in the preparation of financial statements do not relate to questions of fact but rather to questions of judgment. For example, there are choices to be made by the board of directors in deciding on the accounting policies to be adopted by the entity: the directors have to select the ones that they consider most appropriate and this decision can have a material impact on the financial statements. Furthermore, many items included in the financial statements cannot be measured with absolute precision and certainty. In many cases, estimates have to be made and the directors may have to choose one value from a range of possible outcomes. When exercising discretion in these areas, the directors have regard to the applicable financial reporting framework. If the directors, whether deliberately or inadvertently, make a biased judgment or an otherwise inappropriate decision, the financial statements may be misstated or misleading.

11 It is against this background that the auditor is required to express an opinion on the financial statements. The audit involves considering the process followed and the choices made by the directors in preparing the financial statements and concluding whether the result gives a true and fair view. The auditor's objectivity requires that an impartial opinion is expressed in the light of all the available audit evidence and the auditor's professional judgment. Objectivity also requires that the auditor adopts a rigorous and robust approach and is prepared to disagree, where necessary, with the directors' judgments.

[2] *The fundamental principle of confidentiality is addressed in the ethical guidance issued by the auditor's professional accountancy body. This principle does not constrain the proper communication between the auditor and shareholders of the audited entity (or equivalent).*

Independence

Independence is freedom from situations and relationships which make it probable that a reasonable and informed third party would conclude that objectivity either is impaired or could be impaired. Independence is related to and underpins objectivity. However, whereas objectivity is a personal behavioural characteristic concerning the auditor's state of mind, independence relates to the circumstances surrounding the audit, including the financial, employment, business and personal relationships between the auditor and the audited entity.

12

The need for independence arises because, in most cases, users of the financial statements and other third parties do not have all the information necessary for judging whether the auditor is, in fact, objective. Although the auditor may be satisfied that its objectivity is not impaired by a particular situation, a third party may reach a different conclusion. For example, if a third party were aware that the auditor had certain financial, employment, business or personal relationships with the audited entity, that individual might reasonably conclude that the auditor could be subject to undue influence from the directors or would not be impartial or unbiased. Public confidence in the auditor's objectivity could therefore suffer as a result of this perception, irrespective of whether there is any actual impairment.

13

Accordingly, in evaluating the likely consequences of such situations and relationships, the test to be applied is not whether the auditor considers that the auditor's objectivity is impaired but whether it is probable that a reasonable and informed third party would conclude that the auditor's objectivity either is impaired or is likely to be impaired. There are inherent threats to the level of independence (both actual and perceived) that the auditor can achieve as a result of the influence that the board of directors and management have over the appointment and remuneration of the auditor. The audit engagement partner considers the application of safeguards where there are threats to auditor independence (both actual and perceived).

14

Compliance with Ethical Standards

The audit firm shall establish policies and procedures, appropriately documented and communicated, designed to ensure that, in relation to each audit engagement, the audit firm, and all those who are in a position to influence the conduct and outcome of the audit, act with integrity, objectivity and independence.

15

For the purposes of APB Ethical Standards, a person in a position to influence the conduct and outcome of the audit is:

16

(a) any person who is directly involved in the audit ('the engagement team'), including:
  (i) the audit partners, audit managers and audit staff ('the audit team');
  (ii) professional personnel from other disciplines involved in the audit (for example, lawyers, actuaries, taxation specialists, IT specialists, treasury management specialists);[3]
  (iii) those who provide quality control or direct oversight of the audit;
(b) any person who forms part of the chain of command for the audit within the audit firm;
(c) any person within the audit firm who, due to any other circumstances, may be in a position to exert such influence.

---

[3] *Where external consultants are involved in the audit, ISA (UK and Ireland) 620 'Using the work of an Expert'* states that the auditor should evaluate the objectivity of the expert.

17 Compliance with the requirements regarding the auditor's integrity, objectivity and independence is a responsibility of both the audit firm and of individual partners and professional staff. The audit firm establishes policies and procedures, appropriate to the size and nature of the audit firm, to promote and monitor compliance with those requirements by any person who is in a position to influence the conduct and outcome of the audit.[4,5]

18 **The leadership of the audit firm shall take responsibility for establishing a control environment within the firm that places adherence to ethical principles and compliance with APB Ethical Standards above commercial considerations.**

19 The leadership of the audit firm influences the internal culture of the firm by its actions and by its example ('the tone at the top'). Achieving a robust control environment requires that the leadership gives clear, consistent and frequent messages, backed up by appropriate actions, which emphasise the importance of compliance with APB Ethical Standards.

20 In order to promote a strong control environment, the audit firm establishes policies and procedures that include:

(a) requirements for partners and staff to report where applicable:
- family and other personal relationships involving an entity audited by the firm;
- financial interests in an entity audited by the firm;
- decisions to join an audited entity.

(b) monitoring of compliance with the firm's policies and procedures relating to integrity, objectivity and independence. Such monitoring procedures include, on a test basis, periodic review of the audit engagement partners' documentation of the consideration of the auditor's objectivity and independence, addressing, for example:
- financial interests in audited entities;
- economic dependence on audited entities;
- the performance of non-audit services;
- audit partner rotation;

(c) identification of the audited entities which partners in the chain of command and their immediate family need to be independent from[6];

(d) prompt communication of possible or actual breaches of the firm's policies and procedures to the relevant audit engagement partners;

(e) evaluation by audit engagement partners of the implications of any identified possible or actual breaches of the firm's policies and procedures that are reported to them;

(f) reporting by audit engagement partners of particular circumstances or relationships as required by APB Ethical Standards;

---

[4] *Monitoring of compliance with ethical requirements will often be performed as part of a broader quality control process. ISQC (UK & Ireland) 1 'Quality Control for firms that perform audits and reviews of historical financial information and other assurance and related services engagements' establishes the basic principles and essential procedures in relation to a firm's responsibilities for its system of quality control for audits.*

[5] *In addition, UK legislation provides that each of the Recognised Supervisory Bodies must have adequate rules and practices to ensure that the audit firm has arrangements to prevent any person from being able to exert any influence over the way in which a statutory audit is conducted in circumstances in which that influence would be likely to affect the independence or integrity of the audit.*

[6] *Such identification is necessary for those in the chain of command to understand how their firm responsibilities result in connections with different entities audited by the firm. It can be achieved by listing the individual audited entities or by a broader statement regarding categories of audited entity, for example, those of a certain business unit.*

(g) operation of an enforcement mechanism to promote compliance with policies and procedures;
(h) empowerment of staff to communicate to senior levels within the firm any issue of objectivity or independence that concerns them; this includes establishing clear communication channels open to staff, encouraging staff to use these channels and ensuring that staff who use these channels are not subject to disciplinary proceedings as a result.

Save where the circumstances contemplated in paragraph 23 apply, the audit firm shall designate a partner in the firm ('the ethics partner') as having responsibility for: 21

(a) the adequacy of the firm's policies and procedures relating to integrity, objectivity and independence, its compliance with APB Ethical Standards, and the effectiveness of its communication to partners and staff within the firm; and
(b) providing related guidance to individual partners.

In assessing the effectiveness of the firm's communication of its policies and procedures relating to integrity, objectivity and independence, ethics partners consider whether they are properly covered in induction programmes, professional training and continuing professional development for all partners and staff. Ethics partners also provide guidance on matters referred to them and on matters which they otherwise become aware of, where a difficult and objective judgment needs to be made or a consistent position reached. 22

In audit firms with three or fewer partners who are 'responsible individuals'[7], it may not be practicable for an ethics partner to be designated. In these circumstances all partners will regularly discuss ethical issues amongst themselves, so ensuring that they act in a consistent manner and observe the principles set out in APB Ethical Standards. In the case of a sole practitioner, advice on matters where a difficult and objective judgment needs to be made is obtained through the ethics helpline of the auditor's professional body, or through discussion with a practitioner from another firm. In all cases, it is important that such discussions are documented. 23

To be able to discharge his or her responsibilities, the ethics partner is an individual possessing seniority, relevant experience and authority within the firm and is provided with sufficient staff support and other resources, commensurate with the size of the firm. Alternative arrangements are established to allow for: 24

- the provision of guidance on those audits where the ethics partner is the audit engagement partner; and
- situations where the ethics partner is unavailable, for example due to illness or holidays.

Whenever a possible or actual breach of an APB Ethical Standard, or of policies and procedures established pursuant to the requirements of an APB Ethical Standard, is identified, the audit engagement partner, in the first instance, and the ethics partner, where appropriate, assesses the implications of the breach, determines whether there are safeguards that can be put in place or other actions that can be taken to address any potential adverse consequences and considers whether there is a need to resign from the audit engagement. 25

An inadvertent violation of this Standard does not necessarily call into question the audit firm's ability to give an audit opinion, provided that: 26

---

[7] *A 'responsible individual' is a partner or employee of the audit firm who is responsible for audit work and designated as such under the audit regulations of a Recognised Supervisory Body.*

(a) the audit firm has established policies and procedures that require all partners and staff to report any breach promptly to the audit engagement partner or to the ethics partner, as appropriate;
(b) the audit engagement partner or ethics partner promptly notifies the relevant partner or member of staff that any matter which has given rise to a breach is to be addressed as soon as possible and ensures that such action is taken;
(c) safeguards, where appropriate, are applied, (for example, having another partner review the work done by the relevant partner or member of staff or removing him or her from the engagement team); and
(d) the actions taken and the rationale for them are documented.

Identification and assessment of threats

27 The auditor identifies and assesses the circumstances, which could adversely affect the auditor's objectivity ('threats'), including any perceived loss of independence, and applies procedures ('safeguards'), which will either:

(a) eliminate the threat (for example, by eliminating the circumstances, such as removing an individual from the engagement team or disposing of a financial interest in the audited entity); or
(b) reduce the threat to an acceptable level, that is a level at which it is not probable that a reasonable and informed third party would conclude that the auditor's objectivity is impaired or is likely to be impaired (for example, by having the audit work reviewed by another partner or by another audit firm).

When considering safeguards, where the audit engagement partner chooses to reduce rather than to eliminate a threat to objectivity and independence, he or she recognises that this judgment may not be shared by users of the financial statements and that he or she may be required to justify the decision.

Threats to objectivity and independence

28 **The audit firm shall establish policies and procedures to require persons in a position to influence the conduct and outcome of the audit to be constantly alert to circumstances that might reasonably be considered threats to their objectivity or the perceived loss of independence and, where such circumstances are identified, to report them to the audit engagement partner or to the ethics partner, as appropriate.**

29 Such policies and procedures require that threats to the auditor's objectivity and independence are communicated to the appropriate person, having regard to the nature of the threats and to the part of the firm and the identity of any person involved. The consideration of all threats and the action taken is documented. If the audit engagement partner is personally involved, or is unsure about the action to be taken, the matter is resolved through consultation with the ethics partner.

30 **The audit firm shall establish policies and procedures which require that partners and employees of the firm, including those providing non-audit services to an audited entity, do not take decisions that are the responsibility of management of the audited entity.**

31 It is not possible to specify all types of decision that are the responsibility of management, but they typically involve leading and directing the audited entity, including making significant judgments and taking decisions regarding the acquisition, deployment and control of human, financial, physical and intangible resources. Examples of judgments and decisions that are not made by the auditor include:

- Setting policies and strategic direction;
- Directing and taking responsibility for the actions of the entity's employees;
- Authorising transactions;
- Deciding which recommendations of the audit firm or other third parties should be implemented;
- Taking responsibility for the preparation and fair presentation of the financial statements in accordance with the applicable financial reporting framework; and
- Taking responsibility for designing, implementing and maintaining internal control.

The principal types of threats to the auditor's objectivity and independence are: 32

- *self-interest threat*
  A self-interest threat arises when the auditor has financial or other interests which might cause it to be reluctant to take actions that would be adverse to the interests of the audit firm or any individual in a position to influence the conduct or outcome of the audit (for example, where the auditor has an investment in the audited entity, is seeking to provide additional services to the audited entity or needs to recover long-outstanding fees from the audited entity).
- *self-review threat*
  A self-review threat arises when the results of a non-audit service performed by the auditor or by others within the audit firm are reflected in the amounts included or disclosed in the financial statements (for example, where the audit firm has been involved in maintaining the accounting records, or undertaking valuations that are incorporated in the financial statements). In the course of the audit, the auditor may need to re-evaluate the work performed in the non-audit service. As, by virtue of providing the non-audit service, the audit firm is associated with aspects of the preparation of the financial statements, it may be (or may be perceived to be) unable to take an impartial view of relevant aspects of those financial statements.
- *management threat*
  Paragraph 30 prohibits partners and employees of the audit firm from taking decisions on behalf of the management of the audited entity. A management threat can also arise when the audit firm undertakes an engagement to provide non-audit services in relation to which management are required to make judgments and take decisions based on that work (for example, the design, selection and implementation of a financial information technology system). In such work, the audit firm may become closely aligned with the views and interests of management and the auditor's objectivity and independence may be impaired, or may be perceived to be, impaired.
- *advocacy threat*
  An advocacy threat arises when the audit firm undertakes work that involves acting as an advocate for an audited entity and supporting a position taken by management in an adversarial context (for example, by acting as a legal advocate for the audited entity in litigation or a regulatory investigation). In order to act in an advocacy role, the audit firm has to adopt a position closely aligned to that of management. This creates both actual and perceived threats to the auditor's objectivity and independence.
- *familiarity (or trust) threat*
  A familiarity (or trust) threat arises when the auditor is predisposed to accept or is insufficiently questioning of the audited entity's point of view (for example, where close personal relationships are developed with the audited entity's personnel through long association with the audited entity).
- *intimidation threat*
  An intimidation threat arises when the auditor's conduct is influenced by fear or

threats (for example, where the auditor encounters an aggressive and dominating individual).

These categories may not be entirely distinct: certain circumstances may give rise to more than one type of threat. For example, where an audit firm wishes to retain the fee income from a large audited entity, but encounters an aggressive and dominating individual, there may be a self-interest threat as well as an intimidation threat.

33 Threats to the auditor's objectivity, including a perceived loss of independence, may arise where the audit firm is appointed to a non-audit service engagement for an entity not audited by the firm, but where an audited entity makes this decision. In such cases, even if the entity not audited by the firm pays the fee for the non-audit service engagement, the auditor considers the implication of the threats (especially the self-interest threat) that arise from the appointment.

34 **The audit firm shall establish policies and procedures to require the audit engagement partner to identify and assess the significance of threats to the auditor's objectivity, including any perceived loss of independence:**

  (a) **when considering whether to accept or retain an audit engagement;**[8]
  (b) **when planning the audit;**
  (c) **when forming an opinion on the financial statements;**[9]
  (d) **when considering whether to accept or retain an engagement to provide non-audit services to an audited entity; and**
  (e) **when potential threats are reported to him or her.**

35 An initial assessment of the threats to objectivity and independence is required when the audit engagement partner is considering whether to accept or retain an audit engagement. That assessment is reviewed and updated at the planning stage of each audit. At the end of the audit process, when forming an opinion on the financial statements but before issuing the report, the audit engagement partner draws an overall conclusion as to whether any threats to objectivity and independence have been properly addressed in accordance with APB Ethical Standards. If, at any time, the auditor is invited to accept an engagement to provide non-audit services to an audited entity, the audit engagement partner considers the impact this may have on the auditor's objectivity and independence.

36 When identifying and assessing threats to the auditor's objectivity and independence, the auditor takes into account current relationships with the audited entity (including non-audit service engagements), those that existed prior to the current audit engagement and any known to be in prospect following the current audit engagement. This is because those prior and subsequent relationships may be perceived as likely to influence the auditor in the performance of the audit or as otherwise impairing the auditor's objectivity and independence.

37 Where the audited entity or a third party calls into question the objectivity and independence of the audit firm in relation to a particular audited entity, the ethics partner carries out such investigations as may be appropriate.

---

[8] *Consideration of whether to accept or retain an audit engagement does not arise with those bodies in the public sector where responsibility for the audit is assigned by legislation.*

[9] *In the case of listed companies, the auditor also assesses whether there is any threat to the auditor's objectivity and independence when discharging responsibilities in relation to preliminary announcements and when reporting on interim results.*

Identification and assessment of safeguards

If the audit engagement partner identifies threats to the auditor's objectivity, including any perceived loss of independence, he or she shall identify and assess the effectiveness of the available safeguards and apply such safeguards as are sufficient to eliminate the threats or reduce them to an acceptable level. 38

The nature and extent of safeguards to be applied depend on the significance of the threats. Where a threat is clearly insignificant, no safeguards are needed. 39

Other APB Ethical Standards address specific circumstances which can create threats to the auditor's objectivity or loss of independence. They give examples of safeguards that can, in some circumstances, eliminate the threat or reduce it to an acceptable level. In circumstances where this is not possible, either the auditor does not accept or withdraws from the audit engagement. 40

APB Ethical Standards contain certain additional requirements or prohibitions that apply only in the case of listed company audited entities: 41

- ES 1, paragraphs 46 and 59;
- ES 3, paragraphs 12, 18 and 19;
- ES 4, paragraphs 16, 25 and 29;
- ES 5, paragraphs 56, 63, 78, 88, 95 and 127.

These additional requirements also apply where regulation or legislation requires that the audit of an entity is conducted in accordance with the auditing standards or ethical requirements that are applicable to the audit of listed companies.

The audit firm shall establish policies and procedures which set out the circumstances in which those additional requirements listed in paragraph 41 that apply to listed companies are applied to other audit engagements. 42

Such policies and procedures take into consideration any additional criteria set by the audit firm, such as the nature of the entity's business, its size, the number of its employees and the range of its stakeholders. For example, a firm may decide to extend the additional requirements to audit engagements of certain regulated financial institutions such as large non-listed banks and insurance companies. 43

The audit engagement partner shall not accept or shall not continue an audit engagement if he or she concludes that any threats to the auditor's objectivity and independence cannot be reduced to an acceptable level. 44

Where a reasonable and informed third party would regard ceasing to act as the auditor as detrimental to the shareholders (or equivalent) of the audited entity, then resignation may not be immediate. However, the audit firm discloses full details of the position to those charged with governance of the audited entity, and establishes appropriate safeguards. 45

Engagement quality control review

46 In the case of listed companies the engagement quality control reviewer[10] shall:

(a) consider the audit firm's compliance with APB Ethical Standards in relation to the audit engagement;

(b) form an independent opinion as to the appropriateness and adequacy of the safeguards applied; and

(c) consider the adequacy of the documentation of the audit engagement partner's consideration of the auditor's objectivity and independence.

47 The audit firm's policies and procedures set out whether there are circumstances in which an engagement quality control review is performed for other audit engagements as described in paragraph 42.

Overall conclusion

48 At the end of the audit process, when forming an opinion but before issuing the report on the financial statements, the audit engagement partner shall reach an overall conclusion that any threats to objectivity and independence have been properly addressed in accordance with APB Ethical Standards. If the audit engagement partner cannot make such a conclusion, he or she shall not report and the audit firm shall resign as auditor.

49 If the audit engagement partner remains unable to conclude that any threat to objectivity and independence has been properly addressed in accordance with APB Ethical Standards, or if there is a disagreement between the audit engagement partner and the engagement quality control reviewer, he or she consults the ethics partner.

50 In concluding on compliance with the requirements for objectivity and independence, the audit engagement partner is entitled to rely on the completeness and accuracy of the data developed by the audit firm's systems relating to independence (for example, in relation to the reporting of financial interests by staff), unless informed otherwise by the firm.

Other auditors involved in the audit of group financial statements

51 The group audit engagement partner shall be satisfied that other auditors (whether a network firm or another audit firm) involved in the audit of the group financial statements, who are not subject to APB Ethical Standards, are objective and document the rationale for that conclusion.

52 The group audit engagement partner obtains appropriate evidence[11] that the other auditors have a sufficient understanding of and have complied with the current IFAC

---

[10] *ISA (UK and Ireland) 220* 'Quality control for audits of historical financial information', *requires the audit engagement partner to appoint an engagement quality control reviewer for all audits of listed entities...The engagement quality control review involves consideration of...the engagement team's evaluation of the independence of the firm...'*

[11] *ISA (UK and Ireland) 600* 'Using the Work of Another Auditor' *states that "The principal auditor should perform procedures to obtain sufficient appropriate audit evidence, that the work of the other auditor is adequate for the principal auditor's purposes, in the context of the specific assignment."*

Code of Ethics for Professional Accountants, including the independence requirements[12].

In the case of a listed company, the group audit engagement partner establishes that the company has communicated its policy[13] on the engagement of the external auditor to supply non-audit services to its affiliates and obtains confirmation that the other auditors will comply with this policy. 53

Network firms not involved in the audit

The audit firm shall establish that network firms which are not involved in the audit are required to comply with global policies and procedures that are designed to meet the requirements of the current IFAC Code[12]. 54

The IFAC Code requires all network firms to be independent of the entities audited by other network firms[14]. International audit networks commonly meet this requirement through global independence policies and procedures designed to comply with the current IFAC Code which are supported by appropriate monitoring and compliance processes within the network. 55

Communication with those charged with governance

The audit engagement partner shall ensure that those charged with governance of the audited entity are appropriately informed on a timely basis of all significant facts and matters that bear upon the auditor's objectivity and independence. 56

The audit committee, where one exists, is usually responsible for oversight of the relationship between the auditor and the entity and of the conduct of the audit process. It therefore has a particular interest in being informed about the auditor's ability to express an objective opinion on the financial statements. Where there is no audit committee, this role is undertaken by the board of directors.[15,16] 57

The aim of these communications is to ensure full and fair disclosure by the auditor to those charged with governance of the audited entity on matters in which they have an interest. These will generally include the key elements of the audit engagement partner's consideration of objectivity and independence, such as: 58

---

[12] *The International Federation of Accountants (IFAC) Code of Ethics for Professional Accountants (the IFAC Code) establishes a conceptual framework for applying the fundamental principles of professional ethics for professional accountants. Section 290 of the IFAC Code illustrates the application of the conceptual framework to independence requirements for audit engagements and represents the international standard on which national standards should be based. No Member Body of IFAC is allowed to apply less stringent standards than those stated in that section. In addition, members of the IFAC Forum of Firms have agreed to apply ethical standards, which are at least as rigorous as those of the IFAC Code.*

[13] *The Combined Code on Corporate Governance requires audit committees to develop the company's policy on the engagement of the external auditor to supply non-audit services.*

[14] *Paragraph 290.15 of the IFAC Code, as updated in July 2006*

[15] *Where there is no audit committee, references to communication with the audit committee are to be construed as including communication with the board of directors.*

[16] *Some bodies in the public sector have audit committees but others have different governance models.*

- the principal threats, if any, to objectivity and independence identified by the auditor, including consideration of all relationships between the audited entity, its affiliates and directors and the audit firm;
- any safeguards adopted and the reasons why they are considered to be effective, including any independent partner review;
- the overall assessment of threats and safeguards;
- information about the general policies and processes within the audit firm for maintaining objectivity and independence.

59 In the case of listed companies, the audit engagement partner shall ensure that the audit committee is provided with:

(a) a written disclosure of relationships that bear on the auditor's objectivity and independence, any safeguards that are in place and details of non-audit services provided to the audited entity and the fees charged in relation thereto;
(b) written confirmation that the auditor is independent;
(c) details of any inconsistencies between APB Ethical Standards and the company's policy for the supply of non-audit services by the audit firm and any apparent breach of that policy.
(d) an opportunity to discuss auditor independence issues.

60 The auditor of a listed company discloses in writing details of all relationships between the auditor and the audited entity, its directors and senior management and its affiliates, including all services provided by the audit firm and its network to the audited entity, its directors and senior management and its affiliates, that the auditor considers may reasonably be thought to bear on the auditor's objectivity and independence and the related safeguards that are in place.

61 The auditor ensures that the total amount of fees that the auditor and its network firms have charged to the audited entity and its affiliates for the provision of services during the reporting period, analysed into appropriate categories[17] are disclosed. For each category any contingent fee arrangements[18] and the amounts of any future services which have been contracted, or where a written proposal has been submitted, are also separately disclosed.

62 The written confirmation that the auditor is independent indicates that the auditor considers that it complies with APB Ethical Standards and that, in its professional judgment, it is independent and its objectivity is not compromised. If it is not possible to make such a confirmation, the communication will include any concerns that the auditor has that its objectivity and independence may be compromised (including instances where the group audit engagement partner does not consider an other auditor to be objective) and an explanation of the actions which necessarily follow from this.

63 The most appropriate time for final confirmation of such matters is usually at the conclusion of the audit. However, communications between the auditor and those charged with the governance of the audited entity will also be needed at the planning stage and whenever significant judgments are made about threats to objectivity and independence and the appropriateness of safeguards put in place, for example, when accepting an engagement to provide non-audit services.

[17] *When considering how to present this analysis of fees, the auditor takes account of any applicable legislation and whether the types of non-audit services provided differ substantially.*

[18] *Paragraph 16 of ES 4 requires the audit engagement partner to disclose to the audit committee, in writing, any contingent fee arrangements for non-audit services provided by the auditor or its network firms.*

Documentation

The audit engagement partner shall ensure that his or her consideration of the auditor's objectivity and independence is appropriately documented on a timely basis.   64

The requirement to document these issues contributes to the clarity and rigour of the audit engagement partner's thinking and the quality of his or her judgments. In addition, such documentation provides evidence that the audit engagement partner's consideration of the auditor's objectivity and independence was properly performed and, for listed companies, provides the basis for review by the engagement quality control reviewer.   65

Matters to be documented[19] include all key elements of the process and any significant judgments concerning: 66

- threats identified, other than those which are clearly insignificant, and the process used in identifying them;
- safeguards adopted and the reasons why they are considered to be effective;
- review by an engagement quality control reviewer or an independent partner;
- overall assessment of threats and safeguards; and
- communication with those charged with governance.

Effective date

Save for the requirements of paragraphs 42 and 54, revisions to this Ethical Standard become effective for audits of financial statements for periods commencing on or after 6 April 2008.   67

In the case of paragraphs 42 and 54, audit firms will be in compliance with this Ethical Standard provided they have implemented revisions to their policies and procedures by 30 September 2008.   68

Firms may complete audit engagements relating to periods commencing prior to 6 April 2008 in accordance with existing ethical standards, putting in place any necessary changes in the subsequent engagement period.   69

---

[19] *The necessary working papers can be combined with those prepared pursuant to paragraph 12 of ISA (UK and Ireland) 220* 'Quality control for audits of historical financial information', *which states that:* 'The engagement partner should ... document conclusions on independence and any relevant discussions with the firm that support these conclusions.'

ES2
Financial, business, employment and personal relationships

(Re-issued December 2004)

Contents

	Paragraphs
Introduction	1 - 4
Financial relationships	5 - 24
Business relationships	25 - 31
Employment relationships	32 - 54
Family and other personal relationships	55 – 60
External consultants involved in the audit	61 - 63
Effective date	64 - 68

Preface

APB Ethical Standards apply in the audit of financial statements. They should be read in the context of the Auditing Practices Board's Statement "The Auditing Practices Board – Scope and Authority of Pronouncements (Revised)" which sets out the application and authority of APB Ethical Standards.

The terms used in APB Ethical Standards are explained in the Glossary.

APB Ethical Standards apply to audits of financial statements in both the private and the public sectors. However, auditors in the public sector are subject to more complex ethical requirements than their private sector counterparts. This includes, for example, compliance with legislation such as the Prevention of Corruption Act 1916, concerning gifts and hospitality, and with Cabinet Office guidance.

Introduction

1. APB Ethical Standard 1 requires the audit engagement partner to identify and assess the circumstances which could adversely affect the auditors' objectivity ('threats'), including any perceived loss of independence, and to apply procedures ('safeguards') which will either:

   (a) eliminate the threat; or
   (b) reduce the threat to an acceptable level (that is, a level at which it is not probable that a reasonable and informed third party would conclude that the auditors' objectivity and independence is impaired or is likely to be impaired).
   When considering safeguards, where the audit engagement partner chooses to reduce rather than to eliminate a threat to objectivity and independence, he or she recognises that this judgment may not be shared by users of the financial statements and that he or she may be required to justify the decision.

2. This Standard provides requirements and guidance on specific circumstances arising out of financial, business, employment and personal relationships with the audit client, which may create threats to the auditors' objectivity or perceived loss of independence. It gives examples of safeguards that can, in some circumstances, eliminate the threat or reduce it to an acceptable level. In circumstances where this is not possible, either the relationship in question is not entered into or the auditors either do not accept or withdraw from the audit engagement, as appropriate.

3. Whenever a possible or actual breach of an APB Ethical Standard is identified, the audit engagement partner, in the first instance, and the ethics partner, where appropriate, assesses the implications of the breach, determines whether there are safeguards that can be put in place or other actions that can be taken to address any potential adverse consequences and considers whether there is a need to resign from the audit engagement.

4. An inadvertent violation of this Standard does not necessarily call into question the audit firm's ability to give an audit opinion provided that:

   (a) the audit firm has established policies and procedures that require all partners and staff to report any breach promptly to the audit engagement partner or to the ethics partner as appropriate;
   (b) the audit engagement partner or ethics partner promptly notifies the partner or member of staff that any matter which has given rise to a breach is to be addressed as soon as possible and ensures that such action is taken;

(c) safeguards, if appropriate, are applied (for example, having another partner review the work done by the relevant partner or member of staff or by removing him or her from the engagement team); and
(d) the actions taken and the rationale for them are documented.

Financial relationships

General considerations

5   A financial interest is an equity or other security, debenture, loan or other debt instrument of an entity, including rights and obligations to acquire such an interest and derivatives directly related to such an interest.

6   Financial interests may be:
(a) owned directly, rather than through intermediaries (a 'direct financial interest'); or
(b) owned through intermediaries, for example, an open ended investment company or a pension scheme (an 'indirect financial interest').

7   **The audit firm, any partner in the audit firm, a person in a position to influence the conduct and outcome of the audit or an immediate family member of such a person should not hold:**
   (a) any direct financial interest in an audit client or an affiliate of an audit client; or
   (b) any indirect financial interest in an audit client or an affiliate of an audit client, where the investment is material to the audit firm or the individual and to the intermediary; or
   (c) any indirect financial interest in an audit client or an affiliate of an audit client, where the person holding it has both:
      (i) the ability to influence the investment decisions of the intermediary; and
      (ii) actual knowledge of the existence of the underlying investment in the audit client.

8   The threats to the auditors' objectivity and independence, where a direct financial interest or a material indirect financial interest in the audit client is held by the audit firm or by one of the individuals specified in paragraph 7 are such that no safeguards can eliminate them or reduce them to an acceptable level.

9   For the purposes of paragraph 7, where holdings in an authorised unit or investment trust, an open ended investment company or an equivalent investment vehicle which is audited by the audit firm, are held by a partner in the audit firm, who is not in a position to influence the conduct and outcome of the audit, or an immediate family member of such a partner, these are to be treated as indirect financial interests. Such interests can therefore be held as long as:

(a) they are not material to the individual; and
(b) the individual has no influence over the investment decisions of the audit client.

10 Where a person in a position to influence the conduct and outcome of the audit, or a partner in the audit firm, or any of their immediate family members, are members or shareholders of an audit client, as a result of membership requirements, or equivalent, the audit firm ensures that no more than the minimum number of shares necessary to comply with the requirement are held and that this shareholding is not material to either the audit client or the individual. Disclosure of such shareholdings

will be made to those charged with governance of the audit client, in accordance with APB Ethical Standard 1, paragraph 49.

Where one of the financial interests specified in paragraph 7 is held by: 11

(a) *the audit firm, a partner in the audit firm or an immediate family member of such a partner:* the entire financial interest is disposed of, a sufficient amount of an indirect financial interest is disposed of so that the remaining interest is no longer material, or the firm does not accept (or withdraws from) the audit engagement;

(b) *a person in a position to influence the conduct and outcome of the audit:* the entire financial interest is disposed of, a sufficient amount of an indirect financial interest is disposed of so that the remaining interest is no longer material, or that person does not retain a position in which they exert such influence on the audit engagement;

(c) *an immediate family member of a person in a position to influence the conduct and outcome of the audit:* the entire financial interest is disposed of, a sufficient amount of an indirect financial interest is disposed of so that the remaining interest is no longer material, or the person in a position to influence the conduct and outcome of the audit does not retain a position in which they exert such influence on the audit engagement.

Where one of the financial interests specified in paragraph 7 is acquired unintentionally, as a result of an external event (for example, inheritance, gift, or merger of firms or companies), the disposal of the financial interest is required immediately, or as soon as possible after the relevant person has actual knowledge of and the right to dispose of the interest. 12

Where the disposal of a financial interest does not take place immediately, the audit firm adopts safeguards to preserve its objectivity until the financial interest is disposed. These may include the temporary exclusion of the person in a position to influence the conduct and outcome of the audit from such influence on the audit or a review of the relevant person's audit work by an audit partner having sufficient experience and authority to fulfill the role, who is not involved in the audit engagement. 13

Where the audit firm or one of the individuals specified in paragraph 7 holds an indirect financial interest but does not have both: 14

(a) the ability to influence the investment decisions of the intermediary; and
(b) actual knowledge of the existence of the underlying investment in the audit client,

there may not be a threat to the auditors' objectivity and independence. For example, where the indirect financial interest takes the form of an investment in a pension fund, the composition of the funds and the size and nature of any underlying investment in the audit client may be known but there is unlikely to be any influence on investment decisions, as the fund will generally be managed independently on a discretionary basis. In the case of an 'index tracker' fund, the investment in the audit client is determined by the composition of the relevant index and there may be no threat to objectivity. As long as the person holding the indirect interest is not directly involved in the audit of the intermediary, nor able to influence the individual investment decisions of the intermediary, any threat to the auditors' objectivity and independence may be regarded as insignificant.

Where the audit firm or one of the individuals specified in paragraph 7 holds a beneficial interest in a properly operated 'blind' trust, they are (by definition) 15 completely unaware of the identity of the underlying investments. If these include an investment in the audit client, this means that they are unaware of the existence of an indirect financial interest. In these circumstances, there is no threat to the auditors' objectivity and independence.

16 Where a person in a position to influence the conduct and outcome of the audit or a partner in the audit firm becomes aware that a close family member holds one of the financial interests specified in paragraph 7, that individual should report the matter to the audit engagement partner to take appropriate action. If it is a close family member of the audit engagement partner, or if the audit engagement partner is in doubt as to the action to be taken, the audit engagement partner should resolve the matter through consultation with the ethics partner.

Financial interests held as trustee

17 Where a direct or an indirect financial interest in the audit client or its affiliates is held in a trustee capacity by a person in a position to influence the conduct and outcome of the audit, or an immediate family member of such a person, a self-interest threat may be created because either the existence of the trustee interest may influence the conduct of the audit or the trust may influence the actions of the audit client. Accordingly, such a trustee interest is only held when:

- the relevant person is not an identified potential beneficiary of the trust; and
- the financial interest held by the trust in the audit client is not material to the trust; and
- the trust is not able to exercise significant influence over the audit client or an affiliate of the audit client; and
- the relevant person does not have significant influence over the investment decisions made by the trust, in so far as they relate to the financial interest in the audit client.

18 Where it is not clear whether the financial interest held by the trust in the audit client is material to the trust or whether the trust is able to exercise significant influence over the audit client, the financial interest is reported to the ethics partner, so that a decision can be made as to the steps that need to be taken.

Financial interests held by audit firm pension schemes

19 Where the pension scheme of an audit firm has a financial interest in an audit client or its affiliates and the firm has any influence over the trustees' investment decisions (other than indirect strategic and policy decisions), the self-interest threat created is such that no safeguards can eliminate it or reduce it to an acceptable level. In other cases (for example, where the pension scheme invests through a collective investment scheme and the firm's influence is limited to investment policy decisions, such as the allocation between different categories of investment), the ethics partner considers the acceptability of the position, having regard to the materiality of the financial interest to the pension scheme.

Loans and guarantees

20 Where audit firms, persons in a position to influence the conduct and outcome of the audit or immediate family members of such persons:

(a) accept a loan[1] or a guarantee of their borrowings from an audit client; or
(b) make a loan to or guarantee the borrowings of an audit client,

a self-interest threat and an intimidation threat to the auditors' objectivity can be created or there may be a perceived loss of independence. In a number of situations, no safeguards can eliminate this threat or reduce it to an acceptable level.

Audit firms, persons in a position to influence the conduct and outcome of the audit and immediate family members of such persons should not make a loan to, or guarantee the borrowings of, an audit client or its affiliates unless this represents a deposit made with a bank or similar deposit taking institution in the ordinary course of business and on normal business terms. 21

Audit firms should not accept a loan from, or have their borrowings guaranteed by, the audit client or its affiliates unless: 22

(a) the audit client is a bank or similar deposit taking institution; and
(b) the loan or guarantee is made in the ordinary course of business on normal business terms; and
(c) the loan or guarantee is not material to both the audit firm and the audit client.

Persons in a position to influence the conduct and outcome of the audit and immediate family members of such persons should not accept a loan from, or have their borrowings guaranteed by, the audit client or its affiliates unless: 23

(a) the audit client is a bank or similar deposit taking institution; and
(b) the loan or guarantee is made in the ordinary course of business on normal business terms; and
(c) the loan or guarantee is not material to the audit client.

Loans by an audit client that is a bank or similar institution to a person in a position to influence the conduct and outcome of the audit, or an immediate family member of such a person (for example, home mortgages, bank overdrafts or car loans), do not create an unacceptable threat to objectivity and independence, provided that normal business terms apply. However, where such loans are in arrears by a significant amount, this creates an intimidation threat that is unacceptable. Where such a situation arises, the person in a position to influence the conduct and outcome of the audit reports the matter to the audit engagement partner, or to the ethics partner, as appropriate and ceases to have any involvement with the audit. The audit engagement partner or, where appropriate, the ethics partner considers whether any audit work is to be reperformed. 24

Business relationships

A business relationship between: 25

(a) the audit firm or a person who is in a position to influence the conduct and outcome of the audit, or an immediate family member of such a person, and
(b) the audit client or its affiliates, or its management

involves the two parties having a common commercial interest. Business relationships may create self-interest, advocacy or intimidation threats to the auditors' objectivity and perceived loss of independence. Examples include:

---

[1] For the purpose of this standard, the term 'loan' does not include ordinary trade credit arrangements or deposits placed for goods or services, unless they are material to either party (see paragraph 26).

- joint ventures with the audit client or with a director, officer or other individual who performs senior managerial functions for the client;
- arrangements to combine one or more services or products of the audit firm with one or more services or products of the audit client and to market the package with reference to both parties;
- distribution or marketing arrangements under which the audit firm acts as a distributor or marketer of any of the audit client's products or services, or the audit client acts as the distributor or marketer of any of the products or services of the audit firm;
- other commercial transactions, such as the audit firm leasing its office space from the audit client.

26   **Audit firms, persons in a position to influence the conduct and outcome of the audit and immediate family members of such persons should not enter into business relationships with an audit client or its affiliates except where they involve the purchase of goods and services from the audit firm or the audit client in the ordinary course of business and on an arm's length basis and the value involved is not material to either party.**

27   Where a business relationship is not in the ordinary course of business, or where it is not on an arm's length basis, or where the value involved is material, and has been entered into by:

   (a)   *the audit firm:* either the relationship is terminated or the firm does not accept (or withdraws from) the audit engagement;
   (b)   *a person in a position to influence the conduct and outcome of the audit:* either the relationship is terminated or that person does not retain a position in which they exert such influence on the audit engagement;
   (c)   *an immediate family member of a person in a position to influence the conduct and outcome of the audit:* either the relationship is terminated or that person does not retain a position in which they exert such influence on the audit engagement.

   Where there is an unavoidable delay in the termination of a business relationship, the audit firm adopts safeguards to preserve its objectivity until the relationship is terminated. These may include a review of the relevant person's audit work or a temporary exclusion of the relevant person from influence on conduct and outcome of the audit.

28   Where a person in a position to influence the conduct and outcome of the audit becomes aware that a close family member has entered into one of the business relationships specified in paragraph 25, that individual should report the matter to the audit engagement partner to take appropriate action. If it is a close family member of the audit engagement partner or if the audit engagement partner is in doubt as to the action to be taken, the audit engagement partner should resolve the matter through consultation with the ethics partner.

29   Where there are doubts as to whether a transaction or series of transactions are either in the ordinary course of business and on an arm's length basis or of such materiality that they constitute a threat to the audit firm's objectivity and independence, the audit engagement partner reports the issue:

- to the ethics partner, so that a decision can be made as to the appropriate action that needs to be taken to ensure that the matter is resolved; and
- to those charged with governance of the audit client, together with other significant facts and matters that bear upon the auditors' objectivity and independence, to obtain their views on the matter.

An audit firm should not provide audit services to any entity or person able to influence the affairs of the audit firm or the performance of any audit engagement undertaken by the audit firm. 30

This prohibition applies to: 31

(a) any entity that owns any significant part of an audit firm, or is an affiliate of such an entity; or
(b) any shareholder, director or other person in a position to direct the affairs of such an entity or its affiliate.

A significant ownership is one that carries the ability materially to influence the policy of an entity.[2]

Employment relationships

Management role with audit client

An audit firm should not admit to the partnership or employ a person to undertake audit work if that person is also employed by the audit client or its affiliates ('dual employment'). 32

Loan staff assignments

An audit firm should not enter into an agreement with an audit client to provide a partner or employee to work for a temporary period as if that individual were an employee of the audit client or its affiliates (a 'loan staff assignment') unless the audit client: 33

(a) agrees that the individual concerned will not hold a management position; and
(b) acknowledges its responsibility for directing and supervising the work to be performed, which will not include such matters as:
- making management decisions; or
- exercising discretionary authority to commit the audit client to a particular position or accounting treatment.

Where an audit firm agrees to assist an audit client by providing loan staff, threats to objectivity and independence may be created. A management threat may arise if the employee undertakes work that involves making judgments and taking decisions that are properly the responsibility of management. Thus, for example, interim management arrangements involving participation in the financial reporting function are not acceptable. 34

A self-review threat may also arise if the individual, during the loan staff assignment, is in a position to influence the preparation of the client's financial statements and then, on completion of that assignment, is assigned to the engagement team for that client, with responsibility to report on matters for which he or she was responsible whilst on that loan staff assignment. 35

Where a partner or employee returns to the firm on completion of a loan staff assignment, that individual should not be given any role on the audit involving any function or activity that he or she performed or supervised during that assignment. 36

[2] *For companies, competition authorities have generally treated a 15% shareholding as sufficient to provide a material ability to influence policy.*

37 In considering for how long this restriction is to be observed, the need to realise the potential value to the effectiveness of the audit of the increased knowledge of the client's business gained through the assignment has to be weighed against the potential threats to objectivity and independence. Those threats increase with the length of the assignment and with the intended level of responsibility of the individual within the engagement team. As a minimum, this restriction will apply to at least the first audit of the financial statements following the completion of the loan staff assignment.

Partners and engagement team members joining an audit client

38 **Where a former partner in the audit firm joins the audit client, the audit firm should take action as quickly as possible - and, in any event, before any further work is done by the audit firm in connection with the audit - to ensure that no significant connections remain between the firm and the individual.**

39 Ensuring that no significant connections remain between the firm and the individual requires that:

- all capital balances and similar financial interests be fully settled (including retirement benefits) unless these are made in accordance with pre-determined arrangements that cannot be influenced by any remaining connections between the individual and the firm; and
- the individual does not participate or appear to participate in the audit firm's business or professional activities.

40 **Audit firms should establish policies and procedures that require:**

(a) **all partners in the audit firm to notify the firm of any situation involving their potential employment with any audit client of the firm; and**
(b) **senior members of any engagement team to notify the audit firm of any situation involving their potential employment with the relevant audit client; and**
(c) **other members of any engagement team to notify the audit firm of any situation involving their probable employment with the relevant audit client; and**
(d) **anyone who has given such notice to be removed from the engagement team; and**
(e) **a review of the audit work performed by the resigning or former engagement team member in the current and, where appropriate, the most recent audit.**

41 Objectivity and independence may be threatened where a director, an officer or an employee of the audit client who is in a position to exert direct and significant influence over the preparation of the financial statements has recently been a partner in the audit firm or a member of the engagement team. Such circumstances may create self-interest, familiarity and intimidation threats, particularly when significant connections remain between the individual and the audit firm. Similarly, objectivity and independence may be threatened when an individual knows, or has reason to believe that he or she will or may be joining the audit client at some time in the future.

42 Where a partner in the audit firm or a member of the engagement team for a particular audit client has left the audit firm and taken up employment with that audit client, the significance of the self-interest, familiarity and intimidation threats is assessed and normally depends on such factors as:

- the position that individual had in the engagement team or firm;
- the position that individual has taken at the audit client;
- the amount of involvement that individual will have with the engagement team (especially where it includes former colleagues with whom he or she worked);

- the length of time since that individual was a member of the engagement team or employed by the audit firm.

Following the assessment of any such threats, appropriate safeguards are applied where necessary.

Any review of audit work is performed by a more senior audit professional. If the individual joining the client is an audit partner, the review is performed by an audit partner who is not involved in the audit engagement. Where, due to its size, the audit firm does not have a partner who was not involved in the audit engagement, it seeks either a review by another audit firm or advice from its professional body. 43

Where a partner leaves the firm and is appointed as a director (including as a non-executive director) or to a key management position with an audit client, having acted as audit engagement partner (or as an independent partner, key audit partner or a partner in the chain of command) at any time in the two years prior to this appointment, the firm should resign as auditors.[3] The firm should not accept re-appointment as auditors until a two-year period, commencing when the former partner ceased to act for the client, has elapsed or the former partner ceases employment with the former client, whichever is the sooner. 44

Where a former member of the engagement team (other than an audit engagement partner, a key audit partner or a partner in the chain of command) leaves the audit firm and, within two years of ceasing to hold that position, joins the audit client as a director (including as a non-executive director) or in a key management position, the audit firm should consider whether the composition of the audit team is appropriate. 45

In such circumstances, the audit firm evaluates the appropriateness of the composition of the audit team by reference to the factors listed in paragraph 42 and alters or strengthens the audit team to address any threat to the auditors' objectivity and independence that may be identified. 46

Family members employed by an audit client

Where a person in a position to influence the conduct and outcome of the audit, or a partner in the audit firm, becomes aware that an immediate or close family member is employed by an audit client in a position to exercise influence on the accounting records or financial statements, that individual should either: 47

(a) in the case of an immediate family member of a person in a position to influence the conduct and outcome of the audit, cease to hold a position in which they exert such influence on the audit; or
(b) in the case of a close family member of a person in a position to influence the conduct and outcome of the audit, or any family member of a partner in the audit firm, report the matter to the audit engagement partner to take appropriate action. If it is a close family member of the audit engagement partner or if the audit engagement partner is in doubt as to the action to be taken, the audit engagement partner should resolve the matter in consultation with the ethics partner.

---

[3] *The timing of the audit firm's resignation as auditors is determined in accordance with paragraph 40 of APB Ethical Standard 1. In the case of those public sector bodies where the responsibility for the audit is assigned by legislation, the auditors cannot resign from the audit engagement and they consider alternative safeguards that they can put in place.*

Governance role with audit client

48 Paragraphs 49 to 51 are supplementary to certain statutory or regulatory provisions that prohibit directors of entities from being appointed as their auditors.[4]

49 A partner or employee of the audit firm who undertakes audit work should not accept appointment:

(a) to the board of directors of the audit client;
(b) to any subcommittee of that board; or
(c) to such a position in an entity which holds directly or indirectly more than 20% of the voting rights in the audit client, or in which the audit client holds directly or indirectly more than 20% of the voting rights.

50 Where a person in a position to influence the conduct and outcome of the audit has an immediate or close family member who holds a position described in paragraph 49, the audit firm should take appropriate steps to ensure that the relevant person does not retain a position in which they exert influence on the conduct and outcome of the audit engagement.

51 Where a partner or employee of the audit firm, not being a member of the engagement team, has an immediate or close family member who holds a position described in paragraph 49, that individual should report that fact to the audit engagement partner, who should consider whether the relationship might be regarded by a reasonable and informed third party as impairing, or being thought to impair, the auditors' objectivity. If the audit engagement partner concludes that the auditors' objectivity may be impaired, that individual should consult with the ethics partner to determine whether appropriate safeguards exist. If no such safeguards exist, the audit firm withdraws from the audit engagement.

Employment with audit firm

52 Objectivity and independence may be threatened where a former director or employee of the audit client becomes a member of the engagement team. Self-interest, self-review and familiarity threats may be created where a member of the engagement team has to report on, for example, financial statements which he or she prepared, or elements of the financial statements for which he or she had responsibility, while with the audit client.

53 Where a former director or a former employee of an audit client, who was in a position to exert significant influence over the preparation of the financial statements, joins the audit firm, that individual should not be assigned to a position in which he or she is able to influence the conduct and outcome of the audit for that client or its affiliates for a period of two years following the date of leaving the audit client.

54 In certain circumstances, a longer period of exclusion from the engagement team may be appropriate. For example, threats to objectivity and independence may exist in relation to the audit of the financial statements of any period which are materially

---

[4] In the case of limited companies, for example, section 27 of the Companies Act 1989 contains detailed provisions. Amongst other things, these state that:

'...A person is ineligible for appointment as company auditor of a company if he is (a) an officer or employee of the company, or (b) a partner or employee of such a person, or a partnership of which such a person is a partner, or if he is ineligible by virtue of paragraph (a) or (b) for appointment as company auditor of any associated undertaking of the company.'

affected by the work of that person whilst occupying his or her former position of influence with the audit client. The significance of these threats depends on factors such as:

- the position the individual held with the audit client;
- the length of time since the individual left the audit client;
- the position the individual holds in the engagement team.

Family and other personal relationships

A relationship between a person who is in a position to influence the conduct and outcome of the audit and another party does not generally affect the consideration of the auditors' objectivity and independence. However, if it is a family relationship, and if the family member also has a financial, business or employment relationship with the audit client, then self-interest, familiarity or intimidation threats to the auditors' objectivity and independence may be created. The significance of any such threats depends on such factors as: 55

- the relevant person's involvement in the audit;
- the nature of the relationship between the relevant person and his or her family member;
- the family member's relationship with the audit client.

A distinction is made between immediate family relationships and close family relationships. Immediate family members comprise an individual's spouse (or equivalent) and dependents, whereas close family members comprise parents, non-dependent children and siblings. While an individual can usually be presumed to be aware of matters concerning his or her immediate family members and to be able to influence their behaviour, it is generally recognised that the same levels of knowledge and influence do not exist in the case of close family members. 56

When considering family relationships, it needs to be acknowledged that, in an increasingly secular, open and inclusive society, the concept of what constitutes a family is evolving and relationships between individuals which have no status formally recognised by law may nevertheless be considered as significant as those which do. It may therefore be appropriate to regard certain other personal relationships, particularly those that would be considered close personal relationships, as if they are family relationships. 57

The audit firm should establish policies and procedures that require: 58

(a) partners and professional staff to report to the audit firm any immediate family, close family and other personal relationships involving an audit client of the firm, to which they are a party and which they consider might create a threat to the auditors' objectivity or a perceived loss of independence;
(b) the relevant audit engagement partners to be notified promptly of any immediate family, close family and other personal relationships reported by partners and other professional staff.

The audit engagement partner should: 59

(a) assess the threats to the auditors' objectivity and independence arising from immediate family, close family and other personal relationships on the basis of the information reported to the firm by persons in a position to influence the conduct and outcome of the audit;

(b) apply appropriate safeguards to eliminate the threat or reduce it to an acceptable level; and
(c) where there are unresolved matters or the need for clarification, consult with the ethics partner.

60 Where such matters are identified or reported, the audit engagement partner or the ethics partner assesses the information available and the potential for there to be a threat to the auditors' objectivity and independence, treating any personal relationship as if it were a family relationship.

External consultants involved in the audit

61 Audit firms may employ external consultants as experts in order to obtain sufficient appropriate audit evidence regarding certain financial statement assertions.[5] There is a risk that an expert's objectivity and independence will be impaired if the expert is related to the entity, for example by being financially dependent upon or having an investment in, the entity.

62 **The audit engagement partner should be satisfied that any external consultant involved in the audit will be objective and document the rationale for that conclusion.**

63 The audit engagement partner obtains information from the external consultant as to the existence of any connections that they have with the audit client including:

- financial interests;
- business relationships;
- employment (past, present and future);
- family and other personal relationships.

Effective date

64 Effective for audits of financial statements for periods commencing on or after 15 December 2004.

65 Firms may complete audit engagements relating to periods commencing prior to 15 December 2004 in accordance with existing ethical guidance from the relevant professional body, putting in place any necessary changes in the subsequent engagement period.

66 Financial interests held at 15 December 2004 that were permissible in accordance with existing ethical guidance (including transitional arrangements) from the relevant professional body, but are prohibited by the requirements of paragraphs 5 to 24, may continue to be held for up to twelve months after that date provided that:

- no new interest is acquired; and
- the audit firm satisfies itself that there are adequate safeguards in place to reduce the threat to acceptable levels.

67 Business relationships existing at 15 December 2004 that were permissible in accordance with existing ethical guidance (including transitional arrangements) from

[5] ISA (UK and Ireland) 620 'Using the work of an Expert' states that the auditor should evaluate the objectivity of the expert.

the relevant professional body, but are prohibited by the requirements of paragraphs 25 to 31, may continue to exist for up to twelve months after that date provided that:
- no new contracts under the business relationship are entered into; and
- the audit firm satisfies itself that there are adequate safeguards in place to reduce the threat to acceptable levels.

The requirements of paragraph 44 in respect of employment with the audit client do not apply if: **68**
- the relevant person has notified an intention to join the client prior to 5 October 2004 or has entered into contractual arrangements prior to that date; and
- the continuation of the audit relationship was permitted by existing ethical guidance (including transitional arrangements) from the relevant professional body.

ES2 (Revised)*
Financial, business, employment and personal relationships

(Revised April 2008)

Contents

	Paragraph
Introduction	1 – 4
Financial relationships	5 – 26
Business relationships	27 – 35
Employment relationships	36 – 58
Family and other personal relationships	59 – 64
External consultants involved in the audit	65 – 67
Effective date	68 – 71

---

* *Revisions to this Standard became effective for audits of financial statements for periods commencing on or after 6 April 2008. The Standard effective before this date is available from the APB website.*

Preface

APB Ethical Standards apply in the audit of financial statements. They are read in the context of the Auditing Practices Board's Statement "The Auditing Practices Board – Scope and Authority of Pronouncements (Revised)" which sets out the application and authority of APB Ethical Standards.

The terms used in APB Ethical Standards are explained in the Glossary.

APB Ethical Standards apply to audits of financial statements in both the private and the public sectors. However, auditors in the public sector are subject to more complex ethical requirements than their private sector counterparts. This includes, for example, compliance with legislation such as the Prevention of Corruption Act 1916, concerning gifts and hospitality, and with Cabinet Office guidance.

Introduction

1 APB Ethical Standard 1 requires the audit engagement partner to identify and assess the circumstances which could adversely affect the auditor's objectivity ('threats'), including any perceived loss of independence, and to apply procedures ('safeguards') which will either:

(a) eliminate the threat; or
(b) reduce the threat to an acceptable level (that is, a level at which it is not probable that a reasonable and informed third party would conclude that the auditor's objectivity and independence is impaired or is likely to be impaired).
(c) When considering safeguards, where the audit engagement partner chooses to reduce rather than to eliminate a threat to objectivity and independence, he or she recognises that this judgment may not be shared by users of the financial statements and that he or she may be required to justify the decision.

2 This Standard provides requirements and guidance on specific circumstances arising out of financial, business, employment and personal relationships with the audited entity, which may create threats to the auditor's objectivity or perceived loss of independence. It gives examples of safeguards that can, in some circumstances, eliminate the threat or reduce it to an acceptable level. In circumstances where this is not possible, either the relationship in question is not entered into or the auditor either does not accept or withdraws from the audit engagement, as appropriate.

3 Whenever a possible or actual breach of an APB Ethical Standard is identified, the audit engagement partner, in the first instance, and the ethics partner, where appropriate, assesses the implications of the breach, determines whether there are safeguards that can be put in place or other actions that can be taken to address any potential adverse consequences and considers whether there is a need to resign from the audit engagement.

4 An inadvertent violation of this Standard does not necessarily call into question the audit firm's ability to give an audit opinion provided that:

(a) the audit firm has established policies and procedures that require all partners and staff to report any breach promptly to the audit engagement partner or to the ethics partner as appropriate;
(b) the audit engagement partner or ethics partner promptly notifies the partner or member of staff that any matter which has given rise to a breach is to be addressed as soon as possible and ensures that such action is taken;

(c) safeguards, if appropriate, are applied (for example, having another partner review the work done by the relevant partner or member of staff or by removing him or her from the engagement team); and
(d) the actions taken and the rationale for them are documented.

Financial relationships

General considerations

5 A financial interest is an equity or other security, debenture, loan or other debt instrument of an entity, including rights and obligations to acquire such an interest and derivatives directly related to such an interest.

6 Financial interests may be:

(a) owned directly, rather than through intermediaries (a 'direct financial interest'); or
(b) owned through intermediaries, for example, an open ended investment company or a pension scheme (an 'indirect financial interest').

7 **Save where the circumstances contemplated in paragraphs 9, 11, 18 or 20 apply, the audit firm, any partner in the audit firm, a person in a position to influence the conduct and outcome of the audit or an immediate family member of such a person shall not hold:**

(a) **any direct financial interest in an audited entity or an affiliate of an audited entity; or**
(b) **any indirect financial interest in an audited entity or an affiliate of an audited entity, where the investment is material to the audit firm or the individual, or to the intermediary; or**
(c) **any indirect financial interest in an audited entity or an affiliate of an audited entity, where the person holding it has both:**
   (i) **the ability to influence the investment decisions of the intermediary; and**
   (ii) **actual knowledge of the existence of the underlying investment in the audited entity.**

8 The threats to the auditor's objectivity and independence, where a direct financial interest or a material indirect financial interest in the audited entity is held by the audit firm or by one of the individuals specified in paragraph 7 are such that no safeguards can eliminate them or reduce them to an acceptable level.

9 Where an immediate family member of a partner who is not in a position to influence the conduct and outcome of the audit holds a financial interest in an audited entity or an affiliate of an audited entity as a consequence of:

- their compensation arrangements (for example, a share option scheme, where the shares have not vested), or
- a decision made, or a transaction undertaken, by an entity with whom that immediate family member has a contractual business or employment arrangement (for example, a partnership agreement),

such financial interests are not generally considered to threaten the auditor's objectivity and independence. However, where such interests are significant or the relevant partner has close working contacts with the engagement team, the ethics partner considers whether any safeguards need to be put in place.

For the purposes of paragraph 7, where holdings in an authorised unit or investment trust, an open ended investment company or an equivalent investment vehicle which is audited by the audit firm, are held by a partner in the audit firm, who is not in a position to influence the conduct and outcome of the audit, or an immediate family member of such a partner, these are to be treated as indirect financial interests. Such interests can therefore be held as long as:

(a) they are not material to the individual; and
(b) the individual has no influence over the investment decisions of the audited entity.

Where a person in a position to influence the conduct and outcome of the audit or a partner in the audit firm, or any of their immediate family members are members or shareholders of an audited entity, as a result of membership requirements, or equivalent, the audit firm ensures that no more than the minimum number of shares necessary to comply with the requirement are held and that this shareholding is not material to either the audited entity or the individual. Disclosure of such shareholdings will be made to those charged with governance of the audited entity, in accordance with APB Ethical Standard 1, paragraph 56.

Where one of the financial interests specified in paragraph 7 is held by:

(a) *the audit firm, a partner in the audit firm or an immediate family member of such a partner:* the entire financial interest is disposed of, a sufficient amount of an indirect financial interest is disposed of so that the remaining interest is no longer material, or the firm does not accept (or withdraws from) the audit engagement;
(b) *a person in a position to influence the conduct and outcome of the audit:* the entire financial interest is disposed of, a sufficient amount of an indirect financial interest is disposed of so that the remaining interest is no longer material, or that person does not retain a position in which they exert such influence on the audit engagement;
(c) *an immediate family member of a person in a position to influence the conduct and outcome of the audit:* the entire financial interest is disposed of, a sufficient amount of an indirect financial interest is disposed of so that the remaining interest is no longer material, or the person in a position to influence the conduct and outcome of the audit does not retain a position in which they exert such influence on the audit engagement.

Where one of the financial interests specified in paragraph 7 is acquired unintentionally, as a result of an external event (for example, inheritance, gift, or merger of firms or companies), the disposal of the financial interest is required immediately, or as soon as possible after the relevant person has actual knowledge of and the right to dispose of the interest.

Where the disposal of a financial interest does not take place immediately, the audit firm adopts safeguards to preserve its objectivity until the financial interest is disposed. These may include the temporary exclusion of the person in a position to influence the conduct and outcome of the audit from such influence on the audit or a review of the relevant person's audit work by an audit partner having sufficient experience and authority to fulfill the role, who is not involved in the audit engagement.

Where the audit firm or one of the individuals specified in paragraph 7 holds an indirect financial interest but does not have both:

(a) the ability to influence the investment decisions of the intermediary; and

(b) actual knowledge of the existence of the underlying investment in the audited entity,

there may not be a threat to the auditor's objectivity and independence. For example, where the indirect financial interest takes the form of an investment in a pension fund, the composition of the funds and the size and nature of any underlying investment in the audited entity may be known but there is unlikely to be any influence on investment decisions, as the fund will generally be managed independently on a discretionary basis. In the case of an 'index tracker' fund, the investment in the audited entity is determined by the composition of the relevant index and there may be no threat to objectivity. As long as the person holding the indirect interest is not directly involved in the audit of the intermediary, nor able to influence the individual investment decisions of the intermediary, any threat to the auditor's objectivity and independence may be regarded as insignificant.

16 Where the audit firm or one of the individuals specified in paragraph 7 holds a beneficial interest in a properly operated 'blind' trust, they are (by definition) completely unaware of the identity of the underlying investments. If these include an investment in the audited entity, this means that they are unaware of the existence of an indirect financial interest. In these circumstances, there is no threat to the auditor's objectivity and independence.

17 **Where a person in a position to influence the conduct and outcome of the audit or a partner in the audit firm becomes aware that a close family member holds one of the financial interests specified in paragraph 7, that individual shall report the matter to the audit engagement partner to take appropriate action. If it is a close family member of the audit engagement partner, or if the audit engagement partner is in doubt as to the action to be taken, the audit engagement partner shall resolve the matter through consultation with the ethics partner.**

Financial interests held as trustee

18 Where a direct or an indirect financial interest in the audited entity or its affiliates is held in a trustee capacity by a person in a position to influence the conduct and outcome of the audit, or an immediate family member of such a person, a self-interest threat may be created because either the existence of the trustee interest may influence the conduct of the audit or the trust may influence the actions of the audited entity. Accordingly, such a trustee interest is only held when:

- the relevant person is not an identified potential beneficiary of the trust; and
- the financial interest held by the trust in the audited entity is not material to the trust; and
- the trust is not able to exercise significant influence over the audited entity or an affiliate of the audited entity; and
- the relevant person does not have significant influence over the investment decisions made by the trust, in so far as they relate to the financial interest in the audited entity.

19 Where it is not clear whether the financial interest held by the trust in the audited entity is material to the trust or whether the trust is able to exercise significant influence over the audited entity, the financial interest is reported to the ethics partner, so that a decision can be made as to the steps that need to be taken.

20 A direct or an indirect financial interest in the audited entity or its affiliates held in a trustee capacity by the audit firm or by a partner in the audit firm (other than a partner in a position to influence the conduct and outcome of the audit), or an

immediate family member of such a person, can only be held when the relevant person is not an identified potential beneficiary of the trust.

Financial interests held by audit firm pension schemes

Where the pension scheme of an audit firm has a financial interest in an audited entity or its affiliates and the firm has any influence over the trustees' investment decisions (other than indirect strategic and policy decisions), the self-interest threat created is such that no safeguards can eliminate it or reduce it to an acceptable level. In other cases (for example, where the pension scheme invests through a collective investment scheme and the firm's influence is limited to investment policy decisions, such as the allocation between different categories of investment), the ethics partner considers the acceptability of the position, having regard to the materiality of the financial interest to the pension scheme.   21

Loans and guarantees

Where audit firms, persons in a position to influence the conduct and outcome of the audit or immediate family members of such persons: 22

(a) accept a loan[1] or a guarantee of their borrowings from an audited entity; or
(b) make a loan to or guarantee the borrowings of an audited entity,

a self-interest threat and an intimidation threat to the auditor's objectivity can be created or there may be a perceived loss of independence. In a number of situations, no safeguards can eliminate this threat or reduce it to an acceptable level.

Audit firms, persons in a position to influence the conduct and outcome of the audit and immediate family members of such persons shall not make a loan to, or guarantee the borrowings of, an audited entity or its affiliates unless this represents a deposit made with a bank or similar deposit taking institution in the ordinary course of business and on normal business terms.   23

Audit firms shall not accept a loan from, or have their borrowings guaranteed by, the audited entity or its affiliates unless: 24

(a) the audited entity is a bank or similar deposit taking institution; and
(b) the loan or guarantee is made in the ordinary course of business on normal business terms; and
(c) the loan or guarantee is not material to both the audit firm and the audited entity.

Persons in a position to influence the conduct and outcome of the audit and immediate family members of such persons shall not accept a loan from, or have their borrowings guaranteed by, the audited entity or its affiliates unless: 25

(a) the audited entity is a bank or similar deposit taking institution; and
(b) the loan or guarantee is made in the ordinary course of business on normal business terms; and
(c) the loan or guarantee is not material to the audited entity.

Loans by an audited entity that is a bank or similar institution to a person in a position to influence the conduct and outcome of the audit, or an immediate family member of such a person (for example, home mortgages, bank overdrafts or car   26

---

[1] *For the purpose of this standard, the term 'loan' does not include ordinary trade credit arrangements or deposits placed for goods or services, unless they are material to either party (see paragraph 28).*

loans), do not create an unacceptable threat to objectivity and independence, provided that normal business terms apply. However, where such loans are in arrears by a significant amount, this creates an intimidation threat that is unacceptable. Where such a situation arises, the person in a position to influence the conduct and outcome of the audit reports the matter to the audit engagement partner or to the ethics partner, as appropriate and ceases to have any involvement with the audit. The audit engagement partner or, where appropriate, the ethics partner considers whether any audit work is to be reperformed.

Business relationships

27 A business relationship between:

(a) the audit firm or a person who is in a position to influence the conduct and outcome of the audit, or an immediate family member of such a person, and
(b) the audited entity or its affiliates, or its management

involves the two parties having a common commercial interest. Business relationships may create self-interest, advocacy or intimidation threats to the auditor's objectivity and perceived loss of independence. Examples include:

- joint ventures with the audited entity or with a director, officer or other individual who performs a management role for the audited entity;
- arrangements to combine one or more services or products of the audit firm with one or more services or products of the audited entity and to market the package with reference to both parties;
- distribution or marketing arrangements under which the audit firm acts as a distributor or marketer of any of the audited entity's products or services, or the audited entity acts as the distributor or marketer of any of the products or services of the audit firm;
- other commercial transactions, such as the audit firm leasing its office space from the audited entity.

28 **Audit firms, persons in a position to influence the conduct and outcome of the audit and immediate family members of such persons shall not enter into business relationships with an audited entity, its management or its affiliates except where they:**

- **involve the purchase of goods and services from the audit firm or the audited entity in the ordinary course of business and on an arm's length basis and which are not material to either party; or**
- **are clearly inconsequential to either party.**

29 Where a business relationship exists, that is not permitted under paragraph 28, and has been entered into by:

(a) *the audit firm:* either the relationship is terminated or the firm does not accept (or withdraws from) the audit engagement;
(b) *a person in a position to influence the conduct and outcome of the audit:* either the relationship is terminated or that person does not retain a position in which they exert such influence on the audit engagement;
(c) *an immediate family member of a person in a position to influence the conduct and outcome of the audit:* either the relationship is terminated or the person in a position to influence the conduct and outcome of the audit does not retain such a position.

Financial, business, employment and personal relationships ES2 (Revised) 61

Where there is an unavoidable delay in the termination of a business relationship, the audit firm adopts safeguards to preserve its objectivity until the relationship is terminated. These may include a review of the relevant person's audit work or a temporary exclusion of the relevant person from influence on conduct and outcome of the audit.

Compliance with paragraph 28 is not intended to prevent an audit firm giving advice in accordance with regulatory requirements[2] to a third party in relation to investment products or services, including those supplied by an audited entity. In such circumstances, the audit firm considers the advocacy and self-interest threats that might be created by the provision of this advice where it gives rise to commission or similar payments by the audited entity to the audit firm and assesses whether any safeguards are required. 30

Where a person in a position to influence the conduct and outcome of the audit becomes aware that a close family member has entered into one of the business relationships specified in paragraph 27, that individual shall report the matter to the audit engagement partner to take appropriate action. If it is a close family member of the audit engagement partner or if the audit engagement partner is in doubt as to the action to be taken, the audit engagement partner shall resolve the matter through consultation with the ethics partner. 31

Where there are doubts as to whether a transaction or series of transactions are either in the ordinary course of business and on an arm's length basis or of such materiality that they constitute a threat to the audit firm's objectivity and independence, the audit engagement partner reports the issue: 32

- to the ethics partner, so that a decision can be made as to the appropriate action that needs to be taken to ensure that the matter is resolved; and
- to those charged with governance of the audited entity, together with other significant facts and matters that bear upon the auditor's objectivity and independence, to obtain their views on the matter.

Where there are doubts about whether a reasonable and informed third party would conclude that a business relationship is clearly inconsequential to either party and would not therefore present a threat to independence, then it is not clearly inconsequential. 33

An audit firm shall not provide audit services to any entity or person able to influence the affairs of the audit firm or the performance of any audit engagement undertaken by the audit firm. 34

This prohibition applies to: 35

(a) any entity that owns any significant part of an audit firm, or is an affiliate of such an entity; or
(b) any shareholder, director or other person in a position to direct the affairs of such an entity or its affiliate.

A significant ownership is one that carries the ability materially to influence the policy of an entity.[3]

---

[2] *Firms providing such services will be authorised either by the Financial Services Authority or by their professional accountancy body acting as a Designated Professional Body.*

[3] *For companies, competition authorities have generally treated a 15% shareholding as sufficient to provide a material ability to influence policy.*

Employment relationships

Management role with an audited entity

36 **An audit firm shall not admit to the partnership, or employ a person to undertake audit work, if that person is also employed by the audited entity or its affiliates ('dual employment').**

Loan staff assignments

37 **An audit firm shall not enter into an agreement with an audited entity to provide a partner or employee to work for a temporary period as if that individual were an employee of the audited entity or its affiliates (a 'loan staff assignment') unless:**

   (a) **the agreement is for a short period of time and does not involve staff or partners performing non-audit services that would not be permitted under APB Ethical Standard 5; and**
   (b) **the audited entity agrees that the individual concerned will not hold a management position, and acknowledges its responsibility for directing and supervising the work to be performed, which will not include such matters as:**
   - **making management decisions; or**
   - **exercising discretionary authority to commit the audited entity to a particular position or accounting treatment.**

38 Where an audit firm agrees to assist an audited entity by providing loan staff, threats to objectivity and independence may be created. A management threat may arise if the employee undertakes work that involves making judgments and taking decisions that are properly the responsibility of management. Thus, for example, interim management arrangements involving participation in the financial reporting function are not acceptable.

39 A self-review threat may also arise if the individual, during the loan staff assignment, is in a position to influence the preparation of the audited entity's financial statements and then, on completion of that assignment, is assigned to the engagement team for that entity, with responsibility to report on matters for which he or she was responsible whilst on that loan staff assignment.

40 **Where a partner or employee returns to the firm on completion of a loan staff assignment, that individual shall not be given any role on the audit involving any function or activity that he or she performed or supervised during that assignment.**

41 In considering for how long this restriction is to be observed, the need to realise the potential value to the effectiveness of the audit of the increased knowledge of the audited entity's business gained through the assignment has to be weighed against the potential threats to objectivity and independence. Those threats increase with the length of the assignment and with the intended level of responsibility of the individual within the engagement team. As a minimum, this restriction will apply to at least the first audit of the financial statements following the completion of the loan staff assignment.

Partners and engagement team members joining an audited entity

42 **Where a former partner in the audit firm joins the audited entity, the audit firm shall take action as quickly as possible – and, in any event, before any further work is done**

Financial, business, employment and personal relationships ES2 (Revised)

by the audit firm in connection with the audit – to ensure that no significant connections remain between the firm and the individual.

Ensuring that no significant connections remain between the firm and the individual requires that:

- all capital balances and similar financial interests be fully settled (including retirement benefits) unless these are made in accordance with pre-determined arrangements that cannot be influenced by any remaining connections between the individual and the firm; and
- the individual does not participate or appear to participate in the audit firm's business or professional activities.

43

Audit firms shall establish policies and procedures that require:

44

(a) all partners in the audit firm to notify the firm of any situation involving their potential employment with any entity audited by the firm; and
(b) senior members of any engagement team to notify the audit firm of any situation involving their potential employment with the relevant audited entity; and
(c) other members of any engagement team to notify the audit firm of any situation involving their probable employment with the relevant audited entity; and
(d) anyone who has given such notice to be removed from the engagement team; and
(e) a review of the audit work performed by the resigning or former engagement team member in the current and, where appropriate, the most recent audit.

Objectivity and independence may be threatened where a director, an officer or an employee of the audited entity who is in a position to exert direct and significant influence over the preparation of the financial statements has recently been a partner in the audit firm or a member of the engagement team. Such circumstances may create self-interest, familiarity and intimidation threats, particularly when significant connections remain between the individual and the audit firm. Similarly, objectivity and independence may be threatened when an individual knows, or has reason to believe that he or she will or may be joining the audited entity at some time in the future.

45

Where a partner in the audit firm or a member of the engagement team for a particular audited entity has left the audit firm and taken up employment with that entity, the significance of the self-interest, familiarity and intimidation threats is assessed and normally depends on such factors as:

46

- the position that individual had in the engagement team or firm;
- the position that individual has taken at the audited entity;
- the amount of involvement that individual will have with the engagement team (especially where it includes former colleagues with whom he or she worked);
- the length of time since that individual was a member of the engagement team or employed by the audit firm.

Following the assessment of any such threats, appropriate safeguards are applied where necessary.

Any review of audit work is performed by a more senior audit professional. If the individual joining the audited entity is an audit partner, the review is performed by an audit partner who is not involved in the audit engagement. Where, due to its size, the audit firm does not have a partner who was not involved in the audit engagement, it seeks either a review by another audit firm or advice from its professional body.

47

48 Where a partner leaves the firm and is appointed as a director (including as a non-executive director) or to a key management position with an audited entity[4], having acted as audit engagement partner (or as an engagement quality control reviewer, key partner involved in the audit or a partner in the chain of command) at any time in the two years prior to this appointment, the firm shall resign as auditor.[5] The firm shall not accept re-appointment as auditor until a two-year period, commencing when the former partner ceased to have an ability to influence the conduct and outcome of the audit, has elapsed or the former partner ceases employment with the former audited entity, whichever is the sooner.

49 Where a former member of the engagement team (other than an audit engagement partner, a key partner involved in the audit or a partner in the chain of command) leaves the audit firm and, within two years of ceasing to hold that position, joins the audited entity as a director (including as a non-executive director) or in a key management position, the audit firm shall consider whether the composition of the audit team is appropriate.

50 In such circumstances, the audit firm evaluates the appropriateness of the composition of the audit team by reference to the factors listed in paragraph 46 and alters or strengthens the audit team to address any threat to the auditor's objectivity and independence that may be identified.

Family members employed by an audited entity

51 Where a person in a position to influence the conduct and outcome of the audit, or a partner in the audit firm, becomes aware that an immediate or close family member is employed by an audited entity in a position to exercise influence on the accounting records or financial statements, that individual shall either:

(a) in the case of an immediate family member of a person in a position to influence the conduct and outcome of the audit, cease to hold a position in which they exert such influence on the audit; or

(b) in the case of a close family member of a person in a position to influence the conduct and outcome of the audit, or any family member of a partner in the audit firm, report the matter to the audit engagement partner to take appropriate action. If it is a close family member of the audit engagement partner or if the audit engagement partner is in doubt as to the action to be taken, the audit engagement partner shall resolve the matter in consultation with the ethics partner.

---

[4] *UK legislation provides that each of the Recognised Supervisory Bodies must have adequate rules and practices to ensure that a key audit partner (the individual responsible for the statutory audit and individuals responsible for a parent undertaking or a material subsidiary undertaking) of a firm appointed by a public interest entity as auditor is prohibited from being appointed as a director or other officer of the entity during a period of two years commencing on the date on which his work as key audit partner ended.*

[5] *The timing of the audit firm's resignation as auditor is determined in accordance with paragraph 45 of APB Ethical Standard 1. In the case of those public sector bodies where the responsibility for the audit is assigned by legislation, the auditor cannot resign from the audit engagement and considers alternative safeguards that can be put in place.*

Governance role with an audited entity

Paragraphs 53 to 55 are supplementary to certain statutory or regulatory provisions that prohibit directors of entities from being appointed as their auditor.[6]   **52**

A partner, or employee of the audit firm who undertakes audit work, shall not accept appointment: **53**

(a) to the board of directors of the audited entity;
(b) to any subcommittee of that board; or
(c) to such a position in an entity which holds directly or indirectly more than 20% of the voting rights in the audited entity, or in which the audited entity holds directly or indirectly more than 20% of the voting rights.

Where a person in a position to influence the conduct and outcome of the audit becomes aware that an immediate or close family member holds a position described in paragraph 53, the audit firm shall take appropriate steps to ensure that the relevant person does not retain a position in which they exert influence on the conduct and outcome of the audit engagement.   **54**

Where a partner or employee of the audit firm, not being a member of the engagement team, becomes aware that an immediate or close family member holds a position described in paragraph 53, that individual shall report that fact to the audit engagement partner, who shall consider whether the relationship might be regarded by a reasonable and informed third party as impairing, or being thought to impair, the auditor's objectivity. If the audit engagement partner concludes that the auditor's objectivity may be impaired, that individual shall consult with the ethics partner to determine whether appropriate safeguards exist. If no such safeguards exist, the audit firm withdraws from the audit engagement.   **55**

Employment with audit firm

Objectivity and independence may be threatened where a former director or employee of the audited entity becomes a member of the engagement team. Self-interest, self-review and familiarity threats may be created where a member of the engagement team has to report on, for example, financial statements which he or she prepared, or elements of the financial statements for which he or she had responsibility, while with the audited entity.   **56**

Where a former director or a former employee of an audited entity, who was in a position to exert significant influence over the preparation of the financial statements, joins the audit firm, that individual shall not be assigned to a position in which he or she is able to influence the conduct and outcome of the audit for that entity or its affiliates for a period of two years following the date of leaving the audited entity.   **57**

In certain circumstances, a longer period of exclusion from the engagement team may be appropriate. For example, threats to objectivity and independence may exist in relation to the audit of the financial statements of any period which are materially affected by the work of that person whilst occupying his or her former position of   **58**

---

[6] *For example, in the case of limited companies and certain other organisations, section 1214 of the Companies Act 2006 contains detailed provisions. Amongst other things, these state that:*

'...A person may not act as statutory auditor of an audited person if [he] is (a) an officer or employee of the audited person, or (b) a partner or employee of such a person, or a partnership of which such a person is a partner.'

influence with the audited entity. The significance of these threats depends on factors such as:

- the position the individual held with the audited entity;
- the length of time since the individual left the audited entity;
- the position the individual holds in the engagement team.

Family and other personal relationships

59 A relationship between a person who is in a position to influence the conduct and outcome of the audit and another party does not generally affect the consideration of the auditor's objectivity and independence. However, if it is a family relationship, and if the family member also has a financial, business or employment relationship with the audited entity, then self-interest, familiarity or intimidation threats to the auditor's objectivity and independence may be created. The significance of any such threats depends on such factors as:

- the relevant person's involvement in the audit;
- the nature of the relationship between the relevant person and his or her family member;
- the family member's relationship with the audited entity.

60 A distinction is made between immediate family relationships and close family relationships. Immediate family members comprise an individual's spouse (or equivalent) and dependents, whereas close family members comprise parents, non-dependent children and siblings. While an individual can usually be presumed to be aware of matters concerning his or her immediate family members and to be able to influence their behaviour, it is generally recognised that the same levels of knowledge and influence do not exist in the case of close family members.

61 When considering family relationships, it needs to be acknowledged that, in an increasingly secular, open and inclusive society, the concept of what constitutes a family is evolving and relationships between individuals which have no status formally recognised by law may nevertheless be considered as significant as those which do. It may therefore be appropriate to regard certain other personal relationships, particularly those that would be considered close personal relationships, as if they are family relationships.

62 The audit firm shall establish policies and procedures that require:

   (a) partners and professional staff to report to the audit firm any immediate family, close family and other personal relationships involving an entity audited by the firm, to which they are a party and which they consider might create a threat to the auditor's objectivity or a perceived loss of independence;

   (b) the relevant audit engagement partners to be notified promptly of any immediate family, close family and other personal relationships reported by partners and other professional staff.

63 The audit engagement partner shall:

   (a) assess the threats to the auditor's objectivity and independence arising from immediate family, close family and other personal relationships on the basis of the information reported to the firm by persons in a position to influence the conduct and outcome of the audit;

   (b) apply appropriate safeguards to eliminate the threat or reduce it to an acceptable level; and

(c) where there are unresolved matters or the need for clarification, consult with the ethics partner.

Where such matters are identified or reported, the audit engagement partner or the ethics partner assesses the information available and the potential for there to be a threat to the auditor's objectivity and independence, treating any personal relationship as if it were a family relationship.

External consultants involved in the audit

Audit firms may employ external consultants as experts in order to obtain sufficient appropriate audit evidence regarding certain financial statement assertions.[7] There is a risk that an expert's objectivity and independence will be impaired if the expert is related to the entity, for example by being financially dependent upon or having an investment in, the entity.

The audit engagement partner shall be satisfied that any external consultant involved in the audit will be objective and document the rationale for that conclusion.

The audit engagement partner obtains information from the external consultant as to the existence of any connections that they have with the audited entity including:

- financial interests;
- business relationships;
- employment (past, present and future);
- family and other personal relationships.

Effective date

Revisions to this Ethical Standard become effective for audits of financial statements for periods commencing on or after 6 April 2008.

Firms may complete audit engagements relating to periods commencing prior to 6 April 2008 in accordance with existing ethical standards, putting in place any necessary changes in the subsequent engagement period.

On appointment as auditor to an entity, an audit firm may continue in a business relationship or a loan staff arrangement which is already contracted at the date of appointment, until the earlier of either:

(i) the completion of the specific obligations under the contract or the end of the contract term, where this is set out in the contract; or

(ii) one year after the date of appointment, where obligations or a term are not defined,

provided that the need for additional safeguards is assessed and if considered necessary, those additional safeguards are applied.

The requirements of paragraph 48 in respect of employment with the audited entity for partners becoming a key partner involved in the audit as a result of the change in definition introduced with effect from 6 April 2008 do not apply if:

---

[7] *ISA (UK and Ireland) 620* 'Using the work of an Expert' *states that the auditor should evaluate the objectivity of the expert.*

- the relevant person has notified an intention to join the audited entity prior to 6 April 2008 or has entered into contractual arrangements prior to that date; and
- the continuation of the audit relationship was permitted by existing ethical standards.

ES3
Long association with the audit engagement
(Re-issued December 2004)

Contents

	Paragraphs
Introduction	1 - 4
General provisions	5 - 11
Additional provisions related to audits of listed companies	12 - 18
Effective date	19 - 22

Preface

APB Ethical Standards apply in the audit of financial statements. They should be read in the context of the Auditing Practices Board's Statement "The Auditing Practices Board – Scope and Authority of Pronouncements (Revised)" which sets out the application and authority of APB Ethical Standards.

The terms used in APB Ethical Standards are explained in the Glossary.

APB Ethical Standards apply to audits of financial statements in both the private and the public sectors. However, auditors in the public sector are subject to more complex ethical requirements than their private sector counterparts. This includes, for example, compliance with legislation such as the Prevention of Corruption Act 1916, concerning gifts and hospitality, and with Cabinet Office guidance.

Introduction

1. APB Ethical Standard 1 requires the audit engagement partner to identify and assess the circumstances which could adversely affect the auditors' objectivity ('threats'), including any perceived loss of independence, and to apply procedures ('safeguards') which will either:

    (a) eliminate the threat; or
    (b) reduce the threat to an acceptable level (that is, a level at which it is not probable that a reasonable and informed third party would conclude that the auditors' objectivity and independence either is impaired or is likely to be impaired).

    When considering safeguards, where the audit engagement partner chooses to reduce rather than to eliminate a threat to objectivity and independence, he or she recognises that this judgment may not be shared by users of the financial statements and that he or she may be required to justify the decision.

2. This Standard provides requirements and guidance on specific circumstances arising out of long association with the audit engagement, which may create threats to the auditors' objectivity or perceived loss of independence. It gives examples of safeguards that can, in some circumstances, eliminate the threat or reduce it to an acceptable level. In circumstances where this is not possible, the auditors either do not accept or withdraw from the audit engagement, as appropriate.

3. Whenever a possible or actual breach of an APB Ethical Standard is identified, the audit engagement partner, in the first instance, and the ethics partner, where appropriate, assesses the implications of the breach, determines whether there are safeguards that can be put in place or other actions that can be taken to address any potential adverse consequences and considers whether there is a need to resign from the audit engagement.

4. An inadvertent violation of this Standard does not necessarily call into question the audit firm's ability to give an audit opinion provided that:

    (a) the audit firm has established policies and procedures that require all partners and staff to report any breach promptly to the audit engagement partner or to the ethics partner, as appropriate;
    (b) the audit engagement partner or ethics partner ensures that any matter which has given rise to a breach is addressed as soon as possible;

(c) safeguards, if appropriate, are applied (for example, by having another partner review the work done by the relevant partner or member of staff or by removing him or her from the engagement team): and
(d) the actions taken and the rationale for them are documented.

General provisions

The audit firm should establish policies and procedures to monitor the length of time that audit engagement partners, key audit partners and staff in senior positions serve as members of the engagement team for each audit. 5

Where audit engagement partners, key audit partners and staff in senior positions have a long association with the audit, the audit firm should assess the threats to the auditors' objectivity and independence and, where the threats are other than clearly insignificant, should apply safeguards to reduce the threats to an acceptable level. Where appropriate safeguards cannot be applied, the audit firm should either resign as auditors or not stand for reappointment, as appropriate.[1] 6

Where audit engagement partners, key audit partners and staff in senior positions have a long association with the audit client, self-interest, self-review and familiarity threats to the auditors' objectivity may arise. Similarly, such circumstances may result in an actual or perceived loss of independence. The significance of such threats depends upon factors such as: 7

- the role of the individual in the engagement team;
- the proportion of time that the audit client contributes to the individual's annual billable hours;
- the length of time that the individual has been associated with that audit engagement.

In order to address such threats, audit firms apply safeguards. Appropriate safeguards may include: 8

- removing ('rotating') the audit partners and the other senior members of the engagement team after a pre-determined number of years;
- involving an additional partner, who is not and has not recently been a member of the engagement team, to review the work done by the audit partners and the other senior members of the engagement team and to advise as necessary;
- applying independent internal quality reviews to the engagement in question.

Once an audit engagement partner has held this role for a continuous period of ten years, careful consideration is given as to whether a reasonable and informed third party would consider the audit firm's objectivity and independence to be impaired. Where the individual concerned is not rotated after ten years, it is important that: 9

(a) alternative safeguards such as those noted in paragraph 8 are applied; or
(b) (i) the reasoning as to why the individual continues to participate in the audit engagement is documented; and
(ii) the facts are communicated to those charged with governance of the audit client in accordance with paragraphs 49-53 of APB Ethical Standard 1.

The audit firm's policies and procedures set out the circumstances in which the audit engagement partners responsible for the audits of non-listed clients are subject to 10

---

[1] In the case of those public sector bodies where the responsibility for the audit is assigned by legislation, the auditors cannot resign from the audit engagement.

accelerated rotation requirements, such as those set out in paragraph 12. These policies take into consideration the nature of the entity's business, its size, the number of its employees and the range of its stakeholders in addition to the factors set out in paragraph 7.

11 Any scheme of rotation of audit partners and other senior members of the engagement team needs to take into account the factors which affect the quality of the audit work, including the experience and continuity of members of the engagement team and the need to ensure appropriate succession planning.

Additional provisions related to audits of listed companies

The audit engagement partner and the independent partner

12 In the case of listed companies, save where the circumstances contemplated in paragraph 13 and 14 apply, the audit firm should establish policies and procedures to ensure that:
   (a) no one should act as audit engagement partner or as independent partner for a continuous period longer than five years;
   (b) where an independent partner becomes the audit engagement partner, the combined period of service in these positions should not exceed five years; and
   (c) anyone who has acted as the audit engagement partner or the independent partner, or held a combination of such positions, for a particular audit client for a period of five years, whether continuously or in aggregate, should not hold any position of responsibility in relation to the audit engagement, until a further period of five years has elapsed.

13 When an audit client becomes a listed company, the length of time the audit engagement partner has served the audit client in that capacity is taken into account in calculating the period before the audit engagement partner is rotated off the engagement team. However, where the audit engagement partner has already served for four or more years, that individual may continue to serve as the audit engagement partner for not more than two years after the audit client becomes a listed company.

14 Some degree of flexibility over the timing of rotation may be necessary in circumstances where a reasonable and informed third party would regard the audit engagement partner's continuity as being especially important to the shareholders of the audit client. For example, where major changes to the audit client's structure or its senior management are expected that would otherwise coincide with the rotation of the audit engagement partner. In these circumstances alternative safeguards are applied to reduce any threats to an acceptable level. Such safeguards may include ensuring that an expanded review of the audit work is undertaken by an audit partner, who is not involved in the audit engagement.

15 In the case of joint audit arrangements for listed companies, audit firms will make arrangements for changes of audit engagement partners and independent partners over a five-year period so that the familiarity threat is avoided, whilst also taking into consideration factors that affect the quality of the audit work.

Key audit partners

In the case of listed companies, the audit firm should establish policies and procedures to ensure that: 16

(a) no one should act as a key audit partner for a continuous period longer than seven years;
(b) where a key audit partner becomes the audit engagement partner, the combined period of service in these positions should not exceed seven years; and
(c) anyone who has acted as a key audit partner for a particular audit client for a period of seven years, whether continuously or in aggregate, should not hold any position of responsibility in relation to the audit engagement until a further period of two years has elapsed.

Other partners and staff in senior positions

In the case of listed companies, the audit engagement partner should review the safeguards put in place to address the threats to the auditors' objectivity and independence arising where: 17

(a) partners have been responsible for significant affiliates (but not as key audit partners); or
(b) staff have been involved in the audit in senior positions;
for a continuous period longer than seven years and should discuss those situations with the independent partner. Any unresolved problems or issues should be referred to the ethics partner.

Such safeguards might include the removal of the member of staff from, or the rotation of roles within, the engagement team.   18

Effective date

Effective for audits of financial statements for periods commencing on or after 15 December 2004.   19

Firms may complete audit engagements relating to periods commencing prior to 15 December 2004 in accordance with existing ethical guidance from the relevant professional body, putting in place any necessary changes in the subsequent engagement period.   20

Firms may implement revisions to their policies and procedures as required under paragraph 5 during the year commencing 15 December 2004.   21

Where the provisions of paragraphs 12 and 16 require audit partners to rotate off the audit engagement prior to the period allowed by existing ethical guidance (including transitional arrangements) from the relevant professional body, they may continue where a change would impair audit quality. However, this extension beyond the period permitted by paragraphs 12 and 16 can be applied only for audits of financial statements for periods commencing on or prior to 15 December 2006.   22

ES3 (Revised)*
Long association with the audit engagement

(Revised April 2008)

Contents

	Paragraph
Introduction	1 – 4
General provisions	5 – 11
Additional provisions related to audits of listed companies	12 – 20
Effective date	21 – 24

---

* Revisions to this Standard became effective for audits of financial statements for periods commencing on or after 6 April 2008. The Standard effective before this date is available from the APB website.

Preface

APB Ethical Standards apply in the audit of financial statements. They are read in the context of the Auditing Practices Board's Statement "The Auditing Practices Board – Scope and Authority of Pronouncements (Revised)" which sets out the application and authority of APB Ethical Standards.

The terms used in APB Ethical Standards are explained in the Glossary.

APB Ethical Standards apply to audits of financial statements in both the private and the public sectors. However, auditors in the public sector are subject to more complex ethical requirements than their private sector counterparts. This includes, for example, compliance with legislation such as the Prevention of Corruption Act 1916, concerning gifts and hospitality, and with Cabinet Office guidance.

Introduction

APB Ethical Standard 1 requires the audit engagement partner to identify and assess the circumstances which could adversely affect the auditor's objectivity ('threats'), including any perceived loss of independence, and to apply procedures ('safeguards') which will either:

(a) eliminate the threat; or
(b) reduce the threat to an acceptable level (that is, a level at which it is not probable that a reasonable and informed third party would conclude that the auditor's objectivity and independence either is impaired or is likely to be impaired).

When considering safeguards, where the audit engagement partner chooses to reduce rather than to eliminate a threat to objectivity and independence, he or she recognises that this judgment may not be shared by users of the financial statements and that he or she may be required to justify the decision.

This Standard provides requirements and guidance on specific circumstances arising out of long association with the audit engagement, which may create threats to the auditor's objectivity or perceived loss of independence. It gives examples of safeguards that can, in some circumstances, eliminate the threat or reduce it to an acceptable level. In circumstances where this is not possible, the auditor either does not accept or withdraws from the audit engagement, as appropriate.

Whenever a possible or actual breach of an APB Ethical Standard is identified, the audit engagement partner, in the first instance, and the ethics partner, where appropriate, assesses the implications of the breach, determines whether there are safeguards that can be put in place or other actions that can be taken to address any potential adverse consequences and considers whether there is a need to resign from the audit engagement.

An inadvertent violation of this Standard does not necessarily call into question the audit firm's ability to give an audit opinion provided that:

(a) the audit firm has established policies and procedures that require all partners and staff to report any breach promptly to the audit engagement partner or to the ethics partner, as appropriate;
(b) the audit engagement partner or ethics partner ensures that any matter which has given rise to a breach is addressed as soon as possible;

(c) safeguards, if appropriate, are applied (for example, by having another partner review the work done by the relevant partner or member of staff or by removing him or her from the engagement team); and
(d) the actions taken and the rationale for them are documented.

General provisions

5 The audit firm shall establish policies and procedures to monitor the length of time that audit engagement partners, key partners involved in the audit and partners and staff in senior positions, including those from other disciplines, serve as members of the engagement team for each audit.

6 Where audit engagement partners, key partners involved in the audit, and partners and staff in senior positions have a long association with the audit, the audit firm shall assess the threats to the auditor's objectivity and independence and shall apply safeguards to reduce the threats to an acceptable level. Where appropriate safeguards cannot be applied, the audit firm shall either resign as auditor or not stand for reappointment, as appropriate.[1]

7 Where audit engagement partners, key partners involved in the audit, other partners and staff in senior positions have a long association with the audited entity, self-interest, self-review and familiarity threats to the auditor's objectivity may arise. Similarly, such circumstances may result in an actual or perceived loss of independence. The significance of such threats depends upon factors such as:

- the role of the individual in the engagement team;
- the proportion of time that the audited entity contributes to the individual's annual billable hours;
- the length of time that the individual has been associated with that audit engagement.

8 In order to address such threats, audit firms apply safeguards. Appropriate safeguards may include:

- removing ('rotating') the partners and the other senior members of the engagement team after a pre-determined number of years;
- involving an additional partner, who is not and has not recently been a member of the engagement team, to review the work done by the partners and the other senior members of the engagement team and to advise as necessary;
- applying independent internal quality reviews to the engagement in question.

9 Once an audit engagement partner has held this role for a continuous period of ten years, careful consideration is given as to whether a reasonable and informed third party would consider the audit firm's objectivity and independence to be impaired. Where the individual concerned is not rotated after ten years, it is important that:

(a) safeguards other than rotation, such as those noted in paragraph 8, are applied; or
(b) (i) the reasoning as to why the individual continues to participate in the audit engagement without any safeguards is documented; and
(ii) the facts are communicated to those charged with governance of the audited entity in accordance with paragraphs 56 – 63 of APB Ethical Standard 1.

[1] In the case of those public sector bodies where the responsibility for the audit is assigned by legislation, the auditor cannot resign from the audit engagement and considers alternative safeguards that can be put in place.

The audit firm's policies and procedures set out whether there are circumstances in which the audit engagement partners, engagement quality control reviewers and key partners involved in the audit of non-listed entities are subject to accelerated rotation requirements, such as those set out in paragraph 12, as described in paragraph 42 of APB Ethical Standard 1. 10

Any scheme of rotation of partners and other senior members of the engagement team needs to take into account the factors which affect the quality of the audit work, including the experience and continuity of members of the engagement team and the need to ensure appropriate succession planning. 11

Additional provisions related to audits of listed companies

The audit engagement partner and the engagement quality control reviewer

In the case of listed companies, save where the circumstances contemplated in paragraph 15 and 16 apply, the audit firm shall establish policies and procedures to ensure that: 12

(a) no one shall act as audit engagement partner or as engagement quality control reviewer for a continuous period longer than five years;
(b) where an engagement quality control reviewer becomes the audit engagement partner, the combined period of service in these positions shall not exceed five years; and
(c) anyone who has acted as the audit engagement partner or the engagement quality control reviewer, or held a combination of such positions, for a particular audited entity for a period of five years, whether continuously or in aggregate, shall not participate in the audit engagement until a further period of five years has elapsed.

The roles that constitute participating in an audit engagement for the purposes of paragraph 12(c), include providing quality control for the engagement, advising or consulting with the engagement team or the client regarding technical or industry specific issues, transactions or events, or otherwise directly influencing the outcome of the audit engagement. This does not include responding to queries in relation to any completed audit engagement. This is not intended to preclude partners whose primary responsibility within a firm is to be consulted on technical or industry specific issues from providing such consultation to the engagement team or client after a period of two years has elapsed from their ceasing to act as audit engagement partner or engagement quality control reviewer, provided that such consultation is in respect of new issues or new types of transactions or events that were not previously required to be considered by that individual in the course of acting as audit engagement partner or engagement quality control reviewer. 13

Where an audit engagement partner or engagement quality control reviewer continues in a non-audit role having been rotated off the engagement team, the new audit engagement partner and the individual concerned ensure that that person, while acting in this new role, does not exert any influence on the audit engagement. Positions in which an individual is responsible for the firm's client relationship with the particular audited entity would not be an acceptable non-audit role. 14

When an audited entity becomes a listed company, the length of time the audit engagement partner has served the audited entity in that capacity is taken into account in calculating the period before the audit engagement partner is rotated off the engagement team. However, where the audit engagement partner has already served for four or more years, that individual may continue to serve as the audit 15 engagement partner for not more than two years after the audited entity becomes a listed company.

16 Some degree of flexibility over the timing of rotation may be necessary in circumstances where a reasonable and informed third party would regard the audit engagement partner's continuity as being especially important to the shareholders of the audited entity. For example, where major changes to the audited entity's structure or its senior management are expected that would otherwise coincide with the rotation of the audit engagement partner. In these circumstances alternative safeguards are applied to reduce any threats to an acceptable level. Such safeguards may include ensuring that an expanded review of the audit work is undertaken by an audit partner, who is not involved in the audit engagement.

17 In the case of joint audit arrangements for listed companies, audit firms will make arrangements for changes of audit engagement partners and engagement quality control reviewers over a five-year period so that the familiarity threat is avoided, whilst also taking into consideration factors that affect the quality of the audit work.

Key partners involved in the audit

18 In the case of listed companies, the audit firm shall establish policies and procedures to ensure that:
   (a) no one shall act as a key partner involved in the audit for a continuous period longer than seven years;
   (b) where a key partner involved in the audit becomes the audit engagement partner, the combined period of service in these positions shall not exceed seven years; and
   (c) anyone who has acted as a key partner involved in the audit for a particular audited entity for a period of seven years, whether continuously or in aggregate, shall not participate in the audit engagement until a further period of two years has elapsed.

Other partners and staff in senior positions

19 In the case of listed companies, the audit engagement partner shall review the safeguards put in place to address the threats to the auditor's objectivity and independence arising where partners and staff have been involved in the audit in senior positions for a continuous period longer than seven years and shall discuss those situations with the engagement quality control reviewer. Any unresolved problems or issues shall be referred to the ethics partner.

20 Safeguards that address the threats arising from such a situation might include the removal of the member of staff from, or the rotation of roles within, the engagement team.

Effective date

21 Revisions to this Ethical Standard become effective for audits of financial statements for periods commencing on or after 6 April 2008.

22 Firms may complete audit engagements relating to periods commencing prior to 6 April 2008 in accordance with existing ethical standards, putting in place any necessary changes in the subsequent engagement period.

Save where the circumstances contemplated in paragraph 24 apply, where a partner currently participating in an audit (other than in the role of audit engagement partner or engagement quality control reviewer) becomes a key partner involved in the audit as a result of the change in definition introduced with effect from 6 April 2008, he or she may continue to participate in the audit engagement, provided that the period of service as a key partner involved in the audit (both before and after 6 April 2008) does not exceed nine years in aggregate. If such a partner is appointed as audit engagement partner after 6 April 2008, the combined period of service as a key partner involved in the audit and audit engagement partner (both before and after 6 April 2008) does not exceed nine years in aggregate. **23**

Where a partner becomes a key partner involved in the audit as a result of the change in definition introduced with effect from 6 April 2008 and has already held such a position for more than nine years, such a partner can continue in the role for one further year. **24**

ES4
Fees, remuneration and evaluation policies, litigation, gifts and hospitality

(Re-issued December 2004)

Contents

	Paragraphs
Introduction	1 - 4
Fees	5 - 35
Remuneration and evaluation policies	36 - 38
Threatened and actual litigation	39 - 41
Gifts and hospitality	42 - 50
Effective date	51 - 54

Preface

APB Ethical Standards apply in the audit of financial statements. They should be read in the context of the Auditing Practices Board's Statement "The Auditing Practices Board – Scope and Authority of Pronouncements (Revised)" which sets out the application and authority of APB Ethical Standards.

The terms used in APB Ethical Standards are explained in the Glossary.

APB Ethical Standards apply to audits of financial statements in both the private and the public sectors. However, auditors in the public sector are subject to more complex ethical requirements than their private sector counterparts. This includes, for example, compliance with legislation such as the Prevention of Corruption Act 1916, concerning gifts and hospitality, and with Cabinet Office guidance.

Introduction

APB Ethical Standard 1 requires the audit engagement partner to identify and assess the circumstances which could adversely affect the auditors' objectivity ('threats'), including any perceived loss of independence, and to apply procedures ('safeguards') which will either:

(a) eliminate the threat; or
(b) reduce the threat to an acceptable level (that is, a level at which it is not probable that a reasonable and informed third party would conclude that the auditors' objectivity and independence either is impaired or is likely to be impaired).

When considering safeguards, where the audit engagement partner chooses to reduce rather than to eliminate a threat to objectivity and independence, he or she recognises that this judgment may not be shared by users of the financial statements and that he or she may be required to justify the decision.

This Standard provides requirements and guidance on specific circumstances arising out of fees, economic dependence, litigation, remuneration and evaluation of partners and staff, and gifts and hospitality, which may create threats to the auditors' objectivity or perceived loss of independence. It gives examples of safeguards that can, in some situations, eliminate the threat or reduce it to an acceptable level. In circumstances where this is not possible, either the situation is avoided or the auditors either do not accept or withdraw from the audit engagement, as appropriate.

Whenever a possible or actual breach of an APB Ethical Standard is identified, the audit engagement partner, in the first instance, and the ethics partner, where appropriate, assesses the implications of the breach, determines whether there are safeguards that can be put in place or other actions that can be taken to address any potential adverse consequences and considers whether there is a need to resign from the audit engagement.

An inadvertent violation of this Standard does not necessarily call into question the audit firm's ability to give an audit opinion provided that:

(a) the audit firm has established policies and procedures that require all partners and staff to report any breach promptly to the audit engagement partner or to the ethics partner, as appropriate;

(b) the audit engagement partner or ethics partner ensures that any matter which has given rise to a breach is addressed as soon as possible;
(c) safeguards, if appropriate, are applied (for example, having another partner review the work done by the relevant partner or member of staff or by removing him or her from the engagement team); and
(d) the actions taken and the rationale for them are documented.

Fees

5 **The audit engagement partner should be satisfied and able to demonstrate that the audit engagement has assigned to it sufficient partners and staff with appropriate time and skill to perform the audit in accordance with all applicable Auditing and Ethical Standards, irrespective of the audit fee to be charged.**

6 Paragraph 5 is not intended to prescribe the approach to be taken by audit firms to the setting of audit fees, but rather to emphasise that there are no circumstances where the amount of the audit fee can justify any lack of appropriate resource or time taken to perform a proper audit in accordance with applicable Auditing and Ethical Standards.

7 **An audit should not be undertaken on a contingent fee basis.**

8 A contingent fee basis is any arrangement made at the outset of an engagement under which a pre-determined amount or a specified commission on or percentage of any consideration or saving is payable to the audit firm upon the happening of a specified event or the achievement of an outcome (or alternative outcomes). Differential hourly fee rates, or arrangements under which the fee payable will be negotiated after the completion of the engagement, do not constitute contingent fee arrangements.

9 Contingent fee arrangements in respect of audit engagements create self-interest threats to the auditors' objectivity and independence that are so significant that they cannot be eliminated or reduced to an acceptable level by the application of any safeguards.

10 The audit fee ordinarily reflects the time spent and the skills and experience of the personnel performing the audit in accordance with all the relevant requirements. It does not depend on whether the auditors' report on the financial statements is qualified or unqualified.

11 The basis for the calculation of the audit fee is agreed with the audit client each year before significant audit work is undertaken. The audit engagement partner explains to the audit client that the estimated audit fee is based on the expected level of audit work required and that, if unforeseen problems are encountered, the cost of any additional audit work found to be necessary will be reflected in the audit fee actually charged. This is not a contingent fee arrangement.

12 **The audit firm should establish policies and procedures to ensure that the audit engagement partner and the ethics partner are notified where others within the audit firm propose to adopt contingent fee arrangements in relation to the provision of non-audit services to the audit client or its affiliates.**

13 Contingent fee arrangements in respect of non-audit services provided by the auditors to an audit client may create a threat to the auditors' objectivity and

independence. The circumstances in which such fee arrangements are not permitted for such non-audit services are dealt with in APB Ethical Standard 5.

In the case of listed companies the audit engagement partner should disclose to the audit committee, in writing, any contingent fee arrangements for non-audit services provided by the auditors or their network firms. 14

In the case of a group audit of a listed company, which involves other auditors, the letter of instruction sent by the group audit engagement partner to the other auditors requests disclosure of any contingent fees for non-audit services charged or proposed to be charged by the other auditors. 15

The actual amount of the audit fee for the previous audit and the arrangements for its payment should be agreed with the audit client before the audit firm formally accepts appointment as auditors in respect of the following period. 16

Ordinarily, any outstanding fees for the previous audit period are paid before the audit firm commences any new audit work. Where they are not, it is important for the audit engagement partner to understand the nature of any disagreement or other issue. 17

Where fees for professional services from the audit client are overdue and the amount cannot be regarded as trivial, the audit engagement partner, in consultation with the ethics partner, should consider whether the audit firm can continue as auditors or whether it is necessary to resign. 18

Where fees due from an audit client, whether for audit or for non-audit services, remain unpaid for a long time - and, in particular, where a significant part is not paid before the auditors' report on the financial statements for the following year is due to be issued - a self-interest threat to the auditors' objectivity and independence is created because the issue of an unqualified audit report may enhance the audit firm's prospects of securing payment of such overdue fees. 19

Where the outstanding fees are in dispute and the amount involved is significant, the threats to the auditors' objectivity and independence may be such that no safeguards can eliminate them or reduce them to an acceptable level. The audit engagement partner therefore considers whether the audit firm can continue with the audit engagement. 20

Where the outstanding fees are unpaid because of exceptional circumstances (including financial distress), the audit engagement partner considers whether the audit client will be able to resolve its difficulties. In deciding what action to take, the audit engagement partner weighs the threats to the auditors' objectivity and independence, if the audit firm were to remain in office, against the difficulties the audit client would be likely to face in finding a successor, and therefore the public interest considerations, if the audit firm were to resign. 21

In any case where the audit firm does not resign from the audit engagement, the audit engagement partner applies appropriate safeguards (such as a review by an audit partner who is not involved in the audit engagement) and notifies the ethics partner of the facts concerning the overdue fees. 22

Where it is expected that the total fees for both audit and non-audit services receivable from a listed audit client and its subsidiaries audited by the audit firm[1] will regularly 23

---

[1] Total fees will include those billed by others where the audit firm is entitled to the fees, but will not include fees billed by the audit firm where it is acting as agent for another party.

exceed 10% of the annual fee income of the audit firm or, where profits are not shared on a firm-wide basis, of the part of the firm by reference to which the audit engagement partner's profit share is calculated, the firm should not act as the auditors of that entity and should either resign as auditors or not stand for reappointment, as appropriate.[2]

24 Where it is expected that the total fees for both audit and non-audit services receivable from a non-listed audit client and its subsidiaries audited by the audit firm will regularly exceed 15% of the annual fee income of the audit firm or, where profits are not shared on a firm-wide basis, of the part of the firm by reference to which the audit engagement partner's profit share is calculated, the firm should not act as the auditors of that entity and should either resign as auditors or not stand for reappointment, as appropriate.

25 Where it is expected that the total fees for both audit and non-audit services receivable from an audit client and its subsidiaries that are audited by the audit firm will regularly exceed 10% in the case of listed companies and 15% in the case of non-listed entities of the annual fee income of the part of the firm by reference to which the audit engagement partner's profit share is calculated, it may be possible to assign the audit client to another part of the firm.

26 Paragraphs 23 and 24 are not intended to require the audit firm to resign as auditors or not stand for reappointment as a result of an individual event or engagement, the nature or size of which was unpredictable and where a reasonable and informed third party would regard ceasing to act as detrimental to the shareholders (or equivalent) of the audit client. However, in such circumstances, the audit firm discloses full details of the position to the ethics partner and to those charged with governance of the audit client and discusses with both what, if any, safeguards may be appropriate.

27 Where it is expected that the total fees for both audit and non-audit services receivable from a listed audit client and its subsidiaries audited by the audit firm will regularly exceed 5% of the annual fee income of the audit firm or the part of the firm by reference to which the audit engagement partner's profit share is calculated, but will not regularly exceed 10%, the audit engagement partner should disclose that expectation to the ethics partner and to those charged with governance of the audit client and consider whether appropriate safeguards should be applied to eliminate or reduce to an acceptable level the threat to the auditors' objectivity and independence.

28 It is fundamental to the auditors' objectivity that they be willing and able, if necessary, to disagree with the directors and management, regardless of the consequences to their own position. Where the auditors are, to any significant extent, economically dependent on the audit client, this may inhibit their willingness or constrain their ability to express a qualified opinion on the financial statements, since this could be viewed as likely to lead to them losing the audit client.

29 An audit firm is deemed to be economically dependent on a listed audit client if the total fees for audit and all other services from that client and its subsidiaries which are audited by the audit firm represent 10% of the total fees of the audit firm or the part of the firm by reference to which the audit engagement partner's profit share is calculated. Where such fees are between 5% and 10%, the audit engagement partner and the ethics partner consider the significance of the threat and the need for appropriate safeguards.

30 Such safeguards might include:

[2] *Paragraphs 23 to 32 do not apply to the audits of those public sector bodies where the responsibility for the audit is assigned by legislation. In such cases, the auditors cannot resign from the audit engagement, irrespective of considerations of economic dependence.*

- taking steps to reduce the non-audit work to be undertaken and therefore the fees earned from the audit client;
- applying independent internal quality control reviews.

Where it is expected that the total fees for both audit and non-audit services receivable from a non-listed audit client and its subsidiaries audited by the audit firm will regularly exceed 10% of the annual fee income of the audit firm or the part of the firm by reference to which the audit engagement partner's profit share is calculated, but will not regularly exceed 15%, the audit engagement partner should disclose that expectation to the ethics partner and to those charged with governance of the audit client and the firm should arrange an external independent quality control review of the audit engagement to be undertaken before the auditors' report is finalised[3]. 31

A quality control review involves discussion with the audit engagement partner, a review of the financial statements and the auditors' report, and consideration of whether the report is appropriate. It also involves a review of selected working papers relating to the significant judgments the engagement team has made and the conclusions they have reached. The extent of the review depends on the complexity of the engagement and the risk that the report might not be appropriate in the circumstances. The review includes considering the following: 32

- Significant risks identified during the audit and the responses to those risks.
- Judgments made, particularly with respect to materiality and significant risks.
- Whether appropriate consultation has taken place on matters involving differences of opinion or other difficult or contentious matters, and the conclusions arising from those consultations.
- The significance and disposition of corrected and uncorrected misstatements identified during the audit.
- The appropriateness of the report to be issued.

Where the quality control reviewer makes recommendations that the audit engagement partner does not accept and the matter is not resolved to the reviewer's satisfaction, the report is not issued until the matter is resolved by following the audit firm's procedures for dealing with differences of opinion.

A new audit firm seeking to establish itself may find the requirements relating to economic dependence difficult to comply with in the short term. In these circumstances, such firms would: 33

(a) not undertake any audits of listed companies, where fees from such a client would represent 10% or more of the annual fee income of the firm; and
(b) for a period not exceeding two years, require external independent quality control reviews of those audits of unlisted entities that represent more than 15% of the annual fee income before the audit opinion is issued.

The firm might also develop its practice by accepting work from non-audit clients so as to bring the fees payable by each audit client below 15%.

A self-interest threat may also be created where an audit partner in the engagement team: 34

- is employed exclusively or principally on that audit engagement;
- is remunerated on the basis of the performance of part of the firm which is substantially dependent on fees from that audit client.

---

[3] As provided in APB Ethical Standard – Provisions Available for Small Entities, auditors of Small Entities are not required to comply with this paragraph.

35   Where the circumstances described in paragraph 34 arise, the audit firm assesses the significance of the threat and, if it is other than clearly insignificant, applies safeguards to reduce the threat to an acceptable level. Such safeguards might include:

- reducing the dependence of the office, partner or person in a position to influence the conduct and outcome of the audit by reallocating the work within the practice;
- a review by an audit partner who is not involved with the audit engagement to ensure that the auditors' objectivity and independence is not affected by the self-interest threat.

Remuneration and evaluation policies

36   **The audit firm should establish policies and procedures to ensure that, in relation to each audit client:**

   (a) the objectives of the members of the audit team do not include selling non-audit services to the audit client;
   (b) the criteria for evaluating the performance of members of the audit team do not include success in selling non-audit services to the audit client; and
   (c) no specific element of the remuneration of a member of the audit team and no decision concerning promotion within the audit firm is based on his or her success in selling non-audit services to the audit client.

37   Where auditors identify areas for possible improvement in a client they may provide general business advice, which might include suggested solutions to problems. Before discussing any non-audit service that might be provided by the audit firm or effecting any introductions to colleagues from outside the audit team, the audit engagement partner considers the threats that such a service would have on the audit engagement, in line with the requirements of APB Ethical Standard 5.

38   The policies and procedures required for compliance with paragraph 36 are not intended to inhibit normal profit-sharing arrangements. However, such policies and procedures are central to an audit firm's ability to demonstrate its objectivity and independence and to rebut any suggestion that an audit that it has undertaken and the opinion that it has given are influenced by the nature and extent of any non-audit services that it has provided to that audit client. Because it is possible that, despite such policies and procedures, such factors may be taken into account in the evaluation and remuneration of members of an audit team, the ethics partner pays particular attention to the actual implementation of those policies and procedures and makes himself or herself available for consultation when needed.

Threatened and actual litigation

39   **Where litigation in relation to audit or non-audit services between the audit client or its affiliates and the audit firm, which is other than insignificant, is already in progress, or where the audit engagement partner considers such litigation to be probable, the audit firm should either not continue with or not accept the audit engagement.**[4]

40   Where litigation (in relation to audit or non-audit services) actually takes place between the audit firm (or any person in a position to influence the conduct and

---

[4] *Paragraphs 39 to 41 do not apply to the audits of those public sector bodies where the responsibility for the audit is assigned by legislation. In such cases, the auditors cannot resign from the audit engagement: the auditors report significant litigation to the relevant legislative authority.*

outcome of the audit) and the audit client, or where litigation is threatened and there is a realistic prospect of such litigation being commenced, self-interest, advocacy and intimidation threats to the auditors' objectivity and independence are created because the audit firm's interest will be the achievement of an outcome to the dispute or litigation that is favourable to itself. In addition, an effective audit process requires complete candour and full disclosure between the audit client management and the engagement team: such disputes or litigation may place the two parties in opposing adversarial positions and may affect management's willingness to make complete disclosure of relevant information. Where the auditors can foresee that such a threat may arise, they inform the audit committee of their intention to resign or, where there is no audit committee, the board of directors.

The auditors are not required to resign immediately in circumstances where a reasonable and informed third party would not regard it as being in the interests of the shareholders for them to do so. Such circumstances might arise, for example, where: 41

- the litigation was commenced as the audit was about to be completed and shareholder interests would be adversely affected by a delay in the audit of the financial statements;
- on appropriate legal advice, the audit firm deems that the threatened or actual litigation is vexatious or designed solely to bring pressure to bear on the opinion to be expressed by the auditors.

Gifts and hospitality

The audit firm, those in a position to influence the conduct and outcome of the audit and immediate family members of such persons should not accept gifts from the audit client, unless the value is clearly insignificant. 42

Those in a position to influence the conduct and outcome of the audit and immediate family members of such persons should not accept hospitality from the audit client, unless it is reasonable in terms of its frequency, nature and cost. 43

Where gifts or hospitality are accepted from an audit client, self-interest and familiarity threats to the auditors' objectivity and independence are created. Familiarity threats also arise where gifts or hospitality are offered to an audit client. 44

Gifts from the audit client, unless their value is clearly insignificant, create threats to objectivity and independence which no safeguards can eliminate or reduce. 45

Hospitality is a component of many business relationships and can provide valuable opportunities for developing an understanding of the client's business and for gaining the insight on which an effective and successful working relationship depends. Therefore, the auditors' objectivity and independence is not necessarily impaired as a result of accepting hospitality from the audit client, provided it is reasonable in terms of its frequency, its nature and its cost. 46

The audit firm should establish policies on the nature and value of gifts and hospitality that may be accepted from and offered to audit clients, their directors, officers and employees, and should issue guidance to assist partners and staff to comply with such policies. 47

In assessing the acceptability of gifts and hospitality, the test to be applied is not whether the auditors consider that their objectivity is impaired but whether it is 48 probable that a reasonable and informed third party would conclude that it is or is likely to be impaired.

49 Where there is any doubt as to the acceptability of gifts or hospitality offered by the audit client, members of the engagement team discuss the position with the audit engagement partner. If there is any doubt as to the acceptability of gifts or hospitality offered to the audit engagement partner, or if the audit engagement partner has any residual doubt about the acceptability of gifts or hospitality to other individuals, the audit engagement partner reports the facts to the ethics partner, for further consideration regarding any action to be taken.

50 Where the cumulative amount of gifts or hospitality accepted from the audit client appears abnormally high, the audit engagement partner reports the facts to both:

- the ethics partner; and
- the audit committee (or, where there is no audit committee, the board of directors),

together with other significant facts and matters that bear upon the auditors' objectivity and independence.

Effective date

51 Effective for audits of financial statements for periods commencing on or after 15 December 2004.

52 Firms may complete audit engagements relating to periods commencing prior to 15 December 2004 in accordance with existing ethical guidance from the relevant professional body, putting in place any necessary changes in the subsequent engagement period.

53 Firms may implement revisions to their policies and procedures as required under paragraphs 12, 36 and 47 during the year commencing 15 December 2004.

54 Where the requirements of paragraph 23 or 24 would result in an audit firm being required to resign from providing one or more services to an entity, the firm may continue to provide services under existing arrangements, until the appointment as auditors for the first period commencing on or after 15 December 2005 is considered, provided that:

- the engagements held at 15 December 2004 were permitted by existing ethical guidance from the relevant professional body;
- the level of dependence on the audit client is not increased from that in existence at 15 December 2004;
- any safeguards required by existing ethical guidance continue to be applied; and
- the need for additional safeguards is assessed and, if considered necessary, those additional safeguards are applied.

ES4 (Revised)*
Fees, remuneration and evaluation policies, litigation, gifts and hospitality

(Revised April 2008)

Contents

	Paragraph
Introduction	1 – 4
Fees	5 – 37
Remuneration and evaluation policies	38 – 40
Threatened and actual litigation	41 – 43
Gifts and hospitality	44 – 52
Effective date	53

---

* *Revisions to this Standard became effective for audits of financial statements for periods commencing on or after 6 April 2008. The Standard effective before this date is available from the APB website.*

Preface

APB Ethical Standards apply in the audit of financial statements. They are read in the context of the Auditing Practices Board's Statement "The Auditing Practices Board – Scope and Authority of Pronouncements (Revised)" which sets out the application and authority of APB Ethical Standards.

The terms used in APB Ethical Standards are explained in the Glossary.

APB Ethical Standards apply to audits of financial statements in both the private and the public sectors. However, auditors in the public sector are subject to more complex ethical requirements than their private sector counterparts. This includes, for example, compliance with legislation such as the Prevention of Corruption Act 1916, concerning gifts and hospitality, and with Cabinet Office guidance.

Introduction

1   APB Ethical Standard 1 requires the audit engagement partner to identify and assess the circumstances which could adversely affect the auditor's objectivity ('threats'), including any perceived loss of independence, and to apply procedures ('safeguards') which will either:

    (a) eliminate the threat; or
    (b) reduce the threat to an acceptable level (that is, a level at which it is not probable that a reasonable and informed third party would conclude that the auditor's objectivity and independence either is impaired or is likely to be impaired).

    When considering safeguards, where the audit engagement partner chooses to reduce rather than to eliminate a threat to objectivity and independence, he or she recognises that this judgment may not be shared by users of the financial statements and that he or she may be required to justify the decision.

2   This Standard provides requirements and guidance on specific circumstances arising out of fees, economic dependence, litigation, remuneration and evaluation of partners and staff, and gifts and hospitality, which may create threats to the auditor's objectivity or perceived loss of independence. It gives examples of safeguards that can, in some situations, eliminate the threat or reduce it to an acceptable level. In circumstances where this is not possible, either the situation is avoided or the auditor either does not accept or withdraws from the audit engagement, as appropriate.

3   Whenever a possible or actual breach of an APB Ethical Standard is identified, the audit engagement partner, in the first instance, and the ethics partner, where appropriate, assesses the implications of the breach, determines whether there are safeguards that can be put in place or other actions that can be taken to address any potential adverse consequences and considers whether there is a need to resign from the audit engagement.

4   An inadvertent violation of this Standard does not necessarily call into question the audit firm's ability to give an audit opinion provided that:

    (a) the audit firm has established policies and procedures that require all partners and staff to report any breach promptly to the audit engagement partner or to the ethics partner, as appropriate;
    (b) the audit engagement partner or ethics partner ensures that any matter which has given rise to a breach is addressed as soon as possible;

(c) safeguards, if appropriate, are applied (for example, having another partner review the work done by the relevant partner or member of staff or by removing him or her from the engagement team); and

(d) the actions taken and the rationale for them are documented.

Fees

The audit engagement partner shall be satisfied and able to demonstrate that the audit engagement has assigned to it sufficient partners and staff with appropriate time and skill to perform the audit in accordance with all applicable Auditing and Ethical Standards, irrespective of the audit fee to be charged. 5

Paragraph 5 is not intended to prescribe the approach to be taken by audit firms to the setting of audit fees, but rather to emphasise that there are no circumstances where the amount of the audit fee can justify any lack of appropriate resource or time taken to perform a proper audit in accordance with applicable Auditing and Ethical Standards. 6

The audit engagement partner shall ensure that audit fees are not influenced or determined by the provision of non-audit services to the audited entity. 7

The audit fee ordinarily reflects the time spent and the skills, the experience of the personnel performing the audit in accordance with all the relevant requirements and the competitive situation in the audit market. Paragraph 7 is intended to prevent any relationship between the appropriate cost of the audit and the actual or potential provision of non-audit services. 8

Paragraph 7 is not intended to prohibit proper cost savings that can be achieved as a result of providing non-audit services in accordance with APB Ethical Standard 5 to the audited entity, for example, where information gained through undertaking a non-audit service is referred to by audit staff when carrying out the audit of the financial statements. 9

An audit shall not be undertaken on a contingent fee basis. 10

A contingent fee basis is any arrangement made at the outset of an engagement under which a pre-determined amount or a specified commission on or percentage of any consideration or saving is payable to the audit firm upon the happening of a specified event or the achievement of an outcome (or alternative outcomes). Differential hourly fee rates, or arrangements under which the fee payable will be negotiated after the completion of the engagement, do not constitute contingent fee arrangements. 11

Contingent fee arrangements in respect of audit engagements create self-interest threats to the auditor's objectivity and independence that are so significant that they cannot be eliminated or reduced to an acceptable level by the application of any safeguards. 12

The audit fee does not depend on whether the auditor's report on the financial statements is qualified or unqualified. The basis for the calculation of the audit fee is agreed with the audited entity each year before significant audit work is undertaken. The audit engagement partner explains to the audited entity that the estimated audit fee is based on the expected level of audit work required and that, if unforeseen problems are encountered, the cost of any additional audit work found to be 13 necessary will be reflected in the audit fee actually charged. This is not a contingent fee arrangement.

14 **The audit firm shall establish policies and procedures to ensure that the audit engagement partner and the ethics partner are notified where others within the audit firm propose to adopt contingent fee arrangements in relation to the provision of non-audit services to the audited entity or its affiliates.**

15 Contingent fee arrangements in respect of non-audit services provided by the auditor to an audited entity may create a threat to the auditor's objectivity and independence. The circumstances in which such fee arrangements are not permitted for such non-audit services are dealt with in APB Ethical Standard 5.

16 **In the case of listed companies the audit engagement partner shall disclose to the audit committee, in writing, any contingent fee arrangements for non-audit services provided by the auditor or its network firms.**

17 In the case of a group audit of a listed company, which involves other auditors, the letter of instruction sent by the group audit engagement partner to the other auditors requests disclosure of any contingent fees for non-audit services charged or proposed to be charged by the other auditors.

18 **The actual amount of the audit fee for the previous audit and the arrangements for its payment shall be agreed with the audited entity before the audit firm formally accepts appointment as auditor in respect of the following period.**

19 Ordinarily, any outstanding fees for the previous audit period are paid before the audit firm commences any new audit work. Where they are not, it is important for the audit engagement partner to understand the nature of any disagreement or other issue.

20 **Where fees for professional services from the audited entity are overdue and the amount cannot be regarded as trivial, the audit engagement partner, in consultation with the ethics partner, shall consider whether the audit firm can continue as auditor or whether it is necessary to resign.**

21 Where fees due from an audited entity, whether for audit or for non-audit services, remain unpaid for a long time – and, in particular, where a significant part is not paid before the auditor's report on the financial statements for the following year is due to be issued – a self-interest threat to the auditor's objectivity and independence is created because the issue of an unqualified audit report may enhance the audit firm's prospects of securing payment of such overdue fees.

22 Where the outstanding fees are in dispute and the amount involved is significant, the threats to the auditor's objectivity and independence may be such that no safeguards can eliminate them or reduce them to an acceptable level. The audit engagement partner therefore considers whether the audit firm can continue with the audit engagement.

23 Where the outstanding fees are unpaid because of exceptional circumstances (including financial distress), the audit engagement partner considers whether the audited entity will be able to resolve its difficulties. In deciding what action to take, the audit engagement partner weighs the threats to the auditor's objectivity and independence, if the audit firm were to remain in office, against the difficulties the audited entity would be likely to face in finding a successor, and therefore the public interest considerations, if the audit firm were to resign.

In any case where the audit firm does not resign from the audit engagement, the audit engagement partner applies appropriate safeguards (such as a review by an audit partner who is not involved in the audit engagement) and notifies the ethics partner of the facts concerning the overdue fees. 24

Where it is expected that the total fees for both audit and non-audit services receivable from a listed audited entity and its subsidiaries audited by the audit firm[1] will regularly exceed 10% of the annual fee income of the audit firm[2] or, where profits are not shared on a firm-wide basis, of the part of the firm by reference to which the audit engagement partner's profit share is calculated, the firm shall not act as the auditor of that entity and shall either resign as auditor or not stand for reappointment, as appropriate.[3] 25

Where it is expected that the total fees for both audit and non-audit services receivable from a non-listed audited entity and its subsidiaries audited by the audit firm will regularly exceed 15% of the annual fee income of the audit firm or, where profits are not shared on a firm-wide basis, of the part of the firm by reference to which the audit engagement partner's profit share is calculated, the firm shall not act as the auditor of that entity and shall either resign as auditor or not stand for reappointment, as appropriate. 26

Where it is expected that the total fees for both audit and non-audit services receivable from an audited entity and its subsidiaries that are audited by the audit firm will regularly exceed 10% in the case of listed companies and 15% in the case of non-listed entities of the annual fee income of the part of the firm by reference to which the audit engagement partner's profit share is calculated, it may be possible to assign the engagement to another part of the firm. 27

Paragraphs 25 and 26 are not intended to require the audit firm to resign as auditor or not stand for reappointment as a result of an individual event or engagement, the nature or size of which was unpredictable and where a reasonable and informed third party would regard ceasing to act as detrimental to the shareholders (or equivalent) of the audited entity. However, in such circumstances, the audit firm discloses full details of the position to the ethics partner and to those charged with governance of the audited entity and discusses with both what, if any, safeguards may be appropriate. 28

Where it is expected that the total fees for both audit and non-audit services receivable from a listed audited entity and its subsidiaries audited by the audit firm will regularly exceed 5% of the annual fee income of the audit firm or the part of the firm by reference to which the audit engagement partner's profit share is calculated, but will not regularly exceed 10%, the audit engagement partner shall disclose that expectation to the ethics partner and to those charged with governance of the audited entity and consider whether appropriate safeguards need to be applied to eliminate or reduce to an acceptable level the threat to the auditor's objectivity and independence. 29

It is fundamental to the auditor's objectivity that it be willing and able, if necessary, to disagree with the directors and management, regardless of the consequences to its 30

---

[1] Total fees will include those billed by others where the audit firm is entitled to the fees, but will not include fees billed by the audit firm where it is acting as agent for another party.

[2] In the case of a sole practitioner, annual fee income of the audit firm includes all earned income received by the individual.

[3] Paragraphs 25 to 34 do not apply to the audits of those public sector bodies where the responsibility for the audit is assigned by legislation. In such cases, the auditor cannot resign from the audit engagement, irrespective of considerations of economic dependence.

own position. Where the auditor is, to any significant extent, economically dependent on the audited entity, this may inhibit the auditor's willingness or constrain the auditor's ability to express a qualified opinion on the financial statements, since this could be viewed as likely to lead to it losing the audit engagement and the entity as a client.

31 An audit firm is deemed to be economically dependent on a listed audited entity if the total fees for audit and all other services from that entity and its subsidiaries which are audited by the audit firm represent 10% of the total fees of the audit firm or the part of the firm by reference to which the audit engagement partner's profit share is calculated. Where such fees are between 5% and 10%, the audit engagement partner and the ethics partner consider the significance of the threat and the need for appropriate safeguards.

32 Such safeguards might include:
- taking steps to reduce the non-audit work to be undertaken and therefore the fees earned from the audited entity;
- applying independent internal quality control reviews.

33 **Where it is expected that the total fees for both audit and non-audit services receivable from a non-listed audited entity and its subsidiaries audited by the audit firm will regularly exceed 10% of the annual fee income of the audit firm or the part of the firm by reference to which the audit engagement partner's profit share is calculated, but will not regularly exceed 15%, the audit engagement partner shall disclose that expectation to the ethics partner and to those charged with governance of the audited entity and the firm shall arrange an external independent quality control review of the audit engagement to be undertaken before the auditor's report is finalised.**

34 A quality control review involves discussion with the audit engagement partner, a review of the financial statements and the auditor's report, and consideration of whether the report is appropriate. It also involves a review of selected working papers relating to the significant judgments the engagement team has made and the conclusions they have reached. The extent of the review depends on the complexity of the engagement and the risk that the report might not be appropriate in the circumstances. The review includes considering the following:
- Significant risks identified during the audit and the responses to those risks.
- Judgments made, particularly with respect to materiality and significant risks.
- Whether appropriate consultation has taken place on matters involving differences of opinion or other difficult or contentious matters, and the conclusions arising from those consultations.
- The significance and disposition of corrected and uncorrected misstatements identified during the audit.
- The appropriateness of the report to be issued.

Where the quality control reviewer makes recommendations that the audit engagement partner does not accept and the matter is not resolved to the reviewer's satisfaction, the report is not issued until the matter is resolved by following the audit firm's procedures for dealing with differences of opinion.

35 A new audit firm seeking to establish itself may find the requirements relating to economic dependence difficult to comply with in the short term. In these circumstances, such firms would:
(a) not undertake any audits of listed companies, where fees from such an audited entity would represent 10% or more of the annual fee income of the firm; and

(b) for a period not exceeding two years, require external independent quality control reviews of those audits of unlisted entities that represent more than 15% of the annual fee income before the audit opinion is issued.

The firm might also develop its practice by accepting work from entities not audited by the firm so as to bring the fees payable by each audited entity below 15%.

A self-interest threat may also be created where an audit partner in the engagement team: 36

- is employed exclusively or principally on that audit engagement; and
- is remunerated on the basis of the performance of part of the firm which is substantially dependent on fees from that audited entity.

Where the circumstances described in paragraph 36 arise, the audit firm assesses the significance of the threat and applies safeguards to reduce the threat to an acceptable level. Such safeguards might include: 37

- reducing the dependence of the office, partner or person in a position to influence the conduct and outcome of the audit by reallocating the work within the practice;
- a review by an audit partner who is not involved with the audit engagement to ensure that the auditor's objectivity and independence is not affected by the self-interest threat.

Remuneration and evaluation policies

The audit firm shall establish policies and procedures to ensure that, in relation to each audited entity: 38

(a) the objectives of the members of the audit team do not include selling non-audit services to the audited entity;
(b) the criteria for evaluating the performance or promotion of members of the audit team do not include success in selling non-audit services to the audited entity; and
(c) no specific element of the remuneration of a member of the audit team is based on his or her success in selling non-audit services to the audited entity.

Where the auditor identifies areas for possible improvement in an audited entity it may provide general business advice, which might include suggested solutions to problems. Before discussing any non-audit service that might be provided by the audit firm or effecting any introductions to colleagues from outside the audit team, the audit engagement partner considers the threats that such a service would have on the audit engagement, in line with the requirements of APB Ethical Standard 5. 39

The policies and procedures required for compliance with paragraph 38 are not intended to inhibit normal profit-sharing arrangements. However, such policies and procedures are central to an audit firm's ability to demonstrate its objectivity and independence and to rebut any suggestion that an audit that it has undertaken and the opinion that it has given are influenced by the nature and extent of any non-audit services that it has provided to that audited entity. Because it is possible that, despite such policies and procedures, such factors may be taken into account in the evaluation and remuneration of members of an audit team, the ethics partner pays particular attention to the actual implementation of those policies and procedures and makes himself or herself available for consultation when needed. 40

Threatened and actual litigation

41 Where litigation in relation to audit or non-audit services between the audited entity or its affiliates and the audit firm, which is other than insignificant, is already in progress, or where the audit engagement partner considers such litigation to be probable, the audit firm shall either not continue with or not accept the audit engagement.[4]

42 Where litigation (in relation to audit or non-audit services) actually takes place between the audit firm (or any person in a position to influence the conduct and outcome of the audit) and the audited entity, or where litigation is threatened and there is a realistic prospect of such litigation being commenced, self-interest, advocacy and intimidation threats to the auditor's objectivity and independence are created because the audit firm's interest will be the achievement of an outcome to the dispute or litigation that is favourable to itself. In addition, an effective audit process requires complete candour and full disclosure between the audited entity's management and the engagement team: such disputes or litigation may place the two parties in opposing adversarial positions and may affect management's willingness to make complete disclosure of relevant information. Where the auditor can foresee that such a threat may arise, it informs the audit committee of its intention to resign or, where there is no audit committee, the board of directors.

43 The auditor is not required to resign immediately in circumstances where a reasonable and informed third party would not regard it as being in the interests of the shareholders for it to do so. Such circumstances might arise, for example, where:

- the litigation was commenced as the audit was about to be completed and shareholder interests would be adversely affected by a delay in the audit of the financial statements;
- on appropriate legal advice, the audit firm deems that the threatened or actual litigation is vexatious or designed solely to bring pressure to bear on the opinion to be expressed by the auditor.

Gifts and hospitality

44 The audit firm, those in a position to influence the conduct and outcome of the audit and immediate family members of such persons shall not accept gifts from the audited entity, unless the value is clearly insignificant.

45 Those in a position to influence the conduct and outcome of the audit and immediate family members of such persons shall not accept hospitality from the audited entity, unless it is reasonable in terms of its frequency, nature and cost.

46 Where gifts or hospitality are accepted from an audited entity, self-interest and familiarity threats to the auditor's objectivity and independence are created. Familiarity threats also arise where gifts or hospitality are offered to an audited entity.

47 Gifts from the audited entity, unless their value is clearly insignificant, create threats to objectivity and independence which no safeguards can eliminate or reduce.

---

[4] Paragraphs 41 to 43 do not apply to the audits of those public sector bodies where the responsibility for the audit is assigned by legislation. In such cases, the auditor cannot resign from the audit engagement: the auditor reports significant litigation to the relevant legislative authority.

Hospitality is a component of many business relationships and can provide valuable opportunities for developing an understanding of the audited entity's business and for gaining the insight on which an effective and successful working relationship depends. Therefore, the auditor's objectivity and independence is not necessarily impaired as a result of accepting hospitality from the audited entity, provided it is reasonable in terms of its frequency, its nature and its cost. **48**

The audit firm shall establish policies on the nature and value of gifts and hospitality that may be accepted from and offered to audited entities, their directors, officers and employees, and shall issue guidance to assist partners and staff to comply with such policies. **49**

In assessing the acceptability of gifts and hospitality, the test to be applied is not whether the auditor considers that the auditor's objectivity is impaired but whether it is probable that a reasonable and informed third party would conclude that it is or is likely to be impaired. **50**

Where there is any doubt as to the acceptability of gifts or hospitality offered by the audited entity, members of the engagement team discuss the position with the audit engagement partner. If there is any doubt as to the acceptability of gifts or hospitality offered to the audit engagement partner, or if the audit engagement partner has any residual doubt about the acceptability of gifts or hospitality to other individuals, the audit engagement partner reports the facts to the ethics partner, for further consideration regarding any action to be taken. **51**

Where the cumulative amount of gifts or hospitality accepted from the audited entity appears abnormally high, the audit engagement partner reports the facts to both: **52**

- the ethics partner; and
- the audit committee (or, where there is no audit committee, the board of directors),

together with other significant facts and matters that bear upon the auditor's objectivity and independence.

Effective date

Revisions to this Ethical Standard become effective for audits of financial statements for periods commencing on or after 6 April 2008. **53**

ES5
Non-audit services provided to audit clients

(Re-issued December 2004)

Contents

Paragraphs

Introduction   1 - 4

General approach to non-audit services   5 - 38

   Identification and assessment of threats and safeguards   12 - 34
   Communication with those charged with governance   35 - 36
   Documentation   37 - 38

Application of general principles to specific non-audit services   39 - 125

   Internal audit services   39 - 47
   Information technology services   48 - 53
   Valuation services   54 - 58
   Actuarial valuation services   59 - 61
   Tax services   62 - 77
   Litigation support services   78 - 80
   Legal services   81 - 82
   Recruitment and remuneration services   83 - 93
   Corporate finance services   94 - 105
   Transaction related services   106 - 112
   Accounting services   113 - 125

Effective date   126 - 129

Preface

APB Ethical Standards apply in the audit of financial statements. They should be read in the context of the Auditing Practices Board's Statement "The Auditing Practices Board – Scope and Authority of Pronouncements (Revised)" which sets out the application and authority of APB Ethical Standards.

The terms used in APB Ethical Standards are explained in the Glossary.

APB Ethical Standards apply to audits of financial statements in both the private and the public sectors. However, auditors in the public sector are subject to more complex ethical requirements than their private sector counterparts. This includes, for example, compliance with legislation such as the Prevention of Corruption Act 1916, concerning gifts and hospitality, and with Cabinet Office guidance.

Introduction

APB Ethical Standard 1 requires the audit engagement partner to identify and assess the circumstances which could adversely affect the auditors' objectivity ('threats'), including any perceived loss of independence, and to apply procedures ('safeguards') which will either:

(a) eliminate the threat; or
(b) reduce the threat to an acceptable level (that is, a level at which it is not probable that a reasonable and informed third party would conclude that the auditors' objectivity and independence either is impaired or is likely to be impaired).

When considering safeguards, where the audit engagement partner chooses to reduce rather than to eliminate a threat to objectivity and independence, he or she recognises that this judgment may not be shared by users of the financial statements and that he or she may be required to justify the decision.

This Standard provides requirements and guidance on specific circumstances arising from the provision of non-audit services by audit firms to their audit clients, which may create threats to the auditors' objectivity or perceived loss of independence. It gives examples of safeguards that can, in some circumstances, eliminate the threat or reduce it to an acceptable level. In circumstances where this is not possible, either the non-audit service engagement in question is not undertaken or the auditors either do not accept or withdraw from the audit engagement, as appropriate.

Whenever a possible or actual breach of an APB Ethical Standard is identified, the audit engagement partner, in the first instance, and the ethics partner, where appropriate, assess the implications of the breach, determine whether there are safeguards that can be put in place or other actions that can be taken to address any potential adverse consequences and consider whether there is a need to resign from the audit engagement.

An inadvertent violation of this Standard does not necessarily call into question the audit firm's ability to give an audit opinion provided that:

(a) the audit firm has established policies and procedures that require all partners and staff to report any breach promptly to the audit engagement partner or to the ethics partner, as appropriate;

(b) the audit engagement partner promptly notifies the partner or member of staff that any matter which has given rise to a breach is to be addressed as soon as possible and ensures that such action is taken;
(c) safeguards, if appropriate, are applied (for example, by having another partner review the work done by the relevant partner or member of staff or by removing him or her from the engagement team); and
(d) the actions taken and the rationale for them are documented.

General approach to non-audit services

5 Paragraphs 6 to 38 of this Standard set out the general approach to be adopted by audit firms and auditors in relation to the provision of non-audit services to their audit clients. This approach is applicable irrespective of the nature of the non-audit services, which may be in question in a given case. (Paragraphs 39 to 125 of this Standard illustrate the application of the general approach to a number of common non-audit services.)

6 In this Standard, 'non-audit services' comprise any engagement in which an audit firm provides professional services to an audit client other than pursuant to:

(a) the audit of financial statements; and
(b) those other roles which legislation or regulation specify can be performed by the auditors of the entity (for example, considering the preliminary announcements of listed companies, complying with the procedural and reporting requirements of regulators, such as requirements relating to the audit of the client's internal controls and reports in accordance with Section 151 or 173 of the Companies Act 1985).

7 There may be circumstances where the audit firm is engaged to provide a non-audit service and where that engagement and its scope are determined by a client which is not an audit client. However, it might be contemplated that an audit client may gain some benefit from that engagement[1]. In these circumstances, whilst there may be no threat to the audit firm's objectivity and independence at the time of appointment, the audit firm considers how the engagement may be expected to develop, whether there are any threats that the audit firm may be subject to if additional relevant parties which are audit clients are identified and whether any safeguards should be put in place.

8 In the case of a group, non-audit services, for the purposes of this Standard, include:

- services provided by the audit firm, to the parent company or to any affiliate;
- services provided by a network firm to the audit client or any of its significant affiliates; and
- services provided by the audit firm of a significant affiliate to the parent company.

9 **The audit firm should establish policies and procedures that require others within the firm, and its network, when considering whether to accept a proposed engagement to provide a non-audit service to an audit client or any of its affiliates, to communicate details of the proposed engagement to the audit engagement partner.**

[1] *For example, in a vendor due diligence engagement, the engagement is initiated and scoped by the vendor before the purchaser is identified. If an audit client of the firm undertaking the due diligence engagement is the purchaser, that audit client may gain the benefit of the report issued by its auditor, it may be a party to the engagement letter and it may pay an element of the fee.*

The audit firm establishes appropriate channels of internal communication to ensure that, in relation to an existing audit client, the audit engagement partner (or their delegate) is informed about any proposed engagement to provide a non-audit service to the audit client or any of its affiliates and that he or she considers the implications for the auditors' objectivity and independence before the engagement is accepted.

In the case of a listed company, the group audit engagement partner establishes that the company has communicated its policy on the engagement of external auditors to supply non-audit services to its affiliates and obtains confirmation that the auditors of the affiliates will comply with this policy.[2]

Identification and assessment of threats and safeguards

Before the audit firm accepts a proposed engagement to provide a non-audit service to an audit client, the audit engagement partner should:

(a) consider whether it is probable that a reasonable and informed third party would regard the objectives of the proposed engagement as being inconsistent with the objectives of the audit of the financial statements; and
(b) identify and assess the significance of any related threats to the auditors' objectivity, including any perceived loss of independence; and
(c) identify and assess the effectiveness of the available safeguards to eliminate the threats or reduce them to an acceptable level.

The objective of the audit of financial statements is to express an opinion on the preparation and presentation of those financial statements. For example, in the case of a limited company, legislation requires the auditors to make a report to the members on all annual accounts laid before the company in general meeting during their tenure of office. The report must state whether, in the auditors' opinion, the accounts have been properly prepared in accordance with the requirements of the legislation, and, in particular, whether they give a true and fair view in accordance with the relevant financial reporting framework.

Where the audit engagement partner considers that it is probable that a reasonable and informed third party would regard the objectives of the proposed non-audit service engagement as being inconsistent with the objectives of the audit of the financial statements, the audit firm should either:

(a) not undertake the non-audit service engagement; or
(b) not accept or withdraw from the audit engagement.

The objectives of engagements to provide non-audit services vary and depend on the specific terms of the engagement. In some cases these objectives may be inconsistent with those of the audit, and, in such cases, this may give rise to a threat to the auditors' objectivity and to the appearance of their independence. Audit firms do not undertake non-audit service engagements where the objectives of such engagements are inconsistent with the objectives of the audit, or do not accept or withdraw from the audit engagement.

Similarly, in relation to a possible new audit client, consideration needs to be given to recent, current and potential engagements to provide non-audit services by the audit firm for the prospective audit client and whether the scope and objectives of those engagements are consistent with the proposed audit engagement. In the case of listed

---

[2] *The Combined Code on Corporate Governance requires audit committees to develop the company's policy on the engagement of the external auditors to supply non-audit services.*

companies, when tendering for a new audit engagement, the audit firm ensures that relevant information on recent non-audit services is drawn to the attention of the audit committee, including:

- when recent non-audit services were provided to the potential client;
- the materiality of those non-audit services to the proposed audit engagement;
- whether those non-audit services would have been prohibited if the client had been an audit client at the time when they were undertaken; and
- the extent to which the outcomes of non-audit services have been audited or reviewed by another audit firm.

Threats to objectivity and independence

17 The principal types of threats to the auditors' objectivity and independence are:

- self-interest threat;
- self-review threat;
- management threat;
- advocacy threat;
- familiarity (or trust) threat; and
- intimidation threat.

The auditors remain alert to the possibility that any of these threats may occur in connection with non-audit services. However, the threats most commonly associated with non-audit services are self-interest threat, self-review threat, management threat and advocacy threat.

18 A **self-interest threat** exists when auditors have financial or other interests which might cause them to be reluctant to take actions that would be adverse to the interests of the audit firm or any individual in a position to influence the conduct or outcome of the audit. In relation to non-audit services, the main self-interest threat concerns fees and economic dependence and these are addressed in APB Ethical Standard 4.

19 Where substantial fees are regularly generated from the provision of non-audit services, and the fees for non-audit services are significantly greater than the annual audit and audit-related fees, the audit firm has regard to the possibility that there may be perceived to be a loss of independence. The audit firm addresses such perceived loss of independence by determining whether there is any risk that there will be an actual loss of independence and objectivity by the audit engagement team. The audit firm ensures that those charged with governance are informed of the position on a timely basis.

20 Where fees for non-audit services are calculated on a contingent fee basis, the perception may be that the audit firm's interests are so closely aligned with the audit client that it threatens the auditor's objectivity and independence. Any contingent fee that is material to the audit firm, or that part of the firm by reference to which the audit engagement partner's profit share is calculated, will create an unacceptable self-interest threat and the audit firm does not undertake such an engagement.

21 A **self-review threat** exists when the results of a non-audit service performed by the engagement team or by others within the audit firm are reflected in the amounts included or disclosed in the financial statements.

22 A threat to objectivity and independence arises because, in the course of the audit, the auditors may need to re-evaluate the work performed in the non-audit service.

As, by virtue of providing the non-audit service, the audit firm is associated with aspects of the preparation of the financial statements, it may be (or may appear to be) unable to take an impartial view of relevant aspects of those financial statements.

In assessing the significance of the self-review threat, the auditors consider the extent to which the non-audit service will: 23

- involve a significant degree of subjective judgment; and
- have a material effect on the preparation and presentation of the financial statements.

Where a significant degree of judgment relating to the financial statements is involved in a non-audit service engagement, the auditors may be inhibited from questioning that judgment in the course of the audit. Whether a significant degree of subjective judgment is involved will depend upon whether the non-audit service involves the application of well-established principles and procedures, and whether reliable information is available. If such circumstances do not exist because the non-audit service is based on concepts, methodologies or assumptions that require judgment and are not established by the client or by authoritative guidance, the auditors' objectivity and the appearance of their independence may be adversely affected. Where the provision of a proposed non-audit service would also have a material effect on the financial statements, it is unlikely that any safeguard can eliminate or reduce to an acceptable level the self-review threat. 24

A **management threat** exists when the audit firm undertakes work that involves making judgments and taking decisions that are properly the responsibility of management. 25

A threat to objectivity and independence arises because, by making judgments and taking decisions that are properly the responsibility of management, the audit firm erodes the distinction between the audit client and the audit firm. The auditors may become closely aligned with the views and interests of management and this may, in turn, impair or call into question the auditors' ability to apply a proper degree of professional scepticism in auditing the financial statements. The auditors' objectivity and the appearance of their independence therefore may be, or may be perceived to be, impaired. 26

Factors to be considered in determining whether a non-audit service does or does not give rise to a management threat include whether: 27

- the non-audit service results in recommendations by the audit firm justified by objective and transparent analyses or the client being given the opportunity to decide between reasonable alternatives;
- the auditors are satisfied that a member of management (or senior employee of the audit client) has been designated by the audit client to receive the results of the non-audit service and make any judgments and decisions that are needed; and
- that member of management has the capability to make independent management judgments and decisions on the basis of the information provided ('informed management').

Where there is 'informed management', the auditors assess whether there are safeguards that can be introduced that would be effective to avoid a management threat or to reduce it to a level at which it can be disregarded. In the absence of such circumstances, it is unlikely that any safeguards can eliminate the management threat or reduce it to an acceptable level. 28

29   An **advocacy threat** exists when the audit firm undertakes work that involves acting as an advocate for an audit client and supporting a position taken by management in an adversarial context.

30   A threat to objectivity and independence arises because, in order to act in an advocacy role, the audit firm has to adopt a position closely aligned to that of management. This creates both actual and perceived threats to the auditors' objectivity and independence. For example, where the audit firm, acting as advocate, has supported a particular contention of management, it may be difficult for the auditors to take an impartial view of this in the context of the audit of the financial statements.

31   Where the provision of a non-audit service would require the auditors to act as advocates for the audit client in relation to matters that are material to the financial statements, it is unlikely that any safeguards can eliminate or reduce to an acceptable level the advocacy threat that would exist.

Safeguards

32   Where any threat to the auditors' objectivity and the appearance of their independence is identified, the audit engagement partner assesses the significance of that threat and considers whether there are safeguards that could be applied and which would be effective to eliminate the threat or reduce it to an acceptable level. If such safeguards can be identified and are applied, the non-audit service may be provided. However, where no such safeguards are applied, the only course is for the audit firm either not to undertake the engagement to provide the non-audit service in question or not to accept (or to withdraw from) the audit engagement.

33   **Where the audit engagement partner concludes that no appropriate safeguards are available to eliminate or reduce to an acceptable level the threats to the auditors' objectivity, including any perceived loss of independence, related to a proposed engagement to provide a non-audit service to an audit client, he or she should inform the others concerned within the audit firm of that conclusion and the firm should either:**

   (a)   not undertake the non-audit service engagement; or
   (b)   not accept or withdraw from the audit engagement.

   If the audit engagement partner is in doubt as to the appropriate action to be taken, he or she should resolve the matter through consultation with the ethics partner.

34   An initial assessment of the threats to objectivity and independence and the safeguards to be applied is required when the audit engagement partner is considering the acceptance of an engagement to provide a non-audit service. That assessment is reviewed whenever the scope and objectives of the non-audit service change significantly. If such a review suggests that safeguards cannot reduce the threat to an acceptable level, the audit firm withdraws from the non-audit service engagement, or does not accept re-appointment or withdraws from the audit engagement.

Communication with those charged with governance

35   **The audit engagement partner should ensure that those charged with governance of the audit client are appropriately informed on a timely basis of:**

(a) all significant facts and matters that bear upon the auditors' objectivity and independence, related to the provision of non-audit services, including the safeguards put in place; and
(b) for listed companies, any inconsistencies between APB Ethical Standards and the company's policy for the supply of non-audit services by the audit firm and any apparent breach of that policy.²

Transparency is a key element in addressing the issues raised by the provision of non-audit services by audit firms to their audit clients. This can be facilitated by timely communication with those charged with governance of the audit client (see APB Ethical Standard 1, paragraphs 49 to 53). Such communications are addressed to the audit committee, where there is one; in other circumstances, they are addressed to the board of directors (or those in an equivalent position). In the case of listed companies, ensuring that the audit committee is properly informed about the issues associated with the provision of non-audit services will assist them to comply with the provisions of the Combined Code on Corporate Governance relating to reviewing and monitoring the external auditors' independence and objectivity and to developing a policy on the engagement of external auditors to supply non-audit services. This will include discussion of any inconsistencies between the company's policy and APB Ethical Standards and ensuring that the policy is communicated to affiliates.

Documentation

The audit engagement partner should ensure that the reasoning for a decision to undertake an engagement to provide non-audit services to an audit client, and any safeguards adopted, is appropriately documented.

Matters to be documented include any significant judgments concerning:

- threats identified;
- safeguards adopted and the reasons why they are considered to be effective; and
- communication with those charged with governance.

Application of general principles to specific non-audit services

Internal audit services

The range of 'internal audit services' is wide and they may not be termed as such by the audit client. For example, the audit firm may be engaged:

- to outsource the audit client's entire internal audit function; or
- to supplement the audit client's internal audit function in specific areas (for example, by providing specialised technical services or resources in particular locations); or
- to provide occasional internal audit services to the audit client on an *ad hoc* basis.

All such engagements would fall within the term 'internal audit services'.

The main threats to the auditors' objectivity and independence arising from the provision of internal audit services are the self-review threat and the management threat.

41 Engagements to provide internal audit services - other than those prohibited in paragraph 43 - may be undertaken, provided that the auditors are satisfied that 'informed management'[3] has been designated by the audit client and provided that appropriate safeguards are applied.

42 Examples of safeguards that may be appropriate when internal audit services are provided to an audit client include ensuring that:
- internal audit projects undertaken by the audit firm are performed by partners and staff who have no involvement in the external audit of the financial statements;
- the audit of the financial statements is reviewed by an audit partner who is not involved in the audit engagement, to ensure that the internal audit work performed by the audit firm has been properly and effectively assessed in the context of the audit of the financial statements.

43 **The audit firm should not undertake an engagement to provide internal audit services to an audit client where it is reasonably foreseeable that:**
   (a) for the purposes of the audit of the financial statements, the auditors would place significant reliance on the internal audit work performed by the audit firm; or
   (b) for the purposes of the internal audit services, the audit firm would undertake part of the role of management.

44 The self-review threat is unacceptably high where the auditors cannot perform the audit of the financial statements without placing significant reliance on the work performed for the purposes of the internal audit services engagement. For example, the provision of internal audit services on the internal financial controls for an audit client which is a large bank, is likely to be unacceptable as the external audit team is likely to place significant reliance on the work performed by the internal audit team in relation to the bank's internal financial controls.

45 The management threat is unacceptably high where the audit firm provides internal audit services that involve audit firm personnel taking decisions or making judgments, which are properly the responsibility of management. For example, such situations can arise where the nature of the internal audit work involves the audit firm in taking decisions as to:
- the scope and nature of the internal audit services to be provided to the audit client, or
- the design of internal controls or implementing changes thereto.

46 During the course of the audit the auditors generally evaluate the design and test the operating effectiveness of some of the entity's internal financial controls, including the operation of any internal audit function and provide management with observations on matters that have come to their attention, including comments on weaknesses in the internal control systems (including the internal audit function) and suggestions for addressing them. This work is a by-product of the audit service rather than the result of a specific engagement to provide non-audit services and therefore does not constitute internal audit services for the purposes of this Standard.

47 In some circumstances, additional internal financial controls work is performed during the course of the audit in response to a specific request for an extended scope to the external audit. Whether it is appropriate for this work to be undertaken by the audit firm will depend on the extent to which it gives rise to a management threat to

---

[3] *The nature of 'informed management' is discussed in paragraph 27.*

the auditor's objectivity and independence. The audit engagement partner reviews the scope and objectives of the proposed work and assesses the threats to which it gives rise and the safeguards available.

Information technology services

48 Design, provision and implementation of information technology (including financial information technology) systems by audit firms for their audit clients creates threats to the auditors' objectivity and independence. The principal threats are the self-review threat and the management threat.

49 Engagements to design, provide or implement information technology systems that are not important to any significant part of the accounting system or to the production of the financial statements and do not have significant reliance placed on them by the auditors, may be undertaken, provided that 'informed management'[3] has been designated by the audit client and provided that appropriate safeguards are applied.

50 Examples of safeguards that may be appropriate when information technology services are provided to an audit client include ensuring that:

- information technology projects undertaken by the audit firm are performed by partners and staff who have no involvement in the external audit of the financial statements;
- the audit of the financial statements is reviewed by an audit partner who is not involved in the audit engagement to ensure that the information technology work performed has been properly and effectively assessed in the context of the audit of the financial statements.

51 **The audit firm should not undertake an engagement to design, provide or implement information technology systems for an audit client where:**

(a) the systems concerned would be important to any significant part of the accounting system or to the production of the financial statements and the auditors would place significant reliance upon them as part of the audit of the financial statements; or

(b) for the purposes of the information technology services, the audit firm would undertake part of the role of management.

52 Where it is reasonably apparent that, having regard to the activities and size of the audit client and the range and complexity of the proposed system, the management lacks the expertise required to take responsibility for the systems concerned, it is unlikely that any safeguards would be sufficient to eliminate these threats or to reduce them to an acceptable level. In particular, formal acceptance by management of the systems designed and installed by the audit firm is unlikely to be an effective safeguard when, in substance, the audit firm have been retained by management as experts and they make important decisions in relation to the design or implementation of systems of internal control and financial reporting.

53 The provision and installation of information technology services associated with a standard 'off the shelf accounting package' (including basic set-up procedures to make the package operate on the client's existing platform and peripherals, setting up the chart of accounts and the entry of standard data such as the client's product names and prices) is unlikely to create a level of threat to the auditor's objectivity and independence that cannot be addressed through applying appropriate safeguards.

Valuation services

54 The audit firm should not undertake an engagement to provide a valuation to an audit client where the valuation would both:

(a) involve a significant degree of subjective judgment; and
(b) have a material effect on the financial statements.

55 The main threats to the auditors' objectivity and independence arising from the provision of valuation services are the self-review threat and the management threat. The self-review threat is considered too high to allow the provision of valuation services which involve the valuation of amounts with a significant degree of subjectivity that may have a material effect on the financial statements.

56 This restriction does not apply in circumstances where the auditors are designated by legislation or regulation as being eligible to carry out a valuation.[4] In such circumstances, the audit engagement partner applies relevant safeguards.

57 It is usual for the auditors to provide the management with accounting advice in relation to valuation matters that have come to their attention during the course of the audit. Such matters might typically include:

- comments on valuation assumptions and their appropriateness;
- errors identified in a valuation calculation and suggestions for correcting them;
- advice on accounting policies and any valuation methodologies used in their application.

Advice on such matters does not constitute valuation services for the purpose of this Standard.

58 Where auditors are engaged to collect and verify the accuracy of data to be used in a valuation to be performed by others, such engagements do not constitute valuation services under this Standard.

Actuarial valuation services

59 The audit firm should not undertake an engagement to provide actuarial valuation services to an audit client, unless the firm is satisfied that either:

(a) all significant judgments, including the assumptions, are made by 'informed management'; or
(b) the valuation has no material effect on the financial statements.

60 Actuarial valuation services are subject to the same general principles as other valuation services. Where they involve the audit firm in making a subjective judgment and have a material effect on the financial statements, actuarial valuations give rise to an unacceptable level of self-review threat and so may not be performed by audit firms for their audit clients.

61 However, in cases where all significant judgments concerning the assumptions, methodology and data for the actuarial valuation are made by 'informed management' and the audit firm's role is limited to applying proven methodologies using the

---

[4] For example, Section 103 of the Companies Act 1985 requires a public company to obtain a report on the value of assets to be received in payment for shares to be allotted from independent accountants who either are the auditors or are qualified to act as auditors, of the allotting company.

given data, for which the management takes responsibility, it may be possible to establish effective safeguards to protect the auditors' objectivity and the appearance of their independence.

Tax services

The range of activities encompassed by the term 'tax services' is wide. Three broad categories of tax service can be distinguished. They are where the audit firm: 62
(a) provides advice to the audit client on one or more specific matters at the request of the audit client; or
(b) undertakes a substantial proportion of the tax planning or compliance work for the audit client; or
(c) promotes tax structures or products to the audit client, the effectiveness of which is likely to be influenced by the manner in which they are accounted for in the financial statements.

Whilst it is possible to consider tax services under broad headings, such as tax planning or compliance, in practice these services are often interrelated and it is impracticable to analyse services in this way for the purposes of attempting to identify generically the threats to which specific engagements give rise. As a result, audit firms need to identify and assess, on a case-by-case basis, the potential threats to the auditors' objectivity and independence before deciding whether to undertake a proposed engagement to provide tax services to an audit client.

The provision of tax services by audit firms to their audit clients may give rise to a number of threats to the auditors' objectivity and independence, including the self-interest threat, the management threat, the advocacy threat and, where the work involves a significant degree of subjective judgment and has a material effect on the financial statements, the self-review threat. 63

Where the audit firm provides advice to the audit client on one or more specific matters at the request of the audit client, a self-review threat may be created. This self-review threat is more significant where the audit firm undertakes a substantial proportion of the tax planning and compliance work for the audit client. However, the auditors may be able to adopt appropriate safeguards. 64

Examples of such safeguards that may be appropriate when tax services are provided to an audit client include ensuring that: 65
- the tax services are provided by partners and staff who have no involvement in the audit of the financial statements;
- the tax services are reviewed by an independent tax partner, or other senior tax employee;
- external independent advice is obtained on the tax work;
- tax computations prepared by the audit team are reviewed by a partner or senior staff member with appropriate expertise who is not a member of the audit team; or
- an audit partner not involved in the audit engagement reviews whether the tax work has been properly and effectively addressed in the context of the audit of the financial statements.

The audit firm should not promote tax structures or products or undertake an engagement to provide tax advice to an audit client where the audit engagement partner has, or ought to have, reasonable doubt as to the appropriateness of the related 66 accounting treatment involved, having regard to the requirement for the financial statements to give a true and fair view in accordance with the relevant financial reporting framework.

67   Where the audit firm promotes tax structures or products or undertakes an engagement to provide tax advice to the audit client, it may be necessary to adopt an accounting treatment about which there is reasonable doubt as to its appropriateness, in order to achieve the desired result. A self-review threat arises in the course of an audit because the auditors may be unable to form an impartial view of the accounting treatment to be adopted for the purposes of the proposed arrangements. Accordingly, this Standard does not permit the promotion of tax structures or products by audit firms to their audit clients where, in the view of the audit engagement partner, after such consultation as is appropriate, the effectiveness of the tax structure or product depends on an accounting treatment about which there is reasonable doubt as to its appropriateness.

68   The audit firm should not undertake an engagement to provide tax services to an audit client wholly or partly on a contingent fee basis where:

(a)   the engagement fees are material to the audit firm or the part of the firm by reference to which the audit engagement partner's profit share is calculated; or
(b)   the outcome of those tax services (and, therefore, the entitlement to the fee) is dependent on:
   (i)   the application of tax law which is uncertain or has not been established; and
   (ii) a future or contemporary audit judgment relating to a material balance in the financial statements of the audit client.

69   Where tax services, such as advising on corporate structures and structuring transactions to achieve a particular effect, are undertaken on a contingent fee basis, self-interest threats to the auditors' objectivity and independence may arise. The auditors may have, or may appear to have, an interest in the success of the tax services, causing them to make an audit judgment about which there is reasonable doubt as to its appropriateness. Where the contingent fee is determined by the outcome of the application of tax law, which is uncertain or has not been established, and where the tax implications are material to the financial statements, the self-interest threat cannot be eliminated or reduced to an acceptable level by the application of any safeguards.

70   The audit firm should not undertake an engagement to provide tax services to an audit client where the engagement would involve the audit firm undertaking a management role.

71   When providing tax services to an audit client, there is a risk that the audit firm undertakes a management role, unless the firm is working with 'informed management'[3] and appropriate safeguards are applied.

72   For entities other than listed companies or significant affiliates of listed companies, auditors may undertake an engagement to prepare accounting entries relating to tax and deferred tax calculations, provided that:

(a)   such services:
   (i)   do not involve initiating transactions or taking management decisions; and
   (ii) are of a technical, mechanical or an informative nature; and
(b)   appropriate safeguards are applied.

The audit firm should not undertake an engagement to provide tax services to an audit 73
client where this would involve acting as an advocate for the audit client, before an
appeals tribunal or court[5] in the resolution of an issue:

(a) **that is material to the financial statements; or**
(b) **where the outcome of the tax issue is dependent on a future or contemporary audit judgment.**

Where the tax services to be provided by the audit firm include representing the client 74
in any negotiations or proceedings involving the tax authorities, advocacy threats to
the auditors' objectivity and independence may arise.

The audit firm is not acting as an advocate where the tax services involve the pro- 75
vision of information to the tax authorities (including an explanation of the
approach being taken and the arguments being advanced by the audit client). In such
circumstances effective safeguards may exist and the tax authorities will undertake
their own review of the issues.

Where the tax authorities indicate that they are minded to reject the audit client's 76
arguments on a particular issue and the matter is likely to be determined by an
appeals tribunal or court, the audit firm may become so closely identified with
management's arguments that the auditors are inhibited from forming an impartial
view of the treatment of the issue in the financial statements. In such circumstances,
if the issue is material to the financial statements or is dependent on a future or
contemporary audit judgment, the audit firm discusses the matter with the audit
client and makes it clear to the client that it will have to withdraw from that element
of the engagement to provide tax services that requires it to act as advocate for the
audit client, or resign from the audit engagement from the time when the matter is
formally listed for hearing before the appeals tribunal.

The audit firm is not, however, precluded from having a continuing role (for 77
example, responding to specific requests for information) for the audit client in
relation to the appeal. The audit firm assesses the threat associated with any continuing role in accordance with the provisions of paragraphs 78 to 80 of this
Standard.

Litigation support services

The audit firm should not undertake an engagement to provide litigation support ser- 78
vices to an audit client where this would involve the estimation by the audit firm of the
likely outcome of a pending legal matter that could be material to the amounts to be
included or the disclosures to be made in the financial statements and there is a sig-
nificant degree of subjectivity involved.

Although management and advocacy threats may arise in litigation support services, 79
such as acting as an expert witness, the primary issue is that a self-review threat will
arise where such services involve a subjective estimation of the likely outcome of a
matter that is material to the amounts to be included or the disclosures to be made in
the financial statements.

---

[5] *The restriction applies to the first level of Tax Court that is independent of the tax authorities and to more authoritative bodies. In the UK this would be the General or Special Commissioners of the Inland Revenue or the VAT and Duties Tribunal.*

80   Litigation support services that do not involve such subjective estimations are not prohibited, provided that the audit firm has carefully considered the implications of any threats and established appropriate safeguards.

Legal services

81   The audit firm should not undertake an engagement to provide legal services to an audit client where this would involve acting as the solicitor formally nominated to represent the client in the resolution of a dispute or litigation which is material to the amounts to be included or the disclosures to be made in the financial statements.

82   Although the provision by auditors of certain types of legal services to their audit clients may create advocacy, self-review and management threats, this Standard does not impose a general prohibition on the provision of legal services. However, in view of the degree of advocacy involved in litigation or other types of dispute resolution procedures and the potential importance of any assessment by the auditors of the merits of the audit client's position when auditing its financial statements, this Standard prohibits an audit firm from acting as the formally nominated representative for an audit client in the resolution of a dispute or litigation which is material to the financial statements (either in terms of the amounts recognised or disclosed in the financial statements).

Recruitment and remuneration services

83   The audit firm should not undertake an engagement to provide recruitment services to an audit client that would involve the firm taking responsibility for the appointment of any director or employee of the audit client.

84   A management threat arises where audit firm personnel take responsibility for any decision as to who should be appointed by the audit client.

85   For an audit client that is a listed company, the audit firm should not undertake an engagement to provide recruitment services in relation to a key management position of the audit client, or a significant affiliate of such an entity.

86   A familiarity threat arises if the audit firm plays a significant role in relation to the identification and recruitment of senior members of management within the company, as the audit engagement team may be less likely to be critical of the information or explanations provided by such individuals than might otherwise be the case. Accordingly, for listed companies, and for significant affiliates of such entities, the audit firm does not undertake engagements that involve the recruitment of individuals for key management positions.

87   The audit firm's policies and procedures will set out circumstances in which recruitment services are not undertaken for non-listed audit clients. These policies will take into consideration the nature of the entity's business, its size, the number of its employees and the range of its stakeholders.

88   Recruitment services involve a specifically identifiable, and separately remunerated, engagement. Audit firms and engagement teams may contribute to an entity's recruitment process in less formal ways. The prohibition set out in paragraph 85 does not extend to senior members of an audit team interviewing prospective employees of

the audit client or to the audit entity using information gathered by the audit firm, including that relating to salary surveys.

The audit firm should not undertake an engagement to provide advice on the quantum of the remuneration package or the measurement criteria on which the quantum is calculated, for a director or key management position of an audit client. 89

The provision of advice on remuneration packages (including bonus arrangements, incentive plans and other benefits) to existing or prospective employees of the audit client gives rise to familiarity threats. The significance of the familiarity threat is considered too high to allow advice on the overall amounts to be paid or on the quantitative measurement criteria included in remuneration packages for directors and key management positions. 90

For other employees, these threats can be adequately addressed by the application of safeguards, such as the advice being provided by partners and staff who have no involvement in the audit of the financial statements. 91

In cases where all significant judgments concerning the assumptions, methodology and data for the calculation of remuneration packages for directors and key management are made by 'informed management' or a third party and the audit firm's role is limited to applying proven methodologies using the given data, for which the management takes responsibility, it may be possible to establish effective safeguards to protect the auditors' objectivity and independence. 92

Advice on tax, pensions and interpretation of accounting standards relating to remuneration packages for directors and key management can be provided by the audit firm, provided they are not prohibited by the requirements of this Standard relating to tax, actuarial valuations and accounting services. Disclosure of the provision of any such advice would be made to those charged with governance of the audit client (see APB Ethical Standard 1, paragraphs 49 to 53). 93

Corporate finance services

The range of services encompassed by the term 'corporate finance services' is wide. For example, the audit firm may be engaged: 94

- to identify possible purchasers for parts of the audit client's business and provide advisory services in the course of such sales; or
- to identify possible 'targets' for the audit client to acquire; or
- to advise the audit client on how to fund its financing requirements, including advising on debt restructuring and securitisation programmes; or
- to act as sponsor on admission to listing on the London Stock Exchange, or as Nominated Advisor on the admission of the audit client on the Alternative Investments Market (AIM); or
- to act as financial adviser to audit client offerors or offerees in connection with public takeovers.

The potential for the auditors' objectivity and independence to be impaired through the provision of corporate finance services varies considerably depending on the precise nature of the service provided. The main threats to auditors' objectivity and independence arising from the provision of corporate finance services are the self-review, management and advocacy threats. Self-interest threats may also arise, especially in situations where the audit firm is paid on a contingent fee basis. 95

96 When providing corporate finance services to an audit client, there is a risk that the audit firm undertakes a management role, unless the firm is working with 'informed management'[3] and appropriate safeguards are applied.

97 Examples of safeguards that may be appropriate when corporate finance services are provided to an audit client include ensuring that:

- the corporate finance advice is provided by partners and staff who have no involvement in the audit of the financial statements;
- any advice provided is reviewed by an independent corporate finance partner within the audit firm;
- external independent advice on the corporate finance work is obtained;
- an audit partner who is not involved in the audit engagement reviews the audit work performed in relation to the subject matter of the corporate finance services provided to ensure that such audit work has been properly and effectively reviewed and assessed in the context of the audit of the financial statements.

98 Where the audit firm undertakes an engagement to provide corporate finance services to an audit client in connection with conducting the sale or purchase of a material part of the audit client's business, the audit engagement partner should inform the audit committee (or equivalent) about the engagement, as set out in paragraphs 49 to 53 of APB Ethical Standard 1.

99 **The audit firm should not undertake an engagement to provide corporate finance services to an audit client where:**

(a) **the engagement would involve the audit firm taking responsibility for dealing in, underwriting or promoting shares; or**
(b) **the audit engagement partner has, or ought to have, reasonable doubt as to the appropriateness of an accounting treatment that is related to the advice provided, having regard to the requirement for the financial statements to give a true and fair view in accordance with the relevant financial reporting framework; or**
(c) **such corporate finance services are to be provided on a contingent fee basis and:**
  (i) **the engagement fees are material to the audit firm or the part of the firm by reference to which the audit engagement partner's profit share is calculated; or**
  (ii) **the outcome of those corporate finance services (and, therefore, the entitlement to the fee) is dependent on a future or contemporary audit judgment relating to a material balance in the financial statements of the audit client; or**
(d) **the engagement would involve the audit firm undertaking a management role.**

100 An unacceptable advocacy threat arises where, in the course of providing a corporate finance service, the audit firm promotes the interests of the audit client by taking responsibility for dealing in, underwriting, or promoting shares.

101 Where the audit firm acts as a sponsor under the Listing Rules[6], or as Nominated Adviser on the admission of the audit client to the AIM, the audit firm is required to confirm that the audit client has satisfied all applicable conditions for listing and other relevant requirements of the listing (or AIM) rules. Where there is, or there ought to be, reasonable doubt that the audit firm will be able to give that confirmation, it does not enter into such an engagement.

---

[6] *In the United Kingdom, the UK Listing Authority's publication the 'Listing Rules'. In the Republic of Ireland, the United Kingdom 'Listing Rules' as modified by the 'Notes on the Listing Rules' published by the Irish Stock Exchange.*

102 A self-review threat arises where the outcome or consequences of the corporate finance service provided by the audit firm may be material to the financial statements of the audit client, which are, or will be, subject to audit by the same firm. Where the audit firm provides corporate finance services, for example advice to the audit client on financing arrangements, it may be necessary to adopt an accounting treatment about which there is reasonable doubt as to its appropriateness in order to achieve the desired result. A self-review threat is created because the auditors may be unable to form an impartial view of the accounting treatment to be adopted for the purposes of the proposed arrangements. Accordingly, this Standard does not permit the provision of advice by audit firms to their audit clients where there is reasonable doubt about the appropriateness of the related accounting treatments.

103 Advice to audit clients on funding issues and banking arrangements, where there is no reasonable doubt as to the appropriateness of the accounting treatment, is not prohibited provided this does not involve the audit firm in taking decisions or making judgments which are properly the responsibility of management.

104 Where a corporate finance engagement is undertaken on a contingent fee basis, self-interest threats to the auditors' objectivity and independence also arise as the auditors may have, or may appear to have, an interest in the success of the corporate finance services. The significance of the self-interest threat is primarily determined by the materiality of the contingent fee to the audit firm, or to the part of the firm by reference to which the audit engagement partner's profit share is calculated. Where the contingent fee and the outcome of the corporate finance services is dependent on a future or contemporary audit judgment relating to a material balance included in the financial statements of the audit client, the self-interest threat cannot be eliminated or reduced to an acceptable level by the application of any safeguards.

105 These restrictions do not apply in circumstances where the auditors are designated by legislation or regulation as being eligible to carry out a particular service. In such circumstances, the audit engagement partner establishes appropriate safeguards.

Transaction related services

106 In addition to corporate finance services, there are other non-audit services associated with transactions that an audit firm may undertake for an audit client. For example:

- investigations into possible acquisitions or disposals ('due diligence' investigations); or
- investigations into the tax affairs of possible acquisitions or disposals; or
- the provision of information to sponsors in relation to prospectuses and other investment circulars (for example, long form reports, comfort letters on the adequacy of working capital).

107 When providing transaction related services to an audit client, unless the firm is working with 'informed management'[3] and appropriate safeguards are applied, there is a risk that the audit firm undertakes a management role.

108 Examples of safeguards that may be appropriate when transaction related services are provided to an audit client include ensuring that:

- the transaction related advice is provided by partners and staff who have no involvement in the audit of the financial statements;

- any advice provided is reviewed by an independent transactions partner within the audit firm;
- external independent advice on the transaction related work is obtained;
- an audit partner who is not involved in the audit engagement reviews the audit work performed in relation to the subject matter of the transaction related service provided to ensure that such audit work has been properly and effectively reviewed and assessed in the context of the audit of the financial statements.

109 **The audit firm should not undertake an engagement to provide transaction related services to an audit client where:**

(a) **the audit engagement partner has, or ought to have, reasonable doubt as to the appropriateness of an accounting treatment that is related to the advice provided, having regard to the requirement for the financial statements to give a true and fair view in accordance with the relevant financial reporting framework; or**

(b) **such transaction related services are to be provided on a contingent fee basis and:**
  (i) **the engagement fees are material to the audit firm or the part of the firm by reference to which the audit engagement partner's profit share is calculated; or**
  (ii) **the outcome of those transaction related services (and, therefore, the entitlement to the fee) is dependent on a future or contemporary audit judgment relating to a material balance in the financial statements of the audit client; or**

(c) **the engagement would involve the audit firm undertaking a management role.**

110 A self-review threat arises where the outcome of the transaction related service undertaken by the audit firm may be material to the financial statements of the audit client which are, or will be, subject to audit by the same firm. Where the audit client proposes to undertake a transaction, it may be necessary to adopt an inappropriate accounting treatment in order to achieve the desired result. A self-review threat is created if the auditors undertake transaction related services in connection with such a transaction. Accordingly, this Standard does not permit the provision of advice by audit firms to their audit clients where there is reasonable doubt about the appropriateness of the accounting treatments related to the transaction advice given.

111 Where a transaction related services engagement is undertaken on a contingent fee basis, self-interest threats to the auditors' objectivity and independence also arise as the auditors may have, or may appear to have, an interest in the success of the transaction. The significance of the self-interest threat is primarily determined by the materiality of the contingent fee to the audit firm, or to the part of the firm by reference to which the audit engagement partner's profit share is calculated. Where the contingent fee and the outcome of the transaction related services is dependent on a future or contemporary audit judgment on a material balance included in the financial statements of the audit client, the self-interest threat cannot be eliminated or reduced to an acceptable level by the application of any safeguards, other than where the transaction is subject to a pre-established dispute resolution procedure.

112 These restrictions do not apply in circumstances where the auditors are designated by legislation or regulation as being eligible to carry out a particular service. In such circumstances, the audit engagement partner establishes appropriate safeguards.

Accounting services

113 In this Standard, the term 'accounting services' is defined as the provision of services that involve the maintenance of accounting records or the preparation of financial

statements that are then subject to audit. Advice on the implementation of current and proposed accounting standards is not included in the term 'accounting services'.

The range of activities encompassed by the term 'accounting services' is wide. In some cases, the audit client may ask the audit firm to provide a complete service including maintaining all of the accounting records and the preparation of the financial statements. Other common situations are: 114

- the audit firm may take over the provision of a specific accounting function on an outsourced basis (for example, payroll);
- the audit client maintains the accounting records, undertakes basic bookkeeping and prepares a year-end trial balance and asks the audit firm to assist with the preparation of the necessary adjustments and the financial statements.

The provision of accounting services by the audit firm to the audit client creates threats to the auditors' objectivity and independence, principally self-review and management threats, the significance of which depends on the nature and extent of the accounting services in question and upon the level of public interest in the audit client. 115

When providing accounting services to an audit client, unless the firm is working with 'informed management'[3], there is a risk that the audit firm undertakes a management role. 116

The audit firm should not undertake an engagement to provide accounting services to: 117

(a) an audit client that is a listed company or a significant affiliate of such an entity, save where the circumstances contemplated in paragraph 121 apply; or

(b) any other audit client, where those accounting services would involve the audit firm undertaking part of the role of management.

Even where there is no engagement to provide any accounting services, it is usual for the auditors to provide the management with accounting advice on matters that have come to their attention during the course of the audit. Such matters might typically include: 118

- comments on weaknesses in the accounting records and suggestions for addressing them;
- errors identified in the accounting records and in the financial statements and suggestions for correcting them;
- advice on the accounting policies in use and on the application of current and proposed accounting standards.

This advice is a by-product of the audit service rather than the result of any engagement to provide non-audit services. Consequently, as it is part of the audit service, such advice cannot be regarded as giving rise to any threat to the auditors' objectivity and independence.

For listed companies or significant affiliates of such entities, the threats to the auditors' objectivity and independence that would be created are too high to allow the audit firm to undertake an engagement to provide any accounting services, save where the circumstances contemplated in paragraph 121 apply. 119

The audit firm's policies and procedures will set out circumstances in which accounting services are not undertaken for non-listed audit clients. These policies will take into consideration the nature of the entity's business, its size, the number of its employees and the range of its stakeholders. 120

121 In emergency situations, the audit firm may provide a listed audit client, or a significant affiliate of such a company, with accounting services to assist the company in the timely preparation of its financial statements. This might arise when, due to external and unforeseeable events, the audit firm personnel are the only people with the necessary knowledge of the audit client's systems and procedures. A situation could be considered an emergency where the audit firm's refusal to provide these services would result in a severe burden for the audit client (for example, withdrawal of credit lines), or would even threaten its going concern status. In such circumstances, the audit firm ensures that:

(a) any staff involved in the accounting services have no involvement in the audit of the financial statements; and
(b) the engagement would not lead to any audit firm staff or partners taking decisions or making judgments which are properly the responsibility of management.

122 For entities other than listed companies or significant affiliates of listed companies, auditors may undertake an engagement to provide accounting services, provided that:

(a) such services:
 (i) do not involve initiating transactions or taking management decisions; and
 (ii) are of a technical, mechanical or an informative nature; and
(b) appropriate safeguards are applied.

123 The maintenance of the accounting records and the preparation of the financial statements are the responsibility of the management of the audit client. Accordingly, in any engagement to provide the audit client with accounting services, the audit firm does not initiate any transactions or take any decisions or make any judgments, which are properly the responsibility of the management. These include:

- authorising or approving transactions;
- preparing originating data (including valuation assumptions);
- determining or changing journal entries, or the classifications for accounts or transactions, or other accounting records without management approval.

124 Examples of accounting services of a technical or mechanical nature or of an informative nature include:

- recording transactions for which management has determined the appropriate account classification, posting coded transactions to the general ledger, posting entries approved by management to the trial balance or providing certain data-processing services (for example, payroll);
- assistance with the preparation of the financial statements where management takes all decisions on issues requiring the exercise of judgment and has prepared the underlying accounting records.

125 Examples of safeguards that may be appropriate when accounting services are provided to an audit client include:

- accounting services provided by the audit firm are performed by partners and staff who have no involvement in the external audit of the financial statements;
- the accounting services are reviewed by a partner or other senior staff member with appropriate expertise who is not a member of the audit team;
- the audit of the financial statements is reviewed by an audit partner who is not involved in the audit engagement to ensure that the accounting services performed have been properly and effectively assessed in the context of the audit of the financial statements.

Effective date

Effective for audits of financial statements for periods commencing on or after 15 December 2004. — 126

Firms may complete audit engagements relating to periods commencing prior to 15 December 2004 in accordance with existing ethical guidance from the relevant professional body, putting in place any necessary changes in the subsequent engagement period. — 127

Where compliance with the requirements of ES 5 would result in a service not being supplied, services contracted before 5 October 2004 may continue to be provided until either: — 128

(a) the completion of the specific task or the end of the contract term, where this is set out in the contract; or
(b) 15 December 2005, where a task or term is not defined,

as long as the following apply:

- the engagement was permitted by existing ethical guidance (including transitional provisions) from the relevant professional body;
- any safeguards required by existing ethical guidance continue to be applied; and
- the need for additional safeguards is assessed, including where possible any additional safeguards specified by ES5, and if considered necessary, those additional safeguards are applied.

In the first year of appointment as auditors to an audit client, an audit firm may continue to provide non-audit services which are already contracted at the date of appointment, until either: — 129

(i) the completion of the specific task or the end of the contract term, where this is set out in the contract; or
(ii) one year after the date of appointment, where a task or term is not defined,

provided that the need for additional safeguards is assessed and if considered necessary, those additional safeguards are applied.

ES5 (Revised)*
Non-audit services provided to audited entities

(Revised April 2008)

Contents

	Paragraph
Introduction	1 – 4
General approach to non-audit services	5 – 39
Identification and assessment of threats and safeguards	11 – 34
Communication with those charged with governance	35 – 36
Documentation	37 – 39
Application of general principles to specific non-audit services	40 – 135
Internal audit services	40 – 48
Information technology services	49 – 54
Valuation services	55 – 62
Actuarial valuation services	63 – 67
Tax services	68 – 86
Litigation support services	87 – 90
Legal services	91 – 92
Recruitment and remuneration services	93 – 103
Corporate finance services	104 – 115
Transaction related services	116 – 122
Accounting services	123 – 135
Effective date	136 – 139

---

* *Revisions to this Standard became effective for audits of financial statements for periods commencing on or after 6 April 2008. The Standard effective before this date is available from the APB website.*

Preface

APB Ethical Standards apply in the audit of financial statements. They are read in the context of the Auditing Practices Board's Statement "The Auditing Practices Board – Scope and Authority of Pronouncements (Revised)" which sets out the application and authority of APB Ethical Standards.

The terms used in APB Ethical Standards are explained in the Glossary.

APB Ethical Standards apply to audits of financial statements in both the private and the public sectors. However, auditors in the public sector are subject to more complex ethical requirements than their private sector counterparts. This includes, for example, compliance with legislation such as the Prevention of Corruption Act 1916, concerning gifts and hospitality, and with Cabinet Office guidance.

Introduction

APB Ethical Standard 1 requires the audit engagement partner to identify and assess the circumstances which could adversely affect the auditor's objectivity ('threats'), including any perceived loss of independence, and to apply procedures ('safeguards') which will either:

(a) eliminate the threat; or
(b) reduce the threat to an acceptable level (that is, a level at which it is not probable that a reasonable and informed third party would conclude that the auditor's objectivity and independence either is impaired or is likely to be impaired).

When considering safeguards, where the audit engagement partner chooses to reduce rather than to eliminate a threat to objectivity and independence, he or she recognises that this judgment may not be shared by users of the financial statements and that he or she may be required to justify the decision.

This Standard provides requirements and guidance on specific circumstances arising from the provision of non-audit services by audit firms to entities audited by them, which may create threats to the auditor's objectivity or perceived loss of independence. It gives examples of safeguards that can, in some circumstances, eliminate the threat or reduce it to an acceptable level. In circumstances where this is not possible, either the non-audit service engagement in question is not undertaken or the auditor either does not accept or withdraws from the audit engagement, as appropriate.

Whenever a possible or actual breach of an APB Ethical Standard is identified, the audit engagement partner, in the first instance, and the ethics partner, where appropriate, assess the implications of the breach, determine whether there are safeguards that can be put in place or other actions that can be taken to address any potential adverse consequences and consider whether there is a need to resign from the audit engagement.

An inadvertent violation of this Standard does not necessarily call into question the audit firm's ability to give an audit opinion provided that:

(a) the audit firm has established policies and procedures that require all partners and staff to report any breach promptly to the audit engagement partner or to the ethics partner, as appropriate;

(b) the audit engagement partner promptly notifies the partner or member of staff that any matter which has given rise to a breach is to be addressed as soon as possible and ensures that such action is taken;
(c) safeguards, if appropriate, are applied (for example, by having another partner review the work done by the relevant partner or member of staff or by removing him or her from the engagement team); and
(d) the actions taken and the rationale for them are documented.

General approach to non-audit services

5 Paragraphs 6 to 39 of this Standard set out the general approach to be adopted by audit firms and auditors in relation to the provision of non-audit services to entities audited by them. This approach is applicable irrespective of the nature of the non-audit services, which may be in question in a given case. (Paragraphs 40 to 135 of this Standard illustrate the application of the general approach to a number of common non-audit services.)

6 In this Standard, 'non-audit services' comprise any engagement in which an audit firm provides professional services to an audited entity other than:

(a) the audit of financial statements; and
(b) pursuant to those other roles which legislation or regulation specify can be performed by the auditor of the entity (for example, considering the preliminary announcements of listed companies, complying with the procedural and reporting requirements of regulators, such as requirements relating to the audit of the audited entity's internal controls and a report in accordance with Section 714 of the Companies Act 2006).

In the case of a group, non-audit services include services provided by the audit firm, to the parent company or to any affiliate.

7 There may be circumstances where the audit firm is engaged to provide a non-audit service and where that engagement and its scope are determined by an entity which is not audited by the firm. However, it might be contemplated that an audited entity may gain some benefit from that engagement[1]. In these circumstances, whilst there may be no threat to the audit firm's objectivity and independence at the time of appointment, the audit firm considers how the engagement may be expected to develop, whether there are any threats that the audit firm may be subject to if additional relevant parties which are audited entities are identified and whether any safeguards need to be put in place.

8 **The audit firm shall establish policies and procedures that require others within the firm, when considering whether to accept a proposed engagement to provide a non-audit service to an audited entity or any of its affiliates, to communicate details of the proposed engagement to the audit engagement partner.**

9 The audit firm establishes appropriate channels of internal communication to ensure that, in relation to an entity audited by the firm, the audit engagement partner (or their delegate) is informed about any proposed engagement to provide a non-audit service to the audited entity or any of its affiliates and that he or she considers the

---

[1] For example, in a vendor due diligence engagement, the engagement is initiated and scoped by the vendor before the purchaser is identified. If an entity audited by the firm undertaking the due diligence engagement is the purchaser, that audited entity may gain the benefit of the report issued by its auditor, it may be a party to the engagement letter and it may pay an element of the fee.

implications for the auditor's objectivity and independence before the engagement is accepted.

In the case of a listed company, the group audit engagement partner establishes that the company has communicated its policy on the engagement of the external auditor to supply non-audit services to its affiliates and obtains confirmation that the auditors of the affiliates will comply with this policy.[2] The group audit engagement partner also requires that relevant information on non-audit services provided by network firms is communicated on a timely basis.   10

Identification and assessment of threats and safeguards

Before the audit firm accepts a proposed engagement to provide a non-audit service to an audited entity, the audit engagement partner shall: 11

(a) **consider whether it is probable that a reasonable and informed third party would regard the objectives of the proposed engagement as being inconsistent with the objectives of the audit of the financial statements; and**
(b) **identify and assess the significance of any related threats to the auditor's objectivity, including any perceived loss of independence; and**
(c) **identify and assess the effectiveness of the available safeguards to eliminate the threats or reduce them to an acceptable level.**

The objective of the audit of financial statements is to express an opinion on the preparation and presentation of those financial statements. For example, in the case of a limited company, legislation requires the auditor to make a report to the members on all annual accounts laid before the company in general meeting during its tenure of office. The report must include a statement as to whether, in the auditor's opinion, the accounts have been properly prepared in accordance with the requirements of the legislation, and, in particular, whether they give a true and fair view of the state of the affairs and profit or loss for the year   12

Where the audit engagement partner considers that it is probable that a reasonable and informed third party would regard the objectives of the proposed non-audit service engagement as being inconsistent with the objectives of the audit of the financial statements, the audit firm shall either: 13

(a) **not undertake the non-audit service engagement; or**
(b) **not accept or withdraw from the audit engagement.**

The objectives of engagements to provide non-audit services vary and depend on the specific terms of the engagement. In some cases these objectives may be inconsistent with those of the audit, and, in such cases, this may give rise to a threat to the auditor's objectivity and to the appearance of its independence. Audit firms do not undertake non-audit service engagements where the objectives of such engagements are inconsistent with the objectives of the audit, or do not accept or withdraw from the audit engagement.   14

Similarly, in relation to a possible new audit engagement, consideration needs to be given to recent, current and potential engagements to provide non-audit services by the audit firm for the prospective audited entity and whether the scope and objectives of those engagements are consistent with the proposed audit engagement. In the case of listed companies, when tendering for a new audit engagement, the audit firm   15

---

[2] *The Combined Code on Corporate Governance requires audit committees to develop the company's policy on the engagement of the external auditor to supply non-audit services.*

ensures that relevant information on recent non-audit services is drawn to the attention of the audit committee, including:

- when recent non-audit services were provided to the entity;
- the materiality of those non-audit services to the proposed audit engagement;
- whether those non-audit services would have been prohibited if the entity had been an audited entity at the time when they were undertaken; and
- the extent to which the outcomes of non-audit services have been audited or reviewed by another audit firm.

Threats to objectivity and independence

16   The principal types of threats to the auditor's objectivity and independence are:

- self-interest threat;
- self-review threat;
- management threat;
- advocacy threat;
- familiarity (or trust) threat; and
- intimidation threat.

The auditor remains alert to the possibility that any of these threats may occur in connection with non-audit services. However, the threats most commonly associated with non-audit services are self-interest threat, self-review threat, management threat and advocacy threat.

17   A **self-interest threat** exists when the auditor has financial or other interests which might cause the auditor to be reluctant to take actions that would be adverse to the interests of the audit firm or any individual in a position to influence the conduct or outcome of the audit. In relation to non-audit services, the main self-interest threat concerns fees and economic dependence and these are addressed in APB Ethical Standard 4.

18   Where substantial fees are regularly generated from the provision of non-audit services, and the fees for non-audit services are significantly greater than the annual audit and audit-related fees, the audit firm has regard to the possibility that there may be perceived to be a loss of independence. The audit firm addresses such perceived loss of independence by determining whether there is any risk that there will be an actual loss of independence and objectivity by the audit engagement team. The audit firm ensures that those charged with governance are informed of the position on a timely basis.

19   Where fees for non-audit services are calculated on a contingent fee basis, the perception may be that the audit firm's interests are so closely aligned with the audited entity that it threatens the auditor's objectivity and independence. Any contingent fee that is material to the audit firm, or that part of the firm by reference to which the audit engagement partner's profit share is calculated, will create an unacceptable self-interest threat and the audit firm does not undertake such an engagement.

20   A **self-review threat** exists when the results of a non-audit service performed by the engagement team or by others within the audit firm are reflected in the amounts included or disclosed in the financial statements.

21   A threat to objectivity and independence arises because, in the course of the audit, the auditor may need to re-evaluate the work performed in the non-audit service. As, by virtue of providing the non-audit service, the audit firm is associated with aspects

of the preparation of the financial statements, it may be (or may appear to be) unable to take an impartial view of relevant aspects of those financial statements.

In assessing the significance of the self-review threat, the auditor considers the extent to which the non-audit service will: 22

- involve a significant degree of subjective judgment; and
- have a material effect on the preparation and presentation of the financial statements.

Where a significant degree of judgment relating to the financial statements is involved in a non-audit service engagement, the auditor may be inhibited from questioning that judgment in the course of the audit. Whether a significant degree of subjective judgment is involved will depend upon whether the non-audit service involves the application of well-established principles and procedures, and whether reliable information is available. If such circumstances do not exist because the non-audit service is based on concepts, methodologies or assumptions that require judgment and are not established by the audited entity or by authoritative guidance, the auditor's objectivity and the appearance of its independence may be adversely affected. Where the provision of a proposed non-audit service would also have a material effect on the financial statements, it is unlikely that any safeguard can eliminate or reduce to an acceptable level the self-review threat. 23

A **management threat** exists when the audit firm undertakes work that involves making judgments and taking decisions that are properly the responsibility of management. 24

Paragraph 30 of APB Ethical Standard 1 prohibits partners and employees of the audit firm from taking decisions on behalf of the management of the audited entity. A threat to objectivity and independence also arises where the audit firm undertakes an engagement to provide non-audit services in relation to which management are required to make judgments and take decisions based on that work. The auditor may become closely aligned with the views and interests of management and this may erode the distinction between the audited entity and the audit firm, in turn, impairing or calling into question the auditor's ability to apply a proper degree of professional scepticism in auditing the financial statements. The auditor's objectivity and the appearance of its independence therefore may be, or may be perceived to be, impaired. 25

In determining whether a non-audit service does or does not give rise to a management threat, the auditor considers whether there is informed management. Informed management exists when: 26

- the auditor is satisfied that a member of management (or senior employee of the audited entity) has been designated by the audited entity to receive the results of the non-audit service and has been given the authority to make any judgments and decisions of the type set out in paragraph 31 of APB Ethical Standard 1 that are needed;
- the auditor concludes that that member of management has the capability to make independent management judgments and decisions on the basis of the information provided; and
- the results of the non-audit service are communicated to the audited entity and, where judgments or decisions are to be made they are supported by an objective analysis of the issues to consider and the audited entity is given the opportunity to decide between reasonable alternatives.

27 In the absence of such informed management it is unlikely that any other safeguards can eliminate a management threat or reduce it to an acceptable level.

28 An **advocacy threat** exists when the audit firm undertakes work that involves acting as an advocate for an audited entity and supporting a position taken by management in an adversarial context.

29 A threat to objectivity and independence arises because, in order to act in an advocacy role, the audit firm has to adopt a position closely aligned to that of management. This creates both actual and perceived threats to the auditor's objectivity and independence. For example, where the audit firm, acting as advocate, has supported a particular contention of management, it may be difficult for the auditor to take an impartial view of this in the context of the audit of the financial statements.

30 Where the provision of a non-audit service would require the auditor to act as an advocate for the audited entity in relation to matters that are material to the financial statements, it is unlikely that any safeguards can eliminate or reduce to an acceptable level the advocacy threat that would exist.

31 Threats to the auditor's objectivity, including a perceived loss of independence, may arise where a non-audit service is provided by the audit firm to an entity not audited by the firm, but which is connected in some way to an audited entity, and the outcome of that service has a material impact on the financial statements of the audited entity. For example, if the audit firm provides actuarial services to the pension scheme of an audited entity, which is in deficit and the audit firm subsequently gives an opinion on financial statements that include judgements given in connection with that service. The audit engagement partner assesses the significance of any related threats to the auditor's objectivity and independence and the effectiveness of the available safeguards to eliminate these threats or reduce them to an acceptable level.

Safeguards

32 Where any threat to the auditor's objectivity and the appearance of its independence is identified, the audit engagement partner assesses the significance of that threat and considers whether there are safeguards that could be applied and which would be effective to eliminate the threat or reduce it to an acceptable level. If such safeguards can be identified and are applied, the non-audit service may be provided. However, where no such safeguards are applied, the only course is for the audit firm either not to undertake the engagement to provide the non-audit service in question or not to accept (or to withdraw from) the audit engagement.

33 **Where the audit engagement partner concludes that no appropriate safeguards are available to eliminate or reduce to an acceptable level the threats to the auditor's objectivity, including any perceived loss of independence, related to a proposed engagement to provide a non-audit service to an audited entity, he or she shall inform the others concerned within the audit firm of that conclusion and the firm shall either:**

(a) **not undertake the non-audit service engagement; or**
(b) **not accept or withdraw from the audit engagement.**

If the audit engagement partner is in doubt as to the appropriate action to be taken, he or she shall resolve the matter through consultation with the ethics partner.

An initial assessment of the threats to objectivity and independence and the safeguards to be applied is required when the audit engagement partner is considering the acceptance of an engagement to provide a non-audit service. The assessment of the threats and the safeguards applied is reviewed whenever the scope and objectives of the non-audit service change significantly. If such a review suggests that safeguards cannot reduce the threat to an acceptable level, the audit firm withdraws from the non-audit service engagement, or does not accept re-appointment or withdraws from the audit engagement.

Communication with those charged with governance

The audit engagement partner shall ensure that those charged with governance of the audited entity are appropriately informed on a timely basis of:

(a) **all significant facts and matters that bear upon the auditor's objectivity and independence, related to the provision of non-audit services, including the safeguards put in place; and**
(b) **for listed companies, any inconsistencies between APB Ethical Standards and the company's policy for the supply of non-audit services by the audit firm and any apparent breach of that policy.**[2]

Transparency is a key element in addressing the issues raised by the provision of non-audit services by audit firms to the entities audited by them. This can be facilitated by timely communication with those charged with governance of the audited entity (see APB Ethical Standard 1, paragraphs 56 to 63). Such communications are addressed to the audit committee, where there is one; in other circumstances, they are addressed to the board of directors (or those in an equivalent position). In the case of listed companies, ensuring that the audit committee is properly informed about the issues associated with the provision of non-audit services will assist them to comply with the provisions of the Combined Code on Corporate Governance relating to reviewing and monitoring the external auditor's independence and objectivity and to developing a policy on the engagement of the external auditor to supply non-audit services. This will include discussion of any inconsistencies between the company's policy and APB Ethical Standards and ensuring that the policy is communicated to affiliates.

Documentation

The audit engagement partner shall ensure that the reasoning for a decision to undertake an engagement to provide non-audit services to an audited entity, and any safeguards adopted, is appropriately documented.

Matters to be documented include any significant judgments concerning:

- threats identified;
- safeguards adopted and the reasons why they are considered to be effective; and
- communication with those charged with governance.

In situations where a management threat is identified in connection with the provision of non-audit services, this documentation will include the auditor's assessment of whether there is informed management. The documentation of communications with the audited entity where judgments and decisions are made by management may take a variety of forms, for example an informal meeting note covering the matters discussed.

Application of general principles to specific non-audit services

Internal audit services

40 The range of 'internal audit services' is wide and they may not be termed as such by the audited entity. For example, the audit firm may be engaged:

- to outsource the audited entity's entire internal audit function; or
- to supplement the audited entity's internal audit function in specific areas (for example, by providing specialised technical services or resources in particular locations); or
- to provide occasional internal audit services to the audited entity on an *ad hoc* basis.

All such engagements would fall within the term 'internal audit services'.

41 The main threats to the auditor's objectivity and independence arising from the provision of internal audit services are the self-review threat and the management threat.

42 Engagements to provide internal audit services – other than those prohibited in paragraph 44 – may be undertaken, provided that the auditor is satisfied that there is informed management and appropriate safeguards are applied to reduce the self-review threat to an acceptable level.

43 Examples of safeguards that may be appropriate when internal audit services are provided to an audited entity include ensuring that:

- internal audit projects undertaken by the audit firm are performed by partners and staff who have no involvement in the external audit of the financial statements;
- the audit of the financial statements is reviewed by an audit partner who is not involved in the audit engagement, to ensure that the internal audit work performed by the audit firm has been properly and effectively assessed in the context of the audit of the financial statements.

44 **The audit firm shall not undertake an engagement to provide internal audit services to an audited entity where it is reasonably foreseeable that:**

(a) **for the purposes of the audit of the financial statements, the auditor would place significant reliance on the internal audit work performed by the audit firm; or**

(b) **for the purposes of the internal audit services, the audit firm would undertake part of the role of management.**

45 The self-review threat is unacceptably high where the auditor cannot perform the audit of the financial statements without placing significant reliance on the work performed for the purposes of the internal audit services engagement. For example, the provision of internal audit services on the internal financial controls for an audited entity which is a large bank, is likely to be unacceptable as the external audit team is likely to place significant reliance on the work performed by the internal audit team in relation to the bank's internal financial controls.

46 The management threat is unacceptably high where the audit firm provides internal audit services that involve audit firm personnel taking decisions or making judgments, which are properly the responsibility of management. For example, such situations can arise where the nature of the internal audit work involves the audit firm in taking decisions as to:

- the scope and nature of the internal audit services to be provided to the audited entity, or
- the design of internal controls or implementing changes thereto.

During the course of the audit the auditor generally evaluates the design and tests the operating effectiveness of some of the entity's internal financial controls, including the operation of any internal audit function and provide management with observations on matters that have come to the attention of the auditor, including comments on weaknesses in the internal control systems (including the internal audit function) and suggestions for addressing them. This work is a by-product of the audit service rather than the result of a specific engagement to provide non-audit services and therefore does not constitute internal audit services for the purposes of this Standard. 47

In some circumstances, additional internal financial controls work is performed during the course of the audit in response to a specific request for an extended scope to the external audit. Whether it is appropriate for this work to be undertaken by the audit firm will depend on the extent to which it gives rise to a management threat to the auditor's objectivity and independence. The audit engagement partner reviews the scope and objectives of the proposed work and assesses the threats to which it gives rise and the safeguards available. 48

Information technology services

Design, provision and implementation of information technology (including financial information technology) systems by audit firms for entities audited by them creates threats to the auditor's objectivity and independence. The principal threats are the self-review threat and the management threat. 49

Engagements to design, provide or implement information technology systems that are not important to any significant part of the accounting system or to the production of the financial statements and do not have significant reliance placed on them by the auditor, may be undertaken, provided that there is informed management and appropriate safeguards are applied to reduce the self-review threat to an acceptable level. 50

Examples of safeguards that may be appropriate when information technology services are provided to an audited entity include ensuring that: 51

- information technology projects undertaken by the audit firm are performed by partners and staff who have no involvement in the external audit of the financial statements;
- the audit of the financial statements is reviewed by an audit partner who is not involved in the audit engagement to ensure that the information technology work performed has been properly and effectively assessed in the context of the audit of the financial statements.

The audit firm shall not undertake an engagement to design, provide or implement information technology systems for an audited entity where: 52

(a) the systems concerned would be important to any significant part of the accounting system or to the production of the financial statements and the auditor would place significant reliance upon them as part of the audit of the financial statements; or
(b) for the purposes of the information technology services, the audit firm would undertake part of the role of management.

53 Where it is reasonably apparent that, having regard to the activities and size of the audited entity and the range and complexity of the proposed system, the management lacks the expertise required to take responsibility for the systems concerned, it is unlikely that any safeguards would be sufficient to eliminate these threats or to reduce them to an acceptable level. In particular, formal acceptance by management of the systems designed and installed by the audit firm is unlikely to be an effective safeguard when, in substance, the audit firm have been retained by management as experts and it makes important decisions in relation to the design or implementation of systems of internal control and financial reporting.

54 The provision and installation of information technology services associated with a standard 'off the shelf accounting package' (including basic set-up procedures to make the package operate on the audited entity's existing platform and peripherals, setting up the chart of accounts and the entry of standard data such as the audited entity's product names and prices) is unlikely to create a level of threat to the auditor's objectivity and independence that cannot be addressed through applying appropriate safeguards.

Valuation services

55 A valuation comprises the making of assumptions with regard to future developments, the application of appropriate methodologies and techniques, and the combination of both to compute a certain value, or range of values, for an asset, a liability or for a business as a whole.

56 **The audit firm shall not undertake an engagement to provide a valuation to:**

   (a) **an audited entity that is a listed company or a significant affiliate of such an entity, where the valuation would have a material effect on the listed company's financial statements, either separately or in aggregate with other valuations provided; or**

   (b) **any other audited entity, where the valuation would both involve a significant degree of subjective judgment and have a material effect on the financial statements either separately or in aggregate with other valuations provided.**

57 The main threats to the auditor's objectivity and independence arising from the provision of valuation services are the self-review threat and the management threat. In all cases, the self-review threat is considered too high to allow the provision of valuation services which involve the valuation of amounts with a significant degree of subjectivity and have a material effect on the financial statements.

58 For listed companies, or significant affiliates of such entities, the threats to the auditor's objectivity and independence that would be perceived to be created are too high to allow the audit firm to undertake any valuation that has a material effect on the listed company's financial statements.

59 The audit firm's policies and procedures will set out whether there are circumstances in which valuation services are not undertaken for non-listed audited entities as described in paragraph 42 of APB Ethical Standard 1.

60 In circumstances where the auditor is designated by legislation or regulation as being eligible to carry out a valuation[3] the restrictions in paragraph 56 do not apply as such

---

[3] For example, Section 593 of the Companies Act 2006 requires a public company to obtain an independent valuation on assets to be received in full or part payment for shares to be allotted from a person who is eligible for appointment as a statutory auditor.

a valuation would not be a non-audit service, as provided by paragraph 6. In such circumstances, the audit engagement partner applies relevant safeguards.

It is usual for the auditor to provide the management with accounting advice in relation to valuation matters that have come to the auditor's attention during the course of the audit. Such matters might typically include: 61

- comments on valuation assumptions and their appropriateness;
- errors identified in a valuation calculation and suggestions for correcting them;
- advice on accounting policies and any valuation methodologies used in their application.

Advice on such matters does not constitute valuation services for the purpose of this Standard.

Where the auditor is engaged to collect and verify the accuracy of data to be used in a valuation to be performed by others, such engagements do not constitute valuation services under this Standard. 62

Actuarial valuation services

The audit firm shall not undertake an engagement to provide actuarial valuation services to: 63

(a) an audited entity that is a listed company or a significant affiliate of such an entity, unless the firm is satisfied that the valuation has no material effect on the listed company's financial statements, either separately or in aggregate with other valuations provided; or

(b) any other audited entity, unless the firm is satisfied that either all significant judgments, including the assumptions, are made by informed management or the valuation has no material effect on the financial statements, either separately or in aggregate with other valuations provided.

Actuarial valuation services are subject to the same general principles as other valuation services. In all cases, where they involve the audit firm in making a subjective judgment and have a material effect on the financial statements, actuarial valuations give rise to an unacceptable level of self-review threat and so may not be performed by audit firms for entities audited by them. 64

In the case of non-listed companies where all significant judgments concerning the assumptions, methodology and data for the actuarial valuation are made by informed management and the audit firm's role is limited to applying proven methodologies using the given data, for which the management takes responsibility, it may be possible to establish effective safeguards to protect the auditors' objectivity and the appearance of its independence. 65

For listed companies, or significant affiliates of such entities, the threats to the auditor's objectivity and independence that would be perceived to be created are too high to allow the audit firm to undertake any actuarial valuation unless the firm is satisfied that the valuation has no material effect on the listed company's financial statements. 66

The audit firm's policies and procedures will set out whether there are circumstances in which actuarial valuation services are not undertaken for non-listed audited entities as described in paragraph 42 of APB Ethical Standard 1. 67

Tax services

68 The range of activities encompassed by the term 'tax services' is wide. Three broad categories of tax service can be distinguished. They are where the audit firm:

(a) provides advice to the audited entity on one or more specific matters at the request of the audited entity; or
(b) undertakes a substantial proportion of the tax planning or compliance work for the audited entity; or
(c) promotes tax structures or products to the audited entity, the effectiveness of which is likely to be influenced by the manner in which they are accounted for in the financial statements.

Whilst it is possible to consider tax services under broad headings, such as tax planning or compliance, in practice these services are often interrelated and it is impracticable to analyse services in this way for the purposes of attempting to identify generically the threats to which specific engagements give rise. As a result, audit firms need to identify and assess, on a case-by-case basis, the potential threats to the auditor's objectivity and independence before deciding whether to undertake a proposed engagement to provide tax services to an audited entity.

69 The provision of tax services by audit firms to entities audited by them may give rise to a number of threats to the auditor's objectivity and independence, including the self-interest threat, the management threat, the advocacy threat and, where the work involves a significant degree of subjective judgment and has a material effect on the financial statements, the self-review threat.

70 Where the audit firm provides advice to the audited entity on one or more specific matters at the request of the audited entity, a self-review threat may be created. This self-review threat is more significant where the audit firm undertakes a substantial proportion of the tax planning and compliance work for the audited entity. However, the auditor may be able undertake such engagements, provided that there is informed management and appropriate safeguards are applied to reduce the self-review threat to an acceptable level.

71 Examples of such safeguards that may be appropriate when tax services are provided to an audited entity include ensuring that:

- the tax services are provided by partners and staff who have no involvement in the audit of the financial statements;
- the tax services are reviewed by an independent tax partner, or other senior tax employee;
- external independent advice is obtained on the tax work;
- tax computations prepared by the audit team are reviewed by a partner or senior staff member with appropriate expertise who is not a member of the audit team; or
- an audit partner not involved in the audit engagement reviews whether the tax work has been properly and effectively addressed in the context of the audit of the financial statements.

72 **The audit firm shall not promote tax structures or products or undertake an engagement to provide tax advice to an audited entity where the audit engagement partner has, or ought to have, reasonable doubt as to the appropriateness of the related accounting treatment involved, having regard to the requirement for the financial statements to give a true and fair view in accordance with the relevant financial reporting framework.**

Where the audit firm promotes tax structures or products or undertakes an engagement to provide tax advice to the audited entity, it may be necessary to adopt an accounting treatment about which there is reasonable doubt as to its appropriateness, in order to achieve the desired result. A self-review threat arises in the course of an audit because the auditor may be unable to form an impartial view of the accounting treatment to be adopted for the purposes of the proposed arrangements. Accordingly, this Standard does not permit the promotion of tax structures or products by audit firms to entities audited by them where, in the view of the audit engagement partner, after such consultation as is appropriate, the effectiveness of the tax structure or product depends on an accounting treatment about which there is reasonable doubt as to its appropriateness. 73

The audit firm shall not undertake an engagement to provide tax services wholly or partly on a contingent fee basis where: 74

(a) the services are provided to an audited entity and the engagement fees are material to the audit firm or the part of the firm by reference to which the audit engagement partner's profit share is calculated; or

(b) the outcome of those tax services (and, therefore, the amount of the fee) is dependent on:
  (i) the application of tax law which is uncertain or has not been established; and
  (ii) a future or contemporary audit judgment relating to a material matter in the financial statements of an audited entity.

Where tax services, such as advising on corporate structures and structuring transactions to achieve a particular effect, are undertaken on a contingent fee basis, self-interest threats to the auditor's objectivity and independence may arise. The auditor may have, or may appear to have, an interest in the success of the tax services, causing the audit firm to make an audit judgment about which there is reasonable doubt as to its appropriateness. Where the contingent fee is determined by the outcome of the application of tax law, which is uncertain or has not been established, and where the tax implications are material to the financial statements, the self-interest threat cannot be eliminated or reduced to an acceptable level by the application of any safeguards. 75

The audit firm shall not undertake an engagement to provide tax services to an audited entity where the engagement would involve the audit firm undertaking a management role. 76

When providing tax services to an audited entity, there is a risk that the audit firm undertakes a management role, unless the firm is working with informed management. 77

For an audited entity that is a listed company or a significant affiliate of such an entity, the audit firm shall not undertake an engagement to prepare current or deferred tax calculations for the purpose of preparing accounting entries that are material to the relevant financial statements, save where the circumstances contemplated in paragraph 131 apply. 78

For listed companies or significant affiliates of such entities, the threats to the auditor's objectivity and independence that would be created are too high to allow the audit firm to undertake an engagement to prepare calculations of current or deferred tax liabilities (or assets) for the purpose of preparing accounting entries that are material to the relevant financial statements, together with associated disclosure notes, save where the circumstances contemplated in paragraph 131 apply. 79

80 For entities other than listed companies or significant affiliates of listed companies, the auditor may undertake an engagement to prepare current or deferred tax calculations for the purpose of preparing accounting entries, provided that:

    (a) such services:
        (i) do not involve initiating transactions or taking management decisions; and
        (ii) are of a technical, mechanical or an informative nature; and
    (b) appropriate safeguards are applied.

81 The audit firm's policies and procedures will set out whether there are circumstances in which current or deferred tax calculations for the purpose of preparing accounting entries are not prepared for non-listed audited entities as described in paragraph 42 of APB Ethical Standard 1.

82 **The audit firm shall not undertake an engagement to provide tax services to an audited entity where this would involve acting as an advocate for the audited entity, before an appeals tribunal or court[4] in the resolution of an issue:**

    (a) that is material to the financial statements; or
    (b) where the outcome of the tax issue is dependent on a future or contemporary audit judgment.

83 Where the tax services to be provided by the audit firm include representing the audited entity in any negotiations or proceedings involving the tax authorities, advocacy threats to the auditor's objectivity and independence may arise.

84 The audit firm is not acting as an advocate where the tax services involve the provision of information to the tax authorities (including an explanation of the approach being taken and the arguments being advanced by the audited entity). In such circumstances effective safeguards may exist and the tax authorities will undertake their own review of the issues.

85 Where the tax authorities indicate that they are minded to reject the audited entity's arguments on a particular issue and the matter is likely to be determined by an appeals tribunal or court, the audit firm may become so closely identified with management's arguments that the auditor is inhibited from forming an impartial view of the treatment of the issue in the financial statements. In such circumstances, if the issue is material to the financial statements or is dependent on a future or contemporary audit judgment, the audit firm discusses the matter with the audited entity and makes it clear that it will have to withdraw from that element of the engagement to provide tax services that requires it to act as advocate for the audited entity, or resign from the audit engagement from the time when the matter is formally listed for hearing before the appeals tribunal.

86 The audit firm is not, however, precluded from having a continuing role (for example, responding to specific requests for information) for the audited entity in relation to the appeal. The audit firm assesses the threat associated with any continuing role in accordance with the provisions of paragraphs 87 to 90 of this Standard.

---

[4] The restriction applies to the first level of Tax Court that is independent of the tax authorities and to more authoritative bodies. In the UK this would be the General or Special Commissioners of HM Revenue & Customs or the VAT and Duties Tribunal.

Litigation support services

Although management and advocacy threats may arise in litigation support services, such as acting as an expert witness, the primary issue is that a self-review threat will arise in all cases where such services involve a subjective estimation of the likely outcome of a matter that is material to the amounts to be included or the disclosures to be made in the financial statements. 87

The audit firm shall not undertake an engagement to provide litigation support services to: 88

(a) an audited entity that is a listed company or a significant affiliate of such an entity, where this would involve the estimation by the audit firm of the likely outcome of a pending legal matter that could be material to the amounts to be included or the disclosures to be made in the listed company's financial statements, either separately or in aggregate with other estimates and valuations provided; or

(b) any other audited entity, where this would involve the estimation by the audit firm of the likely outcome of a pending legal matter that could be material to the amounts to be included or the disclosures to be made in the financial statements, either separately or in aggregate with other estimates and valuations provided and there is a significant degree of subjectivity involved.

In the case of non-listed entities, litigation support services that do not involve such subjective estimations are not prohibited, provided that the audit firm has carefully considered the implications of any threats and established appropriate safeguards. 89

The audit firm's policies and procedures will set out whether there are circumstances in which litigation support services are not undertaken for non-listed audited entities as described in paragraph 42 of APB Ethical Standard 1. 90

Legal services

The audit firm shall not undertake an engagement to provide legal services to an audited entity where this would involve acting as the solicitor formally nominated to represent the audited entity in the resolution of a dispute or litigation which is material to the amounts to be included or the disclosures to be made in the financial statements. 91

Although the provision by the auditor of certain types of legal services to its audited entities may create advocacy, self-review and management threats, this Standard does not impose a general prohibition on the provision of legal services. However, in view of the degree of advocacy involved in litigation or other types of dispute resolution procedures and the potential importance of any assessment by the auditor of the merits of the audited entity's position when auditing its financial statements, this Standard prohibits an audit firm from acting as the formally nominated representative for an audited entity in the resolution of a dispute or litigation which is material to the financial statements (either in terms of the amounts recognised or disclosed in the financial statements). 92

Recruitment and remuneration services

The audit firm shall not undertake an engagement to provide recruitment services to an audited entity that would involve the firm taking responsibility for the appointment of any director or employee of the audited entity. 93

136 *APB Ethical Standards*

94 A management threat arises where audit firm personnel take responsibility for any decision as to who is appointed by the audited entity.

95 **For an audited entity that is a listed company, the audit firm shall not undertake an engagement to provide recruitment services in relation to a key management position of the audited entity, or a significant affiliate of such an entity.**

96 A familiarity threat arises if the audit firm plays a significant role in relation to the identification and recruitment of senior members of management within the company, as the audit engagement team may be less likely to be critical of the information or explanations provided by such individuals than might otherwise be the case. Accordingly, for listed companies, and for significant affiliates of such entities, the audit firm does not undertake engagements that involve the recruitment of individuals for key management positions.

97 The audit firm's policies and procedures will set out whether there are circumstances in which recruitment services are not undertaken for non-listed audited entities as described in paragraph 42 of APB Ethical Standard 1.

98 Recruitment services involve a specifically identifiable, and separately remunerated, engagement. Audit firms and engagement teams may contribute to an entity's recruitment process in less formal ways. The prohibition set out in paragraph 95 does not extend to:

- senior members of an audit team interviewing prospective directors or employees of the audited entity and advising on the candidate's technical financial competence; or
- the audit entity using information gathered by the audit firm, including that relating to salary surveys.

99 **The audit firm shall not undertake an engagement to provide advice on the quantum of the remuneration package or the measurement criteria on which the quantum is calculated, for a director or key management position of an audited entity.**

100 The provision of advice on remuneration packages (including bonus arrangements, incentive plans and other benefits) to existing or prospective employees of the audited entity gives rise to familiarity threats. The significance of the familiarity threat is considered too high to allow advice on the overall amounts to be paid or on the quantitative measurement criteria included in remuneration packages for directors and key management positions.

101 For other employees, these threats can be adequately addressed by the application of safeguards, such as the advice being provided by partners and staff who have no involvement in the audit of the financial statements.

102 In cases where all significant judgments concerning the assumptions, methodology and data for the calculation of remuneration packages for directors and key management are made by informed management or a third party and the audit firm's role is limited to applying proven methodologies using the given data, for which the management takes responsibility, it may be possible to establish effective safeguards to protect the auditor's objectivity and independence.

103 Advice on tax, pensions and interpretation of accounting standards relating to remuneration packages for directors and key management can be provided by the audit firm, provided they are not prohibited by the requirements of this Standard relating to tax, actuarial valuations and accounting services. Disclosure of the

provision of any such advice would be made to those charged with governance of the audited entity (see APB Ethical Standard 1, paragraphs 56 to 63).

Corporate finance services

The range of services encompassed by the term 'corporate finance services' is wide. For example, the audit firm may be engaged: 104

- to identify possible purchasers for parts of the audited entity's business and provide advisory services in the course of such sales; or
- to identify possible 'targets' for the audited entity to acquire; or
- to advise the audited entity on how to fund its financing requirements, including advising on debt restructuring and securitisation programmes; or
- to act as sponsor on admission to listing on the London Stock Exchange, or as Nominated Advisor on the admission of the audited entity on the Alternative Investments Market (AIM); or
- to act as financial adviser to audited entity offerors or offerees in connection with public takeovers.

The potential for the auditor's objectivity and independence to be impaired through the provision of corporate finance services varies considerably depending on the precise nature of the service provided. The main threats to auditor's objectivity and independence arising from the provision of corporate finance services are the self-review, management and advocacy threats. Self-interest threats may also arise, especially in situations where the audit firm is paid on a contingent fee basis. 105

When providing corporate finance services to an audited entity, there is a risk that the audit firm undertakes a management role, unless the firm is working with informed management. Appropriate safeguards are applied to reduce the self-review threat to an acceptable level. 106

Examples of safeguards that may be appropriate when corporate finance services are provided to an audited entity include ensuring that: 107

- the corporate finance advice is provided by partners and staff who have no involvement in the audit of the financial statements,
- any advice provided is reviewed by an independent corporate finance partner within the audit firm,
- external independent advice on the corporate finance work is obtained,
- an audit partner who is not involved in the audit engagement reviews the audit work performed in relation to the subject matter of the corporate finance services provided to ensure that such audit work has been properly and effectively reviewed and assessed in the context of the audit of the financial statements.

Where the audit firm undertakes an engagement to provide corporate finance services to an audited entity in connection with conducting the sale or purchase of a material part of the audited entity's business, the audit engagement partner informs the audit committee (or equivalent) about the engagement, as set out in paragraphs 56 to 63 of APB Ethical Standard 1. 108

The audit firm shall not undertake an engagement to provide corporate finance services in respect of an audited entity where: 109

(a) **the engagement would involve the audit firm taking responsibility for dealing in, underwriting or promoting shares; or**

(b) the audit engagement partner has, or ought to have, reasonable doubt as to the appropriateness of an accounting treatment that is related to the advice provided, having regard to the requirement for the financial statements to give a true and fair view in accordance with the relevant financial reporting framework; or

(c) such corporate finance services are to be provided on a contingent fee basis and:
   (i) the engagement fees are material to the audit firm or the part of the firm by reference to which the audit engagement partner's profit share is calculated; or
   (ii) the outcome of those corporate finance services (and, therefore, the amount of the fee) is dependent on a future or contemporary audit judgment relating to a material matter in the financial statements of an audited entity; or

(d) the engagement would involve the audit firm undertaking a management role in the audited entity.

110 An unacceptable advocacy threat arises where, in the course of providing a corporate finance service, the audit firm promotes the interests of the audited entity by taking responsibility for dealing in, underwriting, or promoting shares.

111 Where the audit firm acts as a sponsor under the Listing Rules[5], or as Nominated Adviser on the admission of the audited entity to the AIM, the audit firm is required to confirm that the audited entity has satisfied all applicable conditions for listing and other relevant requirements of the listing (or AIM) rules. Where there is, or there ought to be, reasonable doubt that the audit firm will be able to give that confirmation, it does not enter into such an engagement.

112 A self-review threat arises where the outcome or consequences of the corporate finance service provided by the audit firm may be material to the financial statements of the audited entity, which are, or will be, subject to audit by the same firm. Where the audit firm provides corporate finance services, for example advice to the audited entity on financing arrangements, it may be necessary to adopt an accounting treatment about which there is reasonable doubt as to its appropriateness in order to achieve the desired result. A self-review threat is created because the auditor may be unable to form an impartial view of the accounting treatment to be adopted for the purposes of the proposed arrangements. Accordingly, this Standard does not permit the provision of advice by audit firms to entities audited by them where there is reasonable doubt about the appropriateness of the related accounting treatments.

113 Advice to audited entities on funding issues and banking arrangements, where there is no reasonable doubt as to the appropriateness of the accounting treatment, is not prohibited provided this does not involve the audit firm in taking decisions or making judgments which are properly the responsibility of management.

114 Where a corporate finance engagement is undertaken on a contingent fee basis, self-interest threats to the auditor's objectivity and independence also arise as the auditor may have, or may appear to have, an interest in the success of the corporate finance services. The significance of the self-interest threat is primarily determined by the materiality of the contingent fee to the audit firm, or to the part of the firm by reference to which the audit engagement partner's profit share is calculated. Where the contingent fee and the outcome of the corporate finance services is dependent on a future or contemporary audit judgment relating to a material matter included in the financial statements of an audited entity, the self-interest threat cannot be eliminated or reduced to an acceptable level by the application of any safeguards.

---

[5] In the United Kingdom, the UK Listing Authority's publication the 'Listing Rules'. In the Republic of Ireland, the United Kingdom 'Listing Rules' as modified by the 'Notes on the Listing Rules' published by the Irish Stock Exchange.

These restrictions do not apply in circumstances where the auditor is designated by legislation or regulation as being eligible to carry out a particular service, since such a service would not be a non-audit service, as provided by paragraph 6. In such circumstances, the audit engagement partner establishes appropriate safeguards.

Transaction related services

In addition to corporate finance services, there are other non-audit services associated with transactions that an audit firm may undertake for an audited entity. For example:
- investigations into possible acquisitions or disposals ('due diligence' investigations); or
- investigations into the tax affairs of possible acquisitions or disposals; or
- the provision of information to sponsors in relation to prospectuses and other investment circulars (for example, long form reports, comfort letters on the adequacy of working capital).

When providing transaction related services to an audited entity, there is a risk that the audit firm may face a management threat, unless the firm is working with informed management. Appropriate safeguards are applied to reduce the self-review threat to an acceptable level.

Examples of safeguards that may be appropriate when transaction related services are provided to an audited entity include ensuring that:
- the transaction related advice is provided by partners and staff who have no involvement in the audit of the financial statements,
- any advice provided is reviewed by an independent transactions partner within the audit firm,
- external independent advice on the transaction related work is obtained,
- an audit partner who is not involved in the audit engagement reviews the audit work performed in relation to the subject matter of the transaction related service provided to ensure that such audit work has been properly and effectively reviewed and assessed in the context of the audit of the financial statements.

The audit firm shall not undertake an engagement to provide transaction related services in respect of an audited entity where:

(a) the audit engagement partner has, or ought to have, reasonable doubt as to the appropriateness of an accounting treatment that is related to the advice provided, having regard to the requirement for the financial statements to give a true and fair view in accordance with the relevant financial reporting framework; or
(b) such transaction related services are to be provided on a contingent fee basis and:
   (i) the engagement fees are material to the audit firm or the part of the firm by reference to which the audit engagement partner's profit share is calculated; or
   (ii) the outcome of those transaction related services (and, therefore, the amount of the fee) is dependent on a future or contemporary audit judgment relating to a material matter in the financial statements of an audited entity; or
(c) the engagement would involve the audit firm undertaking a management role in the audited entity.

A self-review threat arises where the outcome of the transaction related service undertaken by the audit firm may be material to the financial statements of the audited entity which are, or will be, subject to audit by the same firm. Where the audited entity proposes to undertake a transaction, it may be necessary to adopt an inappropriate accounting treatment in order to achieve the desired result. A self-review threat is created if the auditor undertakes transaction related services in connection with such a transaction. Accordingly, this Standard does not permit the provision of advice by audit firms to entities audited by them where there is reasonable doubt about the appropriateness of the accounting treatments related to the transaction advice given.

121 Where a transaction related services engagement is undertaken on a contingent fee basis, self-interest threats to the auditor's objectivity and independence also arise as the auditor may have, or may appear to have, an interest in the success of the transaction. The significance of the self-interest threat is primarily determined by the materiality of the contingent fee to the audit firm, or to the part of the firm by reference to which the audit engagement partner's profit share is calculated. Where the contingent fee and the outcome of the transaction related services is dependent on a future or contemporary audit judgment on a material matter included in the financial statements of an audited entity, the self-interest threat cannot be eliminated or reduced to an acceptable level by the application of any safeguards, other than where the transaction is subject to a pre-established dispute resolution procedure.

122 These restrictions do not apply in circumstances where the auditor is designated by legislation or regulation as being eligible to carry out a particular service, since such a service would not be a non-audit service, as provided by paragraph 6. In such circumstances, the audit engagement partner establishes appropriate safeguards.

Accounting services

123 In this Standard, the term 'accounting services' is defined as the provision of services that involve the maintenance of accounting records or the preparation of financial statements that are then subject to audit. Advice on the implementation of current and proposed accounting standards is not included in the term 'accounting services'.

124 The range of activities encompassed by the term 'accounting services' is wide. In some cases, the audited entity may ask the audit firm to provide a complete service including maintaining all of the accounting records and the preparation of the financial statements. Other common situations are:

- the audit firm may take over the provision of a specific accounting function on an outsourced basis (for example, payroll);
- the audited entity maintains the accounting records, undertakes basic book-keeping and prepares a year-end trial balance and asks the audit firm to assist with the preparation of the necessary adjustments and the financial statements.

125 The provision of accounting services by the audit firm to the audited entity creates threats to the auditor's objectivity and independence, principally self-review and management threats, the significance of which depends on the nature and extent of the accounting services in question and upon the level of public interest in the audited entity.

126 When providing accounting services to an audited entity, unless the firm is working with informed management, there is a risk that the audit firm undertakes a management role.

127 **The audit firm shall not undertake an engagement to provide accounting services to:**

(a) an audited entity that is a listed company or a significant affiliate of such an entity, save where the circumstances contemplated in paragraph 131 apply; or
(b) any other audited entity, where those accounting services would involve the audit firm undertaking part of the role of management.

Even where there is no engagement to provide any accounting services, it is usual for the auditor to provide the management with accounting advice on matters that have come to the auditor's attention during the course of the audit. Such matters might typically include: 128

- comments on weaknesses in the accounting records and suggestions for addressing them;
- errors identified in the accounting records and in the financial statements and suggestions for correcting them;
- advice on the accounting policies in use and on the application of current and proposed accounting standards.

This advice is a by-product of the audit service rather than the result of any engagement to provide non-audit services. Consequently, as it is part of the audit service, such advice is not regarded as giving rise to any threat to the auditor's objectivity and independence.

For listed companies or significant affiliates of such entities, the threats to the auditor's objectivity and independence that would be created are too high to allow the audit firm to undertake an engagement to provide any accounting services, save where the circumstances contemplated in paragraph 131 apply. 129

The audit firm's policies and procedures will set out whether there are circumstances in which accounting services are not undertaken for non-listed audited entities as described in paragraph 42 of APB Ethical Standard 1. 130

In emergency situations, the audit firm may provide a listed audited entity, or a significant affiliate of such a company, with accounting services to assist the company in the timely preparation of its financial statements. This might arise when, due to external and unforeseeable events, the audit firm personnel are the only people with the necessary knowledge of the audited entity's systems and procedures. A situation could be considered an emergency where the audit firm's refusal to provide these services would result in a severe burden for the audited entity (for example, withdrawal of credit lines), or would even threaten its going concern status. In such circumstances, the audit firm ensures that: 131

(a) any staff involved in the accounting services have no involvement in the audit of the financial statements; and
(b) the engagement would not lead to any audit firm staff or partners taking decisions or making judgments which are properly the responsibility of management.

For entities other than listed companies or significant affiliates of listed companies, the auditor may undertake an engagement to provide accounting services, provided that: 132

(a) such services:
  (i) do not involve initiating transactions or taking management decisions; and
  (ii) are of a technical, mechanical or an informative nature; and
(b) appropriate safeguards are applied to reduce the self-review threat to an acceptable level.

133 The maintenance of the accounting records and the preparation of the financial statements are the responsibility of the management of the audited entity. Accordingly, in any engagement to provide the audited entity with accounting services, the audit firm does not initiate any transactions or take any decisions or make any judgments, which are properly the responsibility of the management. These include:
- authorising or approving transactions;
- preparing originating data (including valuation assumptions);
- determining or changing journal entries, or the classifications for accounts or transactions, or other accounting records without management approval.

134 Examples of accounting services of a technical or mechanical nature or of an informative nature include:
- recording transactions for which management has determined the appropriate account classification, posting coded transactions to the general ledger, posting entries approved by management to the trial balance or providing certain data-processing services (for example, payroll);
- assistance with the preparation of the financial statements where management takes all decisions on issues requiring the exercise of judgment and has prepared the underlying accounting records.

135 Examples of safeguards that may be appropriate when accounting services are provided to an audited entity include:
- accounting services provided by the audit firm are performed by partners and staff who have no involvement in the external audit of the financial statements;
- the accounting services are reviewed by a partner or other senior staff member with appropriate expertise who is not a member of the audit team;
- the audit of the financial statements is reviewed by an audit partner who is not involved in the audit engagement to ensure that the accounting services performed have been properly and effectively assessed in the context of the audit of the financial statements.

Effective date

136 Revisions to this Ethical Standard become effective for audits of financial statements for periods commencing on or after 6 April 2008.

137 Firms may complete audit engagements relating to periods commencing prior to 6 April 2008 in accordance with existing ethical standards, putting in place any necessary changes in the subsequent engagement period.

138 Where compliance with the requirements of ES 5 would result in a service not being supplied, services contracted before 6 April 2008 may continue to be provided until the earlier of either:

(a) the completion of the specific task or the end of the contract term, where this is set out in the contract; or
(b) 6 April 2009, where a task or term is not defined,

as long as the following apply:

- the engagement was permitted by existing ethical standards (including transitional provisions);
- any safeguards required by existing ethical standards continue to be applied; and

- the need for additional safeguards is assessed, including where possible any additional safeguards specified by ES 5, and if considered necessary, those additional safeguards are applied.

In the first year of appointment as auditor to an audited entity, an audit firm may continue to provide non-audit services which are already contracted at the date of appointment, until the earlier of either:

(i) the completion of the specific task or the end of the contract term, where this is set out in the contract; or
(ii) one year after the date of appointment, where a task or term is not defined,

provided that the need for additional safeguards is assessed and if considered necessary, those additional safeguards are applied.

APB Ethical Standard
Provisions available for small entities

(Issued December 2004)

Contents

	Paragraphs
Introduction	1 - 4
Alternative provisions	
Economic dependence	5 - 6
Self review threat – non-audit services	7 - 11
Exemptions	
Management threat - non-audit services	12 – 14
Advocacy threat – tax services	15 - 17
Partners joining an audit client	18 – 21
Disclosure requirements	22 – 24
Effective date	25

Appendix: Illustrative disclosures

Preface

APB Ethical Standards apply in the audit of financial statements. They should be read in the context of the Auditing Practices Board's Statement "The Auditing Practices Board – Scope and Authority of Pronouncements (Revised)" which sets out the application and authority of APB Ethical Standards.

The terms used in APB Ethical Standards are explained in the Glossary.

The criteria for a 'Small Entity' established in paragraph 4 of this Standard relate to UK entities. Separate guidance will be provided for entities in the Republic of Ireland.

Introduction

The APB issues Ethical Standards which set out the standards that auditors are required to comply with in order to discharge their responsibilities in respect of their integrity, objectivity and independence. The Ethical Standards issued in October 2004 address such matters as: 1

- How audit firms set policies and procedures to ensure that, in relation to each audit, the audit firm and all those who are in a position to influence the conduct and outcome of an audit act with integrity, objectivity and independence;
- Financial, business, employment and personal relationships;
- Long association with the audit engagement;
- Fees, remuneration and evaluation policies, litigation, gifts and hospitality;
- Non-audit services provided to audit clients.

Such Ethical Standards apply to all audit firms and to all audits and must be read in order to understand the alternative provisions and exemptions contained in this Standard.

The APB is aware that a limited number of the requirements in Ethical Standards 1 to 5 are difficult for certain audit firms to comply with, particularly when auditing a small entity. Whilst the APB is clear that those standards are appropriate in the interests of establishing the integrity, objectivity and independence of auditors, it accepts that certain dispensations, as set out in this Standard, are appropriate to facilitate the cost effective audit of the financial statements of Small Entities (as defined below). 2

This Standard provides alternative provisions for auditors of Small Entities to apply in respect of the threats arising from economic dependence and where tax or accounting services are provided and allows the option of taking advantage of exemptions from certain of the requirements in APB Ethical Standards 1 to 5 for a Small Entity audit engagement. Where an audit firm takes advantage of the exemptions within this Standard, it is required to: 3

(a) take the steps described in this Standard; and
(b) disclose in the audit report the fact that the firm has applied APB Ethical Standard – Provisions Available for Small Entities.

In this Standard, a 'Small Entity'[1] is: 4

---

[1] *The criteria for a 'Small Entity' established in paragraph 4 of this Standard relate to UK entities. Separate guidance will be provided for entities in the Republic of Ireland.*

(a) any company, which is not a UK or Irish listed company or an affiliate thereof, that meets two or more of the following requirements in both the current financial year and the preceding financial year:
- not more than £5.6 million turnover;
- not more than £2.8 million balance sheet total;
- not more than 50 employees.

(b) any charity with an income of less than £5.6 million;

(c) any pension fund with less than 1,000 members (including active, deferred and pensioner members)[2];

(d) any firm regulated by the FSA, which is not required to appoint an auditor in accordance with chapter 3 of the FSA Supervision Manual which forms a part of the FSA Handbook[3];

(e) any credit union which is a mutually owned financial co-operative established under the Credit Unions Act 1979 and the Industrial and Provident Societies Act 1965 (or equivalent legislation), which meets the criteria set out in (a) above;

(f) any entity registered under the Industrial and Provident Societies Act 1965, incorporated under the Friendly Societies Act 1992 or registered under the Friendly Societies Act 1974 (or equivalent legislation), which meets the criteria set out in (a) above;

(g) any registered social landlord with less than 250 units; and

(h) any other entity, such as a club, which would be a Small Entity if it were a company.

Where an entity falls into more than one of the above categories, it is only regarded as a 'Small Entity' if it meets the criteria of all relevant categories.

Alternative provisions

Economic dependence

5   When auditing the financial statements of a Small Entity an audit firm is not required to comply with the requirement in APB Ethical Standard 4, paragraph 31 that an external independent quality control review is performed.

6   APB Ethical Standard 4, paragraph 31 provides that, where it is expected that the total fees for both audit and non-audit services receivable from a non-listed audit client and its subsidiaries audited by the audit firm will regularly exceed 10% of the annual fee income of the audit firm or the part of the firm by reference to which the audit engagement partner's profit share is calculated, but will not regularly exceed 15% the firm should arrange an external independent quality control review of the audit engagement to be undertaken before the auditors' report is finalised. Although an external independent quality control review is not required, nevertheless the audit engagement partner discloses the expectation that fees will amount to between 10% and 15% of the firm's annual fee income to the ethics partner and to those charged with governance of the audit client

---

[2] *In cases where a scheme with more than 1,000 members has been in wind-up over a number of years, such a scheme does not qualify as a Small Entity, even where the remaining number of members falls below 1,000.*

[3] *This relates to those firms that are not required to appoint an auditor under rule 3.3.2 of the FSA Supervision Manual.*

Self-review threat – non-audit services

When undertaking non-audit services for a Small Entity audit client, the audit firm is not required to apply safeguards to address a self-review threat provided: 7

(a) the audit client has 'informed management'; and
(b) the audit firm extends the cyclical inspection of completed engagements that is performed for quality control purposes.

APB Ethical Standard 5 requires that, when an audit firm provides non-audit services to an audit client, appropriate safeguards are applied in order to reduce any self-review threat to an acceptable level. APB Ethical Standard 5 provides examples of safeguards that may be appropriate when non-audit services are provided to an audit client (for example in paragraphs 65 for tax services and 125 for accounting services). In the case of an audit of a Small Entity, alternative procedures involve discussions with 'informed management', supplemented by an extension of the firm's cyclical inspection of completed engagements that is performed for quality control purposes. 8

The audit firm extends the number of engagements inspected under the requirements of ISQC (UK and Ireland) 1 *'Quality control for firms that perform audits and reviews of historical financial information, and other assurance and related services engagements'*[4] to include a random selection of audit engagements where non-audit services have been provided. Particular attention is given to ensuring that there is documentary evidence that 'informed management' has made such judgments and decisions that are needed in relation to the presentation and disclosure of information in the financial statements. 9

Those inspecting the engagements are not involved in performing the engagement. Small audit firms may wish to use a suitably qualified external person or another firm to carry out engagement inspections. 10

In addition to the documentation requirements of ISQC (UK and Ireland) 1, those inspecting the engagements document their evaluation of whether the documentary evidence that 'informed management' made such judgments and decisions that were needed in relation to the presentation and disclosure of information in the financial statements. 11

Exemptions

Management threat – non-audit services

When undertaking non-audit services for Small Entity audit clients, the audit firm is not required to adhere to the prohibitions in APB Ethical Standard 5, relating to providing non-audit services that involve the audit firm undertaking part of the role of management, provided that: 12

(a) it discusses objectivity and independence issues related to the provision of non-audit services with those charged with governance; and
(b) it discloses the fact that it has applied this Standard in accordance with paragraph 22.

---

[4] *ISQC (UK and Ireland) 1 requires audit firms to establish policies and procedures which include a periodic inspection of a selection of completed engagements. Engagements selected for inspection include at least one engagement for each engagement partner over the inspection cycle, which ordinarily spans no more than three years.*

13 APB Ethical Standard 5, paragraph 28 provides that where an audit firm provides non-audit services to an audit client that does not have 'informed management', it is unlikely that any safeguards can eliminate the management threat or reduce it to an acceptable level with the consequence that such non-audit services may not be provided to that audit client. This is because the absence of a capable member of management, who has been designated by the audit client to:

- receive the results of the non-audit services provided by the audit firm; and
- make any judgments and decisions that are needed, on the basis of the information provided,

means that there is an increased threat that the audit firm takes certain decisions and makes certain judgments, which are properly the responsibility of management.

14 An audit firm auditing a Small Entity is exempted from the requirements of APB Ethical Standard 5, paragraphs 43(b) (internal audit services), 51(b) (information technology services), 70 (tax services), 99(d) (corporate finance services) 109(c) (transaction related services) and 117(b) (accounting services) in circumstances when there is no 'informed management' as envisioned by APB Ethical Standard 5, provided it discusses objectivity and independence issues related to the provision of non-audit services with those charged with governance and discloses the fact that it has applied this Standard in accordance with paragraph 22.

Advocacy threat – tax services

15 The audit firm of a Small Entity is not required to comply with APB Ethical Standard 5, paragraph 73 provided that it discloses the fact that it has applied this Standard in accordance with paragraph 22.

16 APB Ethical Standard 5, paragraph 73 provides that 'the audit firm should not undertake an engagement to provide tax services to an audit client where this would involve acting as an advocate for the audit client, before an appeals tribunal or court in the resolution of an issue:

(a) that is material to the financial statements; or
(b) where the outcome of the tax issue is dependent on a future or contemporary audit judgment'.

Such circumstances may create an advocacy threat which it is unlikely any safeguards can eliminate or reduce to an acceptable level.

17 Where an audit firm auditing a Small Entity takes advantage of the dispensation in paragraph 15, it discloses the fact that it has applied this Standard in accordance with paragraph 22.

Partners joining an audit client

18 The audit firm of a Small Entity is not required to comply with APB Ethical Standard 2, paragraph 44 provided that:

(a) it takes appropriate steps to determine that there has been no significant threat to the audit team's integrity, objectivity and independence; and
(b) it discloses the fact that it has applied this Standard in accordance with paragraph 22.

APB Ethical Standard 2, paragraph 44 provides that 'where a former partner is appointed as a director or to a key management position with an audit client, having acted as audit engagement partner (or as an independent partner, key audit partner or a partner in the chain of command) at any time in the two years prior to this appointment, the firm should resign as auditors and should not accept re-appointment until a two-year period, commencing when the former partner ceased to act for the client, has elapsed or the former partner ceases employment with the former client, whichever is the sooner'. Such circumstances may create self-interest, familiarity and intimidation threats.

19

An audit firm takes appropriate steps to determine that there has been no significant threat to the audit team's integrity, objectivity and independence as a result of the former partner's employment by an audit client that is a Small Entity by:

20

(a) assessing the significance of the self-interest, familiarity or intimidation threats, having regard to the following factors:
  - the position the individual has taken at the audit client;
  - the nature and amount of any involvement the individual will have with the audit team or the audit process;
  - the length of time that has passed since the individual was a member of the audit team or firm; and
  - the former position of the individual within the audit team or firm, and
(b) if the threat is other than clearly insignificant, applying alternative procedures such as:
  - considering the appropriateness or necessity of modifying the audit plan for the audit engagement;
  - assigning an audit team to the subsequent audit engagement that is of sufficient experience in relation to the individual who has joined the audit client;
  - involving an audit partner or senior staff member with appropriate expertise, who was not a member of the audit team, to review the work done or otherwise advise as necessary; or
  - undertaking an engagement quality control review of the audit engagement.

When an audit firm auditing a Small Entity takes advantage of paragraph 18 it discloses the fact that it has applied this Standard in accordance with paragraph 22 and documents the steps that it has taken to comply with this Standard.

21

Disclosure requirements

Where the audit firm has taken advantage of an exemption provided in paragraphs 12, 15 or 18 of this Standard, the audit engagement partner should ensure that:

22

(a) the auditors' report discloses this fact, and
(b) either the financial statements, or the auditors' report, discloses the type of non-audit services provided to the audit client or the fact that a former audit engagement partner has joined the client.

The fact that an audit firm has taken advantage of an exemption from APB Ethical Standard – Provisions Available for Small Entities is set out in a separate paragraph of the audit report as part of the Basis of audit opinion. It does not affect the Opinion paragraph. An illustrative example of such disclosure is set out in the Appendix.

23

24 The audit engagement partner ensures that within the financial statements reference is made to the type of non-audit services provided to the audit client or the fact that a former partner has joined the client. An illustration of possible disclosures is set out in the Appendix. Where such a disclosure is not made within the financial statements it is included in the auditors' report.

Effective date

25 Effective for audits of financial statements for periods commencing on or after 15 December 2004.

Appendix: Illustrative disclosures

(a) Illustrative disclosure of the fact that the audit firm has taken advantage of an exemption within the auditors' report

Basis of audit opinion

We conducted our audit in accordance with United Kingdom Auditing Standards issued by the Auditing Practices Board. An audit includes examination, on a test basis, of evidence relevant to the amounts and disclosures in the financial statements. It also includes an assessment of the significant estimates and judgments made by [the directors] in the preparation of the financial statements, and of whether the accounting policies are appropriate to the [company's] circumstances, consistently applied and adequately disclosed.

We planned and performed our audit so as to obtain all the information and explanations which we considered necessary in order to provide us with sufficient evidence to give reasonable assurance that the financial statements are free from material misstatement, whether caused by fraud or other irregularity or error. In forming our opinion we also evaluated the overall adequacy of the presentation of information in the financial statements.

We have undertaken the audit in accordance with the requirements of APB Ethical Standards including APB Ethical Standard – Provisions Available for Small Entities, in the circumstances set out in note [x] to the financial statements.

Opinion

In our opinion the financial statements give a true and fair view of the state of the [company's] affairs as at ..... .

[Date of the auditors' report, a*uditors' signature and* address]

(b) Illustrative disclosure of relevant circumstances within the financial statements

Note [x]   In common with many other businesses of our size and nature we use our auditors to prepare and submit returns to the tax authorities and assist with the preparation of the financial statements[5].

---

[5] *Where exemption in paragraph 12 (Management threat in relation non-audit services) is applied.*

Note [x]   In common with many other businesses of our size and nature we use our auditors to provide tax advice and to represent us, as necessary, at tax tribunals[6].

Note [x]   XYZ, a former partner of [audit firm] joined [audit client] as [a director] on [date][7].

---

[6] *Where exemption in paragraph 15 (Advocacy threat – tax services) is applied.*

[7] *Where exemption in paragraph 18 (Partners joining an audit client) is applied.*

APB Ethical Standards
Glossary of terms
(Issued December 2004)

accounting services	The provision of services that involve the maintenance of accounting records or the preparation of financial statements that are then subject to audit
affiliate	Any undertaking which is connected to another by means of common ownership, control or management.
audit client	The entity whose financial statements are subject to audit.
audit engagement partner	The partner or other person in the firm who is responsible for the audit engagement and its performance and for the report that is issued on behalf of the firm, and who, where required, has the appropriate authority from a professional, legal or regulatory body.
audit firm	The sole practitioner, partnership, limited liability partnership or other corporate entity engaged in the provision of audit services. For the purpose of APB Ethical Standards, audit firm includes network firms in the UK and Ireland, which are controlled by the audit firm or its partners.
audit team	All audit professionals who, regardless of their legal relationship with the auditor or audit firm, are assigned to a particular audit engagement in order to perform the audit task (e.g. audit partner(s), audit manager(s) and audit staff).
chain of command	All persons who have a direct supervisory, management or other oversight responsibility over either any audit partner of the audit team or over the conduct of audit work in the audit firm. This includes all partners, principals and shareholders who may prepare, review or directly influence the performance appraisal of any audit partner of the audit team as a result of that partner's involvement with the audit engagement.
close family	A non-dependent parent, child or sibling.
contingent fee basis	Any arrangement made at the outset of an engagement under which a pre-determined amount or a specified commission on or percentage of any consideration or saving is payable to the audit firm upon the happening of a specified event or the achievement of an outcome (or alternative outcomes). Differential hourly fee rates, or arrangements under which the fee payable will be negotiated after the completion of the engagement, do not constitute contingent fee arrangements.
engagement team	All persons who are directly involved in the acceptance and performance of a particular audit. This includes the audit team, professional personnel from other disciplines involved in the audit engagement and those who provide quality control or direct oversight of the audit engagement.
ethics partner	The partner or other person in the audit firm having responsibility for the adequacy of the firm's policies and procedures relating to integrity, objectivity and independence,

Glossary of terms 153

their compliance with APB Ethical Standards and the effectiveness of their communication to partners and staff within the firm and providing related guidance to individual partners.

financial interest An equity or other security, debenture, loan or other debt instrument of an entity, including rights and obligations to acquire such an interest and derivatives directly related to such an interest.

immediate family A spouse (or equivalent) or dependent.

independent partner A partner or other person performing the function of a partner who is not a member of the audit team (but who may be the person who undertakes an engagement quality control review to meet the requirements of Proposed ISA (UK & Ireland) 220 'Quality control for audits of historical financial information'). The experience required of the independent partner is determined by the nature of the audit engagement and the seniority and experience of the audit engagement partner.

key audit partner An audit partner, or other person performing the function of an audit partner, of the engagement team (other than the audit engagement partner) who is involved at the group level and is responsible for key decisions or judgments on significant matters, such as on significant subsidiaries or divisions of the audit client, or on significant risk factors that relate to the audit of that client.

key management position Any position at the audit client which involves the responsibility for fundamental management decisions at the audit client (e.g. as a CEO or CFO), including an ability to influence the accounting policies and the preparation of the financial statements of the audit client. A key management position also arises where there are contractual and factual arrangements which in substance allow an individual to participate in exercising such a management function in a different way (e.g. via a consulting contract).

listed company An entity whose shares, stock or debt are quoted or listed on a recognised stock exchange, or are marketed under the regulations of a recognised stock exchange or other equivalent body.

network firm Any entity:

(i) controlled by the audit firm; or

(ii) under common control, ownership or management; or

(iii) otherwise affiliated or associated with the audit firm through the use of a common name or through the sharing of significant common professional resources.

person in a position to influence the conduct and outcome of the audit:

(a) Any person who is directly involved in the audit (the engagement team), including:

(i) the audit partners, audit managers and audit staff (the audit team);

(ii) professional personnel from other disciplines involved in the audit (for example, lawyers, actuaries, taxation specialists, IT specialists, treasury management specialists);

(iii) those who provide quality control or direct oversight of the audit;

(b) Any person, who forms part of the chain of command for the audit within the audit firm;

(c) Any person within the audit firm who, due to any other circumstances, may be in a position to exert such influence.

APB Ethical Standard
Provisions available for small entities (Revised)*

(Revised April 2008)

Contents

	Paragraph
Introduction	1 – 4
Alternative provisions	
Economic dependence	5 – 6
Self review threat – non-audit services	7 – 11
Exemptions	
Management threat – non-audit services	12 – 14
Advocacy threat – tax services	15 – 17
Partners joining an audited entity	18 – 21
Disclosure requirements	22 – 24
Effective date	25
Appendix: Illustrative disclosures	

---

* *Revisions to this Standard became effective for audits of financial statements for periods commencing on or after 6 April 2008. The Standard effective before this date is available from the APB website.*

Preface

APB Ethical Standards apply in the audit of financial statements. They are read in the context of the Auditing Practices Board's Statement "The Auditing Practices Board – Scope and Authority of Pronouncements (Revised)" which sets out the application and authority of APB Ethical Standards.

The terms used in APB Ethical Standards are explained in the Glossary.

Introduction

1   The APB issues Ethical Standards which set out the standards that auditors are required to comply with in order to discharge their responsibilities in respect of their integrity, objectivity and independence. The Ethical Standards 1 to 5 address such matters as:

- How audit firms set policies and procedures to ensure that, in relation to each audit, the audit firm and all those who are in a position to influence the conduct and outcome of an audit act with integrity, objectivity and independence;
- Financial, business, employment and personal relationships;
- Long association with the audit engagement;
- Fees, remuneration and evaluation policies, litigation, gifts and hospitality;
- Non-audit services provided to audited entities.

These Ethical Standards apply to all audit firms and to all audits and must be read in order to understand the alternative provisions and exemptions contained in this Standard.

2   The APB is aware that a limited number of the requirements in Ethical Standards 1 to 5 are difficult for certain audit firms to comply with, particularly when auditing a small entity. Whilst the APB is clear that those standards are appropriate in the interests of establishing the integrity, objectivity and independence of auditors, it accepts that certain dispensations, as set out in this Standard, are appropriate to facilitate the cost effective audit of the financial statements of Small Entities (as defined below).

3   This Standard provides alternative provisions for auditors of Small Entities to apply in respect of the threats arising from economic dependence and where tax or accounting services are provided and allows the option of taking advantage of exemptions from certain of the requirements in APB Ethical Standards 1 to 5 for a Small Entity audit engagement. Where an audit firm takes advantage of the exemptions within this Standard, it is required to:

(a) take the steps described in this Standard; and
(b) disclose in the audit report the fact that the firm has applied APB Ethical Standard – Provisions Available for Small Entities.

4   (i)   In this Standard, for the UK a 'Small Entity' is:
   (a) any company, which is not a UK listed company or an affiliate thereof, that qualifies as a small company under Section 382 of the Companies Act 2006;
   (b) where group accounts are produced, any group that qualifies as small under Section 383 of the Companies Act 2006;
   (c) any charity with an income of less than the turnover threshold applicable to small companies as identified in Section 382 of the Companies Act 2006;

Exemptions

Management threat – non-audit services

When undertaking non-audit services for Small Entity audited entities, the audit firm is not required to adhere to the prohibitions in APB Ethical Standard 5, relating to providing non-audit services that involve the audit firm undertaking part of the role of management, provided that:

(a) it discusses objectivity and independence issues related to the provision of non-audit services with those charged with governance, confirming that management accept responsibility for any decisions taken; and
(b) it discloses the fact that it has applied this Standard in accordance with paragraph 22.

APB Ethical Standard 5, paragraph 27 provides that where an audit firm provides non-audit services to an audited entity where there is no 'informed management', it is unlikely that any other safeguards can eliminate a management threat or reduce it to an acceptable level with the consequence that such non-audit services may not be provided to that audited entity. This is because the absence of a member of management, who has the authority and capability to:

- receive the results of the non-audit services provided by the audit firm; and
- make any judgments and decisions that are needed, on the basis of the information provided,

means that there is an increased management threat since the audit firm will be closer to those decisions and judgments which are properly the responsibility of management and more aligned with the views and interests of management.

An audit firm auditing a Small Entity is exempted from the requirements of APB Ethical Standard 5, paragraphs 44(b) (internal audit services), 52(b) (information technology services), 76 (tax services), 109(d) (corporate finance services) 119(c) (transaction related services) and 127(b) (accounting services) in circumstances when there is no 'informed management' as envisioned by APB Ethical Standard 5, provided it discusses objectivity and independence issues related to the provision of non-audit services with those charged with governance, confirming that management accept responsibility for any decisions taken and discloses the fact that it has applied this Standard in accordance with paragraph 22.

Advocacy threat – tax services

The audit firm of a Small Entity is not required to comply with APB Ethical Standard 5, paragraph 82 provided that it discloses the fact that it has applied this Standard in accordance with paragraph 22.

APB Ethical Standard 5, paragraph 82 provides that 'the audit firm shall not undertake an engagement to provide tax services to an audited entity where this would involve acting as an advocate for the audited entity, before an appeals tribunal or court in the resolution of an issue:

(a) that is material to the financial statements; or
(b) where the outcome of the tax issue is dependent on a future or contemporary audit judgment'.

Such circumstances may create an advocacy threat which it is unlikely any safeguards can eliminate or reduce to an acceptable level.

17 Where an audit firm auditing a Small Entity takes advantage of the dispensation in paragraph 15, it discloses the fact that it has applied this Standard in accordance with paragraph 22.

Partners joining an audited entity

18 **The audit firm of a Small Entity is not required to comply with APB Ethical Standard 2, paragraph 48 provided that:**

   (a) **it takes appropriate steps to determine that there has been no significant threat to the audit team's integrity, objectivity and independence; and**

   (b) **it discloses the fact that it has applied this Standard in accordance with paragraph 22.**

19 APB Ethical Standard 2, paragraph 48 provides that 'where a former partner is appointed as a director or to a key management position with an audited entity, having acted as audit engagement partner (or as an engagement quality control reviewer, key partner involved in the audit or a partner in the chain of command) at any time in the two years prior to this appointment, the firm shall resign as auditors and shall not accept re-appointment until a two-year period, commencing when the former partner ceased to have an ability to influence the conduct and outcome of the audit, has elapsed or the former partner ceases employment with the former audited entity, whichever is the sooner'. Such circumstances may create self-interest, familiarity and intimidation threats.

20 An audit firm takes appropriate steps to determine that there has been no significant threat to the audit team's integrity, objectivity and independence as a result of the former partner's employment by an audited entity that is a Small Entity by:

   (a) assessing the significance of the self-interest, familiarity or intimidation threats, having regard to the following factors:
   - the position the individual has taken at the audited entity;
   - the nature and amount of any involvement the individual will have with the audit team or the audit process;
   - the length of time that has passed since the individual was a member of the audit team or firm; and
   - the former position of the individual within the audit team or firm, and

   (b) if the threat is other than clearly insignificant, applying alternative procedures such as:
   - considering the appropriateness or necessity of modifying the audit plan for the audit engagement;
   - assigning an audit team to the subsequent audit engagement that is of sufficient experience in relation to the individual who has joined the audited entity;
   - involving an audit partner or senior staff member with appropriate expertise, who was not a member of the audit team, to review the work done or otherwise advise as necessary; or
   - undertaking an engagement quality control review of the audit engagement.

21 When an audit firm auditing a Small Entity takes advantage of paragraph 18 it discloses the fact that it has applied this Standard in accordance with paragraph 22 and documents the steps that it has taken to comply with this Standard.

Disclosure requirements

Where the audit firm has taken advantage of an exemption provided in paragraphs 12, 15 or 18 of this Standard, the audit engagement partner shall ensure that: 22

(a) the auditors' report discloses this fact, and
(b) either the financial statements, or the auditors' report, discloses the type of non-audit services provided to the audited entity or the fact that a former audit engagement partner has joined the audited entity.

The fact that an audit firm has taken advantage of an exemption from APB Ethical Standard – Provisions Available for Small Entities is set out in a separate paragraph of the audit report as part of the Basis of audit opinion. It does not affect the Opinion paragraph. An illustrative example of such disclosure is set out in the Appendix. 23

The audit engagement partner ensures that within the financial statements reference is made to the type of non-audit services provided to the audited entity or the fact that a former partner has joined the audited entity. An illustration of possible disclosures is set out in the Appendix. Where such a disclosure is not made within the financial statements it is included in the auditors' report. 24

Effective date

Revisions to this Ethical Standard become effective for audits of financial statements for periods commencing on or after 6 April 2008. 25

Appendix: Illustrative disclosures

(a) Illustrative disclosure of the fact that the audit firm has taken advantage of an exemption within the auditors' report

Basis of audit opinion

We conducted our audit in accordance with United Kingdom Auditing Standards issued by the Auditing Practices Board. An audit includes examination, on a test basis, of evidence relevant to the amounts and disclosures in the financial statements. It also includes an assessment of the significant estimates and judgments made by [the directors] in the preparation of the financial statements, and of whether the accounting policies are appropriate to the [company's] circumstances, consistently applied and adequately disclosed.

We planned and performed our audit so as to obtain all the information and explanations which we considered necessary in order to provide us with sufficient evidence to give reasonable assurance that the financial statements are free from material misstatement, whether caused by fraud or other irregularity or error. In forming our opinion we also evaluated the overall adequacy of the presentation of information in the financial statements.

We have undertaken the audit in accordance with the requirements of APB Ethical Standards including APB Ethical Standard – Provisions Available for Small Entities, in the circumstances set out in note [x] to the financial statements.

Opinion

In our opinion the financial statements give a true and fair view of the state of the [company's] affairs as at .... .

[Date of the auditors' report, *auditors' signature and* address]

(b) Illustrative disclosure of relevant circumstances within the financial statements

Note [x]   In common with many other businesses of our size and nature we use our auditors to prepare and submit returns to the tax authorities and assist with the preparation of the financial statements[5].

Note [x]   In common with many other businesses of our size and nature we use our auditors to provide tax advice and to represent us, as necessary, at tax tribunals[6].

Note [x]   XYZ, a former partner of [audit firm] joined [audited entity] as [a director] on [date][7].

---

[5] *Where exemption in paragraph 12 (Management threat in relation non-audit services) is applied.*

[6] *Where exemption in paragraph 15 (Advocacy threat – tax services) is applied.*

[7] *Where exemption in paragraph 18 (Partners joining an audited entity) is applied.*

APB Ethical Standards
Glossary of terms

(Revised April 2008)

accounting services	The provision of services that involve the maintenance of accounting records or the preparation of financial statements that are then subject to audit
affiliate	Any undertaking which is connected to another by means of common ownership, control or management.
audit engagement partner	The partner or other person in the firm who is responsible for the audit engagement and its performance and for the report that is issued on behalf of the firm, and who, where required, has the appropriate authority from a professional, legal or regulatory body.
audit firm	The sole practitioner, partnership, limited liability partnership or other corporate entity engaged in the provision of audit services. For the purpose of APB Ethical Standards, audit firm includes network firms in the UK and Ireland, which are controlled by the audit firm or its partners.
audit team	All audit professionals who, regardless of their legal relationship with the auditor or audit firm, are assigned to a particular audit engagement in order to perform the audit task (e.g. audit partner(s), audit manager(s) and audit staff).
audited entity	The entity whose financial statements are subject to audit by the audit firm.
chain of command	All persons who have a direct supervisory, management or other oversight responsibility over either any audit partner of the audit team or over the conduct of audit work in the audit firm. This includes all partners, principals and shareholders who may prepare, review or directly influence the performance appraisal of any audit partner of the audit team as a result of that partner's involvement with the audit engagement. It does not include any non-executive individuals on a supervisory or equivalent board.
close family	A non-dependent parent, child or sibling.
contingent fee basis	Any arrangement made under which a fee is calculated on a pre-determined basis relating to the outcome or result of a transaction or the result of the work performed. Differential hourly fee rates, or arrangements under which the fee payable will be negotiated after the completion of the engagement, do not constitute contingent fee arrangements.
engagement quality control reviewer	A partner or other person in the firm or a suitably qualified external person, with sufficient and appropriate experience and authority to objectively evaluate, before the auditor's report is issued, the significant judgments which the engagement team has made and the conclusions reached in formulating the auditor's report. This may be the person who undertakes an engagement quality control review to meet the requirements of

Proposed ISA (UK & Ireland) 220 *'Quality control for audits of historical financial information'*.

engagement team All persons who are directly involved in the acceptance and performance of a particular audit. This includes the audit team, professional personnel from other disciplines involved in the audit engagement and those who provide quality control or direct oversight of the audit engagement.

ethics partner The partner or other person in the audit firm having responsibility for the adequacy of the firm's policies and procedures relating to integrity, objectivity and independence, their compliance with APB Ethical Standards and the effectiveness of their communication to partners and staff within the firm and providing related guidance to individual partners.

financial interest An equity or other security, debenture, loan or other debt instrument of an entity, including rights and obligations to acquire such an interest and derivatives directly related to such an interest.

immediate family A spouse (or equivalent) or dependent.

informed management Member of management (or senior employee) of the audited entity who has the authority and capability to make independent management judgments and decisions in relation to non-audit services on the basis of information provided by the audit firm.

key management position Any position at the audited entity which involves the responsibility for fundamental management decisions at the audited entity (e.g. as a CEO or CFO), including an ability to influence the accounting policies and the preparation of the financial statements of the audited entity. A key management position also arises where there are contractual and factual arrangements which in substance allow an individual to participate in exercising such a management function in a different way (e.g. via a consulting contract).

key partner involved in the audit A partner, or other person in the engagement team (other than the audit engagement partner or engagement quality control reviewer), who either:

- is involved at the group level and is responsible for key decisions or judgments on significant matters or risk factors that relate to the audit of that audited entity, or

- is primarily responsible for the audit of a significant affiliate or division[1] of the audited entity.

listed company An entity whose shares, stock or debt are quoted or listed on a UK or Irish recognised stock exchange, or are marketed under the regulations of a UK or Irish recognised stock exchange or other equivalent body. This includes any company in which the public can trade shares on the open market, such as those listed on the London Stock Exchange (including those

---

[1] *For the purposes of this definition, a significant affiliate or division is an affiliate or division which in the judgment of the group auditor, is individually likely to be of financial significance to the group, including those affiliates or divisions located outside the UK and Ireland.*

Glossary of terms

admitted to trade on the Alternative Investments Market), PLUS Markets and the Irish Stock Exchange (including those admitted to trade on the Irish Enterprise Exchange).

network firm Any entity which is part of a larger structure that is aimed at co-operation and which is:

(i) controlled by the audit firm; or

(ii) under common control, ownership or management; or

(iii) part of a larger structure that is clearly aimed at profit or cost sharing; or

(iv) otherwise affiliated or associated with the audit firm through common quality control policies and procedures, common business strategy, the use of a common name or through the sharing of significant common professional resources.

non-audit services Any engagement in which an audit firm provides professional services to an audited entity other than pursuant to:

(a) the audit of financial statements; and

(b) those other roles which relevant legislation or regulation specify can be performed by the auditor of the entity.

In the case of a group, non-audit services include services provided by the audit firm, to the parent company or to any affiliate.

person in a position to influence the conduct and outcome of the audit:

(a) Any person who is directly involved in the audit (the engagement team), including:

(i) the audit partners, audit managers and audit staff (the audit team);

(ii) professional personnel from other disciplines involved in the audit (for example, lawyers, actuaries, taxation specialists, IT specialists, treasury management specialists);

(iii) those who provide quality control or direct oversight of the audit;

(b) Any person, who forms part of the chain of command for the audit within the audit firm;

(c) Any person within the audit firm who, due to any other circumstances, may be in a position to exert such influence.

Ethical Standard for Reporting Accountants

(Issued October 2006)

Contents

	Paragraph
Section 1	
Introduction	1.1 – 1.14
Compliance with ethical standards	1.15 – 1.27
Identification and assessment of threats	1.28 – 1.54
Identification and assessment of safeguards	1.55 – 1.59
Engagement Quality Control Review	1.60 – 1.62
Overall conclusion	1.63 – 1.65
Other accountants involved in an investment circular reporting engagement	1.66 – 1.67
Communication with those charged with governance	1.68 – 1.76
Documentation	1.77 – 1.79
Section 2 – Specific circumstances creating threats to a reporting accountant's objectivity and independence	
Introduction	2.1 – 2.2
Financial relationships	2.3 – 2.18
Business relationships	2.19 – 2.25
Employment relationships	2.26 – 2.46
Family and other personal relationships	2.47 – 2.52
External consultants involved in an investment circular reporting engagement	2.53 – 2.55
Association with an engagement client	2.56 – 2.62
Fees	2.63 – 2.78
Threatened and actual litigation	2.79 – 2.81
Gifts and hospitality	2.82 – 2.89
Section 3 - The provision of other services	
Introduction	3.1 – 3.12
Internal audit services	3.13 - 3.21
Information technology services	3.22 – 3.27
Valuation services	3.28 – 3.31
Actuarial valuation services	3.32 – 3.34
Tax services	3.35 – 3.49
Litigation support services	3.50 – 3.52
Legal services	3.53 – 3.54
Recruitment and remuneration services	3.55 – 3.63
Corporate finance services	3.64 – 3.76
Transaction related services	3.77 – 3.82
Accounting services	3.83 – 3.89
Section 4 - Effective date	4.1 – 4.6

Appendix 1 – Glossary of terms

Section 1

Introduction

APB Ethical Standards for Auditors require an auditor to be independent from the entity that it is appointed to audit. There is a substantial degree of similarity between an audit opinion and the nature of assurance provided by accountants reporting for the purposes of an investment circular prepared in accordance with the statutory or regulatory requirements of a recognised stock exchange. Accordingly, the Auditing Practices Board (APB) believes that users of investment circulars will expect an equivalent standard of independence of reporting accountants to that required of auditors. 1.1

This standard is based on the APB Ethical Standards for Auditors and applies to all engagements: 1.2

- that are subject to the requirements of the Standards for Investment Reporting (SIRs) issued by the APB, and
- which are in connection with an investment circular in which a report from the reporting accountant is to be published.

This standard applies to all public reporting engagements undertaken in accordance with the SIRs. It also applies to all private reporting engagements that are directly linked to such public reporting engagements.

Where a private reporting engagement is undertaken, but it is not intended that the reporting accountant will issue a public report, the reporting accountant follows the ethical guidance issued by the professional accountancy body of which the reporting accountant is a member. The APB is not aware of any significant instances where the relevant parts of the ethical guidance issued by professional accountancy bodies in the UK and Ireland are more restrictive than this standard. 1.3

An investment circular is a document issued by an entity pursuant to statutory or regulatory requirements relating to securities on which it is intended that a third party should make an investment decision, including a prospectus, listing particulars, a circular to shareholders or similar document. 1.4

Public confidence in the operation of the capital markets and in the conduct of public interest entities depends, in part, upon the credibility of the opinions and reports issued by reporting accountants in connection with investment circulars. Such credibility depends on beliefs concerning the integrity, objectivity and independence of reporting accountants and the quality of work they perform. The APB establishes quality control, investment reporting[1] and ethical standards to provide a framework for the practice of reporting accountants. 1.5

Reporting Accountants should conduct an investment circular reporting engagement with integrity, objectivity and independence. 1.6

Integrity

Integrity is a prerequisite for all those who act in the public interest. It is essential that reporting accountants act, and are seen to act, with integrity, which requires not 1.7

---

[1] SIR 1000 paragraph 18 states 'In the conduct of an engagement involving an investment circular, the reporting accountant should comply with the applicable ethical standards issued by the Auditing Practices Board'.

only honesty but a broad range of related qualities such as fairness, candour, courage, intellectual honesty and confidentiality.

1.8 It is important that the directors and management of an engagement client can rely on the reporting accountant to treat the information obtained during an engagement as confidential, unless they have authorised its disclosure, it is already known to third parties or the reporting accountant has a legal right or duty to disclose it. Without this, there is a danger that the directors and management will fail to disclose such information to the reporting accountant and that the outcome of the engagement will thereby be impaired.

Objectivity

1.9 Objectivity is a state of mind that excludes bias, prejudice and compromise and that gives fair and impartial consideration to all matters that are relevant to the task in hand, disregarding those that are not. Objectivity requires that the reporting accountant's judgment is not affected by conflicts of interests. Like integrity, objectivity is a fundamental ethical principle.

1.10 The need for reporting accountants to be objective arises from the fact that the important issues involved in an engagement are likely to relate to questions of judgment rather than to questions of fact. For example, in relation to historical financial information included in an investment circular directors have to form a view as to whether it is necessary to make adjustments to previously published financial statements. If the directors, whether deliberately or inadvertently, make a biased judgment or an otherwise inappropriate decision, the financial information may be misstated or misleading.

1.11 It is against this background that reporting accountants are engaged to undertake an investment circular reporting engagement. The reporting accountant's objectivity requires that it expresses an impartial opinion in the light of all the available information and its professional judgment. Objectivity also requires that the reporting accountant adopts a rigorous and robust approach and is prepared to disagree, where necessary, with the directors' judgments.

Independence

1.12 Independence is freedom from situations and relationships which make it probable that a reasonable and informed third party would conclude that objectivity either is impaired or could be impaired. Independence is related to and underpins objectivity. However, whereas objectivity is a personal behavioural characteristic concerning the reporting accountant's state of mind, independence relates to the circumstances surrounding the engagement, including the financial, employment, business and personal relationships between the reporting accountant and its engagement client and other parties who are connected with the investment circular.

1.13 The need for independence arises because, in most cases, users of the financial information and other third parties do not have all the information necessary to assess whether reporting accountants are, in fact, objective. Although reporting accountants themselves may be satisfied that their objectivity is not impaired by a particular situation, a third party may reach a different conclusion. For example, if a third party were aware that the reporting accountant had certain financial, employment, business or personal relationships with the engagement client, that individual might reasonably conclude that the reporting accountant could be subject to undue influence from the engagement client or would not be impartial or unbiased. Public confidence in the reporting accountant's objectivity could therefore suffer as a result of this perception, irrespective of whether there is any actual impairment.

Accordingly, in evaluating the likely consequences of such situations and relationships, the test to be applied is not whether the reporting accountant considers that its objectivity is impaired but whether it is probable that a reasonable and informed third party would conclude that the reporting accountant's objectivity either is impaired or is likely to be impaired. There are inherent threats to the level of independence (both actual and perceived) that the reporting accountant can achieve as a result of the influence that the board of directors and management have over its appointment and remuneration. The reporting accountant considers the application of safeguards where there are threats to their independence (both actual and perceived). 1.14

Compliance with ethical standards

The reporting accountant should establish policies and procedures, appropriately documented and communicated, designed to ensure that, in relation to each investment circular reporting engagement, the firm, and all those who are in a position directly to influence the conduct and outcome of the investment circular reporting engagement, act with integrity, objectivity and independence. 1.15

For the purposes of the APB Ethical Standard for Reporting Accountants, a person in a position directly to influence the conduct and outcome of the investment circular reporting engagement is: 1.16

(a) any person within the firm who is directly involved in the investment circular reporting engagement ('the engagement team'), including:
  (i) the partners, managers and staff from assurance and other disciplines involved in the engagement (for example, taxation specialists, IT specialists, treasury management specialists, lawyers, actuaries);[2]
  (ii) those who provide quality control or direct oversight of the engagement;
(b) any person within the firm who can directly influence the conduct and outcome of the investment circular reporting engagement through the provision of direct supervisory, management or other oversight of the engagement team in the context of the investment circular reporting engagement.

Because investment circulars may relate to transactions that are price sensitive and therefore confidential, the fact that a firm has been engaged to undertake an investment circular reporting engagement is likely to be known by only a limited number of individuals within the firm. For this reason, the requirements of this standard apply only to: 1.17

(a) individuals within the engagement team and those with a direct supervisory, management or other oversight responsibility for the engagement team who have actual knowledge of the investment circular reporting engagement; and
(b) where required by this Standard, the firm.

Compliance with the requirements regarding the reporting accountant's integrity, objectivity and independence is a responsibility of both the firm and of individual partners and professional staff. The firm establishes policies and procedures, 1.18

---

[2] Where external consultants are engaged by the reporting accountant and involved in the engagement, the reporting accountant should evaluate the objectivity of the expert in accordance with paragraphs 2.53 to 2.55 of this Standard.

appropriate to the size and nature of the firm, to promote and monitor compliance with those requirements by any person who is in a position directly to influence the conduct and outcome of the investment circular reporting engagement.[3]

1.19 **The leadership of the firm should take responsibility for establishing a control environment within the firm that places adherence to ethical principles and compliance with the APB Ethical Standard for Reporting Accountants above commercial considerations.**

1.20 The leadership of the firm influences the internal culture of the organisation by its actions and by its example ('the tone at the top'). Achieving a robust control environment requires that the leadership gives clear, consistent and frequent messages, backed up by appropriate actions, which emphasise the importance of compliance with the APB Ethical Standard for Reporting Accountants.

1.21 In order to promote a strong control environment, the firm establishes policies and procedures (including the maintenance of appropriate records) that include:

(a) reporting by partners and staff as required by the APB Ethical Standard for Reporting Accountants of particular circumstances including:
- family and other personal relationships involving an engagement client of the firm;
- financial interests in an engagement client of the firm; and
- decisions to join an engagement client;

(b) monitoring of compliance with the firm's policies and procedures relating to integrity, objectivity and independence. Such monitoring procedures include, on a test basis, periodic review of the engagement partners' documentation of their consideration of the reporting accountant's objectivity and independence, addressing, for example:
- financial interests in engagement clients;
- contingent fee arrangements;
- economic dependence on clients;
- the performance of other service engagements for the engagement client;

(c) a mechanism for prompt communication of possible or actual breaches of the firm's policies and procedures to the relevant engagement partners;

(d) evaluation by engagement partners of the implications of any identified possible or actual breaches of the firm's policies and procedures that are reported to them;

(e) prohibiting members of the engagement team from making, or assuming responsibility for, management decisions for the engagement client;

(f) operation of an enforcement mechanism to promote compliance with policies and procedures; and

(g) empowerment of staff to communicate to senior levels within the firm any issue of objectivity or independence that concerns them; this includes establishing clear communication channels open to staff, encouraging staff to use these channels and ensuring that staff who use these channels are not subject to disciplinary proceedings as a result.

---

[3] *Monitoring of compliance with ethical requirements will often be performed as part of a broader quality control process. ISQC (UK & Ireland) 1 'Quality Control for firms that perform audits and reviews of historical financial information and other assurance and related services engagements*' establishes the basic principles and essential procedures in relation to a firm's responsibilities for its system of quality control for engagements in connection with an investment circular.

Save where the circumstances contemplated in paragraph 1.24 apply, the firm should designate a partner in the firm ('the ethics partner'[4]) as having responsibility for: **1.22**

(a) the adequacy of the firm's policies and procedures relating to integrity, objectivity and independence, their compliance with the APB Ethical Standard for Reporting Accountants, and the effectiveness of their communication to partners and staff within the firm; and
(b) providing related guidance to individual partners.

In assessing the effectiveness of the firm's communication of its policies and procedures relating to integrity, objectivity and independence, ethics partners consider whether these matters are properly covered in induction programmes, professional training and continuing professional development for all partners and staff with direct involvement in investment circular reporting engagements. Ethics partners also provide guidance on matters referred to them and on matters which they otherwise become aware of, where a difficult and objective judgment needs to be made or a consistent position reached.   **1.23**

In firms with three or less partners, it may not be practicable for an ethics partner to be designated. In these circumstances all partners will regularly discuss ethical issues amongst themselves, so ensuring that they act in a consistent manner and observe the principles set out in the APB Ethical Standard for Reporting Accountants. In the case of a sole practitioner, advice on matters where a difficult and objective judgment needs to be made is obtained through the ethics helpline of their professional body, or through discussion with a practitioner from another firm. In all cases, it is important that such discussions are documented.   **1.24**

To be able to discharge his or her responsibilities, the ethics partner is an individual possessing seniority, relevant experience and authority within the firm and is provided with sufficient staff support and other resources, commensurate with the size of the firm. Alternative arrangements are established to allow for: **1.25**

- the provision of guidance on those engagements where the ethics partner is the engagement partner; and
- situations where the ethics partner is unavailable, for example due to illness or holidays.

Whenever a possible or actual breach of the APB Ethical Standard for Reporting Accountants, or of policies and procedures established pursuant to the requirements of the APB Ethical Standard for Reporting Accountants, is identified, the engagement partner, in the first instance, and the ethics partner, where appropriate, assesses the implications of the breach, determines whether there are safeguards that can be put in place or other actions that can be taken to address any potential adverse consequences and considers whether there is a need to withdraw from the investment circular reporting engagement.   **1.26**

An inadvertent violation of this Standard does not necessarily call into question the firm's ability to undertake an investment circular reporting engagement, provided that: **1.27**

(a) the firm has established policies and procedures that require all partners and staff to report any breach promptly to the engagement partner or to the ethics partner, as appropriate;

---

[4] *This individual may be the same person who is designated as the ethics partner for the purposes of the APB Ethical Standards for Auditors.*

(b) the engagement partner or ethics partner promptly notifies the relevant partner or member of staff that any matter which has given rise to a breach is to be addressed as soon as possible and ensures that such action is taken;

(c) safeguards, where appropriate, are applied, (for example, having another partner review the work done by the relevant partner or member of staff or removing him or her from the engagement team); and

(d) the actions taken and the rationale for them are documented.

Identification and assessment of threats

1.28 Reporting accountants identify and assess the circumstances, which could adversely affect their objectivity ('threats'), including any perceived loss of independence, and apply procedures ('safeguards'), which will either:

(a) eliminate the threat (for example, by eliminating the circumstances, such as removing an individual from the engagement team or disposing of a financial interest in the engagement client); or

(b) reduce the threat to an acceptable level; that is a level at which it is not probable that a reasonable and informed third party would conclude that the reporting accountant's objectivity is impaired or is likely to be impaired (for example, by having the work reviewed by another partner or by another firm).

When considering safeguards, where the engagement partner chooses to reduce rather than to eliminate a threat to objectivity and independence, he or she recognises that this judgment may not be shared by third parties and that he or she may be required to justify the decision.

Threats to objectivity and independence

1.29 The principal types of threats to the reporting accountant's objectivity and independence are:

- self-interest threat;
- self-review threat;
- management threat;
- advocacy threat;
- familiarity (or trust) threat; and
- intimidation threat.

1.30 A **self-interest threat** arises when reporting accountants have financial or other interests which might cause them to be reluctant to take actions that would be adverse to the interests of the firm or any individual in a position directly to influence the conduct or outcome of the engagement (for example, when the engagement partner has a financial interest in the company issuing the investment circular).

1.31 A **self-review threat** arises when the results of a service performed by the engagement team or others within the firm are reflected in the amounts included or disclosed in the financial information that is the subject of the investment circular reporting engagement (for example, when reporting in relation to an initial public offering for a company where the firm has been involved in maintaining the accounting records of that company). A threat to objectivity arises because, in the course of the investment circular reporting engagement, the reporting accountant may need to re-evaluate the work performed in the course of the other service previously provided by the firm. As, by virtue of providing the other service, the firm is associated with aspects of the financial information being reported upon, the reporting accountant engagement client may constitute one or more parties, dependent on the circumstances of the transaction which is the subject of the investment circular[5]. Where the party responsible for issuing the investment circular is different from the party whose financial information is included in the investment circular, the reporting accountant makes an assessment of independence with respect to both these parties, applying the alternative procedures set out in paragraph 1.44 as necessary.

Where either: 1.44

- an investment circular reporting engagement is undertaken to provide a report on the financial information relating to an audit client but the reporting accountant's report is to be published in an investment circular issued by another entity that is not an audit client; or
- the reporting accountant's report is to be published in an investment circular issued by an audit client but the reporting accountant's report is on financial information relating to another entity that is not an audit client,

it may not be practicable in the time available to identify all relationships and other service engagements recently undertaken by the firm for the non-audit client and its significant affiliates. In such instances the reporting accountant undertakes those enquiries[6] that are practical in the time available into the relationships and other service engagements that the firm has with the non-audit client and, having regard to its obligations to maintain confidentiality, addresses any identified threats. Having done so, the reporting accountant discloses to those charged with governance of the issuing engagement client that a consideration of all known threats has been undertaken and, where appropriate, safeguards applied, but this does not constitute a full evaluation of all relationships and other services provided to the non-audit client.

The firm should establish policies and procedures to require persons in a position directly to influence the conduct and outcome of the investment circular reporting engagement to be constantly alert to circumstances and relationships with: 1.45

(a) **the engagement client, and**
(b) **other parties who are connected with the investment circular,**

that might reasonably be considered threats to their objectivity or the perceived loss of their independence, and, where such circumstances or relationships are identified, to report them to the engagement partner or to the ethics partner, as appropriate.

Such policies and procedures require that threats to the reporting accountant's objectivity and independence are communicated to the appropriate person, having regard to the nature of the threats and the part of the firm and the identity of any person involved. The consideration of all threats and the action taken is documented. If the engagement partner is personally involved, or if he or she is unsure about the action to be taken, the matter is resolved through consultation with the ethics partner. 1.46

In addition to considering independence in the context of the engagement client, the reporting accountant also considers relationships with other parties who are 1.47

---

[5] For example, where a report on a target company's financial statements is included in the acquiring company's investment circular.

[6] For example, these enquiries are likely to include reviewing the list of engagements recorded in the firm's accounting systems and an enquiry of individuals within the firm who are responsible for maintaining such systems as to whether any confidentially coded engagements could be relevant.

connected with the investment circular. These parties will include the sponsor or nominated advisor, other parties from whom, in accordance with the engagement letter, the reporting accountant takes instructions and other entities directly involved in the transaction which is the subject of the investment circular.[7] The reporting accountant considers the circumstances involved and uses judgment to assess whether it is probable that a reasonable and informed third party would conclude that the reporting accountant's objectivity either is impaired or is likely to be impaired as a result of relationships held with any of these parties.

1.48 In the case of established financial institutions or advisers, the reporting accountant may have extensive relationships with these parties, including for the provision of other services or the purchase of goods and services in the ordinary course of business. These relationships will not generally give rise to a significant threat to the reporting accountant's objectivity.

1.49 Relationships with other parties who are connected with the investment circular which are outside the ordinary course of business or which are material to any party are more likely to give rise to a significant threat to the reporting accountant's objectivity. Consideration of the threats to the reporting accountant's objectivity in relation to other entities will primarily be concerned with matters that could give rise to self-interest and intimidation threats, for example:

- where there is financial dependence on the relationship with the other party arising from fees (including any contingent element) for investment circular reporting engagements undertaken by the firm as a result of connections with the other parties;
- joint ventures or similar relationships with the other party or with a senior member of their management;
- significant purchases of goods or services which are not in the ordinary course of business or are not on an arm's length basis;
- personal relationships between engagement team members and individuals in senior positions within the other party; or
- large direct financial interests in, or loans made by, the other party.

1.50 **The firm should establish policies and procedures to require the engagement partner to identify and assess the significance of threats to the reporting accountant's objectivity, including any perceived loss of independence:**

  (a) **when considering whether to accept an investment circular reporting engagement and planning the work to be undertaken;**
  (b) **when signing the report;**
  (c) **when considering whether the firm can accept or retain an engagement to provide other services to an engagement client during the relevant period; and**
  (d) **when potential threats are reported to him or her.**

1.51 An initial assessment of the threats to objectivity and independence is required when the engagement partner is considering whether to accept an investment circular reporting engagement and planning the engagement. At the end of the engagement, when reporting on the work undertaken but before issuing the report, the engagement partner draws an overall conclusion as to whether any threats to objectivity and independence have been properly addressed in accordance with the APB Ethical Standard for Reporting Accountants. If, at any time, the reporting accountant is invited to accept an engagement to provide other services to an engagement client for which the firm is undertaking an investment circular reporting engagement, the

---

[7] *Where such entities are part of a complex group or corporate structure, the reporting accountant considers issues relating to the wider group and not just the entity directly involved in the transaction.*

engagement partner considers the impact this new engagement may have on the reporting accountant's objectivity and independence.

When identifying and assessing threats to their objectivity and independence, reporting accountants take into account their current relationships with the engagement client (including other service engagements) and those that existed prior to the current engagement in the relevant period. The relevant period covers the period during which the engagement is undertaken and any additional period before the engagement period but subsequent to the balance sheet date of the most recent audited financial statements[8]. This is because those prior relationships may be perceived as likely to influence the reporting accountant in the performance of the investment circular reporting engagement or as otherwise impairing the reporting accountant's objectivity and independence.

1.52

A firm's procedures will include reference to records of past and current engagements whenever a new investment circular reporting engagement is proposed.

1.53

Where the engagement client or a third party calls into question the objectivity and independence of the firm in relation to a particular client, the ethics partner carries out such investigations as may be appropriate.

1.54

Identification and assessment of safeguards

If the engagement partner identifies threats to the reporting accountant's objectivity, including any perceived loss of independence, he or she should identify and assess the effectiveness of the available safeguards and apply such safeguards as are sufficient to eliminate the threats or reduce them to an acceptable level.

1.55

The nature and extent of safeguards to be applied depend on the significance of the threats. Where a threat is clearly insignificant, no safeguards are needed.

1.56

Sections 2 and 3 of this Standard address specific circumstances which can create threats to the reporting accountant's objectivity or loss of independence. They give examples of safeguards that can, in some circumstances, eliminate the threat or reduce it to an acceptable level. In circumstances where this is not possible, either the reporting accountant does not accept (or withdraws from) the investment circular reporting engagement or, in the case of threats arising from the current provision of other services, does not undertake the engagement to provide the other service.

1.57

The engagement partner should not accept or should not continue an investment circular reporting engagement if he or she concludes that any threats to the reporting accountant's objectivity and independence cannot be reduced to an acceptable level.

1.58

1.59 If during the conduct of the investment circular reporting engagement the engagement partner becomes aware of a threat and concludes that it cannot be reduced to an acceptable level, the firm withdraws immediately from the engagement, save in circumstances where a reasonable and informed third party would regard ceasing to act as the reporting accountant would be contrary to the public interest. In such cases withdrawal from the investment circular reporting engagement may not be appropriate. The firm discloses on a timely basis full details of the position to those charged with governance of the issuing

---

[8] *In the case of newly incorporated clients (not part of an established group of companies), where there has been no financial statement audit, this period is from the date of incorporation.*

engagement client and those the reporting accountant is instructed to advise, as set out in paragraphs 1.68 to 1.76, and establishes appropriate safeguards.

Engagement Quality Control Review

1.60 Paragraph 22 of SIR 1000 requires the reporting accountant to comply with applicable standards and guidance set out in ISQC (UK and Ireland) 1 *'Quality control for firms that perform audits and reviews of historical financial information and other assurance and related services engagements'* and ISA (UK and Ireland) 220 *'Quality control for audits of historical financial information'*. This includes the appointment of an engagement quality control reviewer for all public reporting engagements.

1.61 The engagement quality control reviewer should:

  (a) consider the firm's compliance with the APB Ethical Standard for Reporting Accountants in relation to the investment circular reporting engagement;
  (b) form an independent opinion as to the appropriateness and adequacy of the safeguards applied; and
  (c) consider the adequacy of the documentation of the engagement partner's consideration of the reporting accountant's objectivity and independence.

1.62 The requirements of paragraph 1.61 supplement the requirements relating to the engagement quality control review established by ISA (UK and Ireland) 220. The engagement quality control reviewer will be a partner or other person performing the function of a partner who is not otherwise involved in the engagement. The experience required of the engagement quality control reviewer is determined by the nature of the engagement and the seniority and experience of the engagement partner.

Overall conclusion

1.63 **At the end of the investment circular reporting engagement, when reporting on the work undertaken but before issuing the report, the engagement partner should reach an overall conclusion that any threats to objectivity and independence have been properly addressed in accordance with the APB Ethical Standard for Reporting Accountants. If the engagement partner cannot make such a conclusion, he or she should not report and the firm should withdraw from the investment circular reporting engagement.**

1.64 If the engagement partner remains unable to conclude that any threat to objectivity and independence has been properly addressed in accordance with the APB Ethical Standard for Reporting Accountants, or if there is a disagreement between the engagement partner and the engagement quality control reviewer, he or she consults the ethics partner.

1.65 In concluding on compliance with the requirements for objectivity and independence, the engagement partner is entitled to rely on the completeness and accuracy of the data developed by the firm's systems relating to independence (for example, in relation to the reporting of financial interests by staff), unless informed otherwise by the firm.

Other accountants involved in an investment circular reporting engagement

The engagement partner should be satisfied that other accountants (whether a network firm or another firm) involved in the investment circular reporting engagement, who are not subject to the APB Ethical Standard for Reporting Accountants, are objective and document the rationale for that conclusion.   1.66

The engagement partner obtains written confirmation from the other accountants that they have a sufficient understanding of and have complied with the applicable provisions of the IFAC Code of Ethics for Professional Accountants, including the independence requirements.[9]   1.67

Communication with those charged with governance

The engagement partner should ensure that those charged with governance of the issuing engagement client, and any other persons or entities the reporting accountant is instructed to advise, are appropriately informed on a timely basis of all significant facts and matters that bear upon the reporting accountant's objectivity and independence.   1.68

Those charged with governance of the issuing engagement client are responsible for oversight of the relationship between the reporting accountant and the entity and of the conduct of the investment circular reporting engagement. This group therefore has a particular interest in being informed about the reporting accountant's ability to report objectively on the engagement.   1.69

The aim of these communications by the reporting accountant is to ensure full and fair disclosure to those charged with governance of the issuing engagement client and to those from whom, in accordance with the engagement letter, the reporting accountant takes instructions of matters in which they have an interest.   1.70

It may be that all of the parties to the engagement letter wish to be informed about all significant facts and matters that bear upon the reporting accountant's objectivity and independence. In other cases, however, the parties to the engagement letter (other than the engagement client) may not wish to be directly involved and may appoint one or more of their number to review these matters on their behalf. At the time of appointment, the reporting accountant ensures that it is clear in the engagement letter to whom these communications are provided. If no such provision is included in the engagement letter, the reporting accountant will make disclosures to all those from whom, in accordance with the engagement letter, the reporting accountant takes instructions.   1.71

Matters communicated will generally include the key elements of the engagement partner's consideration of objectivity and independence, such as: 1.72

- the principal threats, if any, to objectivity and independence identified by the reporting accountant, including consideration of relationships between the firm and:
    - the engagement client, its affiliates and directors, and

---

[9] The International Federation of Accountants Code of Ethics for Professional Accountants (the IFAC Code) establishes a conceptual framework for ethical requirements for professional accountants and includes independence requirements for assurance engagements. No Member Body of IFAC is allowed to apply less stringent standards than those stated in the IFAC Code. In addition, members of the IFAC Forum of Firms have agreed to apply ethical standards, which are at least as rigorous as those of the IFAC Code.

- the sponsor and such other parties from whom the reporting accountant takes instructions, and
- other entities directly involved in the transaction which is the subject of the investment circular;
• any safeguards adopted and the reasons why they are considered to be effective;
• the considerations of the engagement quality control review;
• the overall assessment of threats and safeguards;
• information about the general policies and processes within the firm for maintaining objectivity and independence.

1.73 The reporting accountant, as a minimum:

(a) discloses in writing to those charged with governance of the issuing engagement client, and any other persons or entities the reporting accountant is instructed to advise:
   (i) details of all relationships that the reporting accountant considers may reasonably be thought to bear on the objectivity and independence of the reporting accountant,[10] having regard to its relationships with the engagement client, its directors and senior management and its affiliates;
   (ii) details of all relationships that the reporting accountant considers give rise to a threat to its objectivity between the reporting accountant and:
      • the sponsor and such other parties from whom the reporting accountant takes instructions[11];
      • other entities directly involved in the transaction which is the subject of the investment circular;
   (iii) whether the total amount of fees that the reporting accountant is likely to charge to the engagement client and its significant affiliates for the provision of services relating to the transaction which is the subject of the investment circular during the relevant period is greater than 5% of the fee income of the firm in the relevant period or the part of the firm by reference to which the engagement partner's profit share is calculated during the relevant period; and
   (iv) the related safeguards that are in place;
(b) confirms in writing that:
   (i) it complies with the APB Ethical Standard for Reporting Accountants and that it is independent and its objectivity is not compromised, and
   (ii) where relevant, the circumstances contemplated in paragraph 1.44 exist and a consideration of all known threats and safeguards has been undertaken, but this does not constitute a full evaluation of all business relationships and other services provided to the entity.

1.74 The reporting accountant seeks to discuss these matters with those charged with governance of the issuing engagement client and those others the reporting accountant is instructed to advise.

1.75 The most appropriate time for final confirmation of such matters is usually at the conclusion of the investment circular reporting engagement. However,

---

[10] Relationships include significant services previously provided by the firm and network firms involved in the investment circular reporting engagement to the engagement client and its significant affiliates. In considering the significance of such services the reporting accountant takes into account whether those services have been the subject of independent review after they were provided.

[11] Where a party to the engagement letter is an established financial institution or adviser, a generic disclosure that the firm has extensive relationships entered into in the ordinary course of business with these parties is sufficient with specific disclosure only being made in the case of relationships which are outside the ordinary course of business or which are material to any party.

client is held by the firm or by one of the individuals specified in paragraph 2.5 are such that no safeguards can eliminate them or reduce them to an acceptable level. If the existence of the transaction which is connected with the investment circular is price sensitive information then disposal of the financial interest may not be possible and the firm either does not accept the engagement or the relevant individuals are not included in the engagement team. Where a partner with one of the financial interests specified normally has direct supervisory or management responsibility over the engagement team, he or she is excluded from this responsibility for the purposes of the particular investment circular reporting engagement.

Where one of the financial interests specified in paragraph 2.5 is held by: 2.7

(a) *the firm:* the entire financial interest is disposed of, a sufficient amount of an indirect financial interest is disposed of so that the remaining interest is no longer material, or the firm does not accept (or withdraws from) the investment circular reporting engagement;
(b) *a person in a position directly to influence the conduct and outcome of the investment circular reporting engagement:* the entire financial interest is disposed of, a sufficient amount of an indirect financial interest is disposed of so that the remaining interest is no longer material, or that person does not retain a position in which they exert such direct influence on the investment circular reporting engagement;
(c) *an immediate family member of a person in a position directly to influence the conduct and outcome of the investment circular reporting engagement:* the entire financial interest is disposed of, a sufficient amount of an indirect financial interest is disposed of so that the remaining interest is no longer material, or the person in a position directly to influence the conduct and outcome of the investment circular reporting engagement does not retain a position in which they exert such direct influence on the investment circular reporting engagement.

Where the firm or one of the individuals specified in paragraph 2.5 holds an indirect financial interest but does not have both: 2.8

(a) the ability to influence the investment decisions of the intermediary; and
(b) actual knowledge of the existence of the underlying investment in the engagement client,

there may not be a threat to the reporting accountant's objectivity and independence. For example, where the indirect financial interest takes the form of an investment in a pension fund, the composition of the funds and the size and nature of any underlying investment in the engagement client may be known but there is unlikely to be any influence on investment decisions, as the fund will generally be managed independently on a discretionary basis. In the case of an 'index tracker' fund, the investment in the engagement client is determined by the composition of the relevant index and there may be no threat to objectivity. As long as the person holding the indirect interest is not directly involved in an investment circular reporting engagement involving the intermediary, nor able to influence the individual investment decisions of the intermediary, any threat to the reporting accountant's objectivity and independence may be regarded as insignificant.

Where the firm or one of the individuals specified in paragraph 2.5 holds a beneficial interest in a properly operated 'blind' trust, they are (by definition) completely unaware of the identity of the underlying investments. If these include an investment in the engagement client, this means that they are unaware of the existence of an indirect financial interest. In these circumstances, there is no threat to the reporting accountant's objectivity and independence. 2.9

2.10 Where a person in a position directly to influence the conduct and outcome of the investment circular reporting engagement becomes aware that a close family member holds one of the financial interests specified in paragraph 2.5, that individual should report the matter to the engagement partner to take appropriate action. If it is a close family member of the engagement partner, or if the engagement partner is in doubt as to the action to be taken, the engagement partner should resolve the matter through consultation with the ethics partner.

Financial interests held as trustee

2.11 Where a direct or an indirect financial interest in the engagement client or its affiliates is held in a trustee capacity by a person in a position directly to influence the conduct and outcome of the investment circular reporting engagement, or an immediate family member of such a person, a self-interest threat may be created because either the existence of the trustee interest may influence the conduct of the investment circular reporting engagement or the trust may influence the actions of the engagement client. Accordingly, such a trustee interest is only held when:

- the relevant person is not an identified potential beneficiary of the trust; and
- the financial interest held by the trust in the engagement client is not material to the trust; and
- the trust is not able to exercise significant influence over the engagement client or an affiliate of the engagement client; and
- the relevant person does not have significant influence over the investment decisions made by the trust, in so far as they relate to the financial interest in the engagement client.

2.12 Where it is not clear whether the financial interest held by the trust in the engagement client is material to the trust or whether the trust is able to exercise significant influence over the engagement client, the financial interest is reported to the ethics partner, so that a decision can be made as to the steps that need to be taken.

Financial interests held by firm pension schemes

2.13 Where the pension scheme of a firm has a financial interest in an engagement client or its affiliates and the firm has any influence over the trustees' investment decisions (other than indirect strategic and policy decisions), the self-interest threat created is such that no safeguards can eliminate it or reduce it to an acceptable level. In other cases (for example, where the pension scheme invests through a collective investment scheme and the firm's influence is limited to investment policy decisions, such as the allocation between different categories of investment), the ethics partner considers the acceptability of the position, having regard to the materiality of the financial interest to the pension scheme.

Loans and guarantees

2.14 Where reporting accountants, persons in a position directly to influence the conduct and outcome of the investment circular reporting engagement or immediate family members of such persons:

(a) accept a loan[13] or a guarantee of their borrowings from an engagement client; or
(b) make a loan to or guarantee the borrowings of an engagement client,

---

[13] *For the purpose of this standard, the term 'loan' does not include ordinary trade credit arrangements or deposits placed for goods or services (see paragraph 2.20).*

a self-interest threat and an intimidation threat to the reporting accountant's objectivity can be created or there may be a perceived loss of independence. No safeguards can eliminate this threat or reduce it to an acceptable level.

The firm, persons in a position directly to influence the conduct and outcome of the investment circular reporting engagement and immediate family members of such persons should not during the engagement period have a loan outstanding to, or guarantee the borrowings of, an engagement client or its affiliates unless this represents a deposit made with a bank or similar deposit taking institution in the ordinary course of business and on normal business terms. 2.15

The firm should not during the engagement period have a loan from, or have its borrowings guaranteed by, the engagement client or its affiliates unless: 2.16

(a) the engagement client is a bank or similar deposit taking institution; and
(b) the loan or guarantee is made in the ordinary course of business on normal business terms; and
(c) the loan or guarantee is not material to both the firm and the engagement client.

Persons in a position directly to influence the conduct and outcome of the investment circular reporting engagement and immediate family members of such persons should not during the engagement period have a loan from, or have their borrowings guaranteed by, the engagement client or its affiliates unless: 2.17

(a) the engagement client is a bank or similar deposit taking institution; and
(b) the loan or guarantee is made in the ordinary course of business on normal business terms; and
(c) the loan or guarantee is not material to the engagement client.

Loans by an engagement client that is a bank or similar institution to a person in a position directly to influence the conduct and outcome of the investment circular reporting engagement, or an immediate family member of such a person (for example, home mortgages, bank overdrafts or car loans), do not create an unacceptable threat to objectivity and independence, provided that normal business terms apply. However, where such loans are in arrears by a significant amount, this creates an intimidation threat that is unacceptable. Where such a situation arises, the person in a position directly to influence the conduct and outcome of the investment circular reporting engagement reports the matter to the engagement partner, or to the ethics partner, as appropriate and ceases to have any involvement with the investment circular reporting engagement. The engagement partner or, where appropriate, the ethics partner considers whether any work is to be reperformed. 2.18

Business relationships

A business relationship between: 2.19

(a) the firm or a person who is in a position directly to influence the conduct and outcome of the investment circular reporting engagement, or an immediate family member of such a person, and
(b) the engagement client or its affiliates, or its management

involves the two parties having a common commercial interest. Business relationships may create self-interest, advocacy or intimidation threats to the reporting accountant's objectivity and perceived loss of independence. Examples include:

- joint ventures with the engagement client or with a director, officer or other individual who performs senior managerial functions for the client;
- arrangements to combine one or more services or products of the firm with one or more services or products of the engagement client and to market the package with reference to both parties;
- distribution or marketing arrangements under which the firm acts as a distributor or marketer of any of the engagement client's products or services, or the engagement client acts as the distributor or marketer of any of the products or services of the firm;
- other commercial transactions, such as the firm leasing its office space from the engagement client.

Subject to the alternative procedures outlined in paragraphs 1.44, a firm will identify all business relationships entered into by the firm, persons in a position directly to influence the conduct and outcome of the investment circular reporting engagement, or an immediate family member of such a person.

2.20 Where a firm is engaged to undertake an investment circular reporting engagement for a client, the firm, persons in a position directly to influence the conduct and outcome of the investment circular reporting engagement and immediate family members of such persons should not have business relationships with the engagement client, its management or its affiliates during the relevant period except where they:

- **are entered into in the ordinary course of business and are clearly trivial; or**
- **involve the purchase of goods and services from the firm or the engagement client in the ordinary course of business and on an arm's length basis.**

2.21 Where a business relationship exists, that is not permitted under paragraph 2.20, and has been entered into by:

(a) *the firm:* either the relationship is terminated before the start of the relevant period or the firm does not accept (or withdraws from) the investment circular reporting engagement;

(b) *a person in a position directly to influence the conduct and outcome of the investment circular reporting engagement:* either the relationship is terminated before the start of the relevant period or that person does not retain a position in which they exert such direct influence on the investment circular reporting engagement[14];

(c) *an immediate family member of a person in a position directly to influence the conduct and outcome of the investment circular reporting engagement:* either the relationship is terminated before the start of the relevant period or that person does not retain a position in which they exert such direct influence on the investment circular reporting engagement[14].

2.22 Where a person in a position directly to influence the conduct and outcome of the investment circular reporting engagement becomes aware that a close family member has one of the business relationships specified in paragraph 2.20, that individual should report the matter to the engagement partner to take appropriate action. If it is a close family member of the engagement partner or if the engagement partner is in doubt as to

---

[14] *If the existence of the transaction which is connected with the investment circular is price sensitive information then termination of the business relationship may not be possible and the firm either does not accept the engagement or the relevant individuals are not included in the engagement team. Where a partner with one of the business relationships specified normally has direct supervisory or management responsibility over the engagement team, he or she is excluded from this responsibility for the purposes of the particular investment circular reporting engagement.*

the action to be taken, the engagement partner should resolve the matter through consultation with the ethics partner.

Where there are doubts as to whether a transaction or series of transactions are either in the ordinary course of business or on an arm's length basis, the engagement partner reports the issue to the ethics partner, so that a decision can be made as to the appropriate action that needs to be taken to ensure that the matter is resolved. 2.23

A firm should not act as reporting accountant to any entity or person able to influence the affairs of the firm or the performance of any investment circular reporting engagement undertaken by the firm. 2.24

This prohibition applies to: 2.25

(a) any entity that owns any significant part of a firm, or is an affiliate of such an entity; or
(b) any shareholder, director or other person in a position to direct the affairs of such an entity or its affiliate.

A significant ownership is one that carries the ability materially to influence the policy of an entity.[15]

Employment relationships

Management role with engagement client

A firm undertaking an investment circular reporting engagement should not have as a partner or employ a person in a position directly to influence the conduct and outcome of the investment circular reporting engagement any person who is also employed by the engagement client or its affiliates ('dual employment'). 2.26

Loan staff assignments

A reporting accountant should not enter into an agreement with an engagement client to provide a partner or employee to work for a temporary period as if that individual were an employee of the engagement client or its affiliates (a 'loan staff assignment') during the relevant period or for a period of one year before it, unless the client: 2.27

(a) agrees that the individual concerned will not hold a management position in relation to the transaction or the financial information that is the subject of the investment circular reporting engagement, and
(b) acknowledges its responsibility for directing and supervising the work to be performed, which will not include such matters as:
   • making management decisions; or
   • exercising discretionary authority to commit the engagement client to a particular position or accounting treatment.

Where a firm agrees to assist an engagement client by providing loan staff, threats to objectivity and independence may be created. A management threat may arise if the employee undertakes work that involves making judgments and taking decisions that are properly the responsibility of management of the engagement client in relation to the transaction or the financial information that is the subject of the investment 2.28

---

[15] *For companies, competition authorities have generally treated a 15% shareholding as sufficient to provide a material ability to influence policy.*

circular reporting engagement. Thus, for example, interim management arrangements involving participation in the financial reporting function involved in producing the financial information that is the subject of the investment circular reporting engagement are not acceptable.

2.29 A self-review threat may also arise if the individual, during the loan staff assignment, is in a position directly to influence the preparation of the engagement client's financial information and then, on completion of that assignment, is assigned to the engagement team for that client.

2.30 **Where a partner or employee returns to the firm on completion of a loan staff assignment, that individual should not be given any role on an investment circular reporting engagement for the engagement client which involves a review of, or any work in relation to, any function or activity that he or she performed or supervised during that assignment.**

2.31 In considering for how long this restriction is to be observed, the need to realise the potential value to the effectiveness of the investment circular reporting engagement of the increased knowledge of the client's business gained through the assignment has to be weighed against the potential threats to objectivity and independence. Those threats increase with the length of the assignment and with the intended level of responsibility of the individual within the engagement team. As a minimum, this restriction will apply to at least the period until an audit has been undertaken of the financial statements following the completion of the loan staff assignment.

Partners and engagement team members joining an engagement client

2.32 **Where a former partner in the firm joins the engagement client, the firm should take action before any further work is done by the firm in connection with the investment circular reporting engagement to ensure that no significant connections remain between the firm and the individual.**

2.33 Ensuring that no significant connections remain between the firm and the individual requires that:

- all capital balances and similar financial interests be fully settled (including retirement benefits) unless these are made in accordance with pre-determined arrangements that cannot be influenced by any remaining connections between the individual and the firm; and
- the individual does not participate or appear to participate in the firm's business or professional activities.

2.34 **Reporting accountants should establish policies and procedures that require:**

(a) senior members of the engagement team to notify the firm of any situation involving their potential employment with the engagement client; and

(b) other members of the engagement team to notify the firm of any situation involving their probable employment with the engagement client; and

(c) anyone who has given such notice to be removed from the engagement team; and

(d) a review of the work performed by the resigning or former engagement team member in relation to the investment circular reporting engagement.

2.35 Objectivity and independence may be threatened where a director, an officer or an employee of the engagement client who is in a position to exert direct and significant influence over the preparation of the financial information has recently been a partner in the firm or a member of an engagement team. Such circumstances may create self-interest, familiarity and intimidation threats, particularly when significant connections remain between the individual and the firm. Similarly, objectivity and independence may be threatened when an individual knows, or has reason to believe that he or she will or may be joining the engagement client at some time in the future.

Where a partner in the firm or a member of the engagement team for a particular client has left the firm and taken up employment with that client, the significance of the self-interest, familiarity and intimidation threats is assessed and normally depends on such factors as: 2.36

- the position that individual had in an engagement team or the firm;
- the position that individual has taken at the engagement client;
- the amount of involvement that individual will have with the engagement team (especially where it includes former colleagues with whom he or she worked);
- the length of time since that individual was a member of an engagement team or employed by the firm.

Following the assessment of any such threats, appropriate safeguards are applied where necessary.

Any review of work is performed by a more senior professional. If the individual joining the engagement client is a partner, the review is performed by a partner who is not involved in the engagement. Where, due to its size, the firm does not have a partner who was not involved in the engagement, it seeks either a review by another firm or advice from its professional body. 2.37

Where a partner leaves the firm and is appointed as a director (including as a non-executive director) or to a key management position with an engagement client, having acted as an audit engagement partner, engagement quality control reviewer, key audit partner, reporting accountant or a partner in the chain of command at any time in the two years prior to such appointment, the firm should not accept an appointment as reporting accountant for a period of two years commencing when the former partner ceased to act for the engagement client or the former partner ceases employment with the engagement client, whichever is the sooner. 2.38

Where a partner (other than as specified in paragraph 2.38) or an employee joins the engagement client as a director (including as a non-executive director) or in a key management position, the firm should consider whether the composition of the engagement team is appropriate. 2.39

In such circumstances, the firm evaluates the appropriateness of the composition of the engagement team by reference to the factors listed in paragraph 2.36 and alters or strengthens the team to address any threat to the reporting accountant's objectivity and independence that may be identified. 2.40

Family members employed by an engagement client

Where a person in a position directly to influence the conduct and outcome of the investment circular reporting engagement becomes aware that an immediate or close family member is employed by the engagement client in a position to exercise influence on the accounting records or financial information, that individual should either: 2.41

(a) in the case of an immediate family member, cease to hold a position in which they exert such direct influence on the investment circular reporting engagement; or
(b) in the case of a close family member, report the matter to the engagement partner to take appropriate action. If it is a close family member of the engagement

partner or if the engagement partner is in doubt as to the action to be taken, the engagement partner should resolve the matter in consultation with the ethics partner.

Governance role with engagement client

2.42 A firm that undertakes an investment circular reporting engagement should not have as a partner or employ a person who during the engagement period is:

(a) on the board of directors of the engagement client;
(b) on any subcommittee of that board; or
(c) in such a position in an entity which holds directly or indirectly more than 20% of the voting rights in the engagement client, or in which the engagement client holds directly or indirectly more than 20% of the voting rights.

2.43 Where a person in a position directly to influence the conduct and outcome of the investment circular reporting engagement has an immediate or close family member who holds a position described in paragraph 2.42, the firm should take appropriate steps to ensure that the relevant person does not retain a position in which they exert direct influence on the conduct and outcome of the investment circular reporting engagement.

Employment with firm

2.44 Objectivity and independence may be threatened where a former director or employee of the engagement client becomes a member of the engagement team. Self-interest, self-review and familiarity threats may be created where a member of the engagement team has to report on, for example, financial information which he or she prepared, or elements of the financial information for which he or she had responsibility, while with the client.

2.45 Where a former director or a former employee of an engagement client, who was in a position to exert significant influence over the preparation of the financial information, joins the firm, that individual should not be assigned to a position in which he or she is able directly to influence the conduct and outcome of an investment circular reporting engagement for that client or its affiliates for a period of two years following the date of leaving the client.

2.46 In certain circumstances, a longer period of exclusion from the engagement team may be appropriate. For example, threats to objectivity and independence may exist in relation to an investment circular reporting engagement relating to the financial information of any period which was materially affected by the work of that person whilst occupying his or her former position of influence with the engagement client. The significance of these threats depends on factors such as:

- the position the individual held with the engagement client;
- the length of time since the individual left the engagement client;
- the position the individual holds in the engagement team.

Family and other personal relationships

2.47 A relationship between a person who is in a position directly to influence the conduct and outcome of the investment circular reporting engagement and another party does not generally affect the consideration of the reporting accountant's objectivity and independence. However, if it is a family relationship, and if the family member also has a financial, business or employment relationship with the engagement client, then self-interest, familiarity or intimidation threats to the reporting accountant's objectivity and independence may be created. The significance of any such threats depends on such factors as:

- the relevant person's involvement in the investment circular reporting engagement;
- the nature of the relationship between the relevant person and his or her family member;
- the family member's relationship with the engagement client.

A distinction is made between immediate family relationships and close family relationships. Immediate family members comprise an individual's spouse (or equivalent) and dependents, whereas close family members comprise parents, non-dependent children and siblings. While an individual can usually be presumed to be aware of matters concerning his or her immediate family members and to be able to influence their behaviour, it is generally recognised that the same levels of knowledge and influence do not exist in the case of close family members. 2.48

When considering family relationships, it needs to be acknowledged that, in an increasingly secular, open and inclusive society, the concept of what constitutes a family is evolving and relationships between individuals which have no status formally recognised by law may nevertheless be considered as significant as those which do. It may therefore be appropriate to regard certain other personal relationships, particularly those that would be considered close personal relationships, as if they are family relationships. 2.49

The reporting accountant should establish policies and procedures that require: 2.50

(a) partners and professional staff to report to the firm where they become aware of any immediate family, close family and other relationships involving an engagement client of the firm and which they consider might create a threat to the reporting accountant's objectivity or a perceived loss of independence;

(b) the relevant engagement partners to be notified promptly of any immediate family, close family and other personal relationships reported by partners and other professional staff.

The engagement partner should: 2.51

(a) assess the threats to the reporting accountant's objectivity and independence arising from immediate family, close family and other personal relationships on the basis of the information reported to the firm;

(b) apply appropriate safeguards to eliminate the threat or reduce it to an acceptable level; and

(c) where there are unresolved matters or the need for clarification, consult with the ethics partner.

Where such matters are identified or reported, the engagement partner or the ethics partner assesses the information available and the potential for there to be a threat to the reporting accountant's objectivity and independence, treating any personal relationship as if it were a family relationship. 2.52

External consultants involved in an investment circular reporting engagement

2.53 Reporting accountants may employ external consultants as part of their investment circular reporting engagement. There is a risk that an expert's objectivity and independence will be impaired if the expert is related to the entity, for example by being financially dependent upon or having an investment in, the entity.

2.54 **The engagement partner should be satisfied that any external consultant engaged by the reporting accountant in the investment circular reporting engagement will be objective and document the rationale for that conclusion.**

2.55 The engagement partner obtains information from the external consultant as to the existence of any connections that they have with the engagement client including:

- financial interests;
- business relationships;
- employment (past, present and future);
- family and other personal relationships.

Association with an engagement client

2.56 Where partners and staff in senior positions have been part of engagement teams acting for a client on a number of audit, corporate finance or other transaction related engagements they gain a deep knowledge of the client and its operations. This association may also create close personal relationships with client personnel, which may create threats to the reporting accountant's objectivity or perceived loss of independence.

2.57 **The firm should establish policies and procedures to monitor the extent of involvement of partners and staff in senior positions where the firm acts in connection with investment circulars on a regular basis for an engagement client.**

2.58 **Where partners and staff in senior positions in the engagement team have had extensive involvement with the engagement client, the firm should assess the threats to the reporting accountant's objectivity and independence and, where the threats are other than clearly insignificant, should:**

- **disclose the engagements previously undertaken by the reporting accountant for the engagement client to those charged with governance of the issuing engagement client and any other persons or entities the reporting accountant is instructed to advise, and**
- **apply safeguards to reduce the threats to an acceptable level.**

Where appropriate safeguards cannot be applied, the firm should either not accept or withdraw from the investment circular reporting engagement as appropriate.

2.59 Where partners and staff in senior positions in the engagement team have had extensive involvement with a particular engagement client, self-interest, self-review and familiarity threats to the reporting accountant's objectivity may arise. Similarly, such circumstances may result in an actual or perceived loss of independence.

Where fees due from an engagement client, whether for audit, investment circular reporting engagements or for other professional services, remain unpaid for a long time a self-interest threat to the reporting accountant's objectivity and independence is created because the signing of a report may enhance the firm's prospects of securing payment of such overdue fees. 2.75

Where the outstanding fees are in dispute and the amount involved is significant, the threats to the reporting accountant's objectivity and independence may be such that no safeguards can eliminate them or reduce them to an acceptable level. The engagement partner therefore considers whether the firm can continue with the investment circular reporting engagement. 2.76

Where the outstanding fees are unpaid because of exceptional circumstances (including financial distress), the engagement partner considers whether the engagement client will be able to resolve its difficulties. In deciding what action to take, the engagement partner weighs the threats to the reporting accountant's objectivity and independence if the firm were to continue with the investment circular reporting engagement, against the difficulties the engagement client would be likely to face in finding a successor, and therefore the public interest considerations, if the firm were to withdraw from the investment circular reporting engagement. 2.77

In any case where the firm does not withdraw from the investment circular reporting engagement, the engagement partner applies appropriate safeguards (such as a review by a partner who is not involved in the engagement) and notifies the ethics partner of the facts concerning the overdue fees. 2.78

Threatened and actual litigation

Where litigation in relation to professional services between the engagement client or its affiliates and the firm, which is other than insignificant, is already in progress, or where the engagement partner considers such litigation to be probable, the reporting accountant should either not continue with or not accept the investment circular reporting engagement. 2.79

Where litigation actually takes place between the firm (or any person in a position directly to influence the conduct and outcome of the investment circular reporting engagement) and the engagement client, or where litigation is threatened and there is a realistic prospect of such litigation being commenced, self-interest, advocacy and intimidation threats to the reporting accountant's objectivity and independence are created because the firm's interest will be the achievement of an outcome to the dispute or litigation that is favourable to itself. In addition, an effective investment circular reporting engagement requires complete candour and full disclosure between the engagement client management and the engagement team: such disputes or litigation may place the two parties in opposing adversarial positions and may affect management's willingness to make complete disclosure of relevant information. Where the reporting accountant can foresee that such a threat may arise, it informs those charged with governance of the issuing engagement client and any other persons or entities the reporting accountant is instructed to advise of its intention to withdraw from the investment circular reporting engagement. 2.80

The reporting accountant is not required to withdraw from the investment circular reporting engagement in circumstances where a reasonable and informed third party would not regard it as being in the public interest for it to do so. Such circumstances might arise, for example, where: 2.81

- the litigation was commenced as the investment circular reporting engagement was about to be completed and stakeholder interests would be adversely affected by a delay in the completion of the work (for example where the engagement relates to the restructuring of a company to avoid its imminent collapse);
- on appropriate legal advice, the firm deems that the threatened or actual litigation is vexatious or designed solely to bring pressure to bear on the opinion to be expressed by the reporting accountant.

Gifts and hospitality

2.82 The reporting accountant, those in a position directly to influence the conduct and outcome of the investment circular reporting engagement and immediate family members of such persons should not accept gifts from the engagement client, unless the value is clearly insignificant.

2.83 Those in a position directly to influence the conduct and outcome of the investment circular reporting engagement and immediate family members of such persons should not accept hospitality from the engagement client, unless it is reasonable in terms of its frequency, nature and cost.

2.84 Where gifts or hospitality are accepted from an engagement client, self-interest and familiarity threats to the reporting accountant's objectivity and independence are created. Familiarity threats also arise where gifts or hospitality are offered to an engagement client.

2.85 Gifts from the engagement client, unless their value is clearly insignificant, create threats to objectivity and independence which no safeguards can eliminate or reduce.

2.86 Hospitality is a component of many business relationships and can provide valuable opportunities for developing an understanding of the client's business and for gaining the insight on which an effective and successful working relationship depends. Therefore, the reporting accountant's objectivity and independence is not necessarily impaired as a result of accepting hospitality from the engagement client, provided it is reasonable in terms of its frequency, its nature and its cost.

2.87 The firm should establish policies on the nature and value of gifts and hospitality that may be accepted from and offered to clients, their directors, officers and employees, and should issue guidance to assist partners and staff to comply with such policies.

2.88 In assessing the acceptability of gifts and hospitality, the test to be applied is not whether the reporting accountant considers that its objectivity is impaired but whether it is probable that a reasonable and informed third party would conclude that it is or is likely to be impaired.

2.89 Where there is any doubt as to the acceptability of gifts or hospitality offered by the engagement client, members of the engagement team discuss the position with the engagement partner. If the cumulative amount of gifts or hospitality accepted from the engagement client appears abnormally high or there is any doubt as to the acceptability of gifts or hospitality offered to the engagement partner, or if the engagement partner has any residual doubt about the acceptability of gifts or hospitality to other individuals, the engagement partner reports the facts to the ethics partner, for further consideration regarding any action to be taken.

('threats'), including any perceived loss of independence, and to apply procedures ('safeguards') which will either:

(a) eliminate the threat; or
(b) reduce the threat to an acceptable level (that is, a level at which it is not probable that a reasonable and informed third party would conclude that the reporting accountant's objectivity and independence is impaired or is likely to be impaired).

When considering safeguards, where the engagement partner chooses to reduce rather than to eliminate a threat to objectivity and independence, he or she recognises that this judgment may not be shared by third parties and that he or she may be required to justify the decision.

2.2 This section of the APB Ethical Standard for Reporting Accountants provides requirements and guidance on specific circumstances arising out of relationships with the engagement client, which may create threats to the reporting accountant's objectivity or a perceived loss of independence. It gives examples of safeguards that can, in some circumstances, eliminate the threat or reduce it to an acceptable level. In circumstances where this is not possible, either the relationship in question is not entered into or the reporting accountant either does not accept or withdraws from the investment circular reporting engagement, as appropriate.

Financial relationships

General considerations

2.3 A financial interest is an interest in an equity or other security, debenture, loan or other debt instrument of an entity, including rights and obligations to acquire such an interest and derivatives directly related to such an interest.

2.4 Financial interests may be:
- owned directly, rather than through intermediaries (a 'direct financial interest'); or
- owned through intermediaries, for example, an open ended investment company or a pension scheme (an 'indirect financial interest').

2.5 Where a firm is engaged to undertake an investment circular reporting engagement for a client, the firm, a person in a position directly to influence the conduct and outcome of the investment circular reporting engagement or an immediate family member of such a person should not hold during the engagement period:

(a) any direct financial interest in the engagement client or an affiliate of the engagement client; or
(b) any indirect financial interest in the engagement client or an affiliate of the engagement client, where the investment is material to the firm or the individual and to the intermediary; or
(c) any indirect financial interest in the engagement client or an affiliate of the engagement client, where the person holding it has both:
  (i) the ability to influence the investment decisions of the intermediary; and
  (ii) actual knowledge of the existence of the underlying investment in the engagement client.

2.6 The threats to the reporting accountant's objectivity and independence, where a direct financial interest or a material indirect financial interest in the engagement

communications between the reporting accountant and those charged with governance of the issuing engagement client and those others the reporting accountant is instructed to advise will also be needed at the planning stage and whenever significant judgments are made about threats to objectivity and independence and the appropriateness of safeguards put in place, for example, when accepting an engagement to provide other services.

Transparency is a key element in addressing the issues raised by the provision of other services by reporting accountants to their clients. This can be facilitated by timely communication with those charged with governance of the issuing engagement client. In the case of companies that are seeking a listing, ensuring that the audit committee is properly informed about the issues associated with the provision of other services will assist the audit committee to comply on an ongoing basis with the provisions of the Combined Code on Corporate Governance[12] relating to reviewing and monitoring the external auditors' independence and objectivity. 1.76

Documentation

The engagement partner should ensure that his or her consideration of the reporting accountant's objectivity and independence is appropriately documented on a timely basis. 1.77

The requirement to document these issues contributes to the clarity and rigour of the engagement partner's thinking and the quality of his or her judgments. In addition, such documentation provides evidence that the engagement partner's consideration of the reporting accountant's objectivity and independence was properly performed and provides the basis for the engagement quality control review. 1.78

Matters to be documented include all key elements of the process and any significant judgments concerning: 1.79

- threats identified (in relation to the engagement client, those from whom, in accordance with the engagement letter, the reporting accountant takes instructions and other entities directly involved in the transaction which is the subject of the investment circular) and the process used in identifying them;
- safeguards adopted and the reasons why they are considered to be effective;
- the engagement quality control review;
- overall assessment of threats and safeguards; and
- communication with those charged with governance of the issuing engagement client and those others the reporting accountant is instructed to advise.

Section 2 - Specific circumstances creating threats to a reporting accountant's objectivity and independence

Introduction

Paragraphs 1.50 and 1.55 require the engagement partner to identify and assess the circumstances which could adversely affect the reporting accountant's objectivity 2.1

---

[12] *Provision C.3.2 provides that 'the main role and responsibilities of the audit committee should be set out in written terms of reference and should include ... to develop and implement a policy on the engagement of the external auditor to supply non-audit services ...'*

2.66 A contingent fee basis is any arrangement made at the outset of an engagement under which a pre-determined amount or a specified commission on or percentage of any consideration or saving is payable to the firm upon the happening of a specified event or the achievement of an outcome (or alternative outcomes). Differential hourly fee rates, or arrangements under which the fee payable will be negotiated after the completion of the engagement, do not constitute contingent fee arrangements.

2.67 Contingent fee arrangements in respect of investment circular reporting engagements create self-interest threats to the reporting accountant's objectivity and independence that are so significant that they cannot be eliminated or reduced to an acceptable level by the application of any safeguards.

2.68 The fee ordinarily reflects the time spent and the skills and experience of the personnel performing the engagement in accordance with all the relevant requirements.

2.69 The basis for the calculation of the fee is agreed with the engagement client prior to the commencement of the engagement. The engagement partner explains to the engagement client that the estimated fee is based on the expected level of work required and that, if unforeseen problems are encountered, the cost of any additional work found to be necessary will be reflected in the fee actually charged. This is not a contingent fee arrangement.

2.70 Investigations into possible acquisitions or disposals ('due diligence engagements'), particularly those performed in relation to a prospective transaction, typically involve a high level of risk and responsibility. A firm carrying out a due diligence engagement may charge a higher fee for work relating to a completed transaction than for the same transaction if it is not completed, for whatever reason, provided that the difference is related to such additional risk and responsibility and not the outcome of the due diligence engagement.

2.71 Where the reporting accountant is aware that the engagement client has a record of seeking substantial discounts to the fee payable where a transaction is unsuccessful or abortive, the engagement partner discusses the position with the ethics partner. An appropriate safeguard may involve arranging an engagement quality control review of the investment circular reporting engagement.

2.72 **The firm should establish policies and procedures to ensure that the engagement partner and the ethics partner are notified where others within the firm have agreed contingent fee arrangements in relation to the provision of other services to the engagement client or its affiliates.**

2.73 Contingent fee arrangements in respect of other services provided by the firm to an engagement client may create a threat to the reporting accountant's objectivity and independence. Where fees for other services are calculated on a contingent fee basis, the perception may be that the firm's interests are so closely aligned with the engagement client that it threatens the reporting accountant's objectivity and independence. Any contingent fee that is material to the firm, or that part of the firm by reference to which the engagement partner's profit share is calculated, will create an unacceptable self-interest threat and the firm does not undertake such an engagement at the same time as an investment circular reporting engagement.

2.74 **Where fees for professional services from the engagement client are overdue and the amount cannot be regarded as trivial, the engagement partner, in consultation with the ethics partner, should consider whether the firm should not accept or should withdraw from the investment circular reporting engagement.**

To evaluate such threats, the reporting accountant gives careful consideration to which individual is appointed as the engagement partner on an investment circular reporting engagement. This consideration will reflect the need for relevant expertise[16] as well as factors such as: 2.60

- the nature of the investment circular reporting engagement and whether it will involve the reappraisal of previously audited financial information,
- the length of time that the audit engagement partner has been associated with the audit engagement,
- the length of time that other partners have acted for the client on corporate finance and other transaction related engagements,
- whether the objectivity of the engagement partner on a subsequent audit could be adversely affected by an opinion on a profit forecast included in the investment circular, and
- the scope of the engagement quality control review.

A self-interest threat may be created where a partner in the engagement team: 2.61

- is employed exclusively or principally on an investment circular reporting engagement that extends for a significant period of time; or
- is remunerated on the basis of the performance of a part of the firm which is substantially dependent on fees from that engagement client.

In order to address those threats that are identified, firms apply safeguards to reduce the threat to an acceptable level. Appropriate safeguards may include: 2.62

- appointing a partner who has no previous involvement with the engagement client as the engagement partner;
- arranging an engagement quality control review of the investment circular reporting engagement by a partner who is not involved with the client and, if relevant, is not remunerated on the basis of the performance of part of the firm which is substantially dependent on fees from that client;
- arranging an external engagement quality control review of the investment circular reporting engagement.

Fees

The engagement partner should be satisfied and able to demonstrate that the investment circular reporting engagement has assigned to it sufficient partners and staff with appropriate time and skill to perform the investment circular reporting engagement in accordance with all applicable Investment Reporting and Ethical Standards, irrespective of the fee to be charged. 2.63

Paragraph 2.63 is not intended to prescribe the approach to be taken by reporting accountants to the setting of fees, but rather to emphasise that there are no circumstances where the amount of the fee can justify any lack of appropriate resource or time taken to perform an investment circular reporting engagement in accordance with applicable Investment Reporting and Ethical Standards. 2.64

An investment circular reporting engagement should not be undertaken on a contingent fee basis. 2.65

---

[16] *Paragraph 25 of SIR 1000 requires that a partner with appropriate experience should be involved in the conduct of the work.*

Section 3 - The provision of other services

Introduction

The provision of other services by reporting accountants to the engagement client may create threats to their objectivity or perceived loss of independence. The threats and safeguards approach set out in Section 1 sets out the general approach to be adopted by reporting accountants in relation to the provision of other services to their clients. This approach is applicable irrespective of the nature of the services, which may be in question in a given case. This Section illustrates the application of the general approach to a number of commonly provided services. 3.1

In this Standard, 'other services' comprise any engagement in which a reporting accountant provides professional services to an engagement client other than pursuant to: 3.2

(a) any investment circular reporting engagement;
(b) the audit of financial statements; and
(c) those other roles which legislation or regulation specify can be performed by the auditors of the entity (for example, considering the preliminary announcements of listed companies, complying with the procedural and reporting requirements of regulators, such as requirements relating to the audit of the client's internal controls and reports in accordance with Section 151 or 173 of the Companies Act 1985).

Where the engagement client is a member of a group, other services, for the purposes of this Standard, include: 3.3

- services provided by the firm, to the parent company or to any of its significant affiliates; and
- services provided by a network firm which is involved in the investment circular reporting engagement to the engagement client or any of its significant affiliates.

The provisions of this section apply only to those other services provided by the reporting accountant to the engagement client during the relevant period. The relevant period covers the period during which the engagement is undertaken and any additional period subsequent to the date of the most recent audited financial statements. Other services provided prior to that date are unlikely to create threats to the reporting accountant's objectivity because: 3.4

- where the reporting accountant undertook the last audit of the engagement client's financial statements and complied with the APB Ethical Standards for Auditors, the requirements applicable to the provision of other services will have been observed; or
- where the last audit of the engagement client's financial statements was undertaken by a different firm, the work done by the reporting accountant in providing other services will have been the subject of independent review in the course of the audit.

The firm should establish policies and procedures, including the alternative procedures outlined in paragraphs 1.44, that enable it to identify circumstances where others within the firm and network firms involved in the investment circular reporting engagement have accepted an engagement to provide during the relevant period, an other service to an engagement client or any of that client's significant affiliates. 3.5

3.6 The firm establishes appropriate policies and procedures to ensure that, in relation to an engagement client, any engagement to provide an other service to the client or any of its significant affiliates during the relevant period is identified so that the engagement partner can consider the implications for the reporting accountant's objectivity and independence before the investment circular reporting engagement is accepted. Such policies and procedures are likely to involve:

i) enquiries of the engagement client;
ii) reference to records of past and current other service engagements provided by the firm;
iii) enquiries of network firms involved in the investment circular reporting engagement as to whether they have provided any other service engagement to the client or any of its significant affiliates during the relevant period.

Such enquiries are undertaken in a manner which seeks to protect confidentiality.

3.7 **Where the engagement partner considers that it is probable that a reasonable and informed third party would regard the objectives of an other service engagement[17] undertaken during the relevant period as being inconsistent with the objectives of the investment circular reporting engagement, the firm should not accept or withdraw from the investment circular reporting engagement.**

3.8 The objectives of engagements to provide other services vary and depend on the specific terms of the engagement. In some cases these objectives may be inconsistent with those of the investment circular reporting engagement, and, in such cases, this may give rise to a threat to the reporting accountant's objectivity and to the appearance of its independence. Firms do not undertake other service engagements during the relevant period, where the objectives of such engagements are inconsistent with the objectives of the investment circular reporting engagement, or do not accept or withdraw from the investment circular reporting engagement.

3.9 Similarly, in relation to a possible new investment circular reporting engagement, consideration needs to be given to recent and current engagements to provide other services by the firm to the client and whether the scope and objectives of those engagements are consistent with the proposed investment circular reporting engagement. In making this assessment, the engagement partner gives consideration to the provisions and guidance given on specific other services in paragraphs 3.13 to 3.89.

3.10 When tendering for a new investment circular reporting engagement, the firm ensures that relevant information on recent other services is drawn to the attention of those charged with governance of the issuing engagement client and any other persons or entities the reporting accountant is instructed to advise, including:

- when recent services were provided to the client;
- the materiality of those services to the proposed investment circular reporting engagement;
- whether those services would have been prohibited if the firm had been undertaking an investment circular reporting engagement at the time when they were undertaken; and
- the extent to which the outcomes of other services have been reviewed by another firm.

---

[17] *This includes consideration of any private reporting engagements associated with the transaction which is the subject of the investment circular that were undertaken before the investment circular was contemplated.*

Where both an investment circular reporting engagement and an engagement to 3.11
undertake other services are provided concurrently the initial assessment of the
threats to objectivity and independence and the safeguards to be applied are reviewed
whenever the scope and objectives of the other service or the investment circular
reporting engagement change significantly. If such a review suggests that safeguards
cannot reduce the threat to an acceptable level, the firm withdraws from the other
service engagement, or withdraws from the investment circular reporting
engagement.

The following paragraphs provide requirements and guidance on the provision of 3.12
specific other services by the reporting accountant during the relevant period to the
engagement client once the assessment of threats to independence and objectivity at
the time of appointment has been made.

Internal audit services

The range of 'internal audit services' is wide and they may not be termed as such by 3.13
the engagement client. For example, the firm may be engaged:

- to outsource the engagement client's entire internal audit function; or
- to supplement the engagement client's internal audit function in specific areas (for example, by providing specialised technical services or resources in particular locations); or
- to provide occasional internal audit services to the engagement client on an *ad hoc* basis.

All such engagements would fall within the term 'internal audit services'.

The main threats to the reporting accountant's objectivity and independence arising 3.14
from the provision of internal audit services are the self-review threat and the
management threat.

Engagements to provide internal audit services - other than those prohibited in 3.15
paragraph 3.17 - may be undertaken, provided that the reporting accountant is
satisfied that 'informed management'[18] has been designated by the client and provided that appropriate safeguards are applied.

Examples of safeguards that may be appropriate when internal audit services are 3.16
provided to an engagement client include ensuring that:

- internal audit projects undertaken by the firm are performed by partners and staff who have no involvement in the investment circular reporting engagement;
- the work of the reporting accountant is reviewed by a partner who is not involved in the engagement, to ensure that the internal audit work performed by the firm has been properly and effectively assessed in the context of the investment circular reporting engagement.

The firm should not undertake an engagement to provide internal audit services to an 3.17
engagement client where it is reasonably foreseeable that:

(a) for the purposes of the investment circular reporting engagement, the reporting accountant would place significant reliance on the internal audit work performed by the firm; or

---

[18] See paragraph 1.36.

(b) for the purposes of the internal audit services, the firm would undertake part of the role of management of the engagement client in relation to the transaction or the financial information that is the subject of the investment circular reporting engagement.

3.18 The self-review threat is unacceptably high where the reporting accountant cannot perform the investment circular reporting engagement without placing significant reliance on the work performed for the purposes of the internal audit services engagement. For example, the provision of internal audit services on the internal financial controls for an engagement client which is a large bank, is likely to be unacceptable as the reporting accountant is likely to place significant reliance on the work performed by the internal audit team in relation to the bank's internal financial controls.

3.19 The management threat is unacceptably high where the firm provides internal audit services that involve firm personnel taking decisions or making judgments which are properly the responsibility of management. For example, such situations can arise where the nature of the internal audit work involves the firm in taking decisions in relation to the transaction or the financial information that is the subject of the investment circular reporting engagement, as to:

- the scope and nature of the internal audit services to be provided to the engagement client, or
- the design of internal controls or implementing changes thereto.

3.20 During the course of an investment circular reporting engagement the reporting accountant may evaluate the design and test the operating effectiveness of some of the entity's internal financial controls, including the operation of any internal audit function and provide management with observations on matters that have come to their attention, including comments on weaknesses in the internal control systems (including the internal audit function) and suggestions for addressing them. This work is a by-product of the investment circular reporting engagement rather than the result of a specific engagement to provide other services and therefore does not constitute internal audit services for the purposes of this Standard.

3.21 In some circumstances, additional internal financial controls work is performed during the course of the investment circular reporting engagement in response to a specific request. Whether it is appropriate for this work to be undertaken by the firm will depend on the extent to which it gives rise to a management threat to the reporting accountant's objectivity and independence. The engagement partner reviews the scope and objectives of the proposed work and assesses the threats to which it gives rise and the safeguards available.

Information technology services

3.22 Design, provision and implementation of information technology (including financial information technology) systems by firms for their clients creates threats to the reporting accountant's objectivity and independence. The principal threats are the self-review threat and the management threat.

3.23 Engagements to design, provide or implement information technology systems that are not important to any significant part of the accounting system or to the production of the financial information that is the subject of the investment circular reporting engagement and do not have significant reliance placed on them by the reporting accountant, may be undertaken, provided that 'informed management'[18] has been designated by the engagement client and provided that appropriate safeguards are applied.

Examples of safeguards that may be appropriate when information technology services are provided to an engagement client include ensuring that: 3.24

- information technology projects undertaken by the firm are performed by partners and staff who have no involvement in the investment circular reporting engagement;
- the work undertaken in the course of the investment circular reporting engagement is reviewed by a partner who is not involved in the engagement to ensure that the information technology work performed has been properly and effectively assessed.

The firm should not undertake an engagement to design, provide or implement information technology systems for an engagement client where: 3.25

(a) the systems concerned would be important to any significant part of the accounting system or to the production of the financial information that is the subject of an investment circular reporting engagement and the reporting accountant would place significant reliance upon them as part of the investment circular reporting engagement; or
(b) for the purposes of the information technology services, the firm would undertake part of the role of management of the engagement client in relation to the transaction or the financial information that is the subject of the investment circular reporting engagement.

Where it is reasonably apparent that, having regard to the activities and size of the engagement client and the range and complexity of the system, the management lacks the expertise required to take responsibility for the systems concerned, it is unlikely that any safeguards would be sufficient to eliminate these threats or to reduce them to an acceptable level. In particular, formal acceptance by management of the systems designed and installed by the firm is unlikely to be an effective safeguard when, in substance, the firm has been retained by management for its expertise and has made important decisions in relation to the design or implementation of systems of internal control and financial reporting in relation to the transaction or the financial information that is the subject of the investment circular reporting engagement. 3.26

The provision and installation of information technology services associated with a standard 'off the shelf accounting package' (including basic set-up procedures to make the package operate on the client's existing platform and peripherals, setting up the chart of accounts and the entry of standard data such as the client's product names and prices) is unlikely to create a level of threat to the reporting accountant's objectivity and independence that cannot be addressed through applying appropriate safeguards. 3.27

Valuation services

The firm should not undertake an engagement to provide a valuation to an engagement client where the valuation would both: 3.28

(a) involve a significant degree of subjective judgment; and
(b) have a material effect on the financial information that is the subject of the investment circular reporting engagement.

3.29 The main threats to the reporting accountant's objectivity and independence arising from the provision of valuation services are the self-review threat and the management threat. The self-review threat is considered too high to allow the provision of valuation services which involve the valuation of amounts with a significant degree of subjectivity that may have a material effect on the financial information that is the subject of the investment circular reporting engagement.

3.30 It is usual for the reporting accountant to provide the management with accounting advice in relation to valuation matters that have come to its attention during the course of the investment circular reporting engagement. Such matters might typically include:
- comments on valuation assumptions and their appropriateness;
- errors identified in a valuation calculation and suggestions for correcting them;
- advice on accounting policies and any valuation methodologies used in their application.

Advice on such matters does not constitute valuation services for the purpose of this Standard.

3.31 Where reporting accountants are engaged to collect and verify the accuracy of data to be used in a valuation to be performed by others, such engagements do not constitute valuation services under this Standard.

Actuarial valuation services

3.32 **The firm should not undertake an engagement to provide actuarial valuation services to an engagement client, unless the firm is satisfied that either:**

(a) **all significant judgments, including the assumptions, are made by 'informed management'[18]; or**

(b) **the valuation has no material effect on the financial information that is the subject of the investment circular reporting engagement.**

3.33 Actuarial valuation services are subject to the same general principles as other valuation services. Where they involve the firm in making a subjective judgment and have a material effect on the financial information that is the subject of the investment circular reporting engagement, actuarial valuations give rise to an unacceptable level of self-review threat and so may not be performed by reporting accountants for their clients.

3.34 However, in cases where all significant judgments concerning the assumptions, methodology and data for the actuarial valuation are made by 'informed management' and the firm's role is limited to applying proven methodologies using the given data, for which the management takes responsibility, it may be possible to establish effective safeguards to protect the reporting accountant's objectivity and the appearance of its independence.

Tax services

3.35 The range of activities encompassed by the term 'tax services' is wide. Three broad categories of tax service can be distinguished. They are where the firm:

(a) provides advice to the engagement client on one or more specific matters at the request of the client; or

(b) undertakes a substantial proportion of the tax planning or compliance work for the engagement client; or
(c) promotes tax structures or products to the engagement client, the effectiveness of which is likely to be influenced by the manner in which they are accounted for in the financial information that is the subject of the investment circular reporting engagement.

Whilst it is possible to consider tax services under broad headings, such as tax planning or compliance, in practice these services are often interrelated and it is impracticable to analyse services in this way for the purposes of attempting to identify generically the threats to which specific engagements give rise. As a result, firms need to identify and assess, on a case-by-case basis, the potential threats to the reporting accountant's objectivity and independence before deciding whether to undertake an engagement to provide tax services to an engagement client.

The provision of tax services by firms to their engagement clients may give rise to a number of threats to the reporting accountant's objectivity and independence, including the self-interest threat, the management threat, the advocacy threat and, where the work involves a significant degree of subjective judgment and has a material effect on the financial information that is the subject of the investment circular reporting engagement, the self-review threat. 3.36

Where the firm provides advice to the engagement client on one or more specific matters at the request of the client, a self-review threat may be created. This self-review threat is more significant where the firm undertakes a substantial proportion of the tax planning and compliance work for the engagement client. However, the reporting accountant may be able to adopt appropriate safeguards. 3.37

Examples of such safeguards that may be appropriate when tax services are provided to an engagement client include ensuring that: 3.38

- the tax services are provided by partners and staff who have no involvement in the investment circular reporting engagement;
- the tax services are reviewed by an independent tax partner, or other senior tax employee;
- external independent advice is obtained on the tax work;
- tax computations prepared by the firm are reviewed by a partner or senior staff member with appropriate expertise who is not a member of the investment circular reporting engagement team; or
- a partner not involved in the engagement reviews whether the tax work has been properly and effectively addressed in the context of the investment circular reporting engagement.

The firm should not promote tax structures or products or undertake an engagement to provide tax advice to an engagement client where the engagement partner has, or ought to have, reasonable doubt as to the appropriateness of the related accounting treatment involved, having regard to the requirement for the financial information to give a true and fair view, in the context of the relevant financial reporting framework. 3.39

Where the firm promotes tax structures or products or undertakes an engagement to provide tax advice to the engagement client, it may be necessary to adopt an accounting treatment about which there is reasonable doubt as to its appropriateness, in order to achieve the desired result. A self-review threat arises in the course of an investment circular reporting engagement because the reporting accountant may be unable to form an impartial view of the accounting treatment to be adopted for the purposes of the proposed arrangements. Accordingly, this Standard does not 3.40

permit the promotion of tax structures or products by firms to their engagement clients where, in the view of the engagement partner, after such consultation as is appropriate, the effectiveness of the tax structure or product depends on an accounting treatment about which there is reasonable doubt as to its appropriateness.

3.41 The firm should not undertake an engagement to provide tax services to an engagement client wholly or partly on a contingent fee basis where:

(a) the engagement fees are material to the firm or the part of the firm by reference to which the engagement partner's profit share is calculated; or
(b) the outcome of those tax services (and, therefore, the entitlement to the fee) is dependent on:
   (i) the application of tax law which is uncertain or has not been established; and
   (ii) a judgment made by the reporting accountant in relation to a material aspect of the investment circular reporting engagement.

3.42 Where tax services, such as advising on corporate structures and structuring transactions to achieve a particular effect, are undertaken on a contingent fee basis, self-interest threats to the reporting accountant's objectivity and independence may arise. The reporting accountant may have, or may appear to have, an interest in the success of the tax services, causing it to make a judgment about which there is reasonable doubt as to its appropriateness. Where the contingent fee is determined by the outcome of the application of tax law, which is uncertain or has not been established, and a judgment made by the reporting accountant in relation to a material aspect of the investment circular reporting engagement, the self-interest threat cannot be eliminated or reduced to an acceptable level by the application of any safeguards.

3.43 The firm should not undertake an engagement to provide tax services to an engagement client where the engagement would involve the firm undertaking a management role for the engagement client in relation to the transaction or the financial information that is the subject of the investment circular reporting engagement.

3.44 When providing tax services to an engagement client, there is a risk that the reporting accountant undertakes a management role, unless the firm is working with 'informed management'[18] and appropriate safeguards are applied, such as the tax services being provided by partners and staff who have no involvement in the investment circular reporting engagement.

3.45 The firm should not undertake an engagement to provide tax services to an engagement client where this would involve acting as an advocate for the client, before an appeals tribunal or court[19] in the resolution of an issue:

(a) that is material to the financial information that is the subject of the investment circular reporting engagement; or
(b) where the outcome of the tax issue is dependent on a judgment made by the reporting accountant in relation to a material aspect of the investment circular reporting engagement.

3.46 Where the tax services to be provided by the firm include representing the client in any negotiations or proceedings involving the tax authorities, advocacy threats to the reporting accountant's objectivity and independence may arise.

---

[19] The restriction applies to the first level of Tax Court that is independent of the tax authorities and to more authoritative bodies. In the UK this would be the General or Special Commissioners of the Inland Revenue or the VAT and Duties Tribunal.

3.47 The firm is not acting as an advocate where the tax services involve the provision of information to the tax authorities (including an explanation of the approach being taken and the arguments being advanced by the client). In such circumstances effective safeguards may exist and the tax authorities will undertake their own review of the issues.

3.48 Where the tax authorities indicate that they are minded to reject the client's arguments on a particular issue and the matter is likely to be determined by an appeals tribunal or court, the firm may become so closely identified with management's arguments that the reporting accountant is inhibited from forming an impartial view of the treatment of the issue in the financial information that is the subject of the investment circular reporting engagement. In such circumstances, if the issue is material to the financial information or is dependent on a judgment made by the reporting accountant in relation to a material aspect of the investment circular reporting engagement, the firm discusses the matter with the engagement client and makes it clear to the engagement client that it will have to withdraw from that element of the engagement to provide tax services that requires it to act as advocate for the engagement client, or withdraw from the investment circular reporting engagement from the time when the matter is formally listed for hearing before the appeals tribunal.

3.49 The firm is not, however, precluded from having a continuing role (for example, responding to specific requests for information) for the engagement client in relation to the appeal. The firm assesses the threat associated with any continuing role in accordance with the provisions of paragraphs 3.50 to 3.52 of this Standard.

Litigation support services

3.50 **The firm should not undertake an engagement to provide litigation support services to an engagement client where this would involve the estimation by the firm of the likely outcome of a pending legal matter that could be material to the amounts to be included or the disclosures to be made in the financial information that is the subject of the investment circular reporting engagement and there is a significant degree of subjectivity involved.**

3.51 Although management and advocacy threats may arise in litigation support services, such as acting as an expert witness, the primary issue is that a self-review threat will arise where such services involve a subjective estimation of the likely outcome of a matter that is material to the amounts to be included or the disclosures to be made in the financial information that is the subject of the investment circular reporting engagement.

3.52 Litigation support services that do not involve such subjective estimations are not prohibited, provided that the firm has carefully considered the implications of any threats and established appropriate safeguards.

Legal services

3.53 **The firm should not undertake an engagement to provide legal services to an engagement client where this would involve acting as the solicitor formally nominated to represent the client in the resolution of a dispute or litigation which is material to the amounts to be included or the disclosures to be made in the financial information that is the subject of the investment circular reporting engagement.**

3.54 Although the provision by reporting accountants of certain types of legal services to their clients may create advocacy, self-review and management threats, this Standard does not impose a general prohibition on the provision of legal services. However, in view of the degree of advocacy involved in litigation or other types of dispute resolution procedures and the potential importance of any assessment by the reporting accountant of the merits of the client's position when reviewing the financial information, this Standard prohibits a reporting accountant from acting as the formally nominated representative for an engagement client in the resolution of a dispute or litigation which is material to the financial information that is the subject of the investment circular reporting engagement (either in terms of the amounts recognised or disclosed in the financial information).

Recruitment and remuneration services

3.55 **The firm should not undertake an engagement to provide recruitment services to an engagement client in relation to the appointment of:**

- **any director or**
- **any employee of the engagement client who will be involved in an area that is directly concerned with the transaction which is the subject of the investment circular.**

3.56 A management threat arises where firm personnel take responsibility for any decision as to who should be appointed by the engagement client. Furthermore, a familiarity threat arises if the firm plays a significant role in relation to the identification and recruitment of senior members of management within the company, as the engagement team may be less likely to be critical of the information or explanations provided by such individuals than might otherwise be the case. Accordingly, the firm does not undertake engagements that involve the recruitment of individuals for key management positions during the relevant period.

3.57 Where the firm has played a significant role in relation to the identification and recruitment of a senior member of management within the company, including all directors, prior to the relevant period, the engagement partner considers whether a familiarity threat exists, taking account of factors such as:

- the closeness of personal relationships between the firm's partners and staff and client personnel;
- the length of time since the recruitment of the individual in question;
- the position held by the individual at the engagement client;
- the extent of involvement that the individual will have with the transaction which is the subject of the investment circular;
- whether the individual is in a position to exercise influence on the accounting records or financial information.

Following the assessment of any such threats, appropriate safeguards are applied where necessary, such as ensuring that the engagement team does not include individuals with a close relationship to the senior member of management or who were involved in the recruitment exercise.

3.58 Recruitment services involve a specifically identifiable, and separately remunerated, engagement. Reporting accountants may contribute to an entity's recruitment process in less formal ways. The prohibition set out in paragraph 3.55 does not extend to senior members of an engagement team interviewing prospective employees of the engagement client or to the entity using information gathered by the firm, including that relating to salary surveys.

The firm should not undertake an engagement to provide advice on the quantum of the remuneration package or the measurement criteria on which the quantum is calculated, for a director or key management position of an engagement client. 3.59

The provision of advice on remuneration packages (including bonus arrangements, incentive plans and other benefits) to existing or prospective employees of the engagement client gives rise to familiarity threats. The significance of the familiarity threat is considered too high to allow advice on the overall amounts to be paid or on the quantitative measurement criteria included in remuneration packages for directors and key management positions. 3.60

For other employees, these threats can be adequately addressed by the application of safeguards, such as the advice being provided by partners and staff who have no involvement in the investment circular reporting engagement. 3.61

In cases where all significant judgments concerning the assumptions, methodology and data for the calculation of remuneration packages for directors and key management are made by 'informed management'[18] or a third party and the firm's role is limited to applying proven methodologies using the given data, for which the management takes responsibility, it may be possible to establish effective safeguards to protect the reporting accountant's objectivity and independence. 3.62

Advice on tax, pensions and interpretation of accounting standards relating to remuneration packages for directors and key management can be provided by the firm, provided they are not prohibited by the requirements of this Standard relating to tax, actuarial valuations and accounting services. 3.63

Corporate finance services

The range of services encompassed by the term 'corporate finance services' is wide. For example, the firm may be engaged: 3.64
- to identify possible purchasers for parts of the client's business and provide advisory services in the course of such sales; or
- to identify possible 'targets' for the client to acquire; or
- to advise the client on how to fund its financing requirements, including advising on debt restructuring and securitisation programmes; or
- to act as sponsor on admission to listing on the London Stock Exchange or the Irish Stock Exchange, as Nominated Advisor on the admission of the client on the Alternative Investments Market (AIM); or as an IEX Adviser on the admission of the client to the Irish Enterprise Exchange (IEX) of the Irish Stock Exchange; or
- to act as financial adviser to client offerors or offerees in connection with public takeovers.

The potential for the reporting accountant's objectivity and independence to be impaired through the provision of corporate finance services varies considerably depending on the precise nature of the service provided. The main threats to reporting accountant's objectivity and independence arising from the provision of corporate finance services are the self-review, management and advocacy threats. Self-interest threats may also arise, especially in situations where the firm is paid on a contingent fee basis. 3.65

3.66 When providing corporate finance services to an engagement client, there is a risk that the firm undertakes a management role, unless the firm is working with 'informed management'[18] and appropriate safeguards are applied.

3.67 Examples of safeguards that may be appropriate when corporate finance services are provided to an engagement client include ensuring that:
- the corporate finance advice is provided by partners and staff who have no involvement in the investment circular reporting engagement,
- any advice provided is reviewed by an independent corporate finance partner within the firm,
- external independent advice on the corporate finance work is obtained,
- a partner who is not involved in the investment circular reporting engagement or the corporate finance services reviews the work performed in the investment circular reporting engagement.

3.68 Where the firm undertakes an engagement to provide corporate finance services to an engagement client in connection with conducting the sale or purchase of a material part of the client's business, the engagement partner should inform those charged with governance of the issuing engagement client and any other person or entity the reporting accountant is instructed to advise about the engagement, as set out in paragraphs 1.68 to 1.76.

3.69 **The firm should not undertake an engagement to provide corporate finance services to an engagement client where:**
  (a) **the engagement would involve the firm taking responsibility for dealing in, underwriting or promoting shares; or**
  (b) **the engagement partner has, or ought to have, reasonable doubt as to the appropriateness of an accounting treatment that is related to the advice provided, having regard to the requirement for the financial information to give a true and fair view in accordance with the relevant financial reporting framework; or**
  (c) **such corporate finance services are to be provided on a contingent fee basis and:**
    (i) **the engagement fees are material to the firm or the part of the firm by reference to which the engagement partner's profit share is calculated; or**
    (ii) **the outcome of those corporate finance services (and, therefore, the entitlement to the fee) is dependent on a judgment made by the reporting accountant in relation to a material aspect of the investment circular reporting engagement[20]; or**
  (d) **the engagement would involve the firm undertaking a management role for the engagement client in relation to the transaction or the financial information that is the subject of the investment circular reporting engagement.**

3.70 An unacceptable advocacy threat arises where, in the course of providing a corporate finance service, the firm promotes the interests of the engagement client by taking responsibility for dealing in, underwriting, or promoting shares.

3.71 Where the firm acts as a Sponsor under the Listing Rules[21], as Nominated Adviser on the admission of the engagement client to the AIM or as IEX Adviser on the

---

[20] *A reporting accountant judgment made in relation to a material aspect of the investment circular reporting engagement would be one which could adversely affect the successful completion of the transaction to which the investment circular relates, for example, where a reporting accountant is considering a qualification to an accountant's report as a result of a disagreement in relation to an accounting treatment which would affect revenue recognition and where a qualified opinion would be likely to render the company unsuitable for listing.*

[21] *In the United Kingdom, the UK Listing Authority's publication the 'Listing Rules'. In the Republic of Ireland, the Irish Stock Exchange's publication the 'Listing Rules'.*

admission of the engagement client to IEX, the firm is required to confirm that the client has satisfied all applicable conditions for listing and other relevant requirements of the Listing Rules, AIM Rules or IEX Rules, respectively. Where there is, or there ought to be, reasonable doubt that the firm will be able to give that confirmation, it does not enter into such an engagement.

A self-review threat arises where the outcome or consequences of the corporate finance service provided by the firm may be material to the financial information that is the subject of the investment circular reporting engagement. Where the firm provides corporate finance services, for example advice to the engagement client on financing arrangements, it may be necessary to adopt an accounting treatment about which there is reasonable doubt as to its appropriateness in order to achieve the desired result. A self-review threat is created because the reporting accountant may be unable to form an impartial view of the accounting treatment to be adopted for the purposes of the proposed arrangements. Accordingly, this Standard does not permit the provision of advice by firms to their engagement clients where there is reasonable doubt about the appropriateness of the related accounting treatments. 3.72

Advice to engagement clients on issues such as funding and banking arrangements, where there is no reasonable doubt as to the appropriateness of the accounting treatment, is not prohibited provided this does not involve the firm in taking decisions or making judgments which are properly the responsibility of management. 3.73

Where a corporate finance engagement is undertaken on a contingent fee basis, self-interest threats to the reporting accountant's objectivity and independence also arise as the reporting accountant may have, or may appear to have, an interest in the success of the corporate finance services. The significance of the self-interest threat is primarily determined by the materiality of the contingent fee to the firm, or to the part of the firm by reference to which the engagement partner's profit share is calculated. Where the contingent fee and the outcome of the corporate finance services is dependent on a judgment made by the reporting accountant in relation to a material aspect of the investment circular reporting engagement, the self-interest threat cannot be eliminated or reduced to an acceptable level by the application of any safeguards. 3.74

In situations where a reporting accountant can see at the outset of the investment circular reporting engagement that there is likely to be a judgment that will be made in relation to a material aspect of the investment circular reporting engagement which could adversely affect the successful completion of the transaction to which the investment circular relates, the firm will not agree to undertake any corporate finance engagements in relation to the transaction on a contingent fee basis, or will not accept the investment circular reporting engagement. Where corporate finance engagements are entered into on a contingent fee basis and a judgment needs to be made in relation to a material aspect of the investment circular reporting engagement during the course of an investment circular reporting engagement, then the firm changes the terms of the corporate finance engagement so that it no longer involves a contingent fee or withdraws from either the relevant corporate finance engagement or the investment circular reporting engagement. 3.75

Where the firm provides a range of corporate finance services to the engagement client, including acting as a Sponsor, Nominated Advisor or IEX Adviser on terms that involve a contingent fee, and that firm also undertakes a public reporting engagement for the engagement client, the self-interest threat caused by contingent fee arrangements may be reduced to an acceptable level by the application of safeguards, such as the corporate finance services being provided by partners and staff who have no involvement in the investment circular reporting engagement. In such 3.76

circumstances the reporting accountant ensures that the situation is fully disclosed to the Financial Services Authority, the Irish Stock Exchange or the London Stock Exchange and any related regulatory requirements have been complied with.[22]

Transaction related services

3.77 In addition to corporate finance services, there are other services associated with transactions that a firm may undertake for an engagement client. For example:

- investigations into possible acquisitions or disposals ('due diligence' engagements); or
- investigations into the tax implications of possible acquisitions or disposals.

3.78 When providing transaction related services to an engagement client, unless the firm is working with 'informed management'[18] and appropriate safeguards are applied, there is a risk that the firm undertakes a management role.

3.79 Examples of safeguards that may be appropriate when transaction related services are provided to an engagement client include ensuring that:

- the transaction related advice is provided by partners and staff who have no involvement in the investment circular reporting engagement,
- any advice provided is reviewed by an independent transactions partner within the firm,
- external independent advice on the transaction related work is obtained,
- a partner who is not involved in the investment circular reporting engagement reviews the work performed in relation to the subject matter of the transaction related service provided to ensure that such work has been properly and effectively reviewed and assessed in the context of the investment circular reporting engagement.

3.80 **The reporting accountant should not undertake an engagement to provide transaction related services to an engagement client where:**

(a) the engagement partner has, or ought to have, reasonable doubt as to the appropriateness of an accounting treatment that is related to the advice provided, having regard to the requirement for the financial information to give a true and fair view in accordance with the relevant financial reporting framework; or

(b) such transaction related services are to be provided on a contingent fee basis and:
  (i) the engagement fees are material to the firm or the part of the firm by reference to which the engagement partner's profit share is calculated; or
  (ii) the outcome of those transaction related services (and, therefore, the entitlement to the fee) is dependent on a judgment made by the reporting

---

[22] *At the date of issue:*
- FSA Listing Rule 8.7.12 states that a sponsor must provide written confirmation to the UKLA that it is independent of the issuer or new applicant by way of a 'Sponsor's Confirmation of Independence' form.
- Irish Stock Exchange Listing Rule 2.2.1(2) requires that for each transaction in respect of which a firm acts as sponsor in accordance with the listing rules, the sponsor must submit to the Exchange at an early stage a confirmation of independence in the form set out in 'Schedule 1'.
- Part Two of the *AIM Nominated Adviser eligibility criteria* states that a nominated adviser may not act as both reporting accountant and nominated adviser to an AIM company unless it has satisfied the London Stock Exchange that appropriate safeguards are in place.
- Part Two of the *IEX Adviser Eligibility Criteria* states that an IEX adviser may not act as both reporting accountant and IEX adviser to an IEX company unless it has satisfied the Irish Stock Exchange that appropriate safeguards are in place.

accountant in relation to a material aspect of the investment circular reporting engagement; or

(c) the engagement would involve the firm undertaking a management role for the engagement client in relation to the transaction or the financial information that is the subject of the investment circular reporting engagement.

A self-review threat arises where the outcome of the transaction related service undertaken by the firm may be material to the financial information that is the subject of the investment circular reporting engagement. Where the engagement client proposes to undertake a transaction, it may be necessary to adopt an inappropriate accounting treatment in order to achieve the desired result. A self-review threat is created if the reporting accountant undertakes transaction related services in connection with such a transaction. Accordingly, this Standard does not permit the provision of advice by firms to their engagement clients where there is reasonable doubt about the appropriateness of the accounting treatments related to the transaction advice given. 3.81

Where a transaction related services engagement is undertaken on a contingent fee basis, self-interest threats to the reporting accountant's objectivity and independence also arise as the reporting accountant may have, or may appear to have, an interest in the success of the transaction. The significance of the self-interest threat is primarily determined by the materiality of the contingent fee to the firm, or to the part of the firm by reference to which the engagement partner's profit share is calculated. Where the contingent fee and the outcome of the transaction related services is dependent on a judgment made by the reporting accountant in relation to a material aspect of the investment circular reporting engagement, the self-interest threat cannot be eliminated or reduced to an acceptable level by the application of any safeguards, other than where the transaction is subject to a pre-established dispute resolution procedure. 3.82

Accounting services

In this Standard, the term 'accounting services' is defined as the provision of services that involve the maintenance of accounting records or the preparation of financial statements or information that is then subject to review in an investment circular reporting engagement. Advice on the implementation of current and proposed accounting standards is not included in the term 'accounting services'. 3.83

The range of activities encompassed by the term 'accounting services' is wide. In some cases, the client may ask the firm to provide a complete service including maintaining all of the accounting records and the preparation of the financial information. Other common situations are: 3.84

- the firm may take over the provision of a specific accounting function on an outsourced basis (for example, payroll);
- the client maintains the accounting records, undertakes basic bookkeeping and prepares trial balance information and asks the firm to assist with the preparation of the necessary adjustments and financial information.

The provision of accounting services by the firm to the engagement client creates threats to the reporting accountant's objectivity and independence, principally self-review and management threats, the significance of which depends on the nature and extent of the accounting services in question and upon the level of public interest in the client. 3.85

3.86 The firm should not undertake an engagement to provide accounting services in relation to the financial information that is the subject of the investment circular reporting engagement save where the circumstances contemplated in paragraph 3.89 apply.

3.87 Even where there is no engagement to provide any accounting services, it is usual for the reporting accountant to provide the management with accounting advice on matters that have come to its attention during the course of an engagement. Such matters might typically include:

- comments on weaknesses in the accounting records and suggestions for addressing them;
- errors identified in the accounting records and in the financial information and suggestions for correcting them;
- advice on the accounting policies in use and on the application of current and proposed accounting standards.

This advice is a by-product of the investment circular reporting engagement rather than the result of any engagement to provide other services. Consequently, as it is part of the reporting accountant's engagement, such advice cannot be regarded as giving rise to any threat to the reporting accountant's objectivity and independence.

3.88 The threats to the reporting accountant's objectivity and independence that would be created are too high to allow the firm to undertake an engagement to provide any accounting services in relation to the financial information that is the subject of the investment circular reporting engagement, save where the circumstances contemplated in paragraph 3.89 apply.

3.89 In emergency situations, the firm may provide an engagement client, or a significant affiliate of such a company, with accounting services to assist the company in the timely preparation of its financial statements or information. This might arise when, due to external and unforeseeable events, the firm personnel are the only people with the necessary knowledge of the client's systems and procedures. A situation could be considered an emergency where the firm's refusal to provide these services would result in a severe burden for the client (for example, withdrawal of credit lines), or would even threaten its going concern status. In such circumstances, the firm ensures that:

(a) any staff involved in the accounting services have no involvement in the investment circular reporting engagement; and
(b) the engagement would not lead to any firm staff or partners taking decisions or making judgments which are properly the responsibility of management.

Section 4 - Effective date

4.1 Effective for investment circular reporting engagements commencing on or after 1 April 2007.

4.2 Firms may complete investment circular reporting engagements commenced prior to 1 April 2007 in accordance with existing ethical guidance applicable to them at the time of their engagement from the relevant professional body.

4.3 Business relationships existing at 31 October 2006 that were permissible in accordance with existing ethical guidance from the relevant professional body, but are prohibited by the requirements of paragraph 2.20, may continue until 31 December 2007 provided that:

- no new contracts (or extensions of contracts) under the business relationship are entered into;
- the reporting accountant satisfies itself that there are adequate safeguards in place to reduce the threat to acceptable levels; and
- disclosure is made to those charged with governance of the issuing engagement client and those the reporting accountant is instructed to advise.

Loan staff assignments existing at 31 October 2006 that are prohibited by the requirements of paragraph 2.27, may continue until the earlier of: **4.4**

(a) the completion of the specific task or the end of the contract term, where this is set out in the contract; or
(b) 31 December 2007, where a task or term is not defined,

as long as the following apply:

- the investment circular reporting engagement was permitted by existing ethical guidance from the relevant professional body;
- any safeguards required by existing ethical guidance continue to be applied;
- the need for additional safeguards is assessed, including where possible safeguards specified in section 3, and if considered necessary, those additional safeguards are applied; and
- disclosure is made to those charged with governance of the issuing engagement client and those the reporting accountant is instructed to advise.

The requirements of paragraph 2.38 in respect of employment with the engagement client do not apply if: **4.5**

- the relevant person has notified an intention to join the client, or has entered into contractual arrangements, prior to 31 October 2006;
- undertaking the investment circular reporting engagement was permitted by existing ethical guidance from the relevant professional body; and
- disclosure is made to those charged with governance of the issuing engagement client and those the reporting accountant is instructed to advise.

Where compliance with the requirements of section 3 would result in an investment circular reporting engagement or other service not being supplied, other services contracted before 31 October 2006 may continue to be provided until the earlier of: **4.6**

(a) the completion of the specific task or the end of the contract term, where this is set out in the contract; or
(b) 31 December 2007, where a task or term is not defined,

as long as the following apply:

- the investment circular reporting engagement was permitted by existing ethical guidance from the relevant professional body;
- any safeguards required by existing ethical guidance continue to be applied;
- the need for additional safeguards is assessed, including where possible safeguards specified in section 3, and if considered necessary, those additional safeguards are applied; and
- disclosure is made to those charged with governance of the issuing engagement client and those the reporting accountant is instructed to advise.

Appendix 1

Glossary of terms

accounting services	The provision of services that involve the maintenance of accounting records or the preparation of financial statements or information that is then subject to review in an investment circular reporting engagement
affiliate	Any undertaking which is connected to another by means of common ownership, control or management.
audit engagement partner	The partner or other person in the firm who is responsible for the audit engagement and its performance and for the report that is issued on behalf of the firm, and who, where required, has the appropriate authority from a professional, legal or regulatory body.
chain of command	All persons who have a direct supervisory, management or other oversight responsibility for the engagement team who have actual knowledge of the investment circular reporting engagement. This includes all partners, principals and shareholders who prepare, review or directly influence the performance appraisal of any partner of the engagement team as a result of their involvement with the investment circular reporting engagement.
close family	A non-dependent parent, child or sibling.
contingent fee basis	Any arrangement made at the outset of an engagement under which a pre-determined amount or a specified commission on or percentage of any consideration or saving is payable to the firm upon the happening of a specified event or the achievement of an outcome (or alternative outcomes). Differential hourly fee rates, or arrangements under which the fee payable will be negotiated after the completion of the engagement, do not constitute contingent fee arrangements.
engagement client	The party responsible for issuing the investment circular containing the financial information[23] (the issuing engagement client) and, if different the party on whose financial information the firm is reporting.
engagement partner	The partner or other person in the firm who is responsible for the investment circular reporting engagement and its performance and for the report that is issued on behalf of the firm, and who, where required, has the appropriate authority from a professional, legal or regulatory body.
engagement period	The engagement period starts when the firm accepts the investment circular reporting engagement and ends on the date of the report.

---

[23] The financial information is described in SIR 1000 as being the 'outcome' of a reporting engagement.

engagement team	All professional personnel who are directly involved in the acceptance and performance of a particular investment circular reporting engagement. This includes those who provide quality control or direct oversight of the engagement.
ethics partner	The partner or other person in the firm having responsibility for the adequacy of the firm's policies and procedures relating to integrity, objectivity and independence, their compliance with APB Ethical Standards and the effectiveness of their communication to partners and staff within the firm and providing related guidance to individual partners.
financial interest	An interest in an equity or other security, debenture, loan or other debt instrument of an entity, including rights and obligations to acquire such an interest and derivatives directly related to such an interest.
firm	The sole practitioner, partnership, limited liability partnership or other corporate entity engaged as a reporting accountant. For the purpose of APB Ethical Standards, the firm includes network firms in the UK and Ireland, which are controlled by the firm or its partners.
immediate family	A spouse (or equivalent) or dependent.
issuing engagement client	The party responsible for issuing the investment circular containing the financial information being reported on.
investment circular	An investment circular is a document issued by an entity pursuant to statutory or regulatory requirements relating to securities on which it is intended that a third party should make an investment decision, including a prospectus, listing particulars, a circular to shareholders or similar document.
investment circular reporting engagement	Any public or private reporting engagement in connection with an investment circular where the engagement is undertaken in accordance with Standards for Investment Reporting (SIRs).
key audit partner	An audit partner, or other person performing the function of an audit partner, of the engagement team (other than the audit engagement partner) who is involved at the group level and is responsible for key decisions or judgments on significant matters, such as on significant subsidiaries or divisions of the audit client, or on significant risk factors that relate to the audit of that client.
key management position	Any position at the engagement client which involves the responsibility for fundamental management decisions at the client (e.g. as a CEO or CFO), including an ability to influence the accounting policies and the preparation of the financial statements of the client. A key management position also arises where there are contractual and factual arrangements which in substance allow an individual to participate in exercising such a management function in a different way (e.g. via a consulting contract).

network firm Any entity:
(i) controlled by the firm or
(ii) under common control, ownership or management or
(iii) otherwise affiliated or associated with the firm through the use of a common name or through the sharing of significant common professional resources.

person in a position directly to influence the conduct and outcome of the investment circular reporting engagement:

(a) Any person who is directly involved in the investment circular reporting engagement (the engagement team), including:

(i) professional personnel from all disciplines involved in the engagement, for example, lawyers, actuaries, taxation specialists, IT specialists, treasury management specialists;

(ii) those who provide quality control or direct oversight of the engagement;

(b) Any person within the firm who can directly influence the conduct and outcome of the investment circular reporting engagement through the provision of direct supervisory, management or other oversight of the engagement team in the context of the investment circular reporting engagement.

private reporting engagement An engagement, in connection with an investment circular, in which a reporting accountant does not express a conclusion that is published in an investment circular

public reporting engagement An engagement in which a reporting accountant expresses a conclusion that is published in an investment circular and which is designed to enhance the degree of confidence of the intended users of the report about the 'outcome' of the directors' evaluation or measurement of 'subject matter' (usually financial information) against 'suitable criteria'.

relevant period The engagement period and any additional period before the engagement period but subsequent to the balance sheet date of the most recent audited financial statements of the engagement client.

reporting accountant An accountant engaged to prepare a report for inclusion in, or in connection with, an investment circular. The reporting accountant may or may not be the auditor of the entity issuing the investment circular. The term "reporting accountant" is used to describe either the engagement partner or the engagement partner's firm[24]. The reporting accountant could be a limited company or a principal employed by the company.

---

[24] *Where the term applies to the engagement partner, it describes the responsibilities or obligations of the engagement partner. Such obligations or responsibilities may be fulfilled by either the engagement partner or another member of the engagement team.*

Consultation Paper
Revised Draft Ethical Standards for Auditors

(Issued March 2009)

Contents

Invitation to Comment

Consultation Paper

Appendix 1 – Exposure Draft of Revisions to APB Ethical Standards for Auditors and ISA (UK and Ireland) 610

Extracts from ES 2 Financial, business, employment and personal relationships
Extracts from ES 3 Long association with the audit engagement
Extracts from ES 4 Fees, remuneration and evaluation policies, litigation, gifts and hospitality
Extracts from ES 5 Non-audit services provided to audit clients
Extracts from ES – Provisions Available for Small Entities
Extracts from Glossary of terms
Extracts from ISA (UK and Ireland) 610

1 Background

1.1 The Auditing Practices Board (APB)'s first Ethical Standards for Auditors (ESs) applied for audits of financial statements for periods commencing on or after 15 December 2004.

1.2 The APB undertook a review of the ESs in 2007, after they had applied for two audit cycles. This review indicated that the standards appeared to be meeting the needs of stakeholders and were working in practice. However, a small number of amendments were made to:

- Implement legislation arising from the EU Statutory Audit Directive[1];
- Allow continued adherence to the principles of the International Federation of Accountants' Code of Ethics for Professional Accountants (the IFAC Code);
- Add to the clarity of the ESs and assist their implementation in practice.

1.3 Revised ESs were issued in April 2008. In its feedback paper on this exercise the APB stated that further dialogue was needed on the issue of partner rotation for listed company audits and that a small number of new issues had arisen during the consultation period which required further work to be completed during 2008.

1.4 The APB has discussed these issues in detail and its current view on each of them is set out in sections 2 to 9 of this paper. Views of commentators are requested on a number of specific questions in relation to each issue, as well as on the detailed amendments that the APB proposes should be made to the ESs, which are set out as a mark up to the current Revised ESs in Appendix 1 to this paper.

1.5 A formal Regulatory Impact Assessment has not been undertaken for the proposed revisions to the ESs. The amendments proposed are largely to clarify the current position or to ease aspects of the ESs. The APB does not therefore believe that the amendments proposed will have an impact on the costs of an audit, but invites the views of commentators on this point.

> **Question 1: Do you believe that any of the proposed changes will add to audit costs? If so, which changes and why?**

1.6 The APB plans that any changes to the ESs as a result of this review will apply to audits of financial statements for periods commencing on or after 15 December 2009. This timing is expected to broadly align with changes that are currently being made to the IFAC Code[2].

> **Question 2: Are there any changes to the ESs proposed by the APB which will be difficult to implement for audits of financial statements for periods commencing on or after 15 December 2009?**

---

[1] *Directive 2006/43/EC on Statutory Audits of Annual and Consolidated Accounts (8th Company Law Directive).*

[2] *Changes to the auditor independence requirements in the IFAC Code have been finalised, but their effective date is still under discussion within the context of the Drafting Conventions project which is being undertaken by the International Ethics Standards Board for Accountants. It is currently thought that the effective date will be for audit reports issued after 1 January 2011. The ESs apply to audits of financial statements for accounting periods commencing on or after a certain date and therefore both sets of requirements would apply to calendar 2010 audits.*

2 Partner rotation requirements

Five or seven year rotation period for the audit engagement partner

The threats to auditor independence that arise from long association with the audit engagement are addressed in ES 3 (Revised). The APB's approach is to set out general provisions requiring firms to monitor the length of time that staff in senior positions serve as members of the engagement team for each audit and then to assess the threats arising from long association and apply safeguards as necessary. Additionally, for listed companies: 2.1

- Paragraph 12 requires audit engagement partners and engagement quality control reviewers to rotate after five years and not then participate in the audit engagement, until a further period of five years has elapsed.
- Paragraph 18 requires key partners involved in the audit to rotate after seven years and not then participate in the audit engagement until a further period of two years has elapsed.

One of the key issues identified during the APB's review of the ESs in 2007 was the question of whether the rotation periods for partners involved in listed company audits strike the right balance between auditor objectivity and relevant knowledge and experience.   2.2

The APB asked for commentators' views on this question as part of the 2007 consultation. This confirmed that stakeholders hold differing views on this issue. Some commentators supported a continuation of the existing requirement for audit engagement partners on listed companies to rotate after five years, while others took the view that this period should be extended to seven years. Many of the arguments for and against a change in the rotation period for audit engagement partners focussed on audit quality. Because of the differing views, the APB made no changes to the rotation periods in the ESs issued in April 2008 but agreed to undertake further work in this area.   2.3

A stakeholder meeting was held on 1st July 2008 to discuss this issue and the APB has also obtained further input from both investors and audit committee chairs on various options. This work has indicated that the relevant arguments on this issue remain finely balanced: 2.4

(a) *Audit quality.* Some believe that less frequent changes of audit partner increases the overall knowledge of the audited entity within the engagement team about past issues and the scope of the entity's activities, thereby enabling the audit engagement partner to give greater focus and scrutiny to the key judgments, and contributing to audit quality over the period of tenure. Alternatively, others believe that changing the audit partner can help maintain audit quality as a fresh view is taken on the key judgments and the new partner can be more questioning of management.

(b) *Stability in an audit engagement.* It is argued that a five year rotation period can create difficulties in practice for audit firms, particularly in the provision of audit services to specialised industries, such as banks and insurance companies. Additionally, some in the corporate community argue that frequent rotation of the audit partner can have a disruptive effect on the audited entity. However, others argue that that there are ample opportunities for continuity to be maintained by retaining managers on the audit of a listed company and, when they are promoted to partner, involving them at some stage as a key partner involved in the audit or as the audit engagement partner.

(c) **International harmonisation.** There is a growing body of opinion that there should be worldwide harmonisation of ethical standards; however, not all countries adopt a consistent rotation period:
- Both the IFAC Code and the European Statutory Audit Directive have a seven year rotation period for audit engagement partners on listed companies,
- A five year partner rotation period applies for the audit of listed companies in the USA, South Africa and Australia.

2.5 Investors in particular continue to express the view that they believe that a five year rotation period provides an important bastion for auditor independence and that there needs to be a strong public interest case before changes are made to it.

Greater flexibility in the rotation period

2.6 Audit committee chairs of some of the largest listed companies and audit firms believe that more flexibility should be introduced on the largest, most complex listed companies. These audit committee chairs believe that in some circumstances extending the rotation period of the current audit engagement partner could safeguard audit quality. Furthermore they believe that considering this matter would closely link in with their review of audit effectiveness under the Combined Code on Corporate Governance.[3]

2.7 Some of the respondents to the 2007 consultation paper who expressed a preference for maintaining the current five year rotation period also recognised that there may be circumstances where mandatory rotation after five years could act against the interests of the audited entity. Although some latitude on audit partner rotation is already provided for in ES 3 (Revised)[4], the APB understands that this flexibility is rarely used in practice.

2.8 It has therefore been suggested that the flexibility currently permitted in ES 3 (Revised) might usefully be extended to more situations provided that any extension of the rotation period is discussed with, and approved by, the audit committee. However, the APB recognises that there are a number of disadvantages to providing such flexibility, including the potential for uncertainty and inconsistency which it may create.

2.9 Following extensive discussion with a number of stakeholders on this proposal, the APB has developed a possible amendment to paragraph 16 of ES 3 (Revised) which clarifies the existing options and adds that an audit committee may extend the tenure of an audit engagement partner of a large listed company which is also either complex or diverse where the audit committee is satisfied with the objectivity of the audit engagement partner and considers that the quality of the audit will be safeguarded by extending the rotation period from five to seven years.

---

[3] *The review and monitoring of the external auditor's independence and objectivity and the effectiveness of the audit process is included in the role and responsibilities of the audit committee as set out in provision C.3.2 of the Combined Code on Corporate Governance, published in June 2008.*

[4] *ES 3 (Revised), paragraph 15 allows individuals to continue for a further two years when a company becomes listed. ES 3 (Revised), paragraph 16 enables a degree of flexibility where a reasonable and informed third party would regard the audit engagement partner's continuity as being especially important to the shareholders (e.g. where there are major changes to the client's structure or its senior management).*

> **Question 3:** The APB would appreciate commentators' views on whether it would be appropriate to provide greater flexibility to ES 3 (Revised) to permit in certain circumstances, and with the prior approval of the audit committee, the rotation period to be extended from five to seven years?

> **Question 4:** In addition to large listed companies which are also complex or diverse, are there any other circumstances where some flexibility as regards the rotation period for audit engagement partners on listed companies would be appropriate? If so, please explain the rationale for your views.

2.10 The APB considers that if more flexibility is to be introduced into the ESs relating to partner rotation it would need to be accompanied by disclosure to shareholders where it is utilised, together with the reasons for the extension from five years. In discussions with investors and audit committee chairs, these stakeholders agreed that such disclosure would be essential.

2.11 To achieve this disclosure the APB is exploring possible mechanisms by which such a disclosure might be made a requirement, including a possible change to the Combined Code on Corporate Governance. However any such change is unlikely in the near future. In the meantime a possible amendment to ES 3 (Revised) is illustrated in Appendix 1 which provides that:

- Where the audit committee and the audit firm agree that a rotation period will be extended, it is also agreed that the company will disclose this fact and the reasons for it to the shareholders; and
- If the company does not agree to make this disclosure, then the audit engagement partner does not continue in this role.

2.12 It is anticipated that such guidance on disclosure would be adhered to by companies and audit firms as non-disclosure would be brought to light by any inspections of individual audits and by the fact that the audit engagement partner is now required to sign the auditor's report in their own name.[5]

> **Question 5:** Do you agree that if an audit committee is able to decide to extend the period of rotation, this fact and the reasons for it should be disclosed to shareholders?

Managers with a long association becoming key partners involved in the audit

2.13 In the feedback paper to the 2007 review of the ESs, the APB noted that some commentators had requested further guidance on the safeguards to be applied when managers with a long association with an audited entity become key partners involved in the audit, in order to promote consistency in approach.

2.14 Currently where a partner or staff member in a senior position has been involved in the audit of a listed company for a continuous period longer than seven years, there

---

[5] Section 503(3) of the UK Companies Act 2006 requires that, where the auditor is a firm, the auditor's report must be signed by the "senior statutory auditor" in his own name for and on behalf of the auditor. Bulletin 2008/06 sets out guidance that the term "Senior Statutory Auditor" has the same meaning as the term "Engagement Partner". [6] ES 3 (Revised), paragraph 19.

is a requirement[6] that the audit engagement partner reviews the safeguards applied to reduce the self-interest, self-review and familiarity threats to an acceptable level. The APB understands that individual firms have adopted their own policies to cover such circumstances, the details of which differ.

2.15 The APB does not propose to prevent managers with a long association with an audited entity becoming key partners on the same audit. Indeed the APB is of the view that this practice can be an important mechanism in enabling continuity within the audit firm.

2.16 The current guidance on the safeguards to be applied in such situations is brief and additional guidance is proposed, referring to the factors that will affect the significance of the threats and some further examples of safeguards that might be applied where partners and staff are in senior positions on an audit engagement for a continuous period longer than seven years.

> **Question 6:** Do you agree that the APB should retain the existing requirement and provide additional guidance in respect of partners and staff in senior positions for a continuous period longer than seven years?

Rotation of Engagement Quality Control Reviewer

2.17 This issue was discussed at the stakeholder meeting held on 1st July 2008. Most parties at that meeting felt that the requirement for the engagement quality control reviewer (EQCR) on listed company audits to rotate after five years could be relaxed as the familiarity threat associated with their involvement is less than for the audit engagement partner and the other threats to objectivity and independence are less likely to apply. The APB agrees that a seven year rotation period is appropriate for the EQCR. In the draft amendments to the revised ESs, this is effected by switching the requirements relating to EQCRs from the paragraphs relating to the audit engagement partner into the paragraphs relating to the key partners involved in the audit.

> **Question 7:** Do you support the proposed extension of the rotation period for the EQCR on listed company audits to seven years?

3 Internal audit staff working directly for the audit team

3.1 The APB understands that there are instances where personnel from a company's internal audit function directly assist the external auditor in carrying out external audit procedures. This situation is not covered in ISA (UK and Ireland) 610, although it would seem that the same threats to independence that might arise would also exist where the auditor:

- relies on work already undertaken by internal audit function; or
- agrees that the internal audit function should undertake certain work and then places reliance on that work.

However, directly involving individual internal audit staff in the audit means that these individuals fall within the definition of the audit team[6]. Some believe that this results in dual employment which is not permitted under paragraph 36 of ES 2 (Revised). | 3.2

The APB considered a number of options associated with this issue and believes that including guidance in ISA (UK and Ireland) 610 would be an appropriate response, with a cross reference to this material in ES 2 (Revised). The APB believes that the threats associated with using internal audit staff to carry out external audit procedures are similar to situations where reliance is placed on other work carried out by the internal audit function. Accordingly the proposed amendment to ISA (UK and Ireland) 610 takes a similar approach by requiring members of the audit team to review the work undertaken, as well as agreeing the approach with those charged with governance in advance. | 3.3

IAASB has announced that it will be reviewing ISA 610 in the near future. One of the issues likely to be addressed as part of this review is internal audit staff working directly for the audit team and the APB intends to promote its approach to this issue to the IAASB at this time. The revision of ISA 610 will also provide an opportunity to explore other issues in connection with placing reliance on work undertaken by the internal audit function. | 3.4

> **Question 8:** Do you support the proposed approach of the APB towards internal audit staff working directly for the audit team?

4 Restructuring services

The consultation on revisions to the ESs identified a concern that there is a conflict of interest where the same firm provides both an audit and restructuring advice to the same company. In particular, any decision over whether to include an emphasis of matter paragraph with regard to going concern in the auditor's report could be influenced by the position taken in relation to the restructuring services. | 4.1

The recent sharp deterioration in economic conditions in the UK and Ireland suggest that in the coming year accounting firms are increasingly likely to be requested to provide restructuring advice to companies, including those to whom they provide audit services. | 4.2

The APB issued *Bulletin 2008/10: Going Concern Issues during the Current Economic Conditions* in December 2008, which included guidance on the ethical issues associated with the provision of non-audit services in relation to restructuring. These paragraphs were based on material already included in the ESs. The APB considers that there is value in bringing this material together in ES 5 (Revised) so as to clarify how the general approach to non-audit services applies to restructuring services. A new section to ES 5 (Revised) is therefore proposed, providing examples of the type of services included in the category of restructuring services and setting out the requirements and guidance associated with their provision to an audited entity. | 4.3

In order to meet concerns that a change to ES 5 (Revised) might disadvantage smaller companies in their negotiations with banks, the APB also proposes to make | 4.4

---

[6] All audit professionals who, regardless of their legal relationship with the auditor or audit firm, are assigned to a particular audit engagement in order to perform the audit task.

it clear in ES – Provisions Available for Small Entities (Revised) that a similar exemption to the advocacy threat associated with tax services would also apply to restructuring services.

> Question 9: Do you support the proposed approach of the APB towards the provision of restructuring services by the external auditor?

5 Securitisation services

5.1 During the Treasury Committee's inquiry into Northern Rock questions were asked about the nature of non-audit services provided by its auditor in 2006 and the impact that these had on auditor independence.

5.2 The non-audit services in question were described in the Northern Rock accounts as 'verification of historical financial information and the performance of certain agreed upon assurance procedures for securitisation transactions'. The APB understands that such services comprised work to verify that analyses of mortgage characteristics contained in prospectuses or investor presentations had been properly extracted from original documentation and were accurately collated. Additionally the SEC requires further work to be performed to confirm that controls and other administrative procedures have been performed for securitisations marketed in the US. The work is therefore similar in nature to both audit work and the work which a reporting accountant performs on prospectuses used by companies raising external finance by way of bond or rights issues.

5.3 The APB considers that such securitisation services are currently covered by the requirements in ES 5 (Revised) relating to transaction related services. In particular ES 5 (Revised), paragraph 119 prohibits transaction related services where:
- There is reasonable doubt as to the appropriateness of a related accounting treatment;
- Such services are provided on a contingent fee basis and:
  - The fees are material to the firm; or
  - The outcome is dependent on a future or contemporary audit judgment; or
- The engagement would involve the firm undertaking a management role.

5.4 In respect of the securitisation services supplied to Northern Rock, an analysis of the threats to auditor independence would suggest that:
- There do not appear to be any significant accounting judgments impacted by the securitisation process as the mortgages involved were included in the consolidated accounts;
- The fees for securitisation services are less than the group audit fees and the APB understands that there were no contingency fee or other special billing arrangements;
- In the prospectus, management made the assertions regarding characteristics of the mortgages in the mortgage pool that were then validated by the auditor. In these circumstances no management threat appears to arise.

5.5 As a result of the above analysis of the threats to auditor independence, the APB believes that there is no need to strengthen the current requirements of ES 5 (Revised) in respect of securitisation services.

> **Question 10: Do respondents support the APB's analysis and conclusion in relation to securitisation services?**

> **Question 11: ES 5 (Revised) paragraph 119 sets out the circumstances in which securitisation services would be prohibited. Are there other circumstances that should result in a prohibition?**

In order to make it clear where assurance services on transactions, such as those relating to securitisations are covered, the APB believes that adding a further example to paragraph 116 (and deleting one from paragraph 104) would clarify that any agreed upon procedures in connection with a transaction (including securitisations) are dealt with under transaction related services. These amendments are included in the extracts from ES 5 (Revised) in Appendix 1. 5.6

6 Financial interests of new partners joining the firm

In the feedback paper to the 2007 consultation the APB agreed to give further consideration to the 'all partner' prohibition on financial interests in audited entities[7]. In particular the APB has discussed the concern of some audit firms that they are restricted in their ability to appoint new partners from outside the firm where these individuals have existing financial interests involving entities that the firm audits which they are unable to unwind without significant penalties. 6.1

The APB proposes to insert an additional paragraph providing relief in respect of this prohibition, so as to permit financial interests of new partners joining the firm where there is no market for disposal in such financial interests, provided that the new partner is not involved in the provision of any services to the entity concerned and that they work in a different part of the firm to the audit engagement partner. 6.2

> **Question 12: Do you support the proposed relaxation of the ESs with respect to financial interests of new partners joining the firm?**

7 Amendments to align with agreed IFAC Code revisions

Governance roles

In its Scope and Authority of Pronouncements the APB states that it is not aware of any significant instances where the relevant parts of the IFAC Code are more restrictive than the ESs. However, the International Ethics Standards Board for Accountants is currently revising aspects of the IFAC Code and the APB has reviewed the draft revised IFAC Code to identify areas where it appears to be more stringent than the ESs. As a result of this review, the APB believes that it is necessary to make one amendment to the ESs in respect of governance roles. 7.1

The subject of governance roles with an audited entity is covered in ES 2 (Revised), paragraphs 52 to 55. IFAC has a prohibition on <u>all partners and employees</u> of the audit firm from serving as a director or officer of an audit client. The prohibition in 7.2

[7] *ES 2 (Revised), paragraph 7.*

ES 2 (Revised) is narrower, relating to all partners and employees of the audit firm who undertake audit work. It is proposed that the scope of paragraph 53 of ES 2 (Revised) be extended to all partners and employees of the audit firm.

> **Question 13: Do you support the proposed strengthening of the ESs with respect to governance roles with an audited entity?**

Definition of an affiliate of an audited entity

7.3 Additionally, in the feedback paper on the 2007 review of the ESs, the APB agreed to reconsider what actions might be taken with a view to bringing the definition of an affiliate more into line with the IFAC Code definition of a related entity[8].

7.4 While the APB believes that its current definition of an affiliate is in substance equivalent to the definition of a related entity in the IFAC Code, it understands that audit firms find the APB definition difficult to apply in practice.

7.5 However, the APB is uncomfortable with adopting the IFAC Code definition as it establishes a materiality test for some entities. The APB believes that in some circumstances the materiality test used does not provide an appropriate criterion as to whether an entity should be included in the scope of the definition of an affiliate. For example, in relation to the provision of non-audit services the significance of self-interest threats does not depend on the size of the entity to whom they are provided, but rather on a variety of other factors related to auditor independence, such as the nature of the non-audit service and the amount of fees.

7.6 The APB has therefore developed a proposed definition of an affiliate that uses a different term (clearly insignificant in relation to auditor independence), for determining those entities that should be treated as affiliates for the purposes of the ESs. The APB believes that the proposed definition uses clearer language and the clearly insignificant test minimises the scope for subjectivity, since the burden of proof is reversed so as to guide audit firms towards a more cautious approach.

7.7 The current APB definition of affiliate does not contain a 'materiality' test. Adding the proposed 'clearly insignificant' test moves the APB definition some way towards the IFAC Code definition.

7.8 This proposal not to align the definition for affiliates precisely with that used in the IFAC Code does not detract from the APB's support for the international harmonisation of ethical standards for accountants. Whilst the APB recognises that its proposed definition will result in a tougher standard than the IFAC Code, it believes that its analysis of the issues will be helpful in achieving a common international definition. The APB intends to communicate to the International Ethics Standards

---

[8] *Related entity* – An entity that has any of the following relationships with the client:
 (a) An entity that has direct or indirect control over the client if the client is material to such entity;
 (b) An entity with a direct financial interest in the client if that such entity has significant influence over the client and the interest in the client is material to such entity;
 (c) An entity over which the client has direct or indirect control;
 (d) An entity in which the client, or an entity related to the client under (c) above, has a direct financial interest that gives it significant influence over such entity and the interest is material to the client and its related entity in (c); and
 (e) An entity which is under common control with the client (a "sister entity") if the sister entity and the client are both material to the entity that controls both the client and sister entity.

Board for Accountants its views on their definition of a related entity with a view to improving the IFAC Code in the future.

> Question 14: Do you support the APB's proposed definition of an affiliate?

8 Remuneration and evaluation policies

The requirement for remuneration and evaluation policies in ES 4 (Revised) applies to the audit team, which only includes audit professionals. As part of its inspection work in 2007/08, the FRC's Audit Inspection Unit (AIU) identified that some firms permit senior specialist personnel from outside the audit function who are involved in audits to be rewarded for selling non-audit services to audited entities or for their performance to be evaluated based on their success in selling non-audit services to audited entities.   8.1

The APB has considered this matter and agrees with the view of the AIU that, although the ESs do not explicitly address the issue, the inclusion of key partners involved in the audit in such reward and performance evaluation processes is not in line with the underlying principles of the ESs. In the draft amendments to the ESs the APB has therefore extended the requirement for remuneration and evaluation policies and procedures to key partners involved in the audit.   8.2

> Question 15: Do you support the proposed change to the ESs with respect to extending the requirements relating to remuneration and evaluation policies to key partners involved in the audit?

The APB has also considered whether this requirement should be extended to partners (other than key partners involved in the audit) and staff from non-audit disciplines who are assigned to the audit and who undertake a substantial part of some of the audit procedures. However, the APB doubts whether a significant threat to independence arises from this and therefore believes that further restriction through the ESs is likely to be disproportionate.   8.3

> Question 16: Do you believe that the requirement for remuneration and evaluation policies should be applied to other partners and staff from non-audit disciplines?

9 Valuation of non-cash consideration for shares

During the development of the APB Bulletin, *Miscellaneous Reports by Auditors required by the UK Companies Act 2006*, the APB discussed whether paragraph 60 in ES 5 (Revised)[9] and the footnote to it remained appropriate.   9.1

Further exploration of this topic suggested that the material in ES 5 (Revised) seemed to provide more encouragement for a company's auditor to undertake a valuation required by Section 593 of the Companies Act 2006 than is offered by the   9.2

---
[9] This paragraph states: 'In circumstances where the auditor is designated by legislation or regulation as being eligible to carry out a valuation... such a valuation would not be a non-audit service, ...' A footnote gives Section 593 of the Companies Act 2006 as an example of a circumstance when this guidance might apply.

law. This seems to conflict with international developments which are generally becoming more restrictive with regard to auditors undertaking valuations.

9.3 The APB therefore proposes that ES 5 (Revised) should be amended, so that the auditor is only permitted to undertake a valuation that is otherwise prohibited under ES 5 (Revised), where this is required by legislation or regulation.

9.4 The amendments associated with this change apply not only to valuations, but to other non-audit services. Amendments are therefore also proposed to the general approach to non-audit services and where specific reference is made to this provision.

> **Question 17: Do you support the proposed strengthening of the ESs with respect to valuations and other non-audit services where legislation provides that the auditor is eligible to carry out a non-audit service, but does not require the auditor to undertake such work?**

Appendix 1 – Exposure Draft of Revisions to APB Ethical Standards for Auditors and ISA (UK and Ireland) 610

Extracts from ES 2 (Revised): Financial, business, employment and personal relationships

7   Save where the circumstances contemplated in paragraphs [A], 9, 11, 18 or 20 apply, the audit firm, any partner in the audit firm, a person in a position to influence the conduct and outcome of the audit or an immediate family member of such a person shall not hold:
   (a) any direct financial interest in an audited entity or an affiliate of an audited entity; or
   (b) any indirect financial interest in an audited entity or an affiliate of an audited entity, where the investment is material to the audit firm or the individual, or to the intermediary; or
   (c) any indirect financial interest in an audited entity or an affiliate of an audited entity, where the person holding it has both:
      (i) the ability to influence the investment decisions of the intermediary; and
      (ii) actual knowledge of the existence of the underlying investment in the audited entity.

[A] Where a person joins the audit firm as a partner, he or she is not required to dispose of financial interests held where there is no market for such interests, or the individual has no entitlement to sell the interest, and the individual is not able to influence the affairs of the entity, provided:
   (a) The financial interests were acquired before the individual joined the audit firm; and
   (b) The partner in question:
      • is not in a position to influence the conduct and outcome of the audit;
      • does not work in the same part of the firm as the audit engagement partner; and
      • is not involved in the provision of a non-audit service to the audit client.
   Such a financial interest is disposed of as soon as possible after the individual becomes able to make a disposal. The audit firm maintains a record of individuals with such financial interests containing a description of the circumstances.

36 **An audit firm shall not admit to the partnership, or employ a person to undertake audit work, if that person is also employed by the audited entity or its affiliates ('dual employment').**
   [B] This requirement is not intended to preclude internal audit personnel directly assisting the external auditor in carrying out external audit procedures provided that appropriate quality control arrangements are established, as described in ISA (UK and Ireland) 610.

53 A partner, or employee of the audit firm ~~who undertakes audit work~~, shall not accept appointment:
   (a) to the board of directors of the audited entity;
   (b) to any subcommittee of that board; or
   (c) to such a position in an entity which holds directly or indirectly more than 20% of the voting rights in the audited entity, or in which the audited entity holds directly or indirectly more than 20% of the voting rights.

Extracts from ES 3 (Revised): Long association with the audit engagement

ADDITIONAL PROVISIONS RELATED TO AUDITS OF LISTED COMPANIES

The audit engagement partner and the engagement quality control reviewer

12   In the case of listed companies, save where the circumstances contemplated in paragraph 15 and 16 apply, the audit firm shall establish policies and procedures to ensure that:
   (a) no one shall act as audit engagement partner ~~or as engagement quality control reviewer~~ for ~~a period longer~~more than five years;
   ~~(b) where an engagement quality control reviewer becomes the audit engagement partner, the combined period of service in these positions shall not exceed five years; and~~
   (<u>b</u>e) anyone who has acted as the audit engagement partner ~~or the engagement quality control reviewer~~, or held a ~~combination of such positions,~~ for a particular audited entity for ~~a period of~~ five years, ~~whether continuously or in aggregate,~~ shall not <u>subsequently</u> participate in the audit engagement until a further period of five years has elapsed.

13   The roles that constitute participating in an audit engagement for the purposes of paragraph 12(<u>b</u>e), ... This is not intended to preclude partners whose primary responsibility within a firm is to be consulted on technical or industry specific issues from providing such consultation to the engagement team or client after a period of two years has elapsed from their ceasing to act as audit engagement partner ~~or engagement quality control reviewer~~, provided that such consultation is in respect of new issues or new types of transactions or events that were not previously required to be considered by that individual in the course of acting as audit engagement partner ~~or engagement quality control reviewer~~.

14   Where an audit engagement partner ~~or engagement quality control reviewer~~ continues in a non-audit role having been rotated off the engagement team, ...

15   When an audited entity becomes a listed company, the length of time the audit engagement partner has served the audited entity in that capacity is taken into account in calculating the period before the audit engagement partner is rotated off the engagement team. However, where the audit engagement partner has already served for four or more years, that individual may continue to serve as the audit engagement partner for not more than two years after the audited entity becomes a listed company.

16   <u>In circumstances where the audit committee (or equivalent) of the audited entity and the audit firm have agreed that a</u>~~Some~~ degree of flexibility over the timing of rotation ~~may be~~<u>would</u> safeguard the quality of the audit ~~necessary~~, the audit engagement partner may continue in this position for an additional period of up to two years, so that no longer than seven years in total is spent in the position of audit engagement partner~~in circumstances where a reasonable and informed third party would regard the audit engagement partner's continuity as being especially important to the shareholders of the audited entity. For example,~~ <u>An audit committee and the audit firm may consider that such flexibility safeguards the quality of the audit, for example, where</u>:
   • the audited entity is so large and either complex or diverse that the audit partner's cumulative knowledge of the business is critical to the audit; or

- ~~major~~ substantial change has recently been made or will soon be made to the nature or ~~audited entity's~~ structure of the audited entity's business; or
- there are unexpected changes in the~~ir~~ senior management of the audited entity ~~are expected that would otherwise coincide with the rotation of the audit engagement partner~~.

In these circumstances alternative safeguards are applied to reduce any threats to an acceptable level. Such safeguards may include ensuring that an expanded review of the audit work is undertaken by an audit partner, who is not involved in the audit engagement.

[C] Where it has been determined that the audit engagement partner may act for a further period (not to exceed two years), this fact and the reasons for it, are to be disclosed to the audited entity's shareholders, (preferably in the corporate governance statement within the annual report). If the audited entity is not prepared to make such a disclosure, the audit firm does not permit the audit engagement partner to continue in this role.

17 In the case of joint audit arrangements for listed companies, audit firms will make arrangements for changes of audit engagement partners ~~and engagement quality control reviewers~~ over a five-year period so that the familiarity threat is avoided, whilst also taking into consideration factors that affect the quality of the audit work.

Key partners involved in the audit

18 In the case of listed companies, the audit firm shall establish policies and procedures to ensure that:
   (a) no one shall act as the engagement quality control reviewer or a key partner involved in the audit for a ~~continuous~~ period longer than seven years;
   (b) where a~~n~~ engagement quality control reviewer or key partner involved in the audit becomes the audit engagement partner, the combined period of service in these positions shall not exceed seven years; and
   (c) anyone who has acted:
      (i) as an engagement quality control reviewer or key partner involved in the audit, or held a combination of such positions, for a particular audited entity for a period of seven years, whether continuously or in aggregate, shall not participate in the audit engagement until a further period of two years has elapsed;
      (ii) in a combination of roles as:
         - an engagement quality control reviewer or a key partner involved in the audit, and
         - the audit engagement partner
      for a particular audited entity for a period of seven years, whether continuously or in aggregate, shall not participate in the audit engagement until a further period of five years has elapsed.

Other partners and staff in senior positions

19 In the case of listed companies, the audit engagement partner shall review the safeguards put in place to address the threats to the auditor's objectivity and independence arising where partners and staff have been involved in the audit in senior positions for a continuous period longer than seven years and shall discuss those situations with the engagement quality control reviewer. Any unresolved problems or issues shall be referred to the ethics partner.

20 The significance of the threats arising where partners and staff have been involved in the audit in senior positions for a continuous period longer than seven years will depend on:
- the total period of time that the individual has been involved in the audit;
- changes in the nature of the work and the role performed by the individual during that period; and
- the portion of time the individual has spent on the audit and non-audit engagements with the audited entity during that period.

[D] Following the assessment of any such threats, appropriate safeguards are applied where necessary. Safeguards that address these threats arising from such a situation might include: the removal of the member of staff from, or
- the rotation of changes in the roles within, the engagement team;
- an additional review of the work done by the individual by the audit engagement partner or other partners in the engagement team;
- additional procedures carried out as part of the engagement quality control review.

If such safeguards do not reduce the threats to an acceptable level, the partner or member of staff is removed from the engagement team.

Extracts from ES 4 (Revised): Fees, remuneration and evaluation policies, litigation, gifts and hospitality

38 The audit firm shall establish policies and procedures to ensure that, in relation to each audited entity:
- (a) the objectives of the members of the audit team and key partners involved in the audit do not include selling non-audit services to the audited entity;
- (b) the criteria for evaluating the performance or promotion of members of the audit team and key partners involved in the audit do not include success in selling non-audit services to the audited entity; and
- (c) no specific element of the remuneration of a member of the audit team and key partners involved in the audit is based on his or her success in selling non-audit services to the audited entity.

Extracts from ES 5 (Revised): Non-audit services provided to audit clients

6 In this Standard, 'non-audit services' comprise any engagement in which an audit firm provides professional services to an audited entity other than:
- (a) the audit of financial statements; and
- (b) pursuant to those other roles which are required by legislation or regulation specify can to be performed by the auditor of the entity (for example, considering the preliminary announcements of listed companies, complying with the procedural and reporting requirements of regulators, such as requirements relating to the audit of the audited entity's internal controls and a report in accordance with Section 714 of the Companies Act 2006).

In the case of a group, non-audit services include services provided by the audit firm, to the parent company or to any affiliate.

60 In circumstances where the auditor is designated by legislation or regulation as being ~~eligible~~ required to carry out a valuation[10] the restrictions in paragraph 56 do not apply as such a valuation would not be a non-audit service, as provided by paragraph 6. In such circumstances, the audit engagement partner applies relevant safeguards.

CORPORATE FINANCE SERVICES

104 The range of services encompassed by the term 'corporate finance services' is wide. For example, the audit firm may be engaged:
- to identify possible purchasers for parts of the audited entity's business and provide advisory services in the course of such sales; or
- to identify possible 'targets' for the audited entity to acquire; or
- to advise the audited entity on how to fund its financing requirements, including advising on debt restructuring and ~~securitisation programmes~~; or
- to act as sponsor on admission to listing on the London Stock Exchange, or as Nominated Advisor on the admission of the audited entity on the Alternative Investments Market (AIM); or
- to act as financial adviser to audited entity offerors or offerees in connection with public takeovers.

115 These restrictions do not apply in circumstances where the auditor is designated by legislation or regulation as being ~~eligible~~ required to carry out a particular service, since such a service would not be a non-audit service, as provided by paragraph 6. In such circumstances, the audit engagement partner establishes appropriate safeguards.

TRANSACTION RELATED SERVICES

116 In addition to corporate finance services, there are other non-audit services associated with transactions that an audit firm may undertake for an audited entity. For example:
- investigations into possible acquisitions or disposals ('due diligence' investigations); or
- investigations into the tax affairs of possible acquisitions or disposals; or
- the provision of information to management or sponsors in relation to prospectuses and other investment circulars (for example, long form reports, comfort letters on the adequacy of working capital); or
- agreed upon procedures or reports provided to management in relation to particular transactions (for example, securitisations).

122 These restrictions do not apply in circumstances where the auditor is designated by legislation or regulation as being ~~eligible~~ required to carry out a particular service, since such a service would not be a non-audit service, as provided by paragraph 6. In such circumstances, the audit engagement partner establishes appropriate safeguards.

---

[10] ~~For example, Section 593 of the Companies Act 2006 requires a public company to obtain an independent valuation on assets to be received in full or part payment for shares to be allotted from a person who is eligible for appointment as a statutory auditor.~~

RESTRUCTURING SERVICES

[E] The potential for the auditor's objectivity and independence to be impaired through the provision of non-audit services in relation to a refinancing or restructuring engagement varies depending on the nature of the service provided. The main threats to auditor objectivity and independence arising from the provision of restructuring services are the self-review, management and advocacy threats.

[F] Examples of restructuring services that the audit firm may be requested to undertake and which may give rise to threats to the auditor's independence and objectivity include:
- Undertaking a review of the business with a view to advising the audited entity on restructuring options.
- Advising on forecasts or projections, for presentation to lenders and other stakeholders, including assumptions.
- Advising the audited entity on how to fund its financing requirements, including debt restructuring programmes.

[G] **The audit firm shall not undertake an engagement to provide restructuring services in respect of an audited entity where:**
   (a) **the engagement would involve the audit firm undertaking a management role in the audited entity; or**
   (b) **the engagement would require**
      the auditor to act as an advocate for the entity in relation to matters that are material to the financial statements.

[H] When providing restructuring services to an audited entity, there is a self-review threat associated with any advice provided to assist the audited entity in that regard and the auditor's assessment of whether it is appropriate for the financial statements to be prepared on a going concern basis. Appropriate safeguards are applied to reduce the self-review threat to an acceptable level.

[I] Examples of safeguards that may be appropriate when restructuring services are provided to an audited entity include:
- The restructuring advice is provided by partners and staff who have no involvement in the audit of the financial statements.
- A review by a partner or other senior staff member with appropriate expertise who has no involvement in the audit of the financial statements of the assessment as to whether it is appropriate for the financial statements to be prepared on a going concern basis.
- Additional procedures undertaken as part of an Engagement Quality Control Review.

[J] Where the audit firm is engaged to provide restructuring services to an audited entity there is a threat that the audit firm undertakes a management role, unless the audit firm ensures that the entity has informed management[11] capable of taking responsibility for the decisions to be made.

[K] If the audit firm attends meetings with the entity's bank or other interested parties it takes particular care to avoid assuming responsibility for the entity's proposals or being regarded as negotiating on behalf of the entity or advocating the appropriateness of the proposals such that its independence is compromised.

---

[11] 'ES – Provisions Available for Small Entities' provides exemptions relating to informed management for auditors of small entities.

Extracts from ES – Provisions Available for Small Entities (Revised)

15   The audit firm of a Small Entity is not required to comply with APB Ethical Standard 5, paragraphs 82 and [G](b) provided that it discloses the fact that it has applied this Standard in accordance with paragraph 22.

16   APB Ethical Standard 5, paragraph 82 provides that 'the audit firm shall not undertake an engagement to provide tax services to an audited entity where this would involve acting as an advocate for the audited entity, before an appeals tribunal or court in the resolution of an issue:
(a)   that is material to the financial statements; or
(b)   where the outcome of the tax issue is dependent on a future or contemporary audit judgment'.

[L]   APB Ethical Standard 5, paragraph [G](b) provides that 'the audit firm shall not undertake an engagement to provide restructuring services in respect of an audited entity where the engagement would require the auditor to act as an advocate for the entity in relation to matters that are material to the financial statements'.

[M]   Such circumstances may create an advocacy threat which it is unlikely any safeguards can eliminate or reduce to an acceptable level.

17   Where an audit firm auditing a Small Entity takes advantage of the dispensation in paragraph 15, it discloses the fact that it has applied this Standard in accordance with paragraph 22.

Extracts from Glossary of terms

affiliate   Any entity~~undertaking~~ which, directly or indirectly,:

(a)   is ~~connected to another by means of common ownership,~~ controlled or significantly influenced by the audited entity;

(b)   has control or significant influence over the audited entity;

(c)   is under common control with the audited entity; except where, in (b) or (c) above, the relationship between the audited entity and the other entity, or between the audit firm and the relevant entity, is clearly insignificant[12] in relation to auditor independence. ~~or management.~~

Extracts from ISA (UK and Ireland) 610

1   The purpose of this International Standard on Auditing (UK and Ireland) (ISA (UK and Ireland)) is to establish standards and provide guidance to external auditors in considering the work of internal auditing. This ISA (UK and Ireland) ~~does not deal with~~ provides guidance on instances when personnel from internal auditing assist the external auditor in carrying out external audit procedures. The audit procedures noted in this ISA (UK and Ireland) need only be applied to internal auditing activities which are relevant to the audit of the financial statements.

---

[12] *Whenever there is any uncertainty about whether a relationship is 'clearly insignificant', then the presumption would be that the relevant entity should be included as an affiliate.*

16 **When the external auditor intends to use specific work of internal auditing, the external auditor should evaluate and perform audit procedures on that work to confirm its adequacy for the external auditor's purposes.**

17 The evaluation of specific work of internal auditing involves consideration of the adequacy of the scope of work and related programs and whether the assessment of the internal auditing remains appropriate. This evaluation may include consideration of whether ...

17-1 In addition to using specific work of an internal audit function, the external auditor may obtain direct assistance from individuals from the internal audit function. In addition to the considerations set out in paragraph 17, when direct assistance is provided by individuals from the internal audit function, the external auditor:
  (a) obtains a written confirmation from such individuals that they agree to follow the instructions of staff of the audit firm in relation to the work performed and that, where applicable, they will keep confidential specific matters as instructed by the audit team;
  (b) directly supervises, reviews and evaluates the work performed;
  (c) ensures that such individuals are only involved in work where self-review or judgment is not an important part of the audit procedure; and
  (d) communicates the details of the planned arrangements with those charged with governance at the planning stage of the audit, so as to agree this approach, as described in paragraph 11-9 of ISA (UK and Ireland) 260.

Part Three

*International Standards on Quality Control
(UK & Ireland)*

Part Three

International Standards on Quality Control
(U.K. & Ireland)

International Standard on Quality Control (UK and Ireland) 1

Quality control for firms that perform audits and reviews of historical financial information, and other assurance and related services engagements*

Contents

	Paragraphs
Introduction	1 – 5
Definitions	6
Elements of a System of Quality Control	7 – 8
Leadership Responsibilities for Quality Within the Firm	9 – 13
Ethical Requirements	14 – 27
Acceptance and Continuance of Client Relationships and Specific Engagements	28 – 35
Human Resources	36 – 45
Engagement Performance	46 – 73
Engagement Documentation	73a – 73l
Monitoring	74 – 93
Documentation	94 – 97
Effective Date	**98**

International Standard on Quality Control (UK and Ireland) (ISQC (UK and Ireland)) 1 "Quality Control for Firms that Perform Audits and Reviews of Historical Financial Information, and Other Assurance and Related Services Engagements" should be read in the context of the Auditing Practices Board's Statement "The Auditing Practices Board – Scope and Authority of Pronouncements (Revised)" which sets out the application and authority of ISQCs (UK and Ireland).

---

* Paragraphs 6(a) and 73a – 73l are conforming amendments introduced by ISA (UK and Ireland) 230 (Revised); associated changes to systems to be established by June 15, 2006.

Introduction

1 The purpose of this International Standard on Quality Control (UK and Ireland) (ISQC (UK and Ireland)) is to establish standards and provide guidance regarding a firm's responsibilities for its system of quality control for audits and reviews of historical financial information, and for other assurance and related services engagements. This ISQC (UK and Ireland) is to be read in conjunction with Parts A and B of the IFAC *Code of Ethics for Professional Accountants* (the IFAC Code).

1-1 In the UK and Ireland the relevant ethical pronouncements with which the auditor complies are the APB's Ethical Standards and the ethical pronouncements relating to the work of auditors issued by the auditor's relevant professional body -see the Statement "The Auditing practices Board – Scope and Authority of Pronouncements".

2 Additional standards and guidance on the responsibilities of firm personnel regarding quality control procedures for specific types of engagements are set out in other pronouncements of the International Auditing and Assurance Standards Board (IAASB). ISA (UK and Ireland) 220, "Quality Control for Audits of Historical Financial Information," for example, establishes standards and provides guidance on quality control procedures for audits of historical financial information.

3 **The firm should establish a system of quality control designed to provide it with reasonable assurance that the firm and its personnel comply with professional standards and regulatory and legal requirements, and that reports issued by the firm or engagement partners are appropriate in the circumstances.**

4 A system of quality control consists of policies designed to achieve the objectives set out in paragraph 3 and the procedures necessary to implement and monitor compliance with those policies.

5 This ISQC (UK and Ireland) applies to all firms. The nature of the policies and procedures developed by individual firms to comply with this ISQC (UK and Ireland) will depend on various factors such as the size and operating characteristics of the firm, and whether it is part of a network.

Definitions

6 In this ISQC (UK and Ireland), the following terms have the meanings attributed below:

(a) "Engagement documentation"–the record of work performed, results obtained, and conclusions the practitioner reached (terms such as "working papers" or "workpapers" are sometimes used). The documentation for a specific engagement is assembled in an engagement file;

(b) "Engagement partner" – the partner or other person in the firm who is responsible for the engagement and its performance, and for the report that is issued on behalf of the firm, and who, where required, has the appropriate authority from a professional, legal or regulatory body;

(c) "Engagement quality control review" – a process designed to provide an objective evaluation, before the report is issued, of the significant judgments the engagement team made and the conclusions they reached in formulating the report;

(d) "Engagement quality control reviewer" – a partner, other person in the firm, suitably qualified external person, or a team made up of such individuals, with sufficient and appropriate experience and authority to objectively evaluate, before the report is issued, the significant judgments the engagement team made and the conclusions they reached in formulating the report;
(e) "Engagement team" – all personnel performing an engagement, including any experts contracted by the firm in connection with that engagement;
(f) "Firm"* – a sole practitioner, partnership, corporation or other entity of professional accountants;
(g) "Inspection" – in relation to completed engagements, procedures designed to provide evidence of compliance by engagement teams with the firm's quality control policies and procedures;
(h) "Listed entity"* – an entity whose shares, stock or debt are quoted or listed on a recognized stock exchange, or are marketed under the regulations of a recognized stock exchange or other equivalent body;
(i) "Monitoring" – a process comprising an ongoing consideration and evaluation of the firm's system of quality control, including a periodic inspection of a selection of completed engagements, designed to enable the firm to obtain reasonable assurance that its system of quality control is operating effectively;
(j) "Network firm"* – an entity under common control, ownership or management with the firm or any entity that a reasonable and informed third party having knowledge of all relevant information would reasonably conclude as being part of the firm nationally or internationally;
(k) "Partner" – any individual with authority to bind the firm with respect to the performance of a professional services engagement;
(l) "Personnel" – partners and staff;
(m) "Professional standards" – IAASB Engagement Standards, as defined in the IAASB's "Preface to the International Standards on Quality Control, Auditing, Assurance and Related Services," and relevant ethical requirements, which ordinarily comprise Parts A and B of the IFAC Code and relevant national ethical requirements[1];
(n) "Reasonable assurance" – in the context of this ISQC (UK and Ireland), a high, but not absolute, level of assurance;
(o) "Staff" – professionals, other than partners, including any experts the firm employs; and
(p) "Suitably qualified external person" – an individual outside the firm with the capabilities and competence to act as an engagement partner, for example a partner of another firm, or an employee (with appropriate experience) of either a professional accountancy body whose members may perform audits and reviews of historical financial information, or other assurance or related services engagements, or of an organization that provides relevant quality control services.

Elements of a System of Quality Control

The firm's system of quality control should include policies and procedures addressing each of the following elements:

(a) **Leadership responsibilities for quality within the firm.**

7

---

* As defined in the IFAC Code published in November 2001.

[1] In the UK and Ireland the relevant ethical pronouncements with which the auditor complies are the APB's Ethical Standards and the ethical pronouncements relating to the work of auditors issued by the auditor's relevant professional body – see the Statement "The Auditing Practices Board – Scope and Authority of Pronouncements".

(b) **Ethical requirements.**
(c) **Acceptance and continuance of client relationships and specific engagements.**
(d) **Human resources.**
(e) **Engagement performance.**
(f) **Monitoring.**

8 **The quality control policies and procedures should be documented and communicated to the firm's personnel.** Such communication describes the quality control policies and procedures and the objectives they are designed to achieve, and includes the message that each individual has a personal responsibility for quality and is expected to comply with these policies and procedures. In addition, the firm recognizes the importance of obtaining feedback on its quality control system from its personnel. Therefore, the firm encourages its personnel to communicate their views or concerns on quality control matters.

Leadership Responsibilities for Quality Within the Firm

9 **The firm should establish policies and procedures designed to promote an internal culture based on the recognition that quality is essential in performing engagements. Such policies and procedures should require the firm's chief executive officer (or equivalent) or, if appropriate, the firm's managing board of partners (or equivalent), to assume ultimate responsibility for the firm's system of quality control.**

10 The firm's leadership and the examples it sets significantly influence the internal culture of the firm. The promotion of a quality-oriented internal culture depends on clear, consistent and frequent actions and messages from all levels of the firm's management emphasizing the firm's quality control policies and procedures, and the requirement to:

(a) Perform work that complies with professional standards and regulatory and legal requirements; and
(b) Issue reports that are appropriate in the circumstances.

Such actions and messages encourage a culture that recognizes and rewards high quality work. They may be communicated by training seminars, meetings, formal or informal dialogue, mission statements, newsletters, or briefing memoranda. They are incorporated in the firm's internal documentation and training materials, and in partner and staff appraisal procedures such that they will support and reinforce the firm's view on the importance of quality and how, practically, it is to be achieved.

11 Of particular importance is the need for the firm's leadership to recognize that the firm's business strategy is subject to the overriding requirement for the firm to achieve quality in all the engagements that the firm performs. Accordingly:

(a) The firm assigns its management responsibilities so that commercial considerations do not override the quality of work performed;
(b) The firm's policies and procedures addressing performance evaluation, compensation, and promotion (including incentive systems) with regard to its personnel, are designed to demonstrate the firm's overriding commitment to quality; and
(c) The firm devotes sufficient resources for the development, documentation and support of its quality control policies and procedures.

12 **Any person or persons assigned operational responsibility for the firm's quality control system by the firm's chief executive officer or managing board of partners should have**

sufficient and appropriate experience and ability, and the necessary authority, to assume that responsibility.

Sufficient and appropriate experience and ability enables the responsible person or persons to identify and understand quality control issues and to develop appropriate policies and procedures. Necessary authority enables the person or persons to implement those policies and procedures. 13

Ethical Requirements

The firm should establish policies and procedures designed to provide it with reasonable assurance that the firm and its personnel comply with relevant ethical requirements. 14

Ethical requirements relating to audits and reviews of historical financial information, and other assurance and related services engagements ordinarily comprise Parts A and B of the IFAC Code together with national requirements that are more restrictive[1]. The IFAC Code establishes the fundamental principles of professional ethics, which include: 15

(a) Integrity;
(b) Objectivity;
(c) Professional competence and due care;
(d) Confidentiality; and
(e) Professional behavior.

Part B of the IFAC Code includes a conceptual approach to independence for assurance engagements that takes into account threats to independence, accepted safeguards and the public interest[1]. 16

The firm's policies and procedures emphasize the fundamental principles, which are reinforced in particular by (a) the leadership of the firm, (b) education and training, (c) monitoring and (d) a process for dealing with non-compliance. Independence for assurance engagements is so significant that it is addressed separately in paragraphs 18-27 below. These paragraphs need to be read in conjunction with the IFAC Code[1]. 17

Independence

The firm should establish policies and procedures designed to provide it with reasonable assurance that the firm, its personnel and, where applicable, others subject to independence requirements (including experts contracted by the firm and network firm personnel), maintain independence where required by the IFAC Code and national ethical requirements[1]. Such policies and procedures should enable the firm to: 18

(a) Communicate its independence requirements to its personnel and, where applicable, others subject to them; and
(b) Identify and evaluate circumstances and relationships that create threats to independence, and to take appropriate action to eliminate those threats or reduce them to an acceptable level by applying safeguards, or, if considered appropriate, to withdraw from the engagement.

Such policies and procedures should require: 19

(a) Engagement partners to provide the firm with relevant information about client engagements, including the scope of services, to enable the firm to evaluate the overall impact, if any, on independence requirements;

(b) Personnel to promptly notify the firm of circumstances and relationships that create a threat to independence so that appropriate action can be taken; and
(c) The accumulation and communication of relevant information to appropriate personnel so that:
    (i) The firm and its personnel can readily determine whether they satisfy independence requirements;
    (ii) The firm can maintain and update its records relating to independence; and
    (iii) The firm can take appropriate action regarding identified threats to independence.

20 The firm should establish policies and procedures designed to provide it with reasonable assurance that it is notified of breaches of independence requirements, and to enable it to take appropriate actions to resolve such situations. The policies and procedures should include requirements for:

(a) All who are subject to independence requirements to promptly notify the firm of independence breaches of which they become aware;
(b) The firm to promptly communicate identified breaches of these policies and procedures to:
    (i) The engagement partner who, with the firm, needs to address the breach; and
    (ii) Other relevant personnel in the firm and those subject to the independence requirements who need to take appropriate action; and
(c) Prompt communication to the firm, if necessary, by the engagement partner and the other individuals referred to in subparagraph (b)(ii) of the actions taken to resolve the matter, so that the firm can determine whether it should take further action.

21 Comprehensive guidance on threats to independence and safeguards, including application to specific situations, is set out in Section 8 of the IFAC Code¹.

22 A firm receiving notice of a breach of independence policies and procedures promptly communicates relevant information to engagement partners, others in the firm as appropriate and, where applicable, experts contracted by the firm and network firm personnel, for appropriate action. Appropriate action by the firm and the relevant engagement partner includes applying appropriate safeguards to eliminate the threats to independence or to reduce them to an acceptable level, or withdrawing from the engagement. In addition, the firm provides independence education to personnel who are required to be independent.

23 At least annually, the firm should obtain written confirmation of compliance with its policies and procedures on independence from all firm personnel required to be independent by the IFAC Code and national ethical requirements¹.

24 Written confirmation may be in paper or electronic form. By obtaining confirmation and taking appropriate action on information indicating noncompliance, the firm demonstrates the importance that it attaches to independence and makes the issue current for, and visible to, its personnel.

25 The IFAC Code¹ discusses the familiarity threat that may be created by using the same senior personnel on an assurance engagement over a long period of time and the safeguards that might be appropriate to address such a threat. **Accordingly, the firm should establish policies and procedures:**

(a) **Setting out criteria for determining the need for safeguards to reduce the familiarity threat to an acceptable level when using the same senior personnel on an assurance engagement over a long period of time; and**

(b) For all audits of financial statements of listed entities, requiring the rotation of the engagement partner after a specified period in compliance with the IFAC Code and national ethical requirements that are more restrictive[1].

Using the same senior personnel on assurance engagements over a prolonged period may create a familiarity threat or otherwise impair the quality of performance of the engagement. Therefore, the firm establishes criteria for determining the need for safeguards to address this threat. In determining appropriate criteria, the firm considers such matters as (a) the nature of the engagement, including the extent to which it involves a matter of public interest, and (b) the length of service of the senior personnel on the engagement. Examples of safeguards include rotating the senior personnel or requiring an engagement quality control review. 26

The IFAC Code[1] recognizes that the familiarity threat is particularly relevant in the context of financial statement audits of listed entities. For these audits, the IFAC Code[1] requires the rotation of the engagement partner after a pre-defined period, normally no more than seven years[2], and provides related standards and guidance. National requirements may establish shorter rotation periods. 27

Acceptance and Continuance of Client Relationships and Specific Engagements

The firm should establish policies and procedures for the acceptance and continuance of client relationships and specific engagements, designed to provide it with reasonable assurance that it will only undertake or continue relationships and engagements where it: 28

(a) Has considered the integrity of the client and does not have information that would lead it to conclude that the client lacks integrity;
(b) Is competent to perform the engagement and has the capabilities, time and resources to do so; and
(c) Can comply with ethical requirements.

The firm should obtain such information as it considers necessary in the circumstances before accepting an engagement with a new client, when deciding whether to continue an existing engagement, and when considering acceptance of a new engagement with an existing client. Where issues have been identified, and the firm decides to accept or continue the client relationship or a specific engagement, it should document how the issues were resolved.

With regard to the integrity of a client, matters that the firm considers include, for example: 29

- The identity and business reputation of the client's principal owners, key management, related parties and those charged with its governance.
- The nature of the client's operations, including its business practices.
- Information concerning the attitude of the client's principal owners, key management and those charged with its governance towards such matters as aggressive interpretation of accounting standards and the internal control environment.
- Whether the client is aggressively concerned with maintaining the firm's fees as low as possible.

---

[2] *APB Ethical Standard 3, "Long Association With The Audit Engagement," requires that, save for particular circumstances described therein, no one should act as audit engagement partner or as independent partner for a listed company for a continuous period longer than 5 years.*

- Indications of an inappropriate limitation in the scope of work.
- Indications that the client might be involved in money laundering or other criminal activities.
- The reasons for the proposed appointment of the firm and non-reappointment of the previous firm.

The extent of knowledge a firm will have regarding the integrity of a client will generally grow within the context of an ongoing relationship with that client.

30 Information on such matters that the firm obtains may come from, for example:

- Communications with existing or previous providers of professional accountancy services to the client in accordance with the IFAC Code[1], and discussions with other third parties.
- Inquiry of other firm personnel or third parties such as bankers, legal counsel and industry peers.
- Background searches of relevant databases.

31 In considering whether the firm has the capabilities, competence, time and resources to undertake a new engagement from a new or an existing client, the firm reviews the specific requirements of the engagement and existing partner and staff profiles at all relevant levels. Matters the firm considers include whether:

- Firm personnel have knowledge of relevant industries or subject matters;
- Firm personnel have experience with relevant regulatory or reporting requirements, or the ability to gain the necessary skills and knowledge effectively;
- The firm has sufficient personnel with the necessary capabilities and competence;
- Experts are available, if needed;
- Individuals meeting the criteria and eligibility requirements to perform engagement quality control review are available, where applicable; and
- The firm is able to complete the engagement within the reporting deadline.

32 The firm also considers whether accepting an engagement from a new or an existing client may give rise to an actual or perceived conflict of interest. Where a potential conflict is identified, the firm considers whether it is appropriate to accept the engagement.

33 Deciding whether to continue a client relationship includes consideration of significant matters that have arisen during the current or previous engagements, and their implications for continuing the relationship. For example, a client may have started to expand its business operations into an area where the firm does not possess the necessary knowledge or expertise.

34 **Where the firm obtains information that would have caused it to decline an engagement if that information had been available earlier, policies and procedures on the continuance of the engagement and the client relationship should include consideration of:**

  (a) **The professional and legal responsibilities that apply to the circumstances, including whether there is a requirement for the firm to report to the person or persons who made the appointment or, in some cases, to regulatory authorities; and**

  (b) **The possibility of withdrawing from the engagement or from both the engagement and the client relationship.**

35 Policies and procedures on withdrawal from an engagement or from both the engagement and the client relationship address issues that include the following:

- Discussing with the appropriate level of the client's management and those charged with its governance regarding the appropriate action that the firm might take based on the relevant facts and circumstances.
- If the firm determines that it is appropriate to withdraw, discussing with the appropriate level of the client's management and those charged with its governance withdrawal from the engagement or from both the engagement and the client relationship, and the reasons for the withdrawal.
- Considering whether there is a professional, regulatory or legal requirement for the firm to remain in place, or for the firm to report the withdrawal from the engagement, or from both the engagement and the client relationship, together with the reasons for the withdrawal, to regulatory authorities.
- Documenting significant issues, consultations, conclusions and the basis for the conclusions.

Human Resources

The firm should establish policies and procedures designed to provide it with reasonable assurance that it has sufficient personnel with the capabilities, competence, and commitment to ethical principles necessary to perform its engagements in accordance with professional standards and regulatory and legal requirements, and to enable the firm or engagement partners to issue reports that are appropriate in the circumstances. 36

Such policies and procedures address the following personnel issues: 37

- Recruitment;
- Performance evaluation;
- Capabilities;
- Competence;
- Career development;
- Promotion;
- Compensation; and
- The estimation of personnel needs.

Addressing these issues enables the firm to ascertain the number and characteristics of the individuals required for the firm's engagements. The firm's recruitment processes include procedures that help the firm select individuals of integrity with the capacity to develop the capabilities and competence necessary to perform the firm's work.

Capabilities and competence are developed through a variety of methods, including the following: 38

- Professional education.
- Continuing professional development, including training.
- Work experience.
- Coaching by more experienced staff, for example, other members of the engagement team.

The continuing competence of the firm's personnel depends to a significant extent on an appropriate level of continuing professional development so that personnel maintain their knowledge and capabilities. The firm therefore emphasizes in its policies and procedures the need for continuing training for all levels of firm personnel, and provides the necessary training resources and assistance to enable personnel to develop and maintain the required capabilities and competence. Where 39 internal technical and training resources are unavailable, or for any other reason, the firm may use a suitably qualified external person for that purpose.

40 The firm's performance evaluation, compensation and promotion procedures give due recognition and reward to the development and maintenance of competence and commitment to ethical principles. In particular, the firm:

(a) Makes personnel aware of the firm's expectations regarding performance and ethical principles;
(b) Provides personnel with evaluation of, and counseling on, performance, progress and career development; and
(c) Helps personnel understand that advancement to positions of greater responsibility depends, among other things, upon performance quality and adherence to ethical principles, and that failure to comply with the firm's policies and procedures may result in disciplinary action.

41 The size and circumstances of the firm will influence the structure of the firm's performance evaluation process. Smaller firms, in particular, may employ less formal methods of evaluating the performance of their personnel.

Assignment of Engagement Teams

42 **The firm should assign responsibility for each engagement to an engagement partner. The firm should establish policies and procedures requiring that:**

(a) **The identity and role of the engagement partner are communicated to key members of client management and those charged with governance;**
(b) **The engagement partner has the appropriate capabilities, competence, authority and time to perform the role; and**
(c) **The responsibilities of the engagement partner are clearly defined and communicated to that partner.**

43 Policies and procedures include systems to monitor the workload and availability of engagement partners so as to enable these individuals to have sufficient time to adequately discharge their responsibilities.

44 **The firm should also assign appropriate staff with the necessary capabilities, competence and time to perform engagements in accordance with professional standards and regulatory and legal requirements, and to enable the firm or engagement partners to issue reports that are appropriate in the circumstances.**

45 The firm establishes procedures to assess its staff's capabilities and competence. The capabilities and competence considered when assigning engagement teams, and in determining the level of supervision required, include the following:

- An understanding of, and practical experience with, engagements of a similar nature and complexity through appropriate training and participation.
- An understanding of professional standards and regulatory and legal requirements.
- Appropriate technical knowledge, including knowledge of relevant information technology.
- Knowledge of relevant industries in which the clients operate.
- Ability to apply professional judgment.
- An understanding of the firm's quality control policies and procedures.

Engagement Performance

46 The firm should establish policies and procedures designed to provide it with reasonable assurance that engagements are performed in accordance with professional standards and regulatory and legal requirements, and that the firm or the engagement partner issue reports that are appropriate in the circumstances.

47 Through its policies and procedures, the firm seeks to establish consistency in the quality of engagement performance. This is often accomplished through written or electronic manuals, software tools or other forms of standardized documentation, and industry or subject matter-specific guidance materials. Matters addressed include the following:

- How engagement teams are briefed on the engagement to obtain an understanding of the objectives of their work.
- Processes for complying with applicable engagement standards.
- Processes of engagement supervision, staff training and coaching.
- Methods of reviewing the work performed, the significant judgments made and the form of report being issued.
- Appropriate documentation of the work performed and of the timing and extent of the review.
- Processes to keep all policies and procedures current.

48 It is important that all members of the engagement team understand the objectives of the work they are to perform. Appropriate team-working and training are necessary to assist less experienced members of the engagement team to clearly understand the objectives of the assigned work.

49 Supervision includes the following:

- Tracking the progress of the engagement.
- Considering the capabilities and competence of individual members of the engagement team, whether they have sufficient time to carry out their work, whether they understand their instructions and whether the work is being carried out in accordance with the planned approach to the engagement.
- Addressing significant issues arising during the engagement, considering their significance and modifying the planned approach appropriately.
- Identifying matters for consultation or consideration by more experienced engagement team members during the engagement.

50 Review responsibilities are determined on the basis that more experienced engagement team members, including the engagement partner, review work performed by less experienced team members. Reviewers consider whether:

(a) The work has been performed in accordance with professional standards and regulatory and legal requirements;
(b) Significant matters have been raised for further consideration;
(c) Appropriate consultations have taken place and the resulting conclusions have been documented and implemented;
(d) There is a need to revise the nature, timing and extent of work performed;
(e) The work performed supports the conclusions reached and is appropriately documented;
(f) The evidence obtained is sufficient and appropriate to support the report; and
(g) The objectives of the engagement procedures have been achieved.

Consultation

51 The firm should establish policies and procedures designed to provide it with reasonable assurance that:

   (a) Appropriate consultation takes place on difficult or contentious **matters;**
   (b) **Sufficient resources are available to enable appropriate consultation to take place;**
   (c) **The nature and scope of such consultations are documented; and**
   (d) **Conclusions resulting from consultations are documented and implemented.**

52 Consultation includes discussion, at the appropriate professional level, with individuals within or outside the firm who have specialized expertise, to resolve a difficult or contentious matter.

53 Consultation uses appropriate research resources as well as the collective experience and technical expertise of the firm. Consultation helps to promote quality and improves the application of professional judgment. The firm seeks to establish a culture in which consultation is recognized as a strength and encourages personnel to consult on difficult or contentious matters.

54 Effective consultation with other professionals requires that those consulted be given all the relevant facts that will enable them to provide informed advice on technical, ethical or other matters. Consultation procedures require consultation with those having appropriate knowledge, seniority and experience within the firm (or, where applicable, outside the firm) on significant technical, ethical and other matters, and appropriate documentation and implementation of conclusions resulting from consultations.

55 A firm needing to consult externally, for example, a firm without appropriate internal resources, may take advantage of advisory services provided by (a) other firms, (b) professional and regulatory bodies, or (c) commercial organizations that provide relevant quality control services. Before contracting for such services, the firm considers whether the external provider is suitably qualified for that purpose.

56 The documentation of consultations with other professionals that involve difficult or contentious matters is agreed by both the individual seeking consultation and the individual consulted. The documentation is sufficiently complete and detailed to enable an understanding of:

   (a) The issue on which consultation was sought; and
   (b) The results of the consultation, including any decisions taken, the basis for those decisions and how they were implemented.

Differences of Opinion

57 The firm should establish policies and procedures for dealing with and resolving differences of opinion within the engagement team, with those consulted and, where applicable, between the engagement partner and the engagement quality control reviewer. Conclusions reached should be documented and implemented.

58 Such procedures encourage identification of differences of opinion at an early stage, provide clear guidelines as to the successive steps to be taken thereafter, and require documentation regarding the resolution of the differences and the implementation of the conclusions reached. **The report should not be issued until the matter is resolved.**

A firm using a suitably qualified external person to conduct an engagement quality   59
control review recognizes that differences of opinion can occur and establishes
procedures to resolve such differences, for example, by consulting with another
practitioner or firm, or a professional or regulatory body.

Engagement Quality Control Review

**The firm should establish policies and procedures requiring, for appropriate engage-   60
ments, an engagement quality control review that provides an objective evaluation of the
significant judgments made by the engagement team and the conclusions reached in
formulating the report. Such policies and procedures should:**

(a) **Require an engagement quality control review for all audits of financial statements
of listed entities;**
(b) **Set out criteria against which all other audits and reviews of historical financial
information, and other assurance and related services engagements should be
evaluated to determine whether an engagement quality control review should be
performed; and**
(c) **Require an engagement quality control review for all engagements meeting the
criteria established in compliance with subparagraph (b).**

**The firm's policies and procedures should require the completion of the engagement   61
quality control review before the report is issued.**

Criteria that a firm considers when determining which engagements other than audits   62
of financial statements of listed entities are to be subject to an engagement quality
control review include the following:

- The nature of the engagement, including the extent to which it involves a matter
  of public interest.
- The identification of unusual circumstances or risks in an engagement or class of
  engagements.
- Whether laws or regulations require an engagement quality control review.

The firm should establish policies and procedures setting out: 63

(a) **The nature, timing and extent of an engagement quality control review;**
(b) **Criteria for the eligibility of engagement quality control reviewers; and**
(c) **Documentation requirements for an engagement quality control review.**

Nature, Timing and Extent of the Engagement Quality Control Review

An engagement quality control review ordinarily involves discussion with the   64
engagement partner, a review of the financial statements or other subject matter
information and the report, and, in particular, consideration of whether the report is
appropriate. It also involves a review of selected working papers relating to the
significant judgments the engagement team made and the conclusions they reached.
The extent of the review depends on the complexity of the engagement and the risk
that the report might not be appropriate in the circumstances. The review does not
reduce the responsibilities of the engagement partner.

An engagement quality control review for audits of financial statements of listed   65
entities includes considering the following:

- The engagement team's evaluation of the firm's independence in relation to the
  specific engagement.

- Significant risks identified during the engagement and the responses to those risks.
- Judgments made, particularly with respect to materiality and significant risks.
- Whether appropriate consultation has taken place on matters involving differences of opinion or other difficult or contentious matters, and the conclusions arising from those consultations.
- The significance and disposition of corrected and uncorrected misstatements identified during the engagement.
- The matters to be communicated to management and those charged with governance and, where applicable, other parties such as regulatory bodies.
- Whether working papers selected for review reflect the work performed in relation to the significant judgments and support the conclusions reached.
- The appropriateness of the report to be issued.

Engagement quality control reviews for engagements other than audits of financial statements of listed entities may, depending on the circumstances, include some or all of these considerations.

66 The engagement quality control reviewer conducts the review in a timely manner at appropriate stages during the engagement so that significant matters may be promptly resolved to the reviewer's satisfaction before the report is issued.

67 Where the engagement quality control reviewer makes recommendations that the engagement partner does not accept and the matter is not resolved to the reviewer's satisfaction, the report is not issued until the matter is resolved by following the firm's procedures for dealing with differences of opinion.

Criteria for the Eligibility of Engagement Quality Control Reviewers

68 **The firm's policies and procedures should address the appointment of engagement quality control reviewers and establish their eligibility through:**

   (a) **The technical qualifications required to perform the role, including the necessary experience and authority; and**
   (b) **The degree to which an engagement quality control reviewer can be consulted on the engagement without compromising the reviewer's objectivity.**

69 The firm's policies and procedures on the technical qualifications of engagement quality control reviewers address the technical expertise, experience and authority necessary to perform the role. What constitutes sufficient and appropriate technical expertise, experience and authority depends on the circumstances of the engagement. In addition, the engagement quality control reviewer for an audit of the financial statements of a listed entity is an individual with sufficient and appropriate experience and authority to act as an audit engagement partner on audits of financial statements of listed entities.

70 The firm's policies and procedures are designed to maintain the objectivity of the engagement quality control reviewer. For example, the engagement quality control reviewer:

   (a) Is not selected by the engagement partner;
   (b) Does not otherwise participate in the engagement during the period of review;
   (c) Does not make decisions for the engagement team; and
   (d) Is not subject to other considerations that would threaten the reviewer's objectivity.

The engagement partner may consult the engagement quality control reviewer during the engagement. Such consultation need not compromise the engagement quality control reviewer's eligibility to perform the role. Where the nature and extent of the consultations become significant, however, care is taken by both the engagement team and the reviewer to maintain the reviewer's objectivity. Where this is not possible, another individual within the firm or a suitably qualified external person is appointed to take on the role of either the engagement quality control reviewer or the person to be consulted on the engagement. The firm's policies provide for the replacement of the engagement quality control reviewer where the ability to perform an objective review may be impaired.

71

Suitably qualified external persons may be contracted where sole practitioners or small firms identify engagements requiring engagement quality control reviews. Alternatively, some sole practitioners or small firms may wish to use other firms to facilitate engagement quality control reviews. Where the firm contracts suitably qualified external persons, the firm follows the requirements and guidance in paragraphs 68-71.

72

Documentation of the Engagement Quality Control Review

Policies and procedures on documentation of the engagement quality control review should require documentation that:

73

(a) The procedures required by the firm's policies on engagement quality control review have been performed;
(b) The engagement quality control review has been completed before the report is issued; and
(c) The reviewer is not aware of any unresolved matters that would cause the reviewer to believe that the significant judgments the engagement team made and the conclusions they reached were not appropriate.

Engagement Documentation

Completion of the Assembly of Final Engagement Files

The firm should establish policies and procedures for engagement teams to complete the assembly of final engagement files on a timely basis after the engagement reports have been finalized.

73a

Law or regulation may prescribe the time limits by which the assembly of final engagement files for specific types of engagement should be completed. Where no such time limits are prescribed in law or regulation, the firm establishes time limits appropriate to the nature of the engagements that reflect the need to complete the assembly of final engagement files on a timely basis. In the case of an audit, for example, such a time limit is ordinarily not more than 60 days after the date of the auditor's report.

73b

Where two or more different reports are issued in respect of the same subject matter information of an entity, the firm's policies and procedures relating to time limits for the assembly of final engagement files address each report as if it were for a separate engagement. This may, for example, be the case when the firm issues an auditor's report on a component's financial information for group consolidation purposes and, at a subsequent date, an auditor's report on the same financial information for statutory purposes.

73c

Confidentiality, Safe Custody, Integrity, Accessibility and Retrievability of Engagement Documentation

73d **The firm should establish policies and procedures designed to maintain the confidentiality, safe custody, integrity, accessibility and retrievability of engagement documentation.**

73e Relevant ethical requirements establish an obligation for the firm's personnel to observe at all times the confidentiality of information contained in engagement documentation, unless specific client authority has been given to disclose information, or there is a legal or professional duty to do so. Specific laws or regulations may impose additional obligations on the firm's personnel to maintain client confidentiality, particularly where data of a personal nature are concerned.

73f Whether engagement documentation is in paper, electronic or other media, the integrity, accessibility or retrievability of the underlying data may be compromised if the documentation could be altered, added to or deleted without the firm's knowledge, or if it could be permanently lost or damaged. Accordingly, the firm designs and implements appropriate controls for engagement documentation to:

(a) Enable the determinination of when and by whom engagement documentation was created, changed or reviewed;
(b) Protect the integrity of the information at all stages of the engagement, especially when the information is shared within the engagement team or transmitted to other parties via the Internet;
(c) Prevent unauthorized changes to the engagement documentation; and
(d) Allow access to the engagement documentation by the engagement team and other authorized parties as necessary to properly discharge their responsibilities.

73g Controls that the firm may design and implement to maintain the confidentiality, safe custody, integrity, accessibility and retrievability of engagement documentation include, for example:

- The use of a password among engagement team members to restrict access to electronic engagement documentation to authorized users.
- Appropriate back-up routines for electronic engagement documentation at appropriate stages during the engagement.
- Procedures for properly distributing engagement documentation to the team members at the start of engagement, processing it during engagement, and collating it at the end of engagement.
- Procedures for restricting access to, and enabling proper distribution and confidential storage of, hardcopy engagement documentation.

73h For practical reasons, original paper documentation may be electronically scanned for inclusion in engagement files. In that case, the firm implements appropriate procedures requiring engagement teams to:

(a) Generate scanned copies that reflect the entire content of the original paper documentation, including manual signatures, cross-references and annotations;
(b) Integrate the scanned copies into the engagement files, including indexing and signing off on the scanned copies as necessary; and
(c) Enable the scanned copies to be retrieved and printed as necessary.

The firm considers whether to retain original paper documentation that has been scanned for legal, regulatory or other reasons.

Retention of Engagement Documentation

The firm should establish policies and procedures for the retention of engagement documentation for a period sufficient to meet the needs of the firm or as required by law or regulation. 73i

The needs of the firm for retention of engagement documentation, and the period of such retention, will vary with the nature of the engagement and the firm's circumstances, for example, whether the engagement documentation is needed to provide a record of matters of continuing significance to future engagements. The retention period may also depend on other factors, such as whether local law or regulation prescribes specific retention periods for certain types of engagements, or whether there are generally accepted retention periods in the jurisdiction in the absence of specific legal or regulatory requirements. In the specific case of audit engagements, the retention period ordinarily is no shorter than five years from the date of the auditor's report, or, if later, the date of the group auditor's report. 73j

Procedures that the firm adopts for retention of engagement documentation include those that: 73k

- Enable the retrieval of, and access to, the engagement documentation during the retention period, particularly in the case of electronic documentation since the underlying technology may be upgraded or changed over time.
- Provide, where necessary, a record of changes made to engagement documentation after the engagement files have been completed.
- Enable authorized external parties to access and review specific engagement documentation for quality control or other purposes.

Ownership of Engagement Documentation

Unless otherwise specified by law or regulation, engagement documentation is the property of the firm. The firm may, at its discretion, make portions of, or extracts from, engagement documentation available to clients, provided such disclosure does not undermine the validity of the work performed, or, in the case of assurance engagements, the independence of the firm or its personnel. 73l

Monitoring

The firm should establish policies and procedures designed to provide it with reasonable assurance that the policies and procedures relating to the system of quality control are relevant, adequate, operating effectively and complied with in practice. Such policies and procedures should include an ongoing consideration and evaluation of the firm's system of quality control, including a periodic inspection of a selection of completed engagements. 74

The purpose of monitoring compliance with quality control policies and procedures is to provide an evaluation of: 75

(a) Adherence to professional standards and regulatory and legal requirements;
(b) Whether the quality control system has been appropriately designed and effectively implemented; and
(c) Whether the firm's quality control policies and procedures have been appropriately applied, so that reports that are issued by the firm or engagement partners are appropriate in the circumstances.

76 The firm entrusts responsibility for the monitoring process to a partner or partners or other persons with sufficient and appropriate experience and authority in the firm to assume that responsibility. Monitoring of the firm's system of quality control is performed by competent individuals and covers both the appropriateness of the design and the effectiveness of the operation of the system of quality control.

77 Ongoing consideration and evaluation of the system of quality control includes matters such as the following:
- Analysis of:
  - New developments in professional standards and regulatory and legal requirements, and how they are reflected in the firm's policies and procedures where appropriate;
  - Written confirmation of compliance with policies and procedures on independence;
  - Continuing professional development, including training; and
  - Decisions related to acceptance and continuance of client relationships and specific engagements.
- Determination of corrective actions to be taken and improvements to be made in the system, including the provision of feedback into the firm's policies and procedures relating to education and training.
- Communication to appropriate firm personnel of weaknesses identified in the system, in the level of understanding of the system, or compliance with it.
- Follow-up by appropriate firm personnel so that necessary modifications are promptly made to the quality control policies and procedures.

78 The inspection of a selection of completed engagements is ordinarily performed on a cyclical basis. Engagements selected for inspection include at least one engagement for each engagement partner over an inspection cycle, which ordinarily spans no more than three years. The manner in which the inspection cycle is organized, including the timing of selection of individual engagements, depends on many factors, including the following:
- The size of the firm.
- The number and geographical location of offices.
- The results of previous monitoring procedures.
- The degree of authority both personnel and offices have (for example, whether individual offices are authorized to conduct their own inspections or whether only the head office may conduct them).
- The nature and complexity of the firm's practice and organization.
- The risks associated with the firm's clients and specific engagements.

79 The inspection process includes the selection of individual engagements, some of which may be selected without prior notification to the engagement team. Those inspecting the engagements are not involved in performing the engagement or the engagement quality control review. In determining the scope of the inspections, the firm may take into account the scope or conclusions of an independent external inspection program. However, an independent external inspection program does not act as a substitute for the firm's own internal monitoring program.

80 Small firms and sole practitioners may wish to use a suitably qualified external person or another firm to carry out engagement inspections and other monitoring procedures. Alternatively, they may wish to establish arrangements to share resources with other appropriate organizations to facilitate monitoring activities.

81 **The firm should evaluate the effect of deficiencies noted as a result of the monitoring process and should determine whether they are either:**

(a) Instances that do not necessarily indicate that the firm's system of quality control is insufficient to provide it with reasonable assurance that it complies with professional standards and regulatory and legal requirements, and that the reports issued by the firm or engagement partners are appropriate in the circumstances; or
(b) Systemic, repetitive or other significant deficiencies that require prompt corrective action.

The firm should communicate to relevant engagement partners and other appropriate personnel deficiencies noted as a result of the monitoring process and recommendations for appropriate remedial action. 82

The firm's evaluation of each type of deficiency should result in recommendations for one or more of the following: 83

(a) Taking appropriate remedial action in relation to an individual engagement or member of personnel;
(b) The communication of the findings to those responsible for training and professional development;
(c) Changes to the quality control policies and procedures; and
(d) Disciplinary action against those who fail to comply with the policies and procedures of the firm, especially those who do so repeatedly.

Where the results of the monitoring procedures indicate that a report may be inappropriate or that procedures were omitted during the performance of the engagement, the firm should determine what further action is appropriate to comply with relevant professional standards and regulatory and legal requirements. It should also consider obtaining legal advice. 84

At least annually, the firm should communicate the results of the monitoring of its quality control system to engagement partners and other appropriate individuals within the firm, including the firm's chief executive officer or, if appropriate, its managing board of partners. Such communication should enable the firm and these individuals to take prompt and appropriate action where necessary in accordance with their defined roles and responsibilities. Information communicated should include the following: 85

(a) A description of the monitoring procedures performed.
(b) The conclusions drawn from the monitoring procedures.
(c) Where relevant, a description of systemic, repetitive or other significant deficiencies and of the actions taken to resolve or amend those deficiencies.

The reporting of identified deficiencies to individuals other than the relevant engagement partners ordinarily does not include an identification of the specific engagements concerned, unless such identification is necessary for the proper discharge of the responsibilities of the individuals other than the engagement partners. 86

Some firms operate as part of a network and, for consistency, may implement some or all of their monitoring procedures on a network basis. Where firms within a network operate under common monitoring policies and procedures designed to comply with this ISQC (UK and Ireland), and these firms place reliance on such a monitoring system: 87

(a) At least annually, the network communicates the overall scope, extent and results of the monitoring process to appropriate individuals within the network firms;
(b) The network communicates promptly any identified deficiencies in the quality control system to appropriate individuals within the relevant network firm or firms so that the necessary action can be taken; and

(c) Engagement partners in the network firms are entitled to rely on the results of the monitoring process implemented within the network, unless the firms or the network advises otherwise.

88 Appropriate documentation relating to monitoring:

(a) Sets out monitoring procedures, including the procedure for selecting completed engagements to be inspected;
(b) Records the evaluation of:
 (i) Adherence to professional standards and regulatory and legal requirements;
 (ii) Whether the quality control system has been appropriately designed and effectively implemented; and
 (iii) Whether the firm's quality control policies and procedures have been appropriately applied, so that reports that are issued by the firm or engagement partners are appropriate in the circumstances; and
(c) Identifies the deficiencies noted, evaluates their effect, and sets out the basis for determining whether and what further action is necessary.

Complaints and Allegations

89 **The firm should establish policies and procedures designed to provide it with reasonable assurance that it deals appropriately with:**

(a) **Complaints and allegations that the work performed by the firm fails to comply with professional standards and regulatory and legal requirements; and**
(b) **Allegations of non-compliance with the firm's system of quality control.**

90 Complaints and allegations (which do not include those that are clearly frivolous) may originate from within or outside the firm. They may be made by firm personnel, clients or other third parties. They may be received by engagement team members or other firm personnel.

91 As part of this process, the firm establishes clearly defined channels for firm personnel to raise any concerns in a manner that enables them to come forward without fear of reprisals.

92 The firm investigates such complaints and allegations in accordance with established policies and procedures. The investigation is supervised by a partner with sufficient and appropriate experience and authority within the firm but who is not otherwise involved in the engagement, and includes involving legal counsel as necessary. Small firms and sole practitioners may use the services of a suitably qualified external person or another firm to carry out the investigation. Complaints, allegations and the responses to them are documented.

93 Where the results of the investigations indicate deficiencies in the design or operation of the firm's quality control policies and procedures, or noncompliance with the firm's system of quality control by an individual or individuals, the firm takes appropriate action as discussed in paragraph 83.

Documentation

94 **The firm should establish policies and procedures requiring appropriate documentation to provide evidence of the operation of each element of its system of quality control.**

How such matters are documented is the firm's decision. For example, large firms may use electronic databases to document matters such as independence confirmations, performance evaluations and the results of monitoring inspections. Smaller firms may use more informal methods such as manual notes, checklists and forms. **95**

Factors to consider when determining the form and content of documentation evidencing the operation of each of the elements of the system of quality control include the following: **96**

- The size of the firm and the number of offices.
- The degree of authority both personnel and offices have.
- The nature and complexity of the firm's practice and organization.

The firm retains this documentation for a period of time sufficient to permit those performing monitoring procedures to evaluate the firm's compliance with its system of quality control, or for a longer period if required by law or regulation. **97**

Effective Date

Systems of quality control in compliance with this ISQC (UK and Ireland) are required to be established by firms in the UK and Ireland by 15 June 2005 (15 June 2006 for paragraphs 6(a) and 73a – 73l). Firms consider the appropriate transitional arrangements for engagements in process at these dates. **98**

Public Sector Perspective

This ISQC (UK and Ireland) is applicable in all material respects to the public sector. **1**

Some of the terms in the ISQC (UK and Ireland), such as "engagement partner" and "firm," should be read as referring to their public sector equivalents. However, with limited exceptions, there is no public sector equivalent of "listed entities," although there may be audits of particularly significant public sector entities which should be subject to the listed entity requirements of mandatory rotation of the engagement partner (or equivalent) and engagement quality control review. There are no fixed objective criteria on which this determination of significance should be based. However, such an assessment should encompass an evaluation of all factors relevant to the audited entity. Such factors include size, complexity, commercial risk, parliamentary or media interest and the number and range of stakeholders affected. **2**

ISQC (UK and Ireland) 1, paragraph 70, states that "The firm's policies and procedures are designed to maintain the objectivity of the engagement quality control reviewer." Subparagraph (a) notes as an example that the engagement quality control reviewer is not selected by the engagement partner. In many jurisdictions there is a single statutorily appointed auditor-general. In such circumstances, where applicable, the engagement reviewer should be selected having regard to the need for independence and objectivity. **3**

In the public sector, auditors may be appointed in accordance with statutory procedures. Accordingly, considerations regarding the acceptance and continuance of client relationships and specific engagements, as set out in paragraphs 28-35 of ISQC (UK and Ireland) 1, may not apply. **4**

260 *International Standards on Quality Control (UK & Ireland)*

5   *Similarly, the independence of public sector auditors may be protected by statutory measures, with the consequence that certain of the threats to independence of the nature envisaged by paragraphs 18-27 of ISQC (UK and Ireland) 1 are unlikely to occur.*

Part Four

International Standards on Auditing (UK & Ireland)

[200]
Objective and general principles governing an audit of financial statements

Contents

	Paragraphs
Introduction	1 - 1-4
Objective of an Audit	2 - 3
General Principles of an Audit	4 - 6
Scope of an Audit	7 - 7-1
Reasonable Assurance	8 - 12
Audit Risk and Materiality	13 - 23
Responsibility for the Financial Statements	24
Effective Date	25

International Standard on Auditing (UK and Ireland) (ISA (UK and Ireland)) 200 "Objective and General Principles Governing an Audit of Financial Statements" should be read in the context of the Auditing Practices Board's Statement "The Auditing Practices Board - Scope and Authority of Pronouncements (Revised)" which sets out the application and authority of ISAs (UK and Ireland).

Introduction

1. The purpose of this International Standard on Auditing (UK and Ireland) (ISA (UK and Ireland)) is to establish standards and provide guidance on the objective and general principles governing an audit of financial statements.

1-1. This ISA (UK and Ireland) uses the terms 'those charged with governance' and 'management'. The term 'governance' describes the role of persons entrusted with the supervision, control and direction of an entity. Ordinarily, those charged with governance are accountable for ensuring that the entity achieves its objectives, and for the quality of its financial reporting and reporting to interested parties. Those charged with governance include management only when they perform such functions.

1-2. In the UK and Ireland, those charged with governance include the directors (executive and non-executive) of a company or other body, the members of an audit committee where one exists, the partners, proprietors, committee of management or trustees of other forms of entity, or equivalent persons responsible for directing the entity's affairs and preparing its financial statements.

1-3. 'Management' comprises those persons who perform senior managerial functions.

1-4. In the UK and Ireland, depending on the nature and circumstances of the entity, management may include some or all of those charged with governance (e.g. executive directors). Management will not normally include non-executive directors.

Objective of an Audit

2. The objective of an audit of financial statements is to enable the auditor to express an opinion whether the financial statements are prepared, in all material respects, in accordance with an applicable financial reporting framework. The phrases used to express the auditor's opinion are "give a true and fair view" or "present fairly, in all material respects," which are equivalent terms.

2-1. The "applicable financial reporting framework" comprises those requirements of accounting standards, law and regulations applicable to the entity that determine the form and content of its financial statements.

3. Although the auditor's opinion enhances the credibility of the financial statements, the user cannot assume that the audit opinion is an assurance as to the future viability of the entity nor the efficiency or effectiveness with which management has conducted the affairs of the entity.

General Principles of an Audit

4. The auditor should comply with the *Code of Ethics for Professional Accountants* issued by the International Federation of Accountants. Ethical principles governing the auditor's professional responsibilities are:

   (a) Independence;

(b) Integrity;
(c) Objectivity;
(d) Professional competence and due care;
(e) Confidentiality;
(f) Professional behavior; and
(g) Technical standards.

> In the UK and Ireland the relevant ethical pronouncements with which the auditor should comply are the APB's Ethical Standards and the ethical pronouncements relating to the work of auditors issued by the auditor's relevant professional body.   4-1
>
> Auditors in the UK and Ireland are subject to ethical requirements from two sources: the Ethical Standards established by APB concerning the integrity, objectivity and independence of the auditor, and the ethical pronouncements established by the auditor's relevant professional body. The APB is not aware of any significant instances where the relevant parts of the IFAC Code of Ethics are more restrictive than the Ethical Standards.   4-2

The auditor should conduct an audit in accordance with ISAs (UK and Ireland). These contain basic principles and essential procedures together with related guidance in the form of explanatory and other material.   5

The auditor should plan and perform an audit with an attitude of professional skepticism recognizing that circumstances may exist that cause the financial statements to be materially misstated. An attitude of professional skepticism means the auditor makes a critical assessment, with a questioning mind, of the validity of audit evidence obtained and is alert to audit evidence that contradicts or brings into question the reliability of documents or management representations. For example, an attitude of professional skepticism is necessary throughout the audit process for the auditor to reduce the risk of overlooking suspicious circumstances, of over generalizing when drawing conclusions from audit observations, and of using faulty assumptions in determining the nature, timing, and extent of the audit procedures and evaluating the results thereof. In planning and performing an audit, the auditor neither assumes that management is dishonest nor assumes unquestioned honesty. Accordingly, representations from management are not a substitute for obtaining sufficient appropriate audit evidence to be able to draw reasonable conclusions on which to base the audit opinion.   6

Scope of an Audit

The term "scope of an audit" refers to the audit procedures deemed necessary in the circumstances to achieve the objective of the audit. **The audit procedures required to conduct an audit in accordance with ISAs (UK and Ireland) should be determined by the auditor having regard to the requirements of ISAs (UK and Ireland), relevant professional bodies, legislation, regulations and, where appropriate, the terms of the audit engagement and reporting requirements.**   7

> Although the basic principles of auditing are the same in the public and the private sectors, the auditor of a public service body often has wider objectives and additional duties and statutory responsibilities, laid down in legislation, directives or codes of practice.   7-1

Reasonable Assurance

8   An audit in accordance with ISAs (UK and Ireland) is designed to provide reasonable assurance that the financial statements taken as a whole are free from material misstatement. Reasonable assurance is a concept relating to the accumulation of the audit evidence necessary for the auditor to conclude that there are no material misstatements in the financial statements taken as a whole. Reasonable assurance relates to the whole audit process.

9   An auditor cannot obtain absolute assurance because there are inherent limitations in an audit that affect the auditor's ability to detect material misstatements. These limitations result from factors such as:

- The use of testing.
- The inherent limitations of internal control (for example, the possibility of management override or collusion).
- The fact that most audit evidence is persuasive rather than conclusive.
- The impracticality of examining all items within a class of transactions or account balance.
- The possibility of collusion or misrepresentation for fraudulent purposes.

9-1   The view given in financial statements is itself based on a combination of fact and judgment and, consequently, cannot be characterized as either 'absolute' or 'correct'. A degree of imprecision is inevitable in the preparation of all but the simplest of financial statements because of inherent uncertainties and the need to use judgment in making accounting estimates and selecting appropriate accounting policies.

10   Also, the work undertaken by the auditor to form an audit opinion is permeated by judgment, in particular regarding:

(a) The gathering of audit evidence, for example, in deciding the nature, timing, and extent of audit procedures; and
(b) The drawing of conclusions based on the audit evidence gathered, for example, assessing the reasonableness of the estimates made by management[1a] in preparing the financial statements.

11   Further, other limitations may affect the persuasiveness of audit evidence available to draw conclusions on particular assertions[1] (for example, transactions between related parties). In these cases certain ISAs (UK and Ireland) identify specified audit procedures which will, because of the nature of the particular assertions, provide sufficient appropriate audit evidence in the absence of:

(a) Unusual circumstances which increase the risk of material misstatement beyond that which would ordinarily be expected; or
(b) Any indication that a material misstatement has occurred.

12   Accordingly, because of the factors described above, an audit is not a guarantee that the financial statements are free of material misstatement.

[1a] In the UK and Ireland, those charged with governance are responsible for the preparation of the financial statements.

[1] Paragraphs 15-18 of ISA (UK and Ireland) 500, "Audit Evidence" discuss the use of assertions in obtaining audit evidence.

Audit Risk and Materiality

Entities pursue strategies to achieve their objectives, and depending on the nature of their operations and industry, the regulatory environment in which they operate, and their size and complexity, they face a variety of business risks.[2] Management[1a] is responsible for identifying such risks and responding to them. However, not all risks relate to the preparation of the financial statements. The auditor is ultimately concerned only with risks that may affect the financial statements. 13

The auditor obtains and evaluates audit evidence to obtain reasonable assurance about whether the financial statements give a true and fair view (or are presented fairly, in all material respects) in accordance with the applicable financial reporting framework. The concept of reasonable assurance acknowledges that there is a risk the audit opinion is inappropriate. The risk that the auditor expresses an inappropriate audit opinion when the financial statements are materially misstated is known as "audit risk".[3] 14

The auditor should plan and perform the audit to reduce audit risk to an acceptably low level that is consistent with the objective of an audit. The auditor reduces audit risk by designing and performing audit procedures to obtain sufficient appropriate audit evidence to be able to draw reasonable conclusions on which to base an audit opinion. Reasonable assurance is obtained when the auditor has reduced audit risk to an acceptably low level. 15

Audit risk is a function of the risk of material misstatement of the financial statements (or simply, the "risk of material misstatement") (*i.e.*, the risk that the financial statements are materially misstated prior to audit) and the risk that the auditor will not detect such misstatement ("detection risk"). The auditor performs audit procedures to assess the risk of material misstatement and seeks to limit detection risk by performing further audit procedures based on that assessment (see ISA (UK and Ireland) 315, "Understanding the Entity and Its Environment and Assessing the Risks of Material Misstatement" and ISA (UK and Ireland) 330, "The Auditor's Procedures in Response to Assessed Risks"). The audit process involves the exercise of professional judgment in designing the audit approach, through focusing on what can go wrong (*i.e.*, what are the potential misstatements that may arise) at the assertion level (see ISA (UK and Ireland) 500, "Audit Evidence") and performing audit procedures in response to the assessed risks in order to obtain sufficient appropriate audit evidence. 16

The auditor is concerned with material misstatements, and is not responsible for the detection of misstatements that are not material to the financial statements taken as a whole. The auditor considers whether the effect of identified uncorrected misstatements, both individually and in the aggregate, is material to the financial statements taken as a whole. Materiality and audit risk are related (see ISA (UK and Ireland) 320, "Audit Materiality"). In order to design audit procedures to determine whether there are misstatements that are material to the financial statements taken as a whole, 17

---

[2] *Paragraphs 30-34 of ISA (UK and Ireland) 315, "Understanding the Entity and Its Environment and Assessing the Risks of Material Misstatement," discuss the concept of business risks and how they relate to risks of material misstatement.*

[3] *This definition of audit risk does not include the risk that the auditor might erroneously express an opinion that the financial statements are materially misstated.*

the auditor considers the risk of material misstatement at two levels: the overall financial statement level and in relation to classes of transactions, account balances, and disclosures and the related assertions.[4]

18   The auditor considers the risk of material misstatement at the overall financial statement level, which refers to risks of material misstatement that relate pervasively to the financial statements as a whole and potentially affect many assertions. Risks of this nature often relate to the entity's control environment (although these risks may also relate to other factors, such as declining economic conditions), and are not necessarily risks identifiable with specific assertions at the class of transactions, account balance, or disclosure level. Rather, this overall risk represents circumstances that increase the risk that there could be material misstatements in any number of different assertions, for example, through management override of internal control. Such risks may be especially relevant to the auditor's consideration of the risk of material misstatement arising from fraud. The auditor's response to the assessed risk of material misstatement at the overall financial statement level includes consideration of the knowledge, skill, and ability of personnel assigned significant engagement responsibilities, including whether to involve experts; the appropriate levels of supervision; and whether there are events or conditions that may cast significant doubt on the entity's ability to continue as a going concern.

19   The auditor also considers the risk of material misstatement at the class of transactions, account balance, and disclosure level because such consideration directly assists in determining the nature, timing, and extent of further audit procedures at the assertion level.[5] The auditor seeks to obtain sufficient appropriate audit evidence at the class of transactions, account balance, and disclosure level in such a way that enables the auditor, at the completion of the audit, to express an opinion on the financial statements taken as a whole at an acceptably low level of audit risk. Auditors use various approaches to accomplish that objective.[6]

20   The discussion in the following paragraphs provides an explanation of the components of audit risk. The risk of material misstatement at the assertion level consists of two components as follows:

- "Inherent risk" is the susceptibility of an assertion to a misstatement that could be material, either individually or when aggregated with other misstatements, assuming that there are no related controls. The risk of such misstatement is greater for some assertions and related classes of transactions, account balances, and disclosures than for others. For example, complex calculations are more likely to be misstated than simple calculations. Accounts consisting of amounts derived from accounting estimates that are subject to significant measurement uncertainty pose greater risks than do accounts consisting of relatively routine, factual data. External circumstances giving rise to business risks may also influence inherent risk. For example, technological developments might make a particular product obsolete, thereby causing inventory to be more susceptible to

---

[4] *ISA (UK and Ireland) 315, "Understanding the Entity and Its Environment and Assessing the Risks of Material Misstatement" provides additional guidance on the auditor's requirement to assess risks of material misstatement at the financial statement level and at the assertion level.*

[5] *ISA (UK and Ireland) 330, "The Auditor's Procedures in Response to Assessed Risks" provides additional guidance on the requirement for the auditor to design and perform further audit procedures in response to the assessed risks at the assertion level.*

[6] *The auditor may make use of a model that expresses the general relationship of the components of audit risk in mathematical terms to arrive at an appropriate level of detection risk. Some auditors find such a model to be useful when planning audit procedures to achieve a desired audit risk though the use of such a model does not eliminate the judgment inherent in the audit process.*

overstatement. In addition to those circumstances that are peculiar to a specific assertion, factors in the entity and its environment that relate to several or all of the classes of transactions, account balances, or disclosures may influence the inherent risk related to a specific assertion. These latter factors include, for example, a lack of sufficient working capital to continue operations or a declining industry characterized by a large number of business failures.

- "Control risk" is the risk that a misstatement that could occur in an assertion and that could be material, either individually or when aggregated with other misstatements, will not be prevented, or detected and corrected, on a timely basis by the entity's internal control. That risk is a function of the effectiveness of the design and operation of internal control in achieving the entity's objectives relevant to preparation of the entity's financial statements. Some control risk will always exist because of the inherent limitations of internal control.

Inherent risk and control risk are the entity's risks; they exist independently of the audit of the financial statements. The auditor is required to assess the risk of material misstatement at the assertion level as a basis for further audit procedures, though that assessment is a judgment, rather than a precise measurement of risk. When the auditor's assessment of the risk of material misstatement includes an expectation of the operating effectiveness of controls, the auditor performs tests of controls to support the risk assessment. The ISAs (UK and Ireland) do not ordinarily refer to inherent risk and control risk separately, but rather to a combined assessment of the "risk of material misstatement." Although the ISAs (UK and Ireland) ordinarily describe a combined assessment of the risk of material misstatement, the auditor may make separate or combined assessments of inherent and control risk depending on preferred audit techniques or methodologies and practical considerations. The assessment of the risk of material misstatement may be expressed in quantitative terms, such as in percentages, or in non-quantitative terms. In any case, the need for the auditor to make appropriate risk assessments is more important than the different approaches by which they may be made.

"Detection risk" is the risk that the auditor will not detect a misstatement that exists in an assertion that could be material, either individually or when aggregated with other misstatements. Detection risk is a function of the effectiveness of an audit procedure and of its application by the auditor. Detection risk cannot be reduced to zero because the auditor usually does not examine all of a class of transactions, account balance, or disclosure and because of other factors. Such other factors include the possibility that an auditor might select an inappropriate audit procedure, misapply an appropriate audit procedure, or misinterpret the audit results. These other factors ordinarily can be addressed through adequate planning, proper assignment of personnel to the engagement team, the application of professional skepticism, and supervision and review of the audit work performed.

Detection risk relates to the nature, timing, and extent of the auditor's procedures that are determined by the auditor to reduce audit risk to an acceptably low level. For a given level of audit risk, the acceptable level of detection risk bears an inverse relationship to the assessment of the risk of material misstatement at the assertion level. The greater the risk of material misstatement the auditor believes exists, the less the detection risk that can be accepted. Conversely, the less risk of material misstatement the auditor believes exist, the greater the detection risk that can be accepted.

Responsibility for the Financial Statements

24 While the auditor is responsible for forming and expressing an opinion on the financial statements, the responsibility for preparing and presenting the financial statements in accordance with the applicable financial reporting framework is that of the management of the entity, with oversight from those charged with governance.[71a] The audit of the financial statements does not relieve management or those charged with governance of their responsibilities.

Effective Date

25 This ISA (UK and Ireland) is effective for audits of financial statements for periods commencing on or after 15 December 2004.

---

[7] *The structures of governance vary from country to country reflecting cultural and legal backgrounds. Therefore, the respective responsibilities of management and those charged with governance vary depending on the legal responsibilities in the particular jurisdiction.*

[210]
Terms of audit engagements
(Issued December 2004)

Contents

	Paragraphs
Introduction	1 - 4
Audit Engagement Letters	5 - 9-1
Recurring Audits	10 - 11
Acceptance of a Change in Engagement	12 - 19-1
Effective Date	**19-2**

Appendix: Example of an Audit Engagement Letter

Appendix 2: Illustrative wording to describe the responsibilities of the directors and the auditor and the scope of the audit, for a limited (non-listed) company client for an audit conducted in accordance with ISAs (UK and Ireland)

International Standard on Auditing (UK and Ireland) (ISA (UK and Ireland)) 210 "Terms of Audit Engagements" should be read in the context of the Auditing Practices Board's Statement "The Auditing Practices Board – Scope and Authority of Pronouncements (Revised)" which sets out the application and authority of ISAs (UK and Ireland).

Introduction

1. The purpose of this International Standard on Auditing (UK and Ireland) (ISA (UK and Ireland)) is to establish standards and provide guidance on:

   (a) agreeing the terms of the engagement with the client; and
   (b) the auditor's response to a request by a client to change the terms of an engagement to one that provides a lower level of assurance.

1-1 This ISA (UK and Ireland) uses the terms 'those charged with governance' and 'management'. The term 'governance' describes the role of persons entrusted with the supervision, control and direction of an entity. Ordinarily, those charged with governance are accountable for ensuring that the entity achieves its objectives, and for the quality of its financial reporting and reporting to interested parties. Those charged with governance include management only when they perform such functions.

1-2 In the UK and Ireland, those charged with governance include the directors (executive and non-executive) of a company or other body, the members of an audit committee where one exists, the partners, proprietors, committee of management or trustees of other forms of entity, or equivalent persons responsible for directing the entity's affairs and preparing its financial statements.

1-3 'Management' comprises those persons who perform senior managerial functions.

1-4 In the UK and Ireland, depending on the nature and circumstances of the entity, management may include some or all of those charged with governance (e.g. executive directors). Management will not normally include non-executive directors.

1-5 For the purpose of this ISA (UK and Ireland) 'client' means the addressees of the auditor's report or, when as often will be the case it is not practical to agree such terms with the addressees, the entity itself through those charged with governance.

2. **The auditor and the client should agree on the terms of the engagement.** The agreed terms would need to be recorded in an audit engagement letter or other suitable form of contract.

2-1 **The terms of the engagement should be recorded in writing.**

3. This ISA is intended to assist the auditor in the preparation of engagement letters relating to audits of financial statements. The guidance is also applicable to related services. When other services such as tax, accounting, or management advisory services are to be provided, separate letters may be appropriate.

4. In some countries, the objective and scope of an audit and the auditor's obligations are established by law. Even in those situations the auditor may still find audit engagement letters informative for their clients.

Audit Engagement Letters

It is in the interest of both client and auditor that the auditor sends an engagement letter, preferably before the commencement of the engagement, to help in avoiding misunderstandings with respect to the engagement. The engagement letter documents and confirms the auditor's acceptance of the appointment, the objective and scope of the audit, the extent of the auditor's responsibilities to the client and the form of any reports.

5

> In the UK and Ireland, the auditor should ensure that the engagement letter documents and confirms the auditor's acceptance of the appointment, and includes a summary of the responsibilities of those charged with governance and of the auditor, the scope of the engagement and the form of any reports.

5-1

> Appendix 2 sets out illustrative wording to describe the responsibilities of the directors and the auditor and the scope of the audit, for a limited (non-listed) company client for an audit conducted in accordance with ISAs (UK and Ireland).

5-2

Principal Contents

The form and content of audit engagement letters may vary for each client, but they would generally include reference to:

6

- The objective of the audit of financial statements.
- Management's responsibility for the financial statements[1].
- The scope of the audit, including reference to applicable legislation, regulations, or pronouncements of professional bodies to which the auditor adheres.
- The form of any reports or other communication of results of the engagement.
- The fact that because of the test nature and other inherent limitations of an audit, together with the inherent limitations of internal control, there is an unavoidable risk that even some material misstatement may remain undiscovered.
- Unrestricted access to whatever records, documentation and other information requested in connection with the audit.

The auditor may also wish to include in the letter:

7

- Arrangements regarding the planning and performance of the audit.
- Expectation of receiving from management written confirmation concerning representations made in connection with the audit.
- Request for the client to confirm the terms of the engagement by acknowledging receipt of the engagement letter.[2]
- Description of any other letters or reports the auditor expects to issue to the client.

---

[1] In the UK and Ireland, those charged with governance are responsible for the preparation of the financial statements.

[2] Acceptance by the client of the terms of the engagement is normally evidenced by signature by a person at an appropriate level within the entity, for example the finance director or equivalent.

- Any confidentiality of other letters or reports to be issued and, where appropriate, the conditions, if any, on which permission might be given to those charged with governance to make those reports available to others.

- Basis on which fees are computed and any billing arrangements.

8   When relevant, the following points could also be made:
- Arrangements concerning the involvement of other auditors and experts in some aspects of the audit.
- Arrangements concerning the involvement of internal auditors and other client staff.
- Arrangements to be made with the predecessor auditor, if any, in the case of an initial audit.
- Any restriction of the auditor's liability when such possibility exists.
- A reference to any further agreements between the auditor and the client.

An example of an audit engagement letter is set out in the Appendix.[1]

Audits of Components

9   When the auditor of a parent entity is also the auditor of its subsidiary, branch or division (component), the factors that influence the decision whether to send a separate engagement letter to the component include:
- Who appoints the auditor of the component.
- Whether the terms for each component are the same.
- Whether a separate audit report is to be issued on the component.
- Legal requirements.
- Regulatory requirements.
- The extent of any work performed by other auditors.
- Degree of ownership by parent.
- Degree of independence of the component's management.

9-1 If the auditor sends one letter relating to the group as a whole, it identifies the components for which the auditor is appointed as auditor. Those charged with governance of the parent entity are requested to forward the letter to those charged with governance of the components concerned. Each board is requested to confirm that the terms of the engagement letter are accepted.

Recurring Audits

10   On recurring audits, the auditor should consider whether circumstances require the terms of the engagement to be revised and whether there is a need to remind the client of the existing terms of the engagement.

11   The auditor may decide not to send a new engagement letter each period. However, the following factors may make it appropriate to send a new letter:
- Any indication that the client misunderstands the objective and scope of the audit.

---

[1] The example letter in the Appendix is not tailored for the United Kingdom and Ireland.

- Any revised or special terms of the engagement.
- A recent change of senior management or those charged with governance.
- A significant change in ownership.
- A significant change in nature or size of the client's business.
- Legal or regulatory requirements.

Acceptance of a Change in Engagement

An auditor who, before the completion of the engagement, is requested to change the engagement to one which provides a lower level of assurance, should consider the appropriateness of doing so.   12

A request from the client for the auditor to change the engagement may result from a change in circumstances affecting the need for the service, a misunderstanding as to the nature of an audit or related service originally requested or a restriction on the scope of the engagement, whether imposed by management or caused by circumstances. The auditor would consider carefully the reason given for the request, particularly the implications of a restriction on the scope of the engagement.   13

A change in circumstances that affects the entity's requirements or a misunderstanding concerning the nature of service originally requested would ordinarily be considered a reasonable basis for requesting a change in the engagement. In contrast a change would not be considered reasonable if it appeared that the change relates to information that is incorrect, incomplete or otherwise unsatisfactory.   14

Before agreeing to change an audit engagement to a related service, an auditor who was engaged to perform an audit in accordance with ISAs (UK and Ireland) would consider, in addition to the above matters, any legal or contractual implications of the change.   15

If the auditor concludes, that there is reasonable justification to change the engagement and if the audit work performed complies with the ISAs (UK and Ireland) applicable to the changed engagement, the report issued would be that appropriate for the revised terms of engagement. In order to avoid confusing the reader, the report would not include reference to: 16

(a) The original engagement; or
(b) Any procedures that may have been performed in the original engagement, except where the engagement is changed to an engagement to undertake agreed-upon procedures and thus reference to the procedures performed is a normal part of the report.

Where the terms of the engagement are changed, the auditor and the client should agree on the new terms.   17

The auditor should not agree to a change of engagement where there is no reasonable justification for doing so. An example might be an audit engagement where the auditor is unable to obtain sufficient appropriate audit evidence regarding receivables and the client asks for the engagement to be changed to a review engagement to avoid a qualified audit opinion or a disclaimer of opinion.   18

If the auditor is unable to agree to a change of the engagement and is not permitted to continue the original engagement, the auditor should withdraw and consider whether there is any obligation, either contractual or otherwise, to report to other parties, such   19 as those charged with governance or shareholders, the circumstances necessitating the withdrawal.

19-1 The auditor of a limited company in Great Britain who ceases to hold office as auditor is required to comply with the requirements of section 394 of the Companies Act 1985 regarding the statement to be made by the auditor in relation to ceasing to hold office. Equivalent requirements for Northern Ireland are contained in Article 401A of the Companies (Northern Ireland) Order 1986 and, for the Republic of Ireland, are contained in section 185 of the Companies Act 1990.

Effective Date

19-2 This ISA (UK and Ireland) is effective for audits of financial statements for periods commencing on or after 15 December 2004.

Public Sector Perspective

Additional guidance for auditors of public sector bodies in the UK and Ireland is given in:

- Practice Note 10 "Audit of Financial Statements of Public Sector Entities in the United Kingdom (Revised)"
- Practice Note 10(I) "The Audit of Central Government Financial Statements in Ireland"

1 *The purpose of the engagement letter is to inform the auditee of the nature of the engagement and to clarify the responsibilities of the parties involved. The legislation and regulations governing the operations of public sector audits generally mandate the appointment of a public sector auditor and the use of audit engagement letters may not be a widespread practice. Nevertheless, a letter setting out the nature of the engagement or recognizing an engagement not indicated in the legislative mandate may be useful to both parties. Public sector auditors have to give serious consideration to issuing audit engagements letters when undertaking an audit.*

2 *Paragraphs 12-19 of this ISA (UK and Ireland) deal with the action a private sector auditor may take when there are attempts to change an audit engagement to one which provides a lower level of assurance. In the public sector specific requirements may exist within the legislation governing the audit mandate; for example, the auditor may be required to report directly to a minister, the legislature or the public if management (including the department head) attempts to limit the scope of the audit.*

Appendix

The example letter in this Appendix is not tailored for the UK and Ireland. Appendix 2 sets out illustrative wording to describe the responsibilities of the directors and the auditor and the scope of the audit, for a limited (non-listed) company client for an audit conducted in accordance with ISAs (UK and Ireland).

Example of an Audit Engagement Letter

The following letter is for use as a guide in conjunction with the considerations outlined in this ISA and will need to be varied according to individual requirements and circumstances.

To the Board of Directors or the appropriate representative of senior management:

You have requested that we audit the balance sheet of .... as of ...., and the related statements of income and cash flows for the year then ending. We are pleased to confirm our acceptance and our understanding of this engagement by means of this letter. Our audit will be made with the objective of our expressing an opinion on the financial statements.

We will conduct our audit in accordance with International Standards on Auditing (or refer to relevant national standards or practices). Those Standards require that we plan and perform the audit to obtain reasonable assurance about whether the financial statements are free of material misstatements. An audit includes examining, on a test basis, evidence supporting the amounts and disclosures in the financial statements. An audit also includes assessing the accounting principles used and significant estimates made by management, as well as evaluating the overall financial statement presentation.

Because of the test nature and other inherent limitations of an audit, together with the inherent limitations of any accounting and internal control system, there is an unavoidable risk that even some material misstatements may remain undiscovered.

In addition to our report on the financial statements, we expect to provide you with a separate letter concerning any material weaknesses in accounting and internal control systems which come to our notice.

We remind you that the responsibility for the preparation of financial statements including adequate disclosure is that of the management of the company. This includes the maintenance of adequate accounting records and internal controls, the selection and application of accounting policies, and the safeguarding of the assets of the company. As part of our audit process, we will request from management written confirmation concerning representations made to us in connection with the audit.

We look forward to full cooperation with your staff and we trust that they will make available to us whatever records, documentation and other information are requested in connection with our audit. Our fees, which will be billed as work progresses, are based on the time required by the individuals assigned to the engagement plus out-of-pocket expenses. Individual hourly rates vary according to the degree of responsibility involved and the experience and skill required.

This letter will be effective for future years unless it is terminated, amended or superseded.

Please sign and return the attached copy of this letter to indicate that it is in accordance with your understanding of the arrangements for our audit of the financial statements.

XYZ & Co.
Acknowledged on behalf of
ABC Company by

(signed)
....
Name and Title
Date

Appendix 2 – Illustrative wording to describe the responsibilities of the directors and the auditor and the scope of the audit, for a limited (non-listed) company client for an audit conducted in accordance with ISAs (UK and Ireland)

The illustrative wording set out below is not necessarily comprehensive or appropriate to be used in relation to every non-listed company, and it must be tailored to specific circumstances - for example, to the special reporting requirements of regulated entities *(note 1)*, or of small companies to which certain exemptions are given.

The wording reflects legal and professional responsibilities as at 15 December 2004. The wording should be amended as necessary to take account of changes in the responsibilities of the directors and the auditor after that date, for example as a result of changes in company legislation.

The auditor includes other wording as appropriate to address the matters set out in paragraphs 6 to 9-1 of this ISA (UK and Ireland).

Responsibilities of directors and auditors

As directors of xxxxxx, you are responsible for ensuring that the company maintains proper accounting records and for preparing financial statements which give a true and fair view and have been prepared in accordance with the Companies Act 1985 *(or other relevant legislation - note 2)*. You are also responsible for making available to us, as and when required, all the company's accounting records and all other relevant records and related information, including minutes of all management and shareholders' meetings. We are entitled to require from the company's officers such other information and explanations as we think necessary for the performance of our duties as auditors.

We have a statutory responsibility to report to the members whether in our opinion the financial statements give a true and fair view and whether they have been properly prepared in accordance with the Companies Act 1985 *(or other relevant legislation)*. In arriving at our opinion, we are required to consider the following matters, and to report on any in respect of which we are not satisfied *(note 3)*:

(a) Whether proper accounting records have been kept by the company *(note 4)* and proper returns adequate for our audit have been received from branches not visited by us;
(b) Whether the company's *(note 4)* balance sheet and profit and loss account are in agreement with the accounting records and returns;
(c) Whether we have obtained all the information and explanations which we consider necessary for the purposes of our audit; and
(d) Whether the information given in the directors' report is consistent with the financial statements.

In addition, there are certain other matters which, according to the circumstances, may need to be dealt with in our report. For example, where the financial statements do not give details of directors' remuneration or of their transactions with the company, the Companies Act 1985 requires us to disclose such matters in our report.

We have a professional responsibility to report if the financial statements do not comply in any material respect with applicable accounting standards, unless in our opinion the non-compliance is justified in the circumstances. In determining whether or not the departure is justified we consider:

(a) Whether the departure is required in order for the financial statements to give a true and fair view; and
(b) Whether adequate disclosure has been made concerning the departure.

Our professional responsibilities also include:

- Including in our report a description of the directors' responsibilities for the financial statements where the financial statements or accompanying information do not include such a description; and
- Considering whether other information in documents containing audited financial statements is consistent with those financial statements.

(note 5)

Scope of audit

Our audit will be conducted in accordance with the International Auditing Standards (UK and Ireland) issued by the Auditing Practices Board, and will include such tests of transactions and of the existence, ownership and valuation of assets and liabilities as we consider necessary. We shall obtain an understanding of the accounting and internal control systems in order to assess their adequacy as a basis for the preparation of the financial statements and to establish whether proper accounting records have been maintained by the company. We shall expect to obtain such appropriate evidence as we consider sufficient to enable us to draw reasonable conclusions therefrom.

The nature and extent of our procedures will vary according to our assessment of the company's accounting system and, where we wish to place reliance on it, the internal control system, and may cover any aspect of the business's operations that we consider appropriate. Our audit is not designed to identify all significant weaknesses in the company's systems but, if such weaknesses come to our notice during the course of our audit which we think should be brought to your attention, we shall report them to you. Any such report may not be provided to third parties without our prior written consent. Such consent will be granted only on the basis that such reports are not prepared with the interests of anyone other than the company in mind and that we accept no duty or responsibility to any other party as concerns the reports.

As part of our normal audit procedures, we may request you to provide written confirmation of certain oral representations which we have received from you during the course of the audit on matters having a material effect on the financial statements. In connection with representations and the supply of information to us generally, we draw your attention to section 389A of the Companies Act 1985 *(note 6)* under which it is an offence for an officer of the company to mislead the auditors.

In order to assist us with the examination of your financial statements, we shall request sight of all documents or statements, including the chairman's statement, operating and financial review and the directors' report, which are due to be issued with the financial statements. We are also entitled to attend all general meetings of the company and to receive notice of all such meetings.

The responsibility for safeguarding the assets of the company and for the prevention and detection of fraud, error and non-compliance with law or regulations rests with yourselves. However, we shall endeavour to plan our audit so that we have a reasonable expectation of detecting material misstatements in the financial statements or accounting records (including those resulting from fraud, error or non-compliance with law or regulations), but our examination should not be relied upon to disclose all such material misstatements or frauds, errors or instances of non-compliance as may exist.

(Where appropriate - note 7) We shall not be treated as having notice, for the purposes of our audit responsibilities, of information provided to members of our firm other than those engaged on the audit (for example information provided in connection with accounting, taxation and other services).

Once we have issued our report we have no further direct responsibility in relation to the financial statements for that financial year. However, we expect that you will inform us of any material event occurring between the date of our report and that of the Annual General Meeting which may affect the financial statements.

Notes

1   Additional guidance is provided in APB Practice Notes.
2   Relevant legislation for the Republic of Ireland is the Companies Acts 1963 to 2003 and for Northern Ireland is the Companies (Northern Ireland) Order 1986.
3   In the Republic of Ireland, auditors are required to report additionally on matters (a) to (d) as identified in the section 'Responsibilities of directors and auditors' of the example engagement letter, and on whether there existed at the balance sheet date a financial situation which, under section 40(1) of the Companies (Amendment) Act 1983, would require the convening of an extraordinary general meeting of the company. Hence this sentence would read: '... we are required to consider the following matters and to report on:'
4   The reference to 'company' does not need to be altered in the case of groups as section 237 of the Companies Act 1985 refers only to the company being audited and not to any parent company or subsidiary or associated undertaking.
5   In the Republic of Ireland, auditors have the following additional legal responsibilities which are set out in the engagement letter:

Company law

To report whether, in their opinion, proper books of account have been kept by the entity.

Where suspected indictable offences under the Companies Acts come to the attention of auditors, while carrying out their audit examination, they are obliged to report these to the Director of Corporate Enforcement. This reporting obligation imposed by Section 194, Companies Act, 1990, as amended by Section 74, Company Law Enforcement Act, 2001, applies regardless of the apparent materiality of the suspected offence, or whether the suspected offence has already been reported to the relevant authorities.

Criminal law

Where, in the course of conducting professional work, it comes to the attention of certain "relevant persons" defined), that information or documents indicate that an offence may have been committed under Section 59 Criminal Justice (Theft and Fraud Offences) Act 2001, auditors have a reporting obligation to the Garda Siochana. This applies regardless of the apparent materiality of the suspected offence, or whether the suspected offence has already been reported to the relevant authorities.

Taxation

Auditors must report material relevant offences, as defined in Section 1079 of the Taxes Consolidation Act 1997, to the directors of the company in writing, requesting them to rectify the matter or notify an appropriate officer of the Revenue Commissioners of the offence within 6 months. In the event that the auditors request is not complied with, the auditor must cease to act as auditor to the company or to assist the company in any taxation matter. The auditor must also send a copy of the auditor's notice of resignation to an appropriate officer of the Revenue Commissioners within 14 days

6   Relevant references for the Republic of Ireland are sections 193(3), 196 and 197 of the Companies Act 1990. The relevant reference for Northern Ireland is Article 397A of the Companies (Northern Ireland) Order 1986.
7   When accounting, taxation or other services are undertaken on behalf of an audit client, information may be provided to members of the audit firm other than those engaged on the audit. In such cases, it may be appropriate for the audit engagement letter to include this or a similar paragraph to indicate that the auditors are not to be treated as having notice, for the purposes of their audit responsibilities, of such information, to make it clear that a company would not be absolved from informing the auditors directly of a material matter.

[220]
Quality control for audits of historical financial information

(Issued December 2004)

Contents

	Paragraphs
Introduction	1 - 4
Definitions	5 - 5-4
Leadership Responsibilities for Quality on Audits	6 - 7
Ethical Requirements	8 - 13
Acceptance and Continuance of Client Relationships and Specific Audit Engagements	14 - 18
Assignment of Engagement Teams	19 - 20
Engagement Performance	21 - 40
Monitoring	41 - 42
Effective Date	**43**

International Standard on Auditing (UK and Ireland) (ISA (UK and Ireland)) 220 "Quality Control for Audits of Historical Financial Information" should be read in the context of the Auditing Practices Board's Statement "The Auditing Practices Board - Scope and Authority of Pronouncements (Revised)" which sets out the application and authority of ISAs (UK and Ireland).

Introduction

The purpose of this International Standard on Auditing (UK and Ireland) (ISA(UK and Ireland)) is to establish standards and provide guidance on specific responsibilities of firm personnel regarding quality control procedures for audits of historical financial information, including audits of financial statements. This ISA (UK and Ireland) is to be read in conjunction with Parts A and B of the IFAC *Code of Ethics for Professional Accountants* (the IFAC Code). 1

In the UK and Ireland the relevant ethical pronouncements with which the auditor complies are the APB's Ethical Standards and the ethical pronouncements relating to the work of auditors issued by the auditor's relevant professional body – see the Statement "The Auditing practices Board – Scope and Authority of Pronouncements." 1-1

The engagement team should implement quality control procedures that are applicable to the individual audit engagement. 2

Under International Standard on Quality Control (UK and Ireland) (ISQC (UK and Ireland)) 1, "Quality Control for Firms that Perform Audits and Reviews of Historical Financial Information, and Other Assurance and Related Services Engagements," a firm has an obligation to establish a system of quality control designed to provide it with reasonable assurance that the firm and its personnel comply with professional standards and regulatory and legal requirements, and that the auditors' reports issued by the firm or engagement partners are appropriate in the circumstances. 3

Engagement teams: 4

(a) Implement quality control procedures that are applicable to the audit engagement;
(b) Provide the firm with relevant information to enable the functioning of that part of the firm's system of quality control relating to independence; and
(c) Are entitled to rely on the firm's systems (for example in relation to capabilities and competence of personnel through their recruitment and formal training; independence through the accumulation and communication of relevant independence information; maintenance of client relationships through acceptance and continuance systems; and adherence to regulatory and legal requirements through the monitoring process), unless information provided by the firm or other parties suggests otherwise.

Definitions

In this ISA (UK and Ireland), the following terms have the meanings attributed below: 5

(a) "Engagement partner" – the partner or other person in the firm who is responsible for the audit engagement and its performance, and for the auditor's report that is issued on behalf of the firm, and who, where required, has the appropriate authority from a professional, legal or regulatory body;
(b) "Engagement quality control review" – a process designed to provide an objective evaluation, before the auditor's report is issued, of the significant judgments the engagement team made and the conclusions they reached in formulating the auditor's report;

(c) "Engagement quality control reviewer" – a partner, other person in the firm, suitably qualified external person, or a team made up of such individuals, with sufficient and appropriate experience and authority to objectively evaluate, before the auditor's report is issued, the significant judgments the engagement team made and the conclusions they reached in formulating the auditor's report;

(d) "Engagement team" – all personnel performing an audit engagement, including any experts contracted by the firm in connection with that audit engagement;

(e) "Firm"* – a sole practitioner, partnership, corporation or other entity of professional accountants;

(f) "Inspection" – in relation to completed audit engagements, procedures designed to provide evidence of compliance by engagement teams with the firm's quality control policies and procedures;

(g) "Listed entity"* – an entity whose shares, stock or debt are quoted or listed on a recognized stock exchange, or are marketed under the regulations of a recognized stock exchange or other equivalent body;

(h) "Monitoring" – a process comprising an ongoing consideration and evaluation of the firm's system of quality control, including a periodic inspection of a selection of completed engagements, designed to enable the firm to obtain reasonable assurance that its system of quality control is operating effectively;

(i) "Network firm"* – an entity under common control, ownership or management with the firm or any entity that a reasonable and informed third party having knowledge of all relevant information would reasonably conclude as being part of the firm nationally or internationally;

(j) "Partner" – any individual with authority to bind the firm with respect to the performance of a professional services engagement;

(k) "Personnel" – partners and staff;

(l) "Professional standards" – IAASB Engagement Standards, as defined in the IAASB's "Preface to the International Standards on Quality Control, Auditing, Assurance and Related Services," and relevant ethical requirements, which ordinarily comprise Parts A and B of the IFAC Code and relevant national ethical requirements¹;

(m) "Reasonable assurance" – in the context of this ISA (UK and Ireland), a high, but not absolute, level of assurance;

(n) "Staff" – professionals, other than partners, including any experts the firm employs; and

(o) "Suitably qualified external person" – an individual outside the firm with the capabilities and competence to act as an engagement partner, for example a partner of another firm, or an employee (with appropriate experience) of either a professional accountancy body whose members may perform audits of historical financial information or of an organization that provides relevant quality control services.

5-1 This ISA (UK and Ireland) uses the terms 'those charged with governance' and 'management'. The term 'governance' describes the role of persons entrusted with the supervision, control and direction of an entity. Ordinarily, those charged with governance are accountable for ensuring that the entity achieves its objectives, and for the quality of its financial reporting and reporting to interested parties. Those charged with governance include management only when they perform such functions.

* As defined in the IFAC Code published in November 2001.

¹ In the UK and Ireland the relevant ethical pronouncements with which the auditor complies are the APB's Ethical Standards and the ethical pronouncements relating to the work of auditors issued by the auditor's relevant professional body - see the Statement "The Auditing practices Board – Scope and Authority of Pronouncements."

Where issues arise out of any of these considerations, the engagement team conducts the appropriate consultations set out in paragraphs 30-33, and documents how issues were resolved.

Deciding whether to continue a client relationship includes consideration of significant matters that have arisen during the current or previous audit engagement, and their implications for continuing the relationship. For example, a client may have started to expand its business operations into an area where the firm does not possess the necessary knowledge or expertise. 17

Where the engagement partner obtains information that would have caused the firm to decline the audit engagement if that information had been available earlier, the engagement partner should communicate that information promptly to the firm, so that the firm and the engagement partner can take the necessary action. 18

Assignment of Engagement Teams

The engagement partner should be satisfied that the engagement team collectively has the appropriate capabilities, competence and time to perform the audit engagement in accordance with professional standards and regulatory and legal requirements, and to enable an auditor's report that is appropriate in the circumstances to be issued. 19

The appropriate capabilities and competence expected of the engagement team as a whole include the following: 20

- An understanding of, and practical experience with, audit engagements of a similar nature and complexity through appropriate training and participation.
- An understanding of professional standards and regulatory and legal requirements.
- Appropriate technical knowledge, including knowledge of relevant information technology.
- Knowledge of relevant industries in which the client operates.
- Ability to apply professional judgment.
- An understanding of the firm's quality control policies and procedures.

Engagement Performance

The engagement partner should take responsibility for the direction, supervision and performance of the audit engagement in compliance with professional standards and regulatory and legal requirements, and for the auditor's report that is issued to be appropriate in the circumstances. 21

The engagement partner directs the audit engagement by informing the members of the engagement team of: 22

(a) Their responsibilities;
(b) The nature of the entity's business;
(c) Risk-related issues;
(d) Problems that may arise; and
(e) The detailed approach to the performance of the engagement.

The engagement team's responsibilities include maintaining an objective state of mind and an appropriate level of professional skepticism, and performing the work delegated to them in accordance with the ethical principle of due care. Members of the engagement team are encouraged to raise questions with more experienced team members. Appropriate communication occurs within the engagement team.

23 It is important that all members of the engagement team understand the objectives of the work they are to perform. Appropriate team-working and training are necessary to assist less experienced members of the engagement team to clearly understand the objectives of the assigned work.

24 Supervision includes the following:

- Tracking the progress of the audit engagement.
- Considering the capabilities and competence of individual members of the engagement team, whether they have sufficient time to carry out their work, whether they understand their instructions, and whether the work is being carried out in accordance with the planned approach to the audit engagement.
- Addressing significant issues arising during the audit engagement, considering their significance and modifying the planned approach appropriately.
- Identifying matters for consultation or consideration by more experienced engagement team members during the audit engagement.

25 Review responsibilities are determined on the basis that more experienced team members, including the engagement partner, review work performed by less experienced team members. Reviewers consider whether:

(a) The work has been performed in accordance with professional standards and regulatory and legal requirements;
(b) Significant matters have been raised for further consideration;
(c) Appropriate consultations have taken place and the resulting conclusions have been documented and implemented;
(d) There is a need to revise the nature, timing and extent of work performed;
(e) The work performed supports the conclusions reached and is appropriately documented;
(f) The evidence obtained is sufficient and appropriate to support the auditor's report; and
(g) The objectives of the engagement procedures have been achieved.

26 **Before the auditor's report is issued, the engagement partner, through review of the audit documentation and discussion with the engagement team, should be satisfied that sufficient appropriate audit evidence has been obtained to support the conclusions reached and for the auditor's report to be issued.**

27 The engagement partner conducts timely reviews at appropriate stages during the engagement. This allows significant matters to be resolved on a timely basis to the engagement partner's satisfaction before the auditor's report is issued. The reviews cover critical areas of judgment, especially those relating to difficult or contentious matters identified during the course of the engagement, significant risks, and other areas the engagement partner considers important. The engagement partner need not review all audit documentation. However, the partner documents the extent and timing of the reviews. Issues arising from the reviews are resolved to the satisfaction of the engagement partner.

28 A new engagement partner taking over an audit during the engagement reviews the work performed to the date of the change. The review procedures are sufficient to satisfy the new engagement partner that the work performed to the date of the review has been planned and performed in accordance with professional standards and regulatory and legal requirements.

Where more than one partner is involved in the conduct of an audit engagement, it is important that the responsibilities of the respective partners are clearly defined and understood by the engagement team.

Consultation

The engagement partner should:

(a) **Be responsible for the engagement team undertaking appropriate consultation on difficult or contentious matters;**
(b) **Be satisfied that members of the engagement team have undertaken appropriate consultation during the course of the engagement, both within the engagement team and between the engagement team and others at the appropriate level within or outside the firm;**
(c) **Be satisfied that the nature and scope of, and conclusions resulting from, such consultations are documented and agreed with the party consulted; and**
(d) **Determine that conclusions resulting from consultations have been implemented.**

Effective consultation with other professionals requires that those consulted be given all the relevant facts that will enable them to provide informed advice on technical, ethical or other matters. Where appropriate, the engagement team consults individuals with appropriate knowledge, seniority and experience within the firm or, where applicable, outside the firm. Conclusions resulting from consultations are appropriately documented and implemented.

It may be appropriate for the engagement team to consult outside the firm, for example, where the firm lacks appropriate internal resources. They may take advantage of advisory services provided by other firms, professional and regulatory bodies, or commercial organizations that provide relevant quality control services.

The documentation of consultations with other professionals that involve difficult or contentious matters is agreed by both the individual seeking consultation and the individual consulted. The documentation is sufficiently complete and detailed to enable an understanding of:

(a) The issue on which consultation was sought; and
(b) The results of the consultation, including any decisions taken, the basis for those decisions and how they were implemented.

Differences of Opinion

Where differences of opinion arise within the engagement team, with those consulted and, where applicable, between the engagement partner and the engagement quality control reviewer, the engagement team should follow the firm's policies and procedures for dealing with and resolving differences of opinion.

As necessary, the engagement partner informs members of the engagement team that they may bring matters involving differences of opinion to the attention of the engagement partner or others within the firm as appropriate without fear of reprisals.

Engagement Quality Control Review

For audits of financial statements of listed entities, the engagement partner should:

(a) **Determine that an engagement quality control reviewer has been appointed;**

(b) Discuss significant matters arising during the audit engagement, including those identified during the engagement quality control review, with the engagement quality control reviewer; and
(c) Not issue the auditor's report until the completion of the engagement quality control review.

For other audit engagements where an engagement quality control review is performed, the engagement partner follows the requirements set out in subparagraphs (a) to (c).

37 Where, at the start of the engagement, an engagement quality control review is not considered necessary, the engagement partner is alert for changes in circumstances that would require such a review.

38 An engagement quality control review should include an objective evaluation of:

(a) The significant judgments made by the engagement team; and
(b) The conclusions reached in formulating the auditor's report.

39 An engagement quality control review ordinarily involves discussion with the engagement partner, a review of the financial information and the auditor's report, and, in particular, consideration of whether the auditor's report is appropriate. It also involves a review of selected audit documentation relating to the significant judgments the engagement team made and the conclusions they reached. The extent of the review depends on the complexity of the audit engagement and the risk that the auditor's report might not be appropriate in the circumstances. The review does not reduce the responsibilities of the engagement partner.

40 An engagement quality control review for audits of financial statements of listed entities includes considering the following:

- The engagement team's evaluation of the firm's independence in relation to the specific audit engagement.
- Significant risks identified during the engagement (in accordance with ISA (UK and Ireland) 315, "Understanding the Entity and its Environment and Assessing the Risks of Material Misstatement"), and the responses to those risks (in accordance with ISA (UK and Ireland) 320, "Auditor's Procedures in Response to Assessed Risks"), including the engagement team's assessment of, and response to, the risk of fraud.
- Judgments made, particularly with respect to materiality and significant risks.
- Whether appropriate consultation has taken place on matters involving differences of opinion or other difficult or contentious matters, and the conclusions arising from those consultations.
- The significance and disposition of corrected and uncorrected misstatements identified during the audit.
- The matters to be communicated to management and those charged with governance and, where applicable, other parties such as regulatory bodies.
- Whether audit documentation selected for review reflects the work performed in relation to the significant judgments and supports the conclusions reached.
- The appropriateness of the auditor's report to be issued.

Engagement quality control reviews for audits of historical financial information other than audits of financial statements of listed entities may, depending on the circumstances, include some or all of these considerations.

Monitoring

ISQC 1 requires the firm to establish policies and procedures designed to provide it with reasonable assurance that the policies and procedures relating to the system of quality control are relevant, adequate, operating effectively and complied with in practice. The engagement partner considers the results of the monitoring process as evidenced in the latest information circulated by the firm and, if applicable, other network firms. The engagement partner considers: 41

(a) Whether deficiencies noted in that information may affect the audit engagement; and
(b) Whether the measures the firm took to rectify the situation are sufficient in the context of that audit.

A deficiency in the firm's system of quality control does not indicate that a particular audit engagement was not performed in accordance with professional standards and regulatory and legal requirements, or that the auditor's report was not appropriate. 42

Effective Date

For firms in the UK and Ireland, this ISA (UK and Ireland) is effective for audits of financial statements for periods commencing on or after 15 December 2004. For network firms outside the UK and Ireland, this ISA (UK and Ireland) is effective for audits of financial statements for periods commencing on or after 15 June 2005. 43

Public Sector Perspective

Additional guidance for auditors of public sector bodies in the UK and Ireland is given in:

- Practice Note 10 "Audit of Financial Statements of Public Sector Entities in the United Kingdom (Revised)"
- Practice Note 10(I) "The Audit of Central Government Financial Statements in Ireland"

Some of the terms in the ISA (UK and Ireland), such as "engagement partner" and "firm," should be read as referring to their public sector equivalents. However, with limited exceptions, there is no public sector equivalent of "listed entities," although there may be audits of particularly significant public sector entities which should be subject to the listed entity requirements of mandatory rotation of the engagement partner (or equivalent) and engagement quality control review. There are no fixed objective criteria on which this determination of significance should be based. However, such an assessment should encompass an evaluation of all factors relevant to the audited entity. Such factors include size, complexity, commercial risk, parliamentary or media interest and the number and range of stakeholders affected. 1

In many jurisdictions there is a single statutorily appointed auditor-general. In such circumstances, where applicable, the engagement reviewer should be selected having regard to the need for independence and objectivity. 2

In the public sector, auditors may be appointed in accordance with statutory procedures. Accordingly, certain of the considerations regarding the acceptance and continuance of 3 client relationships and specific engagements, as set out in paragraphs 16-17 of this ISA (UK andIreland), may not be relevant.

4   Similarly, the independence of public sector auditors may be protected by statutory measures. However, public sector auditors or audit firms carrying out public sector audits on behalf of the statutory auditor may, depending on the terms of the mandate in a particular jurisdiction, need to adapt their approach in order to ensure compliance with the spirit of paragraphs 12 and 13. This may include, where the public sector auditor's mandate does not permit withdrawal from the engagement, disclosure through a public report, of circumstances that have arisen that would, if they were in the private sector, lead the auditor to withdraw.

5   Paragraph 20 sets out capabilities and competence expected of the engagement team. Additional capabilities may be required in public sector audits, dependent upon the terms of the mandate in a particular jurisdiction. Such additional capabilities may include an understanding of the applicable reporting arrangements, including reporting to parliament or in the public interest. The wider scope of a public sector audit may include, for example, some aspects of performance auditing or a comprehensive assessment of the arrangements for ensuring legality and preventing and detecting fraud and corruption.

[230] Revised
Audit Documentation

(Effective for audits of financial information for periods beginning on or after June 15, 2006)

Contents

	Paragraph
Introduction	1 - 5
Definitions	6
Nature of Audit Documentation	7 - 8
Form, Content and Extent of Audit Documentation	9 - 24
Documentation of the Identifying Characteristics of Specific Items or Matters Being Tested	12 - 13
Significant Matters	14 - 19
Documentation of Departures from Basic Principles or Essential Procedures	20 - 22
Identification of Preparer and Reviewer	23 - 24
Assembly of the Final Audit File	25 - 30
Changes to Audit Documentation in Exceptional Circumstances after the Date of the Auditor's Report	31 - 32
Effective Date	33

Appendix: Specific Audit Documentation Requirements and Guidance in Other ISAs (UK and Ireland)

Conforming Amendments to Other Pronouncements

International Standard on Auditing (UK and Ireland) (ISA (UK and Ireland)) 230 (Revised), "Audit Documentation," should be read in the context of the Auditing Practices Board's Statement "The Auditing Practices Board – Scope and Authority of Pronouncements (Revised)" which sets out the application and authority of ISAs (UK and Ireland).

This ISA (UK and Ireland) adopts the text of ISA 230 (Revised) issued by the International Auditing and Assurance Standards Board. Supplementary material added by the APB is differentiated by the use of grey shading.

Introduction

1. The purpose of this International Standard on Auditing (UK and Ireland) (ISA (UK and Ireland)) is to establish standards and provide guidance on audit documentation. The Appendix lists other ISAs (UK and Ireland) containing subject matter-specific documentation requirements and guidance. Laws or regulations may establish additional documentation requirements.

2. **The auditor should prepare, on a timely basis, audit documentation that provides:**
   (a) **A sufficient and appropriate record of the basis for the auditor's report; and**
   (b) **Evidence that the audit was performed in accordance with ISAs (UK and Ireland) and applicable legal and regulatory requirements.**

3. Preparing sufficient and appropriate audit documentation on a timely basis helps to enhance the quality of the audit and facilitates the effective review and evaluation of the audit evidence obtained and conclusions reached before the auditor's report is finalized. Documentation prepared at the time the work is performed is likely to be more accurate than documentation prepared subsequently.

4. Compliance with the requirements of this ISA (UK and Ireland) together with the specific documentation requirements of other relevant ISAs (UK and Ireland) is ordinarily sufficient to achieve the objectives in paragraph 2.

5. In addition to these objectives, audit documentation serves a number of purposes, including:
   (a) Assisting the audit team to plan and perform the audit;
   (b) Assisting members of the audit team responsible for supervision to direct and supervise the audit work, and to discharge their review responsibilities in accordance with ISA (UK and Ireland) 220, "Quality Control for Audits of Historical Financial Information;"
   (c) Enabling the audit team to be accountable for its work;
   (d) Retaining a record of matters of continuing significance to future audits;
   (e) Enabling an experienced auditor to conduct quality control reviews and inspections[1] in accordance with ISQC (UK and Ireland) 1, "Quality Control for Firms that Perform Audits and Reviews of Historical Financial Information, and Other Assurance and Related Services Engagements;" and
   (f) Enabling an experienced auditor to conduct external inspections in accordance with applicable legal, regulatory or other requirements.

Definitions

6. In this ISA (UK and Ireland):
   (a) "Audit documentation" means the record of audit procedures performed,[2] relevant audit evidence obtained, and conclusions the auditor reached (terms such as "working papers" or "workpapers" are also sometimes used); and
   (b) "Experienced auditor" means an individual (whether internal or external to the firm) who has a reasonable understanding of (i) audit processes, (ii) ISAs (UK and Ireland) and applicable legal and regulatory requirements, (iii) the business

---

[1] As defined in ISA (UK and Ireland) 220.

[2] Audit procedures performed include audit planning, as addressed in ISA (UK and Ireland) 300, "Planning an Audit of Financial Statements."

environment in which the entity operates, and (iv) auditing and financial reporting issues relevant to the entity's industry.

Nature of Audit Documentation

Audit documentation may be recorded on paper or on electronic or other media. It includes, for example, audit programs, analyses, issues memoranda, summaries of significant matters, letters of confirmation and representation, checklists, and correspondence (including e-mail) concerning significant matters. Abstracts or copies of the entity's records, for example, significant and specific contracts and agreements, may be included as part of audit documentation if considered appropriate. Audit documentation, however, is not a substitute for the entity's accounting records. The audit documentation for a specific audit engagement is assembled in an audit file. 7

The auditor ordinarily excludes from audit documentation superseded drafts of working papers and financial statements, notes that reflect incomplete or preliminary thinking, previous copies of documents corrected for typographical or other errors, and duplicates of documents. 8

Form, Content and Extent of Audit Documentation

The auditor should prepare the audit documentation so as to enable an experienced auditor, having no previous connection with the audit, to understand: 9

(a) **The nature, timing, and extent of the audit procedures performed to comply with ISAs (UK and Ireland) and applicable legal and regulatory requirements;**
(b) **The results of the audit procedures and the audit evidence obtained; and**
(c) **Significant matters arising during the audit and the conclusions reached thereon.**

The form, content and extent of audit documentation depend on factors such as: 10

- The nature of the audit procedures to be performed;
- The identified risks of material misstatement;
- The extent of judgment required in performing the work and evaluating the results;
- The significance of the audit evidence obtained;
- The nature and extent of exceptions identified;
- The need to document a conclusion or the basis for a conclusion not readily determinable from the documentation of the work performed or audit evidence obtained; and
- The audit methodology and tools used.

It is, however, neither necessary nor practicable to document every matter the auditor considers during the audit.

Oral explanations by the auditor, on their own, do not represent adequate support for the work the auditor performed or conclusions the auditor reached, but may be used to explain or clarify information contained in the audit documentation. 11

Documentation of the Identifying Characteristics of Specific Items or Matters Being Tested

12 In documenting the nature, timing and extent of audit procedures performed, the auditor should record the identifying characteristics of the specific items or matters being tested.

13 Recording the identifying characteristics serves a number of purposes. For example, it enables the audit team to be accountable for its work and facilitates the investigation of exceptions or inconsistencies. Identifying characteristics will vary with the nature of the audit procedure and the item or matter being tested. For example:

- For a detailed test of entity-generated purchase orders, the auditor may identify the documents selected for testing by their dates and unique purchase order numbers.
- For a procedure requiring selection or review of all items over a specific amount from a given population, the auditor may record the scope of the procedure and identify the population (for example, all journal entries over a specified amount from the journal register).
- For a procedure requiring systematic sampling from a population of documents, the auditor may identify the documents selected by recording their source, the starting point and the sampling interval (for example, a systematic sample of shipping reports selected from the shipping log for the period from April 1 to September 30, starting with report number 12345 and selecting every 125th report).
- For a procedure requiring inquiries of specific entity personnel, the auditor may record the dates of the inquiries and the names and job designations of the entity personnel.
- For an observation procedure, the auditor may record the process or subject matter being observed, the relevant individuals, their respective responsibilities, and where and when the observation was carried out.

Significant Matters

14 Judging the significance of a matter requires an objective analysis of the facts and circumstances. Significant matters include, amongst others:

- Matters that give rise to significant risks (as defined in ISA (UK and Ireland) 315, "Understanding the Entity and its Environment and Assessing the Risks of Material Misstatement").
- Results of audit procedures indicating (a) that the financial information could be materially misstated, or (b) a need to revise the auditor's previous assessment of the risks of material misstatement and the auditor's responses to those risks.
- Circumstances that cause the auditor significant difficulty in applying necessary audit procedures.
- Findings that could result in a modification to the auditor's report.

15 The auditor may consider it helpful to prepare and retain as part of the audit documentation a summary (sometimes known as a completion memorandum) that describes the significant matters identified during the audit and how they were addressed, or that includes cross-references to other relevant supporting audit documentation that provides such information. Such a summary may facilitate effective and efficient reviews and inspections of the audit documentation, particularly for large and complex audits. Further, the preparation of such a summary may assist the auditor's consideration of the significant matters.

The auditor should document discussions of significant matters with management and others on a timely basis. 16

The audit documentation includes records of the significant matters discussed, and when and with whom the discussions took place. It is not limited to records prepared by the auditor but may include other appropriate records such as agreed minutes of meetings prepared by the entity's personnel. Others with whom the auditor may discuss significant matters include those charged with governance, other personnel within the entity, and external parties, such as persons providing professional advice to the entity. 17

If the auditor has identified information that contradicts or is inconsistent with the auditor's final conclusion regarding a significant matter, the auditor should document how the auditor addressed the contradiction or inconsistency in forming the final conclusion. 18

The documentation of how the auditor addressed the contradiction or inconsistency, however, does not imply that the auditor needs to retain documentation that is incorrect or superseded. 19

Documentation of Departures from Basic Principles or Essential Procedures

The basic principles and essential procedures in ISAs (UK and Ireland) are designed to assist the auditor in meeting the overall objective of the audit. Accordingly, other than in exceptional circumstances, the auditor complies with each basic principle and essential procedure that is relevant in the circumstances of the audit. 20

Where, in exceptional circumstances, the auditor judges it necessary to depart from a basic principle or an essential procedure that is relevant in the circumstances of the audit, the auditor should document how the alternative audit procedures performed achieve the objective of the audit, and, unless otherwise clear, the reasons for the departure. This involves the auditor documenting how the alternative audit procedures performed were sufficient and appropriate to replace that basic principle or essential procedure. 21

The documentation requirement does not apply to basic principles and essential procedures that are not relevant in the circumstances, i.e., where the circumstances envisaged in the specified basic principle or essential procedure do not apply. For example, in a continuing engagement, nothing in ISA (UK and Ireland) 510, "Initial Engagements – Opening Balances and Continuing Engagements – Opening Balances," related to intial engagements is relevant. Similarly, if an ISA (UK and Ireland) includes conditional requirements, they are not relevant if the specified conditions do not exist (for example, the requirement to modify the auditor's report where there is a limitation of scope). 22

Identification of Preparer and Reviewer

In documenting the nature, timing and extent of audit procedures performed, the auditor should record: 23

(a) **Who performed the audit work and the date such work was completed; and**
(b) **Who reviewed the audit work performed and the date and extent of such review.**[3]

---

[3] *Paragraph 26 of ISA (UK and Ireland) 220 establishes the requirement for the auditor to review the audit work performed through review of the audit documentation, which involves the auditor documenting the extent and timing of the reviews. Paragraph 25 of ISA (UK and Ireland) 220 describes the nature of a review of work performed.*

24 The requirement to document who reviewed the audit work performed does not imply a need for each specific working paper to include evidence of review. The audit documentation, however, evidences who reviewed specified elements of the audit work performed and when.

Assembly of the Final Audit File

25 **The auditor should complete the assembly of the final audit file on a timely basis after the date of the auditor's report.**

26 ISQC (UK and Ireland) 1 requires firms to establish policies and procedures for the timely completion of the assembly of audit files. As ISQC (UK and Ireland) 1 indicates, 60 days after the date of the auditor's report is ordinarily an appropriate time limit within which to complete the assembly of the final audit file.

27 The completion of the assembly of the final audit file after the date of the auditor's report is an administrative process that does not involve the performance of new audit procedures or the drawing of new conclusions. Changes may, however, be made to the audit documentation during the final assembly process if they are administrative in nature. Examples of such changes include:

- Deleting or discarding superseded documentation.
- Sorting, collating and cross-referencing working papers.
- Signing off on completion checklists relating to the file assembly process.
- Documenting audit evidence that the auditor has obtained, discussed and agreed with the relevant members of the audit team before the date of the auditor's report.

28 **After the assembly of the final audit file has been completed, the auditor should not delete or discard audit documentation before the end of its retention period.**

29 ISQC (UK and Ireland) 1 requires firms to establish policies and procedures for the retention of engagement documentation. As ISQC (UK and Ireland) 1 indicates, the retention period for audit engagements ordinarily is no shorter than five years from the date of the auditor's report, or, if later, the date of the group auditor's report.[3a]

30 **When the auditor finds it necessary to modify existing audit documentation or add new audit documentation after the assembly of the final audit file has been completed, the auditor should, regardless of the nature of the modifications or additions, document:**

(a) **When and by whom they were made, and (where applicable) reviewed;**

[3a] *In the UK and Republic of Ireland this requirement is applied having regard to specific requirements of the Audit Regulations.*

Audit Regulation 3.08b states that "A Registered Auditor must keep all audit working papers which auditing standards require for a period of at least six years. The period starts with the end of the accounting period to which the papers relate."

Audit Regulation 7.06 states that "In carrying out its responsibilities under regulation 7.03, the Registration Committee, any sub-committee, the secretariat, or a monitoring unit may, to the extent necessary for the review of a firm's audit work or how it is complying or intends to comply with these regulations, require a Registered Auditor or an applicant for registration to provide any information, held in whatsoever form (including electronic), about the firm or its clients and to allow access to the firm's systems and personnel."

The Audit Regulations referred to above were originally published in December 1995 and updated in June 2005 (Audit News 40).

(b) The specific reasons for making them; and
(c) Their effect, if any, on the auditor's conclusions.

Changes to Audit Documentation in Exceptional Circumstances after the Date of the Auditor's Report

When exceptional circumstances arise after the date of the auditor's report that require the auditor to perform new or additional audit procedures or that lead the auditor to reach new conclusions, the auditor should document: 31

(a) The circumstances encountered;
(b) The new or additional audit procedures performed, audit evidence obtained, and conclusions reached; and
(c) When and by whom the resulting changes to audit documentation were made, and (where applicable) reviewed.

Such exceptional circumstances include the discovery of facts regarding the audited financial information that existed at the date of the auditor's report that might have affected the auditor's report had the auditor then been aware of them.   32

Effective Date

This ISA (UK and Ireland) is effective for audits of financial information for periods beginning on or after June 15, 2006.   33

Appendix

Specific Audit Documentation Requirements and Guidance in Other ISAs (UK and Ireland)

The following lists the main paragraphs that contain specific documentation requirements and guidance in other ISAs (UK and Ireland):

- ISA (UK and Ireland) 210, "Terms of Audit Engagements" – Paragraph 5–5-2;
- ISA (UK and Ireland) 220, "Quality Control for Audits of Historical Financial Information" – Paragraphs 11–14, 16, 25, 27, 30, 31 and 33;
- ISA (UK and Ireland) 240, "The Auditor's Responsibility to Consider Fraud in an Audit of Financial Statements" – Paragraphs 60 and 107–111;
- ISA (UK and Ireland) 250, Section A "Consideration of Laws and Regulations" – Paragraph 28; Section B "The Auditor's Right and Duty to Report to Regulators in the Financial Sector" – Paragraph 46;
- ISA (UK and Ireland) 260, "Communication of Audit Matters with Those Charged with Governance" – Paragraph 16;
- ISA (UK and Ireland) 300, "Planning an Audit of Financial Statements" – Paragraphs 22-26;
- ISA (Ireland) 315, "Understanding the Entity and its Environment and Assessing the Risks of Material Misstatement" – Paragraphs 122 and 123;
- ISA (UK and Ireland) 330, "The Auditor's Procedures in Response to Assessed Risks" – Paragraphs 73 and 74;
- ISA (UK and Ireland) 402, "Audit Considerations in Relation to Entities using Service Organizations" – Paragraphs 5-3 and 9-13;
- ISA (UK and Ireland) 505, "External Confirmations" – Paragraph 33;
- ISA (UK and Ireland) 570, "Going Concern" – Paragraph 30-1;
- ISA (UK and Ireland) 580, "Management Representations" – Paragraph 10; and
- ISA (UK and Ireland) 600, "Using the Work of Another Auditor" – Paragraph 14.

Amendments to ISA (UK and Ireland) 200, ISA (UK and Ireland) 330, ISQC (UK and Ireland) 1, and the APB Statement "The Auditing Practices Board – Scope and Authority of Pronouncements (Revised)" as a Result of ISA (UK and Ireland) 230 (Revised)

ISA (UK and Ireland) 200, "Objective and General Principles Governing an Audit of Financial Statements"

The following paragraph is added as 7a.*

The auditor may, in exceptional circumstances, judge it necessary to depart from a basic principle or an essential procedure that is relevant in the circumstances of the audit, in order to achieve the objective of the audit. In such a case, the auditor is not precluded from representing compliance with ISAs (UK and Ireland), provided the departure is appropriately documented as required by ISA (UK and Ireland) 230 (Revised), "Audit Documentation."

This amendment is effective for audits of financial statements for periods beginning on or after June 15, 2006.

---

* *This conforming change is inserted in a different location to that indicated by the IAASB to take account of the fact that the APB has not promulgated ISA 700 (Revised), relating to auditor's reports, and the conforming changes releted to that standard.*

ISA (UK and Ireland) 330, "The Auditor's Procedures in Response to Assessed Risks"

The following paragraphs in ISA (UK and Ireland) 330 are amended as marked:

The auditor's substantive procedures should include the following audit procedures related to the financial statement closing process: 50

- Agreeing or reconciling the financial statements with to the underlying accounting records; and
- Examining material journal entries and other adjustments made during the course of preparing the financial statements.

The nature and extent of the auditor's examination of journal entries and other adjustments depends on the nature and complexity of the entity's financial reporting process and the associated risks of material misstatement.

The auditor should document the overall responses to address the assessed risks of material misstatement at the financial statement level and the nature, timing, and extent of the further audit procedures, the linkage of those procedures with the assessed risks at the assertion level, and the results of those audit procedures, including the conclusions where these are not otherwise clear. In addition, if the auditor plans to use audit evidence about the operating effectiveness of controls obtained in prior audits, the auditor should document the conclusions reached with regard to relying on such controls that were tested in a prior audit. The manner in which these matters are documented is based on the auditor's professional judgment. ISA (UK and Ireland) 230, "Documentation" establishes standards and provides guidance regarding documentation in the context of the audit of financial statements.   73

The following paragraphs are added to ISA (UK and Ireland) 330:

The auditor's documentation should demonstrate that the financial statements agree or reconcile with the underlying accounting records.   73a

The manner in which the matters referred to in paragraphs 73 and 73a are documented is based on the auditor's professional judgment. ISA (UK and Ireland) 230 (Revised), "Audit Documentation" establishes standards and provides guidance regarding documentation in the context of the audit of financial statements.   73b

These amendments to ISA (UK and Ireland) 330 are effective for audits of financial statements for periods beginning on or after June 15, 2006.

ISQC (UK and Ireland) 1, "Quality Control for Firms that Perform Audits and Reviews of Historical Financial Information and Other Assurance and Related Services Engagements"

The following definition is added to ISQC (UK and Ireland) 1:

(a) "Engagement documentation"–the record of work performed, results obtained, and conclusions the practitioner reached (terms such as "working papers" or "workpapers" are sometimes used). The documentation for a specific engagement is assembled in an engagement file;   6

Existing subparagraphs (a)-(o) of paragraph 6 will be renumbered accordingly.

The following new subheader and paragraphs are added to ISQC (UK and Ireland) 1 as a subsection within the "Engagement Performance" section, after paragraph 73.

Engagement Documentation

Completion of the Assembly of Final Engagement Files

73a The firm should establish policies and procedures for engagement teams to complete the assembly of final engagement files on a timely basis after the engagement reports have been finalized.

73b Law or regulation may prescribe the time limits by which the assembly of final engagement files for specific types of engagement should be completed. Where no such time limits are prescribed in law or regulation, the firm establishes time limits appropriate to the nature of the engagements that reflect the need to complete the assembly of final engagement files on a timely basis. In the case of an audit, for example, such a time limit is ordinarily not more than 60 days after the date of the auditor's report.

73c Where two or more different reports are issued in respect of the same subject matter information of an entity, the firm's policies and procedures relating to time limits for the assembly of final engagement files address each report as if it were for a separate engagement. This may, for example, be the case when the firm issues an auditor's report on a component's financial information for group consolidation purposes and, at a subsequent date, an auditor's report on the same financial information for statutory purposes.

Confidentiality, Safe Custody, Integrity, Accessibility and Retrievability of Engagement Documentation

73d The firm should establish policies and procedures designed to maintain the confidentiality, safe custody, integrity, accessibility and retrievability of engagement documentation.

73e Relevant ethical requirements establish an obligation for the firm's personnel to observe at all times the confidentiality of information contained in engagement documentation, unless specific client authority has been given to disclose information, or there is a legal or professional duty to do so. Specific laws or regulations may impose additional obligations on the firm's personnel to maintain client confidentiality, particularly where data of a personal nature are concerned.

73f Whether engagement documentation is in paper, electronic or other media, the integrity, accessibility or retrievability of the underlying data may be compromised if the documentation could be altered, added to or deleted without the firm's knowledge, or if it could be permanently lost or damaged. Accordingly, the firm designs and implements appropriate controls for engagement documentation to:

(a) Enable the determinination of when and by whom engagement documentation was created, changed or reviewed;
(b) Protect the integrity of the information at all stages of the engagement, especially when the information is shared within the engagement team or transmitted to other parties via the Internet;
(c) Prevent unauthorized changes to the engagement documentation; and
(d) Allow access to the engagement documentation by the engagement team and other authorized parties as necessary to properly discharge their responsibilities.

73g Controls that the firm may design and implement to maintain the confidentiality, safe custody, integrity, accessibility and retrievability of engagement documentation include, for example:

- The use of a password among engagement team members to restrict access to electronic engagement documentation to authorized users.
- Appropriate back-up routines for electronic engagement documentation at appropriate stages during the engagement.
- Procedures for properly distributing engagement documentation to the team members at the start of engagement, processing it during engagement, and collating it at the end of engagement.
- Procedures for restricting access to, and enabling proper distribution and confidential storage of, hardcopy engagement documentation.

For practical reasons, original paper documentation may be electronically scanned for inclusion in engagement files. In that case, the firm implements appropriate procedures requiring engagement teams to: **73h**

(a) Generate scanned copies that reflect the entire content of the original paper documentation, including manual signatures, cross-references and annotations;
(b) Integrate the scanned copies into the engagement files, including indexing and signing off on the scanned copies as necessary; and
(c) Enable the scanned copies to be retrieved and printed as necessary.

The firm considers whether to retain original paper documentation that has been scanned for legal, regulatory or other reasons.

Retention of Engagement Documentation

The firm should establish policies and procedures for the retention of engagement documentation for a period sufficient to meet the needs of the firm or as required by law or regulation. **73i**

The needs of the firm for retention of engagement documentation, and the period of such retention, will vary with the nature of the engagement and the firm's circumstances, for example, whether the engagement documentation is needed to provide a record of matters of continuing significance to future engagements. The retention period may also depend on other factors, such as whether local law or regulation prescribes specific retention periods for certain types of engagements, or whether there are generally accepted retention periods in the jurisdiction in the absence of specific legal or regulatory requirements. In the specific case of audit engagements, the retention period ordinarily is no shorter than five years from the date of the auditor's report, or, if later, the date of the group auditor's report. **73j**

Procedures that the firm adopts for retention of engagement documentation include those that: **73k**

- Enable the retrieval of, and access to, the engagement documentation during the retention period, particularly in the case of electronic documentation since the underlying technology may be upgraded or changed over time.
- Provide, where necessary, a record of changes made to engagement documentation after the engagement files have been completed.
- Enable authorized external parties to access and review specific engagement documentation for quality control or other purposes.

Ownership of Engagement Documentation

Unless otherwise specified by law or regulation, engagement documentation is the property of the firm. The firm may, at its discretion, make portions of, or extracts from, engagement documentation available to clients, provided such disclosure does **73l** not undermine the validity of the work performed, or, in the case of assurance engagements, the independence of the firm or its personnel.

The effective date paragraph in ISQC (UK and Ireland) 1 is amended as marked:

98 Systems of quality control in compliance with this ISQC (UK and Ireland) are required to be established by firms in the UK and Ireland by 15 June 2005 (15 June 2006 for paragraphs 6(a) and 73a–73l). Firms consider the appropriate transitional arrangements for engagements in process at th~~at~~ese dates.

APB Statement: "The Auditing Practices Board – Scope and Authority of Pronouncements (Revised)"

The following paragraph in the APB Statement is amended as marked:

22 The nature of APB standards and associated guidance requires professional accountants to exercise professional judgment in applying them. Where, in exceptional circumstances, auditors and reporting accountants ~~may~~ judge it necessary to depart from a basic principle or essential procedure that is relevant in the circumstances ~~of a standard to achieve more effectively the objective~~ of the engagement. ~~When such a situation arises,~~ the auditor or reporting accountant documents how the alternative procedures performed achieve the objective of the engagement and, unless otherwise clear, the reasons for the departure.

This amendment is effective for engagements performed by auditors and reporting accountants for periods beginning on or after June 15, 2006.

[240]
The auditor's responsibility to consider fraud in an audit of financial statements

(Issued December 2004)

Contents

	Paragraphs
Introduction	1 - 3
Characteristics of Fraud	4 - 12
Responsibilities of Those Charged With Governance and of Management	13 - 16
Inherent Limitations of an Audit in the Context of Fraud	17 - 20
Responsibilities of the Auditor for Detecting Material Misstatement Due to Fraud	21 - 22
Professional Skepticism	23 - 26
Discussion Among the Engagement Team	27 - 32
Risk Assessment Procedures	33 - 56
Identification and Assessment of the Risks of Material Misstatement Due to Fraud	57 - 60
Responses to the Risks of Material Misstatement Due to Fraud	61 - 82
Evaluation of Audit Evidence	83 - 89
Management Representations	90 - 92
Communications With Management and Those Charged With Governance	93 - 101
Communications to Regulatory and Enforcement Authorities	102
Auditor Unable to Continue the Engagement	103 - 106
Documentation	107 - 111
Effective Date	112

Appendix 1: Examples of Fraud Risk Factors

Appendix 2: Examples of Possible Audit Procedures to Address the Assessed Risks of Material Misstatement Due to Fraud

Appendix 3: Examples of Circumstances that Indicate the Possibility of Fraud

International Standard on Auditing (UK and Ireland) (ISA (UK and Ireland)) 240 "The Auditor's Responsibility to Consider Fraud in an Audit of Financial Statements" should be read in the context of the Auditing Practices Board's Statement "The Auditing Practices Board - Scope and Authority of Pronouncements (Revised)" which sets out the application and authority of ISAs (UK and Ireland).

Introduction

The purpose of this International Standard on Auditing (UK and Ireland) (ISA (UK and Ireland)) is to establish standards and provide guidance on the auditor's responsibility to consider fraud in an audit of financial statements[1] and expand on how the standards and guidance in ISA (UK and Ireland) 315, "Understanding the Entity and its Environment and Assessing the Risks of Material Misstatement" and ISA (UK and Ireland) 330, "The Auditor's Procedures in Response to Assessed Risks" are to be applied in relation to the risks of material misstatement due to fraud. The standards and guidance in this ISA (UK and Ireland) are intended to be integrated into the overall audit process. 1

This ISA (UK and Ireland) uses the terms 'those charged with governance' and 'management'. The term 'governance' describes the role of persons entrusted with the supervision, control and direction of an entity. Ordinarily, those charged with governance are accountable for ensuring that the entity achieves its objectives, and for the quality of its financial reporting and reporting to interested parties. Those charged with governance include management only when they perform such functions. 1-1

In the UK and Ireland, those charged with governance include the directors (executive and non-executive) of a company or other body, the members of an audit committee where one exists, the partners, proprietors, committee of management or trustees of other forms of entity, or equivalent persons responsible for directing the entity's affairs and preparing its financial statements. 1-2

'Management' comprises those persons who perform senior managerial functions. 1-3

In the UK and Ireland, depending on the nature and circumstances of the entity, management may include some or all of those charged with governance (e.g. executive directors). Management will not normally include non-executive directors. 1-4

This standard: 2
- Distinguishes fraud from error and describes the two types of fraud that are relevant to the auditor, that is, misstatements resulting from misappropriation of assets and misstatements resulting from fraudulent financial reporting; describes the respective responsibilities of those charged with governance and the management of the entity for the prevention and detection of fraud, describes the inherent limitations of an audit in the context of fraud, and sets out the responsibilities of the auditor for detecting material misstatements due to fraud;
- Requires the auditor to maintain an attitude of professional skepticism recognizing the possibility that a material misstatement due to fraud could exist, notwithstanding the auditor's past experience with the entity about the honesty and integrity of management and those charged with governance;
- Requires members of the engagement team to discuss the susceptibility of the entity's financial statements to material misstatement due to fraud and requires the engagement partner to consider which matters are to be communicated to members of the engagement team not involved in the discussion;

---

[1] The auditor's responsibility to consider laws and regulations in an audit of financial statements is established in ISA (UK and Ireland) 250, "Consideration of Laws and Regulations."

- Requires the auditor to:
  - Perform procedures to obtain information that is used to identify the risks of material misstatement due to fraud;
  - Identify and assess the risks of material misstatement due to fraud at the financial statement level and the assertion level; and for those assessed risks that could result in a material misstatement due to fraud, evaluate the design of the entity's related controls, including relevant control activities, and to determine whether they have been implemented;
  - Determine overall responses to address the risks of material misstatement due to fraud at the financial statement level and consider the assignment and supervision of personnel; consider the accounting policies used by the entity and incorporate an element of unpredictability in the selection of the nature, timing and extent of the audit procedures to be performed;
  - Design and perform audit procedures to respond to the risk of management override of controls;
  - Determine responses to address the assessed risks of material misstatement due to fraud;
  - Consider whether an identified misstatement may be indicative of fraud;
  - Obtain written representations from management[1a] relating to fraud; and
  - Communicate with management and those charged with governance;
- Provides guidance on communications with regulatory and enforcement authorities;
- Provides guidance if, as a result of a misstatement resulting from fraud or suspected fraud, the auditor encounters exceptional circumstances that bring into question the auditor's ability to continue performing the audit; and
- Establishes documentation requirements.

3   In planning and performing the audit to reduce audit risk to an acceptably low level, the auditor should consider the risks of material misstatements in the financial statements due to fraud.

Characteristics of Fraud

4   Misstatements in the financial statements can arise from fraud or error. The distinguishing factor between fraud and error is whether the underlying action that results in the misstatement of the financial statements is intentional or unintentional.

5   The term "error" refers to an unintentional misstatement in financial statements, including the omission of an amount or a disclosure, such as the following:

- A mistake in gathering or processing data from which financial statements are prepared.
- An incorrect accounting estimate arising from oversight or misinterpretation of facts.
- A mistake in the application of accounting principles relating to measurement, recognition, classification, presentation or disclosure.

6   The term "fraud" refers to an intentional act by one or more individuals among management, those charged with governance, employees, or third parties, involving the use of deception to obtain an unjust or illegal advantage. Although fraud is a broad legal concept, for the purposes of this ISA (UK and Ireland), the auditor is concerned with fraud that causes a material misstatement in the financial statements. Auditors do not make legal determinations of whether fraud has actually occurred.

[1a] In the UK and Ireland, the auditor obtains written representations from those charged with governance.

Fraud involving one or more members of management or those charged with governance is referred to as "management fraud;" fraud involving only employees of the entity is referred to as "employee fraud." In either case, there may be collusion within the entity or with third parties outside of the entity.

Two types of intentional misstatements are relevant to the auditor, that is, misstatements resulting from fraudulent financial reporting and misstatements resulting from misappropriation of assets. 7

Fraudulent financial reporting involves intentional misstatements including omissions of amounts or disclosures in financial statements to deceive financial statement users. Fraudulent financial reporting may be accomplished by the following: 8

- Manipulation, falsification (including forgery), or alteration of accounting records or supporting documentation from which the financial statements are prepared.
- Misrepresentation in, or intentional omission from, the financial statements of events, transactions or other significant information.
- Intentional misapplication of accounting principles relating to amounts, classification, manner of presentation, or disclosure.

Fraudulent financial reporting often involves management override of controls that otherwise may appear to be operating effectively. Fraud can be committed by management overriding controls using such techniques as: 9

- Recording fictitious journal entries, particularly close to the end of an accounting period, to manipulate operating results or achieve other objectives;
- Inappropriately adjusting assumptions and changing judgments used to estimate account balances;
- Omitting, advancing or delaying recognition in the financial statements of events and transactions that have occurred during the reporting period;
- Concealing, or not disclosing, facts that could affect the amounts recorded in the financial statements;
- Engaging in complex transactions that are structured to misrepresent the financial position or financial performance of the entity; and
- Altering records and terms related to significant and unusual transactions.

Fraudulent financial reporting can be caused by the efforts of management to manage earnings in order to deceive financial statement users by influencing their perceptions as to the entity's performance and profitability. Such earnings management may start out with small actions or inappropriate adjustment of assumptions and changes in judgments by management. Pressures and incentives may lead these actions to increase to the extent that they result in fraudulent financial reporting. Such a situation could occur when, due to pressures to meet market expectations or a desire to maximize compensation based on performance, management intentionally takes positions that lead to fraudulent financial reporting by materially misstating the financial statements. In some other entities, management may be motivated to reduce earnings by a material amount to minimize tax or to inflate earnings to secure bank financing. 10

Misappropriation of assets involves the theft of an entity's assets and is often perpetrated by employees in relatively small and immaterial amounts. However, it can also involve management who are usually more able to disguise or conceal misappropriations in ways that are difficult to detect. Misappropriation of assets can be accomplished in a variety of ways including: 11

- Embezzling receipts (for example, misappropriating collections on accounts receivable or diverting receipts in respect of written-off accounts to personal bank accounts);
- Stealing physical assets or intellectual property (for example, stealing inventory for personal use or for sale, stealing scrap for resale, colluding with a competitor by disclosing technological data in return for payment);
- Causing an entity to pay for goods and services not received (for example, payments to fictitious vendors, kickbacks paid by vendors to the entity's purchasing agents in return for inflating prices, payments to fictitious employees); and
- Using an entity's assets for personal use (for example, using the entity's assets as collateral for a personal loan or a loan to a related party).

Misappropriation of assets is often accompanied by false or misleading records or documents in order to conceal the fact that the assets are missing or have been pledged without proper authorization.

12 Fraud involves incentive or pressure to commit fraud, a perceived opportunity to do so and some rationalization of the act. Individuals may have an incentive to misappropriate assets for example, because the individuals are living beyond their means. Fraudulent financial reporting may be committed because management is under pressure, from sources outside or inside the entity, to achieve an expected (and perhaps unrealistic) earnings target – particularly since the consequences to management for failing to meet financial goals can be significant. A perceived opportunity for fraudulent financial reporting or misappropriation of assets may exist when an individual believes internal control can be overridden, for example, because the individual is in a position of trust or has knowledge of specific weaknesses in internal control. Individuals may be able to rationalize committing a fraudulent act. Some individuals possess an attitude, character or set of ethical values that allow them knowingly and intentionally to commit a dishonest act. However, even otherwise honest individuals can commit fraud in an environment that imposes sufficient pressure on them.

Responsibilities of Those Charged With Governance and of Management

13 The primary responsibility for the prevention and detection of fraud rests with both those charged with governance of the entity and with management. The respective responsibilities of those charged with governance and of management may vary by entity and from country to country. In some entities, the governance structure may be more informal as those charged with governance may be the same individuals as management of the entity.

14 It is important that management, with the oversight of those charged with governance, place a strong emphasis on fraud prevention, which may reduce opportunities for fraud to take place, and fraud deterrence, which could persuade individuals not to commit fraud because of the likelihood of detection and punishment. This involves a culture of honesty and ethical behavior. Such a culture, based on a strong set of core values, is communicated and demonstrated by management and by those charged with governance and provides the foundation for employees as to how the entity conducts its business. Creating a culture of honesty and ethical behavior includes setting the proper tone; creating a positive workplace environment; hiring, training and promoting appropriate employees; requiring periodic confirmation by

employees of their responsibilities and taking appropriate action in response to actual, suspected or alleged fraud.

It is the responsibility of those charged with governance of the entity to ensure, through oversight of management, that the entity establishes and maintains internal control to provide reasonable assurance with regard to reliability of financial reporting, effectiveness and efficiency of operations and compliance with applicable laws and regulations. Active oversight by those charged with governance can help reinforce management's commitment to create a culture of honesty and ethical behavior. In exercising oversight responsibility, those charged with governance consider the potential for management override of controls or other inappropriate influence over the financial reporting process, such as efforts by management to manage earnings in order to influence the perceptions of analysts as to the entity's performance and profitability. **15**

It is the responsibility of management, with oversight from those charged with governance, to establish a control environment and maintain policies and procedures to assist in achieving the objective of ensuring, as far as possible, the orderly and efficient conduct of the entity's business. This responsibility includes establishing and maintaining controls pertaining to the entity's objective of preparing financial statements that give a true and fair view (or are presented fairly in all material respects) in accordance with the applicable financial reporting framework and managing risks that may give rise to material misstatements in those financial statements. Such controls reduce but do not eliminate the risks of misstatement. In determining which controls to implement to prevent and detect fraud, management considers the risks that the financial statements may be materially misstated as a result of fraud. As part of this consideration, management may conclude that it is not cost effective to implement and maintain a particular control in relation to the reduction in the risks of material misstatement due to fraud to be achieved. **16**

Inherent Limitations of an Audit in the Context of Fraud

As described in ISA (UK and Ireland) 200, "Objective and General Principles Governing an Audit of Financial Statements," the objective of an audit of financial statements is to enable the auditor to express an opinion whether the financial statements are prepared, in all material respects, in accordance with an applicable financial reporting framework. Owing to the inherent limitations of an audit, there is an unavoidable risk that some material misstatements of the financial statements will not be detected, even though the audit is properly planned and performed in accordance with ISAs (UK and Ireland). **17**

The risk of not detecting a material misstatement resulting from fraud is higher than the risk of not detecting a material misstatement resulting from error because fraud may involve sophisticated and carefully organized schemes designed to conceal it, such as forgery, deliberate failure to record transactions, or intentional misrepresentations being made to the auditor. Such attempts at concealment may be even more difficult to detect when accompanied by collusion. Collusion may cause the auditor to believe that audit evidence is persuasive when it is, in fact, false. The auditor's ability to detect a fraud depends on factors such as the skillfulness of the perpetrator, the frequency and extent of manipulation, the degree of collusion involved, the relative size of individual amounts manipulated, and the seniority of those individuals involved. While the auditor may be able to identify potential opportunities for fraud to be perpetrated, it is difficult for the auditor to determine **18** whether misstatements in judgment areas such as accounting estimates are caused by fraud or error.

19 Furthermore, the risk of the auditor not detecting a material misstatement resulting from management fraud is greater than for employee fraud, because management is frequently in a position to directly or indirectly manipulate accounting records and present fraudulent financial information. Certain levels of management may be in a position to override control procedures designed to prevent similar frauds by other employees, for example, by directing subordinates to record transactions incorrectly or to conceal them. Given its position of authority within an entity, management has the ability to either direct employees to do something or solicit their help to assist in carrying out a fraud, with or without the employees' knowledge.

20 The subsequent discovery of a material misstatement of the financial statements resulting from fraud does not, in and of itself, indicate a failure to comply with ISAs (UK and Ireland). This is particularly the case for certain kinds of intentional misstatements, since audit procedures may be ineffective for detecting an intentional misstatement that is concealed through collusion between or among one or more individuals among management, those charged with governance, employees, or third parties, or that involves falsified documentation. Whether the auditor has performed an audit in accordance with ISAs (UK and Ireland) is determined by the audit procedures performed in the circumstances, the sufficiency and appropriateness of the audit evidence obtained as a result thereof and the suitability of the auditor's report based on an evaluation of that evidence.

Responsibilities of the Auditor for Detecting Material Misstatement Due to Fraud

21 An auditor conducting an audit in accordance with ISAs (UK and Ireland) obtains reasonable assurance that the financial statements taken as a whole are free from material misstatement, whether caused by fraud or error. An auditor cannot obtain absolute assurance that material misstatements in the financial statements will be detected because of such factors as the use of judgment, the use of testing, the inherent limitations of internal control and the fact that much of the audit evidence available to the auditor is persuasive rather than conclusive in nature.

22 When obtaining reasonable assurance, an auditor maintains an attitude of professional skepticism throughout the audit, considers the potential for management override of controls and recognizes the fact that audit procedures that are effective for detecting error may not be appropriate in the context of an identified risk of material misstatement due to fraud. The remainder of this ISA (UK and Ireland) provides additional guidance on considering the risks of fraud in an audit and designing procedures to detect material misstatements due to fraud.

Professional Skepticism

23 As required by ISA (UK and Ireland) 200, the auditor plans and performs an audit with an attitude of professional skepticism recognizing that circumstances may exist that cause the financial statements to be materially misstated. Due to the characteristics of fraud, the auditor's attitude of professional skepticism is particularly important when considering the risks of material misstatement due to fraud. Professional skepticism is an attitude that includes a questioning mind and a critical assessment of audit evidence. Professional skepticism requires an ongoing

questioning of whether the information and audit evidence obtained suggests that a material misstatement due to fraud may exist.

The auditor should maintain an attitude of professional skepticism throughout the audit, recognizing the possibility that a material misstatement due to fraud could exist, notwithstanding the auditor's past experience with the entity about the honesty and integrity of management and those charged with governance. 24

As discussed in ISA (UK and Ireland) 315, the auditor's previous experience with the entity contributes to an understanding of the entity. However, although the auditor cannot be expected to fully disregard past experience with the entity about the honesty and integrity of management and those charged with governance, the maintenance of an attitude of professional skepticism is important because there may have been changes in circumstances. When making inquiries and performing other audit procedures, the auditor exercises professional skepticism and is not satisfied with less-than-persuasive audit evidence based on a belief that management and those charged with governance are honest and have integrity. With respect to those charged with governance, maintaining an attitude of professional skepticism means that the auditor carefully considers the reasonableness of responses to inquiries of those charged with governance, and other information obtained from them, in light of all other evidence obtained during the audit. 25

An audit performed in accordance with ISAs (UK and Ireland) rarely involves the authentication of documents, nor is the auditor trained as or expected to be an expert in such authentication. Furthermore, an auditor may not discover the existence of a modification to the terms contained in a document, for example through a side agreement that management or a third party has not disclosed to the auditor. During the audit, the auditor considers the reliability of the information to be used as audit evidence including consideration of controls over its preparation and maintenance where relevant. Unless the auditor has reason to believe the contrary, the auditor ordinarily accepts records and documents as genuine. However, if conditions identified during the audit cause the auditor to believe that a document may not be authentic or that terms in a document have been modified, the auditor investigates further, for example confirming directly with the third party or considering using the work of an expert to assess the document's authenticity. 26

Discussion Among the Engagement Team

Members of the engagement team should discuss the susceptibility of the entity's financial statements to material misstatement due to fraud. 27

ISA (UK and Ireland) 315 requires members of the engagement team to discuss the susceptibility of the entity to material misstatement of the financial statements. This discussion places particular emphasis on the susceptibility of the entity's financial statements to material misstatement due to fraud. The discussion includes the engagement partner who uses professional judgment, prior experience with the entity and knowledge of current developments to determine which other members of the engagement team are included in the discussion. Ordinarily, the discussion involves the key members of the engagement team. The discussion provides an opportunity for more experienced engagement team members to share their insights about how and where the financial statements may be susceptible to material misstatement due to fraud. 28

29 **The engagement partner should consider which matters are to be communicated to members of the engagement team not involved in the discussion.** All of the members of the engagement team do not necessarily need to be informed of all of the decisions reached in the discussion. For example, a member of the engagement team involved in audit of a component of the entity may not need to know the decisions reached regarding another component of the entity.

30 The discussion occurs with a questioning mind setting aside any beliefs that the engagement team members may have that management and those charged with governance are honest and have integrity. The discussion ordinarily includes:

- An exchange of ideas among engagement team members about how and where they believe the entity's financial statements may be susceptible to material misstatement due to fraud, how management could perpetrate and conceal fraudulent financial reporting, and how assets of the entity could be misappropriated;
- A consideration of circumstances that might be indicative of earnings management and the practices that might be followed by management to manage earnings that could lead to fraudulent financial reporting;
- A consideration of the known external and internal factors affecting the entity that may create an incentive or pressure for management or others to commit fraud, provide the opportunity for fraud to be perpetrated, and indicate a culture or environment that enables management or others to rationalize committing fraud;
- A consideration of management's involvement in overseeing employees with access to cash or other assets susceptible to misappropriation;
- A consideration of any unusual or unexplained changes in behavior or lifestyle of management or employees which have come to the attention of the engagement team;
- An emphasis on the importance of maintaining a proper state of mind throughout the audit regarding the potential for material misstatement due to fraud;
- A consideration of the types of circumstances that, if encountered, might indicate the possibility of fraud;
- A consideration of how an element of unpredictability will be incorporated into the nature, timing and extent of the audit procedures to be performed;
- A consideration of the audit procedures that might be selected to respond to the susceptibility of the entity's financial statement to material misstatements due to fraud and whether certain types of audit procedures are more effective than others;
- A consideration of any allegations of fraud that have come to the auditor's attention; and
- A consideration of the risk of management override of controls.

31 Discussing the susceptibility of the entity's financial statements to material misstatement due to fraud is an important part of the audit. It enables the auditor to consider an appropriate response to the susceptibility of the entity's financial statements to material misstatement due to fraud and to determine which members of the engagement team will conduct certain audit procedures. It also permits the auditor to determine how the results of audit procedures will be shared among the engagement team and how to deal with any allegations of fraud that may come to the auditor's attention. Many small audits are carried out entirely by the engagement partner (who may be a sole practitioner). In such situations, the engagement partner, having personally conducted the planning of the audit, considers the susceptibility of the entity's financial statements to material misstatement due to fraud.

It is important that after the initial discussion while planning the audit, and also at intervals throughout the audit, engagement team members continue to communicate and share information obtained that may affect the assessment of risks of material misstatement due to fraud or the audit procedures performed to address these risks. For example, for some entities it may be appropriate to update the discussion when reviewing the entity's interim financial information.

Risk Assessment Procedures

As required by ISA (UK and Ireland) 315, to obtain an understanding of the entity and its environment, including its internal control, the auditor performs risk assessment procedures. As part of this work the auditor performs the following procedures to obtain information that is used to identify the risks of material misstatement due to fraud:

(a) Makes inquiries of management, of those charged with governance, and of others within the entity as appropriate and obtains an understanding of how those charged with governance exercise oversight of management's processes for identifying and responding to the risks of fraud and the internal control that management has established to mitigate these risks.
(b) Considers whether one or more fraud risk factors are present.
(c) Considers any unusual or unexpected relationships that have been identified in performing analytical procedures.
(d) Considers other information that may be helpful in identifying the risks of material misstatement due to fraud.

Inquiries and Obtaining an Understanding of Oversight Exercised by Those Charged With Governance

When obtaining an understanding of the entity and its environment, including its internal control, the auditor should make inquiries of management regarding:

(a) Management's assessment of the risk that the financial statements may be materially misstated due to fraud;
(b) Management's process for identifying and responding to the risks of fraud in the entity, including any specific risks of fraud that management has identified or account balances, classes of transactions or disclosures for which a risk of fraud is likely to exist;
(c) Management's communication, if any, to those charged with governance regarding its processes for identifying and responding to the risks of fraud in the entity; and
(d) Management's communication, if any, to employees regarding its views on business practices and ethical behavior.

As management[1b] is responsible for the entity's internal control and for the preparation of the financial statements, it is appropriate for the auditor to make inquiries of management regarding management's own assessment of the risk of fraud and the controls in place to prevent and detect it. The nature, extent and frequency of management's assessment of such risk and controls vary from entity to entity. In some entities, management may make detailed assessments on an annual basis or as part of continuous monitoring. In other entities, management's assessment may be less formal and less frequent. In some entities, particularly smaller entities, the focus of the assessment may be on the risks of employee fraud or

---

[1b] In the UK and Ireland, those charged with governance are responsible for the preparation of the financial statements.

misappropriation of assets. The nature, extent and frequency of management's assessment are relevant to the auditor's understanding of the entity's control environment. For example, the fact that management has not made an assessment of the risk of fraud may in some circumstances be indicative of the lack of importance that management places on internal control.

36 In a small owner managed entity, the owner-manager may be able to exercise more effective oversight than in a larger entity, thereby compensating for the generally more limited opportunities for segregation of duties. On the other hand, the owner-manager may be more able to override controls because of the informal system of internal control. This is taken into account by the auditor when identifying the risks of material misstatement due to fraud.

37 When making inquiries as part of obtaining an understanding of management's process for identifying and responding to the risks of fraud in the entity, the auditor inquires about the process to respond to internal or external allegations of fraud affecting the entity. For entities with multiple locations, the auditor inquires about the nature and extent of monitoring of operating locations or business segments and whether there are particular operating locations or business segments for which a risk of fraud may be more likely to exist.

38 **The auditor should make inquiries of management, internal audit, and others within the entity as appropriate, to determine whether they have knowledge of any actual, suspected or alleged fraud affecting the entity.**

39 Although the auditor's inquiries of management may provide useful information concerning the risks of material misstatements in the financial statements resulting from employee fraud, such inquiries are unlikely to provide useful information regarding the risks of material misstatement in the financial statements resulting from management fraud. Making inquiries of others within the entity, in addition to management, may be useful in providing the auditor with a perspective that is different from management and those responsible for the financial reporting process. Such inquiries may provide individuals with an opportunity to convey information to the auditor that may not otherwise be communicated. The auditor uses professional judgment in determining those others within the entity to whom inquiries are directed and the extent of such inquiries. In making this determination the auditor considers whether others within the entity may be able to provide information that will be helpful to the auditor in identifying the risks of material misstatement due to fraud.

40 The auditor makes inquiries of internal audit personnel, for those entities that have an internal audit function. The inquiries address the views of the internal auditors regarding the risks of fraud, whether during the year the internal auditors have performed any procedures to detect fraud, whether management has satisfactorily responded to any findings resulting from these procedures, and whether the internal auditors have knowledge of any actual, suspected or alleged fraud.

41 Examples of others within the entity to whom the auditor may direct inquiries about the existence or suspicion of fraud include:
   - Operating personnel not directly involved in the financial reporting process;
   - Employees with different levels of authority;
   - Employees involved in initiating, processing or recording complex or unusual transactions and those who supervise or monitor such employees;
   - In-house legal counsel;
   - Chief ethics officer or equivalent person; and

- The person or persons charged with dealing with allegations of fraud.

When evaluating management's responses to inquiries, the auditor maintains an attitude of professional skepticism recognizing that management is often in the best position to perpetrate fraud. Therefore, the auditor uses professional judgment in deciding when it is necessary to corroborate responses to inquiries with other information. When responses to inquiries are inconsistent, the auditor seeks to resolve the inconsistencies. 42

The auditor should obtain an understanding of how those charged with governance exercise oversight of management's processes for identifying and responding to the risks of fraud in the entity and the internal control that management has established to mitigate these risks. 43

Those charged with governance of an entity have oversight responsibility for systems for monitoring risk, financial control and compliance with the law. In many countries, corporate governance practices are well developed and those charged with governance play an active role in oversight of the entity's assessment of the risks of fraud and of the internal control the entity has established to mitigate specific risks of fraud that the entity has identified. Since the responsibilities of those charged with governance and management may vary by entity and by country, it is important that the auditor understands their respective responsibilities to enable the auditor to obtain an understanding of the oversight exercised by the appropriate individuals.[2] Those charged with governance include management when management performs such functions, such as may be the case in smaller entities. 44

Obtaining an understanding of how those charged with governance exercise oversight of management's processes for identifying and responding to the risks of fraud in the entity, and the internal control that management has established to mitigate these risks, may provide insights regarding the susceptibility of the entity to management fraud, the adequacy of such internal control and the competence and integrity of management. The auditor may obtain this understanding by performing procedures such as attending meetings where such discussions take place, reading the minutes from such meetings or by making inquiries of those charged with governance. 45

The auditor should make inquiries of those charged with governance to determine whether they have knowledge of any actual, suspected or alleged fraud affecting the entity. 46

The auditor makes inquiries of those charged with governance in part to corroborate the responses to the inquiries from management. When responses to these inquiries are inconsistent, the auditor obtains additional audit evidence to resolve the inconsistencies. Inquiries of those charged with governance may also assist the auditor in identifying risks of material misstatement due to fraud. 47

Consideration of Fraud Risk Factors

When obtaining an understanding of the entity and its environment, including its internal control, the auditor should consider whether the information obtained indicates that one or more fraud risk factors are present. 48

---

[4] ISA (UK and Ireland) 260, "Communication of Audit Matters With Those Charged With Governance," paragraph 8, discusses with whom the auditor communicates when the entity's governance structure is not well defined.

49   The fact that fraud is usually concealed can make it very difficult to detect. Nevertheless, when obtaining an understanding of the entity and its environment, including its internal control, the auditor may identify events or conditions that indicate an incentive or pressure to commit fraud or provide an opportunity to commit fraud. Such events or conditions are referred to as "fraud risk factors." For example:

- The need to meet expectations of third parties to obtain additional equity financing may create pressure to commit fraud;
- The granting of significant bonuses if unrealistic profit targets are met may create an incentive to commit fraud; and

An ineffective control environment may create an opportunity to commit fraud. While fraud risk factors may not necessarily indicate the existence of fraud, they have often been present in circumstances where frauds have occurred. The presence of fraud risk factors may affect the auditor's assessment of the risks of material misstatement.

50   Fraud risk factors cannot easily be ranked in order of importance. The significance of fraud risk factors varies widely. Some of these factors will be present in entities where the specific conditions do not present risks of material misstatement. Accordingly, the auditor exercises professional judgment in determining whether a fraud risk factor is present and whether it is to be considered in assessing the risks of material misstatement of the financial statements due to fraud.

51   Examples of fraud risk factors related to fraudulent financial reporting and misappropriation of assets are presented in Appendix 1 to this ISA (UK and Ireland). These illustrative risk factors are classified based on the three conditions that are generally present when fraud exists: an incentive or pressure to commit fraud; a perceived opportunity to commit fraud; and an ability to rationalize the fraudulent action. Risk factors reflective of an attitude that permits rationalization of the fraudulent action may not be susceptible to observation by the auditor. Nevertheless, the auditor may become aware of the existence of such information. Although the fraud risk factors described in Appendix 1 cover a broad range of situations that may be faced by auditors, they are only examples and other risk factors may exist. The auditor also has to be alert for risk factors specific to the entity that are not included in Appendix 1. Not all of the examples in Appendix 1 are relevant in all circumstances, and some may be of greater or lesser significance in entities of different size, with different ownership characteristics, in different industries, or because of other differing characteristics or circumstances.

52   The size, complexity, and ownership characteristics of the entity have a significant influence on the consideration of relevant fraud risk factors. For example, in the case of a large entity, the auditor ordinarily considers factors that generally constrain improper conduct by management, such as the effectiveness of those charged with governance and of the internal audit function and the existence and enforcement of a formal code of conduct. Furthermore, fraud risk factors considered at a business segment operating level may provide different insights than the consideration thereof at an entity-wide level. In the case of a small entity, some or all of these considerations may be inapplicable or less important. For example, a smaller entity may not have a written code of conduct but, instead, may have developed a culture that emphasizes the importance of integrity and ethical behavior through oral communication and by management example. Domination of management by a single individual in a small entity does not generally, in and of itself, indicate a failure by management to display and communicate an appropriate attitude regarding internal control and the financial reporting process. In some entities, the need for

management authorization can compensate for otherwise weak controls and reduce the risk of employee fraud. However, domination of management by a single individual can be a potential weakness since there is an opportunity for management override of controls.

Consideration of Unusual or Unexpected Relationships

When performing analytical procedures to obtain an understanding of the entity and its environment, including its internal control, the auditor should consider unusual or unexpected relationships that may indicate risks of material misstatement due to fraud.   53

Analytical procedures may be helpful in identifying the existence of unusual transactions or events, and amounts, ratios, and trends that might indicate matters that have financial statement and audit implications. In performing analytical procedures the auditor develops expectations about plausible relationships that are reasonably expected to exist based on the auditor's understanding of the entity and its environment, including its internal control. When a comparison of those expectations with recorded amounts, or with ratios developed from recorded amounts, yields unusual or unexpected relationships, the auditor considers those results in identifying risks of material misstatement due to fraud. Analytical procedures include procedures related to revenue accounts with the objective of identifying unusual or unexpected relationships that may indicate risks of material misstatement due to fraudulent financial reporting, such as, for example, fictitious sales or significant returns from customers that might indicate undisclosed side agreements.   54

Consideration of Other Information

When obtaining an understanding of the entity and its environment, including its internal control, the auditor should consider whether other information obtained indicates risks of material misstatement due to fraud.   55

In addition to information obtained from applying analytical procedures, the auditor considers other information obtained about the entity and its environment that may be helpful in identifying the risks of material misstatement due to fraud. The discussion among team members described in paragraphs 27-32 may provide information that is helpful in identifying such risks. In addition, information obtained from the auditor's client acceptance and retention processes, and experience gained on other engagements performed for the entity, for example engagements to review interim financial information, may be relevant in the identification of the risks of material misstatement due to fraud.   56

Identification and Assessment of the Risks of Material Misstatement Due to Fraud

When identifying and assessing the risks of material misstatement at the financial statement level, and at the assertion level for classes of transactions, account balances and disclosures, the auditor should identify and assess the risks of material misstatement due to fraud. Those assessed risks that could result in a material misstatement due to fraud are significant risks and accordingly, to the extent not already done so, the auditor should evaluate the design of the entity's related controls, including relevant control activities, and determine whether they have been implemented.   57

58   To assess the risks of material misstatement due to fraud the auditor uses professional judgment and:
   (a) Identifies risks of fraud by considering the information obtained through performing risk assessment procedures and by considering the classes of transactions, account balances and disclosures in the financial statements;
   (b) Relates the identified risks of fraud to what can go wrong at the assertion level; and
   (c) Considers the likely magnitude of the potential misstatement including the possibility that the risk might give rise to multiple misstatements and the likelihood of the risk occurring.

59   It is important for the auditor to obtain an understanding of the controls that management has designed and implemented to prevent and detect fraud because in designing and implementing such controls, management may make informed judgments on the nature and extent of the controls it chooses to implement, and the nature and extent of the risks it chooses to assume. The auditor may learn, for example, that management has consciously chosen to accept the risks associated with a lack of segregation of duties. This may often be the case in small entities where the owner provides day-to-day supervision of operations. Information from obtaining this understanding may also be useful in identifying fraud risk factors that may affect the auditor's assessment of the risks that the financial statements may contain material misstatement due to fraud.

Risks of Fraud in Revenue Recognition

60   Material misstatements due to fraudulent financial reporting often result from an overstatement of revenues (for example, through premature revenue recognition or recording fictitious revenues) or an understatement of revenues (for example, through improperly shifting revenues to a later period). Therefore, the auditor ordinarily presumes that there are risks of fraud in revenue recognition and considers which types of revenue, revenue transactions or assertions may give rise to such risks. Those assessed risks of material misstatement due to fraud related to revenue recognition are significant risks to be addressed in accordance with paragraphs 57 and 61. Appendix 3 includes examples of responses to the auditor's assessment of the risk of material misstatement due to fraudulent financial reporting resulting from revenue recognition. If the auditor has not identified, in a particular circumstance, revenue recognition as a risk of material misstatement due to fraud, the auditor documents the reasons supporting the auditor's conclusion as required by paragraph 110.

Responses to the Risks of Material Misstatement Due to Fraud

61   The auditor should determine overall responses to address the assessed risks of material misstatement due to fraud at the financial statement level and should design and perform further audit procedures whose nature, timing and extent are responsive to the assessed risks at the assertion level.

62   ISA (UK and Ireland) 330 requires the auditor to perform substantive procedures that are specifically responsive to risks that are assessed as significant risks.

63   The auditor responds to the risks of material misstatement due to fraud in the following ways:

(a) A response that has an overall effect on how the audit is conducted, that is, increased professional skepticism and a response involving more general considerations apart from the specific procedures otherwise planned.
(b) A response to identified risks at the assertion level involving the nature, timing and extent of audit procedures to be performed.
(c) A response to identified risks involving the performance of certain audit procedures to address the risks of material misstatement due to fraud involving management override of controls, given the unpredictable ways in which such override could occur.

The response to address the assessed risks of material misstatement due to fraud may affect the auditor's professional skepticism in the following ways: 64

(a) Increased sensitivity in the selection of the nature and extent of documentation to be examined in support of material transactions.
(b) Increased recognition of the need to corroborate management explanations or representations concerning material matters.

The auditor may conclude that it would not be practicable to design audit procedures that sufficiently address the risks of material misstatement due to fraud. In such circumstances the auditor considers the implications for the audit (see paragraphs 89 and 103). 65

Overall Responses

In determining overall responses to address the risks of material misstatement due to fraud at the financial statement level the auditor should: 66

(a) **Consider the assignment and supervision of personnel;**
(b) **Consider the accounting policies used by the entity; and**
(c) **Incorporate an element of unpredictability in the selection of the nature, timing and extent of audit procedures.**

The knowledge, skill and ability of the individuals assigned significant engagement responsibilities are commensurate with the auditor's assessment of the risks of material misstatement due to fraud for the engagement. For example, the auditor may respond to identified risks of material misstatement due to fraud by assigning additional individuals with specialized skill and knowledge, such as forensic and IT experts, or by assigning more experienced individuals to the engagement. In addition, the extent of supervision reflects the auditor's assessment of risks of material misstatement due to fraud and the competencies of the engagement team members performing the work. 67

The auditor considers management's selection and application of significant accounting policies, particularly those related to subjective measurements and complex transactions. The auditor considers whether the selection and application of accounting policies may be indicative of fraudulent financial reporting resulting from management's effort to manage earnings in order to deceive financial statement users by influencing their perceptions as to the entity's performance and profitability. 68

Individuals within the entity who are familiar with the audit procedures normally performed on engagements may be more able to conceal fraudulent financial reporting. Therefore, the auditor incorporates an element of unpredictability in the selection of the nature, extent and timing of audit procedures to be performed. This can be achieved by, for example, performing substantive procedures on selected account balances and assertions not otherwise tested due to their materiality or risk, 69 adjusting the timing of audit procedures from that otherwise expected, using different sampling methods, and performing audit procedures at different locations or at locations on an unannounced basis.

Audit Procedures Responsive to Risks of Material Misstatement Due to Fraud at the Assertion Level

70 The auditor's responses to address the assessed risks of material misstatement due to fraud at the assertion level may include changing the nature, timing, and extent of audit procedures in the following ways:

- The nature of audit procedures to be performed may need to be changed to obtain audit evidence that is more reliable and relevant or to obtain additional corroborative information. This may affect both the type of audit procedures to be performed and their combination. Physical observation or inspection of certain assets may become more important or the auditor may choose to use computer-assisted audit techniques to gather more evidence about data contained in significant accounts or electronic transaction files. In addition, the auditor may design procedures to obtain additional corroborative information. For example, if the auditor identifies that management is under pressure to meet earnings expectations, there may be a related risk that management is inflating sales by entering into sales agreements that include terms that preclude revenue recognition or by invoicing sales before delivery. In these circumstances, the auditor may, for example, design external confirmations not only to confirm outstanding amounts, but also to confirm the details of the sales agreements, including date, any rights of return and delivery terms. In addition, the auditor might find it effective to supplement such external confirmations with inquiries of non-financial personnel in the entity regarding any changes in sales agreements and delivery terms.
- The timing of substantive procedures may need to be modified. The auditor may conclude that performing substantive testing at or near the period end better addresses an assessed risk of material misstatement due to fraud. The auditor may conclude that, given the risks of intentional misstatement or manipulation, audit procedures to extend audit conclusions from an interim date to the period end would not be effective. In contrast, because an intentional misstatement, for example a misstatement involving improper revenue recognition, may have been initiated in an interim period, the auditor may elect to apply substantive procedures to transactions occurring earlier in or throughout the reporting period.
- The extent of the procedures applied reflects the assessment of the risks of material misstatement due to fraud. For example, increasing sample sizes or performing analytical procedures at a more detailed level may be appropriate. Also, computer-assisted audit techniques may enable more extensive testing of electronic transactions and account files. Such techniques can be used to select sample transactions from key electronic files, to sort transactions with specific characteristics, or to test an entire population instead of a sample.

71 If the auditor identifies a risk of material misstatement due to fraud that affects inventory quantities, examining the entity's inventory records may help to identify locations or items that require specific attention during or after the physical inventory count. Such a review may lead to a decision to observe inventory counts at certain locations on an unannounced basis or to conduct inventory counts at all locations on the same date.

72 The auditor may identify a risk of material misstatement due to fraud affecting a number of accounts and assertions, including asset valuation, estimates relating to specific transactions (such as acquisitions, restructurings, or disposals of a segment of

the business), and other significant accrued liabilities (such as pension and other post-employment benefit obligations, or environmental remediation liabilities). The risk may also relate to significant changes in assumptions relating to recurring estimates. Information gathered through obtaining an understanding of the entity and its environment may assist the auditor in evaluating the reasonableness of such management estimates and underlying judgments and assumptions. A retrospective review of similar management judgments and assumptions applied in prior periods may also provide insight about the reasonableness of judgments and assumptions supporting management estimates.

Examples of possible audit procedures to address the assessed risks of material misstatement due to fraud are presented in Appendix 2 to this ISA (UK and Ireland). The appendix includes examples of responses to the auditor's assessment of the risks of material misstatement resulting from both fraudulent financial reporting and misappropriation of assets.   73

Audit Procedures Responsive to Management Override of Controls

As noted in paragraph 19, management is in a unique position to perpetrate fraud because of management's ability to directly or indirectly manipulate accounting records and prepare fraudulent financial statements by overriding controls that otherwise appear to be operating effectively. While the level of risk of management override of controls will vary from entity to entity, the risk is nevertheless present in all entities and is a significant risk of material misstatement due to fraud. Accordingly, in addition to overall responses to address the risks of material misstatement due to fraud and responses to address the assessed risks of material misstatement due to fraud at the assertion level, the auditor performs audit procedures to respond to the risk of management override of controls.   74

Paragraphs 76-82 set out the audit procedures required to respond to risk of management override of controls. However, the auditor also considers whether there are risks of management override of controls for which the auditor needs to perform procedures other than those specifically referred to in these paragraphs.   75

To respond to the risk of management override of controls, the auditor should design and perform audit procedures to: 76

(a) Test the appropriateness of journal entries recorded in the general ledger and other adjustments made in the preparation of financial statements;
(b) Review accounting estimates for biases that could result in material misstatement due to fraud; and
(c) Obtain an understanding of the business rationale of significant transactions that the auditor becomes aware of that are outside of the normal course of business for the entity, or that otherwise appear to be unusual given the auditor's understanding of the entity and its environment.

Journal Entries and Other Adjustments

Material misstatements of financial statements due to fraud often involve the manipulation of the financial reporting process by recording inappropriate or unauthorized journal entries throughout the year or at period end, or making adjustments to amounts reported in the financial statements that are not reflected in formal journal entries, such as through consolidating adjustments and reclassifications. In designing and performing audit procedures to test the appropriateness of   77 journal entries recorded in the general ledger and other adjustments made in the preparation of the financial statements the auditor:

(a) Obtains an understanding of the entity's financial reporting process and the controls over journal entries and other adjustments;
(b) Evaluates the design of the controls over journal entries and other adjustments and determines whether they have been implemented;
(c) Makes inquiries of individuals involved in the financial reporting process about inappropriate or unusual activity relating to the processing of journal entries and other adjustments;
(d) Determines the timing of the testing; and
(e) Identifies and selects journal entries and other adjustments for testing.

78 For the purposes of identifying and selecting journal entries and other adjustments for testing, and determining the appropriate method of examining the underlying support for the items selected, the auditor considers the following:

- *The assessment of the risks of material misstatement due to fraud* – the presence of fraud risk factors and other information obtained during the auditor's assessment of the risks of material misstatement due to fraud may assist the auditor to identify specific classes of journal entries and other adjustments for testing.
- *Controls that have been implemented over journal entries and other adjustments* – effective controls over the preparation and posting of journal entries and other adjustments may reduce the extent of substantive testing necessary, provided that the auditor has tested the operating effectiveness of the controls.
- *The entity's financial reporting process and the nature of evidence that can be obtained* – for many entities routine processing of transactions involves a combination of manual and automated steps and procedures. Similarly, the processing of journal entries and other adjustments may involve both manual and automated procedures and controls. When information technology is used in the financial reporting process, journal entries and other adjustments may exist only in electronic form.
- *The characteristics of fraudulent journal entries or other adjustments* – inappropriate journal entries or other adjustments often have unique identifying characteristics. Such characteristics may include entries (a) made to unrelated, unusual, or seldom-used accounts, (b) made by individuals who typically do not make journal entries, (c) recorded at the end of the period or as post-closing entries that have little or no explanation or description, (d) made either before or during the preparation of the financial statements that do not have account numbers, or (e) containing round numbers or consistent ending numbers.
- *The nature and complexity of the accounts* – inappropriate journal entries or adjustments may be applied to accounts that (a) contain transactions that are complex or unusual in nature, (b) contain significant estimates and period-end adjustments, (c) have been prone to misstatements in the past, (d) have not been reconciled on a timely basis or contain unreconciled differences, (e) contain inter-company transactions, or (f) are otherwise associated with an identified risk of material misstatement due to fraud. In audits of entities that have several locations or components, consideration is given to the need to select journal entries from multiple locations.
- *Journal entries or other adjustments processed outside the normal course of business* – non standard journal entries may not be subject to the same level of internal control as those journal entries used on a recurring basis to record transactions such as monthly sales, purchases and cash disbursements.

79 The auditor uses professional judgment in determining the nature, timing and extent of testing of journal entries and other adjustments. Because fraudulent journal

entries and other adjustments are often made at the end of a reporting period, the auditor ordinarily selects the journal entries and other adjustments made at that time. However, because material misstatements in financial statements due to fraud can occur throughout the period and may involve extensive efforts to conceal how the fraud is accomplished, the auditor considers whether there is also a need to test journal entries and other adjustments throughout the period.

Accounting Estimates

In preparing financial statements, management is responsible for making a number of judgments or assumptions that affect significant accounting estimates and for monitoring the reasonableness of such estimates on an ongoing basis. Fraudulent financial reporting is often accomplished through intentional misstatement of accounting estimates. In reviewing accounting estimates for biases that could result in material misstatement due to fraud the auditor: 80

(a) Considers whether differences between estimates best supported by audit evidence and the estimates included in the financial statements, even if they are individually reasonable, indicate a possible bias on the part of the entity's management, in which case the auditor reconsiders the estimates taken as a whole; and
(b) Performs a retrospective review of management judgments and assumptions related to significant accounting estimates reflected in the financial statements of the prior year. The objective of this review is to determine whether there is an indication of a possible bias on the part of management, and it is not intended to call into question the auditor's professional judgments made in the prior year that were based on information available at the time.

If the auditor identifies a possible bias on the part of management in making accounting estimates, the auditor evaluates whether the circumstances producing such a bias represent a risk of material misstatement due to fraud. The auditor considers whether, in making accounting estimates, management's actions appear to understate or overstate all provisions or reserves in the same fashion so as to be designed either to smooth earnings over two or more accounting periods, or to achieve a designated earnings level in order to deceive financial statement users by influencing their perceptions as to the entity's performance and profitability. 81

Business Rationale for Significant Transactions

The auditor obtains an understanding of the business rationale for significant transactions that are outside the normal course of business for the entity, or that otherwise appear to be unusual given the auditor's understanding of the entity and its environment and other information obtained during the audit. The purpose of obtaining this understanding is to consider whether the rationale (or the lack thereof) suggests that the transactions may have been entered into to engage in fraudulent financial reporting or to conceal misappropriation of assets. In gaining such an understanding the auditor considers the following: 82

- Whether the form of such transactions appears overly complex (for example, the transaction involves multiple entities within a consolidated group or multiple unrelated third parties).
- Whether management has discussed the nature of and accounting for such transactions with those charged with governance of the entity, and whether there is adequate documentation.
- Whether management is placing more emphasis on the need for a particular accounting treatment than on the underlying economics of the transaction.

- Whether transactions that involve non-consolidated related parties, including special purpose entities, have been properly reviewed and approved by those charged with governance of the entity.
- Whether the transactions involve previously unidentified related parties or parties that do not have the substance or the financial strength to support the transaction without assistance from the entity under audit.

Evaluation of Audit Evidence

83 As required by ISA (UK and Ireland) 330, the auditor, based on the audit procedures performed and the audit evidence obtained, evaluates whether the assessments of the risks of material misstatement at the assertion level remain appropriate. This evaluation is primarily a qualitative matter based on the auditor's judgment. Such an evaluation may provide further insight about the risks of material misstatement due to fraud and whether there is a need to perform additional or different audit procedures. As part of this evaluation, the auditor considers whether there has been appropriate communication with other engagement team members throughout the audit regarding information or conditions indicative of risks of material misstatement due to fraud.

84 An audit of financial statements is a cumulative and iterative process. As the auditor performs planned audit procedures information may come to the auditor's attention that differs significantly from the information on which the assessment of the risks of material misstatement due to fraud was based. For example, the auditor may become aware of discrepancies in accounting records or conflicting or missing evidence. Also, relationships between the auditor and management may become problematic or unusual. Appendix 3 to this ISA (UK and Ireland) contains examples of circumstances that may indicate the possibility of fraud.

85 **The auditor should consider whether analytical procedures that are performed at or near the end of the audit when forming an overall conclusion as to whether the financial statement as a whole are consistent with the auditor's knowledge of the business indicate a previously unrecognized risk of material misstatement due to fraud.** Determining which particular trends and relationships may indicate a risk of material misstatement due to fraud requires professional judgment. Unusual relationships involving year-end revenue and income are particularly relevant. These might include, for example, uncharacteristically large amounts of income being reported in the last few weeks of the reporting period or unusual transactions; or income that is inconsistent with trends in cash flow from operations.

86 **When the auditor identifies a misstatement, the auditor should consider whether such a misstatement may be indicative of fraud and if there is such an indication, the auditor should consider the implications of the misstatement in relation to other aspects of the audit, particularly the reliability of management[1a] representations.**

87 The auditor cannot assume that an instance of fraud is an isolated occurrence. The auditor also considers whether misstatements identified may be indicative of a higher risk of material misstatement due to fraud at a specific location. For example, numerous misstatements at a specific location, even though the cumulative effect is not material, may be indicative of a risk of material misstatement due to fraud.

88 If the auditor believes that a misstatement is or may be the result of fraud, but the effect of the misstatement is not material to the financial statements, the auditor evaluates the implications, especially those dealing with the organizational position

of the individual(s) involved. For example, fraud involving a misappropriation of cash from a small petty cash fund normally would be of little significance to the auditor in assessing the risks of material misstatement due to fraud because both the manner of operating the fund and its size would tend to establish a limit on the amount of potential loss, and the custodianship of such funds normally is entrusted to a non-management employee. Conversely, if the matter involves higher-level management, even though the amount itself is not material to the financial statements, it may be indicative of a more pervasive problem, for example, implications about the integrity of management. In such circumstances, the auditor re-evaluates the assessment of the risks of material misstatement due to fraud and its resulting impact on the nature, timing, and extent of audit procedures to respond to the assessed risks. The auditor also reconsiders the reliability of evidence previously obtained since there may be doubts about the completeness and truthfulness of representations made and about the genuineness of accounting records and documentation. The auditor also considers the possibility of collusion involving employees, management or third parties when reconsidering the reliability of evidence.

When the auditor confirms that, or is unable to conclude whether, the financial statements are materially misstated as a result of fraud, the auditor should consider the implications for the audit. ISA (UK and Ireland) 320, "Audit Materiality" and ISA (UK and Ireland) 700, "The Auditor's Report on Financial Statements" provide guidance on the evaluation and disposition of misstatements and the effect on the auditor's report.

Management Representations

The auditor should obtain written representations from management[1a] **that:**

(a) **It acknowledges its responsibility for the design and implementation of internal control to prevent and detect fraud;**
(b) **It has disclosed to the auditor the results of its assessment of the risk that the financial statements may be materially misstated as a result of fraud;**
(c) **It has disclosed to the auditor its knowledge of fraud or suspected fraud affecting the entity involving:**
   (i) **Management**[2a]
   (ii) **Employees who have significant roles in internal control; or**
   (iii) **Others where the fraud could have a material effect on the financial statements; and**
(d) **It has disclosed to the auditor its knowledge of any allegations of fraud, or suspected fraud, affecting the entity's financial statements communicated by employees, former employees, analysts, regulators or others.**

ISA (UK and Ireland) 580, "Management Representations" provides guidance on obtaining appropriate representations from management[1a] in the audit. In addition to acknowledging its responsibility for the financial statements, it is important that, irrespective of the size of the entity, management acknowledges its responsibility for internal control designed and implemented to prevent and detect fraud.

Because of the nature of fraud and the difficulties encountered by auditors in detecting material misstatements in the financial statements resulting from fraud, it is important that the auditor obtains a written representation from management[1a] confirming that it has disclosed to the auditor the results of management's

---
[2a] In the UK and Ireland, and those charged with governance.

assessment of the risk that the financial statements may be materially misstated as a result of fraud and its knowledge of actual, suspected or alleged fraud affecting the entity.

Communications With Management and Those Charged With Governance

93 If the auditor has identified a fraud or has obtained information that indicates that a fraud may exist, the auditor should communicate these matters as soon as practicable to the appropriate level of management.

94 When the auditor has obtained evidence that fraud exists or may exist, it is important that the matter be brought to the attention of the appropriate level of management as soon as practicable. This is so even if the matter might be considered inconsequential (for example, a minor defalcation by an employee at a low level in the entity's organization). The determination of which level of management is the appropriate one is a matter of professional judgment and is affected by such factors as the likelihood of collusion and the nature and magnitude of the suspected fraud. Ordinarily, the appropriate level of management is at least one level above the persons who appear to be involved with the suspected fraud.

95 If the auditor has identified fraud involving:

  (a) **Management;**
  (b) **Employees who have significant roles in internal control; or**
  (c) **Others where the fraud results in a material misstatement in the financial statements,**

  the auditor should communicate these matters to those charged with governance as soon as practicable.

96 The auditor's communication with those charged with governance may be made orally or in writing. ISA (UK and Ireland) 260, "Communication of Audit Matters With Those Charged With Governance" identifies factors the auditor considers in determining whether to communicate orally or in writing. Due to the nature and sensitivity of fraud involving senior management, or fraud that results in a material misstatement in the financial statements, the auditor reports such matters as soon as practicable and considers whether it is necessary to also report such matters in writing. If the auditor suspects fraud involving management, the auditor communicates these suspicions to those charged with governance and also discusses with them the nature, timing and extent of audit procedures necessary to complete the audit.

97 If the integrity or honesty of management or those charged with governance is doubted, the auditor considers seeking legal advice to assist in the determination of the appropriate course of action.

98 At an early stage in the audit, the auditor reaches an understanding with those charged with governance about the nature and extent of the auditor's communications regarding fraud that the auditor becomes aware of involving employees other than management that does not result in a material misstatement.

99 **The auditor should make those charged with governance and management aware, as soon as practicable, and at the appropriate level of responsibility, of material**

weaknesses in the design or implementation of internal control to prevent and detect fraud which may have come to the auditor's attention.

If the auditor identifies a risk of material misstatement of the financial statements due to fraud, which management has either not controlled, or for which the relevant control is inadequate, or if in the auditor's judgment there is a material weakness in management's risk assessment process, the auditor includes such internal control deficiencies in the communication of audit matters of governance interest (see ISA (UK and Ireland) 260).   100

The auditor should consider whether there are any other matters related to fraud to be discussed with those charged with governance of the entity.[3] Such matters may include for example: 101

- Concerns about the nature, extent and frequency of management's assessments of the controls in place to prevent and detect fraud and of the risk that the financial statements may be misstated.
- A failure by management to appropriately address identified material weaknesses in internal control.
- A failure by management to appropriately respond to an identified fraud.
- The auditor's evaluation of the entity's control environment, including questions regarding the competence and integrity of management.
- Actions by management that may be indicative of fraudulent financial reporting, such as management's selection and application of accounting policies that may be indicative of management's effort to manage earnings in order to deceive financial statement users by influencing their perceptions as to the entity's performance and profitability.
- Concerns about the adequacy and completeness of the authorization of transactions that appear to be outside the normal course of business.

Communications to Regulatory and Enforcement Authorities

The auditor's professional duty to maintain the confidentiality of client information may preclude reporting fraud to a party outside the client entity. The auditor considers obtaining legal advice to determine the appropriate course of action in such circumstances. The auditor's legal responsibilities vary by country[3a] and in certain circumstances, the duty of confidentiality may be overridden by statute, the law or courts of law. For example, in some countries, the auditor of a financial institution has a statutory duty to report the occurrence of fraud to supervisory authorities. Also, in some countries the auditor has a duty to report misstatements to authorities in those cases where management and those charged with governance fail to take corrective action.   102

---

[6] *For a discussion of these matters, see ISA (UK and Ireland) 260, "Communication of Audit Matters With Those Charged With Governance," paragraphs 11-12.*

[3a] *In the UK and Ireland, anti-money laundering legislation (see footnote 15 to ISA (UK and Ireland) 250, "Consideration of laws and regulations") imposes a duty on auditors to report all suspicions that a criminal offence giving rise to any direct or indirect benefit from criminal conduct has been committed regardless of whether that offence has been committed by a client or a third party. Suspicions relating to fraud are likely to be required to be reported under this legislation.*

Auditor Unable to Continue the Engagement

103 If, as a result of a misstatement resulting from fraud or suspected fraud, the auditor encounters exceptional circumstances that bring into question the auditor's ability to continue performing the audit the auditor should:

(a) Consider the professional and legal responsibilities applicable in the circumstances, including whether there is a requirement for the auditor to report to the person or persons who made the audit appointment or, in some cases, to regulatory authorities;
(b) Consider the possibility of withdrawing from the engagement; and
(c) If the auditor withdraws:
  (i) Discuss with the appropriate level of management and those charged with governance the auditor's withdrawal from the engagement and the reasons for the withdrawal; and
  (ii) Consider whether there is a professional or legal requirement to report to the person or persons who made the audit appointment or, in some cases, to regulatory authorities, the auditor's withdrawal from the engagement and the reasons for the withdrawal.

104 Such exceptional circumstances can arise, for example, when:

(a) The entity does not take the appropriate action regarding fraud that the auditor considers necessary in the circumstances, even when the fraud is not material to the financial statements;
(b) The auditor's consideration of the risks of material misstatement due to fraud and the results of audit tests indicate a significant risk of material and pervasive fraud; or
(c) The auditor has significant concern about the competence or integrity of management or those charged with governance.

105 Because of the variety of the circumstances that may arise, it is not possible to describe definitively when withdrawal from an engagement is appropriate. Factors that affect the auditor's conclusion include the implications of the involvement of a member of management or of those charged with governance (which may affect the reliability of management[1a] representations) and the effects on the auditor of a continuing association with the entity.

106 The auditor has professional and legal responsibilities in such circumstances and these responsibilities may vary by country. In some countries, for example, the auditor may be entitled to, or required to, make a statement or report to the person or persons who made the audit appointment or, in some cases, to regulatory authorities. Given the exceptional nature of the circumstances and the need to consider the legal requirements, the auditor considers seeking legal advice when deciding whether to withdraw from an engagement and in determining an appropriate course of action, including the possibility of reporting to shareholders, regulators or others.[4]

---

[8] The *IFAC* Code of Ethics for Professional Accountants *provides guidance on communications with a proposed successor auditor.*

In the UK and Ireland the relevant ethical guidance on proposed communications with a successor auditor is provided by the ethical pronouncements relating to the work of auditors issued by the auditor's relevant professional body.

Documentation

The documentation of the auditor's understanding of the entity and its environment and the auditor's assessment of the risks of material misstatement required by paragraph 122 of ISA (UK and Ireland) 315 should include: 107

(a) The significant decisions reached during the discussion among the engagement team regarding the susceptibility of the entity's financial statements to material misstatement due to fraud; and
(b) The identified and assessed risks of material misstatement due to fraud at the financial statement level and at the assertion level.

The documentation of the auditor's responses to the assessed risks of material misstatement required by paragraph 73 of ISA (UK and Ireland) 330 should include: 108

(a) The overall responses to the assessed risks of material misstatements due to fraud at the financial statement level and the nature, timing and extent of audit procedures, and the linkage of those procedures with the assessed risks of material misstatement due to fraud at the assertion level; and
(b) The results of the audit procedures, including those designed to address the risk of management override of controls.

The auditor should document communications about fraud made to management, those charged with governance, regulators and others.   109

When the auditor has concluded that the presumption that there is a risk of material misstatement due to fraud related to revenue recognition is not applicable in the circumstances of the engagement, the auditor should document the reasons for that conclusion.   110

The extent to which these matters are documented is for the auditor to determine using professional judgment.   111

Effective Date

This ISA (UK and Ireland) is effective for audits of financial statements for periods commencing on or after 15 December 2004.   112

Public Sector Perspective

> Additional guidance for auditors of public sector bodies in the UK and Ireland is given in:
> - Practice Note 10 "Audit of Financial Statements of Public Sector Entities in the United Kingdom (Revised)"
> - Practice Note 10(I) "The Audit of Central Government Financial Statements in Ireland"

ISA (UK and Ireland) 240 is applicable in all material respects to audits of public sector entities.   1

In the public sector the scope and nature of the audit relating to the prevention and detection of fraud may be affected by legislation, regulation, ordinances or ministerial   2 directives. The terms of the mandate may be a factor that the auditor needs to take into account when exercising judgment.

3   Requirements for reporting fraud, whether or not discovered through the audit process often may be subject to specific provisions of the audit mandate or related legislation or regulation in line with paragraph 102 of the ISA (UK and Ireland).

4   In many cases in the public sector the option of withdrawing from the engagement as suggested in paragraph 103 of the ISA (UK and Ireland) may not be available to the auditor due to the nature of the mandate or public interest considerations.

Appendix 1 – Examples of Fraud Risk Factors

The fraud risk factors identified in this Appendix are examples of such factors that may be faced by auditors in a broad range of situations. Separately presented are examples relating to the two types of fraud relevant to the auditor's consideration, that is, fraudulent financial reporting and misappropriation of assets. For each of these types of fraud, the risk factors are further classified based on the three conditions generally present when material misstatements due to fraud occur: (a) incentives/pressures, (b) opportunities, and (c) attitudes/rationalizations. Although the risk factors cover a broad range of situations, they are only examples and, accordingly, the auditor may identify additional or different risk factors. Not all of these examples are relevant in all circumstances, and some may be of greater or lesser significance in entities of different size or with different ownership characteristics or circumstances. Also, the order of the examples of risk factors provided is not intended to reflect their relative importance or frequency of occurrence.

Risk Factors Relating to Misstatements Arising from Fraudulent Financial Reporting

The following are examples of risk factors relating to misstatements arising from fraudulent financial reporting.

Incentives/Pressures

1   Financial stability or profitability is threatened by economic, industry, or entity operating conditions, such as (or as indicated by) the following:

   - High degree of competition or market saturation, accompanied by declining margins.
   - High vulnerability to rapid changes, such as changes in technology, product obsolescence, or interest rates.
   - Significant declines in customer demand and increasing business failures in either the industry or overall economy.
   - Operating losses making the threat of bankruptcy, foreclosure, or hostile takeover imminent.
   - Recurring negative cash flows from operations or an inability to generate cash flows from operations while reporting earnings and earnings growth.
   - Rapid growth or unusual profitability especially compared to that of other companies in the same industry.
   - New accounting, statutory, or regulatory requirements.

2   Excessive pressure exists for management to meet the requirements or expectations of third parties due to the following:

- Profitability or trend level expectations of investment analysts, institutional investors, significant creditors, or other external parties (particularly expectations that are unduly aggressive or unrealistic), including expectations created by management in, for example, overly optimistic press releases or annual report messages.
- Need to obtain additional debt or equity financing to stay competitive, including financing of major research and development or capital expenditures.
- Marginal ability to meet exchange listing requirements or debt repayment or other debt covenant requirements.
- Perceived or real adverse effects of reporting poor financial results on significant pending transactions, such as business combinations or contract awards.

Information available indicates that the personal financial situation of management or those charged with governance is threatened by the entity's financial performance arising from the following:

- Significant financial interests in the entity.
- Significant portions of their compensation (for example, bonuses, stock options, and earn-out arrangements) being contingent upon achieving aggressive targets for stock price, operating results, financial position, or cash flow.[5]
- Personal guarantees of debts of the entity.

There is excessive pressure on management or operating personnel to meet financial targets established by those charged with governance, including sales or profitability incentive goals.

Opportunities

The nature of the industry or the entity's operations provides opportunities to engage in fraudulent financial reporting that can arise from the following:

- Significant related-party transactions not in the ordinary course of business or with related entities not audited or audited by another firm.
- A strong financial presence or ability to dominate a certain industry sector that allows the entity to dictate terms or conditions to suppliers or customers that may result in inappropriate or non-arm's length transactions.
- Assets, liabilities, revenues, or expenses based on significant estimates that involve subjective judgments or uncertainties that are difficult to corroborate.
- Significant, unusual, or highly complex transactions, especially those close to period end that pose difficult "substance over form" questions.
- Significant operations located or conducted across international borders in jurisdictions where differing business environments and cultures exist.
- Use of business intermediaries for which there appears to be no clear business justification.
- Significant bank accounts or subsidiary or branch operations in tax-haven jurisdictions for which there appears to be no clear business justification.

There is ineffective monitoring of management as a result of the following:

- Domination of management by a single person or small group (in a non owner-managed business) without compensating controls.
- Ineffective oversight by those charged with governance over the financial reporting process and internal control.

---

[9] *Management incentive plans may be contingent upon achieving targets relating only to certain accounts or selected activities of the entity, even though the related accounts or activities may not be material to the entity as a whole.*

3   There is a complex or unstable organizational structure, as evidenced by the following:

- Difficulty in determining the organization or individuals that have controlling interest in the entity.
- Overly complex organizational structure involving unusual legal entities or managerial lines of authority.
- High turnover of senior management, legal counsel, or those charged with governance.

4   Internal control components are deficient as a result of the following:

- Inadequate monitoring of controls, including automated controls and controls over interim financial reporting (where external reporting is required).
- High turnover rates or employment of ineffective accounting, internal audit, or information technology staff.
- Ineffective accounting and information systems, including situations involving material weaknesses in internal control.

Attitudes/Rationalizations

- Ineffective communication, implementation, support, or enforcement of the entity's values or ethical standards by management or the communication of inappropriate values or ethical standards.
- Nonfinancial management's excessive participation in or preoccupation with the selection of accounting policies or the determination of significant estimates.
- Known history of violations of securities laws or other laws and regulations, or claims against the entity, its senior management, or those charged with governance alleging fraud or violations of laws and regulations.
- Excessive interest by management in maintaining or increasing the entity's stock price or earnings trend.
- A practice by management of committing to analysts, creditors, and other third parties to achieve aggressive or unrealistic forecasts.
- Management failing to correct known material weaknesses in internal control on a timely basis.
- An interest by management in employing inappropriate means to minimize reported earnings for tax-motivated reasons.
- Low morale among senior management.
- The owner-manager makes no distinction between personal and business transactions.
- Dispute between shareholders in a closely held entity.
- Recurring attempts by management to justify marginal or inappropriate accounting on the basis of materiality.
- The relationship between management and the current or predecessor auditor is strained, as exhibited by the following:
  - Frequent disputes with the current or predecessor auditor on accounting, auditing, or reporting matters.
  - Unreasonable demands on the auditor, such as unreasonable time constraints regarding the completion of the audit or the issuance of the auditor's report.
  - Formal or informal restrictions on the auditor that inappropriately limit access to people or information or the ability to communicate effectively with those charged with governance.
  - Domineering management behavior in dealing with the auditor, especially involving attempts to influence the scope of the auditor's work or the

selection or continuance of personnel assigned to or consulted on the audit engagement.

Risk Factors Arising from Misstatements Arising from Misappropriation of Assets

Risk factors that relate to misstatements arising from misappropriation of assets are also classified according to the three conditions generally present when fraud exists: (a) incentives/pressures, (b) opportunities, and (c) attitudes/rationalizations. Some of the risk factors related to misstatements arising from fraudulent financial reporting also may be present when misstatements arising from misappropriation of assets occur. For example, ineffective monitoring of management and weaknesses in internal control may be present when misstatements due to either fraudulent financial reporting or misappropriation of assets exist. The following are examples of risk factors related to misstatements arising from misappropriation of assets.

Incentives/Pressures

Personal financial obligations may create pressure on management or employees with access to cash or other assets susceptible to theft to misappropriate those assets.

Adverse relationships between the entity and employees with access to cash or other assets susceptible to theft may motivate those employees to misappropriate those assets. For example, adverse relationships may be created by the following:

- Known or anticipated future employee layoffs.
- Recent or anticipated changes to employee compensation or benefit plans.
- Promotions, compensation, or other rewards inconsistent with expectations.

Opportunities

Certain characteristics or circumstances may increase the susceptibility of assets to misappropriation. For example, opportunities to misappropriate assets increase when there are the following:

- Large amounts of cash on hand or processed.
- Inventory items that are small in size, of high value, or in high demand.
- Easily convertible assets, such as bearer bonds, diamonds, or computer chips.
- Fixed assets which are small in size, marketable, or lacking observable identification of ownership.

Inadequate internal control over assets may increase the susceptibility of misappropriation of those assets. For example, misappropriation of assets may occur because there is the following:

- Inadequate segregation of duties or independent checks.
- Inadequate oversight of senior management expenditures, such as travel and other re-imbursements.
- Inadequate management oversight of employees responsible for assets, for example, inadequate supervision or monitoring of remote locations.
- Inadequate job applicant screening of employees with access to assets.
- Inadequate record keeping with respect to assets.
- Inadequate system of authorization and approval of transactions (for example, in purchasing).
- Inadequate physical safeguards over cash, investments, inventory, or fixed assets.
- Lack of complete and timely reconciliations of assets.

- Lack of timely and appropriate documentation of transactions, for example, credits for merchandise returns.
- Lack of mandatory vacations for employees performing key control functions.
- Inadequate management understanding of information technology, which enables information technology employees to perpetrate a misappropriation.
- Inadequate access controls over automated records, including controls over and review of computer systems event logs.

Attitudes/Rationalizations

- Disregard for the need for monitoring or reducing risks related to misappropriations of assets.
- Disregard for internal control over misappropriation of assets by overriding existing controls or by failing to correct known internal control deficiencies.
- Behavior indicating displeasure or dissatisfaction with the entity or its treatment of the employee.
- Changes in behavior or lifestyle that may indicate assets have been misappropriated.
- Tolerance of petty theft.

Appendix 2 – Examples of Possible Audit Procedures to Address the Assessed Risks of Material Misstatement Due to Fraud

The following are examples of possible audit procedures to address the assessed risks of material misstatement due to fraud resulting from both fraudulent financial reporting and misappropriation of assets. Although these procedures cover a broad range of situations, they are only examples and, accordingly they may not be the most appropriate nor necessary in each circumstance. Also the order of the procedures provided is not intended to reflect their relative importance.

Consideration at the Assertion Level

Specific responses to the auditor's assessment of the risks of material misstatement due to fraud will vary depending upon the types or combinations of fraud risk factors or conditions identified, and the account balances, classes of transactions and assertions they may affect.

The following are specific examples of responses:

- Visiting locations or performing certain tests on a surprise or unannounced basis. For example, observing inventory at locations where auditor attendance has not been previously announced or counting cash at a particular date on a surprise basis.
- Requesting that inventories be counted at the end of the reporting period or on a date closer to period end to minimize the risk of manipulation of balances in the period between the date of completion of the count and the end of the reporting period.
- Altering the audit approach in the current year. For example, contacting major customers and suppliers orally in addition to sending written confirmation, sending confirmation requests to a specific party within an organization, or seeking more or different information.

- Performing a detailed review of the entity's quarter-end or year-end adjusting entries and investigating any that appear unusual as to nature or amount.
- For significant and unusual transactions, particularly those occurring at or near year-end, investigating the possibility of related parties and the sources of financial resources supporting the transactions.
- Performing substantive analytical procedures using disaggregated data. For example, comparing sales and cost of sales by location, line of business or month to expectations developed by the auditor.
- Conducting interviews of personnel involved in areas where a risk of material misstatement due to fraud has been identified, to obtain their insights about the risk and whether, or how, controls address the risk.
- When other independent auditors are auditing the financial statements of one or more subsidiaries, divisions or branches, discussing with them the extent of work necessary to be performed to address the risk of material misstatement due to fraud resulting from transactions and activities among these components.
- If the work of an expert becomes particularly significant with respect to a financial statement item for which the risk of misstatement due to fraud is high, performing additional procedures relating to some or all of the expert's assumptions, methods or findings to determine that the findings are not unreasonable, or engaging another expert for that purpose.
- Performing audit procedures to analyze selected opening balance sheet accounts of previously audited financial statements to assess how certain issues involving accounting estimates and judgments, for example an allowance for sales returns, were resolved with the benefit of hindsight.
- Performing procedures on account or other reconciliations prepared by the entity, including considering reconciliations performed at interim periods.
- Performing computer-assisted techniques, such as data mining to test for anomalies in a population.
- Testing the integrity of computer-produced records and transactions.
- Seeking additional audit evidence from sources outside of the entity being audited.

Specific Responses—Misstatement Resulting from Fraudulent Financial Reporting

Examples of responses to the auditor's assessment of the risk of material misstatements due to fraudulent financial reporting are as follows:

Revenue recognition

- Performing substantive analytical procedures relating to revenue using disaggregated data, for example, comparing revenue reported by month and by product line or business segment during the current reporting period with comparable prior periods. Computer-assisted audit techniques may be useful in identifying unusual or unexpected revenue relationships or transactions.
- Confirming with customers certain relevant contract terms and the absence of side agreements, because the appropriate accounting often is influenced by such terms or agreements and basis for rebates or the period to which they relate are often poorly documented. For example, acceptance criteria, delivery and payment terms, the absence of future or continuing vendor obligations, the right to return the product, guaranteed resale amounts, and cancellation or refund provisions often are relevant in such circumstances.
- Inquiring of the entity's sales and marketing personnel or in-house legal counsel regarding sales or shipments near the end of the period and their knowledge of any unusual terms or conditions associated with these transactions.

- Being physically present at one or more locations at period end to observe goods being shipped or being readied for shipment (or returns awaiting processing) and performing other appropriate sales and inventory cutoff procedures.
- For those situations for which revenue transactions are electronically initiated, processed, and recorded, testing controls to determine whether they provide assurance that recorded revenue transactions occurred and are properly recorded.

Inventory Quantities

- Examining the entity's inventory records to identify locations or items that require specific attention during or after the physical inventory count.
- Observing inventory counts at certain locations on an unannounced basis or conducting inventory counts at all locations on the same date.
- Conducting inventory counts at or near the end of the reporting period to minimize the risk of inappropriate manipulation during the period between the count and the end of the reporting period.
- Performing additional procedures during the observation of the count, for example, more rigorously examining the contents of boxed items, the manner in which the goods are stacked (for example, hollow squares) or labeled, and the quality (that is, purity, grade, or concentration) of liquid substances such as perfumes or specialty chemicals. Using the work of an expert may be helpful in this regard.
- Comparing the quantities for the current period with prior periods by class or category of inventory, location or other criteria, or comparison of quantities counted with perpetual records.
- Using computer-assisted audit techniques to further test the compilation of the physical inventory counts—for example, sorting by tag number to test tag controls or by item serial number to test the possibility of item omission or duplication.

Management estimates

- Using an expert to develop an independent estimate for comparison to management's estimate.
- Extending inquiries to individuals outside of management and the accounting department to corroborate management's ability and intent to carry out plans that are relevant to developing the estimate.

Specific Responses—Misstatements Due to Misappropriation of Assets

Differing circumstances would necessarily dictate different responses. Ordinarily, the audit response to a risk of material misstatement due to fraud relating to misappropriation of assets will be directed toward certain account balances and classes of transactions. Although some of the audit responses noted in the two categories above may apply in such circumstances, the scope of the work is to be linked to the specific information about the misappropriation risk that has been identified.

Examples of responses to the auditor's assessment of the risk of material misstatements due to misappropriation of assets are as follows:

- Counting cash or securities at or near year-end.
- Confirming directly with customers the account activity (including credit memo and sales return activity as well as dates payments were made) for the period under audit.

- Analyzing recoveries of written-off accounts.
- Analyzing inventory shortages by location or product type.
- Comparing key inventory ratios to industry norm.
- Reviewing supporting documentation for reductions to the perpetual inventory records.
- Performing a computerized match of the vendor list with a list of employees to identify matches of addresses or phone numbers.
- Performing a computerized search of payroll records to identify duplicate addresses, employee identification or taxing authority numbers or bank accounts
- Reviewing personnel files for those that contain little or no evidence of activity, for example, lack of performance evaluations.
- Analyzing sales discounts and returns for unusual patterns or trends.
- Confirming specific terms of contracts with third parties.
- Obtaining evidence that contracts are being carried out in accordance with their terms.
- Reviewing the propriety of large and unusual expenses.
- Reviewing the authorization and carrying value of senior management and related party loans.
- Reviewing the level and propriety of expense reports submitted by senior management.

Appendix 3 – Examples of Circumstances that Indicate the Possibility of Fraud

The following are examples of circumstances that may indicate the possibility that the financial statements may contain a material misstatement resulting from fraud.

Discrepancies in the accounting records, including the following:

- Transactions that are not recorded in a complete or timely manner or are improperly recorded as to amount, accounting period, classification, or entity policy.
- Unsupported or unauthorized balances or transactions.
- Last-minute adjustments that significantly affect financial results.
- Evidence of employees' access to systems and records inconsistent with that necessary to perform their authorized duties.
- Tips or complaints to the auditor about alleged fraud.

Conflicting or missing evidence, including the following:

- Missing documents.
- Documents that appear to have been altered.
- Unavailability of other than photocopied or electronically transmitted documents when documents in original form are expected to exist.
- Significant unexplained items on reconciliations.
- Unusual balance sheet changes, or changes in trends or important financial statement ratios or relationships, for example receivables growing faster than revenues.
- Inconsistent, vague, or implausible responses from management or employees arising from inquiries or analytical procedures.
- Unusual discrepancies between the entity's records and confirmation replies.

- Large numbers of credit entries and other adjustments made to accounts receivable records.
- Unexplained or inadequately explained differences between the accounts receivable sub-ledger and the control account, or between the customer statements and the accounts receivable sub-ledger.
- Missing or non-existent cancelled checks in circumstances where cancelled checks are ordinarily returned to the entity with the bank statement.
- Missing inventory or physical assets of significant magnitude.
- Unavailable or missing electronic evidence, inconsistent with the entity's record retention practices or policies.
- Fewer responses to confirmations than anticipated or a greater number of responses than anticipated.
- Inability to produce evidence of key systems development and program change testing and implementation activities for current-year system changes and deployments.

Problematic or unusual relationships between the auditor and management, including the following:

- Denial of access to records, facilities, certain employees, customers, vendors, or others from whom audit evidence might be sought.
- Undue time pressures imposed by management to resolve complex or contentious issues.
- Complaints by management about the conduct of the audit or management intimidation of engagement team members, particularly in connection with the auditor's critical assessment of audit evidence or in the resolution of potential disagreements with management.
- Unusual delays by the entity in providing requested information.
- Unwillingness to facilitate auditor access to key electronic files for testing through the use of computer-assisted audit techniques.
- Denial of access to key IT operations staff and facilities, including security, operations, and systems development personnel.
- An unwillingness to add or revise disclosures in the financial statements to make them more complete and understandable.
- An unwillingness to address identified weaknesses in internal control on a timely basis.

Other includes the following:

- Unwillingness by management to permit the auditor to meet privately with those charged with governance.
- Accounting policies that appear to be at variance with industry norms.
- Frequent changes in accounting estimates that do not appear to result from changes circumstances.
- Tolerance of violations of the entity's code of conduct.

[250]
Section A – Consideration of laws and regulations in an audit of financial statements
Section B – The auditor's right and duty to report to regulators in the financial sector

(Issued December 2004)

Contents

Section A – Consideration of Laws and Regulations in an Audit of Financial Statements

	Paragraph
Introduction	1 - 8-1
Responsibility of Management for the Compliance With Laws and Regulations	9 - 10-3
The Auditor's Consideration of Compliance With Laws and Regulations	11 - 31
Reporting of Noncompliance	32 - 38-12
Withdrawal From the Engagement	39 - 40
Effective Date	40-1 - 40-2

Appendix: Indications that Noncompliance May Have Occurred

Section B – The Auditor's Right and Duty to Report to Regulators in the Financial Sector

Introduction	1 - 16
Appointment as Auditor and Ceasing to Hold Office	17 - 20
Conduct of the Audit	21 - 49
Reporting	50 - 71
Effective Date	72

Note on Legal Requirements

Appendix 1: The Regulatory Framework

Appendix 2: The Application of the Statutory Duty to Report Regulators

Appendix 3: Action by the Auditor on Discovery of a Breach of a Regulator's Requirements

International Standard on Auditing (UK and Ireland) (ISA (UK and Ireland)) 250 "Consideration of Laws and Regulations in an Audit of Financial Statements" should be read in the context of the Auditing Practices Board's Statement "The Auditing Practices Board - Scope and Authority of Pronouncements" which sets out the application and authority of ISAs (UK and Ireland).

Section A

Introduction

The purpose of this International Standard on Auditing (UK and Ireland) (ISA (UK and Ireland)) is to establish standards and provide guidance on the auditor's responsibility to consider laws and regulations in an audit of financial statements. 1

This ISA (UK and Ireland) uses the terms 'those charged with governance' and 'management'. The term 'governance' describes the role of persons entrusted with the supervision, control and direction of an entity. Ordinarily, those charged with governance are accountable for ensuring that the entity achieves its objectives, and for the quality of its financial reporting and reporting to interested parties. Those charged with governance include management only when they perform such functions. 1-1

In the UK and Ireland, those charged with governance include the directors (executive and non-executive) of a company or other body, the members of an audit committee where one exists, the partners, proprietors, committee of management or trustees of other forms of entity, or equivalent persons responsible for directing the entity's affairs and preparing its financial statements. 1-2

'Management' comprises those persons who perform senior managerial functions. 1-3

In the UK and Ireland, depending on the nature and circumstances of the entity, management may include some or all of those charged with governance (e.g. executive directors). Management will not normally include non-executive directors. 1-4

When designing and performing audit procedures and in evaluating and reporting the results thereof, the auditor should recognize that noncompliance by the entity with laws and regulations may materially affect the financial statements. However, an audit cannot be expected to detect noncompliance with all laws and regulations. Detection of noncompliance, regardless of materiality, requires consideration of the implications for the integrity of management[1] or employees and the possible effect on other aspects of the audit. 2

The term "noncompliance" as used in this ISA (UK and Ireland) refers to acts of omission or commission by the entity being audited, either intentional or unintentional, which are contrary to the prevailing laws or regulations. Such acts, include transactions entered into by, or in the name of, the entity or on its behalf by its management[2] or employees. For the purpose of this ISA (UK and Ireland), noncompliance does not include personal misconduct (unrelated to the business activities of the entity) by the entity's management or employees. 3

Whether an act constitutes noncompliance is a legal determination that is ordinarily beyond the auditor's professional competence. The auditor's training, experience and understanding of the entity and its industry may provide a basis for recognition that 4

---

[1] In the UK and Ireland, the auditor also considers the implications for the integrity of those charged with governance.

[2] In the UK and Ireland, such acts include transactions entered into by, or in the name of, the entity or on its behalf by those charged with governance.

some acts coming to the auditor's attention may constitute noncompliance with laws and regulations. The determination as to whether a particular act constitutes or is likely to constitute noncompliance is generally based on the advice of an informed expert qualified to practice law but ultimately can only be determined by a court of law.

5   Laws and regulations vary considerably in their relation to the financial statements. Some laws or regulations determine the form or content of an entity's financial statements or the amounts to be recorded or disclosures to be made in financial statements. Other laws or regulations are to be complied with by management[3] or set the provisions under which the entity is allowed to conduct its business. Some entities operate in heavily regulated industries (such as banks and chemical companies). Others are only subject to the many laws and regulations that generally relate to the operating aspects of the business (such as those related to occupational safety and health and equal employment). Noncompliance with laws and regulations could result in financial consequences for the entity such as fines, litigation, etc. Generally, the further removed noncompliance is from the events and transactions ordinarily reflected in financial statements, the less likely the auditor is to become aware of it or to recognize its possible noncompliance.

5-1   When determining the type of procedures necessary in a particular instance the auditor takes account of the particular entity concerned and the complexity of the regulations with which it is required to comply. In general, a small company which does not operate in a regulated area will require few specific procedures compared with a large multinational corporation carrying on complex, regulated business.

6   Laws and regulations vary from country to country. National accounting and auditing standards are therefore likely to be more specific as to the relevance of laws and regulations to an audit.

7   This ISA (UK and Ireland) applies to audits of financial statements and does not apply to other engagements in which the auditor is specifically engaged to test and report separately on compliance with specific laws or regulations.

8   Guidance on the auditor's responsibility to consider fraud and error in an audit of financial statements is provided in ISA (UK and Ireland) 240, "The Auditor's Responsibility to Consider Fraud in an Audit of Financial Statements."

8-1   Guidance on the auditor's responsibility to report direct to regulators in the financial sector is provided in Section B of this ISA (UK and Ireland).

Responsibility of Management[4] for the Compliance With Laws and Regulations

9   It is management's responsibility to ensure that the entity's operations are conducted in accordance with laws and regulations[4]. The responsibility for the prevention and detection of noncompliance rests with management[4].

---

[3] *In the UK and Ireland, there are also laws or regulations that are to be complied with by those charged with governance.*

[4] *In the UK and Ireland, this responsibility rests with those charged with governance.*

The following policies and procedures, among others, may assist management[5] in discharging its responsibilities for the prevention and detection of noncompliance:

- Monitoring legal requirements and ensuring that operating procedures are designed to meet these requirements.
- Instituting and operating appropriate internal control.
- Developing, publicizing and following a code of conduct.
- Ensuring employees are properly trained and understand the code of conduct.
- Monitoring compliance with the code of conduct and acting appropriately to discipline employees who fail to comply with it.
- Engaging legal advisors to assist in monitoring legal requirements.
- Maintaining a register of significant laws with which the entity has to comply within its particular industry and a record of complaints.

In larger entities, these policies and procedures may be supplemented by assigning appropriate responsibilities to the following:

- An internal audit function.
- An audit committee.
- A legal department.
- A compliance function.

In the UK and Ireland, in certain sectors or activities (for example financial services), there are detailed laws and regulations that specifically require directors to have systems to ensure compliance. These laws and regulations could, if breached, have a material effect on the financial statements. In addition, the directors are required to report certain instances of non-compliance to the proper authorities on a timely basis.

In the UK and Ireland, it is the directors' responsibility to prepare financial statements that give a true and fair view of the state of affairs of a company or group and of its profit or loss for the financial year. Accordingly it is necessary, where possible non-compliance with law or regulations has occurred which may result in a material misstatement in the financial statements, for them to ensure that the matter is appropriately reflected and/or disclosed in the financial statements.

In the UK and Ireland, in addition, directors and officers of companies have responsibility to provide information required by the auditor, to which they have a legal right of access[6]. Such legislation also provides that it is a criminal offence to give to the auditor information or explanations which are misleading, false or deceptive.

The Auditor's Consideration of Compliance With Laws and Regulations

The auditor is not, and cannot be held responsible for preventing noncompliance. The fact that an annual audit is carried out may, however, act as a deterrent.

---

[5] *In the UK and Ireland, the policies and procedures may also assist those charged with governance in discharging their responsibilities for the prevention and detection of noncompliance.*

[6] *In the UK under Section 389A of the Companies Act 1985 or Sections 193(3) and 197 of the Companies Act, 1990 in Ireland.*

12 An audit is subject to the unavoidable risk that some material misstatements of the financial statements will not be detected, even though the audit is properly planned and performed in accordance with ISAs (UK and Ireland). This risk is higher with regard to material misstatements resulting from noncompliance with laws and regulations due to factors such as the following:

- There are many laws and regulations, relating principally to the operating aspects of the entity, that typically do not have a material effect on the financial statements and are not captured by the entity's information systems relevant to financial reporting.
- The effectiveness of audit procedures is affected by the inherent limitations of internal control and by the use of testing.
- Much of the audit evidence obtained by the auditor is persuasive rather than conclusive in nature.
- Noncompliance may involve conduct designed to conceal it, such as collusion, forgery, deliberate failure to record transactions, senior management[7] override of controls or intentional misrepresentations being made to the auditor.

13 In accordance with ISA (UK and Ireland) 200, "Objective and General Principles Governing an Audit of Financial Statements" the auditor should plan and perform the audit with an attitude of professional skepticism recognizing that the audit may reveal conditions or events that would lead to questioning whether an entity is complying with laws and regulations.

14 In accordance with specific statutory requirements, the auditor may be specifically required to report as part of the audit of the financial statements whether the entity complies with certain provisions of laws or regulations[8]. In these circumstances, the auditor would plan to test for compliance with these provisions of the laws and regulations.

15 In order to plan the audit, the auditor should obtain a general understanding of the legal and regulatory framework applicable to the entity and the industry and how the entity is complying with that framework.

15-1 **In the UK and Ireland, the auditor should obtain a general understanding of the procedures followed by the entity to ensure compliance with that framework.**

16 In obtaining this general understanding, the auditor would particularly recognize that some laws and regulations may give rise to business risks that have a fundamental effect on the operations of the entity. That is, noncompliance with certain laws and regulations may cause the entity to cease operations, or call into question the entity's continuance as a going concern. For example, noncompliance with the requirements of the entity's license or other title to perform its operations could have

---

[7] *In the UK and Ireland, an additional factor is override of controls by those charged with governance.*

[8] *In Ireland, the Companies (Auditing and Accounting) Act 2003 contains provisions that will require, when commenced, directors of "large" companies to make statements regarding compliance with the Companies Acts, tax laws and any other elements that provide a legal framework within which the company operates and that may materially affect the company's financial statements. Auditors of such companies will be required to review the statements to determine whether they are fair and reasonable having regard to information obtained by the auditor in the course of the audit or other work undertaken for the company. The auditors' review requirements are not addressed in this ISA (UK and Ireland)).*

such an impact (for example, for a bank, noncompliance with capital or investment requirements)[9].

To obtain the general understanding of laws and regulations, the auditor would ordinarily: 17

- Use the existing understanding of the entity's industry, regulatory and other external factors;
- Inquire of management[10] concerning the entity's policies and procedures regarding compliance with laws and regulations;
- Inquire of management[10] as to the laws or regulations that may be expected to have a fundamental effect on the operations of the entity;
- Discuss with management[11] the policies or procedures adopted for identifying, evaluating and accounting for litigation claims and assessments; and
- Discuss the legal and regulatory framework with auditors of subsidiaries in other countries (for example, if the subsidiary is required to adhere to the securities regulations of the parent company).

After obtaining the general understanding, the auditor should perform further audit procedures to help identify instances of noncompliance with those laws and regulations where noncompliance should be considered when preparing financial statements, specifically: 18

(a) **Inquiring of management as to whether the entity is in compliance with such laws and regulations;** ~~and~~

(b) **Inspecting correspondence with the relevant licensing or regulatory authorities.**

(c) Enquiring of those charged with governance as to whether they are on notice of any such possible instances of non-compliance with law or regulations.

In the UK and Ireland, the auditor's procedures should be designed to help identify possible or actual instances of non-compliance with those laws and regulations which provide a legal framework within which the entity conducts its business and which are central to the entity's ability to conduct its business and hence to its financial statements. 18-1

Further, the auditor should obtain sufficient appropriate audit evidence about compliance with those laws and regulations generally recognized by the auditor to have an effect on the determination of material amounts and disclosures in financial statements. The auditor should have a sufficient understanding of these laws and regulations in order to consider them when auditing the assertions related to the determination of the amounts to be recorded and the disclosures to be made. 19

Such laws and regulations would be well established and known to the entity and within the industry; they would be considered on a recurring basis each time financial statements are issued. These laws and regulations, may relate, for example, to the form and content of financial statements[12], including industry specific requirements; 20

---

[9] *Such requirements exist in the UK under the Financial Services and Markets Act 2000 and in Ireland under the Investment Intermediaries Act 1995, the Central Bank Acts 1942 to 1989 and the Credit Union Act , 1997.*

[10] *In the UK and Ireland, the auditor makes inquiries of such matters with those charged with governance.*

[11] *In the UK and Ireland, the auditor discusses such matters with those charged with governance.*

[12] *In the UK under Schedule 4 to the Companies Act 1985 or The Companies (Amendment) Act, 1986 in Ireland.*

accounting for transactions under government contracts; or the accrual or recognition of expenses for income taxes or pension costs.

20-1 In the UK and Ireland, these laws and regulations include:

- Those which determine the circumstances under which a company is prohibited from making a distribution except out of profits available for the purpose[13].
- Those laws which require auditors expressly to report non-compliance, such as the requirements relating to the maintenance of proper accounting records or the disclosure of particulars of directors' remuneration in a company's financial statements[14].

21 Other than as described in paragraphs 18-20, the auditor does not perform other audit procedures on the entity's compliance with laws and regulations since this would be outside the scope of an audit of financial statements.

22 The auditor should be alert to the fact that audit procedures applied for the purpose of forming an opinion on the financial statements may bring instances of possible non-compliance with laws and regulations to the auditor's attention. For example, such audit procedures include reading minutes; inquiring of the entity's management[10] and legal counsel concerning litigation, claims and assessments; and performing substantive tests of details of classes of transactions, account balances, or disclosures.

22-1 In the UK and Ireland, when carrying out procedures for the purpose of forming an opinion on the financial statements, the auditor should be alert for those instances of possible or actual noncompliance with laws and regulations that might incur obligations for partners and staff in audit firms to report money laundering offences.

22-3 There may be a wide range of laws and regulations falling into this category, many of which fall outside the expertise of individuals trained in financial auditing. There can therefore be no assurance that the auditor appointed to report on an entity's statements will detect all material breaches of such laws and regulations. However, when the auditor suspects the existence of breaches which could be material, the auditor needs to consider whether and how the matter ought to be reported, as set out later in this ISA (UK and Ireland).

22-4 Anti-money laundering legislation[15] in the UK and Ireland extends further than the laundering of money that is derived from drug trafficking or is related to

---

[13] In the UK under Section 263 of the Companies Act 1985 or Section 45 of the Companies (Amendment) Act, 1983 in Ireland.

[14] In the UK under Sections 237(2) and 237(4)(a) of the Companies Act 1985 or Section 193 and 194 of the Companies Act, 1990 in Ireland.

[15] In the UK, with effect from 1 March 2004 The Money Laundering Regulations 2003 replaced the 1993 and 2001 regulations and the requirements of the Proceeds of Crime Act 2002 were extended to the provision by way of business of audit services by a person who is eligible for appointment as a company auditor under section 25 of the Companies Act 1989.
In Ireland, with effect from 15 September 2003 the Criminal Justice Act 1994 (Section 32) Regulations 2003 designate accountants, auditors, and tax advisors and others for the purposes of the anti-money laundering provisions of the Criminal Justice Act, 1994, as amended.

terrorist[16] offences and has specific auditor reporting responsibilities[17]. The new anti-money laundering legislation imposes a duty to report money laundering in respect of the proceeds of all crime. The detailed legislation in both countries differs but the impact on the auditor can broadly be summarised as follows:

- Money laundering includes concealing, disguising, converting, transferring, removing, using, acquiring or possessing property[18] which constitutes or represents a benefit from criminal conduct[19]. Although the anti-money laundering legislation does not contain de minimis concessions in the UK the National Criminal Intelligence Service ("NCIS") has introduced guidance on reports of limited intelligence value.
- Partners and staff in audit firms are required to report suspicions[20] that a criminal offence, giving rise to direct or indirect benefit has been committed, regardless of whether that offence has been committed by a client or by a third party.

---

[16] In the UK, the Terrorism Act 2000 (as amended by the Anti-terrorism, Crime and Security Act 2001) and associated regulations. The duty to report drug trafficking related money laundering has been subsumed into the general requirement to report the proceeds of crime.
In Ireland, there is similar proposed legislation that the auditor will need to consider in due course.

[17] Anti-money laundering legislation differs in the UK and Ireland, references to such legislation in the main body of the SAS uses generalised wording with the specific requirements of the UK and Irish legislation described in footnotes.

[18] In the UK, "property" is criminal property if it constitutes a person's benefit from criminal conduct or it represents such a benefit (in whole or part and whether directly or indirectly), and the alleged offender knows or suspects that it constitutes or represents such a benefit.
In Ireland, "property" is defined as including money and all other property, real or personal, heritable or moveable, including choses in action and other intangible or incorporeal property.

[19] In the UK, "criminal conduct" is defined as conduct which constitutes an offence in any part of the UK or would constitute such an offence if it occurred in any part of the UK.
In Ireland, "criminal conduct" means conduct which constitutes an 'indictable offence', or where the conduct occurs outside the State, would constitute such an offence if it occurred within the State and also constitutes an offence under the law of the country or territorial unit in which it occurs, and includes participation in such conduct.

[20] In the UK, as a result of the Proceeds of Crime Act 2002 and the 2003 Money Laundering Regulations auditors are required to report where they know or suspect, or have reasonable grounds to know or suspect, that another person is engaged in money laundering. Partners and staff in audit firms discharge their responsibilities by reporting to their Money Laundering Reporting Officer ("MLRO") or, in the case of sole practitioners, to NCIS.
In Ireland, the Criminal Justice Act, 1994, as amended, and the Criminal Justice Act, 1994 (Section 32) Regulations, 2003 require auditors and other defined persons to report to the Garda Síochána and the Revenue Commissioners where they suspect that an offence, as defined in the legislation, in relation to the business of that person has been or is being committed. Two further reporting duties exist in Irish law, Section 74 of the Company Law Enforcement Act 2001 requires auditors to report to the Director of Corporate Enforcement instances of the suspected commission of indictable offences under the Companies Acts and Section 59 of the Criminal Justice (Theft and Fraud Offences) Act, 2001 requires 'relevant persons', as defined in the section and which includes auditors of companies, to report 'indications' that specified offences under the Act have been committed to the Garda Síochána. Additionally, auditors may report direct to the Revenue Commissioners certain offences under Section 1079 of the Taxes Consolidation Act, 1997.

- Partners and staff in audit firms need to be alert to the dangers of making disclosures that are likely to tip off a money launderer or prejudice an investigation ('tipping-off'[21]), as this will constitute a criminal offence under the anti-money laundering legislation.

23 The auditor should obtain written representations that management[22] has disclosed to the auditor all known actual or possible noncompliance with laws and regulations whose effects should be considered when preparing financial statements.

23-1 Where applicable, the written representations should include the actual or contingent consequences which may arise from the non-compliance.

24 In the absence of audit evidence to the contrary, the auditor is entitled to assume the entity is in compliance with these laws and regulations.

Compliance with Tax Legislation

24-1 In the UK and Ireland, the auditor's responsibility to express an opinion on an entity's financial statements does not extend to determining whether the entity has complied in every respect with applicable tax legislation. The auditor needs to obtain sufficient appropriate evidence to give reasonable assurance that the amounts included in the financial statements in respect of taxation are not materially misstated. This will usually include making appropriate enquiries of those advising the entity on taxation matters (whether within the audit firm or elsewhere).

24-2 In the UK and Ireland, if the auditor becomes aware that the entity has failed to comply with the requirements of tax legislation, the auditor follows the procedures for reporting set out in paragraphs 38 to 38-1 of this ISA (UK and Ireland).

Audit Procedures When Noncompliance is Discovered

25 The Appendix to this ISA (UK and Ireland) sets out examples of the type of information that might come to the auditor's attention that may indicate noncompliance.

---

[21] *In the UK, 'tipping off' is an offence under section 333 of the Proceeds of Crime Act 2002. It arises when an individual discloses matters where:*
(a) There is knowledge or suspicion that a report has already been made, and
(b) That disclosure is likely to prejudice any investigation which might be conducted following the report.
Whilst "tipping off" requires a person to have knowledge or suspicion that a report has been or will be made, a further offence of prejudicing an investigation is included in section 342 of POCA. Under this provision, it is an offence to make any disclosure which may prejudice an investigation of which a person has knowledge or suspicion, or to falsify, conceal, destroy or otherwise dispose of, or cause or permit the falsification, concealment, destruction or disposal of, documents relevant to such an investigation.
In Ireland Section 58 of the Criminal Justice Act, 1994, as amended, establishes the offence of "prejudicing an investigation". This relates both to when a person, knowing or suspecting that an investigation is taking place, makes any disclosure likely to prejudice the investigation or when a person, knowing that a report has been made, makes any disclosure likely to prejudice any investigation arising from the report.

[22] *In the UK and Ireland the auditor obtains this written representation from those charged with governance.*

When the auditor becomes aware of information concerning a possible instance of noncompliance, the auditor should[23] obtain an understanding of the nature of the act and the circumstances in which it has occurred, and sufficient other information to evaluate the possible effect on the financial statements.   26

When evaluating the possible effect on the financial statements, the auditor considers: 27

- The potential financial consequences, such as fines, penalties, damages, threat of expropriation of assets[24], enforced discontinuation of operations and litigation.
- Whether the potential financial consequences require disclosure.
- Whether the potential financial consequences are so serious as to call into question the true and fair view (fair presentation) given by the financial statements.

As the consideration of compliance with laws and regulations may involve consideration of matters which do not lie within the competence and experience of individuals trained in the audit of financial information, it may be necessary for the auditor to obtain appropriate expert advice (whether through the entity or independently) in order to evaluate the possible effect on the entity's financial statements. Where this is the case, the auditor is required to meet the Standards set out in ISA (UK and Ireland) 620 "Using the work of an expert".   27-1

When the auditor believes there may be noncompliance, the auditor should document the findings and discuss them with management[11]. Documentation of findings would include copies of records and documents and making minutes of conversations, if appropriate.   28

Any discussion of findings with those charged with governance and with management should be subject to compliance with legislation relating to 'tipping off' and any requirement to report the findings direct to a third party.   28-1

If management[25] does not provide satisfactory information that it is in fact in compliance, the auditor would consult with the entity's lawyer about the application of the laws and regulations to the circumstances and the possible effects on the financial statements. When it is not considered appropriate to consult with the entity's lawyer or when the auditor is not satisfied with the opinion, the auditor would consider consulting the auditor's own lawyer as to whether a violation of a law or regulation is involved, the possible legal consequences and what further action, if any, the auditor would take.   29

When adequate information about the suspected noncompliance cannot be obtained, the auditor should consider the effect of the lack of sufficient appropriate audit evidence on the auditor's report.   30

---

[23] *Subject to compliance with legislation relating to 'tipping off'. See footnote 21.*

[24] *The Proceeds of Crime Act 2002 ("POCA") establishes an independent Government Department, the Assets Recovery Agency.*
In Ireland, the Criminal Assets Bureau, a similar agency responsible for the confiscation of assets was established by the Criminal Assets Bureau Act, 1996.

[25] *In the UK and Ireland, the auditor obtains such information from those charged with governance.*

31 The auditor should consider the implications of noncompliance in relation to other aspects of the audit, particularly the reliability of management[26] representations. In this regard, the auditor reconsiders the risk assessment and the validity of management representations, in case of noncompliance not detected by the entity's internal controls or not included in management representations. The implications of particular instances of noncompliance discovered by the auditor will depend on the relationship of the perpetration and concealment, if any, of the act to specific control activities and the level of management or employees involved.

Reporting of Noncompliance

To Management

32 The auditor should, as soon as practicable, either communicate with those charged with governance, or obtain audit evidence that they are appropriately informed, regarding noncompliance that comes to the auditor's attention. However, the auditor need not do so for matters that are clearly inconsequential or trivial and may reach agreement in advance on the nature of such matters to be communicated.

33 If in the auditor's judgment the noncompliance is believed to be intentional and material, the auditor should communicate the finding without delay.

33-1 In the UK and Ireland the auditor should communicate the finding where the non-compliance is material or is believed to be intentional. The non-compliance does not have to be both material and intentional.

33-2 Any communication with those charged with governance, or action by the auditor to obtain evidence that they are appropriately informed is subject to compliance with legislation relating to 'tipping off'.

34 If the auditor suspects that members of senior management, including members of the board of directors[27], are involved in noncompliance, the auditor should report the matter to the next higher level of authority at the entity, if it exists, such as an audit committee or a supervisory board. Where no higher authority exists, or if the auditor believes that the report may not be acted upon or is unsure as to the person to whom to report, the auditor would consider seeking legal advice.

34-1 In the case of suspected Money Laundering it may be appropriate to report the matter direct to the appropriate authority.

To the Users of the Auditor's Report on the Financial Statements

35 If the auditor concludes that the noncompliance has a material effect on the financial statements, and has not been properly reflected in the financial statements, the auditor should[23] express a qualified or an adverse opinion.

---

[26] In the UK and Ireland, the auditor also considers the reliability of representations from those charged with governance.

[27] In the UK and Ireland, the auditor also reports such matters if those charged with governance are suspected of being involved in non compliance.

If the auditor is precluded by the entity from obtaining sufficient appropriate audit evidence to evaluate whether noncompliance that may be material to the financial statements, has, or is likely to have, occurred, the auditor should[23] express a qualified opinion or a disclaimer of opinion on the financial statements on the basis of a limitation on the scope of the audit.	36
If the auditor is unable to determine whether noncompliance has occurred because of limitations imposed by the circumstances rather than by the entity, the auditor should[23] consider the effect on the auditor's report.	37
In the UK and Ireland, if the auditor concludes that the view given by the financial statements could be affected by a level of uncertainty concerning the consequences of a suspected or actual noncompliance which, in the auditor's opinion, is significant, the auditor, subject to compliance with legislation relating to 'tipping off', includes an explanatory paragraph referring to the matter in the auditor's report.	37-1
In the UK and Ireland, in determining whether disclosures concerning the matter are adequate, or whether an explanatory paragraph needs to be included in the auditor's report, the auditor bases the decision primarily on the adequacy of the overall view given by the financial statements. Steps taken to regularize the position (for example, where there has been an unauthorized material transaction for which authority has subsequently been obtained), or the possible consequences of qualification, are not, on their own, grounds on which the auditor may refrain from expressing a qualified opinion or from including an explanatory paragraph reflecting a significant uncertainty.	37-2
In the UK and Ireland, when determining whether a suspected or actual instance of non-compliance with laws or regulations requires disclosure in the financial statements, the auditor has regard to whether shareholders require the information to enable them to assess the performance of the company and any potential implications for its future operations or standing. Where a suspected or actual instance of non-compliance needs to be reflected in the financial statements, a true and fair view will require that sufficient particulars are provided to enable users of the financial statements to appreciate the significance of the information disclosed. This would usually require the full potential consequences to be disclosed and, in some cases, it may be necessary for this purpose that the financial statements indicate that non-compliance with laws or regulations is or may be involved.	37-3
In the UK and Ireland, when considering whether the financial statements reflect the possible consequences of any suspected or actual non-compliance, the auditor has regard to the requirements of FRS 12 "Provisions, contingent liabilities and contingent assets"/IAS 37, "Provisions, contingent liabilities and contingent assets". Suspected or actual non-compliance with laws or regulations may require disclosure in the financial statements because, although the immediate financial effect on the entity may not be material, there could be future material consequences such as fines or litigation. For example, an illegal payment may not itself be material but may result in criminal proceedings against the entity or loss of business which could have a material effect on the true and fair view given by the financial statements.	37-4

To Regulatory and Enforcement Authorities

38 The auditor's duty of confidentiality would ordinarily preclude reporting non-compliance to a third party. However, in certain circumstances, that duty of confidentiality is overridden by statute, law or by courts of law (for example, in some countries the auditor is required to report noncompliance by financial institutions to the supervisory authorities). The auditor may need to seek legal advice in such circumstances, giving due consideration to the auditor's responsibility to the public interest.

38-1 **If the auditor becomes aware of a suspected or actual non-compliance with law and regulations which gives rise to a statutory duty to report, the auditor should, subject to compliance with legislation relating to "tipping off", make a report to the appropriate authority without undue delay.**

38-2 Legislation in the UK and Ireland establishes specific responsibilities for the auditor to report suspicions regarding certain criminal offences. In addition, the auditor of entities subject to statutory regulation[28], has separate responsibilities to report certain information direct to the relevant regulator. Standards and guidance on these responsibilities is given in Section B of this ISA (UK and Ireland) and relevant APB Practice Notes.

38-3 The procedures and guidance in Section B of this ISA (UK and Ireland) can be adapted to circumstances in which the auditor of other types of entity becomes aware of a suspected instance of non-compliance with laws or regulations which the auditor is under a statutory duty to report.

38-4 Where the auditor becomes aware of a suspected or actual instance of non-compliance with law or regulations which does not give rise to a statutory duty to report to an appropriate authority the auditor considers whether the matter may be one that ought to be reported to a proper authority in the public interest and, where this is the case, except in the circumstances covered in paragraph 38-6 below, discusses the matter with those charged with governance, including any audit committee.

38-5 If, having considered any views expressed on behalf of the entity and in the light of any legal advice obtained, the auditor concludes that the matter ought to be reported to an appropriate authority in the public interest, the auditor notifies those charged with governance in writing of the view and, if the entity does not voluntarily do so itself or is unable to provide evidence that the matter has been reported, the auditor reports it.

38-6 The auditor reports a matter direct to a proper authority in the public interest and without discussing the matter with the entity if the auditor concludes that the suspected or actual instance of non-compliance has caused the auditor no longer to have confidence in the integrity of the those charged with governance.

38-7 Examples of circumstances which may cause the auditor no longer to have confidence in the integrity of those charged with governance include situations:

---

[28] *Auditors of financial service entities, pension schemes and, in the UK, charities have a statutory responsibility, subject to compliance with legislation relating to "tipping off", to report matters that are likely to be of material significance to the regulator.*

- Where the auditor suspects or has evidence of the involvement or intended involvement of those charged with governance in possible non-compliance with law or regulations which could have a material effect on the financial statements; or
- Where the auditor is aware that those charged with governance are aware of such non-compliance and, contrary to regulatory requirements or the public interest, have not reported it to a proper authority within a reasonable period.

Determination of where the balance of public interest lies requires careful consideration. An auditor whose suspicions have been aroused uses professional judgment to determine whether the auditor's misgivings justify the auditor in carrying the matter further or are too insubstantial to deserve reporting. The auditor is protected from the risk of liability for breach of confidence or defamation provided that:

38-8

- In the case of breach of confidence, disclosure is made in the public interest, and such disclosure is made to an appropriate body or person[29], and there is no malice motivating the disclosure; and
- In the case of defamation disclosure is made in the auditor's capacity as auditor of the entity concerned, and there is no malice motivating the disclosure.

In addition, the auditor is protected from such risks where the auditor is expressly permitted or required by legislation to disclose information.

'Public interest' is a concept that is not capable of general definition. Each situation must be considered individually. Matters to be taken into account when considering whether disclosure is justified in the public interest may include:

38-9

- The extent to which the suspected or actual non-compliance with law or regulations is likely to affect members of the public;
- Whether those charged with governance have rectified the matter or are taking, or are likely to take, effective corrective action;
- The extent to which non-disclosure is likely to enable the suspected or actual non-compliance with law or regulations to recur with impunity;
- The gravity of the matter;
- Whether there is a general ethos within the entity of disregarding law or regulations; and
- The weight of evidence and the degree of the auditor's suspicion that there has been an instance of non-compliance with law or regulations.

An auditor who can demonstrate having acted reasonably and in good faith in informing an authority of a breach of law or regulations which the auditor thinks has been committed would not be held by the court to be in breach of duty to the client even if, an investigation or prosecution having occurred, it were found that there had been no offence.

38-10

---

[29] In the UK, proper authorities could include the Serious Fraud Office, the Crown Prosecution Service, police forces, the Financial Services Authority the Panel on Takeovers and Mergers, the Society of Lloyd's, local authorities, the Charity Commissioners for England and Wales, the Scottish Office For Scottish Charities, the Inland Revenue, HM Customs and Excise, the Department of Trade and Industry and the Health and Safety Executive.
In Ireland, comparable bodies could include the Garda Bureau of Fraud Investigation, the Revenue Commissioners, the Irish Stock Exchange, the Irish Financial Services Regulatory Authority, the Pensions Board, the Director of Corporate Enforcement and the Department of Enterprise Trade and Employment.

38-11   The auditor needs to remember that the auditor's decision as to whether to report, and if so to whom, may be called into question at a future date, for example on the basis of:

- What the auditor knew at the time;
- What the auditor to have known in the course of the audit;
- What the auditor ought to have concluded; and
- What the auditor ought to have done.

The auditor may also wish to consider the possible consequences if financial loss is occasioned by non-compliance with law or regulations which the auditor suspects (or ought to suspect) has occurred but decided not to report.

38-12   The auditor may need to take legal advice before making a decision on whether the matter needs to be reported to a proper authority in the public interest.

Withdrawal From the Engagement

39   The auditor may conclude that withdrawal from the engagement is necessary when the entity does not take the remedial action that the auditor considers necessary in the circumstances, even when the noncompliance is not material to the financial statements. Factors that would affect the auditor's conclusion include the implications of the involvement of the highest authority within the entity which may affect the reliability of management[26] representations, and the effects on the auditor of continuing association with the entity. In reaching such a conclusion, the auditor would ordinarily seek legal advice.

39-1   Resignation by the auditor is a step of last resort. It is normally preferable for the auditor to remain in office to fulfil the auditor's statutory duties, particularly where minority interests are involved. However, there are circumstances where there may be no alternative to resignation, for example where the directors of a company refuse to issue its financial statements or the auditor wishes to inform the shareholders or creditors of the company of the auditor's concerns and there is no immediate occasion to do so.

40   As stated in the *Code of Ethics for Professional Accountants*[30] **issued by the International Federation of Accountants, on receipt of an inquiry from the proposed auditor, the existing auditor should advise whether there are any professional reasons why the proposed auditor should not accept the appointment.** The extent to which an existing auditor can discuss the affairs of a client with a proposed auditor will depend on whether the client's permission to do so has been obtained and/or the legal or ethical requirements that apply in each country relating to such disclosure. If there are any such reasons or other matters which need to be disclosed, the existing auditor would, taking account of the legal and ethical constraints, including where appropriate permission of the client, give details of the information and discuss freely with the proposed auditor all matters relevant to the appointment. **If permission from the client to discuss its affairs with the proposed auditor is denied by the client, that fact should be disclosed to the proposed auditor.**

---

[30] *In the UK and Ireland the relevant ethical pronouncements with which the auditor complies are the APB's Ethical Standards and the ethical pronouncements relating to the work of auditors issued by the auditor's relevant professional body — see the Statement "The Auditing practices Board — Scope and Authority of Pronouncements.*

Effective Date

This ISA (UK and Ireland) is effective for audits of financial statements for periods commencing on or after 15 December 2004. **40-1**

In the UK, the Money Laundering Regulations 2003 came into force on 1 March 2004. In Ireland, the Criminal Justice Act 1994 (Section 32) Regulations 2003 are effective from 15 September 2003. **40-2**

Public Sector Perspective

Additional guidance for auditors of public sector bodies in the UK and Ireland is given in:

- Practice Note 10 "Audit of Financial Statements of Public Sector Entities in the United Kingdom (Revised)"
- Practice Note 10(I) "The Audit of Central Government Financial Statements in Ireland"

Many public sector engagements include additional audit responsibilities with respect to consideration of laws and regulations. Even if the auditor's responsibilities do not extend beyond those of the private sector auditor, reporting responsibilities may be different as the public sector auditor may be obliged to report on instances of noncompliance to governing authorities or to report them in the audit report. In respect to public sector entities, the Public Sector Committee (PSC) has supplemented the guidance included in this ISA (UK and Ireland) in its Study 3, "Auditing for Compliance with Authorities – A Public Sector Perspective." 1

Appendix – Indications That Noncompliance May Have Occurred

Examples of the type of information that may come to the auditor's attention that may indicate that noncompliance with laws or regulations has occurred are listed below:

- Investigation by government departments.
- Payment of fines or penalties.
- Payments for unspecified services or loans to consultants, related parties, employees or government employees.
- Sales commissions or agent's fees that appear excessive in relation to those ordinarily paid by the entity or in its industry or to the services actually received.
- Purchasing at prices significantly above or below market price.
- Unusual payments in cash, purchases in the form of cashiers' checks payable to bearer or transfers to numbered bank accounts.
- Complex corporate structures including offshore companies where ownership cannot be identified.
- Unusual transactions with companies registered in tax havens.
- Tax evasion such as the under declaring of income and over claiming of expenses.
- Payments for goods or services made other than to the country from which the goods or services originated.

- Payments without proper exchange control documentation.
- Existence of an information system which fails, whether by design or by accident, to provide an adequate audit trail or sufficient evidence.
- Unauthorized transactions or improperly recorded transactions.
- Media comment.
- Transactions undertaken by the entity that have no apparent purpose or that make no obvious economic sense.
- Where those charged with governance of the entity refuse to provide necessary information and explanations to support transactions and other dealings of the company.

Section B

The Auditor's Right and Duty to Report to Regulators in the Financial Sector

Introduction

The purpose of this Section of this ISA (UK and Ireland) is to establish standards and provide guidance on the circumstances in which the auditor of a financial institution subject to statutory regulation (a 'regulated entity') is required to report direct to a regulator information which comes to the auditor's attention in the course of the work undertaken in the auditor's capacity as auditor of the regulated entity. This may include work undertaken to express an opinion on the entity's financial statements, other financial information or on other matters specified by legislation or by a regulator.

The auditor of a regulated entity should bring information of which the auditor has become aware in the ordinary course of performing work undertaken to fulfil the auditor's audit responsibilities to the attention of the appropriate regulator without delay when:

(a) **The auditor concludes that it is relevant to the regulator's functions having regard to such matters as may be specified in statute or any related regulations; and**
(b) **In the auditor's opinion there is reasonable cause to believe it is or may be of material significance to the regulator.**

The auditor of a regulated entity generally has special reporting responsibilities in addition to the responsibility to report on financial statements. These special reporting responsibilities take two forms:

(a) *A responsibility to provide a report on matters specified in legislation or by a regulator.* This form of report is often made on an annual or other routine basis and does not derive from another set of reporting responsibilities. The auditor is required to carry out appropriate procedures sufficient to form an opinion on the matters concerned. These procedures may be in addition to those carried out to form an opinion on the financial statements; and
(b) *A statutory duty to report certain information, relevant to the regulators' functions, that come to the auditor's attention in the course of the audit work.* The auditor has no responsibility to carry out procedures to search out the information relevant to the regulator. This form of report is derivative in nature, arising only in the context of another set of reporting responsibilities, and is initiated by the auditor on discovery of a reportable matter.

The statutory duty to report to a regulator applies to information which comes to the attention of the auditor in the auditor's capacity as auditor. In determining whether information is obtained in that capacity, two criteria in particular need to be considered: first, whether the person who obtained the information also undertook the audit work; and if so, whether it was obtained in the course of or as a result of undertaking the audit work. Appendix 2 to this section of this ISA (UK and Ireland) sets out guidance on the application of these criteria.

The auditor may have a statutory right to bring information to the attention of the regulator in particular circumstances which lie outside those giving rise to a statutory duty to initiate a direct report. Where this is so, the auditor may use that right to make a direct report relevant to the regulator on a specific matter which comes to the auditor's attention when the auditor concludes that doing so is necessary to protect the interests of those for whose benefit the regulator is required to act.

6   This section of this ISA (UK and Ireland) deals with both forms of direct reports. Guidance on the auditor's responsibility to provide special reports on a routine basis on other matters specified in legislation or by a regulator is given in the Practice Notes dealing with regulated business, for example banks, building societies, investment businesses and insurers.

7   The standards and explanatory material in this section of this ISA (UK and Ireland) complement but do not replace the legal and regulatory requirements applicable to each regulated entity. Where the application of those requirements, taking into account any published interpretations, is insufficiently clear for the auditor to determine whether a particular circumstance results in a legal duty to make a report to a regulator, or a right to make such a report, it may be appropriate to take legal advice.

Definitions

8   **The Act**: In the United Kingdom, this comprises the Financial Services and Markets Act 2000 and regulations made under that Act, and any future legislation including provisions relating to the duties of auditors similar to those contained in that statute.

9   In the Republic of Ireland, *the Acts* comprise the Central Bank Acts 1942 to 1989, the Building Societies Act 1989, The Central Bank and Financial Services Authority of Ireland Act, 2003, the Trustees Savings Bank Act 1989, the Insurance Act 1989, the European Communities (Undertakings for Collective Investment in Transferable Securities) Regulations 1989, the Unit Trusts Act 1990, the ICC Bank Act (section 3) Regulations 1993 and, in the case of investment companies, the Companies Act 1990 and any future legislation[1] including provisions relating to the duties of auditors similar to those contained in those Acts, together with other regulations made under them.

10 **Audit**: for the purpose of this Section of this ISA (UK and Ireland), the term *audit* refers both to an engagement to report on the financial statements of a regulated entity and to an engagement to provide a report on other matters specified by statute or by a regulator undertaken in the capacity of auditor.

11 **Auditor**: the term 'auditor' should be interpreted in accordance with the requirements of the Acts. Guidance on its interpretation is contained in Practice Notes relating to each area of the financial sector to which the duty applies.

12 **Control environment**: the overall attitude, awareness and actions of those charged with governance and management regarding internal controls and their importance in the entity. Factors reflected in the control environment include:

    • Management's philosophy and operating style;

---

[1] *Specifically, the Central Bank and Financial Services Authority of Ireland (no. 2) Bill published in December 2003 is also likely to introduce changes to the duties of auditors.*

- The entity's organisational structure and methods of assigning authority and responsibility (including segregation of duties and management supervisory controls); and
- Management's methods of imposing control including the internal audit function, the functions of those charged with governance and personnel policies and procedures.

Those charged with governance: In the UK and Ireland, those charged with governance include the directors (executive and non-executive) of a company or other body, the members of an audit committee where one exists, the partners, proprietors, committee of management or trustees of other forms of entity, or equivalent persons responsible for directing the entity's affairs and preparing its financial statements. 13

Material significance: the term 'material significance' requires interpretation in the context of the specific legislation applicable to the regulated entity. A matter or group of matters is normally of material significance to a regulator's functions when, due either to its nature or its potential financial impact, it is likely of itself to require investigation by the regulator. Further guidance on the interpretation of the term in the context of specific legislation is contained in Practice Notes dealing with the rights and duties of auditors of regulated entities to report direct to regulators. 14

Regulated entity: an individual, company or other type of entity authorised to carry on business in the financial sector which is subject to statutory regulation. 15

Regulator: such persons as are empowered by the Act to regulate business in the financial sector. The term includes the Financial Services Authority (FSA), Irish Financial Services Regulatory Authority (IFSRA) and such other bodies as may be so empowered in future legislation. 16

Appointment as Auditor and Ceasing to Hold Office

Before accepting appointment, the auditor follows the procedures identified in the APB's Ethical Standards and the ethical pronouncements and Audit Regulations issued by the auditor's relevant professional body. 17

In the case of regulated entities, the auditor would in particular obtain an understanding of the appropriate statutory and regulatory requirements and a preliminary knowledge of the management and operations of the entity, so as to enable the auditor to determine whether a level of knowledge of the business adequate to perform the audit can be obtained. The procedures carried out by the auditor in seeking to obtain this preliminary understanding may include discussion with the previous auditor and, in some circumstances, with the regulator. 18

On ceasing to hold office, the auditor may be required by statute or by regulation to make specific reports concerning the circumstances relating to that event, and would also follow the procedures identified in the ethical guidance issued by the relevant professional body. 19

In addition, the auditor of a regulated entity would assess whether it is appropriate to bring any matters of which the auditor is then aware to the notice of the regulator. Under legislation in the UK, this may be done either before or after ceasing to hold office, as the auditor's statutory right to disclose to a regulator 20 information obtained in the course of the auditor's appointment is not affected by the auditor's removal, resignation or otherwise ceasing to hold office.

Conduct of the Audit

21   The duty to make a report direct to a regulator does not impose upon the auditor a duty to carry out specific work: it arises solely in the context of work carried out to fulfil other reporting responsibilities. Accordingly, no auditing procedures in addition to those carried out in the normal course of auditing the financial statements, or for the purpose of making any other specified report, are necessary for the fulfilment of the auditor's responsibilities.

22   It will, however, be necessary for the auditor to take additional time in carrying out a financial statement audit or other engagement to assess whether matters which come to the auditor's attention should be included in a direct report and, where appropriate, to prepare and submit the report. These additional planning and follow-up procedures do not constitute an extension of the scope of the financial statement audit or of other work undertaken to provide a specified report relating to a regulated entity. They are necessary solely in order to understand and clarify the reporting responsibility and, where appropriate, to make a report.

23   The circumstances in which the auditor is required by statute to make a report direct to a regulator include matters which are not considered as part of the audit of financial statements or of work undertaken to discharge other routine responsibilities. For example, the duty to report would apply to information of which the auditor became aware in the course of the auditor's work which is relevant to the FSA's criteria for approved persons, although the auditor is not otherwise required to express an opinion on such matters. However, the legislation imposing a duty to make reports direct to regulators does not require the auditor to change the scope of the audit work, nor does it place on the auditor an obligation to conduct the audit work in such a way that there is reasonable certainty that the auditor will discover all matters which regulators might consider as being of material significance. Therefore, whilst the auditor of a regulated entity is required to be alert to matters which may require a report, the auditor is not expected to be aware of all circumstances which, had the auditor known of them, would have led the auditor to make such a report. It is only when the auditor becomes aware of such a matter during the conduct of the normal audit work that the auditor has an obligation to determine whether a report to the regulator is required by statute or appropriate for other reasons.

24   Similarly, the auditor is not responsible for reporting on a regulated entity's overall compliance with rules with which it is required to comply nor is the auditor required to conduct the audit work in such a way that there is reasonable certainty that the auditor will discover breaches. Nevertheless, breaches of rules with which a regulated entity is required to comply may have implications for the financial statements and, accordingly, the auditor of a regulated entity needs to consider whether any actual or contingent liabilities may have arisen from breaches of regulatory requirements. Breaches of a regulator's requirements may also have consequences for other matters on which the auditor of a regulated entity is required to express an opinion and, if such breaches represent criminal conduct, could give rise to the need to report to specified authorities.

Planning

When gaining a knowledge of the business for the purpose of the audit, the auditor of a regulated entity should obtain an understanding of its current activities, the scope of its authorisation and the effectiveness of its control environment. 25

ISAs (UK and Ireland) require the auditor to gain a sufficient understanding of the reporting entity's business to plan and perform the audit effectively and to assess the risk of material misstatements in the financial statements. 26

In the context of a regulated entity, the auditor's understanding of its business needs to extend to the applicable statutory provisions, the rules of the regulator concerned and any guidance issued by the regulator on the interpretation of those rules, together with other guidance issued by the APB. 27

The auditor is also required to assess the risk of misstatements in the financial statements, or of other errors in relation to other matters on which the auditor is required to report. In making such an assessment the auditor takes into account the control environment, including the entity's higher level procedures for complying with the requirements of its regulator. Such a review gives an indication of the extent to which the general atmosphere and controls in the regulated entity are conducive to compliance, for example through consideration of *inter alia:* 28

- The adequacy of procedures and training to inform staff of the requirements of relevant legislation and the rules or other regulations of the regulator;
- The adequacy of procedures for authorisation of transactions;
- Procedures for internal review of the entity's compliance with regulatory or other requirements;
- The authority of, and any resources available to, the compliance officer/ Money Laundering Reporting Officer ('MLRO'); and
- Procedures to ensure that possible breaches of requirements are investigated by an appropriate person and are brought to the attention of senior management.

In some areas of the financial sector, conducting business outside the scope of the entity's authorisation is a serious regulatory breach, and therefore of material significance to the regulator. In addition, it may result in fines, suspension or loss of authorisation. 29

Where the auditor's review of the reporting entity's activities indicates that published guidance by the regulator may not be sufficiently precise to enable the auditor to identify circumstances in which it is necessary to initiate a report, the auditor would consider whether it is necessary to discuss the matters specified in legislation with the appropriate regulator with a view to reaching agreement on its interpretation. 30

Similarly, where a group includes two or more companies separately regulated by different regulators, there may be a need to clarify the regulators' requirements in any overlapping areas of activity. However, the statutory duty to make a report as presently defined arises only in respect of the legal entity subject to regulation. Therefore the auditor of an unregulated company in a group that includes one or more other companies which are authorised by regulators would not have a duty to report matters to the regulators of those companies. 31

When a regulated entity is subject to provisions of two or more regulators, the auditor needs to take account of the separate reporting requirements in planning 32 and conducting the audit work. Arrangements may exist for one regulatory body to rely on financial monitoring being carried out by another body (the 'lead regulator') and where this is the case, routine reports by the regulated entity's auditor may be made to the lead regulator alone.

33 However, the auditor's statutory duty to report cannot be discharged by reliance on the lead regulator informing others. Therefore, where the auditor concludes that a matter is of material significance to one regulator, the auditor needs to assess the need for separate reports informing each regulator of matters which the auditor concludes are or may be of material significance to it.

Supervision and Control

34 **The auditor should ensure that all staff involved in the audit of a regulated entity have an understanding of:**
   (a) **The provisions of applicable legislation;**
   (b) **The regulator's rules and any guidance issued by the regulator; and**
   (c) **Any specific requirements which apply to the particular regulated entity, appropriate to their role in the audit and sufficient (in the context of that role) to enable them to identify situations which may give reasonable cause to believe that a matter should be reported to the regulator.**

35 ISAs (UK and Ireland) require the auditor to exercise adequate control and supervision over staff conducting work on an audit. Consequently, in planning and conducting the audit of a regulated entity the auditor needs to ensure that staff are alert to the possibility that a report to its regulator may be required.

36 Auditing firms also need to establish adequate procedures to ensure that any matters which are discovered in the course of or as a result of audit work and may give rise to a duty to report are brought to the attention of the partner responsible for the audit on a timely basis.

37 The right and duty to report to a regulator applies to information of which the auditor becomes aware in the auditor's capacity as such. They do not extend automatically to any information obtained by an accounting firm regardless of its source. Consequently partners and staff undertaking work in another capacity are not required to have detailed knowledge of the regulator's requirements (unless necessary for that other work) nor to bring information to the attention of the partner responsible for the audit on a routine basis.

38 However, as discussed further in Appendix 2, firms need to establish lines of communications, commensurate with their size and complexity, sufficient to ensure that non-audit work undertaken for a regulated entity which is likely to have an effect on the audit is brought to the attention of the partner responsible for the audit, who will need to determine whether the results of non-audit work undertaken for a regulated entity ought to be assessed as part of the audit process.

Identifying Matters Requiring a Report Direct to Regulators

39 **Where an apparent breach of statutory or regulatory requirements comes to the auditor's attention, the auditor should:**
   (a) **Obtain such evidence as is available to assess its implications for the auditor's reporting responsibilities;**

(b) **Determine whether, in the auditor's opinion, there is reasonable cause to believe that the breach is of material significance to the regulator; and**
(c) **Consider whether the apparent breach is criminal conduct that gives rise to criminal property and, as such, should be reported to the specified authorities.**

The precise matters which give rise to a statutory duty on auditors to make a report to a regulator derive from the relevant Acts. Broadly, such matters fall into three general categories:

(a) The financial position of the regulated entity;
(b) Its compliance with requirements for the management of its business; and
(c) The status of those charged with governance as fit and proper persons.

Further detailed guidance on the interpretation of these matters in the context of specific legislation applicable to each type of regulated entity is contained in Practice Notes dealing with the rights and duties of auditors of regulated entities to report direct to regulators.

In assessing the effect of an apparent breach, the auditor takes into account the quantity and type of evidence concerning such a matter which may reasonably be expected to be available. If the auditor concludes that the auditor has been prevented from obtaining all such evidence concerning a matter which may give rise to a duty to report, the auditor would normally make a report direct to the regulator without delay.

An apparent breach of statutory or regulatory requirements may not of itself give rise to a statutory duty to make a report to a regulator. There will normally be a need for some further investigation and discussion of the circumstances surrounding the apparent breach with the directors in order to obtain sufficient information to determine whether it points to a matter which is or may be of material significance to the regulator. For example, a minor breach which has been corrected by the regulated entity and reported (if appropriate) to the regulator, and which from the evidence available to the auditor appears to be an isolated occurrence, would not normally give the auditor reasonable cause to believe that it is or may be of material significance to the regulator. However a minor breach that results in a criminal offence that gave rise to the criminal property would be reportable to the specified authorities under the anti-money laundering legislation.

When determining whether a breach of statutory or regulatory requirements gives rise to a statutory duty to make a report direct to a regulator, the auditor considers factors such as:

- Whether the breach, though minor, is indicative of a general lack of compliance with the regulator's requirements or otherwise casts doubt on the status of those charged with governance as fit and proper persons;
- Whether a breach which occurred before the auditor's visit to the regulated entity was reported by the entity itself and has since been corrected, such that, at the date of the auditor's discovery, no breach exists;
- Whether the circumstances giving rise to a breach which occurred before the auditors visit to the regulated entity continue to exist, or those charged with governance have not taken corrective action, or the breach has re-occurred; and
- Whether the circumstances suggest that an immediate report to the regulator is necessary in order to protect the interests of depositors, investors, policyholders, clients of the entity or others in whose interests the regulator is required to act.

44   The auditor would normally seek evidence to assess the implications of a suspected breach before reporting a matter to the regulator. However, the auditor's responsibility to make a report does not require the auditor to determine the full implications of a matter before reporting: the auditor is required to exercise professional judgment as to whether or not there is reasonable cause to believe that a matter is or may be of material significance to the regulator. In forming that judgment, the auditor undertakes appropriate investigations to determine the circumstances but does not require the degree of evidence which would be a normal part of forming an opinion on financial statements. Such investigations, subject to compliance with legislation relating to 'tipping off'[2], would normally include:

- Enquiry of appropriate level of staff;
- Review of correspondence and documents relating to the transaction or event concerned; and
- Discussion with those charged with governance, or other senior management where appropriate.

In the case of a life company, it would also be appropriate to consult with the appointed actuary, who also has various statutory duties under insurance companies legislation.

45   The potential gravity of some apparent breaches may be such that an immediate report to the regulator is essential in order to enable the regulator to take appropriate action: in particular, prompt reporting of a loss of client assets may be necessary to avoid further loss to investors or others in whose interests the regulator is required to act. The auditor is therefore required to balance the need for further investigation of the matter with the need, subject to compliance with legislation relating to 'tipping off', for prompt reporting.

46   On completion of the auditor's investigations, the auditor needs to ensure that the facts and the basis for the auditor's decision (whether to report or not) is adequately documented such that the reasons for that decision may be clearly demonstrated should the need to do so arise in future.

Reliance on Other Auditors

47   An auditor with responsibilities for reporting on financial statements including financial information of one or more components audited by other auditors is required to obtain sufficient appropriate audit evidence that the work of the other auditors is adequate for the purposes of the audit. The same principle applies to reliance on another auditor in a different type of engagement. The auditor of a

---

[2] In the UK, 'tipping off' is an offence under section 333 of the Proceeds of Crime Act 2002 (POCA). It arises when an individual discloses matters where:
(a) There is knowledge or suspicion that a report has already been made; and
(b) That disclosure is likely to prejudice any investigation which might be conducted following the report.
Whilst 'tipping off' requires a person to have knowledge or suspicion that a report has been or will be made, a further offence of prejudicing an investigation is included in section 342 of POCA. Under this provision, it is an offence to make any disclosure which may prejudice an investigation of which a person has knowledge or suspicion, or to falsify, conceal, destroy or otherwise dispose of, or cause or permit the falsification, concealment, destruction or disposal of, documents relevant to such an investigation.
In Ireland, Section 58 of the Criminal Justice Act, 1994, as amended, establishes the offence of 'prejudicing an investigation'. This relates both to when a person, knowing or suspecting that an investigation is taking place, makes any disclosure likely to prejudice the investigation or when a person, knowing that a report has been made, makes any disclosure likely to prejudice any investigation arising from the report.

regulated entity who relies on work undertaken by other auditors needs to establish reporting arrangements such that the other auditors bring to the attention of the auditor of the regulated entity matters arising from their work which may give rise to a duty to report to a regulator.

The nature of the reporting arrangements will depend on the nature of the work undertaken by the other auditors. For example, the statutory duty to make a report relates to the legal entity subject to regulation rather than to the entire group to which that entity may belong. Consequently, the auditor of a holding company authorised by one regulator would not be expected to have knowledge of all matters which come to the attention of a subsidiary's auditor. The auditor of the regulated entity would, however, have a duty to report, where appropriate, matters which arise from the audit of the regulated entity's own financial statements and of the consolidated group figures. | 48

Where the audit of a regulated entity is undertaken by joint auditors, knowledge obtained by one auditing firm is likely to be deemed to be known by the other. Care will therefore be needed in agreeing and implementing arrangements to exchange information relating to matters which may give rise to a duty to report to a regulator including compliance with legislation relating to tipping off. | 49

Reporting

The Auditor's Statutory Duty to Report Direct to Regulators

When the auditor concludes, after appropriate discussion and investigations, that a matter which has come to the auditor's attention gives rise to a statutory duty to make a report, subject to compliance with legislation relating to 'tipping off', the auditor should bring the matter to the attention of the regulator without undue delay in a form and manner which will facilitate appropriate action by the regulator. When the initial report is made orally, the auditor should make a contemporaneous written record of the oral report and should confirm the matter in writing to the regulator. | 50

Except in the circumstances referred to in paragraph 54 the auditor seeks to reach agreement with those charged with governance on the circumstances giving rise to a report direct to the regulator. However, where a statutory duty to report arises, the auditor is required to make such a report regardless of: | 51

(a) Whether the matter has been referred to the regulator by other parties (including the company, whether by those charged with governance or otherwise); and
(b) Any duty owed to other parties, including the those charged with governance of the regulated entity and its shareholders (or equivalent persons).

Except in the circumstances set out in paragraph 54, the auditor sends a copy of the auditor's written report to those charged with governance and (where appropriate) audit committee of the regulated entity. | 52

In normal circumstances, the auditor would wish to communicate with the regulator with the knowledge and agreement of those charged with governance of the regulated entity. However, in some circumstances immediate notification of the discovery of a matter giving reasonable grounds to believe that a reportable matter exists will be necessary – for example, a phone call to alert the regulator followed by a meeting to discuss the circumstances. | 53

54 When the matter giving rise to a statutory duty to make a report direct to a regulator casts doubt on the integrity of those charged with governance or their competence to conduct the business of the regulated entity, the auditor should, subject to compliance with legislation relating to 'tipping off', make the report to the regulator without delay and without informing those charged with governance in advance.

55 Speed of reporting is essential where the circumstances cause the auditor no longer to have confidence in the integrity of those charged with governance. In such circumstances, there may be a serious and immediate threat to the interests of depositors or other persons for whose protection the regulator is required to act; for example where the auditor believes that a fraud or other irregularity may have been committed by, or with the knowledge of, those charged with governance, or have evidence of the intention of those charged with governance to commit or condone a suspected fraud or other irregularity.

56 In circumstances where the auditor no longer has confidence in the integrity of those charged with governance, it is not appropriate to provide those charged with governance with copies of the auditor's report. Since such circumstances will be exceptional and extreme, the auditor may wish to seek legal advice as to the auditor's responsibilities and the appropriate course of action.

Money Laundering

57 For a number of years auditors in the UK have been required to report to an appropriate authority where they suspect the laundering of money which either derived from drug trafficking or was related to terrorist offences. In the UK, partners and staff in audit firms must continue to report non-compliance with certain laws related to terrorism[3] but new anti-money laundering legislation[4] in the UK and Ireland has extended both the definition of what money laundering comprises and the auditor's reporting responsibilities[5]. The anti-money laundering legislation now imposes a duty to report money laundering in respect of the proceeds of all crime. The detailed legislation in both countries differs but common features include:

---

[3] *In the UK, the Terrorism Act 2000 (as amended by the Anti-terrorism, Crime and Security Act 2001) and associated regulations. The duty to report drug trafficking related money laundering has been subsumed into the general requirement to report the proceeds of crime.*
In Ireland, there is similar proposed legislation that auditors will need to consider in due course.

[4] *In the UK, with effect from 1 March 2004 The Money Laundering Regulations 2003 replaced the 1993 and 2001 regulations and the requirements of the Proceeds of Crime Act 2002 were extended to the provision by way of business of audit services by a person who is eligible for appointment as a company auditor under section 25 of the Companies Act 1989 or Article 28 of the Companies (Northern Ireland) Order 1990.*
In Ireland, with effect from 15 September 2003 the Criminal Justice Act 1994 (Section 32) Regulations 2003 designate accountants, auditors, and tax advisors and others for the purposes of the anti-money laundering provisions of the Criminal Justice Act, 1994, as amended.

[5] *Anti-money laundering legislation differs in the UK and Ireland, references to such legislation in the main body of this ISA (UK and Ireland) use generalised wording with the specific requirements of the UK and Irish legislation described in footnotes.*

- Money laundering includes concealing, disguising, converting, transferring, removing, using, acquiring or possessing property[6] which constitutes or represents a benefit from criminal conduct[7]. Although the anti-money laundering legislation does not contain de minimis concessions in the UK the National Criminal Intelligence Service (NCIS) has introduced guidance on reports of limited intelligence value;
- Partners and staff in audit firms are required to report all suspicions[8] that a criminal offence, giving rise to any direct or indirect benefit has been committed, regardless of whether that offence has been committed by a client or by a third party;
- Partners and staff in audit firms need to be alert to the dangers of making disclosures that are likely to tip off a money launderer or prejudice an investigation ('tipping off'), as this will constitute a criminal offence under the anti-money laundering legislation.

This ISA (UK and Ireland) does not address these responsibilities although, when reporting to a regulator (whether under a statutory duty or right) the auditor has regard to the offence of 'tipping off'.

The Auditor's Right to Report Direct to Regulators

When a matter comes to the auditor's attention which the auditor concludes does not give rise to a statutory duty to report but nevertheless may be relevant to the regulator's exercise of its functions, the auditor should, subject to compliance with legislation relating to 'tipping off':

(a) **Consider whether the matter should be brought to the attention of the regulator under the terms of the appropriate legal provisions enabling the auditor to report direct to the regulator; and, if so**

58

---

[6] *In the UK, 'property' is criminal property if it constitutes a person's benefit from criminal conduct or it represents such a benefit (in whole or part and whether directly or indirectly), and the alleged offender knows or suspects that it constitutes or represents such a benefit.*
In Ireland, 'property' is defined as including money and all other property, real or personal, heritable or moveable, including choses in action and other intangible or incorporeal property.

[7] *In the UK, 'criminal conduct' is defined as conduct which constitutes an offence in any part of the United Kingdom or would constitute such an offence if it occurred in any part of the UK.*
In Ireland, 'criminal conduct' means conduct which constitutes an 'indictable offence', or where the conduct occurs outside the State, would constitute such an offence if it occurred within the State and also constitutes an offence under the law of the country or territorial unit in which it occurs, and includes participation in such conduct.

[8] *In the UK, as a result of the Proceeds of Crime Act 2002 and the 2003 Money Laundering Regulations auditors are required to report where they know or suspect or have reasonable grounds to know or suspect that another person is engaged in money laundering. Partners and staff in audit firms discharge their responsibilities by reporting to their Money Laundering Reporting Officer ('MLRO') or, in the case of sole practitioners, to the National Criminal Intelligence Service.*
In Ireland, the Criminal Justice Act, 1994, as amended, and the Criminal Justice Act, 1994 (Section 32) Regulations, 2003 require auditors and other defined persons to report to the Garda Síochána and the Revenue Commissioners where they suspect that an offence as defined in the legislation in relation to the business of that person has been or is being committed. Two further reporting duties exist in Irish law, Section 74 of the Company Law Enforcement Act 2001 requires auditors to report to the Director of Corporate Enforcement instances of the suspected commission of indictable offences under the Companies Acts and Section 59 of the Criminal Justice (Theft and Fraud Offences) Act, 2001 requires 'relevant persons', as defined in the section and which includes auditors of companies, to report 'indications' that specified offences under the Act have been committed to the Garda Síochána. Additionally, auditors may report direct to the Revenue Commissioners certain offences under Section 1079 of the Taxes Consolidation Act, 1997.

(b) Advise those charged with governance that in the auditor's opinion the matter should be drawn to the regulators' attention.

Where the auditor is unable to obtain, within a reasonable period, adequate evidence that those charged with governance have properly informed the regulator of the matter, the auditor should, subject to compliance with legislation relating to 'tipping off', make a report direct to the regulator without undue delay.

59 The auditor may become aware of matters which the auditor concludes are relevant to the exercise of the regulator's functions even though they fall outside the statutory definition of matters which must be reported to a regulator. In such circumstances, the Acts provide the auditor with protection for making disclosure of the matter to the appropriate regulator.

60 Where the auditor considers that a matter which does not give rise to a statutory duty to report is nevertheless, in the auditor's professional judgment, such that it should be brought to the attention of the regulator, it is normally appropriate for the auditor to request those charged with governance of the regulated entity in writing to draw it to the attention of the regulator.

Contents of a Report Initiated by the Auditor

61 **When making or confirming in writing a report direct to a regulator, the auditor should:**

(a) **State the name of the regulated entity concerned;**
(b) **State the statutory power under which the report is made;**
(c) **State that the report has been prepared in accordance with ISA (UK and Ireland) 250, Section B 'The auditor's Right and Duty to Report to Regulators in the Financial Sector';**
(d) **Describe the context in which the report is given;**
(e) **Describe the matter giving rise to the report;**
(f) **Request the regulator to confirm that the report has been received; and**
(g) **State the name of the auditor, the date of the written report and, where appropriate, the date on which an oral report was made to the regulator and the name and title of the individual to whom the oral report was made.**

62 Such a report is a by-product of other work undertaken by the auditor. As a result it is not possible for the auditor or the regulator to conclude that all matters relevant to the regulator were encountered in the course of the auditor's work. The auditor's report therefore sets out the context in which the information reported was identified and indicates the extent to which the matter has been investigated and discussed with those charged with governance.

Context of a Report

63 Matters to which the auditor may wish to refer when describing the context in which a report is made direct to a regulator include:

- The nature of the appointment from which the report derives. For example, it may be appropriate to distinguish between a report made in the course of an audit of financial statements and one which arises in the course of a more limited engagement, such as an appointment to report on specified matters by the FSA or IFSRA;
- The applicable legislative requirements and interpretations of those requirements which have informed the auditor's judgment;

- The extent to which the auditor has investigated the circumstances giving rise to the matter reported;
- Whether the matter reported has been discussed with those charged with governance;
- Whether steps to rectify the matter have been taken.

Communication of Information by the Regulator

64 The Acts provide that, in certain exceptional circumstances, regulators may pass confidential information to another party. The precise circumstances in which regulators may disclose information varies, but in general they may do so if considered necessary to fulfil their own obligations under the appropriate Act, or, in some cases, to enable the auditor to fulfil the auditor's duties either to the regulated entity or, in other cases, to the regulator. Confidential information remains confidential in the hands of the recipient.

65 In so far as the law permits, regulators have confirmed that they will consider taking the initiative in bringing a matter to the attention of the auditor of a regulated entity in circumstances where:

(a) They believe the matter is of such importance that the auditor's knowledge of it could significantly affect the form of the auditor's report on the entity's financial statements or other matters on which the auditor is required to report, or the way in which the auditor discharges the auditor's reporting responsibilities; and
(b) The disclosure is for the purpose of enabling or assisting the regulator to discharge its functions under the Acts.

66 The auditor needs to be aware that there may be circumstances in which the regulators are unable to disclose such information. Where the auditor of a regulated entity is not informed by the regulator of any matter, therefore, the auditor cannot assume that there are no matters known to the regulator which could affect the auditor's judgment as to whether information is of material significance. However, in the absence of disclosure by the regulator, the auditor can only form a judgment in the light of evidence to which the auditor has access.

Relationship With Other Reporting Responsibilities

67 **When issuing a report expressing an opinion on a regulated entity's financial statements or on other matters specified by legislation or a regulator, the auditor:**

(a) **Should consider whether there are consequential reporting issues affecting the auditor's opinion which arise from any report previously made direct to the regulator in the course of the auditor's appointment; and**
(b) **Should assess whether any matters encountered in the course of the audit indicate a need for a further direct report.**

68 The circumstances which give rise to a report direct to a regulator may involve an uncertainty or other matter which requires disclosure in the financial statements. The auditor will therefore need to consider whether the disclosures made in the financial statements are adequate for the purposes of giving a true and fair view of the regulated entity's state of affairs and profit or loss. Where the auditor concludes that an uncertainty which has resulted in such a report is significant, the auditor is required by ISA (UK and Ireland) 700 "The Auditor's Report on Financial Statements" to consider whether to add an explanatory paragraph drawing attention to the matter in the auditor's report.

69 Similarly, circumstances giving rise to a report direct to a regulator may also require reflection in the auditor's reports on other matters required by legislation or another regulator.

70 In fulfilling the responsibility to report direct to a regulator, it is important that the auditor not only assess the significance of individual transactions or events but also consider whether a combination of such items over the course of the work undertaken for the auditor's primary reporting responsibilities may give the auditor reasonable grounds to believe that they constitute a matter of material significance to the regulator, and so give rise to a statutory duty to make a report.

71 As there is no requirement for the auditor to extend the scope of the audit work to search for matters which may give rise to a statutory duty to report, such an assessment of the cumulative effect of evidence obtained in the course of an audit would be made when reviewing the evidence in support of the opinions to be expressed in the reports the auditor has been appointed to make. Where such a review leads to the conclusion that the cumulative effect of matters noted in the course of the audit is of material significance to the regulator, it will be appropriate for a report to be made as set out in paragraph 61 above. However, reports indicating a 'nil return' are not appropriate.

Effective Date

72 In the United Kingdom, the Money Laundering Regulations 2003 came into force on 1 March 2004. In Ireland, the Criminal Justice Act 1994 (Section 32) Regulations 2003 are effective from 15 September 2003. This Section of this ISA (UK and Ireland) is effective for audits of financial statements for periods commencing on or after 15 December 2004.

Note on Legal Requirements

i Reference should be made to the legislation itself for an understanding of the relevant points of law. In interpreting the legal requirements it is also appropriate to refer to guidance published by the regulators and that contained in Practice Notes issued by the Auditing Practices Board.

Legal Requirements in the United Kingdom

ii The auditor's right to report to a regulator is contained in The Financial Services and Markets Act 2000, sections 342 and 343.

iii The auditor's duty to report to a regulator is set out in the Statutory Instrument The Financial Services and Markets Act 2000 (Communication by Auditors) Regulations 2001.

Legal Requirements in the Republic of Ireland

iv The auditor's duty to report to a regulator is set out in:
   (a) The Building Societies Act 1989, section 89(i);
   (b) The Central Bank Act 1989, section 47;
   (c) The Trustee Savings Bank Act 1989, section 38(i);
   (d) The Insurance Act 1989, section 35(i);

(e) The European Communities (Undertakings for Collective Investment in Transferable Securities) Regulations 1989, sections 83(2) to (7);
(f) The Unit Trusts Act 1990, section 15;
(g) The Stock Exchange Act 1995, section 34;
(h) The Investment Intermediaries Act 1995, section 33 (applicable to investment and insurance intermediaries;
(i) The Pensions (Amendment) Act 1996, section 83;
(j) The Credit Unions Act 1997, section 122; and
(k) The Companies Act 1990, section 258.

Further reporting duties are included in the Central Bank and Financial Services Authority of Ireland (no. 2) Bill published in December 2003.

Appendix 1 – The Regulatory Framework

In both the UK and Ireland, legislation exists in the principal areas of financial services to protect the interests of investors, depositors in banks and other users of financial services. Regulated entities operating in the financial sector are required to comply with legal and regulatory requirements concerning the way their business is conducted. Compliance with those rules is monitored in four principal ways:

- Internal monitoring by those charged with governance of the regulated entity;
- Submission of regular returns by the regulated entity to the regulator;
- Monitoring and, in some cases, inspection of the entity by the regulator;
- Subject to compliance with legislation relating to 'tipping off', reports by the reporting entity's auditor on its financial statements and other specified matters required by legislation or by the regulator.

Responsibility for Ensuring Compliance

Ensuring compliance with the requirements with which a regulated entity is required to comply in carrying out its business is the responsibility of those charged with governance of a regulated entity. It requires adequate organisation and systems of controls. The regulatory framework provides that adequate procedures for compliance must be established and maintained. Those charged with governance of a regulated entity are also normally required to undertake regular reviews of compliance and to inform the regulator of any breach of the rules and regulations applicable to its regulated business. In addition, regulators may undertake compliance visits.

The auditor of regulated entity normally has responsibilities for reporting, subject to compliance with legislation relating to 'tipping off', on particular aspects of its compliance with the regulator's requirements. However, the auditor has no direct responsibility for expressing an opinion on an entity's overall compliance with the requirements for the conduct of its business, nor does an audit provide any assurance that breaches of requirements which are not the subject of regular auditors' reports will be detected.

The Role of Auditors

4 Those charged with governance of regulated entities have primary responsibility for ensuring that all appropriate information is made available to regulators. Normal reporting procedures (including auditor's reports on records, systems and returns, and regular meetings with those charged with governance and/or management and auditors) supplemented by any inspection visits considered necessary by the regulators should provide the regulators with all the information they need to carry out their responsibilities under the relevant Act.

Routine Reporting by Auditors

5 Regulators' requirements for reports by auditors vary. In general terms, however, such reports may include opinions on:
- The regulated entity's annual financial statements;
- The regulated entity's compliance with requirements for financial resources; and
- The adequacy of the regulated entity's system of controls over its transactions and in particular over its clients' money and other property.

6 As a result of performing the work necessary to discharge their routine reporting responsibilities, or those arising from an appointment to provide a special report required by the regulator, the auditor of a regulated entity may become aware of matters which the auditor considers need to be brought to the regulator's attention sooner than would be achieved by routine reports by the entity or its auditor.

7 The auditor of a regulated entity normally has a right to communicate in good faith, subject to compliance with legislation relating to 'tipping off', information the auditor considers is relevant to the regulators' functions.

The Auditor's Statutory Duty to Report to the Regulator

8 In addition, the auditor is required by law to report, subject to compliance with legislation relating to 'tipping off', direct to a regulator when the auditor concludes that there is reasonable cause to believe that a matter is or may be of material significance to the regulator. The precise matters which result in a statutory duty to make such a report vary, depending upon the specific requirements of relevant legislation and the regulator's rules. In general, however, a duty to report to a regulator arises when the auditor becomes aware that:
- The regulated entity is in serious breach of:
  - Requirements to maintain adequate financial resources; or
  - Of requirements for those charged with governance to conduct its business in a sound and prudent manner (including the maintenance of systems of control over transactions and over any clients' assets held by the business); or
- There are circumstances which give reason to doubt the status of those charged with governance or senior management as fit and proper persons.

Confidentiality

Confidentiality is an implied term of the auditor's contracts with client entities. However, subject to compliance with legislation relating to 'tipping off', in the circumstances leading to a right or duty to report, the auditor is entitled to communicate to regulators in good faith information or opinions relating to the business or affairs of the entity or any associated body without contravening the duty of confidence owed to the entity and, in the case of a bank, building society and friendly society, its associated bodies. 9

The statutory provisions permitting the auditor to communicate information to regulators relate to information obtained in the auditor's capacity as auditor of the regulated entity concerned. Auditors and regulators therefore should be aware that confidential information obtained in other capacities may not normally be disclosed to another party. 10

Appendix 2 – The Application of the Statutory Duty to Report to Regulators

Introduction

The statutory duty to report to a regulator, subject to compliance with legislation relating to 'tipping off', applies to information which comes to the attention of the auditor in the auditor's capacity as auditor. However, neither the term 'auditor' nor the phrase "in the capacity of auditor" are defined in the legislation, nor has the court determined how these expressions should be construed. 1

As a result, it is not always clearly apparent when an accounting firm should regard itself as having a duty to report to a regulator. For example, information about a regulated entity may be obtained when partners or staff of the firm which is appointed as its auditor carry out work for another client entity; or when the firm undertakes other work for the regulated entity. Auditors, regulated entities and regulators need to be clear as to when the normal duty of confidentiality will be overridden by the auditor's statutory duty to report to the regulator. 2

In order to clarify whether or not an accounting firm should regard itself as bound by the duty, the APB has developed, in conjunction with HM Treasury, the IFSRA and the regulators, guidance on the interpretation of the key conditions for the existence of that duty, namely that the firm is to be regarded as auditor of a regulated entity and that information is obtained in the capacity of auditor. 3

Guidance on the interpretation of the term 'auditor' in the context of each Act is contained in the separate Practice Notes dealing with each area affected by the legislation. 4

This appendix sets out guidance on the interpretation of the phrase "in the capacity of auditor". The Board nevertheless continues to hold the view that the meaning of the phrase should be clarified in legislation in the longer term. 5

In the Capacity of Auditor

6 In determining whether information is obtained in the capacity of auditor, two criteria in particular should be considered:

(a) Whether the person who obtained the information also undertook the audit work; and if so
(b) Whether it was obtained in the course of or as a result of undertaking the audit work.

7 It is then necessary to apply these criteria to information about a regulated entity which may become known from a number of sources, and by a number of different individuals within an accounting firm. Within a large firm, for example, information may come to the attention of the partner responsible for the audit of a regulated entity, a partner in another office who undertakes a different type of work, or members of the firm's staff at any level. In the case of a sole practitioner who is the auditor of a regulated entity, information about a regulated entity may also be obtained by the practitioner in the course of work other than its audit.

Non-Audit Work Carried out in Relation to a Regulated Entity

8 Where partners or staff involved in the audit of a regulated entity carry out work other than its audit (non-audit work) information about the regulated entity will be known to them as individuals. In circumstances which suggest that a matter would otherwise give rise to a statutory duty to report, subject to compliance with legislation relating to 'tipping off', if obtained in the capacity of auditor, it will be prudent for them to make enquiries in the course of their audit work in order to establish whether this is the case from information obtained in that capacity.

9 However where non-audit work is carried out by other partners or staff, neither of the criteria set out in paragraph 6 is met in respect of information which becomes known to them. Nevertheless the firm should take proper account of such information when it could affect the audit so that it is treated in a responsible manner, particularly since in partnership law the knowledge obtained by one partner in the course of the partnership business may be imputed to the entire partnership. In doing so, two types of work may be distinguished: first, work which could affect the firm's work as auditor and, secondly, work which is undertaken purely in an advisory capacity.

10 A firm appointed as auditor of a regulated entity needs to have in place appropriate procedures to ensure that the partner responsible for the audit function is made aware of any other relationship which exists between any department of the firm and the regulated entity when that relationship could affect the firm's work as auditor. Common examples of such work include accounting work, particularly for smaller entities, and provision of tax services to the regulated entity.

11 *Prima facie*, information obtained in the course of non-audit work is not covered by either the right or the duty to report to a regulator. However, the firm appointed as auditor needs to consider whether the results of other work undertaken for a regulated entity need to be assessed as part of the audit process. In principle, this is no different to seeking to review a report prepared by outside consultants on, say, the entity's accounting systems so as to ensure that the auditor makes a proper assessment of the risks of misstatement in the financial statements and of the work needed to form an opinion. Consequently, the partner responsible for the audit needs to make appropriate enquiries in the process of

planning and completing the audit (see paragraph 67 above). Such enquiries would be directed to those aspects of the non-audit work which might reasonably be expected to be relevant to the audit. When, as a result of such enquiries, those involved in the audit become aware of issues which may be of material significance to a regulator such issues should be considered, and if appropriate reported, subject to compliance with legislation relating to 'tipping off, following the requirements set out in this Section of this ISA (UK and Ireland).

Work which is undertaken in an advisory capacity, for example to assist the directors of a regulated entity to determine effective and efficient methods of discharging their duties, would not normally affect the work undertaken for the audit. Nevertheless, in rare instances, the partner responsible for such advisory work may conclude that steps considered necessary in order to comply with the regulator's requirements have not been taken by the directors or that the directors intend in some respect not to comply with the regulator's requirements. Such circumstances would require consideration in the course of work undertaken for the audit, both to consider the effect on the auditor's routine reports and to determine whether the possible non-compliance is or is likely to be of material significance to the regulator. 12

Work Relating to a Separate Entity

Information obtained in the course of work relating to another entity audited by the same firm (or the same practitioner) is confidential to that other entity. The auditor is not required, and has no right, to report to a regulator confidential information which arises from work undertaken by the same auditing firm for another client. However, as a matter of sound practice, individuals involved in the audit of a regulated entity who become aware (in a capacity other than that of auditor of a regulated entity) of a matter which could otherwise give rise to a statutory duty to report would normally make enquiries in the course of their audit of the regulated entity to establish whether the information concerned is substantiated. 13

In carrying out the audit work, the auditor is required to have due regard to whether disclosure of non-compliance with laws and regulations to a proper authority is appropriate in the public interest. standards and guidance on this general professional obligation is set out in Section A of this ISA (UK and Ireland). 14

Conclusion

The phrase "in his capacity as auditor" limits information subject to the duty to report to matters of which the auditor becomes aware in the auditor's capacity as such. Consequently, it is unlikely that a partnership can be said to be acting in its capacity as auditor of a particular regulated entity whenever any apparently unrelated material comes to the attention of a partner or member of staff not engaged in that audit, particularly if that material is confidential to another client. 15

The statutory duty to report to a regulator, subject to compliance with legislation relating to 'tipping off', therefore does not extend automatically to any information obtained by an accounting firm regardless of its source. Accounting firms undertaking audits of regulated entities need, however, to establish lines of communication, commensurate with their size and organisational structure, 16 sufficient to ensure that non-audit work undertaken for a regulated entity which is likely to have an effect on the audit is brought to the attention of the partner responsible for the audit and to establish procedures for the partner responsible for the audit to make appropriate enquiries of those conducting such other work as part of the process of planning and completing the audit.

Appendix 3 – Action by the Auditor on Discovery of a Breach of a Regulator's Requirements

1 This appendix sets out in the form of a flowchart the steps involved in assessing whether a report to a regulator is required when a breach of the regulator's requirements comes to the attention of the auditor.

2 The flowchart is intended to provide guidance to readers in understanding this Section of this ISA (UK and Ireland). It does not form part of the auditing standards contained in the ISA (UK and Ireland).

8-1   In order to ensure that effective two-way communication is established, the expectations both of the auditor and those charged with governance regarding the form, level of detail and timing of communications are established at an early stage in the audit process. The manner in which these expectations are established will vary, reflecting the size and nature of the entity and the manner in which those charged with governance operate.

8-2   **The auditor should ensure that those charged with governance are provided with a copy of the audit engagement letter on a timely basis.**

9   To avoid misunderstandings, an audit engagement letter may explain that the auditor will communicate only those matters of governance interest that come to attention as a result of the performance of an audit and that the auditor is not required to design audit procedures for the specific purpose of identifying matters of governance interest. The engagement letter may also:

- Describe the form in which any communications on audit matters of governance interest will be made.
- Identify the relevant persons with whom such communications will be made.
- Identify any specific audit matters of governance interest that it has been agreed are to be communicated.

9-1   ISA (UK and Ireland) 210, "Terms of Audit Engagements," requires that the auditor and the client should agree on the terms of the engagement. "Client" means the addressees of the of the auditor's report or, when as often will be the case it is not practical to agree such terms with the addressees, the entity itself through those charged with governance.

9-2   The provision of copies of the audit engagement letter to those charged with governance facilitates the review and agreement of the audit engagement letter by the Audit Committee, as recommended by the Combined Code Guidance on Audit Committees. As part of their review, the guidance further recommends the audit committee to consider whether the audit engagement letter has been updated to reflect changes in circumstances since the previous year.

10   The effectiveness of communications is enhanced by developing a constructive working relationship between the auditor and those charged with governance. This relationship is developed while maintaining an attitude of professional independence and objectivity.

Groups

10-1   Where a parent undertaking is preparing group financial statements, the auditor of the parent undertaking communicates to those charged with governance of the parent undertaking such matters brought to the attention of those charged with governance of its subsidiary undertakings, by the auditors of the subsidiary undertakings, as they judge to be of significance in the context of the group (e.g. weaknesses in systems of internal control that have resulted, or could result, in material errors in the group financial statements).

10-2   There are statutory obligations on corporate subsidiary undertakings, and their auditors, in the UK and Ireland to provide the auditor of a corporate parent

and any relevant legislation. The auditor also considers the legal responsibilities of those persons. For example, in entities with supervisory boards or with audit committees, the relevant persons may be those bodies. However, in entities where a unitary board has established an audit committee, the auditor may decide to communicate with the audit committee, or with the whole board, depending on the importance of the audit matters of governance interest.

7-1 In most UK and Irish entities a board or equivalent governing body comprises individuals who are collectively charged with governance, including financial reporting. In some smaller entities a single individual may be charged with governance. In other cases, committees of a board or individual members of it may be charged with specific tasks in order to assist a board to meet its governance responsibilities (e.g. there may be an audit committee, a remuneration committee or a nomination committee).

7-2 When considering communicating with a committee the auditor considers whether the committee is in a position to provide the information and explanations the auditor needs for the purpose of the audit, whether the committee has the authority to act on the auditor's findings and whether there may be a need to repeat the communication to the board or governing body. Irrespective of what may be agreed, the auditor may judge it necessary to communicate directly with the board or governing body when a matter is sufficiently important.

7-3 The establishment of audit committees by the boards of listed companies, many public sector bodies and some other organizations has meant that communication with the audit committee[2], where one exists, has become a key element in the auditor's communication with those charged with governance. It is to be expected that the engagement partner will be invited regularly to attend meetings of the audit committee and that the audit committee chairman, and to a lesser extent the other members of the audit committee, will wish to liaise on a continuing basis with the engagement partner.

7-4 The audit committee ordinarily will, at least annually, meet the auditor, without management, to discuss matters relating to the audit committee's remit and issues arising from the audit.

7-5 As part of obtaining an understanding of the control environment, the auditor obtains an understanding of how the audit committee operates, including the particular remit given to the committee by the entity's board and its role in relation to governance matters such as reviewing the identification, evaluation and management of business risks. An entity's board and its auditor bear in mind that communication to audit committees forms only part of the auditor's overall obligation to communicate effectively with those charged with governance.

8 When the entity's governance structure is not well defined, or those charged with governance are not clearly identified by the circumstances of the engagement, or by legislation, the auditor comes to an agreement with the entity about with whom audit matters of governance interest are to be communicated. Examples include some owner-managed entities, some not for profit organizations, and some government agencies.

---

[2] *The Combined Code on Corporate Governance, and the Guidance on Audit Committees (The Smith Guidance) appended to it, contain, inter alia, recommendations about the conduct of the audit committee's relationship with the auditor.*

opinion of the auditor, are both important and relevant to those charged with governance in overseeing the financial reporting and disclosure process. Audit matters of governance interest include only those matters that have come to the attention of the auditor as a result of the performance of the audit. The auditor is not required, in an audit in accordance with ISAs (UK and Ireland), to design audit procedures for the specific purpose of identifying matters of governance interest.

4-1 The principal purposes of communications with those charged with governance are to:
(a) Reach a mutual understanding of the scope of the audit and the respective responsibilities of the auditor and those charged with governance;
(b) Share information to assist both the auditor and those charged with governance fulfill their respective responsibilities; and
(c) Provide to those charged with governance constructive observations arising from the audit process.

4-2 Although the requirements of this ISA (UK and Ireland) focus on the auditor's communications to those charged with governance, it is important that there is effective two-way communication (see paragraphs 2-1 and 2-2). The auditor reasonably expects those charged with governance to give the auditor such information and explanations as the auditor requires for the purposes of the audit[1a].

4-3 The extent, form and frequency of communications with those charged with governance will vary, reflecting the size and nature of the entity and the manner in which those charged with governance operate, as well as the auditor's views as to the importance of the audit matters of governance interest relating to the audit. In particular, communications with those charged with governance of listed companies might be more formal than communications with those charged with governance of smaller entities, or of subsidiary undertakings.

Relevant Persons

5 **The auditor should determine the relevant persons who are charged with governance and with whom audit matters of governance interest are communicated.**

6 The structures of governance vary from country to country reflecting cultural and legal backgrounds. For example, in some countries, the supervision function, and the management function are legally separated into different bodies, such as a supervisory (wholly or mainly non-executive) board and a management (executive) board. In other countries, both functions are the legal responsibility of a single, unitary board, although there may be an audit committee that assists that board in its governance responsibilities with respect to financial reporting.

7 This diversity makes it difficult to establish a universal identification of the persons who are charged with governance and with whom the auditor communicates audit matters of governance interest. The auditor uses judgment to determine those persons with whom audit matters of governance interest are communicated, taking into account the governance structure of the entity, the circumstances of the engagement

---

[1a] *Section 389A of the Companies Act 1985 sets legal requirements in relation to the communication of information to the auditor. (For Northern Ireland and the Republic of Ireland, relevant requirements are set out in Article 245(3) of the Companies (Northern Ireland) Order 1986 and Section 193(3), Companies Act 1990, respectively.)*

Introduction

The purpose of this International Standard on Auditing (UK and Ireland) (ISA (UK and Ireland)) is to establish standards and provide guidance on communication of audit matters arising from the audit of financial statements between the auditor and those charged with governance of an entity. These communications relate to audit matters of governance interest as defined in this ISA (UK and Ireland). This ISA (UK and Ireland) does not provide guidance on communications by the auditor to parties outside the entity, for example, external regulatory or supervisory agencies. — 1

The auditor should communicate audit matters of governance interest arising from the audit of financial statements with those charged with governance of an entity. — 2

For the purposes of this ISA (UK and Ireland) the term "communicate" is used in the sense of an active two-way communication (dialogue) between the auditor and those charged with governance. Effective communication is unlikely to be achieved when the auditor communicates with those charged with governance solely by means of formal written reports. — 2-1

The auditor discusses issues clearly and unequivocally with those charged with governance so that the implications of those issues are likely to be fully comprehended by them. — 2-2

For the purposes of this ISA (UK and Ireland), "governance" is the term used to describe the role of persons entrusted with the supervision, control and direction of an entity.[1] Those charged with governance ordinarily are accountable for ensuring that the entity achieves its objectives, with regard to reliability of financial reporting, effectiveness and efficiency of operations, compliance with applicable laws, and reporting to interested parties. Those charged with governance include management only when it performs such functions. — 3

In the UK and Ireland, those charged with governance include the directors (executive and non-executive) of a company or other body, the members of an audit committee where one exists, the partners, proprietors, committee of management or trustees of other forms of entity, or equivalent persons responsible for directing the entity's affairs and preparing its financial statements. — 3-1

'Management' comprises those persons who perform senior managerial functions. — 3-2

In the UK and Ireland, depending on the nature and circumstances of the entity, management may include some or all of those charged with governance (e.g. executive directors). Management will not normally include non-executive directors. — 3-3

For the purpose of this ISA (UK and Ireland), "audit matters of governance interest" are those that arise from the audit of financial statements and, in the — 4

---

[1] *Principles of corporate governance have been developed by many countries as a point of reference for the establishment of good corporate behavior. Such principles generally focus on publicly traded companies; however, they may also serve to improve governance in other forms of entities. There is no single model of good corporate governance. Board structures and practices vary from country to country. A common principle is that the entity should have in place a governance structure which enables the board to exercise objective judgment on corporate affairs, including financial reporting, independent in particular from management.*

[260]*
Communication of audit matters with those charged with governance

(Issued December 2004)

Contents

	Paragraphs
Introduction	1 - 4-3
Relevant Persons	5 - 10
Groups	10-1 - 10-3
Audit Matters of Governance Interest to be Communicated	11 - 12
Timing of Communications	13 - 14-1
Forms of Communications	15 - 17-1
Effectiveness of Communications	17-2 - 17-4
Other Matters	18 - 19-1
Confidentiality	20 - 20-3
Laws and Regulations	21
Effective Date	22

Appendix: Other ISAs (UK and Ireland) Referring to Communication With Those Charged With Governance and With Management

---

International Standard on Auditing (UK and Ireland) (ISA (UK and Ireland)) 260 "Communication of Audit Matters With Those Charged With Governance" should be read in the context of the Auditing Practices Board's Statement "The Auditing Practices Board – Scope and Authority of Pronouncements (Revised)" which sets out the application and authority of ISAs (UK and Ireland).

Editor's note: *The text of an Exposure Draft which is proposed to replace this standard is printed on page 2061.*

Action by the Auditor on Discovery of a Breach of a Regulator's Requirements

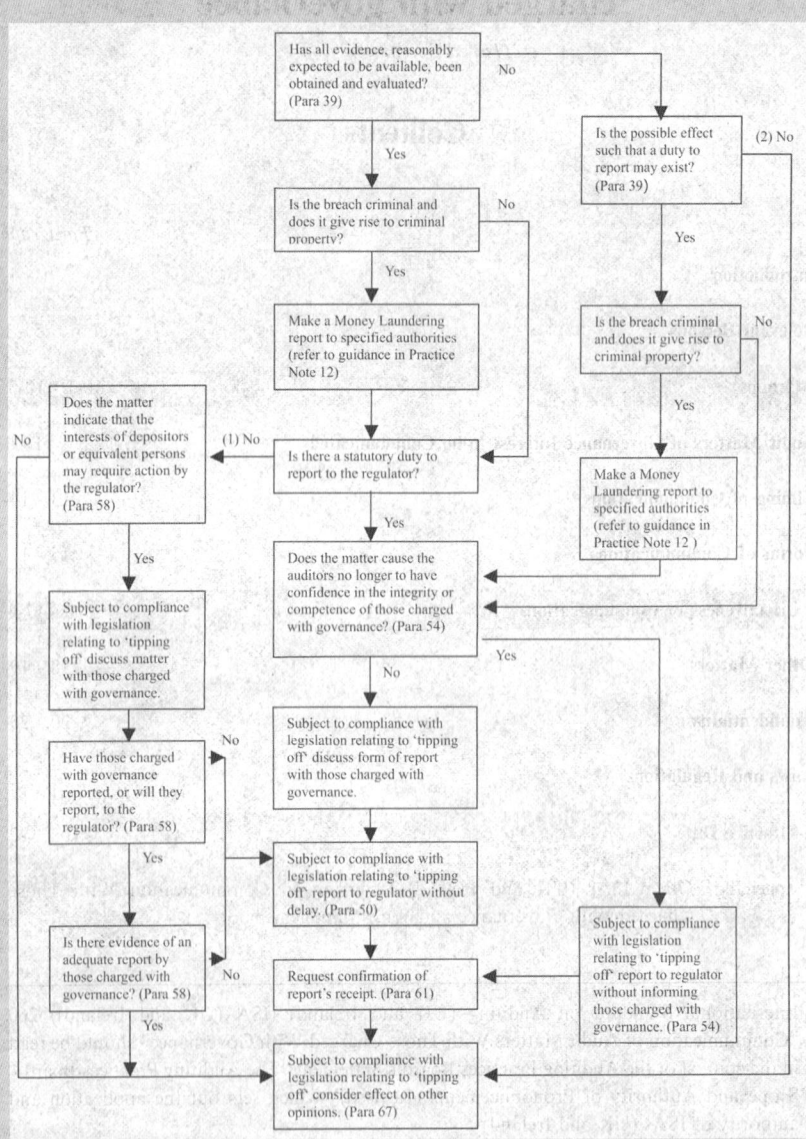

(1) This note would only be followed when a distinct right to report to the regulator exists. Otherwise, where no duty to report exists, the auditor would next consider the effect on other opinions.
(2) Where the auditor considers that a distinct right to report to the regulator exists, the auditor would next consider the question marked (1).

may be (or may be perceived to be) unable to take an impartial view of relevant aspects of that financial information.

1.32 There is a self-review threat where a firm prepares an accountant's report on historical financial information which has been included in, or formed part of, financial statements which have already been subject to audit by the same firm. In such situations, where the two engagement teams are not completely independent of each other, the engagement partner evaluates the significance of the self-review threat created. If this is other than clearly insignificant, safeguards are applied, such as the appointment of an engagement quality control reviewer who has not been involved in the audit.

1.33 In assessing the significance of the self-review threat in relation to an investment circular reporting engagement, the reporting accountant considers the extent to which the other service will:

- involve a significant degree of subjective judgment; and
- have a material effect on the preparation and presentation of the financial information that is the subject of the investment circular reporting engagement.

1.34 Where a significant degree of subjective judgment relating to the financial information is involved in an other service engagement, the reporting accountant may be inhibited from questioning that judgment in the course of the investment circular reporting engagement. Whether a significant degree of subjective judgment is involved will depend upon whether the other service involves the application of well-established principles and procedures, and whether reliable information is available. If such circumstances do not exist because the other service is based on concepts, methodologies or assumptions that require judgment and are not established by the engagement client or by authoritative guidance, the reporting accountant's objectivity and the appearance of its independence may be adversely affected. Where the provision of the other service during the relevant period also has a material effect on the financial information that is the subject of the investment circular reporting engagement, it is unlikely that any safeguard can eliminate or reduce to an acceptable level the self-review threat.

1.35 A **management threat** arises when the firm undertakes work that involves making judgments and taking decisions, which are the responsibility of the management of the party responsible for issuing the investment circular containing the financial information or the party on whose financial information the firm is reporting (the engagement client) in relation to:

- the transaction (for example, where it has been working closely with a company in developing a divestment strategy); or
- the financial information that is the subject of the investment circular reporting engagement (for example, deciding on the assumptions to be used in a profit forecast).

A threat to objectivity and independence arises because, by making judgments and taking decisions that are properly the responsibility of management, the firm erodes the distinction between the engagement client and the reporting accountant. The firm may become closely aligned with the views and interests of management and this may, in turn, impair or call into question the reporting accountant's ability to apply a proper degree of professional scepticism in performing the investment circular reporting engagement. The reporting accountant's objectivity and independence therefore may be impaired, or may be perceived to be, impaired.

1.36 Factors to be considered in determining whether an other service does or does not give rise to a management threat include whether:

- the other service results in recommendations by the firm justified by objective and transparent analyses or the engagement client being given the opportunity to decide between reasonable alternatives;
- the reporting accountant is satisfied that a member of management (or senior employee) has been designated by the engagement client to receive the results of the other service and make any judgments and decisions that are needed; and
- that member of management has the capability to make independent management judgments and decisions on the basis of the information provided ('informed management').

1.37 Where there is 'informed management', the reporting accountant assesses whether there are safeguards that can be introduced that would be effective to avoid a management threat or to reduce it to a level at which it can be disregarded. Such safeguards would include the investment circular reporting engagement being provided by partners and staff who have no involvement in those other services. In the absence of 'informed management', it is unlikely that any safeguards can eliminate the management threat or reduce it to an acceptable level.

1.38 An **advocacy threat** arises when the firm undertakes work that involves acting as an advocate for an engagement client and supporting a position taken by management in an adversarial context (for example, by undertaking an active responsibility for the marketing of an entity's shares). In order to act in an advocacy role, the firm has to adopt a position closely aligned to that of management. This creates both actual and perceived threats to the reporting accountant's objectivity and independence. For example, where the firm, acting as advocate, has supported a particular contention of management, it may be difficult for the reporting accountant to take an impartial view of this in the context of its review of the financial information.

1.39 Where the provision of an other service would require the reporting accountant to act as an advocate for the engagement client in relation to matters that are material to the financial information that is the subject of the investment circular reporting engagement, it is unlikely that any safeguards can eliminate or reduce to an acceptable level the advocacy threat that would exist.

1.40 A **familiarity threat** arises when reporting accountants are predisposed to accept or are insufficiently questioning of the engagement client's point of view (for example, where they develop close personal relationships with client personnel through long association with the engagement client).

1.41 An **intimidation threat** arises when the conduct of reporting accountants is influenced by fear or threats (for example, where they encounter an aggressive and dominating party).

1.42 These categories may not be entirely distinct: certain circumstances may give rise to more than one type of threat. For example, where a firm wishes to retain the fee income from a large client, but encounters an aggressive and dominating individual, there may be a self-interest threat as well as an intimidation threat.

1.43 When identifying threats to objectivity and independence, reporting accountants consider circumstances and relationships with a number of different parties. The

undertaking with such information and explanations as that auditor may reasonably require for the purposes of the audit[3]. Where there is no such statutory obligation (e.g. for non corporate entities and overseas subsidiary undertakings), permission may be needed by the auditors of the subsidiary undertakings, from those charged with governance of the subsidiary undertakings, to disclose the contents of any communication to them to the auditor of the parent undertaking and also for the auditor of the parent undertaking to pass those disclosures onto those charged with governance of the parent undertaking. The auditor of the parent undertaking seeks to ensure that appropriate arrangements are made at the planning stage for these disclosures. Normally, such arrangements for groups are recorded in the instructions to the auditors of subsidiary undertakings and relevant engagement letters.

The auditor of the parent undertaking considers the manner in which the group is managed and the wishes of those charged with governance of the parent undertaking when deciding with whom the auditor should communicate in the group about particular matters. In recognition of the responsibilities of those charged with governance of subsidiary undertakings, the auditors of those subsidiary undertakings communicate audit matters of governance interest to those charged with governance of the subsidiary undertakings.

10-3

Audit Matters of Governance Interest to be Communicated

The auditor should consider audit matters of governance interest that arise from the audit of the financial statements and communicate them with those charged with governance. Ordinarily such matters include the following:

11

- Relationships that may bear on the firm's independence and the integrity and objectivity of the audit engagement partner and audit staff.

  See paragraphs 11-2 – 11-6 below.

- The general approach and overall scope of the audit, including any expected limitations thereon, or any additional requirements.

  See paragraphs 11-7 – 11-11 below.

- The selection of, or changes in, significant accounting policies and practices that have, or could have, a material effect on the entity's financial statements.

  See paragraph 11-13 – 11-14 below.

- The potential effect on the financial statements of any material risks and exposures, such as pending litigation, that are required to be disclosed in the financial statements.

---

[3] Section 389A of the Companies Act 1985 requires a subsidiary undertaking which is a body corporate incorporated in Great Britain, and its auditors, to give to the auditors of any parent company of the undertaking such information and explanations as they may reasonably require for the purposes of their duties as auditors of that company. If a parent company has a subsidiary undertaking which is not a body corporate incorporated in Great Britain, section 389A requires that it shall, if required by its auditors to do so, take all such steps as are reasonably open to it to obtain from the subsidiary undertaking such information and explanations as the parent company auditors may reasonably require for the purposes of their duties as auditors of that company. (Similar obligations regarding companies incorporated in Northern Ireland and the Republic of Ireland are set out in Article 397A of the Companies (Northern Ireland) Order 1986 and Section 196, Companies Act 1990, respectively.)

- Audit adjustments, whether or not recorded by the entity that have, or could have, a material effect on the entity's financial statements.

    See paragraphs 11-16 – 11-20 below.

- Material uncertainties related to events and conditions that may cast significant doubt on the entity's ability to continue as a going concern.
- Disagreements with management about matters that, individually or in aggregate, could be significant to the entity's financial statements or the auditor's report. These communications include consideration of whether the matter has, or has not, been resolved and the significance of the matter.
- Expected modifications to the auditor's report.

    See paragraph 11-21 below.

- Other matters warranting attention by those charged with governance, such as material weaknesses in internal control, questions regarding management integrity, and fraud involving management.

    See paragraph 11-22 – 11-23 below.

- Any other matters agreed upon in the terms of the audit engagement.

11.a   The auditor should inform those charged with governance of those uncorrected misstatements aggregated[4] by the auditor during the audit that were determined by management to be immaterial, both individually and in the aggregate, to the financial statements taken as a whole.

11.b   The uncorrected misstatements communicated to those charged with governance need not include the misstatements below a designated amount[5].

11-1   Additional standards and guidance, for auditors in the UK and Ireland, relating to the communication of uncorrected misstatements are set out in paragraphs 11-16 to 11-20 below.

Integrity, Objectivity and Independence

11-2   APB Ethical Standard 1, "Integrity, objectivity and independence" requires the audit engagement partner to ensure that those charged with the governance of the audit client are appropriately informed on a timely basis of all significant facts and matters that bear upon the auditor's objectivity and independence.

11-3   The audit committee where one exists, is usually responsible for oversight of the relationship between the auditor and the entity and of the conduct of the audit process. It therefore has a particular interest in being informed about the auditor's ability to express an objective opinion on the financial statements. Where there is no audit committee, this role is taken by the board of directors.

11-4   The aim of these communications is to ensure full and fair disclosure by the auditor to those charged with governance of the audit client on matters in which

---

[4] In the UK and Ireland, the term "aggregated" used in this particular context is taken to mean "identified".

[5] In the UK and Ireland, the auditor communicates all uncorrected misstatements other than those that the auditor believes are clearly trivial (see paragraph 11-16).

they have an interest. These will generally include the key elements of the audit engagement partner's consideration of objectivity and independence such as:

- The principal threats, if any to objectivity and independence identified by the auditor, including consideration of all relationships between the audit client, its affiliates and directors and the audit firm.
- Any safeguards adopted and the reasons why they are considered to be effective.
- Any independent partner review.
- The overall assessment of threats and safeguards.
- Information about the general policies and processes within the audit firm for maintaining objectivity and independence.

In the case of listed companies, the auditor, as a minimum: **11-5**

(a) Discloses in writing:
   (i) Details of all relationships between the auditor and the client, its directors and senior management and its affiliates, including all services provided by the audit firm and its network to the client, its directors and senior management and its affiliates, that the auditor considers may reasonably be thought to bear on the auditor's objectivity and independence;
   (ii) The related safeguards that are in place; and
   (iii) The total amount of fees that the auditor and the auditor's network firms have charged to the client and its affiliates for the provision of services during the reporting period, analyzed into appropriate categories, for example, statutory audit services, further audit services, tax advisory services and other non-audit services. For each category, the amounts of any future services which have been contracted or where a written proposal has been submitted, are separately disclosed;
(b) Confirms in writing that the auditor complies with APB Ethical Standards and that, in the auditor's professional judgment, the auditor is independent and the auditor's objectivity is not compromised, or otherwise declare that the auditor has concerns that the auditor's objectivity and independence may be compromised (including instances where the group audit engagement partner does not consider the other auditors to be objective); and explaining the actions which necessarily follow from this; and
(c) Seeks to discuss these matters with the audit committee.

The most appropriate time for such communications is usually at the conclusion   **11-6**
of the audit. However, communications between the auditor and those charged with governance of the audit client will also be needed at the planning stage and whenever significant judgments are made about threats to objectivity and the appropriateness of safeguards put in place, for example, when accepting an engagement to provide non audit services.

Planning Information

The auditor should communicate to those charged with governance an outline of the   **11-7**
nature and scope, including, where relevant, any limitations thereon, of the work the auditor proposes to undertake and the form of the reports the auditor expects to make.

The nature and detail of the planning information communicated will reflect the   **11-8**
size and nature of the entity and the manner in which those charged with governance operate.

11-9 The auditor communicates in outline the principal ways in which the auditor proposes to address the risks of material misstatement, with particular reference to areas of higher risk. As part of the two-way communication process the auditor seeks to gain an understanding of the attitude of those charged with governance to the business risks of the entity. When describing the planned approach to addressing the risk of material misstatement, the auditor does not describe the plan in such detail that the "surprise" element of the audit is lost. Other matters that might be communicated in outline include:

- The concept of materiality and its application to the audit approach.
- The auditor's approach to the assessment of, and reliance on, internal controls.
- The extent, if any, to which reliance will be placed on the work of internal audit and on the way in which the external and internal auditors can best work together on a constructive and complementary basis.
- Where relevant, the work to be undertaken by any other firms of auditors (including related firms) and how the principal auditor intends to obtain assurance as to the adequacy of the other auditors' procedures in so far as it relates to the principal auditor's role.

11-10 In any particular year, the auditor may decide that there are no significant changes from audit matters of governance interest that have been communicated previously and judge that it is unnecessary to remind those charged with governance of all or part of that information. In these circumstances, the auditor need only make those charged with governance aware that the auditor has no new audit matters of governance interest to communicate. Matters that are included in the audit engagement letter need not be repeated.

11-11 Other matters that the auditor may, for the purpose of the audit, find beneficial to discuss with those charged with governance include:

- The views of those charged with governance of the nature and extent of significant internal and external operational, financial, compliance and other risks facing the entity which might affect the financial statements, including the likelihood of those risks materializing and how they are managed.
- The control environment within the entity, including the attitude of management to controls, and whether those charged with governance have a process for keeping under review the effectiveness of the system of internal control and, where a review of the effectiveness of internal control has been carried out, the results of that review.
- Actions those charged with governance plan to take in response to matters such as developments in law, accounting standards, corporate governance reporting, Listing Rules, and other developments relevant to the entity's financial statements and annual report.

Findings From the Audit

11-12 The auditor should communicate the following findings from the audit to those charged with governance:

(a) The auditor's views about the qualitative aspects of the entity's accounting practices and financial reporting;

(b) The final draft of the representation letter, that the auditor is requesting management and those charged with governance to sign. The communication should specifically refer to any matters where management is reluctant to make the representations requested by the auditor;

(c) Uncorrected misstatements;

(d) Expected modifications to the auditor's report;
(e) Material weaknesses in internal control identified during the audit;
(f) Matters specifically required by other ISAs (UK and Ireland) to be communicated to those charged with governance; and
(g) Any other audit matters of governance interest.

Qualitative Aspects of Accounting Practices and Financial Reporting

11-13 The accounting requirements of company law, accounting standards and interpretations issued by the relevant accounting standard setters, permit a degree of choice in some areas as to the specific accounting policies and practices that may be adopted by an entity. Additionally, there are matters for which those charged with governance have to make accounting estimates and judgments.

11-14 In the course of the audit of the financial statements, the auditor considers the qualitative aspects of the financial reporting process, including items that have a significant impact on the relevance, reliability, comparability, understandability and materiality of the information provided by the financial statements. The auditor discusses in an open and frank manner with those charged with governance the auditor's views on the quality and acceptability of the entity's accounting practices and financial reporting. Such discussions may include:

- The appropriateness of the accounting policies to the particular circumstances of the entity, judged against the objectives of relevance, reliability, comparability and understandability but having regard also to the need to balance the different objectives and the need to balance the cost of providing information with the likely benefit to users of the entity's financial statements.
  The auditor explains to those charged with governance why the auditor considers any accounting policy not to be appropriate, and requests those charged with governance to make appropriate changes. If those charged with governance decline to make the changes on the grounds that the effect is not material, the auditor informs them that the auditor will consider qualifying the auditor's report when the effect of not using an appropriate policy can reasonably be expected to influence the economic decisions of users of the financial statements.
- The timing of transactions and the period in which they are recorded.
- The appropriateness of accounting estimates and judgments, for example in relation to provisions, including the consistency of assumptions and degree of prudence reflected in the recorded amounts.
- The potential effect on the financial statements of any material risks and exposures, such as pending litigation, that are required to be disclosed in the financial statements.
- Material uncertainties related to events and conditions that may cast significant doubt on the entity's ability to continue as a going concern.
- The extent to which the financial statements are affected by any unusual transactions including non-recurring profits and losses recognized during the period and the extent to which such transactions are separately disclosed in the financial statements.
- Apparent misstatements in the other information in the document containing the audited financial statements or material inconsistencies between it and the audited financial statements.
- The overall balance and clarity of the information contained in the annual report.

- Disagreements about matters that, individually or in aggregate, could be significant to the entity's financial statements or the auditor's report. These communications include consideration of whether the matters have, or have not, been resolved and the significance of the matters.

Management Representation Letter

11-15   The auditor reviews the content of management's representation letter with those charged with governance. The auditor explains the significance of representations that have been requested relating to non-standard issues.

Uncorrected Misstatements

11-16   The auditor communicates all uncorrected misstatements, other than those that the auditor believes are clearly trivial[6], to the entity's management and requests that management correct them. When communicating misstatements, the auditor distinguishes between misstatements that are errors of fact and misstatements that arise from differences in judgment and explain why the latter are considered misstatements. When such misstatements identified by the auditor are not corrected by management the auditor communicates the misstatements to those charged with governance, in accordance with the requirement set out in paragraph 11a, and requests them to make the corrections. Where those charged with governance refuse to make some or all of the corrections, the auditor discusses with them the reasons for, and appropriateness of, not making those corrections, having regard to qualitative as well as quantitative considerations, and considers the implications for their audit report of the effect of misstatements that remain uncorrected.

11-17   If management have corrected material misstatements, the auditor considers whether those corrections of which the auditor is aware should be communicated to those charged with governance so as to assist them to fulfill their governance responsibilities, including reviewing the effectiveness of the system of internal control.

11-18   Paragraph 5a.(b) of ISA (UK and Ireland) 580, "Management Representations," requires the auditor to obtain written representations from management that it believes the effects of those uncorrected misstatements identified by the auditor during the audit are immaterial, both individually and in the aggregate, to the financial statements taken as a whole. A summary of such misstatements is required to be included in or attached to the written representations.

11-19   **The auditor should seek to obtain a written representation from those charged with governance that explains their reasons for not correcting misstatements brought to their attention by the auditor.**

11-20   If those charged with governance refuse to make some or all of the corrections the auditor has requested, a representation is obtained to reduce the possibility of

---

[6] *This is not another expression for 'immaterial'. Matters which are 'clearly trivial' will be of an wholly different (smaller) order of magnitude than the materiality thresholds used in the audit, and will be matters that are clearly inconsequential, whether taken individually or in aggregate and whether judged by any quantitative and/ or qualitative criteria. Further, whenever there is any uncertainty about whether one or more items are 'clearly trivial' (in accordance with this definition), the presumption should be that the matter is not 'clearly trivial'.*

misunderstandings concerning their reasons for not making the corrections. A summary of the uncorrected misstatements[7] is included in, or attached to, the representation letter. Obtaining the representation does not relieve the auditor of the need to form an independent opinion as to the materiality of uncorrected misstatements.

Expected Modifications to the Auditor's Report

The auditor discusses expected modifications to the auditor's report on the financial statements with those charged with governance to ensure that: 11-21

(a) Those charged with governance are aware of the proposed modification and the reasons for it before the report is finalized;
(b) There are no disputed facts in respect of the matter(s) giving rise to the proposed modification (or that matters of disagreement are confirmed as such); and
(c) Those charged with governance have an opportunity, where appropriate, to provide the auditor with further information and explanations in respect of the matter(s) giving rise to the proposed modification.

Material Weaknesses in Internal Control

A material weakness in internal control is a deficiency in design or operation which could adversely affect the entity's ability to record, process, summarize and report financial and other relevant data so as to result in a material misstatement in the financial statements. The auditor normally does not need to communicate information concerning a material weakness of which those charged with governance are aware and in respect of which, in the view of the auditor, appropriate corrective action has been taken, unless the weakness is symptomatic of broader weaknesses in the overall control environment and there is a risk that other material weaknesses may occur. Material weaknesses of which the auditor is aware are communicated where they have been corrected by management without the knowledge of those charged with governance. 11-22

The auditor explains to those charged with governance that the auditor has not provided a comprehensive statement of all weaknesses which may exist in internal control or of all improvements which may be made, but has addressed only those matters which have come to the auditor's attention as a result of the audit procedures performed. 11-23

As part of the auditor's communications, those charged with governance are informed that: 12

- The auditor's communications of matters include only those audit matters of governance interest that have come to the attention of the auditor as a result of the performance of the audit.
- An audit of financial statements is not designed to identify all matters that may be relevant to those charged with governance. Accordingly, the audit does not ordinarily identify all such matters.

---

[7] *The summary need not include any misstatements that the auditors believe are 'clearly trivial' (see footnote 6).*

Timing of Communications

13   The auditor should communicate audit matters of governance interest on a timely basis. This enables those charged with governance to take appropriate action.

13-1   **The auditor should plan with those charged with governance the form and timing of communications to them.**

14   In order to achieve timely communications, the auditor discusses with those charged with governance the basis and timing of such communications. In certain cases, because of the nature of the matter, the auditor may communicate that matter sooner than previously agreed.

14-1   In certain circumstances the auditor may identify matters that need to be communicated to those charged with governance without delay (e.g. the existence of a material weakness in internal control). Findings from the audit that are relevant to the financial statements, including the auditor's views about the qualitative aspects of the entity's accounting and financial reporting, are communicated to those charged with governance before they approve the financial statements.

Forms of Communications

15   The auditor's communications with those charged with governance may be made orally or in writing. The auditor's decision whether to communicate orally or in writing is affected by factors such as:

- The size, operating structure, legal structure, and communications processes of the entity being audited;
- The nature, sensitivity and significance of the audit matters of governance interest to be communicated;
- The arrangements made with respect to periodic meetings or reporting of audit matters of governance interest;
- The amount of on-going contact and dialogue the auditor has with those charged with governance.
- Statutory and regulatory requirements.

15-1   As stated in paragraph 10-3, in relation to the audit of groups, the auditor of the parent undertaking considers the manner in which the group is managed and the wishes of those charged with governance of the parent undertaking when deciding with whom the auditor should communicate in the group about particular matters. These considerations include whether it is necessary and appropriate to communicate in writing with those charged with governance of subsidiary undertakings.

16   When audit matters of governance interest are communicated orally, the auditor documents in the working papers the matters communicated and any responses to those matters. This documentation may take the form of a copy of the minutes of the auditor's discussion with those charged with governance. In certain circumstances, depending on the nature, sensitivity, and significance of the matter, it may be

advisable for the auditor to confirm in writing with those charged with governance any oral communications on audit matters of governance interest.

> **In the UK and Ireland, the auditor should communicate in writing with those charged with governance regarding the significant findings from the audit.** 16-1
>
> This written communication is issued even if its content is limited to explaining that there is nothing the auditor wishes to draw to the attention of those charged with governance. To avoid doubt where there are no matters the auditor wishes to communicate in writing, the auditor communicates that fact in writing to those charged with governance. 16-2

Ordinarily, the auditor initially discusses audit matters of governance interest with management, except where those matters relate to questions of management competence or integrity. These initial discussions with management are important in order to clarify facts and issues, and to give management an opportunity to provide further information. If management agrees to communicate a matter of governance interest with those charged with governance, the auditor may not need to repeat the communications, provided that the auditor is satisfied that such communications have effectively and appropriately been made. 17

> The auditor incorporates in the communication of audit matters of governance interest to those charged with governance comments made by management, where those comments will aid the understanding of those charged with governance, and any actions management have indicated that they will take. 17-1

Effectiveness of Communications

> **The auditor should consider whether the two-way communication between the auditor and those charged with governance has been adequate for an effective audit and, if it has not, should take appropriate action.** 17-2
>
> Paragraph 69 of ISA 315 "Understanding the Entity and Its Environment and Assessing the Risks of Material Misstatement", identifies participation by those charged with governance, including their interaction with internal and external auditors, as an element the auditor considers when evaluating the design of the entity's control environment. Inadequate two-way communication may indicate an unsatisfactory control environment, which will influence the auditor's assessment of the risks of material misstatements. Examples of evidence about the adequacy of the two-way communication process may include: 17-3
>
> - The appropriateness and timeliness of actions taken by those charged with governance in response to the recommendations made by the auditor. (See also paragraph 19-1 regarding significant matters raised in previous communications.)
> - The apparent openness of those charged with governance in their communications with the auditor.
> - The willingness and capacity of those charged with governance to meet with the auditor without management present.
> - The apparent ability of those charged with governance to fully comprehend the recommendations made by the auditor. For example, the extent to which those charged with governance probe issues and question recommendations made to them.

17-4 If the two-way communication between the auditor and those charged with governance is inadequate, there is a risk that the auditor may not obtain all the audit evidence required to form an opinion on the financial statements. In such a situation, the auditor considers taking actions such as:

- Obtaining legal advice about the consequences of different courses of action.
- Communicating with third parties (e.g. an appropriate regulator), or higher authority in the governance structure that is outside the entity (such as the owners of a small business).

If the auditor concludes that the two way communication is unlikely to become adequate for the purposes of the audit, the auditor considers withdrawing from the engagement.

Other Matters

18 If the auditor considers that a modification of the auditor's report on the financial statements is required, as described in ISA (UK and Ireland) 700, "The Auditor's Report on Financial Statements," communications between the auditor and those charged with governance cannot be regarded as a substitute.

19 The auditor considers whether audit matters of governance interest previously communicated may have an effect on the current year's financial statements. The auditor considers whether the point continues to be a matter of governance interest and whether to communicate the matter again with those charged with governance.

19-1 The auditor considers the actions taken by those charged with governance in response to previous communications. Where significant matters raised in previous communications to those charged with governance have not been dealt with effectively, the auditor enquires as to why appropriate action has not been taken. If the auditor considers that a matter raised previously has not been adequately addressed, consideration is given to repeating the point in a current communication; otherwise there is a risk that the auditor may give an impression that the auditor is satisfied that the matter has been adequately addressed or is no longer significant.

Confidentiality

20 The requirements of national professional accountancy bodies, legislation or regulation may impose obligations of confidentiality that restrict the auditor's communications of audit matters of governance interest. The auditor refers to such requirements, laws and regulations before communicating with those charged with governance. In some circumstances, the potential conflicts with the auditor's ethical and legal obligations of confidentiality and reporting may be complex. In these cases, the auditor may wish to consult with legal counsel.

20-1 Occasionally those charged with governance may wish to provide third parties, for example bankers or certain regulatory authorities, with copies of a written communication from the auditor. It is appropriate to ensure that third parties who see the communication understand that it was not prepared with third parties in mind. Furthermore, where the written communications contain open and frank discussion of aspects of the entity's accounting and financial reporting practices, it may not be appropriate for such communications to be disclosed to third parties.

Thus the auditor normally states in the communication to those charged with governance that:

(a) The report has been prepared for the sole use of the entity and, where appropriate, any parent undertaking and its auditor;
(b) It must not be disclosed to a third party, or quoted or referred to, without the written consent of the auditor; and
(c) No responsibility is assumed by the auditor to any other person.

In the public or regulated sectors, the auditor may have a duty to submit a report to those charged with governance annually, and also to submit copies of the report to relevant regulatory or funding bodies. In the public sector, there may also be a requirement or expectation that reports will be made public and in such circumstances some or all of the restrictions set out in the preceding paragraph may not be appropriate. **20-2**

Any communication with those charged with governance is confidential information. Thus, when the auditor communicates in writing with those charged with governance, the auditor requires the prior consent of those charged with governance if the auditor is to provide a copy of the communication to a third party. **20-3**

Laws and Regulations

The requirements of national professional accountancy bodies, legislation or regulation may impose obligations on the auditor to make communications on governance related matters. These additional communications requirements are not covered by this ISA (UK and Ireland); however, they may affect the content, form and timing of communications with those charged with governance. **21**

Effective Date

This ISA (UK and Ireland) is effective for audits of financial statements for periods commencing on or after 15 December 2004. **22**

Public Sector Perspective

Additional guidance for auditors of public sector bodies in the UK and Ireland is given in:

- Practice Note 10 "Audit of Financial Statements of Public Sector Entities in the United Kingdom (Revised)"
- Practice Note 10(I) "The Audit of Central Government Financial Statements in Ireland"

While the basic principles contained in this ISA (UK and Ireland) apply to the audit of financial statements in the public sector, the legislation giving rise to the audit mandate may specify the nature, content and form of the communications with those charged with governance of the entity. **1**

For public sector audits, the types of matters that may be of interest to the governing body may be broader than the types of matters discussed in the ISA (UK and Ireland), **2** which are directly related to the audit of financial statements. Public sector auditors' mandates may require them to report matters that come to their attention that relate to:

- Compliance with legislative or regulatory requirements and related authorities;
- Adequacy of internal control;
- Economy, efficiency and effectiveness of programs, projects and activities.

3   For public sector auditors, the auditors' written communications may be placed on the public record. For that reason, the public sector auditor needs to be aware that their written communications may be distributed to a wider audience than solely those persons charged with governance of the entity.

Appendix – Other ISAs (UK and Ireland) Referring to Communication With Those Charged With Governance and With Management

210 - TERMS OF AUDIT ENGAGEMENTS

2   The auditor and the client should agree on the terms of the engagement.

2-1 The terms of the engagement should be recorded in writing.

5-1 In the UK and Ireland, the auditor should ensure that the engagement letter documents and confirms the auditor's acceptance of the appointment, and includes a summary of the responsibilities of those charged with governance and of the auditor, the scope of the engagement and the form of any reports.

10   On recurring audits, the auditor should consider whether circumstances require the terms of the engagement to be revised and whether there is a need to remind the client of the existing terms of the engagement.

17   Where the terms of the engagement are changed, the auditor and the client should agree on the new terms.

19   If the auditor is unable to agree to a change of the engagement and is not permitted to continue the original engagement, the auditor should withdraw and consider whether there is any obligation, either contractual or otherwise, to report to other parties, such as those charged with governance or shareholders, the circumstances necessitating the withdrawal.

240 - FRAUD

90   The auditor should obtain written representations from management[8] that:

(a) It acknowledges its responsibility for the design and implementation of internal control to prevent and detect fraud;
(b) It has disclosed to the auditor the results of its assessment of the risk that the financial statements may be materially misstated as a result of fraud;
(c) It has disclosed to the auditor its knowledge of fraud or suspected fraud affecting the entity involving:

---

[8] In the UK and Ireland, the auditor obtains written representations from those charged with governance.

(i) Management[9];
(ii) Employees who have significant roles in internal control; or
(iii) Others where the fraud could have a material effect on the financial statements; and
(d) It has disclosed to the auditor its knowledge of any allegations of fraud, or suspected fraud, affecting the entity's financial statements communicated by employees, former employees, analysts, regulators or others.

If the auditor has identified a fraud or has obtained information that indicates that a fraud may exist, the auditor should communicate these matters as soon as practicable to the appropriate level of management.   93

If the auditor has identified fraud involving: 95

(a) Management;
(b) Employees who have significant roles in internal control; or
(c) Others where the fraud results in a material misstatement in the financial statements,
the auditor should communicate these matters to those charged with governance as soon as practicable.

The auditor should make those charged with governance and management aware, as soon as practicable, and at the appropriate level of responsibility, of material weaknesses in the design or implementation of internal control to prevent and detect fraud which may have come to the auditor's attention.   99

The auditor should consider whether there are any other matters related to fraud to be discussed with those charged with governance of the entity.   101

If, as a result of a misstatement resulting from fraud or suspected fraud, the auditor encounters exceptional circumstances that bring into question the auditor's ability to continue performing the audit the auditor should: 103

(a) Consider the professional and legal responsibilities applicable in the circumstances, including whether there is a requirement for the auditor to report to the person or persons who made the audit appointment or, in some cases, to regulatory authorities;
(b) Consider the possibility of withdrawing from the engagement; and
(c) If the auditor withdraws:
  (i) Discuss with the appropriate level of management and those charged with governance the auditor's withdrawal from the engagement and the reasons for the withdrawal; and
  (ii) Consider whether there is a professional or legal requirement to report to the person or persons who made the audit appointment or, in some cases, to regulatory authorities, the auditor's withdrawal from the engagement and the reasons for the withdrawal.

---

[9] In the UK and Ireland, and those charged with governance.

250 SECTION A - CONSIDERATION OF LAWS AND REGULATIONS

23 The auditor should obtain written representations that management[10] has disclosed to the auditor all known actual or possible noncompliance with laws and regulations whose effects should be considered when preparing financial statements.

23-1 Where applicable, the written representations should include the actual or contingent consequences which may arise from the non-compliance.

28 When the auditor believes there may be noncompliance, the auditor should document the findings and discuss them with management[11].

28-1 Any discussion of findings with those charged with governance and with management should be subject to compliance with legislation relating to 'tipping off' and any requirement to report the findings direct to a third party.

32 The auditor should, as soon as practicable, either communicate with those charged with governance, or obtain evidence that they are appropriately informed, regarding noncompliance that comes to the auditor's attention.

33 If in the auditor's judgment the noncompliance is believed to be intentional and material, the auditor should communicate the finding without delay.

33-1 In the UK and Ireland the auditor should communicate the finding where the non-compliance is material or is believed to be intentional. The non-compliance does not have to be both material and intentional.

34 If the auditor suspects that members of senior management, including members of the board of directors[12], are involved in noncompliance, the auditor should report the matter to the next higher level of authority at the entity, if it exists, such as an audit committee or a supervisory board.

315 - UNDERSTANDING THE ENTITY AND ITS ENVIRONMENT AND ASSESSING THE RISKS OF MATERIAL MISSTATEMENT

120 The auditor should make those charged with governance or management aware, as soon as practicable, and at an appropriate level of responsibility, of material weaknesses in the design or implementation of internal control which have come to the auditor's attention.

320 – AUDIT MATERIALITY

17 If the auditor has identified a material misstatement resulting from error, the auditor should communicate the misstatement to the appropriate level of management on a timely basis, and consider the need to report it to those charged with governance in accordance with ISA (UK and Ireland) 260, "Communication of Audit Matters to Those Charged with Governance."

---

[10] In the UK and Ireland the auditor obtains this written representations from those charged with governance.

[11] In the UK and Ireland, the auditor discusses such matters with those charged with governance.

[12] In the UK and Ireland, the auditor also reports such matters if those charged with governance are suspected of being involved in non compliance.

545 - FAIR VALUE MEASUREMENTS AND DISCLOSURES

The auditor should obtain written representations from management regarding the reasonableness of significant assumptions, including whether they appropriately reflect management's intent and ability to carry out specific courses of action on behalf of the entity where relevant to the fair value measurements or disclosures. 63

550 - RELATED PARTIES

The auditor should obtain a written representation from management[13] concerning: 15

(a) The completeness of information provided regarding the identification of related parties; and
(b) The adequacy of related party disclosures in the financial statements.

The auditor should obtain a written representation from management[14] concerning: 115

(a) The completeness of information provided regarding the identification of related parties; and
(b) The adequacy of related party disclosures in the financial statements.

560 - SUBSEQUENT EVENTS

When, after the date of the auditor's report but before the financial statements are issued, the auditor becomes aware of a fact which may materially affect the financial statements, the auditor should consider whether the financial statements need amendment, should discuss the matter with management[15], and should take the action appropriate in the circumstances. 9

When, after the financial statements have been issued, the auditor becomes aware of a fact which existed at the date of the auditor's report and which, if known at that date, may have caused the auditor to modify the auditor's report, the auditor should consider whether the financial statements need revision[16], should discuss the matter with management[15], and should take the action appropriate in the circumstances. 14

570 - GOING CONCERN

When events or conditions have been identified which may cast significant doubt on the entity's ability to continue as a going concern, the auditor should: 26

(a) Review management's[17] plans for future actions based on its going concern assessment;

---

[13] In the UK and Ireland the auditor obtains written representations from those charged with governance.

[14] In the UK and Ireland the auditor obtains written representations from those charged with governance.

[15] In the UK and Ireland the auditor discusses these matters with those charged with governance. Those charged with governance are responsible for the preparation of the financial statements.

[16] In the UK the detailed regulations governing revised financial statements and directors' reports, where the revision is voluntary, are set out in sections 245 to 245C of the Companies Act 1985 and in the Articles 253 to 253C of the Companies (Northern Ireland) Order 1986. There are no provisions in the Companies Acts of the Republic of Ireland for revising financial statements

[17] In the UK and Ireland, those charged with governance are responsible for the preparation of the entity's financial statements and the assessment of the entity's ability to continue as a going concern.

- (b) Gather sufficient appropriate audit evidence to confirm or dispel whether or not a material uncertainty exists through carrying out procedures considered necessary, including considering the effect of any plans of management and other mitigating factors; and
- (c) Seek written representations from management[18] regarding its plans for future action.

26-1 The auditor should consider the need to obtain written confirmations of representations from those charged with governance regarding:

- (a) The assessment of those charged with governance that the company is a going concern;
- (b) Any relevant disclosures in the financial statements.

580 - MANAGEMENT REPRESENTATIONS

2 The auditor should obtain appropriate representations from management.

2-1 Written confirmation of appropriate representations from management, as required by paragraph 4 below, should be obtained before the audit report is issued.

3-1 In the UK and Ireland, the auditor should obtain evidence that those charged with governance acknowledge their collective responsibility for the preparation of the financial statements and have approved the financial statements.

4 The auditor should obtain written representations from management on matters material to the financial statements when other sufficient appropriate audit evidence cannot reasonably be expected to exist.

5.a The auditor should obtain written representations from management that:

- (a) It acknowledges its responsibility for the design and implementation of internal control to prevent and detect error; and
- (b) It believes the effects of those uncorrected financial statements misstatements aggregated by the auditor during the audit are immaterial, both individually and in the aggregate, to the financial statements taken as a whole. A summary of such items should be included in or attached to the written representations.

15 If management refuses to provide a representation that the auditor considers necessary, this constitutes a scope limitation and the auditor should express a qualified opinion or a disclaimer of opinion.

720 - OTHER INFORMATION

11-1 If the auditor identifies a material inconsistency the auditor should seek to resolve the matter through discussion with those charged with governance.

16 If the auditor becomes aware that the other information appears to include a material misstatement of fact, the auditor should discuss the matter with the entity's management[19].

---

[18] In the UK and Ireland the auditor obtains written representations from those charged with governance.

[19] In the UK and Ireland the auditor discusses such matters with, and obtains responses from, those charged with governance.

[300]
Planning an audit of financial statements

(Issued December 2004)

Contents

	Paragraphs
Introduction	1 - 5
Preliminary Engagement Activities	6 - 7
Planning Activities	8 - 27
The Overall Audit Strategy	8 - 12
The Audit Plan	13 - 15
Changes to Planning Decisions During the Course of the Audit	16 - 17
Direction, Supervision and Review	18 - 21
Documentation	22 - 26
Communications With Those Charged With Governance and Management	27
Additional Considerations in Initial Audit Engagements	28 - 29
Effective Date	30

Appendix: Examples of Matters the Auditor May Consider in Establishing the Overall Audit Strategy

> International Standard on Auditing (UK and Ireland) (ISA (UK and Ireland)) 300 "Planning an Audit of Financial Statements" should be read in the context of the Auditing Practices Board's Statement "The Auditing Practices Board – Scope and Authority of Pronouncements" which sets out the application and authority of ISAs (UK and Ireland).

Introduction

1   The purpose of this International Standard on Auditing (UK and Ireland) (ISA (UK and Ireland)) is to establish standards and provide guidance on the considerations and activities applicable to planning an audit of financial statements. This ISA (UK and Ireland) is framed in the context of recurring audits. In addition, matters the auditor considers in initial audit engagements are included in paragraphs 28 and 29.

1-1   This ISA (UK and Ireland) uses the terms 'those charged with governance' and 'management'. The term 'governance' describes the role of persons entrusted with the supervision, control and direction of an entity. Ordinarily, those charged with governance are accountable for ensuring that the entity achieves its objectives, and for the quality of its financial reporting and reporting to interested parties. Those charged with governance include management only when they perform such functions.

1-2   In the UK and Ireland, those charged with governance include the directors (executive and non-executive) of a company or other body, the members of an audit committee where one exists, the partners, proprietors, committee of management or trustees of other forms of entity, or equivalent persons responsible for directing the entity's affairs and preparing its financial statements.

1-3   'Management' comprises those persons who perform senior managerial functions.

1-4   In the UK and Ireland, depending on the nature and circumstances of the entity, management may include some or all of those charged with governance (e.g. executive directors). Management will not normally include non-executive directors.

2   **The auditor should plan the audit so that the engagement will be performed in an effective manner.**

3   Planning an audit involves establishing the overall audit strategy for the engagement and developing an audit plan, in order to reduce audit risk to an acceptably low level. Planning involves the engagement partner and other key members of the engagement team to benefit from their experience and insight and to enhance the effectiveness and efficiency of the planning process.

4   Adequate planning helps to ensure that appropriate attention is devoted to important areas of the audit, that potential problems are identified and resolved on a timely basis and that the audit engagement is properly organized and managed in order to be performed in an effective and efficient manner. Adequate planning also assists in the proper assignment of work to engagement team members, facilitates the direction and supervision of engagement team members and the review of their work, and assists, where applicable, in coordination of work done by auditors of components and experts. The nature and extent of planning activities will vary according to the size and complexity of the entity, the auditor's previous experience with the entity, and changes in circumstances that occur during the audit engagement.

5   Planning is not a discrete phase of an audit, but rather a continual and iterative process that often begins shortly after (or in connection with) the completion of the previous audit and continues until the completion of the current audit engagement. However, in planning an audit, the auditor considers the timing of certain planning activities and audit procedures that need to be completed prior to the performance of

further audit procedures. For example, the auditor plans the discussion among engagement team members,[1] the analytical procedures to be applied as risk assessment procedures, the obtaining of a general understanding of the legal and regulatory framework applicable to the entity and how the entity is complying with that framework, the determination of materiality, the involvement of experts and the performance of other risk assessment procedures prior to identifying and assessing the risks of material misstatement and performing further audit procedures at the assertion level for classes of transactions, account balances, and disclosures that are responsive to those risks.

Preliminary Engagement Activities

The auditor should perform the following activities at the beginning of the current audit engagement: 6

- **Perform procedures regarding the continuance of the client relationship and the specific audit engagement** (see ISA (UK and Ireland) 220, "Quality Control for Audits of Historical Financial Information" for additional guidance).
- **Evaluate compliance with ethical requirements, including independence** (see ISA (UK and Ireland) 220 for additional guidance).
- **Establish an understanding of the terms of the engagement** (see ISA (UK and Ireland) 210, "Terms of Audit Engagements" for additional guidance).

The auditor's consideration of client continuance and ethical requirements, including independence, occurs throughout the performance of the audit engagement as conditions and changes in circumstances occur. However, the auditor's initial procedures on both client continuance and evaluation of ethical requirements (including independence) are performed prior to performing other significant activities for the current audit engagement. For continuing audit engagements, such initial procedures often occur shortly after (or in connection with) the completion of the previous audit.

The purpose of performing these preliminary engagement activities is to help ensure   7
that the auditor has considered any events or circumstances that may adversely affect the auditor's ability to plan and perform the audit engagement to reduce audit risk to an acceptably low level. Performing these preliminary engagement activities helps to ensure that the auditor plans an audit engagement for which:

- The auditor maintains the necessary independence and ability to perform the engagement.
- There are no issues with management integrity[2] that may affect the auditor's willingness to continue the engagement.
- There is no misunderstanding with the client as to the terms of the engagement.

---

[1] ISA (UK and Ireland) 315, "Understanding the Entity and Its Environment and Assessing the Risks of Material Misstatement" paragraphs 14-19 provide guidance on the engagement team's discussion of the susceptibility of the entity to material misstatements of the financial statements. ISA (UK and Ireland) 240, "The Auditor's Responsibility to Consider Fraud in an Audit of Financial Statements" paragraphs 27-32 provide guidance on the emphasis given during this discussion to the susceptibility of the entity's financial statements to material misstatement due to fraud.

[2] In the UK and Ireland, the auditor is also concerned to establish that there are no issues with the integrity of those charged with governance that may affect the auditor's willingness to continue the engagement.

Planning Activities

The Overall Audit Strategy

8   The auditor should establish the overall audit strategy for the audit.

9   The overall audit strategy sets the scope, timing and direction of the audit, and guides the development of the more detailed audit plan. The establishment of the overall audit strategy involves:

(a) Determining the characteristics of the engagement that define its scope, such as the financial reporting framework used, industry-specific reporting requirements and the locations of the components of the entity;
(b) Ascertaining the reporting objectives of the engagement to plan the timing of the audit and the nature of the communications required, such as deadlines for interim and final reporting, and key dates for expected communications with management and those charged with governance; and
(c) Considering the important factors that will determine the focus of the engagement team's efforts, such as determination of appropriate materiality levels, preliminary identification of areas where there may be higher risks of material misstatement, preliminary identification of material components and account balances, evaluation of whether the auditor may plan to obtain evidence regarding the effectiveness of internal control, and identification of recent significant entity-specific, industry, financial reporting or other relevant developments.

In developing the overall audit strategy, the auditor also considers the results of preliminary engagement activities (see paragraphs 6 and 7) and, where practicable, experience gained on other engagements performed for the entity. The Appendix to this ISA (UK and Ireland) lists examples of matters the auditor may consider in establishing the overall audit strategy for an engagement.

10 The process of developing the audit strategy helps the auditor to ascertain the nature, timing and extent of resources necessary to perform the engagement. The overall audit strategy sets out clearly, in response to the matters identified in paragraph 9, and subject to the completion of the auditor's risk assessment procedures:

(a) The resources to deploy for specific audit areas, such as the use of appropriately experienced team members for high risk areas or the involvement of experts on complex matters;
(b) The amount of resources to allocate to specific audit areas, such as the number of team members assigned to observe the inventory count at material locations, the extent of review of other auditors' work in the case of group audits, or the audit budget in hours to allocate to high risk areas;
(c) When these resources are deployed, such as whether at an interim audit stage or at key cut-off dates; and
(d) How such resources are managed, directed and supervised, such as when team briefing and debriefing meetings are expected to be held, how engagement partner and manager reviews are expected to take place (for example, on-site or off-site), and whether to complete engagement quality control reviews.

11 Once the audit strategy has been established, the auditor is able to start the development of a more detailed audit plan to address the various matters identified in the overall audit strategy, taking into account the need to achieve the audit objectives through the efficient use of the auditor's resources. Although the auditor ordinarily establishes the overall audit strategy before developing the detailed audit plan, the

two planning activities are not necessarily discrete or sequential processes but are closely inter-related since changes in one may result in consequential changes to the other. Paragraphs 14 and 15 provide further guidance on developing the audit plan.

In audits of small entities, the entire audit may be conducted by a very small audit team. Many audits of small entities involve the audit engagement partner (who may be a sole practitioner) working with one engagement team member (or without any engagement team members). With a smaller team, co-ordination and communication between team members are easier. Establishing the overall audit strategy for the audit of a small entity need not be a complex or time-consuming exercise; it varies according to the size of the entity and the complexity of the audit. For example, a brief memorandum prepared at the completion of the previous audit, based on a review of the working papers and highlighting issues identified in the audit just completed, updated and changed in the current period based on discussions with the owner-manager, can serve as the basis for planning the current audit engagement. 12

The Audit Plan

The auditor should develop an audit plan for the audit in order to reduce audit risk to an acceptably low level. 13

The audit plan is more detailed than the audit strategy and includes the nature, timing and extent of audit procedures to be performed by engagement team members in order to obtain sufficient appropriate audit evidence to reduce audit risk to an acceptably low level. Documentation of the audit plan also serves as a record of the proper planning and performance of the audit procedures that can be reviewed and approved prior to the performance of further audit procedures. 14

The audit plan includes: 15

- A description of the nature, timing and extent of planned risk assessment procedures sufficient to assess the risks of material misstatement, as determined under ISA (UK and Ireland) 315, "Understanding the Entity and Its Environment and Assessing the Risks of Material Misstatement;"
- A description of the nature, timing and extent of planned further audit procedures at the assertion level for each material class of transactions, account balance, and disclosure, as determined under ISA (UK and Ireland) 330, "The Auditor's Procedures in Response to Assessed Risks." The plan for further audit procedures reflects the auditor's decision whether to test the operating effectiveness of controls, and the nature, timing and extent of planned substantive procedures; and
- Such other audit procedures required to be carried out for the engagement in order to comply with ISAs (UK and Ireland) (for example, seeking direct communication with the entity's lawyers).

Planning for these audit procedures takes place over the course of the audit as the audit plan for the engagement develops. For example, planning of the auditor's risk assessment procedures ordinarily occurs early in the audit process. However, planning of the nature, timing and extent of specific further audit procedures depends on the outcome of those risk assessment procedures. In addition, the auditor may begin the execution of further audit procedures for some classes of transactions, account balances and disclosures before completing the more detailed audit plan of all remaining further audit procedures.

Changes to Planning Decisions During the Course of the Audit

16   The overall audit strategy and the audit plan should be updated and changed as necessary during the course of the audit.

17   Planning an audit is a continual and iterative process throughout the audit engagement. As a result of unexpected events, changes in conditions, or the audit evidence obtained from the results of audit procedures, the auditor may need to modify the overall audit strategy and audit plan, and thereby the resulting planned nature, timing and extent of further audit procedures. Information may come to the auditor's attention that differs significantly from the information available when the auditor planned the audit procedures. For example, the auditor may obtain audit evidence through the performance of substantive procedures that contradicts the audit evidence obtained with respect to the testing of the operating effectiveness of controls. In such circumstances, the auditor re-evaluates the planned audit procedures, based on the revised consideration of assessed risks at the assertion level for all or some of the classes of transactions, account balances or disclosures.

Direction, Supervision and Review

18   The auditor should plan the nature, timing and extent of direction and supervision of engagement team members and review of their work.

19   The nature, timing and extent of the direction and supervision of engagement team members and review of their work vary depending on many factors, including the size and complexity of the entity, the area of audit, the risks of material misstatement, and the capabilities and competence of personnel performing the audit work. ISA (UK and Ireland) 220 contains detailed guidance on the direction, supervision and review of audit work.

20   The auditor plans the nature, timing and extent of direction and supervision of engagement team members based on the assessed risk of material misstatement. As the assessed risk of material misstatement increases, for the area of audit risk, the auditor ordinarily increases the extent and timeliness of direction and supervision of engagement team members and performs a more detailed review of their work. Similarly, the auditor plans the nature, timing and extent of review of the engagement team's work based on the capabilities and competence of the individual team members performing the audit work.

21   In audits of small entities, an audit may be carried out entirely by the audit engagement partner (who may be a sole practitioner). In such situations, questions of direction and supervision of engagement team members and review of their work do not arise as the audit engagement partner, having personally conducted all aspects of the work, is aware of all material issues. The audit engagement partner (or sole practitioner) nevertheless needs to be satisfied that the audit has been conducted in accordance with ISAs (UK and Ireland). Forming an objective view on the appropriateness of the judgments made in the course of the audit can present practical problems when the same individual also performed the entire audit. When particularly complex or unusual issues are involved, and the audit is performed by a sole practitioner, it may be desirable to plan to consult with other suitably-experienced auditors or the auditor's professional body.

Documentation

The auditor should document the overall audit strategy and the audit plan, including any significant changes made during the audit engagement. 22

The auditor's documentation of the overall audit strategy records the key decisions considered necessary to properly plan the audit and to communicate significant matters to the engagement team. For example, the auditor may summarize the overall audit strategy in the form of a memorandum that contains key decisions regarding the overall scope, timing and conduct of the audit. 23

The auditor's documentation of the audit plan is sufficient to demonstrate the planned nature, timing and extent of risk assessment procedures, and further audit procedures at the assertion level for each material class of transaction, account balance, and disclosure in response to the assessed risks. The auditor may use standard audit programs or audit completion checklists. However, when such standard programs or checklists are used, the auditor appropriately tailors them to reflect the particular engagement circumstances. 24

The auditor's documentation of any significant changes to the originally planned overall audit strategy and to the detailed audit plan includes the reasons for the significant changes and the auditor's response to the events, conditions, or results of audit procedures that resulted in such changes. For example, the auditor may significantly change the planned overall audit strategy and the audit plan as a result of a material business combination or the identification of a material misstatement of the financial statements. A record of the significant changes to the overall audit strategy and the audit plan, and resulting changes to the planned nature, timing and extent of audit procedures, explains the overall strategy and audit plan finally adopted for the audit and demonstrates the appropriate response to significant changes occurring during the audit. 25

The form and extent of documentation depend on such matters as the size and complexity of the entity, materiality, the extent of other documentation, and the circumstances of the specific audit engagement. 26

Communications With Those Charged With Governance and Management

The auditor may discuss elements of planning with those charged with governance and the entity's management. These discussions may be a part of overall communications required to be made to those charged with governance of the entity or may be made to improve the effectiveness and efficiency of the audit. Discussions with those charged with governance ordinarily include the overall audit strategy and timing of the audit, including any limitations thereon, or any additional requirements[3]. Discussions with management often occur to facilitate the conduct and management of the audit engagement (for example, to coordinate some of the planned audit procedures with the work of the entity's personnel). Although these discussions often occur, the overall audit strategy and the audit plan remain the auditor's responsibility. When discussions of matters included in the overall audit strategy or audit plan occur, care is required in order to not compromise the effectiveness of the audit. For example, the auditor considers whether discussing the 27

---

[3] ISA (UK and Ireland) 260, "Communication of Audit Matters With Those Charged With Governance," requires the auditor to communicate to those charged with governance an outline of the nature and scope, including, where relevant, any limitations thereon, of the work the auditor proposes to undertake. Examples are given of planning information that might be communicated.

nature and timing of detailed audit procedures with management compromises the effectiveness of the audit by making the audit procedures too predictable.

Additional Considerations in Initial Audit Engagements

28 The auditor should perform the following activities prior to starting an initial audit:
    (a) **Perform procedures regarding the acceptance of the client relationship and the specific audit engagement (see ISA (UK and Ireland) 220 for additional guidance).**
    (b) **Communicate with the previous auditor, where there has been a change of auditors, in compliance with relevant ethical requirements.**

29 The purpose and objective of planning the audit are the same whether the audit is an initial or recurring engagement. However, for an initial audit, the auditor may need to expand the planning activities because the auditor does not ordinarily have the previous experience with the entity that is considered when planning recurring engagements. For initial audits, additional matters the auditor may consider in developing the overall audit strategy and audit plan include the following:

- Unless prohibited by law or regulation, arrangements to be made with the previous auditor, for example, to review the previous auditor's working papers.
- Any major issues (including the application of accounting principles or of auditing and reporting standards) discussed with management in connection with the initial selection as auditors, the communication of these matters to those charged with governance and how these matters affect the overall audit strategy and audit plan.
- The planned audit procedures to obtain sufficient appropriate audit evidence regarding opening balances (see paragraph 2 of ISA (UK and Ireland) 510, "Initial Engagements - Opening Balances").
- The assignment of firm personnel with appropriate levels of capabilities and competence to respond to anticipated significant risks.
- Other procedures required by the firm's system of quality control for initial audit engagements (for example, the firm's system of quality control may require the involvement of another partner or senior individual to review the overall audit strategy prior to commencing significant audit procedures or to review reports prior to their issuance).

Effective Date

30 This ISA (UK and Ireland) is effective for audits of financial statements for periods commencing on or after 15 December 2004.

Public Sector Perspective

Additional guidance for auditors of public sector bodies in the UK and Ireland is given in:
- Practice Note 10 "Audit of Financial Statements of Public Sector Entities in the United Kingdom (Revised)"
- Practice Note 10(I) "The Audit of Central Government Financial Statements in Ireland"

This ISA (UK and Ireland) is applicable in all material respects to audits of public   1
sector entities.

Some of the terms used in this ISA (UK and Ireland) such as "engagement partner"   2
and "firm" should be read as referring to their public sector equivalents.

Paragraph 6 of this ISA (UK and Ireland) refers to ISA (UK and Ireland) 210,   3
"Terms of Audit Engagements," and ISA (UK and Ireland) 220, "Quality Control for
Audits of Historical Financial Information." The Public Sector Perspectives to those
ISAs (UK and Ireland) contain a discussion of their applicability to audits of public
sector entities, and are therefore relevant to the application of this ISA (UK and
Ireland) in the public sector.

Appendix – Examples of Matters the Auditor May Consider in Establishing the Overall Audit Strategy

This appendix provides examples of matters the auditor may consider in establishing the overall audit strategy. Many of these matters will also influence the auditor's detailed audit plan. The examples provided cover a broad range of matters applicable to many engagements. While some of the matters referred to below may be required to be performed by other ISAs (UK and Ireland), not all matters are relevant to every audit engagement and the list is not necessarily complete. In addition, the auditor may consider these matters in an order different from that shown below.

Scope of the Audit Engagement

The auditor may consider the following matters when establishing the scope of the audit engagement:

- The financial reporting framework on which the financial information to be audited has been prepared, including any need for reconciliations to another financial reporting framework.
- Industry-specific reporting requirements such as reports mandated by industry regulators.
- The expected audit coverage, including the number and locations of components to be included.
- The nature of the control relationships between a parent and its components that determine how the group is to be consolidated.
- The extent to which components are audited by other auditors.
- The nature of the business segments to be audited, including the need for specialized knowledge.
- The reporting currency to be used, including any need for currency translation for the financial information audited.
- The need for a statutory audit of standalone financial statements in addition to an audit for consolidation purposes.
- The availability of the work of internal auditors and the extent of the auditor's potential reliance on such work.
- The entity's use of service organizations and how the auditor may obtain evidence concerning the design or operation of controls performed by them.
- The expected use of audit evidence obtained in prior audits, for example, audit evidence related to risk assessment procedures and tests of controls.
- The effect of information technology on the audit procedures, including the availability of data and the expected use of computer-assisted audit techniques.

- The coordination of the expected coverage and timing of the audit work with any reviews of interim financial information and the effect on the audit of the information obtained during such reviews.
- The discussion of matters that may affect the audit with firm personnel responsible for performing other services to the entity.
- The availability of client personnel and data.

Reporting Objectives, Timing of the Audit and Communications Required

The auditor may consider the following matters when ascertaining the reporting objectives of the engagement, the timing of the audit and the nature of communications required:

- The entity's timetable for reporting, such as at interim and final stages.
- The organization of meetings with management and those charged with governance to discuss the nature, extent and timing of the audit work.
- The discussion with management and those charged with governance regarding the expected type and timing of reports to be issued and other communications, both written and oral, including the auditor's report, management letters and communications to those charged with governance.
- The discussion with management regarding the expected communications on the status of audit work throughout the engagement and the expected deliverables resulting from the audit procedures.
- Communication with auditors of components regarding the expected types and timing of reports to be issued and other communications in connection with the audit of components.
- The expected nature and timing of communications among engagement team members, including the nature and timing of team meetings and timing of the review of work performed.
- Whether there are any other expected communications with third parties, including any statutory or contractual reporting responsibilities arising from the audit.

Direction of the Audit

The auditor may consider the following matters when setting the direction of the audit:

- With respect to materiality:
  - Setting materiality for planning purposes.
  - Setting and communicating materiality for auditors of components.
  - Reconsidering materiality as audit procedures are performed during the course of the audit.
  - Identifying the material components and account balances.
- Audit areas where there is a higher risk of material misstatement.
- The impact of the assessed risk of material misstatement at the overall financial statement level on direction, supervision and review.
- The selection of the engagement team (including, where necessary, the engagement quality control reviewer) and the assignment of audit work to the team members, including the assignment of appropriately experienced team members to areas where there may be higher risks of material misstatement.
- Engagement budgeting, including considering the appropriate amount of time to set aside for areas where there may be higher risks of material misstatement.
- The manner in which the auditor emphasizes to engagement team members the need to maintain a questioning mind and to exercise professional skepticism in gathering and evaluating audit evidence.

- Results of previous audits that involved evaluating the operating effectiveness of internal control, including the nature of identified weaknesses and action taken to address them.
- Evidence of management's[4] commitment to the design and operation of sound internal control, including evidence of appropriate documentation of such internal control.
- Volume of transactions, which may determine whether it is more efficient for the auditor to rely on internal control.
- Importance attached to internal control throughout the entity to the successful operation of the business.
- Significant business developments affecting the entity, including changes in information technology and business processes, changes in key management, and acquisitions, mergers and divestments.
- Significant industry developments such as changes in industry regulations and new reporting requirements.
- Significant changes in the financial reporting framework, such as changes in accounting standards.
- Other significant relevant developments, such as changes in the legal environment affecting the entity.

[4] *In the UK and Ireland, the auditor also considers evidence of the commitment of those charged with governance to the design and operation of sound internal control.*

[315]
Understanding the entity and its environment and assessing the risks of material misstatement

(Issued December 2004)

Contents

	Paragraphs
Introduction	1 - 5
Risk Assessment Procedures and Sources of Information About the Entity and Its Environment, Including Its Internal Control	6
Risk Assessment Procedures	7 - 13
Discussion Among the Engagement Team	14 - 19
Understanding the Entity and Its Environment, Including Its Internal Control	20 - 21
Industry, Regulatory and Other External Factors, Including the Applicable Financial Reporting Framework	22 - 24
Nature of the Entity	25 - 29
Objectives and Strategies and Related Business Risks	30 - 34
Measurement and Review of the Entity's Financial Performance	35 - 40
Internal Control	41 - 99
Assessing the Risks of Material Misstatement	100 - 107
Significant Risks That Require Special Audit Consideration	108 - 114
Risks for Which Substantive Procedures Alone Do Not Provide Sufficient Appropriate Audit Evidence	115 - 118
Revision of Risk Assessment	119
Communicating With Those Charged With Governance and Management	120 - 121
Documentation	122 - 123
Effective Date	124

Appendix 1: Understanding the Entity and Its Environment

Appendix 2: Internal Control Components

Appendix 3: Conditions and Events That May Indicate Risks of Material Misstatement

---

International Standard on Auditing (UK and Ireland) (ISA (UK and Ireland)) 315 "Understanding the Entity and its Environment and Assessing the Risks of Material Misstatement" should be read in the context of the Auditing Practices Board's Statement "The Auditing Practices Board - Scope and Authority of Pronouncements (Revised)" which sets out the application and authority of ISAs (UK and Ireland).

Introduction

The purpose of this International Standard on Auditing (UK and Ireland) (ISA (UK and Ireland)) is to establish standards and provide guidance on obtaining an understanding of the entity and its environment, including its internal control, and on assessing the risks of material misstatement in a financial statement audit. The importance of the auditor's risk assessment as a basis for further audit procedures is discussed in the explanation of audit risk in ISA (UK and Ireland) 200, "Objective and General Principles Governing an Audit of Financial Statements." 1

This ISA (UK and Ireland) uses the terms 'those charged with governance' and 'management'. The term 'governance' describes the role of persons entrusted with the supervision, control and direction of an entity. Ordinarily, those charged with governance are accountable for ensuring that the entity achieves its objectives, and for the quality of its financial reporting and reporting to interested parties. Those charged with governance include management only when they perform such functions. 1-1

In the UK and Ireland, those charged with governance include the directors (executive and non-executive) of a company or other body, the members of an audit committee where one exists, the partners, proprietors, committee of management or trustees of other forms of entity, or equivalent persons responsible for directing the entity's affairs and preparing its financial statements. 1-2

'Management' comprises those persons who perform senior managerial functions. 1-3

In the UK and Ireland, depending on the nature and circumstances of the entity, management may include some or all of those charged with governance (e.g. executive directors). Management will not normally include non-executive directors. 1-4

The auditor should obtain an understanding of the entity and its environment, including its internal control, sufficient to identify and assess the risks of material misstatement of the financial statements whether due to fraud or error, and sufficient to design and perform further audit procedures. ISA (UK and Ireland) 500, "Audit Evidence," requires the auditor to use assertions in sufficient detail to form a basis for the assessment of risks of material misstatement and the design and performance of further audit procedures. This ISA (UK and Ireland) requires the auditor to make risk assessments at the financial statement and assertion levels based on an appropriate understanding of the entity and its environment, including its internal control. ISA (UK and Ireland) 330, "The Auditor's Procedures in Response to Assessed Risks" discusses the auditor's responsibility to determine overall responses and to design and perform further audit procedures whose nature, timing, and extent are responsive to the risk assessments. The requirements and guidance of this ISA (UK and Ireland) are to be applied in conjunction with the requirements and guidance provided in other ISAs (UK and Ireland). In particular, further guidance in relation to the auditor's responsibility to assess the risks of material misstatement due to fraud is discussed in ISA (UK and Ireland) 240, "The Auditor's Responsibility to Consider Fraud in an Audit of Financial Statements." 2

The following is an overview of the requirements of this standard: 3

- *Risk assessment procedures and sources of information about the entity and its environment, including its internal control.* This section explains the audit

procedures that the auditor is required to perform to obtain the understanding of the entity and its environment, including its internal control (risk assessment procedures). It also requires discussion among the engagement team about the susceptibility of the entity's financial statements to material misstatement.
- *Understanding the entity and its environment, including its internal control.* This section requires the auditor to understand specified aspects of the entity and its environment, and components of its internal control, in order to identify and assess the risks of material misstatement.
- *Assessing the risks of material misstatement.* This section requires the auditor to identify and assess the risks of material misstatement at the financial statement and assertion levels. The auditor:
  - Identifies risks by considering the entity and its environment, including relevant controls, and by considering the classes of transactions, account balances, and disclosures in the financial statements;
  - Relates the identified risks to what can go wrong at the assertion level; and
  - Considers the significance and likelihood of the risks.

This section also requires the auditor to determine whether any of the assessed risks are significant risks that require special audit consideration or risks for which substantive procedures alone do not provide sufficient appropriate audit evidence. The auditor is required to evaluate the design of the entity's controls, including relevant control activities, over such risks and determine whether they have been implemented.

- *Communicating with those charged with governance and management.* This section deals with matters relating to internal control that the auditor communicates to those charged with governance and management.
- *Documentation.* This section establishes related documentation requirements.

4 Obtaining an understanding of the entity and its environment is an essential aspect of performing an audit in accordance with ISAs (UK and Ireland). In particular, that understanding establishes a frame of reference within which the auditor plans the audit and exercises professional judgment about assessing risks of material misstatement of the financial statements and responding to those risks throughout the audit, for example when:

- Establishing materiality and evaluating whether the judgment about materiality remains appropriate as the audit progresses;
- Considering the appropriateness of the selection and application of accounting policies, and the adequacy of financial statement disclosures;
- Identifying areas where special audit consideration may be necessary, for example, related party transactions, the appropriateness of management's use of the going concern assumption, or considering the business purpose of transactions;
- Developing expectations for use when performing analytical procedures;
- Designing and performing further audit procedures to reduce audit risk to an acceptably low level; and
- Evaluating the sufficiency and appropriateness of audit evidence obtained, such as the appropriateness of assumptions and of management's oral and written representations[1a].

5 The auditor uses professional judgment to determine the extent of the understanding required of the entity and its environment, including its internal control. The auditor's primary consideration is whether the understanding that has been obtained is sufficient to assess the risks of material misstatement of the financial statements and

---

[1a] *In the UK and Ireland, the auditor obtains written representations from those charged with governance.*

walk-throughs of systems, to determine whether changes have occurred that may affect the relevance of such information.

When relevant to the audit, the auditor also considers other information such as that obtained from the auditor's client acceptance or continuance process or, where practicable, experience gained on other engagements performed for the entity, for example, engagements to review interim financial information. 13

Discussion Among the Engagement Team

The members of the engagement team should discuss the susceptibility of the entity's financial statements to material misstatements. 14

The objective of this discussion is for members of the engagement team to gain a better understanding of the potential for material misstatements of the financial statements resulting from fraud or error in the specific areas assigned to them, and to understand how the results of the audit procedures that they perform may affect other aspects of the audit including the decisions about the nature, timing, and extent of further audit procedures. 15

The discussion provides an opportunity for more experienced engagement team members, including the engagement partner, to share their insights based on their knowledge of the entity, and for the team members to exchange information about the business risks[1] to which the entity is subject and about how and where the financial statements might be susceptible to material misstatement. As required by ISA (UK and Ireland) 240, particular emphasis is given to the susceptibility of the entity's financial statements to material misstatement due to fraud. The discussion also addresses application of the applicable financial reporting framework to the entity's facts and circumstances. 16

Professional judgment is used to determine which members of the engagement team are included in the discussion, how and when it occurs, and the extent of the discussion. The key members of the engagement team are ordinarily involved in the discussion; however, it is not necessary for all team members to have a comprehensive knowledge of all aspects of the audit. The extent of the discussion is influenced by the roles, experience, and information needs of the engagement team members. In a multi-location audit, for example, there may be multiple discussions that involve the key members of the engagement team in each significant location. Another factor to consider in planning the discussions is whether to include experts assigned to the engagement team. For example, the auditor may determine that including a professional possessing specialist information technology (IT)[2] or other skills is needed on the engagement team and therefore includes that individual in the discussion. 17

As required by ISA (UK and Ireland) 200, the auditor plans and performs the audit with an attitude of professional skepticism. The discussion among the engagement team members emphasizes the need to maintain professional skepticism throughout the engagement, to be alert for information or other conditions that indicate that a material misstatement due to fraud or error may have occurred, and to be rigorous in following up on such indications. 18

---

[1] See paragraph 30.

[2] Information technology (IT) encompasses automated means of originating, processing, storing and communicating information, and includes recording devices, communication systems, computer systems (including hardware and software components and data), and other electronic devices.

19 Depending on the circumstances of the audit, there may be further discussions in order to facilitate the ongoing exchange of information between engagement team members regarding the susceptibility of the entity's financial statements to material misstatements. The purpose is for engagement team members to communicate and share information obtained throughout the audit that may affect the assessment of the risks of material misstatement due to fraud or error or the audit procedures performed to address the risks.

Understanding the Entity and Its Environment, Including Its Internal Control

20 The auditor's understanding of the entity and its environment consists of an understanding of the following aspects:

(a) Industry, regulatory, and other external factors, including the applicable financial reporting framework.
(b) Nature of the entity, including the entity's selection and application of accounting policies.
(c) Objectives and strategies and the related business risks that may result in a material misstatement of the financial statements.
(d) Measurement and review of the entity's financial performance.
(e) Internal control.

Appendix 1 contains examples of matters that the auditor may consider in obtaining an understanding of the entity and its environment relating to categories (a) through (d) above. Appendix 2 contains a detailed explanation of the internal control components.

21 The nature, timing, and extent of the risk assessment procedures performed depend on the circumstances of the engagement such as the size and complexity of the entity and the auditor's experience with it. In addition, identifying significant changes in any of the above aspects of the entity from prior periods is particularly important in gaining a sufficient understanding of the entity to identify and assess risks of material misstatement.

Industry, Regulatory and Other External Factors, Including the Applicable Financial Reporting Framework

22 **The auditor should obtain an understanding of relevant industry, regulatory, and other external factors including the applicable financial reporting framework.** These factors include industry conditions such as the competitive environment, supplier and customer relationships, and technological developments; the regulatory environment encompassing, among other matters, the applicable financial reporting framework, the legal and political environment, and environmental requirements affecting the industry and the entity; and other external factors such as general economic conditions. See ISA (UK and Ireland) 250, "Consideration of Laws and Regulations in an Audit of Financial Statements" for additional requirements related to the legal and regulatory framework applicable to the entity and the industry.

23 The industry in which the entity operates may give rise to specific risks of material misstatement arising from the nature of the business or the degree of regulation. For example, long-term contracts may involve significant estimates of revenues and costs that give rise to risks of material misstatement. In such cases, the auditor considers

Smaller entities often do not set their objectives and strategies, or manage the related 34
business risks, through formal plans or processes. In many cases there may be no
documentation of such matters. In such entities, the auditor's understanding is
ordinarily obtained through inquiries of management and observation of how the
entity responds to such matters.

Measurement and Review of the Entity's Financial Performance

The auditor should obtain an understanding of the measurement and review of the 35
entity's financial performance. Performance measures and their review indicate to the
auditor aspects of the entity's performance that management and others consider to
be of importance. Performance measures, whether external or internal, create pressures on the entity that, in turn, may motivate management to take action to improve
the business performance or to misstate the financial statements. Obtaining an
understanding of the entity's performance measures assists the auditor in considering
whether such pressures result in management actions that may have increased the
risks of material misstatement.

Management's measurement and review of the entity's financial performance is to be 36
distinguished from the monitoring of controls (discussed as a component of internal
control in paragraphs 96-99), though their purposes may overlap. Monitoring of
controls, however, is specifically concerned with the effective operation of internal
control through consideration of information about the control. The measurement
and review of performance is directed at whether business performance is meeting the
objectives set by management (or third parties), but in some cases performance
indicators also provide information that enables management to identify deficiencies
in internal control.

Internally-generated information used by management for this purpose may include 37
key performance indicators (financial and non-financial), budgets, variance analysis,
segment information and divisional, departmental or other level performance
reports, and comparisons of an entity's performance with that of competitors.
External parties may also measure and review the entity's financial performance. For
example, external information such as analysts' reports and credit rating agency
reports may provide information useful to the auditor's understanding of the entity
and its environment. Such reports often are obtained from the entity being audited.

Internal measures may highlight unexpected results or trends requiring manage- 38
ment's inquiry of others in order to determine their cause and take corrective action
(including, in some cases, the detection and correction of misstatements on a timely
basis). Performance measures may also indicate to the auditor a risk of misstatement
of related financial statement information. For example, performance measures may
indicate that the entity has unusually rapid growth or profitability when compared to
that of other entities in the same industry. Such information, particularly if combined with other factors such as performance-based bonus or incentive
remuneration, may indicate the potential risk of management[2a] bias in the preparation of the financial statements.

Much of the information used in performance measurement may be produced by the 39
entity's information system. If management assumes that data used for reviewing the
entity's performance are accurate without having a basis for that assumption, errors
may exist in the information, potentially leading management to incorrect conclusions about performance. When the auditor intends to make use of the performance
measures for the purpose of the audit (for example, for analytical procedures), the
auditor considers whether the information related to management's review of the

entity's performance provides a reliable basis and is sufficiently precise for such a purpose. If making use of performance measures, the auditor considers whether they are precise enough to detect material misstatements.

40   Smaller entities ordinarily do not have formal processes to measure and review the entity's financial performance. Management nevertheless often relies on certain key indicators which knowledge and experience of the business suggest are reliable bases for evaluating financial performance and taking appropriate action.

Internal Control

41   **The auditor should obtain an understanding of internal control relevant to the audit.** The auditor uses the understanding of internal control to identify types of potential misstatements, consider factors that affect the risks of material misstatement, and design the nature, timing, and extent of further audit procedures. Internal control relevant to the audit is discussed in paragraphs 47-53 below. In addition, the depth of the understanding is discussed in paragraphs 54-56 below.

42   Internal control is the process designed and effected by those charged with governance, management, and other personnel to provide reasonable assurance about the achievement of the entity's objectives with regard to reliability of financial reporting, effectiveness and efficiency of operations and compliance with applicable laws and regulations. It follows that internal control is designed and implemented to address identified business risks that threaten the achievement of any of these objectives.

43   Internal control, as discussed in this ISA (UK and Ireland), consists of the following components:

   (a) The control environment.
   (b) The entity's risk assessment process.
   (c) The information system, including the related business processes, relevant to financial reporting, and communication.
   (d) Control activities.
   (e) Monitoring of controls.

   Appendix 2 contains a detailed discussion of the internal control components.

44   The division of internal control into the five components provides a useful framework for auditors to consider how different aspects of an entity's internal control may affect the audit. The division does not necessarily reflect how an entity considers and implements internal control. Also, the auditor's primary consideration is whether, and how, a specific control prevents, or detects and corrects, material misstatements in classes of transactions, account balances, or disclosures, and their related assertions, rather than its classification into any particular component. Accordingly, auditors may use different terminology or frameworks to describe the various aspects of internal control, and their effect on the audit than those used in this ISA (UK and Ireland), provided all the components described in this ISA (UK and Ireland) are addressed.

45   The way in which internal control is designed and implemented varies with an entity's size and complexity. Specifically, smaller entities may use less formal means and simpler processes and procedures to achieve their objectives. For example, smaller entities with active management involvement in the financial reporting process may not have extensive descriptions of accounting procedures or detailed written policies. For some entities, in particular very small entities, the owner-

manager[3] may perform functions which in a larger entity would be regarded as belonging to several of the components of internal control. Therefore, the components of internal control may not be clearly distinguished within smaller entities, but their underlying purposes are equally valid.

For the purposes of this ISA (UK and Ireland), the term "internal control" encompasses all five components of internal control stated above. In addition, the term "controls" refers to one or more of the components, or any aspect thereof.   46

Controls Relevant to the Audit

There is a direct relationship between an entity's objectives and the controls it implements to provide reasonable assurance about their achievement. The entity's objectives, and therefore controls, relate to financial reporting, operations and compliance; however, not all of these objectives and controls are relevant to the auditor's risk assessment.   47

Ordinarily, controls that are relevant to an audit pertain to the entity's objective of preparing financial statements for external purposes that give a true and fair view (or are presented fairly, in all material respects) in accordance with the applicable financial reporting framework and the management of risk that may give rise to a material misstatement in those financial statements. It is a matter of the auditor's professional judgment, subject to the requirements of this ISA (UK and Ireland), whether a control, individually or in combination with others, is relevant to the auditor's considerations in assessing the risks of material misstatement and designing and performing further procedures in response to assessed risks. In exercising that judgment, the auditor considers the circumstances, the applicable component and factors such as the following: 48

- The auditor's judgment about materiality.
- The size of the entity.
- The nature of the entity's business, including its organization and ownership characteristics.
- The diversity and complexity of the entity's operations.
- Applicable legal and regulatory requirements.
- The nature and complexity of the systems that are part of the entity's internal control, including the use of service organizations.

Controls over the completeness and accuracy of information produced by the entity may also be relevant to the audit if the auditor intends to make use of the information in designing and performing further procedures. The auditor's previous experience with the entity and information obtained in understanding the entity and its environment and throughout the audit assists the auditor in identifying controls relevant to the audit. Further, although internal control applies to the entire entity or to any of its operating units or business processes, an understanding of internal control relating to each of the entity's operating units and business processes may not be relevant to the audit.   49

Controls relating to operations and compliance objectives may, however, be relevant to an audit if they pertain to data the auditor evaluates or uses in applying audit procedures. For example, controls pertaining to non-financial data that the auditor uses in analytical procedures, such as production statistics, or controls pertaining to detecting non-compliance with laws and regulations that may have a direct and   50

---

[3] This ISA (UK and Ireland) uses the term "owner-manager" to indicate the proprietors of entities who are involved in the running of the entity on a day-to-day basis.

material effect on the financial statements, such as controls over compliance with income tax laws and regulations used to determine the income tax provision, may be relevant to an audit.

51 An entity generally has controls relating to objectives that are not relevant to an audit and therefore need not be considered. For example, an entity may rely on a sophisticated system of automated controls to provide efficient and effective operations (such as a commercial airline's system of automated controls to maintain flight schedules), but these controls ordinarily would not be relevant to the audit.

52 Internal control over safeguarding of assets against unauthorized acquisition, use, or disposition may include controls relating to financial reporting and operations objectives. In obtaining an understanding of each of the components of internal control, the auditor's consideration of safeguarding controls is generally limited to those relevant to the reliability of financial reporting. For example, use of access controls, such as passwords, that limit access to the data and programs that process cash disbursements may be relevant to a financial statement audit. Conversely, controls to prevent the excessive use of materials in production generally are not relevant to a financial statement audit.

53 Controls relevant to the audit may exist in any of the components of internal control and a further discussion of controls relevant to the audit is included under the heading of each internal control component below. In addition, paragraphs 113 and 115 discuss certain risks for which the auditor is required to evaluate the design of the entity's controls over such risks and determine whether they have been implemented.

Depth of Understanding of Internal Control

54 Obtaining an understanding of internal control involves evaluating the design of a control and determining whether it has been implemented. Evaluating the design of a control involves considering whether the control, individually or in combination with other controls, is capable of effectively preventing, or detecting and correcting, material misstatements. Further explanation is contained in the discussion of each internal control component below. Implementation of a control means that the control exists and that the entity is using it. The auditor considers the design of a control in determining whether to consider its implementation. An improperly designed control may represent a material weakness[4] in the entity's internal control and the auditor considers whether to communicate this to those charged with governance and management as required by paragraph 120.

55 Risk assessment procedures to obtain audit evidence about the design and implementation of relevant controls may include inquiring of entity personnel, observing the application of specific controls, inspecting documents and reports, and tracing transactions through the information system relevant to financial reporting. Inquiry alone is not sufficient to evaluate the design of a control relevant to an audit and to determine whether it has been implemented.

56 Obtaining an understanding of an entity's controls is not sufficient to serve as testing the operating effectiveness of controls, unless there is some automation that provides for the consistent application of the operation of the control (manual and automated elements of internal control relevant to the audit are further described below). For example, obtaining audit evidence about the implementation of a manually operated

---

[4] *A material weakness in internal control is one that could have a material effect on the financial statements.*

control at a point in time does not provide audit evidence about the operating effectiveness of the control at other times during the period under audit. However, IT enables an entity to process large volumes of data consistently and enhances the entity's ability to monitor the performance of control activities and to achieve effective segregation of duties by implementing security controls in applications, databases, and operating systems. Therefore, because of the inherent consistency of IT processing, performing audit procedures to determine whether an automated control has been implemented may serve as a test of that control's operating effectiveness, depending on the auditor's assessment and testing of controls such as those over program changes. Tests of the operating effectiveness of controls are further described in ISA (UK and Ireland) 330.

Characteristics of Manual and Automated Elements of Internal Control Relevant to the Auditor's Risk Assessment

Most entities make use of IT systems for financial reporting and operational purposes. However, even when IT is extensively used, there will be manual elements to the systems. The balance between manual and automated elements varies. In certain cases, particularly smaller, less complex entities, the systems may be primarily manual. In other cases, the extent of automation may vary with some systems substantially automated with few related manual elements and others, even within the same entity, predominantly manual. As a result, an entity's system of internal control is likely to contain manual and automated elements, the characteristics of which are relevant to the auditor's risk assessment and further audit procedures based thereon. 57

The use of manual or automated elements in internal control also affects the manner in which transactions are initiated, recorded, processed, and reported.[5] Controls in a manual system may include such procedures as approvals and reviews of activities, and reconciliations and follow-up of reconciling items. Alternatively, an entity may use automated procedures to initiate, record, process, and report transactions, in which case records in electronic format replace such paper documents as purchase orders, invoices, shipping documents, and related accounting records. Controls in IT systems consist of a combination of automated controls (for example, controls embedded in computer programs) and manual controls. Further, manual controls may be independent of IT, may use information produced by IT, or may be limited to monitoring the effective functioning of IT and of automated controls, and to handling exceptions. When IT is used to initiate, record, process or report transactions, or other financial data for inclusion in financial statements, the systems and programs may include controls related to the corresponding assertions for material accounts or may be critical to the effective functioning of manual controls that depend on IT. An entity's mix of manual and automated controls varies with the nature and complexity of the entity's use of IT. 58

Generally, IT provides potential benefits of effectiveness and efficiency for an entity's internal control because it enables an entity to: 59

- Consistently apply predefined business rules and perform complex calculations in processing large volumes of transactions or data;
- Enhance the timeliness, availability, and accuracy of information;
- Facilitate the additional analysis of information;
- Enhance the ability to monitor the performance of the entity's activities and its policies and procedures;

---
[5] *Paragraph 9 of Appendix 2 defines initiation, recording, processing, and reporting as used throughout this ISA (UK and Ireland).*

- Reduce the risk that controls will be circumvented; and
- Enhance the ability to achieve effective segregation of duties by implementing security controls in applications, databases, and operating systems.

60   IT also poses specific risks to an entity's internal control, including the following:

- Reliance on systems or programs that are inaccurately processing data, processing inaccurate data, or both.
- Unauthorized access to data that may result in destruction of data or improper changes to data, including the recording of unauthorized or non-existent transactions, or inaccurate recording of transactions. Particular risks may arise where multiple users access a common database.
- The possibility of IT personnel gaining access privileges beyond those necessary to perform their assigned duties thereby breaking down segregation of duties.
- Unauthorized changes to data in master files.
- Unauthorized changes to systems or programs.
- Failure to make necessary changes to systems or programs.
- Inappropriate manual intervention.
- Potential loss of data or inability to access data as required.

61   Manual aspects of systems may be more suitable where judgment and discretion are required such as for the following circumstances:

- Large, unusual or non-recurring transactions.
- Circumstances where errors are difficult to define, anticipate or predict.
- In changing circumstances that require a control response outside the scope of an existing automated control.
- In monitoring the effectiveness of automated controls.

62   Manual controls are performed by people, and therefore pose specific risks to the entity's internal control. Manual controls may be less reliable than automated controls because they can be more easily bypassed, ignored, or overridden and they are also more prone to simple errors and mistakes. Consistency of application of a manual control element cannot therefore be assumed. Manual systems may be less suitable for the following:

- High volume or recurring transactions, or in situations where errors that can be anticipated or predicted can be prevented or detected by control parameters that are automated.
- Control activities where the specific ways to perform the control can be adequately designed and automated.

63   The extent and nature of the risks to internal control vary depending on the nature and characteristics of the entity's information system. Therefore in understanding internal control, the auditor considers whether the entity has responded adequately to the risks arising from the use of IT or manual systems by establishing effective controls.

Limitations of Internal Control

64   Internal control, no matter how well designed and operated, can provide an entity with only reasonable assurance about achieving the entity's financial reporting objectives. The likelihood of achievement is affected by limitations inherent to internal control. These include the realities that human judgment in decision-making can be faulty and that breakdowns in internal control can occur because of human failures, such as simple errors or mistakes. For example, if an entity's information system personnel do not completely understand how an order entry system processes

whether the engagement team includes members with sufficient relevant knowledge and experience.

Legislative and regulatory requirements often determine the applicable financial reporting framework to be used by management[2a] in preparing the entity's financial statements. In most cases, the applicable financial reporting framework will be that of the jurisdiction in which the entity is registered or operates and the auditor is based, and the auditor and the entity will have a common understanding of that framework. In some cases there may be no local financial reporting framework, in which case the entity's choice will be governed by local practice, industry practice, user needs, or other factors. For example, the entity's competitors may apply International Financial Reporting Standards (IFRS) and the entity may determine that IFRS are also appropriate for its financial reporting requirements. The auditor considers whether local regulations specify certain financial reporting requirements for the industry in which the entity operates, since the financial statements may be materially misstated in the context of the applicable financial reporting framework if management[2a] fails to prepare the financial statements in accordance with such regulations.

Nature of the Entity

The auditor should obtain an understanding of the nature of the entity. The nature of an entity refers to the entity's operations, its ownership and governance, the types of investments that it is making and plans to make, the way that the entity is structured and how it is financed. An understanding of the nature of an entity enables the auditor to understand the classes of transactions, account balances, and disclosures to be expected in the financial statements.

The entity may have a complex structure with subsidiaries or other components in multiple locations. In addition to the difficulties of consolidation in such cases, other issues with complex structures that may give rise to risks of material misstatement include: the allocation of goodwill to business segments, and its impairment; whether investments are joint ventures, subsidiaries, or investments accounted for using the equity method; and whether special-purpose entities are accounted for appropriately.

An understanding of the ownership and relations between owners and other people or entities is also important in determining whether related party transactions have been identified and accounted for appropriately. ISA (UK and Ireland) 550, "Related Parties" provides additional guidance on the auditor's considerations relevant to related parties.

The auditor should obtain an understanding of the entity's selection and application of accounting policies and consider whether they are appropriate for its business and consistent with the applicable financial reporting framework and accounting polices used in the relevant industry. The understanding encompasses the methods the entity uses to account for significant and unusual transactions; the effect of significant accounting policies in controversial or emerging areas for which there is a lack of authoritative guidance or consensus; and changes in the entity's accounting policies. The auditor also identifies financial reporting standards and regulations that are new to the entity and considers when and how the entity will adopt such requirements. Where the entity has changed its selection of or method of applying a significant accounting policy, the auditor considers the reasons for the change and whether it is

---

[2a] *In the UK and Ireland, those charged with governance are responsible for preparing the financial statements.*

appropriate and consistent with the requirements of the applicable financial reporting framework.

29 The presentation of financial statements in conformity with the applicable financial reporting framework includes adequate disclosure of material matters. These matters relate to the form, arrangement, and content of the financial statements and their appended notes, including, for example, the terminology used, the amount of detail given, the classification of items in the statements, and the basis of amounts set forth. The auditor considers whether the entity has disclosed a particular matter appropriately in light of the circumstances and facts of which the auditor is aware at the time.

Objectives and Strategies and Related Business Risks

30 **The auditor should obtain an understanding of the entity's objectives and strategies, and the related business risks that may result in material misstatement of the financial statements.** The entity conducts its business in the context of industry, regulatory and other internal and external factors. To respond to these factors, the entity's management or those charged with governance define objectives, which are the overall plans for the entity. Strategies are the operational approaches by which management intends to achieve its objectives. Business risks result from significant conditions, events, circumstances, actions or inactions that could adversely affect the entity's ability to achieve its objectives and execute its strategies, or through the setting of inappropriate objectives and strategies. Just as the external environment changes, the conduct of the entity's business is also dynamic and the entity's strategies and objectives change over time.

31 Business risk is broader than the risk of material misstatement of the financial statements, though it includes the latter. Business risk particularly may arise from change or complexity, though a failure to recognize the need for change may also give rise to risk. Change may arise, for example, from the development of new products that may fail; from an inadequate market, even if successfully developed; or from flaws that may result in liabilities and reputational risk. An understanding of business risks increases the likelihood of identifying risks of material misstatement. However, the auditor does not have a responsibility to identify or assess all business risks.

32 Most business risks will eventually have financial consequences and, therefore, an effect on the financial statements. However, not all business risks give rise to risks of material misstatement. A business risk may have an immediate consequence for the risk of misstatement for classes of transactions, account balances, and disclosures at the assertion level or the financial statements as a whole. For example, the business risk arising from a contracting customer base due to industry consolidation may increase the risk of misstatement associated with the valuation of receivables. However, the same risk, particularly in combination with a contracting economy, may also have a longer-term consequence, which the auditor considers when assessing the appropriateness of the going concern assumption. The auditor's consideration of whether a business risk may result in material misstatement is, therefore, made in light of the entity's circumstances. Examples of conditions and events that may indicate risks of material misstatement are given in Appendix 3.

33 Usually management identifies business risks and develops approaches to address them. Such a risk assessment process is part of internal control and is discussed in paragraphs 76-79.

toward hiring competent financial, accounting, and IT personnel may not mitigate a strong bias by top management to overstate earnings. Changes in the control environment may affect the relevance of information obtained in prior audits. For example, management's decision to commit additional resources for training and awareness of financial reporting activities may reduce the risk of errors in processing financial information. Alternatively, management's failure to commit sufficient resources to address security risks presented by IT may adversely affect internal control by allowing improper changes to be made to computer programs or to data, or by allowing unauthorized transactions to be processed.

The existence of a satisfactory control environment can be a positive factor when the auditor assesses the risks of material misstatement and as explained in paragraph 5 of ISA (UK and Ireland) 330, influences the nature, timing, and extent of the auditor's further procedures. In particular, it may help reduce the risk of fraud, although a satisfactory control environment is not an absolute deterrent to fraud. Conversely, weaknesses in the control environment may undermine the effectiveness of controls and therefore be negative factors in the auditor's assessment of the risks of material misstatement, in particular in relation to fraud. 74

The control environment in itself does not prevent, or detect and correct, a material misstatement in classes of transactions, account balances, and disclosures and related assertions. The auditor, therefore, ordinarily considers the effect of other components along with the control environment when assessing the risks of material misstatement; for example, the monitoring of controls and the operation of specific control activities. 75

The Entity's Risk Assessment Process

The auditor should obtain an understanding of the entity's process for identifying business risks relevant to financial reporting objectives and deciding about actions to address those risks, and the results thereof. The process is described as the "entity's risk assessment process" and forms the basis for how management determines the risks to be managed. 76

In evaluating the design and implementation of the entity's risk assessment process, the auditor determines how management identifies business risks relevant to financial reporting, estimates the significance of the risks, assesses the likelihood of their occurrence, and decides upon actions to manage them. If the entity's risk assessment process is appropriate to the circumstances, it assists the auditor in identifying risks of material misstatement. 77

The auditor inquires about business risks that management has identified and considers whether they may result in material misstatement. During the audit, the auditor may identify risks of material misstatement that management failed to identify. In such cases, the auditor considers whether there was an underlying risk of a kind that should have been identified by the entity's risk assessment process, and if so, why that process failed to do so and whether the process is appropriate to its circumstances. If, as a result, the auditor judges that there is a material weakness in the entity's risk assessment process, the auditor communicates to those charged with governance as required by paragraph 120. 78

In a smaller entity, management may not have a formal risk assessment process described in paragraph 76. For such entities, the auditor discusses with management how risks to the business are identified by management and how they are

Information System, Including the Related Business Processes, Relevant to Financial Reporting, and Communication

80   The information system relevant to financial reporting objectives, which includes the accounting system, consists of the procedures and records established to initiate, record, process, and report entity transactions (as well as events and conditions) and to maintain accountability for the related assets, liabilities, and equity.

81   **The auditor should obtain an understanding of the information system, including the related business processes, relevant to financial reporting, including the following areas:**
   - **The classes of transactions in the entity's operations that are significant to the financial statements.**
   - **The procedures, within both IT and manual systems, by which those transactions are initiated, recorded, processed and reported in the financial statements.**
   - **The related accounting records, whether electronic or manual, supporting information, and specific accounts in the financial statements, in respect of initiating, recording, processing and reporting transactions.**
   - **How the information system captures events and conditions, other than classes of transactions, that are significant to the financial statements.**
   - **The financial reporting process used to prepare the entity's financial statements, including significant accounting estimates and disclosures.**

82   In obtaining this understanding, the auditor considers the procedures used to transfer information from transaction processing systems to general ledger or financial reporting systems. The auditor also understands the entity's procedures to capture information relevant to financial reporting for events and conditions other than transactions, such as the depreciation and amortization of assets and changes in the recoverability of accounts receivables.

83   An entity's information system typically includes the use of standard journal entries that are required on a recurring basis to record transactions such as sales, purchases, and cash disbursements in the general ledger, or to record accounting estimates that are periodically made by management, such as changes in the estimate of uncollectible accounts receivable.

84   An entity's financial reporting process also includes the use of non-standard journal entries to record non-recurring, unusual transactions or adjustments. Examples of such entries include consolidating adjustments and entries for a business combination or disposal or non-recurring estimates such as an asset impairment. In manual, paper-based general ledger systems, non-standard journal entries may be identified through inspection of ledgers, journals, and supporting documentation. However, when automated procedures are used to maintain the general ledger and prepare financial statements, such entries may exist only in electronic form and may be more easily identified through the use of computer-assisted audit techniques.

85   Preparation of the entity's financial statements include procedures that are designed to ensure information required to be disclosed by the applicable financial reporting framework is accumulated, recorded, processed, summarized and appropriately reported in the financial statements.

86   In obtaining an understanding, the auditor considers risks of material misstatement associated with inappropriate override of controls over journal entries and the controls surrounding non-standard journal entries. For example, automated processes and controls may reduce the risk of inadvertent error but do not overcome the risk that individuals may inappropriately override such automated processes, for

example, by changing the amounts being automatically passed to the general ledger or financial reporting system. Furthermore, the auditor maintains an awareness that when IT is used to transfer information automatically, there may be little or no visible evidence of such intervention in the information systems.

The auditor also understands how the incorrect processing of transactions is resolved, for example, whether there is an automated suspense file and how it is used by the entity to ensure that suspense items are cleared out on a timely basis, and how system overrides or bypasses to controls are processed and accounted for. 87

The auditor obtains an understanding of the entity's information system relevant to financial reporting in a manner that is appropriate to the entity's circumstances. This includes obtaining an understanding of how transactions originate within the entity's business processes. An entity's business processes are the activities designed to develop, purchase, produce, sell and distribute an entity's products and services; ensure compliance with laws and regulations; and record information, including accounting and financial reporting information. 88

The auditor should understand how the entity communicates financial reporting roles and responsibilities and significant matters relating to financial reporting. Communication involves providing an understanding of individual roles and responsibilities pertaining to internal control over financial reporting and may take such forms as policy manuals and financial reporting manuals. It includes the extent to which personnel understand how their activities in the financial reporting information system relate to the work of others and the means of reporting exceptions to an appropriate higher level within the entity. Open communication channels help ensure that exceptions are reported and acted on. The auditor's understanding of communication pertaining to financial reporting matters also includes communications between management and those charged with governance, particularly the audit committee, as well as external communications such as those with regulatory authorities. 89

Control Activities

The auditor should obtain a sufficient understanding of control activities to assess the risks of material misstatement at the assertion level and to design further audit procedures responsive to assessed risks. Control activities are the policies and procedures that help ensure that management directives are carried out; for example, that necessary actions are taken to address risks that threaten the achievement of the entity's objectives. Control activities, whether within IT or manual systems, have various objectives and are applied at various organizational and functional levels. Examples of specific control activities include those relating to the following: 90

- Authorization.
- Performance reviews.
- Information processing.
- Physical controls.
- Segregation of duties.

In obtaining an understanding of control activities, the auditor's primary consideration is whether, and how, a specific control activity, individually or in combination with others, prevents, or detects and corrects, material misstatements in classes of transactions, account balances, or disclosures. Control activities relevant to the audit are those for which the auditor considers it necessary to obtain an understanding in order to assess risks of material misstatement at the assertion level and to design and perform further audit procedures responsive to the assessed risks. 91

An audit does not require an understanding of all the control activities related to each significant class of transactions, account balance, and disclosure in the financial statements or to every assertion relevant to them. The auditor's emphasis is on identifying and obtaining an understanding of control activities that address the areas where the auditor considers that material misstatements are more likely to occur. When multiple control activities achieve the same objective, it is unnecessary to obtain an understanding of each of the control activities related to such objective.

92   The auditor considers the knowledge about the presence or absence of control activities obtained from the understanding of the other components of internal control in determining whether it is necessary to devote additional attention to obtaining an understanding of control activities. In considering whether control activities are relevant to the audit, the auditor considers the risks the auditor has identified that may give rise to material misstatement. Also, control activities are relevant to the audit if the auditor is required to evaluate them as discussed in paragraphs 113 and 115.

93   **The auditor should obtain an understanding of how the entity has responded to risks arising from IT.** The use of IT affects the way that control activities are implemented. The auditor considers whether the entity has responded adequately to the risks arising from IT by establishing effective general IT-controls and application controls. From the auditor's perspective, controls over IT systems are effective when they maintain the integrity of information and the security of the data such systems process.

94   General IT-controls are policies and procedures that relate to many applications and support the effective functioning of application controls by helping to ensure the continued proper operation of information systems. General IT-controls that maintain the integrity of information and security of data commonly include controls over the following:

- Data center and network operations.
- System software acquisition, change and maintenance.
- Access security.
- Application system acquisition, development, and maintenance.

They are generally implemented to deal with the risks referred to in paragraph 60 above.

95   Application controls are manual or automated procedures that typically operate at a business process level. Application controls can be preventative or detective in nature and are designed to ensure the integrity of the accounting records. Accordingly, application controls relate to procedures used to initiate, record, process and report transactions or other financial data. These controls help ensure that transactions occurred, are authorized, and are completely and accurately recorded and processed. Examples include edit checks of input data, and numerical sequence checks with manual follow-up of exception reports or correction at the point of data entry.

Monitoring of Controls

96   **The auditor should obtain an understanding of the major types of activities that the entity uses to monitor internal control over financial reporting, including those related to those control activities relevant to the audit, and how the entity initiates corrective actions to its controls.**

Monitoring of controls is a process to assess the effectiveness of internal control performance over time. It involves assessing the design and operation of controls on a timely basis and taking necessary corrective actions modified for changes in conditions. Management accomplishes monitoring of controls through ongoing activities, separate evaluations, or a combination of the two. Ongoing monitoring activities are often built into the normal recurring activities of an entity and include regular management and supervisory activities. 97

In many entities, internal auditors or personnel performing similar functions contribute to the monitoring of an entity's activities. See ISA (UK and Ireland) 610, "Considering the Work of Internal Auditing" for additional guidance. Management's monitoring activities may also include using information from communications from external parties such as customer complaints and regulator comments that may indicate problems or highlight areas in need of improvement. 98

Much of the information used in monitoring may be produced by the entity's information system. If management assumes that data used for monitoring are accurate without having a basis for that assumption, errors may exist in the information, potentially leading management to incorrect conclusions from its monitoring activities. The auditor obtains an understanding of the sources of the information related to the entity's monitoring activities, and the basis upon which management considers the information to be sufficiently reliable for the purpose. When the auditor intends to make use of the entity's information produced for monitoring activities, such as internal auditor's reports, the auditor considers whether the information provides a reliable basis and is sufficiently detailed for the auditor's purpose. 99

Assessing the Risks of Material Misstatement

The auditor should identify and assess the risks of material misstatement at the financial statement level, and at the assertion level for classes of transactions, account balances, and disclosures. For this purpose, the auditor: 100

- Identifies risks throughout the process of obtaining an understanding of the entity and its environment, including relevant controls that relate to the risks, and by considering the classes of transactions, account balances, and disclosures in the financial statements;
- Relates the identified risks to what can go wrong at the assertion level;
- Considers whether the risks are of a magnitude that could result in a material misstatement of the financial statements; and
- Considers the likelihood that the risks could result in a material misstatement of the financial statements.

The auditor uses information gathered by performing risk assessment procedures, including the audit evidence obtained in evaluating the design of controls and determining whether they have been implemented, as audit evidence to support the risk assessment. The auditor uses the risk assessment to determine the nature, timing, and extent of further audit procedures to be performed. 101

The auditor determines whether the identified risks of material misstatement relate to specific classes of transactions, account balances, and disclosures and related assertions, or whether they relate more pervasively to the financial statements as a whole and potentially affect many assertions. The latter risks (risks at the financial statement level) may derive in particular from a weak control environment. 102

103 The nature of the risks arising from a weak control environment is such that they are not likely to be confined to specific individual risks of material misstatement in particular classes of transactions, account balances, and disclosures. Rather, weaknesses such as management's lack of competence may have a more pervasive effect on the financial statements and may require an overall response by the auditor.

104 In making risk assessments, the auditor may identify the controls that are likely to prevent, or detect and correct, material misstatement in specific assertions. Generally, the auditor gains an understanding of controls and relates them to assertions in the context of processes and systems in which they exist. Doing so is useful because individual control activities often do not in themselves address a risk. Often only multiple control activities, together with other elements of internal control, will be sufficient to address a risk.

105 Conversely, some control activities may have a specific effect on an individual assertion embodied in a particular class of transactions or account balance. For example, the control activities that an entity established to ensure that its personnel are properly counting and recording the annual physical inventory relate directly to the existence and completeness assertions for the inventory account balance.

106 Controls can be either directly or indirectly related to an assertion. The more indirect the relationship, the less effective that control may be in preventing, or detecting and correcting, misstatements in that assertion. For example, a sales manager's review of a summary of sales activity for specific stores by region ordinarily is only indirectly related to the completeness assertion for sales revenue. Accordingly, it may be less effective in reducing risk for that assertion than controls more directly related to that assertion, such as matching shipping documents with billing documents.

107 The auditor's understanding of internal control may raise doubts about the auditability of an entity's financial statements. Concerns about the integrity of the entity's management may be so serious as to cause the auditor to conclude that the risk of management misrepresentation in the financial statements is such that an audit cannot be conducted. Also, concerns about the condition and reliability of an entity's records may cause the auditor to conclude that it is unlikely that sufficient appropriate audit evidence will be available to support an unqualified opinion on the financial statements. In such circumstances, the auditor considers a qualification or disclaimer of opinion, but in some cases the auditor's only recourse may be to withdraw from the engagement.

Significant Risks That Require Special Audit Consideration

108 **As part of the risk assessment as described in paragraph 100, the auditor should determine which of the risks identified are, in the auditor's judgment, risks that require special audit consideration (such risks are defined as "significant risks").** In addition, ISA (UK and Ireland) 330, paragraphs 44 and 51 describe the consequences for further audit procedures of identifying a risk as significant.

109 The determination of significant risks, which arise on most audits, is a matter for the auditor's professional judgment. In exercising this judgment, the auditor excludes the effect of identified controls related to the risk to determine whether the nature of the risk, the likely magnitude of the potential misstatement including the possibility that the risk may give rise to multiple misstatements, and the likelihood of the risk occurring are such that they require special audit consideration. Routine, non-complex transactions that are subject to systematic processing are less likely to give rise to significant risks because they have lower inherent risks. On the other hand,

significant risks are often derived from business risks that may result in a material misstatement. In considering the nature of the risks, the auditor considers a number of matters, including the following:

- Whether the risk is a risk of fraud.
- Whether the risk is related to recent significant economic, accounting or other developments and, therefore, requires specific attention.
- The complexity of transactions.
- Whether the risk involves significant transactions with related parties.
- The degree of subjectivity in the measurement of financial information related to the risk especially those involving a wide range of measurement uncertainty.
- Whether the risk involves significant transactions that are outside the normal course of business for the entity, or that otherwise appear to be unusual.

Significant risks often relate to significant non-routine transactions and judgmental matters. Non-routine transactions are transactions that are unusual, either due to size or nature, and that therefore occur infrequently. Judgmental matters may include the development of accounting estimates for which there is significant measurement uncertainty. 110

Risks of material misstatement may be greater for risks relating to significant non-routine transactions arising from matters such as the following: 111

- Greater management intervention to specify the accounting treatment.
- Greater manual intervention for data collection and processing.
- Complex calculations or accounting principles.
- The nature of non-routine transactions, which may make it difficult for the entity to implement effective controls over the risks.

Risks of material misstatement may be greater for risks relating to significant judgmental matters that require the development of accounting estimates, arising from matters such as the following: 112

- Accounting principles for accounting estimates or revenue recognition may be subject to differing interpretation.
- Required judgment may be subjective, complex or require assumptions about the effects of future events, for example, judgment about fair value.

For significant risks, to the extent the auditor has not already done so, the auditor should evaluate the design of the entity's related controls, including relevant control activities, and determine whether they have been implemented. An understanding of the entity's controls related to significant risks is required to provide the auditor with adequate information to develop an effective audit approach. Management ought to be aware of significant risks; however, risks relating to significant non-routine or judgmental matters are often less likely to be subject to routine controls. Therefore, the auditor's understanding of whether the entity has designed and implemented controls for such significant risks includes whether and how management responds to the risks and whether control activities such as a review of assumptions by senior management or experts, formal processes for estimations or approval by those charged with governance have been implemented to address the risks. For example, where there are one-off events such as the receipt of notice of a significant lawsuit, consideration of the entity's response will include such matters as whether it has been referred to appropriate experts (such as internal or external legal counsel), whether an assessment has been made of the potential effect, and how it is proposed that the circumstances are to be disclosed in the financial statements. 113

114 If management has not appropriately responded by implementing controls over significant risks and if, as a result, the auditor judges that there is a material weakness in the entity's internal control, the auditor communicates this matter to those charged with governance as required by paragraph 120. In these circumstances, the auditor also considers the implications for the auditor's risk assessment.

Risks for Which Substantive Procedures Alone Do Not Provide Sufficient Appropriate Audit Evidence

115 As part of the risk assessment as described in paragraph 100, the auditor should evaluate the design and determine the implementation of the entity's controls, including relevant control activities, over those risks for which, in the auditor's judgment, it is not possible or practicable to reduce the risks of material misstatement at the assertion level to an acceptably low level with audit evidence obtained only from substantive procedures. The consequences for further audit procedures of identifying such risks are described in paragraph 25 of ISA (UK and Ireland) 330.

116 The understanding of the entity's information system relevant to financial reporting enables the auditor to identify risks of material misstatement that relate directly to the recording of routine classes of transactions or account balances, and the preparation of reliable financial statements; these include risks of inaccurate or incomplete processing. Ordinarily, such risks relate to significant classes of transactions such as an entity's revenue, purchases, and cash receipts or cash payments.

117 The characteristics of routine day-to-day business transactions often permit highly automated processing with little or no manual intervention. In such circumstances, it may not be possible to perform only substantive procedures in relation to the risk. For example, in circumstances where a significant amount of an entity's information is initiated, recorded, processed, or reported electronically such as in an integrated system, the auditor may determine that it is not possible to design effective substantive procedures that by themselves would provide sufficient appropriate audit evidence that relevant classes of transactions or account balances, are not materially misstated. In such cases, audit evidence may be available only in electronic form, and its sufficiency and appropriateness usually depend on the effectiveness of controls over its accuracy and completeness. Furthermore, the potential for improper initiation or alteration of information to occur and not be detected may be greater if information is initiated, recorded, processed or reported only in electronic form and appropriate controls are not operating effectively.

118 Examples of situations where the auditor may find it impossible to design effective substantive procedures that by themselves provide sufficient appropriate audit evidence that certain assertions are not materially misstated include the following:

- An entity that conducts its business using IT to initiate orders for the purchase and delivery of goods based on predetermined rules of what to order and in what quantities and to pay the related accounts payable based on system-generated decisions initiated upon the confirmed receipt of goods and terms of payment. No other documentation of orders placed or goods received is produced or maintained, other than through the IT system.
- An entity that provides services to customers via electronic media (for example, an Internet service provider or a telecommunications company) and uses IT to create a log of the services provided to its customers, initiate and process its billings for the services and automatically record such amounts in electronic accounting records that are part of the system used to produce the entity's financial statements.

Revision of Risk Assessment

The auditor's assessment of the risks of material misstatement at the assertion level is based on available audit evidence and may change during the course of the audit as additional audit evidence is obtained. In particular, the risk assessment may be based on an expectation that controls are operating effectively to prevent, or detect and correct, a material misstatement at the assertion level. In performing tests of controls to obtain audit evidence about their operating effectiveness, the auditor may obtain audit evidence that controls are not operating effectively at relevant times during the audit. Similarly, in performing substantive procedures the auditor may detect misstatements in amounts or frequency greater than is consistent with the auditor's risk assessments. In circumstances where the auditor obtains audit evidence from performing further audit procedures that tends to contradict the audit evidence on which the auditor originally based the assessment, the auditor revises the assessment and modifies the further planned audit procedures accordingly. See paragraphs 66 and 70 of ISA (UK and Ireland) 330 for further guidance.

Communicating With Those Charged With Governance and Management

The auditor should make those charged with governance or management aware, as soon as practicable, and at an appropriate level of responsibility, of material weaknesses in the design or implementation of internal control which have come to the auditor's attention.

If the auditor identifies risks of material misstatement which the entity has either not controlled, or for which the relevant control is inadequate, or if in the auditor's judgment there is a material weakness in the entity's risk assessment process, then the auditor includes such internal control weaknesses in the communication of audit matters of governance interest. See ISA (UK and Ireland) 260, "Communications of Audit Matters with Those Charged with Governance."

Documentation

The auditor should document:

(a) The discussion among the engagement team regarding the susceptibility of the entity's financial statements to material misstatement due to error or fraud, and the significant decisions reached;
(b) Key elements of the understanding obtained regarding each of the aspects of the entity and its environment identified in paragraph 20, including each of the internal control components identified in paragraph 43, to assess the risks of material misstatement of the financial statements; the sources of information from which the understanding was obtained; and the risk assessment procedures;
(c) The identified and assessed risks of material misstatement at the financial statement level and at the assertion level as required by paragraph 100; and
(d) The risks identified and related controls evaluated as a result of the requirements in paragraphs 113 and 115.

The manner in which these matters are documented is for the auditor to determine using professional judgment. In particular, the results of the risk assessment may be documented separately, or may be documented as part of the auditor's documentation of further procedures (see paragraph 73 of ISA (UK and Ireland) 330 for additional guidance). Examples of common techniques, used alone or in combination include narrative descriptions, questionnaires, check lists and flow charts. Such techniques may also be useful in documenting the auditor's assessment of the risks of material misstatement at the overall financial statement and assertions level. The form and extent of this documentation is influenced by the nature, size and complexity of the entity and its internal control, availability of information from the entity and the specific audit methodology and technology used in the course of the audit. For example, documentation of the understanding of a complex information system in which a large volume of transactions are electronically initiated, recorded, processed, or reported may include flowcharts, questionnaires, or decision tables. For an information system making limited or no use of IT or for which few transactions are processed (for example, long-term debt), documentation in the form of a memorandum may be sufficient. Ordinarily, the more complex the entity and the more extensive the audit procedures performed by the auditor, the more extensive the auditor's documentation will be. ISA (UK and Ireland) 230, "Documentation" provides guidance regarding documentation in the context of the audit of financial statements.

Effective Date

124   This ISA (UK and Ireland) is effective for audits of financial statements for periods commencing on or after 15 December 2004.

Public Sector Perspective

> Additional guidance for auditors of public sector bodies in the UK and Ireland is given in:
>
> - Practice Note 10 "Audit of Financial Statements of Public Sector Entities in the United Kingdom (Revised)"
> - Practice Note 10(I) "The Audit of Central Government Financial Statements in Ireland"

1   *When carrying out audits of public sector entities, the auditor takes into account the legislative framework and any other relevant regulations, ordinances or ministerial directives that affect the audit mandate and any other special auditing requirements. Therefore in obtaining an understanding of the regulatory framework as required in paragraph 22 of this ISA (UK and Ireland), auditors will have regard to the legislation and proper authority governing the operation of an entity. Similarly in respect of paragraph 30 of this ISA (UK and Ireland) the auditor should be aware that the "management objectives" of public sector entities may be influenced by concerns regarding public accountability and may include objectives which have their source in legislation, regulations, government ordinances, and ministerial directives.*

2   *Paragraphs 47-53 of this ISA UK and Ireland) explain the controls relevant to the audit. Public sector auditors often have additional responsibilities with respect to internal controls, for example to report on compliance with an established Code of Practice. Public sector auditors can also have responsibilities to report on the compliance with legislative authorities. Their review of internal controls may be broader and more detailed.*

3   *Paragraphs 120 and 121 of this ISA (UK and Ireland) deals with communication of weaknesses. There may be additional communication or reporting requirements for*

public sector auditors. For example, internal control weaknesses may have to be reported to the legislature or other governing body.

Appendix 1 – Understanding the Entity and Its Environment

This appendix provides additional guidance on matters the auditor may consider when obtaining an understanding of the industry, regulatory, and other external factors that affect the entity, including the applicable financial reporting framework; the nature of the entity; objectives and strategies and related business risks; and measurement and review of the entity's financial performance. The examples provided cover a broad range of matters applicable to many engagements; however, not all matters are relevant to every engagement and the list of examples is not necessarily complete. Additional guidance on internal control is contained in Appendix 2.

Industry, Regulatory and Other External Factors, Including The Applicable Financial Reporting Framework

Examples of matters an auditor may consider include the following:

- Industry conditions
    - The market and competition, including demand, capacity, and price competition
    - Cyclical or seasonal activity
    - Product technology relating to the entity's products
    - Energy supply and cost
- Regulatory environment
    - Accounting principles and industry specific practices
    - Regulatory framework for a regulated industry
    - Legislation and regulation that significantly affect the entity's operations
        - Regulatory requirements
        - Direct supervisory activities
    - Taxation (corporate and other)
    - Government policies currently affecting the conduct of the entity's business
        - Monetary, including foreign exchange controls
        - Fiscal
        - Financial incentives (for example, government aid programs)
        - Tariffs, trade restrictions
    - Environmental requirements affecting the industry and the entity's business
- Other external factors currently affecting the entity's business
    - General level of economic activity (for example, recession, growth)
    - Interest rates and availability of financing
    - Inflation, currency revaluation

Nature of the Entity

Examples of matters an auditor may consider include the following:

Business Operations

- Nature of revenue sources (for example, manufacturer, wholesaler, banking, insurance or other financial services, import/export trading, utility, transportation, and technology products and services)
- Products or services and markets (for example, major customers and contracts, terms of payment, profit margins, market share, competitors, exports, pricing policies, reputation of products, warranties, order book, trends, marketing strategy and objectives, manufacturing processes)
- Conduct of operations (for example, stages and methods of production, business segments, delivery or products and services, details of declining or expanding operations)
- Alliances, joint ventures, and outsourcing activities

Involvement in electronic commerce, including Internet sales and marketing activities

- Geographic dispersion and industry segmentation
- Location of production facilities, warehouses, and offices
- Key customers
- Important suppliers of goods and services (for example, long-term contracts, stability of supply, terms of payment, imports, methods of delivery such as "just-in-time")
- Employment (for example, by location, supply, wage levels, union contracts, pension and other post employment benefits, stock option or incentive bonus arrangements, and government regulation related to employment matters)
- Research and development activities and expenditures
- Transactions with related parties

Investments

- Acquisitions, mergers or disposals of business activities (planned or recently executed)
- Investments and dispositions of securities and loans
- Capital investment activities, including investments in plant and equipment and technology, and any recent or planned changes
- Investments in non-consolidated entities, including partnerships, joint ventures and special-purpose entities

Financing

- Group structure – major subsidiaries and associated entities, including consolidated and non-consolidated structures
- Debt structure, including covenants, restrictions, guarantees, and off-balance-sheet financing arrangements
- Leasing of property, plant or equipment for use in the business
- Beneficial owners (local, foreign, business reputation and experience)
- Related parties
- Use of derivative financial instruments

Financial Reporting

- Accounting principles and industry specific practices
- Revenue recognition practices
- Accounting for fair values

- Inventories (for example, locations, quantities)
- Foreign currency assets, liabilities and transactions
- Industry-specific significant categories (for example, loans and investments for banks, accounts receivable and inventory for manufacturers, research and development for pharmaceuticals)
- Accounting for unusual or complex transactions including those in controversial or emerging areas (for example, accounting for stock-based compensation)
- Financial statement presentation and disclosure

Objectives and Strategies and Related Business Risks

Examples of matters an auditor may consider include the following:

- Existence of objectives (*i.e.*, how the entity addresses industry, regulatory and other external factors) relating to, for example, the following:
  - Industry developments (a potential related business risk might be, for example, that the entity does not have the personnel or expertise to deal with the changes in the industry)
  - New products and services (a potential related business risk might be, for example, that there is increased product liability)
  - Expansion of the business (a potential related business risk might be, for example, that the demand has not been accurately estimated)
  - New accounting requirements (a potential related business risk might be, for example, incomplete or improper implementation, or increased costs)
  - Regulatory requirements (a potential related business risk might be, for example, that there is increased legal exposure)
  - Current and prospective financing requirements (a potential related business risk might be, for example, the loss of financing due to the entity's inability to meet requirements)
  - Use of IT (a potential related business risk might be, for example, that systems and processes are incompatible)
- Effects of implementing a strategy, particularly any effects that will lead to new accounting requirements (a potential related business risk might be, for example, incomplete or improper implementation)

Measurement and review of the Entity's Financial Performance

Examples of matters an auditor may consider include the following:

- Key ratios and operating statistics
- Key performance indicators
- Employee performance measures and incentive compensation policies
- Trends
- Use of forecasts, budgets and variance analysis
- Analyst reports and credit rating reports
- Competitor analysis
- Period-on-period financial performance (revenue growth, profitability, leverage)

Appendix 2 – Internal Control Components

As set out in paragraph 43 and described in paragraphs 67-99, internal control consists of the following components:

(a) The control environment;
(b) The entity's risk assessment process;

(c) The information system, including the related business processes, relevant to financial reporting, and communication;
(d) Control activities; and
(e) Monitoring of controls.

This appendix further explains the above components as they relate to a financial statement audit.

Control Environment

2   The control environment includes the attitudes, awareness, and actions of management and those charged with governance concerning the entity's internal control and its importance in the entity. The control environment also includes the governance and management functions and sets the tone of an organization, influencing the control consciousness of its people. It is the foundation for effective internal control, providing discipline and structure.

3   The control environment encompasses the following elements:
   (a) *Communication and enforcement of integrity and ethical values.* The effectiveness of controls cannot rise above the integrity and ethical values of the people who create, administer, and monitor them. Integrity and ethical values are essential elements of the control environment which influence the effectiveness of the design, administration, and monitoring of other components of internal control. Integrity and ethical behavior are the product of the entity's ethical and behavioral standards, how they are communicated, and how they are reinforced in practice. They include management's actions to remove or reduce incentives and temptations that might prompt personnel to engage in dishonest, illegal, or unethical acts. They also include the communication of entity values and behavioral standards to personnel through policy statements and codes of conduct and by example.
   (b) *Commitment to competence.* Competence is the knowledge and skills necessary to accomplish tasks that define the individual's job. Commitment to competence includes management's consideration of the competence levels for particular jobs and how those levels translate into requisite skills and knowledge.
   (c) *Participation by those charged with governance.* An entity's control consciousness is influenced significantly by those charged with governance. Attributes of those charged with governance include independence from management, their experience and stature, the extent of their involvement and scrutiny of activities, the appropriateness of their actions, the information they receive, the degree to which difficult questions are raised and pursued with management, and their interaction with internal and external auditors. The importance of responsibilities of those charged with governance is recognized in codes of practice and other regulations or guidance produced for the benefit of those charged with governance. Other responsibilities of those charged with governance include oversight of the design and effective operation of whistle blower procedures and the process for reviewing the effectiveness of the entity's internal control.
   (d) *Management's philosophy and operating style.* Management's philosophy and operating style encompass a broad range of characteristics. Such characteristics may include the following: management's approach to taking and monitoring business risks; management's attitudes and actions toward financial reporting (conservative or aggressive selection from available alternative accounting principles, and conscientiousness and conservatism with which accounting estimates are developed); and management's attitudes toward information processing and accounting functions and personnel.

(e) *Organizational structure.* An entity's organizational structure provides the framework within which its activities for achieving entity-wide objectives are planned, executed, controlled, and reviewed. Establishing a relevant organizational structure includes considering key areas of authority and responsibility and appropriate lines of reporting. An entity develops an organizational structure suited to its needs. The appropriateness of an entity's organizational structure depends, in part, on its size and the nature of its activities.
(f) *Assignment of authority and responsibility.* This factor includes how authority and responsibility for operating activities are assigned and how reporting relationships and authorization hierarchies are established. It also includes policies relating to appropriate business practices, knowledge and experience of key personnel, and resources provided for carrying out duties. In addition, it includes policies and communications directed at ensuring that all personnel understand the entity's objectives, know how their individual actions interrelate and contribute to those objectives, and recognize how and for what they will be held accountable.
(g) *Human resource policies and practices.* Human resource policies and practices relate to recruitment, orientation, training, evaluating, counseling, promoting, compensating, and remedial actions. For example, standards for recruiting the most qualified individuals – with emphasis on educational background, prior work experience, past accomplishments, and evidence of integrity and ethical behavior – demonstrate an entity's commitment to competent and trustworthy people. Training policies that communicate prospective roles and responsibilities and include practices such as training schools and seminars illustrate expected levels of performance and behavior. Promotions driven by periodic performance appraisals demonstrate the entity's commitment to the advancement of qualified personnel to higher levels of responsibility.

Application to Small Entities

Small entities may implement the control environment elements differently than larger entities. For example, small entities might not have a written code of conduct but, instead, develop a culture that emphasizes the importance of integrity and ethical behavior through oral communication and by management example. Similarly, those charged with governance in small entities may not include an independent or outside member.

Entity's Risk Assessment Process

An entity's risk assessment process is its process for identifying and responding to business risks and the results thereof. For financial reporting purposes, the entity's risk assessment process includes how management identifies risks relevant to the preparation of financial statements that give a true and fair view (or are presented fairly, in all material respects) in accordance with the entity's applicable financial reporting framework, estimates their significance, assesses the likelihood of their occurrence, and decides upon actions to manage them. For example, the entity's risk assessment process may address how the entity considers the possibility of unrecorded transactions or identifies and analyzes significant estimates recorded in the financial statements. Risks relevant to reliable financial reporting also relate to specific events or transactions.

Risks relevant to financial reporting include external and internal events and circumstances that may occur and adversely affect an entity's ability to initiate, record, process, and report financial data consistent with the assertions of management in the financial statements. Once risks are identified, management considers their significance, the likelihood of their occurrence, and how they should be managed. Management may initiate plans, programs, or actions to address specific risks or it may decide to accept a risk because of cost or other considerations. Risks can arise or change due to circumstances such as the following:

- *Changes in operating environment.* Changes in the regulatory or operating environment can result in changes in competitive pressures and significantly different risks.
- *New personnel.* New personnel may have a different focus on or understanding of internal control.
- *New or revamped information systems.* Significant and rapid changes in information systems can change the risk relating to internal control.
- *Rapid growth.* Significant and rapid expansion of operations can strain controls and increase the risk of a breakdown in controls.
- *New technology.* Incorporating new technologies into production processes or information systems may change the risk associated with internal control.
- *New business models, products, or activities.* Entering into business areas or transactions with which an entity has little experience may introduce new risks associated with internal control.
- *Corporate restructurings.* Restructurings may be accompanied by staff reductions and changes in supervision and segregation of duties that may change the risk associated with internal control.
- *Expanded foreign operations.* The expansion or acquisition of foreign operations carries new and often unique risks that may affect internal control, for example, additional or changed risks from foreign currency transactions.
- *New accounting pronouncements.* Adoption of new accounting principles or changing accounting principles may affect risks in preparing financial statements.

Application to Small Entities

7   The basic concepts of the entity's risk assessment process are relevant to every entity, regardless of size, but the risk assessment process is likely to be less formal and less structured in small entities than in larger ones. All entities should have established financial reporting objectives, but they may be recognized implicitly rather than explicitly in small entities. Management may be aware of risks related to these objectives without the use of a formal process but through direct personal involvement with employees and outside parties.

Information System, Including the Related Business Processes, Relevant To Financial Reporting, And Communication

8   An information system consists of infrastructure (physical and hardware components), software, people, procedures, and data. Infrastructure and software will be absent, or have less significance, in systems that are exclusively or primarily manual. Many information systems make extensive use of information technology (IT).

9   The information system relevant to financial reporting objectives, which includes the financial reporting system, consists of the procedures and records established to initiate, record, process, and report entity transactions (as well as events and conditions) and to maintain accountability for the related assets, liabilities, and equity. Transactions may be initiated manually or automatically by programmed procedures. Recording includes identifying and capturing the relevant information for transactions or events. Processing includes functions such as edit and validation, calculation, measurement, valuation, summarization, and reconciliation, whether

performed by automated or manual procedures. Reporting relates to the preparation of financial reports as well as other information, in electronic or printed format, that the entity uses in measuring and reviewing the entity's financial performance and in other functions. The quality of system-generated information affects management's ability to make appropriate decisions in managing and controlling the entity's activities and to prepare reliable financial reports.

Accordingly, an information system encompasses methods and records that:

- Identify and record all valid transactions.
- Describe on a timely basis the transactions in sufficient detail to permit proper classification of transactions for financial reporting.
- Measure the value of transactions in a manner that permits recording their proper monetary value in the financial statements.
- Determine the time period in which transactions occurred to permit recording of transactions in the proper accounting period.
- Present properly the transactions and related disclosures in the financial statements.

Communication involves providing an understanding of individual roles and responsibilities pertaining to internal control over financial reporting. It includes the extent to which personnel understand how their activities in the financial reporting information system relate to the work of others and the means of reporting exceptions to an appropriate higher level within the entity. Open communication channels help ensure that exceptions are reported and acted on.

Communication takes such forms as policy manuals, accounting and financial reporting manuals, and memoranda. Communication also can be made electronically, orally, and through the actions of management.

Application to Small Entities

Information systems and related business processes relevant to financial reporting in small entities are likely to be less formal than in larger entities, but their role is just as significant. Small entities with active management involvement may not need extensive descriptions of accounting procedures, sophisticated accounting records, or written policies. Communication may be less formal and easier to achieve in a small entity than in a larger entity due to the small entity's size and fewer levels as well as management's greater visibility and availability.

Control Activities

Control activities are the policies and procedures that help ensure that management directives are carried out, for example, that necessary actions are taken to address risks that threaten the achievement of the entity's objectives. Control activities, whether within IT or manual systems, have various objectives and are applied at various organizational and functional levels.

Generally, control activities that may be relevant to an audit may be categorized as policies and procedures that pertain to the following:

- *Performance reviews.* These control activities include reviews and analyses of actual performance versus budgets, forecasts, and prior period performance; relating different sets of data – operating or financial – to one another, together with analyses of the relationships and investigative and corrective actions; comparing internal data with external sources of information; and review of

functional or activity performance, such as a bank's consumer loan manager's review of reports by branch, region, and loan type for loan approvals and collections.
- *Information processing.* A variety of controls are performed to check accuracy, completeness, and authorization of transactions. The two broad groupings of information systems control activities are application controls and general IT-controls. Application controls apply to the processing of individual applications. These controls help ensure that transactions occurred, are authorized, and are completely and accurately recorded and processed. Examples of application controls include checking the arithmetical accuracy of records, maintaining and reviewing accounts and trial balances, automated controls such as edit checks of input data and numerical sequence checks, and manual follow-up of exception reports. General IT-controls are polices and procedures that relate to many applications and support the effective functioning of application controls by helping to ensure the continued proper operation of information systems. General IT-controls commonly include controls over data center and network operations; system software acquisition, change and maintenance; access security; and application system acquisition, development, and maintenance. These controls apply to mainframe, miniframe, and end-user environments. Examples of such general IT-controls are program change controls, controls that restrict access to programs or data, controls over the implementation of new releases of packaged software applications, and controls over system software that restrict access to or monitor the use of system utilities that could change financial data or records without leaving an audit trail.
- *Physical controls.* These activities encompass the physical security of assets, including adequate safeguards such as secured facilities over access to assets and records; authorization for access to computer programs and data files; and periodic counting and comparison with amounts shown on control records (for example comparing the results of cash, security and inventory counts with accounting records). The extent to which physical controls intended to prevent theft of assets are relevant to the reliability of financial statement preparation, and therefore the audit, depends on circumstances such as when assets are highly susceptible to misappropriation. For example, these controls would ordinarily not be relevant when any inventory losses would be detected pursuant to periodic physical inspection and recorded in the financial statements. However, if for financial reporting purposes management relies solely on perpetual inventory records, the physical security controls would be relevant to the audit.
- *Segregation of duties.* Assigning different people the responsibilities of authorizing transactions, recording transactions, and maintaining custody of assets is intended to reduce the opportunities to allow any person to be in a position to both perpetrate and conceal errors or fraud in the normal course of the person's duties. Examples of segregation of duties include reporting, reviewing and approving reconciliations, and approval and control of documents.

16 Certain control activities may depend on the existence of appropriate higher level policies established by management or those charged with governance. For example, authorization controls may be delegated under established guidelines, such as investment criteria set by those charged with governance; alternatively, non-routine transactions such as major acquisitions or divestments may require specific high level approval, including in some cases that of shareholders.

Application to Small Entities

17 The concepts underlying control activities in small entities are likely to be similar to those in larger entities, but the formality with which they operate varies. Further,

small entities may find that certain types of control activities are not relevant because of controls applied by management. For example, management's retention of authority for approving credit sales, significant purchases, and draw-downs on lines of credit can provide strong control over those activities, lessening or removing the need for more detailed control activities. An appropriate segregation of duties often appears to present difficulties in small entities. Even companies that have only a few employees, however, may be able to assign their responsibilities to achieve appropriate segregation or, if that is not possible, to use management oversight of the incompatible activities to achieve control objectives.

Monitoring of Controls

An important management responsibility is to establish and maintain internal control on an ongoing basis. Management's monitoring of controls includes considering whether they are operating as intended and that they are modified as appropriate for changes in conditions. Monitoring of controls may include activities such as management's review of whether bank reconciliations are being prepared on a timely basis, internal auditors' evaluation of sales personnel's compliance with the entity's policies on terms of sales contracts, and a legal department's oversight of compliance with the entity's ethical or business practice policies. 18

Monitoring of controls is a process to assess the quality of internal control performance over time. It involves assessing the design and operation of controls on a timely basis and taking necessary corrective actions. Monitoring is done to ensure that controls continue to operate effectively. For example, if the timeliness and accuracy of bank reconciliations are not monitored, personnel are likely to stop preparing them. Monitoring of controls is accomplished through ongoing monitoring activities, separate evaluations, or a combination of the two. 19

Ongoing monitoring activities are built into the normal recurring activities of an entity and include regular management and supervisory activities. Managers of sales, purchasing, and production at divisional and corporate levels are in touch with operations and may question reports that differ significantly from their knowledge of operations. 20

In many entities, internal auditors or personnel performing similar functions contribute to the monitoring of an entity's controls through separate evaluations. They regularly provide information about the functioning of internal control, focusing considerable attention on evaluating the design and operation of internal control. They communicate information about strengths and weaknesses and recommendations for improving internal control. 21

Monitoring activities may include using information from communications from external parties that may indicate problems or highlight areas in need of improvement. Customers implicitly corroborate billing data by paying their invoices or complaining about their charges. In addition, regulators may communicate with the entity concerning matters that affect the functioning of internal control, for example, communications concerning examinations by bank regulatory agencies. Also, management may consider communications relating to internal control from external auditors in performing monitoring activities. 22

Application to Small Entities

Ongoing monitoring activities of small entities are more likely to be informal and are typically performed as a part of the overall management of the entity's operations. 23

Management's close involvement in operations often will identify significant variances from expectations and inaccuracies in financial data leading to corrective action to the control.

Appendix 3 – Conditions and Events That May Indicate Risks of Material Misstatement

The following are examples of conditions and events that may indicate the existence of risks of material misstatement. The examples provided cover a broad range of conditions and events; however, not all conditions and events are relevant to every audit engagement and the list of examples is not necessarily complete.

- Operations in regions that are economically unstable, for example, countries with significant currency devaluation or highly inflationary economies.
- Operations exposed to volatile markets, for example, futures trading.
- High degree of complex regulation.
- Going concern and liquidity issues including loss of significant customers.
- Constraints on the availability of capital and credit.
- Changes in the industry in which the entity operates.
- Changes in the supply chain.
- Developing or offering new products or services, or moving into new lines of business.
- Expanding into new locations.
- Changes in the entity such as large acquisitions or reorganizations or other unusual events.
- Entities or business segments likely to be sold.
- Complex alliances and joint ventures.
- Use of off-balance-sheet finance, special-purpose entities, and other complex financing arrangements.
- Significant transactions with related parties.
- Lack of personnel with appropriate accounting and financial reporting skills.
- Changes in key personnel including departure of key executives.
- Weaknesses in internal control, especially those not addressed by management.
- Inconsistencies between the entity's IT strategy and its business strategies.
- Changes in the IT environment.
- Installation of significant new IT systems related to financial reporting.
- Inquiries into the entity's operations or financial results by regulatory or government bodies.
- Past misstatements, history of errors or a significant amount of adjustments at period end.
- Significant amount of non-routine or non-systematic transactions including intercompany transactions and large revenue transactions at period end.
- Transactions that are recorded based on management's intent, for example, debt refinancing, assets to be sold and classification of marketable securities.
- Application of new accounting pronouncements.
- Accounting measurements that involve complex processes.
- Events or transactions that involve significant measurement uncertainty, including accounting estimates.
- Pending litigation and contingent liabilities, for example, sales warranties, financial guarantees and environmental remediation.

[320]*
Audit materiality

(Issued December 2004)

Contents

	Paragraphs
Introduction	1 - 3
Materiality	4 - 8
The Relationship between Materiality and Audit Risk	9 - 11
Evaluating the Effect of Misstatements	12 - 16
Communication of errors	17
Effective Date	**17-1**

> International Standard on Auditing (UK and Ireland) (ISA (UK and Ireland)) 320 "Audit Materiality" should be read in the context of the Auditing Practices Board's Statement "The Auditing Practices Board – Scope and Authority of Pronouncements (Revised)" which sets out the application and authority of ISAs (UK and Ireland).

Editor's note: The text of an Exposure Draft which is proposed to replace this Standard is printed on page 2085.

Introduction

1 The purpose of this International Standard on Auditing (UK and Ireland) (ISA (UK and Ireland)) is to establish standards and provide guidance on the concept of materiality and its relationship with audit risk.

1-1 This ISA (UK and Ireland) uses the terms 'those charged with governance' and 'management'. The term 'governance' describes the role of persons entrusted with the supervision, control and direction of an entity. Ordinarily, those charged with governance are accountable for ensuring that the entity achieves its objectives, and for the quality of its financial reporting and reporting to interested parties. Those charged with governance include management only when they perform such functions.

1-2 In the UK and Ireland, those charged with governance include the directors (executive and non-executive) of a company or other body, the members of an audit committee where one exists, the partners, proprietors, committee of management or trustees of other forms of entity, or equivalent persons responsible for directing the entity's affairs and preparing its financial statements.

1-3 'Management' comprises those persons who perform senior managerial functions.

1-4 In the UK and Ireland, depending on the nature and circumstances of the entity, management may include some or all of those charged with governance. (e.g. executive directors). Management will not normally include non-executive directors.

2 **The auditor should consider materiality and its relationship with audit risk when conducting an audit.**

3 "Materiality" is defined in the International Accounting Standards Board's "Framework for the Preparation and Presentation of Financial Statements" in the following terms:

> "Information is material if its omission or misstatement could influence the economic decisions of users taken on the basis of the financial statements. Materiality depends on the size of the item or error judged in the particular circumstances of its omission or misstatement. Thus, materiality provides a threshold or cut-off point rather than being a primary qualitative characteristic which information must have if it is to be useful."

Materiality

4 **The objective of an audit of financial statements is to enable the auditor to express an opinion whether the financial statements are prepared, in all material respects, in accordance with an applicable financial reporting framework.** The assessment of what is material is a matter of professional judgment.

5 In designing the audit plan, the auditor establishes an acceptable materiality level so as to detect quantitatively material misstatements. However, both the amount (quantity) and nature (quality) of misstatements need to be considered. Examples of qualitative misstatements would be the inadequate or improper description of an accounting policy when it is likely that a user of the financial statements would be

misled by the description, and failure to disclose the breach of regulatory requirements when it is likely that the consequent imposition of regulatory restrictions will significantly impair operating capability.

The auditor needs to consider the possibility of misstatements of relatively small amounts that, cumulatively, could have a material effect on the financial statements. For example, an error in a month end procedure could be an indication of a potential material misstatement if that error is repeated each month.

6

The auditor considers materiality at both the overall financial statement level and in relation to classes of transactions, account balances, and disclosures. Materiality may be influenced by considerations such as legal and regulatory requirements and considerations relating to classes of transactions, account balances, and disclosures and their relationships. This process may result in different materiality levels depending on the aspect of the financial statements being considered.

7

> For example, in the UK and Ireland, the expected degree of accuracy of certain statutory disclosures, such as directors' emoluments, may make normal materiality considerations irrelevant.

7-1

Materiality should be considered by the auditor when:

8

(a) **Determining the nature, timing and extent of audit procedures; and**
(b) **Evaluating the effect of misstatements.**

The Relationship between Materiality and Audit Risk

When planning the audit, the auditor considers what would make the financial statements materially misstated. The auditor's understanding of the entity and its environment establishes a frame of reference within which the auditor plans the audit and exercises professional judgment about assessing the risks of material misstatement of the financial statements and responding to those risks throughout the audit. It also assists the auditor to establish materiality and in evaluating whether the judgment about materiality remains appropriate as the audit progresses. The auditor's assessment of materiality, related to classes of transactions, account balances, and disclosures helps the auditor decide such questions as what items to examine and whether to use sampling and substantive analytical procedures. This enables the auditor to select audit procedures that, in combination, can be expected to reduce audit risk to an acceptably low level.

9

> If the auditor identifies factors which result in the revision of the preliminary materiality assessment, the auditor considers the implications for the audit approach and may modify the nature, timing and extent of planned audit procedures.

9-1

There is an inverse relationship between materiality and the level of audit risk, that is, the higher the materiality level, the lower the audit risk and vice versa. The auditor takes the inverse relationship between materiality and audit risk into account when determining the nature, timing and extent of audit procedures. For example, if, after planning for specific audit procedures, the auditor determines that the acceptable materiality level is lower, audit risk is increased. The auditor would compensate for this by either:

10

(a) Reducing the assessed risk of material misstatement, where this is possible, and supporting the reduced level by carrying out extended or additional tests of control; or
(b) Reducing detection risk by modifying the nature, timing and extent of planned substantive procedures.

Materiality and Audit Risk in Evaluating Audit Evidence

11 The auditor's assessment of materiality and audit risk may be different at the time of initially planning the engagement from at the time of evaluating the results of audit procedures. This could be because of a change in circumstances or because of a change in the auditor's knowledge as a result of performing audit procedures. For example, if audit procedures are performed prior to period end, the auditor will anticipate the results of operations and the financial position. If actual results of operations and financial position are substantially different, the assessment of materiality and audit risk may also change. Additionally, the auditor may, in planning the audit work, intentionally set the acceptable materiality level at a lower level than is intended to be used to evaluate the results of the audit. This may be done to reduce the likelihood of undiscovered misstatements and to provide the auditor with a margin of safety when evaluating the effect of misstatements discovered during the audit.

Evaluating the Effect of Misstatements

12 **In evaluating whether the financial statements are prepared, in all material respects, in accordance with an applicable financial reporting framework, the auditor should assess whether the aggregate of uncorrected misstatements that have been identified during the audit is material.**

12-1 In the UK and Ireland the auditor ordinarily evaluates whether the financial statements give a true and fair view.

13 The aggregate of uncorrected misstatements comprises:

(a) Specific misstatements identified by the auditor including the net effect of uncorrected misstatements identified during the audit of previous periods; and
(b) The auditor's best estimate of other misstatements which cannot be specifically identified (*i.e.*, projected errors).

14 The auditor needs to consider whether the aggregate of uncorrected misstatements is material. If the auditor concludes that the misstatements may be material, the auditor needs to consider reducing audit risk by extending audit procedures or requesting management to adjust the financial statements. In any event, management may want to adjust the financial statements for the misstatements identified.

15 **If management refuses to adjust the financial statements and the results of extended audit procedures do not enable the auditor to conclude that the aggregate of uncorrected misstatements is not material, the auditor should consider the appropriate modification to the auditor's report in accordance with ISA (UK and Ireland) 700 "The Auditor's Report on Financial Statements."**

16 If the aggregate of the uncorrected misstatements that the auditor has identified approaches the materiality level, the auditor would consider whether it is likely that

undetected misstatements, when taken with aggregate uncorrected misstatements could exceed materiality level. Thus, as aggregate uncorrected misstatements approach the materiality level the auditor would consider reducing audit risk by performing additional audit procedures or by requesting management to adjust the financial statements for identified misstatements.

Communication of Errors

If the auditor has identified a material misstatement resulting from error, the auditor should communicate the misstatement to the appropriate level of management on a timely basis, and consider the need to report it to those charged with governance in accordance with ISA (UK and Ireland) 260, "Communication of Audit Matters to Those Charged with Governance." 17

Effective Date

This ISA (UK and Ireland) is effective for audits of financial statements for periods commencing on or after 15 December 2004. 17-1

Public Sector Perspective

Additional guidance for auditors of public sector bodies in the UK and Ireland is given in:

- Practice Note 10 "Audit of Financial Statements of Public Sector Entities in the United Kingdom (Revised)"
- Practice Note 10(I) "The Audit of Central Government Financial Statements in Ireland"

In assessing materiality, the public sector auditor must, in addition to exercising professional judgment, consider any legislation or regulation which may impact that assessment. In the public sector, materiality is also based on the "context and nature" of an item and includes, for example, sensitivity as well as value. Sensitivity covers a variety of matters such as compliance with authorities, legislative concern or public interest. 1

[330]
The auditor's procedures in response to assessed risks

(Issued December 2004)

Contents

	Paragraphs
Introduction	1 - 3
Overall Responses	4 - 6
Audit Procedures Responsive to Risks of Material Misstatement at the Assertion Level	7 - 9
Considering the Nature, Timing, and Extent of Further Audit Procedures	10 - 21
Tests of Controls	22 - 47
Substantive Procedures	48 - 64
Adequacy of Presentation and Disclosure	65
Evaluating the Sufficiency and Appropriateness of Audit Evidence Obtained	66 - 72
Documentation	73
Effective Date	74

> International Standard on Auditing (UK and Ireland) (ISA (UK and Ireland)) 330 "The Auditor's Procedures in Response to Assessed Risks" should be read in the context of the Auditing Practices Board's Statement "The Auditing Practices Board – Scope and Authority of Pronouncements (Revised)" which sets out the application and authority of ISAs (UK and Ireland).

Introduction

The purpose of this International Standard on Auditing (UK and Ireland) (ISA (UK and Ireland)) is to establish standards and provide guidance on determining overall responses and designing and performing further audit procedures to respond to the assessed risks of material misstatement at the financial statement and assertion levels in a financial statement audit. The auditor's understanding of the entity and its environment, including its internal control, and assessment of the risks of material misstatement are described in ISA (UK and Ireland) 315, "Understanding the Entity and Its Environment and Assessing the Risks of Material Misstatement."   **1**

> This ISA (UK and Ireland) uses the terms 'those charged with governance' and 'management'. The term 'governance' describes the role of persons entrusted with the supervision, control and direction of an entity. Ordinarily, those charged with governance are accountable for ensuring that the entity achieves its objectives, and for the quality of its financial reporting and reporting to interested parties. Those charged with governance include management only when they perform such functions.   **1-1**
>
> In the UK and Ireland, those charged with governance include the directors (executive and non-executive) of a company or other body, the members of an audit committee where one exists, the partners, proprietors, committee of management or trustees of other forms of entity, or equivalent persons responsible for directing the entity's affairs and preparing its financial statements.   **1-2**
>
> 'Management' comprises those persons who perform senior managerial functions.   **1-3**
>
> In the UK and Ireland, depending on the nature and circumstances of the entity, management may include some or all of those charged with governance (e.g. executive directors). Management will not normally include non-executive directors.   **1-4**

The following is an overview of the requirements of this standard: **2**

- *Overall responses.* This section requires the auditor to determine overall responses to address risks of material misstatement at the financial statement level and provides guidance on the nature of those responses.
- *Audit procedures responsive to risks of material misstatement at the assertion level.* This section requires the auditor to design and perform further audit procedures, including tests of the operating effectiveness of controls, when relevant or required, and substantive procedures, whose nature, timing, and extent are responsive to the assessed risks of material misstatement at the assertion level. In addition, this section includes matters the auditor considers in determining the nature, timing, and extent of such audit procedures.
- *Evaluating the sufficiency and appropriateness of audit evidence obtained.* This section requires the auditor to evaluate whether the risk assessment remains appropriate and to conclude whether sufficient appropriate audit evidence has been obtained.
- *Documentation.* This section establishes related documentation requirements.

In order to reduce audit risk to an acceptably low level, the auditor should determine overall responses to assessed risks at the financial statement level, and should design and perform further audit procedures to respond to assessed risks at the assertion level. The overall responses and the nature, timing, and extent of the further audit   **3**

procedures are matters for the professional judgment of the auditor. In addition to the requirements of this ISA (UK and Ireland), the auditor also complies with the requirements and guidance in ISA (UK and Ireland) 240, "The Auditor's Responsibility to Consider Fraud in an Audit of Financial Statements" in responding to assessed risks of material misstatement due to fraud.

Overall Responses

4   **The auditor should determine overall responses to address the risks of material misstatement at the financial statement level.** Such responses may include emphasizing to the audit team the need to maintain professional skepticism in gathering and evaluating audit evidence, assigning more experienced staff or those with special skills or using experts,[1] providing more supervision, or incorporating additional elements of unpredictability in the selection of further audit procedures to be performed. Additionally, the auditor may make general changes to the nature, timing, or extent of audit procedures as an overall response, for example, performing substantive procedures at period end instead of at an interim date.

5   The assessment of the risks of material misstatement at the financial statement level is affected by the auditor's understanding of the control environment. An effective control environment may allow the auditor to have more confidence in internal control and the reliability of audit evidence generated internally within the entity and thus, for example, allow the auditor to conduct some audit procedures at an interim date rather than at period end. If there are weaknesses in the control environment, the auditor ordinarily conducts more audit procedures as of the period end rather than at an interim date, seeks more extensive audit evidence from substantive procedures, modifies the nature of audit procedures to obtain more persuasive audit evidence, or increases the number of locations to be included in the audit scope.

6   Such considerations, therefore, have a significant bearing on the auditor's general approach, for example, an emphasis on substantive procedures (substantive approach), or an approach that uses tests of controls as well as substantive procedures (combined approach).

Audit Procedures Responsive to Risks of Material Misstatement at the Assertion Level

7   **The auditor should design and perform further audit procedures whose nature, timing, and extent are responsive to the assessed risks of material misstatement at the assertion level.** The purpose is to provide a clear linkage between the nature, timing, and extent of the auditor's further audit procedures and the risk assessment. In designing further audit procedures, the auditor considers such matters as the following:

- The significance of the risk.
- The likelihood that a material misstatement will occur.
- The characteristics of the class of transactions, account balance, or disclosure involved.
- The nature of the specific controls used by the entity and in particular whether they are manual or automated.

---

[1] *The assignment of engagement personnel to the particular engagement reflects the auditor's risk assessment, which is based on the auditor's understanding of the entity.*

- Whether the auditor expects to obtain audit evidence to determine if the entity's controls are effective in preventing, or detecting and correcting, material misstatements.

The nature of the audit procedures is of most importance in responding to the assessed risks.

The auditor's assessment of the identified risks at the assertion level provides a basis for considering the appropriate audit approach for designing and performing further audit procedures. In some cases, the auditor may determine that only by performing tests of controls may the auditor achieve an effective response to the assessed risk of material misstatement for a particular assertion. In other cases, the auditor may determine that performing only substantive procedures is appropriate for specific assertions and, therefore, the auditor excludes the effect of controls from the relevant risk assessment. This may be because the auditor's risk assessment procedures have not identified any effective controls relevant to the assertion, or because testing the operating effectiveness of controls would be inefficient. However, the auditor needs to be satisfied that performing only substantive procedures for the relevant assertion would be effective in reducing the risk of material misstatement to an acceptably low level. Often the auditor may determine that a combined approach using both tests of the operating effectiveness of controls and substantive procedures is an effective approach. Irrespective of the approach selected, the auditor designs and performs substantive procedures for each material class of transactions, account balance, and disclosure as required by paragraph 49. 8

In the case of very small entities, there may not be many control activities that could be identified by the auditor. For this reason, the auditor's further audit procedures are likely to be primarily substantive procedures. In such cases, in addition to the matters referred to in paragraph 8 above, the auditor considers whether in the absence of controls it is possible to obtain sufficient appropriate audit evidence. 9

Considering the Nature, Timing, and Extent of Further Audit Procedures

Nature

The nature of further audit procedures refers to their purpose (tests of controls or substantive procedures) and their type, that is, inspection, observation, inquiry, confirmation, recalculation, reperformance, or analytical procedures. Certain audit procedures may be more appropriate for some assertions than others. For example, in relation to revenue, tests of controls may be most responsive to the assessed risk of misstatement of the completeness assertion, whereas substantive procedures may be most responsive to the assessed risk of misstatement of the occurrence assertion. 10

The auditor's selection of audit procedures is based on the assessment of risk. The higher the auditor's assessment of risk, the more reliable and relevant is the audit evidence sought by the auditor from substantive procedures. This may affect both the types of audit procedures to be performed and their combination. For example, the auditor may confirm the completeness of the terms of a contract with a third party, in addition to inspecting the document. 11

In determining the audit procedures to be performed, the auditor considers the reasons for the assessment of the risk of material misstatement at the assertion level for each class of transactions, account balance, and disclosure. This includes considering both the particular characteristics of each class of transactions, account balance, or disclosure (*i.e.*, the inherent risks) and whether the auditor's risk 12 assessment takes account of the entity's controls (*i.e.*, the control risk). For example, if the auditor considers that there is a lower risk that a material misstatement may occur because of the particular characteristics of a class of transactions without consideration of the related controls, the auditor may determine that substantive analytical procedures alone may provide sufficient appropriate audit evidence. On the other hand, if the auditor expects that there is a lower risk that a material misstatement may arise because an entity has effective controls and the auditor intends to design substantive procedures based on the effective operation of those controls, then the auditor performs tests of controls to obtain audit evidence about their operating effectiveness. This may be the case, for example, for a class of transactions of reasonably uniform, non-complex characteristics that are routinely processed and controlled by the entity's information system.

13　The auditor is required to obtain audit evidence about the accuracy and completeness of information produced by the entity's information system when that information is used in performing audit procedures. For example, if the auditor uses non-financial information or budget data produced by the entity's information system in performing audit procedures, such as substantive analytical procedures or tests of controls, the auditor obtains audit evidence about the accuracy and completeness of such information. See ISA (UK and Ireland) 500, "Audit Evidence" paragraph 11 for further guidance.

Timing

14　Timing refers to when audit procedures are performed or the period or date to which the audit evidence applies.

15　The auditor may perform tests of controls or substantive procedures at an interim date or at period end. The higher the risk of material misstatement, the more likely it is that the auditor may decide it is more effective to perform substantive procedures nearer to, or at, the period end rather than at an earlier date, or to perform audit procedures unannounced or at unpredictable times (for example, performing audit procedures at selected locations on an unannounced basis). On the other hand, performing audit procedures before the period end may assist the auditor in identifying significant matters at an early stage of the audit, and consequently resolving them with the assistance of management or developing an effective audit approach to address such matters. If the auditor performs tests of controls or substantive procedures prior to period end, the auditor considers the additional evidence required for the remaining period (see paragraphs 37-38 and 56-61).

16　In considering when to perform audit procedures, the auditor also considers such matters as the following:

- The control environment.
- When relevant information is available (for example, electronic files may subsequently be overwritten, or procedures to be observed may occur only at certain times).
- The nature of the risk (for example, if there is a risk of inflated revenues to meet earnings expectations by subsequent creation of false sales agreements, the auditor may wish to examine contracts available on the date of the period end).
- The period or date to which the audit evidence relates.

17　Certain audit procedures can be performed only at or after period end, for example, agreeing the financial statements to the accounting records and examining adjustments made during the course of preparing the financial statements. If there is a risk that the entity may have entered into improper sales contracts or transactions may not have been finalized at period end, the auditor performs procedures to respond to that specific risk. For example, when transactions are individually material or an error in cutoff may lead to a material misstatement, the auditor ordinarily inspects transactions near the period end.

Extent

Extent includes the quantity of a specific audit procedure to be performed, for example, a sample size or the number of observations of a control activity. The extent of an audit procedure is determined by the judgment of the auditor after considering the materiality, the assessed risk, and the degree of assurance the auditor plans to obtain. In particular, the auditor ordinarily increases the extent of audit procedures as the risk of material misstatement increases. However, increasing the extent of an audit procedure is effective only if the audit procedure itself is relevant to the specific risk; therefore, the nature of the audit procedure is the most important consideration. 18

The use of computer-assisted audit techniques (CAATs) may enable more extensive testing of electronic transactions and account files. Such techniques can be used to select sample transactions from key electronic files, to sort transactions with specific characteristics, or to test an entire population instead of a sample. 19

Valid conclusions may ordinarily be drawn using sampling approaches. However, if the quantity of selections made from a population is too small, the sampling approach selected is not appropriate to achieve the specific audit objective, or if exceptions are not appropriately followed up, there will be an unacceptable risk that the auditor's conclusion based on a sample may be different from the conclusion reached if the entire population was subjected to the same audit procedure. ISA (UK and Ireland) 530, "Audit Sampling and Other Means of Testing" contains guidance on the use of sampling. 20

This standard regards the use of different audit procedures in combination as an aspect of the nature of testing as discussed above. However, the auditor considers whether the extent of testing is appropriate when performing different audit procedures in combination. 21

Tests of Controls

The auditor is required to perform tests of controls when the auditor's risk assessment includes an expectation of the operating effectiveness of controls or when substantive procedures alone do not provide sufficient appropriate audit evidence at the assertion level. 22

When the auditor's assessment of risks of material misstatement at the assertion level includes an expectation that controls are operating effectively, the auditor should perform tests of controls to obtain sufficient appropriate audit evidence that the controls were operating effectively at relevant times during the period under audit. See paragraphs 39-44 below for discussion of using audit evidence about the operating effectiveness of controls obtained in prior audits. 23

The auditor's assessment of risk of material misstatement at the assertion level may include an expectation of the operating effectiveness of controls, in which case the auditor performs tests of controls to obtain audit evidence as to their operating effectiveness. Tests of the operating effectiveness of controls are performed only on those controls that the auditor has determined are suitably designed to prevent, or 24 detect and correct, a material misstatement in an assertion. Paragraphs 104-106 of ISA (UK and Ireland) 315 discuss the identification of controls at the assertion level likely to prevent, or detect and correct, a material misstatement in a class of transactions, account balance or disclosure.

25 **When, in accordance with paragraph 115 of ISA (UK and Ireland) 315, the auditor has determined that it is not possible or practicable to reduce the risks of material misstatement at the assertion level to an acceptably low level with audit evidence obtained only from substantive procedures, the auditor should perform tests of relevant controls to obtain audit evidence about their operating effectiveness.** For example, as discussed in paragraph 115 of ISA (UK and Ireland) 315, the auditor may find it impossible to design effective substantive procedures that by themselves provide sufficient appropriate audit evidence at the assertion level when an entity conducts its business using IT and no documentation of transactions is produced or maintained, other than through the IT system.

26 Testing the operating effectiveness of controls is different from obtaining audit evidence that controls have been implemented. When obtaining audit evidence of implementation by performing risk assessment procedures, the auditor determines that the relevant controls exist and that the entity is using them. When performing tests of the operating effectiveness of controls, the auditor obtains audit evidence that controls operate effectively. This includes obtaining audit evidence about how controls were applied at relevant times during the period under audit, the consistency with which they were applied, and by whom or by what means they were applied. If substantially different controls were used at different times during the period under audit, the auditor considers each separately. The auditor may determine that testing the operating effectiveness of controls at the same time as evaluating their design and obtaining audit evidence of their implementation is efficient.

27 Although some risk assessment procedures that the auditor performs to evaluate the design of controls and to determine that they have been implemented may not have been specifically designed as tests of controls, they may nevertheless provide audit evidence about the operating effectiveness of the controls and, consequently, serve as tests of controls. For example, the auditor may have made inquiries about management's use of budgets, observed management's comparison of monthly budgeted and actual expenses, and inspected reports pertaining to the investigation of variances between budgeted and actual amounts. These audit procedures provide knowledge about the design of the entity's budgeting policies and whether they have been implemented, and may also provide audit evidence about the effectiveness of the operation of budgeting policies in preventing or detecting material misstatements in the classification of expenses. In such circumstances, the auditor considers whether the audit evidence provided by those audit procedures is sufficient.

Nature of Tests of Controls

28 The auditor selects audit procedures to obtain assurance about the operating effectiveness of controls. As the planned level of assurance increases, the auditor seeks more reliable audit evidence. In circumstances when the auditor adopts an approach consisting primarily of tests of controls, in particular related to those risks where it is not possible or practicable to obtain sufficient appropriate audit evidence only from substantive procedures, the auditor ordinarily performs tests of controls to obtain a higher level of assurance about their operating effectiveness.

29 **The auditor should perform other audit procedures in combination with inquiry to test the operating effectiveness of controls.** Although different from obtaining an

understanding of the design and implementation of controls, tests of the operating effectiveness of controls ordinarily include the same types of audit procedures used to evaluate the design and implementation of controls, and may also include reperformance of the application of the control by the auditor. Since inquiry alone is not sufficient, the auditor uses a combination of audit procedures to obtain sufficient appropriate audit evidence regarding the operating effectiveness of controls. Those controls subject to testing by performing inquiry combined with inspection or reperformance ordinarily provide more assurance than those controls for which the audit evidence consists solely of inquiry and observation. For example, an auditor may inquire about and observe the entity's procedures for opening the mail and processing cash receipts to test the operating effectiveness of controls over cash receipts. Because an observation is pertinent only at the point in time at which it is made, the auditor ordinarily supplements the observation with inquiries of entity personnel, and may also inspect documentation about the operation of such controls at other times during the audit period in order to obtain sufficient appropriate audit evidence.

The nature of the particular control influences the type of audit procedure required to obtain audit evidence about whether the control was operating effectively at relevant times during the period under audit. For some controls, operating effectiveness is evidenced by documentation. In such circumstances, the auditor may decide to inspect the documentation to obtain audit evidence about operating effectiveness. For other controls, however, such documentation may not be available or relevant. For example, documentation of operation may not exist for some factors in the control environment, such as assignment of authority and responsibility, or for some types of control activities, such as control activities performed by a computer. In such circumstances, audit evidence about operating effectiveness may be obtained through inquiry in combination with other audit procedures such as observation or the use of CAATs. 30

In designing tests of controls, the auditor considers the need to obtain audit evidence supporting the effective operation of controls directly related to the assertions as well as other indirect controls on which these controls depend. For example, the auditor may identify a user review of an exception report of credit sales over a customer's authorized credit limit as a direct control related to an assertion. In such cases, the auditor considers the effectiveness of the user review of the report and also the controls related to the accuracy of the information in the report (for example, the general IT-controls). 31

In the case of an automated application control, because of the inherent consistency of IT processing, audit evidence about the implementation of the control, when considered in combination with audit evidence obtained regarding the operating effectiveness of the entity's general controls (and in particular, change controls) may provide substantial audit evidence about its operating effectiveness during the relevant period. 32

When responding to the risk assessment, the auditor may design a test of controls to be performed concurrently with a test of details on the same transaction. The objective of tests of controls is to evaluate whether a control operated effectively. The objective of tests of details is to detect material misstatements at the assertion level. Although these objectives are different, both may be accomplished concurrently through performance of a test of controls and a test of details on the same transaction, also known as a dual-purpose test. For example, the auditor may examine an invoice to determine whether it has been approved and to provide substantive audit evidence of a transaction. The auditor carefully considers the design and evaluation of such tests to accomplish both objectives. 33

34　The absence of misstatements detected by a substantive procedure does not provide audit evidence that controls related to the assertion being tested are effective. However, misstatements that the auditor detects by performing substantive procedures are considered by the auditor when assessing the operating effectiveness of related controls. A material misstatement detected by the auditor's procedures that was not identified by the entity ordinarily is indicative of the existence of a material weakness in internal control, which is communicated to management and those charged with governance.

Timing of Tests of Controls

35　The timing of tests of controls depends on the auditor's objective and determines the period of reliance on those controls. If the auditor tests controls at a particular time, the auditor only obtains audit evidence that the controls operated effectively at that time However, if the auditor tests controls throughout a period, the auditor obtains audit evidence of the effectiveness of the operation of the controls during that period.

36　Audit evidence pertaining only to a point in time may be sufficient for the auditor's purpose, for example, when testing controls over the entity's physical inventory counting at the period end. If, on the other hand, the auditor requires audit evidence of the effectiveness of a control over a period, audit evidence pertaining only to a point in time may be insufficient and the auditor supplements those tests with other tests of controls that are capable of providing audit evidence that the control operated effectively at relevant times during the period under audit. Such other tests may consist of tests of the entity's monitoring of controls.

37　**When the auditor obtains audit evidence about the operating effectiveness of controls during an interim period, the auditor should determine what additional audit evidence should be obtained for the remaining period.** In making that determination, the auditor considers the significance of the assessed risks of material misstatement at the assertion level, the specific controls that were tested during the interim period, the degree to which audit evidence about the operating effectiveness of those controls was obtained, the length of the remaining period, the extent to which the auditor intends to reduce further substantive procedures based on the reliance of controls, and the control environment. The auditor obtains audit evidence about the nature and extent of any significant changes in internal control, including changes in the information system, processes, and personnel that occur subsequent to the interim period.

38　Additional audit evidence may be obtained, for example, by extending the testing of the operating effectiveness of controls over the remaining period or testing the entity's monitoring of controls.

39　**If the auditor plans to use audit evidence about the operating effectiveness of controls obtained in prior audits, the auditor should obtain audit evidence about whether changes in those specific controls have occurred subsequent to the prior audit. The auditor should obtain audit evidence about whether such changes have occurred by performing inquiry in combination with observation or inspection to confirm the understanding of those specific controls.** Paragraph 23 of ISA (UK and Ireland) 500 states that the auditor performs audit procedures to establish the continuing relevance of audit evidence obtained in prior periods when the auditor plans to use the audit evidence in the current period. For example, in performing the prior audit, the auditor may have determined that an automated control was functioning as intended. The auditor obtains audit evidence to determine whether changes to the automated control have been made that affect its continued effective functioning, for example, through inquiries of management and the inspection of logs to indicate what controls have been changed. Consideration of audit evidence about these changes may support either increasing or decreasing the expected audit evidence to be obtained in the current period about the operating effectiveness of the controls.

If the auditor plans to rely on controls that have changed since they were last tested, the auditor should test the operating effectiveness of such controls in the current audit. Changes may affect the relevance of the audit evidence obtained in prior periods such that there may no longer be a basis for continued reliance. For example, changes in a system that enable an entity to receive a new report from the system probably do not affect the relevance of prior period audit evidence; however, a change that causes data to be accumulated or calculated differently does affect it. 40

If the auditor plans to rely on controls that have not changed since they were last tested, the auditor should test the operating effectiveness of such controls at least once in every third audit. As indicated in paragraphs 40 and 44, the auditor may not rely on audit evidence about the operating effectiveness of controls obtained in prior audits for controls that have changed since they were last tested or controls that mitigate a significant risk. The auditor's decision on whether to rely on audit evidence obtained in prior audits for other controls is a matter of professional judgment. In addition, the length of time period between retesting such controls is also a matter of professional judgment, but cannot exceed two years. 41

In considering whether it is appropriate to use audit evidence about the operating effectiveness of controls obtained in prior audits, and, if so, the length of the time period that may elapse before retesting a control, the auditor considers the following: 42

- The effectiveness of other elements of internal control, including the control environment, the entity's monitoring of controls, and the entity's risk assessment process.
- The risks arising from the characteristics of the control, including whether controls are manual or automated (see ISA (UK and Ireland) 315, paragraphs 57-63 for a discussion of specific risks arising from manual and automated elements of a control).
- The effectiveness of general IT-controls.
- The effectiveness of the control and its application by the entity, including the nature and extent of deviations in the application of the control from tests of operating effectiveness in prior audits.
- Whether the lack of a change in a particular control poses a risk due to changing circumstances.
- The risk of material misstatement and the extent of reliance on the control.

In general, the higher the risk of material misstatement, or the greater the reliance on controls, the shorter the time period elapsed, if any, is likely to be. Factors that ordinarily decrease the period for retesting a control, or result in not relying on audit evidence obtained in prior audits at all, include the following:

- A weak control environment.
- Weak monitoring of controls.
- A significant manual element to the relevant controls.
- Personnel changes that significantly affect the application of the control.
- Changing circumstances that indicate the need for changes in the control.
- Weak general IT-controls.

When there are a number of controls for which the auditor determines that it is appropriate to use audit evidence obtained in prior audits, the auditor should test the operating effectiveness of some controls each audit. The purpose of this requirement is 43 to avoid the possibility that the auditor might apply the approach of paragraph 41 to all controls on which the auditor proposes to rely, but test all those controls in a single audit period with no testing of controls in the subsequent two audit periods. In addition to providing audit evidence about the operating effectiveness of the controls being tested in the current audit, performing such tests provides collateral evidence about the continuing effectiveness of the control environment and therefore contributes to the decision about whether it is appropriate to rely on audit evidence obtained in prior audits. Therefore, when the auditor determines in accordance with paragraphs 39-42 that it is appropriate to use audit evidence obtained in prior audits for a number of controls, the auditor plans to test a sufficient portion of the controls in that population in each audit period, and at a minimum, each control is tested at least every third audit.

44 When, in accordance with paragraph 108 of ISA (UK and Ireland) 315, the auditor has determined that an assessed risk of material misstatement at the assertion level is a significant risk and the auditor plans to rely on the operating effectiveness of controls intended to mitigate that significant risk, the auditor should obtain the audit evidence about the operating effectiveness of those controls from tests of controls performed in the current period. The greater the risk of material misstatement, the more audit evidence the auditor obtains that relevant controls are operating effectively. Accordingly, although the auditor often considers information obtained in prior audits in designing tests of controls to mitigate a significant risk, the auditor does not rely on audit evidence obtained in a prior audit about the operating effectiveness of controls over such risks, but instead obtains the audit evidence about the operating effectiveness of controls over such risks in the current period.

Extent of Tests of Controls

45 The auditor designs tests of controls to obtain sufficient appropriate audit evidence that the controls operated effectively throughout the period of reliance. Matters the auditor may consider in determining the extent of the auditor's tests of controls include the following:

- The frequency of the performance of the control by the entity during the period.
- The length of time during the audit period that the auditor is relying on the operating effectiveness of the control.
- The relevance and reliability of the audit evidence to be obtained in supporting that the control prevents, or detects and corrects, material misstatements at the assertion level.
- The extent to which audit evidence is obtained from tests of other controls related to the assertion.
- The extent to which the auditor plans to rely on the operating effectiveness of the control in the assessment of risk (and thereby reduce substantive procedures based on the reliance of such control).
- The expected deviation from the control.

46 The more the auditor relies on the operating effectiveness of controls in the assessment of risk, the greater is the extent of the auditor's tests of controls. In addition, as the rate of expected deviation from a control increases, the auditor increases the extent of testing of the control. However, the auditor considers whether the rate of expected deviation indicates that the control will not be sufficient to reduce the risk of material misstatement at the assertion level to that assessed by the auditor. If the rate of expected deviation is expected to be too high, the auditor may determine that tests of controls for a particular assertion may not be effective.

Because of the inherent consistency of IT processing, the auditor may not need to increase the extent of testing of an automated control. An automated control should function consistently unless the program (including the tables, files, or other permanent data used by the program) is changed. Once the auditor determines that an automated control is functioning as intended (which could be done at the time the control is initially implemented or at some other date), the auditor considers performing tests to determine that the control continues to function effectively. Such tests might include determining that changes to the program are not made without being subject to the appropriate program change controls, that the authorized version of the program is used for processing transactions, and that other relevant general controls are effective. Such tests also might include determining that changes to the programs have not been made, as may be the case when the entity uses packaged software applications without modifying or maintaining them. For example, the auditor may inspect the record of the administration of IT security to obtain audit evidence that unauthorized access has not occurred during the period. 47

Substantive Procedures

Substantive procedures are performed in order to detect material misstatements at the assertion level, and include tests of details of classes of transactions, account balances, and disclosures and substantive analytical procedures. The auditor plans and performs substantive procedures to be responsive to the related assessment of the risk of material misstatement. 48

Irrespective of the assessed risk of material misstatement, the auditor should design and perform substantive procedures for each material class of transactions, account balance, and disclosure. This requirement reflects the fact that the auditor's assessment of risk is judgmental and may not be sufficiently precise to identify all risks of material misstatement. Further, there are inherent limitations to internal control including management override. Accordingly, while the auditor may determine that the risk of material misstatement may be reduced to an acceptably low level by performing only tests of controls for a particular assertion related to a class of transactions, account balance or disclosure (see paragraph 8), the auditor always performs substantive procedures for each material class of transactions, account balance, and disclosure. 49

The auditor's substantive procedures should include the following audit procedures related to the financial statement closing process: 50

- Agreeing the financial statements to the underlying accounting records; and
- Examining material journal entries and other adjustments made during the course of preparing the financial statements.

The nature and extent of the auditor's examination of journal entries and other adjustments depends on the nature and complexity of the entity's financial reporting process and the associated risks of material misstatement.

When, in accordance with paragraph 108 of ISA (UK and Ireland) 315, the auditor has determined that an assessed risk of material misstatement at the assertion level is a significant risk, the auditor should perform substantive procedures that are specifically responsive to that risk. For example, if the auditor identifies that management is under pressure to meet earnings expectations, there may be a risk that management is inflating sales by improperly recognizing revenue related to sales agreements with terms that preclude revenue recognition or by invoicing sales before shipment. In these circumstances, the auditor may, for example, design external confirmations not only to confirm outstanding amounts, but also to confirm the details of the sales agreements, including date, any rights of return and delivery terms. In addition, the 51 auditor may find it effective to supplement such external confirmations with inquiries of non-financial personnel in the entity regarding any changes in sales agreements and delivery terms.

52 When the approach to significant risks consists only of substantive procedures, the audit procedures appropriate to address such significant risks consist of tests of details only, or a combination of tests of details and substantive analytical procedures The auditor considers the guidance in paragraphs 53-64 in designing the nature, timing, and extent of substantive procedures for significant risks. In order to obtain sufficient appropriate audit evidence, the substantive procedures related to significant risks are most often designed to obtain audit evidence with high reliability.

Nature of Substantive Procedures

53 Substantive analytical procedures are generally more applicable to large volumes of transactions that tend to be predictable over time. Tests of details are ordinarily more appropriate to obtain audit evidence regarding certain assertions about account balances, including existence and valuation. In some situations, the auditor may determine that performing only substantive analytical procedures may be sufficient to reduce the risk of material misstatement to an acceptably low level. For example, the auditor may determine that performing only substantive analytical procedures is responsive to the assessed risk of material misstatement for a class of transactions where the auditor's assessment of risk is supported by obtaining audit evidence from performance of tests of the operating effectiveness of controls. In other situations, the auditor may determine that only tests of details are appropriate, or that a combination of substantive analytical procedures and tests of details are most responsive to the assessed risks.

54 The auditor designs tests of details responsive to the assessed risk with the objective of obtaining sufficient appropriate audit evidence to achieve the planned level of assurance at the assertion level. In designing substantive procedures related to the existence or occurrence assertion, the auditor selects from items contained in a financial statement amount and obtains the relevant audit evidence. On the other hand, in designing audit procedures related to the completeness assertion, the auditor selects from audit evidence indicating that an item should be included in the relevant financial statement amount and investigates whether that item is so included. For example, the auditor might inspect subsequent cash disbursements to determine whether any purchases had been omitted from accounts payable.

55 In designing substantive analytical procedures, the auditor considers such matters as the following:
- The suitability of using substantive analytical procedures given the assertions.
- The reliability of the data, whether internal or external, from which the expectation of recorded amounts or ratios is developed.
- Whether the expectation is sufficiently precise to identify a material misstatement at the desired level of assurance.
- The amount of any difference in recorded amounts from expected values that is acceptable.

The auditor considers testing the controls, if any, over the entity's preparation of information used by the auditor in applying analytical procedures. When such controls are effective, the auditor has greater confidence in the reliability of the information and, therefore, in the results of analytical procedures. Alternatively, the auditor may consider whether the information was subjected to audit testing in the current or prior period. In determining the audit procedures to apply to the information upon which the expectation for substantive analytical procedures is based, the auditor considers the guidance in paragraph 11 of ISA (UK and Ireland) 500.

Timing of Substantive Procedures

When substantive procedures are performed at an interim date, the auditor should perform further substantive procedures or substantive procedures combined with tests of controls to cover the remaining period that provide a reasonable basis for extending the audit conclusions from the interim date to the period end.   56

In some circumstances, substantive procedures may be performed at an interim date.   57
This increases the risk that misstatements that may exist at the period end are not detected by the auditor. This risk increases as the remaining period is lengthened. In considering whether to perform substantive procedures at an interim date, the auditor considers such factors as the following:

- The control environment and other relevant controls.
- The availability of information at a later date that is necessary for the auditor's procedures.
- The objective of the substantive procedure.
- The assessed risk of material misstatement.
- The nature of the class of transactions or account balance and related assertions.
- The ability of the auditor to perform appropriate substantive procedures or substantive procedures combined with tests of controls to cover the remaining period in order to reduce the risk that misstatements that exist at period end are not detected.

Although the auditor is not required to obtain audit evidence about the operating effectiveness of controls in order to have a reasonable basis for extending audit conclusions from an interim date to the period end, the auditor considers whether performing only substantive procedures to cover the remaining period is sufficient. If the auditor concludes that substantive procedures alone would not be sufficient, tests of the operating effectiveness of relevant controls are performed or the substantive procedures are performed as of the period end.   58

In circumstances where the auditor has identified risks of material misstatement due to fraud, the auditor's response to address those risks may include changing the timing of audit procedures. For example, the auditor might conclude that, given the risks of intentional misstatement or manipulation, audit procedures to extend audit conclusions from an interim date to the period end would not be effective. In such circumstances, the auditor might conclude that substantive procedures need to be performed at or near the end of the reporting period to address an identified risk of material misstatement due to fraud (see ISA (UK and Ireland) 240).   59

Ordinarily, the auditor compares and reconciles information concerning the balance at the period end with the comparable information at the interim date to identify amounts that appear unusual, investigates any such amounts, and performs substantive analytical procedures or tests of details to test the intervening period. When the auditor plans to perform substantive analytical procedures with respect to the intervening period, the auditor considers whether the period end balances of the particular classes of transactions or account balances are reasonably predictable with respect to amount, relative significance, and composition. The auditor considers whether the entity's procedures for analyzing and adjusting such classes of transactions or account balances at interim dates and for establishing proper accounting   60 cutoffs are appropriate. In addition, the auditor considers whether the information system relevant to financial reporting will provide information concerning the balances at the period end and the transactions in the remaining period that is sufficient to permit investigation of: significant unusual transactions or entries (including those at or near period end); other causes of significant fluctuations, or expected fluctuations that did not occur; and changes in the composition of the classes of transactions or account balances. The substantive procedures related to the remaining period depend on whether the auditor has performed tests of controls.

61   If misstatements are detected in classes of transactions or account balances at an interim date, the auditor ordinarily modifies the related assessment of risk and the planned nature, timing, or extent of the substantive procedures covering the remaining period that relate to such classes of transactions or account balances, or extends or repeats such audit procedures at the period end.

62   The use of audit evidence from the performance of substantive procedures in a prior audit is not sufficient to address a risk of material misstatement in the current period. In most cases, audit evidence from the performance of substantive procedures in a prior audit provides little or no audit evidence for the current period. In order for audit evidence obtained in a prior audit to be used in the current period as substantive audit evidence, the audit evidence and the related subject matter must not fundamentally change. An example of audit evidence obtained from the performance of substantive procedures in a prior period that may be relevant in the current year is a legal opinion related to the structure of a securitization to which no changes have occurred during the current period. As required by paragraph 23 of ISA (UK and Ireland) 500, if the auditor plans to use audit evidence obtained from the performance of substantive procedures in a prior audit, the auditor performs audit procedures during the current period to establish the continuing relevance of the audit evidence.

Extent of the Performance of Substantive Procedures

63   The greater the risk of material misstatement, the greater the extent of substantive procedures. Because the risk of material misstatement takes account of internal control, the extent of substantive procedures may be increased as a result of unsatisfactory results from tests of the operating effectiveness of controls. However, increasing the extent of an audit procedure is appropriate only if the audit procedure itself is relevant to the specific risk.

64   In designing tests of details, the extent of testing is ordinarily thought of in terms of the sample size, which is affected by the risk of material misstatement. However, the auditor also considers other matters, including whether it is more effective to use other selective means of testing, such as selecting large or unusual items from a population as opposed to performing representative sampling or stratifying the population into homogeneous subpopulations for sampling. ISA (UK and Ireland) 530 contains guidance on the use of sampling and other means of selecting items for testing. In designing substantive analytical procedures, the auditor considers the amount of difference from the expectation that can be accepted without further investigation. This consideration is influenced primarily by materiality and the consistency with the desired level of assurance. Determination of this amount involves considering the possibility that a combination of misstatements in the specific account balance, class of transactions, or disclosure could aggregate to an unacceptable amount. In designing substantive analytical procedures, the auditor increases the desired level of assurance as the risk of material misstatement increases.

ISA (UK and Ireland) 520, "Analytical Procedures" contains guidance on the application of analytical procedures during an audit.

Adequacy of Presentation and Disclosure

The auditor should perform audit procedures to evaluate whether the overall presentation of the financial statements, including the related disclosures, are in accordance with the applicable financial reporting framework. The auditor considers whether the individual financial statements are presented in a manner that reflects the appropriate classification and description of financial information. The presentation of financial statements in conformity with the applicable financial reporting framework also includes adequate disclosure of material matters. These matters relate to the form, arrangement, and content of the financial statements and their appended notes, including, for example, the terminology used, the amount of detail given, the classification of items in the statements, and the bases of amounts set forth. The auditor considers whether management should have disclosed a particular matter in light of the circumstances and facts of which the auditor is aware at the time. In performing the evaluation of the overall presentation of the financial statements, including the related disclosures, the auditor considers the assessed risk of material misstatement at the assertion level. See paragraph 17 of ISA (UK and Ireland) 500 for a description of the assertions related to presentation and disclosure.

65

Evaluating the Sufficiency and Appropriateness of Audit Evidence Obtained

Based on the audit procedures performed and the audit evidence obtained, the auditor should evaluate whether the assessments of the risks of material misstatement at the assertion level remain appropriate.

66

An audit of financial statements is a cumulative and iterative process. As the auditor performs planned audit procedures, the audit evidence obtained may cause the auditor to modify the nature, timing, or extent of other planned audit procedures. Information may come to the auditor's attention that differs significantly from the information on which the risk assessment was based. For example, the extent of misstatements that the auditor detects by performing substantive procedures may alter the auditor's judgment about the risk assessments and may indicate a material weakness in internal control. In addition, analytical procedures performed at the overall review stage of the audit may indicate a previously unrecognized risk of material misstatement. In such circumstances, the auditor may need to reevaluate the planned audit procedures, based on the revised consideration of assessed risks for all or some of the classes of transactions, account balances, or disclosures and related assertions. Paragraph 119 of ISA (UK and Ireland) 315 contains further guidance on revising the auditor's risk assessment.

67

The concept of effectiveness of the operation of controls recognizes that some deviations in the way controls are applied by the entity may occur. Deviations from prescribed controls may be caused by such factors as changes in key personnel, significant seasonal fluctuations in volume of transactions and human error. When such deviations are detected during the performance of tests of controls, the auditor makes specific inquiries to understand these matters and their potential consequences, for example, by inquiring about the timing of personnel changes in key internal control functions. The auditor determines whether the tests of controls performed provide an appropriate basis for reliance on the controls, whether

68

additional tests of controls are necessary, or whether the potential risks of misstatement need to be addressed using substantive procedures.

69 The auditor cannot assume that an instance of fraud or error is an isolated occurrence, and therefore considers how the detection of a misstatement affects the assessed risks of material misstatement. Before the conclusion of the audit, the auditor evaluates whether audit risk has been reduced to an acceptably low level and whether the nature, timing, and extent of the audit procedures may need to be reconsidered. For example, the auditor reconsiders the following:
- The nature, timing, and extent of substantive procedures.
- The audit evidence of the operating effectiveness of relevant controls, including the entity's risk assessment process.

70 **The auditor should conclude whether sufficient appropriate audit evidence has been obtained to reduce to an acceptably low level the risk of material misstatement in the financial statements.** In developing an opinion, the auditor considers all relevant audit evidence, regardless of whether it appears to corroborate or to contradict the assertions in the financial statements.

71 The sufficiency and appropriateness of audit evidence to support the auditor's conclusions throughout the audit are a matter of professional judgment. The auditor's judgment as to what constitutes sufficient appropriate audit evidence is influenced by such factors as the following:
- Significance of the potential misstatement in the assertion and the likelihood of its having a material effect, individually or aggregated with other potential misstatements, on the financial statements.
- Effectiveness of management's responses and controls to address the risks.
- Experience gained during previous audits with respect to similar potential misstatements.
- Results of audit procedures performed, including whether such audit procedures identified specific instances of fraud or error.
- Source and reliability of the available information.
- Persuasiveness of the audit evidence.
- Understanding of the entity and its environment, including its internal control.

72 **If the auditor has not obtained sufficient appropriate audit evidence as to a material financial statement assertion, the auditor should attempt to obtain further audit evidence. If the auditor is unable to obtain sufficient appropriate audit evidence, the auditor should express a qualified opinion or a disclaimer of opinion.** See ISA (UK and Ireland) 700, "The Auditor's Report on Financial Statements" for further guidance.

Documentation

73 **The auditor should document the overall responses to address the assessed risks of material misstatement at the financial statement level and the nature, timing, and extent of the further audit procedures, the linkage of those procedures with the assessed risks at the assertion level, and the results of the audit procedures.** In addition, if the auditor plans to use audit evidence about the operating effectiveness of controls obtained in prior audits, the auditor should document the conclusions reached with regard to relying on such controls that were tested in a prior audit. The manner in which these matters are documented is based on the auditor's professional judgment. ISA (UK and Ireland) 230, "Documentation" establishes standards and provides guidance regarding documentation in the context of the audit of financial statements.

Effective Date

This ISA (UK and Ireland) is effective for audits of financial statements for periods commencing on or after 15 December 2004.

74

Public Sector Perspective

> Additional guidance for auditors of public sector bodies in the UK and Ireland is given in:
> - Practice Note 10 "Audit of Financial Statements of Public Sector Entities in the United Kingdom (Revised)"
> - Practice Note 10(I) "The Audit of Central Government Financial Statements in Ireland"

When carrying out audits of public sector entities, the auditor takes into account the legislative framework and any other relevant regulations, ordinances or ministerial directives that affect the audit mandate and any other special auditing requirements. Such factors might affect, for example, the extent of the auditor's discretion in establishing materiality and judgments on the nature and scope of audit procedures to be applied. Paragraph 3 of this ISA (UK and Ireland) may have to be applied only after giving consideration to such restrictions.

1

[402]
Audit considerations relating to entities using service organizations

(Issued December 2004)

Contents

	Paragraphs
Introduction	1 - 3-1
Additional Statutory or Regulatory Reporting Responsibilities	3-2
Definitions	3-3 - 3-4
Understanding the Entity and its Environment	
Service Organization Activities Relevant to the Audit	4 - 5-2
Understanding the Contractual Terms and Monitoring Arrangements	5-3 - 5-4
Considering Access to Sources of Audit Evidence	6 - 6-3
Indemnities	6-4
Compliance with Laws and Regulations	6-5
Assessing Risks	7 - 9-7
Designing Audit Procedures	9-8 - 9-11
Accounting Records	9-12 - 9-17
Obtaining Audit Evidence	9-18 - 10
Service Organization Auditor's Report	11 - 18
Reporting	18-1 - 18-2
Effective Date	18-3
Appendix Examples of Factors Relating to Activities Undertaken by Service Organizations Which May Increase the Risk of Material Misstatements	

International Standard on Auditing (UK and Ireland) (ISA (UK and Ireland)) 402, "Audit Considerations Relating to Entities Using Service Organizations" should be read in the context of the Auditing Practices Board's Statement "The Auditing Practices Board – Scope and Authority of Pronouncements (Revised)" which sets out the application and authority of ISAs (UK and Ireland).

Introduction

The purpose of this International Standard on Auditing (UK and Ireland) (ISA (UK and Ireland)) is to establish standards and provide guidance to an auditor where the entity uses a service organization. This ISA (UK and Ireland) also describes the service organization auditor's reports which may be obtained by the entity's auditors. 1

> This ISA (UK and Ireland) uses the terms 'those charged with governance' and 'management'. The term 'governance' describes the role of persons entrusted with the supervision, control and direction of an entity. Ordinarily, those charged with governance are accountable for ensuring that the entity achieves its objectives, and for the quality of its financial reporting and reporting to interested parties. Those charged with governance include management only when they performs such functions. 1-1
>
> In the UK and Ireland, those charged with governance include the directors (executive and non-executive) of a company or other body, the members of an audit committee where one exists, the partners, proprietors, committee of management or trustees of other forms of entity, or equivalent persons responsible for directing the entity's affairs and preparing its financial statements. 1-2
>
> 'Management' comprises those persons who perform senior managerial functions. 1-3
>
> In the UK and Ireland, depending on the nature and circumstances of the entity, management may include some or all of those charged with governance (e.g. executive directors). Management will not normally include non-executive directors. 1-4

The auditor should consider how an entity's use of a service organization affects the entity's internal control so as to identify and assess the risk of material misstatement and to design and perform further audit procedures. 2

A client may use a service organization such as one that executes transactions and maintains related accountability or records transactions and processes related data (for example, a computer systems service organization). If the entity uses a service organization, certain policies, procedures and records maintained by the service organization may be relevant to the audit of the financial statements of the client. 3

> Use of a service organisation does not diminish the ultimate responsibility of those charged with governance for conducting its business in a manner which meets their legal responsibilities, including those of safeguarding the entity's assets, maintaining proper accounting records and preparing financial statements which provide information about its economic activities and financial position. Practical issues, including the way in which accounting records will be kept and the manner in which those charged with governance assess the quality of the service, need to be addressed. 3-1

Additional Statutory or Regulatory Responsibilities

3-2 An auditor appointed to report on a client's financial statements may have additional reporting responsibilities, which could be affected by the client's use of a service organisation (for example, reporting on compliance with the requirement of company law concerning maintenance of adequate accounting records; or the expression of an opinion on reports by the entity to its regulator).

Definitions

3-3 *Service organisation*: the term 'service organisation' is used in this ISA (UK and Ireland) to refer to any entity that provides services to another. Service organisations undertake a wide variety of activities, including:

- Information processing.
- Maintenance of accounting records.
- Facilities management.
- Maintenance of safe custody of assets, such as investments.
- Initiation or execution of transactions on behalf of the other entity.

Service organisations may undertake activities on a dedicated basis for one entity, or on a shared basis, either for members of a single group of entities or for unrelated customers.

3-4 *Relevant activities*: this term is used to refer to activities undertaken by a service organisation that are relevant to the audit. Relevant activities are those that:

(a) Relate directly to:
   (i) The preparation of the entity's financial statements, including the maintenance of material elements of its accounting records which form the basis for those financial statements; and
   (ii) The reporting of material assets, liabilities and transactions which are required to be included or disclosed in the financial statements (excluding the charge for provision of the service concerned); or
(b) Are subject to law and regulations that are central to the entity's ability to conduct its business.[1]

Understanding the entity and its environment

Service Organization Activities Relevant to the Audit

4 A service organization may establish and execute policies and procedures that affect the entity's internal control. These policies and procedures are physically and operationally separate from the entity. When the services provided by the service organization are limited to recording and processing the entity's transactions and the entity retains authorization and maintenance of accountability, the entity may be able to implement effective policies and procedures within its organization. When the service organization executes the entity's transactions and maintains accountability, the entity may deem it necessary to rely on policies and procedures at the service organization.

---

[1] *ISA (UK and Ireland) 250, paragraph 18-1.*

In obtaining an understanding of the entity and its environment, the auditor should determine the significance of service organization activities to the entity and the relevance to the audit. In doing so, the auditor obtains an understanding of the following, as appropriate:

- Nature of the services provided by the service organization.
- Terms of contract and relationship between the entity and the service organization.
- Extent to which the entity's internal control interact with the systems at the service organization.
- The entity's internal control relevant to the service organization activities such as:
  - Those that are applied to the transactions processed by the service organization.
  - How the entity identifies and manages risks related to use of the service organization.
- Service organization's capability and financial strength, including the possible effect of the failure of the service organization on the entity.
- Information about the service organization such as that reflected in user and technical manuals.
- Information available on controls relevant to the service organization's information systems such as general IT controls and application controls.

5

Examples of service organisation activities that are relevant to the audit include:

- Maintenance of the entity's accounting records.
- Other finance functions (such as the computation of tax liabilities, or debtor management and credit risk analysis) which involve establishing the carrying value of items in the financial statements.
- Management of assets.
- Undertaking or making arrangements for transactions as agent of the entity.

5-1

Other types of services, for example facilities management, may involve activities which do not fall within the definition of relevant activities.

5-2

Understanding the Contractual Terms and Monitoring Arrangements

The auditor should obtain and document an understanding of the contractual terms which apply to relevant activities undertaken the service organization and the way that the entity monitors those activities so as to ensure that it meets its fiduciary and other legal responsibilities.

5-3

Matters which the auditor may consider include:

- Whether the terms contain an adequate specification of the information to be provided to the entity and responsibilities for initiating transactions relating to the activity undertaken by the service organization.
- The way that accounting records relating to relevant activities are maintained.
- Whether the entity has rights of access to accounting records prepared by the service organisation concerning the activities undertaken, and relevant underlying information held by it, and the conditions in which such access may be sought.
- Whether the terms take proper account of any applicable requirements of regulatory bodies concerning the form of records to be maintained, or access to them.

5-4

- The nature of relevant performance standards.
- The way in which the entity monitors performance of relevant activities and the extent to which its monitoring process relies on controls operated by the service organization.
- Whether the service organisation has agreed to indemnify the entity in the event of a performance failure.
- Whether the contractual terms permit the auditor access to sources of audit evidence, including accounting records of the entity and other information necessary for the conduct of the audit.

Considering Access to Sources of Evidence

6 The auditor would also consider the existence of third-party reports from service organization auditors, internal auditors, or regulatory agencies as a means of obtaining information about the internal control of the service organization and about its operation and effectiveness. When the auditor intends to use work of the internal auditor, ISA (UK and Ireland) 610, "Considering the Work of Internal Auditing" provides guidance on evaluating the adequacy of the internal auditor's work for the auditor's purposes.

6a The understanding obtained may lead the auditor to decide that the control risk assessment of the risk of material misstatement will not be affected by controls at the service organization; if so, further consideration of this ISA (UK and Ireland) is unnecessary.

6-1 Access to information held by the service organisation is not always necessary in order to obtain sufficient appropriate audit evidence: sufficient evidence may, depending on the nature of activities undertaken by the service organisation, be available at the client itself. If the auditor concludes that access to information or records held by the service organisation is necessary for the purposes of the audit, and the contract terms do not provide for such access, the auditor requests those charged with governance to make appropriate arrangements to obtain it.

6-2 The auditor evaluates the efficiency and effectiveness of visiting the service organisation or using evidence provided by the service organisation's auditor, by:

(a) Requesting the service organisation auditor or the entity's internal audit function to perform specified procedures: where information necessary to form an opinion on the entity's financial statements is not available without access to the service organisation's underlying records, its auditor may conclude that the most effective manner to obtain that information is to request the service organisation's auditor or the entity's internal audit function (where the function is established on a suitable basis[2]) to do so. The feasibility of this approach will depend on whether the contractual arrangements with the service organisation entitle the entity to obtain supplementary information when considered necessary;

(b) Reviewing information from the service organisation and its auditor concerning the design and operation of its controls systems: those charged with

---

[2] The auditor determines whether this is the case by applying the criteria set out in ISA (UK and Ireland) 610 'Considering the work of internal auditing'.

governance may use such information as part of their arrangements for monitoring the activities undertaken by a service organisation. Where this is the case, those charged with governance of the entity periodically obtain reports from the service organisation, its auditor, or both, confirming that controls have operated as agreed. Such reports may provide information on the operation of controls at the service organisation relevant to the auditor's judgment as to the extent to which controls reduce the necessity to obtain evidence from substantive procedures.

Where the contractual terms do not provide for access to information held by the service organisation which the auditor considers necessary in order to report on the entity's financial statements, the auditor discusses with the those charged with governance at the entity the way in which such information may be obtained and, unless it is made available, qualify the auditor's opinion on the entity's financial statements. If, following discussions with those charged with governance, the auditor concludes that necessary changes in arrangements agreed between the entity and service organisation will not be made in the future, the auditor considers withdrawing from the engagement.

6-3

Indemnities

Agreement by a service organisation to provide an indemnity does not provide information directly relevant to the auditor's assessment of the risk of material misstatements relating to financial statement assertions. However, such agreements may help to inform the auditor's judgment concerning the effect of performance failure on the entity's financial statements: this may be relevant in instances of performance failure, when the existence of an indemnity may help to ensure that the entity's status as a going concern is not threatened. Where the auditor wishes to rely on the operation of the indemnity for this purpose, the resources available to the service organisation also need to be considered.

6-4

Compliance with Law and Regulations

Additionally, the auditor considers whether the activities undertaken by the service organisation are in an area in which the entity is required to comply with requirements of law and regulations. In such circumstances, non-compliance may have a significant effect on the financial statements. The auditor therefore determines whether the law and regulations concerned are to be regarded as relevant to the audit[3] in order to meet the requirements of ISA (UK and Ireland) 250 "Consideration of laws and regulations in an audit of financial statements" and undertake procedures to assess the risk of a misstatement arising from non-compliance as set out in that ISA (UK and Ireland).

6-5

Assessing Risks

If the auditor concludes that the activities of the service organization are significant to the entity and relevant to the audit, the auditor should obtain a sufficient understanding of the entity and its environment, including its internal control, to identify and assess the risks of material misstatement and design further audit procedures in response to the

7

---

[3] *Laws and regulations are relevant to the audit when they either relate directly to the preparation of the financial statements of the entity, or are central to its ability to conduct its business - [ISA (UK and Ireland) 250 – Section A, paragraphs 18-1 and 19]*

assessed risk. The auditor assesses the risk of material misstatement at the financial statement level and at the assertion level for classes of transactions, account balances and disclosures.

8   If the understanding obtained is insufficient, the auditor would consider the need to request the service organization to have its auditor perform such risk assessment procedures to supply the necessary information, or the need to visit the service organization to obtain the information. An auditor wishing to visit a service organization may advise the entity to request the service organization to give the auditor access to the necessary information.

9   The auditor may be able to obtain a sufficient understanding of internal control affected by the service organization by reading the third-party report of the service organization auditor. In addition, when assessing the risks of material misstatement, for assertions affected by the service organization's internal controls, the auditor may also use the service organization auditor's report. **If the auditor uses the report of a service organization auditor, the auditor should consider making inquiries concerning that auditor's professional competence in the context of the specific assignment undertaken by the service organization auditor.**

9-1   **The auditor should determine the effect of relevant activities on their assessment of risk and the client's control environment.**

9-2   The auditor assesses risk in relation to financial statement assertions. An entity's decision to commission a service organisation to undertake activities which are relevant to the audit (as defined in paragraph 3-4) affects risk in relation to financial statement assertions about material account balances and classes of transactions arising from those activities. The auditor's assessment of risk will be affected inter alia by:

- *The nature of the services provided*: the complexity of activities undertaken by the service organisation may affect the auditor's assessment of risk. For example, outsourcing the treasury function involves a considerably greater degree of risk than straightforward custody of investments.
- *The degree to which authority is delegated to the service organisations*: the provision of accounting services consisting of maintenance of accounting records limited to recording completed transactions carries a relatively low risk of error compared with accounting services which involve initiating transactions (for example, VAT payments). In some cases, the entity may delegate wide powers of decision-making to the service provider, as is the case where an investment manager is given discretionary powers in relation to an entity's investment portfolio.
- *The arrangements for ensuring quality of the service provided*: such arrangements may vary considerably, depending upon the nature of the service and the degree of delegation involved. In general, the greater degree of delegation, the more likely it is that the entity's management will rely on controls operated by the service organisation over the completeness and integrity of information and records of the entity.
- *Whether the activities involve assets which are susceptible to loss or misappropriation*.
- *The reputation for integrity of those responsible for direction and management of the service organisation*: the extent to which a service organisation has a proven record for ensuring quality both of service and of information may provide indicative factors relating to the likely reliability of information it provides to the entity. The auditor therefore considers the extent and

frequency of errors in and adjustments to information provided by the service organisation.

Some outsourced activities are the subject of regulation, notably investment management. However, the existence of regulation does not eliminate the need for the auditor to obtain independent evidence because controls required by regulators, and inspection work undertaken by them in service organisations, may not be relevant to or sufficiently focussed on aspects of importance to the entity. Furthermore, reports from the service organisation's auditor required by its regulator are not ordinarily available to an entity or its auditor.

9-3

The financial standing of a service organisation is relevant to the audit insofar as the auditor considers it necessary to rely on the operation of an indemnity from the service organisation in assessing the entity's status as a going concern (see paragraph 6-4). However, a service organisation whose cash and/or capital resources are low in relation to the nature of services provided or the volume of its customers may be susceptible to pressures resulting in errors or deliberate misstatements in reporting to the entity, or fraud. If the auditor considers that this factor may be relevant to the assessment of risk, the auditor also takes into account the existence of binding arrangements to provide resources to the service organisations from a holding company or other group company, and the financial strength of the group as a whole.

9-4

The arrangements made by those charged with governance to monitor the way in which activities are undertaken by a service organisation may include a number of factors relevant to the auditor's assessment of risk. These include:

9-5

- The extent and nature of controls operated by the entity's personnel.
- Undertakings by the service organisation for the operation of internal controls, and whether such controls are adequately specified, having regard to the size and complexity of the activities undertaken by the service organization.
- Actual experience of adjustments to, or errors and omissions in, reports received from the service organization.
- The way in which the entity determines whether the service organisation complies with its contractual undertakings, in particular the way in which it monitors compliance with applicable law and regulations.
- Whether the service organisation provides information on the design and operation of systems of controls, possibly accompanied by reports from its external auditor.

When a service organisation undertakes maintenance of accounting records, factors of particular importance to the auditor's assessment of risk include the following:

9-6

- The knowledge and expertise of service organisation staff in matters relevant to the entity's business.
- The practicability of control by the entity's management, and the nature of controls actually implemented. Some types of business facilitate the use of analytical control techniques subsequent to completion of transactions (for example payroll processing); others need detailed processing controls operated on a concurrent basis (for example, distribution centres which hold stock belonging to the entity and arrange deliveries for the entity).
- The use of quality assurance processes by the service organisation (e.g. its internal audit function).

9-7 Examples of ways in which different activities undertaken by service organisations can affect the risk of misstatement are given in the Appendix to this ISA (UK and Ireland).

Designing Audit Procedures

9-8 Following the assessment of risk, the auditor determines the nature, timing and extent of tests of control and substantive procedures required to provide sufficient appropriate audit evidence as to whether the financial statements are free of material misstatement.

9-9 Assessing the sufficiency and appropriateness of audit evidence as a basis for reporting on financial statements requires the auditor to exercise judgment concerning both the quantity of evidence required and its quality. This judgment is affected by the degree of risk of material misstatements in the financial statements, the quality of the entity's accounting and internal control systems and the reliability of information available.

9-10 The reliability of information for use as audit evidence is determined by a number of factors, including its source. In general terms, evidence supporting an item in an entity's financial statements is more reliable when it is obtained from an independent source; similarly, documentary evidence is normally regarded as more reliable than oral representations.

9-11 The use of service organisations to undertake particular activities introduces an additional element in the auditor's judgment as to whether evidence can be regarded as coming from an independent source. Whilst the service organisation is a third party, the nature of the activities undertaken or the arrangements for their management may mean that information it provides concerning transactions initiated, processed or recorded on behalf of the entity cannot be regarded as independent for audit purposes. Hence the auditor needs to assess carefully the nature and source of information available in order to establish the most effective way to obtain evidence competent to support an independent opinion on its financial statements.

Accounting Records

9-12 **If a service organisation maintains all or part of an entity's accounting records, the auditor should assess whether the arrangements affect the auditor's reporting responsibilities in relation to accounting records arising from law or regulation.**

9-13 For each relevant activity involving maintenance of material elements of the entity's accounting records by a service organisation, the auditor obtains and documents an understanding as to the way that the accounting records are maintained, including the way in which those charged with governance ensure that its accounting records meet any relevant legal obligations. Such obligations may arise under statute, regulation (for example, specific requirements apply to authorised investment businesses) or under the terms of the entity's governing document (for example, the trust deed establishing a charity may require it to maintain particular records).

9-14 Key obligations of entities incorporated under company law are:

(a) To maintain accounting records which are sufficient to:

(i) Disclose with reasonable accuracy, at any time, the financial position of the company at that time, and
(ii) Enable the directors to ensure that the company's financial statements meet statutory requirements;
(b) To guard against falsification; and
(c) To provide its directors, officers and auditor with access to its accounting records at any time[4].

When an entity incorporated under company law arranges for a service organisation to maintain its accounting records, the contractual arrangements can only be regarded as appropriate if they establish the company's legal ownership of the records and provide for access to them at any time by those charged with governance of the company and by its auditor.

9.15

An auditor of entities incorporated under company law has statutory reporting obligations relating to compliance with requirements for companies to maintain proper accounting records. Where such an entity outsources the preparation of its accounting records to a service organisation, issues relating to whether the arrangements with the service organisation are such as to permit the entity to meet its statutory obligations may require careful consideration, by both those charged with governance and the auditor. Where there is doubt, the auditor may wish to encourage the those charged with governance to take legal advice before issuing their report on its financial statements.

9-16

A particular issue arises in relation to companies incorporated in the United Kingdom. The wording of UK company law appears to be prescriptive and to require the company itself to keep accounting records. Consequently, whether a company 'keeps' records (as opposed to 'causes records to be kept') will depend upon the particular terms of the outsourcing arrangements and, in particular, the extent to which the company retains ownership of, has access to, or holds copies of, those records[5].

9-17

Obtaining Audit Evidence.

Based on the auditor's understanding of the aspects of the entity's accounting system and control environment relating to relevant activities, the auditor should:

9-18

(a) **Assess whether sufficient appropriate audit evidence concerning the relevant financial statement assertions is available from records held at the entity; and if not,**
(b) **Determine effective procedures to obtain evidence necessary for the audit, either by direct access to records kept by service organisations or through information obtained from the service organisations or their auditor.**

In general, the most cost effective audit approach is likely to be based on information obtained from the entity, together with confirmations from the service organisation, where these provide independent evidence. However, such an approach may not always be feasible, particularly in instances where the service

9-19

---

[4] In the UK, Companies Act 1985, sections 221, 222, 389A and 722 and in Ireland, Companies Act 1963, section 378 and Companies Act 1990, sections 193 and 202.

[5] In Ireland, company law requires that companies shall cause records to be kept in accordance with its requirements.

organisation can initiate transactions or payments on the entity's behalf without prior agreement or approval.

9-20 When the service organisation maintains material elements of the accounting records of the entity, the auditor may require direct access to those records in order to obtain sufficient appropriate audit evidence relating to the operation of controls over those records or to substantiate transactions and balances recorded in them, or both. Such access may involve either physical inspection of records at the service organisation's premises or interrogation of records maintained electronically from the entity or another location, or both. Where direct access is achieved electronically, the auditor may also need to consider obtaining evidence as to the adequacy of controls operated by the service organisation over the completeness and integrity of the entity's data for which it is responsible.

9-21 In determining the extent and nature of audit evidence to be obtained in relation to balances representing assets held or transactions undertaken by service organisations undertaking relevant activities, the auditor evaluates the efficiency and effectiveness of the following procedures:

(a) Inspecting records and documents held by the entity: the effectiveness of this source of evidence is determined by the nature and extent of the accounting records and supporting documentation retained by the entity. In some cases the entity may not maintain detailed records or documentation initiating transactions, nor will it receive documentation confirming specific transactions undertaken on its behalf;

(b) Establishing the effectiveness of controls: entities may monitor performance of activities undertaken by a service organisation in a variety of ways. Where a entity has established direct controls over such activities, its auditor may, if the auditor proposes to place reliance on their operation, undertake tests of those controls. Alternatively, the arrangements for monitoring the activity concerned may include obtaining an undertaking from the service organisation that its control systems will provide assurance as to the reliability of financial information;

(c) Obtaining representations to confirm balances and transactions from the service organisation: where the entity maintains independent records of balances and transactions and a service organisation executes transactions only at the specific authorisation of the entity or acts as a simple custodian of assets, confirmation from the service provider corroborating those records usually constitutes reliable audit evidence concerning the existence of the transactions and assets concerned.

If the entity does not maintain independent records, information obtained in representations from the service provider is merely a statement of what is reflected in the records maintained by the service organisation. Hence such representations do not, taken alone, constitute reliable audit evidence. In these circumstances, the auditor considers whether there is a separation of functions for the services provided such that an alternative source of independent evidence can be identified. For example:

- When one service organisation initiates transactions and another independent organisation holds related documents of title or other records (for example an investment manager initiates trades and another entity acts as custodian), the auditor may confirm year end balances with the latter, apply other substantive procedures to transactions reported by the first service organisation and review the reconciliation of differences between the records of the two organizations.
- If one organisation both initiates transactions on behalf of the entity and also holds related documents of title, all the information available

> to the auditor is based on that organisation's information. In such circumstances, the auditor is unable to obtain reliable audit evidence to corroborate representations from the service organisation unless effective separation of functions exists, for example where there are separate departments to provide the investment management and custodian services, which operate independently and whose records are independently generated and maintained.
> (d) Performing analytical review procedures on the records maintained by the entity or on the returns received from the service organisation: the effectiveness of analytical procedures is likely to vary by assertion and will be affected by the extent and detail of information available;
> (e) Inspecting records and documents held by the service organisation: the auditor's access to the records of the service organisation is likely to be established as part of the contractual arrangements between the entity and the service organisation.

The auditor obtains audit evidence about the operating effectiveness of controls when the auditor's risk assessment includes an expectation of the operating effectiveness of the service organization's controls or when substantive procedures alone do not provide sufficient appropriate audit evidence at the assertion level. The auditor may also conclude that it would be efficient to obtain audit evidence from tests of controls. Audit evidence about the operating effectiveness of controls may be obtained by the following: 10

- Performing tests of the entity's controls over activities of the service organization.
- Obtaining a service organization auditor's report that expresses an opinion as to the operating effectiveness of the service organization's internal control for the service organization activities relevant to the audit.
- Visiting the service organization and performing tests of controls.

Service Organization Auditor's Reports

When using a service organization auditor's report, the auditor should consider the nature of and content of that report. 11

The report of the service organization auditor will ordinarily be one of two types as follows: 12

Type A—Report on the Design and Implementation of Internal Control

(a) A description of the service organization's internal control, ordinarily prepared by the management of the service organization; and
(b) An opinion by the service organization auditor that:
   (i) The above description is accurate;
   (ii) The internal control is suitably designed to achieve their stated objectives; and
   (iii) The internal controls have been implemented.

Type B—Report on the Design, Implementation and Operating Effectiveness of Internal Control

(a) A description of the service organization's internal control, ordinarily prepared by the management of the service organization; and
(b) An opinion by the service organization auditor that:
   (i) The above description is accurate;
   (ii) The internal controls is suitably designed to achieve their stated objectives;
   (iii) The internal controls have been implemented; and
   (iv) The internal controls are operating effectively based on the results from the tests of controls. In addition to the opinion on operating effectiveness, the service organization auditor would identify the tests of controls performed and related results.

The report of the service organization auditor will ordinarily contain restrictions as to use (generally to management, the service organization and its customers, and the entity's auditors).

13 **The auditor should consider the scope of work performed by the service organization auditor and should evaluate the usefulness and appropriateness of reports issued by the service organization auditor.**

13-1 **The auditor should consider whether the report issued by the service organization auditor is sufficient for its intended use.**

13-2 In assessing the relevance of reports from the auditor of the service organisation or from the client's internal audit function regarding the operation of its accounting and internal control systems, the auditor considers whether the report:

(a) Addresses controls and procedures concerning financial statement assertions that are relevant to the auditor's examination;
(b) Provides an adequate level of information concerning relevant aspects of the systems' design, implementation and operation over a specified period, including:
   (i) The way in which the service organization monitors the completeness and integrity of data relating to reports to its customers; and
   (ii) Whether the service organization auditor's testing of operational effectiveness of controls was undertaken in relation to all customers (or all customers of a specified type, that includes the entity) and addressed transactions and balances that could be expected to be representative of the population as a whole; and
(c) Covers the period during which the entity auditor intends to rely on an assessment of control risk at the service organization.

14 While Type A reports may be useful to the auditor in obtaining an understanding of the internal control, an auditor would not use such reports as audit evidence about the operating effectiveness of controls.

15 In contrast, Type B reports may provide such audit evidence since tests of control have been performed. When a Type B report is to be used as audit evidence about operating effectiveness of controls, the auditor would consider whether the controls tested by the service organization auditor are relevant to the entity's transactions, account balances, and disclosures, and related assertions, and whether the service organization auditor's tests of control and the results are adequate. With respect to the latter, two key considerations are the length of the period covered by the service organization auditor's tests and the time since the performance of those tests.

If the service organization auditor's Type B reports do not fully cover the period during which the auditor intends to rely on internal control at the service organization, the auditor determines whether additional auditing procedures or a change in audit strategy are necessary. In making this determination, the length of the period not covered by the report is considered. 15-1

Additional auditing procedures which may be carried out with respect to a period not covered by such test include: 15-2

- Review of stewardship reports or any other correspondence from the service organization to the client relating to the intervening period.
- Consideration of any previous or subsequent reports issued by the service organization's auditor.
- Consideration of the reputation of the service organization as a provider of reliable information (in order to form a judgment about the risk of error in the 'stub period').
- A request for assurance from the service organization, or possibly its auditor, that there were no significant changes in the intervening period to the stated control objectives or control procedures designed to achieve those objectives that are relevant to the auditor.

For those specific tests of control and results that are relevant, the auditor should consider whether the nature, timing and extent of such tests provide sufficient appropriate audit evidence about the operating effectiveness of the internal control to support the auditor's assessed risks of material misstatement. 16

The auditor of a service organization may be engaged to perform substantive procedures that are of use to the entity's auditor. Such engagements may involve the performance of procedures agreed upon by the entity and its auditor and by the service organization and its auditor. 17

When the auditor uses a report from the auditor of a service organization, no reference should be made in the entity's auditor's report to the auditor's report on the service organization. 18

Reporting

If an auditor concludes that evidence from records held by a service organization is necessary in order to form an opinion on the client's financial statements and the auditor is unable to obtain such evidence, the auditor should include a description of the factors leading to the lack of evidence in the basis of opinion section of their report and qualify their opinion or issue a disclaimer of opinion on the financial statements. 18-1

The auditor is unlikely to be able to obtain sufficient appropriate evidence to express an unqualified opinion if all of the following three conditions exist: 18-2

(a) The client does not maintain adequate records of, or controls over, the activities undertaken by the service organisation or cause such records to be maintained independently of the service organisation;

(b) The service organization has not made available a report from its auditor concerning the operation of aspects of its systems of controls which the auditor considers sufficient for the purposes of their audit; and
(c) The auditor is unable to carry out such tests as the auditor considers appropriate at the service organization itself, nor has it been possible for those tests to be undertaken by the service organization's auditor.

In such circumstances, the auditor issues a disclaimer of opinion when the possible effect of the resulting limitation on the scope of their work is so material or pervasive that the auditor is unable to express an opinion. When the effect of the limitation is not so material or pervasive, the auditor indicates that the auditor's opinion is qualified as to the possible adjustments to the financial statements that might have been determined to be necessary had the limitation not existed.

Effective Date

18-3 This ISA (UK and Ireland) is effective for audits of financial statements for periods commencing on or after 15 December 2004.

Appendix – Examples of Factors Relating to Activities Undertaken by Service Organizations Which May Increase the Risk of Material Misstatements

1 Outsourced Accounting Functions

Degree of risk	Characteristics	Examples
High	• Complex transactions • Those undertaking accounting work need extensive business or specialist knowledge • Delegated authority to initiate and execute transactions • Effective controls only possible on 'real time' basis • Reversal of outsourcing costly/difficult • High cost of performance failure (e.g. misleading management reports leading to poor decision making) • High proportion of finance functions outsourced	• Maintenance of both accounting records and preparation of budgets and control reports • Accounting records of retail business
Medium	• Some business knowledge needed but parameters for necessary judgements can be identified and agreed in advance • Transactions can be initiated but execution requires approval from entity • Execution of transactions on instruction from entity • Analytical techniques insufficient for adequate degree of control	• Outsourcing of accounting records by a supplier of raw materials • Credit control • Leasing arrangements

Degree of risk	Characteristics	Examples
	• Discrete functions outsourced.	
Low	• Little requirement for judgment in processing transactions • Non-complex transactions • Little business knowledge required • Analytical control techniques effective • Effects of failure can be contained. • Easy to rearrange/ find alternate service organisations • Low proportion of discrete functions outsourced	• Processing salary payments • Preparation of invoices • Data entry

2 Outsourced Investment Custody and Management

Degree of risk	Characteristics	Examples
High	- Transactions can be initiated on a discretionary basis - Entity does not maintain and cannot generate independent records of assets and interest, dividends or other income - Complex financial instruments - Custody and investment management undertaken by two separate entities but records are not independently generated, or one combined report is provided to the entity	- Discretionary trading, same custodian
Medium	- Combination of custody and execution of transactions/ collection of income but entity maintains or can generate (for example by reference to Extel) independent records of income - Custody and investment management undertaken by two unrelated entities which maintain independently generated records (i.e. derived from different source data) and report separately direct to the entity	- Custodian responsible for collection of dividends and reporting of income: entity reviews information - Independent custodian and investment manager

Degree of risk	Characteristics	Examples
Low	<ul><li>Entity initiates and maintains records of transactions</li><li>Separation of execution and custody functions</li><li>Low frequency of transactions and/or counterparties</li><li>Non-complex financial instruments</li><li>Analytical control techniques effective</li></ul>	<ul><li>Custody of assets only</li><li>Execution of investment transactions pursuant to entity's instructions</li></ul>

[500]
Audit evidence
(Issued December 2004)

Contents

	Paragraphs
Introduction	1 - 2
Concept of Audit Evidence	3 - 6
Sufficient Appropriate Audit Evidence	7 - 14
The Use of Assertions in Obtaining Audit Evidence	15 - 18
Audit Procedures for Obtaining Audit Evidence	19 - 38
Inspection of Records or Documents	26 - 27
Inspection of Tangible Assets	28
Observation	29
Inquiry	30 - 34
Confirmation	35
Recalculation	36
Reperformance	37
Analytical Procedures	38
Effective Date	39

International Standard on Auditing (UK and Ireland) (ISA (UK and Ireland)) 500 "Audit Evidence" should be read in the context of the Auditing Practices Board's Statement "The Auditing Practices Board – Scope and Authority of Pronouncements (Revised)" which sets out the application and authority of ISAs (UK and Ireland).

Introduction

1. The purpose of this International Standard on Auditing (UK and Ireland) (ISA (UK and Ireland)) is to establish standards and provide guidance on what constitutes audit evidence in an audit of financial statements, the quantity and quality of audit evidence to be obtained, and the audit procedures that auditors use for obtaining that audit evidence.

1-1 This ISA (UK and Ireland) uses the terms 'those charged with governance' and 'management'. The term 'governance' describes the role of persons entrusted with the supervision, control and direction of an entity. Ordinarily, those charged with governance are accountable for ensuring that the entity achieves its objectives, and for the quality of its financial reporting and reporting to interested parties. Those charged with governance include management only when they perform such functions.

1-2 In the UK and Ireland, those charged with governance include the directors (executive and non-executive) of a company or other body, the members of an audit committee where one exists, the partners, proprietors, committee of management or trustees of other forms of entity, or equivalent persons responsible for directing the entity's affairs and preparing its financial statements.

1-3 'Management' comprises those persons who perform senior managerial functions.

1-4 In the UK and Ireland, depending on the nature and circumstances of the entity, management may include some or all of those charged with governance (e.g. executive directors). Management will not normally include non-executive directors.

2. **The auditor should obtain sufficient appropriate audit evidence to be able to draw reasonable conclusions on which to base the audit opinion.**

Concept of Audit Evidence

3. "Audit evidence" is all the information used by the auditor in arriving at the conclusions on which the audit opinion is based, and includes the information contained in the accounting records underlying the financial statements and other information. Auditors are not expected to address all information that may exist.[1] Audit evidence, which is cumulative in nature, includes audit evidence obtained from audit procedures performed during the course of the audit and may include audit evidence obtained from other sources such as previous audits and a firm's quality control procedures for client acceptance and continuance.

4. Accounting records generally include the records of initial entries and supporting records, such as checks and records of electronic fund transfers; invoices; contracts; the general and subsidiary ledgers, journal entries and other adjustments to the financial statements that are not reflected in formal journal entries; and records such as work sheets and spreadsheets supporting cost allocations, computations, reconciliations and disclosures. The entries in the accounting records are often initiated, recorded, processed and reported in electronic form. In addition, the accounting

---

[1] See paragraph 14.

records may be part of integrated systems that share data and support all aspects of the entity's financial reporting, operations and compliance objectives.

Management[1a] is responsible for the preparation of the financial statements based upon the accounting records of the entity. The auditor obtains some audit evidence by testing the accounting records, for example, through analysis and review, reperforming procedures followed in the financial reporting process, and reconciling related types and applications of the same information. Through the performance of such audit procedures, the auditor may determine that the accounting records are internally consistent and agree to the financial statements. However, because accounting records alone do not provide sufficient audit evidence on which to base an audit opinion on the financial statements, the auditor obtains other audit evidence.

Other information that the auditor may use as audit evidence includes minutes of meetings; confirmations from third parties; analysts' reports; comparable data about competitors (benchmarking); controls manuals; information obtained by the auditor from such audit procedures as inquiry, observation, and inspection; and other information developed by, or available to, the auditor that permits the auditor to reach conclusions through valid reasoning.

Sufficient Appropriate Audit Evidence

Sufficiency is the measure of the quantity of audit evidence. Appropriateness is the measure of the quality of audit evidence; that is, its relevance and its reliability in providing support for, or detecting misstatements in, the classes of transactions, account balances, and disclosures and related assertions. The quantity of audit evidence needed is affected by the risk of misstatement (the greater the risk, the more audit evidence is likely to be required) and also by the quality of such audit evidence (the higher the quality, the less may be required). Accordingly, the sufficiency and appropriateness of audit evidence are interrelated. However, merely obtaining more audit evidence may not compensate for its poor quality.

A given set of audit procedures may provide audit evidence that is relevant to certain assertions, but not others. For example, inspection of records and documents related to the collection of receivables after the period end may provide audit evidence regarding both existence and valuation, although not necessarily the appropriateness of period-end cutoffs. On the other hand, the auditor often obtains audit evidence from different sources or of a different nature that is relevant to the same assertion. For example, the auditor may analyze the aging of accounts receivable and the subsequent collection of receivables to obtain audit evidence relating to the valuation of the allowance for doubtful accounts. Furthermore, obtaining audit evidence relating to a particular assertion, for example, the physical existence of inventory, is not a substitute for obtaining audit evidence regarding another assertion, for example, the valuation of inventory.

The reliability of audit evidence is influenced by its source and by its nature and is dependent on the individual circumstances under which it is obtained. Generalizations about the reliability of various kinds of audit evidence can be made; however, such generalizations are subject to important exceptions. Even when audit evidence is obtained from sources external to the entity, circumstances may exist that could affect the reliability of the information obtained. For example, audit evidence

---

[1a] In the UK and Ireland, the auditor obtains written representations from those charged with governance.

obtained from an independent external source may not be reliable if the source is not knowledgeable. While recognizing that exceptions may exist, the following generalizations about the reliability of audit evidence may be useful:

- Audit evidence is more reliable when it is obtained from independent sources outside the entity.
- Audit evidence that is generated internally is more reliable when the related controls imposed by the entity are effective.
- Audit evidence obtained directly by the auditor (for example, observation of the application of a control) is more reliable than audit evidence obtained indirectly or by inference (for example, inquiry about the application of a control).
- Audit evidence is more reliable when it exists in documentary form, whether paper, electronic, or other medium (for example, a contemporaneously written record of a meeting is more reliable than a subsequent oral representation of the matters discussed).
- Audit evidence provided by original documents is more reliable than audit evidence provided by photocopies or facsimiles.

10 An audit rarely involves the authentication of documentation, nor is the auditor trained as or expected to be an expert in such authentication. However, the auditor considers the reliability of the information to be used as audit evidence, for example, photocopies, facsimiles, filmed, digitized or other electronic documents, including consideration of controls over their preparation and maintenance where relevant.

11 **When information produced by the entity is used by the auditor to perform audit procedures, the auditor should obtain audit evidence about the accuracy and completeness of the information.** In order for the auditor to obtain reliable audit evidence, the information upon which the audit procedures are based needs to be sufficiently complete and accurate. For example, in auditing revenue by applying standard prices to records of sales volume, the auditor considers the accuracy of the price information and the completeness and accuracy of the sales volume data. Obtaining audit evidence about the completeness and accuracy of the information produced by the entity's information system may be performed concurrently with the actual audit procedure applied to the information when obtaining such audit evidence is an integral part of the audit procedure itself. In other situations, the auditor may have obtained audit evidence of the accuracy and completeness of such information by testing controls over the production and maintenance of the information. However, in some situations the auditor may determine that additional audit procedures are needed. For example, these additional procedures may include using computer-assisted audit techniques (CAATs) to recalculate the information.

12 The auditor ordinarily obtains more assurance from consistent audit evidence obtained from different sources or of a different nature than from items of audit evidence considered individually. In addition, obtaining audit evidence from different sources or of a different nature may indicate that an individual item of audit evidence is not reliable. For example, corroborating information obtained from a source independent of the entity may increase the assurance the auditor obtains from a management[1a] representation. Conversely, when audit evidence obtained from one source is inconsistent with that obtained from another, the auditor determines what additional audit procedures are necessary to resolve the inconsistency.

13 The auditor considers the relationship between the cost of obtaining audit evidence and the usefulness of the information obtained. However, the matter of difficulty or expense involved is not in itself a valid basis for omitting an audit procedure for which there is no alternative.

In forming the audit opinion the auditor does not examine all the information available because conclusions ordinarily can be reached by using sampling approaches and other means of selecting items for testing. Also, the auditor ordinarily finds it necessary to rely on audit evidence that is persuasive rather than conclusive; however, to obtain reasonable assurance,[2] the auditor is not satisfied with audit evidence that is less than persuasive. The auditor uses professional judgment and exercises professional skepticism in evaluating the quantity and quality of audit evidence, and thus its sufficiency and appropriateness, to support the audit opinion.

14

The Use of Assertions in Obtaining Audit Evidence

Management[3] is responsible for the fair presentation of financial statements that reflect the nature and operations of the entity. In representing that the financial statements give a true and fair view (or are presented fairly, in all material respects) in accordance with the applicable financial reporting framework, management implicitly or explicitly makes assertions regarding the recognition, measurement, presentation and disclosure of the various elements of financial statements and related disclosures.

15

The auditor should use assertions for classes of transactions, account balances, and presentation and disclosures in sufficient detail to form a basis for the assessment of risks of material misstatement and the design and performance of further audit procedures. The auditor uses assertions in assessing risks by considering the different types of potential misstatements that may occur, and thereby designing audit procedures that are responsive to the assessed risks. Other ISAs (UK and Ireland) discuss specific situations where the auditor is required to obtain audit evidence at the assertion level.

16

Assertions used by the auditor fall into the following categories:

17

(a) Assertions about classes of transactions and events for the period under audit:
  (i) Occurrence – transactions and events that have been recorded have occurred and pertain to the entity.
  (ii) Completeness – all transactions and events that should have been recorded have been recorded.
  (iii) Accuracy – amounts and other data relating to recorded transactions and events have been recorded appropriately.
  (iv) Cutoff – transactions and events have been recorded in the correct accounting period.
  (v) Classification – transactions and events have been recorded in the proper accounts.
(b) Assertions about account balances at the period end.
  (i) Existence – assets, liabilities, and equity interests exist.
  (ii) Rights and obligations – the entity holds or controls the rights to assets, and liabilities are the obligations of the entity.
  (iii) Completeness – all assets, liabilities and equity interests that should have been recorded have been recorded.

---

[2] Paragraphs 8-12 of ISA (UK and Ireland) 200, "Objective and General Principles Governing an Audit of Financial Statements," provide discussion of reasonable assurance as it relates to an audit of financial statements.

[3] In the UK and Ireland, those charged with governance are responsible for the preparation of the financial statements.

(iv) Valuation and allocation – assets, liabilities, and equity interests are included in the financial statements at appropriate amounts and any resulting valuation or allocation adjustments are appropriately recorded.
(c) Assertions about presentation and disclosure:
  (i) Occurrence and rights and obligations – disclosed events, transactions, and other matters have occurred and pertain to the entity.
  (ii) Completeness – all disclosures that should have been included in the financial statements have been included.
  (iii) Classification and understandability – financial information is appropriately presented and described, and disclosures are clearly expressed.
  (iv) Accuracy and valuation – financial and other information are disclosed fairly and at appropriate amounts.

18 The auditor may use the assertions as described above or may express them differently provided all aspects described above have been covered. For example, the auditor may choose to combine the assertions about transactions and events with the assertions about account balances. As another example, there may not be a separate assertion related to cutoff of transactions and events when the occurrence and completeness assertions include appropriate consideration of recording transactions in the correct accounting period.

Audit Procedures for Obtaining Audit Evidence

19 The auditor obtains audit evidence to draw reasonable conclusions on which to base the audit opinion by performing audit procedures to:

(a) Obtain an understanding of the entity and its environment, including its internal control, to assess the risks of material misstatement at the financial statement and assertion levels (audit procedures performed for this purpose are referred to in the ISAs (UK and Ireland) as "risk assessment procedures");

(b) When necessary or when the auditor has determined to do so, test the operating effectiveness of controls in preventing, or detecting and correcting, material misstatements at the assertion level (audit procedures performed for this purpose are referred to in the ISAs (UK and Ireland) as "tests of controls"); and

(c) Detect material misstatements at the assertion level (audit procedures performed for this purpose are referred to in the ISAs (UK and Ireland) as "substantive procedures" and include tests of details of classes of transactions, account balances, and disclosures and substantive analytical procedures).

20 The auditor always performs risk assessment procedures to provide a satisfactory basis for the assessment of risks at the financial statement and assertion levels. Risk assessment procedures by themselves do not provide sufficient appropriate audit evidence on which to base the audit opinion, however, and are supplemented by further audit procedures in the form of tests of controls, when necessary, and substantive procedures.

21 Tests of controls are necessary in two circumstances. When the auditor's risk assessment includes an expectation of the operating effectiveness of controls, the auditor is required to test those controls to support the risk assessment. In addition, when substantive procedures alone do not provide sufficient appropriate audit evidence, the auditor is required to perform tests of controls to obtain audit evidence about their operating effectiveness.

22 The auditor plans and performs substantive procedures to be responsive to the related assessment of the risks of material misstatement, which includes the results of

tests of controls, if any. The auditor's risk assessment is judgmental, however, and may not be sufficiently precise to identify all risks of material misstatement. Further, there are inherent limitations to internal control, including the risk of management override, the possibility of human error and the effect of systems changes. Therefore, substantive procedures for material classes of transactions, account balances, and disclosures are always required to obtain sufficient appropriate audit evidence.

23 The auditor uses one or more types of audit procedures described in paragraphs 26-38 below. These audit procedures, or combinations thereof, may be used as risk assessment procedures, tests of controls or substantive procedures, depending on the context in which they are applied by the auditor. In certain circumstances, audit evidence obtained from previous audits may provide audit evidence where the auditor performs audit procedures to establish its continuing relevance.

24 The nature and timing of the audit procedures to be used may be affected by the fact that some of the accounting data and other information may be available only in electronic form or only at certain points or periods in time. Source documents, such as purchase orders, bills of lading, invoices, and checks, may be replaced with electronic messages. For example, entities may use electronic commerce or image processing systems. In electronic commerce, the entity and its customers or suppliers use connected computers over a public network, such as the Internet, to transact business electronically. Purchase, shipping, billing, cash receipt, and cash disbursement transactions are often consummated entirely by the exchange of electronic messages between the parties. In image processing systems, documents are scanned and converted into electronic images to facilitate storage and reference, and the source documents may not be retained after conversion. Certain electronic information may exist at a certain point in time. However, such information may not be retrievable after a specified period of time if files are changed and if backup files do not exist. An entity's data retention policies may require the auditor to request retention of some information for the auditor's review or to perform audit procedures at a time when the information is available.

25 When the information is in electronic form, the auditor may carry out certain of the audit procedures described below through CAATs.

Inspection of Records or Documents

26 Inspection consists of examining records or documents, whether internal or external, in paper form, electronic form, or other media. Inspection of records and documents provides audit evidence of varying degrees of reliability, depending on their nature and source and, in the case of internal records and documents, on the effectiveness of the controls over their production. An example of inspection used as a test of controls is inspection of records or documents for evidence of authorization.

27 Some documents represent direct audit evidence of the existence of an asset, for example, a document constituting a financial instrument such as a stock or bond. Inspection of such documents may not necessarily provide audit evidence about ownership or value. In addition, inspecting an executed contract may provide audit evidence relevant to the entity's application of accounting policies, such as revenue recognition.

Inspection of Tangible Assets

28 Inspection of tangible assets consists of physical examination of the assets. Inspection of tangible assets may provide reliable audit evidence with respect to their

existence, but not necessarily about the entity's rights and obligations or the valuation of the assets. Inspection of individual inventory items ordinarily accompanies the observation of inventory counting.

Observation

29   Observation consists of looking at a process or procedure being performed by others. Examples include observation of the counting of inventories by the entity's personnel and observation of the performance of control activities. Observation provides audit evidence about the performance of a process or procedure, but is limited to the point in time at which the observation takes place and by the fact that the act of being observed may affect how the process or procedure is performed. See ISA (UK and Ireland) 501, "Audit Evidence – Additional Considerations for Specific Items" for further guidance on observation of the counting of inventory.

Inquiry

30   Inquiry consists of seeking information of knowledgeable persons, both financial and non-financial, throughout the entity or outside the entity. Inquiry is an audit procedure that is used extensively throughout the audit and often is complementary to performing other audit procedures. Inquiries may range from formal written inquiries to informal oral inquiries. Evaluating responses to inquiries is an integral part of the inquiry process.

31   Responses to inquiries may provide the auditor with information not previously possessed or with corroborative audit evidence. Alternatively, responses might provide information that differs significantly from other information that the auditor has obtained, for example, information regarding the possibility of management override of controls. In some cases, responses to inquiries provide a basis for the auditor to modify or perform additional audit procedures.

32   The auditor performs audit procedures in addition to the use of inquiry to obtain sufficient appropriate audit evidence. Inquiry alone ordinarily does not provide sufficient audit evidence to detect a material misstatement at the assertion level. Moreover, inquiry alone is not sufficient to test the operating effectiveness of controls.

33   Although corroboration of evidence obtained through inquiry is often of particular importance, in the case of inquiries about management intent, the information available to support management's intent may be limited. In these cases, understanding management's past history of carrying out its stated intentions with respect to assets or liabilities, management's stated reasons for choosing a particular course of action, and management's ability to pursue a specific course of action may provide relevant information about management's intent.

34   In respect of some matters, the auditor obtains written representations from management[1a] to confirm responses to oral inquiries. For example, the auditor ordinarily obtains written representations from management[1a] on material matters when other sufficient appropriate audit evidence cannot reasonably be expected to exist or when the other audit evidence obtained is of a lower quality. See ISA (UK and Ireland) 580, "Management Representations" for further guidance on written representations.

Confirmation

Confirmation, which is a specific type of inquiry, is the process of obtaining a representation of information or of an existing condition directly from a third party. For example, the auditor may seek direct confirmation of receivables by communication with debtors. Confirmations are frequently used in relation to account balances and their components, but need not be restricted to these items. For example, the auditor may request confirmation of the terms of agreements or transactions an entity has with third parties; the confirmation request is designed to ask if any modifications have been made to the agreement and, if so, what the relevant details are. Confirmations also are used to obtain audit evidence about the absence of certain conditions, for example, the absence of a "side agreement" that may influence revenue recognition. See ISA (UK and Ireland) 505, "External Confirmations" for further guidance on confirmations. 35

Recalculation

Recalculation consists of checking the mathematical accuracy of documents or records. Recalculation can be performed through the use of information technology, for example, by obtaining an electronic file from the entity and using CAATs to check the accuracy of the summarization of the file. 36

Reperformance

Reperformance is the auditor's independent execution of procedures or controls that were originally performed as part of the entity's internal control, either manually or through the use of CAATs, for example, reperforming the aging of accounts receivable. 37

Analytical Procedures

Analytical procedures consist of evaluations of financial information made by a study of plausible relationships among both financial and non-financial data. Analytical procedures also encompass the investigation of identified fluctuations and relationships that are inconsistent with other relevant information or deviate significantly from predicted amounts. See ISA (UK and Ireland) 520, "Analytical Procedures," for further guidance on analytical procedures. 38

Effective Date

This ISA (UK and Ireland) is effective for audits of financial statements for periods commencing on or after 15 December 2004. 39

Public Sector Perspective

> Additional guidance for auditors of public sector bodies in the UK and Ireland is given in:
> - Practice Note 10 "Audit of Financial Statements of Public Sector Entities in the United Kingdom (Revised)"
> - Practice Note 10(I) "The Audit of Central Government Financial Statements in Ireland"

500   *International Standards on Auditing (UK & Ireland)*

1   *When carrying out audits of public sector entities, the auditor takes into account the legislative framework and any other relevant regulations, ordinances or ministerial directives that affect the audit mandate and any other special auditing requirements. In making assertions about the financial statements, management asserts that transactions and events have been in accordance with legislation or proper authority in addition to the assertions in paragraph 15 of this ISA (UK and Ireland).*

[501]
Audit evidence – additional considerations for specific items
(Issued December 2004)

Contents

	Paragraphs
Introduction	1 - 3
Attendance at Physical Inventory Counting	4 - 18-7
Superceded by ISA (UK and Ireland) 505	
Procedures Regarding Litigation and Claims	31 - 37
Valuation and Disclosure of Long-term Investments	38 - 41
Segment Information	42 - 45
Effective Date	45-1

International Standard on Auditing (UK and Ireland) (ISA (UK and Ireland)) 501, "Audit Evidence – Additional Considerations for Specific Items" should be read in the context of the Auditing Practices Board's Statement "The Auditing Practices Board – Scope and Authority of Pronouncements (Revised)" which sets out the application and authority of ISAs (UK and Ireland).

Introduction

1 The purpose of this International Standard on Auditing (UK and Ireland) (ISA (UK and Ireland)) is to establish standards and provide guidance additional to that contained in ISA (UK and Ireland) 500, "Audit Evidence" with respect to certain specific financial statement account balances and other disclosures.

1-1 This ISA (UK and Ireland) uses the terms 'those charged with governance' and 'management'. The term 'governance' describes the role of persons entrusted with the supervision, control and direction of an entity. Ordinarily, those charged with governance are accountable for ensuring that the entity achieves its objectives, and for the quality of its financial reporting and reporting to interested parties. Those charged with governance include management only when they perform such functions.

1-2 In the UK and Ireland, those charged with governance include the directors (executive and non-executive) of a company or other body, the members of an audit committee where one exists, the partners, proprietors, committee of management or trustees of other forms of entity, or equivalent persons responsible for directing the entity's affairs and preparing its financial statements.

1-3 'Management' comprises those persons who perform senior managerial functions.

1-4 In the UK and Ireland, depending on the nature and circumstances of the entity, management may include some or all of those charged with governance (e.g. executive directors). Management will not normally include non-executive directors.

2 Application of the standards and guidance provided in this ISA (UK and Ireland) will assist the auditor in obtaining audit evidence with respect to the specific financial statement account balances and other disclosures addressed.

3 This ISA (UK and Ireland) comprises the following parts:
(a) Attendance at Physical Inventory Counting
(b) Superceded by ISA (UK and Ireland) 505 – Part B has been deleted.
(c) Inquiry Regarding Litigation and Claims
(d) Valuation and Disclosure of Long-term Investments
(e) Segment Information

Attendance at Physical Inventory Counting

4 Management[1] ordinarily establishes procedures under which inventory is physically counted at least once a year to serve as a basis for the preparation of the financial statements or to ascertain the reliability of the perpetual inventory system.

4-1 In accordance with ISA (UK and Ireland) 315, "Understanding the Entity and its Environment and Assessing the Risks of Material misstatement" the auditor uses professional judgment to assess the risks of material misstatement. Risk factors

---

[1] In the UK and Ireland, those charged with governance are responsible for the preparation and presentation of the financial statements.

relating to the existence assertion in the context of the audit of inventory include the:

- Reliability of accounting and inventory recording systems including, in relation to work in progress, the systems that track location, quantities and stages of completion.
- Timing of physical inventory counts relative to the year-end date, and the reliability of records used in any 'roll-forward' of balances.
- Location of inventory, including inventory on 'consignment' and inventory held at third-party warehouses.
- Physical controls over the inventory, and its susceptibility to theft or deterioration.
- Objectivity, experience and reliability of the inventory counters and of those monitoring their work.
- The degree of fluctuation in inventory levels.
- Nature of the inventory, for example whether specialist knowledge is needed to identify the quantity, quality and/or identity of inventory items.
- Difficulty in carrying out the assessment of quantity, for example whether a significant degree of estimation is involved.

4-2 When planning the audit, the auditor also assesses the risk of material misstatements due to fraud. Based on this risk assessment, the auditor designs audit procedures so as to have a reasonable expectation of detecting material misstatements arising from fraud. Fraudulent activities which can occur in relation to inventory include:

- 'False sales' involving the movement of inventory still owned by the entity to a location not normally used for storing inventory.
- Movement of inventory between entity sites with physical inventory counts at different dates.
- The appearance of inventory and work in progress being misrepresented so that they seem to be of a higher value/greater quantity.
- The application of inappropriate estimating techniques.
- Inventory count records prepared during physical inventory counts deliberately being incorrectly completed or altered after the event.
- Additional (false) inventory count records being added to those prepared during the count.

5 **When inventory is material to the financial statements, the auditor should obtain sufficient appropriate audit evidence regarding its existence and condition by attendance at physical inventory counting unless impracticable.** The auditor's attendance serves as a test of controls or substantive procedure over inventory depending on the auditor's risk assessment and planned approach. Such attendance enables the auditor to inspect the inventory, to observe compliance with the operation of management's procedures for recording and controlling the results of the count and to provide audit evidence as to the reliability of management's procedures.

5-1 The principal sources of evidence relating to the existence of inventory are:

(a) Evidence from audit procedures which confirm the reliability of the accounting records upon which the amount in the financial statements is based;
(b) Evidence from tests of the operation of internal controls over inventory, including the reliability of inventory counting procedures applied by the entity; and

(c) Substantive evidence from the physical inspection tests undertaken by the auditor.

6   If unable to attend the physical inventory count on the date planned due to unforeseen circumstances, the auditor should take or observe some physical counts on an alternative date and, when necessary, perform audit procedures on intervening transactions.

7   Where attendance is impracticable, due to factors such as the nature and location of the inventory, the auditor should consider whether alternative procedures provide sufficient appropriate audit evidence of existence and condition to conclude that the auditor need not make reference to a scope limitation. For example, documentation of the subsequent sale of specific inventory items acquired or purchased prior to the physical inventory count may provide sufficient appropriate audit evidence.

8   In planning attendance at the physical inventory count or the alternative procedures, the auditor considers the following:

- The risks of material misstatement related to inventory.
- The nature of the internal control related to inventory.
- Whether adequate procedures are expected to be established and proper instructions issued for physical inventory counting.
- The timing of the count.
- The locations at which inventory is held.
- Whether an expert's assistance is needed.

8-1   The effectiveness of the auditor's attendance at a physical inventory count is increased by the use of audit staff who are familiar with the entity's business and where advance planning has been undertaken. Planning procedures include:

- Performing analytical procedures, and discussing with management any significant changes in inventory over the year and any problems with inventory that have recently occurred, for example unexpected 'stock-out' reports and negative inventory balances.
- Discussing inventory counting arrangements and instructions with management.
- Familiarisation with the nature and volume of the inventory, the identification of high value items, the method of accounting for inventory and the conditions giving rise to obsolescence.
- Assessing the implications of the locations at which inventory is held for inventory control and recording.
- Considering the quantity and nature of work in progress, the quantity of inventory held by third parties, and whether expert valuers or inventory counters will be engaged (further guidance on these issues is set out in paragraphs 8-2 and 8-3 below).
- Reviewing internal control relating to inventory, so as to identify potential areas of difficulty (for example cut-off).
- Considering any internal audit involvement, with a view to deciding the reliance which can be placed on it.
- Considering the results of previous physical inventory counts made by the entity.
- Reviewing the auditor's working papers for the previous year.

8-2   Prior to attending a physical inventory count, the auditor establishes whether expert help, such as that provided by a quantity surveyor, needs to be obtained by management to substantiate quantities, or to identify the nature and condition of the inventories, where they are very specialised. In cases where the entity engages a third party expert the auditor assesses, in accordance with ISA (UK and Ireland) 620 "Using the Work of an Expert", the objectivity and professional qualifications, experience and resources of the expert engaged to carry out this work, and also the instructions given to the expert.

Management may from time to time appoint inventory counters from outside the entity, a practice common for inventory at, for example, farms, petrol stations and public houses. The use of independent inventory counters does not eliminate the need for the auditor to obtain audit evidence as to the existence of inventory. In addition, as well as obtaining satisfaction as to the competence and objectivity of the independent inventory counters, the auditor considers how to obtain evidence as to the procedures followed by them to ensure that the inventory count records have been properly prepared. In this connection, the auditor has regard to the relevant guidance set out in ISA (UK and Ireland) 402, "Auditor's Considerations Relating to Entities Using Service Organizations".	8-3
When the quantities are to be determined by a physical inventory count and the auditor attends such a count, or when the entity operates a perpetual system and the auditor attends a count one or more times during the year, the auditor would ordinarily observe count procedures and perform test counts.	9
The nature of the auditor's procedures during their attendance at a physical inventory count will depend upon the results of the assessment of risks of material misstatements carried out in accordance with ISA (UK and Ireland) 315. In cases where the auditor decides to place reliance on accounting systems and internal controls, the auditor attends a physical inventory count primarily to obtain evidence regarding the design and operating effectiveness of management procedures for confirming inventory quantities.	9-1
Where entities maintain detailed inventory records and check these by regular test counts the auditor performs audit procedures designed to confirm whether management: (a) Maintains adequate inventory records that are kept up-to-date; (b) Has satisfactory procedures for inventory counting and test-counting; and (c) Investigates and corrects all material differences between the book inventory records and the physical counts. The auditor attends a physical inventory count to gain assurance that the inventory checking as a whole is effective in confirming that accurate inventory records are maintained. If the entity's inventory records are not reliable the auditor may need to request management to perform alternative procedures which may include a full count at the year end.	9-2
In entities that do not maintain detailed inventory records the quantification of inventory for financial statement purposes is likely to be based on a full physical count of all inventory held at a date close to the company's year end. In such circumstances the auditor will consider the date of the physical inventory count recognising that the evidence of the existence of inventory provided by the inventory count is greater when the inventory count is carried out at the end of the financial year. Physical inventory counts carried out before or after the year end may also be acceptable for audit purposes provided the auditor is satisfied that the records of inventory movements in the intervening period are reliable.	9-3

10 If the entity uses procedures to estimate the physical quantity, such as estimating a coal pile, the auditor would need to be satisfied regarding the reasonableness of those procedures.

11 When inventory is situated in several locations, the auditor would consider at which locations attendance is appropriate, taking into account the materiality of the inventory and the risk of material misstatement at different locations.

12 The auditor would review management's instructions regarding:
    (a) The application of control activities, for example, collection of used stocksheets, accounting for unused stocksheets and count and re-count procedures;
    (b) Accurate identification of the stage of completion of work in progress, of slow moving, obsolete or damaged items and of inventory owned by a third party, for example, on consignment; and
    (c) Whether appropriate arrangements are made regarding the movement of inventory between areas and the shipping and receipt of inventory before and after the cutoff date.

12-1 The auditor examines the way the physical inventory count is organised and evaluates the adequacy of the client's instructions for the physical inventory count. Such instructions, preferably in writing, should cover all phases of the inventory counting procedures, be issued in good time and be discussed with the person responsible for the physical inventory count to check that the procedures are understood and that potential difficulties are anticipated. If the instructions are found to be inadequate, the auditor seeks improvements to them.

13 To obtain audit evidence that management's control activities are adequately implemented, the auditor would observe employees' procedures and perform test counts. When performing test counts, the auditor performs procedures over both the completeness and the accuracy of the count records by tracing items selected from those records to the physical inventory and items selected from the physical inventory to the count records. The auditor considers the extent to which copies of such count records need to be retained for subsequent audit procedures and comparison.

13-1 If the manner of carrying out the inventory count or the results of the test-counts are not satisfactory, the auditor immediately draws the matter to the attention of the management supervising the inventory count and may have to request a recount of part, or all of the inventory.

13-2 When carrying out test counts, the auditor gives particular consideration to those inventory items which the auditor believes to have a high value either individually or as a category of inventory. The auditor includes in the audit working papers items for any subsequent testing considered necessary, such as copies of (or extracts from) inventory count records and details of the sequence of those records, and any differences noted between the records and the physical inventory counted.

13-3 The auditor determines whether the procedures for identifying damaged, obsolete and slow moving stock operate properly. The auditor obtains (from observation and by discussion e.g. with storekeepers and inventory counters) information about the inventory condition, age, usage and, in the case of work in progress, its stage of completion. Further, the auditor ascertains that stock held on behalf of third parties is separately identified and accounted for.

The auditor also considers cutoff procedures including details of the movement of inventory just prior to, during and after the count so that the accounting for such movements can be checked at a later date. 14

> The auditor considers whether management has instituted adequate cut-off procedures, i.e. procedures intended to ensure that movements into, within and out of inventory are properly identified and reflected in the accounting records in the correct period. The auditor's procedures during the inventory count will depend on the manner in which the year end inventory value is to be determined. For example, where inventory is determined by a full count and evaluation at the year end, the auditor tests the arrangements made to identify inventory that corresponds to sales made before the cut-off point and the auditor identifies goods movement documents for reconciliation with financial records of purchases and sales. Alternatively, where the full count and evaluation is at an interim date and year end inventory is determined by updating such valuation by the cost of purchases and sales, the auditor performs appropriate procedures during attendance at the physical inventory count and in addition tests the financial cut-off (involving the matching of costs with revenues) at the year end. 14-1

For practical reasons, the physical inventory count may be conducted at a date other than period end. This will ordinarily be adequate for audit purposes only when the entity has designed and implemented controls over changes in inventory. The auditor would determine whether, through the performance of appropriate audit procedures, changes in inventory between the count date and period end are correctly recorded. 15

When the entity operates a perpetual inventory system which is used to determine the period end balance, the auditor would evaluate whether, through the performance of additional procedures, the reasons for any significant differences between the physical count and the perpetual inventory records are understood and the records are properly adjusted. 16

The auditor performs audit procedures over the final inventory listing to determine whether it accurately reflects actual inventory counts. 17

When inventory is under the custody and control of a third party, the auditor would ordinarily obtain direct confirmation from the third party as to the quantities and condition of inventory held on behalf of the entity. Depending on materiality of this inventory the auditor would also consider the following: 18

- The integrity and independence of the third party.
- Observing, or arranging for another auditor to observe, the physical inventory count.
- Obtaining another auditor's report on the adequacy of the third party's internal control for ensuring that inventory is correctly counted and adequately safeguarded.
- Inspecting documentation regarding inventory held by third parties, for example, warehouse receipts, or obtaining confirmation from other parties when such inventory has been pledged as collateral.

> - Testing the owner's procedures for investigating the custodian and evaluating the custodian's performance.
> - The guidance set out in ISA (UK and Ireland) 402.

18-1 The auditor's working papers include details of the auditor's observations and tests (for example, of physical quantity, cut-off date and controls over inventory count records), the manner in which points that are relevant and material to the inventory being counted or measured have been dealt with by the entity, instances where the entity's procedures have not been satisfactorily carried out and the auditor's conclusions.

18-2 Although the principal reason for attendance at a physical inventory count is usually to obtain evidence to substantiate the existence of the inventory, attendance can also enhance the auditor's understanding of the business by providing an opportunity to observe the production process and/or business locations at first hand and providing evidence regarding the completeness and valuation of inventory and the entity's internal control. Matters that the auditor may wish to observe whilst attending a physical inventory count include:

Understanding the business

- The production process.
- Evidence of significant pollution and environmental damage.
- Unused buildings and machinery.

Completeness and valuation of inventory

- Physical controls.
- Obsolete inventory (for example goods beyond their sale date).
- Scrap, and goods marked for re-awork.
- Returned goods.

Internal control

- Exceptions identified by the production process (for example missing work tickets).
- The operation of 'shop-floor' disciplines regarding the inputting of data such as inventory movements into the computer systems.

18-3 Some entities use computer-assisted techniques to perform inventory counts; for example hand held scanners can be used to record inventory items which update computerised records. In some situations there are no stock-sheets, no physical count records, and no paper records available at the time of the count. In these circumstances the auditor considers the IT environment surrounding the inventory count and considers the need for specialist assistance when evaluating the techniques used and the controls surrounding them. Relevant issues involve systems interfaces, and the controls over ensuring that the computerised inventory records are properly updated for the inventory count information.

The auditor considers the following aspects of the physical inventory count:

(a) How the test counts (and double counts where two people are checking) are recorded;
(b) How differences are investigated before the computerised inventory records are updated for the counts; and
(c) How the computerised inventory records are updated, and how inventory differences are recorded.

After the Physical Inventory Count

After the physical inventory count, the matters recorded in the auditor's working papers at the time of the count or measurement, including apparent instances of obsolete or deteriorating inventory, are followed up. For example, details of the last serial numbers of goods inwards and outwards records and of movements during the inventory count may be used in order to check cut-off. Further, copies of (or extracts from) the inventory count records and details of test counts, and of the sequence of inventory count records may be used to check that the results of the count have been properly reflected in the accounting records of the entity.

18-4

Where appropriate, the auditor considers whether management has instituted procedures to ensure that all inventory movements between the observed inventory count and the period end have been adjusted in the accounting records, and the auditor tests these procedures to the extent considered necessary to address the assessed risk of material misstatement. In addition, the auditor follows up all queries and notifies senior management of serious problems encountered during the physical inventory count.

18-5

In conclusion, the auditor considers whether attendance at the physical inventory count has provided sufficient reliable audit evidence in relation to relevant assertions (principally existence) and, if not, the other procedures that should be performed.

18-6

Work in Progress

Management may place substantial reliance on internal controls designed to ensure the completeness and accuracy of records of work in progress. In such circumstances there may not be a physical inventory count which can be attended by the auditor. Nevertheless, inspection of the work in progress may assist the auditor in understanding the entity's control systems and processes. It will also assist the auditor in planning further audit procedures, and it may also help on such matters as the determination of the stage of completion of construction or engineering work in progress. For this purpose, the auditor identifies the accounting records that will be used by management to produce the work in progress figure in the year-end accounts and, where unfinished items are uniquely identifiable (for example by reference to work tickets or labels), the auditor physically examine items to obtain evidence that supports the recorded stage of completion. In some cases, for example in connection with building projects, photographic evidence can also be useful evidence as to the state of work in progress at the date of the physical inventory count, particularly if provided by independent third parties or the auditor.

18-7

Superceded by ISA (UK and Ireland) 505 – PART B (paragraphs 19-30) has been deleted.

Procedures Regarding Litigation and Claims

Litigation and claims involving an entity may have a material effect on the financial statements and thus may be required to be disclosed and/or provided for in the financial statements.

31

32   The auditor should carry out audit procedures in order to become aware of any litigation and claims involving the entity which may result in a material misstatement of the financial statements. Such procedures would include the following:
- Make appropriate inquiries of management[2] including obtaining representations.
- Review minutes of those charged with governance and correspondence with the entity's legal counsel.
- Examine legal expense accounts.
- Use any information obtained regarding the entity's business including information obtained from discussions with any in-house legal department.

33   When the auditor assesses a risk of material misstatement regarding litigation or claims that have been identified or when the auditor believes they may exist, the auditor should seek direct communication with the entity's legal counsel. Such communication will assist in obtaining sufficient appropriate audit evidence as to whether potentially material litigation and claims are known and management's[1] estimates of the financial implications, including costs, are reliable. When the auditor determines that the risk of material misstatement is a significant risk, the auditor evaluates the design of the entity's related controls and determines whether they have been implemented. Paragraphs 108-114 of ISA (UK and Ireland) 315, "Understanding the Entity and Assessing the Risks of Material Misstatement" provides further guidance on the determination of significant risks.

34   The letter, which should be prepared by management[3] and sent by the auditor, should request the entity's legal counsel to communicate directly with the auditor. When it is considered unlikely that the entity's legal counsel will respond to a general inquiry[4], the letter would ordinarily specify the following:
- A list of litigation and claims.
- Management's[1] assessment of the outcome of the litigation or claim and its estimate of the financial implications, including costs involved.
- A request that the entity's legal counsel confirm the reasonableness of management's assessments and provide the auditor with further information if the list is considered by the entity's legal counsel to be incomplete or incorrect.

35   The auditor considers the status of legal matters up to the date of the audit report. In some instances, the auditor may need to obtain updated information from entity's legal counsel.

36   In certain circumstances, for example, where the auditor determines that the matter is a significant risk, the matter is complex or there is disagreement between management and the entity's legal counsel, it may be necessary for the auditor to meet with the entity's legal counsel to discuss the likely outcome of litigation and claims. Such meetings would take place with management's[5] permission and, preferably, with a representative of management in attendance.

37   If management[4] refuses to give the auditor permission to communicate with the entity's legal counsel, this would be a scope limitation and should ordinarily lead to a qualified

---

[2] *In the UK and Ireland the auditor makes appropriate enquiries of those charged with governance.*

[3] *In the UK and Ireland the letter should be prepared by those charged with governance.*

[4] *In the UK, the Council of the Law Society has advised solicitors that it is unable to recommend them to comply with non-specific requests for information.*

[5] *In the UK and Ireland the auditor seeks the permission of those charged with governance.*

opinion or a disclaimer of opinion. Where the entity's legal counsel refuses to respond in an appropriate manner and the auditor is unable to obtain sufficient appropriate audit evidence by applying alternative audit procedures, the auditor would consider whether there is a scope limitation which may lead to a qualified opinion or a disclaimer of opinion.

Valuation and Disclosure of Long-term Investments

When long-term investments are material to the financial statements, the auditor should obtain sufficient appropriate audit evidence regarding their valuation and disclosure. 38

Audit procedures regarding long-term investments ordinarily include obtaining audit evidence as to whether the entity has the ability to continue to hold the investments on a long term basis and discussing with management whether the entity will continue to hold the investments as long-term investments and obtaining written representations to that effect. 39

Other audit procedures would ordinarily include considering related financial statements and other information, such as market quotations, which provide an indication of value and comparing such values to the carrying amount of the investments up to the date of the auditor's report. 40

If such values do not exceed the carrying amounts, the auditor would consider whether a write-down is required. If there is an uncertainty as to whether the carrying amount will be recovered, the auditor would consider whether appropriate adjustments and/or disclosures have been made. 41

Segment Information

When segment information is material to the financial statements, the auditor should obtain sufficient appropriate audit evidence regarding its presentation and disclosure in accordance with the applicable financial reporting framework. 42

The auditor considers segment information in relation to the financial statements taken as a whole, and is not ordinarily required to apply audit procedures that would be necessary to express an opinion on the segment information standing alone. However, the concept of materiality encompasses both quantitative and qualitative factors and the auditor's procedures recognize this. 43

Audit procedures regarding segment information ordinarily consist of analytical procedures and other audit procedures as appropriate in the circumstances. 44

The auditor would discuss with management[1] the methods used in determining segment information, and consider whether such methods are likely to result in disclosure in accordance with the applicable financial reporting framework and perform audit procedures over the application of such methods. The auditor would consider sales, transfers and charges between segments, elimination of inter-segment amounts, comparisons with budgets and other expected results, for example, operating profits as a percentage of sales, and the allocation of assets and costs among segments including consistency with prior periods and the adequacy of the disclosures with respect to inconsistencies. 45

Effective Date

45-1 This ISA (UK and Ireland) is effective for audits of financial statements for periods commencing on or after 15 December 2004.

[505]
External confirmations

(Issued December 2004)

Contents

	Paragraphs
Introduction	1 - 6
Relationship of External Confirmation Procedures to the Auditor's Assessments of the Risk of Material Misstatement	7 - 11
Assertions Addressed by External Confirmations	12 - 16
Design of the External Confirmation Request	17 - 19
Use of Positive and Negative Confirmations	20 - 24
Management Requests	25 - 27
Characteristics of Respondents	28 - 29
The External Confirmation Process	30 - 35
Evaluating the Results of the Confirmation Process	36
External Confirmations Prior to the Year-end	37
Effective Date	38

International Standard on Auditing (UK and Ireland) (ISA (UK and Ireland)) 505 "External Confirmations" should be read in the context of the Auditing Practices Board's Statement "The Auditing Practices Board – Scope and Authority of Pronouncements (Revised)" which sets out the application and authority of ISAs (UK and Ireland).

Introduction

1 The purpose of this International Standard on Auditing (UK and Ireland) (ISA (UK and Ireland)) is to establish standards and provide guidance on the auditor's use of external confirmations as a means of obtaining audit evidence.

1-1 This ISA (UK and Ireland) uses the terms 'those charged with governance' and 'management'. The term 'governance' describes the role of persons entrusted with the supervision, control and direction of an entity. Ordinarily, those charged with governance are accountable for ensuring that the entity achieves its objectives, and for the quality of its financial reporting and reporting to interested parties. Those charged with governance include management only when they perform such functions.

1-2 In the UK and Ireland, those charged with governance include the directors (executive and non-executive) of a company or other body, the members of an audit committee where one exists, the partners, proprietors, committee of management or trustees of other forms of entity, or equivalent persons responsible for directing the entity's affairs and preparing its financial statements.

1-3 'Management' comprises those persons who perform senior managerial functions.

1-4 In the UK and Ireland, depending on the nature and circumstances of the entity, management may include some or all of those charged with governance (e.g. executive directors). Management will not normally include non-executive directors.

2 **The auditor should determine whether the use of external confirmations is necessary to obtain sufficient appropriate audit evidence at the assertion level. In making this determination, the auditor should consider the assessed risk of material misstatement at the assertion level and how the audit evidence from other planned audit procedures will reduce the risk of material misstatement at the assertion level to an acceptably low level.**

3 ISA (UK and Ireland) 500, "Audit Evidence" states that the reliability of audit evidence is influenced by its source and by its nature, and is dependent on the individual circumstances under which it is obtained. It indicates that, while recognizing exceptions may exist, the following generalization about the reliability of audit evidence may be useful:

- Audit evidence is more reliable when it is obtained from independent sources outside the entity.
- Audit evidence obtained directly by the auditor is more reliable than audit evidence obtained indirectly or by inference.
- Audit evidence is more reliable when it exists in documentary form.
- Audit evidence provided by original documents is more reliable than audit evidence provided by photocopies or facsimiles.

Accordingly, audit evidence in the form of original written responses to confirmation requests received directly by the auditor from third parties who are not related to the entity being audited, when considered individually or cumulatively with audit evidence from other audit procedures, may assist in reducing the risk of material misstatement for the related assertions to an acceptably low level.

External confirmation is the process of obtaining and evaluating audit evidence through a representation of information or an existing condition directly from a third party in response to a request for information about a particular item affecting assertions in the financial statements or related disclosures. In deciding to what extent to use external confirmations the auditor considers the characteristics of the environment in which the entity being audited operates and the practice of potential respondents in dealing with requests for direct confirmation.

External confirmations are frequently used in relation to account balances and their components, but need not be restricted to these items. For example, the auditor may request external confirmation of the terms of agreements or transactions an entity has with third parties. The confirmation request is designed to ask if any modifications have been made to the agreement, and if so what the relevant details are. External confirmations may also be used to obtain audit evidence about the absence of certain conditions, for example, the absence of a "side agreement" that may influence revenue recognition. Other examples of situations where external confirmations may be used include the following:

- Bank balances and other information from bankers.
- Accounts receivable balances.
- Stocks held by third parties at bonded warehouses for processing or on consignment.
- Property title deeds held by lawyers or financiers for safe custody or as security.
- Investments purchased from stockbrokers but not delivered at the balance sheet date.
- Loans from lenders.
- Accounts payable balances.

The reliability of the audit evidence obtained by external confirmations depends, among other factors, upon the auditor applying appropriate audit procedures in designing the external confirmation request, performing the external confirmation procedures, and evaluating the results of the external confirmation procedures. Factors affecting the reliability of confirmations include the control the auditor exercises over confirmation requests and responses, the characteristics of the respondents, and any restrictions included in the response or imposed by management[1].

Relationship of External Confirmation Procedures to the Auditor's Assessments of the Risk of Material Misstatement

ISA (UK and Ireland) 315, "Understanding the Entity and Its Environment and Assessing the Risks of Material Misstatement" discusses the auditor's responsibility to obtain an understanding of the entity and its environment including its internal control; and to assess the risks of material misstatement. It outlines the audit procedures performed to assess the risks of material misstatements of the financial statements sufficient to design and perform further audit procedures.

ISA (UK and Ireland) 330, "The Auditor's Procedures in Response to Assessed Risks" discusses the auditor's responsibility to determine overall responses and to design and perform further audit procedures whose nature, timing and extent are responsive to the assessed risks of material misstatement at the financial statement and assertion levels. In particular, ISA (UK and Ireland) 330 indicates that the auditor determines the nature and extent of audit evidence to be obtained from the

---

[1] In the UK and Ireland such restrictions might be imposed by those charged with governance.

performance of substantive procedures in response to the related assessment of the risk of material misstatement, and that, irrespective of the assessed risk of material misstatement, the auditor designs and performs substantive procedures for each material class of transactions, account balance, and disclosure. These substantive procedures may include the use of external confirmations for certain assertions.

9   Paragraph 11 of ISA (UK and Ireland) 330 indicates that the higher the auditor's assessment of risk, the more reliable and relevant is the audit evidence sought by the auditor from substantive procedures. Consequently as the assessed risk of material misstatement increases, the auditor designs substantive procedures to obtain more reliable and relevant audit evidence, or more persuasive audit evidence, at the assertion level. In these situations, the use of confirmation procedures may be effective in providing sufficient appropriate audit evidence.

10 The lower the assessed risk of material misstatement, the less assurance the auditor needs from substantive procedures to form a conclusion about an assertion. For example, an entity may have a loan that it is repaying according to an agreed schedule, the terms of which the auditor has confirmed in previous years. If the other work carried out by the auditor (including such tests of controls as are necessary) indicates that the terms of the loan have not changed and has lead to the risk of material misstatement over the balance of the loan outstanding being assessed as lower, the auditor might limit substantive procedures to testing details of the payments made, rather than again confirming the balance directly with the lender.

11 When the auditor has identified a risk as being significant (see paragraph 108 of ISA (UK and Ireland) 315), the auditor may give particular consideration to whether confirmations of certain matters may be an appropriate way of reducing the risk of misstatement. For example, unusual or complex transactions may be associated with higher assessed risk than simple transactions. If the entity has entered into an unusual or complex transaction that results in a higher assessed risk of material misstatement, the auditor considers confirming the terms of the transaction with the other parties in addition to examining documentation held by the entity.

Assertions Addressed by External Confirmations

12 ISA (UK and Ireland) 500 requires the use of assertions in assessing risks and designing and performing audit procedures in response to the assessed risks. ISA (UK and Ireland) 500 categorizes the assertions into those relating to classes of transactions, account balances, and disclosures. While external confirmations may provide audit evidence regarding these assertions, the ability of an external confirmation to provide audit evidence relevant to a particular assertion varies.

13 External confirmation of an account receivable provides reliable and relevant audit evidence regarding the existence of the account as at a certain date. Confirmation also provides audit evidence regarding the operation of cutoff procedures. However, such confirmation does not ordinarily provide all the necessary audit evidence relating to the valuation assertion, since it is not practicable to ask the debtor to confirm detailed information relating to its ability to pay the account.

14 Similarly, in the case of goods held on consignment, external confirmation is likely to provide reliable and relevant audit evidence to support the existence and the rights and obligations assertions, but might not provide audit evidence that supports the valuation assertion.

The relevance of external confirmations to auditing a particular assertion is also affected by the objective of the auditor in selecting information for confirmation. For example, when auditing the completeness assertion for accounts payable, the auditor needs to obtain audit evidence that there is no material unrecorded liability. Accordingly, sending confirmation requests to an entity's principal suppliers asking them to provide copies of their statements of account directly to the auditor, even if the records show no amount currently owing to them, will usually be more effective in detecting unrecorded liabilities than selecting accounts for confirmation based on the larger amounts recorded in the accounts payable subsidiary ledger.

When obtaining audit evidence for assertions not adequately addressed by confirmations, the auditor considers other audit procedures to complement confirmation procedures or to be used instead of confirmation procedures.

Design of the External Confirmation Request

The auditor should tailor external confirmation requests to the specific audit objective. When designing the request, the auditor considers the assertions being addressed and the factors that are likely to affect the reliability of the confirmations. Factors such as the form of the external confirmation request, prior experience on the audit or similar engagements, the nature of the information being confirmed, and the intended respondent, affect the design of the requests because these factors have a direct effect on the reliability of the audit evidence obtained through external confirmation procedures.

Also, in designing the request, the auditor considers the type of information respondents will be able to confirm readily since this may affect the response rate and the nature of the audit evidence obtained. For example, certain respondents' information systems may facilitate the external confirmation of single transactions rather than of entire account balances. In addition, respondents may not always be able to confirm certain types of information, such as the overall accounts receivable balance, but may be able to confirm individual invoice amounts within the total balance.

Confirmation requests ordinarily include management's authorization to the respondent to disclose the information to the auditor. Respondents may be more willing to respond to a confirmation request containing management's authorization, and in some cases may be unable to respond unless the request contains management's authorization.

Use of Positive and Negative Confirmations

The auditor may use positive or negative external confirmation requests or a combination of both.

A positive external confirmation request asks the respondent to reply to the auditor in all cases either by indicating the respondent's agreement with the given information, or by asking the respondent to fill in information. A response to a positive confirmation request is ordinarily expected to provide reliable audit evidence. There is a risk, however, that a respondent may reply to the confirmation request without verifying that the information is correct. The auditor is not ordinarily able to detect whether this has occurred. The auditor may reduce this risk, however, by using positive confirmation requests that do not state the amount (or other information) on the confirmation request, but ask the respondent to fill in the amount or furnish other information. On the other hand, use of this type of "blank" confirmation request may result in lower response rates because additional effort is required of the respondents.

22 A negative external confirmation request asks the respondent to reply only in the event of disagreement with the information provided in the request. However, when no response has been received to a negative confirmation request, the auditor remains aware that there will be no explicit audit evidence that intended third parties have received the confirmation requests and verified that the information contained therein is correct. Accordingly, the use of negative confirmation requests ordinarily provides less reliable audit evidence than the use of positive confirmation requests, and the auditor considers performing other substantive procedures to supplement the use of negative confirmations.

23 Negative confirmation requests may be used to reduce the risk of material misstatement to an acceptable level when:

(a) The assessed risk of material misstatement is lower;
(b) A large number of small balances is involved;
(c) A substantial number of errors is not expected; and
(d) The auditor has no reason to believe that respondents will disregard these requests.

24 A combination of positive and negative external confirmations may be used. For example, where the total accounts receivable balance comprises a small number of large balances and a large number of small balances, the auditor may decide that it is appropriate to confirm all or a sample of the large balances with positive confirmation requests and a sample of the small balances using negative confirmation requests.

Management Requests

25 **When the auditor seeks to confirm certain balances or other information, and management requests the auditor not to do so, the auditor should consider whether there are valid grounds for such a request and obtain audit evidence to support the validity of management's requests. If the auditor agrees to management's request not to seek external confirmation regarding a particular matter, the auditor should apply alternative audit procedures to obtain sufficient appropriate audit evidence regarding that matter.**

26 If the auditor does not accept the validity of management's request and is prevented from carrying out the confirmations, there has been a limitation on the scope of the auditor's work and the auditor should consider the possible impact on the auditor's report.

27 When considering the reasons provided by management, the auditor applies an attitude of professional skepticism and considers whether the request has any implications regarding management's integrity. The auditor considers whether management's request may indicate the possible existence of fraud or error. If the auditor believes that fraud or error exists, the auditor applies the guidance in ISA (UK and Ireland) 240, "The Auditor's Responsibility to Consider Fraud in an Audit of Financial Statements." The auditor also considers whether the alternative audit procedures will provide sufficient appropriate audit evidence regarding that matter.

Characteristics of Respondents

28 The reliability of audit evidence provided by a confirmation is affected by the respondent's competence, independence, authority to respond, knowledge of the matter being confirmed, and objectivity. For this reason, the auditor attempts to ensure, where practicable, that the confirmation request is directed to an appropriate individual. For example, when confirming that a covenant related to an entity's long-term debt has been waived, the auditor directs the request to an official of the creditor who has knowledge about the waiver and has the authority to provide the information.

29 The auditor also assesses whether certain parties may not provide an objective or unbiased response to a confirmation request. Information about the respondent's competence, knowledge, motivation, ability or willingness to respond may come to the auditor's attention. The auditor considers the effect of such information on designing the confirmation request and evaluating the results, including determining whether additional audit procedures are necessary. The auditor also considers whether there is sufficient basis for concluding that the confirmation request is being sent to a respondent from whom the auditor can expect a response that will provide sufficient appropriate audit evidence. For example, the auditor may encounter significant unusual year-end transactions that have a material effect on the financial statements, the transactions being with a third party that is economically dependent upon the entity. In such circumstances, the auditor considers whether the third party may be motivated to provide an inaccurate response.

The External Confirmation Process

30 **When performing confirmation procedures, the auditor should maintain control over the process of selecting those to whom a request will be sent, the preparation and sending of confirmation requests, and the responses to those requests.** Control is maintained over communications between the intended recipients and the auditor to minimize the possibility that the results of the confirmation process will be biased because of the interception and alteration of confirmation requests or responses. The auditor ensures that it is the auditor who sends out the confirmation requests, that the requests are properly addressed, and that it is requested that all replies are sent directly to the auditor. The auditor considers whether replies have come from the purported senders.

No Response to a Positive Confirmation Request

31 **The auditor should perform alternative audit procedures where no response is received to a positive external confirmation request. The alternative audit procedures should be such as to provide audit evidence about the assertions that the confirmation request was intended to provide.**

32 Where no response is received, the auditor ordinarily contacts the recipient of the request to elicit a response. Where the auditor is unable to obtain a response, the auditor uses alternative audit procedures. The nature of alternative audit procedures varies according to the account and assertion in question. In the examination of accounts receivable, alternative audit procedures may include examination of subsequent cash receipts, examination of shipping documentation or other client documentation to provide audit evidence for the existence assertion, and examination of sales near the period-end to provide audit evidence for the cutoff assertion. In the examination of accounts payable, alternative audit procedures may include

examination of subsequent cash disbursements or correspondence from third parties to provide audit evidence of the existence assertion, and examination of other records, such as goods received notes, to provide audit evidence of the completeness assertion.

Reliability of Responses Received

33   The auditor considers whether there is any indication that external confirmations received may not be reliable. The auditor considers the response's authenticity and performs audit procedures to dispel any concern. The auditor may choose to verify the source and contents of a response in a telephone call to the purported sender. In addition, the auditor requests the purported sender to mail the original confirmation directly to the auditor. With ever-increasing use of technology, the auditor considers validating the source of replies received in electronic format (for example, fax or electronic mail). Oral confirmations are documented in the work papers. If the information in the oral confirmations is significant, the auditor requests the parties involved to submit written confirmation of the specific information directly to the auditor.

Causes and Frequency of Exceptions

34   **When the auditor forms a conclusion that the confirmation process and alternative audit procedures have not provided sufficient appropriate audit evidence regarding an assertion, the auditor should perform additional audit procedures to obtain sufficient appropriate audit evidence.**

In forming the conclusion, the auditor considers the:

(a) Reliability of the confirmations and alternative audit procedures;
(b) Nature of any exceptions, including the implications, both quantitative and qualitative of those exceptions; and
(c) Audit evidence provided by other audit procedures.

Based on this evaluation, the auditor determines whether additional audit procedures are needed to obtain sufficient appropriate audit evidence.

35   The auditor also considers the causes and frequency of exceptions reported by respondents. An exception may indicate a misstatement in the entity's records, in which case, the auditor determines the reasons for the misstatement and assesses whether it has a material effect on the financial statements. If an exception indicates a misstatement, the auditor reconsiders the nature, timing and extent of audit procedures necessary to provide the audit evidence required.

Evaluating the Results of the Confirmation Process

36   **The auditor should evaluate whether the results of the external confirmation process together with the results from any other audit procedures performed, provide sufficient appropriate audit evidence regarding the assertion being audited.** In conducting this evaluation the auditor considers the guidance provided by ISA (UK and Ireland) 330 and ISA (UK and Ireland) 530, "Audit Sampling and Other Means of Testing."

External Confirmations Prior to the Year-end

When the auditor uses confirmation as at a date prior to the balance sheet to obtain audit evidence to support an assertion, the auditor obtains sufficient appropriate audit evidence that transactions relevant to the assertion in the intervening period have not been materially misstated. Depending on the assessed risk of material misstatement, the auditor may decide to confirm balances at a date other than the period end, for example, when the audit is to be completed within a short time after the balance sheet date. As with all types of pre-year-end work, the auditor considers the need to obtain further audit evidence relating to the remainder of the period. ISA (UK and Ireland) 330 provides additional guidance when audit procedures are performed at an interim date.   37

Effective Date

This ISA (UK and Ireland) is effective for audits of financial statements for periods commencing on or after 15 December 2004.   38

[510]
Initial engagements – opening balances and continuing engagements – opening balances

(Issued December 2004)

Contents

	Paragraph
Introduction	1 - 3
Audit Procedures	4 - 10-2
Audit Conclusions and Reporting	11 - 14
Effective Date	14 - 1

International Standard on Auditing (UK and Ireland) (ISA (UK and Ireland)) 510 "Initial Engagements – Opening Balances and Continuing Engagements - Opening Balances" should be read in the context of the Auditing Practices Board's Statement "The Auditing Practices Board – Scope and Authority of Pronouncements (Revised)" which sets out the application and authority of ISAs (UK and Ireland).

Initial engagements and continuing engagements – opening balances 510

Introduction

The purpose of this International Standard on Auditing (UK and Ireland) (ISA (UK and Ireland)) is to establish standards and provide guidance regarding opening balances when the financial statements are audited for the first time or when the financial statements for the prior period were audited by another auditor. This ISA (UK and Ireland) would also be considered when the auditor becomes aware of contingencies and commitments existing at the beginning of the period. Guidance on the audit and reporting requirements regarding comparatives is provided in ISA (UK and Ireland) 710 "Comparatives." 1

This ISA (UK and Ireland) also provides guidance regarding opening balances for a continuing auditor (an auditor who audited and reported on the preceding periods financial statements and continues as auditor for the current period). 1-1

This ISA (UK and Ireland) uses the terms 'those charged with governance' and 'management'. The term 'governance' describes the role of persons entrusted with the supervision, control and direction of an entity. Ordinarily, those charged with governance are accountable for ensuring that the entity achieves its objectives, and for the quality of its financial reporting and reporting to interested parties. Those charged with governance include management only when they perform such functions. 1-2

In the UK and Ireland, those charged with governance include the directors (executive and non-executive) of a company or other body, the members of an audit committee where one exists, the partners, proprietors, committee of management or trustees of other forms of entity, or equivalent persons responsible for directing the entity's affairs and preparing its financial statements. 1-3

'Management' comprises those persons who perform senior managerial functions. 1-4

In the UK and Ireland, depending on the nature and circumstances of the entity, management may include some or all of those persons charged with governance (e.g. executive directors). Management will not normally include non-executive directors. 1-5

For initial audit engagements, the auditor should obtain sufficient appropriate audit evidence that: 2

(a) The opening balances do not contain misstatements that materially affect the current period's financial statements;
(b) The prior period's closing balances have been correctly brought forward to the current period or, when appropriate, have been restated; and
(c) Appropriate accounting policies are consistently applied or changes in accounting policies have been properly accounted for and adequately presented and disclosed.

The auditor should also obtain sufficient appropriate audit evidence for the matters set out in paragraph 2 for continuing audit engagements (see paragraphs 10-1 and 10-2). 2-1

"Opening balances" means those account balances which exist at the beginning of the period. Opening balances are based upon the closing balances of the prior period and reflect the effects of: 3

(a) Transactions of prior periods; and
(b) Accounting policies applied in the prior period.

In an initial audit engagement, the auditor will not have previously obtained audit evidence supporting such opening balances.

Audit Procedures

4   The sufficiency and appropriateness of the audit evidence the auditor will need to obtain regarding opening balances depends on such matters as:

- The accounting policies followed by the entity.
- Whether the prior period's financial statements were audited, and if so whether the auditor's report was modified.
- The nature of the accounts and the risk of material misstatement in the current period's financial statements.
- The materiality of the opening balances relative to the current period's financial statements.

5   The auditor will need to consider whether opening balances reflect the application of appropriate accounting policies and that those policies are consistently applied in the current period's financial statements. When there are any changes in the accounting policies or application thereof, the auditor would consider whether they are appropriate and properly accounted for and adequately presented and disclosed.

6   When the prior period's financial statements were audited by another auditor, the current auditor may be able to obtain sufficient appropriate audit evidence regarding opening balances by reviewing the predecessor auditor's working papers. In these circumstances, the current auditor would also consider the professional competence and independence of the predecessor auditor. If the prior period's auditor's report was modified, the auditor would pay particular attention in the current period to the matter which resulted in the modification.

7   Prior to communicating with the predecessor auditor, the current auditor will need to consider the *Code of Ethics for Professional Accountants* issued by the International Federation of Accountants.

7-1   In the UK and Ireland the relevant ethical guidance on proposed communications with a predecessor auditor is provided by the ethical pronouncements relating to the work of auditors issued by the auditor's relevant professional body.

8   When the prior period's financial statements were not audited or when the auditor is not able to be satisfied by using the audit procedures described in paragraph 6, the auditor will need to perform other audit procedures such as those discussed in paragraphs 9 and 10.

9   For current assets and liabilities some audit evidence can ordinarily be obtained as part of the current period's audit procedures. For example, the collection (payment) of opening accounts receivable (accounts payable) during the current period will provide some audit evidence of their existence, rights and obligations, completeness and valuation at the beginning of the period. In the case of inventories, however, it is more difficult for the auditor to be satisfied as to inventory on hand at the beginning of the period. Therefore, additional audit procedures are ordinarily necessary such as

observing a current physical inventory taking and reconciling it back to the opening inventory quantities, performing audit procedures on the valuation of the opening inventory items, and performing audit procedures on gross profit and cutoff. A combination of these procedures may provide sufficient appropriate audit evidence.

For noncurrent assets and liabilities, such as fixed assets, investments and long-term debt, the auditor will ordinarily examine the accounting records and other information underlying the opening balances. In certain cases, the auditor may be able to obtain confirmation of opening balances with third parties, for example, for long-term debt and investments. In other cases, the auditor may need to carry out additional audit procedures.   10

Continuing Auditor

If a continuing auditor issued an unqualified report on the preceding period's financial statements and the audit of the current period has not revealed any matters which cast doubt on those financial statements, the procedures regarding opening balances need not extend beyond ensuring that opening balances have been appropriately brought forward and that current accounting policies have been consistently applied.   10-1

If a qualified report was issued on the preceding period's financial statements the auditor, in addition to carrying out the procedures in paragraph 10-1, considers whether the matter which gave rise to the qualification has been resolved and properly dealt with in the current period's financial statements.   10-2

Audit Conclusions and Reporting

If, after performing audit procedures including those set out above, the auditor is unable to obtain sufficient appropriate audit evidence concerning opening balances, the auditor's report should include: 11

(a) **A qualified opinion,** for example:
"We did not observe the counting of the physical inventory stated at XXX as at December 31, 19X1, since that date was prior to our appointment as auditors. We were unable to satisfy ourselves as to the inventory quantities at that date by other audit procedures.
In our opinion, except for the effects of such adjustments, if any, as might have been determined to be necessary had we been able to observe the counting of physical inventory and satisfy ourselves as to the opening balance of inventory, the financial statements give a true and fair view of (present fairly, in all material respects,) the financial position of ... as at December 31, 19X2 and the results of its operations and its cash flows for the year then ended in accordance with ...;"

> Illustrative examples of auditor's reports tailored for use with audits conducted in accordance with ISAs (UK and Ireland) are given in the most recent version of the APB Bulletin, "Auditor's Reports on Financial Statements".

(b) **A disclaimer of opinion; or**

(c) **In those jurisdictions where it is permitted[1], an opinion which is qualified or disclaimed regarding the results of operations and unqualified regarding financial position,** for example:

"We did not observe the counting of the physical inventory stated at XXX as at December 31, 19X1, since that date was prior to our appointment as auditors. We were unable to satisfy ourselves as to the inventory quantities at that date by other audit procedures.

Because of the significance of the above matter in relation to the results of the Company's operations for the year to December 31, 19X2, we are not in a position to, and do not, express an opinion on the results of its operations and its cash flows for the year then ended.

In our opinion, the balance sheet gives a true and fair view of (or 'presents fairly in all material respects,') the financial position of the Company as at December 31, 19X2, in accordance with ....."

> Illustrative examples of auditor's reports tailored for use with audits conducted in accordance with ISAs (UK and Ireland) are given in the most recent version of the APB Bulletin, "Auditor's Reports on Financial Statements".

12 If the opening balances contain misstatements which could materially affect the current period's financial statements, the auditor would inform management[2] and, after having obtained management's authorization, the predecessor auditor, if any. **If the effect of the misstatement is not properly accounted for and adequately presented and disclosed, the auditor should express a qualified opinion or an adverse opinion, as appropriate.**

13 **If the current period's accounting policies have not been consistently applied in relation to opening balances and if the change has not been properly accounted for and adequately presented and disclosed, the auditor should express a qualified opinion or an adverse opinion as appropriate.**

14 If the entity's prior period auditor's report was modified, the auditor would consider the effect thereof on the current period's financial statements. For example, if there was a scope limitation, such as one due to the inability to determine opening inventory in the prior period, the auditor may not need to qualify or disclaim the current period's audit opinion. **However, if a modification regarding the prior period's financial statements remains relevant and material to the current period's financial statements, the auditor should modify the current auditor's report accordingly.**

Effective Date

14-1 This ISA (UK and Ireland) is effective for audits of financial statements for periods commencing on or after 15 December 2004.

---

[1] *This form of opinion is permitted in the UK and Ireland.*

[2] *In the UK and Ireland the auditor would inform those charged with governance and seek their authorization to inform the predecessor auditor, if any.*

[520]
Analytical procedures

(Issued December 2004)

Contents

	Paragraphs
Introduction	1 - 3-4
Nature and Purpose of Analytical Procedures	4 - 7
Analytical Procedures as Risk Assessment Procedures	8 - 9-1
Analytical Procedures as Substantive Procedures	10 - 12
Analytical Procedures in the Overall Review at the End of the Audit	13 - 13-2
Investigating Unusual Items	17 - 18
Effective Date	**18-1**

International Standard on Auditing (UK and Ireland) (ISA (UK and Ireland)) 520 "Analytical Procedures" should be read in the context of the Auditing Practices Board's Statement "The Auditing Practices Board – Scope and Authority of Pronouncements (Revised)" which sets out the application and authority of ISAs (UK and Ireland).

Introduction

1. The purpose of this International Standard on Auditing (UK and Ireland) (ISA (UK and Ireland)) is to establish standards and provide guidance on the application of analytical procedures during an audit.

2. **The auditor should apply analytical procedures as risk assessment procedures to obtain an understanding of the entity and its environment and in the overall review at the end of the audit.** Analytical procedures may also be applied as substantive procedures.

3. "Analytical procedures" means evaluations of financial information made by a study of plausible relationships among both financial and non-financial data. Analytical procedures also encompass the investigation of identified fluctuations and relationships that are inconsistent with other relevant information or deviate significantly from predicted amounts.

3-1. This ISA (UK and Ireland) uses the terms 'those charged with governance' and 'management'. The term 'governance' describes the role of persons entrusted with the supervision, control and direction of an entity. Ordinarily, those charged with governance are accountable for ensuring that the entity achieves its objectives, and for the quality of its financial reporting and reporting to interested parties. Those charged with governance include management only when they perform such functions.

3-2. In the UK and Ireland, those charged with governance include the directors (executive and non-executive) of a company or other body, the members of an audit committee where one exists, the partners, proprietors, committee of management or trustees of other forms of entity, or equivalent persons responsible for directing the entity's affairs and preparing its financial statements.

3-3. 'Management' comprises those persons who perform senior managerial functions.

3-4. In the UK and Ireland, depending on the nature and circumstances of the entity, management may include some or all of those charged with governance (e.g. executive directors). Management will not normally include non-executive directors.

Nature and Purpose of Analytical Procedures

4. Analytical procedures include the consideration of comparisons of the entity's financial information with, for example:

   - Comparable information for prior periods.
   - Anticipated results of the entity, such as budgets or forecasts, or expectations of the auditor, such as an estimation of depreciation.
   - Similar industry information, such as a comparison of the entity's ratio of sales to accounts receivable with industry averages or with other entities of comparable size in the same industry.

5. Analytical procedures also include consideration of relationships:

   - Among elements of financial information that would be expected to conform to a predictable pattern based on the entity's experience, such as gross margin percentages.

- Between financial information and relevant non-financial information, such as payroll costs to number of employees.

Various methods may be used in performing the above audit procedures. These range from simple comparisons to complex analyses using advanced statistical techniques. Analytical procedures may be applied to consolidated financial statements, financial statements of components (such as subsidiaries, divisions or segments) and individual elements of financial information. The auditor's choice of audit procedures, methods and level of application is a matter of professional judgment.

6

Analytical procedures are used for the following purposes:

7

(a) As risk assessment procedures to obtain an understanding of the entity and its environment (paragraphs 8-9).
(b) As substantive procedures when their use can be more effective or efficient than tests of details in reducing the risk of material misstatement at the assertion level to an acceptably low level (paragraphs 10-19).
(c) As an overall review of the financial statements at the end of the audit (paragraph 13).

Analytical Procedures as Risk Assessment Procedures

The auditor should apply analytical procedures as risk assessment procedures to obtain an understanding of the entity and its environment. Application of analytical procedures may indicate aspects of the entity of which the auditor was unaware and will assist in assessing the risks of material misstatement in order to determine the nature, timing and extent of further audit procedures.

8

Analytical procedures applied as risk assessment procedures use both financial and non-financial information, for example, the relationship between sales and square footage of selling space or volume of goods sold. Paragraph 10 of ISA (UK and Ireland) 315, "Understanding the Entity and Its Environment and Assessing the Risks of Material Misstatement", contains additional guidance on applying analytical procedures as risk assessment procedures.

9

> Analytical procedures at this stage are usually based on interim financial information, budgets and management accounts. However, for those entities with less formal means of controlling and monitoring performance, it may be possible to extract relevant financial information from the accounting system, VAT returns and bank statements. Discussions with management, focused on identifying significant changes in the business since the prior financial period, may also be useful.

9-1

Analytical Procedures as Substantive Procedures

The auditor designs and performs substantive procedures to be responsive to the related assessment of the risk of material misstatement at the assertion level. The auditor's substantive procedures at the assertion level may be derived from tests of details, from substantive analytical procedures, or from a combination of both. The decision about which audit procedures to use to achieve a particular audit objective is based on the auditor's judgment about the expected effectiveness and efficiency of

10

the available audit procedures in reducing the assessed risk of material misstatement at the assertion level to an acceptably low level.

11 The auditor will ordinarily inquire of management as to the availability and reliability of information needed to apply substantive analytical procedures and the results of any such procedures performed by the entity. It may be efficient to use analytical data prepared by the entity, provided the auditor is satisfied that such data is properly prepared.

12 When designing and performing analytical procedures as substantive procedures, the auditor will need to consider a number of factors such as the following:

- The suitability of using substantive analytical procedures given the assertions (paragraphs 12a and 12b).
- The reliability of the data, whether internal or external, from which the expectation of recorded amounts or ratios is developed (paragraphs 12c and 12d).
- Whether the expectation is sufficiently precise to identify a material misstatement at the desired level of assurance (paragraph 112e).
- The amount of any difference of recorded amounts from expected values that is acceptable (paragraph 12f).

Suitability of Using Substantive Analytical Procedures Given the Assertions

12a Substantive analytical procedures are generally more applicable to large volumes of transactions that tend to be predictable over time. The application of substantive analytical procedures is based on the expectation that relationships among data exist and continue in the absence of known conditions to the contrary. The presence of these relationships provides audit evidence as to the completeness, accuracy and occurrence of transactions captured in the information produced by the entity's information system. However, reliance on the results of substantive analytical procedures will depend on the auditor's assessment of the risk that the analytical procedures may identify relationships as expected when, in fact, a material misstatement exists.

12b In determining the suitability of substantive analytical procedures given the assertions, the auditor considers:

(a) *The assessment of the risk of material misstatement.* The auditor considers the understanding of the entity and its internal control, the materiality and likelihood of misstatement of the items involved, and the nature of the assertion in determining whether substantive analytical procedures are suitable. For example, if controls over sales order processing are weak, the auditor may place more reliance on tests of details rather than substantive analytical procedures for assertions related to receivables. As another example, when inventory balances are material, the auditor ordinarily does not rely only on substantive analytical procedures when performing audit procedures on the existence assertion. ISA (UK and Ireland) 330, "The Auditor's Procedures in Response to Assessed Risks" indicates that when the approach to significant risks consists only of substantive procedures, the audit procedures appropriate to address such significant risks consist of tests of details only, or a combination of tests of details and substantive analytical procedures.

(b) *Any tests of details directed toward the same assertion.* Substantive analytical procedures may also be considered appropriate when tests of details are performed on the same assertion. For example, when auditing the collectibility of accounts receivable, the auditor may apply substantive analytical procedures to an aging of customers' accounts in addition to tests of details on subsequent cash receipts.

The Reliability of the Data

The reliability of data is influenced by its source and by its nature and is dependent on the circumstances under which it is obtained. In determining whether data is reliable for purposes of designing substantive analytical procedures, the auditor considers:

(a) *Source of the information available.* For example, information is ordinarily more reliable when it is obtained from independent sources outside the entity.
(b) *Comparability of the information available.* For example, broad industry data may need to be supplemented to be comparable to that of an entity that produces and sells specialized products.
(c) *Nature and relevance of the information available.* For example, whether budgets have been established as results to be expected rather than as goals to be achieved.
(d) *Controls over the preparation of the information.* For example, controls over the preparation, review and maintenance of budgets.
(e) *Prior year knowledge and understanding.* For example, the knowledge gained during previous audits, together with the auditor's understanding of the effectiveness of the accounting and internal control systems and the types of problems that in prior periods have given rise to accounting adjustments.
(f) *Whether the information is produced internally.* For example, if the information is produced internally, its reliability is enhanced if it is produced independently of the accounting system or there are adequate controls over its preparation. The necessity for evidence on the reliability of such information depends on the results of the other audit procedures and on the importance of the results of analytical procedures as a basis for the auditor's opinion.

12c

The auditor considers testing the controls, if any, over the entity's preparation of information used by the auditor in applying substantive analytical procedures. When such controls are effective, the auditor has greater confidence in the reliability of the information and, therefore, in the results of substantive analytical procedures. The controls over non-financial information can often be tested in conjunction with other tests of controls. For example, an entity in establishing controls over the processing of sales invoices may include controls over the recording of unit sales. In these circumstances, the auditor could test the operating effectiveness of controls over the recording of unit sales in conjunction with tests of the operating effectiveness of controls over the processing of sales invoices. Alternatively, the auditor may consider whether the information was subjected to audit testing in the current or prior period. In determining the audit procedures to apply to the information upon which the expectation for substantive analytical procedures is based, the auditor considers the guidance in paragraph 11 of ISA (UK and Ireland) 500, "Audit Evidence."

12d

Whether the Expectation is Sufficiently Precise

In assessing whether the expectation can be developed sufficiently precise to identify a material misstatement at the desired level of assurance, the auditor considers factors such as:

12e

- *The accuracy with which the expected results of substantive analytical procedures can be predicted.* For example, the auditor will ordinarily expect greater consistency in comparing gross profit margins from one period to another than in comparing discretionary expenses, such as research or advertising.
- *The degree to which information can be disaggregated.* For example, substantive analytical procedures may be more effective when applied to financial information on individual sections of an operation or to financial statements of components of a diversified entity, than when applied to the financial statements of the entity as a whole.
- *The availability of the information, both financial and nonfinancial.* For example, the auditor considers whether financial information, such as budgets or forecasts, and non-financial information, such as the number of units produced or sold, is available to design substantive analytical procedures. If the information is available, the auditor also considers the reliability of the information as discussed in paragraphs 12c and 12d above.
- *The frequency with which a relationship is observed.* For example, a pattern repeated monthly as opposed to annually.

Amount of Difference of Recorded Amounts from Expected Values that is Acceptable

12f In designing and performing substantive analytical procedures, the auditor considers the amount of difference from expectation that can be accepted without further investigation. This consideration is influenced primarily by materiality and the consistency with the desired level of assurance. Determination of this amount involves considering the possibility that a combination of misstatements in the specific account balance, class of transactions, or disclosure could aggregate to an unacceptable amount. The auditor increases the desired level of assurance as the risk of material misstatement increases by reducing the amount of difference from the expectation that can be accepted without further investigation. Paragraphs 17 and 18 below discuss the auditor's response when the amount of difference between the expected value and the reported value exceeds the amount that can be accepted without further investigation.

12g When the auditor performs substantive procedures at an interim date and plans to perform substantive analytical procedures with respect to the intervening period, the auditor considers how the matters discussed in paragraphs 12a-12f affect the ability to obtain sufficient appropriate audit evidence for the remaining period. This includes considering whether the period end balances of the particular classes of transactions or account balances are reasonably predictable with respect to amount, relative significance, and composition. See ISA (UK and Ireland) 330 paragraphs 56-61 for additional guidance.

Analytical Procedures in the Overall Review at the End of the Audit

13 **The auditor should apply analytical procedures at or near the end of the audit when forming an overall conclusion as to whether the financial statements as a whole are consistent with the auditor's understanding of the entity.** The conclusions drawn from the results of such audit procedures are intended to corroborate conclusions formed during the audit of individual components or elements of the financial statements and assist in arriving at the overall conclusion as to the reasonableness of the financial statements. However, they may also identify a previously unrecognized risk of material misstatement. In such circumstances, the auditor may need to re-evaluate

the planned audit procedures, based on the revised consideration of assessed risks for all or some of the classes of transactions, account balances, or disclosures and related assertions.

These procedures will also involve consideration of whether the assertions contained in the financial statements are consistent with the auditor's understanding of the entity. **13-1**

The principal considerations when carrying out such procedures are: **13-2**

(a) Whether the financial statements adequately reflect the information and explanations previously obtained and conclusions previously reached during the course of the audit;

(b) Whether the procedures reveal any new factors which may affect the presentation of, or disclosures in, the financial statements;

(c) Whether analytical procedures applied when completing the audit, such as comparing the information in the financial statements with other pertinent data, produce results which assist in arriving at the overall conclusion as to whether the financial statements as a whole are consistent with the auditor's knowledge of the entity's business;

(d) Whether the presentation adopted in the financial statements may have been unduly influenced by the desire of those charged with governance to present matters in a favourable or unfavourable light; and

(e) The potential impact on the financial statements of the aggregate of uncorrected misstatements (including those arising from bias in making accounting estimates) identified during the course of the audit and the preceding period's audit, if any.

[Paragraphs 14-16 were deleted when the audit risk standards[1] became effective.]

Investigating Unusual Items

When analytical procedures identify significant fluctuations or relationships that are inconsistent with other relevant information or that deviate from predicted amounts, the auditor should investigate and obtain adequate explanations and appropriate corroborative audit evidence. **17**

The investigation of unusual fluctuations and relationships ordinarily begins with inquiries of management, followed by: **18**

(a) Corroboration of management's responses, for example, by comparing them with the auditor's understanding of the entity and other audit evidence obtained during the course of the audit; and

(b) Consideration of the need to apply other audit procedures based on the results of such inquiries, if management is unable to provide an explanation or if the explanation is not considered adequate.

---

[1] *The audit risk standards comprise ISA (UK and Ireland) 315, "Understanding the Entity and its Environment and Assessing the Risks of Material Misstatement," ISA (UK and Ireland) 330, "The Auditor's Procedures in Response to Assessed Risks," and ISA (UK and Ireland) 500 (Revised), "Audit Evidence." The audit risk standards gave rise to amendments to this and other ISAs (UK and Ireland).*

Effective Date

18-1 This ISA (UK and Ireland) is effective for audits of financial statements for periods commencing on or after 15 December 2004.

Public Sector Perspective

Additional guidance for auditors of public sector bodies in the UK and Ireland is given in:

- Practice Note 10 "Audit of Financial Statements of Public Sector Entities in the United Kingdom (Revised)"
- Practice Note 10(I) "The Audit of Central Government Financial Statements in Ireland"

1 *The relationships between individual financial statement items traditionally considered in the audit of business entities may not always be appropriate in the audit of governments or other non-business public sector entities; for example, in many such public sector entities there is often little direct relationship between revenues and expenditures. In addition, because expenditure on the acquisition of assets is frequently non-capitalized, there may be no relationship between expenditures on, for example, inventories and fixed assets and the amount of those assets reported in the financial statements. In addition, in the public sector, industry data or statistics for comparative purposes may not be available. However, other relationships may be relevant, for example, variations in the cost per kilometer of road construction or the number of vehicles acquired compared with vehicles retired. Where appropriate, reference has to be made to available private sector industry data and statistics. In certain instances, it may also be appropriate for the auditor to generate an in-house database of reference information.*

[530]
Audit sampling and other means of testing

(Issued December 2004)

Contents

	Paragraphs
Introduction	1 - 2
Definitions	3 - 12
Audit Evidence	13 - 17
Risk Considerations in Obtaining Audit Evidence	18 - 20
Audit Procedures for Obtaining Audit Evidence	21
Selecting Items for Testing to Gather Audit Evidence	22 - 27
Statistical Versus Non-statistical Sampling Approaches	28 - 30
Design of the Sample	31 - 39
Sample Size	40 - 41
Selecting the Sample	42 - 43
Performing the Audit Procedure	44 - 46
Nature and Cause of Errors	47 - 50
Projecting Errors	51 - 53
Evaluating the Sample Results	54 - 56
Effective Date	57

Appendix 1: Examples of Factors Influencing Sample Size for Tests of Controls

Appendix 2: Examples of Factors Influencing Sample Size for Tests of Details

Appendix 3: Sample Selection Methods

> International Standard on Auditing (UK and Ireland) (ISA (UK and Ireland)) 530 "Audit Sampling and Other Means of Testing" should be read in the context of the Auditing Practices Board's Statement "The Auditing Practices Board – Scope and Authority of Pronouncements (Revised)" which sets out the application and authority of ISAs (UK and Ireland).

Introduction

1   The purpose of this International Standard on Auditing (UK and Ireland) (ISA (UK and Ireland)) is to establish standards and provide guidance on the use of audit sampling and other means of selecting items for testing when designing audit procedures to gather audit evidence.

1-1 This ISA (UK and Ireland) applies to any audit using sampling whether related to financial statements or not. Nothing contained in this statement is intended to preclude non-statistically based samples where there are reasonable grounds for believing that the results may be relied on for the purpose of the test. Statistically based sampling involves the use of techniques from which mathematically constructed conclusions about the population can be drawn. An auditor draws a judgmental opinion about the population from non-statistical methods.

1-2 This ISA (UK and Ireland) uses the terms 'those charged with governance' and 'management'. The term 'governance' describes the role of persons entrusted with the supervision, control and direction of an entity. Ordinarily, those charged with governance are accountable for ensuring that the entity achieves its objectives, and for the quality of its financial reporting and reporting to interested parties. Those charged with governance include management only when they perform such functions.

1-3 In the UK and Ireland, those charged with governance include the directors (executive and non-executive) of a company or other body, the members of an audit committee where one exists, the partners, proprietors, committee of management or trustees of other forms of entity, or equivalent persons responsible for directing the entity's affairs and preparing its financial statements.

1-4 'Management' comprises those persons who perform senior managerial functions.

1-5 In the UK and Ireland, depending on the nature and circumstances of the entity, management may include some or all of those charged with governance (e.g. executive directors). Management will not normally include non-executive directors.

2   **When designing audit procedures, the auditor should determine appropriate means for selecting items for testing so as to gather sufficient appropriate audit evidence to meet the objectives of the audit procedures.**

Definitions

3   "Audit sampling" (sampling) involves the application of audit procedures to less than 100% of items within a class of transactions or account balance such that all sampling units have a chance of selection. This will enable the auditor to obtain and evaluate audit evidence about some characteristic of the items selected in order to form or assist in forming a conclusion concerning the population from which the sample is drawn. Audit sampling can use either a statistical or a non-statistical approach.

4   For purposes of this ISA (UK and Ireland), "error" means either control deviations, when performing tests of controls, or misstatements, when performing tests of

details. Similarly, total error is used to mean either the rate of deviation or total misstatement.

"Anomalous error" means an error that arises from an isolated event that has not recurred other than on specifically identifiable occasions and is therefore not representative of errors in the population.

"Population" means the entire set of data from which a sample is selected and about which the auditor wishes to draw conclusions. For example, all of the items in a class of transactions or account balance constitute a population. A population may be divided into strata, or sub-populations, with each stratum being examined separately. The term population is used to include the term stratum.

"Sampling risk" arises from the possibility that the auditor's conclusion, based on a sample may be different from the conclusion reached if the entire population were subjected to the same audit procedure. There are two types of sampling risk:

(a) The risk the auditor will conclude, in the case of a test of controls, that controls are more effective than they actually are, or in the case of a test of details, that a material error does not exist when in fact it does. This type of risk affects audit effectiveness and is more likely to lead to an inappropriate audit opinion; and
(b) The risk the auditor will conclude, in the case of a test of controls, that controls are less effective than they actually are, or in the case of a test of details, that a material error exists when in fact it does not. This type of risk affects audit efficiency as it would usually lead to additional work to establish that initial conclusions were incorrect.

The mathematical complements of these risks are termed confidence levels.

"Non-sampling risk" arises from factors that cause the auditor to reach an erroneous conclusion for any reason not related to the size of the sample. For example, ordinarily the auditor finds it necessary to rely on audit evidence that is persuasive rather than conclusive, the auditor might use inappropriate audit procedures, or the auditor might misinterpret audit evidence and fail to recognize an error.

"Sampling unit" means the individual items constituting a population, for example checks listed on deposit slips, credit entries on bank statements, sales invoices or debtors' balances, or a monetary unit.

"Statistical sampling" means any approach to sampling that has the following characteristics:

(a) Random selection of a sample; and
(b) Use of probability theory to evaluate sample results, including measurement of sampling risk.

A sampling approach that does not have characteristics (a) and (b) is considered non-statistical sampling.

"Stratification" is the process of dividing a population into subpopulations, each of which is a group of sampling units which have similar characteristics (often monetary value).

"Tolerable error" means the maximum error in a population that the auditor is willing to accept.

Audit Evidence

13 In accordance with ISA (UK and Ireland) 500, "Audit Evidence" audit evidence is obtained by performing risk assessment procedures, tests of controls and substantive procedures. The type of audit procedure to be performed is important to an understanding of the application of audit sampling in gathering audit evidence.

Risk Assessment Procedures

13a In accordance with ISA (UK and Ireland) 315, "Understanding the Entity and Its Environment and Assessing the Risks of Material Misstatement," the auditor performs risk assessment procedures to obtain an understanding of the entity and its environment, including its internal control. Ordinarily, risk assessment procedures do not involve the use of audit sampling. However, the auditor often plans and performs tests of controls concurrently with obtaining an understanding of the design of controls and determining whether they have been implemented. In such cases, the following discussion of tests of controls is relevant.

Tests of Control

14 In accordance with ISA (UK and Ireland) 330, "The Auditor's Procedures in Response to Assessed Risks" tests of controls are performed when the auditor's risk assessment includes an expectation of the operating effectiveness of controls.

15 Based on the auditor's understanding of internal control, the auditor identifies the characteristics or attributes that indicate performance of a control, as well as possible deviation conditions which indicate departures from adequate performance. The presence or absence of attributes can then be tested by the auditor.

16 Audit sampling for tests of controls is generally appropriate when application of the control leaves audit evidence of performance (for example, initials of the credit manager on a sales invoice indicating credit approval, or evidence of authorization of data input to a microcomputer based data processing system).

Substantive Procedures

17 Substantive procedures are concerned with amounts and are of two types: tests of details of classes of transactions, account balances, and disclosures and substantive analytical procedures. The purpose of substantive procedures is to obtain audit evidence to detect material misstatements at the assertion level. In the context of substantive procedures, audit sampling and other means of selecting items for testing, as discussed in this ISA (UK and Ireland), relate only to tests of details. When performing tests of details, audit sampling and other means of selecting items for testing and gathering audit evidence may be used to verify one or more assertions about a financial statement amount (for example, the existence of accounts receivable), or to make an independent estimate of some amount (for example, the value of obsolete inventories).

Risk Considerations in Obtaining Audit Evidence

18 In obtaining audit evidence, the auditor should use professional judgment to assess the risk of material misstatement (which includes inherent and control risk) and design further audit procedures to ensure this risk is reduced to an acceptably low level.

[Paragraph 19 was deleted when the audit risk standards[1] became effective.] 19

Sampling risk and non-sampling risk can affect the components of the risk of material misstatement. For example, when performing tests of controls, the auditor may find no errors in a sample and conclude that controls are operating effectively, when the rate of error in the population is, in fact, unacceptably high (sampling risk). Or there may be errors in the sample which the auditor fails to recognize (non-sampling risk). With respect to substantive procedures, the auditor may use a variety of methods to reduce detection risk to an acceptable level. Depending on their nature, these methods will be subject to sampling and/or non-sampling risks. For example, the auditor may choose an inappropriate substantive analytical procedure (non-sampling risk) or may find only minor misstatements in a test of details when, in fact, the population misstatement is greater than the tolerable amount (sampling risk). For both tests of controls and substantive tests of details, sampling risk can be reduced by increasing sample size, while non-sampling risk can be reduced by proper engagement planning supervision and review. 20

Audit Procedures for Obtaining Audit Evidence

Audit procedures for obtaining audit evidence include inspection, observation, inquiry and confirmation, recalculation, reperformance and analytical procedures. The choice of appropriate audit procedures is a matter of professional judgment in the circumstances. Application of these audit procedures will often involve the selection of items for testing from a population. Paragraphs 19-38 of ISA (UK and Ireland) 500 contain additional discussion on audit procedures for obtaining audit evidence. 21

Selecting Items for Testing to Gather Audit Evidence

When designing audit procedures, the auditor should determine appropriate means of selecting items for testing. The means available to the auditor are: 22
(a) Selecting all items (100% examination);
(b) Selecting specific items, and
(c) Audit sampling.

The decision as to which approach to use will depend on the circumstances, and the application of any one or combination of the above means may be appropriate in particular circumstances. While the decision as to which means, or combination of means, to use is made on the basis of the risk of material misstatement related to the assertion being tested and audit efficiency, the auditor needs to be satisfied that methods used are effective in providing sufficient appropriate audit evidence to meet the objectives of the audit procedure. 23

Selecting All Items

The auditor may decide that it will be most appropriate to examine the entire population of items that make up a class of transactions or account balance (or a stratum within that population). 100% examination is unlikely in the case of tests of 24

---

[1] The audit risk standards comprise ISA (UK and Ireland) 315, "Understanding the Entity and its Environment and Assessing the Risks of Material Misstatement," ISA (UK and Ireland) 330, "The Auditor's Procedures in Response to Assessed Risks," and ISA (UK and Ireland) 500 (Revised), "Audit Evidence." The audit risk standards gave rise to amendments to this and other ISAs (UK and Ireland).

controls; however, it is more common for tests of details. For example, 100% examination may be appropriate when the population constitutes a small number of large value items, when there is a significant risk and other means do not provide sufficient appropriate audit evidence, or when the repetitive nature of a calculation or other process performed automatically by an information system makes a 100% examination cost effective, for example, through the use of computer-assisted audit techniques (CAATs).

Selecting Specific Items

25 The auditor may decide to select specific items from a population based on such factors as the auditor's understanding of the entity, the assessed risk of material misstatement, and the characteristics of the population being tested. The judgmental selection of specific items is subject to non-sampling risk. Specific items selected may include:

- *High value or key items*. The auditor may decide to select specific items within a population because they are of high value, or exhibit some other characteristic, for example items that are suspicious, unusual, particularly risk-prone or that have a history of error.
- *All items over a certain amount*. The auditor may decide to examine items whose values exceed a certain amount so as to verify a large proportion of the total amount of class of transactions or account balance.
- *Items to obtain information*. The auditor may examine items to obtain information about matters such as the nature of the entity, the nature of transactions, and internal control.
- *Items to test control activities*. The auditor may use judgment to select and examine specific items to determine whether or not a particular control activity is being performed.

26 While selective examination of specific items from a class of transactions or account balance will often be an efficient means of gathering audit evidence, it does not constitute audit sampling. The results of audit procedures applied to items selected in this way cannot be projected to the entire population. The auditor considers the need to obtain sufficient appropriate audit evidence regarding the remainder of the population when that remainder is material.

Audit Sampling

27 The auditor may decide to apply audit sampling to a class of transactions or account balance. Audit sampling can be applied using either non-statistical or statistical sampling methods. Audit sampling is discussed in detail in paragraphs 30-55.

Statistical Versus Non-statistical Sampling Approaches

28 The decision whether to use a statistical or non-statistical sampling approach is a matter for the auditor's judgment regarding the most efficient manner to obtain sufficient appropriate audit evidence in the particular circumstances. For example, in the case of tests of controls the auditor's analysis of the nature and cause of errors will often be more important than the statistical analysis of the mere presence or absence (that is, the count) of errors. In such a situation, non-statistical sampling may be most appropriate.

When applying statistical sampling, the sample size can be determined using either probability theory or professional judgment. Moreover, sample size is not a valid criterion to distinguish between statistical and non-statistical approaches. Sample size is a function of factors such as those identified in Appendices 1 and 2. When circumstances are similar, the effect on sample size of factors such as those identified in Appendices 1 and 2 will be similar regardless of whether a statistical or non-statistical approach is chosen.

Often, while the approach adopted does not meet the definition of statistical sampling, elements of a statistical approach are used, for example the use of random selection using computer generated random numbers. However, only when the approach adopted has the characteristics of statistical sampling are statistical measurements of sampling risk valid.

Design of the Sample

When designing an audit sample, the auditor should consider the objectives of the audit procedure and the attributes of the population from which the sample will be drawn.

When designing an audit sample the auditor should also consider the sampling and selection methods.

The auditor first considers the specific objectives to be achieved and the combination of audit procedures which is likely to best achieve those objectives. Consideration of the nature of the audit evidence sought and possible error conditions or other characteristics relating to that audit evidence will assist the auditor in defining what constitutes an error and what population to use for sampling.

The auditor considers what conditions constitute an error by reference to the objectives of the audit procedure. A clear understanding of what constitutes an error is important to ensure that all, and only, those conditions that are relevant to the objectives of the audit procedure are included in the projection of errors. For example, in a test of details relating to the existence of accounts receivable, such as confirmation, payments made by the customer before the confirmation date but received shortly after that date by the client are not considered an error. Also, a misposting between customer accounts does not affect the total accounts receivable balance. Therefore, it is not appropriate to consider this an error in evaluating the sample results of this particular audit procedure, even though it may have an important effect on other areas of the audit, such as the assessment of the likelihood of fraud or the adequacy of the allowance for doubtful accounts.

When performing tests of controls, the auditor generally makes an assessment of the rate of error the auditor expects to find in the population to be tested. This assessment is based on the auditor's understanding of the design of the relevant controls and whether they have been implemented or the examination of a small number of items from the population. Similarly, for tests of details, the auditor generally makes an assessment of the expected amount of error in the population. These assessments are useful for designing an audit sample and in determining sample size. For example, if the expected rate of error is unacceptably high, tests of controls will normally not be performed. However, when performing tests of details, if the expected amount of error is high, 100% examination or the use of a large sample size may be appropriate.

Population

35 It is important for the auditor to ensure that the population is:

  (a) *Appropriate* to the objective of the audit procedure, which will include consideration of the direction of testing. For example, if the auditor's objective is to test for overstatement of accounts payable, the population could be defined as the accounts payable listing. On the other hand, when testing for understatement of accounts payable, the population is not the accounts payable listing but rather subsequent disbursements, unpaid invoices, suppliers' statements, unmatched receiving reports or other populations that provide audit evidence of understatement of accounts payable; and

  (b) *Complete.* For example, if the auditor intends to select payment vouchers from a file, conclusions cannot be drawn about all vouchers for the period unless the auditor is satisfied that all vouchers have in fact been filed. Similarly, if the auditor intends to use the sample to draw conclusions about whether a control activity operated effectively during the financial reporting period, the population needs to include all relevant items from throughout the entire period. A different approach may be to stratify the population and use sampling only to draw conclusions about the control activity during, say, the first 10 months of a year, and to use alternative audit procedures or a separate sample regarding the remaining two months. ISA (UK and Ireland) 330 contains additional guidance on performing audit procedures at an interim period.

35a The auditor is required to obtain audit evidence about the accuracy and completeness of information produced by the entity's information system when that information is used in performing audit procedures. When performing audit sampling, the auditor performs audit procedures to ensure that the information upon which the audit sampling is performed is sufficiently complete and accurate. ISA (UK and Ireland) 500 paragraph 11 contains additional guidance on the audit procedures to perform regarding the accuracy and completeness of such information.

Stratification

36 Audit efficiency may be improved if the auditor stratifies a population by dividing it into discrete sub-populations which have an identifying characteristic. The objective of stratification is to reduce the variability of items within each stratum and therefore allow sample size to be reduced without a proportional increase in sampling risk. Sub-populations need to be carefully defined such that any sampling unit can only belong to one stratum.

37 When performing tests of details, a class of transaction or account balance or is often stratified by monetary value. This allows greater audit effort to be directed to the larger value items which may contain the greatest potential monetary error in terms of overstatement. Similarly, a population may be stratified according to a particular characteristic that indicates a higher risk of error, for example, when testing the valuation of accounts receivable, balances may be stratified by age.

38 The results of audit procedures applied to a sample of items within a stratum can only be projected to the items that make up that stratum. To draw a conclusion on the entire population, the auditor will need to consider the risk of material misstatement in relation to whatever other strata make up the entire population. For example, 20% of the items in a population may make up 90% of the value of an account balance. The auditor may decide to examine a sample of these items. The auditor evaluates the results of this sample and reaches a conclusion on the 90% of

value separately from the remaining 10% (on which a further sample or other means of gathering audit evidence will be used, or which may be considered immaterial).

Value Weighted Selection

It will often be efficient in performing tests of details, particularly when testing for overstatements, to identify the sampling unit as the individual monetary units (for example, dollars) that make up a class of transactions or account balance. Having selected specific monetary units from within the population, for example, the accounts receivable balance, the auditor then examines the particular items, for example, individual balances, that contain those monetary units. This approach to defining the sampling unit ensures that audit effort is directed to the larger value items because they have a greater chance of selection, and can result in smaller sample sizes. This approach is ordinarily used in conjunction with the systematic method of sample selection (described in Appendix 3) and is most efficient when selecting items using CAATs. 39

Sample Size

In determining the sample size, the auditor should consider whether sampling risk is reduced to an acceptably low level. Sample size is affected by the level of sampling risk that the auditor is willing to accept. The lower the risk the auditor is willing to accept, the greater the sample size will need to be. 40

The sample size can be determined by the application of a statistically-based formula or through the exercise of professional judgment objectively applied to the circumstances. Appendices 1 and 2 indicate the influences that various factors typically have on the determination of sample size, and hence the level of sampling risk. 41

Selecting the Sample

The auditor should select items for the sample with the expectation that all sampling units in the population have a chance of selection. Statistical sampling requires that sample items are selected at random so that each sampling unit has a known chance of being selected. The sampling units might be physical items (such as invoices) or monetary units. With non-statistical sampling, an auditor uses professional judgment to select the items for a sample. Because the purpose of sampling is to draw conclusions about the entire population, the auditor endeavors to select a representative sample by choosing sample items which have characteristics typical of the population, and the sample needs to be selected so that bias is avoided. 42

The principal methods of selecting samples are the use of random number tables or CAATs, systematic selection and haphazard selection. Each of these methods is discussed in Appendix 3. 43

Performing the Audit Procedure

The auditor should perform audit procedures appropriate to the particular audit objective on each item selected. 44

If a selected item is not appropriate for the application of the audit procedure, the audit procedure is ordinarily performed on a replacement item. For example, a 45 voided check may be selected when testing for evidence of payment authorization. If the auditor is satisfied that the check had been properly voided such that it does not constitute an error, an appropriately chosen replacement is examined.

46 Sometimes however, the auditor is unable to apply the designed audit procedures to a selected item because, for instance, documentation relating to that item has been lost. If suitable alternative audit procedures cannot be performed on that item, the auditor ordinarily considers that item to be in error. An example of a suitable alternative audit procedure might be the examination of subsequent receipts when no reply has been received in response to a positive confirmation request.

Nature and Cause of Errors

47 **The auditor should consider the sample results, the nature and cause of any errors identified, and their possible effect on the particular audit objective and on other areas of the audit.**

48 When performing tests of controls, the auditor is primarily concerned with obtaining audit evidence that controls operated effectively throughout the period of reliance. This includes obtaining audit evidence about how controls were applied at relevant times during the period under audit, the consistency with which they were applied, and by whom or by what means they were applied. The concept of effectiveness of the operation of controls recognizes that some errors in the way controls are applied by the entity may occur. However, when such errors are identified, the auditor makes specific inquiries to understand these matters and also needs to consider matters such as:

(a) The direct effect of identified errors on the financial statements; and
(b) The effectiveness of internal control and their effect on the audit approach when, for example, the errors result from management override of a control.

In these cases, the auditor determines whether the tests of controls performed provide an appropriate basis for use as audit evidence, whether additional tests of controls are necessary, or whether the potential risks of misstatement need to be addressed using substantive procedures.

49 In analyzing the errors discovered, the auditor may observe that many have a common feature, for example, type of transaction, location, product line or period of time. In such circumstances, the auditor may decide to identify all items in the population that possess the common feature, and extend audit procedures in that stratum. In addition, such errors may be intentional, and may indicate the possibility of fraud.

50 Sometimes, the auditor may be able to establish that an error arises from an isolated event that has not recurred other than on specifically identifiable occasions and is therefore not representative of similar errors in the population (an anomalous error). To be considered an anomalous error, the auditor has to have a high degree of certainty that such error is not representative of the population. The auditor obtains this certainty by performing additional audit procedures. The additional audit procedures depend on the situation, but are adequate to provide the auditor with sufficient appropriate audit evidence that the error does not affect the remaining part of the population. One example is an error caused by a computer breakdown that is known to have occurred on only one day during the period. In that case, the auditor assesses the effect of the breakdown, for example by examining specific transactions processed on that day, and considers the effect of the cause of the breakdown on

audit procedures and conclusions. Another example is an error that is found to be caused by use of an incorrect formula in calculating all inventory values at one particular branch. To establish that this is an anomalous error, the auditor needs to ensure the correct formula has been used at other branches.

Projecting Errors

For tests of details, the auditor should project monetary errors found in the sample to the population, and should consider the effect of the projected error on the particular audit objective and on other areas of the audit. The auditor projects the total error for the population to obtain a broad view of the scale of errors, and to compare this to the tolerable error. For tests of details, tolerable error is the tolerable misstatement, and will be an amount less than or equal to the auditor's materiality used for the individual class of transactions or account balances being audited. 51

When an error has been established as an anomalous error, it may be excluded when projecting sample errors to the population. The effect of any such error, if uncorrected, still needs to be considered in addition to the projection of the non-anomalous errors. If a class of transactions or account balance has been divided into strata, the error is projected for each stratum separately. Projected errors plus anomalous errors for each stratum are then combined when considering the possible effect of errors on the total class of transactions or account balance. 52

For tests of controls, no explicit projection of errors is necessary since the sample error rate is also the projected rate of error for the population as a whole. 53

Evaluating the Sample Results

The auditor should evaluate the sample results to determine whether the assessment of the relevant characteristic of the population is confirmed or needs to be revised. In the case of tests of controls, an unexpectedly high sample error rate may lead to an increase in the assessed risk of material misstatement, unless further audit evidence substantiating the initial assessment is obtained. In the case of tests of details, an unexpectedly high error amount in a sample may cause the auditor to believe that a class of transactions or account balance is materially misstated, in the absence of further audit evidence that no material misstatement exists. 54

If the total amount of projected error plus anomalous error is less than but close to that which the auditor deems tolerable, the auditor considers the persuasiveness of the sample results in the light of other audit procedures, and may consider it appropriate to obtain additional audit evidence. The total of projected error plus anomalous error is the auditor's best estimate of error in the population. However, sampling results are affected by sampling risk. Thus when the best estimate of error is close to the tolerable error, the auditor recognizes the risk that a different sample would result in a different best estimate that could exceed the tolerable error. Considering the results of other audit procedures helps the auditor to assess this risk, while the risk is reduced if additional audit evidence is obtained. 55

If the evaluation of sample results indicates that the assessment of the relevant characteristic of the population needs to be revised, the auditor may: 56

(a) Request management to investigate identified errors and the potential for further errors, and to make any necessary adjustments; and/or

(b) Modify the nature, timing and extent of further audit procedures. For example, in the case of tests of controls, the auditor might extend the sample size, test an alternative control or modify related substantive procedures; and/or

(c) Consider the effect on the audit report.

Effective Date

57 This ISA (UK and Ireland) is effective for audits of financial statements for periods commencing on or after 15 December 2004.

Appendix 1 – Examples of Factors Influencing Sample Size for Tests of Controls

The following are factors that the auditor considers when determining the sample size for tests of controls. These factors, which need to be considered together, assume the auditor does not modify the nature or timing of tests of controls or otherwise modify the approach to substantive procedures in response to assessed risks.

FACTOR	EFFECT ON SAMPLE SIZE
An increase in the extent to which the risk of material misstatement is reduced by the operating effectiveness of controls	Increase
An increase in the rate of deviation from the prescribed control activity that the auditor is willing to accept	Decrease
An increase in the rate of deviation from the prescribed control activity that the auditor expects to find in the population	Increase
An increase in the auditor's required confidence level (or conversely, a decrease in the risk that the auditor will conclude that the risk of material misstatement is lower than the actual risk of material misstatement in the population)	Increase
An increase in the number of sampling units in the population	Negligible effect

1 *The extent to which the risk of material misstatement is reduced by the operating effectiveness of controls.* The more assurance the auditor intends to obtain from the operating effectiveness of controls, the lower the auditor's assessment of the risk of material misstatement will be, and the larger the sample size will need to be. When the auditor's assessment of the risk of material misstatement at the assertion level includes an expectation of the operating effectiveness of controls, the auditor is required to perform tests of controls. Other things being equal, the more the auditor relies on the operating effectiveness of controls in the risk assessment, the greater is the extent of the auditor's tests of controls (and therefore, the sample size is increased).

2 *The rate of deviation from the prescribed control activity the auditor is willing to accept (tolerable error).* The lower the rate of deviation that the auditor is willing to accept, the larger the sample size needs to be.

The rate of deviation from the prescribed control activity the auditor expects to find in the population (expected error). The higher the rate of deviation that the auditor expects, the larger the sample size needs to be so as to be in a position to make a reasonable estimate of the actual rate of deviation. Factors relevant to the auditor's consideration of the expected error rate include the auditor's understanding of the business (in particular, risk assessment procedures undertaken to obtain an understanding of internal control), changes in personnel or in internal control, the results of audit procedures applied in prior periods and the results of other audit procedures. High expected error rates ordinarily warrant little, if any, reduction of the assessed risk of material misstatement, and therefore in such circumstances tests of controls would ordinarily be omitted.

The auditor's required confidence level. The greater the degree of confidence that the auditor requires that the results of the sample are in fact indicative of the actual incidence of error in the population, the larger the sample size needs to be.

The number of sampling units in the population. For large populations, the actual size of the population has little, if any, effect on sample size. For small populations however, audit sampling is often not as efficient as alternative means of obtaining sufficient appropriate audit evidence.

Appendix 2 – Examples of Factors Influencing Sample Size for Tests of Details

The following are factors that the auditor considers when determining the sample size for tests of details. These factors, which need to be considered together, assume the auditor does not modify the approach to tests of controls or otherwise modify the nature or timing of substantive procedures in response to the assessed risks.

FACTOR	EFFECT ON SAMPLE SIZE
An increase in the auditor's assessment of the risk of material misstatement	Increase
An increase in the use of other substantive procedures directed at the same assertion	Decrease
An increase in the auditor's required confidence level (or conversely, a decrease in the risk that the auditor will conclude that a material error does not exist, when in fact it does exist)	Increase
An increase in the total error that the auditor is willing to accept (tolerable error)	Decrease
An increase in the amount of error the auditor expects to find in the population	Increase
Stratification of the population when appropriate	Decrease
The number of sampling units in the population	Negligible Effect

[Deleted by IAASB]

The auditor's assessment of the risk of material misstatement. The higher the auditor's assessment of the risk of material misstatement, the larger the sample size needs to be. The auditor's assessment of the risk of material misstatement is affected by inherent risk and control risk. For example, if the auditor does not perform tests of controls, the auditor's risk assessment cannot be reduced for the effective operation of internal controls with respect to the particular assertion. Therefore, in order to reduce audit risk to an acceptably low level, the auditor needs a low detection risk and will rely more on substantive procedures. The more audit evidence that is obtained from tests of details (that is, the lower the detection risk), the larger the sample size will need to be.

3   *The use of other substantive procedures directed at the same assertion.* The more the auditor is relying on other substantive procedures (tests of details or substantive analytical procedures) to reduce to an acceptable level the detection risk regarding a particular class of transactions or account balance, the less assurance the auditor will require from sampling and, therefore, the smaller the sample size can be.

4   *The auditor's required confidence level.* The greater the degree of confidence that the auditor requires that the results of the sample are in fact indicative of the actual amount of error in the population, the larger the sample size needs to be.

5   *The total error the auditor is willing to accept (tolerable error).* The lower the total error that the auditor is willing to accept, the larger the sample size needs to be.

6   *The amount of error the auditor expects to find in the population (expected error).* The greater the amount of error the auditor expects to find in the population, the larger the sample size needs to be in order to make a reasonable estimate of the actual amount of error in the population. Factors relevant to the auditor's consideration of the expected error amount include the extent to which item values are determined subjectively, the results of risk assessment procedures, the results of tests of control, the results of audit procedures applied in prior periods, and the results of other substantive procedures.

7   *Stratification.* When there is a wide range (variability) in the monetary size of items in the population. It may be useful to group items of similar size into separate sub-populations or strata. This is referred to as stratification. When a population can be appropriately stratified, the aggregate of the sample sizes from the strata generally will be less than the sample size that would have been required to attain a given level of sampling risk, had one sample been drawn from the whole population.

8   *The number of sampling units in the population.* For large populations, the actual size of the population has little, if any, effect on sample size. Thus, for small populations, audit sampling is often not as efficient as alternative means of obtaining sufficient appropriate audit evidence. (However, when using monetary unit sampling, an increase in the monetary value of the population increases sample size, unless this is offset by a proportional increase in materiality.)

Appendix 3 – Sample Selection Methods

The principal methods of selecting samples are as follows:

(a) Use of a computerized random number generator (through CAATs) or random number tables.

(b) Systematic selection, in which the number of sampling units in the population is divided by the sample size to give a sampling interval, for example 50, and having determined a starting point within the first 50, each 50th sampling unit thereafter is selected. Although the starting point may be determined haphazardly, the sample is more likely to be truly random if it is determined by use of a computerized random number generator or random number tables. When using systematic selection, the auditor would need to determine that sampling units within the population are not structured in such a way that the sampling interval corresponds with a particular pattern in the population.

(c) Haphazard selection, in which the auditor selects the sample without following a structured technique. Although no structured technique is used, the auditor would nonetheless avoid any conscious bias or predictability (for example, avoiding difficult to locate items, or always choosing or avoiding the first or last entries on a page) and thus attempt to ensure that all items in the population have a chance of selection. Haphazard selection is not appropriate when using statistical sampling.

(d) Block selection involves selecting a block(s) of contiguous items from within the population. Block selection cannot ordinarily be used in audit sampling because most populations are structured such that items in a sequence can be expected to have similar characteristics to each other, but different characteristics from items elsewhere in the population. Although in some circumstances it may be an appropriate audit procedure to examine a block of items, it would rarely be an appropriate sample selection technique when the auditor intends to draw valid inferences about the entire population based on the sample.

[540]*
Audit of accounting estimates

(Issued December 2004)

Contents

	Paragraphs
Introduction	1 - 4-1
The Nature of Accounting Estimates	5 - 7
Audit Procedures Responsive to the Risk of Material Misstatement of the Entity's Accounting Estimates	8 - 10
Reviewing and Testing the Process Used by Management	11 - 21
Use of an Independent Estimate	22
Review of Subsequent Events	23
Evaluation of Results of Audit Procedures	24 - 27
Effective Date	**27-1**

International Standard on Auditing (UK and Ireland) (ISA (UK and Ireland)) 540 "Audit of Accounting Estimates" should be read in the context of the Auditing Practices Board's Statement "The Auditing Practices Board – Scope and Authority of Pronouncements (Revised)" which sets out the application and authority of ISAs (UK and Ireland).

Editor's note: The text of an Exposure Draft which is proposed to replace this Standard is printed on page 2100.

Introduction

The purpose of this International Standard on Auditing (UK and Ireland) (ISA (UK and Ireland)) is to establish standards and provide guidance on the audit of accounting estimates contained in financial statements. This ISA (UK and Ireland) is not intended to be applicable to the examination of prospective financial information, though many of the audit procedures outlined herein may be suitable for that purpose. **1**

This ISA (UK and Ireland) uses the terms 'those charged with governance' and 'management'. The term 'governance' describes the role of persons entrusted with the supervision, control and direction of an entity. Ordinarily, those charged with governance are accountable for ensuring that the entity achieves its objectives, and for the quality of its financial reporting and reporting to interested parties. Those charged with governance include management only when they perform such functions. **1-1**

In the UK and Ireland, those charged with governance include the directors (executive and non-executive) of a company or other body, the members of an audit committee where one exists, the partners, proprietors, committee of management or trustees of other forms of entity, or equivalent persons responsible for directing the entity's affairs and preparing its financial statements. **1-2**

'Management' comprises those persons who perform senior managerial functions. **1-3**

In the UK and Ireland, depending on the nature and circumstances of the entity, management may include some or all of those charged with governance (e.g. executive directors). Management will not normally include non-executive directors. **1-4**

The auditor should obtain sufficient appropriate audit evidence regarding accounting estimates. **2**

"Accounting estimate" means an approximation of the amount of an item in the absence of a precise means of measurement. Examples are: **3**

- Allowances to reduce inventory and accounts receivable to their estimated realizable value.
- Provisions to allocate the cost of fixed assets over their estimated useful lives.
- Accrued revenue.
- Deferred tax.
- Provision for a loss from a lawsuit.
- Losses on construction contracts in progress.
- Provision to meet warranty claims.

Management[1] is responsible for making accounting estimates included in financial statements. These estimates are often made in conditions of uncertainty regarding the outcome of events that have occurred or are likely to occur and involve the use of judgment. As a result, the risk of material misstatement is greater when accounting estimates are involved and in some cases the auditor may determine that the risk of material misstatement related to an accounting estimate is a significant risk that **4**

---

[1] *In the UK and Ireland those charged with governance are responsible for the preparation of the financial statements.*

requires special audit consideration. See paragraphs 108-114 of ISA (UK and Ireland) 315, "Understanding the Entity and Its Environment and Assessing the Risks of Material Misstatement."

4-1 In addition, audit evidence obtained is generally less conclusive when accounting estimates are involved. Consequently, in assessing the sufficiency and appropriateness of audit evidence on which to base the audit opinion, the auditor is more likely to need to exercise judgment when considering accounting estimates than in other areas of the audit.

The Nature of Accounting Estimates

5 The determination of an accounting estimate may be simple or complex depending upon the nature of the item. For example, accruing a charge for rent may be a simple calculation, whereas estimating a provision for slow-moving or surplus inventory may involve considerable analyses of current data and a forecast of future sales. In complex estimates, there may be a high degree of special knowledge and judgment required.

6 Accounting estimates may be determined as part of the routine information system relevant to financial reporting operating on a continuing basis, or may be non-routine, operating only at period end. In many cases, accounting estimates are made by using a formula based on experience, such as the use of standard rates for depreciating each category of fixed assets or a standard percentage of sales revenue for computing a warranty provision. In such cases, the formula needs to be reviewed regularly by management, for example, by reassessing the remaining useful lives of assets or by comparing actual results with the estimate and adjusting the formula when necessary.

7 The uncertainty associated with an item, or the lack of objective data may make it incapable of reasonable estimation, in which case, the auditor needs to consider whether the auditor's report needs modification to comply with ISA (UK and Ireland) 700 "The Auditor's Report on Financial Statements."

Audit Procedures Responsive to the Risk of Material Misstatement of the Entity's Accounting Estimates

8 **The auditor should design and perform further audit procedures to obtain sufficient appropriate audit evidence as to whether the entity's accounting estimates are reasonable in the circumstances and, when required, appropriately disclosed.** The audit evidence available to detect a material misstatement in an accounting estimate will often be more difficult to obtain and less persuasive than audit evidence available to detect a material misstatement in other items in the financial statements. The auditor's understanding of the entity and its environment, including its internal control, assists the auditor in identifying and assessing the risks of material misstatement of the entity's accounting estimates.

9 An understanding of the procedures and methods, including relevant control activities, used by management in making the accounting estimates is important for the auditor to identify and assess risks of material misstatement in order to design the nature, timing and extent of the further audit procedures.

The auditor should adopt one or a combination of the following approaches in the audit of an accounting estimate:

(a) Review and test the process used by management to develop the estimate;
(b) Use an independent estimate for comparison with that prepared by management; or
(c) Review of subsequent events which provide audit evidence of the reasonableness of the estimate made.

Reviewing and Testing the Process Used by Management

The steps ordinarily involved in reviewing and testing of the process used by management are:

(a) Evaluation of the data and consideration of assumptions on which the estimate is based;
(b) Testing of the calculations involved in the estimate;
(c) Comparison, when possible, of estimates made for prior periods with actual results of those periods; and
(d) Consideration of management's approval procedures.

Evaluation of Data and Consideration of Assumptions

The auditor would evaluate whether the data on which the estimate is based is accurate, complete and relevant. When information produced by the entity is used, it will need to be consistent with the data processed through the information system relevant to financial reporting. For example, in substantiating a warranty provision, the auditor would obtain audit evidence that the data relating to products still within the warranty period at period end agree with the sales information within the information system relevant to financial reporting. ISA (UK and Ireland) 500, "Audit Evidence" paragraph 11 provides additional guidance on the requirement to obtain audit evidence about the accuracy and completeness of information produced by the entity when it is used in performing audit procedures.

The auditor may also seek audit evidence from sources outside the entity. For example, when examining a provision for inventory obsolescence calculated by reference to anticipated future sales, the auditor may, in addition to examining internal data such as past levels of sales, orders on hand and marketing trends, seek audit evidence from industry-produced sales projections and market analyses. Similarly, when examining management's estimates of the financial implications of litigation and claims, the auditor would seek direct communication with the entity's lawyers.

The auditor would evaluate whether the data collected is appropriately analyzed and projected to form a reasonable basis for determining the accounting estimate. Examples are the analysis of the age of accounts receivable and the projection of the number of months of supply on hand of an item of inventory based on past and forecast usage.

The auditor would evaluate whether the entity has an appropriate base for the principal assumptions used in the accounting estimate. In some cases, the assumptions will be based on industry or government statistics, such as future inflation rates, interest rates, employment rates and anticipated market growth. In other cases, the assumptions will be specific to the entity and will be based on internally generated data.

16 In evaluating the assumptions on which the estimate is based, the auditor would consider, among other things, whether they are:

- Reasonable in light of actual results in prior periods.
- Consistent with those used for other accounting estimates.
- Consistent with management's plans which appear appropriate.

The auditor would need to pay particular attention to assumptions which are sensitive to variation, subjective or susceptible to material misstatement.

17 In the case of complex estimating processes involving specialized techniques, it may be necessary for the auditor to use the work of an expert, for example, engineers for estimating quantities in stock piles of mineral ores. Guidance on how to use the work of an expert is provided in ISA (UK and Ireland) 620 "Using the Work of an Expert."

18 The auditor would review the continuing appropriateness of formulae used by management in the preparation of accounting estimates. Such a review would reflect the auditor's knowledge of the financial results of the entity in prior periods, practices used by other entities in the industry and the future plans of management as disclosed to the auditor.

Testing of Calculations

19 The auditor would perform audit procedures on the calculation procedures used by management. The nature, timing and extent of the auditor's procedures will depend on the assessed risk of material misstatement, which is impacted by such factors as the complexity involved in calculating the accounting estimate, the auditor's understanding and evaluation of the procedures and methods, including relevant control activities used by the entity in producing the estimate and the materiality of the estimate in the context of the financial statements.

Comparison of Previous Estimates with Actual Results

20 When possible, the auditor would compare accounting estimates made for prior periods with actual results of those periods to assist in:

(a) Obtaining audit evidence about the general reliability of the entity's estimating procedures and methods, including relevant control activities;
(b) Considering whether adjustments to estimating formulae may be required; and
(c) Evaluating whether differences between actual results and previous estimates have been quantified and that, where necessary, appropriate adjustments or disclosures have been made.

Consideration of Management's Approval Procedures

21 Material accounting estimates are ordinarily reviewed and approved by management. The auditor would consider whether such review and approval is performed by the appropriate level of management and that it is evidenced in the documentation supporting the determination of the accounting estimate.

Use of an Independent Estimate

22 The auditor may make or obtain an independent estimate and compare it with the accounting estimate prepared by management. When using an independent estimate the auditor would ordinarily evaluate the data, consider the assumptions and perform audit procedures on the calculation procedures used in its development. It may also be appropriate to compare accounting estimates made for prior periods with actual results of those periods.

Review of Subsequent Events

23 Transactions and events which occur after period end, but prior to completion of the audit, may provide audit evidence regarding an accounting estimate made by management. The auditor's review of such transactions and events may reduce, or even remove, the need for the auditor to review and perform audit procedures on the process used by management to develop the accounting estimate or to use an independent estimate in assessing the reasonableness of the accounting estimate.

Evaluation of Results of Audit Procedures

24 **The auditor should make a final assessment of the reasonableness of the entity's accounting estimates based on the auditor's understanding of the entity and its environment and whether the estimates are consistent with other audit evidence obtained during the audit.**

25 The auditor would consider whether there are any significant subsequent transactions or events which affect the data and the assumptions used in determining the accounting estimates.

26 Because of the uncertainties inherent in accounting estimates, evaluating differences can be more difficult than in other areas of the audit. When there is a difference between the auditor's estimate of the amount best supported by the available audit evidence and the estimated amount included in the financial statements, the auditor would determine whether such a difference requires adjustment. If the difference is reasonable, for example, because the amount in the financial statements falls within a range of acceptable results, it may not require adjustment. However, if the auditor believes the difference is unreasonable, management would be requested to revise the estimate. If management refuses to revise the estimate, the difference would be considered a misstatement and would be considered with all other misstatements in assessing whether the effect on the financial statements is material.

27 The auditor would also consider whether individual differences which have been accepted as reasonable are biased in one direction, so that, on a cumulative basis, they may have a material effect on the financial statements. In such circumstances, the auditor would evaluate the accounting estimates taken as a whole.

Effective Date

27-1 This ISA (UK and Ireland) is effective for audits of financial statements for periods commencing on or after 15 December 2004.

[545]
Auditing fair value measurements and disclosures
(Issued December 2004)

Contents

	Paragraph
Introduction	1 - 9
Understanding the Entity's Process for Determining Fair Value Measurements and Disclosures and Relevant Control Activities, and Assessing Risk	10 - 16
Evaluating the Appropriateness of Fair Value Measurements and Disclosures	17 - 28
Using the Work of an Expert	29 - 32
Audit Procedures Responsive to the Risk of Material Misstatement of the Entity's Fair Value Measurements and Disclosures	33 - 55
Disclosures About Fair Values	56 - 60
Evaluating the Results of Audit Procedures	61 - 62
Management Representations	63 - 64
Communication with Those Charged with Governance	65
Effective Date	66

Appendix: Fair Value Measurements and Disclosures under Different Financial Reporting Frameworks

---

International Standard on Auditing (UK and Ireland) (ISA (UK and Ireland)) 545 "Auditing Fair Value Measurements and Disclosures" should be read in the context of the Auditing Practices Board's Statement "The Auditing Practices Board – Scope and Authority of Pronouncements (Revised)" which sets out the application and authority of ISAs (UK and Ireland).

Introduction

The purpose of this International Standard on Auditing (UK and Ireland) (ISA (UK and Ireland)) is to establish standards and provide guidance on auditing fair value measurements and disclosures contained in financial statements. In particular, this ISA (UK and Ireland) addresses audit considerations relating to the measurement, presentation and disclosure of material assets, liabilities and specific components of equity presented or disclosed at fair value in financial statements. Fair value measurements of assets, liabilities and components of equity may arise from both the initial recording of transactions and later changes in value. Changes in fair value measurements that occur over time may be treated in different ways under different financial reporting frameworks. For example, some financial reporting frameworks may require that such changes be reflected directly in equity, while others may require them to be reflected in income. 1

Many of the examples of accounting principles given in this ISA (UK and Ireland) are based on International Accounting Standards. If other accounting standards are used (e.g. Financial Reporting Standards issued by the UK Accounting Standards Board) the auditor recognizes that, whilst the accounting principles may differ, the audit principles remain the same. 1-1

Paragraph 22 of ISA (UK and Ireland) 315 "Understanding the Entity and its Environment and Assessing the Risks of Material Misstatement" requires that "the auditor should obtain an understanding of ... the applicable financial reporting framework." That understanding includes the requirements of the particular accounting standards that the entity is required or chooses, where a choice is possible, to comply with. The auditor takes that understanding into account when complying with the requirements of this ISA (UK and Ireland). The auditor also takes into account requirements of legislation pertaining to fair value accounting (e.g. Schedule 4 of the UK Companies Act 1985 as amended by "The Companies Act 1985 (International Accounting Standards and Other Accounting Amendments) Regulations 2004"). 1-2

This ISA (UK and Ireland) uses the terms 'those charged with governance' and 'management'. The term 'governance' describes the role of persons entrusted with the supervision, control and direction of an entity. Ordinarily, those charged with governance are accountable for ensuring that the entity achieves its objectives, and for the quality of its financial reporting and reporting to interested parties. Those charged with governance include management only when they perform such functions. 1-3

In the UK and Ireland, those charged with governance include the directors (executive and non-executive) of a company or other body, the members of an audit committee where one exists, the partners, proprietors, committee of management or trustees of other forms of entity, or equivalent persons responsible for directing the entity's affairs and preparing its financial statements. 1-4

'Management' comprises those persons who perform senior managerial functions. 1-5

In the UK and Ireland, depending on the nature and circumstances of the entity, management may include some or all of those charged with governance (e.g. executive directors). Management will not normally include non-executive directors. 1-6

2   While this ISA (UK and Ireland) provides guidance on auditing fair value measurements and disclosures, audit evidence obtained from other audit procedures also may provide audit evidence relevant to the measurement and disclosure of fair values. For example, inspection procedures to verify existence of an asset measured at fair value also may provide relevant audit evidence about its valuation (such as the physical condition of an investment property).

2a ISA (UK and Ireland) 500, "Audit Evidence" paragraph 16 requires the auditor to use assertions in sufficient detail to form a basis for the assessment of risks of material misstatements and the design and performance of further audit procedures in response to the assessed risks. Fair value measurements and disclosures are not in themselves assertions, but may be relevant to specific assertions, depending on the applicable financial reporting framework.

3   **The auditor should obtain sufficient appropriate audit evidence that fair value measurements and disclosures are in accordance with the entity's applicable financial reporting framework.** Paragraph 22 of ISA (UK and Ireland) 315, "Understanding the Entity and Its Environment and Assessing the Risks of Material Misstatement" requires the auditor to obtain an understanding of the entity's applicable financial reporting framework.

4   Management[1] is responsible for making the fair value measurements and disclosures included in the financial statements. As part of fulfilling its responsibility, management needs to establish an accounting and financial reporting process for determining the fair value measurements and disclosures, select appropriate valuation methods, identify and adequately support any significant assumptions used, prepare the valuation and ensure that the presentation and disclosure of the fair value measurements are in accordance with the entity's applicable financial reporting framework.

5   Many measurements based on estimates, including fair value measurements, are inherently imprecise. In the case of fair value measurements, particularly those that do not involve contractual cash flows or for which market information is not available when making the estimate, fair value estimates often involve uncertainty in both the amount and timing of future cash flows. Fair value measurements also may be based on assumptions about future conditions, transactions or events whose outcome is uncertain and will therefore be subject to change over time. The auditor's consideration of such assumptions is based on information available to the auditor at the time of the audit and the auditor is not responsible for predicting future conditions, transactions or events which, had they been known at the time of the audit, may have had a significant effect on management's actions or management's assumptions underlying the fair value measurements and disclosures. Assumptions used in fair value measurements are similar in nature to those required when developing other accounting estimates. ISA (UK and Ireland) 540, "Audit of Accounting Estimates" provides guidance on auditing accounting estimates. This ISA (UK and Ireland), however, addresses considerations similar to those in ISA (UK and Ireland) 540 as well as others in the specific context of fair value measurements and disclosures in accordance with an applicable financial reporting framework.

6   Different financial reporting frameworks require or permit a variety of fair value measurements and disclosures in financial statements. They also vary in the level of guidance that they provide on the basis for measuring assets and liabilities or the

---

[1] In the UK and Ireland, those charged with governance are responsible for the preparation of the financial statements.

related disclosures. Some financial reporting frameworks give prescriptive guidance, others give general guidance, and some give no guidance at all. In addition, certain industry-specific measurement and disclosure practices for fair values also exist. While this ISA (UK and Ireland) provides guidance on auditing fair value measurements and disclosures, it does not address specific types of assets or liabilities, transactions, or industry-specific practices. The Appendix to this ISA (UK and Ireland) discusses fair value measurements and disclosures under different financial reporting frameworks and the prevalence of fair value measurements, including the fact that different definitions of "fair value" may exist under such frameworks. For example, International Accounting Standard (IAS) 39, "Financial Instruments: Recognition and Measurement" defines fair value as "the amount for which an asset could be exchanged, or a liability settled, between knowledgeable, willing parties in an arm's length transaction."

In most financial reporting frameworks, underlying the concept of fair value measurements is a presumption that the entity is a going concern without any intention or need to liquidate, curtail materially the scale of its operations, or undertake a transaction on adverse terms. Therefore, in this case, fair value would not be the amount that an entity would receive or pay in a forced transaction, involuntary liquidation, or distress sale. An entity, however, may need to take its current economic or operating situation into account in determining the fair values of its assets and liabilities if prescribed or permitted to do so by its financial reporting framework and such framework may or may not specify how that is done. For example, management's plan to dispose of an asset on an accelerated basis to meet specific business objectives may be relevant to the determination of the fair value of that asset. 7

The measurement of fair value may be relatively simple for certain assets or liabilities, for example, assets that are bought and sold in active and open markets that provide readily available and reliable information on the prices at which actual exchanges occur. The measurement of fair value for other assets or liabilities may be more complex. A specific asset may not have an active market or may possess characteristics that make it necessary for management to estimate its fair value (for example, an investment property or a complex derivative financial instrument). The estimation of fair value may be achieved through the use of a valuation model (for example, a model premised on projections and discounting of future cash flows) or through the assistance of an expert, such as an independent valuer. 8

The uncertainty associated with an item, or the lack of objective data may make it incapable of reasonable estimation, in which case, the auditor considers whether the auditor's report needs modification to comply with ISA (UK and Ireland) 700, "The Auditor's Report on Financial Statements." 9

Understanding the Entity's Process for Determining Fair Value Measurements and Disclosures and Relevant Control Activities, and Assessing Risk

As part of the understanding of the entity and its environment, including its internal control, the auditor should obtain an understanding of the entity's process for determining fair value measurements and disclosures and of the relevant control activities sufficient to identify and assess the risks of material misstatement at the assertion level and to design and perform further audit procedures. 10

Management[1] is responsible for establishing an accounting and financial reporting process for determining fair value measurements. In some cases, the measurement of 11 fair value and therefore the process set up by management to determine fair value may be simple and reliable. For example, management may be able to refer to published price quotations to determine fair value for marketable securities held by the entity. Some fair value measurements, however, are inherently more complex than others and involve uncertainty about the occurrence of future events or their outcome, and therefore assumptions that may involve the use of judgment need to be made as part of the measurement process. The auditor's understanding of the measurement process, including its complexity, helps identify and assess the risks of material misstatement in order to determine the nature, timing and extent of the further audit procedures.

12   When obtaining an understanding of the entity's process for determining fair value measurements and disclosures, the auditor considers, for example:

- The relevant control activities over the process used to determine fair value measurements, including, for example, controls over data and the segregation of duties between those committing the entity to the underlying transactions and those responsible for undertaking the valuations.
- The expertise and experience of those persons determining the fair value measurements.
- The role that information technology has in the process.
- The types of accounts or transactions requiring fair value measurements or disclosures (for example, whether the accounts arise from the recording of routine and recurring transactions or whether they arise from non-routine or unusual transactions).
- The extent to which the entity's process relies on a service organization to provide fair value measurements or the data that supports the measurement. When an entity uses a service organization, the auditor complies with the requirements of ISA (UK and Ireland) 402, "Audit Considerations Relating to Entities Using Service Organizations."
- The extent to which the entity uses the work of experts in determining fair value measurements and disclosures (see paragraphs 29–32 of this Standard).
- The significant management assumptions used in determining fair value.
- The documentation supporting management's assumptions.
- The methods used to develop and apply management assumptions and to monitor changes in those assumptions.
- The integrity of change controls and security procedures for valuation models and relevant information systems, including approval processes.
- The controls over the consistency, timeliness and reliability of the data used in valuation models.

13   ISA (UK and Ireland) 315, "Understanding the Entity and its Environment and Assessing the Risks of Material Misstatement," requires the auditor to obtain an understanding of the components of internal control. In particular, the auditor obtains a sufficient understanding of control activities related to the determination of the entity's fair value measurements and disclosures in order to identify and assess the risks of material misstatement and to design the nature, timing and extent of the further audit procedures.

14   **After obtaining an understanding of the entity's process for determining fair value measurements and disclosures, the auditor should identify and assess the risks of material misstatement at the assertion level related to the fair value measurements and disclosures in the financial statements to determine the nature, timing and extent of the further audit procedures.**

The degree to which a fair value measurement is susceptible to misstatement is an inherent risk. Consequently, the nature, timing and extent of the further audit procedures will depend upon the susceptibility to misstatement of a fair value measurement and whether the process for determining fair value measurements is relatively simple or complex. 15

Where the auditor has determined that the risk of material misstatement related to a fair value measurement or disclosure is a significant risk that requires special audit considerations, the auditor follows the requirements of ISA (UK and Ireland) 315. 15a

ISA (UK and Ireland) 315 discusses the inherent limitations of internal controls. As fair value determinations often involve subjective judgments by management, this may affect the nature of control activities that are capable of being implemented. The susceptibility to misstatement of fair value measurements also may increase as the accounting and financial reporting requirements for fair value measurements become more complex. The auditor considers the inherent limitations of controls in such circumstances in assessing the risk of material misstatement. 16

Evaluating the Appropriateness of Fair Value Measurements and Disclosures

The auditor should evaluate whether the fair value measurements and disclosures in the financial statements are in accordance with the entity's applicable financial reporting framework. 17

The auditor's understanding of the requirements of the applicable financial reporting framework and knowledge of the business and industry, together with the results of other audit procedures, are used to assess whether the accounting for assets or liabilities requiring fair value measurements is appropriate, and whether the disclosures about the fair value measurements and significant uncertainties related thereto are appropriate under the entity's applicable financial reporting framework. 18

The evaluation of the appropriateness of the entity's fair value measurements under its applicable financial reporting framework and the evaluation of audit evidence depends, in part, on the auditor's knowledge of the nature of the business. This is particularly true where the asset or liability or the valuation method is highly complex. For example, derivative financial instruments may be highly complex, with a risk that differing interpretations of how to determine fair values will result in different conclusions. The measurement of the fair value of some items, for example "in-process research and development" or intangible assets acquired in a business combination, may involve special considerations that are affected by the nature of the entity and its operations if such considerations are appropriate under the entity's applicable financial reporting framework. Also, the auditor's knowledge of the business, together with the results of other audit procedures, may help identify assets for which management[1] needs to recognize an impairment by using a fair value measurement pursuant to the entity's applicable financial reporting framework. 19

Where the method for measuring fair value is specified by the applicable financial reporting framework, for example, the requirement that the fair value of a marketable security be measured using quoted market prices as opposed to using a valuation model, the auditor considers whether the measurement of fair value is consistent with that method. 20

21   Some financial reporting frameworks presume that fair value can be measured reliably for assets or liabilities as a prerequisite to either requiring or permitting fair value measurements or disclosures. In some cases, this presumption may be overcome when an asset or liability does not have a quoted market price in an active market and for which other methods of reasonably estimating fair value are clearly inappropriate or unworkable. When management[1] has determined that it has overcome the presumption that fair value can be reliably determined, the auditor obtains sufficient appropriate audit evidence to support such determination, and whether the item is properly accounted for under the applicable financial reporting framework.

22   **The auditor should obtain audit evidence about management's intent to carry out specific courses of action, and consider its ability to do so, where relevant to the fair value measurements and disclosures under the entity's applicable financial reporting framework.**

23   In some financial reporting frameworks, management's[1] intentions with respect to an asset or liability are criteria for determining measurement, presentation, and disclosure requirements, and how changes in fair values are reported within financial statements. In such financial reporting frameworks, management's intent is important in determining the appropriateness of the entity's use of fair value. Management often documents plans and intentions relevant to specific assets or liabilities and the applicable financial reporting framework may require it to do so. While the extent of audit evidence to be obtained about management's intent is a matter of professional judgment, the auditor's procedures ordinarily include inquiries of management, with appropriate corroboration of responses, for example, by:

- Considering management's past history of carrying out its stated intentions with respect to assets or liabilities.
- Reviewing written plans and other documentation, including, where applicable, budgets, minutes, *etc*.
- Considering management's stated reasons for choosing a particular course of action.
- Considering management's ability to carry out a particular course of action given the entity's economic circumstances, including the implications of its contractual commitments.

The auditor also considers management's ability to pursue a specific course of action if ability is relevant to the use, or exemption from the use, of fair value measurement under the entity's applicable financial reporting framework.

24   **Where alternative methods for measuring fair value are available under the entity's applicable financial reporting framework, or where the method of measurement is not prescribed, the auditor should evaluate whether the method of measurement is appropriate in the circumstances under the entity's applicable financial reporting framework.**

25   Evaluating whether the method of measurement of fair value is appropriate in the circumstances requires the use of professional judgment. When management selects one particular valuation method from alternative methods available under the entity's applicable financial reporting framework, the auditor obtains an understanding of management's rationale for its selection by discussing with management its reasons for selecting the valuation method. The auditor considers whether:

(a) Management has sufficiently evaluated and appropriately applied the criteria, if any, provided in the applicable financial reporting framework to support the selected method;

(b) The valuation method is appropriate in the circumstances given the nature of the asset or liability being valued and the entity's applicable financial reporting framework; and
(c) The valuation method is appropriate in relation to the business, industry and environment in which the entity operates.

Management may have determined that different valuation methods result in a range of significantly different fair value measurements. In such cases, the auditor evaluates how the entity has investigated the reasons for these differences in establishing its fair value measurements. 26

The auditor should evaluate whether the entity's method for its fair value measurements is applied consistently. 27

Once management has selected a specific valuation method, the auditor evaluates whether the entity has consistently applied that basis in its fair value measurement, and if so, whether the consistency is appropriate considering possible changes in the environment or circumstances affecting the entity, or changes in the requirements of the entity's applicable financial reporting framework. If management has changed the valuation method, the auditor considers whether management can adequately demonstrate that the valuation method to which it has changed provides a more appropriate basis of measurement, or whether the change is supported by a change in the requirements of the entity's applicable financial reporting framework or a change in circumstances. For example, the introduction of an active market for a particular class of asset or liability may indicate that the use of discounted cash flows to estimate the fair value of such asset or liability is no longer appropriate. 28

Using the Work of an Expert

The auditor should determine the need to use the work of an expert. The auditor may have the necessary skill and knowledge to plan and perform audit procedures related to fair values or may decide to use the work of an expert. In making such a determination, the auditor considers the matters discussed in paragraph 7 of ISA (UK and Ireland) 620. 29

If the use of such an expert is planned, the auditor obtains sufficient appropriate audit evidence that such work is adequate for the purposes of the audit, and complies with the requirements of ISA (UK and Ireland) 620. 30

When planning to use the work of an expert, the auditor considers whether the expert's understanding of the definition of fair value and the method that the expert will use to determine fair value are consistent with that of management and the requirements of the applicable financial reporting framework. For example, the method used by an expert for estimating the fair value of real estate or a complex derivative, or the actuarial methodologies developed for making fair value estimates of insurance obligations, reinsurance receivables and similar items, may not be consistent with the measurement principles of the applicable financial reporting framework. Accordingly, the auditor considers such matters, often by discussing, providing or reviewing instructions given to the expert or when reading the report of the expert. 31

In accordance with ISA (UK and Ireland) 620, the auditor assesses the appropriateness of the expert's work as audit evidence. While the reasonableness of assumptions and the appropriateness of the methods used and their application are 32 the responsibility of the expert, the auditor obtains an understanding of the significant assumptions and methods used, and considers whether they are appropriate, complete and reasonable, based on the auditor's knowledge of the business and the results of other audit procedures. The auditor often considers these matters by discussing them with the expert. Paragraphs 39-49 discuss the auditor's evaluation of significant assumptions used by management, including assumptions relied upon by management based on the work of an expert.

Audit Procedures Responsive to the Risk of Material Misstatement of the Entity's Fair Value Measurements and Disclosures

33   The auditor should design and perform further audit procedures in response to assessed risks of material misstatement of assertions relating to the entity's fair value measurements and disclosures. ISA (UK and Ireland) 330, "The Auditor's Procedures in Response to Assessed Risks" discusses the auditor's responsibility to design and perform further audit procedures whose nature, timing and extent are responsive to the assessed risk of material misstatement at the assertion level. Such further audit procedures include tests of control and substantive procedures, as appropriate. Paragraphs 34-55 below provide additional specific guidance on substantive procedures that may be relevant in the context of the entity's fair value measurements and disclosures.

34   Because of the wide range of possible fair value measurements, from relatively simple to complex, the auditor's procedures can vary significantly in nature, timing and extent. For example, substantive procedures relating to the fair value measurements may involve (a) testing management's significant assumptions, the valuation model, and the underlying data (see paragraphs 39–49), (b) developing independent fair value estimates to corroborate the appropriateness of the fair value measurement (see paragraph 52), or (c) considering the effect of subsequent events on the fair value measurement and disclosures (see paragraphs 53–55).

35   The existence of published price quotations in an active market ordinarily is the best audit evidence of fair value. Some fair value measurements, however, are inherently more complex than others. This complexity arises either because of the nature of the item being measured at fair value or because of the valuation method required by the applicable financial reporting framework or selected by management. For example, in the absence of quoted prices in an active market, some financial reporting frameworks permit an estimate of fair value based on an alternative basis such as a discounted cash flow analysis or a comparative transaction model. Complex fair value measurements normally are characterized by greater uncertainty regarding the reliability of the measurement process. This greater uncertainty may be a result of:

- Length of the forecast period.
- The number of significant and complex assumptions associated with the process.
- A higher degree of subjectivity associated with the assumptions and factors used in the process.
- A higher degree of uncertainty associated with the future occurrence or outcome of events underlying the assumptions used.
- Lack of objective data when highly subjective factors are used.

36   The auditor's understanding of the measurement process, including its complexity, helps guide the auditor's determination of the nature, timing and extent of audit procedures to be performed. The following are examples of considerations in the development of audit procedures:

- Using a price quotation to obtain audit evidence about valuation may require an understanding of the circumstances in which the quotation was developed. For example, where quoted securities are held for investment purposes, valuation at the listed market price may require adjustment under the entity's applicable financial reporting framework if the holding is significantly large in size or is subject to restrictions in marketability.
- When using audit evidence provided by a third party, the auditor considers its reliability. For example, when information is obtained through the use of external confirmations, the auditor considers the respondent's competence, independence, authority to respond, knowledge of the matter being confirmed, and objectivity in order to be satisfied with the reliability of the evidence. The extent of such audit procedures will vary according to the assessed risk of material misstatement associated with the fair value measurements. The auditor complies with ISA (UK and Ireland) 505, "External Confirmations" in this regard.
- Audit evidence supporting fair value measurements, for example, a valuation by an independent valuer, may be obtained at a date that does not coincide with the date at which the entity is required to measure and report that information in its financial statements. In such cases, the auditor obtains audit evidence that management has taken into account the effect of events, transactions and changes in circumstances occurring between the date of fair value measurement and the reporting date.
- Collateral often is assigned for certain types of investments in debt instruments that either are required to be measured at fair value or are evaluated for possible impairment. If the collateral is an important factor in measuring the fair value of the investment or evaluating its carrying amount, the auditor obtains sufficient appropriate audit evidence regarding the existence, value, rights and access to or transferability of such collateral, including consideration whether all appropriate liens have been filed, and considers whether appropriate disclosures about the collateral have been made under the entity's applicable financial reporting framework.
- In some situations, additional audit procedures, such as the inspection of an asset by the auditor, may be necessary to obtain sufficient appropriate audit evidence about the appropriateness of a fair value measurement. For example, inspection of an investment property may be necessary to obtain information about the current physical condition of the asset relevant to its fair value, or inspection of a security may reveal a restriction on its marketability that may affect its value.

Testing Management's Significant Assumptions, the Valuation Model, and the Underlying Data

The auditor's understanding of the reliability of the process used by management to determine fair value is an important element in support of the resulting amounts and therefore affects the nature, timing, and extent of further audit procedures. A reliable process for determining fair value is one that results in reasonably consistent measurement and, where relevant, presentation and disclosure of fair value when used in similar circumstances. When obtaining audit evidence about the entity's fair value measurements and disclosures, the auditor evaluates whether:

(a) The assumptions used by management are reasonable;
(b) The fair value measurement was determined using an appropriate model, if applicable;
(c) Management used relevant information that was reasonably available at the time.

38   Estimation techniques and assumptions and the auditor's consideration and comparison of fair value measurements determined in prior periods, if any, to results obtained in the current period may provide audit evidence of the reliability of management's processes. However, the auditor also considers whether such variances result from changes in economic circumstances.

39   **Where the auditor determines there is a significant risk related to fair value, or where otherwise applicable, the auditor should evaluate whether the significant assumptions used by management[1] in measuring fair values, taken individually and as a whole, provide a reasonable basis for the fair value measurements and disclosures in the entity's financial statements.**

40   It is necessary for management to make assumptions, including assumptions relied upon by management based upon the work of an expert, to develop fair value measurements. For these purposes, management's assumptions also include those assumptions developed under the guidance of those charged with governance. Assumptions are integral components of more complex valuation methods, for example valuation methods that employ a combination of estimates of expected future cash flows together with estimates of the values of assets or liabilities in the future, discounted to the present. Auditors pay particular attention to the significant assumptions underlying a valuation method and evaluate whether such assumptions are reasonable. To provide a reasonable basis for the fair value measurements and disclosures, assumptions need to be relevant, reliable, neutral, understandable and complete. Paragraph 36 of the "International Framework for Assurance Engagements" describes these characteristics in more detail.

41   Specific assumptions will vary with the characteristics of the asset or liability being valued and the valuation method used (*e.g.*, replacement cost, market or an income-based approach). For example, where discounted cash flows (an income-based approach) are used as the valuation method, there will be assumptions about the level of cash flows, the period of time used in the analysis, and the discount rate.

42   Assumptions ordinarily are supported by differing types of audit evidence from internal and external sources that provide objective support for the assumptions used. The auditor assesses the source and reliability of audit evidence supporting management's assumptions, including consideration of the assumptions in light of historical information and an evaluation of whether they are based on plans that are within the entity's capacity.

43   Audit procedures dealing with management's assumptions are performed in the context of the audit of the entity's financial statements. The objective of the audit procedures is therefore not intended to obtain sufficient appropriate audit evidence to provide an opinion on the assumptions themselves. Rather, the auditor performs audit procedures to consider whether the assumptions provide a reasonable basis in measuring fair values in the context of an audit of the financial statements taken as a whole.

44   Identifying those assumptions that appear to be significant to the fair value measurement requires the exercise of judgment by management. The auditor focuses attention on significant assumptions. Generally, significant assumptions cover matters that materially affect the fair value measurement and may include those that are:

   (a)   Sensitive to variation or uncertainty in amount or nature. For example, assumptions about short-term interest rates may be less susceptible to significant variation compared to assumptions about long-term interest rates;
   (b)   Susceptible to misapplication or bias.

The auditor considers the sensitivity of the valuation to changes in significant 45
assumptions, including market conditions that may affect the value. Where applicable, the auditor encourages management to use such techniques as sensitivity analysis to help identify particularly sensitive assumptions. In the absence of such management analysis, the auditor considers whether to employ such techniques. The auditor also considers whether the uncertainty associated with a fair value measurement, or the lack of objective data may make it incapable of reasonable estimation under the entity's applicable financial reporting framework (see paragraph 9).

The consideration of whether the assumptions provide a reasonable basis for the fair 46
value measurements relates to the whole set of assumptions as well as to each assumption individually. Assumptions are frequently interdependent, and therefore, need to be internally consistent. A particular assumption that may appear reasonable when taken in isolation may not be reasonable when used in conjunction with other assumptions. The auditor considers whether management has identified the significant assumptions and factors influencing the measurement of fair value.

The assumptions on which the fair value measurements are based (for example, the 47
discount rate used in calculating the present value of future cash flows) ordinarily will reflect what management expects will be the outcome of specific objectives and strategies. To be reasonable, such assumptions, individually and taken as a whole, also need to be realistic and consistent with:

(a) The general economic environment and the entity's economic circumstances;
(b) The plans of the entity;
(c) Assumptions made in prior periods, if appropriate
(d) Past experience of, or previous conditions experienced by, the entity to the extent currently applicable;
(e) Other matters relating to the financial statements, for example, assumptions used by management in accounting estimates for financial statement accounts other than those relating to fair value measurements and disclosures; and
(f) If applicable, the risk associated with cash flows, including the potential variability of the cash flows and the related effect on the discounted rate.

Where assumptions are reflective of management's intent and ability to carry out specific courses of action, the auditor considers whether they are consistent with the entity's plans and past experience (see paragraphs 22 and 23).

If management relies on historical financial information in the development of 48
assumptions, the auditor considers the extent to which such reliance is justified. However, historical information might not be representative of future conditions or events, for example, if management intends to engage in new activities or circumstances change.

For items valued by the entity using a valuation model, the auditor is not expected to 49
substitute his or her judgment for that of the entity's management. Rather, the auditor reviews the model, and evaluates whether the model is appropriate and the assumptions used are reasonable. For example, it may be inappropriate to use a discounted cash flow method in valuing an equity investment in a start-up enterprise if there are no current revenues on which to base the forecast of future earnings or cash flows.

The auditor should perform audit procedures on the data used to develop the fair value 50
measurements and disclosures and evaluate whether the fair value measurements have been properly determined from such data and management's assumptions.

51 The auditor evaluates whether the data on which the fair value measurements are based, including the data used in the work of an expert, are accurate, complete and relevant; and whether the fair value measurements have been properly determined using such data and management's assumptions. The auditor's procedures also may include, for example, audit procedures such as verifying the source of the data, mathematical recalculation and reviewing of information for internal consistency, including whether such information is consistent with management's intent to carry out specific courses of action discussed in paragraphs 22 and 23.

Developing Independent Fair Value Estimates for Corroborative Purposes

52 The auditor may make an independent estimate of fair value (for example, by using an auditor-developed model) to corroborate the entity's fair value measurement. When developing an independent estimate using management's assumptions, the auditor evaluates those assumptions as discussed in paragraphs 39-49. Instead of using management's assumptions the auditor may develop separate assumptions to make a comparison with management's fair value measurements. In that situation, the auditor nevertheless understands management's assumptions. The auditor uses that understanding to determine that the auditor's model considers the significant variables and to evaluate any significant difference from management's estimate. The auditor also performs audit procedures on the data used to develop the fair value measurements and disclosures as discussed in paragraphs 50 and 51. The auditor considers the guidance contained in ISA (UK and Ireland) 520, "Analytical Procedures" when performing these procedures during an audit.

Subsequent Events

53 **The auditor should consider the effect of subsequent events on the fair value measurements and disclosures in the financial statements.**

54 Transactions and events that occur after period-end but prior to completion of the audit, may provide appropriate audit evidence regarding the fair value measurements made by management. For example, a sale of investment property shortly after the period-end may provide audit evidence relating to the fair value measurement.

55 In the period after a financial statement period-end, however, circumstances may change from those existing at the period-end. Fair value information after the period-end may reflect events occurring after the period-end and not the circumstances existing at the balance sheet date. For example, the prices of actively traded marketable securities that change after the period-end ordinarily do not constitute appropriate audit evidence of the values of the securities that existed at the period-end. The auditor complies with ISA (UK and Ireland) 560, "Subsequent Events" when evaluating audit evidence relating to such events.

Disclosures About Fair Values

56 **The auditor should evaluate whether the disclosures about fair values made by the entity are in accordance with its financial reporting framework.**

57 Disclosure of fair value information is an important aspect of financial statements in many financial reporting frameworks. Often, fair value disclosure is required because of the relevance to users in the evaluation of an entity's performance and financial position. In addition to the fair value information required by the applicable

financial reporting framework, some entities disclose voluntary additional fair value information in the notes to the financial statements.

When auditing fair value measurements and related disclosures included in the notes to the financial statements, whether required by the applicable financial reporting framework or disclosed voluntarily, the auditor ordinarily performs essentially the same types of audit procedures as those employed in auditing a fair value measurement recognized in the financial statements. The auditor obtains sufficient appropriate audit evidence that the valuation principles are appropriate under the entity's applicable financial reporting framework, are being consistently applied, and the method of estimation and significant assumptions used are properly disclosed in accordance with the entity's applicable financial reporting framework. The auditor also considers whether voluntary information may be inappropriate in the context of the financial statements. For example, management[1] may disclose a current sales value for an asset without mentioning that significant restrictions under contractual arrangements preclude the sale in the immediate future. 58

The auditor evaluates whether the entity has made appropriate disclosures about fair value information as called for by its financial reporting framework. If an item contains a high degree of measurement uncertainty, the auditor assesses whether the disclosures are sufficient to inform users of such uncertainty. For example, the auditor might evaluate whether disclosures about a range of amounts, and the assumptions used in determining the range, within which the fair value is reasonably believed to lie is appropriate under the entity's applicable financial reporting framework, when management[1] considers a single amount presentation not appropriate. Where applicable, the auditor also considers whether the entity has complied with the accounting and disclosure requirements relating to changes in the valuation method used to determine fair value measurements. 59

When disclosure of fair value information under the applicable financial reporting framework is omitted because it is not practicable to determine fair value with sufficient reliability, the auditor evaluates the adequacy of disclosures required in these circumstances. If the entity has not appropriately disclosed fair value information required by the applicable financial reporting framework, the auditor evaluates whether the financial statements are materially misstated by the departure from the applicable financial reporting framework. 60

Evaluating the Results of Audit Procedures

In making a final assessment of whether the fair value measurements and disclosures in the financial statements are in accordance with the entity's applicable financial reporting framework, the auditor should evaluate the sufficiency and appropriateness of the audit evidence obtained as well as the consistency of that evidence with other audit evidence obtained and evaluated during the audit. 61

When assessing whether the fair value measurements and disclosures in the financial statements are in accordance with the entity's applicable financial reporting framework, the auditor evaluates the consistency of the information and audit evidence obtained during the audit of fair value measurements with other audit evidence obtained during the audit, in the context of the financial statements taken as a whole. For example, the auditor considers whether there is or should be a relationship or correlation between the interest rates used to discount estimated future cash flows in determining the fair value of an investment property and interest rates on borrowings currently being incurred by the entity to acquire investment property. 62

Management Representations

63 The auditor should obtain written representations from management regarding the reasonableness of significant assumptions, including whether they appropriately reflect management's intent and ability to carry out specific courses of action on behalf of the entity where relevant to the fair value measurements or disclosures.

64 ISA (UK and Ireland) 580, "Management Representations" discusses the use of management representations as audit evidence. Depending on the nature, materiality and complexity of fair values, management[3] representations about fair value measurements and disclosures contained in the financial statements also may include representations about:

- The appropriateness of the measurement methods, including related assumptions, used by management in determining fair values within the applicable financial reporting framework, and the consistency in application of the methods.
- The basis used by management to overcome the presumption relating to the use of fair value set forth under the entity's applicable financial reporting framework.
- The completeness and appropriateness of disclosures related to fair values under the entity's applicable financial reporting framework.
- Whether subsequent events require adjustment to the fair value measurements and disclosures included in the financial statements.

Communication with Those Charged with Governance

65 ISA (UK and Ireland) 260, "Communication of Audit Matters with Those Charged with Governance" requires auditors to communicate audit matters of governance interest with those charged with governance. Because of the uncertainties often involved with some fair value measurements, the potential effect on the financial statements of any significant risks may be of governance interest. For example, the auditor considers communicating the nature of significant assumptions used in fair value measurements, the degree of subjectivity involved in the development of the assumptions, and the relative materiality of the items being measured at fair value to the financial statements as a whole. The auditor considers the guidance contained in ISA (UK and Ireland) 260 when determining the nature and form of communication.

Effective Date

66 This ISA (UK and Ireland) is effective for audits of financial statements for periods commencing on or after 15 December 2004.

Public Sector Perspective

Additional guidance for auditors of public sector bodies in the UK and Ireland is given in:

- Practice Note 10 "Audit of Financial Statements of Public Sector Entities in the United Kingdom (Revised)"
- Practice Note 10(I) "The Audit of Central Government Financial Statements in Ireland"

Many governments are moving to accrual accounting and are adopting fair value as the basis of valuation for many classes of the assets and liabilities that they hold, or for disclosures of items in the financial statements. The broad principles of this ISA (UK and Ireland) are therefore applicable to the consideration of the audit of fair value measurements and disclosures included in the financial statements of public sector entities.

Paragraph 3 of the ISA (UK and Ireland) states that when fair value measurements and disclosures are material to the financial statements, the auditor should obtain sufficient appropriate audit evidence that such measurements and disclosures are in accordance with the entity's applicable financial reporting framework. The International Public Sector Accounting Standards accounting framework include a number of standards that require or allow the recognition or disclosure of fair values.

As noted in paragraph 8 of the ISA (UK and Ireland), determining the fair value of certain assets or liabilities may be complex where there is no active market. This can be a particular issue in the Public Sector, where entities have significant holdings of specialized assets. Furthermore many assets held by public sector entities do not generate cash flows. In these circumstances a fair value or similar current value may be estimated by reference to other valuation methods including, but not limited to, depreciated replacement cost and indexed price method.

Appendix – Fair Value Measurements and Disclosures under Different Financial Reporting Frameworks

Different financial reporting frameworks require or permit a variety of fair value measurements and disclosures in financial statements. They also vary in the level of guidance that they provide on the basis for measuring assets and liabilities or the related disclosures. Some financial reporting frameworks give prescriptive guidance, others give general guidance, and some give no guidance at all. In addition, certain industry-specific measurement and disclosure practices for fair values also exist.

Different definitions of fair value may exist among financial reporting frameworks, or for different assets, liabilities or disclosures within a particular framework. For example, International Accounting Standard (IAS) 39, "Financial Instruments: Recognition and Measurement" defines fair value as "the amount for which an asset could be exchanged, or a liability settled, between knowledgeable, willing parties in an arm's length transaction". The concept of fair value ordinarily assumes a current transaction, rather than settlement at some past or future date. Accordingly, the process of measuring fair value would be a search for the estimated price at which that transaction would occur. Additionally, different financial reporting frameworks may use such terms as "entity-specific value", "value in use", or similar terms, but may still fall within the concept of fair value in this ISA (UK and Ireland).

Different financial reporting frameworks may treat changes in fair value measurements that occur over time in different ways. For example, a particular financial reporting framework may require that changes in fair value measurements of certain assets or liabilities be reflected directly in equity, while such changes might be reflected in income under another framework. In some frameworks, the determination of whether to use fair value accounting or how it is applied is influenced by management's intent to carry out certain courses of action with respect to the specific asset or liability.

4   Different financial reporting frameworks may require certain specific fair value measurements and disclosures in financial statements and prescribe or permit them in varying degrees. The financial reporting frameworks may:

- Prescribe measurement, presentation and disclosure requirements for certain information included in the financial statements or for information disclosed in notes to financial statements or presented as supplementary information.
- Permit certain measurements using fair values at the option of an entity or only when certain criteria have been met.
- Prescribe a specific method for determining fair value, for example, through the use of an independent appraisal or specified ways of using discounted cash flows.
- Permit a choice of method for determining fair value from among several alternative methods (the criteria for selection may or may not be provided by the financial reporting framework).
- Provide no guidance on the fair value measurements or disclosures of fair value other than their use being evident through custom or practice, for example, an industry practice.

5   Some financial reporting frameworks presume that fair value can be measured reliably for assets or liabilities as a prerequisite to either requiring or permitting fair value measurements or disclosures. In some cases, this presumption may be overcome when an asset or liability does not have a quoted market price in an active market and for which other methods of reasonably estimating fair value are clearly inappropriate or unworkable.

6   Some financial reporting frameworks require certain specified adjustments or modifications to valuation information, or other considerations unique to a particular asset or liability. For example, accounting for investment properties may require adjustments to be made to an appraised market value, such as adjustments for estimated closing costs on sale; adjustments related to the property's condition and location, and other matters. Similarly, if the market for a particular asset is not an active market, published price quotations may have to be adjusted or modified to arrive at a more suitable measure of fair value. For example, quoted market prices may not be indicative of fair value if there is infrequent activity in the market, the market is not well established, or small volumes of units are traded relative to the aggregate number of trading units in existence. Accordingly, such market prices may have to be adjusted or modified. Alternative sources of market information may be needed to make such adjustments or modifications.

Prevalence of Fair Value Measurements

7   Measurements and disclosures based on fair value are becoming increasingly prevalent in financial reporting frameworks. Fair values may occur in, and affect the determination of, financial statements in a number of ways, including the measurement at fair value of:

- Specific assets or liabilities, such as marketable securities or liabilities to settle an obligation under a financial instrument, routinely or periodically "marked-to-market".
- Specific components of equity, for example when accounting for the recognition, measurement and presentation of certain financial instruments with equity features, such as a bond convertible by the holder into common shares of the issuer.

- Specific assets or liabilities acquired in a business combination. For example, the initial determination of goodwill arising on the purchase of an entity in a business combination usually is based on the fair value measurement of the identifiable assets and liabilities acquired and the fair value of the consideration given.
- Specific assets or liabilities adjusted to fair value on a one-time basis. Some financial reporting frameworks may require the use of a fair value measurement to quantify an adjustment to an asset or a group of assets as part of an asset impairment determination, for example, a test of impairment of goodwill acquired in a business combination based on the fair value of a defined operating entity or reporting unit, the value of which is then allocated among the entity's or unit's group of assets and liabilities in order to derive an implied goodwill for comparison to the recorded goodwill.
- Aggregations of assets and liabilities. In some circumstances, the measurement of a class or group of assets or liabilities calls for an aggregation of fair values of some of the individual assets or liabilities in such class or group. For example, under an entity's applicable financial reporting framework, the measurement of a diversified loan portfolio might be determined based on the fair value of some categories of loans comprising the portfolio.
- Transactions involving the exchange of assets between independent parties without monetary consideration. For example, a non-monetary exchange of plant facilities in different lines of business.
- Information disclosed in notes to financial statements or presented as supplementary information, but not recognized in the financial statements.

[550]
Related parties

(Issued December 2004)

Contents

For accounting periods commencing on or after 1 January 2005, the consolidated financial statements of listed companies must be prepared under EU adopted IFRS. Other companies will be able to continue to prepare their financial statements in accordance with UK and Irish accounting standards. Paragraphs 1 to 17 of this ISA (UK and Ireland) apply to the audit of financial statements prepared under IAS 24 and paragraphs 101 to 117 of this ISA (UK and Ireland) apply to the audit of financial statements prepared under FRS 8.

	IAS 24 paragraphs	FRS 8 paragraphs
Introduction	1 - 6-2	101 - 106-2
Existence and Disclosure of Related Parties	6-3 - 8	106-3 - 108
Transactions with Related Parties	9 - 12	109 - 112
Examining Identified Related Party Transactions	13 - 14-2	113 - 114-2
Disclosures Relating to Control of the Entity	14-3 - 14-6	114-3 - 114-5
Management Representations	15 - 15-2	115 - 115-2
Audit Conclusions and Reporting	16 - 16-2	116 - 116-2
Effective Date	16-3	116-3

International Standard on Auditing (UK and Ireland) (ISA (UK and Ireland)) 550 "Related Parties" should be read in the context of the Auditing Practices Board's Statement "The Auditing Practices Board – Scope and Authority of Pronouncements (Revised)" which sets out the application and authority of ISAs (UK and Ireland).

ISA (UK and Ireland) 550 to be used where IAS 24, "Related Party Disclosures" applies

Introduction

The purpose of this International Standard on Auditing (UK and Ireland) (ISA (UK and Ireland)) is to establish standards and provide guidance on the auditor's responsibilities and audit procedures regarding related parties and transactions with such parties regardless of whether International Accounting Standard (IAS) 24, "Related Party Disclosures," or similar requirement, is part of the applicable financial reporting framework. 1

In the UK and Ireland, for accounting periods commencing on or after 1 January 2005, the consolidated financial statements of listed companies must be prepared under EU adopted IFRS. From the same date other companies will be able, either to make an irrevocable election to prepare their financial statements under EU adopted IFRS, or to prepare their financial statements in accordance with UK and Irish accounting standards. Paragraphs 1 to 16-2 of this ISA (UK and Ireland) apply to financial statements prepared under EU adopted IFRS, including IAS 24. Paragraphs 101 to 116-2 of this ISA (UK and Ireland) apply to financial statements prepared under UK and Irish accounting standards, including FRS 8, "Related Party Disclosures". 1-1

This ISA (UK and Ireland) uses the terms 'those charged with governance' and 'management'. The term 'governance' describes the role of persons entrusted with the supervision, control and direction of an entity. Ordinarily, those charged with governance are accountable for ensuring that the entity achieves its objectives, and for the quality of its financial reporting and reporting to interested parties. Those charged with governance include management only when they perform such functions. 1-2

In the UK and Ireland, those charged with governance include the directors (executive and non-executive) of a company or other body, the members of an audit committee where one exists, the partners, proprietors, committee of management or trustees of other forms of entity, or equivalent persons responsible for directing the entity's affairs and preparing its financial statements. 1-3

'Management' comprises those persons who perform senior managerial functions. 1-4

In the UK and Ireland, depending on the nature and circumstances of the entity, management may include some or all of those charged with governance (e.g. executive directors). Management will not normally include non-executive directors. 1-5

The auditor should perform audit procedures designed to obtain sufficient appropriate audit evidence regarding the identification and disclosure by management[1] of related parties and the effect of related party transactions that are material to the financial statements. However, an audit cannot be expected to detect all related party transactions. 2

---

[1] *In the UK and Ireland those charged with governance are responsible for the preparation of the financial statements*

3   As indicated in ISA (UK and Ireland) 200 "Objective and General Principles Governing an Audit of Financial Statements," in certain circumstances there are limitations that may affect the persuasiveness of audit evidence available to draw conclusions on particular assertions. Because of the degree of uncertainty associated with the assertions regarding the completeness of related parties, the audit procedures identified in this ISA (UK and Ireland) will provide sufficient appropriate audit evidence regarding those assertions in the absence of any circumstance identified by the auditor that:

    (a) Increases the risk of material misstatement beyond that which would ordinarily be expected; or
    (b) Indicates that a material misstatement regarding related parties has occurred.

    Where there is any indication that such circumstances exist, the auditor should perform modified, extended or additional audit procedures as are appropriate in the circumstances.

4   Definitions regarding related parties are given in IAS 24 and are adopted for the purposes of this ISA (UK and Ireland)[2]

4-1 IAS 24 does not override the disclosure requirements of either companies legislation or listing rules. Similarly, the requirements of IAS 24 do not override exemptions from disclosures given by law to, and utilized by, certain types of entity. For the purposes of this ISA (UK and Ireland) companies legislation is defined as:

    (a) In Great Britain, the Companies Act 1985;
    (b) In Northern Ireland, The Companies (Northern Ireland) Order 1986; and
    (c) In the Republic of Ireland, the Companies Acts 1963 to 2003 and the European Communities (Companies: Group Accounts) Regulations 1992.

5   Management[1] is responsible for the identification and disclosure of related parties and transactions with such parties. This responsibility requires management to implement adequate internal control to ensure that transactions with related parties are appropriately identified in the information system and disclosed in the financial statements.

5-1 As transactions between related parties may not be on an arm's length basis and there may be an actual, or perceived, conflict of interest those charged with governance usually ensure that such transactions are subject to appropriate approval procedures. The approval of material related party transactions is often recorded in the minutes of meetings of those charged with governance.

5-2 In owner managed entities, as the risks associated with such transactions are the same, similar approval procedures would ideally apply. Often, however, procedures are less formalized because the owner manager is often personally aware of, and implicitly or explicitly approves, all such transactions.

5-3 The definition of a related party is complex and in part subjective and it may not always be self-evident to management whether a party is related. Furthermore, many information systems are not designed to either distinguish or summarize related party transactions and outstanding balances between an entity and its related parties. Management may, therefore, have to carry out additional analysis

[2] Definitions from IAS 24, "Related Party Disclosures," are set out in the Appendix.

of the accounting records to identify related party transactions. Accordingly related party transactions are often inherently difficult for the auditor to detect.

The auditor needs to have a sufficient understanding of the entity and its environment to enable identification of the events, transactions and practices that may result in a risk of material misstatement regarding related parties and transactions with such parties. While the existence of related parties and transactions between such parties are considered ordinary features of business, the auditor needs to be aware of them because:

(a) The applicable financial reporting framework may require disclosure in the financial statements of certain related party relationships and transactions, such as those required by IAS 24;
(b) The existence of related parties or related party transactions may affect the financial statements. For example, the entity's tax liability and expense may be affected by the tax laws in various jurisdictions which require special consideration when related parties exist;
(c) The source of audit evidence affects the auditor's assessment of its reliability. Generally a greater degree of reliance may be placed on audit evidence that is obtained from or created by unrelated third parties;
(d) A related party transaction may be motivated by other than ordinary business considerations, for example, profit sharing or even fraud; and
(e) The entity may be engaged in transfers of goods and services with related parties in accordance with specified transfer pricing policies or under reciprocal trading arrangements, such as barter transactions, which may give rise to accounting recognition and measurement issues. In particular an entity may have received or provided management services at no charge.

The risk that undisclosed related party transactions, or outstanding balances between an entity and its related parties, will not be detected by the auditor is especially high when:

(a) Related party transactions have taken place without charge;
(b) Related party transactions are not self-evident to the auditor;
(c) Transactions are with a party that the auditor could not reasonably be expected to know is a related party;
(d) Transactions undertaken with a related party in an earlier period have remained unsettled for a considerable period of time; or
(e) Active steps have been taken by those charged with governance or management to conceal either the full terms of a transaction or that a transaction is, in substance, with a related party.

Those charged with governance or management may wish to conceal the fact that a transaction, or an outstanding balance is with a related party because.

(a) Its disclosure may be sensitive to the parties involved and they may be reticent about disclosing it; and
(b) The transaction may be motivated by other than ordinary business considerations, for example to enhance the presentation of the financial statements (for example fraud or window dressing).

Related party transactions may be concealed in whole or in part from the auditor for fraudulent or other purposes. The likelihood of detecting fraudulent related party transactions depends upon the nature of the fraud and, in particular, the degree of collusion, the seniority of those involved and the level of deception concerned. ISA (UK and Ireland) 240 "The Auditor's responsibility to Consider Fraud in an Audit of Financial Statements" establishes the standards and provides the guidance on the auditor's responsibility to consider fraud in an audit of financial statements, including related party transactions.

Existence and Disclosure of Related Parties

6-3 When planning the audit the auditor should assess the risk that material undisclosed related party transactions, or undisclosed outstanding balances between an entity and its related parties may exist.

6-4 The responsibility of those charged with governance to identify, approve and disclose related party transactions requires them to implement adequate information systems to identify related parties and internal control to ensure that related party transactions are appropriately identified in the accounting records and disclosed in the financial statements. As part of the risk assessment the auditor obtains an understanding of such information systems and internal control.

6-5 The extent to which formal policies and codes of conduct dealing with relationships with related parties are maintained normally depends on the significance of related parties and on the philosophy and operating style of the management of the entity and of those charged with governance. Such policies often cover the approval, recording and reporting of related party transactions entered into, on behalf of the entity, by employees and those charged with governance.

6-6 In respect of entities that do not have formal policies and codes of conduct concerning related party transactions, for example owner managed entities, the auditor may only be able to perform substantive procedures. If the auditor assesses the risk of undisclosed related party transactions as low such planned substantive procedures may not need to be extensive.

7 The auditor should review information provided by those charged with governance and management identifying the names of all known related parties and should perform the following audit procedures in respect of the completeness of this information:

(a) Review prior year working papers for names of known related parties;
(b) Review the entity's procedures for identification of related parties;
(c) Inquire as to the affiliation of those charged with governance and officers with other entities;
(d) Review shareholder records to determine the names of principal shareholders or, if appropriate, obtain a listing of principal shareholders from the share register;
(e) Review minutes of the meetings of shareholders and those charged with governance and other relevant statutory records such as the register of directors' interests;
(f) Inquire of other auditors currently involved in the audit, or predecessor auditors, as to their knowledge of additional related parties;
(g) Review the entity's income tax returns and other information supplied to regulatory agencies;
(h) Review invoices and correspondence from lawyers for indications of the existence of related parties or related party transactions; and
(i) Inquire of the names of all pension and other trusts established for the benefit of employees and the names of their management.

- Reviewing confirmations of loans receivable and payable and confirmations from banks. Such a review may indicate guarantor relationship and other related party transactions.
- Reviewing investment transactions, for example, purchase or sale of an equity interest in a joint venture or other entity.

Examining Identified Related Party Transactions

13   **In examining the identified related party transactions, the auditor should obtain sufficient appropriate audit evidence as to whether these transactions have been properly recorded and disclosed.**

14   Given the nature of related party relationships, audit evidence of a related party transaction may be limited, for example, regarding the existence of inventory held by a related party on consignment or an instruction from a parent company to a subsidiary to record a royalty expense. Because of the limited availability of appropriate audit evidence about such transactions, the auditor considers performing audit procedures such as:

- Discussing the purpose of the transaction with management or those charged with governance.
- Confirming the terms and amount of the transaction with the related party.
- Inspecting information in possession of the related party.
- Corroborating with the related party the explanation of the purpose of the transaction and, if necessary, confirming that the transaction is bona fide.
- Obtaining information from an unrelated third party.
- Confirming or discussing information with persons associated with the transaction, such as banks, lawyers, guarantors and agents.

14-1   IAS 24 requires that "an entity shall disclose the nature of the related party relationship as well as information about the transactions and outstanding balances necessary for an understanding of the potential effect of the relationship on the financial statements". An example of a disclosure falling within this requirement would be noting that the transfer of a major asset had taken place at an amount materially different from that obtainable on normal commercial terms. The auditor, therefore, is alert for related party transactions that have occurred on other than normal commercial terms. In particular, the auditor is alert for unrecorded transactions such as the receipt or provision of management services at no charge.

14-2   The auditor considers the implications for other aspects of the audit if they identify material related party transactions not included in the information provided by management or those charged with governance. In particular, the auditor considers the impact on their assessment of audit risk and the reliance placed on other representations made by those charged with governance during the audit.

If, in the auditor's judgment, there is a lower risk of significant related parties remaining undetected, these procedures may be modified as appropriate.

7-1 After evaluating the results of:
   (a) Determining the implementation of the entity's internal control with respect to related party transactions; and
   (b) The audit procedures described in the preceding paragraph

The auditor may determine that few additional substantive procedures are required to obtain sufficient appropriate audit evidence that no other material related party transactions have occurred. However, if the auditor assesses the controls with respect to related party transactions as weak, it may be necessary to perform additional substantive procedures to obtain reasonable assurance that no material undisclosed related party transactions have occurred.

8 Where the applicable financial reporting framework requires disclosure of related party relationships, the auditor should be satisfied that the disclosure is adequate.

Transactions with Related Parties

9 The auditor should review information provided by those charged with governance and management identifying related party transactions and should be alert for other material related party transactions.

10 When obtaining an understanding of the entity's internal control, the auditor should consider the adequacy of control activities over the authorization and recording of related party transactions.

11 During the course of the audit, the auditor needs to be alert for transactions which appear unusual in the circumstances and may indicate the existence of previously unidentified related parties. Examples include:

- Transactions which have abnormal terms of trade, such as unusual prices, interest rates, guarantees, and repayment terms.
- Transactions which lack an apparent logical business reason for their occurrence.
- Transactions in which substance differs from form.
- Transactions processed in an unusual manner.
- High volume or significant transactions with certain customers or suppliers as compared with others.
- Unrecorded transactions such as the receipt or provision of management services at no charge.

12 During the course of the audit, the auditor carries out audit procedures which may identify the existence of transactions with related parties. Examples include:

- Performing detailed tests of transactions and balances.
- Reviewing minutes of meetings of shareholders and those charged with governance.
- Reviewing accounting records for large or unusual transactions or balances, paying particular attention to transactions recognized at or near the end of the reporting period.

Disclosures Relating to Control of the Entity

The auditor should obtain sufficient appropriate audit evidence that disclosures in the financial statements relating to control of the entity are properly stated. 14-3

IAS 24 requires "Relationships between parents and subsidiaries shall be disclosed irrespective of whether there have been transactions between those related parties. An entity shall disclose the name of the entity's parent and, if different, the ultimate controlling party. If neither the entity's parent nor the ultimate controlling party produces financial statements available for public use, the name of the next most senior parent that does so shall also be disclosed." Companies legislation contains additional detailed disclosures requirements relating to control of a company[3]. 14-4

The next most senior parent is the first parent in the group above the immediate parent that produces consolidated financial statements available for public use. 14-5

The auditor may only be able to determine the name of the entity's ultimate controlling party through specific inquiry of management or those charged with governance. When the auditor considers it necessary, the auditor obtains corroboration from the ultimate controlling party confirming representations received in this regard. 14-6

Management Representations

The auditor should obtain a written representation from management[4] concerning: 15

(a) **The completeness of information provided regarding the identification of related parties; and**
(b) **The adequacy of related party disclosures in the financial statements.**

The written representations obtained by the auditor include confirmation from those charged with governance that they (and any key managers or other individuals who are in a position to influence, or who are accountable for the stewardship of the reporting entity) have disclosed all transactions relevant to the entity and that they are not aware of any other such matters required to be disclosed in the financial statements, whether under IAS 24 or other requirements. 15-1

An entity may require its management and those charged with governance to sign individual declarations on these disclosure matters. In view of the inherent difficulties of detecting undisclosed related party transactions, and having regard to the conclusions drawn from other audit evidence, the auditor may wish to inspect the individual declarations. For this purpose, it may be helpful if they are addressed jointly to a designated official of the entity and also to the auditor. In other cases, the auditor may wish to obtain representations directly from each of those charged with governance and from members of management. 15-2

---

[3] *In Great Britain these requirements are set out in S. 231 and Schedule 5 Parts I and II of the Companies Act 1985. In Northern Ireland these requirements are set out in Article 239 and Schedule 5 Parts I and II of the Companies (Northern Ireland) Order 1986. In the Republic of Ireland these requirements are set out in S 16 of the Companies (Amendment) Act 1986 and Regulations 36 and 44 of the European Communities (Companies: Group Accounts) Regulations 1992.*

[4] *In the UK and Ireland the auditor obtains written representations from those charged with governance.*

Audit Conclusions and Reporting

16 If the auditor is unable to obtain sufficient appropriate audit evidence concerning related parties and transactions with such parties or concludes that their disclosure in the financial statements is not adequate, the auditor should modify the audit report appropriately.

16-1 If the auditor is unable to obtain sufficient appropriate audit evidence concerning related party transactions and transactions with such parties, this is a limitation on the scope of the audit. Accordingly the auditor considers the need to issue either a qualified opinion or disclaimer of opinion in accordance with eh requirements of ISA (UK and Ireland) 700, "The Auditor's Report on Financial Statements."

16-2 If the auditor concludes that the disclosure of related party transactions is not adequate the auditor considers the need to issue either a qualified or adverse opinion depending on the particular circumstances. Where the auditor is aware of material undisclosed related party transactions or an undisclosed control relationship, that in the auditor's opinion is required to be disclosed, the opinion section of the auditor's report, whenever practicable, includes the information that would have been included in the financial statements had the relevant requirements been followed.

Effective Date

16-3 This ISA (UK and Ireland) is effective for audits of financial statements for, periods commencing on or after 15 December 2004.

Public Sector Perspective

Additional guidance for auditors of public sector bodies in the UK and Ireland is given in:

- Practice Note 10 "Audit of Financial Statements of Public Sector Entities in the United Kingdom (Revised)"
- Practice Note 10(I) "The Audit of Central Government Financial Statements in Ireland"

1 *In applying the audit principles in this ISA (UK and Ireland), auditors have to make reference to legislative requirements which are applicable to public sector entities and employees in respect of related party transactions. Such legislation may prohibit entities and employees from entering into transactions with related parties. There may also be a requirement for public sector employees to declare their interests in entities with which they transact on a professional and/or commercial basis. Where such legislative requirements exist, the audit procedures would need to be expanded to detect instances of noncompliance with these requirements.*

2 *While International Public Sector Guideline 1, "Financial Reporting by Government Business Enterprises," indicates that all International Accounting Standards (IASs) apply to business enterprises in the public sector, IAS 24, Related Party Disclosures does not require that transactions between state controlled enterprises be disclosed.*

Definitions of related parties included in IAS 24 and this ISA (UK and Ireland) do not address all circumstances relevant to public sector entities. For example, the status, for purposes of application of this ISA (UK and Ireland), of the relationship between ministers and departments of state, and departments of state and statutory authorities or government agencies is not discussed.

Appendix – Definitions adopted from IAS 24

<u>Related party</u>. A party is related to an entity if:

(a) directly, or indirectly through one or more intermediaries, the party:
   (i) Controls, is controlled by, or is under common control with, the entity (this includes parents, subsidiaries and fellow subsidiaries);
   (ii) Has an interest in the entity that gives it significant influence over the entity; or
   (iii) Has joint control over the entity;
(b) The party is an associate (as defined in IAS 28 Investments in Associates) of the entity;
(c) The party is a joint venture in which the entity is a venturer (see IAS 31 Interests in Joint Ventures);
(d) The party is a member of the key management personnel of the entity or its parent;
(e) The party is a close member of the family of any individual referred to in (a) or (d);
(f) The party is an entity that is controlled, jointly controlled or significantly influenced by or for which significant voting power in such entity resides with, directly or indirectly, any individual referred to in (d) or (e); or
(g) The party is a post-employment benefit plan for the benefit of employees of the entity, or of any entity that is a related party of the entity.

A <u>related party transaction</u> is a transfer of resources, services or obligations between related parties, regardless of whether a price is charged.

<u>Close members of the family of an individual</u> are those family members who may be expected to influence, or be influenced by, that individual in their dealings with the entity. They may include:

(a) The individual's domestic partner and children;
(b) Children of the individual's domestic partner; and
(c) Dependents of the individual or the individual's domestic partner.

<u>Control</u> is the power to govern the financial and operating policies of an entity so as to obtain benefits from its activities.

<u>Joint control</u> is the contractually agreed sharing of control over an economic activity.

<u>Key management personnel</u> are those persons having authority and responsibility for planning, directing and controlling the activities of the entity, directly or indirectly, including any director (whether executive or otherwise) of that entity.

<u>Significant influence</u> is the power to participate in the financial and operating policy decisions of an entity, but is not control over those policies. Significant influence may be gained by share ownership, statute or agreement.

ISA (UK and Ireland) 550 to be used where FRS 8, "Related Party Disclosures" applies

Introduction

101 The purpose of this International Standard on Auditing (UK and Ireland) (ISA (UK and Ireland)) is to establish standards and provide guidance on the auditor's responsibilities and audit procedures regarding related parties and transactions with such parties regardless of whether International Accounting Standard (IAS) 24, "Related Party Disclosures," or similar requirement, is part of the applicable financial reporting framework.

101-1 In the UK and Ireland for accounting periods commencing on or after 1 January 2005, the following companies will continue to be able, if they wish, to prepare their financial statements in accordance with UK and Irish accounting standards:

(a) All companies within a listed group for their individual financial statements (and, where a consolidation is prepared by an unlisted subsidiary, for those consolidated financial statements);
(b) Unlisted companies; and
(c) Other entities, including many public benefit entities.

Paragraphs 101 to 116-2 apply to financial statements prepared under UK and Irish accounting standards, including FRS 8, "Related Party Disclosures". Paragraphs 1 to 16-2 of this ISA (UK and Ireland) apply to financial statements prepared under EU adopted IFRS, including IAS 24.

101-2 This ISA (UK and Ireland) uses the terms 'those charged with governance' and 'management'. The term 'governance' describes the role of persons entrusted with the supervision, control and direction of an entity. Ordinarily, those charged with governance are accountable for ensuring that the entity achieves its objectives, and for the quality of its financial reporting and reporting to interested parties. Those charged with governance include management only when they perform such functions.

101-3 In the UK and Ireland, those charged with governance include the directors (executive and non-executive) of a company or other body, the members of an audit committee where one exists, the partners, proprietors, committee of management or trustees of other forms of entity, or equivalent persons responsible for directing the entity's affairs and preparing its financial statements.

101-4 'Management' comprises those persons who perform senior managerial functions.

101-5 In the UK and Ireland, depending on the nature and circumstances of the entity, management may include some or all of those charged with governance (e.g. executive directors). Management will not normally include non-executive directors.

102 The auditor should perform audit procedures designed to obtain sufficient appropriate audit evidence regarding the identification and disclosure by management[1] of related

---

[1] In the UK and Ireland those charged with governance are responsible for the preparation of the financial statements.

parties and the effect of related party transactions that are material to the financial statements. However, an audit cannot be expected to detect all related party transactions.

As indicated in ISA (UK and Ireland) 200 "Objective and General Principles Governing an Audit of Financial Statements," in certain circumstances there are limitations that may affect the persuasiveness of audit evidence available to draw conclusions on particular assertions. Because of the degree of uncertainty associated with the assertions regarding the completeness of related parties, the audit procedures identified in this ISA (UK and Ireland) will provide sufficient appropriate audit evidence regarding those assertions in the absence of any circumstance identified by the auditor that: 103

(a) Increases the risk of material misstatement beyond that which would ordinarily be expected; or
(b) Indicates that a material misstatement regarding related parties has occurred.

Where there is any indication that such circumstances exist, the auditor should perform modified, extended or additional audit procedures as are appropriate in the circumstances.

Definitions regarding related parties are given in FRS 8 and are adopted for the purposes of this ISA (UK and Ireland)[2] 104

> FRS 8 does not override the disclosure requirements of either companies legislation or listing rules. Similarly, the requirements of FRS 8 do not override exemptions from disclosures given by law to, and utilized by, certain types of entity. For the purposes of this ISA (UK and Ireland) companies legislation is defined as:
>
> (a) In Great Britain, the Companies Act 1985;
> (b) In Northern Ireland, The Companies (Northern Ireland) Order 1986; and
> (c) In the Republic of Ireland, the Companies Acts 1963 to 2003 and the European Communities (Companies: Group Accounts) Regulations 1992.

104-1

> FRS 8 exempts the disclosure of certain related party transactions undertaken by an entity. In exceptional circumstances if an entity avails itself of an exemption contained in an accounting standard this may be inconsistent with the overriding requirement for the financial statements to give a true and fair view of the state of the entity's affairs. In the course of an audit the auditor may become aware of transactions that are exempt from disclosure under FRS 8. The auditor assesses whether such related party transactions need to be disclosed in order for the financial statements to give a true and fair view.

104-2

Management[1] is responsible for the identification and disclosure of related parties and transactions with such parties. This responsibility requires management to implement adequate internal control to ensure that transactions with related parties are appropriately identified in the information system and disclosed in the financial statements. 105

> As transactions between related parties may not be on an arm's length basis and there may be an actual, or perceived, conflict of interest those charged with

105-1

---

[2] Definitions from FRS 8, "Related Party Disclosures," are set out in the Appendix.

governance usually ensure that such transactions are subject to appropriate approval procedures. The approval of material related party transactions is often recorded in the minutes of meetings of those charged with governance.

105-2 In owner managed entities, as the risks associated with such transactions are the same, similar approval procedures would ideally apply. Often, however, procedures are less formalized because the owner manager is often personally aware of, and implicitly or explicitly approves, all such transactions.

105-3 The definition of a related party is complex and in part subjective and it may not always be self-evident to management whether a party is related. Furthermore, many information systems are not designed to either distinguish or summarize related party transactions and outstanding balances between an entity and its related parties. Management may, therefore, have to carry out additional analysis of the accounting records to identify related party transactions. Accordingly related party transactions are often inherently difficult for the auditor to detect.

105-4 These difficulties are heightened by the particular perspective to the concept of materiality introduced by FRS 8 which states: "The materiality of related party transactions is to be judged, not only in terms of their significance to the reporting entity, but also in relation to the other related party when that party is:

(a) A director, key manager or other individual in a position to influence, or accountable for stewardship of, the reporting entity; or
(b) A member of the close family of any individual mentioned in (a) above; or
(c) An entity controlled by any individual mentioned in (a) or (b) above".

Although the auditor designs audit procedures so as to have a reasonable expectation of detecting undisclosed related party transactions that are material to the reporting entity, an audit cannot necessarily be expected to detect all such transactions; nor can it be expected to detect transactions that are not material to the entity, even though they may be material to the other related party.

106 The auditor needs to have a sufficient understanding of the entity and its environment to enable identification of the events, transactions and practices that may result in a risk of material misstatement regarding related parties and transactions with such parties. While the existence of related parties and transactions between such parties are considered ordinary features of business, the auditor needs to be aware of them because:

(a) The applicable financial reporting framework may require disclosure in the financial statements of certain related party relationships and transactions, such as those required by FRS 8;
(b) The existence of related parties or related party transactions may affect the financial statements. For example, the entity's tax liability and expense may be affected by the tax laws in various jurisdictions which require special consideration when related parties exist;
(c) The source of audit evidence affects the auditor's assessment of its reliability. Generally a greater degree of reliance may be placed on audit evidence that is obtained from or created by unrelated third parties;
(d) A related party transaction may be motivated by other than ordinary business considerations, for example, profit sharing or even fraud; and

(e) The entity may be engaged in transfers of goods and services with related parties in accordance with specified transfer pricing policies or under reciprocal trading arrangements, such as barter transactions, which may give rise to accounting recognition and measurement issues. In particular an entity may have received or provided management services at no charge.

The risk that undisclosed related party transactions, or outstanding balances between an entity and its related parties, will not be detected by the auditor is especially high when: **106-1**

(a) Related party transactions have taken place without charge;
(b) Related party transactions are not self-evident to the auditor;
(c) Transactions are with a party that the auditor could not reasonably be expected to know is a related party;
(d) Transactions undertaken with a related party in an earlier period have remained unsettled for a considerable period of time; or
(e) Active steps have been taken by those charged with governance or management to conceal either the full terms of a transaction or that a transaction is, in substance, with a related party.

Those charged with governance or management may wish to conceal the fact that a transaction, or an outstanding balance is with a related party because: **106-2**

(a) Its disclosure may be sensitive to the parties involved and they may be reticent about disclosing it; and
(b) The transaction may be motivated by other than ordinary business considerations, for example to enhance the presentation of the financial statements (for example fraud or window dressing).

Related party transactions may be concealed in whole or in part from the auditor for fraudulent or other purposes. The likelihood of detecting fraudulent related party transactions depends upon the nature of the fraud and, in particular, the degree of collusion, the seniority of those involved and the level of deception concerned. ISA (UK and Ireland) 240 "The Auditor's responsibility to Consider Fraud in an Audit of Financial Statements" establishes the standards and provides the guidance on the auditor's responsibility to consider fraud in an audit of financial statements, including related party transactions.

Existence and Disclosure of Related Parties

When planning the audit the auditor should assess the risk that material undisclosed related party transactions, or undisclosed outstanding balances between an entity and its related parties may exist. **106-3**

The responsibility of those charged with governance to identify, approve and disclose related party transactions requires them to implement adequate information systems to identify related parties and internal control to ensure that related party transactions are appropriately identified in the accounting records and disclosed in the financial statements. As part of the risk assessment the auditor obtains an understanding of such information systems and internal control. **106-4**

The extent to which formal policies and codes of conduct dealing with relationships with related parties are maintained normally depends on the significance of related parties and on the philosophy and operating style of the management of the entity and of those charged with governance. Such policies often cover the **106-5** approval, recording and reporting of related party transactions entered into, on behalf of the entity, by employees and those charged with governance.

106-6 In respect of entities that do not have formal policies and codes of conduct concerning related party transactions, for example owner managed entities, the auditor may only be able to perform substantive procedures. If the auditor assesses the risk of undisclosed related party transactions as low such planned substantive procedures may not need to be extensive.

107 The auditor should review information provided by those charged with governance and management identifying the names of all known related parties and should perform the following audit procedures in respect of the completeness of this information:

(a) Review prior year working papers for names of known related parties;
(b) Review the entity's procedures for identification of related parties;
(c) Inquire as to the affiliation of those charged with governance and officers with other entities;
(d) Review shareholder records to determine the names of principal shareholders or, if appropriate, obtain a listing of principal shareholders from the share register;
(e) Review minutes of the meetings of shareholders and those charged with governance and other relevant statutory records such as the register of directors' interests;
(f) Inquire of other auditors currently involved in the audit, or predecessor auditors, as to their knowledge of additional related parties;
(g) Review the entity's income tax returns and other information supplied to regulatory agencies;
(h) Review invoices and correspondence from lawyers for indications of the existence of related parties or related party transactions; and
(i) Inquire of the names of all pension and other trusts established for the benefit of employees and the names of their management.

If, in the auditor's judgment, there is a lower risk of significant related parties remaining undetected, these procedures may be modified as appropriate.

107-1 After evaluating the results of:

(a) Determining the implementation of the entity's internal control with respect to related party transactions; and
(b) The audit procedures described in the preceding paragraph

the auditor may determine that few additional substantive procedures are required to obtain sufficient appropriate audit evidence that no other material related party transactions have occurred. However, if the auditor assesses the controls with respect to related party transactions as weak, it may be necessary to perform additional substantive procedures to obtain reasonable assurance that no material undisclosed related party transactions have occurred.

108 Where the applicable financial reporting framework requires disclosure of related party relationships, the auditor should be satisfied that the disclosure is adequate.

Transactions with Related Parties

The auditor should review information provided by those charged with governance and management identifying related party transactions and should be alert for other material related party transactions.   109

When obtaining an understanding of the entity's internal control, the auditor should consider the adequacy of control activities over the authorization and recording of related party transactions.   110

During the course of the audit, the auditor needs to be alert for transactions which appear unusual in the circumstances and may indicate the existence of previously unidentified related parties. Examples include: 111

- Transactions which have abnormal terms of trade, such as unusual prices, interest rates, guarantees, and repayment terms.
- Transactions which lack an apparent logical business reason for their occurrence.
- Transactions in which substance differs from form.
- Transactions processed in an unusual manner.
- High volume or significant transactions with certain customers or suppliers as compared with others.
- Unrecorded transactions such as the receipt or provision of management services at no charge.

During the course of the audit, the auditor carries out audit procedures which may identify the existence of transactions with related parties. Examples include: 112

- Performing detailed tests of transactions and balances.
- Reviewing minutes of meetings of shareholders and those charged with governance.
- Reviewing accounting records for large or unusual transactions or balances, paying particular attention to transactions recognized at or near the end of the reporting period.
- Reviewing confirmations of loans receivable and payable and confirmations from banks. Such a review may indicate guarantor relationship and other related party transactions.
- Reviewing investment transactions, for example, purchase or sale of an equity interest in a joint venture or other entity.

Examining Identified Related Party Transactions

In examining the identified related party transactions, the auditor should obtain sufficient appropriate audit evidence as to whether these transactions have been properly recorded and disclosed.   113

Given the nature of related party relationships, audit evidence of a related party transaction may be limited, for example, regarding the existence of inventory held by a related party on consignment or an instruction from a parent company to a subsidiary to record a royalty expense. Because of the limited availability of appropriate audit evidence about such transactions, the auditor considers performing audit procedures such as: 114

- Discussing the purpose of the transaction with management or those charged with governance.

- Confirming the terms and amount of the transaction with the related party.
- Inspecting information in possession of the related party.

- Corroborating with the related party the explanation of the purpose of the transaction and, if necessary, confirming that the transaction is bona fide.
- Obtaining information from an unrelated third party.

- Confirming or discussing information with persons associated with the transaction, such as banks, lawyers, guarantors and agents.

114-1 FRS 8 requires "disclosure of any other elements of the [related party] transactions necessary for an understanding of the financial statements. An example falling within this requirement would be the need to give an indication that the transfer of a major asset had taken place at an amount materially different from that obtainable on normal commercial terms". The auditor, therefore, is alert for related party transactions that have occurred on other than normal commercial terms. In particular, the auditor is alert for unrecorded transactions such as the receipt or provision of management services at no charge.

114-2 The auditor considers the implications for other aspects of the audit if they identify material related party transactions not included in the information provided by management or those charged with governance. In particular, the auditor considers the impact on their assessment of audit risk and the reliance placed on other representations made by those charged with governance during the audit.

Disclosures Relating to Control of the Entity

114-3 **The auditor should obtain sufficient appropriate audit evidence that disclosures in the financial statements relating to control of the entity are properly stated.**

114-4 FRS 8 requires, "when the reporting entity is controlled by another party, there should be disclosure of the related party relationship and the name of that party and, if different, that of the ultimate controlling party. If the controlling party or ultimate controlling party of the entity is not known, that fact should be disclosed". Companies legislation contains additional detailed disclosures requirements relating to control of a company[3].

114-5 The auditor may only be able to determine the name of the entity's ultimate controlling party through specific inquiry of management or those charged with governance. When the auditor considers it necessary, the auditor obtains corroboration from the ultimate controlling party confirming representations received in this regard.

---

[3] *In Great Britain these requirements are set out in S. 231 and Schedule 5 Parts I and II of the Companies Act 1985. In Northern Ireland these requirements are set out in Article 239 and Schedule 5 Parts I and II of the Companies (Northern Ireland) Order 1986. In the Republic of Ireland these requirements are set out in S 16 of the Companies (Amendment) Act 1986 and Regulations 36 and 44 of the European Communities (Companies: Group Accounts) Regulations 1992.*

Management Representations

The auditor should obtain a written representation from management[4] concerning: **115**

(a) The completeness of information provided regarding the identification of related parties; and
(b) The adequacy of related party disclosures in the financial statements.

> The written representations obtained by the auditor include confirmation from those charged with governance that they (and any key managers or other individuals who are in a position to influence, or who are accountable for the stewardship of the reporting entity) have disclosed all transactions relevant to the entity and that they are not aware of any other such matters required to be disclosed in the financial statements, whether under FRS 8 or other requirements.
>
> **115-1**
>
> An entity may require its management and those charged with governance to sign individual declarations on these disclosure matters. In view of the inherent difficulties of detecting undisclosed related party transactions (in particular transactions that are not material to the entity), and having regard to the conclusions drawn from other audit evidence, the auditor may wish to inspect the individual declarations. For this purpose, it may be helpful if they are addressed jointly to a designated official of the entity and also to the auditor. In other cases, the auditor may wish to obtain representations directly from each of those charged with governance and from members of management.
>
> **115-2**

Audit Conclusions and Reporting

If the auditor is unable to obtain sufficient appropriate audit evidence concerning related parties and transactions with such parties or concludes that their disclosure in the financial statements is not adequate, the auditor should modify the audit report appropriately. **116**

> If the auditor is unable to obtain sufficient appropriate audit evidence concerning related party transactions and transactions with such parties, this is a limitation on the scope of the audit. Accordingly the auditor considers the need to issue either a qualified opinion or disclaimer of opinion in accordance with eh requirements of ISA (UK and Ireland) 700, "The Auditor's Report on Financial Statements."
>
> **116-1**
>
> If the auditor concludes that the disclosure of related party transactions is not adequate the auditor considers the need to issue either a qualified or adverse opinion depending on the particular circumstances. Where the auditor is aware of material undisclosed related party transactions or an undisclosed control relationship, that in the auditor's opinion is required to be disclosed, the opinion section of the auditor's report, whenever practicable, includes the information that would have been included in the financial statements had the relevant requirements been followed.
>
> **116-2**

---

[4] *In the UK and Ireland the auditor obtains written representations from those charged with governance.*

Effective Date

116-3 This ISA (UK and Ireland) is effective for audits of financial statements for periods commencing on or after 15 December 2004.

Public Sector Perspective

Additional guidance for auditors of public sector bodies in the UK and Ireland is given in:

- Practice Note 10 "Audit of Financial Statements of Public Sector Entities in the United Kingdom (Revised)"
- Practice Note 10(I) "The Audit of Central Government Financial Statements in Ireland"

1 *In applying the audit principles in this ISA (UK and Ireland), auditors have to make reference to legislative requirements which are applicable to public sector entities and employees in respect of related party transactions. Such legislation may prohibit entities and employees from entering into transactions with related parties. There may also be a requirement for public sector employees to declare their interests in entities with which they transact on a professional and/or commercial basis. Where such legislative requirements exist, the audit procedures would need to be expanded to detect instances of noncompliance with these requirements.*

2 *While International Public Sector Guideline 1, "Financial Reporting by Government Business Enterprises," indicates that all International Accounting Standards (IASs) apply to business enterprises in the public sector, IAS 24, Related Party Disclosures does not require that transactions between state controlled enterprises be disclosed. Definitions of related parties included in IAS 24 and this ISA (UK and Ireland) do not address all circumstances relevant to public sector entities. For example, the status, for purposes of application of this ISA (UK and Ireland), of the relationship between ministers and departments of state, and departments of state and statutory authorities or government agencies is not discussed.*

Appendix – Definitions Adopted From FRS 8

Related parties

(a) Two or more parties are related parties when at any time during the financial period:
  (i) One party has direct or indirect control of the other party; or;
  (ii) The parties are subject to common control from the same source; or
  (iii) One party has influence over the financial and operating policies of the other party to an extent that that other party might be inhibited from pursuing at all times its own separate
      interests; or
  (iv) The parties, in entering a transaction, are subject to influence from the same source to such an extent that one of the parties
      to the transaction has subordinated its own separate interests.
(b) For the avoidance of doubt, the following are related parties of the reporting entity;

(i) Its ultimate and intermediate parent undertakings, subsidiary undertakings and fellow subsidiary undertakings;
(ii) Its associates and joint ventures;
(iii) The investor or venturer in respect of which the reporting entity is an associate or a joint venture;
(iv) Directors[1] of the reporting entity and the directors of its ultimate and intermediate parent undertakings; and
(v) Pension funds for the benefit of employees of the reporting entity or of any entity that is a related party of the reporting entity;

(c) And the following are presumed to be related parties of the reporting entity unless it can be demonstrated that neither party has influenced the financial and operating policies of the other in such a way as to inhibit the pursuit of separate interests:
(i) The key management of the reporting entity and the key management of its parent undertaking or undertakings;
(ii) A person owning or able to exercise control over 20 per cent or more of the voting rights of the reporting entity, whether directly or through nominees;
(iii) Each person acting in concert in such a way as to be able to exercise control or influence (in terms of (a) (iii) above) over the reporting entity; and
(iv) An entity managing or managed by the reporting entity under a management contract.

(d) Additionally, because of their relationship with certain parties that are, or are presumed to be, related parties of the reporting entity, the following are also presumed to be related parties of the reporting entity:
(i) Members of the close family of any individual falling under parties mentioned in (a) – (c) above; and
(ii) Partnerships, companies, trusts or other entities in which any individual or member of the close family in (a) – (c) above has a controlling interest.

Sub-paragraphs (b), (c) and (d) are not intended to be an exhaustive list of related parties.

Related party transaction: The transfer of assets or liabilities or the performance of services by, to or for a related party irrespective of whether a price is charged.

Close family: Close members of the family of an individual are those family members, or members of the same household, who may be expected to influence, or be influenced by, that person in their dealings with the reporting entity.

Control: The ability to direct the financial and operating policies of an entity with a view to gaining economic benefits from its activities.

Key management: Those persons in senior positions having authority or responsibility for directing or controlling the major activities and resources of the reporting entity.

Persons acting in concert: Persons who, pursuant to an agreement or understanding (whether formal or informal), actively co-operate, whether by the ownership by any of them of shares in an undertaking or otherwise, to exercise control or influence (in terms of (a) (iii) above in the definition of related parties) over that undertaking.

---

[1] Directors include shadow directors, which are defined in companies legislation as persons in accordance with whose directions or instructions the directors of the company are accustomed to act.

[560]
Subsequent events
(Issued December 2004)

Contents

	Paragraphs
Introduction	1 - 3
Events Occurring Up to the Date of the Auditor's Report	4 - 7
Facts Discovered After the Date of the Auditor's Report But Before the Financial Statements are Issued	8 - 12
Facts Discovered After the Financial Statements Have Been Issued	13 - 18
Offering of Securities to the Public	19
Effective Date	**19-1**

International Standard on Auditing (UK and Ireland) (ISA (UK and Ireland)) 560 "Subsequent Events" should be read in the context of the Auditing Practices Board's Statement "The Auditing Practices Board - Scope and Authority of Pronouncements (Revised)" which sets out the application and authority of ISAs (UK and Ireland).

Introduction

The purpose of this International Standard on Auditing (UK and Ireland) (ISA (UK and Ireland)) is to establish standards and provide guidance on the auditor's responsibility regarding subsequent events. In this ISA (UK and Ireland), the term "subsequent events" is used to refer to both events occurring between period end and the date of the auditor's report, and facts discovered after the date of the auditor's report.

1

This ISA (UK and Ireland) uses the terms 'those charged with governance' and 'management'. The term 'governance' describes the role of persons entrusted with the supervision, control and direction of an entity. Ordinarily, those charged with governance are accountable for ensuring that the entity achieves its objectives, and for the quality of its financial reporting and reporting to interested parties. Those charged with governance include management only when they perform such functions.

1-1

In the UK and Ireland, those charged with governance include the directors (executive and non-executive) of a company or other body, the members of an audit committee where one exists, the partners, proprietors, committee of management or trustees of other forms of entity, or equivalent persons responsible for directing the entity's affairs and preparing its financial statements.

1-2

'Management' comprises those persons who perform senior managerial functions.

1-3

In the UK and Ireland, depending on the nature and circumstances of the entity, management may include some or all of those charged with governance (e.g. executive directors). Management will not normally include non-executive directors.

1-4

In the UK and Ireland the auditor has responsibility for three phases when considering subsequent events. The ISA (UK and Ireland) provides guidance on the auditor's responsibilities in relation to:

(a) Events occurring between period end and the date of the auditor's report;
(b) Facts discovered after the date of the auditor's report but before the financial statements are issued; and
(c) Facts discovered after financial statements have been issued but before the laying of the financial statements before the members, or equivalent.

1-5

These three phases - and auditor's responsibilities in relation to them - leading to the laying of financial statements before members apply to all entities. However, in practice one or more of the phases may be so short as not to require separate consideration by the auditor, for example where the meeting at which those charged with governance of a small owner-managed entity approve the financial statements, and the auditor's report is signed, is immediately followed by the entity's annual general meeting.

1-6

Facts discovered after the laying of the financial statements before the members may result in those charged with governance issuing revised accounts as defined by relevant legislation. The auditor's considerations in relation to revised financial statements are covered in paragraphs 14 to 18 below.

1-7

2   The auditor should consider the effect of subsequent events on the financial statements and on the auditor's report.

3   International Accounting Standard 10, "Events After the Balance Sheet Date" deals with the treatment in financial statements of events, both favorable and unfavorable, that occur between the balance sheet date and the date when the financial statements are authorised for issue and identifies two types of events:

   (a) Those that provide evidence of conditions that existed at the balance sheet date (adjusting events after the balance sheet date); and
   (b) Those that are indicative of conditions that arose after the balance sheet date (non-adjusting events after the balance sheet date).

Events Occurring Up to the Date of the Auditor's Report

4   **The auditor should perform audit procedures designed to obtain sufficient appropriate audit evidence that all events up to the date of the auditor's report that may require adjustment of, or disclosure in, the financial statements have been identified.** These procedures are in addition to procedures which may be applied to specific transactions occurring after period end to obtain audit evidence as to account balances as at period end, for example, the testing of inventory cutoff and payments to creditors. The auditor is not, however, expected to conduct a continuing review of all matters to which previously applied audit procedures have provided satisfactory conclusions.

5   The audit procedures to identify events that may require adjustment of, or disclosure in, the financial statements would be performed as near as practicable to the date of the auditor's report. Such audit procedures take into account the auditor's risk assessment and ordinarily include the following:

   - Reviewing procedures management has established to ensure that subsequent events are identified.
   - Reading minutes of the meetings of shareholders, those charged with governance, including established committees such as relevant executive committees and the audit committee, held after period end and inquiring about matters discussed at meetings for which minutes are not yet available.
   - Reading the entity's latest available interim financial statements and, as considered necessary and appropriate, budgets, cash flow forecasts and other related management reports.
   - Inquiring, or extending previous oral or written inquiries, of the entity's legal counsel concerning litigation and claims.
   - Inquiring of management as to whether any subsequent events have occurred which might affect the financial statements. Examples of inquiries of management on specific matters are:
     - The current status of items that were accounted for on the basis of preliminary or inconclusive data.
     - Whether new commitments, borrowings or guarantees have been entered into.
     - Whether sales or acquisition of assets have occurred or are planned.
     - Whether the issue of new shares or debentures or an agreement to merge or liquidate has been made or is planned.
     - Whether any assets have been appropriated by government or destroyed, for example, by fire or flood.
     - Whether there have been any developments regarding risk areas and contingencies.

- Whether any unusual accounting adjustments have been made or are contemplated.
- Whether any events have occurred or are likely to occur which will bring into question the appropriateness of accounting policies used in the financial statements as would be the case, for example, if such events call into question the validity of the going concern assumption.

In the UK and Ireland the auditor reviews procedures established by those charged with governance and inquires of those charged with governance as to whether any subsequent events have occurred which might affect the financial statements.   5-1

When a component, such as a division, branch or subsidiary, is audited by another auditor, the auditor would consider the other auditor's procedures regarding events after period end and the need to inform the other auditor of the planned date of the auditor's report.   6

When the auditor becomes aware of events which materially affect the financial statements, the auditor should consider whether such events are properly accounted for and adequately disclosed in the financial statements.   7

Facts Discovered After the Date of the Auditor's Report But Before the Financial Statements are Issued

The auditor does not have any responsibility to perform audit procedures or make any inquiry regarding the financial statements after the date of the auditor's report. During the period from the date of the auditor's report to the date the financial statements are issued, the responsibility to inform the auditor of facts which may affect the financial statements rests with management[1].   8

When, after the date of the auditor's report but before the financial statements are issued, the auditor becomes aware of a fact which may materially affect the financial statements, the auditor should consider whether the financial statements need amendment, should discuss the matter with management[2], and should take the action appropriate in the circumstances.   9

When management[3] amends the financial statements, the auditor would carry out the audit procedures necessary in the circumstances and would provide management with a new report on the amended financial statements. The new auditor's report would be dated not earlier than the date the amended financial statements are signed or approved and, accordingly, the audit procedures referred to in paragraphs 4 and 5 would be extended to the date of the new auditor's report.   10

---

[1] *In the UK and Ireland the responsibility to inform the auditor of facts which may affect the financial statements rests with those charged with governance.*

[2] *In the UK and Ireland the auditor discusses these matters with those charged with governance. Those charged with governance are responsible for the preparation of the financial statements.*

[3] *In the UK and Ireland the responsibility for amending the financial statements rests with those charged with governance.*

11 When management³ does not amend the financial statements in circumstances where the auditor believes they need to be amended and the auditor's report has not been released to the entity, the auditor should express a qualified opinion or an adverse opinion.

12 When the auditor's report has been released to the entity, the auditor would notify those charged with governance not to issue the financial statements and the auditor's report thereon to third parties. If the financial statements are subsequently released, the auditor needs to take action to prevent reliance on the auditor's report. The action taken will depend on the auditor's legal rights and obligations and the recommendations of the auditor's lawyer.

Facts Discovered After the Financial Statements Have Been Issued

13 After the financial statements have been issued, the auditor has no obligation to make any inquiry regarding such financial statements.

13-1 For the purposes of this ISA (UK and Ireland), in the UK and the Republic of Ireland the term "after the financial statements have been issued" includes the period after the financial statements have been issued but before they have been laid before members, or equivalent. In the UK or the Republic of Ireland the auditor has a statutory right to attend the AGM and be heard on any part of the business of the meeting which concerns them as auditor, including making a statement about facts discovered after the date of the auditor's report and this implies that where subsequent events come to the attention of the auditor, the auditor needs to consider what to do in relation to them.

14 When, after the financial statements have been issued, the auditor becomes aware of a fact which existed at the date of the auditor's report and which, if known at that date, may have caused the auditor to modify the auditor's report, the auditor should consider whether the financial statements need revision⁴, should discuss the matter with management², and should take the action appropriate in the circumstances.

14-1 Where the auditor becomes aware of a fact relevant to the audited financial statements which did not exist at the date of the auditor's report there are no statutory provisions for revising financial statements. The auditor discusses with those charged with governance whether they should withdraw the financial statements and where those charged with governance decide not to do so the auditor may wish to take advice on whether it might be possible to withdraw their report. In both cases, other possible courses of action include the making of a statement by those charged with governance or the auditor at the annual general meeting. In any event legal advice may be helpful.

15 When management³ revises the financial statements, the auditor would carry out the audit procedures necessary in the circumstances, would review the steps taken by management to ensure that anyone in receipt of the previously issued financial statements together with the auditor's report thereon is informed of the situation, and would issue a new report on the revised financial statements.

⁴ In the UK the detailed regulations governing revised financial statements and directors' reports, where the revision is voluntary, are set out in sections 245 to 245C of the Companies Act 1985 and in the Articles 253 to 253C of the Companies (Northern Ireland) Order 1986. There are no provisions in the Companies Acts of the Republic of Ireland for revising financial statements.

The new auditor's report should include an emphasis of a matter paragraph referring to a note to the financial statements that more extensively discusses the reason for the revision of the previously issued financial statements and to the earlier report issued by the auditor. The new auditor's report would be dated not earlier than the date the revised financial statements are approved and, accordingly, the audit procedures referred to in paragraphs 4 and 5 would ordinarily be extended to the date of the new auditor's report. Local regulations of some countries permit the auditor to restrict the audit procedures regarding the revised financial statements to the effects of the subsequent event that necessitated the revision. In such cases, the new auditor's report would contain a statement to that effect.

16

When issuing a new report the auditor has regard to the regulations relating to reports on revised annual financial statements and directors' reports[5].

16-1

When management[5] does not take the necessary steps to ensure that anyone in receipt of the previously issued financial statements together with the auditor's report thereon is informed of the situation and does not revise the financial statements in circumstances where the auditor believes they need to be revised, the auditor would notify those charged with governance of the entity that action will be taken by the auditor to prevent future reliance on the auditor's report. The action taken will depend on the auditor's legal rights and obligations and the recommendations of the auditor's lawyers.

17

For example, where the financial statements are issued but have not yet been laid before the members or equivalent, or if those charged with governance do not intend to make an appropriate statement at the annual general meeting, then the auditor may consider making an appropriate statement at the annual general meeting. The auditor does not have a statutory right to communicate directly in writing with the members although, if the auditor resigns or is removed or is not reappointed, the auditor has, for example, various duties under company law[6].

17-1

It may not be necessary to revise the financial statements and issue a new auditor's report when issue of the financial statements for the following period is imminent, provided appropriate disclosures are to be made in such statements.

18

Offering of Securities to the Public

In the UK and Ireland, standards and guidance for accountants engaged to prepare a report and/or letter for inclusion in, or in connection with, an investment circular are set out in APB's Statements of Investment Circular Reporting Standards (SIRS).

---

[5] *In the UK and Ireland, those charged with governance have responsibility for taking the steps referred to in paragraph 17.*

[6] *The auditor of a limited company in Great Britain who ceases to hold office as auditor is required to comply with the requirements of section 394 of the Companies Act 1985 regarding the statement to be made by the auditor in relation to ceasing to hold office. Equivalent requirements for Northern Ireland are contained in Article 401A of the Companies (Northern Ireland) Order 1986 and, for the Republic of Ireland, are contained in section 185 of the Companies Act 1990.*

19 In cases involving the offering of securities to the public, the auditor should consider any legal and related requirements applicable to the auditor in all jurisdictions in which the securities are being offered. For example, the auditor may be required to carry out additional audit procedures to the date of the final offering document. These procedures would ordinarily include carrying out the audit procedures referred to in paragraphs 4 and 5 up to a date at or near the effective date of the final offering document and reading the offering document to assess whether the other information in the offering document is consistent with the financial information with which the auditor is associated.

Effective Date

19-1 This ISA (UK and Ireland) is effective for audits of financial statements for periods commencing on or after 15 December 2004.

[570]
Going concern
(Issued December 2004)

Contents

	Paragraph
Introduction	1 - 2-1
Management's Responsibility	3 - 8
Auditor's Responsibility	9 - 10
Planning the Audit and Performing Risk Assessment Procedures	11 - 16
Evaluating Management's Assessment	17 - 21-3
Period Beyond Management's Assessment	22 - 25
Further Audit Procedures When Events or Conditions are Identified	26 - 29
Audit Conclusions and Reporting	30 - 38-1
Significant Delay in the Signature or Approval of Financial Statements	39
Application to Groups	39-1 - 39-2
Effective Date	40

Appendix 1: Preparation of the Financial Statements: Note on Legal and Professional Requirements

Appendix 2: Illustrative Examples of the Auditor's Assessment of Whether Evidence Provided by the Those Charged With Governance, Concerning the Attention They Have Paid to the Period One Year From the Date of Approval of the Financial Statements, is Sufficient

---

International Standard on Auditing (UK and Ireland) (ISA (UK and Ireland)) 570 "Going Concern" should be read in the context of the Auditing Practices Board's Statement "The Auditing Practices Board - Scope and Authority of Pronouncements (Revised)" which sets out the application and authority of ISAs (UK and Ireland).

Introduction

1 The purpose of this International Standard on Auditing (UK and Ireland) (ISA (UK and Ireland)) is to establish standards and provide guidance on the auditor's responsibility in the audit of financial statements with respect to the going concern assumption used in the preparation of the financial statements, including considering management's[1a] assessment of the entity's ability to continue as a going concern.

1-1 This ISA (UK and Ireland) contains standards and guidance for the auditor in relation to the going concern basis that is generally presumed in financial statements which are required to be properly prepared in accordance with the Act[1b], and to give a true and fair view. In the absence of specific legal or other provisions to the contrary, the principles and procedures embodied in the ISA (UK and Ireland) apply also to the audit of the financial statements of other entities. This ISA (UK and Ireland) does not establish standards nor provide guidance about going concern in any other context, such as that of an engagement to report on an entity's future viability.

1-2 This ISA (UK and Ireland) uses the terms 'those charged with governance' and 'management'. The term 'governance' describes the role of persons entrusted with the supervision, control and direction of an entity. Ordinarily, those charged with governance are accountable for ensuring that the entity achieves its objectives, and for the quality of its financial reporting and reporting to interested parties. Those charged with governance include management only when they perform such functions.

1-3 In the UK and Ireland, those charged with governance include the directors (executive and non-executive) of a company or other body, the members of an audit committee where one exists, the partners, proprietors, committee of management or trustees of other forms of entity, or equivalent persons responsible for directing the entity's affairs and preparing its financial statements.

1-4 'Management' comprises those persons who perform senior managerial functions.

1-5 In the UK and Ireland, depending on the nature and circumstances of the entity, management may include some or all of those charged with governance (e.g. executive directors). Management will not normally include non-executive directors.

2 **When planning and performing audit procedures and in evaluating the results thereof, the auditor should consider the appropriateness of management's[1a] use of the going concern assumption in the preparation of the financial statements.**

2-1 **The auditor should consider any relevant disclosures in the financial statements.**

[1a] *In the UK and Ireland, those charged with governance are responsible for the preparation of the financial statements and the assessment of the entity's ability to continue as a going concern.*

[1b] *For Great Britain, 'the Act' refers to the Companies Act 1985. For Northern Ireland, the equivalent legislation is provided by the Companies (Northern Ireland) Order 1986 and for the Republic of Ireland by the Companies Acts 1963 to 2003.*

Management's Responsibility[1a]

The going concern assumption is a fundamental principle in the preparation of financial statements. Under the going concern assumption, an entity is ordinarily viewed as continuing in business for the foreseeable future with neither the intention nor the necessity of liquidation, ceasing trading or seeking protection from creditors pursuant to laws or regulations. Accordingly, assets and liabilities are recorded on the basis that the entity will be able to realize its assets and discharge its liabilities in the normal course of business.   3

Some financial reporting frameworks contain an explicit requirement[1] for management[1a] to make a specific assessment of the entity's ability to continue as a going concern, and standards regarding matters to be considered and disclosures to be made in connection with going concern. For example, International Accounting Standard 1 (revised 2003), "Presentation of Financial Statements," requires management to make an assessment of an enterprise's ability to continue as a going concern.[2]   4

> Appendix 1 to this ISA (UK and Ireland) summarizes, in relation to going concern, the legal and professional accounting requirements in the UK and Ireland with which those charged with governance comply in preparing financial statements.   4-1

> An important consequence of the legal and professional accounting requirements in the UK and Ireland is that, when preparing financial statements, those charged with governance should satisfy themselves as to whether the going concern basis is appropriate. Even if it is appropriate, it may still be necessary for the financial statements to contain additional disclosures, for instance relating to the adoption of that basis, in order to give a true and fair view.   4-2

In other financial reporting frameworks, there may be no explicit requirement for management to make a specific assessment of the entity's ability to continue as a going concern. Nevertheless, since the going concern assumption is a fundamental principle in the preparation of the financial statements, management[1a] has a responsibility to assess the entity's ability to continue as a going concern even if the financial reporting framework does not include an explicit responsibility to do so.   5

---

[1] *The detailed requirements regarding management's responsibility to assess the entity's ability to continue as a going concern and related financial statement disclosures may be set out in accounting standards, legislation or regulation.*

[2] *IAS 1, "Presentation of Financial Statements," paragraphs 23 and 24 state: "When preparing financial statements, management shall make an assessment of an entity's ability to continue as a going concern. Financial statements shall be prepared on a going concern basis unless management either intends to liquidate the entity or to cease trading, or has no realistic alternative but to do so. When management is aware, in making its assessment, of material uncertainties related to events or conditions that may cast significant doubt upon the entity's ability to continue as a going concern, those uncertainties shall be disclosed. When financial statements are not prepared on a going concern basis, that fact shall be disclosed, together with the basis on which the financial statements are prepared and the reasons why the entity is not a going concern.*
In assessing whether the going concern assumption is appropriate, management takes into account all available information about the future, which is at least, but is not limited to, twelve months from the balance sheet date. The degree of consideration depends on the facts in each case. When an entity has a history of profitable operations and ready access to financial resources, a conclusion that the going concern basis of accounting is appropriate may be reached without detailed analysis. In other cases, management may need to consider a wide range of factors relating to current and expected profitability, debt repayment schedules and potential sources of replacement financing before it can satisfy itself that the going concern basis is appropriate."

6   When there is a history of profitable operations and a ready access to financial resources, management[1a] may make its assessment without detailed analysis.

7   Management's[1a] assessment of the going concern assumption involves making a judgment, at a particular point in time, about the future outcome of events or conditions which are inherently uncertain. The following factors are relevant:

- In general terms, the degree of uncertainty associated with the outcome of an event or condition increases significantly the further into the future a judgment is being made about the outcome of an event or condition. For that reason, most financial reporting frameworks that require an explicit management assessment specify the period for which management is required to take into account all available information.
- Any judgment about the future is based on information available at the time at which the judgment is made. Subsequent events can contradict a judgment which was reasonable at the time it was made.
- The size and complexity of the entity, the nature and condition of its business and the degree to which it is affected by external factors all affect the judgment regarding the outcome of events or conditions.

8   Examples of events or conditions, which may give rise to business risks, that individually or collectively may cast significant doubt about the going concern assumption are set out below. This listing is not all-inclusive nor does the existence of one or more of the items always signify that a material uncertainty[3] exists.

Financial

- Net liability or net current liability position.

- Necessary borrowing facilities have not been agreed.

- Fixed-term borrowings approaching maturity without realistic prospects of renewal or repayment; or excessive reliance on short-term borrowings to finance long-term assets.

- Major debt repayment falling due where refinancing is necessary to the entity's continued existence.
- Major restructuring of debt.

- Indications of withdrawal of financial support by debtors and other creditors.
- Negative operating cash flows indicated by historical or prospective financial statements.
- Adverse key financial ratios.
- Substantial operating losses or significant deterioration in the value of assets used to generate cash flows.

- Major losses or cash flow problems which have arisen since the balance sheet date.

- Arrears or discontinuance of dividends.

[3] The phrase "material uncertainty" is used in IAS 1 in discussing the uncertainties related to events or conditions which may cast significant doubt on the enterprise's ability to continue as a going concern that should be disclosed in the financial statements. In other financial reporting frameworks, and elsewhere in the ISA's (UK and Ireland), the phrase "significant uncertainties" is used in similar circumstances.

- Inability to pay creditors on due dates.
- Inability to comply with the terms of loan agreements.
- Reduction in normal terms of trade credit by suppliers.
- Change from credit to cash-on-delivery transactions with suppliers.
- Inability to obtain financing for essential new product development or other essential investments.
- Substantial sales of fixed assets not intended to be replaced.

Operating

- Loss of key management without replacement.
- Loss of key staff without replacement.
- Loss of a major market, franchise, license, or principal supplier.
- Labor difficulties or shortages of important supplies.
- Fundamental changes in the market or technology to which the entity is unable to adapt adequately.
- Excessive dependence on a few product lines where the market is depressed.
- Technical developments which render a key product obsolete.

Other

- Non-compliance with capital or other statutory requirements.
- Pending legal or regulatory proceedings against the entity that may, if successful, result in claims that are unlikely to be satisfied.
- Changes in legislation or government policy expected to adversely affect the entity.
- Issues which involve a range of possible outcomes so wide that an unfavorable result could affect the appropriateness of the going concern basis.

The significance of such events or conditions often can be mitigated by other factors. For example, the effect of an entity being unable to make its normal debt repayments may be counterbalanced by management's plans to maintain adequate cash flows by alternative means, such as by disposal of assets, rescheduling of loan repayments, or obtaining additional capital. Similarly, the loss of a principal supplier may be mitigated by the availability of a suitable alternative source of supply.

Auditor's Responsibility

The auditor's responsibility is to consider the appropriateness of management's[1a] use of the going concern assumption in the preparation of the financial statements, and consider whether there are material uncertainties about the entity's ability to continue as a going concern that need to be disclosed in the financial statements. The auditor considers the appropriateness of management's use of the going concern assumption even if the financial reporting framework used in the preparation of the financial statements does not include an explicit requirement for management to make a specific assessment of the entity's ability to continue as a going concern.

9-1 The auditor also considers whether there are adequate disclosures regarding the going concern basis in the financial statements in order that they give a true and fair view.

9-2 The auditor's procedures necessarily involve a consideration of the entity's ability to continue in operational existence for the foreseeable future. In turn, that necessitates consideration both of the current and the possible future circumstances of the business and the environment in which it operates.

10 The auditor cannot predict future events or conditions that may cause an entity to cease to continue as a going concern. Accordingly, the absence of any reference to going concern uncertainty in an auditor's report cannot be viewed as a guarantee as to the entity's ability to continue as a going concern.

Planning the Audit and Performing Risk Assessment Procedures

11 In obtaining an understanding of the entity, the auditor should consider whether there are events or conditions and related business risks which may cast significant doubt on the entity's ability to continue as a going concern.

12 The auditor should remain alert for audit evidence of events or conditions and related business risks which may cast significant doubt on the entity's ability to continue as a going concern in performing audit procedures throughout the audit. If such events or conditions are identified, the auditor should, in addition to performing the procedures in paragraph 26, consider whether they affect the auditor's assessment of the risks of material misstatement.

13 The auditor considers events and conditions relating to the going concern assumption when performing risk assessment procedures, because this allows for more timely discussions with management, review of management's plans and resolution of any identified going concern issues.

14 In some cases, management[1a] may have already made a preliminary assessment when the auditor is performing risk assessment procedures. If so, the auditor reviews that assessment to determine whether management has identified events or conditions, such as those discussed in paragraph 8, and management's plans to address them.

15 If management[1a] has not yet made a preliminary assessment, the auditor discusses with management the basis for their intended use of the going concern assumption, and inquires of management whether events or conditions, such as those discussed in paragraph 8, exist. The auditor may request management to begin making its assessment, particularly when the auditor has already identified events or conditions relating to the going concern assumption.

16 The auditor considers the effect of identified events or conditions when assessing the risks of material misstatement and, therefore, their existence may affect the nature, timing and extent of the auditor's further procedures in response to the assessed risks.

Evaluating Management's[1a] Assessment

The auditor should evaluate management's[1a] assessment of the entity's ability to continue as a going concern. 17

> The auditor should assess the adequacy of the means by which the those charged with governance have satisfied themselves that: 17-1
>
> (a) It is appropriate for them to adopt the going concern basis in preparing the financial statements; and
> (b) The financial statements include such disclosures, if any, relating to going concern as are necessary for them to give a true and fair view.
>
> For this purpose:
>
> (i) The auditor should make enquiries of those charged with governance and examine appropriate available financial information; and
> (ii) Having regard to the future period to which those charged with governance have paid particular attention in assessing going concern (see paragraphs 18 and 18-1 below), the auditor should plan and perform procedures specifically designed to identify any material matters which could indicate concern about the entity's ability to continue as a going concern.

The auditor should consider the same period as that used by management[1a] in making its assessment under the applicable financial reporting framework. If management's assessment of the entity's ability to continue as a going concern covers less than twelve months from the balance sheet date, the auditor should ask management to extend its assessment period to twelve months from the balance sheet date. 18

> In the UK and Ireland, if the period used by the those charged with governance in making their assessment is less than one year from the date of approval of the financial statements, and they have not disclosed that fact in the financial statements, the auditor does so within the audit report (see paragraphs 31-4 and 31-5). 18-1
>
> In assessing going concern, those charged with governance take account of all relevant information of which they are aware at the time. The nature of the exercise entails that those charged with governance look forward, and there will be some future period to which they will pay particular attention in assessing going concern. It is not possible to specify a minimum length for this period: it is recognized in any case that any such period would be artificial and arbitrary since in reality there is no 'cut off point' after which there should be a sudden change in the approach adopted by those charged with governance. The length of the period is likely to depend upon such factors as: 18-2
>
> - The entity's reporting and budgeting systems; and
> - The nature of the entity, including its size or complexity.
>
> Where the period considered by those charged with governance has been limited, for example, to a period of less than one year from the date of approval of the financial statements, those charged with governance will have determined whether, in their opinion, the financial statements require any additional disclosure to explain adequately the assumptions that underlie the adoption of the going concern basis.

18-3 The basis for the auditor's procedures is the information upon which those charged with governance have based their assessment and the reasoning of those charged with governance. The auditor assesses whether this constitutes sufficient appropriate audit evidence for the purpose of the audit and whether the auditor concurs with the judgment of those charged with governance about the need for additional disclosures.

18-4 The following factors in particular may affect the information available to the auditor, and whether the auditor considers this information constitutes sufficient audit evidence for the purpose of the audit.

(a) *The nature of the entity (its size and the complexity of its circumstances, for instance).* This ISA (UK and Ireland) applies to the audits of the financial statements of all sizes of entity. The larger or more complex the entity the more sophisticated is likely to be the information available and needed to support the assessment of whether it is appropriate to adopt the going concern basis.

(b) *Whether the information relates to future events, and if so how far into the future those events lie.* The information relating to the period falling after one year from the balance sheet date is often prepared in far less detail and subject to a greater degree of estimation than the information relating to periods ending on or before one year from the balance sheet date.

19 Management's[1a] assessment of the entity's ability to continue as a going concern is a key part of the auditor's consideration of the going concern assumption. As noted in paragraph 7, most financial reporting frameworks requiring an explicit management assessment specify the period for which management is required to take into account all available information.[4]

19-1 A determination of the sufficiency of the evidence supplied to the auditor by those charged with governance will depend on the particular circumstances. However, to be sufficient the evidence may not require formal cash flow forecasts and budgets to have been prepared for the period ending one year from the date of approval of the financial statements. Although such forecasts and budgets are likely to provide the most persuasive evidence, alternative sources of evidence may also be acceptable. Often, the auditor through discussion with those charged with governance of their plans and expectations for that period may be able to obtain satisfaction that those charged with governance have in fact paid particular attention to a period of one year from the date of approval of the financial statements. Appendix 2 illustrates circumstances where formal budgets and forecasts have, with justification, not been provided for the entire twelve month period yet the auditor is able to conclude that those charged with governance have paid particular attention to the period ending one year from the date of approval of the financial statements.

20 In evaluating management's[1a] assessment, the auditor considers the process management followed to make its assessment, the assumptions on which the assessment is based and management's plans for future action. The auditor considers whether

---

[4] *For example, IAS 1 defines this as a period that should be at least, but is not limited to, twelve months from the balance sheet date.*

FRS 18 does not specify this period but does require that where the foreseeable future considered by the directors has been limited to a period of less than one year from the <u>date of approval</u> of the financial statements, that fact should be disclosed in the financial statements.

the assessment has taken into account all relevant information of which the auditor is aware as a result of the audit procedures.

> The auditor may need to consider some or all of the following matters: **20-1**
>
> - Whether the period to which those charged with governance have paid particular attention in assessing going concern is reasonable in the entity's circumstances and in the light of the need for those charged with governance to consider the ability of the entity to continue in operational existence for the foreseeable future.
> - The systems, or other means (formal or informal), for timely identification of warnings of future risks and uncertainties the entity might face.
> - Budget and/or forecast information (cash flow information in particular) produced by the entity, and the quality of the systems (or other means, formal or informal) in place for producing this information and keeping it up to date.
> - Whether the key assumptions underlying the budgets and/or forecasts appear appropriate in the circumstances.
> - The sensitivity of budgets and/or forecasts to variable factors both within the control of those charged with governance and outside their control.
> - Any obligations, undertakings or guarantees arranged with other entities (in particular, lenders, suppliers and group companies) for the giving or receiving of support.
> - The existence, adequacy and terms of borrowing facilities, and supplier credit.
> - The plans of those charged with governance for resolving any matters giving rise to the concern (if any) about the appropriateness of the going concern basis. In particular, the auditor may need to consider whether the plans are realistic, whether there is a reasonable expectation that the plans are likely to resolve any problems foreseen and whether those charged with governance are likely to put the plans into practice effectively.
>
> The extent of the procedures is influenced primarily by the excess of the financial **20-2** resources available to the entity over the financial resources that it requires. The entity's procedures (and the auditor's procedures) need not always be elaborate in order to provide sufficient appropriate audit evidence. For example, the auditor may not always need to examine budgets and forecasts for this purpose. This is particularly likely to be the case in respect of entities with uncomplicated circumstances. Many smaller companies fall into this category. Thus for example:
>
> - Regarding the systems or other means for timely identification of warnings of future risks and uncertainties, those charged with governance might consider that it is appropriate simply to keep abreast of developments within their individual business and their business sector. In the circumstances, the auditor might concur with those charged with governance; or
> - Those charged with governance might not, as a matter of course, prepare periodic cash flow and other budgets, forecasts or other management accounts information apart from the accounting records required by law and outline plans for the future. In the view of those charged with governance, this might be acceptable where the business is stable. In the circumstances the auditor might concur with those charged with governance. Hence the auditor's procedures regarding budgets, forecasts and related issues might comprise discussion of the outline plans of those charged with governance in the light of other information available to the auditor.

21   As noted in paragraph 6, when there is a history of profitable operations and a ready access to financial resources, management[1a] may make its assessment without detailed analysis. In such circumstances, the auditor's conclusion about the appropriateness of this assessment normally is also made without the need for performing detailed procedures. When events or conditions have been identified which may cast significant doubt about the entity's ability to continue as a going concern, however, the auditor performs additional audit procedures, as described in paragraph 26.

The Auditor's Examination of Borrowing Facilities

21-1   In examining borrowing facilities the auditor could decide, for example, that it is necessary:

(a) To obtain confirmations of the existence and terms of bank facilities; and
(b) To make an own assessment of the intentions of the bankers relating thereto.

The latter assessment could involve the auditor examining written evidence or making notes of meetings which the auditor would hold with those charged with governance and, occasionally, with those charged with governance and the entity's bankers. In making an assessment of the bankers' intentions the auditor ascertains, normally through enquiries of those charged with governance, whether the bankers are aware of the matters that are causing the auditor to decide that such an assessment is necessary. It is also important that the relationships between the auditor, those charged with governance and the bankers are clarified and understood.

21-2   The auditor might be more likely to decide that it is necessary to obtain confirmations of the existence and terms of bank facilities, and to make an independent assessment of the intentions of the bankers relating thereto, in cases where, for example:

- There is a low margin of financial resources available to the entity.
- The entity is dependent on borrowing facilities shortly due for renewal.
- Correspondence between the bankers and the entity reveals that the last renewal of facilities was agreed with difficulty, or that, since the last review of facilities, the bankers have imposed additional conditions as a prerequisite for continued lending.
- A significant deterioration in cash flow is projected.
- The value of assets granted as security for the borrowings is declining.
- The entity has breached the terms of borrowing covenants, or there are indications of potential breaches.

21-3   The auditor considers whether any inability to obtain sufficient appropriate audit evidence regarding the existence and terms of borrowing facilities and the intentions of the lender relating thereto, and/or the factors giving rise to this inability, need to be:

- Disclosed in the financial statements in order that they give a true and fair view; and/or
- Referred to (by way of an explanatory paragraph or a qualified opinion) in the auditor's report.

Period Beyond Management's[1a] Assessment

The auditor should inquire of management as to its knowledge of events or conditions and related business risks beyond the period of assessment used by management[1a] that may cast significant doubt on the entity's ability to continue as a going concern. 22

The auditor is alert to the possibility that there may be known events, scheduled or otherwise, or conditions that will occur beyond the period of assessment used by management[1a] that may bring into question the appropriateness of management's use of the going concern assumption in preparing the financial statements. The auditor may become aware of such known events or conditions during the planning and performance of the audit, including subsequent events procedures. 23

Since the degree of uncertainty associated with the outcome of an event or condition increases as the event or condition is further into the future, in considering such events or conditions, the indications of going concern issues will need to be significant before the auditor considers taking further action. The auditor may need to ask management[1a] to determine the potential significance of the event or condition on their going concern assessment. 24

The auditor does not have a responsibility to design audit procedures other than inquiry of management to test for indications of events or conditions which cast significant doubt on the entity's ability to continue as a going concern beyond the period assessed by management[1a] which, as discussed in paragraph 18, would be at least twelve months from the balance sheet date. 25

Further Audit Procedures When Events or Conditions are Identified

When events or conditions have been identified which may cast significant doubt on the entity's ability to continue as a going concern, the auditor should: 26

(a) Review management's[1a] plans for future actions based on its going concern assessment;
(b) Gather sufficient appropriate audit evidence to confirm or dispel whether or not a material uncertainty exists through carrying out audit procedures considered necessary, including considering the effect of any plans of management and other mitigating factors; and
(c) Seek written representations from management[5] regarding its plans for future action.

The auditor should consider the need to obtain written confirmations of representations from those charged with governance regarding: 26-1

(a) The assessment of those charged with governance that the company is a going concern;
(b) Any relevant disclosures in the financial statements.

Such written confirmations are necessary in respect of matters material to the financial statements when those representations are critical to obtaining sufficient appropriate audit evidence. In view of their importance, it is appropriate for such confirmations to be provided by those charged with governance, rather than other levels of the entity's management. 26-2

---

[5] *In the UK and Ireland the auditor obtains written representations from those charged with governance.*

26-3 If they are unable to obtain such written confirmations of representations as they consider necessary from those charged with governance, the auditor considers whether:

- There is a limitation on the scope of the auditor's work which requires a qualified opinion or disclaimer of opinion; or
- The failure of those charged with governance to provide the written confirmations could indicate that there is concern.

27 Events or conditions which may cast significant doubt on the entity's ability to continue as a going concern may be identified in performing risk assessment procedures or in the course of performing further audit procedures. The process of considering events or conditions continues as the audit progresses. When the auditor believes such events or conditions may cast significant doubt on the entity's ability to continue as a going concern, certain audit procedures may take on added significance. The auditor inquires of management as to its plans for future action, including its plans to liquidate assets, borrow money or restructure debt, reduce or delay expenditures, or increase capital. The auditor also considers whether any additional facts or information are available since the date on which management[1a] made its assessment. The auditor obtains sufficient appropriate audit evidence that management's plans are feasible and that the outcome of these plans will improve the situation.

28 Audit procedures that are relevant in this regard may include:

- Analyzing and discussing cash flow, profit and other relevant forecasts with management.
- Analyzing and discussing the entity's latest available interim financial statements.
- Reviewing the terms of debentures and loan agreements and determining whether any have been breached.
- Reading minutes of the meetings of shareholders, those charged with governance and relevant committees for reference to financing difficulties.
- Inquiring of the entity's lawyer regarding the existence of litigation and claims and the reasonableness of management's assessments of their outcome and the estimate of their financial implications.
- Confirming the existence, legality and enforceability of arrangements to provide or maintain financial support with related and third parties and assessing the financial ability of such parties to provide additional funds.
- Considering the entity's plans to deal with unfilled customer orders.
- Reviewing events after period end to identify those that either mitigate or otherwise affect the entity's ability to continue as a going concern.

29 When analysis of cash flow is a significant factor in considering the future outcome of events or conditions the auditor considers:

(a) The reliability of the entity's information system for generating such information; and
(b) Whether there is adequate support for the assumptions underlying the forecast.

In addition the auditor compares:

(c) The prospective financial information for recent prior periods with historical results; and
(d) The prospective financial information for the current period with results achieved to date.

Audit Conclusions and Reporting

Based on the audit evidence obtained, the auditor should determine if, in the auditor's judgment, a material uncertainty exists related to events or conditions that alone or in aggregate, may cast significant doubt on the entity's ability to continue as a going concern.   30

The auditor should document the extent of the auditor's concern (if any) about the entity's ability to continue as a going concern.   30-1

The auditor might be more likely to conclude that there is a significant level of concern about the entity's ability to continue as a going concern if, for example, indications such as those in paragraph 8 are present. However, where such indications are present, the auditor may have obtained sufficient appropriate evidence causing the auditor to conclude that there is not a significant level of concern about the entity's ability to continue as a going concern.   30-2

The auditor could consider that there is a significant level of concern about the entity's ability to continue as a going concern, or the auditor could disagree with the preparation of the financial statements on the going concern basis. In such cases (whether or not this is because of potential insolvency) the auditor might decide to write to those charged with governance drawing their attention to the need to consider taking suitable advice. In particular, those charged with governance of an entity may need to obtain advice from specialist accountants or lawyers on the appropriateness and implications of continuing to trade while they know, or ought to know, that the entity is insolvent.   30-3

A material uncertainty exists when the magnitude of its potential impact is such that, in the auditor's judgment, clear disclosure of the nature and implications of the uncertainty is necessary for the presentation of the financial statements not to be misleading.   31

The auditor should consider whether the financial statements are required to include disclosures relating to going concern in order to give a true and fair view.   31-1

In particular, if the future period to which those charged with governance have paid particular attention is, as described in paragraph 18-2, not very long, those charged with governance will have determined whether, in their opinion, the financial statements require any additional disclosures to explain adequately the assumptions that underlie the adoption of the going concern basis. The auditor assesses whether to concur with the judgments of those charged with governance regarding the need for additional disclosures and their adequacy. Disclosure, however, does not eliminate the need to make appropriate judgments about the suitability of the future period as an adequate basis for assessing the position.   31-2

To avoid repetition, the text in the financial statements might refer readers to specific disclosures located elsewhere in the annual report (for instance in the Operating and Financial Review). The auditor takes account of such specified disclosures in considering the adequacy of disclosures in the financial statements.   31-3

If the period to which those charged with governance have paid particular attention in assessing going concern is less than one year from the date of approval of the financial statements, and those charged with governance have not disclosed that fact,   31-4

31-5 Where, in forming their opinion, the auditor's assessment of going concern is based on a period to which those charged with governance have paid particular attention which is less than one year from the date of approval of the financial statements, it is appropriate for the auditor to disclose that fact within the basis of the audit opinion, unless it is disclosed in the financial statements or accompanying information (for example, the Operating and Financial Review). In deciding whether to disclose the fact, the auditor assesses whether the evidence supplied by those charged with governance is sufficient to demonstrate that those charged with governance have, in assessing going concern, paid particular attention to a period of one year from the date of approval of the financial statements.

the auditor should do so within the section of the auditor's report setting out the basis of the audit opinion, unless the fact is clear from any other references in the auditor's report[6].

31-6 The auditor qualifies the audit opinion if the auditor considers that those charged with governance have not taken adequate steps to satisfy themselves that it is appropriate for them to adopt the going concern basis. This might arise, for example, when the auditor does not consider that the future period to which those charged with governance have paid particular attention in assessing going concern is reasonable in the entity's circumstances. This is a limitation on the scope of the auditor's work, as the auditor is unable to obtain all the information and explanations which they consider necessary for the purpose of their audit.

Going Concern Assumption Appropriate but a Material Uncertainty Exists

32 If the use of the going concern assumption is appropriate but a material uncertainty exists, the auditor considers whether the financial statements:

(a) Adequately describe the principal events or conditions that give rise to the significant doubt on the entity's ability to continue in operation and management's plans to deal with these events or conditions; and

(b) State clearly that there is a material uncertainty related to events or conditions which may cast significant doubt on the entity's ability to continue as a going concern and, therefore, that it may be unable to realize its assets and discharge its liabilities in the normal course of business.

33 **If adequate disclosure is made in the financial statements, the auditor should express an unqualified opinion but modify the auditor's report by adding an emphasis of matter paragraph that highlights the existence of a material uncertainty relating to the event or condition that may cast significant doubt on the entity's ability to continue as a going concern and draws attention to the note in the financial statements that discloses the matters set out in paragraph 32.** In evaluating the adequacy of the financial statement disclosure, the auditor considers whether the information explicitly draws the reader's attention to the possibility that the entity may be unable to continue realizing its assets and discharging its liabilities in the normal course of business. The following is an example of such a paragraph when the auditor is satisfied as to the adequacy of the note disclosure:

> "Without qualifying our opinion, we draw attention to Note X in the financial statements which indicates that the Company incurred a net loss of ZZZ during the year ended December 31, 20X1 and, as of that date, the Company's current

---

[6] *If the non-disclosure of the fact in the financial statements is a departure from the requirements of the applicable financial reporting framework, the auditor would give a qualified opinion ("except for").*

liabilities exceeded its total assets by ZZZ. These conditions, along with other matters as set forth in Note X, indicate the existence of a material uncertainty which may cast significant doubt about the Company's ability to continue as a going concern."

In extreme cases, such as situations involving multiple material uncertainties that are significant to the financial statements, the auditor may consider it appropriate to express a disclaimer of opinion instead of adding an emphasis of matter paragraph.

The emphasis of matter paragraph describes clearly the nature of the matters giving rise to the auditor's concern and refers to the relevant disclosures in the financial statements. The auditor uses judgment to decide the extent to which it is necessary for the description in the auditor's report to repeat information taken from the notes to the financial statements. The extent of the auditor's concern is one factor affecting the nature and extent of the description in the auditor's report. The prime consideration is clarity of communication. The description is normally identified within the auditor's report through the use of the sub-heading 'Going concern'. 33-1

The auditor might have concluded that there is a significant level of concern about the entity's ability to continue as a going concern. In these cases the auditor does not normally regard the disclosures as adequate unless (in addition to any disclosures otherwise required, for example by accounting standards) the following matters are included in the financial statements: 33-2

(a) A statement that the financial statements have been prepared on the going concern basis;
(b) A statement of the pertinent facts;
(c) The nature of the concern;
(d) A statement of the assumptions adopted by those charged with governance, which should be clearly distinguishable from the pertinent facts;
(e) (Where appropriate and practicable) a statement regarding the plans of those charged with governance for resolving the matters giving rise to the concern; and
(f) Details of any relevant actions by those charged with governance.

The guidance above regarding disclosures in the financial statements does not constitute an accounting standard.

If adequate disclosure is not made in the financial statements, the auditor should express a qualified or adverse opinion, as appropriate (ISA (UK and Ireland) 700, "The Auditor's Report on Financial Statements," paragraphs 45–46). The report should include specific reference to the fact that there is a material uncertainty that may cast significant doubt about the entity's ability to continue as a going concern. The following is an example of the relevant paragraphs when a qualified opinion is to be expressed: 34

"The Company's financing arrangements expire and amounts outstanding are payable on March 19, 20X1. The Company has been unable to re-negotiate or obtain replacement financing. This situation indicates the existence of a material uncertainty which may cast significant doubt on the Company's ability to continue as a going concern and therefore it may be unable to realize its assets and discharge its liabilities in the normal course of business. The financial statements (and notes thereto) do not disclose this fact.

In our opinion, except for the omission of the information included in the preceding paragraph, the financial statements give a true and fair view of (present fairly, in all material respects,) the financial position of the Company at December 31, 20X0 and the results of its operations and its cash flows for the year then ended in accordance with ..."

> Illustrative examples of auditor's reports tailored for use with audits conducted in accordance with ISAs (UK and Ireland) are given in the most recent version of the APB Bulletin, "Auditor's Reports on Financial Statements".

The following is an example of the relevant paragraphs when an adverse opinion is to be expressed:

"The Company's financing arrangements expired and the amount outstanding was payable on December 31, 20X0. The Company has been unable to re-negotiate or obtain replacement financing and is considering filing for bankruptcy. These events indicate a material uncertainty which may cast significant doubt on the Company's ability to continue as a going concern and therefore it may be unable to realize its assets and discharge its liabilities in the normal course of business. The financial statements (and notes thereto) do not disclose this fact.

In our opinion, because of the omission of the information mentioned in the preceding paragraph, the financial statements do not give a true and fair view of (or do not present fairly) the financial position of the Company as at December 31, 20X0, and of its results of operations and its cash flows for the year then ended in accordance with....(and do not comply with...)..."

> Illustrative examples of auditor's reports tailored for use with audits conducted in accordance with ISAs (UK and Ireland) are given in Appendix 2 and the most recent version of the APB Bulletin, "Auditor's Reports on Financial Statements".

Going Concern Assumption Inappropriate

35 **If, in the auditor's judgment, the entity will not be able to continue as a going concern, the auditor should express an adverse opinion if the financial statements have been prepared on a going concern basis.** If, on the basis of the additional audit procedures carried out and the information obtained, including the effect of management's plans, the auditor's judgment is that the entity will not be able to continue as a going concern, the auditor concludes, regardless of whether or not disclosure has been made, that the going concern assumption used in the preparation of the financial statements is inappropriate and expresses an adverse opinion.

36 When the entity's management[1a] has concluded that the going concern assumption used in the preparation of the financial statements is not appropriate, the financial statements need to be prepared on an alternative authoritative basis. If on the basis of the additional audit procedures carried out and the information obtained the auditor determines the alternative basis is appropriate, the auditor can issue an unqualified opinion if there is adequate disclosure but may require an emphasis of matter in the auditor's report to draw the user's attention to that basis.

In rare circumstances, in order to give a true and fair view, those charged with governance may have prepared the financial statements on a basis other than that of going concern. If the auditor considers this other basis to be appropriate in the specific circumstances, and if the financial statements contain the necessary disclosures, the auditor should not qualify the auditor's report in this respect.   36-1

Some enterprises are formed for a specific purpose, such as a joint venture to undertake a construction project, and are wound up or dissolved when the purpose is achieved. Under these circumstances the financial statements may be prepared on a basis that reflects the fact that assets may need to be realized other than in the ordinary course of operations. In these circumstances the auditor may wish, without qualifying the audit opinion, to refer in the auditor's report to the basis on which the financial statements are prepared; the auditor may do this in the introductory paragraph of the report.   36-2

Management Unwilling to Make or Extend its Assessment

If management[1a] is unwilling to make or extend its assessment when requested to do so by the auditor, the auditor should consider the need to modify the auditor's report as a result of the limitation on the scope of the auditor's work. In certain circumstances, such as those described in paragraphs 15, 18 and 24, the auditor may believe that it is necessary to ask management to make or extend its assessment. If management is unwilling to do so, it is not the auditor's responsibility to rectify the lack of analysis by management, and a modified report may be appropriate because it may not be possible for the auditor to obtain sufficient appropriate evidence regarding the use of the going concern assumption in the preparation of the financial statements.   37

In some circumstances, the lack of analysis by management may not preclude the auditor from being satisfied about the entity's ability to continue as a going concern. For example, the auditor's other procedures may be sufficient to assess the appropriateness of management's[1a] use of the going concern assumption in the preparation of the financial statements because the entity has a history of profitable operations and a ready access to financial resources. In other circumstances, however, the auditor may not be able to confirm or dispel, in the absence of management's assessment, whether or not events or conditions exist which indicate there may be a significant doubt on the entity's ability to continue as a going concern, or the existence of plans management has put in place to address them or other mitigating factors. In these circumstances, the auditor modifies the auditor's report as discussed in ISA (UK and Ireland) 700, "The Auditor's Report on Financial Statements," paragraphs 36–44.   38

Regulated Entities

When the auditor of a regulated financial entity considers that it might be necessary to either qualify the audit opinion or add an explanatory paragraph to the audit report, the auditor may have a duty to inform the appropriate regulator at an early stage in the audit. In such cases the regulator might, if it has not already done so, specify corrective action to be taken by the entity. At the time at which the auditor formulates the audit report, the auditor takes account of matters such as: 38-1

- Any views expressed by the regulator.
- Any legal advice obtained by those charged with governance.
- The actual and planned corrective action.

Significant Delay in the Signature or Approval of Financial Statements

39 When there is significant delay in the signature or approval of the financial statements by management[1a] after the balance sheet date, the auditor considers the reasons for the delay. When the delay could be related to events or conditions relating to the going concern assessment, the auditor considers the need to perform additional audit procedures, as described in paragraph 26, as well as the effect on the auditor's conclusion regarding the existence of a material uncertainty, as described in paragraph 30.

Application to Groups

39-1 The principles and procedures set out in this ISA (UK and Ireland) apply also to the audit of consolidated financial statements.

39-2 It may be appropriate, on the grounds of materiality, for the group financial statements to be prepared on the going concern basis even though it is inappropriate for the individual financial statements of one or more members of the group to be prepared on the going concern basis.

Effective Date

40 This ISA (UK and Ireland) is effective for audits of financial statements for periods commencing on or after 15 December 2004.

Public Sector Perspective

Additional guidance for auditors of public sector bodies in the UK and Ireland is given in:

- Practice Note 10 "Audit of Financial Statements of Public Sector Entities in the United Kingdom (Revised)"
- Practice Note 10(I) "The Audit of Central Government Financial Statements in Ireland"

1 *The appropriateness of the use of the going concern assumption in the preparation of the financial statements is generally not in question when auditing either a central government or those public sector entities having funding arrangements backed by a central government. However, where such arrangements do not exist, or where central government funding of the entity may be withdrawn and the existence of the entity may be at risk, this ISA (UK and Ireland) will provide useful guidance. As governments*

Appendix 2 – Illustrative Examples of the Auditor's Assessment of Whether Evidence Provided by Those Charged With Governance, Concerning the Attention They Have Paid to the Period One Year From the Date of Approval of the Financial Statements, is Sufficient

The appendix is illustrative only and does not form part of the Auditing Standards. The purpose of the appendix is to illustrate the application of the Auditing Standards to assist in clarifying their meaning in a number of commercial situations. The examples focus on particular aspects of the situations illustrated and are not intended to be a comprehensive discussion of all the relevant factors that might influence either the directors' or auditor's assessment of the appropriateness of the going concern basis. As the auditor would need to exercise judgment in the circumstances described it is possible that different auditors may arrive at different conclusions. This does not, however, detract from the examples which demonstrate thought process and the implications for an audit report once certain conclusions have been reached by the auditor. These examples neither modify nor override the Auditing Standards.

Example 1 - A small company producing specialized computer application software

Extract from the auditor's risk assessment

This owner managed company employs a few highly trained and highly paid computer system designers to design application software for use by transportation enterprises, such as airlines and bus companies, in preparing their timetables and fare structures. Few companies are engaged in this field and the supply of suitably trained staff is limited. The system designers, who met at University, have been with the company since its formation. They all have an equity interest in the company.

Although the company has only been in existence for five years it has established a reputation for excellence in its field. Its reputation derives from the skill and expertise of its individual employees rather than from anything attaching to the company itself.

A significant amount of time is spent by the designers in pure research activities developing new products. In addition the time needed to develop individual systems relating to an established product can be considerable. In addition to design of new systems the company maintains those systems it has installed on a contractual basis and undertakes training courses in the use of the systems for the employees of its customers.

The company is thinly capitalized and relies primarily on advances from its customers supplemented by short term bank borrowings for its day to day cash requirements.

The company employs a part time book-keeper to prepare the financial statements, cash flow forecasts and maintain the books of account.

The company has usually been in a position to choose which contracts it accepts and has not had difficulty in recovering its costs. The company is not economically dependent on any one transportation enterprise.

The company updates each month a rolling cash flow projection with a six month time horizon. The company does not prepare projections for a longer period as it perceives its management need is to be able to manage effectively its short term cash flow. The company has negotiated a line of credit with its bankers which it would be able to utilize to overcome short term cash shortages.

Assessment by the auditor of whether there is sufficient evidence that the directors have paid particular attention to a period of twelve months

When the auditor assesses whether the directors have, in assessing going concern, paid particular attention to a period of one year from the expected date of approval of the financial statements the auditor:

(a) Reviews the cash flow forecasts for the six month period from the expected date of approval of the financial statements; and
(b) Then enquires of the directors the steps they have taken to assess the appropriateness of the going concern basis for the subsequent six month period.

The directors inform the auditor that they do not consider there is any need for cash flow forecasts to be prepared beyond six months because:

- The cash flow forecasts show a net cash inflow for the period;
- They have reviewed in detail the assumptions implicit in the forecast with the bookkeeper and concur with them;
- The company has a significant back-log of orders which will occupy half of the designers for at least the next year;
- The company is actively tendering for both systems design and maintenance contracts in the United Kingdom and Europe and is considering expanding into the Americas;
- The company has recently renewed its arrangements with its bankers for a further year;
- The design employees seem to be settled and stimulated and there is no reason to believe that they will leave the company in the foreseeable future; and
- In the unlikely event that the company did not win many of the tenders it could modify its existing expansion plans which have been necessitated by an increase in maintenance contracts. Rather than employ new staff to undertake this work existing staff could be reassigned to it.

The auditor concludes that the directors have paid particular attention to the period ending one year after their approval of the financial statements.

Example 2 - *An enterprise in the fashion industry*

Extract from the auditor's risk assessment

This company employing 1,000 people designs and manufactures ladies fashion wear. Its business is seasonal and it presents two major collections per year: one in the spring and one in the autumn.

The company has attracted established designers and they are regarded as one of the leading manufacturers.

Almost all of the company's sales orders are received from the major retailers when they show their collections. Although some of the garments are manufactured prior to the showing of the collection the majority of them will be manufactured in the four months immediately following the showing.

The company's finance director is a qualified accountant with a staff of 6. Because of the seasonal nature of the business the company prepares its detailed budgets and cash flow forecasts until the end of the next season. The company's year end is 30 June and the directors expect to approve the financial statements during October. Detailed cash flow forecasts are only available to the end of February in the following year a period of only four months from the approval of the financial statements.

The company which has been marginally profitable over the last few years has a small line of credit with its bank but is financed primarily through the factoring of its debtors.

Assessment by the auditor of whether there is sufficient evidence that the directors have paid particular attention to a period of twelve months

When the auditor assesses whether the directors have, in assessing going concern, paid particular attention to a period of one year from the expected date of approval of the financial statements the auditor would:

(a) Review the cash flow forecasts for the four month period from the expected date of approval of the financial statements; and
(b) Then enquire of the directors the steps they have taken to assess the appropriateness of the going concern basis for the subsequent eight month period.

The directors inform the auditor that they do not consider there is any need for additional cash flow forecasts to be prepared beyond the end of February in the following year because:

- The cash flow forecasts show a net cash inflow for the period and the present cash position is strong because of a recent sale of debtors from the present collection;
- The directors have reviewed in detail the assumptions implicit in the forecast and concur with them;
- The designers are working on the next collection and they believe, based on discussions with some of the retailers, that they have some good general ideas

which will appeal to their customers if translated into imaginative detailed designs;
- Discussions with the major retailers indicate that they expect demand to be high next season;
- The company's relationship with its factor is good and they do not expect any difficulties in selling their debtors in the future;
- The company anticipates no major capital expenditures in the next twelve months. Most of the machinery is less than five years old and in any event is financed by lease arrangements rather than by purchase; and
- The company has recently renewed its arrangements with its bankers for a further year.

The auditor concludes that the directors have paid particular attention to the period ending one year after their approval of the financial statements.

The auditor's options when the auditor concludes that the directors have not paid particular attention to the period ending one year after the approval of the financial statements

The two examples above illustrate that the auditor may conclude that the directors have paid particular attention, to the period ending one year after the approval of the financial statements, even though they have not prepared cash flow forecasts for that period.

The auditor may conclude in slightly different situations that the directors have not paid particular attention to the period ending one year after the approval of the financial statements. If this is the case the auditor needs to consider the impact on the auditor's report which may be either:

(a) The auditor may conclude that there is a significant level of concern about the entity's ability to continue as a going concern (but the auditor does not disagree with the use of the going concern basis). In which case the directors include a note to the financial statements and the auditor includes an emphasis of matter paragraph when setting out the basis of their opinion (in accordance with paragraph 33 of the ISA (UK and Ireland)); or, less probably;

(b) The auditor may conclude that the directors have not paid particular attention to the period ending one year from the date of approval of the financial statements but there is no significant level of concern. Then if the directors:
 (i) Refer to the period paid particular attention to, in the annual report, the auditor need not refer to the period in the basis of opinion (in accordance with paragraph 31-5 of the ISA (UK and Ireland)); however
 (ii) If the directors do not refer to the period paid particular attention to, the auditor would do so in the auditor's report in accordance with paragraph 31-4 of the ISA (UK and Ireland)[10]; or

(c) The auditor may conclude that the directors have not taken adequate steps to satisfy themselves that it is appropriate to adopt the going concern basis. Accordingly, there is a limitation of scope which gives rise to a qualified auditor's report (in accordance with paragraph 31-6 of the ISA (UK and Ireland)).

---

[10] *If the non-disclosure in the financial statements of the period paid particular attention to is a departure from the requirements of the applicable financial reporting framework, the auditor would give a qualified opinion ("except for").*

[580]
Management representations

(Issued December 2004)

Contents

	Paragraphs
Introduction	1 - 2-1
Acknowledgment by Management of its Responsibility for the Financial Statements	3 - 3-3
Representations by Management as Audit Evidence	4 - 9-1
Documentation of Representations by Management	10 - 14-1
Action if Management Refuses to Provide Representations	15
Effective Date	15-1

Appendix: Example of a Management Representation Letter

Appendix 2: Specific Management Representations the Auditor is Required by Other ISAs (UK and Ireland) to Obtain

---

International Standard on Auditing (UK and Ireland) (ISA (UK and Ireland)) 580 "Management Representations" should be read in the context of the Auditing Practices Board's Statement "The Auditing Practices Board – Scope and Authority of Pronouncements (Revised)" which sets out the application and authority of ISAs (UK and Ireland).

Introduction

1   The purpose of this International Standard on Auditing (UK and Ireland) (ISA (UK and Ireland)) is to establish standards and provide guidance on the use of management representations as audit evidence, the procedures to be applied in evaluating and documenting management representations and the action to be taken if management refuses to provide appropriate representations.

1-1 This ISA (UK and Ireland) uses the terms 'those charged with governance' and 'management'. The term 'governance' describes the role of persons entrusted with the supervision, control and direction of an entity. Ordinarily, those charged with governance are accountable for ensuring that the entity achieves its objectives, and for the quality of its financial reporting and reporting to interested parties. Those charged with governance include management only when they perform such functions.

1-2 In the UK and Ireland, those charged with governance include the directors (executive and non-executive) of a company or other body, the members of an audit committee where one exists, the partners, proprietors, committee of management or trustees of other forms of entity, or equivalent persons responsible for directing the entity's affairs and preparing its financial statements.

1-3 'Management' comprises officers those persons who perform senior managerial functions.

1-4 In the UK and Ireland, depending on the nature and circumstances of the entity, management may include some or all of those charged with governance (e.g. executive directors). Management will not normally include non-executive directors.

2   **The auditor should obtain appropriate representations from management.**

2-1 **Written confirmation of appropriate representations from management, as required by paragraph 4 below, should be obtained before the audit report is issued.**

Acknowledgment by Management of its Responsibility for the Financial Statements

3   The auditor should obtain audit evidence that management[1a] acknowledges its responsibility for the fair presentation of the financial statements in accordance with the applicable financial reporting framework, and has approved the financial statements. The auditor can obtain audit evidence of management's acknowledgment of such responsibility and approval from relevant minutes of meetings of those charged with governance or by obtaining a written representation from management or a signed copy of the financial statements.

[1a] *In the UK and Ireland, those charged with governance are responsible for the preparation of the financial statements.*

In the UK and Ireland, the auditor should obtain evidence that those charged with governance acknowledge their collective responsibility for the preparation of the financial statements and have approved the financial statements.   3-1

In the UK and Ireland, the directors of a company have a legal collective responsibility to prepare company and, where appropriate, group financial statements that give a true and fair view.   3-2

When the auditor has responsibility for reporting on the financial statements of a group of companies, acknowledgement by the directors of their responsibility for the financial statements applies to both the group financial statements and the financial statements of the parent undertaking.   3-3

Representations by Management as Audit Evidence

The auditor should obtain written representations from management on matters material to the financial statements when other sufficient appropriate audit evidence cannot reasonably be expected to exist. The possibility of misunderstandings between the auditor and management is reduced when oral representations are confirmed by management in writing. Matters which might be included in a letter from management or in a confirmatory letter to management are contained in the example of a management representation letter in the Appendix to this ISA (UK and Ireland).[1b]   4

It is advisable for the auditor to discuss the relevant matters with those responsible for giving written representations before they sign them to ensure that they understand what it is that they are being asked to confirm.   4-1

Written representations requested from management may be limited to matters that are considered either individually or collectively material to the financial statements. Regarding certain items it may be necessary to inform management of the auditor's understanding of materiality.   5

The auditor should obtain written representations from management that: 5.a

(a) **It acknowledges its responsibility for the design and implementation of internal control to prevent and detect error; and**
(b) **It believes the effects of those uncorrected financial statements misstatements aggregated by the auditor during the audit are immaterial, both individually and in the aggregate, to the financial statements taken as a whole. A summary of such items should be included in or attached to the written representations.**

During the course of an audit, management makes many representations to the auditor, either unsolicited or in response to specific inquiries. When such representations relate to matters which are material to the financial statements, the auditor will need to: 6

(a) Seek corroborative audit evidence from sources inside or outside the entity;
(b) Evaluate whether the representations made by management appear reasonable and consistent with other audit evidence obtained, including other representations; and

---

[1b] The example letter does not include all management representations that ISAs (UK and Ireland) require the auditor to obtain. Appendix 2 gives a summary of the management representations the auditor is required by other ISAs (UK and Ireland) to obtain as at 15 December 2004.

(c) Consider whether the individuals making the representations can be expected to be well informed on the particular matters.

7   Representations by management cannot be a substitute for other audit evidence that the auditor could reasonably expect to be available. For example, a representation by management as to the cost of an asset is not a substitute for the audit evidence of such cost that an auditor would ordinarily expect to obtain. If the auditor is unable to obtain sufficient appropriate audit evidence regarding a matter which has, or may have, a material effect on the financial statements and such audit evidence is expected to be available, this will constitute a limitation in the scope of the audit, even if a representation from management has been received on the matter.

8   In certain instances, audit evidence other than that obtained by performing inquiry may not be reasonably expected to be available; therefore the auditor obtains a written representation by management. For example, the auditor may not be able to obtain other audit evidence to corroborate management's intention to hold a specific investment for long-term appreciation.

8-1 In some exceptional cases, the matter may be of such significance the auditor refers to the representations in the auditor's report as being relevant to an understanding of the basis of the audit opinion.

8-2 When the auditor has responsibility for reporting on group financial statements, where appropriate the auditor obtains written confirmation of representations relating to specific matters regarding both the group financial statements and the financial statements of the parent undertaking. The means by which the auditor obtains these representations depends on the group's methods of delegation of management control and authority. The auditor may be able to obtain the required representations regarding the group financial statements from the management of the parent undertaking because of the level of their involvement in the management of the group. Alternatively, the auditor may obtain certain representations regarding matters material to the group financial statements directly from the management of the subsidiary undertakings, or by seeing relevant representations by management to the auditors of those subsidiary undertakings, in addition to those obtained from the management of the parent undertaking.

9   **If a representation by management is contradicted by other audit evidence, the auditor should investigate the circumstances and, when necessary, reconsider the reliability of other representations made by management.**

9-1 The investigation of apparently contradictory audit evidence regarding a representation received usually begins with further enquiries of management, to ascertain whether the representation has been misunderstood or whether the other audit evidence has been misinterpreted, followed by corroboration of management's responses. If management is unable to provide an explanation or if the explanation is not considered adequate, further audit procedures may be required to resolve the matter.

Documentation of Representations by Management

The auditor would ordinarily include in audit working papers evidence of management's representations in the form of a summary of oral discussions with management or written representations from management. **10**

A written representation is ordinarily more reliable audit evidence than an oral representation and can take the form of: **11**

(a) A representation letter from management;
(b) A letter from the auditor outlining the auditor's understanding of management's representations, duly acknowledged and confirmed by management; or
(c) Relevant minutes of meetings of the board of directors or similar body or a signed copy of the financial statements.

> A signed copy of the financial statements for a company may be sufficient evidence of the directors' acknowledgement of their collective responsibility for the preparation of the financial statements where it incorporates a statement to that effect. A signed copy of the financial statements, however, is not, by itself, sufficient appropriate evidence to confirm other representations given to the auditor as it does not, ordinarily, clearly identify and explain the specific separate representations. **11-1**

Basic Elements of a Management Representation Letter

When requesting a management representation letter, the auditor would request that it be addressed to the auditor, contain specified information and be appropriately dated and signed. **12**

A management representation letter would ordinarily be dated the same date as the auditor's report. However, in certain circumstances, a separate representation letter regarding specific transactions or other events may also be obtained during the course of the audit or at a date after the date of the auditor's report, for example, on the date of a public offering. **13**

> Written representations required as audit evidence are obtained before the audit report is issued. **13-1**

A management representation letter would ordinarily be signed by the members of management who have primary responsibility for the entity and its financial aspects (ordinarily the senior executive officer and the senior financial officer) based on the best of their knowledge and belief. In certain circumstances, the auditor may wish to obtain representation letters from other members of management. For example, the auditor may wish to obtain a written representation about the completeness of all minutes of the meetings of shareholders, the board of directors and important committees from the individual responsible for keeping such minutes. **14**

> In the UK and Ireland, it is usually appropriate for the auditor to request that the management representation letter be discussed and agreed by those charged with governance and signed on their behalf by the chairman and secretary, before they approve the financial statements, to ensure that all those charged with governance are aware of the representations on which the auditor intends to rely in expressing the auditor's opinion on those financial statements. For the audit of statutory **14-1**

financial statements, the auditor may also wish to consider whether to take the opportunity to remind the directors that it is an offence to mislead the auditor (UK: Section 389A of the Companies Act 1985; Ireland: Section 197(i), Companies Act, 1990).

Action if Management Refuses to Provide Representations

15   **If management refuses to provide a representation that the auditor considers necessary, this constitutes a scope limitation and the auditor should express a qualified opinion or a disclaimer of opinion.** In such circumstances, the auditor would evaluate any reliance placed on other representations made by management during the course of the audit and consider if the other implications of the refusal may have any additional effect on the auditor's report.

Effective Date

15-1   This ISA (UK and Ireland) is effective for audits of financial statements for periods commencing on or after 15 December 2004.

Appendix

This example letter does not include all representations that ISAs (UK and Ireland) require the auditor to obtain. A summary of such representations as at 15 December 2004 is included in Appendix 2. Additionally, in the UK and Ireland representations from those charged with governance would include acknowledgment of any responsibilities they may have in law in relation to the preparation of financial statements and providing information to the auditor. An example of such a representation for directors of a UK company incorporated under the Companies Act 1985 is:

> "We acknowledge as directors our responsibilities under the Companies Act 1985 for preparing financial statements which give a true and fair view and for making accurate representations to you. All the accounting records have been made available to you for the purpose of your audit and all the transactions undertaken by the company have been properly reflected and recorded in the accounting records. All other records and related information, including minutes of all management and shareholders meetings, have been made available to you."

In the Republic of Ireland reference would be made to the Companies Acts 1963 – 2003.

Example of a Management Representation Letter

The following letter is not intended to be a standard letter. Representations by management will vary from one entity to another and from one period to the next.

Although seeking representations from management on a variety of matters may serve to focus management's attention on those matters, and thus cause management to specifically address those matters in more detail than would otherwise be the case, the auditor needs to be cognizant of the limitations of management representations as audit evidence as set out in this ISA (UK and Ireland).

(Entity Letterhead)

(To Auditor) (Date)

This representation letter is provided in connection with your audit of the financial statements of ABC Company for the year ended December 31, 19X1 for the purpose of expressing an opinion as to whether the financial statements give a true and fair view of (present fairly, in all material respects,) the financial position of ABC Company as of December 31, 19X1 and of the results of its operations and its cash flows for the year then ended in accordance with (indicate applicable financial reporting framework).

We acknowledge our responsibility for the fair presentation of the financial statements in accordance with (indicate applicable financial reporting framework).[1]

We confirm, to the best of our knowledge and belief, the following representations:

Include here representations relevant to the entity. Such representations may include:

- There have been no irregularities involving management or employees who have a significant role in internal control or that could have a material effect on the financial statements.
- We have made available to you all books of account and supporting documentation and all minutes of meetings of shareholders and the board of directors (namely those held on March 15, 19X1 and September 30, 19X1, respectively).
- We confirm the completeness of the information provided regarding the identification of related parties.
- The financial statements are free of material misstatements, including omissions.
- The Company has complied with all aspects of contractual agreements that could have a material effect on the financial statements in the event of noncompliance. There has been no noncompliance with requirements of regulatory authorities that could have a material effect on the financial statements in the event of noncompliance.
- The following have been properly recorded and when appropriate, adequately disclosed in the financial statements:
  (a) The identity of, and balances and transactions with, related parties.
  (b) Losses arising from sale and purchase commitments.
  (c) Agreements and options to buy back assets previously sold.
  (d) Assets pledged as collateral.
- We have no plans or intentions that may materially alter the carrying value or classification of assets and liabilities reflected in the financial statements.
- We have no plans to abandon lines of product or other plans or intentions that will result in any excess or obsolete inventory, and no inventory is stated at an amount in excess of net realizable value.
- The Company has satisfactory title to all assets and there are no liens or encumbrances on the company's assets, except for those that are disclosed in Note X to the financial statements.
- We have recorded or disclosed, as appropriate, all liabilities, both actual and contingent, and have disclosed in Note X to the financial statements all guarantees that we have given to third parties.

[1] If required add "On behalf of the board of directors (or similar body)."

- Other than ... described in Note X to the financial statements, there have been no events subsequent to period end which require adjustment of or disclosure in the financial statements or Notes thereto.
- The ... claim by XYZ Company has been settled for the total sum of XXX which has been properly accrued in the financial statements. No other claims in connection with litigation have been or are expected to be received.
- There are no formal or informal compensating balance arrangements with any of our cash and investment accounts. Except as disclosed in Note X to the financial statements, we have no other line of credit arrangements.
- We have properly recorded or disclosed in the financial statements the capital stock repurchase options and agreements, and capital stock reserved for options, warrants, conversions and other requirements.

(Senior Executive Officer)

(Senior Financial Officer)

5   Accordingly, directors cannot assume that preparing the financial statements on the going concern basis and in accordance with the other provisions of the Act will necessarily result in the financial statements giving a true and fair view. Whilst, in general, compliance with accounting standards is also necessary to meet the requirement to prepare financial statements giving a true and fair view, such compliance is not of itself sufficient to ensure that a true and fair view is given in all cases.

Accounting Standards and the Definition of 'Going Concern'

6   FRS 18 states that "The information provided by financial statements is usually most relevant if prepared on the hypothesis that the entity is able to continue in existence for the foreseeable future. This hypothesis is commonly referred to as the going concern assumption."

7   FRS 18 requires that:

"An entity should prepare its financial statements on a going concern basis, unless

(a) the entity is being liquidated or has ceased trading, or
(b) the directors have no realistic alternative but to liquidate the entity or to cease trading,

in which circumstances the entity may, if appropriate, prepare its financial statements on a basis other than that of going concern."

8   FRS 18 also requires that "When preparing financial statements, directors should assess whether there are significant doubts about an entity's ability to continue as a going concern." and, in relation to that assessment, the following information should be disclosed in the financial statements:

"(a) any material uncertainties of which the directors are aware in making their assessment, related to events or conditions that may cast significant doubt upon the entity's ability to continue as a going concern.
(b) where the foreseeable future considered by the directors has been limited to a period of less than one year from the date of approval of the financial statements, that fact.
(c) when the financial statements are not prepared on a going concern basis, that fact, together with the basis on which the financial statements are prepared and the reason why the entity is not regarded as a going concern."

9   The requirements of IAS 1 are consistent with those of FRS 18 with the exception that, if the foreseeable future considered by the directors has been limited to a period of less than one year from the date of approval of the financial statements, IAS 1 does not require disclosure of that fact. IAS 1 states that "In assessing whether the going concern assumption is appropriate, management takes into account all available information about the future, which is at least, but not limited to, twelve months from the balance sheet date.

corporatize and privatize government entities, going concern issues will become increasingly relevant to the public sector.

Appendix 1 – Preparation of the Financial Statements: Note on Legal and Professional Requirements

Company Law and Accounting Standards

The UK Companies Act 1985 specifies certain accounting principles which should normally be adopted in preparing the financial statements of a company. One of these principles is that:

'the company shall be presumed to be carrying on business as a going concern' (paragraph 10 of Schedule 4 to the Act).[7]

However such a presumption is not conclusive and may be disregarded if the facts of the particular situation so require. The term 'going concern' is not defined in the Act but, as discussed below, is explained in International Accounting Standard (IAS) 1 'Presentation of Financial Statements' and Financial Reporting Standard (FRS) 18 'Accounting Policies'.

Paragraph 15 of Schedule 4 to the UK Companies Act 1985 states that departures from the Act's accounting principles *may* be made if it appears to the directors that there are 'special reasons' for doing so.[8] The financial statements must disclose any such departure, the reasons for it and its effect. 'Special reasons' would include circumstances where the directors conclude, on the basis of the facts as they appear to them, that it is appropriate to depart from the going concern presumption.

Furthermore, in addition to that particular provision of the UK Companies Act 1985, section 226 of the Act contains an overriding requirement for directors to prepare financial statements which give a true and fair view of the state of affairs of the company as at the end of the financial year and of its profit or loss for the financial year[9].

If compliance with the provisions of the Act would not be *sufficient* to give a true and fair view, the Act requires the directors to give the necessary additional information in the financial statements. If, in 'special circumstances', compliance with the provisions of the Act is *inconsistent* with the requirement to give a true and fair view, the Act requires the directors to depart from the particular provision to the extent necessary to give a true and fair view. The financial statements must disclose the particulars of any such departure, the reasons for it and its effect.

---

[7] *In the Republic of Ireland the equivalent is Section 5(a), Companies (Amendment) Act, 1986.*

[8] *In the Republic of Ireland the equivalent is Section 6, Companies (Amendment) Act 1986.*

[9] *In the Republic of Ireland the equivalent is Section 3(b), Companies (Amendment) Act 1986.*

Appendix 2

Specific Management Representations the Auditor is Required by Other ISAs (UK and Ireland) to Obtain

This appendix sets out the specific management representations required by ISAs (UK and Ireland) in issue at 15 December 2004. It is not a comprehensive list of the only representations that the auditor needs to obtain. As stated in paragraph 4 of this ISA (UK and Ireland), the auditor should obtain written representations from management on matters material to the financial statements when other sufficient appropriate audit evidence cannot reasonably be expected to exist. Also, as stated in paragraph 14-1, in the UK and Ireland, it is usually appropriate for the auditor to request that the management representation letter be discussed and agreed by those charged with governance and signed on their behalf by the chairman and secretary, before they approve the financial statements, to ensure that all those charged with governance are aware of the representations on which the auditor intends to rely in expressing the auditor's opinion on those financial statements.

240 - THE AUDITOR'S RESPONSIBILITY TO CONSIDER FRAUD IN AN AUDIT OF FINANCIAL STATEMENTS

The auditor should obtain written representations from management[2] that:

(a) It acknowledges its responsibility for the design and implementation of internal control to prevent and detect fraud;
(b) It has disclosed to the auditor the results of its assessment of the risk that the financial statements may be materially misstated as a result of fraud;
(c) It has disclosed to the auditor its knowledge of fraud or suspected fraud affecting the entity involving:
 (i) Management[3];
 (ii) Employees who have significant roles in internal control; or
 (iii) Others where the fraud could have a material effect on the financial statements; and
(d) It has disclosed to the auditor its knowledge of any allegations of fraud, or suspected fraud, affecting the entity's financial statements communicated by employees, former employees, analysts, regulators or others.

250 SECTION A - CONSIDERATION OF LAWS AND REGULATIONS IN AN AUDIT OF FINANCIAL STATEMENTS

The auditor should obtain written representations that management[4] has disclosed to the auditor all known actual or possible noncompliance with laws and regulations whose effects should be considered when preparing financial statements.

---

[2] In the UK and Ireland the auditor obtains written representations from those charged with governance.

[3] In the UK and Ireland, and those charged with governance.

[4] In the UK and Ireland the auditor obtains this written representation from those charged with governance.

23-1	Where applicable, the written representations should include the actual or contingent consequences which may arise from the non-compliance.

260 - COMMUNICATION OF AUDIT MATTERS WITH THOSE CHARGED WITH GOVERNANCE

11-19	The auditor should seek to obtain a written representation from those charged with governance that explains their reasons for not correcting misstatements brought to their attention by the auditor.

545 - AUDITING FAIR VALUE MEASUREMENTS AND DISCLOSURES

63	The auditor should obtain written representations from management regarding the reasonableness of significant assumptions, including whether they appropriately reflect management's intent and ability to carry out specific courses of action on behalf of the entity where relevant to the fair value measurements or disclosures.

550 - RELATED PARTIES

15/115	The auditor should obtain a written representation from management[5] concerning: (a) The completeness of information provided regarding the identification of related parties; and (b) The adequacy of related party disclosures in the financial statements.

570 - GOING CONCERN

26	When events or conditions have been identified which may cast significant doubt on the entity's ability to continue as a going concern, the auditor should: .... (c) Seek written representations from management[6] regarding its plans for future action.
26-1	The auditor should consider the need to obtain written confirmations of representations from those charged with governance regarding: (a) The assessment of those charged with governance that the company is a going concern; (b) Any relevant disclosures in the financial statements.

---

[5] In the UK and Ireland the auditor obtains written representations from those charged with governance.

[6] In the UK and Ireland the auditor obtains written representations from those charged with governance.

600 (Revised)*
Using the work of another auditor

(Issued April 2008)

Contents

	Paragraph
Introduction	1 - 5-4
Acceptance as Principal Auditor	6
The Principal Auditor's Procedures	7 – 14-1
Cooperation Between Auditors	15 - 15-5
Reporting Considerations	16 - 17-1
Division of Responsibility	18 - 18-1
Effective Date	18-2
Appendix: Statutory Framework	

International Standard on Auditing (UK and Ireland) (ISA (UK and Ireland)) 600 "Using the Work of Another Auditor" should be read in the context of the Auditing Practices Board's Statement "The Auditing Practices Board - Scope and Authority of Pronouncements (Revised)" which sets out the application and authority of ISAs (UK and Ireland).

---

* *This revision was issued in April 2008 and introduces a new requirement in paragraph 14-1 which is applicable for audits of financial statements for periods commencing on or after 6 April 2008. Footnote 1 to paragraph 15-1 was also added and the summary in the Appendix of the statutory framework updated for the Companies Act 2006.*

Introduction

1   The purpose of this International Standard on Auditing (UK and Ireland) (ISA (UK and Ireland)) is to establish standards and provide guidance when an auditor, reporting on the financial statements of an entity, uses the work of another auditor on the financial information of one or more components included in the financial statements of the entity. This ISA (UK and Ireland) does not deal with those instances where two or more auditors are appointed as joint auditors nor does it deal with the auditor's relationship with a predecessor auditor. Further, when the principal auditor concludes that the financial statements of a component are immaterial, the standards in this ISA (UK and Ireland) do not apply. When, however, several components, immaterial in themselves, are together material, the procedures outlined in this ISA (UK and Ireland) would need to be considered.

1-1   The statutory requirements relating to companies incorporated in the UK and Ireland for other auditors to co-operate with principal auditors are explained in more detail in paragraphs 15-1 to 15-5 below and in the attached Appendix. In certain parts of the public sector where the responsibilities of principal and other auditors are governed by statutory provisions, these override the provisions of this ISA (UK and Ireland). This ISA (UK and Ireland) does not deal with those instances where two or more auditors are appointed as joint auditors nor does it deal with the auditor's relationship with predecessor auditors.

2   **When the principal auditor uses the work of another auditor, the principal auditor should determine how the work of the other auditor will affect the audit.**

3   "Principal auditor" means the auditor with responsibility for reporting on the financial statements of an entity when those financial statements include financial information of one or more components audited by another auditor.

4   "Other auditor" means an auditor, other than the principal auditor, with responsibility for reporting on the financial information of a component which is included in the financial statements audited by the principal auditor. Other auditors include affiliated firms, whether using the same name or not, and correspondents, as well as unrelated auditors.

5   "Component" means a division, branch, subsidiary, joint venture, associated company or other entity whose financial information is included in financial statements audited by the principal auditor

5-1   This ISA (UK and Ireland) uses the terms 'those charged with governance' and 'management'. The term 'governance' describes the role of persons entrusted with the supervision, control and direction of an entity. Ordinarily, those charged with governance are accountable for ensuring that the entity achieves its objectives, and for the quality of its financial reporting and reporting to interested parties. Those charged with governance include management only when they perform such functions.

5-2   In the UK and Ireland, those charged with governance include the directors (executive and non-executive) of a company or other body, the members of an audit committee where one exists, the partners, proprietors, committee of management or trustees of other forms of entity, or equivalent persons responsible for directing the entity's affairs and preparing its financial statements.

'Management' comprises those persons who perform senior managerial functions. 5-3

In the UK and Ireland, depending on the nature and circumstances of the entity, management may include some or all of those charged with governance (e.g. executive directors). Management will not normally include non-executive directors. 5-4

Acceptance as Principal Auditor

The auditor should consider whether the auditor's own participation is sufficient to be able to act as the principal auditor. For this purpose the principal auditor would consider: 6

(a) The materiality of the portion of the financial statements which the principal auditor audits;
(b) The principal auditor's degree of knowledge regarding the business of the components;
(c) The risk of material misstatements in the financial statements of the components audited by the other auditor; and
(d) The performance of additional procedures as set out in this ISA (UK and Ireland) regarding the components audited by the other auditor resulting in the principal auditor having significant participation in such audit; and
(e) The nature of the principal auditor's relationship with the firm acting as other auditor.

The Principal Auditor's Procedures

When planning to use the work of another auditor, the principal auditor should consider the professional competence of the other auditor in the context of the specific assignment. Some of the sources of information for this consideration could be common membership of a professional organization, common membership of, or affiliation, with another firm or reference to the professional organization to which the other auditor belongs. These sources can be supplemented when appropriate by inquiries with other auditors, bankers, *etc.* and by discussions with the other auditor. 7

In the UK and Ireland, when planning to use the work of another auditor, the principal auditor's consideration of the professional competence of the other auditor should include consideration of the professional qualifications, experience and resources of the other auditor in the context of the specific assignment. 7-1

The principal auditor considers the standing of any firm with which the other auditor is affiliated and also considers making reference to the other auditor's professional organization. The principal auditor's assessment may be influenced by the review of the previous work of the other auditor. 7-2

The principal auditor should perform procedures to obtain sufficient appropriate audit evidence, that the work of the other auditor is adequate for the principal auditor's purposes, in the context of the specific assignment. 8

The principal auditor would advise the other auditor of: 9

(a) The independence requirements regarding both the entity and the component and obtain written representation as to compliance with them;
(b) The use that is to be made of the other auditor's work and report and make sufficient arrangements for the coordination of their efforts at the initial planning stage of the audit. The principal auditor would inform the other auditor of matters such as areas requiring special consideration, procedures for the identification of intercompany transactions that may require disclosure and the timetable for completion of the audit; and
(c) The accounting, auditing and reporting requirements and obtain written representation as to compliance with them.

10 The principal auditor might also, for example, discuss with the other auditor the audit procedures applied, review a written summary of the other auditor's procedures (which may be in the form of a questionnaire or checklist) or review working papers of the other auditor. The principal auditor may wish to perform these procedures during a visit to the other auditor. The nature, timing and extent of procedures will depend on the circumstances of the engagement and the principal auditor's knowledge of the professional competence of the other auditor. This knowledge may have been enhanced from the review of previous audit work of the other auditor.

11 The principal auditor may conclude that it is not necessary to apply procedures such as those described in paragraph 10 because sufficient appropriate audit evidence previously obtained that acceptable quality control policies and procedures are complied with in the conduct of the other auditor's practice. For example, when they are affiliated firms the principal auditor and the other auditor may have a continuing, formal relationship providing for procedures that give that audit evidence such as periodic inter-firm review, tests of operating policies and procedures and review of working papers of selected audits.

12 **The principal auditor should consider the significant findings of the other auditor.**

13 The principal auditor may consider it appropriate to discuss with the other auditor and the management of the component, the audit findings or other matters affecting the financial information of the component and may also decide that supplementary tests of the records or the financial information of the component are necessary. Such tests may, depending on the circumstances, be performed by the principal auditor or the other auditor.

13-1 In the UK and Ireland, the principal auditor may also consider it appropriate to discuss with those charged with governance of the component the audit findings or other matters affecting the financial information of the component. The principal auditor may consider it appropriate to request copies of reports to management or those charged with governance issued by the other auditor.

14 The principal auditor would document in the audit working papers the components whose financial information was audited by other auditors, their significance to the financial statements of the entity as a whole, the names of the other auditors and any conclusions reached that individual components are immaterial. The principal auditor would also document the procedures performed and the conclusions reached. For example, working papers of the other auditor that have been reviewed would be identified and the results of discussions with the other auditor would be recorded. However, the principal auditor need not document the reasons for limiting the procedures in the circumstances described in paragraph 11, provided those reasons

are summarized elsewhere in documentation maintained by the principal auditor's firm.

> In the UK and Ireland, the principal auditor should document any review that it undertakes, for the purpose of the group audit, of the audit work conducted by other auditors.

14-1

Cooperation Between Auditors

The other auditor, knowing the context in which the principal auditor will use the other auditor's work, should cooperate with the principal auditor. For example, the other auditor would bring to the principal auditor's attention any aspect of the other auditor's work that cannot be carried out as requested. Similarly, subject to legal and professional considerations, the other auditor will need to be advised of any matters that come to the attention of the principal auditor which may have an important bearing on the other auditor's work.

15

> In the UK and Ireland, the other auditor carries out the audit work in the knowledge that the financial information on which the other auditor reports is to be included within the financial statements which are reported on by the principal auditor. In many circumstances when the component is a subsidiary undertaking, there is a statutory obligation on the other auditor, and the component which the other auditor audits, to give the principal auditor such information and explanations as the principal auditor may reasonably require for the purpose of the principal auditor's audit. Where there is no statutory obligation on the other auditor and the principal auditor advises that the principal auditor intends to use the other auditor's work, the other auditor may require permission from the component to communicate with the principal auditor on matters pertaining to the component's audit. If the component refuses such permission, the other auditor brings this to the attention of the principal auditor so that the principal auditor can discuss and agree an appropriate course of action with those charged with governance of the entity which they audit.[1]

15-1

> If the other auditor identifies a matter which the other auditor considers likely to be relevant to the principal auditor's work, the other auditor may communicate directly with the principal auditor, providing consent is obtained by the component or there exists a statutory obligation, or it may require reference to the matter to be made within the other auditor's audit report.

15-2

> In the UK and Ireland the other auditor has sole responsibility for the other auditor's audit opinion on the financial statements of the component which the other auditor audits. Accordingly, the other auditor plans and executes the audit in a manner which enables the other auditor to report on the component without placing reliance on the principal auditor necessarily informing the other auditor of matters which have come to the principal auditor's attention and which may have an important bearing on the financial statements of the component. This may involve the other auditor seeking representations directly from the management or those charged with governance of the entity audited by the principal auditor.

15-3

---

[1] Schedule 10, paragraph 10A, to the Companies Act 2006 includes provisions relating to arrangements to enable Recognised Supervisory Bodies and other bodies involved in monitoring audits to have access to the audit documentation of certain other auditors involved in the group audit. These provisions are addressed in audit regulations not in ISAs (UK and Ireland).

15-4   In the UK and Ireland there is no obligation, statutory or otherwise, on the principal auditor to provide information to the other auditor. However, in undertaking the audit work the principal auditor may identify matters which the principal auditor considers to be relevant to the other auditor's work. In these circumstances, the principal auditor discusses and agrees an appropriate course of action with those charged with governance of the entity which they audit.

15-5   The course of action agreed with those charged with governance may involve the principal auditor communicating directly with the other auditor, or those charged with governance informing the component or the other auditor. However, there may be circumstances where sensitive commercial considerations dictate that information cannot be passed on to the component or the other auditor. In this event, the principal auditor is not required to take further action as to do so would be in breach of the principle of client confidentiality.

Reporting Considerations

16   When the principal auditor concludes that the work of the other auditor cannot be used and the principal auditor has not been able to perform sufficient additional procedures regarding the financial information of the component audited by the other auditor, the principal auditor should express a qualified opinion or disclaimer of opinion because there is a limitation in the scope of the audit.

17   If the other auditor issues, or intends to issue, a modified auditor's report, the principal auditor would consider whether the subject of the modification is of such a nature and significance, in relation to the financial statements of the entity on which the principal auditor is reporting, that a modification of the principal auditor's report is required.

17-1   When the principal auditor is satisfied that the work of the other auditors is adequate for the purposes of the audit, no reference to the other auditors is made in the principal auditor's report.

Division of Responsibility

18   While compliance with the guidance in the preceding paragraphs is considered desirable, the local regulations of some countries permit a principal auditor to base the audit opinion on the financial statements taken as a whole solely upon the report of another auditor regarding the audit of one or more components. **When the principal auditor does so, the principal auditor's report should state this fact clearly and should indicate the magnitude of the portion of the financial statements audited by the other auditor.** When the principal auditor makes such a reference in the auditor's report, audit procedures are ordinarily limited to those described in paragraphs 7 and 9.

18-1   In the UK and Ireland the principal auditor has sole responsibility for the principal auditor's audit opinion and a reference to the other auditor in the principal auditor's report may be misunderstood and interpreted as a qualification of the principal auditor's opinion or a division of responsibility, which is not acceptable.

Effective Date

This ISA (UK and Ireland) is effective for audits of financial statements for periods commencing on or after 15 December 2004. The requirement in paragraph 14-1 is effective for audits of financial statements for periods commencing on or after 6 April 2008.

18-2

Public Sector Perspective

Additional guidance for auditors of public sector bodies in the UK and Ireland is given in:

- Practice Note 10 "Audit of Financial Statements of Public Sector Entities in the United Kingdom (Revised)"
- Practice Note 10(I) "The Audit of Central Government Financial Statements in Ireland"

The basic principles in this ISA (UK and Ireland) apply to the audit of financial statements in the public sector, however, supplementary guidance on additional considerations when using the work of other auditors in the public sector is needed. For example, the principal auditor in the public sector has to ensure that, where legislation has prescribed compliance with a particular set of auditing standards, the other auditor has complied with those standards. In respect to public sector entities, the Public Sector Committee has supplemented the guidance included in this ISA (UK and Ireland) in its Study 4 "Using the Work of Other Auditors—A Public Sector Perspective."

1

Appendix

This Appendix provides a summary of the legal rights of parent company auditors to obtain information from subsidiary undertakings and the auditors of those undertakings. It is not intended to be an authoritative guide to all of the legal provisions relevant to auditors' rights to information. For complete guidance reference should be made to the relevant legislation.

Statutory Framework at 15 December 2004[2]

If a parent company and its subsidiary undertaking are companies incorporated in Great Britain, section 389A(3) of the Companies Act 1985 imposes a duty on the subsidiary undertaking and its auditors to 'give to the auditors of any parent company of the undertaking such information and explanations as they may reasonably require for the purposes of their duties as auditors of that company'. Similar obligations regarding companies incorporated in Northern Ireland and the Republic of Ireland are set out in Article 397A(3) of the Companies (Northern Ireland) Order 1986 and section 196(1) of the Companies Act 1990 respectively.

1

---

[2] *A revision of section 389A of the UK Companies Act 1985 came into effect in 2005 which strengthened the rights of auditors to obtain information and explanations from other parties as well as subsidiary undertakings and their auditors.*

2. Where a parent company is incorporated in Great Britain but its subsidiary undertaking is not, section 389A(4) of the Companies Act 1985 imposes a duty on the parent company, if required by its auditors to do so, to 'take all such steps as are reasonably open to it to obtain from the subsidiary undertaking such information and explanations as they may reasonably require for the purposes of their duties as auditors of that company'. Similar obligations on parent companies incorporated in Northern Ireland and the Republic of Ireland are set out in Article 397A(4) of the Companies (Northern Ireland) Order 1986 and section 196(2) of the Companies Act 1990 respectively.

Companies Act 2006

3. Under the UK Companies Act 2006, the auditor's rights to information are addressed in sections 499 and 500.

4. Section 499 addresses the auditor's general right to information and identifies persons the auditor of a company may require to "provide him with such information or explanations as he thinks necessary for the performance of his duties as auditor." These persons include:

   - any subsidiary undertaking of the company which is a body corporate incorporated in the United Kingdom; and
   - any officer, employee or auditor of any such subsidiary undertaking or any person holding or accountable for any books, accounts or vouchers of any such subsidiary undertaking,

   including any persons who fell in these categories at a time to which the information required by the auditor relates or relate.

5. Section 500 addresses the auditor's rights to information from overseas subsidiaries. It provides that where a parent company has a subsidiary undertaking that is not a body corporate incorporated in the United Kingdom, the auditor of the parent company may require it to "take all such steps as are reasonably open to it" to obtain such information or explanations from particular persons as the parent company auditor may reasonably require for the purposes of his duties as auditor. Those persons are:

   (a) the undertaking;
   (b) any officer, employee or auditor of the undertaking;
   (c) any person holding or accountable for any of the undertaking's books, accounts or vouchers;
   (d) any person who fell within paragraph (b) or (c) at a time to which the information or explanations relates or relate.

6. The rights to information provided for in sections 499 and 500 are subject to any restrictions imposed by rights to legal privilege.

[610]
Considering the work of internal audit

(Issued December 2004)

Contents

	Paragraphs
Introduction	1 - 4
Scope and Objectives of Internal Auditing	5
Relationship Between Internal Auditing and the External Auditor	6 - 8
Understanding and Assessment of Internal Auditing	9 - 13
Timing of Liaison and Coordination	14 - 15
Evaluating the Work of Internal Auditing	16 - 19-1
Effective Date	**19-2**

International Standard on Auditing (UK and Ireland) (ISA (UK and Ireland)) 610 "Considering the Work of Internal Audit" should be read in the context of the Auditing Practices Board's Statement "The Auditing Practices Board – Scope and Authority of Pronouncements (Revised)" which sets out the application and authority of ISAs (UK and Ireland).

Introduction

1   The purpose of this International Standard on Auditing (UK and Ireland) (ISA (UK and Ireland)) is to establish standards and provide guidance to external auditors in considering the work of internal auditing. This ISA (UK and Ireland) does not deal with instances when personnel from internal auditing assist the external auditor in carrying out external audit procedures. The audit procedures noted in this ISA (UK and Ireland) need only be applied to internal auditing activities which are relevant to the audit of the financial statements.

1-1   This ISA (UK and Ireland) uses the terms 'those charged with governance' and 'management'. The term 'governance' describes the role of persons entrusted with the supervision, control and direction of an entity. Ordinarily, those charged with governance are accountable for ensuring that the entity achieves its objectives, and for the quality of its financial reporting, and reporting to interested parties. Those charged with governance include management only when they perform such functions.

1-2   In the UK and Ireland, those charged with governance include the directors (executive and non-executive) of a company or other body, the members of an audit committee where one exists, the partners, proprietors, committee of management or trustees of other forms of entity, or equivalent persons responsible for directing the entity's affairs and preparing its financial statements.

1-3   'Management' comprises those persons who perform senior managerial functions.

1-4   In the UK and Ireland, depending on the nature and circumstances of the entity, management may include some or all of those charged with governance (e.g. executive directors). Management will not normally include non-executive directors.

2   **The external auditor should consider the activities of internal auditing and their effect, if any, on external audit procedures.**

3   "Internal auditing" means an appraisal activity established within an entity as a service to the entity. Its functions include, amongst other things, monitoring internal control.

4   While the external auditor has sole responsibility for the audit opinion expressed and for determining the nature, timing and extent of external audit procedures, certain parts of internal auditing work may be useful to the external auditor.

Scope and Objectives of Internal Auditing

5   The scope and objectives of internal auditing vary widely and depend on the size and structure of the entity and the requirements of its management. Ordinarily, internal auditing activities include one or more of the following:

- Monitoring of internal control. The establishment of adequate internal control is a responsibility of management which demands proper attention on a continuous basis. Internal auditing is ordinarily assigned specific responsibility by management for reviewing controls, monitoring their operation and recommending improvements thereto.

- Examination of financial and operating information. This may include review of the means used to identify, measure, classify and report such information and specific inquiry into individual items including detailed testing of transactions, balances and procedures.
- Review of the economy, efficiency and effectiveness of operations including non-financial controls of an entity.
- Review of compliance with laws, regulations and other external requirements and with management policies and directives and other internal requirements.

- Special investigations into particular areas, for example, suspected fraud.

Relationship Between Internal Auditing and the External Auditor

The role of internal auditing is determined by management[1], and its objectives differ from those of the external auditor who is appointed to report independently on the financial statements. The internal audit function's objectives vary according to management's requirements[2]. The external auditor's primary concern is whether the financial statements are free of material misstatements.   6

Nevertheless some of the means of achieving their respective objectives are often similar and thus certain aspects of internal auditing may be useful in determining the nature, timing and extent of external audit procedures.   7

Internal auditing is part of the entity. Irrespective of the degree of autonomy and objectivity of internal auditing, it cannot achieve the same degree of independence as required of the external auditor when expressing an opinion on the financial statements. The external auditor has sole responsibility for the audit opinion expressed, and that responsibility is not reduced by any use made of internal auditing. All judgments relating to the audit of the financial statements are those of the external auditor.   8

Understanding and Preliminary Assessment of Internal Auditing

The external auditor should obtain a sufficient understanding of internal audit activities to identify and assess the risks of material misstatement of the financial statements and to design and perform further audit procedures.   9

Effective internal auditing will often allow a modification in the nature and timing, and a reduction in the extent of audit procedures performed by the external auditor but cannot eliminate them entirely. In some cases, however, having considered the activities of internal auditing, the external auditor may decide that internal auditing will have no effect on external audit procedures.   10

The effectiveness of internal auditing may be an important factor in the external auditor's evaluation of the control environment and assessment of audit risk.   10-1

The external auditor should perform an assessment of the internal audit function when internal auditing is relevant to the external auditor's risk assessment.   11

[1] *In the UK and Ireland those charged with governance, rather than management, are usually responsible for determining the role of internal auditing.*

[2] *For Listed Companies in the UK and Ireland, "The Combined Code on Corporate Governance" (FRC 2003) contains guidance to assist company boards in making suitable arrangements for their audit committees.*

12 The external auditor's preliminary assessment of the internal audit function will influence the external auditor's judgment about the use which may be made of internal auditing in making risk assessments and thereby modifying the nature, timing and extent of further external audit procedures.

13 When obtaining an understanding and performing an assessment of the internal audit function, the important criteria are:
   (a) Organizational Status: specific status of internal auditing in the entity and the effect this has on its ability to be objective. In the ideal situation, internal auditing will report to the highest level of management and be free of any other operating responsibility. Any constraints or restrictions placed on internal auditing by management would need to be carefully considered. In particular, the internal auditors will need to be free to communicate fully with the external auditor.
   (b) Scope of Function: the nature and extent of internal auditing assignments performed. The external auditor would also need to consider whether management acts on internal audit recommendations and how this is evidenced.
   (c) Technical Competence: whether internal auditing is performed by persons having adequate technical training and proficiency as internal auditors. The external auditor may, for example, review the policies for hiring and training the internal auditing staff and their experience and professional qualifications.
   (d) Due Professional Care: whether internal auditing is properly planned, supervised, reviewed and documented. The existence of adequate audit manuals, work programs and working papers would be considered.

Timing of Liaison and Coordination

14 When planning to use the work of internal auditing, the external auditor will need to consider internal auditing's tentative plan for the period and discuss it at as early a stage as possible. Where the work of internal auditing is to be a factor in determining the nature, timing and extent of the external auditor's procedures, it is desirable to agree in advance the timing of such work, the extent of audit coverage, materiality levels and proposed methods of sample selection, documentation of the work performed and review and reporting procedures.

15 Liaison with internal auditing is more effective when meetings are held at appropriate intervals during the period. The external auditor would need to be advised of and have access to relevant internal auditing reports and be kept informed of any significant matter that comes to the internal auditor's attention which may affect the work of the external auditor. Similarly, the external auditor would ordinarily inform the internal auditor of any significant matters which may affect internal auditing.

Evaluating the Work of Internal Auditing

16 **When the external auditor intends to use specific work of internal auditing, the external auditor should evaluate and perform audit procedures on that work to confirm its adequacy for the external auditor's purposes.**

17 The evaluation of specific work of internal auditing involves consideration of the adequacy of the scope of work and related programs and whether the assessment of the internal auditing remains appropriate. This evaluation may include consideration of whether:

(a) The work is performed by persons having adequate technical training and proficiency as internal auditors and the work of assistants is properly supervised, reviewed and documented;
(b) Sufficient appropriate audit evidence is obtained to be able to draw reasonable conclusions;
(c) Conclusions reached are appropriate in the circumstances and any reports prepared are consistent with the results of the work performed; and
(d) Any exceptions or unusual matters disclosed by internal auditing are properly resolved.

The nature, timing and extent of the audit procedures performed on the specific work of internal auditing will depend on the external auditor's judgment as to the risk of material misstatement of the area concerned, the assessment of internal auditing and the evaluation of the specific work by internal auditing. Such audit procedures may include examination of items already examined by internal auditing, examination of other similar items and observation of internal auditing procedures. 18

In the event that the external auditor concludes that the work of internal auditing is not adequate for the external auditor's purposes, the external auditor extends the audit procedures beyond those originally planned to ensure that sufficient appropriate audit evidence is obtained to support the conclusions reached. 18-1

The external auditor would record conclusions regarding the specific internal auditing work that has been evaluated and the audit procedures performed on the internal auditor's work. 19

The auditor considers whether amendments to the external audit program are required as a result of matters identified by internal auditing. 19-1

Effective Date

This ISA (UK and Ireland) is effective for audits of financial statements for periods commencing on or after 15 December 2004. 19-2

Public Sector Perspective

Additional guidance for auditors of public sector bodies in the UK and Ireland is given in:

- Practice Note 10 "Audit of Financial Statements of Public Sector Entities in the United Kingdom (Revised)"
- Practice Note 10(I) "The Audit of Central Government Financial Statements in Ireland"

The basic principles in this ISA (UK and Ireland) apply to the audit of financial statements in the public sector. Supplementary guidance on additional considerations, when considering the work of internal auditing in the public sector is provided in the Public Sector Committee's Study 4 "Using the Work of Other Auditors – A Public Sector Perspective."[1] 1

[620]
Using the work of an expert

(Issued December 2004)

Contents

	Paragraphs
Introduction	1 - 5-2
Determining the Need to Use the Work of an Expert	6 - 7
Competence and Objectivity of the Expert	8 - 10-1
Scope of the Expert's Work	11
Evaluating the Work of the Expert	12 - 15
Reference to an Expert in the Auditor's Report	16 - 17
Effective Date	**17-1**

International Standard on Auditing (UK and Ireland) (ISA (UK and Ireland)) 620 "Using the Work of an Expert" should be read in the context of the Auditing Practices Board's Statement "The Auditing Practices Board – Scope and Authority of Pronouncements (Revised)" which sets out the application and authority of ISAs (UK and Ireland).

Introduction

The purpose of this International Standard on Auditing (UK and Ireland) (ISA (UK and Ireland)) is to establish standards and provide guidance on using the work of an expert as audit evidence.   **1**

> This ISA (UK and Ireland) uses the terms 'those charged with governance' and 'management'. The term 'governance' describes the role of persons entrusted with the supervision, control and direction of an entity. Ordinarily, those charged with governance are accountable for ensuring that the entity achieves its objectives, and for the quality of its financial reporting, and reporting to interested parties. Those charged with governance include management only when they perform such functions.   **1-1**
>
> In the UK and Ireland, those charged with governance include the directors (executive and non-executive) of a company or other body, the members of an audit committee where one exists, the partners, proprietors, committee of management or trustees of other forms of entity, or equivalent persons responsible for directing the entity's affairs and preparing its financial statements.   **1-2**
>
> 'Management' comprises those persons who perform senior managerial functions.   **1-3**
>
> In the UK and Ireland, depending on the nature and circumstances of the entity, management may include some or all of those charged with governance (e.g. executive directors). Management will not normally include non-executive directors.   **1-4**

When using the work performed by an expert, the auditor should obtain sufficient appropriate audit evidence that such work is adequate for the purposes of the audit.   **2**

"Expert" means a person or firm possessing special skill, knowledge and experience in a particular field other than accounting and auditing.   **3**

The auditor's education and experience enable the auditor to be knowledgeable about business matters in general, but the auditor is not expected to have the expertise of a person trained for or qualified to engage in the practice of another profession or occupation, such as an actuary or engineer.   **4**

An expert may be: **5**

(a) Contracted by the entity;
(b) Contracted by the auditor;
(c) Employed by the entity; or
(d) Employed by the auditor.

When the auditor uses the work of an expert employed by the audit firm, the auditor will be able to rely on the firm's systems for recruitment and training that determine that expert's capabilities and competence, as explained in ISA (UK and Ireland) 220, "Quality Control for Audits of Historical Financial Information" instead of needing to evaluate them for each audit engagement.

> If the auditor determines that it is appropriate to seek to use the work of an expert, the auditor considers whether an appropriate expert is already employed by the auditor or the entity. If neither the auditor or the entity employ an   **5-1**

appropriate expert, the auditor considers asking those charged with governance to engage an appropriate expert subject to the auditor being satisfied as to the expert's competence and objectivity (see paragraphs 8 to 10-1 below). If those charged with governance are unable or unwilling to engage an expert, the auditor may consider engaging an expert or whether sufficient appropriate audit evidence can be obtained from other sources. If unable to obtain sufficient appropriate audit evidence, the auditor considers the possible need to modify the auditor's report.

5-2   Although the auditor may use the work of an expert, the auditor has sole responsibility for the audit opinion.

Determining the Need to Use the Work of an Expert

6   In obtaining an understanding of the entity and performing further procedures in response to assessed risks, the auditor may need to obtain, in conjunction with the entity or independently, audit evidence in the form of reports, opinions, valuations and statements of an expert. Examples are:

- Valuations of certain types of assets, for example, land and buildings, plant and machinery, works of art, and precious stones.
- Determination of quantities or physical condition of assets, for example, minerals stored in stockpiles, underground mineral and petroleum reserves, and the remaining useful life of plant and machinery.
- Determination of amounts using specialized techniques or methods, for example, an actuarial valuation.
- The measurement of work completed and to be completed on contracts in progress.
- Legal opinions concerning interpretations of agreements, statutes and regulations.

7   When determining the need to use the work of an expert, the auditor would consider:

(a) The engagement team's knowledge and previous experience of the matter being considered;
(b) The risk of material misstatement based on the nature, complexity, and materiality of the matter being considered; and
(c) The quantity and quality of other audit evidence expected to be obtained.

Competence and Objectivity of the Expert

8   When planning to use the work of an expert, the auditor should evaluate the professional competence of the expert. This will involve considering the expert's:

(a) Professional certification or licensing by, or membership in, an appropriate professional body; and
(b) Experience and reputation in the field in which the auditor is seeking audit evidence.

8-1   In the UK and Ireland, when planning to use the work of an expert the auditor should assess the professional qualifications, experience and resources of the expert.

9   The auditor should evaluate the objectivity of the expert.

The risk that an expert's objectivity will be impaired increases when the expert is: 10
(a) Employed by the entity; or
(b) Related in some other manner to the entity, for example, by being financially dependent upon or having an investment in the entity.

If the auditor is concerned regarding the competence or objectivity of the expert, the auditor needs to discuss any reservations with management and consider whether sufficient appropriate audit evidence can be obtained concerning the work of an expert. The auditor may need to undertake additional audit procedures or seek audit evidence from another expert (after taking into account the factors in paragraph 7).

> If the auditor is unable to obtain sufficient appropriate audit evidence concerning the work of an expert, the auditor considers the possible need to modify the auditor's report.   10-1

Scope of the Expert's Work

The auditor should obtain sufficient appropriate audit evidence that the scope of the expert's work is adequate for the purposes of the audit. Audit evidence may be obtained through a review of the terms of reference which are often set out in written instructions from the entity to the expert. Such instructions to the expert may cover matters such as: 11

- The objectives and scope of the expert's work.
- A general outline as to the specific matters the auditor expects the expert's report to cover.
- The intended use by the auditor of the expert's work, including the possible communication to third parties of the expert's identity and extent of involvement.
- The extent of the expert's access to appropriate records and files.
- Clarification of the expert's relationship with the entity, if any.
- Confidentiality of the entity's information.
- Information regarding the assumptions and methods intended to be used by the expert and their consistency with those used in prior periods.

In the event that these matters are not clearly set out in written instructions to the expert, the auditor may need to communicate with the expert directly to obtain audit evidence in this regard. In obtaining an understanding of the entity, the auditor also considers whether to include the expert during the engagement team's discussion of the susceptibility of the entity's financial statements to material misstatement.

Evaluating the Work of the Expert

The auditor should evaluate the appropriateness of the expert's work as audit evidence regarding the assertion being considered. This will involve evaluation of whether the substance of the expert's findings is properly reflected in the financial statements or supports the assertions, and consideration of: 12

- Source data used.
- Assumptions and methods used and their consistency with prior periods.
- When the expert carried out the work.

- Results of the expert's work in the light of the auditor's overall knowledge of the business and of the results of other audit procedures.

13 When considering whether the expert has used source data which is appropriate in the circumstances, the auditor would consider the following procedures:

(a) Making inquiries regarding any procedures undertaken by the expert to establish whether the source data is relevant and reliable; and
(b) Reviewing or testing the data used by the expert.

14 The appropriateness and reasonableness of assumptions and methods used and their application are the responsibility of the expert. The auditor does not have the same expertise and, therefore, cannot always challenge the expert's assumptions and methods. However, the auditor will need to obtain an understanding of the assumptions and methods used and to consider whether they are appropriate and reasonable, based on the auditor's knowledge of the business and the results of other audit procedures.

15 **If the results of the expert's work do not provide sufficient appropriate audit evidence or if the results are not consistent with other audit evidence, the auditor should resolve the matter.** This may involve discussions with the entity and the expert, applying additional audit procedures, including possibly engaging another expert, or modifying the auditor's report.

Reference to an Expert in the Auditor's Report

16 **When issuing an unmodified auditor's report, the auditor should not refer to the work of an expert.** Such a reference might be misunderstood to be a qualification of the auditor's opinion or a division of responsibility, neither of which is intended.

17 If, as a result of the work of an expert, the auditor decides to issue a modified auditor's report, in some circumstances it may be appropriate, in explaining the nature of the modification, to refer to or describe the work of the expert (including the identity of the expert and the extent of the expert's involvement). In these circumstances, the auditor would obtain the permission of the expert before making such a reference. If permission is refused and the auditor believes a reference is necessary, the auditor may need to seek legal advice.

Effective Date

17-1 This ISA (UK and Ireland) is effective for audits of financial statements for periods commencing on or after 15 December 2004.

[700]*
The auditor's report on financial statements

(Issued December 2004)

Contents

	Paragraphs
Introduction	1 - 4
Basic Elements of the Auditor's Report	5 - 26-1
The Auditor's Report	27 - 28
Modified Reports	29 - 40-1
Circumstances That May Result in Other Than an Unqualified Opinion	41 - 46
Effective Date	**47**
Appendix: Flowchart - Forming an opinion on financial statements	

International Standard on Auditing (UK and Ireland) (ISA (UK and Ireland)) 700 "The Auditor's Report on Financial Statements" should be read in the context of the Auditing Practices Board's Statement "The Auditing Practices Board – Scope and Authority of Pronouncements (Revised)" which sets out the application and authority of ISAs (UK and Ireland).

Editor's note:
i) *Example audit reports, to be applied in conjunction with this Standard are contained in APB Audit Bulletins 2005/4 'Audit Report on Financial Statements in Great Britain and Northern Ireland' and 2006/1 'Audit Reports on Financial Statements in the Republic of Ireland'. These Bulletins are printed on pages 1809 and 1917.*
ii) *The Exposure Draft of a proposed replacement for this Standard is printed on page 2161.*

Introduction

1 The purpose of this International Standard on Auditing (UK and Ireland) (ISA (UK and Ireland)) is to establish standards and provide guidance on the form and content of the auditor's report issued as a result of an audit performed by an independent auditor of the financial statements of an entity. Much of the guidance provided can be adapted to auditor reports on financial information other than financial statements.

1-1 This ISA (UK and Ireland) uses the terms 'those charged with governance' and 'management'. The term 'governance' describes the role of persons entrusted with the supervision, control and direction of an entity. Ordinarily, those charged with governance are accountable for ensuring that the entity achieves its objectives, and for the quality of its financial reporting and reporting to interested parties. Those charged with governance include management only when they perform such functions.

1-2 In the UK and Ireland, those charged with governance include the directors (executive and non-executive) of a company or other body, the members of an audit committee where one exists, the partners, proprietors, committee of management or trustees of other forms of entity, or equivalent persons responsible for directing the entity's affairs and preparing its financial statements.

1-3 'Management' comprises those persons who perform senior managerial functions.

1-4 In the UK and Ireland, depending on the nature and circumstances of the entity, management may include some or all of those charged with governance (e.g. executive directors). Management will not normally include non-executive directors.

2 **The auditor should review and assess the conclusions drawn from the audit evidence obtained as the basis for the expression of an opinion on the financial statements.**

3 This review and assessment involves considering whether the financial statements have been prepared in accordance with an acceptable financial reporting framework[1] being either International Accounting Standards (IASs) or relevant national standards or practices. It may also be necessary to consider whether the financial statements comply with statutory requirements.

4 **The auditor's report should contain a clear written expression of opinion on the financial statements taken as a whole.**

Basic Elements of the Auditor's Report

5 The auditor's report includes the following basic elements, ordinarily in the following layout:

(a) Title;
(b) Addressee;

---

[1] The Framework of International Standards on Auditing also identifies another authoritative and comprehensive financial reporting framework. Reporting in accordance with this third type of framework is covered in ISA 800, "The Auditor's Report on Special Purpose Audit Engagements."

(c) *Opening or introductory paragraph*
    (i) Identification of the financial statements audited;
    (ii) A statement of the responsibility of the entity's management[2] and the responsibility of the auditor;
(d) *Scope paragraph (describing the nature of an audit)*
    (i) A reference to the ISAs or relevant national standards or practices;
    (ii) A description of the work the auditor performed;
(e) *Opinion paragraph* containing
    (i) A reference to the financial reporting framework used to prepare the financial statements (including identifying the country of origin[3] of the financial reporting framework when the framework used is not International Accounting Standards); and
    (ii) An expression of opinion on the financial statements;
(f) Date of the report;
(g) Auditor's address; and
(h) Auditor's signature.

A measure of uniformity in the form and content of the auditor's report is desirable because it helps to promote the reader's understanding and to identify unusual circumstances when they occur.

Title

The auditor's report should have an appropriate title. It may be appropriate to use the term "Independent Auditor" in the title to distinguish the auditor's report from reports that might be issued by others, such as by officers of the entity, the board of directors, or from the reports of other auditors who may not have to abide by the same ethical requirements as the independent auditor.

6

Addressee

The auditor's report should be appropriately addressed as required by the circumstances of the engagement and local regulations. The report is ordinarily addressed either to the shareholders or the board of directors of the entity whose financial statements are being audited.

7

> In the UK and Ireland, the Companies Act requires that the auditor's report on the financial statements of a company is addressed to its members because the audit is undertaken on their behalf. The auditor's report on financial statements of other types of reporting entity is addressed to the appropriate person or persons, as defined by statute or by the terms of the individual engagement.

7-1

Opening or Introductory Paragraph

The auditor's report should identify the financial statements of the entity that have been audited, including the date of and period covered by the financial statements.

8

[2] *In the UK and Ireland, those charged with governance are responsible for the preparation of the financial statements.*

[3] *In some circumstances it also may be necessary to refer to a particular jurisdiction within the country of origin to identify clearly the financial reporting framework used.*

9   The report should include a statement that the financial statements are the responsibility of the entity's management[4] and a statement that the responsibility of the auditor is to express an opinion on the financial statements based on the audit.

9-1   In the UK and Ireland:

(a) The auditor should distinguish between the auditor's responsibilities and the responsibilities of those charged with governance by including in the auditor's report a reference to a description of the relevant responsibilities of those charged with governance when that description is set out elsewhere in the financial statements or accompanying information; or

(b) Where the financial statements or accompanying information do not include an adequate description of the relevant responsibilities of those charged with governance, the auditor's report should include a description of those responsibilities.

9-2   An appreciation of the interrelationship between the responsibilities of those who prepare financial statements and those who audit them is also necessary to achieve an understanding of the nature and context of the opinion expressed by the auditor. Readers need to be aware that it is those charged with governance of the reporting entity and not the auditor who determines the accounting policies followed. In the UK and Ireland, the auditor's report therefore also sets out the respective responsibilities of those charged with governance and the auditor.

10   Financial statements are the representations of management[2]. The preparation of such statements requires management[2] to make significant accounting estimates and judgments, as well as to determine the appropriate accounting principles and methods used in preparation of the financial statements. This determination will be made in the context of the financial reporting framework that management[2] chooses, or is required, to use. In contrast, the auditor's responsibility is to audit these financial statements in order to express an opinion thereon.

11   An illustration of these matters in an opening (introductory) paragraph is:

"We have audited the accompanying[5] balance sheet of the ABC Company as of December 31, 20X1, and the related statements of income and cash flows for the year then ended. These financial statements are the responsibility of the Company's management. Our responsibility is to express an opinion on these financial statements based on our audit."

Illustrative examples of auditor's reports tailored for use with audits conducted in accordance with ISAs (UK and Ireland) are given in the most recent version of the APB Bulletin, "Auditor's Reports on Financial Statements".

---

[4] *The level of management responsible for the financial statements will vary according to the legal situation in each country.*

In the UK and Ireland, those charged with governance are responsible for the preparation of the financial statements. Thus it is the directors of a company who are required by law to prepare annual accounts which consist of a balance sheet and profit and loss account together with accompanying notes and which give a true and fair view of the state of affairs of the company (or group) at the end of the financial year and of the profit or loss of the company (or group) for that year.

[5] *The reference can be by page numbers.*

Scope Paragraph

The auditor's report should describe the scope of the audit by stating that the audit was conducted in accordance with ISAs (UK and Ireland) or in accordance with relevant national standards or practices as appropriate. "Scope" refers to the auditor's ability to perform audit procedures deemed necessary in the circumstances. The reader needs this as an assurance that the audit has been carried out in accordance with established standards or practices. Unless otherwise stated, the auditing standards or practices followed are presumed to be those of the country indicated by the auditor's address. 12

The report should include a statement that the audit was planned and performed to obtain reasonable assurance about whether the financial statements are free of material misstatement. 13

> In the UK and Ireland, the auditor's statement that the audit was planned and performed to obtain reasonable assurance about whether the financial statements are free of material misstatement, includes reference to material misstatement caused by fraud or other irregularity or error. 13-1

The auditor's report should describe the audit as including: 14

(a) Examining, on a test basis, evidence to support the financial statement amounts and disclosures;
(b) Assessing the accounting principles used in the preparation of the financial statements;
(c) Assessing the significant estimates made by management[2] in the preparation of the financial statements; and
(d) Evaluating the overall financial statement presentation.

> In the UK and Ireland, the accounting principles used in the preparation of financial statements are established by legislation. The auditor should consider whether the accounting policies are appropriate to the reporting entity's circumstances, consistently applied and adequately disclosed. 14-1

The report should include a statement by the auditor that the audit provides a reasonable basis for the opinion. 15

An illustration of these matters in a scope paragraph is: 16

> "We conducted our audit in accordance with International Standards on Auditing (or refer to relevant national standards or practices). Those Standards require that we plan and perform the audit to obtain reasonable assurance about whether the financial statements are free of material misstatement. An audit includes examining, on a test basis, evidence supporting the amounts and disclosures in the financial statements. An audit also includes assessing the accounting principles used and significant estimates made by management, as well as evaluating the overall financial statement presentation. We believe that our audit provides a reasonable basis for our opinion."

> Illustrative examples of auditor's reports tailored for use with audits conducted in accordance with ISAs (UK and Ireland) are given in the most recent version of the APB Bulletin, "Auditor's Reports on Financial Statements".

16-1 In the UK and Ireland:
  (a) In some circumstances, the auditor may be required to report whether the financial statements have been properly prepared in accordance with regulations or other requirements, but is not required to report on whether they give a true and fair view. Where the special circumstances of the reporting entity require or permit the adoption of policies or accounting bases which do not normally permit a true and fair view to be given, the auditor refers to those circumstances in the paragraphs dealing with the respective responsibilities of those charged with governance and the auditor (unless the matter is included in a separate statement given by those charged with governance) and may draw attention to them in the basis of opinion section of the report.
  (b) The auditor may wish to include additional comment in this part of the auditor's report to highlight matters which they regard as relevant to a proper understanding of the basis of their opinion.

Opinion Paragraph

17 **The opinion paragraph of the auditor's report should clearly indicate the financial reporting framework used to prepare the financial statements (including identifying the country of origin of the financial reporting framework when the framework used is not International Accounting Standards) and state the auditor's opinion as to whether the financial statements give a true and fair view (or are presented fairly, in all material respects,) in accordance with that financial reporting framework and, where appropriate, whether the financial statements comply with statutory requirements.**

18 The terms used to express the auditor's opinion are "give a true and fair view"[6] or "present fairly, in all material respects," and are equivalent. Both terms indicate, amongst other things, that the auditor considers only those matters that are material to the financial statements.

19 The financial reporting framework is determined by IASs, rules issued by recognized standard setting bodies, and the development of general practice within a country, with an appropriate consideration of fairness and with due regard to local legislation. To advise the reader of the context in which the auditor's opinion is expressed, the auditor's opinion indicates the framework upon which the financial statements are based. The auditor refers to the financial reporting framework in such terms as:

  "...in accordance with International Accounting Standards (or [title of financial reporting framework with reference to the country of origin])..."

Illustrative examples of auditor's reports tailored for use with audits conducted in accordance with ISAs (UK and Ireland) are given in the most recent version of the APB Bulletin, "Auditor's Reports on Financial Statements".

This designation will help the user to better understand which financial reporting framework was used in preparing the financial statements. When reporting on financial statements that are prepared specifically for use in another country, the auditor considers whether appropriate disclosure has been made in the financial statements about the financial reporting framework that has been used.

---

[6] *In the UK and Ireland, the auditor ordinarily is required by law or regulations to evaluate whether the financial statements give a true and fair view.*

For accounting periods commencing on or after 1 January 2005, the consolidated financial statements of UK companies that are admitted to trading on a regulated market and Irish listed companies must be prepared under EU adopted IFRS. Other companies may choose to use EU adopted IFRS; those who do not will be able to continue to prepare their financial statements in accordance with UK and Irish standards.

19-1

In addition to an opinion on the true and fair view (or fair presentation, in all material respects,), the auditor's report may need to include an opinion as to whether the financial statements comply with other requirements specified by relevant statutes or law.

20

An illustration of these matters in an opinion paragraph is:

21

"In our opinion, the financial statements give a true and fair view of (or 'present fairly, in all material respects,') the financial position of the Company as of December 31, 20X1, and of the results of its operations and its cash flows for the year then ended in accordance with International Accounting Standards (or [title of financial reporting framework with reference to the country of origin[7]]) (and comply with ...[8])."

Illustrative examples of auditor's reports tailored for use with audits conducted in accordance with ISAs (UK and Ireland) are given in the most recent version of the APB Bulletin, "Auditor's Reports on Financial Statements".

[9]

22

Other requirements specified by relevant statutes and law in the UK and Ireland

Further opinions or information to be included in the auditor's report may be determined by specific statutory requirements applicable to the reporting entity, or, in some circumstances, by the terms of the auditor's engagement. Such matters may be required to be dealt with by a positive statement in the auditor's report or only by exception. For example, in the Republic of Ireland the auditor is required to state whether, in the auditor's opinion, proper books of account have been kept, whereas company legislation in the United Kingdom requires the auditor to report only when a company has not maintained proper accounting records.

22-1

Where further opinions are required by statute or other regulation, matters which result in qualification of such an opinion may also result in a qualification of the auditor's opinion on the financial statements. For example, if proper accounting records have not been maintained and as a result it proves impracticable for the auditor to obtain sufficient evidence concerning material matters in the financial statements, the auditor's report indicates that the scope of the examination was limited and includes a qualified opinion or disclaimer of opinion on the financial statements arising from that limitation, as required by paragraphs 37 and 38.

22-2

[7] *See footnote 3.*

[8] *Refer to relevant statutes or law.*

[9] *Deleted by the IAASB.*

Date of Report

23 **The auditor should date the report as of the completion date of the audit.** This informs the reader that the auditor has considered the effect on the financial statements and on the report of events and transactions of which the auditor became aware and that occurred up to that date.

23-1 **In the UK and Ireland, the date of an auditor's report on a reporting entity's financial statements is the date on which the auditor signed the report expressing an opinion on those statements.**

24 Since the auditor's responsibility is to report on the financial statements as prepared and presented by management^2, the auditor should not date the report earlier than the date on which the financial statements are signed or approved by management[10].

24-1 **In the UK and Ireland, the auditor should not date the report earlier than the date on which all other information contained in a report of which the audited financial statements form a part have been approved by those charged with governance and the auditor has considered all necessary available evidence.**

24-2 The auditor is not in a position to form the opinion until the financial statements (and any other information contained in a report of which the audited financial statements form a part) have been approved by those charged with governance and the auditor has completed the assessment of all the evidence the auditor considers necessary for the opinion or opinions to be given in the auditor's report. This assessment includes events occurring up to the date the opinion is expressed. The auditor therefore plans the conduct of audits to take account of the need to ensure, before expressing an opinion on financial statements, that those charged with governance have approved the financial statements and any accompanying financial information and that the auditor has completed a sufficient review of post balance sheet events.

24-3 The date of the auditor's report is, therefore, the date on which, following:

(a) receipt of the financial statements and accompanying documents in the form approved by those charged with governance for release;
(b) review of all documents which the auditor is required to consider in addition to the financial statements (for example the directors' report, chairman's statement or other review of an entity's affairs which will accompany the financial statements); and
(c) completion of all procedures necessary to form an opinion on the financial statements (and any other opinions required by law or regulation) including a review of post balance sheet events the auditor signs (in manuscript) the auditor's report expressing an opinion on the financial statements for distribution with those statements.

24-4 The form of the financial statements and other financial information approved by those charged with governance, and considered by the auditor when signing a report expressing the auditor's opinion, may be in the form of final drafts from which printed documents will be prepared. Subsequent production of printed copies of the financial statements and auditor's report does not constitute the creation of a new document. Copies of the report produced for circulation to

---

[10] *In the UK and Ireland, the financial statements are signed or approved by those charged with governance.*

shareholders or others may therefore reproduce a printed version of the auditor's signature showing the date of actual signature.

If the date on which the auditor signs the report is later than that on which those charged with governance approved the financial statements, the auditor takes such steps as are appropriate: 24-5

(a) to obtain assurance that those charged with governance would have approved the financial statements on that later date (for example, by obtaining confirmation from specified individual members of the board to whom authority has been delegated for this purpose); and
(b) to ensure that their procedures for reviewing subsequent events cover the period up to that date.

The copy of the auditor's report that is delivered to the registrar of companies is required to state the name of the auditor and be signed by the auditor. Where the auditor signs the auditor's report in a form from which a final printed version is produced, the auditor may sign copies for identification purposes in order to provide the registrar with appropriately signed copies. No further active procedures need be followed at that later date. 24-6

Auditor's Address

The report should name a specific location, which is ordinarily the city where the auditor maintains the office that has responsibility for the audit. 25

Auditor's Signature

The report should be signed in the name of the audit firm, the personal name of the auditor or both, as appropriate. The auditor's report is ordinarily signed in the name of the firm because the firm assumes responsibility for the audit. 26

In the UK and Ireland, where required by relevant law and regulations, the report also states the auditor's status as a registered auditor. 26-1

The Auditor's Report

An *unqualified opinion* should be expressed when the auditor concludes that the financial statements give a true and fair view (or are presented fairly, in all material respects,) in accordance with the identified financial reporting framework. An unqualified opinion also indicates implicitly that any changes in accounting principles or in the method of their application, and the effects thereof, have been properly determined and disclosed in the financial statements. 27

In the UK and Ireland, an unqualified opinion entails concluding whether inter alia: 27-1

- The financial statements have been prepared using appropriate accounting principles, which have been consistently applied;
- Any departures from relevant legislation, regulations or the identified financial reporting framework are justified and adequately explained in the financial statements; and

- There is adequate disclosure of all information relevant to the proper understanding of the financial statements.

28 The following is an illustration of the entire auditor's report incorporating the basic elements set forth and illustrated above. This report illustrates the expression of an unqualified opinion.

"AUDITOR'S REPORT

(APPROPRIATE ADDRESSEE)

We have audited the accompanying[11] balance sheet of the ABC Company as of December 31, 20X1, and the related statements of income, and cash flows for the year then ended. These financial statements are the responsibility of the Company's management. Our responsibility is to express an opinion on these financial statements based on our audit.

We conducted our audit in accordance with International Standards on Auditing (or refer to relevant national standards or practices). Those Standards require that we plan and perform the audit to obtain reasonable assurance about whether the financial statements are free of material misstatement. An audit includes examining, on a test basis, evidence supporting the amounts and disclosures in the financial statements. An audit also includes assessing the accounting principles used and significant estimates made by management, as well as evaluating the overall financial statement presentation. We believe that our audit provides a reasonable basis for our opinion.

In our opinion, the financial statements give a true and fair view of (or 'present fairly, in all material respects,') the financial position of the Company as of December 31, 20X1, and of the results of its operations and its cash flows for the year then ended in accordance with International Accounting Standards (or [title of financial reporting framework with reference to the country of origin[12]]) (and comply with ...[13]).

AUDITOR

Date

Address"

Illustrative examples of auditor's reports tailored for use with audits conducted in accordance with ISAs (UK and Ireland) are given in the most recent version of the APB Bulletin, "Auditor's Reports on Financial Statements".

Modified Reports

29 An auditor's report is considered to be modified in the following situations:

Matters That Do Not Affect the Auditor's Opinion

(a) Emphasis of matter

---

[11] See footnote 5.

[12] See footnote 3.

[13] See footnote 8.

Matters That Do Affect the Auditor's Opinion

(b) Qualified opinion,
(c) Disclaimer of opinion, or
(d) Adverse opinion.

Uniformity in the form and content of each type of modified report will further the user's understanding of such reports. Accordingly, this ISA (UK and Ireland) includes suggested wording to express an unqualified opinion as well as examples of modifying phrases for use when issuing modified reports.

> Illustrative examples of auditor's reports tailored for use with audits conducted in accordance with ISAs (UK and Ireland) are given in the most recent version of the APB Bulletin, "Auditor's Reports on Financial Statements".

Matters That Do Not Affect the Auditor's Opinion

In certain circumstances, an auditor's report may be modified by adding an emphasis of matter paragraph to highlight a matter affecting the financial statements which is included in a note to the financial statements that more extensively discusses the matter. The addition of such an emphasis of matter paragraph does not affect the auditor's opinion. The paragraph would preferably be included after the opinion paragraph and would ordinarily refer to the fact that the auditor's opinion is not qualified in this respect. 30

The auditor should modify the auditor's report by adding a paragraph to highlight a material matter regarding a going concern problem. 31

The auditor should consider modifying the auditor's report by adding a paragraph if there is a significant uncertainty (other than a going concern problem), the resolution of which is dependent upon future events and which may affect the financial statements. An uncertainty is a matter whose outcome depends on future actions or events not under the direct control of the entity but that may affect the financial statements. 32

> The emphasis of matter paragraph describes the matter giving rise to the significant uncertainty and its possible effects on the financial statements, including (where practicable) quantification. Where it is not possible to quantify the potential effects of the resolution of the uncertainty, the auditor includes a statement to that effect. Reference may be made to notes in the financial statements but such a reference is not a substitute for sufficient description of the significant uncertainty so that a reader can appreciate the principal points at issue and their implications. 32-1

> Communication with the reader is enhanced by the use of an appropriate subheading differentiating the emphasis of matter paragraph from other matters included in the section describing the basis of the auditor's opinion. 32-2

> In determining whether an uncertainty is significant, the auditor considers: 32-3
>
> (a) the risk that the estimate included in financial statements may be subject to change;
> (b) the range of possible outcomes; and
> (c) the consequences of those outcomes on the view shown in the financial statements.

32-4 Uncertainties are regarded as significant when they involve a significant level of concern about the validity of the going concern basis or other matters whose potential effect on the financial statements is unusually great. A common example of a significant uncertainty is the outcome of major litigation.

32-5 An unqualified opinion indicates that the auditor considers that appropriate estimates and disclosures relating to significant uncertainties are made in the financial statements. It remains unqualified notwithstanding the inclusion of an emphasis of matter paragraph describing a significant uncertainty.

32-6 When the auditor concludes that the estimate of the outcome of a significant uncertainty is materially misstated or that the disclosure relating to it is inadequate, the auditor issues a qualified opinion.

33 An illustration of an emphasis of matter paragraph for a significant uncertainty in an auditor's report follows:

"In our opinion ... (remaining words are the same as illustrated in the opinion paragraph—paragraph 28 above).

Without qualifying our opinion we draw attention to Note X to the financial statements. The Company is the defendant in a lawsuit alleging infringement of certain patent rights and claiming royalties and punitive damages. The Company has filed a counter action, and preliminary hearings and discovery proceedings on both actions are in progress. The ultimate outcome of the matter cannot presently be determined, and no provision for any liability that may result has been made in the financial statements."

Illustrative examples of auditor's reports tailored for use with audits conducted in accordance with ISAs (UK and Ireland) are given in the most recent version of the APB Bulletin, "Auditor's Reports on Financial Statements".

(An illustration of an emphasis of matter paragraph relating to going concern is set out in ISA (UK and Ireland) 570, "Going Concern.")

34 The addition of a paragraph emphasizing a going concern problem or significant uncertainty is ordinarily adequate to meet the auditor's reporting responsibilities regarding such matters. However, in extreme cases, such as situations involving multiple uncertainties that are significant to the financial statements, the auditor may consider it appropriate to express a disclaimer of opinion instead of adding an emphasis of matter paragraph.

35 In addition to the use of an emphasis of matter paragraph for matters that affect the financial statements, the auditor may also modify the auditor's report by using an emphasis of matter paragraph, preferably after the opinion paragraph, to report on matters other than those affecting the financial statements. For example, if an amendment to other information in a document containing audited financial statements is necessary and the entity refuses to make the amendment, the auditor would consider including in the auditor's report an emphasis of matter paragraph describing the material inconsistency. An emphasis of matter paragraph may also be used when there are additional statutory reporting responsibilities.

Matters That Do Affect the Auditor's Opinion

An auditor may not be able to express an unqualified opinion when either of the following circumstances exist and, in the auditor's judgment, the effect of the matter is or may be material to the financial statements:

(a) There is a limitation on the scope of the auditor's work; or
(b) There is a disagreement with management[2] regarding the acceptability of the accounting policies selected, the method of their application or the adequacy of financial statement disclosures.

The circumstances described in (a) could lead to a qualified opinion or a disclaimer of opinion. The circumstances described in (b) could lead to a qualified opinion or an adverse opinion. These circumstances are discussed more fully in paragraphs 41–46.

36

In the UK and Ireland, when the auditor concludes that the financial statements of a company do not comply with accounting standards, the auditor assesses:

(a) Whether there are sound reasons for the departure;
(b) Whether adequate disclosure has been made concerning the departure from accounting standards;
(c) Whether the departure is such that the financial statements do not give a true and fair view of the state of affairs and profit or loss.

In normal cases, a departure from accounting standards will result in the issue of a qualified or adverse opinion on the view given by the financial statements.

36-1

In the UK and Ireland, where no explanation is given for a departure from accounting standards, its absence may of itself impair the ability of the financial statements to give a true and fair view of the company's state of affairs and profit or loss. When the auditor concludes that this is so, a qualified or adverse opinion on the view given by the financial statements is appropriate, in addition to a reference (where appropriate) to the departure from accounting standards and the reasons for the departure.

36-2

A *qualified opinion* should be expressed when the auditor concludes that an unqualified opinion cannot be expressed but that the effect of any disagreement with management[2], or limitation on scope is not so material and pervasive as to require an adverse opinion or a disclaimer of opinion. A qualified opinion should be expressed as being 'except for' the effects of the matter to which the qualification relates.

37

A *disclaimer of opinion* should be expressed when the possible effect of a limitation on scope is so material and pervasive that the auditor has not been able to obtain sufficient appropriate audit evidence and accordingly is unable to express an opinion on the financial statements.

38

An *adverse opinion* should be expressed when the effect of a disagreement is so material and pervasive to the financial statements that the auditor concludes that a qualification of the report is not adequate to disclose the misleading or incomplete nature of the financial statements.

39

Whenever the auditor expresses an opinion that is other than unqualified, a clear description of all the substantive reasons should be included in the report and, unless impracticable, a quantification of the possible effect(s) on the financial statements. Ordinarily, this information would be set out in a separate paragraph preceding the

40

opinion or disclaimer of opinion and may include a reference to a more extensive discussion, if any, in a note to the financial statements.

40-1 Whilst reference may be made to relevant notes in the financial statements, such reference is not a substitute for sufficient description of the circumstances in the auditor's report so that a reader can appreciate the principal points at issue and their implications for an understanding of the financial statements.

Circumstances That May Result in Other Than an Unqualified Opinion

Limitation on Scope

41 A limitation on the scope of the auditor's work may sometimes be imposed by the entity (for example, when the terms of the engagement specify that the auditor will not carry out an audit procedure that the auditor believes is necessary). However, when the limitation in the terms of a proposed engagement is such that the auditor believes the need to express a disclaimer of opinion exists, the auditor would ordinarily not accept such a limited engagement as an audit engagement, unless required by statute. Also, a statutory auditor would not accept such an audit engagement when the limitation infringes on the auditor's statutory duties.

Limitation of scope imposed by the entity before accepting an audit engagement in the UK and Ireland

41-1 If the auditor is aware, before accepting an audit engagement, that those charged with governance of the entity, or those who appoint its auditor, will impose a limitation on the scope of the audit work which the auditor considers likely to result in the need to issue a disclaimer of opinion on the financial statements, the auditor should not accept that engagement, unless required to do so by statute[14].

41-2 Agreeing to such a restriction on the scope of the audit work would seriously threaten the auditor's independence and make it impossible for the auditor to meet with integrity and rigour the requirements of ISAs (UK and Ireland). The acceptance of such a limited engagement as an audit engagement would be incompatible with the auditor's obligations to:

- Conduct any audit of financial statements in accordance with applicable legislation;

---

[14] There are certain circumstances in which (regardless of any limitation imposed on the scope of the audit work) the auditor is required by statute to accept an audit engagement, for example the majority of appointments of the national audit agencies to audit the accounts of certain public sector bodies. However, in general, there is no such requirement in the private sector; there may be a statutory requirement for the entity to appoint auditors, but this does not create an obligation for any auditors to accept appointment.

- Conduct any audit of financial statements in accordance with Auditing Standards contained in the ISAs (UK and Ireland); and
- Comply with the APB ethical standards.

Furthermore, the auditor, by accepting the engagement on such restricted terms, might be regarded as complicit in an arrangement to enable the entity to observe the form of any legal or regulatory audit requirements but to evade complying with the substance of those obligations.

Limitation on scope imposed by the entity after accepting an audit engagement in the UK and Ireland

If the auditor becomes aware, after accepting an audit engagement, that those charged with governance of the entity, or those who appointed them as its auditor, have imposed a limitation on the scope of the audit work which they consider likely to result in the need to issue a disclaimer of opinion on the financial statements, the auditor should request the removal of the limitation. If the limitation is not removed, the auditor should consider resigning from the audit engagement. 41-3

If the limitation is not removed, the auditor considers the factors discussed in paragraph 41-2 above and may often decide that resignation from the audit engagement is appropriate. If, after careful consideration of all the circumstances (for example, where third party interests are involved), the auditor concludes that it is appropriate to continue with the engagement, the auditor includes in the audit report a full description of the events which led to the disclaimer. On completion of the audit for that year, however, the auditor will follow the requirements of paragraph 41-1 when deciding whether to undertake the audit for the following period[15]. 41-4

In cases where the auditor resigns immediately, or continues with the audit for that year but does not seek reappointment, the auditor needs to comply with: 41-5

(a) Any statutory or regulatory requirements for a statement of the circumstances of ceasing to hold office;[16] and
(b) The requirements of APB ethical standards concerning the response to enquiries from any proposed successor auditor seeking information which could affect the decision whether or not they may properly accept appointment.

The fact that such a limitation has been imposed on the scope of the auditor's work may be a matter to which the auditor refers in both cases.

Where a significant limitation of scope has arisen during the course of the audit work the auditor should consider whether an obligation arises under statute, as discussed in ISA (UK and Ireland) 250, Part B, to make a report to the appropriate regulators. 41-6

---

[15] *Auditors in the Republic of Ireland are required by the Companies Act 1963 (section 160, para 2(c)) to give the company notice in writing of their unwillingness to be re-appointed, where this is the case.*

[16] *For example, in the case of a limited company incorporated in the United Kingdom, on ceasing to hold office for any reason, the auditor is required under section 394(1) Companies Act 1985 (or Article 58(1) Companies (No 2) (Northern Ireland) Order 1990) to make '... a statement of any circumstances connected with his ceasing to hold office which he considers should be brought to the attention of the members or creditors of the company or, if he considers that there are no such circumstances, a statement that there are none.' Similar requirements exist in the Republic of Ireland (section 185 Companies Act, 1990).*

Limitation on scope imposed by circumstances

42 A scope limitation may be imposed by circumstances (for example, when the timing of the auditor's appointment is such that the auditor is unable to observe the counting of physical inventories). It may also arise when, in the opinion of the auditor, the entity's accounting records are inadequate or when the auditor is unable to carry out an audit procedure believed to be desirable. In these circumstances, the auditor would attempt to carry out reasonable alternative procedures to obtain sufficient appropriate audit evidence to support an unqualified opinion.

43 When there is a limitation on the scope of the auditor's work that requires expression of a qualified opinion or a disclaimer of opinion, the auditor's report should describe the limitation and indicate the possible adjustments to the financial statements that might have been determined to be necessary had the limitation not existed.

43-1 In the UK and Ireland, in considering whether a limitation of scope results in a lack of evidence necessary to form an opinion, the auditor assesses:

(a) The quantity and type of evidence which may reasonably be expected to be available to support the particular figure or disclosure in the financial statements; and
(b) The possible effect on the financial statements of the matter for which insufficient evidence is available. When the possible effect is, in the opinion of the auditor, material to the financial statements, there will be insufficient evidence to support an unqualified opinion.

44 Illustrations of these matters are set out below.

Limitation on Scope—Qualified Opinion

"We have audited ... (remaining words are the same as illustrated in the introductory paragraph—paragraph 28 above).

Except as discussed in the following paragraph, we conducted our audit in accordance with ... (remaining words are the same as illustrated in the scope paragraph—paragraph 28 above).

We did not observe the counting of the physical inventories as of December 31, 20X1, since that date was prior to the time we were initially engaged as auditors for the Company. Owing to the nature of the Company's records, we were unable to satisfy ourselves as to inventory quantities by other audit procedures.

In our opinion, except for the effects of such adjustments, if any, as might have been determined to be necessary had we been able to satisfy ourselves as to physical inventory quantities, the financial statements give a true and ... (remaining words are the same as illustrated in the opinion paragraph—paragraph 28 above).

Illustrative examples of auditor's reports tailored for use with audits conducted in accordance with ISAs (UK and Ireland) are given in the most recent version of the APB Bulletin, "Auditor's Reports on Financial Statements".

Limitation on Scope—Disclaimer of Opinion

"We were engaged to audit the accompanying balance sheet of the ABC Company as of December 31, 20X1, and the related statements of income and cash flows for the year then ended. These financial statements are the responsibility of the Company's management. (Omit the sentence stating the responsibility of the auditor).

(The paragraph discussing the scope of the audit would either be omitted or amended according to the circumstances.)

(Add a paragraph discussing the scope limitation as follows:)

We were not able to observe all physical inventories and confirm accounts receivable due to limitations placed on the scope of our work by the Company.

Because of the significance of the matters discussed in the preceding paragraph, we do not express an opinion on the financial statements.

> Illustrative examples of auditor's reports tailored for use with audits conducted in accordance with ISAs (UK and Ireland) are given in the most recent version of the APB Bulletin, "Auditor's Reports on Financial Statements".

Disagreement with Management[2]

The auditor may disagree with management[2] about matters such as the acceptability of accounting policies selected, the method of their application, or the adequacy of disclosures in the financial statements. **If such disagreements are material to the financial statements, the auditor should express a qualified or an adverse opinion.**

45

Illustrations of these matters are set out below.

46

Disagreement on Accounting Policies-Inappropriate Accounting Method—Qualified Opinion

"We have audited ... (remaining words are the same as illustrated in the introductory paragraph—paragraph 28 above).

We conducted our audit in accordance with ... (remaining words are the same as illustrated in the scope paragraph—paragraph 28 above).

As discussed in Note X to the financial statements, no depreciation has been provided in the financial statements which practice, in our opinion, is not in accordance with International Accounting Standards. The provision for the year ended December 31, 20X1, should be xxx based on the straight-line method of depreciation using annual rates of 5% for the building and 20% for the equipment. Accordingly, the fixed assets should be reduced by accumulated depreciation of xxx and the loss for the year and accumulated deficit should be increased by xxx and xxx, respectively.

In our opinion, except for the effect on the financial statements of the matter referred to in the preceding paragraph, the financial statements give a true and ... (remaining words are the same as illustrated in the opinion paragraph—paragraph 28 above)."

> Illustrative examples of auditor's reports tailored for use with audits conducted in accordance with ISAs (UK and Ireland) are given in the most recent version of the APB Bulletin, "Auditor's Reports on Financial Statements".

670   *International Standards on Auditing (UK & Ireland)*

Disagreement on Accounting Policies—Inadequate Disclosure—Qualified Opinion

"We have audited ... (remaining words are the same as illustrated in the introductory paragraph—paragraph 28 above).

We conducted our audit in accordance with ... (remaining words are the same as illustrated in the scope paragraph—paragraph 28 above).

On January 15, 20X2, the Company issued debentures in the amount of xxx for the purpose of financing plant expansion. The debenture agreement restricts the payment of future cash dividends to earnings after December 31, 19X1. In our opinion, disclosure of this information is required by ...[17].

In our opinion, except for the omission of the information included in the preceding paragraph, the financial statements give a true and ... (remaining words are the same as illustrated in the opinion paragraph—paragraph 28 above)."

> Illustrative examples of auditor's reports tailored for use with audits conducted in accordance with ISAs (UK and Ireland) are given in the most recent version of the APB Bulletin, "Auditor's Reports on Financial Statements".

Disagreement on Accounting Policies—Inadequate Disclosure—Adverse Opinion

"We have audited ... (remaining words are the same as illustrated in the introductory paragraph—paragraph 28 above).

We conducted our audit in accordance with ... (remaining words are the same as illustrated in the scope paragraph—paragraph 28 above).

(Paragraph(s) discussing the disagreement).

In our opinion, because of the effects of the matters discussed in the preceding paragraph(s), the financial statements do not give a true and fair view of (or do not 'present fairly') the financial position of the Company as of December 20, 19X1, and of the results of its operations and its cash flows for the year then ended in accordance with International Accounting Standards (or [title of financial reporting framework with reference to the country of origin[18]]) (and do not comply with ...[19])."

> Illustrative examples of auditor's reports tailored for use with audits conducted in accordance with ISAs (UK and Ireland) are given in the most recent version of the APB Bulletin, "Auditor's Reports on Financial Statements".

Effective Date

47 This ISA (UK and Ireland) is effective for audits of financial statements for periods commencing on or after 15 December 2004.

---

[17] See footnote 8.

[18] See footnote 3.

[19] See footnote 8.

Public Sector Perspective

Additional guidance for auditors of public sector bodies in the UK and Ireland is given in:

- Practice Note 10 "Audit of Financial Statements of Public Sector Entities in the United Kingdom (Revised)"
- Practice Note 10(I) "The Audit of Central Government Financial Statements in Ireland"

While the basic principles contained in this ISA (UK and Ireland) apply to the audit of financial statements in the public sector, the legislation giving rise to the audit mandate may specify the nature, content and form of the auditor's report. 1

This ISA (UK and Ireland) does not address the form and content of the auditor's report in circumstances where financial statements are prepared in conformity with a disclosed basis of accounting, whether mandated by legislation or ministerial (or other) directive, and that basis results in financial statements which are misleading. 2

Paragraph 17 of this standard requires the auditor to indicate clearly the financial reporting framework used to prepare the financial statements. Where a public sector entity has adopted International Public Sector Accounting Standards as the financial reporting framework, the auditor should clearly state that fact in the audit opinion. For example: 3

> "In our opinion, the financial statements present fairly, in all material respects, the financial position of the [public sector entity] as of December 31, 20X1 and of its financial performance and its cash flows for the year then ended in accordance with International Public Sector Accounting Standards."

Appendix

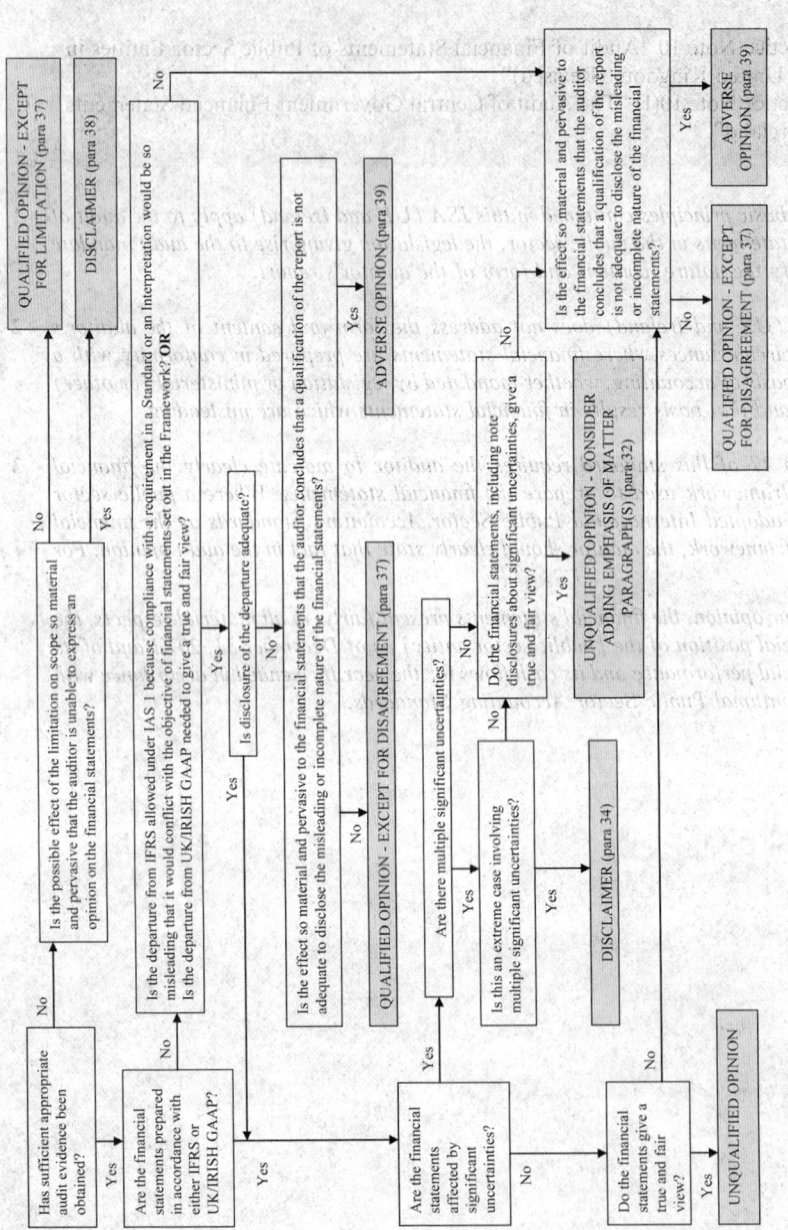

[1] This flowchart does not cover modified reports involving going concern problems. Refer to the most recent version of the APB Bulletin, "Auditor's Reports on Financial Statements".

[700] (Revised)
The auditor's report on financial statements

(Issued March 2009)

Contents

An explanation of APB's approach to revising ISA (UK and Ireland) 700 to facilitate more concise auditor's reports

ISA (UK and Ireland) 700 (Revised)

Illustrative Auditor's Reports[1]

1. UK publicly traded company using IFRSs as adopted by the European Union, where the scope of the audit is described on the APB web-site or elsewhere in the annual report
2. UK publicly traded company using IFRSs as adopted by the European Union, where the scope of the audit is described within the auditor's report
3. UK non-publicly traded company using UK GAAP, where the scope of the audit is described on the APB web-site or elsewhere in the annual report
4. UK non-publicly traded company using UK GAAP, where the scope of the audit is described within the auditor's report

---

[1] The illustrative auditor's reports do not form part of ISA (UK and Ireland) 700 (Revised).

An explanation of APB's approach to revising ISA (UK and Ireland) 700 to facilitate more concise auditor's reports

Background

In December 2007 the Auditing Practices Board (APB) issued the Discussion Paper "The Auditor's Report: A time for change?" In this APB sought views on what steps it should take to reflect, in the standard auditor's report, the coming into force of the Companies Act 2006, and also on whether more wide ranging changes should be made to the content of the auditor's report.

Institutional investors, preparer organizations, public sector bodies and some auditing firms expressed strong support for a shorter auditor's report. They observed that there were opportunities for streamlining the current report especially in relation to the current descriptions of the auditor's and directors' responsibilities and the summarised description
of the scope of an audit.

Many of the institutional investors also called for the auditor's report to be made more informative. Views on how this could be achieved varied. Some called for the auditor's report to provide more of an insight into the quality of the work which the auditor has carried out; others suggested much greater use of emphasis of matter paragraphs.

How ISA (UK and Ireland) 700 (Revised) will facilitate more concise auditor's reports

Improving the conciseness of the auditor's report is the first phase of APB's work to respond to these views. The requirements of the attached revision of ISA (UK and Ireland) 700 will enable auditors to provide shorter auditor's reports as illustrated by the illustrative examples provided on pages 24 to 31.

A significant change relates to what was previously described as the "basis of opinion". ISA (UK and Ireland) 700 (Revised) changes the heading of this section to "Scope of the audit" and allows three alternatives. In the case of UK companies, the report can:

- cross refer to a "Statement of the Scope of an Audit" that is maintained on APB's web site (See Example 1 on page 24 and Example 3 on page 28); or
- cross refer to a "Statement of the Scope of an Audit" that is included elsewhere within the Annual Report (See Example 1 on page 24 and Example 3 on page 28); or
- include a prescribed description of the scope of an audit (See Example 2 on page 26 and Example 4 on page 30).

Where auditors decide to include a description of the scope of the audit within the auditor's report, APB believes the description should be as short as possible and use the prescribed words.

A further significant change relates to the description of the auditor's responsibilities which has been both reduced in length and in part re-distributed to the second part of the auditor's report that addresses other reporting matters.

Making auditor's reports more informative

The second phase is for APB to undertake research to better understand what can realistically be done to make auditor's reports more informative. APB believes that this work is best coordinated on an international basis and wishes to support work that the International Auditing and Assurance Standards Board (IAASB) may undertake.

In the short term, pending future possible changes to the standards in this area, APB wishes to make clear that ISA (UK and Ireland) 700 (Revised) does not preclude auditors from including additional comment in the auditor's report to highlight matters which they regard as relevant to a proper understanding of their work. To facilitate the inclusion of such additional comments in the auditor's report APB has introduced into the revised ISA (UK and Ireland) the requirement relating to "Other Matter Paragraphs in the Auditor's Report" from ISA 706 "Emphasis of Matter Paragraphs and Other Matter Paragraphs in the Independent Auditor's Report" (see paragraph 55 of ISA (UK and Ireland) 700 (Revised)).

Based on comments received in response to the Discussion Paper, APB also believes that providing a fuller description of the scope of an audit on its website will be informative to users.

Discussing the alternatives with those charged with governance

APB encourages auditors to discuss the proposed content of the auditor's report with those charged with governance. The following matters in particular might usefully be the subject of such discussions:

- the advantages and disadvantages of the various alternative approaches to the description of the scope of the audit, permitted by ISA (UK and Ireland) 700 (Revised); and
- matters that auditors may wish to include in the auditor's report under the heading "Other Matter".

APB believes that those charged with governance have a legitimate interest in understanding why an auditor has chosen a particular approach to describing the scope of the audit and why the auditor considers it necessary to report the "Other Matter".

A window of opportunity to influence international developments

The form and content of the auditor's report is a matter of active consideration internationally. In particular, the European Commission has yet to decide on the form and content of auditor's reports within the EU and the IAASB has agreed to consider recent research and developments with regard to the auditor's report. APB continues to believe that there is a "window of opportunity" during which it can influence international decisions on the auditor's report, especially if its ideas are implemented in practice and are found to be beneficial by the investor community.

APB will therefore monitor reaction to the changes it has made to ISA (UK and Ireland) 700 and, in particular, the extent to which:

- reference is made to the longer version of the Scope of an Audit on APB's website;
- reference is made to the Scope of an Audit elsewhere within the annual report; and

- auditors decide to provide additional comment in the auditor's report to highlight matters which they regard as relevant to a proper understanding of their work in 'Other Matter' paragraphs.

Focus on UK companies

The catalyst for change was the implementation of the Companies Act 2006 and APB is also responding, in part, to the views of institutional investors. It therefore seems appropriate to focus, initially, on UK companies. Consequently APB has established a two-stage implementation plan:

- The effective date of ISA (UK and Ireland) 700 (Revised) for UK companies will be for accounting periods ending on or after 5 April 2009.
- For other UK entities the effective date is for periods ending on or after 15 December 2010 (ie the same effective date as will apply to the clarified ISAs (UK and Ireland).

Consistent with this approach APB will initially provide descriptions of the scope of an audit on APB's web-site with respect to UK companies only. If there is a strong take up of cross referring to its web site APB will, in due course, consider the need to provide examples applicable to other types of entity.

Republic of Ireland

With respect to Irish companies and entities APB is monitoring developments in Irish Law which may have an effect on the content or structure of auditor's reports issued in accordance with Irish legal requirements. APB will make an announcement concerning the applicability of ISA (UK and Ireland) 700 (Revised) in the Republic of Ireland when there is more certainty about the legal position. In the meantime the version of ISA (UK and Ireland) 700 that was effective for periods commencing on or after 15 December 2004 remains in effect with respect to Irish auditor's reports.

[700] (Revised)
The auditor's report on financial statements
(Issued March 2009)

Contents

	Paragraph
Introduction	1 – 5
Basic Elements of the Auditor's Report	6 – 41
The Auditor's Report	42 – 44
Modified Reports	45 – 76
Effective Date	77

International Standard on Auditing (UK and Ireland) (ISA (UK and Ireland)) 700 "The Auditor's Report on Financial Statements" (Revised) should be read in the context of the Auditing Practices Board's Statement "The Auditing Practices Board - Scope and Authority of Pronouncements (Revised)" which sets out the application and authority of ISAs (UK and Ireland).

Introduction

1. This International Standard on Auditing (UK and Ireland) (ISA (UK and Ireland)) establishes standards and provides guidance on the form and content of the auditor's report issued as a result of an audit performed by an independent auditor of the financial statements of:

    (a) UK companies, except for those that are charities, for periods commencing on or after 6 April 2008 and ending on or after 5 April 2009[1]; and
    (b) all other UK entities for periods ending on or after 15 December 2010.

    For earlier accounting periods and for audits carried out in the Republic of Ireland the previous version of ISA (UK and Ireland) 700 is applicable[2].

2. This ISA (UK and Ireland) is written to address both "true and fair frameworks[3]" and "compliance frameworks". A "true and fair framework" is one that requires compliance with the framework but which acknowledges that to achieve a true and fair view:

    (a) it may be necessary to provide disclosures additional to those specifically required by the framework[4]; and
    (b) it may be necessary to depart from a requirement of the framework[5].

    A "compliance framework" is one that requires compliance with the framework and does not contain the acknowledgements in (a) or (b) above.

3. In this ISA (UK and Ireland) the term "those charged with governance" is defined as: The person(s) or organization(s) (e.g., a corporate trustee) with responsibility for overseeing the strategic direction of the entity and obligations related to the accountability of the entity. This includes overseeing the financial reporting process. For some entities in some jurisdictions, those charged with governance may include management personnel, for example, executive members of a governance board of a private or public sector entity, or an owner-manager. In the UK and Ireland, those charged with governance include the directors (executive and non-executive) of a company or other body, the members of an audit committee where one exists, the partners, proprietors, committee of management or trustees of other forms of entity, or equivalent persons responsible for directing the entity's affairs and preparing its financial statements.

4. **The auditor's report on the financial statements should contain a clear written expression of opinion on the financial statements taken as a whole, based on the auditor evaluating the conclusions drawn from the audit evidence obtained, including evaluating whether.**

[1] For UK Companies issuing financial statements for periods commencing on or after 6 April 2008 and ending before 5 April 2009 guidance on the wording of auditor's reports is provided by Bulletin 2008/8 "Auditor's Reports for Short Accounting Periods in Compliance with the United Kingdom Companies Act 2006".

[2] That version was effective for periods commencing on or after 15 December 2004.

[3] True and fair frameworks are sometimes referred to as "fair presentation frameworks".

[4] In the IFRS Framework this is acknowledged in paragraph 17(c) of IAS 1. In UK GAAP this is acknowledged in Sections 396(4) and 404(4) of the Companies Act 2006.

[5] This is sometimes referred to as the "true and fair override". In the IFRS Framework this is acknowledged in paragraph 19 of IAS 1. In UK GAAP this is acknowledged in Sections 396(5) and 404(5) of the Companies Act 2006.

(a) sufficient appropriate audit evidence has been obtained;
(b) uncorrected misstatements are material, individually or in aggregate;
(c) in respect of a true and fair framework, the financial statements, including the related notes, give a true and fair view; and
(d) in respect of all frameworks, the financial statements have been prepared in all material respects in accordance with the framework, including the requirements of applicable law.

In particular, the auditor should evaluate whether: 5

(a) the financial statements adequately refer to or describe the relevant financial reporting framework;
(b) the financial statements adequately disclose the significant accounting policies selected and applied;
(c) the accounting policies selected and applied are consistent with the applicable financial reporting framework, and are appropriate in the circumstances;
(d) accounting estimates are reasonable;
(e) the information presented in the financial statements is relevant, reliable, comparable and understandable;
(f) the financial statements provide adequate disclosures to enable the intended users to understand the effect of material transactions and events on the information conveyed in the financial statements; and
(g) the terminology used in the financial statements, including the title of each financial statement, is appropriate.

Basic Elements of the Auditor's Report

Title

The auditor's report should have an appropriate title. 6

The term "Independent Auditor" is usually used in the title in order to distinguish 7 the auditor's report from reports that might be issued by others, such as by those charged with governance, or from the reports of other auditors who may not have to comply with the Auditing Practices Board's (APB's) Ethical Standards for Auditors.

Addressee

The auditor's report should be appropriately addressed as required by the circumstances 8 **of the engagement.**

The Companies Acts[6] require the auditor to report to the company's members 9 because the audit is undertaken on their behalf. Such auditor's reports are, therefore, typically addressed to either the members or the shareholders of the company. The auditor's report on financial statements of other types of reporting entity is addressed to the appropriate person or persons, as defined by statute or by the terms of the individual engagement.

---

[6] *In the United Kingdom the Companies Act 2006 establishes this requirement. In the Republic of Ireland the Companies Acts 1963 to 2005 establish this requirement.*

Introductory Paragraph

10   The auditor's report should identify the financial statements of the entity that have been audited, including the date of, and period covered by, the financial statements.

Respective responsibilities of those charged with governance and the auditor

11   The auditor's report should include a statement that those charged with governance are responsible for the preparation of the financial statements and a statement that the responsibility of the auditor is to audit and express an opinion on the financial statements in accordance with applicable legal requirements and International Standards on Auditing (UK and Ireland). The report should also state that those standards require the auditor to comply with the APB's Ethical Standards for Auditors.

12   An appreciation of the interrelationship between the responsibilities of those who prepare financial statements and those who audit them facilitates an understanding of the nature and context of the opinion expressed by the auditor.

13   The preparation of financial statements requires those charged with governance to make significant accounting estimates and judgments, as well as to determine the appropriate accounting principles and methods used in preparation of the financial statements. This determination will be made in the context of the financial reporting framework that those charged with governance choose, or are required, to use. In contrast, the auditor's responsibility is to audit the financial statements in order to express an opinion on them.

Scope of the audit of the financial statements

14   The auditor's report should either:

   (a)   cross refer to a "Statement of the Scope of an Audit" that is maintained on the APB's web site; or
   (b)   cross refer to a "Statement of the Scope of an Audit" that is included elsewhere within the Annual Report; or
   (c)   include the following description of the scope of an audit.

   "An audit involves obtaining evidence about the amounts and disclosures in the financial statements sufficient to give reasonable assurance that the financial statements are free from material misstatement, whether caused by fraud or error. This includes an assessment of: whether the accounting policies are appropriate to the *[describe nature of entity]* circumstances and have been consistently applied and adequately disclosed; the reasonableness of significant accounting estimates made by *[describe those charged with governance]*; and the overall presentation of the financial statements".

15   The APB maintains on its web site example descriptions of the scope of an audit of the financial statements of various categories of United Kingdom company.[7]

16   Where the scope of the audit is described within the Annual Report but not in the auditor's report, such description includes the prescribed text set out in paragraph 14. The content of the description of the scope of the audit is determined by the

---

[7] A description of the scope of an audit of the financial statements of a UK publicly traded company or group can be found at www.frc.org.uk/apb/scope/UKP. The description for a UK non-publicly traded company or group can be found at www.frc.org.uk/apb/scope/UKNP.

auditor regardless of whether it is incorporated into the auditor's report or published as a separate statement elsewhere in the annual report.

Opinion on the financial statements

The opinion paragraph of the auditor's report should clearly state the auditor's opinion as required by the relevant financial reporting framework used to prepare the financial statements, including applicable law.   17

When expressing an unqualified opinion on financial statements prepared in accordance with a true and fair framework the opinion paragraph should clearly state that the financial statements give a true and fair view. It is not sufficient for the auditor to conclude that the financial statements give a true and fair view solely on the basis that the financial statements were prepared in accordance with accounting standards and any other applicable legal requirements.   18

Although the "true and fair" concept has been central to accounting and auditing practice in the UK and Ireland for many years it is not defined in legislation. In 2008, the Financial Reporting Council published a legal opinion, that it had commissioned, entitled "The true and fair requirement revisited" (The Opinion)[8]. The Opinion confirms the overarching nature of the true and fair requirement to the preparation of financial statements in the United Kingdom, whether they are prepared in accordance with international or national accounting standards.   19

The Opinion states that "The preparation of financial statements is not a mechanical process where compliance with relevant accounting standards will automatically ensure that those financial statements show a true and fair view, or a fair presentation. Such compliance may be highly likely to produce such an outcome; but it does not guarantee it".   20

To advise the reader of the context in which the auditor's opinion is expressed, the auditor's opinion indicates the financial reporting framework upon which the financial statements are based. In the UK and Ireland subject to certain restrictions, these normally comprise: 21

- "International Financial Reporting Standards (IFRSs) as adopted by the European Union", and the national law that is applicable when using IFRSs and, in the case of consolidated financial statements of publicly traded companies[9], Article 4 of the IAS Regulation (1606/2002/EC); or
- "UK Generally Accepted Accounting Practice", which comprises applicable UK company law and UK Accounting Standards as issued by the Accounting Standards Board (ASB); or
- "Generally Accepted Accounting Practice in Ireland", which comprises applicable Irish company law and the Accounting Standards issued by the ASB and promulgated by the Institute of Chartered Accountants in Ireland.

Opinion in respect of an additional financial reporting framework

When an auditor is engaged to issue an opinion on the compliance of the financial statements with an additional financial reporting framework the second opinion should   22

---

[8] The Opinion can be downloaded from the FRC website at www.frc.org.uk/about/trueandfair.cfm

[9] A publicly traded company is one whose securities are admitted to trading on a regulated market in any Member State in the European Union".

be clearly separated from the first opinion on the financial statements, by use of an appropriate heading.

23 The financial statements of some entities may comply with two financial reporting frameworks (for example "IFRSs as issued by the IASB" and "IFRSs as adopted by the European Union") and those charged with governance may engage the auditor to express an opinion in respect of both frameworks. If the auditor is satisfied that there are no differences between the two financial reporting frameworks that affect the financial statements being reported on, the auditor states a second separate opinion with regard to the other financial reporting framework.

Requirement specific to public sector entities where an opinion on regularity is given

24 For the audit of certain public sector entities the audit mandate may require the auditor to express an opinion on regularity[10]. Regularity is the requirement that financial transactions are in accordance with the legislation authorising them.

25 **Where the auditor has a reporting responsibility with respect to regularity the opinion arising from this responsibility should be set out in a separate section of the auditor's report following the opinion[s] on the financial statements.**

Opinion on other matters

26 **The auditor should address other reporting responsibilities in [a] separate section[s] of the auditor's report following the opinion[s] on the financial statements and, where there is one, the opinion on regularity.**

27 The auditor sets out its opinion[s] on these other reporting responsibilities in [a] separate section[s] of the report in order to clearly distinguish it from the auditor's opinion[s] on the financial statements.

28 Other reporting responsibilities may be determined by specific statutory requirements applicable to the reporting entity, or, in some circumstances, by the terms of the auditor's engagement[11]. Such matters may be required to be dealt with by either:

(a) a positive statement in the auditor's report; or
(b) by exception.

An example of (a) arises in the United Kingdom where the auditor of a company is required to state whether, in the auditor's opinion, the information given in the directors' report for the financial year for which the accounts are prepared is consistent with those accounts[12]. An example of (b) arises in the United Kingdom where company legislation requires the auditor of a company to report if a company has not maintained adequate accounting records[13].

[10] Guidance for auditors of public sector bodies in the UK and Ireland is given in Practice Note 10 "Audit of Financial Statements of Public Sector Bodies in the United Kingdom (Revised)" and Practice Note 10(1) "Audit of Central Governent Financial Statements in the Republic of Ireland (Revised)".

[11] An example of a reporting responsibility determined by the terms of the auditor's engagement is where the directors of a listed company are required by the rules of a Listing Authority to ensure that the auditor reviews certain statements made by the directors before the annual report is published.

[12] Section 496 of the Companies Act 2006.

[13] Section 498(2)(a) of the Companies Act 2006.

If the auditor is required to report on certain matters by exception the auditor should describe its responsibilities under the heading "Matters on which we are required to report by exception" and incorporate a suitable conclusion in respect of such matters. 29

Where the auditor has discharged such responsibilities and has nothing to report in respect of them, the conclusion could be expressed in the form of the following phrase:"We have nothing to report in respect of the following:". 30

Where the auditor expresses a modified conclusion in respect of other reporting responsibilities (including those on which they are required to report by exception) this may give rise to a modification of the auditor's opinion on the financial statements. For example, if adequate accounting records have not been maintained and as a result it proves impracticable for the auditor to obtain sufficient appropriate evidence concerning material matters in the financial statements, the auditor's report on the financial statements includes a qualified opinion or disclaimer of opinion arising from that limitation. 31

Date of Report

The date of an auditor's report on a reporting entity's financial statements should be the date on which the auditor signed the report expressing an opinion on those statements. 32

This informs the reader that the auditor has considered the effect on the financial statements and on the auditor's report of events and transactions of which the auditor became aware and that occurred up to that date. 33

The auditor should not sign, and hence date, the report earlier than the date on which all other information contained in a report of which the audited financial statements form a part have been approved by those charged with governance and the auditor has considered all necessary available evidence. 34

The auditor is not in a position to form the opinion until the financial statements (and any other information contained in a report of which the audited financial statements form a part) have been approved by those charged with governance and the auditor has completed the assessment of all the evidence the auditor considers necessary for the opinion or opinions to be given in the auditor's report. This assessment includes events occurring up to the date the opinion is expressed. The auditor, therefore, plans the conduct of an audit to take account of the need to ensure, before expressing an opinion on financial statements, that those charged with governance have approved the financial statements and any accompanying other information and that the auditor has completed a sufficient review of post balance sheet events. 35

The date of the auditor's report is, therefore, the date on which the auditor signs the auditor's report expressing an opinion on the financial statements for distribution with those financial statements, following: 36

(a) receipt of the financial statements and accompanying documents in the form approved by those charged with governance for release;
(b) review of all documents which the auditor is required to consider in addition to the financial statements (for example the directors' report, chairman's statement or other review of an entity's affairs which will accompany the financial statements); and
(c) completion of all procedures necessary to form an opinion on the financial statements (and any other opinions required by law or regulation) including a review of post balance sheet events.

37 The form of the financial statements and other information approved by those charged with governance, and considered by the auditor when signing a report expressing the auditor's opinion, may be in the form of final drafts from which printed documents will be prepared. Subsequent production of printed copies of the financial statements and the auditor's report does not constitute the creation of a new document. Copies of the report produced for circulation to shareholders or others may, therefore, reproduce a printed version of the auditor's signature showing the date of actual signature.

38 If the date on which the auditor signs the report is later than that on which those charged with governance approved the financial statements, the auditor takes such steps as are appropriate:

(a) to obtain assurance that those charged with governance would have approved the financial statements on that later date (for example, by obtaining confirmation from specified individual members of the board to whom authority has been delegated for this purpose); and

(b) to ensure that their procedures for reviewing subsequent events cover the period up to that date.

Location of Auditor's Office

39 **The report should name the location of the office where the auditor is based.**

Auditor's Signature

40 **The auditor's report should state the name of the auditor and be signed and dated.**

41 The report is signed in the name of the audit firm, the personal name of the auditor or both, as required by law. In the case of a UK company, where the auditor is an individual the report is required to be signed by the individual. Where the auditor of a UK company is a firm the report is required to be signed by the senior statutory auditor[14] in his or her own name, for and on behalf of the auditor.

The Auditor's Report

42 **With respect to compliance frameworks an unqualified opinion on the financial statements should be expressed only when the auditor concludes that they have been prepared in accordance with the identified financial reporting framework, including the requirements of applicable law.**

43 **With respect to true and fair frameworks, in addition to the requirement in paragraph 42, an unqualified opinion on the financial statements should be expressed only when the auditor concludes that the financial statements give a true and fair view.**

44 Illustrative examples of auditor's reports tailored for use with audits conducted in accordance with ISAs (UK and Ireland) are given in various Bulletins and Practice Notes issued by the APB. With respect to companies examples are provided in the most recent versions of the APB Bulletins, "Auditor's Reports on Financial Statements in the United Kingdom"/"Auditor's Reports on Financial Statements in the Republic of Ireland".

---

[14] *See Bulletin 2008/6 "The "Senior Statutory Auditor" under the United Kingdom Companies Act 2006". This Bulletin, at paragraphs 8-10 also explains the meaning of "signing the auditor's report" in a UK context.*

Modified Reports

An auditor's report is considered to be modified in the following situations: 45

Matters That Do Not Affect the Auditor's Opinion

(a) Emphasis of matter

Matters That Do Affect the Auditor's Opinion

(b) Qualified opinion,
(c) Disclaimer of opinion, or
(d) Adverse opinion.

The APB Bulletins referred to in paragraph 44 include examples of modified auditor's reports illustrating each of these situations.

Matters That Do Not Affect the Auditor's Opinion

An auditor's report may be modified by adding an emphasis of matter paragraph to highlight a matter affecting the financial statements which is included in a note to the financial statements that more extensively discusses the matter. The addition of such an emphasis of matter paragraph does not affect the auditor's opinion. The emphasis of matter paragraph usually follows the opinion paragraph on the financial statements and refers to the fact that the auditor's opinion is not qualified in this respect. Communication with the reader is enhanced by the use of an appropriate subheading. 46

The auditor should consider modifying the auditor's report by adding a paragraph if there is a significant uncertainty, the resolution of which is dependent upon future events and which may affect the financial statements. In accordance with the requirements of ISA (UK and Ireland) 570 "Going Concern" the auditor should always modify the auditor's report by adding a paragraph to highlight a material uncertainty relating to an event or condition that may cast significant doubt on the entity's ability to continue as a going concern. 47

An uncertainty is a matter whose outcome depends on future actions or events not under the direct control of the entity but that may affect the financial statements. 48

The emphasis of matter paragraph describes the matter giving rise to the significant uncertainty and its possible effects on the financial statements, including (where practicable) quantification. Where it is not possible to quantify the potential effects of the resolution of the uncertainty, the auditor includes a statement to that effect. Reference may be made to notes in the financial statements but such a reference is not a substitute for sufficient description of the significant uncertainty so that a reader can appreciate the principal points at issue and their implications. 49

In determining whether an uncertainty is significant, the auditor considers: 50

(a) the risk that the estimate included in financial statements may be subject to change;
(b) the range of possible outcomes; and
(c) the consequences of those outcomes on the view shown in the financial statements.

51 Uncertainties are regarded as significant when they involve a significant level of concern about the validity of the going concern basis or other matters whose potential effect on the financial statements is unusually great. An example of a significant uncertainty may be the outcome, either beneficial or detrimental, of major litigation.

52 An unqualified opinion indicates that the auditor considers that appropriate estimates and disclosures relating to significant uncertainties are made in the financial statements. It remains unqualified notwithstanding the inclusion of an emphasis of matter paragraph describing a significant uncertainty.

53 When the auditor concludes that the estimate of the outcome of a significant uncertainty is materially misstated or that the disclosure relating to it is inadequate, the auditor issues a qualified opinion.

54 The addition of a paragraph emphasising a going concern problem or other significant uncertainty is ordinarily adequate to meet the auditor's reporting responsibilities regarding such matters. However, in extreme cases, such as situations involving multiple uncertainties that are significant to the financial statements, the auditor may consider it appropriate to express a disclaimer of opinion instead of adding an emphasis of matter paragraph.

55 **If the auditor considers it necessary to communicate a matter other than those that are presented or disclosed in the financial statements that, in the auditor's judgment, is relevant to users' understanding of the audit, the auditor's responsibilities or the auditor's report and this is not prohibited by law or regulation, the auditor should do so in a paragraph in the auditor's report, with the heading "Other Matter," or other appropriate heading.**

56 "Other Matter" paragraphs may be used by the auditor in an number of different circumstances, for example:

- To provide further explanation of the auditor's responsibilities in the audit of the financial statements or of the auditor's report thereon.
- Where reporting by exception on corporate governance matters[15].
- If an amendment to other information in a document containing audited financial statements is necessary to correct a material inconsistency and the entity refuses to make the amendment, the auditor would consider including in the auditor's report an emphasis of matter paragraph describing the material inconsistency.

Matters That Do Affect the Auditor's Opinion

57 An auditor may not be able to express an unqualified opinion when either of the following circumstances exist and, in the auditor's judgment, the effect of the matter is or may be material to the financial statements:

(a) there is a disagreement with those charged with governance regarding the acceptability of the accounting policies selected, the method of their application or the adequacy of financial statement disclosures; or

(b) there is a limitation on the scope of the auditor's work

The circumstances described in (a) could lead to a qualified opinion or an adverse opinion. The circumstances described in (b) could lead to a qualified opinion or a

---

[15] See Bulletin 2006/5 paragraph 55.

disclaimer of opinion. These circumstances are discussed more fully in paragraphs 66–76.

The three financial reporting frameworks described in paragraph 21 (which are all true and fair frameworks) recognise that a departure from an accounting standard may be necessary where compliance with that standard would produce a result so misleading that it would conflict with the objective of financial statements. IAS 1 states that the circumstances in which there should be such a conflict are "extremely rare", FRS 18 uses the word "exceptional". As discussed in The Opinion described in paragraph 19, both of these terms contemplate departures from a relevant standard in circumstances that compliance therewith would be inconsistent with the basic objective of fair presentation or the true and fair view. Against this background, therefore, the circumstances in which departure from an accounting standard is appropriate are very limited.   58

In almost all cases, therefore, a departure from accounting standards will result in the issuance of a qualified or adverse opinion on the view given by the financial statements. When the auditor concludes that the financial statements of a company do not comply with accounting standards, the auditor assesses whether: 59

(a) the departure is necessary in order to show a true and fair view; and
(b) adequate disclosure has been made concerning the departure from accounting standards.

Where an explanation is not given for a departure from accounting standards, its absence may of itself impair the ability of the financial statements to give a true and fair view of the company's state of affairs and profit or loss. When the auditor concludes that this is so, a qualified or adverse opinion on the view given by the financial statements is appropriate, in addition to a reference (where appropriate) to the departure from accounting standards and the reasons for the departure.   60

A qualified opinion should be expressed when the auditor concludes that an unqualified opinion cannot be expressed but that the effect of any disagreement with those charged with governance, or limitation on scope is not so material and pervasive as to require an adverse opinion or a disclaimer of opinion. A qualified opinion should be expressed as being "except for" the effects of the matter to which the qualification relates.   61

A disclaimer of opinion should be expressed when the possible effect of a limitation on scope is so material and pervasive that the auditor has not been able to obtain sufficient appropriate audit evidence and accordingly is unable to express an opinion on the financial statements.   62

An adverse opinion should be expressed when the effect of a disagreement is so material and pervasive to the financial statements that the auditor concludes that a qualification of the report is not adequate to disclose the misleading or incomplete nature of the financial statements.   63

Whenever the auditor expresses an opinion that is other than unqualified, a clear description of all the substantive reasons should be included in the report and, unless impracticable, a quantification of the possible effect(s) on the financial statements. Ordinarily, this information would be set out in a separate paragraph preceding the opinion or disclaimer of opinion and may include a reference to a more extensive discussion, if any, in a note to the financial statements.   64

Whilst reference may be made to relevant notes in the financial statements, such reference is not a substitute for sufficient description of the circumstances in the   65 auditor's report so that a reader can appreciate the principal points at issue and their implications for an understanding of the financial statements.

Disagreement with Those Charged with Governance

66 The auditor may disagree with those charged with governance about matters such as the acceptability of accounting policies selected, the method of their application, or the adequacy of disclosures in the financial statements. **If such disagreements are material to the financial statements, the auditor should express a qualified or an adverse opinion.**

Limitation on Scope

67 A limitation on the scope of the auditor's work may sometimes be imposed by the entity (for example, when the terms of the engagement specify that the auditor will not carry out an audit procedure that the auditor believes is necessary). However, when the limitation in the terms of a proposed engagement is such that the auditor believes the need to express a disclaimer of opinion exists; the auditor would ordinarily not accept such a limited engagement as an audit engagement, unless required to by statute. Also, a statutory auditor would not accept such an audit engagement when the limitation infringes on the auditor's statutory duties.

Limitation on scope imposed by the entity before accepting an audit engagement

68 **If the auditor is aware, before accepting an audit engagement, that those charged with governance of the entity, or those who appoint its auditor, will impose a limitation on the scope of the audit work which the auditor considers likely to result in the need to issue a disclaimer of opinion on the financial statements, the auditor should not accept that engagement, unless required to do so by statute[16].**

69 Agreeing to such a restriction on the scope of the audit work would seriously threaten the auditor's independence and make it impossible for the auditor to meet with integrity and rigour the requirements of ISAs (UK and Ireland). The acceptance of such a limited engagement as an audit engagement would be incompatible with the auditor's obligations to conduct any audit of financial statements in accordance with:

(a) applicable legislation; and
(b) Auditing Standards contained in the ISAs (UK and Ireland).

Furthermore, the auditor, by accepting the engagement on such restricted terms, might be regarded as complicit in an arrangement to enable the entity to observe the form of any legal or regulatory audit requirements but to evade complying with the substance of those obligations.

Limitation on scope imposed by the entity after accepting an audit engagement

70 **If the auditor becomes aware, after accepting an audit engagement, that those charged with governance of the entity, or those who appointed them as its auditor, have imposed a limitation on the scope of the audit work which they consider likely to result in the**

---

[16] *There are certain circumstances in which (regardless of any limitation imposed on the scope of the audit work) the auditor is required by statute to accept an audit engagement, for example the majority of appointments of the national audit agencies to audit the accounts of certain public sector bodies. However, in general, there is no such requirement in the private sector; there may be a statutory requirement for the entity to appoint an auditor, but this does not create an obligation for any auditor to accept appointment.*

need to issue a disclaimer of opinion on the financial statements, the auditor should request the removal of the limitation. If the limitation is not removed, the auditor should consider resigning from the audit engagement.

If the limitation is not removed, the auditor considers the factors discussed in paragraph 69 above and may often decide that resignation from the audit engagement is appropriate. If, after careful consideration of all the circumstances (for example, where third party interests are involved), the auditor concludes that it is appropriate to continue with the engagement, the auditor includes in the audit report a full description of the events which led to the disclaimer. On completion of the audit for that year, however, the auditor will follow the requirements of paragraph 68 when deciding whether to undertake the audit for the following period[17].

In cases where the auditor resigns immediately, or continues with the audit for that year but does not seek reappointment, the auditor needs to comply with any statutory, regulatory or professional requirements for a statement of the circumstances of ceasing to hold office.[18] The fact that such a limitation has been imposed on the scope of the auditor's work may be a matter to which the auditor refers in both cases.

Where a significant limitation on scope has arisen during the course of the audit work the auditor considers whether an obligation arises under statute, as discussed in ISA (UK and Ireland) 250, Section B, to make a report to the appropriate regulators.

Limitation on scope imposed by circumstances

A scope limitation may be imposed by circumstances (for example, when the timing of the auditor's appointment is such that the auditor is unable to observe the counting of physical inventories). It may also arise when, in the opinion of the auditor, the entity's accounting records are inadequate or when the auditor is unable to carry out an audit procedure believed to be desirable. In these circumstances, the auditor would attempt to carry out reasonable alternative procedures to obtain sufficient appropriate audit evidence to support an unqualified opinion.

When there is a limitation on the scope of the auditor's work that requires expression of a qualified opinion or a disclaimer of opinion, the auditor's report should describe the limitation and indicate the possible adjustments to the financial statements that might have been determined to be necessary had the limitation not existed.

In considering whether a limitation on scope results in a lack of evidence necessary to form an opinion, the auditor assesses:

(a) the quantity and type of evidence which may reasonably be expected to be available to support the particular figure or disclosure in the financial statements; and
(b) the possible effect on the financial statements of the matter for which insufficient evidence is available. When the possible effect is, in the opinion of the auditor, material to the financial statements, there will be insufficient evidence to support an unqualified opinion.

---

[17] *Auditors in the Republic of Ireland are required by the Companies Act 1963 (section 160, para 2(c)) to give the company notice in writing of their unwillingness to be re-appointed, where this is the case.*

[18] *For example, in the case of a quoted company incorporated in the United Kingdom, on ceasing to hold office for any reason, the auditor is required under section 519(3) Companies Act 2006 to make'... a statement of the circumstances connected with his ceasing to hold office.' Similar requirements exist in the Republic of Ireland (section 185 Companies Act, 1990).*

Effective Date

77 This ISA (UK and Ireland) is effective for audits of financial statements of:

(a) UK companies, except for those that are charities, for periods commencing on or after 6 April 2008 and ending on or after 5 April 2009; and

(b) all other UK entities for periods ending on or after 15 December 2010.

For earlier accounting periods and for audits carried out in the Republic of Ireland the previous version of ISA (UK and Ireland) 700 is applicable[19].

---

[19] *That version was effective for periods commencing on or after 15 December 2004.*

Illustrative auditor's reports

The four Illustrative auditor's reports set out on the following pages do not form part of ISA (UK and Ireland) 700 (Revised).

Example 1 – UK publicly traded company using IFRSs as adopted by the European Union, where the scope of the audit is described on the APB web-site or elsewhere in the annual report

- Group and parent company financial statements not presented separately
- IFRSs as adopted by the European Union used for both group and parent company financial statements
- Company does meet the Companies Act definition of a quoted company
- Section 408 exemption relating to parent company's own income statement not taken

INDEPENDENT AUDITOR'S REPORT TO THE MEMBERS OF XYZ PLC

We have audited the financial statements of (name of entity) for the year ended ... which comprise [specify the financial statements, such as the Group and Parent Company Statements of Financial Position, the Group and Parent Company Statements of Comprehensive Income, the Group and Parent Company Statements of Cash Flows, the Group and Parent Company Statements of Changes in Equity,] and the related notes[20]. The financial reporting framework that has been applied in their preparation is applicable law and International Financial Reporting Standards (IFRSs) as adopted by the European Union.

Respective responsibilities of directors and auditors

As explained more fully in the Directors' Responsibilities Statement [set out [on pages...]], the directors are responsible for the preparation of the financial statements and for being satisfied that they give a true and fair view. Our responsibility is to audit the financial statements in accordance with applicable law and International Standards on Auditing (UK and Ireland). Those standards require us to comply with the Auditing Practices Board's (APB's) Ethical Standards for Auditors.

Scope of the audit of the financial statements

A description of the scope of an audit of financial statements is [provided on the APB's web-site at www.frc.org.uk/apb/scope/UKP] / [set out [on page x] of the Annual Report].

Opinion on financial statements

In our opinion the financial statements:

- give a true and fair view of the state of the group's and the parent company's affairs as at ... and of the group's and the parent company's profit [loss] for the year then ended;
- have been properly prepared in accordance with IFRSs as adopted by the European Union; and
- have been prepared in accordance with the requirements of the Companies Act 2006 and, as regards the group financial statements, Article 4 of the IAS Regulation.

---

[20] Auditor's reports of entities that do not publish their financial statements on a web site or publish them using "PDF" format may refer to the financial statements by reference to page numbers.

Opinion on other matters prescribed by the Companies Act 2006
In our opinion:

- the part of the Directors' Remuneration Report to be audited has been properly prepared in accordance with the Companies Act 2006; and
- the information given in the Directors' Report for the financial year for which the financial statements are prepared is consistent with the financial statements.

Matters on which we are required to report by exception
We have nothing to report in respect of the following:

Under the Companies Act 2006 we are required to report to you if, in our opinion:

- adequate accounting records have not been kept, or returns adequate for our audit have not been received from branches not visited by us; or
- the parent company financial statements and the part of the Directors' Remuneration Report to be audited are not in agreement with the accounting records and returns; or
- certain disclosures of directors' remuneration specified by law are not made; or
- we have not received all the information and explanations we require for our audit.

Under the Listing Rules we are required to review:

- the directors' statement, [set out [on page]], in relation to going concern; and
- the parts of the Corporate Governance Statement relating to the company's compliance with the nine provisions of the [2006] [June 2008][21] Combined Code specified for our review.

[Signature]   *Address*
John Smith (Senior statutory auditor)   *Date*
for and on behalf of ABC LLP, Statutory Auditor

---

[21] *The June 2008 Combined Code applies to accounting periods beginning on or after 29 June 2008; the 2006 Combined Code applies before that date.*

Example 2 – UK publicly traded company using IFRSs as adopted by the European Union, where the scope of the audit is described within the auditor's report

- Group and parent company financial statements not presented separately
- IFRSs as adopted by the European Union used for both group and parent company financial statements
- Company does meet the Companies Act definition of a quoted company
- Section 408 exemption relating to parent company's own income statement not taken

INDEPENDENT AUDITOR'S REPORT TO THE MEMBERS OF XYZ PLC

We have audited the financial statements of (name of entity) for the year ended ... which comprise [specify the financial statements, such as the Group and Parent Company Statements of Financial Position, the Group and Parent Company Statements of Comprehensive Income, the Group and Parent Company Statements of Cash Flows, the Group and Parent Company Statements of Changes in Equity,] and the related notes[22]. The financial reporting framework that has been applied in their preparation is applicable law and International Financial Reporting Standards (IFRSs) as adopted by the European Union.

Respective responsibilities of directors and auditors

As explained more fully in the Directors' Responsibilities Statement [set out [on pages...]], the directors are responsible for the preparation of the financial statements and for being satisfied that they give a true and fair view. Our responsibility is to audit the financial statements in accordance with applicable law and International Standards on Auditing (UK and Ireland). Those standards require us to comply with the Auditing Practices Board's Ethical Standards for Auditors.

Scope of the audit

An audit involves obtaining evidence about the amounts and disclosures in the financial statements sufficient to give reasonable assurance that the financial statements are free from material misstatement, whether caused by fraud or error. This includes an assessment of: whether the accounting policies are appropriate to the group's and the parent company's circumstances and have been consistently applied and adequately disclosed; the reasonableness of significant accounting estimates made by the directors; and the overall presentation of the financial statements.

Opinion on financial statements

In our opinion the financial statements:

- give a true and fair view of the state of the group's and the parent company's affairs as at ... and of the group's and the parent company's profit [loss] for the year then ended;
- have been properly prepared in accordance with IFRSs as adopted by the European Union; and
- have been prepared in accordance with the requirements of the Companies Act 2006 and, as regards the group financial statements, Article 4 of the IAS Regulation.

Opinion on other matters prescribed by the Companies Act 2006

In our opinion:

---

[22] Auditor's reports of entities that do not publish their financial statements on a web site or publish them using "PDF" format may refer to the financial statements by reference to page numbers.

- the part of the Directors' Remuneration Report to be audited has been properly prepared in accordance with the Companies Act 2006; and
- the information given in the Directors' Report for the financial year for which the financial statements are prepared is consistent with the financial statements.

Matters on which we are required to report by exception
We have nothing to report in respect of the following:

Under the Companies Act 2006 we are required to report to you if, in our opinion:

- adequate accounting records have not been kept, or returns adequate for our audit have not been received from branches not visited by us; or
- the parent company financial statements and the part of the Directors' Remuneration Report to be audited are not in agreement with the accounting records and returns; or
- certain disclosures of directors' remuneration specified by law are not made; or
- we have not received all the information and explanations we require for our audit.

Under the Listing Rules we are required to review:

- the directors' statement, [set out [on page]], in relation to going concern; and
- the parts of the Corporate Governance Statement relating to the company's compliance with the nine provisions of the [2006] [June 2008][23] Combined Code specified for our review.

[Signature]   Address
John Smith (Senior statutory auditor)   Date
for and on behalf of ABC LLP, Statutory Auditor

---

[23] The June 2008 Combined Code applies to accounting periods beginning on or after 29 June 2008; the 2006 Combined Code applies before that date.

Example 3 – UK Non-publicly traded company using UK GAAP, where the scope of the audit is described on the apb web-site or elsewhere in the annual report

- Group and parent company financial statements not presented separately
- Company prepares group financial statements
- Company is not a quoted company
- UK GAAP used for group and parent company financial statements
- Section 408 exemption taken for parent company's own profit and loss account

INDEPENDENT AUDITOR'S REPORT TO THE MEMBERS OF XYZ LIMITED

We have audited the financial statements of (name of entity) for the year ended ... which comprise [specify the financial statements, such as the Group Profit and Loss Account, the Group and Parent Company Balance Sheets, the Group Cash Flow Statement, the Group Statement of Total Recognised Gains and Losses,] and the related notes[24]. The financial reporting framework that has been applied in their preparation is applicable law and United Kingdom Accounting Standards (United Kingdom Generally Accepted Accounting Practice).

Respective responsibilities of directors and auditors

As explained more fully in the Directors' Responsibilities Statement [set out [on pages...]], the directors are responsible for the preparation of the financial statements and for being satisfied that they give a true and fair view. Our responsibility is to audit the financial statements in accordance with applicable law and International Standards on Auditing (UK and Ireland). Those standards require us to comply with the Auditing Practices Board's (APB's) Ethical Standards for Auditors.

Scope of the audit

A description of the scope of an audit of financial statements is [provided on the APB's web-site at www.frc.org.uk/apb/scope/UKNP] / [set out [on page x] of the Annual Report].

Opinion on financial statements

In our opinion the financial statements:

- give a true and fair view of the state of the group's and the parent company's affairs as at ... and of the group's profit [loss] for the year then ended;
- have been properly prepared in accordance with United Kingdom Generally Accepted Accounting Practice; and
- have been prepared in accordance with the requirements of the Companies Act 2006.

Opinion on other matter prescribed by the Companies Act 2006

In our opinion the information given in the Directors' Report for the financial year for which the financial statements are prepared is consistent with the financial statements.

Matters on which we are required to report by exception

We have nothing to report in respect of the following matters where the Companies Act 2006 requires us to report to you if, in our opinion:

---

[24] Auditor's reports of entities that do not publish their financial statements on a web site or publish them using "PDF" format may refer to the financial statements by reference to page numbers.

- adequate accounting records have not been kept, or returns adequate for our audit have not been received from branches not visited by us; or
- the parent company financial statements are not in agreement with the accounting records and returns; or
- certain disclosures of directors' remuneration specified by law are not made; or
- we have not received all the information and explanations we require for our audit.

[Signature]
John Smith (Senior statutory auditor)
for and on behalf of ABC LLP, Statutory Auditor

Address
Date

Example 4 – UK Non-publicly traded company using UK GAAP, where the scope of the audit is described within the auditor's report

- Group and parent company financial statements not presented separately
- Company prepares group financial statements
- Company is not a quoted company
- UK GAAP used for group and parent company financial statements
- Section 408 exemption taken for parent company's own profit and loss account

INDEPENDENT AUDITOR'S REPORT TO THE MEMBERS OF XYZ LIMITED

We have audited the financial statements of (name of entity) for the year ended ... which comprise [specify the financial statements, such as the Group Profit and Loss Account, the Group and Parent Company Balance Sheets, the Group Cash Flow Statement, the Group Statement of Total Recognised Gains and Losses,] and the related notes[25]. The financial reporting framework that has been applied in their preparation is applicable law and United Kingdom Accounting Standards (United Kingdom Generally Accepted Accounting Practice).

Respective responsibilities of directors and auditors

As explained more fully in the Directors' Responsibilities Statement [set out [on pages...]], the directors are responsible for the preparation of the financial statements and for being satisfied that they give a true and fair view. Our responsibility is to audit the financial statements in accordance with applicable law and International Standards on Auditing (UK and Ireland). Those standards require us to comply with the Auditing Practices Board's Ethical Standards for Auditors.

Scope of the audit

An audit involves obtaining evidence about the amounts and disclosures in the financial statements sufficient to give reasonable assurance that the financial statements are free from material misstatement, whether caused by fraud or error. This includes an assessment of: whether the accounting policies are appropriate to the group's and the parent company's circumstances and have been consistently applied and adequately disclosed; the reasonableness of significant accounting estimates made by the directors; and the overall presentation of the financial statements.

Opinion on financial statements

In our opinion the financial statements:

- give a true and fair view of the state of the group's and the parent company's affairs as at ... and of the group's profit [loss] for the year then ended;
- have been properly prepared in accordance with United Kingdom Generally Accepted Accounting Practice; and
- have been prepared in accordance with the requirements of the Companies Act 2006.

Opinion on other matter prescribed by the Companies Act 2006

In our opinion the information given in the Directors' Report for the financial year for which the financial statements are prepared is consistent with the financial statements.

---

[25] Auditor's reports of entities that do not publish their financial statements on a web site or publish them using "PDF" format may refer to the financial statements by reference to page numbers.

Matters on which we are required to report by exception
We have nothing to report in respect of the following matters where the Companies Act 2006 requires us to report to you if, in our opinion:

- adequate accounting records have not been kept, or returns adequate for our audit have not been received from branches not visited by us; or
- the parent company financial statements are not in agreement with the accounting records and returns; or
- certain disclosures of directors' remuneration specified by law are not made; or
- we have not received all the information and explanations we require for our audit.

[Signature]   *Address*
John Smith (Senior statutory auditor)   *Date*
for and on behalf of ABC LLP, Statutory Auditor

[710]
Comparatives
(Issued December 2004)

Contents

	Paragraphs
Introduction	1 - 5-1
Corresponding Figures	6 - 19
Comparative Financial Statements	20 - 31
Effective Date	32

Appendix 1: Discussion of Financial Reporting Frameworks for Comparatives

Appendix 2: Example Auditor's Reports

International Standard on Auditing (UK and Ireland) (ISA (UK and Ireland)) 710 "Comparatives" should be read in the context of the Auditing Practices Board's Statement "The Auditing Practices Board – Scope and Authority of Pronouncements (Revised)" which sets out the application and authority of ISAs (UK and Ireland).

Introduction

1 The purpose of this International Standard on Auditing (UK and Ireland) (ISA (UK and Ireland)) is to establish standards and provide guidance on the auditor's responsibilities regarding comparatives. It does not deal with situations when summarized financial statements are presented with the audited financial statements (for guidance see ISA (UK and Ireland) 720 "Other Information in Documents Containing Audited Financial Statements," and ISA 800 "The Auditor's Report on Special Purpose Audit Engagements").

1-1 This ISA (UK and Ireland) uses the terms 'those charged with governance' and 'management'. The term 'governance' describes the role of persons entrusted with the supervision, control and direction of an entity. Ordinarily, those charged with governance are accountable for ensuring that the entity achieves its objectives, and for the quality of its financial reporting and reporting to interested parties. Those charged with governance include management only when they perform such functions.

1-2 In the UK and Ireland, those charged with governance include the directors (executive and non-executive) of a company or other body, the members of an audit committee where one exists, the partners, proprietors, committee of management or trustees of other forms of entity, or equivalent persons responsible for directing the entity's affairs and preparing its financial statements.

1-3 'Management' comprises those persons who perform senior managerial functions.

1-4 In the UK and Ireland, depending on the nature and circumstances of the entity, management may include some or all of those charged with governance (e.g. executive directors). Management will not normally include non-executive directors.

1-5 ISA (UK and Ireland) 510 "Opening Balances" establishes standards and guidance regarding opening balances, including when the financial statements are audited for the first time or when the financial statements for the prior period were audited by another auditor.

2 **The auditor should determine whether the comparatives comply in all material respects with the financial reporting framework applicable to the financial statements being audited.**

2-1 **The auditor should obtain sufficient appropriate audit evidence that amounts derived from the preceding period's financial statements are free from material misstatements and are appropriately incorporated in the financial statements for the current period.**

3 The existence of differences in financial reporting frameworks between countries results in comparative financial information being presented differently in each framework. Comparatives in financial statements, for example, may present amounts (such as financial position, results of operations, cash flows) and appropriate disclosures of an entity for more than one period, depending on the framework. The frameworks and methods of presentation are referred to in this ISA (UK and Ireland) as follows:

(a) *Corresponding figures* where amounts and other disclosures for the preceding period are included as part of the current period financial statements, and are intended to be read in relation to the amounts and other disclosures relating to the current period (referred to as "current period figures" for the purpose of this ISA (UK and Ireland)). These corresponding figures are not presented as complete financial statements capable of standing alone, but are an integral part of the current period financial statements intended to be read only in relationship to the current period figures; and
(b) *Comparative financial statements* where amounts and other disclosures for the preceding period are included for comparison with the financial statements of the current period, but do not form part of the current period financial statements.

(Refer to Appendix 1 to this ISA (UK and Ireland) for discussion of these different reporting frameworks.)

Comparatives are presented in compliance with the applicable financial reporting framework. The essential audit reporting differences are that:

(a) For corresponding figures, the auditor's report only refers to the financial statements of the current period; whereas
(b) For comparative financial statements, the auditor's report refers to each period that financial statements are presented.

This ISA (UK and Ireland) provides guidance on the auditor's responsibilities for comparatives and for reporting on them under the two frameworks in separate sections.

> In the UK and Ireland the corresponding figures method of presentation is usually required.

Corresponding Figures

The Auditor's Responsibilities

The auditor should obtain sufficient appropriate audit evidence that the corresponding figures meet the requirements of the applicable financial reporting framework. The extent of audit procedures performed on the corresponding figures is significantly less than for the audit of the current period figures and is ordinarily limited to ensuring that the corresponding figures have been correctly reported and are appropriately classified. This involves the auditor evaluating whether:

(a) Accounting policies used for the corresponding figures are consistent with those of the current period or whether appropriate adjustments and/or disclosures have been made; and
(b) Corresponding figures agree with the amounts and other disclosures presented in the prior period or whether appropriate adjustments and/or disclosures have been made.

> In the UK and Ireland, the auditor should obtain sufficient appropriate audit evidence that:
>
> (a) **The accounting policies used for the corresponding amounts are consistent with those of the current period and appropriate adjustments and disclosures have been made where this is not the case;**

> (b) The corresponding amounts agree with the amounts and other disclosures presented in the preceding period and are free from errors in the context of the financial statements of the current period; and
> (c) Where corresponding amounts have been adjusted as required by relevant legislation and accounting standards, appropriate disclosures have been made.

7 When the financial statements of the prior period have been audited by another auditor, the incoming auditor evaluates whether the corresponding figures meet the conditions specified in paragraph 6 above and also follows the guidance in ISA (UK and Ireland) 510 "Initial Engagements – Opening Balances."

8 When the financial statements of the prior period were not audited, the incoming auditor nonetheless assesses whether the corresponding figures meet the conditions specified in paragraph 6 above and also follows the guidance in ISA (UK and Ireland) 510 "Initial Engagements – Opening Balances."

9 If the auditor becomes aware of a possible material misstatement in the corresponding figures when performing the current period audit, the auditor performs such additional audit procedures as are appropriate in the circumstances.

Reporting

10 When the comparatives are presented as corresponding figures, the auditor should issue an audit report in which the comparatives are not specifically identified because the auditor's opinion is on the current period financial statements as a whole, including the corresponding figures.

11 The auditor's report would make specific reference to the corresponding figures only in the circumstances described in paragraphs 12, 13, 15(b), and 16 through 19.

12 When the auditor's report on the prior period, as previously issued, included a qualified opinion, disclaimer of opinion, or adverse opinion and the matter which gave rise to the modification is:

(a) Unresolved, and results in a modification of the auditor's report regarding the current period figures, the auditor's report should also be modified regarding the corresponding figures; or

(b) Unresolved, but does not result in a modification of the auditor's report regarding the current period figures, the auditor's report should be modified regarding the corresponding figures.

> 12-1 With respect to situations described in 12(b), if corresponding amounts are required by law or regulation, the reference is in the form of a qualification on the grounds of non-compliance with that requirement. If corresponding amounts are presented solely as good practice, the reference is made in the auditor's report in the form of an explanatory paragraph.

13 When the auditor's report on the prior period, as previously issued, included a qualified opinion, disclaimer of opinion, or adverse opinion and the matter which gave rise to the modification is resolved and properly dealt with in the financial statements, the current report does not ordinarily refer to the previous modification. However, if the matter is material to the current period, the auditor may include an emphasis of matter paragraph dealing with the situation.

In some circumstances the auditor may consider it appropriate to qualify the audit opinion on the current period's financial statements. For example, if a provision which the auditor considered should have been made in the previous period is made in the current period.	13-1

In performing the audit of the current period financial statements, the auditor, in certain unusual circumstances, may become aware of a material misstatement that affects the prior period financial statements on which an unmodified report has been previously issued.   **14**

In such circumstances, the auditor should consider the guidance in ISA (UK and Ireland) 560 "Subsequent Events" and: **15**

(a) **If the prior period financial statements have been revised and reissued with a new auditor's report, the auditor should obtain sufficient appropriate audit evidence that the corresponding figures agree with the revised financial statements; or**
(b) **If the prior period financial statements have not been revised and reissued, and the corresponding figures have not been properly restated and/or appropriate disclosures have not been made, the auditor should issue a modified report on the current period financial statements modified with respect to the corresponding figures included therein.**

If, in the circumstances described in paragraph 14, the prior period financial statements have not been revised and an auditor's report has not been reissued, but the corresponding figures have been properly restated and/or appropriate disclosures have been made in the current period financial statements, the auditor may include an emphasis of matter paragraph describing the circumstances and referencing to the appropriate disclosures. In this regard, the auditor also considers the guidance in ISA (UK and Ireland) 560 "Subsequent Events."   **16**

Incoming Auditor – Additional Requirements

Prior Period Financial Statements Audited by Another Auditor

In some jurisdictions, the incoming auditor is permitted to refer to the predecessor auditor's report on the corresponding figures in the incoming auditor's report for the current period. **When the auditor decides to refer to another auditor, the incoming auditor's report should indicate:**   **17**

(a) **That the financial statements of the prior period were audited by another auditor;**
(b) **The type of report issued by the predecessor auditor and, if the report was modified, the reasons therefor; and**
(c) **The date of that report.**

In the UK and Ireland the incoming auditor does not refer to the predecessor auditor's report on the corresponding figures in the incoming auditor's report for the current period. The incoming auditor assumes audit responsibility for the corresponding figures only in the context of the financial statements as a whole. The incoming auditor reads the preceding period's financial statements and, using the knowledge gained during the current audit, considers whether they have been properly reflected as corresponding figures in the current period's financial statements.	17-1

17-2 Although the incoming auditor is not required to re-audit the financial statements of the preceding period, if the incoming auditor becomes aware of a possible material misstatement of corresponding figures, the procedures in paragraphs 14 - 16 apply.

Prior Period Financial Statements Not Audited

18 **When the prior period financial statements are not audited, the incoming auditor should state in the auditor's report that the corresponding figures are unaudited.** Such a statement does not, however, relieve the auditor of the requirement to perform appropriate audit procedures regarding opening balances of the current period. Clear disclosure in the financial statements that the corresponding figures are unaudited is encouraged.

18-1 If the auditor is not able to obtain sufficient appropriate audit evidence regarding the corresponding figures, or if there is not adequate disclosure, the auditor considers the implications for the auditor's report.

19 **In situations where the incoming auditor identifies that the corresponding figures are materially misstated, the auditor should request management[1a] to revise the corresponding figures or if management refuses to do so, appropriately modify the report.**

Comparative Financial Statements

The Auditor's Responsibilities

20 **The auditor should obtain sufficient appropriate audit evidence that the comparative financial statements meet the requirements of the applicable financial reporting framework.** This involves the auditor evaluating whether:

(a) Accounting policies of the prior period are consistent with those of the current period or whether appropriate adjustments and/or disclosures have been made; and
(b) Prior period figures presented agree with the amounts and other disclosures presented in the prior period or whether appropriate adjustments and disclosures have been made.

21 When the financial statements of the prior period have been audited by another auditor, the incoming auditor evaluates whether the comparative financial statements meet the conditions in paragraph 20 above and also follows the guidance in ISA (UK and Ireland) 510 "Initial Engagements – Opening Balances."

22 When the financial statements of the prior period were not audited, the incoming auditor nonetheless evaluates whether the comparative financial statements meet the conditions specified in paragraph 20 above and also follows the guidance in ISA (UK and Ireland) 510 "Initial Engagements – Opening Balances."

[1a] *In The UK and Ireland, those charged with governance are responsible for the preparation of the financial statements.*

If the auditor becomes aware of a possible material misstatement in the prior year figures when performing the current period audit, the auditor performs such additional audit procedures as are appropriate in the circumstances. 23

Reporting

When the comparatives are presented as comparative financial statements, the auditor should issue a report in which the comparatives are specifically identified because the auditor's opinion is expressed individually on the financial statements of each period presented. Since the auditor's report on comparative financial statements applies to the individual financial statements presented, the auditor may express a qualified or adverse opinion, disclaim an opinion, or include an emphasis of matter paragraph with respect to one or more financial statements for one or more periods, while issuing a different report on the other financial statements. 24

When reporting on the prior period financial statements in connection with the current year's audit, if the opinion on such prior period financial statements is different from the opinion previously expressed, the auditor should disclose the substantive reasons for the different opinion in an emphasis of matter paragraph. This may arise when the auditor becomes aware of circumstances or events that materially affect the financial statements of a prior period during the course of the audit of the current period. 25

Incoming Auditor – Additional Requirements

Prior Period Financial Statements Audited by Another Auditor

When the financial statements of the prior period were audited by another auditor, 26
(a) **The predecessor auditor may reissue the audit report on the prior period with the incoming auditor only reporting on the current period; or**
(b) **The incoming auditor's report should state that the prior period was audited by another auditor and the incoming auditor's report should indicate:**
   (i) **That the financial statements of the prior period were audited by another auditor;**
   (ii) **The type of report issued by the predecessor auditor and if the report was modified, the reasons therefor; and**
   (iii) **The date of that report.**

In performing the audit on the current period financial statements, the incoming auditor, in certain unusual circumstances, may become aware of a material misstatement that affects the prior period financial statements on which the predecessor auditor had previously reported without modification. 27

In these circumstances, the incoming auditor should discuss the matter with management and, after having obtained management's authorization, contact the predecessor auditor and propose that the prior period financial statements be restated. If the predecessor agrees to reissue the audit report on the restated financial statements of the prior period, the auditor should follow the guidance in paragraph 26. 28

If, in the circumstances discussed in paragraph 27, the predecessor does not agree with the proposed restatement or refuses to reissue the audit report on the prior period financial statements, the introductory paragraph of the auditor's report may indicate that the predecessor auditor reported on the financial statements of the prior period before restatement. In addition, if the incoming auditor is engaged to audit 29 and applies sufficient audit procedures to be satisfied as to the appropriateness of the restatement adjustment, the auditor may also include the following paragraph in the report:

> We also audited the adjustments described in Note X that were applied to restate the 19X1 financial statements. In our opinion, such adjustments are appropriate and have been properly applied.

Prior Period Financial Statements Not Audited

30   **When the prior period financial statements are not audited, the incoming auditor should state in the auditor's report that the comparative financial statements are unaudited.** Such a statement does not, however, relieve the auditor of the requirement to carry out appropriate audit procedures regarding opening balances of the current period. Clear disclosure in the financial statements that the comparative financial statements are unaudited is encouraged.

31   **In situations where the incoming auditor identifies that the prior year unaudited figures are materially misstated, the auditor should request management to revise the prior year's figures or if management refuses to do so, appropriately modify the report.**

Effective Date

32   This ISA (UK and Ireland) is effective for audits of financial statements for periods commencing on or after 15 December 2004.

Appendix 1 – Discussion of Financial Reporting Frameworks for Comparatives

1   Comparatives covering one or more preceding periods provide the users of financial statements with information necessary to identify trends and changes affecting an entity over a period of time.

2   Under financial reporting frameworks (both implicit and explicit) prevailing in a number of countries, comparability and consistency are desirable qualities for financial information. Defined in broadest terms, comparability is the quality of having certain characteristics in common and comparison is normally a quantitative assessment of the common characteristics. Consistency is a quality of the relationship between two accounting numbers. Consistency (for example, consistency in the use of accounting principles from one period to another, the consistency of the length of the reporting period, *etc.*) is a prerequisite for true comparability.

3   There are two broad financial reporting frameworks for comparatives: the corresponding figures and the comparative financial statements.

4   Under the corresponding figures framework, the corresponding figures for the prior period(s) are an integral part of the current period financial statements and have to be read in conjunction with the amounts and other disclosures relating to the current period. The level of detail presented in the corresponding amounts and disclosures is dictated primarily by its relevance to the current period figures.

Under the comparative financial statements framework, the comparative financial statements for the prior period(s) are considered separate financial statements. Accordingly, the level of information included in those comparative financial statements (including all statement amounts, disclosures, footnotes and other explanatory statements to the extent that they continue to be of significance) approximates that of the financial statements of the current period.

Appendix 2 – Example Auditor's Reports

Illustrative examples of auditor's reports tailored for use with audits conducted in accordance with ISAs (UK and Ireland) are given in the most recent version of the APB Bulletin, "Auditor's Reports on Financial Statements".

Example A   Corresponding Figures: Example Report for the circumstances described in paragraph 12a

AUDITOR'S REPORT

(APPROPRIATE ADDRESSEE)

We have audited the accompanying[1] balance sheet of the ABC Company as of December 31, 19X1, and the related statements of income and cash flows for the year then ended. These financial statements are the responsibility of the Company's management. Our responsibility is to express an opinion on these financial statements based on our audit.

We conducted our audit in accordance with International Standards on Auditing (or refer to applicable national standards or practices). Those Standards require that we plan and perform the audit to obtain reasonable assurance about whether the financial statements are free of material misstatement. An audit includes examining, on a test basis, evidence supporting the amounts and disclosures in the financial statements. An audit also includes assessing the accounting principles used and significant estimates made by management, as well as evaluating the overall financial statement presentation. We believe that our audit provides a reasonable basis for our opinion.

As discussed in Note X to the financial statements, no depreciation has been provided in the financial statements which practice, in our opinion, is not in accordance with International Accounting Standards (or refer to applicable national standards). This is the result of a decision taken by management at the start of the preceding financial year and caused us to qualify our audit opinion on the financial statements relating to that year. Based on the straight-line method of depreciation and annual rates of 5% for the building and 20% for the equipment, the loss for the year should be increased by XXX in 19X1 and XXX in 19X0, the fixed assets should be reduced by accumulated depreciation of XXX in 19X1 and XXX in 19X0, and the accumulated loss should be increased by XXX in 19X1 and XXX in 19X0.

In our opinion, except for the effect on the financial statements of the matter referred to in the preceding paragraph, the financial statements give a true and fair view of (or 'present fairly, in all material respects,') the financial position of the Company as of

---

[1] The reference can be by page numbers.

December 31, 19X1, and of the results of its operations and its cash flows for the year then ended in accordance with ...[2] (and comply with ...[3]).

AUDITOR
Date
Address

---

[2] Indicate International Accounting Standards or applicable national standards.

[3] Reference to applicable statutes or laws.

Example B *Corresponding Figures: Example Report for the circumstances described in paragraph 12b*

AUDITOR'S REPORT

(APPROPRIATE ADDRESSEE)

We have audited the accompanying[4] balance sheet of the ABC Company as of December 31, 19X1, and the related statements of income and cash flows for the year then ended. These financial statements are the responsibility of the Company's management. Our responsibility is to express an opinion on these financial statements based on our audit.

We conducted our audit in accordance with International Standards on Auditing (or refer to applicable national standards or practices). Those Standards require that we plan and perform the audit to obtain reasonable assurance about whether the financial statements are free of material misstatement. An audit includes examining, on a test basis, evidence supporting the amounts and disclosures in the financial statements. An audit also includes assessing the accounting principles used and significant estimates made by management, as well as evaluating the overall financial statement presentation. We believe that our audit provides a reasonable basis for our opinion.

Because we were appointed auditors of the Company during 19X0, we were not able to observe the counting of the physical inventories at the beginning of that (period) or satisfy ourselves concerning those inventory quantities by alternative means. Since opening inventories enter into the determination of the results of operations, we were unable to determine whether adjustments to the results of operations and opening retained earnings might be necessary for 19X0. Our audit report on the financial statements for the (period) ended (balance sheet date) 19X0 was modified accordingly.

In our opinion, except for the effect on the corresponding figures for 19X0 of the adjustments, if any, to the results of operations for the (period) ended 19X0, which we might have determined to be necessary had we been able to observe beginning inventory quantities as at ..., the financial statements give a true and fair view of (or 'present fairly, in all material respects,') the financial position of the Company as of December 31, 19X1, and of the results of its operations and its cash flows for the year then ended in accordance with ...[5] (and comply with ....[6]).

AUDITOR

Date
Address

---

[4] The reference can be by page numbers.

[5] Indicate International Accounting Standards or applicable national standards.

[6] Reference to applicable statutes or laws.

Example C *Comparative Financial Statements: Example Report for the circumstances described in paragraph 24*

AUDITOR'S REPORT

(APPROPRIATE ADDRESSEE)

We have audited the accompanying[7] balance sheets of the ABC Company as of December 31, 19X1 and 19X0, and the related statements of income and cash flows for the years then ended. These financial statements are the responsibility of the Company's management. Our responsibility is to express an opinion on these financial statements based on our audits.

We conducted our audits in accordance with International Standards on Auditing (or refer to applicable national standards or practices). Those Standards require that we plan and perform the audit to obtain reasonable assurance about whether the financial statements are free of material misstatement. An audit includes examining, on a test basis, evidence supporting the amounts and disclosures in the financial statements. An audit also includes assessing the accounting principles used and significant estimates made by management, as well as evaluating the overall financial statement presentation. We believe that our audits provide a reasonable basis for our opinion.

As discussed in Note X to the financial statements, no depreciation has been provided in the financial statements which practice, in our opinion, is not in accordance with International Accounting Standards (or refer to applicable national standards). Based on the straight-line method of depreciation and annual rates of 5% for the building and 20% for the equipment, the loss for the year should be increased by XXX in 19X1 and XXX in 19X0, the fixed assets should be reduced by accumulated depreciation of XXX in 19X1 and XXX in 19X0, and the accumulated loss should be increased by XXX in 19X1 and XXX in 19X0.

In our opinion, except for the effect on the financial statements of the matter referred to in the preceding paragraph, the financial statements give a true and fair view of (or 'present fairly, in all material respects,') the financial position of the Company as of December 31, 19X1 and 19X0, and of the results of its operations and its cash flows for the years then ended in accordance with ...[8] (and comply with ....[9]).

AUDITOR

Date
Address

---

[7] *The reference can be by page numbers.*

[8] *Indicate International Accounting Standards or applicable national standards.*

[9] *Reference to applicable statutes or laws.*

Example D *Corresponding Figures: Example Report for the circumstances described in paragraph 17*

AUDITOR'S REPORT

(APPROPRIATE ADDRESSEE)

We have audited the accompanying[10] balance sheet of the ABC Company as of December 31, 19X1, and the related statements of income and cash flows for the year then ended. These financial statements are the responsibility of the Company's management. Our responsibility is to express an opinion on these financial statements based on our audit. The financial statements of the Company as of December 31, 19X0, were audited by another auditor whose report dated March 31, 19X1, expressed an unqualified opinion on those statements.

We conducted our audit in accordance with International Standards on Auditing (or refer to applicable national standards or practices). Those Standards require that we plan and perform the audit to obtain reasonable assurance about whether the financial statements are free of material misstatement. An audit includes examining, on a test basis, evidence supporting the amounts and disclosures in the financial statements. An audit also includes assessing the accounting principles used and significant estimates made by management, as well as evaluating the overall financial statement presentation. We believe that our audit provides a reasonable basis for our opinion.

In our opinion, the financial statements give a true and fair view of (or 'present fairly, in all material respects,') the financial position of the Company as of December 31, 19X1, and of the results of its operations and its cash flows for the year then ended in accordance with ...[11] (and comply with ...[12]).

AUDITOR

Date
Address

---

[10] *The reference can be by page numbers.*

[11] *Indicate International Accounting Standards or applicable national standards.*

[12] *Reference to applicable statutes or laws.*

Example E *Comparative Financial Statements: Example Report for the circumstances described in paragraph 26b*

AUDITOR'S REPORT

(APPROPRIATE ADDRESSEE)

We have audited the accompanying[13] balance sheet of the ABC Company as of December 31, 19X1, and the related statements of income and cash flows for the year then ended. These financial statements are the responsibility of the Company's management. Our responsibility is to express an opinion on these financial statements based on our audit. The financial statements of the Company as of December 31, 19X0, were audited by another auditor whose report dated March 31, 19X1, expressed a qualified opinion due to their disagreement as to the adequacy of the provision for doubtful receivables.

We conducted our audit in accordance with International Standards on Auditing (or refer to applicable national standards or practices). Those Standards require that we plan and perform the audit to obtain reasonable assurance about whether the financial statements are free of material misstatement. An audit includes examining, on a test basis, evidence supporting the amounts and disclosures in the financial statements. An audit also includes assessing the accounting principles used and significant estimates made by management, as well as evaluating the overall financial statement presentation. We believe that our audit provides a reasonable basis for our opinion.

The receivables referred to above are still outstanding at December 31, 19X1 and no provision for potential loss has been made in the financial statements. Accordingly, the provision for doubtful receivables at December 31, 19X1 and 19X0 should be increased by XXX, the net profit for 19X0 decreased by XXX and the retained earnings at December 31, 19X1 and 19X0 reduced by XXX.

In our opinion, except for the effect on the financial statements of the matter referred to in the preceding paragraph, the 19X1 financial statements referred to above give a true and fair view of (or 'present fairly, in all material respects,') the financial position of the Company as of December 31, 19X1, and of the results of its operations and its cash flows for the year then ended in accordance with ...[14] (and comply with ...[15]).

AUDITOR

Date
Address

---

[13] *The reference can be by page numbers.*

[14] *Indicate International Accounting Standards or applicable national standards.*

[15] *Reference to applicable statutes or laws.*

International standard on auditing (UK and Ireland) 720 (revised)
Section A – Other information in documents containing audited financial statements
Section B – The auditor's statutory reporting responsibility in relation to directors' reports

Contents

Section A

	Paragraph
Introduction	1 - 8
Access to Other Information	9
Consideration of Other Information	10
Material Inconsistencies	11 - 13-1
Material Misstatements of Fact	14 - 18-4
Further Actions Available to the Auditor	18-5 - 18-6
Availability of Other Information After the Date of the Auditor's Report	19 - 23
Effective Date	23-1
Appendix: Electronic Publication of the Auditor's Report	

Section B

Introduction	1 - 4
The Auditor's Procedures	5 - 11
Documentation	12
Effective Date	13
Appendix: Illustrative Wording for the Auditor's Report	

International Standard on Auditing (UK and Ireland) (ISA (UK and Ireland)) 720 "Other Information in Documents Containing Audited Financial Statements" should be read in the context of the Auditing Practices Board's Statement "The Auditing Practices Board – Scope and Authority of Pronouncements (Revised)" which sets out the application and authority of ISAs (UK and Ireland).

This ISA (UK and Ireland) adopts the text of ISA 720 issued by the International Auditing and Assurance Standards Board. Supplementary material added by the APB is differentiated by the use of grey shading.

Section A – Other information in documents containing audited financial statements

Introduction

The purpose of this Section of this International Standard on Auditing (UK and Ireland) (ISA (UK and Ireland)) is to establish standards and provide guidance on the auditor's consideration of other information, on which the auditor has no obligation to report, in documents containing audited financial statements. This ISA (UK and Ireland) applies when an annual report is involved; however, it may also apply to other documents, such as those used in securities offerings[1].   **1**

The standards and guidance in this Section apply to all other information included in documents containing audited financial statements, including the directors' report. Further standards and guidance on the auditor's statutory reporting obligations in relation to directors' reports are set out in Section B.   **1-1**

This Section of this ISA (UK and Ireland) is primarily directed towards the auditor's consideration of other information contained in an entity's published annual report. It is not intended to address issues which may arise if financial information is extracted from that document.   **1-2**

This ISA (UK and Ireland) uses the terms 'those charged with governance' and 'management'. The term 'governance' describes the role of persons entrusted with the supervision, control and direction of an entity. Ordinarily, those charged with governance are accountable for ensuring that the entity achieves its objectives, and for the quality of its financial reporting and reporting to interested parties. Those charged with governance include management only when they perform such functions.   **1-3**

In the UK and Ireland, those charged with governance include the directors (executive and non-executive) of a company or other body, the members of an audit committee where one exists, the partners, proprietors, committee of management or trustees of other forms of entity, or equivalent persons responsible for directing the entity's affairs and preparing its financial statements.   **1-4**

'Management' comprises those persons who perform senior managerial functions.   **1-5**

In the UK and Ireland, depending on the nature and circumstances of the entity, management may include some or all of those charged with governance (e.g. executive directors). Management will not normally include non-executive directors.   **1-6**

The auditor should read the other information to identify material inconsistencies with the audited financial statements.   **2**

If, as a result of reading the other information, the auditor becomes aware of any apparent misstatements therein, or identifies any material inconsistencies with the audited financial statements, the auditor should seek to resolve them.   **2-1**

---

[1] *The guidance in this ISA (UK and Ireland) is limited to Annual Reports and statutory audits. Guidance on other information issued with investment circulars is covered in Statement of Investment Reporting Standard (SIR) 1000.*

3   A "material inconsistency" exists when other information contradicts information contained in the audited financial statements. A material inconsistency may raise doubt about the audit conclusions drawn from audit evidence previously obtained and, possibly, about the basis for the auditor's opinion on the financial statements.

4   An entity ordinarily issues on an annual basis a document which includes its audited financial statements together with the auditor's report thereon. This document is frequently referred to as the "annual report." In issuing such a document, an entity may also include, either by law or custom, other financial and non-financial information. For the purpose of this ISA (UK and Ireland), such other financial and non-financial information is called "other information."

4-1   When the auditor reads the other information, the auditor does so in the light of the knowledge the auditor has acquired during the audit. The auditor is not expected to verify any of the other information. The audit engagement partner (and, where appropriate, other senior members of the engagement team who can reasonably be expected to be aware of the more important matters arising during the audit and to have a general understanding of the entity's affairs), reads the other information with a view to identifying significant misstatements therein or matters which are inconsistent with the financial statements.

4-2   Guidance to auditors in the UK and Ireland on the consideration of other information where the annual financial statements accompanied by the auditor's report are published on an entity's website, or in Great Britain where companies can meet their statutory reporting obligations to shareholders by distributing annual financial statements and certain other reports electronically, is given in the Appendix to this Section[2].

5   Examples of other information include a report by management or those charged with governance on operations, financial summaries or highlights, employment data, planned capital expenditures, financial ratios, names of officers and directors and selected quarterly data.

5-1   Further examples relevant in the UK and Ireland are a directors' report required by statute (see Section B), statements relating to corporate governance, as required by the Listing Rules, a chairman's statement, a voluntary Operating and Financial Review and non-statutory financial information included within the annual report[3].

---

[2] *In Great Britain The Companies Act (Electronic Communications) Order 2000 enables companies to meet, subject to certain conditions, their statutory reporting obligations to shareholders by distributing annual financial statements and certain other reports electronically, or to post their financial statements on their web site and advise shareholders of this.*

[3] *The APB recognises that in some circumstances the presentation of non-statutory financial information and associated narrative explanations with the statutory results may help shareholders understand better the financial performance of a company. However, the APB is concerned that in other circumstances such non-statutory information in annual reports has the potential to be misleading and shareholders may sometimes be misinformed by the manner in which non-statutory information is presented. The APB believes that the potential for non-statutory information to be misleading is considerable when undue and inappropriate prominence is given to the non-statutory information, when there is no description of the non-statutory information and, where appropriate, the adjusted numbers are not reconciled to the statutory financial information.*

If the auditor believes that the other information is misleading, and the auditor is unable to resolve the matter with management and those charged with governance, the auditor considers the implications for the auditor's report and what further actions may be appropriate. The auditor has regard to the guidance in paragraphs 18-5 and 18-6 below. 5-2

In certain circumstances, the auditor has a statutory or contractual obligation to report specifically on other information. In other circumstances, the auditor has no such obligation. However, the auditor needs to give consideration to such other information when issuing a report on the financial statements, as the credibility of the audited financial statements may be undermined by inconsistencies which may exist between the audited financial statements and other information. 6

The credibility of the audited financial statements may also be undermined by misstatements within the other information. 6-1

Some jurisdictions require the auditor to apply specific procedures to certain of the other information, for example, required supplementary data and interim financial information. If such other information is omitted or contains deficiencies, the auditor may be required to refer to the matter in the auditor's report. 7

In the UK and Ireland an example of this type of work for a listed company would include the auditor's review of whether the Corporate Governance Statement reflects the company's compliance with the provisions of the Combined Code specified by the Listing Rules for review by the auditor. 7-1

When there is an obligation to report specifically on other information, the auditor's responsibilities are determined by the nature of the engagement and by local legislation and professional standards. When such responsibilities involve the review of other information, the auditor will need to follow the guidance on review engagements in the appropriate ISAs (UK and Ireland). 8

Access to Other Information

In order that an auditor can consider other information included in the annual report, timely access to such information will be required. The auditor therefore needs to make appropriate arrangements with the entity to obtain such information prior to the date of the auditor's report[4]. In certain circumstances, all the other information may not be available prior to such date. In these circumstances, the auditor would follow the guidance in paragraphs 20-23[5]. 9

---

[4] *ISA (UK and Ireland) 700 requires that "The auditor should not date the report earlier than the date on which all other information contained in a report of which the audited financial statements form a part have been approved by those charged with governance and the auditor has considered all necessary available evidence.'*

[5] *Paragraphs 19 to 23 are not applicable in an audit conducted in compliance with ISAs (UK and Ireland).*

Consideration of Other Information

10 The objective and scope of an audit of financial statements are formulated on the premise that the auditor's responsibility is restricted to information identified in the auditor's report. Accordingly, the auditor has no specific responsibility to determine that other information is properly stated.

Material Inconsistencies

11 If, on reading the other information, the auditor identifies a material inconsistency, the auditor should determine whether the audited financial statements or the other information needs to be amended.

11-1 **If the auditor identifies a material inconsistency the auditor should seek to resolve the matter through discussion with those charged with governance.**

11-2 If the auditor concludes that the other information contains inconsistencies with the financial statements, and the auditor is unable to resolve them through discussion with those charged with governance, the auditor considers requesting those charged with governance to consult with a qualified third party, such as the entity's legal counsel and considers the advice received.

12 **If an amendment is necessary in the audited financial statements and the entity refuses to make the amendment, the auditor should express a qualified or adverse opinion.**

13 **If an amendment is necessary in the other information and the entity refuses to make the amendment, the auditor should consider including in the auditor's report an emphasis of matter paragraph describing the material inconsistency or taking other actions.** The actions taken, such as not issuing the auditor's report or withdrawing from the engagement, will depend upon the particular circumstances and the nature and significance of the inconsistency. The auditor would also consider obtaining legal advice as to further action.

13-1 In circumstances where the auditor has no issues with the financial statements themselves, and the emphasis of matter is being used to report on matters other than those affecting the financial statements, an emphasis of matter paragraph in relation to a material inconsistency does not give rise to a qualified audit opinion.

Material Misstatements of Fact

14 While reading the other information for the purpose of identifying material inconsistencies, the auditor may become aware of an apparent material misstatement of fact.

15 For the purpose of this ISA (UK and Ireland), a "material misstatement of fact" in other information exists when such information, not related to matters appearing in the audited financial statements, is incorrectly stated or presented.

15-1 A material misstatement of fact in other information would potentially include an inconsistency between information obtained by the auditor during the audit (such as information obtained as part of the planning process or analytical procedures, or as management representations) and information which is included in the other information.

If the auditor becomes aware that the other information appears to include a material misstatement of fact, the auditor should discuss the matter with the entity's management.[6] When discussing the matter with the entity's management, the auditor may not be able to evaluate the validity of the other information and management's responses to the auditor's inquiries, and would need to consider whether valid differences of judgment or opinion exist.   16

The auditor should consider whether the other information requires to be amended.   16-1

When the auditor still considers that there is an apparent misstatement of fact, the auditor should request management[7] **to consult with a qualified third party, such as the entity's legal counsel and should consider the advice received.**   17

If the auditor concludes that there is a material misstatement of fact in the other information which management refuses to correct, the auditor should consider taking further appropriate action. The actions taken could include such steps as notifying those charged with governance in writing of the auditor's concern regarding the other information and obtaining legal advice.   18

In the UK and Ireland the auditor requests those charged with governance to correct any material misstatements of fact in the other information.   18-1

If an amendment is necessary in the other information and the entity refuses to make the amendment, the auditor should consider including in the auditor's report an emphasis of matter paragraph describing the material misstatement.   18-2

In circumstances where the auditor has no issues with the financial statements, and the emphasis of matter is being used to report on matters other than those affecting the financial statements, an emphasis of matter paragraph in relation to a material misstatement of fact in the other information does not give rise to a qualified audit opinion.   18-3

The auditor has regard to the nature of the inconsistency or misstatement that in the auditor's opinion exists. A distinction may be drawn between a matter of fact and one of judgment. It is generally more difficult for the auditor to take issue with a matter of judgment (such as the view of those charged with governance of the likely out-turn for the following year) than a factual error. Although an auditor does not substitute the auditor's judgment for that of those charged with governance in such matters, there may be circumstances in which the auditor is aware that the expressed view of those charged with governance is significantly at variance with the entity's internal assessment or is so unreasonable as not to be credible to someone with the auditor's knowledge.   18-4

---

[6] *In the UK and Ireland the auditor discusses such matters with, and obtains responses from, those charged with governance.*

[7] *In the UK and Ireland the auditor requests those charged with governance to consult with a qualified third party.*

Further Actions Available to the Auditor

18-5 The auditor of a limited company in the United Kingdom or the Republic of Ireland may use the auditor's right to be heard at any general meeting of the members on any part of the business of the meeting which concerns the auditor as auditor[8].

18-6 The auditor may also consider resigning from the audit engagement. In the case of auditors of limited companies in the United Kingdom or the Republic of Ireland, the requirements for the auditor to make a statement on ceasing to hold office as auditor apply[9]. When making a statement in these circumstances, the considerations set out in paragraph 18-4 above would normally be applicable.

Availability of Other Information After the Date of the Auditor's Report

Paragraphs 19 to 23 are not applicable in an audit conducted in accordance with ISAs (UK and Ireland). ISA (UK and Ireland) 700, "The Auditor's Report on Financial Statements" requires that "The auditor should not date the report earlier than the date on which all other information contained in a report of which the audited financial statements forma part have been approved by those charged with governance and the auditor has considered all necessary available evidence.".

19 When all the other information is not available to the auditor prior to the date of the auditor's report, the auditor would read the other information at the earliest possible opportunity thereafter to identify material inconsistencies.

20 If, on reading the other information, the auditor identifies a material inconsistency or becomes aware of an apparent material misstatement of fact, the auditor would determine whether the audited financial statements or the other information need revision.

21 When revision of the audited financial statements is appropriate, the guidance in ISA (UK and Ireland) 560, "Subsequent Events" would be followed.

22 When revision of the other information is necessary and the entity agrees to make the revision, the auditor would carry out the audit procedures necessary under the circumstances. The audit procedures may include reviewing the steps taken by management to ensure that individuals in receipt of the previously issued financial statements, the auditor's report thereon and the other information are informed of the revision.

23 **When revision of the other information is necessary but management refuses to make the revision, the auditor should consider taking further appropriate action.** The actions taken could include such steps as notifying those charged with governance in writing of the auditor's concern regarding the other information and obtaining legal advice.

[8] *The relevant reference for Great Britain is section 390 of the Companies Act 1985, for Northern Ireland is Article 398 of the Companies (Northern Ireland) Order 1986 and for the Republic of Ireland is section 193(5) of the Companies Act 1990.*

[9] *The relevant reference for Great Britain is section 394 of the Companies Act 1985, for Northern Ireland is Article 401A of the Companies (Northern Ireland) Order 1986 and for the Republic of Ireland is section 185 of the Companies Act 1990.*

Effective Date

23-1

This Section of this ISA (UK and Ireland) is effective for audits of financial statements for periods commencing on or after 1 April 2005 and ending on or after 31 March 2006.

Public Sector Perspective

Additional guidance for auditors of public sector bodies in the UK and Ireland is given in:

- Practice Note 10 "Audit of Financial Statements of Public Sector Bodies in the United Kingdom (Revised)"
- Practice Note 10(I) "The Audit of Central Government Financial Statements in Ireland"

This ISA (UK and Ireland) is applicable in the context of the audit of financial statements. In the public sector, the auditor may often have a statutory or contractual obligation to report specifically on other information. As paragraph 8 of Section A of this ISA (UK and Ireland) indicates, the procedures stated in this ISA (UK and Ireland) would not be adequate to satisfy legislative or other audit requirements related to, for example, the expression of an opinion on the reliability of performance indicators and other information contained in the annual report. It would be inappropriate to apply this ISA (UK and Ireland) in circumstances where the auditor does have an obligation to express an opinion on such information. In the absence of specific auditing requirements in relation to "other information," the broad principles contained in this ISA (UK and Ireland) are applicable.

1

Appendix – Electronic Publication of the Auditor's Report

Introduction

1. In Great Britain The Companies Act 1985 (Electronic Communications) Order 2000 (the Electronic Communications Order) enables companies to meet, subject to certain conditions, their statutory reporting obligations to shareholders by distributing annual financial statements and certain other reports[10] electronically, or to post their financial statements on their web site and advise shareholders of this.

2. Various types of financial information can be found on web sites including information that has been audited (for example the annual financial statements), information which the auditor may have reviewed (for example interim financial information) and information with which the auditor has had no direct involvement, such as financial highlights from a company's Annual Report or may never have seen, such as presentations for analysts. In addition, web sites typically contain a considerable amount of non-financial information.

3. The purpose of this Appendix is to provide guidance to auditors on the consideration of other information not only if companies decide to take advantage of the Electronic Communications Order, but also in the more common current situation where the annual financial statements accompanied by the auditor's report are published on an entity's web site[11].

The Auditor's Consideration of Other Information Issued with the Annual Report

Checking Information Presented Electronically

4. When companies include the annual financial statements and the auditor's report on their web site or, in Great Britain, decide to distribute annual financial statements to their shareholders electronically, the auditor:

    (a) Reviews the process by which the financial statements to be published electronically are derived from the financial information contained in the manually signed accounts;
    (b) Checks that the proposed electronic version is identical in content with the manually signed accounts; and
    (c) Checks that the conversion of the manually signed accounts into an electronic format has not distorted the overall presentation of the financial information, for example, by highlighting certain information so as to give it greater prominence.

---

[10] Other reports include Summary Financial Statements.

[11] This guidance is generally applicable both to auditors in Great Britain (where the Electronic Communications Order applies) and in Northern Ireland and the Republic of Ireland (where it does not).

It is recommended that the auditor retains a printout or disk of the final electronic version for future reference if necessary.

Auditor's Report Wording

The auditor considers whether the wording of the auditor's report is suitable for electronic distribution. Issues include:

- Identifying the financial statements that have been audited and the information that has been reviewed, or read, by the auditor.
- Identifying the nationality of the accounting and auditing standards applied.
- Limiting the auditor's association with any other information distributed with the Annual Report.

Identification of the Financial Statements That Have Been Audited

In Annual Reports produced in a hard copy format, the auditor's report usually identifies the financial statements which have been audited by reference to page numbers. The use of page numbers is often not a suitable method of identifying particular financial information presented on a web site[12] The auditor's report therefore needs to specify in another way the location and description of the information that has been audited.

The APB recommends that the auditor's report describes, by name, the primary statements that comprise the financial statements. The same technique can also be used to specify the information that has been reviewed or, because it is included in the Annual Report, read by the auditor.

The auditor ensures that the auditor's statutory report on the full financial statements is not associated with extracts from, or summaries of, those audited financial statements.

Identification of the Nationality of the Accounting and Auditing Standards Applied

Auditor's reports on web sites will be accessible internationally, and it is therefore important that the auditor's report indicates clearly the nationality of the accounting standards used in the preparation of the financial statements and the nationality of the auditing standards applied. For the same reason, the auditor ensures that the auditor's report discloses sufficient of the auditor's address to enable readers to understand in which country the auditor is located.

Limitation of the Auditor's Association With any Other Information Distributed With the Annual Report

In addition to the Annual Report many companies publish on their web sites a considerable volume of financial and non-financial information. This information could take the form of additional analyses or alternative presentations of audited financial information. Users of the web site are likely to find it difficult to distinguish financial information which the auditor has audited, or read, from other

---

[12] *The audited financial statements can be presented on the web site using a variety of webfile formats. As at the date of this Bulletin, examples of these are the Portable Document Format (PDF) or Hypertext Mark-up Language (HTML). Page numbers generally continue to be an effective referencing mechanism for PDF files but this is not always the case when data is represented in HTML.*

data. This issue is exacerbated when there are hyperlinks which allow users to move easily from one area of the web site to another.

12   The auditor gives careful consideration to the use of hyperlinks between the audited financial statements and information contained on the web site that has not been subject to audit or 'reading' by the auditor ('other information'). To avoid possible misunderstandings concerning the scope of the audit, the auditor requests those charged with governance to ensure that hyperlinks contain warnings that the linkage is from audited to unaudited information.

13   Sometimes audited information is not included in the financial statements themselves (e.g. certain information relating to directors' remuneration may be set out as part of a company's corporate governance disclosures). The APB is of the view that companies should be encouraged to make disclosures that are required to be audited, as part of the financial statements or included in the Annual Report in such a way that it is clear which elements of it have been audited. In other circumstances the auditor assesses whether the scope of the audit will be capable of being clearly described. If this cannot be achieved to the satisfaction of the auditor it may be necessary to describe the particulars that have been audited within the auditor's report.

14   The auditor is concerned to establish that the auditor's report on the financial statements is not inappropriately associated with other information. The auditor takes steps to satisfy themselves that information that they have audited or, because it is included in the Annual Report, read, is distinguished from other information in a manner appropriate to the electronic format used by the entity. Techniques that can be used to differentiate material within a web site include

- Icons or watermarks.
- Colour borders.
- Labels/banners such as 'annual report' or 'audited financial statements'.

The appropriate mode of differentiation between audited and unaudited information will be dependent on the electronic format selected, and the nature and extent of other information presented on the web site. The method of differentiation would normally also be clearly stated in an introduction page within the web site.

15   During the course of the audit, the auditor discusses with the those charged with governance or, where appropriate, the audit committee how the financial statements and auditor's report will be presented on the entity's web site with a view to minimizing the possibility that the auditor's report is inappropriately associated with other information. If the auditor is not satisfied with the proposed electronic presentation of the audited financial statements and auditor's report, the auditor requests that the presentation be amended. If the presentation is not amended the auditor will, in accordance with the terms of the engagement, not give consent for the electronic release of the audit opinion.

16   If the auditor's report is used without the auditor's consent, and the auditor has concerns about the electronic presentation of the audited financial statements or the auditor's report and appropriate action is not taken by those charged with governance, the auditor seeks legal advice as necessary. The auditor also considers whether it would be appropriate to resign.

Section B – The auditor's statutory reporting responsibility in relation to directors' reports

Introduction

The purpose of this Section of this International Standard on Auditing (UK and Ireland) (ISA (UK and Ireland)) is to establish standards and provide guidance on the auditor's statutory reporting responsibility in relation to directors' reports.

In the United Kingdom and the Republic of Ireland, legislation[1] requires the auditor of a company to state in the auditor's report whether, in the auditor's opinion, the information given in the directors' report is consistent with the financial statements.

"Information given in the directors' report" includes information that is included by way of cross reference to other information presented separately from the directors' report. For example, a UK company may decide to present a voluntary Operating and Financial Review (OFR) which includes some or all of the matters required for the Business Review section of the directors' report. Rather than duplicate the information, the company may cross refer from the Business Review section in the directors' report to the relevant information provided in the OFR.

The auditor is not required to verify, or report on, the completeness of the information in the directors' report. If, however, the auditor becomes aware that information that is required by law or regulations to be in the directors' report has been omitted the auditor communicates the matter to those charged with governance. This communication includes situations where the required information is presented separately from the directors' report without appropriate cross references.

The Auditor's Procedures

The auditor should read the information in the directors' report and assess whether it is consistent with the financial statements.

Much of the information in the directors' report is likely to be extracted or directly derived from the financial statements and will therefore be directly comparable with them. Some financial information may, however, be more detailed or prepared on a different basis from that in the financial statements. Where the financial information is more detailed, the auditor agrees the information to the auditor's working papers or the entity's accounting records. Where the financial information has been prepared on a different basis, the auditor

---

[1] *Relevant legislation includes:*
- *In Great Britain, with effect for financial years that commence on after 1 April 2005, section 235 of the Companies Act 1985 as amended by "The Companies Act 1985 (Operating and Financial Review and Directors' Report etc.) Regulations 2005" (SI 2005/1011).*
- *In Northern Ireland, with effect for financial years that commence on after 1 April 2005, Article 243 of the Companies (Northern Ireland) Order 1986 as amended by "The Companies (1986 Order) (Operating and Financial Review and Directors' Report etc.) Regulations (Northern Ireland) 2005" (Statutory Rule 2005 No.61).*
- *In the Republic of Ireland, Section 15 of the Companies (Amendment) Act 1986.*

considers whether there is adequate disclosure of the differences in the bases of preparation to enable an understanding of the differences in the information, and checks the reconciliation of the information to the financial statements.

7 **If the auditor identifies any inconsistencies between the information in the directors' report and the financial statements the auditor should seek to resolve them.**

8 Inconsistencies include:

- Differences between amounts or narrative appearing in the financial statements and the directors' report.
- Differences between the bases of preparation of related items appearing in the financial statements and the directors' report, where the figures themselves are not directly comparable and the different bases are not disclosed.
- Contradictions between figures contained in the financial statements and narrative explanations of those figures in the directors' report.

The auditor ordinarily seeks to resolve inconsistencies through discussion with management and those charged with governance.

9 **If the auditor is of the opinion that the information in the directors' report is materially inconsistent[2] with the financial statements, and has been unable to resolve the inconsistency, the auditor should state that opinion and describe the inconsistency in the auditor's report.**

10 **If an amendment is necessary to the financial statements and management and those charged with governance refuse to make the amendment, the auditor should express a qualified or adverse opinion on the financial statements.**

11 The Appendix to this Section includes illustrative wording for the auditor's report. Example A, where the auditor has concluded that information in the directors' report is consistent with the information in the financial statements. Example B, where the auditor has concluded that information in the directors' report is not consistent with the information in the financial statements.

Documentation

12 **The auditor should document:**

(a) **The results of those procedures performed to assess whether the information in the directors' report is consistent with the financial statements, including details of any material inconsistencies identified and how they were resolved; and**

(b) **The conclusion reached as to whether the information in the directors' report is consistent with the financial statements.**

Effective Date

13 This Section of this ISA (UK and Ireland) is effective for audits of financial statements for periods commencing on or after 1 April 2005 and ending on or after 31 March 2006.

---

[2] *Materiality is addressed in ISA (UK and Ireland) 320 "Audit Materiality". An inconsistency is "material" if it could influence the economic decisions of users.*

Appendix – Illustrative Wording for the Auditor's Report

Example A. Extracts from an auditor's report with an unmodified opinion on the directors' report

Respective responsibilities of directors and auditors

[Details of other responsibilities as are applicable – for examples see the illustrative reports in the APB Bulletin "Auditor's Reports on Financial Statements in Great Britain and Northern Ireland"[3]]

We report to you whether in our opinion the information given in the directors' report is consistent with the financial statements. [The information given in the directors' report includes that specific information presented in the Operating and Financial Review that is cross referred from the Business Review section of the directors' report.[4]]

Basis of audit opinion
.....

Opinion

In our opinion:

[● *Opinion on the financial statements and other opinions, if any, that are required.*]
● The information given in the directors' report is consistent with the financial statements.

Example B – Extracts from an auditor's report with a modified opinion on the directors' report (financial statements prepared under UK GAAP)

Respective responsibilities of directors and auditors

[Details of other responsibilities as are applicable – for examples see the illustrative reports in the APB Bulletin "Auditor's Reports on Financial Statements in Great Britain and Northern Ireland"[3]]

We report to you whether in our opinion the information given in the directors' report is consistent with the financial statements. [The information given in the directors' report includes that specific information presented in the Operating and Financial Review that is cross referred from the Business Review section of the directors' report.[4]]

---

[3] *Illustrative reports for the Republic of Ireland are given in the APB Bulletin "Auditor's Reports on Financial Statements in the Republic of Ireland".*

[4] *Include and tailor as necessary to clarify the information covered by the auditor's opinion.*

Basis of audit opinion
.....

Opinion

In our opinion:

[• *Opinion on the financial statements and other opinions, if any, that are required.*]

Material inconsistency between the financial statements and the directors' report

In our opinion, the information given in the seventh paragraph of the Business Review in the directors' report is not consistent with the financial statements. That paragraph states without amplification that "the company's trading for the period resulted in a 10% increase in profit over the previous period's profit". The profit and loss account, however, shows that the company's profit for the period includes a profit of £Z which did not arise from trading but arose from the disposal of assets of a discontinued operation. Without this profit on the disposal of assets the company would have reported a profit for the year of £Y, representing a reduction in profit of 25% over the previous period's profit on a like for like basis. Except for this matter, in our opinion the information given in the directors' report is consistent with the financial statements.

Glossary of terms[1]

This Glossary defines terms used in the ISAs (UK and Ireland), the ISQC (UK and Ireland) and APB Ethical Standards for Auditors. It is based on the IAASB glossary of terms, with supplemental definitions used in the APB Ethical Standards for Auditors shown in grey highlighted text.

Separate glossaries are used in connection with the SIRs and the draft Ethical Standard for Reporting Accountants. These are included in SIR 1000 at Appendix 4 and in the draft ESRA at Appendix 1.

Access controls—Procedures designed to restrict access to on-line terminal devices, programs and data. Access controls consist of "user authentication" and "user authorization." "User authentication" typically attempts to identify a user through unique logon identifications, passwords, access cards or biometric data. "User authorization" consists of access rules to determine the computer resources each user may access. Specifically, such procedures are designed to prevent or detect:

(a) Unauthorized access to on-line terminal devices, programs and data;
(b) Entry of unauthorized transactions;
(c) Unauthorized changes to data files;
(d) The use of computer programs by unauthorized personnel; and
(e) The use of computer programs that have not been authorized.

Accounting estimate—An approximation of the amount of an item in the absence of a precise means of measurement.

Accounting records—Generally include the records of initial entries and supporting records, such as checks and records of electronic fund transfers; invoices; contracts; the general and subsidiary ledgers; journal entries and other adjustments to the financial statements that are not reflected in formal journal entries; and records such as work sheets and spreadsheets supporting cost allocations, computations, reconciliations and disclosures.

Accounting services—The provision of services that involve the maintenance of accounting records or the preparation of financial statements that are then subject to audit.

Adverse opinion—(see Modified auditor's report)

Affiliate—Any undertaking which is connected to another by means of common ownership, control or management.

Agreed-upon procedures engagement—An engagement in which an auditor is engaged to carry out those procedures of an audit nature to which the auditor and the entity and any appropriate third parties have agreed and to report on factual findings. The

---

[1] Where accounting terms have not been defined in the IAASB pronouncements, reference should be made to the Glossary of Terms published by the International Accounting Standards Board.

recipients of the report form their own conclusions from the report by the auditor. The report is restricted to those parties that have agreed to the procedures to be performed since others, unaware of the reasons for the procedures may misinterpret the results.

Analytical procedures—Evaluations of financial information made by a study of plausible relationships among both financial and non-financial data. Analytical procedures also encompass the investigation of identified fluctuations and relationships that are inconsistent with other relevant information or deviate significantly from predicted amounts.

Annual report—A document issued by an entity, ordinarily on an annual basis, which includes its financial statements together with the auditor's report thereon.

Anomalous error—(see Audit sampling)

Application controls in information technology— Manual or automated procedures that typically operate at a business process level. Application controls can be preventative or detective in nature and are designed to ensure the integrity of the accounting records. Accordingly, application controls relate to procedures used to initiate, record, process and report transactions or other financial data.

Appropriateness—The measure of the quality of evidence, that is, its relevance and reliability in providing support for, or detecting misstatements in, the classes of transactions, account balances, and disclosures and related assertions.

Assertions—Representations by management, explicit or otherwise, that are embodied in the financial statements.

Assess—Analyze identified risks of to conclude on their significance. "Assess," by convention, is used only in relation to risk. (also see Evaluate)

Assistants—Personnel involved in an individual audit other than the auditor.

Association—(see Auditor association with financial information)

Assurance—(see Reasonable assurance)

Assurance engagement—An engagement in which a practitioner expresses a conclusion designed to enhance the degree of confidence of the intended users other than the responsible party about the outcome of the evaluation or measurement of a subject matter against criteria. The outcome of the evaluation or measurement of a subject matter is the information that results from applying the criteria (also see Subject matter information). Under the "International Framework for Assurance Engagements" there are two types of assurance engagement a practitioner is permitted to perform: a reasonable assurance engagement and a limited assurance engagement.

> *Limited assurance engagement*—The objective of a limited assurance engagement is a reduction in assurance engagement risk to a level that is acceptable in the circumstances of the engagement, but where that risk is greater than for a reasonable assurance engagement, as the basis for a negative form of expression of the practitioner's conclusion.
>
> *Reasonable assurance engagement*—The objective of a reasonable assurance engagement is a reduction in assurance engagement risk to an acceptably low

level in the circumstances of the engagement as the basis for a positive form of expression of the practitioner's conclusion.

Assurance engagement risk—The risk that the practitioner expresses an inappropriate conclusion when the subject matter information is materially misstated.

Attendance—Being present during all or part of a process being performed by others; for example, attending physical inventory taking will enable the auditor to inspect inventory, to observe compliance of management's procedures to count quantities and record such counts and to test-count quantities.

Audit Documentation—The record of audit procedures performed, relevant audit evidence obtained, and conclusions the auditor reached (terms such as "working papers" or "workpapers" are also sometimes used.

Audit evidence—All of the information used by the auditor in arriving at the conclusions on which the audit opinion is based. Audit evidence includes the information contained in the accounting records underlying the financial statements and other information.

Audit firm—(see Firm)

Audit matters of governance interest—Those matters that arise from the audit of financial statements and, in the opinion of the auditor, are both important and relevant to those charged with governance in overseeing the financial reporting and disclosure process. Audit matters of governance interest include only those matters that have come to the attention of the auditor as a result of the performance of the audit.

Audit of financial statements—The objective of an audit of financial statements is to enable the auditor to express an opinion whether the financial statements are prepared, in all material respects, in accordance with an applicable financial reporting framework. An audit of financial statements is an assurance engagement (see Assurance engagement).

Audit opinion—(see Opinion)

Audit risk—Audit risk is the risk that the auditor expresses an inappropriate audit opinion when the financial statements are materially misstated. Audit risk is a function of the risk of material misstatement (or simply, the "risk of material misstatement") (i.e., the risk that the financial statements are materially misstated prior to audit) and the risk that the auditor will not detect such misstatement ("detection risk"). The risk of material misstatement has two components: inherent risk and control risk (as described at the assertion level below). Detection risk is the risk that the auditor's procedures will not detect a misstatement that exists in an assertion that could be material, individually or when aggregated with other misstatements.

Inherent risk—Inherent risk is the susceptibility of an assertion to a misstatement, that could be material, individually or when aggregated with other misstatements assuming that there were no related internal controls.

Control risk—Control risk is the risk that a misstatement that could occur in an assertion and that could be material, individually or when aggregated with other misstatements, will not be prevented or detected and corrected on a timely basis by the entity's internal control.

Audit sampling—The application of audit procedures to less than 100% of items within an account balance or class of transactions such that all sampling units have a chance of selection. This will enable the auditor to obtain and evaluate audit evidence about some characteristic of the items selected in order to form or assist in forming a conclusion concerning the population from which the sample is drawn. Audit sampling can use either a statistical or a non-statistical approach.

Anomalous error—An error that arises from an isolated event that has not recurred other than on specifically identifiable occasions and is therefore not representative of errors in the population.

Confidence levels—The mathematical complements of sampling risk.

Expected error—The error that the auditor expects to be present in the population.

Non-sampling risk—Arises from factors that cause the auditor to reach an erroneous conclusion for any reason not related to the size of the sample. For example, most audit evidence is persuasive rather than conclusive, the auditor might use inappropriate procedures, or the auditor might misinterpret evidence and fail to recognize an error.

Non-statistical sampling—Any sampling approach that does not have the characteristics of statistical sampling.

Population—The entire set of data from which a sample is selected and about which the auditor wishes to draw conclusions. A population may be divided into strata, or sub-populations, with each stratum being examined separately. The term population is used to include the term stratum.

Sampling risk—Arises from the possibility that the auditor's conclusion, based on a sample may be different from the conclusion reached if the entire population were subjected to the same audit procedure.

Sampling unit—The individual items constituting a population, for example checks listed on deposit slips, credit entries on bank statements, sales invoices or debtors' balances, or a monetary unit.

Statistical sampling—Any approach to sampling that has the following characteristics:
(a) Random selection of a sample; and
(b) Use of probability theory to evaluate sample results, including measurement of sampling risk.

Stratification—The process of dividing a population into subpopulations, each of which is a group of sampling units which have similar characteristics (often monetary value).

Tolerable error—The maximum error in a population that the auditor is willing to accept.

Total error—Either the rate of deviation or total misstatement.

Audit team—All audit professionals who, regardless of their legal relationship with the auditor or audit firm, are assigned to a particular audit engagement in order to perform the audit task (e.g. audit partner(s), audit manager(s) and audit staff).

Audited entity – The entity whose financial statements are subject to audit by the audit firm.

Auditor—The engagement partner. The term "auditor" is used to describe either the engagement partner or the audit firm. Where it applies to the engagement partner, it describes the obligations or responsibilities of the engagement partner. Such obligations or responsibilities may be fulfilled by either the engagement partner or a member of the audit team. Where it is expressly intended that the obligation or responsibility be fulfilled by the engagement partner, the term "engagement partner" rather than "auditor" is used. (The term "auditor" may be used when describing related services and assurance engagements other than audits. Such reference is not intended to imply that a person performing a related service or assurance engagement other than an audit need necessarily be the auditor of the entity's financial statements.)

Existing auditor—The auditor of the financial statements of the current period.

External auditor—Where appropriate the term "external auditor" is used to distinguish the external auditor from an internal auditor.

Incoming auditor—The auditor of the financial statements of the current period, where either the financial statements of the prior period have been audited by another auditor (in this case the incoming auditor also known as a successor auditor), or the audit is an initial audit engagement.

Internal auditor—A person performing an internal audit.

Other auditor—An auditor, other than the principal auditor, with responsibility for reporting on the financial information of a component, which is included in the financial statements audited by the principal auditor. Other auditors include affiliated firms, whether using the same name or not, and correspondents, as well as unrelated auditors.

Predecessor auditor—The auditor who was previously the auditor of an entity and who has been replaced by an incoming auditor.

Principal auditor—The auditor with responsibility for reporting on the financial statements of an entity when those financial statements include financial information of one or more components audited by another auditor.

Proposed auditor—An auditor who is asked to replace an existing auditor.

Successor auditor—An auditor replacing an existing auditor (also known as an incoming auditor).

Auditor association with financial information—An auditor is associated with financial information when the auditor attaches a report to that information or consents to the use of the auditor's name in a professional connection.

Chain of command—All persons who have a direct supervisory, management or other oversight responsibility over either any audit partner of the audit team or over the conduct of audit work in the audit firm. This includes all partners, principals and shareholders who may prepare, review or directly influence the performance appraisal of any audit partner of the audit team as a result of that partner's involvement with the audit engagement. It does not include any non-executive individuals on a supervisory or equivalent board.

Close family—Any non-dependent parent, child or sibling.

Comparatives—Comparatives in financial statements, may present amounts (such as financial position, results of operations, cash flows) and appropriate disclosures of an entity for more than one period, depending on the framework. The frameworks and methods of presentation are as follows:

(a) Corresponding figures where amounts and other disclosures for the preceding period are included as part of the current period financial statements, and are intended to be read in relation to the amounts and other disclosures relating to the current period (referred to as "current period figures"). These corresponding figures are not presented as complete financial statements capable of standing alone, but are an integral part of the current period financial statements intended to be read only in relationship to the current period figures.
(b) Comparative financial statements where amounts and other disclosures for the preceding period are included for comparison with the financial statements of the current period, but do not form part of the current period financial statements.

Comparative financial statements—(see Comparatives)

Compilation engagement—An engagement in which accounting expertise, as opposed to auditing expertise, is used to collect, classify and summarize financial information.

Component—A division, branch, subsidiary, joint venture, associated company or other entity whose financial information is included in financial statements audited by the principal auditor.

Comprehensive basis of accounting—A comprehensive basis of accounting comprises a set of criteria used in preparing financial statements which applies to all material items and which has substantial support.

Computer-assisted audit techniques—Applications of auditing procedures using the computer as an audit tool (also known as CAATs).

Computer information systems (CIS) environment—Exists when a computer of any type or size is involved in the processing by the entity of financial information of significance to the audit, whether that computer is operated by the entity or by a third party.

Confidence levels—(see Audit sampling)

Confirmation—A specific type of inquiry that is the process of obtaining a representation of information or of an existing condition directly from a third party.

Contingent fee basis—Any arrangement made under which a fee is calculated on a pre-determined basis relating to the outcome or result of a transaction or the result of the work performed. Differential hourly fee rates, or arrangements under which the fee payable will be negotiated after the completion of the engagement, do not constitute contingent fee arrangements.

Control activities—Those policies and procedures that help ensure that management directives are carried out. Control activities are a component of internal control.

Control environment—Includes the governance and management functions and the attitudes, awareness and actions of those charged with governance and management concerning the entity's internal control and its importance in the entity. The control environment is a component of internal control.

Control risk—(see Audit risk)

Corporate governance—(see Governance)

Corresponding figures—(see Comparatives)

Criteria—The benchmarks used to evaluate or measure the subject matter including, where relevant, benchmarks for presentation and disclosure. Criteria can be formal or less formal. There can be different criteria for the same subject matter. Suitable criteria are required for reasonably consistent evaluation or measurement of a subject matter within the context of professional judgment.

> *Suitable criteria*—Exhibit the following characteristics:
> - Relevance: relevant criteria contribute to conclusions that assist decision-making by the intended users.
> - Completeness: criteria are sufficiently complete when relevant factors that could affect the conclusions in the context of the engagement circumstances are not omitted. Complete criteria include, where relevant, benchmarks for presentation and disclosure.
> - Reliability: reliable criteria allow reasonably consistent evaluation or measurement of the subject matter including, where relevant, presentation and disclosure, when used in similar circumstances by similarly qualified practitioners.
> - Neutrality: neutral criteria contribute to conclusions that are free from bias.
> - Understandability: understandable criteria contribute to conclusions that are clear, comprehensive, and not subject to significantly different interpretations.

Current period figures—Amounts and other disclosures relating to the current period.

Database—A collection of data that is shared and used by a number of different users for different purposes.

Detection risk—(see Audit risk)

Disclaimer of opinion—(see Modified auditor's report)

Electronic Data Interchange (EDI)—The electronic transmission of documents between organizations in a machine-readable form.

Emphasis of matter paragraph(s)—(see Modified auditor's report)

Employee fraud—Fraud involving only employees of the entity subject to the audit.

Encryption (cryptography)—The process of transforming programs and information into a form that cannot be understood without access to specific decoding algorithms (cryptographic keys). For example, the confidential personal data in a payroll system may be encrypted against unauthorized disclosure or modification. Encryption can provide an effective control for protecting confidential or sensitive programs and information from unauthorized access or modification. However, effective security depends upon proper controls over access to the cryptographic keys.

Engagement documentation—The record of work performed, results obtained, and conclusions reached (terms such as "working papers" or "workpapers" are sometimes used). The documentation for a specific engagement is assembled in an engagement file.

Engagement partner—The partner or other person in the firm who is responsible for the engagement and its performance, and for the report that is issued on behalf of the firm, and who, where required, has the appropriate authority from a professional, legal or regulatory body.

Engagement letter—An engagement letter documents and confirms the auditor's acceptance of the appointment, the objective and scope of the audit, the extent of the auditor's responsibilities to the client and the form of any reports.

Engagement quality control review—A process designed to provide an objective evaluation, before the report is issued, of the significant judgments the engagement team made and the conclusions they reached in formulating the report.

Engagement quality control reviewer—A partner, other person in the firm, suitably qualified external person, or a team made up of such individuals, with sufficient and appropriate experience and authority to objectively evaluate, before the report is issued, the significant judgments the engagement team made and the conclusions they reached in formulating the report.

Engagement team—All personnel performing an engagement, including any experts contracted by the firm in connection with that engagement.

> For the purposes of APB Ethical Standards, engagement team comprises all persons who are directly involved in the acceptance and performance of a particular audit. This includes the audit team, professional personnel from other disciplines involved in the audit engagement and those who provide quality control or direct oversight of the audit engagement, but it does not include experts contracted by the firm.

Entity's risk assessment process—A component of internal control that is the entity's process for identifying business risks relevant to financial reporting objectives and deciding about actions to address those risks, and the results thereof.

Environmental matters—

(a) Initiatives to prevent, abate, or remedy damage to the environment, or to deal with conservation of renewable and non-renewable resources (such initiatives may be required by environmental laws and regulations or by contract, or they may be undertaken voluntarily);
(b) Consequences of violating environmental laws and regulations;
(c) Consequences of environmental damage done to others or to natural resources; and
(d) Consequences of vicarious liability imposed by law (for example, liability for damages caused by previous owners).

Environmental performance report—A report, separate from the financial statements, in which an entity provides third parties with qualitative information on the entity's commitments towards the environmental aspects of the business, its policies and targets in that field, its achievement in managing the relationship between its business processes and environmental risk, and quantitative information on its environmental performance.

Environmental risk—In certain circumstances, factors relevant to the assessment of inherent risk for the development of the overall audit plan may include the risk of material misstatement of the financial statements due to environmental matters.

Error—An unintentional misstatement in financial statements, including the omission of an amount or a disclosure.

Ethics partner—The partner or other person in the audit firm having responsibility for the adequacy of the firm's policies and procedures relating to integrity, objectivity and independence, their compliance with APB Ethical Standards and the effectiveness of their communication to partners and staff within the firm and providing related guidance to individual partners.

Evaluate—Identify and analyze the relevant issues, including performing further procedures as necessary, to come to a specific conclusion on a matter. "Evaluation," by convention, is used only in relation to a range of matters, including evidence, the results of procedures and the effectiveness of management's response to a risk. (also see Assess)

Existing auditor—(see Auditor)

Expected error— (see Audit sampling)

Experienced auditor—An individual (whether internal or external to the firm) who has a reasonable understanding of (i) audit processes, (ii) ISAs (UK and Ireland) and applicable legal and regulatory requirements, (iii) the business environment in which the entity operates, and (iv) auditing and financial reporting issues relevant to the entity's industry.

Expert—A person or firm possessing special skill, knowledge and experience in a particular field other than accounting and auditing.

External audit—An audit performed by an external auditor.

External auditor—(see Auditor)

External confirmation—The process of obtaining and evaluating audit evidence through a direct communication from a third party in response to a request for information about a particular item affecting assertions made by management in the financial statements.

Fair value—The amount for which an asset could be exchanged, or a liability settled, between knowledgeable, willing parties in an arm's length transaction.

Financial interest—An equity or other security, debenture, loan or other debt instrument of an entity, including rights and obligations to acquire such an interest and derivatives directly related to such an interest.

Firewall—A combination of hardware and software that protects a WAN, LAN or PC from unauthorized access through the Internet and from the introduction of unauthorized or harmful software, data or other material in electronic form.

Firm—A sole practitioner, partnership or corporation or other entity of professional accountants.

> For the purpose of APB Ethical Standards, audit firm includes network firms in the UK and Ireland which are controlled by the audit firm or its partners.

Forecast—Prospective financial information prepared on the basis of assumptions as to future events which management expects to take place and the actions management expects to take as of the date the information is prepared (best-estimate assumptions).

Fraud—An intentional act by one or more individuals among management, those charged with governance, employees, or third parties, involving the use of deception to obtain an unjust or illegal advantage. Two types of intentional misstatement are relevant to the auditor: misstatements resulting from fraudulent financial reporting and misstatements resulting from misappropriation of assets (also see Fraudulent financial reporting and Misappropriation of assets).

Fraudulent financial reporting—Involves intentional misstatements, including omissions of amounts or disclosures in financial statements, to deceive financial statement users.

General IT-controls— Policies and procedures that relate to many applications and support the effective functioning of application controls by helping to ensure the continued proper operation of information systems. General IT-controls commonly include controls over data center and network operations; system software acquisition, change and maintenance; access security; and application system acquisition, development, and maintenance.

Going concern assumption—Under this assumption, an entity is ordinarily viewed as continuing in business for the foreseeable future with neither the intention nor the necessity of liquidation, ceasing trading or seeking protection from creditors pursuant to laws or regulations. Accordingly, assets and liabilities are recorded on the basis that the entity will be able to realize its assets and discharge its liabilities in the normal course of business.

Governance—Describes the role of persons entrusted with the supervision, control and direction of an entity. Those charged with governance ordinarily are accountable for ensuring that the entity achieves its objectives, financial reporting, and reporting to interested parties. Those charged with governance include management only when it performs such functions.

> In the UK and Ireland, those charged with governance include the directors (executive and non-executive) of a company or other body, the members of an audit committee where one exists, the partners, proprietors, committee of management or trustees of other forms of entity, or equivalent persons responsible for directing the entity's affairs and preparing its financial statements.

Government business enterprises—Businesses that operate within the public sector ordinarily to meet a political or social interest objective. They are ordinarily required to operate commercially, that is, to make profits or to recoup, through user charges a substantial proportion of their operating costs.

Immediate family—A spouse (or equivalent) or dependent.

Incoming auditor—(see Auditor)

Independence[2]—Comprises:

(a) Independence of mind—the state of mind that permits the provision of an opinion without being affected by influences that compromise professional judgment, allowing an individual to act with integrity, and exercise objectivity and professional judgment; and
(b) Independence in appearance—the avoidance of facts and circumstances that are so significant a reasonable and informed third party, having knowledge of all relevant information, including any safeguards applied, would reasonably conclude a firm's, or a member of the assurance team's, integrity, objectivity or professional skepticism had been compromised.

Information system relevant to financial reporting—A component of internal control that includes the financial reporting system, and consists of the procedures and records established to initiate, record, process and report entity transactions (as well as events and conditions) and to maintain accountability for the related assets, liabilities and equity.

Informed management – Member of management (or senior employee) of the audited entity who has the authority and capability to make independent management judgments and decisions in relation to non-audit services on the basis of information provided by the audit firm.

Inherent risk—(see Audit risk)

Initial audit engagement—An audit engagement in which either the financial statements are audited for the first time; or the financial statements for the prior period were audited by another auditor.

Inquiry—Inquiry consists of seeking information of knowledgeable persons, both financial and non-financial, throughout the entity or outside the entity.

Inspection (as an audit procedure)—Examining records or documents, whether internal or external, or tangible assets.

Inspection (in relation to completed engagements)—Procedures designed to provide evidence of compliance by engagement teams with the firm's quality control policies and procedures;

Intended users—The person, persons or class of persons for whom the practitioner prepares the assurance report. The responsible party can be one of the intended users, but not the only one.

---

[2] *As defined in the IFAC Code of Ethics for Professional Accountants.* APB Ethical Standard 1 defines independence as freedom from situations and relationships which make it probable that a reasonable and informed third party would conclude that objectivity either is impaired or could be impaired. Independence is related to and underpins objectivity. However, whereas objectivity is a personal behavioural characteristic concerning the auditor's state of mind, independence relates to the circumstances surrounding the audit, including the financial, employment, business and personal relationships between the auditor and the audited entity.

Interim financial information or statements—Financial information (which may be less than a complete set of financial statements as defined above) issued at interim dates (usually half-yearly or quarterly) in respect of a financial period.

Internal auditing—An appraisal activity established within an entity as a service to the entity. Its functions include, amongst other things, examining, evaluating and monitoring the adequacy and effectiveness of internal control.

Internal auditor—(see Auditor)

Internal control—The process designed and effected by those charged with governance, management and other personnel to provide reasonable assurance about the achievement of the entity's objectives with regard to reliability of financial reporting, effectiveness and efficiency of operations and compliance with applicable laws and regulations. Internal control consists of the following components:

(a) The control environment;
(b) The entity's risk assessment process;
(c) The information system, including the related business processes, relevant to financial reporting, and communication;
(d) Control activities; and
(e) Monitoring of controls.

Investigate—Inquire into matters arising from other procedures to resolve them.

IT environment—The policies and procedures that the entity implements and the IT infrastructure (hardware, operating systems, etc.) and application software that it uses to support business operations and achieve business strategies.

Key management position—Any position at the audited entity which involves the responsibility for fundamental management decisions at the audited entity (e.g. as a CEO or CFO), including an ability to influence the accounting policies and the preparation of the financial statements of the audited entity. A key management position also arises where there are contractual and factual arrangements which in substance allow an individual to participate in exercising such a management function in a different way (e.g. via a consulting contract).

Key partner involved in the audit—An audit partner, or other person in the engagement team (other than the audit engagement partner or engagement quality control reviewer) who either:

- is involved at the group level and is responsible for key decisions or judgments on significant matters or risk factors that relate to the audit of that audited entity, or
- is primarily responsible for the audit of a significant affiliate or division[3] of the audited entity.

Limited assurance engagement—(see Assurance engagement)

Limitation on scope—A limitation on the scope of the auditor's work may sometimes be imposed by the entity (for example, when the terms of the engagement specify that

---

[3] *For the purposes of this definition, a significant affiliate or division is an affiliate or division which in the judgment of the group auditor, is individually likely to be of financial significance to the group, including those affiliates or divisions located outside the UK and Ireland.*

the auditor will not carry out an audit procedure that the auditor believes is necessary). A scope limitation may be imposed by circumstances (for example, when the timing of the auditor's appointment is such that the auditor is unable to observe the counting of physical inventories). It may also arise when, in the opinion of the auditor, the entity's accounting records are inadequate or when the auditor is unable to carry out an audit procedure believed desirable.

Listed entity[4]—An entity whose shares, stock or debt are quoted or listed on a recognized stock exchange, or are marketed under the regulations of a recognized stock exchange or other equivalent body.

> For the purpose of APB Ethical Standards, listed company includes any company in which the public can trade shares on the open market, such as those listed on the London Stock Exchange (including those admitted to trade on the Alternative Investments Market), PLUS Markets and the Irish Stock Exchange (including those admitted to trade on the Irish Enterprise Exchange).

Local Area Network (LAN)—A communications network that serves users within a confined geographical area. LANs were developed to facilitate the exchange and sharing of resources within an organization, including data, software, storage, printers and telecommunications equipment. They allow for decentralized computing. The basic components of a LAN are transmission media and software, user terminals and shared peripherals.

Management—Comprises officers and others who also perform senior managerial functions. Management includes those charged with governance only in those instances when they perform such functions.

> In the UK and Ireland, depending on the nature and circumstances of the entity, management may include some or all of those charged with governance (e.g. executive directors). Management will not normally include non-executive directors.

Management fraud—Fraud involving one or more members of management or those charged with governance.

Management representations—Representations made by management to the auditor during the course of an audit, either unsolicited or in response to specific inquiries.

Material inconsistency—Exists when other information contradicts information contained in the audited financial statements. A material inconsistency may raise doubt about the audit conclusions drawn from audit evidence previously obtained and, possibly, about the basis for the auditor's opinion on the financial statements.

Material misstatement of fact—Exists in other information when such information, not related to matters appearing in the audited financial statements, is incorrectly stated or presented.

Material weakness—A weakness in internal control that could have a material effect on the financial statements.

---
[4] *As defined in the IFAC Code of Ethics for Professional Accountants.*

Materiality—Information is material if its omission or misstatement could influence the economic decisions of users taken on the basis of the financial statements. Materiality depends on the size of the item or error judged in the particular circumstances of its omission or misstatement. Thus, materiality provides a threshold or cutoff point rather than being a primary qualitative characteristic which information must have if it is to be useful.

Misappropriation of assets—Involves the theft of an entity's assets and is often perpetrated by employees in relatively small and immaterial amounts. However, it can also involve management who are usually more capable of disguising or concealing misappropriations in ways that are difficult to detect.

Misstatement—A misstatement of the financial statements that can arise from fraud or error (also see Fraud and Error).

Modified auditor's report—An auditor's report is considered to be modified if either an emphasis of matter paragraph(s) is added to the report or if the opinion is other than unqualified:

Matters that Do Not Affect the Auditor's Opinion
Emphasis of matter paragraph(s)—An auditor's report may be modified by adding an emphasis of matter paragraph(s) to highlight a matter affecting the financial statements which is included in a note to the financial statements that more extensively discusses the matter. The addition of such an emphasis of matter paragraph(s) does not affect the auditor's opinion. The auditor may also modify the auditor's report by using an emphasis of matter paragraph(s) to report matters other than those affecting the financial statements.

Matters that Do Affect the Auditor's Opinion
Qualified opinion—A qualified opinion is expressed when the auditor concludes that an unqualified opinion cannot be expressed but that the effect of any disagreement with management, or limitation on scope is not so material and pervasive as to require an adverse opinion or a disclaimer of opinion.

Disclaimer of opinion—A disclaimer of opinion is expressed when the possible effect of a limitation on scope is so material and pervasive that the auditor has not been able to obtain sufficient appropriate audit evidence and accordingly is unable to express an opinion on the financial statements.

Adverse opinion—An adverse opinion is expressed when the effect of a disagreement is so material and pervasive to the financial statements that the auditor concludes that a qualification of the report is not adequate to disclose the misleading or incomplete nature of the financial statements.

Monitoring (in relation to quality control)—A process comprising an ongoing consideration and evaluation of the firm's system of quality control, including a periodic inspection of a selection of completed engagements, designed to enable the firm to obtain reasonable assurance that its system of quality control is operating effectively.

Monitoring of controls—A process to assess the effectiveness of internal control performance over time. It includes assessing the design and operation of controls on a timely basis and taking necessary corrective actions modified for changes in conditions. Monitoring of controls is a component of internal control.

National practices (auditing)—A set of guidelines not having the authority of standards defined by an authoritative body at a national level and commonly applied by auditors in the conduct of an audit, review, other assurance or related services.

National standards (auditing)—A set of standards defined by law or regulations or an authoritative body at a national level, the application of which is mandatory in conducting an audit, review, other assurance or related services.

Network firm[5]—An entity under common control, ownership or management with the firm or any entity that a reasonable and informed third party having knowledge of all relevant information would reasonably conclude as being part of the firm nationally or internationally.

> For the purpose of APB Ethical Standards, a network firm is any entity which is part of a larger structure that is aimed at co-operation and which is:
>
> (i) controlled by the audit firm; or
> (ii) under common control, ownership or management; or
> (iii) part of a larger structure that is clearly aimed at profit sharing; or
> (iv) otherwise affiliated or associated with the audit firm through common quality control policies and procedures, common business strategy, the use of a common name or through the sharing of significant common professional resources.
>
> *Non-audit services* – Any engagement in which an audit firm provides professional services to an audited entity other than pursuant to:
>
> (a) the audit of financial statements; and
> (b) those other roles which relevant legislation or regulation specify can be performed by the auditor of the entity.
>
> In the case of a group, non-audit services include services provided by the audit firm, to the parent company or to any affiliate.

Noncompliance—Refers to acts of omission or commission by the entity being audited, either intentional or unintentional, that are contrary to the prevailing laws or regulations.

Non-sampling risk—(see Audit sampling)

Non-statistical sampling—(see Audit sampling)

Observation—Consists of looking at a process or procedure being performed by others, for example, the observation by the auditor of the counting of inventories by the entity's personnel or the performance of control activities.

Opening balances—Those account balances which exist at the beginning of the period. Opening balances are based upon the closing balances of the prior period and reflect the effects of transactions of prior periods and accounting policies applied in the prior period.

Opinion—The auditor's report contains a clear written expression of opinion on the financial statements as a whole. An unqualified opinion is expressed when the auditor concludes that the financial statements give a true and fair view (or are presented fairly, in all material respects,) in accordance with the applicable financial reporting framework. (also see Modified auditor's report)

---

[5] *As defined in the IFAC Code of Ethics for Professional Accountants.*

Other auditor—(see Auditor)

Other information—Financial or non-financial information (other than the financial statements or the auditor's report thereon) included – either by law or custom – in the annual report.

Overall audit strategy—Sets the scope, timing and direction of the audit, and guides the development of the more detailed audit plan.

Partner—Any individual with authority to bind the firm with respect to the performance of a professional services engagement.

PCs or personal computers (also referred to as microcomputers)—Economical yet powerful self-contained general purpose computers consisting typically of a monitor (visual display unit), a case containing the computer electronics and a keyboard (and mouse). These features may be combined in portable computers (laptops). Programs and data may be stored internally on a hard disk or on removable storage media such as CDs or floppy disks. PCs may be connected to on-line networks, printers and other devices such as scanners and modems.

> *Person in a position to influence the conduct and outcome of the audit*—This is:
> (a) Any person who is directly involved in the audit (the engagement team), including:
>   (i) the audit partners, audit managers and audit staff (the audit team);
>   (ii) professional personnel from other disciplines involved in the audit (for example, lawyers, actuaries, taxation specialists, IT specialists, treasury management specialists);
>   (iii) those who provide quality control or direct oversight of the audit;
> (b) Any person, who forms part of the chain of command for the audit within the audit firm;
> (c) Any person within the audit firm who, due to any other circumstances, may be in a position to exert such influence.

Personnel—Partners and staff.

Planning—Involves establishing the overall audit strategy for the engagement and developing an audit plan, in order to reduce audit risk to an acceptably low level.

Population—(see Audit sampling)

Post balance sheet events—(see Subsequent events)

Practitioner—A professional accountant in public practice.

Predecessor auditor—(see Auditor)

Principal auditor—(see Auditor)

> *Professional accountant*—Those persons who are members of a professional accountancy body, whether in public practice (including a sole practitioner, partnership or corporate body), industry, commerce, the public sector or education.

Professional accountant in public practice[6]—A professional accountant, irrespective of functional classification (e.g. audit, tax or consulting) in a firm that provides professional services. This term is also used to refer to a firm of professional accountants in public practice.

Professional skepticism—An attitude that includes a questioning mind and a critical assessment of evidence.

Professional standards—IAASB engagement standards, as defined in the IAASB's "Preface to the International Standards on Quality Control, Auditing, Assurance and Related Services," and relevant ethical requirements, which ordinarily comprise Parts A and B of the IFAC *Code of Ethics for Professional Accountants* and relevant national ethical requirements.[7]

Programming controls—Procedures designed to prevent or detect improper changes to computer programs that are accessed through on-line terminal devices. Access may be restricted by controls such as the use of separate operational and program development libraries and the use of specialized program library software. It is important for on-line changes to programs to be adequately documented, controlled and monitored.

Projection—Prospective financial information prepared on the basis of:

(a) Hypothetical assumptions about future events and management actions which are not necessarily expected to take place, such as when some entities are in a start-up phase or are considering a major change in the nature of operations; or
(b) A mixture of best-estimate and hypothetical assumptions.

Proposed auditor—(see Auditor)

Prospective financial information—Financial information based on assumptions about events that may occur in the future and possible actions by an entity. Prospective financial information can be in the form of a forecast, a projection or a combination of both. (see Forecast and Projection)

Public sector—National governments, regional (for example, state, provincial, territorial) governments, local (for example, city, town) governments and related governmental entities (for example, agencies, boards, commissions and enterprises).

Qualified opinion—(see Modified auditor's report)

Quality controls—The policies and procedures adopted by a firm designed to provide it with reasonable assurance that the firm and its personnel comply with professional standards and regulatory and legal requirements, and that reports issued by the firm or engagement partners are appropriate in the circumstances.

Reasonable assurance (in the context of quality control)—A high, but not absolute, level of assurance.

---

[6] As defined in the IFAC Code of Ethics for Professional Accountants.

[7] In the UK and Ireland the relevant ethical pronouncements with which the auditor complies are the APB's Ethical Standards and the ethical pronouncements relating to the work of auditors issued by the auditor's relevant professional body – see the Statement "The Auditing Practices Board – Scope and Authority of Pronouncements".

Reasonable assurance (in the context of an audit engagement)—A high, but not absolute, level of assurance, expressed positively in the auditor's report as reasonable assurance, that the information subject to audit is free of material misstatement.

Reasonable assurance engagement—(see Assurance engagement)

Recalculation—Consists of checking the mathematical accuracy of documents or records.

Related party—Related party and related party transaction are defined in International Accounting Standard (IAS) 24, "Related Party Disclosures" as:

> *Related party*— A party is related to an entity if:
> (a) Directly, or indirectly through one or more intermediaries, the party:
>   (i) Controls, is controlled by, or is under common control with, the entity (this includes parents, subsidiaries and fellow subsidiaries);
>   (ii) Has an interest in the entity that gives it significant influence over the entity; or
>   (iii) Has joint control over the entity;
> (b) The party is an associate (as defined in IAS 28, "Investments in Associates") of the entity;
> (c) The party is a joint venture in which the entity is a venturer (see IAS 31, "Interest in Joint Ventures");
> (d) The party is a member of the key management personnel of the entity or its parent;
> (e) The party is a close member of the family of any individual referred to in (a) or (d);
> (f) The party is an entity that is controlled, jointly controlled or significantly influenced by, or for which significant voting power in such entity resides with, directly or indirectly, any individual referred to in (d) or (e); or,
> (g) The party is a post-employment benefit plan for the benefit of employees of the entity, or of any entity that is a related party of the entity.
>
> *Related party transaction*— A transfer of resources, services or obligations between related parties, regardless of whether a price is charged.

The above definitions of "related party" and "related party transaction" apply when the financial statements being audited are intended to comply with IAS 24. If the financial statements being audited are intended to comply with Financial Reporting Standard 8, "Related Party Disclosures", the definitions included therein are used (see the Appendix to ISA (UK and Ireland) 550, "Related Parties").

Related services—Comprise agreed-upon procedures and compilations.

Reperformance—The auditor's independent execution of procedures or controls that were originally performed as part of the entity's internal controls, either manually or through the use of CAATs.

Responsible party—The person (or persons) who:

(a) In a direct reporting engagement, is responsible for the subject matter; or
(b) In an assertion-based engagement, is responsible for the subject matter information (the assertion), and may be responsible for the subject matter.

The responsible party may or may not be the party who engages the practitioner (the engaging party).

Review (in relation to quality control)—Appraising the quality of the work performed and conclusions reached by others.

Review engagement—The objective of a review engagement is to enable an auditor to state whether, on the basis of procedures which do not provide all the evidence that would be required in an audit, anything has come to the auditor's attention that causes the auditor to believe that the financial statements are not prepared, in all material respects, in accordance with an applicable financial reporting framework.

Review procedures—The procedures deemed necessary to meet the objective of a review engagement, primarily inquiries of entity personnel and analytical procedures applied to financial data.

Risk assessment procedures—The audit procedures performed to obtain an understanding of the entity and its environment, including its internal control, to assess the risks of material misstatement at the financial statement and assertion levels.

Risk of material misstatement—(see Audit Risk)

Sampling risk—(see Audit sampling)

Sampling unit—(see Audit sampling)

Scope of an audit—The audit procedures deemed necessary in the circumstances to achieve the objective of the audit.

Scope of a review—The review procedures deemed necessary in the circumstances to achieve the objective of the review.

Scope limitation—(see Limitation on scope)

Segment information—Information in the financial statements regarding distinguishable components or industry and geographical aspects of an entity.

Significance—The relative importance of a matter, taken in context. The significance of a matter is judged by the practitioner in the context in which it is being considered. This might include, for example, the reasonable prospect of its changing or influencing the decisions of intended users of the practitioner's report; or, as another example, where the context is a judgment about whether to report a matter to those charged with governance, whether the matter would be regarded as important by them in relation to their duties. Significance can be considered in the context of quantitative and qualitative factors, such as relative magnitude, the nature and effect on the subject matter and the expressed interests of intended users or recipients.

Significant risk—A risk that requires special audit consideration.

Small entity—Any entity in which:
(a) There is concentration of ownership and management in a small number of individuals (often a single individual); and
(b) One or more of the following are also found:
   (i) Few sources of income;
   (ii) Unsophisticated record-keeping; and

(iii) Limited internal controls together with the potential for management override of controls.

Small entities will ordinarily display characteristic (a), and one or more of the characteristics included under (b).

> In the UK and Ireland, company law provides a lighter reporting regime for companies that are defined, by legislation, as small. A company qualifies as "small" if it meets particular thresholds in respect of turnover, balance sheet total/ gross assets and number of employees and certain other criteria. The thresholds and other criteria are subject to change and reference to the relevant legislation should be made to determine what they are in respect of a particular accounting period.
>
> For the purpose of the APB Ethical Standards, a Small Entity is defined in "APB Ethical Standard – Provisions Available for Small Entities".

Special purpose auditor's report—A report issued in connection with the independent audit of financial information other than an auditor's report on financial statements, including:

(a) Financial statements prepared in accordance with a comprehensive basis of accounting other than International Accounting Standards or national standards;
(b) Specified accounts, elements of accounts, or items in a financial statement;
(c) Compliance with contractual agreements; and
(d) Summarized financial statements.

Staff—Professionals, other than partners, including any experts the firm employs.

Statistical sampling—(see Audit sampling)

Stratification—(see Audit sampling)

Subject matter information—The outcome of the evaluation or measurement of a subject matter. It is the subject matter information about which the practitioner gathers sufficient appropriate evidence to provide a reasonable basis for expressing a conclusion in an assurance report.

Subsequent events—International Accounting Standard (IAS) 10, "Events After the Balance Sheet Date," deals with the treatment in financial statements of events, both favourable and unfavourable, that occur between the date of the financial statements (referred to as the "balance sheet date" in the IAS) and the date when the financial statements are authorized for issue and identifies two types of events:

(a) Those that provide further evidence of conditions that existed at period end; and
(b) Those that are indicative of conditions that arose subsequent to period end.

Substantive procedures—Audit procedures performed to detect material misstatements at the assertion level; they include:

(a) Tests of details of classes of transactions, account balances; and disclosures and
(b) Substantive analytical procedures.

Successor auditor—(see Auditor)

Sufficiency—Sufficiency is the measure of the quantity of audit evidence. The quantity of the audit evidence needed is affected by the risk of misstatement and also by the quality of such audit evidence.

Suitable criteria—(see Criteria)

Suitably qualified external person (for the purpose of ISQC 1)—An individual outside the firm with the capabilities and competence to act as an engagement partner, for example a partner of another firm, or an employee (with appropriate experience) of either a professional accountancy body whose members may perform audits and reviews of historical financial information, other assurance or related services engagements, or of an organization that provides relevant quality control services.

Summarized financial statements—Financial statements summarizing an entity's annual audited financial statements for the purpose of informing user groups interested in the highlights only of the entity's financial performance and position.

Supreme Audit Institution—The public body of a State which, however designated, constituted or organized, exercises by virtue of law, the highest public auditing function of that State.

Test—The application of procedures to some or all items in a population.

Tests of control—Tests performed to obtain audit evidence about the operating effectiveness of controls in preventing, or detecting and correcting, material misstatements at the assertion level.

Those charged with governance—(see Governance)

Tolerable error—(see Audit sampling)

Total error—(see Audit sampling)

Transaction logs—Reports that are designed to create an audit trail for each on-line transaction. Such reports often document the source of a transaction (terminal, time and user) as well as the transaction's details.

Uncertainty— A matter whose outcome depends on future actions or events not under the direct control of the entity but that may affect the financial statements.

Understanding of the entity and its environment—The auditor's understanding of the entity and its environment consists of the following aspects:

(a) Industry, regulatory, and other external factors, including the applicable financial reporting framework.
(b) Nature of the entity, including the entity's selection and application of accounting policies.
(c) Objectives and strategies and the related business risks that may result in a material misstatement of the financial statements.
(d) Measurement and review of the entity's financial performance.
(e) Internal control.

Unqualified opinion—(see Opinion)

Walk-through test—Involves tracing a few transactions through the financial reporting system.

Wide Area Network (WAN)—A communications network that transmits information across an expanded area such as between plant sites, cities and nations. WANs allow for on-line access to applications from remote terminals. Several LANs can be interconnected in a WAN.

Working papers—The material prepared by and for, or obtained and retained by, the auditor in connection with the performance of the audit. Working papers may be in the form of data stored on paper, film, electronic media or other media.

Introduction
Standards for Investment Reporting (SIRs)

SIRs contain basic principles and essential procedures with which reporting accountants are required to comply in the conduct of an engagement in connection with an investment circular (eg a prospectus listing particulars circular to shareholders or similar documents) prepared for issue in connection with a securities transaction governed wholly or in part by the laws and regulations of the United Kingdom or Republic of Ireland.

[1000]
Investment reporting standards applicable to all engagements in connection with an investment circular

Contents

	Paragraphs
Introduction	1 - 5
Engagement acceptance and continuance	6 - 9
Agreeing the terms of the engagement	10 - 17
Ethical requirements	18 - 19
Legal and regulatory requirements	20 - 21
Quality control	22 - 27
Planning and performing the engagement	28 - 45
Documentation	46 - 49
Professional scepticism	50 - 52
Reporting	53 - 61
Modified opinions	62 - 64
Pre-existing financial information	65
Consent	66 - 74
Events occurring between the date of the reporting accountant's report and the completion date of the transaction	75 - 77
Effective date	78

Appendices

1 Summary of possible reporting accountant's public reporting engagements under the Prospectus Rules
2 Principal legal and regulatory requirements
3 Example of a consent letter
4 Glossary of terms

Investment reporting standards applicable to all engagements in connection with an investment circular

SIR 1000 contains basic principles and essential procedures ("Investment Reporting Standards"), indicated by paragraphs in bold type, with which a reporting accountant is required to comply in the conduct of all engagements in connection with an investment circular prepared for issue in connection with a securities transaction governed wholly or in part by the laws and regulations of the United Kingdom.

SIR 1000 also includes explanatory and other material, including appendices, in the context of which the basic principles and essential procedures are to be understood and applied. It is necessary to consider the whole text of the SIR to understand and apply the basic principles and essential procedures.

The definitions in the glossary of terms set out in Appendix 4 are to be applied in the interpretation of this and all other SIRs. Terms defined in the glossary are underlined the first time that they occur in the text.

This SIR replaces SIR 100 "Investment circulars and reporting accountants" issued in December 1997.

To assist readers, SIRs contain references to, and extracts from, certain legislation and chapters of the Rules of the UK Listing Authority. Readers are cautioned that these references may change subsequent to publication.

Introduction

The application of Standards for Investment Reporting (SIRs) is best understood by reference to the following four defined terms used throughout the SIRs:

(a) **investment circular** is a generic term defined as "*Any document issued by an entity pursuant to statutory or regulatory requirements relating to securities on which it is intended that a third party should make an investment decision, including a prospectus, listing particulars, a circular to shareholders or similar document*";

(b) **reporting accountant** is defined as "*An accountant engaged to prepare a report for inclusion in, or in connection with, an investment circular. The reporting accountant may or may not be the auditor of the entity issuing the investment circular. The term "reporting accountant" is used to describe either the engagement partner or the engagement partner's firm*[1]. *The reporting accountant could be a limited company or an engagement principal employed by the company;*

(c) **public reporting engagement** is defined as "*An engagement in which a reporting accountant expresses a conclusion that is published in an investment circular, and which is designed to enhance the degree of confidence of the intended users of the report about the 'outcome*[2]' *of the directors' evaluation or measurement of 'subject matter' against 'suitable criteria'*"; and

(d) **private reporting engagement** is defined as "*An engagement, in connection with an investment circular, in which a reporting accountant does not express a conclusion that is published in an investment circular*". Private reporting engagements are

1

---

[1] Where the term applies to the engagement partner, it describes the responsibilities or obligations of the engagement partner. Such obligations or responsibilities may be fulfilled by either the engagement partner or a member of the engagement partner's team.

[2] The "outcome" is sometimes described as "subject matter information."

likely to involve the reporting accountant reporting privately to one or more of an issuer, sponsor or regulator.

2   In order to provide flexibility to develop SIRs for a wide range of possible public reporting engagements, the description of public reporting engagement includes three generic terms. Their meanings are as follows:

(a) the "**subject matter**" of the engagement is that which is being evaluated or measured against suitable criteria. Examples of subject matter are the entity's financial position and the directors' expectation of the issuer's profit for the period covered by a profit forecast;
(b) criteria are the benchmarks used to evaluate or measure the subject matter. "**Suitable criteria**" are usually derived from laws and regulations and are required by directors to enable them to make reasonably consistent evaluations or measurements of the subject matter. With respect to public reporting engagements the suitable criteria for specific types of engagement are described in the individual SIR dealing with such engagements. Where the reporting accountant's engagement requires it to consider only certain criteria, such criteria are described as "reporting accountant's criteria". Reporting accountant's criteria are set out in the SIRs. Where a SIR has not been issued with respect to a particular type of reporting engagement, the reporting accountant uses those criteria that are specified by legislation or regulation. The evaluation or measurement of a subject matter solely on the basis of the reporting accountant's own expectations, judgments and individual experience would not constitute suitable criteria; and
(c) the "**outcome**" of the evaluation or measurement of a subject matter is the information that results from the directors applying the suitable criteria to the subject matter. Examples of outcomes are historical financial information and a directors' profit forecast and related disclosures that are included in an investment circular.

3   Not all engagements performed by a reporting accountant are public reporting engagements. Examples of engagements that are not public reporting engagements include:

- Engagements involving the preparation of a comfort letter.
- Engagements involving the preparation of a long form report.

Such engagements are private reporting engagements.

4   This SIR establishes basic principles and essential procedures for the work of reporting accountants that are common to all reporting engagements (both public and private) relating to investment circulars. Other SIRs set out basic principles and essential procedures to address the particular issues and requirements arising on specific public reporting engagements. These comprise:

(a) SIR 2000 "Investment reporting standards applicable to public reporting engagements on historical financial information";
(b) SIR 3000 "Investment reporting standards applicable to public reporting engagements on profit forecasts"; and
(c) SIR 4000 "Investment reporting standards applicable to public reporting engagements on pro forma financial information.

5   Appendix 1 summarises public reporting engagements that reporting accountants may be required to undertake under the Prospectus Rules.

Engagement acceptance and continuance

The reporting accountant should accept (or continue where applicable) a reporting engagement only if, on the basis of a preliminary knowledge of the engagement circumstances, nothing comes to the attention of the reporting accountant to indicate that the requirements of relevant ethical standards and guidance, issued by the Auditing Practices Board and the professional bodies of which the reporting accountant is a member, will not be satisfied. (SIR 1000.1) 6

The reporting accountant should accept (or continue where applicable) a reporting engagement only if: 7

(a) the scope of the engagement is expected to be sufficient to support the required report;
(b) the reporting accountant expects to be able to carry out the procedures required by the SIRs; and
(c) those persons who are to perform the engagement collectively possess the necessary professional competencies. (SIR 1000.2)

In determining whether the scope of the engagement is expected to be sufficient to support the required report, the reporting accountant considers whether there appear to be any significant limitations on the scope of the reporting accountant's work. 8

A reporting accountant may be requested to perform reporting engagements on a wide range of matters. Some engagements may require specialised skills and knowledge. In these circumstances the reporting accountant considers using internal or external specialists having the appropriate skills. 9

Agreeing the terms of the engagement

The reporting accountant should agree the terms of the engagement with those from whom they accept instructions. All the terms of the engagement should be recorded in writing. (SIR 1000.3) 10

Generally, a letter is prepared by the reporting accountant, covering all aspects of the engagement, and accepted in writing by the directors of the issuer and, where relevant, the sponsor. With respect to a public reporting engagement the letter will record the reporting accountant's understanding of what constitutes the subject matter of the engagement, the suitable criteria, and the information that constitutes the outcome of the evaluation or measurement of the subject matter against the suitable criteria. 11

As an alternative to a letter drafted by the reporting accountant, an instruction letter may be issued by the directors and, where relevant, the sponsor. In these circumstances, its terms are formally acknowledged by the reporting accountant in writing, clarifying particular aspects of the instructions and covering any matters that may not have been addressed. 12

This letter, or exchange of letters (together referred to as "the engagement letter"), provides evidence of the contractual relationship between the reporting accountant, the entity and, where relevant, the sponsor. It sets out clearly the scope and limitations of the work to be performed by the reporting accountant. It also confirms the reporting accountant's acceptance of the engagement and includes a summary of the reporting accountant's responsibilities and those of the directors and, where relevant, the sponsor as they relate to the reporting accountant's role. 13

14 The engagement letter establishes a direct responsibility to the other parties from the reporting accountant. It is also the mechanism by which the scope of the reporting accountant's contribution is defined and agreed. If in the course of the engagement the terms of the engagement are changed, such changes are similarly agreed, and recorded in writing.

15 The engagement letter will usually set out the form of any reports (public or private) required (including, in each case, the nature of any opinion to be expressed by the reporting accountant). Accordingly, it is important to clarify those from whom the reporting accountant has agreed to accept instructions including, where relevant, sponsors, and determine their requirements and the scope of such reports, at an early stage.

16 **The engagement letter should specify those reports that are intended for publication in the investment circular and any other reports that are required. The engagement letter should specify, in respect of each report, to whom it is to be addressed. (SIR 1000.4)**

17 The engagement letter sets out the express terms governing the reporting accountant's contractual responsibilities in connection with the transaction to those instructing them. Reporting accountants do not accept responsibility beyond the matters or entities in respect of which they are specifically instructed. Nor are they expected to comment or report on matters which more properly fall within the skill and experience of other experts or advisers. They understand, however, the need to apply their own professional skill and experience in interpreting and carrying out their instructions. The reporting accountant may find information outside the defined scope of the engagement that it believes should be disclosed, because, in its view such information is material to the purpose of the investment circular or to the proposed transaction. The reporting accountant discusses such matters with the directors of the issuer and the sponsor, where relevant, and agrees a course of action.

Ethical requirements

18 **In the conduct of an engagement involving an investment circular, the reporting accountant should comply with the applicable ethical standards issued by the Auditing Practices Board. The reporting accountant should also adhere to the relevant ethical guidance of the professional bodies of which the reporting accountant is a member. (SIR 1000.5)**

19 While it is not the responsibility of the reporting accountant to judge the appropriateness, or otherwise, of a proposed transaction, in respect of which they have been engaged, there may be rare circumstances where a reporting accountant considers the proposed transaction, or their proposed association with the transaction, to be so inappropriate that the reporting accountant cannot properly commence work or continue to act.

Legal and regulatory requirements

20 **The reporting accountant should be familiar with the applicable laws and regulations governing the report which is to be given. (SIR 1000.6)**

21 The principal legal and regulatory requirements applicable to reporting accountants in the United Kingdom are summarised in Appendix 2. Readers are cautioned that these references may change subsequent to publication of this SIR.

Quality control

The reporting accountant should comply with the applicable standards and guidance set out in International Standard on Quality Control (UK and Ireland) 1 and ISA (UK and Ireland) 220. (SIR 1000.7)   22

International Standard on Quality Control (UK and Ireland) 1 "Quality control for firms that perform audits and reviews of historical financial information, and other assurance and related services engagements" provides standards and guidance on the system of quality control that a firm establishes.   23

The quality control procedures that an engagement partner applies are those set out in ISA (UK and Ireland) 220 "Quality control for audits of historical financial information". In applying ISA (UK and Ireland) 220, the terms "audit" and "audit engagement" are read as "reporting accountant's engagement" and the term "auditor's report" is read as "reporting accountant's report".   24

When undertaking any engagement involving an investment circular a partner with appropriate experience should be involved in the conduct of the work. (SIR 1000.8)   25

Reporting accountants are frequently from a firm that is also the auditor of the entity. The audit partner, although having knowledge of the entity, may not have the necessary experience to take responsibility for all aspects of an engagement involving an investment circular. The extent of involvement of a partner with the requisite experience of dealing with investment circulars is determined, for example, by the expertise required to make the reports that the reporting accountant has agreed to provide and the experience of the audit partner.   26

In some cases it may be appropriate for the partner with the requisite experience of dealing with investment circulars to act as a second partner. In other cases it may be appropriate for such a partner to be the lead engagement partner.   27

Planning and performing the engagement

28. The reporting accountant should develop and document a plan for the work so as to perform the engagement in an effective manner. (SIR 1000.9)

Planning is an essential component of all reporting accountant's engagements. Examples of the main matters to be considered include: 29

- The terms of the engagement.
- Ethical considerations.
- Whether the timetable is realistic.
- The reporting accountant's understanding of the entity and its environment.
- Identifying potential problems that could impact the performance of the engagement.
- The need for the involvement of specialists.

Planning is not a discrete phase, but rather an iterative process throughout the engagement. As a result of unexpected events, changes in conditions or the evidence obtained from the results of evidence-gathering procedures, the reporting accountant may need to revise the overall strategy and engagement plan, and thereby the resulting planned nature, timing and extent of further procedures.   30

31 A preliminary review of the available information may provide an indication of potential issues that might need to be addressed in carrying out the engagement. If the preliminary review indicates that there are factors which may give rise to a qualification or other modification of any report, then such factors are reported immediately to the directors and, where relevant, the sponsor.

32 Changes in circumstances, or unexpected results of work carried out, may require the plan to be amended as work progresses. Any such amendments are documented. Where the changes affect the work set out in the engagement letter, the engagement letter is also amended as necessary following agreement with the directors, and where relevant, the sponsor.

33 **The reporting accountant should consider materiality in planning its work in accordance with its instructions and in determining the effect of its findings on the report to be issued. (SIR 1000.10)**

34 Matters are material if their omission or misstatement could, individually or collectively, influence the economic decisions of users of the outcome. Materiality depends on the size and nature of the omission or misstatement judged in light of the surrounding circumstances. The size or nature of the matter, or a combination of both, could be the determining factor.

35 In certain circumstances, such as private reporting engagements to report the results of agreed-upon procedures, materiality may have been determined for the reporting accountant within the scope of the engagement.

36 **The reporting accountant should obtain sufficient appropriate evidence on which to base the report provided. (SIR 1000.11)**

37 The reporting accountant, either directly or indirectly, will seek to obtain evidence derived from one or more of the following procedures: inspection, observation, enquiry, confirmation, computation and analytical procedures. The choice of which of these, or which combination, is appropriate will depend on the circumstances of each engagement and on the form of opinion (if any) to be given. Guidance on considerations applicable in particular circumstances is given in other SIRs which address the particular issues and requirements arising on specific engagements.

38 The evidence gathered in support of an individual report takes account of the information gathered and conclusions drawn in support of other reporting engagements in connection with the transaction.

39 **If the reporting accountant becomes aware of any withholding, concealment or misrepresentation of information, it should take steps, as soon as practicable, to consider its obligation to report such findings and, if necessary, take legal advice to determine the appropriate response. (SIR 1000.12)**

40 In preparing any report the reporting accountant relies on information supplied to it by the directors, employees or agents of the entity that is the subject of the reporting accountant's enquiries. The engagement letter may limit the extent of the reporting accountant's responsibility where information which is material to the report has been withheld from, concealed from or misrepresented to the reporting accountant. Notwithstanding any such limitation, the reporting accountant does not accept such information without further inquiry where, applying its professional skill and experience to the engagement, the information provided, prima facie, gives rise to doubts about its validity.

The reporting accountant normally informs the directors of the issuer and the sponsor, where relevant, as soon as practicable, of any withholding, concealment or misrepresentation of information. The reporting accountant's duty of confidentiality would ordinarily preclude reporting to a third party. However, in certain circumstances, that duty of confidentiality is overridden by law, for example, in the case of suspected money laundering it may be appropriate to report the matter direct to the appropriate authority. The reporting accountant may need to seek legal advice in such circumstances, giving due consideration to any public interest considerations. 41

The reporting accountant should obtain appropriate written confirmation of representations from the directors of the entity. (SIR 1000.13) 42

Written confirmation of representations made by the directors on matters material to the reporting accountant's report is ordinarily obtained. These representations also encompass statements or opinions attributed to directors, management, employees or agents of an entity, which are relied upon by the reporting accountant. 43

This may be achieved by the directors confirming that they have read a final draft of the report and that to the best of their knowledge and belief: 44

(a) they have made available to the reporting accountant all significant information, relevant to the report, of which they have knowledge;
(b) the report is factually accurate, no material facts have been omitted and the report is not otherwise misleading; and
(c) the report accurately reflects any opinion or statements attributed therein to the directors, management, employees or agents of the entity.

Representations by the directors of the entity cannot replace the evidence that the reporting accountant could reasonably expect to be available to support any opinion given, if any. An inability to obtain sufficient appropriate evidence regarding a matter could represent a limitation of scope even if a representation has been received on the matter. 45

Documentation

The reporting accountant should document matters that are significant in providing evidence that supports the report provided and in providing evidence that the engagement was performed in accordance with SIRs. (SIR 1000.14) 46

The reporting accountant should record in the working papers (or, if applicable, the report) the reporting accountant's reasoning on all significant matters that require the exercise of judgment, and related conclusions. (SIR 1000.15) 47

The information to be recorded in working papers is a matter of professional judgment since it is neither necessary nor practical to document every matter considered by the reporting accountant. When applying professional judgment in assessing the extent of documentation to be prepared and retained, the reporting accountant may consider what is necessary to provide an understanding of the work performed and the basis of the principal decisions taken to another person, such as a reporting accountant, who has no previous experience with the engagement. That other person may, however, only be able to obtain an understanding of detailed aspects of the engagement by discussing them with the reporting accountant who prepared the documentation. 48

The form and content of working papers are affected by matters such as: 49

- The nature and scope of the engagement.
- The form of the report and the opinion, if any, to be given.
- The nature and complexity of the entity's business.
- The nature and condition of the entity's accounting and internal control systems.
- The needs in the particular circumstances for direction, supervision and review of the work of members of the reporting accountant's team.
- The specific methodology and technology that the reporting accountant uses.

Professional scepticism

50 The reporting accountant should plan and perform an engagement with an attitude of professional scepticism. (SIR 1000.16)

51 An attitude of professional scepticism is essential to ensure that the reporting accountant makes a critical assessment, with a questioning mind, of the validity of evidence obtained and is alert to evidence that contradicts or brings into question the reliability of documents or representations.

52 Whilst the reporting accountant may proceed on the basis that information and explanations provided by the directors and management of the issuer are reliable, it assesses them critically and considers them in the context of its knowledge and findings derived from other areas of its work. The reporting accountant is alert for, and, where appropriate reports, on a timely basis, to the directors and sponsors, where relevant, any inconsistencies it considers to be significant. The extent to which the reporting accountant is required to perform further procedures on the information and explanations received will depend upon the reporting accountant's specific instructions, and the level of assurance, if any, it is to provide and the requirements of relevant SIRs.

Reporting

53 In all reports the reporting accountant should:

(a) address reports only to those parties who are party to the engagement letter (and on the basis agreed in the engagement letter) or to a relevant regulatory body;
(b) identify the matters to which the report relates;
(c) address all matters that are required by the engagement letter;
(d) explain the basis of the reporting accountant's work;
(e) give, where applicable, a clear expression of opinion;
(f) include the reporting accountant's manuscript or printed signature;
(g) include the reporting accountant's address; and
(h) date the report. (SIR 1000.17)

54 In all public reporting engagements the reporting accountant should explain the basis of the reporting accountant's opinion by including in its report:

(a) a statement as to the reporting accountant's compliance, or otherwise, with applicable Standards for Investment Reporting; and
(b) a summary description of the work performed by the reporting accountant. (SIR 1000.18)

55 Certain of the reports prepared in connection with investment circulars are public reporting engagements and, therefore, intended for publication in the investment

circular. Examples of such reports are accountant's reports, reports on profit forecasts and reports on pro forma financial information. Additional basic principles and essential procedures on the expression of opinions or conclusions relating to these example public reporting engagements are provided as follows:

(a) accountant's reports on historical financial information, in SIR 2000;
(b) reports on profit forecasts, in SIR 3000; and
(c) reports on pro forma financial information, in SIR 4000.

In private reporting engagements the reporting accountant would ordinarily include in its report: 56
    (a) a statement of compliance with this SIR; and
    (b) either a summary description of the work performed or a cross reference to the description of work to be performed in the engagement letter.

In some private reporting engagements those engaging the reporting accountant agree with the reporting accountant the procedures to be performed[3]. In such cases it may be unnecessary for the report of the reporting accountant to repeat the description of the procedures that is set out in the engagement letter.

Before signing the report, the reporting accountant should consider whether it is appropriate to make the required report, having regard to the scope of the work performed and the evidence obtained. (SIR 1000.19) 57

The date of a report is the date on which the reporting accountant signs the report as being suitable for release. However, the reporting accountant should not sign the report (whether modified or not) unless sufficient appropriate evidence has been obtained and all relevant procedures have been finalised. Such procedures include the review procedures of both the engagement partner and the engagement quality control reviewer. 58

As noted in paragraph 15 above, the engagement letter usually sets out the form of the report to be issued, including, where applicable, the form of opinion to be expressed. The reporting accountant ensures that the form of report or opinion is consistent with the terms of the engagement letter. 59

The level of assurance, if any, provided by the reporting accountant may vary from engagement to engagement. This reflects the wide range of characteristics of the matters to which the engagements undertaken by reporting accountants relate. To avoid any misunderstanding by the user of the report as to the scope of the opinion or the level of assurance provided, it is important that the matters to which the engagements undertaken by reporting accountants relate are clearly identified and that the reporting accountant's opinion or other assurance is expressed in terms that are appropriate to the particular engagement. Standards and guidance on the form and scope of reports appropriate in particular circumstances is given in other SIRs which address particular issues and requirements relevant to individual reports. 60

In certain circumstances the Prospectus Rules require, "a declaration by those responsible for certain parts of the registration document that, having taken all reasonable care to ensure that such is the case, the information contained in the part of the registration document for which they are responsible is, to the best of their knowledge, in accordance with the facts and contains no omission likely to affect its import". The reporting accountant is responsible for its reports included in investment circulars and ordinarily includes this declaration (when satisfied it is able to do 61

---

[3] These are often referred to as "agreed-upon procedures engagements".

Modified opinions

62 The reporting accountant should not express an unmodified opinion when the following circumstances exist and, in the reporting accountant's judgment, the effect of the matter is or may be material:

(a) there is a limitation on the scope of the reporting accountant's work, that is, circumstances prevent, or there are restrictions imposed that prevent, the reporting accountant from obtaining evidence required to reduce engagement risk to the appropriate level; or

(b) the outcome is materially misstated. (SIR 1000.20)

63 Where not precluded by regulation, the reporting accountant expresses a qualified opinion when the effect of a matter described in paragraph 62 is not so material or pervasive as to require an adverse opinion or a disclaimer of opinion. When giving a qualified opinion, the opinion is expressed "except for" the matter to which the qualification relates.

64 Some regulations require a positive and unmodified opinion. Consequently, in the event that the reporting accountant is unable to report in the manner prescribed it considers, with the parties to whom it is to report, whether the outcome can be amended to alleviate its concerns, or whether the outcome should be omitted from the investment circular.

Pre-existing financial information

65 With respect to historical financial information, where the issuer already has available:

(a) audited annual financial statements; or

(b) audited or reviewed financial information, which meet the requirements of the applicable rules in respect of the preparation and presentation of historical financial information to be included in the investment circular,

it may choose to include these financial statements, or financial information, in the investment circular together with the pre-existing reports of the auditor. In these circumstances the audit firm is not required by the Prospectus Rules to consent to the inclusion of its reports in the investment circular.

Consent

66 Where the reporting accountant is required to give consent to the inclusion of its public report, or references to its name, in an investment circular the reporting accountant should, before doing so, consider its public report in the form and context in which it appears, or is referred to, in the investment circular as a whole by:

(a) comparing its public report together with the information being reported on to the other information in the rest of the investment circular and assessing whether the reporting accountant has any cause to believe that such other information is inconsistent with the information being reported on; and

(b) assessing whether the reporting accountant has any cause to believe that any information in the investment circular is misleading.

When the reporting accountant believes information in the investment circular is either inconsistent with its public report, together with the information being reported on, or misleading, the reporting accountant should withhold its consent until the reporting accountant is satisfied that its concerns are unwarranted or until the investment circular has been appropriately amended. (SIR 1000.21)

The reporting accountant should give consent to the inclusion of any report in an investment circular only when all relevant reports that it has agreed to make, in that investment circular, have been finalised. (SIR 1000.22) 67

In order to comply with the relevant legislation or regulations, the issuer of an investment circular may ask a reporting accountant to provide a consent letter, consenting to the inclusion of public reports in investment circulars in a number of different circumstances. An example consent letter is set out in Appendix 3. The various circumstances include: 68

(a) under the Prospectus Rules. These relate to a prospectus issued by an issuer (other than under the Listing Rules). No consent is required to the inclusion of previously issued reports. Where a reporting accountant prepares an accountant's report on a financial information table for the purposes of the prospectus, the reporting accountant's consent must be obtained. A statement referring to the reporting accountant's consent to the inclusion of such report in the prospectus is required, by item 23.1 of Annex I of the Prospectus Rules, to be included in the Prospectus;
(b) under the Listing Rules. Where these relate to listing particulars prepared in connection with an application for admission of securities to listing, the same consent requirements, that is item 23.1 of Annex I of the Prospectus Rules, apply;
(c) under the Listing Rules. Where these relate to a Class 1 circular, paragraph 13.4.1 (6) of the Listing Rules sets out similar consent requirements;
(d) under the City Code. In connection with a takeover, Rule 28.4 requires a similar consent requirement in respect of a public report on a profit forecast. Rule 28.5 requires a similar consent in connection with a subsequent document issued in connection with the offer; and
(e) under the AIM Rules. The consent requirements of item 23.1 of Annex I of the Prospectus Rules apply.

Whilst the reporting accountant's reporting responsibilities do not extend beyond its report, the process of giving consent involves an awareness of the overall process whereby the investment circular is prepared, and may entail discussions with those responsible for the document as a whole in relation to its contents. 69

In deciding whether to give its consent, a reporting accountant reads the final version of the investment circular with a view to assessing the overall impression given by the document, having regard to the purposes for which it has been prepared, as well as considering whether there are any inconsistencies between its report and the information in the rest of the document. As part of this process the reporting accountant considers whether it has any cause to believe that any information in the investment circular may be misleading such that the reporting accountant would not wish to be associated with it. 70

For this purpose the engagement partner uses the knowledge of the partners and professional staff working on the engagement. If particular issues are identified the 71 engagement partner may make enquiries of partners and professional staff previously engaged on the audit of financial statements that are the basis of financial information in the investment circular, and any other partners and professional staff who may have been previously consulted regarding such issues, including the engagement quality review partner who is independent of the engagement. The engagement partner is not expected to make enquiries more widely within the reporting accountant's firm.

72 Because of the degree of knowledge required and the increased responsibility that may be assumed, it is inappropriate for a reporting accountant to provide consent unless the reporting accountant has been commissioned to undertake work specifically in connection with the relevant document in relation to the matter for which consent is sought. Hence, if an investment circular includes a reference to a report or opinion, previously provided by the reporting accountant, which is already in the public domain, the reporting accountant is not expected to provide consent to the inclusion of that information and does not generally do so. As discussed in paragraph 65, an example would be the inclusion or incorporation by reference in a prospectus of a previously published audit report or interim review report.

73 An exception to this general rule would be where the reporting accountant has previously consented to the inclusion in an investment circular of that earlier report or opinion and it is being repeated or referred to in connection with the same transaction in respect of which it was originally issued. For example, as noted in paragraph 68 above, Rule 28.5 of the City Code requires a profit forecast made and reported on in one document to be confirmed in any subsequent document in connection with the same offer, and for the reporting accountant to indicate that it has no objection to its report continuing to apply. In such a case, before issuing its consent the reporting accountant makes enquiries as to whether there have been any material events subsequent to the date of its original report which might require modification of or disclosure in that report.

74 Letters of consent are dated the same date as the relevant document. The City Code requires the letter of consent to be available for public inspection. The letter of consent may be made available for public inspection in other cases.

Events occurring between the date of the reporting accountant's report and the completion date of the transaction

75 **If, in the period between the date of the reporting accountant's report and the completion date of the transaction, the reporting accountant becomes aware of events and other matters which, had they occurred and been known at the date of the report, might have caused it to issue a different report or withhold consent, the reporting accountant should discuss the implications of them with those responsible for the investment circular and take additional action as appropriate. (SIR 1000.23)**

76 If, as a result of discussion with those responsible for the investment circular concerning an event that occurred prior to the completion date of the transaction, the reporting accountant is either uncertain about or disagrees with the course of action proposed, it may consider it necessary to take legal advice with respect to its responsibilities in the particular circumstances.

77 After the date of its report, the reporting accountant has no obligation to perform procedures or make enquiries regarding the investment circular.

Effective date

A reporting accountant is required to comply with the Investment Reporting Standards contained in this SIR for reports signed after 31 August 2005. Earlier adoption is encouraged.

78

Appendix 1 – Summary of possible reporting accountant's public reporting engagements under the prospectus rules

In the following table possible reporting accountant's responsibilities, as set out in the Prospectus Rules, are shaded.

	Shares	Debt, units < €50k	Debt, units =/> €50k	Derivatives, units < €50k	Derivatives, units =/> €50k	Asset backed securities, units < €50k	Asset backed securities, units =/> €50k	Depository receipts, units < €50k	Depository receipts, units =/> €50k	Banks issuing anything other than equity securities
Applicable annex:										
Registration document	I, II	IV	IX	IV	IX	VII	VII	X	X	XI
Securities note	III	V	XIII	XII	XII	VIII	VIII	X	X	As relevant instrument type
Historical financial information	I, 20.1	IV, 13.1	IX, 11.1	IV, 13.1	IX, 11.1	VII, 8.2	VII, 8.2 bis	X, 20.1	X, 20.1 bis	XI, 11.1
Number of years	3 years with latest 2 years on new GAAP	2 years with latest year on new GAAP	2 years with latest year on new GAAP	2 years with latest year on new GAAP	2 years with latest year on new GAAP	2 years with latest year on new GAAP	2 years with latest year on new GAAP	3 years with latest 2 years on new GAAP	3 years with latest 2 years on new GAAP	2 years with latest year on new GAAP
GAAP	National GAAP or IFRS[1] as applicable to EU issuer. IFRS or GAAP equivalent to IFRS for non-EU issuers	National GAAP or IFRS[1] as applicable to EU issuer. IFRS or GAAP equivalent to IFRS for non-EU issuers	National GAAP or IFRS[1] as applicable to EU issuer. Non-EU issuers may use local GAAP with a narrative description of differences	National GAAP or IFRS[1] as applicable to EU issuer. IFRS or GAAP equivalent to IFRS for non-EU issuers	National GAAP or IFRS[1] as applicable to EU issuer. Non-EU issuers may use local GAAP with a narrative description of differences	National GAAP or IFRS[1] as applicable to EU issuer. IFRS or GAAP equivalent to IFRS for non-EU issuers	National GAAP or IFRS[1] as applicable to EU issuer. Non-EU issuers may use local GAAP with a narrative description of differences	National GAAP or IFRS[1] as applicable to EU issuer. IFRS or GAAP equivalent to IFRS for non-EU issuers	National GAAP or IFRS[1] as applicable to EU issuer. Non-EU issuers may use local GAAP with a narrative description of differences	National GAAP or IFRS[1] as applicable to EU issuer. IFRS or GAAP equivalent to IFRS for non-EU issuers

	Shares	Debt, units < €50k	Debt, units =/> €50k	Derivatives, units < €50k	Derivatives, units =/> €50k	Asset backed securities, units < €50k	Asset backed securities, units =/> €50k	Depository receipts, units < €50k	Depository receipts, units =/> €50k	Banks issuing anything other than equity securities
Issuers operating less than one year	Special purpose financial information must be included	Special purpose financial information must be included	No additional requirements	Special purpose financial information must be included	No additional requirements	Special purpose financial information must be included	No additional requirements	Special purpose financial information must be included	No additional requirements	Special purpose financial information must be included
Report on financial information	Auditor's report or accountant's report as applicable	Auditor's report or accountant's report as applicable	Auditor's report or accountant's report as applicable	Auditor's report or accountant's report as applicable	Auditor's report or accountant's report as applicable	Auditor's report or accountant's report as applicable	Auditor's report or accountant's report as applicable	Auditor's report or accountant's report as applicable	Auditor's report or accountant's report as applicable	Auditor's report or accountant's report as applicable

1 In this table the expression IFRS is intended to refer to "those IFRSs as adopted for use in the European Union".

	Shares	Debt, units < €50k	Debt, units =/> €50k	Derivatives, units < €50k	Derivatives, units =/> €50k	Asset backed securities, units < €50k	Asset backed securities, units =/> €50k	Depository receipts, units < €50k	Depository receipts, units =/> €50k	Banks issuing anything other than equity securities
Age of latest financial information	I, 20.5	IV, 13.4	IX, 11.4	IV, 13.4	IX, 11.4	-	-	X, 20.4	X, 20.4	XI, 11.4
Age of audited information	No more than 15 months if unaudited interims or 18 months if audited interims	No more than 18 months	No more than 18 months	No more than 18 months	No more than 18 months	No requirements	No requirements	No more than 15 months if unaudited interims or 18 months if audited interims	No more than 15 months if unaudited interims or 18 months if audited interims	No more than 18 months
Pro forma financial information	I, 20.2 & II	-	-	-	-	-	-	-	-	-
Information	Required to show effect of significant gross changes	No requirements	No requirements	No requirements	No requirements	No requirements	No requirements	No requirements	No requirements	No requirements
Report on proper compilation	Required, where pro forma included	No requirements	No requirements	No requirements	No requirements	No requirements	No requirements	No requirements	No requirements	No requirements
Profit forecasts and estimates	I, 13	IV, 9	IX, 8	IV, 9	IX, 8	-	-	X, 13	X, 13	XI, 8
Disclosure of assumptions	Required	Required	Required	Required	Required	No requirements	No requirements	Required	Required	Required
Report on proper compilation	Required	Required	No requirements	Required	No requirements	No requirements	No requirements	Required	Required	Required
Outstanding forecasts	Update statement required	No requirements	No requirements	No requirements	No requirements	No requirements	No requirements	Update statement required	Update statement required	No requirements

Appendix 2 – Principal legal and regulatory requirements

The description of legal and regulatory requirements provided in this appendix is intended to be a guide and not intended to be a definitive interpretation of such requirements.

The FSA Handbook

1 In July 2005 the then existing listing rules were modified to take account of the implementation of the Prospectus Directive in the United Kingdom. At the same time the opportunity was taken to revise the rules applying to the continuing obligations of listed companies.

2 The FSA Handbook now includes three parts relevant to securities and their issuers, namely: the "Prospectus Rules", the "Listing Rules" and the "Disclosure Rules".

3 The Prospectus Rules effect the practical implementation of the Prospectus Directive. They apply to all prospectuses required to be issued by UK companies either offering securities to the public or seeking admission of securities to a regulated market. The annexes to the PD Regulation provide detailed rules on prospectuses and, in particular, the content requirements of prospectuses. In respect of prospectus content requirements, the Prospectus Rules reproduce the Annexes to the PD Regulation. Accordingly, references to the contents requirements in Annexes to the Prospectus Rules are also references to the Annexes to the PD Regulation.

4 The Prospectus Rules also make it clear that the FSA expect "CESR's recommendations for the consistent implementation of the European Commission's Regulation on Prospectuses no. 809/2004"[1] to be followed by issuers when preparing a prospectus.

5 The Listing Rules provide the rules and guidance applicable to issuers of securities both seeking admission to, and once admitted to, the Official List. They include the conditions for admission to listing, the requirements concerning Sponsors under the Listing Rules, Class 1 and related party transactions and the requirements for listing particulars when a prospectus is not required to be prepared.

6 The Disclosure Rules contain rules and guidance in relation to the publication and control of "inside information" and the disclosure of transactions by persons discharging managerial responsibilities and their connected persons.

7 The annexes to the Prospectus Rules provide that historical financial information for the last three completed financial years, where it exists, is to be included in a prospectus. This information can either be extracted or incorporated by reference from the issuer's annual financial statements or presented in the prospectus specifically for that purpose. The Prospectus Rules provide that where the accounting framework to be applied in an issuer's next annual financial statements is different from that previously applied, at least some of the historical financial information must be represented on the basis of those new policies. The historical financial information must either be accompanied by the auditor's report on the statutory financial

---

[1] *"CESR" is the Committee of European Securities Regulators. Its recommendations were issued in February 2005 and are sometimes referred to as the "Level 3 Guidance of the Lamfalussy Process". This guidance can be accessed on the CESR website www.cesr-eu.org.*

statements or by a new opinion by reporting accountants where the information has been presented for the purpose of the prospectus.

8   Where an issuer with listed equity securities proposes to undertake a Class 1 acquisition, Listing Rule 13.5 requires that certain historical financial information is presented in relation to the target and, where relevant, the target's subsidiary undertakings. The last three years historical financial information must be presented in a financial information table on a basis consistent with accounting policies of the issuer. Unless the target is itself admitted to trading on an EU regulated market or on an overseas regulated market or listed on an overseas investment exchange, the financial information table must be reported on by a reporting accountant. However, if there is no report by reporting accountants on the financial information table itself, it is necessary for the issuer to consider whether any material adjustment is required to achieve consistency between the target's historical financial information and the accounting policies of the issuer, in which event a reconciliation of key financial statement components must be presented and the reconciliation reported on by reporting accountants.

9   If an issuer chooses to include a profit forecast or profit estimate in a prospectus the registration document may be required to contain the following information:
   (a) a statement setting out the principal assumptions upon which the issuer has based its forecast or estimate. See item 13.1 of Annex I to the Prospectus Rules for more detailed requirements regarding assumptions; and
   (b) a report prepared by independent accountants or auditors stating that in the opinion of the independent accountants or auditors the forecast or estimate has been properly compiled on the basis stated and that the basis of accounting used for the profit forecast or estimate is consistent with the accounting policies of the issuer.

The profit forecast or estimate must be prepared on a basis comparable with the historical financial information.

10 If a profit forecast in a prospectus has been published which is still outstanding, the issuer must provide a statement setting out whether or not that forecast is still correct as at the time of the registration document, and an explanation of why such forecast is no longer valid if that is the case.

11 Where an issuer includes pro forma financial information in a prospectus, (relating to shares, transferable securities equivalent to shares and certain other securities convertible into shares), Annex I item 20.2 and Annex II of the Prospectus Rules require any such information to be reported on by the reporting accountants. The Listing Rules also require a reporting accountant's report on any pro forma financial information that an issuer chooses to include in a Class 1 circular.

12 Where a statement or report attributed to an expert (including reporting accountants) is included in a prospectus at the issuer's request, the Prospectus Rules require a statement of consent from the expert. This is discussed in more detail in paragraphs 66 to 74 in the body of this SIR. The consent of the auditor is not required where reports (audit or review) previously issued by the auditor are included in a prospectus.

13 Other rules apply in particular circumstances. By replication of the Prospectus Rules requirements an expert is required, by the Listing Rules, to consent to the inclusion of any report in any listing particulars. However, the consent of the auditor is not

required where reports (audit or review) previously issued by the auditor are included in the listing particulars.

The Listing Rules also require pro forma financial information in a Class 1 circular to be reported on by an issuer's reporting accountants and to contain provisions requiring an expert's consent to any report included in a Class 1 circular.

Admission to the Main Market of the London Stock Exchange

A two-stage admission process applies to companies who want to have their securities admitted to the Main Market for listed securities of the London Stock Exchange. The securities need to be admitted to the Official List by the UK Listing Authority (UKLA), a division of the Financial Services Authority, and also admitted to trading by the London Stock Exchange. To be admitted to trading the Admission and Disclosure Standards need to be met. Once both processes are complete the securities are officially listed on the Exchange.

AIM requirements

Under the AIM Rules of the London Stock Exchange, companies seeking admission to AIM must publish an AIM admission document. This is the case whether or not they are required by the Prospectus Rules to prepare a prospectus (because they are also making an offer of securities to the public which is not exempt from the requirement to produce a prospectus).

The AIM Rules provide that the content of an admission document should be based on the share disclosure requirements in the Prospectus Rules, modified to allow issuers to elect not to include certain financial information where no prospectus is required, notably profit forecasts and pro forma financial information. However, if such information is included the Prospectus Rules requirements must be followed.

The Professional Securities Market

From 1 July 2005, issuers listing debt, convertibles or depository receipts in London will have a choice of being admitted to a regulated market or the Professional Securities Market, which is a market operated and regulated by the London Stock Exchange. Issuers listing on the Professional Securities Market will not be required to report historical financial information under IFRSs or an EU approved equivalent standard either in listing documents or as a continuing obligation requirement.

The City Code

Where a document sent to shareholders in connection with an offer falling within the scope of the City Code contains a profit forecast or estimate, with certain exceptions, Rule 28.3 of the City Code requires that forecast or estimate to be reported on by reporting accountants and by the financial advisers. The City Code's requirements for such reports are similar to those under the Prospectus Rules. In certain circumstances, the City Code also provides for a reporting accountant to report on merger benefit statements (Rule 19.1) and interim financial information (Rule 28.6 (c)).

Companies legislation

20   In the United Kingdom, financial information presented in an investment circular may constitute "non statutory accounts" within the meaning of section 240 of the Companies Act 1985. The document in which the financial information is presented will usually, therefore, contain a statement complying with section 240(3) of the Companies Act 1985. However, this statement is only appropriate where the financial information comprises non-statutory accounts of the company issuing the document. No statement is needed in respect of financial information on a target company in an acquisition circular, for example, unless the directors of the target company explicitly accept responsibility for that part of the document. The statement is also the responsibility of the directors of the company publishing the document, not the reporting accountants.

Financial Services and Markets Act 2000

21   Upon implementation of the Prospectus Directive into UK law with effect from 1 July 2005, the existing regime regarding the issue of prospectuses in the UK whether in connection with an official listing of securities or a <u>public offer</u> was repealed.

22   Under Part VI, the FSA's function is a statutory one. Part VI covers not only the whole process by which securities are admitted to official listing but also the obligations to which companies are subject once they have obtained listing. The Listing Rules represent listing rules for the purposes of Part VI.

23   Prospectus Rule 5.5 (in relation to prospectuses), and regulation 6 of The Financial Services and Markets Act 2000 (Official Listing of Securities) Regulations 2001 (in relation to listing particulars, i.e. not prospectuses within the meaning of the Prospectus Directive) provide that each person:

   (a) who accepts, and is stated in the particulars as accepting, responsibility for the particulars or for any part of the particulars; or
   (b) who has authorised the contents of, or any part of, the particulars;
   is deemed to accept responsibility for the particulars (or that part of them).

24   This raises potential issues for reporting accountants, for example:

   - If they are involved in advising on an investment circular but are not named in it.
   - If they issue a report or letter which is included in the investment circular.

25   In the first example the Prospectus Rules and The Financial Services and Markets Act 2000 (Official Listing of Securities) Regulations 2001 relieve professional advisers from responsibility for the circular where they are solely giving advice as to the contents of the listing particulars in a professional capacity.

26   In the second example the Prospectus Rules and The Financial Services and Markets Act 2000 (Official Listing of Securities) Regulations 2001 limit the responsibility of experts, including reporting accountants, to the part for which they accept responsibility and only if the part for which they accept responsibility is included in (or substantially in) the form and context to which they have agreed.

Appendix 3 – Example of a consent letter

The Directors
ABC plc

Dear Sirs

We hereby give our consent to the inclusion in the [describe Investment Circular] dated [ ] issued by ABC plc of [our accountant's report]/[our report relating to the profit estimate for the year ended 20 ,]/[our report relating to the profit forecast for the year ending 20 ,]/[our report relating to the pro forma financial information for the year ended 20] dated [ ] [[and] the references to our name[2]] in the form and context in which [it]/[they] are included, as shown in the enclosed proof of the [describe Investment Circular] which we have signed for identification.

[We also hereby authorise the contents of the [report[s]] referred to above which [is/are] included in the Prospectus for the purposes of Prospectus Rule [5.5.3R (2)(f)] [5.5.4R (2)(f)] **OR** [We also hereby authorise the contents of the [report[s]] referred to above which [is/are] included in the Listing Particulars for the purposes of Regulation 6(1)(e) of The Financial Services and Markets Act 2000 (Official Listing of Securities) Regulations 2001.] **OR** [We also hereby authorise the contents of the report[s] referred to above which [is/are] included in the Admission Document for the purposes of the Schedule Two to the AIM Rules][3]

Yours faithfully

Reporting accountant

---

[2] *This is required only when a statement is attributed to a reporting accountant as an expert outside the context of a report from the reporting accountant included in the investment circular.*

[3] *This paragraph is not required in respect of a Class 1 Circular.*

Appendix 4 – Glossary of terms

Accountant's report - A report by a reporting accountant included in an investment circular, in which the reporting accountant normally expresses a "true and fair, for the purposes of the investment circular" opinion on historical financial information relating to the issuer and its subsidiaries in accordance with SIR 2000 "Investment Reporting Standards applicable to public reporting engagements on historical financial information ".

Admission and Disclosure Standards - The Admission and Disclosure Standards published by the London Stock Exchange, for companies admitted or seeking to be admitted to trading by the Exchange.

Agreed-upon procedures [engagements] - An engagement where the reporting accountant is engaged to carry out procedures of an audit or assurance nature, that the reporting accountant, the entity and any appropriate third parties have agreed, and to report on factual findings. The recipients of the report must form their own conclusions from the report by the reporting accountant. The report is restricted to those parties that have agreed to the procedures to be performed, since others, unaware of the reasons for the procedures, may misinterpret the results.

AIM - The Alternative Investment Market operated by the London Stock Exchange plc. The market is for smaller growing companies. Securities admitted to AIM are unlisted.

AIM Admission Document - The document prepared in connection with an application for admission of an issuer's securities to trading on AIM. If upon admission a prospectus is required in accordance with the Prospectus Rules, such prospectus may serve as the AIM Admission Document.

AIM Rules - The Rules of the Alternative Investment Market.

CESR - The Committee of European Securities Regulators.

Circular - A circular issued by any company to its shareholders and/or holders of its debt securities in connection with a transaction, which does not constitute a prospectus, listing particulars or AIM admission document.

City Code - The City Code on Takeovers and Mergers, published by the Panel on Takeovers and Mergers.

Class 1 circular - A circular relating to a Class 1 transaction.

Class 1 transaction - A transaction where one or more of a number of specified percentage ratios exceed a predetermined level as specified in Chapter 10 of the Listing Rules.

Comfort letter - A private letter from the reporting accountant, usually prepared at the request of the issuer and/or the sponsor, where relevant. It is intended to provide the addressees with comfort (in the form of an opinion or a report on the results of specific procedures carried out by the reporting accountants) regarding matters relevant to the addressees' responsibilities.

Completion date of the transaction - The date by which any offer contained in the circular must have been accepted or application made for shares or other securities to be issued, or the date on which shareholders vote to approve the transaction.

Consent letter - A letter whereby the reporting accountant consents to the inclusion in an investment circular of references to its name or the inclusion of any of its reports or letters which are to be published therein.

Due diligence - The process whereby the directors of the issuer and other parties, whether as principal or in an advisory capacity, satisfy themselves that the transaction is entered into after due and careful enquiry and that all relevant regulatory and/or legal requirements have been properly complied with. There is no generally accepted definition of required procedures for this purpose and where others (such as reporting accountants) are engaged to carry out work that will form part of the process, it is for the instructing parties to make clear what is required of those others in the particular circumstances.

Engagement partner - The partner or other person in the firm who is responsible for the engagement and its performance, and for reports that are issued on behalf of the firm, and who, where required, has the appropriate authority from a professional, legal or regulatory body.

Financial information - The term is used to signify the specific information presented in the form of a table upon which a reporting accountant reports. Typically, this information encompasses a number of accounting periods.

Financial statements - A balance sheet, profit and loss account (or other form of income statement), statement of cash flow, and statement of total recognised gains and losses (or statement of changes in equity), notes and other statements and explanatory material. In order to avoid confusion the term financial information is used throughout the SIRs to refer to the information upon which the reporting accountant reports. When the term financial statements is used within the SIRs this refers to financial statements from which the financial information has been derived by the issuer.

FSA - Financial Services Authority.

FSMA - Financial Services and Markets Act 2000.

IFRSs - International Financial Reporting Standards issued by the International Accounting Standards Board. This term incorporates all International Financial Reporting Standards, International Accounting Standards (IASs) and Interpretations originated by the International Financial Reporting Interpretations Committee (IFRIC) or the former Standards Interpretation Committee of the IASC.

Investment circular - A generic term describing any document issued by an entity pursuant to statutory or regulatory requirements relating to securities on which it is intended that a third party should make an investment decision, including a prospectus, listing particulars, circular to shareholders or similar document.

ISAs (UK and Ireland) - International Standards on Auditing (UK and Ireland) issued by the Auditing Practices Board.

Issuer - For the purposes of the Prospectus Rules "A legal person who issues or proposes to issue securities". For the purposes of the Listing Rules "Any company or other legal person or undertaking (including a public sector issuer), any class of whose securities has been admitted to listing, or is the subject of an application for admission to listing".

Listing particulars - A document not being a Prospectus prepared in connection with an admission of securities to the Official List.

Listing Rules - The part of the FSA's Handbook entitled "Listing Rules" governing the conduct of companies whose securities are admitted to the Official List.

London Stock Exchange - The London Stock Exchange plc.

Long form report - A private report with a restricted circulation, normally prepared by the reporting accountants on the instructions of, and addressed to, the sponsor, where relevant, and the directors of the issuer as part of their due diligence, dealing with agreed matters including commentary on financial and other information in an orderly and relevant form for a specific purpose.

Main Market - The London Stock Exchange's market for larger and established companies. Securities admitted to the Main Market are listed.

Nominated adviser - A corporate broker, investment banker or other professional adviser approved by the London Stock Exchange to act as a nominated adviser to an AIM company under the AIM Rules.

Ofex - An independent, self regulated, UK market for smaller companies.

Official List - The Official List maintained by the FSA.

Outcome - The outcome of the evaluation or measurement of a subject matter is the information that results from the directors applying the suitable criteria to the subject matter. Examples of outcomes are historical financial information and a directors' profit forecast and related disclosures that are included in an investment circular.

Partner - Any individual with authority to bind a firm of reporting accountants with respect to the performance of any engagement in connection with an investment circular.

PD Regulation - the implementing EU Regulation 809/2004 that provides the detailed rules concerning Prospectuses and their contents. Much of the text of this regulation is included within the Prospectus Rules.

Private reporting engagement - An engagement in which a reporting accountant does not express a conclusion that is published in an investment circular.

Professional Securities Market - A market for debt, convertibles and depository receipts, which is operated and regulated by the London Stock Exchange. This is not a regulated market as defined by the Prospectus and Transparency Directives.

Profit estimate - Historical financial information for a financial period which has expired but for which the results have not yet been published.

Profit forecast - The PD Regulation defines a profit forecast as "a form of words which expressly states or by implication indicates a figure or a minimum or maximum figure for the likely level of profits or losses for the current financial period and/or financial periods subsequent to that period, or contains data from which calculation of such a figure for future profits or losses may be made, even if no particular figure is mentioned and the word "profit" is not used. Where a profit forecast relates to an extended period and/or is subject to significant uncertainty it is sometimes referred to as a projection.

Pro forma financial information - Financial information such as net assets, profit or cash flow statements that demonstrate the impact of a transaction on previously published financial information together with the explanatory notes thereto.

Projection - See "Profit forecast".

Prospectus - The document issued in accordance with the Prospectus Rules in connection with either a public offer or an admission of securities to trading on a regulated market.

Prospectus Regulations - The UK statutory instrument which makes amendments to Part VI of FSMA and to certain secondary legislation.

Prospectus Rules - The FSA's Handbook part "Prospectus Rules" which together with the PD Regulation and the changes to FSMA Part VI made by the Prospectus Regulations, implement the Prospectus Directive into UK law. In respect of Prospectus content requirements, the Prospectus Rules reproduce the Annexes to the PD Regulation. Accordingly, references to the contents requirements in Annexes to the Prospectus Rules are also references to the Annexes to the PD Regulation.

Public offer - An offer to the public in any form to subscribe for securities in an issuer.

Public reporting engagement - An engagement in which a reporting accountant expresses a conclusion that is published in an investment circular and which is designed to enhance the degree of confidence of the intended users of the report about the "outcome" of the directors' evaluation or measurement of "subject matter" (usually financial information) against "suitable criteria".

Report - This term encompasses letters that the reporting accountant may be required to send by regulation or arising from the terms of the engagement.

Reporting accountant - An accountant engaged to prepare a report for inclusion in, or in connection with, an investment circular. The reporting accountant may or may not be the auditor of the entity issuing the investment circular. The term "reporting accountant" is used to describe either the engagement partner or the engagement partner's firm. The reporting accountant could be a limited company or an engagement principal employed by the company.

Reporting accountant's criteria - A subset of suitable criteria which the reporting accountant's engagement requires the reporting accountant to consider. Reporting accountant's criteria are set out in appendices to the SIRs.

Securities - Are as defined by Article 4 of the EU's Markets in Financial Instruments Directive with the exception of money-market instruments having a maturity of less than twelve months.

Sponsor - For the purposes of SIRs, "sponsor" is a generic term which includes any one or more of the following to whom the reporting accountant has agreed, in its engagement letter, to address a relevant report:

(a) a person approved, under section 88 of FSMA, by the FSA as a sponsor. The FSA's sponsor regime applies to applications for admission to listing and major transactions. The sponsor regime is designed to ensure that effective due diligence is undertaken on issuers and transactions to ensure that issuers are eligible for listing, that major transactions are properly evaluated and that all relevant information has been included in the investment circular. Listing Rule 8.2.1 sets out the circumstances when an issuer must appoint a sponsor;
(b) a nominated adviser approved by the London Stock Exchange in connection with an application for admission to AIM and subsequent transactions by a company with securities traded on AIM; and
(c) in connection with any transaction, any party, other than the issuer, who may have specific responsibility for the preparation and/or contents of an investment circular.

Subject matter - The subject matter of an engagement is that which is being evaluated or measured against "suitable criteria". Examples of subject matter are the entity's financial position and the directors' expectation of the issuer's profit for the period covered by a profit forecast.

Suitable criteria - Criteria are the benchmarks used to evaluate or measure the subject matter. Suitable criteria are usually derived from laws and regulations and are required by directors to enable them to make reasonably consistent evaluations or measurements of the subject matter. With respect to public reporting engagements the suitable criteria for specific types of engagement are described in the individual SIR dealing with such engagements.

[2000]
Investment reporting standards applicable to public reporting engagements on historical financial information

Contents

	Paragraphs
Introduction	1 - 15
Pre-existing financial information	16 - 17
True and fair view, for the purposes of the investment circular	18 - 23
General professional considerations	24 - 27
Planning	28 - 31
Understanding of the entity, its environment and risk assessment	32 - 38
Materiality	39
The reporting accountant's procedures	40 - 46
Evidence	47 - 54
Obtaining access to information in audit working papers	55 - 58
Related parties	59
Events occurring up to the date of the accountant's report	60
Events occurring between the date of the accountant's report and the completion date of the transaction	61 - 64
Going concern	65 - 66
Representations	67 - 70
Joint reporting accountants	71
Reporting	72 - 76
Other information – references to previous audit opinions	77
Comparatives	78
Consent in the context of investment circulars containing a report by a reporting accountant	79

Effective date 80

Appendices

1 Bold letter paragraphs included in ISAs (UK and Ireland) that are unlikely to apply to the reporting accountant's exercise in relation to historical financial information in investment circulars
2 Examples of engagement letter clauses
3 Example of an accountant's report on historical financial information

ANNEXURE

Accounting conventions commonly used in the preparation of historical financial information in investment circulars[1]

---

[1] The Annexure has been compiled by the APB from a number of sources. It does not include either basic principles, essential procedures or guidance promulgated by the APB.

Investment reporting standards applicable to public reporting engagements on historical financial information

SIR 2000 contains basic principles and essential procedures ("Investment Reporting Standards") indicated by paragraphs in bold type, with which a reporting accountant is required to comply in the conduct of an engagement involving the examination of historical financial information which is intended to give a true and fair view, for the purposes of the relevant investment circular, included within an investment circular prepared for issue in connection with a securities transaction governed wholly or in part by the laws and regulations of the United Kingdom.

SIR 2000 also includes explanatory and other material, including appendices, in the context of which the basic principles and essential procedures are to be understood and applied. It is necessary to consider the whole text of the SIR to understand and apply the basic principles and essential procedures.

For the purposes of the SIRs, an investment circular is defined as: "any document issued by an entity pursuant to statutory or regulatory requirements relating to listed or unlisted securities on which it is intended that a third party should make an investment decision, including a prospectus, listing particulars, circular to shareholders or similar document".

SIR 1000 "Investment reporting standards applicable to all engagements in connection with an investment circular" contains basic principles and essential procedures that are applicable to all engagements involving an investment circular. The definitions in the glossary of terms set out in Appendix 4 of SIR 1000 are to be applied in the interpretation of this and all other SIRs. Terms defined in the glossary are underlined the first time that they occur in the text.

This SIR replaces SIR 200 "Accountants' reports on historical financial information in investment circulars" issued in December 1997.

To assist readers, SIRs contain references to, and extracts from, certain legislation and chapters of the Rules of the UK Listing Authority. Readers are cautioned that these references may change subsequent to publication.

Introduction

1   The purpose of this Standard for Investment Reporting (SIR) is to establish standards and provide guidance on the reporting accountant's responsibilities and procedures when preparing an "accountant's report" on historical financial information. The work required to prepare an "accountant's report" is referred to in this SIR as the "reporting accountant's exercise". The objective of the reporting accountant's exercise is to enable the reporting accountant to express an opinion as to whether, for the purposes of the relevant investment circular, the financial information gives a true and fair view of the state of affairs and profits, cash flows and statements of changes in equity of the issuer, or where applicable the target.

2   **When the reporting accountant is engaged to prepare an accountant's report, the reporting accountant should obtain sufficient appropriate evidence to express an opinion as to whether the financial information presents a true and fair view, for the purposes of the investment circular. (SIR 2000.1)**

3   An engagement to prepare an accountant's report is a public reporting engagement as described in SIR 1000. The description of a public reporting engagement includes three generic terms having the following meanings in the context of an engagement to report on historical financial information:

   (a) with respect to historical financial information the "**subject matter**" is the entity's financial position for the periods being reported on;
   (b) the "**suitable criteria**" are the requirements of the applicable financial reporting framework, the PD Regulation, and Listing Rules together with any "accepted conventions", as set out in the Annexure, that are applicable; and
   (c) with respect to historical financial information the "**outcome**" is the directors' historical financial information that is included in the investment circular and which has resulted from the directors applying the suitable criteria to the subject matter. The reporting accountant expresses an opinion (in the "**accountant's report**") as to whether the historical financial information gives, for the purposes of the investment circular, a true and fair view.

4   The Prospectus Rules set out certain requirements, derived from the PD Regulation, relating to the presentation of historical financial information in a prospectus. Annex I of the PD Regulation (and there are equivalent requirements in a number of the other annexes) requires that historical financial information is either audited or "reported on as to whether or not, for the purposes of the registration document, it gives a true and fair view, in accordance with auditing standards applicable in a Member State or an equivalent standard." SIR 2000 is regarded as an equivalent standard for the purposes of the PD Regulation[2].

5   With respect to Class 1 acquisitions, Chapter 13 of the Listing Rules sets out requirements for a financial information table relating to a target company and the accountant's opinion on that table. The accountant's opinion is required to state whether, for the purposes of the Class 1 circular, the financial information table gives a true and fair view of the financial matters set out in it, and whether the financial information table has been prepared in a form that is consistent with the accounting policies adopted in the listed company's latest annual accounts.

6   In this SIR, accountant's opinions on such financial information tables are described as "accountant's reports".

7   An accountant's report is likely to be used where the issuer's audited annual financial statements do not meet the standards of preparation and presentation prescribed in the applicable rules and need, therefore, to be adjusted in order that historical financial information which complies with the applicable rules can be presented. For example, where the entity is seeking a listing, the financial information for the last two years is required to be prepared and presented in a form consistent with that which will be adopted in the issuer's next published annual financial statements, having regard to accounting standards and policies and legislation applicable to such annual financial statements. In the context of Class 1 circulars, the objective may be to present the financial information of the target for all periods in a form which is consistent and comparable with the accounting policies adopted by the listed company in its latest annual accounts.

8   In addition, an accountant's report is used where the issuer has a complex financial history and there are no underlying financial statements that have been audited.

---

[2] *In respect of prospectus content requirements, the Prospectus Rules reproduce the Annexes to the PD Regulation. Accordingly, references to the contents requirements in the Annexes to the Prospectus Rules are also references to the Annexes to the PD Regulation.*

Conventions for accounting where there are complex financial histories are described in the Annexure.

9 The nature of the accountant's report is such that the objective of the reporting accountant's exercise does not differ in essence from that of an auditor. The underlying requirement of this SIR is that the reporting accountant will, in conducting the work necessary to provide the accountant's report, perform or rely on work that meets those requirements of ISAs (UK and Ireland) that are applicable to the reporting accountant's exercise. The reporting accountant applies ISAs (UK and Ireland) on the basis set out in this SIR in the context of the following:

(a) the reporting accountant is often reporting on financial information that has been included in, or formed part of, financial statements which have themselves already been subject to audit by an independent auditor. In consequence, there may be available to the reporting accountant a body of independent evidence relating to the historical financial information which would not be available to an auditor examining the financial information for the first time;

(b) the financial information being examined may relate to accounting periods in circumstances where financial statements for one, and possibly two, subsequent periods have been prepared and audited. These circumstances mean that in assessing risks that may affect the historical financial information in relation to earlier periods the reporting accountant has the benefit of information relating to uncertainties affecting the financial information which would not have been available to an auditor auditing the information for the first time; and

(c) the reporting accountant does not have the statutory reporting responsibilities of an auditor.

10 This SIR provides standards that address those aspects of the reporting accountant's exercise that require the reporting accountant to perform procedures directly, for example risk assessment procedures. It also provides guidance on the application of ISAs (UK and Ireland) to the reporting accountant's exercise.

11 This SIR recognises that the reporting accountant may wish to use evidence previously obtained by the auditor who audited the historical financial statements for the relevant period covered by the reporting accountant's exercise. Guidance is provided on the steps that the reporting accountant undertakes, including initial planning considerations, in order to assess the suitability of the audit evidence for this purpose.

12 Subject to the considerations set out in this SIR, references in the ISAs (UK and Ireland) to the auditor performing audit procedures or obtaining audit evidence may be read as references to the reporting accountant being satisfied that the procedures have been performed, or the evidence obtained, either by the reporting accountant or an auditor.

13 Certain requirements of ISAs (UK and Ireland) will not apply to the reporting accountant's exercise, for example, when the requirement of an ISA (UK and Ireland) is predicated on a continuing relationship between an auditor and the entity being audited, or because of the specific nature of the reporting accountant's responsibilities, under applicable regulations, as discussed in this SIR. A summary of the bold letter paragraphs included in ISAs (UK and Ireland) that are unlikely to apply to the reporting accountant's exercise is included in Appendix 1 of this SIR.

14 This SIR also provides guidance to the reporting accountant in the context of assessing whether the financial information shows a true and fair view, for the purposes of the investment circular. In situations where the issuer has a historical

record of audited financial statements, the true and fair view for the purposes of the investment circular may be a financial reporting framework such as International Financial Reporting Standards. In situations where the issuer has a complex financial history the conventions to support the true and fair view for the purposes of the investment circular are set out in the Annexure.

15 The structure of this SIR reflects the order of the ISAs (UK and Ireland) and the contents are intended to be read in conjunction with the ISAs (UK and Ireland).

Pre-existing financial information

16 With respect to historical financial information, where the issuer already has available:

(a) audited annual financial statements; or
(b) audited or reviewed interim financial information,

which meet the requirements of the applicable rules in respect of the preparation and presentation of historical financial information to be included in the investment circular, it may choose to include these financial statements, or financial information, in the investment circular together with the pre-existing reports of the auditor. In these circumstances an accountant's report is not prepared and this SIR does not apply to such circumstances. Furthermore, in these circumstances the audit firm is not required by the Prospectus Rules to consent to the inclusion of its reports in the investment circular.

17 Notwithstanding that the audit firm is not required to give consent, a reporting accountant that is also the auditor of the company may become aware that the financial statements are defective. For example a material error may have been detected in the original financial statements. If the reporting accountant does become aware that the financial statements are defective and that the directors have not revised them as required by the Companies Act 1985, it discusses the matter with those charged with governance. If the directors do not decide to revise the financial statements the reporting accountant considers the need to take legal advice.

True and fair view, for the purposes of the investment circular

18 The reporting accountant should:

(a) obtain an understanding of the purpose of the investment circular;
(b) ascertain which financial reporting framework is required to be used by the applicable regulations and which, if any, accepted conventions as to the preparation and presentation of historical financial information for inclusion in investment circulars are to be applied; and
(c) review the appropriateness of the accounting policies,

in order to determine whether the proposed historical financial information prepared by the issuer is capable of giving a true and fair view, for the purposes of the investment circular. (SIR 2000.2)

19 Where historical financial information is presented in a prospectus the Prospectus Rules generally determine the applicable financial reporting framework. The Prospectus Rules require the most recent year's financial information to be presented in a form consistent with that which will be adopted in the issuer's next published

annual financial statements, having regard to the accounting standards, policies and legislation applicable to such annual financial statements.

The reporting accountant satisfies itself that the directors have performed a thorough review of the accounting policies used in preparing the historical financial information in determining the accounting policies appropriate for the business following the transaction that is the subject of the prospectus. The reporting accountant also considers whether the policies are consistent with the applicable financial reporting framework, and accounting policies used in the relevant industry. Where the reporting accountant does not agree with the directors' final proposed accounting policies they refer to the guidance on reporting set out in paragraphs 72 to 76 of this SIR. 20

Where information is presented in a Class 1 circular, the suitable criteria are those set out in the Listing Rules. These rules require financial information to be presented in a form consistent with the accounting policies adopted in the issuer's latest annual consolidated accounts. 21

The directors have regard to, and make appropriate disclosure of, accepted conventions which have been developed for the preparation and presentation of historical financial information in investment circulars (including those relating to additional disclosures). These conventions have been developed to assist the directors, to the extent consistent with established accounting principles, to fulfil the criteria set out in the relevant regulations, present the information in an easily analysable form, and give a true and fair view for the purposes of the applicable investment circular. 22

The Annexure provides a summary of these conventions including, among others, conventions that address: 23

- Making adjustments to previously published financial statements and dealing with entities which have not previously prepared consolidated accounts.
- Carve outs.
- Acquisitions.
- Newly formed issuers.

In certain circumstances applying the conventions may result in combined or aggregated, rather than consolidated, financial information being presented in order to meet the requirement to present financial information that gives a true and fair view, for the purposes of the investment circular.

General professional considerations

SIR 1000.3 and SIR 1000.4 set out basic principles and essential procedures applicable to agreeing the terms of the engagement. Paragraphs 11 to 15 and paragraph 17 of SIR 1000 provide guidance with respect to these basic principles and essential procedures. SIR 1000.5 sets out the basic principles and essential procedures with respect to the ethical requirements that apply to a reporting accountant. 24

Where the evidence used by the reporting accountant includes that contained within the working papers of an auditor, the working papers of the reporting accountant identify the papers reviewed and the nature of the work performed. Whilst it is not necessary for the working papers to replicate all of the detailed findings contained in the auditor's working papers reporting accountants do document the basis on which the auditor addressed the particular risks identified in the reporting accountant's risk assessment procedures. 25

26 In considering the requirements of ISA (UK and Ireland) 240 "The auditor's responsibility to consider fraud in an audit of financial statements" and ISA (UK and Ireland) 250 "Section A - Consideration of Laws and Regulations in an audit of financial statements. Section B - The auditor's right and duty to report to regulators in the financial sector" for the auditor to report any matters arising to certain authorities, the reporting accountant will need to assess the effect of these requirements when reporting in terms of the true and fair view, for the purposes of the investment circular. Where matters arise which may potentially require disclosure by the reporting accountant and the reporting accountant is unsure how to proceed, the reporting accountant takes legal advice.

27 In applying ISAs (UK and Ireland) 240, 250 and 260 "Communication of audit matters with those charged with governance", the reporting accountant considers who, in relation to the investment circular, should be regarded as a person charged with governance. Where the issuer has already formed an audit committee, the reporting accountant communicates with the audit committee in accordance with the guidance set out in this SIR. In the absence of an audit committee those responsible for governance will usually be the directors of the issuer.

Planning

28 **The reporting accountant should perform and document risk assessment procedures to support the reporting accountant's exercise. (SIR 2000.3)**

29 In addition to those matters that a reporting accountant considers when applying SIR 1000, a reporting accountant may consider:

- Any previous modifications to the audit report on underlying financial statements and the potential impact on the approach to the reporting accountant's exercise.
- The nature of adjustments to previously published historical financial information which may be proposed by the preparer of the historical financial information (for example as a result of changing the applicable accounting framework) and the sources of evidence to support an examination of the adjustments.
- The interaction with other roles undertaken by the reporting accountant in connection with the transaction, for example preparing a long form report.
- Staffing, including relevant experience and skills linked to investment circular reporting, and sources of consultation.
- Liaison with the auditor and arrangements for terms of access to the auditor's working papers, or equivalent evidence if maintained in machine readable form.
- The nature and timing of procedures to support any decision to rely on evidence obtained by the auditor.
- Whether the financial reporting framework applicable to the audited financial statements is the same as that applicable to the financial information contained in the investment circular.
- Whether there are any special circumstances concerning the appointment, resignation or reporting responsibilities of the auditor.
- Whether there is evidence of any limitation having been placed on the work of the auditor.
- Whether corrections or adjustments to subsequent financial statements indicate possible inadequacies in the audits of earlier periods.

30 **Where the reporting accountant is considering using audit evidence obtained by an auditor as part of the evidence for the reporting accountant's exercise, the reporting**

accountant should consider the professional qualification, independence and professional competence of the auditor and the quality control systems applied by the audit firm to that engagement. (SIR 2000.4)

Matters that the reporting accountant considers include: 31

- The integrity and experience of the auditor.
- Whether the auditor was required to apply ISAs (UK and Ireland) or equivalent standards.
- Whether there is any evidence that the auditor has not complied with applicable independence requirements.

Understanding of the entity, its environment and risk assessment

The reporting accountant should obtain an understanding of the entity and its environment, including its internal control, sufficient to identify and assess the risks of material misstatement of the historical financial information covered by the accountant's report whether due to fraud or error, and sufficient to design and perform further procedures. (SIR 2000.5) 32

Such an understanding is ordinarily obtained by: 33

(a) meeting the directors and management of the entity;
(b) visiting the entity's premises;
(c) discussing the financial information and recent results with management;
(d) applying analytical procedures to the financial information; and
(e) obtaining from management an understanding of the principal transaction flows, internal controls and reporting arrangements of the business.

If this process indicates that there are factors which may give rise to a modification of the accountant's report then such factors are reported immediately to those responsible for the investment circular, usually the directors and any other responsible parties. 34

In considering areas of risk in relation to the periods for which historical financial information is presented, the reporting accountant has regard to the probability that misstatements in earlier periods, if they exist, are likely to have been detected in subsequent periods. Account is also taken of the fact that other uncertainties, particularly those affecting subjective matters in the historical financial information, may have been resolved with the passage of time. 35

When performing the risk assessment, the reporting accountant should take into account all other relevant work performed in connection with the investment circular. (SIR 2000.6) 36

The reporting accountant may be undertaking other relevant work related to the transaction giving rise to the accountant's report. For example, the reporting accountant may have been commissioned to prepare a long form report, or a comfort letter on a statement of sufficiency of working capital. 37

If other relevant work has been performed by another firm the reporting accountant requests the issuer to provide access to such work. If the reporting accountant is not allowed access to such work they consider the implications for their report. 38

Materiality

39 The reporting accountant determines materiality for the purposes of the reporting accountant's work independently from the auditor, if any, who audited the underlying financial statements, and accordingly the reporting accountant's assessment of materiality may differ from that of the auditor. In determining materiality for the purposes of reporting on historical financial information, regard is had to the context in which the opinion is to be given (which includes the fact that the information may relate to a trend of results over a three year period).

The reporting accountant's procedures

40 **The reporting accountant should perform procedures to obtain sufficient appropriate evidence as to whether the work of an auditor, which the reporting accountant plans to use, is adequate for the reporting accountant's purposes. Where the reporting accountant concludes that the auditor's work is not adequate, does not have access to the auditor's working papers, or an audit has not previously been performed, the reporting accountant should perform procedures that compensate for this. The procedures of the auditor and the reporting accountant, taken together, should meet the requirements of ISAs (UK and Ireland) unless:**

(a) **a requirement is not applicable to the reporting accountant's engagement; or**
(b) **it is not practicable for the reporting accountant to undertake such procedures.**

If the reporting accountant decides not to meet a requirement of ISAs (UK and Ireland) that is not listed in Appendix 1, it should document the reason for not meeting the requirement and why its omission does not have an impact on its opinion. (SIR 2000.7)

41 In determining the procedures to be performed in response to the assessed risk of material misstatement at the assertion level, the reporting accountant considers the extent to which the procedures that the reporting accountant wishes to perform have previously been performed by an auditor. Where such procedures have been performed by an auditor, the reporting accountant may, subject to the considerations discussed in this SIR, use the evidence obtained by the auditor from those procedures as part of the reporting accountant's own evidence.

42 The nature of ISAs (UK and Ireland) requires reporting accountants to exercise professional judgment in applying them. In exceptional circumstances reporting accountants may judge it necessary to depart from a basic principle or essential procedure of a standard to achieve more effectively the objective of the engagement. When such a situation arises the reporting accountant documents the reason for the departure unless the basic principle or essential procedure is one of those set out in Appendix 1. Appendix 1 identifies bold letter paragraphs that are unlikely to apply to the reporting accountant's exercise and sets out some of the generic reasons why a bold letter paragraph may not be applicable.

43 Where applicable auditing standards have changed during the period covered by the historical financial information, or it is not practicable for the reporting accountant to undertake procedures that meet the requirements of ISAs (UK and Ireland), the reporting accountant considers the implications for the reporting accountant's exercise, having regard to its risk assessment. The reporting accountant may be able to conclude that it is unnecessary to apply certain bold letter paragraphs in the ISAs (UK and Ireland) throughout the three year period covered by the accountant's report because:

(a) it is sufficient to apply them with respect to the latest period only, because sufficient appropriate evidence relating to earlier periods can be obtained from the latest period; or
(b) the auditing standards that were applicable at the time met the same objectives as the requirements of ISAs (UK and Ireland)[3].

In such cases the reporting accountant documents the reason or justification for not meeting the requirement and why omitting it does not have an impact on its opinion.

When the reporting accountant intends to use audit evidence obtained by the auditor, it should evaluate whether the audit procedures performed by the auditor adequately respond to the reporting accountant's assessment of the risks (including significant risks requiring special audit consideration) of material misstatement of the financial information to be included in the investment circular. (SIR 2000.8) 44

The reporting accountant's procedures should include: 45

(a) **examining material adjustments from previously published historical financial statements made during the course of preparing the historical financial information and considering the responsible party's basis for satisfying itself that the adjustments are necessary and whether they have been correctly determined;**
(b) **evaluating whether all necessary adjustments to previously published historical financial statements have been made; and**
(c) **where the information is based on previously published financial statements, comparing the historical financial information to those financial statements and assessing whether the information has been accurately extracted therefrom. (SIR 2000.9)**

In certain areas, use of the work of the auditor may be the only practicable means of obtaining the evidence necessary to support the reporting accountant's opinion[4]. The timing of the reporting accountant's own work will inevitably be dictated by the timing of the preparation of the historical financial information and the related investment circular and this may be some time after the end of the periods to which the report relates. 46

Evidence

The reporting accountant reconsiders the matters considered at the planning stage as described in paragraphs 29 and 31. 47

Where the financial information to be reported on has previously been subject to audit, the auditor's working papers will be a useful source for the evidence which the reporting accountant may need to support its opinion on the financial information. 48

If planning to use the work of the auditor, the reporting accountant considers whether: 49

(a) the work of the auditor was conducted to an appropriate materiality level; and

---

[3] Prior to the adoption of ISAs (UK and Ireland) applicable auditing standards in the United Kingdom were "Statements of Auditing Standards" (SASs) issued by the Auditing Practices Board. For the purposes of SIR 2000 the SASs are deemed to meet the same objectives as the requirements of ISAs (UK and Ireland).

[4] Procedures which require the reporting accountant to be physically present at a client site at a relevant date (for example attendance at physical inventory counting) will clearly be impossible to perform.

(b) the auditor appears to have complied with the auditing standards applicable to the auditor's work.

50 The reporting accountant accepts evidence in audit working papers as being prima facie truthful and genuine, but in considering that evidence adopts an attitude of professional scepticism, whether the audit working paper was produced by an auditor from the reporting accountant's own firm or by another auditor. However, with respect to audit working papers obtained from the reporting accountant's own firm, the reporting accountant is more familiar with the detailed quality control procedures that will have been applied in the conduct of the audit. The application of professional scepticism will include considering the evidence contained in the audit working papers in the light of the understanding of the entity and its environment, including its internal control and such other evidence as the reporting accountant obtains directly.

51 The extent to which independent testing of the evidence obtained by the auditor (for example, reperformance of tests performed by the auditor) will be necessary is a matter for the reporting accountant's judgment on the basis of the information available at the time, including the reporting accountant's evaluation of the auditor's work.

52 **The reporting accountant should evaluate the quality of the audit evidence obtained by the auditor that the reporting accountant intends to rely on. Where the reporting accountant concludes that such audit evidence is either not sufficient or is inappropriate for the purposes of the reporting accountant's exercise the reporting accountant should obtain evidence directly. Where the evidence is not available, the reporting accountant should consider the implications for its report. (SIR 2000.10)**

53 Where the reporting accountant intends to rely on internal controls, the reporting accountant performs tests of control when unable to rely on the auditor's tests of such internal controls. This is likely to arise when:

(a) the auditor has not performed tests of those internal controls; or
(b) the auditor has performed tests of internal controls but the internal controls have subsequently changed.

54 Where relevant information is not available from the audit working papers, the reporting accountant will need to obtain the relevant evidence directly. The audit working papers are unlikely for example, to contain information concerning post balance sheet events up to the date of signing the accountant's report or to contain evidence relating to any adjustments made to the financial statements in preparing the historical financial information.

Obtaining access to information in audit working papers

55 When the company's auditor, or former auditor, is not appointed as the reporting accountant, the auditor will be aware that the reporting accountant may need access to information contained in the audit working papers. The auditor or former auditor is normally prepared, in accordance with relevant professional guidance, to make the audit working papers available to reporting accountants for the purpose of work under this SIR.

56 Access may be granted only on the basis that the auditor accepts no responsibility or liability to the reporting accountant in connection with the use of the audit working

papers by the reporting accountant. This has no effect on the reporting accountant's judgment regarding the extent to which reliance is placed on the working papers.

In cases where the reporting accountant is not able to obtain access to information in audit working papers, the reporting accountant will have no option other than to obtain the relevant evidence directly.   57

Irrespective of whether the reporting accountant has access to the auditor's working papers, the reporting accountant seeks to obtain, either from the directors or from the auditor, copies of all relevant communications sent by the auditor to those charged with governance of the entity, including those required to be sent by auditing standards applicable at the time, and copies of any responses to such communications made by management. A relevant communication would, for example, be one that discussed internal control and other weaknesses.   58

Related parties

Paragraphs 7(a) and 107(a) of ISA (UK and Ireland) 550 "Related Parties" require prior years' working papers to be reviewed for names of known related parties. These paragraphs do not apply in respect of the earliest period where more than one period is to be reported on.   59

Events occurring up to the date of the accountant's report

Unless a post balance sheet event indicates that there has been an error in the preparation of the historical financial information in an earlier period, the reporting accountant will, having regard to the convention for treating post balance sheet events for the purposes of historical financial information in an investment circular (as referred to in the Annexure), only consider the impact of post balance sheet events occurring up to the date of the accountant's report on the final period presented.   60

Events occurring between the date of the accountant's report and the completion date of the transaction

If, in the period between the date of the accountant's report and the <u>completion date of the transaction</u>, the reporting accountant becomes aware of events and other matters which, had they occurred and been known at the date of the report, might have caused it to issue a different report or to withhold consent, the reporting accountant should discuss the implications of them with those responsible for the investment circular and take additional action as appropriate. (SIR 2000.11)   61

After the date of the accountant's report, the reporting accountant has no obligation to perform procedures or make enquiries regarding the investment circular.   62

Under Chapter 3 of the Prospectus Rules, a supplementary prospectus must be prepared if, after the date the prospectus has been formally approved by the <u>FSA</u> and before the final closing of the offer of <u>securities</u> to the public or the commencement of trading in the relevant securities, there is a significant change affecting any matter contained in the document or a significant new matter has arisen (or a material mistake or inaccuracy is noted).   63

64 If, as a result of discussions with those responsible for the investment circular concerning a subsequent event that occurred prior to the completion date of the transaction, the reporting accountant is either uncertain about or disagrees with the course of action proposed, the reporting accountant may consider it necessary to take legal advice with respect to an appropriate course of action.

Going concern

65 References to an emphasis of matter relating to a material uncertainty regarding going concern that is relevant at the time the accountant's report is signed, and which will not be resolved by a satisfactory outcome to the transaction to which the investment circular relates, will be included in the basis of opinion section of the reporting accountants' report.

66 Where the matter or uncertainty will be resolved if the outcome of transactions to which the investment circular containing the report relates is satisfactory (for example the successful raising of money through a share issue or shareholder approval of a transaction), the reporting accountant will consider whether adequate disclosure of that matter or uncertainty is made in the basis of preparation note to the historical financial information. If adequate disclosure is made in the historical financial information it is unlikely to be necessary for the reporting accountant to include an emphasis of matter in the basis of opinion section of its report.

Representations

67 SIR 1000.13 sets out the basic principles and essential procedures with respect to obtaining written confirmation of representations from the directors of the entity.

68 A number of specific representations are required by ISAs (UK and Ireland). Where representations have been obtained by the auditor, subject to the considerations set out in this SIR, it may not be necessary for the reporting accountant to seek further representations covering the same matters, other than in relation to the period since the audit opinion relating to the final period included in the historical financial information was given.

69 Representations additional to those pursuant to ISAs (UK and Ireland) that a reporting accountant may consider for incorporation in the letter of representation or board minute include:
- Confirmation from the directors or management of the entity that they are responsible for the preparation of the historical financial information.
- Confirmation that any adjustments made to historical financial statements for the purposes of preparing the historical financial information are necessary, have been correctly determined and that there are no other adjustments that are necessary.

70 In relation to a Class 1 acquisition, the acquirer may not be in a position to make representations in relation to the historical financial information of the target entity on matters such as fraud, non-compliance with laws and regulation and related parties. In such circumstances representations may be sought from the management of the target entity.

Joint reporting accountants

71 When joint reporting accountants are appointed, the division of work as between them is a matter for agreement. The arrangements between the joint reporting accountants may form part of the engagement letter. Irrespective of any such arrangement, the joint reporting accountants are jointly and severally responsible for the report to be given. Each of the joint reporting accountants participates in the planning of the engagement and they agree upon the scope of work and any changes subsequently found to be necessary thereto. Each of the joint reporting accountants has regard to the considerations set out in this SIR in respect of using the work of an auditor in determining the extent to which it is appropriate to rely on the evidence obtained by the other reporting accountants or the extent to which they consider it necessary to carry out their own work. Each of the joint reporting accountants reviews the work of the other to the extent considered necessary and records the results of that review. A common set of working papers is normally maintained.

Reporting

72 SIRs 1000.17, 1000.18, 1000.19 and 1000.20 set out the basic principles and essential procedures with respect to reporting.

73 The reporting accountant's opinion is usually expressed in terms of whether, for the purpose of the relevant investment circular, the financial information gives a true and fair view of the state of affairs and profits, cash flows and statement of changes in equity.

74 When there is a limitation on the scope of the reporting accountant's work, the reporting accountant considers whether the limitation results in a lack of evidence necessary to form an opinion. When the possible effect is, in the opinion of the reporting accountant, material to the financial information, there will be insufficient evidence to support an unqualified opinion. The nature of the work of reporting accountants is such that in the absence of reliable contemporary evidence relating to significant accounts and balances it may not be possible to form an opinion on the financial information. This might be the case where there has been no audit of the underlying financial information in the past or where the auditor has given a qualified opinion because of a limitation in the scope of work.

75 As a consequence of the purpose for which financial information is presented and the importance which may be attached to it by readers of the document, a reporting accountant does not normally agree to be associated with financial information where a disclaimer of opinion needs to be given on the information for the entire period.

76 The reporting accountant needs to be satisfied that the financial information adequately describes the applicable financial reporting framework in the description of the basis of preparation, and makes reference to this in the report.

Other information – references to previous audit opinions

77 The reporting accountant's opinion is arrived at independently of any audit opinion previously given on the financial statements which form the basis for the financial information to be reported on. It is not part of the reporting accountant's role to explain (where this is the case) why the reporting accountant's opinion differs from

the opinion of the auditor. In some cases, however, there may be an obligation on an issuer to disclose details of qualifications or disclaimers contained in audit reports prepared by the statutory auditor. In such cases, the reporting accountant considers the disclosures made by the issuer relating to such qualifications or disclaimers and whether any matters disclosed might give rise to questions as to how the reporting accountant has dealt with matters giving rise to the qualifications or disclaimers. If the reporting accountant is not satisfied with the disclosures, the reporting accountant discusses the matter with those responsible for the investment circular and ensures that the appropriate information is included by the issuer or is included in the accountant's report. Where the audit has been undertaken by another firm, the reporting accountant does not normally refer to the name of the auditor in the accountant's report.

Comparatives

78 The reporting accountant is required to provide a report on each period included in the historical financial information to which the reporting requirement relates. In consequence the financial information does not constitute "comparatives" as contemplated by ISA (UK and Ireland) 710 "Comparatives". Accordingly ISA (UK and Ireland) 710 is not applicable to the work of the reporting accountant.

Consent in the context of investment circulars containing a report by a reporting accountant

79 Paragraphs 66 to 74 of SIR 1000 deal with consent in relation to the inclusion of an accountant's report in an investment circular.

Effective date

80 A reporting accountant is required to comply with the Investment Reporting Standards contained in this SIR for reports signed after 31 August 2005. Earlier adoption is encouraged.

Appendix 1 – Bold letter paragraphs included in ISAs (UK and Ireland) that are unlikely to apply to the reporting accountant's exercise in relation to historical financial information in investment circulars.

This summary is illustrative and is included as a convenient source of reference only. It should not be used as a substitute for a reading of the full text of SIR 2000. The summary identifies bold letter paragraphs that are unlikely to apply to the reporting accountant's exercise. The Appendix either cross-refers to paragraphs within SIR 2000 which discuss aspects of ISAs (UK and Ireland) or includes separate discussion below.

ISAs (UK and Ireland) are regularly revised and from time to time new ISAs (UK and Ireland) are issued. Also, there may be extant bold letter paragraphs that, for one reason or another, are not applicable to a particular engagement. Particular bold letter paragraphs in ISAs (UK and Ireland) are unlikely to apply to the reporting accountant's exercise for the following reasons, among others:

- Equivalent and overriding requirements are set out in SIRs, for example ethical requirements.
- The concept of a recurring engagement, or an ongoing relationship with a client, although relevant to audits is usually not relevant to engagements to report on an investment circular.
- The requirement for the reporting accountant to report on three years may remove the need to consider prior years' working papers for the first year reported on.
- With respect to an Initial Public Offering (IPO) there may be no practical distinction between management and those charged with corporate governance.

ISA (UK and Ireland)	SIR 2000 Reference or comment
200 Objective and General Principles Governing an Audit of Financial Statements	
"The auditor should comply with the Code of Ethics for Professional Accountants issued by the International Federation of Accountants." (4)	Paragraph 24 (Paragraph 18 of SIR 1000).
"In the UK and Ireland the relevant ethical pronouncements with which the auditor should comply are the APB's Ethical Standards and the ethical pronouncements relating to the work of auditors issued by the auditor's relevant professional body." (4-1)	Paragraph 24 (Paragraph 18 of SIR 1000).
210 Terms of Audit Engagements	
"On recurring audits, the auditor should consider whether circumstances require the terms of the engagement to be revised and whether there is a need to remind the client of the existing terms of the engagement." (10)	The concept of recurring audits does not apply to investment circulars.
"An auditor who, before the completion of the engagement, is requested to change the engagement to one which provides a lower level of assurance, should consider the appropriateness of doing so." (12)	Changing the engagement to one which provides a lower level of assurance is not permitted by the PD Regulation.

ISA (UK and Ireland)	SIR 2000 Reference or comment
"The auditor should not agree to a change of engagement where there is no reasonable justification for doing so." (18)	The regulation does not provide the opportunity to vary the nature of the engagement.
300 Planning an Audit of Financial Statements	
"The auditor should perform the following activities prior to starting an initial audit: (b) Communicate with the previous auditor, where there has been a change of auditors, in compliance with relevant ethical requirements. (28)	Not applicable as there is not an ongoing relationship.
330 The Auditor's Procedures in Response to Assessed Risks	
"If the auditor plans to use audit evidence about the operating effectiveness of controls obtained in prior audits, the auditor should obtain audit evidence about whether changes in those specific controls have occurred subsequent to the prior audit. The auditor should obtain audit evidence about whether such changes have occurred by performing inquiry in combination with observation or inspection to confirm the understanding of those specific controls". (39)	Paragraphs 52 and 53.
"If the auditor plans to rely on controls that have changed since they were last tested, the auditor should test the operating effectiveness of such controls in the current audit". (40)	Paragraphs 52 and 53.
"If the auditor plans to rely on controls that have not changed since they were last tested, the auditor should test the operating effectiveness of such controls at least once in every third audit." (41)	Paragraphs 52 and 53.
"When there are a number of controls for which the auditor determines that it is appropriate to use audit evidence obtained in prior audits, the auditor should test the operating effectiveness of some controls each audit." (43)	Paragraphs 52 and 53.
510 Initial engagements – Opening Balances and Continuing Engagements – Opening Balances	
"The auditor should also obtain sufficient appropriate audit evidence for the matters set out in paragraph 2 for continuing audit engagements (see paragraphs 10-1 and 10-2". (2-1)	Not applicable as the reporting accountant's exercise is not a continuing engagement.

ISA (UK and Ireland)	SIR 2000 Reference or comment
550 Related Parties	
IAS 24	
"The auditor should review information provided by those charged with governance and management identifying the names of all known related parties and should perform the following audit procedures in respect of the completeness of this information: (a) Review prior year working papers for names of known related parties;" (7)	Paragraph 59 explains that this does not apply in respect of the earliest period where more than one period is to be reported on.
FRS 8	
"(a) Review prior year working papers for names of known related parties;" (107)	Paragraph 59 explains that this does not apply in respect of the earliest period where more than one period is to be reported on.
560 Subsequent Events	
"When, after the date of the auditor's report but before the financial statements are issued, the auditor becomes aware of a fact which may materially affect the financial statements, the auditor should consider whether the financial statements need amendment, should discuss the matter with management and should take the action appropriate in the circumstances." (9)	Paragraphs 61 to 64.
"When management does not amend the financial statements in circumstances where the auditor believes they need to be amended and the auditor's report has not been released to the entity, the auditor should express a qualified opinion or an adverse opinion." (11)	Paragraphs 61 to 64.
"When, after the financial statements have been issued, the auditor becomes aware of a fact which existed at the date of the auditor's report and which, if known at that date, may have caused the auditor to modify the auditor's report, the auditor should consider whether the financial statements need revision, should discuss the matter with management, and should take the action appropriate in the circumstances." (14)	Paragraphs 61 to 64.
"The new auditor's report should include an emphasis of a matter paragraph referring to a note to the financial statements that more extensively discusses the reason for the revision of the previously issued financial statements and to the earlier report issued by the auditor." (16)	Paragraphs 61 to 64.
710 Comparatives	
All paragraphs.	Paragraph 78.

Appendix 2 – Examples of engagement letter clauses

These examples of engagement letter clauses are intended for consideration in the context of an accountant's report. They should be tailored to the specific circumstances and supplemented by such other clauses as are relevant and appropriate.

For a prospectus

Financial information upon which the report is to be given

We understand that the directors of ABC plc will include in the Prospectus historical financial information for the [three] years ended [ ] in relation to ABC plc, the last [two years] of which will be presented and prepared in a form consistent with that which will be adopted in ABC plc's next published annual financial statements, having regard to accounting standards and policies and legislation applicable to such annual financial statements in accordance with the requirements of Annex I item 20.1 of the Prospectus Rules.

Responsibilities

The directors of ABC plc are responsible for the historical financial information.

It is our responsibility to form an opinion as to whether the financial information gives a true and fair view for the purposes of the Prospectus and to report our opinion to the directors of ABC plc.

Scope of work

We shall expect to obtain such relevant and reliable evidence as we consider sufficient to enable us to draw reasonable conclusions therefrom. The nature and extent of our procedures will vary according to our assessment of the appropriate sources of evidence. Our work will be directed to those matters which in our view materially affect the overall financial information upon which our opinion is to be given, and will not be directed to the discovery of errors or misstatements which we consider to be immaterial.

It is expected that a substantial part of the evidence which we may require will be contained in the audit files of LMN Accountants. ABC plc has agreed that it will use its best endeavours to ensure that the relevant audit files are made available to us.

Our work may also depend upon receiving without undue delay full co-operation from all relevant officials of ABC plc and their disclosure to us of all the accounting records of ABC plc and all other records and related information (including certain representations) as we may need for the purposes of our examination.

For a Class 1 circular

Financial information upon which the report is to be given

We understand that the directors of ABC plc will include in the Class 1 Circular a historical financial information table for the [three] years ended [ ] in relation to XYZ Limited which will be presented and prepared in a form consistent with the accounting policies adopted in ABC plc's latest annual consolidated accounts in accordance with the requirements of chapter 13 of the Listing Rules.

Responsibilities

The directors of ABC plc are responsible for the historical financial information table.

It is our responsibility to form an opinion as to whether the financial information gives a true and fair view for the purposes of the Class 1 circular and whether the financial information table has been prepared in a form that is consistent with the accounting policies adopted in ABC plc's latest annual accounts and to report our opinion to the directors of ABC plc.

Scope of work

We shall expect to obtain such relevant and reliable evidence as we consider sufficient to enable us to draw reasonable conclusions therefrom. The nature and extent of our procedures will vary according to our assessment of the appropriate sources of evidence. Our work will be directed to those matters which in our view materially affect the overall financial information upon which our opinion is to be given, and will not be directed to the discovery of errors or misstatements which we consider to be immaterial.

It is expected that a substantial part of the evidence which we may require will be contained in the audit files of LMN Accountants. ABC plc has agreed that it will use its best endeavours to ensure that the relevant audit files are made available to us.

Our work may also depend upon receiving without undue delay full co-operation from all relevant officials of ABC plc and XYZ Limited and their disclosure to us of all the accounting records of XYZ Limited and all other records and related information (including certain representations) as we may need for the purposes of our examination.

Appendix 3 – Example of an accountant's report on historical financial information

Date

Reporting accountant's address

Addressees, as agreed between the parties in the engagement letter

Dear Sirs

[ABC plc]/[XYZ Limited]

We report on the financial information set out [in paragraphs .... to ....]. This financial information has been prepared for inclusion in the [describe document[1]] dated..........of ABC plc on the basis of the accounting policies set out in paragraph [ ]. This report is required by [Relevant Regulation] and is given for the purpose of complying with that [Relevant Regulation] and for no other purpose.

Responsibilities

[As described in paragraph [ ]] [T/t]he Directors of ABC plc are responsible for preparing the financial information [on the basis of preparation set out in [*note x to the financial information*]] [and in accordance with [*the applicable financial reporting framework*]].

It is our responsibility to form an opinion [on the financial information] [as to whether the financial information gives a true and fair view, for the purposes of the [describe document], and to report our opinion to you.

Basis of opinion

We conducted our work in accordance with Standards for Investment Reporting issued by the Auditing Practices Board in the United Kingdom. Our work included an assessment of evidence relevant to the amounts and disclosures in the financial information. It also included an assessment of significant estimates and judgments made by those responsible for the preparation of the financial information and whether the accounting policies are appropriate to the entity's circumstances, consistently applied and adequately disclosed.

We planned and performed our work so as to obtain all the information and explanations which we considered necessary in order to provide us with sufficient evidence to give reasonable assurance that the financial information is free from material misstatement whether caused by fraud or other irregularity or error.

Opinion

In our opinion, the financial information gives, for the purposes of the [describe document] dated ......, a true and fair view of the state of affairs of [ABC plc]/[XYZ Limited] as at the dates stated and of its profits, cash flows and [recognised gains and losses] [changes in equity] for the periods then ended in accordance with the basis of preparation set out in note x and in accordance with [*the applicable financial*

---

[1] For example, "prospectus", "listing particulars", "Class 1 circular" and "AIM admission document."

reporting framework] as described in note y] [and has been prepared in a form that is consistent with the accounting policies adopted in [ABC plc's] latest annual accounts²].

Declaration³

For the purposes of [Prospectus Rule [5.5.3R(2)(f)] [5.5.4R (2)(f)]] [Paragraph a of Schedule Two of the AIM Rules] we are responsible for [this report as part] [the following part(s)] of the [prospectus] [registration document] [AIM admission document] and declare that we have taken all reasonable care to ensure that the information contained [in this report][those parts] is, to the best of our knowledge, in accordance with the facts and contains no omission likely to affect its import. This declaration is included in the [prospectus] [registration document] [AIM admission document] in compliance with [item 1.2 of annex I of the PD Regulation] [item 1.2 of annex III of the PD Regulation] [Schedule Two of the AIM Rules].

Yours faithfully

Reporting accountant

---

² *The wording in these square brackets is appropriate for inclusion where the report relates to historical financial information included in a Class 1 circular.*

³ *This declaration is a requirement of the Prospectus Rules and is appropriate for inclusion when the report is included in a Prospectus, see Appendix 2 of SIR 1000. It is also appropriate for inclusion in an AIM admission document under Schedule Two of the AIM Rules.*

Annexure

ACCOUNTING CONVENTIONS COMMONLY USED IN THE PREPARATION OF HISTORICAL FINANCIAL INFORMATION IN INVESTMENT CIRCULARS

This Annexure has been compiled by the APB from a number of sources to describe conventions commonly used for the preparation of historical financial information intended to show a true and fair view for the purposes of an investment circular. It does not include either basic principles, essential procedures, or guidance promulgated by the APB.

Introduction

1 Preparers[1] have regard to accepted conventions which have been developed for the preparation and presentation of historical financial information in investment circulars. They seek to assist preparers, to the extent consistent with established accounting principles, to meet the obligation that the historical financial information should give a true and fair view for the purposes of the relevant investment circular. These conventions also take into account the requirement contained in the Prospectus Directive that the information should be presented in an easily analysable and comprehensible form. The conventions are described in the material presented below.

Disclosure of the financial reporting framework adopted

2 Preparers summarise the applicable financial reporting framework within the notes to the financial information. Where one of the conventions described in this Annexure is applied and its application has a material effect on the financial information or is necessary for an understanding of the basis of preparation of the financial information, it is appropriate to describe the treatment adopted in the basis of preparation note in the historical financial information.

Adjustments to the financial information

3 Preparers make adjustments, only in respect of material items, in order to:

(a) present the financial information for all relevant years on the basis of consistent, acceptable and appropriately applied accounting policies, in accordance with the applicable requirements;
(b) correct errors; and
(c) record adjusting post balance sheet events where appropriate (see paragraph 13 below).

4 The historical financial information presented will be based on the records of the entity whose historical financial information is presented in the investment circular (referred to as "the entity" throughout this Annexure), for the periods reported on. These records reflect the representations and intentions of the

---

[1] *The directors and management of an entity are responsible for the preparation and presentation of the financial statements of an entity. In this Annexure they are collectively referred to as "the preparers".*

entity's management at the time the underlying financial information was drawn up. Matters such as the selection of accounting policies, accounting estimates and valuation judgments form part of the responsibilities of management in compiling a record of their stewardship.

In presenting historical financial information in an investment circular, except insofar as necessary to achieve the objectives set out above, preparers do not seek to replace accounting policies, accounting estimates or valuation judgments with alternatives subsequently selected by themselves. They consider whether the specific application of the basis of accounting originally adopted by management falls within an acceptable range of alternatives (if not, the conclusion will usually be that an error has occurred, which may need to be adjusted). Furthermore, it is not normally appropriate for adjustments to be made to eliminate items of earned income or expenses incurred, nor, in any circumstances, to recognise notional items of income or expense. The historical financial information presented in the investment circular is thus a version of the historical record as presented by the entity's management and adjustments are introduced only to achieve those specific objectives set out in paragraph 3 of this Annexure.

Trend of results

The historical financial information included in an investment circular presents a trend of results for the relevant period. In this respect the financial information may be distinguished from the financial information contained in statutory accounts.

Notional, or other, adjustments that impact net profits or net assets are not introduced in order to make the "track record" more consistent with the entity's expected operations or structure following the transaction. Such adjustments would anticipate future events and are not consistent with the principle that the historical financial information should record the events which actually occurred during the period of the historical financial information.

Adjustments for change in basis of accounting

Adjustments are made to ensure that, wherever practicable, the financial information is stated on the basis of consistent accounting policies. Under the PD Regulation (subject to certain transitional provisions in Article 35 of the PD Regulation), the financial information for the most recent year (where audited historical financial information is required for the latest 2 financial years) or most recent 2 years (where audited historical financial information is required for the latest 3 financial years) is required to be prepared and presented in a form consistent with that which will be adopted in the issuer's next published annual financial statements (having regard to accounting standards and policies and legislation applicable to such annual financial statements). The requirements do not prevent entities from presenting the financial information for all periods in a form which is consistent with that which will be adopted in the next published financial statements if they so choose. In other contexts such as in a Class 1 transaction, the objective may be for the financial information for all periods to be presented in a form consistent with the accounting policies adopted by the acquirer in its latest annual consolidated accounts.

9   When considering the adjustments that may be necessary where a new International Financial Reporting Standard or other relevant accounting standard has been introduced during, or (where applicable under the regulations) subsequent to, the period to which the regulations apply, a relevant factor will be whether the requirements for implementing the new accounting standard provide that it should be applied retroactively once adopted. Where adoption of a new accounting standard leads to the inclusion of a prior year adjustment in the accounts, adjustments are made, to the extent practicable, to reflect the effect of the policy in any relevant earlier period. Where the adoption of a new accounting standard does not lead to the inclusion of a prior year adjustment, for example where the accounting standard is stated to apply to transactions first accounted for after a certain date; no such adjustment is made to the financial information. Where an entity chooses to adopt a new accounting standard early and this is permitted or encouraged, although not required, by that standard, the financial information reflects the same treatment as adopted by the entity.

10 Although adjustments may be made for changes in accounting policies, adjustments are not normally made for changes in the methods of applying an accounting policy (whether a one-off change or a series of gradual refinements) or otherwise to correct the entity's accounting estimates, provided that there were no errors. The effect of correcting an estimate in a later period is normally reflected in the result of that period. Consideration may be given to whether an understanding of the trend of results would be assisted by separate or additional disclosure in relation to changes in the methods of applying accounting policies or the impact of a correction of an accounting estimate.

11 Occasionally, an accounting policy may have been applied on the basis of considerations other than relevant economic ones (for example where financial statements measure the carrying amount of depreciable fixed assets in accordance with depreciation policies which are influenced by taxation considerations - as is the case in certain jurisdictions). Those presenting historical financial information in an investment circular may determine that an adjustment is necessary in order for the financial information to present a true and fair view, for the purposes of the relevant investment circular.

Audit qualifications relating to non-compliance with accounting standards

12 Where the auditor's report(s) on the underlying financial statements was qualified on grounds, for example, of failure to comply with an applicable accounting standard or disagreement over an accounting treatment, it may be possible to make adjustments so as to remove the need for a similar qualification in a report on the adjusted historical financial information.

Post balance sheet events

13 In determining whether adjustment is to be made for post balance sheet events, subject to the guidance set out above, it is normal practice to consider events only up to the date on which the audit report on the relevant underlying financial statements was originally signed by the auditors except in relation to the final period presented. In respect of this final period, it will be necessary for post balance sheet events to be reflected up to the date on which the historical financial information to be presented in the investment circular is approved by the

responsible party. Where the financial information is based upon financial records which were not audited, the relevant date for post balance sheet event considerations in the earlier periods is normally taken to be the date at which the underlying balance sheet was finalised.

Presentation of the financial information

Subject to the requirements of any applicable regulation, the financial information is presented on a consistent and comparable basis from period to period and includes such presentational changes to the financial information as are necessary in order to achieve this.

Presentational changes might be made to:

(a) present the financial information in a comparable way; and
(b) give due prominence to matters of particular importance in the context of the document in which the financial information is included.

The financial information contained in the entity's records may not have been presented on a comparable basis from period to period because the convention for presenting financial information adopted in earlier periods may have been different from that adopted in later periods.

Whenever practicable, financial information is presented in such a way that information which a user of the investment circular might wish to compare, is in fact comparable. Presentational changes of this nature may be categorised as follows:

(a) reclassifications (for example, cost of sales reclassified as distribution costs);
(b) re-analyses (for example, restatements of analyses between continuing and discontinued activities);
(c) grossing up of items netted off in earlier periods (for example, matched assets and liabilities previously left off balance sheet);
(d) derivation or computation of information undisclosed in earlier periods (for example, profit and loss account subtotals or cash flow statements); and
(e) harmonisation of note disclosures (for example the editing of notes for earlier periods to integrate them with notes for later periods).

For example, a business classed as a continuing operation in one year may have been designated a discontinued activity in financial statements drawn up for a later period. It will be desirable for the relevant information within continuing operations in the earlier periods to be reclassified as discontinued. Where separate disclosure of information relating to entities acquired during the period has been presented in the financial statements, it is customary to reclassify such information for the purposes of the historical financial information as continuing activities, other than in respect of acquisitions made in the final period of the track record.

Changes are not, however, made to the presentation adopted in the financial statements on which the financial information is based, unless such changes are consistent with the requirement to give a true and fair view for the purposes of the investment circular.

Where it is considered that the significance of certain items to an understanding of the financial information may be obscured by the presentation adopted in the financial statements, it is usually appropriate for that presentation to be changed, relevant disclosures to be made or relevant explanations to be introduced to highlight their significance. This approach may be adopted for example to highlight certain categories of expense, such as proprietors' remuneration, in the trading record of a company seeking flotation. It may also be adopted to highlight the results of different classes of business, particularly in cases where there are proposals that a class of business is to be discontinued.

21 However, in all cases, changes in presentation would be inappropriate if they are in conflict with applicable accounting standards.

22 As noted above, in certain cases regulatory requirements stipulate that information for the most recent two of the three years is to be presented on a basis comparable with that which would be adopted in an issuer's next annual financial statements. In such cases, in order that the reader is able to relate the first year's information to the final two years, preparers may present financial information for the second year on the basis originally reported (and thus comparable with the first year) as well as on the adjusted basis required by the regulation.

Issues connected with underlying financial statements

23 Where the entity has prepared accounts consolidating all its subsidiaries during the period, the financial information will, subject to any adjustments made, be the information set out in the consolidated accounts.

24 There may be cases where historical financial information is to be prepared for an entity in circumstances where consolidated financial statements do not exist. This may arise for example where the business is a sub-group, the parent company of which was exempt from the requirement to prepare consolidated accounts, or where the business comprises companies under common ownership but which were not constituted as a legal sub-group.

Unconsolidated accounts

25 Where there has been a legal sub-group it will usually be appropriate, for ease of analysis and comprehension, for the accounts of the subsidiaries to be consolidated into the accounts of the parent company. For this purpose, specially prepared consolidated accounts may be compiled by the relevant entity, applying the normal conventions for consolidation.

Entities under common management and control

26 Where the entities have been under common management and control but do not form a legal group, the historical financial information will normally be presented on a combined or aggregated basis. Under this method, the results and net assets of the relevant entities are aggregated (with eliminations for intercompany transactions and balances), as are the related share capital balances and reserves. If the information is not presented on a combined or aggregated basis then separate historical financial information for entities accounting for substantially the whole of the historical revenue earning record is likely to be required.

Carve outs

Where a business has formed part of a larger group ("overall group") during the three year period, but has not been accounted for separately, it may be desirable to present a separate track record (a "carve out") for that business ("carve out business"), derived from the records of the overall group. This approach may be preferable to the alternative approach of presenting the track record of the overall group, with appropriate disclosures of operations discontinuing or not acquired. Circumstances where a carve out approach might be followed include flotations of businesses in a demerger and Class 1 acquisitions of divisions of a selling group.

27

When considering whether it is appropriate to present carve out financial information, the following factors will be relevant:

28

(a) the extent to which the carve out business has been separately managed and financially controlled within the overall group; and
(b) the extent to which it is practicable to identify the historical financial information attributable to the carve out business.

Where the omission of the results and assets of those operations not the subject of the transaction concerned would be misleading in the context of the circumstances in which the historical financial information is to be presented, it will generally be appropriate to adopt the approach of presenting financial information on the overall group. Disclosures are made to assist the user to understand the contribution made by the operations not the subject of the transaction concerned. However, each case will need to be assessed on its own facts and circumstances.

29

In preparing the track record for the carve out business, the guidance in paragraph 5 of this Annexure will be relevant. The objective will be, so far as possible, to present a historical record reflecting the events which actually occurred in the reporting period. Whilst it may be possible to identify certain transactions and balances which clearly relate to the carve out business, there will often be cases where the accounting records do not differentiate between items which relate to the carve out business and items which relate to the remainder of the overall group's business. Examples include management overheads, funding arrangements and shared assets. The guidance below discusses some of the elements typically encountered in preparing a carve out track record.

30

Clear and comprehensive disclosure in the notes to the historical financial information will normally be needed in the basis of preparation in order for the nature of the historical financial information to be clearly understood. The description would be expected to give a general indication of the process adopted for the preparation of the historical financial information, and describe any factors which are particularly important to an understanding of the manner in which the information has been prepared.

31

The accounting policies to be adopted in the carve out accounts will need to reflect the requirements relating to the presentation of historical financial information and may differ from those previously adopted. The question of functional currency is also considered having regard to the economic environment of the carve out business, which may lead to the adoption of a different functional currency from that of the overall group.

32

Allocations

33 Where transactions or balances are not accounted for within the overall group in a manner which clearly attributes them to the carve out business, it will generally be desirable for a method for allocating the relevant amounts to the carve out business to be identified with a view to providing the fairest approximation to the amounts actually attributable to the carve out business. The method adopted is applied on a rational and consistent basis. It will not, however, be appropriate to make allocations where there is no rational or consistent basis for doing so.

Bases for allocating transactions and balances

34 The appropriate basis for allocating group income and expenditure to a carve out business will vary according to the circumstances. It may, for example, be appropriate to allocate centrally accounted-for human resources costs on the basis of headcount (but account might be taken also of relative levels of staff turnover or other factors which indicate greater or less than average use in deciding whether the approach was in fact appropriate). The costs of a head office accounts department might be allocated by reference to the relevant sizes of the carve out business and remaining group. Again if other factors suggest that size is not a good indicator – if for example a disproportionate number of the accounting team are engaged in work for one part of the business and not the other – refinements to the approach might be considered appropriate.

35 It is important to recognise that the purpose of the allocation is to attribute an appropriate element of the overall group record to the carve out business. As a consequence, the position shown will frequently not be that which might have existed if the carve out business had been a stand-alone business. The position will be affected by the arrangements which apply to the group as a whole, which are a matter of historical fact and which it is not the purpose of the carve out financial information to alter. Frequently, disclosure will be made accompanying the financial information highlighting that the information presented may not be representative of the position which may prevail after the transaction.

36 Where an element of overall group third party debt is to be assumed by the carve out business, it may be appropriate to allocate an appropriate element of such debt to the carve out business during the historical track record period. The basis for such an allocation may be by reference to the terms of the separation agreement. In other cases, the debt may be treated as part of the carve out business' balance with the overall group. Finance lease borrowings would be expected to be allocated in line with the allocation of the related asset. The allocation of interest income/costs would follow the way in which the related debt and debt instruments have been apportioned.

Relationship with the remaining group

37 In addition to transactions with 'third parties', the results of the business will also include transactions with the part of the overall group which is not part of the carve out business (the "remaining group"). Hence, for example, sales which were previously regarded as 'intra group' will need to be re-examined to determine whether they relate to entities within the carve out business or outside it.

38 The remaining group will normally also be regarded as a related party for the purposes of disclosing related party transactions, and it will normally be necessary to identify the extent of the relationships between the carve out business and

the remaining group. Balances with the remaining group may have comprised elements of trading balances and short term or long term funding balances, which may or may not have been interest bearing. Balances of a trading nature will normally be presented as an element of debtors or creditors. Balances which are considered to be funding in nature (having regard inter alia to the use made of the balances, the period for which they remain outstanding and the level of other capital) will normally be classified according to their general nature. Where the balance is interest bearing and has other characteristics of debt, it will be presented in the manner of debt financing. Where the balance does not have the characteristics of debt, it will be re-classified from creditors into capital and be presented in the manner of equity, typically aggregated with the share capital and reserves of companies comprising the carve out business, as 'parent company net investment' in the carve out business.

Balances with the remaining group may also contain elements of third party debtors or creditors which have been accounted for on behalf of the carve out business by the remaining group. Examples might be VAT costs, payroll taxes, certain customers or suppliers common to the carve out business and the remaining group, and external funding balances. Such elements of the balance with the remaining group would be expected to be reallocated to the appropriate third party captions. 39

Consolidation journals within the overall group accounting records will need to be analysed and, if appropriate, allocated to the carve out business. 40

Pension costs

Where employees of the carve out business participate in a pension scheme relating to the overall group, the track record of the carve out business would reflect the apportioned costs applicable to the carve out business. The accounting implications of any pension surplus/deficit attributable to the carve out business would also normally be expected to be reflected in the track record. 41

Acquisitions

Acquisitions will be treated in accordance with the guidance in paragraphs 50 to 52 of this Annexure. It should be noted that acquisitions previously regarded as too small for separate disclosure in the overall group accounts may become sufficiently material to require separate disclosure in the context of the carve out business. 42

Disposals, non recurring and exceptional items

Non recurring and exceptional items are generally allocated to the carve out business and accounted for in accordance with the applicable accounting standard. The treatment of disposals follows that described in paragraph 53 of this Annexure. 43

Taxation

Tax charges are generally allocated to the carve out business to reflect the proportion of the overall group charge attributable to the carve out business. The approach will typically involve the aggregation of the tax charges actually incurred by the companies within the carve out business (and will therefore reflect 44 the benefits, reliefs and charges arising as a result of membership of the overall group), after taking account of the tax effects of any adjustments. Where the information relating to the tax charges actually incurred is not available, the tax charge may be recomputed on the basis of the results of the carve out business. The tax rate applied is selected having regard to the tax position of the overall group and might thus include the impact of benefits, reliefs and charges arising as a result of membership of the overall group, to the extent that they would have been available to or imposed upon the carve out business.

Cash flow statements

45 A cash flow statement is prepared for the carve out business based on the carve out information. Where the overall group operates a central cash account, cash flows relating to centrally settled costs are allocated to the carve out business to the extent that the related balances are allocated to the carve out business.

Investments in subsidiaries, joint ventures and associates

46 The status of an entity in the overall group's accounts (that is, whether it is recorded as a subsidiary, joint venture or associate) may be the result of investments in the relevant entity by more than one group company. If not all the investing companies are to be part of the carve out business, this may mean that the status of the entity in the track record of the carve out business is different from that within the overall group. Additional or new disclosures may therefore be required.

Treatment of other items

47 Dividends are expected to be reflected in the track record of the carve out business where companies within the carve out business have paid dividends to members of the remaining group.

48 In relation to the disclosure of directors' remuneration, it is normal to present information for those individuals who are to be directors of the carve out business or who were employed by the overall group in a capacity equivalent to that of a director of the carve out business. The information disclosed will reflect the salaries and benefits paid in respect of services to the carve out business by any member of the overall group to those individuals (irrespective of whether the individuals were directors or not) during the period covered by the track record. No information is presented for proposed directors of the carve out business who were not employed by the overall group, or for individuals who served as directors of companies within the carve out group but who are not to be directors of the carve out group's holding company following the transaction.

49 A segmental analysis is prepared for the carve out business to reflect the segments which the carve out business has decided to adopt.

Acquisitions

50 Entities acquired during the period covered by the historical financial information will typically be accounted for, in the records of the acquiring entity, in accordance with the accounting treatment applicable, having regard to the set of accounting standards adopted. Hence, for example, if the accounting standards

require acquisition accounting, the acquired subsidiary will be accounted for from the date of acquisition by the acquiring entity.

Chapter 13 of the Listing Rules states that, in the case of a Class 1 acquisition when, during the three year period to be covered by the historical financial information (or in the lesser period up to the date of the acquisition if the target's business has been in operation for less than 3 years), the target has acquired or has agreed to acquire an undertaking which would have been classified, at the date of the acquisition, as a Class 1 acquisition, financial information on that undertaking must be given, which covers as a minimum the period from the beginning of the three year period to the date of acquisition. 51

Generally (and typically where the acquisition has been or will be accounted for under the acquisition method), the requirement outlined in paragraph 50 of this Annexure leads to a separate table of historical financial information covering the results of the acquired subsidiary undertaking during the period prior to acquisition. The Listing Rules contain no express contents requirements for acquisitions which would have been classified as smaller than Class 1 (ie a Class 2 or Class 3 transaction), although Listing Rule 13.3 contains contents requirements applicable to all circulars. Additional financial information may be required where the financial information presented in the entity's own track record does not account for substantially all of the track record of the business during the three year period. 52

Disposals

Disposals of subsidiaries or a discontinuation of a material section of the business are reflected by separate analysis between the continuing business and the disposed or discontinued business, either under the relevant headings in the profit and loss table or in the notes to the historical financial information. It is not normally appropriate to make adjustments to eliminate the results of subsidiaries that have been disposed of or discontinued operations from the trading record. However, it may not be necessary to introduce the results of a subsidiary that has been disposed of or a discontinued operation into specially prepared consolidated accounts or combined accounts prepared having regard to the considerations set out in paragraphs 25 to 49 of this Annexure, unless the inclusion of such information is relevant to an understanding of the business to which the historical financial information relates. 53

Financial information on newly formed issuers

In many cases, investment circulars are prepared in relation to newly formed companies (for example start up businesses, investment trusts, newly formed holding companies etc). Generally such companies will not have prepared accounts for a financial year at the time the investment circular is to be issued and consequently financial statements will need to be prepared for the purposes of the investment circular. 54

Unincorporated entities and entities producing limited accounting information

Acquisitions may involve entities which do not prepare financial information which meets the standards required for statutory accounts in the UK (and additionally may not have been subject to the disciplines of an external audit). The accounting conventions adopted may be devised for internal management 55 accounting purposes rather than to meet more generally applicable accounting standards. In such cases, it may not be possible to present financial information meeting the requirements of the relevant regulations. The decision as to what information to present will depend upon the degree to which the information can be regarded as sufficiently relevant and reliable having regard to the purpose for which it is presented. Frequently the purpose will be to assist shareholders in a decision; it is for those responsible for the investment circular to weigh up the balance between depriving shareholders of information which may be relevant to a decision and being satisfied that the information presented is of sufficient quality to be properly used as the basis for a decision. Where there is significant doubt about the quality of the financial information available, those responsible for the investment circular would be advised not to present it in the investment circular. This may lead to very limited financial information appearing in the relevant investment circular. In the case of an investment circular regulated by the UK Listing Authority, the position should be discussed in advance with the UK Listing Authority.

Changes in the legal form of entities

56 There may be circumstances where businesses have been carried on during the period covered by the report by different legal entities with the consequence that the relevant financial information may be found in the accounts of different legal entities. A typical example is a management buy-out, where prior to the buy-out, the business might have been accounted for in the financial statements of a subsidiary undertaking of the vendor, but, following the buy-out, the financial information may be that of the entity formed to effect the acquisition.

57 In cases where the legal entity accounting for the business has changed (for example where a business has been transferred from one entity to another – typically a newly formed company) but where there is no essential change in the underlying business, it is normal for the financial information to be presented as part of a single table, with the results of the predecessor entity shown next to those of the successor entity (generally on a combined basis in the period during which the transaction took place).

58 A consequence of the change in legal entity may be a change in the capital structure. Frequently, where there is a management buy-out, debt becomes a significant part of the capitalisation of the business. In order to highlight for the reader the potential lack of comparability between periods, a statement is often included within the introduction or beneath the profit and loss account (and in the relevant notes) referring to the change in capital structure and alerting the reader to the fact that the information relating to financing costs may not be comparable throughout the period. In certain cases, where the effect is material to an appreciation of the figures, it may also be necessary to draw attention to a discontinuity in values attributed to balance sheet items. In circumstances where, as in the case of a management buy-out, fair value adjustments have been made during the period covered by the historical financial information, it is inappropriate to attempt to show the impact of such adjustments on the results prior to the acquisition.

However, the impact of the fair value adjustments is, where practicable, highlighted in respect of the post-acquisition results.

Earnings per share

In cases where there has been a capital reorganisation since the date at which the last balance sheet was drawn up, it will usually be appropriate for the earnings per share figures disclosed to be adjusted to reflect the reorganisation (to the extent that it involves issues of shares for no consideration, issues containing a bonus element, share splits etc). In such cases, the number of shares used in the earnings per share calculation is adjusted so that the shares originally in issue are replaced by the number of new shares, representing the shares originally in issue, following the reorganisation. Where shares have been issued during the period, this is taken into account in calculating the equivalent weighted average number of post-reorganisation shares. Where the reconstruction involves conversions, for example of preference shares or loan stock, the earnings figures used in the calculation of earnings per share may also need to be adjusted to eliminate the effect of any related preference dividends or interest. 59

Difficulties may also arise over the relevance of the earnings per share figure in certain cases, for example where prior to flotation a new holding company has been created. In such cases an earnings per share figure based on the share capital of the subsidiary may be of limited significance to investors. Accordingly, it is usually appropriate to include a supplementary earnings per share figure, in addition to the historical earnings per share figure, based on the relevant number of shares in the new parent company (before the issue of shares to raise new funds). This approach is also generally adopted in the case of a carve out business which did not have share capital during the reporting period. Where the effect is material and where practicable, the number of shares used for the purposes of the calculation is adjusted to reflect variations in the levels of capital funding the operations arising, for example, from issues of equity for cash during the period under review. In some circumstances, such as where there has been a management buy out during the period reported on, the differences in the capital structure may be such that a comparison of the earnings per share figures is not meaningful. Where this is the case, the statement to be included beneath the profit and loss table mentioned above generally refers also to the lack of comparability of the earnings per share information. 60

Reporting currency

Where historical financial information is to be presented on a target entity, and that target has reported historically in a currency other than that of the acquiring entity, it is normal to present the financial information in the target's original reporting currency. 61

Extraction without material adjustment

In a Class 1 circular, the listed company must (in addition to citing the source of the information) state whether the financial information that has been extracted from audited accounts was extracted without material adjustment. It is not possible to prescribe conditions for determining whether an adjustment will be a material adjustment in any given case, although presentational changes which do not have the effect of altering net assets, are normally permitted to be made. The UK Listing Authority will need to agree the approach in individual cases. 62

[3000]
Investment reporting standards applicable to public reporting engagements on profit forecasts

Contents

	Paragraphs
Introduction	1 - 5
The nature of profit forecasts	6 - 17
Reliability	*13 - 14*
Understandability	*15*
Comparability	*16*
Compilation process	*17*
Engagement acceptance and continuance	18 - 19
Agreeing the terms of the engagement	20
Ethical requirements	21
Legal and regulatory requirements	22 - 24
Quality control	25
Planning and performing the engagement	26 - 61
Materiality	*34 - 38*
Public reporting engagement risk	*39 - 45*
Historical financial information	*46 - 50*
Consistent accounting policies	*51 - 53*
Presentation of the profit forecast	*54 - 59*
Representation letter	*60 - 61*
Documentation	62
Professional scepticism	63
Reporting	64 - 73
Responsibilities	*65*
Basis of preparation of the profit forecast	*66 - 67*
Basis of opinion	*68 - 70*
Expression of opinion	*71 - 73*
Modified opinions	74 - 77
Consent	78 - 79

Public reporting engagements on profit forecasts 3000 817

Events occurring between the date of the reporting accountant's report and the completion date of the transaction 80 - 83

Effective date 84

Appendices

1 The regulatory background
2 Reporting accountant's criteria
3 Other regulatory provisions relevant to the preparers of profit forecasts
4 Examples of engagement letter clauses
5 Examples of management representation letter clauses
6 Example of a report on a profit forecast
7 Example of a report on a profit estimate that is not subject to assumptions

Investment reporting standards applicable to public reporting engagements on profit forecasts

SIR 3000 contains basic principles and essential procedures ("Investment Reporting Standards"), indicated by paragraphs in bold type, with which a reporting accountant is required to comply in the conduct of an engagement to report on a profit forecast which is included within an investment circular prepared for issue in connection with a securities transaction governed wholly or in part by the law and regulations of the United Kingdom.

SIR 3000 also includes explanatory and other material, including appendices, in the context of which the basic principles and essential procedures are to be understood and applied. It is necessary to consider the whole text of the SIR to understand and apply the basic principles and essential procedures.

For the purposes of SIRs, an investment circular is defined as: "any document issued by an entity pursuant to statutory or regulatory requirements relating to listed or unlisted securities on which it is intended that a third party should make an investment decision, including a prospectus, listing particulars, circular to shareholders or similar document".

SIR 1000 "Investment reporting standards applicable to all engagements involving an investment circular" contains basic principles and essential procedures that are applicable to all engagements involving an investment circular. The definitions in the Glossary of terms set out in Appendix 4 of SIR 1000 are to be applied in the interpretation of this and all other SIRs. Terms defined in the glossary are underlined the first time that they occur in the text.

To assist readers, SIRs contain references to, and extracts from, certain legislation and chapters of the Rules of the UK Listing Authority. Readers are cautioned that these references may change subsequent to publication.

Introduction

1 Standard for Investment Reporting (SIR) 1000 "Investment Reporting Standards applicable to all engagements in connection with an investment circular" establishes the Investment Reporting Standards applicable to all engagements involving investment circulars. The purpose of this SIR is to establish specific additional Investment Reporting Standards and provide guidance for a reporting accountant engaged to report publicly on profit forecasts to be included in an investment circular under the PD Regulation, other regulations with similar requirements[1], the City Code, or if required by the London Stock Exchange in respect of an AIM Admission Document.

2 An engagement to report publicly on the proper compilation of a profit forecast is a public reporting engagement as described in SIR 1000. The description of a public reporting engagement includes three generic terms having the following meanings in the context of an engagement to report on the proper compilation of a profit forecast:

---

[1] *In the UK the Prospectus Directive is implemented into law through amendments to Part VI of FSMA and to certain secondary legislation. The Annexes to the PD Regulation have been incorporated into the Prospectus Rules issued by the FSA..*

(a) with respect to a profit forecast the "**subject matter**" is the directors' expectation of the issuer's profit for the period of the forecast;
(b) "**suitable criteria**" to be used by directors in the preparation of the profit forecast are provided by the requirements of the PD Regulation and the guidance[2] issued by CESR (CESR Recommendations). In forming its opinion as to whether the profit forecast has been properly compiled the reporting accountant considers whether certain of those criteria ("**reporting accountant's criteria**") have been properly applied. Reporting accountant's criteria are set out in Appendix 2 of this SIR; and
(c) with respect to a profit forecast the "**outcome**"[3] is the directors' profit forecast and related disclosures, that is included in the investment circular, and on which the reporting accountant expresses an opinion (in the "**reporting accountant's report**") as to whether that forecast is properly compiled on the basis stated and the basis of accounting used is consistent with the accounting policies of the issuer.

The PD Regulation defines a profit forecast as "a form of words which expressly states or by implication indicates a figure or a minimum or maximum figure for the likely level of profits or losses for the current financial period and/or financial periods subsequent to that period, or contains data from which a calculation of such a figure for future profits or losses may be made, even if no particular figure is mentioned and the word "profit" is not used"[4]. Where a profit forecast relates to an extended period and/or is subject to significant uncertainty it is sometimes referred to as a projection. 3

A profit forecast may include historical financial information relating to a past period. For example, a forecast made on 15 October 20xx for the profit for the year ended 31 December 20xx may include the profit for the six months ended 30 June 20xx included in the issuer's half yearly report and amounts extracted from management accounts for July and August. A profit estimate is historical financial information for a financial period which has expired but for which the results have not yet been published. 4

In this SIR requirements relating to "profit forecasts" also apply to statements typically referred to as "profit estimates" or "projections". The Investment Circular Reporting Standards in this SIR are applied to the whole period of the profit forecast including historical financial information included therein. 5

The nature of profit forecasts

A profit forecast is, by definition, uncertain because events and circumstances may not occur as expected or may not be predicted at all, or because the directors may take actions different to those previously intended. A profit forecast will usually include disclosures which provide information to assist the intended users understand the uncertainties involved. 6

A profit forecast is usually based on assumptions, relating to the expected outcome of future events and possible actions by the entity. As assumptions on which any forward-looking element of a profit forecast is based are a critical element of the 7

---

[2] CESR issued "CESR's Recommendations for the Consistent Implementation of the European Commission's Regulation on Prospectuses No. 809/2004" in February 2005.

[3] The "outcome" is sometimes described as "subject matter information".

[4] The definition of a profit forecast in the City Code is similar to that used by the PD Regulation.

profit forecast, the various regulations require, among other things, the disclosure of the principal assumptions which could have a material effect on the achievement of the profit forecast including those within the influence and control of the directors.

8   The extent to which a profit forecast will differ materially from the actual out-turn will depend on a profit forecast's particular circumstances. The length of the period into the future to which the profit forecast relates is only one, and not necessarily the most significant, factor. For example, an established business may be able to predict with greater certainty its results for the following year, particularly if it operates in a very stable environment, than a start-up business or an established business entering a new field.

9   Profit forecasts are inherently uncertain and the probability that a profit forecast will correctly predict the actual out-turn is dependent upon the many factors which determine that uncertainty. The fact that a profit forecast does not correctly predict the actual out-turn does not mean that the profit forecast was not properly compiled.

10 The Institute of Chartered Accountants in England and Wales issued guidance entitled "Prospective Financial Information – Guidance for UK directors" in September 2003 ("ICAEW Guidance") to assist directors in meeting the needs of the intended users of such information and of regulators and to promote the production of high quality prospective financial information, including profit forecasts.

11 As explained in Appendix 1 of this SIR the CESR Recommendations state that profit forecasts should be:

   (a) reliable;
   (b) understandable;
   (c) comparable; and
   (d) relevant.

Directors are required to form a judgment as to whether the profit forecast is relevant to the purpose of the investment circular[5] and, therefore, whether or not it is appropriate for the profit forecast to be included in the investment circular. The directors' judgment in this regard will be influenced by the applicable regulatory requirements. The role of the reporting accountant is to report on whether a profit forecast, that the directors have decided to include in an investment circular, has been properly compiled. The role of the reporting accountant does not include questioning the directors' decision to include a profit forecast in an investment circular.

12 In order to provide an opinion on the proper compilation of a profit forecast the reporting accountant carries out the procedures required by this SIR and SIR 1000, and any others it considers necessary, to satisfy itself that the profit forecast is:

   (a) reliable[6];

---

[5] The ICAEW Guidance considers that a profit forecast will only be "relevant" if it:
   (a) has the ability to influence economic decisions of investors;
   (b) is provided in time to influence the economic decisions of investors; and
   (c) has predictive value or, by helping to confirm or correct past evaluations or assessments, it has confirmatory value.

[6] The business analysis principle in the ICAEW Guidance.

(b) understandable[7]; and
(c) comparable[8].

Consequently, these three principles are considered to be suitable criteria for the evaluation of profit forecasts by the reporting accountant (see Appendix 2 of this SIR).

Reliability

The ICAEW Guidance explains that to be **reliable** a profit forecast will possess the following attributes:

(a) it can be depended upon by the intended users as a faithful representation of what it either purports to represent or could reasonably be expected to represent;
(b) it is neutral because it is free from deliberate or systematic bias intended to influence a decision or judgment to achieve a predetermined result;
(c) it is free from material error;
(d) it is complete within the bounds of what is material; and
(e) it is prudent in that a degree of caution is applied in making judgments under conditions of uncertainty.

The ICAEW Guidance explains that a profit forecast will be a faithful representation where it reflects an entity's strategies, plans and risk analysis in a way that is appropriate for the purpose for which the profit forecast is being prepared. The fact that a profit forecast does not correctly predict the actual out-turn once reported, does not necessarily mean that it was not reliable when made.

A profit forecast, including the assumptions used, is more likely to possess the above attributes when the issuer has undertaken an analysis of the underlying business and its strategies, plans and risks (the directors' business analysis) and when the forecast is prepared as a faithful representation of that business analysis, taking prudent account of the risk analysis. The reliability of a profit forecast is, therefore, a function of: 14

(a) the quality of the analysis undertaken; and
(b) the degree to which that analysis is reflected in the profit forecast.

Understandability

To be **understandable** a profit forecast contains the information necessary for intended users to appreciate the degree of uncertainty attaching to the information and how that uncertainty might impact it. This requires the disclosure of assumptions and other matters relevant to the basis of preparation of the profit forecast which are of importance in assisting the intended users' understanding of the profit forecast. The omission of important information may prevent a profit forecast from being understandable and equally, if the disclosure is too complex or too extensive the understandability of the profit forecast may be also impaired. What constitutes reasonable disclosure will therefore depend upon the particular circumstances of each profit forecast but will need to take into consideration: 15

---

[7] *The reasonable disclosure principle in the ICAEW Guidance.*

[8] *The subsequent validation principle in the ICAEW Guidance.*

(a) sources of uncertainty and the related assumptions made relating to uncertainties;
(b) the factors that will affect whether assumptions will be borne out in practice; and
(c) alternative outcomes, being the consequences of assumptions not being borne out.

Comparability

16   The usefulness of a profit forecast is derived partly from its **comparability**, namely the expectation that it will be possible to compare it to the actual results and that it can be compared to equivalent information for other reporting periods. For this to be the case profit forecasts need to be prepared and presented on a basis comparable with the actual financial information for that period and will involve the application of the accounting policies used by the entity in preparing the historical financial information included in the investment circular.

Compilation process

17   The compilation of a profit forecast is the gathering, classification and summarisation of relevant financial information. The process followed by the preparer would be expected to include:

(a) an appropriate analysis of the business (what is appropriate will depend on a number of factors including the complexity and predictability of the business and the length of the period being forecast and accordingly the content, degree of detail and presentation of such analyses may vary significantly);
(b) identification of material uncertainties;
(c) selection of appropriate assumptions;
(d) where relevant, identification of and reference to, appropriate third party information (eg. market research reports);
(e) arithmetic computation of the profit forecast;
(f) appropriate sensitivity analysis;
(g) appropriate disclosures to enable the intended users to understand the profit forecast; and
(h) appropriate consideration of the profit forecast and approval of it by the directors of the entity.

Engagement acceptance and continuance

18   SIR 1000.1 and SIR 1000.2 set out the basic principles and essential procedures, with respect to engagement acceptance and continuance, which are applicable to all engagements involving an investment circular.

19   When accepting or continuing an engagement to report publicly on a profit forecast, the reporting accountant ascertains whether the directors intend to comply with all relevant regulatory requirements, in particular those that are the basis of the reporting accountant's criteria set out in Appendix 2 of this SIR.

Agreeing the terms of the engagement

20 SIR 1000.3 and SIR 1000.4 set out the basic principles and essential procedures with respect to agreeing the terms of the engagement. Examples of engagement letter clauses are set out in Appendix 4 of this SIR.

Ethical requirements

21 SIR 1000.5 sets out the basic principles and essential procedures with respect to the ethical requirements that apply to a reporting accountant[9].

Legal and regulatory requirements

22 The PD Regulation requires any profit forecast or estimate included in a prospectus to be reported on by independent accountants or auditors (referred to in this SIR as "a reporting accountant") and specifies the form of opinion to be given[10]. The City Code contains provisions in relation to profit forecasts included in offer documents and requires reports from the auditors or reporting accountants in certain circumstances.

23 SIR 1000.6 sets out the basic principles with respect to the legal and regulatory requirements applicable to a reporting accountant.

24 Appendices 1, 2 and 3 to this SIR set out those provisions of the PD Regulation, the CESR Recommendations relating to the implementation of the PD Regulation, and the City Code, that provide the suitable criteria for directors. Those provisions that are the basis of criteria for a reporting accountant expressing an opinion on whether the profit forecast has been properly compiled are set out in Appendix 2 of this SIR.

Quality control

25 SIR 1000.7 and SIR 1000.8 set out the basic principles and essential procedures with respect to the quality control of engagements to report on profit forecasts.

Planning and performing the engagement

26 SIR 1000.9 and SIR 1000.10 set out the basic principles and essential procedures with respect to the planning of all reporting engagements. Additional essential procedures and guidance are set out below.

27 **The reporting accountant should obtain an understanding of the key factors affecting the subject matter sufficient to identify and assess the risk of the profit forecast not being properly compiled and sufficient to design and perform evidence gathering procedures including:**

(a) the background to and nature of the circumstances in which the profit forecast, which is included in the investment circular, was made;

---

[9] *In January 2006 the APB issued an Exposure Draft of an Ethical Standard for Reporting Accountants (ESRA).*

[10] *The PD Regulation requirements are reproduced verbatim in the Prospectus Rules issued by the FSA.*

(b) the entity's business; and
(a) the procedures adopted, or planned to be adopted, by the directors for the preparation of the profit forecast. (SIR 3000.1)

28 The reporting accountant gains an understanding of the background to and nature of the circumstances in which the profit forecast is being prepared, by discussion with the directors or management of the issuer and by reading relevant supporting documentation. In particular, the reporting accountant ascertains whether the profit forecast is being made for the first time or whether it is a forecast that has previously been made by the issuer that may be required to be updated by the directors.

29 The reporting accountant uses professional judgment to determine the extent of the understanding required of the entity's business. In a start-up situation or where an established business is entering a new field the reporting accountant's understanding of the prospective business is necessarily limited to general knowledge of the field being entered and an understanding of the business analysis undertaken by the entity.

30 Reporting on the proper compilation of a profit forecast generally requires an understanding of the entity's management accounting, budgeting and forecasting systems and procedures beyond that normally considered necessary for an audit of historical financial statements.

31 Discussion with the preparers of a profit forecast will identify the process by which the profit forecast has been, or will be prepared, the extent to which the ICAEW guidance has been followed, the sources of information used, areas of significant uncertainty where assumptions have been made and the basis for those assumptions and how those assumptions have been documented. Specific matters for consideration include:

- The organisational structure of the entity and the extent to which subsidiaries or local operating units have been involved in the preparation of the profit forecast.
- Whether the profit forecast is prepared on a basis comparable with the most recent historical financial information in the investment circular.
- The extent to which the period of the forecast includes historical financial information.
- Whether the profit forecast will be capable of comparison to subsequently published historical financial information.

32 Where profit forecasts are regularly prepared by the entity either for internal management purposes or for publication, the reporting accountant considers the closeness to actual out-turns achieved in previous forecasts and the analysis of any variances. As well as helping to provide an understanding of the entity's business this may be helpful in identifying those aspects of the business which are subject to significant uncertainty.

33 **The reporting accountant should consider materiality and public reporting engagement risk in planning its work in accordance with its instructions and in determining the effect of its findings on the report to be issued. (SIR 3000.2)**

Materiality

34 The ICAEW Guidance states that in order for a profit forecast to be *reliable* it will, amongst other things, be free of material error. An error in the context of the proper compilation of a profit forecast includes:

- Assumptions that are not consistent with the analysis of the business.
- Mathematical or clerical mistakes in the compilation of the profit forecast.
- Misapplication of accounting policies.
- Misapplication of a stated assumption.
- Known misstatements in historical financial information embodied in the forecast without adjustment.

Additionally, there may be deficiencies in the presentation of a profit forecast which may impair the understandability or comparability of the forecast in a way that is material. An error could, therefore, also include: 35

(a) failure to disclose an assumption or other explanation which is necessary for an understanding of the forecast; or
(b) presenting the forecast in a way that it is not capable of being compared with subsequent published results.

Matters are material if their omission or misstatement could, individually or collectively, influence the economic decisions of the intended users of the profit forecast. Materiality depends on the size and nature of the omission or misstatement judged in light of the surrounding circumstances. The size or nature of the matter, or a combination of both, could be the determining factor. 36

Evaluating whether an omission or misstatement could influence economic decisions of the intended users of the profit forecast, and so be material, requires consideration of the characteristics of those intended users. The intended users are assumed to: 37

(a) have a reasonable knowledge of business and economic activities and accounting and a willingness to study the profit forecast with reasonable diligence; and
(b) make reasonable economic decisions on the basis of the profit forecast.

The determination of materiality, therefore, takes into account how intended users with such characteristics could reasonably be expected to be influenced in making economic decisions.

The fact that the out-turn differs from the forecast does not necessarily mean that the forecast was not properly compiled as, for example, actual economic conditions may have differed from those reasonably assumed in the preparation of the profit forecast. 38

Public reporting engagement risk

"Public reporting engagement risk" is the risk that the reporting accountant expresses the positive and unmodified opinion required by the PD Regulation or the City Code when the profit forecast has not been properly compiled on the basis stated or the basis of accounting used for the profit forecast is not consistent with the accounting policies of the issuer. 39

SIR 1000.11 and SIR 1000.12 set out the basic principles and essential procedures, with respect to obtaining evidence, that are applicable to all engagements involving an investment circular. Additional basic principles, essential procedures and guidance relating to engagements to report on profit forecasts are set out below. 40

To form an opinion that the profit forecast has been properly compiled, the reporting accountant should obtain sufficient appropriate evidence that the forecast is free from material error in its compilation by: 41

(a) obtaining evidence that the directors have applied the criteria set out in Appendix 2 of this SIR;
(b) checking that the profit forecast has been accurately computed based upon the disclosed assumptions and the preparer's accounting policies;
(c) considering whether the assumptions used are consistent with the directors' business analysis and the reporting accountant's own knowledge of the business; and
(d) where applicable, evaluating the basis on which any historical financial information included in the profit forecast has been prepared. (SIR 3000.3)

42 The reporting accountant considers the business analysis carried out by the preparer of the profit forecast and whether there is prima facie evidence that it has been used by the directors in compiling the profit forecast. The extent and nature of the analysis that is necessary to support a forecast, and therefore the extent of the reporting accountant's consideration of such analysis, will be dependent upon the specific circumstances in which the forecast is being prepared. The reporting accountant discusses the preparer's plans, strategies and risk analysis with the preparer of the profit forecast, considers documentary support for them and assesses whether they are consistent with the analysis of the business. Where the outcome is dependent upon the intent of the directors and management the reporting accountant will ordinarily obtain representations from the directors concerning such matters.

43 The preparer can be expected to document the assumptions that have been made relating to matters significant to the profit forecast. The reporting accountant will, therefore, obtain from preparers of the profit forecast details of those assumptions identified as being relevant to the compilation of the profit forecast. It will usually be the case that not all of the assumptions made in support of the profit forecast will be published. This is because only those that are material to an understanding of the profit forecast are required to be disclosed.

44 There may be a range of appropriate assumptions which can be used as the basis for a profit forecast and the resulting forecast may differ significantly depending on which assumptions are adopted. The reporting accountant is not required to express an opinion on the appropriateness of the assumptions used or the achievability of the results reflected in a profit forecast. The reporting accountant does however:

(a) consider if any of the assumptions adopted by the directors which, in the opinion of the reporting accountant are necessary for a proper understanding of the profit forecast, have not been adequately disclosed; and
(b) consider whether any material assumption made by the directors appears to be unrealistic.

45 When checking whether the profit forecast has been accurately computed the reporting accountant considers whether cash flow statements and balance sheets have been prepared to act as checks against omissions and inconsistencies. If cash flow statements and balance sheets have not been prepared, in circumstances where the reporting accountant considers this to be necessary, the reporting accountant discusses with the directors whether their preparation is necessary in order to properly compile the profit forecast.

Historical financial information

46 When evaluating the basis on which any historical financial information included in the profit forecast has been prepared the reporting accountant should:

(a) consider whether any element of that historical financial information has been audited or reviewed by the auditors and, if so, the results of that audit or review;

(b) evaluate the suitability of unaudited historical financial information included in the profit forecast;
(c) evaluate how the historical financial information has been embodied into the profit forecast; and
(d) if adjustments have been made to previously published historical financial information evaluate whether the adjustments appear appropriate in the circumstances. (SIR 3000.4)

If historical financial information has been audited or reviewed the reporting accountant evaluates the scope of the audit or review procedures performed. In performing such an evaluation the reporting accountant ordinarily seeks access to the working papers of the auditor or reviewer and considers whether the results of those procedures indicate that the historical financial information may be unreliable or reveal uncertainties that ought to require the directors to make and disclose assumptions in the forecast. 47

In order to evaluate the suitability of unaudited historical financial information included in the profit forecast the reporting accountant[11]: 48

(a) understands the internal control environment of the entity relevant to the historical financial information;
(b) discusses with the management of the issuer the accounting policies applied and any differences from the method of preparing the entity's published financial statements;
(c) enquires of management, including internal audit, whether there have been any changes in the financial reporting systems or internal controls, or any breakdowns in systems and controls, which might affect the reliability of the financial information;
(d) enquires about changes in the entity's procedures for recording, classifying and summarising transactions, accumulating information for disclosure, and preparing the financial information;
(e) considers the accuracy of unaudited historical financial information by comparing it to audited financial statements for the same period;
(f) compares the historical financial information to previous budgets or forecasts prepared by the entity in respect of the period covered by the historical financial information and gains an understanding of the reasons for any significant differences; and
(g) checks the historical financial information used in the profit forecast agrees to, or reconciles with, the underlying accounting records of the entity.

Where the reporting accountant determines that it is not able to obtain sufficient appropriate evidence from the above procedures to indicate that the financial information for the expired part of the forecast period forms a suitable basis for inclusion in the profit forecast the reporting accountant discusses the matter with the directors of the issuer and, if appropriate, the issuer's advisers. 49

In considering historical financial information included in a profit forecast, it is important that the reporting accountant understands the manner in which such information has been included in the profit forecast. Where different systems or processes have been used to produce prospective financial information and the historical information, there is a risk that there may be inconsistencies in the cut-off between these two sources of information which could lead to a material error in the compilation of the profit forecast. 50

---

[11] *Some of these procedures may already have been performed as part of a review.*

Consistent accounting policies

51   The reporting accountant should compare the accounting policies used in connection with the profit forecast with those used by the entity in preparing the most recent historical financial information in the investment circular, and evaluate whether they are consistent with each other and continue to be appropriate so far as concerns the profit forecast. (SIR 3000.5)

52   Where the profit forecast relates to the expansion of an existing business the reporting accountant's primary consideration is the consistency of the accounting policies used. However, the reporting accountant also considers the ongoing appropriateness of the accounting policies in the light of the business plans underlying the profit forecast.

53   Where the profit forecast relates to a start-up situation the reporting accountant considers the appropriateness of the accounting policies chosen.

Presentation of the profit forecast

54   The reporting accountant should consider whether it has become aware of anything to cause it to believe that:
   (a)   the profit forecast is presented in a way that is not understandable;
   (b)   a material assumption is unrealistic;
   (c)   an assumption or other information which appears to it to be material to a proper understanding of the profit forecast has not been disclosed; or
   (d)   the profit forecast is not capable of subsequently being compared with historical financial information.

   If the reporting accountant is aware of such matters it should discuss them with the parties responsible for the profit forecast and with those persons to whom its report is to be addressed and consider whether it is able to issue its opinion. (SIR 3000.6)

55   The ICAEW Guidance provides guidance to directors with regard to the matters that should be disclosed in connection with a profit forecast. This covers both the manner in which the profit forecast is presented and the use of disclosure to deal with uncertainty. It is important that useful information is not obscured through the inclusion of immaterial items or the use of headings or financial measures which are not meaningful to, or may be misunderstood by, the intended users.

56   When evaluating the presentation of a profit forecast the reporting accountant considers whether the components of the profit forecast are clearly described and whether the descriptions are adequate to allow an intended user to understand the profit forecast. For example, if a profit forecast is presented as a single figure for profit before tax, and this was to be achieved by the inclusion of a significant non-recurring profit from the sale of a fixed asset, consideration is given as to whether additional disclosure is necessary to make the profit forecast understandable.

57   When evaluating whether the disclosures made in respect of a profit forecast are sufficient to make it understandable, the reporting accountant considers whether the degree of uncertainty inherent in the information is clearly disclosed. Disclosure of an assumption may not make the profit forecast understandable if the significance of that assumption is not apparent from the disclosure made.

58   Where a profit forecast is subject to significant uncertainty it is common practice for the preparers to perform a sensitivity analysis in respect of those assumptions which

are either believed to be subject to the greatest uncertainty and/or where the profit forecast is most sensitive to variations in such assumptions. The reporting accountant considers such sensitivity analysis, as it may assist in the identification of material assumptions or other aspects of the profit forecast where the uncertainty requires additional disclosure to enable it to be understood.

The manner in which the profit forecast is presented in the investment circular will also be considered in respect of whether the profit forecast is capable of being compared with subsequent historical financial information. The choice of captions and disclosure or emphasis of particular numbers or attributes may determine how the profit forecast will be interpreted and consideration is given as to whether this is consistent with the purpose for which the profit forecast has been prepared. 59

Representation letter

SIR 1000.13 sets out the basic principles and essential procedures, with respect to representation letters, that are applicable to all engagements involving an investment circular. Examples of representation letter clauses are set out in Appendix 5 of this SIR. 60

Some of the assumptions used in the compilation of a profit forecast will be dependent on the intent of the directors and management. Consequently the representations of directors and management as to their intent are a particularly important source of evidence for the reporting accountant. 61

Documentation

SIR 1000.14 and SIR 1000.15 set out the basic principles and essential procedures with respect to the reporting accountant's working papers. 62

Professional scepticism

SIR 1000.16 sets out the basic principle with respect to the attitude of professional scepticism adopted by the reporting accountant in planning and performing an engagement. 63

Reporting

SIR 1000.17, SIR 1000.18 and SIR 1000.19 set out the basic principles and essential procedures, with respect to reporting, that are applicable to all engagements involving an investment circular. Additional basic principles and essential procedures relating to engagements to report on profit forecasts are set out below. 64

Responsibilities

In all reports on profit forecasts in investment circulars the reporting accountant should explain the extent of its responsibility in respect of the profit forecast by including in its report: 65

(a) a statement that the reporting accountant's responsibility is to form an opinion (as required by the relevant regulatory requirement) on the compilation of the profit forecast and to report its opinion to the addressees of the report; and

(b) a statement that the profit forecast and the assumptions on which it is based are the responsibility of the directors. (SIR 3000.7)

Basis of preparation of the profit forecast

66 The reporting accountant should include a basis of preparation section of its report that cross refers to disclosures that explain the basis of preparation of the profit forecast including:

(a) assumptions made;
(b) the accounting policies applied; and
(c) where appropriate, the source of historical financial information embodied in the profit forecast. (SIR 3000.8)

67 Where the entity is reporting on the expansion of an established business it is usual for it to report that the basis of accounting is consistent with the existing accounting policies. Where the accounting policies used in the profit forecast differ from those previously published a more detailed explanation of the accounting policies used in the preparation of the profit forecast will be appropriate.

Basis of opinion

68 SIR 1000.18 sets out the basic principles and essential procedures, with respect to the basis of the reporting accountant's opinion, that are applicable to all engagements involving an investment circular. Additional basic principles and essential procedures relating to engagements to report on profit forecasts are set out below.

69 The reporting accountant should explain the basis of its opinion by including in its report a statement that where the profit forecast and any assumptions on which it is based relate to the future and may, therefore, be affected by unforeseen events, the reporting accountant does not express any opinion as to whether the actual results achieved will correspond to those shown in the profit forecast. (SIR 3000.9)

70 By its nature financial information relating to the future is inherently uncertain. For a profit forecast to be understandable sufficient information must be disclosed to allow an intended user to understand this uncertainty. As the reporting accountant is not required to form or express an opinion on the achievability of the result shown in the profit forecast, it is inappropriate for the reporting accountant to include in the basis of preparation section of its report cautionary language relating to uncertainty beyond that referred to above.

Expression of opinion

71 The report should contain a clear expression of opinion that complies with applicable regulatory requirements. (SIR 3000.10)

72 In forming its opinion the reporting accountant takes account of those events or information which the reporting accountant becomes aware of occurring up to the date on which the reporting accountant signs the report, that affect the opinion expressed in the report.

73 The investment circular in which the reporting accountant's report is included may be made available in other countries, such as the United States of America, which have their own standards for accountants when reporting on profit forecasts. In such circumstances, the reporting accountant considers whether to include a reference to

the fact that a report issued in accordance with the SIRs should not be relied upon as if it had been issued in accordance with the standards applicable in that other country. An example of such a reference is included in the example reports set out in Appendices 6 and 7 of this SIR.

Modified opinions

SIR 1000.20 sets out the basic principles and essential procedures, with respect to modified opinions, that are applicable to all engagements involving an investment circular. Additional basic principles and essential procedures relating to engagements to report on profit forecasts are set out below. 74

The reporting accountant should not express an unmodified opinion when the directors have not applied the criteria set out in Appendix 2 of this SIR and in the reporting accountant's judgment the effect of not doing so is, or may be, material. (SIR 3000.11) 75

The PD and other regulations, such as the City Code, usually require a positive and unmodified opinion. Consequently, in the event that the reporting accountant concludes that it is unable to report in the manner prescribed it invites those responsible for the profit forecast to consider whether the profit forecast can be amended to alleviate its concerns or whether the profit forecast should be omitted from the investment circular. 76

Examples of reports on a profit forecast and a profit estimate expressing such positive and unmodified opinions are set out in Appendices 6 and 7 of this SIR. 77

Consent

SIR 1000.21 and SIR 1000.22 set out the basic principles and essential procedures with respect to the giving of consent by the reporting accountant. 78

The reporting accountant considers whether disclosures in the investment circular, such as those in the "Risk Factors" section, are consistent with the assumptions and other disclosures made in connection with the profit forecast before consent is given by the reporting accountant to its report on the profit forecast being included in the investment circular. 79

Events occurring between the date of the reporting accountant's report and the completion date of the transaction

SIR 1000.23 sets out the basic principles and essential procedures with respect to events occurring between the date of the reporting accountant's report and the completion date of the transaction. 80

Under Sections 81 and 87G of the FSMA, Prospectus Rule 3.4, and Listing Rule 4.4.1, a supplementary investment circular must be prepared if, after the date the investment circular has been formally approved by a regulator and before dealings in the relevant securities commence, the issuer becomes aware that there has been a significant change affecting any matter contained in the document or a significant new matter has arisen, the inclusion of information in respect of which would have been required if it had arisen at the time of its preparation. A similar obligation arises under Article 16 of the Prospectus Directive in respect of the period following 81 registration of the investment circular during which an agreement in respect of the securities can be entered into in pursuance of the offer contained in the investment circular.

82 If, as a result of discussion with those responsible for the investment circular concerning an event that occurred prior to the completion date of the transaction, the reporting accountant is either uncertain about or disagrees with the course of action proposed the reporting accountant may consider it necessary to take legal advice with respect to its responsibilities in the particular circumstances.

83 After the date of its report, the reporting accountant has no obligation to perform procedures or make enquiries regarding the investment circular.

Effective date

84 A reporting accountant is required to comply with the Investment Reporting Standards contained in this SIR for reports signed after 31 March 2006. Earlier adoption is encouraged.

Appendix 1 – The regulatory background

Prospectus Directive Requirements

The **Prospectus Directive** and **PD Regulation** determine the requirements for the content of a prospectus. In determining whether the PD Regulation has been complied with, the FSA will take into account whether a person has complied with the CESR Recommendations.

The PD Regulation requires that where an issuer chooses to include a profit forecast (including a profit estimate) in a prospectus it must:

(a) be prepared on a basis comparable with the historical financial information in the prospectus;
(b) include a statement setting out the principal assumptions upon which the issuer has based its forecast or estimate. There must be a clear distinction between assumptions about factors which the members of the administrative, management or supervisory bodies can influence and assumptions about factors which are exclusively outside the influence of the members of the administrative, management or supervisory bodies; the assumptions must be readily understandable by investors, be specific and precise and not relate to the general accuracy of the estimates underlying the forecast; and
(c) other than for issuers of high denomination debt and derivative securities, include a report prepared by independent accountants or auditors stating that in their opinion the forecast or estimate has been properly compiled on the basis stated and that the basis of accounting used for the profit forecast or estimate is consistent with the accounting policies of the issuer.

The CESR Recommendations provide further guidance concerning the principles that should be applied in preparing a profit forecast in a prospectus. In addition to due care and diligence being taken to ensure that profit forecasts or estimates are not misleading to investors, the following principles should be taken into consideration when profit forecasts are being compiled. Profit forecasts and estimates should be:

(a) *reliable* – they should be supported by a thorough analysis of the issuer's business and should represent factual and not hypothetical strategies, plans and risk analysis; (a criterion for a reporting accountant see Appendix 2 of this SIR)
(b) *understandable* - they should contain disclosure that is not too complex or extensive for investors to understand; (a criterion for a reporting accountant see Appendix 2 of this SIR)
(c) *comparable* – they should be capable of justification by comparison with outcomes in the form of historical financial information (a criterion for a reporting accountant see Appendix 2 of this SIR); and
(d) *relevant* – they must have an ability to influence economic decisions of investors and provided on a timely basis so as to influence such decisions and assist in confirming or correcting past evaluations or assessments. (Not a criterion for a reporting accountant see paragraph 11 of this SIR).

The City Code

The City Code requires that:

(a) all communications to shareholders in an offer, including forecasts, must maintain the highest standard of accuracy and fair presentation;

(b) assumptions should be drafted in a way that allows shareholders to understand their implications; and

(c) the forecast is compiled with due care and consideration by the directors and the disclosure of assumptions should provide useful information to assist shareholders to help them to form a view as to the reasonableness and reliability of the forecast.

Notes 1(c) and (d) to Rule 28.2 of the City Code state:

"The forecast and the assumptions on which it is based are the sole responsibility of the directors. However, a duty is placed on the financial advisers to discuss the assumptions with their client and to satisfy themselves that the forecast has been made with due care and consideration. Auditors or consultant accountants must satisfy themselves that the forecast, so far as the accounting policies and calculations are concerned, has been properly compiled on the basis of the assumptions made.

Although the accountants have no responsibility for the assumptions, they will as a result of their review be in a position to advise the company on what assumptions should be listed in the circular and the way in which they should be described. The financial advisers and accountants obviously have substantial influence on the information about assumptions to be given in the circular; neither should allow an assumption to be published which appears to be unrealistic, or one to be omitted which appears to be important, without commenting appropriately in its report".

Whilst the City Code does not explicitly identify the principles contained in the CESR Recommendations those principles are consistent with the requirement of the Code.

Appendix 2 – Reporting accountant's criteria

PD Regulation	Annex 1[1] of PD Regulation	CESR Recommendations
A statement setting out the principal assumptions upon which the issuer has based its forecast or estimate.	13.1	
There must be a clear distinction between assumptions about factors which the members of the administrative, management or supervisory bodies can influence and assumptions about factors which are exclusively outside the influence of the members of the administrative, management or supervisory bodies; the assumptions must be readily understandable by investors, be specific and precise and not relate to the general accuracy of the estimates underlying the forecast.	13.1	
The profit forecast or estimate must be prepared on a basis comparable with the historical financial information.	13.3	
The following principles should be taken into consideration when profit forecasts or estimates are being compiled. Profit forecasts or estimates should be • **Understandable**, ie Profit forecasts or estimates should contain disclosure that is not too complex or extensive for investors to understand; • **Reliable**, ie Profit forecasts should be supported by a thorough analysis of the issuer's business and should represent factual and not hypothetical strategies, plans and risk analysis; • **Comparable**, ie Profit forecasts or estimates should be capable of justification by comparison with outcomes in the form of historical financial information;		para 41

[1] The column illustrates Annex I as an example. Other annexes to the PD Regulation contain identical requirements with respect to profit forecasts. See Appendix 1 of SIR 1000.

Appendix 3 – Other regulatory provisions relevant to the preparers of profit forecasts

PD Regulation	Annex 1 of PD Regulation	CESR Recommendations
(8) Voluntary disclosure of profit forecasts in a share registration document should be presented in a consistent and comparable manner and accompanied by a statement prepared by independent accountants or auditors. This information should not be confused with the disclosure of known trends or other factual data with material impact on the issuer's prospects. Moreover, they should provide an explanation of any changes in disclosure policy relating to profit forecasts when supplementing a prospectus or drafting a new prospectus. Recital 8		
Profit forecast means a form of words which expressly states or by implication indicates a figure or a minimum or maximum figure for the likely level of profits or losses for the current financial period and/or financial periods subsequent to that period, or contains data from which a calculation of such a figure for future profits or losses may be made, even if no particular figure is mentioned and the word "profit" is not used. Article 2		
Profit estimate means a profit forecast for a financial period which has expired and for which results have not yet been published. Article 2		
If an issuer chooses to include a profit forecast or profit estimate the registration document must contain the information set out in items 13.1 and 13.2.	13	
A report prepared by independent accountants or auditors stating that in the opinion of the independent accountants or auditors the forecast or estimate has been properly compiled on the basis stated and that the basis of accounting used for the profit forecast or estimate is consistent with the accounting policies of the issuer.	13.2	
If a profit forecast in a prospectus has been published which is still outstanding, then provide a statement setting out whether or not that forecast is still correct as at the time of the registration document, and an explanation of why such forecast is no longer valid if that is the case.	13.4	

	PD Regulation	Annex I of PD Regulation	CESR Recommendations
The inclusion of a profit forecast or estimate in a prospectus is the responsibility of the issuer and persons responsible for the prospectus and due care and diligence must be taken to ensure that profit forecasts or estimates are not misleading to investors.			para 40
The following principles should be taken into consideration when profit forecasts or estimates are being compiled. Profit forecasts or estimates should be • **Relevant**, ie profit forecasts and estimates must have an ability to influence economic decisions of investors and provided on a timely basis so as to influence such decisions and assist in confirming or correcting past evaluations or assessments.			para 41
Where an issuer provides a profit forecast or estimate in a registration document, if the related schedules so requires, it must be reported on by independent accountants or auditors in the registration document (as described in item 13.2 of Annex I of the Regulation). Where the issuer does not produce a single prospectus, upon the issuance of the securities note and summary at a later time, the issuer should either: • Confirm the profit forecasts or estimates; or • State that the profit forecasts or estimates are no longer valid or correct; or • Make appropriate alteration of profit forecasts or estimates. In this case they must be reported upon as described in item 13.2 of Annex I of the Regulation.			para 42
If an issuer has made a statement other than in a previous prospectus that would constitute a profit forecast or estimate if made in a prospectus, for instance, in a regulatory announcement, and that statement is still outstanding at the time of publication of the prospectus, the issuer should consider whether the forecasts or estimates are still material and valid and choose whether or not to include them in the prospectus. CESR considers that there is a presumption that an outstanding forecast made other than in a previous prospectus will be material in the case of share issues (especially in the context of an IPO). This is not necessarily the presumption in case of non-equity securities.			paras 43 & 44
When there is an outstanding profit forecast or estimate in relation to a material undertaking which the issuer has acquired, the issuer should consider whether it is appropriate to make a statement as to whether or not the profit forecast or estimate is still valid or correct. The issuer should also evaluate the effects of the acquisition and the profit forecast made by that undertaking on its own financial position and report on it as it would have done if the profit forecast or estimate had been made by the issuer.			paras 45 & 46

	PD Regulation	Annex I of PD Regulation	CESR Recommendations
The forecast or estimate should normally be of profit before tax (disclosing separately any non-recurrent items and tax charges if they are expected to be abnormally high or low). If the forecast or estimate is not of profit before tax, the reasons for presenting another figure from the profit and loss account must be disclosed and clearly explained. Furthermore the tax effect should be clearly explained. When the results are published relating to a period covered by a forecast or estimate, the published financial statements must disclose the relevant figure so as to enable the forecast and actual results to be directly compared.			paras 47 & 48
CESR recognises that often in practice, there is a fine line between what constitutes a profit forecast and what constitutes trend information as detailed in item 12 of Annex I of the Regulation. A general discussion about the future or prospects of the issuer under trend information will not normally constitute a profit forecast or estimate as defined in Articles 2.10 and 2.11 of the Regulation. Whether or not a statement constitutes profit forecasts or estimates is a question of fact and will depend upon the circumstances of the particular issuer.			para 49
This is a non-exhaustive list of factors that an issuer is expected to take into consideration when preparing forecasts: • Past results, market analysis, strategic evolutions, market share and position of the issuer • Financial position and possible changes therein • Description of the impact of an acquisition or disposal, change in strategy or any major change in environmental matters and technology • Changes in legal and tax environment • Commitments towards third parties.			para 50

Appendix 4 – Examples of engagement letter clauses

The examples of engagement letter clauses are intended for consideration in the context of a public reporting engagement on a profit forecast. They should be tailored to the specific circumstances and supplemented by such other clauses as are relevant and appropriate.

Financial information upon which the report is to be given

The [investment circular] will contain a profit [forecast] [estimate] for the company for the period [ending] [ended] [date] (the "PFI") prepared and presented in accordance with [item 13 of Annex I of the PD Regulation] [the requirements of the City Code] [other applicable regulation]. We will prepare a report on the profit [forecast] [estimate] addressed to [...] expressing our opinion on the profit [forecast] [estimate], in the form described below, to be included in the [investment circular].

We will ask the Directors to make certain representations to us regarding the PFI. If the PFI is intended only to be a hypothetical illustration, or the Directors are unable to make such representations to us, we will not wish to be associated with the PFI and accordingly, will be unable to report publicly on it.

Responsibilities

The preparation and presentation of the profit forecast will be the responsibility solely of the Directors. [This responsibility includes the identification and disclosure of the assumptions underlying the profit forecast. (omit if no assumptions)] The Directors are also responsible for ensuring that the PFI is prepared and presented in accordance with [item 13 of Annex I of the PD Regulation] [the requirements of the City Code] [other applicable regulation].

We will require the Directors to formally adopt the PFI before we report on it. We understand that the Directors will have regard to the guidance issued by The Institute of Chartered Accountants in England & Wales entitled "Prospective Financial Information – Guidance for UK directors" in preparing the PFI.

It is our responsibility to form an opinion as to whether the profit [forecast] [estimate] has been properly compiled on the basis stated and whether such basis is consistent with the accounting policies normally adopted by ABC plc.

If the results of our work are satisfactory, and having regard to the requirements of [item 13.2 of Annex I of the PD Regulation] [the City Code] [other applicable regulation], we shall prepare a report on the profit [forecast] [estimate] for inclusion in the [investment circular]. An illustration of the form of our report is attached.

Scope of work

Our work will be undertaken in accordance with Standard for Investment Reporting (SIR) 3000 "Investment Reporting Standards Applicable to Public Reporting Engagements on Profit Forecasts" issued by the Auditing Practices Board and will be subject to the limitations described therein.

We draw your attention in particular to paragraph 75 of SIR 3000 which would preclude us from expressing any opinion if the Directors have not complied with the regulatory requirements set out in Appendix 2 of that SIR.

As the purpose of our engagement is restricted as described above and since the PFI and the assumptions on which it is based relate to the future and may be affected by unforeseen events, we will not provide any opinion as to how closely the actual result achieved will correspond to the profit [forecast] [estimate]. Accordingly we neither confirm nor otherwise accept responsibility for the ultimate accuracy and achievability of the PFI.

Assumptions

We will discuss the assumptions with the persons responsible for preparing the PFI together with the evidence they have to support the assumptions, but we will not seek to independently verify or audit those assumptions. We are not responsible for identifying the assumptions.

In the event that anything comes to our attention to indicate that any of the assumptions adopted by the Directors which, in our opinion, are necessary for a proper understanding of the PFI have not been disclosed or if any material assumption made by the Directors appears to us to be unrealistic we will inform the directors so that steps can be taken to resolve the matter. However, we are required to comment in our report if an assumption is published which appears to us to be unrealistic or an assumption is omitted which appears to us to be important to an understanding of the PFI.

Appendix 5 – Examples of management representation letter clauses

Similar clauses to those below could be amended to be used in connection with a report on a profit estimate.

Introduction

We refer to the forecast of *[insert description of items forecast]*, profit for the financial year and earnings per share of ABC plc ("the Company") and its subsidiaries together ("the ABC Group") for the year ending [*date*] ("the profit forecast") set out on page [●] of the [Prospectus]/[Circular]/[Offer Document] to be issued on [*date*]. We acknowledge that we are solely responsible for the profit forecast and the assumptions on which it is based as set out on page [●] and confirm on behalf of the Directors [and Proposed Directors] of the Company to the best of our knowledge and belief, having made appropriate enquiries of officials of the Company, the following representations made to you in the course of your work:

Specific representations

- The profit forecast is based on our assessment of the financial position and results of operations and cash flow for the period and is presented on a basis consistent with the accounting policies [normally] [to be] adopted by the ABC Group and has been prepared in accordance with relevant legislative requirements.[1]
- We believe the forecast results are likely to be achieved although achievement of the forecast may be favourably or unfavourably affected by unforeseeable and uncontrollable events.
- We have made available to you all significant information relevant to the profit forecast of which we have knowledge.
- All significant assumptions have been disclosed and the assumptions underlying the profit forecast are reasonable and appropriate.
- The results shown in the [audited/unaudited] financial results for the six months ended [*date*] and the unaudited management accounts for the [●] months ended [*date*] which are included in the profit forecast have been prepared in accordance with the accounting policies [normally] [to be] adopted by the ABC Group and are free from material misstatement.
- There are no contingencies, (other than those which have been taken into account in making the forecast), that are material in the context of the profit forecast which should be disclosed or taken into account in the profit forecast.
- The profit forecast is presented in a manner which is balanced and fair and not misleading and contains all information necessary for a proper understanding of the profit forecast.
- The profit forecast together with the assumptions and the representations in this letter have been approved by the board of directors.

---

[1] *The reporting accountant may also wish to obtain a representation that the profit forecast has been prepared in accordance with 'Prospective Financial Information - Guidance for UK directors' published by the Institute of Chartered Accountants in England and Wales.*

Representations in respect of specific assumptions such as;

- The assumed like for like increase in sales of 5% in the last quarter of 200X incorporates expected price increases of 2% based on preliminary discussions with three of our major customers.
- The assumed increase in gross margin of 2 percentage points from 1 July 200X is based on manufacturing cost savings as a result of the realisation of efficiencies resulting from the factory reorganisation which we expect to be completed by the end of May 200X.
- The assumed increase in sales prices by 2% more than the general level of inflation in 200Y is based upon the expectation that our major competitor will announce a price increase of at least that amount in November 200X. Our expectation takes account of similar timing of increases in previous years and information derived from conversations with mutual customers.
- The opening of two new sales outlets in the current financial year assumes that negotiations to agree a lease on one out of the three potential units in Guildford will be completed and that refitting and pre-opening will be completed within 10 weeks which is 25% longer than the historical average due to additional building works being required in one of the potential sites.
- The profit forecast assumes that a forward sale of $x million will be designated as a hedge against expected US$ income.

Appendix 6 – Example of a report on a profit forecast

Date

Reporting accountant's address

Addressees, as agreed between the parties in the engagement letter

Dear Sirs

[ABC plc]

We report on the profit forecast comprising [*insert description of items comprising the prospective financial information, e.g.* [*forecast of turnover, operating profit, profit before tax and earnings per share*]/[*projected profit and loss account*]] of ABC plc ("the Company") and its subsidiaries (together "the ABC Group") for the [*specify period*] ending [*date*] (the "Profit Forecast"). The Profit Forecast, and the material assumptions upon which it is based, are set out on pages [•] to [•] of the [*describe document*] ("the [Document]") issued by the Company dated [*date*]. This report is required by [Relevant Regulation] [guidance issued by the London Stock Exchange with respect to the AIM market] and is given for the purpose of complying with that [Relevant Regulation] [guidance issued by the London Stock Exchange] and for no other purpose.

[*Substitute the following text for the last sentence of the immediately preceding paragraph, where a profit forecast is made by an offeree in the context of a takeover.* This report is required by Rule 28.3(b) of the City Code and is given for the purpose of complying with that rule and for no other purpose. Accordingly, we assume no responsibility in respect of this report to the Offeror or any person connected to, or acting in concert with, the Offeror or to any other person who is seeking or may in future seek to acquire control of the Company (an "Alternative Offeror") or to any other person connected to, or acting in concert with, an Alternative Offeror.]

Responsibilities

It is the responsibility of the Directors of ABC plc to prepare the Profit Forecast in accordance with the requirements of the [PD Regulation]/[Listing Rules]/[City Code] [guidance issued by the London Stock Exchange].

It is our responsibility to form an opinion as required by the [PD Regulation]/ [Listing Rules]/[City Code] [guidance issued by the London Stock Exchange] as to the proper compilation of the Profit Forecast and to report that opinion to you.

Basis of preparation of the Profit Forecast

The Profit Forecast has been prepared on the basis stated on page [ ] of the [Document][1] and is based on the [audited/unaudited] interim financial results for the [six] months ended [date], the unaudited management accounts for the [x] months

---

[1] *The disclosures presented with the profit forecast should explain the basis on which the forecast has been prepared. This will include identification of the accounting policies used and the financial information used in compiling the forecast. Typically this may include reference to audited/unaudited financial statements of the entity for an interim period, unaudited management accounts and management's forecast for the period for which no management accounts are available.*

ended [date] and a forecast to [date]. The Profit Forecast is required to be presented on a basis consistent with the accounting policies of the ABC Group.

Basis of opinion

We conducted our work in accordance with the Standards for Investment Reporting issued by the Auditing Practices Board in the United Kingdom. Our work included [evaluating the basis on which the historical financial information included in the Profit Forecast has been prepared and] considering whether the Profit Forecast has been accurately computed based upon the disclosed assumptions and the accounting policies of the ABC Group. Whilst the assumptions upon which the Profit Forecast are based are solely the responsibility of the Directors, we considered whether anything came to our attention to indicate that any of the assumptions adopted by the Directors which, in our opinion, are necessary for a proper understanding of the Profit Forecast have not been disclosed and whether any material assumption made by the Directors appears to us to be unrealistic.

We planned and performed our work so as to obtain the information and explanations we considered necessary in order to provide us with reasonable assurance that the Profit Forecast has been properly compiled on the basis stated.

Since the Profit Forecast and the assumptions on which it is based relate to the future and may therefore be affected by unforeseen events, we can express no opinion as to whether the actual results reported will correspond to those shown in the Profit Forecast and differences may be material.

[*This paragraph may be omitted if the document is not to be distributed outside the UK* - Our work has not been carried out in accordance with auditing or other standards and practices generally accepted in the United States of America [or other jurisdictions] and accordingly should not be relied upon as if it had been carried out in accordance with those standards and practices.]

Opinion

In our opinion, the Profit Forecast has been properly compiled on the basis [stated] [of the assumptions made by the Directors/][2] and the basis of accounting used is consistent with the accounting policies of the ABC Group[3].

Declaration[4]

For the purposes of [Prospectus Rule [5.5.3R(2)(f)] [5.5.4R(2)(f)] [guidance issued by the London Stock Exchange] we are responsible for [this report as part] [the following part(s) of the [prospectus] [registration document] [AIM admission document] and declare that we have taken all reasonable care to ensure that the information contained [in this report] [those parts] is, to the best of our knowledge, in

---

[2] *The City Code requires 'on the basis of the assumptions made by the Directors' but the PD Regulation requires 'on the basis stated'.*

[3] *Where the accounting policies used in the profit forecast either differ from those used by the company in its latest published financial statements or where the company has never published financial statements reference should be made to the accounting policies which have been used.*

[4] *This declaration is a requirement of the PD Regulation and is appropriate for inclusion when the report is included in a Prospectus, see Appendix 2 of SIR 1000.*

accordance with the facts and contains no omission likely to affect its import. This declaration is included in the [prospectus] [registration document] [AIM admission document] in compliance with [item 1.2 of annex I of the PD Regulation] [item 1.2 of annex III of the PD Regulation] [guidance issued by the London Stock Exchange].

Yours faithfully

Reporting Accountant

Appendix 7 – Example of a report on a profit estimate that is not subject to assumptions

Date

Reporting accountant's address

Addressees, as agreed between the parties in the engagement letter

Dear Sirs

[ABC plc]

We report on the profit estimate comprising [*insert description of items comprising the prospective financial information, e.g.* [estimate of turnover, operating profit, profit before tax and earnings per share]/[estimated profit and loss account]] of ABC plc ("the Company") and its subsidiaries (together "the ABC Group") for the [*specify period*] ended [*date*] (the "Profit Estimate"). The Profit Estimate and the basis on which it is prepared is set out on pages [●] to [●] of the [*describe document*] ("the [Document]") issued by the Company dated [*date*]. This report is required by [Relevant Regulation] [guidance issued by the London Stock Exchange with respect to the AIM market] and is given for the purpose of complying with that [Relevant Regulation] [guidance issued by the London Stock Exchange] and for no other purpose.

[*Substitute the following text for the last sentence of the immediately preceding paragraph, where a profit estimate is made by an offeree in the context of a takeover.* This report is required by Rule 28.3(b) of the City Code and is given for the purpose of complying with that rule and for no other purpose. Accordingly, we assume no responsibility in respect of this report to the Offeror or any person connected to, or acting in concert with, the Offeror or to any other person who is seeking or may in future seek to acquire control of the Company (an "Alternative Offeror") or to any other person connected to, or acting in concert with, an Alternative Offeror.]

Responsibilities

It is the responsibility of the directors of ABC plc to prepare the Profit Estimate in accordance with the requirements of the [PD Regulation]/[Listing Rules]/[City Code]. In preparing the Profit Estimate the directors of ABC plc are responsible for correcting errors that they have identified which may have arisen in unaudited financial results and unaudited management accounts used as the basis of preparation for the Profit Estimate.

It is our responsibility to form an opinion as required by the [PD Regulation]/ [Listing Rules]/[City Code] as to the proper compilation of the Profit Estimate and to report that opinion to you.

Basis of preparation of the Profit Estimate

The Profit Estimate has been prepared on the basis stated on page [ ] of the [Document][1] and is based on the [audited/unaudited] interim financial results for the [six] months ended [date], the unaudited management accounts for the [x] months ended [date] and an estimate for the [month] to [date]. The Profit Estimate is required to be presented on a basis consistent with the accounting policies of the ABC Group.

Basis of opinion

We conducted our work in accordance with the Standards for Investment Reporting issued by the Auditing Practices Board in the United Kingdom. Our work included evaluating the basis on which the historical financial information for the [x] months to [date] included in the Profit Estimate has been prepared and considering whether the Profit Estimate has been accurately computed using that information and whether the basis of accounting used is consistent with the accounting policies of the ABC Group.

We planned and performed our work so as to obtain the information and explanations we considered necessary in order to provide us with reasonable assurance that the Profit Estimate has been properly compiled on the basis stated.

However, the Profit Estimate has not been audited. The actual results reported, therefore, may be affected by revisions required to accounting estimates due to changes in circumstances, the impact of unforeseen events and the correction of errors in the [interim financial results] [management accounts]. Consequently we can express no opinion as to whether the actual results achieved will correspond to those shown in the Profit Estimate and the difference may be material.

[*This paragraph may be omitted if the document is not to be distributed outside the UK* Our work has not been carried out in accordance with auditing or other standards and practices generally accepted in the United States of America [or other jurisdictions] and accordingly should not be relied upon as if it had been carried out in accordance with those standards and practices.]

Opinion

In our opinion, the Profit Estimate has been properly compiled on the basis stated and the basis of accounting used is consistent with the accounting policies of the ABC Group[2].

---

[1] *The disclosures presented with the profit estimate should explain the basis on which the estimate has been prepared. This will include identification of the accounting policies used and the financial information used in compiling the estimate. Typically this may include reference to audited/unaudited financial statements of the entity for an interim period, unaudited management accounts and management's estimate (which may itself be based on other forms of management information for the period for which no management accounts are available.*

[2] *Where the accounting policies used in the profit estimate either differ from those used by the company in its latest published financial statements or where the company has never published financial statements reference should be made to the accounting policies which have been used.*

Declaration[3]

For the purposes of [Prospectus Rule [5.5.3R(2)(f)] [5.5.4R(2)(f)] [guidance issued by the London Stock Exchange] we are responsible for [this report as part] [the following part(s) of the [prospectus] [registration document] [AIM admission document] and declare that we have taken all reasonable care to ensure that the information contained [in this report] [those parts] is, to the best of our knowledge, in accordance with the facts and contains no omission likely to affect its import. This declaration is included in the [prospectus] [registration document] [AIM admission document] in compliance with [item 1.2 of annex I of the PD Regulation] [item 1.2 of annex III of the PD Regulation] [guidance issued by the London Stock Exchange].

Yours faithfully

Reporting Accountant

---

[3] *This declaration is a requirement of the PD Regulation and is appropriate for inclusion when the report is included in a Prospectus, see Appendix 2 of SIR 1000.*

[4000]
Investment reporting standards applicable to public reporting engagements on pro forma financial information

Contents

	Paragraphs
Introduction	1 - 2
The nature of pro forma financial information	3 - 5
Compilation process	5
Engagement acceptance and continuance	6 - 7
Agreeing the terms of the engagement	8
Ethical requirements	9
Legal and regulatory requirements	10 - 12
Quality control	13
Planning and performing the engagement	14 - 48
Materiality	20 - 22
Public reporting engagement risk	23 - 26
Unadjusted financial information of the issuer	27 - 29
Adjustments	30 - 38
Omitted adjustments	39 - 41
Checking the calculations	42
Consistent accounting policies	43 - 45
Presentation of pro forma financial information	46 - 47
Representation letter	48
Documentation	49
Professional scepticism	50
Reporting	51 - 59
Responsibilities	52 - 53
Basis of preparation of the pro forma financial information	54 - 55
Expression of opinion	56 - 59
Modified opinions	60 - 63
Consent	64

Events occurring between the date of the reporting accountant's report and the completion date of the transaction   65 - 68

Effective date   69

Appendices

1   Reporting accountant's criteria
2   Other regulatory provisions relevant to the preparers of pro forma financial information
3   Examples of engagement letter clauses
4   Examples of management representation letter clauses
5   Example report on pro forma financial information in accordance with the PD Regulation or the Listing Rules

ANNEXURE

Sections of TECH 18/98 "Pro forma financial information – Guidance for preparers under the Listing Rules" (published by the Institute of Chartered Accountants in England & Wales) that remain relevant

Investment reporting standards applicable to public reporting engagements on pro forma financial information

SIR 4000 contains basic principles and essential procedures ("Investment Reporting Standards"), indicated by paragraphs in bold type, with which a reporting accountant is required to comply in the conduct of an engagement to report on pro forma financial information, which is included within an investment circular prepared for issue in connection with a securities transaction governed wholly or in part by the laws and regulations of the United Kingdom.

SIR 4000 also includes explanatory and other material, including appendices, in the context of which the basic principles and essential procedures are to be understood and applied. It is necessary to consider the whole text of the SIR to understand and apply the basic principles and essential procedures.

For the purposes of the SIRs, an investment circular is defined as: "any document issued by an entity pursuant to statutory or regulatory requirements relating to listed or unlisted securities on which it is intended that a third party should make an investment decision, including a prospectus, listing particulars, circular to shareholders or similar document".

SIR 1000 "Investment reporting standards applicable to all engagements involving an investment circular" contains basic principles and essential procedures that are applicable to all engagements involving an investment circular. The definitions in the glossary of terms set out in Appendix 4 of SIR 1000 are to be applied in the interpretation of this and all other SIRs. Terms defined in the glossary are underlined the first time that they occur in the text.

To assist readers, SIRs contain references to, and extracts from, certain legislation and chapters of the Rules of the UK Listing Authority. Readers are cautioned that these references may change subsequent to publication.

Introduction

1 Standard for Investment Reporting (SIR) 1000 "Investment Reporting Standards applicable to all engagements in connection with an investment circular" establishes the Investment Reporting Standards applicable to all engagements involving investment circulars. The purpose of this SIR is to establish specific additional Investment Reporting Standards and provide guidance for a reporting accountant engaged to report publicly on pro forma financial information to be included in an investment circular under the PD Regulation, the Listing Rules[1], or if required by the London Stock Exchange in respect of an AIM Admission Document.

2 An engagement to report publicly on the proper compilation of pro forma financial information is a public reporting engagement as described in SIR 1000. The description of a public reporting engagement includes three generic terms having the following meanings in the context of an engagement to report on the proper compilation of pro forma financial information:

---

[1] In the UK the Prospectus Directive is implemented into law through amendments to Part VI of FSMA and to certain secondary legislation. The Annexes to the PD Regulation have been incorporated into the Prospectus Rules issued by the FSA.

(a) with respect to pro forma financial information the "**subject matter**", is the impact that the transaction, that is the subject of the investment circular, would have had on the earnings of the issuer (assuming that the transaction had been undertaken at the commencement of the financial period used for the illustration) or on the assets and liabilities of the issuer (assuming that the transaction had been undertaken at the end of the financial period used for the illustration);

(b) "**suitable criteria**" to be used by directors in the preparation of the pro forma financial information are provided by the requirements of the PD Regulation and the guidance issued by CESR[2] (CESR Recommendations). In forming its opinion as to whether the pro forma financial information has been properly compiled the reporting accountant considers whether certain of those criteria ("**reporting accountant's criteria**") have been properly applied. Reporting accountant's criteria are set out in Appendix 1 of this SIR; and

(c) with respect to pro forma financial information the "**outcome**"[3] is the pro forma financial information and related disclosures that are included in the investment circular and on which the reporting accountant expresses an opinion (in the "**reporting accountant's report**") as to whether that information is properly compiled on the basis stated and whether such basis is consistent with the accounting policies of the issuer.

The nature of pro forma financial information

3   For the purpose of this SIR "pro forma financial information" is defined to include financial information such as net assets, profit or cash flow statements that demonstrate the impact of a transaction on previously published financial information together with the explanatory notes thereto. Under item 1 of Annex II of the PD Regulation the pro forma financial information must be accompanied by introductory text describing the transaction, the businesses or entities involved, the period to which it refers and its purpose and limitations.

4   The Institute of Chartered Accountants in England and Wales (ICAEW) issued guidance entitled "Pro forma financial information - Guidance for preparers under the Listing Rules"[4] in September 1998 (the "ICAEW Guidance") to assist directors when preparing pro forma financial information for inclusion in documents subject to approval by the FSA prior to their issue. While aspects of this guidance remain of assistance to directors there are differences between the requirements of the PD Regulation, the CESR Recommendations and the requirements on which the ICAEW guidance was based. The Annexure has been prepared to assist in determining which parts of the ICAEW guidance continue to be relevant.

Compilation process

5   The compilation of pro forma information is the gathering, classification and summarisation of relevant financial information. The process followed by the preparer would be expected to include the following:

(a) the accurate extraction of information from sources permitted under the PD Regulation;

---

[2] *CESR issued "CESR's Recommendations for the Consistent Implementation of the European Commission's Regulation on Prospectuses No. 809/2004" in February 2005.*

[3] *The "outcome" is sometimes described as "subject matter information".*

[4] *TECH 18/98*

(b) the making of adjustments to the source information that are arithmetically correct, appropriate and complete for the purpose for which the pro forma financial information is presented;
(c) arithmetic computation of the pro forma information;
(d) consideration of accounting policies;
(e) appropriate disclosure to enable the intended users to understand the pro forma financial information; and
(f) appropriate consideration of the pro forma financial information and approval by the directors of the entity.

Engagement acceptance and continuance

SIR 1000.1 and SIR 1000.2 set out the basic principles and essential procedures, with respect to engagement acceptance and continuance, that are applicable to all engagements involving an investment circular.   6

When accepting or continuing an engagement to report publicly on pro forma information, the reporting accountant ascertains whether the directors intend to comply with all relevant regulatory requirements, in particular those that constitute the reporting accountant's criteria set out in Appendix 1 of this SIR.   7

Agreeing the terms of the engagement

SIR 1000.3 and SIR 1000.4 set out the basic principles and essential procedures with respect to agreeing the terms of the engagement. Examples of engagement letter clauses are set out in Appendix 3 of this SIR.   8

Ethical requirements

SIR 1000.5 sets out the basic principles and essential procedures with respect to the ethical requirements that apply to a reporting accountant[5].   9

Legal and regulatory requirements

The PD Regulation requires any pro forma financial information included in a prospectus to be reported on by independent accountants or auditors (referred to in this SIR as the "reporting accountant") and specifies the form of opinion to be given. The Listing Rules require any pro forma financial information included in a Class 1 circular to be reported on in the same way. References in the SIR to the PD Regulation apply equally to the Listing Rules where those Rules apply.   10

SIR 1000.6 sets out the basic principles with respect to the legal and regulatory requirements applicable to a reporting accountant.   11

Appendices 1 and 2 to this SIR set out those provisions of the PD Regulation and the CESR Recommendations, relating to the implementation of the Regulation, that provide the suitable criteria for directors. Those provisions that constitute criteria for   12

---

[5] In January 2006 the APB issued an Exposure Draft of an Ethical Standard for Reporting Accountants (ESRA).

a reporting accountant expressing an opinion on whether the pro forma information has been properly compiled are set out in Appendix 1 of this SIR.

Quality control

13   SIR 1000.7 and SIR 1000.8 set out the basic principles and essential procedures with respect to the quality control of engagements to report on pro forma financial information.

Planning and performing the engagement

14   SIR 1000.9 and SIR 1000.10 set out the basic principles and essential procedures with respect to the planning of all reporting engagements. Additional basic principles, essential procedures and guidance are set out below.

15   **The reporting accountant should obtain an understanding of the key factors affecting the subject matter sufficient to identify and assess the risk of the pro forma financial information not being properly compiled and sufficient to design and perform evidence gathering procedures including:**

   (a) the nature of the transaction being undertaken by the issuer;
   (b) the entity's business; and
   (c) the procedures adopted, or planned to be adopted, by the directors for the preparation of the pro forma financial information. (SIR 4000.1)

16   The reporting accountant gains an understanding of the transaction, in respect of which the pro forma financial information is being prepared, by discussion with the directors or management of the issuer and by reading relevant supporting documentation.

17   The reporting accountant uses professional judgment to determine the extent of the understanding required of the entity's business.

18   Other matters for consideration by the reporting accountant include the availability of evidence to provide factual support for the proposed adjustments and the accounting policies that will form the basis of the adjustments to the pro forma financial information.

19   **The reporting accountant should consider materiality and public reporting engagement risk in planning its work in accordance with its instructions and in determining the effect of its findings on the report to be issued. (SIR 4000.2)**

Materiality

20   Matters are material if their omission or misstatement could, individually or collectively, influence the economic decisions of the intended users of the pro forma financial information. Materiality depends on the size and nature of the omission or misstatement judged in light of the surrounding circumstances. The size or nature of the matter, or a combination of both, could be the determining factor.

21   A misstatement in the context of the compilation of pro forma financial information includes, for example:

   • Use of an inappropriate source for the unadjusted financial information.

- Incorrect extraction of the unadjusted financial information from an appropriate source.
- In relation to adjustments, the misapplication of accounting policies or failure to use the accounting policies adopted in the last, or to be adopted in the next, financial statements.
- Failure to make an adjustment required by the PD regulation.
- Making an adjustment that does not comply with the PD regulation.
- A mathematical or clerical mistake.
- Inadequate, or incorrect, disclosures.

Evaluating whether an omission or misstatement could influence economic decisions of the intended users of the pro forma financial information, and so be material, requires consideration of the characteristics of those intended users. The intended users are assumed to: 22

(a) have a reasonable knowledge of business and economic activities and accounting and a willingness to study the pro forma financial information with reasonable diligence; and
(a) make reasonable economic decisions on the basis of the pro forma financial information.

The determination of materiality, therefore, takes into account how intended users with such characteristics could reasonably be expected to be influenced in making economic decisions.

Public reporting engagement risk

"Public reporting engagement risk" is the risk that the reporting accountant expresses an inappropriate opinion when the pro forma financial information has not been properly compiled on the basis stated or that basis is not consistent with the accounting policies of the issuer[6]. 23

SIR 1000.11 and SIR 1000.12 set out the basic principles and essential procedures, with respect to obtaining evidence, that are applicable to all engagements involving an investment circular. Additional basic principles, essential procedures and guidance relating to engagements to report on pro forma financial information are set out below. 24

The reporting accountant should obtain sufficient appropriate evidence that the pro forma financial information is free from material error in its compilation by: 25

(a) checking that the unadjusted financial information of the issuer has been accurately extracted from a source that is both appropriate and in accordance with the relevant regulation;
(b) obtaining evidence that the directors have applied the criteria set out in Appendix 1 of this SIR and, therefore, that the adjustments are appropriate and complete for the purpose for which the pro forma financial information is presented; and
(c) checking that the calculations within the pro forma financial information are arithmetically correct. (SIR 4000.3)

Item 5 of Annex II of the PD Regulation permits pro forma financial information to be published only in respect of: 26

(a) the current financial period;

---

[6] *The PD Regulation requires a positive and unmodified opinion – for this reason there is no risk that the reporting accountant will inappropriately modify its opinion.*

(b) the most recently completed financial period; and
(c) the most recent interim period for which relevant unadjusted information has been or will be published or is being published in the same investment circular.

Unadjusted financial information of the issuer

27 The reporting accountant considers whether the period in respect of which the pro forma financial information is proposed to be published is permitted under the PD Regulation. The reporting accountant also considers whether the source of the unadjusted financial information for the issuer is appropriate and whether the source of the unadjusted financial information is clearly stated.

28 The reporting accountant is not required to perform specific procedures on the unadjusted financial information of the issuer other than as described in paragraph 27. However, if the reporting accountant has reason to believe that the unadjusted financial information is, or may be, unreliable, or if a report thereon has identified any uncertainties or disagreements, the reporting accountant considers the effect on the pro forma financial information.

29 The reporting accountant checks the extraction of the unadjusted financial information from the source concerned.

Adjustments

30 Item 6 of Annex II to the PD Regulation requires pro forma adjustments to be:

(a) clearly shown and explained;
(b) directly attributable to the transaction; and
(c) factually supportable.

31 In addition, in respect of a pro forma profit and loss or cash flow statement, they must be clearly identified as to those adjustments which are expected to have a continuing impact on the issuer and those which are not.

32 More detailed guidance for directors concerning the implementation of these requirements is provided by the CESR Recommendations and those parts of the ICAEW Guidance that remain relevant (see Annexure).

33 The reporting accountant considers the way in which the directors have fulfilled their responsibilities. With its understanding of the transaction and the entity's business as background the reporting accountant discusses with the directors the steps the directors have taken to identify relevant adjustments and whether such adjustments are permitted to be made.

34 If, as a result of these enquiries, the reporting accountant becomes aware of a significant adjustment which, in its opinion, ought to be made for the purposes of the pro forma financial information it discusses the position with the directors of the issuer and, if necessary, the issuer's advisers. If the reporting accountant is not able to agree with the directors and the issuer's advisers as to how the matter is to be resolved it considers the consequences for its report.

35 The reporting accountant considers the adjustments to assess whether they are "directly attributable" to the transaction whose impact is being illustrated by the pro forma financial information, that is, they are an integral part of the transaction concerned. If a potential adjustment is not directly attributable to the transaction or

transactions described in the investment circular, it cannot be made (although it may be appropriate to disclose by way of note to the pro forma financial information the nature of a prohibited potential adjustment and the effect it would have had if it had been permissible to include it).

In assessing whether adjustments are directly attributable to the transaction the reporting accountant considers whether the adjustments relate to future events and/or decisions. This is because adjustments that are related to the transaction being illustrated but which are dependent on actions to be taken once the transaction has been completed, cannot be said to be "directly attributable". 36

The reporting accountant considers whether the adjustments have been clearly shown and explained and, in respect of a pro forma profit and loss or cash flow statement, whether they have been clearly identified as to those which are expected to have a continuing impact on the issuer (that is, relate to events or circumstances that are expected to recur) and to those which are not. 37

The reporting accountant obtains appropriate evidence that the directors of the issuer have factual support for each adjustment. Sources of such evidence would include published financial statements, other financial information or valuations disclosed elsewhere in the investment circular, purchase and sale agreements and other agreements relating to the transaction. 38

Omitted adjustments

In view of the specific restrictions on the nature of the adjustments permitted to be made under item 6 of Annex II of the PD Regulation, the directors may not be permitted to make all the adjustments that they would otherwise wish to. For example, an adjustment which is directly attributable but which is not factually supportable could not be included in pro forma financial information. 39

If any adjustments are excluded because of the requirement in item 6 of Annex II of the PD Regulation for adjustments to be factually supportable, the reporting accountant considers the effect on the pro forma financial information and in particular whether the exclusion renders the pro forma financial information misleading. In such circumstances, the reporting accountant may consider that disclosure in the notes to the pro forma financial information of the fact that such an adjustment has not been made is sufficient in the context of the overall purpose of the pro forma financial information. 40

However, if the reporting accountant concludes that an omitted adjustment is so fundamental as to render the pro forma statement misleading in the context of the investment circular, it discusses the matter with the directors and, if necessary, the issuer's advisers and in the event that acceptable changes to the disclosures are not made, considers whether it is able to issue its report. 41

Checking the calculations

The reporting accountant ascertains whether the adjustments made in the pro forma financial information are included under the appropriate financial statement caption as well as the arithmetical accuracy of the calculations within the pro forma financial information itself. 42

Consistent accounting policies

43 The reporting accountant should evaluate whether the adjustments made to the unadjusted financial information are consistent with the accounting policies adopted in the last, or to be adopted in the next, financial statements of the entity presenting the pro forma financial information. (SIR 4000.4)

44 It is the responsibility of the directors of the issuer to ensure that in accordance with item 4 of Annex II of the PD Regulation the pro forma financial information is prepared in a manner consistent with either the accounting policies adopted in the last, or to be adopted in the next, financial statements of the issuer.

45 Where the reporting accountant is not the auditor of the issuer or has not otherwise reported on the financial information relating to the subject of the transaction, it evaluates the steps taken to ensure that the pro forma financial information has been prepared in a manner consistent with the accounting policies of the issuer. Guidance for directors with respect to the consistency of accounting policies is provided by the ICAEW Guidance.

Presentation of pro forma financial information

46 The reporting accountant should consider whether it has become aware of anything to cause it to believe that the pro forma financial information is presented in a way that is not understandable or is misleading in the context in which it is provided. If the reporting accountant is aware of such matters it should discuss them with the parties responsible for the pro forma financial information and with those persons to whom its report is to be addressed, and consider whether it is able to issue its report. (SIR 4000.5)

47 The reporting accountant reads the pro forma financial information to assess whether:

(a) as required by item 1 of Annex II of the PD Regulation, the pro forma financial information includes a description of the transaction, the businesses or entities involved and the period to which it refers and clearly states the purpose for which it has been prepared, that it has been prepared for illustrative purposes only and that, because of its nature, it addresses a hypothetical situation and, therefore, does not represent the company's actual financial position or results;
(b) in accordance with the normal form of presentation under item 3 of Annex II of the PD Regulation, the pro forma financial information is presented in columnar format composed of (a) the historical unadjusted information, (b) the pro forma adjustments and (c) the resulting pro forma financial information in the final column; and
(c) disclosures, in the notes to the pro forma financial information, concerning omitted adjustments are satisfactory (see paragraphs 40 and 41 above).

Representation letter

48 SIR 1000.13 sets out the basic principles and essential procedures, with respect to representation letters, that are applicable to all engagements involving an investment circular. Examples of management representation letter clauses are set out in Appendix 4 of this SIR.

Documentation

SIR 1000.14 and SIR 1000.15 set out the basic principles and essential procedures with respect to the reporting accountant's working papers.   49

Professional scepticism

SIR 1000.16 sets out the basic principle with respect to the attitude of professional scepticism adopted by the reporting accountant in planning and performing an engagement.   50

Reporting

SIRs 1000.17, SIR 1000.18 and SIR 1000.19 set out the basic principles and essential procedures, with respect to reporting, that are applicable to all engagements involving an investment circular. Additional basic principles and essential procedures relating to engagements to report on pro forma financial information are set out below.   51

Responsibilities

In all reports on pro forma financial information in investment circulars the reporting accountant should explain the extent of its responsibility in respect of the pro forma financial information by including in its report: 52

(a) a statement that the reporting accountant's responsibility is to form an opinion (as required by the applicable regulatory requirements) on the proper compilation of the pro forma financial information and to report its opinion to the addressees of the report; and
(b) a statement that the pro forma financial information is the responsibility of the directors. (SIR 4000.6)

The reporting accountant's responsibility in relation to the opinion required by the PD Regulation is limited to the provision of the report and the opinion expressed.   53

Basis of preparation of the pro forma financial information

The reporting accountant should include a basis of preparation section of its report that cross refers to disclosures that explain the basis of preparation of the pro forma financial information. (SIR 4000.7)   54

The basis of preparation section of the report will make clear whether the accounting policies applied in the preparation of the pro forma information are those adopted by the entity in preparing the last published financial statements or those that it plans to adopt in the next published financial statements.   55

Expression of opinion

The report on the pro forma financial information should contain a clear expression of opinion that complies with applicable regulatory requirements. (SIR 4000.8)   56

57 In forming its opinion the reporting accountant takes account of those events which the reporting accountant becomes aware of occurring up to the date on which the reporting accountant signs the report, that affect the opinion expressed in the report.

58 In providing the opinion required by the PD Regulation the reporting accountant is not providing any assurance in relation to any source financial information on which the pro forma financial information is based beyond that opinion. In particular, the reporting accountant is not refreshing or updating any opinion that it may have given in any other capacity on that source financial information.

59 The investment circular in which the reporting accountant's report is included may be made available in other countries, such as the United States of America, which have their own standards for accountants when reporting on pro forma financial information. In such circumstances, the reporting accountant considers whether to include a reference to the fact that a report issued in accordance with the SIRs should not be relied upon as if it had been issued in accordance with the standards applicable in that other country. An example of such a reference is included in the example report set out in Appendix 5 of this SIR.

Modified opinions

60 SIR 1000.20 sets out the basic principles and essential procedures, with respect to modified opinions, that are applicable to all engagements involving an investment circular. Additional basic principles and essential procedures relating to engagements to report on pro forma financial information are set out below.

61 In the event that the reporting accountant concludes that it is unable to report in the manner prescribed it considers, with the parties to whom it is to report, whether the pro forma financial information can be amended to alleviate its concerns or whether the pro forma information should be omitted from the investment circular and the requirement for information to be given on the effect of the transaction satisfied in some other way.

62 **As the PD Regulation requires a positive and unmodified opinion, the reporting accountant should not express an opinion when the directors have not applied the criteria set out in Appendix 1 of this SIR and, in the reporting accountant's judgment the effect of not doing so is, or may be, material. (SIR 4000.9)**

63 An example of a report on pro forma financial information expressing a positive and unmodified opinion, pursuant to the PD Regulation, is set out in Appendix 5 of this SIR.

Consent

64 SIR 1000.21 and SIR 1000.22 set out the basic principles and essential procedures with respect to the giving of consent by the reporting accountant.

Events occurring between the date of the reporting accountant's report and the completion date of the transaction

SIR 1000.23 sets out the basic principles and essential procedures with respect to events occurring between the date of the reporting accountant's report and the completion date of the transaction. 65

Under Section 81 and 87G of the FSMA, Prospectus Rule 3.4 and Listing Rule 4.4.1, a supplementary investment circular must be prepared if, after the date the investment circular has been formally approved by a regulator and before dealings in the relevant securities commence, the issuer becomes aware that there has been a significant change affecting any matter contained in the document or a significant new matter has arisen, the inclusion of information in respect of which would have been required if it had arisen at the time of its preparation. A similar obligation arises, under Article 16 of the Prospectus Directive, in respect of the period following registration of the investment circular during which an agreement in respect of the securities can be entered into in pursuance of the offer contained in the investment circular. 66

If, as a result of discussions with those responsible for the investment circular concerning an event that occurred prior to the completion date of the transaction, the reporting accountant is either uncertain about or disagrees with the course of action proposed it may consider it necessary to take legal advice with respect to its responsibilities in the particular circumstances. 67

After the date of its report, the reporting accountant has no obligation to perform procedures or make enquiries regarding the investment circular. 68

Effective date

A reporting accountant is required to comply with the Investment Reporting Standards contained in this SIR for reports signed after 31 March 2006. Earlier adoption is encouraged. 69

Appendix 1 – Reporting accountant's criteria

	Annex I of PD Regulation	Annex II of PD Regulation	CESR Recommendations
In the case of a significant gross change, a description of how the transaction might have affected the assets and liabilities and earnings of the issuer, had the transaction been undertaken at the commencement of the period being reported on or at the date reported. This requirement will normally be satisfied by the inclusion of pro forma financial information.	20.2		
The pro forma information must normally be presented in columnar format composed of: a) the historical unadjusted information; b) the pro forma adjustments; and c) the resulting pro forma financial information in the final column		3	
The sources of the pro forma financial information have to be stated.		3	
The pro forma information must be prepared in a manner consistent with the accounting policies adopted by the issuer in its last or next financial statements and shall identify the following: a) the basis upon which it is prepared; b) the source of each item of information and adjustment.		4	
Pro forma adjustments related to the pro forma financial information must be: a) clearly shown and explained.		6	
Pro forma adjustments related to the pro forma financial information must be: b) directly attributable to the transaction.		6	

	Annex I of PD Regulation	Annex II of PD Regulation	CESR Recommendations
"Directly attributable to transactions". Pro forma information should only reflect matters that are an integral part of the transactions which are described in the prospectus. In particular, pro forma financial information should not include adjustments which are dependent on actions to be taken once the current transactions have been completed, even where such actions are central to the issuer's purpose in entering into the transactions.			Para 88
Pro forma adjustments related to the pro forma financial information must be: c) factually supportable.		6	
"Factually supportable". The nature of the facts supporting an adjustment will vary according to the circumstances. Nevertheless, facts are expected to be capable of some reasonable degree of objective determination. Support might typically be provided by published accounts, management accounts, other financial information and valuations contained in the document, purchase and sale agreements and other agreements to the transaction covered by the prospectus. For instance in relation to management accounts, the interim figures for an undertaking being acquired may be derived from the consolidation schedules underlying that undertaking's interim statements.			Para 87
In respect of a pro forma profit and loss or cash flow statement, the adjustments must be clearly identified as to those expected to have a continuing impact on the issuer and those which are not.		6	
The accounting treatment applied to adjustments should be presented and prepared in a form consistent with the policy the issuer would adopt in its last or next published financial statements.			Para 89[1]

---

[1] Paragraph 89 of the CESR guidance also makes recommendations that do not constitute criteria but provide useful guidance with respect to this criterion.

Appendix 2 – Other regulatory provisions relevant to the preparers of pro forma financial information

PD Regulation	Annex I of PD Regulation	Annex II of PD Regulation	CESR Recommendations
Recital 9			
(9) Pro forma financial information is needed in case of significant gross change, i.e. a variation of more than 25% relative to one or more indicators of the size of the issuer's business, in the situation of an issuer due to a particular transaction, with the exception of those situations where merger accounting is required.			
For these purposes, "Significant gross change" is described in recital 9 of the PD Regulation. Thus, in order to assess whether the variation to an issuer's business as a result of a transaction is more than 25%, the size of the transaction should be assessed relative to the size of the issuer by using appropriate indicators of size prior to the relevant transaction. A transaction will constitute a significant gross change where at least one of the indicators of size is more than 25%. A non-exhaustive list of indicators of size is provided below: - Total assets - Revenue - Profit or loss Other indicators of size can be applied by the issuer especially where the stated indicators of size produce an anomalous result or are inappropriate to the specific industry of the issuer, in these cases the issuers should address these anomalies by agreement of the competent authority. The appropriate indicators of size should refer to figures from the issuer's last or next published annual financial statements.			Paras 90 to 94
Article 5 Pro forma financial information should be preceded by an introductory explanatory paragraph that states in clear terms the purpose of including this information in the prospectus			
This pro forma financial information is to be presented as set out in Annex II and must include the information indicated therein. Pro forma financial information must be accompanied by a report prepared by independent accountants or auditors.	20.2		

PD Regulation	Annex I of PD Regulation	Annex II of PD Regulation	CESR Recommendations
The pro forma information must include a description of the transaction, the businesses or entities involved and the period to which it refers.		1	
The pro forma information must clearly state the purpose to which it has been prepared		1	
The pro forma information must clearly state that it has been prepared for illustrative purposes only		1	
The pro forma information must clearly state that, because of its nature, it addresses a hypothetical situation and, therefore, does not represent the company's actual financial position or results.		1	
In order to present pro forma financial information, a balance sheet and profit and loss account, and accompanying explanatory notes, depending on the circumstances may be included		2	
Where applicable the financial statements of the acquired businesses or entities must be included in the prospectus.		3	
Pro forma information may only be published in respect of: a) the current financial period; b) the most recently completed financial period; and/or c) the most recent interim period for which relevant unadjusted information has been or will be published or is being published in the same document		5	

Appendix 3 – Examples of engagement letter clauses

The examples of engagement letter clauses are intended for consideration in the context of a public reporting engagement on pro forma financial information. They should be tailored to the specific circumstances and supplemented by such other clauses as are relevant and appropriate.

Financial information upon which the report is to be given

The [investment circular] will include a pro forma [balance sheet/profit and loss account] together with a description of the basis of presentation (including the accounting policies used) and supporting notes to illustrate how the transaction might have affected the financial information of the company had the transaction been undertaken at the beginning of the period[s] concerned or as at the date[s] stated (the "pro forma financial information").

Responsibilities

The pro forma financial information, which will be the responsibility solely of the directors, will be prepared for illustrative purposes only. This is required to be prepared in accordance with items 1 to 6 of Annex II of the PD Regulation.

It is our responsibility to form an opinion as to whether the pro forma financial information has been properly compiled on the basis stated and that such basis is consistent with the accounting policies of ABC plc.

If the results of our work are satisfactory, and having regard to the requirements of item 7 of Annex II of the PD Regulation, we shall prepare a report on the pro forma financial information for inclusion in the [*describe document*]. An illustration of the form of our report is attached.

Scope of work

Our work will be undertaken in accordance with Standard for Investment Reporting (SIR) 4000 "Investment Reporting Standards Applicable to Public Reporting Engagements on Pro Forma Financial Information" issued by the Auditing Practices Board and will be subject to the limitations described therein.

We draw your attention in particular to paragraph 62 of SIR 4000 which would preclude us from expressing any opinion if the directors have not complied with the regulatory requirements set out in Appendix 1 of that SIR.

Appendix 4 – Examples of management representation letter clauses

The following are examples of management representation letter clauses relating to a report on pro forma financial information, issued pursuant to the PD Regulation or Listing Rules, which may be obtained from the issuer. Alternatively they may form the basis for a board minute.

Introduction

We refer to the pro forma financial information set out in Part [...] of the [investment circular] dated...to be issued in connection with [...] dated. We acknowledge that we are solely responsible for the pro forma financial information and confirm on behalf of the Directors of the Company to the best of our knowledge and belief, having made appropriate enquiries of officials of the Company [and the directors and officials of the target company], the following representations made to you in the course of your work.

Specific representations

- We acknowledge as duly appointed officials of the Company our responsibility for the pro forma financial information (which has been prepared in accordance with [CESR's Recommendations for the Consistent Implementation of the European Commission's Regulation on Prospectuses No. 809/2004"] [and, to the extent applicable, with Technical Release TECH 18/98 published by the Institute of Chartered Accountants in England and Wales].
- We have considered the pro forma financial information and we confirm that, in our opinion, as required by item 20.2 of Annex I of the PD Regulation, the pro forma financial information provides investors with information about the impact of the transaction by illustrating how that transaction might have affected the [assets and liabilities] [and] [earnings] of the issuer, had the transaction been undertaken at the commencement of the period being reported on or at the date reported. Furthermore, we confirm that, in our opinion, the pro forma financial information is not misleading.
- We have considered the adjustments included in the pro forma financial information. We confirm that, in our opinion, the pro forma financial information includes all appropriate adjustments permitted by item 6 of Annex II of the PD Regulation, of which we are aware, necessary to give effect to the transaction as if the transaction had been undertaken [at the date reported on] [at the commencement of the period being reported on].
- [We have considered those adjustments which have been omitted by virtue of not being permitted to be included by item 6 of Annex II of the PD Regulation and the disclosures made in respect thereof. In our opinion the omission of these adjustments does not render the pro forma financial information misleading.]
- [*Where the accounting policies in the issuer's next financial statements are used.* The accounting policies used in compiling the pro forma financial information are those to be adopted in the Company's next financial statements, and all changes necessary to reflect those policies have been made.]
- [*Any specific representations relating to information included in the pro forma financial information.*]

Appendix 5 – Example report on pro forma financial information in accordance with the pd regulation or the listing rules

Date

Reporting accountant's address

Addressees, as agreed between the parties in the engagement letter

Dear Sirs,

[ABC plc]

We report on the pro forma [financial information] (the "Pro forma financial information") set out in Part [...] of the [investment circular] dated........, which has been prepared on the basis described [in note x], for illustrative purposes only, to provide information about how the [transaction] might have affected the financial information presented on the basis of the accounting policies [adopted/to be adopted[1]] by ABC plc in preparing the financial statements for the period [ended/ending] [*date*]. This report is required by [Relevant Regulation] [guidance issued by the London Stock Exchange with respect to the AIM market] and is given for the purpose of complying with that [Relevant Regulation] [guidance issued by the London Stock Exchange] and for no other purpose.

Responsibilities

It is the responsibility of the directors of ABC plc to prepare the Pro forma financial information in accordance with [item 20.2 of Annex I of the PD Regulation] [guidance issued by the London Stock Exchange].

It is our responsibility to form an opinion, as required by [item 7 of Annex II of the PD Regulation] [guidance issued by the London Stock Exchange], as to the proper compilation of the Pro forma financial information and to report that opinion to you.

In providing this opinion we are not updating or refreshing any reports or opinions previously made by us on any financial information used in the compilation of the Pro forma financial information, nor do we accept responsibility for such reports or opinions beyond that owed to those to whom those reports or opinions were addressed by us at the dates of their issue.

Basis of Opinion

We conducted our work in accordance with the Standards for Investment Reporting issued by the Auditing Practices Board in the United Kingdom. The work that we performed for the purpose of making this report, which involved no independent examination of any of the underlying financial information, consisted primarily of comparing the unadjusted financial information with the source documents, considering the evidence supporting the adjustments and discussing the Pro forma financial information with the directors of ABC plc.

---

[1] *See paragraph 44 of SIR 4000*

We planned and performed our work so as to obtain the information and explanations we considered necessary in order to provide us with reasonable assurance that the Pro forma financial information has been properly compiled on the basis stated and that such basis is consistent with the accounting policies of ABC plc.

[*This paragraph may be omitted if the document is not to be distributed outside the UK* - Our work has not been carried out in accordance with auditing or other standards and practices generally accepted in the United States of America [or other jurisdictions] and accordingly should not be relied upon as if it had been carried out in accordance with those standards and practices.]

Opinion

In our opinion:

(a) the Pro forma financial information has been properly compiled on the basis stated; and
(b) such basis is consistent with the accounting policies of ABC plc.

Declaration[2]

For the purposes of [Prospectus Rule [5.5.3R(2)(f)] [5.5.4R(2)(f)]] [guidance issued by the London Stock Exchange] we are responsible for [this report as part] [the following part(s)] of the [prospectus] [registration document] [AIM Admission Document] and declare that we have taken all reasonable care to ensure that the information contained [in this report] [those parts] is, to the best of our knowledge, in accordance with the facts and contains no omission likely to affect its import. This declaration is included in the [prospectus] [registration document] [AIM Admission Document] in compliance with [item 1.2 of Annex I of the PD Regulation] [item 1.2 of Annex III of the Prospectus Regulation] [guidance issued by the London Stock Exchange].

Yours faithfully

Reporting accountant

---

[2] *This declaration is a requirement of the Prospectus Rules and is appropriate for inclusion when the report is included in a Prospectus, see Appendix 2 of SIR 1000. It is also appropriate for inclusion in an AIM admission document under Schedule Two of the AIM Rules.*

Annexure

SECTIONS OF TECH 18/98 "PRO FORMA FINANCIAL INFORMATION – GUIDANCE FOR PREPARERS UNDER THE LISTING RULES"[1] (PUBLISHED BY THE INSTITUTE OF CHARTERED ACCOUNTANTS IN ENGLAND & WALES) THAT REMAIN RELEVANT

This Annexure has been compiled by the APB to indicate those paragraphs of TECH 18/98 that continue to be relevant. (There are differences between the requirements of the PD Regulation and the CESR Recommendations compared to the requirements on which TECH 18/98 was based.) The Annexure does not include either basic principles, essential procedures, or guidance promulgated by the APB.

Paragraphs in TECH 18/98	Application under the PD Regulation
1 to 5	Not applicable
6	Principles still applicable, save that under Item 20.2 of Annex I of the PD Regulation inclusion of pro forma information is now normally included where there has been a "significant gross change" (as defined in Recital (9))
7 and 8	Principles still applicable
9	Not applicable – replaced by the following: Item 20.2 of Annex I of the PD Regulation. In the case of a significant gross change, a description of how the transaction might have affected the assets and liabilities and earnings of the issuer, had the transaction been undertaken at the commencement of the period being reported on or at the date reported. This requirement will normally be satisfied by the inclusion of pro forma financial information. This pro forma financial information is to be presented as set out in Annex II and must include the information indicated therein. Pro forma financial information must be accompanied by a report prepared by independent accountants or auditors.
10 and 11	Principles still applicable
12 to 19	Principles still applicable save that there is no express requirement under the PD Regulation for all appropriate adjustments to be included, nor for the pro forma financial information not to be misleading
20	Not applicable – replaced by the following (the words **emphasised** are additional to the original Listing Rule and certain other words have been deleted): Item 1 of Annex II of the PD Regulation. The pro forma information **must include a description of the transaction, the businesses or entities involved and the period to which it refers**, and must clearly state the following: a) the purpose **to** which it has been prepared; b) the fact that it has been prepared for illustrative purposes only; c) the fact that because of its nature, **the pro forma financial information addresses a hypothetical situation and, therefore, does not represent the company's actual financial position or results.** Item 2 of Annex II of the PD Regulation **In order to present pro forma financial information, a balance sheet and profit and loss account, and accompanying explanatory notes, depending on the circumstances may be included.**
21 to 24	Principles still applicable
25	Not applicable – replaced by the following:

---

[1] This Annexure applies to TECH 18/98 which was published by the ICAEW in 1998 and is available for download from its website. The ICAEW has indicated that it intends to update and reissue TECH 18/98. When it is reissued this Annexure will no longer be applicable and should not be used.

	Item 3 of Annex II of the PD Regulation. Pro forma financial information must **normally** be presented in columnar format, **composed of**: a) the **historical** unadjusted information; b) the pro forma adjustments; and c) the **resulting** pro forma financial information **in the final column**. **The sources of the pro forma financial information have to be stated and, if applicable, the financial statements of the acquired businesses or entities must be included in the prospectus** Item 4 of Annex II of the PD Regulation. The pro forma information must be prepared in a manner consistent with the accounting policies adopted by the issuer in its **last or next** financial statements and shall identify the following: a) the basis upon which it is prepared; b) the source of each item of information and adjustment.
26	Principles still applicable
27	Principles still applicable, save that the accounting policies to be used in the next financial statements may also be applied
28 to 29	Principles still applicable
30	Not applicable
31 and 32	Principles still applicable
33	Not applicable
34	Applicable, save that the words "*and, in the case of a pro forma balance sheet or net asset statement, as at the date on which such periods end or ended*" are omitted
35 to 43	Principles still applicable
44 and 45	Not applicable
46 to 71	Principles still applicable
72 to 74	Not applicable

[5000]
Investment reporting standards applicable to public reporting engagements on financial information reconciliations under the listing rules

Contents

	Paragraphs
Introduction	1 – 4
The nature of financial information reconciliations	5 – 9
Engagement acceptance and continuance	10 – 14
Agreeing the terms of the engagement	15
Ethical requirements	16
Legal and regulatory requirements	17 – 19
Quality control	20
Planning and performing the engagement	21 – 51
Materiality	*28 – 32*
Public reporting engagement risk	*33 – 35*
Consideration of directors' procedures and controls	*36 – 38*
Unadjusted financial information of the target	*39 – 41*
Completeness of adjustments and consistency of accounting policies	*42 – 46*
Checking the calculations	*47 – 48*
Presentation of the financial information reconciliation	*49 – 50*
Representation letter	*51*
Documentation	52
Professional scepticism	53
Reporting	54 – 60
Responsibilities	*55 – 57*
Basis of preparation of the financial information reconciliation	*58*
Expression of opinion	*59 – 60*
Modified opinions	61 – 63
Consent	64
Events occurring between the date of the reporting accountant's report and the completion date of the transaction	65
Effective date	66

Appendices

1. Regulatory provisions applicable to Class 1 circulars
2. Examples of engagement letter clauses
3. Examples of management representation letter clauses
4. Example report on a financial information reconciliation in accordance with the Listing Rules

ANNEXURE

Accounting conventions and processes used in preparing financial information reconciliations for inclusion in Class 1 circulars.

Investment reporting standards applicable to public reporting engagements on financial information reconciliations under the listing rules

SIR 1000 "Investment reporting standards applicable to all engagements in connection with an investment circular" contains basic principles and essential procedures ("Investment Reporting Standards") that are applicable to all engagements involving an investment circular. The definitions in the glossary of terms set out in Appendix 4 of SIR 1000 are to be applied in the interpretation of this and all other SIRs. Terms defined in the glossary are underlined the first time that they occur in the text.

SIR 5000 contains additional Investment Reporting Standards, indicated by paragraphs in bold type, with which a reporting accountant is required to comply in the conduct of an engagement to report on financial information reconciliations which are included within a Class 1 circular prepared for issue in connection with a securities transaction governed wholly or in part by the laws and regulations of the United Kingdom or the Republic of Ireland.

SIR 5000 also includes explanatory and other material, including appendices, in the context of which the Investment Reporting Standards are to be understood and applied. It is necessary to consider the whole text of the SIR to understand and apply the basic principles and essential procedures.

To assist readers, SIRs contain references to, and extracts from, certain legislation and chapters of the Rules of the UK Listing Authority (UKLA) and the Listing Rules of the Irish Stock Exchange Limited (ISE) (together "the Listing Rules"). Readers are cautioned that these references may change subsequent to publication.

Introduction

1   Standard for Investment Reporting (SIR) 1000 "Investment Reporting Standards applicable to all engagements in connection with an Investment Circular" establishes the Investment Reporting Standards applicable to all engagements involving investment circulars. The purpose of SIR 5000 is to establish specific additional Investment Reporting Standards and provide guidance for a reporting accountant engaged to report publicly on reconciliations of the financial information of a target[1] to the accounting policies of an issuer (financial information reconciliations) to be included in a Class 1 circular under the Listing Rules.

2   Financial information reconciliations (sometimes referred to as GAAP reconciliations) may be included in investment circulars other than Class 1 circulars. If the reporting accountant is requested to report in similar terms to those for a Class 1 circular in such a context, and agrees to do so, the guidance in this SIR may be helpful. However, this SIR is not intended to be used in connection with GAAP reconciliations that are included within a note to financial statements included in an investment circular.

3   An engagement to report on the proper compilation of financial information reconciliations is a public reporting engagement as described in SIR 1000. The description of a public reporting engagement includes three generic terms having the

---

[1] Under UKLA LR 13.5.1R(1): ISE LR 10.5.1(1) where a listed company is seeking to acquire an interest in another company, that company is described as a "target".

following meanings in the context of an engagement to report on the proper compilation of financial information reconciliations:

(a) the "**subject matter**" is the target's financial information for the periods being reported on, presented in accordance with the target's accounting policies (ie the target's unadjusted financial information);
(b) the "**suitable criteria**" are the requirements of the financial reporting framework adopted by the issuer, the accounting policies of the issuer and any "accepted conventions", as set out in the Annexure, that have been applied; and
(c) the "**outcome**[2]" is the financial information of the target, as adjusted, together with the adjustments, that is included in the Class 1 circular and which has resulted from the directors applying the suitable criteria to the subject matter. The reporting accountant expresses an opinion as to whether that financial information (as adjusted) is properly compiled on the basis stated and whether the adjustments are appropriate for presenting the financial information (as adjusted) on a basis consistent in all material respects with the issuer's accounting policies.

In order to express an opinion on the reconciliation the reporting accountant is not required to re-assess any judgments or estimates underlying the subject matter or provide an opinion on the subject matter.

The nature of financial information reconciliations

Paragraph 5 of SIR 2000 "Investment Reporting Standards Applicable to Public Reporting Engagements on Historical Financial Information" describes, with respect to Class 1 acquisitions, the requirements of the Listing Rules for a Class 1 circular to include a financial information table relating to the target and an accountant's opinion on that table.

However, under the Listing Rules, when an issuer seeks to acquire a publicly traded company (a target) a financial information table is not required to be presented on the basis of the issuer's accounting policies but is presented on the basis of the target's accounting policies. Consequently the accountant's opinion described in SIR 2000 is not required and there are additional Listing Rules that apply[3].

Under these additional rules (see Appendix 1), where a material adjustment needs to be made to the financial information presented in respect of the target in the Class 1 circular to achieve consistency with the issuer's accounting policies, the issuer is required to include the following in the Class 1 circular[4]:

(a) a reconciliation of financial information on the target, for all periods covered by the financial information table, normally on the basis of the accounting policies used in the issuer's last published accounts[5];
(b) an accountant's opinion that sets out:

---

[2] *The "outcome" is sometimes described as "subject matter information".*

[3] *These rules are UKLA LR 13.5.27R and 13.5.28R; ISE LR 10.5.27 and 10.5.28.*

[4] *Under UKLA LR 13.5.30R(2) and ISE LR 10.5.30(2) similar requirements apply where the target has published half yearly or quarterly financial information subsequent to the end of its last financial year and a material adjustment needs to be made to the financial information presented in respect of the relevant interim period of the target in the Class 1 circular to achieve consistency with the issuer's accounting policies.*

[5] *The UKLA's publication "List!" 16 at paragraph 2.5 discusses certain circumstances where accounting policies other than those used in the issuer's last published accounts are used.*

(i) whether the reconciliation of financial information in the financial information table has been properly compiled on the basis stated; and
(ii) whether the adjustments are appropriate for the purpose of presenting the financial information (as adjusted) on a basis consistent in all material respects with the issuer's accounting policies.

If no material adjustment needs to be made to the target's financial information, in order to achieve consistency with the issuer's accounting policies, then the Class 1 circular is not required to include a financial information reconciliation.

8   The need for a financial information reconciliation usually arises because the target and the issuer prepare their respective financial statements in accordance with different financial reporting frameworks (for example, the issuer may prepare its financial statements in accordance with International Financial Reporting Standards as adopted by the European Union and the target may prepare its financial statements in accordance with United States Generally Accepted Accounting Principles) but may also arise through different choices made within the same financial reporting framework.

9   Other than the need for the financial information to be presented on a basis consistent in all material respects with the listed company's accounting policies, the Listing Rules contain no further requirements regarding the proper compilation of the financial information reconciliation, or the appropriateness of adjustments. In particular, the Listing Rules do not specify the individual financial statements or financial statement components that should comprise "financial information" for this purpose. Consequently the directors have regard to accepted conventions which have developed for the preparation and presentation of financial information reconciliations in Class 1 circulars. The Annexure provides a summary of these accepted conventions.

Engagement acceptance and continuance

10   SIR 1000.1 and SIR 1000.2 set out the Investment Reporting Standards with respect to engagement acceptance and continuance that are applicable to all engagements involving an investment circular. Additional Investment Reporting Standards and guidance are set out below.

11   When accepting or continuing an engagement to report publicly on financial information reconciliations, the reporting accountant ascertains whether the directors intend to comply with the relevant regulatory requirements.

12   In determining whether the persons who are to perform the engagement collectively possess the necessary professional competence the reporting accountant should:

(a) assess whether the engagement team[6], or those with whom the engagement team intend to consult, have sufficient knowledge and experience of the issuer's financial reporting framework; and

[6] *The "engagement team" is any person within the reporting accountant's firm who is directly involved in the engagement including:*
   (a) the partners, managers and staff from assurance and other disciplines involved in the engagement (for example, taxation specialists, IT specialists, treasury management specialists, lawyers, actuaries); and
   (b) those who provide quality control or direct oversight of the engagement

(b) consider the extent to which the engagement team requires knowledge of the target's financial reporting framework or are able to consult with those having such knowledge having regard to management's processes. (SIR 5000.1)

Where the target's or the issuer's financial information has been prepared in accordance with a financial reporting framework other than that of the country in which the reporting accountant practises[7], the reporting accountant determines whether it has, or can obtain, the necessary professional competence to evaluate whether the financial information reconciliation has been prepared in accordance with the requirements of the Listing Rules.

The successful completion of the reporting accountant's engagement will depend on receiving, on a timely basis, the co-operation of the management and directors both of the issuer and of the target including their disclosure to the reporting accountant of all the pertinent accounting records and any other relevant records and related information. In a hostile bid, or other limited access situation, the reporting accountant is unlikely to obtain the necessary access to the officials and records of the target and, therefore, is unlikely to be in a position to report on a financial information reconciliation. In such situations the circumstances are discussed with the UK Listing Authority[8] (UKLA) or the Irish Stock Exchange (ISE).

Agreeing the terms of the engagement

SIR 1000.3 and SIR 1000.4 set out the Investment Reporting Standards with respect to agreeing the terms of the engagement. Examples of engagement letter clauses are set out in Appendix 2 of this SIR.

Ethical requirements

SIR 1000.5 sets out the Investment Reporting Standard with respect to the ethical requirements that apply to a reporting accountant[9].

Legal and regulatory requirements

The legal and regulatory requirements relating to financial information reconciliations in Class 1 circulars are set out in Chapter 13 of the UKLA Listing Rules and Chapter 10 of the ISE Listing Rules. These chapters also set out the requirements for the inclusion of financial information tables in Class 1 circulars.

SIR 1000.6 sets out the Investment Reporting Standards with respect to the legal and regulatory requirements applicable to a reporting accountant.

---

[7] UKLA LR 13.5.23R and ISE LR 10.5.23 require that the accountant's opinion must be given by an independent accountant who is qualified to act as an auditor. With the exception of paragraph 56, this SIR is drafted on the presumption that the opinion is provided by the issuer's reporting accountant or auditor. However, this need not be the case.

[8] The UKLA generally encourages advisers or issuers preparing an investment circular in a limited access situation to contact them as soon as possible to discuss the exact disclosure requirements. In certain circumstances it may be appropriate for a financial information reconciliation to be published in a supplementary circular within 28 days of a contested offer becoming unconditional.

[9] In October 2006 the APB issued the Ethical Standard for Reporting Accountants (ESRA).

19 Appendix 1 summarises the relevant requirements of the Listing Rules and illustrates those requirements that are dealt with by SIR 2000 and those dealt with by SIR 5000.

Quality control

20 SIR 1000.7 and SIR 1000.8 set out the Investment Reporting Standards with respect to the quality control of engagements to report on financial information reconciliations.

Planning and performing the engagement

21 SIR 1000.9 and SIR 1000.10 set out the Investment Reporting Standards with respect to the planning of all reporting engagements. Additional Investment Reporting Standards and guidance are set out below.

22 The reporting accountant should obtain an understanding of those factors affecting the subject matter sufficient to identify and assess the risk of the financial information reconciliation not being properly compiled and the adjustments being inappropriate for the purpose of presenting the financial information (as adjusted) on a basis consistent in all material respects with the issuer's accounting policies. The reporting accountant's understanding should be sufficient to design and perform evidence gathering procedures and in particular should include:

(a) the nature of the target's and the issuer's businesses;
(b) the accounting policies of the target and of the issuer and the application of those policies;
(c) the requirements of the issuer's financial reporting framework;
(d) the extent to which the issuer has employees with the requisite knowledge of the financial reporting framework used by the target, or the ability to consult with those having such knowledge; and
(e) the procedures and controls adopted, or planned to be adopted, by the directors for the preparation of the financial information reconciliation. (SIR 5000.2)

23 The reporting accountant may gain an understanding of the nature of the target's business in a number of ways, for example:

- Reviewing publicly available information on the target.
- Through discussion with the issuer's directors or management.
- Through discussion with the target's directors or management.
- Through discussion with the target's auditor, where that auditor is prepared to assist the reporting accountant to gain a wider understanding of the target, its financial reporting procedures and the way in which its accounting policies are applied.

24 In obtaining an understanding of the target's and the issuer's businesses the reporting accountant may consider the following, for example:

- Business operations:
  - Conduct of operations and nature of revenue sources.
  - Products or services and markets.
- Financing and Investments:
  - Group structure.
  - Finance structure.
  - Investments in non-consolidated entities, including partnerships, joint ventures and special purpose entities.

- Financial reporting:
  - Industry specific practices.
  - Revenue recognition practices.
  - Accounting for unusual or complex transactions including those in emerging areas.

Under the Listing Rules the financial information reconciliation on the target is required to be prepared on the basis of the accounting policies of the issuer[10]. Guidance in the Listing Rules indicates that "accounting policies" includes accounting standards and accounting disclosures[11]. A financial information reconciliation, therefore, is not confined to a reconciliation to the published accounting policies of an issuer but also to those accounting standards comprising the issuer's financial reporting framework, regardless of whether they are articulated within the issuer's statement of accounting policies, even if they have not previously been relevant to the issuer. Accordingly, both the issuer and the reporting accountant consider the extent to which they will need access to expertise in the target's financial reporting framework. However financial information reconciliations do not normally extend to reconciling note disclosures.

Other matters for consideration by the reporting accountant include the availability of evidence to support the proposed adjustments and the accounting policies that will form the basis of the adjustments to the target's financial information.

The reporting accountant should consider materiality and public reporting engagement risk in planning its work in accordance with its instructions and in determining the effect of its findings on the report to be issued. (SIR 5000.3)

Materiality

The Listing Rules require a financial information reconciliation to be included in a Class 1 circular only when a material adjustment needs to be made to the target's financial information to achieve consistency with the listed company's accounting policies[12]. The judgment concerning materiality to comply with the Listing Rules is the responsibility of the issuer. The reporting accountant is not required to evaluate this determination of materiality made by the issuer. However, if the reporting accountant becomes aware that a material adjustment may need to be made to the target's financial statements to achieve consistency with the listed company's accounting policies, and the issuer has not prepared a financial information reconciliation, it discusses the matter with the directors of the issuer.

The following guidance on materiality addresses the reporting accountant's responsibilities with respect to a financial information reconciliation once the issuer is satisfied that the preparation of a financial information reconciliation is required under the Listing Rules.

Matters are material if their omission or misstatement could, individually or collectively, influence the economic decisions of the intended users of the financial information reconciliation. Materiality depends on the size and nature of the omission or misstatement judged in the light of the surrounding circumstances.

[10] *UKLA LR 13.5.4R and ISE LR10.5.4*

[11] *UKLA LR 13.5.5G and ISE LR 10.5.5.*

[12] *UKLA LRs 13.5.27R and 13.5.28R and ISE LRs 10.5.27 and 10.5.28.*

Materiality is determined by reference to the financial information of the target, as adjusted in the financial information reconciliation.

31 A misstatement in the context of the compilation of a financial information reconciliation includes, for example:

- Use of an inappropriate source for the target's financial information.
- Incorrect extraction of the target's financial information from an appropriate source.
- In relation to adjustments, the misapplication of accounting policies or failure to use the issuer's accounting policies.
- Failure to make an adjustment necessary for the purpose of presenting the financial information (as adjusted) on a basis consistent in all material respects with the issuer's accounting policies.
- Disclosing as an adjustment the rectification of an error in the underlying financial information of the target[13].
- A mathematical or clerical mistake.

32 If the reporting accountant becomes aware of a material misstatement in the financial information reconciliation it discusses the matter with the directors of the issuer. If the reporting accountant is not able to agree with the directors as to how the matter is to be resolved it considers the consequences for its opinion.

Public reporting engagement risk

33 "Public reporting engagement risk" is the risk that the reporting accountant expresses an inappropriate opinion when the financial information reconciliation has not been properly compiled on the basis stated or when the adjustments are not appropriate for the purpose of presenting the financial information (as adjusted) on a basis consistent, in all material respects, with the accounting policies of the issuer.

34 SIR 1000.11 and SIR 1000.12 set out the Investment Reporting Standards with respect to obtaining evidence that are applicable to all engagements involving an investment circular. Additional Investment Reporting Standards and guidance relating to engagements to report on financial information reconciliations are set out below.

35 **The reporting accountant should assess whether the reconciliation of financial information in the financial information table has been properly compiled on the basis stated and whether the adjustments are appropriate for the purpose of presenting the financial information (as adjusted) on a basis consistent in all material respects with the issuer's accounting policies. In making these assessments the reporting accountant should, having regard to the procedures and controls adopted by the directors:**

(a) **check whether the financial information of the target has been accurately extracted from an appropriate source;**
(b) **assess whether all adjustments necessary for the purpose of presenting the financial information (as adjusted) on a basis consistent in all material respects with the issuer's accounting policies have been made; and**
(c) **check the arithmetical accuracy of the calculations within the financial information reconciliation. (SIR 5000.4)**

---

[13] See discussion in paragraph 12 of Annexure concerning the manner in which a rectification of a misstatement in the underlying financial information may be disclosed.

Consideration of directors' procedures and controls

In assessing whether the financial information reconciliation has been properly compiled on the basis stated and whether the adjustments are appropriate the reporting accountant has regard to the procedures and controls adopted by the issuer. Such procedures and controls may encompass both high-level internal controls over the reconciliation process and lower level accounting control activities.

High-level internal controls over the reconciliation process that the reporting accountant may wish to assess include, whether:

- Employees (or outside experts utilised by the issuer), have the requisite knowledge and experience to prepare and monitor the preparation of the reconciliation.
- The directors of the issuer have been involved to an appropriate extent in the preparation of the financial information reconciliation.
- Where applicable, management has compared the reconciliation to any that may have been made before.

Examples of accounting control activities that the reporting accountant may wish to assess include, whether:

- When making adjustments management sought to ensure that the principles of double-entry bookkeeping were followed such that "one-sided" entries were not made.
- Management considered the tax effects of the adjustments and assessed whether the resultant effective tax rate is understandable and meaningful.
- Management analysed the differences between the opening and closing equity account balances, as adjusted. (This is sometimes referred to as an equity roll forward reconciliation.) Such an analysis would have assisted management in seeking to ensure that the principles of double-entry bookkeeping have been followed where the other side of an adjustment is to an equity account.
- Management considered whether the cash and cash equivalent position, as adjusted, is (and should be) the same as that shown by the unadjusted financial statements. If there is a difference between the cash position reported on the two bases management should be able to explain how the difference arises and, in particular, to have considered whether the difference may reflect an error in the double-entry bookkeeping applied to the reconciliation process.

Unadjusted financial information of the target

The reporting accountant assesses whether the unadjusted financial information has been extracted from an appropriate source: namely the financial information table of the target included in the Class 1 circular or such published half yearly or quarterly financial information that is required, by the Listing Rules[14], to be reproduced in the Class 1 circular.

The reporting accountant is not required to perform specific procedures on the unadjusted financial information of the target other than as described in paragraph 39, and in particular is not required to audit the unadjusted financial information. However, if the reporting accountant has reason to believe that the unadjusted financial information is, or may be, unreliable, or if a report thereon has identified any uncertainties or disagreements, the reporting accountant considers the effect on the financial information reconciliation.

[14] *UKLA LR13.5.30R(1) and ISE LR10.5.30(1)*

41 When the directors have identified an error in the underlying financial information that does not reflect a genuine difference between the accounting policies of the target and the issuer it is not rectified by being presented as an adjustment. The issuer would discuss the proposed presentation of the rectification of the error with the UKLA or the ISE. The reporting accountant would wish to see evidence, based on such discussions, of the agreement of the UKLA or the ISE to the proposed presentation of the rectification of the error.

Completeness of adjustments and consistency of accounting policies

42 In assessing the completeness of the adjustments and whether the adjustments are appropriate for the purpose of presenting the financial information (as adjusted) on a basis consistent, in all material respects, with the issuer's accounting policies, the reporting accountant utilises its expertise, and the expertise of those with whom they have consulted, in the issuer's financial reporting framework.

43 The reporting accountant assesses the thoroughness with which the directors have fulfilled their responsibility for ensuring the completeness of adjustments. In view of the importance of the accuracy of a financial reconciliation to potential investors the directors will be expected to have carefully analysed the target's accounting policies and prepared an "impact analysis" of the effect of applying the issuer's accounting policies to the target's financial information. With its understanding of the target and the issuer's business as background (see paragraph 24) the reporting accountant discusses with the directors the steps the directors have taken to identify relevant adjustments.

44 As described in paragraph 25 the definition of accounting policies in the Listing Rules encompasses the accounting standards of the applicable financial reporting framework. The reporting accountant's assessment of the completeness of adjustments is likely to include gaining an understanding of the differences between the financial reporting frameworks of the target and the issuer and, in particular:

(a) identifying those accounting standards in the issuer's or the target's financial reporting framework that may have a particular impact on the target's or issuer's industries;
(b) assessing the adequacy of the directors' impact analysis;
(c) considering the adequacy of the process followed by the issuer in ensuring the completeness of the adjustments, in particular the depth of involvement of senior management in the preparation of the reconciliation. Paragraphs 23 to 33 of the Annexure describe in more detail the processes that management may use when preparing a financial information reconciliation; and
(d) assessing whether the reconciliation, taken as a whole, appears to have any material omissions.

45 **The reporting accountant should obtain sufficient appropriate evidence that the issuer can support each adjustment (including the detailed calculation of the adjustment) and that, where appropriate, such support has been obtained from the appropriate level of management of the target. (SIR 5000.5)**

46 If the reporting accountant becomes aware of an adjustment which:

(a) in its opinion, ought to be made for the purposes of the financial information reconciliation; or
(b) in its opinion, ought not to have been made for the purposes of the financial information reconciliation; or

(c) the directors of the issuer cannot support (either in principle or in matters of detail and computation),

it discusses the position with the directors of the issuer and, if necessary, the issuer's advisers. If the reporting accountant is not able to agree with the directors of the issuer and the issuer's advisers as to how the matter is to be resolved it considers the consequences for its report.

Checking the calculations

The reporting accountant ascertains whether the adjustments made in the financial information reconciliation are included under the appropriate financial statement captions as well as the arithmetical accuracy of the calculations within the financial information reconciliation itself. 47

In respect of the adjustments the reporting accountant checks the calculation of the effect on the target's financial information of applying the accounting policy of the issuer rather than the accounting policies of the target. 48

Presentation of the financial information reconciliation

The reporting accountant should consider whether it has become aware of anything to cause it to believe that the financial information reconciliation is presented in a way that is not understandable or is misleading in the context in which it is provided. If the reporting accountant is aware of such matters it should discuss them with the directors of the issuer and any other persons to whom its report is to be addressed, and consider whether it is able to issue its opinion. (SIR 5000.6) 49

The underlying principle is that a reader of the Class 1 circular will be able to understand how the adjustments that have been made affect the underlying financial information. The reporting accountant may wish to assess whether, for example, there is adequate disclosure of the specific line items of the income statement or balance sheet that give rise to an adjustment. 50

Representation letter

SIR 1000.13 sets out the Investment Reporting Standard with respect to representation letters that is applicable to all engagements involving an investment circular. Examples of representation letter clauses applicable to financial information reconciliations are set out in Appendix 3. 51

Documentation

SIR 1000.14 and SIR 1000.15 set out the Investment Reporting Standards with respect to the reporting accountant's working papers. 52

Professional scepticism

SIR 1000.16 sets out the Investment Reporting Standard with respect to the attitude of professional scepticism adopted by the reporting accountant in planning and performing an engagement. 53

Reporting

54 SIR 1000.17, SIR 1000.18 and SIR 1000.19 set out the Investment Reporting Standards with respect to reporting that are applicable to all engagements involving an investment circular. Additional Investment Reporting Standards relating to engagements to report on financial information reconciliations are set out below. An example report on a financial information reconciliation prepared in accordance with the Listing Rules is set out in Appendix 4.

Responsibilities

55 In all reports on financial information reconciliations in Class 1 circulars the reporting accountant should explain the extent of its responsibility in respect of the reconciliations by including in its report:

(a) a statement that the reporting accountant's responsibility is to form an opinion as to whether the reconciliations have been properly compiled on the basis stated and the adjustments are appropriate for the purpose of presenting the financial information (as adjusted) on a basis consistent in all material respects with the accounting policies of the issuer and to report its opinion to the addressees of the report; and

(b) a statement that the financial information reconciliation is the responsibility of the directors. (SIR 5000.7)

56 The reporting accountant's responsibility in relation to the opinion required by the Listing Rules is limited to the provision of the report and the opinion expressed. Where an audit or other opinion has been expressed on the financial information of the target by a firm other than the reporting accountant, the reporting accountant may state in the responsibilities section that it does not accept any responsibility for any of the historical financial statements of the target and that it expresses no opinion on those financial statements. An example of such a reference is included in the example report in Appendix 4.

57 Where the reporting accountant has provided an audit or other opinion on the financial information of the target the reporting accountant may state in the responsibilities section that:

(a) it is not updating or refreshing any reports or opinions previously made by it on any financial information used in the compilation of the reconciliations; and

(b) it accepts no responsibility for such reports or opinions beyond that owed to those to whom those reports or opinions were addressed at the date of their issue.

An example of such a reference is included in the example report in Appendix 4.

Basis of preparation of the financial information reconciliation

58 The reporting accountant should, in its report, cross refer to disclosures that explain the basis of preparation of the financial information reconciliation (SIR 5000.8).

Expression of opinion

59 The report on the financial information reconciliation should contain a clear expression of opinion that complies with the requirements of the Listing Rules. (SIR 5000.9)

The Class 1 circular in which the reporting accountant's report is included may be made available in other countries, such as the United States of America, which have their own standards for accountants when reporting on financial information reconciliations. In such circumstances, the reporting accountant considers whether to include a reference to the fact that a report issued in accordance with the SIRs should not be relied upon as if it had been issued in accordance with the standards applicable in that other country. An example of such a reference is included in the example report in Appendix 4.

Modified opinions

SIR 1000.20 sets out the Investment Reporting Standard, with respect to modified opinions, that is applicable to all engagements involving an investment circular.

With respect to the compilation of a financial information reconciliation, the reporting accountant may conclude that the outcome is materially misstated, (for example, in the circumstances described in paragraph 31 above), and in such circumstances considers the impact of such misstatements on its opinion.

In the event that the reporting accountant concludes that it is necessary to express a modified opinion it explains the circumstances to the directors of the issuer and any other parties to whom it is to report so that the issuer has an opportunity to amend the financial information reconciliation to alleviate the reporting accountant's concerns.

Consent

SIR 1000.21 and SIR 1000.22 set out the Investment Reporting Standards with respect to the giving of consent by the reporting accountant.

Events occurring between the date of the reporting accountant's report and the completion date of the transaction

After the date of its report, the reporting accountant has no obligation to perform procedures or make enquiries regarding the Class 1 circular. However, the reporting accountant may become aware of events and other matters which, had they occurred and been known at the date of the report, might have caused it to issue a different report or to withhold consent. SIR 1000.23 sets out the Investment Reporting Standards with respect to such events occurring between the date of the reporting accountant's report and the completion date of the transaction.

Effective date

A reporting accountant is required to comply with the Investment Reporting Standards contained in this SIR for reports signed after 31 May 2008. Earlier adoption is encouraged.

Appendix 1 – Regulatory provisions applicable to class 1 circulars

Type of Class 1 Transaction	SIR 2000 – Requirement for a financial information table	SIR 2000 – Requirement for an accountant's opinion in true and fair terms	SIR 2000 – Possibility of a modified opinion	SIR 5000 – Requirement for a financial information reconciliation	SIR 5000 – Requirement for an accountant's opinion in properly compiled terms	SIR 5000 – Possibility of a modified opinion
Class 1 Acquisition of a target that is neither admitted to trading, listed on an overseas investment exchange, nor admitted to trading on an overseas regulated market.	✓ UKLA 13.5.12R UKLA 13.5.14R ISE 10.5.12 ISE 10.5.14	✓ UKLA 13.5.21R UKLA 13.5.22R ISE 10.5.21 ISE 10.5.22	✓ UKLA 13.5.25R ISE 10.5.25	✗	✗	n/a
Class 1 Acquisition of a target that is admitted to trading …and a material adjustment needs to be made.	✓ UKLA 13.5.12R UKLA 13.5.14R ISE 10.5.12 ISE 10.5.14	✗ UKLA 13.5.21R ISE 10.5.21	n/a	UKLA 13.5.27R(2)(a) UKLA 13.5.30R(2) ISE 10.5.27(2)(a) ISE 10.5.30(2)	UKLA 13.5.27R(2)(b) UKLA 13.5.30R(2) ISE 10.5.27(2)(b) ISE 10.5.30(2)	UKLA 13.5.27R(2)(b) UKLA 13.5.30R ISE 10.5.27(2)(b) ISE 10.5.30
Class 1 Acquisition of a target that is admitted to trading … and NO material adjustment needs to be made	✓ UKLA 13.5.12R UKLA 13.5.14R ISE 10.5.12 ISE 10.5.14	✓ UKLA 13.5.21R ISE 10.5.21	n/a	✗ If no material adjustment required then not in scope of UKLA 13.5.27R: ISE 10.5.27	UKLA 13.5.28R ISE 10.5.28	n/a
Class 1 disposal	✓ UKLA 13.5.12R UKLA 13.5.19R ISE 10.5.12 ISE 10.5.19	✗ UKLA 13.5.21R UKLA 13.5.29G ISE 10.5.21 ISE 10.5.29	n/a	✗	✗	n/a

Note 1: Within Chapter 13 of the UKLA Listing Rules and Chapter 10 of the ISE Listing Rules the terms "financial information" and "financial information table" are used. The terms have different meanings in that the requirements for a financial information table are set out in UKLA LR 13.5.18R and ISE 10.5.18 whereas the term financial information is not defined.
Note 2: Within Chapter 13 of the UKLA Listing Rules and Chapter 10 of the ISE Listing Rules two different types of accountant's opinion are discussed. The opinion relevant to financial information reconciliations is set out in UKLA 13.5.27R (2)(b) and ISE 10.5.27(2)(b) and is dealt with in this SIR. The other opinion which is relevant to opinions on financial information tables is set out in UKLA LR 13.5.22R and ISE 10.5.22 and dealt with in SIR 2000.
Note 3: UKLA LR13.5.30R(2) and ISE 10.5.30(2) require a financial information reconciliation of a target to be produced with respect to subsequent half yearly or quarterly financial information

Appendix 2 – Examples of engagement letter clauses

The examples of engagement letter clauses are intended for consideration in the context of a public reporting engagement on a financial information reconciliation in a Class 1 circular. They should be tailored to the specific circumstances and supplemented by such other clauses as are relevant and appropriate.

Financial information upon which the report is to be given

The Class 1 circular will include a financial information table relating to ABC Inc. prepared in accordance with the requirements of Listing Rule [13.5.18R] [10.5.18] [and interim financial information relating to ABC Inc. reproduced in accordance with Listing Rule [13.5.30R(2)] [10.5.30(2)]].

We understand that the Class 1 circular will also include a financial information reconciliation of ABC Inc. for the three years ended [31 December 200X] [and the interim period ended [*date*]] (the "Reconciliation"). The Reconciliation will comprise [the income statements] and [balance sheets] of ABC Inc. showing the adjustments necessary to restate them to conform to XYZ plc's stated accounting policies. The Reconciliation will include supporting notes to explain the adjustments made.

Responsibilities

The preparation of the Reconciliation in accordance with the requirements of the Listing Rules will be the responsibility solely of the directors.

It is our responsibility to form an opinion as to whether the Reconciliation has been properly compiled on the basis stated and the adjustments are appropriate for the purpose of presenting the financial information (as adjusted) on a basis consistent in all material respects with the accounting policies of XYZ plc.

If the results of our work are satisfactory, and having regard to the requirements of Listing Rule [13.5.27R (2)(b)] [10.5.27(2)(b)] [and Listing Rule [13.5.30(2)] [10.5.30(2)]], we shall prepare a report on the Reconciliation for inclusion in the Class 1 circular. An illustration of the form of our report if the results of our work are satisfactory is attached.

Scope of work

Our work will be undertaken in accordance with the Standards for Investment Reporting issued by the Auditing Practices Board and will be subject to the limitations described therein.

In performing this engagement we will expect to receive, without undue delay, such:

(a) co-operation from all relevant officials of XYZ plc and ABC Inc. [including its auditors];
(b) access to all the pertinent accounting records of XYZ plc and ABC Inc. and any other relevant records and related information; [and]
(c) representations from XYZ plc[; and]
(d) [access to the files of the auditors of ABC Inc.],

as we may need for the purposes of our examination.

Appendix 3 – Examples of management representation letter clauses

The following are examples of management representation letter clauses relating to reports on financial information reconciliations, issued pursuant to the Listing Rules, which may be obtained from the issuer. Alternatively they may form the basis for a board minute.

Introduction

We refer to the financial information reconciliation set out in Part [...] of the [Class 1 circular] dated...(the "Reconciliation"). We acknowledge that we are solely responsible for the Reconciliation and confirm on behalf of the directors of the company to the best of our knowledge and belief, having made appropriate enquiries of officials of the company [and the directors and officials of the [target]], the following representations made to you in the course of your work.

Specific representations

- We acknowledge as duly appointed officials of the company our responsibility for the Reconciliation which has been prepared in accordance with the requirements of the Listing Rules of [the United Kingdom Listing Authority] [the Irish Stock Exchange Limited].
- We have considered the adjustments included in the Reconciliation. We confirm that, in our opinion, the Reconciliation includes all adjustments that are appropriate for the purpose of presenting the financial information (as adjusted) on a basis consistent in all material respects with the accounting policies of XYZ plc.
- We have made available to you all significant information relevant to the Reconciliation of which we have knowledge.
- [...*Any specific representations relating to information included in the Reconciliations (for example representations concerning accounting policies in greater detail than that included in the published financial statements).*]

Appendix 4 – Example report on a financial information reconciliation in accordance with the listing rules

Date

Reporting accountant's address

Addressees, as agreed between the parties in the engagement letter

Dear Sirs,

XYZ plc (the "Company"): proposed acquisition of ABC Inc (the "Target")

We report on the reconciliation of [*describe items reconciled* the consolidated income statement for each of the years in the three-year period ended [*date*] [and the interim period ended [*date*]], and of *describe items reconciled* the consolidated balance sheet as at[*dates*]], together the "financial information", as previously reported in the financial statements of the Target prepared under [United States Generally Accepted Accounting Principles], showing the adjustments necessary to restate it on the basis of the Company's accounting policies [specify the accounting policies e.g. those used in preparing the Company's last set of annual financial statements] (the "Reconciliation"), set out in Part [ ] of the Class 1 circular of the Company dated [*date*]. This report is required by Listing Rule[s] [13.5.27R(2)(b) [and 13.5.30R(2)] of the United Kingdom Listing Authority] [10.5.27(2)(b) [and 10.5.30(2) of the Irish Stock Exchange Limited]] and is given for the purpose of complying with [that] [those] Listing Rule[s] and for no other purpose.

Responsibilities

It is the responsibility of the directors of the Company (the "Directors") to prepare the Reconciliation in accordance with Listing Rule[s] [13.5.27R(2)(a) [and 13.5.30R(2)]] [10.5.27(2)(a) [and 10.5.30(2)]].

It is our responsibility to form an opinion, as required by Listing Rule[s] [13.5.27R(2)(b) [and 13.5.30R(2)]] [10.5.27(2)(a) and 10.5.30(2)]], as to whether:

(a) the Reconciliation has been properly compiled on the basis stated; and
(b) the adjustments are appropriate for the purpose of presenting the financial information (as adjusted) on a basis consistent in all material respects with the Company's accounting policies,

and to report that opinion to you.

[*Insert where an audit or other opinion has been expressed on the financial statements of the Target upon which the Reconciliation is based by a firm other than the reporting accountant, or where such information is unaudited:* The Reconciliation is based on the [un]audited balance sheet[s] as at [*dates*] and income statement[s] for [each of] the [year[s]]/[period[s]] then ended of [the Target] which were the responsibility of the directors of [the Target] [and were audited by another firm of accountants]. We do not accept any responsibility for any of the historical financial statements of [the Target], nor do we express any opinion on those financial statements.]

[*Insert where the reporting accountant has provided an audit or other opinion on the financial statements of the Target upon which the Reconciliation is based:* In providing this opinion we are not updating or refreshing any reports or opinions previously made by us on any financial information used in the compilation of the Reconciliation, nor do we accept responsibility for such reports or opinions beyond that owed to those to whom those reports or opinions were addressed at the date of their issue.]

Basis of Opinion

We conducted our work in accordance with the Standards for Investment Reporting issued by the Auditing Practices Board in [the United Kingdom] [Ireland]. The work that we performed for the purpose of making this report, which involved no independent examination of any of the underlying financial information, consisted primarily of checking whether the unadjusted financial information of [the Target] has been accurately extracted from an appropriate source, assessing whether all adjustments necessary for the purpose of presenting the financial information on a basis consistent in all material respects with [the Company's] accounting policies have been made, examination of evidence supporting the adjustments in the Reconciliation and checking the arithmetical accuracy of the calculations within the Reconciliation.

We planned and performed our work so as to obtain the information and explanations we considered necessary in order to provide us with reasonable assurance that the Reconciliation has been properly compiled on the basis stated and that the adjustments are appropriate for the purpose of presenting the financial information (as adjusted) on a basis consistent in all material respects with the Company's accounting policies.

[*This paragraph may be omitted if the document is not to be distributed outside [the UK] [Ireland]* – Our work has not been carried out in accordance with auditing or other standards and practices generally accepted in the United States of America [or other jurisdictions] and accordingly should not be relied upon as if it had been carried out in accordance with those standards and practices.]

Opinion

In our opinion:

(a) the Reconciliation has been properly compiled on the basis stated; and
(b) the adjustments are appropriate for the purpose of presenting the financial information (as adjusted) on a basis consistent in all material respects with the Company's accounting policies.

Declaration

[*This paragraph is only included if the investment circular is also a prospectus.* For the purposes of [Prospectus Rule [5.5.3R(2)(f)] [5.5.4R(2)(f)]] /[Paragraph 2(2)(f) of Schedule 1 to "The Prospectus (Directive 2003/71/EC) Regulations 2005"] [Paragraph 3(2)(f) of Schedule 1 to "the Prospectus (Directive 2003/71/EC) Regulations 2005"] we are responsible for this report as part of the [prospectus] [registration document] and declare that we have taken all reasonable care to ensure that the information contained [in this report] [those parts] is, to the best of our knowledge, in accordance with the facts and contains no omission likely to affect its import. This declaration is included in the [prospectus] [registration document] in compliance with [item 1.2 of Annex I of the PD Regulation] [item 1.2 of Annex III of the PD Regulation].]

Yours faithfully

Reporting accountant

Annexure

ACCOUNTING CONVENTIONS AND PROCESSES USED IN PREPARING FINANCIAL INFORMATION RECONCILIATIONS FOR INCLUSION IN CLASS 1 CIRCULARS

This Annexure has been compiled by the APB from a number of sources to describe conventions and processes commonly used for the proper compilation of financial information reconciliations. It does not constitute basic principles, essential procedures, or guidance promulgated by the APB.

Introduction

Financial information tables

1   With respect to Class 1 acquisitions, Chapter 13 of the Listing Rules of the UK Listing Authority (UKLA) and Chapter 10 of the Listing Rules of the Irish Stock Exchange Limited (ISE) set out requirements for a financial information table relating to targets[1].

2   A financial information table is required to include, for each of the periods covered by the table:

   (a) a balance sheet and its explanatory notes;
   (b) an income statement and its explanatory notes;
   (c) a cash flow statement and its explanatory notes;
   (d) a statement showing either all changes in equity or changes in equity other than those arising from capital transactions with owners and distributions to owners;
   (e) the accounting policies; and
   (f) any additional explanatory notes.

3   When an issuer seeks to acquire a target that is not publicly traded[2], the financial information table is presented on the basis of the issuer's accounting policies. However, when an issuer seeks to acquire a publicly traded target the financial information table is presented on the basis of the target's accounting policies.

4   With respect to a target that is not publicly traded a reporting accountant's opinion is required as to whether, for the purposes of the Class 1 circular, the financial information table gives a true and fair view of the financial matters set out in it, and whether the financial information table has been prepared in a form that is consistent with the accounting policies adopted in the listed company's latest annual consolidated accounts.

Financial information of publicly traded targets

5   With respect to targets that are publicly traded a reporting accountant's opinion on the financial information table is not required. However, with respect to a publicly traded target, if a material adjustment needs to be made to the target's financial

---

[1] Where a listed company is seeking to acquire an interest in another company, that company is described as a target.

[2] A target that is not publicly traded is one that is neither admitted to the Official List nor admitted to trading, listed on an overseas investment exchange nor admitted to trading on an overseas regulated market.

statements to achieve consistency with the issuer's accounting policies there are additional requirements.

Therefore, with respect to a publicly traded target, the issuer is required to make a determination as to whether material adjustments need to be made to the target's financial statements in order to achieve consistency with the issuer's accounting policies. Such a determination will need to be made by a staff member or outside expert having appropriate qualifications (see paragraph 23) and involve the identification of material differences (if any) between the accounting policies of the issuer and the accounting policies of the target (see paragraph 24).

Where such a material adjustment does need to be made the issuer is required to include the following in the Class 1 circular in addition to the financial information table referred to above[3]:

(a) a reconciliation of "financial information" on the target, for all periods covered by the financial information table, normally on the basis of the accounting policies used in the issuer's last published accounts[4];
(b) a reporting accountant's opinion on that reconciliation that sets out:
 (i) whether the reconciliation of financial information in the financial information table has been properly compiled on the basis stated; and
 (ii) whether the adjustments are appropriate for the purpose of presenting the financial information (as adjusted) on a basis consistent in all material respects with the issuer's accounting policies.

The need for accounting conventions

The term "financial information" is not defined by the Listing Rules nor are there any detailed rules regarding the "proper compilation" of a financial information reconciliation. The directors, therefore, have regard to accepted conventions which have developed for the preparation and presentation of financial information reconciliation tables in Class 1 circulars. These conventions are summarised in paragraphs 9 to 22 that follow. In paragraphs 23 to 33 there is a discussion of processes that the issuer may adopt when preparing financial information reconciliations.

Conventions

Format of financial information reconciliations

The overriding principle regarding the format of the presentation of a financial information reconciliation is that the presentation discloses all the material adjustments that are required to be made in order to present the financial information (as adjusted) on a basis consistent with the issuer's accounting policies. The relevant accounting policies of the issuer are normally those adopted by the issuer in its last published accounts.

---

[3] Under UKLA LR 13.5.30R(2) and ISE LR 10.5.30(2) similar requirements apply where the target has published half yearly or quarterly financial information subsequent to the end of its last financial year and a material adjustment needs to be made to the financial information presented in respect of the relevant interim period of the target in the Class 1 circular to achieve consistency with the issuer's accounting policies.

[4] The UKLA's publication "List!" 16 at paragraph 2.5 discusses certain circumstances where accounting policies other than those used in the issuer's last published accounts are used.

10 Financial information reconciliations typically address the balance sheet and income statement or extracts of the balance sheet and income statement. However, if there is a material adjustment required, for example, to the cash flow statement or the Statement of Changes in Equity then relevant financial information from the relevant statement may also be presented. A material adjustment may arise to the cash flow statement where the target and the issuer use different definitions of the composition of cash and cash equivalents.

11 There is no prescribed format for the presentation of the reconciliation. Sometimes they are presented in columnar form using as a basis the descriptions of financial statement items in the target's financial information. However, alternative presentations are commonly used and the underlying principle is that the reader of the Class 1 circular should be able to understand how the adjustments affect the underlying financial information.

Errors in the underlying financial information

12 Where an error in the underlying financial information is identified that does not reflect a genuine difference between the accounting policies of the target and the issuer it is not rectified by being presented as an adjustment. The issuer discusses the proposed presentation of the rectification of the error with the UKLA or the ISE.

13 What constitutes an error will be defined by the financial reporting framework used by the issuer. In the case of International Financial Reporting Standards (IFRSs) as adopted by the EU, for example, an error is defined as: "omissions from, and misstatements in, the target's financial statements, for one or more prior periods arising from a failure to use, or misuse of, reliable information that:

(a) was available when financial statements for those periods were authorised for issue; and
(b) could reasonably be expected to have been obtained and taken into account in the preparation and presentation of those financial statements.

Such errors include the effects of mathematical mistakes, mistakes in applying accounting policies, oversights or misinterpretations of fact and fraud".

Accounting policies

14 Guidance in UKLA Listing Rule 13.5.5G and ISE Listing Rule 10.5.5 indicates that "accounting policies include accounting standards and accounting disclosures". A financial information reconciliation, therefore, is not confined to a reconciliation to the stated accounting policies of an issuer but to those policies and the accounting standards comprising the financial reporting framework of the issuer regardless of whether they are articulated within the issuer's statement of accounting policies. However, reconciliations do not normally extend to reconciling note disclosures.

15 Under many financial reporting frameworks, such as IFRSs as adopted by the EU, the application of different measurement bases to financial statement items is evidence that different accounting policies have been applied. IAS 8 states "A change in the measurement basis applied is a change in an accounting policy and is not a change in an accounting estimate"[5]. Examples of measurement bases, described in

---

[5] *IAS 8 "Accounting Policies, Changes in Accounting Estimates and Errors" paragraph 35*

IFRSs as adopted by the EU are: historical cost, current cost, net realisable value, fair value or recoverable amount[6].

In the process of applying the entity's accounting policies, management makes various judgments, apart from those involving estimations (see paragraph 19) that can have a significant effect on the amounts recognised in the financial statements. Under IFRSs as adopted by the EU the entity is required to disclose those judgments that have the most significant effect on the amounts recognised in the financial statements[7]. 16

Examples of such judgments are: 17

- Whether financial assets are held-to-maturity investments.
- When substantially all the significant risks and rewards of ownership of financial assets and lease assets are transferred to other entities.
- Whether, in substance, particular sales of goods are financing arrangements and therefore do not give rise to revenue.
- Whether the substance of the relationship between the entity and a special purpose entity indicates that the special purpose entity is controlled by the entity.

Where the target and the issuer have made, or would make, different judgments in similar circumstances this gives rise to the need for an adjustment.

Accounting estimates

Although adjustments are made for differences in accounting policies (as defined), adjustments are not made to replace the target's accounting estimates with new estimates made by the issuer. However, in rare circumstances the effect of a difference from applying an accounting estimate may be material to the adjusted financial information and the issuer may consider that it is necessary to explain this through supplemental disclosure to allow the financial information reconciliation to be considered in context. An example of such a circumstance is where the issuer and the target both have a policy of depreciating a particular class of property, plant and equipment on a straight line basis over its expected useful life. However, the target's estimate of the expected useful life differs significantly from the issuer's estimated useful life and the effect of the difference in estimate is material to the financial information reconciliation. 18

Distinguishing between accounting policies and accounting estimates

Many financial reporting frameworks recognise that it can be difficult to distinguish changes in accounting policies from changes in accounting estimates and that in such instances of uncertainty the change is treated as a change in accounting estimate[8]. A similar principle applies when determining whether a target uses different accounting policies to those used by the issuer. 19

---

[6] IAS 1 "Presentation of financial statements" paragraph 109

[7] IAS 1 paragraphs 113 and 114

[8] IAS 8 paragraph 35

Explanation of adjustments

20 The overriding principle that the issuer follows is to ensure that the adjustments are clearly shown and explained.

21 The convention is that material adjustments are presented on a disaggregated basis (that is offsetting adjustments are not netted off) as such presentation enhances the understanding of the users of the reconciliation.

Material adjustments

22 The requirement for a reconciliation arises where a material adjustment needs to be made to the target's financial statements to achieve consistency with the listed company's accounting policies. It is not possible to prescribe conditions for determining whether an adjustment will be a material adjustment in any given case, although presentational accounting policy differences, which do not have the effect of altering net assets, net income or cash flows are not normally treated as material. The UKLA or the ISE will usually wish to agree the approach in individual cases.

Processes for preparing a financial information reconciliation

Identification of all material differences

23 In order to identify all material differences between the accounting policies of the issuer and the accounting policies of the target the issuer's staff responsible for preparation of the reconciliation will need to have (or acquire) a requisite degree of expertise with respect to both financial reporting frameworks. Such expertise may be augmented by the use of appropriate reference material and technical guides. In complex cases the issuer may have to employ an outside expert having appropriate qualifications.

Preparing a financial information reconciliation

24 There are four basic steps involved in preparing a financial information reconciliation. These are:
   (a) identification of all material differences between the accounting policies of the issuer and the accounting policies of the target (See paragraph 6);
   (b) performing an "impact analysis" by performing a detailed analysis of the application of those policies and gathering the relevant data to enable either:
       (i) the adjustments to be calculated; or
       (ii) a determination to be made that no adjustments are required.
   (c) in respect of each material difference calculating the effect on the target's financial information of applying the accounting policies of the issuer rather than the accounting policies of the target; and
   (d) ensuring that the bookkeeping underpinning the financial information reconciliation is complete and accurate.

25 In practice these steps will need to be undertaken by the issuer's staff responsible for preparation of the reconciliation in consultation with, and with the cooperation of, the relevant finance staff of the target. It is unlikely that the issuer's staff will be able to achieve the necessary understanding of the target's financial information without a high degree of involvement of the target's finance staff in the process. In a hostile bid,

or other limited access situation, the issuer is unlikely to be in a position to prepare a financial information reconciliation. In such situations the circumstances are discussed with the UKLA or the ISE.

The UKLA generally encourages issuers preparing an investment circular in a limited access situation to contact them as soon as possible to discuss the exact disclosure requirements. In certain circumstances it may be appropriate for a financial information reconciliation to be published in a supplementary circular within 28 days of a contested offer becoming unconditional. 26

Identification of all material differences between the accounting policies of the issuer and the target

As explained in paragraph 14 the identification is not confined to the stated accounting policies of the issuer or the target but also encompasses differences between those accounting standards that affect the financial statements of the issuer or the target regardless of whether the application of the accounting standards has been articulated in the statement of accounting policies. 27

Impact analysis

The issuer, therefore, gains an understanding of the differences between the financial reporting frameworks of the target and the issuer and may prepare an "impact analysis". Such an impact analysis may be prepared in conjunction with, or as a development of, the initial determination prepared by the issuer referred to in paragraph 6. 28

The impact analysis should in particular identify those accounting standards in the issuer's or target's financial reporting frameworks that may have a particular impact on the target's or issuer's industries. 29

Using proprietary checklists or synopses of the requirements of accounting standards may assist issuers in preparing an impact analysis. 30

Calculating the effect on the target's financial information of applying the issuer's accounting policies

In order to calculate the adjustments required to be made in respect of each identified difference, between the accounting policies of the target and the issuer, the issuer is likely to require access to the accounting records and related information of the target. To provide support for the calculation of each adjustment the issuer retains appropriate documented evidence. 31

Ensuring that the bookkeeping is complete and accurate

When preparing a financial information reconciliation there are a number of accounting controls that an issuer may apply, for example: 32

- Ensuring, when making adjustments, that the principles of double-entry bookkeeping are followed. The risk of making one-sided adjustments is mitigated to a great extent if working papers are prepared covering an adjusted income statement, an adjusted balance sheet and an adjusted statement of equity, even if not all of these are to be published.

- Considering the income, and other, tax effects of the adjustments and assessing whether the resultant effective tax rate is understandable and meaningful.
- Analysing the differences between the (adjusted) opening and closing equity account balances. (This is sometimes referred to as an equity roll forward reconciliation.) Such an analysis will be of assistance in checking that the principles of double-entry bookkeeping have been followed where the other side of an adjustment is to an equity account.
- Proving that the cash and cash equivalent position, as adjusted, is the same as that shown by the unadjusted financial statements (unless there is a reason for there being a difference). If there is a difference between the cash position reported on the two bases the issuer should understand how this difference arises and consider whether it may reflect an error in the double-entry bookkeeping applied to the reconciliation process[9].

Internal controls over the reconciliation

33 The following high level internal controls should typically be in place:

- The issuer should have employees (or access to outside experts), and other technical resources, with requisite knowledge and experience to prepare and monitor the preparation of the financial information reconciliation.
- The directors of the issuer should be committed to the proper preparation of financial information reconciliations as evidenced by a careful review of the financial information reconciliations being performed.
- Where applicable, comparing the reconciliation to those made in earlier periods. This may be applicable where the listed company has made an unsuccessful bid for the target in a previous period or a bid for other targets that use the same financial reporting framework.

---

[9] *Cash flow statements are usually not published as part of a financial information reconciliation. Nevertheless, comparing the resultant cash position from moving from the target's financial reporting framework to that of the issuer may be a useful accounting control.*

Part Six

APB Practice Notes

Part Six

APB Practice Notes

[PN 9]
Reports by auditors under company legislation in the Republic of Ireland*

(Issued August 1994)

Contents

	Paragraphs
Introduction	1 - 3
Annual financial statements	4
Form and content of auditors' reports	5
Opinion on the financial statements	6 - 9
Other information required by the Companies Acts	10 - 17
Dating the audit report	18
Other reports arising from the financial statements	19
Abridged financial statements (section 18 of the 1986 Act)	20 - 23
The report under section 18(4) of the 1986 Act	24 - 31
The special report for the purposes of section 18(3) of the 1986 Act	32 - 33
Distributions (section 49(3)(c) of the 1983 Act)	34 - 37
Re-registration of a private company as a public limited company (section 9(3)(b) of the 1983 Act)	38 - 40
Other reports	
Allotment of shares by a public limited company otherwise than for cash (section 30(1) of the 1983 Act)	41 - 46
Transfer of non-cash assets to a public limited company by a member of the company (section 32(2)(b) of the 1983 Act)	47 - 48
Distributions by public limited companies: the use of initial accounts (section 49(6) of the 1983 Act)	49 - 51
Statutory declarations of solvency by companies (section 128(4) of the 1990 Act)	52 - 54
Special report on 'proper books of account' (section 194 of the 1990 Act)	55 - 62
Resignation as auditor (section 185 of the 1990 Act)	63 - 66
Use of the term 'registered auditors'	67 - 69

Appendix 1 – Examples of auditors' reports expressing an unqualified opinion

Appendix 2 – Examples of auditors' reports expressing qualified opinions

Appendix 3 – Examples of other reports required by the Companies Acts

---

* ***Editor's note:*** *The guidance in paragraphs 4–18 on the form and content of the auditor's report on annual financial statements has been superseded by the content of Audit Bulletin 2006/1 'Auditor's Reports on Financial Statements in the Republic of Ireland'.*

Appendix 4 – Example wording of a description of the directors' responsibilities for inclusion in a company's financial statements

Reports by auditors under company legislation in the Republic of Ireland

Introduction

This Practice Note describes how the principles of the Statement of Auditing Standards 'Auditors' reports on financial statements' – 600 – should be applied to reports by auditors issued under the Companies Acts, 1963 to 1990, and the European Communities (Companies: Group Accounts) Regulations, 1992 – S.I. 201 of 1992 – in the Republic of Ireland ('the Companies Acts'). It should be read in conjunction with the Statement 'The scope and authority of APB pronouncements'. Examples of audit reports are given in the Appendices to this Practice Note.

References in this Practice Note are as follows:

1963 Act	– Companies Act, 1963
1983 Act	– Companies (Amendment) Act, 1983
1986 Act	– Companies (Amendment) Act, 1986
1990 Act	– Companies Act, 1990
1992 Regulations	– European Communities (Companies: Group Accounts) Regulations, 1992

The guidance given in this Practice Note takes account of the law as at 31 May 1994.

Annual financial statements

The auditors of a company have a duty under the Companies Acts to make a report to the members of the company on the financial statements[1] examined by them. Specifically, they are required to report on every balance sheet and profit and loss account and on all group financial statements laid before the company in general meeting during their tenure of office.

Form and content of auditors' reports

Standards and guidance on the form and content of auditors' reports issued following the audit of a company's financial statements are contained in the Statement of Auditing Standards 'Auditors' reports on financial statements' – 600.

Opinion on the financial statements

The Companies Acts require the auditors to state in their report whether, in their opinion a true and fair view is given:

(a) in the balance sheet, of the state of the company's affairs at the end of the financial year;

---

[1] In this Practice Note, the expression 'financial statements' is used to denote annual accounts, the contents of which are defined:-
(a) for company accounts in Section 3 of the 1986 Act, and
(b) for group accounts in Regulation 13 of the 1992 Regulations,
unless the company is governed by later legislation specific to credit institutions and insurance undertakings. For companies excluded from the scope of the 1986 Act, under Section 2 of that Act, the contents of individual accounts are governed by Section 149 of the 1963 Act.

(b) in the profit and loss account (if not framed as a consolidated account), of the company's profit or loss for the financial year; and

(c) in the case of group financial statements, of the state of affairs and profit or loss of the company and its subsidiaries dealt with by those financial statements.

7 Accounting standards set out in Financial Reporting Standards ('FRSs') require, in certain circumstances, further 'primary statements' in addition to the balance sheet and profit and loss account. These further primary statements are normally necessary in order that the annual accounts give a true and fair view. The Companies Acts do not require the auditors to refer to those 'primary statements' in their report.

8 The auditors are also required to state whether, in their opinion, the financial statements have been properly prepared in accordance with the Companies Acts. In this context, the expression 'properly prepared' includes compliance with the requirements of the Companies Acts with respect to the form and content of the balance sheet and profit and loss account and any additional information to be provided by way of notes to the accounts, subject to an overriding requirement that the financial statements should give a true and fair view.

9 The auditors of a company incorporated in the Republic of Ireland refer in their report to the Companies Acts, 1963 to 1990, to the Companies (Amendment) Act, 1983, and to the European Communities (Companies: Group Accounts) Regulations, 1992. If the company is incorporated in Great Britain, the auditors refer to the Companies Act, 1985. Where a company is incorporated in the Republic of Ireland and the auditors are based in Great Britain, they consider whether it would be helpful to adapt the wording of their report so that there can be no doubt as to which country's law is being referred to (e.g. by referring to 'the Companies Acts, 1963 to 1990, in the Republic of Ireland', or 'the Companies (Amendment) Act, 1983, in the Republic of Ireland').

Other information required by the Companies Acts

10 Other matters required to be expressly stated in the auditors' report, under Section 193 of the 1990 Act, Section 15 of the 1986 Act, and under Regulation 38 of the 1992 Regulations include the following expressions of opinion by the auditors:

(i) whether, in their opinion, proper books of account have been kept by the company;

(ii) whether, in their opinion, proper returns adequate for their audit have been received from branches of the company not visited by them;

(iii) whether, in their opinion, there exists at the balance sheet date a financial situation in the context of Section 40 of the 1983 Act (see paragraphs 11 to 13 below);

(iv) whether, in their opinion, the information given in the directors' report is consistent with the financial statements. (see paragraphs 14 and 15 below).

In addition, the following statements are required of the auditors:

(v) whether the company's balance sheet and (if not consolidated) its profit and loss account are in agreement with the books of account and returns; and

(vi) whether the auditors have obtained all the information and explanations which, to the best of their knowledge and belief, are necessary for the purposes of their audit (see paragraph 13 below).

11 Paragraph 10(iii) above outlines the requirement for the auditors to express their opinion as to whether or not a particular financial situation exists at the balance

sheet date. Section 40 of the 1983 Act refers to the financial situation where net assets are 'half or less of the company's called-up share capital' which in certain circumstances requires the convening of an extraordinary general meeting ('EGM'). Matters to be considered by the auditors in this context include:

(a) they base their opinion, as to whether a financial situation exists, solely on the amounts of the assets (whether at cost or valuation) and liabilities included in the balance sheet on which they are reporting. Reporting on the financial situation shown in the balance sheet means that the auditors ignore disclosure of the market values of property and investments that is made merely by way of note to the balance sheet. Furthermore, post-balance sheet events that are defined by Statement of Standard Accounting Practice No. 17 as 'non-adjusting' are not taken into account;
(b) Section 40 of the 1983 Act does not apply to situations which existed and were known by the directors to exist before 13 October 1983, the day on which the Act came into force. In such situations, there is no obligation on the auditors to report as to whether or not a financial situation existed;
(c) even though the balance sheet shows that a financial situation exists, there may be additional circumstances which avoid the need to convene an EGM. The auditors' responsibility is confined to reporting on the existence of the financial situation regardless of whether an EGM has been or will be held. Auditors need not comment in the audit report on such additional circumstances.

12 Where the auditors have added an explanatory paragraph to their unqualified opinion referring to inherent uncertainties which, in their opinion, are fundamental, it will be possible to express the separate 'financial situation' opinion.

13 Where the auditors cannot report without qualification to the effect that in their opinion the financial statements give a true and fair view, this may have an impact on the further 'financial situation' opinion referred to above at paragraph 10(iii), since that further opinion is based on the amounts shown in the balance sheet.

The impact of audit qualifications in this context may be summarised as follows:

(a) Where the auditors have qualified their opinion because of the effect of a limitation on the scope of their work, they should consider whether the adjustments which might be required, had there been no limitation of scope, could result in the net assets of the company altering from more than half of the called-up share capital to half or less (or vice versa). Except where the adjustments could result in the financial situation being affected in this way, it should be possible to express the separate 'financial situation' opinion.
(b) Where the auditors have disclaimed an opinion because the possible effect of a limitation on the scope of their work is so material or pervasive that the auditors have not been able to obtain sufficient evidence to support, and accordingly are unable to express, an opinion on the financial statements, it will be necessary for them to give a disclaimer of opinion in relation to the separate 'financial situation'.
(c) Finally, where the auditors have qualified their opinion due to disagreement affecting balance sheet amounts, they express the further special opinion based on the assumption that the balance sheet is adjusted for the amounts in disagreement.

14 Section 15 of the 1986 Act requires the auditors to state whether, in their opinion, the information given in the report of the directors relating to the financial year concerned is consistent with the accounts prepared by the company for that year. A similar obligation for group accounts is imposed by Regulation 38 of the 1992

Regulations. The auditors are not required to form an opinion on the directors' report itself.

15   Although the auditors have no statutory responsibilities in respect of items in the directors' report which, in their opinion, are misleading but not inconsistent with the financial statements, there may be occasions when a matter is potentially so misleading to the users of these financial statements that it would be inappropriate for the auditors to remain silent. In these circumstances the auditors should consider seeking legal and other professional advice. The [draft] Statement of Auditing Standards 'Other Information in Documents containing Audited Financial Statements' – 160 – gives detailed guidance on this area.

16   As noted in paragraph 10 (vi) above, the auditors must state whether they have obtained all the information and explanations necessary for the purpose of their audit. In particular circumstances, for example where there has been a limitation of the scope of the audit giving rise to a qualification of the audit report, the auditors should consider whether they can make that statement.

17   Other requirements of the Companies Acts give the auditors additional reporting responsibilities. These responsibilities, which may or may not affect the wording of their report, are set out below. In the circumstances specified in (i) and (ii) below the auditors must set out the required particulars in their report, so far as they are reasonably able to do so.

(i) *Section 191(8) of the 1963 Act.*
   If the financial statements do not comply with the requirements of Section 191 which deals with 'Particulars of directors' salaries and payments to be given in accounts'.

(ii) *Section 46 of the 1990 Act.*
   If the financial statements do not comply with the requirements of Section 41 or 43 which deal with particulars of substantial contracts, loans and other transactions with directors, together with particulars of related amounts outstanding at the balance sheet date.

(iii) *Section 149(5) of the 1963 Act.*
   Section 149(5) provides that in a holding company's financial statements the pre-acquisition profits or losses attributable to any shares in a subsidiary shall not be treated as revenue profits or losses, and that profits for a subsidiary's financial year are to be apportioned to the periods before and after the dates of its acquisition for this purpose. It is further provided, however, that where the directors and the auditors are satisfied and so certify that it would be fair and reasonable and would not prejudice the rights and interests of any person, the treatment required by Section 149(5) need not be followed.

(iv) *Section 63 of the 1990 Act.*
   Section 63 of the 1990 Act requires disclosure in the directors' report, or in the notes to the financial statements, of directors' interests in shares or debentures of the company, as well as interests (where applicable) in shares or debentures of its subsidiary or fellow-subsidiary, or of its holding company (see paragraph 22 below).

Dating of the audit report

18   The Companies Acts require that both the balance sheet and the profit and loss account are signed by two of the directors of the company on behalf of the board. The auditors may not sign and date their report until the financial statements have been so approved and they have considered all necessary available evidence. The Statement of Auditing Standards 'Auditors' reports on financial statements' – 600 –

and [draft] Statement 'Subsequent Events' – 150 – give detailed guidance on this area.

Other reports arising from the financial statements

The Companies Acts require the auditors to give other reports arising from their normal report of a company's financial statements. The Statement of Auditing Standards 'Auditors' reports on financial statements' – 600, which indicates 'Much of the guidance provided can be adapted to auditors' reports on financial information other than financial statements', will normally be applicable when giving these reports. Auditors' reports on other information therefore follow the structure set out in SAS 600 and include a description of the basis of the opinion expressed. A statement of the respective responsibilities ought ordinarily also to be included, unless: 19

(a) the directors have no responsibilities concerning the presentation to shareholders of information on which the auditors report, so that the auditors report direct to the shareholders rather than attesting to a report made by the directors; or
(b) the auditors' report is addressed to the company or the directors, and is intended primarily for private use. However, where the auditors are aware that their report is intended for wide distribution, they may nevertheless wish to include a description of respective responsibilities so that a third party reader of their report is aware of the general nature of those responsibilities.

Abridged financial statements (Section 18 of the 1986 Act)

The 1986 Act entitles certain companies to exemption from filing the financial statements laid before the AGM, if instead abridged financial statements are filed with the Registrar of Companies. The abridged financial statements are required to give a true and fair view (see paragraph 25 below). 20

Whether companies may file abridged financial statements depends upon their qualifying as small or medium-sized. The copy of the abridged financial statements annexed to the annual return must contain a statement by the directors that: 21

(a) they have relied on specified exemptions contained in Sections 10 to 12 of the 1986 Act; and
(b) they have done so on the ground that the company is entitled to the benefit of those exemptions as a small or medium-sized company.

Section 63 of the 1990 Act requires disclosure in the directors' report, or in the notes to the financial statements, of directors' interests in shares or debentures of the company, as well as interests (where applicable) in shares or debentures of its subsidiary or fellow-subsidiary, or of its holding company. Small companies, as defined in Section 8 of the 1986 Act, are not required to file a copy of their directors' report. Where such companies avail of the option not to file a directors' report they must disclose the 'Section 63' information in the notes to the financial statements laid before the AGM and in the notes to the filed accounts. 22

Where abridged financial statements are annexed to the annual return the auditors will make two separate reports: 23

(a) a report to the directors required under Section 18(4) of the 1986 Act (see paragraphs 24 to 31 below), and

(b) a special report which, under Section 18(3) of the 1986 Act, must accompany the abridged financial statements annexed to the annual return (see paragraphs 32 and 33 below). This report includes, *inter alia*, a copy of the auditors' report under Section 18(4) of the Act.

The report under Section 18(4) of the 1986 Act

24   If the directors propose to annex abridged financial statements to the annual return, and if the auditors are satisfied both that the directors are so entitled and that the abridged financial statements have been properly prepared, pursuant to the exemption provisions of Sections 10 to 12 of the 1986 Act, it is the auditors' duty under Section 18(4) of the 1986 Act to provide the directors with a report in writing stating that in their opinion:

- the directors of the company are entitled to annex those abridged financial statements to the annual return, and
- the abridged financial statements have been properly prepared pursuant to the exemption provisions.

This report will incorporate the following elements:

(a) Addressee – the report is addressed to the directors.
(b) Introductory Paragraph – the report covers only the abridged financial statements which the directors propose to annex to the annual return.
(c) Respective Responsibilities – a statement that it is the directors' responsibility to properly prepare abridged financial statements. The auditors are required to form an opinion thereon.
(d) Basis of Opinion – the auditors indicate that their work is limited to an examination of the abridged financial statements to be annexed to the annual return and the financial statements to be laid before the AGM, which should form the basis for those abridged financial statements, so as to confirm compliance with Section 18 of the 1986 Act.
(e) Opinion – the auditors state that in their opinion:
    (i) the directors are entitled to annex the abridged financial statements to the annual return; and
    (ii) the abridged financial statements have been properly prepared pursuant to the exemption provisions of Sections 10 to 12 of the 1986 Act (see paragraph 26 below).
(f) Date – the report is be dated on or as soon as possible after the date of the report on the financial statements to be laid before the AGM (but not before the date of the statement by the directors described in paragraph 21 above). The impression must not be given that this report in any way 'updates' the audit report on the financial statements to be laid before the AGM.

If the auditors cannot make the positive statements indicated at (e)(i) and (ii) above, they do not issue any report to the directors and the company cannot then file the abridged financial statements with the Registrar of Companies.

25   Legal advice received states that the abridged financial statements prepared by a company for annexation to its annual return for filing with the Registrar of Companies must give a true and fair view.

26   However, in order to form the opinion that abridged financial statements prepared for filing purposes have been 'properly prepared' (see paragraph 24(e)(ii) above), the auditors need only be satisfied that the process of abridging the financial statements has been carried out in the manner permitted by the 1986 Act. For this purpose the auditors do not have a statutory duty to consider whether the abridged financial

statements give a true and fair view, but legal advice received states that where in the auditors' opinion the abridgement process has impaired the true and fair view the auditors should outline their reservations in this regard (see paragraph 30 below).

27 The auditors may form the opinion that the abridged financial statements to be annexed to the annual return do not give a true and fair view because either:

(a) the auditors' report on the financial statements to be laid before the AGM was qualified (see paragraphs 28 and 29 below);

or

(b) in the auditors' opinion the process of abridgement for filing purposes has itself impaired the true and fair view, for example by the omission from those abridged financial statements of certain information contained in the financial statements to be laid before the AGM (see paragraph 30 below).

28 If the report on the financial statements to be laid before the AGM is qualified, the abridged financial statements annexed to the annual return may nevertheless be deemed to be properly prepared so long as the auditors are satisfied that the process of abridging the financial statements has been carried out in the manner permitted by the 1986 Act. In such cases the auditors will state in their special report under Section 18(3) that their report on the financial statements to be laid before the AGM was a qualified report (see paragraph 32 below).

29 If, however, the qualification of the auditors' report on the financial statements to be laid before the AGM relates to one of the determinants for exemption the auditors will consider whether the maximum effect of the matter giving rise to the qualification would cause the turnover, employee numbers or balance sheet totals to exceed the exemption limits. If the qualification is in the form of a disclaimer or an adverse opinion, the auditors need to consider whether they can properly assess the determinants for exemption on the basis of financial statements which in their opinion are, or could be, misleading as a whole.

30 If in the auditors' opinion the abridgement process has impaired the true and fair view given by the financial statements to be laid before the AGM, but the auditors can conclude that the abridgement process has been properly carried out, the auditors can make the section 18(4) report but they state their opinion that the abridgement process has impaired the true and fair view and outline the nature of their reservations in this regard.

31 Where there is to be a change of auditors, it is desirable to plan for the auditors who reported on the financial statements to be laid before the AGM to report on the abridged financial statements to be annexed to the annual return. If this is not possible, the new auditors performing the latter function can accept the financial statements to be laid before the AGM as a basis for their work unless they have grounds to doubt the accuracy of the determinants for exemption, for example because of a qualified opinion. The new auditors indicate in their report by whom the audit of the financial statements to be laid before the AGM was carried out.

The special report for the purposes of Section 18(3) of the 1986 Act

32 The abridged financial statements annexed to the annual return and filed with the Registrar of Companies must, under Section 18(3) of the 1986 Act, be accompanied by a special report by the auditors containing:

a copy of the auditors' report to the directors under Section 18(4) of the 1986 Act, and

– a copy of the auditors' report to the members under Section 193 of the 1990 Act on the financial statements to be laid before the AGM.

This special report will include the following elements:

(a) Addressee – the 1986 Act does not state to whom the special report should be addressed; in the absence of any other requirement it may be addressed to the directors.
(b) Scope of report – the special report is restricted to reproducing the auditors' reports under Section 18(4) of the 1986 Act and Section 193 of the 1990 Act.
(c) Opinion – apart from the opinions included in the two reports which are to be reproduced, no further opinion is required by statute in this special report.
(d) Date – the special report is dated on the same date as the report under Section 18(4).

On the basis of legal advice received, where the report on the financial statements to be laid before the AGM was qualified the auditors should so state in this special report (see paragraph 28 above).

33 If the report under Section 193 of the 1990 Act is qualified the auditors need to ensure that a reader of the special report will be able to understand the circumstances giving rise to that qualification. Usually this will be achieved satisfactorily by reproducing the qualified report, as required by Section 18(3) of the 1986 Act (see paragraph 32). But where the qualification includes a reference to a note to the financial statements to be laid before the AGM, without stating explicitly all the relevant information contained in that note, it is recommended that the auditors also reproduce the full text of the note in their special report, immediately following the text of their qualified report under Section 193 of the 1990 Act.

Distributions (Section 49(3)(c) of the 1983 Act)

34 The 1983 Act prohibits all companies from making a distribution otherwise than out of profits available for the purpose.

35 Where the auditors have issued a 'qualified report' on the last annual financial statements the company's ability to make a distribution, by reference to those financial statements, could be in doubt. In such circumstances, the company may not proceed to do so unless the auditors have made a statement under Section 49(3)(c) of the 1983 Act concerning the company's ability to make the distribution. For the purpose of this additional statement, an 'unqualified report' is specified by Section 49(9) of the 1983 Act as a report which is without qualification to the effect that in the auditors' opinion the financial statements have been properly prepared in accordance with the Companies Acts. Accordingly, circumstances where the auditors' report refers to the existence of a 'financial situation' in the context of Section 40(1) of the 1983 Act, or to inconsistency/ies in the directors' report by reference to the financial statements, are, for the purposes of Section 49 of the 1983 Act, reports 'without qualification'.

36 The auditors' statement under Section 49(3)(c) of the 1983 Act will incorporate the following elements:

(a) Addressee – the statement required of the auditors can be included as a separate paragraph in the audit report to the members on the financial statements. If, instead, a separate statement is made then it would be appropriate for it to be addressed to the members and sent to the company secretary.

(b) Introductory Paragraph – the auditors refer to their audit which will have been carried out in accordance with Auditing Standards issued by the Auditing Practices Board and state the date on which their opinion was expressed and that their opinion was qualified.
(c) Basis of Opinion – the statement is restricted to an evaluation of the auditors' qualified report on the last annual financial statements in the context of distributable profits.
(d) Opinion – the auditors are required to state whether in their opinion the subject matter of the qualification is material for the purpose of determining whether proposed distributions, and those which have not yet been proposed, are permitted. A qualification is not material for this purpose if the financial effect of the matters giving rise to qualification could not be such as to reduce the distributable profits below the levels required for the purpose of such distributions. The level of the proposed or potential distribution will always be quantified in the opinion.
Where the maximum effect of a qualification cannot be quantified, it would normally be material for distribution purposes unless the auditors can conclude that the effect of the qualification on the distributable profits could only be favourable. A disclaimer of opinion on the financial statements as a whole would be material as the auditors would be unable to form an opinion on the amount at which the company's distributable profits are stated.
(e) Date – if a separate statement is made, the date used is that on which the statement is completed. In any case the statement must be available to be laid before the company in general meeting before the distribution in question is made, and so the report will have to be completed by that date.

On a change of auditors, the report under Section 49(3) of the 1983 Act can only be made by the auditors who reported on the last annual financial statements. 37

Re-registration of a private company as a public limited company (Section 9(3)(b) of the 1983 Act)

A private company applying to re-register as a public limited company is required to deliver certain documents to the Registrar of Companies including a copy of a balance sheet (together with related notes) of the company prepared as at a date not more than 7 months before the application, together with an audit report thereon without material qualification, and a further written statement by the company's auditors concerning the amount of the company's net assets. 38

The written statement will incorporate the following elements: 39

(a) Addressee – The 1983 Act does not state to whom the report should be addressed; in the absence of any other requirement it may be addressed to the directors.
(b) Introductory Paragraph – the report is restricted to the relevant audited balance sheet of the company.
(c) Basis of Opinion – the auditors indicate that their work is limited to an examination of the relationship between the company's net assets and its called-up share capital and undistributable reserves stated in the balance sheet already audited, so that it is clear that no further audit work has been carried out.
(d) Opinion – the auditors express an opinion that as at the balance sheet date the balance sheet shows that the amount of the company's net assets was not less than the aggregate of its called-up share capital and undistributable reserves.
(e) Other information required – the 1983 Act requires that the audit report on the relevant balance sheet should be without any material qualification. For a qualified report to be acceptable, the auditors are required to state in their

report that the matter giving rise to the qualification is not material for determining (by reference to the balance sheet) whether at the balance sheet date the net assets of the company were not less than the aggregate of its called-up share capital and undistributable reserves.

In determining whether a qualification is not material for the above purpose, the considerations are similar to those outlined in paragraph 36(d) above.

(f) Date – the statement by the auditors is dated when it is signed, which cannot be earlier than the date of the audit report on the relevant balance sheet.

If there is a change in auditors, the new auditors can accept the balance sheet audited by their predecessors as a basis for the work referred to at (c) above, unless the audit report thereon contains a material qualification. The new auditors indicate in their report by whom the audit of the relevant balance sheet was carried out.

40 Illustrative wording for use when the company's financial statements were prepared within seven months before the application, is shown in example 4 of Appendix 3. If the latest financial statements are not eligible for use, it will be necessary for the company to prepare a balance sheet. This balance sheet is required to be audited and the auditors' report should be prepared based on Statement of Auditing Standards 'Auditors' reports on financial statements' – 600.

Other reports

Allotment of shares by public limited company otherwise than for cash (Section 30(1) of the 1983 Act)

41 Companies may allot shares and receive payment for them in a form other than cash. Where a public limited company proposes to allot shares for such non-cash consideration it must, subject to certain exceptions, obtain during the 6 months before the date of the allotment a report on the value of the assets to be received in payment for the shares. This will not apply to an allotment of bonus shares capitalised from reserves.

42 The report must be made by independent accountants who either are the auditors, or are qualified to act as auditors, of the allotting company. They are entitled, however, to rely on another person, a specialist, who appears to them to have the requisite knowledge and experience and who is not, *inter alia*, an officer or a servant of the company, to make the valuation of all or part of the assets.

43 Guidance on the work to be carried out when relying on a specialist is contained in the [draft] Statement of Auditing Standards 'Using the work of an expert' – 520. In such circumstances, the specialist must report directly to the reporting accountant.

44 The independent accountants' report will incorporate the following elements:

   (a) Addressee – the report is made to the company itself and sent to the company secretary for circulation to the proposed allottees.
   (b) Introductory Paragraph/s – as well as expressing the opinion set out in (d) below, the report must include the following information:
       (i) the nominal value of the shares in question;
       (ii) any premium payable on them;
       (iii) a description of the consideration;
       (iv) a description of the part of the consideration valued by the independent accountants, the method used and the date of the valuation; and

(v) the extent to which the nominal value of the shares and any premium are to be treated as paid up:
(1) by the consideration;
(2) in cash.
(c) Basis of Opinion – the report indicates the basis of valuation of the consideration for the allotment of shares.
(d) Opinion – the independent accountants must state that in their opinion:
(i) if the valuation has been made by another person, it appears to be reasonable to accept or arrange for such a valuation. In this case, the report also states the specialist's name and what knowledge and experience he has to carry out the valuation, and describe the part of the consideration valued by him, the method used to value it and specify the date of the valuation;
(ii) the method of valuation was reasonable in all the circumstances;
(iii) there appears to have been no material change in the value of the asset in question since the valuation; and
(iv) on the basis of the valuation, the value of the consideration including any cash to be paid, is not less than the total amount to be treated as paid up on the shares together with the whole of any premium.
(e) Date – the date used is that on which the report is signed.

There is no provision for the report to be qualified. The independent accountants cannot issue any report unless their opinion is unqualified.

In certain circumstances the allotment of shares may represent only a part of the consideration for the transfer of a non-cash asset to the allotting company (e.g. cash may also be paid). In such cases, the independent accountants' report must apply to so much of the value of the non-cash asset as is attributable to paying up the full value of the shares (i.e. nominal value and any premium). The report must also state: 45

(a) what valuations have been made in order to determine that proportion of the consideration;
(b) the reason for those valuations;
(c) the method and date of any such valuation; and
(d) any other relevant matters.

Before the independent accountants can make a statement that there appears to have been no material change in the value of the asset since the valuation, they may have to perform additional work. If the period of time between the making of the valuation and the date of the report is such that there may have been a change in the value, the independent accountants will need to reconsider the valuation. If they made arrangements for someone else to perform the valuation they need to obtain written confirmation from that person as to whether there has been a change in value. 46

Transfer of non-cash assets to a public[2] limited company by a member of the company (Section 32(2)(b) of the 1983 Act)

During the first two years following its registration (or re-registration if it was previously a private company) a public limited company may not lawfully purchase from certain of its members a non-cash asset for a consideration worth one-tenth or more of the nominal value of the company's issued share capital unless the terms of the transfer have been approved by an ordinary resolution. Similar restrictions apply where a third party acquires a non-cash asset for which the company pays. 47

---

[2] In accordance with Section 155 of the 1990 Act the provisions of Sections 32 to 36 of the 1983 Act shall apply to private companies in certain circumstances.

48 In addition to approval by an ordinary resolution, a valuation report (similar to that described in paragraphs 42 to 46 above) on the asset purchased by the company (and on any asset given by the company in payment) must have been made to the company during the six months preceding the transfer. The report must be made by independent accountants qualified to act as the company's auditors and will incorporate the following elements:

(a) Addressee – the report is made to the company itself and sent to the company secretary for circulation to the members of the company and to the person selling the asset.

(b) Introductory Paragraph/s – as well as expressing the opinion set out in (d) below, the report must include the following information:
  (i) the consideration to be received by the company, describing the asset in question, and the consideration to be given by the company and specifying any amounts to be received or given in cash; and
  (ii) the method and date of valuation.

(c) Basis of Opinion – the report indicates the basis of valuation of the consideration.

(d) Opinion – the independent accountants must state that in their opinion:
  (i) if the valuation has been made by another person, it appears to be reasonable to accept such a valuation. In this case, the report also states the specialist's name and what knowledge and experience he has to carry out the valuation, and describe the part of the consideration valued by him, the method used to value it and the date of the valuation;
  (ii) the method of valuation was reasonable in all the circumstances;
  (iii) there appears to have been no material change in the value of the asset in question since the valuation (see paragraph 46 above); and
  (iv) on the basis of the valuation used, the value of the consideration to be received by the company is not less than the value of the consideration to be given by it.

(e) Date – the date used is that on which the report is signed. Circulation of the report must not be later than the notice calling the meeting at which the resolution to approve the transfer is proposed.

There is no provision for the report to be qualified. The independent accountants cannot issue any report unless their opinion is unqualified.

Distributions by public limited companies: the use of initial accounts (Section 49(6) of the 1983 Act)

49 Paragraphs 34 to 37 of this Practice Note describe the statement required where a company wishes to make a distribution and a qualified audit report has been given on the annual financial statements. A company may wish to make a distribution during its first accounting period or after the end of that period but before the accounts for that period have been laid before a general meeting or delivered to the Registrar of Companies.

50 'Initial accounts' must be prepared for this purpose. The initial accounts, in the case of a public limited company, are required to comply with Section 149 of the 1963 Act, as amended by the 1986 Act, with respect to the form and contents of the balance sheet and profit and loss account and any additional information to be provided by way of notes to the accounts. The initial accounts must be approved by and signed on behalf of the directors in the same manner as annual financial statements, and must be delivered to the Registrar of Companies. Group accounts are not required.

In the case of a public limited company, the auditors are required to make a report on the initial accounts. The report will incorporate the following elements: 51

(a) Addressee – the Companies Acts do not state to whom the report should be addressed; in the absence of any other requirement it may be addressed to the directors.
(b) Introductory Paragraph/s – the report is concerned with the initial accounts. The period covered by the initial accounts will be identified.
(c) Basis of Opinion – the audit of the initial accounts should be carried out in accordance with Auditing Standards issued by the Auditing Practices Board. The report contains the relevant paragraphs from Example 2 of Appendix 2 of the Statement of Auditing Standards 'Auditors' reports on financial statements' – 600 – dealing with the respective responsibilities of directors and auditors and with the basis of opinion.
(d) Opinion – the auditors must state whether, in their opinion, the accounts have been properly prepared within the meaning of Section 49(9) of the 1983 Act. For these purposes, the term 'properly prepared' means that the accounts must give a true and fair view of the state of the company's affairs as at the balance sheet date and of its profit or loss for the relevant period, and must comply with the provisions of Section 149 of the 1963 Act, as amended by the 1986 Act, subject to such modifications as are necessary because the accounts do not relate to a financial year.If the opinion above is qualified, the auditors must state (Section 49(6)(c)) whether the distribution is permitted (see paragraph 36 above).
(e) Date – the same principles apply for initial accounts as for annual financial statements.

Statutory declarations of solvency by companies (Section 128(4) of the 1990 Act)

Where it is proposed to wind up a company by a member's voluntary liquidation the company's directors are obliged to make a statutory declaration of solvency to the effect that they have made a full inquiry into the affairs of the company and have formed the opinion that the company will be able to pay its debts in full within a specified period which cannot exceed 12 months from the commencement of the winding up. 52

The declaration of solvency must include a statement of the company's assets and liabilities as at a specified date which cannot be more than 3 months before the date of the declaration. 53

In addition to the requirement for the directors to prepare this statutory declaration a report is required to be made by independent accountants qualified to act as the company's auditors. This report will incorporate the following elements: 54

(a) Addressee – the 1990 Act does not state to whom the report is addressed; in the absence of any other requirement it may be addressed to the directors.
(b) Introductory Paragraph/s – the report is restricted to the statement of assets and liabilities and to the directors' opinion thereon.
(c) Respective Responsibilities – a statement that it is the directors' responsibility to form the opinion that the company will be able to pay its debts in full within 12 months and to draw up the appropriate Statement of Affairs. The auditors' will state their responsibility to form an independent opinion as to the reasonableness of the Statement of Affairs.
(d) Opinion – the independent accountants must state whether, in their opinion and to the best of their information and according to the explanations given to them, the statement of assets and liabilities and the directors' opinion are reasonable.

(e) Date – the date used is that on which the directors approve the statement of assets and liabilities.

Special report on 'proper books of account' (Section 194 of the 1990 Act)

55 Legal advice received states that the auditors are obliged to notify the company if, at any time that they are discharging their functions as auditors, information is acquired which causes them to form the opinion that the company is contravening, or has contravened, Section 202 of the 1990 Act. Section 202 obliges a company to keep 'proper books of account' and specifies detailed requirements in that regard.

56 It should be noted that the auditors' duty to comply with the provisions of this Act is personal to them and, accordingly, it is recommended that they obtain independent legal advice when in doubt or where deemed necessary in particular circumstances.

57 Where the auditors form the opinion that 'proper books of account' are not being or have not been kept, they shall

'(a) serve a notice on the company as soon as may be stating their opinion, and
(b) not later than 7 days after the service of such notice on the company, notify the Registrar of Companies in the prescribed form of the notice.'

The notification to the Registrar of Companies is made on Form H4.

58 The auditors should ensure that they are made aware of any other relationships between any department of their firm and the company which could affect their work. They should ensure that they are informed of potential 'Section 194' matters by all of the departments within the firm which have relationships with the company. It would, therefore, be prudent for such firms to establish adequate systems of inter-departmental communication so that any such matters are brought to the attention of the appropriate partner responsible for the audit.

59 The auditors are not obliged to make a report under Section 194 where, in their opinion, the contraventions of Section 202 '. . . are minor or otherwise immaterial in nature'. In determining whether contraventions uncovered can be so described the auditors must assess the quantum in financial terms that is involved as a result of the failure, together with the impact of those contraventions upon the accounting system.

60 Where the auditors form the opinion that the company's directors '. . . have taken the necessary steps to ensure that proper books of account are kept . . . .' they are not obliged to notify the Registrar of Companies of the contravention of Section 202 – which they would otherwise be obliged to do within 7 days of so notifying the company.

61 It is theoretically possible for the company's directors, up to the seventh day following the receipt of the notice from the auditors of a contravention of Section 202, to take those necessary steps. Although it may frequently be possible to do so, this does not mean that the proper books of account have to be put in place but merely that the necessary steps have been taken within 7 days. For example, the nature of the contravention may be such that the company is obliged to advertise for and engage new competent staff to deal with its accounting records, while in the meantime arranging for some other party to maintain proper books of account for the company. In determining whether the appropriate steps have been taken by the company's directors, the auditors will have to assess the competence of the directors and the bona fides and extent of their actions within this 7 day period.

The auditors' special report under Section 194 will incorporate the following elements:

(a) Addressee – the 1990 Act does not state to whom the report is addressed; in the absence of any other agreement it may be addressed to the directors.
(b) Introductory Paragraphs – no introductory paragraph is necessary as the report's title refers to a specific statutory requirement.
(c) Opinion – the report is restricted to the statement of the auditors' opinion regarding the failure by the company to maintain proper books of account.
In the particular circumstances of each case the auditors should outline to the directors, in a separate letter, the nature and extent of the deficiency/deficiencies in the company's records which have caused them to issue this report.
(d) Date – the date used is that on which the necessary work to form the opinion that a Section 194 report is required has been completed.
Prompt issuance of this report assists the directors in taking the necessary steps to ensure that proper books of account are kept.

Resignation as auditor (Section 185 of the 1990 Act)

Section 185 of the 1990 Act requires auditors who resign, or by notice under Section 160(2)(c) of the 1963 Act indicate their unwillingness to be re-appointed, to serve notice in writing on the company to that effect. The auditors must send, within 14 days, a copy of their notice to the Registrar of Companies.

Section 185(2) provides that the auditors' notice shall contain either:

'a) A statement to the effect that there are no circumstances connected with the resignation to which it relates that the auditor concerned considers should be brought to the notice of the members or creditors of the company, or
b) A statement of any such circumstances as aforesaid.'

Where the 'Section 185 notice' contains a statement of particular circumstances the company must, within 14 days, circulate copies of that notice to all those entitled under Section 159 of the 1963 Act to receive copies of the company's financial statements.

Where a statement in accordance with Section 185(2)(b) is made, the resigning auditors are entitled to requisition the convening by the directors of a general meeting of the company.

Use of the term 'registered auditors'

When issuing reports under company legislation, auditors follow the principles established in SAS 600. This requires reports on financial statements to include the manuscript or printed signature of the auditors (SAS 600.2). The signature is normally that of the firm because the firm as a whole assumes responsibility for the report. To assist identification, the report normally also includes the location of the auditors' office and, where appropriate, indicates their status as registered auditors.

Where appointed as auditors of a company (or of another entity required to appoint registered auditors) auditors therefore include the words 'registered auditors' in their reports on financial statements. Other reports required under company legislation are commonly required to be given by the appointed auditors of the company concerned; in all such cases, the words 'registered auditor(s)' appear after the auditors' signature.

69 Reports relating to the transfer of non-cash assets to a public limited company or allotment of shares by a public limited company otherwise than for cash, may be given either by the company's appointed auditors or independent accountants who are qualified to be appointed as auditors. Where company law does not require a report to be given by the appointed auditors, that report need not include the words 'registered auditors'.

Appendix 1 – Examples of auditors' reports expressing an unqualified opinion

Example 1 – Unqualified audit report – company without subsidiaries

AUDITORS' REPORT TO THE SHAREHOLDERS OF XYZ LIMITED

We have audited the financial statements on pages . . . to . . . which have been prepared under the historical cost convention (as modified by the revaluation of certain fixed assets) and the accounting policies set out on page . . . .

Respective responsibilities of directors and auditors

As described on page . . . the company's directors are responsible for the preparation of financial statements. It is our responsibility to form an independent opinion, based on our audit, on those statements and to report our opinion to you.

Basis of opinion

We conducted our audit in accordance with Auditing Standards issued by the Auditing Practices Board. An audit includes examination, on a test basis, of evidence relevant to the amounts and disclosures in the financial statements. It also includes an assessment of the significant estimates and judgements made by the directors in the preparation of the financial statements, and of whether the accounting policies are appropriate to the company's circumstances, consistently applied and adequately disclosed.

We planned and performed our audit so as to obtain all the information and explanations which we considered necessary in order to provide us with sufficient evidence to give reasonable assurance that the financial statements are free from material misstatement, whether caused by fraud or other irregularity or error. In forming our opinion we also evaluated the overall adequacy of the presentation of information in the financial statements.

Opinion

In our opinion the financial statements give a true and fair view of the state of the company's affairs at 31 December 19. . . and of its profit for the year then ended and have been properly prepared in accordance with the Companies Acts, 1963 to 1990.

We have obtained all the information and explanations we consider necessary for the purposes of our audit.[3] In our opinion proper books of account have been kept by the company. The financial statements are in agreement with the books of account.

In our opinion the information given in the directors' report on pages . . . to . . . is consistent with the financial statements.

The net assets of the company, as stated in the balance sheet on page . . ., are more than half of the amount of its called-up share capital and, in our opinion, on that basis there did not exist at 31 December 19.. a financial situation which under Section 40(1) of the Companies (Amendment) Act 1983 would require the convening of an extraordinary general meeting of the company.[4]

Registered Auditors   Address
Date

Example 2 – Unqualified audit report – company submitting group accounts

AUDITORS' REPORT TO THE SHAREHOLDERS OF XYZ LIMITED

We have audited the financial statements on pages . . . to . . . which have been prepared under the historical cost convention (as modified by the revaluation of certain fixed assets) and the accounting policies set out on page . . . .

Respective responsibilities of directors and auditors

As described on page . . . the company's directors are responsible for the preparation of financial statements. It is our responsibility to form an independent opinion, based on our audit, on those statements and to report our opinion to you.

Basis of opinion

We conducted our audit in accordance with Auditing Standards issued by the Auditing Practices Board. An audit includes examination, on a test basis, of evidence

---

[3] *Where returns from branches are material in the context of the auditors forming their opinion as to whether the financial statements give a true and fair view, in the further opinion relating to the books of account the following wording is used:*

'In our opinion proper books of account have been kept by the company and proper returns adequate for our audit have been received from branches of the company not visited by us.'

[4] a) *Where a financial situation did exist at the balance sheet date the following wording is used:*

'The net assets of the company, as stated in the balance sheet on page..., are not more than half of the amount of its called-up share capital and, in our opinion, on that basis there did exist at 31 December 19.. a financial situation which under Section 40(1) of the Companies (Amendment) Act 1983 may require the convening of an extraordinary general meeting of the company'.

b) *In cases where the balance sheet shows an excess of liabilities over assets the following wording is used:*

'The balance sheet on page ... shows an excess of liabilities over assets and, in our opinion, on that basis there did exist at 31 December 19..., a financial situation which under Section 40(1) of the Companies (Amendment) Act 1983 may require the convening of an extraordinary general meeting of the company.'

relevant to the amounts and disclosures in the financial statements. It also includes an assessment of the significant estimates and judgements made by the directors in the preparation of the financial statements, and of whether the accounting policies are appropriate to the company's circumstances, consistently applied and adequately disclosed.

We planned and performed our audit so as to obtain all the information and explanations which we considered necessary in order to provide us with sufficient evidence to give reasonable assurance that the financial statements are free from material misstatement, whether caused by fraud or other irregularity or error. In forming our opinion we also evaluated the overall adequacy of the presentation of information in the financial statements.

Opinion

In our opinion the financial statements give a true and fair view of the state of affairs of the company and the group at 31 December 19.. and of the profit of the group for the year then ended and have been properly prepared in accordance with the Companies Acts, 1963 to 1990, and the European Communities (Companies: Group Accounts) Regulations, 1992.

We have obtained all the information and explanations we consider necessary for the purposes of our audit.[5] In our opinion proper books of account have been kept by the company. The company's balance sheet is in agreement with the books of account.

In our opinion the information given in the directors' report on pages . . . to . . . is consistent with the financial statements.

The net assets of the company, as stated in the balance sheet on page . . ., are more than half of the amount of its called-up share capital and, in our opinion, on that basis there did not exist at 31 December 19.. a financial situation which under Section 40(1) of the Companies (Amendment) Act 1983 would require the convening of an extraordinary general meeting of the company.[6]

Registered Auditors   Address
Date

---

[5] *Where returns from branches are material in the context of the auditors forming their opinion as to whether the financial statements give a true and fair view, in the further opinion relating to the books of account the following wording is used:*
'In our opinion proper books of account have been kept by the company and proper returns adequate for our audit have been received from branches of the company not visited by us.'

[6] a)   *Where a financial situation did exist at the balance sheet date the following wording is used:*

    'The net assets of the company, as stated in the balance sheet on page..., are not more than half of the amount of its called-up share capital and, in our opinion, on that basis there did exist at 31 December 19.. a financial situation which under Section 40(1) of the Companies (Amendment) Act 1983 may require the convening of an extraordinary general meeting of the company.'

  b)   *In cases where the balance sheet shows an excess of liabilities over assets the following wording is used:*

    'The balance sheet on page ... shows an excess of liabilities over assets and, in our opinion, on that basis there did exist at 31 December 19.., a financial situation which under Section 40(1) of the Companies (Amendment) Act 1983 may require the convening of an extraordinary general meeting of the company'.

Example 3 – Unqualified audit report – fundamental uncertainty

AUDITORS' REPORT TO THE SHAREHOLDERS OF XYZ LIMITED

We have audited the financial statements on pages . . . to . . . which have been prepared under the historical cost convention (as modified by the revaluation of certain fixed assets) and the accounting policies set out on page . . ..

Respective responsibilities of directors and auditors

As described on page . . . the company's directors are responsible for the preparation of financial statements. It is our responsibility to form an independent opinion, based on our audit, on those statements and to report our opinion to you.

Basis of opinion

We conducted our audit in accordance with Auditing Standards issued by the Auditing Practices Board. An audit includes examination, on a test basis, of evidence relevant to the amounts and disclosures in the financial statements. It also includes an assessment of the significant estimates and judgements made by the directors in the preparation of the financial statements, and of whether the accounting policies are appropriate to the company's circumstances, consistently applied and adequately disclosed.

We planned and performed our audit so as to obtain all the information and explanations which we considered necessary in order to provide us with sufficient evidence to give reasonable assurance that the financial statements are free from material misstatement, whether caused by fraud or other irregularity or error. In forming our opinion we also evaluated the overall adequacy of the presentation of information in the financial statements.

Fundamental uncertainty

In forming our opinion, including our opinion as required by Section 40(1) of the Companies (Amendment) Act, 1983, we have considered the adequacy of the disclosures made in the financial statements concerning the possible outcome of negotiations for additional finance being made available to replace an existing loan of IR£. . . which is repayable on 30 April 19.. . .. The financial statements have been prepared on a going concern basis, the validity of which depends upon funding being available. The financial statements do not include any adjustments that would result from a failure to obtain funding. Details of this fundamental uncertainty are described in note. . . .. Our opinion is not qualified in this respect.

Opinion

In our opinion the financial statements give a true and fair view of the state of the company's affairs at 31 December 19.. and of its profit for the year then ended and have been properly prepared in accordance with the Companies Acts, 1963 to 1990.

We have obtained all the information and explanations we consider necessary for the purposes of our audit. In our opinion proper books of account have been kept by the company. The financial statements are in agreement with the books of account.

In our opinion the information given in the directors' report on pages . . . to . . . is consistent with the financial statements.

The net assets of the company, as stated in the balance sheet on page . . ., are more than half of the amount of its called-up share capital and, in our opinion, on that basis there did not exist at 31 December 19.. a financial situation which under Section 40(1) of the Companies (Amendment) Act 1983 would require the convening of an extraordinary general meeting of the company.

Registered Auditors   Address
Date

Appendix 2 – Examples of auditors' reports expressing qualified opinions

The purpose of this Appendix is to illustrate some of the principles described in the Statement of Auditing Standards 'Auditors' Reports on Financial Statements' – 600 – as they relate to qualified audit reports for companies in the Republic of Ireland.

In particular the examples in this Appendix show how various forms of qualification of the audit opinion may affect the other information which the Companies Acts require to be included in the audit report on the annual financial statements (for example, the 'financial situation' opinion).

Example 1 – Qualified opinion – scope limitation

AUDITORS' REPORT TO THE SHAREHOLDERS OF XYZ LIMITED

We have audited the financial statements on pages . . . to . . . which have been prepared under the historical cost convention (as modified by the revaluation of certain fixed assets) and the accounting policies set out on page . . . .

Respective responsibilities of directors and auditors

As described on page . . . the company's directors are responsible for the preparation of financial statements. It is our responsibility to form an independent opinion, based on our audit, on those statements and to report our opinion to you.

Basis of opinion

We conducted our audit in accordance with Auditing Standards issued by the Auditing Practices Board, except that the scope of our work was limited as explained below.

An audit includes examination, on a test basis, of evidence relevant to the amounts and disclosures in the financial statements. It also includes an assessment of the significant estimates and judgements made by the directors in the preparation of the financial statements, and of whether the accounting policies are appropriate to the company's circumstances, consistently applied and adequately disclosed.

We planned our audit so as to obtain all the information and explanations which we considered necessary in order to provide us with sufficient evidence to give reasonable assurance that the financial statements are free from material misstatement, whether caused by fraud or other irregularity or error. However, the evidence available to us was limited because IR£. . . of the company's recorded turnover comprises cash sales, over which there was no system of control on which we could rely for the purpose of our audit. There were no other satisfactory audit procedures that we could adopt to confirm that cash sales were properly recorded.

In forming our opinion we also evaluated the overall adequacy of the presentation of information in the financial statements.

Qualified opinion arising from limitation in audit scope

Except for any adjustments that we might have found to be necessary had we been able to obtain sufficient evidence concerning cash sales, in our opinion the financial statements give a true and fair view of the state of the company's affairs at 31 December 19.. and of its profit for the year then ended and have been properly prepared in accordance with the Companies Acts, 1963 to 1990.

As indicated above we were unable to satisfy ourselves that all cash sales were properly recorded. In all other respects:

(1) we have obtained all the information and explanations we consider necessary for the purpose of our audit; and
(2) in our opinion proper books of account have been kept by the company.

The financial statements are in agreement with the books of account.

In our opinion the information given in the directors' report on pages . . . to . . . is consistent with the financial statements.

The net assets of the company, as stated in the balance sheet on page . . ., are more than half of the amount of its called-up share capital and, in our opinion, on that basis there did not exist at 31 December 19.. a financial situation which under Section 40(1) of the Companies (Amendment) Act 1983 would require the convening of an extraordinary general meeting of the company.

Registered Auditors   Address
Date

Note: If the impact of the scope limitation had been regarded as so material or pervasive that the auditors were unable to express an opinion on the financial statements (which is not the case in this example) a disclaimer of opinion would be required.

Example 2 – Qualified opinion – failure to keep proper books of account

AUDITORS' REPORT TO THE SHAREHOLDERS OF XYZ LIMITED

We have audited the financial statements on pages . . . to . . . which have been prepared under the historical cost convention (as modified by the revaluation of certain fixed assets) and the accounting policies set out on page . . . .

Respective responsibilities of directors and auditors

As described on page . . . . the company's directors are responsible for the preparation of financial statements. It is our responsibility to form an independent opinion, based on our audit, on those statements and to report our opinion to you.

Basis of opinion

We conducted our audit in accordance with Auditing Standards issued by the Auditing Practices Board. An audit includes examination, on a test basis, of evidence relevant to the amounts and disclosures in the financial statements. It also includes an assessment of the significant estimates and judgements made by the directors in the preparation of the financial statements, and of whether the accounting policies are appropriate to the company's circumstances, consistently applied and adequately disclosed.

We planned and performed our audit so as to obtain all the information and explanations which we considered necessary in order to provide us with sufficient evidence to give reasonable assurance that the financial statements are free from material misstatement, whether caused by fraud or other irregularity or error. In forming our opinion we also evaluated the overall adequacy of the presentation of information in the financial statements.

Opinion, including a qualified opinion arising from failure to keep proper books of account

In our opinion the financial statements give a true and fair view of the state of the company's affairs at 31 December 19... and of its profit for the year then ended and have been properly prepared in accordance with the Companies Acts, 1963 to 1990.

We have obtained all the information and explanations we consider necessary for the purposes of our audit. On 20 September 19.. we issued a special report expressing our opinion that the company had failed to maintain proper books of account. The directors then took the necessary steps to ensure proper books of account are kept by the company. In all other respects, in our opinion proper books of account have been kept by the company. The financial statements are in agreement with the books of account.

In our opinion the information given in the directors' report on pages . . . to . . . is consistent with the financial statements.

The net assets of the company, as stated in the balance sheet on page . . . , are more than half of the amount of its called-up share capital and, in our opinion, on that basis there did not exist at 31 December 19.. a financial situation which under Section

40(1) of the Companies (Amendment) Act, 1983 would require the convening of the extraordinary general meeting of the company.

Registered Auditors Address
Date

Example 3 – Qualified opinion – disagreement, except for

AUDITORS' REPORT TO THE SHAREHOLDERS OF XYZ LIMITED

We have audited the financial statements on pages . . . to . . . which have been prepared under the historical cost convention (as modified by the revaluation of certain fixed assets) and the accounting policies set out on page . . ..

Respective responsibilities of directors and auditors

As described on page . . . the company's directors are responsible for the preparation of financial statements. It is our responsibility to form an independent opinion, based on our audit, on those statements and to report our opinion to you.

Basis of opinion

We conducted our audit in accordance with Auditing Standards issued by the Auditing Practices Board. An audit includes examination, on a test basis, of evidence relevant to the amounts and disclosures in the financial statements. It also includes an assessment of the significant estimates and judgements made by the directors in the preparation of the financial statements, and of whether the accounting policies are appropriate to the company's circumstances, consistently applied and adequately disclosed.

We planned and performed our audit so as to obtain all the information and explanations which we considered necessary in order to provide us with sufficient evidence to give reasonable assurance that the financial statements are free from material misstatement, whether caused by fraud or other irregularity or error. In forming our opinion we also evaluated the overall adequacy of the presentation of information in the financial statements.

Qualified opinion arising from disagreement on accounting treatment

Included in the debtors shown on the balance sheet is an amount of IR£x owing by a company which has ceased trading. XYZ Limited has no security for this debt. In our opinion XYZ Limited, as an unsecured creditor, will not receive full payment and a provision of IR£y should have been made, reducing profits before tax and net assets by that amount.

Except for the absence of this provision, in our opinion the financial statements give a true and fair view of the state of the company's affairs at 31 December 19.. and of its profit for the year then ended and have been properly prepared in accordance with the Companies Acts, 1963 to 1990.

We have obtained all the information and explanations we consider necessary for the purposes of our audit. In our opinion proper books of account have been kept by the company. The financial statements are in agreement with the books of account.

In our opinion, the information given in the directors' report on pages . . . to . . . is consistent with the financial statements.

The net assets of the company, as stated in the balance sheet on page . . . ., are more than half of the amount of its called-up share capital and, in our opinion, on that basis there did not exist at 31 December 19.. a financial situation which under Section 40(1) of the Companies (Amendment) Act, 1983 would require the convening of the extraordinary general meeting of the company.

Registered Auditors   Address
Date

Notes
1   Since the effect of the disagreement can be quantified in this example, it is appropriate to take the amount involved into account for the purpose of the 'financial situation' opinion.
2   Although the amount of IR£x is shown in the debtors ledger without any provision in respect of its irrecoverability, on the presumption that other company documentation (for example, correspondence with the debtor company, correspondence with the liquidator, etc) referring to that irrecoverability is available within the company, the auditors can express the opinion that 'proper books of account' have been kept.

Example 4 – Qualified opinion – uncertainty, disclaimer of opinion

AUDITORS' REPORT TO THE MEMBERS OF XYZ LIMITED

We have audited the financial statements on pages . . . to . . . which have been prepared under the historical cost convention (as modified by the revaluation of certain fixed assets) and the accounting policies set out on page . . . .

Respective responsibilities of directors and auditors

As described on page . . . the company's directors are responsible for the preparation of financial statements. It is our responsibility to form an independent opinion, based on our audit, on those statements and to report our opinion to you.

Basis of opinion

We conducted our audit in accordance with Auditing Standards issued by the Auditing Practices Board, except that the scope of our work was limited as explained below.

An audit includes examination, on a test basis, of evidence relevant to the amounts and disclosures in the financial statements. It also includes an assessment of the significant estimates and judgements made by the directors in the preparation of the financial statements, and of whether the accounting policies are appropriate to the company's circumstances, consistently applied and adequately disclosed.

We planned our audit so as to obtain all the information and explanations which we considered necessary in order to provide us with sufficient evidence to give reasonable assurance that the financial statements are free from material misstatement, whether caused by fraud or other irregularity or error. However, the evidence available was limited because, as indicated in note . . ., the estimates of losses to completion of long-term construction contracts depend on a number of assumptions including those relating to substantially increased productivity which has yet to be achieved. In view of this uncertainty we are unable to confirm that the provision for losses of IR£. . . is adequate. Any adjustment to this figure could have a significant effect on the profit for the year.

In forming our opinion we also evaluated the overall adequacy of the presentation of information in the financial statements

Opinion: disclaimer on view given by financial statements

Because of the possible effect of the limitation in evidence available to us, we are unable to form an opinion as to:

(i) whether the financial statements give a true and fair view of the state of the company's affairs at 31 December 19.. and of its profit for the year then ended, or
(ii) whether there did or did not exist at 31 December 19.. a financial situation which under Section 40(1) of the Companies (Amendment) Act 1983 would require the convening of an extraordinary general meeting of the company.

In all other respects, in our opinion the financial statements have been properly prepared in accordance with the Companies Acts 1963 to 1990.

As indicated above we were unable to obtain sufficient evidence in relation to the estimates of losses to completion of long-term construction contracts. In all other respects:

(1) we have obtained all the information and explanations we consider necessary for the purpose of our audit; and
(2) in our opinion proper books of account have been kept by the company.

The financial statements are in agreement with the books of account.

In our opinion the information given in the directors' report on pages . . . to . . . is consistent with the financial statements.

Registered Auditors   Address
Date

Notes
1 In this example it is assumed that the potential impact of the uncertainties relating to estimates of losses on long-term construction contracts is so material or pervasive in relation to the company's balance sheet and profit and loss account, that the auditors are unable to form an opinion on the true and fair view.
2 In this case the area in relation to which the scope of the auditors' work was limited is well defined so that the auditors are able to reach an opinion as to whether the financial statements in all other respects have been properly prepared in accordance with the Companies Acts, 1963 to 1990. Such a conclusion would not normally be possible where more pervasive uncertainties are involved.

3 The disclaimer of opinion emphasises that the auditors are unable to state whether the balance sheet gives a true and fair view of the state of the company's affairs at the balance sheet date. The balance sheet is, therefore, not a reliable basis on which to compare net assets to called-up share capital. A disclaimer is accordingly required for the 'financial situation' opinion.

Example 5 – Qualified opinion – disagreement, adverse opinion

AUDITORS' REPORT TO THE SHAREHOLDERS OF XYZ LIMITED

We have audited the financial statements on pages . . . to . . . which have been prepared under the historical cost convention (as modified by the revaluation of certain fixed assets) and the accounting policies set out on page . . .

Respective responsibilities of directors and auditors

As described on page . . . the company's directors are responsible for the preparation of financial statements. It is our responsibility to form an independent opinion, based on our audit, on those statements and to report our opinion to you.

Basis of opinion

We conducted our audit in accordance with Auditing Standards issued by the Auditing Practices Board. An audit includes examination, on a test basis, of evidence relevant to the amounts and disclosures in the financial statements. It also includes an assessment of the significant estimates and judgements made by the directors in the preparation of the financial statements, and of whether the accounting policies are appropriate to the company's circumstances, consistently applied and adequately disclosed.

We planned and performed our audit so as to obtain all the information and explanations which we considered necessary in order to provide us with sufficient evidence to give reasonable assurance as to whether the financial statements are free from material misstatement, whether caused by fraud or other irregularity or error. In forming our opinion we also evaluated the overall adequacy of the presentation of information in the financial statements.

Adverse opinion

As more fully explained in note . . . no provision has been made for losses expected to arise on certain long-term contracts currently in progress because the directors consider that such losses should be off-set against expected but unearned future profits on other long-term contracts. In our opinion provision should be made for such foreseeable losses on individual contracts as required by Statement of Standard Accounting Practice No 9. If losses had been so recognised the effect would have been to reduce the profit before tax for the year and the value of contract work in progress (net assets) at 31 December 19.. by IR£. . . .

In view of the effect of the failure to provide for the losses referred to above, in our opinion the financial statements do not give a true and fair view of the state of the company's affairs at 31 December 19.. and of its profit for the year then ended. In all other respects in our opinion the financial statements have been properly prepared in accordance with the Companies Acts, 1963 to 1990.

We have obtained all the information and explanations we consider necessary for the purposes of our audit. In our opinion proper books of account have been kept by the company. The financial statements are in agreement with the books of account.

In our opinion the information given in the directors' report on pages . . . to . . . is consistent with the financial statements.

The net assets of the company, as stated in the balance sheet on page . . ., are more than half of the amount of its called-up share capital and, in our opinion, on that basis there did not exist at 31 December 19.. a financial situation which under Section 40(1) of the Companies (Amendment) Act 1983 would require the convening of an extraordinary general meeting of the company.

Registered Auditors   Address
Date

Notes
1   In this example it is assumed that the impact of the disagreement is fundamental in relation to the company's balance sheet and profit and loss account.
2   Since the effect of the disagreement can be quantified in this example, it is appropriate to take the amount involved into account for the purpose of the 'financial situation' opinion.

Appendix 3 – Examples of other reports required by the Companies Acts

Example 1 – Report on abridged financial statements

AUDITORS' REPORT TO THE DIRECTORS OF XYZ LIMITED PURSUANT TO SECTION 18(4) OF THE COMPANIES (AMENDMENT) ACT 1986

We have examined:
(i)   the abridged financial statements for the year ended 31 December 19.. on pages . . . to . . . which the directors of XYZ Limited propose to annex to the annual return of the company; and
(ii) the financial statements to be laid before the Annual General Meeting, which form the basis for those abridged financial statements.

Respective responsibilities of directors and auditors

It is your responsibility properly to prepare the abridged financial statements. It is our responsibility to form an independent opinion on those abridged financial statements and to report our opinion to you.

Basis of opinion

The scope of our work for the purpose of this report was limited to confirming that the directors are entitled to annex abridged financial statements to the annual return and that those abridged financial statements have been properly prepared, pursuant to Sections 10 to 12 of the Companies (Amendment) Act 1986, from the financial statements to be laid before the Annual General Meeting. The scope of our work for the purpose of this report does not include examining or dealing with events after the date of our report on the full financial statements.

Opinion

In our opinion the directors are entitled under Section 18 of the Companies (Amendment) Act 1986 to annex to the annual return of the company abridged financial statements and those abridged financial statements have been properly prepared pursuant to the provisions of Sections 10 to 12 of that Act (exemptions available to small and medium-sized companies).[7]

Registered Auditors   Address
Date

Example 2 – Report on abridged financial statements annexed to the annual return

AUDITORS' SPECIAL REPORT TO THE DIRECTORS OF XYZ LIMITED PURSUANT TO SECTION 18(3) OF THE COMPANIES (AMENDMENT) ACT 1986

On . . . (date) we reported, as auditors of XYZ Limited, to the directors of the company on the copy of the abridged financial statements for the year ended 31 December 19.. on pages . . . to . . ., and our report was as follows:

'We have examined:

(i) The abridged financial statements for the year ended 31 December 19.. on pages . . . to . . . which the directors of XYZ Limited propose to annex to the annual return of the company; and
(ii) the financial statements to be laid before the Annual General Meeting, which form the basis for those abridged financial statements.

Respective responsibilities of directors and auditors

It is your responsibility properly to prepare the abridged financial statements. It is our responsibility to form an independent opinion on those abridged financial statements and to report our opinion to you.

Basis of opinion

The scope of our work for the purpose of this report was limited to confirming that the directors are entitled to annex abridged financial statements to the annual return and that those abridged financial statements have been properly

---

[7] Where, in the auditors' opinion, the abridgement process has impaired the true and fair view given by the financial statements to be laid before the Annual General Meeting the following additional paragraph should be included.

'In our opinion the abridged financial statements do not give a true and fair view because... (outlining the auditors' reservations).'

prepared, pursuant to Sections 10 to 12 of the Companies (Amendment) Act, 1986, from the financial statements to be laid before the Annual General Meeting. The scope of our work for the purpose of this report does not include examining or dealing with events after the date of our report on the full financial statements.

Opinion

In our opinion the directors are entitled under Section 18 of the Companies (Amendment) Act 1986 to annex to the annual return of the company abridged financial statements and those abridged financial statements have been properly prepared pursuant to the provisions of Sections 10 to 12 of that Act (exemptions available to small and medium-sized companies).'

Other information

(The abridged financial statements have been prepared from the financial statements to be laid before the Annual General Meeting, in respect of which our audit report, as detailed below, was qualified.)[8]

On . . . (date) we reported, as auditors of XYZ Limited[9], to the members on the company's financial statements for the year ended 31 December 19.. to be laid before its Annual General Meeting, and our report was as follows:

'We have audited the financial statements on pages . . . to . . . which have been prepared under the historical cost convention (as modified by the revaluation of certain fixed assets) and the accounting policies set out on page . . .'

Respective responsibilities of directors and auditors

As described on page . . . the company's directors are responsible for the preparation of financial statements. It is our responsibility to form an independent opinion, based on our audit, on those statements and to report our opinion to you.

Basis of opinion

We conducted our audit in accordance with Auditing Standards issued by the Auditing Practices Board. An audit includes examination, on a test basis, of evidence relevant to the amounts and disclosures in the financial statements. It also includes an assessment of the significant estimates and judgements made by the directors in the preparation of the financial statements, and of whether the accounting policies are appropriate to the company's circumstances, consistently applied and adequately disclosed.

We planned and performed our audit so as to obtain all the information and explanations which we considered necessary in order to provide us with

---

[8] For inclusion as necessary (see paragraphs 28 and 30).

[9] Where the financial statements to be laid before the AGM have been reported on by the previous auditors of the company, this paragraph would be reworded as follows:
'On . . . (date) ABC and Co. reported, as auditors of XYZ Limited, to the members on the company's financial statements. . . .'

sufficient evidence to give reasonable assurance that the financial statements are free from material misstatement, whether caused by fraud or other irregularity or error. In forming our opinion we also evaluated the overall adequacy of the presentation of information in the financial statements.

Opinion

In our opinion the financial statements give a true and fair view of the state of the company's affairs at 31 December 19 . . . and of its profit for the year then ended and have been properly prepared in accordance with the Companies Acts, 1963 to 1990.

We have obtained all the information and explanations we consider necessary for the purposes of our audit. In our opinion proper books of account have been kept by the company. The financial statements are in agreement with the books of account.

In our opinion the information given in the directors' report on pages . . . to . . . is consistent with the financial statements.

The net assets of the company, as stated in the balance sheet on page ....., are more than half of the amount of its called-up share capital and, in our opinion, on that basis there did not exist at 31 December 19.. a financial situation which under Section 40(1) of the Companies (Amendment) Act 1983 would require the convening of an extraordinary general meeting of the company.'

Registered Auditors   Address
Date

Example 3 – Statement on a company's ability to make a distribution

AUDITORS' STATEMENT TO THE MEMBERS OF XYZ LIMITED PURSUANT TO SECTION 49(3)(c) OF THE COMPANIES (AMENDMENT) ACT 1983

We have audited the financial statements of XYZ Limited for the year ended 31 December 19.. in accordance with Auditing Standards issued by the Auditing Practices Board and have expressed a qualified opinion thereon in our report dated . . ..

Basis of opinion

We have carried out such procedures as we considered necessary to evaluate the effect of the qualified opinion for the determination of profits available for distribution.

Opinion

In our opinion the subject matter of that qualification is not material for determining, by reference to those financial statements, whether the distribution (interim dividend for the year ended. . .) of IR£. . . proposed by the company is permitted under Section 49 of the Companies (Amendment) Act, 1983.

Registered Auditors   Address
Date

Notes

1 Where the amount of the dividend has not yet been determined, the auditors' statement is expressed in terms of the company's ability to make potential distributions up to a specific level. The opinion paragraph will be worded as follows:

'In our opinion the subject matter of the foregoing qualification is not material for determining, by reference to those financial statements, whether a distribution of not more than IR£. . . by the company would be permitted under Section 49 of the Companies (Amendment) Act 1983.'

2 This example assumes that a separate report is given regarding the company's ability to make a distribution. This matter is sometimes referred to in the statutory audit report by adding a separate paragraph. That paragraph might be worded as follows:

'In our opinion the subject matter of the foregoing qualification is not material for determining whether the distribution of IR£.. proposed by the company is permitted under Section 49 of the Companies (Amendment) Act 1983.'

Example 4 – Statement when a private company wishes to re-register as a public limited company

AUDITORS' STATEMENT TO THE DIRECTORS OF XYZ LIMITED PURSUANT TO SECTION 9(3)(b) OF THE COMPANIES (AMENDMENT) ACT 1983

We have examined the balance sheet of XYZ Limited as at 31 December 19.. which formed part of the financial statements for the year then ended audited by us/ABC and Co.

Basis of opinion

The scope of our work for the purpose of this statement was limited to an examination of the relationship between the company's net assets and its called-up share capital and undistributable reserves stated in the audited balance sheet in connection with the company's proposed re-registration as a public limited company.

Opinion

In our opinion the balance sheet shows that at 31 December 19.. the amount of the company's net assets was not less than the aggregate of its called-up share capital and undistributable reserves.

We audited the financial statements of XYZ Limited for the year ended 31 December 19.. in accordance with Auditing Standards issued by the Auditing Practices Board and expressed a qualified opinion thereon. The matter giving rise to our qualification is not material for determining by reference to the balance sheet at 31 December 19.. whether at that date the net assets of the company were not less than the aggregate of its called-up share capital and undistributable reserves.[10]

---

[10] *For inclusion as necessary.*

Registered Auditors　　　　　　　　　　　　　　　　　　　　　　　　　　　　Address
Date

Example 5 – Report when a public limited company wishes to allot shares otherwise than for cash

INDEPENDENT ACCOUNTANTS' REPORT TO XYZ PUBLIC LIMITED COMPANY FOR THE PURPOSES OF SECTION 30(1)(b) OF THE COMPANIES (AMENDMENT) ACT 1983

We report on the value of the consideration for the allotment to. . . (name of allottee) of . . .(number) shares, having a nominal value of IR£1 each, to be issued at a premium of. . . pence per share. The shares and share premium are to be treated as fully paid up.

The consideration for the allotment to. . . (name of allottee) is the freehold building situated at . . .(address) and . . . (number) shares, having a nominal value of IR£1 each, in LMN public limited company.

Basis of opinion

The freehold building was valued on the basis of its open market value by . . .(name of specialist), a Fellow of the Royal Institution of Chartered Surveyors, on. . .(date) and in our opinion it is reasonable to accept such a valuation.

The shares in LMN public limited company were valued by us on. . .(date) on the basis of the price shown in the Stock Exchange Daily Official List at. . .(date).

Opinion

In our opinion, the methods of valuation of the freehold building and the shares in LMN public limited company were reasonable in all the circumstances. There appears to have been no material change in the value of either part of the consideration since the valuations were made. On the basis of the valuations, in our opinion, the value of the total consideration is not less than IR£. . .(being the total amount to be treated as paid up on the shares allotted together with the share premium).

Registered Auditors　　　　　　　　　　　　　　　　　　　　　　　　　　　　Address
Date

Note: a similar form of report is required pursuant to Section 32 of the 1983 Act when a public limited company purchases non-cash assets from certain of its members.

Example 6 – Report on initial accounts when a public limited company wishes to make a distribution

AUDITORS' REPORT TO THE DIRECTORS OF XYZ PLC PURSUANT TO SECTION 49(6)(b) OF THE COMPANIES (AMENDMENT) ACT 1983

We have audited the initial accounts of XYZ plc on pages . . . to . . . which have been prepared under the historical cost convention (as modified by the revaluation of certain fixed assets) and the accounting policy set out on page . . . .

Respective responsibilities of directors and auditors

As described on page . . . you are responsible for the preparation of the initial accounts. It is our responsibility to form an independent opinion, based on our audit, of those initial accounts and to report our opinion to you.

Basis of opinion

We conducted our audit in accordance with Auditing Standards issued by the Auditing Practices Board. An audit includes examination, on a test basis, of evidence relevant to the amounts and disclosures in the financial statements. It also includes an assessment of the significant estimates and judgements made by the directors in the preparation of the initial accounts, and of whether the accounting policies are appropriate to the company's circumstances, consistently applied and adequately disclosed.

We planned and performed our audit so as to obtain all the information and explanations which we considered necessary in order to provide us with sufficient evidence to give reasonable assurance that the initial accounts are free from material misstatement, whether caused by fraud or other irregularity or error. In forming our opinion we also evaluated the overall adequacy of the presentation of information in the initial accounts.

Opinion

In our opinion the initial accounts for the period from . . . to . . . have been properly prepared within the meaning of Section 49(9) of the Companies (Amendment) Act 1983.

Registered Auditors   Address
Date

Example 7 – Report when a company is required to prepare a statutory declaration of solvency

INDEPENDENT ACCOUNTANTS REPORT TO THE DIRECTORS OF XYZ LIMITED PURSUANT TO SECTION 128 OF THE COMPANIES ACT, 1990

We have examined the statement of the assets and liabilities of XYZ Limited as at 31 December 19.. which forms part of the statutory declaration of solvency made by the directors on 15 February 19.

Basis of opinion

The scope of our work for the purpose of this report was limited to confirming that:

(i) the statement of the company's assets and liabilities at 31 December 19..; and
(ii) the opinion of the directors that the company will be able to pay its debts in full within the period specified in the statutory declaration of solvency

are reasonable.

Opinion

In our opinion, and to the best of our information and according to the explanations given to us, the statement of the company's assets and liabilities at 31 December 19.., and the opinion of the directors that the company will be able to pay its debts in full within the stated period, are reasonable.

Registered Auditors/Independent Accountants   Address
Date

Example 8 – Report where a company has failed to keep 'proper books of account'

AUDITORS SPECIAL REPORT TO THE DIRECTORS OF XYZ LIMITED PURSUANT TO SECTION 194 OF THE COMPANIES ACT, 1990

In our opinion, the company has failed/is failing to keep proper books of account in accordance with Section 202 of the Companies Act, 1990.

Registered Auditors   Address
Date

Note: In circumstances where the company has failed to keep 'proper books of account', and the directors have not taken the necessary steps to rectify the situation within 7 days, the auditor is obliged to make a report to the Companies Registration Office. That further report is made on Form H4.

Appendix 4 – Example wording of a description of the directors' responsibilities for inclusion in a company's financial statements

STATEMENT OF DIRECTORS' RESPONSIBILITIES

Company law requires the directors to prepare financial statements for each financial year which give a true and fair view of the state of affairs of the company and of the profit or loss for that period. In preparing those financial statements, the directors are required to:

- select suitable accounting policies and then apply them consistently;
- make judgements and estimates that are reasonable and prudent;
- state whether applicable accounting standards have been followed, subject to any material departures disclosed and explained in the financial statements;[11]
- prepare the financial statements on the going concern basis unless it is inappropriate to presume that the company will continue in business.[12]

The directors are responsible for keeping proper books of account which disclose with reasonable accuracy at any time the financial position of the company and to enable them to ensure that the financial statements comply with the Companies Acts, 1963 to 1990 (and the European Communities (Companies: Group Accounts) Regulations 1992).[13] They are also responsible for safeguarding the assets of the company and hence for taking reasonable steps for the prevention and detection of fraud and other irregularities.

---

[11] *Statutory obligation in Britain and in Northern Ireland for plcs and 'large companies.'*

[12] *If no separate statement on going concern is made by the directors.*

[13] *For insertion if the company is a parent undertaking.*

[PN 10]
Audit of Financial Statements of Public Sector Bodies in the United Kingdom

Contents

	Paragraphs
Foreword – the role of the public sector auditor	3
International Standard on Quality Control (UK and Ireland) 1	10
ISA (UK and Ireland) 200: Objective and General Principles Governing an Audit of Financial Statements	12
ISA (UK and Ireland) 210: Terms of Audit Engagements	14
ISA (UK and Ireland) 220: Quality Control for Audits of Historical Financial Information	20
ISA (UK and Ireland) 230: Documentation	23
ISA (UK and Ireland) 240: The Auditor's Responsibility to Consider Fraud in an Audit of Financial Statements	25
ISA (UK and Ireland) 250: Consideration of Laws and Regulations in an Audit of Financial Statements	33
ISA (UK and Ireland) 260: Communication of Audit Matters with Those Charged With Governance	36
ISA (UK and Ireland) 300: Planning an Audit of Financial Statements	41
ISA (UK and Ireland) 315: Obtaining an Understanding of the Entity and its Environment and Assessing the Risks of Material Misstatement	43
ISA (UK and Ireland) 320: Audit Materiality	49
ISA (UK and Ireland) 330: The Auditor's Procedures in Response to Assessed Risks	51
ISA (UK and Ireland) 402: Audit Considerations Relating to Entities Using Service Organisations	53
ISA (UK and Ireland) 500: Audit Evidence	55
ISA (UK and Ireland) 501: Audit Evidence – Additional Considerations for Specific Items	56
ISA (UK and Ireland) 505: External Confirmations	57
ISA (UK and Ireland) 510: Initial Engagements – Opening Balances	58

ISA (UK and Ireland) 520: Analytical Procedures   61

ISA (UK and Ireland) 530: Audit Sampling and Other Selective Testing Procedures   63

ISA (UK and Ireland) 540: Audit of Accounting Estimates   64

ISA (UK and Ireland) 545: Auditing Fair Value Measurements and Disclosures   65

ISA (UK and Ireland) 550: Related Party Disclosures   66

ISA (UK and Ireland) 560: Subsequent Events   67

ISA (UK and Ireland) 570: Going Concern   72

ISA (UK and Ireland) 580: Management Representations   83

ISA (UK and Ireland) 600: Using the Work of Another Auditor   85

ISA (UK and Ireland) 610: Considering the Work of Internal Audit   88

ISA (UK and Ireland) 620: Using the Work of an Expert   91

ISA (UK and Ireland) 700: The Auditor's Report   92

ISA (UK and Ireland) 710: Comparatives   99

ISA (UK and Ireland) 720: Other Information in Documents Containing Audited Financial Statements   101

The Audit of Regularity   105

Appendix 1: Glossary of Terms   129

Appendix 2: The legislative framework governing the audit of public sector bodies in the UK   138

Appendix 3: Risks to regularity and possible control procedures   142

Foreword – the role of the public sector auditor

1 Those who are responsible for the conduct of public business and for spending public money are accountable for ensuring that this business is conducted in accordance with the law and proper standards of accounting and governance and that public money is used economically, efficiently and effectively.

2 External auditors in the public sector give an independent opinion on the financial statements and may review and, where appropriate, report on aspects of the arrangements set in place by the audited body to ensure the proper conduct of its financial affairs and to manage its performance and use of resources. As such, external audit is an essential element in the process of accountability and makes an important contribution to the stewardship of public money and the corporate governance of public services.

3 The standards governing the conduct and reporting of the audit of financial statements in the public sector are a matter for the national audit agencies and certain regulators to determine. However, the heads of the national audit agencies in the UK have chosen to adopt the Auditing Practices Board's engagement standards and quality control standards as the basis of their approach to the audit of financial statements. ISAs (UK and Ireland) apply to all audits of financial statements for periods commencing on or after 15 December 2004.

Definitions

4 For the purpose of this Practice Note, the following terms are defined:
- An **auditor** of a public sector body (a **public sector auditor**) can be:
  - a person, or persons appointed under statute or agreement (such as the Comptroller and Auditor General); or
  - a person or persons appointed by, employed by or acting as the agent of a national audit agency, a secretary of state or a government department acting under statute or by agreement (such as a firm of auditors appointed by the Audit Commission); or
  - a person or persons appointed as auditor to a body regulated by an independent regulator which has determined that this Practice Note applies (such as Monitor, the independent regulator of NHS Foundation Trusts).
- A **national audit agency** is one of the United Kingdom public audit agencies responsible for carrying out the audit of the financial statements of public sector bodies for a public sector auditor (the National Audit Office for the Comptroller and Auditor General, Wales Audit Office for the Auditor General for Wales, Audit Scotland for the Auditor General for Scotland and the Accounts Commission, and the Northern Ireland Audit Office for the Comptroller and Auditor General for Northern Ireland) or for the appointment and regulation of auditors of public sector bodies (the Accounts Commission, the Auditor General for Scotland, the Audit Commission and the Auditor General for Wales);
- **Parliament** includes the United Kingdom Parliament and the Scottish Parliament, but not the National Assembly for Wales or the Northern Ireland Assembly.
- The **public sector**[1]
  - government departments and their executive agencies;

---

[1] *There is more than one generally accepted definition of the* **public sector** *and the inclusion of any particular category of entities will depend on the purposes for which the definition is being applied. This is also the case with the definition of central government. comprises:*

- the Scottish Executive and its sponsored and associated bodies, National Assembly for Wales, the Northern Ireland Executive and their sponsored bodies;
- trading funds;
- bodies not administered as government departments but which are subject to Ministerial and departmental control, for example non-departmental public bodies (NDPBs);
- local authorities and other local government bodies (such as police and fire authorities);
- National Health Service bodies, including:
  - strategic health authorities, primary care trusts, NHS trusts, special health authorities and NHS Foundation Trusts in England;
  - local health boards and NHS trusts in Wales;
  - health boards and special health boards in Scotland; and
  - health boards, trusts and special agencies in Northern Ireland.
- in Scotland, further education colleges and the water authority.

It does not include other public corporations or the nationalised industries. The first four parts of the definition can collectively be regarded as **central government**.

Responsibilities of Public Sector Auditors

Public sector auditors act and report in accordance with the mandates that govern their activities and provide the authority for the auditor to carry out and to report the results of the audit work. These mandates are embodied in legislation and, in some circumstances, set out in codes of audit practice established in accordance with legislation.

The mandates of public sector auditors vary in accordance with the requirements laid down in the legislation relevant to each jurisdiction within the public sector and within each geographical area. The legislative framework governing the audit of public sector bodies UK wide and in England, Wales, Scotland and Northern Ireland is summarised in Appendix 2. These mandates establish broadly similar responsibilities for each jurisdiction in relation to:

- the financial statements (see paragraphs 8-9);
- compliance with legislative and other authorities (sometimes referred to as 'regularity') (see paragraphs 10-15); and
- economy, efficiency and effectiveness (sometimes referred to as 'value for money' or 'use of resources') (see paragraph 16).

In some parts of the UK, English is not the primary language used by public bodies for the conduct of business including preparation of the accounts, for example as a result of applying options available under the Welsh Language Act 1993. Where this occurs, the auditor ensures that the auditor's responsibilities under auditing standards can be properly discharged through, for example, including staff with the appropriate language skills in the engagement team and the use of translation services.

The financial statements

The legislative framework governing public sector bodies sets out the requirements on the public bodies in relation to the preparation of financial statements. For example, the Government Resources and Accounts Act 2000 requires government departments to prepare resource accounts for each financial year and send them within a specified period to the Comptroller and Auditor General. The Comptroller and Auditor General is required to examine the accounts with a view to reaching an opinion as to whether they present a true and fair view; to certify and issue a report on them; and to send them to HM Treasury to lay before the House of Commons.

9   This Practice Note provides public sector auditors with further guidance on the application of ISAs (UK and Ireland) to the audit of financial statements, including the regularity opinion where appropriate, in the public sector. The standards governing other reporting assignments in the public sector are a matter for the national audit agencies and certain regulators to determine.

Compliance with legislative and other authorities

10 For central government bodies, public sector auditors express an opinion on whether transactions included in the financial statements conform, where appropriate, with the legislation that authorises them; regulations issued by a body with the power to do so; Parliamentary authority; and HM Treasury authority. The requirement derives from the Exchequer and Audit Departments Act 1921 (and the Government Resources and Accounts Act 2000), whereby the Comptroller and Auditor General has to satisfy himself that expenditure and income (money and other resources provided by Parliament, in the 2000 Act) have been applied in accordance with Parliament's intentions and conforms to governing authorities[2]

11 In Scotland, the Public Finance and Accountability (Scotland) Act 2000 requires audits of accounts for which the Auditor General is responsible to include an auditor's report that sets out findings on whether the expenditure and receipts shown in the account were incurred or applied in accordance with relevant statutory provisions and with any applicable guidance (whether as to propriety or otherwise) issued by Scottish Ministers.

12 There is also a requirement deriving from that set out in paragraph 10 to provide an explicit opinion on regularity in relation to specified National Health Service entities in England and all National Health Service entities in Wales which are to be consolidated in the financial statements of the Department of Health and National Assembly for Wales. This requirement also exists in relation to specified health and social services entities in Northern Ireland.

13 In other health entities and in local government there is no requirement for auditors to express an opinion on the regularity of transactions, (except in Northern Ireland where the Comptroller and Auditor General does express an opinion on the regularity of transactions for entities in the health sector). However, auditors are required by the Audit Commission's and Audit Scotland's Codes of Audit Practice and the Auditor General for Wales' Code of Audit and Inspection Practice to be alert to the question of legality and review the arrangements set in place by the audited body to ensure compliance with laws and regulations. Where unlawful transactions or events come to the auditor's attention the auditor is empowered under legislation to report to the appropriate authorities.

14 Where expenditure in any part of the public sector involves the application of European Union funds, the European Court of Auditors has a right to audit the final

---

[2] *In Wales, the equivalent authority comes from section 97(6) of the Government of Wales Act 1998. In Northern Ireland, it comes from the Exchequer and Audit Act (Northern Ireland) 1921, the Northern Ireland Act 1998, the Government Resources and Accounts Act (Northern Ireland) 2001 and the Audit and Accountability (Northern Ireland) Order 2003.. Accordingly, he provides Parliament with an explicit, separate, opinion on the regularity of transactions included in the financial statements of central government bodies.*

use of monies, wherever they have ultimately been spent. The Court will normally address the regularity with which funds have been applied.

This Practice Note provides public sector auditors with guidance on the audit of regularity in the section at paragraphs 277-383 below. 15

Other review and reporting assignments

Public sector auditors may also be required to review and report on other information prepared by public bodies. Practice Note 10 does not provide guidance to the auditor on conducting these other review and reporting assignments. The standards governing other review assignments in the public sector are a matter for the national audit agencies or certain regulators to determine. Such other information on which public sector auditors may be required to review and report may include aspects of their corporate governance or on their arrangements to secure economy, efficiency and effectiveness in the use of resources, including: 16

- **performance information**. The Audit Commission Act 1998, the Public Audit (Wales) Act 2004 and the Local Government (Scotland) Act 1973 require the Audit Commission's, the Auditor General for Wales's and the Accounts Commission's appointed auditors to obtain satisfaction that, where appropriate, the body has made the necessary arrangements for collecting, recording and publishing specified performance information. In practice, an Audit Commission appointed auditor's responsibilities in relation to performance information derive from the auditor's general responsibility to obtain satisfaction that the audited body has put in place proper arrangements to secure economy, efficiency and effectiveness in their use of resources, which are defined in the Code of Audit Practice to include arrangements to ensure data quality. In central government, there is no statutory requirement for public sector auditors to review and report on non-financial performance information published by departments, agencies and non-departmental public bodies or the adequacy of supporting systems. Public sector auditors may nevertheless be invited to carry out an assignment to review Executive Agency or NDPB performance indicators where the Minister responsible decides this is required. The Comptroller and Auditor General was invited by Government in 2002 to review the adequacy of data systems supporting Departments Public Service Agreement targets.
- **grant claims**. Public bodies in receipt of government grants may be required to provide assurance about the extent to which a grant claim or return has been prepared in accordance with the requirements of the government entity and that the figures presented are properly supported and fairly presented. Auditors of local government and NHS bodies (excluding NHS Foundation Trusts) in England may examine and report on audited bodies' government grant claims and returns in accordance with a framework prescribed by the Audit Commission. In carrying out this work, auditors in England act as agents of the Audit Commission. In Wales, a similar arrangement applies to the whole of the devolved public sector under the Government of Wales Act 1998. In Scotland similar arrangements apply.
- **corporate governance**. Public sector auditors are required to review and report on the corporate governance statements that public sector bodies are required to include with their financial statements.
- **best value performance plans.** Auditors of local government bodies in England and Wales are required to consider and report on audited bodies' Best Value

Performance Plans, giving a conclusion as to whether the plan has been prepared and published in accordance with legislation and statutory guidance[3]
- **economy, efficiency and effectiveness.** The nature of the auditor's responsibilities varies between different parts of the public sector. The National Audit Act 1983 empowers the Comptroller and Auditor General to carry out examinations into the economy, efficiency and effectiveness with which Departments have used their resources in discharging their functions. The Government of Wales Act 1998 and the Public Audit (Wales) Act 2004 provide the Auditor General for Wales with similar powers as does the Audit (Northern Ireland) Order 1987 and the Northern Ireland Act 1998 for the Comptroller and the Auditor General for Northern Ireland and the Public Finance and Accountability (Scotland) Act 2000 for the Auditor General for Scotland. Under the Local Government (Scotland) Act 1973 the Accounts Commission appointed auditor is required to obtain satisfaction that the audited body has made proper arrangements for securing best value and is complying with its duties with regard to community planning. Under the Audit Commission Act 1998, an Audit Commission appointed auditor is required to obtain satisfaction that the audited body has made proper arrangements for securing economy, efficiency and effectiveness in its use of resources. The Public Audit (Wales) Act 2004 contains a similar requirement for local government auditors appointed by the Auditor General in Wales and the Health and Social Care (Community Health and Standards) Act 2003 contains a similar requirement for auditors of NHS Foundation Trusts. Legislation in Northern Ireland also gives local government auditors a role in relation to economy, efficiency and effectiveness.
- **standards of financial conduct.** Public sector auditors are required to review and, where appropriate, to report, on issues relating to standards of financial conduct in public bodies and aspects of the arrangements set in place by the audited body to ensure the proper conduct of its financial affairs. In central government, the Comptroller and Auditor General has regard to and reports to Parliament on matters of propriety. The Auditor General for Wales, the Comptroller and Auditor General for Northern Ireland and the Auditor General for Scotland have a similar responsibility. In local government and the National Health Service in England and the health service in Northern Ireland the auditor's work on propriety is covered both by the auditor's work on the accounts, and as part of the auditor's work in relation to the use of resources, specifically in relation to arrangements to safeguard the financial standing of the audited body and arrangements to ensure that the audited body's affairs are managed in accordance with proper standards of conduct and to prevent and detect fraud and corruption.

The conduct of assignments undertaken by public sector auditors

17 The standards governing the conduct and reporting of the audit of financial statements in the public sector are a matter for the national audit agencies and certain regulators to determine. However, the heads of the national audit agencies in the UK have chosen to adopt the Auditing Practices Board's engagement standards and quality control standards as the basis of their approach to the audit of financial statements. Where appropriate this is embodied in codes of audit practice which also deal with other responsibilities. For example, the Audit Commission Act 1998 requires the Commission to prepare and keep under review a Code of Audit Practice

---

[3] *In Wales, the Best Value regime is known as the 'Wales Programme for Improvement'. Under the Local Government (Scotland) Act 1973 the Accounts Commission may initiate studies into economy, efficiency and effectiveness. Also the Controller of Audit may make reports to the Accounts Commission on the performance of a local authority of its duties relating to best value and community planning..*

prescribing the way in which auditors are to carry out their functions. The Code embodies the Commission's view of best professional practice with respect to the standards, procedures and techniques to be adopted by auditors in discharging their functions, and as such serves to define the scope and form of local authority and health entity audits, reflecting the statutory requirements and the wider aims and objectives of the audits of local government and health bodies. Audit Scotland issues a single non-statutory Code of Audit Practice approved by the Accounts Commission and the Auditor General for Scotland that covers the whole of the public sector in Scotland. The Auditor General for Wales has issued a Code of Audit and Inspection Practice under section 16 of the Public Audit Wales Act (2004) for local government appointed auditors. This has been extended on a non-statutory basis to cover the whole of the Welsh public sector and includes Value for Money audit and Wales Programme for Improvement work. The new Auditor General for Wales' Code of Audit and Inspection Practice will apply from the 2005-06 financial year. Where an independent regulator prescribes the way in which auditors are to carry out their functions, possibly in an Audit Code, the auditor follows these requirements.

International Standard on Quality Control (UK and Ireland) 1

Background Note

The purpose of this International Standard on Quality Control (UK and Ireland) is to establish standards and provide guidance regarding a firm's responsibilities for its system of quality control for audits and reviews of historical financial information and for other assurance and related services engagements. This ISQC (UK and Ireland) is to be read in conjunction with the APB's ethical standards and the ethical pronouncements relating to the work of auditors issued by the auditor's relevant professional body.

Introduction

The auditor reads the guidance in this section of the Practice Note in conjunction with ISQC (UK and Ireland) 1. The purpose of the guidance contained in this section of the Practice Note is to highlight the key areas where public sector practice differs from that of the private sector. In particular, this section of the Practice Note clarifies terms used in ISQC (UK and Ireland) 1 in the context of the public sector and provides guidance on withdrawing from an engagement.

In the context of the audit of public sector entities the following clarification of terms used in ISQC (UK and Ireland) 1 is relevant:

- "firm" may be taken as a general reference to the organisation, including the national audit agencies, of which the auditor is a partner or employee; and
- "engagement partner" may be taken as a general reference to the individual identified as being responsible for the conduct of the audit.

All the requirements of ISQC (UK and Ireland) 1 are relevant to the audit of financial statements of public sector entities. However, the following additional guidance is required:

(a) Withdrawing from an engagement

In the public sector, where the auditor is appointed under statute the auditor cannot decline or withdraw from the engagement. Where public sector auditors are not appointed by statute there are still a number of avenues open to the auditor other than withdrawing from the engagement. In most cases public sector auditors have the statutory authority to report publicly matters that may otherwise have caused withdrawal from the engagement. For example, in the central government sector such matters can be reported to Parliament.

(b) Taking appropriate action to address threats to auditor independence

When allocating an in-house engagement team to a particular audit, a national audit agency evaluates auditor independence in accordance with the requirements of ISQC (UK and Ireland) 1. Where appointed by statute, a national audit agency will not have the opportunity to decline or withdraw from an engagement where threats to independence are identified. However, the national audit agency may take alternative steps to reduce threats to an acceptable level. Such steps may include changing the membership of the engagement team.

Where an audit firm is appointed by, employed by or is acting as the agent of a national audit agency, the national audit agency will assess the firm's independence when the firm is appointed. In conducting the public sector audit work the firm complies with the requirements of ISQC (UK and Ireland) 1 on independence.

21 The APB's ethical standards and the ethical pronouncements relating to the work of auditors issued by the auditor's relevant professional body apply in the public sector to the extent that they are relevant. Public sector auditors also comply with additional ethical requirements, such as restrictions on political activities or requirements contained in the Audit Commission's 'Statement of Independence'.

ISA (UK and Ireland) 200: Objective and General Principles Governing an Audit of Financial Statements

Background Note

The purpose of this International Standard on Auditing (UK and Ireland) is to establish standards and provide guidance on the objective and general principles governing an audit of financial statements.

Introduction

22 The auditor reads the guidance in this section of the Practice Note in conjunction with ISA (UK and Ireland) 200. The purpose of the guidance contained in this section of the Practice Note is to highlight the key areas where public sector practice differs from that of the private sector. In particular, this section of the Practice Note highlights the requirement for many public sector auditors to report on the regularity of transactions undertaken by the audited entity in the period covered by the financial statements.

Scope of an Audit

> The audit procedures required to conduct an audit in accordance with ISAs (UK and Ireland) should be determined by the auditor having regard to the requirements of ISAs (UK and Ireland), relevant professional bodies, legislation, regulations and, where appropriate, the terms of the audit engagement and reporting requirements. (ISA (UK and Ireland) 200 para 7)

23. Although the basic principles of auditing are the same in the public and private sectors, the auditor of a public service body often has wider objectives and additional duties and statutory responsibilities, laid down in legislation, directives or codes of practice.

The Regularity Opinion

24. In observing the requirements of ISA (UK and Ireland) 200, the auditor is aware that:

- for central government, specified health entities and probation boards[4]
- in recognition of the importance of regularity to the audit of these entities, the structure of the auditor's report includes an explicit opinion on the regularity of transactions.

25. The auditor also considers propriety. It is a related concept but propriety is not covered by the regularity opinion. Further guidance on propriety is provided in paragraphs 282 to 284 of this Practice Note.

26. As set out in the section of this Practice Note on ISQC (UK and Ireland) 1, public sector auditors comply with the relevant ethical requirements.

27. Further guidance on regularity and the reporting of regularity in the audit opinion is included in the separate section of this Practice Note on regularity.

ISA (UK and Ireland) 210: Terms of Audit Engagements

Background Note

The purpose of this International Standard on Auditing (UK and Ireland) is to establish standards and provide guidance on:

(a) agreeing the terms of engagement with the client; and
(b) the auditor's response to a request by a client to change the terms of an engagement to one that provides a lower level of assurance.

Introduction

28. The auditor reads the guidance in this section of the Practice Note in conjunction with ISA (UK and Ireland) 210. The purpose of the guidance contained in this

---

[4] In England and Wales, a probation board is a body corporate. In Northern Ireland, the probation board is an NDPB. In Scotland, the probation service is undertaken by the social services departments of local authorities, there is a requirement to obtain evidence on compliance with authorities; and

section of the Practice Note is to highlight the key areas where public sector practice differs from that of the private sector. This section of the Practice Note provides guidance to the auditor on the legislative framework surrounding the terms of public sector audit engagements.

29   In this section of the Practice Note, the client is considered to be the audited body.

> The auditor and the client should agree on the terms of the engagement. (ISA (UK and Ireland) 210 para 2)

30   Engagements in the public sector normally differ substantially from those addressed in ISA (UK and Ireland) 210. In the public sector there are normally at least three parties with an interest in the terms of an engagement: the auditor, the audited entity and the relevant national audit agency (or Secretary of State, if responsible for the appointment of the auditor). In most instances, the statutory framework allows a substantial part of the scope and objectives of the audit to be mandated by the national audit agency.

31   For this reason, engagement letters are not normally concluded between the auditor and the audited entity. Either an engagement letter is agreed between the auditor and the national audit agency (or Secretary of State, or regulator) or is made unnecessary because the terms of the engagement have been set out comprehensively in letters of appointment and associated documents such as Codes of Audit Practice.

32   The auditor determines whether agreement about the responsibilities of the entity and of the auditor, the scope of the engagement and the form of reports can be understood without formally being recorded in writing. This will normally only be possible where the relevant national audit agency has, in the opinion of the auditor, issued letters of appointment, letters of understanding, Codes of Audit Practice and associated documents of audit requirements or guidance that contain all the provisions required by paragraph 6 of ISA (UK and Ireland) 210 which sets out the principal contents of an engagement letter.

33   The auditor may find it appropriate to conclude letters of understanding with the audited entity to confirm the auditor's understanding of the roles of the three parties with an interest in the engagement, the requirements of the audit, the responsibilities of each party, how the responsibilities will be met, and the expectations that each party can have of the other. However, such a document is not intended to be a substitute for the clarification of any uncertainties in the auditing framework that will need to be resolved with the relevant national audit agency. In circumstances where roles, requirements and responsibilities mandated by the national audit agency are not clear or are debatable, the auditor requests that the national audit agency provides greater clarity in the terms of its appointment; auditor and audited entities do not seek to interpret the intentions behind the uncertainties.

> The terms of the engagement should be recorded in writing. (ISA (UK and Ireland) 210 para 2-1)

34   In the public sector, the terms of engagement are usually recorded in the letter of understanding, Codes of Audit Practice and any relevant audit requirements or guidance issued by a regulatory body.

Central Government

In central government, the audit of many entities is provided for in legislation or by Royal Charter. Such legislation will usually directly appoint, on behalf of the Houses of Parliament, the Comptroller and Auditor General as auditor. In the public sector auditors take due account of the legislative requirements on the appointment of the auditor and the arrangements under which an engagement is defined. 35

For UK-wide entities and those covering England, the Comptroller and Auditor General is appointed by statute to audit all government departments, agencies and all non-departmental public bodies (except those that are companies). 36

In Wales, the Auditor General is appointed by statute or agreement to audit the accounts of the National Assembly, its sponsored and other related public bodies and all NHS Wales entities. The Auditor General for Wales also appoints the auditors of local government bodies in Wales. In Scotland, the Auditor General appoints the auditor of the Scottish Executive and most of its sponsored bodies. For Northern Ireland, the framework is similar to that applicable in England, with legislation applicable to specific entities providing directly for the appointment of the Comptroller and Auditor General for Northern Ireland or for sponsoring departments to appoint auditors. For health entities in Northern Ireland responsibility for the audit is covered by the Audit and Accountability (Northern Ireland) Order 2003. 37

For financial statements produced by central government departments, including those of executive agencies, the auditor's duties are set out in legislation. As an example, the Government Resources and Accounts Act 2000 prescribes the duties of the Comptroller and Auditor General to examine, on behalf of Parliament, the accounts of government departments. Because the auditor's responsibilities for these financial statements are set out in detail in legislation, the auditor does not need to agree on the terms of the engagement with the government department or agency concerned. Nevertheless, in these cases the auditor normally sets out in a letter the auditor's understanding of the respective responsibilities of the auditor and of management and provides details of the scope and nature of the audit. 38

Legislation governing the establishment of non-departmental public bodies and the appointment of the auditor has not to date prescribed in detail the auditor's responsibilities. 39

Where the financial statements are laid before Parliament, either by statute or command, and there is no letter of appointment from the sponsor department setting out the auditor's responsibilities or the responsibilities are not clearly set out in legislation, an engagement letter is required. The auditor agrees the terms of engagement with the Chief Executive or Accounting Officer of the audited entity. The areas that may be covered in such a letter of engagement are set out in the annex to this section of the Practice Note. 40

The auditor also considers whether HM Treasury agreement of these terms may be required. Where the financial statements are not laid before Parliament, the auditor agrees the terms of the audit engagement with the addressee of the auditor's report. 41

Local Government and Health Entities

The appointment of auditors to local government and health entities (excluding NHS Foundation Trusts) is made within a statutory framework where audits are required to be executed in accordance with the applicable Code of Audit Practice. The Codes 42 deal with many of those matters that would in the private sector context have been dealt with in a letter of engagement. The Audit Commission and Audit Scotland supply a copy of the relevant Code to all audited bodies and writes to inform them of the statutory appointment, the fee arrangements and any general matters that might affect the audit.

43 The Audit Commission also writes a letter of appointment and provides a copy of the Statement of Responsibilities to all local government and health entities in England, to help improve understanding of the terms upon which the Commission appoints auditors, and their responsibilities and duties.

44 In the case of NHS Foundation Trusts, the Board of Governors is responsible, under the Health and Social Care (Community Health and Standards) Act 2003, for the appointment of auditors. Auditors must comply with the Audit Code for NHS Foundation Trusts, as published by Monitor. As part of this Audit Code, the auditor agrees an engagement letter with the NHS Foundation Trust and in doing so complies with ISA (UK and Ireland) 210.

45 In Wales, the Auditor General for Wales' Code of Audit and Inspection Practice is statutory for local government auditors and extended on a non-statutory basis to cover the whole of the Welsh public sector.

46 Audit Scotland also issues a Statement of Responsibilities.

47 In Northern Ireland, responsibility for the audit of all health entities has been allocated, under the Audit and Accountability (Northern Ireland) Order 2003, to the Comptroller and Auditor General for Northern Ireland. Such audits are therefore governed by the relevant statutes and by auditing standards. Local government auditors work to a non-statutory Code of Audit Practice although draft legislation is under consultation that will provide for the Code to have a statutory base.

48 The arrangements set out in paragraphs 42 to 47 above meet the substance and intent of ISA (UK and Ireland) 210 and therefore auditors of local government and health entities do not need to agree a separate engagement letter for the audit of the financial statements (except in Northern Ireland health bodies, for which paragraph 40 is applicable).

Acceptance of a Change in Engagement

> An auditor who, before the completion of the engagement, is requested to change the engagement to one which provides a lower level of assurance, should consider the appropriateness of doing so. (ISA (UK and Ireland) 210 para 12)

49 Where the auditor's responsibilities are set out in statute or relevant codes of practice, the terms of the engagement cannot be changed to provide a lower level of assurance.

> If the auditor is unable to agree to a change of the engagement and is not permitted to continue the original engagement, the auditor should withdraw and consider whether there is any obligation, either contractual or otherwise, to report to other parties, such as those charged with governance or shareholders, the circumstances necessitating the withdrawal. (ISA (UK and Ireland) 210 para 19)

(c) Not issue the auditor's report until the completion of the engagement quality control review. (ISA (UK and Ireland) 220 para 36)

The ISA (UK and Ireland) requires that engagement quality control review is undertaken for all audit engagements where the entity is a listed company, and that firms establish policies setting out the circumstances in which an engagement quality control review is performed for other audit engagements, whether on the grounds of the public interest or risk.

In the public sector, the auditor[5]

ISA (UK and Ireland) 230: Documentation

Background Note

The purpose of this International Standard on Auditing (UK and Ireland) is to establish standards and provide guidance regarding documentation in the context of the audit of financial statements.

Introduction

The auditor reads the guidance in this section of the Practice Note in conjunction with ISA (UK and Ireland) 230. The purpose of the guidance contained in this section of the Practice Note is to highlight the key areas where public sector practice differs from that of the private sector. Although the requirements of ISA (UK and Ireland) 230 are applied in full in the public sector, this section of the Practice Note identifies some additional consideration for the public sector auditor.

The auditor should adopt appropriate procedures for maintaining the confidentiality and safe custody of the working papers and for retaining them for a period sufficient to meet the needs of the practice and in accordance with legal and professional requirements of record retention. (ISA (UK and Ireland) 230 para 13)

Although public sector auditors apply the provisions of ISA (UK and Ireland) 230 in full, auditors may also have additional statutory obligations relating to confidentiality. For example, when carrying out central government assignments auditors are aware of, and comply with, any applicable provisions of the Official Secrets Act 1989. Auditors of local government and health entities (excluding NHS Foundation Trusts) in England are bound by the requirements for confidentiality contained in section 49 of the Audit Commission Act 1998 and auditors of local government entities in Wales are bound by the provisions of Section 54 of the Public Audit (Wales) Act 2004. Auditors of NHS Foundation Trusts are bound by the same

---

[5] *The auditor, in the public sector context, is defined in paragraph 4 of the Foreword. considers the circumstances in which an engagement quality control review of the audit is necessary. In doing so the auditor will need to consider the size and characteristics of the entity. Generally engagement quality control reviews are more likely to be appropriate to larger, more complex, entities than smaller ones, and to higher profile entities than lower profile entities. An engagement quality control review may be appropriate for smaller entities with a high profile, for example if there is a particularly high level of Parliamentary, public or media interest in the entity.*

requirements, set out in section 8 of schedule 5 of the Health and Social Care (Community Health and Standards) Act 2003.

60 The auditor also considers whether there are specific statutory requirements for the retention of working papers. For instance, the Public Records Act 1958 and the Public Records (Scotland) Act 1937 could apply to the audit of a central government entity. Advice is provided on the implications of these statutory provisions for the retention of financial records in Government Accounting. Where the auditor is uncertain as to the auditor's statutory duties, the auditor considers seeking legal advice.

61 The acceptance of most appointments in the public sector requires the auditor to acknowledge that the auditor's working papers may be subject to inspection by the national audit agency that appointed the auditor or that is responsible for the audit of a higher tier entity and by review agencies that have statutory rights of access to information relevant to the auditor's duties. If not bound by a specific statutory requirement, ethical considerations normally entail that the national audit agency acquires the duty of confidentiality that is held by the auditor.

62 Whilst the auditor is expected to comply with statutory obligations relating to confidentiality, the auditor is also aware that the audit work may be potentially disclosable under the Freedom of Information Act 2000.

63 The Freedom of Information Act 2000 and the Freedom of Information (Scotland) Act 2002 introduce a statutory right of access to all information held by public authorities. All individuals have this right of access from 1 January 2005.

64 In December 2002, the Public Audit Forum published a consultation paper *Freedom of Information and Public Sector Audit*. In this paper, the national audit agencies accepted their obligations as public authorities under the Acts and made clear their intention to publish as much information as possible where there is known to be public interest. There is no over-riding exemption relating to the disclosure of information acquired in the course of an audit. However, on a case by case basis the auditor considers whether exemptions may be applied. The Acts provide a number of exemptions where the public interest in withholding information is greater than the public interest in disclosing it, for example:

- prejudicing the audit function; and
- disclosure prior to publication.

As case law develops further guidance will be published by the Information Commissioner.

65 In all cases the auditor consults with relevant parties (such as the audited body to which the request relates) before making a decision on disclosure under the Act.

ISA (UK and Ireland) 240: The Auditor's Responsibility to Consider Fraud in an Audit of Financial Statements

Background Note

The purpose of this International Standard on Auditing (UK and Ireland) is to establish basic principles and essential procedures and to provide guidance on the auditor's responsibility to consider fraud in an audit of financial statements.

Introduction

66 The auditor reads the guidance in this section of the Practice Note in conjunction with ISA (UK and Ireland) 240. The purpose of the guidance contained in this section of the Practice Note is to highlight the key areas where public sector practice differs from that of the private sector. Details are provided below regarding certain additional responsibilities of the public sector auditor in relation to fraud and the auditor's duty to report instances of fraud to specified third parties. This guidance also highlights some specific issues the auditor considers when understanding the risk of fraud in an entity.

> In planning and performing the audit to reduce audit risk to an acceptably low level, the auditor should consider the risks of material misstatements in the financial statements due to fraud. (ISA (UK and Ireland) 240 para 3)

67 The public sector auditor's responsibilities under ISA (UK and Ireland) 240 are not any different from those of private sector auditors as regards the audit of the financial statements (although in some instances they are different with respect to the other responsibilities relating to fraud as set out in paragraphs 68 and 69 below).

68 Further details regarding the requirements of public sector auditors with regard to fraud are given in the following documents:

- central government auditors have regard to HM Treasury (or Department of Finance and Personnel in Northern Ireland) and other appropriate guidance on corporate governance;
- the Audit Commission's Code of Audit Practice requires auditors of local government and health entities (excluding NHS Foundation Trusts) in England to review and, where appropriate, examine evidence that is relevant to the audited body's corporate performance management and financial management arrangements and report on these arrangements. This review will include consideration of the arrangements in place for ensuring that the audited body's affairs are managed in accordance with proper standards of conduct and to prevent and detect fraud and corruption. Such reviews are also carried out by auditors of health entities in Northern Ireland;
- the Auditor General for Wales' Code of Audit and Inspection Practice requires auditors of local government entities in Wales to form a view on the adequacy of aspects of the body's stewardship and governance arrangements; and
- Audit Scotland's Code of Audit Practice requires auditors of public sector entities in Scotland to consider and assess the arrangements in place for the prevention and detection of fraud and corruption.

69 These other responsibilities are different from and wider than those to which ISA (UK and Ireland) 240 is directly relevant. The auditor is concerned, to a greater or lesser extent, with reviewing and reporting upon the entity's arrangements for the prevention and detection of fraud. ISA (UK and Ireland) 240 is concerned with ensuring that the auditor considers the risks of material misstatement in the financial statements due to fraud and designs and performs further audit procedures whose nature, timing and extent are responsive to assessed risks.

Fraud in the Context of the Regularity Opinion

70 Fraudulent transactions cannot, by definition, be regular since they are without proper authority. Where the auditor has a duty to give a regularity opinion, fraud that is material always results in a qualification of the regularity part of the opinion, regardless of the manner or extent of disclosure in the financial statements. Guidance on fraud in the context of regularity is set out in the separate section in this Practice Note on regularity.

> The auditor should obtain an understanding of how those charged with governance exercise oversight of management's processes for identifying and responding to the risks of fraud in the entity and the internal control that management has established to mitigate these risks. (ISA (UK and Ireland) 240 para 43)

71 The responsibilities of public sector entities in relation to the prevention and detection of fraud and error are set out in statute, standards and other guidance:

| Central government entities | Under "Government Accounting" the *Accounting Officer* has a personal responsibility for the proper presentation of financial statements for which he or she is answerable and for ensuring that:

• proper financial procedures are followed;

• public funds are properly and well managed and safeguarded;

• assets are similarly controlled and safeguarded; and

• funds are applied only to the extent and for the purposes authorised by Parliament.

"Government Accounting" also states that *departments* are expected to develop and maintain effective controls to prevent fraud and to ensure that when it does occur it is detected promptly.

In Wales, the Accounting Officer follows the guidance set out in the "Accounting Officer Memorandum" of the National Assembly for Wales, issued by HM Treasury.

In Scotland, the functions of *Accountable Officers* are set out in the |

	Public Finance and Accountability (Scotland) Act 2000, and include: • signing the financial statements; and • ensuring the propriety and regularity of the finances. In Northern Ireland, the responsibilities of an Accounting Officer are contained in "Government Accounting Northern Ireland", issued by the Department of Finance and Personnel.
Local government entities	*Entities* have a statutory duty to make arrangements for the proper administration of their financial affairs. An *officer* is appointed to have responsibility for the administration of these arrangements. In addition, in England, the Accounts and Audit Regulations 2003 require the *"responsible financial officer"* to determine accounting control systems that include measures to enable the prevention and detection of inaccuracies and fraud. In Wales, the Accounts and Audit (Wales) Regulations 2005 have been made by the National Assembly for Wales under section 39 of the Public Audit (Wales) Act 2004.
Health entities	In England, Secretary of State directions require NHS bodies to take all necessary steps to counter fraud in the NHS. In addition, *the Chief Executive* and *the Director of Finance* of health bodies (excluding NHS Foundation Trusts) in England are required by the Secretary of State to monitor and ensure compliance with the directions. In NHS Foundation Trusts, the Accounting Officer is required by the regulator to ensure a high standard of financial management. In Wales, the arrangements are similar to those in England, with Accountable Officers being designated by the National Assembly for Wales.

	In Scotland, under the Public Finance and Accountability (Scotland) Act 2000, NHS Accountable Officers have a personal responsibility for the propriety and regularity of financial transactions and for signing the accounts of their entities. In Scotland, minimum financial control standards required for the Statement of Internal Financial Control also require that: • a fraud and corruption policy and response plan are in place; and • systems are in place that produce reliable financial information and proper accounting records. The position in Northern Ireland is broadly similar to England and Wales.

Consideration of Fraud Risk Factors

> When obtaining an understanding of the entity and its environment, including its internal control, the auditor should consider whether the information obtained indicates that one or more fraud risk factors are present. (ISA (UK and Ireland) 240 para 48)

72   Public sector auditors consider whether fraud risk factors are present when obtaining an understanding of audited entities. The risk of external fraud may be particularly high where a body is involved in issuing grants or benefits to the public or collecting tax revenues.

73   ISA (UK and Ireland) 240 describes 2 types of fraud that are relevant to the auditor:
• misstatements resulting from the misappropriation of assets; and
• misstatements resulting from fraudulent financial reporting.

74   A public sector auditor needs to consider misstatements that may arise from fraudulent financial reporting where the audited body may manipulate its results to meet externally set targets e.g. the achievement of a statutory break-even duty by an NHS Trust or where financial results affect performance ratings by an inspectorate.

Auditor Unable to Continue the Engagement

> If, as a result of a misstatement resulting from fraud or suspected fraud, the auditor encounters exceptional circumstances that bring into question the auditor's ability to continue performing the audit the auditor should:
> (a) Consider the professional and legal responsibilities applicable in the circumstances, including whether there is a requirement for the auditor to

> report to the person or persons who made the audit appointment or, in some cases, to regulatory authorities;
> (b) Consider the possibility of withdrawing from the engagement; and
> (c) If the auditor withdraws:
>   (i) Discuss with the appropriate level of management and those charged with governance the auditor's withdrawal from the engagement and the reasons for the withdrawal; and
>   (ii) Consider whether there is a professional or legal requirement to report to the person or persons who made the audit appointment or, in some cases, to regulatory authorities, the auditor's withdrawal from the engagement and the reasons for the withdrawal. (ISA (UK and Ireland) 240 para 103)

75 In the public sector, where the auditor is appointed under statute the auditor cannot decline or withdraw from the engagement. Where the public sector auditor is not appointed by statute there are still a number of avenues open to the auditor other than withdrawing from the engagement. In most cases a public sector auditor has the statutory authority to report publicly matters that may otherwise have caused withdrawal from the engagement. For example, in the central government sector such matters can be reported to Parliament.

Documentation

> The auditor should document communications about fraud made to management, those charged with governance, regulators and others. (ISA (UK and Ireland) 240 para 109)

76 In considering whether to report a suspected or actual instance of fraud to a proper authority, the auditor of a public sector entity has regard to paragraph 102 of ISA (UK and Ireland) 240 and to:

- the provisions relevant to the entity that set out in the responsibilities of those charged with governance for the reporting of misconduct, fraud or other irregularity; and
- the duties which the auditor may have under the terms of engagement to report to a third party.

77 Where, in accordance with ISA (UK and Ireland) 240, the auditor considers that there is a duty to report to a third party (because of the implication of those charged with governance in the matter or their refusal to report), the proper authorities to whom the auditor is initially expected to report instances of suspected or actual fraud may differ:

UK wide departments and central government departments covering England and Wales	HM Treasury.
National Assembly for Wales and its sponsored public bodies	The Compliance Officer of the National Assembly for Wales.
Central government departments in Scotland	The Auditor General for Scotland.

Central government departments in Northern Ireland	The Department of Finance and Personnel.
Non-departmental public bodies and executive agencies	The sponsor department.
Local government entities	A relevant authority as set out in ISA (UK and Ireland) 240, such as the Police.
Health entities	Counter Fraud and Security Management Service In Northern Ireland, reports are made to the Department of Health, Social Services and Public Safety.

78 Because the public sector is covered by separate legislation on corruption[6]

79 The auditor is also aware of the responsibilities in relation to reporting money laundering offences (see guidance in paragraphs 89 to 91 of this Practice Note), including those relating to 'tipping-off'.

80 The terms of engagement for the auditor of a non-departmental public body may require the auditor to report to the sponsor department on acts of misconduct, fraud or other irregularity irrespective of whether the entity's directors have themselves reported the matter to the sponsor department.

> When the auditor has concluded that the presumption that there is a risk of material misstatement due to fraud related to revenue recognition is not applicable in the circumstances of the engagement, the auditor should document the reasons for that conclusion. (ISA (UK and Ireland) 240 para 110)

81 ISA (UK and Ireland) 240 states, in paragraph 60, that material misstatements due to fraudulent financial reporting often result from an overstatement of revenues (for

---

[6] *Specific legislation on corruption applies to United Kingdom public bodies of all descriptions and their agents, where an agent is a person serving under a public body. The generally applicable legislation comprises:*
- *the Public Bodies Corruption Act 1889;*
- *the Prevention of Corruption Act 1906; and*
- *the Prevention of Corruption Act 1916.*

Section 117(2) of the Local Government Act 1972 is also relevant to local authorities in England and Wales: it prescribes that officers shall not accept any fee or reward under colour of their office or employment other than proper remuneration. In Northern Ireland, section 47 of the Local Government (Northern Ireland) Act 1972 applies to the same effect.

Section 2 of the Prevention of Corruption Act 1916 states that:
'any money, gift or other consideration paid to or received by a person in the employment of any...government department or public body by or from a person, or agent of a person, holding or seeking to obtain a contract from any...government department or public body shall be deemed to have been paid corruptly...unless the contrary is proved.'

The importance of this particular provision is that, where a person employed by a public body has received any money, gift or consideration from a contractor or tenderer, the burden of proof is on that person to establish that such consideration was not paid or received corruptly., the auditor considers to whom the auditor may report suspected or actual acts of corruption, irrespective of whether, in the auditor's opinion, the consequences of the corruption could have a material effect on the financial statements. In the first instance, the auditor normally brings the matter to the attention of those charged with governance. It is then the responsibility of those charged with governance to report the matter to the proper authorities. If the auditor of an entity identifies a suspected or actual instance of corruption, and if, having reported the matter to those charged with governance the auditor is unable to establish whether those charged with governance have reported the matter to the relevant third party, the auditor takes the steps set out in paragraph 102 of ISA (UK and Ireland) 240.

example, through premature revenue recognition or recording fictitious revenues) or an understatement of revenues (for example, through improperly shifting revenues to a later period). Therefore, the auditor ordinarily presumes that there are risks of fraud in revenue recognition and considers which types of revenue, revenue transactions or assertions may give rise to such risks. Those assessed risks of material misstatement due to fraud related to revenue recognition are significant risks. For some public sector bodies this presumption regarding the risk of fraud relating to revenue recognition may not apply. The public sector auditor needs to consider whether there is a risk of material misstatement due to fraud related to revenue recognition where the audited body is required to meet externally set targets.

ISA (UK and Ireland) 250: Consideration of Laws and Regulations in an Audit of Financial Statements

Background Note

The purpose of this International Auditing Standard (UK and Ireland) is to establish standards and provide guidance on the auditor's responsibility to consider laws and regulations in an audit of financial statements.

Introduction

The auditor reads the guidance in this section of the Practice Note in conjunction with ISA (UK and Ireland) 250. The purpose of the guidance contained in this section of the Practice Note is to highlight the key areas where public sector practice differs from that of the private sector. In relation to the auditor's consideration of laws and regulations, the guidance below advises the public sector auditor of the additional laws and regulations the auditor needs to consider in the audit of a public sector entity. 82

Section A – Consideration of Laws and Regulations in an Audit of Financial Statements

An audit of financial statements in the public sector is similar in scope and nature to an entity in the private sector. The auditor has regard to the risk that financial statements might be materially affected by the entity's non-compliance with laws and regulation. For auditors of central government, specified health entities and probation boards there is a specific reporting requirement commonly known as regularity. 83

ISA (UK and Ireland) 250 is concerned with laws and regulations that, if not complied with, may materially affect the financial statements of any entity. Such laws and regulations fall into two categories: 84

- those which determine the form or contents of an entity's financial statements; and
- those which are to be complied with by those charged with governance or set the provisions under which an entity is allowed to conduct its business.

In order to plan the audit, the auditor should obtain a general understanding of the legal and regulatory framework applicable to the entity and the industry and

> how the entity is complying with that framework. (ISA (UK and Ireland) 250 para 15)

85 Furthermore, as ISA (UK and Ireland) 250 states, where statutory requirements exist which requires the auditor to report, as part of the audit of the financial statements, whether the entity complies with certain provisions of laws or regulations, the auditor needs:

- to obtain a *general understanding* of such legal and regulatory framework applicable to the entity and how the entity is complying with that framework; and
- to *test compliance* with provisions of laws and regulations.

86 Where the auditor is required to examine and report on the regularity of transactions, the auditor applies the guidance on law and regulations in the context of the regularity opinion set out in the separate section in this Practice Note on regularity.

The Auditor's Consideration of Compliance With Laws and Regulations

> In the UK and Ireland, the auditor should obtain a general understanding of the procedures followed by the entity to ensure compliance with that framework (ISA (UK and Ireland) 250 para 15-1)

87 Auditors of local government and health entities are required to have a wider regard to law and regulations than the potential impact of non-compliance on the financial statements:

- auditors of local government and health entities (excluding NHS Foundation Trusts) have separate statutory responsibilities to take specific action and/or to report in relation to matters that come to the auditor's attention that indicate that unlawful expenditure has been or will be incurred or a financial loss or deficiency has arisen or will arise;
- the Audit Commission's Code of Audit Practice requires auditors of local government and health entities (excluding NHS Foundation Trusts) in England to review and, where appropriate, examine evidence that is relevant to the audited body's corporate performance management and financial management arrangements and report on these arrangements. This review will include consideration of the arrangements in place for compliance with laws and regulations;
- The Auditor General for Wales' Code of Audit and Inspection Practice contains a similar requirement;
- Audit Scotland's Code of Audit Practice requires auditors of local government entities to consider whether there are any matters relating to failure to comply with laws and regulations to be brought to the attention of the Controller of Audit;
- in Northern Ireland, auditors of health entities review and, where appropriate, report on the financial aspects of the audited entity's corporate governance arrangements as they relate to the legality of transactions that might have a significant financial consequence; and
- requirements may also be established by other regulators such as Monitor who issue the Code of Audit Practice for NHS Foundation Trusts.

These other responsibilities are different from those to which ISA (UK and Ireland) 88
250 is directly relevant and assign particular duties to the auditor in relation to the
entity's arrangements to prevent non-compliance and to matters that come to the
auditor's attention, irrespective of the potential for a material impact on the financial
statements. The auditor takes care to ensure that, where matters come to the auditor's attention in relation to the auditor's other responsibilities relating to legality,
these findings are properly reviewed under the framework of ISA (UK and Ireland)
250 for their potential impact on the financial statements.

> In the UK and Ireland, when carrying out procedures for the purpose of forming
> an opinion on the financial statements, the auditor should be alert for those
> instances of possible or actual noncompliance with laws and regulations that
> might incur obligations for partners and staff in audit firms to report money
> laundering offences. (ISA (UK and Ireland) 250 para 22-1)

Where a public sector auditor works for a firm or a national audit agency that is 89
subject to the Money Laundering Regulations 2003, then knowledge or suspicion of
money laundering offences must be reported to the relevant Money Laundering
Reporting Officer(s) (MLRO) who will decide whether or not the matter is reported
to the National Criminal Intelligence Service.

The impact of the Money Laundering Regulations 2003 on Departments is set out in 90
HM Treasury Guidance.

The auditor considers the guidance in paragraph 22-4 of the ISA (UK and Ireland) 91
regarding 'tipping-off', which also applies in the public sector.

Withdrawal from the Engagement

Further guidance on withdrawing from engagements in the public sector is provided 92
in paragraph 75 of this Practice Note.

ISA (UK and Ireland) 260: Communication of Audit Matters with Those Charged With Governance

> **Background Note**
>
> The purpose of this International Standard on Auditing (UK and Ireland) is to
> establish standards and provide guidance on communication of audit matters
> arising from the audit of financial statements between the auditor and those
> charged with governance of an entity.

Introduction

The auditor reads the guidance in this section of the Practice Note in conjunction 93
with ISA (UK and Ireland) 260. The purpose of the guidance contained in this
section of the Practice Note is to highlight the key areas where public sector practice
differs from that of the private sector. In particular, this section of the Practice Note
identified who "those charged with governance" are in the public sector and the
framework in place for reporting to sponsor departments and third parties.

> The auditor should communicate audit matters of governance interest arising from the audit of financial statements with those charged with governance of an entity. (ISA (UK and Ireland) 260 para 2)

94   In common with other parts of the public sector, Accounting Officers in central government and NHS Foundation Trusts[7]

Relevant Persons

> The auditor should determine the relevant persons who are charged with governance and with whom audit matters of governance interest are communicated. (ISA (UK and Ireland) 260 para 5)

95   For further information on governance arrangements in the public sector, and their associated responsibilities, the auditor refers to the following Auditing Practices Board Bulletins:

     2003/01   Corporate Governance: Requirements of Public Sector Auditors (Central Government)

     2003/02   Corporate Governance: Requirements of Public Sector Auditors (National Health Service)

     2004/02   Corporate Governance: Requirements of Public Sector Auditors (Local Government Bodies)

Central Government

96   In central government the Accounting Officer has personal responsibilities (as set out in Government Accounting Chapter 4 and Government Accounting Northern Ireland Chapter 4) for:

- ensuring that effective management systems appropriate for the achievement of the organisation's objectives including financial monitoring and control systems have been put in place;
- keeping proper accounts;
- ensuring internal audit is established and organised in accordance with the Government Internal Audit Standards; and
- ensuring the regularity and propriety of public finances.

97   Audit committees are not mandatory in central government. However, HM Treasury strongly encourages the establishment of audit committees in all central government bodies. Where a body elects not to have an audit committee, HM Treasury expects

---

[7] *Auditors are not, however, required to report on the regularity of financial transactions of NHS Foundation Trusts, and Accountable Officers of specified health entities are responsible not only for maintaining adequate internal controls, but also for the regularity of the public funds for which they are accountable. Guidance on reporting to those charged with governance in the context of regularity is set out in the separate section of this Practice Note on the audit of regularity.*

the circumstances justifying the decision to be clearly identified. Audit committees have a role in advising the accounting officer on governance issues[8]

Local Government Bodies

Local government bodies are governed by democratically elected or appointed members who are supported by professional officers. It is the responsibility of the body to ensure that sound systems of financial management and internal control are in place and to designate the appropriate committee to fulfil the role of those charged with governance. Local authorities also have three designated statutory officers each of whom has a specific role in relation to accountability and control and have roles that are consistent with "management" as defined in the ISA (UK and Ireland): 98

- Head of Paid Service – usually the Chief Executive, responsible to the full council for the corporate and overall strategic management of the authority;
- Monitoring Officer[9]
- Chief Financial Officer – local authorities are required to appoint an officer with responsibility for the proper administration of their financial affairs.

Audit committees are not mandatory for local government bodies with the exception of police authorities in England and Wales. 99

National Health Service Bodies and Health Entities in Northern Ireland

Personal responsibility of Accountable Officers as set out in the Accountable Officer Memorandum for: 100

- ensuring that the body operates effective management systems;
- achieving value for money from the available resources;
- keeping proper accounts; and
- ensuring the regularity and propriety of expenditure.

Audit committees are mandatory for NHS bodies as specified in the Codes of Conduct and Accountability (1994) and for health entities in Northern Ireland. They have an advisory role in that they report to and advise the full board and audit committee on audit and governance matters. Best practice guidance is set out in the Audit Committee Handbook. 101

Other Bodies

Other bodies may have other governance arrangements as specified by the relevant regulator. For example, in NHS Foundation Trusts it is the Accounting Officer who has responsibility for governance issues as set out in the Accounting Officer memorandum issued by Monitor. 102

---

[8] *Further information on the Corporate Governance arrangements in Central Government can be found in the Corporate Governance Code for Central Government Departments* (http://www.hm-treasury.gov.uk/media/5DF/7D/corpgovernancecode280705.pdf).

[9] *Local authorities in Northern Ireland do not have Monitoring Officers – responsible for reporting to the authority any actual or potential breaches of the law or any maladministration, and for ensuring that procedures for recording and reporting key decisions are operating effectively;*

Reports to Sponsoring Bodies

103   Special arrangements have developed for reporting to those charged with governance by auditors of non-departmental public bodies (known as Assembly Sponsored Public Bodies in Wales) and other similar entities sponsored by government departments. In such cases the Accounting Officer of the sponsor department must obtain assurance that the financial and other management controls applied by the non-departmental public body or similar entity are adequate to ensure regularity and propriety. Reports from the auditor of the lower tier entity may assist the Accounting Officer in obtaining such assurance. Sponsor departments generally require auditors of their non-departmental public bodies to:

- provide the sponsor department with copies of management letters and other relevant correspondence; and
- report significant matters arising out of the audit work to the sponsor department, including:
  - failures of internal control, misconduct, fraud or other irregularity;
  - occasions where the Board, Chief Executive or any other official has fallen short of the high standards of financial integrity expected of those responsible for the management of public assets; or
  - occasions where the entity has incurred expenditure of an extravagant or wasteful nature.

104   The auditors of NHS bodies (excluding NHS Foundation Trusts) in England have a specific duty under the Audit Commission Act 1998 to refer a matter to the Secretary of State where they have reason to believe that the body or an officer of the body:

- is about to make, or has made, a decision which involves or would involve the incurring of expenditure which is unlawful;
- is about to take, or has taken, a course of action which, if pursued to its conclusion, would be unlawful and likely to cause loss or deficiency.

105   These and any other matters on which the auditor may be required to report to management are normally specified in the terms of appointment or engagement letter or Codes of Audit Practice.

Third Parties Interested in Reports to Those Charged With Governance

106   In the public sector the auditor generally has a responsibility to submit an annual audit letter and there may be a requirement that such letters are made public as described in paragraph 20-2 of ISA (UK and Ireland). Even where such reports are not made public, it remains possible that a third party may seek to place reliance on a report to those charged with governance made by a public sector auditor, even though such reliance was not foreseen when the audit was undertaken. It is appropriate to ensure that third parties who see the communication understand that it was not prepared with third parties in mind. In such instances the auditor uses the guidance contained in paragraph 20-1 of ISA (UK and Ireland) 260.

107   Limitations in reports to those charged with governance on responsibilities to other parties are amplified in the Audit Commission's "Statement of Responsibilities of Auditors and Audited Bodies", provided to all audited bodies in England, the Code of Audit Practice in Scotland and the Auditor General for Wales' Code of Audit and Inspection Practice. Effective reference to these documents, as appropriate, in any report to those charged with governance achieves the purpose intended in the ISAs (UK and Ireland).

ISA (UK and Ireland) 300: Planning an Audit of Financial Statements

Background Note

The purpose of this International Standard on Auditing (UK and Ireland) is to establish standards and provide guidance on the considerations and activities applicable to planning an audit of financial statements. This ISA (UK and Ireland) is framed in the context of recurring audits. In addition, matters the auditor considers in initial engagements are included in paragraphs 28 and 29 of ISA (UK and Ireland) 300.

Introduction

108 The auditor reads the guidance in this section of the Practice Note in conjunction with ISA (UK and Ireland) 300. The purpose of the guidance contained in this section of the Practice Note is to highlight the key areas where public sector practice differs from that of the private sector. In particular, the public sector auditor considers the requirement to provide an opinion on the regularity of transactions.

The auditor should plan the audit so that the engagement will be performed in an effective manner. (ISA (UK and Ireland) 300 para 2)

109 Effective working by the public sector auditor requires that the evidence needed to satisfy each responsibility and meet each duty (whether laid down in statute, relevant Codes of Audit Practice, or letters of appointment) is collected and considered in a structured way that contributes with greatest effect to the objectives of the audit considered as a whole. Where the auditor has completed work in relation to other responsibilities and duties, the auditor considers whether the work meets the requirements of ISAs (UK and Ireland) before seeking to place reliance on it for the purposes of the audit of the financial statements.

Preliminary Engagement Activities

The auditor should perform the following activities at the beginning of the current audit engagement:

- Perform procedures regarding the continuance of the client relationship and the specific audit engagement.
- Evaluate compliance with ethical requirements, including independence.
- Establish an understanding of the terms of the engagement. (ISA (UK and Ireland) 300 para 6)

110 Further guidance on declining or withdrawing from engagements in the public sector is provided in paragraph 75 of this Practice Note.

111 When establishing an understanding of the terms of the engagement, the auditor will need to consider the requirement to provide an opinion on the regularity of transactions. For further guidance on the audit of regularity, please see the separate section of this Practice Note on regularity.

Planning Activities

> The auditor should establish the overall audit strategy for the audit. (ISA (UK and Ireland) 300 para 8)

112 Where the auditor has a duty to give a regularity opinion, in developing the overall audit strategy the auditor obtains a sufficient understanding of the framework of authorities governing the audited entity and its activities that is sufficient to enable the auditor to identify events, transactions and practices that may have a significant effect on the regularity of transactions in the financial statements. Guidance on planning the audit of regularity is set out in the separate section in this Practice Note on regularity.

ISA (UK and Ireland) 315: Obtaining an Understanding of the Entity and its Environment and Assessing the Risks of Material Misstatement

Background Note

> The purpose of this International Standard on Auditing (UK and Ireland) is to establish standards and provide guidance on obtaining an understanding of the entity and its environment, including internal control, and on assessing the risks of material misstatement in a financial statement audit.

Introduction

113 The auditor reads the guidance in this section of the Practice Note in conjunction with ISA (UK and Ireland) 315. The purpose of the guidance contained in this section of the Practice Note is to highlight the key areas where public sector practice differs from that of the private sector. The public sector auditor gains an understanding of the legislative background of the audited entity and considers the relevant reporting requirements. This guidance also outlines some additional business risks the public sector auditor may consider.

> The auditor should obtain an understanding of the entity and its environment, including its internal control, sufficient to identify and assess the risks of material misstatement of the financial statements whether due to fraud or error, and sufficient to design and perform further audit procedures. (ISA (UK and Ireland) 315 para 2)

114 This ISA (UK and Ireland) requires the auditor to make risk assessments at the financial statement and assertion levels based on an appropriate understanding of the entity and its environment. In the public sector, the auditor of specified entities has to consider the additional assertion of regularity. At the planning stage, the public sector auditor therefore needs to obtain an understanding of the framework of authorities specific to the entity. For further guidance on obtaining an understanding of the framework of authorities, the auditor may refer to the separate section of this Practice Note on regularity.

Industry, Regulatory and Other External Factors, Including the Applicable Financial Reporting Framework

> The auditor should obtain an understanding of relevant industry, regulatory, and other external factors including the applicable financial reporting framework. (ISA (UK and Ireland) 315 para 22)

The auditor obtains an understanding of the financial reporting framework and regulatory factors under which the financial statements are prepared and their impact on the audit. The financial reporting framework and other regulations for the public sector include those set out in:

- the specific legislation that has established the audited entity and determines its activities;
- standards that constitute UK GAAP;
- accounts directions;
- Government Accounting[10].
- other HM Treasury guidance on the application of accounting standards, the Companies Acts and the disclosure of information;
- manuals for accounts for NHS entities and subsequent instructions issued by the Department of Health, Monitor, the Scottish Executive Health Department, the National Assembly for Wales and the Department of Health, Social Services and Public Safety in Northern Ireland; and
- the Code of Practice on Local Authority Accounting (SORP), the Charities SORP and the Pensions SORP as well as the Further Education SORP for Scotland.

115

When considering compliance with the applicable financial reporting framework, the public sector auditor's procedures are performed in the knowledge that entities have their own legislative framework and accounting provisions that prescribe the form and content of financial statements. The financial reporting requirements for each type of public sector entity are summarised below:

116

Government departments	Prescribed by HM Treasury under section 5 of the Government Resources and Accounts Act 2000 or, in Northern Ireland, by the Department of Finance and Personnel under section 9 of the Government Resources and Accounts Act (Northern Ireland) 2001.
Trading Funds	Accounts direction issued by HM Treasury to each fund in pursuance of section 4(6) of the Government Trading Funds Act 1973 or, in Northern Ireland, by the Department of Finance and Personnel under Article 8(6) of the Financial Provisions (Northern Ireland) Order 1993.
Supply financed executive agencies	Accounts direction issued by HM Treasury to each agency in pursuance of section 7 of the Government Resources and Accounts Act 2000 or, in Northern Ireland, by the Department of Finance and Personnel under section 11 of the Government

---

[10] In Scotland, the Scottish Public Finance Manual serves the same purpose as Government Accounting. In Northern Ireland there is a Government Accounting Northern Ireland manual. and the Government Financial Reporting Manual;

	Resources and Accounts Act (Northern Ireland) 2001.
National Assembly for Wales and its executive agencies	Accounts directions issued by HM Treasury under the Government of Wales Act 1998.
Non-departmental public bodies (and Assembly Sponsored Public Bodies in Wales)	Provided for in specific legislation or Royal Charter, with the sponsoring body being empowered to issue directions, with HM Treasury or Northern Ireland Department of Finance and Personnel consent.
Central government entities in Scotland including Executive Agencies, NDPBs and Trading Funds	Prescribed by directions issued by Scottish Ministers.
Local government entities	In England, the Local Government Act 1972, Local Government Finance Act 1988, Local Government and Housing Act 1989, School Standards and Framework Act 1998, Building Control Act 1984, Building (Local Authority Charges) Regulations 1998, Accounts and Audit Regulations 2003, Local Government Act 2003, Superannuation Act 1972, and the Code of Practice on Local Authority Accounting (SORP). In Wales, the Accounts and Audit (Wales) Regulations 2005 issued under the Public Audit (Wales) Act 2004, the Local Authority (Capital Finance and Accounting) (Wales) Regulations 2003 and the Code of Practice on Local Authority Accounting (SORP). In Scotland, the Local Authority Accounts (Scotland) Regulations 1985, the Code of Practice on Local Authority Accounting (SORP), and statements issued by the Local Authorities (Scotland) Accounts Advisory Committee. In Northern Ireland, the Local Government Act (Northern Ireland) 1972, Accounts Direction issued by the Department of Environment and the Code of Practice on Local Authority Accounting (SORP).
Health entities	In England, for health entities (excluding NHS Foundation Trusts) Accounts direction issued by the Secretary of State under the National Health Service Act 1977, with the approval of HM Treasury, supplemented by the relevant Manual for Accounts. For NHS Foundation Trusts, Accounts Directions issued by Monitor, with the approval of HM Treasury, supplemented by the relevant manual for accounts. In Wales, the National Health Service Act 1977 and directions issued by the National Assembly of Wales, with the approval of HM Treasury, supplemented by the relevant Manual for Accounts.

	In Scotland, Accounts direction issued by Scottish Ministers, supplemented by the relevant Manual for Accounts. In Northern Ireland, Accounts direction issued by the Department of Health, Social Services and Public Safety with the approval of the Department of Finance and Personnel, supplemented by the relevant Manual for Accounts.
Probation Boards in England and Wales	Criminal Justice and Court Services Act 2000 and directions issued by the Secretary of State.
Further education colleges in Scotland	Directions issued under the Further and Higher Education (Scotland) Act 1992.
The water authority in Scotland	Directions issued under the Water Industry (Scotland) Act 2002.

117 Each of these items is potentially subject to change between financial years and securing an understanding of the applicable financial reporting requirements is an important element in planning an audit in the public sector.

118 Where a report is given on statements made by those charged with governance relating to corporate governance, this is outside the scope of the audit of the financial statements, even though it may be based on work carried out for that audit. In preparing a report on the statement reference is made to APB guidance on disclosures relating to corporate governance rather than to ISA (UK and Ireland) 315, as well as to relevant guidance issued by the national audit agencies.

Nature of the Entity

> The auditor should obtain an understanding of the nature of the entity. (ISA (UK and Ireland) 315 para 25)

119 In the public sector this will include obtaining an understanding of the legislative background of the body and the way in which it is funded.

Objectives and Strategies and Related Business Risks

> The auditor should obtain an understanding of the entity's objectives and strategies, and the related business risks that may result in material misstatement of the financial statements. (ISA (UK and Ireland) 315 para 30)

120 There are a number of additional factors that may be considered by the auditor when assessing business risks for public sector entities. These arise from the particular coincidence in the public sector of a closely regulated regime, a large volume of transactions processed and a public reporting process. These additional factors may arise where:

- major new legislation or expenditure programmes have been introduced;
- there is the possibility of manipulation by management to achieve performance or other targets;
- an entity is likely to be wound up, reorganised, merged, sold or privatised;

- there is political pressure on an entity to complete transactions quickly; and
- the final form of account does not reflect the underlying management and accounting processes.

121 Where entities are required to work to annual limits on resources, the risk of transactions being recorded in the wrong accounting period is increased, since there is a temptation for an entity in surplus to bring forward payments and for an entity in deficit to delay them.

Assessing the Risks of Material Misstatement

> The auditor should identify and assess the risks of material misstatement at the financial statement level, and at the assertion level for classes of transactions, account balances, and disclosures. (ISA (UK and Ireland) 315 para 100)

122 Guidance on the assessment of regularity risks within the financial statements audit is set out in the separate section of this Practice Note on regularity.

> As part of the risk assessment as described in paragraph 100, the auditor should determine which of the risks identified are, in the auditor's judgment, risks that require special audit consideration (such risks are defined as "significant risks"). (ISA (UK and Ireland) 315 para 108)

123 Possible significant risks in the public sector include the risks that:
- financial transactions entered into by the entity in the period do not conform to the authorities that govern them (known as "regularity"). For further guidance on possible risks to regularity, refer to appendix 3;
- organisations issuing grants may have been subject to fraudulent grant claims;
- the financial statements may have been manipulated to meet externally set targets; and
- Private Finance Initiative transactions have not been accounted for in accordance with UK GAAP and guidance issued by HM Treasury.

For significant risks, to the extent the auditor has not already done so, the auditor should evaluate the design of the entity's related controls, including relevant control activities, and determine whether they have been implemented. (ISA (UK and Ireland) 315 para 113)

124 For further guidance on possible control procedures relating to the identified risks to regularity, the auditor may refer to appendix 3.

ISA (UK and Ireland) 320: Audit Materiality

> **Background Note**
>
> The purpose of this International Standard on Auditing (UK and Ireland) is to establish standards and provide guidance on the concept of materiality and its relationship with audit risk.

Introduction

125 The auditor reads the guidance in this section of the Practice Note in conjunction with ISA (UK and Ireland) 320. The purpose of the guidance contained in this section of the Practice Note is to highlight the key areas where public sector practice differs from that of the private sector. In particular, public sector auditors consider additional responsibilities and duties.

> The auditor should consider materiality and its relationship with audit risk when conducting an audit. (ISA (UK and Ireland) 320 para 2)

126 The auditor makes an assessment of materiality with reference to the auditor's understanding of the expectations of the users of the financial statements. However, in the consideration of materiality, the assessment remains the auditor's own and is not dictated directly by any explicit or implicit interest expressed by any individual (such as a member of the public) with an interest in the financial statements.

127 When assessing the materiality of uncorrected misstatements, the public sector auditor considers them individually as well as in aggregate, because there may be special considerations applying to the reporting of certain classes of misstatement.

> The objective of an audit of financial statements is to enable the auditor to express an opinion whether the financial statements are prepared, in all material respects, in accordance with an applicable financial reporting framework. (ISA (UK and Ireland) 320 para 4)

128 A public sector auditor may have other specific responsibilities and duties under statute or be required under the terms of engagement to make reports on matters that do not affect the opinion on the financial statements. Where this is the case, the auditor may adopt a level of significance appropriate to these other responsibilities and duties which differs from the materiality level applied to the audit of the financial statements. There is no necessary connection between the materiality of an item to the financial statements and its significance to one of the auditor's other responsibilities or duties.

129 For example, in the course of carrying out work relating to other responsibilities and duties, the auditor may detect errors, omissions or weaknesses in accounting arrangements. In these instances the auditor considers the materiality of the findings for the audit of the financial statements and reviews the risk assessments on which the audit was based to ensure that they remain valid.

130 Where the auditor has a duty to give a regularity opinion, the qualitative considerations applying to the assessment of materiality may reflect the interests expressed by principal users in the regularity of transactions. Guidance on the interaction between the regularity aspects and the audit of the financial statements is given in the separate section of this Practice Note on regularity.

Evaluating the Effect of Misstatements

> In evaluating whether the financial statements are prepared, in all material respects, in accordance with an applicable financial reporting framework, the

> auditor should assess whether the aggregate of uncorrected misstatements that have been identified during the audit is material. (ISA (UK and Ireland) 320 para 12)
>
> In the UK and Ireland the auditor evaluates whether the financial statements give a true and fair view. (ISA (UK and Ireland) 320 para 12-1)

131   Across the public sector, most financial statements include an opinion as to whether the financial statements give a true and fair view. However, there are instances where the auditing framework requires an opinion as to whether the financial statements present fairly or properly present the entity's transactions or balances. In particular, local authority accounts include an opinion as to whether the financial statements present fairly the entity's transactions or balances. Whichever wording is used for the opinion on the financial statements, this will not have an impact on the extent to which the auditor observes the requirements of ISAs (UK and Ireland).

ISA (UK and Ireland) 330: The Auditor's Procedures in Response to Assessed Risks

> **Background Note**
>
> The purpose of this International Standard on Auditing (UK and Ireland) is to establish standards and provide guidance on determining overall responses and designing and performing further audit procedures in response to assessed risks of material misstatement at the financial statement and assertion levels in a financial statement audit.

Introduction

132   The auditor reads the guidance in this section of the Practice Note in conjunction with ISA (UK and Ireland) 330. The purpose of the guidance contained in this section of the Practice Note is to highlight the key areas where public sector practice differs from that of the private sector.

Audit Procedures to Risks of Material Misstatement at the Assertion Level

> The auditor should design and perform further audit procedures whose nature, timing, and extent are responsive to the assessed risks of material misstatement at the assertion level. (ISA (UK and Ireland) 330 para 7)
>
> When, in accordance with paragraph 108 of ISA (UK and Ireland) 315, the auditor has determined that an assessed risk of material misstatement at the assertion level is a significant risk and the auditor plans to rely on the operating effectiveness of controls intended to mitigate that significant risk, the auditor should obtain the audit evidence about the operating effectiveness of those controls from tests of controls performed in the current period. (ISA (UK and Ireland) 330 para 44)
>
> When, in accordance with paragraph 108 of ISA (UK and Ireland) 315, the auditor has determined that an assessed risk of material misstatement at the assertion level is a significant risk, the auditor should perform substantive

procedures that are specifically responsive to that risk. (ISA (UK and Ireland) 330 para 51)

133 Paragraph 123 in this Practice Note outlines the issues the public sector auditor considers when assessing significant risks. The section of this Practice Note on regularity provides further guidance on planning the audit of regularity and responding to assessed risks. Where the auditor has identified a risk that results may have been manipulated to meet externally set targets, the auditor performs audit procedures to address this risk such as analytical procedures to identify anomalies in results, reviewing unusual transactions and reviewing significant judgements made by those charged with governance when preparing the financial statements.

ISA (UK and Ireland) 402: Audit Considerations Relating to Entities Using Service Organisations

Background Note

The purpose of this International Standard on Auditing (UK and Ireland) is to establish standards and provide guidance to an auditor where the entity uses a service organization. This ISA (UK and Ireland) also describes the service organization auditor's reports which may be obtained by the entity's auditors.

Introduction

134 The auditor reads the guidance in this section of the Practice Note in conjunction with ISA (UK and Ireland) 402. The purpose of the guidance contained in this section of the Practice Note is to highlight the key areas where public sector practice differs from that of the private sector. In particular, this section of the Practice Note outlines the procedures in place for allowing the public sector auditor access to records maintained by service organisations.

Understanding the Entity and its Environment

In obtaining an understanding of the entity and its environment, the auditor should determine the significance of service organization activities to the entity and the relevance to the audit. (ISA (UK and Ireland) 402 para 5)

135 The responsibilities of an auditor in the public sector go beyond those in the private sector by virtue of statutory or other prescribed duties and obligations. This includes the need for an auditor of central government, specified health bodies and probation boards to give an opinion on the regularity of expenditure. This may require the public sector auditor to inspect records maintained by service organisations in relation to activities undertaken on behalf of public sector entities. Guidance on the audit of regularity is set out in the separate section in this Practice Note on regularity.

Understanding the Contractual Terms and Monitoring Arrangements

> The auditor should obtain and document an understanding of the contractual terms which apply to relevant activities undertaken by the service organization and the way that the entity monitors those activities so as to ensure that it meets its fiduciary and other legal responsibilities. (ISA (UK and Ireland) 402 para 5-3)

136 ISA (UK and Ireland) 402 in itself is not sufficient to secure access rights for the public sector auditor, and it is important that such access rights and the purpose of such rights are recognised and provided for in the contract between the service organisation and the public sector entity.

137 In respect of central government entities in England, section 8 of the Government Resources and Accounts Act 2000 gives the Comptroller and Auditor General statutory access to any documents relating to a department's accounts which are managed by service organisations compiling or handling the financial records of any entity that he audits. In Wales, inspection rights are prescribed in section 95 of the Government of Wales Act 1998 as amended by the Public Audit (Wales) Act 2004. In Scotland, access rights are prescribed in section 24 of the Public Finance and Accountability (Scotland) Act 2000. In Northern Ireland, section 3 of the Audit and Accountability (Northern Ireland) Order 2003 provides the Comptroller and Auditor General for Northern Ireland with similar statutory access.

138 HM Treasury guidance on *Standardisation of PFI Contracts version 3 (April 2004)*, requires an access clause to be included in all Private Finance Initiative (PFI) contracts.

139 In addition, there are other sources of guidance such as the Office of Government Commerce's *Successful Delivery Toolkit* which provides guidance on model conditions of contract.

140 In the local government and health sectors, section 6 of the Audit Commission Act 1998 provides the appointed auditor in England with a right of access at all reasonable times to every document relating to an entity subject to audit which appears to the auditor necessary for the purposes of the auditor's functions under the Act. The auditor may also require a person holding or accountable for any such document to give the auditor such information and explanation as the auditor thinks necessary for the purposes of the auditor's functions under the Act. Similar rights are available to the auditor in Wales under section 18 of the Public Audit (Wales) Act 2004 and section 95 of the Government of Wales Act 1998, in Scotland under section 100 of the Local Government (Scotland) Act 1973 and section 24 of the Public Finance and Accountability (Scotland) Act 2000, and in Northern Ireland under section 3 of the Audit and Accountability (Northern Ireland) Order 2003.

ISA (UK and Ireland) 500: Audit Evidence

Background Note

The purpose of this International Standard on Auditing (UK and Ireland) is to establish standards and provide guidance on what constitutes audit evidence in an audit of financial statements, the quantity and quality of audit evidence to be obtained, and the audit procedures that auditors use for obtaining that audit evidence.

Introduction

The auditor reads the guidance in this section of the Practice Note in conjunction with ISA (UK and Ireland) 500. The purpose of the guidance contained in this section of the Practice Note is to highlight the key areas where public sector practice differs from that of the private sector. In particular, the public sector auditor obtains sufficient audit evidence to support the regularity assertion.

141

> The auditor should obtain sufficient appropriate audit evidence to be able to draw reasonable conclusions on which to base the audit opinion. (ISA (UK and Ireland) 500 para 2)

Entities will usually have established internal controls designed to secure the regularity of transactions. However, where the audited entity is responsible for giving grants or other financial assistance to other parties, it is often the case that the regularity of the transaction will depend on the other parties satisfying the criteria and meeting the terms for receiving assistance. Evidence might then be required on the entity's exercise of its responsibilities to satisfy itself about the transactions of these other parties. Guidance on audit evidence for regularity work is set out in the separate section in this Practice Note on regularity.

142

The Use of Assertions in Obtaining Audit Evidence

> The auditor should use assertions for classes of transactions, account balances, and presentation and disclosures in sufficient detail to form a basis for the assessment of risks of material misstatement and the design and performance of further audit procedures. (ISA (UK and Ireland) 500 para16)

In addition to the assertions set out in paragraph 17 (a) of ISA (UK and Ireland) 500, the public sector auditor considers the additional assertion of regularity.

143

ISA (UK and Ireland) 501: Audit Evidence – Additional Considerations for Specific Items

> **Background Note**
>
> The purpose of this International Standard on Auditing (UK and Ireland) is to establish standards and provide guidance additional to that contained in ISA (UK and Ireland) 500, "Audit Evidence" with respect to certain specific financial statement account balances and other disclosures.
>
> The ISA (UK and Ireland) comprises the following parts:
> - Attendance at physical inventory counting;
> - Inquiry regarding litigation and claims;
> - Valuation and disclosure of long-term investments; and
> - Segment information.

144 No additional guidance is required to apply ISA (UK and Ireland) 501 to the audit of financial statements in the public sector.

ISA (UK and Ireland) 505: External Confirmations

> **Background Note**
>
> The purpose of this International Standard on Auditing (UK and Ireland) is to establish standards and provide guidance on the auditor's use of external confirmation as a means of obtaining audit evidence.

145 No additional guidance is required to apply ISA (UK and Ireland) 505 to the audit of financial statements in the public sector.

ISA (UK and Ireland) 510: Initial Engagements – Opening Balances and Continuing Engagements – Opening Balances

> **Background Note**
>
> The purpose of this International Standard on Auditing (UK and Ireland) is to establish standards and provide guidance regarding opening balances when the financial statements are audited for the first time or when the financial statements for the prior period were audited by another auditor. This ISA (UK and Ireland) would also be considered when the auditor becomes aware of contingencies and commitments existing at the beginning of the period. Guidance on the audit and reporting requirements regarding comparatives is provided in ISA (UK and Ireland) 710 "Comparatives". This ISA (UK and Ireland) also provides guidance regarding opening balances for a continuing engagement.

Introduction

146 The auditor reads the guidance in this section of the Practice Note in conjunction with ISA (UK and Ireland) 510. The purpose of the guidance contained in this section of the Practice Note is to highlight the key areas where public sector practice differs from that of the private sector.

147 All of the requirements of ISA (UK and Ireland) 510 are relevant to the public sector auditor. However, the variety of circumstances in which ISA (UK and Ireland) 510 will apply will be different from that in the private sector. New legislation and changes in Government policies mean that new audit appointments will arise from the imposed breaking-up or bringing-together of existing public sector entities or changes in public sector audit arrangements.

> For initial audit engagements, the auditor should obtain sufficient appropriate audit evidence that:
>
> (a) The opening balances do not contain misstatements that materially affect the current period's financial statements;
>
> (b) The prior period's closing balances have been correctly brought forward to the current period or, when appropriate, have been restated; and

(c) Appropriate accounting policies are consistently applied or changes in accounting policies have been properly accounted for and adequately presented and disclosed. (ISA (UK and Ireland) 510 para 2)

ISA (UK and Ireland) 510 is concerned with the opening balances when financial statements are audited for the first time or when the financial statements for the prior period were audited by another auditor.

In the public sector, the following additional guidance may be relevant:

Nature of Opening Balances	Additional Guidance
Opening balance amounts are identifiable from the preceding period's audited financial statements for another entity	This will require that the balances are clearly identifiable. Additional procedures may also be necessary to confirm that there are no aspects to the change in status of the new entity that result in changes to the basis on which the balances were prepared.
Opening balance amounts are not identifiable from the preceding period's audited financial statements for another entity, but have been derived from balances contained in those statements.	Subject to the arrangements for co-operation, the auditor may discuss with the outgoing auditor whether information is available that would provide substantive evidence for the opening balances. Such evidence would be considered in the context of the requirements of ISA (UK and Ireland) 600. In the absence of evidence available through such co-operation, the auditor considers carrying out substantive testing of opening balances.
Opening balances have been calculated as part of a separate disaggregation/ merger exercise, subject to a separate specific review and report by an auditor	The auditor considers the scope of the specific review and report in the context of the requirements of ISA (UK and Ireland) 600 as if the auditor was the principal auditor. Where the work from the separate specific review cannot be used, the auditor considers carrying out substantive testing of opening balances.
Opening balances have been calculated as part of a separate disaggregation/ merger exercise, but not subject to separate specific review and report	The auditor considers carrying out substantive testing of opening balances.

150 Where, after performing the procedures described in paragraph 2 of ISA (UK and Ireland) 510 and the table above, the auditor is unable to obtain sufficient appropriate audit evidence concerning the opening balances of the entity, the auditor considers the implications for the auditor's report.

The Audit of Opening Balances by the Incoming Auditor

151 In the audit of central government entities, the incoming auditor to a new audit assignment is normally able to obtain audit evidence about the opening balances from the procedures outlined in the guidance supporting ISA (UK and Ireland) 510.

152 Paragraph 6 of ISA (UK and Ireland) 510 states that when the prior period's financial statements were audited by another auditor, the current auditor may be able to obtain sufficient audit evidence regarding opening balances by reviewing the predecessor auditor's working papers. In the public sector, in the interests of efficiency and reducing the audit burden, the predecessor auditor is expected by the national audit agencies to adopt a co-operative approach in dealing with enquiries and requests for information from the incoming auditor. This expectation is normally formalised in a letter of appointment or associated document.

153 The auditor of a local government or health entity is required as a result of the acceptance of an appointment to make available copies of certain specified documentation to the incoming auditor on request when the appointment comes to an end. Arrangements will include an agreement on access to particular reports or papers that may be required by the incoming auditor rather than the transfer of all the relevant papers or data. This requirement for co-operation does not diminish the incoming auditor's responsibilities for meeting the requirements of ISA (UK and Ireland) 510, but may provide additional supporting documentation that will facilitate the meeting of these responsibilities.

ISA (UK and Ireland) 520: Analytical Procedures

Background Note

The purpose of this International Standard on Auditing (UK and Ireland) is to establish standards and provide guidance on the application of analytical procedures during an audit.

Introduction

154 The auditor reads the guidance in this section of the Practice Note in conjunction with ISA (UK and Ireland) 520. The purpose of the guidance contained in this section of the Practice Note is to highlight the key areas where public sector practice differs from that of the private sector. In particular, guidance is provided on the data relationships the public sector auditor may consider when performing analytical procedures.

The auditor should apply analytical procedures as risk assessment procedures to obtain an understanding of the entity and its environment and in the overall review at the end of the audit. (ISA (UK and Ireland) 520 para 2)

All public sector entities produce a comprehensive range of information and data. Much of the information is consolidated and published by Government entities and other bodies, particularly performance indicators. The auditor can use this information both in performing analytical procedures that compare the activities of a single entity from one year to another and in making comparisons between similar entities.   **155**

Examples of Data Relationships

Paragraph 4 of ISA (UK and Ireland) 520 sets out examples of data relationships that may be considered by the auditor. The public sector auditor also considers relationships: **156**

- between elements of financial information that would be expected to conform to a predictable pattern based on the entity's experience, such as staff costs; and
- where expenditure and income are expected to conform to a demand pattern that can be deduced from other related data, such as the number of people within a certain age range.

The public sector auditor may also divide the financial information the auditor considers into two classes: **157**

- programme expenditure and income; and
- administrative expenditure and income.

Each has a number of essential features that influence the nature of the analytical procedures that may be undertaken.   **158**

Programme expenditure and income relate to the actual function of the audited entity, and are disclosed in the financial statements as, for example, appropriations in aid, grant payments and healthcare treatments. Features of such transactions are that: **159**

- they may be closely related to non-financial information such as the number of bodies in receipt of grant or persons receiving hospital treatment;
- they may not always be directly comparable to prior periods because of changes in eligibility rules and Government policy; and
- they are comparable to published departmental/entity strategy and expenditure plans.

Administrative costs relate to the running of the audited entity and can be distinguished from programme expenditure because they are: **160**

- usually closely related to comparable information for prior periods and are less likely to experience significant fluctuation owing to changes in Government policy and the entity's strategy;
- closely related to information such as number of locations, number of employees and size of buildings; and
- usually directly comparable to other entities with similar establishment sizes.

Analytical procedures might assist the auditor in assessing the internal consistency of the financial statements, but on their own are unlikely to provide the auditor with sufficient appropriate evidence in support of a regularity opinion. Guidance on analytical procedures and regularity is set out in the separate section in this Practice Note on regularity.   **161**

ISA (UK and Ireland) 530: Audit Sampling and Other Selective Testing Procedures

Background Note

The purpose of this International Standard on Auditing (UK and Ireland) is to establish standards and provide guidance on the use of audit sampling and other means of selecting items for testing when designing audit procedures to gather audit evidence.

162 No additional guidance is required to apply ISA (UK and Ireland) 530 to the audit of financial statements in the public sector.

ISA (UK and Ireland) 540: Audit of Accounting Estimates

Background Note

The purpose of this International Standard on Auditing (UK and Ireland) is to establish standards and provide guidance on the audit of accounting estimates contained in the financial statements. This ISA (UK and Ireland) is not intended to be applicable to the examination of prospective financial information, though many of the audit procedures outlined herein may be suitable for that purpose.

163 No additional guidance is required to apply ISA (UK and Ireland) 540 to the audit of financial statements in the public sector.

ISA (UK and Ireland) 545: Auditing Fair Value Measurements and Disclosures

Background Note

The purpose of this International Standard on Auditing (UK and Ireland) is to establish standards and provide guidance on auditing fair value measurements and disclosures contained in financial statements.

164 No additional guidance is required to apply ISA (UK and Ireland) 545 to the audit of financial statements in the public sector.

ISA (UK and Ireland) 550: Related Party Disclosures

Background Note

The purpose of this International Standard on Auditing (UK and Ireland) is to establish standards and provide guidance on the auditor's responsibilities and audit procedures regarding related parties and transactions with such parties.

Introduction

The auditor reads the guidance in this section of the Practice Note in conjunction with ISA (UK and Ireland) 550. The purpose of the guidance contained in this section of the Practice Note is to highlight the key areas where public sector practice differs from that of the private sector. In particular, information is provided on the additional accounting guidance available on the identification of related parties in the public sector.

165

> The auditor should perform audit procedures designed to obtain sufficient appropriate audit evidence regarding the identification and disclosure by management[11]

The related parties of public sector entities are subject to specific restrictions on the nature and scope of the relationships that they can enter into with the entity. The restrictions proscribe practices that might be permissible in relationships outside the public sector.

166

Each part of the public sector has developed guidance on the restrictions on relationships between entities and related parties. Accounting guidance on the identification of related parties and related party transactions with regard to FRS 8 has also been developed:

167

Central government entities and the National Assembly for Wales	The Government Financial Reporting Manual or other applicable advice from HM Treasury, the Scottish Executive or the Northern Ireland Department of Finance and Personnel.
Local government entities	Code of Practice on Local Authority Accounting (SORP).
Health entities	The relevant manual for accounts and the NHS Finance Manual.

ISA (UK and Ireland) 560: Subsequent Events

Background Note

The purpose of this International Standard on Auditing (UK and Ireland) is to establish standards and provide guidance on the auditor's responsibility regarding subsequent events. In this ISA (UK and Ireland), the term "subsequent events" is used to refer to both events occurring between period end and the date of the auditor's report, and facts discovered after the date of the auditor's report.

Introduction

The auditor reads the guidance in this section of the Practice Note in conjunction with ISA (UK and Ireland) 560. The purpose of the guidance contained in this

168

---

[11] In the UK and Ireland those charged with governance are responsible for the preparation of the financial statements. Paragraphs 95 – 102 set out who those charged with governance are in the public sector. of related parties and the effect of related party transactions that are material to the financial statements. (ISA (UK and Ireland) 550 para 102)

section of the Practice Note is to highlight the key areas where public sector practice differs from that of the private sector. Information is provided below regarding when financial statements of public sector entities are considered to be "issued".

Events Occurring Up to the Date of the Auditor's Report

> The auditor should perform audit procedures designed to obtain sufficient appropriate audit evidence that all events up to the date of the auditor's report that may require adjustment of, or disclosure in, the financial statements have been identified. (ISA (UK and Ireland) 560 para 4)

169 In addition to the procedures described in paragraph 5 of ISA (UK and Ireland) 560, the auditor considers matters arising from relevant proceedings of Parliament and other related entities which the auditor may have become aware of during the course of the audit as being scheduled to take place at or after the period end, the outcome of which may have an impact on the audited entity.

> When, after the date of the auditor's report but before the financial statements are issued, the auditor becomes aware of a fact which may materially affect the financial statements, the auditor should consider whether the financial statements need amendment, should discuss the matter with management[12]

170 In interpreting the requirements of ISA (UK and Ireland) 560, the financial statements of central government entities are considered to be "issued" on the following dates:

Central government entities where the statutory auditor is responsible for the printing of the document containing the audited financial statements	Date of despatch by the auditor to the Clerk of the House of Commons or House of Lords for laying before Parliament.
Central government entities where the financial statements are laid before the Houses of Parliament by the Secretary of State of the sponsoring department or by HM Treasury, and where the statements are considered by an intermediate body before being laid before Parliament	Date of despatch by those charged with governance to the Secretary of State of the sponsoring department or HM Treasury, or to the Members of the intermediate body, whichever is the earlier.

---

[12] *In the UK and Ireland the auditor would discuss these matters with those charged with governance. Those charged with governance are responsible for the preparation of the financial statements, and should take the action appropriate in the circumstances. (ISA (UK and Ireland) 560 para 9)*

National Assembly for Wales and its sponsored and related public bodies, and NHS Wales entities	Date of despatch by the Auditor General to the Table Office of the National Assembly.
Central government entities in Scotland	Date of despatch by the Auditor General to Scottish Ministers for laying before Parliament.
Central government and health entities in Northern Ireland	Date of despatch by the department, body or person specified in the relevant legislation for laying before the Northern Ireland Assembly.

Date financial statements are laid before members or equivalent

For central government entities, the date that the financial statements are laid before members or their equivalent is taken to refer to the date that they are laid before the Parliament or the Assembly. **171**

In central government, the financial statements of most reporting entities are generally laid before: the House of Commons; the House of Lords; both of these Houses of Parliament; the National Assembly for Wales, the Northern Ireland Assembly or the Scottish Parliament. However, for certain entities, usually non-departmental public bodies, the financial statements may also be considered by an intermediate body (often a board, trustees or equivalent) before being formally laid before Parliament, either by the intermediate body, by the Secretary of State of the department responsible for the entity, or by HM Treasury. Where such a reporting hierarchy exists, the auditor considers subsequent events that the auditor becomes aware of and that occur from the date of the auditor's report until the date on which the financial statements are laid before Parliament. **172**

The financial statements of some central government entities are not formally laid before the Houses of Parliament but may be deposited in the libraries of the House of Commons and House of Lords by the sponsor department. Because the financial statements of these entities are not formally laid before Parliament, the auditor only considers subsequent events that occur up to the date on which the financial statements are issued. Otherwise, the auditor of a central government entity follows the requirements of ISA (UK and Ireland) 560 for subsequent events occurring between the dates of issue and of laying before the Parliament or the Assembly. **173**

Subsequent Events in the Audit of Local Government and Health Entities (Excluding Health Entities in Wales and Northern Ireland)

For the auditor of a local government or health entity, the concept of subsequent events is restricted by the status that the auditor's report is given by statute. In order to fulfil statutory requirements, the audit opinion and audit certificate have to be issued when the audit has been concluded. The issue of the audit certificate marks the closure of the audit and the end of the exercise of the auditor's powers and duties in respect of that audit. **174**

In local government the date of closure of an audit can be delayed for a significant time after the audit of the financial statements has been completed whilst the auditor satisfies other statutory responsibilities and duties. In England and Wales, it is therefore common practice for the auditor to give an opinion in advance of closure. However, this is not the opinion that the auditor is required to enter on the relevant statement of accounts in accordance with section 9 of the Audit Commission Act **175**

1998 (the statutory opinion). Prior to issuing this advance opinion the auditor considers whether an adverse conclusion to outstanding questions or objections could result in a material impact on the financial statements and hence on an opinion that they present fairly the financial position of the audited entity. In such circumstances, the auditor considers whether it is appropriate to issue such an advance opinion. Where an advance opinion is given, the auditor makes it clear that it is an opinion given in advance of closure of the audit.

176   If an opinion is given in advance of the closure of the audit, this opinion will be revisited to establish whether it is still appropriate at the time the audit is concluded and the statutory audit opinion and certificate are issued. The auditor carries out a subsequent events review from the date of issue of the advance opinion up to the date when the audit is concluded and the statutory opinion and certificate are issued.

177   As the statutory opinion can only be given when the audit is concluded, it is necessary formally to issue an opinion at the same time that the completion certificate is issued. The auditor refers to the advance opinion and to any additional work the auditor has carried out since it was issued in order to reach the auditor's current view (i.e. post balance sheet event procedures).

Facts Discovered After the Date of the Auditor's Report But Before the Financial Statements are Issued

> When, after the date of the auditor's report but before the financial statements are issued, the auditor becomes aware of a fact which may materially affect the financial statements, the auditor should consider whether the financial statements need amendment, should discuss the matter with management[13]

178   If the Accounting Officer or Chief Executive decides not to amend the financial statements, where the auditor believes that they need to be revised, the auditor considers taking appropriate steps on a timely basis to prevent reliance on the auditor's report. For example:

- if the financial statements are considered by an intermediate body before being despatched to the Secretary of State of the sponsor department and before being laid before Parliament, the auditor considers making a statement to that body, depending on the auditor's relationship with the intermediate body as may be set out in the auditor's terms of engagement, and in the light of any legal advice on the auditor's position; and
- if there is no intermediate body, and the entity has despatched the financial statements to the Secretary of State of the sponsor department but they have yet to be laid before Parliament, then subject to any legal advice on the auditor's position, the auditor considers reporting the auditor's concerns to the department. If the content of the auditor's letter of appointment is based on the guidance issued by HM Treasury, the auditor normally has right of access to report to the department any matters of importance arising out of the auditor's work.

179   Where the financial statements are produced by an entity which is audited by the Comptroller and Auditor General, the auditor has the possibility, in addition to the

---

[13] *In the UK and Ireland the auditor would discuss these matters with those charged with governance. Those charged with governance are responsible for the preparation of the financial statements., and should take the action appropriate in the circumstances. (ISA (UK and Ireland) 560 para 9)*

options described in paragraph 178, of reporting separately to Parliament on the implications of the subsequent event for the financial statements and the auditor's report. Similar arrangements enable the Auditor General for Wales to report separately to the National Assembly and for the C&AG for Northern Ireland to the Northern Ireland Assembly.

Where the subsequent event occurred after the date of the auditor's report, the auditor may, in addition to seeking legal advice, discuss the matter with the entity's Chief Executive and with the sponsor department to establish whether it might be possible to withdraw the auditor's report before the financial statements are laid before the Parliament or the Assembly. 180

Facts Discovered After the Financial Statements Have Been Issued

> The new auditor's report should include an emphasis of a matter paragraph referring to a note to the financial statements that more extensively discusses the reason for the revision of the previously issued financial statements and to the earlier report issued by the auditor. (ISA (UK and Ireland) 560 para (16)

In the public sector, the issue of the auditor's statutory audit opinion marks the end of the audit and once the financial statements have been issued they cannot be revised and the auditor's report cannot be re-issued. 181

If a matter that needs to be drawn to the attention of stakeholders arises once the financial statements have been issued, the auditor has other mechanisms available for making a public statement. For example, in the central government sector the Comptroller and Auditor General can report to Parliament and the auditor of a local government or a health entity can consider the issue of a public interest report. 182

ISA (UK and Ireland) 570: Going Concern

Background Note

> The purpose of this International Standard on Auditing (UK and Ireland) is to establish standards and provide guidance on the auditor's responsibility in the audit of financial statements with respect to going concern assumptions used in the preparation of the financial statements, including considering management's assessment of the entity's ability to continue as a going concern.

Introduction

The auditor reads the guidance in this section of the Practice Note in conjunction with ISA (UK and Ireland) 570. The purpose of the guidance contained in this section of the Practice Note is to highlight the key areas where public sector practice differs from that of the private sector. This guidance outlines the additional responsibilities a public sector auditor may have to review and report upon an 183 entity's arrangements to maintain its general financial health and the circumstances in which cessation of business may arise and the appropriate audit response.

> When planning and performing audit procedures and in evaluating the results thereof, the auditor should consider the appropriateness of management's[14]

184 The public sector auditor may have other responsibilities relating to going concern different from those to which ISA (UK and Ireland) 570 is directly relevant. The public sector auditor may be required to review and report upon the entity's arrangements to maintain its general financial health.

185 The auditor of a local government or a health entity (excluding NHS Foundation Trusts) in England is required by the Audit Commission's Code of Audit Practice to review and, where appropriate, examine evidence that is relevant to the audited body's corporate performance management and financial management arrangements and report on these arrangements. This review will include consideration of the arrangements to safeguard the financial standing of the audited body. The auditor of a local government entity in Scotland is also expected to consider such matters. The auditor of an NHS Foundation Trust should follow guidance issued by the regulator, Monitor.

186 The auditor of a local government or a health entity in Northern Ireland and Wales also assesses the general financial standing of the audited entity.

187 For entities where the form of financial statements prepared is determined by an accounts direction issued by HM Treasury (for central government departments and executive agencies) or a Secretary of State of a sponsor department (for non-departmental public bodies and NHS entities) by reference to the Government Financial Reporting Manual or equivalent guidance, the Government Financial Reporting Manual (or equivalent guidance) indicates the circumstances in which the going concern basis may or may not be adopted by the entity.

188 Where there is no reference in the direction to the Government Financial Reporting Manual, the direction will normally require such financial statements to be prepared on a going concern basis.

189 Where central government entities prepare financial statements on a cash basis, ISA (UK and Ireland) 570 does not apply to the audit as the going concern basis is not used in the preparation of the statements. However, the auditor still considers whether there are any matters affecting the audited entity's ability to continue as a going concern. Where the auditor identifies such matters, the auditor considers the need to report separately to Parliament on those matters and may include an explanatory paragraph in the auditor's report. The auditor does not, however, qualify the audit opinion on the proper presentation of the financial statements.

190 For local government entities, there is an explicit requirement in the Code of Practice on Local Authority Accounting (SORP) for the financial statements to be prepared on the going concern basis.

---

[14] *In the UK and Ireland, those charged with governance are responsible for the preparation of the financial statements and the assessment of the entity's ability to continue as a going concern. use of the going concern assumption in the preparation of the financial statements. (ISA (UK and Ireland) 570 para 2)*

Planning the Audit and Performing Risk Assessment Procedures

> In obtaining an understanding of the entity, the auditor should consider whether there are events or conditions and related business risks which may cast significant doubt on the entity's ability to continue as a going concern. (ISA (UK and Ireland) 570 para 11)

To apply ISA (UK and Ireland) 570 in the public sector, the auditor considers the circumstances in which a public sector entity may cease to continue in its operational existence. 191

It is not uncommon in the public sector for entities to spend more in one year than they have resources to cover or to become overstretched in their commitments, such that they might have a deficit of income over expenditure or an excess of liabilities over assets. However, it is less common that the operational existence of a public sector entity will cease or its scale of operations be subject to a forced reduction as a result of an inability to finance its operations or of net liabilities (although this is possible where a central government entity operates at arm's length from Government, particularly in a trading capacity). The reasons for this are: 192

- local government entities carry out functions essential to the local communities and are themselves revenue-raising bodies (without a specified limit on revenue-raising powers), and have the possibility, on application, of recovering losses over a period;
- for health entities (excluding NHS Foundation Trusts), there is a general assumption that no part of the NHS will be allowed to cease operations other than by deliberate closure by central government, announced in advance. Legislation is in place under which the liabilities of NHS trusts are transferred to another public entity if the trust is closed; the position of Health Trusts in Northern Ireland is also covered by legislation; and
- ultimately government departments can act to avoid financial failures by individual entities in central government and other parts of the public sector and thus secure continuation of the delivery of public services (although this may require Parliamentary authority).

Cessation is most likely to result from a Government policy decision. A policy decision may be taken to: 193

- wind up and dissolve an entity in its entirety where the Government determines that its functions are no longer required;
- wind up and dissolve all or part of an entity, but transfer some or all of its functions to another entity in the same sector or another sector;
- merge the entity, or some part of it, with another in the same sector; or
- privatise an entity, or some part of it, where the Government decides that certain functions would be better delivered by the private sector.

In each of these cases the operational existence of all or part of the entity ceases, but only in the case of dissolution without any continuation of operations would the going concern basis cease clearly to be appropriate. In the other cases the auditor considers the basis on which the activities are transferred, from the viewpoint of the entity that is relinquishing the assets and liabilities at the accounting date. 194

Consideration of the foreseeable future

195   ISA (UK and Ireland) 570 specifies that, in assessing whether the going concern assumption is appropriate, those charged with governance take into account all available information for the foreseeable future, which is at least twelve months from the balance sheet date. If the period to which those charged with governance have paid particular attention in assessing going concern is less than one year from the date of approval of the financial statements, and those charged with governance have not disclosed the fact, the auditor complies with the requirements of paragraph 31-4 of ISA (UK and Ireland) 570.

196   Government policy is inherently subject to political uncertainty. Changes of Government or ministerial positions can have a significant impact on the status and functions of public sector entities. However, it is rare that the future cannot be predicted with some certainty for the period up to one year from the date of approval of the financial statements. Political decisions are often no more uncertain than those completely unforeseeable risks faced by all private sector companies, of which neither the directors nor the auditor could be aware. The provisions of paragraphs 4 of ISA (UK and Ireland) 570 are therefore applied by the auditor.

Auditor's responsibilities for the consideration of the appropriateness of the going concern basis

197   In forming a view on the entity's ability to continue its operations, public sector auditor's consideration of going concern embraces two separate, but sometimes overlapping, factors:

- the greater risk associated with changes in policy direction (for example, where there is a change in Government); and
- the less common operational, or business, risk (for example, where an entity has insufficient working capital to continue its operations at its existing level).

198   To minimise the risk of it not coming to the auditor's attention that the Government has made, or is likely to make, a decision on policy direction which could impact on the going concern assumption, the auditor ascertains whether:

- the Government has a known intention to review an area of policy affecting the audited entity, for example as a result of a manifesto commitment;
- a review has been announced and is in progress;
- a review has indicated that the audited entity could be rationalised or that an entity's future may be re-examined; or
- there is a known intention to privatise the activities of the audited entity.

199   When the auditor becomes aware of information which indicates that the Government has made, or plans to make, a policy decision which is likely to impact on the entity's continued operational existence, the auditor first establishes whether the entity's operational activities are likely to be transferred elsewhere in the public sector. If they are, going concern will not generally be an issue. If not, then in considering the going concern assumption, the auditor may decide to request that the audited entity secures from the relevant department or executive body a letter of financial support, confirming that the entity continues to have financial backing for the foreseeable future.

Further Audit Procedures When Events or Conditions are Identified

> When events or conditions have been identified which may cast significant doubt on the entity's ability to continue as a going concern, the auditor should:
> (a) Review management's plans for future actions based on its going concern assessment;
> (b) Gather sufficient appropriate audit evidence to confirm or dispel whether or not a material uncertainty exists through carrying out audit procedures considered necessary, including considering the effect of any plans of management and other mitigating factors; and
> (c) Seek written representations from management regarding its plans for future action. (ISA (UK and Ireland) 570 para 26)

200 Paragraphs 26-1 to 26-3 of ISA (UK and Ireland) 570 suggest that the auditor considers the need to obtain written confirmations of representations from those charged with governance regarding their assessment that an entity is a going concern and any relevant disclosures in the financial statements.

201 However, given that a key consideration in the public sector is Government policy, the public sector auditor considers whether to request that the entity secures direct confirmation from the department or executive body responsible for providing financial backing to the entity. In such circumstances, a representation provided by the Accounting Officer, Accountable Officer or responsible financial officer of the entity that financial backing will continue to be received may not be sufficient as meaningful assurance on the future of an entity. This is because the representation could be based upon presumption of knowledge of facts about the intentions of the financial backer that might not be possessed by the entity or judgements about future conditions for support that the entity is not capable of making.

202 Where the auditor judges that the going concern basis is appropriate for the preparation of a public sector entity's financial statements substantially on the basis of third party confirmations received from the department or executive body responsible for providing financial backing, the auditor considers whether this is a matter of such significance that the confirmations are referred to in the financial statements and in the auditor's report as being relevant to a proper understanding of the basis of the auditor's opinion.

203 If no appropriate representations or confirmations can be obtained, the auditor considers whether there is a limitation on the scope of the audit work that requires a qualified opinion or a fundamental uncertainty that requires an explanatory paragraph in the auditor's report.

Annex

Illustrative Examples of Audit Procedures and Auditor's Reports

Example – A supply financed executive agency where the Secretary of State of the parent department has announced a review of its operations

Situation 1

- The auditor considers that the probability of any change in the nature of operations is remote.
- An unqualified auditor's report without an added explanatory paragraph.

204 When planning the audit, the auditor becomes aware of the following matters:

- the Secretary of State of the parent department has recently announced a review of the agency's operations. The review will examine the services provided by the agency and consider whether, together with the services provided by two other agencies, they could be better provided by one trading fund; and
- the Chief Executive believes that the agency's services would be more expensive to provide under the new proposed arrangements and that the review is unlikely to recommend any significant change in operations.

205 The auditor's initial assessment might be that there is some uncertainty about the ability of the agency to continue as a going concern. The auditor plans to monitor the progress of the review by liaising with the Chief Executive and reconsider the position when the auditor has completed the audit.

206 Having completed all other aspects of the audit, the auditor considers the progress of the review:

- the Chief Executive knows that the review is almost completed and the department has begun to consider its findings. The Chief Executive has been told that it is unlikely that the Secretary of State will recommend the closure of the agency;
- the auditor informs the Chief Executive that the auditor intends to contact the department to confirm this understanding;
- on behalf of the Principal Accounting Officer, the Finance Director of the parent department gives a written representation to the auditor that, while the recommendations arising from the review have not been finalised, it is now unlikely that the agency would be significantly affected by them; and
- the auditor therefore considers that the probability of the agency not being a going concern is remote.

207 The Chief Executive considers that no special disclosures are required in the financial statements. The auditor agrees and accordingly does not consider it necessary to qualify the audit opinion or to add an explanatory paragraph to the auditor's report.

Situation 2

- The auditor considers that there is significant uncertainty as to the future of the agency, but as yet the Secretary of State has made no decision on the agency's future.
- An unqualified auditor's report with an added explanatory paragraph.

208 The circumstances and audit work are as in Situation 1 except as follows.

Having completed all other aspects of the audit, the auditor considers the progress of the review:

- the Chief Executive knows that the review is almost completed and the department has begun to consider its findings. He does not know what the Secretary of State's recommendation might be on the future of the agency;
- the Chief Executive arranges a meeting between himself, the auditor and officials of the parent department to discuss the situation;
- the departmental officials indicate that preliminary studies showed a merger might result in efficiencies and that a further cost benefit study is ongoing. Its results will not be known for some months; and
- in view of this uncertainty, the parent department's Finance Director, acting for the Principal Accounting Officer, is not willing to provide any written representation about the future of the agency.

The auditor believes there is significant uncertainty as to the future of the agency and discusses the concerns with the Chief Executive. The Chief Executive has already decided to make appropriate disclosures in the financial statements as follows.

Extract from the notes to the financial statements

Note 1 Basis of preparing financial statements

On 1 September 20XX the Secretary of State for XXXX announced a review of the operations of the agency which would examine the different ways in which its current services can be provided in the future. The review is considering several options, including the possible merger of the agency with other entities. The Secretary of State has not yet announced the outcome of the review and therefore the Chief Executive considers that it is appropriate to prepare financial statements on the going concern basis. The financial statements do not include any adjustments that would result from a decision to alter the operations of the agency, or to transfer its activities to another entity.

In these circumstances, the auditor considers an audit opinion can be formed but has a significant level of concern about the ability of the agency to continue as a going concern. Hence, while the auditor does not qualify the audit opinion, the auditor includes a suitable explanatory paragraph when setting out the basis of the opinion, as set out below.

Paragraph 33 of ISA (UK and Ireland) 570 requires that:

"the auditor should express an unqualified opinion but modify the auditor's report by adding an emphasis of matter paragraph that highlights the existence of a material uncertainty relating to the event or condition that may cast significant doubt on the entity's ability to continue as a going concern and draws attention to the note in the financial statements that discloses the matters set out in paragraph 32."

In this example, the auditor does not disagree with the preparation of the financial statements on the going concern basis.

Extract from the 'Basis of opinion' section of the auditor's report

Going concern

In forming our opinion, we have considered the adequacy of the disclosures made in Note 1 of the financial statements concerning the uncertainty as to the continuation of the agency in its present form. In view of the significance of this uncertainty to the financial statements, we consider that it should be drawn to your attention, but our opinion is not qualified in this respect.

Situation 3

- The Secretary of State has announced that the agency will cease operations at the end of the next financial year and its activities will be transferred to a new trading fund.
- The auditor is satisfied that the agency has made appropriate adjustments to, and disclosures in, its financial statements.
- An unqualified auditor's report without an added explanatory paragraph.

213 The circumstances and audit work are as in Situation 2 except as follows.

214 During the audit the Secretary of State announces that the review has been completed and that the agency will cease operations and be wound up at the end of the next financial year. Its activities will be transferred to a new trading fund, together with the activities of two other executive agencies.

215 The auditor obtains further details of the restructuring plans through the Chief Executive. The auditor ascertains that all assets and liabilities will be transferred for nil consideration to the new trading fund. The majority of staff will be transferred to the trading fund, but a number will be made redundant. The costs of redundancy will be borne by the agency in the next financial year. All operating leases will be transferred to the trading fund for nil consideration and there are no other contingent liabilities.

216 The Chief Executive considers that the agency cannot prepare financial statements on the going concern basis. The financial statements therefore show:

- full provision for the redundancy and early retirement costs expected to be incurred over the next year and the fact that the decision has been communicated to employees before the year-end; and
- all fixed assets written down to the fair value at which they will be taken into the new entity's books. The Chief Executive's budget for the next financial year shows the agency will break even and so no provision for future losses need be considered.

217 The auditor reviews these treatments and audits the values attributed to fixed assets and the provision for redundancy costs. The auditor concludes that appropriate adjustments have been made.

218 The financial statements contain the following note.

Extract from the notes to the financial statements

Note 1 Basis of preparing financial statements

On 1 July 20XX the Secretary of State for XXXX announced that the agency would be wound up on 31 March 20XY and its activities transferred to a new trading fund, the JKL Centre. The operations of the agency will not transfer to the JKL Centre as a going concern and the Chief Executive considers it inappropriate for the financial statements to be prepared on a going concern basis. Appropriate adjustments have been made to the values of fixed assets to bring them into line with the bases of measurement applicable to the trading fund (see Note Z) and full provision has been made for the cost of redundancy and early retirement for staff who will not transfer to the JKL Centre.

219 The auditor concludes that the agency have made appropriate disclosures in the financial statements. The auditor issues an unqualified opinion in the auditor's report.

Situation 4

- As for situation 3, except that the auditor is not satisfied as to the appropriateness of adjustments and disclosures made and considers that the financial statements are materially misstated.
- A qualified auditor's report - disagreement with accounting treatment.

220 The circumstances and audit work are as in Situation 3 except as follows.

221 The Chief Executive believes it is inappropriate to adjust the values of fixed assets, as they are being transferred with all other assets and liabilities for nil consideration. The Chief Executive does not believe it appropriate to provide for redundancy costs on the grounds that the agency will receive specific additional funding in the following financial year.

222 The auditor disagrees, as the audit determines:

- some fixed assets will be surplus to the requirements of the trading fund and will have no value to it; and
- the decision on making some staff redundant was taken and communicated before the year-end and therefore full provision is made.

223 If the auditor cannot persuade the Chief Executive to make appropriate adjustments to the financial statements, the auditor will qualify the audit opinion on the grounds of disagreement. As the opinion has been qualified, there is no need to include an explanatory paragraph in the Basis of Opinion section.

ISA (UK and Ireland) 580: Management Representations

Background Note

The purpose of this International Standard on Auditing (UK and Ireland) is to establish standards and provide guidance on the use of management representations as audit evidence, the procedures to be applied in evaluating and documenting management representations and the action to be taken if management refuses to provide appropriate representations.

Introduction

224 The auditor reads the guidance in this section of the Practice Note in conjunction with ISA (UK and Ireland) 580. The purpose of the guidance contained in this section of the Practice Note is to highlight the key areas where public sector practice differs from that of the private sector. In particular, this section of the Practice Note provides guidance to public sector auditors in relation to obtaining management representations in respect of additional responsibilities.

Acknowledgement by Management of its Responsibility for the Financial Statements

> The auditor should obtain audit evidence that management[15]

225 In addition to the representations made relating to the financial statements in accordance with ISA (UK and Ireland) 580 the auditor of a public sector entity may be required to meet other responsibilities additional to giving a true and fair opinion on the financial statements. For example, the auditor may be required to report on the regularity of transactions entered into by the entity. The auditor may wish to obtain representations relevant to these additional responsibilities in the same letter or statement from the entity.

> In the UK and Ireland, the auditor should obtain evidence that those charged with governance acknowledge their collective responsibility for the preparation of the financial statements and have approved the financial statements. (ISA (UK and Ireland) 580 para 3-1)

226 Paragraphs 3 to 3-3 of ISA (UK and Ireland) 580 requires the auditor to obtain evidence that those charged with governance acknowledge their individual or collective responsibility for the preparation of the financial statements and that they have approved them. Paragraphs 95 to 102 of this Practice Note provide guidance on who "those charged with governance" are in the public sector.

227 The auditor takes care to ensure that representations are only accepted from those competent to give them, such that:

- acknowledgement of the responsibilities of "directors" for the financial statements is made by those in whom the responsibilities are vested; and
- management representations on matters material to the financial statements are made by persons who have knowledge of the facts or who are authorised to make the judgement or express the opinion (for instance, a legal officer may be best placed to make representations about contingent liabilities) – this may be particularly relevant where the financial statements comprise a consolidation of information from lower tier accounts.

228 In central government and health entities, representations will usually be obtained from the Accounting Officer or the Accountable Officer. In Local Government, the responsible finance officer has statutory responsibility for the proper administration of the entity's financial affairs. The auditor of a local government entity may therefore obtain representations from the responsible finance officer.

Representations by Management as Audit Evidence

> The auditor should obtain written representations from management that:
>
> (a) It acknowledges its responsibility for the design and implementation of internal control to prevent and detect error; and

---

[15] *In the UK and Ireland, those charged with governance are responsible for the preparation of the financial statements. acknowledges its responsibility for the fair presentation of the financial statements in accordance with the applicable financial reporting framework, and has approved the financial statements. (ISA (UK and Ireland) 580 para 3)*

> (b) It believes the effects of those uncorrected financial statements misstatements aggregated by the auditor during the audit are immaterial, both individually and in the aggregate, to the financial statements taken as a whole. A summary of such items should be included in or attached to the written representations. (ISA (UK and Ireland) 580 para 5a)

Where the auditor has a responsibility to give a regularity opinion, it may be necessary to obtain representations about knowledge and opinions relevant to the duty, such as the application of any grants or other financial assistance given by the audited entity to other parties. Guidance on the role of representations in the audit of regularity is set out in the separate section in this Practice Note on regularity. 229

ISA (UK and Ireland) 600: Using the Work of Another Auditor

> **Background Note**
>
> The purpose of this International Standard on Auditing (UK and Ireland) is to establish standards and provide guidance when an auditor, reporting on the financial statements of an entity, uses the work of another auditor on the financial information of one or more components included in the financial statements of the entity.

Introduction

The auditor reads the guidance in this section of the Practice Note in conjunction with ISA (UK and Ireland) 600. The purpose of the guidance contained in this section of the Practice Note is to highlight the key areas where public sector practice differs from that of the private sector. In particular, this guidance outlines the situations in the public sector where the requirements of ISA (UK and Ireland) 600 need to be considered. 230

> When the principal auditor uses the work of another auditor, the principal auditor should determine how the work of the other auditor will affect the audit. (ISA (UK and Ireland) 600 para 2)

All national audit agencies have agreed to work within the principles set out in the Public Audit Forum document *What Public Sector Bodies can Expect from their Auditors* published in March 2000. 231

There are five generally applicable situations in which the public sector auditor may encounter another auditor and become principal auditor, as described below, such that the requirements of ISA (UK and Ireland) 600 need to be considered: 232

- The audit of Whole of Government Accounts by the Comptroller and Auditor General. This situation is analogous to the audit of a group of companies. The National Audit Office considers the work of auditors of local authorities and health entities appointed by the other national audit agencies, and private sector auditors of public corporations, non-departmental public bodies that are companies and NHS Foundation Trusts.
- Where the auditor audits an entity that consolidates or summarises the financial statements of lower tier bodies. Two examples are: the audit of a local authority

that has interests in companies that require disclosures in the financial statements where the auditor of the authority considers the work of the auditor to the company; and the audit of the National Health Service summarised accounts prepared by the Department of Health, where the National Audit Office consider the work of the auditor appointed to audit the individual authorities, boards and trusts that make up the summarised accounts.

- Where the auditor audits an entity that has pooled budgets or shared services audited by another auditor.
- Where the auditor audits an entity that has contracted out services to another party. In this situation, whether the auditor needs access to the contractor and/or to the contractor's auditor depends on the particular nature of the service provided, the information available at the principal entity and the terms of engagement of the other auditor. The guidance on ISA (UK and Ireland) 402 discusses the requirements of an auditor in this position.
- Where the auditor has a duty to give a regularity opinion, it will be necessary to obtain assurance about the application of any material grants or other financial assistance given by the audited entity to other parties. Guidance on using the work of another auditor for this purpose is set out in the separate section in this Practice Note on regularity. In the audit of regularity, the auditor may seek to use the work of the auditor of the grant recipient and reduce the extent of the auditor's own audit procedures. In some cases the auditor does not have a right of access to the lower tier entity and may have no alternative source of audit evidence outside the work of the other auditor – an auditor in such a situation considers carefully whether there is a limitation of scope that impacts on the auditor's acceptance of an appointment, the auditor's procedures or the auditor's report in accordance with this ISA (UK and Ireland).

233 In the situations described above, the other auditor whose work the principal auditor may seek to use might also be a public sector auditor. In this case, the requirements of ISA (UK and Ireland) 600 are equally applicable to the work of this other auditor.

The Principal Auditor's Procedures

> When planning to use the work of another auditor, the principal auditor should consider the professional competence of the other auditor in the context of the specific assignment. (ISA (UK and Ireland) 600 para 7)
>
> In the UK and Ireland, when planning to use the work of another auditor, the principal auditor's consideration of the professional competence of the other auditor should include consideration of the professional qualifications, experience and resources of the other auditor in the context of the specific assignment. (ISA (UK and Ireland) 600 para 7-1)

234 Where the auditor is appointed by a national audit agency, the appointed auditor will have had to demonstrate professional qualifications, experience and resources to the national audit agency. Whilst this does not mean that the principal auditor can then assume the competence of this auditor, it provides a clear framework within which the assessment required by paragraphs 7 and 7-1 can be made.

ISA (UK and Ireland) 610: Considering the Work of Internal Audit

Background Note

The purpose of this International Standard on Auditing (UK and Ireland) is to establish standards and provide guidance to external auditors in considering the work of internal auditing.

Introduction

The auditor reads the guidance in this section of the Practice Note in conjunction with ISA (UK and Ireland) 610. The purpose of the guidance contained in this section of the Practice Note is to highlight the key areas where public sector practice differs from that of the private sector.   235

The external auditor should consider the activities of internal auditing and their effect, if any, on external audit procedures. (ISA (UK and Ireland) 610 para 2)

A distinctive feature of internal audit in the public sector is that it is normally a mandatory element of any entity's framework of internal control. Details of the role and responsibilities of internal audit, and applicable internal auditing standards and practices are set out in paragraph 240.   236

In applying the standards and guidance contained in ISA (UK and Ireland) 610 the public sector external auditor considers whether the performance of the internal audit function enables the external auditor to use the work of the internal auditor.   237

Understanding and Preliminary Assessment of Internal Auditing

The external auditor should obtain a sufficient understanding of internal audit activities to identify and assess the risks of material misstatement of the financial statements and to design and perform further audit procedures. (ISA (UK and Ireland) 610 para 9)

Where the auditor has other responsibilities in relation to systems of internal control, the work of internal audit may be considered as a part of that framework. An assessment of the internal audit function may be carried out for such purposes, even if the auditor considers that it may not be possible or desirable to rely on its work in specific areas for the purpose of the external audit of the financial statements. For example, where the auditor has a responsibility to provide a negative assurance on the Statement on Internal Control and has assessed internal audit's work in this area, the auditor will often rely on the Head of Internal Audit's annual assurance report.   238

The work of internal audit may also be considered in relation to the auditor's other responsibilities. The auditor takes care to ensure that, where matters come to the auditor's attention relating to the work of internal audit in relation to the auditor's other responsibilities, these findings are properly reviewed in accordance with ISA (UK and Ireland) 610 for their potential impact on the audit of the financial statements.   239

> The external auditor should perform an assessment of the internal audit function when internal auditing is relevant to the external auditor's risk assessment. (ISA (UK and Ireland) 610 para 11)

240 Role and responsibilities of internal audit, and applicable internal auditing standards and practices

	Roles and responsibilities of internal audit	Internal auditing standards and practices
Central government entities	The precise responsibilities of an internal audit unit are determined by the permanent head of a department as Accounting Officer (Accountable Officer in Scotland), or by the Chief Executive of an executive agency or non-departmental public body. These include, the provision of assurance on risk management, internal control and governance established by management to: • achieve the entity's objectives; • ensure the economical, effective and efficient use of resources; • ensure compliance with established policies, procedures, laws and regulations; • safeguard the entity's assets and interests from losses of all kinds, including those arising from fraud, irregularity or corruption; and • ensure the integrity and reliability of information and data.	An Accounting Officer (Accountable Officer in Scotland) is charged with making arrangements for internal audit to accord with the objectives, standards and practices set out in the Government Internal Audit Standards. Under Government Accounting, the internal audit arrangements for non-departmental public bodies must be approved by the sponsor departments.
Local government entities	There is a statutory responsibility for authorities in England and Wales to maintain an adequate and	Local government entities in England are required to maintain an adequate and effective system of internal audit

	effective system of internal audit. There is no direct statutory requirement for authorities in Scotland or Northern Ireland, but internal audit is an implicit element of the administrative arrangements to be made by the responsible financial officer under section 95 of the Local Government (Scotland) Act 1973 and section 54 of the Local Government Act (Northern Ireland) 1972. No detailed specification for internal audit is imposed on local government entities.	in accordance with 'proper internal audit practices' which are contained in the CIPFA Code of Practice for Internal Auditors in Local Government in the UK. This Code of Practice is also followed by local government entities in Wales and Scotland.
Health entities (excluding NHS Foundation Trusts)	The Accountable Officer has responsibility for ensuring that the arrangements for internal audit comply with those described in the NHS Internal Audit Standards. The Head of Internal Audit is accountable to the Accountable Officer although this accountability may be discharged via a designated Director, e.g. the Director of Finance.	The NHS Internal Audit Standards set out mandatory standards and guidelines for the internal audit function. The Audit Committee has a responsibility to agree plans, monitor performance and evaluate the extent to which the internal audit function complies with the mandatory standards and guidelines.

ISA (UK and Ireland) 620: Using the Work of an Expert

Background Note

The purpose of this International Standard on Auditing (UK and Ireland) is to establish standards and provide guidance on using the work of an expert as audit evidence.

241 No additional guidance is required to apply ISA (UK and Ireland) 620 to the audit of financial statements in the public sector.

ISA (UK and Ireland) 700: The Auditor's Report

Background Note

The purpose of this International Standard on Auditing (UK and Ireland) is to establish standards and provide guidance on the form and content of the auditor's report issued as a result of an audit performed by an independent auditor of the financial statements of an entity.

Introduction

242 The auditor reads the guidance in this section of the Practice Note in conjunction with ISA (UK and Ireland) 700. The purpose of the guidance contained in this section of the Practice Note is to highlight the key areas where public sector practice differs from that of the private sector. In particular, this section of the Practice Note provides guidance to the public sector auditor on the appropriate addressee of the auditor's report and other sector-specific references that may be made in the auditor's report.

243 Illustrative auditor's reports for public sector entities are provided in the most recent APB Bulletin on public sector audit reports.

Basic Elements of the Auditor's Report

The auditor's report should be appropriately addressed as required by the circumstances of the engagement and local regulations. (ISA (UK and Ireland) 700 para 7)

244 ISA (UK and Ireland) 700 requires the title of an auditor's report to identify the person or persons to whom it is addressed. This is normally the person or persons on whose behalf the audit is undertaken.

245 For central government entities, audits are normally undertaken on behalf of a Parliament or an Assembly. The principle that the auditor is working on behalf of Parliament means that in most instances the auditor's report is addressed to the Parliament. The only exceptions to this are:

- where legislation requires the appointment of the auditor and specifies the person or persons to whom the auditor shall report. For example, for some non-

departmental public bodies the governing legislation requires the auditor to report to the relevant Secretary of State; and
- where the audited financial statements are not required to be laid before Parliament. In such cases the auditor considers on whose behalf the audit is undertaken. Although this is normally the person or persons making the appointment, the auditor may need to look behind this. For example, HM Treasury may appoint the auditor on behalf of a Secretary of State.

246 For local government entities, the relevant legislation does not specify the person to whom the auditor shall report. The auditor takes into account the advice of the Audit Commission, the Auditor General for Wales and the Accounts Commission in addressing the auditor's report. It is normally expected that the auditor's report is addressed to the authority as a corporate entity. The Accounts Commission's Code of Audit Practice also expects that the report will be addressed to the members of the Accounts Commission. In Northern Ireland, the report is addressed to the Department of the Environment.

247 In England, the auditor's report on health entities is addressed to directors of the board. In Scotland the auditor's report on health entities is addressed to the members of the entity, the Auditor General for Scotland and the Scottish Parliament. In Northern Ireland, the report is addressed to the Northern Ireland Assembly. In Wales, the Auditor General for Wales addresses the report to the Members of the National Assembly for Wales.

> The auditor's report should identify the financial statements of the entity that have been audited, including the date of and period covered by the financial statements. (ISA (UK and Ireland) 700 para 8)

248 For certain entities there is a requirement to certify that the audit has been carried out or to certify that the audit has been completed. The former is a fundamental part of the audit opinion as required by the legislation for specific non-departmental public bodies and is incorporated into the wording of the introductory paragraph. The latter is a wider responsibility for auditors of local government in England and Wales and health entities in England and its link with the opinion on the financial statements needs to be understood. Auditors refer to paragraphs 174 to 177 of this Practice Note and to the separate guidance on this issue that is published from time to time by the Audit Commission and the Auditor General for Wales.

> The report should include a statement that the financial statements are the responsibility of the entity's management and a statement that the responsibility of the auditor is to express an opinion on the financial statements based on the audit. (ISA (UK and Ireland) 700 para 9)

249 For public sector entities, the responsibilities equivalent to those of directors may lie with different individuals or groups.

250 In all entities required to have their accounts laid before a Parliament (or an Assembly), responsibility for the financial statements rests with either an Accounting Officer or in some cases a Principal Accounting Officer and one or more Additional Accounting Officers. The financial statements are required to include a statement of those responsibilities. In all such entities the statement of responsibilities draws attention to the responsibilities of the Accounting Officer separately from those of

any board members. Where appropriate, it also refers to any joint responsibilities of the Accounting Officer, board members and their equivalents.

251 Local government entities are required by the Code of Practice on Local Authority Accounting (SORP) to include in their statement of accounts a statement of responsibilities which sets out the respective responsibilities of the authority and the chief financial officer for the accounts. An illustrative example is given in an appendix to the SORP, but the mandatory minimum information requirement for the statement is a disclosure of:

- the authority's responsibilities for the accounts under local government legislation and other requirements; and
- the Chief Financial Officer's legal and professional responsibility for the accounts.

252 For health entities, the statements of responsibilities are required to set out separately the responsibilities of the Chief Executive as Accountable Officer for the entity and the responsibilities of the directors / Board members in respect of the accounts. A pro forma for the statement is published each year in the relevant Manual for Accounts.

253 Expected disclosures in a public sector entity's Statement of Responsibilities are set out on the annex to this section of the Practice note.

> The opinion paragraph of the auditor's report should clearly indicate the financial reporting framework used to prepare the financial statements (including identifying the country of origin of the financial reporting framework when the framework used is not International Accounting Standards) and state the auditor's opinion as to whether the financial statements give a true and fair view (or are presented fairly, in all material respects,) in accordance with that financial reporting framework and, where appropriate, whether the financial statements comply with statutory requirements. (ISA (UK and Ireland) 700 para 17)

254 The applicable financial reporting frameworks are set out in paragraph 115 of this Practice Note.

255 Where the requirement to audit an entity's financial statements is provided for under statute, the auditor may refer to the relevant Act of Parliament when identifying the financial statements have been audited:

Government departments and supply financed executive agencies	The Government Resources and Accounts Act 2000; in Wales, the Government of Wales Act 1998; in Scotland, the Public Finance and Accountability (Scotland) Act 2000; and, in Northern Ireland, the Government Resources and Accounts Act (Northern Ireland) 2001.
Trading Funds	Government Trading Funds Act 1973; in Scotland, the Public Finance and Accountability (Scotland) Act 2000; and, in Northern Ireland, the Government Resources and Accounts Act (Northern Ireland) 2001.

Non-departmental public bodies and public bodies sponsored by the National Assembly for Wales	Legislation establishing the audit requirement for the particular entity (and orders made under devolved powers of the National Assembly).
Local government	In England, the Audit Commission Act 1998 and the Code of Audit Practice issued by the Audit Commission. In Wales, the Public Audit (Wales) Act 2004 and the Auditor General's Code of Audit and Inspection Practice. In Scotland, Part VII of the Local Government (Scotland) Act 1973 and the Code of Audit Practice approved by the Accounts Commission. In Northern Ireland, the Local Government Act (Northern Ireland) 1972 and the Code of Audit Practice issued by the Department of the Environment[16]
Health entities (and social services entities in Northern Ireland)	In England for health entities excluding NHS Foundation Trusts, the Audit Commission Act 1998 and the Code of Audit Practice issued by the Audit Commission. For NHS Foundation Trusts, the Health and Social Care (Community Health and Standards) Act 2003 and the Audit Code issued by Monitor. In Wales, the Public Audit (Wales) Act 2004. In Scotland, the National Health Service (Scotland) Act 1978. In Northern Ireland, the Health and Personal Social Services (Northern Ireland) Order 1972 as amended and directions issued by the Department of Health, Social Services and Public Safety.
Probation Boards	In England, the Audit Commission Act 1998 In Wales, the Public Audit (Wales) Act 2004.
Further education colleges in Scotland	The Further and Higher Education (Scotland) Act 1992.
The water authority in Scotland	The Water Industry (Scotland) Act 2002.

In central government, these requirements are usually set out in an accounts direction issued by HM Treasury, the Northern Ireland Department of Finance and Personnel, Scottish Ministers or a Secretary of State, the National Assembly for Wales, or in guidance provided by the Government Financial Reporting Manual. Where such an accounts direction refers to primary statements required by the Companies Acts (or in Northern Ireland, the Companies (Northern Ireland) Orders) and the further primary statements required by accounting standards, the auditor refers to all such statements when expressing the audit opinion.

---

[16] *The Local Government (Northern Ireland) Order 2005 is being taken forward by the Department of Environment and when enacted will replace the audit provisions within the Local Government Act (Northern Ireland) 1972.*

257 Health entities are also required to prepare their financial statements in accordance with an accounts direction issued by the Secretary of State, Monitor, the National Assembly for Wales, Scottish Ministers or the relevant department.

258 For local government entities, the financial statements are to be prepared in accordance with the Code of Practice on Local Authority Accounting (SORP). The statutory framework for this is established for England by the Audit Commission Act 1998 and the Accounts and Audit Regulations 2003 and for Scotland by the Local Government (Scotland) Act 1973 and the Local Authority Accounts (Scotland) Regulations 1985 and for Wales by the Public Audit (Wales) Act 2004 and the Accounts and Audit (Wales) Regulations 2005 issued under section 39 of that Act. However, the standard audit opinions recommended by the Auditor General for Wales expects the auditor to refer only to the accounts having been prepared "in accordance with the accounting policies relevant to local authorities" as set out in the statement of accounting policies. In Northern Ireland, the Local Government Act (Northern Ireland) 1972 provides for the Department of the Environment to give a direction on the form and content of the accounts to be kept by district councils.

259 Across the public sector, most financial statements include an opinion as to whether the financial statements give a true and fair view. However, there are instances where the auditing framework requires an opinion as to whether the financial statements present fairly or properly present the entity's transactions or balances. Whichever wording is used for the opinion on the financial statements, this will not have an impact on the extent to which the auditor observes the requirements of Auditing Standards.

The regularity part of the auditor's opinion

260 Further guidance on the reporting of regularity in the audit opinion is included in the separate section of this Practice Note on regularity.

If the auditor becomes aware, after accepting an audit engagement, that those charged with governance of the entity, or those who appointed them as its auditor, have imposed a limitation on the scope of the audit work which they consider likely to result in the need to issue a disclaimer of opinion on the financial statements, the auditor should request the removal of the limitation. If the limitation is not removed, the auditor should consider resigning from the audit engagement. (ISA (UK and Ireland) 700 para 41-3)

261 Guidance on withdrawing from engagements in the public sector is provided in paragraph 75 of this Practice Note.

Annex

Contents of the Statement of Responsibilities

The examples in this Annex are based on particular assumptions about the adequacy of the disclosures made in the financial statements about the responsibilities of the entity, directors and officers for keeping accounting records and preparing the financial statements. Where these disclosures are not adequate, then the sections for respective responsibilities in the example auditor's reports might need to be extended.

Statements of responsibilities includes disclosures with regard to the following matters:

Responsibility for:	
1	Proper accounting records that disclose with reasonable accuracy at any time the financial position of the entity and enable the entity to ensure that financial statements are prepared to comply with statutory requirements.
2	Safeguarding the assets of the entity and for taking reasonable steps for the prevention and detection of fraud and other irregularities.
3	Preparation of financial statements for each financial year that give a true and fair view of/present fairly view of the state of affairs of the entity and its performance for that period.
4	In preparing financial statements: • selecting suitable accounting policies and then applying them consistently; • making judgements and estimates that are reasonable and prudent; • stating whether applicable accounting standards have been followed, subject to any material departures disclosed and explained in the financial statements; and • preparing the financial statements on the going concern basis, unless it is inappropriate to presume that the entity will continue in business.
5	Where a regularity opinion is given, responsibility for the regularity of the public finances for which the Accounting/Accountable Officer is answerable.

ISA (UK and Ireland) 710: Comparatives

Background Note

The purpose of this International Standard on Auditing (UK and Ireland) is to establish standards and provide guidance on the auditor's responsibilities regarding comparatives.

Introduction

The auditor reads the guidance in this section of the Practice Note in conjunction with ISA (UK and Ireland) 710. The purpose of the guidance contained in this section of the Practice Note is to highlight the key areas where public sector practice differs from that of the private sector. In particular, guidance is provided on the requirement to disclose comparatives in the public sector.

The Auditor's Responsibilities

In the UK and Ireland, the auditor should obtain sufficient appropriate audit evidence that:

> (a) The accounting policies used for the corresponding amounts are consistent with those of the current period and appropriate adjustments and disclosures have been made where this is not the case;
> (b) The corresponding amounts agree with the amounts and other disclosures presented in the preceding period and are free from errors in the context of the financial statements of the current period; and
> (c) Where corresponding amounts have been adjusted as required by relevant legislation and accounting standards, appropriate disclosures have been made. (ISA (UK and Ireland) 710 para 6-1)

263 All parts of the public sector have a requirement for the disclosure of comparatives:
- the Government Financial Reporting Manual requires certain central government entities to disclose comparatives in their financial statements - disclosure of comparatives may also be referred to in the accounts directions issued under the legislative authority governing the bodies, trading funds, and executive agencies concerned;
- local government entities are required by the Code of Practice on Local Authority Accounting (SORP) to disclose comparatives; and
- health entities are required by the relevant Manual for Accounts to disclose comparative figures.

ISA (UK and Ireland) 720: Other Information in Documents Containing Audited Financial Statements

Background Note

The purpose of this International Standard on Auditing (UK and Ireland) is to establish standards and provide guidance on the auditor's consideration of other information, on which the auditor has no obligation to report, in documents containing audited financial statements.

Introduction

264 The auditor reads the guidance in this section of the Practice Note in conjunction with ISA (UK and Ireland) 720. The purpose of the guidance contained in this section of the Practice Note is to highlight the key areas where public sector practice differs from that of the private sector. In particular, guidance is provided on the other information that might be included with the audited financial statements and the auditor's responsibilities with regard to that information.

> The auditor should read the other information to identify material inconsistencies with the audited financial statements. (ISA (UK and Ireland) 720 para 2)

The foreword

265 Most public sector entities are required to include a foreword in the same documents as the financial statements:

Entity	Requirements
Central government departments and supply financed executive agencies	Accounts direction issued under the Government Resources and Accounts Act 2000, the Public Finance and Accountability (Scotland) Act 2000 or the Government Resources and Accounts Act (Northern Ireland) 2001 and relevant guidance (notably the Government Financial Reporting Manual).
Supply financed executive agencies	Accounts direction issued under the Government Trading Funds Act 1973, the Public Finance and Accountability (Scotland) Act 2000 or the Government Resources and Accounts Act (Northern Ireland) 2001 and relevant guidance.
The National Assembly for Wales and its executive agencies	Accounts directions issued under the Government of Wales Act 1998 and relevant guidance.
Non-departmental public bodies and Assembly-sponsored public bodies	Accounts direction issued under the specific legislation setting up the entities concerned and relevant guidance such as the Government Financial Reporting Manual.
Local government bodies	The Accounts and Audit Regulations 2003 (England only), the 2005 regulations issued by the National Assembly for Wales and/or the Code of Practice on Local Authority Accounting (SORP).
Health bodies	Accounts direction issued under the relevant legislation and the relevant Manual for Accounts.

There is no requirement that the auditor's opinion on the financial statements extends to the foreword, and the information contained within it is then considered in accordance with the requirements of ISA (UK and Ireland) 720.

266

In most cases, the accounts direction requires the foreword to contain the information that the Companies Acts requires to be disclosed in the directors' report, to the extent that such disclosures are appropriate to the entity concerned.

267

Other information

The requirements for publishing other information outside the foreword but in documents containing financial statements will vary, depending on the nature of the entity's operations, and the reporting requirements imposed by the accounts direction or SORP. Typically, they may include a statement setting out the responsibilities of the Accounting Officer or equivalent and a corporate governance statement.

268

Increasingly, however, entities are required, usually under a provision of the accounts direction, to provide information on performance. This may cover, for example, performance against financial, quality of service, volume of work and efficiency targets. Such performance information may be taken directly from the audited financial statements, or derived in part through calculation using data taken from the accounting or other records.

269

270 Health entities are exceptional in the amount of additional information that is required to be associated with the financial statements. There is a separate requirement for health entities to produce an annual report, usually accompanied by summary financial statements (subject to separate report, based on the work carried out for the audit of the financial statements). There is a requirement for the annual report to include the information required by the Companies Acts to be disclosed in the Directors' Report. However, if entities do not take the option of publishing summary financial statements with the annual report, then the full accounts must be published with it, bringing the annual report within the scope of ISA (UK and Ireland) 720 for the audit of the financial statements.

271 Health entities are required to submit a number of other statements as part of the annual reporting cycle, including summarisation schedules for consolidation of the NHS accounts, financial statements for charitable and non-charitable funds held on trust and a corporate governance statement. In Northern Ireland, health entities are also required to include other financial statements including those for endowments and other property held in trust and accounts for monies held on behalf of patients or residents.

272 Each of these statements is subject to separate requirements for reporting outside the scope of the audit of the main financial statements.

> If, as a result of reading the other information, the auditor becomes aware of any apparent misstatements therein, or identifies any material inconsistencies with the audited financial statements, the auditor should seek to resolve them. (ISA (UK and Ireland) 720 para (2-1)

273 Where the auditor:

- identifies an inconsistency between the other information and corresponding or related amounts or disclosures in the audited financial statements; and
- concludes that, under the circumstances, the other information needs to be amended,

the auditor considers whether to take action as recommended by ISA (UK and Ireland) 720.

274 In taking action, the auditor's concern is to ensure that the credibility of the financial statements and the related auditor's report is not undermined. Possible steps that might be taken to protect the auditor's report include:

- no further action - subject to management agreeing to amend the other information, either after communicating concerns to the responsible officer or, where appropriate, to the sponsoring government department or other entity to which the entity might be accountable - requests might also be made that the responsible officer consults an appropriate third party if disagreement persists;
- consider the implications for the auditor's report - the impact on the opinion itself will only be considered where doubt remains that an amendment might be required to the financial statements themselves; or
- resigning from the appointment.

275 Where audits are conducted under statute by the Comptroller and Auditor General, (including NHS bodies in Wales audited by the Auditor General for Wales and health entities in Northern Ireland which are audited by the Comptroller and Auditor General of Northern Ireland) the resignation option is not available and the

auditor's reports attract specific legal privileges. In these cases, if the information is not corrected, the auditor's report includes an explanatory paragraph.

For local government and health entities, the options for action additionally include reporting in the annual audit letter or its equivalent or, if the matter is significant, making a report in the public interest (England and Wales or referring the matter to the Controller of Audit (Scotland)). In Northern Ireland, the Comptroller and Auditor General is able to report on any issue to the Northern Ireland Assembly. Local government auditors in Northern Ireland make a report to the Department of the Environment and can include matters of significance. This report is forwarded to the local government entity and made available to the public.

The Audit of Regularity

The concept of regularity reflects Parliament's concern that public money raised through taxation on the public is used only for those purposes approved by Parliament. The preparation of financial statements by public bodies is an important means by which they are accountable for the use of public funds made available to them by Parliament. This leads to the financial statements for bodies directly accountable to Parliament including an implied assertion regarding the regularity of financial transactions, in addition to the financial statement assertions identified in ISA (UK and Ireland) 500.

Regularity can be defined as the requirement that a financial transaction is in accordance with:

- authorising legislation;
- regulations issued under governing legislation;
- Parliamentary authorities; and (where relevant)
- HM Treasury authorities.

As noted in the Foreword, in central government and for specified health entities (including special health authorities, strategic health authorities and primary care trusts) and probation boards there is an explicit statutory requirement on the auditor to provide an additional statement on the regularity of the transactions underlying the entity's financial statements. This is discharged through the audit of the financial statements and is reported in a separate part of the audit opinion on the financial statements. Regularity adds an additional dimension to the audit of financial statements in the public sector. Nevertheless the auditor, as far as possible, adopts an integrated audit approach covering the audit of the financial statements and of regularity.

The auditor is expected to comply with the Auditing Practices Board's engagement standards and quality control standards on all audits of public sector financial statements. These standards apply equally to the auditor's work in relation to the regularity assertion. The objective of this section is to provide an auditor who has a duty to provide an additional statement on regularity of transactions underlying the entities financial statements with practical guidance on the audit of regularity and to expand on:

- obtaining an understanding of the framework of authorities;
- gathering evidence on compliance with authorities; and
- giving an explicit opinion on the regularity of transactions (where this is required).

281 In considering the framework of laws and regulations auditors of central government, specified health entities and probation boards distinguish between those authorities which are specific to the entity and provide specific direct authority for its financial transactions and those laws and regulations which provide the general framework within which it conducts its activities. Laws and regulations that fall within the general framework include those relating to health and safety, environmental protection and employment. While non-compliance with those laws and regulations that provide the general legal framework would not affect the auditor's opinion on the regularity of transactions it may nevertheless have financial consequences for the entity.

The guidance is supplementary to, and intended to be read in conjunction with, the relevant engagement standards and quality control standards and the guidance set out elsewhere in this Practice Note.

Propriety – a Related Concept

282 Whereas regularity is concerned with compliance with appropriate authorities, propriety is concerned more with standards of conduct, behaviour and corporate governance. It includes matters such as fairness, integrity, the avoidance of personal profit from public business, even-handedness in the appointment of staff, open competition in the letting of contracts and the avoidance of waste and extravagance. In central government, propriety is defined in Government Accounting.

283 Propriety is not readily susceptible to objective verification and is not expressly covered in the opinion on financial statements. When issues of propriety come to light in the course of the audit of financial statements, the auditor considers whether and, if so, how, they may be reported. Where propriety is part of the wider statutory role, as it is for the Comptroller and Auditor General, the auditor considers whether a matter is of such significance that it needs to be reported to Parliament. In other cases, where propriety falls within the terms of the auditor's engagement, reporting may be to management. In Scotland, the Public Finance and Accountability (Scotland) Act 2000 requires audits of accounts for which the Auditor General is responsible to include auditor's reports that set out findings on whether the expenditure and receipts shown in the account were incurred or applied in accordance with relevant statutory provisions and with any applicable guidance (whether as to propriety or otherwise) issued by Scottish Ministers.

284 The concept of propriety is discussed further in the Public Audit Forum's document *Propriety and Audit in the Public Sector*.

The Audit of Regularity - an Overview

285 As ISA (UK and Ireland) 250 states, where statutory requirements exist which requires the auditor to report, as part of the audit of the financial statements, whether the entity complies with certain provisions of laws or regulations, the auditor needs:

- to obtain a general understanding of the legal and regulatory framework applicable to the entity and the industry and how the entity is complying with that framework; and
- to test compliance with these provisions of the laws and regulations.

This provides the basis for the auditor's approach to the audit of the regularity 286
assertion on the financial statements of public sector entities, which can be summarised as:

- **obtaining a sufficient understanding of the framework of authorities**. The auditor identifies laws and regulations that are specific to the entity. The auditor obtains a broad understanding that is sufficient to enable identification of transactions or events that may have a significant effect on the regularity of transactions in the financial statements. The auditor also considers the systems and procedures in place to ensure compliance with authorities. The auditor obtains an understanding of the internal control environment to enable a preliminary assessment of control risk in relation to, where appropriate, the regularity assertion;
- *testing for regularity*. To obtain sufficient appropriate evidence to substantiate assertions about regularity, the auditor will usually have to perform substantive procedures on transactions. The extent of these procedures will depend on the auditor's assessment of the effectiveness of the design of systems in translating authorities into controls and the extent to which tests of those controls support an assessment of moderate or low control risk. Tests are usually integrated with those relating to the audit of the financial statements. In complex regulatory environments this may involve an examination of the translation of authorities into relevant rules and procedures; and
- *reporting on regularity*. Auditors in the central government and health sectors and auditors of probation boards give a separate and explicit opinion on regularity. Auditors may also provide separate reports to Parliament, Assemblies or the Secretary of State on regularity issues.

These steps in the audit of regularity are considered in more detail in the rest of this section.

Obtaining a Sufficient Understanding of the Framework of Authorities

An auditor in the public sector has, or obtains, an understanding of the framework 287
of authorities governing the audited body and its activities which is sufficient to
enable identification of events, transactions and practices which may have a material
effect on the regularity of transactions in the financial statements. The extent of the
auditor's work in relation to obtaining a sufficient understanding of the regulatory
framework will depend on the complexity of the laws and regulations. In complex
regulatory environments the auditor will consider the translation of authorities into
relevant rules and procedures. In obtaining a sufficient understanding of the framework of authorities, the auditor may seek representations from the entity about
the authorities that govern its operations, but any representations received are
reviewed critically in accordance with ISA (UK and Ireland) 580.

In all regards, the audited entity retains the responsibility for ensuring the regularity 288
of its transactions and for disclosing these transactions in the financial statements.
Where the environment is complex, this will include a responsibility for translating
authorities into local procedures and to monitor adherence to those procedures.
However, the auditor has a responsibility for understanding the framework of
authorities and cannot rely wholly on management representations about the framework, as the auditor's opinion on regularity must be based on evidence of
compliance with authorities, rather than on evidence of compliance with the entity's
understanding of the framework.

Identifying laws and regulations which form the framework of authorities

289 The governing authorities which the auditor considers when obtaining a knowledge of the entity's activities and identifying the framework of authorities will include:

- authorising legislation;
- regulations issued under governing legislation;
- Parliamentary authorities; and (where relevant)
- HM Treasury authorities.

290 The auditor can identify the framework of authorities governing public sector entities from a number of sources, for example:

- previous experience with the entity or similar entities;
- discussions with the staff employed by the entity (finance officers, internal audit, policy and legal branches); and
- documents produced by the entity (for example minutes of board and other principal committee meetings, correspondence and minutes of meetings with HM Treasury and sponsor departments (for central government bodies), prior years' financial and annual reports, budgets, internal management reports, management policy manuals, manuals of accounting and internal control, scheme control plans).

Obtaining an understanding of the framework of authorities

291 Understanding the framework of authorities and using this information appropriately will assist the auditor in developing the audit plan and in identifying potential material irregularity in the financial statements, for example, from new and complex legislation or from a misinterpretation of legislation and its scope. The auditor's understanding of the authorities includes knowledge of the reasons for the legislation and its objectives as this will aid the auditor's understanding of any secondary legislation or subsidiary regulations. For central government entities this may be obtained from discussions with the department and, where appropriate, by reference to the relevant departmental papers and notes on clauses within an Act or Statutory Instrument. Where the auditor is uncertain whether legislation has been properly interpreted and the effect could be material, it may be necessary to seek a legal opinion (see paragraphs 354 to 358 below). In the case of executive agencies and non-departmental public bodies this may involve consultation with the sponsor department.

292 For some public sector entities the authorities governing their nature and activities may not change from year to year. In these circumstances, the auditor may already have sufficient knowledge of those authorities from previous audits. Where the authorities change, the auditor obtains sufficient knowledge of any new or amended authorities which are likely to be material to the financial statements and the regularity opinion.

Extent of auditor's work on the framework of authorities

293 The nature and complexity of the relevant legislation and other authorities can vary significantly between different entities (see paragraphs 295 to 296 below). These authorities will in turn determine the extent of the auditor's work on regularity. In the case of specified health entities the same legislative and regulatory framework may be applicable to a number of entities, for example all strategic health authorities operate within a common legislative framework.

In some entities, such as the Ministry of Defence and the Foreign and Commonwealth Office, many activities are conducted under the common law powers of the Crown and subject only to the limitations of the Supply grant and the ambit in the Appropriation Act, which may be set out in general and wide-ranging terms. In these entities the auditor's primary concern will be that the activities financed by supply fall within the provisions of the Estimate. 294

In other central government entities, such as the Department for Work and Pensions the regulatory framework is complex with a wide range of statutory authorities governing the administration of individual schemes and hence the individual transaction. For example, eligibility for specific Social Security benefits will vary from benefit to benefit and are often set out in supplementary regulations issued by the Secretary of State. It remains the audited body's responsibility to ensure that legislation and regulations are appropriately reflected at all stages through to operational guidance. In these entities the auditor's work on regularity will involve obtaining sufficient appropriate evidence regarding whether transactions are in accordance with authorities governing individual schemes. This evidence can be obtained through tests of controls and from substantive procedures. Where the regulations are complex this work will usually involve reviewing the process for translation of authorities into the entity's detailed operating instructions and procedures relating to financial transactions. The extent of the auditor's work will have regard to judgements on materiality (see paragraphs 309–311 below). 295

For specified health entities, there are a number of direct statutory authorities that enable Primary Care Trusts to perform functions such as commissioning healthcare from providers and making payments to general practitioners. However, many of the constraints over the regularity of transactions will derive from the Secretary of State's discretions written into the relevant legislation. For instance, the terms of payments to general practitioners in England are set out in the relevant contract, consolidating directions issued by the Secretary of State. In these circumstances, the auditor's work on regularity is restricted to those governing authorities that directly affect the audited entity's powers and duties, and excludes the Parliamentary or HM Treasury authorities that might overlie the direct authorities. Thus, the auditor has an interest in a Primary Care Trust's arrangements for ensuring that payments meet the terms of the relevant contract and in whether the contract complies with the Secretary of State's directions, but not in whether the directions themselves have the proper authorities. 296

Consideration of systems and procedures designed to ensure compliance

Public sector entities will usually have installed internal controls to ensure regularity. In obtaining a general understanding of the framework of authorities and risks to regularity, the auditor considers how the entity's management complies with the framework and seeks to mitigate the risk of material irregularity through controls. The auditor's consideration of the controls over regularity will involve an assessment of the general control environment at the entity level and control procedures relating to individual transaction streams. 297

As part of the auditor's review of the control environment in public sector entities the auditor also considers the general control framework for ensuring regularity, including: 298

- the entity's organisational structure and the extent to which the responsibility for ensuring regularity is devolved from, for example in central government, the Accounting Officer (Accountable Officer in Scotland and in specified health

entities) or Chief Executive to, for example, the Principal Finance Officer or Finance Director;
- the Accounting Officer's or Chief Executive's methods of controlling those officers, departments or agents responsible for ensuring regularity;
- the results of that part of internal audit's work programme which covers controls over compliance with laws and regulations; and
- the entity's corporate governance arrangements, in so far as the arrangements address compliance with regulations.

In considering the general control framework the auditor may also take account of the work carried out by the entity to support the corporate governance statements, and the auditor's own work in reviewing the statement.

299 Controls and procedures which the audited body operates to ensure regularity of individual transaction streams may include:
- application of desk instructions for staff which translate statutory requirements into a set of operating procedures;
- appointment of an officer responsible for ensuring that desk instructions are kept up-to-date and reflect any legislative changes;
- guidance set out in financial memoranda between the sponsor department and the entity in receipt of grants;
- monitoring of compliance with financial memoranda; and
- receipt of reports on compliance from auditors of other entities.

Translation of authorities into relevant rules and procedures

300 It is sometimes necessary for the auditor to consider major or new legislation affecting the financial transactions or to consider whether regulations are appropriately translated into relevant rules and procedures. The auditor's work on legislation or regulations need only focus on those authorities that are relevant to the entity's financial transactions, such as those that govern the powers of the entity to make payments or receive money, or set out the value of such payments or receipts. It is not concerned with administrative rules or regulations that are not directly linked to financial transactions.

301 The auditor's consideration of the translation of authorities may involve reviewing the legislation to identify the provisions that authorise activities and reviewing the process for their translation and interpretation in subsidiary regulations and guidelines. It may also extend to the process for translation of those regulations into working manuals or other key documentation. In conducting this review the auditor pays particular attention to the statutory authorities which govern, for example:
- the powers of Ministers and their departments and HM Treasury to determine the rules and procedures under delegated authority;
- the controls to be operated by the entity responsible for the administration of a scheme;
- the eligibility of beneficiaries to receive grants or other kinds of financial support under a scheme;
- the calculation of grant or any other payments; and
- the setting of fees and charges and other revenues.

302 In considering relevant rules and procedures relating to schemes, the auditor also identifies those controls that are designed to prevent and detect material irregularities.

Where the volume of laws or regulations is significant, entities may have systems for the design and monitoring of procedures and controls to ensure that they are appropriate and meet legislative requirements. Internal audit units may also have their own programme of work for reviewing controls to ensure compliance with regulations and authorities. The auditor may seek to place reliance on the entity's systems governing the translation of authorities and the design of rules and procedures by testing the controls over this process. The testing of controls may involve a review of the work of those charged with governance or internal audit on compliance with rules and procedures. 303

Where only minor changes in legislation occur it may not be necessary to carry out a re-assessment of regulations. The auditor nevertheless remains alert for significant problems encountered by the audited body relating to the interpretation of new and existing legislation or the application of regulations. The auditor considers such problems and records, as necessary, any impact on the audit. 304

In the case of lower tier entities, such as strategic health authorities, the auditor is entitled to rely on the regulations that the entities receive from higher tier bodies and are concerned only with the arrangements put in place by the entity to implement them. The auditor does not consider whether those regulations are, themselves, a proper reflection of a higher regulation or statute. 305

Testing for Regularity

Where specific authorities govern transactions of the entity, the auditor plans and performs procedures to determine whether in all material respects the entity's expenditure and income (payments and receipts) comply with those authorities. The principles and procedures applied to obtain sufficient appropriate evidence to support an opinion on the regularity of transactions in the financial statements of an entity in central government, specified health entities and probation boards are the same as those applied to the audit of any other financial statement assertion. Thus, in forming an opinion on regularity, the auditor seeks to provide reasonable assurance that the financial statements are free from material irregularity 306

There may however be particular considerations in respect of the auditor's assessment of materiality, risk and the design of audit procedures in relation to the regularity assertion (as set out below). In addition to these considerations the auditor may have particular regard to the regularity of receipts, the disclosure of transactions in accordance with appropriate authorities, and securing management representations. This section also considers using the work of others in the audit of regularity. 307

Materiality

The concept of materiality applies to the audit of regularity as to the other assertions in relation to the financial statements. The auditor is therefore only required to obtain sufficient appropriate evidence to give an opinion, in central government and for specified health entities and probation boards, on whether expenditure and income (payments and receipts) have been applied for the purposes intended by Parliament and conform with the authorities which govern them "in all material respects". This explicitly recognises the fact that the auditor cannot detect all occurrences of irregularity through the audit work. In determining whether individually material items require detailed testing, the auditor will have regard to the auditor's assessment of inherent and control risk. In some circumstances the auditor's assessment of risk may necessitate that all individually material transactions are tested in detail. 308

309 The auditor's assessment of what is material is a matter of judgement and includes both quantitative (value) and qualitative (nature) considerations. Materiality affects both the way in which the auditor plans and designs the audit work on regularity and how the auditor evaluates and reports the results of that work. The assessment of materiality at the planning stage is likely to be at the same value for regularity as for other aspects of the audit of the financial statements.

310 Auditors of central government, of specified health entities and of probation boards may also have to consider whether and how auditors may report irregularities that have been identified and which may not be quantitatively material. This is because Parliament has an interest in breaches of authority even where the sums of money involved may be small in relation to the overall expenditure in the financial statements. For example, in the context of regularity, the auditor applies separate qualitative assessments in relation to breaches of Parliamentary authority where:

- expenditure incurred is in excess of the amounts authorised by Parliament. An Excess Vote will automatically result in qualification irrespective of the amount involved; and
- expenditure incurred is outside the ambit of the Vote or without HM Treasury authority. An ex-gratia payment made by central government body to a staff member leaving the organisation, without prior HM Treasury approval, is an example of this type of irregular expenditure.

311 The auditor remains alert to the nature of irregularities and considers their significance having regard to Parliament's interest in the matter. The auditor may adopt specific procedures where the auditor considers there is a risk of an Excess Vote or to identify activities or transactions that may not be in accordance with Parliament's intentions as set out in the framework of authorities.

Assessment of risk

312 In central government, for specified health entities and for probation boards the auditor considers the risk that an inappropriate audit opinion will be given on:

- whether the expenditure and income (or payments and receipts) have been applied for the purposes intended by Parliament and conform to the authorities which govern them; and
- whether there is proper disclosure in the financial statements of any transactions which are not in compliance with the appropriate authorities.

In this context, the auditor considers the components of audit risk. Audit risk is a function of the risk of material misstatement of the financial statements and the risk that the auditor will not detect such a misstatement ("detection risk"). The risk of material misstatement at the assertion level consists of two components: "inherent risk" and "control risk". The risk of an auditor giving an inappropriate opinion where transactions that are not in compliance with authorities are not properly disclosed is considered in paragraphs 335 and 336.

313 To assess the inherent risk of an irregularity occurring, the auditor will use judgement to evaluate a range of factors. In the context of the regularity opinion specific factors include:

- the complexity of the regulations;
- the introduction of major new legislation or changes in existing regulations;
- services and programmes administered under European Union authorities, where the framework of authorities can be complex;
- services and programmes delivered through third parties; and

- payments and receipts made on the basis of claims or declarations.

Control risk in the context of regularity is the risk that an irregularity that could occur in an account balance or class of transactions and that could be material would not be prevented, or detected and corrected on a timely basis, by the accounting and control systems. Where the auditor expects to be able to rely on the auditor's assessment of control risk to reduce the extent of substantive procedures relating to regularity, the auditor makes a preliminary assessment of control risk and plan and perform tests of controls to support that assessment. 314

Some of the risk factors and the possible mitigating controls the auditor may consider in relation to regularity are summarised in Appendix 3. 315

The auditor considers the significance of inherent and control risk of material irregularity in determining the nature, timing and extent of substantive procedures required to reduce audit risk to an acceptable level. As part of the risk assessment, the auditor determines which of the risks identified require special audit consideration. 316

The auditor remains aware that risks may be specific to one financial statement assertion. A high inherent risk to regularity would not necessarily mean that high inherent risk applies to all other aspects of the audit of the financial statements. 317

Audit procedures

Audit procedures designed to test regularity will usually be based on a mix of tests of controls and substantive audit procedures. 318

Tests of controls

The auditor may identify specific risks to regularity that leads to an assessment that the inherent risk of material breach is high. In these circumstances it is likely that the same risks will have been recognised by management and controls put in place to mitigate the risk. The table at Appendix 3 sets out some of the control procedures that might be used in relation to the main inherent risks. 319

The auditor may seek to reduce the extent of substantive procedures for the regularity assertion where the auditor obtains satisfactory evidence as to the effectiveness of the entity's accounting and internal control systems. In doing so the auditor may also have regard to work carried out on the auditor's review of the statement on internal control. However, when the auditor concludes that the controls to ensure regularity are not effective, the auditor will not rely on them. 320

The auditor plans and performs the audit of the internal controls designed to ensure regularity as the auditor would for the audit of any other aspect of the audit financial statements. 321

Substantive audit procedures

The auditor will usually have to perform some substantive procedures to confirm that expenditure incurred conforms to governing authorities, the range and scope being dependent on the extent to which evidence from tests of control support a moderate to low assessment of control risk. The extent of substantive procedures will also be determined with regard to any evidence relating directly to regularity or 322 irregularity provided by tests of controls. Evidence in support of the regularity assertion will often go some way towards satisfying other financial statement assertions, and will usually be gathered as part of an integrated approach to the audit of an account balance.

323 The auditor may encounter difficulties obtaining sound audit evidence regarding certain aspects of regularity, for instance eligibility for grants. In such cases, the auditor considers the reliability of the audit evidence available. Ideally, the auditor requires direct evidence to satisfy the objective of the test. Where this is not available the auditor considers how the entity satisfied itself as to regularity. This may be through the work of a separate inspection function or by receiving advice or assurance from an independent third party.

324 Rather than pay grants directly to the recipients intended by Parliament, public sector bodies may fund other bodies that are responsible for the administration of a scheme. Where this is the case, and insofar as it is consistent with the objective of giving an opinion on the financial statements based on independent audit evidence, the auditor of the body may seek to make use of the financial reporting arrangements put in place by the body to ensure proper accountability for such grants. This includes consideration of any work undertaken by the auditor of the other body on the regularity of expenditure.

325 The auditor may adopt more extensive procedures where there is a potential Excess Vote. An Excess Vote can arise when a department exceeds the cash, resource or administration budget set down in their Estimates. Such procedures might involve detailed tests to confirm:

- that income and expenditure has been recorded in the correct period and is valid;
- that income has been correctly categorised as Appropriations in Aid or Consolidated Fund Extra Receipts (CFER); and
- the accuracy and completeness of administrative costs recorded in the accounts.

326 The auditor may also carry out specific tests to identify activities and transactions that may not be in accordance with Parliament's intention. These tests might involve:

- the review of Accounts against the Estimates and the Appropriation Act and any specific legislation to identify transactions which may be outside Parliament's intention;
- the review of the entity's management accounts to identify any unusual transaction streams or account balances or any incorrect analysis of transactions; and
- the substantive testing of transactions and account balances.

Analytical procedures

327 Analytical procedures on their own are unlikely to provide the auditor with sufficient appropriate evidence in support of regularity. They may nevertheless, in certain circumstances, assist the auditor in assessing whether amounts recorded in financial statements are consistent with expectations. For example, where allowances under a scheme are subject to a maximum value and the number of recipients is known the auditor may use analytical procedures to identify whether the permitted maximum may have been breached.

Auditing compliance with European Union authorities

An auditor engaged in the examination of expenditure on schemes funded by the European Union considers the compliance of transactions with the governing European legislation. In particular, the auditor obtains satisfaction that any regulations established in delegated legislation are consistent with the provisions in the governing European Council or Commission Regulation and that these provisions are properly translated into departmental instructions and procedures. Any expenditure outside the provisions in the governing Regulation is irregular.

328

European Directives allow the national authorities discretion in the choice of form and methods of implementation. However, delays or inconsistencies in the implementation of Directives may leave the national enacting legislation and any related expenditure open to legal challenge in the European Court of Justice. The auditor obtains satisfaction that those central government departments responsible for enacting laws relative to Directives have taken appropriate action to ensure that the national law is enacted and that the legislation is consistent with the Directives concerned. This may form part of the auditor's review of the overall control environment to ensure compliance with legislation.

329

The auditor also remains alert to any legal actions that challenge the provisions of Acts or delegated legislation implementing European legislation by making enquiries of the entity and obtaining representations. The auditor enquires of the management of public sector bodies whether the Commission has, for any reason, instituted legal action or infringement proceedings against the United Kingdom on the implementation of European legislation.

330

Regularity of receipts

The auditor approaches the audit of regularity of receipts, including revenues from taxation, in the same way the auditor would approach the audit of the regularity of expenditure. There may, nevertheless, be particular considerations when auditing the regularity of fees and charges levied by public sector entities. These involve:

331

- reviewing the relevant primary legislation to confirm that it provides appropriate authority for Ministers, departments or other public sector bodies to levy fees and charges for the services concerned;
- confirming that fee orders and other types of Statutory Instrument issued under the governing legislation are in accordance with those authorities;
- for supply funded activities, confirming that the Appropriation Act provides the appropriate Parliamentary authority for the receipts to be applied in aid of expenditure; and
- for specified National Health Service entities, that income generation activities fall within the scope of the NHS and Community Care Act 1990.

In addition to these considerations, an auditor in central government will also obtain satisfaction that fees and charges levied for services reflect the appropriate costs for those services. In particular, the auditor obtains satisfaction that Ministers or their departments are not abusing their powers to deliberately set fees and charges at levels that would generate a surplus, unless exceptionally an order under Section 102 of the Finance (No 2) Act 1987 is in force allowing fees to be set at a level to recover past deficits. Equally, where fees are waived or deliberately set at a level to incur a deficit the auditor confirms that the entity has the authority to waive fees or not recover all appropriate costs.

332

333 The treatment of surplus receipts and deficits by a Trading Fund must be considered in the light of the Fund's financial objectives. The fact that a body is a Trading Fund does not relieve it of the need to obtain a Section 102 order to recover a deficit for statutory services.

334 As well as determining the authorities for levying fees and charges, the auditor also confirms that receipts are properly utilised and disclosed in financial statements as authorised by Parliament in the appropriate legislation.

Disclosure and regularity

335 In addition to the risk of giving an inappropriate opinion on the regularity assertion, auditors in central government, of specified health entities and of probation boards also consider the risk that irregularities may not be properly disclosed in financial statements. This component of audit risk can be defined as "the risk that the auditor will give an inappropriate opinion on whether there is proper disclosure in the financial statements of any (financial) transactions which are not in compliance with the appropriate authorities". Even where a breach of regularity is disclosed, auditors in central government still consider the implications for the audit opinion on regularity and the need to present a separate report on the matter to parliament. In doing so the auditor will need to consider the materiality of the matter at issue.

336 Specific disclosure risks faced by auditors in central government include:

- inappropriate treatment of expenditure and receipts in relation to an Excess Vote;
- the failure to obtain HM Treasury or other appropriate authority for virement (i.e. transfer of expenditure) between Estimate lines or;
- the failure to note special payments, write-offs or any other losses in the financial statements.

The auditor may adopt particular procedures to address these risks, as part of the auditor's overall review of the financial statements. In determining the appropriate treatment of receipts the auditor will consider, for example:

- amounts appropriated in aid do not exceed the gross provisions on the Request for Resources;
- that any excess receipts are surrendered to the Consolidated Fund; and
- that receipts are not netted-off against expenditure, except in the limited circumstances prescribed in Government Accounting. The auditor may also perform detailed substantive procedures in relation to losses incurred and special payments made by the entity.

Representations on regularity

337 Audit evidence on regularity will be gathered from the auditor's substantive procedures and tests of control. However, because of the importance of regularity in central government, to specified health entities and to probation boards, the auditor will also seek representations from Accounting Officers (for central government sector entities and probation boards) or Accountable Officers (in Scotland and for specified health entities) on the discharge of their responsibility for the regularity of transactions. This is particularly important in areas, such as certain benefit and grant schemes, where direct evidence is not available to the auditor.

338 Accounting or Accountable Officers are normally expected to provide a formal statement on the discharge of their responsibility each year. Where this statement is

included in the financial statements, the auditor makes reference to it in the responsibilities section of the auditor's report; where the statement is not included or is not comprehensive in setting out responsibilities, the auditor makes the disclosures in the responsibilities section of the auditor's report. The length and formality of management representations on regularity do not influence the scope of the auditor's procedures in obtaining evidence to support the regularity assertion.

Regularity and using the work of others

The auditor of a public sector entity may use the work of auditors in other entities when examining the application of grants. The auditor may also consult, in central government, with HM Treasury or the sponsor department on issues of regularity and seek independent legal advice. 339

Using the work of internal audit

The auditor of a public sector entity may wish to make use of the work of the internal auditor to obtain sufficient appropriate evidence in support of the regularity assertion. Where the auditor considers internal audit work the auditor applies ISA (UK and Ireland) 610. 340

Using the work of another auditor

There are three main situations where the auditor of a central government entity or specified health entity may encounter the work of another auditor, where the entity: 341

- consolidates or summarises the financial statements of other bodies;
- has paid a grant to another entity; or
- has contracted out services to a service organisation.

Whenever possible, and in so far as it is consistent with the objective of giving an opinion on the financial statements based on independent audit evidence, the auditor of a central government entity, a specified health entity or a probation board in the interests of efficiency and to reduce the overall burden of audit, seeks to use the work of the auditor of the other entity. 342

Where the entity consolidates or summarises the financial statements of other bodies

The auditor may be responsible for reporting on the financial statements of a public sector entity where those financial statements include financial information from one or more components (or other entities). An example of this is the Resource Account prepared by the Department of Health that consolidates the results of individual health bodies. 343

Where the financial statements of public sector entities consolidate or summarise the financial information of other entities, the auditor of the higher entity determines how the work of the other auditor will affect the audit of regularity. Where the auditor of a public sector entity wishes to use the work of another auditor in testing the regularity assertion, the auditor follows the standards and guidance in ISA (UK and Ireland) 600. 344

The principal auditor obtains representations from another auditor as to that auditor's independence from the entity and their compliance with the relevant auditing and reporting requirements. This also applies if the principal auditor uses 345 audited financial statements, signed by the other auditor, which contain a specific opinion on regularity.

<u>Where the public sector entity has paid a grant-in-aid or other grant to another entity.</u>

346 Examples of this situation include grants-in-aid paid by central government departments to fund most non-departmental public bodies and the grants paid by other government departments to local authorities.

347 The central government department or principal entity will usually establish controls designed to ensure that the recipient or other entity complies with the grant conditions. It is common practice for financial memoranda and grant conditions to require a report or certificate on regularity to be sent by the other entity's auditor to the principal entity's management or for the entity to prepare financial statements including grant transactions and submit these to the principal entity together with the auditor's report on the statements. For example, the Office of the Deputy Prime Minister requires local authorities to secure auditor's certification of expenditure against grants made to local authorities.

348 The auditor of a public sector entity is usually able to audit most assertions by reference to the entity alone, but the auditor may need to examine the application of grants paid to other entities. The auditor can do this through:

- examination of the evidence available in the principal entity including reports by their own internal audit function;
- using the work of the other entity's external auditor;
- consideration of the work of the other entity's internal audit function; and
- direct access to the other entity and performance of appropriate audit procedures.

In some cases the auditor of a public sector entity does not have a right of access to the other entity and will have no alternative but to use the work of the other auditor.

349 Where the auditor seeks to use the evidence available to the principal entity, where this includes the work of another auditor, the auditor exercises professional judgement as to whether sufficient appropriate evidence to support the regularity assertion has been obtained.

350 Where the auditor seeks to use the work of the internal auditor to obtain sufficient appropriate evidence in relation to grants paid to other entities, the auditor may do this through:

- examining the scope, nature and extent of evidence available from the internal auditor of the principal entity, from the audit of grant payments to the other entity;
- examining, from the information available in the principal entity, the scope, nature and extent of the evidence available from the internal auditor of the other entity. In examining this work, the public sector external auditor has regard to:
  - the results of any effectiveness monitoring performed by the principal entity on the internal audit function of the other entity; and
  - any assessment of the internal audit function of the other entity as may have been performed by the external auditor of the entity and as may have been reported to the principal entity.

351 The Audit Commission issues detailed instructions to the auditor concerning the certification of grants to local authorities and NHS bodies including detailed

checklists covering the statutory requirements. The central government auditor may use the certificate and reports issued by the auditor of other entities on grants and subsidies by:

- confirming that the instructions issued to the auditor of the other entity address the regularity considerations satisfactorily; and
- agreeing the scope and reviewing the results of the quality control review programmes by the Audit Commission and Audit Scotland.

352 Where another auditor is required to provide a report or certificate on regularity to the principal entity, it is often the case that this is done a considerable time after the financial period being audited. Reports or certificates are sometimes provided as late as one year after the period end. However, central government sector and specified health entity auditors ensure that only the evidence available to the principal entity relating to the period for which the principal auditor is reporting an opinion on regularity is used. Where this is not possible, or if the principal and other entities have different year end dates, then the principal auditor may have to perform additional procedures, including the exercise of inspection rights where appropriate.

Where the public sector entity has contracted out services to a service organisation.

353 In this situation, whether the public sector auditor needs access to the service organisation and/or the contractor's auditor to audit the regularity assertion depends on the nature of the services provided, the information available at the principal entity, and the terms of engagement of the other auditor.

Obtaining legal advice

354 It is reasonable for the auditor to rely on legal opinions obtained by the entity concerning the regularity of schemes or transactions where such opinions are provided by an appropriate independent expert and where there are no factors, other than those on which legal opinions have been obtained, which may lead the auditor to question the regularity of expenditure. In such circumstances, the auditor applies the principles of ISA (UK and Ireland) 620.

355 Where the auditor is uncertain about the regularity of schemes or individual transactions the auditor may seek legal advice. Where a public sector auditor is considering the need to obtain legal opinions concerning the interpretation of statutes or regulations the auditor follows the standards and guidance in ISA (UK and Ireland) 620.

356 When determining whether to seek legal advice on a matter of regularity the auditor considers:

- the materiality of the matter in the context of the financial statements;
- the risk of irregularity based on the nature and complexity of the governing authorities; and
- the availability of other relevant audit evidence. In particular, the auditor determines whether the entity has sought its own legal advice at the time the scheme was designed or, where the uncertainty relates to a particular group of transactions, at the time the transactions occurred.

357 Where the auditor determines that it is appropriate to seek a legal opinion, and the entity has not taken legal advice on the matter, the approach is discussed and the point on which the opinion is required agreed with the entity. Usually where the entity accepts there is doubt about the regularity of transactions it will be willing to

seek clarification of the legal position. Where the entity is unwilling to seek legal advice or where the auditor has concerns about the legal advice given to the entity, the auditor may wish to seek a separate legal opinion.

358 When planning to seek a legal opinion, the auditor assesses the objectivity, professional qualifications, experience and resources of the expert. When planning to rely on the opinion of the entity's own legal advisers, the auditor pays particular attention to the objectivity of advice given.

Consulting HM Treasury and sponsors

359 Where the auditor is uncertain about the regularity of expenditure in relation to conditions of grant or HM Treasury authority the auditor may seek advice from the sponsoring department or from HM Treasury. In these circumstances the auditor follows similar steps to those the auditor would take when seeking legal advice.

360 The auditor first determines whether the entity sought clarification or, where necessary, obtained the appropriate authorities from the sponsoring department or HM Treasury at the time the expenditure was incurred. If the entity has not sought appropriate advice or authorisation the auditor asks it to do so.

Regularity and Reporting

361 Auditors in central government and of specified health entities and probation boards are required to give a separate and explicit opinion on the regularity of transactions in the entity's financial statements. In addition, the auditor may provide separate reports, other than through audit opinions, on issues of regularity. In certain circumstances the auditor may be required to report matters relating to regularity to third parties. For example, the auditor of other entities may be required to report to sponsor departments on the regularity of the activities and the transactions of those entities.

Response to breaches of regularity

362 Where non-compliance with regulations is suspected or discovered, the auditor considers the wider implications for the financial statements as a whole. This will also include consideration of the implications for the auditor's assessment of risks and controls in relation to material irregularities and the reliance the auditor can place on the overall control environment and representations from management.

363 The auditor will consider the nature and extent of any non-compliance and, in particular, whether it arises from a fundamental misinterpretation of legislation or a misapplication of departmental rules. The most likely course is that the auditor will obtain further evidence, for example, by carrying out additional testing of a particular category of transactions.

364 Cases of non-compliance with regulations will usually be reported to the management of the entity to allow corrective action to be taken, for example, by recovering overpayments of grant. Where it is not possible for the entity to take corrective action the auditor may encourage it to disclose the non-compliance in its financial statements by outlining the circumstances surrounding the breach of regulations and the possible extent of irregular transactions. Even where a breach of regularity is disclosed, auditors in central government still consider the implications for the audit opinion on regularity and the need to present a separate report on the matter to

Parliament. In doing so the auditor will need to consider the materiality of the matter at issue.

In most cases of suspected irregularity which are material, the auditor is able to reach agreement with management on whether the relevant transactions were in compliance with the authorities which govern them. However, if the entity's management does not accept the auditor's opinion that the relevant transactions are not in compliance with the appropriate authorities, then the auditor: 365

- communicates in a report to the appropriate level of management, the board of directors or the audit committee the findings from the auditor's investigations into the circumstances surrounding the suspected irregularity and the conclusions drawn therefrom;
- for central government bodies, considers whether, under the terms of Government Accounting or, for a non-departmental public body, the financial memorandum, the matter is one which management is required to report to the sponsor department or HM Treasury and if so, request in writing that management notify the appropriate proper authority;
- reports direct to the sponsor department or to HM Treasury (as appropriate) the circumstances of the non-compliance with authority if management are required to do so and the auditor is unable to establish whether management have complied with the requirement; and
- for a non-departmental public body, considers whether, under the terms of the auditor's engagement the matter is one which the auditor is required to report to the sponsor department and if so, report the matter to the department.

If, after taking these steps, management continue to take the view that the relevant transactions are in accordance with the appropriate authorities, and decline to apply the accounting treatment and to make the disclosures in the financial statements which the auditor considers necessary in the circumstances, then the auditor issues an adverse or qualified opinion, in accordance with the guidance described in paragraph 89 of ISA (UK and Ireland) 240. Further guidance on fraud and regularity is provided in paragraphs 368 to 373 below. 366

Auditors of specified health bodies in England also have a responsibility under section 19 of the Audit Commission Act to refer forthwith to the Secretary of State any matter where it is believed that a decision by the body or an officer has incurred or would involve unlawful expenditure or that some action by the body or an officer has been or would be unlawful and likely to cause loss or deficiency. Qualification of the regularity opinion will normally trigger a section 19 report, but not vice versa if the matter is not judged material. 367

Fraud and irregularity

Only a court of law can determine whether a particular transaction is fraudulent. However, the auditor often encounters situations where there is suspicion of fraud, identified by management, internal audit, third parties or the auditor. Although the auditor does not have the authority to determine whether or not a fraud has actually occurred, the auditor does have a responsibility to determine whether, in the auditor's opinion, the transactions concerned are in compliance with the authorities that govern them. 368

Fraudulent transactions cannot, by definition, be regular since they are without proper authority. Since central government and specified health entity auditors are required to express an opinion on regularity, fraud which is material always results in qualification of the regularity part of the opinion, regardless of the manner or extent 369 of disclosure in the financial statements. Fraud in the context of the auditor's opinion on the regularity of transactions may embrace suspected as well as proven fraud.

370 The definition of fraud in ISA (UK and Ireland) 240 includes acts committed by individuals both inside and outside the audited entity. Guidance in the ISA (UK and Ireland) is, however, primarily concerned with internal fraud as it is this type of fraud which is considered most likely to lead to material misstatements in the financial statements. The responsibility that the public sector auditor has to reach an opinion on regularity means that the auditor is also concerned with the extent of fraud perpetrated from outside the entity.

371 The guidance in appendix 1 of ISA (UK and Ireland) 240 provides examples of fraud risk factors. These are all relevant to central government and specified health entities and probation boards, but in addition, the auditor considers those conditions and events which increase the risk of external fraud.

372 Paragraph 61 of ISA (UK and Ireland) 240 requires the auditor to determine overall responses to address the assessed risks of material misstatement due to fraud at the financial statement level and design and perform further audit procedures whose nature, timing and extent are responsive to the assessed risks at the assertion level. However, as explained in paragraph 17 of ISA (UK and Ireland) 240, owing to the inherent limitations of an audit, there is an unavoidable risk that some material misstatements of the financial statements will not be detected, even though the audit is properly planned and performed in accordance with ISAs (UK and Ireland). In addition, the likelihood of the auditor detecting material fraud, and in particular external fraud, is always lower than a reasonable expectation of detecting error, since fraud is usually accompanied by acts specifically designed to conceal its existence, or involving collusion between employees, or employees and third parties, or falsification of records. The auditor cannot be expected to identify forged documentation in support of claims for grants or other benefits, other than the most obvious forgeries, and generally do not have investigative powers or rights of access to individuals or organisations making claims.

373 Both for practical reasons and in recognition of the responsibilities of those charged with governance in this area, the auditor is likely to focus on the adequacy of the entity's internal controls for preventing and detecting fraud.

Regularity opinion on financial statements

374 Central government and specified health entity auditors provide an additional expression of opinion on the regularity of transactions. Depending on the basis on which the financial statements are prepared[17]

- for financial statements prepared on a cash basis

---

[17] *The equivalent wording in Scotland is slightly different. The statutory requirement is set out in Section 22(1)(c) of the Public Finance and Accountability (Scotland) Act 2000, and refers to the auditor reporting "whether the expenditure and receipts shown in the accounts were incurred or applied in accordance with any applicable guidance (whether as to propriety or otherwise) issued by the Scottish Ministers." In Wales, the statutory authority is section 97 of the Government of Wales Act 1998 and section 61(3) of the Public Audit (Wales) Act 2004 for NHS bodies. In Northern Ireland, the relevant legislation is the Exchequer and Audit Act (Northern Ireland) 1921, the Northern Ireland Act 1998 the Government Resources and Accounts Act (Northern Ireland) 2001 and the Audit and Accountability (Northern Ireland) Order 2003., the form of words used in the regularity part of the opinion is:*

"in all material respects the payments (expenditure) and receipts have been applied to the purposes intended by Parliament"[18]

- for financial statements prepared on an accruals basis

"in all material respects the expenditure and income have been applied to the purposes intended by Parliament and the financial transactions conform to the authorities which govern them".

The provisions of individual engagements may require the auditor to make reference to specific legislation, rather than the generic term "authorities".

The standard wording is designed to be consistent with the statutory requirements[19]   375

- disclosure of the Accounting Officer/Accountable Officer's responsibilities in relation to regularity in the statement of responsibilities and a reference to the disclosure in the responsibilities section of the auditor's report; or, full disclosure in the responsibilities section; and
- inclusion of the overall work performed with regard to regularity in the scope of the basis of opinion section of the auditor's report.

Where the auditor concludes that material financial transactions are not in com-   376
pliance with the appropriate authorities, that is, that expenditure (payments) or income (receipts) have not been applied to the purposes intended by Parliament and that the financial transactions are not in conformity with the authorities which govern them, the auditor qualifies the regularity part of the opinion. Where the auditor is unable to obtain sufficient evidence to reach an opinion on regularity the auditor qualifies the regularity part of the opinion on the grounds of a limitation in audit scope.

A qualified opinion on regularity does not in itself lead to a qualification of the truth   377
and fairness, fair presentation or proper presentation part of the opinion. However, the auditor considers whether the matter is properly disclosed in the financial statements and whether it is so pervasive as to make the financial statements misleading. Examples of qualifications to the regularity part of the opinion are provided in the APB Bulletin on public sector audit reports.

Published reports other than audit opinions

Auditors of central government entities consider the need for reporting other than   378
through the audit opinion where the audit opinion is qualified as a consequence of a material irregularity. The purpose of a separate report is to provide Parliament with a detailed explanation beyond that given in the audit opinion and which could form the basis of a hearing by the Committee of Public Accounts (or the Audit Committee

---

[18] In Northern Ireland and Wales, the reference is to the Assembly, rather than Parliament, and conform to the authorities which govern them".

[19] The Exchequer and Audit Departments Act 1921 refers to the Comptroller and Auditor General having to "satisfy himself that the money expended has been applied to the purpose or purposes for which the grants made by Parliament were intended to provide and that the expenditure conforms to the authority which governs it". More recently the Government Resources and Accounts Act 2000 refers to the Comptroller and Auditor General satisfying himself "that resources authorised by Parliament to be used have been used for the purposes in relation to which the use was authorised; and that the department's financial transactions are in accordance with any relevant authority" and is not intended to extend the auditor's responsibilities beyond those set out in the statutory provisions. The wording also needs to be accompanied by:

of the National Assembly in Wales or other Parliamentary Committees in Scotland or Public Accounts Committee of the Northern Ireland Assembly).

379 In England auditors of specified health entities may consider the issue of a public interest report on any matter which comes to the auditor's attention in the course of the audit in order that it may be considered by the entity concerned or brought to the attention of the public.

380 In central government a separate report will always be required where there is an Excess Vote on a Resource Account. An excess constitutes a breach of Parliamentary control and, regardless of the amounts involved, the Committee of Public Accounts has to be informed of the background and reasons. In such circumstances Parliament must be requested to give retrospective approval to the additional expenditure.

381 In Wales, the Auditor General for Wales may report in the public interest on any body where he is the statutory auditor. Any such reports must be laid before the Assembly which ensures that they are published and come within the remit of the Audit Committee.

382 The auditor may in some cases identify irregularities during the course of the audit which are not material to the financial statements but which need, in the auditor's judgement, to be drawn to the attention of Parliament or the addressees of the auditor's report. An example of this may be where expenditure in previous years is retrospectively deemed to be irregular by virtue of a legal challenge to the provisions of an Act.

Reporting to sponsors

383 As stated in paragraph 347 above, the auditors of other bodies may be required as part of the engagement to submit reports to sponsoring departments that cover compliance with authorities. The form and scope of these reports may be determined by the sponsoring department as part of a specific condition of the grant or subsidy and, in the case of payments to local authorities, will be subject to specific instructions to the auditor. In other entities, the auditor may be required to submit a more general report on the entities' compliance with regulations. Again the nature and scope of such reports will be determined by the auditor's terms of engagement.

Appendix 1

Glossary of Terms

Accountable Officer (1) – members of the staff of the Scottish Administration designated by the Principal Accountable Officer with responsibility for parts of the Administration, bodies or office-holders as regards signing the accounts of the entity and ensuring the propriety and regularity of its finances.

Accountable Officer (2) – the officer (directed as the Chief Executive) responsible for the propriety and regularity of the public finances of health entities, and for the keeping of proper records, as set out in the Accountable Officers' Memorandum issued by the Department of Health. In Northern Ireland, the Accountable Officers' Memorandum is issued by the Department of Health, Social Services and Public Safety.

Accounting Officer – usually the permanent head or senior full-time official of a central government entity or an NHS Foundation Trust, appointed or designated as the Accounting Officer for that entity and with a personal responsibility for, amongst other things, signing of the financial statements, ensuring that proper financial procedures are followed and accounting records maintained, ensuring that public funds and assets are properly managed and safeguarded and all relevant financial considerations, including issues on propriety, regularity or value for money are taken into account. See also **Principal Accounting Officer**.

Accounts Commission – the independent body with statutory responsibilities for securing the audit of local government entities in Scotland, and to assist such entities in achieving best value. In relation to the audit of the financial statements, the Commission is responsible for appointing auditors, setting the required standards for its appointed auditors and regulating the quality of audits.

Accounts direction – the document issued by HM Treasury or the Secretary of State of a parent or sponsor department, or by the National Assembly for Wales or Scottish Ministers which sets out the accounting and disclosure requirements to be applied in preparing the entity's financial statements. In Northern Ireland, the Department of Finance and Personnel is responsible for issuing accounts for central government departments and executive agencies whilst normally the sponsoring department is empowered to direct the form of accounts for non-departmental public bodies and health service entities, with the consent of the Department of Finance and Personnel.

Additional Accounting Officer – the senior full-time official, usually the Chief Executive, of a supply financed executive agency who is designated by the appropriate Accounting Officer of the parent department to assume personal responsibility for the management of the entity's activities.

Administration Budget – the budget set in the Estimates. An Excess Vote qualification will usually be required if a department exceeds its Administration Budget.

Ambit – the description, in Part I of a Supply Estimate, of departmental operations funded through Supply. The ambit can only be extended or otherwise modified by the presentation of a Revised or Supplementary Supply Estimate. The ambit is structured in a way that relates directly to the individual Requests for Resources contained in the Estimate.

Appropriation Act – annual acts which give legal standing to the limits set out in Supply Estimates for Resource Expenditure, Net Cash Requirement and Appropriations in Aid and the purposes to which expenditure may be applied (the ambit). The Appropriation Act also authorises issues from the Consolidated Fund and prescribes the overall sum to be appropriated to particular Estimates in order to finance specified services.

Appropriations in aid – income that, with the authority of Parliament, is used to finance some of the gross expenditure of the department. Amounts that may be appropriated in aid are voted separately in relation to income related to each Request for Resources and for a single amount for non-operating income.

Assembly – the National Assembly for Wales or the Northern Ireland Assembly[20]

---

[20] This Practice Note has been prepared on the premise that devolved administration is operating in Northern Ireland in the form of the Northern Ireland Assembly. When Section 1 of the Northern Ireland Act 2000 is in force (i.e. the Assembly is suspended) references to the Assembly should be substituted with "Parliament".

Assembly Sponsored Public Bodies (ASPBs) – In Wales, non-departmental public bodies are known as assembly sponsored public bodies. The Assembly's Principal Accounting Officer appoints the Chief Executives as the ASPB's accounting officers and the Assembly issues the ASPB's financial memorandum.

Audit Commission – the independent body with statutory responsibilities to regulate the audit of local government and health entities (excluding NHS Foundation Trusts) in England, and to promote improvements in the economy, efficiency and effectiveness of local government and NHS services. In relation to the audit of the financial statements, the Commission is responsible for appointing auditors, setting the required standards for its appointed auditors and regulating the quality of audits.

Auditor General for Scotland – the individual responsible for authorising the issue of public funds from the Scottish Consolidated Fund to government departments and other public sector bodies; for examining or ensuring the examination of parliamentary accounts (which includes determining whether sums paid out of the Fund have been paid out and applied in accordance with statute), and certifying and reporting on them; for carrying out or ensuring the carrying out of examinations into the economy, efficiency and effectiveness with which the Scottish Ministers and the Lord Advocate have used their resources in discharging their functions; and for carrying out or ensuring the carrying out of examinations into the economy, efficiency and effectiveness with which other persons determined under Scottish legislation to whom sums are paid out of the Fund have used those sums in discharging their functions.

Auditor General for Wales (AGW) – the individual responsible for examining and certifying the accounts of the National Assembly for Wales, its sponsored and other related public bodies and NHS Wales entities. The AGW also appoints the auditors of local government bodies in Wales, undertakes performance and value for money studies and best value inspections (known as the Wales Programme for Improvement). The AGW and his staff form the Wales Audit Office (see below).

Auditor's report – any auditor's report expressing an opinion on the truth and fairness, fair presentation or proper presentation of financial statements and, in specified cases, on the regularity of the financial transactions included in them and any other legal and regulatory requirements. In central government, the auditor's report may also be referred to as a **Certificate**.

Audit Scotland – the body that supports the Auditor General for Scotland and the Accounts Commission (under their direction) in the exercise of their functions and, in particular, provides them, or ensures that they are provided, with the property, staff and services which they require for the exercise of those functions. Audit Scotland may make arrangements with any public body or office-holder for the provision of administrative, professional or technical services in connection with the conduct of audits.

Authorities – relevant Acts of Parliament, Statutory Instruments, directions, regulations, or other statutory guidance, and authorities issued by HM Treasury and by sponsoring departments using powers given in statute with which entities are required to comply.

Central government (sector) auditors – any external auditors or audit firm, from the public or private sectors, responsible for the external audit of an entity in central government.

Central government entities – defined as government departments and their executive agencies, any entity which operates as a trading fund (a government department, part of a department or an executive agency) and non-departmental public bodies. For the purposes of this Practice Note, central government does not include National Health Service bodies, local authorities, public corporations or nationalised industries.

Certificate (1) – the title of an audit report containing the opinion of the Comptroller and Auditor General, the Auditor General for Wales and the Comptroller and Auditor General for Northern Ireland on financial statements audited under statute where there is a statutory requirement for his examination to be certified, usually on the resource and other accounts produced by government departments (and on accounts produced by health entities in Wales and Northern Ireland). Use of the word 'certificate' clearly differentiates the audit report from any other report of the Comptroller and Auditor General, Auditor General for Wales and the Auditor General for Northern Ireland.

Certificate (2) – the declaration by auditors under the Audit Commission Act 1998 that the audit of a local government or health entity has been completed in accordance with the Act. The certificate is normally, but not necessarily, incorporated in the audit report. A similar certificate is issued by local government auditors in Wales under the Public Audit (Wales) Act 2004.

Chief Executive – the title applied to the senior official of an executive agency or non-departmental public body or an Assembly-sponsored public body accountable to the Secretary of State or Scottish Minister of the parent or sponsor department or National Assembly for Wales for the management and operations of that agency.

Code of Audit Practice – any document identified as such, issued by a national audit agency, that prescribes the way in which the auditor is to carry out their functions in respect of the audits of specified entities, embodying what the national audit agency considers to be the best professional practice with respect to the standards, procedures and techniques to be adopted by the auditor.

Code of Practice on Local Authority Accounting (SORP) – the document specifying the principles and practices of accounting required to prepare a Statement of Accounts which 'presents fairly' the financial position and transactions of a local government entity in the United Kingdom. Prepared by a joint committee of the Chartered Institute of Public Finance and Accountancy and the Local Authorities (Scotland) Accounts Advisory Committee, and endorsed by the Accounting Standards Board as a Statement of Recommended Practice.

Committee of Public Accounts – the Select Committee of the House of Commons empowered to inquire into the financial administration of government departments and examine their accounts. The Committee reports on its findings to the House of Commons. Similar committees exist in the Scottish Parliament and the Wales and Northern Ireland Assemblies.

Comptroller and Auditor General (the C&AG) – the head of the National Audit Office, appointed by the Crown and an Officer of the House of Commons. As Comptroller, the C&AG's duties are to authorise the issue by HM Treasury of public funds from the Consolidated Fund and National Loans Fund to government departments and others; as Auditor General, the C&AG certifies the accounts of all government departments and some other public bodies, and carries out value-for-money examinations.

Comptroller and Auditor General for Northern Ireland –the individual responsible for authorising the issue of public funds to Northern Ireland departments and other public sector bodies, for carrying out the audit of the financial statements of Northern Ireland central government and health entities (which includes satisfying himself that expenditure and income have been applied in accordance with the Assembly's intentions and conforms to governing authorities) and for examining the economy, efficiency and effectiveness with which Northern Ireland central government entities have discharged their functions.

Consolidated Fund – the central fund into which receipts from taxation and certain miscellaneous revenue are paid and from which comes money voted by Parliament by annual Supply procedures.

Consolidated Fund (Appropriation) Act – the Act that authorises issues from the Consolidated Fund and prescribes the overall sum to be appropriated to particular Estimates in order to finance specified services.

Corruption – the offering, giving, soliciting or acceptance of any inducement or reward that may influence the actions taken by an entity, its members or its officers.

Department of Finance and Personnel – the government department responsible for carrying out the HM Treasury role in Northern Ireland. Government Accounting Northern Ireland, issued by the Department of Finance and Personnel, sets out the overall rules and requirements for accountability and accounting in central government in Northern Ireland.

Entity – the generic term used in the Practice Note for any government department, executive agency, trading fund, non-departmental public body, company or other body or organisation which produces audited financial statements.

Excess vote (1) – audit qualifications where a department's expenditure has exceeded the resources or cash voted; or exceeded the Administration Budget set in the Estimate.

Excess vote (2) – the voting by Parliament to retrospectively approve additional resources or cash where the expenditure on a Resource Account exceeded the funds previously approved by Parliament or to amend the Ambit previously voted by Parliament.

Executive agency – an entity established to carry out the executive functions of government as distinct from providing policy advice. The term executive agency is a generic one that encompasses both bodies financed by departmental Supply Estimates and trading funds. See also **supply financed executive agency** and **Trading Fund**.

Financial memorandum – the document issued by the Secretary of State of a parent or sponsor department of an executive agency or a non-departmental public body which sets out the accounting and other rules governing the use of funds provided by Parliament for the entity's activities.

Government Accounting – the manual published by HM Treasury through The Stationery Office, which sets out the overall rules and requirements for accountability in central government.

Government Departments – these represent the top tier of central government. Parliament provides money annually to each department to spend for purposes that are specified in Supply Estimates. Each government department is headed by an

Accounting Officer who is responsible to Parliament for the application and expenditure of the funds provided in the Supply Estimates.

Government Financial Reporting Manual – the manual which sets out the principles applicable to the accounting and disclosure requirements for the preparation and presentation of accounts by central government entities.

Grant – payments made by departments to outside bodies to reimburse expenditure on agreed items or functions.

Grant-in-Aid – regular payments made by departments to outside bodies (usually non-departmental public bodies) to finance expenditure on agreed items or functions.

Health entities – individual corporate entities that are part of the National Health Service but that do not form part of a department or are constituted as executive agencies, non-departmental public bodies or public corporations. Includes strategic health authorities, NHS trusts and primary care trusts. In Wales, health entities are NHS Trusts and Local Health Boards. In Northern Ireland health entities are Health and Social Services Boards, Trusts and Special Agencies.

Legislation – Acts of Parliament and delegated or subordinate legislation including, for example, Statutory Instruments, or Rules and Orders issued by Ministers and submitted to Parliament. The term legislation also includes Regulations, Directives and Decisions issued by the European Council of Ministers and the European Commission.

Local Government Auditors – local government auditors in Northern Ireland are appointed to audits by the Department of the Environment under the Local Government Act (NI) 1972. The Audit and Accountability (Northern Ireland) Order 2003 provides for the Department of the Environment to designate persons who are members of staff of the Northern Ireland Audit Office as local government auditors with the consent of the Comptroller and Auditor General for Northern Ireland

Local government entities – entities whose auditors are subject to appointment by the Audit Commission (other than health entities), the Auditor General for Wales, the Accounts Commission or the Northern Ireland Department of the Environment. Includes local authorities, police authorities, fire authorities, National Park authorities, joint committees and joint boards.

Manual for Accounts – the documents produced by the Department of Health and Monitor for health entities each financial year giving more detailed instructions as to the meeting of the obligations set out in the relevant accounts direction. In Northern Ireland the Department of Health, Social Services and Public Safety produces manuals of accounts which are updated annually with Statement of Accounts guidance.

Members – the individuals of a local government or health entity, who have either been elected, nominated or appointed to non-executive positions or who are officers who have been appointed as board directors (health entities only).

Monitor - a non-departmental public body established under the Health and Social Care (Community Health and Standards) Act 2003. Monitor is the independent regulator of NHS Foundation Trusts and is responsible for authorising, monitoring and regulating NHS Foundation Trusts.

National audit agency – one of the United Kingdom agencies responsible for carrying out the audit of the financial statements of public sector bodies for a public sector auditor (the National Audit Office for the Comptroller and Auditor General, the Wales Audit Office for the Auditor General for Wales, Audit Scotland for the Auditor General for Scotland, the Accounts Commission, and the Northern Ireland Audit Office for the Comptroller and Auditor General for Northern Ireland) or for the appointment and regulation of auditors of public sector bodies (the Accounts Commission and the Auditor General for Scotland, the Audit Commission and the Auditor General for Wales). National audit agencies may also have responsibilities under statute or agreement for carrying out other assignments in their own right, such as examinations of economy, efficiency and effectiveness.

National Audit Office – the office that carries out the audit of the accounts of government departments and a wide range of public bodies on behalf of the Comptroller and Auditor General.

Non-departmental public body – an entity that has a role in the process of government but is neither a government department nor forms part of a department. It is established at arm's length from departments and may carry out executive, regulatory, administrative or commercial functions. (For Wales, see Assembly sponsored public bodies.)

Northern Ireland Audit Office – the office that carries out the audit of the accounts of central government departments, health entities and other public bodies on behalf of the Comptroller and Auditor General for Northern Ireland.

Officers – individuals employed by an entity to be responsible for the administration and operations of the entity.

Other responsibilities – any function, other than the audit of the financial statements and the giving of an opinion on regularity, that public sector auditors take on whether as a result of statutory prescriptions or direction by the relevant national audit agency.

Parent department – used in the context of executive agencies, in contrast with the term "sponsor department" as used for non-departmental public bodies, to refer to the government department which any individual executive agency remains a part of, both in terms of Parliamentary funding and accountability.

Parliament – the United Kingdom Parliament and the Scottish Parliament, but not the National Assembly for Wales or the Northern Ireland Assembly.

Principal Accountable Officer – the most senior member of the staff of the Scottish Administration, responsible for signing the accounts of the expenditure and receipts of the Scottish Administration or any part of it (so far as it is not a function of any Accountable Officer) and for ensuring the propriety and regularity of the finances of the Scottish Administration.

Principal Accounting Officer – the permanent head of a government department appointed by HM Treasury in compliance with section 5 of the Government Resources and Accounts Act 2000, as the Accounting Officer for the resource accounts of that department. In Wales, the Principal Accounting Officer for the National Assembly for Wales is appointed by HM Treasury under section 98 of the Government of Wales Act 1998. In Northern Ireland, the appointment is made by the Department of Finance and Personnel in compliance with section 9 of the Government Resources and Accounts Act (Northern Ireland) 2001.

Propriety – concerned with Parliament's intentions as to the way in which public business should be conducted, including the conventions agreed with Parliament and in particular, the Committee of Public Accounts.

Public Authorities – the Freedom of Information Act 2000 applies to approximately 100,000 public authorities. These public authorities are either listed as such in schedule 1 of the Act or have subsequently been designated as public authorities under Schedule 5 of the Act.

Regularity – the requirement that financial transactions are in accordance with the legislation authorising them, regulations issued by a body with the power to do so under governing legislation, Parliamentary authority and HM Treasury authority.

Request for Resources (RfR) – the functional level into which departmental Estimates may be split. RfRs contain a number of functions being carried out by the department in pursuit of one or more of that department's objectives.

Responsible financial officer – the officer appointed by a local government entity under section 151 of the Local Government Act 1972 to be responsible for the proper administration of its financial affairs.

Sponsor department – normally the department through which Parliamentary funding and accountability is made for non–departmental public bodies.

Subhead – individual elements of departmental expenditure identifiable in Estimates as single cells, for example A1 being administration costs within a particular line of departmental spending.

Supply - the money voted by Parliament to meet the services shown in Supply Estimates.

Supply Estimates – the detailed expenditure plans produced annually by and for government departments which are laid before Parliament and voted upon by the House of Commons.

Supply Financed Executive Agency – an executive agency which is either a department in its own right, or forms part of a government ('parent') department and is financed as a Supply service through an Estimate.

Tier – any level in a series of entities through which grant is passed down from Parliament to the intended recipients. Top tier entities are usually government departments. Lower tier entities comprise agencies, non-departmental public bodies and non-central government sector organisations.

Trading Fund – a department, and/or an executive agency established under the Government Trading Funds Act 1973 as amended by the Government Trading Act 1990. It is financed outside the Supply system and operates within a financing framework covering its operating costs and receipts, capital expenditure, borrowings and cash flows.

Virement – the transfer of savings on one subhead to meet excess expenditure on another subhead within the same Request for Resources, subject to HM Treasury approval.

Vote – this term refers to the process by which Parliament approves funds in response to Supply Estimates.

Wales Audit Office – The body established following the passing of the Public Audit (Wales) Act 2004 consisting of the Auditor General for Wales and his staff.

Appendix 2

The legislative framework governing the audit of public sector bodies in the UK

1. The Comptroller and Auditor General and the National Audit Office

The requirement for the Comptroller and Auditor General to carry out **financial statement audit** is set out in the Government Resources and Accounts Act 2000 (for central government) and also the Trading Funds Act 1973. The requirements for central government bodies other than departments and trading funds to prepare financial statements and the associated audit arrangements are covered in the legislation establishing the bodies.

For central government, the Government Resources and Accounts Act 2000 requires the Comptroller and Auditor General to satisfy himself that money provided by Parliament has been expended for the purposes intended by Parliament, that resources authorised by Parliament to be used have been used for the purposes in relation to which the use was authorised and that the department's financial transactions are in accordance with any relevant authority. This is known as **compliance with legislative authorities (regularity)**.

The National Audit Act 1983 empowers the Comptroller and Auditor General to carry out examinations into the **economy, efficiency and effectiveness** with which departments have used their resources in discharging their functions.

2. The Audit Commission

Under the Audit Commission Act 1998 the **audit of financial statements** in local government and NHS entities in England (excluding NHS Foundation Trusts) is the responsibility of the Audit Commission and its appointed auditors.

Auditors appointed under the Audit Commission Act 1998 are required to obtain satisfaction that the accounts have been prepared in accordance with relevant directions and regulations and comply with all other applicable statutory requirements.

Auditors of local government bodies are also specifically required to:

- consider applying to the Courts for a declaration that an item of account is unlawful; and
- consider whether to issue and, if appropriate, to issue an advisory notice or an application for judicial review.

Auditors of NHS bodies appointed under the Audit Commission Act 1998 are required to refer to a matter to the Secretary of State if there is reason to believe that NHS bodies have made or are about to make decisions involving potentially unlawful expenditure or have taken or are about to take potentially unlawful action likely to cause a loss or deficiency.

The Audit Commission Act 1998 requires that the Commission's appointed auditors obtain satisfaction that the audited body has made proper arrangements for securing **economy, efficiency and effectiveness** in its use of resources.

3. Monitor

Monitor was established under the Health and Social Care (Community Health and Standards) Act 2003. Monitor is the independent regulator of NHS Foundation Trust and is responsible for authorising, monitoring and regulating NHS Foundation Trusts.

4. The Auditor General for Wales and the Wales Audit Office

The office of Auditor General for Wales was established under the terms of the Government of Wales Act 1998. Under that Act, arrangements were made for the Auditor General to **examine and certify the accounts** of the National Assembly for Wales, and its sponsored and other related public bodies and to undertake economy, efficiency and effectiveness examinations. In examining and accounts, the AGW is required to satisfy himself that the expenditure has been incurred lawfully and in accordance with the authority which governs it.

The Public Audit (Wales) Act 2004, extended the Auditor General's functions by:

- appointing him as the external auditor of the accounts of all NHS Wales entities;
- giving him the responsibility for appointing the auditors of and undertaking value for money/performance studies on local government bodies in Wales; and
- giving him responsibility for undertaking best value inspections under the Local Government Act 1999 (known as the Wales Programme for Improvement).

The Auditor General and his staff form the Wales Audit Office.

The responsibilities of local government auditors in Wales are similar to those appointed by the Audit Commission in England (see above).

5. The Accounts Commission, the Auditor General for Scotland and Audit Scotland

The Accounts Commission for Scotland has a statutory duty under the Local Government (Scotland) Act 1973 to secure the audit of the accounts of local authorities in Scotland. The Act requires that the appointed auditor:

- satisfies himself that the financial statements of the body have been prepared in accordance with all statutory requirements applicable to the accounts;
- considers certain matters relating to legality, loss and deficiency;
- satisfies himself that the body has made proper arrangements for securing **best value and is complying with its duties for community planning**; and
- satisfies himself that a local authority has made adequate arrangements for collecting, recording and publishing prescribed performance standards.

Devolution in Scotland has had a major impact on this framework of responsibility, with the establishment of the Scottish Parliament, an Auditor General for Scotland and the formation of a public audit agency, Audit Scotland. Beyond the establishment of the office of the Auditor General for Scotland (contained in the Scotland Act 1998) detailed legislative provisions regarding the responsibilities of the Auditor General and accounting and audit arrangements are contained in the Public Finance and Accountability (Scotland) Act 2000. The Auditor General's responsibilities cover devolved central government bodies, health bodies, further education institutions and the water authority.

The Act provides for the establishment of Audit Scotland to support the Auditor General and the Accounts Commission in exercise of their respective functions. The Act also provides for the audit of accounts by the Auditor General. Under the Act, the auditor's report on such accounts must set out the auditor's findings on a number of matters. These include whether the expenditure and receipts shown in the account were incurred or applied in accordance with the appropriate authority or in accordance with applicable guidance issued by Scottish Ministers (whether as to propriety or otherwise).

The Act also provides for the Auditor General to initiate examinations into the economy, efficiency and effectiveness with which bodies and office holders referred to in the Act have used their resources in discharging their functions.

6. Northern Ireland

The Comptroller and Auditor General and the Northern Ireland Audit Office

The principal legislative authorities for the responsibility of the Comptroller and Auditor General in Northern Ireland, including the requirement to carry out the audit of the financial statements of Northern Ireland departments, executive agencies, trading funds and health entities, are the Exchequer and Audit Act (NI) 1921, the Northern Ireland Act 1998, the Government Resources and Accounts Act (Northern Ireland) 2001 and the Audit and Accountability (Northern Ireland) Order 2003. The requirement for other Northern Ireland central government bodies to prepare financial statements and the associated audit arrangements are covered in the legislation establishing the bodies.

For central government departments the Exchequer and Audit Act (NI) 1921, the Northern Ireland Act 1998, the Government Resources and Accounts Act (Northern Ireland) 2001 and the Audit and Accountability (Northern Ireland) Order 2003 require the Comptroller and Auditor General for Northern Ireland to satisfy himself that expenditure and income have been applied in accordance with the Assembly's intentions and conform to governing authorities (regularity).

The Audit (Northern Ireland) Order 1987 established the Northern Ireland Audit Office as an organisation independent of government. The Order also provided for the Comptroller and Auditor General for Northern Ireland to carry out **examinations into the economy, efficiency and effectiveness** with which any department, authority or other body to which the Order applies has used its resources in discharging its functions. This was extended by Section 60(2) of the Northern Ireland Act 1998, section 23 of the Resources and Accounts Act (Northern Ireland) 2001 and section 3 of the Audit and Accountability (Northern Ireland) Order 2003.

Local Government

The principal legislative authority for the responsibilities of local government auditors is contained in the Local Government Act (NI) Act 1972[21]

- consider applying to the court for a declaration that an item of account is unlawful;
- certify a sum due arising from any failure to account and certify losses caused by wilful misconduct; and

---

[21] *The Local Government (Northern Ireland) Order 2005 is being taken forward by the Department of Environment and when enacted will replace the audit provisions within the Local Government Act (Northern Ireland) 1972. and includes the audit of every district, borough and city council in Northern Ireland. Auditors of these local government audits are also specifically required to:*

- consider and, if appropriate, issue a prohibition order and an application for judicial review.

A local government auditor shall, if required by the Department of the Environment, carry out comparative and other studies aimed at making recommendations for improving economy, efficiency and effectiveness in the provision of services by councils.

Appendix 3

Risks to regularity and possible control procedures

Risk	Description	Mitigating Controls
Complexity of Regulations	The more complex the regulations the greater the risk of error. This may occur either through a misunderstanding or misinterpretation of the regulation or through an error in application.	• Formal procedures for the translation of statutory requirements into operating instructions. • Formal control plans prepared and monitored by scheme managers. • Review of scheme control plans and operating manuals by internal audit or some other independent audit.
New Legislation	New legislation may require the introduction of new administrative and control procedures. This may result in errors in either the design or operation of controls required to ensure regularity.	The controls identified above involving formal procedures for the translation of statutory requirements into scheme rules. Formal control plans and the independent review of operating instructions and control plans will also apply where schemes are introduced following new legislation.
European Union Schemes	Where legislation is developed by the European Commission there is a risk that regulations and guidance may be misinterpreted or omitted from internal instructions.	The mitigating controls identified in connection with the complexity of regulations apply equally to EU funded schemes.

Services and programmes delivered through third parties	Where programmes are administered by agents, departments lose a degree of direct control and may have to rely on agents to ensure compliance with authorities.	Formal agreements between the entity and the agent defining control procedures to be applied in the administration of services. • Management control and monitoring of third party activities. • Inspection visits by internal audit to third parties to review systems and procedures, including those relevant to regularity. • Independent certification of payments and receipts by the third parties' auditor.
Payments and receipts made on the basis of claims or declarations	An entity's ability to confirm compliance with authorities may be restricted where, for example, criteria specified for receipt of grant are not subject to direct verification.	• Established criteria for making claims, clearly set out in departmental instructions and guidance to claimants. • Standard requirements for documentation evidencing entitlement to be submitted in support of claims. (This may be a condition of payment of grant or a requirement once the activity supported by the grant has been completed). • Physical inspection of claimants' records etc., to confirm eligibility. • Procedures for assessing the financial standing of claimants before awarding a grant and for monitoring continuing solvency. • Independent certification of the application of grant by external auditor.

[PN 11]
The audit of charities in the United Kingdom (Revised)

(Issued December 2008)

Contents

	Page
Preface	3
Introduction	5
Special features of charities	10
Governance	
Operating structures and branches	
Sources of income	
Restricted funds	
Trading income	
The audit of financial statements	
ISAs (UK and Ireland)	16
200 Objective and General Principles Governing the Audit of Financial Statements	16
210 Terms of Audit Engagement	18
220 Quality Control for Audits of Historical Financial Information	20
240 The Auditor's Responsibility to Consider Fraud in an Audit of Financial Statements	22
250 Section A – Consideration of Laws and Regulations in an Audit of Financial Statements	25
Section B – The Auditors' Right and Duty to Report to Regulators in the Financial Sector	32
260 Communication of Audit Matters with Those Charged with Governance	40
300 Planning an Audit of Financial Statements	42
315 Obtaining an Understanding of the Entity and Its Environment and Assessing the Risks of Material Misstatement	44
320 Audit Materiality	52
330 The Auditor's Procedures in response to Assessed Risks	54
402 Audit Considerations Relating to Entities Using Service Organisations	59
505 External Confirmations	62
510 Opening Balances	63
520 Analytical Procedures	64
540 Audit of Accounting Estimates	65
545 Auditing Fair Value Measurements and Disclosures	67
550 Related Parties	69
560 Subsequent Events	71
570 The Going Concern Basis in Financial Statements	72
580 Management Representations	76
600 Using the Work of Another Auditor (Revised)	78
700 The Auditor's Report on Financial Statements	80

720 Section A – Other Information in Documents Containing Audited Financial
     Statements   84
     Section B – The Auditor's Statutory Reporting Responsibility in Relation to
     Directors' Reports

Summary Financial Information and Summarised Financial Statements   87

Appendices

1. Charity accounting and audit regulations in the United Kingdom
2. Publications
3. Example paragraphs for insertion into an engagement letter
4. Illustrative example statements of trustees' responsibilities
5. The duty of auditors to report matters of material significance to the Charity
   Commission and OSCR
6. Control activities
7. Definitions
8. Some significant topics relevant to audits of charities

Preface

This Practice Note contains guidance on the application of Auditing Standards issued by the Auditing Practices Board (APB) to the audit of charities in the United Kingdom.

The Practice Note is supplementary to, and should be read in conjunction with, International Standards on Auditing (ISAs) (UK and Ireland), which apply to all audits undertaken in the United Kingdom. It sets out the special considerations relating to the audit of charities which arise from individual ISAs (UK and Ireland). The Practice Note does not, and is not intended to, provide detailed guidance on the audits of charities, so where no special considerations arise from a particular ISA (UK and Ireland), no material is included.

This Practice Note supersedes the guidance included in Practice Note 11 'The audit of charities in the United Kingdom' (Revised) issued by the APB in April 2002, and takes account of significant regulatory and other developments affecting charities since that date, including:

- the replacement of Statements of Auditing Standards by ISAs (UK and Ireland),
- the implementation of the Companies Act 2006 for accounting periods commencing on or after 6 April 2008,
- changes to the Charities Act 1993 which apply to charities in England and Wales for accounting periods commencing on or after 1 April 2008
- changes arising from the introduction of the Charities and Trustee Investment (Scotland) Act 2005 which apply to charities in Scotland for accounting periods commencing 1 April 2006 and
- the establishment of the Office of the Scottish Charity Regulator (OSCR).

The legal framework for charities is complex and different requirements exist depending on the charity's constitution, the part of the UK in which it is established and the type of activity it undertakes. The Practice Note contains guidance for auditors; the APB's intention is not to provide a comprehensive commentary on all aspects of law that may apply to a charity's operations, and the Practice Note should not be used as a substitute for appropriate consultation with legal advisers.

The Practice Note is based on the legislation and regulations that are effective at 1 November 2008. Further changes to the legislative framework are anticipated but are not addressed in this guidance including:

- The introduction of a new form of charity, a Charitable Incorporated Organisation (CIO),
- Changes to the regulation of charities in Northern Ireland, and
- Changes to reporting thresholds.

This Practice Note has been prepared with advice and assistance from staff of the Charity Commission for England and Wales, the Office of the Scottish Charity Regulator (OSCR), and the Department for Social Development in Northern Ireland.

Introduction

The purpose of this Practice Note is to give guidance on the application of ISAs (UK and Ireland) to the audit of charities in the United Kingdom. ISAs (UK and Ireland) contain the basic principles and essential procedures, referred to as Auditing Standards, which are indicated in the text of the ISAs (UK and Ireland) by bold type and with which auditors are required to comply, except where otherwise stated in the conduct of any audit of financial statements.

2   Audits of charities required by legislation in the United Kingdom may only be carried out by a registered auditor, or other persons authorised by statute or to whom, in England and Wales, the Charity Commission may grant dispensation[1]. Registered auditors are required to comply with Auditing Standards when conducting audits. This principle applies to charity audits, irrespective of their size, but the way in which Auditing Standards are applied needs to be adapted to suit the particular characteristics of the entity audited.

3   Where an audit is being performed on an entity within the Public Sector in the United Kingdom this Practice Note complements Practice Note 10: the Audit of Financial Statements of Public Sector Bodies in the United Kingdom (Revised).

4   Audit exemption thresholds are established in UK legislation and an independent examination will often be permitted instead of an audit. Guidance on the conduct of independent examinations in England & Wales has been published by The Charity Commission[2]. OSCR has yet to prepare guidance specifically for independent examiners of charities registered in Scotland; however, example independent examiners reports are available within the accounts guidance on its website. An independent examination is significantly different from an audit, and is often not required to be undertaken by a registered auditor or indeed, by a qualified accountant. This Practice Note does not provide guidance on independent examinations.

Legislative and regulatory framework

5   The legal framework for charities is complex, and different requirements exist depending on the charity's constitution, the part of the United Kingdom in which the charity is established, or is active, and the type of activity which it undertakes. In addition, charities are affected by the whole range of national legislation applicable to business entities, such as employment, tax and pensions law and health and safety regulations.

6   The main laws that relate to a charity's financial statements and audit are:
   - All company charities: the Companies Act 2006 (CA 2006);
   - Charities in England and Wales: the Charities Act 1993 (as amended by the Charities Act 2006);
   - All charities registered in Scotland with OSCR: the Charities and Trustee Investment (Scotland) Act 2005 (2005 Act (Scotland));
   - Non-company charities in Northern Ireland: the Charities Act (Northern Ireland) 1964.

7   The legal requirements in relation to accounting and audit for charities in Scotland and Northern Ireland differ in some respects from that applicable in England and

---

[1] *The dispensation arises where a charity is audited under another statutory regime which is considered sufficiently similar to the audit requirements of the Charities Act or audited under arrangements which are sufficiently similar. The Charity Commission can also give a dispensation from audit in exceptional circumstances allowing an independent examination in place of an audit.*

[2] *Independent Examination of Charity Accounts, Directions and Guidance Notes.*

Wales, and it is important for auditors to understand what legislation applies. The legislation relating to accounting and audit applicable to each jurisdiction in the United Kingdom is summarised in Appendix 1 – Charity accounting and audit regulations in the United Kingdom.

The regulatory framework is also complex. The principal regulators for charities (which are referred to as 'the charity regulators' in this Practice Note) are: 8

- England and Wales: the Charity Commission;
- Scotland: Office of the Scottish Charity Regulator (OSCR);
- Northern Ireland: Department for Social Development.

Appendix 1 to this Practice Note provides a summary of the regulatory framework for each of these jurisdictions.

The Charity Commission has powers under legislation to act for the protection of charity property where in the course of an inquiry it is satisfied that there has been misconduct or mismanagement in the administration of a charity, or that it is necessary to act for the purposes of protecting the property of a charity or to secure its proper application for the purposes of the charity. These powers include: 9

- issuing directions to the trustees;
- suspension of any trustee, officer, agent or employee;
- appointment of additional trustees;
- removal of a trustee, officer, agent or employee;
- freezing of property, restrictions on transactions or payments; and
- appointment of an interim manager.

In Scotland, OSCR has similar powers under sections 28, 31 and 34 of the Charities and Trustee Investment (Scotland) Act 2005. In Northern Ireland the Department for Social Development also has some, though more restricted, powers to intervene in a charity's affairs.

Charities with significant operations in Scotland but established in another jurisdiction are required to register separately with OSCR and to comply with the 2005 Act (Scotland) and regulations made thereunder. OSCR has prepared guidance on registration entitled 'Guidance on Registration with OSCR for England and Wales Charities' (September 2006)[3]. The Guidance includes a number of self-assessment questions to assist in determining whether registration with OSCR is required and, although it refers to English and Welsh charities, the principles apply to Northern Irish charities with operations in Scotland. OSCR has formally delayed the monitoring of English and Welsh charities with operations in Scotland while it discusses with the Charity Commission how best to minimise the regulatory burden of dual regulation and monitoring[4]. 10

In addition to relevant charities legislation and regulations, charities may be subject to other regulatory regimes. Examples of bodies which, when constituted as charities, may be subject to additional and/or different accounting and audit requirements include companies, registered social landlords, friendly societies, non-departmental public bodies (NDPBs), universities and further education colleges. Statements of 11

---

[3] *'Guidance on Registration with OSCR for England and Wales Charities' (September 2006) is available on the OSCR website.*

[4] *OSCR will be carrying out a consultation in late 2008 on the proposed monitoring regime for dual registration charities with a view to implementing a monitoring programme in Spring 2009.*

Recommended Practice (SORPs) are issued in relation to a number of such sectors, and need to be taken into account in preparing charities' financial statements.

Charity governing documents

12 The governing document of the charity establishes the purpose and constitution of the charity. It may also require an audit to be undertaken (which may supplement, but not derogate from, a statutory requirement for an audit). There is no such thing as a standard charity; the governing document of each charity is individual and will need careful consideration to identify matters relevant to the audit such as particular charitable objects and any special powers conferred on the trustees.

13 The terms of charities' governing documents tend to be narrower than those for commercial entities, the objects of which are usually very generally phrased. This means that the auditors are much more likely to be faced with a situation where a client charity has acted ultra vires or in breach of trust than would be the case with an entity in the commercial sector.

14 Any transaction by a charity that is undertaken outside its objects and powers is potentially a breach of trust. Such transactions require particular consideration. Non-compliance with the governing document is also likely to have financial implications for the charity, and thus needs to be taken into account in determining whether the financial statements give a true and fair view. Charities are broadly exempt from direct tax on their charitable activities and therefore if transactions are outside the objects, or involve substantial donors, there may also be tax implications. In addition such transactions may give rise to a need to report the matter to the charity regulator.

Accounting and auditing requirements

15 The financial statements of a charity which are prepared to give a true and fair view[5] under the requirements of either the Charities Act 1993 or the 2005 Act (Scotland) and/or companies legislation are required to be prepared in accordance with applicable law and regulations, and UK accounting standards.

16 UK Generally Accepted Accounting Practice (UK GAAP) comprises law and accounting standards issued by the Accounting Standards Board, including where applicable the FRSSE. Charities cannot currently apply International Financial Reporting Standards.

17 The Statement of Recommended Practice 'Accounting and Reporting by Charities' (the Charities SORP) is an interpretation of UK accounting standards for the charity sector and is intended to apply to the accounts of all charities in the United Kingdom required to give a true and fair view (unless a separate SORP exists for a particular class of charities[6]). The Charities SORP issued in March 2005 by the Charity Commission is likely to be replaced by an updated Charities SORP issued by the Charity Commission and OSCR, which is anticipated once the ASB has determined the convergence timetable of UK GAAP with IFRS.

---

[5] *Trustees of small non-company charities in England and Wales and Scotland which are within the income thresholds defined by legislation may elect to prepare financial statements on a receipts and payments basis. Financial statements prepared on a receipts and payments basis are not required to give a true and fair view.*

[6] *Where sector specific SORPs exist eg. for Registered Social Landlords, and Further and Higher Educational Institutions, the specialist SORP takes precedence).*

18 FRS 18- Accounting Policies- requires a statement that financial statements have been prepared in accordance with the relevant SORP, and details of any departures from the recommended practice and disclosures. Consequently, it is normally necessary to follow the guidance set out in the Charities SORP in order to give a true and fair view, as required by legislation.

19 Apart from any requirement for audit in the governing document, the statutory requirement for audit depends on the size of the charity, as defined in relevant legislation or regulations. Audit exemption thresholds are described in Appendix 1. For company charities the interaction between the thresholds established in the CA 2006, the Charities Act 1993 and the 2005 Act (Scotland) need to be considered.

20 A number of non-departmental public bodies are charities. The auditors of such bodies are responsible for expressing an opinion on both the view given by the body's financial statements and on whether the expenditure of the body is in accordance with the purposes intended by Parliament[7]. Furthermore, for some bodies where the auditor is appointed by the Secretary of State, there may be a requirement in the auditor's terms of engagement for them to report to the sponsor department any significant matters arising out of their audit work, including losses incurred owing to failures of internal control, misconduct, fraud or other irregularity.

Reports to third parties

21 In addition to the auditor's report on the financial statements, auditors of charities may be requested to provide additional reports in relation to grant-funded projects, giving assurance on matters such as the proper use of money and costs to completion. This Practice Note does not cover such additional engagements[8].

Reporting direct to the charity regulators

22 In addition to their primary objective of reporting on financial statements, auditors of charities may have an additional statutory duty to report in certain circumstances to the relevant charity regulator. This duty is discussed in the section giving guidance on ISA (UK and Ireland) 250 section B: The auditor's right and duty to report to regulators in the financial sector.

Special features of charities

23 There is a great diversity of charities in terms of constitution, activity and size. The smallest are local, single activity operations sometimes run by trustees with limited financial expertise, whereas the largest are international organisations with multiple activities, employing many full-time professional staff and operating sophisticated accounting systems. Despite this diversity there are special features of charities which will influence the planning and performance of all charity audits.

---

[7] Practice Note 10 (Revised) provides guidance for auditors of public bodies on reporting on the regularity of expenditure.

[8] Guidance has been provided by ICAEW in Audit 3/03 – Public sector special reporting engagements – grant claims.

Governance

24 Although the detail of regulation differs between different parts of the United Kingdom, the general principles governing the duties of trustees are the same regardless of what they are called in the charity's governing document[9]. They must comply with the charity's governing document. Trustees:

- have the general duty of protecting all the charity's property;
- are responsible for the solvency and continuing effectiveness of the charity and the preservation of any permanent endowments; and
- must exercise control over the charity's financial affairs.

25 Trustee duties and responsibilities[10] include, but are not limited to:

- where a particular function is delegated to staff or third parties, monitoring the performance of the delegated function and clearly setting out the scope and limits of the delegated authority;
- acting in accordance with the charity's governing document, in particular, the income and property of the charity must be applied for the purposes set out in the governing document and, in the case of any restricted fund, within the particular trusts attaching to that fund, and for no other purpose;
- acting reasonably and prudently in the charity's interests only and without regard to their own private interests;
- not deriving remuneration or benefit personally from the charity unless explicit powers exist to do so;
- maintaining proper accounting records and preparation of accounts required by the regulatory regime under which they operate;
- being able and willing to give time to the efficient administration of the charity and the fulfillment of its trusts.

In addition, trustees are required to have regard to the regulators' guidance on how charities meet their public benefit requirement.

26 Trustees may not profit out of transactions with the charity or receive any remuneration or benefit from it unless there is express provision for this in the charity's governing document[11], the transaction is authorised by the relevant public authority, (in England and Wales usually the Charity Commission), or the conditions set out in paragraph 211 below apply.

27 It is possible for employees to be appointed as trustees if this is provided for in a charity's governing document or, in England and Wales, is otherwise authorised. Typically, the authority will draw a clear distinction between their functions as employees, conducting the operations of the charity in accordance with the trustees' policy, for which they may be paid, and time spent acting as trustees, to which the remuneration authority would not usually extend[12]. Similarly, professionally qualified trustees may only charge the charity for their firm's or their own professional services if the conditions set out above are applicable.

[9] *Charity trustees are defined in legislation as "the persons having the general control and management of the administration of a charity".*

[10] *Comprehensive information regarding trustees' duties and responsibilities is set out in guidance issued by the charity regulators.*

[11] *For charities registered in Scotland, the authorising provision would have to have been in force on 15 November 2004.*

[12] *In Scotland the authority applies to all services as there is no distinction drawn.*

The Charities SORP and the Regulations in both England and Wales and Scotland require the accounts of a charity to disclose most transactions between the trustees and the charity, and trustee remuneration/benefits from the charity, whether authorised or not. The disclosure requirements are widely drawn to include a person connected with a charity trustee and companies or institutions connected with the charity. 28

Charity trustees are usually unpaid and part time, and governance structures can be very varied. In planning the audit, the auditor needs to understand the nature of the charity's governance and the influence that this has on the control environment of the charity (see ISA (UK and Ireland) 315) and on reporting to those charged with governance (see ISA (UK and Ireland) 260). 29

Operating structures and branches

Charities can adopt a variety of organisational structures including: 30

- a single centrally-administered organisation,
- a centrally-administered organisation with branches both in the UK and overseas, and
- a parent charity with a group structure including subsidiaries, joint ventures and associates.

A charity may operate through branches to raise funds or carry out particular aspects of its charitable activities. The auditor needs to understand whether entities in the wider structure adopted by a charity fall within the definition of branches in the Charities SORP as such branches will be accounted for as part of the charity. The principles set out in the Charities SORP apply whether operations are carried out in the UK or overseas. In England and Wales separate charities may account as one entity where a uniting direction has been issued by the Charity Commission. Such entities will normally be listed as subsidiary registrations by the Charity Commission.

The auditor also needs to be aware that some charities will use the term "branches" outside of its Charities SORP meaning to describe a network of charities which are administratively autonomous and as such are separate accounting entities. The constitutional provisions in such cases may require careful consideration. Audits of independent (or autonomous) branches should be regarded as separate engagements. 31

Joint venture situations whereby two or more charities jointly control an entity or undertake joint arrangements in partnership to carry out an activity sometimes exist. The auditor needs to understand the structure adopted in such arrangements and how they are differentiated from participating interests in associates. The Charities SORP provides guidance on this issue and the accounting methods to be adopted. 32

The auditor will also need to consider the terms on which branches raise funds. Local appeals may be for specific purposes, and where this is the case such funds will be restricted in the accounts of the main charity. The Charities SORP requires non autonomous branches (see definition in Appendix 7 of this Practice Note) to be accounted for in the entity's financial statements and for consolidated financial statements to be prepared in group situations. 33

Sources of income

Sources of income (other than trading income) giving rise to particular audit issues include: 34

- cash donations,
- legacies,
- gifts in kind and donated services,
- contractual income, and
- grants, for example from public authorities or other charities.

Donations may be made tax effectively, through gift aid, payroll giving, and gifts of land and shares. For most tax effective schemes, and especially for gift aid, there are detailed requirements relating to the procedures to be followed by donors and recipient charities, as well as detailed rules designed to prevent abuse (for instance the substantial donor rules or reciprocal benefit limits). Auditors consider the implications of the significance of these income streams and adapt their procedures accordingly.

35 Obtaining assurance as to the completeness of recorded donation income can be difficult as such income will not always be supported by invoices or equivalent documentation. Where cash donations are received, the trustees need to make arrangements to institute appropriate controls, to the extent practicable, to ensure that all income is properly accounted for. Auditors are likely to rely on evidence concerning such controls in order to form a view on the completeness of the income shown in its financial statements.

36 The use of autonomous branches, agents or loosely affiliated volunteer groups for fund-raising needs to be considered when determining the appropriate method of income recognition for donations[13].

37 Trustees need to understand the terms attaching to legacies in order to consider the application of the charity's income recognition policies, and the valuation of donations in kind.

38 An understanding of the conditions underlying contractual or grant income is also necessary to determine the proper accounting treatment. As well as distinguishing whether the income is restricted or not, the nature of the terms and conditions may affect taxation considerations (for example the Value Added Tax (VAT) treatment).

39 Income received under contract is unrestricted income while grants for the provision of a specific service normally give rise to restricted income. However the terminology used to describe funding arrangements can differ, particularly in respect to international charities, and the auditor seeks to understand the nature of all significant funding arrangements to determine the proper accounting treatment.

40 Grants are often made for specific purposes and are subject to conditions, breach of which can have serious implications for the charity. Developments in the public sector mean that auditors of a public authority donor may have, or seek, the right of access to the charity's records to follow through and verify the use made of the grant. In addition grants from public bodies are increasingly subject to claw back provisions requiring repayment if a charity breaches specified conditions.

Restricted funds

41 Restricted funds are subject to specific trusts, which may be declared by the donor or created through legal process. They may be restricted income funds (which are

---

[13] *The Charities SORP states that income recognition is dependent on entitlement, certainty of receipt and the monetary value being measurable with sufficient reliability.*

expendable at the discretion of the trustees in furtherance of some particular aspect of the objects of the charity) or they may be endowments (where the assets are required to be invested or retained for actual use rather than expended) (see SORP definition in Appendix 7). If restricted funds are used other than in the way specified, the trustees of the charity will have breached their duty.

The Charities SORP indicates that restricted funds are to be separately disclosed in the charity's financial statements. Consequently, auditors consider whether restrictions are likely to exist as part of their planning process and when assessing the presentation of funds in a charity's balance sheet. Auditors also establish whether they may be requested to issue a special report to the donor organisation in respect of grants or restricted funds. 42

Trading income

Whilst charities do not enjoy a general exemption from direct taxation, there are significant tax exemptions available to charities both in relation to income and chargeable gains. Auditors need to have an understanding of these statutory exemptions and extra-statutory concessions in order to identify incoming resources that may fall outside their scope. Where income is receivable that does not fall within such reliefs, a charity can be exposed to significant tax liabilities. 43

The existence of trading activities can affect the charity's compliance with laws and regulations, potential tax liabilities and, in some cases, can give rise to matters to be reported to the relevant charity regulator as a result of the auditors' statutory duty to report. Trading by charities falls into two main categories 44

- primary purpose trading (also known as charitable trading) which is generally exempt from direct taxation, and
- trading to raise funds for charitable purposes, which is generally not exempt from direct taxation.

Primary purpose trading is the exercise of a trade in the course of the actual carrying out of a primary purpose of a charity, for example the charging of fees by a school which is established as a charity for the advancement of education. The tax exemption available on primary purpose trading also extends to trades where the work is mainly carried out by the beneficiaries of the charity and the remedial or educational value of the work to the beneficiaries can be demonstrated. 45

Charitable trading may also extend beyond primary purpose activities to incorporate 'ancillary trading'. Ancillary trading, which contributes indirectly to the successful furtherance of the purposes of the charity, is treated as part of 'primary purpose trading' for both charity law and tax purposes. An example of ancillary trading is the sale of food and drink in a restaurant or bar by a theatre charity to members of an audience. The level of annual turnover which is said to be ancillary may have a bearing on the question whether the trading really is ancillary, but there is no specific level of annual turnover beyond which trading will definitely not be regarded as ancillary. 46

Trading for fund-raising purposes and other non-charitable trading activities, where undertaken directly by a charity on a substantial or regular basis, may be contrary to charity law and the profits may be liable to income or corporation tax. If a relevant power exists a charity may trade on a small scale for fund-raising purposes. The usual test for permissibility (although not invariably) is whether the trades fall within the tax exemptions for small trading activities or the concessional relief for fund-raising events. 47

48 Substantial permanent trading for fund-raising purposes would also be incompatible with charitable status, and generally such trades would be hived off to a wholly-owned subsidiary company. Similarly, a failure to apply such income or gains for charitable purposes only can result in loss of tax relief. The impact of a tax assessment, perhaps going back a number of years, may affect a charity's ability to conduct its business.

49 Charities enjoy no general exemption from VAT which can apply to a range of goods and services supplied in the course of business. Certain primary purpose trading activities as well as trading for fund-raising purposes can fall within the wider meaning of business activity for VAT purposes. Many areas in which charities operate, such as the supply of certain educational, health and welfare services, or cross-charging for services, may be exempt from VAT, and a number of special reliefs also apply specifically to charities[14]. Non-compliance or errors could have adverse financial consequences for the charity.

The audit of financial statements

ISAs (UK and Ireland) apply to the conduct of all audits. This includes audits of the financial statements of charities. The purpose of the following paragraphs is to identify the special considerations arising from the application of certain 'bold letter' requirements to the audit of charities, and to suggest ways in which these can be addressed (extracts from ISAs (UK and Ireland) are indicated by grey-shaded boxes below). This Practice Note does not contain commentary on all of the bold letter requirements included in the ISAs (UK and Ireland) and reading it should not be seen as an alternative to reading the relevant ISAs (UK and Ireland) in their entirety. In addition, where no special considerations arise from a particular ISA (UK and Ireland), no material is included.

ISA (UK AND IRELAND) 200: OBJECTIVE AND GENERAL PRINCIPLES GOVERNING THE AUDIT OF THE FINANCIAL STATEMENTS

Background note

The purpose of this ISA (UK and Ireland) is to establish standards and provide guidance on the objective and general principles governing an audit of financial statements.

The auditor should plan and perform an audit with an attitude of professional scepticism, recognising that circumstances may exist that cause the financial statements to be materially misstated. (paragraph 6)

50 A fundamental principle is that practitioners should not accept or perform work which they are not competent to undertake. The importance of technical competence is also underlined in the Auditor's Code, issued by the APB, which states that the necessary degree of professional skill demands an understanding of financial reporting and business. Practitioners should not undertake the audit of a charity

---

[14] *A number of specific exemptions and zero-rating treatments may be available in relation to supplies by and to a charity.*

unless they are satisfied that they have, or can obtain, the necessary level of competence. The auditor's responsibilities in this respect are not related to the level of fee charged for the audit. For example, the same levels of rigour are required in respect of audits carried out on an honorary basis as for audits carried out for a commercial fee.

Auditing Standards include a requirement for auditors to comply with relevant ethical requirements relating to audit engagements. In the United Kingdom, the auditor should comply with the APB's Ethical Standards (ESs) and relevant ethical guidance relating to the work of auditors issued by the auditor's professional body. 51

Particular issues that the audit engagement partner of a charity has regard to when assessing possible threats to the independence and objectivity and the nature and extent of the safeguards to be applied include: 52

- self interest – in addition to financial interests, the auditor needs to be aware of other interests in a charity which may affect the conduct or outcome of the audit. The auditor therefore ensures that none of the audit team is in any way dependant upon the charity or are involved in providing significant support to the charity.
- self review – auditors will often be asked to provide additional help and advice, often on a pro bono basis. The provision of this service is regarded in the same way as other non-audit services in assessing whether there is a threat to objectivity.

The ESs include a small number of additional requirements that apply to the audits of listed companies[15]. ES1 establishes that an audit firm's policies and procedures will set out the circumstances in which these additional requirements apply to the audits of non-listed clients (which may include some charities), taking into consideration the nature of the entity's business, its size, the number of its employees and the range of its stakeholders.

Where safeguards include the review by an engagement quality control reviewer, that individual should have sufficient knowledge of the charity regulatory framework to enable a meaningful review to be completed. 53

ISA (UK AND IRELAND) 210: TERMS OF AUDIT ENGAGEMENT

Background note

The purpose of this ISA (UK and Ireland) is to establish standards and provide guidance on agreeing the terms of the engagement with the client.

The auditor and the client should agree on the terms of the engagement. (paragraph 2)

The auditor should ensure that the engagement letter documents and confirms the auditor's acceptance of the appointment, and includes a summary of the responsibilities of those charged with governance and of the auditor, the scope of the engagement and the form of any reports. (paragraph 5-1)

---

[15] These are set out in paragraph 41 of ES 1 (Revised).

54 The same basic principles used in drafting engagement letters apply in relation to the audit of charities as to the audit of any entity. Practical considerations arising from the particular characteristics of charities are considered below.

55 Paragraph 1-5 of ISA (UK and Ireland) 210 indicates that the term 'client' used in paragraph 1 means the addressee of the auditor's report (the client is the trustee(s)). Consequently, the auditor agrees the terms of the engagement with the trustees of the charity and addresses the letter of engagement to the trustees.

56 The auditor may consider checking that all the trustees receive a copy of the letter. If the trustees are not engaged in the day-to-day running of the charity, the auditor may wish to send a copy of the engagement letter to the chief executive or the persons responsible for its day-to-day management, together with a more detailed description of the audit work to be undertaken and any client assistance to be given.

57 Matters that will normally be included in an engagement letter for a charity are:
- the legislative framework under which the financial statements are prepared and the audit is conducted[16];
- the statutory duty to report to the charity regulators any matters of which auditors become aware that may be of material significance to the respective regulators;
- access to information, recognising that not all charities are constituted as limited companies (for which auditors' rights of access are enshrined in company law).

58 Trustees may issue other reports to stakeholders in addition to the annual report required by statute. For example, they may provide summary reports and financial statements, and periodic newsletters. Where this is the case, the engagement letter also sets out the auditor's responsibilities, if any, in respect of such other reports.

59 It is the responsibility of the trustees to identify the need for any additional reports required by funders and to instruct the auditor accordingly: it will not be practicable for the auditor to check the documentation relating to all funds received by the charity to identify any conditions requiring special reports. However the auditor may consider it appropriate to enquire of the trustees whether any reports are required in addition to the auditor's report on the charity's financial statements. Separate engagement letters will be obtained for non-audit work undertaken on behalf of the charity or its trustees.

> On recurring audits, the auditor should consider whether circumstances require the terms of the engagement to be revised and whether there is a need to remind the client of the existing terms of the engagement. (paragraph 10)

60 ISA (UK and Ireland) 210 sets out a number of reasons as to why an engagement letter should be revised on a recurring audit. In the case of charities, these reasons are also applicable including changes in the legal and regulatory framework or a new SORP.

Appendix 3 sets out example paragraphs for an engagement letter for the audit of:

---

[16] At present, the Charities Accounts (Scotland) Regulations 2006 also include the Trustees' Annual Report within the statement of account which is subject to audit. To address this unintended effect of the Regulations, the APB understands that the Scottish Government intends to amend the Regulations in order to remove any disparity with other UK jurisdictions.

- England and Wales: non-company (accruals basis)
- England and Wales: non-company (receipts and payments basis)
- England and Wales: company
- Scotland: non-company (accruals basis)
- Scotland: non-company (receipts and payments basis)
- Scotland: company
- Cross-border charity.

ISA (UK AND IRELAND) 220: QUALITY CONTROL FOR AUDITS OF HISTORICAL FINANCIAL INFORMATION

Background note

The purpose of this ISA (UK and Ireland) is to establish standards and provide guidance on specific responsibilities of firm personnel regarding quality control procedures for audits of historical financial information, including audits of financial statements.

The engagement team should implement quality control procedures that are applicable to the individual audit engagement.(paragraph 2)

The engagement partner should be satisfied that the engagement team collectively has the appropriate capabilities, competence and time to perform the audit engagement in accordance with professional standards and regulatory and legal requirements, and to enable an auditor's report that is appropriate in the circumstances to be issued. (paragraph 19)

61 The requirements of International Standard on Quality Control (UK and Ireland) 1 – Quality Control for Firms that Perform Audits and Reviews of Historical Financial Information, and other Assurance and Related Services Engagements apply to all audits. Matters of particular relevance to charity audits are:

- the requirement in paragraph 36 regarding the need for sufficient staff with the capabilities, competence and commitment to ethical principles necessary to perform audit engagements;
- the requirement in paragraph 42 (b) that the engagement partner has the appropriate capabilities, competence, authority and time to perform the role;
- the requirement in paragraph 51 that the firm should establish policies and procedures designed to provide it with reasonable assurance that appropriate consultation takes place and is documented; and
- the requirement in paragraph 60(b) that audit firms establish policies and procedures for determining when an engagement quality control review should be performed on audits other than listed companies.

Staff capabilities, competence

62 As explained in paragraph 50 of this Practice Note competence is emphasised in the Auditor's Code. As well as ensuring that the engagement team has an appropriate level of knowledge of the charity sector, the engagement partner also satisfies himself that the members of the engagement team have sufficient knowledge, commensurate with their roles in the engagement, of:

(a) the Charities SORP;
(b) the governing document of the charity;
(c) the legal responsibilities and duties of charity trustees; and
(d) the regulatory framework within which charities operate

to identify situations which may give them reasonable cause to believe that a matter should be reported to a charity regulator.

Engagement Quality Control Reviews

63   ISQC (UK and Ireland) 1 requires audit firms to establish policies and procedures which set out criteria to determine whether engagement quality control reviews should be performed. Guidance to ISQC 1 notes that one of the criteria that a firm considers when determining whether to require completion of an engagement quality control review includes the nature of the engagement, including the extent to which it involves a matter of public interest. What is a matter of public interest is difficult to define: factors that may apply to a charity include:

- the size of the charity;
- its national or local profile;
- its sources of funds (including the extent to which the charity receives public funds).

ISA (UK AND IRELAND) 240: THE AUDITOR'S RESPONSIBILITY TO CONSIDER FRAUD IN AN AUDIT OF FINANCIAL STATEMENTS

Background note

The purpose of this ISA(UK and Ireland) is to establish standards and to provide guidance on the auditor's responsibility to consider fraud in an audit of financial statements and expand on how the standards and guidance in ISA (UK and Ireland) 315 and ISA (UK and Ireland) 330 are to be applied in relation to the risks of material misstatement due to fraud.

In planning and performing the audit to reduce audit risk to an acceptably low level, the auditor should consider the risks of material misstatements in the financial statements due to fraud. (paragraph 3)

The auditor should maintain an attitude of professional scepticism throughout the audit, recognising the possibility that a material misstatement due to fraud could exist, notwithstanding the auditor's past experience with the entity about the honesty and integrity of management and those charged with governance. (paragraph 24)

The auditor should make inquiries of management, internal audit, and others within the entity as appropriate, to determine whether they have knowledge of any actual, suspected or alleged fraud affecting the entity. (paragraph 38)

The auditor should make inquiries of those charged with governance to determine whether they have knowledge of any actual, suspected or alleged fraud affecting the entity. (paragraph 46)

The trustees of a charity are responsible for the prevention and detection of fraud in relation to the charity, even if they have delegated some of their executive functions to senior staff. They are expected to safeguard charity assets and reserves through the implementation of appropriate systems of control. The auditor of a charity is responsible for forming an opinion as to whether financial statements show a true and fair view and to this end the auditor plans, performs and evaluates audit work in order to have a reasonable expectation of detecting material misstatements in the financial statements arising from error or fraud. 64

Many charities receive funds which have restrictions placed upon them. These funds are held on trust and must be applied to the purpose for which they were given. The misappropriation or misapplication of funds constitutes a breach of trust, whether it was intentional or accidental. In planning, performing and evaluating the audit work the auditor considers the risk of material misstatement arising from breaches of trust. 65

The auditor considers the possibility that the charity's records of incoming resources to which it is legally entitled may be incomplete as a result of fraud. A common type of fraud against charities is the diversion of donations to bank or building society accounts which the charity does not control. Sources of audit evidence as to whether incoming resources from appeals and other 'non-routine' sources have been fully recorded can involve the assessment and testing of internal controls, and comparison of donations actually received by the charity to past results for similar appeals, to budgets and to statistics for response rates for charities in general. 66

> When obtaining an understanding of the entity and its environment, including its internal control, the auditor should consider whether the information obtained indicates that one or more fraud risk factors are present. (paragraph 48)

A list of features which may increase the risk of fraud is contained in Appendix 1 to ISA (UK and Ireland) 240. Additional charity specific factors include: 67
(a) the limited involvement of trustees in key decision making or monitoring transactions, and limited engagement with charity staff;
(b) widespread branches or operations, such as those established in response to emergency appeals in countries where there is no effective system of law and order;
(c) the management or supervision of volunteer staff;
(d) transactions (income and expenditure) often undertaken in cash;
(e) unpredictable patterns of giving (in cash, by cheque, and through donations in kind) by members of the public, both in terms of timing and point of donation;
(f) informal banking or cash transfer methods used in areas remote from conventional banking systems;
(g) inconsistent regulation across international borders;
(h) international transfer of funds.

The auditor is not required to review or conclude on the adequacy of the approach taken by trustees to assess and address risks faced by their charity. However, where the trustees have produced documentation that sets out their assessment of the various risks facing the charity, and how they believe those risks are controlled and managed, the auditor has regard to that documentation (and any fraud register where maintained) when performing his own assessment of the risk of material misstatements to financial reporting resulting from fraud. 68

In assessing the risk of misstatement arising from fraud, auditors also consider the extent of the trustees' involvement in the day-to-day administration of the charity, 69 their access to its resources and their ability, collectively or individually, to override any internal controls. Additionally, they consider the arrangements the trustees have put in place to monitor work undertaken by third parties, for example custodianship of investments and fundraising.

> If the auditor has identified a fraud or has obtained information that indicates that a fraud may exist, the auditor should communicate these matters as soon as practicable to the appropriate level of management (paragraph 93).
>
> The auditor should document communications about fraud made to management, those charged with governance, regulators and others. (paragraph 109)

70 The appropriate level of management for most charities will be the board of trustees.

71 However, where there is a suspected or actual instance suggesting dishonesty or fraud involving a significant loss of or major risk to charitable funds or assets, the auditor should make a report direct to a proper authority without delay, and without informing the trustees in advance if they are suspected of being involved (see also the guidance in the section on ISA (UK and Ireland) 250 section B).

72 In the case of charities, the proper authorities include the Serious Organised Crime Agency (SOCA) where there is a suspicion of money laundering (see ISA (UK and Ireland) 250A section) and the appropriate charity regulator.

ISA (UK AND IRELAND) 250: SECTION A – CONSIDERATION OF LAWS AND REGULATIONS IN AN AUDIT OF FINANCIAL STATEMENTS

> **Background note**
>
> The purpose of this ISA (UK and Ireland) is to establish standards and provide guidance on the auditor's responsibility to consider laws and regulations in the audit of financial statements.

> When designing and performing audit procedures and in evaluating and reporting the results thereof, the auditor should recognise that non-compliance by the entity with laws and regulations may materially affect the financial statements. (paragraph 2)
>
> In accordance with ISA (UK and Ireland) 200, "Objective and General Principles Governing an Audit of Financial Statements" the auditor should plan and perform the audit with an attitude of professional scepticism recognising that the audit may reveal conditions or events that would lead to questioning whether an entity is complying with laws and regulations. (paragraph 13)
>
> In order to plan the audit, the auditor should obtain a general understanding of the legal and regulatory framework applicable to the entity and the industry and how the entity is complying with that framework. (paragraph 15)

Paragraph 2 of ISA (UK and Ireland) 250 states that auditors should recognise that non-compliance by the entity with laws and regulations may materially affect the financial statements. In the case of charities, relevant laws and regulations include trust law, and hence include requirements as to the use of restricted funds and preservation of any permanent endowments (capital funds). 73

The regulatory framework and charity governing documents

The legal framework for charities is complex, and different requirements exist depending on the charity's constitution, the part of the United Kingdom in which the charity is established and the type of activity which it undertakes. In addition, charities are affected by the whole range of national legislation applicable to business entities, such as employment, tax and pensions law and health and safety regulations. 74

The trustees of a charity are responsible for ensuring that the necessary controls are in place to ensure compliance with applicable law and regulations, and to detect and correct any breaches that have occurred, even if they have delegated some of their executive functions to professional staff or advisers. 75

> After obtaining the general understanding, the auditor should perform further audit procedures to help identify instances of non-compliance with those laws and regulations where non-compliance should be considered when preparing financial statements, specifically:
>
> (a) Inquiring of management as to whether the entity is in compliance with such laws and regulations;
> (b) Inspecting correspondence with the relevant licensing or regulatory authorities; and
> (c) Enquiring of those charged with governance as to whether they are on notice of any such possible instances of non-compliance with law or regulations. (paragraph 18)
>
> In the UK and Ireland, the auditor's procedures should be designed to help identify possible or actual instances of non-compliance with those laws and regulations which provide a legal framework within which the entity conducts its business and which are central to the entity's ability to conduct its business and hence to its financial statements. (paragraph 18-1)

Classification of laws and regulations

Laws and regulations relevant to the audit can be regarded as falling into two main categories: 76

(a) those relating directly to the preparation of the entity's financial statements, or the inclusion or disclosure of specific items in the financial statements; and
(b) those which provide a legal framework within which the entity conducts its business and which are central to the entity's ability to conduct its business and hence to its financial statements.

Laws and regulations which do not fall into either category need not be taken into account in planning audit work to be undertaken: however, auditors are required to remain alert to the possibility of breaches of other requirements and to investigate any which come to their attention. 77

Laws relating directly to the preparation of the financial statements

78   In addition to requiring the auditors to obtain sufficient appropriate audit evidence about compliance with laws and regulations relating directly to the preparation of the financial statements, the ISA (UK and Ireland) also indicates that where there is a statutory duty for auditors to report, in their opinion on the financial statements, on whether the entity complies with certain laws and regulations the auditors need to obtain evidence of that compliance.

79   Laws and regulations which relate directly to the preparation of financial statements for unincorporated charities are contained in the relevant legislation and subordinate regulations[17] relating to the particular UK jurisdiction in which the charity operates. Where individual charities are subject to legislation other than specific charity legislation, for example charitable companies or charitable registered social landlords, there may be certain additional disclosure requirements.

80   Auditors also check whether charities' governing documents contain any special provisions as to the disclosure of information in the financial statements or reporting requirements for the auditors. Users of the financial statements of a charity reasonably expect that the transactions recorded within them are authorised by the governing document of the charity and in furtherance of the charity's objects. In order to give a true and fair view, due regard needs to be given to disclosure of any significant non-compliance with the governing document.

81   Auditors therefore familiarise themselves with charities' governing documents and in planning and conducting their audit:

- ensure that their audit procedures cover compliance with the governing document;
- consider any changes in the charity's activities to ensure that these comply with the governing document; and
- are alert to new or unusual transactions which may not be in accordance with the governing document.

Laws which are central to the charity's conduct of its business

82   The ISA (UK and Ireland) requires auditors to carry out specified steps to help identify possible or actual instances of non-compliance with those laws and regulations which fall into the category of those central to the entity's ability to conduct its business, that is those laws and regulations where:

(a) compliance is a pre-requisite of obtaining a licence to operate; or
(b) non-compliance may reasonably be expected to result in the entity ceasing operations, or call into question the entity's status as a going concern.

83   Determination of which laws and regulations are central to a particular charity requires consideration of its governing document, the activities it undertakes and any laws and regulations specifically applicable to those activities, as well as the requirements of charity law. To assist in identifying possible or actual instances of non-compliance with these laws and regulations, auditors inspect any recent correspondence between the charity and the relevant charity regulator in accordance with the provisions of the ISA (UK and Ireland).

---

[17] See Appendix 1.

84 In addition, each charity is bound to comply with the terms of its governing document, which may, for example, take the form of a trust deed, a will, a constitution or the Articles of Association of a company.

85 The charity sector is diverse in terms of activities undertaken and hence the requirements of laws and regulations that are central to a charity's ability to operate are likely to be derived from the activities undertaken as well as arising from charitable status. For example charities providing residential care in England and Wales will be subject to the requirements of the Registered Homes Act 1984, as amended by the Registered Homes (Amendment) Act 1991, and those in England and Wales providing residential accommodation for children will be subject to the provisions of the Children Act 1989. Similarly, many care services in Scotland are regulated by the Scottish Commission for the Regulation of Care under the Regulation of Care (Scotland) Act 2001. Significant regulatory breaches can result in loss of registration and hence ability to undertake particular activities. Similar legislative requirements can affect charitable operations in different parts of the sector and in the different parts of the United Kingdom.

86 The auditor will therefore also consider the impact of that particular activity on the overall ability of the charity to operate effectively in terms of the charity's current objectives. Where a particular activity, whilst subject to laws and regulations, is not central to a charity's ability to achieve its objectives and to operate then the auditor has no responsibility for considering whether such laws and regulations have been observed.

87 Breaches of laws and regulations which apply to a particular type of activity may also result in fines, the financial consequences of which may, in particular instances, be significant. Severe financial consequences may also arise from failure to comply with grant conditions or taxation law.

Money laundering

> In the UK and Ireland, when carrying out procedures for the purpose of forming an opinion on the financial statements, the auditor should be alert for those instances of possible or actual non-compliance with laws and regulations that might incur obligations for partners and staff in audit firms to report money laundering offences. (paragraph 22-1)

88 Auditors in the UK have reporting obligations under the Proceeds of Crime Act 2002 and the Money Laundering Regulations 2007 to report knowledge or suspicion of money laundering offences, including those arising from fraud and thefts, to SOCA. The impact of the detailed legislation on auditors can broadly be summarised as follows:

- money laundering includes concealing, disguising, converting, transferring, removing, using, acquiring or possessing property[18] resulting from criminal conduct[19];
- the anti-Money Laundering legislation contains no de minimis concessions;

---

[18] "Property" is criminal property if it constitutes a person's benefit from criminal conduct or it represents such a benefit (in whole or part and whether directly or indirectly), and the alleged offender knows or suspects that it constitutes or represents such a benefit.

[19] "Criminal conduct" is defined as conduct which constitutes an offence in any part of the UK or would constitute such an offence if it occurred in any part of the UK.

- partners and staff in audit firms are required to report suspicions[20] that a criminal offence, giving rise to direct or indirect benefit from criminal conduct has been committed, regardless of whether that offence has been committed by a client or by a third party;
- partners and staff in audit firms need to be alert to the dangers of making disclosures that are likely to prejudice an investigation ('tipping off'[21]) as this will constitute a criminal offence under the anti-Money Laundering legislation.

89 Trustees of charities have no specific statutory responsibilities in connection with money laundering over and above those which apply generally to individuals and organisations although, for certain charities, there are 'serious incident reporting' obligations.

90 Failure by an auditor to report knowledge or suspicion of money laundering is a criminal offence. Auditors are required to report through their Money Laundering Reporting Officer ('MLRO') to SOCA suspicions of criminal conduct that give rise to criminal property. Partners and staff in audit firms discharge their responsibilities by reporting to their MLRO.

91 Further guidance on the matters to be considered by auditors is set out in Practice Note 12 'Money laundering – Interim guidance for auditors in the United Kingdom' (Revised).

92 For the purpose of this guidance, money laundering includes activities relating to terrorist financing (including attempts to commit a financing offence under the Terrorism Act 2000). This extends the money laundering reporting requirements for partners and staff in audit firms to terrorist fund-raising, the use of money or other property for the purposes of terrorism, or the possession of money or other property and arrangements where money or other property is to be made available to another, where a person intends or has reasonable cause to suspect that it may be used for the purposes of terrorism irrespective of whether those funds come from a legitimate source or not.

93 Any knowledge or suspicions of involvement of a charity's trustees in money laundering would normally be regarded as being of material significance to the charity regulators and so give rise to a statutory duty to report in addition to making any necessary report required by legislation relating to money laundering offences.

Reporting non-compliance with laws and regulations

> The auditor should, as soon as practicable, either communicate with those charged with governance, or obtain audit evidence that they are appropriately informed, regarding non-compliance that comes to the auditor's attention. (paragraph 32)

[20] *Auditors are required to report where they know or suspect or have reasonable grounds to know or suspect that another person is engaged in money laundering.*

[21] *'Tipping off' is an offence under the Proceeds of Crime Act 2002. It arises when an individual discloses matters where*
(a) there is knowledge or suspicion that a report has already been made, and
(b) that disclosure is likely to prejudice any investigation which might be conducted following the report.

The ISA (UK and Ireland) provides guidance on action to be taken by the auditor when possible non-compliance with laws and regulations is discovered. The procedures described in paragraphs 26 to 38 of the ISA (UK and Ireland) apply to the audit of charities as to other entities, but there may be special reporting considerations, as set out below. 94

(1) Reporting to management

The ISA (UK and Ireland) requires auditors to communicate their findings to the appropriate level of management, unless they conclude that the suspected or actual instance of non-compliance ought to be reported to a 'proper authority' and that they no longer have confidence in the trustees. In this case, the auditors make a report direct to a proper authority, without delay and without informing the trustees in advance. 95

In those cases where the trustees are not involved in the day-to-day management of the charity, having delegated this function to staff, and it is the latter who are suspected of involvement in the breach of law or regulations, the auditors may consider that it is appropriate to communicate with the trustees in the first instance. 96

(2) Reporting to the addressees of the auditors' report on the financial statements

The auditor's report on a non-company charity's financial statements is usually addressed to its trustees. Although an actual or suspected breach of relevant law or regulations may already have been reported to the trustees as managers of the charity, the auditor's report on the financial statements is nevertheless required to include details of any fundamental uncertainty, or disagreement over disclosure of a suspected or actual instance of non-compliance having a material effect on the financial statements. 97

(3) Reporting to third parties

ISA (UK and Ireland) 250 B deals with the reporting of actual or suspected non-compliance to third parties, in particular reporting to a 'proper authority' in the public interest. The ISA (UK and Ireland) states that the auditors only report to an authority 'with a proper interest to receive the information'. In the case of registered charities this will be the Charity Commission or OSCR as appropriate. 98

ISA (UK AND IRELAND) 250: SECTION B – THE AUDITOR'S RIGHT AND DUTY TO REPORT TO REGULATORS IN THE FINANCIAL SECTOR

> The auditor of a regulated entity should bring information of which the auditor has become aware in the ordinary course of performing work undertaken to fulfil the auditor's audit responsibilities to the attention of the appropriate regulator without delay when:
>
> (a) The auditor concludes that it is relevant to the regulator's functions having regard to such matters as may be specified in statute or any related regulations; and
> (b) In the auditor's opinion there is reasonable cause to believe it is or may be of material significance to the regulator. (paragraph 2)
>
> Where an apparent breach of statutory or regulatory requirements comes to the auditor's attention, the auditor should:

> (a) Obtain such evidence as is available to assess its implications for the auditor's reporting responsibilities;
> (b) Determine whether, in the auditor's opinion, there is reasonable cause to believe that the breach is of material significance to the regulator; and
> (c) Consider whether the apparent breach is criminal conduct that gives rise to criminal property and, as such, should be reported to the specified authorities. (paragraph 39)

99 Although the title of ISA (UK and Ireland) 250 section B refers to reports to regulators in the financial sector, the principles and essential procedures included in ISA (UK and Ireland) 250 section B apply in respect of the statutory duty and the discretionary right to report to charity regulators in England and Wales and Scotland.

100 The legislative basis for the charity auditors statutory duty to report is:

- England and Wales: sections 44A and 68A of the Charities Act 1993 require auditors to communicate to the Charity Commission certain matters of which they become aware in their capacity as auditors of a charity. The statutory duty to report to the Charity Commission extends to charities excepted from registration but does not extend to exempt charities[22].
- Scotland: Section 46 of the Charities and Trustee Investment (Scotland) Act 2005, which sets out the duty of the auditors of all forms of charity registered in Scotland to report to OSCR. OSCR has similar investigative powers to those of the Charity Commission.

These provisions also establish the right to report a matter to the charity regulator which does not appear to fall within the scope of the duty to report but which the auditor has reasonable cause to believe is likely to be relevant to the charity regulator for the purposes of the exercise of any of its functions. The right to report, like the duty to report, applies to charitable companies and to non-company charities.

101 The Charities Act 1993 and the 2005 Act (Scotland) specify the matters which give rise to a duty to make an immediate report to the relevant regulator as those:

(a) which relate to the activities or affairs of the charity or of any connected institution or body, and
(b) which the auditor has reasonable cause to believe is, or is likely to be, of material significance for the exercise, in relation to the charity, of the relevant regulator's functions[23]

102 Auditors of charities required to register in England and Wales and Scotland are required to report matters they believe may be of material significance to the regulators to both the Charity Commission and OSCR.

103 Neither the Charities Act 1993 nor the 2005 Act (Scotland) require the auditor to perform any additional audit work as a result of the statutory duty nor is the auditor required specifically to seek out breaches of the requirements applicable to a

---

[22] 'Exempt' charities are excluded at present from the Charity Commission's supervision and monitoring, and consequently their auditors are not covered by the duty to report to the Commission. There is however no disapplication of the reporting duty for exempt company charities.

[23] For the Charity Commission this is section 8 (general power to institute inquiries) or 18 (power to act for protection of charities) of the Charities Act 1993 and for OSCR this is sections 28 (inquiries about charities), 30 (removal from the Register of a charity which no longer meets the test) and 31 (powers of OSCR following enquiries).

particular charity. However, in circumstances where the auditor identifies that a reportable matter may exist, the auditor carries out such extra work, as considered necessary, to determine whether the facts and circumstances give 'reasonable cause to believe' that the matter does in fact exist. It should be noted that the auditor's work does not need to prove that the reportable matter exists.

Where possible, it is Charity Commission practice to seek to resolve issues collaboratively with a charity. However if the charity declines to co-operate or assist, under section 8 of the Charities Act 1993, the Charity Commission has the power to institute inquiries with regard to charities or a particular charity or class of charities, either generally or for particular purposes. For the purposes of any inquiry instituted under this section, the Charity Commission has powers to obtain information, which include the power to call for documents and require persons to give evidence. The charity's auditors may also be required to provide information. OSCR has similar powers and approach and under sections 28 and 29 of the 2005 Act (Scotland); the powers of investigation are extended to include a body that may be holding itself out as a charity. 104

The Charity Commission's usual practice, when instituting an inquiry under section 8 of the 1993 Act, is to send a notice of this to the charity trustees. However, in rare cases this is not done as sending a formal notice of the institution of an inquiry to the trustees would have an adverse effect on the conduct of the inquiry. OSCR undertakes investigative inquiries under its enquiry and intervention policy and also sends a notice of this to the charity trustees. 105

Criteria for determining the existence of a duty to report to the Charity Regulators

Determining whether a matter is reportable under the Charities Act 1993 or section 46 of the 2005 Act (Scotland) involves consideration both of whether the auditor has a 'reasonable cause to believe' and that the matter in question 'is, or is likely to be of material significance' to the charity regulators. 106

'Material significance' is defined by ISA (UK and Ireland) 250 section B as follows: 107

> "*The term 'material significance' requires interpretation in the context of the specific legislation applicable to the regulated entity. A matter or group of matters is normally of material significance to a regulator's function when, due either to its nature or its potential financial impact, it is likely of itself to require investigation by the regulator.*"

'Material significance' does not have the same meaning as materiality in the context of the audit of financial statements. Whilst a particular event may be trivial in terms of its possible effect on the financial statements of an entity, it may be of a nature or type that is likely to change the perception of the regulator. For example, dishonesty by a trustee may not be significant in financial terms in comparison with the income of the charity but would have a significant effect on the relevant charity regulator's consideration of whether the person concerned should be allowed to continue to act as a charity trustee. 108

Matters which the Charity Commission and OSCR have indicated are likely to be of material significance are set out on the charity regulators' websites and in Appendix 5 of this Practice Note. Other sources of information include: 109

- the Charity Commission's Directions and guidance for independent examinations[24];
- Annual Returns (in Scotland, Supplementary Monitoring Returns[25]) which signpost a number of the areas that the relevant regulator considers significant; and
- in England and Wales, any serious incident report made by the trustees to the Charity Commission.

110 The determination of whether a matter is, or is likely to be, of material significance to the Charity Commission or OSCR inevitably requires auditors to exercise their judgment. In forming such judgments, auditors need to consider not simply the facts of the matter but also their implications. In addition, it is possible that a matter, which is not materially significant in isolation, may become so when other possible breaches are considered, together with other reported and unreported breaches of which the auditor is aware.

111 Auditors of charities base their judgment of 'material significance' to the charity regulator solely on their understanding of the facts of which they are aware without making any assumptions about the information available to the charity regulator in connection with any particular charity.

112 Minor breaches of trustees' obligations, or isolated administrative errors that are unlikely to jeopardise the charity's assets or amount to misconduct or mismanagement would not normally be of 'material significance'. ISA (UK and Ireland) 250 section B however requires auditors of regulated entities, when reporting on their financial statements, to review information obtained in the course of the audit and to assess whether the cumulative effect is of 'material significance' such as to give rise to a duty to report to the regulator. In circumstances where auditors are uncertain whether they may be required to make a report or not, they consider taking legal advice.

113 Where a situation is identified and the auditors, having considered the guidance provided in this section of the Practice Note and in Appendix 5, remain uncertain as to whether the matter is likely to be of 'material significance' the auditors may wish to discuss the circumstances giving rise to their concern with the charity regulators. Whilst such discussions may help inform auditors in reaching their conclusion as to whether a particular matter is likely to fall within the charity regulator's regulatory function, it is not used as substitute for the auditors' own judgment. Such discussions do not remove the need to report where the matter is considered to be reportable.

114 On completion of their investigations, auditors ensure that the facts and circumstances, and the basis for their conclusion as to whether these are, or are likely to be of 'material significance' to the charity regulator, are adequately documented such that the reasons for their decision to report may be clearly demonstrated should the need to do so arise in future.

115 Whilst confidentiality is an implied term of auditors' contracts with a charity or other entity, in the circumstances described in section 44A Charities Act 1993 and section 46 of the 2005 Act in Scotland, it does not prevail. Subject to compliance with legislation regarding tipping off, in the circumstances leading to a right or duty to report auditors are required to communicate information or opinions on a matter

---

[24] *CC 31: Independent examination of charity accounts. Examples of matters to be reported to the Charity Commission are set out in Appendix 5 of this publication.*

[25] *Completed by charities with gross income over £25,000.*

relating to the affairs of the charity or any connected institution or body. The defence afforded to auditors from any potential breach of duty is given in respect of information obtained in their capacity as auditors.

In addition, auditors who cease to hold office, for any reason, as a charity's auditors are required by paragraph 35 of the 2008 Regulations (E&W) and Regulation 10(6) of the 2006 Regulations (Scotland) to make a statement as to whether there are any matters concerning their ceasing to hold office which should be brought to the attention of the trustees and to send a copy of their statement to the charity regulator. 116

Conduct of the audit

ISA (UK and Ireland) 250 section B requires auditors to ensure that all staff involved in the audit of a regulated entity 'have an understanding of: 117

(a) the provisions of applicable legislation,
(b) the regulator's rules and any guidance issued by the regulator, and
(c) any specific requirements which apply to the particular regulated entity,

appropriate to their role in the audit and sufficient (in the context of that role) to enable them to identify situations which may give reasonable cause to believe that a matter should be reported to the regulator.'

Auditors include procedures within their planning process to ensure that members of the audit team have sufficient understanding (in the context of their role) to enable them to recognise breaches, and that such matters are reported to the audit engagement partner without delay so that a decision may be made as to whether a duty to report arises. 118

Connected entities

Auditors need to be aware that the duty to report extends to any institution or body corporate connected with the charity[26]. 119

The charity auditors decide whether there are any matters to be reported to the Charity Commission or OSCR relating to the affairs of the charity in the light of the information that they receive about the connected entity for the purpose of auditing the financial statements of the charity. If the charity auditors are aware of possible circumstances that may fall due to be reported, they have a right under section 44A (3) of the Charities Act 1993 to obtain further information direct from the management or auditors of the connected entity to ascertain whether the matter should be reported. To facilitate such possible discussions, at the planning stage of the audit, the auditors of the charity will have considered whether arrangements need to be put in place to allow them to communicate with the management and auditors of the connected entity. If the auditors of the charity are unable to communicate with the management and auditors of the connected entity to obtain further information concerning the circumstances they have identified they report the circumstances, and the fact that they have been unable to obtain further information, direct to the charity regulator. 120

---

[26] *'Connected' includes any institution controlled by the charity or a body corporate in which the charity has a substantial interest (20% or more of the share capital or voting rights) (section 44A (6) of the Charities Act 1993).*

Discussing matters of material significance with trustees

121 The trustees are the persons principally responsible for the management of the charity. Unless the matters arising are related to trustee fraud and subject to the tipping off provisions of the Money Laundering Regulations, auditors will normally bring a matter of "material significance" to the attention of the trustees and seek agreement on the facts and circumstances. However, ISA (UK and Ireland) 250 section B stresses that where the auditors conclude that a duty to report arises they should bring the matter to the attention of the regulator without undue delay. The trustees may wish to report the matters identified to the charity regulator themselves and detail the actions taken or to be taken. Whilst such a report from the trustees may provide valuable information, it does not relieve the auditors of the statutory duty to report directly to the charity regulator.

Contents of a report to the charity regulators

122 ISA (UK and Ireland) 250 section B provides details of the information that should be included in a report to a regulator. The Charity Commission and OSCR have indicated that a report should follow the format as set out in Appendix 5 of this Practice Note.

123 The report to the Charity Commission is required to be in writing. This can include making a report by email. Auditors are not relieved of their duty to make a written report where an oral report has been previously made to the Charity Commission or by any informal discussions of the issue with Charity Commission staff. Similarly, auditors are not relieved of their duty to report on the basis that any other party has provided relevant information, whether written or oral, to the Charity Commission.

124 In Scotland, there is no legislative requirement to make the report in writing but it is recommended that a written report or record of any verbal report is forwarded to OSCR.

125 Where trustees wish to make a submission to the charity regulators as to the circumstances and steps being taken to address a reportable matter, the auditors may attach such a memorandum or report prepared by the trustees to their report.

126 Where such additional information is provided auditors refer to the additional information in their report, and indicate whether or not they have undertaken additional procedures to determine whether any remedial actions described have been taken.

Timing of a report

127 The duty to report arises once auditors have concluded that there is reasonable cause to believe that the matter is or is likely to be of material significance to the relevant regulator's regulatory function. In reaching their conclusion auditors may wish to take appropriate advice and consult with colleagues or lawyers.

128 The report should be made without undue delay once a conclusion has been reached. Unless the matter casts doubt on the integrity of the trustees this should not preclude discussion of the matter with trustees and seeking such further advice as is necessary, so that a decision can be made on whether or not a duty to report exists. Such consultations and discussions are however undertaken on a timely basis to enable auditors to conclude on the matter without undue delay.

Information received in a capacity other than as auditor

There may be circumstances where it is not clear whether information about a charity coming to the attention of the auditors is received in the capacity of auditor or in some other capacity, for example as general adviser to the charity. Appendix 2 to ISA (UK and Ireland) 250 section B provides guidance as to how information obtained may be relevant to the auditors in the planning and conduct of the audit and the steps that need to be taken to ensure the communication of information that is relevant to the audit. Matters that are potentially of material significance to the regulator, and which arise in this context should be considered and if appropriate reported, in accordance with ISA (UK and Ireland) 250 section B.

Failure to fulfil the statutory duty to report

Failure to comply with sections 44A or 68A of the Charities Act 1993 or section 46 of the 2005 Act (Scotland) is regarded as a matter for the professional bodies to deal with pursuant to their own disciplinary procedures. For cases where the charity regulators have decided to make a complaint they have indicated that, within any legal restrictions that may apply, they will make available to those professional bodies any relevant information in its possession.

Auditors' right to report to the Charity Regulator

In the case of charities in England and Wales and Scotland, the circumstances giving rise to a duty to report are equivalent to those applicable to regulated entities in the financial sector. Auditors also have a separate right to report where there is no statutory duty. This right in England and Wales is set out for non-company charities in section 44A(3) of the Charities Act 1993. Section 68A extends this section to company charities. This right is given by section 46 of the 2005 Act (Scotland) to auditors of charities registered in Scotland.

Auditors' right to report in relation to charities in Northern Ireland

The statutory duty to report to the relevant charity regulator, and hence the statutory protection with respect to duties of confidentiality, do not extend to auditors of charities in Northern Ireland. In the absence of the statutory duty auditors consider whether a matter identified may be one that ought to be reported to a proper authority[27] in the public interest. Guidance on the factors to be taken into account when exercising their right to report in the public interest is set out in ISA (UK and Ireland) 250 section A. When considering whether to exercise their right to report to an appropriate authority, auditors of charities established in Northern Ireland will have regard to the examples of matters that would be of material significance to the Charity Commission and OSCR which are included in Appendix 6 of this Practice Note. Auditors may need to take legal advice before making a decision on whether a matter should be reported in the public interest.

---

[27] At the time of publication of this Practice Note, this would normally be the Department for Social Development.

ISA (UK AND IRELAND) 260: COMMUNICATION OF AUDIT MATTERS WITH THOSE CHARGED WITH GOVERNANCE

Background note

The purpose of this ISA (UK and Ireland) is to establish standards and provide guidance on communication of audit matters arising from the audit of financial statements between the auditor and those charged with governance of an entity. These communications relate to audit matters of governance interest as defined in this ISA (UK and Ireland). This ISA (UK and Ireland) does not provide guidance on communications by the auditor to parties outside the entity, for example, external regulatory or supervisory agencies.

The auditor should communicate audit matters of governance interest arising from the audit of financial statements with those charged with governance of an entity. (paragraph 2)

133 The auditor always issues written communication even if its content is limited to explaining there is nothing the auditor wishes to draw to the attention of those charged with governance. However, ISA (UK and Ireland) 260 also stresses that communication should be active, two-way communication between the auditor and those charged with governance. Effective communication is unlikely to be achieved when the auditor communicates with those charged with governance solely by means of formal written reports.

134 The auditor's consideration of the system of internal control is undertaken as part of the steps necessary to form an opinion on the entity's financial statements. There is no statutory or regulatory requirement for a separate report on the design or operation of a charity's system of internal control. Nevertheless, the auditor's work may identify information on the systems which would assist the trustees in seeking to establish and maintain effective and efficient systems.

135 Findings from the audit to be communicated to those charged with governance include any material weaknesses in the internal control systems identified during the audit.

136 Charity auditors notify trustees of all breaches discovered in the course of their work of duties relevant to the administration of the charity imposed by any enactment or rule of law on the trustees or managers or any professional adviser, regardless of whether the matter gave rise to a statutory duty to report to the charity regulators. Such notification normally takes place in the course of assessing the consequences of each particular breach. However, auditors may also summarise such breaches in their report of audit matters to those charged with governance.

The auditor should determine the relevant persons who are charged with governance and with whom audit matters of governance interest are communicated. (paragraph 5)

137 Those charged with governance include the directors (non executive and executive) of a company. In relation to a charity this will include at a minimum the board of trustees who are collectively charged with governance. For larger charities where

there are sub-committees of the board, for example an audit committee, the sub-committee may be charged with specific tasks in order to assist the board in meeting its governance responsibilities.

138 Those charged with the governance of a charity have responsibilities at least as onerous as those of full-time, paid directors of commercial enterprises in relation to the security of a charity's income, assets and their proper application and, in the case of larger charities, are required by the Charities SORP to make a statement in their Annual Report concerning risks to which a charity is exposed and their management.

139 Where the trustees employ staff to whom certain executive functions are delegated, auditors consider the persons to whom it would be most appropriate to address their reports. Whilst staff may play a central role in the direction and management of a charity, it must be remembered that such powers are delegated from the trustee body.

ISA (UK AND IRELAND) 300: PLANNING AN AUDIT OF FINANCIAL STATEMENTS

Background note

The purpose of this ISA (UK and Ireland) is to establish standards and provide guidance on the considerations and activities applicable to planning an audit of financial statements. This ISA (UK and Ireland) is framed in the context of recurring audits. In addition, matters the auditor considers in initial audit engagements are included in paragraphs 28 and 29.

The auditor should plan the audit so that the engagement will be performed in an effective manner. (paragraph 2)

The auditor should develop an audit plan for the audit in order to reduce audit risk to an acceptably low level. (paragraph 13)

140 In developing the audit plan, the auditor considers the responsibilities as set out in statute and the letter of engagement to ensure that the scope of the audit plan is sufficient and includes, where appropriate, reports required by statute.

141 Particular issues auditors consider, at the planning stage, include:

- the applicable reporting framework including:
  - the legislative requirements, for example companies legislation or, in England and Wales the Charities Act 1993 or, in Scotland the 2005 Act (Scotland);
  - the Charities SORP (or a sector specific SORP where one applies);
  - The governing document for the charity, which may also include specific reporting requirements;
- governance arrangements, including planning with the trustees the form and timing of communications;
- operating structures, branches and overseas operations including:
  - the extent to which the charity's activities (either of a fundraising or a charitable nature) are undertaken through branches or overseas activities and the impact this has on the auditors' required knowledge of the business

(for example taxation and employment law), their risk assessments and sources of audit evidence, and
- the structure and management of any related or connected entities, in particular the degree to which the entities are managed and controlled by the trustees and management of the charity;
- the charity's activities in the context of its stated objects and powers, including any limitations of the charity's governing document, or terms and restrictions placed on material gifts or donations received;
- the likely impact on the financial statements of the charity of the activities of any related or connected entities (for example, a separate limited company set up to undertake commercial activities for the charity);
- the statutory duty to report matters to the charity regulators including whether members of the audit team have sufficient understanding (in the context of their role) to enable them to identify situations which may give reasonable cause to believe that a matter should be reported to the regulator;
- whether other auditors' reports are required, for example special reports to funders of the charity, grant donors or EU agencies.

142 At an early stage in planning the audit, auditors seek agreement with the trustees for necessary access to third parties, when appropriate, and the timing and extent of the information required from them. The principal requirements are normally set out in the auditors' engagement letter. More detailed arrangements for obtaining access and information are likely to be one of the main subjects of discussion with the trustees, whether at a planning meeting or more informally, before the auditors complete their audit plan.

ISA (UK AND IRELAND) 315: OBTAINING AN UNDERSTANDING OF THE ENTITY AND ITS ENVIRONMENT AND ASSESSING THE RISKS OF MATERIAL MISSTATEMENT

Background note
The purpose of this ISA (UK and Ireland) is to establish standards and to provide guidance on obtaining an understanding of the entity and its environment, including its internal control, and on assessing the risks of material misstatement in a financial statement audit.

The auditor should obtain an understanding of relevant industry, regulatory, and other external factors including the applicable financial reporting framework. (paragraph 22)

The regulatory framework

143 As described in the introduction to this Practice Note the legal framework for charities is complex, and different requirements exist depending on the charity's constitution, the part of the United Kingdom in which the charity is established and the type of activity which it undertakes. The auditor needs to ascertain and understand the applicable law and regulations of the jurisdiction within which the charity operates. This involves keeping up to date with laws and regulations relating to charities generally, and to the client charity in particular.

The accounting requirements under which charities report depend on how they are 144
constituted and the relevant national jurisdiction within the United Kingdom. The
principal categories are set out in Appendix 1.

> The auditor should obtain an understanding of the nature of the entity. (paragraph 25)

Knowledge of the charity's activities, governance, operating structure, sources of 145
income and the existence of restricted funds is essential for ascertaining the risk of
material misstatement arising from fraud, error, or non-compliance with applicable
law and regulations and in order to plan and carry out audit work effectively and
efficiently. Certain special features of charities are outlined in the introduction section of this Practice Note.

The auditor also needs to understand the charity's governing document. There are 146
many different types of governing instrument or constitution which will determine
the objects of the charity and the powers of its trustees, and the audit approach needs
to be adapted accordingly. Particular issues include:

- any limitations in objectives placed on the charity by its governing document, or
- terms and restrictions placed on material gifts or donations received.

> The auditor should obtain an understanding of the entity's selection and application of accounting policies and consider whether they are appropriate for its business and consistent with the applicable financial reporting framework and accounting policies used in the relevant industry. (paragraph 28)
>
> The auditor should obtain an understanding of the entity's objectives and strategies, and the related business risks that may result in material misstatement of the financial statements. (paragraph 30)

The auditor reviews accounting policies and considers the application of the Cha- 147
rities SORP. Accounting policies adopted may have a significant effect on the
recognition of assets and liabilities or their presentation within financial statements.
Policies that may require particularly careful consideration include those for the
recognition of:

- legacies receivable;
- grants receivable as voluntary income;
- grants receivable or payable on performance related conditions;
- liabilities resulting from constructive obligations;
- gifts in kind and donated services; and
- heritage assets.

The auditor considers what steps have been taken by trustees and senior management in respect of cost allocations. Policies that affect the allocation of costs between
charitable activities and income generation may have a significant impact on how
costs are presented in the statement of financial activities.

The auditor also considers the key performance indicators used to monitor the 148
performance of the charity especially those used by the trustees.

> The auditor should obtain an understanding of internal control relevant to the audit. (paragraph 41)

149 There is a wide variation between different charities in terms of size, activity and organisation. Smaller charities may be administered by volunteer staff or by third party administrators. Larger charities may directly employ professionally qualified, full-time staff. However, the responsibilities of trustees for ensuring that the charity has adequate internal controls and therefore is properly administered and its assets properly safeguarded apply irrespective of a charity's size or administrative arrangements, and the attitude, role and involvement of each charity's trustees are likely to be fundamental in determining the effectiveness of its control environment.

150 The maintenance of an effective system of internal control is at least as important, if not more so, for charities as it is for other entities, since it is a fundamental duty of charity trustees to protect the property of their charity and to secure its application for the objects of the charity. Failure to do so can render the trustees personally liable for any loss occasioned to the charity[28]. Auditors of certain charities, for example registered friendly societies and registered social landlords, are subject to specific reporting requirements in respect of internal controls. Where there is such a requirement, auditors plan their work bearing in mind the need to report if a satisfactory system of control over transactions has not been maintained.

Control environment

151 The role, attitude and actions of the trustees are fundamental in shaping the control environment of a charity. Factors to consider include:

- the amount of time committed by trustees to the charity's affairs;
- the skills and qualifications of individual trustees;
- trustees' understanding of the charity and its legal and regulatory environment;
- the regularity and effectiveness of trustee meetings and the level of attendance at these meetings;
- the adequacy of minutes of trustee meetings;
- the independence of trustees from each other;
- the policy on dealing with trustee conflicts;
- the processes for managing trustee conflicts of interest;
- the supervision by the trustees of relatively informal working arrangements which are common when using volunteers;
- the degree of involvement in key decision making or monitoring transactions and engagement with charity staff;
- the attitude of trustees to previously identified control weaknesses;
- the level of delegation by trustees to senior management and the formality of this delegation; and
- the committee structure of the organisation.

152 Other features of the control environment will depend on the size, activities, organisation and corporate governance structures of the charity but might include:

- a recognised plan of the charity's structure showing clearly the areas of responsibility and lines of authority and reporting. Where the charity does not have staff, and is administered entirely by the trustees, there can still be an

---

[28] Guidance leaflets entitled 'Internal financial controls for charities' and 'The hallmarks of an effective charity' have been published by the Charity Commission, and OSCR has published 'Guidance for charity trustees – acting with care and diligence'.

- agreed division of duties, provided there is adequate monitoring by the body of trustees as a whole;
- segregation of duties where charities have more than one member of staff (whether paid or not). In larger charities, such segregation could include involvement of staff from outside the finance department in certain transactions, for example in providing a first signatory for cheques;
- supervision by trustees of activities of staff where segregation of duties is not practical;
- competence, training and qualification of paid staff and any volunteers appropriate to the tasks they have to perform;
- involvement of the trustees in the recruitment, appointment and supervision of senior executives;
- access of trustees to independent professional advice where necessary;
- budgetary controls in the form of estimates of income and expenditure for each financial year and comparison of actual results with the estimates on a regular basis; and
- communication of results of such reviews to the trustees on a regular basis so as to facilitate their review of performance and enable them to initiate action where necessary.

> The auditor should obtain an understanding of the entity's process for identifying business risks relevant to financial reporting objectives and deciding about actions to address those risks, and the results thereof. (paragraph 76)

The Charities SORP requires charities that are subject to a statutory audit to include a statement in the annual trustees' report confirming that the major risks to which the charity is exposed, as identified by the trustees, have been reviewed and systems have been established to manage those risks. In addition, the companies legislation requires medium and large sized charitable companies to disclose what key risks and uncertainties the charity faces. As a result of this, charities will often maintain a risk register.

> The auditor should obtain an understanding of the information system, including the related business processes, relevant to financial reporting, including the following areas:
> - The classes of transactions in the entity's operations that are significant to the financial statements.
> - The procedures, within both IT and manual systems, by which those transactions are initiated, recorded, processed and reported in the financial statements.
> - The related accounting records, whether electronic or manual, supporting information, and specific accounts in the financial statements, in respect of initiating, recording, processing and reporting transactions.
> - How the information system captures events and conditions, other than classes of transactions, that are significant to the financial statements.
> - The financial reporting process used to prepare the entity's financial statements, including significant accounting estimates and disclosures. (paragraph 81)

For charities it is particularly important that the systems in place are able to capture accurately any restrictions placed on income (whether imposed by the donor or as a result of the charity's fundraising initiatives). The charity also needs to ensure the documentation supporting the restrictions on the income is retained and easily accessible; this includes any deeds of covenant.

> The auditor should obtain a sufficient understanding of control activities to assess the risks of material misstatement at the assertion level and to design further audit procedures responsive to assessed risks. (paragraph 90)

155 Some of the control activities which are special to charities are set out in Appendix 6 of this Practice Note.

> The auditor should obtain an understanding of how the entity has responded to risks arising from IT. (paragraph 93)

156 Many charities have websites which provide facilities for online giving. These may support a donation by credit card, sponsorship or legacy making. Auditors consider whether adequate controls exist over the IT supporting these websites and the financial systems in respect of gifts made or pledged using these facilities.

> *Assessing the Risks of Material Misstatement*
>
> The auditor should identify and assess the risks of material misstatement at the financial statement level, and at the assertion level for classes of transactions, account balances, and disclosures. (paragraph 100)

157 There is a wide variation between different charities in terms of size, activity and organisation, so that there can be no standard approach to internal controls and risk. Auditors assess risk and the adequacy of controls in relation to the circumstances of each charity.

158 Factors considered by the auditor in assessing whether there may be an increased level of risk of material misstatement at the financial statement level include:

- evidence of failure to act in accordance with those objects and powers in the charity's governing document;
- the strength of the control environment;
- the complexity and extent of regulation;
- the significance of donations and cash receipts including whether donations are received over the internet or by credit card;
- the treatment of legacy income;
- the valuation of gifts in kind and donated services;
- difficulties of the charity in establishing ownership and timing of voluntary income where funds are raised by non-controlled bodies;
- lack of predictable income or a precisely defined relationship between expenditure and income which makes it difficult for the charity to ensure that income to which it is entitled is actually received;
- uncertainty of future income which can make consideration of future operations and viability of the charity difficult;
- restricted funds which require special considerations as to use and accounting;
- the extent and nature of trading activities;
- the complexity of tax rules (whether Income Tax, Capital Gains Tax, VAT or business rates) relating to charities;

- difficulties in identification and quantification of liabilities arising from constructive obligations[29];
- the sensitivity of certain key statistics, such as the proportion of resources used in administration and fund-raising;
- the need to maintain adequate resources for future expenditure while avoiding the build up of reserves which could appear excessive to potential donors or be incompatible with the entity's charitable status;
- the valuation of heritage or unusual fixed assets.

Overseas activities may give rise to additional risks including:

159

- significant aspects of a charity's business may be conducted in conditions or locations which impede access to the accounting records;
- the transactions may be in a number of different and volatile currencies;
- conduit funding[30] or informal banking arrangements may be used;
- due to the location of the activities management may have reduced oversight and limited ability to monitor activities and transactions;
- governance, responsibility and accountability may be unclear regarding branches, joint ventures and the use of partners in overseas locations.

In these circumstances auditors will need to ensure that they are able to assess the full extent of the activities, and have the necessary understanding of the regulatory environment in which significant activities are carried out – for example in relation to taxation and employment law[31].

> As part of the risk assessment, the auditor should determine which of the risks identified are, in the auditor's judgment, risks that require special audit consideration (such risks are defined as "significant risks"). (paragraph 108)
>
> For significant risks, to the extent the auditor has not already done so, the auditor should evaluate the design of the entity's related controls, including relevant control activities, and determine whether they have been implemented. (paragraph 113)

Issues concerning the completeness of incoming resources, the existence of restricted funds and overseas operations are likely to give rise to significant risks affecting charity audits, and audit procedures in respect of these are commented on further in the section on ISA (UK and Ireland) 330 below.

160

ISA (UK AND IRELAND) 320: AUDIT MATERIALITY

Background note

The purpose of this ISA (UK and Ireland) is to establish standards and provide guidance on the concept of materiality and its relationship with audit risk.

---

[29] See also paragraph 148 of the Charities SORP.

[30] Resources received and distributed by a charity as agent for another entity, usually another charity. The principal in the arrangement is the charity providing the resources who retains the legal responsibility for the charitable application of the funds.

[31] The Charity Commission has issued guidance on charities working internationally.

> The auditor should consider materiality and its relationship with audit risk when conducting an audit. (paragraph 2)
>
> Materiality should be considered by the auditor when:
> (a) Determining the nature, timing and extent of audit procedures; and
> (b) Evaluating the effect of misstatements. (paragraph 8)

161 The auditors consider materiality in planning an audit and when assessing whether the accounts give a true and fair view from the point of view of the addressees of the report (in most cases, the trustees). The principles underlying this consideration of materiality are no different from those involved in the audit of other entities and are explained in the ISA (UK and Ireland).

162 ISA (UK and Ireland) 320 indicates that materiality is considered at both the overall financial statement level and in relation to individual account balances, classes of transactions and disclosures. This can result in different materiality considerations being applied depending on the item of the accounts being considered, for example the degree of accuracy expected in the case of certain statutory disclosures e.g. transactions with trustees are likely to be considered to be material. Also particular disclosures or expenditure categories may be sensitive and warrant extra attention, for example, restricted funds and costs of generating funds.

Branches

163 The auditors clarify with management which entities will form part of the financial statements being produced by the charity. Where a charity operates through branches or subsidiaries, their contribution to the results and financial position of the charity may not be known at the time of planning the audit. In this case, the auditors consider how to decide the likely results of branches or subsidiaries by reference to procedures such as:

- discussion with management; consideration of problems or particular issues encountered in previous years to see whether there is an identifiable pattern suggestive of weak management or fraud, for example;
- consideration of prior year figures; and
- any budgeted or preliminary results;

and incorporate the resulting best estimate into the materiality calculation for the audit as a whole. Further guidance on consolidated financial statements is given in the section on ISA (UK and Ireland) 600 below.

Restricted funds

164 Many charities receive funds subject to specific trusts, which must be accounted for separately (unless grouped together if, individually, they are comparatively small) in accordance with the Charities SORP. It is not necessary in every case to set a different monetary materiality level for such funds: however, the ISA (UK and Ireland) indicates that materiality may be influenced by considerations such as legal and regulatory requirements, which may result in different materiality considerations being applied to particular aspects of the financial statements.

165 Any breaches of the terms of trusts relating to restricted funds which come to the auditors' attention in the course of their work, regardless of materiality to the

financial statements as a whole, need to be considered in terms of their significance to the auditors' report on the financial statements and brought to the attention of trustees, as a failure on their part to comply with the terms of trusts may place them in breach of their responsibilities.

Auditors also consider the disclosure of restricted funds which are subject to specific trusts as to their application, paying particular attention to: 166

- any funds that are in deficit;
- any income funds which are held in illiquid assets (including inter-fund loans) thereby preventing application of the fund; and
- any expenditure of the capital of a permanently endowed fund.

ISA (UK AND IRELAND) 330: THE AUDITOR'S PROCEDURES IN RESPONSE TO ASSESSED RISKS

> **Background note**
>
> The purpose of this ISA (UK and Ireland) is to establish standards and provide guidance on determining overall responses and designing and performing further audit procedures to respond to the assessed risks of material misstatement at the financial statement and assertion levels in a financial statement audit.

> When, in accordance with paragraph 115 of ISA (UK and Ireland) 315, the auditor has determined that it is not possible or practicable to reduce the risks of material misstatement at the assertion level to an acceptably low level with audit evidence obtained only from substantive procedures, the auditor should perform tests of relevant controls to obtain audit evidence about their operating effectiveness (paragraph 25).
>
> When, in accordance with paragraph 108 of ISA (UK and Ireland) 315, the auditor has determined that an assessed risk of material misstatement at the assertion level is a significant risk, the auditor should perform substantive procedures that are specifically responsive to that risk (paragraph 51).

Completeness of incoming resources

The incoming resources of charities often involve a number of different sources, ranging from grants from government departments to occasional cash donations by members of the public in response to street collections. Whilst it is the trustees' responsibility to safeguard the assets and incoming resources of the charity, the voluntary nature of some elements of its incoming resources raises considerations concerning the methods available to the trustees for the purposes of ensuring that all incoming resources to which the charity is entitled are correctly accounted for. 167

The amount of voluntary donations cannot in many cases be determined in advance, nor can a charity be regarded as necessarily entitled to funds, even when the amounts can be predicted, before they are donated to it. Trustees of a charity cannot be held responsible for the security of money or other assets which are intended for its use until that money or assets are, or should be, within the control of the charity. Trustees should, however, establish procedures to ensure appropriate recording and safeguarding as soon as such assets come within their control. 168

169 The Charities SORP reflects the position described in the previous paragraph. Discussing the criteria for recognising incoming resources, it states:

> "Incoming resources – both for income and endowment funds – should be recognised in the Statement of Financial Activities when the effect of a transaction or other event results in an increase in the charity's assets. This will be dependent on the following three factors being met:
> (a) entitlement – normally arises when there is control over the rights or other access to the resource, enabling the charity to determine its future application;
> (b) certainty – when it is virtually certain that the incoming resource will be received;
> (c) measurement – when the monetary value of the incoming resource can be measured with sufficient reliability".

170 The auditor considers the following factors when addressing the completeness of incoming resources:

- *loss of incoming resources through fraud*: auditors consider the possibility that the charity's records of incoming resources to which it is legally entitled may be incomplete as a result of fraud. A common type of fraud against charities is the diversion of donations to bank or building society accounts which the charity trustees do not control. Sources of audit evidence as to whether incoming resources from appeals and other 'non-routine' sources have been fully recorded can involve the assessment and testing of the sort of internal controls described in Appendix 6, and comparison of donations actually received by the charity to past results for similar appeals and statistics for response rates for charities in general;
- *recognition of incoming resources from third party fund-raisers:* income recognition can be a complex issue where a charity obtains resources by means of fund-raising organisations[32]. The auditor considers the agreement (between the charity and the fund-raiser) and other documents relating to the transaction to see whether all donations received in the charity's name have been transmitted to it or otherwise accounted for and that amounts have been accounted for gross where appropriate instead of having been netted off at source;
- *recognition of incoming resources from branches, associates or subsidiaries:* if charities use branches, associates or subsidiaries to raise funds, the auditor considers the arrangements made by the main charity to determine at what point incoming resources are recognised;
- *recognition of legacy income:* legacy income is recognised on a receivable basis when there is sufficient evidence to provide necessary certainty that the legacy will be received and the value of the incoming resources can be measured with sufficient reliability (SORP, paras 123-124). These criteria will normally be met following probate and once the executor(s) of the estate have established that there are sufficient assets in the estate, after settling liabilities, to pay the legacy. Evidence that the executors have determined that a payment can be made may arise on the agreement of the estate accounts or notification that the payment will be made. Where notification is received after the year end but it is clear that the executor(s) have agreed prior to the year end that the legacy can be paid, then it is accrued (SORP, para 127). The certainty and measurability of the receipt may be affected by subsequent events such as valuations and disputes. The auditor therefore reviews information available up to when the accounts are approved for evidence relating to legacies receivable existing at the balance sheet date. The auditor also considers the consistent application of legacy recognition

---

[32] *The Charities Act 1992 Section 59 requires there to be an agreement between the charity and the fund-raiser in a prescribed form.*

policies and the adequacy of their disclosure in accounting policy notes (SORP, para 363(a)) and considers the implications for the audit report of policies that closely equate to recognition on receipt. Sources of audit evidence as to whether legacy income has been correctly recorded include probate information, estate accounts, correspondence from executors or solicitors, and legacy fundraising agencies.
- *informal fund-raising groups:* where informal fund-raising groups raise money or other resources for charitable purposes on a voluntary basis, without knowledge of any particular charity, criteria for recognising income are not met until the funds raised are notified to the recipient charity. In general neither trustees nor auditors have an obligation to estimate the extent of income from such sources before this point. Even if a legal entitlement on the part of the charity to the resulting income may arise under trust law, it would normally be inappropriate for the charity to account for income from such sources since its ultimate cash realisation, so far as the charity itself is concerned, cannot be determined with sufficient certainty;
- *grants or contractual funding:* in the case of grant or contractual funded charities, an examination of the grant applications or contract and correspondence can assist in confirming completeness of incoming resources. The auditor considers obtaining direct confirmation of the amounts receivable from the grant provider; and
- *non-cash donations:* satisfactory operation of internal controls may enable the auditor to obtain sufficient appropriate audit evidence as to the recognition and measurement of gifts in kind or donated services or facilities. The basis of any valuation of non-cash donations should be clearly stated in the notes to the financial statements and consistently applied. The auditor considers whether the policy is reasonable in the circumstances and has been properly applied.

Analytical procedures may also be used as a source of audit evidence about the completeness of incoming resources. Whilst the degree of inherent uncertainty affecting donated incoming resources may restrict the reliance which can be placed on such techniques in respect of donations, they nevertheless provide a source of additional corroborative evidence to supplement that drawn from the auditor's consideration of relevant controls over completeness of incoming resources from donations. The auditor therefore undertakes analytical procedures to assess whether such incoming resources are consistent with his knowledge of the charity and its activities over the period, and considers undertaking other forms of analytical review. 171

In the case of larger charities with more complex operations, there are specialist publications and sources of information which can be referred to for general information about charities as well as comparative figures and statistics. These sources include 'trade' journals, umbrella organisations, and the charity regulators. Available statistics include responses to mail shots (i.e. donations received), and industry norms such as sales per square foot for trading operations in different areas. 172

Restricted funds

Restricted funds (including endowments) which are subject to specific trusts as to their application may give rise to a significant risk of misstatement. 173

Audit procedures may include: 174
- consideration of internal control procedures put in place by the charity to identify restricted funds whether imposed by the donor or as a result of the charity's fund raising initiatives;

- consideration of the methods used in cost allocation to ensure that the expenditure is allocated in accordance with the terms or conditions attaching to restricted funds ;
- comparison of expenditure (whether out of income or capital) with the terms of the restricted fund, and appeal documentation, bid submissions and related reports to donors;
- consideration of future funding to cover negative balances;
- consideration of the validity of transfers between funds;
- consideration of the ability of the fund to meet its obligations in view of the liquidity of its underlying assets; and
- consideration of whether the capital of an endowed fund has been expended without express authority.

Overseas operations

175 Overseas activities can be undertaken through a number of different structures including branches, joint ventures with other charities, projects managed by local agents or partners through to the grant funding of autonomous local organisations. Auditors of a charity are responsible for forming an opinion on the financial statements reflecting all of the charity's operations, including UK and overseas branches.

176 Audit procedures on overseas operations may include:
- auditors obtaining an understanding of how trustees control overseas operations. Management procedures may involve the vetting of applications, reviewing project reports received, setting thresholds for site visits to projects involving significant grant funding, confirmation of grant receipts, reviewing accounts and the local certification of expenditure;
- obtaining evidence from field officers' reports as to work undertaken;
- comparison of accounting returns of expenditure with field reports and plans for consistency and reasonableness;
- analytical review of accounting returns received from overseas branches or local agents;
- consideration of any inspection or internal control visit reports undertaken by any internal audit function;
- consideration of audit work undertaken by local auditors, and consideration of any audit reports carried out on behalf of international donors for example government departments; and
- evidence from the audit work of another audit firm.

177 Where material assets are held or material funds are applied by overseas branches or subsidiaries auditors may seek observational evidence by way of site visits.

178 Such visits may provide valuable evidence of the existence of tangible fixed assets and of project work being undertaken by the charity. Auditors need to be aware of the logistical arrangements which may be needed were site visits to remote areas to be considered.

179 Where a charity makes a significant grant to an overseas organisation that is autonomous from the charity, the auditors seek evidence to support receipt of funding by that organisation, and that the charity has exercised reasonable diligence in ensuring application of the funds for appropriate charitable purposes.

180 Where the overseas operations are part of the charity, the transfer of funds by itself does not give rise to expenditure as such funds remain under the control of the

charity. However, an understanding of the structure of the charity will be needed in determining at what point expenditure is incurred, and audit evidence will be required to support material expenditure of money in the field.

ISA (UK AND IRELAND) 402: AUDIT CONSIDERATIONS RELATING TO ENTITIES USING SERVICE ORGANISATIONS

Background note

The purpose of this ISA (UK and Ireland) is to establish standards and provide guidance to an auditor where the entity uses a service organisation

In obtaining an understanding of the entity and its environment, the auditor should determine the significance of service organization activities to the entity and the relevance to the audit. (paragraph 5)

181 The auditor identifies whether the charity uses service organisations and assesses the effect of any such use on the procedures necessary to obtain sufficient and appropriate audit evidence to determine with reasonable assurance whether the financial statements are free of material misstatement.

182 Use of a service organisation does not diminish the ultimate responsibility of the trustees for conducting the affairs of the charity in a manner which meets their legal responsibilities, including those of safeguarding the assets, maintaining proper accounting records and preparing financial statements.

183 Similarly, an entity's use of a service organisation does not alter the auditor's responsibilities when reporting on its financial statements, but may have a significant effect on the nature of procedures undertaken to obtain sufficient appropriate audit evidence to determine whether a user entity's financial statements are free from material misstatement.

184 The auditor of a charity needs to consider the nature and extent of activity undertaken by service organisations to determine whether those activities are relevant to the audit, and what their effect is on audit risk.

185 Service organisations undertake a range of activities within the charity sector including:

- Maintenance of accounting records, payroll services,
- Fundraising,
- Custodianship of assets, and investment management services.

If the auditor concludes that the activities of the service organisation are significant to the entity and relevant to the audit, the auditor should obtain a sufficient understanding of the entity and its environment, including its internal control to identify and assess the risks of material misstatement and design further audit procedures in response to the assessed risk. (paragraph 7)

186 If the auditor is able to obtain a sufficient understanding of risk on which to base his planning of audit procedures by considering the charity's controls and information

available to the charity, for example by reviewing a report produced in accordance with AAF 01/06[33], the auditor will not need to supplement that understanding and assessment by making further enquiries about the control arrangements of relevant service providers.

187 If the auditor is unable to obtain a sufficient understanding of risk by considering information and controls at the entity level, the auditor takes steps to obtain a more detailed understanding of the control arrangements of relevant service providers by such means as visiting the service organisation or requesting the service organisation's auditor or the entity's internal audit function to perform specified procedures. The feasibility of this approach will depend on whether the contractual arrangements between the trustees and the service provider entitle the trustees to obtain supplementary information when considered necessary.

188 Where controls are poor or absent, the auditor also considers whether the status of the charity's internal control arrangements should be the subject of a report to the relevant charity regulator.

189 For charities in England and Wales, the charity's governing document may set out powers for the trustees to delegate activities to outside service organisations, who may not be charities themselves. Auditors review such documents where practicable, or alternatively hold discussions with the trustees, to determine whether there is authority, or presumed authority, for outsourcing.

190 It is not uncommon for charities to share an accounting function. In such cases the auditors consider the control arrangements for allocation of costs between such connected entities.

191 Where investment management arrangements exist, the auditors consider how trustees set investment objectives and monitor performance. The auditors also discuss with the trustees how they ensure that the level of delegation is consistent with the charity's powers and that the investment powers are being properly exercised.

192 PN 15: The audit of occupational pension schemes in the United Kingdom (Revised)[34] sets out guidance on the auditor's considerations and sources of audit evidence in circumstances where investment management and custody functions are outsourced. This guidance may also be relevant to certain charity audits.

193 Certain arrangements may also involve a service organisation providing facilities and services direct to a charity's beneficiaries. Examples include:

- management of a recreational facility such as a sports centre, provision of services to beneficiaries such as the management of a care facility, and
- provision of ancillary catering facilities e.g. a museum restaurant.

---

[33] 'Assurance reports on internal controls of service organisations made available to third parties', issued by the ICAEW.

[34] Paragraphs 247-259.

ISA (UK AND IRELAND) 505: EXTERNAL CONFIRMATIONS

Background note

The purpose of this ISA (UK and Ireland) is to establish standards and provide guidance on the auditor's use of external confirmations as a means of obtaining audit evidence.

The auditor should determine whether the use of external confirmations is necessary to obtain sufficient appropriate audit evidence at the assertion level. In making this determination, the auditor should consider the assessed risk of material misstatement at the assertion level and how the audit evidence from other planned audit procedures will reduce the risk of material misstatement at the assertion level to an acceptably low level. (paragraph 2)

194 External confirmations can provide reliable audit evidence of the amounts recoverable from grant providers and sources of contractual income. However some sources of such income, for example local authorities and some government funding bodies may not respond to confirmation requests and alternative procedures will be required to obtain appropriate audit evidence.

195 For bank balances held in overseas locations the auditor considers the format of the request for information sent to the overseas bank to ensure that the request will be fully understood by the bank.

196 The auditor considers the implications of failures of overseas banks to reply to requests for information, and whether these should be included in a report to those charged with governance.

ISA (UK AND IRELAND) 510: INITIAL ENGAGEMENTS – OPENING BALANCES AND CONTINUING ENGAGEMENTS – OPENING BALANCES

Background note

The purpose of this ISA (UK and Ireland) is to establish standards and provide guidance regarding opening balances when the financial statements are audited for the first time or when the financial statements for the prior period were audited by another auditor.

For initial audit engagements, the auditor should obtain sufficient appropriate audit evidence that :

(a) The opening balances do not contain misstatements that materially affect the current period's financial statements;
(b) The prior period's closing balances have been correctly brought forward to the current period or, when appropriate, have been restated; and
(c) Appropriate accounting policies are consistently applied or changes in accounting policies have been properly accounted for and adequately presented and disclosed. (paragraph 2)

197 Special considerations will apply where a non-company charity changes its basis of accounting from a receipts and payments to an accruals basis, or where the financial statements become subject to an audit, having previously been subject to a report by an independent examiner.

198 When there has been a change in the basis of accounting, procedures may include checking bank statements, reviewing receipts and payments after the year end, and physically checking any tangible fixed assets. For analytical procedures performed in the current year the auditors are likely to need to adjust the prior year management information prepared on a receipts and payments basis to enable a proper comparison.

ISA (UK AND IRELAND) 520: ANALYTICAL PROCEDURES

Background note

The purpose of this ISA (UK and Ireland) is to establish standards and provide guidance on the application of analytical procedures during an audit.

The auditor should apply analytical procedures as risk assessment procedures to obtain an understanding of the entity and its environment and in the overall review at the end of the audit. (paragraph 2)

199 A particular difficulty in applying analytical procedures to the audit of charities is that certain items in the financial statements can be very difficult to predict. For example, the level of income from donations and legacies cannot always be forecast with any great accuracy, as people's pattern of giving may change unpredictably. It is also difficult to establish a relationship between donations and other figures in the financial statements, as expenditure levels other than fundraising costs may not have any direct relationship with such income.

200 The usefulness of individual procedures depends on the scale and nature of activities undertaken, but examples of measures that can be adopted include:

- comparison of actual income and expenditure to prior years' figures and trends;
- comparison of actual to budgeted results;
- comparison of actual income to successful bids, legacy notifications and potential legacies reported in the minutes;
- comparison of actual expenditure to the auditors' own estimate of the expenditure that would be reasonable for the particular transaction under review;
- comparison of results of an individual branch to those of similar branches of the main charity;
- checking charity shops' sales revenue between different periods (eg monthly) and to other shops operating in similar locations;
- analysis of efficiency ratios such as staff or administration costs as a percentage of benefits delivered or grants made, or the ratio of costs to income generated for material categories of fundraising; and
- comparison of actual donations received as a result of fund-raising activities to the amount which could be expected on the basis of charity statistics, if any are available.

ISA (UK AND IRELAND) 540: AUDIT OF ACCOUNTING ESTIMATES

> **Background note**
>
> The purpose of this ISA (UK and Ireland) is to establish standards and provide guidance on the audit of accounting estimates contained in financial statements.
>
> The auditor should obtain sufficient appropriate audit evidence regarding accounting estimates (paragraph 2)
>
> The auditor should adopt one or a combination of the following approaches in the audit of an accounting estimate:
>
> (a) Review and test the process used by management to develop the estimate;
> (b) Use an independent estimate for comparison with that prepared by management; or
> (c) Review subsequent events which provide audit evidence of the reasonableness of the estimate made. (paragraph 10)

201 The Charities SORP provides detailed guidance on appropriate accounting policies and measurement bases. In applying these policies and bases the use of estimates and estimation techniques will be necessary to determine the monetary value of assets and liabilities and to determine the allocation of costs within the Statement of Financial Activities (SoFA). In order to comply with FRS 18 'Accounting Policies' and the Charities SORP, a charity's financial statements discloses a description of the estimation techniques adopted, including underlying principles, that are significant.

202 Evidence to support accounting estimates may frequently be obtained as part of the auditors' review of the post balance sheet period, for example by checking the subsequent expenditure of designated funds, or recoverability of accruals in respect of, for example, tax claims, grant awards and legacies.

203 Evidence relating to cost allocations across the cost categories of the SoFA may sometimes be obtained through observation, for example by observing the key duties of staff and internal departments to determine whether staff costs are reasonably allocated between the categories of charitable expenditure and the costs of generating funds. Where material estimates are required to allocate joint costs between the expenditure categories of the SoFA, auditors consider the requirements of FRS 18 – Accounting Policies, that the accounting policies adequately explain the estimation techniques adopted.

204 Where expenditure by a charity relates to a project which is of uncertain duration, because it is subject to external circumstances beyond the control of the trustees, it may be difficult to determine matters such as the expected useful economic life of fixed assets used in the project (for example, vehicles or other capital equipment used to provide emergency aid in a war zone may have an uncertain future, or the trustees may consider that the economic costs of redeploying equipment exceed its book value). The auditors use their knowledge of the charity's activities and accounting policies to assess whether the periods for write-down of fixed assets are reasonable and in line with any estimate of service potential.

> The auditor should make a final assessment of the reasonableness of the entity's accounting estimates based on the auditor's understanding of the entity and its environment and whether the estimates are consistent with other audit evidence obtained during the audit. (paragraph 24)

205 On occasions evidence obtained on an accounting estimate from post balance sheet review and observation may be insufficiently conclusive. Where such estimates are likely to be material auditors review the process by which the estimate was arrived at and consider the basis of the calculation in terms of its reasonableness, justifiability and consistency. In so doing, auditors will draw heavily on their knowledge of the charity in testing the consistency of principles adopted. Estimates of this nature may include:

- the quantification of future charitable commitments and constructive liabilities;
- valuations of gifts in kind received, particularly property;
- valuation of assets received for onward distribution;
- valuation of fixed asset investments where no market price exists e.g. unlisted securities and trading subsidiaries of the parent charity;
- valuation of heritage assets;
- valuation of intangible income derived from donated services or use of facilities;
- estimates of on-going service potential of fixed assets, in the absence of a cash flow, in an impairment review;
- recoverability of loans made to beneficiaries in the furtherance of a charity's objects.

ISA (UK AND IRELAND) 545: AUDITING FAIR VALUE MEASUREMENTS AND DISCLOSURES

> **Background note**
>
> The purpose of this ISA (UK and Ireland) is to establish standards and provide guidance on auditing fair value measurements and disclosures contained in financial statements.

> The auditor should obtain sufficient appropriate audit evidence that fair value measurements and disclosures are in accordance with the entity's applicable financial reporting framework. (paragraph 3)
>
> As part of the understanding of the entity and its environment, including its internal control, the auditor should obtain an understanding of the entity's process for determining fair value measurements and disclosures and of the relevant control activities sufficient to identify and assess the risks of material misstatement at the assertion level and to design and perform further audit procedures. (paragraph 10)
>
> The auditor should evaluate whether the fair value measurements and disclosures in the financial statements are in accordance with the entity's applicable financial reporting framework. (paragraph 17)

206 It is becoming increasing common for accounting standards to require assets and liabilities to be reflected in the balance sheet at fair value, being the amount for which

an asset or liability could be exchanged between knowledgeable, willing parties in an arm's length transaction.

While there are few references in the SORP to fair value, there are a number of areas where the application of ISA (UK and Ireland) 545 may be helpful, including: 207

- the valuation of defined benefit pension schemes. Charities also have the specific complexities of allocating pension deficits/assets between funds and the effect of these deficits/assets on their free reserves;
- the need to recognise material grant commitments at their present value in the balance sheet;
- the need to recognise all investments (apart from programme related investments) at market value;
- the option to recognise tangible fixed assets at valuation;
- the valuation of heritage assets;
- the need to fair value the assets and liabilities acquired where acquisition accounting is applied (in this situation, the due diligence process may only provide limited information on the fair value of some assets such as land and buildings and heritage assets);
- the need to recognise gifts in kind (apart from second hand goods donated for resale) at a reasonable estimate of their gross value to the charity and donated services and facilities at a reasonable estimate of the value to the charity of the service or facility received.

The auditor considers the processes management have adopted for determining the fair values of these assets and liabilities and the reasonableness of these valuations. The auditor assesses the reasonableness of the valuations by comparisons with the sales value of similar assets (where these values are publicly available), gains or losses being recognised by other charities which hold similar assets, sector indices and market trends.   208

The Charities SORP allows certain valuations to be undertaken by trustees or employees of a charity, provided that in the case of property valuations they are suitably qualified. In this situation, the auditor assesses the employees/trustees relevant experience by, for example, determining their professional qualifications, and/or discussing their experience of valuing similar items.   209

ISA (UK AND IRELAND) 550: RELATED PARTIES

Background note

The purpose of this ISA (UK and Ireland) is to establish standards and provide guidance on the auditor's responsibilities and audit procedures regarding related parties and transactions with such parties regardless of whether International Accounting Standard (IAS) 24, "Related Party Disclosures," or similar requirement, is part of the applicable financial reporting framework.

The auditor should perform audit procedures designed to obtain sufficient appropriate audit evidence regarding the identification and disclosure by management[35] of related parties and the effect of related party transactions that are material to the financial statements. (paragraph 102)

---

[35] *In the UK and Ireland those charged with governance are responsible for the preparation of the financial statements.*

> Where there is any indication that such circumstances exist, the auditor should perform modified, extended or additional audit procedures as are appropriate in the circumstances. (paragraph 103)
>
> When planning the audit the auditor should assess the risk that material undisclosed related party transactions, or undisclosed outstanding balances between an entity and its related parties may exist. (paragraph 106-3)

210 The auditors consider the steps taken by the trustees to identify and record transactions with related parties and remain alert, in carrying out their audit, for evidence of such transactions which are not included in the information provided by the trustees.

211 Charity trustees, or those connected to them, may receive payment for providing goods or services to the charity where there is a clear benefit to the charity. The Charities Act 2006 and the 2005 Act (Scotland) allow for trustees to be paid for providing goods or services to a charity if certain conditions are satisfied. These provisions do not allow payment for being a trustee or for any type of contractual employment within the charity unless explicit authority exists. The following conditions must be met before a trustee can be paid for providing goods or services:

- the amount of the remuneration must be set out in writing between the charity and the relevant person and must not be unreasonable for the services in question;
- it must be in the best interests of the charity for the services to be provided by the relevant person;
- if more than one person who is a trustee is entitled to receive the remuneration, they must constitute a minority of the trustees; and
- the constitution of the charity must not contain an express provision prohibiting the relevant person from receiving the remuneration.

Accounting disclosure is still required of any remuneration or benefit received by trustees or those connected to them notwithstanding that the payment is authorised and/or falls within the conditions set out above.

212 This apart, neither charity trustees nor persons connected with them should transact business with the charity (or with any company owned by the charity), other than meeting or reimbursing properly incurred expenses, except where the transaction, and any benefit (including remuneration) derived from it, is either expressly permitted by the charity's governing document or, in England and Wales, permission has been obtained from the Charity Commission. In Scotland, the authorising provision within the governing document must have been in force on 15 November 2004.

213 The Charities SORP provides further information and examples of related party transactions and disclosures required which includes remuneration or benefits paid to trustees or persons connected with them. The Charities SORP related party disclosures are also required by the 2008 Regulations (E&W). For charities registered in Scotland, the SORP definition of related parties is extended in the 2005 Act (Scotland) section 68(2).

ISA (UK AND IRELAND) 560: SUBSEQUENT EVENTS

Background note

The purpose of this ISA (UK and Ireland) is to establish standards and provide guidance on the auditor's responsibility regarding subsequent events.

The auditor should perform audit procedures designed to obtain sufficient appropriate audit evidence that all events up to the date of the auditor's report that may require adjustment of, or disclosure in, the financial statements have been identified
(paragraph 4)

214 The Charities SORP indicates that the determination after the balance sheet date of the amount of a gift aid payment to a parent charity by a subsidiary undertaking, if the subsidiary had a present legal or constructive obligation at the balance sheet date, is an adjusting post balance sheet event.

ISA (UK AND IRELAND) 570: THE GOING CONCERN BASIS IN FINANCIAL STATEMENTS

Background note

The purpose of this ISA (UK and Ireland) is to establish standards and provide guidance on the auditor's responsibility in the audit of financial statements with respect to the going concern assumption used in the preparation of the financial statements, including considering management's assessment[36] of the entity's ability to continue as a going concern.

When planning and performing audit procedures and in evaluating the results thereof, the auditor should consider the appropriateness of management's use of the going concern assumption in the preparation of the financial statements.
(paragraph 2)

The auditor should consider any relevant disclosures in the financial statements.
(paragraph 2-1)

215 A charity should prepare its accounts on a going concern basis unless it is being liquidated or has ceased operating or there is no realistic alternative but to liquidate or to cease its activities.

216 The Charities SORP reiterates the relevance of this concept in the preparation of charity accounts which are intended to show a true and fair view. FRS 18 requires trustees, when preparing financial statements, to assess whether there are significant doubts as to the charity's ability to continue as a going concern.

---

[36] In the UK and Ireland, those charged with governance are responsible for the preparation of the financial statements and the assessment of the entity's ability to continue as a going concern.

217 Although the most significant factor ensuring the future viability of many charities is public goodwill, it is difficult, if not impossible, to value and cannot be included in the balance sheet, nor can auditors rely solely on the existence of goodwill as evidence to support the going concern assumption.

218 The auditor has no duty to assess whether the charity's activities are for the public benefit in order to establish that the charity is a going concern. However, persistent failure by a charity to meet its public benefit requirement may have an implication for the auditor's assessment of going concern.

Basis for preparation of financial statements

219 In considering factors relating to a charity's status as a going concern, it is necessary to take account of the particular circumstances of that charity which may affect its ability to continue its activities. Auditors consider the availability of future funding and whether uncertainties exist which require disclosure in the financial statements. The charity's purpose may also require consideration: some charitable activities are focused on a specific purpose, and once this is achieved, the charity may cease to operate.

220 Where the going concern basis within a charity group involves support between entities, the auditor considers the extent to which such support is within the charitable objects and powers.

Circumstances where a charity may not be a going concern

221 The examples of indicators contained in the ISA (UK and Ireland) apply as much to charities as to commercial entities and include pointers such as an excess of current liabilities over current assets. Charity specific indicators include:

   – inability to finance its operations from its own resources or unrestricted funds;
   – decision by the trustees to curtail or cease activities;
   – transfer to, or take-over by, another entity of the charity's activities;
   – loss of essential resources or key staff;
   – existence of tax liabilities which cannot be met from existing resources;
   – deficits on unrestricted funds;
   – loss of clients, for example where a public authority ends a practice or contract to refer (and pay for) clients to the charity;
   – loss of operating licence (for example, for a residential care home);
   – significant changes in strategy of major funders, and significant decline in donations by the public;
   – investigation by a charity regulator;
   – loans made to subsidiaries which cannot be repaid;
   – claw-back of grant received and gift-aid refunds;
   – reliance on major donors;
   – failure to meet reserves policy targets;
   – persistent failure to meet the requirement for public benefit, leading to withdrawal of funding or tax liabilities.

Where a charity fails to meet the public benefit requirement either in whole or in part, the auditor also considers the implication of actions taken, or likely to be taken, by the regulator, and assesses the implications on his opinion.

The operations of charities

Assessment of the going concern basis can be complicated by the uncertainty as to future income streams to which many charities are subject. In considering projections of income the auditors consider the income sources, their regularity and predictability and the degree of risk attaching to such sources. 222

Restrictions placed on the use of particular funds held by a charity may be relevant to the consideration of its going concern status. An understanding of unrestricted and restricted income, and capital or permanently endowed funds is relevant both in relation to the consideration of balance sheet funds held at the year end and to the impact that such restrictions may have on the understanding of future cash-flows. Factors the auditors consider may include: 223

- the nature and impact of the restrictions placed on the use of any material restricted income funds,
- the liquidity of assets held within restricted income funds,
- the nature of the restrictions placed on expenditure of any endowed funds, the impact such restrictions have on the ability to fund planned activities, the nature of any restrictions to be placed on future appeals or other projected income, and
- the operational ability to withdraw from projects or activities which have been subject to fund designations or restrictions.

Charities receiving grants of public funds (including lottery funds) are normally required to meet certain specified conditions. Expenditure outside grant conditions can lead to disallowance and repayment. Many charities rely on public authorities for grant support. Where the financial effect of withdrawal of funding would be fundamental to a particular charity, auditors assess whether compliance with grant conditions has been achieved or otherwise obtain evidence about steps taken by the trustees to ensure compliance. 224

The timing of cash flows may also be relevant for certain categories of charities. Factors that can impact on a charity's cash flows include: 225

- reliance on annual votes of monies from governmental or central funding bodies, reliance on grant funding that reimburses expenditure only once incurred, or delays in the approval or payment of such funding,
- grant funding provided for specific projects but not for central administrative costs, or funding of long-term projects based only on short-term commitments as to funding receivable,
- the cash flow impact of any constructive liabilities accrued in the balance sheet, or on conditions being met for any contingent grants disclosed within contingent liabilities, and
- constructive obligations, such as grant payables or other funding commitments, that are recognised as liabilities but are payable over a number of years,

Obtaining evidence, audit conclusions and reporting

In considering going concern, it may be helpful for the auditors to include the following points in discussions with trustees: 226

- the reliability of the budget and cash-flow forecast for the coming year, based on past experience and the certainty of inflows and outflows ;
- the nature of management information systems covering future income and expenditure; where the charity relies for a significant part of its funding on one or more major institutional donors or granting authorities such as local

authorities, whether it would be practical to obtain a degree of comfort from such funders as to their future support for the charity;
- any shortfall of identifiable future income on forecast expenditure needing to be made up by voluntary donations of cash or other resources;
- lists of projects supported or awards made in the year and planned for the following year;
- the level of uncommitted reserves remaining available to the charity;
- any reliance on support by the charity's bankers, major donors, or public authorities; concentration on the provision of services to a particular category of beneficiaries or objects for which future funding or demand may be limited; and
- any special operating licences or similar conditions.

ISA (UK AND IRELAND) 580: MANAGEMENT REPRESENTATIONS

Background note

The purpose of this ISA (UK and Ireland) is to establish standards and provide guidance on the use of management representations as audit evidence, the procedures to be applied in evaluating and documenting management representations and the action to be taken if management refuses to provide appropriate representations.

The auditor should obtain appropriate representations from management. (paragraph 2)

227 An important principle is that auditors do not accept the unsupported representations of trustees or senior management of the charity where these relate to matters which are material to the financial statements. Moreover, representations cannot substitute for evidence that the auditors reasonably expect to be available.

Written confirmation of appropriate representations from management, as required by paragraph 4 below, should be obtained before the audit report is issued. (paragraph 2-1)

In the UK and Ireland, the auditor should obtain evidence that those charged with governance acknowledge their collective responsibility for the preparation of the financial statements and have approved the financial statements. (paragraph 3-1)

The auditor should obtain written representations from management on matters material to the financial statements when other sufficient appropriate audit evidence cannot reasonably be expected to exist. (paragraph 4)

228 ISA (UK and Ireland) 580 requires auditors to obtain written confirmation of appropriate representations from management. These commonly take the form of a representation letter and normally include a representation concerning the completeness of information made available to the auditors, including minutes of trustee meetings and correspondence with the charity regulators. In addition, ISA (UK and Ireland) 250 and ISA (UK and Ireland) 550 require auditors to obtain written confirmation in respect of the completeness of disclosure to the auditors of:

- known events which involve possible non-compliance with laws and regulations, together with the actual or contingent consequences which may arise there from; and
- information provided regarding the identification of related parties and the adequacy of related party disclosures.

229 The trustees as a body are responsible for the contents and presentation of the financial statements. Consequently, discussion of the content of any written representation by the trustee body as a whole may be appropriate before it is signed on behalf of the trustees.

230 For charities where there are executive staff, it is likely that in practice there are some representations that necessitate discussion with those persons. Auditors often find it useful to attend the meeting at which trustees consider the financial statements and representation letter, to encourage discussion of significant items or matters, including unadjusted errors, arising in the course of the audit.

231 In addition to the examples of other representations given in ISA (UK and Ireland) 580, the auditor of a charity also considers obtaining confirmation that:
- all income has been recorded,
- the restricted funds have been properly applied,
- constructive obligations for grants have been recognised, and
- all correspondence with regulators has been made available to the auditor including, in England and Wales, any serious incident reports.

232 Timely communication by auditors with the trustees on significant issues on which representations will be required is important in this sector, which relies primarily on unpaid (voluntary) trustees who are not involved in the day-to-day running of the affairs of the charity.

233 If there is a delay between the approval of the financial statements by the trustees and their receipt by the auditor for the approval of the audit report, the auditor considers whether to obtain an update of the trustees' representations, either by enquiry of the trustees about any changes to the charity's circumstances or by requesting the trustees to provide an updated representation letter.

ISA (UK AND IRELAND) 600 (REVISED): USING THE WORK OF ANOTHER AUDITOR

Background note

The purpose of this ISA (UK and Ireland) is to establish standards and provide guidance when an auditor, reporting on the financial statements of an entity, uses the work of another auditor on the financial information of one or more components included in the financial statements of the entity.

When the principal auditor uses the work of another auditor, the principal auditor should determine how the work of the other auditor will affect the audit. (paragraph 2)

In the UK and Ireland, when planning to use the work of another auditor, the principal auditor's consideration of the professional competence of the other

> auditor should include consideration of the professional qualifications, experience and resources of the other auditor in the context of the specific assignment. (paragraph 7-1)

234 Where auditors use the services of other auditors in the audit of a charity's financial statements, then the auditors advise the other auditors of the use that is to be made of their work and make the necessary arrangements for the co-ordination of their efforts at the initial planning stage of the audit.

235 Some charities operate through local branches, subsidiaries or other units whose financial reports are audited or examined by subsidiary auditors. In these circumstances, the principal auditors' planning of the audit of the charity as a whole includes the following considerations:

- the materiality of the results of the branches to the financial statements;
- the quality, nature and timing of information produced by the branches;
- the extent of the work undertaken by the subsidiary auditor, or other person making a report in connection with the branch or subsidiary financial reports and the reliance that may be placed on the other's work.

236 Where the charity is a limited company, there is a statutory obligation on any subsidiary undertaking which is a company incorporated in Great Britain, and on its auditor, to give to the auditor of the parent company such information and explanations as they may reasonably require for the purposes of their duties.

237 Auditors of non-company charities in England & Wales have, under section 44(1)(d) of the 1993 Act, a right of access to books, documents and records which relate to the charity. This access right extends beyond those records which are in the ownership of the charity and, under the 2008 Regulations, includes the records of any subsidiaries of the charity. In Scotland this right applies to all legal forms of charity registered in Scotland and is given under Regulation 13 of the 2006 Regulations (Scotland).

238 Where returns from a subsidiary auditor indicate a potential problem (such as a qualified opinion) which could be material, the principal auditors seek to obtain authority from the trustees to discuss the issue with the auditor(s) involved to explore whether, with additional procedures, it would be possible to obtain further evidence such that an unqualified opinion can be given on the group financial statements.

ISA (UK AND IRELAND) 700: THE AUDITOR'S REPORT ON FINANCIAL STATEMENTS

> **Background note**
>
> The purpose of this ISA (UK and Ireland) is to establish standards and provide guidance on the form and content of the auditor's report issued as a result of an audit performed by an independent auditor of the financial statements of an entity. Much of the guidance provided can be adapted to auditor reports on financial information other than financial statements.

> The auditor's report should contain a clear written expression of opinion on the financial statements taken as a whole. (paragraph 4)

> The auditor should consider modifying the auditor's report by adding a paragraph if there is a significant uncertainty (other than a going concern problem), the resolution of which is dependent on future events and which may affect the financial statements (paragraph 32)

The auditor reviews and assesses the conclusions drawn from the audit evidence obtained as the basis for the expression of an opinion on the financial statements. Examples of points that the auditor considers as part of this assessment include: 239

- the consistency of accounting policies adopted with the Charities SORP;
- the adequacy of analysis of incoming resources;
- the allocation of costs between SoFA expenditure headings;
- accounting treatment of heritage assets;
- capitalisation of expenditure on fixed assets;
- service potential of impaired assets;
- accounting for constructive obligations for grant payments.

Auditors' reports

The form and content of auditors' reports on the financial statements of charities follow the basic principles and procedures established by the ISA (UK and Ireland). However, because of the complexity of the legal framework, auditors need to ensure descriptions of the legislative basis and responsibilities of auditors and trustees are precise to the circumstances of the body audited. 240

Example auditor's reports are set out in Bulletins issued by the APB, which are supplementary to this Practice Note, differentiating between reports on company and non-company charities in England and Wales, charities in Scotland, and cross border charities. 241

Addressee of the report

Audit reports made under company legislation are addressed to members (in Scotland – members and trustees) whilst reports made under charity law are made to the trustees. 242

Statement of trustees' responsibilities

ISA (UK and Ireland) 700 requires auditors to include a statement distinguishing between their responsibilities and those of the entity's directors (in the case of a charity, its trustees) and to refer to a description of the latter's responsibilities set out in the financial statements or accompanying information. If no adequate description is given, the ISA (UK and Ireland) requires the auditors to provide details in their report. 243

The responsibilities of the trustees will vary according to the constitution of the particular charity, for example the duties of trustees of charitable companies derive from both company and charity law. Some example wordings for trustees' responsibilities are set out in Appendix 4. 244

Auditors need to be aware that where charities are required to prepare accounts under both Scottish and English law, both sets of legal requirements must be adhered to. 245

Compliance with relevant legal and accounting requirements

246 The auditor's opinion on a charity's financial statements is expressed in the context of the particular legislation and accounting requirements applicable to the charity concerned.

247 Auditors are also aware that the trust deed establishing a charity may establish additional requirements concerning the contents of its financial statements (but cannot derogate from the statutory requirements). The auditors therefore assess whether any such requirements are met. Where the auditors become aware of information which indicates that a transaction or transactions undertaken by the charity may have breached any terms of its trust deed, they consider the implications for their reporting responsibilities following the guidance in the sections dealing with ISA (UK and Ireland) 250.

248 As far as charitable companies in England, Wales and Scotland[37] are concerned care needs to be taken to understand the interaction between the CA 2006, the Charities Act 1993 (as amended by the Charities Act 2006) and the 2005 Act (Scotland). The effect of orders[38] made under company and charity law is that for charitable companies below the audit exemption threshold established in the CA 2006, the legal requirements for audit scrutiny are provided in England and Wales by the Charities Act 1993 and in Scotland by the 2005 Act (Scotland). Accordingly, the audit arrangements referred to in the auditor's reports are the Charities Act 1993 and the 2005 Act (Scotland). This assumes that the charitable company has complied with section 475 (2) of CA 2006 which, for the company to be exempt from the audit requirement, requires a statement on the face of the balance sheet that the company is entitled to audit exemption. For charitable companies below the CA 2006 threshold but above the Charities Act 1993/2005 Act (Scotland) threshold this could be achieved by a statement such as 'The directors consider that the charity is exempt from an audit in accordance with the Companies Act 2006 but is required to have a statutory audit under the Charities Act 1993 / the 2005 Act (Scotland).' CA 2006 continues to apply to the responsibilities of the charitable company for accounts preparation.

Trustees' Annual Reports

249 Audits under companies legislation include consideration of whether the Trustees' Annual Report is consistent with the financial statements.

250 The 2006 Regulations (Scotland) require the auditor to include in their report a statement where they have identified that information contained in the Trustees' Annual Report is inconsistent with the financial statements[39].

---

[37] In Northern Ireland the special rules for the audit of small charitable companies provided by the Companies Act is currently retained.

[38] Relevant orders are:
- The Companies Act 2006 (Commencement No. 6, Saving and Commencement Nos. 3 and 5 (Amendment)) Order 2008
- The Charities Act 2006 (Charitable Companies Audit and Group Accounts Provisions) Order 2008 SI 2008 / 527.

[39] At present, the 2006 Regulations (Scotland) also include the Trustees' Annual Report within the statement of account which is subject to audit. To address this unintended effect of the Regulations, the APB understands that the Scottish Government intends to amend the Regulations in order to remove any disparity with other UK jurisdictions.

Other matters

Auditors of charities in England and Wales and Scotland are required to include an additional statement in their report on the financial statements if they conclude that: 251

(a) the charity has failed to keep accounting records in accordance with the relevant Act; or
(b) the financial statements are not in agreement with the accounting records; or
(c) necessary information and explanations have not been made available to them.

ISA (UK AND IRELAND) 720 (REVISED): SECTION A – OTHER INFORMATION IN DOCUMENTS CONTAINING AUDITED FINANCIAL STATEMENTS AND SECTION B – THE AUDITOR'S STATUTORY REPORTING RESPONSIBILITY IN RELATION TO DIRECTORS' REPORTS

Background note

The purpose of this ISA (UK and Ireland) is to establish standards and provide guidance on the auditor's consideration of other information, on which the auditor has no obligation to report, in documents containing audited financial statements. This ISA (UK and Ireland) applies when an annual report is involved; however, it may also apply to other documents.

The auditor should read the other information to identify material inconsistencies with the audited financial statements. (paragraph 2)

If as a result of reading the other information, the auditor becomes aware of any apparent misstatement therein, or identifies any material inconsistencies with the audited financial statements the auditor should seek to resolve them. (paragraph 2-1)

If, on reading the other information, the auditor identifies a material inconsistency, the auditor should determine whether the audited financial statements or the other information needs to be amended. (paragraph 11)

As noted above, audits of charitable companies include consideration of whether the Trustees' Annual Report is consistent with the financial statements. ISA (UK and Ireland) 720 Section B applies in such circumstances. ISA (UK and Ireland) 720 Section A applies to: 252

- Trustees' annual reports of non-company charities, and
- Other information disclosed in the annual reports of all charities.

One of the fundamental principles set out in The Auditors' Code is that auditors do not allow their reports to be included in documents containing other information if they consider that the additional information is in conflict with the matters covered by their report and they have cause to believe it to be misleading.   253

Auditors read the other information contained in the annual report in the light of the knowledge they have acquired during the audit. The auditors are not expected to verify any of the other information. They read the other information with a view to identifying whether there are any apparent misstatements therein or matters which   254 are inconsistent with the financial statements. It is important to ensure that the trustees are aware of the auditors' responsibilities in respect of the other information, as set out in ISA (UK and Ireland) 720 and the extent of those responsibilities is specifically outlined in the engagement letter.

255 An Annual Report may include:

- statements by the patron, president, chairman of the trustees and/or chief executive of the charity;
- an operating and financial review;
- an investment policy and performance report;
- a statement of grant making policies;
- a statement of reserves policy;
- a statement of achievements against objectives;
- a risk management statement by trustees (based on the Charities SORP or expanded and based on the Combined Code for listed companies);
- a treasurer's report;
- financial summaries; and
- projections of future expenditure based on planned activity.

Additional care will be needed where, for example, the annual report and the financial statements are prepared at the same time but by different personnel, so that their content is largely independent. The Charities SORP requires that where the charity is subject to a statutory audit, the charity trustees should state in their report that the major identified risks to which the charity is exposed have been reviewed and that systems have been established to manage such risks. Whilst this is not mandatory for charities that are not subject to statutory audit, some will choose to make such a statement.

256 The ISA (UK and Ireland) requires auditors who become aware of any apparent material misstatements or inconsistencies in other information published together with the audited financial statements to seek to resolve them. Whilst auditors are not expected to verify any risk management statement made by trustees they are likely to become aware of the steps taken by the trustees to identify and manage identified financial risks through their work in assessing audit risk under ISA (UK and Ireland) 315. They may also become aware of non-financial risks during the course of their audit.

257 If, after discussion with the trustees, any material misstatement or inconsistency identified by auditors in relation to a corporate governance or risk management statement remains in a Trustees' Report, the auditors consider reporting this in the opinion section of their report. It should be noted that, as this does not give rise to a qualified audit opinion on the financial statements, the auditors' comments may be included under the heading 'other matter' as illustrated in the APB Bulletin 2006/5.

258 Charity trustees may request auditors specifically to review a corporate governance or risk management statement made by them in their annual report or contained in "other information" presented with the financial statements. Providing guidance on a review of this nature is beyond the scope of this Practice Note.

Summary Financial Information and Summarised Financial Statements

259 Many charities publish financial information in a format different from the statutory financial statements. This is usually in the annual report, impact statement, or annual

review, but may also occur in other instances such as fund raising literature or local branch literature. In this connection it should be noted that the auditor's report on the full financial statements is not reproduced in conjunction with any accounts other than the complete financial statements reported on by the auditor.

260 The accounting requirements of the legislation do not extend to such summarised information. Trustees of charities which are not limited companies may therefore produce summarised financial statements on an extra-statutory basis, whilst in the case of charitable companies the specific provisions of section 435 of the Companies Act 2006 concerning non-statutory financial statements apply.

261 The Charities SORP distinguishes between summary financial information, and summarised financial statements. The table below sets out the differences:

Characteristics of :

Summarised financial statements	Summary financial information
Includes a summary of the Statement of Financial Activities (SoFA) and Balance Sheet	Draws information from only parts of the accounts.
The summary is derived from statutory accounts.	May be based on interim accounts or other financial information as well as statutory accounts.
A financial statement that purports to be a Statement of Financial Activities or Balance Sheet or summary thereof.	Makes no reference to either of these primary statements.
Represents the entire finances of a charity or a charity group.	Represents analysis, for example of a particular activity or region.

Non-company charities

262 The Charities SORP (paragraphs 371 to 376) sets out general principles for the preparation of summarised financial statements.

263 Summarised financial statements are to be accompanied by a statement, signed on behalf of the trustees, indicating:

- that they are not the statutory accounts but a summary of information relating both to the SoFA and the balance sheet,
- whether or not the full financial statements from which the summary is derived have as yet been externally scrutinised,
- where they have been externally scrutinised, whether the audit report is modified,
- where the audit report is modified, sufficient details should be provided in the summarised financial statements to enable the reader to appreciate the significance of the report,
- where accounts are produced only for a branch of the charity, it must be clearly stated that the summarised financial statements are for the branch only and have been extracted from the full accounts of the reporting charity (giving its name),
- details of how the full annual accounts, the external scrutiny report (as applicable) and the Trustees' Annual Report can be obtained,
- the date on which the annual accounts were approved, and

- for charities registered in England and Wales, whether or not the annual report and accounts have been submitted to the Charity Commission.

There is no statutory requirement for the auditors of a non-company charity to report on summarised financial statements. However, If the full financial statements have been externally scrutinised the Charities SORP requires a statement from the external scrutinisers giving an opinion as to whether or not the summarised financial statements are consistent with the full financial statements to be attached.

264 When a report on summarised financial statements is to be provided in addition to a report on the full financial statements, auditors carry out procedures to establish that the summarised financial statements are consistent with the full financial statements.

265 Matters which may give rise to an inconsistency include:
- information which has been inaccurately extracted from the annual financial statements and Trustees' Report;
- the use of headings in the summarised financial statements that are incompatible with the statutory headings in the full annual financial statements from which they are derived;
- information which, in the auditors' opinion, has been summarised in a manner which is not consistent with the annual financial statements (for example, if the summary is unduly selective); and
- the omission from the summarised financial statements of information which is not specifically required by any regulations but which, in the auditors' opinion, is necessary to ensure consistency with the annual financial statements (for example, omission of information relating to an exceptional item or a non-adjusting subsequent event which the auditors consider fundamental to a reader's understanding of the charity's results or financial position).

266 If the auditor's report on the full financial statements was modified, the auditors consider whether the trustees' statement accompanying the summarised financial statements gives enough details to enable the reader to understand the significance of the auditors' report. They will also include an explanatory paragraph in their report on the summarised financial statements.

267 If the auditors are not satisfied, after discussion with the trustees, that the description given in the trustees' statement describes their report adequately, the principle of association in The Auditors' Code published by the APB indicates that the auditors will not issue a report to be included with the summarised financial statements in respect of which they consider that any qualification or explanatory paragraph in the original audit report is inadequately described.

268 If, in the auditors' opinion, the summarised financial statements are inconsistent with the full financial statements they state this fact in their report. An example of the auditors' statement on summarised financial statements is set out at the end of this section. In addition, either where trustees publish inconsistent summarised financial statements, or the auditors' statement on these is to be qualified, the auditors consider whether this is a matter reportable to the relevant charity regulator in accordance with ISA (UK and Ireland) 250 section B.

269 Charities may issue other summary financial information which is not based on the full financial statements approved by trustees. This may include, for example, interim figures on a fund-raising appeal or on a project. Whilst the Charities SORP requires a statement by the trustees to accompany such financial information, there is no requirement for auditors to review such information and they will only do so if their

names are to be associated with it in any way, in accordance with the principles discussed in the section on ISA (UK and Ireland) 720. However auditors may find it useful to refer to these documents as part of the process of obtaining knowledge of the charity in accordance with ISA (UK and Ireland) 315.

Where a charity prepares summary financial information which does not purport to be summarised financial statements, then the trustees may ask the auditors to prepare a form of report other than that specified in this Practice Note and the SORP. The form of such wording is beyond the scope of this Practice Note. 270

Charitable companies – statutory summary financial statements

All companies have the option under CA 2006 Section 426 to provide summary financial statements instead of copies of the full accounts and reports to the members of the company under companies legislation. Section 427 sets out the form and content for statutory summary financial statements prepared by unquoted companies, and includes the requirements of the auditors. Bulletin 2008/3 contains a summary of the requirements of CA 2006 for the contents of the summary financial statement for different types of company and for the auditor's statement thereon. 271

Industrial and Provident Societies

There are no statutory provisions in respect of summary financial information or statements produced by industrial and provident societies. However the Charities SORP generally applies to all charities in the United Kingdom and therefore the principles applying to non-company charities are applicable. 272

Illustrative example (Non-statutory summarised financial statements): Independent auditor's statement to the trustees of XYZ charity

We have examined the summarised financial statements [for the year ended...] [set out on pages...].

Respective responsibilities of the trustees and the auditor

The trustees are responsible for preparing the [summarised financial statements] [summarised annual report] in accordance with applicable United Kingdom law and the recommendations of the charities SORP.

Our responsibility is to report to you our opinion on the consistency of the summarised financial statements [within the summarised annual report] with the full annual financial statements and the Trustees' Annual Report.

[We also read the other information contained in the summarised annual report and consider the implications for our report if we become aware of any apparent misstatements or material inconsistencies with the summarised financial statements.]

We conducted our work in accordance with Bulletin 2008/3 issued by the Auditing Practices Board.

Opinion

In our opinion the summarised financial statements are consistent with the full annual financial statements and the Trustees' Annual Report of XYZ charity for the year ended....

Or

Qualified opinion

In our opinion the summarised financial statements are not consistent with the full annual financial statements and the Trustee's Annual Report of XYZ charity for the year ended ... in the following respects. ...

Statutory auditor   *Address*
Date

Appendix 1 – Charity accounting and audit regulations in the United Kingdom (updated for the Companies Act 2006)

> The information set out in this Appendix is an overview of the legal framework only, and is likely to be amended over time. Reference should also be made directly to the relevant legislation and regulations as considered necessary.

The Regulatory Framework

England and Wales

1   In England and Wales the Charities Act 1993 as amended by the Charities Act 2006 provides the primary legislative framework for charity regulation by the Charity Commission. In particular the Charity Commission is responsible for the registration, supervision and regulation of charities that are not exempt. A public register of charities is maintained. All charities, except some of the very smallest, exempt charities and certain other classes of charity that have been excepted from registration must register with the Charity Commission.

2   Under the 1993 Act as amended, the Charity Commission may by order require any person to furnish them with any information in their possession which relates to any charity and is relevant to the discharge of their functions. These powers extend to all charities whatever their legal form. Certain types of charity may also be monitored by other bodies, for example by the Housing Corporation in the case of charitable Registered Social Landlords in England.

Excepted charities

3   Certain charities in England and Wales are excepted from registration with the Charity Commission by order or regulation. Examples include certain religious charities, armed forces charities wholly or mainly concerned with the promotion of efficiency of the armed forces and some Scout and Guide groups. Excepted charities do not usually have to submit accounts to the Charity Commission (except on

request) or annual returns, but in most other respects are fully within the Charity Commission's jurisdiction. They are required to prepare accounts and are subject to the same audit or examination requirements as they would be if registered and can be required under s.46 of the Charities Act 1993 to prepare an annual report and submit it together with the accounts for the year.

Exempt charities

Exempt charities in England and Wales are excluded from the Charity Commission's supervision and monitoring, subject to the charity's primary regulator being able to ensure due compliance with trust law. Exempt charities do not register with the Charity Commission, nor do they submit accounts and annual returns. Such charities can seek advice and apply for Schemes and most enabling orders. Exempt charities are listed in Schedule 2 of the Charities Act 1993 and are generally subject to their own statutory and regulatory provisions. Examples include universities, many maintained schools, and many national museums and galleries.

Registered charitable societies within the meaning of the Friendly Societies Act 1974 or the Industrial and Provident Societies Act 1965 in England and Wales were also exempt charities under Schedule 2 of the 1993 Act. These formerly exempt charities, friendly societies or industrial and provident societies are required to register unless they are subject to regulation by another regulator. For those covered by other regulators specific accounting and auditing requirements are provided by the legislative framework applicable to such societies.

The reporting rights and duties of exempt charities will be dependent on how such charities are constituted and any specific statutes or regulations applying to them. If constituted as companies then reporting rights and duties will be under the Companies Act 2006. If constituted as a friendly or industrial and provident society then the legislation applicable to such societies will apply.

Scotland

In Scotland the main primary legislation is the Charities and Trustee Investment (Scotland) Act 2005. Supervision of charities registered in Scotland is carried out by OSCR. OSCR's statutory functions are to:
- maintain the Scottish Charity Register (including granting charitable status),
- encourage, facilitate and monitor compliance with the 2005 Act (Scotland), and
- identify and investigate apparent misconduct, following which it has the power to take remedial action.

Northern Ireland

In Northern Ireland the Charities Branch of the Voluntary and Community Unit of the Department for Social Development is the body responsible for charities. The regulatory framework under which charities operate is provided primarily by the Charities Act (Northern Ireland) 1964 and the Charities (Northern Ireland) Order 1987. Under section 3 of the Charities Act (Northern Ireland) 1964 the Department for Social Development (formerly the Department of Health and Social Services) may, with the consent of the Attorney-General, require any person having in his possession any documents relating to a charity to give the documents (or copies) to the Department if it has reason to believe that the charity's property may have been concealed, misapplied or withheld. The legislation is widely drawn and would cover both audit clients' documents held and auditors' own working papers.

9   There is no requirement for audit under current charities legislation in Northern Ireland. Therefore there are no statutory provisions relating to auditors' rights to information and explanations. As full access to information is fundamental to the proper conduct of an audit in accordance with Auditing Standards, auditors who are unable to obtain all the information and explanations they consider necessary for the purposes of forming an opinion will qualify their report accordingly. Similarly no legislation covers auditors' reports to trustees.

Friendly and Industrial and Provident Societies

10   There are relatively few remaining charitable friendly societies – the Financial Services Authority regulates those that remain. The primary legislation relating to charitable societies is the Friendly Societies Act 1974, although new registrations under this Act are not permitted. Societies can be incorporated under the Friendly Societies Act 1992 but the purposes defined in Schedule 2 of this Act are unlikely to be charitable. A charitable incorporated society is not an exempt charity. A number of charities, primarily Registered Social Landlords, are constituted as industrial and provident societies.

11   The accounting requirements for industrial and provident societies are set out in the Friendly and Industrial and Provident Societies Act 1968, which require accounts to be prepared giving a true and fair view. All industrial and provident societies are required to submit an annual return, including the accounts, which are public records. Similar provisions apply to charitable societies registered under the Friendly Societies Act 1974.

12   In Scotland, charities which are registered under the Friendly Societies Act or the Industrial and Provident Societies Act are still subject to the provisions of the 2005 Act (Scotland) and 2006 Regulations (Scotland). Registered Social Landlords in Northern Ireland register under the Industrial & Provident Societies Act (Northern Ireland) 1969, and are also required to register with the Department of the Environment.

Primary legislation applicable to charities

UK-wide	England & Wales	Scotland	N. Ireland
Companies Act 2006 or N. Ireland equivalent	Charities Acts 1992, 1993 (as amended by 2006)	The Charities and Trustee Investment (Scotland) Act 2005	Charities Act (Northern Ireland) 1964
Friendly Societies Acts 1974 to 1992		Trusts (Scotland) Acts 1921 and 1961	
Industrial & Provident Societies Acts 1965 to 1978 or N. Ireland equivalent		Housing (Scotland) Act 2001	
Housing Associations Act 1985			
Housing Acts 1988 and 1996			

Principal secondary legislation

England & Wales	Scotland	N. Ireland
The Charities (Accounts & Reports) Regulations 2008	The Charities Accounts (Scotland) Regulations 2006	The Charities (Northern Ireland) Order 1987
The Charities (Exemption from Registration) Regulations 1996	The Charities Accounts (Scotland) Amendment Regulations 2007	
The Charities (Exemption of Universities from Registration) Regulations 1966	The Charities References in Documents (Scotland) Regulations 2007	
The Charities (Exemption from Registration and Accounts) Regulations 1965	The Charities Reorganisation (Scotland) Regulations 2007	
The Charities (Exception of Voluntary Schools from Registration) Regulations 1960 and section 23 School Standards and Framework Act 1998		

Accounting and reporting requirements

Charitable company	Industrial & Provident Society	Unincorporated charity		
UK-wide	UK-wide	England & Wales[40]	Scotland	N. Ireland
Accruals basis; true and fair view required		Gross income no more than £100,000, option to prepare Receipts and Payments accounts	Gross income less than £100,000, should prepare Receipts and Payments	Charities choose either annual Receipts and Payments or Income and Expenditure account.
		Accruals basis and true and fair view required where income £100,000 and more		

[40] Registered charities with gross income of £10,000 or less, and excepted charities which are not registered, are not required to submit annual reports or accounts to the Charity Commission, unless requested to do so. All registered charities must prepare an annual report, even if they are not requested to submit it to the Charity Commission.

The Charities SORP and UK Legal Requirements

13 The Charities SORP applies to all charities in the United Kingdom whose financial statements are required to give a true and fair view, and for whom no more specialist SORP applies. So far as the preparation of accounts is concerned, falling within more than one regulated sector may influence the accounting requirements for a charity. Paragraph 5 of the Charities SORP (reissued in March 2005) states that, where a Statement of Recommended Practice exists for a particular class of charities, the trustees of charities in that class should adhere to that SORP instead.

14 Whilst the Charities SORP is generally compatible with the requirements of UK law, it is recognised that where necessary, its recommendations should be adapted to meet any statutory requirements relating to the form and content of accounts, such as are contained in companies legislation, the Industrial and Provident Societies Acts 1965 to 1978, or registered social landlord accounting regulations for England, Wales or Scotland. The recommendations of the Charities SORP should also be adapted to meet any special requirements of the charity's own governing document.

15 It is not envisaged that the requirements of different regimes will be incompatible. For example, there is a general requirement under companies and friendly societies legislation in the United Kingdom for financial statements to give a true and fair view. The aim of SORPs, including the Charities SORP, is to assist entities in achieving a true and fair view appropriate to their circumstances.

16 All charities in England & Wales as defined in the 1993 Act are affected in some respects by the accounting and reporting provisions of Part VI of the 1993 Act. However the way in which they are affected will depend on their constitution, size and whether they are registered, excepted or exempt.

Charitable Companies (United Kingdom)

17 Charitable companies are generally incorporated as companies limited by guarantee and the requirements of CA 2006 applicable to such companies apply throughout Great Britain. CA 2006 requires directors of companies to approve accounts only if they give a true and fair view of the assets, liabilities, financial position and of the net income or expenditure for the year. The accounts must be prepared in accordance with section 396 of CA 2006. Section 396 allows for the adaption of formats enabling Charities SORP compliant accounts to be prepared by charitable companies. Paragraphs 419 to 428 of the Charities SORP provide a detailed analysis of the impact of the Companies Act requirements on SORP compliant accounts.

18 CA 2006 requires annual accounts to give a true and fair view, which means that charitable companies, however small, must prepare their accounts on an accruals basis.

19 Charitable companies registered in England & Wales are also subject to certain provisions of the 1993 Act. Likewise, charitable companies registered in Scotland are also subject to the provisions of the 2005 Act (Scotland).

Requirements for external scrutiny of financial statements

(The constitution of the charity may impose more demanding requirements than, but cannot derogate from, the following rules)

Charitable companies

England & Wales	Scotland	N.Ireland
Independent Examination where gross income is between £10,000 and £500,000. Where gross income is over £250,000, the Examiner must be a member of a specified body.	Independent examination required where gross income is less than £500,000. The Examiner must be a member of a specified body.	Audit required under the Companies (Northern Ireland) Order 1986
Audit required where: • gross income is over £500,000 or • gross assets are over £2.8 million <u>and</u> gross income is over £100,000[41] Audit must be undertaken by a registered auditor unless the Charity Commission gives a dispensation	Audit required where: • gross income is £500,000 or more or • gross assets are over £2.8 million Audit must be undertaken by a registered auditor or by the Auditor General for Scotland	

20 Section 1175 and Schedule 9 to the CA 2006 removes from company law special rules about the audit of smaller companies that are charities. The effect is that as far as accounts scrutiny is concerned audits will be undertaken under the requirements of charity law. In England and Wales the audit of group accounts prepared by small company parent charities is also undertaken under the provisions of charity law. In Northern Ireland the special rules for the audit of small charitable companies provided by the Companies Act is currently retained.

21 Limited company charities which fall below the statutory audit threshold under CA 2006 are potentially exempt from the Companies Act audit requirement.

Differences between an audit undertaken in accordance with CA 2006 and an audit undertaken in accordance with charity legislation include:

- to qualify for exemption from CA 2006 the directors must make the prescribed statement on the company balance sheet;
- CA 2006 requires that the auditor explicitly reports on the consistency of the annual report with the financial statements. Audit reports under charity law do not;
- the CA 2006 audit report is signed by a senior statutory auditor. Audit reports under charity law can be signed in the name of the firm;
- the CA 2006 permits the auditor to limit liability. There is no such provision in charity law.

---

[41] These limits apply to accounting periods beginning on or after 1 April 2008.

22 In both cases limited company charities which fall below the statutory audit threshold are not required to file an audit report with Companies House.

Industrial and Provident Societies

23 In England & Wales, charitable Industrial and Provident Societies are exempt from audit if turnover is less than £90,000. An audit exemption report is required if turnover is more than £90,000 and less than £250,000 and total assets are less than £2.8 million. An audit is required above this threshold (exemption not available if there is a subsidiary). In Scotland, all charitable Industrial and Provident Societies are also subject to the provisions of the 2005 Act (Scotland). They must prepare accounts on the accruals basis which must be audited where gross income is £500,000 or more or where gross assets are at least £2.8 million. Below these thresholds, independent examination by a member of a specified body must be carried out.

Non-company charities

England & Wales	Scotland	N.Ireland
Independent Examination where gross income is between £10,000 and £500,000. Where gross income is over £250,000 the Examiner must be a member of a specified body.	Independent examination required where gross income is less than £500,000. Where gross income is £100,000 or more, the Examiner must be a member of a specified body.	No statutory requirements in N.Ireland.
Audit required where: • gross income is over £500,000 or • gross assets are over £2.8 million <u>and</u> gross income is over £100,000[42] Audit must be undertaken by a registered auditor unless the Charity Commission gives a dispensation	Audit required where: • gross income is £500,000 or more or • gross assets are over £2.8 million <u>and</u> accruals accounts are prepared Audit must be undertaken by a registered auditor or by the Auditor General for Scotland	

24 A charity's governing document may require an audit, even though the charity may be below the threshold and therefore only require an Independent Examination. In such circumstances the trustees may wish to approach the Charity Commission/ OSCR with a view to amending the requirement of the governing document to bring it in line with statutory provisions. Where the intention of the governing document is ambiguous in terms of the level of scrutiny required the trustees may seek the advice

---

[42] *These limits apply to accounting periods beginning on or after 1 April 2008.*

of the Charity Commission or seek to amend the relevant clause in line with the requirements of charity law.

Other aspects of law relevant to auditors

England and Wales

Content of Auditor's Report

The 2008 Regulations set out the matters to be included in the audit report. In addition to giving an opinion on the state of affairs and incoming resources and their application and compliance with the Regulations, additional statements in the auditor's report are required where the opinion is formed that: 25

- proper accounting records have not been kept in accordance with section 41 of the 1993 Act;
- the statement of accounts does not accord with those records;
- any information contained in the statement of accounts is inconsistent in any material respect with any report of the charity trustees prepared under section 45 of the 1993 Act in respect of the financial year in question; or
- information and explanations considered necessary have not been provided.

Access to information and explanations

Auditors or independent examiners have a right of access with respect to books, documents and other records (however and wherever kept) relating to the charity concerned and any subsidiaries; the auditor or independent examiner is entitled to require, in relation to the charity, information and explanations from past or present charity trustees, or from past or present officers or employees of the charity. 26

Other Reporting Rights and Duties

Auditors are required by section 44 of the Charities Act 1993 to report to the Charity Commission in writing if, in connection with an audit of a charity, they become aware of a matter of material significance to the Charity Commission's regulatory functions under sections 8 or 18 of the 1993 Act. A similar reporting duty is imposed on independent examiners. Detailed guidance on the audit implications of this duty is provided in the section of this Practice Note on ISA (UK and Ireland) 250 B. 27

In addition when auditors cease for any reason to hold office they must send to the charity trustees a statement of circumstances connected with their ceasing to hold office, which they consider should be brought to the trustees' attention or, if they consider that there are no such circumstances, a statement that there are none. A copy of the statement should be sent to the Charity Commission unless there are no such circumstances to report. 28

Scotland

Content of Auditor's Report

The 2006 Regulations (Scotland) set out the matters to be included in the audit report. The auditor must give an opinion as follows: 29

- Where regulation 8 (of the 2006 Regulations (Scotland)) applies, the statement of account complies with the regulatory requirements, gives a true and fair view of the state of affairs of the charity at the year end and of the incoming resources and application of resources during the year;
- Where regulation 9 applies, the statement of account complies with the regulatory requirements and properly presents the receipts and payments of the charity for the year and its statement of balances at the year end.

In addition, the auditor is required to make a statement where the opinion is formed that:

- the accounting records have not been kept in accordance with the 2005 Act (Scotland) and 2006 Regulations (Scotland);
- the statement of account does not accord with those records;
- any information contained in the statement of account is inconsistent in any material respect with any report of the charity trustees prepared under section 44 (1) (b) of the 2005 Act (Scotland) in respect of the financial year;
- any information or explanation to which the auditor is entitled under regulation 13 has not been afforded to them.

Access to information and explanations

30 The 2006 Regulations provide that the auditors shall have the right of access at all times to the records of the relevant charity and shall be entitled to require such information and explanations from the present or former trustees as they think necessary for the performance of their duties.

Other Reporting Rights and duties

31 Where auditors cease to hold office for any reason, Regulation 10 of 2006 Regulations (Scotland) states that they must include in their notice of resignation a statement as to any circumstances connected with their resignation which they consider should be brought to the trustees' attention, or a statement that there are none. If there are circumstances which they consider should be brought to the trustees' attention, they should send a copy of the statement to OSCR.

32 Auditors are required by section 46 of the 2005 Act (Scotland) to report to OSCR if, in connection with an audit of a charity, they become aware of a matter of material significance to OSCR's regulatory functions under sections 28, 30 or 31 of the 2005 Act (Scotland). A similar reporting duty is placed on independent examiners. Guidance on the audit implications of this duty is provided in the section of this Practice Note on ISA (UK and Ireland) 250 B.

Appendix 2 – Publications

The Charities SORP

Accounting and Reporting by Charities – Statement of Recommended Practice (Charities SORP) was published in March 2005. This publication can be viewed and downloaded for free from the Charity Commission's web site.

The Charity Commission

For charities registered in England and Wales the Charity Commission produces a range of publications, audio-cassettes and a video, which provide information about the Commission's role, the duties of charity trustees, and charity law. The list of current publications is available on the Charity Commission's web site – www.charitycommission.gov.uk and the publications are available for download from the website or by ordering from Charity Commission Direct. The web site also provides access to model governing documents, a series of publications in relation to the current review of the register as well as useful guidance on a variety of current topics and issues.

OSCR

For charities registered in Scotland, further reading matter is available from OSCR. All of its publications are available on the website www.oscr.org.uk and some are also available in hard copy by request.

Northern Ireland

Northern Ireland Department for Social Development – Charities Branch Voluntary Activity Unit

- Northern Ireland Charities: A guide for trustees

Northern Ireland Council for Voluntary Action charity advice service

- Notes on charitable status Lotteries: a guidance for voluntary groups

Charity Regulators:

England and Wales

Charity Commission Direct
PO Box 1227
Liverpool
L69 3UG

0845 3000 218
0845 3000 219 Textphone service for hearing and speech impaired callers
Email enquiries@charitycommission.gov.uk

Scotland

The Office of the Scottish Charity Regulator
2nd floor
Quadrant House
9 Riverside Drive
Dundee DD1 4NY

01382 220446

Email info@oscr.org.uk

Northern Ireland

Charities Branch
The Department for Social Development
Lighthouse Building,

1 Cromac Place,
Gasworks Business Park,
Ormeau Road,
Belfast BT7 2JB

028 90 829427

Appendix 3 – Example paragraphs for insertion into an engagement letter[43]

England and Wales

Non-company (accruals basis)

The following paragraphs should be inserted into the auditor's standard letter of engagement for non- company charities in England & Wales which are preparing financial statements on an accruals basis:

Para 1: As trustees of the charity, you are responsible for maintaining proper accounting records and an appropriate system of internal control for the charity. You are also responsible for preparing the annual report and financial statements which give a true and fair view and have been prepared in accordance with applicable accounting standards and the Charities Act 1993 ("the Act") and regulations there under.

Para 2: As trustees of a charity, you are under a duty to prepare an annual report for each financial year complying in its form and content with regulations made under the Charities Act 1993. You should also have regard to the SORP, issued by the Charity Commission for England & Wales and any subsequent amendments or variations to this statement.

Para 3: Under the Charities Act 1993 we have a statutory responsibility to report to you as trustees whether in our opinion the financial statements comply with the requirements of regulations made under that Act and whether they give a true and fair view of the state of affairs of the charity at the end of the financial year and of the incoming resources and application of the resources of the charity in that year. In arriving at our opinion, we are required to consider the following matters, and report on any in respect of which we are not satisfied:
- whether proper accounting records have been kept by the charity and proper returns adequate for our audit have been received from branches not visited by us in accordance with Section 41 of the Charities Act 1993;
- whether the charity's balance sheet and income and expenditure account are in agreement with the accounting records and returns;
- whether we have obtained all the information and explanations which we consider necessary for the purpose of our audit; and
- whether the information given in the trustees' annual report is consistent with the financial statements.

Para 4: Under the Charities (Accounts and Reports) Regulations 2008 and the SORP you are required to report as to whether you have given consideration to the major risks to which the charity is exposed, and to the

---

[43] These example paragraphs take account of changes introduced by the Companies Act 2006 and the Charities Act 2006. As a result, they are appropriate for accounting periods beginning on or after 6 April 2008.

Para 5: systems designed to manage those risks. We are not required to audit this statement, or to form an opinion on the effectiveness of the risk management and control procedures.

Para 5: We have a statutory duty to report to the Charity Commission such matters (concerning the activities or affairs of the charity or any connected institution or body corporate) of which we become aware during the course of our audit which are (or are likely to be) of material significance to the Commission in the exercise of their powers of inquiry into, or acting for the protection of, charities (The Charities (Accounts and Reports) Regulations 2008).

Para 6: From time to time we may have to rely on oral representations by management which are uncorroborated by other audit evidence. Where they relate to matters which are material to the financial statements, we will request that you provide written confirmation of them. In particular, where misstatements in the financial statements that we bring to your attention are not adjusted, we are required to obtain your reasons in writing.

Non-company (receipts and payments basis)

Alternative paragraphs for a non-company charity in England & Wales which prepares accounts on a receipts and payments basis:

1. New paragraph. In accordance with the Charities Act 1993 Section 42(3), where the charity's gross income in any financial year does not exceed £100,000, the charity's trustees may elect to prepare a receipts and payments account and a statement of assets and liabilities [as its annual statement of accounts]. [You have elected to prepare such an account and statement].
2. References in paragraphs 3 and 6 above will be to the 'account and statement' rather than to 'statement of account/financial statement'.
3. The statutory requirement to report on the major risks does not apply, so paragraph 4 is dropped.

Charitable company

Alternative paragraphs for a charity in England and Wales which is incorporated under the Companies Act 2006 and does not exceed the small company thresholds (as defined by the Companies Act 2006):

For all paragraphs, the term charity can be replaced with charitable company.
1. References in paragraph 1 above to the "Charities Act 1993" should be replaced with "Companies Act 2006".
2. Paragraph 2 above should be replaced with "As trustees of a charity, you have a duty under the Companies Act 2006 to prepare a directors' report for each financial year and also an annual report complying in its form and content with regulations made under the Charities Act 1993. You should also have regard to the Statement of Recommended Practice 'Accounting and Reporting by Charities (revised 2005)' ("SORP"), issued by the Charity Commission for England & Wales and any subsequent amendments or variations to this statement".
3. In the first section of paragraph 3 above replace "you as trustees" with "the members". In the first section, also replace "comply with the requirements of regulations made under that Act" with "have been properly prepared in accordance with the Companies Act 2006" In the first bullet point delete "in accordance with Section 41 of the Charities Act 1993".

Alternative paragraphs where the charity is incorporated under the Companies Act 2006, and exceeds the small company thresholds (as defined by the Companies Act 2006):

> The changes applicable for company charities which do not exceed the small company thresholds as defined by companies legislation will also apply to these charities.
>
> In addition, in paragraph 3 "Under the Charities Act 1993" should be replaced with "Under the Companies Act 2006".

Scotland

Non-company (accruals basis)

Alternative paragraphs for non-company charities registered in Scotland preparing accounts on an accruals basis:

1: References in paragraphs 1 and 2 above to the "Charities Act 1993" should be replaced with "Charities and Trustee Investment (Scotland) Act 2005".
2: References in the first section of paragraph 3 above to the "Charities Act 1993" should be replaced with "Charities and Trustee Investment (Scotland) Act 2005". In the first bullet point of paragraph 3 above, "Section 41 of the Charities Act 1993" should be replaced with "Section 44 of the Charities and Trustee Investment (Scotland) Act 2005".
3: In paragraph 4 above, "Charities (Accounts and Reports) Regulations 2007 and the SORP" should be deleted so that the paragraph reads "Under the SORP you are required to ...."
4: References in paragraph 5 above to "the Charity Commission" should be replaced with "OSCR". In addition, the reference at the end of the paragraph to "(The Charities (Accounts and Reports) Regulations 2008)" should be replaced with "(section 46 of the Charities and Trustee Investment (Scotland) Act 2005)".
5 New paragraph – "The Charity and Trustee Investment (Scotland) Act 2005 currently requires the trustees' report to be subject to external audit. The Scottish Government has indicated that this is a technical error which will be corrected by legislation in the future. Therefore, you agree that we will not be expressing a true and fair opinion on the trustees' report. As a result, this engagement letter has been produced on the basis that the trustees' report does not need to be audited, and hence is consistent with the example audit reports issued by the Institute of Chartered Accountants of Scotland."

Non-company (receipts and payments basis)

Alternative paragraphs for a non- company charity in Scotland which prepares accounts on a receipts and payments basis:

1. In paragraph 1, replace "You are also responsible for preparing the annual report and financial statements which give a true and fair view and have been prepared in accordance with applicable accounting standards and the Charities and Trustee Investment (Scotland) Act 2005 and regulations thereunder." with "In accordance with the Charities and Trustee Investment (Scotland) Act 2005 and regulations thereunder, where the charity's gross income in any financial year does not exceed £100,000, the charity's trustees may elect to prepare a receipts and payments account, a statement of balances, notes and annual report. You have elected to prepare such a statement of account."

2. Reference in Paragraph 2 to the SORP is not applicable so the whole of the second sentence should be removed.
3. In paragraph 3 the opinion expressed as "the financial statements comply with the requirements of regulations made under that Act and whether they give a true and fair view of the state of affairs of the charity at the end of the financial year and of the incoming resources and application of the resources of the charity in that year." should be replaced with "the statement of account properly presents the receipts and payments of the charity for the financial year in question and its statement of balances as at the end of that year".
4. In paragraph 3 above, the second bullet point should be replaced with "whether the accounts and statement are in agreement with the accounting records and returns".

Charitable company

Alternative paragraphs for a charity in Scotland which is incorporated under the Companies Act 2006:

1. For all paragraphs, the term "charity" can be replaced with "charitable company".
2. References to "Charities and Trustee Investment (Scotland) Act 2005" should be replaced with "Companies Act 2006 and the Charities and Trustee Investment (Scotland) Act 2005".
3. For large companies, in paragraph 3, the auditor has a duty to report to both the trustees and the members. So the first sentence should be amended from "to report to you as trustees" to read "to report to the members and to you as trustees".
4. In paragraph 3 replace "that Act" with "the Charities and Trustee Investment (Scotland) Act 2005 and have been properly prepared in accordance with the Companies Act 2006".

Cross-border charity

Alternative paragraph for a charity registered in England and Wales and which has operations in Scotland:

The relevant changes noted above for Scotland need to be combined with the English and Welsh requirements. For example, paragraph 1 should read "As trustees of the charity, you are responsible for maintaining proper accounting records and an appropriate system of internal control for the charity. You are also responsible for preparing the annual report and financial statements which give a true and fair view and have been prepared in accordance with applicable accounting standards, the Charities Act 1993 ("the Act") and regulations thereunder and the Charities and Trustee Investment (Scotland) Act 2005 and regulations thereunder".

Appendix 4 – Illustrative example statements of trustees' responsibilities

The general duties of trustees in relation to financial reporting are set out in Appendix 1, but these need to be adapted to the circumstances of individual entities. Examples are given below of statements for:

1. a charity which is subject only to the regulation generally applicable to charities in the country where it is based (England & Wales, or Scotland, or Northern Ireland);
2. a charitable company which is subject to the requirements of the Companies Act 2006 (this example also illustrates wording appropriate to consolidated accounts);
3. a public sector entity.

1 Statement of trustees' responsibilities

The trustees are responsible for preparing the Trustees' Report and the financial statements in accordance with applicable law and United Kingdom Accounting Standards (United Kingdom Generally Accepted Accounting Practice).

The law applicable to charities in [England & Wales/Scotland/Northern Ireland][44] requires the trustees to prepare financial statements for each financial year which give a true and fair view of the state of affairs of the charity and of the incoming resources and application of resources of the charity for that period. In preparing these financial statements, the trustees are required to:

- select suitable accounting policies and then apply them consistently;
- observe the methods and principles in the Charities SORP;
- make judgments and estimates that are reasonable and prudent;
- state whether applicable accounting standards have been followed, subject to any material departures disclosed and explained in the financial statements;
- prepare the financial statements on the going concern basis unless it is inappropriate to presume that the charity will continue in business.

The trustees are responsible for keeping proper accounting records that disclose with reasonable accuracy at any time the financial position of the charity and enable them to ensure that the financial statements comply with the [Charities Act 1993, the Charity (Accounts and Reports) Regulations 2008 and the provisions of the trust deed][45]. They are also responsible for safeguarding the assets of the charity and hence for taking reasonable steps for the prevention and detection of fraud and other irregularities.

The trustees are responsible for the maintenance and integrity of the charity and financial information included on the charity's website. Legislation in the United Kingdom governing the preparation and dissemination of financial statements may differ from legislation in other jurisdictions.[46]

2. Statement of trustees' responsibilities – Charitable company

The trustees (who are also directors of [name of charity] for the purposes of company law) are responsible for preparing the Trustees' Report and the financial statements

---

[44] For Scottish charities, the references should be supplemented by the Charities and Trustee Investment (Scotland) Act 2005, the Charities Accounts (Scotland) Regulations 2006 and the provisions of the charity's constitution.

[45] For Scottish charities, the references should be supplemented by the Charities and Trustee Investment (Scotland) Act 2005, the Charities Accounts (Scotland) Regulations 2006 and the provisions of the charity's constitution.

[46] Only required if the accounts are included on the entity's website.

in accordance with applicable law and United Kingdom Accounting Standards (United Kingdom Generally Accepted Accounting Practice).

Company law requires the trustees to prepare financial statements for each financial year which give a true and fair view of the state of affairs of the charitable company [**and the group**[47]] and of the incoming resources and application of resources, including the income and expenditure, of the charitable [**company/group**] for that period. In preparing these financial statements, the trustees are required to:

- select suitable accounting policies and then apply them consistently;
- observe the methods and principles in the Charities SORP;
- make judgments and estimates that are reasonable and prudent;
- state whether applicable UK Accounting Standards have been followed, subject to any material departures disclosed and explained in the financial statements;
- prepare the financial statements on the going concern basis unless it is inappropriate to presume that the charitable company will continue in business.

The trustees are responsible for keeping proper accounting records that disclose with reasonable accuracy at any time the financial position of the charitable company and enable them to ensure that the financial statements comply with the Companies Act 2006[48]. They are also responsible for safeguarding the assets of the charitable company [and the group] and hence for taking reasonable steps for the prevention and detection of fraud and other irregularities.

In so far as the trustees are aware:

- there is no relevant audit information of which the charitable company's auditor is unaware; and
- the trustees have taken all steps that they ought to have taken to make themselves aware of any relevant audit information and to establish that the auditor is aware of that information.[49]

The trustees are responsible for the maintenance and integrity of the corporate and financial information included on the charitable company's website. Legislation in the United Kingdom governing the preparation and dissemination of financial statements may differ from legislation in other jurisdictions.[50]

3 Statement of trustees' responsibilities – public sector entity accounts

Law applicable to Public Sector entities in England & Wales/Scotland/Northern Ireland requires the trustees to prepare financial statements for each financial year which give a true and fair view of the charity's financial activities during the year and of its financial position at the end of the year. In preparing those financial statements, the trustees are required to:

- select suitable accounting policies and then apply them consistently;
- make judgments and estimates that are reasonable and prudent;

---

[47] *In England and Wales group accounts prepared by small company parent charities are prepared under the accounting provisions of the Charities Act.*

[48] *For Scottish charities, the references should be supplemented by the Charities and Trustee Investment (Scotland) Act 2005 and the Charities Accounts (Scotland) Regulations 2006.*

[49] *These two bullet points are required if subject to audit.*

[50] *Only required if the accounts are included on the entity's website.*

- state whether applicable accounting standards and statements of recommended practice have been followed, subject to any material departures disclosed and explained in the financial statements; and
- prepare the financial statements on the going concern basis unless it is inappropriate to presume that the charity will continue in operation.

The trustees are required to follow the accounts direction issued by the Secretary of State/Scottish Ministers, and are responsible for ensuring that proper accounting records are maintained which disclose with reasonable accuracy at any time the financial position of the charity and which enable them to ensure that the financial statements comply with (applicable law, regulations and trust deed). They are also responsible for safeguarding the assets of the charity and hence for taking reasonable steps for the prevention and detection of fraud and other irregularities.

The trustees have a responsibility to ensure that the entity's system of internal control complies with the obligations placed on the entity by the relevant Secretary of State/Scottish Ministers.

Where an Accounting Officer has been appointed the financial statements must include a statement of the scope of their responsibilities in respect of the internal controls and the financial statements along the following lines:

X has been designated as Accounting Officer for the charity. His/her relevant responsibilities as Accounting Officer, including his/her responsibility for the propriety and regularity of the public finances for which he/she is answerable and for the keeping of proper records, are set out in Managing Public Money issued by the Treasury.

If the entity is required to comply with the Companies Act the annual report must contain a statement to the effect that:

(a) so far as the Accounting Officer (or equivalent) is aware, there is no relevant audit information of which the entity's auditors are unaware, and
(b) the Accounting Officer (or equivalent) has taken all the steps that s/he ought to have taken to make him/herself aware of any relevant audit information and to establish that the entity's auditors are aware of that information.

Appendix 5 – The duty of Auditors to report matters of Material Significance to the Charity Commission and OSCR.

Introduction

The Charity Commission and OSCR value the objectivity and independence that auditors bring to their work and the assurance that the audit process provides makes an important contribution to maintaining public trust and confidence in charities. Auditors in both England and Wales and Scotland have a common statutory duty to report matters of material significance to charity regulators. This important duty will be a key contribution to the ability of charity regulators to take timely action and so they have agreed a common list of matters of material significance to assist the auditor in reporting important matters on a timely basis. The sooner the charity regulators are made aware of a matter the sooner it can be considered and, where appropriate, regulatory action taken to protect a charity, its beneficiaries and its charitable assets.

Guidance

The Charities Act 1993 section 44, as amended by the Charities Act 2006, places a duty on the auditors of both a non-company charity and a company charity to report matters of "material significance" to the Commission. Section 46 of the Charities and Trustee Investment (Scotland) Act 2005 places a similar duty on auditors of Scottish charities to report matters of "material significance" to OSCR.

The duty to report arises where the auditor, in the course of their audit, identifies a matter, which relates to the activities or affairs of the charity or of any connected institution or body, and which the auditor has reasonable cause to believe is likely to be of material significance for the purposes of the exercise by the Commission of its functions under section 8 or 18 of the Charities Act 1993 or the exercise by OSCR of its functions under sections 28, 30 or 31 of the Charities and Trustee Investment (Scotland) Act 2005.

Subject to compliance with money laundering legislation regarding "tipping off", in the circumstances leading to a right or duty to report, the auditor is entitled to communicate to charity regulators in good faith information or opinions relating to the business or affairs of the entity or any associated body without contravening the duty of confidence owed to the entity. In addition, in England and Wales, the Charities Act 1993 provides additional statutory protection for the auditor as no duty, for example confidentiality, is regarded as contravened merely because of any information or opinion contained in the report.

The reporting of a matter of material significance is a separate report from the auditor's report on the accounts. The Charities Act 1993 and the Charities and Trustee Investment (Scotland) Act 2005 require the report to be made immediately the matter comes to the auditor's attention and in England and Wales the Charities Act 1993 requires that this is done in writing. There is no requirement under Scottish law for a report to be made in writing but it is recommended to do so.

It is not part of the reporting duty to require auditors to perform any additional scrutiny work as a result of the statutory duty nor are they required specifically to seek out reportable matters. Auditors do however include procedures within their planning processes to ensure that members of the audit team have sufficient understanding (in the context of their role) to enable them to identify situations which may give reasonable cause to believe that a matter should be reported to the regulator. Where a matter comes to light relating to a previous financial year which would give rise to a duty to report, then the auditor should still make a report.

In order to recognise whether a situation is likely to be of material significance to a regulator's function an understanding is needed of those matters which either due to their nature or potential financial impact are likely to require evaluation and, where appropriate, investigation by the regulator.

Both the Charity Commission and OSCR will always consider the following to be of material significance and hence reportable:

- matters suggesting dishonesty or fraud involving a significant loss of, or a major risk to, charitable funds or assets;
- failure(s) of internal controls, including failure(s) in charity governance, that resulted in a significant loss or misappropriation of charitable funds, or which leads to significant charitable funds being put at major risk;

- matters leading to the knowledge or suspicion that the charity or charitable funds have been used for money laundering or such funds are the proceeds of serious organised crime or that the charity is a conduit for criminal activity;
- matters leading to the belief or suspicion that the charity, its trustees, employees or assets, have been involved in or used to support terrorism or proscribed organisations in the UK or outside of the UK;
- evidence suggesting that in the way the charity carries out its work relating to the care and welfare of beneficiaries, the charity's beneficiaries have been or were put at significant risk of abuse or mistreatment;
- significant or recurring breach(es) of either a legislative requirement or of the charity's trusts;
- a deliberate or significant breach of an order or direction made by a charity regulator under statutory powers including suspending a charity trustee, prohibiting a particular transaction or activity or granting consent on particular terms involving significant charitable assets or liabilities; and
- the notification on ceasing to hold office or resigning from office, of those matters reported to the charity's trustees.

These matters are considered central to the integrity of a charity and as such will require evaluation and where appropriate investigation by the regulators. The Charity Commission and OSCR consider all such reports to have a very high intelligence value. Both take a risk based and proportionate approach to inquiry work when deciding whether to open an inquiry. The duty to report applies to the auditor who must make a report whether or not the matter has already been notified to other regulators or agencies and whether or not the trustees have already advised the charity regulators, for example, by making a serious incident report to the Charity Commission.

Matters which the Charity Commission and OSCR have indicated are likely to be of material significance are set out on the charity regulators' websites. Other sources of information include:

- the Charity Commission's Directions and guidance for independent examinations;
- Annual Returns (in Scotland, Supplementary Monitoring Returns[51]) which signpost a number of the areas that the relevant regulator considers significant; and
- in England and Wales, any serious incident report made by the trustees to the Charity Commission.

The list of "serious incidents" is principally concerned with serious criminal or unlawful activity, or very serious incidents concerning a charity that may affect its funds, property, beneficiaries or reputation. Some of the incidents listed may not actually be criminal activity, but do flag up a risk of potential criminal activity or other risks, which if realised, would have a serious detrimental impact on the charity.

There is no serious incident reporting requirement placed on trustees in Scotland.

Where auditors make a report, they may not have all the information but should be prepared to provide as much relevant information as possible about the matter(s) they are reporting.

---

[51] Completed by charities with gross income over £25,000.

The auditor's right to report to charity regulators under the Charities Act 1993 Act and the Charities and Trustee Investment (Scotland) Act 2005

The auditor also has a broad discretionary right to report matters that they believe may be relevant to the work of the charity regulators but they are not under a duty to report such matters.

The Charity Commission and OSCR consider such reports to have considerable intelligence value and welcome these submissions. Given the broad discretion permitted it is not appropriate to list instances for reporting but the auditor may usefully review matters which were not considered material relating to the statutory duty and matters upon which trustees are requested to provide additional information as part of the annual return process.

Matters falling within this discretionary category are likely to be indicative of significant risks to charitable funds or their proper application and would therefore normally be relevant to the work of the regulators. Where such a matter arises, the auditor may discuss the matter with the trustees to identify whether it remains a matter of concern and whether the trustees have taken or are taking action which can reasonably be expected to remedy or mitigate the effect on the current or future years.

Although the auditor enjoys a discretion as to whether to make a report of a matter relevant to the work of the Charity Commission and OSCR, it is recommended that auditors document any relevant matters identified in the course of the audit and document the basis of any decision not to report a matter falling within this discretionary category.

Ceasing to hold office

In addition to the duty to report matters of material significance, Regulations under the Charities Act 1993 and the Charities and Trustee Investment (Scotland) Act 2005 provide that 'Where an auditor appointed by charity trustees ceases for any reason to hold office he shall send to the charity trustees a statement of any circumstances connected with his ceasing to hold office which he considers should be brought to their attention or, if he considers that there are no such circumstances, a statement that there are none; and the auditor shall send a copy of any statement sent to the charity trustees under this paragraph (except a statement that there are no such circumstances) to..." the Charity Commission and/or OSCR.

Matters that may require consideration in relation to this duty include:

- disagreement over opinions expressed or to be expressed in an auditors' report;
- disagreement over any disclosure made or to be made to the Commission in respect of a matter of material significance;
- disagreement over any accounting policy, assumption, financial judgment or disclosure made in the accounts or in the preparation of the accounts;
- concerns over any matter which is believed to give rise to a material risk of a loss of charitable funds; and
- lack of co-operation or obstruction in the context of an audit.

Cross Border Charities

Where a charity registered in England & Wales also operates in Scotland it will need to be registered with OSCR as well as the Charity Commission. For such cross border charities neither regulator is considered to be the principal regulator and both will have an interest in receiving reports. The auditor should therefore make a report to both regulators who will determine which regulator takes forward the issues raised by the report.

Reporting gateways

To ensure reports are handled efficiently and immediately, auditors should make reports to the regulators as follows:

- To the Charity Commission by e-mail
  – whistleblowing@charitycommission.gsi.gov.uk
- To OSCR by e-mail – info@oscr.org.uk

Within the body of the e-mail, or in an attachment thereto, the following information should be provided:

- the auditor's name and contact address, telephone number and/or e-mail address;
- the charity's name and registration number (if applicable);
- whether the auditor is reporting a matter of material significance, or is exercising his right to report;
- under which of the eight headings of reportable matters the report is being made;
- a description of the matter giving rise to concern and the information available on the matter reported, where possible providing an estimate of the financial implications;
- where the trustees are attempting to deal with the situation, a brief description of any steps being taken by the trustees of which the auditor has been made aware;
- if the report concerns terrorist, money laundering or criminal activity confirmation that the auditor has already notified the Serious Organised Crime Agency and/or the Police as appropriate;
- if the report concerns the abuse of vulnerable beneficiaries details of whether the auditor has contacted the Police and/or Social Services.

In England and Wales the Charities Act 1993 requires the report to be in writing and therefore a hard copy of any report made orally should also be forwarded to:

Charity Commission Direct
PO Box 1227
Liverpool
L69 3UG

In Scotland, there is no legislative requirement to make the report in writing, but it is recommended that a written report or record of any verbal report is forwarded to:

OSCR
Quadrant House
9 Riverside Drive
Dundee
DD1 4NY

Appendix 6 – Control activities

The following tables set out some of the control activities which are special to charities. The tables are not intended to be comprehensive: there may be other control activities which will be relevant to a particular charity's activities and control activities which are of general application (such as segregation of duties or physical security of tangible assets) which are not included in the examples given below. The nature and extent of the control activities will clearly depend on the size of the charity.

Table 1: cash donations

Source	Examples of controls
Collecting boxes and tins	• numerical control over boxes and tins • satisfactory sealing of boxes and tins so that any opening prior to recording cash is apparent • regular collection and recording of proceeds from collecting boxes • dual control over counting and recording of proceeds • public collections are undertaken within legal requirements for public collections
Other cash receipts	• clear directions to staff on how to handle cash donations • advice to donors on where to make donations securely
Postal receipts	• unopened mail kept securely • dual control over the opening of mail • immediate recording of donations on opening of mail or receipt • agreement of bank paying-in slips to record of receipts by an independent person • rotation of post opening staff
Receipts over the internet	• sending a confirmation of receipt to the donor • controls over the writing up of daybooks
Text giving	• IT controls to ensure texts received are processed correctly with a full audit trail maintained

Table 2: other donations

Source	Examples of controls
Gift aid	• establish procedures to ensure donations are initially recorded correctly with tax compliance issues being met • regular checks and follow-up procedures to ensure due amounts are received • regular checks to ensure all tax repayments have been obtained • structured archive system in place to ensure documentation is retained for 7 years • procedures for the sale of donated goods on behalf of donors where gift aid is to be claimed on the sale proceeds.

Legacies	• comprehensive correspondence files maintained in respect of each legacy, and numerically controlled searches of agency reports of legacies receivable • regular reports and follow-up procedures undertaken in respect of outstanding legacies • security of chattels received as legacies and procedures to establish their value and proper realisation
Donations in kind/ donated services	• in case of charity shops, separation of recording, storage and sale of stock • immediate recording of donated assets for use by the charity • procedures for recording donated services • logging of donated goods for distribution received which are only recognised in the accounts when distributed.

Table 3: other income

Source	Examples of controls
Fund-raising activities	• records maintained for each fund-raising event • other controls maintained over receipts appropriate to the type of activity and receipt (as set out in tables 1 and 2) • prenumbered tickets for ticket income • controls maintained over expenses as for administrative expenses • reconciliation of financial aspects of the fundraising database to the general ledger
Grants and loans, including those from government bodies	• regular checks that all sources of income or funds are fully utilised and appropriate claims made • ensuring income or funds are correctly applied in accordance with the terms of the grant or loan • comprehensive records of applications made and follow-up procedures for those not discharged • appropriate controls procedures if stipulated by the funding agreement

Table 4: fixed assets

Source	Examples of controls
Existence of assets	• a register of fixed assets, including donated assets
Valuation	• donated tangible fixed assets recorded at their current value at the date of the gift and then depreciated in line with other assets • donated fixed asset investments recorded at their marketable value at the time of the gift

Table 5: use of funds

	Examples of controls
Restricted funds	• records maintained to identify relevant income, expenditure and assets • appropriate allocation of income generated by restricted funds • terms controlling application of funds • oversight of application of fund monies by independent personnel or trustees
Grants to beneficiaries	• records maintained, as appropriate, of requests for material grants received not paid to beneficiaries and their treatment • appropriate checks made on applications and applicants for grants, and that amounts paid are intra vires • records maintained of all grant decisions, checking that proper authority exists, that adequate documentation is presented to decision-making meetings, and that any conflicts of interest are recorded • controls to ensure grants made are properly spent by the recipient for the specified purpose, for example requirements for returns with supporting documentation or auditor's reports concerning expenditure, or monitoring visits.
Related party transactions	• annual declarations of interests received from all trustees • Register of interests maintained

Table 6: Branch operations

Location	
Head office	• regular reports or returns to the charity's head office by any branch, office or individual representative of the charity, checks to ensure that all these are received, and a mechanism for monitoring branch activities, for example by comparison of expenditure to budget • prompt investigation of any report of the misuse of the charity's name • proper acknowledgements of remittances to and from abroad • clarity of instructions and guidelines as to receipt and transfer of income to identify the point at which it belongs to the main charity • controls over recruitment and appointment of staff to run branch operations • controls regarding the opening of bank accounts and the transfer of funds between bank accounts • defined authorisation limits and responsibilities for local staff in ordering and paying for goods and services • if the amounts involved are material, periodic checks by internal audit or head office personnel.

Branch	<ul><li>internal controls of equivalent standard to those of the main charity in any branch where the trustees of the charity have direct control</li><li>existence of an accounts manual and the standardisation of procedures at all branches</li><li>proper acknowledgements of remittances to and from abroad</li><li>retention of documents for local inspection (for example at overseas locations if local law requires this) or for periodic transmission to the head office, and</li><li>in the case of overseas branches, controls over treasury operations, for example to ensure that unspent cash balances are held in hard currencies and in secure holdings where the overseas economy is inflationary and conditions are unstable.</li></ul>

Appendix 7 – Definitions

Abbreviations and frequently used terms in this Practice Note are set out below:

Branches	Entities or administrative bodies set up, for example, to conduct a particular aspect of the business of the charity, or to conduct the business of the charity in a particular geographical area and which are included within the individual accounts of a charity. For the purpose of the Charities SORP a branch is:<ul><li>simply part of the administrative machinery of the charity, or</li><li>a fund shown in the accounts as a restricted or endowment fund. This may include:</li></ul>a separate trust which is administered by or on behalf of the charity and whose funds are held for specific charitable purposes which are within the general purposes of the charity. in England and Wales, a separate trust (or legal entity) not falling within the above which the Charity Commission has united by a direction under section 96(5) or 96(6), Charities Act 1993.
Charity	Any institution, corporate or not, which is established for charitable purposes and is subject to the control of the High Court in the exercise of the Court's jurisdiction with respect to charities.
Charitable purposes	When referred to in the context of Charity Commission and HMRC UK-wide matters, this means purposes that are exclusively charitable according to the law of England & Wales. Charitable purposes for Scottish Registered Charities are as defined within the Charities and Trustee Investment (Scotland) Act 2005.
Charity Regulators	The principal regulators for charities in the UK are, for; England and Wales – The Charity Commission Scotland – Office of the Scottish Charity Regulator Northern Ireland – Department for Social Development.

| Charitable company | A company:
• formed and registered under the Companies Act 2006 and
• which is established for exclusively charitable purposes. |
|---|---|
| Charity trustees | The persons having the general control and management of the administration of a charity, regardless of what they are called.

For example, in the case of an unincorporated association the executive or management committee are its charity trustees, and in the case of a charitable company it is the directors who are the charity trustees. |
Charities SORP	Statement of Recommended practice –'Accounting and Reporting by Charities', originally issued by the Charity Commission under the auspices of the Accounting Standards Board in March 2005.
CA 2006	The Companies Act 2006.
Directors	The ISAs (UK and Ireland) which are considered in sections of the Practice Note use the word 'directors' to describe the persons who are legally responsible for a reporting entity's affairs, including the preparation of its financial statements. The equivalent persons for a charity are its trustees and the directors of a charitable company are, by virtue of their office, its trustees. This Practice Note therefore uses the term 'trustees' rather than 'directors'.
Excepted charity	One which does not have to register with the Charity Commission, but in most other respects is fully within its jurisdiction. Under section 3(5) of the Charities Act 1993, the following charities fall into this category :
• any charity which is excepted by an Order or by Regulations,
• any charity which has neither
any permanent endowment, nor
the use or occupation of any land, and and
whose annual income from all sources doe does not amount to more than £5000,
• places of worship registered under the Places of Worship Registration Act 1855.
Exempt charities	Exempt charities in England and Wales are specifically excluded from the Charity Commission's supervision and monitoring. Exempt charities do not register with the Charity Commission, nor do they submit accounts and annual returns. These are
charities listed in Schedule 2 to the Charities Act 1993 as amended by Chapter 3 of the Charities Act 2006 (every institution listed is not necessarily a charity; the Act grants exempt status only "so far as they are charities").
FSA	The Financial Services Authority.
Gift Aid	Tax relief for certain payments made to charity.

Management	References in the Practice Note to 'management' are to those persons, who may include trustees, who have executive responsibility for the conduct of the entity's operation. Care needs to be taken to identify the legal position of senior staff. Many charities call their salaried chief executive 'Director' which is not to be confused with the term of Company Director in company law. In most cases, whilst accountable only to the trustee body and having responsibility for the execution of that body's policy, a salaried chief executive is not a trustee and therefore holds a position whose legal status is significantly different from that of a company director.
NDPB	A Non-departmental public body is an entity that has a role in the process of government but is neither a government department nor forms part of a department. It is established at arm's length from departments and may carry out executive, regulatory, administrative or commercial functions (see also Practice Note 10).
Non-company charities	Non-company charities mean charities other than those which are formed and registered under the Companies Act 2006 or to which the provisions of that Act apply. The term includes charities incorporated by Royal Charter or by special Act of Parliament. Charities incorporated under general legislation other than the Companies Act 2006, such as Industrial and Provident Societies Acts, are referred to separately as appropriate.
OSCR	Office of the Scottish Charity Regulator.
1964 Act (NI)	The Charities Act (Northern Ireland) 1964.
1987 Order (NI)	The Charities (Northern Ireland) Order 1987.
2005 Act (Scotland)	The Charities and Trustee Investment (Scotland) Act 2005.
2006 Regulations (Scotland)	The Charities Accounts (Scotland) Regulations 2006.
2008 Regulations (E&W)	The Charities (Accounts and Reports) Regulations 2008.
Restricted funds	Restricted funds are defined in Appendix 3 to the Charities SORP as: 'funds subject to specific trusts, which may be declared by the donor(s), or with their authority (for example in a public appeal), or created through legal process but still within the wider objects of the charity. [They] may be restricted income funds, which are expendable at the discretion of the trustees in furtherance of some particular aspect(s) of the objects of the charity. Or they may be capital (i.e. endowment) funds, where the assets are required to be invested, or retained for actual use, rather than expended.'

Serious Incident Reports	Information provided to the Charity Commission by the trustees of a charity about serious incidents which have caused or could cause harm to their charity including any necessary declaration made by them as part of their Charity's Annual Return concerning the reporting of such matters.
SOCA	Serious Organised Crime Agency. Contact details – www.soca.gov.uk
SoFA	A Statement of Financial Activities. A charity's SoFA shows all the incoming resources becoming available during the year and all its expenditure for the year, and reconciles all the changes in its funds. The SoFA should account for all the funds of the charity and should be presented in columns representing the different types of funds.

Appendix 8 – Some significant topics relevant to audits of charities

TOPIC	PARAGRAPH NUMBERS	SECTION
Branches	30-33 67 163	Introduction ISA (UK&I) 240 ISA (UK&I) 320 Appendix 6
Charity Governing Documents	12-14 80-81 141 146 189 247	Introduction ISA (UK&I) 250A ISA (UK&I) 300 ISA (UK&I) 315 ISA (UK&I) 402 ISA (UK&I) 700
Cash Donations and Donations in Kind	34-35 67 199 207	Introduction ISA (UK&I) 240 ISA (UK&I) 520 ISA (UK&I) 545 Appendix 6
Completeness of Income	35 66 158 167 172	Introduction ISA (UK&I) 240 ISA (UK&I) 315 ISA (UK&I) 330
Grant Income	38-40 147 194 224-225	Introduction ISA (UK&I) 315 ISA (UK&I) 505 ISA (UK&I) 570 Appendix 6
Overseas Operations	141 159 175-180	ISA (UK&I) 300 ISA (UK&I) 315 ISA (UK&I) 330

Restricted Funds	41-42	Introduction
	164-166	ISA (UK&I) 320
	173-174	ISA (UK&I) 330
	223	ISA (UK&I) 570
		Appendix 6
Trading Activities	43-46	Introduction
Trustees' Responsibilities	24-29	Introduction
	64,69	ISA (UK&I) 240
	75	ISA (UK&I) 250
	137-138	ISA (UK&I) 260
	149-151	ISA (UK&I) 315
	211-212	ISA (UK&I) 550
	229	ISA (UK&I) 580
Trustees' Report on Risks	68	ISA (UK&I) 240
	153	ISA (UK&I) 315
Taxation	47-49	Introduction
	158	ISA (UK&I) 315
	221	ISA (UK&I) 570

[PN 12 (Revised)]
Money laundering legislation – interim guidance for auditors in the United Kingdom

Contents

	Paragraph
Introduction	1-13

Key legal requirements
The Proceeds of Crime Act 2002
The Terrorism Act 2000
The Money Laundering Regulations 2007

Firm-wide practices   14-23

Client identification and on-going monitoring of business relationships
Money Laundering Reporting Officer
Training

Impact of legislation on audit procedures   24-60

Identification of knowledge or suspicions
Further enquiry
Reporting to the MLRO and to SOCA
Legal privilege
'Tipping off' and prejudicing an investigation
Reporting to obtain appropriate consent
Reporting to regulators
The auditor's report on financial statements
Resignation and communication with successor auditors

Appendices

Appendix 1   Examples of situations that may give rise to money laundering offences that auditors may encounter during the course of the audit

Appendix 2   Guidance as to whom the anti-money laundering legislation applies

Introduction

1. Practice Note 12 (Revised), "Money Laundering", was last issued as interim guidance in January 2007. This version has been updated to take account of recent changes including the issuance of the Money Laundering Regulations 2007 and the Terrorism Act 2000 and Proceeds of Crime Act 2002 (Amendment) Regulations 2007. This version of Practice Note 12 (Revised) has been submitted to HM Treasury for approval in accordance with sections 330 and 331 of the Proceeds of Crime Act 2002 ("POCA") and section 21A of the Terrorism Act 2000 ("TA 2000"). It reflects the legislation effective at 31 January 2008. Auditors need to be alert to subsequent changes in legislative requirements.

2. Practice Note 12 (Revised) focuses on the impact of the UK anti-money laundering legislation on auditors' responsibilities when auditing and reporting on financial statements. It does not provide general guidance on the legislation. The Consultative Committee of Accountancy Bodies has issued "Anti-Money Laundering Guidance for the Accountancy Sector" ("CCAB Guidance") which provides general guidance on the legislation for all entities providing audit, accountancy, tax advisory or insolvency related services[1].

3. The anti-money laundering legislation is complex and some uncertainty still exists as to how the courts will interpret it in practice. Notwithstanding this, it is expected that the courts will take into account guidance issued by authoritative bodies. To obtain a full understanding of the legal requirements auditors refer to the relevant provisions of the legislation and, if necessary, obtain legal advice.

4. The use of the term 'auditor' in this Practice Note means anyone who is part of the engagement team (not necessarily only those employed by an audit firm). The engagement team comprises all persons who are directly involved in the acceptance and performance of a particular audit. This includes the audit team, professional personnel from other disciplines involved in the audit engagement and those who provide quality control or direct oversight of the audit engagement, but it does not include experts contracted by the firm.

Key legal requirements

5. The key legal requirements introduced by POCA (as subsequently amended by the Serious and Organised Crime and Police Act 2006 (SOCPA)), TA 2000 and the Money Laundering Regulations 2007 (the "ML Regulations") are as follows:

   - Part 7 of POCA consolidated, updated and reformed criminal law in the UK with regard to money laundering. The definition of money laundering[2]

---

[1] *Cross references in the Practice Note to "CCAB Guidance" are to the guidance issued by the CCAB in December 2007. This is published by the ICAEW as TECH 07/07.*

[2] *Section 340(11) of POCA states that "Money laundering is an act which:*
   (a) constitutes an offence under section 327, 328 or 329,
   (b) constitutes an attempt, conspiracy or incitement to commit an offence specified in paragraph (a),
   (c) constitutes aiding, abetting, counselling or procuring the commission of an offence specified in paragraph (a), or
   (d) would constitute an offence specified in paragraph (a), (b) or (c) if done in the UK."

comprises three principal money laundering offences[3] (behaviour that directly constitutes money laundering). These include possessing, or in any way dealing with, or concealing, the proceeds of any crime and includes crime committed by an entity or an individual.
- TA 2000 contains similar offences for the laundering of terrorist funds, although in such cases, the funds involved include any funds that are likely to be used for the financing of terrorism. There is no need for funds to have been obtained from a previous criminal offence for them to be terrorist funds.
- POCA and the ML Regulations do not extend the scope of the audit, but auditors are within the regulated sector and are required to report where:
  - they know or suspect, or have reasonable grounds to know or suspect, that another person is engaged in money laundering;
  - they can identify the other person or the whereabouts of any of the laundered property or that they believe, or it is reasonable to expect them to believe that information that they have obtained will or may assist in identifying that other person or the whereabouts of the laundered property; and
  - the information has come to the auditors in the course of their 'regulated' business.
- Failure by an auditor to report knowledge or suspicion of, or reasonable grounds to know or suspect, money laundering in relation to the proceeds of any crime is a criminal offence[4]. Auditors (partners and staff) will face criminal penalties[5] if they breach the requirements.
- The requirement to report is not just related to matters that might be considered material to the financial statements; auditors have to report knowledge or suspicion, or reasonable grounds for knowledge or suspicion, of crimes that potentially have no material financial statement impact. POCA does not contain de minimis concessions.
- Firms must take appropriate measures so that partners and staff are made aware of the provisions of POCA, the ML Regulations and the TA 2000 and are given training in how to recognise and deal with actual or suspected money laundering activities.

---

[3] *The principal money laundering offences defined under POCA are:*
- *s327 "Concealing" criminal property (including concealing or disguising its nature, source, location, disposition, movement, ownership or rights attaching; converting, transferring or removing from any part of the UK).*
- *s328 "Arranging" (entering into or becoming concerned in an arrangement which the business or an individual knows or suspects facilitates the acquisition, retention, use or control of criminal property by or on behalf of another person).*
- *s329 "Acquiring, using or possessing criminal property".*

[4] *Subject to the provisions of POCA section 330(6) relating to legal professional privilege and section 330(7A) relating to offences committed overseas.*

[5] *Criminal penalties are covered under sections 334 and 336(6) of POCA. The maximum penalty for the three principal money laundering offences on conviction on indictment is fourteen years imprisonment. The maximum penalty on conviction on indictment is five years imprisonment for the following offences:*
- *a person in the regulated sector other than a nominated officer failing to disclose (section 330),*
- *the nominated officer failure to disclose offences (section 331 for the regulated sector, section 332 for those outside this sector),*
- *the giving of consent by a nominated officer inappropriately to prohibited acts (section 336(5)), and*
- *the 'tipping off' offence (sections 333A to 333E).*

Furthermore in all cases, an unlimited fine can be imposed.
On summary conviction, the maximum penalty for all the above offences is six months' imprisonment and/or a fine not exceeding the statutory maximum. A person guilty of an offence under section 339(1A) of making a disclosure under section 330, 331, 332 or 338 otherwise than in the form prescribed by the Secretary of State or otherwise than in the manner so prescribed is liable on summary conviction to a fine not exceeding level 5 on the standard scale.

- Auditors are required to adopt rigorous client identification procedures and appropriate anti-money laundering procedures.

The Proceeds of Crime Act 2002

6 POCA defines both the money laundering offences and the auditor's reporting responsibilities. The anti-money laundering legislation imposes a duty to report money laundering in respect of all criminal property. Property is criminal property if:

(a) It constitutes a person's benefit from criminal conduct or it represents such a benefit (in whole or in part and whether directly or indirectly); and
(b) The alleged offender knows or suspects that it constitutes or represents such a benefit.

7 There are three principal money laundering offences[3] which define money laundering to encompass offences relating to the possession, acquisition, use, concealment or conversion of criminal property and involvement in arrangements relating to criminal property. These principal offences apply to all persons and businesses whether or not they are within the regulated sector.

8 In addition, under section 330 of POCA persons working in the regulated sector are required to report knowledge or suspicion, or reasonable grounds for knowledge or suspicion, that another person is engaged in money laundering to a nominated officer where that knowledge or suspicion, or reasonable grounds for knowledge or suspicion, came to those persons in the course of their business or employment in the regulated sector. In audit firms the nominated officer is usually known as a Money Laundering Reporting Officer ("MLRO") and is referred to as such in this Practice Note.[6] If as a result of that report the MLRO has knowledge or suspicion of, or reasonable grounds to know or suspect money laundering, the MLRO then has a responsibility to report to the Serious Organised Crime Agency (SOCA). POCA does not contain de minimis concessions that affect the reporting requirements of auditors with the result that reports need to be made irrespective of the quantum of the benefits derived from, or the seriousness of, the offence. Partners and staff in audit firms need to be alert to the dangers of disseminating information that is likely to 'tip off' a money launderer or prejudice an investigation[7] as this may constitute a criminal offence under the anti-money laundering legislation.

9 Auditors who consider that the actions they plan to take, or may be asked to take, will result in themselves committing a principal money laundering offence are required to obtain prior consent to those actions from their MLRO and the MLRO is required to seek appropriate prior consent from SOCA (see paragraphs 48 to 50).

The Terrorism Act 2000

10 For the purposes of this guidance, money laundering includes activities relating to terrorist financing. This extends the money laundering reporting requirements for partners and staff in audit firms to terrorist fund-raising, the use of money or other

---

[6] Section 20(3) of the ML Regulations recognises that the requirements relating to internal reporting procedures do not apply to sole practitioners, but the external reporting obligations under POCA remain. There is no obligation on a sole practitioner to appoint an MLRO where the sole practitioner does not employ any staff, or act in association with any other person. Where no MLRO is appointed and a sole practitioner has knowledge or suspicion of, or reasonable grounds to know or suspect, money laundering the sole practitioner has a responsibility to report to SOCA.

[7] See guidance on 'tipping off' and prejudicing an investigation in paragraphs 44 to 47.

property for the purposes of terrorism, or the possession of money or other property and arrangements where money or other property is to be made available to another, where a person intends, knows or has reasonable cause to suspect that it may be used for the purposes of terrorism irrespective of whether those funds come from a legitimate source or not.

The Money Laundering Regulations 2007

The Money Laundering Regulations 2007 replace the Money Laundering Regulations 2003. The ML Regulations define the 'regulated sector' as including persons, acting in the course of business as a statutory auditor within the meaning of Part 42 of the Companies Act 2006[8], when carrying out statutory audit work within the meaning of section 1210 of the Companies Act 2006[9]. For the purposes of this Practice Note "person" is interpreted as referring to a UK audit firm that is designated as a "Registered Auditor" to which the ML Regulations apply. All partners and staff within a UK audit firm who are involved in providing audit services in the UK are subject to the audit firm's requirements under the ML Regulations (see guidance in Appendix 2).

Where a Registered Auditor is not carrying out statutory audit work the ML Regulations will nevertheless often apply as they also cover "a firm or sole practitioner who by way of business provides accountancy services to other persons, when providing such services"[10].

The ML Regulations impose requirements on businesses in the regulated sector relating to systems and training to prevent money laundering, identification procedures for clients, record keeping procedures and internal reporting procedures.

Firm-wide practices

The ML Regulations requires businesses in the regulated sector to establish risk-sensitive policies and procedures relating to:

- Customer identification and on-going monitoring of business relationships;
- Reporting internally and to SOCA[11];
- Record keeping;
- Internal control, risk assessment and management;
- Training for all relevant employees; and
- Monitoring and management of compliance with and the internal communication of such policies and procedures.

In addition, audit firms need to ensure sufficient senior management oversight of the systems used for monitoring compliance with these procedures. It may be helpful for this to be co-ordinated with the responsibility for the firm's quality control systems under ISQC (UK and Ireland) 1. Detailed guidance on developing and applying a risk based approach is given in section 4 of the CCAB Guidance.

---

[8] *Before the entry into force of Part 42 of the Companies Act 2006, this applies to a person who is eligible for appointment as a company auditor under Section 25 of the Companies Act 1989 or Article 28 of the Companies (Northern Ireland) Order 1990.*

[9] *Regulation 3(4) of the Money Laundering Regulations 2007.*

[10] *Regulation 3(7) of the Money Laundering Regulations 2007.*

[11] *Whilst a risk based approach is appropriate when devising policies and procedures, the auditor will not adopt a risk based approach to making reports either internally or to SOCA.*

Client identification and on-going monitoring of business relationships

15 Appropriate identification procedures, as required by the ML Regulations, are mandatory when accepting appointment as auditor. The extent of information collected about the client and verification of identity undertaken will depend on the client risk assessment. Guidance on identification procedures is given in section 5 of the CCAB Guidance.

16 Auditing standards on quality control for audits state that acceptance of client relationships and specific audit engagements includes considering the integrity of the principal owners, key management and those charged with governance of the entity. This involves the auditor making appropriate enquiries and may involve discussions with third parties, the obtaining of written references and searches of relevant databases. These procedures may provide some of the relevant client identification information but may need to be extended to comply with the ML Regulations.

17 It may be helpful for the auditor to explain to the client the reason for requiring evidence of identity and this can be achieved by including an additional paragraph in the audit engagement letter. Where client identification procedures start before the engagement letter is drafted it might be helpful for the auditor to address this in pre-engagement letter communications with the potential client. The following is an illustrative paragraph that could be included for this purpose:

"*Client identification*
As with other professional services firms, we are required to identify our clients for the purposes of the UK anti-money laundering legislation. We are likely to request from you, and retain, some information and documentation for these purposes and/or to make searches of appropriate databases. If we are not able to obtain satisfactory evidence of your identity within a reasonable time, there may be circumstances in which we are not able to proceed with the audit appointment."

18 It may also be helpful to inform clients of the auditor's responsibilities under POCA to report knowledge or suspicion, or reasonable grounds to know or suspect, that a money laundering offence has been committed and the restrictions created by the 'tipping off' rules on the auditor's ability to discuss such matters with their clients. The following is an illustrative paragraph that could be included in the audit engagement letter for this purpose:

"*Money laundering disclosures*
The provision of audit services is a business in the regulated sector under the Proceeds of Crime Act 2002 and, as such, partners and staff in audit firms have to comply with this legislation which includes provisions that may require us to make a money laundering disclosure in relation to information we obtain as part of our normal audit work. It is not our practice to inform you when such a disclosure is made or the reasons for it because of the restrictions imposed by the 'tipping off' provisions of the legislation."

19 Whether or not to include these illustrative paragraphs in the audit engagement letter is a policy decision to be taken by individual firms.

20 The activities of and the relationship with the audit client will be monitored on an on-going basis. For example, if there has been a change in the client's circumstances, such as changes in beneficial ownership, control or directors, and this information was relied upon originally as part of the client identification procedures then, depending on the auditor's assessment of risk, the procedures may need to be re-performed and documented. However, annual reappointment as auditor does not, in itself, require the client identification procedures to be re-performed.

Money Laundering Reporting Officer

The ML Regulations require relevant businesses to appoint a nominated officer (usually known as the MLRO). A sole practitioner who does not employ any staff, or act in association with any other person, is by default an MLRO. Auditors are required to report where they know or suspect, or have reasonable grounds to know or suspect, that another person is engaged in money laundering or, for the purposes of obtaining consent, where they know or suspect that they are involved in money laundering. Partners and staff in audit firms discharge their responsibilities by reporting to their MLRO or, in the case of sole practitioners, to SOCA and, where appropriate, by obtaining consent from the MLRO or SOCA to continue with any prohibited activities. The MLRO is responsible for deciding, on the basis of the information provided by the partners and staff, whether further enquiry is required, whether the matter should be reported to SOCA and for making the report to SOCA. Partners and staff may seek advice from the MLRO who will often act as the main source of guidance and if necessary act as the liaison point for communication with lawyers, SOCA and the relevant law enforcement agency. More detailed guidance on the role of the MLRO is given in section 7 of the CCAB Guidance. 21

Training

Firms are required to take appropriate measures so that partners and staff are made aware of the relevant provisions of POCA, the ML Regulations and the TA 2000 and are given training in how to recognise and deal with activities which may be related to money laundering. Guidance on training is given in section 3 of the CCAB Guidance. The level of training provided to individuals needs to be appropriate to both the level of exposure of the individual to money laundering risk and their role and seniority within the firm. Senior members of the firm whatever their role need to understand the requirements of POCA and the ML Regulations. 22

Apart from the training referred to in paragraph 22 above, additional training or expertise in criminal law is not required under POCA. However, ISA (UK and Ireland) 250 'Consideration of laws and regulations in an audit of financial statements' requires an auditor to obtain a general understanding of the legal and regulatory framework applicable to the entity and the industry to help identify possible or actual instances of non-compliance with those laws and regulations which provide a legal framework within which the entity conducts its business and which are central to the entity's ability to conduct its business and hence to its financial statements. 23

Impact of legislation on audit procedures

Identification of knowledge or suspicions

ISA (UK and Ireland) 250 establishes standards and provides guidance on the auditor's responsibility to consider law and regulations in an audit of financial statements. The anti-money laundering legislation does not require the auditor to extend the scope of the audit, save as referred to in paragraph 32 below, but the normal audit work could give rise to knowledge or suspicion, or reasonable grounds for knowledge or suspicion, that will need to be reported. Such knowledge or suspicion may arise in relation to: 24

- law and regulations relating directly to the preparation of the financial statements;

- law and regulations which provide a legal framework within which the entity conducts its business; and
- other law and regulations.

25 Auditing standards on law and regulations require the auditor to obtain sufficient appropriate audit evidence about compliance with those laws and regulations that have an effect on the determination of material amounts and disclosures in the financial statements. This may cause the auditor to be suspicious that, for example, breaches of the Companies Act or tax offences have taken place, which may be criminal offences resulting in criminal property.

26 Auditing standards on law and regulations also require the auditor to perform procedures to help identify possible or actual instances of non-compliance with those laws and regulations which provide a legal framework within which the entity conducts its business and which are central to the entity's ability to conduct its business[12] and hence to its financial statements. These procedures consist of:

- obtaining a general understanding of the legal and regulatory framework applicable to the entity and the industry and of the procedures followed to ensure compliance with that framework;
- inspecting correspondence with the relevant licensing or regulatory authorities;
- enquiring of those charged with governance as to whether they are on notice of any such possible instances of non-compliance with law or regulations; and
- obtaining written representation that those charged with governance have disclosed to the auditor all known actual or possible non-compliance with laws and regulations whose effects should be considered when preparing financial statements, together with, where applicable, the actual or contingent consequences which may arise from the non-compliance.

This work may give the auditor grounds to suspect that criminal offences have been committed.

27 Laws relating to money laundering will be central to an entity's business, if that business is within the regulated sector as defined by POCA and the ML Regulations[13]. When auditing the financial statements of businesses within the regulated sector the auditor reviews the steps taken by the entity to comply with the ML

---

[12] *For example, non-compliance with certain laws and regulations may cause the entity to cease operations, or call into question the entity's status as a going concern.*

[13] *For the purposes of this Practice Note this includes (but is not restricted to) the following persons acting in the course of business in the United Kingdom:*
- *credit institutions;*
- *financial institutions (including money service operators);*
- *auditors, insolvency practitioners, external accountants and tax advisers;*
- *independent legal professionals;*
- *trust or company service providers;*
- *estate agents;*
- *high value dealers when dealing in goods of any description which involves accepting a total cash payment of 15,000 euro or more*
- *casinos.*

The legislation from which this list is derived is complicated and comprises two sources. If in doubt, an auditor refers to the definitions of:
- *the regulated sector, defined in the Proceeds of Crime Act 2002 Schedule 9 Part 1 (as amended by Statutory Instrument 2003/3074 "The Proceeds of Crime Act 2002 (Business in the Regulated Sector and Supervisory Authorities) Order 2003" and Statutory Instrument 2007/3287 "The Proceeds of Crime Act 2002 (Business in the Regulated Sector and Supervisory Authorities) Order 2007); and*
- *relevant businesses as defined in paragraph 3(1) of the ML Regulations.*

Regulations, assesses their effectiveness and obtains management representations concerning compliance with the ML Regulations. If the client's systems are thought to be ineffective the auditor considers whether there is a responsibility to report 'a matter of material significance' to the regulator and the possible impact of fines, following non-compliance with the ML Regulations or POCA. Where the entity's business is outside the regulated sector, although the auditor's reporting responsibilities under the money laundering legislation are unchanged, the entity's management is not required to implement the ML Regulations. Whilst the principal money laundering offences apply to these entities, the laws relating to money laundering are unlikely to be considered by the auditor to be central to an entity's business for the purposes of ISA (UK and Ireland) 250.

In relation to other laws and regulations, auditing standards on laws and regulations require the auditor to be alert to the fact that audit procedures applied for the purpose of forming an opinion on the financial statements may bring instances of possible non-compliance with laws and regulations to the auditor's attention and to be alert for those instances that might incur obligations for partners and staff in audit firms to report money laundering offences. 28

The auditor also gives consideration to whether any contingent liabilities might arise in this area. For example, there may be regulatory or criminal fines for offences under POCA or the ML Regulations. In certain circumstances, even where no offence under POCA has been committed, civil claims may arise or recovery actions by the Assets Recovery Agency (which is to be incorporated within SOCA with effect from 1st April 2008) may give rise to contingent liabilities. The auditor will remain alert to the fact that discussions with the client on such matters may give rise to a risk of 'tipping off' (see paragraphs 44 to 47). 29

In some situations the audit client may have obtained legal advice to the effect that certain actions or circumstances do not give rise to criminal conduct and therefore cannot give rise to criminal property. As explained in auditing standards on law and regulations, whether an act constitutes non-compliance with law or regulations may involve consideration of matters which do not lie within the competence and experience of individuals trained in the audit of financial information. Provided that the auditor considers that the advice has been obtained from a suitably qualified and independent lawyer and that the lawyer was made aware of all relevant circumstances known to the auditor, the auditor may rely on such advice, provided the auditor has complied with auditing standards on using the work of an expert. 30

The anti-money laundering legislation requires UK auditors to report the laundering of the proceeds of conduct which takes place overseas if that conduct would constitute an offence in any part of the UK. The anti-money laundering legislation does not change the scope of the audit and does not therefore impose any requirement for the UK parent company auditor to change or add to the normal instructions to auditors of overseas subsidiaries. However, when considering non-UK parts of the group audit the UK parent company auditor will need to consider whether information obtained as part of the group audit procedures (for example reports made by non-UK subsidiary auditors, discussions with non-UK subsidiary auditors or discussions with UK and non-UK directors) gives rise to knowledge or suspicion, or reasonable grounds for knowledge or suspicion, such that there is a requirement for the UK parent company auditor to report to SOCA. 31

Further enquiry

32 Once the auditor suspects a possible breach of law or regulations, the auditor will need to make further enquiries to assess the implications of this for the audit of the financial statements. Auditing standards on laws and regulations require that when the auditor becomes aware of information concerning a possible instance of non-compliance, the auditor should obtain an understanding of the nature of the act and the circumstances in which it has occurred, and sufficient other information to evaluate the possible effect on the financial statements. Where the auditor knows or suspects, or has reasonable grounds to know or suspect, that another person is engaged in money laundering, a disclosure must be made to the firm's MLRO or, for sole practitioners, to SOCA. The anti-money laundering legislation does not require the auditor to undertake any additional enquiries to determine further details of the predicate criminal offence. If the auditor is genuinely uncertain as to whether or not there are grounds to make a disclosure, the auditor will bring the matter to the attention of the audit engagement partner who may wish to seek advice from the MLRO.

33 In performing any further enquiries in the context of the audit of the financial statements the auditor takes care not to alert a money launderer to the possibility that a report will be or has been made, especially if management and/or the directors are themselves involved in the suspected criminal activity.

Reporting to the MLRO and to SOCA

34 In the UK, auditors report to their MLRO or, in the case of sole practitioners, to SOCA where they know or suspect, or have reasonable grounds to know or suspect, that another person is engaged in money laundering. Money laundering reports need to be made irrespective of the quantum of the benefits derived from, or the seriousness of, the offence. There are no de minimis concessions applicable to the auditor contained in POCA, the ML Regulations or the TA 2000. There is no provision for the auditor not to make a report even where the auditor considers that the matter has already been reported (although in such cases the 'limited intelligence value' report may be appropriate).

35 However, the auditor is not required to report where:

- the auditor does not have the information to identify the money launderer and the whereabouts of any of the laundered property, or
- the auditor does not believe, and it is unreasonable to expect the auditor to believe, that any information held by the auditor will or may assist in identifying the money launderer or the whereabouts of any of the laundered property.

For example, a company involved in the retail business is likely to have been the victim of shoplifting offences, but information that the auditor has is unlikely to be able to identify the money launderer or the whereabouts of any of the laundered property, and the auditor is not required to report knowledge or suspicion of money laundering arising from such a crime.

36 Where suspected money laundering occurs wholly or partially overseas in relation to conduct that is lawful in the country where it occurred, the position is more complicated, and the auditor needs to be careful to ensure that the strict requirements of POCA have been satisfied if no report is to be made to the MLRO or to SOCA. In these circumstances, the auditor considers two questions:

- where the client or third party's money laundering is occurring wholly overseas; is the money laundering lawful there? If it is, a report is not required. However, auditors need to be careful to ensure that no consequences of the criminal conduct are, in fact, occurring in the UK;
- where the client or third party's money laundering is occurring in the UK in relation to underlying conduct which occurred overseas and was lawful there, would it amount to a 'serious offence' under English law[14] if the conduct had occurred here? If it would have amounted to such an offence, a report is required.

The duties to report on overseas money laundering activity are complex as they rely on knowledge of both overseas and UK law. In practice auditors may choose to report all overseas money laundering activity to their MLRO.

During the course of the audit work the auditor might obtain knowledge or form a suspicion about a prohibited act that would be a criminal offence under POCA sections 327, 328 or 329 but it has yet to occur. Because attempting or conspiring to commit a money laundering offence is in itself a money laundering offence, it is possible that in some circumstances a report might need to be made. 37

Where the auditor has made a report to the MLRO and the MLRO has decided that further enquiry is necessary, the auditor will need to be made aware of the outcome of the enquiry to determine whether there are any implications for the audit report or the decision to accept reappointment as auditor. 38

The format of the internal report made to the MLRO is not specified by the ML Regulations. MLROs determine the form in which partners and staff in audit firms report knowledge or suspicion of, or reasonable grounds to know or suspect, money laundering offences internally to their MLRO, although this will need to provide the MLRO with sufficient information to enable a report to be made to SOCA if necessary. Reporting as soon as is practicable to the MLRO is the individual responsibility of the partner or audit staff member and although suspicions would normally be discussed within the engagement team before deciding whether or not to make an internal report to the MLRO this should not delay the report to the MLRO and, even where the rest of the engagement team disagrees, an individual should not be dissuaded from reporting to the MLRO if the individual still considers that it is necessary. In the case of a sole practitioner, who is not required to appoint an MLRO, the sole practitioner reports directly to SOCA. 39

The MLRO makes the decision as to whether a report is made by the audit firm to SOCA. Suspicious Activity Reports may be made using one of SOCA's forms and methods of submission (http://www.soca.gov.uk/financialIntel/suspectActivity.html# forms). The SOCA reporting guidance permits aggregated reporting of suspicious activity that meets the SOCA criteria for 'limited intelligence value' reporting. These criteria are defined in SOCA guidance notes for completing the 'limited intelligence value' report form available on the SOCA website. The forms can be completed either electronically or typed and sent as a hard copy version. Hard copies are available to be downloaded from the website or direct from SOCA. 40

---

[14] A 'serious offence' is conduct that would constitute an offence punishable by imprisonment for a maximum term in excess of 12 months if it occurred in any part of the UK, with the exception of:
(a) an offence under the Gaming Act 1968;
(b) an offence under the Lotteries and Amusements Act 1976; or
(c) an offence under section 23 or 25 of the Financial Services and Markets Act 2000.

41 The timing of reporting by the MLRO to SOCA, or in the case of a sole practitioner their report to SOCA, is governed by section 331(4) of POCA which requires the disclosure to be made "as soon as is practicable" after the information or other matter comes to the attention of the MLRO. In practice this does not always mean "immediately". The timing of reports will be influenced by whether:

- the information includes time sensitive information (that may, for example, allow the recovery of proceeds of crime if communicated immediately) in which case the report will be made quickly;
- further information is required before a report can be made to SOCA, in which case, a report will be made as soon as all the required information has been obtained;
- the information indicates a minor irregularity but there is nothing to suggest dishonest behaviour, in which case a 'limited intelligence value' report can be made as soon as possible after the completion of the audit[15].

Guidance on the reporting of knowledge and suspicions by the MLRO to SOCA is given in section 7 of the CCAB Guidance.

42 Partners and staff in audit firms follow their firm's internal documentation procedures when considering whether to include documentation relating to money laundering reporting in the audit working papers. However, in order to prevent 'tipping off' where another auditor or professional advisor has access to the audit file, the auditor may wish to have all details of internal reports held by the MLRO and exclude these from client files.

Legal privilege

43 Legal privilege can provide a defence for a professional legal adviser to a charge of failing to report knowledge or suspicion of money laundering and is generally available to the legal profession when giving legal advice to a client or acting in relation to litigation.[16] If the auditor is given access to client information over which legal professional privilege may be asserted (for example, correspondence between clients and solicitors in relation to legal advice or litigation) and that information gives grounds to suspect money laundering, the auditor considers whether the auditor is nevertheless obliged to report to the MLRO. There is some ambiguity about how the issue of legal privilege is interpreted and a prudent approach is to assume that legal privilege does not extend to the auditor and where the auditor is in possession of client information which is clearly privileged (for example, a solicitor's advice to an audit client), the auditor seeks legal advice to determine whether that privilege can be extended to the auditor.

---

[15] *For the purposes of this Practice Note 'completion of the audit' is interpreted as being no later than the date the auditor's report is signed, although if there is likely to be a significant period between the date the audit work is completed and the date the auditor's report is signed the auditor considers submitting relevant reports earlier.*

[16] *Statutory Instrument 2006/308 "The Proceeds of Crime Act 2002 and Money Laundering Regulations 2003 (Amendment) Order 2006" extended this defence to accountants, auditors or tax advisers who satisfy certain conditions where the information on which their suspicion of money laundering is based comes to their attention in privileged circumstances (as defined in POCA section 330(10)). Examples may be where a client provides information in connection with the provision by the auditor of advice on legal issues such as tax or company law. The giving of such advice would not normally arise as a result of an audit engagement, but may arise where the auditor has an additional contract with the client, to provide advisory services. In such circumstances, the auditor may discuss their money laundering suspicions with the MLRO without requiring the MLRO to make a disclosure to SOCA. Guidance on privilege reporting exemption is given in paragraphs 7.26 to 7.46 of the CCAB Guidance.*

'Tipping off' and prejudicing an investigation

In the UK, 'tipping off' is an offence for individuals in the regulated sector under section 333A of POCA. This offence arises: 44

(a) When an individual discloses that a disclosure (internal or external) has already been made where the disclosure is based on information that came to that individual in the course of a business in the regulated sector and the disclosure by the individual is likely to prejudice an investigation which might be conducted following the internal or external disclosure that has been made; or
(b) When an individual discloses that an investigation is being contemplated or is being carried out into allegations that a money laundering offence has been committed and the disclosure by the individual is likely to prejudice that investigation and the information on which the disclosure is based came to a person in the course of a business in the regulated sector.

There are a number of exceptions to this offence under sections 333B, 333C and 333D of POCA, including where disclosures are made: 45

- to a fellow auditor employed by a firm that shares common ownership, management or control with the audit firm (some network firms may not meet this test);
- to an auditor in another firm in the EEA (or an equivalent jurisdiction for money laundering purposes, where both are subject to equivalent confidentiality and data protection obligations), in relation to the same client or a transaction or service involving them both, for the purpose of preventing a money laundering offence;
- to a supervisory authority for the person making the disclosure;
- for the purpose of the prevention, detection or investigation of a criminal offence where the auditor is acting as a relevant professional adviser (whether in the UK or elsewhere);
- to the client, for the purpose of dissuading the client from engaging in an offence; or
- in circumstances where the person making the disclosure does not know or suspect that the disclosure is likely to prejudice an investigation.

A further offence of prejudicing an investigation is included in section 342 of POCA. Under this provision, it is an offence to make any disclosure which is likely to prejudice an investigation of which a person has knowledge or suspicion, or to falsify, conceal, destroy or otherwise dispose of, or cause or permit the falsification, concealment, destruction or disposal of, documents relevant to such an investigation. 46

ISA (UK and Ireland) 260 requires the auditor to communicate audit matters of governance interest arising from the audit of the financial statements with those charged with governance of an entity. The auditor will consider whether there is a need to communicate suspicions of money laundering to those charged with governance of an entity. As set out above, under section 333D of POCA a tipping off offence is not committed by an auditor (when he or she is acting as a relevant professional adviser) where a disclosure is made to the client in order to dissuade the client from engaging in a money laundering offence (for example, where an employee is engaged in money laundering using the client's financial systems, the auditor may inform the client of the situation in order to prevent the client from committing a money laundering offence). However, care will be taken as to whom the disclosure is made where senior management of the client or those charged with governance are or are suspected to be involved in the money laundering activity or complicit with it. For example, where a client develops a policy approved by the directors that duplicate payments on its invoices will not be returned to customers and that no 47 credit is given against further invoices, the company may be committing a criminal offence (see Example 2 in Appendix 1 of this Practice Note).

Reporting to obtain appropriate consent

48   In addition to the auditor's duty to report knowledge or suspicion of, or reasonable grounds to know or suspect, money laundering under POCA sections 330 and 331, the auditor may need to obtain appropriate consent to perform an act which could otherwise constitute a principal money laundering offence (subject to the SOCPA amendments to sections 327, 328 and 329 for overseas activities[17]). For example, if the auditor suspected that the audit report was necessary in order for financial statements to be issued in connection with a transaction involving the proceeds of crime, or if the auditor was to sign off an auditor's report on financial statements for a company that was a front for illegal activity, the auditor might be involved in an arrangement which facilitated the acquisition, retention, use or control of criminal property under section 328 of POCA. In these circumstances, in addition to the normal procedures, the auditor would generally need to obtain appropriate consent from SOCA via the MLRO as soon as is practicable. Consent may be given expressly or may be deemed to have been given following the expiry of certain time limits specified in section 336 of POCA. Where applicable the auditor understands the applicable time limits. Further guidance on seeking appropriate consent is given in section 8 of the CCAB Guidance.

49   The auditor will also need to consider whether continuing to act for the company could itself constitute money laundering, for example if it amounted to aiding or abetting the commission of one of the principal money laundering offences in sections 327, 328 or 329 of POCA, or if it amounted to one of the principal money laundering offences itself, in particular the offence of becoming involved in an arrangement under section 328 of POCA. In those circumstances the auditor may want to consider whether to resign, but should firstly contact the MLRO, both to report the suspicions and to seek guidance in respect of 'tipping off'. If the auditor wishes to continue to conduct the audit the auditor, through the MLRO, may need to seek appropriate consent from SOCA for such an action to be taken.

50   Appropriate consent from SOCA will protect the auditor from committing a principal money laundering offence but will not relieve the auditor from any civil liability or other professional, legal or ethical obligations. As an alternative to seeking appropriate consent, the auditor may wish to consider resignation from the audit but, in such circumstances, is still required to disclose suspicions to the MLRO. Further guidance on resignation is given in paragraphs 56 to 60 below.

Reporting to regulators

51   Reporting to SOCA does not relieve the auditor from other statutory duties. Examples of statutory reporting responsibilities include:

- *audits of entities in the financial sector*: the auditor has a statutory duty to report matters of 'material significance' to the FSA which come to the auditor's attention in the course of the audit work;

---

[17] It is not a money laundering offence for a person to deal with the proceeds of conduct which that person knows, or believes on reasonable grounds, occurred in a particular country or territory outside the UK, and which was known to be lawful, at the time it occurred, under the criminal law then applying in that country or territory, and does not constitute a 'serious offence' under English law (see footnote 14).

- *audits of entities in the public sector*: auditors of some public sector entities may be required to report on the entity's compliance with requirements to ensure the regularity and propriety of financial transactions. Activity connected with money laundering may be a breach of those requirements; and
- *audits of other types of entity:* auditors of some other entities are also required to report matters of 'material significance' to regulators (for example, charities and occupational pension schemes).

Knowledge or suspicion, or reasonable grounds for knowledge or suspicion, of involvement of the entity's directors in money laundering, or of a failure of a regulated business to comply with the ML Regulations would normally be regarded as being of material significance to a regulator and so give rise to a statutory duty to report to the regulator in addition to the requirement to report to SOCA. In determining whether such a duty arises, the auditor follows the requirements of auditing standards on reporting to regulators in the financial sector and considers the specific guidance dealing with each area set out in related Practice Notes. A tipping off offence is not committed when a report is made to that person's supervisory authority or in any other circumstances where a disclosure is not likely to prejudice an investigation. 52

The auditor's report on financial statements

Where it is suspected that money laundering has occurred the auditor will need to apply the concept of materiality when considering whether the auditor's report on the financial statements needs to be qualified or modified, taking into account whether: 53

- the crime itself has a material effect on the financial statements;
- the consequences of the crime have a material effect on the financial statements; or
- the outcome of any subsequent investigation by the police or other investigatory body may have a material effect on the financial statements.

If it is known that money laundering has occurred and that directors or senior staff of the company were knowingly involved, the auditor will need to consider whether the auditor's report is likely to include a qualified opinion on the financial statements. In such circumstances the auditor considers whether disclosure in the report on the financial statements, either through qualifying the opinion or referring to fundamental uncertainty, could alert a money launderer. 54

Timing may be the crucial factor. Any delay in issuing the audit report pending the outcome of an investigation is likely to be impracticable and could in itself alert a money launderer. The auditor seeks advice from the MLRO who acts as the main source of guidance and if necessary is the liaison point for communication with lawyers, SOCA and the relevant law enforcement agency. 55

Resignation and communication with successor auditors

The auditor may wish to resign from the position as auditor if the auditor believes that the client or an employee is engaged in money laundering or any other illegal act, particularly where a normal relationship of trust can no longer be maintained. Where the auditor intends to cease to hold office there may be a conflict between the requirements under section 519 of the Companies Act 2006 for the auditor to deposit a statement at a company's registered office of any circumstances that the auditor believes need to be brought to the attention of members or creditors and the risk of 56 'tipping off'. This may arise if, for example, the circumstances connected with the resignation of the auditor include knowledge or suspicion of money laundering and an internal or external disclosure being made. See section 9 of CCAB Guidance for guidance on cessation of work and resignation.

57   Where such disclosure of circumstances may amount to 'tipping off', the auditor seeks to agree the wording of the section 519 disclosure with the relevant law enforcement agency and, failing that, seeks legal advice. The auditor seeks advice from the MLRO who acts as the main source of guidance and if necessary is the liaison point for communication with lawyers, SOCA and the relevant law enforcement agency. The auditor may as a last resort need to apply to the court for direction as to what is included in the section 519 statement.

58   The offence of 'tipping off' may also cause a conflict with the need to communicate with the prospective successor auditor in accordance with legal and ethical requirements relating to changes in professional appointment. For example, the existing auditor might feel obliged to mention knowledge or suspicion regarding suspected money laundering and any external disclosure made to SOCA. Under section 333C of POCA this would not constitute 'tipping off' if it was done to prevent the incoming auditor from committing a money laundering offence. However, as an audit opinion is rarely used for money laundering purposes, this is unlikely to apply in an audit situation.

59   If information about internal and external reports made by the auditor is considered relevant information for the purposes of paragraph 9 of Schedule 10 of the Companies Act 2006[18], the auditor considers whether the disclosure of that information would constitute a 'tipping off' offence under section 333A, because it may prejudice an investigation. If the auditor considers a 'tipping off' offence might be committed, the auditor speaks to SOCA to see if they are content that disclosure in those circumstances would not prejudice any investigation. The auditor may, as a last resort, need to apply to the Court for directions as to what is disclosed to the incoming auditor.

60   Where the only information which needs to be disclosed is the underlying circumstances which gave rise to the disclosure, there are two scenarios to consider:

- Where the auditor only wishes to disclose the suspicions about the underlying criminal conduct and the basis for those suspicions, the auditor will not commit an offence under POCA if that information only is disclosed. For example, if audit files are made available to the incoming auditor containing working papers that detail circumstances which have lead the audit team to suspect the management of a fraud and this suspicion is noted on the file, this will not constitute a 'tipping off' offence.
- If the auditor wishes to disclose any suspicions specifically about money laundering (for example, if the working papers in the example above indicated that the suspected fraud also constituted a suspicion of money laundering), then as a matter of prudence, the approach adopted follows that described in paragraphs 56 and 57 in relation to the section 519 statement.

---

[18] *Statutory Instrument 2007/3494 "The Statutory Auditors and Third Country Auditors Regulations 2007" comes into force on 6th April 2008 and requires the auditor to make available all relevant information held in relation to holding the office as auditor to a successor auditor.*

Appendix 1 – Examples of situations that may give rise to money laundering offences that auditors may encounter during the course of the audit

These are examples of some of the situations that auditors may encounter during the course of the audit and some of the factors that auditors may wish to bear in mind when considering reporting suspicions of money laundering. They are intended to demonstrate the breadth of the money laundering legislation. This is not an exhaustive list of offences, nor a guide as to how such offences must be dealt with. The best way to deal with suspected money laundering will vary according to the particular facts of each case and should be dealt with in accordance with the firm's procedures.

The examples are based on the legislation and SOCA guidance current at the time the Practice Note was finalised. Auditors will wish to consider whether SOCA guidance has been updated as well as the extent to which they are prepared to follow any SOCA guidance, particularly if SOCA states in its guidance that in a particular type of case no report at all is required.

1. Offences where the client is the victim (for example, shoplifting)

The auditor acts for a large retail client. The auditor discovers there has been significant stock shrinkage in a number of stores. The client attributes at least some of this to shoplifting. In addition, the auditor is aware that some of the stores hold files detailing instances when the police have been called to deal with shoplifters caught by the security guards.

POCA does not require the auditor to undertake further enquiry outside the auditor's normal audit work to determine whether an offence has occurred or to find out further details of the offence. Accordingly, the auditor does not need to review the files containing the details of the police being called, unless the auditor would otherwise have done so for the purposes of the audit.

Where the auditor does not believe that the information will or may assist in identifying the shoplifter or the whereabouts of any of the goods stolen by the shoplifter, for example where the identity of the shoplifters cannot be deduced from the information and the proceeds have disappeared without trace, the auditor decides not to make a report to the MLRO.

In the circumstances where the information possessed by the client will assist in identifying the shoplifter or the whereabouts of any of the goods stolen by the shoplifter, the auditor must make a report to the MLRO briefly describing the situation and stating where the information on the identity of shoplifters may be found.

2. Offences that indicate dishonest behaviour (for example, overpayments not returned)

Some customers of the audit client have overpaid their invoices and some have paid twice. The auditor discovers that the audit client has a policy of retaining all overpayments by customers and crediting them to the profit and loss account if they are not claimed within a year.

The auditor considers whether the retention of the overpayments might amount to theft by the audit client from its customer. If so, the client will be in possession of the proceeds of its crime, a money laundering offence.

In the case of minor irregularities where there is nothing to suggest dishonest behaviour, (for example where the client attempted to return the overpayments to its customers, or if the overpayments were mistakenly overlooked), the person making the report may be satisfied that no criminal property is involved and therefore a report is not required.

If there are no such indications that the company has acted honestly, the auditor concludes that the client may have acted dishonestly. Following the firm's procedures, which take into account the SOCA guidance about minor irregularities where dishonest behaviour is suspected, and about multiple suspicions of limited intelligence value which arise during the course of one audit, the auditor must make a report to the MLRO at the end of the audit, briefly describing the situation and any other matters of limited intelligence value.

3. Companies Act offences that are civil offences (for example, illegal dividend payments)

During the course of the audit, the auditor discovers that the audit client has paid a dividend based on draft accounts. Audit adjustments subsequently reduce distributable reserves to the extent that the dividend is now illegal under the Companies Act.

The auditor recognises that the payment of an illegal dividend is not per se a criminal offence because the Companies Act imposes only civil sanctions on companies making illegal distributions and decides not to report the matter to the MLRO.

4. Offences that involve saved costs (for example, environmental offences)

The client has a factory which manufactures some of the goods sold in its retail business. In the course of reviewing board minutes, the auditor discovers that the client has been disposing of waste from the factory without a proper licence. There are concerns that pollutants from the waste have been leaking into a nearby river. The client is currently in discussion with the relevant licensing authorities to try to get proper authorisation.

The auditor has reasonable grounds to suspect that the client may have committed offences of disposing of waste without the relevant licence and of polluting the nearby river. The client has saved the costs of applying for a licence. It is also apparent that its methods of disposing of the waste are cheaper than processing it properly. These saved costs may represent the benefit of the client's crime. The client is in possession of the benefit of a crime and the auditor therefore suspects that it has committed a money laundering offence.

The firm's procedures take into account the SOCA guidance which states that in the case of regulatory matters, where the relevant government agency is already aware of an offence which also happens to be an instance of suspected money laundering, a limited intelligence value report can be made. A limited intelligence value report can also be made where the only benefit from criminal conduct is in the form of cost savings.

The authorities are aware of the licensing issue and the pollution of the nearby river. As the only benefit to the company is in the form of cost savings, the auditor decides to include this matter in the limited intelligence value report to the MLRO at the end of the audit.

Alternatively, if the client has accrued for back licence fees, fines and/or restitution costs, there may be no remaining proceeds to the original offence and therefore no need to report.

5. Conduct committed overseas that is a criminal offence under English law (for example, bribery, because English Law on bribery applies to overseas conduct)

The client plans to expand its retail operations into a country where it has not operated before. Construction of its first outlets is underway and it is in consultation with the overseas Government about obtaining the necessary permits to sell its goods (although these negotiations are proving difficult). The client has engaged a consultancy firm to oversee the implementation of its plans and liaise 'on the ground', although it is not clear to the auditor exactly what the firm's role is. The auditor notices that the payments made to the firm are very large, particularly in comparison to the services provided. The auditor reviews the expenses claimed by the consultant and notes that some of these are for significant sums to meet government officials' expenses.

The auditor considers whether the payments may be for the consultant to use in paying bribes, for example to obtain the necessary permits. The country is one where corruption and facilitation payments are known to be widespread. The auditor makes some enquiries about the consultancy firm but cannot establish that it is a reputable business.

Taking into account compliance with legislation relating to 'tipping off' the auditor questions the client's Finance Director about the matter and the FD admits that the consultant has told him that some 'facilitation payments' will be necessary to move the project along and the FD agreed that some payments should be made to get the local officials to do the jobs that they should be doing anyway; for example, to get the traffic police to let the construction vehicles through nearby road blocks. The FD thought that such payments were acceptable in the country in question.

The auditor suspects that bribes have been paid and the auditor is aware that bribery, including the bribery of government officials, is a criminal offence under UK law. Bribery of foreign public officials, by UK nationals and corporations, is a criminal offence even where it occurs wholly outside the UK, under Part 12 of the Anti-terrorism Crime and Security Act 2001 Accordingly, the auditor decides to make a full report to the MLRO.

6. Lawful Conduct Overseas which would amount to a serious offence if it occurred in England and Wales (for example, a cartel operation)

The client's overseas subsidiary is one of three key suppliers of goods to a particular market in Europe. The subsidiary has recently significantly increased its prices and margins and its principal competitors have done the same. There has been press speculation that the suppliers acted in concert, but publicly they have cited increased costs of production as driving the increase. Whilst this explains part of the reason for the increase, it is not the only reason because of the increase in margins.

On reviewing the accounting records, the auditor sees significant payments for consultancy services. He seeks an explanation for these costs and is informed that these relate to the recent price increase. Apparently, this related to an assessment of the impact of the price increase on the market as well as some compensation for any losses the competitors suffered on their business outside of Europe. Some of the increased profits have flowed back to the client parent company. The client informs the auditor that there is not a criminal cartel offence under local law.

The auditor has a number of concerns:

- The subsidiary may be engaged in conduct amounting to money laundering overseas. However, because the conduct is not criminal there it also does not constitute money laundering under local law. No report is therefore required about the subsidiary.
- The parent company has received profits from the subsidiary and may therefore be engaged in money laundering in England. The auditor suspects that the subsidiary's conduct, whilst lawful where it occurred, would be unlawful under English law if it was committed here, since the auditor suspects that the agreement to fix prices would have been dishonest. The auditor therefore makes a full disclosure to the MLRO.

In rare circumstances where the auditor is also concerned about being involved in a prohibited arrangement, the auditor also needs to consider whether the overseas conduct would amount to a serious criminal offence if it was committed in England and Wales. As a cartel offence is serious a report would be made to the MLRO and the auditor would await consent from the MLRO before proceeding further.

7. Offences committed overseas that are not criminal offences under UK law (for example, breach of exchange controls and importing religious material)

During the course of the audit, the auditor forms a suspicion that one of the overseas subsidiaries has been in breach of a number of local laws. In particular:

- Dividends have been paid to the parent company in breach of local exchange control requirements.
- The subsidiary has imported religious materials intended for the preaching of a particular faith, which is contrary to the laws of that jurisdiction.

Money laundering offences include conduct occurring overseas which would constitute an offence if it had occurred in the UK. Because the UK has no exchange control legislation and the preaching of any faith is allowed it is possible that neither of the offences committed by the overseas subsidiary constitute offences under UK law. The auditor considers whether any other offence might have been committed if this conduct took place in the UK, but the auditor decides not to make a report to the MLRO in these circumstances.

Appendix 2 – Guidance as to whom the anti-money laundering legislation applies

To whom does the reporting requirement apply?

The requirement to make a report under section 330 and 331 of POCA applies to information which comes to a person in the course of a business, or an MLRO, in the regulated sector. That information may relate to money laundering by persons or businesses inside or outside the regulated sector.

The offence of failing to report that another person is engaged in money laundering applies to all money laundering, including conduct taking place overseas that would be an offence if it took place in the UK (see paragraph 36 of this Practice Note). For that reason there may be an obligation to report information arising from the audit of non-UK companies or their subsidiaries.

When is an auditor in the UK regulated sector?

The regulated sector includes any firm or individual who acts in the course of a business carried on in the UK as an auditor.

A person is eligible for appointment as an auditor if the person is a member of a recognised supervisory body, (which is a body established in the UK which maintains and enforces rules as to the eligibility of persons to seek appointment as an auditor and the conduct of audit work, and which is recognised by the Secretary of State by Order) and is eligible for appointment under the rules of that body.

For the purposes of this Practice Note the AML reporting requirements apply to all partners and staff within a UK audit firm who are involved in audit work in the UK. Where they become involved in audit work in the UK, such persons may include:

- Experts from other disciplines within the UK audit firm.
- Experts from outside the UK audit firm.
- Employees of non-UK audit firms for example, an auditor from an overseas office of an international firm.

Where they are not involved in audit work in the UK such persons may fall within other parts of the regulated sector, for example the provision of accountancy services to other persons by way of business is within the regulated sector regardless of whether the person providing the services is or is not a member of a UK professional auditing/accountancy body.

It is unlikely that it will be practicable or desirable for a UK audit firm which is within the regulated sector to distinguish for reporting purposes between partners and staff who are providing services in the regulated sector and those who are not. Accordingly, UK audit firms may choose to impose procedures across the firm requiring all partners and staff to report to the firm's MLRO[19].

The following table illustrates how the reporting requirements might apply to a number of different audit/client scenarios.[20] This table is intended as a guide and it is recognised that there may be factual scenarios which do not fall within the categories above. In case of any doubt, auditors should refer to the provisions of POCA and the ML Regulations, which take precedence over any guidance in this Appendix.

---

[19] *Persons outside the regulated sector are not obliged to report to their MLRO under POCA section 330 and section 331 (the 'failure to report' offence), but can make voluntary reports under POCA section 337 of information they obtain in the course of their trade, profession, business or employment which causes them to know or suspect, or gives reasonable grounds for knowing or suspecting, that another person is engaged in money laundering. Such reports are protected from breach of client confidentiality in the same way as reports made under POCA section 330 and section 331.*

[20] *The audit/client reporting scenarios do not take into account the exemptions for activities occurring outside the UK.*

Persons	Offence discovered as part of audit of:	
	UK companies (including UK subsidiaries of UK or non-UK companies)	Non-UK companies (including non-UK subsidiaries of UK or non-UK companies)
• working in UK for UK audit firm	Yes	Yes
• working in UK for non-UK audit firm[21]	Possibly. Where the auditor or audit firm is not eligible for appointment as a UK auditor, in practice, it is likely that the auditor or firm would be providing accountancy services and therefore fall within the UK regulated sector.	
• seconded to UK audit firm	Yes	Yes
• working temporarily outside UK or on foreign secondments, or working permanently outside UK but employed by a UK audit firm	The position of an auditor working temporarily outside the UK or on foreign secondments, or working permanently outside the UK but still within a UK audit firm (but not necessarily employed by the UK firm), is more difficult. For example the duty to report may be influenced by the terms of the secondment. The following is a non-exhaustive list of issues to consider and firms may wish to take legal advice in relation to the need for their employees to comply with the UK's money laundering reporting regime as well as any local legal requirements. Issues to consider include: • If the auditor's work outside the UK is part of a UK audit then in some circumstances that information may have come to the auditor's attention in the course of engaging in UK regulated activities and therefore be reportable. • In the case of an auditor working permanently outside the UK for a UK firm, it may be appropriate to consider whether the auditor is working at a separate firm or at a branch office of a UK firm. • An auditor should be particularly cautious about any decision not to make a report on their return to the UK if the information relates to work that the auditor is undertaking in the UK. • Regardless of the strict legal position, firms may wish to consider putting in place a business-wide anti-money laundering strategy to protect their global reputation and UK regulated business. • An auditor working permanently or temporarily outside the UK considers the anti-money laundering legislation in their host country.	
• working permanently outside UK for non-UK audit firm	No	No

[21] It is recognised that it would not be possible for a non-UK audit firm or auditor to be appointed as the auditor of a UK company. However, these categories have been included for completeness.

[PN 14]
The audit of registered social landlords in the United Kingdom (Revised)

Contents

		Paragraphs
Preface		3
Introduction		4
Special considerations arising from auditing standards – ISAs (UK and Ireland)		10
200	Objective and General Principles Governing an Audit of Financial Statements	10
210	Terms of Audit Engagements	11
220	Quality Control for Audits of Historical Financial Information	13
240	The Auditor's Responsibility to Consider Fraud in an Audit of Financial Statements	14
250	Section A – Consideration of Laws and Regulations in an Audit of Financial Statements	17
250	Section B – The Auditors' Right and Duty to Report to Regulators in the Financial Sector	20
260	Communication of Audit Matters With Those Charged With Governance	22
300	Planning an Audit of Financial Statements	24
315	Obtaining an Understanding of the Entity and Its Environment and Assessing the Risks of Material Misstatement	26
320	Audit Materiality	38
330	The Auditor's Procedures in response to Assessed Risks	39
402	Audit Considerations Relating to Entities Using Service Organisations	41
500	Audit Evidence	43
505	External Confirmations	44
520	Analytical Procedures	45
540	Audit of Accounting Estimates	47
545	Auditing Fair Value Measurements and Disclosures	49
550	Related Parties	51
560	Subsequent Events	53
570	Going Concern	54
580	Management Representations	57
610	Considering the Work of Internal Audit	59
620	Using the Work of an Expert	60
700	The Independent Auditor's Report on a Complete Set of General Purpose Financial Statements	61
720	Other Information in Documents Containing Audited Financial Statements	66
Reports on service charge statements		68

Appendices

1. Regulation of Registered Social Landlords
2. Constitution of Registered Social Landlords
3. Legislative Framework
4. Codes of audit practice and good practice notes

5 Example paragraphs for inclusion in an engagement letter for an RSL that is an Industrial and Provident Society
6 A statement of the board's responsibilities for an RSL that is an Industrial and Provident Society
7 Illustrative example of auditors' report on the financial statements of an RSL that is an Industrial and Provident Society
8 Definitions
9 Some significant topics relevant to audits of RSLs

The audit of registered social landlords in the United Kingdom (Revised)

Preface

This Practice Note contains guidance on the application of auditing standards issued by the Auditing Practices Board (the APB) to the audit of Registered Social Landlords (RSLs) in the United Kingdom. The Practice Note is also indicative of good practice for the audit of other social landlords which are not subject to the regulatory regime applicable to RSLs.

The Practice Note is supplementary to, and should be read in conjunction with, International Standards on Auditing (ISAs) (UK and Ireland), which apply to all audits undertaken in the United Kingdom in respect of periods commencing on or after 15 December 2004.

This Practice Note supersedes the guidance included in Practice Note 14 'The audit of registered social landlords in the United Kingdom' issued by the APB in November 2003, and takes account of regulatory and other developments affecting RSLs since PN 14 was issued, principally the replacement of Statements of Auditing Standards (SASs) by ISAs (UK and Ireland).

Certain RSLs may be constituted as charities in which case auditors also refer to the APB's Practice Note 11 The Audit of Charities in the United Kingdom (Revised).

The Practice Note is based on legislation (including the Housing Act 2004) and regulations in effect at 31 December 2005. The regulatory framework of RSLs differs in the various jurisdictions of the United Kingdom and the Practice Note has been prepared with advice and assistance from staff of The Housing Corporation, the Department for Social Development in Northern Ireland, Communities Scotland and the National Assembly for Wales.

'Registered Social Landlords' (RSLs) in England and Wales include registered housing associations, registered housing charitable trusts and local housing companies. In this Practice Note, the term RSL is also used to apply to housing associations in Scotland and Northern Ireland. RSLs are registered with the relevant regulatory body, that is, the Housing Corporation in England, the Department for Social Development in Northern Ireland, Communities Scotland in Scotland and the National Assembly for Wales in Wales.

Introduction

1 This introduction summarises the key features of RSLs which require special consideration by auditors, and explains the environment within which auditors operate. More detailed information, specific to each UK jurisdiction, is provided in the appendices.

The nature of registered social landlords

2 RSLs provide social housing (accommodation usually made available at less than market rates and allocated to applicants in greatest housing need) and other related services. RSLs provide an alternative to local authority and private sector rented housing, either by acquiring existing dwellings, acquiring and rehabilitating existing

dwellings or by undertaking new building, with the aim of providing rented accommodation in perpetuity or until purchased by the tenant.

3   RSLs vary in size and constitution but there are certain identifying factors which both unite them and make them unique in their method of operation. RSLs are not-for-profit organisations and are managed under the oversight of a board or committee of management ('the board'). RSLs operate independently of both central and local government, although they are frequently in receipt of substantial sums of public funds and local authorities may have nomination rights in relation to certain rented properties.

The Constitution of registered social landlords

4   RSLs may be constituted in various ways and can be highly complex as a result of the legal and regulatory frameworks under which they operate. It is important that auditors understand the statutory framework within which RSLs operate (Appendix 2 sets out the different types of legal entities – for example industrial and provident societies, limited companies, unincorporated organisations such as charities – and the applicable regulatory regimes).

Responsibilities and powers of the regulators

5   RSLs are registered with the relevant regulatory body, that is, the Housing Corporation in England, the Department for Social Development in Northern Ireland, Communities Scotland in Scotland and the National Assembly for Wales in Wales. RSLs are registered in the jurisdiction where their registered office is situated. Registration brings with it significant regulatory requirements with which RSLs must comply. Once an RSL is registered, the board must ensure that certain conditions, determined by the regulatory body, are observed. For example, the Housing Corporation's Regulatory Code and Communities Scotland's Performance Standards require the RSLs which they regulate to be viable, well governed and well managed.

6   The regulatory bodies presently have dual roles of regulating the RSLs which are registered with them and investing funds in social housing related activities. The regulatory bodies maintain a register of RSLs which is open to public inspection. The regulatory bodies have no direct powers over unregistered social landlords, but if they operate within groups which include RSLs they will be able to influence how the group as a whole is run.

7   RSLs are eligible to apply for grant from the publicly funded social housing programme. They must provide documents and other information to the regulatory body as required. They also have to obtain the regulator's agreement before they can undertake certain courses of action, for example disposing of housing assets including land, entering into charges over such assets or land or changing their rules.

8   RSLs are governed by boards which are made up mainly of non-executive voluntary members (which may include tenants), but which may also include a limited number of paid and/or staff members.

9   Regulatory staff review information provided by RSLs and may request further information or make periodic visits or inspections to follow up any specific concerns. The regulatory bodies have a range of powers where serious concerns have been identified and the RSL is unable or unwilling to address those concerns. These include powers to make appointments to governing bodies, to direct an inquiry into the affairs of an RSL and to intervene where an RSL is threatened with insolvency.

Responsibilities of the board

Boards[1] have the legal responsibility for the running of an RSL. They retain ultimate control and responsibility over all aspects of the activities of the RSL and must ensure that the financial and legal responsibilities are fulfilled properly. The powers of boards are wide and, although particular functions may be delegated to sub-committees or to staff, boards retain the responsibility for seeing that those functions are carried out properly.

The roles and responsibilities of boards normally include:

- defining and monitoring compliance with the governing documents, values and objectives of the RSL;
- establishing plans to achieve those objectives;
- approving each year's budget and financial statements prior to publication;
- establishing and overseeing an appropriate framework of delegation and effective systems of control;
- taking key decisions on matters that will, or might, create significant risks for the RSL;
- monitoring the performance of the RSL in relation to these plans, budgets and decisions;
- appointing and, if necessary, dismissing the chief executive and being represented in the appointment of key second tier managers;
- appointing and agreeing the remuneration of the auditors;
- satisfying themselves that the affairs of the RSL are conducted lawfully and in accordance with performance standards set by the regulators; and
- overseeing the RSL's relationship with its regulatory body.

In larger RSLs, the oversight of systems of control and liaison with the external auditors is usually delegated by the board to an audit committee.

Part III of Schedule 1 to the Housing Act 1996[2] has widened the responsibility for ensuring compliance with the accounting requirements set out in the schedule to include 'every responsible person who is concerned with the conduct and management of the affairs on an RSL, and is in that capacity responsible for the preparation of the accounts'.

The regulatory bodies in each of the UK jurisdictions have issued codes of audit practice (see Appendix 4) or good practice notes relating to external audit. The codes, good practice notes, circulars and other relevant documents provide guidance to boards on, and define their responsibilities for, amongst other things, the appointment of auditors and the nature of the RSL's working relationship with the auditors.

---

[1] Also referred to as Committees of Management.

[2] In Scotland, part 3 of Schedule 7 to the Housing (Scotland) Act 2001.

14 In 2001 the Housing Corporation issued Circular 25/01 'Internal controls assurance', which replaced a previous Circular 18/96 in England[3]. Circular 25/01 does not require external auditors to report on the board's published statement which will cover the complete internal control system rather than merely financial controls. The auditors' responsibilities for other information in documents containing audited financial statements, such as the internal control statement, are covered in the ISA (UK and Ireland) 720 section later in this Practice Note. In addition, the board is free to request their auditors to conduct further work on the statement on internal control if they wish to do so. Further guidance on external auditor responsibilities in such circumstances is covered below under 'Responsibilities and rights of auditors'.

Responsibilities and rights of auditors

15 Every RSL is required under the various social housing legislation to have an annual independent audit. However, provisions in the Housing Act 2004 will enable the Housing Corporation and the National Assembly for Wales to exempt smaller RSLs from audit. Auditors of RSLs must be registered auditors.

16 The statutory duties of auditors in relation to the financial statements are to:

(a) express an opinion as to whether the financial statements give a 'true and fair view' and have been properly prepared in accordance with the appropriate statutory requirements; and
(b) state, in the auditors' report:
   (i) where proper books of account have not been kept;
   (ii) where a satisfactory system of control over transactions has not been maintained in accordance with the relevant legislation; and
   (iii) if the financial statements are not in agreement with the books and records of the RSL.

Auditors may also be required to report on certain returns of RSLs to the relevant regulatory body.

17 Under Housing Corporation Circular 25/01, 'Internal Controls Assurance', the board of an RSL in England is required to include a statement in the annual financial statements in respect of internal control. RSLs are free to request their auditors to conduct further work on the statement of internal control if they wish to do so. In this instance, RSLs might require the external auditors to form an opinion on three questions:

- does the statement reflect the process defined by the board for its review of the effectiveness of internal control?
- does the documentation prepared by or for the board provide sound support for the statement?
- is the statement made by the board in accordance with the auditors' knowledge of the RSL obtained during the audit of the financial statements?

---

[3] *In 1996 the Housing Corporation issued Circular 18/96 'Internal financial control and financial reporting' which tailored the 'Cadbury' guidance for directors of listed companies to RSLs in England, and provided guidance to boards consistent with that for directors of listed companies. Circular 18/96 required the RSL to publish a statement on its internal financial control system (if it has over 50 units) and the external auditors to report on that statement. Communities Scotland issued Guidance Note 97/02, and this guidance is now contained in chapter 10 of the SFHA's publication 'Raising Standards', and applies to RSLs with more than 150 units. HAC 10/96 and Circular 8/97 were issued in Northern Ireland and Wales respectively. All these publications contain the same requirements as Circular 18/96.*

The auditors' relationship with the regulators

18 Auditors have no formal requirement to report directly to the social housing regulators[4]. There is, however, an indirect relationship because the regulatory bodies provide guidance to RSLs on dealing with their auditors and require RSLs to forward to them copies of audited financial statements and management letters.

Principal special features of RSL audits

19 Regulations and guidance – The auditor may need to consider codes of audit practice or guidance notes issued by regulatory bodies[5] which advise RSLs on their relationship with them and require RSLs to submit copies of auditors' management letters together with the RSL's response to the regulatory body. The auditor may be requested to report on certain returns to the regulatory body, for example in connection with grants, or to funders, for example in connection with covenant compliance.

20 Other guidance – The auditor considers as necessary other guidance issued by the three Housing Federations, for example guidance relating to corporate governance and accounting for Supported Housing.

21 Internal controls – Legislation requires auditors of most RSLs to state in their report on the financial statements if the RSL has failed to maintain a satisfactory system of internal control. This, together with the fact that RSLs are in receipt of substantial amounts of public funding in the form of social housing grant and other public sector grants, means that internal controls are particularly relevant.

22 The long-term nature of the business – The main source of income of most RSLs, rents, is generally predictable. As a result analytical procedures are often a useful audit tool.

23 Substantial debt financing – RSLs typically raise significant funds through borrowing, and must be able to demonstrate that future income will be sufficient to meet outgoings. Auditors consider this when reviewing the appropriateness of the use of the going concern assumption in the preparation of the financial statements.

24 Valuation of housing properties – A significant number of RSLs including those established by means of Large Scale Voluntary Transfers, carry their housing properties at an existing use valuation. This is obtained by means of a professional valuation and, as set out in ISA (UK and Ireland) 620: Using the work of an expert, auditors consider the proper inclusion of the valuation in the accounts, the information on which the valuer has relied and the reasons for any changes in the valuation from the previous period.

25 The potentially complex direct tax, indirect tax and employee tax rules – The nature of RSL operations means that corporation tax and other tax computations for RSLs may be complex. Examples of complexities include:

---

[4] *Those RSLs that are charities may have reporting responsibilities to charity regulators – see the section below on ISA (UK and Ireland) 250 B. In addition, a provision in the Housing Act 2004 permits disclosure of information to the regulator in certain circumstances.*

[5] *In Scotland SEDD Circular 5/2002 explains the Housing (Scotland) Act 2001 and, in particular, the Right to Buy legislation. Also in Scotland, guidance notes SHGN 2001/10 and CSGN 2002/05 cover financial reporting by RSLs, and requirements for providing information for the purposes of financial scrutiny by Communities Scotland.*

- group structures which, because of the nature of the organisations involved, may not be capable of being grouped for tax purposes;
- conflict between the accounting standards and recommended practice and the tax treatment, particularly in relation to enhancements to property;
- partial exemption treatment for VAT purposes;
- possible difficulties for Large Scale Voluntary Transfers in claiming input VAT on certain property refurbishment costs; and
- the impact of employee tax for employees transferring from local authorities.

26 Supported housing – There are differing sources of funding for supported housing and care activities (such as, in England, 'Supporting people'). Auditors consider whether RSLs have systems in place to ensure compliance with contracts and quality standards. Failure to comply with contractual arrangements could result in a clawback of grant.

Application of this Practice Note

27 This Practice Note provides auditors of RSLs with guidance which is designed to ensure the consistent application of ISAs (UK and Ireland) across the sector. It is not in itself, however, sufficient to provide all the detailed knowledge required by auditors dealing with RSLs under all circumstances which may arise. Other relevant material includes the legislation governing the activities of individual RSLs and the audit of their financial statements and the Statement of Recommended Practice (SORP). Auditors may also consider relevant codes of governance, circulars and guidance on financial reporting issued by the regulatory bodies and housing federations from time to time.

Directors

28 The following sections of the Practice Note use the term 'directors' to describe the persons who are charged with governance of an RSL, including the preparation of its financial statements. For the purpose of this Practice Note, 'directors' should be taken to mean the members of the Board of an RSL.

Special considerations arising from Auditing Standards

ISAs (UK and Ireland) apply to the conduct of all audits in respect of accounting periods commencing on or after 15 December 2004. This includes audits of the financial statements of RSLs. The purpose of the following paragraphs is to identify the special considerations arising from the application of certain 'bold letter' requirements (which are indicated by grey-shaded boxes below) to the audit of RSLs, and to suggest ways in which these can be addressed. This Practice Note does not contain commentary on all of the bold letter requirements included in the ISAs (UK and Ireland) and reading it should not be seen as an alternative to reading the relevant ISAs (UK and Ireland) in their entirety. In addition, where no special considerations arise from a particular ISA (UK and Ireland), no material is included.

ISA (UK AND IRELAND) 200: OBJECTIVE AND GENERAL PRINCIPLES GOVERNING AN AUDIT OF FINANCIAL STATEMENTS

> **Background note**
>
> The purpose of this ISA (UK and Ireland) is to establish standards and provide guidance on the objective and general principles governing an audit of financial statements.

Auditing standards include a requirement for auditors to comply with relevant ethical requirements relating to audit engagements. In the UK, the auditor should comply with the APB's Ethical Standards and relevant ethical guidance relating to the work of auditors issued by the auditor's professional body. A fundamental principle is that practitioners should not accept or perform work which they are not competent to undertake. The importance of technical competence is also underlined in the Auditors' Code, issued by the APB, which states that the necessary degree of professional skill demands an understanding of financial reporting and business. Practitioners should not undertake the audit of RSLs unless they are satisfied that they have, or can obtain, the necessary level of competence.   29

ISA (UK AND IRELAND) 210: TERMS OF AUDIT ENGAGEMENTS

> **Background note**
>
> The purpose of this ISA (UK and Ireland) is to establish standards and provide guidance on agreeing the terms of the engagement with the client.

> The auditor and the client should agree on the terms of the engagement. (para 2)

The basic principles used in drafting engagement letters apply in relation to the audit of RSLs as to the audit of any entity.   30

> The auditor should confirm that the engagement letter documents and confirms the auditor's acceptance of the appointment, and includes a summary of the responsibilities of those charged with governance and of the auditor, the scope of the engagement and the form of any reports. (para 5-1)

Auditors may accept additional responsibilities as part of the terms of their engagement. Such responsibilities are recorded in the audit engagement letter or in a separate engagement letter.   31

Additional responsibilities may arise: 32
- under statute;
- from recommendations issued to RSLs within the various codes and other recommendations from the relevant regulatory body or relevant housing federation; or
- by agreement with the RSL.

33 Under statute there may be additional statutory returns which are required to be reviewed or signed by auditors. For example, in England and Wales reports may be required under the Landlord and Tenant Act 1985[6] (where variable service charges are registered and applied as part of, or in addition to, rent). Tenants may be entitled to request a summary of service costs on which an independent qualified accountant has issued a report.

34 The recommendations made to all RSLs by their regulatory bodies are not themselves binding on auditors. However, RSLs are likely to want to comply with best practice and with recommendations made by their regulatory bodies or relevant housing federations. Accordingly, RSLs and their auditors take account of such recommendations when agreeing the work which the auditors will undertake and the form of report which the auditors will issue.

35 Reports may also be requested by RSLs as part of a commercial agreement with lenders or on an ad hoc basis, for example an investigation into a possible fraud or irregularity. The terms of engagement for such reports are not addressed by ISA (UK and Ireland) 210 nor by this Practice Note.

36 Considerations where regulators or boards require reporting on internal controls and other aspects of corporate governance are discussed in paragraphs 109–110 below.

37 There are various legislative and regulatory requirements to report on specific information. These requirements can be included either in the main engagement letter or in a separate one(s), to emphasise that they are separate engagements. Topics set out in an engagement letter normally include:

- the responsibilities of the board and the auditors;
- the scope of the audit;
- reliance on internal audit;
- management representations;
- the detection of fraud and error;
- reports to management; and
- other audit requirements.

Example paragraphs for a letter of engagement for an RSL that is an Industrial and Provident Society are set out in Appendix 5. This may be tailored for RSLs that are companies or charities.

> On recurring audits, the auditor should consider whether circumstances require the terms of the engagement to be revised and whether there is a need to remind the client of the existing terms of the engagement. (para 10)

38 ISA (UK and Ireland) 210 sets out a number of reasons as to why an engagement letter should be revised on a recurring audit. In the case of RSLs, these reasons are also applicable. For example, changes in regulatory requirements or a new accounting determination, may indicate the need to reissue engagement letters.

---

[6] Parts of this Act are being superseded by the Commonhold and Leasehold Reform Act 2002.

ISA (UK AND IRELAND) 220: QUALITY CONTROL FOR AUDITS OF HISTORICAL FINANCIAL INFORMATION

Background note

The purpose of this ISA (UK and Ireland) is to establish standards and provide guidance on specific responsibilities of firm personnel regarding quality control procedures for audits of historical financial information, including audits of financial statements.

Reference should also be made to ISQC (UK and Ireland) 1 – Quality Control for Firms that Perform Audits and Reviews of Historical Financial Information, and other Assurance and Related Services Engagements.

The engagement partner should be satisfied that the engagement team collectively has the appropriate capabilities, competence and time to perform the audit engagement in accordance with professional standards and regulatory and legal requirements, and to enable an auditor's report that is appropriate in the circumstances to be issued (para 19).

Before commencing the audit of an RSL a firm ensures that it has enough staff who have adequate knowledge and experience of such audits. Staff involved in an audit of an RSL will have a broad understanding, commensurate with the individual's role and responsibilities in the audit process, of:

- the scope and nature of the activities of the RSL;
- the most significant parts of the relevant regulator's guidance; and
- the relevant general principles of the Statement of Recommended Practice (SORP).

ISA (UK AND IRELAND) 240: THE AUDITOR'S RESPONSIBILITY TO CONSIDER FRAUD IN AN AUDIT OF FINANCIAL STATEMENTS

Background note

The purpose of this ISA(UK and Ireland) is to establish basic principles and essential procedures and to provide guidance on the auditor's responsibility to consider fraud in an audit of financial statements and expand on how the standards and guidance in ISA (UK and Ireland) 315 and ISA (UK and Ireland) 330 are to be applied in relation to the risks of material misstatement due to fraud. The standards and guidance in this ISA (UK and Ireland) are intended to be integrated into the overall audit process.

In planning and performing the audit to reduce audit risk to an acceptably low level, the auditor should consider the risks of material misstatements in the financial statements due to fraud (para 3).

> The auditor should make inquiries of management, internal audit, and others within the entity as appropriate, to determine whether they have knowledge of any actual, suspected or alleged fraud affecting the entity (para 38).
>
> The auditor should make inquiries of those charged with governance to determine whether they have knowledge of any actual, suspected or alleged fraud affecting the entity (para 46).

> When obtaining an understanding of the entity and its environment, including its internal control, the auditor should consider whether the information obtained indicates that one or more fraud risk factors are present (para 48).

40 ISA (UK and Ireland) 240 states that two types of intentional misstatements are relevant to the auditor – misstatements resulting from fraudulent financial reporting and misstatements resulting from misappropriation of assets.

41 RSLs have been encouraged by their respective regulatory bodies to establish adequate internal controls. For example, the Housing Corporation's Circular 25/01 'Internal controls assurance' not only confirms that the board should maintain a sound system of internal control, but also requires all RSLs to maintain a register of all incidents of actual or attempted fraud and to advise it of all frauds in excess of £5,000 or equivalent in value (£1,000 for smaller RSLs) immediately on discovery and any fraud or corrupt act perpetrated or attempted by a board member or member of the senior management team of the RSL. As part of the risk assessment, the auditor reviews this register and enquires as to whether the register has been commented upon by the regulatory body during a monitoring or compliance visit.

42 In the case of RSLs, fraudulent financial reporting involving intentional misstatements to deceive financial statement users by influencing their perceptions as to the entity's performance and profitability, is less likely than in commercial entities due to the absence of trading in shares or significant management bonus arrangements. However, areas where the board might, where relevant, be expected to introduce strong internal controls to avoid the occurrence of fraud or error include purchasing (for development and maintenance), the holding of cash for residents (for example in supported housing), the collection of rent in cash and the major fund flows (for example the draw down and repayment of loans and grants).

43 There are a number of external issues which are likely to influence an RSL's objectives and strategies. For example, in the current move in England towards consolidation within the sector, there is increased focus on efficiency and cost control, and the desire to become/stay a Housing Corporation development partner. The strategies being adopted by RSLs to manage these issues may result in an incentive for material misstatement of the financial statements. RSLs often also have significant borrowings with covenants attached (generally interest cover and gearing covenants). This may create pressures on the entity that, in turn, may motivate management to take action to improve the reported business performance or to misstate the financial statements.

> The auditor should consider whether analytical procedures that are performed at or near the end of the audit when forming an overall conclusion as to whether the financial statements as a whole are consistent with the auditor's knowledge of the

business indicate a previously unrecognised risk of material misstatement due to fraud (para 85).

Determining which particular trends and relationships may indicate risks of material misstatement due to fraud requires professional judgement. Unusual fluctuations in major works expenditures or excessive payments to contractors may indicate fraudulent activity. 44

If the auditor has identified a fraud or has obtained information that indicates that a fraud may exist, the auditor should communicate these matters as soon as practicable to the appropriate level of management (para 93).

The auditor should document communications about fraud made to management, those charged with governance, regulators and others (para 109).

When auditors become aware of, or suspect that there may be, any matter which might warrant inclusion within the register, they document their findings and, subject to any requirement to report them directly to a third party, discuss the matter with senior management or a board member as soon as is practicable. After discussing the matter to ensure that they are aware of the circumstances, auditors consider reporting the matter to the board and the audit committee, ensuring that such discussions and reporting are carried out without delay. Auditors take account of the management structure of the RSL in determining with whom to discuss a matter in the first instance and to whom such a report should be given. In certain circumstances, it may be appropriate not to report or discuss the matter with the management or officers of the RSL but to refer the matter directly to the board. Auditors document communications about fraud made to management or the board. 45

There is currently no requirement for auditors to report suspected instances of fraud to a regulatory body unless they consider it a matter of public interest or, in the case of an unincorporated, non-exempt charity, unless they consider it a matter of material significance for the exercise of the Charity Commission's functions under sections 8 or 18 of the Charities Act 1993[7]. Guidance is given in the APB's Practice Note 11 The Audit of Charities in the United Kingdom (Revised). 46

ISA (UK AND IRELAND) 250: CONSIDERATION OF LAWS AND REGULATIONS IN AN AUDIT OF FINANCIAL STATEMENTS

Background note

The purpose of this ISA (UK and Ireland) is to establish standards and provide guidance on the auditor's responsibility to consider laws and regulations in the audit of financial statements.

---

[7] Further guidance on this matter is set out in the section below on ISA (UK and Ireland) 250 B. Footnote 8 refers to likely changes in legislation relating to charities.

Section A

> In order to plan the audit, the auditor should obtain a general understanding of the legal and regulatory framework applicable to the entity and the industry and how the entity is complying with that framework. (para 15)

47   Laws and regulations which relate directly to the presentation of the financial statements of RSLs are contained in Accounting Orders or Determinations issued under the relevant statutes, and in Circulars and other guidance issued by regulators. The precise nature of those requirements is determined by two factors:

   (a)   whether the RSL is constituted as a registered charity, a society registered under the Industrial and Provident Societies Act 1965 or as a non-profit making company; and
   (b)   which regulatory body has granted registration to the RSL (and the jurisdiction in which that body operates).

   Key requirements of applicable laws and regulations are set out in Appendix 3.

48   However, in general, all RSLs are required to prepare financial statements which give a true and fair view of the state of affairs at the end of the accounting period and the surplus or deficit at the end of that period, and hence are expected to meet the requirements of Financial Reporting Standards and Statements of Standard Accounting Practice issued by the Accounting Standards Board (ASB).

49   The SORP interprets for social landlords how present best accounting practice (as set out in the ASB Standards) applies to them. The development of a SORP in accordance with the ASB's code of practice provides authoritative guidance, at the time of issue, on the application of accounting standards (compliance with which is considered necessary, in all save exceptional cases to meet the requirement to give a true and fair view) in a manner which takes account of the particular circumstances of the sector concerned. Financial Reporting Standard (FRS) 18 'Accounting policies' requires the use of the most appropriate accounting policies and provides that the inclusion of industry practice in a SORP will be persuasive (but not conclusive) evidence that practice represents the most appropriate policy. FRS 18 also requires entities whose financial statements fall within the scope of this SORP to state the title of the SORP and whether its financial statements have been prepared in accordance with those of the SORP's provisions currently in effect. In the event of a departure, the auditors check that the specific requirements of paragraph 58 of FRS 18 have been met.

50   The auditor also checks whether the governing documents of certain charitable RSLs contain any special provisions as to any additional disclosure of information in the financial statements or reporting requirements for auditors. The auditor considers whether transactions undertaken accord with the objects of the charity and are within the powers conferred by the governing document. In order to give a true and fair view, due regard needs to be given to disclosure of any non compliance with the governing document.

> After obtaining the general understanding, the auditor should perform further audit procedures to help identify instances of non-compliance with those laws and regulations where non-compliance should be considered when preparing financial statements, specifically:

on this topic, for auditors of unincorporated charitable RSLs, is given in the APB's Practice Note 11: The Audit of Charities in the United Kingdom (Revised).

Auditors of other RSLs, which are not unincorporated charities, do not have a statutory duty to report suspected or actual instances of non-compliance with the law or regulations to an appropriate authority. ISA (UK and Ireland) 250, however, requires auditors of all entities to consider whether a suspected instance of non-compliance with law and regulations should be reported to the appropriate authority in the public interest[9]. The auditor may need to take legal advice before making a decision on whether a matter should be reported in the public interest.

ISA (UK and Ireland) 250 gives examples of bodies which could constitute the proper and appropriate authorities. In the context of RSLs, the proper authority is ordinarily the relevant regulatory body (the Housing Corporation, the Department for Social Development (Northern Ireland), Communities Scotland and the National Assembly for Wales), and, in any part of the United Kingdom, the Police.

ISA (UK AND IRELAND) 260: COMMUNICATION OF AUDIT MATTERS WITH THOSE CHARGED WITH GOVERNANCE

Background note

The purpose of this ISA (UK and Ireland) is to establish standards and provide guidance on communication of audit matters arising from the audit of financial statements between the auditor and those charged with governance of an entity. These communications relate to audit matters of governance interest as defined in this ISA (UK and Ireland). This ISA (UK and Ireland) does not provide guidance on communications by the auditor to parties outside the entity, for example, external regulatory or supervisory agencies.

The auditor should communicate audit matters of governance interest arising from the audit of financial statements with those charged with governance of an entity. (para 2)

The principal purposes of communication to those charged with governance are for the auditor to:

- ensure that there is a mutual understanding of the scope of the audit and the respective responsibilities of the auditor and those charged with governance;
- share information to assist both auditor and those charged with governance to fulfil their respective responsibilities; and
- provide to those charged with governance observations arising from the audit process.

Relevant matters relating to the audit include: relationships that may bear on the auditors' independence and objectivity; audit planning information; and the findings from the audit, including the auditors' views on the qualitative aspects of the entity's accounting and reporting.

---

[9] For example, a failure to report a significant fraud or misappropriation of grant monies.

> The auditor should determine the relevant persons who are charged with governance and with whom audit matters of governance interest are communicated. (para 5)

63 Because responsibilities in RSLs are delegated by the board to the management team, the auditor considers to whom it would be most appropriate to address reports. Whilst the management team may play a central role in the direction and management of RSLs, its powers are delegated from the board. The auditor therefore usually addresses reports to the board, with a copy to the management team.

> The auditor should communicate audit matters of governance interest on a timely basis. (para 13)

64 The auditor considers the requirement in ISA (UK and Ireland) 260 to communicate the following to those charged with governance at or near the completion of the audit:
- expected modifications to the auditor's report;
- unadjusted misstatements;
- material weaknesses in the accounting and internal control systems;
- views about the qualitative aspects of the RSL's accounting practices and financial reporting;
- matters specifically required by other auditing standards to be communicated to those charged with governance (such as fraud and error); and
- any other relevant matters relating to the audit.

65 All four UK regulators require RSLs to send them copies of auditors' management letters, together with the RSL's response. It is recognised that the management letter addresses only those matters which have come to the attention of the auditors in the course of their audit. This should be filed within six months of the year end.

66 Submitting a management letter does not affect the auditor's responsibilities for giving an opinion on the financial statements or the statutory requirement to make reference within the auditor's report where a satisfactory system of internal control has not been maintained.

> The auditor should plan with those charged with governance the form and timing of communications to them. (para 13-1)

67 ISA (UK and Ireland) 260 stresses that communication should be active two way communication between the auditor and those charged with governance and it notes that this is unlikely to be achieved if communication is only by way of written reports. It encourages dialogue.

ISA (UK AND IRELAND) 300: PLANNING AN AUDIT OF FINANCIAL STATEMENTS

> **Background note**
>
> The purpose of this ISA (UK and Ireland) is to establish standards and provide guidance on the considerations and activities applicable to planning an audit of financial statements. This ISA (UK and Ireland) is framed in the context of recurring audits. In addition, matters the auditor considers in initial audit engagements are included in paragraphs 28 and 29.

> The auditor should plan the audit so that the engagement will be performed in an effective manner. (para 2)

In developing the audit plan, the auditor considers the responsibilities as set out in statute and the letter of engagement to ensure that the scope of the audit plan is sufficient and includes, where appropriate, reports required by statute or by the regulatory bodies. **68**

The auditor obtains an understanding of the accounting principles under which the financial statements are prepared and their impact on the audit. Accounting principles for RSLs include those set out in: **69**

- specific legislation;
- accounting and other recommendations issued by the regulators;
- accounting standards; and
- the SORP.

> The auditor should develop an audit plan for the audit in order to reduce audit risk to an acceptably low level. (para 13)

In designing the audit procedures the auditor seeks, as far as practicable, to make use of the internal controls, work of internal audit and financial reporting arrangements which are in place at the RSL. **70**

It may be appropriate at the planning stage to identify any additional procedures or evidence which may be necessary for the work on other reports, for example on service charges or reports under the Landlord and Tenant Act 1985, to assist in discharging such additional reporting responsibilities. **71**

> The auditor should document the overall audit strategy and the audit plan, including any significant changes made during the audit engagement (para 22).

The auditor may report to, and discuss elements of planning with, the audit committee or board and with management, including the overall strategy and timing of the audit together with any additional requirements which may be agreed. Notwithstanding these discussions, the overall strategy and audit plan remain the auditor's responsibility. **72**

ISA (UK AND IRELAND) 315: OBTAINING AN UNDERSTANDING OF THE ENTITY AND ITS ENVIRONMENT AND ASSESSING THE RISKS OF MATERIAL MISSTATEMENT

Background note

The purpose of this ISA (UK and Ireland) is to establish standards and to provide guidance on obtaining an understanding of the entity and its environment, including its internal control, and on assessing the risks of material misstatement in a financial statement audit.

Understanding the Entity and Its Environment, Including Its Internal control

The auditor should obtain an understanding of relevant industry, regulatory, and other external factors including the applicable financial reporting framework (para 22).

The Constitution of registered social landlords

73 RSLs may be constituted in various ways. It is important that the auditor understands the legal framework within which the RSL operates. Appendix 2 provides information on the different types of legal entities – for example industrial and provident societies, charities and limited companies.

Regulation

74 Auditors understand the regulatory framework applicable to the RSL and consider relevant communications from the regulator, for example in England the Annual Viability Review, the HCA assessment and inspection reports from the Audit Commission.

Financial reporting requirements

75 RSLs are subject to accounting requirements through Determinations or Statutory Instruments and the Companies Act 1985, the Industrial and Provident Societies Acts 1965-2002, the Housing (Scotland) Act 2001 or the Charities Act 1993[10]. The precise application of those requirements is determined by whether the RSL is constituted as a registered charity, a society registered under the Industrial and Provident Societies Act 1965 or as a non-profit making company limited by guarantee under the Companies Act 1985.

76 Details of applicable laws and regulations are set out in Appendix 3. However, in general, all RSLs are required to prepare financial statements which give a true and fair view of the state of affairs at the end of the accounting period and the surplus or deficit at the end of that period, and hence are expected to meet the requirements of Financial Reporting Standards, Statements of Standard Accounting Practice and UITF Abstracts issued or adopted by the ASB.

---

[10] *In addition, from 2006, the Charities Act 2005 in England and Wales and the Charity and Trustee Investment (Scotland) Act 2005 in Scotland.*

77 The SORP 'Accounting by Registered Social Landlords'[11] interprets for social landlords how present best accounting practice (as set out in the ASB Standards) applies to them. While there is no specific legal requirement that RSLs should comply with accounting standards or with the SORP, legislation[12] requires the board of an RSL to state whether its financial statements have been prepared in accordance with applicable accounting standards and statements of recommended practice. In addition, the Accounting Determinations in England and Wales require disclosure to be made of compliance with the SORP where appropriate.

> The auditor should obtain an understanding of the nature of the entity (para 25).

78 The auditor seeks to understand the overall structure, activities, finances and governance of the RSL. Examples of areas the auditor may wish to consider include:

- the structure /changes in structure of the RSL, including its group members and subsidiaries (e.g. charitable or non-charitable);
- the main activities of the RSL and any significant developments since the previous audit, for example new development activity, acquisitions or disposals and organic growth areas;
- the financing and funding structure which supports the RSL's activities and any significant internal or external developments which may impact on the entity;
- the overall governance arrangements which support the systems of internal control including audit committee, risk management and internal audit arrangements;
- the framework for business planning, financial and performance management: and
- significant issues raised by external regulators and the entity's response.

79 RSLs may participate in complex projects, such as schemes developed under the Private Finance Initiative (PFI). Here the RSL may undertake the renovation and management of properties or provide other services, such as residential care, over a defined period without having ownership of the properties. Auditors consider the accounting for such schemes in accordance with Application Note F of FRS 5.

80 Some RSLs are involved in the development of both social housing and housing for outright sale, sometimes as part of the same overall scheme. Under such arrangements, surpluses generated on the sale of properties may be used to subsidise other social housing which may be developed without recourse to social housing grant or with lower levels of grant than would normally be the case. In such circumstances, auditors consider the appropriate carrying value of these social housing properties.

> The auditor should obtain an understanding of the entity's selection and application of accounting policies and consider whether they are appropriate for its business and consistent with the applicable financial reporting framework and accounting policies used in the relevant industry (para 28).

---

[11] Issued originally in 1999, and updated in December 2002 and May 2005 jointly by the National Housing Federation, the Welsh Federation of Housing Associations and the Scottish Federation of Housing Associations (the Three Federations) in accordance with the ASB's code of practice for the development and issue of SORPs.

[12] The 2000 Accounting Determination, the Registered Housing Associations (Accounting Requirements) (Scotland) Order 1999, the Accounting Requirements for RSLs registered in Wales – General Determination 2000 and the Registered Housing Associations (Accounting Requirements) (Northern Ireland) Order 1993.

81 Accounting policies that are especially relevant to RSLs include:
- depreciation;
- capitalisation of building costs; and
- impairment.

82 Under FRS 15 RSLs are required to depreciate their housing properties. As a result judgments need to be made on the useful economic lives of properties which depend on matters such as property type, method of construction and location. In addition, the depreciation to properties carried at a valuation, and the need to depreciate only the value of the buildings (as distinct from the land on which they are situated) results in additional complexity.

83 In respect of capitalisation of building costs, the revised SORP states that works which result in an increase in the net rental income, either as a result of an increase in rental income or a reduction in future maintenance costs or a significant extension of the life of the property are deemed to be improvements and should be capitalised. The SORP also requires disclosure of the total works to properties which have been both expensed and capitalised. In addition, under FRS 15, only costs which are directly attributable to bringing properties into working condition for intended use may be capitalised.

84 FRS 11 requires that impairments resulting from a major reduction in the service potential of a property which might, for example, result from a reduction in demand in the local community, should be recognised in the Income and Expenditure Account. As a result judgments need to be made regarding the likely future service potential of the property.

> The auditor should obtain an understanding of the entity's objectives and strategies, and the related business risks that may result in material misstatement of the financial statements (para 30).

85 Each RSL will have its own objectives and strategies. The Housing Corporation's regulatory requirements have resulted in nearly all RSLs having well established risk management procedures that highlight the more significant risks faced by the RSL. The auditor gains an overview of the main risks identified and considers the implications for the audit.

86 There are also a number of external issues which are likely to influence the ability of the RSL to achieve its objectives and strategies. For example, with the current move towards consolidation within the sector, there is a pronounced focus by the regulator on efficiency and cost control. Many, particularly the larger, RSLs have strong desires to become/stay a Housing Corporation development partner, a key ingredient of which is the continuing demonstration of financial strength. RSLs face a number of pressures on the strength of their financial position. These include rising maintenance costs (resulting from a number of factors including health and safety issues, Government regulations, and deterioration through age of the housing stock), fluctuations in demand for housing in some locations, high salary inflation for some posts (including also rising pension costs) and cuts in Supporting People funding. Consequently, there may be pressures on the RSL to improve the reported business performance, and this could lead to an incentive to misstate the financial statements.

> The auditor should obtain an understanding of the measurement and review of the entity's financial performance (para 35).

In addition to internal performance measures used by individual RSLs, RSLs are 87
subject to considerable external benchmarking and performance review including,
for example, participation in benchmarking clubs, other comparative information
published by the Housing Corporation and various league tables in the housing
press.

> The auditor should obtain an understanding of internal control relevant to the audit (para 41).

The responsibility for the establishment and proper operation of a system of internal 88
control lies with the board of each RSL. It is the board's responsibility to determine
what is appropriate for the RSL.

Relevant factors for the auditor to consider when planning the work that will be 89
performed on internal controls in the audit of a RSL include:

- the statutory requirement to report if the RSL has not maintained a satisfactory system of control[13];
- the expectation (in Wales, the requirement) that the management letter will be passed on to the regulatory body; and
- any additional procedures that have been agreed with the client.

Requirements of auditors in relation to control systems

Legislation requires auditors of RSLs that are Industrial and Provident Societies 90
and/or charities to state in their report on the financial statements if the RSL has
failed to maintain a satisfactory system of internal control. In forming a view as to
whether a system of internal control is satisfactory, the auditor obtains sufficient
appropriate evidence that material weaknesses in control have not existed during the
year. A material weakness is defined as 'a condition which may result in a material
misstatement in the financial statements'.

The legislation does not establish the criteria by which auditors assess whether a 91
system of control is satisfactory; this is a matter for the auditors' judgment. In
forming a judgment, auditors consider:

(a) evidence obtained in relation to compliance with ISAs (UK and Ireland);
(b) their knowledge of the control procedures adopted by the entity;

---

[13] **Requirements for registered social landlords to have control systems**
RSLs that are subject to the requirements of the Friendly and Industrial and Provident Societies Act 1968 s.9(4)(b) or, in Northern Ireland, the Industrial and Provident Societies Act (Northern Ireland) 1969 are required to establish and maintain satisfactory systems of control of their books of account, their cash holdings and all their receipts and remittances. Auditors of such RSLs are required, under the same legislation, to carry out such investigations as will enable them to form an opinion as to whether the RSL has maintained a satisfactory system of control over its transactions and, if they are of the opinion that the RSL has failed in any respect to comply with this requirement, to state that fact in their report. In England and Wales the Housing Act 1996 Schedule 1 Part III s.18 (1) extends these requirements to RSLs which are not Industrial and Provident Societies but are registered charities. Similar provisions apply to registered charities in Northern Ireland and Scotland.

(c) the board's latest published corporate governance statement as required by Housing Corporation Circular 25/01 'Internal controls assurance'[14], together with the annual report of the chief executive (or executive team) to the board concerning the effectiveness of the systems of internal control. Circular 25/01 requires an RSL owning or managing more than 250 units to disclose in its published statement 'information on the process that the board has adopted in addressing material internal control aspects of any significant problems disclosed in the annual report and accounts'. In addition the Circular says that 'Reference to regulatory concerns should also be considered, where these have led [the Corporation] to intervene in the affairs of the association'; and

(d) their knowledge of 'reportable weaknesses'. A reportable weakness is defined in the SFHA's publication – Raising Standards as ' a weakness that has resulted in material loss, contingencies or uncertainties which require disclosure in the audited accounts'.

92 The regulatory bodies in each of the UK jurisdictions have issued codes of audit practice or good practice notes relating to external audit. The codes, good practice notes, circulars and other relevant documents provide guidance to boards on, and define their responsibilities for, amongst other things, the appointment of auditors and the nature of the RSL's working relationship with the auditors.

93 In November 2001 the Housing Corporation issued Circular 25/01 'Internal controls assurance', which replaced Circular 18/96 in England. Circular 25/01 does not require external auditors to report on the board's published statement which will cover the complete internal control system rather than merely financial controls. The board is free to request their auditor to conduct further work on the statement on internal control if they wish to do so.

> The auditor should obtain an understanding of the control environment (para 67).

Control environment

94 The role, attitude and actions of the board members are fundamental in shaping the control environment of a RSL. Factors to consider include:

- the amount of time committed by board members;
- the skills and qualifications of individual board members;
- the frequency and regularity of board meetings;
- the form and content of board meetings; and
- the degree of involvement in, or supervision of, the RSL's transactions on the part of individual board members.

95 Other features of the control environment depend on the size, activity and organisation of the RSL but might include:

- segregation of duties, for example, other than in very small RSLs, it is usual for housing management activities to be separated from the finance department;
- a recognised plan of the structure showing clearly the areas of responsibility and lines and levels of authority and accountability;

---

[14] *In Scotland, the requirement is established by Guidance Note 97/02-Code of Audit Practice for Registered Housing Associations. Information on the practical application of this Guidance Note is contained in chapter 10 of the SFHA's publication – Raising Standards. In Wales the requirement is established by Circular 8/97 and in Northern Ireland by Housing Association Guide Part 1-Appendix 12 Annex D-E as revised in 2005.*

- the existence of a medium term plan setting out financial projections;
- evidence of a commitment to comply with the obligations agreed with the regulator in the RSL's Regulatory Plan;
- the role of any internal audit function;
- the competence, training and qualification of staff appropriate to the tasks they have to perform;
- involvement of the board in the recruitment, appointment and supervision of senior executives;
- access of board members to independent professional advice where necessary;
- budgetary controls in the form of estimates of income and expenditure for each financial year and comparison of actual results with the estimates on a regular basis; and
- communication of the results of such reviews to the board on a regular basis so as to facilitate their review of performance and to enable them to initiate action where necessary.

The auditor should obtain an understanding of the entity's process for identifying business risks relevant to financial reporting objectives and deciding about actions to address those risks, and the results thereof (para 76).

Since 2000, the Housing Corporation has issued guidance and a series of topic papers encouraging best practice on key elements for a risk management framework covering:

- identifying risk;
- linking risk assessment to business planning;
- review of business activities;
- ongoing risk identification and monitoring;
- managing risk;
- governance – the role of the Board, executive management, operational management and internal audit.

The auditor understands the entity's approach to risk management and assesses the effectiveness of the risk management process, including how management identifies risks relevant to the preparation of financial statements, estimates their significance, assesses the likelihood of their occurrence, and decides upon actions to manage them.

The auditor should obtain a sufficient understanding of control activities to assess the risks of material misstatement at the assertion level and to design further audit procedures responsive to assessed risks (para 90).

Control activities

The following paragraphs list some of the control activities which are of particular significance to RSLs. The list is not intended to be exhaustive as there may be other control procedures that are relevant to the activities of a particular RSL. Control procedures that are of general application, such as segregation of duties or physical security of tangible assets, are not included in the examples given below.

Rents:

- periodic checking (by an official other than a rent collector) of notifications of voids, of changes in rent and the housing stock to the rent ledger and to tenants' rent books or equivalent;

- reconciliation of rents receivable to the number of units, rents and the incidence of voids;
- review of housing benefits under/over payments;
- controls to ensure that all housing accommodation is recorded and that all changes are reflected in the records;
- arrears procedures performed by a person who is not responsible for collecting or handling rent moneys including aged analysis of rents outstanding; and
- regular comparisons between the rent ledger and the banking records.

99 Service charges:

- reconciliation of service charges receivable with the number of units, the service charges and the incidence of voids;
- arrears procedures performed by a person who is not responsible for collecting or handling service charge monies.

100 Property development:

- project appraisal process;
- proper tendering procedures;
- list of approved suppliers;
- involvement of the board in the appointment of significant contractors, external advisers and consultants;
- ensuring approval of grant funding prior to accepting tender;
- liaison with appropriate planning and authorising bodies and, where appropriate, the regulatory body;
- authorisation procedures, involving the board, before material purchases of properties are made; and
- inspection and approval procedures before payment.

101 Fixed assets and depreciation:

- a register of fixed assets;
- a register of property title deeds;
- depreciation calculated and recorded as the accounting policy requires;
- authorisation procedures, involving the board, for material disposals; and
- procedures to ensure that, where appropriate, the consent of the regulatory body has been obtained for disposals and that proceeds have been received and accounted for properly.

102 Grants and loans:

- regular checks that all sources of income or funds are fully utilised and appropriate claims made;
- periodic review to ensure loan covenants are met;
- procedures to ensure that income or funds are applied correctly in accordance with the terms of the grant or loan;
- development of an approved treasury and borrowing policy;
- register of properties to show location of title deed and security; and
- comprehensive records of applications made and follow-up procedures.

103 Repairs:

- procedures for obtaining tenders or quotations, particularly in respect of major repair work;
- inspection and approval procedures before payment to ensure adequate segregation of duties between responsible officials in the RSL; and
- comparison of repair costs against budgets.

Cash:

- controls over cash held on behalf of residents, for example in supported housing.

Treasury operations:

- controls over the authorisation of capital instruments;
- budgeting and monitoring of cash flow projections; and
- procedures to ensure investment risks on surplus funds are minimised.

Governance:

- recognition and application of good governance structures;
- consideration of risks and risk management;
- process for implementation and review of systems of internal control; and
- appropriate relationships with key stakeholders.

> The auditor should obtain an understanding of how the entity has responded to risks arising from IT (para 93).

Auditors consider whether adequate IT controls exist over both financial systems and other systems relevant to the audit including in particular housing management systems which record rents charged and collected and housing properties.

Assessing the Risks of Material Misstatement

> The auditor should identify and assess the risks of material misstatement at the financial statement level, and at the assertion level for classes of transactions, account balances, and disclosures (para 100).

Relevant risks may include:

- non-compliance with financial covenants;
- changes in government policy, for example, the level of government grants or the rules governing the payment of housing benefit;
- the large number of and changing sources of revenue funding which have different and often restricted application;
- deteriorating condition of housing stock combined with regulatory requirement to meet the decent homes standard;
- limited financial, personnel and other resources in a growing sector;
- the increased use of treasury management activities, for example derivatives;
- restrictions on certain funds which require special considerations as to use and accounting, for example the Disposal Proceeds Fund;
- the complexity of tax rules (corporation tax and VAT);
- the need to determine appropriate splits between land and buildings for the purposes of depreciation, particularly where properties were acquired rather than built or when carried at a valuation;
- the need to maintain adequate resources and the ability to raise finance for future expenditure on repairs and developments;
- instances of non compliance with regulations due to their complexity and extent; and
- falling property values due to increasing voids and 'hard to let' properties.

> As part of the risk assessment, the auditor should determine which of the risks identified are, in the auditor's judgment, risks that require special audit consideration (such risks are defined as 'significant risks') (para 108).
>
> For significant risks, to the extent the auditor has not already done so, the auditor should evaluate the design of the entity's related controls, including relevant control activities, and determine whether they have been implemented. (para 113)

108 Significant risks may include, for example:

- incorrect capitalisation of major works on properties;
- incorrect accounting for significant property development work; and
- complex transactions such as PFI, mixed developments and joint ventures.

Examples of substantive procedures to address these risks are described in the section on ISA (UK and Ireland) 330.

Reporting on internal controls

Scotland, Wales and Northern Ireland

109 As noted earlier, Communities Scotland has issued Guidance Note 97/02[15] which contains the same requirements as Circular 18/96 'Internal financial control and financial reporting'. In Northern Ireland HAC 10/96, and in Wales Circular 8/97 provide similar guidance.

Guidance Note 97/02 requires RSLs with more than 150 units to include, within their annual reports, a statement about the RSL's system of internal financial control and for auditors to review the statement in order to enable them to conclude that:

(a) the board has provided the disclosure required by the guidance; and
(b) the board's comments are not inconsistent with the information of which they are aware from their audit of the financial statements.

110 In reporting on internal financial controls and other corporate governance disclosures, auditors follow the guidance set out in Bulletin 2004/3. Reports by auditors are addressed to the RSL and therefore are not normally included in the auditors' report on the financial statements. Auditors' letters of engagement normally include a reference to any review of the board's statements associated with corporate governance.

ISA (UK AND IRELAND) 320: AUDIT MATERIALITY

> **Background note**
>
> The purpose of this ISA (UK and Ireland) is to establish standards and provide guidance on the concept of materiality and its relationship with audit risk.
>
> Materiality should be considered by the auditor when:
>
> (a) Determining the nature, timing and extent of audit procedures; and
> (b) Evaluating the effect of misstatements. (para 8)

---

[15] *This guidance is now included in chapter 10 of the SFHA's publication – Raising Standards.*

ISA 320 makes a distinction between the auditor's consideration of materiality in planning the audit, and that in evaluating the results of audit procedures. The assessment of materiality at the planning stage influences the nature, timing and extent of audit tests. The materiality of matters found in the course of audit work is considered both in relation to their possible impact on the financial statements, and in relation to applicable regulations and other factors governing the conduct of individual RSLs. In the case of RSLs particular disclosures or expenditure categories may be sensitive and warrant extra attention, for example the Chief Executive's remuneration, restricted funds and bad debt provision. In view of RSLs' social objectives and the requirement not to distribute surplus, it will not normally be appropriate to base materiality on the surplus made by the RSL during the accounting period. More relevant bases for planning materiality are likely to be gross revenues or net assets. 111

The auditor considers materiality in assessing whether the accounts give a true and fair view from the point of view of the addressees of the report. The principles underlying this consideration of materiality are no different from those involved in the audit of other entities and are explained in ISA 320. 112

ISA (UK AND IRELAND) 330: THE AUDITOR'S PROCEDURES IN RESPONSE TO ASSESSED RISKS

Background note

The purpose of this ISA (UK and Ireland) is to establish standards and provide guidance on determining overall responses and designing and performing further audit procedures to respond to the assessed risks of material misstatement at the financial statement and assertion levels in a financial statement audit.

When the auditor has determined that it is not possible to reduce the risks of material misstatement at the assertion level to an acceptably low level with audit evidence obtained only from substantive procedures, the auditor should perform tests of relevant controls to obtain audit evidence about their operating effectiveness (para 25)

A significant proportion of RSLs' activities involve a large number of small transactions such as rental income. Auditors seek evidence to determine the completeness and accuracy of rental income. Where auditors are satisfied, through evaluation and testing, that there are appropriate and effective controls including, for example, the effective reconciliation of housing management and finance systems, they can use the results of this internal control testing as a source of audit evidence about the completeness and accuracy of recorded transactions. 113

When the auditor has determined that an assessed risk of material misstatement at the assertion level is a significant risk, the auditor should perform substantive procedures that are specifically responsive to that risk (para 51).

Possible significant risks in the context of RSLs are listed in the section on ISA (UK and Ireland) 315. In respect of a significant risk arising from capitalisation, the auditor considers whether the RSL's policy, for example on the types of works to be capitalised, as well as the approach to the capitalisation of internal development 114 costs and interest, is in compliance with FRS 15 and the detailed interpretation set out in the SORP. The auditor will then carry out detailed checks to ensure compliance with the policy.

115 For RSLs undertaking significant property development work, this presents particular audit risks, such as:

- incorrect allocation of costs to schemes
- cost overruns due to poor budgeting or unauthorised expenditure leading to costs in excess of the original project appraisal; here the auditor considers risk of impairment to the carrying value
- fraud risks arising from purchasing frauds, such as payment for services not supplied, or collusion.

Although controls are likely to exist over the authorisation and allocation of costs, if there is material expenditure on property development auditors perform substantive procedures such as the examination of invoices and post project appraisal reports.

116 Risks relating to complex transactions are also likely to be assessed as significant due to:

- lack of experience of RSL staff in carrying out such non core activities
- the complexity of the transactions eg: legal structures, tax, accounting and funding arrangements
- involvement of, and reliance on, third parties
- viability arising from cost over runs
- issues relating to the vires of the RSL.

The auditor reviews such arrangements and considers whether they are accounted for appropriately. In addition, if the auditor identifies that management is under pressure to decrease costs reported, such as in order to meet an interest cover covenant, the risk of management over capitalising maintenance and repairs expenditure may be assessed as significant. The auditor reviews the capitalisation policy for compliance with FRS 15 and the SORP and reviews the items capitalised to ensure compliance with the agreed policy.

ISA (UK AND IRELAND) 402: AUDIT CONSIDERATIONS RELATING TO ENTITIES USING SERVICE ORGANISATIONS

Background note

The purpose of this ISA (UK and Ireland) is to establish standards and provide guidance to an auditor where the entity uses a service organisation

In obtaining an understanding of the entity and its environment, the auditor should determine the significance of service organization activities to the entity and the relevance to the audit. (para 5)

117 The auditor identifies whether the reporting RSL uses service organisations and assesses the effect of any such use on the procedures necessary to obtain sufficient and appropriate audit evidence to determine with reasonable assurance whether the financial statements are free of material misstatement.

118 Use of a service organisation does not diminish the ultimate responsibility of the board or the audit committee for conducting its business in a manner which meets

their legal responsibilities, including those of safeguarding the assets, maintaining proper accounting records and preparing financial statements.

Similarly, an entity's use of a service organisation does not alter the auditor's responsibilities when reporting on its financial statements, but may have a significant effect on the nature of procedures undertaken to obtain sufficient appropriate audit evidence to determine whether a user entity's financial statements are free from material misstatement. 119

Service organisations undertake a wide range of activities within the RSL sector. Many of these are capable of having a significant effect on the financial statements. Consequently the auditor of an RSL needs to consider the nature and extent of activity undertaken by service organisations to determine whether those activities are relevant to the audit, and what their effect is on audit risk. 120

Examples of potential activities undertaken by service organisations may include: 121
- maintenance of the RSL accounting records;
- processing of the payroll;
- management of assets, including outsourcing of repairs, maintenance and development work;
- management of agency schemes.

> Based on the auditor's understanding of the aspects of the entity's accounting system and control environment relating to relevant activities, the auditor should:
>
> (a) Assess whether sufficient appropriate audit evidence concerning the relevant financial statement assertions is available from records held at the entity; and if not,
> (b) Determine effective procedures to obtain evidence necessary for the audit, either by direct access to records kept by service organisations or through information obtained from the service organisations or their auditor. (9-18)

Some outsourced activities are the subject of regulation, notably investment management. However, regulation does not by itself eliminate the need for RSL auditors to obtain independent evidence because controls required by regulators, and inspection work undertaken by them in service organisations, may not be relevant to or sufficiently focussed on aspects of importance to the RSL organisations. Furthermore, reports from the service organisation's auditors required by its regulator are not ordinarily available to a RSL or its auditors. 122

ISA (UK AND IRELAND) 500: AUDIT EVIDENCE

> **Background note**
>
> The purpose of this ISA (UK and Ireland) is to establish standards and provide guidance on what constitutes audit evidence in an audit of financial statements, the quantity and quality of audit evidence to be obtained, and the audit procedures that auditors use for obtaining that audit evidence.

> When information produced by the entity is used by the auditor to perform audit procedures, the auditor should obtain audit evidence about the accuracy and completeness of the information (para 11).

123 The audit of RSLs often involves reliance on non-financial systems, and testing controls over such systems may therefore be appropriate. For example, in auditing bad debt provisions, the auditor considers the accuracy of the ageing of rental debtors derived from the housing management system. In some situations the auditor may determine that additional audit procedures are needed, for example, using computer-assisted audit techniques (CAATs) to recalculate the information.

Inspection of Housing Properties

124 Given the large number of housing properties owned and managed by RSLs, physical inspection alone is unlikely to be an appropriate means of testing existence, and the auditor considers obtaining confirmation of title from the Land Registry. Such tests do not however establish that the valuation of properties is appropriate.

ISA (UK AND IRELAND) 505: EXTERNAL CONFIRMATIONS

Background note

The purpose of this ISA (UK and Ireland) is to establish standards and provide guidance on the auditor's use of external confirmations as a means of obtaining audit evidence.

The auditor should determine whether the use of external confirmations is necessary to obtain sufficient appropriate audit evidence at the assertion level. In making this determination, the auditor should consider the assessed risk of material misstatement at the assertion level and how the audit evidence from other planned audit procedures will reduce the risk of material misstatement at the assertion level to an acceptably low level (para 2).

125 Situations in which external confirmations may be used by RSL auditors normally include:
   - Bank balances and other information from bankers;
   - Loan balances and terms and conditions; and
   - Ownership of properties.

Other situations where confirmations may be obtained by auditors include:
   - Balances with local authorities, agencies and other partners; and
   - Land Registry details confirmed by lawyers.

Confirmations are unlikely to be appropriate as a means of checking balances with tenants and leaseholders given the volume and size of individual balances.

ISA (UK AND IRELAND) 520: ANALYTICAL PROCEDURES

Background note

The purpose of this ISA (UK and Ireland) is to establish standards and provide guidance on the application of analytical procedures during an audit.

> The auditor should apply analytical procedures as risk assessment procedures to obtain an understanding of the entity and its environment and in the overall review at the end of the audit. (para 2)

RSLs are required to submit returns to their regulator and many publish a comprehensive range of information and data which may assist auditors by providing an indication of trends and current ratios. In addition, there is typically financial information produced internally by RSLs, for management information and for use in compiling regulatory returns and published information, which may provide a valuable source of evidence. The auditor ascertains the most appropriate data for comparison and the most useful sources of such data (for example, in England the Housing Corporation's website benchmarking statistics and the Annual Viability Returns), depending on the tests and comparisons which are to be carried out and the nature of the client.

Parts of the income and expenditure of RSLs, and in particular interest payable and rental income, are predictable. Consequently, certain analytical procedures are capable of being used as substantive analytical procedures. This facilitates comparison with budgets, comparison with other developments within the sector, and proofs in total. The majority of RSLs produce cash flow projections and annual budgets and may also produce some or all of the following which the auditor may utilise in the course of the audit:

- business plan projections;
- expenditure profiles for development programmes;
- statistical data concerning the administration and operation of RSLs;
- quarterly financial returns;
- performance indicators; and
- publicly available databases.

In the context of capital, major and routine repairs and maintenance expenditure, the auditor may wish to consider:

- movements and unexpected or unusual relationships between current and prior year capital programmes, allocations, budgeted amounts and cash planning targets for acquisitions and disposals;
- comparison of the level of development department activity and professional fees with recorded additions to housing properties;
- major repairs grants and repairs costs in comparison to budget and previous years' costs;
- the ratio of repairs and maintenance to the cost of housing land and buildings;
- comparison against prior year and expected amounts for construction costs per property;
- comparison of actual expenditure against costs in stock condition surveys;
- for special needs housing, comparison of the ratio of care staff to the number of bed spaces;
- review of amount of grant as a percentage of development cost;
- movements on any suspense or construction in progress accounts;
- comparison of interest and overheads capitalised with prior years; and
- comparison with external benchmark indicators.

In terms of rental income, the auditor may wish to consider:

- the relationship between the number of housing units available for occupation, the incidence of empty units and rents receivable;

- movements, and any unexpected or unusual relationships, between current and prior year budgets for rents received or service charges;
- movements, and unexpected or unusual relationships, between current year, prior year and budget for voids and bad debts as a percentage of rents; and
- rents and service charges for each month.

128 Much of the other income and administrative expenditure relates to the day to day operations of RSLs (as opposed to being part of programmed expenditure) and may have the following features:

- amounts are usually related to comparable information for prior periods;
- amounts are usually directly comparable to other RSLs of similar size and nature; and
- some amounts are closely related to non-financial information such as the number of units, the number of employees and the size of office buildings.

ISA (UK AND IRELAND) 540: AUDIT OF ACCOUNTING ESTIMATES

Background note

The purpose of this ISA (UK and Ireland) is to establish standards and provide guidance on the audit of accounting estimates contained within the financial statements.

The auditor should design and perform further audit procedures to obtain sufficient appropriate audit evidence as to whether the entity's accounting estimates are reasonable in the circumstances and, when required, appropriately disclosed. (para 8)

129 In common with most reporting entities, RSLs need to make a number of accounting estimates whilst preparing their financial statements. The main areas where estimates are likely to be required concern:

(a) depreciation of housing properties, and especially the estimated useful economic life;
(b) the level of bad and doubtful debt provisions against tenant arrears;
(c) impairment provisions, including situations where existing use valuations are below net cost but the RSL assesses the net realisable value of the property, after deducting any grants that would need to be repaid or recycled, to be higher than net cost. Further judgments may be required in order to determine whether an alternative measure of service potential may be more appropriate where assets are held for social purposes.

The auditor should adopt one or a combination of the following approaches in the audit of an accounting estimate:

(a) Review and test the process used by management to develop the estimate;
(b) Use an independent estimate for comparison with that prepared by management; or
(c) Review of subsequent events which provide audit evidence of the reasonableness of the estimate made. (para 10)

> The auditor should make a final assessment of the reasonableness of the entity's accounting estimates based on the auditor's understanding of the entity and its environment and whether the estimates are consistent with other audit evidence obtained during the audit. (para 24)

Depreciation

130 Depreciation charges are difficult to assess because of the length of the useful economic life of the property. Taking into account any special factors affecting the particular RSL, such as type, location and method of construction, the auditor compares the estimated useful economic lives adopted by the RSL with those prevalent in the sector. If the RSL is out of line, the auditor considers whether the reasons for the variance are plausible.

Bad and doubtful debt provisions

131 When evaluating whether adequate provision has been made for bad and doubtful debts, an effective approach is likely to involve consideration of applicable ratios and trends together with an evaluation of the effectiveness of the housing management system. Analytical procedures are likely to be an effective technique because of the large volume of relatively small amounts due to an RSL. Furthermore, complexities arising from housing benefit payments from local authorities may mean that an approach based on consideration of individual debtors is time consuming. When reliance is placed on analytical procedures the auditor considers whether past ratios and trends continue to be applicable in current economic circumstances.

132 The legal position of the RSL is often such that enforcement procedures in relation to the debt are more expensive to carry out than the amounts involved, are uncertain given the attitudes of the courts, and even if successful may only lead to payment over a prolonged period. In some cases, non-payment of a disputed balance may not be the cause, but external factors such as arrears stemming from delays in processing genuine housing benefit claims. In other cases the arrears may stem from rejected or invalid housing benefit claims.

Valuation

133 Existing use value-social housing (EUV-SH) and other bases of valuation usually involve an element of judgment. In both cases, the RSL may choose to use the services of an external specialist, such as a qualified surveyor, to arrive at the estimate. Where they do not, the auditor assesses whether the estimates have nevertheless been arrived at in a reasonable manner under the circumstances.

ISA (UK AND IRELAND) 545: AUDITING FAIR VALUE MEASUREMENTS AND DISCLOSURES

> **Background note**
>
> The purpose of this ISA (UK and Ireland) is to establish standards and provide guidance on auditing fair value measurements and disclosures contained in financial statements.

> The auditor should obtain sufficient appropriate audit evidence that fair value measurements and disclosures are in accordance with the entity's applicable financial reporting framework. (para 3)

134 In RSLs, fair value measurements and disclosures are most likely to apply to those RSLs who hold fixed assets at valuation. Valuers are reliant on information provided to them by the RSL in order to perform the valuation, and this matter is discussed further in the section on ISA (UK and Ireland) 620 below.

135 Under acquisition accounting, the identifiable assets and liabilities of the RSL acquired should be included in the acquirer's balance sheet at their fair value at the date of acquisition. The auditor ensures that the valuation method and amount adopted is appropriately supported and properly reflected in the financial statements.

136 In principle the fair value of housing properties is the Existing Use Value Social Housing (EUV-SH) of these properties. The fair value of other assets and liabilities can be assessed in accordance with the requirements of FRS 7. The auditor considers whether the information provided is consistent with the financial records subject to audit.

> As part of the understanding of the entity and its environment, including its internal control, the auditor should obtain an understanding of the entity's process for determining fair value measurements and disclosures and of the relevant control activities sufficient to identify and assess the risks of material misstatement at the assertion level and to design and perform further audit procedures. (para 10)

137 Fair values for all assets and liabilities of an acquired entity should be determined in accordance with FRS 7. Generally, RSLs obtain a valuation based on EUV-SH from a specialist valuer. RSLs should assess the recoverability of arrears in the acquired entity, taking into consideration their own provisions policy. Fixed rate loans should be revalued in the light of interest rates at the time of acquisition.

> The auditor should evaluate whether the fair value measurements and disclosures in the financial statements are in accordance with the entity's applicable financial reporting framework. (para 17)

138 For RSLs the fair value measurements and disclosures in the financial statements should be in accordance with the SORP and the General Determination 2000[16].

ISA (UK AND IRELAND) 550: RELATED PARTIES

Background note

> The purpose of this ISA (UK and Ireland) is to establish standards and provide guidance on the auditor's responsibilities and audit procedures regarding related parties and transactions with such paries regardless of whether International

---

[16] As at the date of publication of this Practice Note, the General Determination is in the process of being revised.

> Accounting Standard (IAS) 24, 'Related Party Disclosures,' or similar requirement, is part of the applicable financial reporting framework.

ISA (UK and Ireland) 550 is split according to whether IAS 24 or FRS 8 applies.   139

> The auditor should perform audit procedures designed to obtain sufficient appropriate audit evidence regarding the identification and disclosure by management [17] of related parties and the effect of related party transactions that are material to the financial statements. (para 102)

The principles and procedures set out in ISA (UK and Ireland) 550 apply to the audit of RSLs as for other entities. In addition, those RSLs that are companies need to comply with relevant sections of the Companies Acts.   140

Subject to certain exemptions, members of the board and those associated with them, and those associated with senior managers, are not allowed to benefit financially from their connection with the RSL.[18] If there is any evidence of the existence of such related party transactions, then both ISA (UK and Ireland) 550 and ISA (UK and Ireland) 250 Consideration of law and regulations applies.   141

> Where there is any indication that such circumstances exist, the auditor should perform modified, extended or additional audit procedures as are appropriate in the circumstances. (para 103)

In England, auditors may take account of the results of any examination of related party transactions undertaken by the Housing Corporation's review teams. However, such examinations do not remove the requirement for auditors to obtain sufficient and appropriate audit evidence that material, identified related party transactions are properly recorded and disclosed.   142

> When planning the audit the auditor should assess the risk that material undisclosed related party transactions, or undisclosed outstanding balances between an entity and its related parties may exist. (para 106-3)

The auditor considers in particular whether appropriate disclosure, as required by Financial Reporting Standard (FRS) 8 – Related Party Disclosures, is made in the financial statements of transactions between the RSL and board members.   143

The provisions of FRS 8 in the context of related parties and RSL management, are applied to all members of 'key management' not just members of the board. Key management may be taken to include those persons having authority and responsibility for planning, directing and controlling the activities of the RSL, directly or indirectly, including any director (whether executive or otherwise) or officer of that RSL.   144

---

[17] In the UK those charged with governance are responsible for the preparation of the financial statements.

[18] Tenant representatives are an exception to this, because they enjoy below-market rents. However they should not obtain any benefits which are not available to other tenants.

ISA (UK AND IRELAND) 560: SUBSEQUENT EVENTS

> **Background note**
>
> The purpose of this ISA (UK and Ireland) is to establish standards and provide guidance on the auditor's responsibility regarding subsequent events.

> The auditor should perform audit procedures designed to obtain sufficient appropriate audit evidence that all events up to the date of the auditor's report that may require adjustment of, or disclosure in, the financial statements have been identified (para 4)

145 In most RSLs, the non-executive board plays a crucial role in approving the financial statements. This often takes place a number of weeks after the on-site audit work has been completed, and may in some cases (such as when an Audit Committee meeting occurs in between) be a significant time after the formal audit clearance meeting has taken place.

146 In addition to normal procedures, the auditor ensures that any information relating to the current period provided to the board meeting at which the financial statements for the previous year are due to be approved does not provide indications of any subsequent events which might require disclosure in or adjustment of the financial statements. If any indications exist, then the auditor clarifies the position, and considers whether adjustments or amendments need to be made. Examples of potential adjustments or disclosures include difficulties with the recoverability of material debtors.

ISA (UK AND IRELAND) 570: GOING CONCERN

> **Background note**
>
> The purpose of this ISA (UK and Ireland) is to establish standards and provide guidance on the auditor's responsibility on the audit of financial statements with respect to the going concern assumption used in the preparation of the financial statements, including management's assessment of the entity's ability to continue as a going concern.

> When planning and performing audit procedures and in evaluating the results thereof, the auditor should consider the appropriateness of management's[19] use of the going concern assumption in the preparation of the financial statements. (para 2)

> The auditor should consider any relevant disclosures in the financial statements. (para 2-1)

---

[19] *In the UK those charged with governance are responsible for the preparation of the financial statements and the assessment of the entity's ability to continue as a going concern.*

Financial statements of RSLs are normally prepared on a going concern basis. For example, in England, the 2000 Accounting Determination requires disclosure where accounts are prepared other than on a going concern basis. 147

To obtain registration, a social landlord must be able to demonstrate that it is operating, or will operate, on a sound and proper financial basis and must be able to demonstrate that its capital commitments can be financed fully (whether by way of loans or from other resources) and that its income will be sufficient to meet its outgoings and to ensure its future financial stability. 148

> In obtaining an understanding of the entity, the auditor should consider whether there are events or conditions and related business risks which may cast significant doubt on the entity's ability to continue as a going concern. (para 11)
>
> The auditor should remain alert for audit evidence of events or conditions and related business risks which may cast significant doubt on the entity's ability to continue as a going concern in performing audit procedures throughout the audit. If such events or conditions are identified, the auditor should consider whether they affect the auditor's assessment of the risks of material misstatement. (para 12)

To apply ISA (UK and Ireland) 570 to RSLs, auditors consider the circumstances in which RSLs may cease to continue in operational existence. 149

Growing RSLs may be a particular risk because of the necessity to finance developments which may have short term negative cash flows. This issue requires an understanding of: 150

- commitments and future development intentions;
- the availability of finance through loan facilities etc;
- the amount of available security to underpin a necessary loan facility;
- the ability to repay the loans, which normally means consideration of a long term financial plan; and
- covenant compliance.

Some of the particular factors which may indicate a potential going concern problem at an RSL are: 151

- transfers of the entire housing stock, or a significant proportion of it;
- potential action from the regulatory body;
- for a transferee RSL, transfers of housing stock where the acquisition cost or carrying value is not covered by the long-term projected net rental income;
- onerous contract terms; this may be particularly relevant where the RSL has entered into Public Finance Initiative or Public Private Partnership contracts which may transfer significant risk to the RSL;
- inability to service interest payments;
- contracts under 'supporting people', joint ventures or outsourcing agreements becoming unsustainable;
- a significant amount of variable interest rate borrowings at a time when interest rates are rising or are predicted to rise;
- a significant short-term repair liability that the RSL will have difficulty in meeting from its own resources;
- a fundamental change in the level of demand for the RSL's properties leading to significant void rates and a substantial fall in income;

- loan repayments or refinancing which cannot be met from the RSL's own resources;
- likely changes in long term revenues as a result of the need to reduce rents in line with government targets as part of rent restructuring;
- breaches of loan covenants; and
- significant loans to subsidiaries involved in activities such as shared ownership or developments for sale in a housing market where sales prices are falling.

> The auditor should evaluate management's assessment of the entity's ability to continue as a going concern.
>
> The auditor should assess the adequacy of the means by which those charged with governance have satisfied themselves that:
>
> (a) It is appropriate for them to adopt the going concern basis in preparing the financial statements; and
> (b) The financial statements include such disclosures, if any, relating to going concern as are necessary for them to give a true and fair view.
>
> For this purpose:
>
> (i) The auditor should make enquiries of those charged with governance and examine appropriate available financial information; and
> (ii) Having regard to the future period to which those charged with governance have paid particular attention in assessing going concern (see paragraphs 18 and 18-1 in the ISA), the auditor should plan and perform procedures specifically designed to identify any material matters which could indicate concern about the entity's ability to continue as a going concern. (para 17-1)

152 In assessing going concern, the board considers the extent to which there may be adverse variations from anticipated funding or revenue, or additional unexpected costs, and any uncertainties as to whether or not the RSL can continue in operational existence for the foreseeable future.

153 Typically, RSLs acquire properties with the assistance of grants or long term borrowings. This method of financing leads to predictable cash flows in that loan repayments can be predicted and, accordingly, the RSL should be able to plan to meet its obligations from available resources. RSLs have a relatively long business cycle and, in preparing its medium term financial forecasts, the board may consider a longer period of time than for entities with a shorter business cycle.

154 If there are any indications that a particular source of funds or revenue may need to be renewed or renegotiated, the auditor may elect to request the RSL to contact the source of such funds for confirmation that the facility, or grant, will continue to be made available to the RSL. Where there continues to be uncertainty, it may be necessary for the board to disclose the circumstances in the financial statements and for the auditors to draw attention to the matter within their report.

ISA (UK AND IRELAND) 580: MANAGEMENT REPRESENTATIONS

Background note

The purpose of this ISA (UK and Ireland) is to establish standards and provide guidance on the use of management representations as audit evidence, the

RSLs day to day management may be delegated to a chief executive and other senior managers. Where representations are taken from such senior staff the auditor will ensure such staff have the necessary authority and that such representations are considered and approved by the directors. In larger RSLs approval may come from a finance or audit committee properly authorised by the directors and including director members with a reporting line back to the main board.

158 Communication with the directors on significant issues on which representations are required remains of particular relevance in a sector which relies primarily on voluntary directors who are not involved in the day-to-day running of the business.

ISA (UK AND IRELAND) 610: CONSIDERING THE WORK OF INTERNAL AUDIT

> **Background note**
>
> The purpose of this ISA (UK and Ireland) is to establish standards and provide guidance to external auditors in considering the work of internal auditing. This ISA (UK and Ireland) does not deal with instances when personnel from internal auditing assist the external auditor in carrying out external audit procedures. The audit procedures noted in this ISA (UK and Ireland) need only be applied to internal auditing activities which are relevant to the audit of the financial statements.

> The external auditor should consider the activities of internal auditing and their effect, if any, on external audit procedures. (para 2)
>
> The external auditor should obtain a sufficient understanding of internal audit activities to identify and assess the risks of material misstatement of the financial statements and to design and perform further audit procedures (para 9).
>
> The external auditor should perform an assessment of the internal audit function when internal auditing is relevant to the external auditor's risk assessment (para 11).

159 It is common practice for larger RSLs to establish an internal audit function. Where this is the case it is for the board of each RSL to determine what is an appropriate internal audit function, taking account of the size of the RSL and the diversity, complexity and pace of change of its activities. In England the Housing Corporation's Circular 25/01 leaves the decision to have an internal audit function completely to the RSL, but does note that many RSLs will find it difficult, if not impossible, to meet the requirements on internal controls assurance without an internal audit function. The Housing Corporation therefore recommends that RSLs owning and/or managing more than 250 units consider annually the need for an internal audit function if they do not have one.

160 Audit committees of RSLs are often concerned to avoid duplication of work, and hence cost, between external and internal audit. However, although it is expected that liaison with any internal audit function, in certain circumstances, could reduce the extent of the procedures of the external auditor, this is a matter for the professional judgment of the external auditor, taking account of the particular circumstances of the individual RSL and the assessment of the internal audit

procedures to be applied in evaluating and documenting management representations and the action to be taken if management refuses to provide appropriate representations.

The auditor should obtain appropriate representations from management. (para 2)

An important principle underlying ISA (UK and Ireland) 580 is that representations by management cannot be a substitute for other audit evidence that the auditor expects to be available.

155

Written confirmation of appropriate representations from management, as required by paragraph 4 below, should be obtained before the audit report is issued. (para 2-1)

The auditor should obtain written representations from management on matters material to the financial statements when other sufficient appropriate audit evidence cannot reasonably be expected to exist. (para 4)

The auditor should obtain written representations from management that:

(a) It acknowledges its responsibility for the design and implementation of internal control to prevent and detect error; and
(b) It believes the effects of those uncorrected financial statements misstatements aggregated by the auditor during the audit are immaterial, both individually and in the aggregate, to the financial statements taken as a whole. A summary of such items should be included in or attached to the written representations. (para 5a)

Examples of instances when the auditor of an RSL may require a representation letter (or other written confirmation such as a board minute) include cases where the auditor wishes to obtain evidence:

156

- about the board's acknowledgement of its responsibilities for the financial statements;
- in relation to ISA (UK and Ireland) 250, ISA (UK and Ireland) 570 and ISA (UK and Ireland) 550; and
- that all minutes and correspondence with the regulatory body have been made available to the auditor.

In the UK and Ireland, the auditor should obtain evidence that those charged with governance acknowledge their collective responsibility for the preparation of the financial statements and have approved the financial statements. (para 3-1)

The board of directors of an RSL as a whole is responsible for the contents and presentation of the financial statements. Consequently, discussion of the content of any written representation by the board of directors as a whole may be appropriate before it is signed on behalf of the directors, often by one of their members. In many

157

function. There is normally, however, regular liaison between the internal audit function and the RSL's external auditor.

ISA (UK AND IRELAND) 620: USING THE WORK OF AN EXPERT

Background note

The purpose of this ISA (UK and Ireland) is to establish standards and provide guidance on using the work of an expert as audit evidence.

When using the work performed by an expert, the auditor should obtain sufficient appropriate audit evidence that such work is adequate for the purposes of the audit. (para 2)

161 There are two areas where it is likely that for some audits of RSL financial statements, use will be made of the work of an expert. The two areas are: valuations of housing and other properties and defined benefit pension schemes.

Valuations

162 Under FRS 15 and the SORP RSLs are permitted to carry housing properties at a valuation. Valuers are reliant on information provided to them by the RSL in order to perform the valuation. If management decide to include properties at a valuation, the auditors need to ensure that the final valuation is properly reflected in the financial statements[20]. The auditor considers whether the information provided is consistent with the financial records subject to audit. The auditor also confirms that any accounting or other errors arising from the audit, and which may have a material bearing on the valuation, have been drawn to the attention of the valuer and reflected in the valuation. The auditor considers the reasons for any changes in valuation from the previous period and consider the conclusions in the light of the auditors' overall knowledge of the business and the results of other audit procedures.

163 The auditor considers overall whether the information provided to the valuer or other relevant professionals to enable them to perform their valuation is complete, accurate and appropriate for their purposes.

Pension schemes

164 A number of RSL financial statements reflect the position in respect of surpluses and deficits on defined benefit pension schemes. The information is usually provided directly by the actuary to the scheme. The auditor follows the guidance set out in PN 22 – The auditors' consideration of FRS 17 'Retirement benefits'-Defined benefit schemes.

---

[20] The SORP requires that valuations should be on the 'Existing Use Value Social Housing' basis, as recognised by the Royal Institution of Chartered Surveyors, and that any departure from the existing use basis, the reasons for it and its effect should be disclosed in the financial statements.

ISA (UK AND IRELAND) 700: THE INDEPENDENT AUDITOR'S REPORT ON A COMPLETE SET OF GENERAL PURPOSE FINANCIAL STATEMENTS

Background note

The purpose of this ISA (UK and Ireland) is to establish standards and provide guidance on the form and content of the auditor's report issued as a result of an audit performed by an independent auditor of the financial statements of an entity. Much of the guidance provided can be adapted to auditor reports on financial information other than financial statements.

The auditor's report should contain a clear written expression of opinion on the financial statements taken as a whole. (para 4)

165 There are particular factors that the auditors of an RSL need to consider in reporting on their audits of the financial statements of RSLs concerning:

- the report – title and addressee;
- statements of responsibility;
- the basis of opinion;
- compliance with relevant accounting requirements; and
- further matters required by statute or other regulations.

166 An example of an auditor's report on the financial statements of an RSL which is an Industrial and Provident Society[21], together with an example of a statement of responsibilities, are included as Appendices. Given the complexity of the legal and regulatory requirements for RSLs, auditors take care to ensure that the correct legislation governing the preparation of the financial statements is referred to.

The auditor's report should be appropriately addressed as required by the circumstances of the engagement and local regulations. (para 7)

167 ISA (UK and Ireland) 700 requires the title of an auditor's report to identify the person or persons to whom it is addressed. These are the person or persons on whose behalf the audit is undertaken. In the RSL sector, audits are normally undertaken on behalf of the members, so auditor's reports are normally addressed to the members of RSLs, although paragraph 9 of the Friendly and Industrial and Provident Societies Act 1968 states that the auditors should report to the society. In the case of an RSL which is a non-exempt charity, other than a charitable company, the Regulations made under Part VI of the Charities Act 1993 require the auditors' report to be addressed to the charity trustees as the persons responsible under the Act for the appointment of the auditor.

In the UK and Ireland:

(a) The auditor should distinguish between the auditor's responsibilities and the responsibilities of those charged with governance by including in their report a reference to a description of the relevant responsibilities of those charged

---

[21] The wording in the example can be tailored for RSLs that are companies or charities.

> with governance when that description is set out elsewhere in the financial statements or accompanying information; or
> (b) Where the financial statements or accompanying information do not include an adequate description of relevant responsibilities of those charged with governance, the auditor's report should include a description of those responsibilities. (para 9-1)

168 ISA (UK and Ireland) 700 requires the auditors to distinguish in their reports between their responsibilities and those of the directors or equivalent persons. For RSLs, the responsibilities equivalent to those of the directors of a limited company lie with the board. An example statement of responsibility is given in Appendix 6.

> The auditor's report should describe the scope of the audit by stating that the audit was conducted in accordance with ISAs (UK and Ireland) or in accordance with relevant national standards or practices as appropriate. (para 12)

169 RSLs are required to prepare financial statements in accordance with statutory requirements, which include the requirement to give a true and fair view. Auditors of RSLs are required to state whether, in their opinion, the financial statements meet those requirements.

170 The specific statutory requirements for form and content of financial statements are determined in accordance with the laws and regulations applicable to the particular RSL, taking account of whether it is constituted as a registered charity, as a society registered under the Industrial and Provident Societies Act 1965 or as a non-profit making company; and whether it is registered in England, Scotland, Wales or Northern Ireland.

171 There is no specific legal requirement that RSLs should comply with accounting standards or with the SORP: however, the 2000 Accounting Determination, the Registered Housing Associations (Accounting Requirements) (Scotland) Order 1999, the Accounting Requirements for RSLs registered in Wales – General Determination 2000 and the Registered Housing Associations (Accounting Requirements) (Northern Ireland) Order 1993 all require the board of an RSL to state whether its financial statements have been prepared in accordance with applicable accounting standards and statements of recommended practice. In addition, the Accounting Determinations in England and Wales require disclosure to be made in accordance with the SORP where appropriate.

172 The SORP has been developed in accordance with the code of practice established by the ASB for the production and issue of SORPs. Consequently, it provides authoritative guidance, at the time of issue, on the application of accounting standards (compliance with which is considered necessary, in all save exceptional circumstances, to meet the requirement to give a true and fair view) in a manner which takes account of the particular circumstances of providers of social housing registered with one of the regulatory bodies in the UK.

173 Furthermore FRS 18 requires the use of the most appropriate accounting policies and provides that the inclusion of an industry practice in a SORP will be persuasive (but not conclusive) evidence that practice represents the most appropriate policy. Whilst the statutory requirements for disclosure do not refer specifically to the SORP, it may normally be assumed to be the applicable SORP in terms of the disclosure requirement referred to above. Consequently, in order to meet the

statutory requirement to give a true and fair view, financial statements of RSLs will normally follow its provisions, taking into account any amendment judged to be necessary as a result of changes in accounting standards since its issue[22].

Further matters required by statute or other regulations

> The opinion paragraph of the auditor's report should clearly indicate the financial reporting framework used to prepare the financial statements (including identifying the country of origin of the financial reporting framework when the framework used is not International Accounting Standards) and state the auditor's opinion as to whether the financial statements give a true and fair view (or are presented fairly, in all material respects,) in accordance with that financial reporting framework and, where appropriate, whether the financial statements comply with statutory requirements. (para 17)

174 The auditor's report should contain any further matters required by statute or other requirements applicable to the particular engagement. For any RSL, such further matters are set out in the Housing Act 1996[23], together with any relevant Statutory Instrument or Accounting Determination or Order issued under the Act. Other relevant statutes include the Industrial and Provident Societies Acts 1965 to 2002[24], the Companies Act 1985[25] and the Charities Act 1993[26], depending on the legal form and jurisdiction of the RSL. As well as referring to these statutes as appropriate, the auditors' report may also need to refer to a trust deed where the RSL is a charitable trust.

175 Depending on the legislation under which they are formed (Appendix 3), there are various requirements for RSLs to maintain adequate books and records and satisfactory systems of internal control and for auditors to report if this is not the case. For example, for RSLs formed under the Industrial and Provident Societies Act 1965, section 9 of the Friendly and Industrial Provident Societies Act 1968 (or, for RSLs that are registered charities, Schedule 1 to the Housing Act 1996) requires auditors to state in their report, where in their opinion:

(a) proper books of account have not been kept in accordance with the requirements of section 1(1)(a) of that Act;
(b) a satisfactory system of control over transactions has not been maintained in accordance with the requirements of section 1(1)(b) of that Act;
(c) the revenue account or accounts, the other accounts (if any) to which the report relates, or the balance sheet are not in agreement with the books of account; or
(d) they have not obtained all the information and explanations they considered necessary.

---

[22] *The financial statements of every RSL in Scotland are required to comply with Schedule 7, part 3, of the Housing (Scotland) Act 2001 and the auditors' report must state whether in the auditors' opinion the financial statements do so comply. SHGN 2001/10 also requires Scottish RSLs to comply with the Housing SORP.*

[23] **Northern Ireland** – *The Housing (Northern Ireland) Order 1992.* **Scotland** – *Part II of the Housing Associations Act 1985 and the Housing (Scotland) Act 2001.*

[24] *Industrial and Provident Societies Act (Northern Ireland) 1969 to 1976. Applies only to RSLs that are industrial and provident societies.*

[25] *Companies (Northern Ireland) Order 1986.*

[26] *In addition, from 2006, the Charities Act 2005 in England and Wales and the Charity and Trustee Investment (Scotland) Act 2005 in Scotland.*

Reports on Service Charge Statements

Under the Commonhold and Leasehold Reform Act 2002 various amendments were made to the Landlord and Tenant Act 1985. These include provisions for the preparation of annual service charge statements, including making these mandatory rather than upon request by a tenant. As at the date of issue of this Practice Note, the provisions relating to annual service charge statements have yet to come into force.

The auditor may be required to report on tenants' or leaseholders' service charge statements, for example either as a requirement of the lease or by the Landlord and Tenant Act 1985 (LTA 1985)[29] or on request where the social landlord prepares such statements voluntarily. 187

As the landlord's obligation under LTA 1985 is only applicable where a request for a summary of costs is made by a tenant, in practice it is very rare that a service charge statement will be prepared by the landlord to fulfil obligations under LTA 1985. Accordingly, landlords generally prepare service charge statements either voluntarily or because they are required to contractually by the lease. 188

For service charge statements prepared under LTA 1985 or under the requirements of the relevant lease, the auditor considers whether all requirements of the lease and relevant legislation in respect of the service charge statement have been met. The form of the auditor's report will be determined by the format of the service charge statement itself. 189

If the service charge statement is prepared under LTA 1985 and covers service charges levied upon four or more leaseholders, the legislation requires that the summary shall be 'certified by a qualified accountant as in his opinion a fair summary complying with the requirements of the LTA 1985 s21 (5); and being sufficiently supported by the accounts, receipts and other documents which have been produced to him.' 190

Where a service charge statement is prepared as a result of a requirement within the lease or voluntarily, there are different possibilities for the audit report depending upon the contents of the service charge statement. Where the service charge statement includes all the disclosures required by LTA 1985, the report referred to in the paragraph above will be of relevance to the form of the actual report, though it will not be the same report. Alternatively, if the service charge statement does not provide these disclosures, the wording of the report will need to be further amended to that referred to below. 191

The auditor's report is addressed to the landlord or managing agent and clarifies that it is the responsibility of RSLs to prepare the financial statements and the responsibility of the auditors to express an opinion on those statements. In addition to the opinion on whether the statements are a 'fair summary', the report states whether the statements are in agreement with the financial records of the RSL and whether the relevant statutory and lease requirements relating to the service charge have been complied with. 192

It is important that the auditors communicate clearly the basis and scope of the opinion which they are expressing, both in their report and in a separate engagement letter. Leaseholders and tenants should understand that they are not receiving any 193

---

[29] As amended by other legislation such as the LTA 1987 and the Commonhold and Leasehold Reform Act 2002.

assurance regarding whether they are being charged a reasonable amount for services or whether those services have been provided effectively.

194 Below is an example of the auditor's report on tenants' and leaseholders' service charge statements prepared either in accordance with LTA 1985, or in accordance with the requirements of a lease or voluntarily.

Independent auditors' report on service charge statement

Report of the auditors to the Landlord/Managing Agent of [property]

In accordance with our engagement letter dated [date], we have examined the service charge statement set out on pages...to....in respect of [property] for the year ended [date] together with the books and records maintained by [Landlord/managing agent] in so far as they relate to [property].

Under the terms of this engagement, we were not required to, and did not, form any opinion as to either the reasonableness of the costs included within the service charge statement or the standard of the services or works provided.

Respective responsibilities of the Landlord and auditors

Under the Landlord and Tenant Act 1985/ Under clause [ ] of the tenancy agreement (or lease) dated [ ] between the Landlord and [*the tenant*], the Landlord is responsible for the preparation of this service charge statement in respect of the costs in respect of [property]. [The Managing Agent has undertaken responsibility for the preparation of the service charge statement on behalf of the Landlord.] It is our responsibility to form an independent opinion, based on our examination, on the service charge account and to report our opinion exclusively to the Landlord / Managing Agent.

Basis of opinion

Our work included examination, on a test basis, of evidence relevant to the amounts included in the statement and their disclosure. [It also included an assessment of the significant estimates and judgments made by the Landlord/Managing Agent in the preparation of the service charge statement.]

We planned and performed our examination so as to obtain all the information and explanations which we considered necessary in order to provide us with sufficient evidence to give reasonable assurance that the service charge statement is a fair summary of the costs relating to [property] and is sufficiently supported by accounts, receipts and other documents which have been made available to us. In view of the purpose for which this service charge statement has been prepared, however, we did not evaluate the overall adequacy of the presentation of the information which would have been required if we were to express an audit opinion under International Standards on Auditing (UK and Ireland) issued by the Auditing Practices Board.

Opinion

In our opinion the service charge statement presents a fair summary of the income and expenditure for the year ended [ ], is sufficiently supported by accounts, receipts and other documents and has been prepared in accordance with [section 21 (5) of the

Landlord and Tenant Act 1985 and] clause [ ] of the tenancy agreement (or lease) dated [ ] between the tenant (leaseholders) and XYZ Registered Social Landlord.

Appendix 1 – Regulation of Registered Social Landlords

RSLs are subject to monitoring and regulation by a regulatory body and need to meet various conditions concerning their objects and constitution. The regulatory bodies are the Housing Corporation (in England), the Department for Social Development (Northern Ireland), Communities Scotland and the National Assembly for Wales.

The regulatory bodies typically have objectives based around:

- the viability, governance and management of RSLs;
- social justice and inclusion;
- sustainable communities;
- value for money;
- protection of public funds; and
- service delivery to tenants.

The regulatory bodies set down their expectations in regulatory codes and circulars, supported by good practice notes and other publications.

The regulatory bodies take regulatory action where performance concerns are identified. In most cases the RSL will be able and willing to address those concerns. Where very serious concerns are identified however the regulatory bodies have a range of other powers at their disposal including:

- power to make appointments to the RSL's Board;
- power to direct an inquiry into the affairs of an RSL; and
- power to intervene where an RSL is threatened with insolvency.

ENGLAND

The Housing Act 1996 sets out the powers of the Housing Corporation which include powers to:

- register and de-register social landlords;
- consent to the disposal of land;
- obtain information from an RSL;
- intervene in the case of insolvency;
- direct the transfer of land; and
- freeze an RSL's assets.

In *How We Regulate 2: Risk based regulation*, published in February 2005, the Housing Corporation introduced a new style of regulation, based on a risk assessment of all lead regulated associations, to determine the planning and delivery of regulatory engagement with each association.

NORTHERN IRELAND

The Housing (Northern Ireland) Order 1976 introduced a system of funding for RSLs through loans and housing association grant (HAG). In contrast to the situation in England and Wales, charities and not-for-profit companies cannot obtain HAG in Northern Ireland because the Housing (Northern Ireland) Order

1992 specifies that only Industrial and Provident Societies can be registered and HAG can only be paid to such RSLs.

8   The Department for Social Development is the regulator for all RSLs in Northern Ireland. It also acts as a paying agent for the government, making grants and subsidies to RSLs.

SCOTLAND

9   The Housing (Scotland) Act 2001 replaced Scottish Homes with Communities Scotland, an agency of the Scottish Executive, as the regulator for all RSLs in Scotland. In addition to being the regulatory body, Communities Scotland also acts as a paying agent for the government, making grants and subsidies to RSLs. Communities Scotland can also pay grants to unregistered organisations, however, these payments are more limited and less generous than for RSLs. The Regulation and Inspection Division of Communities Scotland is responsible for inspecting RSLs.

10 All the social housing legislation up to 1985 was consolidated into the Housing Association Act 1985 and the Housing (Scotland) Acts 1987 and 1988. From July 2001 the Housing (Scotland) Act 2001 came into force, repealing certain sections of previous housing legislation.

11 The regulatory powers of Communities Scotland are similar to those outlined above under the England section.

WALES

12 The Housing Act 1988 established Housing for Wales as the regulator for RSLs in Wales. The legislation gives Housing for Wales powers identical to those of the Housing Corporation in England. These powers are now administered by the National Assembly for Wales.

13 The National Assembly for Wales (previously Housing for Wales) produces circulars for RSLs from time to time and issues publications and Accounting Determinations. Under a new Regulatory Code applying from April 2005 larger RSLs will be required to produce rolling thirty year financial projections in a prescribed format.

ELIGIBILITY TO REGISTER

England and Wales

14 Section 2 of the Housing Act 1996 ('the 1996 Act') provides that a body is eligible for registration as a social landlord if it falls into one of the following categories:

 • a registered charity[30] which is a housing association;
 • a society registered under the Industrial and Provident Societies Act 1965 which satisfies the conditions in section 2(2) of the 1996 Act; or

---

[30] Under the *Housing Associations Act 1985* a housing association is eligible for registration if it is
 – a registered charity; or
 – a society registered under the Industrial and Provident Societies Act 1965 which fulfils the conditions set out in section 4(2) of the Housing Associations Act 1985.
However the term 'a registered charity' has no application in Northern Ireland nor in Scotland as the Charities Act applies only to England and Wales. Scottish charities are only defined in terms of tax exemptions in the Law Reform (Miscellaneous Provisions) (Scotland) Act 1990. A Scottish industrial and provident society may, therefore, have charitable status although it will not be a 'registered charity'.

- a company registered under the Companies Act 1985 which satisfies the conditions in section 2(2) of the 1996 Act.

Northern Ireland

In Northern Ireland, all RSLs must be industrial and provident societies and their objects must accord with the definitions given respectively in the Housing (Northern Ireland) Order 1992 and the Housing Associations Act 1985. 15

Scotland

Chapter 1 of Part 3 of the Housing (Scotland) Act 2001 (the 2001 Act) provides that a body is eligible for registration as a social landlord if it is – 16

- A society registered under the Industrial and Provident Societies Act 1965 which has its registered office in Scotland and satisfies the conditions in paragraph 58(2) of the 2001 Act, or
- A company registered under the Companies Act 1985 which has its registered office in Scotland and satisfies those conditions.

In addition to being eligible for admission to the register of Social Landlords, RSLs must also satisfy criteria set by Communities Scotland in accordance with Section 61 of the 2001 Act.

Appendix 2 – Constitution of Registered Social Landlords

The constitution of every RSL (or the legal rules relating to it) must prohibit it from distributing any surplus funds or assets to either its members or board (for example the payment of dividends or a distribution on a winding up)[31]. Each RSL remains an independent and self governing body which is not a public body and does not exist to serve government. 1

All RSLs in Northern Ireland, and the majority of RSLs in England and Wales and Scotland, are industrial and provident societies. Many of these have charitable status. 2

RSLs may also be incorporated under the Companies Act 1985 as companies limited by guarantee with charitable status or as unincorporated charitable trusts. 3

The objects of an RSL which is a registered charity must satisfy the definition of a housing association given in the Housing Associations Act 1985 which is as follows: 4

'...a society, body of trustees or company:
- which is established for the purpose of, or amongst whose objects or powers are included those of, providing, constructing, improving or managing, or facilitating or encouraging the construction or improvement of housing accommodation, and
- which does not trade for profit or whose constitution or rules prohibit the issue of capital with interest or dividend exceeding such rates as may be prescribed by the Treasury, whether with or without differentiation as between share and loan capital.'

---

[31] *Certain RSLs are able to make payments to their Board members in accordance with the rules of the regulatory bodies.*

5   RSLs that are industrial and provident societies or companies do not have to be housing associations and they do not have to satisfy the definition of a housing association contained in the Housing Associations Act 1985. They do, however, have to have amongst their objects those matters set out in Section 2(2) of the 1996 Act (which replicates the provisions of section 4(2) of the Housing Associations Act 1985):

the conditions are that the body is non-profit making and is established for the purpose of, or has among its objects or powers, the provision, construction, improvements or management of

- houses to be kept available for letting;
- houses for occupation by members of the body, where the rules of the body restrict membership to persons entitled or prospectively entitled (as tenants or otherwise) to occupy a house provided or managed by the body; or
- hostels

and that any additional purposes or objects are among those specified in subsection (4), as follows:

the permissible additional purposes or objects are:

- providing land, amenities or services, or providing, constructing, repairing or improving buildings, for its residents, either exclusively or together with other persons;
- acquiring, or repairing and improving, or creating by the conversion of houses or other property, houses to be disposed of on sale, on lease or on shared ownership terms;
- constructing houses to be disposed of on shared ownership terms;
- managing houses held on leases or other lettings (not being houses within subsection (2)(a) or (b) or blocks of flats);
- providing services of any description for owners or occupiers of houses in arranging or carrying out works of maintenance, repair or improvement, or encouraging or facilitating the carrying out of such works; and
- encouraging and giving advice on the forming of housing associations or providing services for, and giving advice on the running of, such associations and other voluntary organisations concerned with housing, or matters connected with housing.

INDUSTRIAL AND PROVIDENT SOCIETIES

The United Kingdom

6   As stated above, all RSLs in Northern Ireland, and the majority of RSLs in England and Wales and Scotland, are industrial and provident societies. The most recent consolidating legislation is the Industrial and Provident Societies Act 1965 ('the 1965 Act'), and RSLs registered under previous Acts are deemed (under section 4 of the 1965 Act) to be registered under the 1965 Act without further formalities. They are therefore often referred to as '1965 Act' associations.

7   Industrial and Provident societies have a number of features in common, for example:
- they are subject to the administrative jurisdiction of the Financial Services Authority (FSA)[32];

---

[32] *Northern Ireland* – *The Registrar of Credit Unions*

- their constitution comprises a book of rules which must be registered with the FSA;
- they must comply with these rules;
- they are governed by a board, which is elected by the members; and
- the members of the board act in a voluntary capacity.

The FSA has a duty to ensure that the activities of RSLs continue to fall within the terms of the Industrial and Provident Societies Act 1965. Control is exercised chiefly by receiving an annual return, which must be filed with the FSA. This return deals primarily with the finances of the RSL. Any member of the RSL, or any member of the public, may apply for a free copy of the latest annual return, together with a copy of the auditor's report on the accounts and a copy of the balance sheet included in the return. 8

RSLs must also keep registers of members and of the particulars noted in the rules which are open to inspection by the FSA and by any member of the public. 9

As well as being responsible for initial registration, the FSA is responsible for registration of any subsequent changes, for example change of registered office, name or alteration of borrowing powers and limits. Similarly, the FSA must be involved in any dissolution or transfer of assets. All such rule changes must be registered. They take effect, not on application, but on approval and registration by the FSA. 10

RSLs that are industrial and provident societies are subject to the audit requirements of the Industrial and Provident Societies Acts, and in Scotland they are also subject to the requirements of Housing (Scotland) Act 2001, Schedule 7, Part 3. As such they are required to keep proper books of account and submit their financial statements for audit at least once a year. 11

Whilst there are exemptions available to certain small industrial and provident societies from the requirement to appoint auditors, RSLs are not entitled to take advantage of this exemption. RSLs are required to submit their audited financial statements to the Registrar with their annual return and present an audited revenue account and balance sheet at the annual general meeting for approval by the members. 12

COMPANIES

England, Scotland and Wales

Charitable companies limited by guarantee

Some RSLs are incorporated under the Companies Act 1985 as companies limited by guarantee but also have charitable status. As companies, their constitutions are their memorandum and articles of association. Companies are governed, on behalf of their members, by boards of directors and are required to submit annual returns and accounts, drawn up in accordance with the Companies Act 1985, to the Registrar of Companies. 13

RSLs which are charitable companies must operate in accordance with the Companies Acts and their memorandum and articles of association are filed with the Registrar of Companies. As charities, they are also subject to regulation by the Charity Commission. All such RSLs must comply with the relevant provisions of charities and companies legislation as well as of legislation relating to RSLs so that, 14 for example, they are unable to take advantage of the exemptions from audit available to small charities and to small companies under the Companies Act 1985.

Non-charitable companies

15 Part I of the Housing Act 1996 enables non-charitable non-profit-making companies to register with the relevant regulatory body (the Housing Corporation in England or the National Assembly for Wales in Wales).

16 The 1996 Act makes no specific reference to local housing companies or the nature of their legal constitution. Local housing companies may, therefore, be incorporated or unincorporated and, if incorporated, limited by guarantee or by shares, or set up as an industrial and provident society. Local housing companies must be not-for-profit if they are to be eligible for registration with the relevant regulatory body as an RSL.

CHARITIES

England and Wales

17 Many RSLs in England and Wales are charities and are often constituted by a trust deed, unless they have been established as charitable companies (see above) or charitable industrial and provident societies. The majority of charitable RSLs are industrial and provident societies and are therefore exempt charities which, although subject to the Charities Act, are not currently regulated by the Charity Commission. Charitable RSLs that are unincorporated bodies (in other words, not industrial and provident societies or companies) are subject to regulation and monitoring by the Charity Commission and are governed by boards who are responsible for ensuring that the charity operates within its objects. RSL charitable companies are regulated by both the Registrar of Companies and the Charity Commission.

18 The activities of certain non-charitable RSLs may be similar to those of charitable RSLs. However, in order to be 'charitable' RSLs, their constitutions must have objects that are wholly charitable and the wholly charitable constitution documents (see below) must have been registered at the appropriate registry.

19 The constitutions of charitable RSLs normally provide that they must act for the 'relief of the aged, impotent or poor people', but RSLs that act for the relief of such people are only 'charitable' if they also have charitable constitutions. Charitable status brings certain benefits:

- their status in the eyes of the general public may be different;
- potential donors may be more inclined to help the RSL;
- some charities make donations only to organisations with charitable status;
- rate relief – or relief on the uniform business rate – may be obtainable on property occupied by a charity;
- exemption is available from liability to Corporation Tax and Capital Gains Tax; and
- exemption is available from stamp duty on purchases of land or property.

20 Because of the benefits of charitable status it is considered important that such organisations are subject to regulation and they are therefore required to register. The Charities Acts provide for a central register of charities in England and Wales to be maintained by the Charity Commission. For most charities registration with the Charity Commission is compulsory but, as stated above, Industrial and Provident Societies are exempt from registration, although still subject to charity law. RSLs

which are charities but which are not industrial and provident societies are subject to the regulatory requirements of the Charity Commissioners and to charity law (and of company law if they are companies).

Charitable trusts must operate in accordance with their trust deeds, as approved by the Charity Commission. RSLs with charitable status which are limited companies must also comply with companies legislation. Charitable status does not remove the overriding requirement for an RSL to comply with relevant legislation, for example the requirement for an external audit irrespective of size. 21

Scotland

In Scotland, charitable status has historically been approved by the Inland Revenue. A new regulator, the Office of the Scottish Charity Regulator, is currently being set up and will assume this responsibility when the Charity and Trustee Investment (Scotland) Act 2005 comes into force. Right to Buy (RTB) is a major and complex issue. RSLs which were already charities when the Housing (Scotland) Act 2001 was implemented are exempt from RTB legislation, but those tenants with an existing RTB will not lose this right (while they remain in the same property) in the event of their RSL converting to charitable status. Those tenants who are not currently entitled to RTB and any new tenants allocated properties after conversion will not be covered by RTB legislation. The Housing (Scotland) Act 2001 has granted a 10 year exemption from offering RTB to all RSLs, outwith any rights attaching to existing tenancies. 22

Appendix 3 – Legislative framework

INTRODUCTION

This appendix refers to certain key requirements but does not constitute an exhaustive list of all enactments or legislative requirements which may have a bearing on RSLs. 1

INDUSTRIAL AND PROVIDENT SOCIETIES ACTS 1965-2002 AND THE FRIENDLY AND INDUSTRIAL AND PROVIDENT SOCIETIES ACT 1968

England, Scotland and Wales

The Industrial and Provident Societies Act 1965 (the 1965 Act) sets out important matters related to Industrial and Provident Societies. Section 37 of the 1965 Act sets out some basic requirements in relation to the audit of the accounts of an Industrial and Provident Society. In particular it requires that auditors should satisfy themselves that proper records have been kept of all transactions, assets and liabilities. The Friendly and Industrial and Provident Societies Act 1968, which sets out the main accounting and audit requirements, requires proper financial records to be kept and that all financial statements agree with those records, that there is satisfactory internal control over transactions and that the financial statements show a true and fair view of the RSL's financial position. 2

The Industrial and Provident Societies Act 1978 simply altered Section 7(3) of the 1965 Act. More importantly, the 1978 Act sets out that the 1978 Act and the 1965 3

Act should be construed as one. It is for this reason that the audit reports make reference to the Industrial & Provident Societies Acts 1965 to 1978.

4 The Industrial and Provident Societies Act 2002 substantially amended the 1965 Act in relation to the conversion of a Registered Society into a Company. In addition, it gave power to the Treasury to modify the relevant statutory provisions in the 1965 Act for the purpose of assimilating the law relating to companies and the law relating to Industrial & Provident Societies. That power includes the power to change, by order, Section 37 of the 1965 Act. No such change has been made as at the date of issue of this Practice Note. Because of this power it is necessary when referring to the 1965 Act also to refer to the 2002 Act. As a consequence, the accounts of an Industrial and Provident Society must comply with the Industrial & Provident Societies Acts 1965 to 2002 and the audit report should cover those Acts.

THE HOUSING ACTS 1974, 1980 AND 1985

England, Scotland and Wales

5 The Housing Acts provide a comprehensive system of grants for registered RSLs and set up the regulator's dual tasks of controlling and financing[33] RSLs.

6 The 1974 Act established the housing association grant regime; the 1980 Act was concerned mainly with the management of property and the legal position of tenants; whilst the 1985 Act was a consolidating Act.

THE HOUSING ACTS 1988, 1996 AND 2004

England and Wales

7 The 1988 Act launched the Government's mixed funding initiative which has increasingly become the normal method of financing new housing schemes.

8 The Housing Act 1996 has amended, replaced or repealed various sections of the Housing Associations Act 1985 and Part II of the Housing Act 1988.

9 The Act introduces the definition of 'registered social landlords' which includes existing registered housing associations, but also includes local housing companies formed from local authority stock. It also introduces the term 'social housing grant' to replace the term 'housing association grant'. The 1996 Act has also made changes to the Housing Corporation's powers and responsibilities. In particular, it allows the Housing Corporation and the National Assembly for Wales to determine the accounting requirements for RSLs.

10 The requirements on registered social landlords to provide the Corporation and the National Assembly for Wales with general and performance information about their activities are now put on a statutory basis. The new regulatory regime gives the Housing Corporation and the National Assembly for Wales significant increases to their inquiry powers, as well as the power to intervene and seek to secure transfer of social housing stock in the event of threatened insolvency.

11 The Act also introduces a range of changes to houses in multiple occupancy, tenancy allocation and homelessness matters.

---

[33] *In Scotland the financing function is in certain cases being transferred to local authorities.*

The 2004 Act extends the power of the Housing Corporation and the National Assembly for Wales to give social housing grant to organisations other than registered social landlords. It also paves the way for the removal of the requirement for smaller associations to have their accounts audited, and sets out circumstances in which the auditor may disclose information to the regulator without breaching the duty of confidentiality to client associations[34]. The Act also introduces a range of changes relating to health and safety, home information packs, the right to buy, tenancy deposit schemes and accommodation for gypsies and travellers.

THE HOUSING (NORTHERN IRELAND) ORDER 1992

The Housing (Northern Ireland) Order 1992 provides the framework for the accounting practice of RSLs and every registered RSL is required, under the Order, to have an annual independent external audit.

Article 13 of the Order details the circumstances in which all RSLs must obtain consent from the regulator before disposing of land and property. RSLs must also meet the regulator's administrative rules on taxation and the rights of tenants.

Articles 19 and 20 provide for the accounting and auditing requirements for registered RSLs, together with enforcement measures.

Under Articles 23 and 24 of the Order, the regulators have specific powers to appoint a person to conduct an inquiry into the affairs of a registered RSL or to audit the RSL. Such action is only taken in extreme cases, normally where mismanagement or maladministration is suspected. The person appointed to carry out the audit must be a registered auditor.

Where mismanagement or maladministration is suspected, Articles 25 and 26 provide for the regulator to take appropriate remedial action, including removing and appointing board members or staff and directing that property be transferred to another RSL.

Article 31 of the Order prevents board members, and their related parties, from obtaining benefits from it except as determined by the Department.

HOUSING ASSOCIATIONS ACT 1985

England, Scotland and Wales

In England and Wales many of the provisions of this Act have been repealed or amended by the Housing Act 1996. In Scotland, the Housing (Scotland) Act 2001

---

[34] *The Housing Act 2004 section 19A states:*

'Disclosure of information by auditors etc. to the Relevant Authority

(1) A person who is, or has been, an auditor of a registered social landlord does not contravene any duty to which he is subject merely because he gives to the Relevant Authority –
  (a) information on a matter of which he became aware in his capacity as auditor of the registered social landlord, or
  (b) his opinion on such a matter,
if he is acting in good faith and he reasonably believes that the information or opinion is relevant to any functions of the Relevant Authority.
(2) Sub-paragraph (1) applies whether or not the person is responding to a request from the Relevant Authority.'

has also modified or repealed certain parts of the 1985 legislation. Reference should be made to the Housing (Scotland) Act 2001, Schedule 10 paragraph 11.

20   The Housing Associations Act 1985 (HAA 1985), together with the Housing Act 1985 and the Landlord and Tenant Act 1985, consolidates all existing legislation up to 1985. No new principles are introduced but the previous legislation has been brought together in a more logical order.

21   The HAA 1985 provides the overall framework for the accounting practice of RSLs. It requires every RSL to have an annual independent external audit.

22   Section 9 details the circumstances in which all RSLs must obtain consent from the regulatory body before disposing of land, or when mortgages are given over, and property. RSLs are also required to meet the regulatory body's rules on taxation and the rights of tenants.

23   Section 15 prevents board members, and their related parties, from being employed by the RSL, or obtaining benefits from it.

24   Under sections 16, 17 and 30, where mismanagement or maladministration is suspected, there are provisions for appropriate remedial action to be taken by the regulatory body, if necessary including the removal and appointment of board members.

25   Section 19 requires RSLs to notify the regulator of any change in name or registered office and to obtain written consent to any other rule change.

26   Section 21 requires that an RSL obtains the consent of the regulator to any amalgamation or dissolution.

27   Under sections 28 and 29 of the Act, the regulatory body has specific powers to appoint a person to conduct an inquiry into the affairs of an RSL or to audit the RSL. Such action is only taken in extreme cases, normally where mismanagement or maladministration is suspected.

THE HOUSING (SCOTLAND) ACTS 1987, 1988 AND 2001

28   The Housing (Scotland) Act 2001 has made extensive amendments to both these earlier Acts. Reference should be made to Housing (Scotland) Act 2001, Schedule 10, para 13 for changes to the 1987 Act and para 14 for the changes to the 1988 Act.

29   The Housing (Scotland) Act 1988 set up Scottish Homes as, among other things, the funding and registration authority for RSLs in Scotland. The 2001 Act transferred all of its functions to Communities Scotland.

30   Under powers given to Communities Scotland to enable relaxation of Schedule 7 Part 1 of the Housing (Scotland) Act 2001, the following exceptions are permitted:
- granting of tenancies to committee members, staff or their close relatives, providing the RSL can provide evidence that the applicant meets the allocation criteria;
- entering into a contract of employment with a close relative of an employee or former employee, subject to the RSL being able to demonstrate that selection criteria were fair; and
- making a payment of RSL Grant under the Scottish Homes Tenants Incentive Scheme to a person covered by section 15, subject to specific criteria being met.

In all the above cases the full committee must authorise the decision, record it appropriately in the minutes and in a section 15 Register maintained by the RSL.

RSLs in Scotland must now comply with the all the relevant provisions of the Housing (Scotland) Act 2001 including– 31

- where a local authority requests an RSL which holds houses for housing purposes in its area to provide accommodation for a homeless person, the RSL must within a reasonable period comply with such a request unless it has a good reason for not doing so;
- the Housing (Scotland) Act 2001 defines Scottish Secure Tenancy and governs restrictions on termination; proceedings for possession; succession to tenancy and variations to the tenancy;
- chapter 2 of the Housing (Scotland) Act 2001 has modernised the Right to Buy legislation contained in the Housing (Scotland) Act 1987.

THE LANDLORD AND TENANT ACT 1985

England and Wales

The Landlord and Tenant Act 1985 is a consolidated Act as amended by the Landlord and Tenant Act 1987. The Act details information RSLs are required to give to tenants, such as the landlord's identity and the provision of rent books (for weekly tenants), and contains provisions regarding the fitness of homes for human habitation, landlords repairing obligations and the levying of service charges. 32

RENT (SCOTLAND) ACT 1984

This Act provides the framework for the fair rent system and for registering rents with the rent officer. (This is not applicable to new RSL lettings after 2 January 1989). The Housing (Scotland) Act 2001 has made amendments to the Rent (Scotland) Act 1984. Reference should be made to the Housing (Scotland) Act, schedule 10, para 9. 33

THE CHARITIES ACTS 1960 AND 1993

England and Wales

The Charities Acts 1960 and 1993 provide for a central register of charities in England and Wales to be maintained by the Charity Commission. For most charities registration is compulsory, but certain classes of charity are 'exempt'. Charities registered under the Industrial and Provident Societies Acts, including social landlords registered under the NHF's charitable model rules, are 'exempt'. 34

Northern Ireland and Scotland

There is no charities' registry in Northern Ireland, although there is a proposal to establish a Northern Ireland Charity Commission. In Scotland, registration is being established by the new regulator, OSCR. 35

THE COMPANIES ACTS 1985 AND 1989

England, Scotland and Wales

36 The Companies Act 1985[35] Requires the auditors' report to state whether or not the financial statements show a true and fair view and comply with accounting standards. It must be attached to the published accounts.

37 Only persons who are eligible for appointment as auditors under the Companies Act 1989[36], and are registered with a supervisory body recognised under this Act, may be appointed as external auditors of registered RSLs.

THE ACCOUNTING REQUIREMENTS FOR REGISTERED SOCIAL LANDLORDS GENERAL DETERMINATION 2000

38 The Accounting Requirements for Registered Social Landlords General Determination 2000[37], sets out the reporting requirements for publishing the financial statements of RSLs in England. The Determination details the required form of financial statements of RSLs. Similar requirements for Scotland are contained in the Registered Housing Associations (Accounting Requirements) (Scotland) Order 1999. The Accounting Requirements for social landlords registered in Wales – General Determination 2000, sets out similar requirements for Wales.

THE COMMONHOLD AND LEASEHOLD REFORM ACT

39 The Commonhold and Leasehold Reform Act 2002 is intended to strengthen residential leaseholders' rights in relation to their landlords, and to address some of the long-standing difficulties of the leasehold tenure. As at the time of publication of this revised Practice Note, many of the provisions of this Act have yet to come into force.

Appendix 4 – Codes of audit practice and good practice notes

THE UNITED KINGDOM

1 The regulatory bodies in each of the UK jurisdictions have issued codes of audit practice and good practice notes. The codes, good practice notes and other relevant circulars provide guidance to RSLs on, and define their responsibilities for, amongst other things, effective audit coverage, the appointment of auditors and the nature of the working relationship with the auditors. They also set out or give guidance on the

---

[35] *The Companies (Northern Ireland) Order 1986 extends the true and fair view required of financial statements to the auditors' report which must be attached to the published accounts and it requires auditors to state that accounts comply with accounting standards.*

[36] *The Companies (Northern Ireland) Order 1969 states that only persons who are eligible for appointment as auditors under the Companies (Northern Ireland) Order 1969, and are registered with a supervisory body recognised under this Order, may be appointed as external auditors of registered RSLs.*

[37] **Northern Ireland**
The Registered Housing Association Accounting Requirements (Northern Ireland) Order 1993.
Scotland
The Registered Housing Association (Accounting Requirements)(Scotland) Order 1999.
Wales
The Accounting Requirements for Social Landlords registered in Wales General Determination 2000.

- select suitable accounting policies and then apply them consistently;
- make judgements and estimates that are reasonable and prudent;
- state whether applicable accounting standards have been followed, subject to any material departures disclosed and explained in the financial statements; and
- prepare the financial statements on the going concern basis unless it is inappropriate to presume that the RSL will continue in business.

The Board is responsible for keeping proper accounting records which disclose with reasonable accuracy at any time the financial position of the RSL and to enable it to ensure that the financial statements comply with the Industrial and Provident Societies Acts 1965 to 2002, Schedule 1 to the Housing Act 1996[39] and the Accounting Requirements for Registered Social Landlords General Determination 2000[40]. It has general responsibility for taking reasonable steps to safeguard the assets of the RSL and to prevent and detect fraud and other irregularities.

As Board members, you are under a duty to prepare an annual report for each financial year complying in its form and content with regulations as made under the Accounting Requirements for Registered Social Landlords General Determination 2000[41]. You are also required to have regard to the Statement of Recommended Practice, Accounting by Registered Social Landlords, (the SORP) issued in December 2002, and updated in May 2005, jointly by the National Housing Federation in England, the Scottish Federation of Housing Associations and the Welsh Federation of Housing Associations. RSL financial statements and accounting practices are expected to comply fully, where appropriate, with the SORP.   1.2

We have a statutory responsibility to report to the members whether in our opinion the financial statements give a true and fair view of the state of the RSL's affairs and of the surplus or deficit for the year, and whether they have been properly prepared in accordance with the Industrial and Provident Societies Acts 1965 to 2002, Schedule 1 to the Housing Act 1996 and the Accounting Requirements for Registered Social Landlords General Determination 2000, as amended, (or other relevant legislation). In arriving at our opinion, we are required to consider the following matters, and to report on any in respect of which we are not satisfied: 1.3

- whether proper accounting records have been kept by the RSL;
- whether the RSL's balance sheet and income and expenditure account are in agreement with the accounting records;
- whether the RSL has maintained a satisfactory system of control over its transactions;
- whether we have obtained all the information and explanations which we consider necessary for the purposes of our audit; and
- whether the information in the Board's report is consistent with that in the audited financial statements[42].

We have a professional responsibility to report if the financial statements do not comply in any material respect with applicable accounting standards, unless in our opinion the non-compliance is justified in the circumstances. In determining whether or not the departure is justified we consider: 1.4

---

[39] **Scotland** – Section 254(1) of the Housing Association Act 1985.

[40] As relevant, insert equivalent requirements for Scotland, Wales and Northern Ireland.

[41] The 1992 Order in Northern Ireland requires accounts and an auditor's report.

[42] Not applicable in Northern Ireland.

- whether the departure is required in order for the financial statements to give a true and fair view; and
- whether adequate disclosure has been made concerning the departure.

1.5 Our professional responsibilities include:

- providing in our report a description of the Committee of Management's responsibilities for the financial statements where the financial statements or accompanying information do not include such a description; and
- considering whether other information in documents containing audited financial statements is consistent with the financial statements.

2. **Scope of audit**

2.1 Our audit will be conducted in accordance with International Standards on Auditing (UK and Ireland) issued by the Auditing Practices Board (APB) and will have particular regard to the APB's Practice Note 'The audit of registered social landlords in the United Kingdom (Revised)' and the Housing Corporation's Good Practice Note 'External audit of housing associations'. It will include such tests of transactions and of the existence, ownership and valuation of assets and liabilities as we consider necessary.

2.2 We shall obtain an understanding of the accounting and internal financial control systems in order to assess their adequacy as a basis for the preparation of the financial statements and to establish whether proper accounting records have been maintained by the RSL.

2.3 We shall expect to obtain such appropriate evidence as we consider sufficient to enable us to draw reasonable conclusions therefrom. The nature and extent of our tests will vary according to our assessment of the RSL's accounting system and where we wish to place reliance on it, the system of internal control, and may cover any aspect of the business operations.

2.4 Our work will be planned in advance and incorporated into an audit plan. This may be varied on the basis of our findings during the course of an audit and from year to year. Accordingly, we may modify our audit scope, rotate our audit emphasis and propose matters of special audit emphasis, as the circumstances dictate.

2.5 Our audit includes assessing the significant estimates and judgements made by the Board in the preparation of the financial statements and whether the accounting policies are appropriate to the RSL's circumstances, consistently applied and adequately disclosed.

2.6 The concept of materiality affects our audit planning and our consideration of matters arising from our audit. We take into account both qualitative and quantitative factors when assessing materiality.

2.7 In forming our opinion we will also evaluate the overall presentation of information in the financial statements.

3. **Internal audit**

3.1 In developing our audit plan, we will liaise with your internal auditors to ensure that our work is properly co-ordinated with theirs. It is our policy to rely upon internal audit work whenever possible, while ensuring that adequate audit coverage is achieved of all significant areas.

Management representations 4.

The information used by the Board in preparing the financial statements will invariably include facts or judgements which are not themselves recorded in the accounting records. As part of our normal audit procedures, we shall request appropriate Board members, or senior officials/management to provide written confirmation each year of such facts or judgements and any other oral representations which we have received during the course of the audit on matters having a material effect on the financial statements. We will also ask you to confirm in that letter that all important and relevant information has been brought to our attention. In addition, we shall present to the Board a schedule of any unadjusted misstatements that have come to our attention in the course of our audit work, and if you decide not to adjust the financial statements for these misstatements we shall request you to explain in writing your reasons for not making the adjustments. 4.1

Detection of fraud, error and non-compliance with laws and regulations 5.

The responsibility for safeguarding the assets of the RSL and for the prevention and detection of fraud, error and non-compliance with law or regulations rests with yourselves. However, we shall endeavour to plan our audit so that we have a reasonable expectation of detecting material misstatements in the financial statements or accounting records (including any material misstatements resulting from fraud, error or non-compliance with law or regulations), but our examination should not be relied upon to disclose all such material misstatements or frauds, errors or instances of non-compliance as may exist. 5.1

Reports to management 6.

At the conclusion of the audit, or sooner if appropriate, we shall prepare a report to The Board that will include comments on: 6.1

- any expected modification of the auditors' report,
- unadjusted misstatements,
- material weaknesses to the accounting and internal control systems identified during the audit,
- the qualitative aspects of the RSL's accounting practices and financial reporting,
- matters specifically required by other Auditing Standards, and
- any other relevant matters relating to the audit.

Our audit is not designed to identify all significant weaknesses in the RSL's system of internal controls. Our review of internal control systems is only performed to the extent required to express an opinion on the RSL's financial statements and therefore our comments on these systems will not necessarily address all possible improvements which might be suggested as a result of a more extensive special examination. 6.2

Other requirements 7.

In order to assist us with the examination of your financial statements, we shall request early sight of all documents or statements (including the Chairman's statement, operating and financial review and the Board report) which are due to be issued with the financial statements. We are also entitled to attend all general meetings of the RSL and to receive notice of all such meetings. 7.1

Once we have issued our report we have no further direct responsibility in relation to the financial statements for that financial year. However, we expect that you will 7.2

inform us of any material event occurring between the date of our report and that of the Annual General Meeting which may affect the financial statements.

8. Summary Financial Statements

8.1 As Board members of the RSL, you are responsible for any summary financial statements. Our responsibility is to report to the members whether in our opinion the summary financial statement is consistent with the full financial statements and report of the RSL for the year. Our work will be conducted in accordance with Bulletin 1999/6 'The auditors' statement on the summary financial statement' issued by the Auditing Practices Board.

9. Adoption of Housing Corporation Circular R2-25/01

9.1 We are not required to report on your compliance with the requirements of Circular R2-25/01. Our responsibilities in respect of this statement on internal control are governed by ISA (UK and Ireland) 720 'Other information in documents containing audited financial statements' which requires that;

- We should read the other information. If as a result we become aware of any apparent misstatements therein, or identify any material inconsistencies with the audited financial statements, we should seek to resolve these with you;
- If we identify an inconsistency between the financial statements and the other information, or a misstatement within the other information, we should consider whether an amendment is required to the financial statements or to the other information and should seek to resolve the matter through discussion with the directors;

If, after discussion with the directors, we conclude that:

- The financial statements require amendment and no such amendment is made, we should consider the implications for our reports;
- The other information requires amendment and no such amendment is made, we should consider appropriate action including the implications for our report.

10. Electronic communications

10.1 We acknowledge that as the Board of the RSL you may wish to publish the RSL's financial statements and the auditors' report on the RSL's website or distribute them to shareholders by means such as e-mail. Your responsibilities concerning the preparation, dissemination and signing of the financial statements do not change simply because the financial statements are reproduced or distributed electronically; it is your responsibility to ensure that any such publication properly presents the financial information and any auditors' report. We request that you advise us of any intended electronic publication before it occurs.

10.2 As auditors, we will review the process by which the financial statements to be published electronically are derived from the financial information contained in the manually signed accounts, check that the proposed electronic version is identical in content with the manually signed accounts and check that the conversion of the manually signed accounts into an electronic format has not distorted the overall presentation of the financial information, for example by highlighting certain information so as to give it greater prominence.

10.3 In accordance with the guidance in 'the electronic publication of the auditor's report' issued by the Auditing Practices Board, we reserve the right to withhold consent to the electronic publication of our report if the audited financial statements or the auditors' report are to be published in an inappropriate manner or to request amendments to the electronic auditors' report if we are not satisfied with the proposed wording or its presentation in the context of the financial statements.

Appendix 6 – A statement of the board's responsibilities for an RSL that is an Industrial and Provident Society

The Industrial and Provident Societies Acts and registered social housing legislation require the board to prepare financial statements for each financial year which give a true and fair view of the state of affairs of the RSL and of the surplus or deficit for that period. In preparing these financial statements, the board is required to:

- select suitable accounting policies and then apply them consistently;
- make judgements and estimates that are reasonable and prudent;
- state whether applicable accounting standards have been followed, subject to any material departures disclosed and explained in the financial statements; and
- prepare the financial statements on the going concern basis unless it is inappropriate to presume that the RSL will continue in business.

The board is responsible for keeping proper accounting records which disclose with reasonable accuracy at any time the financial position of the RSL and to enable it to ensure that the financial statements comply with the Industrial and Provident Societies Acts 1965 to 2002[43], Schedule 1 to the Housing Act 1996 and the Accounting Requirements for Registered Social Landlords Determination 2000 as amended. It has general responsibility for taking reasonable steps to safeguard the assets of the RSL and to prevent and detect fraud and other irregularities.

Appendix 7 – Illustrative example of auditors' report on the financial statements of an RSL that is an Industrial and Provident Society

EXAMPLE – UNQUALIFIED OPINION

Independent auditors' report to the members of [Registered Social Landlord]

We have audited the financial statements of [Registered Social Landlord] for the year ended ....,which comprise (state the primary financial statements such as the Income and Expenditure Account, the Balance Sheet)[44] and the related notes. These financial statements have been prepared under the accounting policies set out therein.

Respective responsibilities of the board and auditors

The board's responsibilities for preparing the financial statements in accordance with applicable law are set out in the Statement of Board's Responsibilities on page ...

---

[43] These references should be amended as necessary for RSLs that are companies or charities.

[44] Auditors' reports on RSLs that do not publish their financial statements on a web site or publish them using 'PDF' format may continue to refer to the financial statements by reference to page numbers.

Our responsibility is to audit the financial statements in accordance with relevant legal and regulatory requirements and International Standards on Auditing (UK and Ireland).

We report to you our opinion as to whether the financial statements give a true and fair view and are properly prepared in accordance with the Industrial and Provident Societies Acts 1965 to 2002, the Housing Act 1996 and the Accounting Requirements for Registered Social Landlords General Determination 2000[45]. We also report to you if, in our opinion, a satisfactory system of control over transactions has not been maintained, if the RSL has not kept proper accounting records, or if we have not received all the information and explanations we require for our audit.

We read other information contained in the Report of the Board and consider whether it is consistent with the audited financial statements. This other information comprises only ..... We consider the implications for our report if we become aware of any apparent misstatements or material inconsistencies with the financial statements. Our responsibilities do not extend to any other information.

Basis of opinion

We conducted our audit in accordance with International Standards on Auditing (UK and Ireland) issued by the Auditing Practices Board. An audit includes examination, on a test basis, of evidence relevant to the amounts and disclosures in the financial statements. It also includes an assessment of the significant estimates and judgements made by the board in the preparation of the financial statements, and of whether the accounting policies are appropriate to [RSL]'s circumstances, consistently applied and adequately disclosed.

We planned and performed our audit so as to obtain all the information and explanations which we considered necessary in order to provide us with sufficient evidence to give reasonable assurance that the financial statements are free from material misstatement, whether caused by fraud or other irregularity or error. In forming our opinion we also evaluated the overall adequacy of the presentation of information in the financial statements.

Opinion

In our opinion the financial statements give a true and fair view of the state of [RSL]'s affairs as at [date] and of its surplus/deficit for the year then ended and have been properly prepared in accordance with the Industrial and Provident Societies Acts, 1965 to 2002, Schedule 1 to the Housing Act 1996 and The Accounting Requirements for Registered Social Landlords General Determination 2000.

Registered auditors   Address

Date

---

[45] For RSLs in Scotland and Wales, the title of the relevant local Determination should be stated.

Appendix 8 – Definitions

Abbreviations and frequently used terms in this Practice Note are set out below:

Registered Social Landlord	'Registered Social Landlords' (RSLs) in England and Wales include registered housing associations, registered housing charitable trusts and local housing companies. In this Practice Note, the term RSL is also used to apply to housing associations in Scotland and Northern Ireland. RSLs are registered with the relevant regulatory body, that is, the Housing Corporation in England, the Department for Social Development in Northern Ireland, Communities Scotland in Scotland and the National Assembly for Wales in Wales.
The Housing Corporation	The principal regulator of RSLs in England.
Communities Scotland	The principal regulator of RSLs in Scotland and an agency of the Scottish Executive. Replaced Scottish Homes as the regulator in 2001.
The National Assembly for Wales	The principal regulator of RSLs in Wales, replacing Housing for Wales in 1999.
The Department for Social Development	The principal regulator of RSLs in Northern Ireland.
The FSA	The Financial Services Authority, the regulator of all businesses in the financial services sector; carries out the registration function for certain RSLs.
The three Federations	The National Housing Federation, the Welsh Federation of Housing Associations and the Scottish Federation of Housing Associations.
Boards	RSLs are governed by boards which are made up mainly of non-executive voluntary members (which may include tenants), but which may also include a limited number of paid and/or staff members. Boards are also referred to as Committees of Management. Boards have the legal responsibility for the running of an RSL. They retain ultimate control and responsibility over all aspects of the activities of the RSL and must ensure that the financial and legal responsibilities are fulfilled properly. The powers of boards are wide and, although particular functions may be delegated to sub-committees or to staff, boards retain the responsibility for seeing that those functions are carried out properly.
SORP	The Statement of Recommended Practice 'Accounting by Registered Social Landlords' (the SORP) was issued originally in 1999, and updated in December 2002 and May 2005 jointly by the National Housing Federation, the Welsh Federation of Housing Associations and the Scottish Federation of Housing Associations (the Three Federations) in accordance with the ASB's

	code of practice for the development and issue of SORPs. The SORP aims to interpret for social landlords how present best accounting practice (as defined by the ASB) can apply to them.
Accounting Determinations	*The Accounting Requirements for Registered Social Landlords General Determination 2000 , sets out the reporting requirements for publishing the financial statements of RSLs in England. The Determination details the required form of financial statements of RSLs. Similar requirements for Scotland are contained in the Registered Housing Associations (Accounting Requirements) (Scotland) Order 1999. The Accounting Requirements for social landlords registered in Wales – General Determination 2000, sets out similar requirements for Wales.*
Directors	*The term 'directors' is used to describe the persons who are charged with governance of an RSL, including the preparation of its financial statements. For the purpose of this Practice Note, 'directors' should be taken to mean the members of the board or committee of management of an RSL.*
Circulars, good practice notes and guidance notes	*The regulatory bodies in each of the UK jurisdictions have issued codes of audit practice and good practice notes. The codes, good practice notes and other relevant circulars provide guidance to RSLs on, and define their responsibilities for, amongst other things, effective audit coverage, the appointment of auditors and the nature of the working relationship with the auditors. They also set out or give guidance on the audit framework and the re-tendering of audits.*

Appendix 9 – Some significant topics relevant to audits of RSLs

TOPIC	PARAGRAPH NUMBER	SECTION
Accounting Determinations	47 147 171	ISA (UK and Ireland) 250 ISA (UK and Ireland) 570 ISA (UK and Ireland) 700 APP 1 APP 3 APP 5
Boards	3, 10-12 94 141-144 145-146 156-158 181	Introduction ISA (UK and Ireland) 315 ISA (UK and Ireland) 550 ISA (UK and Ireland) 560 ISA (UK and Ireland) 580 ISA (UK and Ireland) 720 APP 3 APP 6
Audit Practice Codes/ Good Practice Notes	13	Introduction APP 4
Debt financing and Grants	7, 23 102 153	Introduction ISA (UK and Ireland) 315 ISA (UK and Ireland) 570
Reporting on Internal Control	14, 17, 21 41 90-93, 109-110 159 175 182	Introduction ISA (UK and Ireland) 240 ISA (UK and Ireland) 315 ISA (UK and Ireland) 610 ISA (UK and Ireland) 700 ISA (UK and Ireland) 720 APP 4 APP 5
SORP	39 49 69 77 171-173	ISA (UK and Ireland) 220 ISA (UK and Ireland) 250 ISA (UK and Ireland) 300 ISA (UK and Ireland) 315 ISA (UK and Ireland) 700
Taxation	25 55 107	Introduction ISA (UK and Ireland) 250 ISA (UK and Ireland) 315
Reports to Regulators	18 46 58-60	Introduction ISA (UK and Ireland) 240 ISA (UK and Ireland) 250
Service charge statements	31-34 187-194	ISA (UK and Ireland) 210 Reports on service charge statements
Property Valuation	81-84 114-116 162-163	ISA (UK and Ireland) 315 ISA (UK and Ireland) 330 ISA (UK and Ireland) 620

[PN 15]
The audit of occupational pension schemes in the United Kingdom (revised)

Contents

	Paragraphs
Preface	
Introduction	5
The audit of financial statements	15
ISAs (UK and Ireland)	
200 Objective and General Principles Governing an Audit of Financial Statements	15
210 Terms of Audit Engagements	17
240 The Auditor's Responsibility to Consider Fraud in an Audit of Financial Statements	23
250 Section A – Consideration of Laws and Regulations in an Audit of Financial Statements	29
Section B – The Auditors' Right and Duty to Report to Regulators in the Financial Sector	
260 Communication of Audit Matters With Those Charged With Governance	50
300 Planning an Audit of Financial Statements	51
315 Obtaining an Understanding of the Entity and Its Environment and Assessing the Risks of Material Misstatement	54
320 Audit Materiality	68
330 The Auditor's Procedures in Response to Assessed Risks	70
402 Audit Considerations Relating to Entities Using Service Organisations	72
520 Analytical Procedures	79
550 Related Parties	81
570 Going Concern	83
580 Management Representations	85
600 Considering the Work of Another Auditor	87
620 Using the Work of an Expert	89
700 The Auditor's Report on Financial Statements	90
720 Section A – Other Information in Documents Containing Audited Financial Statements (Revised)	95
The Auditors' Statement about Contributions (the Statement)	97
Liaison with the Scheme Actuary	106
Appendices	
1 List of principal relevant legislation	109
2 The legal and regulatory framework	110
3 List of publications	130
4 Illustrative examples of appointment and resignation letters and paragraphs for engagement letters	132

5	Illustrative example of representation letter	148
6	Illustrative examples of auditors' reports and statements about contributions	152
7	Illustrative example statement of trustees' responsibilities	160
8	Impact of the scheme benefit structure on risk	162
9	Non-statutory audit appointments	166
10	Definitions	170
11	Some significant topics relevant to audits of pension schemes	172

Preface

This Practice Note contains guidance on the application of auditing standards issued by the Auditing Practices Board (APB) to the audit of occupational pension schemes in the United Kingdom. Audits of occupational pension schemes, where required by applicable legislation in the United Kingdom, may only be carried out by registered auditors or other persons approved by the Secretary of State for Work and Pensions.

The Practice Note is supplementary to, and should be read in conjunction with, International Standards on Auditing (ISAs) (UK and Ireland), which apply to all audits undertaken in the United Kingdom in respect of accounting periods commencing on or after 15 December 2004. This Practice Note sets out the special considerations relating to the audit of occupational pension schemes which arise from the individual ISAs (UK and Ireland). The Practice Note does not and is not intended to provide detailed guidance on the audits of pension schemes, so where no special considerations arise from a particular ISA (UK and Ireland), no material is included.

With effect from 6 April 2005 the Pensions Regulator (TPR) became the regulatory body responsible for the regulation of work-based pension schemes, replacing the Occupational Pensions Regulatory Authority (Opra). TPR adopts a risk-based approach to regulation and is able to make use of a wide range of powers, as detailed in the Pensions Act 2004. Previous guidance issued by Opra has been replaced by Codes of Practice and other TPR Guidance will be issued over time. Of particular importance to auditors of occupational schemes is the 'Reporting breaches of the law' Code of Practice[1].

The trustees of occupational pension schemes are required to meet the general provisions of trust law (taking into account the particular circumstances of pension schemes) and to comply with the provisions of the Pension Schemes Act 1993 (PSA 1993) and the Pensions Acts 1995 and 2004 ("PA 1995" and "PA 2004"). In addition, the activities of occupational pension schemes are subject to HM Revenue & Customs (HMRC) and financial services legislation. Scheme auditors need to be aware of the accounting and auditing implications of these requirements. Auditors of public sector schemes (and other statutory schemes established under separate statute) need to be aware of the particular legislative requirements relating to the scheme concerned.

The principal amendments and additions made to Practice Note (PN)15: 'The audit of occupational pension schemes in the United Kingdom' (Revised) to reflect developments since it was originally issued in 2004 are as follows:

- the guidance on the application of Statements of Auditing Standards has been replaced by guidance on the special considerations arising from ISAs (UK and Ireland), including the guidance that was set out in Bulletin 2005/05 "Audit Risk and Fraud – Supplementary Guidance for Auditors of Occupational Pension Schemes",
- references to the role and powers of Opra have been replaced by equivalent material in relation to TPR,
- the guidance on reporting on contributions, including the example auditors' statements in Appendix 6, have been revised to reflect the introduction of materiality as a consideration by The Occupational Pension Schemes

[1] A full list of all Codes of Practice together with any supporting guidance is available at www.thepensionsregulator.gov.uk

(Administration and Audited Accounts) (Amendment) Regulations 2005, (SI 2005 No. 2426) for financial periods beginning on or after 22 September 2005,
- the summary of the legal and regulatory framework in Appendix 2 has been updated to reflect the effects of the Pension Act 2004, Finance Act 2004 and Finance Act 2005,
- new guidance on the accounts required for an actuarial valuation, Pension Protection Fund valuations, and to support an application to the Fraud Compensation Fund has been inserted into Appendix 2,
- new guidance on the particular considerations that apply to non-statutory audit appointments is set out in Appendix 9.

This Practice Note has been prepared with advice and assistance from staff of TPR and is based on the legislation and regulations in effect at 31 January 2007.

Introduction

The purpose of this Practice Note is to give guidance on the application of International Standards on Auditing (ISAs) (UK and Ireland) to the audit of occupational pension schemes in the United Kingdom. They contain the basic principles and essential procedures, referred to as Auditing Standards, which are indicated in the text of the ISAs (UK and Ireland) in bold type, and with which auditors are required to comply in the conduct of any audit of financial statements.   1

Registered auditors are required to comply with Auditing Standards when conducting audits. This principle applies in the context of occupational pension schemes in the same way as to entities in any sector, irrespective of their size, but the way in which Auditing Standards are applied needs to be adapted to suit the particular characteristics of the entity audited. For example, an engagement to provide an auditors' statement about contributions does not constitute an audit but the guidance provided in this Practice Note relating to certain Auditing Standards is still relevant (see paragraph 22 below).   2

There is a variety of ways of providing pensions in the UK. Most occupational pension schemes in the UK are required to produce annual financial statements and to appoint scheme auditors to report on those financial statements and on the payment of contributions to the scheme. There are some exemptions from the statutory audit requirement, including certain small schemes and funded unapproved schemes[2]. In addition, auditors of certain insured schemes are required by statute only to report on contributions paid to the scheme, and do not report on the scheme's financial statements. Where statutory provisions do not require an audit, a scheme's trust deed and rules may still require its financial statements to be audited; however, a trust deed may not derogate from the statutory provisions in this regard.   3

The guidance in this Practice Note is written primarily for audits of financial statements of occupational pension schemes carried out to meet the requirements of pensions legislation. However the guidance is also applicable to audits undertaken solely under the terms of a scheme's trust deed or other agreement requiring auditors to provide a similar report, including requests from trustees where the scheme is otherwise exempt from audit or for financial statements prepared other than at the normal scheme year end.   4

[2] *The Occupational Pension Schemes (Scheme Administration) Regulations 1996 (SI 1996 No.1715) (as amended) define those schemes where the requirements under the PA 1995 to appoint auditors (and actuaries) do not apply.*

5   Where a scheme (often in conjunction with other related schemes) has established a common investment fund ("CIF"), each scheme's interest in the CIF is represented in its financial statements by units or shares in that fund shown at market value. The financial statements should also state the percentage of units in issue owned by the scheme at the beginning and the end of the scheme year and either:

- include the financial statements of the CIF itself within the scheme's annual report; or
- provide equivalent details of the CIF's portfolio and income and state the scheme's proportionate share thereof.

CIFs are normally set up under trust like pension schemes but they are not subject to the statutory audit requirement of the Pensions Act 1995. However, in order to support the valuation of the units and the disclosures by a participating scheme, the audit work on investments that would otherwise have been part of the audit of the scheme will normally need to be performed on the investment portfolio of the CIF, even if an audit of the CIF is not required by its own trust deed.

Legislative and regulatory framework

6   Pension schemes operate within a framework of law and regulation which is complex and differs in a number of respects from that applicable to commercial enterprises. This framework involves both trust law and specific statutory provisions, set out primarily in the PSA 1993, the PA 1995 and the PA 2004 and Regulations made under those Acts. Funded schemes are usually established under trust law or (generally in the case of public sector schemes) under specific statute, and for a non-statutory scheme to obtain registered scheme status it is essential that it is established under 'irrevocable trusts'. To the extent necessary to carry out their audit, it is essential for auditors of occupational pension schemes to have a good understanding of current pensions legislation and associated regulations, including accounting and taxation aspects. In the case of public sector schemes, this extends to the specific requirements applicable to each scheme, which may differ in a number of respects from the requirements of PA 1995 and PA 2004.

Occupational pension schemes – key characteristics

7   The general duties and powers of pension scheme trustees are essentially the same as those of other trustees. The principal elements of their responsibilities under trust law and statute are the proper management of funds provided by employees and their sponsoring employers during the course of their employment so as to provide pension benefits and, subsequently, the payment of these benefits to those entitled to them.

8   Benefits at retirement may be provided by an employer on a funded basis or on an unfunded 'pay-as-you-go' basis. The latter involves payment by the employer of pension commitments out of the employer's available resources when the employee has retired: the provision of pensions in this way involves no advance funding. No requirements exist for the audit of such arrangements (unless they are established under a specific statute), and they are not considered in this Practice Note.

9   Broadly, funded occupational pension schemes fall into two principal types, differentiated by the way in which pensions payable are determined. In defined benefit schemes, the pension to be paid is determined in advance, for example by reference to average or final salary levels. By contrast, in defined contribution schemes (also

called money purchase schemes) the amount to be paid is determined by the extent of funds available when an individual pension commences. Hybrid or mixed benefit schemes may also be established, combining both forms of benefits.

In the case of schemes providing defined benefits, determining the extent of future obligations to pay pensions and of the funding necessary to meet those obligations requires actuarial assessment. Trustees of such schemes are therefore required by statute to appoint a scheme actuary to report on the funding required and the security of accrued and prospective rights of scheme members. 10

Trustees of defined contribution schemes are not normally required to appoint a scheme actuary, although they may take actuarial advice to assess the potential level of benefits available. Some but not all defined contribution schemes buy annuities from third parties to avoid uncertainty and the ongoing obligation to pay pensions. 11

Trustees of nearly all funded occupational schemes, irrespective of the method of funding, are required by regulations made under the PA 1995[3] to make available to members an annual report. The content of the annual report varies with the type of scheme. It generally comprises the following: 12

(a) a trustees' report, giving a review of the management of the scheme, membership statistics and developments during the period;
(b) an investment report, reviewing the investment policy and performance of the scheme;
(c) (i) for schemes that have yet to have a Scheme Specific Funding ("SSF") actuarial valuation, a statement and certificate from the appointed scheme actuary (generally when the scheme provides defined benefits), or
 (ii) for schemes that have had an SSF valuation, a copy of the certificate from the scheme actuary as to the adequacy of contributions and a copy of the latest Summary Funding Statement prepared by the trustees;
(d) financial statements showing a true and fair view of the financial transactions of the scheme during the period and of the disposition of its assets and liabilities at the end of the period;
(e) an independent auditors' report on the financial statements;
(f) a trustees' summary of contributions; and
(g) an independent auditors' statement about contributions payable to the scheme.

The annual report may also include a compliance statement, containing administrative disclosures required by law or made voluntarily.

Although the PA 1995 refers to auditors as 'professional advisers' of the trustees, scheme auditors are required by the Act to be independent of the scheme, and their function is to provide an objective opinion on the scheme's financial statements and a statement about contributions.

As indicated above, the statutory regime applying to occupational schemes is complex and forms of scheme are diverse. In addition, because the activities of a scheme are governed by trust law, the scheme auditors need to be aware of the principal terms of the deed or other instrument establishing the scheme. The statutory regime and trust law have a significant effect on the scheme auditors' work, as do other factors concerning the way in which scheme trustees fulfill their responsibilities. 13

---

[3] *The Occupational Pension Schemes (Disclosure of Information) Regulations 1996, SI 1996 No.1655.*

Financial statements

14 The form and content of a pension scheme's financial statements are specified in the Occupational Pension Schemes (Requirement to obtain Audited Accounts and a Statement from the Auditor) Regulations 1996[4] ('the Audited Accounts Regulations'). These require scheme trustees to obtain financial statements which:

   (a) contain specified information, set out in the Schedule to the Audited Accounts Regulations; and
   (b) show a true and fair view of the financial transactions of the scheme during the scheme year and of the amount and disposition as at the end of the scheme year of its assets and of its liabilities, other than liabilities to pay pensions and benefits after the end of the scheme year.

15 The Audited Accounts Regulations require the trustees to state whether the financial statements have been prepared in accordance with the most recent applicable version of the Statement of Recommended Practice 'Financial Reports of Pension Schemes' ('the Pensions SORP')[5] and to indicate any material departures from its guidance. The Pensions SORP supplements general accounting principles set out in Financial Reporting Standards and Statements of Standard Accounting Practice, indicating best practice in accounting and financial reporting by pension schemes. Consequently it is normally necessary to follow the guidance in the Pensions SORP in order for pension scheme financial statements to show a true and fair view.

16 The nature of applicable accounting requirements and their effect on auditors' reports are considered in more detail in the Practice Note's section on ISA (UK and Ireland) 700 'The auditor's report on financial statements'.

Contents of the auditor's report on pension scheme financial statements

17 The responsibilities of pension scheme auditors reflect the nature of schemes' financial statements.

18 Occupational pension scheme financial statements exclude estimates of future pension benefits payable: in the case of defined benefit schemes, information about the extent of liabilities for future benefits and the adequacy of the scheme's funding are included in the section of the annual report dealing with the actuary's report; the need to assess future liabilities does not arise in defined contribution schemes. Thus the Audited Accounts Regulations do not require scheme auditors to express an opinion as to whether the financial statements of a pension scheme prepared by or on behalf of its trustees show a true and fair view of its state of affairs but whether the financial statements obtained by the trustees show a true and fair view of the scheme's

   (i) financial transactions and assets, and
   (ii) liabilities, other than liabilities to pay pensions and benefits after the end of the scheme year.

19 Scheme auditors' statutory responsibilities under the PA 1995 do not require them to undertake work to determine whether the trustees' report or other sections of the

---

[4] *The Occupational Pension Schemes (Requirement to obtain Audited Accounts and a Statement from the Auditor) Regulations 1996, SI 1996 No.1975, as amended (most recently by The Occupational Pension Schemes (Administration and Audited Accounts) (Amendment) Regulations 2005, SI 2005 No. 2426)*

[5] *Issued by the Pensions Research Accountants Group (PRAG) in accordance with the Accounting Standards Board's code of practice for the development and issue of SORPs.*

This aspect of the scheme auditors' work is discussed further in the section dealing with ISA (UK and Ireland) 570 'Going concern'.

Reliance on third parties

Trustees of occupational pensions schemes – who do not necessarily have first hand actuarial, accounting or other relevant experience – frequently rely on advice or services from experts in order to fulfil their responsibilities to safeguard the interests of scheme members. The PA 1995 also requires trustees to appoint professional advisers in certain areas and to ensure that such advisers are appropriately qualified.

Reliance on third parties – actuaries

To provide the actuarial skills needed to determine funding requirements of a defined benefit scheme, trustees of such schemes are, in all but a few cases, specifically required by statute to appoint a scheme actuary to provide them with necessary valuations and advice. Consideration of the action taken by trustees in response to advice from the scheme actuary consequently forms an important element of the work undertaken by the scheme auditors in order to report on contributions to a defined benefit scheme.

When forming an opinion on the view shown by a scheme's financial statements, scheme auditors are not required to express an opinion as to the completeness or accuracy of the long term liabilities determined by a scheme's actuary; the actuary's certificate and statement are the responsibility of the scheme actuary. However, as set out in the Auditors' Code, scheme auditors do not permit their names to be associated with information inconsistent with their report or which they consider to be misleading. Scheme auditors therefore normally seek to discuss with the scheme actuary any matters of mutual interest.

The statutory duty to report matters of material significance to TPR applies to scheme actuaries, the trustees and all others who are involved in the administration of a scheme, as well as to the scheme auditor. Consequently, scheme auditors who become aware of a matter which may be reportable consider whether to discuss the circumstances with the scheme actuary and/or the trustees where this may assist them in forming their opinion as to whether to report to TPR.

To facilitate effective liaison, scheme auditors and scheme actuaries seek agreement from the trustees of a scheme to communication between them as part of their terms of engagement when accepting appointment. Further commentary concerning liaison with the scheme actuary is set out in a separate section of this Practice Note.

Reliance on third parties – investment managers and custodians

Investments form the principal asset of a pension scheme, and income from investments is an important element in ensuring that the scheme can meet future pension obligations. The level of funds available and the expected future yield are also important elements of the scheme actuary's valuation of a defined benefit scheme.

The PA 1995 provides for trustees to appoint investment managers to undertake the management of the funds available for investment. The trustees nevertheless retain ultimate responsibility for the proper use of the scheme's funds, and are specifically required to determine the investment policy appropriate to a particular scheme's circumstances. This policy is set out in the trustees' Statement of Investment Principles and is often summarised in the annual report to scheme members.

38 Scheme auditors take steps to determine that all investments and income from investments due to the scheme are properly reflected in its financial statements. When trustees have appointed an investment manager or custodian to undertake work on the scheme's behalf, scheme auditors consider the controls operated by the trustees over the service provider.

39 Issues relating to obtaining sufficient appropriate evidence when the trustees have delegated some of their functions to investment managers or custodians are discussed in the section dealing with ISA (UK and Ireland) 402 'Audit Considerations Relating to Entities Using Service Organisations'.

Reliance on third parties – scheme administrators

40 Trustees of pension schemes may delegate aspects of administration (although not ultimate responsibility), including record keeping and matters relating to contributions and benefits to a third party (including the sponsoring employer – see below). In such cases, the scheme auditors normally obtain direct access to the relevant records of the third party in order to obtain relevant audit evidence, as discussed in the section dealing with ISA (UK and Ireland) 402.

Reliance on third parties – sponsoring employers

41 In many cases, the relationship between the scheme and the sponsoring employer may consist only of contractual arrangements relating to the establishment of the scheme. However, in the case of on-going schemes, the sponsoring employer may also provide administrative services. Such services may be the subject of a separate contract between the employer and the trustees.

42 Where trustees delegate administrative work to the sponsoring employer (or to another service provider), scheme auditors assess the controls established by the trustees over the work being carried out to ensure inter alia the completeness and accuracy of records maintained by the sponsoring employer (or other service provider) on behalf of the scheme.

Ethical Standards

43 APB Ethical Standards for Auditors apply to the audit of financial statements, including those of occupational pension schemes. Particular issues that the audit engagement partner of a pension scheme has regard to when assessing possible threats to independence and objectivity and the nature and extent of the safeguards to be applied include:

- any professional relationships that he or his firm have with organisations that contribute to the scheme (eg whether the firm also audits the sponsoring employer);
- non-audit services provided to the trustees of the scheme by the firm (eg accounting, actuarial, administrative and risk management services), and
- non-audit services provided to the sponsoring employer by the firm.

The APB Ethical Standards include a small number of additional requirements that apply to the audits of listed companies[8]. The Ethical Standards require that an audit firm's policies and procedures set out the circumstances in which these additional requirements apply to the audits of non-listed clients, taking into consideration the nature of the entity's business, its size, the number of its employees and the range of its stakeholders. These may include some occupational pension schemes.

The audit of financial statements

ISAs (UK and Ireland) apply to the conduct of all audits in respect of accounting periods commencing on or after 15 December 2004. This includes audits of the financial statements of occupational pension schemes. The purpose of the following paragraphs is to identify the special considerations arising from the application of certain 'bold letter' requirements to the audits of occupational pension schemes, and to suggest ways in which these can be addressed (extracts from ISAs (UK and Ireland) are indicated by grey-shaded boxes below). This Practice Note does not contain commentary on all of the bold letter requirements included in the ISAs (UK and Ireland) and reading it should not be seen as an alternative to reading the relevant ISAs (UK and Ireland) in their entirety. In addition, where no special considerations arise from a particular ISA (UK and Ireland), no material is included.

ISA (UK and Ireland) 200: Objective and General Principles Governing an Audit of Financial Statements

Background note

The purpose of this ISA (UK and Ireland) is to establish standards and provide guidance on the objective and general principles governing an audit of financial statements.

The auditor should plan and perform an audit with an attitude of professional scepticism, recognising that circumstances may exist that cause the financial statements to be materially misstated (paragraph 6).

44 Auditing Standards include a requirement for auditors to comply with the APB's Ethical Standards and relevant ethical guidance issued by the auditor's professional body in the conduct of any audit of financial statements, which apply equally to audits of pension schemes. A fundamental principle is that practitioners should not accept or perform work which they are not competent to undertake. The importance of technical competence is also underlined in The Auditors' Code issued by the APB, that is appended to the APB's Scope and Authority of Pronouncements (Revised) and states that the necessary degree of professional skill demands an understanding of financial reporting and business. Practitioners should not undertake the audit of occupational pension schemes unless they are satisfied that they have or can attain the necessary level of competence.

45 Before commencing the audit of an occupational pension scheme, a firm ensures that it has enough staff who have adequate knowledge and experience of such audits.

---

[8] ES1 paragraph 42, ES3 paragraph 11, ES5 paragraph 87 and ES5 paragraph 120.

Staff involved in an audit of an occupational pension scheme will have a broad understanding, commensurate with the individual's role and responsibilities in the audit process, of:

- the status (e.g. open, closed to new members, closed to future accrual) and nature of the scheme;
- the scheme's trust deed and rules;
- the most significant parts of the relevant regulator's guidance; and
- the relevant general principles of the Pensions SORP.

ISA (UK and Ireland) 210: Terms of Audit Engagements

Background note

The purpose of this ISA (UK and Ireland) is to establish standards and provide guidance on agreeing the terms of the engagement with the client.

The auditor and the client should agree on the terms of the engagement. (paragraph 2)

The auditor should confirm that the engagement letter documents and confirms the auditor's acceptance of the appointment, and includes a summary of the responsibilities of those charged with governance and of the auditor, the scope of the engagement and the form of any reports. (paragraph 5-1)

46 ISA (UK and Ireland) 210 requires that an engagement letter be obtained for all audit appointments. This requirement supplements that included in the PA 1995 whereby trustees are required to appoint the scheme's auditors.

The appointment of scheme auditors

47 Section 47(1)(a) of the PA 1995 requires the trustees or managers of most occupational pension schemes to appoint Statutory Scheme Auditors. The Scheme Administration Regulations (SI 1996 No 1715, regulation 3), as amended, exempt a number of schemes from appointing scheme auditors (see paragraph 61 of Appendix 2).

Method of appointment under statute

48 To be effective, the appointment of scheme auditors (or, where a scheme is exempt from the requirement to appoint a 'scheme auditor', any non-statutory auditor) must be made in accordance with the Regulations[9]. The trustees or managers of the scheme forward a Notice of Appointment to the auditors specifying:

- the date the appointment is due to take effect,
- to whom the auditors are to report, and
- from whom the auditors will take instructions.

---

[9] *The Occupational Pension Schemes (Scheme Administration) Regulations 1996, SI 1996 No. 1715, as amended.*

The date the appointment is due to take effect ('the effective date') is at a future date. The date of appointment does not become effective until the auditors have acknowledged receipt of the Notice of Appointment. This being the case, a practical approach may be for the Notice of Appointment to specify the 'effective date' as being the date of the auditors' acknowledgement.

It is important that the date of the scheme year end should be established. To facilitate this it is desirable for the Notice of Appointment to:

- state the date of the scheme year end. If the appointment is in relation to a scheme year which has already ended the engagement terms should specify which scheme years will be subject to audit, and
- be clear as to the name of the scheme to which the appointment is proposed. In the case of an appointment covering a number of schemes, there should normally be separate Notices of Appointment for each or, if particular circumstances warrant it, a schedule detailing the separate schemes.

For the appointment to be effective, the PA 1995 requires auditors to acknowledge receipt of the Notice of Appointment within one month of its date of receipt. Appointment is not effective unless and until this acknowledgement is sent by the auditors within the one month period. As the acknowledgement makes the appointment effective from the date specified in the Notice of Appointment, auditors consider whether they are aware of any matters which may have arisen since the effective date which may lead to an obligation to make a report to TPR.

The PA 1995 also requires the auditors to state that they will notify the trustees or managers immediately they become aware of the existence of any conflict of interest to which they are subject in relation to the scheme. In order to assist with identifying conflicts of interest, some audit firms request trustees to provide representations on this matter before they accept appointment, and obtain re-confirmation of the position in the annual representation letter.

An example Notice of Appointment and an example letter of acknowledgement of appointment are set out in Appendix 4.

Auditors will not send the acknowledgement until they have completed pre-acceptance procedures including, for example:

- considering their competence to undertake the engagement (including their ability to manage potential conflicts of interest, and knowledge of the laws and regulations to which the scheme is subject),
- establishing requisite knowledge of the client, including the nature of the scheme, the names of the trustees and previous auditors, any investment managers or administrators, the scheme year-end, and obtaining a copy of the trust deed and rules and the last set of audited financial statements, and
- obtaining from the trustees a written notice of resignation made by the previous auditors[10], and corresponding with the previous auditors.

If the auditors do not acknowledge appointment within one month, the Notice of Appointment ceases to be valid. The trustees or managers will then need to provide a new Notice of Appointment.

---

[10] The statement or declaration on resignation is to be given to the succeeding auditors by the trustees rather than by the outgoing auditors. Regulations require that the statement or declaration should be provided to the incoming auditors within fourteen days from the date on which the trustees or managers receive it or the date of the new appointment whichever is the later. In practice, incoming auditors are likely to wish to have access to a statement or declaration before they accept appointment.

55 It will normally be beneficial for the auditors to have undertaken pre-acceptance procedures and, at least in principle, agreed their terms of engagement with the trustees before the Notice of Appointment is sent to them. To facilitate this process, the trustees may decide to notify the auditors of a proposed appointment prior to sending the formal Notice of Appointment under the Regulations. This would allow the auditors to progress their acceptance procedures prior to receiving the formal notification, thereby allowing the acknowledgement of their acceptance to be submitted within the one month of receipt required by the Regulations.

56 Once the appointment is effective (i.e. once the acknowledgement letter has been completed and returned within one month of receipt of the Notice of Appointment), the scheme auditors finalise the engagement terms with the trustees and document these in an engagement letter. For further guidance on this see the section on engagement letters in Appendix 4.

57 If the resignation, removal or death of a scheme auditor occurs, the Scheme Administration Regulations require that a new appointment be made within three months. Failure to appoint new auditors within the three-month period may be a matter of material significance to TPR. If auditors are requested to accept appointment after three months from the date when a previous auditor left office, or if there was no previous auditor appointed under the PA 1995 and the scheme is not a new one[11], the breach will need to be noted and may need to be reported to TPR.

The letter of engagement

58 The same basic principles used in drafting engagement letters apply in relation to the audit of pension schemes as to the audit of any entity. Practical considerations arising from the particular characteristics of pension schemes are considered below.

59 Paragraph 1-5 of ISA (UK and Ireland) 210 indicates that the term 'client' used in paragraph 1 means the addressee of the scheme auditors' report (the client is the trustee(s)). Consequently, the scheme auditors agree the terms of their engagement with the trustees of the scheme and address their letter of engagement to the trustees.

60 The scheme auditors may consider ensuring that all the trustees receive a copy of the letter, and establishing that the trustees agree to the terms of the engagement by asking for a signed copy of the letter to be returned as confirmation of this. If the trustees are not engaged in the day-to-day running of the scheme, the scheme auditors may wish to request the trustees to send a copy of the engagement letter to the administrators, together with a more detailed description of the audit work to be undertaken and any client assistance to be given.

61 Scheme auditors set out the nature and scope of their audit obligations under PA 1995 so as to ensure trustees are aware of the extent of those responsibilities. In particular, they include reference to their responsibility to report on the contributions payable to the scheme and to the statutory duty to report to TPR in certain circumstances, making it clear that the duty is to report matters if found, and does not involve undertaking additional work to identify reportable matters.

62 Scheme auditors do not have a right of access under the PA 1995 to information held by third parties. Consequently, it is necessary for scheme auditors to request such

---

[11] *There is no time period in the PA 1995 for the appointment of auditors by newly-constituted schemes. Schemes are simply required to have one in place. Normally appointments will take place as the scheme is established as one of a series of adviser and service provider appointments by the trustees.*

information, when necessary for their audit, through the trustees. Scheme auditors therefore include in the engagement letter a paragraph relating to access to third parties to whom the trustees delegate particular functions, and to their records relating to the pension scheme. Scheme auditors may require information from the:

- administrator;
- investment manager;
- custodian;
- sponsoring employer – or employers where there is a multi-employer scheme – and the sponsoring employer's auditors;
- scheme actuary.

In view of the importance of the scheme actuary's work to the information contained in a scheme's annual report, it is normally appropriate for scheme auditors to obtain the trustees' agreement to direct dealings with the scheme actuary, both in terms of ongoing liaison regarding the affairs of the scheme and also in respect of the scheme actuary's and scheme auditors' duty to report matters of material significance directly to TPR, and to document this agreement in their engagement letter. 63

Regulations made under the PA 1995 require the employer to notify the trustees, within one month, of the occurrence of any event relating to the employer which there is reasonable cause to believe will be of material significance to the trustees or the scheme's professional advisers in the exercise of their functions. Scheme auditors may wish to include a term in their engagement letter requiring the trustees to undertake to inform the scheme auditors of any matters which come to their attention which may be relevant to the audit. 64

Trustees may issue other reports to scheme members in addition to the annual report required by statute. For example, they may provide summary reports and financial statements, and periodic newsletters. Where this is the case, the engagement letter also sets out the scheme auditors' responsibilities, if any, in respect of such other reports. 65

In certain circumstances, trustees may wish the scheme auditors to provide additional reports, for example reports to the HMRC or the Department for Work and Pensions or to trustees of other schemes. Whilst the scheme auditors may initiate discussion of such additional work, it is the responsibility of the trustees to identify the need for any additional reports and to instruct the scheme auditors accordingly. 66

Appendix 4 gives specimen paragraphs for engagement letters for 67

(a) the audit of an occupational pension scheme required to obtain audited financial statements under section 41 of the PA 1995; and
(b) the auditors' statement about contributions (with additional paragraphs for earmarked pension schemes).

The Appendix also includes details of the procedural matters to be followed when fulfilling the requirements of the PA 1995. 68

Resignation or removal of auditors

The Scheme Administration Regulations require a written notice of resignation by the scheme auditors which should contain either: 69

- a statement specifying the circumstances; or
- a declaration of no circumstances.

70 The statement is made by the outgoing scheme auditors specifying any circumstances connected with their resignation which, in their opinion, significantly affect the interests of the members or prospective members of, or beneficiaries under, the scheme. Under the Disclosure Regulations, the annual report must include a copy of any statement made on resignation or removal in accordance with regulations made under s47(6) PA 1995. Where the auditors know of no such circumstances, and hence make a declaration to that effect, there is no requirement to include this declaration in the annual report, although it is often included for the avoidance of doubt. The trustees are required to provide a copy of the statement or declaration to the succeeding scheme auditors.

> On recurring audits, the auditor should consider whether circumstances require the terms of engagement to be revised and whether there is a need to remind the client of the existing terms of the engagement. (paragraph 10)

71 The auditor considers annually whether changes to the legal and regulatory requirements may require the terms of the engagement letter to be revised.

ISA (UK and Ireland) 240: The Auditor's Responsibility to Consider Fraud in an Audit of Financial Statements

> **Background note**
>
> The purpose of this ISA (UK and Ireland) is to establish basic principles and essential procedures and to provide guidance on the auditor's responsibility to consider fraud in an audit of financial statements and expand on how the standards and guidance in ISA (UK and Ireland) 315 and ISA (UK and Ireland) 330 are to be applied in relation to the risks of material misstatement due to fraud. The standards and guidance in this ISA (UK and Ireland) are intended to be integrated into the overall audit process.

> In planning and performing the audit to reduce audit risk to an acceptably low level, the auditor should consider the risks of material misstatements in the financial statements due to fraud. (paragraph 3)
>
> The auditor should maintain an attitude of professional scepticism throughout the audit, recognising the possibility that a material misstatement due to fraud could exist, notwithstanding the auditor's past experience with the entity about the honesty and integrity of management and those charged with governance. (paragraph 24)
>
> The auditor should make inquiries of management, internal audit, and others within the entity as appropriate, to determine whether they have knowledge of any actual, suspected or alleged fraud affecting the entity. (paragraph 38)

72 Auditors of pension schemes should be aware that the potential for fraud exists in all schemes. Although due to the nature of pension schemes (not profit-making and not trading) the risk of fraudulent financial reporting can generally be considered to be low, the risk of misappropriation of assets remains. Professional scepticism therefore remains key.

> The auditor should make inquiries of those charged with governance to determine whether they have knowledge of any actual, suspected or alleged fraud affecting the entity (paragraph 46).
>
> When obtaining an understanding of the entity and its environment, including its internal control, the auditor should consider whether the information obtained indicates that one or more fraud risk factors are present. (paragraph 48)

73 The trustees of a pension scheme are responsible for ensuring that the assets and revenues of the scheme are adequately safeguarded against the effects of fraud and error through the implementation of appropriate controls. This responsibility remains with trustees even if they have delegated some or all of their executive functions to third parties.

74 Examples of types of fraud which may occur in the context of a pension scheme include:

- misappropriation of assets;
- non-payment of contributions (employee/employer) to the scheme by the employer;
- using assets of the scheme directly or as collateral for borrowing by the employer or an associate of the employer;
- misapplying the assets of a scheme to meet the obligations and expenses of another scheme or of the sponsoring employer;
- buying/selling of scheme assets by the investment manager without the required mandate or authorisation;
- lending of scheme assets by the custodian without authorisation;
- exchange of assets without sufficient valuable consideration (for example, selling assets such as property at below market value);
- assets of the scheme used for the personal preferment of the trustees or used for the personal preferment of an individual scheme member;
- benefit claims by members or their beneficiaries to which they are not entitled – for example, failure to notify a scheme of the death of a true beneficiary;
- creation of fictitious scheme records by the administrator – for example, dummy beneficiary records.

75 These examples are only illustrative and do not cover all situations which may arise. Guidance on the internal control procedures which can be put in place by trustees, and are designed to minimise the risk of fraud or error occurring, is included in the section on ISA (UK and Ireland) 315 'Obtaining an Understanding of the Entity and Its Environment and Assessing the Risks of Material Misstatement'. Instances of actual or suspected fraud are also likely to involve breaches of specific statutory or trust law requirements relating to pension schemes.

76 Examples of conditions or events which may increase the risk of fraud are:

- trustees or scheme management displaying a significant disregard for the various regulatory authorities;
- trustees or scheme management having little or no involvement in the day-to-day administration of the scheme;
- trustees or scheme management having ready access to the scheme's assets and an ability to override any internal controls;
- trustees or scheme management failing to put in place arrangements to monitor activities undertaken by third parties, including the employer;

- trustees or scheme management displaying a lack of candour in dealings with members, the scheme actuary or the scheme auditors on significant matters affecting scheme assets;
- the sponsoring employer operating in an industry with increasing business failures, or itself having financial difficulties;
- significant levels, or unusual types, of related party transactions (including employer-related investments) involving unaudited entities or entities audited by other firms.

77 The audit planning process includes an assessment of the risk of material misstatements, whether arising from fraud or error. Conditions or events which increase the risk of fraud and error include previous experience or incidents which call into question the competence or integrity of persons involved in the operation of the scheme, which include:

- the trustees;
- the sponsoring employer, its directors or staff (and in the case of groups, those of the holding company or subsidiary undertakings);
- third parties to whom the trustees have delegated the conduct of scheme activities, for example:
  - the investment manager (including the insurance company) or investment adviser,
  - the property manager,
  - the scheme administrator,
  - the investment custodian, and
  - payroll administrator (both employee and pensioner payroll);
- professional advisers, principally
  - the actuary, and
  - the lawyer.

78 Section 249A of PA 2004 requires trustees or managers of an occupational pension scheme to establish and operate internal controls which are adequate for the purpose of securing that the scheme is administered and managed in accordance with the scheme's rules and in accordance with the requirements of the law. A Code of Practice – Internal controls, and supporting guidance has been issued by TPR setting out TPR's expectations of how occupational pension schemes should satisfy the legal requirement to have adequate controls in place.

79 The auditor is not required to review or conclude on the adequacy of the approach taken by trustees to assess and address risks faced by their scheme. However, where the trustees have produced documentation that sets out their assessment of the various risks facing the scheme, and how they believe those risks are controlled and mitigated, the auditor has regard to that documentation when performing his own assessment of the risk of material misstatements to financial reporting resulting from fraud.

80 In assessing the risk of misstatement arising from fraud, scheme auditors also consider the extent of the trustees' involvement in the day-to-day administration of the scheme, their access to its resources and their ability, collectively or individually, to override any internal controls. Additionally, they consider the arrangements the trustees have put in place to monitor work undertaken by third parties, for example custodianship of investments or the day-to-day administration of the scheme, including those circumstances where the services are provided by the sponsoring employer.

> When performing analytical procedures to obtain an understanding of the entity and its environment, including its internal control, the auditor should consider unusual or unexpected relationships that may indicate risks of material misstatement due to fraud. (paragraph 53)

> The auditor should consider whether analytical procedures that are performed at or near the end of the audit when forming an overall conclusion as to whether the financial statements as a whole are consistent with the auditor's knowledge of the business indicate a previously unrecognised risk of material misstatement due to fraud. (paragraph 85)

81 Detailed guidance on the analytical techniques that may be applied either to obtain an understanding of a scheme or at or near the end of the audit is set out in the section of this Practice Note dealing with ISA (UK and Ireland) 520.

82 Determining which particular trends and relationships may indicate risks of material misstatement due to fraud requires professional judgement. Unusual fluctuations in benefits and other payments, particularly when not matched by matching changes in the number and status of members, may indicate fraudulent activity.

> If the auditor has identified a fraud or has obtained information that indicates that a fraud may exist, the auditor should communicate these matters as soon as practicable to the appropriate level of management. (paragraph 93)

> The auditor should document communications about fraud made to management, those charged with governance, regulators and others. (paragraph 109)

Reporting to management

83 Scheme auditors communicate their findings to the appropriate level of management, unless it is concluded that the suspected or actual instance of fraud ought to be reported to TPR and/or the Serious Organised Crime Agency (SOCA) (which has taken over the functions of the National Criminal Intelligence Service (NCIS)) in the public interest and that the auditor no longer has confidence in the integrity of the directors or equivalents (in the case of a pension scheme, the trustees or managers). In this case, the scheme auditor makes a report direct to TPR/SOCA in the public interest, without delay and without informing the trustees in advance.

84 In the case of pension schemes where the trustees are not involved in the day-to-day management of the scheme, having delegated this function to staff or a third party, and it is the latter who are suspected of involvement in fraud, the scheme auditor may consider that it is appropriate to communicate with the trustees in the first instance.

Reporting to addressees of the scheme auditor's report on the financial statements

85 The scheme auditor's report on financial statements is addressed to the trustees of the scheme concerned, and to other parties if required by the trust deed or other applicable rules. Even where an actual or suspected fraud has already been communicated fully to the trustees, the scheme auditor's report on the financial

statements includes details of any fundamental uncertainty, or disagreement over disclosure of a suspected or actual instance of fraud having a material effect on the financial statements.

Reporting to third parties

86 Any suspected or actual fraud found at a pension scheme will normally give rise to a statutory duty to report to TPR. Guidance on this area is contained in the section of this Practice Note dealing with Section B of ISA (UK and Ireland) 250.

> When the auditor has concluded that the presumption that there is a risk of material misstatement due to fraud related to revenue recognition is not applicable to the circumstances of the engagement, the auditor should document the reasons for that conclusion. (paragraph 110)

87 Auditors of pension schemes usually rebut the presumption that revenue recognition gives rise to a risk of material misstatement due to fraud. Revenue in a pension scheme is generally contributions and investment income, pension schemes are not profit making entities and pension scheme accounts are not publicly available. Unlike sales revenue of a commercial entity, there is little scope to manipulate revenue of a pension scheme, for example through false invoicing or misuse of credit notes. Given these facts, there is therefore likely to be little incentive for revenue to be fraudulently misstated.

ISA (UK and Ireland) 250: Section A – Consideration of Laws and Regulations in an Audit of Financial Statements

> **Background note**
>
> The purpose of this ISA (UK and Ireland) is to establish standards and provide guidance on the auditor's responsibility to consider laws and regulations in the audit of financial statements.

> When designing and performing audit procedures and in evaluating and reporting the results thereof, the auditor should recognise that non-compliance by the entity with laws and regulations may materially affect the financial statements. (paragraph 2)
>
> In accordance with ISA (UK and Ireland) 200, "Objective and General principles Governing an Audit of Financial Statements" the auditor should plan and perform the audit with an attitude of professional scepticism recognising that the audit may reveal conditions or events that would lead to questioning whether an entity is complying with laws and regulations. (paragraph 13)
>
> In order to plan the audit, the auditor should obtain a general understanding of the legal and regulatory framework applicable to the entity and the industry and how the entity is complying with that framework. (paragraph 15)

Paragraph 2 of ISA (UK and Ireland) 250 states that auditors should recognise that non-compliance by the entity with laws and regulations may materially affect the financial statements. In the case of a pension scheme, relevant laws and regulations include trust law, and hence the specific requirements of the scheme's governing document (usually a trust deed). 88

The regulatory framework

The regulatory framework within which an occupational pension scheme operates does not alter the nature of the scheme auditors' responsibility to consider laws and regulations in an audit of financial statements, as described by ISA (UK and Ireland) 250. 89

The trustees of a pension scheme are responsible for ensuring that the necessary controls are in place to ensure compliance with applicable laws and regulations, and to detect and correct any breaches that have occurred, even if they have delegated some of their executive functions to professional staff or advisers. 90

> After obtaining the general understanding, the auditor should perform further audit procedures to help identify instances of non-compliance with those laws and regulations where non-compliance should be considered when preparing financial statements, specifically:
>
> (a) Inquiring of management as to whether the entity is in compliance with such laws and regulations;
> (b) Inspecting correspondence with the relevant licensing or regulatory authorities; and.
> (c) Enquiring of those charged with governance as to whether they are on notice of any such possible instances of non-compliance with law or regulations. (paragraph 18)
>
> In the UK and Ireland, the auditor's procedures should be designed to help identify possible or actual instances of non-compliance with those laws and regulations which provide a legal framework within which the entity conducts its business and which are central to the entity's ability to conduct its business and hence to its financial statements. (paragraph 18-1)

Classification of laws and regulations

Laws and regulations relevant to the audit of a pension scheme can be regarded as falling into three main categories: 91

(a) those which relate directly to the preparation of the entity's financial statements, or the inclusion or disclosure of specific items in the financial statements,
(b) those which relate to the payment of contributions to the scheme,
(c) those which provide a legal framework[12] within which the entity conducts its business and which are central to the entity's ability to conduct its business and hence to its financial statements.

Examples of items falling into each of these categories are discussed in the following paragraphs. Laws and regulations which do not fall into either category need not be taken into account in planning audit work to be undertaken: however, scheme 92

---

[12] TPR has issued a series of Codes of Practice, which set out the regulator's expectations of how relevant laws and regulations should be complied with in practice.

auditors are required to remain alert to the possibility of breaches of other requirements, including trust law, and to investigate any which come to their attention.

Laws relating directly to the preparation of the financial statements

93 ISA (UK and Ireland) 250 requires auditors to obtain sufficient appropriate audit evidence about compliance with those laws and regulations which relate directly to the preparation of, or the inclusion or disclosure of specific items in, the financial statements. The ISA (UK and Ireland) also requires auditors to obtain evidence relating to compliance with laws and regulations where there is a statutory requirement for auditors to report, as part of the audit of financial statements, on whether the entity complies with those provisions.

94 The laws and regulations which relate directly to the preparation of financial statements of pension schemes, or where there is a statutory duty for scheme auditors to report on compliance as part of the audit, are included in the list of relevant legislation set out in Appendix 1. All staff involved in a scheme's audit need a broad understanding of the requirements of the PSA 1993, PA 1995, PA 2004 and related Regulations, in particular of the principal requirements of the Administration Regulations (SI No 1996/1715) and the Audited Accounts Regulations (SI No 1996/1975), as amended by subsequent regulations, and of the general principles of the Pensions SORP.

95 Further knowledge is required, commensurate with the individual's role and responsibilities in the audit process, of:

- the trust deed and rules of a particular scheme;
- the legal and regulatory framework applicable to occupational pension schemes sufficient to meet the requirements of ISAs (UK and Ireland), including:
  - the responsibilities of pension scheme trustees under general trust law and the Pensions Act 1995 and 2004,
  - responsibilities of pension scheme managers, the sponsoring employer, any professional adviser or any prescribed person acting in connection with the scheme;
- the detailed requirements concerning the preparation of the financial statements and other matters on which scheme auditors are required routinely to report.

96 Scheme auditors also gain an understanding of the pension scheme's trust deed and plan and conduct their audit so as to ensure that their audit procedures cover compliance with any special provisions as to the disclosure of information in the financial statements or reporting requirements. Users of the financial statements of a scheme reasonably expect that the transactions recorded within them are authorised by the governing document: hence, in order to show a true and fair view, due regard needs to be given to disclosure of any material non-compliance with the governing document.

Laws relating to the payment of contributions to the scheme

97 ISA (UK and Ireland) 250 indicates that where statutory requirements exist which require the auditors to report, as part of the audit of the financial statements, whether the entity complies with certain provisions of laws or regulations, the auditors need to have a sufficient understanding of such laws and regulations and to test for compliance with such provisions.

Scheme auditors are required, in addition to their opinion on the financial statements, to give a statement as to whether the scheme has received contributions in accordance with legislative requirements. In the case of ear-marked schemes, which are not required to prepare audited financial statements, auditors are required by statute only to report about contributions. In addition to the statutory requirements, the trust deed and rules of schemes may require auditors to report on whether contributions have been paid to the scheme in accordance with the rules of the scheme and with the recommendations of the actuary, where one is appointed. 98

Further considerations relating to reporting on contributions are set out in paragraphs 312-347 below. 99

Laws which are central to the pension scheme's conduct of its activities and to its financial statements

ISA (UK and Ireland) 250 requires auditors to carry out specified steps to help identify possible or actual instances of non-compliance with those laws and regulations which fall into the category of those that are central to the entity's ability to conduct its business. 100

'Central' is described in the ISA (UK and Ireland) as relating to those laws and regulations where: 101
(a) compliance is a pre-requisite of obtaining a license to operate; or
(b) non-compliance may reasonably be expected to result in the entity ceasing operations, or call into question the entity's status as a going concern.

In the context of pension schemes, these two criteria indicate that laws and regulations are central to a particular scheme when breaches would have any of the following consequences: 102

(a) action by HMRC to rescind registered status (for example, as a result of a change to the constitution or the nature and value of benefits provided which do not comply with the legislation); or
(b) action by TPR under sections 3-9 or 11 of the PA 1995, as amended by the PA 2004:
   – to remove or replace the scheme's trustees. Action to remove trustees can be taken where in TPR's opinion there is serious or persistent breach of their fiduciary duties. TPR has the power to appoint trustees, where necessary, to secure that the trustees as a whole have the necessary skill and knowledge, to secure proper use of assets, or to ensure that there is a sufficient number of trustees for the proper administration of the scheme;
   – to wind up the scheme. This action may be taken where TPR concludes that the scheme ought to be replaced or is no longer required, or that the step is necessary to protect the interests of the generality of members of the scheme.

The Pensions Ombudsman may also make recommendations concerning remedial action necessary in particular cases, which may lead to investigation and action by TPR. Scheme auditors therefore include a review of correspondence with that body, as well as correspondence with TPR and HMRC, as part of their procedures to assess the risk of non-compliance with laws and regulations which are central to a pension scheme. 103

In addition, each scheme is bound to comply with the terms of its governing document. Failure to comply will constitute a breach of trust, which may form 104 grounds for intervention by TPR. Determination of laws and regulations which are central to a particular scheme therefore requires consideration of its governing document, as well as applicable laws and regulations and the requirements of trust law and statute.

Money laundering

> In the UK and Ireland, when carrying out procedures for the purpose of forming an opinion on the financial statements, the auditor should be alert for those instances of possible or actual non-compliance with laws and regulations that might incur obligations for partners and staff in audit firms to report money laundering offences. (paragraph 22-1)

105 Auditors in the United Kingdom have reporting obligations under the Proceeds of Crime Act 2002 and the Money Laundering Regulations 2003 (as amended) to report knowledge or suspicion of money laundering offences, including those arising from fraud and thefts, to the Serious Organised Crime Agency (SOCA). The impact of the detailed legislation on auditors can broadly be summarised as follows:

- money laundering includes concealing, disguising, converting, transferring, removing, using, acquiring or possessing property[13] resulting from criminal conduct[14].
- the anti-Money Laundering legislation contains no de minimis concessions.
- partners and staff in audit firms are required to report suspicions[15] that a criminal offence, giving rise to direct or indirect benefit from criminal conduct has been committed, regardless of whether that offence has been committed by a client or by a third party.
- partners and staff in audit firms need to be alert to the dangers of making disclosures that are likely to prejudice an investigation ('tipping off'[16]) as this will constitute a criminal offence under the anti-Money Laundering legislation.

106 Trustees of pension schemes have no specific statutory responsibilities in connection with money laundering over and above those which apply generally to individuals and organisations.

107 Failure by an auditor to report knowledge or suspicion of money laundering is a criminal offence. Auditors are required to report through their Money Laundering Reporting Officer ('MLRO') to SOCA suspicions of criminal conduct that give rise to criminal property. Partners and staff in audit firms discharge their responsibilities by reporting to their MLRO.

[13] *"Property" is criminal property if it constitutes a person's benefit from criminal conduct or it represents such a benefit (in whole or part and whether directly or indirectly), and the alleged offender knows or suspects that it constitutes or represents such a benefit.*

[14] *"Criminal conduct" is defined as conduct which constitutes an offence in any part of the United Kingdom or would constitute such an offence if it occurred in any part of the UK.*

[15] *Auditors are required to report where they know or suspect or have reasonable grounds to know or suspect that another person is engaged in money laundering.*

[16] *'Tipping off' is an offence under the Proceeds of Crime Act 2002. It arises when an individual discloses matters where*
(a) there is knowledge or suspicion that a report has already been made, and
(b) that disclosure is likely to prejudice any investigation which might be conducted following the report.

- a duty which is relevant to the administration of the scheme in question, and is imposed by or by virtue of an enactment or rule of law has not been or is not being complied with, and
- the failure to comply is likely to be of material significance to the TPR in the exercise of any of its functions.

Although the title of ISA (UK and Ireland) 250: Section B refers to reports to regulators in the financial sector, the principles and essential procedures included in ISA (UK and Ireland) 250 apply in respect of this statutory duty to report to TPR. 118

The obligation to report under section 70 does not require scheme auditors to undertake additional work directed at identifying matters to report over and above that which is necessary to fulfil their obligations under the Audited Accounts Regulations to report on a scheme's financial statements and on the payment of contributions. Scheme auditors are therefore not required to put into place arrangements to detect matters to be reported under section 70; their obligation is limited to reporting those which come to their attention. This applies even where, as in the case of certain ear-marked schemes, the scheme auditors are reporting only about contributions so that the focus of their work is very narrow. Although the scope of their work makes the discovery of reportable items less likely, auditors of such schemes may nevertheless find the guidance in this section of the Practice Note helpful in meeting their statutory duty under section 70[17]. 119

Occupational pension schemes operate within a complex legal framework determined by general trust law and specific statutory provisions. The Pensions Acts 1995 and 2004 and related regulations introduced specific statutory requirements concerning key areas of trustees' responsibilities and scheme administration which supplement, but do not replace, the requirements of trust law. 120

The purpose of the statutory duty to report under section 70 of the PA 2004 is to strengthen the system of regulation of occupational pension schemes in the United Kingdom by requiring the parties listed earlier (including scheme auditors and actuaries) to communicate in particular circumstances with TPR, so assisting the exercise of its statutory objectives. The PA 2004 provides TPR with a variety of powers (set out in Appendix 2 of this Practice Note) that it can use to ensure that trustees and others comply with the legal requirements for the proper administration of occupational pension schemes. 121

TPR has indicated that it does not consider isolated and inconsequential breaches that relate to an otherwise well-run scheme materially significant, because experience has shown that such breaches do not constitute a risk to members' interests. This will particularly be the case where the reaction by the trustees was such that prompt and effective corrective action was taken. For the majority of breaches which occur, TPR will seek to provide assistance and guidance to trustees and others, thus achieving compliance without recourse to punitive action. In those instances where TPR considers there has been, or could be, a materially significant risk to the security of scheme assets or members' benefits, TPR will use its regulatory powers to protect members' interests. 122

---

[17] *TPR has published guidance supporting the 'Reporting breaches of the law' code of practice giving examples of breaches that it considers to be of material significance. Guidance is also included in other Codes.*

Criteria for reporting to TPR

Material significance

123 Scheme auditors conducting activities under the PA 1995 need to assess information of which they become aware in the course of their work which indicates that a breach of law may have taken place so as to determine whether, in their opinion, that information may be relevant to TPR in the context of its powers.

124 In circumstances where scheme auditors identify that a reportable matter may exist, they carry out such extra work, as considered necessary, to determine whether the facts and circumstances give them 'reasonable cause to believe' that the matter does in fact exist. This may require the scheme auditor to seek information from the employer, its auditors or other third parties[18]. TPR has stated that "Having a reasonable cause to believe that a breach has occurred means more than merely having a suspicion that cannot be substantiated." It should be noted that the scheme auditors' work does not need to prove that the reportable matter exists, merely that they have reasonable cause to believe that there was a breach of the law.

125 Paragraph 39 of ISA (UK and Ireland) 250: Section B requires that:

'Where an apparent breach of statutory or regulatory requirements comes to the auditor's attention, the auditor should:
(a) Obtain such evidence as is available to assess its implications for the auditor's reporting responsibilities; and
(b) Determine whether, in the auditor's opinion, there is reasonable cause to believe that the breach is of material significance to the regulator; and
(c) Consider whether the apparent breach is criminal conduct that gives rise to criminal property and, as such, should be reported to the specified authorities.'

126 In the context of pension schemes, scheme auditors are required to assess all breaches which come to their attention of any duty relevant to the administration of the scheme imposed by any enactment or rule of law on not only the trustees or manager of the scheme concerned, but also on the employer, any professional adviser or any prescribed person acting in connection with the scheme. This includes breaches of statute, regulation and trust law.

127 'Material significance' is defined in paragraph 14 of ISA (UK and Ireland) 250: Section B as follows:

A matter or group of matters is normally of material significance to a regulator's functions when, due either to its nature or its potential financial impact, it is likely of itself to require investigation by the regulator.'

128 'Material significance' does not have the same meaning as materiality in the context of the audit of financial statements. Whilst a particular event may be trivial in terms of its possible effect on the financial statements of an entity, it may be of a nature or type which is likely to change the perception of the regulator. For example, dishonesty by a trustee may not be significant in financial terms in comparison with the income of the scheme but could have a significant effect on TPR's consideration of whether to prohibit an individual from being a trustee.

---

[18] *In circumstances where the scheme auditor is uncertain whether an action or an inaction constitutes a breach of the law, they clarify the legal requirements to the extent necessary to decide whether they have a reasonable cause to believe that the law has been broken.*

In interpreting the term 'of material significance' in the context of pension schemes, scheme auditors need to be aware of the specific requirements of relevant legislation, including the role of TPR as established by the PA 2004. TPR's powers enable it to react to information reported to it which indicates a need to intervene to protect the rights of members of a scheme or to safeguard its assets. This includes situations where trustees may be in breach of trust arising from their poor stewardship of the scheme. TPR's approach to regulation is risk based and proportionate; its objectives are clearly set out in statute. TPR will proactively supervise the activities of occupational pension schemes gathering information from a number of sources, including the Scheme Return. 129

As already noted, TPR has issued Code of Practice 01 – Reporting breaches of the law together with Guidance. The supporting guidance gives possible examples of breaches TPR may consider to be materially significant. The examples are designed to aid the reporter by illustrating situations against which the actual breach can be compared thus aiding the reporter in reaching an appropriate decision. Additional guidance is also provided in other Codes. 130

TPR's focus is on the areas it considers critical to protecting members' benefits and security of scheme assets. These are: 131

- dishonesty;
- poor governance, inadequate controls resulting in deficient administration, or slow or inappropriate decision-making practices;
- incomplete or inaccurate advice; or
- acting (or failing to act) in deliberate contravention of the law.

Where the breach is caused by one of the above, it is likely to be of material significance to TPR. TPR has indicated that all such breaches would give rise to thorough investigation and that it expects scheme auditors to report any instances of such breaches which come to their attention. 132

The examples of breaches provided in TPR Guidance have been categorised according to the nature and severity of the breach; i.e. as either 'red, amber or green' breach situations (known as the traffic light framework) and include: 133

- breaches scheme auditors may become aware of in carrying out their professional duties that TPR consider to be materially significant; and
- circumstances which render the breach materially significant.

The determination of whether a matter is, or is likely to be, of material significance to the regulator inevitably requires scheme auditors to exercise their judgment. In forming such judgments, scheme auditors need to consider not simply the facts of the matter but also the reaction by trustees to the breach and the wider implications of the breach. In addition, it is possible that a matter, which is not materially significant in isolation, may become so when other possible breaches are considered, together with other reported and unreported breaches of which the auditor is aware. 134

In forming an opinion as to whether a matter that has been identified is likely to be of material significance, scheme auditors of a defined benefit scheme may wish to liaise with the scheme actuary. This procedure helps to ensure that the cumulative effect of all breaches is considered and not only those identified by one professional adviser. It is important to ensure that the auditors' terms of engagement allow discussions with the scheme actuary in this context. 135

On completion of their investigations, scheme auditors ensure that the facts and circumstances and the basis for their conclusion as to whether to report to TPR are 136 adequately documented such that the reasons for their decision (particularly for a decision not to report) may be clearly demonstrated should the need to do so arise in future.

137 Whilst confidentiality is an implied term of scheme auditors' and actuaries' contracts in respect of a pension scheme or other entity, section 70 (3) of the PA 2004 states:

"No duty to which a person is subject is to be regarded as contravened merely because of any information or opinion contained in a written report under this section".

138 Hence reporting to TPR under section 70 does not contravene the duty of confidentiality, provided that scheme auditors communicate in good faith matters which they have reasonable cause to believe amount to a relevant breach, and which in their view are likely to be of material significance to TPR in the exercise of its functions.

Other considerations

139 In assessing the effect of an apparent breach of duty which has come to their attention, scheme auditors take into account the quantity and type of evidence concerning such a matter which may reasonably be expected to be available. If the scheme auditors conclude that they have been prevented from obtaining all such evidence concerning a matter which may give rise to a duty to report, they consider making a report direct to TPR without further delay.

140 Not every actual or suspected breach of a legal duty relevant to the administration of a scheme which comes to the scheme auditors' attention will give rise to a duty to report to TPR. Scheme auditors need to assess whether a duty to report arises by considering the type of requirement which has been breached and the implications of the breach in relation to the specific circumstances of the scheme.

141 Certain events that would attract sanctions do not constitute breaches of the Pensions Acts 1995 or 2004 if there is a 'reasonable excuse' for them. In the APB's view, whether an excuse is 'reasonable' (and therefore would not give rise to sanctions) is not a matter on which auditors should form a judgment with a view to deciding whether to report a particular matter to TPR. However TPR would expect the auditors to exercise professional discretion in deciding what is materially significant to TPR. Auditors therefore report to TPR all breaches attracting criminal sanctions which come to their attention, without attempting to evaluate whether excuses are 'reasonable'. Auditors may wish to precede the written report by way of a telephone call to TPR in respect of breaches requiring urgent attention.

142 Breaches of other legal duties require careful consideration in the light of both:

(a) the gravity of the matter taken alone; and
(b) its implications when considered with other information known to the scheme auditors.

The potential gravity of some breaches of legal duty may be such that an individual breach is likely of itself to warrant the consideration by TPR of the use of its powers to debar an individual from acting as trustee, to appoint a new trustee or otherwise to intervene in the running of a scheme, to issue an Improvement or Third Party Notice or to impose financial penalties.

143 TPR's powers also cover other important elements of the relationship between the trustees and members. Persistent breaches of these requirements such as communications with scheme members may also be regarded as materially significant to TPR.

144 All breaches of law therefore require careful assessment, irrespective of their apparent individual significance. Breaches which, of themselves, may not be of the gravity described in paragraph 142, may be indicative of a general lack of compliance with legal requirements or of a more significant breach of duty which is likely to be of material significance to TPR. Where the scheme auditors conclude (after further enquiries, if appropriate) that this is the case, a duty to report arises. In addition auditors carry forward a note of unreported and reported breaches from year to year in order to gauge the cumulative effect which might suggest a need to report to TPR.

145 Other individual breaches do not give rise to a duty to report if scheme auditors conclude after their enquiries that they do not immediately or potentially constitute a significant risk to the security of scheme assets or immediately or potentially have any detrimental impact on members' benefits, for example if:

- the matter is an isolated occurrence;
- its occurrence is inconsequential;
- appropriate corrective action was taken immediately on discovery, both in relation to the individual matter (for example, incorrect information provided to a member was followed immediately on discovery by accurate information and an appropriate letter) and in relation to the scheme's systems of controls; and
- the trustees had given proper consideration to bringing the matter to TPR's attention.

TPR has indicated that in these circumstances and where the appropriate course of action has been taken by the trustees, TPR will not regard the breach as materially significant. This is indicated by the easements granted in respect of contributions paid late, for example.

Reporting of late scheme financial statements

146 One of the civil breaches of the PA 1995 is the failure by trustees or managers to obtain audited financial statements within seven months of the end of the scheme year. Although the obtaining of scheme financial statements is the responsibility of the trustees (who may decide to appoint an administrator or other appropriate person to assist them), auditors who are aware of persistent failures by trustees or managers to obtain audited financial statements within seven months of the end of the scheme year (for example where the failures are as a result of poorly maintained records or inadequate administration systems) consider reporting this to TPR.

147 Auditors therefore put in place procedures to establish whether trustees have obtained audited financial statements within the seven month period established by the Regulations. Where they act for a large number of pension schemes, auditors may find it helpful to establish a database or other system to monitor the dates scheme financial statements are obtained. As soon as the auditors conclude that the trustees have failed to obtain audited financial statements within the required timeframe, they consider whether to report the matter to TPR.

148 There are a number of different circumstances in which auditors determine whether a scheme's audited financial statements have been obtained by the trustees within seven months after the scheme's year end date:

- *Where the audit is recurring:* in these circumstances, the auditors will be aware of the date of the year end of the pension schemes for which they have

responsibility. Occasionally, the trustees may change the year end date in which case auditors amend their records on a timely basis once they have been informed.
- *Where the auditors are newly appointed:* in these circumstances and as part of their acceptance procedures prior to appointment, auditors establish the date of the scheme year end and consider whether there are late financial statements in respect of the year(s) for which they are to be appointed. If there are late financial statements in respect of any such period they consider reporting such matters to TPR as soon as their appointment is effective.
- *Where the trustees have not determined the date of the scheme year end at the time the auditors are appointed (for example, in the case of a newly constituted scheme):* in these circumstances the auditors will assume, unless and until they are otherwise informed by the trustees, that the scheme year end will be 31 March following the date of commencement of the scheme or, if this would cause the initial period to be less than six months, then the 31 March in the year following[19].

Conduct of the audit

149 Paragraph 34 of ISA (UK and Ireland) 250: Section B states that: 'The auditor should ensure that all staff involved in the audit of a regulated entity have an understanding of the following:

(a) The provisions of applicable legislation;
(b) The regulator's rules and any guidance issued by the regulator; and
(c) Any specific requirements which apply to the particular regulated entity

appropriate to their role in the audit and sufficient (in the context of that role) to enable them to identify situations which may give reasonable cause to believe that a matter should be reported to the regulator.'

150 As noted above, the PA 2004 does not require scheme auditors to perform any additional work as a result of the statutory duty to report to TPR nor are they required specifically to seek out breaches of the requirements applicable to a particular pension scheme. However, the duty to report is not restricted to rules of law directly relevant to the scheme auditors' routine reporting responsibilities, but extends to non-compliance with any duty relevant to the administration of a scheme imposed by any enactment or rule of law on the trustees or managers, the employer, any professional adviser or any prescribed person, should the scheme auditors become aware of breaches. Scheme auditors therefore include procedures within their planning process to ensure that members of the audit team have sufficient understanding (in the context of their role) to enable them to recognise breaches and that such matters are reported to the audit engagement partner without delay so that a decision may be made as to whether a duty to report arises.

151 The numbers of staff involved in the audit of a pension scheme will vary, depending on its size and complexity. While specific expertise will also vary, all staff will be

---

[19] *The maximum duration of a scheme year is specified in the Occupational Pension Schemes (Requirement to obtain Audited Accounts and a Statement from the Auditor) Regulations 1996 SI 1996 No. 1975:*
"Scheme year means :
(a) a year specified for the purposes of the scheme in any document comprising the scheme or, if none, a period of 12 months commencing on 1st April or on such date as the trustees or managers select; or
(b) such other period (if any) exceeding 6 months but not exceeding 18 months as is selected by the trustees or managers in connection with –
- the commencement or termination of the scheme, or
- a variation of the date on which the year or period referred to in paragraph (a) is to commence".

aware of the main features of a pension scheme audit. In addition, at least the staff who are involved in a scheme's audit team in a supervisory or review role should have an understanding of the following:

- the general principles of the Pensions SORP;
- the principal requirements of the Scheme Administration Regulations (SI no 1996/1715, as amended) and the Audited Accounts Regulations (SI no 1996/1975, as amended);
- TPR's Codes of Practice and the supporting Guidance, in particular Reporting breaches of the law;
- the trust deed and rules of the particular scheme;
- the standards and guidance in Section B of ISA (UK and Ireland) 250.

Further knowledge is required, commensurate with the individual's role and responsibilities in the audit process, of:

- the legal and regulatory framework applicable to occupational pension schemes sufficient to meet the requirements of ISAs (UK and Ireland), including:
    - the responsibilities of pension scheme trustees under general trust law and the PA 1995 and PA 2004;
    - responsibilities of pension scheme managers, the sponsoring employer, any professional adviser, third party administrators or any prescribed person acting in connection with the scheme; and
- the detailed requirements concerning the preparation of the financial statements and other matters on which scheme auditors are required routinely to report.

An overview, which provides a general introduction to the major features of the legal and regulatory framework, is set out in Appendix 2.

Reporting matters of material significance

Section 70(2) of the PA 2004 imposes a duty for reports to be made 'as soon as reasonably practicable'. The duty to report only arises once scheme auditors have concluded that there is reasonable cause to believe that a breach of duty exists and that the breach is likely to be of material significance to TPR in the exercise of its functions. In reaching their conclusion, scheme auditors may wish to take appropriate advice and consult with colleagues or lawyers. The obligation to report as soon as reasonably practicable does not prevent such consultation taking place as part of the process of forming an opinion that a duty to report arises. However, the more serious the nature of the breach, e.g. dishonesty, the more urgently consultation needs to take place.

The trustees are the persons principally responsible for the management of the scheme. In forming their opinion, scheme auditors will therefore normally seek to reach agreement with the trustees on the circumstances giving rise to a report to TPR and to understand whether they intend to make a report. However, paragraph 53 of ISA (UK and Ireland) 250 Section B stresses that in some circumstances, immediate notification of a matter giving reasonable grounds to believe that a reportable matter exists will be necessary. Paragraph 54 of ISA (UK and Ireland) 250: Section B also states that:

'When the matter giving rise to a statutory duty to make a report direct to a regulator casts doubt on the integrity of those charged with governance or their competence to conduct the business of the regulated entity, the auditors should, subject to compliance with legislation relating to "tipping off", make the report to the regulator without delay and without informing those charged with governance in advance.'

Therefore scheme auditors cannot undertake to inform trustees in advance of every matter which they bring to TPR's attention.

155 In certain circumstances joint reporting (i.e. a shared report between the trustees and auditors) of breaches to the regulator may be appropriate. A number of difficulties, however, arise in practice, including:

- delays occurring due to the time taken to agree wording with all the signatories of the joint report, and
- scheme auditors finding it difficult to associate themselves with trustees' descriptions of action plans to avoid further breaches.

In the light of these practical difficulties, the APB recommends that scheme auditors do not delay reporting to TPR in order to participate in a joint report; rather they report to TPR directly once they have concluded that a breach of material significance has occurred.

Contents of a report to TPR

156 When making a report concerning a matter of material significance direct to a regulator, in accordance with Section B of ISA (UK and Ireland) 250, auditors are required to:
  (a) state the name of the regulated entity concerned;
  (b) state the statutory power under which the report is made;
  (c) state that the report has been prepared in accordance with ISA (UK and Ireland) 250, Section B 'The Auditor's Right and Duty to Report to Regulators in the Financial Sector';
  (d) describe the context in which the report is given;
  (e) describe the matter giving rise to the report and why the matter is considered to be of material significance;
  (f) request the regulator to confirm that the report has been received; and
  (g) state the name of the auditor, the date of the written report and, where appropriate, the date on which an oral report was made to the regulator and the name and title of the individual to whom the oral report was made (paragraph 61 of Section B).

The statutory power under which such reports are made to TPR is section 70(2) of the PA 2004.

157 The requirement under section 70(1) of the PA 2004 for reports to be in writing does not preclude oral or electronic reporting to TPR in circumstances where speed of reporting is essential. However, the duty to report is not satisfied until any such report is confirmed in writing.

Describing the context of a report

158 The description of the context in which the report is made sets out information relevant to a proper understanding of its subject matter, primarily concerning the way in which the matter was identified, and the extent to which it has been investigated and discussed with those responsible for stewardship of the scheme. Matters to which pension scheme auditors may wish to refer include:

- The nature of the engagement from which the report derives. For example, it may be appropriate to distinguish between a report made by the auditors of a defined benefit scheme or defined contribution scheme, who are required to

express an opinion on the scheme's financial statements as well as to report on its contributions, and one which arises from the more limited engagement as the auditors of an earmarked scheme who are required to report only on the scheme's contributions;
- The applicable provisions of PA 1995 or PA 2004 and related Regulations and any interpretations of those provisions which have informed the scheme auditors' judgement;
- The extent (if any) to which the scheme auditors have investigated the circumstances giving rise to the matter reported, including (in the case of defined benefit schemes) whether the matter has been discussed with the scheme actuary or other third parties. TPR has also indicated that under normal circumstances it would expect reports to state (to the extent that this information is available) the name, address, telephone and fax numbers of the scheme actuary and the scheme's registration number and HMRC registration number, to assist TPR in identifying the scheme. If the matter has already been considered by TPR and the TPR case number is known, this may also usefully be included, together with information on:
  - whether or not the matter reported has been discussed with the trustees;
  - why the breach is thought to be of material significance; and
  - whether or not the trustees have taken steps to rectify the matter.

It may be difficult for auditors to confirm whether or not the trustees have taken steps to rectify a reported matter. In such circumstances, the auditors may decide to encourage the trustees to report the matter and describe their rectification process.

Where trustees wish to make a submission to TPR as to the circumstances and steps being taken to address a reportable matter, the auditors may attach such a memorandum or report prepared by the trustees to their report. Where such additional information is provided, auditors refer to the additional information in their report, and indicate whether or not they have undertaken additional procedures to determine whether any remedial actions described have been taken. 159

Matters already reported to TPR

The requirement to report applies to all parties who are subject to the reporting duty who become aware of a breach that is likely to be of material significance to TPR and it is not automatically discharged by another party reporting the breach. Where a breach of the legislation has occurred and the matter has already been reported to TPR, the scheme auditors' statutory duty to report should be considered in the light of the nature of the breach, any response by TPR and whether the report fully reflects their own concerns. 160

In order to document the background to a decision whether to make a report, a scheme auditor should obtain a copy of the report already made to TPR and of TPR's response. 161

Unreported breaches of legal duty

If the scheme auditors conclude that a breach of a duty imposed by law is not likely to be of material significance, they have no specific statutory duty to report to TPR. Scheme auditors nevertheless take steps to ensure that such breaches are taken into account for future consideration. 162

Paragraph 70 of Section B of ISA (UK and Ireland) 250 requires auditors of regulated entities, when reporting on their financial statements, not only to assess the 163 significance of individual transactions or events but also to consider whether a combination of such items over the course of their audit work may give them reasonable grounds to believe that they constitute a matter of material significance, so giving rise to a duty to report to TPR.

164 In circumstances where auditors are uncertain whether they may be required to make a report or not, they consider taking legal advice.

165 Information about unreported instances of breaches of the Pensions Acts 1995 and 2004 and related Regulations and breaches of other legal duties relevant to scheme administration is therefore assessed by a scheme's auditors when issuing their report on its financial statements, in order to determine whether the cumulative effect is or is likely to be of material significance to TPR. Where there is evidence of persistent breaches, a duty to report normally arises.

166 Scheme auditors also take steps to ensure that the scheme's trustees are made aware of breaches which have come to their attention in the course of their work, whether or not they have led to a duty to report to TPR, for example by requesting that copies of any management letters dealing with such breaches are circulated to all the trustees.

Information received in a capacity other than as scheme auditor

167 Where an audit firm is appointed as scheme auditor and is also engaged to provide services to the scheme's employer, for example as auditor to the employer, so long as the two engagements are separate (including the staff involved) then the audit firm in its capacity as employer auditor has no duty to consider reporting to TPR. However, if the employer is alerted to a breach by the employer audit engagement team, the employer has a duty to consider reporting it.

168 Similarly, if the audit firm provides services to other entities that provide services to the pension scheme, for example investment managers, custodians and pensions administrators, then so long as the pension scheme audit engagement is separate from these other engagements, the audit firm in its capacity as provider of these other services has no duty to consider reporting to TPR.

Failure to fulfil the statutory duty to report matters of material significance

169 A scheme auditor who is aware of a breach of law and fails to report it to TPR whilst having reasonable grounds to believe that a breach of law had occurred and that breach was, or was likely to be, of material significance to TPR in the exercise of its functions, is in breach of both the statutory requirement to report and of Auditing Standards with which registered auditors are required to comply.

170 Section 70 (4) of the PA 2004 made provision for TPR, under section 10 of the PA 1995, to impose civil penalties for failure to comply with section 70 of the PA 2004, as well as to refer the scheme auditor to his professional body. Within any legal restrictions which may operate, TPR makes available to those bodies all the information in its possession, including copies of correspondence between TPR and the scheme auditors concerned, relevant to such a case.

necessary to obtain sufficient appropriate evidence in order to discharge their statutory obligation to report on the payment of contributions.

Other areas which may have significant impact depending upon the circumstances of the scheme are transfer values paid and received, administration expenses and debtors and creditors. 179

When planning the work to be undertaken the scheme auditor considers the other information available to the scheme auditors, including: 180

- minutes of trustee meetings;
- information in the public domain regarding relevant developments at the sponsoring employer;
- membership records; and
- actuarial valuation.

When planning the audit of a pension scheme's financial statements, scheme auditors also take into account the importance of the work of third parties in the administration and accounting on behalf of the trustees. Such third parties include the: 181

- administrator;
- investment manager;
- investment custodian;
- property manager;
- sponsoring and participating employer(s).

At an early stage in planning the audit, scheme auditors seek agreement with the trustees for necessary access to third parties, when appropriate, and the timing and extent of the information required from them. The principal requirements are normally set out in the scheme auditors' engagement letter. More detailed arrangements for obtaining access and information are likely to be one of the main subjects of discussion with the trustees, whether at a planning meeting or more informally, before the scheme auditors complete their audit plan. 182

In delegating particular matters to third parties, such as investment managers, trustees are legally obliged to do so in a manner which is consistent with their duty to act prudently. Hence, in addition to exercising care in the selection of advisers and other third parties to whom scheme activities are delegated, trustees need to lay down adequate guidelines for the way the third parties undertake those activities and for monitoring their performance. This is frequently achieved by using service agreements. Where significant functions have been delegated to third parties, scheme auditors review any such agreements with third parties as part of the planning process. 183

How such delegation actually works in practice also has an impact on the control environment and the audit plan. Effective segregation of duties between third parties and regular supervision and direction by the trustees can greatly strengthen the control environment while, in contrast, the blurring of responsibilities and poor communication and co-ordination can weaken the control environment. 184

The sections on ISA (UK and Ireland) 315 ' Obtaining an Understanding of the Entity and Its Environment and Assessing the Risks of Material Misstatement', and ISA (UK and Ireland) 402 'Audit Considerations Relating to Entities Using Service Organisations' give guidance on the factors to be considered by scheme auditors when determining the evidence about outsourced functions which is necessary to support their report on the scheme's financial statements. 185

186 Scheme auditors may wish to discuss their audit plan with the trustees so as to enable the trustees to consider whether they require any specific additional procedures to be performed beyond those necessary to support the audit opinion. For example, the trustees may request the scheme auditors to carry out additional tests on the detailed membership records, or on the calculation of individual benefits, to provide the trustees with added assurance that reliable records are being maintained and that the individual payments being made are in accordance with the rules of the scheme.

ISA (UK and Ireland) 315: Obtaining an Understanding of the Entity and its Environment and Assessing the Risks of Material Misstatement

> **Background note**
>
> The purpose of this ISA (UK and Ireland) is to establish standards and to provide guidance on obtaining an understanding of the entity and its environment, including its internal control, and on assessing the risks of material misstatement in a financial statement audit.

187 The principles of obtaining and using knowledge of the scheme to be audited are the same as those applying to the audit of any entity.

188 However, ISA (UK and Ireland) 315 takes little account of the possible use of service organisations by a reporting entity. When planning an audit of a pension scheme, the ISA (UK and Ireland) should be read in conjunction with ISA (UK and Ireland) 402 'Audit Considerations Relating to Entities Using Service Organisations', which is discussed later in this Practice Note. The discussion in this section focuses on the control environment and controls of the entity (i.e. the pension scheme) itself, rather than those service organisations which may be relevant to the audit.

A. Understanding the Entity and Its Environment, Including Its Internal Controls

> The auditor should obtain an understanding of relevant industry, regulatory, and other external factors including the applicable financial reporting framework. (paragraph 22)

Legislative and Regulatory Requirements

189 Pension schemes operate within a framework of law and regulation which is complex and differs in a number of respects from that applicable to commercial enterprises. This framework involves both trust law and specific statutory provisions, set out primarily in the Pension Schemes Act 1993, the Pensions Acts 1995 and 2004, and Regulations made under those Acts. Funded schemes are usually established under trust law or (generally in the case of public sector schemes) under specific statute, and for a non-statutory scheme to register with HMRC it is essential that it is established under 'irrevocable trusts'. It is essential for auditors of occupational pension schemes to have a good understanding of relevant pensions legislation and associated regulations. In the case of public sector schemes, this extends to the specific requirements applicable to each scheme, which may differ in a number of respects from the requirements of the Pensions Acts.

Financial Reporting: Legal Requirements and Accounting Standards

190 The form and content of a pension scheme's financial statements are specified in the Occupational Pension Schemes (Requirement to obtain Audited Accounts and a Statement from the Auditor) Regulations 1996 (SI 1996 No 1975) ('the Audited Accounts Regulations'). These require scheme trustees to obtain financial statements which:

(a) contain specified information, set out in the Schedule to the Audited Accounts Regulations; and
(b) show a true and fair view of the financial transactions of the scheme during the scheme year and of the amount and disposition as at the end of the scheme year of its assets and of its liabilities, other than liabilities to pay pensions and benefits after the end of the scheme year.

191 The Audited Accounts Regulations require the trustees to state whether the financial statements have been prepared in accordance with the Statement of Recommended Practice 'Financial Reports of Pension Schemes' (the Pensions SORP)[20] and to indicate any material departures from its guidance. The Pensions SORP supplements general accounting principles set out in Financial Reporting Standards and Statements of Standard Accounting Practice, indicating best practice in accounting and financial reporting by pension schemes. Consequently it is normally necessary to follow the guidance in the Pensions SORP in order for pension scheme financial statements to show the true and fair view required by legislation.

> The auditor should obtain an understanding of the nature of the entity. (paragraph 25)

192 The scheme auditor's understanding of the nature of the entity usually includes:

(a) **scheme nature and documentation**
   - trust deed and rules
   - the definition of pensionable earnings/pay, where not covered by the above
   - membership numbers
   - nature of the scheme and type of benefits provided
   - scheme booklet
   - documentation of the schemes "registered pension scheme" status
   - correspondence with HMRC relating to registered pension scheme status
   - contracting out documentation

(b) **scheme governance**
   - membership of the trustee body and division of responsibilities
   - outsourcing arrangements and principal terms of contractual agreements with third party service providers
   - correspondence with TPR/Pensions Ombudsman/the Pensions Advisory Service (TPAS)
   - minutes of meetings of the trustee body and key sub-committees
   - internal dispute resolution procedure and any disputes in progress
   - arrangements for agreeing schedule of contributions or payment schedule with the sponsoring employer and taking actuarial advice where necessary

---

[20] The SORP, which was revised in November 2002, was issued by the Pensions Research Accountants Group (PRAG) in accordance with the Accounting Standards Board's code of practice for the development and issue of SORPs.

(c) **sponsoring and participating employers**
   – identity of the sponsoring and other participating employer(s)
   – agreements with employer(s) and related parties, including any relevant covenants or guarantees supporting the scheme
   – details of employer auditors
   – arrangements for payments in accordance with the agreed schedule of contributions or payment schedule and rules of the scheme
   – arrangements for payment of additional voluntary contributions

(d) **scheme actuary** (where appropriate)
   – letter of appointment
   – areas of responsibility
   – valuation reports and details of funding requirements
   – statement of funding principles
   – latest statements and certificates

(e) **scheme administration**
   – responsibilities of pension scheme managers, the sponsoring and participating employer, any prescribed professional adviser or any prescribed person acting in connection with the scheme
   – service agreements
   – division of administrative responsibilities
   – documentation of accounting systems and controls
   – accounting and membership records
   – stewardship reports
   – systems and controls documentation

(f) **investments**
   – statement of funding principles
   – statement of investment principles
   – custody arrangements
   – service agreements with investment managers and custodians
   – investment managers' reports
   – nature of investments and extent of employer-related investment, use of complex financial instruments, stock lending, unquoted investments
   – borrowings
   – common investment fund arrangements
   – subsidiaries
   – AVC arrangements

(g) **other advisers**
   – relationship/contracts with other advisers

> The auditor should obtain an understanding of the entity's selection and application of accounting policies and consider whether they are appropriate for its business and consistent with the applicable financial reporting framework and accounting policies used in the relevant industry. (paragraph 28)

193 The Pensions SORP provides detailed guidance on appropriate accounting policies. Material departures from the Pensions SORP must be disclosed in the financial statements.

In the case of most pension schemes, the following will be the key areas of the financial statements and therefore the choice of accounting policies in these areas will be of most significance to the financial statements:

- contributions
- investments
- investment return
- benefits and transfers

As noted in paragraph 191 above, pension scheme accounts are required to include a statement whether the accounts have been prepared in accordance with the Pensions SORP and if they have not 'an indication of where there are any material departures from those guidelines'.

The principles underlying the Pensions SORP are as follows:

- investment assets are included at their market value
- income and expenditure items are included on the accruals basis.

As a result, trustees are left with little discretion as to the choice of accounting policies. Therefore the auditor's primary concern will be to understand the manner in which these policies have been applied in the particular context of the individual scheme and to ensure that where the trustees have adopted a policy that is not in accordance with the Pensions SORP, such as where some income and expenditure items have been dealt with on the cash basis rather than the accruals basis, either the impact is not material to the financial statements or, where the impact is material, the alternative policy can be justified by the circumstances and is disclosed as a deviation from the Pensions SORP.

> The auditor should obtain an understanding of the entity's objectives and strategies, and the related business risks that may result in material misstatement of the financial statements (ISA (UK and Ireland) 315. (paragraph 30)

Scheme auditors need to be aware of the principal terms of the trust instrument governing the particular scheme. This is usually contained in the Trust Deed and Rules which set out the objectives of the scheme and determine the powers of the trustees, along with the more detailed rules in respect of how the scheme affairs should be conducted. Failure to comply with the Trust Deed and Rules may constitute a breach of trust, and may result in a report to TPR.

Defined contribution schemes

The benefits payable by defined contribution schemes will be directly related to and determined by the assets attributable to an individual member at the date that their pension benefits become payable. The risk that the pension that can be secured with the assets available is inadequate is borne by the member, not the scheme. Therefore in the absence of a loss of the assets due to theft or mismanagement, such a scheme does not face "business risks" that threaten the achievement of the scheme's objective.

Defined benefit schemes

Due to the nature of the commitment of defined benefit schemes to pay benefits related to members' salaries at or close to retirement, such schemes face a risk of being under-funded, and therefore being unable to meet all benefits in full as they fall due for payment. This situation may arise from a number of factors, including:

- inadequate contributions
- inadequate investment returns
- adverse changes in experience affecting the amount and/or duration of benefit payments (e.g. improvements in pensioner survival).

201 Financial statements of pension schemes record the historical levels of contributions, investment return and benefit payments but are not designed to provide measures of the current or future levels of funding: these measures are provided by the outcomes of the work of the actuary, whose statements sit alongside the audited financial statements within the annual report.

> The auditor should obtain an understanding of the measurement and review of the entity's financial performance. (paragraph 35)

202 Conventional measures of financial performance, such as profit, return on capital or cash flow are typically not relevant to pension scheme financial statements. However the trustees should have procedures in place to monitor investment performance, and the auditor considers these as part of their audit work.

> The auditor should obtain an understanding of internal control relevant to the audit. (paragraph 41)

203 There is a wide variation between different schemes in terms of size, activity and organisation. Smaller schemes may be administered by the staff of the sponsoring employer or by third party administrators or a combination of both. Larger schemes may employ directly professionally qualified, full-time staff. However, the responsibilities of trustees for ensuring that the scheme has adequate internal controls and therefore is properly administered and its assets properly safeguarded apply irrespective of a scheme's size or administrative arrangements, and the attitude, role and involvement of each scheme's trustees are likely to be fundamental in determining the effectiveness of its control environment. The Regulator's code of practice on internal controls and supporting Guidance provides trustees with guidelines on their duty to establish and operate adequate internal controls.

204 In addition to reviewing accounting systems and the control environment in order to assess the risk of material misstatement in a pension scheme's financial statements, scheme auditors also undertake a review of the arrangements made by the trustees to implement the contribution rates set out in the payment schedule (for defined contribution schemes) or schedule of contributions certified by the actuary (for defined benefit, hybrid and mixed benefit schemes). The scheme auditor may also undertake work to test the adequacy of internal controls instituted for this purpose.

205 Paragraph 48 of ISA (UK and Ireland) 315 makes it clear that a scheme's use of service organisations is relevant to the auditor's consideration of the controls that are relevant to the audit. For the purpose of compliance with this ISA (UK and Ireland), it is not necessary for the auditor to document and assess the control environment or controls of service organisations so long as his work at entity level has provided him with a sufficient understanding of risk on which to base his planning of audit procedures (see later discussion of ISA (UK and Ireland) 402).

> The auditor should obtain an understanding of the control environment. (paragraph 67)

206 Trustees of a pension scheme are responsible for determining and implementing systems of control appropriate to a particular scheme and sufficient to allow them properly to discharge their legal duties.

207 Where trustees delegate the operation of the detailed controls, the trustees focus on the selection, appointment and monitoring of appropriate third party delegates. In the case of outsourced activities, the responsibility for these functions remains that of the trustees, who should have appropriate controls in place over these arrangements. These may include:

- risk assessment prior to contracting with the service provider, which includes a proper due diligence and periodic review of the appropriateness of the arrangement;
- appropriate contractual agreements or service level agreements;
- contingency plans should the provider fail in delivery of services;
- appropriate management information and reporting from the outsourced provider; and
- appropriate controls over scheme members' information.

208 The maintenance of an effective control environment is as important for pension schemes as it is for other entities, since it is a fundamental duty of pension scheme trustees to protect the assets of the scheme. Failure to do so can render the trustees personally liable for any loss occasioned to the scheme. The scheme auditor's statutory responsibilities do not include any requirement to report to the trustees on the design or operation of a scheme's systems of controls. However, auditing standards require auditors to report any material weaknesses in the accounting and internal control systems identified during the audit to directors (or equivalents) on a timely basis. For pension schemes this would therefore require any such report to be made to the trustees.

209 An effective control environment is likely to include the following features:

(a) appropriate trustee competence, commitment and involvement;
(b) properly trained and qualified staff, in relation to the tasks they have to perform;
(c) adequate segregation of duties. Where the size of the pension scheme does not allow for segregation of duties between administrative staff, supervision by the trustees is especially important;
(d) the trustees have adequate arrangements to obtain independent professional advice; and
(e) in the case of larger schemes, budgetary controls in the form of estimates for each financial year of income, expenditure and (where expenses and benefit payments are significant) cash flows, including regular comparisons of actual figures to the estimates. For smaller schemes and in areas where future income and expenditure are difficult to predict (for example special contributions, death benefits, lump sum withdrawals which arise incidentally) trustees or managers may rely on specific procedures to approve items of expenditure and monitor the nature and levels of income and expenditure.

210 Factors taken into account when considering the attitude, role and involvement of a scheme's trustees include:

- the skills and qualifications of individual trustees;
- the regularity and effectiveness of trustee meetings;
- arrangements to monitor adherence to the scheme's statement of investment principles;
- training undertaken by trustees;
- compliance with industry guidelines (for example the Regulator's Codes of Practice);
- the policy on dealing with trustee conflicts;
- adequacy of minutes of trustee meetings;
- the division of duties between trustees;
- the involvement of trustees in supervision and control procedures, including matters such as cheque-signing arrangements;
- the trustees' attitude towards third parties to whom they delegate the conduct of scheme activities;
- arrangements for trustees to monitor scheme income and expenditure;
- the attitude of trustees to previously identified breaches or control weaknesses.

> The auditor should obtain an understanding of the entity's process for identifying business risks relevant to financial reporting objectives and deciding about actions to address those risks, and the results thereof. (paragraph 76)

211 Where a scheme has a formal process for identifying business risks, (such as maintaining a risk register) the auditor reviews the process and considers its outcomes. For schemes without such a process, which is usually the case with smaller schemes, the auditor refers to paragraph 79 of ISA (UK and Ireland) 315.

212 The key operational risk of a pension scheme is that it will become under-funded and, as a result, be unable to meet its obligations to pay pensions as they fall due for payment in the future. Pension scheme annual financial statements are not designed to provide a view of the adequacy of a scheme's state of funding and, as a result, this risk is not relevant to annual financial reporting by pension schemes.

> The auditor should obtain a sufficient understanding of control activities to assess the risks of material misstatement at the assertion level and to design further audit procedures responsive to assessed risks. (paragraph 90)

213 Aspects of the control activities which are pensions-related are described below. Control activities which are not specific to pension schemes (such as segregation of duties) are not included in the examples, but are relevant to the auditors' assessment of the components of audit risk.

Control activities

214 In any scheme, key activities consist of receiving contributions, and investing scheme funds to generate capital growth and income. Where members have retired, the scheme will be also be involved in securing or paying pension benefits. Examples of controls which trustees may implement in each of these areas where they are material to the financial affairs of the scheme, both to reduce the risk of material misstatements and to minimise the risk of loss of the scheme's assets through fraud, are set out in the table below.

Contributions receivable	controls to monitor and check the accurate and timely receipt of contributions from the employer in accordance with the Schedule of Contributions or Payment Schedule, such as monitoring date received, comparing contributions received to the prior month or carrying out full reconciliations of contributions received to expected amounts using source data
	agreeing special contributions to actuarial advice and employer communications
	agreement of receipts to current membership records
	agreement of receipts to actuary's recommendations
	reviewing reports from administrators on the results of checks that membership records are up-to-date
Benefits payable	agreement of benefits payable to list of current pensioners or beneficiaries
	agreement of benefits payable to scheme rules, actuarial advice, relevant legislation and trust law
	reconciling DC and AVC benefits to provider statements and member records
	scrutiny of claims made on the scheme to determine bona fides
	monitoring of queries arising from benefit statements and monitoring of disputes resolution procedures
Protection of scheme assets and investment return	physical security, where appropriate, over cash, cheques, share certificates, title deeds etc.
	monitoring of compliance with the statement of funding principles
	monitoring of compliance with the statement of investment principles
	monitoring of investment manager's performance against agreed investment objectives and service levels (including property management where significant)
	use of independent benchmarking services to monitor investment return
	obtaining indemnities from third parties providing services
Monitoring of custody arrangements	monitoring of investment cash flows (including use of budgets and forecasts)

ICAEW Technical Release "AAF 01/06 – Assurance reports on internal controls of service organisations made available to third parties" is applicable to the full range of services that trustees may obtain from third party providers (rather than the more limited scope of FRAG 21/94 (revised) which AAF 01/06 replaces). Trustees may therefore seek to obtain (where available) copies of reports issued under AAF 01/06 from investment and/or property managers, custodians, providers of scheme administration and/or fund accounting where these activities are carried out by third parties on behalf of the trustees.

216 Where trustees obtain copies of reports produced under AAF 01/06, these are likely to provide useful information for scheme auditors in obtaining an understanding of risk and the impact of outsourced activities (see paragraph 241).

Accounting records

217 Section 49 of the PA 1995 requires the trustees to maintain books and records of the transactions of the scheme. The nature of the books and records to be maintained are set out in the Scheme Administration Regulations and consist of particular items specified in the Regulations[21]. Further requirements relating to records of contributions for defined benefit schemes are set out in the regulations prescribing the Minimum Funding Requirement (in the case of schemes that have yet to become subject to the scheme funding regime of the PA 2004) and The Occupational Pension Schemes (Scheme Funding) Regulations 2005 (SI 2005 No 3377) (in the case of schemes that have become subject to that regime). (See Appendix 2 for details).

218 The reporting responsibilities of pension scheme auditors do not include a requirement to report a breach of these requirements in their report on financial statements, as is the case for companies and various other entities. However, the auditor considers whether failure by the trustees to ensure that the requirements of section 49 are met is likely to be of material significance to TPR and so give rise to a statutory duty to report.

219 Additionally, HMRC has specified requirements regarding accounting records. Failure to comply may jeopardise a scheme's tax status, with consequential impact on the scheme's assets and liabilities.

> The auditor should obtain an understanding of how the entity has responded to risks arising from IT. (paragraph 93)

220 Auditors consider whether adequate IT controls exist over both financial systems and other systems relevant to the audit, including the administration and membership records.

B. Assessing the Risks of Material Misstatement

> The auditor should identify and assess the risks of material misstatement at the financial statement level, and at the assertion level for classes of transactions, account balances, and disclosures. (paragraph 100)

221 There is a wide variation between different schemes in terms of size, activity and organisation, so that there can be no standard approach to internal controls and risk. Scheme auditors assess risk and the adequacy of controls in relation to the circumstances of each scheme.

222 Factors considered by the auditor in assessing whether there may be an increased level of risk of material misstatement at the financial statement level include:

- complex scheme structure;

---

[21] *These requirements are the minimum. Trustees are likely to require more detailed and historic records for the effective management of their scheme than the minimum set down in legislation.*

- major changes in the operation of the scheme or participating/sponsoring employers;
- outdated trust deed and rules, which have numerous amendments;
- inadequacy of administrative resources;
- informal arrangements for delegation of discretionary decisions;
- employer is the sole trustee;
- cash flow difficulties of the sponsoring or participating employer(s);
- the involvement of the sponsoring employer(s) in corporate acquisitions or disposals;
- previous enquiries by regulatory bodies
- experience from previous years' audits.

Factors considered by the auditor in assessing whether there may be an increased level of risk of material misstatement at the assertion level include:

- complex contribution arrangements, for example:
  - age-related rates;
  - -a complex definition of pensionable earnings;
  - rates which are related to benefit accrual rates (DB arrangements) or which are subject to member choice, possibly with employer matching;
  - rates which are different for different participating employers;
- complex benefit structure, for example:
  - continuous service granted in respect of membership of previous pension arrangements;
  - elements of benefits that are subject to trustees' discretion;
  - "added years" purchased with AVCs;
- membership profile:
  - difficulties in establishing pensioner existence;
  - numbers of members leaving the scheme, giving rise to transfer payments;
  - the death rate among scheme members, and extent of consequential adjustments to benefits payable to surviving spouses
- non compliance with schedule of contributions or payment schedule;
- investment arrangements:
  - investment in volatile markets or in assets that are difficult to value;
  - use of complex financial instruments;
  - insurance policies, including those linked with life-styling arrangements;
  - remote location of assets and unregulated custodial arrangements;
  - non-standard investment classes – works of art, loans;
  - significant levels of employer-related investment.

As part of the risk assessment, the auditor should determine which of the risks identified are, in the auditor's judgment, risks that require special audit consideration (such risks are defined as "significant risks"). (paragraph 108)

For significant risks, to the extent the auditor has not already done so, the auditor should evaluate the design of the entity's related controls, including relevant control activities, and determine whether they have been implemented. (paragraph 113)

Significant risks may arise from significant changes to the scheme. For example:

- changes in third party service providers (such as a change in the scheme administrator or investment manager);
- a scheme reconstruction;

- changes in sponsoring or participating employers; or
- changes in funding arrangements by the employer.

225 Significant risks may also be presented by the following:

- investment types that are illiquid and difficult to value;
- benefits whose calculation are particularly complex and/or involve significant exercise of discretion in individual cases;
- contributions whose rates depend on the identity of the employing company within a group, member age and/or members' management status or are variable at the discretion of the member and/or the employer.

226 Where the use of service organisations is relevant to material aspects of the scheme's financial statements, the scheme auditor needs to have a sufficient understanding of the possible impact of the involvement of the service organisation(s) on financial information in order to assess the risks of material misstatement in the financial statements that might be controlled by the entity i.e. the trustees.

ISA (UK and Ireland) 320: Audit Materiality

Background note

The purpose of this ISA (UK and Ireland) is to establish standards and provide guidance on the concept of materiality and its relationship with audit risk.

Materiality should be considered by the auditor when:

(a) Determining the nature, timing and extent of audit procedures; and
(b) Evaluating the effect of misstatements. (paragraph 8)

227 The principles of assessing materiality of a pension scheme to be audited are the same as those applying to the audit of any entity. However, the focus of attention in a set of financial statements of a pension scheme does not correspond to that of a commercial trading entity: net earnings or level of working capital are not among the prime indicators for a pension scheme and therefore when considering materiality the focus is directed at contributions receivable, benefits payable, returns on investment, the levels of other items of income and expenditure and the disposition of the scheme assets.

228 ISA (UK and Ireland) 320 indicates that materiality is considered at both the overall financial statement level and in relation to individual account balances, classes of transactions and disclosures. In the context of pension schemes, materiality is usually based on:

- a percentage of the total value of the assets in the scheme, or
- a percentage of the inflows or outflows from dealings with members.

229 Materiality for pension schemes may vary with the nature of the scheme – defined benefit/defined contribution – and needs to be assessed for each individual scheme rather than applying any general guidelines. It is also important to distinguish, especially for the benefit of the trustees, that materiality in relation to the audit of the pension scheme's financial statements will not necessarily coincide with the expectations of materiality of an individual member of the scheme in relation to his or her

expected benefits. Even in the case of defined contribution arrangements, the scheme auditors' judgments about materiality are made in the context of the financial statements as a whole and the account balances and classes of transactions reported in those statements, rather than in the context of an individual member's designated assets, contributions or benefits.

The scheme auditors' statement about contributions requires assessment of whether specific conditions have been met. This narrower and more factual focus of the report entails close consideration of payment dates and amounts, and hence a different level of materiality to that used in relation to the scheme's financial statements is likely to be appropriate. 230

Scheme auditors have a duty under the PA 1995, if they become aware of breaches of law which they have reasonable grounds to believe are 'of material significance' to the exercise of the functions of the regulator, TPR, to report such matters to the regulator. The meaning of the term 'of material significance' differs from 'materiality' in the context of forming an opinion as to whether financial statements show a true and fair view, and is considered in more detail in the section commenting on the application of ISA (UK and Ireland) 250, Section B 'The Auditors' Right and Duty to Report to Regulators in the Financial Sector'. 231

Neither the scope of the audit, nor the scheme auditors' assessment of materiality for planning purposes, are affected by the duty to report matters that are likely to be of material significance to TPR. 232

ISA (UK and Ireland) 330: The Auditor's Procedures in Response to Assessed Risks

Background note

The purpose of this ISA (UK and Ireland) is to establish standards and provide guidance on determining overall responses and designing and performing further audit procedures to respond to the assessed risks of material misstatement at the financial statement and assertion levels in a financial statement audit.

When in accordance with paragraph 115 of ISA (UK and Ireland) 315 the auditor has determined that it is not possible to reduce the risks of material misstatement at the assertion level to an acceptably low level with audit evidence obtained only from substantive procedures, the auditor should perform tests of relevant controls to obtain audit evidence about their operating effectiveness. (paragraph 25)

When in accordance with paragraph 108 of ISA (UK and Ireland) 315 the auditor has determined that an assessed risk of material misstatement at the assertion level is a significant risk, the auditor should perform substantive procedures that are specifically responsive to that risk. (paragraph 51)

There are a limited number of circumstances where it may not be possible or practicable to reduce the risks of material misstatement in a pension scheme's financial statements to an appropriate level with only substantive procedures. Some possible examples are: 233

- complex contribution structures or a large number of payroll sites;

- investment re-organisations;
- complex benefit structures.

234 Where the auditor deems such a situation to exist, the operating effectiveness of the controls in place will need to be tested.

235 Possible significant risks in the context of pension schemes are listed in the section on ISA (UK and Ireland) 315. The related substantive procedures that an auditor might apply are as follows:
- Where significant investments are illiquid and difficult to value, the auditor pays particular attention to the basis adopted by the trustees for obtaining a market valuation. Where the trustees have sought the assistance of specialist valuers, the auditor has regard to the requirements of ISA (UK and Ireland) 620 'Using the Work of an Expert' when deciding how much direct testing to apply to the values reflected in the scheme's financial statements.
- Where calculations of significant benefits are particularly complex and/or involve significant exercise of discretion in individual cases, the trustees are likely to have engaged specialists (possibly the scheme actuary) to perform calculations on their behalf. Once again, the auditor has regard to ISA (UK and Ireland) 620 'Using the Work of an Expert' when deciding how much direct testing to apply to benefits reflected in the scheme's financial statements.
- Where calculations of contributions include rates that depend on the identity of the employing company within a group, member age and/or members' management status, the auditor considers the procedures adopted by the trustees for ensuring the correct allocation of members to age bands, employer groups or senior management/staff membership categories. In the case of contribution rates that are variable or discretionary, the auditor pays particular attention to the manner in which the trustees exercise their discretion or monitor the discretion of members to change rates as a basis for ensuring that contributions are received in accordance with the requirements of the Schedule of Contributions or Payment Schedule (as applicable).

ISA (UK and Ireland) 402: Audit Considerations Relating to Entities Using Service Organisations

Background note

The purpose of this ISA (UK and Ireland) is to establish standards and provide guidance to an auditor where the entity uses a service organisation

In obtaining an understanding of the entity and its environment, the auditor should determine the significance of service organisation activities to the entity and the relevance to the audit. (paragraph 5)

236 The auditor identifies whether the pension scheme uses service organisations and assesses the effect of any such use on the procedures necessary to obtain sufficient and appropriate audit evidence to determine with reasonable assurance whether the financial statements are free of material misstatement.

237 Use of a service organisation does not diminish the ultimate responsibility of the trustees for conducting the affairs of the scheme in a manner which meets their legal

responsibilities, including those of safeguarding the assets, maintaining proper accounting records and preparing financial statements.

Similarly, an entity's use of a service organisation does not alter the auditor's responsibilities when reporting on its financial statements, but may have a significant effect on the nature of procedures undertaken to obtain sufficient appropriate audit evidence to determine whether a user entity's financial statements are free from material misstatement. 238

Service organisations undertake a wide range of activities within the pensions sector. Many of these are capable of having a significant effect on the financial statements. Consequently the auditor of a pension scheme needs to consider the nature and extent of activity undertaken by service organisations to determine whether those activities are relevant to the audit, and what their effect is on audit risk. 239

Examples of activities that may be undertaken by service organisations include: 240

- maintenance of the scheme's accounting and/or membership records;
- processing of the pension payroll;
- collection and investment of contributions paid over by the employer;
- custody and management of the scheme's investment assets, including the collection of income and (where possible) the recovery of withholding tax suffered;
- calculation and payment of benefits and transfers.

> If the auditor concludes that the activities of the service organisation are significant to the entity and relevant to the audit, the auditor should obtain a sufficient understanding of the entity and its environment, including its internal control to identify and assess the risks of material misstatement and design further audit procedures in response to the assessed risk. (paragraph 7)

If the auditor is able to obtain a sufficient understanding of risk on which to base his planning of audit procedures by considering the pension fund's controls and information available to the pension fund, for example by reviewing a report produced in accordance with AAF 01/06 (see paragraph 252(c) below), the auditor will not need to supplement that understanding and assessment by making further enquiries about the control arrangements of relevant service providers. 241

If the auditor is unable to obtain a sufficient understanding of risk by considering information and controls at the entity level, the auditor takes steps to obtain a more detailed understanding of the control arrangements of relevant service providers by such means as visiting the service organisation or requesting the service organisation's auditor or the entity's internal audit function to perform specified procedures. The feasibility of this approach will depend on whether the contractual arrangements between the trustees and the service provider entitle the trustees to obtain supplementary information when considered necessary. 242

Where controls are poor or absent, the auditor also considers whether the status of the scheme's internal control arrangements should be the subject of a report to TPR. 243

> Based on the auditor's understanding of the aspects of the entity's accounting system and control environment relating to relevant activities, the auditor should:

> (a) Assess whether sufficient appropriate audit evidence concerning the relevant financial statement assertions is available from records held at the entity; and if not,
> (b) Determine effective procedures to obtain evidence necessary for the audit, either by direct access to records kept by service organisations or through information obtained from the service organisations or their auditor. (paragraph 9-18)

244   Information prepared on behalf of the trustees of a pension scheme by outsourced service providers (e.g. actuaries, investment managers and custodians, and scheme administrators) should be considered as being "produced by the entity" and therefore the auditor is required to obtain audit evidence about the accuracy and completeness of that information (see also ISA (UK and Ireland) 500.

Administration of contributions and benefits

245   When a pension scheme uses another organisation or the sponsoring employer to deal with the administration of contributions and benefits and to maintain membership and financial records, the trustees arrange for the scheme auditors to have direct access to the records and personnel of the relevant organisation acting as scheme administrator.

246   Where particular administrative functions such as the collection of contributions and the payment of benefits are delegated to sponsoring employers, the scheme auditors may, with the agreement of the trustees and the employers, request the employers' auditors or internal auditors to carry out specified procedures and to report their findings to the scheme auditors. Where such auditors are used, the requirements set out in ISA (UK and Ireland) 610 'Considering the work of internal audit' or ISA (UK and Ireland) 600 'Considering the work of another auditor', as applicable, should be followed. If the foregoing methods of obtaining audit evidence are not available to the scheme auditors, they may need to consider whether this will result in a limitation to the scope of their audit which affects their opinions on the financial statements and on the payment of contributions.

Investment management and custody

247   The relationship between the pension scheme and third party investment managers and custodians will often have a significant impact on the source, nature and timing of financial information available to the pension scheme and the accounting records maintained by it.

248   The scheme auditors will wish to consider how the contract(s) between the pension scheme and service organisations, and the manner in which the trustees of the pension scheme ensure compliance with the contract terms, affect audit evidence requirements in relation to the following assertions:

- existence: the investments exist at a given date;
- rights and obligations: the investments pertain to the scheme at the relevant date and any lien or other charge is properly identified;
- occurrence: investment income and purchases and sales of investments pertain to the scheme during the relevant period;
- completeness: there are no unrecorded investments or related assets and liabilities, investment income, transactions or events, or undisclosed items;
- valuation: investments are recorded at an appropriate carrying value;

- measurement: investment transactions are recorded at the proper amount and revenue or expense is allocated to the proper period; and
- presentation and disclosure: investment related items are disclosed, classified and described in accordance with the applicable accounting framework. In the case of occupational pension schemes, the applicable accounting framework is established by PA 1995 and related regulations, accounting standards issued by the ASB and the Pensions SORP.

The principal factors affecting the scheme auditors' judgment as to the extent and nature of audit evidence required in relation to investments managed by a third party are:

(a) The nature and extent of the investment services provided by the third party;
(b) The materiality and inherent risk of the financial statement assertions relating to activities delegated to the service organisations;
(c) The nature and extent of records maintained by the trustees or scheme administrators, and the level of supervision that the trustees exercise over any third parties;
(d) The reputation of the third party for providing accurate and timely information. The reputation of the entity may be enhanced in circumstances where the service provided is subject to regulatory oversight (as is the case in relation to investment management) and there is no evidence of regulatory action against the service organisation having been initiated by the regulator concerned; and
(e) The contract terms between the pension scheme and the various service organisations concerned, and the ways in which the trustees of the pension scheme monitor compliance with the contract terms, including any arrangements for independent check on the actions of one service organisation by another (for example, where duties are segregated between a custodian and investment manager who operate independently of each other).

A contract clause whereby the investment manager or custodian indemnifies the scheme in the event of loss caused by maladministration is unlikely to provide information directly relevant to the scheme auditors' judgment concerning the extent of evidence to be obtained in relation to investments and investment income. However, such a clause may, together with information concerning the financial resources available to the service organisation, be relevant to the auditors' understanding of the effect on the scheme's financial statements of performance failure by the investment manager or custodian.

Sources of evidence

The trustees or scheme administrator may maintain accounting records which are initiated independently from the investment manager and/or custodian, and are sufficient to monitor the transactions undertaken on behalf of the scheme. When such records are kept, and the scheme auditors' assessment of control risk is low, sufficient appropriate audit evidence may ordinarily be obtained by performing procedures on the records maintained by the scheme administrator, and agreeing them to the extent deemed appropriate with independent confirmations from third parties, including the investment manager and/or custodian.

Where trustees or administrators do not maintain accounting records in relation to investments and related transactions which are initiated independently from the investment manager and/ or custodian (for example, where the trustees have given the investment manager discretionary powers) the scheme auditors consider whether sufficient appropriate audit evidence is available from other sources. Alternative sources of audit evidence are:

(a) Returns and/or confirmations from service organisations: reconciliation of representations from independent service organisations may provide valuable audit evidence especially in relation to the ownership and existence assertions. The quality of such evidence is determined by the degree to which there is segregation of responsibility between the custodian and investment manager. Hence such reconciliations form reliable audit evidence only if the scheme auditors can also obtain evidence that the two entities are operated and managed independently of each other and maintain separate records and databases;

(b) Funds reconciliations: analytical review of reconciliations between cash movements and investment transactions, possibly accompanied by more detailed substantive procedures, can provide useful evidence concerning the existence and ownership assertions but provides relatively little evidence in relation to other assertions including completeness of investment income;

(c) Controls reports provided by service organisations: as part of their approach to monitoring the activities of a service organisation, trustees may decide to obtain a 'controls report' from the service organisation covering the design and operating effectiveness of the organisation's accounting and internal control systems relevant to the scheme. Reports prepared under AAF01/06 'Assurance reports on internal controls of service organisations made available to third parties' (a technical release issued by the Audit Faculty of the ICAEW) include an assurance opinion given by the reporting accountant in which they conclude on the fairness of the directors' description and the design and operating effectiveness of control procedures in relation to a specified reporting period.

Scheme auditors may find such an assurance report obtained by the trustees useful audit evidence, especially where:

  (i) the scope of the work performed by the reporting accountants adequately addresses controls relevant to the financial statement assertions concerning the scheme's investments;

  (ii) it contains an unqualified assurance report by the reporting accountant;

  (iii) the scheme auditor has confidence, in the context of the specific assignment undertaken, regarding the professional competence of the reporting accountant;

  (iv) the assurance report covers the full reporting period of the pension scheme or, where this is not the case, the scheme auditors conclude, after taking into account the reputation of the investment manager and/or custodian as a provider of reliable information, that they are able to carry out appropriate additional procedures in order to rely on returns from the investment manager and/or custodian in relation to the remainder of the reporting period;

(d) Agreed-upon procedures performed by service entity auditors: the effectiveness of this method of obtaining audit evidence will depend upon the ways in which the service organisation operates. For example, if investments are held on a pooled basis, confirmation of the specific investments owned by one scheme may be impracticable. In addition, such procedures may involve considerable cost;

(e) Direct inspection of the service provider's records by user auditors: some service contracts provide pension scheme trustees with access to the records of the service organisation. Unless such a contractual agreement exists, there is no right of auditor access to records maintained outside the scheme. If access is obtained, direct inspection, particularly in relation to a comparatively small fund operated by a large investment manager, is likely to give considerable practical difficulties and to involve considerable cost.

253 The above guidance relates to situations where the pension scheme has a portfolio of investments and these investments are disclosed in the financial statements. The guidance is not intended to address the situation where the scheme invests wholly in unitised products such as a managed fund. It is the units in the fund that are shown

in the net assets statement as scheme assets rather than the underlying investments of the managed fund, and consequently the scheme auditors normally obtain evidence as to the existence and value of the units themselves rather than the underlying investments.

Similarly, where a scheme invests in a common investment fund constituted under a trust deed requiring the preparation of audited financial statements, the net assets statement of the scheme reflects the participation in the net assets and investment portfolio of the common investment fund, as reflected in its financial statements, rather than the individual underlying investments. In such cases, the scheme auditors normally agree the amount at which the investment is included in the net assets statement with the common investment funds' audited financial statements, and place reliance on the work of the fund's auditors following the requirements of ISA (UK and Ireland) 600. 254

Some outsourced activities are the subject of regulation, notably investment management. However, regulation does not by itself eliminate the need for pension scheme auditors to obtain independent evidence because controls required by regulators, and inspection work undertaken by them in service organisations, may not be relevant to or sufficiently focussed on aspects of importance to pension schemes. Furthermore, reports from the service organisation's auditors required by its regulator are not ordinarily available to a pension scheme or its auditors. 255

Many pension schemes outsource the maintenance of their accounting records to third parties. Scheme auditors obtain and document an understanding as to the way the accounting records are maintained, including the way in which trustees ensure that their records meet the PA 1995 and trust deed requirements for such records. 256

Scheme auditors may need to obtain audit evidence in relation to information provided by the relevant employer and in this may seek the assistance of the employer's auditors. It is the statutory duty of the employer and the employer's auditors to disclose on request to the trustees such information as is reasonably required for the performance of the duties of the trustees or scheme auditors. The trustees in turn have a statutory duty to disclose such information to the scheme auditors as they reasonably require to perform their duties. If scheme auditors require the assistance of the employer's auditors in providing information or in carrying out certain audit procedures, it is appropriate for the initial request to be made through the trustees and the employer. 257

The Pensions Research Accountants Group (PRAG) has issued guidance for scheme trustees entitled "Outsourcing for trustees"[22], which provides practical guidance on the management of the risks that can arise when functions are carried out by a service provider. As one of the risks concerns access to accounting records, it may be beneficial for scheme auditors to enquire whether trustees have obtained the PRAG guidance and considered its implications. 258

If the scheme auditors conclude that evidence from records held by a service provider is necessary in order to form an opinion on the financial statements of the pension scheme and they are unable to obtain such evidence, they consider how this will affect their audit opinion. If the scheme auditors decide to qualify their opinion due to insufficient audit evidence relating to outsourced activities this situation may need to be reported to TPR under section 70 of the PA 2004. 259

---

[22] Available from the PRAG Administrator, whose contact details may be obtained from PRAG's website – www.prag.org.uk.

ISA (UK and Ireland) 520: Analytical Procedures

Background note

The purpose of this ISA (UK and Ireland) is to establish standards and provide guidance on the application of analytical procedures during an audit.

The auditor should apply analytical procedures as risk assessment procedures to obtain an understanding of the entity and its environment and in the overall review at the end of the audit. (paragraph 2)

260 Analytical review techniques are likely to be particularly useful in the audit of pension schemes, not only at the planning and overall review stages of the audit but also as substantive procedures to supplement other evidence concerning the operation of controls or accuracy of individual balances and transactions.

261 Although pension schemes' income, resources and expenditure may fluctuate from year to year, for most transactions there are still ways in which the scheme auditor can establish whether the figures are internally consistent and reflect the pension scheme's operations during the year. Key techniques include comparison of information shown in the financial statements, for example:

- investment income is usually a substantial proportion of total income and analytical procedures can be used in this context;
- monthly and annual patterns of contribution income can be compared to expected amounts using rates set out in the schedule of contributions or payment schedule. However, difficulties may be encountered when differing rates of contribution are used for different categories of members;
- monthly and annual patterns of pensions payments can be compared to movements in membership statistics and increases to benefits in payment;
- membership statistics and bench-marking reports on investment performance, which ought to correlate to financial information shown in the financial statements;
- non-financial information contained in documents issued by the scheme, such as summary reports, pensions newsletters, or in management information reports concerning scheme membership;
- minutes of trustees' meetings, including committees and sub-committees of the trustees, which can be expected to reflect major issues and events arising during the period under review;
- comparison of actual income and expenditure to prior years' figures and trends;
- comparison of actual expenditure to the scheme auditor's own expectation of expenditure that would be reasonable for the particular transaction under review, for example average pension payment per pensioner;
- comparison with published information, for example in respect of investment income, equity yields and rental income per square foot.

ISA (UK and Ireland) 550: Related Parties

Background note

> The purpose of this ISA (UK and Ireland) is to establish standards and provide guidance on the auditor's responsibilities and audit procedures regarding related parties and transactions with such parties regardless of whether International Accounting Standard (IAS) 24, "Related Party Disclosures," or similar requirement, is part of the applicable financial reporting framework.

> When planning the audit the auditor should assess the risk that material undisclosed related party transactions, or undisclosed outstanding balances between an entity and its related parties may exist. (paragraph 106-3)

The related parties of pension schemes fall into three broad categories: 262

- employer-related;
- trustee-related; or
- officers and managers.

The Pensions SORP recommends that for financial reporting purposes related parties should be deemed also to include other pension schemes for the benefit of employees of companies and businesses related to the employers, or for the benefit of the employees of any entity that is itself a related party of the reporting pension scheme. 263

The same principles and procedures set out in ISA (UK and Ireland) 550 apply to the audit of pension schemes as for other entities. The scheme auditors consider the possibility of related party transactions, for example where a pension scheme contracts with the employer or related third parties for the use of a property or for the supply of goods or services to the scheme, even if these result in more favourable terms for the pension scheme than would otherwise be available. 264

Scheme auditors enquire as to the procedures that the trustees have introduced to identify related parties and to authorise and record any related party transactions, including transactions with or loans to the sponsoring employer. Paragraphs 2.126 to 2.131 of the Pensions SORP provide guidance on the types of transaction that fall into the categories shown above and the form of disclosure recommended. Scheme auditors consider whether the trustees have made appropriate arrangements for identifying, authorising and recording such transactions in the circumstances of the particular scheme. Scheme auditors also obtain written representations from the trustees concerning the completeness of information provided regarding the related party disclosures in the financial statements. 265

It is a fundamental principle of trust law that trustees do not benefit from their trust. In addition, certain forms of employer-related investments are also prohibited or restricted by the legislation. This means that pension scheme trustees are prohibited from transacting directly with the pension scheme, although transactions between pension schemes and businesses in which any of the trustees have an indirect interest (for example as a shareholder or a director) are not necessarily prohibited. The pension scheme trustee who is also a scheme member may, however, benefit as a scheme member from decisions taken as a trustee. 266

ISA (UK and Ireland) 570: Going Concern

> Background note

> The purpose of this ISA (UK and Ireland) is to establish standards and provide guidance on the auditor's responsibility on the audit of financial statements with respect to the going concern assumption used in the preparation of the financial statements, including management's assessment of the entity's ability to continue as a going concern.

> When planning and performing audit procedures and in evaluating the results thereof, the auditor should consider the appropriateness of management's use of the going concern assumption in the preparation of the financial statements. (paragraph 2)
>
> The auditor should consider any relevant disclosures in the financial statements. (paragraph 2-1)
>
> In obtaining an understanding of the entity, the auditor should consider whether there are events or conditions and related business risks which may cast significant doubt on the entity's ability to continue as a going concern. (paragraph 11)
>
> The auditor should evaluate management's assessment of the entity's ability to continue as a going concern (paragraph 17).

267 The scheme auditors' assessment of a scheme's status as a going concern differs from that undertaken in the audit of the financial statements of a commercial entity.

268 As explained in the Pensions SORP, the going concern concept does not play the same fundamental role in the measurement and classification of assets and liabilities in pension scheme financial statements as it does in the financial statements of commercial entities. The basis of preparation of financial statements does not change unless the trustees have taken the decision to wind up the scheme (the Pensions SORP, paragraphs 2.33 to 2.34).

269 The scheme auditors' legal obligation in reporting on financial statements of a pension scheme is to express an opinion as to whether those statements show a true and fair view of the scheme's financial transactions and its assets and liabilities (excluding liabilities to pay pensions and benefits falling due after the scheme year end) rather than a true and fair view of the broader concept of an entity's state of affairs. This form of opinion reflects the nature of pension schemes' financial statements, which exclude long term obligations to meet pension commitments.

270 Information about the continued ability of a scheme to meet future benefits is provided in the actuarial statements and actuarial valuation, neither of which form a basis of the audited financial statements but are included or referred to in the annual report alongside the financial statements. Scheme auditors have no statutory responsibility to report on information contained in the annual report: however, they are required by ISA (UK and Ireland) 720 to read other information included in documents containing audited financial statements and, if they become aware of apparent misstatements or inconsistencies with the audited financial statements, to seek to resolve them. In addition, The Auditors' Code indicates that auditors do not allow their reports to be included in documents containing other information which they consider to be misleading.

Pension scheme auditors make enquiries of the trustees as to whether there are circumstances indicating that it may be appropriate to wind up the scheme. In addition, TPR has power to order a scheme to be wound up and therefore the scheme auditors consider correspondence with TPR in this regard. 271

In all cases where the scheme auditors conclude that there are circumstances which may lead to the scheme being wound up, they consider whether the trustees have provided relevant information in the trustees' report as recommended by the Pensions SORP. If the scheme auditors become aware that the trustees have taken a decision to wind up the scheme, they consider whether appropriate changes have been made in the bases of valuation of assets in the financial statements, as recommended by the Pensions SORP. 272

The trustees' consideration of the appropriateness of the going concern basis when preparing the financial statements does not involve their consideration of prospective financial information. Therefore, the ISA (UK and Ireland) paragraph 17-1 b(ii) requirement for the auditor to identify any material matters which could indicate concern about a scheme's ability to continue as a going concern is not relevant to the audit of a pension scheme. Further, the auditor does not search for circumstances that might, as a result of a future uncertain event, lead to the scheme needing to be wound up. 273

ISA (UK and Ireland) 580: Management Representations

Background note

The purpose of this ISA (UK and Ireland) is to establish standards and provide guidance on the use of management representations as audit evidence, the procedures to be applied in evaluating and documenting management representations and the action to be taken if management refuses to provide appropriate representations.

The auditor should obtain appropriate representations from management. (paragraph 2)

An important principle is that scheme auditors do not accept the unsupported representations of trustees or senior management of the pension scheme where these relate to matters which are material to the financial statements. Moreover, representations cannot substitute for evidence that the scheme auditors reasonably expect to be available. 274

Written confirmation of appropriate representations from management, as required by paragraph 4 below, should be obtained before the audit report is issued. (paragraph 2-1)

In the UK and Ireland, the auditor should obtain evidence that those charged with governance acknowledge their collective responsibility for the preparation of the financial statements and have approved the financial statements. (paragraph 3-1)

> The auditor should obtain written representations from management on matters material to the financial statements when other sufficient appropriate audit evidence cannot reasonably be expected to exist. (paragraph 4)

275 ISA (UK and Ireland) 580 requires auditors to obtain written confirmation of appropriate representations from management. These commonly take the form of a representation letter and normally include a representation concerning the completeness of information made available to the scheme auditors, including minutes of trustee meetings and correspondence with the Pensions Ombudsman, TPAS and TPR. In addition, ISA (UK and Ireland) 250 and ISA (UK and Ireland) 550 require auditors to obtain written confirmation in respect of the completeness of disclosure to the auditors of:

- known events which involve possible non-compliance with laws and regulations, together with the actual or contingent consequences which may arise therefrom; and
- information provided regarding the identification of related parties and the adequacy of related party disclosures.

276 The trustees as a body are responsible for the contents and presentation of the financial statements. Consequently, discussion of the content of any written representation by the trustee body as a whole may be appropriate before it is signed on behalf of the trustees, often by two of their members. The body of trustees as a whole is responsible for the contents and presentation of the financial statements.

277 For larger pension schemes where there is a non-trustee chief executive or pensions manager, it is also likely that in practice there are some representations that necessitate discussion with that person. Scheme auditors often find it useful to attend the meeting at which trustees consider the financial statements and representation letter, to encourage discussion of significant items or matters, including unadjusted errors, arising in the course of the audit.

278 An example of a representation letter is included in Appendix 5.

279 In many pension schemes day to day management may be delegated to a scheme management team, possibly provided by a service organisation. In these circumstances, the trustees may wish scheme management or the third party service organisation to provide a representation to them in relation to some or all aspects of the preparation of the financial statements. This is a relationship matter for the trustees and should not impact on the nature or strength of the representations made by the trustees to the auditor.

280 Timely communication by auditors with the trustees on significant issues on which representations will be required is important in this sector, which relies primarily on unpaid (voluntary) trustees who are not involved in the day-to-day running of the affairs of the scheme.

281 If there is a delay between the approval of the financial statements by the trustees and their receipt by the auditor for the approval of the audit report and the statement about contributions, the auditor considers whether to obtain an update of the trustees' representations, either by enquiry of the secretary to the trustees about any changes to the scheme's circumstances or by requesting the trustees to provide an updated representation letter.

ISA (UK and Ireland) 600: Using the Work of Another Auditor

Background note

The purpose of this ISA (UK and Ireland) is to establish standards and provide guidance when an auditor reporting on the financial statements of an entity ('the principal auditor') uses the work of another auditor ('the other auditor') on the financial information of one or more components included in the financial statements of the entity.

When the principal auditor uses the work of another auditor, the principal auditor should determine how the work of the other auditor will affect the audit. (paragraph 2)

When planning to use the work of another auditor, the principal auditor should consider the professional competence of the other auditor in the context of the specific assignment. (paragraph 7)

282 Where scheme auditors use the services of other auditors in the audit of statutory financial statements, then the scheme auditors advise the other auditors of the use that is to be made of their work and make the necessary arrangements for the co-ordination of their efforts at the initial planning stage of the audit.

283 The Scheme Administration Regulations require sponsoring employers and their auditors to provide trustees with 'such information as is reasonably required' for the scheme auditors to carry out their duties (Appendix 2, paragraph 60). Scheme auditors may therefore request scheme trustees to ask the auditors of the employer to carry out certain work on contributions paid to the scheme by the employer, rather than undertaking such work themselves. Typically this arises in multi-employer schemes, such as industry-wide arrangements.

The principal auditor should perform procedures to obtain sufficient appropriate audit evidence that the work of the other auditor is adequate for the principal auditor's purposes in the context of the specific assignment. (paragraph 8)

284 Scheme auditors specify the procedures to be undertaken and provide these to the trustees. The trustees then pass these to the employer and the employer's auditor, who is engaged by the employer to undertake the work on the understanding that the results will be passed to the scheme trustees purely for the purposes of the scheme audit. If the trustees wish to contract directly with the employer's auditors to undertake work on their behalf, the employer's auditors will need to be appointed as a professional adviser to the scheme under the Scheme Administration Regulations in the same way as scheme auditors.

ISA (UK and Ireland) 620: Using the Work of an Expert

Background note

> The purpose of this ISA (UK and Ireland) is to establish standards and provide guidance on using the work of an expert as audit evidence.

> When using the work performed by an expert, the auditor should obtain sufficient appropriate audit evidence that such work is adequate for the purposes of the audit. (paragraph 2)

285 Areas in which the scheme auditors may, in conjunction with the trustees, use the work of an expert to provide audit evidence include:

- valuations of certain investments, for example unquoted investments, insurance policies, properties and works of art and certain derivatives and alternative investment categories; and
- legal opinions concerning the interpretation of the trust deed and rules.

286 The nature of the scheme auditors' statutory opinion excludes consideration of liabilities to pay pension and benefits after the end of the scheme year. As a result, scheme auditors do not ordinarily rely on the work of the scheme actuary to provide audit evidence to support their report on a scheme's financial statements.

287 Nevertheless, for a defined benefit scheme, the actuary's certificate and/or statement is an important element in the information accompanying the audited financial statements as part of the trustees' annual report. ISA (UK and Ireland) 720 requires scheme auditors to read such accompanying information and, if they become aware of any apparent misstatements or inconsistencies with the audited financial statements, to seek to resolve them. Steps to be taken to facilitate necessary liaison with the scheme actuary are discussed in the section of this Practice Note headed Liaison with the scheme actuary.

ISA (UK and Ireland) 700: The Auditor's Report on Financial Statements

> **Background note**
>
> The purpose of this ISA (UK and Ireland) is to establish standards and provide guidance on the form and content of the auditor's report issued as a result of an audit performed by an independent auditor of the financial statements of an entity. Much of the guidance provided can be adapted to auditors' reports on financial information other than financial statements.

> The auditor's report should contain a clear written expression of opinion on the financial statements taken as a whole. (paragraph 4)
>
> The auditor's report should be appropriately addressed as required by the circumstances of the engagement and local regulations. (paragraph 7)
>
> In the UK and Ireland:
>
> (a) The auditor should distinguish between the auditor's responsibilities and the responsibilities of those charged with governance by including in their report a reference to a description of the relevant responsibilities of those charged

> with governance when that description is set out elsewhere in the financial statements or accompanying information; or
> (b) Where the financial statements or accompanying information do not include an adequate description of relevant responsibilities of those charged with governance, the auditor's report should include a description of those responsibilities. (paragraph 9-1)
>
> The auditor's report should describe the scope of the audit by stating that the audit was conducted in accordance with ISAs (UK and Ireland) or in accordance with relevant national standards or practices as appropriate. (paragraph 12)
>
> The opinion paragraph of the auditor's report should clearly indicate the financial reporting framework used to prepare the financial statements (including identifying the country of origin of the financial reporting framework when the framework used is not International Accounting Standards) and state the auditor's opinion as to whether the financial statements give a true and fair view (or are presented fairly, in all material respects) in accordance with that financial reporting framework and, where appropriate, whether the financial statements comply with statutory requirements. (paragraph 17)

288　The form and content of auditors' reports on the financial statements of occupational pension schemes follow the basic principles and procedures established by ISA (UK and Ireland) 700, supplemented by the particular detailed requirements of the Audited Accounts Regulations which are explained in the following paragraphs.

Addressee of the report

289　The Audited Accounts Regulations require trustees to obtain audited financial statements: hence the scheme auditors address their report on a scheme's financial statements to the trustees of the scheme and to other parties if required by the trust deed or other applicable rules.

Statement of trustees' responsibilities

290　ISA (UK and Ireland) 700 requires auditors to include a statement distinguishing between their responsibilities and those of the entity's directors (in the case of a pension scheme, its trustees) and to refer to a description of the latter's responsibilities set out in the financial statements or accompanying information. If no adequate description is given, the ISA requires the auditors to provide details in their report.

291　The responsibilities of the trustees may vary according to the constitution of the particular pension scheme. Example Trustees' Responsibilities Statements are set out in Appendix 7, which may be adapted to the circumstances of individual schemes.

Compliance with relevant accounting requirements

292　The scheme auditors' opinion on a pension schemes' financial statements is expressed in the context of the particular accounting requirements applicable to the pension scheme concerned. ISA (UK and Ireland) 700 includes commentary on compliance with the requirements of law and accounting standards (see paragraphs 22-1 and 22-2). In general terms, unless exceptional circumstances apply, compliance with accounting standards is necessary to show a true and fair view.

Requirements of the Pensions Act 1995

293 The Audited Accounts Regulations made under the PA 1995 require trustees or managers of certain types of scheme to obtain accounts which contain the information specified in the Schedule to the Regulations and show a true and fair view of the financial transactions of the scheme during the scheme year, the amount and disposition of the assets at the end of the scheme year and the liabilities of the scheme, other than the liabilities to pay pensions and benefits after the end of the scheme year. The Regulations require the scheme auditors to state whether or not in their opinion the financial statements contain the information specified in the Schedule to the Regulations.

294 The Pensions SORP has been developed and issued by PRAG in accordance with the Accounting Standards Board's code of practice for the production and issue of SORPs. The Pensions SORP was last revised in November 2002 and sets out guidance intended to represent best practice on the form and content of the financial statements of pension schemes prepared in accordance with accounting standards current at the time of its issue.

295 The Audited Accounts Regulations require trustees of a scheme to disclose in its financial statements whether those statements have been prepared following the Pensions SORP's guidelines, and, if not, to give details of any material departures. Although the Pensions SORP's guidance is not mandatory, this provision, taken with the general status of a Pensions SORP issued in accordance with the ASB's code, has the effect of establishing a strong presumption that financial statements which meet the PA 1995's requirement to show a true and fair view will normally follow the guidance contained in the Pensions SORP, taking into account any amendment judged to be necessary as a result of changes in financial reporting standards since its issue.

Other considerations

296 The trust deed establishing a scheme may establish additional requirements concerning the contents of its financial statements (but may not derogate from the statutory requirements). The scheme auditors therefore assess whether any such requirements are met. In addition, where the scheme auditors become aware of information which indicates that a transaction or transactions undertaken by the scheme may have breached any terms of its trust deed, they consider the implications for their reporting responsibilities following the guidance in the sections dealing with ISA (UK and Ireland) 250.

Examples of scheme auditors' reports

297 ISA (UK and Ireland) 700 sets out requirements for the content of auditors' reports on financial statements, including the circumstances in which additional explanatory material is necessary or the auditors' opinion is to be qualified. Examples of scheme auditors' reports showing different legislative requirements and illustrating each of the different forms of opinion are set out in Appendix 6.

Relationship with duty to report to TPR

298 When determining the nature of their report, scheme auditors also assess whether the evidence obtained over the audit as a whole indicates that a statutory duty to report direct to TPR exists in addition to any report already made in respect of particular

matters encountered in the course of their work. In making this assessment, the scheme auditors take into account their accumulated knowledge of the scheme and the attitude of the trustees towards regulatory requirements.

In addition, a decision by the scheme auditors either to issue a qualified opinion on the financial statements of the scheme or to qualify their statement about contributions may be of material significance to TPR and, if so, is reported to TPR by the scheme auditors without waiting for the issue of the annual report. The report should take account of the normal reporting guidelines referred to earlier in this Practice Note. 299

Electronic publication of annual reports

An increasing number of pension schemes have made arrangements for members to obtain information about their schemes (including the scheme annual report) electronically: this may be via publicly accessible websites or on corporate intranet sites. 300

Auditors determine through discussion with trustees whether the annual report, and therefore their audit report and statement about contributions, is to be "published" electronically. If electronic publication is proposed, auditors follow the guidance in Appendix 1 of ISA (UK and Ireland) 720 titled 'Electronic Publication of the Auditor's Report'. The main aim of the guidance is to ensure that the auditors' duty of care is not extended solely as a result of their report being published in electronic rather than hard copy form. In addition, as information published on websites is available in many countries with different legal requirements, it must be clear which legislation governs the preparation and dissemination of the financial statements. 301

Summary financial information

Some pension schemes produce statements which summarise financial information based on the full financial statements in their publications. They do this to communicate key financial information without providing the greater detail required in the full accounts with the intention of making this information more accessible to the lay readership of these publications, particularly pension scheme members. 302

There is no requirement for trustees to attach to these summary financial statements a statement from the auditor giving an opinion as to whether the summary financial information is consistent with the full audited accounts. However, the Pensions SORP recommends that as a matter of good practice trustees include the auditor in the distribution of any publications containing summary financial information. 303

Where trustees request auditors to be associated formally with summary financial information, auditors ensure that the nature and presentation of any report that is to be provided for inclusion with the summary financial information is appropriate. In particular, information that is in summarised form or that lacks the analysis contained in full financial statements is unlikely to show a true and fair view; in practice the greatest assurance that the scheme auditor is likely to be able to provide is confirmation that the summarised or selected information has been properly extracted from the full financial statements. 304

The report by the auditor should include the following elements: 305

- Statement of the respective responsibilities of the trustees and the auditor: the summary financial information is the responsibility of the trustees; the auditors

- are only responsible for forming and reporting their opinion on that information.
- Basis of opinion: a description of the steps taken by the auditor to form their opinion. This will normally be a comparison of the information in the summary financial information with the audited financial statements.
- Opinion: a statement that in the opinion of the auditor the summary financial information has been properly extracted from the audited financial statements for the relevant financial period.

ISA (UK and Ireland) 720 (Revised): Section A – Other information in Documents Containing Audited Financial Statements

Background note

The purpose of this ISA (UK and Ireland) is to establish standards and provide guidance on the auditor's consideration of other information, on which the auditor has no obligation to report, in documents containing audited financial statements. This ISA (UK and Ireland) applies when an annual report is involved; however, it may also apply to other documents.

The auditor should read the other information to identify material inconsistencies with the audited financial statements. (paragraph 2)

306 One of the fundamental principles set out in The Auditors' Code is that auditors do not allow their reports to be included in documents containing other information if they consider that the additional information is in conflict with the matters covered by their report or they have cause to believe it to be misleading.

307 Scheme auditors read the other information contained in the annual report in the light of the knowledge they have acquired during the audit. The scheme auditors are not expected to verify any of the other information. They read the other information with a view to identifying whether there are any apparent misstatements therein or matters which are inconsistent with the financial statements. It is important to ensure that the trustees are aware of the scheme auditors' responsibilities in respect of the other information, as set out in ISA (UK and Ireland) 720 and the extent of those responsibilities is specifically outlined in the engagement letter.

308 The 'other information' which may accompany the financial statements of a pension scheme and examples of the areas of potential concern are as follows:

- Trustees' report – membership reconciliation: are the changes in membership numbers consistent with the financial information – number of deaths, new contributors?
- Trustees' report – pension increases: is the rate of increase reflected in the benefit payments?
- Trustees' report: are details of the basis of calculation of transfer payments consistent with the actual basis of the amounts paid?
- Actuary's certificate as to the adequacy of contributions and the actuary's statement (schemes that are still subject to the MFR regime) or Summary Funding Statement (schemes that have had a Scheme Specific Funding Valuation): are the recommended rates of contribution the same as those received by the scheme?

- Investment report: is the asset total and investment income/return reported by the investment manager consistent with the amounts shown in the financial statements?
- Popular report (summary annual report which does not normally accompany the financial statements): are all extracts in the popular report consistent with the audited financial statements?

The trustees may also distribute other documents together with the financial statements such as personal benefit statements, scheme funding statements, new rules booklets or newsletters. The scheme auditors have no statutory responsibility to consider these documents. 309

Practical considerations concerning the timing of work undertaken by the scheme auditors and actuaries are discussed in a subsequent section of this Practice Note, 'Liaison with the scheme actuary'. 310

> If, on reading the other information, the auditor identifies a material inconsistency, the auditor should determine whether the audited financial statements or the other information needs to be amended. (paragraph 11)
>
> If the auditor identifies a material inconsistency the auditor should seek to resolve the matter through discussion with those charged with governance. (paragraph 11-1)

Where the scheme auditors identify inconsistencies or apparent misstatements within the other information they consider whether an amendment is required to the financial statements or to the other information, and discuss the issues with those responsible for preparing the financial statements and annual report, and seek to resolve the situation. If the situation is not resolved, and involves information which the scheme auditors consider to be material, they make reference to the matter in their report on the financial statements and consider whether to report to TPR. 311

The Auditors' Statement about Contributions (the Statement)

Requirement to provide the Statement

Under Regulation 2 of the Audited Accounts Regulations the trustees of an occupational pension scheme are required to obtain, not more than seven months after the end of the scheme year, an auditor's statement about contributions under the scheme. Regulation 4 (as amended) sets out the form and content of the auditor's statement as follows: 312

- a statement as to whether or not in his opinion contributions have in all material respects been paid at least in accordance with the schedule of contributions [for a defined benefit, hybrid or mixed benefit scheme] or payment schedule [for a defined contribution scheme]; and
- if the above statement is negative or qualified, a statement of the reasons.

If the trustees have not put in place a Schedule of Contributions or a Payment Schedule the scheme auditor is required to make a Statement as to whether or not contributions have been paid in accordance with the scheme rules or the contracts under which they were payable and, if applicable, the recommendations of the 313 scheme actuary. If this Statement is negative or qualified, a statement of the reasons must be given.

314 The Statement is not an audit opinion. However it is normal practice for the scheme auditor to provide it at the same time as providing the audit opinion on the overall financial statements. The work to support the Statement will draw on the auditors' work performed in relation to contributions as part of the audit of the scheme's financial statements. Accordingly guidance to auditors on providing the Statement is set out in this Practice Note. For consistency between the various types of scheme (as, for example, in the case of earmarked schemes there are no statutory financial statements), it is recommended that the auditors' statement about contributions is presented separately from the opinion on the financial statements.

SCHEDULES OF CONTRIBUTIONS

Schemes that continue to be subject to the Minimum Funding Requirement regime

315 Under section 58 of the PA 1995 trustees of pension schemes subject to the Minimum Funding Requirement must prepare, maintain and from time to time revise a Schedule of Contributions. The required contents of the Schedule of Contributions are set out in Regulation 17 of the MFR Regulations as follows:

- the rates and due dates of all contributions (other than voluntary contributions) payable by or on behalf of active members of the scheme;
- the rates and due dates of the contributions payable by or on behalf of each person who is an employer in relation to the scheme; and
- if separate contributions to cover expenses which are likely to fall due for payment by the trustees in the schedule period are made to the scheme, the rates and due dates of those contributions.

A Schedule of Contributions is required for any scheme that has an MFR valuation and it needs to cover all sections of the scheme. For example:

- a hybrid scheme with separate sections providing defined benefit and defined contribution benefits would need to include both rates and the due dates on the Schedule of Contributions;
- a hybrid scheme providing the better of a defined benefit and a defined contribution benefit should prepare a Schedule of Contributions which would set out the higher of the defined contribution and the contribution required as a result of an MFR valuation of the defined benefits and the due dates.

A Schedule of Contributions is only legally effective from the date of certification by the Scheme Actuary.

Schemes that are subject to the Scheme Specific Funding requirements

316 Under section 227 of the PA 2004 the trustees or managers of pension schemes subject to the Act's Scheme Specific Funding requirements must prepare and from time to time review and if necessary revise a Schedule of Contributions. The required contents of the Schedule of Contributions are set out in Regulation 10 of the Occupational Pension Schemes (Scheme Funding) Regulations 2005 as follows:

- the rates and due dates of all contributions (other than voluntary contributions) payable by or on behalf of active members of the scheme and the employer;

- if separate contributions to cover expenses which are likely to fall due for payment by the trustees in the schedule period are made to the scheme, the rates and due dates of those contributions;
- where additional contributions are required in order to give effect to a recovery plan, the rates and dates of those contributions must be shown separately from the rates and dates of contributions otherwise payable;
- a note to explain the treatment of the Pension Protection Fund levy.

The Schedule of Contributions must be prepared by the trustees within 15 months of the effective date of the actuarial valuation. The Schedule is generally required to cover a period of five years from the date of certification by the scheme actuary, or the recovery plan if the plan covers a longer period. The schedule must be signed by the trustees and make provision for signature by the employer in order to signify the employer's agreement to the matters included within it.

317 A Schedule of Contributions is required for any scheme that is subject to the PA 2004's funding requirements and it needs to cover all sections of the scheme. For example, a hybrid scheme with separate sections providing defined benefit and defined contribution benefits would need to include both rates and the due dates on the Schedule of Contributions. A Schedule of Contributions is only legally effective from the date of certification by the Scheme Actuary.

318 The content of the Schedule of Contributions is amongst the matters to which trustees are required to obtain the agreement of the employer under section 229 of the PA 2004. There may be instances when TPR imposes a Schedule of Contributions on the parties.

Payment Schedules

319 Under section 87 of the PA 1995 the trustees of most defined contribution pension schemes must prepare, maintain and from time to time revise a Payment Schedule the required contents of which are:

- separate entries for the rates and due dates of contributions (other than voluntary contributions) payable towards the scheme by or on behalf of the employer, and in the case of a scheme in relation to which there is more than one employer, each employer, and the active members of the scheme (Regulation 19 of the Scheme Administration Regulations);
- amounts payable towards the scheme by the employer in respect of expenses likely to be incurred in the scheme year (Regulation 18 of the Scheme Administration Regulations).

320 In the case where an insurance premium is payable, the payment schedule need not contain separate entries identifying the contributions payable by or on behalf of the employer and the active members of the scheme in respect of that premium.

321 The content of the Payment Schedule should be as specified in the scheme documentation or, in the absence of this, as agreed between the trustees and the employer and if agreement cannot be reached with the employer the Payment Schedule should be prepared and put in place by the trustees without the employer's agreement.

Trustee regulatory responsibilities

322 Schedules of Contributions and Payment Schedules are part of a regulatory mechanism to make sure that the employer pays the right contributions on time. If the employer fails to pay contributions in accordance with the Schedule of Contributions or Payment Schedule the trustees need to consider whether to report the matter to TPR. Guidance on reporting late contributions is set out in Code of Practice: Funding defined benefits (for Schedules of Contributions) and Code of Practice: Reporting late payment of contributions to occupational money purchase schemes (for Payment Schedules). Generally, the codes only require the reporting of late contributions by the trustees if the late contributions are likely to be of material significance to the TPR: for example, if contributions due are more than 90 days late or if the late payment involves dishonesty or a misuse of assets or contributions. The trustees must report late contributions to TPR and members within a "reasonable period".

323 The Schedule of Contributions and Payment Schedule are disclosable documents under the PA 1995 and the trustees are therefore required to make them available or provide them to members and others on request.

Scope of contribution schedules

324 In relation to Schedules of Contributions, TPR's Code of Practice: Funding defined benefits comments that the Schedule of Contributions should not refer to the contributions covering individual augmentations or general benefit improvements, unless these were planned and due to be paid when the Schedule of Contributions was certified. However, trustees do sometimes include the requirement for the employer to meet the cost of augmentations in their Schedule of Contributions even when amounts and timing are not certain at the time of preparing the Schedule of Contributions, in which case contributions arising from such matters do fall within the scope of the Schedule of Contributions and the auditors' statement about contributions.

325 In relation to Payment Schedules, Regulation 19 of the Scheme Administration Regulations states that a Payment Schedule should contain "separate entries for the rates and due dates of contributions (other than voluntary contributions) payable towards the scheme by or on behalf of the employer, and ... the active members of the scheme." The law does not state that **all** employee and employer contributions should be included, and the reference to "voluntary contributions" does not distinguish between employee and employer. This lack of clarity is particularly troublesome for defined contribution schemes because contribution arrangements can be complex and flexible. For example, it is becoming increasingly popular for defined contribution schemes to offer members the opportunity to pay additional employee contributions which are matched to some extent by additional employer contributions. These are treated as "normal contributions" in the scheme records but are sometimes regarded as "voluntary" for Payment Schedule purposes. Similarly, special employer contributions, such as salary/bonus sacrifice, are sometimes not included since they are made by the employee/employer on a "voluntary" basis.

326 Auditors are not required to interpret the law in this area. Instead they take account of the analysis in the trustees' summary of contributions between contributions payable under the schedule and contributions not payable under the schedule and consider whether the former have been paid in accordance with the requirements of the schedule. Although AVCs are not required by law to be included in schedules

some trustees do include them. In these cases the auditors' statement about contributions will also cover AVCs.

Effective date for schedules

A Schedule of Contributions is legally effective from the date of certification by the scheme actuary. Contributions received prior to the certification date need to be considered in relation to the Schedule of Contributions applicable at that time or, if no Schedule of Contributions was in place, against the rules of the scheme and, where appropriate, the recommendations of the scheme actuary. 327

The question may arise as to whether it is permissible to backdate an entry on the Schedule of Contributions, for example, to correct the omission of certain contributions due to a drafting error. It is not possible for a Schedule of Contributions to be backdated to include such contributions since this would constitute a change in the rates on the Schedule of Contributions which would require a revision by the Scheme Actuary. As explained above, the Schedule of Contributions is only effective from the certification date. 328

In relation to Payment Schedules, there is no equivalent certification requirement to act as a legal trigger to make a Payment Schedule effective so the picture is not as clear as it is for a Schedule of Contributions. The law does not require a Payment Schedule to be physically signed by the trustees or employer, merely agreed between them, or failing agreement, put in place by the trustees. Auditors therefore satisfy themselves about the date from which the Payment Schedule was "in place". In the absence of legal or other guidance the auditor should regard a Payment Schedule as being effective from the date it is used by the trustees to monitor the receipt of contributions to the scheme from the employer. It therefore follows that a Payment Schedule is not effective for periods prior to its preparation and use. A Payment Schedule can be amended by the trustee and the employer to refer to contribution arrangements that were omitted but the omitted arrangements will only be effective from the date they are included in the Payment Schedule. They cannot have retrospective effect. 329

Based on the comments above it follows that auditors only report against schedules from their effective dates and should not take account of retrospective adjustments made to schedules or to periods referred to in the schedule which pre-date the schedule's effective date. 330

Materiality

Scheme auditors provide Statements in relation to contributions due under the schedule and therefore plan and carry out their work with a reasonable expectation of detecting errors which are material to contributions due under the schedule as a whole rather than, for example, at an individual member level. Therefore scheme auditors do need to consider materiality in relation to the Statement when planning and performing their work. 331

The Statement requires assessment of whether specific conditions have been met. This narrower more factual focus entails close consideration of payment dates and amounts and hence a different level of materiality to that used for the audit of the scheme's financial statements is likely to be appropriate. 332

For financial periods beginning before 22 September 2005, the legislation requires scheme auditors to state whether or not contributions have been paid in accordance 333 with the schedule and does not refer to materiality in relation to the Statement. Therefore in providing his Statement the scheme auditor considers whether or not contributions have been under or over paid against the schedule and qualifies his Statement accordingly. As a result, auditors may be required to issue qualified Statements even in respect of very minor breaches of schedules, either in relation to the amount or timing of payments.

334 As a result of amendments to the Audited Accounts Regulations made by The Occupational Pension Schemes (Administration and Audited Accounts) (Amendment) Regulations 2005 (SI 2005 No. 2426), for financial periods beginning on or after 22 September 2005, auditors provide Statements as to whether contributions have *in all material respects* been paid *at least* in accordance with the schedule. As a result, auditors consider whether any breaches of the schedule in relation to the timing and/or amount of contributions that they have detected from their work require them to qualify their Statement.

335 In circumstances where a schedule is not in place or a schedule has ceased to have effect (for example because the scheme has commenced winding up or been the subject of a scheme failure notice, which causes the schedule to lapse), the Audited Accounts Regulations require the auditor to provide a Statement as to whether or not contributions have been paid in accordance with the scheme rules and, if applicable, the recommendations of the scheme actuary. The amendments made by SI 2005 No. 2426 referred to in paragraph 334 do not amend the relevant clause of the Audited Accounts Regulations, so the auditor is not able to have regard to materiality when framing his statement in these circumstances. However, scheme rules do not normally specify the dates on or before which contributions are required to be paid to a scheme. As a result, in circumstances where a payment of contributions was made during a scheme year at an incorrect amount, and the auditor is reporting by reference to the scheme rules, the requirements of the scheme rules are still likely to be satisfied if a correction to the payment is made before the auditor approves the Statement. Where a correction is not made before the auditor approves the Statement, the auditor will need to qualify his statement appropriately.

336 There can be cases where late contributions do not require to be reported to TPR by the trustees or the auditor but do represent a material breach of the Schedule of Contributions or Payment Schedule. Therefore late contributions which are not required to be reported to TPR may nonetheless result in a qualified auditors' statement about contributions.

Work to be performed

337 In order to report on contributions, scheme auditors obtain either the Schedule of Contributions or the Payment Schedule, and undertake procedures, normally on a test basis, in order to obtain sufficient appropriate evidence to conclude on whether or not contributions payable to the scheme have been paid for the amounts, and at the times, set out in the applicable schedule. In doing this the scheme auditors should have regard to both the amount of contributions received and the timing of those contributions.

338 Some issues that may require consideration include:

- changes in the rates of contributions payable and the timing of the implementation of the change in the employer payroll and the amendment to the schedules;
- changes in the definition of pensionable pay;

- whether the schedule is sufficiently clear in its drafting to allow the auditor to properly assess whether contributions have been paid in accordance with its requirements;
- whether the schedule complies with legal requirements, the requirements of the scheme's trust deed and the relevant TPR Code of Practice and related guidance;
- the scheme's systems of recording and monitoring contributions;
- any reports to TPR by the trustees of late or inaccurate contributions;
- whether there have been any member complaints about incorrect contributions, for example in response to annual benefit statements issued to members.

Reporting

The Statement is not an audit opinion and the work performed by the scheme auditor to provide the Statement is different to that of an audit. It is therefore important that the reader of the Statement does not confuse it with the audit opinion on the financial statements. Therefore it is recommended that the Statement is given separately from the audit opinion for all pension schemes. 339

It is important for the readers of the Statement to understand which contributions are covered by it and which are not. As discussed above some trustees include special contributions and AVCs on their schedules and some do not. It is also important for the scheme auditor to be able to clearly identify which contributions are covered by the Statement. To assist in this the trustees prepare a Summary of Contributions paid to the scheme under the Schedule of Contributions/Payment Schedule and the scheme auditors refer to this in their Statement. Trustees are required by the Disclosure Regulations (SI 1996 No 1655) to give reasons in the annual report where contributions have not been paid in accordance with the schedule. 340

An example Summary of Contributions and Auditors' Statement is set out in Appendix 6.

Non-compliance with a schedule

The legislation requires scheme auditors to state whether or not contributions have been paid in all material respects at least in accordance with the relevant schedule. Therefore in providing his Statement the scheme auditor considers whether or not contributions have been materially under-paid against the schedule and qualifies his Statement accordingly. Similarly, where contributions were paid late at any time during the period covered by the Statement, the auditor judges whether the late payment(s) were material and qualifies his Statement accordingly. 341

Whether underpayments or late payments of contributions are material to the auditors' statement is a matter of professional judgement. Typically the auditor will have regard to the frequency of the breaches and the cumulative, as well as the individual, impact of the breaches. 342

The auditor may encounter circumstances where the schedule omits contributions paid to the scheme which the auditor would expect to be included on the schedule, for example, normal contributions from a new participating employer. The auditor determines whether the omission is an error in the schedule through discussion with the trustees, employer and in the case of defined benefit schemes, the scheme actuary. If it is an error then the scheme auditor considers how he should report: 343

- if the omission is significant such that the schedule is ineffective, then the auditor reports against the scheme rules and, where appropriate, recommendations of the actuary; or
- if the omission is not significant but all parties agree the contribution should have been included on the schedule, then the contribution should be included in the reconciliation of the contributions payable under the schedule and the total contributions reported in the financial statements with an explanatory note explaining the reason why this contribution had to be included in the reconciliation.

As a result of the above it will be possible for the contributions paid under the schedules as set out in the Summary of Contributions to be different from the contributions reported in the financial statements. In these circumstances a reconciliation of contributions paid under the schedules and contributions reported in the financial statements should be included in the Summary of Contributions. In this connection, auditors consider whether any circumstances of non-compliance may require them to make a report to TPR, by reference to the relevant TPR Code of Practice and related Guidance.

Non-compliance with the scheme rules and advice of the actuary

344   In circumstances where the auditor is providing a Statement as to whether or not contributions have been paid in accordance with the scheme rules (and, if applicable, the recommendations of the scheme actuary) apparent breaches in relation to amounts (and possibly timing) need to be considered carefully.

345   If the scheme rules and/or advice of the actuary (where relevant) include requirements in relation to the timing as well as the amount of payments of contributions, the auditor considers whether the payments made to the scheme during the period complied with those requirements and, if they did not, the auditor will normally qualify his Statement.

346   If neither the scheme rules nor the advice of the actuary (where relevant) include requirements in relation to the timing of payments of contributions, and underpayments of contributions appear to have occurred during the financial period, the auditor establishes whether the shortfall was remedied by additional payments made to the scheme before the end of the financial period. If they were, the auditor will normally be able to conclude that the requirements of the scheme rules and the advice of the actuary have been met. Where some or all of the shortfall remains outstanding at the end of the financial period covered by the auditor's statement, the auditor will normally qualify his Statement.

Reporting on contributions as part of a non-statutory audit engagement

347   When a scheme is exempt from the statutory requirement for audited financial statements and/or an auditors' statement about contributions, the trust deed may nonetheless require the trustees to engage an auditor to report on contributions. In these cases, the auditors' responsibilities will be as defined by the trust deed, including the benchmark for reporting (i.e. either the requirements of a schedule or of the trust deed and rules). The wording of the trust deed will also determine whether overpayments or immaterial late payments or underpayments impact on the wording of the auditors' statement.

Liaison with the Scheme Actuary[23]

348 The liability to pay pensions after the scheme year end, and the actuarial valuation of that liability, is not within the scope of the financial statements or of the audit, so the scheme auditor has no responsibility for confirming the accuracy and appropriateness of underlying data used by the actuary.

349 As noted in the discussion of ISA (UK and Ireland) 720, the auditor reads the other information contained in the annual report (which includes the actuarial statements) with a view to identifying whether there are any apparent misstatements therein or matters which are inconsistent with the financial statements. However, this does not require the scheme auditor to carry out any checking of the basis of the actuary's statements.

350 Nonetheless, the scheme auditor may agree (if requested) to undertake additional work to provide assurance to the trustees that information supplied to the scheme actuary is consistent with that used in the preparation of the financial statements. In these circumstances, the additional work will normally be the subject of a separate letter of engagement and will be reported on separately from the financial statements.

351 Auditors and actuaries will look to the scheme trustees (rather than each other) as the primary source of information in relation to their professional roles. However, reference to arrangements for direct communication between the scheme auditor and the scheme actuary is normally included in the engagement letters of both the scheme auditors and the actuary. Such access is relevant to a number of areas of the scheme auditor's responsibility:

(a) in planning the timing of audit procedures in the context of the trustees' timetable for the annual report, the scheme auditor may wish to liaise with the scheme actuary to understand the nature and timing of any planned actuarial statements or certificates;
(b) in relation to the statement about contributions, the scheme auditor may require evidence to confirm that the correct schedule of contributions was being used by the scheme during its financial year, for example where there is doubt about the effective date of a schedule;
(c) in relation to benefit payments during the scheme year, the scheme auditor may seek to understand the nature and extent of the scheme actuary's involvement in the determination of benefits payable;
(d) in relation to any actuarial statement or certificate included in the annual report, the scheme auditor reads the actuarial statement or certificate which accompanies their report on the scheme's financial statements and, if they become aware of any apparent misstatements therein, or identify any material inconsistencies with the audited financial statements, they seek to resolve the situation;
(e) when assessing whether a breach of legal duty discovered by the scheme auditor is likely to be of material significance to TPR, the scheme auditor may wish to consult with the scheme actuary in order to assist in forming his opinion.

Completion of the trustees' annual report

352 A practical consideration in completing the audit is the timing of the issue of the scheme auditors' report, the scheme actuary's certificate and (until the completion of

---

[23] The ICAEW has issued more general guidance on this subject entitled : TECH 45/03 – Protocol: Actuaries' and Auditors' Inter-professional Communication – Pensions. Note that this document is being revised at the time of finalisation of this Practice Note.

the first valuation under the Scheme Funding Regulations) the scheme actuary's statement, all of which are required to be included in the trustees' annual report. ISA (UK and Ireland) 720 requires the scheme auditors to read other information included in the annual report and to seek to resolve any inconsistencies with the financial statements or possible misstatements which they identify, as set out above. ISA (UK and Ireland) 700 requires the financial statements and all other financial information in the annual report to have been approved by the trustees before the audit report is signed.

353 The trustees' annual report must be available within seven months of the end of the scheme year. It should include:

- For schemes that are still subject to the MFR regime:
  - the latest actuarial certificate (which, described briefly, confirms the scheme actuary's opinion that the rates of contribution shown in the schedule of contributions will be adequate to secure compliance with the scheme's funding requirements), and
  - the latest actuarial statement (which, described briefly, gives the scheme actuary's opinion as to whether the resources of the scheme are likely in the normal course of events to meet the liabilities of the scheme as they fall due on the assumption that specified contributions are paid) available at the time the annual report is approved.

  These are not necessarily recent documents. Where a more recent statement or certificate is in the course of preparation, the trustees may wish (providing that there is sufficient time within the statutory time limit of seven months) to delay issue of the annual report until that certificate is available. However, there is no requirement to delay the annual report so that a more recent statement or certificate can be included.

- For schemes that are subject to the Scheme Specific Funding requirements:
  - the latest actuarial certificate, and
  - a copy of the latest Summary Funding Statement prepared by the trustees.

354 Close liaison and a good working relationship between the scheme auditors and the scheme actuary will enable both to carry out the work needed to arrive at their respective professional conclusions within the trustees' overall timetable for the preparation of the annual report.

355 Further guidance relevant to liaison with the scheme actuary is set out in the sections dealing with ISA (UK and Ireland) 210 'Terms of Engagement' and Section B of ISA (UK and Ireland) 250 'The Auditors' Right and Duty to Report to Regulators in the Financial Sector'. Professional guidance issued or adopted by the Board for Actuarial Standards ('BAS') also includes matters on which the actuary will wish to communicate with the auditors.

Appendix 1 – List of principal relevant legislation

Set out below are some of the more important Statutes and Regulations affecting Occupational Pension Schemes in the UK. This is not intended to be a comprehensive list of all relevant legislation.

(Note that some of the statutes and regulations may have been amended subsequently)

Statutes

Trustee Investments Act 1961
Pension Schemes Act 1993
Pensions Act 1995
Trustee Act 2000
Pensions Act 2004Finance Acts 2004 and 2006

Regulations

The Occupational Pension Schemes (Minimum Funding Requirement and Actuarial Valuations) Regulations 1996 SI 1536
The Occupational Pension Schemes (Disclosure of Information) Regulations 1996 SI 1655
The Occupational Pension Schemes (Scheme Administration) Regulations 1996 SI 1715
The Occupational Pension Schemes (Transfer Values) Regulations 1996 SI 1847
The Occupational Pension Schemes (Requirement to Obtain Audited Accounts and a Statement from the Auditor) Regulations 1996 SI 1975
The Occupational Pension Schemes (Winding up) Regulations 1996 SI 3126
The Occupational Pension Schemes (Investment) Regulations 1996 SI 3127
The Occupational Pension Schemes (Deficiency on Winding Up etc.) Regulations 1996 SI 3128
The Register of Occupational and Personal Pension Schemes Regulations 1997 SI 371
The Occupational Pension Schemes (Administration and Audited Accounts) (Amendment) Regulations 2005 SI 2426
The Occupational Pension Schemes (Internal Control) Regulations 2005 SI 3379
The Occupational Pension Schemes (Investment) Regulations 2005 SI 3378
The Occupational Pension Schemes (Scheme Funding) Regulations 2005 SI 3377
The Occupational Pension Schemes (Member Nominated Trustees and Directors) Regulations 2006 SI 714
The Occupational Pension Schemes (Trustees' Knowledge and Understanding) Regulations 2006 SI 686
The Occupational Pension Schemes (Payments to Employer) Regulations 2006 SI 802

Appendix 2 – The legal and regulatory framework

This Appendix sets out a description of the major features of the legal and regulatory framework based on law as at 31 January 2007. It is intended to provide a general introduction for those unfamiliar with these major features and does not deal with any particular aspect in any depth. It is not intended to provide an interpretation of any aspect of the law nor to substitute for direct reference to the legislation.

Types of pension scheme

1. Pension schemes may be divided into two main types: occupational schemes and personal schemes. Occupational schemes are those run by employers for the benefit of their employees and from an employee viewpoint, are linked with employment. On leaving the service of the employer, active membership ceases, though the employee may leave the benefits accrued to date in the scheme.

2. Personal pension schemes are individual arrangements made by individuals. These arrangements are available to those who are self employed, in non pensionable employment and, from 6 April 2006, to those who also contribute to an occupational pension scheme. They may accept contributions from the employer as well as the

employee. Some employers set up group personal pension plans, which are an arrangement for the employees of a particular employer to participate in a personal pension scheme on a grouped basis. These arrangements are subject to different legislation from occupational pension schemes and, with the exception of a stakeholder pension scheme registered as an occupational trust-based scheme, are not subject to the pension scheme audit regime.

3. As outlined above, with effect from 6 April 2006, individuals are able to contribute to both an occupational and personal pension arrangements on a concurrent basis. This change has arisen following the implementation of new tax rules. An overview of the new regime is set out in paragraph 46 of this Appendix.

Occupational pension schemes

4. Pension schemes are very varied in their benefit structure. The main types are as follows:

- defined benefit (or earnings related) – a pension scheme where the benefit is calculated by reference to the member's pensionable earnings usually for a period ending at or before normal pension date or leaving service (hence the common description of such schemes as 'final salary' schemes), usually also based on pensionable service. Because of the uncertainties in determining the extent of future liabilities of such schemes, the trustees of such schemes are required to obtain regular actuarial assessments of the schemes' liabilities and estimated future costs;
- defined contribution (or money purchase) – a pension scheme where the individual member's benefit is determined by reference to contributions paid into the scheme in respect of that member, increased by an amount reflecting the investment return on those contributions. Because the scheme's commitment to pay future pensions is determined by the extent of funds available, no actuarial valuation is normally required;
- hybrid – a pension scheme in which the benefit is usually calculated as the better of two alternatives, for example on a defined contribution and a defined benefit basis; such a term may also be applied to a multiple benefit or mixed benefit scheme – a pension scheme in which there is both a defined benefit and defined contribution section; membership of the different sections need not necessarily be compulsory or complementary.

5. From 6 April 2006 it is not compulsory for employers to offer members a facility to pay additional voluntary contributions (AVCs). Under the new tax regime scheme, members can contribute to however many schemes they wish. Where AVCs are available, these may be on a defined benefit or defined contribution basis. Contributions providing defined benefits are generally paid into the scheme itself and can provide 'added years' at retirement. Defined contribution AVCs may be invested in the main fund or, more usually, invested with a third party such as an insurance company or building society. These investments remain under the control of and are the responsibility of the trustees of the scheme.

6. Members may choose to pay 'free standing AVCs' (FSAVCs) to an independent third party provider. FSAVCs are outside the control of the trustees and do not form part of the assets of the occupational scheme.

Tax status

7. All tax legislation in force at 5 April 2006 was superseded on 6 April 2006 (known as Authorisation Day or 'A' Day) by the new regime. Details of the new regime were set out in the Finance Act 2004 and Finance Act 2005.

8. Where pension schemes had obtained HMRC approval by 5 April 2006, they automatically become Registered Pension Schemes under the tax rules. All new schemes need to register with HMRC to become Registered Pension Schemes. Registered Pension Schemes receive a number of valuable tax reliefs so it is usual for pension schemes in the United Kingdom to seek such status.

Insured schemes

9. Insured schemes are those where the long-term investment is an insurance policy. The trustees enter into a contract with a life assurance company under which premiums are paid to secure the benefits for the members and meet the costs of administering the scheme. Such schemes are generally used by small employers for ease of administration. The contract with the insurance company may be deposit administration or a with profits policy or the underlying investments may be pooled funds. An insured scheme may provide defined benefits or it may be a defined contribution scheme, in which case there may be a series of policies ear-marked for individual members, so that the policy provides all the benefits payable under the scheme for the particular member or their dependants.

10. A fully insured scheme is one under which insurance policies provide benefits corresponding at all times to those promised under the scheme. On retirement, the trustees of insured schemes arrange for an annuity to be purchased to settle the liability for the pension and in most cases, the responsibility for paying the pension is passed to the insurer.

Ear-marked schemes

11. An ear-marked scheme is a particular type of insured scheme under which all the benefits other than death benefits are money purchase benefits and all are secured by one or more policies of insurance or annuity contracts, and such policies or contracts are specifically allocated to the provision of benefits for individual members or any other person who has a right to benefits under the scheme. An ear-marked scheme is required to appoint an auditor to issue a report about contributions but is exempt from having to obtain audited financial statements, unless the deed and rules require them, in which case the statements are non-statutory.

12. Under the Occupational Pension Schemes (Administration and Audited Accounts) (Amendment) Regulations 2005, the exemption of 'relevant' ear-marked schemes (i.e. money purchase schemes where all the members are trustees and under the provisions of which the scheme trustee decisions must be unanimous, disregarding for this purpose any trustees who are not members) from the requirement to appoint an auditor (and therefore from the requirement to obtain an auditor's statement) is restricted to schemes with fewer than 12 members for financial years beginning on or after 22 September 2005 and is removed entirely for financial years beginning on or after 6 April 2006.

13. The Occupational Pension Schemes (Administration and Audited Accounts) (Amendment) Regulations 2005, require that the Trustees and managers of an ear-marked scheme shall upon receiving a written request from a relevant person:

- make available a copy of the most recent accounts published in relation to the insurance companies with which they hold ear marked policies of insurance or annuity contracts in relation to that person
- make that information available to the person who requested it within a reasonable time.

Managed funds

14. Some pension schemes use insurance company pooled funds as their investment vehicle. The arrangement consists essentially of an investment contract by means of which an insurance company offers participation in one or more pooled funds. Such schemes are not insured schemes; however, insured schemes may be invested in internally managed funds of the insurance company.

Self administered schemes

15. Larger schemes generally directly manage the investment of their assets as they can usually achieve better returns and their size means that they are able to manage the long-term investment risks themselves. In such schemes, the trustees are free to invest in any form of investment permitted by the trust deed and legislation. The trustees will invest directly in investments (both UK and overseas) such as equities, fixed interest and index-linked securities, property, managed funds and cash. The composition of the portfolio may be related to the age profile of scheme members and the liability of the scheme to pay pensions. The investment management is usually handled by third party investment managers and custodians. Other functions, such as scheme administration and the operation of the pension payroll, may be handled in-house or by a third party administrator.

Small Schemes

16. A Small Scheme (formerly known as a SSAS) is a scheme generally with fewer than 12 members. Such schemes are almost invariably defined contribution and the level of self-investment in the employer is allowed to be higher than that permitted for other Registered Pension Schemes. SSASs are less regulated than other schemes, particularly where all the members are trustees and decisions require unanimity.

17. Before the Occupational Pension Schemes (Administration and Audited Accounts) (Amendment) Regulations 2005, money purchase SSASs were exempt from appointing a scheme auditor under the PA 1995 if all members were trustees (or trustee directors) and all decisions were made only by the trustees who were members by unanimous agreement (disregarding for this purpose "pensioneer" trustees). The exemption is amended by the regulations and, for financial years beginning on or after 6 April 2006, applies to schemes which meet the following criteria:

- fewer than 12 members where all the members are trustees of the scheme; and
- either:—

the provisions of the scheme provide that all decisions which fall to be made by the trustees are made by unanimous agreement by the trustees who are members of the scheme; or

the scheme has a trustee who is independent in relation to the scheme for the purposes of section 23 of the 1995 Act (power to appoint independent trustees), and is registered in the register maintained by the Authority in accordance with regulations made under subsection (4) of that section.

This exemption therefore does not apply if, for example, there are deferred members who are not trustees. Even if the exemption applies, the scheme's trust deed and rules may still require an audit and HMRC and the scheme actuary may require scheme financial statements. Schemes which are exempt from the requirement to appoint an auditor are also exempt from the requirement to prepare a payment schedule.

Pensions legislation

18. There are three major pieces of legislation relating to pension schemes, the Pension Schemes Act 1993 (PSA 1993), the Pensions Act 1995 (PA 1995) and the Pensions Act 2004 (PA 2004). The PSA 1993 is a consolidating act which brought together the legislation relating to contracting out of the State Earnings Related Pension Scheme (now replaced by the State Second Pension – S2P) and that relating to the requirements for the protection of scheme members, such as disclosure and restrictions on employer-related investment. The PA 1995 was a reforming law which resulted in new and revised regulation of occupational pension schemes. The Act itself is largely enabling legislation, with the detailed requirements set out in Regulations. There are numerous sets of Regulations made under the PA 1995, some of which replace regulations issued under earlier legislation subsequently consolidated into the PSA 1993.

19. The PA 2004, was another piece of reforming law. As with the PA 1995, the Act is largely enabling legislation with detailed requirements set out in Regulations. The changes implemented in the PA 2004 were in part a result of experiences resulting from working with the PA 1995 – for example, replacement of Minimum Funding Requirement with Scheme Specific Funding, the replacement of Opra by TPR – and the need to comply with the EC Directive on the Activities and Supervision of Institutions for Occupational Retirement Provision (commonly known as the 'Occupational Pensions Directive'), which Member States were required to incorporate into their local laws before 23 September 2005.

20. Only a few of the regulations made under the PA 1995 and PA 2004 apply to public service and statutory schemes, many of which are unfunded. Local Authority schemes, which are funded, are subject to separate legislation. Auditors of public sector schemes need to be aware of the legislation which applies to the particular scheme being audited.

Trust law

21. As most funded pension schemes are constituted under trusts they are subject to trust law. A trust is usually established by a legal document, the trust deed, which places the responsibility for the stewardship and custody of the assets on the trustees. The trustees are required to comply with the general requirements of the trust, the general law and legislation which almost entirely applies to pension scheme trusts, such as PSA 1993, PA 1995 and PA 2004 some of whose provisions override those of the trust. The principal powers and duties are as follows:

(a) to act fairly;
(b) to take reasonable care and skill in discharging their powers and duties;
(c) to obtain possession and control of the trust fund;
(d) to act in the beneficiaries' best interests (i.e. of all scheme members);
(e) to act fairly between the interests of different classes of beneficiaries;
(f) to act prudently and diligently like an ordinary man of business, using any special skill they possess;
(g) to invest the scheme's assets;

(h) not to delegate their performance of their duties and powers (but see below);
(i) to appoint professional advisers;
(j) to keep records; and
(k) to provide information.

The above list is not to be taken as being exhaustive.

22. The obligation not to delegate the performance of duties and powers is qualified in that trustees may be permitted to delegate matters either under statute or, if specifically authorised to do so, under the terms of their trust. As statutory provisions are limited, many trust deeds include wide powers of delegation. Permission to delegate does not release trustees from responsibility. Given they are fiduciaries, the trustees must take due care in selecting the delegate, in determining suitable guidelines for the performance of the matter delegated, and in monitoring the delegate's actual performance and compliance with the guidelines set. A distinction needs to be drawn between the delegation of the exercise or the performance of trustees' duties and powers with the employment of agents to carry out necessary activities on their behalf. The law has long recognised that trustees do not have to take all administrative steps themselves and Part IV of the Trustee Act 2000 expressly empowers trustees to employ and pay agents at the expense of the trust fund. However Part IV of the Trustee Act 2000 does not permit trustees to authorise anyone to exercise any of the asset management functions except if there is a policy statement in place and also a written agreement in which the agent agrees to comply with the policy statement.

23. Subject to the provisions of the trust, the PA 1995, the PA 2004 and the Trustee Act 2000, the trustees' main statutory duties and powers of investment are derived from the Trustee Act 1925 and the Trustee Investments Act 1961 (In Northern Ireland, the equivalent legislation is contained in the Trustee Act (Northern Ireland) 1962). Trustees must act in the best interests of beneficiaries of the scheme, and to ensure that no one who is not entitled receives any trust property. Where a trustee is also a director or employee of the sponsoring employer, he should set aside any other concerns, duties or responsibilities when acting in his capacity as a trustee.

Financial reporting

24. Scheme trustees have a statutory duty under the PSA 1993 s113, PA 1995 s41 and The Occupational Pension Schemes (Disclosure of Information) Regulations 1996 (SI 1996/1655) to produce a scheme annual report within 7 months of the end of the scheme year. The report will principally comprise:

- a trustees' report, which provides a review of the management of the scheme, membership statistics and developments during the period;
- an investment report, which reviews the investment policy and performance of the scheme;
- a compliance statement, which contains additional information about the scheme which is required to be disclosed by law or is disclosed voluntarily but which the trustees consider is not of such significance to the users of the annual report that it requires the more prominent disclosure afforded by inclusion in the trustees' report;
- except for schemes that are exempt, the financial statements, (referred to throughout the regulations as 'accounts') which should show a true and fair view of the financial transactions of the scheme during the period and of the disposition of its net assets at the period end, and/or the auditors' statement about contributions;

- a copy of the latest certificate by the actuary as to the adequacy of the contributions payable towards the scheme and either an actuarial statement (schemes that are still subject to the MFR regime) or a copy of the Summary Funding Statement prepared by the trustees (schemes that are subject to the requirements of the Scheme Specific Funding regime).

25. Whilst the individual components of the annual report are separate, it will be necessary for the user to read the whole report to gain a full and proper appreciation of the scheme's financial position.

Audited financial statements

26. Audited financial statements are required in a number of different circumstances. These are outlined below.

Financial statements included in the annual report

27. As noted above, the annual report of a pension scheme should include audited financial statements and the auditors' statement about contributions. The detailed legislation governing audited financial statements for inclusion in the annual report is contained in The Occupational Pension Schemes (Requirement to obtain Audited Accounts and a Statement from the Auditor) Regulations 1996, SI 1996/1975, as amended (most recently by The Occupational Pension Schemes (Administration and Audited Accounts) (Amendment) Regulations 2005, SI 2426).

Accounts for the purposes of an actuarial valuation

28. Trustees must consider obtaining an actuarial valuation earlier than is normal where it appears to them that events have made it unsafe for them to continue to rely on the results of the previous valuation as a basis for the current level of contributions. Some of the circumstances which the trustees may consider are:

- Present recovery plan is significantly inadequate
- Employer ceases to participate in multi-employer scheme
- Bulk transfer into or out of the scheme
- Significant fall in market value of the assets of the scheme
- Significant member movements.

In such circumstances trustees may request scheme auditors to provide an audit opinion for the purpose of a scheme funding valuation.

29. The Occupational Pension Schemes (Minimum Funding Requirement and Actuarial Valuations) Regulations 1996 (SI 1996/1536) required actuaries to adopt the asset values as shown in audited accounts for the purpose of forming an opinion on whether the minimum funding requirement was met. Actuaries may have based their valuation on audited accounts covering a period between one and eighteen months, provided that they complied in all other respects with legislative requirements.

30. Where the scheme actuary was unable to certify the adequacy of the contributions between successive valuations or if there was a relevant minimum funding requirement (MFR) multi-employer event, the scheme was required to undertake an emergency valuation for which audited accounts were required. The new 'Scheme Funding' legislation and The Occupational Pension Schemes (Scheme Funding)

Regulations 2005 (SI 2005/3377) resulted in transitional arrangements which need to be adopted when undertaking these emergency valuations.

31. Emergency valuations with an effective valuation date prior to 22 September 2005 had to be prepared within six months from the date the negative certificate was signed, or for multi-employer events which took place before 30 December 2005 (also with effective valuation date prior to 22 September 2005) then within six months of this event. In both cases the actuary may have produced the emergency valuation in accordance with the minimum funding requirements.

32. For those schemes subject to such an emergency valuation with an effective date after 21 September 2005, the trustees are required to obtain a valuation in accordance with the requirements of The Occupational Pension Schemes (Scheme Funding) Regulations 2005 (SI 2005/3377) 18 months after the negative certificate is signed *or the event*. The eighteen month time limit only applies if the effective date chosen is not more than three years after the effective date of the last formal minimum funding requirement valuation; otherwise the effective date has to be no more than one year after 30 December 2005 and the time limit for completion is fifteen months.

33. Therefore, all valuations with an effective date on or after 22 September 2005 must be prepared in accordance with the 'Scheme Funding' requirements of Part 3 of the Pensions Act 2004 and The Occupational Pension Schemes (Scheme Funding) Regulations 2005 (SI 2005/3377).

34. In most circumstances, trustees will request scheme auditors to provide an audit opinion for the purposes of an emergency scheme specific funding valuation. It is recognised that the trustees do not need to prepare a full annual report. For the purposes of the audit and subsequent valuation the accounts should be prepared in accordance with the requirements of Regulation 3 of The Occupational Pension Schemes (Requirement to obtain Audited Accounts and a Statement from the Auditor) Regulations 1996 (SI 1996/1975). There may be circumstances where, at the request of the scheme actuary, accounts are required for the purposes of calculating a section 75 debt. To satisfy this request, accounts may need to be prepared in accordance with Regulation 3.

Accounts required for the Pension Protection Fund valuations

35. The Pension Protection Fund (PPF) was established to pay compensation to members of eligible defined benefit pension schemes, when there is a qualifying insolvency event in relation to the employer and where there are insufficient assets in the pension scheme to cover Pension Protection Fund levels of compensation.

36. The PPF is a statutory fund run by the Board of the PPF, a statutory corporation established under the provisions of the Pensions Act 2004. The PPF became operational on 6 April 2005.

Section 143 valuations

37. In the event of a qualifying insolvency event, the scheme will enter what is referred to as the assessment period. In determining whether or not the PPF assumes responsibility for a scheme, the PPF must, as soon as reasonably practicable, obtain an actuarial valuation of the scheme as at the relevant time (as required by section 143 PA 2004). The relevant time will depend upon the basis under which the PPF may assume responsibility.

38. For the purposes of obtaining a section 143 valuation, the trustees of the scheme will be required to produce 'relevant accounts', as defined in The Pension Protection Fund (Valuation) Regulations 2005 (S.I. 2005/672) and request the scheme auditors to provide an audit opinion based on these 'relevant accounts'. It should be noted that authoritative interpretation of legislative requirements and definitions is a matter for the Courts to decide upon. For the purposes of this exercise, 'relevant accounts' can be prepared in accordance with the requirements of The Occupational Pension Schemes (Requirement to obtain Audited Accounts and a Statement from the Auditor) Regulations (S.I. 1996/1975) and this approach is supported by the PPF.

Where an application for reconsideration is made to the PPF, it shall be accompanied by audited scheme accounts. The form and content of those accounts is prescribed in paragraph 25 of the Pension Protection Fund (Entry Rules) Regulations 2005 (S.I. 2005/590).

Section 179 valuations

39. Eligible schemes are required to pay a levy to the PPF consisting of a risk based pension protection levy and a scheme based pension protection levy. The calculation of the levy will take account of a number of scheme specific factors including the extent of a funding deficit. For the purposes of enabling the risk based pension protection levy to be calculated in respect of eligible schemes, Regulations make provision requiring scheme trustees to provide the PPF (or TPR on PPF's behalf) with an actuarial valuation.

40. For the purposes of obtaining a section 179 valuation, the trustees of the scheme will be required to produce 'relevant accounts', as defined in The Pension Protection Fund (Valuation) Regulations 2005 (S.I. 2005/672) and request the scheme auditors to provide an audit opinion based on these 'relevant accounts'. It should be noted that authoritative interpretation of legislative requirements and definitions is a matter for the Courts to decide upon. For the purposes of this exercise, 'relevant accounts' can be prepared in accordance with the requirements of The Occupational Pension Schemes (Requirement to obtain Audited Accounts and a Statement from the Auditor) Regulations (S.I. 1996/1975) and this approach is supported by the PPF.

Accounts required during PPF Assessment Period

41. During an assessment period, although the trustees may need to reduce certain benefit payments to PPF levels pending the outcome of the assessment and to recover any overpayments, the trustees continue to operate the scheme and the statutory obligation to obtain audited accounts remains. Trustees of relevant schemes will be required to prepare the full Annual Report and Accounts in accordance with the Occupational Pension Schemes (Requirement to obtain Audited Accounts and a Statement from the Auditor) Regulations 1996 and with the guidelines set out in the Statement of Recommended Practice. In preparing the Annual Report and accounts, and taking account of the need to produce accounts for the purposes of a section 143 valuation, trustees may wish to use the section 143 effective valuation date as a revised statutory accounting reference date, thus consolidating the two audit processes. The trustees may then wish to use the anniversaries of the effective section 143 valuation date for future statutory accounting period ends.

Accounts for applications to the Fraud Compensation Fund (formerly the Pensions Compensation Board)

42. The Pensions Act 1995 established the Pensions Compensation Board. Financed by a levy on occupational pension schemes, the compensation scheme covered most trust based occupational pension schemes where an offence involving dishonesty (such as theft or fraud) had led to a shortfall of assets and the sponsoring employer was insolvent. As a result of the Pensions Act 2004, the Pensions Compensation Board was dissolved with effect from 31 August 2005, and a Fraud Compensation Fund established under the management of the Board of the PPF. On 1 September 2005, the net assets of the Pension Compensation Board, together with applications in process at that date, were transferred to the Fraud Compensation Fund.

43. In order to establish the amount of the loss for the purposes of compensation, the Board of the PPF requires a statement of the value of the scheme assets as at the date immediately before the date of application for compensation. The assets must be valued on the valuation principles set out and adopted as in the most recent audited financial statements and be certified by the scheme's auditor. The assets before the loss should be taken from the latest audited accounts or a PPF valuation adjusted (by an accountant in the case of accounts or an actuary in the case of a PPF valuation) to the date immediately before the loss. If there are no such accounts or valuation then the assets should be "as reported by an accountant". The value of the assets immediately before the application (after the loss) should be "as reported by an accountant".

Taxation

44. The new pension tax regime began on 6 April 2006. The new regime is a radical simplification of the pre April 2006 tax system: there is now a single pension tax system and all schemes will broadly be subject to the same rules. Previously there were eight systems with a wide range of differing rules applying to each of the systems.

45. The background to the changes was set out in the Green Paper published in December 2002 followed by consultation documents in December 2003. The Finance Act 2004 contained the detailed legislative framework and additional legislation was published in the Finance Act 2005.

46. An overview of the tax regime post 6 April 2006 is set out below:

- All schemes need to register with HMRC and will be known as Registered Pension Schemes.
- The maximum annual tax allowable contribution or inflow of value into a member's pension fund is set initially at £215,000 in the first year and will increase in steps of £10,000 per annum to reach £255,000 in 2010/2011. This is known as the annual allowance.
- The maximum annual contribution is the greater of £3,600 or 100% of salary subject to the annual allowance limit.
- The maximum lifetime fund limit is £1.5million initially and will increase annually in predetermined amounts to reach £1.8million in 2010 / 2011.
- Death in service cash benefits are included within the lifetime fund limit but pension schemes may allow for additional dependants' income benefits.
- If the value of the fund exceeds the lifetime limit, the excess will be subject to recovery tax totalling a maximum of 55%, which will have to be paid before the benefits can be drawn.

- A member can take a maximum tax free cash lump sum of 25% of the fund subject to a lifetime limit.
- The minimum age at which retirement benefits can be taken will increase to age 55 from 6 April 2010 from the existing limit of 50.
- There will no longer be a requirement to leave employment before an individual can draw pension benefits.
- Between ages 55 and 75 pension income benefits may be drawn directly from the pension scheme.
- There are transitional reliefs for members with large funds at 6 April 2006. Elections for 'primary' or 'enhanced' protection have to be made within 3 years of the new regime coming into force.
- If a member of the pension scheme leaves early and has more than 3 months' service but less than 2 years' service, the scheme is obliged to offer the choice of a transfer value or a refund of personal contributions.

Statutory rights and responsibilities of the various parties associated with pension schemes

47. The rights and responsibilities of the various parties associated with pension schemes are set out below. Most of the trustees' responsibilities originate in trust law and beneficiaries are able to take action for breach of trust in the civil courts. However, many of the duties and responsibilities of trustees (and also of other parties associated with occupational pension schemes) are now included in the PA 1995 and PA 2004, and there are civil and criminal penalties for failures to comply.

Trustees

Appointment and removal

48. Individual trustees are usually appointed and removed by deed. Where a corporate entity is appointed trustee, directors' appointment and removal is dealt with under the terms of the memorandum and articles of the company. Trustees may be appointed as a result of a statutory requirement as well as the terms of the trust deed and rules of the scheme.

49. Sections 241 to 243 of the Pensions Act 2004 require schemes to make arrangements that provide for at least one third of the Trustees in an occupational pension scheme to be member nominated trustees (MNTs). If the trustee is a company, the arrangements must provide for at least one third of the directors to be member nominated directors (MNDs). These provisions came into force on 6 April 2006.

50. The Occupational Pension Schemes (Member Nominated Trustees and Directors) Regulations 2006 SI 714 prescribe those type of schemes where the requirements do not apply, modify the provisions in certain limited circumstances and contain transitional provisions.

51. In addition, the PA 1995 includes a statutory requirement for an independent trustee in defined benefit schemes where the sponsoring employer is subject to insolvency procedures. However, a non-statutory independent trustee may be appointed in circumstances other than employer insolvency. It is becoming increasingly common for independent, paid trustees to be appointed to the trustee body.

52. A trustee may be removed by court order for misconduct or mismanagement. In accordance with the Pensions Act 1995, as amended, TPR may by order prohibit a person from being a trustee of a particular trust scheme, a particular description of trust schemes or trust schemes in general. TPR may also, by order, suspend a trustee pending consideration being given to a prohibition order. Where TPR prohibits a trustee, TPR may appoint a replacement. TPR may also by order appoint a trustee of a trust scheme where they are satisfied that it is necessary to do so in order to secure that the trustees as a whole have, or exercise, the necessary knowledge and skill for the proper administration of the scheme, to secure that the number of trustees is sufficient for the proper administration of the scheme or to secure the proper use or application of the assets of the scheme.

Eligibility

53. The following are automatically disqualified from acting as trustee:-

- individuals with a conviction for an offence involving dishonesty or deception (unless the conviction is spent);
- undischarged bankrupts and those who have made arrangements with their creditors;
- individuals subject to a disqualification order as a company director; corporate trustees if any of the directors is disqualified from acting as a trustee.

TPR can also disqualify a person from acting as trustee in certain circumstances.

54. TPR maintains a record of trustees it has disqualified and must disclose on request whether an individual is on this register with respect to a scheme specified in the request or all schemes.

55. Where the trustee board consists of one or more corporate trustees, the individual directors of the corporate trustee may be liable as if they were trustees of the scheme for the purposes of the PA 1995.

56. The auditor appointment is that of a firm (or a sole practitioner) and not an individual one: no directors, partners or employees of the audit firm may act as trustee of a scheme that is an audit client of the firm. Any scheme auditor who acts as trustee is guilty of an offence and liable to a fine and/or imprisonment.

Functions of Trustees under the PA 1995

57. The PA 1995 imposes a number of statutory duties on trustees. The Act refers to trustees or managers, so that where there are no trustees because the scheme is not set up under trust, the scheme managers are responsible for compliance with the legislation. These statutory duties include, in general terms:-

- the preparation, maintenance and revision of a statement of investment principles (s35);
- the exercise of their powers of investment in accordance with the legislation (s36);
- adherence to limits on employer related investment (s40);
- obtaining and disclosing audited financial statements and actuarial valuations and certificates (s41);
- the appointment of professional advisers (s47);
- the maintenance of proper books and records (s49);
- drawing up and implementing dispute resolution procedures (s50);

- for defined benefit schemes that have not had their first valuation under the Scheme Funding Regulations (and therefore remain subject to the Minimum Funding Requirement), the obtaining of actuarial valuations (s57) and the agreeing with the sponsoring employer of a schedule of contributions which is then certified by the scheme actuary (s58) and for defined contribution schemes, where scheme rules are silent, agreeing with the sponsoring employer a payment schedule (s87).

58. The Act also gives trustees a number of powers, including:-
- the power of investment and delegation of investment management (s34);
- the power to make payments of surplus to sponsoring employers if the trust deed permits such payments in an ongoing scheme (s37) and on winding up (s76).

Powers relating to payments to employers may now only be exercised by trustees, in accordance with The Occupational Pension Schemes (Payments to Employers) Regulations 2006 SI 2006/802.

Functions and powers of Trustees under PA 2004

59. The PA 2004 has further developed the functions and powers of the trustees. Some of the more significant changes include:
- Monitor investments to ensure scheme objectives are met (s244);
- Statutory duty to report to the Pensions Regulator (s70);
- Employees need to be consulted on pension changes by employer (s262);
- Trustees required to have sufficient knowledge and understanding of pensions and trust law (s249);
- Trustees to establish and operate internal controls which are adequate (s249A);
- Trustees to notify the regulator of certain events (s69);
- For defined benefit schemes that have had a valuation under the Scheme Funding Regulations, trustees to put in place a statement of funding principles (s223), obtain valuations of the scheme liabilities under the scheme funding rules (s224) agree a schedule of contributions with the employer (s227) and, if the scheme is in deficit, agree a recovery plan with the sponsoring company (s226).

Sponsoring employers

60. Sponsoring employers have a number of duties and responsibilities under the legislation. These include the following:
- Payment of contributions in accordance with the schedule of contributions for a defined-benefit scheme or payment schedule for a defined-contribution scheme. The Occupational Pension Schemes (Scheme Administration) Regulations 1996 (SI 1996/1715) stipulate that member contributions are to be paid by the employer to the trustees within 19 days of the end of the month in which they are deducted from the employees' pay. Failure to pay contributions deducted from members' pay within the prescribed time scale is an offence and TPR may fine the employer. In cases of fraudulent evasion, the employer may be prosecuted and, if found guilty, fined or imprisoned or both. In certain circumstances, trustees are required to report failures to pay members' contributions or contributions due under a schedule to TPR and/or scheme members.
- Where the employer operates the pensions payroll on behalf of the pension scheme, the employer must transfer into a separate bank account any payments

of benefit which have not been made to members within two days of receiving it. Failure to comply may attract a penalty in the form of a fine.
- The Scheme Administration Regulations impose on sponsoring employers a duty to disclose to the trustees or managers 'the occurrence of any event relating to the employer which there is reasonable cause to believe will be of material significance in the exercise by the trustees or managers or professional advisers of any of their functions'. The requisite disclosures have to be made within one month of the occurrence.
- The Scheme Administration Regulations also impose on the sponsoring employers and former sponsoring employers a duty to disclose on request to trustees or managers 'such information as is reasonably required for the performance of the duties of trustees or managers or professional advisers'. This includes information for the purpose of the scheme audit.

Auditors

61. Section 47(1)(a) of PA 1995 requires the trustees or managers of every occupational pension scheme to appoint a scheme auditor except where the scheme is exempt from doing so by The Occupational Pension Schemes (Scheme Administration) Regulations 1996, as amended.

As a result of the amendments made by The Occupational Pension Schemes (Administration and Audited Accounts) (Amendment) Regulations 2005 (S.I. 2005 No 2426), the following schemes are exempt from the statutory requirement:

(a) a scheme which is –
　(i)　provided for, or by, or under an enactment (including a local Act);
　(ii)　guaranteed by a Minister of the Crown or other public authority;
(b) an occupational pension scheme which provides relevant benefits and which on or after 6th April 2006 is not a registered scheme;
(c) unfunded occupational pension schemes;
(d) occupational pension schemes with less than 2 members;
(e) a scheme :
　(i)　with fewer than 12 members where all the members are trustees of the scheme and either:
　　(aa) the provisions of the scheme provide that all decisions which fall to be made by the trustees are made by unanimous agreement by the trustees who are members of the scheme; or
　　(bb) the scheme has a trustee who is independent in relation to the scheme for the purposes of section 23 of the 1995 Act (power to appoint independent trustees), and is registered in the register maintained by the Authority in accordance with regulations made under subsection (4) of that section; or
　(ii)　with fewer than 12 members where all the members are directors of a company which is the sole trustee of the scheme, and either:
　　(aa) the provisions of the scheme provide that any decisions made by the company in its capacity as trustee are made by the unanimous agreement of all the directors who are members of the scheme; or
　　(bb) one of the directors of the company is independent in relation to the scheme for the purposes of section 23 of the 1995 Act, and is registered in the register maintained by the Authority in accordance with regulations made under subsection (4) of that section;
(f) occupational pension schemes with a superannuation fund such as is mentioned in section 615(6) of the Taxes Act;
(g) the Devonport Royal Dockyard Pension Scheme;
(h) the AWE Pension Scheme established by a deed made on 29th March 1993;

(i) the Babcock Naval Services Pension Scheme, established by a deed made on 29th August 2002.

Also, in relation to a scheme to which section 47(1)(a) of the Pensions Act 1995 does not apply, the requirement to obtain accounts in accordance with paragraph (1)(a) or an auditor's statement in accordance with paragraph (1)(b) of The Occupational Pension Schemes (Requirement to obtain Audited Accounts and a Statement from the Auditor) Regulations 1996 applies to a scheme which either :

(i) falls within (b) or (f) above and has 100 or more members; or
(ii) falls within (g), (h) or (i) above.

62. The Audited Accounts Regulations require trustees of occupational pension schemes to 'obtain' audited financial statements within seven months of the end of the scheme year. The scheme auditor must be qualified to act as auditor of a company, or be approved by the Secretary of State for Work and Pensions, and must comply with independence requirements set out in The Occupational Pension Schemes (Scheme Administration) Regulations (SI 1996/1715).

63. The audit reporting requirements are set out in The Occupational Pension Schemes (Requirement to obtain Audited Accounts and a Statement from the Auditor) Regulations 1996 (SI 1996/1975). The scheme auditor is required to give an opinion as to whether the financial statements

(i) contain the information specified in the schedule to SI 1996/1975 and
(ii) show a true and fair view of the financial transactions of the scheme during the scheme year and of the amount and disposition, at the end of the scheme year, of the assets and liabilities of the scheme, other than liabilities to pay pensions and benefits after the end of the scheme year.

64. The scheme auditor is also required to provide a statement about contributions, stating whether or not in his opinion contributions have been paid in accordance with the schedule of contributions or payment schedule. If the statement is negative or qualified, the auditor must give his reasons. The trust deeds of some schemes also require the auditors' opinion as to whether contributions have been paid in accordance with the rules of the scheme and the recommendations of the actuary.

65. The requirements for scheme auditors in respect of their statement about contributions was amended by The Occupational Pension Schemes (Administration and Audited Accounts) (Amendment) Regulations 2005 SI 2426, whereby for accounting periods beginning on or after 23 September 2005, the opinion should be whether the contributions have in all material respects been paid at least in accordance with the schedule of contributions or payment schedule.

66. For money purchase insured schemes ('ear-marked schemes'), only the scheme auditors' statement on contributions is required under the legislation. Where the 'ear-marked' scheme has more than 100 members, a copy of the insurance company's accounts should be provided with the summary of contributions and auditors' statement, where a member requests a copy of the financial statements.

67. An ear-marked scheme is defined in the Occupational Pension Schemes (Requirement to Obtain Audited Accounts and Statement from the Auditor) Regulations 1996 SI 1975 as "an occupational pension scheme which is a money purchase scheme where all the benefits are secured by one or more policies of insurance or annuity contracts and such policies or contracts are specifically allocated to the provision of benefits for individual members or any other person who

has a right to benefits under the scheme". The insurer should provide confirmation of whether or not a scheme falls within this definition.

68. The Disclosure Regulations require scheme trustees to explain in the annual report the reasons for any qualified auditors' statement and to state how the situation has been or is likely to be resolved. If such a situation was not resolved in a previous year, the trustees must explain how it has been or is likely to be resolved.

The rights of the auditor in relation to information disclosure

69. The Scheme Administration Regulations require sponsoring employers (and former sponsoring employers), their auditors or actuaries to provide trustees with 'such information as is reasonably required' for the trustees' professional advisers, including the scheme auditors, to carry out their duties. Trustees must provide similar information to their professional advisers and also make the scheme's books, accounts and records available. The statutory requirements relating to the maintenance of scheme records are included in the Scheme Administration Regulations (SI 1996/1715), as amended.

Actuaries

70. The PA 2004 sets out the framework for the legislation relating to the role of the actuary in relation to defined benefit schemes. Section 224, PA 2004 and The Occupational Pension Schemes (Scheme Funding) Regulations (SI2005/3377), hereafter referred to as the Funding Regulations, require ongoing actuarial valuations to be normally undertaken every three years. The valuation has to enable the expected future course of the scheme's contribution rates and funding level to be understood. The Funding Regulations specify the way in which the assets and liabilities of the scheme are to be determined, calculated and verified by the actuary. Asset values are to be those stated in the latest available audited financial statements.

71. The PA 2004 and the Funding Regulations require the preparation of a schedule of contributions within 15 months after the effective date of the first actuarial valuation showing:

- separately the rates of contributions payable towards the scheme by or on behalf of the employer and the active members of the scheme,
- the dates on or before which the contributions must be paid, and where additional contributions are required in order to give effect to a recovery plan, the rates and dates of those contributions must be shown separately from other contributions.

72. The schedule must be signed by the trustees or managers of the scheme and make provision for signature by the employer in order to signify agreement to matters included in it. The schedule must incorporate the actuary's certification, as set out in the regulations.

73. The schedule must be reviewed and where necessary revised from time to time in accordance with the Funding Regulations.

74. Section 226 requires that if an actuarial valuation shows that the scheme does not meet the statutory funding objective, a recovery plan must be put in place by the trustees. The recovery plan sets out how the statutory funding objective is to be met and over what period. When preparing the recovery plan the trustees must obtain the

agreement of the employer and take actuarial advice. A copy of the recovery plan must be sent to TPR.

The Pensions Regulator ("TPR")

75. Whilst not an exhaustive list, the main powers conferred on TPR by the pensions legislation include:

- power to issue Contribution Notices and Financial Support Directions;
- power to issue Third Party Notices and Improvement Notices;
- power to request Skilled Person reports;
- power to issue a Freezing Order;
- power to direct or authorise schemes to be wound up;
- power to make orders for the suspension of persons from office as trustees;
- power to make orders for the prohibition of persons as trustees;
- power to impose financial penalties;
- power to appoint trustees including independent trustees;
- right to apply to the courts for injunctions and interdicts to prevent persons from misappropriating or misusing scheme assets;
- power to apply to the Court for restitution orders;
- power to gather information and obtain warrants in relation to its investigative powers;
- right to share information with other Regulators.

Appendix 3 – List of publications

The Pensions Regulator (TPR)

TPR has issued a number of publications which auditors may find useful in providing amplification of relevant areas of the regulations and in understanding the perspective of the regulator. Publications may be obtained on its website: www.thepensionsregulator.gov.uk or from the TPR helpdesk on 0870 6063636. Alternatively, customer support can be contacted on the following email address: customersupport@thepensionsregulator.gov.uk

In addition to the "Reporting breaches of the law" Code of Practice and supporting guidance, which is referred to earlier in this Practice Note, there have been a number of other Codes of Practice issued by TPR which may be useful to auditors. These publications include the following:

- Notifiable Events – this code of practice covers the duty to notify TPR of specified scheme related events (which trustees/managers must report) and employer-related events (which employers must report). This duty applies to all defined benefit schemes which are eligible for entry to the Pension Protection Fund and to employers who sponsor such schemes.
- Funding Defined Benefits – this code of practice relates to the new scheme funding requirements which replace the MFR (minimum funding requirement). Under the new requirements trustees must specify how the statutory funding objective will be met, obtain regular actuarial valuations, set out an appropriate schedule of contributions, and prepare a recovery plan to meet any funding shortfall.

This code is directed at trustees but will also be of interest to anyone professionally involved in the funding of defined benefit pension schemes.

The Code of Practice and associated guidance set out the new funding process and explain what trustees need to do in order to meet their key obligations.

This code also provides specific guidelines in relation to the monitoring of contributions and the procedures to be followed in the event of a contributions failure for defined benefit schemes.

- Reporting late payment of contributions to occupational money purchase schemes – this code of practice gives guidelines for trustees of occupational money purchase schemes on reporting late payment of contributions to TPR and to scheme members.

Trustees will only be required to report late payment of contributions where the late payment is likely to be of material significance to TPR. Trustees should use their judgement to assess whether they need to make a report – the code provides practical examples of when trustees should and should not report.

- Internal Controls – this Code of Practice provides trustees with guidelines on their duty to establish and operate adequate internal controls. The code is supported by guidance and is intended to assist trustees in undertaking a risk review exercise to identify internal control weaknesses.

These controls must be sufficient to ensure that the scheme is administered and managed in accordance with the scheme rules and the relevant legislation. The code provides practical guidelines on developing a risk management framework, helping trustees to focus on the key risks to their schemes.

This code is primarily for trustees, but will also be of interest to advisers, employers, service providers and scheme administrators.

- Trustee knowledge and understanding – this code of practice sets out practical guidance for trustees on how they can comply with legal requirements introduced from April 2006. Trustees of occupational schemes are required to be conversant with their own scheme documents, and to have knowledge and understanding (appropriate to their role as trustee) of trusts and pensions law and of the principles of funding and investment. These requirements will apply to all trustees. However, newly appointed trustees (other than corporate, professional or expert trustees) are given six months from their date of appointment to meet the requirements.

Accounting guidance

An industry SORP, Financial Reports of Pension Schemes, has been prepared by the Pensions Research Accountants Group (PRAG).

The SORP applies to all pension scheme financial statements which are intended to give a true and fair view and embraces all the information requirements of the Audited Accounts Regulations. These Regulations require the inclusion of a statement whether the financial statements have been prepared in accordance with the SORP 'and, if not, an indication of where there are any material departures from those guidelines'.

Pensions Terminology (Sixth edition)

A glossary of pensions terminology for pension schemes, published by the Pensions Management Institute (PMI) and the Pensions Research Accountants Group

(PRAG). It is available from The Pensions Management Institute, PMI House, 4-10 Artillery Lane, London E1 7LS, Telephone 0207 247 1452, Fax 0207 375 0603

Appendix 4 – Illustrative examples of appointment and resignation letters and paragraphs for engagement letters

The illustrative examples of letters in this appendix have been drafted to apply to an occupational pension scheme that is subject to the requirement to obtain audited financial statements and a statement about contributions imposed under section 41 of the PA 1995 and the Audited Accounts Regulations and to an 'ear-marked scheme' as defined by those regulations. They are not necessarily comprehensive or appropriate to be used in relation to every pension scheme, and must be tailored to specific circumstances – for example, to any special reporting requirements imposed by regulation on particular types of scheme or by the scheme documentation. Note also that certain categories of occupational pension scheme are exempt from individual provisions of the various regulations made under the PA 1995 – the provisions of the regulations described in the following letters therefore do not apply to all occupational pension schemes.

Examples

1 Example notice of appointment as scheme auditor to an occupational pension scheme under section 47 of the PA 1995

2 Example acknowledgment of notice of appointment as scheme auditor

3 Example resignation letter as scheme auditor

4 Example paragraphs for terms of engagement as scheme auditor to an occupational pension scheme that is required to obtain audited financial statements under the PA 1995

5 Example paragraphs for terms of engagement as scheme auditor to an ear-marked scheme

1 Example notice of appointment as auditor[24] to an Occupational Pension Scheme under Section 47 of the Pensions Act 1995

This form of notice of appointment has been drafted to apply to an occupational pension scheme that is subject to the requirement to appoint an auditor under section 47 of the PA 1995.

(To be typed on the scheme's letterhead)

(Addressed to the auditors)

Date

---

[24] *If the audit appointment is of the 'non-statutory' type, then references to 'auditors' in the Notice should be changed to 'Non-Statutory Auditors'.*

Dear Sirs,

Notice of appointment as auditors to the ( ) Pension Scheme

In accordance with section 47 of the Pensions Act 1995 and the Occupational Pension Schemes (Scheme Administration) Regulations 1996, we hereby give you written notice of your appointment as auditors to the ()Pension Scheme.

Your appointment by us under the regulations is to take effect from (the date of your letter of acknowledgement). You will take instructions from .... and report to ....[25] Your appointment is initially in respect of the financial statements to be prepared as at .... , the scheme's year-end. (The scheme's previous auditors were .... (name and address, if applicable) A copy of the previous auditors' statement/declaration on leaving office is attached, and we have authorised them to provide information to you as necessary and appropriate).

We confirm that, under section 27 of the Pensions Act 1995, no trustee of the scheme is connected with, or is an associate of, (firm's name), which would render (firm's name) ineligible to act as auditor to the Scheme.

We would be grateful if you will write to acknowledge receipt of this notice within one month.

Yours faithfully,

Signed for and on behalf of the Trustees of the () Pension Scheme.

2 Example acknowledgement of notice of appointment as Scheme Auditor to an Occupational Pension Scheme

The Trustees,
The () Pension Scheme

Date

Dear Sirs,

Acknowledgement of Appointment as Auditors of the ()Pension Scheme

We write to acknowledge receipt of your Notice of Appointment dated ....

Our appointment as auditors of the scheme is effective from (the date of this letter Note this date cannot be retrospective). We understand that our appointment is initially in respect of the financial statements to be prepared as at .... , the scheme's year-end.

We confirm that we will notify you immediately we become aware of the existence of any conflict of interest to which we may become subject in relation to the scheme.

Yours faithfully,

---

[25] *Auditors' terms of engagement are normally determined by the trustees and the auditors' reports are normally addressed to the trustees although some trust deeds may require otherwise.*

3 Example resignation letter as scheme auditor to an Occupational Pension Scheme

> The Trustees
> The () Pension Scheme
>
> Date
>
> Dear Sirs,
>
> **Notice of resignation as Auditors of the () Pension Scheme**[26]
>
> We acknowledge receipt of your letter dated ...... informing us of your intention to nominate .... as auditors to the scheme.
>
> We hereby give you formal notice of our resignation as auditors of the [name] scheme ("the Scheme") with effect from today *or* the date of this letter.
>
> There are no circumstances connected with our resignation which we consider significantly affect the interests of the members or prospective members of, or beneficiaries under, the Scheme.
>
> The Trustees are reminded of their responsibility to appoint a replacement auditor within 3 months from the date of resignation, as required by Regulation 5(8) of The Occupational Pension Schemes (Scheme Administration) Regulations 1996.
>
> Yours faithfully,

4 Example paragraphs for terms of engagement as scheme auditor to an Occupational Pension Scheme

> *Responsibilities of trustees and auditors*
>
> 1.1 The respective statutory duties of trustees and scheme auditors in regard to financial statements and audit are contained in The Occupational Pension Schemes (Requirement to obtain Audited Accounts and a Statement from the Auditor) Regulations 1996 ['the Audited Accounts Regulations']. In summary, under Regulation 2 of the Audited Accounts Regulations, it is the duty of the trustees to obtain audited financial statements within seven months of the end of the scheme year. It is also the trustees' duty to obtain the auditors' statement about contributions under the scheme within seven months of the end of the scheme year.
>
> 1.2 It is the responsibility of the trustees to make appropriate arrangements to ensure that, in the preparation of the financial statements:
>
> - the most appropriate accounting policies are selected and then applied consistently;

---

[26] *A clean notice of resignation cannot be issued if the auditors are aware of matters which are likely to be of material significance to The Pensions Regulator (TPR). In such circumstances, auditors must report the matter to TPR and refer to them in the notice of resignation. A copy of any statement made on the auditor's resignation or removal which is negative or qualified has to be included in the scheme's annual report.*

- judgments and estimates are made that are reasonable and prudent.

1.3 The Trustees are also responsible for safeguarding the assets of the scheme. The responsibility for the prevention and detection of breaches of trust or statute and fraud rests with the Trustees. However, we shall endeavour to plan our audit so that we have a reasonable expectation of detecting material misstatements in the financial statements or accounting records resulting from such breaches or fraud, but our examination should not be relied upon to disclose any such breaches or frauds which may exist. If at any time the trustees wish us to undertake detailed checking with the specific objective of investigating possible irregularities, we shall be pleased to receive your instructions.

1.4 As trustees of the pension scheme, you are responsible for maintaining records of trustees' meetings and proper accounting records and preparing financial statements which give a true and fair view and comply with the Pensions Act 1995, and its Regulations, in particular the Occupational Pension Schemes (Disclosure of Information) Regulations 1996, Occupational Pension Schemes (Scheme Administration) Regulations 1996 and The Occupational Pension Schemes (Requirement to obtain Audited Accounts and a Statement from the Auditor) Regulations 1996. You are also responsible for making available to us, as and when required, all the scheme's accounting records and all other records and related information, including minutes of all management and trustees' meetings. [Your accounting records are kept by *(name)* and we shall require direct access to those records.] We shall, of course, be pleased to assist with accountancy and administrative matters if requested to do so, but such services are distinct from our function as auditors.

1.5 As Trustees you are responsible for notifying us if you become aware that under Section 27 of the Pensions Act 1995 any trustee of the scheme is connected with, or is an associate of *(firm name)* which would render *(firm name)* ineligible to act as auditor to the scheme.

1.6 Sponsoring employers and their auditors also have statutory obligations to disclose information to both the trustees and ourselves. The Scheme Administration Regulations require any sponsoring employer to notify trustees of the occurrence of events relating to the employer which they believe to be of material significance to the trustees or managers or professional advisers. You hereby undertake to notify us of matters which may be relevant to the financial affairs of the scheme which have been notified to you by the sponsoring employers or have otherwise come to your attention.

1.7 We confirm that we are Registered Auditors, eligible to conduct audits under the Scheme Administration Regulations. We confirm that we will notify you immediately we become aware of the existence of any conflict of interest to which we are subject in relation to the scheme.

1.8 Our duty as scheme auditors is to report to you whether in our opinion:

- the financial statements presented to us for audit show a true and fair view of the financial transactions of the scheme during the scheme year and of the amount and disposition at the end of the scheme year of the scheme assets and of its liabilities, other than liabilities to pay pensions and benefits after the end of the scheme year in accordance with applicable law and United Kingdom Accounting Standards (United Kingdom

Generally Accepted Accounting Practice), and contain the information specified in the Schedule to The Occupational Pension Schemes (Requirement to obtain Audited Accounts and a Statement from the Auditor) Regulations 1996; and
- contributions have, in all material respects, been paid to the scheme during the scheme year at least in accordance with the [schedule of contributions] [or payment schedule] and if not state the reasons.

1.9 We have a professional responsibility to report if the financial statements do not comply in any material respect with applicable accounting standards, unless in our opinion the non-compliance is justified in the circumstances. In determining whether or not the departure is justified we consider:

- whether the departure is required in order that the financial statements may show a true and fair view; and
- whether adequate disclosure has been made concerning the departure.

In addition, under the Audited Accounts Regulations, the financial statements are required to include a statement as to whether they have been prepared in accordance with the Statement of Recommended Practice, 'Financial Reports of Pension Schemes', published by the Pensions Research Accountants Group, and if not to indicate where there are any material departures and the reasons for any such departures. Failure to comply in this respect will require us to qualify our opinion on whether the financial statements contain the information specified in the Regulations.

1.10 In order to assist us with the examination of your financial statements, we shall request sight of all documents or statements which are to be incorporated into the annual report of which the financial statements will form part, including the trustees' report, the actuarial statement, the actuarial certificate, the compliance statement and the investment report. We have a professional responsibility to satisfy ourselves that they are consistent with and do not undermine the credibility of the financial statements. However, our responsibility in relation to reports by the scheme's actuary or by other scheme advisers is limited to understanding the implications of those reports for the scheme's financial statements.

1.11 Our professional responsibilities also require us to mention in our report a description of the trustees' responsibilities for the financial statements where the financial statements or accompanying information do not include such a description.

1.12 Our responsibility as auditors does not extend to the preparation or signature of returns to The Pensions Regulator.

Scope of our work

2.1 Our audit will be conducted in accordance with the International Standards on Auditing (UK and Ireland) issued by the Auditing Practices Board, and will include such tests of transactions and of the existence, ownership and valuation of assets and liabilities as we consider necessary. Our work will include examination, on a test basis, of evidence relevant to the amounts of contributions payable to the scheme and the timing of those payments. We shall obtain an understanding of the accounting and internal control systems in order to assess their adequacy as a basis for the preparation of the financial statements and to establish whether proper accounting records have been maintained by the scheme. We shall expect to obtain such appropriate evidence as we consider sufficient to enable us to draw reasonable conclusions therefrom.

2.2 The nature and extent of our procedures will vary according to our assessment of the scheme's accounting system and, where we wish to place reliance on it, the system of internal control, and may cover any aspect of the scheme's operations that we consider appropriate. Our audit is not designed to identify all significant weaknesses in the scheme's systems but if such weaknesses come to our notice during the course of our audit which we think should be brought to your attention we shall report them to you. Any such report may not be provided to third parties without our prior written consent. Such consent will be granted only on the basis that such reports are not prepared with the interests of anyone other than the scheme in mind and that we accept no duty or responsibility to any other party as concerns the reports. We are not required to perform tests in connection with or report on:

- the scheme's long term pension liabilities;
- the trustees' report, the investment report and any other reports[27] accompanying the financial statements.

Our audit includes assessing the significant estimates and judgments made in the preparation of the financial statements and whether the accounting policies are appropriate to the scheme's circumstances, consistently applied and appropriately disclosed.

In forming our opinion, we shall also evaluate the overall adequacy of the presentation of information in the financial statements.

2.3 The Scheme Administration Regulations also require employers and their auditors or actuaries to furnish you on request with such information as is reasonably required for the performance of our duties as scheme auditors and the Regulations require you in turn to disclose such information to us. In this context, we may require written confirmation of certain matters from scheme employers and their auditors.

2.4 In order to carry out our duties as scheme auditors, we may need to consult with the scheme actuary or other actuarial adviser appointed by you. You hereby authorise us to communicate directly with such persons for the purposes of performing our duties as scheme auditors.

2.5 Once we have issued our report we have no further direct responsibility in relation to the financial statements for that financial year.

Representations by trustees and third parties

3.1 The information used by the trustees in preparing the financial statements will invariably include facts or judgements which are not themselves recorded in the accounting records. As part of our normal audit procedures, we shall request the trustees, those charged with governance, or senior officials/management involved in the administration of the scheme, to provide written confirmation each year of such facts or judgements and any other oral representations that we have received

---

[27] Except where the trustees have chosen to include their summary of contributions in the trustees' report.

during the course of the audit on matters having a material effect on the financial statements.

3.2 In addition, we shall present to the trustees/those charged with governance, a schedule of any unadjusted misstatements that have come to our attention in the course of our audit work and if you decide not to adjust the financial statements for those misstatements we shall request you to explain in writing your reasons for not making the adjustments.

Reporting to those charged with governance

4.1 Our work is not designed to identify all weaknesses in the Scheme's systems but, if such weaknesses come to our attention during the course of our work, which we consider should be brought to your attention, we shall report them to you.

4.2 We will agree with those charged with governance of the Scheme, the timing and form of communication between ourselves.

Reporting to The Pensions Regulator

5.1 We have a statutory duty under section 70 of the Pensions Act 2004 to report immediately to The Pensions Regulator (TPR) if we have reasonable cause to believe that there is or has been some failure to comply with any duty relevant to the administration of the scheme imposed by any enactment or rule of law on the trustees or managers, the employer, any professional adviser or any prescribed person acting in connection with the scheme and that the failure to comply is likely to be of material significance to TPR. We may have to make this report without your knowledge and consent and we cannot undertake to you to fetter this discretion in any manner.

5.2 Section 70 does not require us to undertake work for the sole purpose of identifying breaches likely to be of material significance to TPR. We shall fulfil our duty under this section in accordance with the requirements and guidance set out in Section B of ISA (UK and Ireland) 250 – "The Auditors' Right and Duty to Report to Regulators in the Financial Sector" and Practice Note 15 (Revised) "The Audit of Occupational Pension Schemes in the United Kingdom". In considering the need to make a report, we may decide to consult the scheme actuary. You hereby authorise us to communicate directly with the scheme actuary.

Electronic communications and reporting

6.1 We acknowledge that as Trustees of the Scheme you may wish to publish the Scheme's financial statements and the auditors' report on the Scheme's web site or distribute them to members by means such as e-mail. Should such a need arise, we will require that you advise us of any intended publication/distribution before it occurs and that additional engagement terms are agreed.

6.2 During the engagement we may, from time to time, communicate electronically with each other. However, the electronic transmission of information cannot be guaranteed to be secure or virus or error free and such information could be intercepted, corrupted, lost, destroyed, arrive late or incomplete, or otherwise be adversely affected or unsafe to use. We recognise that systems and procedures cannot be a guarantee that transmissions will be unaffected by such hazard.

6.3 We confirm that we each accept the risks of and authorise electronic communications between us. We each agree to use commercially reasonable procedures to check for the then most commonly known viruses before sending information electronically. We shall each be responsible for protecting our own systems and interests in relation to electronic communications.

Auditors' Statement about Contributions

7.1 The trustees of the scheme are responsible for ensuring that there is prepared, maintained and from time to time revised a Schedule of Contributions/Payment Schedule (the Schedule) showing the rates of contributions payable to the scheme by or on behalf of the employer and the active members of the scheme and the dates on or before which such contributions are to be paid.

The trustees are also responsible for obtaining a statutory auditors' statement about contributions.

7.2 As auditors appointed under the Pensions Act 1995 we have and shall have a statutory responsibility to report to the trustees on whether in our opinion the contributions payable to the scheme have been paid, in all material respects, at least in accordance with the Schedule of Contributions/Payment Schedule ("our Statement"). In arriving at our opinion in our Statement, we shall be required to consider whether we have obtained all the information and explanations which we consider necessary for the purposes of our work.

7.3 Our work will include examination, on a test basis, of evidence relevant to the amounts of contributions payable to the scheme and the timing of those payments. Our work will not constitute an audit of the scheme and will be performed solely for the purposes of giving the required statement about contributions. We will plan and perform our work so as to obtain all the information and explanations which we consider necessary in order to give reasonable assurance that contributions paid to the scheme under the Schedule have been paid, in all material respects, at least in accordance with that Schedule.

Termination of appointment

8.1 Our appointment as scheme auditors may only be terminated, by you or by us, by notice in writing. The notice shall state the date with effect from which the appointment terminates. In the case of a notice of resignation given by us, the notice shall contain either:

(a) a statement specifying any circumstances connected with our resignation which, in our opinion, significantly affect the interests of the members or prospective members of, or beneficiaries under, the scheme; or
(b) a declaration that we know of no such circumstances.

In the case of a notice of termination given by you, we shall provide you with the aforementioned statement or declaration within 14 days of our receiving the written notice of termination of our appointment. You are required by the Scheme Administration Regulations to provide a copy of the statement or declaration to our successors or proposed successors as scheme auditors.

5 Example paragraphs for terms of engagement as scheme auditor to an earmarked pension scheme

The following example has been drafted to apply to an earmarked scheme (other than a 'relevant ear-marked scheme') within the meaning of The Occupational Pension Schemes (Requirement to obtain Audited Accounts and a Statement from the Auditor) Regulations 1996. It may need to be adapted to the particular circumstances of the individual scheme for any special requirements imposed by regulation or by the scheme documentation.

Responsibilities of trustees and scheme auditors

1.1 You have determined that an audit of the financial statements of the Scheme is not required as the Scheme is an 'ear-marked scheme' within the meaning of The Occupational Pension Schemes (Requirement to obtain Audited Accounts and a Statement from the Auditor) Regulations 1996 ['the Audited Accounts Regulations']. This letter therefore only deals with the scheme auditors' statutory statement about contributions under the scheme. Should you instruct us to carry out an audit of the financial statements of the Scheme, a separate letter of engagement will be required.

1.2 The respective statutory duties of trustees and scheme auditors in regard to financial statements and audit are contained in The Occupational Pension Schemes (Disclosure of Information) Regulations 1996 ['the Disclosure Regulations'] and the Audited Accounts Regulations.

1.3 In summary, you are required under Regulation 6 of the Disclosure Regulations to make available an annual report of the Scheme within seven months of the end of the scheme year. This report will principally comprise a trustees' report setting out information specified in Schedule 3 to the Disclosure Regulations together with a Summary of Contributions, as described below, and an auditors' statement about contributions as specified in the Audited Accounts Regulations.

1.4 Under section 87 of the Pensions Act 1995, you are responsible as trustees for ensuring that there is prepared, maintained and from time to time revised a schedule (the payment schedule) showing the rates of contributions payable towards the scheme by or on behalf of the employer and the active members of the scheme and the dates on or before which such contributions are to be paid.

1.5 Trustees are responsible for maintaining books and records in accordance with regulations made under the Pension Schemes Act 1993 and Pensions Act 1995, including The Occupational Pension Schemes (Scheme Administration) Regulations 1996 ['the Scheme Administration Regulations']. These should include written records of trustees' meetings. Under Regulation 12 of the Scheme Administration Regulations, the trustees are responsible for keeping records in respect of contributions received in respect of any active member of the scheme.

1.6 You are also responsible for making available to us any of the scheme's books and records and other information as may reasonably be required for the performance of our duties. For the purposes of our report, in particular, we will require a Summary of Contributions, for inclusion in the trustees' report and approved by you, showing the aggregate amount paid to the scheme during the scheme year in respect of employer and members' contributions (other than any member voluntary and any special contributions). [Your accounting records are kept by (name) and we shall require direct access to those records.]

1.7 As Trustees you are responsible for notifying us if you become aware that under Section 27 of the Pensions Act 1995 any trustee of the scheme is connected with, or is an associate of (firm name) which would render (firm name) ineligible to act as auditor to the scheme.

1.8 We confirm that we are Registered Auditors, eligible to act as scheme auditors under the Scheme Administration Regulations. We confirm that we will notify you immediately we become aware of the existence of any conflict of interest to which we are subject in relation to the scheme.

1.9 Our duty as scheme auditors is to provide you with a statement about contributions under the scheme as required by Regulation 4 of the Audited Accounts Regulations. We shall report to you whether, in our opinion, the contributions payable to the scheme during the scheme year, as reported in the Summary of Contributions, have been paid, in all material respects, at least in accordance with the payment schedule maintained under section 87 of the Pensions Act 1995 [or, where there is no such payment schedule in relation to all or part of the scheme year, whether in our opinion contributions have been paid, in all material respects, at least in accordance with the scheme rules or contracts under which they were payable.] If our opinion is negative or qualified, we shall state the reasons.

Scope of our work

2.1 Our work will include examination, on a test basis, of evidence relevant to the amounts of contributions payable to the scheme and the timing of those payments. Our work will not constitute an audit of the financial transactions and net assets of the scheme and will be performed solely for the purposes of giving the required statement about contributions. We will plan and perform our work so as to obtain all the information and explanations which we consider necessary in order to give reasonable assurance that contributions payable as reported in the Summary of Contributions have been paid, in all material respects, at least in accordance with the payment schedule maintained by you under section 87 of the Pensions Act 1995 [or, where there is no such payment schedule in relation to all or part of the scheme year, contributions payable as reported in the Summary of Contributions have been paid, in all material respects, at least in accordance with the scheme rules or contracts under which they were payable].

2.2 The Scheme Administration Regulations also require employers and their auditors to furnish you on request with such information as is reasonably required for the performance of our duties as scheme auditors and the Regulations require you in turn to disclose such information to us. In this context, we may require written confirmation of certain matters from scheme employers and their auditors.

2.3 The Scheme Administration Regulations require any sponsoring employer to notify trustees of the occurrence of events relating to the employer which they believe to be of material significance to the trustees or managers or professional advisers. You hereby undertake to notify us of matters which may be relevant to the financial affairs of the scheme which have been notified to you by the sponsoring employers or have otherwise come to your attention.

2.4 The responsibility for safeguarding the assets of the scheme and for the prevention and detection of fraud, error and non-compliance with law or regulations rests with yourselves. However, we shall endeavour to plan our work so that we have a reasonable expectation of detecting material misstatements in the Summary of Contributions (including those resulting from fraud, error, non-compliance with law or regulations or breaches of trust), but our examination should not be relied upon to disclose all such material misstatements or frauds, errors or instances of non-compliance or breach of trust as may exist.

2.5 In order to carry out our duties as scheme auditors, we may need to consult with the scheme's actuary or other actuarial adviser appointed by you. You hereby authorise us to communicate directly with such persons for the purposes of performing our duties as scheme auditors.

Representations by trustees and third parties

3.1 Information and explanations from the scheme's personnel are an important part of our work. In order to avoid any misunderstanding and as part of our normal procedures, we may request you to provide written confirmation of certain oral representations which we have received from trustees or your personnel during the course of our work on matters we consider may have a material effect on the auditors' statement.

Reporting to those charged with governance

4.1 Our work is not designed to identify all weaknesses in the Scheme's systems but, if such weaknesses come to our attention during the course of our work, which we consider should be brought to your attention, we shall report them to you.

4.2 We will agree with those charged with governance of the Scheme, the timing and form of communication between ourselves.

Reporting to The Pensions Regulator

5.1 We have a statutory duty under section 70 of the Pensions Act 2004 to report immediately to The Pensions Regulator (TPR) if we have reasonable cause to believe that there is or has been some failure to comply with any duty relevant to the administration of the scheme imposed by any enactment or rule of law on the trustees or managers, the employer, any professional adviser or any prescribed person acting in connection with the scheme and that the failure to comply is likely to be of material significance to TPR. We may have to make this report without your knowledge and consent and we cannot undertake to you to fetter this discretion in any manner.

5.2 Section 70 does not require us to undertake work for the sole purpose of identifying breaches likely to be of material significance to TPR. We shall fulfil our duty under this section in accordance with the requirements and guidance set out in Section B of ISA (UK and Ireland) 250 – "The Auditors' Right and Duty to Report to Regulators in the Financial Sector" and Practice Note 15 (Revised) "The Audit of Occupational Pension Schemes in the United Kingdom". In considering the need to make a report, we may decide to consult the scheme actuary. You hereby authorise us to communicate directly with the scheme actuary.

Electronic communications and reporting

6.1 We acknowledge that as Trustees of the Scheme you may wish to publish the Scheme's Summary of Contributions and the auditors' statement on the Scheme's web site or distribute them to members by means such as e-mail. Should such a need arise, we will require that you advise us of any intended publication/distribution before it occurs and that additional engagement terms are agreed.

6.2 During the engagement we may, from time to time, communicate electronically with each other. However, the electronic transmission of information cannot be guaranteed to be secure or virus or error free and such information could be intercepted, corrupted, lost, destroyed, arrive late or incomplete, or otherwise be adversely affected or unsafe to use. We recognise that systems and procedures cannot be a guarantee that transmissions will be unaffected by such hazard.

We confirm that we each accept the risks of and authorise electronic communications between us. We each agree to use commercially reasonable procedures to check for the then most commonly known viruses before sending information electronically. We shall each be responsible for protecting our own systems and interests in relation to electronic communications.

Termination of appointment

7.1 Our appointment as scheme auditors may only be terminated, by you or by us, by notice in writing. The notice shall state the date with effect from which the appointment terminates. In the case of a notice of resignation given by us, the notice shall contain either:

(a) a statement specifying any circumstances connected with our resignation which, in our opinion, significantly affect the interests of the members or prospective members of, or beneficiaries under, the scheme; or
(b) a declaration that we know of no such circumstances.

In the case of a notice of termination given by you, we shall provide you with the aforementioned statement or declaration within 14 days of our receiving the written notice of termination of our appointment. You are required by the Scheme Administration Regulations to provide a copy of the statement or declaration to our successors or proposed successors as scheme auditors.

Appendix 5 – Illustrative example of representation letter

The following example of a management representation letter from the trustees of a scheme to its scheme auditors is in the form of a letter, but it is not intended to be a standard letter, nor to imply that management representations must necessarily be in the form of a letter from the trustees. Representations by management vary from one entity to another and from one year to the next.

Although seeking representations from the trustees on a variety of matters may serve to focus their attention on those matters, and thus cause them to specifically address those matters in more detail than would otherwise be the case, scheme auditors are aware of the limitations of management representations as audit evidence as set out in ISA (UK and Ireland) 580.

(Scheme letterhead)

(Date)

(To the scheme auditors)

This representation letter is provided in connection with your [audit of the Scheme's financial statements/examination of the Scheme's summary of contributions] for the year ended [date] for the purpose of expressing an opinion as to whether the financial statements give a true and fair view of the financial position of the Scheme in accordance with applicable law and United Kingdom Accounting Standards (United Kingdom Generally Accepted Accounting Practice) and making a statement about contributions.

We acknowledge as trustees our responsibilities for ensuring that financial statements are prepared which give a true and fair view, for keeping records in respect of contributions received in respect of active members of the scheme and for making accurate representations to you.

We confirm to the best of our knowledge and belief the following representations:

1) All the accounting records have been made available to you for the purpose of your audit and all the transactions undertaken by the Scheme have been properly reflected and recorded in the accounting records. All other records and related information, including minutes of all trustee meetings have been made available to you.

2) We acknowledge our responsibilities for the design and implementation of internal control to prevent and detect fraud and error.

3) We have disclosed to you the results of our assessment of the risk that the financial statements may be materially misstated as a result of fraud.

4) [We are not aware of any / We have disclosed to you all] significant facts relating to any frauds or suspected frauds affecting the Scheme involving:

(i) management
(ii) employees who have significant roles in internal control, or
(iii) others where the fraud could have a material effect on the financial statements.

5) We have disclosed to you our knowledge of any allegations of fraud, or suspected fraud, affecting the Scheme's financial statements communicated by members, former members, employers, regulators or others.

6) We have considered the uncorrected misstatements detailed in the appendix to this letter. We believe that no adjustment is required to be made in respect of any of these items as they are individually and in aggregate immaterial having regard to the financial statements taken as a whole. [insert any special reasons which the trustees believe are relevant]

7) Where required, the value at which assets and liabilities are recorded in the net assets statement is, in the opinion of the trustees, the market value. We are responsible for the reasonableness of any significant assumptions underlying the valuation, including consideration of whether they appropriately reflect our intent and ability to carry out specific courses of action on behalf of the Scheme. Any significant changes in those values since the balance sheet date have been disclosed to you.

8) We confirm the completeness of the information provided regarding the identification of related parties, and the adequacy of related party disclosures in the financial statements.

9) There have been no significant transactions with related parties [other than those disclosed to you in our memorandum dated (date)] and we are not aware of any other such matters required to be disclosed in the financial statements in accordance with Financial Reporting Standard 8 and with the recommendations of the Statement of Recommended Practice, 'Financial Reports of Pension Schemes' or any other requirement. We have confirmed this with all key managers and other individuals who are in a position to influence or are accountable for the stewardship of the scheme.

10) *[And if applicable With* regard to (list of specific transactions) we confirm that to the best of our knowledge and belief these transactions are not significant to the related party or to the scheme such that they would influence decisions made by a user of the accounts.]

11) We confirm that the scheme is a Registered Pension Scheme. We are not aware of any reason why the tax status of the scheme should change.

12) We are not aware of any actual or possible instances of non-compliance with laws and regulations, the effects of which should be considered when preparing financial statements, *[except as disclosed below, together with the actual or contingent consequences which may arise therefrom].*

13) We have not made any reports to The Pensions Regulator nor are we aware of any such reports having been made by any of our advisors. We confirm that we are not aware of any late contributions or breaches of the [payment schedule/ schedule of contributions] that have arisen which we considered did not require reporting under the easement introduced under The Occupational Pension Schemes (Miscellaneous Amendments) Regulations 2000. We also confirm that we are not aware of any other matters which have arisen that would require a report to The Pensions Regulator.

There have been no other communications with The Pensions Regulator or other regulatory bodies during the scheme year or subsequently concerning matters of non-compliance with any legal duty. [We have drawn to your attention all correspondence and notes of meetings with regulators.]

14) We have [not] commissioned advisory reports [on the following] which may affect the conduct of your work in relation to the Scheme's financial statements and [schedule of contributions] [payment schedule].

15) There have been no events since the scheme year end which necessitate revision of the figures included in the financial statements or inclusion in the notes thereto. Should further material events occur, which may necessitate revision of the figures included in the financial statements or inclusion in the notes thereto, we will advise you accordingly.

16) We confirm that, under section 27 of the Pensions Act 1995, no trustee of the scheme is connected with, or is an associate of, (Scheme Auditor), which would render (Scheme Auditor) ineligible to act as auditor to the Scheme.

As discussed, approved and minuted by the board of trustees at its meeting on............ (date)

Chairman...................... Secretary......................

Other signatories may include those with specific knowledge of the relevant matters, for example the chief financial officer.

Note

The paragraphs included in the example above relate to a specific set of circumstances. Set out below are some additional issues which, depending on the particular circumstances, the materiality of the amounts concerned to the financial statements and the extent of other audit evidence obtained, may be the subject of representations from management:

- Going concern, when events or conditions have been identified which may cast doubt on the scheme's ability to continue as a going concern;
- Whether scheme documentation is fully up to date [for example: you have been informed of all changes to the scheme rules];
- Confirmation of propriety of transactions [for example: no transactions have been made which are not in the interests of the scheme members or the scheme during the scheme year or subsequently];
- Confirmation of particular disclosures [for example: there has been no 'self-investment' in a scheme employer or stock-lending];
- Material accounting estimates – confirming basis of estimation;
- Lack of evidence – material representations where no other evidence available;
- Trustees' opinions – confirmations of opinions concerning matters dealt with in the financial statements; and
- Accounting policies – confirming most appropriate, appropriately adopted and disclosed as required by Financial Reporting Standard 18.

Appendix 6 – Illustrative examples of auditors' reports and statements about contributions

This appendix includes as example 1 an auditors' report for an occupational pension scheme. It also sets out as example 2 an Auditors' Statement about Contributions.

Example 1: Unqualified opinion on the financial statements of a scheme.

Independent Auditors' report to the Trustees of the ABC Pension Scheme

We have audited the financial statements of the ABC Pension Scheme for the year ended ..... which comprise the fund account, the net assets statement and the related notes. These financial statements have been prepared under the accounting policies set out therein.

Respective responsibilities of Trustees and Auditors

As described in the Statement of Trustees' responsibilities, the scheme's Trustees are responsible for obtaining an annual report, including audited financial statements prepared in accordance with applicable law and United Kingdom

Accounting Standards (United Kingdom Generally Accepted Accounting Practice).

Our responsibility is to audit the financial statements in accordance with relevant legal and regulatory requirements and International Standards on Auditing (UK and Ireland).

We report to you our opinion as to whether the financial statements show a true and fair view and contain the information specified in the schedule to the Occupational Pension Schemes (Requirement to obtain Audited Accounts and a statement from the Auditor) Regulations 1996 made under the Pensions Act 1995. We also report to you if, in our opinion, we have not received all the information and explanations we require for our audit, or if the information specified by law is not disclosed.

We read the other information contained in the annual report and consider the implications for our report if we become aware of any apparent misstatements or material inconsistencies with the financial statements. The other information comprises the Trustees' Report, the Investment Report, (the Actuarial statements[28],) the Compliance Statement and Members' Information (*amend headings as applicable to match the document*).

Basis of audit opinion

We conducted our audit in accordance with International Standards on Auditing (UK and Ireland) issued by the Auditing Practices Board. An audit includes examination, on a test basis, of evidence relevant to the amounts and disclosures in the financial statements. It also includes an assessment of the significant estimates and judgments made by the Trustees in the preparation of the financial statements, and of whether the accounting policies are appropriate to the Scheme's circumstances, consistently applied and adequately disclosed.

We planned and performed our audit so as to obtain all the information and explanations which we considered necessary in order to provide us with sufficient evidence to give reasonable assurance that the financial statements are free from material misstatement, whether caused by fraud or other irregularity or error. In forming our opinion we also evaluated the overall adequacy of the presentation of information in the financial statements.

Opinion

In our opinion:

- the financial statements show a true and fair view, in accordance with United Kingdom Generally Accepted Accounting Practice, of the financial transactions of the Scheme during the year ended [date], and of the amount and disposition at that date of its assets and liabilities, other than the liabilities to pay pensions and benefits after the end of the year; and
- the financial statements contain the information specified in Regulation 3 of and the Schedule to the Occupational Pension Schemes (Requirement to obtain Audited Accounts and a Statement from the Auditor) Regulations 1996.

---

[28] *In the case of a defined benefit scheme only.*

(Chartered Auditors) Address Accountants)Registered

Date

Example 2: Pro-forma trustees' Summary of Contributions and auditors' Statements about Contributions[29]

XYZ Scheme

Summary of Contributions payable in the year

£

Contributions payable under the Schedule of Contributions/Payment Schedule:

Employer normal contributions*

Employer special contributions*

Employer additional contributions*

Employee normal contributions*

Employee additional contributions*

Total contributions payable under the Schedule

Other contributions:

Employee additional voluntary contributions*

Other contributions [describe]*

Total contributions payable to the Scheme:

Signed on behalf of the Trustees:

Date

Note: If the total of contributions reported above is not the same as that reported in the financial statements, provide a reconciliation.

*These descriptions of contributions which could be due under the schedules is for illustrative purposes only and should be replaced with the appropriate description of

---

[29] *The statutory disclosures require any reasons for a qualified auditors' statement to be disclosed in the trustees' report, so it is logical for the trustees' summary of contributions to be included in the report.*

contributions for the scheme.

> ## Unqualified Auditors' Statement about contributions
>
> Independent Auditors' Statement about Contributions, under Regulation 4 of The Occupational Pension Schemes (Requirement to obtain Audited Accounts and a Statement from the Auditor) Regulations 1996, to the trustees of the XYZ Pension Scheme.
>
> We have examined the summary of contributions to the XYZ Pension Scheme for [or 'in respect of'] the scheme year ended [...] to which this statement is attached/ which is set out in the trustees' report on page x.
>
> **Respective responsibilities of trustees and auditors**
>
> As described on page [ ] the scheme's trustees are responsible for ensuring that there is prepared, maintained and from time to time revised a [schedule of contributions/payment schedule] which sets out the rates and due dates of certain contributions payable towards the scheme by or on behalf of the employer and the active members of the scheme. The trustees are also responsible for keeping records in respect of contributions received in respect of any active member of the scheme and for monitoring whether contributions are made to the Scheme by the employer in accordance with the [schedule of contributions/payment schedule].
>
> It is our responsibility to provide a statement about contributions paid under the [schedule of contributions/payment schedule] and to report our opinion to you.
>
> **Basis of statement about contributions**
>
> We planned and performed our work so as to obtain the information and explanations which we considered necessary in order to give reasonable assurance that contributions reported in the attached summary of contributions have{in all material respects}* been paid {at least}* in accordance with the relevant requirements. For this purpose the work that we carried out included examination, on a test basis, of evidence relevant to the amounts of contributions payable to the scheme and the timing of those payments under the [schedule of contributions/payment schedule]. Our Statement about contributions is required to refer to those breaches of the schedule of contributions which come to our attention in the course of our work.
>
> **Statement about contributions**
>
> In our opinion contributions for the scheme year ended .... as reported in the attached summary of contributions have {in all material respects}* been paid {at least}* in accordance with the schedule of contributions certified by the scheme actuary on [ ]/ payment schedule dated [...].
>
> (Chartered Accountants)
> Registered Auditors   Address
>
> Date

* **Note:** These words should be included in auditors' statements for financial periods beginning on or after 22 September 2005. They should be excluded from auditors' statements relating to earlier financial periods.

Qualified auditors' statement about contributions

Because schedules of contributions and payment schedules are specific in relation to dates and rates, it is sometimes necessary to qualify the auditors' statement on contributions under the scheme. An appropriate example for a defined benefit scheme, which may be suitably adapted for a money purchase scheme with a payment schedule, is given below.

> **Defined benefit (final salary) scheme which has prepared a schedule of contributions. Non-compliance with schedule – Extract from an auditors' report including a negative statement about contributions**
>
> *Qualified statement about contributions under the scheme*
>
> As explained on page xx[30], [give brief details of the departure from the schedule including an indication of the frequency of late payments, and quantification of the amounts involved – e.g. 'in relation to three months during the year contributions amounting in total to £X were paid later than the due date set out in the schedule of contributions'.]
>
> In view of the significance of the matter referred to above, in our opinion contributions for the scheme year ended ....as reported in the attached summary of contributions have not {in all material respects}* been paid {at least}* in accordance with the schedule of contributions certified by the actuary on [date].

* **Note:** These words should be included in auditors' statements for financial periods beginning on or after 22 September 2005. They should be excluded from auditors' statements relating to earlier financial periods.

Other reporting situations

Accounts for actuarial valuations

1 As explained in paragraphs 35 to 40 of Appendix 2, there may be occasions when auditors are asked to provide audit reports for the purposes of PPF valuations.

2 The auditor and the trustees agree a separate engagement letter which covers:
- The fact that the audit relates to a set of accounts prepared specifically for the purpose of a PPF valuation, and
- The period the accounts are to cover (normally the period from the last scheme year end to the date of the PPF valuation).

3 Such accounts are statutory accounts required by the Pensions Act 2004 and related regulations. However, the notes to the financial statements should refer to the reason for their preparation and the fact that the financial statements are not the statutory annual financial statements of the scheme. Suggested wording is given

---

[30] This will normally refer to the note in the trustees' report where the trustees give the reasons for the qualified auditors' statement.

below. The audit report and trustees' responsibilities statements should also be drafted to reflect the circumstances under which they are being issued, and examples of these are also given below.

Independent Auditors' Report to the trustees of the XYZ Pension Scheme

We have audited the financial statements of [name of scheme] for the period ended [date] which comprise the fund account, the net assets statement and the related notes. These financial statements have been prepared under the accounting policies set out therein.

Respective responsibilities of trustees and auditors

As described in the statement of trustees' responsibilities on page [number], where the trustees determine that audited financial statements should be obtained for the purposes of a valuation under the Pension Protection Fund (Valuation) Regulations 2005 they have accepted responsibility for obtaining such financial statements prepared in accordance with applicable law and UK Accounting Standards (UK Generally Accepted Accounting Practice).

Our responsibility is to audit the financial statements in accordance with relevant legal and regulatory requirements and International Standards on Auditing (UK and Ireland).

We report to you our opinion as to whether the financial statements show a true and fair view and contain the information specified in the Schedule to the Occupational Pension Schemes (Requirement to obtain Audited Accounts and a Statement from the Auditor) Regulations 1996 made under the Pensions Act 1995, as if those requirements were to apply to these financial statements. We also report to you if, in our opinion, we have not received all the information and explanations we require for our audit.

Basis of audit opinion

We conducted our audit in accordance with International Standards on Auditing (UK and Ireland) issued by the Auditing Practices Board. An audit includes examination, on a test basis, of evidence relevant to the amounts and disclosures in the financial statements. It also includes an assessment of the significant estimates and judgements made by or on behalf of the trustees in the preparation of the financial statements, and of whether the accounting policies are appropriate to the scheme's circumstances, consistently applied and adequately disclosed.

We planned and performed our audit so as to obtain all the information and explanations which we considered necessary in order to provide us with sufficient evidence to give reasonable assurance that the financial statements are free from material misstatement, whether caused by fraud or other irregularity or error. In forming our opinion we also evaluated the overall adequacy of the presentation of information in the financial statements.

Opinion

In our opinion the financial statements:

- show a true and fair view, in accordance with UK Generally Accepted Accounting Practice, of the financial transactions of the scheme during the period from [date] to [date] and of the amount and disposition at that date of its assets and liabilities (other than liabilities to pay pensions and benefits after the end of the period); and
- contain the information specified in Regulation 3 of, and the Schedule to, the Occupational Pension Schemes (Requirement to obtain Audited Accounts and a Statement from the Auditor) Regulations 1996 made under the Pensions Act 1995, as if those requirements applied under the Pension Protection Fund (Valuation) Regulations 2005.

(Chartered Accountants)
Registered Auditors

Date

Address

Notes to the financial statements

The notes to the financial statements should refer to the reason for their preparation and the fact that they are not the statutory annual financial statements of the scheme, as follows:

Note in relation to the financial statements produced for the purposes of a Pension Protection Fund Valuation

These financial statements have been prepared as at [date] for the purposes of a valuation in accordance with the Pension Protection Fund (Valuation) Regulations 2005. The trustees have elected to prepare them in accordance with the Occupational Pension Schemes (Requirement to obtain Audited Accounts and a Statement from the Auditor) Regulations 1996 and with the Statement of Recommended Practice 'Financial Reports of Pension Schemes'.

The financial statements summarise the transactions of the scheme and deal with the net assets at the disposal of the trustees. They do not take account of obligations to pay pensions and benefits which fall due after the end of the period.

They do not constitute the statutory annual financial statements of the scheme, the most recent of which were prepared for the scheme year ended [date].

Appendix 7 – Illustrative example statement of trustees' responsibilities

Statutory audit

The following illustrative wording may be used as the basis for preparing a statement for inclusion in a scheme's annual report. Nothing in this illustration is intended to impose obligations on trustees that do not exist in law.

The financial statements are the responsibility of the Trustees. Pension scheme regulations require the trustees to make available to scheme members, beneficiaries and certain other parties, audited financial statements for each scheme year which:

- show a true and fair view of the financial transactions of the scheme during the scheme year and of the amount and disposition at the end of that year of the assets and liabilities, other than liabilities to pay pensions and benefits after the end of the scheme year, in accordance with applicable law and United Kingdom Accounting Standards (United Kingdom Generally Accepted Accounting Practice), and
- contain the information specified in the Schedule to The Occupational Pension Schemes (Requirement to obtain Audited Accounts and a Statement from the Auditor) Regulations 1996, including a statement whether the financial statements have been prepared in accordance with the Statement of Recommended Practice 'Financial Reports of Pension Schemes' (Revised November 2002).

The trustees have supervised the preparation of the financial statements and have agreed suitable accounting policies, to be applied consistently, making any estimates and judgments on a prudent and reasonable basis.

The trustees are also responsible for making available certain other information about the scheme in the form of an Annual Report.

Defined benefit schemes

The trustees are responsible under pensions legislation for ensuring that there is prepared, maintained and from time to time revised a schedule of contributions showing the rates of contributions payable towards the scheme by or on behalf of the employer and the active members of the scheme and the dates on or before which such contributions are to be paid. The trustees are also responsible for keeping records in respect of contributions received in respect of any active member of the scheme and for monitoring whether contributions are made to the Scheme by the employer in accordance with the schedule of contributions. Where breaches of the schedule occur, the trustees are required by the Pensions Acts 1995 and 2004 to consider making reports to the Pensions Regulator and the members.

Money purchase schemes

The trustees are responsible under pensions legislation for ensuring that there is prepared, maintained and from time to time revised a payment schedule showing the rates of contributions payable towards the scheme by or on behalf of the employer and the active members of the scheme and the dates on or before which such contributions are to be paid. The trustees are also responsible for keeping records in respect of contributions received in respect of any active member of the scheme and for monitoring whether contributions are made to the Scheme by the employer in accordance with the payment schedule. Where breaches of the schedule occur, the trustees are required by the Pensions Act 1995 to consider making reports to the Pensions Regulator and the members.

The trustees also have a general responsibility for ensuring that adequate accounting records are kept and for taking such steps as are reasonably open to them to safeguard the assets of the scheme and to prevent and detect fraud and other irregularities, including the maintenance of an appropriate system of internal control.

Note: further reporting about contributions

In addition to the statutory requirements, the trust deed and rules of many schemes require auditors to report on whether contributions have been paid to the scheme in accordance with the rules of the scheme and with the recommendations of the actuary, where one is appointed. In such cases, to make it clear that compliance with the rules and recommendations is in the first instance a matter for the trustees, references to the "schedule of contributions" or "payment schedule" in the paragraphs set out above will need to be extended to include "the scheme rules and recommendations of the actuary" (if appointed).

Audited financial statements prepared for a PPF valuation

If audited financial statements are being prepared for the purposes of a PPF valuation (S.143 or S.179, as explained further in paragraphs 35-40 of Appendix 2) and there is no accompanying annual report, the opening paragraph of the above Statement of Trustees' Responsibilities will need to be amended to read as follows :

> These audited financial statements, which are the responsibility of the trustees, have been prepared as at [insert date], for the purposes of an actuarial valuation being undertaken in accordance with {Section 143 or Section 179} of the Pensions Act 2004. The trustees have applied the requirements of the Audited Account Regulations so as to:

Appendix 8 – Impact of the scheme benefit structure on risk

The nature of the benefit structure of an individual scheme can affect the nature of the records that are maintained by the scheme administrator, the risks of misstatement of the financial statements or the trustees' summary of contributions, and possibly the trustees' expectations about the audit work required to support the audit opinions. The following sections describe some of the features of the audit of defined contribution, defined benefit and hybrid schemes which may give rise to specific risks.

Defined contribution schemes

In most defined contribution schemes, contributions are received and invested for the benefit of individual members, and there is no pooling or cross-subsidy as there is in defined benefit schemes. Although individual schemes may offer only one type of investment vehicle (such as unitised funds or an insurance arrangement) members will typically be able to make a choice between a range of different investment exposures, for example to UK or foreign investments and to equity or fixed interest instruments.

The ultimate benefit receivable by a member will depend upon their individual history of contributions (and related investments) made by them and/or on their behalf. It is therefore essential that the administration arrangements of defined contribution schemes accurately record the contributions paid in on behalf of each member, and that contributions are allocated according to the scheme's investment arrangements, reflecting members' choices where applicable.

While systematic errors in the administrative records may give rise to a risk of misstatement in the financial statements, individual errors are unlikely to be material. The financial statements present the aggregate position of members' interests in the scheme so the audit opinion, and therefore the work required to support it, is based on an assessment of materiality and risk to the financial statements as a whole, not on the position of individual members.

Trustees may commission auditors to carry out additional work to review the administrative effectiveness and accuracy of individual records and the allocation of contributions. The scope of this work will be subject to discussion and agreement between the auditor and the trustees; it does not have a direct relationship with the auditor's opinion on the financial statements and is not considered further in this Practice Note.

The risk of misstatement to particular audit assertions may arise in the following areas:

Completeness of investment assets

(a) Notionally unitised funds

Where a scheme operates a notionally unitised managed portfolio of investments, errors in the unitisation process may result in the misallocation of interests between members without affecting the overall balance of the fund and the assets disclosed in the financial statements. However, it is vital that the aggregate allocation and revaluation of units is reconciled regularly with the value of actual investments made and held to ensure that the aggregate value of units is supported by an equivalent value of real assets.

(b) Insurance policies or managed fund units

Where trustees invest members' contributions in insurance policies or managed fund units, the auditor will be concerned to ensure that the information about scheme assets that is reported by the insurer or fund manager is complete. Relevant controls include:

- reconciliations carried out of the units (and their values) of individual member allocations with the total units in issue and the value of assets held by the scheme; and
- where third party providers maintain records at an individual member level and not on an aggregated scheme level, with aggregation only for periodic financial reporting purposes, reconciliation of the increase/decrease in the number of members at the beginning and end of the scheme financial period with the joiners and leavers during that period.

Accuracy of contributions reflected in the trustees' summary of contributions

The rules of a defined contribution scheme may permit members to select and change their contribution rate, and the rate of employer contribution may also vary, possibly in tandem with that of the member. Such complexities may increase the risk that contributions are not collected and paid over, with consequential effect on the auditors' statement about contributions.

Proper presentation of additional voluntary contributions (AVCs)

On retirement the funds resulting from AVC contributions are subject to different rules in respect of how they are applied in providing benefits. Accordingly the contributions and, where they are invested separately from normal contributions, the related investments (where material) are required to be disclosed separately in the financial statements. If administration records do not clearly distinguish AVCs from other contributions, the separate disclosure of AVCs in the financial statements may be misstated.

Non-compliance with the timing requirements of the payment schedule

The trustees of a pension scheme will have agreed a payment schedule with the employer. The auditors' statement about contributions gives assurance that this schedule has been adhered to.

Particular features of the payment arrangements of insured schemes that may increase the risk of late payments include the following:

- direct debit payment arrangements may not be adjusted immediately for the effects of changes in pensionable salaries and/or the contribution rates used in making payroll deductions;
- contributions may be deducted from new members' pay but not collected by the insurer until the direct debit is next adjusted; and
- the direct debit may fall on a non-banking day and it is processed on the next available banking day which happens to fall after the date set out in the payment schedule, resulting in a breach of the timing requirements of the schedule and possibly of Section 49 of the PA 1995.

An additional problem may arise if contributions are paid each month on the basis of the actual contribution liability but the insurer's administration systems cannot accept the payments because the amounts do not equal premiums set at the last renewal date.

Defined benefit schemes

Completeness and disclosure of investment assets

Investment assets are not designated to the interests of individual members but are held on a pooled basis. As a result, with the exception of money purchase AVCs, the accurate designation of investments to individual members is not a relevant audit issue.

However, where a scheme participates along with a number of other schemes in a common investment fund, the trustees (and therefore the auditor) of an individual participating scheme will be concerned to ensure that the portion of the common investment fund that is attributed to "their scheme" accurately represents its interest in the fund.

In situations where participating schemes are allocated units in the common investment fund, it is vital that the aggregate allocation and revaluation of units is reconciled regularly with the value of actual investments made and held to ensure that the aggregate value of units is supported by an equivalent value of real assets. In other situations it may be necessary for the auditor to examine the basis on which contributions into the fund, withdrawals (if any) from the fund and investment income and growth are attributed to the scheme's share of the common fund.

Accuracy of contributions reflected in the trustees' summary of contributions

Variable rates of contributions may exist where:

- the scheme offers a range of accrual rates for different rates of member contributions; or
- some members, for example senior executives, pay different rates to the rest of the members; or
- there are variable offsets, such as the NI lower earnings limit.

Such complexities may increase the risk that contributions are not correctly calculated. To address this risk, the auditor considers whether there are controls over the administration records and the employer's payroll, which ensure the accurate identification and application of contribution rates for individual members and the employer.

Hybrid schemes

Hybrid schemes offer both defined benefit and defined contribution benefits. Trustees may permit surplus funds in the defined benefit section to fund employer contributions to the defined contribution section (or vice versa) by means of a transfer of assets between the sections for accounting purposes. Where this occurs, the auditor confirms that the arrangement is permitted by the scheme's deed and rules and supported by the scheme actuary. The auditor also considers whether the transfer in lieu of cash contributions is paid or credited in a timely manner.

Accuracy of the split of assets between the sections of the scheme

The rules of hybrid schemes may allow members to transfer between sections. This gives rise to a risk that members' choices may not be properly reflected in the financial records, and therefore that the analysis of assets between the defined benefit and defined contribution sections may be misstated. In these situations the auditor will consider the controls over the recording of such transfers.

Accuracy of calculation of benefits

Certain hybrid schemes may have an 'underpin', such that the members are entitled to benefits calculated as the higher of those accumulated under the defined contribution and defined benefit rules. When auditing scheme benefits, the auditor pays particular attention to the application of this aspect of the scheme rules in the calculations.

Appendix 9 – Non-statutory audit appointments

This appendix covers the particular considerations that apply when the trustees of a scheme are exempt from the statutory obligation to obtain audited financial statements and an auditors' statement about contributions but the trust deed and rules require the trustees to obtain 'audited' financial statements.

APPLICATION OF ISAs (UK AND IRELAND) AND THE GUIDANCE IN THIS PRACTICE NOTE

Where a true and fair audit opinion is to be issued, the requirements of ISAs (UK and Ireland) and the guidance given in this Practice Note apply. Unless specifically required by the trust deed, auditors do not however produce a statement about contributions, so the guidance in this Practice Note on that subject will not be relevant.

Non-statutory auditors fall within the scope of the definition of "professional adviser", as used in Section 70 of the Pensions Act 2004, so they are subject to the same statutory duty to make reports to TPR as statutory auditors. As a result, ISA (UK and Ireland) 250 Section B applies to non-statutory audits and the related guidance in this Practice Note is also relevant.

APPOINTMENT AND REMOVAL

A non-statutory auditor falls within the definition of the term "professional adviser" used in the Occupational Pension Schemes (Scheme Administration) Regulations, so the provisions relating to the appointment and removal of scheme auditors (as discussed in paragraphs 48 to 57 and 69 to 71) apply equally to the appointment of a non-statutory auditor.

ENGAGEMENT LETTER

The engagement letter will need to be tailored to reflect the particular circumstances of the individual scheme, the nature and scope of the auditor's role (as set out in the trust deed and rules) and the form and content of the annual report and financial statements.

Where the form and content of the financial statements is not specified in the trust deed but a 'true and fair' audit opinion is required, the financial statements fall within the scope of the Pensions SORP so they should be prepared so as to comply in all material respects with its recommendations.

Non-statutory auditors may wish to use the example letter for a statutory audit set out in Example 4 of Appendix 4 as a starting point for the tailoring, but then have regard to the following:

- **Responsibilities of trustees and auditors** – The trustees' responsibility to obtain audited accounts (and therefore to appoint the auditor) arises under the requirements of the trust deed, rather than regulations made under the Pensions Act 1995; also the form and content of the financial statements will be determined by the requirements of the trust deed, rather than regulations. The responsibility of the auditor to audit and report on the financial statements also arises from the trust deed not regulations.
- **Scope of work** – Where the auditor is required to express a "true and fair" audit opinion, his work will be governed by the requirements of Auditing Standards. Whether the auditor is to test and report on contributions to the scheme will depend on the presence of a requirement in the trust deed.
- **Representations by trustees and third parties** – Information and explanations from the scheme's personnel are likely to be an equally important part of the work of a non-statutory auditor, so he is likely to wish to obtain relevant written representations towards the end of the audit.
- **Reporting to those charged with governance** – These paragraphs are likely to be equally relevant to the non-statutory audit.
- **Reporting to The Pensions Regulator** – A non-statutory auditor of an occupational pension scheme falls within the definition of "professional adviser" (as used in Section 70 of the Pensions Act 2004) so (like the statutory auditor) is subject to the duty to report to TPR under Section 70 of the Pensions Act 2004.

- **Electronic communications and reporting** – The non-statutory auditor needs to determine whether the financial statements or the annual report with which his audit report is to be circulated are to be made available electronically.
- **Auditors' Statement about Contributions** – It is unlikely that a non-statutory auditor will be required to report about contributions by reference to a Payment Schedule. However, where the trust deed imposes a requirement (probably to report whether contributions have been paid in accordance with the trust deed and rules), these paragraphs should be carefully tailored to replace references to a statutory statement about contributions with the form of opinion required by the terms of the trust deed.
- **Termination of appointment** – As noted above, the termination of the appointment of a non-statutory auditor is subject to the same legal requirements as the termination of a statutory appointment.

REPORTING

Trustees' responsibilities statement

The first part of the example statement in Appendix 7 will typically need to be amended to read as follows:

> The non-statutory financial statements are the responsibility of the trustees. The trust deed and rules of the scheme require the trustees to prepare audited financial statements for each scheme year which:
> - show a true and fair view of the financial transactions of the scheme during the scheme year and of the amount and disposition at the end of that year of the assets and liabilities, other than liabilities to pay pensions and benefits after the end of the scheme year, and
> - contain the information specified in the Statement of Recommended Practice 'Financial Reports of Pension Schemes (Revised November 2002)' and the Trust Deed.

Audit report

Auditor's reports resulting from non-statutory audits retain the same structure as Example 1 in Appendix 6 but the wording needs to be tailored for the particular circumstances. A tailored example is shown below:

> **Auditors' report to the Trustees of the ABC Pension Scheme**
>
> We have audited the non-statutory financial statements of the ABC Pension Scheme for the year ended .... which comprise the fund account, the net assets statement and the related notes. These financial statements have been prepared under the accounting policies set out therein.
>
> **Respective responsibilities of Trustees and Auditors**
>
> As described in the Statement of Trustees' responsibilities, the scheme's Trustees are responsible under the Trust Deed for obtaining an annual report, including audited financial statements prepared in accordance with the requirements of the

Trust Deed, applicable law and United Kingdom Accounting Standards (United Kingdom Generally Accepted Accounting Practice).

Our responsibility is to audit the financial statements in accordance with the requirements of the Trust Deed and International Standards on Auditing (UK and Ireland).

We report to you our opinion as to whether the financial statements show a true and fair view. We also report to you if, in our opinion, we have not received all the information and explanations we require for our audit, or if the information required to be disclosed by the trust deed is not disclosed.

We read the other information contained in the annual report and consider the implications for our report if we become aware of any apparent misstatements or material inconsistencies with the financial statements. The other information comprises the Trustees' Report, the Investment Report, the Compliance Statement and Members' Information (*include/amend headings as applicable to match the document*).

Basis of audit opinion

We conducted our audit in accordance with International Standards on Auditing (UK and Ireland) issued by the Auditing Practices Board. An audit includes examination, on a test basis, of evidence relevant to the amounts and disclosures in the financial statements. It also includes an assessment of the significant estimates and judgments made by the Trustees in the preparation of the financial statements, and of whether the accounting policies are appropriate to the Scheme's circumstances, consistently applied and adequately disclosed.

We planned and performed our audit so as to obtain all the information and explanations which we considered necessary in order to provide us with sufficient evidence to give reasonable assurance that the financial statements are free from material misstatement, whether caused by fraud or other irregularity or error. In forming our opinion we also evaluated the overall adequacy of the presentation of information in the financial statements.

Opinion

In our opinion:
- the financial statements show a true and fair view, in accordance with United Kingdom Generally Accepted Accounting Practice, of the financial transactions of the Scheme during the year ended [date], and of the amount and disposition at that date of its assets and liabilities, other than the liabilities to pay pensions and benefits after the end of the year; and
- the financial statements contain the information specified in the Trust Deed.

(Chartered Accountants)
Registered Auditors   Address

Date

Appendix 10 – Definitions

Terms in this Practice Note are used as defined in the Glossary of terms issued by the APB in conjunction with Auditing Standards, and Pensions Terminology – a Glossary for Pension Schemes (sixth edition) published by the Pensions Management Institute (PMI) and the Pensions Research Accountants Group (PRAG).

Terms and abbreviations in this Practice Note for frequently used terms are as follows:

Assurance reports on internal controls of service organisations made available to third parties	Reports on internal controls, usually those at service organisations, issued in accordance with guidance published by the Institute of Chartered Accountants in England and Wales in Technical Release AAF 01/06
Audited Accounts Regulations	The Occupational Pension Schemes (Requirement to obtain Audited Accounts and a Statement from the Auditor) Regulations 1996 (SI 1996/1975), as amended
Disclosure Regulations	The Occupational Pension Schemes (Disclosure of Information) Regulations 1996 (SI 1996/1655), as amended
Ear-marked schemes	Money purchase schemes under which all benefits are secured by one or more policies of insurance or annuity contracts specifically allocated to individuals or their dependants. Such schemes are not required by statute to obtain audited financial statements.
FRS	Financial Reporting Standard issued by the Accounting Standards Board, a part of the Financial Reporting Council
Funding Regulations	The Occupational Pension Schemes (Scheme Funding) Regulations 2005 (SI 2005/3377)
HMRC	HM Revenue & Customs
MFR	Minimum funding requirement, now superseded by the scheme specific funding regime
Opra	The regulator of work-based pension schemes in the UK until 5 April 2005, when it was replaced by TPR (see below)
PA 1995; PA 2004	The Pensions Act 1995; The Pensions Act 2004
Pensions SORP	The Statement of Recommended Practice 'Financial reports of pension schemes' (November 2002)
PRAG	The Pensions Research Accountants Group
PSA 1993	The Pension Schemes Act 1993
ISAs (UK and Ireland)	Auditing standards issued by the Auditing Practices Board that are based on International Standards on Auditing issued by the International Auditing and Assurance Standards Board

Scheme	An occupational pension scheme as defined by Part 1 Section 1 of PSA 1993; the activities of occupational pension schemes are defined in s255 of the PA 2004
Scheme Administration Regulations	The Occupational Pension Schemes (Scheme Administration Regulations 1996 (SI 1996/1715), as amended
TPR	The Pensions Regulator

Appendix 11 – Some significant topics relevant to audits of pension schemes

Topic	Paragraph Numbers	Section
Statement about contributions	20-22 230 312-347 64-66 –	Introduction ISA (UK and Ireland) 320 The auditors' Statement about Contributions (the Statement) Appendix 2 Appendix 6
Reports to TPR	24-27 113-115 116-171 348-355 –	Introduction ISA (UK and Ireland) 250A ISA (UK and Ireland) 250B Liaison with the scheme actuary Appendix 3
Liaison with actuaries	32-35 287 348-355 70-74	Introduction ISA (UK and Ireland) 620 Liaison with the scheme actuary Appendix 2
Reliance on third parties	31-42 236-259 285-287	Introduction ISA (UK and Ireland) 402 ISA (UK and Ireland) 620
Reporting to those charged with governance	83-84 110-111 172-173	ISA (UK and Ireland) 240 ISA (UK and Ireland) 250A ISA (UK and Ireland) 260
Trust deed	13 88, 95-96, 104 192, 222 285 296 21-22	Introduction ISA (UK and Ireland) 250A ISA (UK and Ireland) 315 ISA (UK and Ireland) 620 ISA (UK and Ireland) 700 Appendix 2
Taxation	6 219 7-8, 44-46	Introduction ISA (UK and Ireland) 315 Appendix 2

Pensions SORP	15	Introduction
	94	ISA (UK and Ireland) 250A
	151	ISA (UK and Ireland) 250B
	193-197	ISA (UK and Ireland) 315
	248	ISA (UK and Ireland) 402
	263, 265	ISA (UK and Ireland) 550
	268, 272	ISA (UK and Ireland) 570
	294-295, 303	ISA (UK and Ireland) 700
	–	Appendix 3
Appointment of scheme auditors	47-57	ISA (UK and Ireland) 210
	–	Appendix 4
Non-statutory audits	48	ISA (UK and Ireland) 210
	171	ISA (UK and Ireland) 250B
	347	The Auditors' Statement about Contributions (the Statement)
	–	Appendix 9

[PN 16]
Bank reports for audit purposes in the United Kingdom (revised)

Contents

Paragraphs

Preface

Introduction

Planning: risk assessment and audit evidence	1 – 9
Planning: the bank report request	10 – 15
Authority to disclose	16 – 17
Guarantees and other third party securities	18
Bank information	19
Bank report request templates	20 – 25
Timing of requests	26 – 29
Minor omissions or discrepancies	30
Accrued Interest and Charges	31

Appendices

1 Templates for auditor request forms:
 1. *Standard Request (including additional information option)*
 2. *Fast Track Request*
 3. *Incomplete Information Request*
 4. *Acknowledgement template*
2 *Authority to disclose information – illustration*
3 *British Bankers' Association guidance note for banks*

Preface

This Practice Note summarises the process agreed between the UK auditing profession and the British Bankers' Association (BBA) regarding the procedures auditors use when requesting confirmation of balances, transactions or arrangements from the bankers of an entity being audited.

In this Practice Note bank confirmations are described as 'bank reports'.

This Practice Note applies to accounting periods commencing on or after **26 December 2007**. Earlier adoption of the new forms and process is encouraged so that efficiency savings, both for banks and auditors, can be realised as soon as possible. However the new process can only be used with the new forms and the provision of main account number and sort code for each legal entity listed in the request for information.

Introduction

Confirmations provided by banks and other financial institutions of balances and other banking arrangements usually provide the auditor with valuable audit evidence.

Over the years the auditing and banking professions have developed protocols and forms to assist this process and in 1998 the Auditing Practices Board issued Practice Note 16: "Bank reports for audit purposes" to formalise the process that existed at that time.

Banking systems have evolved since PN 16 was first issued and a number of administrative difficulties have been identified both on the part of banks and auditors. Discussions between the auditing profession and banks, facilitated by the British Bankers' Association (BBA), have therefore been held with a view to updating PN 16 to reflect new circumstances and to make the bank report process as efficient and effective as possible.

In October 2005 the APB issued, as a consultation draft, a proposed revision of PN 16 which reflected such discussions. The relatively minor changes proposed to the original Practice Note were to:

- encourage auditors to submit requests for information earlier;
- recommend the provision of a main account name and number by the auditor, to facilitate banks in identifying the appropriate customer more readily; and
- clarify that auditors do not need a new authority to disclose information every time that they ask for confirmation of bank details.

A number of respondents to the October 2005 consultation draft recommended more extensive changes to the process and it was agreed that further discussions would take place between the audit profession and the BBA. As those discussions were incomplete in autumn 2006 the APB concluded that it would be helpful to issue the October 2005 consultation draft as interim guidance to apply to audits of entities with 31 December 2006 year ends.

The most recent discussions have resulted in an agreement that in order for the auditors to benefit from improvements in the speed and accuracy of responses to their requests more extensive changes should be made to PN 16 to:

- encourage auditors to think more about the banking information they ask banks to confirm and to request additional information on trade finance and derivative and commodity trading only when there is a reasonable expectation that the client utilises such facilities. Currently auditors often send a blanket request for information to the bank, rather than a more targeted request based on the auditor's knowledge of banking arrangements that exist, or are likely to exist. This results in delay in auditors receiving responses and considerable added complexity and cost for the banks.
- reflect the fact that most audit requests are now actioned by specialised teams based in banks' regional service centres, rather than at branch level. This means both that audit letters sent to the branch can take time to be redirected to the service centre, and that the client knowledge that would enable a local manager to find most, if not all, the relevant information about a client quickly, can now involve an extensive search across different sections and locations by the regional centre staff.
- better reflect banks' information systems that are not designed to facilitate the production of a bank report. For example, banks' core records are account number based, and that without the main account number for each legal entity the search can be difficult. Entity names are often similar in nature and the identification of the relevant customer is not always straightforward. The provision of account number and sort code details will assist in the identification of the customer.

Main changes to PN 16

As well as confirming the changes made in the October 2005 draft, additional changes have been made to PN 16 to:

- add guidance to put the decision as to whether to obtain a bank report and, if so, what information to be covered by it, into the context of a risk based approach to the audit and to encourage auditors to refer to the annual facilities letter sent by the banks to many of their clients in making their risk assessments;
- introduce new bank report templates for:
    - a Standard Request (including the option of additional information on trade finance and derivative and commodity trading) thereby allowing the bank to respond within its normal timeframe,
    - a Fast-Track Request thereby requesting the bank to respond within an accelerated timeframe, and
    - an Incomplete Information Request to be used when the auditor is not able to provide all of the information required for the Standard Request (main account sort code and account number or where additional information is requested, a sample reference to facility account number);
- explain that the banks have agreed:
    - to publish addresses for the centres to which requests for audit information are to be addressed on the BBA website;
    - either to acknowledge auditor requests for bank reports and provide bank contact details, or where an acknowledgement will not be given to publish on the BBA website details of where contact can be made. This will facilitate the auditor in following up late or missing bank reports, or question information in reports that were received;
- clarify that, with a few exceptions, banks do not need a new authority to disclose information every time that auditors ask for confirmation of bank details;
- request auditors using the Standard Request to provide the main account sort code and account number for each legal entity named in the request and, where additional information is requested, a sample facility account number for trade

finance or derivative and commodity trading information. This helps banks identify the appropriate information;
- remove custodian arrangements from the categories of additional information listed in the Standard Request. The existence and location of the assets held for safe keeping by banks is unlikely to be readily identified from account number details and banks are likely to have to conduct extensive searches which often result in a 'nil return'. If the auditor wishes to confirm the existence and nature of specific assets held for safe keeping or suspects that the entity is concealing assets they make separate arrangements to confirm these or carry out a physical inspection; and
- remove the statement requesting the bank to advise the auditor if the authority is insufficient to allow the bank to provide full disclosure of the information requested. Banks have not been doing this because of data protection regulations and auditors have been taking unwarranted comfort that they are being informed of all details of a banking relationship.

Planning: Risk Assessment and Audit Evidence

1 The following International Standards on Auditing (ISAs) (UK and Ireland) are particularly relevant to the auditor's decisions as to whether to obtain a bank report and, if so, what information is to be covered by it:

- ISA (UK and Ireland) 300, *Planning an audit of financial statements*
- ISA (UK and Ireland) 315, *Understanding the entity and its environment and assessing the risks of material misstatement*
- ISA (UK and Ireland) 500, *Audit evidence*
- ISA (UK and Ireland) 505, *External confirmations*.

2 ISA (UK and Ireland) 300 *Planning an audit of financial statements* requires the auditor to plan the audit so that the engagement will be performed in an effective manner.

3 ISA (UK and Ireland) 315 *Understanding the entity and its environment and assessing the risks of material misstatement* requires the auditor to identify and assess the risks of material misstatement at the financial statement level, and at the assertion level for classes of transactions, account balances, and disclosures. Decisions on whether or not to request a bank report and, if so, the nature of evidence to be obtained are responses to the auditor's assessment of the risks of material misstatement.

4 ISA (UK and Ireland) 500, *Audit evidence* considers the relative reliability of audit evidence obtained from different sources.

5 ISA (UK and Ireland) 505 *External confirmations* states that the auditor should determine whether the use of external confirmations is necessary to obtain sufficient appropriate audit evidence at assertion level.

6 During the planning phase of the audit the auditor therefore considers the risks in relation to relevant financial statement assertions including bank related information to be disclosed in the notes to the financial statements when deciding whether to obtain a bank report.

7 Many banks lay out the facilities the entity uses, or those made available to the entity, in an annual facilities letter. The auditor takes into account the banking facilities provided when assessing the risks in relation to relevant financial statement assertions and when deciding whether to obtain a bank report and what banking

information is to be confirmed. Where there is no facilities letter, the auditor asks the entity's management what banking relationships are in place.

Given the importance of cash to an entity's business and its susceptibility to fraudulent misuse the auditor will usually conclude that, in the absence of a bank report regarding account balances, facilities and securities, it will not normally be practical to obtain sufficient appropriate audit evidence from other sources. 8

In rare circumstances where the banking transactions and relationships are very simple and sufficient appropriate audit evidence is likely to be available from other sources the auditor may consider that obtaining a bank report of account balances, facilities and securities is unnecessary. For example, in circumstances where landlords and tenants agree voluntarily to have an audit of the service charge statement of account for a block of flats sufficient, appropriate audit evidence may be obtained from inspecting bank statements and performing analytical procedures on transactions recorded during the period. 9

Planning: the bank report request

Having decided to obtain a bank report, the auditor plans the submission of the request to the bank including: 10

- determining the date by which the bank report is needed;
- depending on the auditor's risk assessment, determining whether confirmation is needed on additional information such as trade finance transactions and balances;
- deciding what type of report to use i.e. Standard (with or without additional information), Fast Track or Incomplete Information Requests;
- making arrangements for assembling the necessary information to be included in the request including the main account sort code and number for each legal entity (that is, subsidiaries as well as the holding company, where a single letter is sent for all companies in a group). If the auditors have decided to confirm additional information (eg trade finance or derivative and commodity trading transactions and balances) a reference will be needed to a sample facility account number;
- checking that the authorities provided to the banks to allow them to disclose information to the auditors are valid; and
- ascertaining where to send the request. It is standard practice for banks to deal with requests for bank reports through a centralised delivery mechanism, using a dedicated query team. The addresses of units dealing with bank report requests for each bank are published on the BBA website at www.bba.org.uk. The designated unit will either respond on behalf of the bank or forward the request to a specialist department.

The normal purpose of bank reports is to provide confirmation of information already available to the auditors. In these circumstances, auditors send a Standard Request for information, including where appropriate a request for additional information. To assist banks retrieve the necessary information auditors provide the main account sort code and number for each legal entity named in the request and, where additional information is requested, a sample facility account number for trade finance or derivative and commodity trading information. 11

When the auditors are unable to provide the main account sort code and number for all the entities in a group or sufficient references to identify additional information 12 required the auditors make a request using an Incomplete Information Request. Circumstances where such a request might be appropriate include:

- because information is not available from the audited entity perhaps due to a break down in controls;
- because the auditor suspects that full information has not been provided to them by the entity for example where there is prior experience of accounts or banking relationships not notified to the auditor or where the auditor suspects impropriety regarding the entity's use of financial instruments;
- where history shows poor record keeping, particularly of financial instruments that do not require an initial entry in the entity's records.

13   Auditors deciding to use an Incomplete Information Request need to be aware that banks cannot give information about legal entities that are not covered by an existing authority to disclose information. This means that details will be provided by the banks of all accounts and facilities relating to an entity listed on the request for a bank report, for which there is a current authority. The bank is under no obligation to tell the auditor that it holds an account or has other arrangements for an entity that is not listed in the request for information. Nor is the bank obliged to tell the auditor that it has withheld information about an entity not listed. Auditors therefore make enquiries of management and apply their understanding of the business to evaluate whether the list of entities to be included on all requests to banks, including the Incomplete Information Request, is complete.

14   Auditors also need to be aware that, where banks are asked to respond to an Incomplete Information Request, searches for possible relationships or facilities will take longer and the banks may charge their customers an additional fee. It is therefore sensible for auditors to use an Incomplete Information Request only where their knowledge of the entity's business indicates that this is necessary.

15   Where the audit plan shows that a bank report is needed sooner than would be the case under normal procedures, the auditor requests a 'Fast Track' response. Fast Track responses are expected to be exceptional, for example where the entity has to meet a US reporting deadline within a month or less of the accounting year end. The process for Fast Track confirmation requests is considered in more detail in paragraph 29 below.

Authority to disclose

16   Banks require the explicit written authority of their customers to disclose the information requested. The BBA has requested that, where possible, this takes the form of an ongoing standing authority rather than as a separate authority each time information is requested. Auditors need to satisfy themselves that an authority is in place and up to date. A single authority can cover several legal entities provided that each entity is specified and the authorisation signatures are appropriate. Banks and building societies that are not members of the BBA may have different requirements for authority to disclose, which are ascertained by auditors before they submit their requests for information.[1]

17   A new authority will be needed in the case of a new audit entity. An updated authority will be needed if there are entity changes such as new group entities or auditor changes such as reorganisation as a limited liability partnership (LLP) or

---

[1] In addition, the BBA has indicated that it will disclose on its website details of credit institutions that do not currently retain authorities and therefore require an authority with each request.

merger with another practice. An illustrative letter providing authority to a bank to disclose information to the entity's auditor is included as Appendix 2.

Guarantees and other third party securities

The provision of information about guarantees and other third party securities has, on occasion, resulted in significant delays in the completion of bank reports because banks have been unable to release the information sought without specific customer consent because of data protection regulations concerning the counter-parties. When banks do not have sufficient authority to provide full disclosure of the information requested, they advise the auditors of that fact and indicate, where that is the case, that such guarantees or third party securities exist. The auditors can then obtain details of the arrangement from the entity, for example by asking to see the relevant facility letter or loan agreement. In some cases, these procedures will suffice. In other cases, auditors will require further independent evidence, and if so they can ask banks for the specific information to be provided once consent from the guarantor or third party has been received. 18

Bank information

The key steps in the bank report process have been agreed with the BBA. The BBA has written to its members setting out guidance for them to follow in responding to requests for audit confirmations. This guidance note is reproduced in full in Appendix 3. A list of current BBA members may be viewed at the BBA's website, www.bba.org.uk. Where the entity's bank is not a BBA member, the auditor may still be able to get a positive response to a request for information. Where a bank report cannot be obtained, the auditors consider whether this represents a limitation of scope that should be referred to in the audit report. 19

Bank report request templates

The request for a bank report is issued on the auditors' own note paper using the appropriate template in Appendix 1. 20

The BBA's guidance to its members defining the information to be given in response to each type of request is set out in Appendix 3 of this Practice Note. The purpose of providing three different request forms is to reflect auditors' planning decisions as to the nature and timing of the information sought. 21

The Standard and Fast Track request templates specify: 22

- the names of all legal entities covered by the request, together with the main account sort code and number of each entity listed;
- reference to a sample facility account number for any additional information required. This will enable the bank to identify the units providing specialist services which need to be consulted. A full listing of all transactions or balances is not required.
- the date for which the auditor is requesting confirmation (ie the period end date) and the date at which the report request is made;
- a statement that neither the auditor's request nor the bank's response will create a contractual relationship between the bank and the auditor; and
- the auditor's contact details.

23 The template for Fast Track Requests include a space for the auditor to explain the reason for the Fast Track requests and the date by which the reply is needed.

24 The Incomplete Information Request contains:
- the names of all legal entities covered by the request, together with the main account number and sort code of the parent company and for as many group entities as can be obtained by the auditor;
- the period end date for which the auditor is requesting confirmation;
- the date at which the report request is made;
- a statement that neither the auditor's request nor the bank's response will create a contractual relationship between the bank and the auditor; and
- the auditor's contact details.

The auditor accepts that banks will not be able to provide this information on an entity that is not covered by a valid authority to disclose.

25 The APB is of the view that the inclusion of a statement that neither the auditor's request nor the bank's response will create a contractual relationship between the bank and the auditor, does not impair the value of the information given as audit evidence. The information given by a bank ought not to be regarded as inaccurate or likely to be inaccurate simply because the giving of it is not actionable. Accordingly, the auditor can reasonably rely upon information given by the bank, provided it is not clearly wrong, suspicious or inconsistent in itself, ambiguous or in conflict with other evidence gathered in the course of the audit.

Timing of requests

26 Where practicable, the auditor sends the bank report request so as to reach the bank one month in advance of the period end date. It is advisable to allow more time at busy periods such as those covering December and March year ends.

27 The BBA has indicated that banks providing acknowledgements of audit requests, if so required, will endeavour to do so within 5 working days of receipt. As part of the acknowledgement process, banks may indicate either a date by which they expect to send a reply to the auditor, or provide an indication of their standard service level agreement (SLA) for the process. The BBA has advised that no practical purpose is served by an auditor's chasing for a bank report until the expected date of receipt (as stated in the bank's acknowledgement or standard SLA) has passed. Banks that do not acknowledge receipt of audit requests are identified on the BBA's website and contact details given for pursuing enquiries.

28 In straightforward circumstances the bank will endeavour to provide the information within a calendar month of the period end date. Where there is a request using an Incomplete Information Request or where a request has been made asking information about guarantees and other third party securities and specific consent is needed from a third party for such information to be released, a response may take longer.

29 For listed companies and other entities subject to tight reporting deadlines the information may be needed sooner than the normal response time of a particular bank. The BBA has therefore agreed a process for fast track responses whereby auditors state why they need the information within less than a calendar month of the period end date. The Fast Track template in Appendix 1 includes a box to be completed by the auditor when seeking an accelerated response.

Minor omissions or discrepancies

Minor omissions or discrepancies in the information provided by the bank may be dealt with informally by telephone or e-mail, although the auditor may request written confirmation of changes to the information provided.   30

Accrued interest and charges

The provision of information about accrued interest and charges at the year end falls outside the scope of this Practice Note.   31

Appendix 1 – Templates for auditor request forms:

1. Standard Request (including additional information option)
2. Fast Track Request
3. Incomplete Information Request
4. Acknowledgement template

REQUEST FOR BANK REPORT FOR AUDIT PURPOSES – STANDARD

The request for a bank report is issued on the auditors' own note paper

Please note – Complete **section 6** only where additional information is required.

In accordance with the agreed practice for provision of information to auditors, please forward information on our mutual client(s) as detailed below on behalf of the bank, its branches and subsidiaries. This request and your response will not create any contractual or other duty with us.

1. **BANK NAME & ADDRESS**

2. **AUDITOR CONTACT DETAILS**

   Name and address of auditor

   Contact number

   Contact name

   Email address

   Period end date (DD/MM/YYYY)

   Date of request (DD/MM/YYYY)

3. **Companies or other business entities**

Company	Main account sort code	Main account number

4. **Authority to disclose information**

   Authority already held and dated (DD/MM/YYYY)

   OR

   Authority Attached

5. **Acknowledgement**

Please complete this section if an acknowledgement is required.

Acknowledgement required	☐ by email	Reference number to be quoted	
OR	☐ by post	(template attached)	

6. **Additional information required**

Trade Finance	☐	One of the facility account numbers	
Derivative & Commodity Trading	☐	One of the facility account numbers	

REQUEST FOR BANK REPORT FOR AUDIT PURPOSES – FAST TRACK

The request for a bank report is issued on the auditors' own note paper

Please note – Complete **section 6** only where additional information is required.

In accordance with the agreed practice for provision of information to auditors, please forward information on our mutual client(s) as detailed below on behalf of the bank, its branches and subsidiaries. This request and your response will not create any contractual or other duty with us.

1. **BANK NAME & ADDRESS**

2. **AUDITOR CONTACT DETAILS**

   Name and address of auditor

   Contact name

   Contact name

   Email address

   Period end date (DD/MM/YYYY)

   Date response required (DD/MM/YYYY)

   Date of request (DD/MM/YYYY)

   Reason for Fast Track request

3. **Companies or other business entities**

Company	Main account sort code	Main account number

4. **Authority to disclose information**

Authority already held and dated (DD/MM/YYYY) [ ] OR Authority Attached [ ]

5. **Acknowledgement**

Please complete this section if an acknowledgement is required.

Acknowledgement required [ ] by email   Reference number to be quoted [ ]

OR [ ] by post   (template attached)

6. **Additional information required**

Trade Finance [ ] One of the facility account numbers [ ]

Derivative & Commodity Trading [ ] One of the facility account numbers [ ]

REQUEST FOR BANK REPORT FOR AUDIT PURPOSES – INCOMPLETE INFORMATION

The request for a bank report is issued on the auditors' own note paper

Please note – Complete **section 6** only where additional information is required.

In accordance with the agreed practice for provision of information to auditors, please forward information on our mutual client(s) as detailed below on behalf of the bank, its branches and subsidiaries. This request and your response will not create any contractual or other duty with us.

1. **BANK NAME & ADDRESS**

2. **AUDITOR CONTACT DETAILS**

Name and address of auditor

Contact number

Contact number

Email address

Period end date (DD/MM/YYYY)

Date response required (DD/MM/YYYY)

We confirm that there are exceptional circumstances that require us to ask for this request to be processed on the basis of incomplete account numbers, sort code and facility account numbers for all companies in the group and/or a facility account number for additional information.. We understand that this may result in the search taking longer to complete than the standard request.

3. **Companies or other business entities**

Company	Main account sort code	Main account number

4. **Authority to disclose information**

Authority already held [ ] OR Authority Attached [ ]
and dated

5. **Acknowledgement**

Please complete this section if an acknowledgement is required.

Acknowledgement [ ] by email   Reference number to [ ]
required   be quoted

OR   [ ] by post   (template attached)

6. **Additional information required**

Trade Finance   [ ] A facility account number if available [ ]

Derivative &   [ ] A facility account number if available [ ]
Commodity
Trading

REQUEST FOR ACKNOWLEDGEMENT OF BANK REPORT FOR AUDIT PURPOSES

The request is issued on the auditors' own note paper

Please note – Part A is to be completed by the Auditor, Part B is to be completed by the Bank

PART A

This acknowledgement should be returned to:

Name and address of auditor

Please contact _____ if you have any queries on this letter

Contact number

Email Address

PART B

Thank you for your request for a bank report for audit purposes in respect of:

Customer Name	Main account sort code	Main account number

The request was received on (DD/MM/YYYY)

Your request is being processed and the report will be sent to you once we have gathered the information sought. In the event of your needing to contact us, please address any enquiries to:

Name and address of bank

Expected response date

Name of Individual or section responsible

Telephone number

Email address

Appendix 2 – Authority to disclose information – illustration

[xxxxx Bank PLC
25 xxx Street
Warrington
Cheshire WA1 1XQ]

[Parent Company Ltd,
Subsidiary 1 Ltd,
Subsidiary 2 Ltd]

Date

I/ We authorise [xxxx Bank PLC] including all branches and subsidiaries to provide to our auditor [*XXX Accountants*] any information that they may request from you regarding all and any of our accounts and dealings with you.

_____   _____
signature(s)[2]   signature(s)[2]

cc: The auditors

[2] *Signatures according to current bank mandates with full authority to action this authorisation.*

Appendix 3 – British Bankers' Association guidance note for banks

Preface 1

Since the Auditing Practices Board (APB) revision of Practice Note 16 was issued for consultation in November 2005 there have been ongoing discussions between the BBA members and representatives of CCAB bodies.

The banks have found these discussions very useful and it has enabled them to understand the difficulties that the existing process presents to auditors. We have listened to the concerns and issues from the auditors' point of view. In turn, the auditors have listened to the banks. There is now an improved understanding of how auditors and banks can have a better working relationship, which will be to the mutual benefit of the client.

The new process is also expected to support the banks in providing an improved service.

Delivery of the bank confirmation request 1.1

Historically, banks have requested auditors to send the requests to a branch. However, many of the larger banks have now centralised such processes. That said, in the absence of a sort code and account number, the use of a branch address has at least given the banks some information to start the search process.

The acknowledgement, by the Auditing Practices Board, of the importance of providing primary sort codes and account numbers will facilitate the production of the bank response in a small number of service centres. This will enable auditors to send requests directly to a central address where this matches a bank's business model.

Acknowledgements 1.2

Banks providing acknowledgements, if requested, of audit requests will endeavour to do so within 5 working days of receipt. Where banks send acknowledgements via email, the audit firm's reference number for the client – and not the client's name – will be quoted for security reasons. Banks that do not acknowledge receipt of audit requests are identified on the BBA's website and contact details given for pursuing enquiries.

Enquiries 1.3

Many of the enquiries received by banks from auditors are classed as being pre-production, eg confirming receipt of the instruction. Many of these calls result from the acknowledgement process not working as well as it could. As banks receiving audit requests centrally are able to issue an acknowledgement earlier in the process, those operating in this way are likely to experience a reduced volume of pre-production enquiries.

For post-production enquiries, where possible, banks will provide a centralised enquiry point or details of how enquiries can be directed to the appropriate area.

1.4 Cooperation

The collaborative approach adopted by the working party of banks and auditors has been instrumental to the redesign of the request templates which will deliver improvements in the service provided. Having worked hard to discuss and understand the process and issues from both viewpoints, on-going cooperation between banks and auditors is seen as a key component to the smooth operation of the audit enquiry process. It is therefore proposed that the working group should be maintained and that liaison meetings should take place periodically, say once or twice per year, with the aim of providing a forum in which practical issues concerning the audit enquiry process can be raised.

1.5 Speed

The provision of primary account number information will address some of the issues experienced by the banks. It is essential that this information is provided, to enable the banks to commence their process more speedily. Account information is used for ensuring that the search is more robust but is also used to find information such as relationship details and allocate the request to the appropriate unit.

This will enable the banks to action the requests more quickly, not only reducing initial administration time but also the time spent locating the customers across the bank network. The banks are committed to reducing their current SLAs and this revised process will support that aspiration.

1.6 Scope

While the auditors have agreed on a best endeavours basis (see below), until periods commencing on or after 26 December 2007, to provide primary sort code and account number information to subsidiary level, it is important that the banks commit to undertaking thorough searches of their records, in line with an authority to disclose, so that all evidence on a customer connection can be gathered. Auditors are not only looking for confirmation of what they already know but also evidence on what may have been omitted, deliberately or otherwise from information provided to them by their clients.

1.7 Timing

As it will take auditors at least one audit season to collect the main sort codes and account numbers for all group members, the BBA has agreed that banks will answer requests for bank reports on a best endeavours basis, until year ends on or after 26 December 2008. "Best endeavours" means that banks will search for information relating to all entities named on a request even if account numbers are not given.

1.8 Disclaimer from creating a contractual obligation

While information provided under PN16: Bank Reports for Audit Purposes does not constitute a contractual obligation between the bank and the auditor, it is a significant component of the evidence gathered in support of the audit and should be provided on a thorough and accurate basis. It is appropriate however for the bank to include a legal disclaimer in correspondence with auditors to the effect that the reply is given solely for the purpose of their audit without any responsibility on the part of the bank, its employees or agents and that it does not relieve the auditor from any other enquiry nor from the performance of any other duty.

Banks should conduct searches against the legal entities listed on the audit request and accounts which are found as a result of these searches checked against the authority to disclose held on bank records.	4.2
Due to client confidentiality obligations, the bank should only disclose to auditors accounts in the name of entities for which they have an express authority to do so.	4.3
Banks will check a new authority on receipt, or where the auditor indicates the existence of an authority from a previous year, against its records. If the authority cannot be verified it will be returned to the auditor together with any request for information for referral back to the client.	4.4

Service level agreements   5

Service Level Agreements (SLAs) are competitive between banks and are therefore not standard, with each bank having their own arrangements. Banks are committed to reducing their SLAs in line with more information being provided by auditors.	5.1

Enquiries   6

Banks receive a number of enquiries from auditors. The following guidance is intended to facilitate the enquiry process.	6.1

Pre-production enquiries   6.2

Banks should send an acknowledgement to the auditor within 5 working days of receipt by post or by email as requested. Where banks do not send acknowledgements on request, they are expected to publish a central enquiry point/make known who will deal with enquiries via the BBA's public website.

With this in mind, auditors diary for receipt of acknowledgement and if not received, chase the bank to confirm receipt (this will reduce the number of urgent requests after the year-end has passed).

Banks may indicate either an expected date when the auditor will receive the reply or provide an indication of their standard SLA for the process. Auditors have been requested to refrain from chasing for a response until the expected date of receipt has passed.

Post-production enquiries   6.3

Enquiry routes for individual banks will be identified on the BBA's public website. It is for each bank to ensure that the information provided remains up-to-date.

Banks should either provide a centralised enquiry point or make known that requests should be addressed to relationship managers.

Banks may provide a unique reference for each audit letter; where they do, auditors should use this reference when making post-production enquiries.

6.4 Fast track requests

Banks receive many requests from auditors for an urgent response. They appreciate that there are circumstances in which it may be necessary to provide a response for an audit letter in a shortened timescale eg group companies with shorter reporting timescales. This however can only be extended on a best endeavours basis as, with a finite resource, this effectively means that staff are diverted from working on requests which were received earlier. It has therefore been agreed that, where auditors require an urgent response, they state the reason on the information request form.

7 Requirements

7.1 Forms – many BBA member banks use imaging technology for workflow management. Those banks may wish to make arrangements with auditors to use standard forms that have been tested for use in an image environment. These can be obtained from the BBA website or directly from the individual banks concerned. There are barriers at present on both the banking and the auditing side to requests being submitted securely using the internet.

7.2 Submitting requests – PN16 indicates that auditors deliver a request to the bank one month before the year end. The banks have underlined for the auditors the importance of this given the volumes of requests that they receive each month. This time is used to undertake preparatory work in advance of the year-end, such as sending out requests for completion by relevant departments.

7.3 Account information – auditors have been requested to provide, as a minimum, one main sort code and account number for each legal entity listed on the request. It is clearly explained within the practice note that the provision of sort codes and account numbers by legal entity will contribute significantly to the efficiency of the search.

7.4 Authority to disclose – while there is no need to provide an authority each time, the auditors have a responsibility for checking with the client that the authority is up-to-date. Banks should regard authorities as on-going unless rescinded by the client. (In Ireland the banks and auditors have agreed that a new authority to disclose should be provided by the auditors on each occasion.)

7.5 Enquiries – auditors have been encouraged to make use of the bank reference number provided in the bank response to the request. This should improve enquiry handling as banks will be able to locate the file much more quickly.

8 Closed accounts

8.1 Where an account relationship existed at the audit date but has subsequently closed an appropriate fee will be required before the audit letter process can begin. In such cases, the bank should return the request to the auditor with a request for the appropriate fee to be provided. It should be made clear that work will not be carried out on the request until the fee is received. The standard SLA will apply from the date the fee is received or the audit date, whichever is the later.

Addendum – Information provided in bank responses

The following tables set out the information that will be provided by banks in response to auditor requests. The banks are required to give the information in the order shown and if no information is available then this must be stated as 'None' in the response.

STANDARD INFORMATION REQUEST

1 **Account and Balance Details**
   Give full titles of all Bank accounts including loans, (whether in sterling or another currency) together with their account numbers and balances. For accounts closed during the 12 months up to the audit report date give the account details and date of closure.

   Note. Also give details where your Customer's name is joined with that of other parties and where the account is in a trade name.

   State if any account or balances are subject to any restriction(s) whatsoever. Indicate the nature and extent of the restriction e.g. garnishee order.

2 **Facilities**
   Give the following details of all loans, overdrafts, and associated guarantees and indemnities:

   - term
   - repayment frequency and/or review date
   - details of period of availability of agreed finance i.e. finance remaining undrawn
   - detail the facility limit.

3 **Securities**
   With reference to the facilities detailed in (2) above give the following details:

   - Any security formally charged (date, ownership and type of charge). State whether the security supports facilities granted by the Bank to the customer or to another party.

   Note. Give details if a security is limited in amount or to a specific borrowing or if to your knowledge there is a prior, equal or subordinate charge.

   - Where there are any arrangements for set-off of balances or compensating balances e.g. back to back loans, give particulars (i.e. date, type of document and accounts covered) of any acknowledgement of set-off, whether given by specific letter of set-off or incorporated in some other document.

Additional information request

Request for Trade Finance information

1	**Trade Finance** Give the currencies and amounts of the following: (a) Letters of Credit (b) Acceptances (c) Bills discounted with recourse to the customer or any subsidiary or related party of the customer. (d) Bonds, Guarantees, Indemnities or other undertakings given to the Bank by the customer in favour of third parties (including separately any such items in favour of any subsidiary or related party of the customer). Give details of the parties in favour of whom guarantees or undertakings have been given, whether such guarantees or undertakings are written or oral and their nature. (e) Bonds, Guarantees, Indemnities or other undertakings given by you, on your customer's behalf, stating whether there is recourse to your customer and/or to its parent or any other company within the group. (f) Other contingent liabilities not already detailed. *Note. For each item state the nature and extent of any facility limits and details of period of availability of agreed facility.*
2	**Securities** With reference to the facilities detailed in the above section give the following: • Details of any security formally charged (date, ownership and type of charge). State whether the security supports facilities granted by the Bank to the customer or to another party. *Note. Give details if a security is limited in amount or to a specific borrowing or if to your knowledge there is prior, equal or subordinate charge.* • Where there are any arrangements for set-off of balances or compensating balances e.g. back to back loans, give particulars (i.e. date, type of document and accounts covered) of any acknowledgement of set-off, whether given by specific letter of set-off or incorporated in some other document.

Request for Derivatives and Commodity Trading information

On occasion Auditors may request Derivatives and Commodity Trading information. Responses must be given in the order as below and if no information is available then this must be stated as 'None' in the response:

1	**Derivatives and Commodity Trading** Give the currencies, amounts and maturity dates on a contract by contract basis of all outstanding derivative contracts including the following: (a) foreign exchange contracts (b) forward rate agreements (c) financial futures (d) interest rate swaps (e) option contracts (f) bullion contracts (g) commodity contracts (h) swap arrangements (near and far dates) (i) credit derivatives including collateralised debt obligations (CDOs) (j) others (indicate their nature). Note. Indicate the nature and extent of any facility limits, detail period of availability of agreed facilities.
2	**Securities** With reference to facilities detailed in the above section give the following: • Details of any security formally charged (date, ownership and type of charge). State whether the security supports facilities granted by the Bank to the customer or to another party. Note – give details if a security is limited in amount or to a specific borrowing or if to your knowledge there is prior, equal or subordinate charge. • Where there are any arrangements for set-off balances of compensating balances e.g. back to back loans, give particulars (i.e. date, type of document and accounts covered) of any acknowledgement of set-off, whether given by specific letter of set-off or incorporated in some other document.

[PN 19]
The Audit of Banks and Building Societies in the United Kingdom (Revised)

(Issued)

Contents

	Paragraphs
Preface	3
Introduction	4

The audit of financial statements

ISAs (UK and Ireland)		13
200	Objective and general principles governing the audit of the financial statements	13
210	Terms of audit engagement	15
220	Quality control for audits of historical financial information	17
240	The auditor's responsibility to consider fraud in an audit of financial statements	18
250	Section A – Consideration of laws and regulations in an audit of financial statements	
	Section B – The Auditors' Right and Duty to Report to Regulators in the Financial Sector	21
300	Planning an audit of financial statements	33
315	Obtaining an understanding of the entity and its environment and assessing the risks of material misstatement	35
320	Audit materiality	44
330	The auditor's procedures in response to assessed risks	45
402	Audit considerations relating to entities using service organisations	50
505	External confirmations	52
520	Analytical procedures	53
540	Audit of accounting estimates	55
545	Auditing fair value measurements and disclosures	57
550	Related parties	59
560	Subsequent events	61
570	The going concern basis in financial statements	62
580	Management representations	63
600	Using the work of another auditor	64
620	Using the work of an expert	66
700	The auditors' report on financial statements	67

Other reports by the auditor	70
Appendix 1 Illustrative examples of auditor's reports	73
1.1 Auditor's report on financial statements, annual business statement and directors' report – under UK GAAP[1] (Building Societies).	

---

[1] This example has been prepared on the basis that the Group and Society financial statements are not presented separately. Generic examples of separate auditor's reports provided where Group and parent company financial statements are presented separately can be found in Appendix 1 to APB Bulletin 2006/6.

1.2 Auditor's report on financial statements, annual business statement and directors' report – under IFRSs as adopted by the European Union (Building Societies).
 1.3 Auditor's statement on summary financial statement (Building Societies).
 1.4 Auditor's report on the s68 BS Act 1986 statement (Building Societies).
 1.5 Auditor's report on the s.343(4) CA1985 statement (UK Banks).
 1.6 Auditor's review report on interim net profits (UK Banks and Building Societies).

Appendix 2   The main parts of FSMA 2000 relevant to deposit takers   87
Appendix 3   FSMA 2000, BS Act 1986 and related statutory instruments: Important provisions for auditors   89
Appendix 4   The FSA Handbook   92
Appendix 5   Possible factors that may indicate going concern issues   95
Appendix 6   Reporting direct to FSA – statutory right and protection for disclosure under general law   97
Appendix 7   Definitions   99

Preface

This Practice Note contains guidance on the application of auditing standards issued by the Auditing Practices Board ('the APB') to the audit of banks and building societies in the United Kingdom (UK). The term 'deposit taker' in this Practice Note should be taken to refer to both banks and building societies. A deposit taker is also referred to as an 'authorised firm' in the context of regulation under the Financial Services and Markets Act 2000.

The Practice Note is supplementary to, and should be read in conjunction with, International Standards on Auditing (ISAs) (UK and Ireland), which apply to all audits undertaken in the United Kingdom in respect of accounting periods commencing on or after 15 December 2004. This Practice Note sets out the special considerations relating to the audit of deposit takers which arise from individual ISAs (UK and Ireland) listed in the contents. It is not the intention of the Practice Note to provide step-by-step guidance to the audit of deposit takers, so where no special considerations arise from a particular ISA (UK and Ireland), no material is included.

This Practice Note has been prepared with advice and assistance from staff of the FSA and is based on the legislation and regulations in effect at 31 December 2006[2].

Introduction

1 The term 'deposit taker' in this Practice Note should be taken to refer to both banks and building societies. Deposit takers can operate in the UK as:

- a company incorporated in the UK which is authorised[3] by the FSA to accept deposits, which is required to comply with BIPRU[4] and is not a building society ('UK bank');
- a UK branch of an entity incorporated outside the EEA, authorised by the FSA to accept deposits and which is required to comply with BIPRU ('non EEA bank');
- a UK branch of a credit institution incorporated in the EEA which has exercised EEA Passport rights[5] to carry on regulated activities in the UK – ('EEA bank')
- a society incorporated under the Building Societies Act 1986 ('BS Act 1986') – ('building society').

2 This Practice Note addresses the responsibilities and obligations of the auditor concerning:

---

[2] *Certain of the references to the FSA Handbook become effective on 1 January 2007.*

[3] *Authorised under FSMA 2000 to undertake regulated activities.*

[4] *Prior to 1 January 2008 some banks will continue to comply with certain elements of the Interim Prudential sourcebook for banks IPRU(BANK) – see paragraph 17.*

[5] *Exercising passport rights entitles an entity incorporated in one EEA member state ('home country') who is authorised to conduct one or more regulated activities subject to the passport rights in the home country to establish a branch and carry out those regulated activities in another EEA member state ('host country') without the need to be authorised by the host country supervisor, (in the UK the FSA) in respect of activities that are subject to the passport rights.*

- the audit of the financial statements in accordance with the Companies Act 1985[6] ('CA1985') – applicable to UK banks;
- the audit of the financial statements in accordance with BS Act 1986 and Building Societies (Accounts and Related Provisions) Regulations 1998[7] ('BS Accounts Regulations 1998') and related obligations – applicable to building societies;
- the right and duty to report direct to the Financial Services Authority[8] ('FSA') in certain circumstances – applicable to UK banks, non EEA banks, building societies and to EEA banks with top-up permissions[9];
- reporting on interim profits for the purposes of their inclusion in capital resources. This is applicable to UK banks and building societies but required only if requested by the deposit taker; and
- reporting on a statement of particulars of transactions and arrangements concerning directors under either s78(9) BS Act 86 or s343(6) CA1985 – applicable to building societies and may be applicable to UK banks respectively.

Non EEA banks and EEA banks are not subject to the audit provisions of the CA1985 and so the terms of engagement are a matter of contract between the auditor and their client who may, for example, be local or head office management or the EEA/non EEA bank's home country auditor. Such engagements take many different forms: the auditor may be asked to report on the financial statements of the UK branch or only on particular aspects thereof, and the form of their opinion will also vary from case to case. The auditor undertaking such an assignment does not have to apply ISAs (UK and Ireland) but may find some of the guidance in this Practice Note of assistance.

In addition to accepting deposits, deposit takers may also undertake other activities regulated under the Financial Services and Markets Act 2000 (FSMA 2000) for which Part IV permissions[10] from the FSA are required. This may include one of more forms of investment business or insurance intermediation. These regulated activities are subject to FSA conduct of business rules and can give rise to auditor reporting responsibilities concerning client assets. This can occur even where a deposit taker is not authorised to hold client assets – a negative assurance report. These reporting responsibilities are addressed in Practice Note 21: The audit of investment businesses in the United Kingdom (Revised)[11] [12]. In addition, deposit takers may also undertake regulated mortgage activity. While this also requires separate Part IV permissions and is also subject to FSA conduct of business rules, no auditor reporting obligations arise in relation to client assets.

---

[6] *Banks which are incorporated in Great Britain are subject to the provisions of the Companies Act 1985 and those incorporated in Northern Ireland to the provisions of the Companies (Northern Ireland) Order 1986.*

[7] *SI 1998/504.*

[8] *SI 2001/2587 and s342 and s343 FSMA 2000.*

[9] *A Part IV permission granted by the FSA to an EEA bank to enable it to undertake a UK regulated activity in the UK for which authorisation to undertake the activity in the home country is not required by the home country supervisor.*

[10] *A permission granted by FSA under Part IV FSMA 2000 permitting an authorised firm to carry on regulated activities as specified in the FSMA 2000 Regulated Activities Order SI 2001/544 as amended.*

[11] *At the date of issue of this Practice Note, PN21 (Revised) was in issue as a consulation draft.*

[12] *Further guidance is included in ICAEW TECH 1/06: Interim guidance for auditors of insurance intermediaries on client asset reporting requirements.*

5   The scope of the statutory audit of a UK bank's financial statements is no different from that of the generality of companies incorporated in the UK. Concerning a building society, in addition to the financial statements and the directors' report the auditor also reports on an annual business statement which accompanies the financial statements. Further, the auditor of a building society is required to report on the summary financial statement that all building societies are obliged to prepare and send to all those members entitled to receive notice of the Annual General Meeting (an option rather than a requirement available to listed companies including listed UK banks).

Legislative and regulatory framework

6   The legal and regulatory framework within which deposit takers operate in the UK is summarised in the following paragraphs.

Financial statements

7   The form and content of the financial statements of UK banks prepared under UK GAAP is governed by the CA1985, Statements of Standard Accounting Practice ('SSAPs'), Financial Reporting Standards ('FRSs') and UITF Abstracts. The prescribed format for a UK banks' financial statements that comply with UK GAAP is set out in Schedule 9 to the CA1985. However, listed UK groups (including listed UK banking groups) must prepare consolidated financial statements in accordance with those International Financial Reporting Standards adopted by the European Union (EU IFRSs)[13] and those parts of CA1985 applicable to companies reporting under EU IFRSs. UK companies or non listed groups, including UK banks and banking groups, are permitted to voluntarily adopt EU IFRSs for their financial statements.

8   The form and content of a building society's financial statements prepared under UK GAAP are prescribed in the BS Accounts Regulations 1998 made under s72C BS Act 1986. These are similar to Schedule 9 CA1985 applicable to UK banks. As for UK banks, building societies apply FRSs, SSAPs and UITF abstracts when reporting under UK GAAP. Building societies with listed securities, including permanent interest-bearing shares, are also required to apply EU IFRSs in their consolidated financial statements. Like UK companies, building societies may also voluntarily adopt EU IFRSs for their entity financial statements.

9   In addition to financial statements and a directors' report, building societies are also required, by BS Act 1986, to prepare:

- an annual business statement – part of the annual report (s74 BS Act 1986); and
- a summary financial statement (s76 BS Act 1986).

10 The ASB has stated that it intends ultimately to converge UK GAAP with IFRS but the timetable for this has yet to be determined. In the meantime, UK Accounting Standards covering financial instruments that are consistent with IFRS[14] have been issued but are subject to complex rules as to which entities they apply to and when.

---

[13] *Article 4 of EC Regulation 1606/2002 as acknowledged in s227(2) CA1985 – the IAS Regulation.*

[14] *International Financial Reporting Standards.*

As the activities of UK banks and building societies largely comprise financial instruments the auditor considers carefully which of the various accounting standards and BBA SORPs[15] apply to the entity being audited.

Financial Services and Markets Act 2000

FSMA 2000 sets out the high level regulatory framework for the financial sector more generally and not just deposit takers. Appendix 2 sets out the main parts of FSMA 2000 relevant to authorised firms which are deposit takers[16]. 11

The wide scope of FSMA 2000 reflects the FSA's extensive responsibilities. These are set out in FSMA 2000 as regulatory objectives covering: 12

- market confidence;
- public awareness;
- the protection of consumers; and
- the reduction of financial crime

FSMA 2000 covers not only the regulation and supervision of financial sector entities but also other issues such as official listing rules, business transfers, market abuse, compensation and ombudsman schemes, investment exchanges and clearing houses. 13

FSMA 2000 is also supported by a large number of statutory instruments. Significant components of the definition and scope of the regulatory framework are contained in the main statutory instruments. A list of important provisions of FSMA 2000 and a list of statutory instruments relevant to the auditor is included in Appendix 3. 14

Under Part X FSMA 2000 the FSA has the power to make 'rules'. The legal effect of a rule varies depending on the power under which it is made and on the language used in the rule. Rules are mandatory unless a waiver has been agreed with the FSA. If an authorised firm contravenes a rule it may be subject to enforcement action and consequent disciplinary measures under Part XIV FSMA 2000. Furthermore, in certain circumstances an authorised firm may be subject to an action for damages under s150 FSMA 2000. In contrast, guidance is generally issued to throw light on a particular aspect of regulatory requirements, and is not binding. However if an authorised firm acts in accordance with it in the circumstances contemplated by that guidance, the FSA will proceed on the basis that the authorised firm has complied with the rule to which the guidance relates. 15

Rules made by the FSA and associated guidance are set out in the FSA Handbook of Rules and Guidance ('the FSA Handbook') (see Appendix 4). The main FSA systems and control requirements are set out in the Senior management arrangements, systems and controls element of the high level standards block of the FSA Handbook ('SYSC'). 16

As a result of the implementation of the Capital Requirements Directive ('CRD') and the Market in Financial Instruments Directive ('MiFID') in the UK, the FSA Handbook is undergoing significant change and restructuring and is subject to complex transitional arrangements. These changes began to take effect from 1 January 2007. The auditor considers carefully the choices made by the deposit taker 17

---

[15] Statements of Recommended Practice issued by the British Bankers' Association and Irish Bankers' Federation.

[16] An entity which has been granted one of more Part IV permissions by the FSA and so is authorised under FSMA 2000 to undertake regulated activities.

under the transitional arrangements in order to understand which parts of what sourcebook applies to the deposit taker.

18 It is clearly unrealistic to expect all members of an audit engagement team to have detailed knowledge of the entire FSA Handbook; rather ISA (UK and Ireland) 250 Section B requires the level of knowledge to be commensurate with an individual's role and responsibilities in the audit process. ISA (UK and Ireland) 220 requires the auditor to establish procedures to facilitate consultation and, thereby, to draw on the collective expertise and specialist technical knowledge of those beyond the engagement team of the auditor.

Prudential requirements

19 Deposit takers are subject to certain prudential requirements which are detailed in GENPRU[17] and BIPRU. These include capital adequacy, liquidity[18], large exposures (concentration risk) and additional related aspects of systems and controls not covered in SYSC. There are also certain specific prudential measures applied by the FSA which deposit takers are required to report to the FSA via prudential returns. The main measures include:
- capital adequacy – ensuring sufficient capital resources in relation to risk requirements to absorb losses;
- liquidity – ensuring sufficient liquid assets or maturing assets to meet liabilities as they fall due; and
- large exposures – avoiding undue credit risk concentrations.

The Building Societies Act 1986

20 In addition to FSMA 2000 which applies to FSA authorised firms generally, BS Act 1986 applies to building societies. It sets out the legal framework applicable to building societies. A list of important provisions of BS Act 1986 and related statutory instruments relevant to the auditor is included in Appendix 3. In addition, further guidance on constitutional matters and compliance with BS Act 1986 is set out in the Building Societies Regulatory Guide ('BSOG')[19] – part of the FSA Handbook. The BS Act 1986 includes, for example:
- s5 principal purpose (paragraph 21);
- s6 lending limit (paragraphs 22 to 24);
- s7 funding limit (paragraphs 22 to 24);
- s9A restrictions on treasury activities (paragraph 25).

21 A building society's purpose or principal purpose must be to make loans secured on residential property and funded substantially by its members. The lending and funding limits (see paragraph 22 below) are quantitative criteria which help to determine a building society's compliance with this purpose. However, other factors will also be taken into account by the FSA including:
- actual and projected income derived from activities or services that have little or no connection with the making of loans secured on residential property; and

---

[17] *General Prudential sourcebook.*

[18] *Temporarily, pending international/EU consensus, the prudential largely quantitative liquidity requirements remain unchanged and are carried forward in IPRU(BANK) and IPRU(BSOC).*

[19] *BSOG carries forward certain material previously included in IPRU(BSOC) – including all of volume 2 and certain sections of volume 1.*

- actual and projected proportion of a building society's resources (eg financial assets, capital, senior management and staff) that are devoted to other services.

There are particular quantitative limits specified in BS Act 1986 that are used in the assessment of compliance with this principal purpose criterion – collectively known as 'nature limits'. The BS Act 1986 limits are as follows:

- at least 75% of business assets must be loans fully secured on residential property – the lending limit (s6 BS Act 1986);
- at least 50% of total funds (ie total shareholder funds, wholesale deposits and bills of exchange and debt instruments) must be raised in the form of shares (deposits conferring membership rights) held by individual members – the funding limit (s7 BS Act 1986).

These nature limits are additional to the prudential measures referred to in paragraph 19 above. In practice, building societies adopt one of the five approaches to financial risk management set out in the IPRU (BSOC) 4.5.5G which in most cases results in the funding limit being applied more restrictively. In addition most building societies choose to apply the lending limit more restrictively. The funding limit and the lending limit as at the end of the financial year must both be reported to members, together with the statutory limits, in the annual business statement, and are also required to be reported to the FSA in the quarterly prudential monitoring return. The annual business statement is reported on by the auditor and is attached to the annual accounts of the building society (see paragraphs 161 and 162).

Both these limits must be calculated on a group basis where that is appropriate. With reference to the lending limit, business assets means total assets, plus provisions for bad and doubtful debts, less fixed assets, less liquid assets and less any long term insurance funds. Business assets, therefore, typically comprise loans, investments in connected undertakings and sundry debtors and prepayments. Building societies preparing their financial statements in accordance with EU IFRS use the appropriate equivalent balance sheet captions. Residential property is defined as being land at least 40% of which is normally used as, or in connection with, one or more dwellings, or which has been, is being, or is to be developed or adapted for such use.

A building society may undertake almost any activity, provided that such activity is included within its Memorandum[20] and provided that the building society or group as a whole continues to comply with the principal purpose and with the nature limits. However s9A BS Act 1986 includes a number of specific prohibitions on a building society's treasury activities, which are that (subject to certain exceptions) a building society is not permitted to:

- act as a market maker in securities, commodities or currencies;
- trade in commodities or currencies; or
- enter into any transaction involving derivative instruments, except in relation to hedging.

Reporting direct to the FSA – statutory right and duty

Under FSMA 2000 (Communications by Auditors) Regulations 2001 (SI 2001/2587) the auditor of an authorised firm or the auditor of an entity closely linked to an authorised firm who is also the auditor of that authorised firm has a statutory duty to communicate matters of material significance to the FSA. Under s340 FSMA 2000 'the auditor' is defined as one required to be appointed under FSA 'rules' or

---

[20] A Memorandum within the meaning of Sch 2 BS Act 1986.

appointed as a result of another enactment. In addition s342 FSMA 2000 provides that no duty to which the auditor is subject shall be contravened by communicating in good faith to the FSA any information or opinion on a matter that the auditor reasonably believes is relevant to any functions of the FSA. Guidance on the identification of matters to be reported to the regulators is set out in the section dealing with ISA (UK and Ireland) 250 Section B.

27 An EEA bank is not required to appoint an auditor under FSA's rules in respect of its UK branch operations unless it has a top up permission. Furthermore, a UK branch of a bank incorporated outside the UK is not required to appoint an auditor under CA1985. Consequently, if an EEA bank (without top up permissions) appoints an auditor to undertake audit procedures at its UK branch this does not fall within the definition of 'auditor' for the purposes of s342/3 FSMA 2000 and SI 2001/2587. As a result the auditor undertaking such work has neither a statutory right nor statutory duty to report direct to the FSA and may not have relief from its duty of confidentiality to its client if the auditor decides to do so. In the event that an auditor of an EEA bank identifies a matter that would be likely to be of material significance to the FSA, the auditor considers whether they have a responsibility to report such matters to the 'head office' auditors of the EEA bank or to the home country regulator. See Appendix 6 concerning disclosure in the public interest.

28 A non EEA bank is required to appoint an auditor under SUP 3.3.2R in respect of its UK branch operations and therefore an auditor appointed in accordance with this rule has both the right and duty to report. Whilst, in principle, there is a requirement to appoint an auditor, there is no FSA requirement for the auditor to undertake audit procedures and there is no corresponding requirement to report on the results of those procedures. Therefore some non EEA banks with UK operations that are not material to the non EEA bank as a whole may have no need to commission an auditor to undertake audit procedures.

Communication between the FSA and the auditor

29 Within the legal constraints that apply, the FSA may pass on to the auditor any information which it considers relevant to his function. Auditors are bound by the confidentiality provisions set out in Part XXIII of FSMA 2000 (Public record, disclosure of information and co-operation) Regulations in respect of confidential information received from the FSA. An auditor may not pass on such confidential information even to the entity being audited without lawful authority, (for example if an exception applies under the FSMA 2000 (Disclosure of confidential information) Regulations 2001) or with the consent of the person from whom the information was received and, if different, to whom the information relates.

30 Before communicating to an authorised firm any information received from the FSA, the auditor considers carefully whether:

- the auditor has received the FSA's express permission to communicate a particular item of information;
- the information relates to any other party whose permission may need to be obtained before disclosure can be made;
- the information was received by FSA in a capacity other than discharging its functions under FSMA 2000 or from another regulator (in which case the auditor may either be prohibited from disclosure or may need the permission of the party which provided the information to that regulator).

The auditors may however disclose to an authorised firm information they have communicated to the FSA except where to do so would have the effect of disclosing information communicated to them by the FSA. If there is any doubt the auditor considers the matters above.

Matters communicated by the FSA during any bilateral meeting may be conveyed by those representatives of the auditor who were present at the meeting (or otherwise received the communication directly) to other partners, directors and employees of the auditor who need to know the information in connection with the auditor's performance of its duties relating to that authorised firm and without the FSA's express permission. However in the interests of prudence and transparency the auditors inform the FSA that they will be discussing the issues covered with colleagues. 31

Where the FSA passes to the auditors information which it considers is relevant to their function, they consider its implications in the context of their work and may need to amend their approach accordingly. However the fact that they may have been informed of such a matter by the regulator does not, of itself, require auditors to change the scope of the work, nor does it necessarily require them actively to search for evidence in support of the situation communicated by the regulator. 32

The auditor is required to cooperate with the FSA (SUP3.8.2R). This may involve attending meetings and providing the FSA with information about the authorised firm that the FSA may reasonably request in discharging its functions. For example this can arise in relation to FSA ARROW II risk assessments. 33

The auditor must notify the FSA without delay if the auditor is removed from office, resigns before the term of office expires or is not re-appointed by the authorised firm. Notification to the FSA includes communicating any matters connected with this event that the auditor considers ought to be drawn to the FSA's attention or a statement that there are no such matters (s344 FSMA 2000 and SUP3.8.11R and 12R). 34

The audit of financial statements

ISAs (UK and Ireland) apply to the conduct of all audits in respect of accounting periods commencing on or after 15 December 2004. This includes audits of the financial statements of deposit takers. The purpose of the following paragraphs is to identify the special considerations arising from the application of certain 'bold letter' requirements to the audit of deposit takers, and to suggest ways in which these can be addressed (extracts from ISAs (UK and Ireland) are indicated by grey-shaded boxes below). This Practice Note does not contain commentary on all of the bold letter requirements included in the ISAs (UK and Ireland) and reading it should not be seen as an alternative to reading the relevant ISAs (UK and Ireland) in their entirety. In addition, where no special considerations arise from a particular ISA (UK and Ireland), no material is included.

ISA (UK and Ireland) 200: Objective and general principles governing the audit of the financial statements

Background note

The purpose of this ISA (UK and Ireland) is to establish standards and provide guidance on the objective and general principles governing an audit of financial statements.

> The auditor should plan and perform an audit with an attitude of professional scepticism, recognising that circumstances may exist that cause the financial statements to be materially misstated. (paragraph 6)

35 Auditing standards include a requirement for auditors to comply with relevant ethical requirements relating to audit engagements. In the United Kingdom, the auditor should comply with the APB's Ethical Standards and relevant ethical guidance relating to the work of auditors issued by the auditor's professional body. A fundamental principle is that practitioners should not accept or perform work which they are not competent to undertake. The importance of technical competence is also underlined in the Auditors' Code[21], issued by the APB, which states that the necessary degree of professional skill demands an understanding of financial reporting and business. Practitioners should not undertake the audit of deposit takers unless they are satisfied that they have, or can obtain, the necessary level of competence.

Independence

36 Independence issues can be complex for the auditor of a bank, and to a lesser extent a building society because of banking and other relationships that the auditor and/or its partners and staff may have with the bank. The auditor makes careful reference to the APB's Ethical Standard 2 – Financial, business, employment and personal relationships.

ISA (UK and Ireland) 210: Terms of audit engagement

Background note

The purpose of this ISA (UK and Ireland) is to establish standards and provide guidance on agreeing the terms of the engagement with the client.

> The auditor and the client should agree on the terms of the engagement. (paragraph 2)
>
> The terms of the engagement should be recorded in writing. (paragraph 2-1)
>
> The auditor should ensure that the engagement letter documents and confirms the auditor's acceptance of the appointment, and includes a summary of the responsibilities of those charged with governance and of the auditor, the scope of the engagement and the form of any reports. (paragraph 5-1)

37 Matters which the auditor may decide to refer to in the engagement letter are as follows:

- the responsibility of the directors/senior management to comply with applicable FSMA 2000 legislation and FSA Handbook rules and guidance including the need to keep the FSA informed about the affairs of the entity;

---

[21] This is appended to the APB's Scope and Authority of Pronouncements.

- the statutory right and duty of the auditor to report direct to the FSA in certain circumstances (see the section of this Practice Note relating to ISA (UK and Ireland) 250 Section B);
- the requirement to cooperate with the auditor (SUP3.6.1R). This includes taking steps to ensure that, where applicable, each of its appointed representatives and material outsourcers gives the auditor the same right of access to records, information and explanations as the authorised firm itself is required to provide the auditor (s341 FSMA 2000 and SUP 3.6.2G to 3.6.8G). It a criminal offence for a deposit taker or its officers, controllers or managers to provide false or misleading information to the auditor (s346 FSMA 2000);
- the need for the deposit taker to make the auditor aware when it appoints a third party (including another department or office of the same audit firm) to review, investigate or report on any aspects of its business activities that may be relevant to the audit of the financial statements and to provide the auditor with copies of reports by such a third party promptly after their receipt.

In this connection the auditor is aware that:

- the FSA does not need to approve the appointment of an auditor but may seek to satisfy itself that an auditor appointed by a firm is independent and has the necessary skills, resources and experience (SUP 3.4.4G, 3.4.7R and 3.4.8G);
- the auditor is required to cooperate with the FSA (SUP 3.8.2R); and
- the auditor must notify the FSA if the auditor ceases to be the auditor of an authorised firm.

ISA (UK and Ireland) 220: Quality control for audits of historical financial information

Background note

The purpose of this ISA (UK and Ireland) is to establish standards and provide guidance on specific responsibilities of firm personnel regarding quality control procedures for audits of historical financial information, including audits of financial statements.

Reference should also be made to ISQC 1 (UK and Ireland) – Quality Control for Firms that Perform Audits and Reviews of Historical Financial Information, and other Assurance and Related Services Engagements.

The engagement partner should be satisfied that the engagement team collectively has the appropriate capabilities, competence and time to perform the audit engagement in accordance with professional standards and regulatory and legal requirements, and to enable an auditor's report that is appropriate in the circumstances to be issued. (paragraph 19)

The nature of banking business is one of rapidly changing and evolving markets. Often deposit takers develop new products and practices which require specialised auditing and accounting responses. It is therefore important that the auditor is familiar with current practice.

As well as ensuring that the engagement team has an appropriate level of knowledge of the industry and its corresponding products, the engagement partner also satisfies himself that the members of the engagement team have sufficient knowledge of the regulatory framework within which deposit takers operate commensurate with their roles on the engagement.

ISA (UK and Ireland) 240: The auditor's responsibility to consider fraud in an audit of financial statements

Background note

The purpose of this ISA (UK and Ireland) is to establish standards and provide guidance on the auditor's responsibility to consider fraud in an audit of financial statements and expand on how the standards and guidance in ISA (UK and Ireland) 315 and ISA (UK and Ireland) 330 are to be applied in relation to the risks of material misstatement due to fraud.

In planning and performing the audit to reduce audit risk to an acceptably low level, the auditor should consider the risks of material misstatements in the financial statements due to fraud. (paragraph 3)

The auditor should maintain an attitude of professional scepticism throughout the audit, recognising the possibility that a material misstatement due to fraud could exist, notwithstanding the auditor's past experience with the entity about the honesty and integrity of management and those charged with governance. (paragraph 24).

The auditor should make inquiries of management, internal audit, and others within the entity as appropriate, to determine whether they have knowledge of any actual, suspected or alleged fraud affecting the entity (paragraph 38).

When obtaining an understanding of the entity and its environment, including its internal control, the auditor should consider whether the information obtained indicates that one or more fraud risk factors are present (paragraph 48).

41 As with other entities, fraud and deposit takers, either fraudulent financial reporting (for example the manipulation of profits or the concealment of losses) or misappropriation of assets, can occur through a combination of management fraud, employee fraud or fraud perpetrated by third parties. However deposit takers are particularly vulnerable to the misappropriation of assets by third parties, sometimes with the collusion of employees or vice versa. This arises in part due to the nature of their activities, a fraud risk factor, which ordinarily involves high values and volumes of disbursement of funds for a variety of purposes including:

- drawdown on loans (including credit cards);
- repayment of customer deposits;
- settlement of financial transactions; and
- funds transfer.

42 A further fraud risk factor is that deposit takers also have custody of valuable and fungible assets including money. As a result fraud is an inherent cost of undertaking deposit taking business. Frauds relating to most types of transactions can be facilitated by identity theft and so 'know your customer' procedures are an important component of the procedures taken by deposit takers to mitigate the risk of fraud.

43 Whilst remuneration policies can create excessive performance pressures in many industries, in certain types of deposit takers or divisions of large banks (eg investment banking operations) performance related bonuses can be significant both in absolute terms and in relation to base remuneration. In addition significant bonus related remuneration can often extend beyond senior management, further down the organisation of deposit takers, and can lead to more pervasive pressures that cause increased risks of fraud. Other examples of fraud risk factors include:

- valuation of complex financial instruments in an environment where there is inadequate segregation of duties and/or lack of supervision or independent review and/or understanding of the valuation techniques and associated inputs; and
- matters that are subject to significant judgment by management – eg allowances for impairment (particularly collective assessment of impairment) or customer compensation provisioning.

44 Principle 3 of the FSA Principles for Businesses requires a firm to take reasonable care to organise and control its affairs responsibly and effectively with adequate risk management systems. SYSC 3.2.20R(1)[22] requires a firm to make and retain adequate records of matters and dealings (including accounting records) which are the subject of requirements and standards under the regulatory system. Whilst the inherent risk of fraud may continue to exist, the establishment of accounting and internal control systems sufficient to meet these requirements frequently reduces the likelihood of fraud giving rise to material misstatements in the financial statements. Guidance on the auditors' consideration of accounting systems and internal controls is provided in ISA (UK and Ireland) 315. Examples of weaknesses in control that could give rise to fraud risk factors are also set out in that section.

> When obtaining an understanding of the entity and its environment, including its internal control, the auditor should consider whether other information obtained indicates risks of material misstatement due to fraud (paragraph 55).

45 The auditor considers reports or information obtained from the deposit taker's compliance department, legal department, and money laundering reporting officer together with reviews undertaken by third parties such as skilled person's reports prepared under s166 FSMA 2000[23].

> If the auditor has identified a fraud or has obtained information that indicates that a fraud may exist, the auditor should communicate these matters as soon as practicable to the appropriate level of management (paragraph 93).
>
> The auditor should document communications about fraud made to management, those charged with governance, regulators and others (paragraph 109).

46 Reduction of financial crime is one of the FSA's statutory objectives. The FSA's rules require authorised firms to report 'significant' fraud, errors and other

---

[22] *Record keeping requirements are under consideration (CP06/19) – revised requirements will be located in SYSC 9 and expected to be effective from 1 November 2007.*

[23] *Under S166 FSMA 2000 provides the FSA with the power to require a firm to appoint a skilled person to provide a report on any matter that the FSA may reasonably require in connection with the exercise of the functions conferred on it by or under FSMA 2000. The requirements concerning skilled persons are set out in SUP5.*

irregularities to the FSA (SUP 15.3.17R). The auditor is aware of the auditor's duty to report direct to FSA in certain circumstances (see the section of this Practice Note relating to ISA (UK and Ireland) 250 Section B).

ISA (UK and Ireland) 250: Section A – Consideration of laws and regulations in an audit of financial statements

Background note

The purpose of this ISA (UK and Ireland) is to establish standards and provide guidance on the auditors' responsibility to consider laws and regulations in the audit of financial statements.

When designing and performing audit procedures and in evaluating and reporting the results thereof, the auditor should recognize that non compliance by the entity with laws and regulations may materially affect the financial statements. (paragraph 2)

In accordance with ISA (UK and Ireland) 200, "Objective and General Principles Governing an Audit of Financial Statements" the auditor should plan and perform the audit with an attitude of professional scepticism recognising that the audit may reveal conditions or events that would lead to questioning whether an entity is complying with laws and regulations. (paragraph 13)

In order to plan the audit, the auditor should obtain a general understanding of the legal and regulatory framework applicable to the entity and the industry and how the entity is complying with that framework. (paragraph 15)

47   FSMA 2000 and related statutory instruments contain sections that will normally be central to the ability of deposit takers to conduct business. Detailed rules and guidance applicable to authorised firms is set out in the FSA Handbook. An overview of this legislation and the FSA Handbook is set out in paragraphs 11 to 18 and 26 to 34 above (and Appendices 2, 3 and 4). In addition to accepting deposits, a deposit taker may also have one or more Part IV permissions from the FSA to undertake one or more types of investment business, insurance intermediation, regulated mortgage activity or other regulated activities. If this is the case, the auditor also considers the laws and regulations (which includes FSMA 2000 and the FSA Handbook) central to the deposit taker's ability to conduct these additional regulated activities.

48   The auditor is alert to any indication that a deposit taker is conducting business outside the scope of its Part IV permission or the deposit taker is failing to meet FSMA 2000 Threshold Conditions[24] or contravening any Principles for Businesses[25]. Such action may be a serious regulatory breach, which may result in fines, public censure, suspension or loss of authorisation. The auditor compares the current activities of the deposit taker with the Scope of Part IV Permission granted by the FSA and considers ISA (UK and Ireland) 250 Section A and where appropriate ISA

---

[24] *The minimum standards that a firm needs to meet to become and remain authorised by the FSA – see Appendix 4.*

[25] *FSA Handbook defines Principles with which authorised firms must comply – see Appendix 4.*

(UK and Ireland) 250 Section B.

> After obtaining the general understanding, the auditor should perform further audit procedures to help identify instances of non compliance with those laws and regulations where non compliance should be considered when preparing financial statements, specifically:
>
> (a) Inquiring of management as to whether the entity is in compliance with such laws and regulations;
> (b) Inspecting correspondence with the relevant licensing or regulatory authorities; and
> (c) Enquiring of those charged with governance as to whether they are on notice of any such possible instances of non-compliance with law or regulations. (paragraph 18)
>
> The auditor's procedures should be designed to help identify possible or actual instances of non-compliance with those laws and regulations which provide a legal framework within which the entity conducts its business and which are central to the entity's ability to conduct its business and hence to its financial statements. (paragraph 18-1)

Specific areas that auditors' procedures may address include the following:

- obtaining a general understanding of the legal and regulatory framework applicable to the entity and industry, and of the procedures followed to ensure compliance with the framework;
- reviewing the deposit taker's Scope of Part IV Permission (an FSA document which sets out the regulated activities that the firm is permitted to engage in, including any limitations and requirements imposed on those permitted activities);
- reviewing correspondence with the FSA and other regulators (including that relating to any FSA supervisory visits, requests for information by FSA or progress concerning FSA ARROW II risk mitigation programmes);
- holding discussions with the deposit taker's Compliance Officer and other personnel responsible for compliance;
- reviewing compliance reports prepared for the Board, audit committees and other committees; and
- consideration of work on compliance matters performed by internal audit.

Money laundering

> In the UK and Ireland, when carrying out procedures for the purpose of forming an opinion on the financial statements, the auditor should be alert for those instances of possible or actual non compliance with laws and regulations that might incur obligations for partners and staff in audit firms to report money laundering offences. (paragraph 22-1)

Authorised firms including deposit takers are subject to the requirements of the Money Laundering Regulations 2003 (as amended) and the Proceeds of Crime Act 2002 as well as FSA rules. These laws and regulations require institutions to establish and maintain procedures to identify their customers, establish appropriate reporting and investigation procedures for suspicious transactions and maintain appropriate records.

51 Laws and regulations relating to money laundering are integral to the legal and regulatory framework within which deposit takers conduct their business. By the nature of their business, deposit takers are ready targets of those engaged in money laundering activities. The effect of this legislation is to make it an offence to provide assistance to those involved in money laundering and makes it an offence not to report suspicions of money laundering to the appropriate authorities, usually the Serious Organised Crime Agency ('SOCA')[26]. FSA requirements are set out in SYSC 3.2.6AR.– 3.2.6JG[27]. In this context, FSA has due regard to compliance with the relevant provisions of guidance issued by the Joint Money Laundering Steering Group ('JMLSG')(SYSC 3.2.6EG)[28].

52 In addition to considering whether a deposit taker has complied with the money laundering laws and regulations, the auditor has reporting obligations under the Proceeds of Crime Act, 2002 and the Money Laundering Regulations, 2003 (as amended) to report knowledge or suspicion of money laundering offences, including those arising from fraud and theft, to SOCA. The auditor is aware of the prohibition on 'tipping off' when discussing money laundering matters with the deposit taker. Given the nature of deposit taking business and the likely frequency of needing to report to SOCA the auditor is aware of the short-form[29] of reporting to SOCA that can be used in appropriate circumstances to report minor and usually numerous items. Further guidance for auditors is provided in Practice Note 12 Money Laundering – Interim Guidance for Auditors in the United Kingdom (Revised).

53 The auditor, in the context of money laundering, is aware of the auditor's duty to report direct to FSA in certain circumstances (see the section of this Practice Note relating to ISA (UK and Ireland) 250 Section B).

ISA (UK and Ireland) 250: Section B – The Auditor's Right and Duty to Report to Regulators in the Financial Sector

> The auditor of a regulated entity should bring information of which the auditor has become aware in the ordinary course of performing work undertaken to fulfil the auditor's audit responsibilities to the attention of the appropriate regulator without delay when:
>
> (a) The auditor concludes that it is relevant to the regulator's functions having regard to such matters as may be specified in statute or any related regulations; and
>
> (b) In the auditor's opinion there is reasonable cause to believe it is or may be of material significance to the regulator. (paragraph 2)
>
> Where an apparent breach of statutory or regulatory requirements comes to the auditor's attention, the auditor should:
>
> (a) Obtain such evidence as is available to assess its implications for the auditor's reporting responsibilities;

---

[26] Previously National Criminal Intelligence Service ('NCIS').

[27] These rules and guidance move to SYSC 6.3 (SYSC 6.3.1R – 6.3.10R) from 1st November 2007. If deposit takers choose to adopt the common platform earlier in 2007, then deposit takers will follow SYSC6.3 earlier. Though the location of the requirements change, the content is the same.

[28] From 1 November 2007 SYSC 6.3.5G.

[29] These are termed limited intelligence value reports.

> (b) Determine whether, in the auditor's opinion, there is reasonable cause to believe that the breach is of material significance to the regulator; and
> (c) Consider whether the apparent breach is criminal conduct that gives rise to criminal property and, as such, should be reported to the specified authorities. (paragraph 39)

Auditors' duty to report to the FSA

Under FSMA 2000 (Communication by Auditors) Regulations 2001 ('the 2001 Regulations'), auditors have duties in certain circumstances to make reports to the FSA. **The 2001 Regulations do not require auditors to perform any additional audit work as a result of the statutory duty nor are auditors required specifically to seek out breaches of the requirements applicable to a particular authorised person.** Information and opinions to be communicated are those meeting the criteria set out below which relate to matters of which the auditor[30] of the authorised person (also referred to below as a 'regulated entity')[31] has become aware:

(i) in his capacity as auditor of the authorised person, and
(ii) if he is also the auditor of a person who has close links with the authorised person, in his capacity as auditor of that person.

54

The criteria for determining the matters to be reported are as follows:

55

(i) the auditor reasonably believes that there is, or has been, or may be, or may have been a contravention of any 'relevant requirement' that applies to the person[32] concerned and that contravention may be of material significance to the FSA in determining whether to exercise, in relation to that person, any of its functions under FSMA 2000, or
(ii) the auditor reasonably believes that the information on, or his opinion on, those matters may be of material significance to the FSA in determining whether the person concerned satisfies and will continue to satisfy the Threshold Conditions,[33] or
(iii) the auditor reasonably believes that the person concerned is not, may not be, or may cease to be, a going concern, or
(iv) the auditor is precluded from stating in his report that the annual accounts have been properly prepared in accordance with the CA 1985 or, where applicable, give a true and fair view or have been prepared in accordance with relevant rules and legislation[34].

In relation to paragraph 55 (i) above, 'relevant requirement' is a requirement by or under FSMA 2000 which relates to authorisation under FSMA 2000 or to the carrying on of any regulated activity. This includes not only relevant statutory instruments but also the FSA's rules (other than the Listing Rules) including the

56

---

[30] *An 'auditor' is defined for this purpose in the Regulations as a person who is, or has been, an auditor of an authorised person appointed under, or as a result of, a statutory provision including s340 FSMA 2000.*

[31] *In the context of FSA regulation, these terms equate to the term 'authorised firm'.*

[32] *In this context the person is an 'Authorised Person'.*

[33] *The Threshold Conditions are set out in Schedule 6 to FSMA 2000 and represent the minimum conditions that a firm is required to satisfy and continue to satisfy to be given and to retain Part IV permission. The FSA's guidance on compliance with the Threshold Conditions is contained in the COND module of the FSA Handbook.*

[34] *Relevant rules and legislation comprise rules made by the FSA under Section 340 of FSMA 2000, and relevant provisions of, and regulations made under, BS Act 1986.*

Principles for Businesses. The duty to report also covers any requirement imposed by or under any other Act[35] the contravention of which constitutes an offence which the FSA has the power to prosecute under FSMA 2000.

57 In relation to paragraph 55 (ii) above the duty to report relates to either information or opinions held by the auditor which may be of significance to the FSA in determining whether the regulated entity satisfies and will continue to satisfy the Threshold Conditions. The duty to report opinions, as well as information, allows for circumstances where adequate information on a matter may not readily be forthcoming from the regulated entity, and where judgments need to be made.

Material significance

58 Determining whether a contravention of a relevant requirement or a Threshold Condition is reportable under the 2001 Regulations involves consideration both of whether the auditor 'reasonably believes' and that the matter in question 'is, or is likely to be, of material significance' to the regulator.

59 The 2001 Regulations do not require auditors to perform any additional audit work as a result of the statutory duty nor are auditors required specifically to seek out breaches of the requirements applicable to a particular regulated entity. However, in circumstances where auditors identify that a reportable matter may exist, they carry out such extra work, as they consider necessary, to determine whether the facts and circumstances cause them 'reasonably to believe' that the matter does in fact exist. It should be noted that the auditors' work does not need to prove that the reportable matter exists.

60 ISA (UK and Ireland) 250 Section B requires that, where an apparent breach of statutory or regulatory requirements comes to the auditors' attention, they obtain such evidence as is available to assess its implications for their reporting responsibilities and determine whether, in their opinion, there is reasonable cause to believe that the breach has occurred and that it relates to a matter that is of material significance to the regulator.

61 'Material significance' is defined by paragraph 14 of ISA (UK and Ireland) 250 Section B as follows:

"A matter or group of matters is normally of material significance to a regulator's function when, due either to its nature or its potential financial impact, it is likely of itself to require investigation by the regulator."

62 'Material significance' does not have the same meaning as materiality in the context of the audit of financial statements. Whilst a particular event may be trivial in terms of its possible effect on the financial statements of an entity, it may be of a nature or type that is likely to change the perception of the regulator. For example, a failure to reconcile client money accounts may not be significant in financial terms but would have a significant effect on the FSA's consideration of whether the regulated entity was satisfactorily controlled and was behaving properly towards its customers.

63 The determination of whether a matter is, or is likely to be, of material significance to the FSA inevitably requires auditors to exercise their judgment. In forming such judgments, auditors need to consider not simply the facts of the matter but also their

---

[35] *Examples include The Proceeds of Crime Act 2002 and prescribed regulations relating to money laundering.*

implications. In addition, it is possible that a matter, which is not materially significant in isolation, may become so when other possible breaches are considered.

The auditor of a regulated entity bases his judgment of 'material significance' to the FSA solely on his understanding of the facts of which he is aware without making any assumptions about the information available to the FSA in connection with any particular regulated entity. 64

Minor breaches of the FSA's rules that, for example, are unlikely to jeopardise the entity's assets or amount to misconduct or mismanagement would not normally be of 'material significance'. ISA (UK and Ireland) 250 Section B however requires auditors of regulated entities when reporting on their financial statements, to review information obtained in the course of the audit and to assess whether the cumulative effect is of 'material significance' such as to give rise to a duty to report to the regulator. In circumstances where auditors are uncertain whether they may be required to make a report or not, they may wish to consider whether to take legal advice. 65

On completion of their investigations, the auditor ensures that the facts and circumstances, and the basis for his conclusion as to whether these are, or are likely to be, of 'material significance' to the FSA, are adequately documented such that the reasons for his decision to report or not, as the case may be, may be clearly demonstrated. 66

Whilst confidentiality is an implied term of auditors' contracts with a regulated entity, s342 of FSMA 2000 states that an auditor does not contravene that duty if he reports to the FSA information or his opinion, if he is acting in good faith and he reasonably believes that the information or opinion is relevant to any function of the FSA. The protection afforded is given in respect of information obtained in his capacity as auditor. 67

Conduct of the audit

ISA (UK and Ireland) 250 Section B requires auditors to ensure that all staff involved in the audit of a regulated entity 'have an understanding of: 68

(a) The provisions of applicable legislation;
(b) The regulator's rules and any guidance issued by the regulator; and
(c) Any specific requirements which apply to the particular regulated entity

appropriate to their role in the audit and sufficient (in the context of that role) to enable them to identify situations they encounter in the course of the audit which may give reasonable cause to believe that a matter should be reported to the regulator.'

Understanding, commensurate with the individual's role and responsibilities in the audit process, is required of : 69

- the provisions of the 2001 Regulations concerning the auditors' duty to report to the regulator;
- the standards and guidance in ISA (UK and Ireland) 250 Section B, and in this section of this Practice Note; and
- relevant sections of the FSA Handbook including the Principles for Businesses and the Threshold Conditions.

70   The auditor includes procedures within his planning process to ensure that members of the audit team have such understanding (in the context of their role) as to enable them to recognise potentially reportable matters, and that such matters are reported to the audit engagement partner without delay so that a decision may be made as to whether a duty to report arises.

71   An audit firm appointed as auditor of a regulated entity needs to have in place appropriate procedures to ensure that the audit engagement partner is made aware of any other relationship which exists between any department of the firm and the regulated entity when that relationship could affect the firm's work as auditors (this matter is covered in more detail in Appendix 2 of ISA (UK and Ireland) 250 Section B). The auditor also requests the regulated entity to advise him when it appoints a third party (including another department or office of the same firm) to review, investigate or report on any aspects of its business activities that may be relevant to the audit of the financial statements and to provide the auditor with copies of reports by such a third party promptly after their receipt. This matter may usefully be referred to in the engagement letter.

Closely linked entities

72   Where the auditor of a regulated entity is also auditor of a closely linked entity[36], a duty to report arises directly in relation to information relevant to the regulated entity of which he becomes aware in the course of his work as auditor of the closely linked entity.

73   The auditor establishes during audit planning whether the regulated entity has one or more closely linked entities of which the audit firm is also the auditor. If there are such entities the auditor considers the significance of the closely linked entities and the nature of the issues that might arise which may be of material significance to the regulator of the regulated entity. Such circumstances may involve:

- activities or uncertainties within the closely linked entity which might significantly impair the financial position of the regulated entity;
- money laundering and, if the closely linked entity is itself regulated;
- matters that the auditor of the closely linked entity is intending to report to its regulator.

74   Following the risk assessment referred to in paragraph 73, the auditor of the regulated entity identifies the closely related entities for which the procedures in this paragraph are necessary. The engagement team of the regulated entity communicates to the engagement team of the selected closely linked entities the audit firm's responsibilities to report to the FSA under the 2001 Regulations and notifies the engagement team of the circumstances that have been identified which, if they exist, might be of material significance to the FSA as regulator of the regulated entity. Prior to completion the auditor of the regulated entity obtains details from the auditor of the closely linked entity of such circumstances or confirmation, usually in writing, that such circumstances do not exist. Where the closely linked entities are part of the inter-auditor group reporting process these steps can be built into that process.

[36] *An entity has close links with an authorised person for this purpose if the entity is a:*
(a) Parent undertaking of an authorised person;
(b) Subsidiary undertaking of an authorised person;
(c) Parent undertaking of a subsidiary undertaking of an authorised person; or
(d) Subsidiary undertaking of a parent undertaking of an authorised person

Whilst confidentiality is an implied term of auditors' contracts with a regulated entity, s343 FSMA 2000 states that an auditor of an entity closely linked to an authorised person who is also the auditor of that authorised person does not contravene that duty if he reports to the FSA information or his opinion, if he is acting in good faith and he reasonably believes that the information or opinion is relevant to any function of the FSA. The protection afforded is given in respect of information obtained in his capacity as auditor. 75

No duty to report is imposed on the auditor of an entity closely linked to a regulated entity who is not also auditor of the regulated entity. 76

In circumstances where he is not also the auditor of the closely linked entity, the auditor of the regulated entity decides whether there are any matters to be reported to the FSA relating to the affairs of the regulated entity in the light of the information that he receives about a closely linked entity for the purpose of auditing the financial statements of the regulated entity. If the auditor becomes aware of possible matters that may fall to be reported, he may wish to obtain further information from the management or auditor of the closely linked entity to ascertain whether the matter should be reported. To facilitate such possible discussions, at the planning stage of the audit, the auditor of the regulated entity will have considered whether arrangements need to be put in place to allow him to communicate with the management and auditor of the closely linked entity. If the auditor of the regulated entity is unable to communicate with the management and auditor of the closely linked entity to obtain further information concerning the matters he has identified he reports the matters, and that he has been unable to obtain further information, direct to the FSA. 77

Information received in a capacity other than as auditor

There may be circumstances where it is not clear whether information about a firm coming to the attention of the auditor is received in the capacity of auditor or in some other capacity, for example as a general adviser to the entity. Appendix 2 to ISA (UK and Ireland) 250 Section B provides guidance as to how information obtained in non-audit work may be relevant to the auditor in the planning and conduct of the audit and the steps that need to be taken to ensure the communication of information that is relevant to the audit. 78

Discussing matters of material significance with the directors

The directors[37] are the persons principally responsible for the management of the regulated entity. The auditor will therefore normally bring a matter of material significance to the attention of the directors subject to compliance with legislation relating to 'tipping off' and seek agreement on the facts and circumstances. However, ISA (UK and Ireland) 250 Section B emphasises that where the auditor concludes that a duty to report arises, he should bring the matter to the attention of the regulator without undue delay. The directors may wish to report the matters identified to the FSA themselves and detail the actions taken or to be taken. Whilst such a report from the directors may provide valuable information, it does not relieve the auditor of the statutory duty to report directly to the FSA. 79

---

[37] This term would include the senior management of EEA or non EEA banks.

Timing of a report

The duty to report arises once the auditor has concluded that he reasonably believes that the matter is or is likely to be of material significance to the FSA's regulatory function. In reaching his conclusion the auditor may wish to take appropriate legal or other advice and consult with colleagues.

80 The report should be made without undue delay once a conclusion has been reached. Unless the matter casts doubt on the integrity of the directors this should not preclude discussion of the matter with the directors and seeking such further advice as is necessary, so that a decision can be made on whether or not a duty to report exists. Such consultations and discussions are however undertaken on a timely basis to enable the auditor to conclude on the matter without undue delay.

Auditors' right to report to the FSA

81 S342 FSMA 2000 provides that no duty to which an auditor of an authorised person is subject shall be contravened by communicating in good faith to the FSA information or an opinion on a matter that the auditor reasonably believes is relevant to any functions of the FSA.

82 The scope of the duty to report is wide particularly since, under the FSA's Principle for Businesses 11 (and corresponding application rules and guidance in SUP 15.3), an authorised firm must disclose to the FSA appropriately anything relating to the authorised firm of which the FSA would reasonably expect notice. However in circumstances where the auditor concludes that a matter does not give rise to a statutory duty to report but nevertheless should be brought to the attention of the regulator, in the first instance he advises the directors of his opinion. Where the auditor is unable to obtain, within a reasonable period, adequate evidence that the directors have properly informed the FSA of the matter, then the auditor makes a report themselves to the regulator without undue delay.

83 The auditor may wish to take legal advice before deciding whether, and in what form, to exercise his right to make a report direct to the regulator in order to ensure, for example, that only relevant information is disclosed and that the form and content of his report is such as to secure the protection of FSMA 2000. Appendix 6 provides additional guidance on disclosure in the public interest. This is relevant to both the auditor's consideration of the right to report and also where neither the right nor the duty to report exists – as is the case for EEA banks without top up permissions. However, the auditor recognises that legal advice will take time and that speed of reporting is likely to be important in order to protect the interests of customers and/or to enable the FSA to meet its statutory objectives.

ISA (UK and Ireland) 300: Planning an audit of financial statements

Background note

The purpose of this ISA (UK and Ireland) is to establish standards and provide guidance on the considerations and activities applicable to planning an audit of financial statements. This ISA (UK and Ireland) is framed in the context of recurring audits. In addition, matters the auditor considers in initial audit engagements are included in paragraphs 28 and 29.

> The auditor should plan the audit so that the engagement will be performed in an effective manner. (paragraph 2)
>
> The auditor should establish the overall audit strategy for the audit. (paragraph 8)
>
> The auditor should develop an audit plan for the audit in order to reduce audit risk to an acceptably low level. (paragraph 13)

84 Matters the auditor of a deposit taker may consider as part of the planning process for the audit of the financial statements include:

- the nature and scope of the deposit taker's business;
- the extent of head office control over networks of branches;
- the deposit taker's relationships with the FSA and any other regulators;
- changes in applicable laws, regulations and accounting requirements;
- the need to involve specialists in the audit;
- the extent to which controls and procedures are outsourced to a third-party provider; and
- issues relating to the auditor's statutory duty to report.

85 Guidance on the first four of these matters is set out in the section on ISA (UK and Ireland) 315 'Obtaining an understanding of the entity and its environment and assessing the risks of material misstatement' below. Considerations in relation to the other matters in planning the audit are:

- the nature and complexity of deposit taking business increases the likelihood that the auditor may consider it necessary to involve specialists in the audit process. For example, the auditor may wish to utilise the work of an expert in the valuation of derivative and other financial instruments not traded in an active market. The auditor considers the need to involve such specialists at an early stage in planning their work. Where such specialists are to be used, they may be involved in the development of the audit plan and may take part in discussions with the management and staff, in order to assist in the development of knowledge and understanding relating to the business;
- the auditor considers the implications of the outsourcing of functions by the deposit taker, and the sources of evidence available to the auditors for transactions undertaken by service organisations in planning their work. This may include the outsourcing of certain functions, such as the IT function; and
- issues relating to the auditor's statutory duty to report include the adequacy of the audit team's understanding of the law and the identification of closely linked entities.

ISA (UK and Ireland) 315: Obtaining an understanding of the entity and its environment and assessing the risks of material misstatement

Background note

The purpose of this ISA (UK and Ireland) is to establish standards and to provide guidance on obtaining an understanding of the entity and its environment, including its internal control, and on assessing the risks of material misstatement in a financial statement audit.

86 Deposit takers can be complex and the auditor seeks to understand the business and the regulatory regime in which they operate. Generally, there is a close relationship between planning and obtaining an understanding of the business and the control environment, which is covered more fully below.

> The auditor should obtain an understanding of relevant industry, regulatory, and other external factors including the applicable financial reporting framework (paragraph 22).
>
> The auditor should obtain an understanding of the nature of the entity (paragraph 25).

87 When performing procedures to obtain an understanding of the deposit taker's business, the auditor considers:

- the relative importance to the deposit taker of each of its business activities[38]. This includes an understanding of the type and extent of specialised activities, for example:
  - derivatives and other complex trading activities (where both documentation, accounting and valuation aspects can be difficult);
  - trade finance, invoice discounting and factoring (where the documentation used can be complex and highly specialised); and
  - leasing (where there are particular accounting issues, especially relating to income recognition);
- the introduction of new categories of customers, or products or marketing and distribution channels;
- the relevant aspects of the deposit taker's risk management procedures;
- the complexity of the deposit taker's information systems;
- the legal and operational structure of the deposit taker;
- a change in the market environment (for example, a marked increase in competition);
- the complexity of products;
- the consistency of products, methods and operations in different departments or locations; and
- the respective roles and responsibilities attributed to the finance, risk control, compliance and internal audit functions.

88 Many banks and UK banking groups are managed globally on product/business lines rather than focused around legal structure. Such 'matrix management' structures typically involve local reporting (often on a legal entity basis) on operational and compliance matters; and business/product based reporting (often globally) of activities undertaken. In addition, global trading activities may mean that transactions are entered into in one location but are recorded in another; it may even be the case that they are controlled and settled in a third location. Furthermore, parts of deposit takers' operations may be undertaken through special purpose entities which may have structures and features that can mean they are excluded from financial statement consolidation. Given these factors, the auditor gains an understanding of how and where transactions are undertaken, recorded and controlled, in order to plan the audit.

---

[38] *The auditor of a building society is aware of the BS Act 1986 statutory and the FSA regulatory limitations on funding, lending and treasury activities and considers whether the continuing activities of the society are, for example, within the restrictions of section 9A of the BS Act 1986 and are compliant with the limitations within the society's treasury approach set out in IPRU(BSOC)4.5.G – see paragraphs 20-25.*

89 Many deposit takers operate a network of branches. In such instances, the auditor determines the degree of head office control over the business and accounting functions at branch level and the scope and effectiveness of the deposit taker's inspection and/or internal audit visits. The extent and impact of visits from regulators is also relevant. Where branches maintain separate accounting records, the extent of audit visits and work on each branch is also dependent on the materiality of, and risks associated with, the operations of each branch and the extent to which controls over branches are exercised centrally. In the case of smaller branches, the degree to which exceptions to a deposit taker's normal control procedures may be caused by minimal staffing levels (the greater difficulty of ensuring adequate segregation of duties, for example) and the consequent need for an increased level of control from outside the branch are relevant to assessing audit risk.

90 In obtaining an understanding of the regulatory factors the auditor considers:

- any formal communications between the FSA in its capacity as the regulator and the deposit taker, including any new or interim risk assessments issued by the FSA and the results of any other supervisory visits conducted by the FSA;
- the contents of any recent reports prepared by 'skilled persons' under s.166 FSMA 2000 together with any correspondence, minutes or notes of meetings relevant to any recent skilled persons' report;
- any formal communications between the deposit taker and other regulators; and
- discussions with the deposit taker's compliance officer together with others responsible for monitoring regulatory compliance.

> The auditor should obtain an understanding of the entity's selection and application of accounting policies and consider whether they are appropriate for its business and consistent with the applicable financial reporting framework and accounting policies used in the relevant industry (paragraph 28).

91 Accounting policies of particular relevance may include allowances for impairment, hedge accounting, classification of assets and liabilities (and thereby their measurement), embedded derivatives, revenue / expense recognition (including effective interest rates), offsetting and derecognition. The auditor undertakes procedures to consider whether the policies adopted are in compliance with applicable accounting standards and gains an understanding of the procedures, systems and controls applied to maintain compliance with them.

> The auditor should obtain an understanding of the entity's objectives and strategies, and the related business risks that may result in material misstatement of the financial statements (paragraph 30).

92 It is important for the auditor to understand the multi-dimensional nature and extent of the financial and business risks which are integral to the environment, and how the deposit taker's systems record and address these risks. Although they may apply to varying degrees, the risks include (but are not limited to):

- credit risk: at its simplest, this is the risk that a borrower or other counterparty will be unable to meet its obligations. However, where credit risk is traded (in the form of secondary market loan trading or credit derivatives, for example), credit risk is often regarded as having two distinct elements:

- spread risk: the risk arising from day to day changes in the price of a credit instrument because of changes in market perceptions about the credit standing of the debtor;
- default risk: the risk that a debtor will default on its obligations; or settlement risk: the risk that a counterparty will be unable to settle its obligations under a transaction (in a securities settlement or payment system, for example) on the due date;
- liquidity risk: the risk that arises from the possibility that a deposit taker has insufficient liquid funds to meet the demands of depositors or other counterparties;
- interest rate risk: the risk that arises where there is a mismatch between the interest rate reset dates or bases for assets and liabilities;
- currency risk: the risk that arises from the mismatching of assets, liabilities and commitments denominated in different currencies;
- market risk[39]: the risk that changes in the value of assets, liabilities and commitments will occur as a result of movements in relative prices (for example, as a result of changes in the market price of tradable assets). Market risk is a generic term which, in addition to interest rate and currency risk and, in some environments, spread risk, also includes equity risk and commodity price risk;
- operational risk: the risk of loss, arising from inadequate or failed internal processes, people and systems or from external events including legal risk; and
- regulatory risk: the risk of public censure, fines (together with related compensation payments) and restriction or withdrawal of authorisation to conduct some or all of the deposit taker's activities. In the UK this may arise from enforcement activity by the FSA.

Failure to manage the risks outlined above can also cause serious damage to a deposit taker's reputation, potentially leading to loss of confidence in the deposit taker, withdrawal of deposits or problems in maintaining liquidity (this is sometimes referred to as reputational risk or franchise risk).

> The auditor should obtain an understanding of the measurement and review of the entity's financial performance (paragraph 35).

93 The auditor obtains an understanding of the measures used by management to review the deposit taker's performance. Further guidance in respect of key performance indicators is given in the section on ISA (UK and Ireland) 520.

> The auditor should obtain an understanding of internal control relevant to the audit (paragraph 41).
>
> The auditor should obtain an understanding of the control environment (paragraph 67).

94 The quality of the overall control environment is dependent upon management's attitude towards the operation of controls. A positive attitude may be evidenced by an organisational framework which enables proper segregation of duties and

---

[39] *Some forms of market risk are 'non-linear', i.e. there is not a constant relationship between the profit and loss and the movement in the underlying price. For example, the relationship between an option's price and the price of its underlying instrument is 'non-linear'; the 'delta' measures the change in the price of an option for a unit change in the price of the underlying instrument whilst the 'gamma' indicates the extent of the 'non-linearity' (the change in delta for a unit change in the price of the underlying instrument).*

delegation of control functions and which encourages failings to be reported and corrected. Thus, where a lapse in the operation of a control is treated as a matter of concern, the control environment will be stronger and will contribute to effective control systems; whereas a weak control environment will undermine detailed controls, however well designed.

In accordance with the requirements of SYSC and PRIN, senior management has a responsibility for establishing and maintaining such systems and controls as are appropriate to the operations of a deposit taker. The FSA can hold senior managers personally accountable for an area or business for which they are responsible. This responsibility extends to personal behaviour not only by senior management but also to other Approved Persons[40]. Statements of Principle and Codes of Practice for Approved Persons (as set out in the FSA Handbook) include acting with integrity, due skill and care and diligence. The fit and proper test applied to Approved Persons includes competence and capability. 95

The FSA requires authorised firms, including deposit takers, to maintain systems and controls appropriate for its business[41]. These include (but are not limited to): 96

- clear and appropriate reporting lines which are communicated within the deposit taker;
- appropriate controls to ensure compliance with laws and regulations (this may mean a separate Compliance function);
- appropriate risk assessment process;
- appropriate management information;
- controls to ensure suitability of staff;
- controls to manage tensions arising out of remuneration policies;
- documented and tested business continuity plans;
- documented business plans or strategies;
- an internal audit function (where appropriate);
- an audit committee (where appropriate); and
- appropriate record keeping arrangements.

For large deposit takers, the volume of transactions can be so great that it may be extremely difficult for the auditor to express an opinion without obtaining considerable assurance from adequate systems of control. Systems of internal control in a deposit taker are important in ensuring orderly and prudent operations of the deposit taker and in assisting the directors to prepare financial statements which give a true and fair view. The following features of the business of deposit takers may be relevant to the auditor's assessment of such internal controls: 97

- the substantial scale of transactions, both in terms of volume and relative value, makes it important that control systems are in place to ensure that transactions are recorded promptly, accurately and completely and are checked and approved, and that records are reconciled at appropriate intervals in order to identify and investigate differences promptly. Processing and accounting for complex transactions or high volumes of less complex transactions will almost inevitably involve the use of sophisticated technology. For example,

---

[40] Any person performing a Controlled Function (an FSA defined term that includes roles beyond senior management such as the head of internal audit or the non-executive directors) must be approved by the FSA (an Approved Person).

[41] Most FSA systems and control requirements are set out in SYSC, but additional requirements relating to prudential matters also exist in GENPRU, BIPRU and in what remains of IPRU (Bank) and IPRU (BSOC).

transactions subject to 'straight through processing' involve little or no manual intervention after they have been initiated.
- a deposit taker deals in money or near money instruments. In the case of most commercial organisations, most movements of funds are the result of a related movement of goods and some audit assurance may therefore be obtained by reference to this relationship. This is not available, however, in the case of deposit takers and similar financial organisations. Management must therefore establish robust systems of control. As the centralised funds transfer departments which exist in larger deposit takers will often process very high volumes and a high value of transactions each day, the need for strong and effective controls over this area is particularly important;
- the fact that deposit takers deal in money and near money instruments makes proper segregation of duties between and amongst those entering into transactions, those recording the transactions, those settling them and where relevant, those responsible for their physical security particularly important;
- the geographical or organisational dispersal of some deposit takers' operations means that, in order to maintain control over their activities, deposit takers need to ensure not only that there are sufficient controls at each location, but also that there are effective communication and control procedures between the various locations and the centre. It is important that there should be clear, comprehensive reporting and responsibility lines, particularly where the business is managed using a 'matrix' structure;
- the activities of deposit takers can typically result in the creation or use of derivatives and other complex transactions. The fact that the resultant cash flows may not take place for a considerable time creates the risk that wrongly recorded or unrecorded positions may exist and that these may not be detected for some time, thereby exposing the deposit taker to risk of misstatement. The valuation of these instruments also poses risks of misstatement. Consequently, deposit takers will normally have developed important operational controls to mitigate such risks of misstatement;
- the provisions of the UK tax legislation require deposit takers to operate various tax deduction and collection arrangements, such as those relating to paying and collecting agents and lower rate tax deducted from interest paid to individuals. In addition, the VAT position of a deposit taker can be particularly complex. These may give rise to significant liabilities if not properly dealt with. Accordingly, an effective control system is essential to ensure that the record-keeping requirements of UK tax legislation are satisfied, and that tax is accounted for promptly and accurately. Similar measures may be needed to address similar provisions arising in any other jurisdictions where the deposit taker operates; and
- the UK regulatory framework is both complex and evolving for deposit takers. This may give rise to significant liabilities for compensation to clients if not properly dealt with. Accordingly, an effective control system is essential to ensure that the requirements of the UK regulators are satisfied. Measures may also be needed to address regulators in other jurisdictions.

> The auditor should obtain a sufficient understanding of control activities to assess the risks of material misstatement at the assertion level and to design further audit procedures responsive to assessed risks (paragraph 90).

98 There is a wide variation between different deposit takers in terms of size, activity and organisation, so that there can be no standard approach to internal controls and risk. The auditor assesses the adequacy of controls in relation to the circumstances of each entity. Examples of weaknesses that may be relevant to the auditor's assessment of the risk of material misstatement are as follows:

- complex products or processes inadequately understood by management; this includes undue concentration of expertise concerning matters requiring the exercise of significant judgment or capable of manipulation such as valuations of financial instruments or allowances for impairment;
- weaknesses in back office procedures underpinning the completeness and accuracy of accounting records such as:
    - backlogs in key reconciliations, particularly those over correspondent bank accounts, settlement accounts and the custody of assets such as securities (either those held on own account or as collateral);
    - inadequate maintenance of suspense or clearing accounts; and
    - backlogs in confirmation processes relating to financial instrument transactions.
- weaknesses in new product approval procedures;
- lack of segregation of duties such as between critical dealing, operational, control, settlement and accounting functions; and
- weakness over payments systems such as inadequate controls over access to payment systems and data..

99 Controls relating to outsourcing activities are considered in the ISA (UK and Ireland) 402 section.

> The auditor should obtain an understanding of how the entity has responded to risks arising from IT. (paragraph 93)

100 As a result of the type and complexity of transactions undertaken, and records held, by deposit takers and the need for swift and accurate information processing and retrieval, many deposit taking functions are highly automated, including: funds transfer systems, the accounting function, the processing and recording of customer transactions, trading activity, regulatory reporting and the supply of management information.

101 The auditor assesses the extent, nature and impact of automation within the deposit taker and plans and performs work accordingly. In particular the auditor considers:

- the required level of IT knowledge and skills may be extensive and may require the auditor to obtain advice and assistance from staff with specialist skills;
- the extent of the application of audit software and related audit techniques;
- general controls relating to the environment within which IT based systems are developed, maintained and operated; and
- external interfaces susceptible to breaches of security.

A single computer system rarely covers all of the deposit taker's requirements. It is common for deposit takers to employ a number of different systems and, in many cases, use PC-based applications (sometimes involving the use of complex spreadsheets) to generate important accounting and/or internal control information. The auditor identifies and understands the communication between computer systems in order to assess whether appropriate controls are established and maintained to cover all critical systems and the links between them and to identify the most effective audit approach.

> The auditor should identify and assess the risks of material misstatement at the financial statement level, and at the assertion level for classes of transactions, account balances, and disclosures (paragraph 100).
>
> As part of the risk assessment as described in paragraph 100, the auditor should determine which of the risks identified are, in the auditor's judgment, risks that require special audit consideration (such risks are defined as "significant risks") (paragraph 108).
>
> For significant risks, to the extent the auditor has not already done so, the auditor should evaluate the design of the entity's related controls, including relevant control activities, and determine whether they have been implemented. (paragraph 113).

102 Significant risks are likely to arise in those areas that are subject to significant judgment by management or are complex and properly understood by comparatively few people within the deposit taker.

103 Examples of significant risks for deposit takers requiring special audit consideration may include:

- allowances for impairment (particularly collective assessments of impairment) (see paragraphs 138 to 140) or customer compensation provisioning ; and
- valuation of certain derivatives and other financial instruments (see paragraphs 143 and 144).

104 Weaknesses in the control environment and in controls such as those described in paragraph 99 above could increase the risk of fraud.

105 The application of complex accounting standards such as IAS32, IAS39 and IFRS 7 (for deposit takers using EU IFRS) and FRS 25, 26 and 29 (for deposit takers using UK GAAP) may also give rise to significant risk with respect to hedge accounting, classification of assets/liabilities, revenue/expense recognition (effective interest rates) and over the adequacy of financial statement disclosure.

ISA (UK and Ireland) 320: Audit materiality

> **Background note**
>
> The purpose of this ISA (UK and Ireland) is to establish standards and provide guidance on the concept of materiality and its relationship with audit risk.
>
> The auditor should consider materiality and its relationship with audit risk when conducting an audit. (paragraph 2)
>
> Materiality should be considered by the auditor when:
>
> (a) Determining the nature, timing and extent of audit procedures; and
> (b) Evaluating the effect of misstatements. (paragraph 8)

106 The principles of assessing materiality in the audit of a deposit taker are the same as those applying to the audit of any other entity. In particular the auditor's

consideration of materiality is a matter of professional judgment, and is affected by the auditor's perception of the common information needs of users as a group[42].

Most deposit taking organisations are profit orientated and a profit based measure, such as a percentage of profit before tax is likely to be used. However, in applying materiality to the audit and assessment of transactions and balances which do not have a direct impact on profit, consideration is given to the extent any misstatement of these items would influence the economic decisions of users taken on the basis of the financial statements. For example, it is not uncommon in deposit takers to encounter balance sheet misclassifications that do not affect profit, such as the offset of trading balances. 107

ISA (UK and Ireland) 330: The auditor's procedures in response to assessed risks

> **Background note**
>
> The purpose of this ISA (UK and Ireland) is to establish standards and provide guidance on determining overall responses and designing and performing further audit procedures to respond to the assessed risks of material misstatement at the financial statement and assertion levels in a financial statement audit.

> When, in accordance with paragraph 115 of ISA (UK and Ireland) 315, the auditor has determined that it is not possible or practicable to reduce the risks of material misstatement at the assertion level to an acceptably low level with audit evidence obtained only from substantive procedures, the auditor should perform tests of relevant controls to obtain audit evidence about their operating effectiveness (paragraph 25).

In practice the nature and volume of transactions relating to the operations of deposit takers often means that performing tests of relevant controls is the most efficient means of reducing audit risk to an acceptably low level. 108

Whilst some aspects of a deposit taker's income statement and balance sheet lend themselves to the application of analytical procedures, income and expense resulting from trading activities is unlikely to be susceptible to these methods because of its inherent unpredictability. 109

> When in accordance with paragraph 108 of ISA (UK and Ireland) 315 the auditor has determined that an assessed risk of material misstatement at the assertion level is a significant risk, the auditor should perform substantive procedures that are specifically responsive to that risk (paragraph 51).

Examples of significant risks for deposit takers requiring special audit consideration include the valuation of derivative and other financial instruments which are not traded in an active market and for which valuation techniques are required – see the 110

---

[42] *The International Accounting Standards Board's 'Framework for the Preparation and Presentation of Financial Statements' indicates that, for a profit orientated entity, as investors are providers of risk capital to the enterprise, the provision of financial statements that meets their needs will also meet most of the needs of other users that financial statements can satisfy.*

section on ISAs (UK and Ireland) 545, and the section on ISA (UK and Ireland) 540 for estimates of allowances for impairment or customer compensation provisioning.

> The auditor should perform audit procedures to evaluate whether the overall presentation of the financial statements, including the related disclosures, are in accordance with the applicable financial reporting framework. (paragraph 65)

Specific financial reporting standards can require extensive narrative disclosures in the financial statements of deposit takers; for example, in relation to the nature and extent of risks arising from financial instruments. In designing and performing procedures to evaluate these disclosures the auditor obtains audit evidence regarding the assertions about presentation and disclosure described in paragraph 17 of ISA (UK and Ireland) 500 'Audit Evidence'.

Disclosure of market risk information under IFRS 7 and FRS 29

111 IFRS 7/FRS 29 Financial instruments: Disclosures may give rise to particular issues for the auditor, particularly in relation to market risk sensitivity analysis.

Understanding the risk measurement method adopted by the management

112 A deposit taker applying IFRS 7/FRS 29, where appropriate, discloses a sensitivity analysis for each type of market risk to which the entity is exposed. Where a deposit taker uses sensitivity analysis, such as value at risk ('VAR') that reflects interdependencies between risk variables and this is the method used to manage the financial risks of the business, disclosures based on these measures may be used instead of the standard method prescribed by IFRS 7/FRS 29 paragraph 40.

113 The auditor obtains an understanding of the method adopted by the management to develop the market price risk information to be disclosed. This may be done in conjunction with obtaining an understanding of the deposit taker's accounting and internal control systems. For example, the auditor considers the independence of the deposit taker's risk management function from the front office in the context of their understanding of the control environment.

Considering the skills needed by the audit team

114 The audit team is assembled on the basis of the skills needed. The auditor's approach to the market price risk disclosures is normally based on reviewing and testing the process used by the management to develop the information to be disclosed, rather than on re-performing the calculations (or making or obtaining an independent assessment). However, obtaining an understanding of that process and assumptions used may require technical knowledge of risk measurement methodologies; these can be complex, especially where a VAR model is adopted. Accordingly, when planning the audit, the auditor considers the skills needed in order to obtain and evaluate audit evidence in this part of the engagement.

115 The nature and extent of any technical knowledge of risk measurement methodologies that are required depends on the circumstances. The auditor takes into account such factors as the complexity of the model used and whether the model has received regulatory recognition. Where appropriate, the auditor may involve an expert in elements of this work (see ISA (UK and Ireland) 620 section).

Considering the application of the risk measurement method

The auditor considers whether the risk measurement method adopted has been applied reasonably by, for example: **116**

- reviewing, and where necessary testing, the internal controls relating to the operation of the deposit taker's risk management system, in order to obtain evidence that the data used in developing the market price risk information are reliable. This may be done in conjunction with the auditor obtaining an understanding of control procedures including those over the data fed into the risk management system, pricing, and independent review of the algorithms. If the deposit taker has applied for regulatory recognition of the method used, the auditor reviews correspondence with the regulator regarding such matters;
- reviewing, and where necessary testing, the internal controls relating to changes in the deposit taker's risk management system (for example, controls over changes to algorithms and assumptions);
- if a VAR model is used, performing analytical review of the model's predictions during the year against actual outcomes (a process commonly referred to as 'backtesting'). The auditor normally reviews any comparisons made by the deposit taker as part of its own backtesting procedures (for a deposit taker to receive regulatory recognition of the model used it is required to undertake backtesting procedures);
- agreeing the amount disclosed to the output of the risk management system.

If an approach based upon internal controls and backtesting proves to be unsatisfactory, the auditor may wish to consider testing the accuracy of the calculations used to develop the required information. However, this situation may indicate that it would be more appropriate for the deposit taker to make disclosures on the simpler basis described in IFRS 7/FRS 29 paragraph 40. **117**

Considering the adequacy of disclosures

Market price risk information is subject to a number of significant limitations which are inherent in the risk measurement methods used. For example: **118**

- there are different VAR models and methods of presenting sensitivity analyses. It is to be expected that, in any particular case, the management of a deposit taker will make an informed choice of the method that it considers to be most suitable. Normally, for the purpose of developing the market price risk information to be disclosed, the management will use the risk measurement method that is used in the deposit taker's risk management system. It would, for example, be reasonable to expect the appropriateness of this method in the past to be supported by the deposit taker's own backtesting procedures, where such procedures are performed. However, in the absence of recognised industry standards on VAR, there is no objective benchmark against which to assess the future appropriateness of management's choice;
- both VAR models and sensitivity analyses involve the management making a number of important assumptions in order to develop the disclosures. These are, by their nature, hypothetical and based on management's judgment (for example, when using a VAR model, assumptions are made concerning the appropriate holding period, confidence level and data set);
- both VAR models and, to a limited extent, sensitivity analyses are based on historical data and cannot take account of the fact that future market price movements, correlations between markets and levels of market liquidity in conditions of market stress may bear no relation to historical patterns; and

- Each of the methods permitted for developing market price risk information may lead to a deposit taker reporting significantly different information, depending on the choice made by the management. IFRS 7/FRS 29 paragraph 41 requires the market price risk information disclosed to be supplemented by other disclosures, including explanations of:
  - the method used in preparing such sensitivity analysis and of the main parameters and assumptions underlying the data provided in the disclosures; and
  - the objective of the method used and the limitations that may result in the information not fully reflecting the fair values of assets and liabilities involved.

119 The auditor considers the overall adequacy of the disclosures made by the deposit taker in response to the requirements of IFRS 7/FRS 29 and whether the market risk information is presented fairly so that its limitations can be understood. In particular, the auditor considers whether it is sufficiently clear that:
- the market price risk information is a relative estimate of risk rather than a precise and accurate number;
- the market price risk information represents a hypothetical outcome and is not intended to be predictive (in the case of probability-based methods, such as VAR, profits and losses are almost certain to exceed the reported amount with a frequency depending on the confidence interval chosen); and
- future market conditions could vary significantly from those experienced in the past.

120 In many deposit takers and related groups, market price risk is primarily managed at the level of individual business units rather than on a legal entity or group-wide basis. Therefore, the auditor considers the appropriateness of the basis on which the market risk information to be disclosed in the financial statements is to be compiled. It may well be inappropriate simply to aggregate the operating unit information to arrive at the information to be disclosed for the deposit taker or group as a whole.

Considering the consistency of the risk measurement method adopted

121 The main purpose of the disclosure of market price risk information is to provide users of a deposit taker's financial statements with a better understanding of the relationship between the deposit taker's profitability and its exposure to risk. For example, an increase in profitability may be achieved by taking on increased risk. IFRS 7/FRS 29 paragraph 40(c) requires disclosure of any changes in the methods and assumptions used and the reasons for the changes. Therefore, the auditor considers the consistency of the method, the main assumptions and parameters with those used in previous years.

122 If the method used for developing the market risk information is also used in the deposit taker's risk management system, modifications will be made to the method as the need arises. If the deposit taker performs its own backtesting procedures, this may lead to modification of, for example, the algorithm used, the assumptions and parameters specified or the parts of the trading book covered. Where modifications have been made, the auditor considers their effect on the market risk measures and whether appropriate disclosures about the changes have been made.

123 In some cases, re-statement may not be possible if the relevant data for the previous year cannot be constructed and in this case the auditor considers whether the disclosures provide sufficient information about the nature and extent of any change in the entity's risk profile. For example, as well as providing the current year figure on

auditor may consider it more effective to test these controls rather than carry out their own confirmation procedures.

ISA (UK and Ireland) 520: Analytical procedures

Background note

The purpose of this ISA (UK and Ireland) is to establish standards and provide guidance on the application of analytical procedures during an audit.

The auditor should apply analytical procedures as risk assessment procedures to obtain an understanding of the entity and its environment and in the overall review at the end of the audit. (paragraph 2)

Aspects of deposit takers' business where there are high volumes of similar transactions or balances, such as interest receivable/payable or interest margins, may lend themselves to analytical procedures to highlight anomalies. 131

The auditor of a deposit taker may wish to consider applying analytical procedures to the following, if the procedures are expected to yield useful audit evidence or where they are considered more efficient or effective than alternative procedures: 132

- asset quality – eg ratio of non-performing loans to total loans and provisions for loan impairment to non-performing loans (overall and by portfolio type);
- earnings/profitability – eg cost/income ratio, the ratio of interest income or expense to average interest bearing assets or liabilities and the ratio of net interest income to average interest bearing assets;
- the exposure to and degree of mismatching arising from the market risks below and the comparison of the related risk positions to risk limits set by management. The auditor may find it helpful to consider risk information to be disclosed under IFRS 7/FRS 29:
    - liquidity;
    - interest rates;
    - foreign exchange;
    - other market risks, such as equity and commodity prices;
- the structure of the loan portfolio/credit exposure by industrial, geographic or other category, or by loan impairment provision;
- regulatory compliance – eg complaints handling or reporting of suspicious transactions under the Money Laundering regulations; and
- operational risk measures – e.g. failed trade rates, volumes of unreconciled items.

Whilst some aspects of a deposit taker's income statement and balance sheet lend themselves easily to analytical procedures, income and expense resulting from trading activities is unlikely to be susceptible to these methods because of its inherent unpredictability. Analytical procedures on income and expense items such as interest will be most effective if returns are calculated on the basis of average daily (or at least monthly) balance information. 133

When performing their review of the financial statements as a whole for consistency with their knowledge of the entity's business and the results of other audit 134 procedures, the auditor considers transactions occurring either side of the year end, including:

- material short-term deposits which are re-lent on broadly similar terms; loan repayments which are received shortly before the year end then re-advanced shortly afterwards; material sale and repurchase transactions or other financing or linked transactions. Experience and judgment are required to identify and assess the implications, if any, of these transactions; they may, for example, be indicative of 'window dressing' of the balance sheet over the year end date;
- other transactions around the year end, apparently at rates which are significantly off market including those that appear to give rise to significant profits or losses;
- the value and nature of transactions between related parties/associated undertakings around the year end;
- the reclassification of balances and transactions to achieve advantageous income recognition and balance sheet treatment/presentation.

Where non financial information or reports produced from systems or processes outside the financial statements accounting system are used in analytical procedures, the auditor considers the reliability of that information or those reports.

ISA (UK and Ireland) 540: Audit of accounting estimates

Background note

The purpose of this ISA (UK and Ireland) is to establish standards and provide guidance on the audit of accounting estimates contained within the financial statements.

The auditor should obtain sufficient appropriate audit evidence regarding accounting estimates (paragraph 2)

The auditor should adopt one or a combination of the following approaches in the audit of an accounting estimate:

(a) Review and test the process used by management to develop the estimate;
(b) Use an independent estimate for comparison with that prepared by management; or
(c) Review of subsequent events which provide audit evidence of the reasonableness of the estimate made. (paragraph 10)

The auditor should make a final assessment of the reasonableness of the entity's accounting estimates based on the auditor's understanding of the entity and its environment and whether the estimates are consistent with other audit evidence obtained during the audit. (paragraph 24)

135   Accounting estimates are used for valuation purposes in a number of areas: the most common examples are allowances for loan losses, and the fair value measurement of financial instruments not traded on an active market. Estimates of allowances for impairment or customer compensation provisioning may represent significant risks.

> When planning the audit the auditor should assess the risk that material undisclosed related party transactions, or undisclosed outstanding balances between an entity and its related parties may exist. (paragraph 106-3)

Related party transactions are defined in FRS 8/IAS 24 'Related party disclosures'. Paragraph 16 of FRS 8 states that the 'disclosure provisions do not apply where to comply with them conflicts with the reporting entity's duties of confidentiality arising by operation of law'. IAS 24 contains no explicit corresponding exemption. However the potentially overriding impact of law concerning confidentiality in respect of disclosures under IAS 24 still needs to be considered. This is particularly relevant in a deposit taking context: deposit takers are usually under a strict duty of confidentiality (by operation of statute, contract or common law) regarding the affairs of their clients and, in respect of transactions entered into in certain overseas jurisdictions, this may even preclude a foreign entity from disclosing information to its parent, another group company or their auditor. A provider of finance (in the course of a business in that regard) and its customer are not 'related' simply because of that relationship. 142

Both when applying EU IFRS or UK GAAP, under ISA (UK and Ireland) 550, the auditor is required to assess the risk that material undisclosed related party transactions may exist. It is in the nature of deposit taking business that transaction volumes are high but this factor will not, of itself, necessarily lead the auditor to conclude that the inherent risk of material undisclosed related party transactions is high. 143

Deposit takers are required to report to FSA changes in control (in some instances with FSA prior approval), changes in circumstances of existing controlling parties and changes in entities who are closely linked to the authorised firm (SUP 11). In addition, there are annual reporting obligations in respect of controlling parties and entities that are closely linked to the firm (SUP 16). As a result, it will therefore normally be the case that there are controls in place to ensure that this information is properly collated. However, the definition of 'controller and closely linked" for regulatory purposes is not congruent with the 'related party' definition in FRS 8/IAS 24 and the auditor therefore considers what controls have been put in place by management to capture information on those parties which fall within the accounting definition only. 144

In reviewing related party information for completeness, the auditor may compare the proposed disclosures in the financial statements to information prepared for regulatory reporting purposes (bearing in mind that the population may be different, as noted in the preceding paragraph). 145

Whilst related party transactions can arise in respect of deposit takers generally, in the context of UK banks and building societies, they frequently arise in respect of deposits held by directors and/or persons connected with them and in respect of loans and other transactions with directors and/or persons connected with them. They may also arise in respect of the sale or arrangement of insurance products and in respect of the provision of professional and other services. Whilst there are CA1985 provisions relating to transactions by banking companies with directors, there are separate BS Act 1986 requirements for building societies in respect of transactions with directors (s62-69 BS Act 1986). See paragraphs 172 to 174 concerning the related auditor's obligation. 146

147 The auditor is aware that BSOG provides additional emphasis for proper approval procedures concerning loans to and transactions with directors (BSOG 1.3.15G and 16G). In addition, the auditor is required to report on the statement that a building society is required to make under s 68 BS Act 1986 concerning loans, and certain other transactions with directors, that are subject to s65 BS Act 1986. The auditor is also aware that the Sch10A BS Act 1986 contains specific disclosure requirements applicable to building societies as regards loans and certain other transactions with directors.

ISA (UK and Ireland) 560: Subsequent events

Background note

The purpose of this ISA (UK and Ireland) is to establish standards and provide guidance on the auditor's responsibility regarding subsequent events.

The auditor should perform audit procedures designed to obtain sufficient appropriate audit evidence that all events up to the date of the auditor's report that may require adjustment of, or disclosure in, the financial statements have been identified (paragraph 4)

148 Matters specific to deposit takers which auditors may consider in their review of subsequent events include:
- an evaluation of material loans and other receivables identified as being in default or potential default at the period end to provide additional evidence concerning period end loan impairment provisions;
- an assessment of material loans and other receivables identified as (potential) defaults since the period end to consider whether any adjustment to the period end carrying value is required;
- a review of movements in market prices and exchange rates, particularly in illiquid markets or where the deposit taker has very large positions, to consider whether prices or rates used in period end valuations were realistic in relation to the size of positions held;
- a review of correspondence with regulators and enquiries of management to determine whether any significant breaches of regulations or other significant regulatory concerns have come to light since the period end; and
- a consideration of post year end liquidity reports for indications of funding difficulties.

ISA (UK and Ireland) 570: The going concern basis in financial statements

Background note

The purpose of this ISA (UK and Ireland) is to establish standards and provide guidance on the auditor's responsibility in the audit of financial statements with respect to the going concern assumption used in the preparation of the financial statements, including management's assessment of the entity's ability to continue as a going concern.

> When planning and performing audit procedures and in evaluating the results thereof, the auditor should consider the appropriateness of management's use of the going concern assumption in the preparation of the financial statements. (paragraph 2)
>
> The auditor should consider any relevant disclosures in the financial statements. (paragraph 2-1)

149 In reviewing going concern, the auditor may consider the following areas in addition to those set out in ISA (UK and Ireland) 570:

- capital adequacy ratios – e.g. review of management's analysis and rationale for ensuring that the deposit taker is capable of maintaining adequate financial resources in excess of the minimum;
- operations/profitability indicators – eg review of the performance of loans in troubled industry sectors in which the deposit taker has a high concentration of exposure;
- liquidity indicators – eg review of the deposit taker's liquidity management process (eg maturity mismatch ladders) for signs of undue deterioration; and
- reputational and other indicators – eg review of the financial press and other sources of market intelligence for evidence of deteriorating reputation; review of correspondence with regulators.

Further details of possible factors that may indicate going concern issues in these areas are set out in Appendix 5 to this Practice Note.

150 If the auditor has any doubts as to the ability of a deposit taker to continue as a going concern, the auditor considers whether he ought to make a report direct to the FSA on which guidance is set out in the section of this Practice Note relating to ISA (UK and Ireland) 250 Section B.

ISA (UK and Ireland) 580: Management representations

> **Background note**
>
> The purpose of this ISA (UK and Ireland) is to establish standards and provide guidance on the use of management representations as audit evidence, the procedures to be applied in evaluating and documenting management representations and the action to be taken if management refuses to provide appropriate representations.

> Written confirmation of appropriate representations from management, as required by paragraph 4 below, should be obtained before the audit report is issued. (paragraph 2-1)
>
> The auditor should obtain written representations from management on matters material to the financial statements when other sufficient appropriate audit evidence cannot reasonably be expected to exist. (paragraph 4)

ISAs (UK and Ireland) 250 and 550 require auditors to obtain written confirmation in respect of completeness of disclosure to the auditors of:
- all known actual or possible non-compliance with laws and regulations (including breaches of FSMA 2000, FSA rules, the Money Laundering Regulations, other regulatory requirements or any other circumstance that could jeopardise the authorisation of the firm under FSMA 2000) whose effects should be considered when preparing financial statements together with the actual or contingent consequences which may arise therefrom; and
- the completeness of information provided regarding the identification of related parties and the adequacy of related party disclosures in the financial statements.

151 In addition to the examples of other representations given in ISA (UK and Ireland) 580, the auditor also considers obtaining confirmation:
- as to the adequacy of provisions for loan impairment (including provisions relating to individual loans if material) and the appropriateness of other accounting estimates (such as derivatives valuations or adequate provisions for compensation concerning upheld complaints by customers);
- that all contingent transactions or commitments have been adequately disclosed and/or included in the balance sheet as appropriate;
- that all correspondence with regulators has been made available to the auditor.

ISA (UK and Ireland) 600: Using the work of another auditor

Background note

The purpose of this ISA (UK and Ireland) is to establish standards and provide guidance when an auditor, reporting on the financial statements of an entity, uses the work of another auditor on the financial information of one or more components included in the financial statements of the entity. This ISA (UK and Ireland) does not deal with those instances where two or more auditors are appointed as joint auditors nor does it deal with the auditors' relationship with a predecessor auditor. Further, when the principal auditor concludes that the financial statements of a component are immaterial, the standards in this ISA (UK and Ireland) do not apply. When, however, several components, immaterial in themselves, are together material, the procedures outlined in this ISA (UK and Ireland) would need to be considered.

When the principal auditor uses the work of another auditor, the principal auditor should determine how the work of the other auditor will affect the audit. (paragraph 2)

In the UK and Ireland, when planning to use the work of another auditor, the principal auditor's consideration of the professional competence of the other auditor should include consideration of the professional qualifications, experience and resources of the other auditor in the context of the specific assignment. (paragraph 7-1)

The principal auditor considers in particular the competence and capability of the other auditor having regard to the laws, regulation and industry practice relevant to the component to be reported on by the other auditor and, when relevant, whether the other auditor has access to relevant expertise, for example in the valuation of financial instruments, appropriate to the component's business.

Further procedures may be necessary for the auditor of a deposit taker where audit work in support of the audit opinion is undertaken by an audit firm that is not subject to the UK audit regulatory regime. Where an overseas firm of the auditor (or an audit firm independent of the auditor) is undertaking audit procedures on a branch, or division or in-house shared service centre of the deposit taker, the auditor has due regard to the requirements in the Audit Regulations[43] to ensure all relevant members of the engagement team are and continue to be fit and proper, are and continue to be competent and are aware of and follow these Audit Regulations and any related procedures and requirements established by the audit firm. This includes the auditor's duty to report direct to the FSA in certain circumstances. More detailed consideration of the auditors' duty to report to the FSA is set out in the section of this Practice Note dealing with ISA (UK and Ireland) 250. 152

ISA (UK and Ireland) 620: Using the work of an expert

Background note

The purpose of this ISA (UK and Ireland) is to establish standards and provide guidance on using the work of an expert as audit evidence.

When using the work performed by an expert, the auditor should obtain sufficient appropriate audit evidence that such work is adequate for the purposes of the audit. (paragraph 2)

Given the complexity, subjectivity and specialist nature of the valuation of derivative and other financial instruments not traded in an active market, together with VAR (or similarly complex) market risk disclosures, the auditor may involve an expert in elements of the audit of these areas. 153

Where the auditor uses an expert as part of the audit, the auditor remains solely responsible for the audit of the deposit taker's financial statements and does not refer to the work of the expert within the auditor's report. 154

ISA (UK and Ireland) 700: The auditor's report on financial statements

Background note

The purpose of this ISA (UK and Ireland) is to establish standards and provide guidance on the form and content of the auditor's report issued as a result of an audit performed by an independent auditor of the financial statements of an entity. Much of the guidance provided can be adapted to auditor reports on financial information other than financial statements.

---

[43] *Audit Regulations and Guidelines* – December 2005 issued by the Institute of Chartered Accountants in England and Wales, the Institute of Chartered Accountants in Scotland and the Institute of Chartered Accountants in Ireland

> In the UK and Ireland:
>
> (a) The auditor should distinguish between the auditor's responsibilities and the responsibilities of those charged with governance by including in the auditor's report a reference to a description of the relevant responsibilities of those charged with governance when that description is set out elsewhere in the financial statements or accompanying information; or
>
> (b) Where the financial statements or accompanying information do not include an adequate description of the relevant responsibilities of those charged with governance, the auditor's report should include a description of those responsibilities. (paragraph 9-1)

155 The auditor may report on the financial statements of a branch of a bank incorporated outside the UK. ISA (UK and Ireland) 700 (or aspects thereof) may remain applicable in these circumstances. However, in agreeing the form of the opinion for a branch audit, the auditor takes into account matters such as the nature and content of the financial statements to which the report relates, the extent to which transactions recorded in the branch may have been initiated in other locations (and, similarly, whether transactions initiated by the branch may have been recorded elsewhere), the specific terms of the engagement as agreed with the party which has commissioned the work (which may be local and/or head office management or the head office auditor, for example) and whether the report will be public or private.

156 The auditor's reporting responsibilities concerning building societies differ from those applicable to a UK bank as follows:

- a statutory requirement for the publication of income and expenditure accounts (as opposed to profit and loss account/income statements) separately for both the society and its subsidiary undertakings (group accounts) (s72F BS Act 1986) and the society itself (s72B BS Act 1986) where prepared under UK GAAP. s72H and s72D BS Act 1986 respectively apply where prepared under EU IFRS. This contrasts with the s230 CA1985 exemption available to UK companies including UK banks from publishing the profit and loss account of the parent company in group accounts;
- a statutory requirement for an annual business statement to be attached to the annual accounts (s74 BS Act 1986), containing information as prescribed by the BS Accounts Regulations 1998; the prescribed content comprises three sections, being section 1, statutory percentages (the lending and funding limits, see paragraph 20 of this Practice Note), disclosing also the statutory limits and an explanation of the basis for each of these ratios, section 2, other percentages (being five operating ratios with their comparatives and an explanation of each ratio), and section 3, information on the directors and officers of the society. The auditor is required to state whether the annual business statement has been prepared in accordance with BS Act 1986 and regulations made thereunder and whether the information given in the annual business statement (excluding the details of directors and officers) gives a true representation of the matters in respect of which it is given (s78(7)(a) BS Act 1986); and
- a statutory requirement for a directors' report to be produced for each financial year (s75 BS Act 1986), containing information as prescribed in s75 and 75A BS Act 1986 and Sch 8 of the BS Accounts Regulations 1998: in addition to consistency with financial statements the auditor is required to state whether the directors' report has been prepared so as to conform to the requirements of s75 BS Act 1986 and the BS Accounts Regulations 1998 (s78(7) BS Act 1986).

157 In relation to the annual business statement the term 'true representation of the matters in respect of which it is given' referred to in paragraph 161 above is the expression drawn directly from the BS Act 1986. It is not defined in BS Act 1986 nor in any related legislation. The part of the annual business statement covered by this opinion comprises data and ratios (see paragraphs 21 to 24) that are almost all derived from audited information within the annual accounts. Procedures undertaken by the auditor usually involve substantive procedures to ensure that:

- the relevant data has been completely and accurately extracted from audited information or from sources that have been subject to audit procedures; and
- the ratios have been accurately calculated in accordance with the statutory definitions within the BS Accounts Regulations 1998.

There is also a statutory requirement for a summary financial statement for building societies, in a format as prescribed in the BS Accounts Regulations 1998, which must be sent to all members entitled to receive notice of meetings and which must be provided on request to all new shareholders (s76 BS Act 1986): the auditor is required by s76(5) BS Act 1986 to provide an auditor's statement as to the consistency of the summary financial statement with the accounts, the annual business statement and the directors' report and its conformity with the requirements of s76 BS Act 1986 and the BS Accounts Regulations 1998[44].

158 Example auditors' reports concerning building societies are set out in Appendix 1.1-4.

Other reports by the auditor

Auditors' review reports on interim net profits

159 A deposit taker must maintain at all times capital resources equal to or in excess of its capital resources requirement. A deposit taker may include interim net profits in its capital resources, calculated in accordance with GENPRU2 Annex 2R or 3R, provided those interim net profits have been reported on by the external auditor in accordance with the 'relevant Auditing Practices Board's Practice Note' (GENPRU2.2.103G)[45]. For this reason the auditor may be asked to report on interim net profits for inclusion in core tier 1 profits for capital adequacy purposes. Deposit takers with a trading book can include net interim trading book profits in lower tier 3 capital without external review (GENPRU2.2.247R).

160 Interim net profits in this context means, net profits of the deposit taker as at a date specified by the deposit taker after the end of its most recently audited financial year end and up to and including its next financial year end, calculated after deductions for tax, declared dividends and other appropriations (GENPRU2.2.102R).

161 GENPRU 2.2.102R does not include specific guidance as to what constitutes an external verification. However "verification" as used in the context of GENPRU is understood to indicate a degree of assurance which is lower than that given by a full

---

[44] A Listed UK bank may choose to prepare summary financial statements to send to its members, subject to certain conditions.

[45] GENPRU is effective from 1 January 2007. For review reports prepared for periods ending up to and including 31 December 2006 reference is made instead to Section 5.3, Chapter CA of IPRU(BANK) or Volume 1, Chapter 1 – Annex 1E of IPRU(BSOC) as appropriate.

audit[46]. An engagement to "verify" interim profits may therefore be taken to be a review engagement, and an opinion may be given in terms of negative assurance. The report is normally addressed to the directors of the deposit taker.

162   As an external "verification" of interim net profits does not require a full scope audit it will be important for the FSA, in considering the adequacy of the "verification" of interim profits, to be informed of the procedures that have been undertaken by the auditors, in support of their opinion. This is particularly important in the case of deposit takers where no prescribed procedures have been established by the FSA themselves in rules or guidance. Consequently the detailed scope of the work undertaken by the auditor in support of his opinion is listed in the auditors' report or included in the report by reference to the letter of engagement where the programme of work has been laid down.

163   In undertaking the review the auditor normally performs the following procedures:

(a) satisfies himself that the figures forming the basis of the interim net profits have been properly extracted from the underlying accounting records;
(b) reviews the accounting policies used in calculating the interim net profits for the period under review so as to obtain comfort that they are consistent with those normally adopted by the deposit taker in drawing up its annual financial statements and are in accordance with either UK GAAP applicable to deposit takers or EU IFRS, as appropriate;
(c) performs analytical procedures on the results to date which form the basis of calculating interim net profits, including comparisons of actual performance to date with budget and with the results of the prior period(s);
(d) discusses with management the overall performance and financial position of the deposit taker;
(e) obtains adequate comfort that the implications of current and prospective litigation, all known claims and commitments, changes in business activities, allowances for loan losses and other impairment provisions have been properly taken into account in arriving at interim net profits; and
(f) follows up significant matters of which the auditor is already aware in the course of auditing the deposit taker's most recent financial statements.

The auditor may also consider obtaining appropriate representations from management.

164   There may be some circumstances in which the auditor considers that additional work is required, for example:

- if the control environment surrounding the preparation of the interim net profits is evaluated as weak;
- if the results of the procedures undertaken in paragraph 169 above are not fully consistent with the interim net profits as reported; or
- if there has been a significant change to the accounting system.

165   The report is addressed to the directors of the deposit taker. An example auditor's report on interim profits is set out in Appendix 1.6.

---

[46] As evidenced by procedures set out in section 5.3 of Chapter CA of I IPRU(BANK) and Volume 1, Chapter 1 – Annex 1E of IPRU(BSOC).

We also report to you if, in our opinion, the [financial statements]¹ are not in agreement with the accounting records or if we have not received all the information and explanations that we require for our audit.

We read the other information contained in the Annual Report and consider whether it is consistent with the audited [financial statements]¹. The other information comprises only [the Chairman's Statement, Chief Executive's Review, Corporate Governance Report and the Directors' Remuneration Report][4]. We consider the implications for our report if we become aware of any apparent misstatements or material inconsistencies with the [financial statements]¹, Annual Business Statement and Directors' Report. Our responsibilities do not extend to any other information.

Basis of audit opinion

We conducted our audit in accordance with International Standards on Auditing (UK and Ireland) issued by the Auditing Practices Board. An audit includes examination, on a test basis, of evidence relevant to the amounts and disclosures in the [financial statements]¹, and the Annual Business Statement. It also includes an assessment of the significant estimates and judgments made by the directors in the preparation of the [financial statements]¹, and of whether the accounting policies are appropriate to the [Group's and] Society's circumstances, consistently applied and adequately disclosed.

We planned and performed our audit so as to obtain all the information and explanations which we considered necessary in order to provide us with sufficient evidence to give reasonable assurance that the [financial statements]¹ are free from material misstatement, whether caused by fraud or other irregularity or error. In forming our opinion we also evaluated the overall adequacy of the presentation of information in the [financial statements]¹.

Opinion

In our opinion:

a) the [financial statements]¹ give a true and fair view, in accordance with UK Generally Accepted Accounting Practice, of the state of affairs [of the Group and] of the Society as at ... and of the income and expenditure [of the Group and] of the Society for the year then ended;
b) the information given in the Annual Business Statement (other than the information upon which we are not required to report) gives a true representation of the matters in respect of which it is given;
c) the information given in the Directors' Report is consistent with the accounting records and the [financial statements]¹, and
d) the [financial statements]¹, the Annual Business Statement and the Directors' Report have each been prepared in accordance with the applicable requirements of the Building Societies Act 1986 and regulations made under it.

Registered Auditors   *Address*
Date

Notes

1. The Building Societies Act 1986 uses the term "annual accounts" rather than "financial statements". The auditor ordinarily uses the term used by the directors in the Annual Report.

2. Auditor's reports of building societies that do not publish their financial statements on a web site or publish them using "PDF" format may continue to refer to the financial statements by reference to page numbers.
3. Directors' emoluments disclosure required in the notes to the financial statements is specified in BS Act 1986 Sch 10A and is required to be audited. Some building societies present separate Directors' Remuneration Reports which include the audited directors' emoluments disclosures in the report instead of the notes to the financial statements. Such reports frequently include additional voluntary disclosures which are not required to be audited. Such reports are similar to Directors' Remuneration Reports (DRR) presented by listed companies. If the part of the DRR that has been audited is clearly cross-referred to in the notes to the financial statements there is no need for the DRR to be referred to in the auditor's report other than in connection with the read requirement in the last paragraph of the responsibilities section.
4. The other information that is "read" is the content of the printed Annual Report other than the financial statements, Directors' Report and Annual Business Statement. The description of the information that is read is tailored to reflect the terms used in the Annual Report.
5. To be tailored as necessary if the required contents of the Directors' Report are disclosed in, and cross referenced to, other parts of the Annual Report.

1.2 – Auditor's report on financial statements, Annual Business Statement and Directors' Report – under IFRSs AS ADOPTED BY THE EUROPEAN UNION

Independent auditor's report to the members of XYZ Building Society

We have audited the [Group and Society] [financial statements][1] of [   ] Building Society for the year ended ... which comprise [state the primary financial statements such as the [Group and Society] Income Statement[s], the [Group and Society] Statement[s] of Changes in equity/Statement of Recognised Income and Expense[2], the [Group and Society] Balance Sheet[s] and the [Group and Society] Cash Flow Statement[s] and the related notes[3] [4]. These [financial statements][1] have been prepared under the accounting policies set out therein.

We have examined the Annual Business Statement (other than the details of directors and officers upon which we are not required to report) and the Directors' Report.

Respective responsibilities of directors and auditors

The directors' responsibilities for preparing the Annual Report including the Directors' Report, the Annual Business Statement, and the [financial statements][1] in accordance with applicable law and International Financial Reporting Standards (IFRSs) as adopted by the European Union are set out in the Statement of Directors' Responsibilities on page x.

Our responsibility is to audit the [financial statements][1] in accordance with relevant legal and regulatory requirements and International Standards on Auditing (UK and Ireland). We are also responsible for examining the Annual Business Statement (other than the details of directors and officers) and for reading the information in the Directors' Report and assessing whether it is consistent with the accounting records and the [financial statements][1].

We report to you our opinion as to whether the [financial statements][1] give a true and fair view and whether the [financial statements][1] are properly prepared in accordance with the Building Societies Act 1986, regulations made under it and, as regards the group [financial statements][1] [Article 4 of the IAS Regulation][5]. In addition, we report to you our opinion as to whether certain information in the Annual Business Statement gives a true representation of the matters in respect of which it is given, whether the information in the Directors' Report is consistent with the accounting records and the [financial statements][1] and whether the Annual Business Statement and the Directors' Report have each been prepared in accordance with the applicable requirements of the Building Societies Act 1986 and regulations made under it.[The information given in the Directors' Report includes that specific information given in the Chief Executive's Review that is cross referred from the Business Review section of the Directors' Report.][7]

We also report to you if, in our opinion, the [financial statements][1] are not in agreement with the accounting records or if we have not received all the information and explanations that we require for our audit.

We read the other information contained in the Annual Report and consider whether it is consistent with the audited [financial statements][1]. The other information comprises only [the Chairman's Statement, Chief Executive's Review, Corporate Governance Report and the Directors' Remuneration Report][6]. We consider the implications for our report if we become aware of any apparent misstatements or material inconsistencies with the [financial statements][1], Annual Business Statement and Directors' Report. Our responsibilities do not extend to any other information.

Basis of audit opinion

We conducted our audit in accordance with International Standards on Auditing (UK and Ireland) issued by the Auditing Practices Board. An audit includes examination, on a test basis, of evidence relevant to the amounts and disclosures in the [financial statements][1], the Annual Business Statement. It also includes an assessment of the significant estimates and judgments made by the directors in the preparation of the [financial statements][1], and of whether the accounting policies are appropriate to the [Group's and] Society's circumstances, consistently applied and adequately disclosed.

We planned and performed our audit so as to obtain all the information and explanations which we considered necessary in order to provide us with sufficient evidence to give reasonable assurance that the [financial statements][1] are free from material misstatement, whether caused by fraud or other irregularity or error. In forming our opinion we also evaluated the overall adequacy of the presentation of information in the [financial statements][1].

Opinion

In our opinion:
a) the [financial statements][1] give a true and fair view, in accordance with IFRSs as adopted by the European Union, of the state of affairs [of the Group and] of the Society as at ... and of the income and expenditure [of the Group and] of the Society for the year then ended;
b) the information given in the Annual Business Statement (other than the information upon which we are not required to report) gives a true representation of the matters in respect of which it is given;

c) the information given in the Directors' Report is consistent with the accounting records and the [financial statements]¹; and
d) the [financial statements]¹, the Annual Business Statement and the Directors' Report have each been prepared in accordance with the applicable requirements of the Building Societies Act 1986, regulations made under it [and, as regards the group financial statements, Article 4 of the IAS Regulation⁵].

Registered Auditors   *Address*
Date

Notes

1. The Building Societies Act 1986 uses the term "annual accounts" rather than "financial statements". The auditor ordinarily uses the term used by the directors in the Annual Report.
2. The Statement of Changes in Equity is titled a Statement of Recognised Income and Expense "SORIE" when it comprises the items set out in paragraph 96 of IAS1. If the statement comprises other items it is titled a Statement of Changes in Equity.
3. Auditor's reports of building societies that do not publish their financial statements on a web site or publish them using "PDF" format may continue to refer to the financial statements by reference to page numbers.
4. Directors' emoluments disclosure required in the notes to the financial statements is specified in BS Act 1986 Sch 10A and is required to be audited. Some building societies present separate Directors' Remuneration Reports which include the audited directors' emoluments disclosures in the report instead of the notes to the financial statements. Such reports frequently include additional voluntary disclosures which are not required to be audited. Such reports are similar to Directors' Remuneration Reports presented by listed companies. If the part of the Directors' Remuneration Report that has been audited is clearly cross-referred to in the notes to the financial statements there is no need for the DRR to be referred to in the auditor's report other than in connection with the read requirement in the last paragraph of the responsibilities section.
5. Building societies that issue traded securities are required by Article 4 of the IAS Regulation to prepare their group accounts using IAS as adopted by the EU. To work out whether the consolidated accounts of a building society come within the requirements of Article 4 of the IAS Regulation there are two points to consider:
    (i) Are any securities of the building society admitted to trading on a regulated market of any Member State? "Securities" includes debt securities as well as shares.
    (ii) Does the building society have to prepare consolidated accounts by virtue of Section 72E of the Building Societies Act 1986 and regulations 3 and 4 of the 1998 Regulations? A consolidated account is required wherever a building society has one or more subsidiary undertakings.
    If the answer to **both** of these questions is yes the building society is required by Article 4 of the IAS Regulation to use IFRSs with respect to its group accounts and it should be referred to in the auditor's report. Article 4 of the IAS Regulation is not referred to in the auditor's report with respect to the non-consolidated accounts of a building society or group accounts where a society has voluntarily adopted IFRSs.
6. The other information that is "read" is the content of the printed Annual Report other than the financial statements, Directors' Report and Annual Business Statement. The description of the information that is read is tailored to reflect the terms used in the Annual Report.

7. To be tailored as necessary if the required contents of the Directors' Report are disclosed in, and cross referenced to, other parts of the Annual Report.

1.3 – Auditor's statement on summary financial statement (building societies)

Statement of the independent auditor to the members and depositors of [   ] Building Society

Pursuant to Section 76 of the Building Societies Act 1986, we have examined the summary financial statement of [   ] Building Society [set out/above on pages x to x]*.

Respective responsibilities of directors and auditors

The directors are responsible for preparing the [summary financial statement/name of document containing summary financial statement]^{1*}, in accordance with applicable United Kingdom law.

Our responsibility is to report to you our opinion on the consistency of the summary financial statement [within the [name of document containing summary financial statement]]^{1*} with the [full financial statements]², Annual Business Statement and Directors' report and its conformity with the relevant requirements of Section 76 of the Building Societies Act 1986 and regulations made under it. [We also read the other information contained in the [name of document containing summary financial statement] and consider the implications for our report if we become aware of any apparent misstatements or material inconsistencies with the summary financial statement.]^{3*}

Basis of opinion

We conducted our work in accordance with Bulletin 1999/6 'The auditors' statement on the summary financial statement' issued by the Auditing Practices Board for use in the United Kingdom [Our report on the society's [group's] full financial statements [full annual accounts]² describes the basis of our audit opinion on those [financial statements]².

Opinion

In our opinion the summary financial statement is consistent with the [full financial statements]², the Annual Business Statement and Directors' Report of [   ] Building Society for the year ended [   ] and complies with the applicable requirements of Section 76 of the Building Societies Act 1986 and regulations made under it⁴.

Registered Auditors   *Address*
Date

Notes

1. If the summary financial statement is part of a larger document, for example including the Chairman's report or the Chief Executive's Review, then reference is made to the name of that larger document.

2. The Building Societies Act 1986 uses the term "annual accounts" rather than "financial statements". The auditor ordinarily uses the term used by the directors in the Annual Report.
3. If the document comprises only the summary financial statement, then this sentence will not be required.
4. The date of the auditor's statement on the summary financial statement ('SFS') should be the same as the directors' approval of the SFS and the auditor's report on the full accounts.

* delete/amend as applicable

1.4 – Auditor's report on the s68 BS Act 1986 statement (building societies).

Independent auditor's report, under Section 78(9) of the Building Societies Act 1986 ("the Act"), to the members of [ ] Building Society on the statement of particulars of transactions and arrangements included in the Section 68(1) Register at any time during the year ended [ ]

We have examined the foregoing statement of transactions and arrangements with directors and persons connected with them, falling within Section 65(1) of the Act.

Respective responsibilities of directors and auditors

It is the responsibility of the directors, under Section 68(1) of the Act, to maintain a register of every existing transaction and arrangement, as defined in Section 65(1) of the Act, with directors or persons connected with directors. Section 68(3) of the Act requires the directors to prepare, for each financial year, a statement containing particulars of all information in the register for the last complete financial year. It is our responsibility, under Section 78(9) and (10) of the Act, to form an independent opinion as to whether the statement accurately contains all the particulars in the register from the last financial year and to report our opinion to you.

Basis of opinion

We planned and performed our work so as to obtain all the information and explanations which we considered necessary in order to provide us with sufficient evidence that the statement gives the particulars required by Section 68 of the Act.

Opinion

In our opinion the statement contains the requisite particulars, as required by Section 68 of the Act, in relation to those transactions recorded by the society in the register of transactions and arrangements maintained under Section 68(1) of the Act.

Registered Auditors   *Address*
Date

1.5 – Auditor's report on the s343(4) CA1985 statement (UK banks)

Independent auditor's report, pursuant to s343(6) Companies Act 1985 ("the Act"), to the members of [   ] ("the company") on the statement of particulars of transactions, arrangements and agreements required by s343(4) of the Act at any time during the year ended [   ]

We have examined the attached statement of transactions and arrangements with directors and persons connected with them, falling within s330 of the Act.

Respective responsibilities of directors and auditors

In accordance with s343(4) and (5) of the Act the company has made available for inspection of members of the company a statement containing the particulars of transactions, arrangements and agreements which the company would, but for paragraph 2 of Part IV of Schedule 9 of the Act, be required to disclose in its accounts or group accounts for the financial year ended [ ]. This statement, for which the company is solely responsible, is attached to this report.

It is our responsibility, to examine the statement and to make a report to the members on it in accordance with the requirements of the Act.

Basis of opinion

We planned and performed our work so as to obtain all the information and explanations which we considered necessary in order to provide us with sufficient evidence that the statement gives the particulars required by s343(4) of the Act.

Opinion

In our opinion the statement contains the requisite particulars, as required by s343(4) of the Act, in relation to those transactions recorded by the company in the register of transactions, arrangements and agreements maintained under s343(2) of the Act.

Registered Auditor   *Address*
Date

1.6 – Auditor's review report on interim net profits (UK banks and Building Societies)

Review report by the auditors to the board of directors of XYZ Limited ('the company')

In accordance with our engagement letter dated [ ], a copy of which is attached as Appendix A, we have reviewed the company's interim net profits for the period [to] as reported in [FSA003, line 24][1] dated [ ] submitted by the company, a copy of which is attached as Appendix B.

FSA003 is the responsibility of, and has been approved by, the directors. Our review did not constitute an audit and accordingly we do not express an audit opinion on the interim net profits reported therein.

Our review has been carried out having regard to[48] GENPRU 2.2.102R and GENPRU 2.2.103G of the FSA Handbook and Practice Note 19 'The audit of banks and building societies in the United Kingdom (Revised)' issued by the Auditing Practices Board.

On the basis of the results of our review, nothing came to our attention that causes us to believe that:

(a) the interim net profits as reported in [FSA003, line 24] 'have not been calculated on the basis of accounting policies adopted by the company in drawing up its annual financial statements for the year ended [   ] [except for][2];
(b) those accounting policies differ in any material respects from those required by [UK GAAP applicable to [banks/building societies]*[3] [4]/International Financial Reporting Standards adopted by the European Commission in accordance with EC Regulation No 1606/2002]*; and
(c) the interim net profits amounting to £ [   ] as so reported are not reasonably stated.

Registered Auditors   Address
Date

Notes

1. Prior to 1 January 2008 all deposit takers will continue to use Forms BSD3 (UK banks) or QFS1 (building societies) and reference is made to these forms instead, where appropriate.
2. Identify any changes, if any, in accounting policies applied for the first time in the interim period under review.
3. UK GAAP applicable to banks comprises Sch 9 to the CA 1985, UK Financial Reporting Standards and UITF Abstracts.
4. UK GAAP applicable to building societies comprises Building Societies Accounts Regulations 1998, UK Financial Reporting Standards and UITF Abstracts.

* delete as applicable

Appendix 2 – The main parts of FSMA 2000 relevant to deposit takers

Part I (and Sch 1) sets out matters concerning structure and governance of the FSA including its regulatory objectives and the principles to be followed in meeting those objectives.

Part II (and Sch 2) sets out the general prohibition on conducting regulated business unless an entity is either authorised or exempt, including restrictions on financial promotions. Regulated activities are defined in SI 2001/544.

---

[48] *GENPRU is effective from 1 January 2007. For review reports prepared for periods ending up to and including 31 December 2006 reference is made instead to Section 5.3, Chapter CA of IPRU(BANK) or Volume 1, Chapter 1 – Annex 1E of IPRU(BSOC) as appropriate.*

Part III (and Schs 3-5) sets out the requirements to become authorised either by receiving a specific permission from the FSA or through the exercise of EEA passport rights. Exempt persons are listed in SI 2001/1201.

Part IV (and Sch 6) sets out the arrangements for application for a permission to undertake authorised business and the criteria (Threshold Conditions) that must be met. An applicant who is refused can apply to the Financial Services and Markets Tribunal (established under Part IX).

Part V sets out the provisions applying to individuals performing designated functions (controlled functions) in an authorised firm. The FSA can specify controlled functions and authorised firms must take reasonable care to ensure that only persons approved by the FSA can undertake these functions. The FSA can specify qualification, training and competence requirements and approved persons must comply with the FSA's statement of principles and code of conduct for approved persons. Appeals can be made to the Tribunal.

Part VIII gives the FSA powers to impose penalties for market abuse – using information not generally available; creating a false or misleading impression; or, failure to observe normal standards – abuse being judged from the point of view of a regular market user. The FSA's powers extend to all persons – not only authorised firms. The FSA is required to publish a code to provide guidance on behaviours that do and do not constitute market abuse. This forms part of the Market Conduct Sourcebook and is called the Code of Market Conduct.

Part X provides the FSA with general powers to make rules which apply to authorised firms, including rules on specific matters – e.g. client money, money laundering. Rules must be published in draft for consultation. Guidance may be provided individually or generally and may be published. The FSA may modify rules or waive particular rules for particular authorised firms in certain situations.

Part XI allows the FSA to gather information from authorised firms, including use of skilled persons' reports under s166, or to commission investigations into authorised firms.

Part XIV sets out the disciplinary measures available to the FSA which can include public censure, unlimited fines, withdrawal of authorisation.

Part XXII includes provisions relating to auditors and their appointment.

Part XXVI brings together in one place the arrangements applying to warning notices and decision notices concerning possible breaches of various requirements imposed by FSMA 2000 or by FSA rules. A warning notice has to state the reasons for proposed actions and allow reasonable time for representations to be made. This will be followed by a decision notice with a right to appeal to the Tribunal.

Appendix 3 – FSMA 2000, BS Act 1986 and related statutory instruments: Important provisions for auditors

FSMA 2000 provisions and related statutory instruments relevant for the auditors of a deposit taker are set out below. Further details of the legislation can be found on The Office of Public Sector Information website- www.opsi.gov.uk. BS Act 1986 provisions and related statutory instruments relevant only to building societies are also set out below.

FSMA 2000 and statutory instruments as amended

Section/Sch	
19	General prohibition from undertaking regulated activity unless authorised
20	Authorised firms acting without permission
21	Restrictions on financial promotion
41	Threshold Conditions
59	Approval by FSA of persons undertaking controlled functions
165	FSA's power to require information
166	Reports by skilled persons
167	Appointment of persons to carry out general investigations
168	Appointment of persons to carry out investigations in particular cases
178	Obligation to notify FSA concerning controllers of an authorised firm
340	Appointment of auditor or actuary by FSA
341	Access to books etc (by auditor or actuary)
342	Information given by auditor or actuary to the FSA
343	Information given by auditor or actuary to the FSA : entities with close links
344	Duty of auditor or actuary resigning etc to give notice
345	Disqualification (of auditor or actuary from acting by FSA)
346	Provision of false or misleading information to auditor or actuary
348	Restrictions on disclosure of confidential information by FSA etc
349	Exceptions from s348
351	Competition information (offence relating to the disclosure of competition information)
352	Offences (contravention of s348 to 350(5))
398	Misleading the FSA
Sch 6	Threshold Conditions
SI 2001	
544	Regulated Activities Order
1177	Carrying on Regulated Activities by Way of Business Order
1201	Exemption Order
1857	Disclosure of Information by Prescribed Persons
2188	Disclosure of Confidential Information
2587	Communications by Auditors

1376/2511 EEA Passport Rights

BS Act 1986 and statutory instruments as amended

Section/Sch

5	Constitution and powers including principal purpose
6	The lending limit
7	The funding limit
8	Raising funds and borrowing
9A	Restriction on powers including treasury activities
62-69	Dealings with directors and disclosure and record of related businesses of directors
71	Accounting records
72A	Duty to prepare individual accounts
72B	Building Societies Act individual accounts
72C	Form and content of Building Societies Act individual accounts
72D	IAS individual accounts
72E	Duty to prepare group accounts
72F	Building Societies Act group accounts
72G	Form and content of Building Societies Act group accounts
72H	IAS group accounts
72I	Consistency of accounts
72J	Disclosures relating to directors, other officers and employees of societies required in notes to the accounts
72K	Disclosures about related party undertakings required in the notes to the accounts
74	Auditors and audit of accounts
75	Directors' report
75A	Business review
76	Summary financial statements for members and depositors
77	Auditors: appointment, tenure, qualifications etc.
78	Auditors' report
78A	Signature of auditors' report
79	Auditors' duties and powers
80	Signing of balance sheet – documents to be annexed
81	Laying and furnishing accounts, etc to [members and authority]
81A	Requirements in connection with publication of accounts
81B	Interpretation of Part 8

119	Interpretation
Sch 10A	Disclosures about directors' remuneration, compensation payments, loans to directors and their connected persons, auditors' remuneration and employees required in notes to the accounts
Sch 10B	Disclosures about related undertakings required in notes to accounts
SI	
1998/504	BS (Accounts and Related Provisions) Regulations 1998
2001/2617	FSMA 2000 (Mutual Societies) Order 2001

Appendix 4 – The FSA Handbook

170 Not all authorised firms are required to comply with all rules contained within the FSA Handbook. This varies with the type of permission – the regulated activity an authorised firm is permitted to undertake is set out in the authorised firm's Scope of Permission. The following can be viewed on the FSA website:

- contents of the FSA Handbook – www.fsa.gov.uk/Pages/handbook
- FSA register which lists the regulated activities that each authorised firm has permission to undertake – www.fsa.gov.uk/Pages/register

171 In gaining an understanding of the FSA Handbook the auditor bears in mind the four statutory objectives of the FSA, set out in paragraph 12 above, which underpin the content of the FSA Handbook. To facilitate usage the FSA Handbook has been structured into a number of blocks and within each block the material has been subdivided into Sourcebooks, Manuals or Guides. There are Rules, evidential provisions[1] and guidance which are contained within all of the blocks[2]. Contravention of Rules (which includes Principles for Businesses) or evidential provisions can give rise to an obligation on the auditor to report the matter direct to the FSA – see the section of this Practice Note relating to ISA (UK and Ireland) 250 Section B. Outline details of certain elements of the FSA Handbook are set out below.

Principles for Businesses

172 The eleven Principles for Businesses, which are general statements that set out the fundamental obligations of firms under the regulatory system, are set out in the FSA Handbook. They derive their authority from the FSA's rule-making powers as set out in the Act and reflect the regulatory objectives. These Principles are as follows:

- an authorised firm must conduct its business with integrity;
- an authorised firm must conduct its business with due skill, care and diligence;
- an authorised firm must take reasonable care to organise and control its affairs responsibly and effectively with adequate risk management;
- an authorised firm must maintain adequate financial resources;
- an authorised firm must observe proper standards of market conduct;
- an authorised firm must pay due regard to the interests of its customers and treat them fairly;

---

[1] An evidential provision is not binding in its own right, but establishes a presumption of compliance or non-compliance with another rule. Guidance may be used to explain the implications of other provisions, to indicate possible means of compliance, or to recommend a particular course of action or arrangement.

[2] Rules are set out in emboldened type and are marked with the icon 'R', evidential provisions are marked 'E' and guidance 'G'. Further guidance on the status of the Handbook text is set out in the General Provisions (GEN) Sourcebook Chapter 2.2 and Chapter 6 of the Reader' Guide.

- an authorised firm must pay due regard to the information needs of its clients, and communicate information to them in a way which is clear, fair and not misleading;
- an authorised firm must manage conflicts of interest fairly, both between itself and its customers and between a customer and another client;
- an authorised firm must take reasonable care to ensure the suitability of its advice and discretionary decisions for any customer who is entitled to rely on its judgement;
- an authorised firm must arrange adequate protection for clients' assets when it is responsible for them; and
- an authorised firm must deal with its regulators in an open and co-operative way, and must disclose to the FSA appropriately anything relating to the authorised firm of which the FSA would reasonably expect notice (see SUP15 – Notifications to the FSA).

Senior management arrangements, systems and controls

SYSC amplifies Principle for Businesses 3, the requirement for a firm to take reasonable care to organise and control its affairs responsibly and effectively, with adequate risk management systems. The relevant chapters[3, 4] are as follows;

- 2 – senior management arrangements
- 3 – systems and controls[5]
- 4 – general organisational requirements
- 5 – employees, agents and other relevant persons
- 6 – compliance, internal audit and financial crime
- 7 – risk control
- 8 – outsourcing
- 9 – record keeping[6]
- 10 – conflicts of interest
- 11 – liquidity risk systems and controls
- 12 – group risk systems and control requirements
- 18 – guidance on Public Disclosure Act – whistle blowing

Threshold Conditions

Under s41 and Schedule 6 of FSMA 2000 Threshold Conditions are the minimum requirements that must be met at authorisation and must continue to be met. The five statutory Threshold Conditions are:

- legal status: deposit taking business must be conducted through a body corporate or partnership – that is, individuals cannot undertake deposit taking business;
- location of offices: the head office of a body corporate must be in the same territory/member state as the registered office;

---

[3] From 1st November 2007, for common platform firms, SYSC Chapter 3 will be disapplied and replaced by SYSC Chapters 4-10 which form the common platform. Deposit takers may adopt the common platform earlier in 2007 if they wish. They would then comply with all of SYSC Chapters 4-10 (as well as 2, 11, 12, 18) and not SYSC Chapter 3. The common platform comprises the combined systems and controls requirements of the CRD and MiFID. Firms subject to the common platform include those subject to the CRD or MiFID or both.

[4] Chapters 3A and 13-17 apply only to insurers.

[5] Chapter 3 is disapplied for common platform firms from 1 November 2007. This includes deposit takers.

[6] Under consultation (CP 06/19) – expected to be effective from 1 November 2007.

- close links: close links must not prevent effective supervision. Entities are regarded as closely linked if there is a group relationship, i.e. parent/subsidiary/fellow subsidiary (but using the EC 7th Company Law Directive definition of subsidiary). They are also closely linked if one owns or controls 20% or more of the voting rights or capital of the other;
- adequate resources: the authorised firm must have adequate resources (financial and non financial) for the type of business conducted taking into account the impact of other group entities and having regard to provisions made against liabilities (including contingent and future liabilities) and the approach to risk management; and
- suitability: the FSA will consider the fitness and propriety of authorised firms, including whether business is conducted with integrity and in compliance with high standards, and whether there is competent and prudent management and exercise of due skill, care and diligence. This will include consideration of whether those subject to the approved persons regime (i.e. those undertaking controlled functions) are, or will be, approved by the FSA.

Appendix 5 – Possible factors that may indicate going concern issues

Capital adequacy ratios

- the deposit taker operating at or near the limit of its individual capital guidance[7] or limit otherwise set by management under the FSA's capital requirements, either on a group or solo basis;
- unjustified attempts to reduce the size of the buffer over and above that specified in individual capital guidance that management maintains.

Operations/profitability indicators

- marked decline in new lending/dealing volumes during the year or subsequently;
- marked decline in new business margins;
- severe overcapacity in markets leading to low pricing as well as low volumes;
- significant increase in loan defaults or seizure of collateral (e.g. house repossessions);
- excessive exposures to troubled industry sectors;
- unusually aggressive dealing positions and/or regular breaches of dealing or lending limits;
- redundancies, layoffs or failure to replace natural wastage of personnel.

Liquidity indicators

- unusually large maturity mismatch in the short term (say up to 3 months), either in total or across currencies;
- maturity mismatch ladders prepared on a basis which fail to recognise/use:
  - expected (as opposed to contractual) cash flows;
  - narrow gaps for near maturities;
  - anticipated defaults on loan repayments;
  - a cushion for market value of volatile investments; or
  - off balance sheet commitments;

---

[7] *Guidance given to a firm about the amount and quality of capital resources that the FSA considers a firm should hold under GENPRU1.2.26R.*

- failure to put in place or renew sufficient committed standby facilities. (Bear in mind, however, that grounds for withdrawal of even 'committed' facilities can often be found when a deposit taker suffers a major loss of confidence);
- dependence on a few large depositors (which may or may not be connected parties);
- withdrawal of (or reduction in) lines of credit by wholesale counterparties;
- regularly overdrawn nostro accounts;
- difficulty in meeting liquidity standards set on an individual basis by the FSA;
- uncompetitively low rates of interest offered to depositors (causing outflow of funds);
- very high rates of interest offered to depositors (to prevent outflow of funds, regardless of financial loss).

Reputational and other indicators

- adverse publicity which could lead to loss of confidence or reputation, including fines or public censure by FSA;
- lowering of ratings by independent credit agencies;
- urgent attempts to remove assets from the balance sheet, apparently involving material loss of profits or at significant expense;
- deferral of investment plans or capitalisation of expenditure.

Appendix 6 – Reporting direct to FSA – statutory right and protection for disclosure under general law

When the auditor concludes that a matter does not give rise to a statutory duty to report direct to the FSA, the auditor considers the right to report to FSA. The right to report is available to the auditor of a UK bank, building society and a non EEA bank but not to the auditor of an EEA bank which has no top up permissions.

In cases of doubt, general law provides protection for disclosing certain matters to a proper authority in the public interest.

Audit firms are protected from the risk of liability from breach of confidence or defamation under general law even when carrying out work which is not clearly undertaken in the capacity of auditor provided that:

- in the case of breach of confidence:
  (i) disclosure is made in the public interest; and
  (ii) such disclosure is made to an appropriate body or person; and
  (iii) there is no malice motivating the disclosure; and
- in the case of defamation:
  (i) the information disclosed was obtained in a proper capacity; and
  (ii) there is no malice motivating the disclosure.

The same protection is given even if there is only a reasonable suspicion that non-compliance with law or regulations has occurred. Provided that it can be demonstrated that an audit firm, in disclosing a matter in the public interest, has acted reasonably and in good faith, it would not be held by the court to be in breach of duty to the institution even if, an investigation or prosecution having occurred, it were found that there had been no breach of law or regulation.

When reporting to proper authorities in the public interest, it is important that, in order to retain the protection of qualified privilege, the auditor reports only to one who has a proper interest to receive the information. The FSA is the proper authority in the case of an authorised institution.

'Public interest' is a concept which is not capable of general definition. Each situation must be considered individually. In general circumstances, matters to be taken into account when considering whether disclosure is justified in the public interest may include:

- the extent to which the suspected non-compliance with law or regulations is likely to affect members of the public;
- whether the directors (or equivalent) have rectified the matter or are taking, or are likely to take, effective corrective action;
- the extent to which non-disclosure is likely to enable the suspected non-compliance with law or regulations to recur with impunity;
- the gravity of the matter;
- whether there is a general management ethos within the entity of disregarding law or regulations;
- the weight of evidence and the degree of the auditor's suspicion that there has been an instance of non-compliance with law or regulations.

Determination of where the balance of public interest lies requires careful consideration. The auditor needs to weigh the public interest in maintaining confidential client relationships against the public interest of disclosure to a proper authority and to use their professional judgment to determine whether their misgivings justify them in carrying the matter further or are too insubstantial to deserve report.

In cases where it is uncertain whether the statutory duty requires or s342 or s343 FSMA 2000 permits an auditor to communicate a matter to the FSA, it is possible that the auditor may be able to rely on the defence of disclosure in the public interest if it communicates a matter to the FSA which could properly be regarded as having material significance in conformity with the guidance in ISA (UK and Ireland) 250 Section B and this Practice Note, although the auditor may wish to seek legal advice in such circumstances.

Appendix 7 – Definitions

Abbreviations and frequently used terms in this Practice Note are set out below

ARROW II	'Advanced Risk Responsive Operating frameWork'. The term used for FSA's risk assessment process – the application of risk based supervision. It is the mechanism through which the FSA evaluates the risk an authorised firm poses to its statutory objectives enabling it to allocate its resources appropriately and respond to the risks identified.
Authorised firm	An entity which has been granted one of more Part IV permissions by the FSA and so is authorised under FSMA 2000 to undertake regulated activities – an authorised person. Authorised firms include deposit takers.
Authorised person	Term used throughout FSMA 2000 and related statutory instruments to refer to an authorised firm – see above.

Authorised by FSA	Same as authorised firm or authorised person – see above.
BBA SORP	Statements of Recommended Practice issued by the British Bankers' Association and the Irish Bankers' Federation.
Bank	UK bank, EEA bank and non EEA bank.
Banking company	Companies Act 1985 definition s742 B.
BIPRU	Prudential sourcebook for banks, building societies and investment firms.
BS Act 1986	Building Societies Act 1986.
BS Accounts Regulations 1998	Building Societies (Accounts and Related Provisions) Regulations 1998.
BSOG	Building Societies Regulatory Guide.
Building society	A society incorporated under the BS Act 1986.
CA1985	Companies Act 1985.
Closely linked entity	As defined in s343(8) FSMA 2000, an entity has close links with an authorised firm for this purpose if the entity is a: (a) Parent undertaking of an authorised firm; (b) Subsidiary undertaking of an authorised firm; (c) Parent undertaking of a subsidiary undertaking of an authorised firm; or (d) Subsidiary undertaking of a parent undertaking of an authorised firm.
COND	Threshold Conditions element of the high level standards block of the FSA Handbook.
CRD	Capital Requirements Directive.
Credit institution	An undertaking whose business is to receive deposits or other repayable funds from the public and to grant credits for its own account and to which the Banking Consolidation Directive applies.
Deposit taker	Banks and building societies – authorised firms which under FSMA 2000 have a Part IV permission to accept deposits.
EEA	European Economic Area.
EEA Bank	A UK branch of a credit institution incorporated in the EEA which has exercised EEA Passport rights to carry on regulated activities in the UK.
EEA Passport rights	Exercising passport rights, an entity incorporated in one EEA member state ('home country') which is authorised to conduct one or more regulated activities subject to the passport rights in the home country to establish a branch and carry out those regulated activities in another EEA member state ('host country') without the need to be authorised by the host country supervisor, FSA, in respect of activities that are subject to the passport rights.
EU IFRS	International Financial Reporting Standards adopted by the European Union.

FRS	Financial Reporting Statements.
FSA	The Financial Services Authority.
FSMA 2000	Financial Services and Markets Act 2000.
FRSSE	Financial Reporting Standard for Smaller Entities.
GENPRU	General Prudential Sourcebook.
IPRU(BANK)	Interim Prudential Sourcebook for banks.
IPRU(BSOC)	Interim Prudential Sourcebook for building societies.
JMLSG	Joint Money Laundering Steering Group.
MiFID	Markets in Financial Instruments Directive.
Material significance	A matter or group of matters is normally of material significance to a regulator's function when, due either to its nature or its potential financial impact, it is likely of itself to require investigation by the regulator.
Non EEA Bank	a UK branch of an entity incorporated outside the EEA, authorised by the FSA to accept deposits and which is required to comply with BIPRU.
Part IV permission	A permission granted by FSA under Part IV FSMA 2000 permitting an authorised firm to carry on regulated activities as specified in the FSMA 2000 Regulated Activities Order SI 2001/544 as amended.
Permission	Part IV permission under FSMA 2000 to undertake one or more regulated activities.
Principles for Businesses	FSA Handbook defined principles with which an authorised firm must comply. The 11 principles are included in a stand alone element of the high level Standards block of the FSA Handbook – PRIN.
Regulated activities	Activities as defined in the Regulated Activities Order SI 2001/544 as amended.
Relevant requirement	In relation to the auditors' duty to report direct to the FSA – requirement by or under FSMA 2000 which relates to authorisation under FSMA 2000 or to the carrying on of any regulated activity. This includes not only relevant statutory instruments but also the FSA's rules (other than the Listing rules) including the Principles for Businesses. The duty to report also covers any requirement imposed by or under any other Act the contravention of which constitutes an offence which the FSA has the power to prosecute under FSMA 2000.
SOCA	Serious and Organised Crime Agency.
SUP	Supervision manual of the FSA Handbook.
SYSC	Senior management arrangements, systems and controls element of the High Level Standards block of the FSA Handbook.
The 2001 Regulations	SI 2001/2587 – FSMA 2000 (Communications by Auditors) Regulations 2001.

Those charged with governance	ISAs (UK and Ireland) use the term "those charged with governance" to describe the persons entrusted with the supervision, control and direction of an entity, who will normally be responsible for the quality of financial reporting, and the term "management" to describe those persons who perform senior managerial functions. The FSA Handbook of Rules and Guidance (FSA Handbook) uses the term "governing body" to describe collectively those charged with governance. In the context of this Practice Note, references to those charged with governance includes directors of deposit takers.
Threshold Conditions	The minimum standards that an authorised firm needs to meet to become and remain authorised by the FSA. The 5 conditions are included in a stand alone element of the high level Standards block of the FSA Handbook – COND.
Top up permission	A Part IV permission granted by the FSA to an EEA bank to enable it to undertake a UK regulated activity in the UK for which authorisation to undertake the activity in the home country is not required by the home country supervisor.
UK bank	A company incorporated in the UK which is authorised by the FSA to accept deposits, which is required to comply with BIPRU and is not a building society.

[PN 20]
The Audit of Insurers in the United Kingdom (Revised)

(Issued)

Contents

	Paragraphs
Preface	3
Introduction	4

The audit of financial statements
ISAs (UK and Ireland)

		Paragraphs
200	Objective and General Principles Governing the Audit of Financial Statements	13
210	Terms of Audit Engagements	15
220	Quality Control for Audits of Historical Financial Information	17
230	Audit Documentation (Revised)	18
240	The Auditor's Responsibility to Consider Fraud in an Audit of Financial Statements	19
250	Section A – Consideration of Laws and Regulations in an Audit of Financial Statements	23
	Section B – The Auditors' Right and Duty to Report to Regulators in the Financial Sector	
300	Planning an Audit of Financial Statements	39
315	Obtaining an Understanding of the Entity and Its Environment and Assessing the Risks of Material Misstatement	42
320	Audit Materiality	51
330	The Auditor's Procedures in response to Assessed Risks	53
402	Audit Considerations Relating to Entities Using Service Organisations	58
505	External Confirmations	60
520	Analytical Procedures	62
540	Audit of Accounting Estimates	63
545	Auditing Fair Value Measurements and Disclosures	70
550	Related Parties	72
560	Subsequent Events	74
570	The Going Concern Basis in Financial Statements	76
580	Management Representation	78
600	Using the Work of Another Auditor	79
620	Using the Work of an Expert	81
700	The Auditors' Report on Financial Statements	83
720	Section A – Other Information in Documents Containing Audited Financial Statements (Revised)	90

Reporting on regulatory returns — 92

Appendix 1 Illustrative examples of auditor's reports — 113
    Reports on regulatory returns
    1.1 Composite insurance company
    1.2 Life Insurance Company
    1.3 General Insurance Company
    1.4 Statement on the group capital adequacy report
    Reports relating to the financial statements of a Lloyd's syndicate

            1.5 Personal and syndicate MAPA accounts
            1.6 Closed year of account
            1.7 Run-off year of account
            Other reports by the auditor
            1.8 Report on interim net profits
Appendix 2 The main parts of FSMA 2000 relevant to insurers   131
Appendix 3 The FSA Handbook   133
Appendix 4 Reporting direct to FSA – statutory right and protection for disclosure
            under general law   136
Appendix 5 Definitions   138

Preface

This Practice Note contains guidance on the application of auditing standards issued by the Auditing Practices Board (the APB) to the audit of insurers in the United Kingdom. It also contains guidance on auditors' reports in connection with regulatory returns and the auditors' duty to report to the Financial Services Authority (FSA) and to the Council of Lloyd's.

The Practice Note is supplementary to, and should be read in conjunction with, International Standards on Auditing (ISAs) (UK and Ireland), which apply to all audits undertaken in the United Kingdom in respect of accounting periods commencing on or after 15 December 2004. This Practice Note sets out the special considerations relating to the audit of insurers which arise from individual ISAs (UK and Ireland) listed in the contents. It is not the intention of the Practice Note to provide step-by-step guidance to the audit of insurers, so where no special considerations arise from a particular ISA (UK and Ireland), no material is included.

The guidance in this Practice Note is applicable to auditors of insurance companies and of Lloyd's syndicates and corporate members. Particular considerations relating to Lloyd's are shown at the end of each section of text and, to assist clarity, are presented with a coloured background in the Practice Note.

This Practice Note has been prepared with advice and assistance from staff of the FSA and Lloyd's and is based on the legislation and regulations in effect at 31 December 2006.

Introduction

1 The term 'insurers' in this Practice Note should be taken to refer to the following types of entity:-
   - Insurance companies authorised by the FSA,
   - Lloyd's syndicates and corporate members,
   - Branches of overseas insurers.

2 This Practice Note addresses the responsibilities and obligations of the auditor concerning:
   - the audit of the insurers' financial statements, as required by section 235 of the Companies Act 1985 (CA 1985), and in relation to Lloyd's the 2004 Regulations and the Syndicate Accounting Byelaw[1];
   - reporting on parts of the insurers' regulatory returns, as required by rule 9.35 of IPRU(INS), and by the Solvency and Reporting Byelaw (No. 13 of 1990) (the "Solvency Byelaw"). Guidance on the auditors' work in relation to such returns is set out in the section of this Practice Note dealing with regulatory returns;
   - where applicable reporting on the insurer's group capital adequacy report, as required by rule 9.40(3)(c) of IPRU(INS). Guidance on the auditors' work in relation to such reports is set out in the section of this Practice Note dealing with group capital adequacy;
   - the right and duty to report direct to the[2] FSA (and, where appropriate, to Lloyd's) in certain circumstances;

---

[1] Auditors of Lloyd's syndicates are required to be 'recognised accountants', that is, registered auditors who have been approved by Lloyd's and have given an undertaking to the Council of Lloyd's in a prescribed form.

[2] SI2001/2587 and s342 and s343 FSMA 2000.

- reporting on interim profits for the purposes of their inclusion in capital resources.

Overseas insurers operating in the UK through branches are not subject to the audit provisions of the CA 1985 and so the terms of engagement are a matter of contract between the auditor and their client who may, for example, be local or head office management or the insurers' home country auditor.

Such engagements take many different forms: the auditor may be asked to report on the financial statements of the UK branch or only on particular aspects thereof, and the form of their opinion will also vary from case to case. The auditor undertaking such assignments may wish to consider the guidance in this Practice Note where relevant, having regard to the agreed scope of their engagement.

Legislative and regulatory framework

Insurers operate within a complex framework of law and regulation which differs in a number of significant respects from that applicable to the generality of commercial enterprises. This framework involves statutory regulation of insurance activities established by European Directive, under which insurance regulators have powers to establish specific requirements as well as to institute investigations into insurers and to suspend or remove authorisation to conduct insurance business where appropriate.

For the purpose of this Practice Note, references to the auditor of a regulated entity or an authorised person in the context of FSA prudential supervision of insurers includes the auditor of a Lloyd's syndicate or corporate member, unless otherwise stated.

Insurance business may not be carried on in the United Kingdom without authorisation to do so. Insurance may be undertaken by:

(a) companies holding permission under Part IV of FSMA 2000 to carry on the regulated activities of effecting and/or carrying out contracts of insurance (companies incorporated under the CA 1985), companies with their head offices outside the EU and pure reinsurers with their head offices in an EEA state carrying on business in the UK);
(b) members of Lloyd's (see Section 316 of the Financial Services and Markets Act 2000 (FSMA 2000));
(c) insurers authorised by other EEA member states which may conduct insurance business in the UK on a 'freedom of services' basis or through the establishment of branches and which qualify automatically for authorisation under FSMA 2000.

In the case of members of Lloyd's, the FSA applies requirements and reporting obligations at the level of the market as a whole and on managing agents.

As well as needing permission under Part IV of FSMA 2000 to effect or carry out contracts of insurance, an insurer is likely to require additional permissions in respect of its activities relating to marketing, arranging or advising on insurance contracts[3].

---

[3] Further guidance in connection with insurance intermediaries is included in ICAEW TECH 1/06: Interim guidance for auditors of insurance intermediaries on client asset reporting requirements.

8   The principal objective of insurance regulation is to provide appropriate protection to policyholders. The principal responsibilities of the FSA are referred to in Paragraph 27 below.

9   Requirements concerning the auditors' duty to report are set out in The FSMA 2000 (Communications by Auditors) Regulations 2001. Guidance on the auditors' duty to report to the FSA (and, where relevant, to Lloyd's) in the context of current legislation is set out in the section on ISA (UK and Ireland) 250 section B in this Practice Note.

10 An insurer carrying on long-term insurance business is required by SUP 4.3.1R to appoint an actuary to perform the actuarial function. The holder of this function is required inter alia, to advise the entity's governing body on the methods and assumptions to be used for the actuarial investigation, and to carry out that investigation in accordance with the methods and assumptions decided upon by the governing body. The purpose of the investigation, which is required once in every period of twelve months and at any other time when there is to be a distribution of surplus from the long-term fund, is:

(a) to value the liabilities attributable to long-term business; and
(b) to determine any excess over those liabilities of the assets representing the long-term business fund.

11 An insurer which writes with-profits business is also required to appoint an actuary to perform the with-profits actuary function. This actuary is required, inter alia, to advise a firm's management at the appropriate level of seniority on key aspects of the discretion to be exercised in respect of with-profits business.

12 A significant part of the FSA's regulatory framework consists of provisions intended to maintain the solvency of insurers and so ensure their ability to meet future claims from policyholders. Accordingly, insurers are required to comply with statutory solvency requirements and also to submit annual regulatory returns providing information concerning the value and type of assets held, claims arising under policies written and other financial information. These annual returns are public documents.

13 Auditors of insurers need to be familiar with the relevant legal and regulatory requirements. The extent to which auditors consider compliance with regulatory requirements in the course of auditing an insurer's financial statements is discussed in the section dealing with ISA (UK and Ireland) 250 'Consideration of law and regulations'. Guidance on auditors' responsibilities in relation to regulatory reporting is contained in the section 'Reporting on regulatory returns'.

Additional Considerations relating to Lloyd's

14 The FSA oversees Lloyd's regulation to ensure consistency with general standards in financial services. Much of the Lloyd's market rule structure is embedded in a series of byelaws passed by the Council. Changes to regulatory requirements are communicated to the market by means of market bulletins.

15 Members underwrite insurance business at Lloyd's as a member of one or more syndicates, each syndicate being managed by a managing agent. Syndicates have no legal personality and are merely the vehicle through which the members underwrite insurance risk. Technically, each syndicate is an annual venture. The year during which it writes business is described as an 'underwriting year' or a

'year of account'. Members have no liability for business underwritten by the same syndicate in previous years of account unless they were members in those years or unless they have reinsured the members of that syndicate for the previous years. However, for practical business purposes, syndicates are treated as continuing from one year to the next. Lloyd's maintains central assets, including the Central Fund, which are available to meet a member's underwriting liabilities in the event of any default by the member.

16 Arrangements for conducting business at Lloyd's involve requirements for trust funds to be maintained in accordance with various trust deeds, some of which confer various powers and authorities on managing agents.

17 FSA rules require the involvement of an actuary to express an opinion on the general insurance business solvency technical provisions and to determine the life business solvency technical provisions.

18 Lloyd's corporate members are not regulated by the FSA. They are subject to Lloyd's requirements. Each Lloyd's corporate member is required to maintain appropriate assets at Lloyd's or other security in favour of Lloyd's to support insurance underwritten on its behalf at Lloyd's.

Financial statements

19 The form and content of the financial statements of UK insurers prepared under UK GAAP is governed by the CA1985, Statements of Standard Accounting Practice ('SSAPs'), Financial Reporting Standards ('FRSs') and UITF Abstracts. The prescribed format for a UK insurers' financial statements that complies with UK GAAP is set out in sections 226, 226A and 255 of, and Schedule 9A to the CA1985. In addition, financial statements of insurance companies prepared under UK GAAP are expected to be prepared in accordance with the guidance in the Statement of Recommended Practice 'Accounting for insurance business' issued by the Association of British Insurers (ABI), (the Insurance SORP). However, listed UK groups (including listed UK insurance groups) must prepare consolidated financial statements in accordance with those International Financial Reporting Standards adopted by the European Union (EU IFRSs)[4] and those parts of CA1985 applicable to companies reporting under EU IFRSs. UK companies or non listed groups, including UK insurers and insurance groups, are permitted to voluntarily adopt EU IFRSs for their financial statements.

20 If an authorised insurance company preparing financial statements under UK GAAP undertakes long-term business, computation of the technical provision for long-term business to be included in its financial statements must be made by a Fellow of the Institute or Faculty of Actuaries based on recognised actuarial methods with due regard to the actuarial principles laid down in Directive 2002/83/EC of the European Parliament and of the Council concerning life insurance. This requirement does not apply to any other technical provisions of the company or, directly, to the technical provisions shown in the financial statements of a Lloyd's corporate member. The actuary carrying out the computation (known as 'the Reporting Actuary') may, but is not required to, make a report in the financial statements relating to the provision.

---

[4] Article 4 of EC Regulation 1606/2002 as acknowledged in s227(2) CA1985 – the IAS Regulation.

Additional considerations relating to Lloyd's

21 The reporting requirements in respect of syndicate activities are set out in the Insurance Accounts Directive (Lloyd's Syndicate and Aggregate Accounts) Regulations 2004 ("the 2004 Regulations"). The 2004 Regulations require the preparation of :

(a) syndicate annual accounts in accordance with the Companies Act 1985, including Schedule 9A (as modified) showing the performance across all years of account of the syndicate during the calendar year;
(b) syndicate underwriting year accounts at the closure of a year of account (unless all the relevant members of the syndicate agree otherwise); and
(c) aggregate accounts reflecting a cumulation of the syndicate profit and loss accounts and the balance sheets prepared at (a).

In addition, the Syndicate Accounting Byelaw 2005 requires the preparation of syndicate underwriting year accounts at 31 December each year in respect of each run-off account (unless all the relevant members of the syndicate agree otherwise).

22 The requirements for the minimum form and content of syndicate underwriting year accounts (referred to at paragraph 21(b) above), together with other related financial reporting requirements, are set out in the Syndicate Accounting Byelaw 2005. With effect from 1 January 2005, syndicate annual accounts (referred to at paragraph 21(a) above), must be prepared in accordance with UK GAAP on an earned basis of recognition.

23 Since each annual venture is treated as having a unique constitution, a mechanism is necessary to enable each such venture to close, normally at the end of three years. Estimated outstanding liabilities as at the date of closure are reinsured, in consideration for a premium, by a subsequent year of account of the same or another syndicate. This reinsurance arrangement is known as a 'reinsurance to close' ("RITC").

24 In certain circumstances, the managing agent may conclude that significant uncertainties (or other factors) exist such that it is not possible to determine an appropriate premium for a reinsurance to close at the normal date of closure. Therefore, the relevant year of account is not closed but placed into run-off until such time as the managing agent concludes that this requirement can be satisfied. Technical provisions will be determined for each run-off account and carried forward until the year of account is closed or all its liabilities discharged.

25 Where the Lloyd's corporate member is a UK company it is required to prepare its financial statements in accordance with the CA1985 applicable to UK insurance companies whether drawn up in accordance with IFRS or UK GAAP.

Financial Services and Markets Act 2000

26 FSMA 2000 sets out the high level regulatory framework for the financial sector more generally and not just insurers. Appendix 2 sets out the main parts of FSMA 2000 relevant to authorised firms[5] which are insurers.

---

[5] An entity which has been granted one of more Part IV permissions by the FSA and so is authorised under FSMA 2000 to undertake regulated activities.

The wide scope of FSMA 2000 reflects the FSA's extensive responsibilities. These are set out in FSMA 2000 as regulatory objectives covering: 27

- market confidence;
- public awareness;
- the protection of consumers; and
- the reduction of financial crime

FSMA 2000 covers not only the regulation and supervision of financial sector entities but also other issues such as official listing rules, business transfers, market abuse, compensation and ombudsman schemes, investment exchanges and clearing houses. FSMA 2000 is also supported by a large number of statutory instruments. Significant components of the definition and scope of the regulatory framework are contained in the main statutory instruments.   28

Under Part X FSMA 2000 the FSA has the power to make 'rules'. The legal effect of a rule varies depending on the power under which it is made and on the language used in the rule. Rules are mandatory unless a waiver has been agreed with the FSA. If an authorised firm contravenes a rule it may be subject to enforcement action and consequent disciplinary measures under Part XIV FSMA 2000. Furthermore, in certain circumstances an authorised firm may be subject to an action for damages under s150 FSMA 2000. In contrast, guidance is generally issued to throw light on a particular aspect of regulatory requirements, and is not binding. However if an authorised firm acts in accordance with it in the circumstances contemplated by that guidance, the FSA will proceed on the basis that the authorised firm has complied with the rule to which the guidance relates.   29

Rules made by the FSA and associated guidance are set out in the FSA Handbook of Rules and Guidance ('the FSA Handbook') (see Appendix 3). The main FSA systems and control requirements are set out in the Senior management arrangements, systems and controls element of the high level standards block of the FSA Handbook ('SYSC').   30

It is clearly unrealistic to expect all members of an audit engagement team to have detailed knowledge of the entire FSA Handbook; rather ISA (UK and Ireland) 250 Section B requires the level of knowledge to be commensurate with an individual's role and responsibilities in the audit process. ISA (UK and Ireland) 220 requires the auditor to establish procedures to facilitate consultation and, thereby, to draw on the collective expertise and specialist technical knowledge of those beyond the engagement team of the auditor.   31

Prudential requirements

Insurers are subject to certain prudential requirements which are detailed in IPRU(INS)[6], which set out the reporting requirements, certain of the rules relating to long-term insurance business and various definitions, and GENPRU[7], INSPRU[8] and SYSC[9], which set out the rules and guidance on the assessment of risk, capital requirements and capital resources.   32

[6] *Interim Prudential Sourcebook for Insurers.*

[7] *General Prudential Sourcebook.*

[8] *Insurance Prudential Sourcebook.*

[9] *Senior management arrangements, systems and controls.*

33 A significant part of the FSA's regulatory framework consists of provisions intended to maintain the solvency of insurers and so ensure their ability to meet future claims from policyholders. An insurer must maintain Capital Resources equal to or in excess of its Capital Resources Requirement at all times. In order to monitor solvency and assess other risks and exposures, insurers are required to submit returns to the FSA providing:

- information concerning the value and type of assets held, claims arising under policies written and other financial information;
- the determination of the Individual Capital Assessment (an unaudited return not available for public inspection); and
- where applicable, the group capital adequacy calculation.

Reporting direct to the FSA – statutory right and duty

34 Under FSMA 2000 (Communications by Auditors) Regulations 2001 (SI 2001/2587) the auditor of an authorised firm or the auditor of an entity closely linked to an authorised firm who is also the auditor of that authorised firm has a statutory duty to communicate matters of material significance to the FSA. Under section 340 FSMA 2000 'the auditor' is defined as one required to be appointed under FSA 'rules' or appointed as a result of another enactment. In addition section 342 FSMA 2000 provides that no duty to which the auditor is subject shall be contravened by communicating in good faith to the FSA any information or opinion on a matter that the auditor reasonably believes is relevant to any functions of the FSA. There is a similar right and duty of the auditor of a Lloyd's syndicate or corporate member to report direct to Lloyd's by the undertaking required from the auditor of a Lloyd's syndicate or corporate member by the Lloyd's Membership Byelaw No 5 of 2005 and the Lloyd's Audit Arrangements Byelaw 1998. These duties do not require auditors of insurers to undertake additional work directed at identifying matters to report over and above the work necessary to fulfil their obligations to report on financial statements and regulatory returns. Guidance on the identification of matters to be reported to the regulators is set out in the section dealing with ISA (UK and Ireland) 250 Section B.

Communication between the FSA and the auditor

35 Within the legal constraints that apply, the FSA may pass on to the auditor any information which it considers relevant to his function. Auditors are bound by the confidentiality provisions set out in Part XXIII of FSMA 2000 (Public record, disclosure of information and co-operation) Regulations in respect of confidential information received from the FSA. An auditor may not pass on such confidential information, even to the entity being audited, without lawful authority (for example, if an exception applies under FSMA 2000 (Disclosure of Confidential Information) Regulations 2001) or without the consent of the person from whom the information was received and, if different, to whom the information relates.

36 Before communicating to an authorised firm any information received from the FSA, the auditor considers carefully whether:

- the auditor has received the FSA's express permission to communicate a particular item of information;
- the information relates to any other party whose permission may need to be obtained before disclosure can be made;
- the information was received by FSA in a capacity other than discharging its functions under FSMA 2000 or from another regulator (in which case the

auditor may either be prohibited from disclosure or may need permission of the party which provided the information to that regulator).

The auditors may however disclose to an authorised firm information they have communicated to the FSA except where to do so would have the effect of disclosing information communicated to them by the FSA. If there is any doubt the auditor considers the matters above.

37 Matters communicated by the FSA during any bilateral meeting may be conveyed by those representatives of the auditor who were present at the meeting (or otherwise received the communication directly) to other partners, directors and employees of the auditor who need to know the information in connection with the auditor's performance of its duties relating to that authorised firm without the FSA's express permission. However, in the interests of prudence and transparency the auditors inform the FSA that they will be discussing the issues covered with colleagues.

38 Where the FSA passes to the auditors information which it considers is relevant to their function, they consider its implications in the context of their work and may need to amend their approach accordingly. However the fact that they may have been informed of such a matter by the regulator does not, of itself, require auditors to change the scope of the work, nor does it necessarily require them actively to search for evidence in support of the situation communicated by the regulator.

39 The auditor is required to cooperate with the FSA (SUP 3.8.2R). This may involve attending meetings and providing the FSA with information about the authorised firm that the FSA may reasonably request in discharging its functions. For example this can arise in relation to FSA ARROW II risk assessments.

40 The auditor must notify the FSA without delay if the auditor is removed from office, resigns before the term of office expires or is not reappointed by the authorised firm. Notification to the FSA includes communicating any matters connected with this event that the auditor considers ought to be drawn to the FSA's attention or a statement that there are no such matters (section 344 FSMA 2000 and SUP 3.8.11R and 12R).

The audit of financial statements

ISAs (UK and Ireland) apply to the conduct of all audits in respect of accounting periods commencing on or after 15 December 2004. This includes audits of the financial statements of insurers. The purpose of the following paragraphs is to identify the special considerations arising from the application of certain 'bold letter' requirements to the audit of insurers, and to suggest ways in which these can be addressed (extracts from ISAs (UK and Ireland) are indicated by grey-shaded boxes below). This Practice Note does not contain commentary on all of the bold letter requirements included in the ISAs (UK and Ireland) and reading it should not be seen as an alternative to reading the relevant ISAs (UK and Ireland) in their entirety. In addition, where no special considerations arise from a particular ISA (UK and Ireland), no material is included.

ISA (UK and IRELAND) 200: OBJECTIVE AND GENERAL PRINCIPLES GOVERNING THE AUDIT OF THE FINANCIAL STATEMENTS

Background note

The purpose of this ISA (UK and Ireland) is to establish standards and provide guidance on the objective and general principles governing an audit of financial statements.

The auditor should plan and perform an audit with an attitude of professional scepticism, recognising that circumstances may exist that cause the financial statements to be materially misstated. (paragraph 6)

41 Auditing standards include a requirement for auditors to comply with relevant ethical requirements relating to audit engagements. In the United Kingdom, the auditor should comply with the APB's Ethical Standards and relevant ethical guidance relating to the work of auditors issued by the auditor's professional body. A fundamental principle is that practitioners should not accept or perform work which they are not competent to undertake. The importance of technical competence is also underlined in the Auditor's Code[10], issued by the APB, which states that the necessary degree of professional skill demands an understanding of financial reporting and business. Practitioners should not undertake the audit of insurers unless they are satisfied that they have, or can obtain, the necessary level of competence.

Independence

42 Independence issues can be complex for the auditor of an insurer because of insurance contracts that the auditor or its partners and staff may have with the insurer. The auditor makes careful reference to the APB's Ethical Standard 2 – financial, business, employment and personal relationships.

ISA (UK and IRELAND) 210: TERMS OF AUDIT ENGAGEMENTS

Background note

The purpose of this ISA (UK and Ireland) is to establish standards and provide guidance on agreeing the terms of the engagement with the client.

The auditor and the client should agree on the terms of the engagement. (paragraph 2)

The terms of the engagement should be recorded in writing. (paragraph 2-1)

---

[10] This is appended to the APB's Scope and Authority of Pronouncements.

> The auditor should ensure that the engagement letter documents and confirms the auditor's acceptance of the appointment, and includes a summary of the responsibilities of those charged with governance and of the auditor, the scope of the engagement and the form of any reports. (paragraph 5-1)

The auditor may choose to combine into a single letter the terms of engagement in relation to the audit of regulatory returns and the group capital adequacy return (if applicable). Matters which the auditor may decide to refer to in the engagement letter are as follows: 43

- the responsibility of the directors/senior management to comply with applicable FSMA 2000 legislation and FSA Handbook rules and guidance including the need to keep the FSA informed about the affairs of the entity;
- the statutory right and duty of the auditor to report direct to the FSA in certain circumstances (see the section of this Practice Note relating to ISA (UK and Ireland) 250 Section B);
- the requirement to cooperate with the auditor (SUP 3.6.1R). This includes taking steps to ensure that, where applicable, each of its appointed representatives and material outsourcers gives the auditor the same right of access to records, information and explanations as the authorised firm itself is required to provide the auditor (s341 FSMA 2000 and SUP 3.6.2G to 3.6.8G). It a criminal offence for an insurer or its officers, controllers or managers to provide false or misleading information to the auditor (s346 FSMA 2000);
- the need for the insurer to make the auditor aware when it appoints a third party (including another department or office of the same audit firm) to review, investigate or report on any aspects of its business activities that may be relevant to the audit of the financial statements and to provide the auditor with copies of reports by such a third party promptly after their receipt.

In this connection the auditor is aware that: 44

- the FSA does not need to approve the appointment of an auditor but may seek to satisfy itself that an auditor appointed by a firm is independent and has the necessary skills, resources and experience (SUP 3.4.4G, 3.4.7R and 3.4.8G);
- the auditor is required to cooperate with the FSA (SUP3.8.2R); and
- the auditor must notify the FSA if the auditor ceases to be the auditor of an authorised firm.

Additional considerations relating to Lloyd's

Further matters specific to Lloyd's syndicates and Lloyd's corporate members which may be dealt with in the engagement letter include: 45

- the responsibilities of the directors of the managing agent or Lloyd's corporate member to keep Lloyd's informed about the affairs of these businesses;
- the auditors' additional duty to report matters to Lloyd's of which they have become aware in their capacity as auditors which may be of material significance to Lloyd's in its capacity as market supervisor; and
- the auditors' duty to provide access to their working papers by the Council of Lloyd's in certain circumstances.

The engagement letter for a Lloyd's syndicate also refers to the aspects of the auditors' responsibilities, as set out in the Audit Arrangements Byelaw ("AAB") as the syndicate's 'recognised accountant', namely: 46

(a) to report on the syndicate's financial statements and related matters;
(b) to report on any syndicate Annual Return as required by or under the Solvency Byelaw; and
(c) as reporting accountant, if appointed by the Council of Lloyd's to report on other specified matters.

ISA (UK and IRELAND) 220: QUALITY CONTROL FOR AUDITS OF HISTORICAL FINANCIAL INFORMATION

Background note

The purpose of this ISA (UK and Ireland) is to establish standards and provide guidance on specific responsibilities of firm personnel regarding quality control procedures for audits of historical financial information, including audits of financial statements.

Reference should also be made to ISQC 1 (UK and Ireland) – Quality Control for Firms that Perform Audits and Reviews of Historical Financial Information, and other Assurance and Related Services Engagements.

The engagement team should implement quality control procedures that are applicable to the individual audit engagement. (paragraph 2)

47 Quality control procedures cover the work of members of the engagement team with actuarial expertise or other specialist knowledge, and have regard to ISA (UK and Ireland) 620 'Using the work of an expert' in relation to the involvement of external actuarial or other expertise.

The engagement partner should be satisfied that the engagement team collectively has the appropriate capabilities, competence and time to perform the audit engagement in accordance with professional standards and regulatory and legal requirements, and to enable an auditor's report that is appropriate in the circumstances to be issued. (paragraph 19)

48 As well as ensuring that the engagement team has an appropriate level of knowledge of the industry and its corresponding products, the engagement partner also satisfies himself that the members of the engagement team have sufficient knowledge of the regulatory framework within which insurers operate commensurate with their roles on the engagement and that, where appropriate, the team includes members with actuarial expertise or has access to external actuarial expertise appropriate to the entity's insurance business.

ISA (UK and IRELAND) 230 (Revised): AUDIT DOCUMENTATION

Background note

The purpose of this ISA (UK and Ireland) is to establish standards and provide guidance regarding documentation in the context of the audit of financial statements.

The auditor should document matters which are important in providing audit evidence to support the auditor's opinion and evidence that the audit was carried out in accordance with ISAs (UK and Ireland). (paragraph 2)

If the auditor uses in-house actuaries (employed by the audit firm) to assist in the audit process (including in the role of Reviewing Actuary described later in the section on reporting on regulatory returns), their working papers form part of the audit working papers. Where external actuaries are engaged by the auditors, the actuaries' report and notes of any meetings or discussions with them form part of the audit working papers. (See also ISA (UK and Ireland) 620 'Using the work of an expert').

ISA (UK and IRELAND) 240: THE AUDITOR'S RESPONSIBILITY TO CONSIDER FRAUD IN AN AUDIT OF FINANCIAL STATEMENTS

Background note

The purpose of this ISA (UK and Ireland) is to establish standards and provide guidance on the auditor's responsibility to consider fraud in an audit of financial statements and expand on how the standards and guidance in ISA (UK and Ireland) 315 and ISA (UK and Ireland) 330 are to be applied in relation to the risks of material misstatement due to fraud.

In planning and performing the audit to reduce audit risk to an acceptably low level, the auditor should consider the risks of material misstatements in the financial statements due to fraud. (paragraph 3)

The auditor should maintain an attitude of professional scepticism throughout the audit, recognizing the possibility that a material misstatement due to fraud could exist, notwithstanding the auditor's past experience with the entity about the honesty and integrity of management and those charged with governance. (paragraph 24)

The following are considered to be significant fraud risks which insurers may be subject to:

(a) policyholder fraud;
(b) fraud by directors and employees; and

(c) fraud by agents, intermediaries or other related parties.

51 Responsibility for the prevention and detection of fraud and error lies with those charged with governance of an insurance company and of the managing agent of a Lloyd's syndicate, even if they have delegated functions to third parties. In carrying out their responsibilities, the directors have regard to the FSA Principles for Businesses (in particular with regard to the criteria for integrity, skill, care and diligence and management and control) and to requirements issued by the Council of Lloyd's. Equivalent provisions apply to directors of managing agents.

52 Principle 3 requires a firm to take reasonable care to organise and control its affairs responsibly and effectively with adequate risk management systems. SYSC 3.2.20R(1) requires a firm to make and retain adequate records of matters and dealings (including accounting records) which are the subject of requirements and standards under the regulatory system. Whilst the inherent risk of fraud may continue to exist, the establishment of accounting and internal control systems sufficient to meet these requirements (particularly in the case of insurance companies that accept business involving both a high volume of policies and claims of comparatively low value) frequently reduces the likelihood of fraud giving rise to material misstatements in the financial statements. Guidance on the auditors' consideration of accounting systems and internal controls is provided in ISA (UK and Ireland) 315.

> The auditor should make inquiries of management, internal audit, and others within the entity as appropriate, to determine whether they have knowledge of any actual, suspected or alleged fraud affecting the entity. (paragraph 38)
>
> When obtaining an understanding of the entity and its environment, including its internal control, the auditor should consider whether the information obtained indicates that one or more fraud risk factors are present. (paragraph 48)

53 As with other entities fraud on insurers, either fraudulent financial reporting (for example the manipulation of profits or the concealment of losses) or misappropriation of assets, can occur through a combination of management fraud, employee fraud or fraud perpetrated by third parties. However, fraud risk factors particularly relevant to insurers may be due to the following:

- The commission driven nature of arrangements with many business introducers whose interests may be more focused on the volume of business and commission thereon rather than the ultimate profitability and sustainability of the business for the insurer. This may increase the risk of fraud committed by agents and intermediaries.
- The existence of very large estimated liabilities which may not crystallise for many years.
- Complex insurance and reinsurance transactions provide an opportunity to conceal inappropriate pricing of the risks transferred and to apply inappropriate accounting treatments which may have a significant impact on the results for a given period and the balance sheet position.
- The transfer of risk under a contract of insurance is not reflected in the passing of any physical asset which can make it difficult for insurers to ensure that all transactions are recorded completely and accurately.
- The nature of delegated underwriting, coupled with large amounts of cash and near liquid assets often held by agents and other intermediaries with delegated authority, increases the propensity for fraud.

- The practice of insurance contracts incepting before all of the terms are agreed and documented provides the opportunity for fraudulent manipulation of contract wordings.

The examples of weaknesses in control set out in the section on ISA (UK and Ireland) 315 below may be especially relevant when assessing fraud risk.

ISA (UK and Ireland) 240 requires auditors to give particular consideration to the likelihood of fraud in relation to the recognition of revenue. In the context of an insurer, "revenue" for this purpose may reasonably be taken as earned premiums. However auditors will also consider the likelihood of fraud in relation to the recognition of income or costs which may have a close relationship to earned premiums, such as reinsurance costs and acquisition costs. 54

Insurers frequently outsource insurance and accounting functions to service companies. Service companies are considered as agents of the insurance companies and auditors will therefore consider the equivalent risk factors for service companies as they consider for all agents. Further guidance on this issue is contained in the section dealing with ISA (UK and Ireland) 402 'Audit Considerations Relating to Entities Using Service Organisations.' 55

> When obtaining an understanding of the entity and its environment, including its internal control, the auditor should consider whether other information obtained indicates risks of material misstatement due to fraud. (paragraph 55)

The auditor considers reports or information obtained from the insurer's compliance department, legal department, and money laundering reporting officer together with reviews undertaken by third parties such as skilled person's reports prepared under s166 FSMA 2000.[11] 56

> If the auditor has identified a fraud or has obtained information that indicates that a fraud may exist, the auditor should communicate these matters as soon as practicable to the appropriate level of management. (paragraph 93)
>
> The auditor should document communications about fraud made to management, those charged with governance, regulators and others. (paragraph 109)

Reduction of financial crime is one of the FSA's statutory objectives. The FSA's rules require authorised firms to report 'significant' fraud, errors and other irregularities to the FSA (SUP 15.3.17R) (and, where applicable, to the Council of Lloyd's). The auditor is aware of the auditor's duty to report direct to FSA in certain circumstances (see the section of this Practice Note relating to ISA (UK and Ireland) 250 Section B. 57

---

[11] Under S166 FSMA 2000 provides the FSA with the power to require a firm to appoint a skilled person to provide a report on any matter that the FSA may reasonably require in connection with the exercise of the functions conferred on it by or under FSMA 2000. The requirements concerning skilled persons are set out in SUP5.

Additional considerations relating to Lloyd's

58 Examples of fraud by directors or employees of a managing agent include fraudulent recharges of agency expenses to managed syndicates and fraudulent misallocation of transactions to different years of account within those syndicates. Instances of suspected or actual fraud may involve breaches of specific requirements relating to syndicates and their managing agents as prescribed by Lloyd's in its capacity as regulator, and are likely to be regarded as being of material significance. Syndicate auditors have a duty to consider reporting all such instances to the Council of Lloyd's without delay in accordance with their undertaking given to Lloyd's. Guidance on such reporting is contained in the ISA (UK and Ireland) 250 section of this Practice Note.

ISA (UK and IRELAND) 250: SECTION A – CONSIDERATION OF LAWS AND REGULATIONS IN AN AUDIT OF FINANCIAL STATEMENTS

Background note

The purpose of this ISA (UK and Ireland) is to establish standards and provide guidance on the auditors' responsibility to consider laws and regulations in the audit of financial statements.

When designing and performing audit procedures and in evaluating and reporting the results thereof, the auditor should recognize that noncompliance by the entity with laws and regulations may materially affect the financial statements. (paragraph 2)

In accordance with ISA (UK and Ireland) 200, "Objective and General Principles Governing an Audit of Financial Statements" the auditor should plan and perform the audit with an attitude of professional scepticism recognising that the audit may reveal conditions or events that would lead to questioning whether an entity is complying with laws and regulations. (paragraph 13)

In order to plan the audit, the auditor should obtain a general understanding of the legal and regulatory framework applicable to the entity and the industry and how the entity is complying with that framework. (paragraph 15)

59 In the context of insurers, laws and regulations are central to the conduct of business if breaches would have either of the following consequences:

    (a) removal of authorisation to carry out insurance business;

    (b) the imposition of fines or restrictions on business activities whose significance is such that, where relevant, the ability of the insurer to continue as a going concern is threatened.

60 Non-compliance with laws and regulations that are central to an insurer's activities is likely to give rise to a statutory duty to report to the FSA or a duty to report to the Council of Lloyd's. Such reports are made in accordance with the requirements of ISA (UK and Ireland) 250 section B, following the guidance set out in the relevant section of this Practice Note.

61 Insurers are affected by two types of regulation which are central to their activities and of which the auditor needs to obtain a general understanding:

(a) prudential supervision; and
(b) market conduct rules.

62 The principal purpose of prudential supervision is to ensure the protection of policyholders because of the promissory nature of transactions between insurers and the public. Much of the legislation for prudential supervision is based on European Directives.

63 Prudential supervision of insurance companies with their head offices in the UK and UK branches of insurers established outside the EEA and pure reinsurers with their head office in an EEA state is carried out by the FSA under rules made by the FSA under FSMA 2000. Ongoing prudential supervision of authorised insurance companies is conducted in part by means of the annual regulatory returns submitted by all authorised insurance companies and UK branches of non-EEA companies within three months of their balance sheet date for insurers making electronic submissions (otherwise 2 months and 15 days).

64 Market conduct regulation relates to the sale of business and is primarily carried out by the FSA through its rules in respect of COB (designated investment business which includes long-term insurance investment business) and ICOB (general insurance and long-term pure protection business).

65 For Lloyd's syndicates, prudential supervision of the Lloyd's market as a whole and of managing agents is carried out by the FSA. Additional supervision of syndicates and managing agents is conducted by Lloyd's. Ongoing prudential supervision of the Lloyd's market is carried out by the FSA on a similar basis to insurance companies including the review of an annual regulatory return for the market as a whole submitted within six months of its balance sheet date.

66 There are, in addition, compensation schemes set up to protect individual policyholders for certain classes of business under the Financial Services Compensation Scheme (FSCS) (established under FSMA 2000), and the Motor Insurers' Bureau (established under the Road Traffic Act 1988). Insurers may be required to contribute to levies raised by these guarantee funds depending on the type of insurance business carried on.

67 There are also consumer affairs bodies, such as the Financial Ombudsman Service (which handles consumer complaints) and the Office of Fair Trading (a statutory body which applies to both financial services and other retail organisations).

Additional considerations relating to Lloyd's

68 In the context of Lloyd's syndicates, and their management, the principal laws and regulations are those relevant to insurers as set out above modified by the requirements prescribed by the Council of Lloyd's, non-compliance with which may reasonably be expected to result in Lloyd's exercising its powers of intervention so as to require the syndicate to cease accepting new business and procure the close of existing business on an orderly basis into a third party.

After obtaining the general understanding, the auditor should perform further audit procedures to help identify instances of non-compliance with those laws and regulations where non-compliance should be considered when preparing financial statements, specifically:

(a) Inquiring of management as to whether the entity is in compliance with such laws and regulations;
(b) Inspecting correspondence with the relevant licensing or regulatory authorities; and
(c) Enquiring of those charged with governance as to whether they are on notice of any such possible instances of non-compliance with law or regulations. (paragraph 18)

The auditor's procedures should be designed to help identify possible or actual instances of non-compliance with those laws and regulations which provide a legal framework within which the entity conducts its business and which are central to the entity's ability to conduct its business and hence to its financial statements. (paragraph 18-1)

69 Specific areas that auditors' procedures may address include the following:

- obtaining a general understanding of the legal and regulatory framework applicable to the entity and industry, and of the procedures followed to ensure compliance with the framework;
- the insurer's compliance with prudential capital requirements (including applicable group capital requirements), the results of the insurer's Individual Capital Assessment (ICA), and whether any Individual Capital Guidance has been given by the FSA;
- the insurer's compliance with the scope of its permissions or any limits that may be specified in any Permission Notice issued by the FSA;
- reviewing correspondence with the FSA and other regulators (including that relating to any FSA supervisory visits, requests for information by FSA or progress concerning FSA ARROW II risk mitigation programmes);
- holding discussions with the insurer's compliance officer and other personnel responsible for compliance;
- reviewing compliance reports prepared for the Board, audit committee and other committees;
- consideration of work on compliance matters performed by internal audit;
- where an authorised insurer is a parent company, considering the impact of breaches of local laws and regulations on the trading status of the parent company, and of the overseas subsidiary/branch if they are likely to have a material effect on the financial statements of the parent company or group. Regard is also had to the powers of intervention exercisable by the relevant regulatory authorities and the potential impact on the group financial statements.

Additional considerations relating to Lloyd's

70 The process for prudential supervision of the market means that Lloyd's centrally has responsibility for reviewing and agreeing with the managing agent for each syndicate an appropriate amount of prudential capital requirements and for determining how those requirements are to be resourced.

71 In the case of Lloyd's syndicates that undertake business outside the UK, Lloyd's co-ordinates compliance with the requirements of overseas regulatory authorities, and incorporates relevant provisions as necessary in its own regulatory requirements, thus supporting a global operating licence. Auditors of a Lloyd's syndicate

that undertakes business overseas therefore do not need to make a separate assessment of the impact of local laws and regulations over and above those specified by Lloyd's.

Money Laundering

In the UK and Ireland, when carrying out procedures for the purpose of forming an opinion on the financial statements, the auditor should be alert for those instances of possible or actual non compliance with laws and regulations that might incur obligations for partners and staff in audit firms to report money laundering offences. (paragraph 22-1)

72 Authorised firms including insurers are subject to the requirements of the Money Laundering Regulations 2003 (as amended) and the Proceeds of Crime Act 2002 as well as FSA rules. These laws and regulations require institutions to establish and maintain procedures to identify their customers, establish appropriate reporting and investigation procedures for suspicious transactions and maintain appropriate records.

73 Laws and regulations relating to money laundering are integral to the legal and regulatory framework within which insurers conduct their business. By the nature of their business, insurers are ready targets of those engaged in money laundering activities. The effect of this legislation is to make it an offence to provide assistance to those involved in money laundering and makes it an offence not to report suspicions of money laundering to the appropriate authorities, usually the Serious Organised Crime Agency ('SOCA')[12]. FSA requirements are set out in SYSC 3.2.6AR – 3.2.6JG. In this context, FSA has due regard to compliance with the relevant provisions of guidance issued by the Joint Money Laundering Steering Group ('JMLSG')(SYSC 3.2.6EG).

74 In addition to considering whether an insurer has complied with the money laundering laws and regulations, the auditor has reporting obligations under the Proceeds of Crime Act, 2002 and the Money Laundering Regulations, 2003 (as amended) to report knowledge or suspicion of money laundering offences, including those arising from fraud and theft, to SOCA. The auditor is aware of the prohibition on 'tipping off' when discussing money laundering matters with the insurer. Given the nature of insurance business and the likely frequency of needing to report to SOCA the auditor is aware of the short-form[13] of reporting to SOCA that can be used in appropriate circumstances to report minor and usually numerous items. Further guidance for auditors is provided in Practice Note 12 Money Laundering – Interim Guidance for Auditors in the United Kingdom (Revised).

75 The auditor, in the context of money laundering, is aware of the auditor's duty to report direct to FSA in certain circumstances (see the section of this Practice Note relating to ISA (UK and Ireland) 250 Section B).

---

[12] *Previously National Criminal Intelligence Service ('NCIS').*

[13] *These are termed limited intelligence value reports.*

ISA (UK and IRELAND) 250: SECTION B – THE AUDITOR'S RIGHT AND DUTY TO REPORT TO REGULATORS IN THE FINANCIAL SECTOR

> The auditor of a regulated entity should bring information of which the auditor has become aware in the ordinary course of performing work undertaken to fulfil the auditor's audit responsibilities to the attention of the appropriate regulator without delay when:
>
> (a) The auditor concludes that it is relevant to the regulator's functions having regard to such matters as may be specified in statute or any related regulations; and
> (b) In the auditor's opinion there is reasonable cause to believe it is or may be of material significance to the regulator. (paragraph 2)

> Where an apparent breach of statutory or regulatory requirements comes to the auditor's attention, the auditor should:
>
> (a) Obtain such evidence as is available to assess its implications for the auditor's reporting responsibilities;
> (b) Determine whether, in the auditor's opinion, there is reasonable cause to believe that the breach is of material significance to the regulator; and
> (c) Consider whether the apparent breach is criminal conduct that gives rise to criminal property and, as such, should be reported to the specified authorities. (paragraph 39)

Auditors' duty to report to the FSA

76 Under the FSMA 2000 (Communication by Auditors) Regulations 2001 (the 2001 Regulations), auditors have duties in certain circumstances to make reports to the FSA. **The 2001 Regulations do not require auditors to perform any additional audit work as a result of the statutory duty nor are auditors required specifically to seek out breaches of the requirements applicable to a particular authorised person.** Information and opinions to be communicated are those meeting the criteria set out below which relate to matters of which the auditor[14] of the authorised person (also referred to below as a 'regulated entity') has become aware:

(i) in his capacity as auditor of the authorised person, and
(ii) if he is also the auditor of a person who has close links with the authorised person, in his capacity as auditor of that person.

77 The criteria for determining the matters to be reported are as follows:

(i) the auditor reasonably believes that there is, or has been, or may be, or may have been a contravention of any 'relevant requirement' that applies to the person[15] concerned and that contravention may be of material significance to the FSA in determining whether to exercise, in relation to that person, any of its functions under FSMA 2000, or

---

[14] An 'auditor' is defined for this purpose in the Regulations as a person who is, or has been, an auditor of an authorised person appointed under, or as a result of, a statutory provision including Section 340 FSMA 2000.

[15] In this context the person is an 'Authorised Person'.

(ii) the auditor reasonably believes that the information on, or his opinion on, those matters may be of material significance to the FSA in determining whether the person concerned satisfies and will continue to satisfy the 'Threshold Conditions'[16], or

(iii) the auditor reasonably believes that the person concerned is not, may not be, or may cease to be, a going concern, or

(iv) the auditor is precluded from stating in his report that the annual accounts have been properly prepared in accordance with the CA 1985 or, where applicable, give a true and fair view or have been prepared in accordance with relevant rules and legislation.

78 In relation to 77 (i) above, 'relevant requirement' is a requirement by or under FSMA 2000 which relates to authorisation under FSMA 2000 or to the carrying on of any regulated activity. This includes not only relevant statutory instruments but also the FSA's rules (other than the Listing Rules) including the Principles for Businesses. The duty to report also covers any requirement imposed by or under any other Act[17] the contravention of which constitutes an offence which the FSA has the power to prosecute under FSMA 2000.

In relation to 77 (ii) above the duty to report relates to either information or opinions held by the auditor which may be of significance to the FSA in determining whether the regulated entity satisfies and will continue to satisfy the Threshold Conditions. The duty to report opinions, as well as information, allows for circumstances where adequate information on a matter may not readily be forthcoming from the regulated entity, and where judgments need to be made.

Material significance

79 Determining whether a contravention of a relevant requirement or a Threshold Condition is reportable under the 2001 Regulations involves consideration both of whether the auditor 'reasonably believes' and that the matter in question 'is, or is likely to be, of material significance' to the regulator.

80 The 2001 Regulations do not require auditors to perform any additional audit work as a result of the statutory duty nor are auditors required specifically to seek out breaches of the requirements applicable to a particular regulated entity. However, in circumstances where auditors identify that a reportable matter may exist, they carry out such extra work, as they consider necessary, to determine whether the facts and circumstances cause them 'reasonably to believe' that the matter does in fact exist. It should be noted that the auditors' work does not need to prove that the reportable matter exists.

81 ISA (UK and Ireland) 250 Section B requires that, where an apparent breach of statutory or regulatory requirements comes to the auditors' attention, they obtain such evidence as is available to assess its implications for their reporting responsibilities and determine whether, in their opinion, there is reasonable cause to believe that the breach has occurred and that it relates to a matter that is of material significance to the regulator.

---

[16] The Threshold Conditions are set out in Schedule 6 to FSMA 2000 and represent the minimum conditions that a firm is required to satisfy and continue to satisfy to be given and to retain Part IV permission. The FSA's guidance on compliance with the Threshold Conditions is contained in the COND module of the FSA Handbook.

[17] Examples include the Proceeds of Crime Act 2002 and prescribed regulations relating to money laundering.

82 Material significance' is defined by paragraph 14 of ISA (UK and Ireland) 250 Section B as follows:

"A matter or group of matters is normally of material significance to a regulator's function when, due either to its nature or its potential financial impact, it is likely of itself to require investigation by the regulator."

83 'Material significance' does not have the same meaning as materiality in the context of the audit of financial statements. Whilst a particular event may be trivial in terms of its possible effect on the financial statements of an entity, it may be of a nature or type that is likely to change the perception of the regulator. For example, a failure to reconcile client money accounts may not be significant in financial terms but would have a significant effect on the FSA's consideration of whether the regulated entity was satisfactorily controlled and was behaving properly towards its customers.

84 The determination of whether a matter is, or is likely to be, of material significance to the FSA inevitably requires auditors to exercise their judgment. In forming such judgments, auditors need to consider not simply the facts of the matter but also their implications. In addition, it is possible that a matter, which is not materially significant in isolation, may become so when other possible breaches are considered.

85 The auditor of a regulated entity bases his judgment of 'material significance' to the FSA solely on his understanding of the facts of which he is aware without making any assumptions about the information available to the FSA in connection with any particular regulated entity.

86 Minor breaches of the FSA's rules that, for example, are unlikely to jeopardise the entity's assets or amount to misconduct or mismanagement would not normally be of 'material significance'. ISA (UK and Ireland) 250 Section B however requires auditors of regulated entities, when reporting on their financial statements, to review information obtained in the course of the audit and to assess whether the cumulative effect is of 'material significance' such as to give rise to a duty to report to the regulator. In circumstances where auditors are uncertain whether they may be required to make a report or not, they may wish to consider whether to take legal advice.

87 On completion of his investigations, the auditor ensures that the facts and circumstances, and the basis for his conclusion as to whether these are, or are likely to be of 'material significance' to the FSA, are adequately documented such that the reasons for his decision to report or not, as the case may be, may be clearly demonstrated.

88 Whilst confidentiality is an implied term of auditors' contracts with a regulated entity, section 342 FSMA 2000 states that an auditor does not contravene that duty if he reports to the FSA information or his opinion, if he is acting in good faith and he reasonably believes that the information or opinion is relevant to any function of the FSA. The protection afforded is given in respect of information obtained in his capacity as auditor.

Conduct of the audit

89 ISA (UK and Ireland) 250 Section B requires auditors to ensure that all staff involved in the audit of a regulated entity 'have an understanding of:

(a) The provisions of applicable legislation;
(b) The regulator's rules and any guidance issued by the regulator; and
(c) Any specific requirements which apply to the particular regulated entity,

appropriate to their role in the audit and sufficient (in the context of that role) to enable them to identify situations they encounter in the course of the audit which may give reasonable cause to believe that a matter should be reported to the regulator.'

90 Understanding, commensurate with the individual's role and responsibilities in the audit process, is required of :

- the provisions of the 2001 Regulations concerning the auditors' duty to report to the regulator,
- the standards and guidance in ISA (UK and Ireland) 250 Section B, and in this section of this Practice Note,
- relevant sections of the FSA Handbook including the Principles for Businesses and the Threshold Conditions; and
- in the context of Lloyd's syndicates, the AAB, the relevant requirements established by the Council of Lloyd's.

91 The auditor includes procedures within his planning process to ensure that members of the audit team have such understanding (in the context of their role) as to enable them to recognise potentially reportable matters, and that such matters are reported to the audit engagement partner without delay so that a decision may be made as to whether a duty to report arises.

92 An audit firm appointed as auditor of a regulated entity needs to have in place appropriate procedures to ensure that the audit engagement partner is made aware of any other relationship which exists between any department of the firm and the regulated entity when that relationship could affect the firm's work as auditors (this matter is covered in more detail in Appendix 2 of ISA (UK and Ireland) 250 Section B). The auditor also requests the regulated entity to advise him when it appoints a third party (including another department or office of the same firm) to review, investigate or report on any aspects of its business activities that may be relevant to the audit of the financial statements and to provide the auditor with copies of reports by such a third party promptly after their receipt. This matter may usefully be referred to in the engagement letter.

Closely linked entities

93 Where the auditor of a regulated entity is also auditor of a closely linked entity[18], a duty to report arises directly in relation to information relevant to the regulated entity of which he becomes aware in the course of his work as auditor of the closely linked entity.

94 The auditor establishes during audit planning whether the regulated entity has one or more closely linked entities of which the audit firm is also the auditor. If there are such entities the auditor considers the significance of the closely linked entities and the nature of the issues that might arise which may be of material significance to the regulator of the regulated entity. Such circumstances may involve:

- activities or uncertainties within the closely linked entity which might significantly impair the financial position of the regulated entity,
- money laundering and, if the closely linked entity is itself regulated,

---

[18] An entity has close links with an authorised person for this purpose if the entity is a:
(a) Parent undertaking of an authorised person;
(b) Subsidiary undertaking of an authorised person;
(c) Parent undertaking of a subsidiary undertaking of an authorised person; or
(d) Subsidiary undertaking of a parent undertaking of an authorised person

- matters that the auditor of the closely linked entity is intending to report to its regulator.

95 Following the risk assessment referred to in paragraph 94, the auditor of the regulated entity identifies the closely related entities for which the procedures in this paragraph are necessary. The engagement team of the regulated entity communicates to the engagement team of the selected closely linked entities the audit firm's responsibilities to report to the FSA under the 2001 Regulations and notifies the engagement team of the circumstances that have been identified which, if they exist, might be of material significance to the FSA as regulator of the regulated entity. Prior to completion the auditor of the regulated entity obtains details from the auditor of the closely linked entity of such circumstances or confirmation, usually in writing, that such circumstances do not exist. Where the closely linked entities are part of the inter-auditor group reporting process these steps can be built into that process.

96 Whilst confidentiality is an implied term of auditors' contracts with a regulated entity, section 343 FSMA 2000 states that an auditor of an entity closely linked to an authorised person who is also the auditor of that authorised person does not contravene that duty if he reports to the FSA information or his opinion, if he is acting in good faith and he reasonably believes that the information or opinion is relevant to any function of the FSA. The protection afforded is given in respect of information obtained in his capacity as auditor.

97 No duty to report is imposed on the auditor of an entity closely linked to a regulated entity who is not also auditor of the regulated entity.

98 In circumstances where he is not also the auditor of the closely linked entity, the auditor of the regulated entity decides whether there are any matters to be reported to the FSA relating to the affairs of the regulated entity in the light of the information that he receives about a closely linked entity for the purpose of auditing the financial statements of the regulated entity. If the auditor becomes aware of possible matters that may fall to be reported, he may wish to obtain further information from the management or auditor of the closely linked entity to ascertain whether the matter should be reported. To facilitate such possible discussions, at the planning stage of the audit, the auditor of the regulated entity will have considered whether arrangements need to be put in place to allow him to communicate with the management and auditor of the closely linked entity. If the auditor of the regulated entity is unable to communicate with the management and auditor of the closely linked entity to obtain further information concerning the matters he has identified he reports the matters, and that he has been unable to obtain further information, direct to the FSA.

Information received in a capacity other than as auditor

99 There may be circumstances where it is not clear whether information about a regulated entity coming to the attention of the auditor is received in the capacity of auditor or in some other capacity, for example as a general adviser to the entity. Appendix 2 to ISA (UK and Ireland) 250 Section B provides guidance as to how information obtained in non-audit work may be relevant to the auditor in the planning and conduct of the audit and the steps that need to be taken to ensure the communication of information that is relevant to the audit.

Discussing matters of material significance with the directors

The directors are the persons principally responsible for the management of the regulated entity. The auditor will therefore normally bring a matter of material significance to the attention of the directors, subject to compliance with legislation relating to "tipping off", and seek agreement on the facts and circumstances. However, ISA (UK and Ireland) 250 Section B emphasises that where the auditor concludes that a duty to report arises he should bring the matter to the attention of the regulator without undue delay. The directors may wish to report the matters identified to the FSA themselves and detail the actions taken or to be taken. Whilst such a report from the directors may provide valuable information, it does not relieve the auditor of the statutory duty to report directly to the FSA. 100

Timing of a report

The duty to report arises once the auditor has concluded that he reasonably believes that the matter is or is likely to be of material significance to the FSA's regulatory function. In reaching his conclusion the auditor may wish to take appropriate legal or other advice and consult with colleagues. 101

The report should be made without undue delay once a conclusion has been reached. Unless the matter casts doubt on the integrity of the directors this should not preclude discussion of the matter with the directors and seeking such further advice as is necessary, so that a decision can be made on whether or not a duty to report exists. Such consultations and discussions are however undertaken on a timely basis to enable the auditor to conclude on the matter without undue delay. 102

Auditors' right to report to the FSA

Section 342 FSMA 2000 provides that no duty to which an auditor of an authorised person is subject shall be contravened by communicating in good faith to the FSA information or an opinion on a matter that the auditor reasonably believes is relevant to any functions of the FSA. For this purpose, "authorised person" is deemed to include a Lloyd's syndicate. 103

The scope of the duty to report is wide particularly since, under the FSA's Principle for Businesses 11, an authorised firm must disclose to the FSA appropriately anything relating to the authorised firm of which the FSA would reasonably expect notice. However in circumstances where the auditor concludes that a matter does not give rise to a statutory duty to report but nevertheless should be brought to the attention of the regulator, in the first instance he advises the directors of his opinion. Where the auditor is unable to obtain, within a reasonable period, adequate evidence that the directors have properly informed the FSA of the matter, then the auditor makes a report to the regulator without undue delay. 104

The auditor may wish to take legal advice before deciding whether, and in what form, to exercise his right to make a report direct to the regulator in order to ensure, for example, that only relevant information is disclosed and that the form and content of his report is such as to secure the protection of FSMA 2000. However, the auditor recognises that legal advice will take time and that speed of reporting is likely to be important in order to protect the interests of customers and/or to enable the FSA to meet its statutory objectives. 105

Additional considerations relating to Lloyd's

106 Syndicate auditors need to consider whether they are under a duty or right to report on a particular matter to the FSA, to the Council of Lloyd's or to both.

107 The duty to report matters of material significance applies to all engagements carried out by recognised accountants. Recognised accountants are not required to carry out procedures to detect matters of material significance. This applies even when the recognised accountant is reporting on specific issues under paragraph 13 of the AAB such that the focus of the work undertaken is very narrow.

108 The key factor in determining when a duty arises is the existence of circumstances that would either lead to suspension of authorisation to operate in the Lloyd's market or that warrant use of Lloyd's power of intervention in an individual entity's conduct of business.

109 Under paragraph 6(6) of the AAB, any appointment of a recognised accountant shall include the consent and waiver provisions set out in Schedule 3 to the AAB. These require the syndicate's managing agent to acknowledge and declare that no duty which the recognised accountant might owe to the syndicate or managing agent concerned would be contravened by the recognised accountant communicating in good faith to the Council any information in relation to a matter of which it has become aware in the ordinary course of work undertaken to fulfil its responsibilities as syndicate auditor or reporting accountant and which it considers is relevant to any function of the Council under the Lloyd's Act 1982 or any byelaws made thereafter.

110 The undertaking given by the recognised accountant as set out in paragraph 4(3) of Schedule 2 of the AAB provides that the recognised accountant undertakes to report to the Council of Lloyd's without delay information of which it becomes aware in the ordinary course of performing either work undertaken to fulfil its audit responsibilities or work undertaken to fulfil its responsibilities as reporting accountant for a syndicate when in its opinion there is reasonable cause to believe that:

(a) the authorisation of the syndicate could be withdrawn;
(b) there is or may be a failure to fulfil relevant criteria of sound and prudent management which is or may be of material significance to Lloyd's in determining whether any of its powers of intervention should be exercised;
(c) there is or may be breach of the provisions of the Lloyd's Acts 1871 to 1982 (or related byelaws or regulations) which is likely to be of material significance to Lloyd's, such that its powers of intervention should be exercised;
(d) the continuous functioning of the syndicate may be affected; or
(e) the recognised accountant concludes that it cannot issue its report without qualifying its opinion.

111 In accordance with the undertaking given in the form set out in Schedule 2 to the AAB, the recognised accountant agrees to the extent that it may do so lawfully and ethically, to provide the Council with such information, documents and explanations in relation to matters which it has a duty to report of which it has become aware.

112 Taken together, the consent and waiver given by the managing agent of the syndicate and the undertaking given by the recognised accountant provide that a recognised accountant is able to communicate to the Council on any matters

which, in the opinion of the recognised accountant, is or may be relevant to any function of Lloyd's as regulator relating to the entity's affairs arising out of the work carried out to fulfil responsibilities as syndicate auditor or reporting accountant. However, the recognised accountant is not protected from any breach of duty if, in making a report to the Council, the reporting accountant does not act in good faith. Accordingly, recognised accountants may wish to take appropriate legal or other professional advice before taking the decision whether, and if so, in what manner, to report to the Council.

Furthermore, the recognised accountant undertakes to report information of which he becomes aware in the ordinary course of performing the work carried out to fulfil responsibilities as syndicate auditor or reporting accountant which relates to any other entity regulated by the Council. This extends to any other entity having close links arising from a control relationship with the entity in relation to which the recognised accountant is performing that work. 113

If the recognised accountant, after becoming aware of a matter giving rise to a statutory duty to report, fails to report either without delay or at all, the Council can take action under paragraph 5(3) of the AAB to remove them from the list of recognised accountants. Action could also be taken by the recognised accountants' own regulatory body. 114

The Council accords particular importance to timely notification of matters giving rise to such a report to the Council by recognised accountants. ISA (UK and Ireland) 250 acknowledges that recognised accountants will normally seek evidence to assess the implications of a suspected breach before reporting a matter. Once they have identified information as being subject to the duty to report, ISA (UK and Ireland) 250 requires them to bring it to the attention of the regulator without delay. Recognised accountants may fail to discharge their duty to report to the Council if they wait until giving their formal opinion on the financial statements of the syndicate or (in their capacity as reporting accountants on syndicates appointed under paragraph 13 of the AAB) on other ad hoc reports, or if they agree to delay making a report until management has had the opportunity to take remedial action. 115

The auditors of a Lloyd's syndicate is required under paragraph 9 of the AAB to give notice to Lloyd's of their resignation, removal or retirement and under paragraph 10 of the AAB such notice shall be accompanied by a statement signed by the auditor to the effect that there are no circumstances connected with their ceasing to hold office which they consider should be brought to the attention of the members of the syndicate or to the managing agent or by a statement by the auditor specifying all such circumstances. In addition the auditor of a Lloyd's syndicate is required to notify the FSA of their resignation, removal or retirement as set out above. 116

Auditors of Lloyd's corporate members are required by the Lloyd's Membership Byelaw to give an undertaking to Lloyd's that includes the following clause: 117

'The auditor undertakes to use its best endeavours, to the extent that it may do so lawfully and ethically, having regard to any relevant guidance on confidentiality to provide to the Council such information or opinions in relation to matters of which it has become aware in its capacity as auditor of the Lloyd's corporate member for the purpose of the exercise by the Council of powers contained in Lloyd's Acts 1871 to 1982 or in byelaws or regulations made thereunder whether or not in respect to a request by or under the authority of the Council. Therefore, auditors of a Lloyd's corporate member need to consider whether they have a duty or right to report a particular matter to Lloyd's'.

118 Auditors of Lloyd's corporate members are not required to carry out procedures to detect matters that may be of material significance to Lloyd's.

119 The key factor in determining whether a duty to report to Lloyd's arises is the existence of circumstances that would either lead to suspension of the Lloyd's corporate member's authorisation to operate in the Lloyd's market or warrant use of Lloyd's power of intervention in the Lloyd's corporate member's conduct of business.

120 The undertaking for a Lloyd's corporate member does not specify the matters described above. However, if the auditor concludes that he cannot issue his report without qualifying his opinion then a duty to report would arise. Reference to an emphasis of matter without qualification of the opinion expressed does not of itself give rise to a duty to report to Lloyd's: however, the factors giving rise to an emphasis of matter may themselves do so.

121 The auditor is not protected from any breach of duty if, in making a report to the Council, the auditor does not act in good faith. Accordingly, the auditor may wish to take appropriate legal or other professional advice before taking the decision whether, and if so, in what manner, to report to the Council.

122 The duty to report to Lloyd's for auditors of Lloyd's corporate members does not extend to any other entity that has close links with the Lloyd's corporate member.

123 The Council accords particular importance to timely notification of matters giving rise to such a report to the Council by auditors of Lloyd's corporate members. ISA (UK and Ireland) 250 acknowledges that auditors will normally seek evidence to assess the implications of a suspected breach before reporting a matter. Once they have identified information as being subject to the duty to report, ISA (UK and Ireland) 250 requires them to bring it to the attention of the regulator without delay. Auditors may fail to discharge their duty to report to the Council if they wait until giving their formal opinion on the financial statements of the corporate member or on other ad hoc reports, or if they agree to delay making a report until management has had the opportunity to take remedial action.

ISA (UK and IRELAND) 300: PLANNING AN AUDIT OF FINANCIAL STATEMENTS

Background note

The purpose of this ISA (UK and Ireland) is to establish standards and provide guidance on the considerations and activities applicable to planning an audit of financial statements. This ISA (UK and Ireland) is framed in the context of recurring audits. In addition, matters the auditor considers in initial audit engagements are included in paragraphs 28 and 29.

The auditor should plan the audit so that the engagement will be performed in an effective manner. (paragraph 2)

> The auditor should establish the overall audit strategy for the audit. (paragraph 8)
>
> The auditor should develop an audit plan for the audit in order to reduce audit risk to an acceptably low level. (paragraph 13)

In planning the audit of an insurer, the auditor obtains a detailed understanding of the particular types of insurance business undertaken. The planning process includes discussion with the insurer's management and, in particular may include those with responsibility for: 124

- determining, implementing and monitoring underwriting policy;
- technical provisions;
- managing investments; and
- compliance and regulation.

Matters the auditor of an insurer may consider as part of the planning process for the audit of the financial statements include: 125

- the nature and scope of the insurer's business;
- the insurer's relationships with the FSA and any other regulators;
- changes in applicable laws, regulations and accounting requirements; and
- issues relating to the auditor's statutory duty to report.

Guidance on the first three matters is included in the section on ISA (UK and Ireland) 315 and on the fourth matter in the section on ISA (UK and Ireland) 250 section B.

In addition, particular issues likely to require consideration in planning the audit are: 126

(a) the need to involve specialists. The nature and complexity of insurance businesses increase the likelihood that auditors may consider it necessary, in order to obtain sufficient appropriate evidence on which to base their report, to involve specialists in the audit process. For example, auditors may wish to rely on the work of an actuary or a statistician to assist their consideration of an insurer's technical provisions. Similarly, the application of relevant tax legislation is likely to be complex, and hence auditors may wish to involve a tax specialist to assist the consideration of provisions for corporation and other taxes included in an insurer's financial statements. Other specialists the auditor may consider involving include regulatory, investment and systems specialists.
Consequently, auditors of an insurer consider the need to involve such specialists at an early stage in planning their work. Where such specialists are to be used, they may take part in discussions with the insurer's management and staff, in order to assist in the development of knowledge and understanding relating to the insurer's business. As part of the planning process the scope of work of the actuarial members of the audit team (or if applicable external actuarial advisors) and the form and content of their working papers and reports (in respect of external actuarial advisors) is agreed in advance.
(b) the effect of delegated authorities granted by the insurer, and the sources of evidence available to the auditors for transactions undertaken by those to whom such authority has been given. Auditors of insurers consider the implications of delegated authorities in planning their work. This may include the outsourcing of certain functions, such as investment management or the delegation of authority to underwrite and/or administer business, and to process and/or settle claims.

127 In the case of a company reporting under UK financial reporting standards undertaking long-term insurance business (other than a Lloyd's corporate member), its Reporting Actuary plays a central role in advising the company's board on the determination of the long-term business technical provision disclosed in its financial statements. Auditors discuss elements of their audit plan with the Reporting Actuary, in order to ensure that their audit procedures have regard to the Reporting Actuary's work. Where the company appoints a separate actuary to fulfil the duties of the actuarial function holder or the with-profits actuary in relation to the company's regulatory obligations, the auditors also consider the need for liaison with these individuals. Further guidance on the distinction between the Reporting Actuary and the actuarial function holder and with-profits actuary is contained in the section of this Practice Note dealing with ISA (UK and Ireland) 620 'Using the work of an expert'.

128 It is normally advantageous for the Reviewing Actuary to be involved in the planning of the audit of the financial statements. In any case, the scope of the work to be performed for the statutory audit and the audit of the regulatory return by the Reviewing Actuary is agreed and documented during the planning stages of the audit.

129 In view of their responsibilities to report on regulatory returns, auditors of authorised insurers plan their work so as to carry out procedures necessary both to form an opinion on the financial statements and to report on matters included in the regulatory returns in an efficient and effective manner.

Additional considerations relating to Lloyd's

130 Syndicate auditors plan their work so as to carry out procedures necessary both to form an opinion on the financial statements and to report separately as to whether the procedures and controls provide assurance that:

- underwriting members' personal accounts and syndicate MAPA accounts have been prepared in accordance with the Syndicate Accounting Byelaw; and
- net results shown in underwriting members' personal accounts and syndicate MAPA accounts have been calculated in accordance with the applicable agency agreements.

131 Much of the business conducted in the Lloyd's market uses central services in areas such as policy preparation, claims adjustment and transaction settlement. The service provider's Independent Accountant's Report on the operation of systems of control relates to certain of the relevant accounting information systems. As part of audit planning syndicate auditors consider the extent to which they intend to place reliance on such reports.

ISA (UK and IRELAND) 315: OBTAINING AN UNDERSTANDING OF THE ENTITY AND ITS ENVIRONMENT AND ASSESSING THE RISKS OF MATERIAL MISSTATEMENT

Background note

The purpose of this ISA (UK and Ireland) is to establish standards and to provide guidance on obtaining an understanding of the entity and its environment, including its internal control, and on assessing the risks of material misstatement in a financial statement audit.

132 Insurers can be complex and the auditor seeks to understand the business and the regulatory regime in which they operate. Generally, there is a close relationship between planning and obtaining an understanding of the business and the control environment, which is covered more fully below.

The auditor should obtain an understanding of relevant industry, regulatory, and other external factors including the applicable financial reporting framework. (paragraph 22)

The auditor should obtain an understanding of the nature of the entity. (paragraph 25)

133 The extent of knowledge required by the auditor in order to understand the business will vary according to the complexity of the business. This understanding addresses both external factors which affect the business and internal factors relating to the business itself.

134 When performing procedures to obtain an understanding of the insurer's business, the auditor considers:

- the methods by which business is transacted including whether the insurer participates with others in contracts for large commercial risks, and if so whether it transacts business as 'leader' in such contracts or as a 'follower';
- the characteristics of its insurance products, including those written in previous years where exposure remains;
- the introduction of new categories of products or customers or distribution channels;
- the reinsurance arrangements;
- the complexity of the insurer's information systems;
- the legal and operational structure of the insurer;
- the number and location of branches;
- the regulatory capital position;
- a change in the market environment (for example, a marked increase in competition);
- relevant economic developments;
- developments in relevant legislation and changes resulting from new judicial decisions.

135 Insurance policies written in previous years may continue to have an impact upon insurers' financial statements in subsequent years. For example, for general insurance

business the terms of the insurance cover provided and the reinsurance arrangements in force in a previous year are factors involved in the determination of technical provisions not only in the year in which the claims are incurred, but also in subsequent periods if the original estimates of the claims in question change. Similarly for life assurance business guarantees and options and other policyholder promises made on the issue of policies in prior years will be one of the key factors in determining estimates for related technical provisions.

136 In obtaining an understanding of the regulatory factors the auditor considers:

- any formal communications between the FSA in its capacity as the regulator and the insurer, including any new or interim risk assessments issued by the FSA and the results of any other supervisory visits conducted by the FSA;
- the contents of any recent reports prepared by 'skilled persons' under s.166 FSMA 2000 together with any correspondence, minutes or notes of meetings relevant to any recent skilled persons' report;
- any formal communications between the insurer and other regulators;
- discussions with the insurer's compliance officer together with others responsible for monitoring regulatory compliance.

> The auditor should obtain an understanding of the entity's selection and application of accounting policies and consider whether they are appropriate for its business and consistent with the applicable financial reporting framework and accounting policies used in the relevant industry. (paragraph 28)

137 Accounting policies of particular relevance may include those in relation to insurance and investment contracts, embedded derivatives in insurance contracts, deferred acquisition costs, classification of assets and liabilities (and thereby their measurement) and revenue recognition (including investment management service contracts). The auditor undertakes procedures to consider whether the policies adopted are in compliance with applicable accounting standards and gains an understanding of the procedures, systems and controls applied to maintain compliance with them.

> The auditor should obtain an understanding of the entity's objectives and strategies, and the related business risks that may result in material misstatement of the financial statements. (paragraph 30)

138 It is important for the auditor to understand the multi-dimensional nature and extent of the financial and business risks which are integral to the environment, and how the insurer's systems record and address these risks. Although they may apply to varying degrees, the risks include (but are not limited to):

- underwriting or insurance risk: which is inherent in any insurance business but will be influenced by, for example, the classes of business underwritten, new products or services introduced and guarantees given;
- credit risk: at its simplest, this is the risk that a third party will be unable to meet its obligations (for example, recoveries from reinsurers);
- liquidity risk: the risk that arises from the possibility that an insurer has insufficient liquid funds to meet claims;
- interest rate risk: the risk that arises where there is a mismatch between the interest rate reset dates or bases used for asset and liability measurement;
- currency risk: the risk that arises from the mismatching of assets, liabilities and commitments denominated in different currencies;

- market risk: the risk that changes in the value of assets, liabilities and commitments will occur as a result of movements in relative prices (for example, as a result of changes in the market price of tradeable assets);
- operational risk: the risk of loss, arising from inadequate or failed internal processes, people or systems or from external events, including legal risk; and
- regulatory risk: the risk of public censure, fines (together with related compensation payments) and restriction or withdrawal of authorisation to conduct some or all of the insurer's activities. In the UK this may arise from enforcement activity by the FSA.

Failure to manage the risks outlined above can also cause serious damage to an insurer's reputation, potentially leading to loss of confidence in the insurer's business (this is sometimes referred to as reputational risk).

> The auditor should obtain an understanding of the measurement and review of the entity's financial performance (paragraph 35).

139 The auditor obtains an understanding of the measures used by management to review the insurer's performance. Further guidance on key performance indicators is given in the section on ISA (UK and Ireland) 520.

> The auditor should obtain an understanding of internal control relevant to the audit. (paragraph 41)
>
> The auditor should obtain an understanding of the control environment. (paragraph 67)

140 The quality of the overall control environment is dependent upon management's attitude towards the operation of controls. A positive attitude may be evidenced by an organisational framework which enables proper segregation of duties and delegation of control functions and which encourages failings to be reported and corrected. Thus, where a lapse in the operation of a control is treated as a matter of concern, the control environment will be stronger and will contribute to effective control systems; whereas a weak control environment will undermine detailed controls, however well designed. The systems of control need to have regard to the requirements of SYSC and PRIN as well as the provisions of IPRU(INS), INSPRU andGENPRU. Although the directors are required to certify that they are satisfied that throughout the financial year the insurer has complied in all material respects with these requirements, auditors of insurers do not have responsibility for reporting on whether systems of control meet regulatory requirements.

141 The FSA requires authorised firms, including insurers, to maintain systems and controls appropriate for its business[19]. These include (but are not limited to):

- clear and appropriate reporting lines which are communicated within the insurer;
- appropriate controls to ensure compliance with laws and regulations (this may mean a separate Compliance function);
- appropriate risk assessment process;

---

[19] *Most FSA systems and control requirements are set out in SYSC, but additional requirements relating to prudential matters also exist in GENPRU and INSPRU.*

- appropriate management information;
- controls to ensure suitability of staff;
- controls to manage tensions arising out of remuneration policies;
- documented and tested business continuity plans;
- documented business plans or strategies;
- an internal audit function (where appropriate);
- an audit committee (where appropriate); and
- appropriate record keeping arrangements.

142 Systems of internal control in an insurer are important in ensuring orderly and prudent operations of the insurer and in assisting the directors to prepare financial statements which give a true and fair view. The following features of the business of insurers may be relevant to the auditor's assessment of such internal controls:

- the substantial scale of transactions, both in terms of volume and relative value, makes it important that control systems are in place to ensure that transactions are recorded promptly, accurately and completely and are checked and approved, and that records are reconciled at appropriate intervals in order to identify and investigate differences promptly. Processing and accounting for complex transactions or high volumes of less complex transactions will almost inevitably involve the use of sophisticated technology. For example, transactions subject to 'straight through processing' involve little or no manual intervention after they have been initiated;
- proper segregation of duties between and amongst those writing the risks, those responsible for establishing claims provisions, those responsible for claims handling, those responsible for claims settlement and those recording these transactions is particularly important;
- equally as important is the proper segregation of duties between and amongst those responsible for the purchase and sale of investments, those recording these transactions and those responsible for the physical security over the documents of title;
- the geographical or organisational dispersal of some insurers' operations means that, in order to maintain control over its activities, insurers need to ensure not only that there are sufficient controls at each location, but also that there are effective communication and control procedures between the various locations and the centre. It is important that there should be clear, comprehensive reporting and responsibility lines, particularly where the business is managed using a 'matrix' structure;
- the activities of insurers can result in the use of complex insurance or reinsurance transactions. The assessment as to whether such transactions transfer risk pose risks of misstatement. Consequently, insurers will normally have developed important operational controls to mitigate such risks of misstatement;
- the provisions of the UK tax legislation are complex for insurers. These may give rise to significant liabilities if not properly dealt with. Accordingly, an effective control system is essential to ensure that the record-keeping requirements of UK tax legislation are satisfied, and that tax is accounted for promptly and accurately. Similar measures may be needed to address similar provisions arising in any other jurisdictions where the insurer operates; and
- the UK regulatory framework is both complex and evolving for insurers. This may give rise to significant liabilities for compensation to policyholders if not properly dealt with. Accordingly, an effective control system is essential to ensure that the requirements of the UK regulators are satisfied. Measures may also be needed to address regulators in other jurisdictions.

> The auditor should obtain an understanding of the entity's process for identifying business risks relevant to financial reporting objectives and deciding about actions to address those risks, and the results thereof. (paragraph 76)

143 Insurers should undertake appropriate risk assessment procedures as part of their risk management and internal control process under FSA rules. Insurers will normally be required to produce an individual capital assessment (ICA), which is designed to quantify risks specific to the entity and to generate and quantify an estimated capital requirement for the entity. The ICA includes an assessment of operational risk. Auditors will normally review such documentation in assessing the insurer's approach to addressing risks.

> The auditor should obtain a sufficient understanding of control activities to assess the risks of material misstatement at the assertion level and to design further audit procedures responsive to assessed risks (paragraph 90).

144 There is a wide variation between different insurers in terms of size, activity and organisation, so that there can be no standard approach to internal controls and risk. The auditor assesses the adequacy of controls in relation to the circumstances of each entity. Examples of weaknesses that may be relevant to the auditor's assessment of the risk of material misstatement are as follows:

- complex products or processes inadequately understood by management; this includes undue concentration of expertise concerning matters requiring the exercise of significant judgment or capable of manipulation such as valuations of financial instruments, insurance or reinsurance contracts;
- weaknesses in back office procedures undermining the completeness and accuracy of accounting records;
- weaknesses in new product approval procedures;
- backlogs in key reconciliations;
- inadequate maintenance of suspense or clearing accounts; and
- delays in the processing of premiums and claims.

Controls relating to outsourcing activities are considered in the ISA (UK and Ireland) 402 section.

> The auditor should obtain an understanding of how the entity has responded to risks arising from IT (paragraph 93).

145 As a result of the type and complexity of transactions undertaken, and records held, by insurers and the need for swift and accurate information processing and retrieval, many insurers are highly automated, including: the accounting function, the processing of premiums, reinsurance and claims, regulatory reporting and the supply of management information.

146 In addition to providing a basis for preparation of the financial statements and meeting requirements for maintenance of adequate accounting records, a key feature of the information systems maintained by an insurer is the importance of reliable and properly coded historical statistical data to operate the business. Historical statistical data is important, for example, in calculating technical provisions, and for providing analyses for regulatory returns.

147 An effective control system over the administration of insurance business will therefore seek to ensure the accurate collation, processing and storing of large volumes of data relating, for example, to:

- acceptance of risk;
- recording of policy details;
- collection of premiums;
- recording, investigation, evaluation and payment of claims;
- identification of classes of business required to be disclosed in the insurer's regulatory returns, and
- transfer of data from the administration systems to systems used for calculating technical provisions.

148 The auditor assesses the extent, nature and impact of automation within the insurer and plans and performs work accordingly. In particular the auditor considers:

- the required level of IT knowledge and skills may be extensive and may require the auditor to obtain advice and assistance from staff with specialist skills;
- the extent of the application of audit software and related audit techniques;
- general controls relating to the environment within which IT based systems are developed, maintained and operated;
- external interfaces susceptible to breaches of security.

149 A single computer system rarely covers all of the insurer's requirements. It is common for insurers to employ a number of different systems and, in many cases, use PC-based applications, sometimes involving the use of complex spreadsheets, to generate important accounting and/or internal control information. The auditor identifies and understands the communication between computer systems in order to assess whether appropriate controls are established and maintained to cover all critical systems and the links between them and to identify the most effective audit approach.

> The auditor should identify and assess the risks of material misstatement at the financial statement level, and at the assertion level for classes of transactions, account balances, and disclosures. (paragraph 100)
>
> As part of the risk assessment as described in paragraph 100, the auditor should determine which of the risks identified are, in the auditor's judgment, risks that require special audit consideration (such risks are defined as "significant risks"). (paragraph 108)
>
> For significant risks, to the extent the auditor has not already done so, the auditor should evaluate the design of the entity's related controls, including relevant control activities, and determine whether they have been implemented. (paragraph 113)

150 Significant risks are likely to arise in those areas that are subject to significant judgment by management or are complex and properly understood by comparatively few people within the insurer.

151 Examples of significant risks for insurers requiring special audit consideration may include:

- the completeness and accuracy of processing of all insurance transactions (see paragraphs 164-174);

- the structure of the reinsurance protection programme and the recognition of reinsurance cost and reinsurance recoveries, including the accounting treatment of complex reinsurance arrangements (see paragraphs 175-179);
- significant measurement uncertainty with respect to technical provisions (see paragraphs 191-207).

Weaknesses in the control environment and in controls such as those described in paragraph 144 above could increase the risk of fraud. 152

The application of complex accounting standards such as IAS 32 and 39, IFRS 4 and 7, (for insurers using EU IFRS) and FRS 25, 26, 27 and 29 (for insurers using UK GAAP) may also give rise to significant risk. This arises from the classification, recognition and measurement of insurance and investment contracts, the classification and measurement of financial assets, hedge accounting, classification of assets/liabilities, revenue/expense recognition. In addition significant risk may arise from the adequacy of financial statement disclosures, notably in respect of insurance and financial risk management. 153

Additional considerations relating to Lloyd's

Responsibility for the establishment and proper operation of systems of control in a Lloyd's syndicate rests with the board of directors of the managing agent. 154

Syndicate auditors are required to report separately on the adequacy of the controls operated by the managing agent to enable it: 155

- to complete the syndicate's Annual Return; and
- to prepare personal accounts

in accordance with the underlying requirements.

Responsibility for the establishment and proper operation of systems of control for a Lloyd's corporate member rests with its board of directors. In exercising this responsibility, the directors may conclude that it is appropriate to place reliance on the records maintained, and summaries thereof, prepared by the managing agents of the underlying syndicates and on other, third party documentation. Such records and summaries may, therefore, be considered by the directors to form part of the accounting records of the corporate member. In addition, the directors of the corporate member and its auditors may conclude that it is appropriate to have regard to the work done by other auditors (including syndicate auditors) and to the reports they may issue. Guidance on this matter is set out in the section on ISA (UK and Ireland) 600 'Using the work of another auditor'. 156

ISA (UK and IRELAND) 320: AUDIT MATERIALITY

Background note

The purpose of this ISA (UK and Ireland) is to establish standards and provide guidance on the concept of materiality and its relationship with audit risk.

> The auditor should consider materiality and its relationship with audit risk when conducting an audit. (paragraph 2)
>
> Materiality should be considered by the auditor when:
>
> (a) Determining the nature, timing and extent of audit procedures; and
> (b) Evaluating the effect of misstatements. (paragraph 8)

157   The principles of assessing materiality in the audit of an insurer are the same as those applying to the audit of any other entity. In particular the auditor's consideration of materiality is a matter of professional judgment, and is affected by the auditor's perception of the common information needs of users as a group[20].

158   Most insurers are profit orientated and quantitative aspects of materiality may be calculated by applying a percentage to a profit based benchmark. However for some insurers, profit before tax from continuing operations may be volatile and the auditor may conclude it appropriate to determine materiality using a normalised figure based on past results. In other circumstances the auditor may use another benchmark such as net assets.

159   In applying materiality to the audit and assessment of transactions and balances which do not have a direct impact on profit consideration is given to the extent any misstatement of these items would influence the economic decisions of users taken on the basis of the financial statements.

Examples of such items may include:

- reinsurance arrangements that are likely to affect the impact of claims on shareholders' funds. For example, any error in the gross estimate of a claim may have little or no effect on the net amount. The balance sheet of an insurer includes gross amounts of technical provisions within liabilities and any reinsurers' shares of technical provisions within assets; and
- some transactions that will have little or no direct effect on an insurer's profit and loss for the year. For example revenue errors on with-profits business will in most cases have no impact on profit for the year as profit is driven by the bonus distribution.

160   In the case of many classes of insurance business, uncertainty relating to the ultimate cost of claims is an inherent feature of the business. As a result, whilst quantitative measures of materiality are of assistance in directing the focus of the auditors' work, qualitative factors relating to the extent and nature of disclosures in the financial statements will also be of importance. Where such uncertainty is considered to be significant, insurance entity auditors consider the disclosures made in the financial statements, and the effect upon the auditors' report. This matter is dealt with in the section on ISA (UK and Ireland) 540 'Audit of Accounting Estimates' and under ISA (UK and Ireland) 700 'The auditors' report on financial statements'.

---

[20] *The International Accounting Standards Board's 'Framework for the Preparation and Presentation of Financial Statements' indicates that, for a profit orientated entity, as investors are providers of risk capital to the enterprise, the provision of financial statements that meets their needs will also meet most of the needs of other users that financial statements can satisfy.*

ISA (UK and IRELAND) 330: THE AUDITOR'S PROCEDURES IN RESPONSE TO ASSESSED RISKS

> **Background note**
>
> The purpose of this ISA (UK and Ireland) is to establish standards and provide guidance on determining overall responses and designing and performing further audit procedures to respond to the assessed risks of material misstatement at the financial statement and assertion levels in a financial statement audit.

> When, in accordance with paragraph 115 of ISA (UK and Ireland) 315, the auditor has determined that it is not possible or practicable to reduce the risks of material misstatement at the assertion level to an acceptably low level with audit evidence obtained only from substantive procedures, the auditor should perform tests of relevant controls to obtain audit evidence about their operating effectiveness. (paragraph 25)

161 In practice the nature and volume of transactions relating to the operations of insurers often means that performing tests of relevant controls is the most efficient means of reducing audit risk to an acceptably low level.

> When, in accordance with paragraph 108 of ISA (UK and Ireland) 315, the auditor has determined that an assessed risk of material misstatement at the assertion level is a significant risk, the auditor should perform substantive procedures that are specifically responsive to that risk. (paragraph 51)

162 Examples of significant risks for insurers requiring special audit consideration may include:

- the completeness and accuracy of processing of all insurance transactions;
- the structure of the reinsurance protection programme and the recognition of reinsurance cost and reinsurance recoveries, including the accounting treatment of complex reinsurance arrangements.

> The auditor should perform audit procedures to evaluate whether the overall presentation of the financial statements, including the related disclosures, are in accordance with the applicable financial reporting framework. (paragraph 65)

163 Specific financial reporting standards can require extensive narrative disclosures in the financial statements of insurers; for example, in relation to the nature and extent of risks arising from contracts. In designing and performing procedures to evaluate these disclosures the auditor obtains audit evidence regarding the assertions about presentation and disclosure described in paragraph 17 of ISA (UK and Ireland) 500 'Audit Evidence'.

Insurance transactions

164 When considering the completeness and accuracy of processing of insurance transactions, auditors have regard to the multiple purposes for which an insurer will use

data entered into its accounting records. Such data may be used not only for inclusion in the financial statements, but may also be included in the regulatory returns of the insurer and be used as the basis for statistical analysis and extrapolation of past trends and transactions in assessing technical provisions. Errors in the data input may therefore have far reaching impact on the overall reported results. Data input required for such other purposes may therefore require additional detail or higher levels of accuracy of coding and allocation compared with those which might be required solely for the preparation of reliable financial statements.

165 For insurance transactions initiated by the insurer, auditors consider the controls implemented for each material class of business and location, together with overall controls applied by the accounting function and management. Matters for consideration will include the procedures for the setting of and monitoring of compliance with guidelines for underwriting and product development, and controls over completeness of transactions and risks undertaken. Insurers often transact very large volumes of transactions which are subject to extensive IT controls, so the use of computer-assisted audit techniques may be appropriate.

166 Auditors of insurers also have regard to the procedures implemented by the insurer to ensure the completeness, accuracy and reliability of information provided by third parties, including intermediaries and agents. Auditors assess the effectiveness of management's controls implemented to ensure that all risks bound by agents under delegated authorities have been included. Procedures include reviewing the insurer's procedures for the approval of such arrangements and the monitoring of the performance of business introduced through such contracts. These may include inspections by the insurer or third parties of the agent's underwriting activities, records and reports to the insurer.

167 Auditors review the contractual terms, and assess the extent to which such agents are reporting transactions on a regular and prompt basis and whether the insurer has completely and accurately recorded the reported transactions in the accounting records and statistical databases. Specific consideration will be paid to the terms of the agent's remuneration to ensure for example that all profit commission and expenses recovery entitlements have been recognised.

168 Where significant insurance risks are underwritten through treaty reinsurance contracts, the nature and complexity of the risks written may differ substantially from those written by the insurer directly. Auditors ascertain the insurer's procedures for approving such contracts, whether relevant transactions are reported regularly and promptly (commonly monthly or quarterly), and whether the insurer has included all such transactions in the accounting records.

169 Reinsurers maintain records of all treaties and may receive regular statements from the cedant of premiums received, claims paid and other data relating to the treaty. The reinsurer may be reliant upon the cedant's statements to maintain accounting records of the underlying treaty transactions.

170 Although a reinsurer may have contractual rights to inspect a cedant's books, it is not uncommon for directors to construct the financial records of the reinsurer from cedant statements. Auditors may obtain evidence that controls in relation to treaty reinsurance exist to ensure that:

- statements from the ceding insurer are received and processed on a regular basis;
- statements are reconciled to the reinsurer's accounting records where appropriate; and
- a procedure exists for the regular review of major treaty results.

An important aspect of an insurer's controls over completeness and accuracy of processing will often be its procedures for the reconciliation of balances with third parties, the settlement of transactions (including their correction where necessary) and the agreement and clearance of old items. Third parties will include policyholders, brokers, underwriting agents and reinsurers, and procedures may vary for each category. Auditors review the insurer's processes and monitoring procedures established to ascertain whether such reconciliations and settlements are up to date. Auditors pay particular attention to the use of suspense or similar accounts, and to whether they are reconciled and cleared regularly and promptly. 171

A significant issue in the audit of insurers is the assessment of whether or not contracts to which the insurers are party should be accounted for as contracts of insurance (or reinsurance). In forming this assessment accounting conventions may require consideration of the level of insurance risk transferred, although the definition of insurance risk and the level of insurance risk required for a contract to be accounted for as insurance (or reinsurance) may vary dependent on whether the insurer is preparing financial statements in accordance with International Financial Reporting Standards or United Kingdom financial reporting standards and on the financial reporting standards in force from time to time. 172

Auditors obtain sufficient, appropriate audit evidence that insurers have properly assessed the level of insurance risk for the purpose of determining whether material contracts or groups of contracts should be accounted for as insurance (or reinsurance), taking into account the applicable accounting requirements. 173

In evaluating the insurer's mechanism for assessing the level of insurance risk, the auditor may consider the following:- 174

- the process adopted by the insurer,
- the likelihood of loss falling to both insurer and reinsurer under different loss scenarios and the probability of occurrence of the scenarios selected for this exercise,
- the cash flow implications under different loss scenarios,
- any penalty, default or adjustable clauses in the contract,
- the existence and operation of any experience account, and
- the existence and operation of other arrangements, whether or not described as reinsurance, that have the effect of limiting the risk transferred by the reinsurance arrangement under review, either by amending the arrangement (e.g. by means of a 'side letter') or by counteracting it (e.g. by re-assumption of the same risk by a separate contract).

Reinsurance

When considering the impact of the insurer's reinsurance arrangements on the financial statements auditors obtain an understanding of the reinsurance programme, including both facultative and treaty arrangements. Auditors assess the procedures for the approval of reinsurance contracts, both in overall terms and in detail. 175

Reinsurance contracts can be complex, and a detailed understanding of individual significant contracts and their inter-relationship with others, as well as an understanding of the programme in total, will be necessary for the auditor to conclude whether the accounting treatment is appropriate and consistent with the substance of the transactions. 176

177 In addition to considering the controls on the purchasing of reinsurance, auditors consider the controls exercised by the insurer to ensure that all reinsurance recoveries to which it is entitled have been identified, correctly calculated and collected. As with reinsurance cost, auditors use their detailed understanding of the relevant reinsurance contracts to assess whether the appropriate accounting treatment has been followed, particularly for complex reinsurance transactions.

178 An important aspect of the uncertainty to which a particular insurer is exposed is the nature and extent of its reinsurance programme. Auditors consider the nature and coverage of any significant reinsurance programmes and, where material, the procedures adopted by the directors or managing agent to determine the financial stability of reinsurers used. Auditors normally consider the operation of significant reinsurance programmes by reviewing whether the risks ceded and the resulting premium and expense information are in accordance with the reinsurance contract. They may also consider the procedures in place for ensuring that material claims or balances, if any, disputed by reinsurers are resolved. Evidence may be obtained by reviewing correspondence with reinsurers or intermediaries and considering the quality and timeliness of reconciliations of reinsurer balances.

179 Auditors also use their understanding of the insurer's reinsurance protection programme to assess the extent to which it is appropriate to recognise credit for reinsurance recoveries within the technical provisions. In their consideration auditors test the matching of reinsurance recoveries against gross claims provisions to ensure consistency of treatment.

ISA (UK and IRELAND) 402: AUDIT CONSIDERATIONS RELATING TO ENTITIES USING SERVICE ORGANISATIONS

Background note

The purpose of this ISA (UK and Ireland) is to establish standards and provide guidance to an auditor where the entity uses a service organisation

In obtaining an understanding of the entity and its environment, the auditor should determine the significance of service organisation activities to the entity and the relevance to the audit. (paragraph 5)

Based on the auditor's understanding of the aspects of the entity's accounting system and control environment relating to relevant activities, the auditor should:

(a) Assess whether sufficient appropriate audit evidence concerning the relevant financial statement assertions is available from records held at the entity; and if not,
(b) Determine effective procedures to obtain evidence necessary for the audit, either by direct access to records kept by service organisations or through information obtained from the service organisations or their auditor. (paragraph 9-18)

If an auditor concludes that evidence from records held by a service organization is necessary in order to form an opinion on the client's financial statements and the auditor is unable to obtain such evidence, the auditor should include a description of the factors leading to the lack of evidence in the basis of opinion section of their report and qualify their opinion or issue a disclaimer of opinion on the financial statements. (paragraph 18-1)

180 In common with other industries the outsourcing of functions to third parties is becoming increasingly prevalent with insurers. Some of the more common areas, such as customer call centres, may have no direct impact on the audit, while others such as IT functions and binding authorities may have a direct relevance. The auditor therefore gains an understanding of the extent of outsourced functions and their relevance to the financial statements. The insurer is obliged to ensure that the auditor has appropriate access to records, information and explanations from material outsourced operations.

181 Whilst an insurer may outsource functions to third parties the responsibility for these functions remains that of the insurer. The insurer should have appropriate controls in place over these arrangements including:

- risk assessment prior to contracting with the service provider, which includes a proper due diligence and periodic review of the appropriateness of the arrangement;
- appropriate contractual agreements or service level agreements;
- contingency plans should the provider fail in delivery of services;
- appropriate management information and reporting from the outsourced provider;
- appropriate controls over customer information; and
- right of access of the insurer's internal audit to test the internal controls of the service provider.

182 If the auditor is unable to obtain sufficient appropriate audit evidence concerning outsourced operations the auditor considers whether it is necessary to report the matter direct to the FSA – see the section of this Practice Note relating to ISA (UK and Ireland) 250 Section B.

Additional considerations relating to Lloyd's

183 Many syndicates use the centrally operated systems for clearing underwriting transactions. The auditors of those systems provide an Independent Accountant's Report on the operation of these systems each calendar year. Syndicate auditors consider the proposed scope of this work as part of their audit planning process and assess the level of reliance they intend to place on the work performed centrally when determining the extent and nature of procedures to be performed at the syndicate.

ISA (UK & Ireland) 505: EXTERNAL CONFIRMATIONS

Background note

The purpose of this ISA (UK and Ireland) is to establish standards and provide guidance on the auditor's use of external confirmations as a means of obtaining audit evidence.

> The auditor should determine whether the use of external confirmations is necessary to obtain sufficient appropriate audit evidence at the assertion level. In making this determination, the auditor should consider the assessed risk of material misstatement at the assertion level and how the audit evidence from other planned audit procedures will reduce the risk of material misstatement at the assertion level to an acceptably low level. (paragraph 2)

184 In general, external confirmation procedures may be useful as part of the audit of :

- amounts receivable from reinsurers in respect of claims paid or payable by the cedant, and
- premiums receivable from intermediaries.

However, external confirmations may not always provide useful audit evidence in relation to insurance balances due to the relative immateriality of individual policyholder balances or transactions.

185 Amounts receivable from reinsurers may comprise an insurer's calculation of amounts that will be recoverable from reinsurers in respect of the insurer's estimate of incurred claims. The relevant reinsurers are unlikely to be in a position to confirm amounts in relation to these claims until such time as the validity of these claims has been assessed, the amounts payable determined, and this has been communicated to and agreed by the relevant reinsurers. Therefore the relevant reinsurers may not be able to provide sufficient appropriate evidence in response to a confirmation request that includes such amounts. The auditor may though determine that confirmation would be an effective procedure in respect of individual material reinsurance recoveries where the reinsurer has agreed the amount involved but the balance has not yet been paid.

186 In deciding to what extent to use external confirmations in respect of premiums receivable from intermediaries, the auditor considers the assessed risk of misstatement together with the characteristics of the environment in which the insurer operates and the practice of potential respondents in dealing with requests for direct confirmation. For example where a captive insurer's premium income comprises solely an annual premium from its parent company and this is due at the year-end then this may be a significant balance and it may be assessed that the parent undertaking is likely to be able to respond to a confirmation request. In these circumstances the auditor may decide to seek positive confirmation from the parent undertaking. Conversely, where premiums receivable comprise a high volume of low value amounts which may be due from individuals or entities that do not have information systems that facilitate external confirmation, the auditor may decide that confirmation may not be an effective audit procedure and may seek to obtain sufficient appropriate evidence from other sources.

ISA (UK and IRELAND) 520: ANALYTICAL PROCEDURES

Background note

The purpose of this ISA (UK and Ireland) is to establish standards and provide guidance on the application of analytical procedures during an audit.

> The auditor should apply analytical procedures as risk assessment procedures to obtain an understanding of the entity and its environment and in the overall review at the end of the audit. (paragraph 2)

187 The deferral and matching principles applied by insurers mean that there are relationships between the movement in balance sheet items and specific profit and loss items (for example deferred acquisition costs, claims provisions and unearned premiums provisions).

188 There are likely to be expected relationships between a number of profit and loss items such as written and earned premiums, incurred claims and earned premiums and premiums and claims gross and reinsurers' share thereof.

189 Given the nature of insurance business, non financial data plays a significant part in managing the pricing and reserving processes. The auditor may consider the usefulness of non financial data such as policy numbers, sums assured, retention levels and claim numbers and their interrelation with financial data in designing analytical review procedures. In addition the auditor may consider measures relating to regulatory compliance – e.g. complaints handling and breaches of conduct of business rules, and operational risk measures – e.g. volumes of unreconciled items.

190 Where non financial information or reports produced from systems or processes outside the financial statements accounting system are used in analytical procedures, the auditor considers the reliability of that information or those reports.

ISA (UK and IRELAND) 540: AUDIT OF ACCOUNTING ESTIMATES

> **Background note**
>
> The purpose of this ISA (UK and Ireland) is to establish standards and provide guidance on the audit of accounting estimates contained within the financial statements.

> The auditor should obtain sufficient appropriate audit evidence regarding accounting estimates (paragraph 2)
>
> The auditor should adopt one or a combination of the following approaches in the audit of an accounting estimate:
> (a) Review and test the process used by management to develop the estimate;
> (b) Use an independent estimate for comparison with that prepared by management; or
> (c) Review of subsequent events which provide audit evidence of the reasonableness of the estimate made. (paragraph 10)

191 For most insurers, the estimation of technical provisions will involve relatively high estimation uncertainty because it will involve significant assumptions about future conditions, transactions or events that are uncertain at the time of the estimation.

Changes in estimation approach are likely to have a significant effect on the profit figure in the financial statements.

192 Audit teams normally involve actuarial specialists in assessing technical provisions. Their level of involvement in the audit process will depend on matters such as the level of expertise of other members of the audit team, the availability of independent actuarial advice to the insurer, and the nature and complexity of the audit issues. They may be used in the initial assessment of the level of risk of each financial statement caption, in assessing the effectiveness of the control environment, in establishing the audit procedures to be adopted and in obtaining and assessing the audit evidence obtained. Further guidance on the use of an actuary is given in the section on ISA (UK and Ireland) 620 "Using the work of an expert".

193 When designing audit procedures to test the process used by management to develop the technical provisions, the auditor considers:
- the policies for setting such provisions;
- the complexity and nature of the models or measurement techniques used to estimate the technical provisions;
- the source data;
- the assumptions used to develop those provisions.

194 The models used to estimate the technical provisions are dependent upon the accuracy and completeness of financial and non-financial data and accordingly the audit procedures will need to address the effectiveness of management's controls over the use and reliability of such data.

195 The assumptions made by management are intended to provide a reasonable basis for the setting of the technical provisions. The objective of the audit procedures performed for the purpose of evaluating these assumptions is not to obtain sufficient appropriate audit evidence to provide an opinion on the assumptions themselves. Furthermore, the auditor's consideration of management's assumptions is based only on information available to the auditor at the time of the audit. The auditor is not responsible for predicting future conditions, transactions or events that, if they had been known at the time of the audit, might have significantly affected management's actions or management's assumptions underlying the technical provisions and related disclosures.

196 For life insurers, the realistic valuation of with-profits liabilities uses a range of estimation techniques. The provision will comprise both historic (most likely asset share based) and projected (option and guarantee) information. Options and guarantees are often valued using stochastic modelling techniques. Auditors assess whether regulatory requirements have been met and whether sufficient scenarios have been run. Any assertions regarding future management and policyholder actions also require careful consideration, including the extent to which management actions are supported by the PPFM[21] or board resolution.

---

[21] *A document intended to provide information to policyholders and others, in respect of the principles and practices in accordance with which a with-profits fund is managed. The prescribed scope and content of the document are set out in COB 6.10 in the FSA Handbook.*

Paragraph 46 of Schedule 9A to the Companies Act 1985 provides that the computation of the long-term business provision[22] of a life insurer shall be made by a Fellow of the Institute or Faculty of Actuaries "on the basis of recognised actuarial methods, with due regard to the actuarial principles laid down in Council Directive 2002/83/EC of the European Parliament and of the Council of 5 November 2002 concerning life assurance". The actuary carrying out this statutory duty for the insurer has been designated as the 'Reporting Actuary' by Guidance Note ("GN") 7 'The Role of Actuaries in Relation to Financial Statements of Insurers and Insurance Groups writing Long-term Business and their Relationship with Auditors' issued by the Institute and Faculty of Actuaries and now adopted by the Board for Actuarial Standards (BAS). The statutory duty of the Reporting Actuary[23] does not extend to any technical provisions other than the long-term business provision. The auditor understands the approach which the Reporting Actuary has adopted in calculating the long term business provision. 197

For general insurers there will normally be a range of technical provisions that may be appropriate for inclusion in the financial statements. Guidance Note 12 'General Insurance Business: Actuarial Reports' issued by the Institute and Faculty of Actuaries and adopted by the BAS provides guidance to actuaries on the preparation of a formal report on, inter alia, technical provisions or on the financial soundness of a general insurance undertaking. If the actuary has prepared a formal report on the technical provisions or on the financial soundness of a general insurance undertaking the auditor reviews the report to gain a better understanding of the scope of the work performed and of any limitations on any opinions expressed. If such a report has not been prepared, it is necessary for auditors to understand the scope of the work carried out by the insurer's actuary. 198

Given that the calculation of an insurer's technical provisions is such a significant activity in the preparation of the insurer's financial statements, once management has selected a specific estimation method, it is important that the insurer consistently applies it. If management has changed the method for calculating technical provisions, the auditor considers whether the method to which it has been changed provides a more appropriate basis of measurement, or that the change is supported by a change in the applicable financial reporting framework, or a change in circumstances. 199

In obtaining an understanding of whether, and if so how, the insurer has assessed the effect of estimation uncertainty on the technical provisions, the auditor considers matters such as: 200

- whether, and if so how, management has considered alternative assumptions or outcomes by, for example, performing a sensitivity analysis to determine the effect of changes in the assumptions on the level of technical provisions;
- how management determines the ultimate technical provisions when analysis indicates that there may be a number of outcome scenarios;

---

[22] "Long-term business provision" is a term used in Schedule 9A to the Companies Act 1985. Insurers preparing financial statements under IFRS may use different designations for such items. In this Practice Note the term should be interpreted as meaning those items that would fall to be classified as long-term business provisions under Schedule 9A to the Companies Act 1985 regardless of how they are described in the financial statements. It may be noted that 'long-term business provision' in this context does not include provisions in respect of linked long-term contracts.

[23] The statutory duty of a Reporting Actuary arises in Schedule 9A to the Companies Act 1985 and so does not apply to long-term insurers preparing financial statements under IFRS, for those companies the term Reporting Actuary in the Practice Note should be taken to refer to any actuary given responsibility by management for the calculation of policyholder liabilities for the purpose of their inclusion in the financial statements.

- whether management monitors the outcome of technical provisions made in the prior period, and whether management has appropriately responded to the outcome of that monitoring procedure.

201 The review of the outcome or re-estimation of prior period accounting estimates may assist the auditor in identifying circumstances or conditions that could increase the uncertainty of a technical provision.. However, the review is not intended to call into question the auditor's judgments made in the prior year that were based on information available at the time.

202 Management bias, whether unintentional or intentional, can be difficult to detect in a particular technical provision. It may only be identified when there has been a change in the method for calculating technical provisions from the prior period based on a subjective assessment without evidence that there has been a change in circumstances when considered in the aggregate of groups of estimates or all estimates, or when observed over a number of accounting periods. Although some form of management bias is inherent in subjective decisions, management may have no intention of misleading the users of financial statements. If, however, there is intention to mislead through, for example, the intentional use of unreasonable estimates, management bias is fraudulent in nature. ISA 240, "The Auditor's Responsibility to Consider Fraud in an Audit of Financial Statements," provides standards and guidance on the auditor's responsibility to consider fraud in an audit of financial statements.

203 Insurance specific financial reporting standards, which form part of the applicable financial reporting frameworks applying to insurers, take into account the inherent uncertainty within the insurance industry and the needs of users of financial statements regarding disclosure of estimation uncertainty. The auditor considers the required disclosure of estimation uncertainty by the applicable financial reporting framework and whether the disclosure proposed by management is adequate. In making this determination, the auditor considers whether adequate disclosure is given regarding the sensitivities associated with the significant assumptions underlying the technical provisions, in light of the materiality level established for the engagement.

204 Insurance specific financial reporting standards can require extensive narrative disclosures in the financial statements of insurers; for example, in relation to the nature and extent of risks arising from insurance contracts. In designing and performing procedures to evaluate these disclosures the auditor obtains audit evidence regarding the assertions about presentation and disclosure described in paragraph 17 of ISA (UK and Ireland) 500 'Audit Evidence'. Guidance on the types of audit procedures that can be used for obtaining audit evidence can be found in paragraphs 26 to 38 of ISA (UK and Ireland) 500.

205 Consideration of the adequacy of disclosure with regard to sensitivities of significant assumptions is of particular importance where the estimation uncertainty of technical provisions may cast significant doubt about the entity's ability to continue as a going concern. ISA (UK & Ireland) 570 "Going Concern" and ISA (UK and Ireland) 700 "The Auditor's Report on Financial Statements" establish standards and provide guidance in such circumstances.

206 Where the applicable financial reporting framework does not prescribe disclosure of estimation uncertainty, the auditor nevertheless considers management's description, in the notes to the financial statements, of the circumstances relating to the estimation uncertainty. ISA (UK & Ireland) 700, "The Auditor's Report on Financial

Statements" provides guidance on the implications for the auditor's report when the auditor believes that management's disclosure of estimation uncertainty in the financial statements is inadequate or misleading.

> The auditor should make a final assessment of the reasonableness of the entity's accounting estimates based on the auditor's understanding of the entity and its environment and whether the estimates are consistent with other audit evidence obtained during the audit. (paragraph 24)

Based on the audit evidence obtained, the auditor may conclude that the evidence points to an estimate of the required technical provision that differs from management's estimate, and that the difference between the auditor's estimate or range and management's estimate constitutes a financial statement misstatement. In such cases, where the auditor has developed a range, a misstatement exists when management's estimate lies outside the auditor's range. The misstatement is measured as the difference between management's estimate and the nearest point of the auditor's range. 207

Additional considerations relating to Lloyd's

The Lloyd's Valuation of Liabilities Rules require all Lloyd's syndicates writing general insurance business to provide to the Council of Lloyd's, each year, for solvency purposes a Statement of Actuarial Opinion (SAO) on their world-wide reserves, both gross and net of reinsurance. 208

The SAO should cover all the business of the syndicate for all years of account from 1993 to date. Separate figures are required gross and net of reinsurance for each year of account. The Institute and Faculty of Actuaries published Guidance Note 20 'Actuarial Reporting Under the Lloyd's Valuation of Liabilities Rules', which has now been adopted by the BAS. The actuary's report given in the SAO is limited to an opinion as to whether the reserves for solvency purposes established by the agent comply with the Lloyd's valuation of liability rules and are not less than the expected future costs of the liabilities for claims, net of anticipated future premiums, claims handling expenses and bad debts. 209

In carrying out their work on the syndicate Annual Return, auditors consider the extent to which they can use the work of the actuary performed for solvency purposes on general insurance business. In making this assessment, auditors read the entire SAO and, if available, any related reports; they may also, where appropriate, discuss the contents of the SAO and related reports with the actuary. Factors to be taken into account in assessing the extent of reliance that may be placed on the actuary's work include: 210

- any limitations of scope of opinion expressed in the actuary's report;
- the reliability of source data used by the actuary and the adequacy of steps taken by the managing agent to ensure the integrity of that data. Care is necessary to avoid inappropriate reliance if management has supplied data to the actuary, on which reliance has been taken, which has not been considered in the course of the audit of the syndicate's financial statements; and
- the extent of any bias in the actuaries' work as a consequence of the actuarial focus being on sufficiency of reserves.

Auditors are also aware that the SAO relates to the solvency reserves of the syndicate for each year of account. The solvency reserves may be different to the technical provisions recorded in the annual report of the syndicate or used in determining the closed year profit or loss.

211 In giving their opinion on the syndicate Annual Return, syndicate auditors have regard to the appropriateness of the allocation of technical provisions between underlying years of account. In addition, the syndicate auditor has regard to the appropriateness of the determination, and allocation to years of account, of technical provisions to meet FSA solvency requirements. Such provisions must be determined in accordance with requirements prescribed by the FSA and Lloyd's.

212 Where a year of account is closed into a subsequent year of account of the same, or another, syndicate, the Syndicate Accounting Byelaw requires technical provisions of the closed year to be shown as a "premium for a reinsurance to close" (RITC) for that account in the underwriting year accounts as at date of closure. This description has the effect, in accounting terms, of enabling the affairs of that year of account to be drawn to a conclusion and the final result for the relevant joint venture determined. Where the year of account has closed by way of an RITC, the syndicate auditor considers whether, in the context of his opinion on the relevant underwriting year accounts, the relationship between the reinsuring and reinsured members of the syndicate gives rise to further materiality considerations.

213 In situations where the annual venture of a syndicate goes into run off, paragraphs 136-139 of the ABI SORP are applicable such that provision for any additional costs to be included in a syndicate's annual accounts should be made in the accounting period in which the decision to cease underwriting or not to close a year of account is taken.

214 In order to comply with Lloyd's Solvency criteria, technical provisions for life business included in a syndicate Annual Return must be established and certified by an actuary in a prescribed form on a basis set out by Lloyd's. For solvency purposes, the auditor relies on the life technical provisions established and certified by the actuary.

ISA (UK and IRELAND) 545: AUDITING FAIR VALUE MEASUREMENTS AND DISCLOSURES

Background note

The purpose of this ISA (UK and Ireland) is to establish standards and provide guidance on auditing fair value measurements and disclosures contained in financial statements.

The auditor should obtain sufficient appropriate audit evidence that fair value measurements and disclosures are in accordance with the entity's applicable financial reporting framework. (paragraph 3)

As part of the understanding of the entity and its environment, including its internal control, the auditor should obtain an understanding of the entity's process for determining fair value measurements and disclosures and of the relevant control activities sufficient to identify and assess the risks of material

> When planning the audit the auditor should assess the risk that material undisclosed related party transactions, or undisclosed outstanding balances between an entity and its related parties may exist. (paragraph 106-3)

217 Both when applying IFRS or UK GAAP, under ISA (UK and Ireland) 550, the auditor is required to assess the risk that material undisclosed related party transactions may exist. It is in the nature of insurance business that transaction volumes are high but this factor will not, of itself, necessarily lead the auditor to conclude that the inherent risk of material undisclosed related party transactions is high.

218 Insurers are likely to have a particularly wide range of contractual arrangements because the nature of insurance is to spread risk. The directors will, in particular, need to consider how best to obtain information on related party interests in policies issued and reinsurance arrangements. In capturing this data, insurers may decide to establish criteria for evaluating materiality to the individuals concerned; the policies are, in most cases, unlikely to be material to the insurer. Auditors will need to consider the adequacy of these procedures.

219 Insurers are required to report to FSA changes in control (in some instances with FSA prior approval), changes in circumstances of existing controllers and changes in entities that are closely linked to the firm (SUP 11). In addition, there are annual reporting obligations in respect of controllers and entities that are closely linked to the firm (SUP 16). As a result, it will therefore normally be the case that there are controls in place to ensure that this information is properly collated. However, the definition of 'controller and closely linked" for regulatory purposes is not congruent with the 'related party' definition in FRS 8/IAS 24 and the auditor therefore considers what controls have been put in place by management to capture information on those parties which fall within the accounting definition only.

220 In reviewing related party information for completeness, the auditor may compare the proposed disclosures in the financial statements to information prepared for regulatory reporting purposes (bearing in mind that the population may be different, as noted in the preceding paragraph).

ISA (UK and IRELAND) 560: SUBSEQUENT EVENTS

Background note

The purpose of this ISA (UK and Ireland) is to establish standards and provide guidance on the auditor's responsibility regarding subsequent events.

> The auditor should perform audit procedures designed to obtain sufficient appropriate audit evidence that all events up to the date of the auditor's report that may require adjustment of, or disclosure in, the financial statements have been identified (paragraph 4)

221 Matters specific to insurance companies which auditors may consider in their review of subsequent events include:

> misstatement at the assertion level and to design and perform further audit procedures. (paragraph 10)
>
> The auditor should evaluate whether the fair value measurements and disclosures in the financial statements are in accordance with the entity's applicable financial reporting framework. (paragraph 17)

215 The valuation of derivative and other financial instruments which are not traded in an active market and so for which valuation techniques are required is an activity that can give rise to significant audit risk. Such financial instruments are priced using valuation techniques such as discounted cashflow models, options pricing models or by reference to another instrument that is substantially the same as the financial instrument subject to valuation. The auditor reviews the controls, procedures and testing of the valuation techniques used by the insurer. Controls and substantive testing could include focusing on:

- valuation technique approval and testing procedures used by the insurer;
- the independence of review, sourcing and reasonableness of observable market data and other parameters used in the valuation techniques;
- calibration procedures used by the insurer to test the validity of valuation techniques applied by comparing outputs to observable market transactions;
- completeness and appropriate inclusion of all relevant observable market data;
- the observability in practice of data classified by the insurer as observable market data;
- the appropriateness and validity of classification of instruments designated as being traded in a non active and in an active market;
- the appropriateness and validity of the particular valuation technique applied to particular financial instruments;
- the appropriateness and validity of the parameters used by the insurer to designate an instrument as substantially the same as the financial instrument being valued;
- mathematical integrity of the valuation models; and
- access controls over valuation models.

216 In the more subjective areas of valuation the auditor obtains an understanding of the assumptions used and undertakes a review of the estimates involved for reasonableness, consistency and conformity with generally accepted practices. In some cases, the auditor may use his own valuation techniques to assess the insurer's valuations. Given the complexities involved and the subjective nature of the judgments inherent the auditor may involve an expert in elements of this work (see the ISA (UK and Ireland) 620 section of this Practice Note).

ISA (UK and IRELAND) 550: RELATED PARTIES

> **Background note**
>
> The purpose of this ISA (UK and Ireland) is to establish standards and provide guidance on the auditor's responsibilities and audit procedures regarding related parties and transactions with such parties regardless of whether International Accounting Standard (IAS) 24, "Related Party Disclosures," or similar requirement, is part of the applicable financial reporting framework.

- an evaluation of the impact of any material subsequent events on the capital resources requirement for the company;
- an assessment of the influence of new information received relevant to claims provisions;
- an assessment of the impact of any developments in doubtful reinsurance recoveries since the balance sheet date;
- an assessment of the impact of any regulatory developments since the balance sheet date; and
- a review of relevant correspondence with regulators and enquiries of management to determine whether any significant breaches of regulations or other significant regulatory concerns have come to light since the period end.

ISA (UK and Ireland) 560 provides guidance to auditors on facts discovered after the financial statements have been issued. If, in the course of their examination of the insurance company's regulatory return, auditors become aware of subsequent events which, had they occurred or been known of at the date of their report on the financial statements, might have caused them to issue a different report, they and the directors consider whether the financial statements need to be revised following the statutory provisions relating to the revision of company annual financial statements and directors' reports set out in sections 245 to 245C of the Companies Act 1985. Where the auditors conclude that this step is appropriate, the matter concerned is likely to be of material significance to the FSA and so give rise to a duty to report to the FSA. 222

Additional considerations relating to Lloyd's

Currently the syndicate Annual Return is required to be submitted to Lloyd's before the syndicate annual accounts are issued. If there has been a post-balance sheet event after the syndicate Annual Return has been signed but before the syndicate annual accounts and (where relevant) personal accounts are signed which is of such significance that it materially affects the view shown in these accounts, then they should be amended. Lloyd's rules may require that an amendment is also made to the syndicate Annual Return. Paragraph 221 sets out matters specific to insurance companies that auditors may consider in their review of subsequent events. The evaluation of the impact of any material event on the capital resources requirement of the insurance company is not applicable to the audit of syndicate accounts. Accordingly, other matters that auditors may consider in their review of subsequent events include an evaluation of the impact of any material subsequent events on the syndicate's ability to continue to write business in the current annual venture or annual ventures yet to be established for subsequent years. 223

ISA (UK and IRELAND) 570: THE GOING CONCERN BASIS IN FINANCIAL STATEMENTS

Background note

The purpose of this ISA (UK and Ireland) is to establish standards and provide guidance on the auditor's responsibility in the audit of financial statements with respect to the going concern assumption used in the preparation of the financial statements, including management's assessment of the entity's ability to continue as a going concern.

> When planning and performing audit procedures and in evaluating the results thereof, the auditor should consider the appropriateness of management's use of the going concern assumption in the preparation of the financial statements. (paragraph 2)
>
> The auditor should consider any relevant disclosures in the financial statements. (paragraph 2-1)

224 With reference to insurance companies, specific audit procedures may include:
- reviewing the means whereby the board of directors and senior management of an insurance company satisfy themselves that the company will have capital in excess of its capital resources requirement for the foreseeable future, including a review of the insurer's Individual Capital Assessment prepared for regulatory purposes;
- considering whether the key assumptions underlying the budgets and/or forecasts appear appropriate in the circumstances. Key assumptions will normally include claims projections (numbers, cost and timing), the profitability of business written and the level of provisions required;
- considering the liquidity of funds to enable the insurer to meet claims and other liabilities as they fall due;
- for a life insurer, reviewing any financial condition report produced by the holder of the actuarial function and other actuarial reports;
- reviewing correspondence with the regulators, and considering any actions taken (or likely to be taken) by the regulators; and
- considering the potential costs of settling claims (for instance uncertainty resulting from judicial decisions) and additional provisions (for example product misselling).

If the auditor has any doubts as to the ability of an insurer to continue as a going concern, the auditor considers whether he ought to make a report direct to the FSA on which guidance is set out in the section of this Practice Note relating to ISA (UK and Ireland) 250 Section B.

Additional considerations relating to Lloyd's

225 The managing agent's responsibility for preparing syndicate annual accounts includes the requirement for the financial statements to be prepared on the basis that the syndicate will continue to write future business unless it is inappropriate to presume the syndicate will do so. Syndicate annual accounts present the collective participations of the members of the syndicate in one or more annual ventures. The ability of a syndicate to meet its obligations as they fall due will reflect the ability of the members of the syndicate to meet their obligations to the syndicate when calls are made. However, irrespective of whether information on a syndicate member's ability to meet its obligations as they fall due is available, the ability of a syndicate to meet its obligations as they fall due is underpinned by the support provided by Lloyd's solvency process and its chain of security for any syndicate members who are unable to meet their underwriting liabilities.

226 Unless it is in run-off, at the date the annual accounts are approved the syndicate will have commenced underwriting business through Lloyd's for the new underwriting year, but it will not have established an annual venture for subsequent years. Accordingly, it is not necessary to carry out some of the audit procedures set out in paragraph 224; in particular an assessment of the available

capital resources is not applicable to syndicate annual accounts. However, audit procedures include making enquiries of the managing agent on the plans for the underwriting of business in future annual ventures of the syndicate.

ISA (UK and IRELAND) 580: MANAGEMENT REPRESENTATIONS

Background note

The purpose of this ISA (UK and Ireland) is to establish standards and provide guidance on the use of management representations as audit evidence, the procedures to be applied in evaluating and documenting management representations and the action to be taken if management refuses to provide appropriate representations.

Written confirmation of appropriate representations from management, as required by paragraph 4 below, should be obtained before the audit report is issued. (paragraph 2-1)
The auditor should obtain written representations from management on matters material to the financial statements when other sufficient appropriate audit evidence cannot reasonably be expected to exist. (paragraph 4)

ISAs (UK and Ireland) 250 and 550 require auditors to obtain written confirmation in respect of completeness of disclosure to the auditors of:

- all known actual or possible non-compliance with laws and regulations (including breaches of FSMA 2000, FSA rules, the Money Laundering Regulations, other regulatory requirements or any other circumstance that could jeopardise the authorisation of the firm under FSMA 2000) whose effects should be considered when preparing financial statements together with the actual or contingent consequences which may arise therefrom; and
- the completeness of information provided regarding the identification of related parties and the adequacy of related party disclosures in the financial statements.

227

ISA (UK and Ireland) 580 requires that auditors should obtain written confirmation of representations from management on matters material to the financial statements when these representations are critical to obtaining sufficient appropriate audit evidence. For life insurers falling within the FSA's realistic capital regime, representations in relation to the management actions assumed in the valuation of realistic liabilities are likely to be relevant. For other insurers, it may be appropriate to obtain a specific representation confirming that full disclosure has been made in respect of any side letters, any multi-year reinsurance contracts or any reinsurance contracts with unusual adjustable features, as well as the adequacy of the claims provision and the IBNR. Auditors may also obtain written representations from those charged with governance regarding:

- the reasonableness of significant assumptions used by the entity in calculating technical provisions;
- all correspondence with regulators having been made available to the auditor

228

ISA (UK and IRELAND) 600: USING THE WORK OF ANOTHER AUDITOR

Background note

The purpose of this ISA (UK and Ireland) is to establish standards and provide guidance when an auditor, reporting on the financial statements of an entity, uses the work of another auditor on the financial information of one or more components included in the financial statements of the entity. This ISA (UK and Ireland) does not deal with those instances where two or more auditors are appointed as joint auditors nor does it deal with the auditors' relationship with a predecessor auditor. Further, when the principal auditor concludes that the financial statements of a component are immaterial, the standards in this ISA (UK and Ireland) do not apply. When, however, several components, immaterial in themselves, are together material, the procedures outlined in this ISA (UK and Ireland) would need to be considered.

When the principal auditor uses the work of another auditor, the principal auditor should determine how the work of the other auditor will affect the audit. (paragraph 2)

In the UK and Ireland, when planning to use the work of another auditor, the principal auditor's consideration of the professional competence of the other auditor should include consideration of the professional qualifications, experience and resources of the other auditor in the context of the specific assignment. (paragraph 7-1)

229 The principal auditor considers in particular the competence and capability of the other auditor having regard to the laws, regulation and industry practice relevant to the component to be reported on by the other auditor and, where relevant, whether the other auditor has access to actuarial or other expertise appropriate to the component's insurance business.

230 Further procedures may be necessary for the auditor of a UK insurer where audit work in support of the audit opinion is undertaken by an individual or audit firm that is not subject to the UK audit regulatory regime. Where an overseas firm of the auditor (or an audit firm independent of the auditor) is undertaking audit procedures on a branch, or division or in-house shared service centre of the insurer, the auditor has due regard to the requirements in the Audit Regulations[24] to ensure all relevant members of the engagement team are and continue to be fit and proper, are and continue to be competent and are aware of and follow these Audit Regulations and any related procedures and requirements established by the audit firm. This includes the auditor's duty to report direct to the FSA in certain circumstances – see ISA (UK and Ireland) 250 section B.

231 In rare circumstances a branch or other part of a UK authorised insurer may be audited by another firm In these circumstances the other auditor has a duty to report matters of material significance to the FSA rather than via the principal auditor.

---

[24] *Audit Regulations and Guidelines – December 2005 issued by the Institute of Chartered Accountants in England and Wales, the Institute of Chartered Accountants in Scotland and the Institute of Chartered Accountants in Ireland.*

However, it is likely that any such matters would have a direct bearing on the work of the principal auditor and would likely be reported to the principal auditor. In such circumstances the principal auditor would consider also reporting such matters directly to the FSA. More detailed consideration of the auditors' duty to report to the FSA is set out in the section of this Practice Note dealing with ISA (UK and Ireland) 250.

Additional considerations relating to Lloyd's

Lloyd's corporate members

Lloyd's has established a central facility to assist corporate members in preparing their statutory financial statements. The facility accumulates information from underlying syndicates and then calculates and aggregates each corporate member's share of that information. The syndicate information is provided to Lloyd's within the syndicate Annual Return together with a syndicate auditor's report thereon.

232

Where corporate members rely on information provided by way of the central clearing system, auditors of corporate members apply the principles of ISA (UK and Ireland) 600 in considering how the work of syndicate auditors affects their audit. Where auditors of corporate members rely on the work of syndicate auditors, they consider the professional qualifications, experience and resources of the other auditors in the context of their audit of the corporate member in question. They obtain appropriate evidence that the work of the syndicate auditors is sufficient for the purposes of the audit of the corporate member's financial statements.

233

Lloyd's syndicates

Syndicate auditors frequently experience situations where audit evidence is derived from information audited by other auditors, for example, where the audit of the managing agent is carried out by a separate firm from the syndicate's auditors. Consequently, the syndicate's auditors may have regard to the work of the agency's auditors in respect of recharged expenses. Also, in the case of certain service company arrangements, different auditors may review the activities of the service company on behalf of the syndicate from the auditors of the syndicate.

234

ISA (UK and IRELAND) 620: USING THE WORK OF AN EXPERT

Background note

The purpose of this ISA (UK and Ireland) is to establish standards and provide guidance on using the work of an expert as audit evidence.

When using the work performed by an expert, the auditor should obtain sufficient appropriate audit evidence that such work is adequate for the purposes of the audit. (paragraph 2)

235 As stated in the section on ISA (UK and Ireland) 540, given the nature and complexity of insurance business the auditor may involve an actuary in assessing technical provisions in the audit of the financial statements. The FSA requires the auditor of a life insurer to obtain and pay due regard to the advice of a reviewing actuary when reporting on regulatory returns (see 'Reporting on regulatory returns' section). Where the auditor uses an expert as part of the audit, the auditor remains solely responsible for the audit of the insurer's financial statements and will not refer to the work of the expert within the auditor's report.

236 Where the auditor decides to use an actuarial expert in relation to his audit of the insurer's technical provisions, the auditor assesses the following:

- the professional competence of the actuary, taking into consideration his professional qualifications, experience and reputation in the market in which the insurer operates;
- the objectivity of the actuary including whether the actuary is connected in some way to the insurer e.g. being financially dependent on the insurer or having a financial interest in the insurer; and
- the scope of the work to be undertaken and degree of reliance that the auditor can place thereon.

An actuary involved in the audit process, although guided by his own profession's standards and guidance and by BAS standards, designs and performs his work to provide the auditor with the required level of audit comfort.

237 Where the actuary is employed by the audit firm, the auditor will be able to rely on his firm's quality control systems, recruitment and training to determine the actuary's capabilities and competence, rather than having to evaluate them for each audit engagement.

238 Where the auditor plans to use an external actuary, the terms of his engagement are established formally in writing, which may include matters such as the following:

- the objectives and scope of the actuary's work;
- the specific matters that the actuary should report on;
- the extent of reliance to be placed by the auditor on the actuary's work;
- the auditor's access to the working papers produced by the actuary; and
- confidentiality of information arising from the client or the auditor.

239 The auditor does not have the same expertise as the actuary. Nevertheless, the auditor seeks to understand and assess the work performed by the actuarial expert and determine whether the actuary's findings are reasonable, based on the auditor's knowledge of the business and the results of other audit procedures. If the actuary's findings are not consistent with other audit evidence, the auditor attempts to resolve the differences by applying additional audit procedures. If the auditor is not satisfied that there is sufficient appropriate audit evidence to support the audit opinion and there is no satisfactory alternative source of audit evidence, the auditor considers the implications for the audit report.

ISA (UK and IRELAND) 700: THE AUDITOR'S REPORT ON FINANCIAL STATEMENTS

Background note

The purpose of this ISA (UK and Ireland) is to establish standards and provide guidance on the form and content of the auditor's report issued as a result of an audit performed by an independent auditor of the financial statements of an entity. Much of the guidance provided can be adapted to auditor reports on financial information other than financial statements.

The auditor should consider modifying the auditor's report by adding a paragraph if there is a significant uncertainty (other than a going concern problem), the resolution of which is dependent on future events and which may affect the financial statements (paragraph 32)

240 The basis on which an insurer's financial statements are prepared takes account of the extent of the inherent uncertainty in the types of insurance business it underwrites. Uncertainties arising from insurance contracts may include:

- general uncertainties arising where the outcomes for provisioning are within a range which is not unusual for the nature of the business underwritten;
- specific uncertainties which are material and subject to an unusually wide range of outcomes; and
- uncertainties where financial reporting standards do not require a provision to be established but where a contingent liability disclosure may be appropriate.

241 If the auditor concludes that the technical provisions are materially misstated or that the disclosures relating to those provisions and the relevant uncertainties are inadequate or misleading and consider that the effect is material to the view given by the financial statements, he is required by ISA (UK and Ireland) 700 to qualify his opinion.

242 Determining technical provisions is subject to a high degree of inherent uncertainty and frequently involves statistical techniques. When reporting on an insurer's financial statements, auditors assess whether such uncertainties fall within the category of significant, and so require to be disclosed in their report. In making this assessment, auditors take into account whether the financial statements provide a user with general information about the types of business written such that the overall level of inherent uncertainty likely to apply to those financial statements is apparent.

243 In rare circumstances the auditor may consider a matter disclosed in the financial statements to be of such importance to users' understanding of the financial statements as a whole that it is appropriate to draw their attention to it. The fact that an auditor of an insurer has identified that the high estimation uncertainty associated with the calculation of technical provisions gives rise to a significant risk does not automatically require the auditor to modify his report for the existence of a significant uncertainty.

244 Where high estimation uncertainties involve significant levels of concern about the validity of the going concern basis they will be regarded as significant and require the auditor to modify his report. In these circumstances the auditor takes account of the

guidance in ISA (UK and Ireland) 570 'The going concern basis in financial statements' and considers whether a duty to report to the regulator exists.

Statutory equalisation provisions

245   INSPRU 1.4 sets out the type of general insurance business in respect of which equalisation provisions are required to be established and maintained by authorised insurers and the formulae to be used in calculating the amount of such provisions.

246   Whilst not permitted under IFRS, for general insurers preparing financial statements in accordance with UK financial reporting standards Schedule 9A to the Companies Act 1985 requires equalisation provisions to be included in an authorised insurer's balance sheet as part of 'technical provisions' under the general heading 'liabilities' (Balance sheet format, item C5 and paragraph 50 of Schedule 9A). However such equalisation provisions are not 'liabilities' as normally defined for the purposes of accounting standards. Consequently, the APB has taken legal advice to clarify the position. The advice obtained is to the following effect:

(a) Individual authorised insurers:
    (i) individual authorised insurers are required by statute to include equalisation provisions in financial statements prepared in accordance with Schedule 9A; and
    (ii) the statutory regime does not permit an argument that, in the generality of cases, the inclusion of equalisation provisions would be inconsistent with showing a true and fair view;

(b) Insurance groups:
    (i) any equalisation provisions in the financial statements of those undertakings being consolidated should be included in the consolidated financial statements;
    (ii) such equalisation provisions may not in the generality of cases:
- be excluded from the consolidated financial statements to ensure that those statements conform with generally accepted accounting principles or practice (Schedule 4A, paragraph 1(1));
- be adjusted so as to accord with the rules used for the group financial statements (Schedule 4A, paragraph 3(1) and paragraph 3(1A)); or
- be excluded on the basis that, under section 227 of the Companies Act 1985, the inclusion of such equalisation reserves in the consolidated financial statements would be inconsistent with showing a true and fair view;

    (iii) it would not be appropriate, with the objective of ensuring that accounting policies shall be applied consistently within the same financial statements:
- to include, on consolidation, equalisation provisions in respect of the businesses of those undertakings which are not required by law to establish equalisation provisions; or
- to eliminate all equalisation provisions in the consolidated financial statements.

The legal advice did not extend to the case of individual authorised insurers or groups preparing their financial statements in accordance with IFRS. However, where this is the case equalisation provisions should not be included in the balance sheet.

247   The Insurance SORP recommends that financial statements incorporating equalisation provisions should disclose:

(a) that the amounts provided are in addition to the provisions required to meet the anticipated ultimate cost of settlement of outstanding claims at the balance sheet date, and that notwithstanding this, Schedule 9A to the Companies Act 1985 requires the amounts to be included within technical provisions; and
(b) the impact of equalisation provisions on shareholders' funds and the effect of movements in the provisions on the results of the accounting period (and, if appropriate, an alternative earnings per share figure disregarding equalisation provisions).

248 Provided that adequate disclosure is made in financial statements which contain statutory equalisation provisions (and in the absence of other reasons to conclude that the financial statements do not give a true and fair view), it is appropriate to regard the financial statements incorporating such equalisation provisions as giving, in the particular circumstances, the required true and fair view. Consequently, unless special circumstances exist which are particular to the company or group concerned, auditors are justified in concluding that financial statements including such provisions give a true and fair view, and in expressing an unqualified opinion to that effect.

249 Notwithstanding that an unqualified opinion is expressed, it is appropriate for auditors to include reference to the particular legal requirements concerning equalisation provisions in their report, when the effect of those provisions is material to an insurance company's financial statements, in order to ensure that a reader is aware that their opinion is expressed in the context of those requirements.

250 ISA (UK and Ireland) 700 includes a requirement that auditors explain the basis of their opinion by including certain specified information in their report. ISA (UK and Ireland) 700 also states that auditors may wish to include further comment drawing attention to other information they regard as relevant to a proper understanding of the basis of their opinion. Accordingly, when reporting on financial statements containing equalisation provisions which are material to their opinion, auditors include in the basis of opinion section of their report an additional comment referring to:

(a) the statutory requirements to maintain equalisation provisions; and
(b) information contained in the financial statements concerning their financial effect.

251 In the absence of other reasons to conclude that the financial statements do not give a true and fair view, auditors express an unqualified opinion on the view given by financial statements which incorporate equalisation provisions in the manner required by Schedule 9A. Such an opinion is only appropriate if:

(a) the provisions are established in accordance with the statutory requirements; and
(b) the financial statements include adequate disclosure concerning the provisions.

252 Factors which need to be taken into account in forming a judgment on the adequacy of disclosure include:

- whether the amounts concerned are clearly distinguished from other items in technical provisions;
- whether the reasons for the effects of the accounting treatment followed are adequately described such that a reader would appreciate the special nature of the provisions;
- whether the disclosure includes comment making it clear that the amounts so included in liabilities are over and above the provisions required to meet the

anticipated ultimate cost of settlement of outstanding claims at the balance sheet date; and
- whether a reader is able to identify the financial effect of equalisation provisions on the company's net assets and the effect of movements in the provisions on the results for the period.

253 Auditors issue a qualified opinion on the view given by those statements if they conclude that disclosure concerning the reserves is inadequate.

254 Illustrative wording of a paragraph to be included in an auditors' report on financial statements of authorised insurers, that are prepared in accordance with UK GAAP and include statutory equalisation reserves is as follows:

"Equalisation provisions

Our evaluation of the presentation of information in the financial statements has had regard to the statutory requirement for insurance companies to maintain equalisation provisions. The nature of equalisation provisions, the amounts set aside at (date), and the effect of the movement in those provisions during the year on shareholders' funds, the balance on the general business technical account and profit [loss] before tax, are disclosed in note x."

Additional considerations relating to Lloyd's

255 Auditors of Lloyd's syndicates' financial statements are required to report their opinion as to whether the annual accounts comply with the requirements of the 2004 Regulations, and whether run-off underwriting year accounts comply with the requirements of the Syndicate Accounting Byelaw.

256 In addition, their report on the annual accounts includes their opinion on whether they give a true and fair view of the calendar year result and of the state of affairs at the balance sheet date. The report of the auditor on closed year underwriting year accounts includes their opinion on whether they give a true and fair view of the result of the closed year of account.

257 Lloyd's require that the auditors' report on syndicate underwriting year accounts is to be addressed to the members of the syndicate participating in the year of account to which they relate and not to all members of the syndicate. Different reporting requirements apply to syndicate underwriting year accounts for a closed year of account as apply to syndicate underwriting year accounts for a run-off year of account which is not closing. Syndicates are not required to maintain statutory equalisation provisions.

258 In preparing underwriting accounts for a closed year of a syndicate, compliance with UK financial reporting standards is normally necessary in order to give a true and fair view of the syndicate's closed year result.

259 Inherent uncertainty is also relevant to syndicate underwriting year accounts. Auditors reporting on underwriting accounts therefore consider:

(a) whether the accounts have been prepared on an appropriate basis;
(b) whether appropriate disclosures have been made; and
(c) whether any uncertainties are significant, having regard to the types of business underwritten by the syndicate.

The auditors of the syndicate underwriting year accounts are required to report by exception if: 260

(a) the managing agent has not maintained proper accounting records in respect of the syndicate;
(b) the underwriting year accounts do not agree with the accounting records; and
(c) they have not received all the information and explanations that they require.

Illustrative wording of an auditor's report on the underwriting accounts of Lloyd's syndicates is shown in Appendix 1.

Members' personal accounts (including syndicate MAPA accounts)

Managing agents are required to prepare personal accounts and MAPA accounts where there is a closed and/or run-off year of account of a syndicate if they are required to prepare syndicate underwriting year accounts or run-off accounts. 261

In addition to their report on a syndicate's annual accounts and underwriting year accounts, syndicate auditors are required to report as to whether the managing agent's procedures and controls provide assurance that:

- members' personal accounts and syndicate MAPA accounts have been properly prepared in accordance with the Syndicate Accounting Byelaw; and
- the net results shown in members' personal accounts and syndicate MAPA accounts have been calculated in accordance with the applicable agency agreements.

In order to be in a position to express an opinion that the procedures and controls taken as a whole are adequate to enable the managing agent to comply with the provisions of the Lloyd's Syndicate Accounting Byelaw, syndicate auditors consider the need for additional procedures beyond those undertaken for the audit of the annual accounts and of the underwriting accounts. Illustrative wording of such a report is shown in Appendix 1.

In providing support for their opinion on members' personal accounts syndicate auditors understand management's process for the preparation of accounts of individual Lloyd's syndicate members and identify, and test as appropriate, the controls that management have established to ensure they are operating effectively. Management controls will include controls to ensure that: 262

- records of individual Lloyd's syndicate participations are accurately maintained;
- changes in Lloyd's reporting requirements in respect of personal accounts are identified and, if necessary, systems are updated;
- personal account totals are reconciled with syndicate accounting records; and
- output from the system is monitored to ensure that Lloyd's requirements have been complied with.

The auditors of personal accounts are required to report by exception if: 263

(a) the managing agent has not maintained proper accounting records in respect of the syndicate;
(b) the personal accounts do not agree with the accounting records; and
(c) they have not received all the information and explanations that they require.

ISA (UK and IRELAND) 720 (Revised): Section A – OTHER INFORMATION IN DOCUMENTS CONTAINING AUDITED FINANCIAL STATEMENTS

Background note

The purpose of this ISA (UK and Ireland) is to establish standards and provide guidance on the auditors consideration of other information, on which the auditor has no obligation to report, in documents containing audited financial statements .This ISA (UK and Ireland) applies when an annual report is involved; however, it may also apply to other documents.

The auditor should read the other information to identify material inconsistencies with the audited financial statements. (paragraph 2)

If as a result of reading the other information, the auditor becomes aware of any apparent misstatement therein, or identifies any material inconsistencies with the audited financial statements the auditor should seek to resolve them. (paragraph 2-1)

If, on reading the other information, the auditor identifies a material inconsistency, the auditor should determine whether the audited financial statements or the other information needs to be amended. (paragraph 11)

264   Insurance companies undertaking long-term business may include supplementary financial statements prepared on an alternative basis to that used in drawing up the financial statements. Without adequate explanation, such supplementary statements may appear inconsistent with the audited financial statements. Auditors therefore consider whether an adequate explanation of the assumptions and different methodology has been provided in the annual report, and if not, they consider including an additional comment in their report on the financial statements.

265   Supplementary financial statements showing performance arising on long-term business calculated on an alternative basis are prepared using different assumptions and methodologies from those applied in preparing the primary financial statements. There are many aspects of the supplementary statements not affected by the alternative assumptions and methodologies and where material the auditor considers whether they are treated consistently in both the primary financial statements and supplementary financial statements. For those material items where different assumptions and methodologies are applied to the same data to produce the supplementary statements the auditor considers whether consistent data has been used.

266   The auditor reads the supplementary financial statements in the light of knowledge acquired during the audit and considers whether there are any apparent misstatements therein. The auditor is not expected to verify or audit the information contained in the supplementary financial statements.

267   The work of the auditor in reporting to the directors on supplementary statements prepared on the alternative method of reporting long term business is outside the scope of this Practice Note.

Reporting on regulatory returns

Auditors of insurers are required to report on specified matters in relation to returns required from the insurer by its regulator. This section sets out guidance for auditors reporting on regulatory returns of authorised insurance companies and of Lloyd's syndicates.   **268**

The following regulatory returns are covered by this section:
- Composite, life and general insurance company regulatory returns;
- Report on group capital adequacy;
- Lloyd's syndicate Annual Return.

Auditors reporting on an insurer's regulatory return often also carry out an audit of its financial statements in accordance with ISAs (UK and Ireland). In such cases, the work that auditors perform on regulatory returns does not represent a second audit, but represents a set of additional procedures which, in conjunction with the evidence drawn from the audit work carried out in relation to the financial statements, will enable them to report as required. When undertaking such additional procedures auditors have regard to the Auditors' Code and the general principles set out below.   **269**

General Principles

The general principles applicable to reporting on regulatory returns are as follows: **270**
- Auditors plan the work to be undertaken in relation to the regulatory return so as to perform that work in an effective manner, taking into account their other reporting responsibilities.
- Auditors familiarise themselves with the regulations governing the preparation of the regulatory return.
- Auditors comply, where relevant, with APB Ethical Standards for Auditors and with ethical guidance issued by their relevant professional bodies.
- Auditors agree the terms of the engagement with the insurer and record them in writing. The auditor may choose to combine the audit requirements in relation to regulatory audits with the financial statement engagement letter, for example in relation to the audit of regulatory returns and the group solvency return (if applicable). In the case of an insurer carrying on long-term insurance business (other than a Lloyd's syndicate), this will include reference to the requirement that the auditor will engage a suitably qualified actuary who is independent of the insurer and pay due regard to advice from that actuary. This actuary is referred to as the Reviewing Actuary[25] by the Faculty and Institute of Actuaries, and this term is used in this section of the Practice Note.
- Auditors consider materiality and its relationship with the risk of material misstatement in the regulatory return in planning their work and in determining the effect of their findings on their report.
- Auditors undertake their work with an attitude of professional scepticism and carry out procedures designed to obtain sufficient appropriate evidence on which to base their opinion on the regulatory return. In particular they:
  (a) apply analytical procedures in forming an overall conclusion as to whether the regulatory return as a whole is consistent with their knowledge of the insurer's business; and
  (b) obtain written confirmation of appropriate representations from management before their report is issued.
- Auditors record in their working papers:
  (a) details of the engagement planning;

[25] Defined in GN 39 and GN 42.

- (b) the nature, timing and extent of the procedures performed in relation to their report on the regulatory return, and the conclusions drawn; and
- (c) their reasoning and conclusions on all significant matters which require the exercise of judgment.
• Auditors reporting on regulatory returns which include financial information on which other auditors have reported obtain sufficient appropriate evidence that the work of those other auditors is adequate for their purposes.
• Auditors issue a report containing a clear expression of their opinion on the regulatory return.
• Auditors consider the matters which have come to their attention while performing the procedures on the regulatory return and whether they should be included in a report to directors or management.
• If the auditors become aware of matters of material significance to the regulator, they make a report direct to the FSA and/or Lloyd's. In addition, when issuing their report on the regulatory return, auditors:
- (a) consider whether there are consequential reporting issues affecting their opinion which arise from any report previously made direct to the FSA and/or Lloyd's in the course of their appointment; and
- (b) assess whether any matters encountered in the course of their work indicate a need for a further direct report.

Authorised insurers

(The following paragraphs do not apply to Lloyd's syndicates, guidance on which is set out in paragraphs 309-319)

271 An insurer regulated by the FSA is required by rule 9.6 of IPRU(INS) to submit a return (the regulatory return) to the FSA within three months of the end of each financial year (reduced to two months and fifteen days if the return is not submitted in an approved electronic form). The format of this return is prescribed by Chapter 9 of IPRU(INS) and its related Appendices. UK incorporated insurers and pure reinsurers (wherever incorporated) are required to prepare a global return covering all business undertaken on a world-wide basis, while direct insurers with head offices outside the EEA are required to prepare both a global return and a UK branch return. Special provisions relate to Swiss direct general insurers and to EEA-deposit insurers.

272 Rule 9.5 of IPRU(INS) requires the regulatory return to be audited in accordance with rule 9.35 by a person qualified in accordance with the rules defined in SUP.

The form and content of the Regulatory Return

273 IPRU(INS) Rule 9.3 refers to the central elements of the regulatory return as comprising a revenue account for the year, a balance sheet as at the end of the year and a profit and loss account for the year or, in the case of a company not trading for profit, an income and expenditure account for the year. Much of the return is made up of a series of forms designed to provide information of the insurance business undertaken in the form of detailed analyses of a balance sheet and a profit and loss account, as these terms are normally understood, in a format suitable for computer input.

274 The requirement to prepare a regulatory return is quite separate from the requirement for a UK incorporated insurer to prepare financial statements under the Companies Act 1985; furthermore, the regulatory return may be prepared some time

after the financial statements have been approved. There is, however, a close correlation between the overall figures included in the two documents. Except where over-ridden by the rules in IPRU(INS), words and expressions used in Schedule 9A have the same meaning within IPRU(INS). In general the rules are drafted so as to remove a number of restrictions that previously applied so that insurers can now apply the same accounting policies in both the regulatory return and the financial statements. In particular GENPRU 1.3 effectively requires that, except where a rule in GENPRU or INSPRU provides for a different method of recognition or valuation, whenever a rule in GENPRU or INSPRU refers to an asset, liability, equity or income statement item, then the insurer for the purposes of that rule, recognises the asset, liability, equity or income statement item and measures its value in accordance with UK GAAP or, where IFRS has been adopted, in accordance with IFRS.

The principal differences between the regulatory return and financial statements prepared under the Companies Act 1985 are as follows: **275**

(a) the regulatory return is primarily intended to demonstrate the solvency of an insurer. Copies of the financial statements are also submitted to the regulator;
(b) the balance sheet included in the regulatory return may show items at different values from those shown in the financial statements, arising from the application of prescribed rules in respect of:
 – the assets that can be treated as admissible; assets that are not admissible (for example deferred acquisition costs in respect of long-term business) are left out of account;
 – the basic valuation principles to be applied to admissible assets and to liabilities;
 – restrictions on the value of assets where the value arrived at by applying the basic valuation principles exceeds the permitted market risk or counter-party exposure limits;
 – the determination of long-term insurance business liabilities;
 – the treatment of certain types of hybrid capital; and
 – a provision for reasonable foreseeable adverse variations where certain commitments are not strictly matched;
(c) the income statement, particularly for general business, provides a large volume of detailed segmental information including a breakdown into combined categories and further sub-divisions into material risk categories, which are reported by currency and, in some cases, reporting territory. Deposit accounting must not be used in the income statement for long-term insurance contracts even where these contracts are subject to deposit accounting as investment business in the financial statements;
(d) additional information is provided on a variety of topics including:
 – the Abstract of the valuation, prepared by the actuarial function holder(s) for a company carrying on long-term insurance business;
 – general business reinsurance arrangements;
 – major general business reinsurers and cedants;
 – the use of derivatives;
 – controllers; and
 – the interests of the actuary appointed to perform the with-profits actuary function;
(e) the regulatory return is accompanied by a certificate signed by prescribed officers of the insurer ('the certificate') which contains a number of statements including statements that the return has been properly prepared in accordance with the requirements in IPRU(INS), INSPRU and GENPRU. This statement is outside the scope of the audit.

Auditors' responsibilities

276 Part II of Appendix 9.6 to IPRU(INS) indicates the matters that must be included in the auditors' report. The basic elements prescribed are:

(a) an opinion as to whether Forms 1 to 3 [or 1, 2 and 10], 11 to 32, 34, 36 to 45, 48, 49, 56, 58 and 60 (including the supplementary notes thereto) and the statements, analyses and reports pursuant to rules 9.25 to 9.27, 9.29 and 9.31 of IPRU(INS) have been properly prepared in accordance with the provisions of the Accounts and Statements Rules (IPRU(INS) rules 9.1 to 9.36E and 9.39), GENPRU and INSPRU.

(b) an opinion as to whether the methods and assumptions determined by the insurer and used to perform the actuarial valuation as set out in the valuation reports appropriately reflect the requirements of INSPRU 1.2 and 1.3.

The auditors of a long-term insurer are also required to obtain, and state in their report that they have obtained and paid due regard to advice from a suitably qualified actuary independent of the insurer in respect of any amounts or information abstracted from the actuarial investigation.

277 In addition, IPRU(INS) requires auditors to report by exception on the maintenance of adequate accounting records and other matters specified by section 237 of the Companies Act 1985.

Standards to be applied by auditors

278 In the case of a UK incorporated insurance company, an audit of the financial statements prepared under the Companies Act 1985 will be conducted in accordance with ISAs (UK and Ireland) issued by the APB to enable the report required by section 235 of the Companies Act 1985 to be given. Key areas in which auditors need to undertake procedures additional to those undertaken to report on the financial statements are:

(a) the application of the prescribed valuation and admissibility rules to assets and liabilities for which existence, title, etc. has already been considered as a part of the audit of the insurer's financial statements;
(b) the sub-division of general business revenue information into the prescribed categories;
(c) presentation of the information in the prescribed forms; and
(d) the specific additional disclosures that fall within the scope of the auditors' report.

279 If an audit of financial statements in accordance with ISAs (UK and Ireland) has not been undertaken (as may be the case in relation to the UK branch of an insurance company incorporated outside the UK) the regulatory return will need to have been subjected to an audit in accordance with those Standards in order to achieve an equivalent standard of evidence.

280 Work specific to the auditors' report on an insurance company's regulatory return may be undertaken concurrently with procedures designed to provide evidence for their report on its financial statements or at a later date. In either case, the auditors consider both aspects of their engagement when planning the audit of the financial statements.

281 Although IPRU(INS) does not require the regulatory return to be drawn up to show a true and fair view, rule 9.11 of IPRU(INS) requires that the return:

'must fairly state the information provided on the basis required by the Accounts and Statements Rule'.

This is of a similar qualitative standard to the requirement of company law that financial statements prepared in accordance with UK financial reporting standards give a true and fair view of a company's state of affairs and profit or loss, hence equivalent considerations of materiality apply. In evaluating whether the requirements of rule 9.11 have been met, auditors therefore apply materiality in relation to the business as a whole, rather than in relation to the particular business reporting category within which a particular item is reported. Following this approach, reliance on analytical review techniques is normally appropriate in relation to, for example, the segmental information provided within the regulatory return. 282

The Auditor's Procedures on Regulatory Returns

Long-term business

The auditor's reporting responsibilities are set out in paragraph 276 above. 283

As also noted above, Rules 9.35(1A) of IPRU(INS) requires that where any part of the regulatory return that is subject to audit contains amounts or information abstracted from the actuarial investigation, the auditor is required to obtain and pay due regard to advice from a reviewing actuary who is independent of the insurer and suitably qualified. 284

The actuarial investigation includes: 285

"(a) a determination of the liabilities of the insurer attributable to its long-term insurance business;
(b) a valuation of any excess over those liabilities of the assets representing the long-term insurance fund or funds and, where any rights of any long-term policy holders to participate in profits relate to particular parts of such a fund a valuation of any excess of assets over liabilities in respect of each of those parts; and
(c) for every long-term insurer which is a realistic basis life firm, a calculation of the with-profits insurance capital component."

The FSA Handbook does not set out the nature of the advice to be obtained from the reviewing actuary or provide guidance on the nature or extent of the work to be performed by the reviewing actuary in providing that advice. The responsibility for determining the nature of the advice and, consequently, the scope and extent of the reviewing actuary's work lies with the auditor, although the auditor discusses the proposed scope of work with the reviewing actuary and considers the views of the reviewing actuary before finalising the scope of work. 286

The auditor obtains advice from the reviewing actuary on those elements of the actuarial investigation that the auditor believes, for the purpose of the audit of the annual return, require expert actuarial input to assess. The areas of the actuarial investigation that the auditor will seek advice from a reviewing actuary on include: 287

- whether the methods and assumptions used to calculate the mathematical reserves appropriately reflect the requirements of INSPRU 1.2 ("Mathematical reserves");
- whether the methods and assumptions used to calculate the "With-profits insurance capital component" ("WPICC") appropriately reflect the requirements of INSPRU 1.3 ("With-profits insurance capital component); and

- whether the statement(s) made under rule 9.31 of IPRU(INS) ("Valuation reports on long-term insurance business") are made in accordance with the requirements of Appendix 9.4 and Appendix 9.4A of IPRU(INS).

288 In addition to obtaining advice on the matters set out in the paragraph above, the auditor obtains advice on all other elements of the actuarial investigation to the extent that they are relevant to the auditable parts of the return. The elements of the actuarial investigation, other than those detailed above, that the auditor may also seek to obtain advice from the reviewing actuary on include:

- whether the data underlying the calculation of the mathematical reserves and WPICC are reliable;
- whether the models used to apply the methods and assumptions underlying the mathematical reserves and WPICC are operating appropriately;
- whether the data contained in Forms 18, 19, 48, 49, 56, 58 and 60 have been correctly abstracted from the actuarial valuation.
- whether the data contained in line 51 of Form 11 has been correctly abstracted from the actuarial valuation (for insurers which transact health insurance).

Consideration of the guidance as set out above, is likely to be of particular relevance to auditors where the auditable parts of the return include disclosure of data at the level of type of product or class of contract. Disclosures in this level of detail are included in the Valuation Reports required under rule 9.31 of IPRU(INS).

289 The auditor engages the reviewing actuary to perform work to the scope the auditor, following discussion with the reviewing actuary, determines is appropriate. Whilst the formality of these arrangements may vary depending on whether the reviewing actuary is with a third party firm of actuaries or is an employee or partner of the auditor or his member firms, the auditor will agree in writing the scope of work and reporting by the reviewing actuary. It is expected that this will include, inter alia,

- the scope of work to be performed by the reviewing actuary including the areas of the actuarial investigation and auditable parts of the return on which the reviewing actuary will perform work and details of the nature and scope of the work to be performed;
- the form of the review that the auditor will carry out on the work of the reviewing actuary;
- the form of report to be issued to the auditor containing the advice from the reviewing actuary;
- a requirement that the reviewing actuary will perform their work having due regard to relevant guidance issued by the Faculty and Institute of Actuaries and the BAS and will notify the auditor immediately he becomes aware of any matters that may indicate non-compliance with the guidance;
- protocols for the timely reporting to the auditor of any issues arising in relation to the duty to report matters of material significance to the FSA;
- arrangements for the confirmation of the reviewing actuary's independence and qualifications (if not an employee or partner of the auditor or his member firms); and
- a requirement for the reviewing actuary to notify the auditor immediately of any significant facts and matters that bear upon the reviewing actuary's objectivity and independence.

Establishing the independence of the reviewing actuary

The auditor should be satisfied that any reviewing actuary will be independent and document the rationale for that conclusion. Guidance for the auditor on establishing the independence of the reviewing actuary is set out below. 290

When planning the audit of the regulatory return, the engagement partner obtains information from the reviewing actuary as to the existence of any connections that the reviewing actuary has with the client including: 291

- financial interests;
- business relationships (including the provision of services);
- employment (past, present and future); and
- family and other personal relationships.

The engagement partner assesses the threats to objectivity and independence that arise from any connections disclosed and considers whether the reviewing actuary has implemented safeguards to eliminate the threats or reduce them to an acceptable level. 292

When assessing the threats to objectivity and independence which arise from services provided to the client or its affiliates and the effectiveness of safeguards established by the actuarial firm, the engagement partner will consider the following factors: 293

- whether the reviewing actuary was the person responsible for the service provided;
- the materiality and the nature of the services to the actuarial firm;
- the extent to which the outcomes of services have been reviewed by another actuarial firm.

In certain circumstances, it is unlikely that any safeguards can eliminate the threat to objectivity and independence or reduce it to an acceptable level. Such circumstances are likely to include: 294

- direct financial interests in the client or an affiliate held by the actuarial firm, the reviewing actuary, any member of the reviewing actuary's team, or immediate family members of such persons;
- material business relationships with the client or an affiliate entered into by the actuarial firm, the reviewing actuary, any member of the reviewing actuary's team, or immediate family members of such persons;
- any connection that enables the client to influence the affairs of the actuarial firm, or the performance of any actuarial review engagement undertaken by the firm;
- situations involving any employment[26] of the reviewing actuary or any member of the reviewing actuary's team, in the past two years, or their current or potential employment with the client;
- situations involving employment of immediate family members of the reviewing actuary, or any member of the reviewing actuary's team by the client in a key management position;
- in the case of listed companies, where the reviewing actuary has acted in this role for a continuous period longer than seven years;
- situations where more than 10% of the total fees of the actuarial firm are regularly receivable from the client and its subsidiaries;

---

[26] *Employment includes appointment to the board of directors of the audit client, any sub-committee of the board, or to such a position in an entity that holds, directly or indirectly, more than 20% of the voting rights in the audit client, or in which the audit client holds directly or indirectly more than 20% of the voting rights.*

- any contingent fee arrangements for services provided to the client and its affiliates by the actuarial firm where the fee is dependent on a future or contemporary actuarial judgment;
- any engagement in the current period of the actuarial firm to provide actuarial valuation or financial reporting services to the client[27] or services where the objectives of the engagement are inconsistent with the objectives of the work of the reviewing actuary.

295 The engagement partner requires the reviewing actuary to notify him immediately of changes in the circumstances on which information was obtained at the start of the engagement, or any others that might reasonably be considered a threat to their objectivity.

296 Where the engagement partner identifies a significant threat to objectivity and independence which has not been eliminated or reduced to an acceptable level, he discusses with the FSA the circumstances that give rise to the threat and what course of action would be appropriate, including obtaining a rule waiver from the FSA. In circumstances where the matter cannot be resolved satisfactorily, the engagement partner considers making a reference to the independence of the reviewing actuary in the report made to the FSA.

Reviewing the work of the reviewing actuary

297 When obtaining and paying due regard to the advice of a reviewing actuary auditors have regard to ISA (UK and Ireland) 620 'Using the work of an expert'. In accordance with paragraph 5 of ISA (UK and Ireland) 620, when the auditor uses the work of an expert employed by the audit firm, the auditor will be able to rely on the firm's systems for recruitment and training that determine that expert's capabilities and competence, as explained in ISA (UK and Ireland) 220 'Quality control for audits of historical financial information' instead of needing to evaluate them for each audit engagement.

298 Consistent with the provisions of ISA (UK and Ireland) 620 the auditor assesses the appropriateness of the reviewing actuary's work as evidence regarding the elements of the annual return being considered. This involves assessment of whether the substance of the reviewing actuary's findings is properly reflected in the annual return, and includes consideration of:

- the source data used;
- the assumptions and methods used;
- when the reviewing actuary carried out the work;
- the reasons for any changes in assumptions and methods compared with those used in the prior period; and
- the results of the reviewing actuary's work in the light of the auditor's overall knowledge of the business and the results of other audit procedures.

299 When considering whether the reviewing actuary has used source data which is appropriate in the circumstances, the auditors may consider the following procedures:

(a) making enquiries regarding any procedures undertaken by the reviewing actuary to establish whether the source data is sufficient, relevant and reliable; and
(b) reviewing or testing the data used by the reviewing actuary.

---

[27] *This will include a service to act as Actuarial Function Holder or a With-profits Actuary.*

The auditors do not have the same expertise as the reviewing actuary; however, they seek to obtain an understanding of the assumptions and methods used by the entity and to consider whether they are reasonable, based on their knowledge of the business. If the results of the reviewing actuary's work are not consistent with other audit evidence, the auditor attempts to resolve the inconsistency by discussions with the reviewing actuary. Applying additional procedures, including possibly engaging another reviewing actuary, may also assist in resolving the inconsistency. If the auditors are not satisfied that the work of the reviewing actuary provides sufficient appropriate audit evidence to support their opinion on the regulatory returns and there is no satisfactory alternative source of audit evidence, they consider the implications for their audit report. 300

Reporting

Auditors' reports on regulatory returns normally include the following matters: 301

(a) a title identifying the persons to whom the report is addressed (which will normally be the directors of the insurance company);
(b) an introductory paragraph identifying the documents within the regulatory return which are covered by the report;
(c) separate sections, appropriately headed, dealing with:
 − respective responsibilities of the company and the auditors, and
 − the basis of the auditors' opinion;
(d) the auditors' opinions on the matters required by statute;
(e) the signature of the auditors; and
(f) the date of the auditors' report.

If the FSA has issued any directions to the insurer, waiving or modifying the application of any rules that affect the audited parts of a regulatory return, the auditor refers to this in the report and expresses the opinions by reference to the rules as modified.

Appendix 1 sets out illustrative examples of reports on regulatory returns for composite, long-term and general insurers. These example wordings need to be tailored to reflect particular circumstances. 302

Rule 9.3 of IPRU(INS) requires every insurer to prepare with respect to each financial year a revenue account, a balance sheet and a profit and loss account. While the global regulatory return might be regarded as the responsibility of the board of directors in the same way as for financial statements, in the case of a UK branch regulatory return, it is required to be signed by the principal UK Executive and the UK Authorised Representative. Consequently, the illustrative reports set out in the appendices refer to 'the company' rather than 'the directors', when referring to the respective responsibilities. 303

Subsequent events

There may be a gap between the date on which an insurance company's statutory financial statements are approved and the date on which its regulatory return is signed. Auditors undertake a review of post-balance sheet events up to the date of their report on the regulatory return before signing that report. 304

Qualifications or emphases of matter

305   When reporting on an insurance company's regulatory returns, auditors include an emphasis of matter or qualify their opinions as appropriate, following the principles in ISA 700 'The Auditors' report on financial statements'. It is possible for the auditors' opinion in their report on an insurance company's financial statements to be qualified whilst that on its regulatory return is unqualified, and vice versa. This may occur where the grounds for qualification relate to the treatment of a particular item (for example, if an asset is included in the regulatory return at a value which does not take account of the specific requirements of the rules relating to the valuation or admissibility of assets). Any qualification or emphasis of matter paragraph in respect of technical provisions would (in the absence of exceptional circumstances such as a Court judgment clarifying liability after the signing of the financial statements) be expected to be reflected in both reports.

306   When auditors include a qualification or an emphasis of matter in their report on the regulatory return, Appendix 9.6 of IPRU(INS) requires them to state whether, in their opinion, the uncertainty is material to determining whether the company has available assets in excess of its capital resources requirement.

307   The certificate is outside the scope of the audit and as such the auditor is not required to express an opinion on this statement. Therefore, despite the general requirement for auditors in ISA (UK and Ireland) 720 'Other information in documents containing audited financial statements' the auditor will not normally read the certificate to identify any inconsistencies with the audited elements of the return. If, however, the auditor becomes aware of any apparent misstatements in the certificate or identifies any material inconsistencies with the audited elements of the return, the auditor seeks to resolve them. This procedure should be extended to include any other form, statement, analysis or report required to be included in the return but not subject to audit.

Resubmitted returns

308   The FSA may require the company to resubmit the regulatory return, or part thereof, where the original regulatory return is considered to be inaccurate or incomplete. The auditors are normally required to express an opinion on the amended or additional material. This can be done by either:

   (a) withdrawing the original report and issuing a completely new report under rule 9.35 of IPRU (INS) or
   (b) issuing a supplementary report on the amended material only, but including a reference to the original report.

The first option is preferable where the nature and volume of changes required gives rise to a resubmission of the complete return. The second option is preferable where the amendments are considered to be relatively minor or are few in number and only the amended forms, supplementary notes and/or statements are resubmitted.

Additional considerations relating to Lloyd's

309   The principal differences between the syndicate Annual Return and the annual accounts of the syndicate are as follows:

   (a) the syndicate Annual Return is primarily intended to assist Lloyd's in preparing the market aggregate accounts in accordance with the 2004

Regulations and preparing the regulatory return to the FSA giving an overall view of solvency and performance of the market;
(b) solvency test adjustments are made within the syndicate Annual Return to reflect the application of prescribed assets and liabilities valuation rules in respect of:
- the assets that can be treated as admissible;
- the basic valuation principles to be applied to admissible assets;
- restrictions on the value of assets where the value arrived at by applying the basic valuation principles exceeds the permitted asset exposure limits;
- the basic valuation principles to be applied to the determination of liabilities for solvency test purposes in respect of each year of account included in the syndicate Annual Return;
(c) the profit and loss accounts in the syndicate Annual Return provide a breakdown of information into required accounting classes; and
(d) additional information in the syndicate Annual Return as specified by Lloyd's.

The syndicate Annual Return includes a managing agent's report to be attached to each submission signed by officers of the agency. The scope of these reports is prescribed by Lloyd's. There are no separate requirements for audited regulatory reports in respect of Lloyd's corporate members.

Auditors' responsibilities

Certain of the submissions of the syndicate Annual Return require an auditors' report to be included. The scope of these reports is prescribed by Lloyd's.

310

Standards to be applied by auditors

In the case of a Lloyd's syndicate, the audit of its annual accounts and, where appropriate, underwriting year accounts conducted in accordance with ISAs (UK and Ireland) issued by the APB underlie the relevant reports to be made. Key areas in which auditors need to undertake procedures in relation to the syndicate Annual Return additional to those undertaken to report on the financial statements are:

311

(a) the application of the prescribed valuation and admissibility rules to assets and liabilities for which existence, title, etc. should have already been considered as a part of the audit of the syndicate's financial statements;
(b) the prescribed analysis of accounting information;
(c) presentation of the information in the prescribed form;
(d) the systems and procedures operated by the managing agent; and
(e) any specific additional disclosures that fall within the scope of the auditors' report.

Auditors may report on parts of the syndicate Annual Return before reporting on the annual accounts and underwriting year accounts. If all aspects of audit work on these accounts are not yet complete, they will need to be satisfied that any matters outstanding with respect to that work will be unlikely to result in changes to the information contained in the relevant part of the syndicate Annual Return. This means that the audit of these accounts must be at an advanced stage and that, subject only to unforeseen events, the auditors expect to be in a position to issue their report on these accounts incorporating the information contained in the return, and know what that report will say. This means completing the audit,

312

including any appropriate reviews by personnel not otherwise involved in the audit as described in ISA (UK and Ireland) 220, subject only to the following:

(a) clearing outstanding audit matters which the auditors are satisfied are unlikely to have a material impact on the annual accounts and underwriting year accounts;

(b) completing audit procedures on the detail of note disclosures to the annual accounts and underwriting year accounts that will not have a material impact on those accounts;

(c) updating the subsequent events review to cover the period between reporting on the syndicate Annual Return and reporting on those accounts (if appropriate); and

(d) obtaining written representations, where relevant, from management and establishing that those accounts have been approved by the directors of the managing agent.

313 Lloyd's prescribes from time to time the information to be reported in the syndicate Annual Return, how that information is to be reported (eg format and content of the return and the allocation of information across the various submissions) the scope of agents', actuaries' and auditors' reports, and the timetable for making the various submissions and annexed reports. The syndicate auditor will need to familiarise himself with such requirements as they are prescribed and to consider their impact on his work. In particular, changes by Lloyd's over time to the prescribed scope of his report, or reports, may indicate that changes (including deletions, additions and amendments) are needed to his work programme in order to support the revised opinions.

314 The syndicate Annual Return may be required to report information at a level of detail which goes beyond the level of disclosure in syndicate annual accounts or underwriting accounts. Having regard to the prescribed scope of the auditor's report on the syndicate Annual Return, or different reports on separate submissions thereof, the auditor applies materiality in relation to the business as a whole, rather than in relation to the particular detailed analysis within which a particular item is reported. Following this approach, reliance on analytical review techniques is normally appropriate in relation to, for example, the segmental and other detailed information within the syndicate Annual Return.

The Auditor's Procedures on Regulatory Returns

315 The FSA has sole responsibility for the regulation and supervision of the Lloyd's market in line with the regulation and supervision of other UK insurers. Lloyd's imposes its own regulations and requirements on the market to enable it to comply with its own reporting obligations to the FSA and overseas regulators and to regulate its own rules. The Society and Lloyd's underwriting agents are subject to regulation by the FSA. At the present time, members of Lloyd's are not regulated directly by the FSA although FSMA 2000 enables the FSA to do so.

316 Lloyd's is required to file a full scope regulatory return with the FSA for the market as a whole which incorporates a demonstration that each member has sufficient assets to meet his underwriting liabilities. The overall return is reported on by the auditors to the Society of Lloyd's in terms specified in the FSA Handbook. The FSA Handbook sets out the matters which must be stated by the syndicate auditor in his report to the directors of the managing agent on that part of the syndicate Annual Return which is intended to assist Lloyd's in preparing the market-level regulatory return to the FSA. The matters are whether:

(a) the return has been properly prepared in accordance with the instructions;
(b) the managing agent's certificate has been properly prepared in accordance with the instructions; and
(c) it was or was not unreasonable for the persons giving the certificate to have made the statements in it.

Where the auditor has not received the information or explanations required to allow them to give the opinion at (c) above, the auditor must add an appropriate qualification, amplification or explanation.

In addition, the auditor of a syndicate writing long-term insurance business must state the extent to which he has in his report relied on the work of the syndicate actuary.

The auditor is aware that information contained in returns on which the syndicate auditor has issued a report will be included in the market-level regulatory return to the FSA.

Qualifications or references to an emphasis of matter

When reporting on submissions of syndicate Annual Returns, auditors include an emphasis of matter or qualify their opinions as appropriate following the principles in ISA (UK and Ireland) 700 'The auditor's report on financial statements'. It is possible for the auditors' opinion in their report on a syndicate Annual Return submission to be qualified whilst that on the annual accounts or underwriting accounts is unqualified and vice versa. This may occur where the grounds for qualification relate to the treatment of a particular item (for example, if an asset or a liability is included in the syndicate Annual Return at a value which does not take account of the specific requirements of the Lloyd's Valuation of Liabilities Rules or the Eligible Asset Rules). Any qualification or emphasis of matter paragraph in respect of technical provisions would normally be expected to be reflected in both reports.

Resubmitted returns

As stated above Lloyd's may require the syndicate to resubmit the syndicate Annual Return, or part thereof, where the original return is not considered to continue to meet their criteria; the auditors may be required to express an opinion on the amended or additional material. This can be done by either:

(a) withdrawing the original report and issuing a new report; or
(b) issuing a supplementary report on the amended material only, but including reference to the original report.

The first option is preferable where the nature and volume of changes required gives rise to a resubmission of the complete return. The second option is preferable where the amendments are considered to be relatively minor or are few in number and only the amended pages of the return are resubmitted.

Auditors' statements on Group Capital Adequacy

The EU Insurance Groups Directive requires regulators not only to monitor insurance companies for which they have regulatory responsibility but also to monitor the solvency of insurance groups to which those firms belong. As a consequence rule

9.40(1) of IPRU(INS) requires an insurer to which INSPRU 6.1 applies to provide to the FSA in respect of its ultimate insurance parent undertaking and its ultimate EEA insurance parent undertaking (if different), a report of:

(a) the group capital resources of that undertaking (as calculated in accordance with INSPRU 6.1.36R);
(b) the group capital resources requirement of that undertaking (as calculated in accordance with INSPRU 6.1.33R); and
(c) particulars of any member of the insurance group which is in a position of regulatory solvency deficit.

321 An insurer is not required to submit the report where it is a non-EEA insurer or where under Article 4(2) of the Insurance Groups Directive, the competent authority of an EEA State other than the United Kingdom has agreed to be the competent authority responsible for exercising supplementary supervision[28].

322 The report required in respect of insurance group capital adequacy must include a statement from the auditors of the insurer (or of another insurer submitting the report on behalf of all relevant insurers in the group) that, in their opinion, the report has been properly compiled in accordance with INSPRU 6.1 and rule 9.40 (1) of IPRU (INS) from information provided by members of the insurance group and from the insurer's own records.

323 The information and calculations to be provided by an insurer under rule 9.40(1) of IPRU(INS) is in respect of the insurer and each member of its insurance group[29]. The insurance group consists of the insurer's ultimate insurance parent undertaking and its related undertakings or where the parent is itself an insurer (a participating insurance undertaking) the insurer and its related undertakings. An insurance parent undertaking is:

(a) a participating insurance undertaking which has a subsidiary undertaking that is an insurance undertaking; or
(b) an insurance holding company which has a subsidiary undertaking which is an insurer; or
(c) an insurance undertaking (not within (a)) which has a subsidiary undertaking which is an insurer.

324 The auditor's report under 9.40(3)(c) of IPRU(INS) is prepared following an examination and not a full scope audit. The requirement is that the auditors should state that, in their opinion, the report has been properly compiled in accordance with INSPRU 6.1 from information provided by members of the insurance group and from the insurer's own records. The auditors are not required to perform any independent examination of the underlying financial information upon which the information in the submission to the FSA is based.

325 In performing their work auditors normally carry out the following procedures necessary to enable them to make the statement required by rule 9.40(3)(c) of IPRU(INS):

(a) reading any instructions issued to other members of the insurance group and comparing these with the requirements set out in INSPRU 6.1;

---

[28] A pure reinsurer whose ultimate insurance parent undertaking is the parent undertaking of a group comprised solely of reinsurance undertakings is exempt from these requirements until 10 December 2007.

[29] If the parent is not only a participating insurance undertaking but an insurer with its head office in the UK, its insurance subsidiaries are not required to submit the report, although some ancillary reporting may be required.

(b) comparing on a test basis, the information provided to the insurer by other members of the insurance group and any adjustments made by the insurer thereto, with
  (i) the instructions (if any) issued by the insurer,
  (ii) the basis upon which the information has been produced,
  (iii) the requirements set out in INSPRU 6.1;
(c) comparing, on a test basis, the compilation of the Report with the information provided to the insurer by other members of the insurance group and with information from the insurer's own records;
(d) confirming the mathematical accuracy of the compilation of the financial information contained in the Report; and
(e) identifying any significant areas where the information included in the submission may not comply with the above.

An example auditor's statement in respect of group capital adequacy is set out in Appendix 1.

326 The additional information on group capital adequacy required to be reported to the FSA under rule 9.40(1A) of IPRU(INS) is not within the scope of the auditors' statement on group capital adequacy. Therefore, the group capital adequacy report is structured so that the auditors' statement clearly identifies those parts of the group capital adequacy report within the scope of the auditors' statement.

327 Rule 9.42A of IPRU(INS) requires that insurers make available to the public certain specified information on the group capital adequacy position but do not require auditors to report on this publicly available information.

328 An insurer may be a member of a financial conglomerate and as such may be required to submit a return that is analogous to the group capital adequacy report for an insurance group. Where the financial conglomerate is an insurance conglomerate (other than one to which SUP 16.7.82R (1)(a) applies) SUP 16.7.83 requires auditors to provide a statement on this return in accordance with rule 9.40 (3)(c) of IPRU (INS). Auditors will follow the guidance in this section of this Practice Note, with suitable amendments (e.g. to make reference to the relevant rules in SUP in addition to those in IPRU(INS)).

Other reports by the auditor

Auditors' review reports on interim net profits

329 An insurer must maintain at all times capital resources equal to or in excess of its capital resources requirement. In the case of a composite insurer this requirement applies separately to capital resources in respect of both its long-term insurance business and general insurance business. An insurer may include interim net profits in its capital resources (calculated in accordance with Stage A of the calculation in the Capital Resources Table in GENPRU 2 Annex 1R) only if those interim net profits have been externally verified by a company's auditors. Auditors may, for this reason, be asked to report on the interim net profits of insurers, for capital adequacy purposes.

330 Interim net profits in this context means, net profits of the insurer as at a date specified by the insurer after the end of its most recently audited financial year end and up to and including its next financial year end, calculated after deductions for tax, declared dividends and other appropriations.

331 GENPRU 2.2.102R does not include specific guidance as to what constitutes an external verification. However "verification" as used in the context of GENPRU is understood to indicate a degree of assurance which is lower than that given by a full audit. An engagement to "verify" interim profits may therefore be taken to be a review engagement, and an opinion may be given in terms of negative assurance. The report is normally addressed to the directors of the insurer.

332 As an external "verification" of interim net profits does not require a full scope audit it will be important for the FSA, in considering the adequacy of the "verification" of interim profits, to be informed of the procedures that have been undertaken by the auditors, in support of their opinion. This is particularly important in the case of insurers where no prescribed procedures have been established by the FSA themselves in rules or guidance. Consequently the detailed scope of the work undertaken by the auditor in support of his opinion is listed in the auditors' report or included in the report by reference to the letter of engagement where the programme of work has been laid down.

333 In undertaking the review the auditor normally performs the following procedures:

(a) satisfies himself that the figures forming the basis of the interim net profits have been properly extracted from the underlying accounting records;

(b) reviews the accounting policies used in calculating the interim net profits for the period under review so as to obtain comfort that they are consistent with those normally adopted by the insurer in drawing up its annual financial statements and, as applicable, are in accordance with the Companies Act 1985, IFRS, UK financial reporting standards (FRSs) and the Insurance SORP as applicable;

(c) performs analytical procedures on the results to date which form the basis of calculating the interim net profits, including comparisons of the actual performance to date with budget and with the results of the prior period(s);

(d) discusses with management the overall performance and financial position of the insurer;

(e) obtains adequate comfort that the implications of current and prospective litigation (not in the ordinary course of insurance business), all known contingencies and commitments, changes in business activities and the determination of insurance technical provisions have been properly taken into account in arriving at the interim net profits; and

(f) follows up significant matters of which the auditor is already aware in the course of auditing the insurer's most recent financial statements

The auditor may also consider obtaining appropriate representations from management.

334 Auditors make it clear that the report has been produced for the use of the insurer in meeting the requirements of the FSA for the purposes of the calculation of its capital resources only. This may be clarified in the report and/or in the engagement letter. An example report is included in Appendix 1.

Appendix 1 – Illustrative examples of auditor's reports

This appendix contains the following example auditor's reports:

Reports on regulatory returns

    1.1 Composite insurance company

    1.2 Life Insurance Company

    1.3 General Insurance Company

    1.4 Statement on the group capital adequacy report

Reports relating to the financial statements of a Lloyd's syndicate

    1.5 Personal and syndicate MAPA accounts

    1.6 Closed year of account

    1.7 Run-off year of account

Other reports by the auditor

    1.8 Report on interim net profits

When reporting on an insurer's regulatory return, the example reports set out in this Appendix need to be adapted to meet the circumstances of that individual company, taking account of the notes set out in the Appendix.

In the case of a partial resubmission, the reports will indicate that the documents being reported upon have been prepared as amended documents to replace the corresponding documents on which the auditors reported on [……. XX].

1.1 – Regulatory Report: Composite Insurance Company

........................[COMPOSITE INSURANCE COMPANY LIMITED]

[Global business/UK branch business]

Financial year ended 31 December 20xx

Report to the directors pursuant to rule 9.35

We have examined the following documents prepared by the company pursuant to the Accounts and Statements Rules set out in part I and part IV of Chapter 9 to IPRU(INS) the Interim Prudential Sourcebook for Insurers, GENPRU the General Prudential Sourcebook and INSPRU the Insurance Prudential Sourcebook ("the Rules") made by the Financial Services Authority under section 138 of the Financial Services and Markets Act 2000:

- Forms [1 to 3, 10 to 32, 34, 36 to 45, 48, 49, 56, 58 and 60], (including the supplementary notes) on pages [...] to [...] ("the Forms");
- the statements required by IPRU(INS) rules 9.25, 9.26, 9.27 and 9.29 on pages [...] to [...] ("the Statements");
- the valuation report required by IPRU(INS) rule 9.31(a) on pages [...] to [...] (the valuation report); and
- the statements, analysis and reports required by IPRU(INS) rule 9.31(b) (the realistic valuation report[30]) on pages [...] to [...].

We are not required to examine and do not express an opinion on:

- Forms [46 to 47, 50 to 55, 57, 59A and 59B] (including the supplementary notes) on pages [...] to [...];
- the statements required by IPRU(INS) rules 9.30, 9.32, 9.32A and 9.36[31] on pages [...] to [...]; and
- the certificate required by IPRU(INS) rule 9.34 on pages [...] to [...] ("the certificate").

Respective responsibilities of the company and its auditors

The company is responsible for the preparation of an annual return (including the Forms, the Statements, the valuation report, (the realistic valuation report), the forms and statements not examined by us and the certificate under the provisions of the Rules. [The requirements of the Rules have been modified by [a] waiver(s) issued under section 148 of the Financial Services and Markets Act 2000 on ....200X [and ....200X]. Under IPRU(INS) rule 9.11 the Forms, the Statements, the valuation report, (and the realistic valuation report), the forms and statements not examined by us and the certificate are required to be prepared in the manner specified by the Rules and to state fairly the information provided on the basis required by the Rules. The methods and assumptions determined by the company and used to perform the actuarial investigation as set out in the valuation report (and the realistic valuation report) prepared in accordance with IPRU(INS) rule 9.31 are required to reflect appropriately the requirements of INSPRU 1.2 (and 1.3[32]).

It is our responsibility to form an independent opinion as to whether the Forms, the Statements, the valuation report (and the realistic valuation report) meet these requirements, and to report our opinions to you. We also report to you if, in our opinion, the company has not kept proper accounting records or if we have not received all the information we require for our examination.

Basis of opinion

We conducted our work in accordance with Practice Note 20 'The audit of insurers in the United Kingdom (Revised)' issued by the Auditing Practices Board. Our work included examination, on a test basis, of evidence relevant to the amounts and disclosures in the Forms, the Statements, the valuation report (and the realistic valuation report). The evidence included that previously obtained by us relating to the audit of the financial statements of the company for the financial year. It also included an assessment of the significant estimates and judgements made by the

---

[30] Required for 'Realistic Basis' firms only.

[31] Required where there is a With-Profits Actuary.

[32] Required for 'Realistic Basis' firms only.

company in the preparation of the Forms, the Statements, the valuation report (and the realistic valuation report).

We planned and performed our work so as to obtain all the information and explanations which we considered necessary in order to provide us with sufficient evidence to give reasonable assurance that the Forms, the Statements, the valuation report (and the realistic valuation report) are free from material misstatement, whether caused by fraud or other irregularity or error and comply with IPRU(INS) rule 9.11.

In accordance with IPRU(INS) rule 9.35(1A), to the extent that any document, Form, Statement, analysis or report to be examined under IPRU(INS) rule 9.35(1) contains amounts or information abstracted from the actuarial investigation performed pursuant to IPRU(INS) rule 9.4, we have obtained and paid due regard to advice from a suitably qualified actuary who is independent of the company.

Opinion

In our opinion:

(i) the Forms, the Statements the valuation report (and the realistic valuation report) fairly state the information provided on the basis required by the Rules [**as modified**] and have been properly prepared in accordance with the provisions of those Rules; and
(ii) the methods and assumptions determined by the company and used to perform the actuarial investigation as set out in the valuation report (and the realistic valuation report) prepared in accordance with IPRU(INS) rule 9.31 appropriately reflect the requirements of INSPRU 1.2 (and 1.3).

Name of auditors

Registered Auditors

Date

1.2 – Regulatory Report: Life Insurance Company

.... [LIFE INSURANCE COMPANY LIMITED]

[Global business/UK branch business]

Financial year ended 31 December 20xx

Report to the directors pursuant to rule 9.35

We have examined the following documents prepared by the company pursuant to the Accounts and Statements Rules set out in part I and part IV of Chapter 9 to IPRU(INS) the Interim Prudential Sourcebook for Insurers, GENPRU the General Prudential Sourcebook and INSPRU the Insurance Prudential Sourcebook ("the Rules") made by the Financial Services Authority under section 138 of the Financial Services and Markets Act 2000:

- Forms **[2, 3, 10 to 19, 40 to 45, 48, 49, 56, 58 and 60]**, (including the supplementary notes) on pages [...] to [...] ("the Forms);

- the statement required by IPRU(INS) rule 9.29 on pages [...] to [...] ("the Statement");
- the valuation report required by IPRU(INS) rule 9.31 (a) (the valuation report); and
- the statements, analysis and reports required by IPRU(INS) rule 9.31 (b) (the realistic valuation report[33]) on pages [...] to [...].

We are not required to examine and do not express an opinion on:

- Forms **[46 to 47, 50 to 55, 57, 59A and 59B]** (including the supplementary notes) on pages [...] to [...];
- the statements required by IPRU(INS) rules 9.30 and 9.36[34] on pages [...] to [...]; and
- the certificate required by IPRU(INS) rule 9.34 on pages [...] to [...] ("the certificate").

Respective responsibilities of the company and its auditors

The company is responsible for the preparation of an annual return (including the Forms, the Statement, the valuation report (the realistic valuation report), the forms and statement not examined by us and the certificate under the provisions of the Rules. **[The requirements of the Rules have been modified by [a] waiver(s) issued under section 148 of the Financial Services and Markets Act 2000 on ....200X [and ....200X.]** Under IPRU(INS) rule 9.11 the Forms, the Statement, valuation report,(realistic valuation report), the forms and statement not examined by us and the certificate are required to be prepared in the manner specified by the Rules and to state fairly the information provided on the basis required by the Rules.

The methods and assumptions determined by the company and used to perform the actuarial investigation as set out in the valuation report, (and the realistic valuation report), prepared in accordance with IPRU(INS) rule 9.31 are required to reflect appropriately the requirements of INSPRU 1.2 (and 1.3[35]).

It is our responsibility to form an independent opinion as to whether the Forms, the Statement, the valuation report (and the realistic valuation report) meet these requirements, and to report our opinions to you. We also report to you if, in our opinion, the company has not kept proper accounting records or if we have not received all the information we require for our examination.

Basis of opinion

We conducted our work in accordance with Practice Note 20 'The audit of insurers in the United Kingdom (Revised)' issued by the Auditing Practices Board. Our work included examination, on a test basis, of evidence relevant to the amounts and disclosures in the Forms, the Statement, the valuation report (and the realistic valuation report). The evidence included that previously obtained by us relating to the audit of the financial statements of the company for the financial year. It also included an assessment of the significant estimates and judgements made by the company in the preparation of the Forms, the Statement, the valuation report (and the realistic valuation report).

---

[33] *Required for 'Realistic Basis' firms only.*

[34] *Required where there is a With-Profits Actuary.*

[35] *Required for 'Realistic Basis' firms only.*

We planned and performed our work so as to obtain all the information and explanations which we considered necessary in order to provide us with sufficient evidence to give reasonable assurance that the Forms, the Statement, the valuation report (and the realistic valuation report) are free from material misstatement, whether caused by fraud or other irregularity or error and comply with IPRU(INS) rule 9.11.

In accordance with IPRU(INS) rule 9.35(1A), to the extent that any document, Form, Statement, analysis or report to be examined under IPRU(INS) rule 9.35(1) contains amounts or information abstracted from the actuarial investigation performed pursuant to rule 9.4, we have obtained and paid due regard to advice from a suitably qualified actuary who is independent of the company.

Opinion

In our opinion:

(i) the Forms, the Statement, the valuation report (and the realistic valuation report) fairly state the information provided on the basis required by the Rules **[as modified]** and have been properly prepared in accordance with the provisions of those Rules; and
(ii) the methods and assumptions determined by the company and used to perform the actuarial investigation as set out in the valuation report (and the realistic valuation report) prepared in accordance with IPRU(INS) rule 9.31 appropriately reflect the requirements of INSPRU 1.2 (and 1.3).

Name of auditors

Registered Auditor

Date

1.3 – Regulatory Report: General Insurance Company

..........................[GENERAL INSURANCE COMPANY LIMITED]

[Global business/UK branch business]

Financial year ended 31 December 20xx

Report to the directors pursuant to Rule 9.35

We have examined the following documents prepared by the company pursuant to the Accounts and Statements Rules set out in part I and part IV of Chapter 9 to IPRU(INS) the Interim Prudential Sourcebook for Insurers, GENPRU the General Prudential Sourcebook and INSPRU the Insurance Prudential Sourcebook ("the Rules") made by the Financial Services Authority under section 138 of the Financial Services and Markets Act 2000:

- Forms **[1, 3, 10 to 13, 15 to 17, 20 to 32, 34 and 36 to 39]**, (including the supplementary notes) on pages [...] to [...] ("the Forms"); and
- the statements required by IPRU(INS) rules 9.25, 9.26, 9.27 and 9.29 on pages [...] to [...] ("the Statements").

We are not required to examine and do not express an opinion on:

- the statements required by IPRU(INS) rules 9.30, 9.32 and 9.32A on pages [...] to [...] and
- the certificate required by IPRU(INS) rule 9.34 on pages [...] to [...] ("the certificate").

Respective responsibilities of the company and its auditors

The company is responsible for the preparation of an annual return (including the Forms, the Statements, the statements not examined by us and the certificate) under the provisions of the Rules. **[The requirements of the Rules have been modified by [a] waiver(s) issued under section 148 of the Financial Services and Markets Act 2000 on ....200X [and ....200X.]** Under IPRU(INS) rule 9.11 the Forms, the Statements, the statements not examined by us and the certificate are required to be prepared in the manner specified by the Rules and to state fairly the information provided on the basis required by the Rules.

It is our responsibility to form an independent opinion as to whether the Forms, and the Statements meet these requirements, and to report our opinions to you. We also report to you if, in our opinion, the company has not kept proper accounting records or if we have not received all the information we require for our examination.

Basis of opinion

We conducted our work in accordance with Practice Note 20 'The audit of insurers in the United Kingdom (Revised)' issued by the Auditing Practices Board. Our work included examination, on a test basis, of evidence relevant to the amounts and disclosures in the Forms and the Statements. The evidence included that previously obtained by us relating to the audit of the financial statements of the company for the financial year. It also included an assessment of the significant estimates and judgements made by the company in the preparation of the Forms and statements.

We planned and performed out work so as to obtain all the information and explanations which we considered necessary in order to provide us with sufficient evidence to give reasonable assurance that the Forms and the Statements are free from material misstatement, whether caused by fraud or other irregularity or error and comply with IPRU(INS) rule 9.11.

Opinion

In our opinion the Forms and the Statements fairly state the information provided on the basis required by the Rules **[as modified]** and have been properly prepared in accordance with the provisions of those Rules.

Name of auditors

Registered Auditors

Date

1.4 – Statement on the group capital adequacy report

Independent auditors' statement to the directors pursuant to rule 9.40(3)(c) of the Interim Prudential Sourcebook for Insurers ("IPRU(INS)")

....

Financial year ended 31 December 20XX

We have reviewed the report[36] prepared pursuant to rule 9.40(1) of IPRU(INS) on pages (x) to (x) ("the report") prepared by Example Insurance Company Ltd ("the insurer").

Respective responsibilities of the insurer and its auditors

The insurer is responsible for the preparation of the report under the provisions of rule 9.40 (1) of IPRU(INS) [as modified by a waiver granted under section 148 of the Financial Services and Markets Act 2000].

(The report has been prepared on the basis set out on pages [x] to[x].)

It is our responsibility to carry out the procedures set out below in the basis of opinion section, and to report whether anything of significance has come to our attention to indicate that the report has not been properly compiled in accordance with INSPRU 6.1 [as modified] and rule 9.41(1) of IPRU(INS) from information provided to the insurer by other members of the insurance group and from the insurer's own records.

Our work did not constitute an audit in accordance with International Standards on Auditing (UK and Ireland) issued by the Auditing Practices Board of the information provided to the insurer by other members of the insurance group and included no independent examination by us of any of the underlying financial information therein. It therefore provides a lower level of assurance than an audit.

Basis of opinion

Our work consisted principally of;

- comparing on a test basis, the compilation of the report with the information provided to the insurer by other members of the insurance group and with information from the insurer's own records;
- confirming the mathematical accuracy of the compilation of the financial information contained in the report;
- [reading the instructions issued to other members of the insurance group and comparing these with the requirements set out in INSPRU 6.1;] and
- comparing on a test basis, the information provided to the insurer by other members of the insurance group and any adjustments made by the insurer thereto, with:
  (a) [the instructions issued by the insurer;]
  (b) [the basis of preparation set out on pages [x] to [x]; and

---

[36] IPRU(INS) 9.40(1A) extends the group capital adequacy report to include additional information not required to be included within the scope of the auditors' statement. Consequently the auditors' statement will need to clearly identify those parts of the group capital adequacy report within the scope of the auditors' statement.

(c) the requirements set out in INSPRU 6.1 [as modified], to identify any significant areas where such information may not comply[therewith][with a), b) and c) above].

Opinion

On the basis of the above procedures, nothing of significance has come to our attention to indicate that the report has not been properly compiled in accordance with INSPRU 6.1 and 9.40(1) of IPRU(INS) [as modified] from information provided to the insurer by other members of the insurance group and from the insurer's own records.

Name of auditors

Registered Auditor

Date

1.5 – Lloyd's syndicate – Personal accounts and syndicate MAPA accounts

Report of the auditors to the members of syndicates, the Council of Lloyd's and its auditors

We have reviewed the procedures and controls employed by [managing agent] in producing personal accounts and syndicate MAPA accounts in accordance with the Lloyd's Syndicate Accounting Byelaw.

Respective responsibilities of the Managing Agent and auditors

As described on page... the Managing Agent is responsible for the preparation of personal accounts and syndicate MAPA accounts in accordance with the Lloyd's Syndicate Accounting Byelaw. It is our responsibility to form an independent opinion, based on our review and to report our opinion to you.

Basis of opinion

Our review included such procedures as we considered necessary to evaluate whether the procedures and controls taken as a whole were operating with sufficient effectiveness to provide reasonable, but not absolute, assurance that personal accounts and syndicate MAPA accounts have been properly prepared in accordance with the Lloyd's Syndicate Accounting Byelaw and that the net results shown in personal accounts and syndicate MAPA accounts have been calculated in accordance with the applicable agency agreements.

These procedures included examination on a test basis of evidence of compliance with the procedures and controls in respect of the preparation of personal accounts and syndicate MAPA accounts. Our procedures did not necessarily include tests of transactions for any particular member or MAPA.

Inherent limitation

Procedures and controls are subject to inherent limitations and, accordingly, errors or irregularities may occur and not be detected. Such procedures cannot be proof against fraudulent collusion, especially on the part of those holding positions of authority or trust. Furthermore, this opinion relates only to those procedures and controls operated in connection with the position as at 31 December 20xx, and should not be seen as providing assurance as to any future position, as changes to systems or controls may alter the validity of our opinion.

Opinion

In our opinion, the procedures and controls taken as a whole provide reasonable but not absolute assurance that:

(a) underwriting member personal accounts and syndicate MAPA accounts have been properly prepared in accordance with the Lloyd's Syndicate Accounting Byelaw; and
(b) the net results shown in underwriting member personal accounts and syndicate MAPA accounts have been calculated in accordance with the applicable agency agreements.

Registered Auditors

Address

Date

1.6 – Lloyd's syndicate – Report to the members of syndicate xxx – 200x closed year of account

We have audited the syndicate underwriting year accounts for the three years ended 31 December 200x, which comprise the Profit and Loss Account, Balance Sheet, Cash Flow Statement and the related notes 1 to X. These accounts have been prepared under the accounting policies set out therein.

Respective responsibilities of the managing agent and auditors

As described in the Statement of Managing Agent's Responsibilities, the managing agent is responsible for the preparation of syndicate underwriting year accounts in accordance with applicable United Kingdom Generally Accepted Accounting Practice.

Our responsibility is to audit the syndicate underwriting year accounts in accordance with the relevant legal and regulatory requirements and International Standards on Auditing (UK and Ireland).

We report to you our opinion as to whether the syndicate underwriting year accounts give a true and fair view of the result of the closed year of account in accordance with the Insurance Accounts Directive (Lloyd's Syndicate and Aggregate Accounts) Regulations 2004. We also report to you if, in our opinion, the report of the managing agent is not consistent with the syndicate underwriting year accounts, if the managing agent in respect of the syndicate has not kept proper accounting records, or if we have not received all the information and explanations we require for our audit.

We read the report of the managing agent and consider the implications for our report if we become aware of any apparent misstatements within it.

Basis of audit opinion

We conducted our audit in accordance with International Standards on Auditing (UK and Ireland) issued by the Auditing Practices Board. An audit includes examination, on a test basis, of evidence relevant to the amounts and disclosures in the syndicate underwriting year accounts. It also includes an assessment of the significant estimates and judgements made by the directors of the managing agent in the preparation of the syndicate underwriting year accounts, and of whether the accounting policies are appropriate to the syndicate's circumstances, consistently applied and adequately disclosed.

We planned and performed our audit so as to obtain all the information and explanations which we considered necessary in order to provide us with sufficient evidence to give reasonable assurance that the syndicate underwriting year accounts are free from material misstatement, whether caused by fraud or other irregularity or error. In forming our opinion we also evaluated the overall adequacy of the presentation of information in the syndicate underwriting year accounts.

Opinion

In our opinion the syndicate underwriting year accounts give a true and fair view in accordance with United Kingdom Generally Accepted Accounting Practice of the result of the 200X closed year of account.

Registered Auditor

Address

Date

1.7 – Lloyd's syndicate – Report to the members of syndicate xxx – 200x run-off year of account

We have audited the syndicate underwriting year accounts for the 200X run-off year of account as at 31 December 200Y, which comprise the Profit and Loss Account, Balance Sheet, and the related notes 1 to X. These accounts have been prepared under the accounting policies set out therein.

Respective responsibilities of the managing agent and auditors

As described in the Statement of Managing Agent's Responsibilities, the managing agent is responsible for the preparation of syndicate underwriting year accounts in accordance with applicable United Kingdom Generally Accepted Accounting Practice.

Our responsibility is to audit the syndicate underwriting year accounts in accordance with the relevant legal and regulatory requirements and International Standards on Auditing (UK and Ireland).

We report to you our opinion as to whether the syndicate underwriting year accounts have been properly prepared in accordance with the Lloyd's Syndicate Accounting Byelaw. We also report to you if, in our opinion, the report of the managing agent is not consistent with the syndicate underwriting year accounts, if the managing agent in respect of the syndicate has not kept proper accounting records, or if we have not received all the information and explanations we require for our audit.

We read the managing agent's report and consider the implications for our report if we become aware of any apparent misstatements within it.

Basis of audit opinion

We conducted our audit in accordance with International Standards on Auditing (UK and Ireland) issued by the Auditing Practices Board. An audit includes examination, on a test basis, of evidence relevant to the amounts and disclosures in the syndicate underwriting year accounts. It also includes an assessment of the significant estimates and judgements made by the directors in the preparation of the syndicate underwriting year accounts, and of whether the accounting policies are appropriate to the syndicate's circumstances, consistently applied and adequately disclosed.

We planned and performed our audit so as to obtain all the information and explanations which we considered necessary in order to provide us with sufficient evidence to give reasonable assurance that the syndicate underwriting year accounts are free from material misstatement, whether caused by fraud or other irregularity or error. In forming our opinion we also evaluated the overall adequacy of the presentation of information in the syndicate underwriting year accounts.

Opinion

In our opinion the syndicate underwriting year accounts for the 200X run-off year of account have been properly prepared in accordance with the Lloyd's Syndicate Accounting Byelaw.

Registered Auditor

London

Date

1.8 – Example of report on interim net profits

External verification of interim net profits for the purposes of Stage A of the calculation in the Capital Resources Table in GENPRU 2 Annex 1R (where the detailed scope of the work undertaken is set out in the engagement letter)

Review report by the auditors to the board of directors of XYZ Limited ("the company")

In accordance with our engagement letter dated *[date]*, a copy of which is attached as Appendix A, we have reviewed the company's statement of interim net profits for the period from [ ] to [ ] ("the interim period") as reported in the reporting statement ("the statement") attached as Appendix B and dated *[date]*.

The statement is the responsibility of, and has been approved by, the directors of the company. Our review of the statement did not constitute an audit, and accordingly we do not express an audit opinion on the interim net profits reported therein.

Our review has been carried out having regard to rules and guidance contained in the FSA's General Prudential Sourcebook and Practice Note 20 "The Audit of Insurers in the United Kingdom (Revised)" issued by the Auditing Practices Board.

On the basis of the results of our review, nothing has come to our attention that causes us to believe that:

(a) the interim net profits as reported in the statement have not been calculated on the basis of the accounting policies adopted by the Company in drawing up its annual financial statements for the year ended [date] [except for][1];
(b) those accounting policies differ in any material respects from those required by UK GAAP[2]/International Financial Reporting Standards adopted by the European Commission in accordance with EC Regulation No 1606/2002; and
(c) the interim net profits amounting to £ [ ] as so reported are not reasonably stated.

Date

Notes

1. Identify any changes arising from the adoption of revised accounting policies that will first be applied in the financial statements containing the interim period.
2. UK GAAP comprises Schedule 9A to the Companies Act 1985, UK financial reporting standards and the Statement Of Recommended Practice on Accounting for Insurance Business issued by the Association of British Insurers.

Appendix 2 – The main parts of FSMA 2000 relevant to insurers[37]

Part I (and Schedule 1) sets out matters concerning the structure and governance of the FSA including its regulatory objectives and the principles to be followed in meeting those objectives.

Part II (and Schedule 2) sets out the general prohibition on conducting regulated business unless a person (including in a corporate sense) is either authorised or exempt, including restrictions on financial promotions. Regulated activities are defined in a statutory instrument. (SI 2001/544)

Part III (and Schedules 3-5) sets out the requirements to become authorised either by receiving a specific permission from the FSA or through the EU single market rules. Exempt persons are listed in a separate statutory instrument. (SI 2001/1201)

Part IV (and Schedule 6) sets out the arrangements for application for a permission to undertake authorised business and the criteria (Threshold Conditions) that must

---

[37] Lloyd's corporate members are not subject to FSMA 2000.

be met. An applicant who is refused can apply to the Financial Services and Markets Tribunal (established under Part IX).

Part V sets out the provisions applying to individuals performing designated functions (controlled functions) in an authorised firm. The FSA can specify controlled functions and firms must take reasonable care to ensure that only persons approved by the FSA can undertake these functions. The FSA can specify qualification, training and competence requirements and approved persons must comply with the FSA's statement of principles and code of conduct for approved persons. Appeals can be made to the Tribunal.

Part VIII gives the FSA powers to impose penalties for market abuse – using information not generally available; creating a false or misleading impression; or failure to observe normal standards. Abuse is judged from the point of view of a regular market user. FSA powers extend to all persons – not only authorised persons. The FSA is required to publish a code to give guidance on what is abuse and to provide a 'safe harbour'. This forms part of the Market Conduct Sourcebook and is called the Code of Market Conduct.

Part X provides the FSA with general powers to make rules which apply to authorised persons, including rules on specific matters – e.g. client money, money laundering. Rules must be published in draft for consultation. Guidance may be provided individually or generally and may be published. The FSA may modify rules or waive particular rules for particular persons in certain situations.

Part XI allows the FSA to gather information from authorised persons, including use of skilled persons' reports under section 166, or to commission investigations into authorised persons.

Part XIV sets out the disciplinary measures available to the FSA which can include public censure, unlimited fines, withdrawal of authorisation.

Part XXII includes the provisions relating to auditors and their appointment.

Part XXVI brings together in one place the arrangements applying to warning notices and decision notices concerning possible breaches of various requirements imposed by FSMA 2000 or by FSA rules. A warning notice has to state the reasons for proposed actions and allow reasonable time for representations to be made. This will be followed by a decision notice with a right to appeal to the Tribunal.

Appendix 3 – The FSA Handbook

Not all authorised firms are required to comply with all rules contained within the FSA Handbook. This varies with the type of permission – the regulated activity an authorised firm is permitted to undertake is set out in the authorised firm's Scope of Permission. The following can be viewed on the FSA website: 335

- contents of the FSA Handbook – www.fsa.gov.uk/Pages/handbook
- FSA register which lists the regulated activities that each authorised firm has permission to undertake – www.fsa.gov.uk/Pages/register

In gaining an understanding of the FSA Handbook the auditor bears in mind the four statutory objectives of the FSA set out in paragraph 27 above which underpin the content of the FSA Handbook. To facilitate usage the FSA Handbook has been structured into a number of blocks and within each block the material has been sub- 336 divided into Sourcebooks, Manuals or Guides. There are Rules, evidential provisions[1] and guidance which are contained within all of the blocks[2] Contravention of Rules (which includes Principles for Businesses) or evidential provisions can give rise to an obligation on the auditor to report the matter direct to the FSA – see the section of this Practice Note relating to ISA (UK and Ireland) 250 Section B. Outline details of certain elements of the FSA Handbook are set out below.

Principles for Businesses

337 The eleven Principles for Businesses, which are general statements that set out the fundamental obligations of firms under the regulatory system, are set out in the FSA Handbook. They derive their authority from the FSA's rule-making powers as set out in the Act and reflect the regulatory objectives. These Principles are as follows:

- an authorised firm must conduct its business with integrity;
- an authorised firm must conduct its business with due skill, care and diligence;
- an authorised firm must take reasonable care to organise and control its affairs responsibly and effectively with adequate risk management;
- an authorised firm must maintain adequate financial resources;
- an authorised firm must observe proper standards of market conduct;
- an authorised firm must pay due regard to the interests of its customers and treat them fairly;
- an authorised firm must pay due regard to the information needs of its clients, and communicate information to them in a way which is clear, fair and not misleading;
- an authorised firm must manage conflicts of interest fairly, both between itself and its customers and between a customer and another client;
- an authorised firm must take reasonable care to ensure the suitability of its advice and discretionary decisions for any customer who is entitled to rely on its judgement;
- an authorised firm must arrange adequate protection for clients' assets when it is responsible for them; and
- an authorised firm must deal with its regulators in an open and co-operative way, and must disclose to the FSA appropriately anything relating to the firm of which the FSA would reasonably expect notice.

Senior management arrangements, systems and controls

338 SYSC amplifies Principle for Businesses 3, the requirement for a firm to take reasonable care to organise and control its affairs responsibly and effectively, with adequate risk management systems. The relevant chapters,[3] are as follows:

- 2 – senior management arrangements
- 3 – systems and controls
- 4 – general organisational requirements
- 5 – employees, agents and other relevant persons
- 6 – compliance, internal audit and financial crime

[1] An evidential provision is not binding in its own right, but establishes a presumption of compliance or non-compliance with another rule. Guidance may be used to explain the implications of other provisions, to indicate possible means of compliance, or to recommend a particular course of action or arrangement.

[2] Rules are set out in emboldened type and are marked with the icon 'R', evidential provisions are marked 'E' and guidance 'G'. Further guidance on the status of the Handbook is set out in the General Provisions (GEN) Sourcebook Chapter 2.2 and Chapter 6 of the Reader's Guide.

[3] Chapters 13-17 apply only to insurers.

- 7 – risk control
- 8 – outsourcing
- 9 – record keeping
- 10 – conflicts of interest
- 11 – liquidity risk systems and controls
- 12 – group risk systems and control requirements
- 13 – operational risk
- 14 – prudential risk management
- 15 – credit risk management
- 16 – market risk management
- 17 – insurance risk
- 18 – guidance on Public Disclosure Act – whistle blowing

Threshold conditions

Under Section 41 and Schedule 6 of FSMA 2000, the Threshold Conditions are the minimum requirements that must be met at authorisation and must continue to be met. The Threshold Conditions relevant to an insurer are: 339

- Legal status : contracts of insurance can only be effected and carried out by a body corporate, a registered friendly society or a member of Lloyd's;
- Location of offices : the head office of a body corporate must be in the same territory/member state as the registered office;
- Claims representatives: the carrying on of motor vehicle liability insurance business requires a claims representative to be appointed in each EEA State other than the UK;
- Close links : close links must not prevent effective supervision. Entities are regarded as closely linked if there is a group relationship, i.e. parent/subsidiary/ fellow subsidiary (but using the EC 7th Company Law Directive definition of subsidiary). They are also closely linked if one owns or controls 20% or more of the voting rights or capital of the other;
- Adequate resources : the firm must have adequate resources (financial and non financial) for the type of business conducted taking into account the impact of other group entities and having regard to provisions made against liabilities (including contingent and future liabilities) and the approach to risk management; and
- Suitability : the firm must satisfy the FSA that it is fit and proper to have Part IV permission in all the circumstances. Although the emphasis is on the firm, the FSA will also consider the fitness and propriety of individuals, including whether business is conducted with integrity and in compliance with high standards and whether there is competent and prudent management and exercise of due skill, care and diligence. This will include consideration of whether those subject to the approved persons regime (i.e. those undertaking controlled functions) are, or will be, approved by the FSA.

Appendix 4 – Reporting direct to FSA – statutory right and protection for disclosure under general law

When the auditor concludes that a matter does not give rise to a statutory duty to report direct to the FSA, the auditor considers the right to report to FSA. 340

In cases of doubt, general law provides protection for disclosing certain matters to a proper authority in the public interest. 341

342 Audit firms are protected from the risk of liability from breach of confidence or defamation under general law even when carrying out work which is not clearly undertaken in the capacity of auditor provided that:

- in the case of breach of confidence:
  (i) disclosure is made in the public interest; and
  (ii) such disclosure is made to an appropriate body or person; and
  (iii) there is no malice motivating the disclosure; and
- in the case of defamation:
  (i) the information disclosed was obtained in a proper capacity; and
  (ii) there is no malice motivating the disclosure.

343 The same protection is given even if there is only a reasonable suspicion that non-compliance with law or regulations has occurred. Provided that it can be demonstrated that an audit firm, in disclosing a matter in the public interest, has acted reasonably and in good faith, it would not be held by the court to be in breach of duty to the institution even if, an investigation or prosecution having occurred, it were found that there had been no breach of law or regulation.

344 When reporting to proper authorities in the public interest, it is important that, in order to retain the protection of qualified privilege, auditors report only to one who has a proper interest to receive the information. The FSA is the proper authority in the case of an authorised institution.

345 'Public interest' is a concept which is not capable of general definition. Each situation must be considered individually. In general circumstances, matters to be taken into account when considering whether disclosure is justified in the public interest may include:

- the extent to which the suspected non-compliance with law or regulations is likely to affect members of the public;
- whether the directors (or equivalent) have rectified the matter or are taking, or are likely to take, effective corrective action;
- the extent to which non-disclosure is likely to enable the suspected non-compliance with law or regulations to recur with impunity;
- the gravity of the matter;
- whether there is a general management ethos within the entity of disregarding law or regulations;
- the weight of evidence and the degree of the auditors' suspicion that there has been an instance of non-compliance with law or regulations.

346 Determination of where the balance of public interest lies requires careful consideration. The auditor needs to weigh the public interest in maintaining confidential client relationships against the public interest of disclosure to a proper authority and to use their professional judgment to determine whether their misgivings justify them in carrying the matter further or are too insubstantial to deserve report.

347 In cases where it is uncertain whether the statutory duty requires or section 342 or section 343 FSMA 2000 permits an auditor to communicate a matter to the FSA, it is possible that the auditor may be able to rely on the defence of disclosure in the public interest if it communicates a matter to the FSA which could properly be regarded as having material significance in conformity with the guidance in ISA (UK and Ireland) 250 Section B and this Practice Note, although the auditor may wish to seek legal advice in such circumstances.

Appendix 5 – Definitions

Abbreviations and frequently used terms in this Practice Note are set out below:

AAB	Audit Arrangements Byelaw (applicable to the Lloyd's Insurance Market).
ABI	Association of British Insurers.
Actuarial Function Holder	An Actuary appointed by a company carrying on long-term insurance business to perform the actuarial function.
ARROW II	'Advanced Risk Responsive Operating frameWork'. The term used for FSA's risk assessment process – the application of risk based supervision. It is the mechanism through which the FSA evaluates the risk an authorised firm poses to its statutory objectives enabling it to allocate its resources appropriately and respond to the risks identified.
Authorised firm	An entity which has been granted one of more Part IV permissions by the FSA and so is authorised under FSMA 2000 to undertake regulated activities – an authorised person. Authorised firms include insurers other than Lloyd's corporate members.
Authorised person	Term used throughout FSMA 2000 and related statutory instruments to refer to an authorised firm – see above.
Authorised insurance company	A company registered under Companies Act 1985 that is authorised by the FSA to conduct insurance business, together with UK branches of insurers established outside the EEA, and (until the Reinsurance Directive is implemented across the EEA) pure reinsurers with their head office in an EEA state carrying on business in the UK.
BAS	Board for Actuarial Standards
CA 1985	The Companies Act 1985.
Closely linked entity	As defined in s343(8) FSMA 2000, an entity has close links with an authorised firm for this purpose if the entity is a: (a) Parent undertaking of an authorised firm; (b) Subsidiary undertaking of an authorised firm; (c) Parent undertaking of a subsidiary undertaking of an authorised firm; or (d) Subsidiary undertaking of a parent undertaking of an authorised firm.
Council of Lloyd's	The council constituted by section 3 of Lloyd's Act 1982.
COND	Threshold conditions element of the high level standards block of the FSA Handbook.
EEA	European Economic Area.
EU IFRS	International Financial Reporting Standards adopted by the European Union.
FSA	The Financial Services Authority.

FSMA 2000	The Financial Services and Markets Act 2000.
GENPRU	General Prudential Sourcebook.
IBNR	"Incurred But Not Reported".
Insurance companies	The term is used, where appropriate, to refer both to authorised insurance companies and to Lloyd's corporate members.
Insurers	The term "insurers" is used in this Practice Note to refer to UK insurance companies authorised by the FSA (insurers with their head offices in the UK, UK branches of insurers established outside the EEA and (until the Reinsurance Directive is implemented across the EEA) pure reinsurers with their head offices in an EEA state carrying on business in the UK) as well as to Lloyd's Syndicates and corporate members.
Insurance SORP	The Statement of Recommended Practice "Accounting for insurance business" issued by the Association of British Insurers (ABI).
INSPRU	Insurance Prudential Sourcebook.
IPRU(INS)	Interim Prudential Sourcebook for Insurers
JMLSG	Joint Money Laundering Steering Group
Lloyd's corporate member	A member of the Society which is a body corporate (including limited liability partnerships) or a Scottish limited partnership.
MAPA	Members' Agents Pooling Arrangements.
Material significance	A matter or group of matters is normally of material significance to a regulator's function when, due either to its nature or its potential financial impact, it is likely of itself to require investigation by the regulator.
Part IV permission	A permission granted by FSA under Part IV FSMA 2000 permitting an authorised firm to carry on regulated activities as specified in the FSMA 2000 Regulated Activities Order SI 2001/544 as amended.
PPFM	Principles and Practices of Financial Management.
Principles for Businesses	FSA Handbook defined principles with which an authorised firm must comply. The 11 principles are included in a stand alone element of the high level Standards block of the FSA Handbook – PRIN.
Recognised Accountant	An accountant included on the Council of Lloyds' list of individuals and firms identified as recognised accountants. Recognised accountants are engaged either by a syndicate to perform the annual solvency audit or annual syndicate audit or by a syndicate or Lloyd's underwriting agent to act as reporting accountant.
Relevant requirement	In relation to the auditors' duty to report direct to the FSA – requirement by or under FSMA 2000 which relates to authorisation under FSMA 2000 or to the carrying on of any regulated activity. This includes not only relevant statutory instruments but also the FSA's rules (other than the Listing

	rules) including the Principles for Businesses. The duty to report also covers any requirement imposed by or under any other Act the contravention of which constitutes an offence which the FSA has the power to prosecute under FSMA 2000.
Reporting Accountant	An accountant appointed by a managing agent on behalf of a syndicate or an underwriting agent for the purposes of reporting to the Council pursuant to paragraph 13 of the AAB [under which the Council of Lloyd's can require a report according to a scope that it sets].
Reporting Actuary	An Actuary appointed by an insurance company to report on the long-term technical provisions in the financial statements, as defined in Guidance Note 7 issued by the Institute and Faculty of Actuaries and adopted by the BAS.
RITC	"reinsurance to close".
Run-off account	A syndicate year of account which has not been closed at the normal date of closure and remains open.
2001 Regulations	SI 2001/2587 – FSMA 2000 (Communications by Auditors) Regulations 2001.
2004 Regulations	Insurance Accounts Directive (Lloyd's Syndicate and Aggregate Accounts) Regulations 2004.
SAO	Statement of Actuarial Opinion.
SOCA	Serious Organised Crime Agency.
Society	The Society incorporated by the Lloyd's Act 1871 by the names of Lloyd's.
SUP	Supervision manual of the FSA Handbook.
SYSC	Senior management arrangements, systems and controls.
The Solvency Byelaw	The Solvency and Reporting Byelaw (No 13 of 1990) (applicable to the Lloyd's Insurance Market).
Syndicate	A group of underwriting members underwriting insurance business at Lloyd's through the agency of a managing agent.
Those charged with governance	ISAs (UK and Ireland) use the term "those charged with governance" to describe the persons entrusted with the supervision, control and direction of an entity, who will normally be responsible for the quality of financial reporting, and the term "management" to describe those persons who perform senior managerial functions. The FSA Handbook of Rules and Guidance (FSA Handbook) uses the term "governing body" to describe collectively those charged with governance. In the context of this Practice Note, references to those charged with governance includes directors of insurance companies, directors of Lloyd's managing agents, and the members of the Council of Lloyd's. Directors of Lloyd's corporate members do not fall within the scope of the FSA Handbook as regards insurance matters.
Threshold Conditions	The minimum standards that an authorised firm needs to meet to become and remain authorised by the FSA. The 5

conditions are included in a stand alone element of the high level Standards block of the FSA Handbook – COND.

WPICC   With-Profits Insurance Capital Component.

[PN 21]
The audit of investment businesses in the United Kingdom (Revised)

(Issued December 2007)

Contents

	Page
Preface	3
Introduction	4
The audit of financial statements	
ISA (UK and Ireland)	11
200: Objective and general principles governing the audit of the financial statements	11
210: Terms of audit engagement	13
220: Quality control for audits of historical financial information	15
240: The auditor's responsibility to consider fraud in an audit of financial statements	16
250: Section A – Consideration of laws and regulations in an audit of financial statements	19
Section B – The auditor's right and duty to report to regulators in the financial sector	25
300: Planning an audit of financial statements	33
315: Obtaining an understanding of the entity and its environment and assessing the risks of material misstatement	35
320: Audit materiality	46
330: The auditor's procedures in response to assessed risks	47
402: Audit considerations relating to entities using service organisations	52
505: External confirmations	54
520: Analytical procedures	55
540: Audit of accounting estimates	56
545: Auditing fair value measurements and disclosures	58
550: Related parties	60
560: Subsequent events	61
570: The going concern basis in financial statements	62
580: Management representations	63
600: Using the work of another auditor	65
620: Using the work of an expert	67
700: The auditor's report on financial statements	68
Auditor's report to the FSA	69
Auditor's review reports on interim net profits	87
Appendix 1 – Illustrative examples of auditor's reports:	89
– 1.1 Auditor's report on client assets under SUP 3.10	
– 1.2 Auditor's review report on interim net profits	

Appendix 2 – Client Assets 96
Appendix 3 –The main parts of FSMA 2000 relevant to investment businesses 115
Appendix 4 – The FSA Handbook 117
Appendix 5 – Reporting direct to the FSA – statutory right and protection for disclosure under general law 120
Appendix 6 – The auditor's right and duty to report to the FSA: Examples of reportable items 122
Appendix 7 – Audit reporting requirements 123
Appendix 8 – Definitions 126

Preface

This Practice Note contains guidance on the application of auditing standards issued by the Auditing Practices Board (APB) to the audit of investment businesses in the United Kingdom (UK). In addition, it contains guidance intended to assist the auditors of investment businesses in reporting on matters specified by the Financial Services Authority (the FSA) as regulator. Guidance is also given on the auditors' right and duty to report to the regulator.

The Practice Note is supplementary to, and should be read in conjunction with, International Standards on Auditing (ISAs) (UK and Ireland), which apply to all audits undertaken in the UK. This Practice Note sets out the special considerations relating to the audit of investment businesses which arise from individual ISAs (UK and Ireland) listed in the contents. It is not the intention of the Practice Note to provide step-by-step guidance to the audit of investment businesses, so where no special considerations arise from a particular ISA (UK and Ireland), no material is included.

New guidance has been included in the Practice Note in relation to reporting to the FSA on client assets under SUP 3.10, which is applicable whether or not a statutory audit is also carried out. This guidance is set out in the section on Auditor's reports to the FSA.

This Practice Note has been prepared with advice and assistance from staff of the FSA (in so far as the obligations of investment businesses and their auditors under the FSA Handbook are concerned). It is based on the legislation and regulations which are in effect at 31 December 2007. The Practice Note does not however constitute general guidance given by the FSA or Industry Guidance. It is not an exhaustive list of all the obligations that investment businesses and their auditors may have under FSMA and the FSA Handbook.

Introduction

The term 'investment business' in this Practice Note should be taken to refer to firms regulated by the FSA for the conduct of 'designated investment business', as set out in the Glossary to the FSA's Handbook and based upon the Financial Services and Markets Act (FSMA) 2000. Firm types are defined in the Glossary to the FSA Handbook, but the following summary is intended to provide the reader with a broad understanding of the different types of investment business. Rules requiring the application of the Markets in Financial Instruments Directive (MiFID) are complex, and auditors need to consider whether it applies to each investment business they audit.

Type of firm	Short form description of firm	Relevant Prudential sourcebook
BIPRU investment firm (which includes a UCITS investment firm[1]).	Undertakes business within the scope of MiFID, for example a discretionary investment manager or a stockbroker.	GENPRU[2] and BIPRU[3]
Exempt CAD firm[4]	Undertakes a restricted level of MiFID scope business for example a securities and futures firm, an investment management firm and a personal investment firm which advises and arranges transactions but does not hold client assets.	IPRU (INV)[5] chapters 9 or 13
Securities and futures firm	Undertakes securities and futures business but is not within the scope of MiFID, for example a corporate finance firm which only provides advice.	IPRU (INV) chapter 3
Investment management firm	Undertakes investment management business, which is not within the scope of MiFID, for example the operator of an unregulated collective investment scheme.	IPRU (INV) chapter 5
Personal investment firm	Undertakes investment advisory business for retail clients, which is not within the scope of MIFID, for example an independent financial adviser.	IPRU (INV) chapter 13
UCITS firm [6]	Operates UCITS schemes, for example an authorised unit trust manager.	UPRU[7]

2   Investment businesses also include banks and insurers, but guidance for auditors of these businesses is set out primarily in Practice Note 19 – 'The audit of banks and building societies in the United Kingdom (Revised)' and in Practice Note 20 – 'The Audit of insurers in the United Kingdom (Revised)'. It is important to note that this

[1] See paragraph 21 for further details of UCITS investment firms and UCITS firms (which are types of UCITS management companies) and the UCITS directive

[2] This is the General Prudential sourcebook.

[3] This is the Prudential sourcebook for Banks, Building Societies and Investment Firms.

[4] For the purposes of the table an exempt CAD firm is shown separately whereas the definitions in the Glossary of securities and futures firm, investment management firm and personal investment firm include an exempt CAD firm.

[5] This is the Interim Prudential sourcebook for Investment Businesses.

[6] See footnote 1.

[7] This is the Prudential sourcebook for UCITS Firms.

Practice Note does not include within its scope an audit that is required for an investment fund that is managed or operated by an investment business. This would include for example the audit report to the unit holders of an authorised unit trust that is required under the FSA's Collective Investment Schemes sourcebook (COLL).

The audit reporting requirements of the firms within the scope of this Practice Note are set out in Appendix 7.

This Practice Note addresses the responsibilities and obligations of the auditor concerning:

- the audit of the financial statements in accordance with the Companies Act 1985, Limited Liability Partnership Act 2000 and for those incorporated in Northern Ireland the provisions of the Companies (Northern Ireland) Order 1986 (dealt with in paragraphs 29 to 179).
- the report to the FSA by the investment business's auditors (dealt with in paragraphs 180 to 263).
- reporting on interim net profits for the purposes of their inclusion in regulatory capital (dealt with in paragraphs 264 to 270).
- the right and duty to report direct to the FSA in certain circumstances (dealt with in paragraphs 63 to 93).

3

This Practice Note does not address other types of work that auditors may also be required to carry out on other areas of an investment business. Auditors in the capacity of independent accountants may, for example be asked to carry out work as a part of an application to become an authorised person; as part of a waiver request; or on cessation of investment business.

Whilst they are not classed as investment businesses, the parts of this Practice Note giving guidance on financial resources and client assets may be useful to the auditors of intermediary firms[8] carrying on:

4

- home finance mediation activities[9] in relation to regulated home finance transactions
- insurance mediation activities in relation to 'non-investment' insurance activities

which are regulated by the FSA. In particular there are FSA 'client asset' rules which are applicable to certain insurance intermediaries and on which auditors may be required to report in certain circumstances. Guidance is included in ICAEW TECH 1/06 – Interim guidance for auditors of insurance intermediaries on client asset reporting requirements. The guidance which is included in Appendix 2 of this Practice Note is also likely to be of relevance to the auditors of intermediary firms in relation to the work normally carried out in order to form an opinion on client money in a report to the FSA.

---

[8] *Home finance intermediaries and insurance intermediaries are defined in the Glossary to the FSA Handbook.*

[9] *Home finance mediation activity includes any mortgage mediation activity, home purchase mediation activity or reversion mediation activity.*

Legislative and regulatory framework

Financial Statements

5   The form and content of the financial statements of investment businesses incorporated as limited liability companies in the UK is governed by the Companies Act 1985, Statements of Standard Accounting Practice ('SSAPs'), Financial Reporting Standards ('FRSs') and Urgent Issues Task Force Abstracts ('UITFs'). The mandatory format for investment businesses' financial statements is set out in Schedule 4 to the Companies Act 1985. A Statutory Instrument introduced in 2004 mandates the preparation of consolidated accounts under International Financial Reporting Standards ('IFRS') for listed groups and permits the preparation of accounts under IFRS for other companies.

6   For entities incorporated under the Limited Liability Partnership Act 2000 ('LLPs'), the form and content of the financial statements are governed by the Limited Liability Partnership Regulations. SSAPs, FRSs and UITFs also apply to any financial statements of LLPs intended to give a true and fair view. In addition there is a Statement of Recommended Practice on accounting by LLPs published by the Consultative Committee of Accountancy Bodies. A Statutory Instrument introduced in 2004 permits the preparation of LLP accounts under IFRS.

Financial Services and Markets Act 2000

7   FSMA 2000 sets out the high level regulatory framework for the whole financial sector more generally and not just investment businesses. Appendix 3 sets out the main parts of FSMA 2000 relevant to investment businesses.

8   The wide scope of FSMA 2000 reflects the FSA's extensive responsibilities. These are set out in FSMA 2000 as regulatory objectives covering:

- market confidence;
- public awareness;
- the protection of consumers; and
- the reduction of financial crime.

9   FSMA 2000 covers not only the regulation and supervision of financial sector entities but also other issues such as official listing rules, business transfers, market abuse, compensation and ombudsman schemes, investment exchanges and clearing houses.

10 FSMA 2000 is also supported by a large number of statutory instruments. Significant components of the definition and scope of the regulatory framework are contained in the main statutory instruments.

11 Under Part X FSMA 2000 the FSA has the power to make 'rules'. The legal effect of a rule varies depending on the power under which it is made and on the language used in the rule. Rules are mandatory unless a waiver has been agreed with the FSA. If an authorised firm contravenes a rule it may be subject to enforcement action and consequent disciplinary measures under Part XIV FSMA 2000. Furthermore, in certain circumstances an authorised firm may be subject to an action for damages under s150 FSMA 2000. In contrast, guidance is generally issued to throw light on a particular aspect of regulatory requirements, and is not binding. However if an authorised firm acts in accordance with it in the circumstances contemplated by that guidance, the FSA will proceed on the basis that the authorised firm has complied with the rule to which the guidance relates.

Rules made by the FSA and associated guidance are set out in the FSA Handbook of Rules and Guidance ('the FSA Handbook') (see Appendix 4). The main FSA systems and control requirements are set out in SYSC[10].

European Directives

Markets in Financial Instruments Directive ('MiFID')

MiFID covers specified 'investment services and activities' and specified 'ancillary services'. The scope of MiFID services and activities falls within the scope of FSMA 2000, although there are a number of additional activities which require authorisation in the UK under FSMA 2000.

Where an entity is incorporated in an EEA member state and has obtained authorisation in that state ('home state') for its MiFID investment services, it can provide those authorised services in other EEA member states ('host states') by setting up branches, or by providing services on a cross-border basis, without obtaining separate authorisation in those states. This is referred to as the 'European passport'.

Incoming branches of EEA entities which provide investment services in the UK under their passport do still need to be registered with the FSA as an incoming EEA firm; this is achieved by a process of notification to the FSA by the home state regulator, rather than by means of a full-scope application for authorisation.

Passports are only available for authorised entities with their head office or registered office in an EEA member state. For example, a UK branch of a US investment business cannot obtain a passport to provide services in other EEA states, although a UK subsidiary can. Also, a passport can only be obtained in respect of services, activities and instruments which are authorised in the home state. For example, where the UK branch of a German investment firm wishes to provide investment services in the UK which are not authorised in Germany, the branch must obtain authorisation from the FSA in addition to its registration as an incoming EEA firm.

The home state regulator is responsible for financial supervision of the entity as a whole, i.e. covering head office and any branches. The home state regulator is also responsible for transaction reporting and rules relating to client assets, covering:

- the investment services provided at home by head office; and
- the investment services provided by any branches in other European states, where these services are within the entity's passport.

The host state regulator is responsible for rules relating to conduct of business excluding transaction reporting and client assets. It is also responsible for client asset rules covering any investment services provided in the host state which are outside the entity's passport.

Capital Requirements Directive ('CRD')

MiFID firms will also fall within the scope of CRD which sets out the minimum amounts of regulatory capital MiFID firms must maintain or exceed. CRD also requires MiFID firms to comply with capital adequacy requirements at a group level i.e. they are subject to consolidated supervision.

---

[10] The Senior Management Arrangements, Systems and Controls sourcebook in the FSA Handbook.

Financial Groups Directive ('FGD')

20 Firms that are part of a financial conglomerate are required to comply with separate group reporting rules. The FGD also extends the scope of the FSA's supplementary supervision of firms which are part of third country groups, ie those with non-EEA holding companies, to require consideration of risks associated with being a member of that group.

Undertakings for Collective Investment in Transferable Securities Directive ('UCITS')

21 Under the terms of this directive, firms that are authorised to operate UCITS schemes in an EEA member state are allowed to sell such schemes on a cross border basis in other EEA member states without being authorised in those states. Such firms are UCITS management companies and can be either a UCITS firm or a UCITS investment firm. A UCITS firm is one that is the operator of UCITS schemes and may also operate other collective investment schemes which are not UCITS schemes, but carries on no other regulated activities except those that are in connection with or for the purposes of such schemes, and, with respect to prudential requirements, it is subject to UPRU. A UCITS investment firm is one that, as allowed under the terms of this directive, in addition to operating UCITS schemes and, in some cases, other collective investment schemes that are not UCITS, has a permission to manage MiFID investments (and may also in some circumstances have permission to provide investment advice and safeguard and administer investments). With respect to prudential requirements, such a firm is subject to the requirements of BIPRU and GENPRU.

Reporting direct to the FSA – statutory right and duty

22 Under FSMA 2000 (Communications by Auditors) Regulations 2001 (SI 2001/2587) the auditor of an authorised firm (or someone who has been such an auditor) or the auditor of an entity closely linked to an authorised firm (or who has been such an auditor) has a statutory duty to communicate certain matters to the FSA. In addition s342 FSMA 2000 provides that no duty to which the auditor is subject shall be contravened by communicating in good faith to the FSA any information or opinion on a matter that the auditor reasonably believes is relevant to any functions of the FSA. Guidance on the identification of matters to be reported to the regulators is set out in the section dealing with ISA (UK and Ireland) 250 Section B.

Communication between the FSA and the auditor

23 Within the legal constraints that apply, the FSA may pass on to the auditor any information which it considers relevant to his function. An auditor is bound by the confidentiality provisions set out in Part XXIII of FSMA 2000 (Public record, disclosure of information and co-operation) in respect of confidential information the auditor receives from the FSA. The auditor may not pass on such confidential information without lawful authority, for example if an exception applies under the FSMA 2000 (Disclosure of confidential information) Regulations 2001 (SI 2001/2188) or with the consent of the person from whom that information was received and, if different, to whom the information relates.

24 Before communicating to an authorised firm any information received from the FSA, the auditor considers carefully whether:

- the auditor has received the FSA's express permission to communicate a particular item of information;

- the information relates to any other party whose permission may need to be obtained before disclosure can be made;
- the information was received by the FSA in a capacity other than discharging its functions under FSMA 2000 or from another regulator (in which case the auditor may either be prohibited from disclosure or may need permission of the party which provided the information to that regulator).

The auditor may however disclose to an authorised firm information the auditor has communicated to the FSA except where to do so would have the effect of disclosing information communicated to the auditor by the FSA. If there is any doubt the auditor considers the matters above.

Matters communicated by the FSA during any bilateral meeting may be conveyed by those representatives of the auditor who were present at the meeting (or otherwise received the communication directly) to other partners, directors and employees of the audit firm who need to know the information in connection with the auditor's performance of its duties relating to that authorised firm and without the FSA's express permission. However in the interests of prudence and transparency the auditor should inform the FSA that they will be discussing the issues covered with colleagues. 25

Where the FSA passes to the auditor information which it considers is relevant to his function, the auditor considers its implications in the context of his work and may need to amend his approach accordingly. However the fact that the auditor may have been informed of such a matter by the FSA does not, of itself, require auditors to change the scope of the work, nor does it necessarily require the auditor actively to search for evidence in support of the situation communicated by the FSA. 26

The auditor is required to cooperate with the FSA (SUP3.8.2R). This may involve attending meetings and providing the FSA with information about the authorised firm that the FSA may reasonably request in discharging its functions. For example this can arise in relation to FSA ARROW II assessments. 27

The auditor must notify the FSA without delay if the auditor is removed from office, resigns before the term of office expires or is not re-appointed by the authorised firm. Notification to the FSA includes communicating any matters connected with this event that the auditor considers ought to be drawn to the FSA's attention or a statement that there are no such matters (s344 FSMA 2000 and SUP3.8.11R and 12R). 28

The audit of financial statements

ISAs (UK and Ireland) apply to the conduct of all audits. This includes audits of the financial statements of investment businesses. The purpose of the following paragraphs is to identify the special considerations arising from the application of certain 'bold letter' requirements to the audit of investment businesses, and to suggest ways in which these can be addressed (extracts from ISAs (UK and Ireland) are indicated by grey-shaded boxes below). This Practice Note does not contain commentary on all of the bold letter requirements included in the ISAs (UK and Ireland) and reading it should not be seen as an alternative to reading the relevant ISAs (UK and Ireland) in their entirety. In addition, where no special considerations arise from a particular ISA (UK and Ireland), no material is included.

ISA (UK AND IRELAND) 200: OBJECTIVE AND GENERAL PRINCIPLES GOVERNING THE AUDIT OF THE FINANCIAL STATEMENTS

Background note

The purpose of this ISA (UK and Ireland) is to establish standards and provide guidance on the objective and general principles governing an audit of financial statements.

The auditor should plan and perform an audit with an attitude of professional scepticism, recognising that circumstances may exist that cause the financial statements to be materially misstated. (paragraph 6)

29 Auditing standards include a requirement for the auditor to comply with relevant ethical requirements relating to audit engagements. In the United Kingdom, the auditor should comply with the APB's Ethical Standards and relevant ethical guidance relating to the work of the auditor issued by the auditor's professional body. A fundamental principle is that practitioners should not accept or perform work which they are not competent to undertake. The importance of technical competence is also underlined in the Auditors' Code[11], issued by the APB, which states that the necessary degree of professional skill demands an understanding of financial reporting and business issues. Practitioners should not undertake the audit of investment businesses unless they are satisfied that they have, or can obtain, the necessary level of competence.

Independence

30 Independence issues can be complex for the auditor of an investment business, because of investments held by the auditor and/or its partners and staff. The auditor makes careful reference to the APB's Ethical Standard 2 – Financial, business, employment and personal relationships on investments by partners and staff in investment businesses.

31 In addition to the APB's Ethical Standards and ethical guidance issued to the auditor by their relevant professional bodies there are rules laid down by the FSA which

---

[11] This is appended to the APB's Scope and Authority of Pronouncements.

apply to audit appointments. The FSA rule book (SUP 3.5) sets out circumstances where the auditor would not be viewed by the regulator as independent.

ISA (UK AND IRELAND) 210: TERMS OF AUDIT ENGAGEMENT

Background note

The purpose of this ISA (UK and Ireland) is to establish standards and provide guidance on agreeing the terms of the engagement with the client.

The auditor and the client should agree on the terms of the engagement. (paragraph 2)

The terms of the engagement should be recorded in writing. (paragraph 2-1)

The auditor should ensure that the engagement letter documents and confirms the auditor's acceptance of the appointment, and includes a summary of the responsibilities of those charged with governance and of the auditor, the scope of the engagement and the form of any reports. (paragraph 5-1)

The terms of the engagement in respect of auditors' client assets reports to the FSA could be combined with the engagement letter for the statutory audit. In this respect the engagement letter makes it clear that the client assets report is addressed to the FSA. Matters which the auditor may decide to refer to in the engagement letter are as follows:

- the responsibility of the directors/senior management to comply with applicable FSMA 2000 legislation and FSA Handbook rules and guidance including the need to keep the FSA informed about the affairs of the entity;
- the statutory right and duty of the auditor to report direct to the FSA in certain circumstances (see section of this Practice Note relating to ISA (UK and Ireland) 250 Section B);
- the requirement to cooperate with the auditor (SUP3.6.1R). This includes taking steps to ensure that, where applicable, each of its appointed representatives and material outsourcers gives the auditor the same right of access to records, information and explanations as the authorised firm itself is required to provide the auditor (s341 FSMA 2000 and SUP 3.6.2G to 3.6.8G). It a criminal offence for a investment business or its officers, controllers or managers to provide false or misleading information to the auditor s346 FSMA 2000);
- the need for the investment business to make the auditor aware when it appoints a third party (including another department or office of the same audit firm) to review, investigate or report on any aspects of its business activities that may be relevant to the audit of the financial statements and to provide the auditor with copies of reports by such a third party promptly after their receipt.

In this connection the auditor is aware that:

- the FSA does not need to approve the appointment of an auditor but may seek to satisfy itself that an auditor appointed by a firm is independent and has the necessary skills, resources and experience (SUP 3.4.4G, 3.4.7R and 3.4.8G);
- the auditor is required to cooperate with the FSA (SUP 3.8.2R); and
- the auditor must notify the FSA if the auditor ceases to be the auditor of the authorised firm.

ISA (UK AND IRELAND) 220: QUALITY CONTROL FOR AUDITS OF HISTORICAL FINANCIAL INFORMATION

> **Background note**
>
> The purpose of this ISA (UK and Ireland) is to establish standards and provide guidance on specific responsibilities of firm personnel regarding quality control procedures for audits of historical financial information, including audits of financial statements.
>
> Reference should also be made to ISQC (UK and Ireland) 1 – Quality Control for Firms that Perform Audits and Reviews of Historical Financial Information, and other Assurance and Related Services Engagements.

> The engagement partner should be satisfied that the engagement team collectively has the appropriate capabilities, competence and time to perform the audit engagement in accordance with professional standards and regulatory and legal requirements, and to enable an auditor's report that is appropriate in the circumstances to be issued. (paragraph 19)

34 The nature of investment business is one of rapidly changing and evolving markets. Often investment businesses develop new products and practices which require specialised auditing and accounting responses. It is therefore important that the auditor is familiar with current practice.

35 As well as ensuring that the engagement team has an appropriate level of knowledge of the industry and its corresponding products, the engagement partner also satisfies himself that the members of the engagement team have sufficient knowledge of the regulatory framework within which investment businesses operate commensurate with their roles in the engagement.

ISA (UK AND IRELAND) 240: THE AUDITOR'S RESPONSIBILITY TO CONSIDER FRAUD IN AN AUDIT OF FINANCIAL STATEMENTS

> **Background note**
>
> The purpose of this ISA (UK and Ireland) is to establish basic principles and essential procedures and to provide guidance on the auditor's responsibility to consider fraud in an audit of financial statements and expand on how the standards and guidance in ISA (UK and Ireland) 315 and ISA (UK and Ireland) 330 are to be applied in relation to the risks of material misstatement due to fraud.

> In planning and performing the audit to reduce audit risk to an acceptably low level, the auditor should consider the risks of material misstatements in the financial statements due to fraud. (paragraph 3)
>
> The auditor should maintain an attitude of professional scepticism throughout the audit, recognising the possibility that a material misstatement due to fraud could exist, notwithstanding the auditor's past experience with the entity about

> the honesty and integrity of management and those charged with governance. (paragraph 24).
>
> The auditor should make inquiries of management, internal audit, and others within the entity as appropriate, to determine whether they have knowledge of any actual, suspected or alleged fraud affecting the entity (paragraph 38).
>
> When obtaining an understanding of the entity and its environment, including its internal control, the auditor should consider whether the information obtained indicates that one or more fraud risk factors are present (paragraph 48).

As with other entities, either fraudulent financial reporting (for example the manipulation of profits or the concealment of losses) or misappropriation of assets, can occur through a combination of management fraud, employee fraud or fraud perpetrated by third parties. 36

The following are examples of matters that may be relevant when assessing fraud risk in the audit of investment businesses: 37

- backlogs in key reconciliations, particularly those with brokers and exchanges and for bank accounts and safe custody accounts – both the investment business's own and those relating to its clients;
- inadequate segregation of duties between the front, middle and back office staff;
- inadequate whistle blowing arrangements;
- high management and staff turnover levels;
- ineffective oversight of offshore operations;
- lack of an effective audit committee;
- complex products inadequately understood by management;
- inadequate definition of management responsibilities and supervision of staff;
- ineffective personnel practices and policies, e.g. screening of applicants;
- inadequate communication of information to management;
- scope for inappropriate revenue recognition or concealment of trading losses;
- ineffective regulatory compliance monitoring.

Whilst remuneration policies can create excessive performance pressures in many industries, in certain types of investment businesses performance related bonuses can be significant both in absolute terms and in relation to base remuneration. In addition significant bonus related remuneration can often extend beyond senior management, further down the organisation of investment businesses, and can lead to more pervasive pressures that cause increased risks of fraud. Other examples of fraud risk factors include: 38

- valuation of complex financial instruments in an environment where there is inadequate segregation of duties and/or lack of supervision or independent review and/or understanding of the valuation techniques and associated inputs; and
- matters that are subject to significant judgment by management – eg allowances for impairment (particularly collective assessment of impairment) or customer compensation provisioning.

Principle 3 of the FSA Principles for Businesses requires a firm to take reasonable care to organise and control its affairs responsibly and effectively with adequate risk management systems. SYSC requires a firm to make and retain adequate records of matters and dealings (including accounting records) which are the subject of requirements and standards under the regulatory system. Whilst the inherent risk of fraud may continue to exist, the establishment of accounting and internal control 39 systems sufficient to meet these requirements frequently reduces the likelihood of fraud giving rise to material misstatements in the financial statements. Guidance on the auditors' consideration of accounting systems and internal controls is provided in the section on ISA (UK and Ireland) 315. Examples of weaknesses in control that could give rise to fraud risk factors are also set out in that section.

> When obtaining an understanding of the entity and its environment, including its internal control, the auditor should consider whether other information obtained indicates risks of material misstatement due to fraud (paragraph 55).

40 The auditor considers reports or information obtained from the investment business's compliance department, legal department, and money laundering reporting officer together with reviews undertaken by third parties such as skilled person's reports prepared under s166 FSMA 2000.

> If the auditor has identified a fraud or has obtained information that indicates that a fraud may exist, the auditor should communicate these matters as soon as practicable to the appropriate level of management (paragraph 93).
>
> The auditor should document communications about fraud made to management, those charged with governance, regulators and others (paragraph 109).

41 Reduction of financial crime is one of the FSA's statutory objectives. The FSA's rules require authorised firms to report 'significant' fraud to the FSA (SUP15.3.17R). The auditor is aware of the auditor's duty to report direct to FSA in certain circumstances (see the section of this Practice Note relating to ISA (UK and Ireland) 250 Section B).

ISA (UK AND IRELAND) 250: SECTION A – CONSIDERATION OF LAWS AND REGULATIONS IN AN AUDIT OF FINANCIAL STATEMENTS

> **Background note**
>
> The purpose of this ISA (UK and Ireland) is to establish standards and provide guidance on the auditor's responsibility to consider laws and regulations in the audit of financial statements.

> When designing and performing audit procedures and in evaluating and reporting the results thereof, the auditor should recognize that non-compliance by the entity with laws and regulations may materially affect the financial statements. (paragraph 2)
>
> In accordance with ISA (UK and Ireland) 200, 'Objective and General Principles Governing an Audit of Financial Statements' the auditor should plan and perform the audit with an attitude of professional scepticism recognizing that the audit may reveal conditions or events that would lead to questioning whether an entity is complying with laws and regulations. (paragraph 13)

> In order to plan the audit, the auditor should obtain a general understanding of the legal and regulatory framework applicable to the entity and the industry and how the entity is complying with that framework. (paragraph 15)

42 The legal and regulatory framework within which investment businesses conduct their business is summarised in the Introduction to the Practice Note. ISA (UK and Ireland) 250 Section A defines laws and regulations which are central to the entity's ability to conduct its business as those where either compliance is a prerequisite of obtaining a licence to operate or where non-compliance may reasonably be expected to result in the entity ceasing operations, or call into question the entity's status as a going concern.

> After obtaining the general understanding, the auditor should perform further audit procedures to help identify instances of non-compliance with those laws and regulations where non-compliance should be considered when preparing financial statements, specifically:
>
> (a) Inquiring of management as to whether the entity is in compliance with such laws and regulations; and
> (b) Inspecting correspondence with the relevant licensing or regulatory authorities.
> (c) Enquiring of those charged with governance as to whether they are on notice of any such possible instances of non-compliance with law or regulations. (paragraph 18)
>
> The auditor's procedures should be designed to help identify possible or actual instances of non-compliance with those laws and regulations which provide a legal framework within which the entity conducts its business and which are central to the entity's ability to conduct its business and hence to its financial statements. (paragraph 18-1)

43 In the context of investment businesses, the two criteria set out in paragraph 42 above indicate that laws and regulations are central to an investment business's ability to conduct its business if non-compliance could cause the regulator to revoke or restrict authorisation. In order to help identify possible or actual instances of non-compliance with laws and regulations which are central to an investment business's ability to conduct its business, specific areas that auditors' procedures may address include the following:

- obtaining a general understanding of the legal and regulatory framework applicable to the entity and industry, and of the procedures followed to ensure compliance with the framework;
- reviewing the investment business's Scope of Part IV Permission (an FSA document which sets out the regulated activities that the firm is permitted to engage in, including any limitations and requirements imposed on those permitted activities);
- reviewing correspondence with the FSA and other regulators (including that relating to any FSA supervisory visits, requests for information by the FSA or progress concerning FSA ARROW II risk mitigation programmes);
- holding discussions with the investment business's compliance officer and other personnel responsible for compliance;
- reviewing compliance reports prepared for the Board, audit committees and other committees; and
- consideration of work on compliance matters carried out by internal audit.

> The auditor should obtain sufficient appropriate audit evidence about compliance with those laws and regulations generally recognised by the auditor to have an effect on the determination of material amounts and disclosures in the financial statements. The auditor should have a sufficient understanding of these laws and regulations in order to consider them when auditing the assertions related to the determination of the amounts to be recorded and the disclosures to be made.(-paragraph 19)

44   The auditor obtains sufficient audit evidence regarding compliance with those laws and regulations that can affect the material amounts and disclosures in the financial statements.

45   The auditor is alert to the fact that audit procedures applied for the purpose of forming an opinion on the financial statements may bring instances of possible non-compliance with the laws and regulations to the auditor's attention. For example, such audit procedures include reading minutes; inquiring of the entity's management and legal counsel concerning litigation, claims and assessments; and performing substantive tests of detail of classes of transactions, account balances or disclosures.

46   There are compensation schemes set up to protect individual investors for certain classes of business under the Financial Services Compensation Scheme (FSCS) (established under FSMA 2000). There are also consumer affairs bodies, such as the Financial Ombudsman Service (which handles consumer complaints) and the Office of Fair Trading (a statutory body which applies to both financial services and other retail organisations).

47   Investment businesses are affected by two types of regulation which are central to their activities and of which the auditor needs to obtain a general understanding:

(a) prudential rules; and
(b) conduct of business rules.

Prudential rules

48   The principal purpose of prudential supervision is to ensure the protection of clients because of the nature of transactions between investment businesses and the public. Much of the legislation for prudential supervision is based on European Directives. Prudential supervision of investment businesses is carried out by the FSA under rules made by the FSA under FSMA 2000. Ongoing prudential supervision of authorised investment businesses is conducted in part by means of annual regulatory returns submitted by many authorised investment businesses.

49   Examples of procedures which an auditor considers carrying out in connection with the prudential rules (which are also relevant to a consideration of going concern) during the course of his audit of the financial statements could include:

- enquiring how management ensure that the financial resources calculations are properly prepared and submitted on time;
- enquiring how management ensure that the firm complies with the financial resources requirements including, where relevant, at consolidated level and the large exposure rules;
- examining the returns to see whether they show that the firm/group has a reasonable surplus of regulatory capital. Enquiries should cover the accounting

period being audited and the future period covered by the auditor's work on going concern;
- reviewing relevant correspondence with the FSA, for example waivers.

Conduct of Business Rules

Conduct of business regulation relates to the sale of business and is primarily carried out by the FSA through its rules in respect of COB (Conduct of Business rules).

The auditor has no direct reporting responsibility in respect of the conduct of business rules. However, breaches of such rules may:

- give rise to material fines and/or claims by investors against the investment business; and
- cause the investment business to have its authorisation restricted or, in extreme cases, withdrawn, so threatening its viability as a going concern.

The auditor ensures that the staff involved in the audit have a general understanding of the business and the objectives of conduct of business regulation, sufficient to enable them to be alert to possible breaches which come to their attention.

As part of the normal procedures undertaken for the purposes of the audit of annual financial statements and reporting to the regulator, the auditor gains an understanding of the investment business's operations, including the nature of the investment business carried out.

The auditor also obtains an understanding of the control environment that exists, including the business's higher level procedures for complying with the conduct of business rules.

Such an understanding will provide an indication of the extent to which the general atmosphere and controls in the investment business are conducive to compliance, for example through consideration of:

- the adequacy of procedures and training to inform staff of the requirements of the rules of the regulator to ensure that they meet those requirements;
- adequacy of authorities and supervision;
- the review of compliance by senior management;
- procedures to ensure that possible breaches are investigated by an appropriate person and are brought to the attention of senior management; and
- the authority of, and resources available to, the Compliance Officer.

The auditor is alert to any indication that an investment business is conducting business outside the scope of its authorisation. Such action may be a serious regulatory breach, which may result in fines, suspension or loss of authorisation.

Where an apparent significant breach of the conduct of business rules comes to the auditors' attention, they ensure that its cause and implications for their reporting responsibilities are identified and further investigation may be appropriate.

Money laundering

> In the UK and Ireland, when carrying out procedures for the purpose of forming an opinion on the financial statements, the auditor should be alert for those

> instances of possible or actual non compliance with laws and regulations that might incur obligations for partners and staff in audit firms to report money laundering offences. (paragraph 22-1)

58 Authorised firms including investment businesses are subject to the requirements of the Money Laundering Regulations 2007 and the Proceeds of Crime Act 2002 as well as FSA rules. These laws and regulations require institutions to establish and maintain procedures to identify their customers, establish appropriate reporting and investigation procedures for suspicious transactions and maintain appropriate records.

59 Laws and regulations relating to money laundering are integral to the legal and regulatory framework within which investment businesses conduct their business. By the nature of their business, investment businesses are ready targets of those engaged in money laundering activities.

60 The effect of this legislation is to make it an offence to provide assistance to those involved in money laundering and makes it an offence not to report suspicions of money laundering to the appropriate authorities, usually the Serious Organised Crime Agency (SOCA)[12]. FSA requirements are set out in SYSC3.2.6AR – 6.3.5G[13]. In this context, FSA has due regard to compliance with the relevant provisions of guidance issued by the Joint Money Laundering Steering Group ('JMLSG')(SYSC3.2.6EG).

61 In addition to considering whether an investment business has complied with the money laundering laws and regulations, the auditor has reporting obligations under the Proceeds of Crime Act, 2002 and the Money Laundering Regulations, 2007 to report knowledge or suspicion of money laundering offences, including those arising from fraud and theft, to SOCA. The auditor is aware of the prohibition on 'tipping off' when discussing money laundering matters with the investment business.[14] Further guidance for auditors is provided in PN 12 Money Laundering – Interim Guidance for Auditors in the United Kingdom (Revised).

62 The auditor, in the context of money laundering, is aware of the auditor's duty to report direct to the FSA in certain circumstances (see section relating to ISA (UK and Ireland) 250 Section B).

ISA (UK AND IRELAND) 250: SECTION B – THE AUDITOR'S RIGHT AND DUTY TO REPORT TO REGULATORS IN THE FINANCIAL SECTOR

> The auditor of a regulated entity should bring information of which the auditor has become aware in the ordinary course of performing work undertaken to fulfil the auditor's audit responsibilities to the attention of the appropriate regulator without delay when:
>
> (a) The auditor concludes that it is relevant to the regulator's functions having regard to such matters as may be specified in statute or any related regulations; and

---

[12] Previously National Criminal Intelligence Service ('NCIS').

[13] For common platform firms the relevant references are included in SYSC 6.

[14] 'Tipping off' is an offence for individuals in the regulated sector under POCA section 333A.

(b) In the auditor's opinion there is reasonable cause to believe it is or may be of material significance to the regulator. (paragraph 2)

Where an apparent breach of statutory or regulatory requirements comes to the auditor's attention, the auditor should:

(a) Obtain such evidence as is available to assess its implications for the auditor's reporting responsibilities;
(b) Determine whether, in the auditor's opinion, there is reasonable cause to believe that the breach is of material significance to the regulator; and
(c) Consider whether the apparent breach is criminal conduct that gives rise to criminal property and, as such, should be reported to the specified authorities. (paragraph 39)

Auditors' duty to report to the FSA

Under the FSMA 2000 (Communication by Auditors) Regulations 2001 (the 2001 Regulations), auditors have duties in certain circumstances to make reports to the FSA. **The 2001 Regulations do not require auditors to perform any additional audit work as a result of the statutory duty nor are auditors required specifically to seek out breaches of the requirements applicable to a particular authorised person.** Information and opinions to be communicated are those meeting the criteria set out below which relate to matters of which the auditor[15] of the authorised person (also referred to below as a 'regulated entity') has become aware:

(i) in his capacity as auditor of the authorised person, and
(ii) if he is also the auditor of a person who has close links with the authorised person, in his capacity as auditor of that person.

The criteria for determining the matters to be reported are as follows:

(i) the auditor reasonably believes that there is, or has been, or may be, or may have been a contravention of any 'relevant requirement' that applies to the person[16] concerned and that contravention may be of material significance to the FSA in determining whether to exercise, in relation to that person, any of its functions under FSMA 2000, or
(ii) the auditor reasonably believes that the information on, or his opinion on, those matters may be of material significance to the FSA in determining whether the person concerned satisfies and will continue to satisfy the 'threshold conditions', or
(iii) the auditor reasonably believes that the person concerned is not, may not be, or may cease to be, a going concern, or
(iv) the auditor is precluded from stating in his report that the annual accounts have been properly prepared in accordance with the Companies Act 1985 or, where applicable, give a true and fair view or have been prepared in accordance with relevant rules and legislation[17]

---

[15] *An 'auditor' is defined for this purpose in the Regulations as a person who is, or has been, an auditor of an authorised person appointed under, or as a result of, a statutory provision including Section 340 of FSMA 2000.*

[16] *In this context the person is an 'Authorised Person'.*

[17] *Relevant rules and legislation comprise rules made by the FSA under Section 340 of FSMA 2000, and relevant provisions of, and regulations made under, the Building Societies Act 1986, the Friendly Societies Act 1992, or the Friendly and Industrial and Provident Societies Act 1968.*

65 In relation to 64 (i) above, 'relevant requirement' is a requirement by or under FSMA 2000 which relates to authorisation under FSMA 2000 or to the carrying on of any regulated activity. This includes not only relevant statutory instruments but also the FSA's rules (other than the Listing rules) including the principles for businesses[18]. The duty to report also covers any requirement imposed by or under any other Act[19] the contravention of which constitutes an offence which the FSA has the power to prosecute under FSMA 2000.

66 In relation to 64 (ii) above the duty to report relates to either information or opinions held by the auditor which may be of significance to the FSA in determining whether the regulated entity satisfies and will continue to satisfy the 'Threshold Conditions'. The duty to report opinions, as well as information, allows for circumstances where adequate information on a matter may not readily be forthcoming from the regulated entity, and where judgments need to be made.

Material significance

67 Determining whether a contravention of a relevant requirement or a Threshold Condition is reportable under the 2001 Regulations involves consideration both of whether the auditor 'reasonably believes' and that the matter in question 'is, or is likely to be, of material significance' to the regulator.

68 The 2001 Regulations do not require auditors to perform any additional audit work as a result of the statutory duty nor are auditors required specifically to seek out breaches of the requirements applicable to a particular regulated entity. However, in circumstances where auditors identify that a reportable matter may exist, they carry out such extra work, as they consider necessary, to determine whether the facts and circumstances cause them 'reasonably to believe' that the matter does in fact exist. It should be noted that the auditors' work does not need to prove that the reportable matter exists.

69 ISA (UK and Ireland) 250 Section B requires that, where an apparent breach of statutory or regulatory requirements comes to the auditors' attention, they should obtain such evidence as is available to assess its implications for their reporting responsibilities and determine whether, in their opinion, there is reasonable cause to believe that the breach has occurred and that it relates to a matter that is of material significance to the regulator.

70 'Material significance' is defined by paragraph 14 of ISA (UK and Ireland) 250 as follows:

> 'A matter or group of matters is normally of material significance to a regulator's function when, due either to its nature or its potential financial impact, it is likely of itself to require investigation by the regulator.'

71 'Material significance' does not have the same meaning as materiality in the context of the audit of financial statements. Whilst a particular event may be trivial in terms of its possible effect on the financial statements of an entity, it may be of a nature or type that is likely to change the perception of the regulator. For example, a failure to reconcile client money accounts may not be significant in financial terms but may

---

[18] The status of the FSA's rules and principles for businesses is explained in Appendix 4 – The FSA Handbook.

[19] Examples include Part 5 of the Criminal Justice Act 1993 and prescribed regulations relating to money laundering.

have a significant effect on the FSA's consideration of whether the regulated entity was satisfactorily controlled and was behaving properly towards its customers.

72 The determination of whether a matter is, or is likely to be, of material significance to the FSA inevitably requires the auditor to exercise judgment. In forming such judgments, the auditor needs to consider not simply the facts of the matter but also their implications. In addition, it is possible that a matter, which is not materially significant in isolation, may become so when other possible breaches are considered.

73 The auditor of a regulated entity bases his judgment of 'material significance' to the FSA solely on his understanding of the facts of which he is aware without making any assumptions about the information available to the FSA in connection with any particular regulated entity.

74 Minor breaches of the FSA's rules that, for example, are unlikely to jeopardise the entity's assets or amount to misconduct or mismanagement would not normally be of 'material significance'. However, ISA (UK and Ireland) 250 requires auditors of regulated entities, when reporting on their financial statements, to review information obtained in the course of the audit and to assess whether the cumulative effect is of 'material significance' such as to give rise to a duty to report to the regulator. In circumstances where auditors are uncertain whether they may be required to make a report or not, they may wish to consider whether to take legal advice.

75 On completion of their investigations, the auditor ensures that the facts and circumstances, and the basis for his conclusion as to whether these are, or are likely to be of 'material significance' to the FSA, are adequately documented such that the reasons for his decision to report or not, as the case may be, may be clearly demonstrated.

76 Whilst confidentiality is an implied term of auditors' contracts with a regulated entity, section 342 of FSMA 2000 states that an auditor does not contravene that duty if he reports to the FSA information or his opinion, if he is acting in good faith and he reasonably believes that the information or opinion is relevant to any function of the FSA. The protection afforded is given in respect of information obtained in his capacity as auditor.

Conduct of the audit

77 ISA (UK and Ireland) 250 requires the auditor to ensure that all staff involved in the audit of a regulated entity 'have an understanding of:

(a) the provisions of applicable legislation,
(b) the regulator's rules and any guidance issued by the regulator, and
(c) any specific requirements which apply to the particular regulated entity,

appropriate to their role in the audit and sufficient (in the context of that role) to enable them to identify situations they encounter in the course of the audit which may give reasonable cause to believe that a matter should be reported to the regulator.'

78 Understanding, commensurate with the individual's role and responsibilities in the audit process, is required of:

- the provisions of the 2001 Regulations concerning the auditors' duty to report to the regulator,

- the Standards and guidance in ISA (UK and Ireland) 250, and in this section of this Practice Note, and
- relevant sections of the FSA's Handbook including the Principles for Businesses and the Threshold Conditions.

79   The auditor includes procedures within the planning process to ensure that members of the audit team have such understanding (in the context of their role) as to enable them to recognise potentially reportable matters, and that such matters are reported to the audit engagement partner without delay so that a decision may be made as to whether a duty to report arises.

80   An audit firm appointed as auditor of a regulated entity needs to have in place appropriate procedures to ensure that the audit engagement partner is made aware of any other relationship which exists between any department of the firm and the regulated entity when that relationship could affect the firm's work as auditor. (This matter is covered in more detail in Appendix 2 of ISA (UK and Ireland) 250). The auditor also requests the regulated entity to advise them when it appoints a third party (including another department or office of the same firm) to review, investigate or report on any aspects of its business activities that may be relevant to the audit of the financial statements and to provide the auditor with copies of reports by such a third party promptly after their receipt. This matter may usefully be referred to in the engagement letter.

Closely linked entities

81   Where the auditor of a regulated entity is also the auditor of a closely linked entity[20], a duty to report arises directly in relation to information relevant to the regulated entity of which he becomes aware in the course of his work as auditor of the closely linked entity.

82   The auditor establishes during audit planning whether the regulated entity has one or more closely linked entities of which the audit firm is also the auditor. If there are such entities the auditor considers the significance of the closely linked entities and the nature of the issues that might arise which may be of material significance to the regulator of the regulated entity. Such circumstances may involve:

- activities or uncertainties within the closely linked entity which might significantly impair the financial position of the regulated entity,
- money laundering and, if the closely linked entity is itself regulated,
- matters that the auditor of the closely linked entity are intending to report to its regulator.

83   Following the risk assessment referred to in paragraph 82, the auditor of the regulated entity identifies the closely linked entities for which the procedures in this paragraph are necessary. The engagement team of the regulated entity communicates to the engagement team of the selected closely linked entities the audit firm's responsibilities to report to the FSA under the 2001 Regulations and notifies the engagement team of the circumstances that have been identified which, if they exist, might be of material significance to the FSA as regulator of the regulated entity. Prior to completion the auditor of the regulated entity obtains details from the

---

[20] *An entity has close links with an authorised person for this purpose if the entity is a:*
  (a) Parent undertaking of an authorised person;
  (b) Subsidiary undertaking of an authorised person;
  (c) Parent undertaking of a subsidiary undertaking of an authorised person; or
  (d) Subsidiary undertaking of a parent undertaking of an authorised person.

auditor of the closely linked entity of such circumstances or confirmation, usually in writing, that such circumstances do not exist. Where the closely linked entities are part of the inter-auditor group reporting process these steps can be built into that process.

Whilst confidentiality is an implied term of auditors' contracts with a regulated entity, section 343 of FSMA 2000 states that an auditor of an entity closely linked to an authorised person who is also the auditor of that authorised person does not contravene that duty if he reports to the FSA information or his opinion, if he is acting in good faith and he reasonably believes that the information or opinion is relevant to any function of the FSA. The protection afforded is given in respect of information obtained in their capacity as the auditor. 84

No duty to report is imposed on the auditor of an entity closely linked to a regulated entity who is not also the auditor of the regulated entity. 85

In circumstances where they are not also the auditor of the closely linked entity, the auditor of the regulated entity decides whether there are any matters to be reported to the FSA relating to the affairs of the regulated entity in the light of the information that they receive about a closely linked entity for the purpose of auditing the financial statements of the regulated entity. If the auditor becomes aware of possible matters that may fall due to be reported, they may wish to obtain further information from the management or the auditor of the closely linked entity to ascertain whether the matter should be reported. To facilitate such possible discussions, at the planning stage of the audit, the auditor of the regulated entity will have considered whether arrangements need to be put in place to allow them to communicate with the management and the auditor of the closely linked entity. If the auditor of the regulated entity is unable to communicate with the management and the auditor of the closely linked entity to obtain further information concerning the matters they have identified they report the matters, and that they have been unable to obtain further information, direct to the FSA. 86

Information received in a capacity other than as auditor

There may be circumstances where it is not clear whether information about a regulated entity coming to the attention of the auditor is received in the capacity of auditor or in some other capacity, for example as a general adviser to the entity. Appendix 2 to ISA (UK and Ireland) 250 provides guidance as to how information obtained in non-audit work may be relevant to the auditor in the planning and conduct of the audit and the steps that need to be taken to ensure the communication of information that is relevant to the audit. 87

Discussing matters of material significance with the directors

The directors are the persons principally responsible for the management of the regulated entity. The auditor will therefore normally bring a matter of material significance to the attention of the directors and seek agreement on the facts and circumstances. However, ISA (UK and Ireland) 250 emphasises that where the auditor concludes that a duty to report arises they should bring the matter to the attention of the regulator without undue delay. The directors may wish to report the matters identified to the FSA themselves and detail the actions taken or to be taken. Whilst such a report from the directors may provide valuable information, it does not relieve the auditor of the statutory duty to report directly to the FSA. 88

Timing of a report

89 The duty to report arises once the auditor reasonably believes that the matter is or is likely to be of material significance to the FSA's regulatory function. In reaching a conclusion the auditor may wish to take appropriate legal or other advice and consult with colleagues.

90 The report should be made without undue delay once a conclusion has been reached. Unless the matter casts doubt on the integrity of the directors the matter can be discussed with the directors and further information sought as is necessary, so that a decision can be made on whether or not a duty to report exists. Such consultations and discussions are however undertaken on a timely basis to enable the auditor to conclude on the matter without undue delay.

Auditors' right to report to the FSA

91 Section 342 of FSMA 2000 provides that no duty to which an auditor of an authorised person is subject shall be contravened by communicating in good faith to the FSA information or an opinion on a matter that the auditor reasonably believes is relevant to any functions of the FSA.

92 The scope of the duty to report is wide particularly since, under the FSA's Principle for Businesses 11 (and corresponding application rules and guidance in SUP 15.3), an authorised firm must disclose to the FSA appropriately anything relating to the authorised firm of which the FSA would reasonably expect notice. However in circumstances where the auditor concludes that a matter does not give rise to a statutory duty to report but nevertheless should be brought to the attention of the regulator, in the first instance they advise the directors of their opinion. Where the auditor is unable to obtain, within a reasonable period, adequate evidence that the directors have properly informed the FSA of the matter, then the auditor makes a report to the regulator without undue delay.

93 The auditor may wish to take legal advice before deciding whether, and in what form, to exercise their right to make a report direct to the regulator in order to ensure, for example, that only relevant information is disclosed and that the form and content of their report is such as to secure the protection of FSMA 2000. However, the auditor recognises that legal advice will take time and that speed of reporting is likely to be important in order to protect the interests of customers and/or to enable the FSA to meet its statutory objectives.

ISA (UK AND IRELAND) 300: PLANNING AN AUDIT OF FINANCIAL STATEMENTS

Background note

The purpose of this ISA (UK and Ireland) is to establish standards and provide guidance on the considerations and activities applicable to planning an audit of financial statements. This ISA (UK and Ireland) is framed in the context of recurring audits. In addition, matters the auditor considers in initial audit engagements are included in paragraphs 28 and 29.

> The auditor should plan the audit so that the engagement will be performed in an effective manner (paragraph 2).
>
> The auditor should establish the overall audit strategy for the audit (paragraph 8).
>
> The auditor should develop an audit plan for the audit in order to reduce audit risk to an acceptably low level (paragraph 13).

To avoid potential duplication of audit effort, the audit approach to an investment business normally addresses the audit of the annual financial statements and the work required for the report to the FSA together. 94

Where applicable the auditor seeks to ensure that his audit work on the statutory accounts and the regulatory report is completed within timescales imposed by the FSA. The audit plan for an investment business typically explains the legal and regulatory background and, in order to reduce audit risk, discusses those areas where the auditor's responsibilities are different from those for other types of entity. 95

Matters the auditor of an investment business considers as part of the planning process for the audit of the financial statements include: 96

- the nature and scope of the investment business;
- the investment business's relationships with the FSA and any other regulators;
- changes in applicable laws, regulations and accounting requirements;
- the need to involve specialists in the audit;
- the extent to which controls and procedures are outsourced to a third-party provider; and
- issues relating to the auditor's statutory duty to report.

In general, further guidance on these matters is set out in the section on ISA (UK and Ireland) 315 'Obtaining an understanding of the entity and its environment and assessing the risks of material misstatement' below. Additional considerations in relation to the latter three matters in planning the audit could be: 97

- the nature and complexity of investment business increases the likelihood that the auditor may consider it necessary to involve specialists in the audit process. For example, the auditor may wish to utilise the work of an expert in the valuation of derivative and other financial instruments not traded in an active market. The auditor considers the need to involve such specialists at an early stage in planning his work. Where such specialists are to be used, they may be involved in the development of the audit plan and may take part in discussions with the management and staff, in order to assist in the development of knowledge and understanding relating to the business;
- the auditor considers the implications of the outsourcing of functions by the investment business and the sources of evidence available to the auditor for transactions undertaken by service organisations in planning his work. This may include the outsourcing of certain functions, such as the IT functions. Further guidance is contained in the section of the Practice Note dealing with ISA (UK and Ireland) 402 'Audit Considerations Relating to Entities Using Service Organisations'; and
- issues relating to the auditor's statutory duty to report include the adequacy of the audit team's understanding of relevant laws and regulations and the identification of closely linked entities.

ISA (UK AND IRELAND) 315: OBTAINING AN UNDERSTANDING OF THE ENTITY AND ITS ENVIRONMENT AND ASSESSING THE RISKS OF MATERIAL MISSTATEMENT

> **Background note**
>
> The purpose of this ISA (UK and Ireland) is to establish standards and to provide guidance on obtaining an understanding of the entity and its environment, including its internal control, and on assessing the risks of material misstatement in a financial statement audit.

98 Investment businesses can be complex and the auditor seeks to understand the business and the regulatory regime in which they operate. Generally, there is a close relationship between planning and obtaining an understanding of the business and the control environment, which is covered more fully below.

> The auditor should obtain an understanding of relevant industry, regulatory, and other external factors including the applicable financial reporting framework (paragraph 22).

99 In obtaining an understanding of the regulatory factors the auditor considers:
- any formal communications between the FSA in its capacity as the regulator and the investment business, including any new or interim risk assessments issued by the FSA, the results of any other supervisory visits conducted by FSA, and any rule waivers granted or special conditions imposed;
- the contents of any recent reports prepared by skilled persons under s166 FSMA 2000 together with any correspondence, minutes or notes of meetings relevant to any report;
- any formal communications between the investment business and other regulators;
- discussions with the investment business's compliance officer together with others responsible for monitoring regulatory compliance.

100 In addition in order to help identify the rules and regulations which are central to an investment business's ability to conduct its business, the auditor may:
- obtain a general understanding of the legal and regulatory framework applicable to the entity and industry, and of the procedures followed to ensure compliance with the framework; and
- review the firm's Scope of Permission Notice (this FSA document sets out the regulated activities that the firm is permitted to engage in, including any limitations and requirements imposed on those permitted activities), for example in relation to the holding of client assets and the extent of investment management discretion permitted.

101 For the audit of companies preparing financial statements under UK GAAP various Statements of Recommended Practice (SORPs) supplement the general accounting principles for particular types of investment business. FRS 18 – Accounting Policies requires that where a relevant SORP exists, financial statements state whether or not they have been prepared in accordance with the SORP, together with details of any departures from the recommended practice and disclosures.

> The auditor should obtain an understanding of the nature of the entity (para 25).

As part of the normal procedures undertaken for the purposes of the audit of annual financial statements and reporting to the regulator, the auditor gains an understanding of the investment business's operations, including the nature of the business carried out. 102

When performing procedures to obtain an understanding of the investment business, the auditor considers: 103

- the relative importance to the investment business of each of its business activities. This includes an understanding of the type and extent of specialised activities;
- the introduction of new categories of customers, or products or marketing and distribution channels;
- the relevant aspects of the investment business's risk management procedures;
- the complexity of the investment business's information systems;
- the legal and operational structure of the investment business;
- a change in the market environment (for example, a marked increase in competition);
- the complexity of products;
- the consistency of products, methods and operations in different departments or locations;
- the respective roles and responsibilities attributed to the finance, risk control, compliance and internal audit functions.

Investment businesses can be involved in any of a wide range of market segments and products. The auditor identifies the principal income and expenditure categories, which could include: 104

- Fees and commissions receivable;
- Commissions payable;
- Trading of securities and other instruments and related gains and losses.

Some investment businesses operate a network of sales offices. In such instances, the auditor determines the degree of head office control over the business and accounting functions at the sales offices and the scope and effectiveness of the investment business's inspection and/or internal audit visits. The extent and impact of visits from regulators is also relevant. Where sales offices maintain separate accounting records, the extent of audit visits and work on each sales office is also dependent on the materiality of, and risks associated with, the operations of each sales office and the extent to which controls over sales offices are exercised centrally. In the case of smaller sales offices, the degree to which exceptions to an investment business's normal control procedures may be caused by minimal staffing levels (the greater difficulty of ensuring adequate segregation of duties, for example) and the consequent need for an increased level of control from outside the sales office are relevant to assessing audit risk. 105

Investment businesses, particularly in the retail sector, may use appointed representatives as a distribution channel for their products. Appointed representatives are not authorised in their own right and instead are the responsibility of the investment business. The auditor considers the increase in regulatory risk of monitoring and controlling appointed representatives in planning the audit approach. 106

> The auditor should obtain an understanding of the entity's selection and application of accounting policies and consider whether they are appropriate for its business and consistent with the applicable financial reporting framework and accounting policies used in the relevant industry (paragraph 28).

107 The auditor undertakes procedures to consider whether the policies adopted are in compliance with applicable accounting standards and gains an understanding of the procedures, systems and controls applied to maintain compliance with them. Accounting policies of particular relevance include those for revenue recognition, and the recognition of client assets. Areas that require careful attention are the extent to which income, and related costs, should be deferred and spread over a period or recognised 'up front', and whether client money and custody assets should be shown on the balance sheet of the statutory financial statements in cases where they meet the definition of assets as set out in the relevant accounting framework.

> The auditor should obtain an understanding of the entity's objectives and strategies, and the related business risks that may result in material misstatement of the financial statements (paragraph 30).

108 The auditor seeks to identify the business risks that may have an impact on the financial statements. The auditor seeks to understand how these risks are managed and controlled by the investment business.

109 Depending on the business involved, the business risks the investment business is exposed to may include:

- *operational risk*: the risk of loss arising from inadequate or failed internal processes, people and systems or from external events, including legal risk;
- *credit risk*: the risk that a counterparty will be unable to meet its obligations. One form of credit risk is default risk, which is the risk that a counterparty will be unable to settle its obligations under a transaction (in a securities settlement or payment system, for example) on the due date;
- *market risk*: the risk that changes in the value of assets, liabilities and commitments will occur as a result of movements in relative prices (for example, as a result of changes in the market price of tradeable assets);
- *regulatory risk*: the risk of public censure, fines (together with related compensation payments) and restriction or withdrawal of authorisation to conduct some or all of the investment business's activities. In the UK this may arise from enforcement activity by the FSA.

110 Failure to manage the risks outlined above can also cause serious damage to an investment business's reputation, potentially leading to loss of confidence in the business. (This is sometimes referred to as reputational risk or franchise risk).

111 Investment businesses should undertake appropriate risk assessment procedures as part of their risk management and internal control process under FSA rules. Investment businesses will normally be required to produce an internal capital adequacy assessment (ICAAP), which is designed to quantify risks specific to the entity and to generate and quantify an estimated capital requirement for the entity. The ICAAP includes an assessment of operational risk. Auditors will normally review such documentation in assessing the investment business's approach to addressing risks.

The auditor is alert to any indication that an investment business is conducting business outside the scope of its authorisation. Such action may be a serious regulatory breach, which may result in fines, suspension or loss of authorisation. In this respect the auditor needs to be familiar with the list of activities of the investment business contained in the Scope of Permission Notice agreed with the FSA. 112

> The auditor should obtain an understanding of the measurement and review of the entity's financial performance (paragraph 35).

The auditor obtains an understanding of the measures used by management to review the investment business's performance. This assists the auditor in understanding pressures on the firm that may prompt management to misstate the financial statements. This information may also assist the auditor when performing analytical procedures. 113

Key performance indicators will depend on the type and size of the investment business but may include the following: 114

- profitability ratios (net profit margin and return on equity);
- expense ratios (particularly remuneration ratios as remuneration is usually the largest expense);
- average commission per trade (for agency brokers); and
- assets under management (for investment managers).

Small investment businesses are unlikely to have sophisticated performance review measures but will still rely on some key indicators.

The application of new and complex accounting standards such as IAS 32, IAS 39 and IFRS 7 (for investment businesses using EU IFRS) and FRSs 25, 26 and 29 (for investment businesses using UK GAAP) may also give rise to risks with respect to the recognition, classification and measurement of assets/liabilities, and over the adequacy of financial statement disclosure. 115

> The auditor should obtain an understanding of the control environment (paragraph 67).

The quality of the overall control environment is dependent upon management's attitude towards the operation of controls. A positive attitude may be evidenced by an organisational framework which enables proper segregation of duties and delegation of control functions and which encourages failings to be reported and corrected. Thus, where a lapse in the operation of a control is treated as a matter of concern, the control environment will be stronger and will contribute to effective control systems; whereas a weak control environment will undermine detailed controls, however well designed. 116

In accordance with the requirements of SYSC and PRIN[21] senior management has a responsibility for establishing and maintaining such systems and controls as are 117

---

[21] The Principles for Businesses sourcebook in the FSA Handbook.

appropriate to the operations of an investment business. The FSA can hold senior managers personally accountable for an area or business for which they are responsible. This responsibility extends to personal behaviour not only by senior management but also to other Approved Persons[22]. Statements of Principle and Codes of Practice for Approved Persons include acting with integrity, due skill and care and diligence. The fit and proper test applied to Approved Persons includes competence and capability.

118 The FSA requires an investment business to maintain systems and controls appropriate for its business. These include (but are not limited to):

- clear and appropriate reporting lines which are communicated within the investment business;
- appropriate controls to ensure compliance with laws and regulations (this may mean a separate compliance function);
- appropriate risk assessment process;
- appropriate management information;
- controls to ensure suitability of staff;
- controls to manage tensions arising out of remuneration policies;
- documented and tested business continuity plans;
- documented business plans or strategies (where appropriate);
- an internal audit function (where appropriate);
- an audit committee (where appropriate); and
- appropriate record keeping arrangements.

119 For large investment businesses, the volume of transactions can be so great that it may be extremely difficult for the auditor to express an opinion without obtaining considerable assurance from adequate systems of control. Systems of internal control in an investment business are important in ensuring orderly and prudent operations of the investment business and in assisting the directors to prepare financial statements which give a true and fair view. The following features of the activities of investment businesses may be relevant to the auditor's assessment of such internal controls:

- the substantial scale of transactions, both in terms of volume and relative value, makes it important that control systems are in place to ensure that transactions are recorded promptly, accurately and completely and are checked and approved, and that records are reconciled at appropriate intervals in order to identify and investigate differences promptly. Processing and accounting for complex transactions or high volumes of less complex transactions will almost inevitably involve the use of sophisticated technology. For example, transactions subject to 'straight through processing' involve little or no manual intervention after they have been initiated;
- the fact that investment businesses deal in money and near money instruments makes proper segregation of duties between and amongst those entering into transactions, those recording the transactions, those settling them and where relevant, those responsible for their physical security particularly important;
- the geographical or organisational dispersal of some investment business's operations means that, in order to maintain control over its activities, investment businesses need to ensure not only that there are sufficient controls at each location, but also that there are effective communication and control procedures between the various locations and the centre. It is important that there should be

---

[22] *Anyone performing a Controlled Function (an FSA defined term that includes roles beyond senior management such as the head of internal audit or the non-executive directors) must be approved by the FSA (an Approved Person).*

- clear, comprehensive reporting and responsibility lines, particularly where the business is managed using a 'matrix' structure;
- the activities of investment businesses can typically result in the creation or use of derivatives and other complex transactions. The fact that the resultant cash flows may not take place for a considerable time creates the risk that wrongly recorded or unrecorded positions may exist and that these may not be detected for some time, thereby exposing the investment business to risk of misstatement. The valuation of these instruments also poses risks of misstatement. Consequently, investment businesses will normally have developed strong operational controls to mitigate such risks of misstatement; and
- the UK regulatory framework is both complex and evolving for investment businesses. This may give rise to significant liabilities for compensation to clients if not properly dealt with. Accordingly, an effective control system is essential to ensure that the requirements of the UK regulators are satisfied. Measures may also be needed to address regulators in other jurisdictions.

120 The auditor also obtains an understanding of the investment business's higher level procedures for complying with the rules governing, for example, client money and custody assets. Such an understanding will provide an indication of the extent to which the general atmosphere and controls in the investment business are conducive to compliance, for example through consideration of:

- the adequacy of procedures and training to inform staff of the requirements of the rules of the regulator to ensure that they meet those requirements;
- adequacy of authorities and supervision;
- the review of compliance by senior management;
- procedures to ensure that possible breaches are investigated by an appropriate person and are brought to the attention of senior management;
- the adequacy of procedures for addressing complaints made by customers in relation to information they were provided with at the time they made investments, which could lead to compensation becoming payable for whole classes of customers; and
- the authority of, and resources available to, the compliance officer.

121 The effective operation of a control system may be enhanced by an internal audit department or by specific monitoring performed by a compliance department. The existence of such departments and their scope and objectives are matters for management. In assessing the effectiveness of such departments, the auditor considers the terms of reference of the departments, their independence from operational personnel and management, the quality of staffing and to whom they report in the investment business.

> The auditor should obtain a sufficient understanding of control activities to assess the risks of material misstatement at the assertion level and to design further audit procedures responsive to assessed risks (paragraph 90).

122 There is a wide variation between different investment businesses in terms of size, activity and organisation, so that there can be no standard approach to internal controls and risk. The auditor assesses the adequacy of controls in relation to the circumstances of each entity. Management of a small investment business may have less need to depend on formal controls for the reliability of the records and other information, because of personal contact with, or involvement in, the operation of the business itself.

123 Examples of weaknesses that may be relevant to the auditor's assessment of the risk of material misstatement are as follows:
- complex products or processes inadequately understood by management; this includes undue concentration of expertise concerning matters requiring the exercise of significant judgment or capable of manipulation such as valuations of financial instruments or allowances for impairment;
- weaknesses in back office procedures contributing to completeness and accuracy of accounting records such as:
    - backlogs in key reconciliations, particularly those over bank accounts, settlement accounts and the custody of assets such as securities (either those held on own account or as collateral);
    - inadequate maintenance of suspense or clearing accounts; and
    - backlogs in confirmation processes relating to financial instrument transactions.
- weaknesses in new product approval procedures; and
- lack of segregation of duties such as between dealing, operational, control, settlement and accounting functions.

124 The auditor may assess and test different systems and controls in different investment businesses, if the auditor considers they provide reasonable assurance that certain control objectives have been achieved. In designing the systems and controls, management should address the following general control objectives:

(a) the business is planned and conducted in an orderly, prudent and cost-effective manner in adherence to established and documented policies;
(b) transactions and commitments are entered into only in accordance with management's general or specific authority;
(c) client assets are safeguarded and are completely and accurately recorded;
(d) the assets of the business are safeguarded and the liabilities controlled;
(e) the risk of loss from fraud, other irregularities and error is minimised, and any such losses are promptly and readily identified;
(f) management is able to monitor on a regular and timely basis the investment business's position relative to its risk exposure;
(g) management is able to prepare complete and accurate returns for the regulator on a timely basis in accordance with the rules; and
(h) issues relating to compliance with the rules are resolved in a timely manner to the satisfaction of the FSA.

125 Systems and controls, including the assignment of responsibilities, should be clearly documented if they are to be understood, communicated and operated effectively and consistently. The investment business and its auditor consider appropriate documentation a prerequisite of an adequate system.

126 Where an investment business provides safeguarding and administration of assets and/or holds client money, the auditor's understanding of the relevant internal controls is particularly important due to the potential exposure of the investment business to claims for compensation, and the requirement for the auditor to report on operational controls relating to client assets.

127 Controls relating to outsourcing activities are considered in the ISA (UK and Ireland) 402 section.

> The auditor should obtain an understanding of how the entity has responded to risks arising from IT. (paragraph 93).

Investment businesses rely heavily on information technology to process trades, obtain market data, manage client data etc. Failures in hardware and software can disrupt operations and lead to loss for the investment business. Investment businesses that provide on-line trading facilities have an even greater risk of loss in event of failure. Investment businesses may also rely heavily on spreadsheets for risk modelling, valuation, and profit and loss calculations. **128**

The auditor assesses the extent, nature and impact of automation within the investment business and plans and performs work accordingly. In particular the auditor considers: **129**

- the required level of IT knowledge and skills may be extensive and may require the auditor to obtain advice and assistance from staff with specialist skills;
- the extent of the application of audit software and related audit techniques;
- general controls relating to the environment within which IT based systems are developed, maintained and operated;
- external interfaces susceptible to breaches of security.

A single computer system rarely covers all of the investment business's requirements. It is common for investment businesses to employ a number of different systems and, in many cases, use PC-based applications (sometimes involving the use of complex spreadsheets) to generate important accounting and/or internal control information. The auditor identifies and understands the communication between computer systems in order to assess whether appropriate controls are established and maintained to cover all critical systems and the links between them and to identify the most effective audit approach. **130**

> The auditor should identify and assess the risks of material misstatement at the financial statement level, and at the assertion level for classes of transactions, account balances, and disclosures (paragraph 100).
>
> As part of the risk assessment, the auditor should determine which of the risks identified are, in the auditor's judgment, risks that require special audit consideration (such risks are defined as 'significant risks') (paragraph 108).
>
> For significant risks, to the extent the auditor has not already done so, the auditor should evaluate the design of the entity's related controls, including relevant control activities, and determine whether they have been implemented. (paragraph 113).

Set out below are certain risks that the auditor may determine to be significant. This list is not all encompassing and will vary for each type of investment business: **131**

- the valuation of investments, including derivatives, which could have a significant impact on the financial statements;
- breaches of the regulator's requirements including, but not limited to, the maintenance of adequate financial resources, controls over client money and assets and anti-money-laundering procedures. This could lead to claims from customers, fines imposed by the FSA and, in severe cases, the investment business may risk losing its authorisation;
- breaches of the terms of client mandates could lead to claims from customers and regulatory fines; and
- the calculation of performance fees to be paid by clients.

ISA (UK AND IRELAND) 320: AUDIT MATERIALITY

> **Background note**
>
> The purpose of this ISA (UK and Ireland) is to establish standards and provide guidance on the concept of materiality and its relationship with audit risk.

> The auditor should consider materiality and its relationship with audit risk when conducting an audit (paragraph 2).
>
> Materiality should be considered by the auditor when:
> (a) Determining the nature, timing and extent of audit procedures; and
> (b) Evaluating the effect of misstatements (paragraph 8).

132 The principles of assessing materiality in the audit of an investment business are the same as those applying to the audit of any other entity. In particular the auditor's consideration of materiality is a matter of professional judgment, and is affected by the auditor's perception of the common information needs of users as a group[23].

133 Most investment businesses are profit orientated and a profit based measure, such as a percentage of profit before tax or income is likely to be used. However it is not uncommon in investment businesses to encounter balance sheet misclassifications that do not affect profit. It may be appropriate when scoping audit work specifically addressing the risk of balance sheet only errors, or where such errors are discovered, to use higher materiality thresholds.

ISA (UK AND IRELAND) 330: THE AUDITOR'S PROCEDURES IN RESPONSE TO ASSESSED RISKS

> **Background note**
>
> The purpose of this ISA (UK and Ireland) is to establish standards and provide guidance on determining overall responses and designing and performing further audit procedures to respond to the assessed risks of material misstatement at the financial statement and assertion levels in a financial statement audit.

> When, in accordance with paragraph 115 of ISA (UK and Ireland) 315 the auditor has determined that it is not possible or practicable to reduce the risks of material misstatement at the assertion level to an acceptably low level with audit evidence obtained only from substantive procedures, the auditor should perform tests of relevant controls to obtain audit evidence about their operating effectiveness (paragraph 25).

---

[23] *The International Accounting Standards Board's 'Framework for the Preparation and Presentation of Financial Statements' indicates that, for a profit orientated entity, as investors are providers of risk capital to the enterprise, the provision of financial statements that meets their needs will also meet most of the needs of other users that financial statements can satisfy.*

Investment businesses that deal on their own account may hold positions in investments at the year-end. Investments held may be valued at fair value, in order to derive the gains or losses related to holding the positions during the financial year and to reflect their current value in the balance sheet. Where an investment business has extensive holdings, a wholly substantive approach to auditing their values may not be practicable. In those circumstances, the auditor may wish to perform tests of controls over the valuation methods used within the product control function. 134

Investment businesses that earn fees for conducting business on behalf of clients may be fined if they breach FSA rules. They may also be liable to pay compensation to clients for instances of breach of contract or mandate or for dealing errors. It is possible that at the year-end there are breaches that are not provided for, either unidentified or fraudulently suppressed. The auditor uses substantive procedures, for example examination of breaches and complaints registers, inquiry of relevant employees and officers and review of correspondence to identify liabilities for breaches and errors. The auditor also assesses the likelihood of unidentified material breaches and errors by understanding the procedures for monitoring the conduct of the business and for identifying breaches and errors. The auditor may determine that it is appropriate to review the controls performed by compliance personnel, the functions performed by the Money Laundering Reporting Officer, the procedures intended to ensure compliance with the client money and client assets rules, and the procedures associated with the breaches register. 135

> Irrespective of the assessed risk of material misstatement, the auditor should design and perform substantive procedures for each material class of transactions, account balance, and disclosure (paragraph 49).

The conduct of investment business generates cash movement. As a result, audit procedures based on following up differences identified in bank reconciliations, and on items posted to any related suspense accounts, will provide substantive evidence for many assertions associated with the significant classes of transactions. Further evidence may be required for the completeness of expenses and associated liabilities, the validity of income and associated assets, and for whether the non-cash side of the double entry has been posted to the correct account. Additional substantive procedures that the auditor may perform for the significant classes of income and expense transactions identified above may include: 136

Fees and commissions receivable

- analytical procedures that relate fees and commissions received to the number or value of agency transactions or to the value of funds under management, depending on the basis for their calculation;
- tests of details involving recalculation of performance fees, normal fees and commissions actually charged, and that should have been charged, according to the underlying agreements;
- where there are material amounts receivable at the year-end, analytical procedures and tests of details may be performed on those items, including an assessment of the recoverability of the outstanding amounts.

Commissions payable

- analytical procedures that relate commissions paid to the transactions on which they are based depending on the calculation basis;

- tests of details involving recalculation of commissions paid in accordance with the underlying agreements;
- where there are material amounts payable at the year-end, analytical procedures and tests of detail may be performed specifically on those items;
- tests of the completeness of year-end accruals by reference to the underlying agreements.

Trading of securities and other instruments and related gains and losses.

137　Gains and losses result when securities are traded. Although both cash and securities move when security trades are settled, this movement is normally electronic rather than physical, and settlement success or failure, together with any settlement differences, are reported to the parties concerned. Substantive procedures may include tests of detail based on these reports, in addition to bank reconciliation procedures on the accounts that include securities transactions.

138　Where securities have been traded before the year-end with settlement due after the year-end, tests of details on the security positions and the counterparty balances may be based on reports of the subsequent settlement (or settlement failure).

139　The accuracy of the firm's record of investments held at year-end is normally audited based on tests of the reconciliation ('depot reconciliation') between the firm's records of positions and the details supplied by the custodian. For financial instruments traded 'over the counter' audit procedures may compare records with the underlying contracts.

140　Holding gains and losses result when year-end positions in financial instruments are revalued. Substantive procedures related to the valuation used, and hence the gains and losses themselves, are considered below.

> When the auditor has determined that an assessed risk of material misstatement at the assertion level is a significant risk, the auditor should perform substantive procedures that are specifically responsive to that risk (paragraph 51).

141　For investment businesses, significant risks may include the valuation of investments held, and liabilities for breach of regulations and for breaches of contract or mandate and the calculation of performance fees. These matters are considered below.

Valuation of investments

142　Year-end positions in investments including any derivatives may be valued by being 'marked to market' or at fair value.

143　The prices of frequently traded instruments dealt on a recognised exchange can be identified from authoritative sources and little or no judgment is necessary in valuing these investments. Some unquoted securities may be equated to a closely equivalent quoted security and priced accordingly, in which case the auditor considers whether the identified equivalent is appropriate, whether any adjustments need to be made, and whether those made are appropriate.

144　Other instruments without a readily ascertainable market value may be priced by complex models – 'marked to model'. This may involve significant judgment in the choice or development of the models and in the assumptions used. Further guidance on valuations is set out in the section on ISA (UK and Ireland) 540.

Liabilities for breaches

The auditor may ask for information from the investment business's legal advisors, may inspect correspondence from clients for complaints, and may decide to review the investment business's records to check for compliance with some regulatory requirements. However, there are no substantive procedures that can conclusively identify breaches that the investment business has not itself identified. In the absence of fraudulent collusion, the auditor may rely on consistency of information and explanations between those responsible for the management of operations, the compliance function, and the finance function. The auditor obtains a representation from the management of the investment business on whether they are aware of any actual or potential non-compliance with laws and regulations that could have a material effect on the ability of the investment business to conduct its business and therefore on the results and financial position to be disclosed in the financial statements. 145

Although custody assets and client money are often not part of the audited financial statements, any material deficiency in client assets could have a direct impact on the financial position of the investment business, either because of compensation due to the customer or perhaps regulatory fines. Guidance on the work the auditor needs to perform when reporting to the FSA under SUP 3.10 in the area of client money and custody assets is given in the section on Auditors' report to the FSA and in appendix 2 to this Practice Note. Investment businesses often account for compensation to clients on a cash basis because of the individually small amounts involved. However, material compensation outstanding at the year-end should be provided for in the financial statements. Consideration will also be given to whether these circumstances may also attract a fine for breach of the FSA rules. 146

Performance fees

Performance fees may represent a significant risk for an investment business. The auditor obtains an understanding of the investment business's systems and controls over performance fees. The auditor may also carry out tests of detail on performance fees including: 147

- confirming the basis of the performance fee calculation to the underlying agreement;
- agreeing that figures used in the performance fee calculation have been correctly extracted from the underlying records;
- reviewing the reasonableness of any estimates or underlying assumptions;
- recalculating the performance fees.

Consideration may also be given to any sources of third party information which is available to support the basis of the performance fee calculation.

> The auditor should perform audit procedures to evaluate whether the overall presentation of the financial statements, including the related disclosures, are in accordance with the applicable financial reporting framework. (paragraph 65)

148 Specific financial reporting standards can require extensive narrative disclosures in the financial statements of investment businesses; for example, in relation to the nature and extent of risks arising from financial instruments. In this respect IFRS 7 and FRS 29 are particularly relevant. In designing and performing procedures to evaluate these disclosures the auditor obtains audit evidence regarding the assertions about presentation and disclosure described in paragraph 17 of ISA (UK and Ireland) 500: Audit Evidence. In the specific case of market risk information the auditor refers to the section on ISA (UK and Ireland) 330 in Practice Note 19 'The audit of banks and building societies in the United Kingdom (Revised)'.

ISA (UK AND IRELAND) 402: AUDIT CONSIDERATIONS RELATING TO ENTITIES USING SERVICE ORGANISATIONS

> **Background note**
>
> The purpose of this ISA (UK and Ireland) is to establish standards and provide guidance to an auditor where the entity uses a service organisation.

> In obtaining an understanding of the entity and its environment, the auditor should determine the significance of service organization activities to the entity and the relevance to the audit (paragraph 5).

149 In common with other industries the outsourcing of functions to third parties is becoming increasingly prevalent with investment businesses. Some of the more common areas, such as property management, may have no direct impact on the audit, while others such as IT functions may have a direct relevance. The auditor therefore gains an understanding of the extent of outsourced functions and their relevance to the financial statements. The investment business is obliged to ensure that the auditor has appropriate access to records, information and explanations from material outsourced operations.

150 The auditor considers the nature of services provided by the service organisation, contractual terms and the components of the entity's internal control which are relevant to the service organisation. The auditor documents and understands the contractual terms with the service organisation. In doing this the auditor may consider the information to be provided to the entity, the maintenance of the accounting records, the entity's and external auditor's rights of access to the accounting records and whether the terms take account of relevant requirements of regulatory bodies.

151 Investment businesses commonly outsource a variety of activities. Specific examples, which are relevant activities, include:
- safe custody of investments by a custodian;
- settlement or clearing of trades;
- maintenance of accounting records;
- transfer agency;
- product administration;
- investment management.

> Based on the auditor's understanding of the aspects of the entity's accounting system and control environment relating to relevant activities, the auditor should:
> (a) Assess whether sufficient appropriate audit evidence concerning the relevant financial statement assertions is available from records held at the entity; and if not,
> (b) Determine effective procedures to obtain evidence necessary for the audit, either by direct access to records kept by service organisations or through information obtained from the service organisations or their auditor (paragraph 9-18).
>
> If an auditor concludes that evidence from records held by a service organisation is necessary in order to form an opinion on the client's financial statements and the auditor is unable to obtain such evidence, the auditor should include a description of the factors leading to the lack of evidence in the basis of opinion section of their report and qualify their opinion or issue a disclaimer of opinion on the financial statements (paragraph 18-1).

152 Whilst an investment business may outsource functions to third parties the responsibility of these functions remains that of the investment business. The investment business should have appropriate controls in place over these arrangements which may include:

- risk assessment prior to contracting with the service provider, which includes a proper due diligence and periodic review of the appropriateness of the arrangement;
- appropriate contractual agreements or service level agreements;
- contingency plans should the provider fail in delivery of services;
- appropriate management information and reporting from the outsourced provider;
- appropriate controls over customer information; and
- right of access of the investment business's internal auditor to test the internal controls of the service provider.

153 If the auditor is unable to obtain sufficient audit evidence concerning outsourced operations the auditor considers whether it is necessary to report the matter direct to the FSA – see guidance in the section on ISA (UK and Ireland) 250 Section B.

ISA (UK AND IRELAND) 505: EXTERNAL CONFIRMATIONS

> **Background note**
>
> The purpose of this ISA (UK and Ireland) is to establish standards and provide guidance on the auditor's use of external confirmations as a means of obtaining audit evidence.

> The auditor should determine whether the use of external confirmations is necessary to obtain sufficient appropriate audit evidence at the assertion level. In making this determination, the auditor should consider the assessed risk of material misstatement at the assertion level and how the audit evidence from other planned audit procedures will reduce the risk of material misstatement at the assertion level to an acceptably low level (paragraph 2).

154 Whilst audit evidence is more reliable when obtained directly from a third party the auditor considers whether evidence obtained from other procedures provides sufficient appropriate audit evidence. For investment management fee debtors and settlement balances, given that the balances are normally only outstanding for a very short period of time the testing of invoicing and settlement controls together with substantive testing of after date cash receipts and payments may provide sufficient appropriate audit evidence.

ISA (UK AND IRELAND) 520: ANALYTICAL PROCEDURES

Background note

The purpose of this ISA (UK and Ireland) is to establish standards and provide guidance on the application of analytical procedures during an audit.

The auditor should apply analytical procedures as risk assessment procedures to obtain an understanding of the entity and its environment and in the overall review at the end of the audit (paragraph 2).

155 Relationships between certain financial and non-financial data can be compared to a prior period, auditor expectations and industry averages. Analytical procedures for investment businesses may include, for example, comparison of:

- fees to funds under management and market indices, and
- commission income and expense to transaction volumes.

156 The use of analytical procedures at the planning stage may highlight events or aspects of the clients' business of which the auditor was previously unaware. These procedures will generally be based upon management accounts and other interim financial and non-financial information available. In determining the audit approach the auditor may apply substantive analytical procedures as part of the overall approach. These procedures will generally be more appropriate when there are larger volumes of transactions which tend to be more predictable.

157 In performing analytical procedures the auditor develops an expectation for the account being reviewed. This expectation will be based on the financial and non-financial data being used and the auditor considers whether the accuracy and reliability of the data can provide the desired level of assurance. The auditor determines the amount of the difference from expectation which requires no further investigation in accordance with the assessed materiality.

158 The auditor applies analytical procedures to the overall review of the financial statements towards the end of the audit process. This will support the overall conclusion on the financial statements.

159 Where non financial information or reports produced from systems or processes outside the financial statements accounting system are used in analytical procedures, the auditor considers the reliability of that information or those reports.

ISA (UK AND IRELAND) 540: AUDIT OF ACCOUNTING ESTIMATES

Background note

The purpose of this ISA (UK and Ireland) is to establish standards and provide guidance on the audit of accounting estimates contained within the financial statements.

The auditor should obtain sufficient appropriate audit evidence regarding accounting estimates (paragraph 2)

The auditor should adopt one or a combination of the following approaches in the audit of an accounting estimate:

(a) Review and test the process used by management to develop the estimate;
(b) Use an independent estimate for comparison with that prepared by management; or
(c) Review subsequent events which provide audit evidence of the reasonableness of the estimate made (paragraph 10).

The auditor should make a final assessment of the reasonableness of the entity's accounting estimates based on the auditor's understanding of the entity and its environment and whether the estimates are consistent with other audit evidence obtained during the audit (paragraph 24).

160 Accounting estimates are used for valuation purposes in some investment businesses, for example, over-the-counter derivatives and illiquid trading positions. For various derivative instruments the auditor may not be able readily to substantiate an independent fair market valuation. In these instances the business may arrange for some form of mathematical modelling to be undertaken to provide a valuation for review and testing by the auditor. The auditor reviews the process for developing and testing the model which has been used by the investment business, and in particular the performance of the model in various conditions when compared with prices actually obtained in the market. This involves obtaining an understanding of the assumptions and a review of the estimates involved for reasonableness, consistency and conformity with generally accepted practices. Given the special complexities involved with these types of products it is common practice for a specialist in this area to be involved in the work.

161 Accounting estimates might also be required in connection with, for example, establishing liabilities for compensation payable to clients as a result of fund pricing errors, and for investment management fee repayments where performance fee arrangements provide for potential clawback.

162 Based on the audit evidence obtained, the auditor may conclude that the evidence points to an estimate that differs from management's estimate, and that the difference between the auditor's estimate or range and management's estimate constitutes a financial statement misstatement. In such cases, where the auditor has developed a range, a misstatement exists when management's estimate lies outside the auditor's range. The misstatement is measured as the difference between management's estimate and the nearest point of the auditor's range.

163 Management bias, whether unintentional or intentional, can be difficult to detect in a particular estimate. It may only be identified when there has been a change in the method for calculating estimates from the prior period based on a subjective assessment without evidence that there has been a change in circumstances, when considered in the aggregate of groups of estimates or all estimates, or when observed over a number of accounting periods. Although some form of management bias is inherent in subjective decisions, management may have no intention of misleading the users of financial statements. If, however, there is intention to mislead through, for example, the intentional use of unreasonable estimates, management bias is fraudulent in nature. ISA 240, 'The Auditor's Responsibility to Consider Fraud in an Audit of Financial Statements,' provides standards and guidance on the auditor's responsibility to consider fraud in an audit of financial statements.

ISA (UK AND IRELAND) 545: AUDITING FAIR VALUE MEASUREMENTS AND DISCLOSURES

Background note

The purpose of this ISA (UK and Ireland) is to establish standards and provide guidance on auditing fair value measurements and disclosures contained in financial statements.

The auditor should obtain sufficient appropriate audit evidence that fair value measurements and disclosures are in accordance with the entity's applicable financial reporting framework (paragraph 3).

As part of the understanding of the entity and its environment, including its internal control, the auditor should obtain an understanding of the entity's process for determining fair value measurements and disclosures and of the relevant control activities sufficient to identify and assess the risks of material misstatement at the assertion level and to design and perform further audit procedures (paragraph 10).

The auditor should evaluate whether the fair value measurements and disclosures in the financial statements are in accordance with the entity's applicable financial reporting framework (paragraph 17).

164 The valuation of derivative and other financial instruments which are not traded in an active market and so for which valuation techniques are required is an activity that can give rise to significant audit risk. Such financial instruments are priced using valuation techniques such as discounted cashflow models, options pricing models or by reference to another instrument that is substantially the same as the financial instrument subject to valuation. The auditor reviews the controls, procedures and testing of the valuation techniques used by the investment business. Controls and substantive testing could include focussing on:

- valuation technique approval and testing procedures used by the investment business;
- the independence of review, sourcing and reasonableness of observable market data and other parameters used in the valuation techniques;

- calibration procedures used by the investment business to test the validity of valuation techniques applied by comparing outputs to observable market transactions;
- the extent and quality of sensitivity analyses prepared by management in relation to both market observable data and other assumptions built into the valuations;
- completeness and appropriate inclusion of all relevant observable market data;
- the observability in practice of data classified by the investment business as observable market data;
- the appropriateness and validity of classification of instruments designated as being traded in a non active and in an active market;
- the appropriateness and validity of the particular valuation technique applied to particular financial instruments;
- the appropriateness and validity of the parameters used by the investment business to designate an instrument as substantially the same as the financial instrument being valued;
- mathematical integrity of the valuation model; and
- access controls over valuation models.

In the more subjective areas of valuation the auditor obtains an understanding of the assumptions used and undertakes a review of the estimates involved for reasonableness, consistency and conformity with generally accepted practices. In some cases, the auditor may use his own valuation techniques to assess the investment business's valuations. Given the complexities involved and the subjective nature of the judgments inherent the auditor may involve an expert in elements of this work (see the ISA (UK and Ireland) 620 section of this Practice Note). **165**

ISA (UK AND IRELAND) 550: RELATED PARTIES

Background note

The purpose of this ISA (UK and Ireland) is to establish standards and provide guidance on the auditor's responsibilities and audit procedures regarding related parties and transactions with such parties regardless of whether International Accounting Standard (IAS) 24, 'Related Party Disclosures,' or similar requirement, is part of the applicable financial reporting framework.

When planning the audit the auditor should assess the risk that material undisclosed related party transactions, or undisclosed outstanding balances between an entity and its related parties may exist. (paragraph 106-3)

Related party transactions are defined in FRS 8/IAS 24 'Related party disclosures'. Paragraph 16 of FRS 8 states that the 'disclosure provisions do not apply where to comply with them conflicts with the reporting entity's duties of confidentiality arising by operation of law'. IAS 24 contains no explicit corresponding exemption. However the potentially overriding impact of law concerning confidentiality in respect of disclosures under IAS 24 still needs to be considered. **166**

Both when applying IFRS or UK GAAP, under ISA (UK and Ireland) 550, the auditor is required to assess the risk that material undisclosed related party transactions may exist. It is in the nature of investment business that transaction volumes **167** are high but this factor will not, of itself, necessarily lead the auditor to conclude that the inherent risk of material undisclosed related party transactions is high.

168 Investment businesses are required to report to FSA changes in control (in some instances with FSA prior approval), changes in circumstances of existing controllers and changes in entities who are closely linked to the firm (SUP 11). In addition, there are annual reporting obligations in respect of controllers and entities who are closely linked to the firm (SUP 16). As a result, it will therefore normally be the case that there are controls in place to ensure that this information is properly collated. However, the definition of "controller" and "closely linked" for regulatory purposes is not congruent with the 'related party' definition in FRS 8/IAS 24 and the auditor therefore considers what controls have been put in place by management to capture information on those parties which fall within the accounting definition only.

169 In reviewing related party information for completeness, the auditor may compare the proposed disclosures in the financial statements to information prepared for regulatory reporting purposes (bearing in mind that the population may be different, as noted in the preceding paragraph).

ISA (UK AND IRELAND) 560: SUBSEQUENT EVENTS

Background note

The purpose of this ISA (UK and Ireland) is to establish standards and provide guidance on the auditor's responsibility regarding subsequent events.

The auditor should perform audit procedures designed to obtain sufficient appropriate audit evidence that all events up to the date of the auditor's report that may require adjustment of, or disclosure in, the financial statements have been identified (paragraph 4).

170 In addition to the specific procedures outlined in ISA (UK and Ireland) 560 to identify subsequent events which may require amendment to, or disclosure in the financial statements of an investment business, the auditor reviews correspondence with the FSA and makes enquiries of management to determine whether any breaches of regulations or other regulatory concerns have come to their attention since the period end.

ISA (UK AND IRELAND) 570: THE GOING CONCERN BASIS IN FINANCIAL STATEMENTS

Background note

The purpose of this ISA (UK and Ireland) is to establish standards and provide guidance on the auditor's responsibility on the audit of financial statements with respect to the going concern assumption used in the preparation of the financial statements, including management's assessment of the entity's ability to continue as a going concern.

> When planning and performing audit procedures and in evaluating the results thereof, the auditor should consider the appropriateness of management's[24] use of the going concern assumption in the preparation of the financial statements (paragraph 2).
>
> The auditor should consider any relevant disclosures in the financial statements (paragraph 2-1).
>
> In obtaining an understanding of the entity, the auditor should consider whether there are events or conditions and related business risks which may cast significant doubt on the entity's ability to continue as a going concern (paragraph 11).

171 In reviewing going concern, the auditor of an investment business considers the following areas in addition to those set out in ISA (UK and Ireland) 570, since the attitude of the FSA and the continued authorisation of the business is particularly relevant to the going concern assumption:
- regulatory censure or fines;
- regulatory capital deficits (as at reporting date and forecast for an appropriate period) (see also paragraph 49);
- reputational and other indicators;
- general non-compliance with the rules of the FSA.

172 If the auditor has any doubts as to the ability of an investment business to continue as a going concern, the auditor considers whether he ought to make a report direct to the FSA on which guidance is set out in the section of this Practice Note relating to ISA (UK and Ireland) 250 Section B.

ISA (UK AND IRELAND) 580: MANAGEMENT REPRESENTATIONS

> **Background note**
>
> The purpose of this ISA (UK and Ireland) is to establish standards and provide guidance on the use of management representations as audit evidence, the procedures to be applied in evaluating and documenting management representations and the action to be taken if management refuses to provide appropriate representations.

> Written confirmation of appropriate representations from management should be obtained before the audit report is issued (paragraph 2-1).
>
> The auditor should obtain written representations from management on matters material to the financial statements when other sufficient appropriate audit evidence cannot reasonably be expected to exist (paragraph 4).

173 ISA (UK and Ireland) 580 requires the auditor to obtain written confirmation of appropriate representations from management. These may take a form of a Board meeting minute or a representation letter and normally include a representation

---

[24] In the UK and Ireland, those charged with governance are responsible for the preparation of the financial statements and the assessment of the entity's ability to continue as a going concern.

concerning the completeness of information made available to the auditor, including correspondence with regulators. In addition, ISAs (UK and Ireland) 250 Section A and 550 require the auditor to obtain written confirmation in respect of completeness of disclosure to the auditor of:

- all known actual or possible non-compliance with laws and regulations (including breaches of FSMA 2000, FSA rules, the Money Laundering Regulations, other regulatory requirements or any other circumstance that could jeopardise the authorisation of the firm under FSMA 2000) whose effects should be considered when preparing financial statements together with the actual or contingent consequences which may arise therefrom; and
- the completeness of information provided regarding the identification of related parties and the adequacy of related party disclosures in the financial statements.

174 In addition to the examples of other representations given in ISA (UK and Ireland) 580 the auditor of an investment business also considers obtaining additional confirmations. The letter could cover the following representations:

- acknowledging management's responsibility for establishing and maintaining accounting records and systems of control in accordance with the rules of the regulator and confirming that unadjusted misstatements are immaterial, both individually and in aggregate;
- confirming that management has made available to the auditor all correspondence and notes of meetings with the FSA relevant to the auditor's examination;
- that all complaints have been drawn to the attention of the auditor;
- where applicable, a representation that no client money or custody assets were administered or held by the investment business;
- that where applicable consolidated supervision does not apply.

ISA (UK AND IRELAND) 600: USING THE WORK OF ANOTHER AUDITOR

Background note

The purpose of this ISA (UK and Ireland) is to establish standards and provide guidance when an auditor, reporting on the financial statements of an entity, uses the work of another auditor on the financial information of one or more components included in the financial statements of the entity. This ISA (UK and Ireland) does not deal with those instances where two or more auditors are appointed as joint auditors nor does it deal with the auditors' relationship with a predecessor auditor. Further, when the principal auditor concludes that the financial statements of a component are immaterial, the standards in this ISA (UK and Ireland) do not apply. When, however, several components, immaterial in themselves, are together material, the procedures outlined in this ISA (UK and Ireland) would need to be considered.

When the principal auditor uses the work of another auditor, the principal auditor should determine how the work of the other auditor will affect the audit (paragraph 2).

In the UK and Ireland, when planning to use the work of another auditor, the principal auditor's consideration of the professional competence of the other auditor should include consideration of the professional qualifications, experience

> and resources of the other auditor in the context of the specific assignment. (paragraph 7.1)

The principal auditor considers in particular the competence and capability of the other auditor having regard to the laws, regulation and industry practice relevant to the component to be reported on by the other auditor and whether the other auditor has access to relevant expertise, for example in the valuation of financial instruments, appropriate to the component's business.   **175**

Further procedures may be necessary for the auditor of an investment business where audit work in support of the audit opinion is undertaken by an audit firm that is not subject to the UK audit regulatory regime. Where an overseas firm of the auditor (or an audit firm independent of the auditor) is undertaking audit procedures on a branch, or division or shared service centre of the investment business, the auditor must have due regard to the requirements in the Audit Regulations[25] to ensure all relevant members of the engagement team are and continue to be fit and proper, are and continue to be competent and are aware of and follow these Audit Regulations and any related procedures and requirements established by the audit firm. This includes the auditor's duty to report direct to the FSA in certain circumstances. More detailed consideration of the auditors' duty to report to the FSA is set out in the section of this Practice Note dealing with ISA (UK and Ireland) 250.   **176**

ISA (UK AND IRELAND) 620: USING THE WORK OF AN EXPERT

> **Background note**
>
> The purpose of this ISA (UK and Ireland) is to establish standards and provide guidance on using the work of an expert as audit evidence.

> When using the work performed by an expert, the auditor should obtain sufficient appropriate audit evidence that such work is adequate for the purposes of the audit. (paragraph 2)

Given the complexity, subjectivity and specialist nature of the valuation of derivative and other financial instruments not traded in an active market, the auditor may involve an expert in elements of the audit of these areas.   **177**

Where the auditor uses an expert as part of the audit, the auditor remains solely responsible for the audit of the investment business's financial statements and will not refer to the work of the expert within the auditor's report.   **178**

---

[25] *Audit Regulations and Guidelines* – December 2005 issued by the Institute of Chartered Accountants in England and Wales, the Institute of Chartered Accountants in Scotland and the Institute of Chartered Accountants in Ireland

ISA (UK AND IRELAND) 700: THE AUDITOR'S REPORT ON FINANCIAL STATEMENTS

> **Background note**
>
> The purpose of this ISA (UK and Ireland) is to establish standards and provide guidance on the form and content of the auditor's report issued as a result of an audit performed by an independent auditor of the financial statements of an entity. Much of the guidance provided can be adapted to auditor reports on financial information other than financial statements.

> In the UK and Ireland:
> (a) The auditor should distinguish between the auditor's responsibilities and the responsibilities of those charged with governance by including in the auditor's report a reference to a description of the relevant responsibilities of those charged with governance when that description is set out elsewhere in the financial statements or accompanying information; or
> (b) Where the financial statements or accompanying information do not include an adequate description of the relevant responsibilities of those charged with governance, the auditor's report should include a description of those responsibilities. (paragraph 9-1)

179 If the auditor of an investment business is to include a qualification in the statutory audit report, the auditor considers whether written notice will need to be given in accordance with the relevant Regulations under FSMA 2000. Guidance on such considerations is contained in the section on ISA (UK and Ireland) 250 Section B.

Auditor's report to the FSA

General

180 Auditors making a report on client assets to the FSA under SUP 3.10 usually also carry out an audit of the entity's annual financial statements, which have been prepared for statutory purposes, in accordance with ISAs (UK and Ireland)[26]. Accordingly, the work that auditors perform in respect of their report to the FSA usually represents a set of additional procedures which, in conjunction with the evidence drawn from the audit work carried out in relation to the annual financial statements, will enable them to report as required.

181 When undertaking such additional procedures, auditors have regard to the General Principles set out below.

The auditors' reporting responsibilities

182 The responsibility and scope of auditors reporting to the FSA is determined by the type of firm on which the auditor is reporting. The table in Appendix 7 summarises

---

[26] The Government changed the relevant legislation to allow certain small investment firms that satisfy the size criteria to take advantage of the small companies audit exemption, with effect from 31st December 2006 year ends.

the scope of reporting for the various different types of investment business. Auditors determine the scope of their audit opinion prior to starting their work.

The auditors' report under SUP 3.10 broadly covers the following matters: **183**
- whether the firm has maintained systems adequate to enable it to comply with the relevant client asset rules throughout the period since the last date at which a report was made;
- whether the firm was in compliance with the relevant client asset rules at the date as at which the report has been made;
- when a subsidiary of the firm is a nominee company in whose name custody assets of the firm are registered, whether that nominee company has maintained throughout the year systems for the custody, identification and control of custody assets which:
  - are adequate; and
  - include reconciliations at appropriate intervals between the records maintained (whether by the firm or the nominee company) and statements or confirmations from custodians or from the person who maintains the record of legal entitlement;
- if there has been a secondary pooling event during the period, the firm has complied with the relevant client money distribution rules in relation to that pooling event.

In discharging their reporting responsibilities regarding an investment business, auditors have particular regard to any changes in the requirements of the FSA in force during the period to which the report relates. **184**

General Principles

The General Principles applicable to reporting on client assets are as follows: **185**
- Auditors agree the terms of the engagement with the investment business and record them in writing (Paragraphs 201 to 203).
- Auditors comply with ethical guidance issued by their relevant professional body (Paragraph 204).
- Auditors familiarise themselves with the relevant rules contained in the FSA Handbook (Paragraphs 205 to 208).
- Auditors take steps to ensure that any delegated work is directed, supervised and reviewed in a manner which provides reasonable assurance that such work is performed competently (Paragraphs 209 to 215).
- Auditors plan the work to be undertaken so as to perform that work in an effective manner, taking into account their other reporting responsibilities (Paragraphs 216 to 227).
- Auditors consider materiality and its relationship with the risk of material misstatement in the report to the FSA in planning their work and in determining the effect of their findings on their report (Paragraph 228).
- When using the work of others, auditors assess their objectivity and competence and obtain sufficient appropriate evidence that such work is adequate for the purposes of the report (Paragraphs 229 and 230).
- Auditors carry out procedures designed to obtain sufficient appropriate evidence on which to base their opinions (Paragraph 231 and Appendix 2).
- Auditors obtain written confirmation of appropriate representations from management before their report is issued (Paragraphs 232 and 233).
- Auditors record in their working papers:
  (a) details of the engagement planning;

- (b) the nature, timing and extent of the procedures performed in relation to their auditors' report to the regulator, and the conclusions drawn; and
  - (c) their reasoning and conclusions on all significant matters which require the exercise of judgment (Paragraphs 234 to 239).
- Auditors undertake their work with an attitude of professional scepticism (Paragraphs 240 and 241).
- The auditor addresses his report to the FSA explaining the basis of the auditor's work (including a statement of compliance with this Practice Note) and expressing a clear opinion that complies with the requirements of the FSA rules (Paragraphs 242 to 255).
- Auditors consider the matters which have come to their attention while performing their procedures and whether they should be included in a report to those charged with governance (Paragraphs 256 to 263).
- If the auditor becomes aware of matters of material significance to the FSA, they report such matters directly to the FSA without delay (see paragraphs 63-76 relating to Section B of ISA (UK and Ireland) 250).

The auditor's report

186 The FSA classifies each of its firms into a prudential category depending on the type of business it is permitted to conduct. The category determines the opinions required in the auditors' report.

187 In the case of banks and building societies which undertake designated investment business, the audit report is also limited to that required under SUP 3.10 (which relates to client assets), except that the auditor is not required to provide an opinion on any nominee companies used. The example report set out in Appendix 1.1 is suitable for those firms where reporting is required under SUP 3.10.

188 The FSA's rules place a specific obligation on the auditor to submit the audit report to the FSA directly. Consequently, if the auditor is unable to submit the report within the timeframe specified, he will be in breach of the FSA's rules and is required to notify the FSA of that fact, and provide an explanation of why the deadline cannot be met.

189 It is possible under the rules to prepare the report on client money and custody assets as at a different date to the firm's accounting reference date. The deadline for submission would be four months after the end of the period on which the auditor is reporting. Subsequent client assets reports may be submitted covering any period of up to 53 weeks commencing on the date on which the previous report ended.

Method of submission of reports to the FSA

190 The FSA has made specific rules which apply to all reports submitted to it; these are set out in SUP 16.3.6R to SUP 16.3.13R. Key provisions are:
- the report must contain the firm's FSA reference number and be marked for the attention of its normal supervisory contact;
- the coversheet contained in SUP 16 Ann 13R must be used;
- the report may be submitted by e-mail;
- the return may be faxed by the deadline;
- if the deadline is not a normal business day, then the report can be submitted by the next business day after the due date.

Components of the auditor's opinion

OPINION ON CLIENT MONEY AND CUSTODY ASSETS [SUP3.10]

Introduction

Certain investment businesses are not required to have a statutory audit of their financial statements but are, nevertheless, required to appoint an auditor[27] to make a client asset report to the FSA.

This section has been developed for use by auditors who are appointed to make a client asset report regardless of whether or not they have been appointed statutory auditor of the investment business.

Client Asset Reports

SUP 3.10 of the FSA Handbook 'Duties of auditors: notification and report on client assets' broadly requires the auditors of firms, to which the Section applies, to submit a report to the FSA, signed in its capacity as auditor, which states whether in the auditor's opinion:

(a) the firm has maintained systems adequate to enable it to comply with the custody rules, the collateral rules and the client money rules throughout the period since the last date as at which a report was made;
(b) the firm was in compliance with the custody rules, the collateral rules and the client money rules at the date as at which the report has been made;
(c) if there has been a secondary pooling event during the period, the firm has complied with the rules in CASS 4.4, and/or CASS 7.9 (Client money distribution) in relation to that pooling event[28].

If an investment business claims not to hold client money or custody assets the auditor is required to report whether anything has come to his attention that causes the auditor to believe that the firm held client money or custody assets during the period covered by the report[29]. Guidance for auditors with respect to investment businesses that do not hold client assets is included in Appendix 2.

The period covered by a client asset report is required to end not more than 53 weeks after the period covered by the previous report on such matters or, if none, after the investment business is authorised or becomes a firm to which SUP 3.10 applies[30].

SUP 3.10 also contains rules concerning the timing of the submission of the client assets report and the method of submission of reports.

---

[27] In this guidance the expression 'auditor' is used in order to be consistent with the terminology used in Section 3.10 of the FSA Handbook.

[28] SUP 3.10.4R(1) and 3.10.5R

[29] SUP 3.10.4R(2)

[30] SUP 3.10.6R

Engagement acceptance and continuance

197 In determining whether the scope of the engagement is expected to be sufficient to support the required report, the auditor considers whether there appear to be any significant limitations on the scope of the auditor's work. In particular, the auditor ascertains whether the directors of the investment business intend to comply with the relevant regulatory requirements.

198 The nature of investment businesses is one of rapidly changing and evolving markets. Often investment businesses develop new products and practices which may require specialised auditing and accounting responses. It is, therefore, important that the auditor is familiar with current practice.

199 In determining whether the persons who are to perform the engagement (the proposed engagement team) collectively possess the necessary professional competency the auditor assesses whether they, (and those with whom they intend to consult), have sufficient knowledge of the specific aspect of the investment industry within which the investment business operates and its corresponding products. The auditor also considers the extent to which the engagement team has sufficient knowledge of the regulatory framework within which the investment business operates commensurate with their roles in the engagement.

200 The knowledge requirements regarding aspects of the investment industry and the regulatory framework may vary between different types of investment business such as:

- BIPRU investment firms (including UCITS investment firms);
- Exempt CAD firms;
- Securities and futures firms;
- Investment management firms;
- Personal investment firms;
- UCITS firms.

Agreeing the terms of the engagement

201 Generally, an engagement letter is prepared by the auditor, covering all aspects of the engagement, and accepted in writing by the directors of the investment business[31]. As the FSA does not need to approve the appointment of an auditor the FSA is not usually an addressee of the engagement letter.

202 However, the FSA is entitled to seek to satisfy itself that an auditor appointed by the investment business is independent and has the necessary skills, resources and experience[32]. The auditor is required to co-operate with the FSA[33] and to notify the FSA if the auditor ceases to be the auditor of the investment business.

203 Matters which the auditor may refer to in the engagement letter are:

- the responsibility of the directors/senior management to comply with applicable legislation and FSA Handbook rules and guidance including the need to keep the FSA informed about the affairs of the investment firm;

---

[31] *Where the auditor is also appointed as statutory auditor a combined engagement letter will usually be issued.*

[32] *SUP 3.4.4G, 3.4.7R and 3.4.8G*

[33] *SUP 3.8.2R*

- the statutory right and duty of the auditor to report directly to the FSA in certain circumstances;
- the requirement to co-operate with the auditor (SUP 3.6.1R). This includes taking steps to ensure that, where applicable, each of its appointed representatives and material outsourcers provides the auditor with the same right of access to records, information and explanations as the authorised investment firm itself is required to provide the auditor. It is a criminal offence for an investment business or its officers, controllers or managers to provide misleading information to the auditor;
- the need for the investment business to make the auditor aware when it appoints a third party (including another department or office of the same audit firm) to review, investigate or report on any aspects of its business activities that may be relevant to the audit of the financial statements and to provide the auditor with copies of reports by such a third party promptly after their receipt.

Ethical guidance

As the Ethical Standards (ES1 to ES 5) issued by the APB apply only to the audit of financial statements they do not apply to assurance engagements to make a client assets report. The UK accountancy bodies have issued their own Codes of Ethics that are to be applied in the conduct of, among others, assurance engagements undertaken by professional accountants in public practice.   204

Legal and regulatory requirements

The Financial Services and Markets Act 2000 (FSMA 2000) establishes the high level regulatory framework for the whole financial sector including investment businesses. Appendix 3 of this Practice Note sets out the main parts of FSMA 2000 that are relevant to investment businesses.   205

An auditor that is appointed to make a client asset report to the FSA is subject to the auditor's statutory right and duty to report to the FSA described in paragraph 22 of this Practice Note. Guidance on the identification of matters to be reported to the regulators is set out in the section dealing with ISA (UK and Ireland) 250 Section B.   206

Auditors are also aware of other legislation which investment businesses are required to comply with. The following are examples of such legislation: 207

- Insider dealing (Securities and Regulated Market) Order 1994.
- Criminal Justice Act 1993.
- Proceeds of Crime Act 2002.
- Money Laundering Regulations 2007.

Set out below are the requirements of the FSA Handbook that are directly relevant to engagements for reporting to the FSA on client assets under SUP 3.10.5R (1) and (2). When reporting under SUP 3.10.5R(3) the relevant requirements are CASS 4.4 and 7.9.   208

CASS 1	Application and general provisions
1.1	Application and purpose
1.2	General application: who? what?
1.3	General application: where?
1.4	Application: particular activities
1.5	Application: electronic media and E-Commerce
CASS 2	Non-directive custody rules
2.1	Custody
2.2	Segregation, registration and recording, and holding
2.3	Client agreement and client statements
2.4	Custodian agreement
2.5	Use of a safe custody investment and stock lending
2.6	Operation
CASS 3	Collateral
3.1	Application and Purpose
3.2	Requirements
CASS 4	Non-directive client money rules
4.1	Application and Purpose
4.2	Statutory trust
4.3	Segregation and operation of client money accounts
CASS 6	Custody: MiFID business
6.1	Application
6.2	Holding of client assets
6.3	Depositing assets with third parties
6.4	Use of financial instruments
6.5	Records, accounts and reconciliations
CASS 7	Client money: MiFID business
7.1	Application and Purpose
7.2	Definition of client money
7.3	Organisational requirements: client money
7.4	Segregation of client money
7.5	Transfer of client money to a third party
7.6	Records, accounts and reconciliations
7.7	Statutory trust
7.8	Notification and acknowledgement of trust
7 Annex 1	
CASS 8	Mandates
8.1	Application

Quality control

209   International Standard on Quality Control (UK and Ireland) 1 'Quality control for firms that perform audits and reviews of historical financial information, and other

assurance and related service engagements' provides standards and guidance on the system of quality control that a firm establishes.

Elements of quality control that are relevant to an individual engagement to report on client assets include: 210

Leadership responsibilities for quality on the engagement

The engagement partner takes responsibility for the overall quality on each client asset report engagement to which that partner is assigned. 211

Ethical requirements

The engagement partner evaluates whether members of the engagement team have complied with ethical requirements applicable to the client asset report engagement. 212

Assignment of engagement teams

The engagement partner assesses whether the engagement team collectively has the appropriate capabilities, competence and time to perform the client asset engagement in accordance with the guidance in this Practice Note and regulatory and legal requirements and to enable a report to be made to the FSA that is appropriate in the circumstances. 213

Engagement performance

The engagement partner takes responsibility for the direction, supervision and performance of a client asset engagement. Before the report is issued to the FSA the engagement partner, through review of the engagement documentation and discussion with the engagement team, determines whether sufficient appropriate evidence has been obtained to support the conclusions reached. 214

Consultation

The engagement partner is responsible for the engagement team undertaking appropriate consultation on difficult or contentious matters and assesses whether the nature and scope of and conclusions resulting from such consultations are documented and agreed with the party consulted. The engagement partner also determines that conclusions resulting from consultations have been implemented. 215

Planning and performing the engagement

Planning involves developing an engagement plan consisting of a detailed approach for the nature, timing and extent of evidence gathering procedures to be performed and the reasons for selecting them. The nature and extent of planning activities will vary with the engagement circumstances, for example the size and complexity of the investment business and the auditor's previous experience with it. 216

Examples of the main matters to be considered include: 217

- the terms of the engagement;
- whether the timetable is realistic;
- the auditor's understanding of the investment business and its environment;

- identifying potential problems that could impact the performance of the engagement;
- the need for the involvement of experts.

218 Planning is not a discrete phase, but rather an iterative process throughout the engagement. As a result of unexpected events, changes in conditions or the evidence obtained from the results of evidence-gathering procedures, the auditor may need to revise the overall strategy and engagement plan, and thereby the resulting planned nature, timing and extent of further procedures.

219 A preliminary review of the available information may provide an indication of potential issues that might need to be addressed in carrying out the engagement. If the preliminary review indicates that there are factors that may give rise to a modification of the auditor's report then such factors are reported immediately to those charged with governance of the authorised investment firm and, where required by the FSA's rules, to the FSA[34].

220 Changes in circumstances, or unexpected results of work carried out, may require the plan to be amended as work progresses. Any such amendments are documented. Where the changes affect the work set out in the engagement letter, the engagement letter is also amended as necessary following agreement with the directors.

Risk of non-compliance with FSA Rules

221 A risk is a threat that circumstances, events or actions will adversely affect an investment business's ability to comply with the applicable FSA Rules. A firm's internal organisation and the environment in which it operates may be continually changing. An effective system of internal control, therefore, depends on a thorough and regular evaluation of the nature and extent of the risks to which the firm is exposed.

222 Once identified, risks can then be assessed by the directors in terms of their likelihood (probability) and potential impact (materiality).

Assurance engagement risk

223 'Assurance engagement risk,' in the context of client asset reports, is the risk that the auditor expresses an unmodified opinion that the investment business:

(a) maintained throughout the period since the last date as at which a report was made systems adequate to enable it to comply with the FSA's custody rules, collateral rules and client money rules,

(b) was in compliance with the custody rules, the collateral rules and the client money rules at the date as at which the report was made, and

(c) the firm has complied with the rules in CASS 4.4 and/or CASS 7.9 (Client money distribution) in relation to a secondary pooling event during the period,

when there is insufficient appropriate evidence available to support the making of these statements.

Appendix 2 provides guidance to auditors on the work normally carried out in order to form an opinion on client assets.

[34] See SUP 3.10.8B

Assessing assurance engagement risk

When assessing assurance engagement risk the main factors that will be considered include: **224**

(a) the scope of the investment business's permission in relation to the holding of client assets;
(b) the extent of investment management discretion permitted;
(c) the introduction of new rules;
(d) changes to existing legislation or rules;
(e) rule waivers granted or special conditions imposed by the FSA; and
(f) the auditor's understanding of the systems and controls regarding client assets.

In making an assessment of risks, auditors would normally meet senior management and the Compliance Officer of the investment business. They would also consider the following: **225**

(a) operational manuals;
(b) documentation of systems and controls;
(c) compliance monitoring programmes and results;
(d) the records maintained by the business of any rule breaches and notifications to the regulator that may have occurred during the period;
(e) correspondence with the FSA, relating to financial returns and any other matters;
(f) the results of the most recent inspection visit made by the FSA; and
(g) the register of complaints received from clients during the period.

As compliance by the investment business with the client asset rules is a continuing obligation, the auditor reports on the adequacy of the accounting records and systems throughout the period under review. However the auditor normally tests controls, transactions and reconciliations at particular points in time rather than continuously throughout the accounting period. If the auditor has obtained sufficient evidence from the results of their testing they may rely on this evidence to conclude on the adequacy of records and systems throughout the period.   **226**

If there has been a system change during the period covered by a report, the auditor considers the system in force both before and after the change. If the change occurred early in the period and the evidence of previous audits has produced satisfactory conclusions, the auditor may decide to perform only limited procedures on the system concerned.   **227**

Materiality

The auditors plan and perform their audit so that they obtain sufficient evidence for their opinion. When doing so, they consider materiality, recognising the nature and scale of the investment business concerned. It is not feasible, or necessary, for the auditors to examine every transaction reflected in the records, or to achieve complete satisfaction that the accounting records are maintained accurately and systems operate totally effectively. They have a reasonable expectation of detecting fraud, other irregularities and errors which would be material to the interests of the clients of the investment business, taken as a whole.   **228**

Use of an expert

The auditor should understand the work for which an expert is used to an extent that is sufficient to enable the auditor to accept responsibility for the opinion provided to   **229** the FSA. The auditor also obtains sufficient appropriate evidence that the expert's work is adequate for the purposes of the engagement.

230 If the auditor has also been appointed as statutory auditor of the financial statements of the investment business, when planning and performing the audit, the auditor always keeps in mind the need for audit evidence in relation to the existence of client assets and the accuracy of the investment business's records.

Detailed guidance on control objectives and audit evidence

231 Detailed guidance on the control objectives and audit evidence is set out in Appendix 2. Auditors apply their judgment in determining the extent and nature of their work which is based on the following general requirements:

(a) the auditors understand the business and the environment in which it operates;
(b) the auditors review the firm's systems and consider whether these are adequate for control and accounting purposes;
(c) the auditors test those systems and controls to establish that they are operating effectively.

Representation letter

232 Written confirmation of representations made by the directors on matters material to the auditor's report on client assets is ordinarily obtained. These representations also encompass statements or opinions attributed to directors, management, employees or agents of an investment business that are relied upon by the auditor.

233 Representations by the directors of the investment business cannot replace the evidence that the auditor could reasonably expect to be available to support the opinion given. An inability to obtain sufficient appropriate evidence regarding a matter could represent a limitation of scope even if a representation has been received on the matter.

Documentation

234 The information to be recorded in working papers is a matter of professional judgment since it is neither necessary nor practical to document every matter considered by the auditor. The auditor prepares documentation sufficient to enable an experienced auditor, having no previous connection with the engagement, to understand:

(a) the nature, timing, and extent of the procedures performed to meet the FSA's requirements with respect to client asset reports;
(b) the results of the procedures and the evidence obtained; and
(c) significant matters arising during the engagement, and the conclusions reached thereon and significant professional judgments made in reaching those conclusions.

235 In documenting the nature, timing and extent of procedures performed, the auditor records:

(a) the identifying characteristics of the specific items or matters being tested;
(b) who performed the procedures and the date such procedures were completed; and
(c) who reviewed the work performed and the date and extent of such review.

236 The auditor documents discussions of significant matters with the investment business, the FSA and any experts engaged by the auditor in connection with the engagement, including when and with whom the discussions took place.

237 If the auditor has identified information that is inconsistent with the auditor's final conclusion regarding a significant matter, the auditor documents how the inconsistency was addressed in forming the final conclusion.

238 The auditor completes the assembly of the final engagement file on a timely basis after the date of the auditor's report. Once the final engagement file has been completed documentation is not deleted or discarded before the end of its retention period.

239 If the auditor finds it necessary to modify existing engagement documentation or add new documentation after the final engagement file has been assembled the auditor documents:

(a) when and by whom they were made and (where applicable) reviewed;
(b) the specific reasons for making them; and
(c) their effect, if any, on the auditor's conclusions.

Professional scepticism

240 An attitude of professional scepticism is essential to ensure that the auditor makes a critical assessment, with a questioning mind, of the validity of evidence obtained and is alert to evidence that contradicts or brings into question the reliability of audit evidence such as documents or representations.

241 Whilst the auditor may proceed on the basis that information and explanations provided by the directors and management of the investment business are reliable, he assesses them critically and, where appropriate, considers them in the context of his knowledge and findings derived from any other areas of work undertaken with the same client.

Reporting

242 The auditor addresses his report to the FSA and in the report:

(a) identifies the matters to which the report relates;
(b) addresses all matters that are required by the engagement letter;
(c) explains the basis of the auditor's work and in particular make a statement of compliance with this Practice Note;
(d) contains a clear expression of opinion that complies with the requirements of the FSA Rules;
(e) includes the auditor's manuscript or printed signature;
(f) includes the auditor's address; and
(g) includes the date.

243 The report is not for the use of third parties. Auditors may wish to ensure that the management of the investment business does not provide the report to anyone other than the FSA (for example, in the letter of engagement or a covering letter with which the report is transmitted to the client). The restriction on distribution to third parties could also be mentioned in the body of the report itself.

244 In view of the fact that the auditor reports to the FSA on his client's compliance with the regulator's rules it is not usually necessary for the auditor to include in his report a description of the work performed.

245 Where a firm is placing reliance on any rule waiver, modification or individual guidance given to it, and this is relevant to any opinion given by the auditor, then the auditor satisfies himself that it is appropriate for the firm to do so. Guidance on the circumstances under which a firm may place reliance on such material is given in Chapters 8 and 9 of the Supervision Manual. The auditor specifically mentions such matters in his report.

246 Before signing the report, the auditor considers whether it is appropriate to make the required report, having regard to the scope of the work performed and the audit evidence obtained.

247 The date of the report is the date on which the auditor signs the report as being suitable for release. However, the auditor does not sign the report (whether modified or not) unless sufficient appropriate evidence has been obtained and all planned procedures have been finalised. Such procedures include the review procedures of both the engagement partner and the engagement quality control reviewer.

An example of a report to the FSA on Client Assets under SUP 3.10 expressing an unmodified opinion is set out in Appendix 1.1.

Modified opinions

248 The auditor does not express an unmodified opinion when there has been a limitation on the scope of the auditor's work, that is circumstances prevented, or there were restrictions imposed that prevented, the auditor from obtaining evidence required to reduce engagement risk to the appropriate level.

249 If one or more of the applicable requirements of the FSA Handbook have not been met the auditor should specify in his report those requirements and the respects in which they have not been met[35].

250 If the auditor is unable to form an opinion as to whether one or more of the applicable requirements of the FSA Handbook have been met, the auditor should specify those requirements in the report and the reasons why the auditor has been unable to form an opinion[36].

251 FSMA 2000 defines rules as including evidential provisions such that, for the purposes of an auditor's report to the FSA, a breach of evidential provisions may indicate a breach of rules. If the auditor considers that an investment business has breached the underlying rule, then the auditor must report that fact in respect of both the underlying rule and the evidential provision and should give both references in the report. If the auditor considers that a business has breached an evidential provision but, nevertheless is satisfied that the firm is in compliance with the underlying rule, then the report refers to the breach of the evidential provision.

252 In considering any matter indicating a possible breach of the rules, auditors analyse the circumstances in order to identify its cause, and establish the action management

[35] SUP 3.10.9R
[36] SUP 3.10.10R

has taken or intends to take to correct the matter. If the matter leads to a qualification and appropriate effective action to correct the matter has been taken (and the auditors are satisfied that this is so), they may choose to report this fact to the FSA so as to ensure the FSA is fully informed about the likelihood of any repetition of the breach in question. However, the prime responsibility for reporting corrective action rests with management.

Although the rules do not provide that trivial breaches can be disregarded, where small exceptions are discovered this of itself would not necessarily require the auditor to qualify their opinion. 253

Auditors exercise care in forming a judgment as to whether a particular breach is trivial, particularly bearing in mind the overriding objective of safeguarding client assets. Steps will be taken to ensure that all staff involved in the audit are aware that the judgment of whether a particular matter is trivial depends on different criteria from any quantitative measure of materiality which may be applied to the audit of the investment business's financial statements. 254

Matters giving rise to a significant risk of loss to investors may also require a report to the FSA under the statutory duty provisions. Such reports will normally be made following discussion with the authorised business: however, ISA(UK and Ireland) 250 emphasises that where the auditors conclude that a duty to report arises, they should bring the matter to the attention of the FSA without undue delay. 255

Other reporting responsibilities

The auditor considers other reporting responsibilities, including the appropriateness of communicating relevant matters, arising from making the client asset report, with management and those charged with governance. 256

The FSA Handbook does not require the auditor of an investment business to submit a management letter to an entity commenting on the entity's internal controls. 257

However, where such letters are prepared and submitted they provide a means for the auditor to provide constructive observations arising from the audit work on client assets. Communication on a timely basis enables the entity to take appropriate action particularly in circumstances where uncorrected weaknesses may lead to the auditor modifying his opinion to the FSA on client assets 258

'Those charged with governance' include the directors (executive and non-executive) of a company or other body, the members of an audit committee where one exists, the partners, proprietors, committee of management or trustees of other forms of entity, or equivalent persons responsible for directing the entity's affairs. 259

In this guidance, 'relevant matters of governance interest' are those that arise from the engagement to make the client asset report and, in the auditor's opinion, are both important and relevant to those charged with governance. Relevant matters of governance interest include only those matters that have come to the attention of the auditor while performing the engagement to make the client asset report. 260

Those charged with governance are likely to find particularly relevant information concerning material weaknesses in internal control, particularly weaknesses relevant to the firm's ability to comply with the custody, collateral or client money rules. The auditor does not normally need to communicate information concerning a material 261 weakness of which those charged with governance are aware and in respect of which, in the view of the auditor appropriate corrective action has been taken, unless the weakness is symptomatic of broader weaknesses in the overall control environment and there is a risk that other material weaknesses may occur. Material weaknesses of which the auditor is aware are communicated where they have been corrected by management without the knowledge of those charged with governance.

262 The auditor considers whether the two way communication between the auditor and those charged with governance has been adequate for an effective audit and, if it has not, takes appropriate action.

263 If the two-way communication between the auditor and those charged with governance is inadequate there is a risk that the auditor may not obtain all the evidence required to provide a report on client assets. If the auditor concludes that the two way communication is inadequate for the purposes of the audit, the auditor considers withdrawing from the engagement.

Auditor's review reports on interim net profits

264 The FSA's capital rules for investment business do not permit certain firms to include interim net profits within reserves in tier 1 capital unless they have been externally verified by the auditor. Trading book profits can be included without external review in Tier 3 capital.

265 Interim profits in this context broadly means, net profits of the investment business as at a date specified by the investment business after the end of its most recently audited financial year end and up to and including its next financial year end, calculated after deductions for tax, forseeable dividends and other appropriations.

266 GENPRU does not include specific guidance as to what constitutes an external verification. However 'verification' as used in the context of GENPRU is understood to indicate a degree of assurance which is lower than that given by a full audit. An engagement to 'verify' interim net profits may therefore be taken to be a review engagement, and an opinion may be given in terms of negative assurance.

267 As an external 'verification' of interim net profits does not require a full scope audit it will be important for the FSA, in considering the adequacy of the 'verification' of interim profits, to be informed of the procedures that have been undertaken by the auditors, in support of their opinion. This is particularly important in the case of investment businesses where no prescribed procedures have been established by the FSA in rules or guidance. Consequently the detailed scope of the work undertaken by the auditor in support of his opinion is listed in the auditors' report or included in the report by reference to the letter of engagement where the programme of work has been laid down.

268 In undertaking the review the auditor normally performs the following procedures:

(a) satisfies himself that the figures forming the basis of the interim net profits have been properly extracted from the underlying accounting records (which in the context of groups include consolidation schedules);

(b) reviews the accounting policies used in calculating the interim net profits so as to obtain comfort that they are consistent with those normally adopted by the investment business in drawing up its annual financial statements and are in accordance with either UK GAAP or EU IFRS as appropriate;

Appendix 1 – Illustrative examples of auditor's reports

This appendix contains the following example auditor's reports:

1.1 – Auditor's report on client assets

1.2 – Auditor's review report on interim net profits

1.1 Auditor's Report on Client Assets under SUP 3.10

Independent Auditor's report to the Financial Services Authority ('the FSA') in respect of ABC Limited for the year/period ended [date]

We report in respect of ABC Limited ('the firm') on the matters set out below.

Our report has been prepared in accordance with SUP 3.10.4R and is addressed to the FSA in its capacity as regulator under the Financial Services and Markets Act 2000.

Basis of opinion

We have carried out such procedures as we considered necessary for the purposes of this report having regard to Practice Note 21, 'The audit of investment businesses in the United Kingdom (Revised)' issued by the Auditing Practices Board.

Systems and control procedures relating to client assets are subject to inherent limitations and, accordingly, errors or irregularities may occur and not be detected. Such procedures cannot be proof against fraudulent collusion, especially on the part of those holding positions of authority or trust. Furthermore, this opinion relates only to the year ended on ( ) and should not be seen as providing assurance as to any future position, as changes to systems or control procedures may alter the validity of our opinion.

Opinion

Either

In our opinion:

- the firm has maintained systems adequate to enable it to comply with the custody rules, the collateral rules and the client money rules throughout the period [from.. to..] since the last date at which a report was made [See note];
- the firm was in compliance with the custody rules, the collateral rules and the client money rules [See note] at the date as at which the report has been made[37];
- [if applicable][38] in relation to the secondary pooling event during the period, the firm has complied with the rules in CASS 4.4 and/or CASS 7.9 (Client money distribution) in relation to that pooling event.

Or

---

[37] *In many cases this will be the year end date but need not be.*

[38] *Guidance on secondary pooling events is not within the scope of this Practice Note*

(c) performs analytical procedures on the results to date, including comparisons of actual performance to date with budget and with the results of prior period(s);
(d) discusses with management the overall performance and financial position of the investment business;
(e) obtains adequate comfort that the implications of current and prospective litigation, all known claims and commitments, changes in business activities and impairment provisions have been properly taken into account in arriving at the interim net profits; and
(f) follows up significant matters of which the auditor is already aware in the course of auditing the investment business's financial statements.

The auditor may also consider obtaining appropriate representations from management.

There may be some circumstances in which the auditor considers that additional work is required, for example: 269

- if the control environment surrounding the preparation of the interim net profits is evaluated as weak;
- if the results of the procedures undertaken above are not fully consistent with the interim net profits as reported; or
- if there has been a significant change to the accounting system.

The report is addressed to the directors of the investment business. An example auditor's report on interim net profits is set out in Appendix 1.2. 270

The scope of the firm's permission did not allow it to hold [client money] [or] [custody assets] [delete as required].

The directors have stated that the firm did not hold [client money] [or] [custody assets] [delete as required] during the year. Based on review procedures performed, nothing has come to our attention that causes us to believe that the firm held [client money] [or] [custody assets] during the year.

Nominee companies [if applicable[39]]

In our opinion, [name of nominee companies], subsidiaries of the firm which are nominee companies in whose name custody assets are registered, maintained throughout the year systems for the custody, identification and control of custody assets which:

(a) were adequate and
(b) included reconciliations at appropriate intervals between the records maintained (whether by the firm or the nominee company) and statements or confirmations from custodians or from the person who maintains the record of legal entitlement.

Registered Auditors

Address   *Date*

Note: The requirements of the handbook that apply, and the wording of the opinion differ, depending on whether or not the firm holds both client money and assets or only one of these:		
	Non-MiFID Business	MiFID Business
(i) Where the firm holds both client money and custody assets	CASS 2, CASS 3, CASS 4.1 to 4.3 apply	CASS 3, CASS 6 and CASS 7.1 to 7.8 apply
	Opinion refers to custody, collateral and client money rules	Opinion refers to custody, collateral and client money rules
(ii) Where the firm holds custody assets but not client money	CASS 2 and CASS 3 apply	CASS 3 and CASS 6 apply
	Opinion refers to custody and collateral rules	Opinion refers to custody and collateral rules
(iii) Where the firm holds client money but not custody assets	CASS 3 and CASS 4.1 to 4.3 apply	CASS 3 and CASS 7.1 to 7.8 apply
	Opinion refers to collateral and client money rules	Opinion refers to collateral and client money rules

---

[39] *This paragraph is only applicable in the case of an investment management firm, personal investment firm, a UCITS firm, securities and futures firm or BIPRU investment firm when a subsidiary of the firm is a nominee company in whose name custody assets of the firm are registered.*

CASS 3 and reference to the collateral rules is not applicable in circumstances where the firm does not receive or hold collateral.

1.2 Auditor's review report on interim net profits

Review report by the auditors to the board of directors of XYZ Limited ('the company')

In accordance with our engagement letter dated [...], a copy of which is attached, we have reviewed the company's statement of interim net profits for the period from [...] to [...] set out on pages [...] to [...] of the attached [see Note 1]. That statement is the responsibility of, and has been approved by, the directors.

Our review did not constitute an audit, and accordingly we do not express an audit opinion on the interim profits. It has been carried out having regard to [see Note 2] of the FSA Handbook and Practice Note 21: The audit of investment businesses in the United Kingdom (Revised) issued by the Auditing Practices Board.

On the basis of the results of our review, nothing has come to our attention that causes us to believe that:

- the interim net profits have not been calculated on the basis of the accounting policies adopted by the company in drawing up its annual financial statements for the year ended [...];
- those accounting policies are not in accordance with the principles set out in [see Note 3]; and
- the interim net profits after tax amounting to £[...] as so reported are not reasonably stated.

Date

Note	Wording for BIPRU investment firms[40]	Wording for exempt CAD firms	Wording for investment management firms	Wording for UCITS firms	Wording for personal investment firms
Note 1	Type of firm it was prior to 1st January 2007: Investment management – financial return UCITS management – financial return Personal investment – retail mediation activities return Securities and futures – reporting statement	Type of firm it was prior to 1st January 2007: Investment management – financial return Personal investment – retail mediation activities return Securities and futures – reporting statement	financial return	financial return	retail mediation activities return

[40] *BIPRU investment firms submit key data sheet FSA 009 together with the forms they were required to submit prior to 1st January 2007. Exempt CAD firms submit the forms they were required to submit prior to 1st November 2007.*

Note 2	2.2.102R and 2.2.103G of GENPRU	9.3.4R or 13 1A.9R of IPRU (INV)	Table 5.2.2(1) of Chapter 5 of IPRU (INV)	Table 2.2.1R of UPRU	Appendix 13(1) of Chapter 13 of IPRU (INV)
Note 3	Type of firm it was prior to 1st January 2007: Investment management – Section 4 table 1 of Annex 5R to chapter 16 of SUP UCITS management – Section 3 table 1 of Annex 16R to chapter 16 of SUP Personal investment – Paragraph 15 of the introduction in Annex 18BG to chapter 16 of SUP Securities and futures – Section 6 of Annex 10R to chapter 16 of SUP	Type of firm it was prior to 1st January 2007: Investment management – Section 4 table 1 of Annex 5R to chapter 16 of SUP Personal investment – Paragraph 15 of the introduction in Annex 18BG to chapter 16 of SUP Securities and futures – Section 6 of Annex 10R to chapter 16 of SUP	Section 4 Table 1 of Annex 5R to Chapter 16 of the FSA's Supervision Manual	Section 3 Table 1 of Annex 16R to Chapter 16 of the FSA's Supervision Manual	Section 15 of Annex 18BG to Chapter 16 of the FSA's Supervision Manual

Appendix 2 – Client Assets

1 This Appendix provides more detailed guidance to auditors on the work normally carried out in order to form an opinion on client assets in the auditor's report to the FSA. In particular it provides guidance on FSA's Client Assets Sourcebook ('CASS'). Auditors also need to familiarise themselves with CASS as there are differences between the MiFID and non-MiFID rules which may not be fully reflected in the examples below.

CASS is separated into the following sections:

(a) CASS 1 – Application and general provisions;
(b) CASS 2 – Non-directive custody rules;
(c) CASS 3 – Collateral;
(d) CASS 4 – Non-directive client money rules;
(e) CASS 5 – Client money (insurance mediation activity);
(f) CASS 6 – Custody (MiFID business);
(g) CASS 7 – Client money (MiFID business);
(h) CASS 8 – Mandates.

CASS 6 and 7 became effective on 1 November 2007 and apply to investment business within the scope of the MiFID. If a firm conducts both MiFID and non-

MiFID business it may elect to apply the MiFID CASS rules to both types of activity.

When reporting to the FSA on whether the firm maintained systems adequate to enable it to comply with the rules in CASS the auditors will be reporting on CASS 2 and 4.1 to 4.3 (for non-MiFID business) and/or CASS 6 and 7.1 to 7.8 (for MiFID business) together with CASS 3 if applicable.

2 The main purpose of the rules in CASS is to ensure that the investment business safeguards client assets. The rules aim to minimise errors, make fraud more difficult to perpetrate, and make it easier for both errors and fraud to be detected. A further purpose is to ensure that, in the event of insolvency of the investment business, client assets are protected from the claims of its general creditors and, in the case of client money, from any right of set off by institutions which hold the money. This purpose is also consistent with Principle 10 of the FSA's Principles.

3 The rules require investment businesses to maintain a high standard of custodianship and associated record-keeping. Management of an investment business is responsible for establishing and maintaining adequate accounting records and systems and controls. This recognises the position of trust under which client assets are held.

4 This Appendix is separated into the following sections:

 (a) Custody assets
 (b) Client money
 (c) No client assets

Each section sets out the relevant planning considerations.

5 This Appendix is to assist in determining the scope of the work for each individual audit. However, it is not intended to limit or replace individual judgement, initiative, and vigilance. Audit procedures are designed to meet the requirements of the particular situation, giving careful consideration to the size and type of organisation and the system of internal accounting control; this is a matter that requires the exercise of professional judgement in the light of the circumstances of each particular case.

6 Where the auditors discover that the systems have failed or material differences have arisen, they consider the implications these may have on other areas of their work, on their reporting obligations and, in particular, on the 'truth and fairness' of the financial statements.

CUSTODY ASSETS

Introduction

7 Custody assets comprise safe custody investments along with any other assets which may be held with such investments on a client's behalf. Firms must apply the rules to those assets which are not safe custody investments in a manner appropriate to the nature and value of those assets.

Broadly, safe custody investments are designated investments held for or on behalf of a client. Designated investments are set out in Schedule 2 part 2 to FSMA 2000 and in Part III of the Regulated Activities Order (Specified Investments). Examples of designated investments include:

 (a) shares and stock in the capital of a company;

(b) debentures;
(c) government and public securities;
(d) warrants or other instruments entitling the holder to subscribe for investments;
(e) certificates representing securities;
(f) units in a collective investment scheme;

any of which belong to the client of an investment business. These investments may be held in the form of collateral. In addition, arranging custody for a client as well as providing custody is covered by the legislation.

For the particular investment business, the auditors understand what may constitute custody assets. They consider all situations and transaction types that may be entered into by the investment business, including arranging custody. Although the investment business may consider that a particular area is not covered by the rules relating to custody assets, the auditors are alert to situations where this is incorrect and the investment business is in breach of the rules as a result. 8

Planning the custody assets work

The auditors' work on custody assets will be planned in relation to the three reporting requirements. For custody assets, the main areas that need to be addressed by the auditors, to enable them to fulfil their reporting requirements are: 9

(a) adequate accounting records;
(b) adequate systems and controls for:
    (i) safe custody and proper control of custody assets, including the sending of periodic statements;
    (ii) proper registration and segregation of custody assets;
    (iii) compliance with reconciliation requirements;
(c) compliance with the relevant rules at the year end date.

The control objectives that a business administering or holding custody assets or collateral will need to meet and the evidence that may be available to the auditors upon which they can base their conclusions are outlined below. 10

Not every business, particularly a smaller one, will be able to meet all these objectives through the establishment of formal controls and segregation of duties. In consequence, not all the evidence indicated below will be available in every case. 11

This does not necessarily mean that the business has weak controls or that there is insufficient evidence for the auditors to give an opinion. The business may well have adequate controls due to close supervision by the management, taking into account the low volume of custody assets handled. It may also use the services of a custodian, the requirements for use of which are set out in the rules. 12

In some cases, therefore, the auditors may place greater reliance on observation and enquiry for their audit evidence than inspection of documentation. In doing so, they need to bear in mind that informal systems are more prone to error and fraud, and that their presence and enquiries may influence the manner in which procedures are operated at that time. 13

This Appendix is arranged by reporting requirement as these are what the auditors bear in mind throughout the planning of their audit. 14

Adequate accounting records

Control objectives

15 The main factors that will be considered are:
   (a) proper and prompt recording of the movements of documents (this includes all documents, including those relating to the investment business's own investments as there is a risk of teeming and lading and having client title documents mixed with the investment business's own documents);
   (b) proper and prompt recording of all purchases and sales of investments on behalf of clients;
   (c) proper and prompt recording of other assets held on behalf of clients;
   (d) records in agreement with the statements sent to clients of assets held on their behalf;
   (e) reconciliations carried out in accordance with the rules; and
   (f) proper and prompt accounting for benefits, such as bonus or scrip issues accruing to clients.

Evidence

16 The main factors that will be considered are:
   (a) evidence that documents of title are recorded immediately on receipt;
   (b) evidence that documents of title are not released from the investment business's control to clients, registrars, brokers, etc. without the records being amended;
   (c) records kept in respect of any document clearly setting out the date of receipt and despatch of the document, the nature of the document, the client to whom the document relates, and the nature, amount and nominal value of the investment to which the document relates;
   (d) evidence that statements are sent to clients at the required intervals, made up to the appropriate date, and properly specifying the documents held. In this context, the auditors may consider obtaining direct confirmation from clients;
   (e) evidence that correspondence from clients querying statements and any other queries have been dealt with properly and promptly; and
   (f) evidence that benefits such as dividends or scrip issues are collected and correctly allocated to each client.

Adequate systems and controls – Safekeeping and proper control of custody assets including the sending of periodic statements

Control objectives

17 The main factors that will be considered are:
   (a) satisfactory arrangements for ensuring the physical safe custody of documents;
   (b) satisfactory arrangements for documents to be released only to the client, or to an eligible custodian, or to some other party upon the circumstances or under discretionary powers given in the client agreement;
   (c) any independent custodian used by the investment business to be eligible to act in such a capacity;
   (d) risk assessments to be carried out on all custodians to assess the risk of placing client assets with a third party;
   (e) written arrangements between the investment business and the custodian covering at least the minimum requirements of the rules;
   (f) written notifications to clients covering the notices and warnings required by the rules; and

(g) an adequate system to ensure that statements are sent to clients at required intervals, and that such statements properly reflect the investment business's records.

Evidence

The main factors that will be considered are: 18

(a) a separate custodian area staffed by people independent of any other operations;
(b) qualifications and experience of managers;
(c) strong boxes, fire-proof rooms and safes, restricted access via password controlled doors or limited access to keys;
(d) the areas for receipt and despatch of documents being limited and strictly controlled;
(e) evidence of spot checks of the custodian area by the compliance or internal audit departments;
(f) written procedures stating how custodian staff are to process the movement of documents and what is required in the form of authorisation;
(g) evidence of procedures for selection of external custodians to ensure that they are eligible and suitable;
(h) results of a risk assessment process including external information on credit rating, financial results etc. and internal information on customer service received;
(i) letters of agreement with custodians stating the terms under which they are operating;
(j) standard notifications to clients and controls to ensure all clients receive the required notifications and warnings;
(k) file copies of statements sent to clients, which agree with the records; and
(l) procedures and controls (e.g. completed checklist) to ensure that all clients receive a statement (where required).

Adequate systems and controls – Proper registration and segregation of custody assets

Control objectives

The main factors that will be considered are: 19

(a) registerable safe custody investments registered in a name permitted by the rules;
(b) where safe custody investments are registered in the same name as that used for the investment business's own investments, that the safe custody investments are registered in a designated account (or held physically as a separate certificate) different from that in which its own investments are registered;
(c) for bearer documents of title, that the owner can be identified at all times and that it is readily apparent which investments relate to the investment business and which to the client;
(d) investments held as security can be separately identified;
(e) arrangements for releasing documents under stock lending arrangements are in accordance with the relevant rules; and
(f) other assets held on behalf of clients are distinguishable from assets belonging to the investment business.

Evidence

The main factors that will be considered are: 20

(a) written instructions from clients stating the manner in which their investments are to be registered; these instructions may be set out in standard client documents;
(b) written procedures setting out how each document is to be identified so as to reflect the client's entitlement to that document (e.g. registered in the client's name);
(c) where safe custody investments are registered in the name of a nominee company, that an appropriate record of the interests of individual clients is maintained;
(d) clear segregation of client investment documents from other investment documents;
(e) physical segregation of bearer securities held for clients from those belonging to the investment business and, where practicable, segregation among individual clients;
(f) separate registers maintained of investments held as security;
(g) evidence of appropriate authority to engage in stock lending arrangements, given to the business by the clients concerned;
(h) separate records of all such transactions sufficient to show the details of the stocks lent at any time and the collateral held;
(i) separate records of other assets held on behalf of clients.

Adequate systems and controls – Compliance with reconciliation requirements

21 The requirement to carry out reconciliations of custody assets and the recording of them occurs in the rules on both accounting records and systems and controls. The auditors test these reconciliations to ensure these requirements are satisfied.

22 Safe custody investments may be held in one or more of the following ways:

(a) physically held as certificates by the investment business;
(b) held by a custodian appointed by the investment business; and/or
(c) dematerialised (e.g. CREST; uncertificated units in a collective investment scheme).

Control objectives – physically held safe custody investments

23 The main factors that will be considered are:

(a) inventory counts and reconciliations of all securities performed with at least the frequency and in the manner required by the relevant rules, and by staff (in so far as possible) independent of the custodian department;
(b) procedures planned and implemented to ensure that the count of client title documents is accurate;
(c) timely clearance of reconciling items;
(d) records retained of the dates and results of the inventory counts.

Evidence – physically held safe custody investments

24 The main factors that will be considered are:

(a) detailed instructions for the counts;
(b) an independent function (such as compliance department or internal audit) organising, controlling or participating in carrying out the counts and reconciliations;
(c) sufficient time and resources devoted to the counts and reconciliations;
(d) full and clear documentation of the counts and reconciliations;

(e) counts carried out at the frequency and with the time limits required by the rules;
(f) adequate explanations for reconciling items;
(g) completion of reconciliations (i.e. all items explained) within time limits set out in the rules.

Control objectives – safe custody investments held by a custodian

The main factors that will be considered are: 25

(a) reconciliations for all custodians performed with at least the frequency and in the manner required by the relevant rules;
(b) timely clearance of reconciling items;
(c) the reconciliations undertaken by a person who is not involved with the recording or movement of the assets, if the size of the investment business permits this segregation of duties;
(d) records retained of the dates and results of reconciliations including confirmations from external custodians.

Evidence – safe custody investments held by a custodian

The main factors that will be considered are: 26

(a) an independent function carrying out the reconciliations;
(b) sufficient time and resources devoted to reconciliations;
(c) full and clear documentation of the reconciliations;
(d) reconciliations carried out at the frequency required by the rules;
(e) adequate explanations for reconciling items;
(f) completion of reconciliations (i.e. all items explained) within time limits set out in the rules.

Control objectives – dematerialised investments

The main factors that will be considered are: 27

(a) reconciliations of all dematerialised investments performed with at least the frequency required by the relevant rules;
(b) timely clearance of reconciling items;
(c) the reconciliations undertaken by a person who is not involved with the recording or movement of the investments, if the size of the investment business permits this segregation of duties;
(d) records retained of the dates and results of the reconciliations, including third party confirmations.

Evidence – dematerialised investments

The main factors that will be considered are: 28

(a) an independent function carrying out reconciliations;
(b) sufficient time and resources devoted to the reconciliations;
(c) full and clear documentation of the reconciliations;
(d) reconciliations completed at the frequency required by the rules;
(e) adequate explanations for reconciling items;
(f) completion of reconciliations (i.e. all items explained) within time limits set out in the rules.

Custody assets other than safe custody investments

29   CASS 2 requires investment businesses to apply the rules to those custody assets which are not safe custody investments in a manner appropriate to the nature and value of the custody assets concerned. This will involve consideration of appropriate reconciliation procedures.

Compliance with the rules at year end dates

30   The main factors that will be considered are:

   (a) registerable investments belonging to clients are registered in appropriate names;
   (b) documents of title held by the investment business are held in such a manner that it is readily apparent that they do not belong to the business;
   (c) the owner of the investments can be identified;
   (d) investments held as security can be separately identified;
   (e) investments held outside the business itself are held by eligible custodians or dematerialised as permitted by the rules;
   (f) the requisite arrangements with custodians have been agreed in writing;
   (g) confirmations have been received from all eligible custodians of investments held by them.

31   Where custody assets are physically held by the investment business itself, the auditors may attend part or all of one of the physical counts of client title documents. In reaching a conclusion regarding the extent to which this is necessary, the auditors consider the strength of controls surrounding, and the independence of, the count, reconciliation, day to day processing and custody of client documents of title.

32   The auditors examine confirmations from independent custodians of documents of title held by them and third party records of dematerialised investments.

33   The auditors inspect correspondence and agreements with custodians in order to verify compliance with the appropriate rules.

34   In larger investment businesses, a rolling reconciliation basis of confirming client title documents (similar to a manufacturing company's system of perpetual stock-taking) is sometimes adopted. This is only permitted by the rules where the FSA has been provided with written confirmation from the investment business's auditors on the adequacy of the systems and controls over the rolling reconciliation process. In giving such a report, the auditors have regard both to the detailed rules in this area and also to the general considerations on the adequacy of systems and controls contained in this Practice Note. In particular, care will be taken to ensure that systems and controls are in place to prevent teeming and lading.

Collateral

35   The collateral rules apply where an investment business holds assets to secure a client's obligation in connection with designated investment business. The main factor that will be considered is that the investment business must keep proper records of such assets.

CLIENT MONEY

Introduction

Client money is defined for the purposes of CASS 1-5 as money of any currency which, in the course of carrying on designated investment business, an investment business holds in respect of any investment agreement entered into, or to be entered into, with or for a client or which an investment business treats as client money in accordance with the client money rules. For this purpose, 'holds' is defined to cover situations both where the firm receives money and where money it already holds is required to be treated as client money.

For the particular investment business, the auditors understand what may constitute client money. They consider all situations and transaction types that may be entered into by the investment business. Although the investment business may consider that a particular area is not covered by the rules relating to client money, the auditors are alert to situations where this is incorrect and the investment business is in breach of the rules as a result.

Types of client

The auditors will be aware that different types of client are identified in the rules and the way in which investment businesses must (or may) treat money received from them varies. Generally, all money received from private/retail customers must be treated as client money although the FSA rules provide for certain non-private customers, ('market counterparties' and 'intermediate customers') to agree to be 'opted out' of protection for non-MiFID business. The opt-out is not available in the MiFID chapters of CASS.

Another category of client identified in the rules is 'affiliated companies'. For MiFID and certain non-MiFID business, money received from companies within the same group should be treated in the same way as money from other clients.

Banks carrying out designated investment business

Although the client money rules apply to all authorised persons, their application to banks is limited in certain respects. However, it is incorrect to state that the client money rules do not apply to banks at all.

Where a bank holds the client money of its investment business clients in accounts with itself, it is acting in its capacity as the client's banker and is not considered to be holding client money under the FSA client money rules. If the money is passed outside the bank then the client money rules may apply. Further guidance is contained in the rules.

Client bank accounts

When an investment business holds or expects to hold client money then it must open one or more client bank accounts. These must generally be at an approved bank (as defined in the rules) in the UK or overseas. Certain disclosures may need to be made to and consent obtained from clients whose money is to be held in overseas accounts before their money is paid into such accounts.

43 Before a client bank account is opened the investment business should carry out a risk assessment on the bank. Ongoing risk assessment should be carried out while the bank continues to hold client money. This should include both external information such as financial statements, credit ratings etc and internal information such as customer service received from the bank in the administration of the account.

44 A client bank account can be a current or a deposit account at a bank or a deposit (but not a share) account at a building society. The rules require that such an account in the name of the investment business has a title which makes it clear that the money in the account does not belong to the business, for example by including the term 'client account' in its title. For non-MiFID business the bank must be given written notice that it is not entitled to exercise any right of set-off against any amount owing to it on any other account of the investment business and that the title of the account distinguishes it from any account containing money belonging to the investment business. The bank must acknowledge these terms in writing. In the case of an account opened in the UK, if the bank has failed to make the necessary acknowledgement within 20 business days, the money must be withdrawn and the account closed.

45 Separate client bank accounts may be used for different categories of client money. There are detailed rules relating to the operation of the categories of bank account and it is not within the scope of this Practice Note to explain them. The auditors will need to study the specific rules carefully.

46 The client money bank accounts should not contain money other than client money, except in certain specified circumstances. The main factor that will be considered will be that any money in the client bank account that is not client money does fall within one of the specified exemptions.

47 Under certain conditions, client money for MiFID business may be held in qualifying money market funds.

Planning the client money work

48 The auditors' work on client money will be planned in relation to the three reporting requirements. For client money, the main areas that need to be addressed by the auditors, to enable them to fulfil their reporting requirements, are:

(a) adequate accounting records;
(b) adequate systems and controls as regards:
   (i) proper holding of client money;
   (ii) payment into and withdrawal from client bank accounts;
   (iii) proper accounting for interest;
   (iv) compliance with daily calculation and reconciliation requirements;
(c) compliance with the relevant rules at the year end date.

49 As with custody assets, the control objectives that the auditors would expect to see in a business holding client money, the evidence from which the auditors seek to draw reasonable conclusions, and the procedures they may perform are outlined below. They are only indicative and will not be applicable to all businesses holding client money, especially smaller ones.

Adequate accounting records

Control objectives

The main factors that will be considered are:

(a) proper recording of movements of client money;
(b) interest credited in accordance with the rules;
(c) reconciliations carried out in accordance with the rules;
(d) appropriate titles are given to accounts.

Evidence

The main factors that will be considered are:

(a) adequate details of the day to day entries of money paid into and out of the client bank accounts and individual client accounts including:
  (i) dates of receipts and payments;
  (ii) name of the client;
  (iii) name of the person from whom money was received or to whom it was paid, if other than the client;
  (iv) sub-ledgers with individual client accounts;
  (v) evidence of designation from a client;
(b) records of the interest earned on the client money bank accounts, the determination of the amount of interest payable to clients and the dates and amounts of interest paid to clients;
(c) records maintained on a timely basis;
(d) evidence that reconciliations have been carried out as required and reconciling items have been investigated and cleared promptly;
(e) the records maintained comply with the detailed guidance given by the FSA;
(f) to provide third party evidence of client balances (except settlement balances), the auditors may consider obtaining direct confirmation from clients; in practice, this may be conveniently combined with testing the accuracy of statements of their investments sent to clients.

Adequate systems and controls – Proper holding of client money

Client money held by investment businesses has to be held on trust for clients in one or more separate client bank accounts at an approved bank as defined in the rules.

Control objectives

The main factors that will be considered are:

(a) bank accounts opened with 'approved' banks;
(b) appropriate and continuing risk assessments will be carried out on banks holding client money;
(c) client money is diversified where amounts are of sufficient size;
(d) bank accounts include 'Client Account', or similar words which make it clear that the money in the account does not belong to the investment business in their description;
(e) where designated client bank accounts are used, then these are identifiable as such and contain the word 'designated' in their title;
(f) appropriate written notifications, confirmations and agreements sent to and received from the banks;
(g) systems are adequate to identify all client money;

(h) systems are adequate to ensure that all client money and only client money is paid in (other than where it is specifically allowed by the rules) and withdrawals are made in compliance with the rules;
(i) systems are adequate to ensure that all client money is paid in promptly; and no later than by close of business the next day, unless otherwise disposed of in accordance with the rules;
(j) systems are adequate to ensure that the three day limit for 'delivery versus payment' transactions is adhered to;
(k) (for MiFID business) any transfer of client money to qualifying money market funds is carried out in accordance with the rules.

Evidence

54 The main factors that will be considered are:
(a) documentation of the procedures for opening new accounts;
(b) an up to date list of all bank accounts which identifies those that are client bank accounts;
(c) results of risk assessment process;
(d) letters from banks agreeing to the required conditions;
(e) evidence of the client's consent to holding any money overseas;
(f) evidence that, where necessary, separate accounts are opened for the different categories of client money;
(g) where necessary, written consent from clients for opting out or for other permitted exceptions relating to the handling of client money;
(h) scrutiny of individual client ledger accounts to ensure that they are not overdrawn, or if overdrawn that 'topping up' is taking place as part of the investment business's internal reconciliation/daily client money calculation procedures.

Adequate systems and controls – Payment into and withdrawal from client bank accounts

Control objectives

55 The main factors that will be considered are:
(a) all client money is paid within one business day into a client bank account (or within the extended time limit for special instances, such as collections by representatives and foreign dividends, as set out in the rules);
(b) all withdrawals from client bank accounts are made only for prescribed purposes and in accordance with client mandates.

Evidence

56 The main factors that will be considered are:
(a) clear internal instructions setting out the procedures to be followed in dealing with any potential client money;
(b) suitable levels of staff (i.e. with the appropriate training and experience) responsible for establishing client money accounts and identifying client money within the investment business;
(c) lodgements regularly and promptly made;
(d) lodgements to client money accounts comprise client money only, except as otherwise permitted;
(e) lodgements to non client money accounts do not include client money;
(f) withdrawals properly authorised and for purposes approved by the rules.

Adequate systems and controls – Proper accounting for interest

For non-MiFID business private customers must be paid all of the interest earned on their client money balances unless the investment business notifies such customers in writing of the terms and frequency with which interest is to be paid or that no interest is to be paid. If no interest is payable to a private customer that fact must be separately identified in any agreement or notification.

Control objectives

The main factors that will be considered are:

(a) where necessary, client approval properly obtained for use of the investment business's own interest provisions;
(b) where applicable, interest paid on all money subject to interest calculations (whether or not the investment business has earned interest);
(c) interest payments correctly calculated by reference to the appropriate terms.

Evidence

The main factors that will be considered are:

(a) notification to clients of the interest method to be adopted, where required by the rules;
(b) schedules showing how interest due to clients has been calculated (or equivalent computer processes);
(c) interest credited to client accounts.

Adequate systems and controls – Compliance with daily calculation and reconciliation requirements

Investment businesses are required to reconcile their client money records with bank statements. For MiFID business, this is described as the 'external reconciliation'; for non-MiFID business, the 'reconciliation'.

Investment businesses are also required to perform calculations to check that the client money resources are at least equal to the client money requirement and to 'top up' (by transfer of their own funds) any shortfalls which arise (MiFID business 'internal reconciliation'; non-MiFID business 'daily calculation').

Control objectives

The main factors that will be considered are:

(a) the internal reconciliation/daily client money calculation is carried out in accordance with the rules;
(b) any shortfall is topped up or excess withdrawn;
(c) reconciliations of client money bank accounts with the relevant bank statements are carried out at the frequency and within the time limits set out in the rules;
(d) the reconciliations are properly prepared and adequate explanations given for reconciling items, which should be cleared without delay;
(e) records are retained of the dates and results of the prescribed reconciliations.

Evidence

The main factors that will be considered are:

(a) an up-to-date list of the accounts held that agrees with the accounts being reconciled;
(b) evidence of an independent preparation and review of these reconciliations and calculations;
(c) reconciliations and calculations being carried out regularly over the period under review;
(d) copies of instructions to banks to make transfers.

Unclaimed client money

64 Where client money is identified as due to a particular client but the investment business has not been able to pay the money to that client, the firm must continue to treat that money as client money unless it meets the conditions set out in the rules.

The main factor that will be considered is whether an investment business that ceases to treat allocated but unclaimed funds as client money has taken the steps set out in the rules.

Compliance with the rules at year end date

65 The rules seek to ensure that:

(a) client money balances are lodged with an approved bank (as defined in the rules);
(b) the banks used have acknowledged the trust status of the client bank accounts;
(c) the client money resource is at least equal to the client money requirement;
(d) the required reconciliations have been carried out of bank balances and client records;
(e) reconciliation differences have been properly investigated and promptly cleared.

66 The auditors carry out normal audit tests on bank reconciliations in their audit of client money. Particular attention will be paid to reconciling items, ensuring that outstanding and uncleared items are properly identified and are duly cleared shortly after the reconciliation date. As part of their substantive testing, the auditors examine and where appropriate obtain direct confirmation of bank balances from each bank (or in the case of margined transaction money, each relevant clearing house and intermediate carrying broker) concerned at the relevant date.

67 The investment business should also reconcile its client money bank accounts as often as necessary (at least once every twenty five business days for non-MiFID business). Some investment business need to reconcile client money bank accounts daily if the volume of business is high.

NO CLIENT ASSETS

68 An auditor of an investment business is alert to situations where the business is not permitted under the terms of its authorisation to hold client assets or does not, as a matter of policy, hold client assets. Where this is the case, the investment business should have systems in place to identify and return any money or other assets it receives which are wholly or partly due to a client.

69 Where the auditor is required to give the FSA a statement of negative assurance that an investment business has not administered or held client assets, they consider carrying out the following procedures:

(a) enquire as to what arrangements an investment business has in place to ensure that relevant staff are aware of what constitutes client assets. This could be documented in a procedural manual or internal memorandum and should outline the procedures to be followed if client assets are identified;
(b) enquire as to to how settlements are effected on behalf of clients (references will be made to client documentation and payment instructions on contract notes or statements);
(c) review the cash book in order to confirm that receipts and payments in the cash book only relate to the investment business's own money and that no client money is being received or held;
(d) review the investment businesses client files to see whether they provide any indication that it has held client assets in order to undertake a particular transaction;
(e) review client agreements for statements of how custody is to be operated; as a corollary, review the agreements with any custodians used and the counterparty files (ie the documentation which supports the investment transactions) for correspondence on settlement procedures to ensure that there is no evidence that the investment business has offered client money protection (ie held separately in accordance with the rules);
(f) in the case of an investment business that does not act for private customers, review the client lists to ascertain that clients do not appear to belong to this category. (There must be proper documentation between the investment business and the client in accordance with the FSA's requirements to determine that the client money rules do not apply);
(g) enquire as to how dividends, especially unclaimed dividends, and rights issues are dealt with;
(h) ascertain whether a system of review exists to ensure that client assets are not administered or held. This could constitute periodic review by the internal auditors or compliance officer and encompass substantive review of the investment business's bank accounts and client agreements; and
(i) enquire as to details of any client money the investment business has received and the action taken.

The auditor considers obtaining a written representation from management that the investment business has not handled any client money or custody assets during the year. 70

The report the auditor makes to the FSA where an investment business does not hold client assets is included in Appendix 1. 71

Appendix 3 – The main parts of FSMA 2000 relevant to investment businesses

Part I (and Sch 1) sets out matters concerning structure and governance of the FSA including its regulatory objectives and the principles to be followed in meeting those objectives.

Part II (and Sch 2) sets out the general prohibition on conducting regulated business unless a person (including in a corporate sense) is either authorised or exempt, including restrictions on financial promotions. Regulated activities are defined in a statutory instrument. (SI 2001/544)

Part III (and Schs 3-5) sets out the requirements to become authorised either by receiving a specific permission from the FSA or through the EU single market rules. Exempt persons are listed in a separate statutory instrument. (SI 2001/1201)

Part IV (and Sch 6) sets out the arrangements for application for a permission to undertake authorised business and the criteria (Threshold Conditions) that must be met. An applicant who is refused can apply to the Financial Services and Markets Tribunal (established under Part IX).

Part V sets out the provisions applying to individuals performing designated functions (controlled functions) in an authorised firm. The FSA can specify controlled functions and firms must take reasonable care to ensure that only persons approved by the FSA can undertake these functions. The FSA can specify qualification, and training and competence requirements and approved persons must comply with the FSA's statement of principles and code of conduct for approved persons. Appeals can be made to the Tribunal.

Part VIII gives the FSA powers to impose penalties for market abuse – using information not generally available; creating a false or misleading impression; or, failure to observe normal standards. Abuse is judged from the point of view of a regular market user. FSA powers extend to all persons – not only authorised persons. The FSA is required to publish a code to give guidance on what is abuse and to provide a 'safe harbour'. This forms part of the Market Conduct Sourcebook and is called the Code of Market Conduct.

Part X provides the FSA with general powers to make rules which apply to authorised persons, including rules on specific matters – e.g. client money and money laundering. Rules must be published in draft for consultation. Guidance may be provided individually or generally and may be published. The FSA may modify rules or waive particular rules for particular persons in certain situations.

Part XI allows the FSA to gather information from authorised persons, including use of skilled persons' reports under section 166, or to commission investigations into authorised persons.

Part XIV sets out the disciplinary measures available to the FSA which can include public censure, unlimited fines, withdrawal of authorisation.

Part XXII includes the provisions relating to auditors and their appointment.

Part XXVI brings together in one place the arrangements applying to warning notices and decision notices concerning possible breaches of various requirements imposed by FSMA 2000 or by FSA rules. A warning notice has to state the reasons for proposed actions and allow reasonable time for representations to be made. This will be followed by a decision notice with a right to appeal to the Tribunal.

Appendix 4 – The FSA Handbook

1. Not all authorised firms are required to comply with all rules contained within the FSA Handbook. This varies with the type of permission – the regulated activity an authorised firm is permitted to undertake is set out in the authorised firm's Scope of Permission. The following can be viewed on the FSA website:

    - contents of the FSA Handbook – www.fsa.gov.uk/Pages/handbook

- the FSA Register which lists the regulated activities that each authorised firm has permission to undertake – www.fsa.gov.uk/Pages/register

In gaining an understanding of the Handbook the auditor bears in mind the four statutory objectives of the FSA, set out in paragraph 8 of the main text, which underpin the content of the FSA Handbook. To facilitate usage the FSA Handbook has been structured into a number of blocks and within each block the material has been sub-divided into sourcebooks or manuals. There are rules, evidential provisions[41] and guidance which are contained within all of the blocks[42]. Contravention of rules (which includes Principles for Businesses) or evidential provisions can give rise to an obligation on the auditor to report the matter direct to the FSA – see the section of this Practice Note relating to ISA (UK and Ireland) 250 Section B. Outline details of certain elements of the FSA Handbook are set out below.

Principles for Businesses

The eleven Principles for Businesses, which are general statements that set out the fundamental obligations of firms under the regulatory system, are set out in the FSA Handbook. They derive their authority from the FSA's rule-making powers as set out in the Act and reflect the regulatory objectives. These Principles are as follows:

- an authorised firm must conduct its business with integrity;
- an authorised firm must conduct its business with due skill, care and diligence;
- an authorised firm must take reasonable care to organise and control its affairs responsibly and effectively with adequate risk management;
- an authorised firm must maintain adequate financial resources;
- an authorised firm must observe proper standards of market conduct;
- an authorised firm must pay due regard to the interests of its customers and treat them fairly;
- an authorised firm must pay due regard to the information needs of its clients, and communicate information to them in a way which is clear, fair and not misleading;
- an authorised firm must manage conflicts of interest fairly, both between itself and its customers and between a customer and another client;
- an authorised firm must take reasonable care to ensure the suitability of its advice and discretionary decisions for any customer who is entitled to rely on its judgement;
- an authorised firm must arrange adequate protection for clients' assets when it is responsible for them; and
- an authorised firm must deal with its regulators in an open and co-operative way, and must disclose to the FSA appropriately anything relating to the authorised firm of which the FSA would reasonably expect notice (see SUP15 – Notifications to the FSA).

Senior management arrangements, systems and controls

SYSC amplifies Principle for Businesses 3, the requirement for a firm to take reasonable care to organise and control its affairs responsibly and effectively, with

---

[41] An evidential provision is not binding in its own right, but establishes a presumption of compliance or non-compliance with another rule. Guidance may be used to explain the implications of other provisions, to indicate possible means of compliance, or to recommend a particular course of action or arrangement.

[42] Rules are set out in emboldened type and are marked with the icon 'R', evidential provisions are marked 'E' and guidance 'G'. Further guidance on the status of the Handbook is set out in the General Provisions (GEN) Sourcebook Chapter 2.2 and Chapter 6 of the Reader's Guide.

adequate risk management systems. The relevant chapters[43,44] for investment businesses are as follows;

- 2 – senior management arrangements
- 3 – systems and controls
- 4 – general organisational requirements
- 5 – employees, agents and other relevant persons
- 6 – compliance, internal audit and financial crime
- 7 – risk control
- 8 – outsourcing
- 9 – record keeping
- 10 – conflicts of interest
- 11 – liquidity risk systems and controls
- 12 – group risk systems and control requirements
- 18 – guidance on Public Disclosure Act – whistle blowing.

Threshold Conditions

5   Under s 41 and Schedule 6 of FSMA 2000 Threshold Conditions are the minimum requirements that must be met at authorisation and must continue to be met. The five statutory Threshold Conditions are:

- legal status: investment business may be conducted by a body corporate, a partnership or a sole trader;
- location of offices: a body corporate constituted under the law of the UK must have its head office and its registered office in the UK;
- close links: close links must not prevent effective supervision. Entities are regarded as closely linked if there is a group relationship, i.e. parent/subsidiary/fellow subsidiary (but using the EC 7th Company Law Directive definition of subsidiary). They are also closely linked if one owns or controls 20% or more of the voting rights or capital of the other;
- adequate resources: the authorised firm must have adequate resources (financial and non financial) for the type of business conducted taking into account the impact of other group entities and having regard to provisions made against liabilities (including contingent and future liabilities) and the approach to risk management; and
- suitability: the FSA will consider the fitness and propriety of authorised firms, including whether business is conducted with integrity and in compliance with high standards, and whether there is competent and prudent management and exercise of due skill, care and diligence. This may include consideration of whether those subject to the approved persons regime (i.e. those undertaking controlled functions) are, or will be, approved by the FSA.

Appendix 5 – Reporting direct to the FSA – statutory right and protection for disclosure under general law

1   When the auditor concludes that a matter does not give rise to a statutory duty to report direct to the FSA, the auditor considers the right to report to the FSA.

---

[43] *From 1st November 2007, for common platform firms, SYSC Chapter 3 has been disapplied and replaced by SYSC Chapters 4-10 which form the common platform. The common platform comprises the combined systems and controls requirements of the CRD and MiFID. Firms subject to the common platform include those subject to the CRD or MiFID or both.*

[44] *Chapters 3A and 13-17 apply only to insurers.*

In cases of doubt, general law provides protection for disclosing certain matters to a proper authority in the public interest.

Audit firms are protected from the risk of liability from breach of confidence or defamation under general law even when carrying out work which is not clearly undertaken in the capacity of auditor provided that:

- in the case of breach of confidence:
  (i) disclosure is made in the public interest; and
  (ii) such disclosure is made to an appropriate body or person; and
  (iii) there is no malice motivating the disclosure; and
- in the case of defamation:
  (i) the information disclosed was obtained in a proper capacity; and
  (ii) there is no malice motivating the disclosure.

The same protection is given even if there is only a reasonable suspicion that non-compliance with law or regulations has occurred. Provided that it can be demonstrated that an audit firm, in disclosing a matter in the public interest, has acted reasonably and in good faith, it would not be held by the court to be in breach of duty to the institution even if, an investigation or prosecution having occurred, it were found that there had been no breach of law or regulation.

When reporting to proper authorities in the public interest, it is important that, in order to retain the protection of qualified privilege, auditors report only to one who has a proper interest to receive the information. The FSA is the proper authority in the case of an investment business.

'Public interest' is a concept which is not capable of general definition. Each situation must be considered individually. In general circumstances, matters to be taken into account when considering whether disclosure is justified in the public interest may include:

- the extent to which the suspected non-compliance with law or regulations is likely to affect members of the public;
- whether the directors (or equivalent) have rectified the matter or are taking, or are likely to take, effective corrective action;
- the extent to which non-disclosure is likely to enable the suspected non-compliance with law or regulations to recur with impunity;
- the gravity of the matter;
- whether there is a general management ethos within the entity of disregarding law or regulations;
- the weight of evidence and the degree of the auditors' suspicion that there has been an instance of non-compliance with law or regulations.

Determination of where the balance of public interest lies requires careful consideration. The auditor needs to weigh the public interest in maintaining confidential client relationships against the public interest of disclosure to a proper authority and to use their professional judgement to determine whether their misgivings justify them in carrying the matter further or are too insubstantial to deserve report.

In cases where it is uncertain whether the statutory duty requires or s 342 or s 343 FSMA 2000 permits an auditor to communicate a matter to the FSA, it is possible that the auditor may be able to rely on the defence of disclosure in the public interest if it communicates a matter to the FSA which could properly be regarded as having material significance in conformity with the guidance in ISA (UK and Ireland) 250 Section B and this Practice Note, although the auditor may wish to seek legal advice in such circumstances.

Appendix 6 – The auditor's right and duty to report to the FSA: Examples of reportable items

Although there are a large number of 'relevant requirements' or matters of concern potentially giving rise to a statutory duty to report, these will normally fall within a number of general themes, which the auditor should be aware of:

- Controllers, directors and senior managers who may not be 'fit and proper';
- Serious breaches of law / regulations;
- Potential disciplinary action against the firm or directors;
- Undertaking activities outside the scope of their permission;
- Failure to comply with limitations or restrictions on permission or individual requirements;
- False or misleading information given to the FSA or matters concealed;
- Problems with another 'regulator' e.g. Office of Fair Trading (i.e. regards the Consumer Credit Act) or overseas regulators;
- Breaches of prudential limits and/or any financial limits;
- Significant actual or potential loss by clients e.g. loss of customer assets or breach of client money rules; where there appear to be conflicts of interest; where there appears to be systemic abuse of advice or discretionary decisions; or as identified by complaints or by cases where a customer sues under s150 FSMA;
- Failure to clearly allocate responsibilities between senior managers or to implement clear reporting lines;
- Major systems and control weaknesses (including major reconciliation failures and backlogs);
- Possible 'going-concern' issues.

The above general themes are intended as a guide – any report would need to be made against a specific relevant requirement. If an issue has been identified relating to one of the themes, (which might be materially significant to the FSA and is in a situation where the auditor is under a duty to report), the auditor should identify the relevant requirement. Even if a specific relevant requirement cannot be established, the auditor should consider whether or not the right to report is appropriate.

The audit of investment businesses in the UK (Revised) PN 21

Appendix 7 – Audit reporting requirements

Types of investment firm and the requirement for an auditor

Firm type	Audit of annual accounts	SUP 3.10 audit
(1) BIPRU investment firm (including a UCITS investment firm and an exempt BIPRU commodities firm)		
Incorporated – not small	X	X
Incorporated – small	X	X
Unincorporated	(Note 1)	X (if there is a permission to hold client assets)
(2) Exempt CAD firm (Note 4)		
Incorporated – not small	X	X
Incorporated – small **(Note 5)**	X	X
Unincorporated		
(3) Securities and Futures firm		
Incorporated – not small	X	X
Incorporated – small	Note 2	X (if there is a permission to hold client assets)
Unincorporated		X (if there is a permission to hold client assets)(4)
Investment management firm		
Incorporated – not small	X	X
Incorporated – small	Note 2	X (if there is a permission to hold client assets)
Unincorporated		X (if there is a permission to hold client assets)
(5) Personal investment firm (not small)		
Incorporated – not small	X	X
Incorporated – small	Note 2	X (if there is a permission to hold client assets)
Unincorporated		X (if there is a permission to hold client assets)
(6) Small personal investment firm (Note 3)		
Incorporated – not small	X	
Incorporated – small	Note 2	
Unincorporated		
(7) UCITS firm		
Incorporated – not small	X	X
Incorporated – small	X	X

Other categories

For other categories of firm, such as authorised professional firms and service companies, readers should refer to the table in SUP 3.1.2R of the FSA Handbook.

Note 1
These firms are required by MiFID to have an audit of their annual accounts but only if they hold client assets.

Note 2
No statutory audit is required under CA 2006 for small companies with financial years ending on or after 31st December 2006. In short, the small companies audit exemption is available if the firm:

(a) meets the Companies Act 2006 criteria for the small companies audit exemption; and
(b) does not undertake any activity within the scope of MiFID, UCITS Directive, Banking Consolidation Directive or the Insurance Directives or is an e-money issuer.

Note 3
A small personal investment firm is one which:

- is not a MiFID investment firm;
- is not a network; and
- has fewer that 26 representatives.

Note 4
For the purposes of this table the terms securities and futures firm, investment management firm and personal investment firm have been taken not to include an exempt CAD firm.

Note 5
An exempt CAD firm that has opted into MiFID can benefit from the audit exemption for small companies in the CA 2006 if it fulfils the conditions of regulation 4C(3) of the FSMA 2000 (Markets in Financial Instruments) Regulations 2007. In other words, if such an exempt CAD firm continues to meet the conditions of the article 3 MiFID exemption (notwithstanding it is an exempt CAD), it can benefit from the small companies exemption.

Appendix 8 – Definitions

Abbreviations and frequently used terms in this Practice Note are set out below:

ARROW II   'Advanced Risk Responsive Operating frameWork'. The term used for FSA's risk assessment process – the application of risk based supervision. It is the mechanism through which the FSA evaluates the risk an authorised firm poses to its statutory objectives enabling it to allocate its resources appropriately and respond to the risks identified.

Auditors	Both auditors appointed under company legislation and, where appropriate, accountants appointed other than under company legislation to carry out work of an audit nature. Throughout this Practice Note, therefore, the term is used to indicate auditors of incorporated investment businesses appointed under company legislation or similar statutory provisions; and any other auditors or reporting accountants appointed to report on a routine basis on matters specified by the regulator. Specifically in the circumstances of reporting on client assets, the auditor is defined as someone meeting the criteria under SUP 3.4.2 (R) (eligible for appointment as an auditor under the Companies Act).
Authorised firm	An entity which has been granted one of more Part IV permissions by the FSA and so is authorised under FSMA 2000 to undertake regulated activities – an authorised person. Authorised firms include investment businesses.
Authorised person	Term used throughout FSMA 2000 and related statutory instruments to refer to an authorised firm – see above.
BIPRU	Prudential sourcebook for banks, building societies and investment firms.
CA1985	Companies Act 1985
Client assets	Assets covered by the FSA's custody rules, collateral rules and client money rules.
Client money	For the purposes of CASS 1-5, client money is defined as money of any currency which, in the course of carrying on designated investment business, an investment business holds in respect of any investment agreement entered into, or to be entered into, with or for a client or which an investment business treats as client money in accordance with the client money rules.
Closely linked entity	As defined in s343(8) FSMA 2000, an entity has close links with an authorised firm for this purpose if the entity is a: (a) Parent undertaking of an authorised firm; (b) Subsidiary undertaking of an authorised firm; (c) Parent undertaking of a subsidiary undertaking of an authorised firm; or (d) Subsidiary undertaking of a parent undertaking of an authorised firm
Conduct of business rules	Those rules, regulations or codes of practice of the FSA regarding the maintenance of adequate standards by investment businesses in their dealings with clients.
Custody assets	A designated investment held for or on behalf of a client or any other asset which is or may be held with a designated investment held for, or on behalf of, a client
Directors	Directors of a company or other body, the partners, proprietors, committee of management or trustees of other forms of enterprise or equivalent persons.
EEA	European Economic Area.

EU IFRS	International Financial Reporting Standards adopted by the European Union.
FRS	Financial Reporting Statements
FSA	The Financial Services Authority.
FSMA 2000	Financial Services and Markets Act 2000
ISD	Investment Services Directive (European Directive: 93/22/EEC).
JMLSG	Joint Money Laundering Steering Group
MiFID	Markets in Financial Instruments Directive
Material significance	A matter or group of matters is normally of material significance to a regulator's function when, due either to its nature or its potential financial impact, it is likely of itself to require investigation by the regulator
OEIC	Open Ended Investment Company
Passport	The authorisation for an entity incorporated in an EEA Member State which is established and authorised in that state ('home state') in relation to activities covered by the Single Market Directives to carry on those activities in other EEA Member States ('host states') by setting up branches, or by providing services on a cross-border basis, without obtaining separate authorisation in those states.
Part IV permission	A permission granted by FSA under Part IV FSMA 2000 permitting an authorised firm to carry on regulated activities as specified in the FSMA 2000 Regulated Activities Order SI 2001/544 as amended.
Principles for Businesses	FSA Handbook defined principles with which an authorised firm must comply. The 11 principles are included in a stand alone element of the high level Standards block of the FSA Handbook – PRIN.
Regulated activities	Activities as defined in the Regulated Activities Order SI 2001/544 as amended
Relevant requirement	In relation to the auditors' duty to report direct to the FSA – a requirement imposed by or under FSMA 2000 which relates to authorisation under FSMA 2000 or to the carrying on of any regulated activity. This includes not only requirements set out in relevant statutory instruments but also the FSA's rules (other than the Listing, prospectus and disclosure rules) including the Principles for businesses. The duty to report also covers any requirement imposed by or under any other Act the contravention of which constitutes an offence which the FSA has the power to prosecute under FSMA 2000.
Regulator	The FSA.
SOCA	Serious Organised Crime Agency
SUP	Supervision manual of the FSA Handbook.

SYSC	Senior management arrangements, systems and controls element of the High Level Standards block of the FSA handbook.
The 2001 Regulations	SI 2001/2587 – FSMA 2000 (Communications by Auditors) Regulations 2001
Those charged with governance	ISAs (UK and Ireland) use the term 'those charged with governance' to describe the persons entrusted with the supervision, control and direction of an entity, who will normally be responsible for the quality of financial reporting, and the term 'management' to describe those persons who perform senior managerial functions. The FSA Handbook of Rules and Guidance (FSA Handbook) uses the term 'governing body' to describe collectively those charged with governance. In the context of this Practice Note, references to those charged with governance includes directors of investment businesses.

[PN 22]
The auditors' consideration of FRS 17 'Retirement benefits' – defined benefit schemes

(Issued November 2001)

Contents

	Paragraph
Introduction	
Background	1–5
The audit approach	6–12
Ethical issues	13–15
Planning considerations	
Communication with the entity directors	16–19
Engagement letters	20
Communication with other parties	21–24
Materiality	25–26
Audit evidence	
Obtaining an understanding of the retirement benefit schemes	27–30
Scheme assets	31–32
Using the work of the scheme auditors	33–37
Multi-employer schemes	38–39
Scheme liabilities	
The need to use the work of the actuary	40–42
The competence and objectivity of the actuary	43–46
The scope of the actuary's work	47–50
Assessing the work of the actuary as audit evidence	51
Source data	52–54
Actuarial assumptions	55–56
Assessing the results of the actuary's work	57–60
Materiality and the valuation of the scheme liabilities	61–63
Accounting policies	64–67
Recognition in the balance sheet	68–70
Going concern	71
Recognition in the profit and loss account and the Statement of Total Recognised Gains and Losses (STRGL)	72–73
Expected return on scheme assets and discount rate	74–76
Disclosures	77–78
Distributable profits	79–80
Management representations	81
Public sector considerations	82

Appendix 1 – Consideration of retirement benefits in the review of interim reports
Appendix 2 – Examples of risks of materials misstatement in relation to FRS 17
Appendix 3 – Smaller entities with insured schemes

The auditors' consideration of FRS 17 'Retirement benefits' – defined benefit schemes

Introduction

Background

This Practice Note gives guidance to auditors on their consideration of and response to the risk of material misstatement of the financial statements of a reporting entity in relation to the requirements of Financial Reporting Standard 17 'Retirement benefits' (FRS 17), in the context of an audit of those financial statements in accordance with Auditing Standards.[1]

FRS 17 deals with retirement benefits payable under both defined contribution schemes and defined benefit schemes. However, the Auditing Practices Board considers that the issues raised by defined contribution schemes will normally be less complex than in the case of defined benefit schemes and do not require specific auditing guidance. Accordingly, this Practice Note provides auditing guidance only in relation to defined benefit schemes.[2]

As defined in FRS 17, the term 'retirement benefits' includes not only pensions but all other post-retirement benefits (such as health care, life insurance and disability income), irrespective of whether these arrangements:

- are statutory, contractual or implicit in the employer's actions;
- arise in the United Kingdom and the Republic of Ireland or overseas;
- are funded or unfunded;
- are approved or unapproved.

Accordingly, retirement benefits include not only post-retirement benefits payable under a formal trust but also those payable pursuant to an informal agreement, such as a promise, a public statement or a similar commitment by the employer.

The requirements of FRS 17 are being introduced in three stages, commencing with accounting periods ending on or after 22 June 2001, for which only certain of the disclosures specified by FRS 17 are to be made. The full requirements of FRS 17 are only to be regarded as standard for accounting periods ending on or after 22 June 2003, although the Accounting Standards Board encourages their early adoption.

The requirements of FRS 17 apply only to financial statements. Appendix 1 to this Practice Note gives guidance on the auditors' consideration of retirement benefits in a review of a reporting entity's interim report.

---

[1] *FRS 17 was issued by the Accounting Standards Board in November 2000. It applies to all financial statements that are intended to give a true and fair view of a reporting employer's financial position and profit or loss (or income and expenditure) for a period.*

[2] *The following terms are defined in paragraph 2 of FRS 17:*
- *retirement benefits – all forms of consideration given by an employer in exchange for services rendered by employees that are payable after the completion of employment*
- *defined contribution scheme – a pension or other retirement benefit scheme into which an employer pays regular contributions fixed as an amount or as a percentage of pay and will have no legal or constructive obligation to pay further contributions if the scheme does not have sufficient assets to pay all employee benefits relating to employee service in the current and prior periods*
- *defined benefit scheme – a pension or other retirement benefit scheme other than a defined contribution scheme.*

The audit approach

6 For all defined benefit schemes (other than certain multi-employer defined benefit schemes that are required to be accounted for as defined contribution schemes (see paragraph 38 below)), FRS 17 requires:

   (a) the scheme assets and liabilities to be valued using specified methods;
   (b) the surplus (or deficit) to be recognised as an asset (or liability) by the reporting entity;
   (c) the change in the defined benefit asset or liability (other than that arising from contributions to the scheme) to be analysed into specified components and recognised in the profit and loss account or the statement of total recognised gains and losses; and
   (d) certain additional disclosures to be made in the reporting entity's financial statements.

7 It is the entity directors' responsibility to establish a process that will enable the reporting entity to comply with FRS 17 and to designate the individuals within the reporting entity who are responsible for this process. The entity directors may not have immediate access to the records of the scheme assets and so may not be in a position to value those assets themselves. Furthermore, the entity directors do not normally possess the expertise required to undertake the valuation of scheme liabilities on the actuarial basis specified by FRS 17. Accordingly, the process established by the entity directors may involve:

   (a) the scheme assets being valued by the scheme trustees, who may, in turn, obtain valuations of:
     - quoted securities from the fund managers or investment custodians;
     - insurance policies from the insurers; and
     - other types of asset from experts (for example, property valuers); and
   (b) the scheme liabilities being valued by a qualified actuary.

8 The entity auditors' objective in relation to FRS 17 is to consider the appropriateness of the steps that the entity directors have taken to satisfy themselves that the amounts and disclosures included in the financial statements are sufficiently reliable. In particular, the entity auditors consider the risk that the entity directors may not have devoted sufficient resources to this process. The nature, timing and extent of the entity auditors' procedures depend on their judgement as to the materiality of the amounts involved and the risk of material misstatement of the financial statements.

9 For the scheme assets, the entity auditors may be able to obtain all the audit evidence they consider necessary without performing procedures directly on the records of the scheme assets held by the scheme trustees. In other cases, they may consider that such procedures are necessary and may, where practicable, ask the entity directors to arrange with the scheme trustees for this work to be performed by the scheme auditors. Any procedures in relation to the scheme assets for the purposes of the audit of the reporting entity financial statements are separate from, and additional to, the audit of the scheme financial statements.

10 For the scheme liabilities; the entity auditors normally obtain some of the audit evidence they require by using the results of the work performed by the actuary who has valued the scheme liabilities.

11 The actuary can be expected to co-operate with the entity auditors. Such cooperation is often encouraged in the guidance to actuaries issued by their professional bodies;

in other cases, the entity directors, when appointing an actuary, may be able to obtain the actuary's agreement to cooperate with the entity auditors.[3]

It is not the role of the entity auditors to 'second guess' the work performed by the actuary. However, they need to be able to consider whether the steps taken by the entity directors are appropriate and whether, in the context of the financial statements taken as a whole, the accounting entries and disclosures required by FRS 17 (and the trends reported over time) are consistent with their knowledge of the reporting entity. 12

Ethical issues

SAS 100 'Objective and general principles governing an audit of financial statements' requires auditors to comply with the ethical guidance issued by their relevant professional bodies. This guidance specifically considers the threat to the auditors' independence and objectivity that may exist when the audit firm (or an associated firm or organisation) provides an audit client with other services, particularly when they directly affect amounts or disclosures in the financial statements. 13

The provision by the audit firm of actuarial services for the purpose of FRS 17 may present (or may reasonably be perceived to present) a threat to their independence and objectivity as entity auditors. The provision of some other form of actuarial services (that is, other than for the purpose of FRS 17) may also compromise their independence and objectivity if the entity directors subsequently decide to use the results of that work for the purpose of FRS 17. In such cases, the nature of the actuarial services requested by the reporting entity may be such that the firm concludes that it cannot adopt safeguards that would adequately address the threat to independence and objectivity that would arise. In such circumstances, the firm would not be able to accept both engagements. 14

SAS 610 (revised) 'Communication of audit matters to those charged with governance' requires the auditors of a listed company: 15

(a) to disclose in writing to the audit committee and discuss as appropriate:
- all relationships that may reasonably be thought to bear upon the firm's independence and the objectivity of the audit engagement partner and the audit staff;
- and the related safeguards that are in place; and

(b) to confirm in writing to the audit committee that, in their professional judgement, the firm is independent and that the objectivity of the audit engagement partner and the audit staff is not impaired.[4]

Planning Considerations

Communication with the entity directors

At the planning stage of the audit, the entity auditors make enquiries in order to understand and assess the process established by the entity directors to enable the 16

---

[3] The Institute and Faculty of Actuaries have jointly developed professional guidance (exposure draft at time of printing) for their members when advising clients in connection with FRS 17.

[4] SAS 610 (revised) was issued in June 2001 and auditors are required to comply with it in respect of audits of financial statements for periods commencing on or after 23 December 2001.

financial statements to be prepared in compliance with FRS 17. Issues to be covered in these discussions include ascertaining:

- who is responsible for the process;
- what arrangements have been made for identifying those schemes that are significant to the reporting entity's compliance with FRS 17;
- who is valuing the scheme assets;
- what arrangements have been made for identifying matters of significance affecting the actuarial valuation (for example, matching the treatment in the scheme assets and in the scheme liabilities of large bulk transfers in or out);
- who is valuing the scheme liabilities;
- how the actuarial assumptions are to be developed and approved;
- whether there is a realistic, coordinated timetable, that takes into account the time needed for the entity auditors to complete their work in connection with retirement benefits;
- whether there are arrangements in place to enable effective communication between all of the parties involved.

17 The entity auditors also discuss with the entity directors the risk of material misstatement of the financial statements in relation to the requirements of FRS 17, with particular reference to areas of higher risk. Appendix 2 to this Practice Note gives some illustrative examples of risks of material misstatement of the financial statements in relation to the requirements of FRS 17.

18 Enabling effective communication between all of the parties involved in complying with FRS 17 is the responsibility of the entity directors and an important aspect of the process established by them. Facilitating dialogue between these parties before any of the work is commenced assists the entity directors to ensure that there is a common understanding as to the work each party is to perform and the timetable for its completion. Appendix 3 to this Practice Note gives guidance on some issues that may of particular relevance in the context of smaller reporting entities with insured schemes.

19 Although it is the responsibility of the entity directors to ensure compliance with FRS 17, they normally delegate to one or more members of management the responsibility for managing the process established to achieve this. Accordingly, in this Practice Note, references to the entity auditors communicating with, making enquiries of or holding discussions with the entity directors are to be construed as referring to the relevant members of management, whenever appropriate.

Engagement letters

20 The issuance of FRS 17 does not represent a fundamental change in legal or professional requirements, but it does underline the need for a clear understanding between the entity directors and the entity auditors about, for example, the involvement of other auditors and experts in the audit. These matters can often be satisfactorily addressed in discussion with the entity directors, or clarified with them in writing, at the planning stage of the audit.

Communication with other parties

21 At the planning stage of the audit, having obtained the permission of the entity directors, the entity auditors normally communicate with the actuary who will be valuing the scheme liabilities for the purpose of complying with FRS 17. Depending on the circumstances, they may also communicate with the scheme auditors

(particularly if they will be assisting the entity auditors with the audit procedures relating to the scheme assets) and with any fund manager, investment custodian, insurer or expert who will be valuing the scheme assets.

Such communications provide the entity auditors with an early opportunity to: 22

(a) assess the objectivity, qualifications, experience and resources of the actuary (see paragraphs 43 to 46 below); and
(b) (where appropriate) consider the qualifications, experience and resources of the scheme auditors and to inform them how their work will be used (see paragraph 37 below).

It also enables them to explore on a preliminary basis the scope of the actuary's work and any specific issues concerning the actuary's work that are of interest to them (see paragraphs 47 to 50 below).

The entity auditors consider any engagement letter, correspondence or other document that contains the entity directors' instructions to the actuary or specifies any limitations on the scope of the actuary's work, or that otherwise defines the relationship between the reporting entity and the actuary. 23

Where the reporting entity is preparing consolidated financial statements, there may be a large number of schemes and consequently many different trustees and actuaries with whom the entity auditors might wish to communicate concerning the audit evidence that is needed. Some of the responsibility for this may in practice be passed to the auditors of the subsidiary undertakings, although (in the case of overseas subsidiaries) it will be important to establish that those auditors are familiar with FRS 17. In some cases, a 'lead actuary' may be identified by the reporting entity, to take on the role of communicating with those involved in the various schemes and of collating the information required under FRS 17. 24

Materiality

SAS 220 requires auditors to consider materiality when determining the nature, timing and extent of their procedures. A matter is material if its omission or misstatement would reasonably influence the decisions of those to whom the auditors' report is addressed. SAS 220 acknowledges that different materiality considerations may be applied depending on the aspect of the financial statements being considered. For example, the auditors may judge that the expected degree of accuracy of note disclosures is lower than for figures included in the primary financial statements and, accordingly, that the level at which an omission or misstatement becomes material is rather higher. 25

These considerations may be of relevance in the two year transitional period during which FRS 17 is being introduced.[5] In the first two years, the entity auditors' judgements of materiality relating to the required note disclosures may be based principally on the relative significance of the amounts involved in the context of the reporting entity's balance sheet. In making such judgements, however, they recognise that figures in the note disclosures in the first two years will provide the basis of the comparative figures in the financial statements for the third year. 26

---

[5] *The full requirements of FRS 17 are to be regarded as standard for accounting periods ending on or after 22 June 2003, but for accounting periods ending before that date (but on or after 22 June 2001 and 22 June 2002), only certain of the disclosures required by FRS 17 are to be made. In the first year, these disclosures relate to the closing balance sheet only (without comparative figures for the previous period).*

Audit evidence

Obtaining an understanding of the retirement benefit schemes

27 The accounting and disclosure requirements of FRS 17 could have a material impact on the financial statements of some reporting entities. Knowledge of the existence of retirement benefit schemes and familiarity with the general nature of their provisions is therefore important to the entity auditors when assessing the financial statement assertions related to scheme assets and liabilities and the cost of providing retirement benefits.

28 To ascertain the arrangements made for providing retirement benefits, the entity auditors make enquiries of the entity directors and obtain an understanding of the rules of any schemes that appear to be significant to the reporting entity's compliance with FRS 17.

29 An understanding of the rules of a scheme may, in some cases, enable the entity auditors to identify obligations to pay retirement benefits. However, there may also be benefits payable that are not recorded in the rules. For example, there may be:

- legal obligations to pay retirement benefits, which arise from informal agreements rather than from a formal contract;
- 'constructive obligations' (for example, where pension benefits are regularly enhanced beyond the minimum required by statute);[6] or
- statutory requirements that over-ride the original provisions of a scheme.

The entity auditors make enquiries of the entity directors in order to understand and assess how these issues have been addressed by the process established by the entity directors to enable them to capture the information needed to prepare financial statements in compliance with FRS 17.

30 Procedures performed by the entity auditors to satisfy other objectives of the audit, for example, reviewing minutes of meetings of the board of directors, may also assist them to identify obligations to pay retirement benefits. Depending on the entity auditors' assessment of the risk of material misstatement of the financial statements, they may plan and perform additional procedures specifically designed to identify obligations to pay retirement benefits, for example, reviewing minutes of meetings of the reporting entity's human resources or remuneration committees, or its communications with trades unions and employees (including contracts of employment).

Scheme assets

31 The scheme assets include current assets such as cash deposits, as well as investments: any liabilities, such as accrued expenses, are to be deducted. Investments normally comprise one or more of the following:

- quoted securities (equity and non-equity shares, bonds);
- unquoted securities;
- unitised securities;
- insurance policies;
- loans and debt instruments; and
- freehold or leasehold properties.

---

[6] *Constructive obligations are dealt with at greater length in Financial Reporting Standard 12 'Provisions, contingent liabilities and contingent assets'.*

Investments occasionally include futures and options, works of art and antiques.

The entity auditors may be able to obtain all the audit evidence they consider necessary in relation to the scheme assets without procedures being performed directly on the records of the scheme assets held by the scheme trustees. For example, if the period between the most recent scheme year-end date and the reporting entity balance sheet date is short and if the audited scheme financial statements are available, the entity auditors may consider that sufficient audit evidence can be obtained by: 32

- asking the entity directors to prepare a reconciliation of the scheme assets valuation at the scheme year-end date with the portfolio valuation at the reporting entity balance sheet date which is being used for FRS 17 purposes;
- obtaining direct confirmation of the scheme assets from the investment custodian; and
- examining the principal reconciling items, such as contributions received; benefits paid; large bulk transfers in and out and estimated investment returns.

Using the work of the scheme auditors

In other cases, the entity auditors may consider that procedures do need to be performed directly on the records of scheme assets. They may be able to undertake such procedures themselves, if the entity directors give their permission and if the scheme trustees are willing to allow them access. Alternatively, when planning the audit, the entity auditors may, where practicable, ask the entity directors to arrange with the scheme trustees for the necessary procedures to be performed by the scheme auditors. The entity auditors use the work of the scheme auditors in accordance with SAS 510 'The relationship between principal auditors and other auditors'.[7] 33

Using the work of the scheme auditors may be necessary if the scheme trustees stipulate that only the scheme auditors may have access to the records of the scheme assets. However, the decision to use the scheme auditors may also result from considerations of efficiency and effectiveness. The scheme auditors normally will be particularly well-placed to assist the entity auditors to obtain audit evidence relating to, for example, the financial statement assertions regarding the: 34

- existence;
- completeness;
- ownership; and
- valuation

of the scheme assets. They can also be expected to be familiar with the scheme assets and the accounting records held by the scheme trustees and, therefore, to be able to perform the necessary procedures in a cost-effective manner.

The scheme auditors may also be able to use some of their work on the audit of the scheme financial statements as a source of evidence for this purpose. In the course of their audit, the scheme auditors will have complied with the requirements of SAS 480 'Service organisations', where applicable. SAS 480 establishes standards and provides guidance on procedures to obtain sufficient appropriate audit evidence where 35

---

[7] *SAS 510 establishes standards and guidance regarding the use by principal auditors, reporting on the financial statements of an entity, of other auditors' work on the financial information of one or more components included in the financial statements of the entity. 'Component' is defined as 'a division, branch, subsidiary undertaking, joint venture, associated undertaking or other entity whose financial information is included in financial statements audited by the principle auditors'. The principles of SAS 510 apply to the entity auditors' use of the scheme auditors' work on the scheme assets.*

an entity uses service organisations, such as investment custodians. Most scheme assets are held by investment custodians. The procedures include:

- understanding and documenting the contractual terms that apply to investment custodians; and
- assessing whether sufficient appropriate audit evidence concerning the relevant financial statement assertions is available from records held by the scheme and, if it is not, obtaining such evidence either by direct access to the records of the investment custodian or by obtaining information from the investment custodian or reports by its auditors.

The scheme auditors normally also obtain direct confirmation in writing from fund managers or investment custodians of the scheme assets as at the scheme year-end date.

36 The scheme auditors will need to perform procedures in addition to those performed for the audit of the scheme financial statements. For example:

- if the reporting entity and the scheme do not share the same accounting period, additional procedures may be needed to update their work on the audit of the scheme financial statements to the reporting entity's balance sheet date; and
- if the reporting entity and the scheme do share the same accounting period but the financial statements of the scheme will not be prepared and audited to the same timetable as those of the reporting entity, additional procedures may be necessary to obtain the evidence needed by the entity auditors on a timely basis.

The scheme auditors may wish to agree a separate engagement letter with the scheme trustees before undertaking this work.

37 Having obtained the permission of the entity directors and the scheme trustees, the entity auditors communicate with the scheme auditors at the planning stage of the audit to agree on the audit work to be undertaken by the scheme auditors. In accordance with SAS 510, the entity auditors obtain sufficient appropriate audit evidence that the work of the scheme auditors is adequate for the entity auditors' purposes. The entity auditors confirm in writing the nature and extent of the procedures to be undertaken by the scheme auditors and the level of materiality to be applied. The entity auditors agree with the scheme auditors, and with the scheme trustees and the entity directors, when the results of that work are to be reported to the entity auditors and the manner in which they are to be reported. Where practicable, the entity auditors require the scheme auditors to provide a report on the factual findings resulting from performing the specified procedures.

Multi-employer schemes

38 When more than one employer participates in a defined benefit scheme, it is known as a 'multi-employer scheme'. In some cases the scheme assets are not clearly allocated to specific employers and it may be difficult to identify the share of the underlying assets and liabilities attributable to each participant on a consistent and reasonable basis. In such circumstances, FRS 17 requires the contributions to be accounted for as if the scheme were a defined contribution scheme, provided that there is disclosure in the financial statements of:

(a) the fact that the scheme is a defined benefit scheme but that the reporting entity is unable to identify its share of the scheme assets and liabilities; and
(b) any available information about the existence of a surplus or deficit in the scheme and the implications of that surplus or deficit for the reporting entity.

In such circumstances, the entity auditors make enquiries of the entity directors regarding the basis for their conclusion that the entity's share of the scheme assets and liabilities cannot be identified and consider any relevant professional advice (for example actuarial or legal advice) that the entity directors may have obtained on this issue. Where different contribution rates apply to different employers participating in the scheme, this may indicate that an allocation of the underlying assets and liabilities is possible. The entity auditors obtain an understanding of the principal provisions of the scheme and of any circumstances (such as the winding-up of the scheme) in which a deficit in the scheme may give rise to either: 39

- a liability (or contingent liability) in the reporting entity; or
- concern about the reporting entity's ability to continue as a going concern.

Scheme liabilities

The need to use the work of the actuary

The scheme liabilities represent the discounted present value of the accrued future retirement benefit obligations based on service up to the reporting entity's balance sheet date. They may be based either on a full actuarial valuation or a more recent actuarial assessment, as at the reporting entity's balance sheet date, or on an update (as at that date) of the most recent full valuation or assessment. (In this Practice Note, 'valuation' refers to a full actuarial valuation, an actuarial assessment or an update.) A full actuarial valuation by a professionally qualified actuary is normally required every three years but will rarely be available as at the reporting entity's balance sheet date. Accordingly, for FRS 17, the actuary will normally review and update the most recent full valuation or subsequent actuarial assessment.[8] 40

The entity auditors are not expected to have the expertise of a person trained for, or qualified to engage in, the practice of another profession or occupation, such as that of a qualified actuary. 41

Except where retirement benefits are not material to the financial statements, the entity auditors will normally use the work of the actuary as audit evidence. SAS 520 'Using the work of an expert' states that auditors, when determining whether to use the work of an expert, review: 42

(a) the importance of the matter being considered in the context of the financial statements;
(b) the risk of misstatement based on the nature and complexity of the matter being considered; and
(c) the quantity and quality of other available relevant audit evidence.

The competence and objectivity of the actuary

SAS 520 requires auditors, when planning to use the work of an expert, to assess the expert's objectivity, qualifications, experience and resources. It indicates that this normally involves considering the expert's: 43

(a) professional certification, or licensing by, or membership of, an appropriate professional body; and
(b) experience and reputation.

---

[8] *The most recent full actuarial valuation will normally have been performed as at the scheme's year-end date in conjunction with the statutory triennial Minimum Funding Requirement valuation.*

44   The entity auditors therefore consider whether the actuary is a member of the Institute of Actuaries, the Faculty of Actuaries or the Society of Actuaries, or of a similar professional body of actuaries practising in countries other than the UK and the Republic of Ireland. The Institute, the Faculty and the Society can provide advice on the acceptability of the standards of professional bodies to which foreign actuaries belong.

45   The entity auditors also consider whether there is a risk that the actuary's objectivity may be impaired when the actuary is an employee of, or related in some other manner to, the reporting entity.

46   If the entity auditors are concerned about the competence or objectivity of the actuary they may discuss their reservations with the entity directors and consider whether sufficient appropriate audit evidence can be obtained. They may undertake additional procedures or may request the entity directors to obtain evidence from another actuary. If unable to obtain sufficient appropriate evidence, they consider the implications for their report.

The scope of the actuary's work

47   SAS 520 requires auditors to obtain sufficient appropriate audit evidence that the expert's scope of work is adequate for the purposes of their audit.

48   Having obtained the permission of the entity directors, the entity auditors communicate with the actuary at the planning stage of the audit:
- to inform the actuary that the entity auditors intend to use the work of the actuary as audit evidence;
- to discuss the scope of the actuary's work as agreed between the actuary and the entity directors, for example:
  - the steps required to achieve the degree of accuracy required in the valuation within the reporting timescale;[9]
  - the procedures to establish the accuracy, authorisation and completeness of the source data to be used;
  - the possible variation in the liability and costs which the actuary is estimating;[10]
  - the impact on the valuation of any significant events of which the entity auditors or the actuary are aware; and
  - the extent to which any events or circumstances indicate that a fuller or more recent valuation might be necessary
- to ascertain the form and content of any reports which the actuary expects to issue for the purpose of FRS 17;
- to obtain confirmation that the actuary:
  - will comply with the requirements of FRS 17 and with the relevant requirements and guidance of the actuary's professional body;
  - will include all retirement benefits payable under schemes which the actuary has been engaged to advise upon;
  - understands the timetable for the entity directors to prepare the financial statements and for the entity auditors to complete their work in connection with retirement benefits;

[9] *Actuarial guidance (exposure draft) requires the actuary to consult with the reporting entity on this matter.*

[10] *Actuarial guidance (exposure draft) requires the actuary to advise the reporting entity on any aspect of the update likely to lead to material misstatement of liabilities or costs.*

- will advise the entity auditors of any matters which come to the actuary's attention which occur in the period from the reporting entity's balance sheet date up to date on which the valuation is completed that would have a material effect on the valuation of the scheme liabilities; and
- is content for the entity directors to make available to the entity auditors copies of any draft or final reports for the purpose of FRS 17 that the actuary may provide to them.

The actuary is not under a professional obligation to agree an engagement letter with the entity directors. However, if the actuary's terms of reference have been confirmed in writing, the entity auditors may find it helpful to review this documentation in order to obtain an understanding of the actuary's scope of work.

As noted above, for most FRS 17 calculations, the most recent full valuation for the scheme will be updated by the actuary to the reporting entity's balance sheet date to reflect current conditions. FRS 17 notes that some aspects of the valuation will need to be updated at each balance sheet date (for example, the financial assumptions, such as the discount rate); other assumptions may not need to be up-dated annually (for example, the mortality rate).[11]

49

In many cases, the changes since the most recent full actuarial valuation (for example, routine changes in benefits and market conditions) can be adequately reflected by updating that valuation. However, where significant changes have taken place (for example, large bulk transfers in or out, or major new early retirement programmes) or where there is a significant level of uncertainty relating to aspects of the valuation (for example, as a result of a court decision or a change in legislation), the actuary may not be confident that the resulting figures will fall within the materiality limits specified by the entity.[12] If the entity auditors become aware of events or circumstances that appear to indicate that there might be material misstatement of liability or costs, they discuss their concerns with the entity directors and with the actuary and, if necessary, request the entity directors to instruct the actuary to undertake the additional work.

50

Assessing the work of the actuary as audit evidence

SAS 520 requires auditors to assess the appropriateness of the expert's work as audit evidence regarding the financial statement assertions being considered. It states that this involves consideration of, amongst other matters:

51

- the source data used;
- the assumptions and methods used; and
- the results of the expert's work in the light of the auditors' overall knowledge of the business and the results of other audit procedures.

Source data

Source data used by the actuary usually include:

52

---

[11] *Similar requirements exist for a triennial funding valuation of the scheme. However the assumptions and measurement methods used for the funding valuation may be different from those for the actuarial valuation required by the FRS.*

[12] *Actuarial guidance (exposure draft) requires the actuary to advise the reporting entity on any aspect of the update likely to lead to material misstatement of liabilities or costs.*

- information as to eligibility, including the number and types of participants covered (active, inactive and former members or beneficiaries), their ages, length of service and gender, salary and earnings history of participants and employee contributions (if any), turnover data and employee future benefit credits accrued since the previous valuation; and
- scheme assets, their values, underlying cash transactions, and items of income and expense.

53 The entity directors are responsible for the source data used by the actuary. The entity auditors make enquiries of the entity directors and of the actuary regarding the procedures undertaken to establish the sufficiency, relevance and reliability of the source data used.[13] If the entity auditors have concerns about the scope of these procedures, they discuss their concerns with the directors and with the actuary and may decide to perform their own procedures.

54 The entity auditors' procedures relating to source data are a matter of judgement; factors they would consider in deciding on the nature, extent and timing of procedures include:

- the nature of the data and sensitivity of the actuarial valuation to the data;
- the source of the data, whether supplied to the actuary by the reporting entity client or by a service organisation, and the extent to which the source data have already been subjected to audit procedures, the nature of those audit procedures (tests of controls or substantive procedures) and by whom (external or internal auditor or the service organisation's auditor) those audit procedures have been applied; and
- the approach taken by the actuary with respect to verifying the validity and completeness of the data.

Actuarial assumptions

55 Actuarial assumptions are estimates of future events that will affect the valuation of the scheme liabilities and the reporting entity's costs of retirement benefits. Examples include such items as mortality rates, termination rates, disability claim rates, retirement age, changes in salary and benefit levels, administrative expenses, discount rates to reflect the time value of money, and return on scheme assets. FRS 17 states that the assumptions are ultimately the responsibility of the entity directors but should be set upon advice given by the actuary.

56 The entity auditors do not have the same expertise as the actuary and cannot necessarily challenge the appropriateness and reasonableness of the assumptions. However, through discussion with the entity directors and, where practicable, with the actuary, the entity auditors:

- obtain a general understanding of the assumptions and review the process used to develop them;
- compare the assumptions with those used by the entity directors in prior years; and
- consider whether, based on their knowledge of the business of the reporting entity and of the scheme and on the results of other audit procedures, the assumptions appear to be reasonable and compatible with those used for the preparation of the financial statements.

[13] For members of the Institute of Actuaries and of the Faculty of Actuaries undertaking any actuarial valuation, the Professional Conduct Standards state that the actuary must carry out appropriate investigations to assess the accuracy and reasonableness of any data being used or state why this has not been done.

Assessing the results of the actuary's work

The entity auditors consider whether the results of the actuary's work are consistent with their overall knowledge of the business and the results of other procedures. 57

There is no prescribed form of report for the actuary to deliver to the entity the results of the work performed: normally the figures required for inclusion in the balance sheet, the profit and loss account and the notes to the financial statements are provided in some form of letter or written report. The actuary may also provide a commentary on other matters, such as: 58

- the movements since the previous valuation in the figures required for inclusion in the balance sheet and the profit and loss account;
- the possible variation in the valuation of the scheme liabilities and the implications for the financial statements and the audit; and
- the sensitivity of the results, funding level, scheme maturity and investments to variations in the source data and assumptions.

The entity auditors obtain copies of all written communications from the actuary to the entity directors concerning the findings of the work performed.

The entity auditors enquire of the entity directors whether the actuary has indicated to them that: 59

- any matters came to his or her attention which occurred in the period from the reporting entity's balance sheet date up to date on which the valuation was completed that would have a material effect on the valuation; or
- he or she had to depart from relevant professional requirements or guidance issued by his or her professional body.

The entity auditors may request the actuary to provide specific confirmation on these points and may enquire as to his or her views on the degree of precision attaching to the valuation and factors giving rise to potential material misstatement. They may also ask the actuary to indicate whether he or she is satisfied that the amounts and disclosures included in the financial statements that relate to retirement benefits adequately reflect the results of his or her work.[14]

If the results of the actuary's work are not consistent with other audit evidence, the entity auditors attempt to resolve the inconsistency by discussions with the entity directors and with the actuary. Applying additional procedures, including requesting the entity directors to obtain evidence from another actuary, may also assist in resolving the inconsistency. 60

Materiality and the valuation of the scheme liabilities

The defined benefit asset (or liability) is based on the surplus (or deficit) of the value of the scheme assets over the value of scheme liabilities. Although the value of the scheme liabilities may sometimes be material to the financial statements, the figure is an estimate and cannot be stated with certainty. Using generally accepted actuarial techniques, there may be a range of acceptable values. In some circumstances, the entity auditors may not be satisfied that the risk of the scheme liabilities being materially misstated has been reduced to an acceptable level. This might occur, for example, if: 61

---

[14] *Actuarial guidance (exposure draft) requires that a clear statement of 'remit, information provided all relevant assumptions, results and analysis are made available to assist the auditor'.*

- events or circumstances give rise to an irreducible inherent uncertainty in the valuation; or
- the entity directors have not established an appropriate process with the necessary resources to enable the reporting entity to comply with FRS 17 with the consequence that the actuary has not, in the time available, been able to perform all the procedures that might be necessary to develop a more precise valuation.

62 Where events or circumstances give rise to an irreducible inherent uncertainty in the valuation, this may represent a fundamental uncertainty. In this case, provided the entity auditors are satisfied that the entity directors have included an adequate description of the fundamental uncertainty in the notes to the financial statements, the entity auditors consider adding an explanatory paragraph referring to the fundamental uncertainty in the section of their report setting out the basis of their opinion (see SAS 600 'The auditors' report on financial statements' (paragraphs 54 to 67)).

63 Where the actuary could, in principle, develop a more precise valuation but has not had sufficient time to do so, this absence of audit evidence may be critical and may represent a limitation in the scope of the audit. This may result in the entity auditors issuing a qualified opinion or a disclaimer of opinion (see SAS 600 'The auditors' report on financial statements' (paragraphs 68 to 73)).

Accounting policies

64 Financial Reporting Standard 18 'Accounting policies' (FRS 18) requires disclosures in the financial statements concerning the accounting policies adopted by the reporting entity, including a description of those estimation techniques adopted that are significant in terms of the range of reasonable monetary amounts. FRS 18 states that this description will include details of those underlying assumptions to which the monetary amount is particularly sensitive.

65 FRS 17 itself specifically requires each of the main financial assumptions used to be disclosed, including:

- the inflation assumption;
- the rate of increase in salaries;
- the rate of increase for pensions in payment and deferred pensions; and
- the rate used to discount liabilities.

22 In many cases, these disclosures will be sufficient to meet any disclosure requirements arising from FRS 18. In some circumstances, however, additional disclosures may be made, for example:

- to provide additional information regarding the estimation techniques used (such as in the case of certain insured schemes (see Appendix 3)); or
- to provide additional contextual information regarding where the estimate falls in relation to the range of reasonable monetary amounts.

The entity auditors carefully consider the adequacy of all such disclosures.

66 Where the entity directors present an Operating and Financial Review (OFR), this may include discussion of the overall performance for the year, including any significant pensions-related gains and losses recognised in the STRGL, and of the principal risks and uncertainties in the business, including any relating to the reporting entity's pension arrangements Thus, for example, in the case of a deficit in

a scheme, the OFR may include the directors' comments on the reasons for the deficit and details of any actions they intend to take. The entity auditors' consideration of the OFR is governed by SAS 160 'Other information in documents containing audited financial statements' (revised).

If the entity auditors have concerns regarding the disclosures in the financial statements or in the OFR, they discuss their views with the directors. If this does not lead to the matter being resolved, the entity auditors may decide to communicate their concerns to those charged with governance, in accordance with SAS 610 (revised) 'Communication of audit matters to those charged with governance' and consider the effect on their audit opinion. 67

Recognition in the balance sheet

FRS 17 requires that a surplus of the value of scheme assets over the value of scheme liabilities be recognised in the reporting entity's balance sheet as an asset; any related deferred tax liability is offset against this asset, rather than included with other deferred tax liabilities. However, the amount that may be recognised as an asset is restricted to the amount of the surplus that can be recovered by the reporting entity, either through reduced contributions or through refunds from the scheme that have been agreed by the scheme trustees. 68

This restriction will typically arise in circumstances where: 69

- the scheme is a closed scheme; or
- there are only a small number of active members.

A deficit in the value of scheme assets below the value of the scheme liabilities is to be recognised as a liability, to the extent that it reflects a legal or constructive obligation; any related deferred tax asset is offset against this liability. If the scheme rules require members' contributions to be increased to help fund a deficit, the present value of the required additional contributions are treated as reducing the deficit to be recognised by the reporting entity.[15] 70

Going concern

In considering going concern, the entity directors take account of all relevant information of which they are aware at the time they approve the financial statements, including events known or expected to occur more than a year beyond the date on which they approve the financial statements. This would include, for example, the fact that a scheme is inadequately funded to a significant extent (or an arrangement is entirely unfunded) and the defined benefit liability to be recognised in the balance sheet may be material. In such circumstances, the entity auditors: 71

- make enquiries into the expected timing of the cash flows likely to arise as result of this liability and into the entity directors' plans for funding these payments, whether from the reporting entity's own resources or otherwise; and
- consider whether the recognition of the defined benefit liability may cause the reporting entity to breach any existing loan covenant, such that the loan creditor might take immediate steps to recover the loan.

[15] *For the purpose of the report required by auditors under section 40, Companies (Amendment) Act, 1983, in the Republic of Ireland, the assets and liabilities recorded in the balance sheet determine whether a financial situation exists. No differentiation is made between pension liabilities and other liabilities.*

In accordance with SAS 130 'The going concern basis in financial statements', the entity auditors assess the adequacy of the means by which the directors have satisfied themselves that the going concern basis and any related disclosures are appropriate.

Recognition in the profit and loss account and the Statement of Total Recognised Gains and Losses (STRGL)

72 The change in the defined benefit asset or liability is required to be analysed into a number of specified components. The nature, timing and extent of the entity auditors' procedures in relation to these components depend on their judgement as to the materiality of the amounts involved and the risk of material misstatement of the financial statements:

(a) charged to operating profit (current service cost, past service cost, gains and losses on settlements and curtailments)
The entity auditors discuss with the entity directors and with the actuary the factors that affect current service cost. For example, it may increase year on year as a percentage of pay if the average age of the workforce is increasing, as is likely where the scheme is closed to new entrants. Benefit improvements may result in higher current service costs and an increased liability for past service relating to current and former employees of the entity.

(b) charged/credited to finance costs/income (expected return on scheme assets, interest on scheme liabilities)
The entity auditors consider whether the interest costs reflect an average of the liabilities at the beginning of the year and movements during the year. They also discuss with the entity directors and with the actuary whether the discount rate reflects the appropriate high quality corporate bond rate at the start of the year and is the same as the rate at which the scheme liabilities were measured at the end of the previous year.

For quoted fixed interest and index-linked securities, the entity auditors compare the expected return with market indices. Where the trustees have significantly changed the risk profile of the investments (switching from equities to corporate bonds, for example), this will be reflected in the expected rate of return calculations. Where the actual return shows a consistent pattern (for example, always less than the expected return) the auditor may wish to discuss with the entity directors and with the actuary whether the equity risk premium (in a scheme with a majority of equities) is being over-estimated in the current year.

(c) recognised in the STRGL (actuarial gains and losses, comprising: actual return less expected return on scheme assets, experience gains and losses arising on scheme liabilities, effects of changes in assumptions underlying scheme liabilities)
The external auditors discuss with the entity directors and with the actuary the underlying reasons for actuarial gains and losses: relevant factors may include employee turnover rates, mortality, early retirements, unexpected changes in salaries or medical costs, and changes in the discount rate.

73 The analysis of the change in the defined benefit asset or liability into these components is usually supplied by the actuary. The entity auditors apply analytical procedures to these figures, for example by comparing them with the corresponding amounts for previous periods and make such enquiries of the entity directors and of the actuary as may be necessary to be satisfied that the figures are consistent with the entity auditors' knowledge of the business of the reporting entity and of the scheme

and that any significant changes can be adequately explained in terms of changes in the scheme.

Expected return on scheme assets and discount rate

The entity auditors pay particular attention to the amounts to be disclosed as the expected return on scheme assets and the rate used to discount the scheme liabilities. These figures are determined by the entity directors' judgement as to the expected rate of return over the long term for each category of scheme assets and the current rate of return on a high quality corporate bond of equivalent currency and term to the scheme liabilities. 74

FRS 17 states that the rate of return expected over the long term will vary according to market conditions, but that it is expected that the amount of the return will be reasonably stable. The expected rate of return is required to be set by the entity directors having taken advice from an actuary. This decision involves a degree of subjectivity and effectively determines the amount of the actual return on scheme assets and interest cost which pass into the profit and loss account and the amounts that are recognised in the STRGL, and can have an important influence on total finance costs in the profit and loss account. Similarly, the entity directors will seek the advice of the actuary when selecting the discount rate. 75

FRS 17 requires disclosure of a 5-year table of the history of amounts recognised in the STRGL: a review of this table may help the entity auditors to identify any systematic bias in the assumptions regarding the expected rate of return. The entity auditors therefore obtain explanations from the entity directors and the actuary to support the expected rate of return for all significant asset categories and consider whether any changes are consistent with, for example, changes in investment strategy. They also discuss the choice of discount rate and seek explanations for any change in the rate from one year to the next. 76

Disclosures

FRS 17 allows that, where a reporting entity has more than one defined benefit scheme, disclosures may be made in total, separately for each scheme or in such groupings as are considered to be most useful. It suggests that useful groupings, for this purpose, may be based on: 77

(a) the geographical location of the schemes; and
(b) whether the schemes are subject to significantly different risks.

FRS 17 allows aggregated disclosure of amounts and assumptions relating to different schemes, although surpluses and deficits must be shown separately. The entity auditors consider whether such aggregation results in: 78

- surpluses and deficits of different schemes being 'netted-off';
- important information about arrangements whose costs are significantly different or more volatile compared with others being 'lost' by the presentation of averaged rates or aggregated values.

The entity auditors consider whether disaggregation is necessary in order for the financial statements to give a true and fair view.

Distributable profits

79 Whether a surplus (or deficit) in a scheme represented by a defined benefit asset (or liability) recognised in the balance sheet in accordance with FRS 17 is a realised profit (or loss) for the purposes of determining the amount of profits available for distribution is an accounting and (in some cases) a legal matter that is beyond the scope of this Practice Note (and beyond the remit of the Auditing Practices Board). FRS 17 suggests that a problem will arise only when the individual financial statements of the reporting entity show a defined benefit liability so large that it reduces realised profits below that needed to cover any intended distribution.[16]

80 SAS 120 'Consideration of law and regulations' requires auditors to obtain sufficient appropriate audit evidence about compliance with those laws and regulations which relate directly to the preparation of, or the inclusion or disclosure of specific items in, the financial statements. Such laws and regulations include those which specify that a distribution cannot be made except out of profits available for the purpose (for example, in the case of a limited company, section 263 of the Companies Act 1985[17]). If the entity auditors become aware that there may not be sufficient realised profits to make a proposed distribution, they normally communicate their concerns to the entity directors and advise them of the potential consequences of making what may be an unlawful distribution. The entity directors and the entity auditors may wish to consult their respective legal advisers. If the entity directors are unable to dispel the entity auditors' concerns and do not modify the proposed distribution, the entity auditors consider the implications of this disagreement for their report on the financial statements. This may result in the entity auditors issuing a qualified or adverse opinion (see SAS 600 'The auditors' report on the financial statements' (paragraphs 74 to 75)).[18]

Management representations

81 SAS 440 'Management representations' requires auditors to obtain written confirmation of representations from management on matters material to the financial statements when those representations are critical to obtaining sufficient appropriate audit evidence. However, management representations cannot be a substitute for other audit evidence that the entity auditors expect to be available. With regard to retirement benefits, the entity auditors obtain the entity directors' written confirmation that, on the basis of the process established by them and having made appropriate enquiries, they are satisfied that the actuarial assumptions underlying the valuation of scheme liabilities are consistent with their knowledge of the business. They may also obtain such confirmation that:

- all significant retirement benefits, including any arrangements that:
  - are statutory, contractual or implicit in the employer's actions;
  - arise in the UK and the Republic of Ireland or overseas;
  - are funded or unfunded;
  - are approved or unapproved

---

[16] *The FRS advises that the entity directors find appropriate solutions with the help of their legal advisers; actuarial advice may also be helpful.*

[17] *The equivalent statutory reference for Northern Ireland is Article 271 of the Companies (Northern Ireland) Order, 1986 and for the Republic of Ireland is section 45 of the Companies (Amendment) Act, 1983.*

[18] *In the case of limited companies in both the United Kingdom and the Republic of Ireland, where the auditors have issued a 'qualified report' on the last financial statements, company legislation states that the company cannot proceed to make a distribution by reference to those financial statements unless the auditors have made a statement in the form specified by the legislation on the company's ability to do so.*

have been identified and properly accounted for; and
- all settlements and curtailments have been identified and properly accounted for.

Public Sector Considerations

The requirements of FRS 17 apply equally to reporting entities in the public sector and the guidance in this Practice Note is intended to apply to the auditors of all such entities. However, there is a wide range of schemes in the public sector, many of which are unfunded; these can give rise to complex accounting issues which require careful consideration.[19]

Appendix 1 – Consideration of retirement benefits in the review of interim reports

The Accounting Standards Board's Statement on Interim Reports (paragraph 27) states that 'it should not usually be necessary to obtain a new actuarial valuation for pension costs, unless a significant event, such as a change in benefits, has rendered the previous estimate misleading. If, however, a more recent actuarial valuation is available at an interim date, this should be used in the interim accounts.'

The Statement, which was published in September 1997 (thus pre-dating FRS 17), is non-mandatory; it is designed to be a guide to best practice. Auditors are often asked by listed companies to review their interim reports and guidance for auditors is given by the Auditing Practices Board in Bulletins 1999/4 and 2001/2.

Where the entity auditors become aware that there has been a significant event affecting the measurement of assets or liabilities in the interim report, they discuss with the entity directors the steps they have taken to review, with the actuary's advice, the impact of that event and how the impact is to be reflected in the interim report.

Appendix 2 – Examples of risks of materials misstatement in relation to FRS 17

The following are examples of how a risk of material misstatement of the financial statements might arise in relation to the requirements of FRS 17. The risks illustrated will not necessarily exist in every case, nor is this intended to be comprehensive listing of all the risks that could exist.

General

The entity directors may not have devoted sufficient resources to establishing a process that will enable the reporting entity to comply with FRS 17.

---

[19] *The Auditing Practices Board is aware that the method of application of FRS 17 to specific types of public sector entity is currently under debate and will consider the need for additional guidance for auditors when the outcome of these discussions is known.*

Completeness of retirement benefit arrangements

The entity directors may not be aware of all schemes and obligations to pay retirement benefits.

Information in respect of overseas schemes may not be well documented or understood by the entity directors.

Subsidiary entities

The requirements of FRS 17 may not be fully understood by the directors of subsidiary entities (or, in the case of overseas subsidiary entities, by their auditors).

Scheme changes

Important changes in schemes (e.g. changes in benefit structures) may not be adequately identified and notified to the actuary.

Consistency

The treatment of scheme assets and liabilities related to bulk transfers and any other settlements or curtailments may be inconsistent (leading to 'cut-off' errors).

Actuarial assumptions

Key assumptions may not be consistent (e.g. the discount rate and the expected return on assets) or may be inappropriate (e.g. benefit improvements).

There may be pressure on the actuary to modify assumptions.

Timetable

The timetable for providing information for scheme asset and liability valuations may not be compatible with the reporting entity's reporting timetable.

Surpluses

The entity directors may not have considered the recoverability of a surplus or may argue that it will be used for future benefit improvements and so should not be accounted for in full.

Deficits

The entity may be in breach of loan covenants when the deficit is taken into account and this may bring the going concern basis into question.

Distributable profits

The entity directors may not have considered the impact of any deficits in the group on distributable profits.

Where an asset is recognised in an individual company, the entity directors may not have considered whether an equivalent amount of reserves can be considered a realised profit available for distribution.

Actuarial updates

There is a risk of imprecise calculations of liabilities in the actuarial update due to changes since the most recent full actuarial valuation.

Source data

There is a risk that the source data used by the actuary (in particular, the membership records) may be inaccurate or incomplete.

Asset values

The scheme trustees may not provide a timely, appropriate report on scheme assets (e.g. investments may not be complete or may not be stated at their fair value).

Multi-employer schemes

In a multi-employer scheme, the assets and liabilities may be capable of allocation to an individual reporting entity within that scheme but this may have not been identified.

Measurement and disclosure

There may be misallocation between the profit and loss account and the STRGL.

Deferred taxation

The entity directors may not have considered how to allocate deferred tax between the profit and loss account and the STRGL.

Appendix 3 – Smaller entities with insured schemes

The guidance in this Practice Note is intended to apply to the auditors of all reporting entities and all types and sizes of defined benefit scheme, although some of the guidance may be more relevant to the auditors of larger reporting entities with significant and complex retirement benefit arrangements. Such entities often have available well-resourced actuaries but are often also subject to tight reporting deadlines (for example, in the case of listed companies).

The circumstances of smaller reporting entities are often quite different. On the one hand, their retirement benefit arrangements are often less complex and they generally enjoy a more relaxed reporting timetable: this may allow more time for the entity and the actuary to perform the work required in order to comply with FRS 17; this also allows the entity auditors more time to obtain the audit evidence they require.

However, in the case of smaller reporting entities, the occupational pension scheme may be administered by an insurance company and the only scheme asset may be an insurance policy (a 'fully insured scheme'); typically, the scheme actuary will be an employee of the insurance company and it is likely that the entity directors will look to the insurance company and its in-house actuary to provide the information required for compliance with FRS 17.

In such circumstances, the entity auditors consider such matters as whether:

- the insurance company will be able to supply the entity directors with values of the scheme assets and liabilities as at the entity balance sheet date, where that differs from the scheme year-end date; and
- it will be appropriate for them to communicate with the insurance company's actuary, as envisaged in this Practice Note;
- the basis to be used by the insurance company to value the insurance policies will represent 'the best approximation to fair value', as envisaged by FRS 17: for this purpose, a surrender value will not suffice unless the trustees have taken the decision to surrender the policy or to wind up the scheme;
- 'earmarked' insurance policies which are excluded from the accounts of the scheme in accordance with statutory exemptions, for example, deferred annuity policies, will have been valued and included in the fair value of scheme assets for the purpose of compliance with FRS 17; and
- evidence will be available to support the basis of valuation of the insurance policy as at the reporting entity balance sheet date.

Where the insurance company cannot provide a valuation of an insurance policy as at the reporting entity balance sheet date, the directors might decide to adjust the most recently obtained valuation for contributions received and benefits paid, with allowance also being made for investment returns. The basis of this technique would need to be clearly disclosed in the notes to the financial statements (see paragraphs 64 to 67).

The fact that the entity auditors were not able to discuss matters with the actuary, does not of itself give rise to a need to qualify the auditors' opinion on the financial statements.

[PN 23]
Auditing derivative financial instruments

(Issued April 2002)

Contents

Introduction	1 - 2
Derivative instruments and activities	3 - 9
Responsibilities of management and those charged with governance	10 - 12
The auditors' responsibility	13 - 17
Knowledge of the business	18 - 22
Key financial risks	23
Assertions to address	24
Risk assessment and internal control	25 - 67
Substantive procedures	68 - 78
Substantive procedures related to assertions	79 - 93
Management representations	94 - 95
Communications with those charged with governance	96
Glossary of Terms	

Introduction

1   The purpose of Practice Note 23 is to provide guidance to auditors in planning and performing auditing procedures for financial statement assertions related to derivative financial instruments[1]. It is based on International Auditing Practice Statement 1012; the main differences being that the Practice Note is written with regard to the financial reporting framework in the United Kingdom and the Republic of Ireland and without reference to International Accounting Standard 39 'Financial Instruments: Recognition and Measurement'. In addition, references to International Standards on Auditing (ISAs) have been replaced with appropriate references to Statements of Auditing Standards (SASs), and there have been some other minor consequential wording changes.

2   The Practice Note focuses primarily on auditing derivatives held by end users, including banks and other financial sector entities when they are the end users. An end user is an entity that enters into a financial transaction, through either an organised exchange or a broker, for the purpose of hedging, asset/liability management or speculating. End users consist primarily of corporations, government entities, institutional investors and financial institutions. An end user's derivative activities often are related to the entity's production or use of a commodity. The accounting systems and internal control issues associated with writing or trading derivatives may be different from those associated with using derivatives.

Derivative instruments and activities

3   Derivative financial instruments are becoming more complex, their use is becoming more commonplace and the accounting requirements to provide information about them in financial statement presentations and disclosures are expanding. Values of derivatives may be volatile. Large and sudden decreases in their value may increase the risk that a loss to an entity using derivatives may exceed the amount, if any, recorded on the balance sheet. Furthermore, because of the complexity of derivative activities, management may not fully understand the risks of using derivatives.

4   For many entities, the use of derivatives has reduced exposures to changes in exchange rates, interest rates and commodity prices, as well as other risks. On the other hand, the inherent characteristics of derivative activities and derivative financial instruments also may result in increased business risk in some entities, in turn increasing audit risk and presenting new challenges to auditors.

5   Financial Reporting Standard (FRS) 13 'Derivatives and Other Financial Instruments: Disclosures' defines a derivative financial instrument as a financial instrument that derives its value from the price or rate of some underlying item[2]. Underlying items include equities, bonds, commodities, interest rates, exchange rates and stock market and other indices. Derivative financial instruments include futures, options, forward contracts, interest rate and currency swaps, interest rate caps, collars and floors, forward interest rate agreements, commitments to purchase shares or bonds, note issuance facilities and letters of credit.

[1] *Practice Note 23 provides guidance on issues related to the audit of derivative financial instruments generally. It does not provide specific guidance on the different types of derivatives that may be encountered in practice.*

[2] *FRS 13 applies to all entities, other than insurance companies, which have one or more of their capital instruments listed or publicly traded on a stock exchange or market, and all banks and similar institutions. The guidance in Practice Note 23 will be of relevance to the audit of any entity that uses derivative financial instruments, not just those entities that are required to comply with FRS 13.*

Derivative financial instruments require no initial net investment or little net investment relative to other types of contracts that have a similar response to changes in market conditions. Derivative contracts are settled at future dates and can be linear or non-linear. They are contracts that either involve obligatory cash flows at a future date (linear) or have option features where one party has the right but not the obligation to demand that another party deliver the underlying item to it (non-linear). The most common linear contracts are forward contracts (for example, foreign exchange contracts and forward rate agreements), futures contracts (for example, a futures contract to purchase a commodity such as oil or power) and swaps. The most common non-linear contracts are options, caps, floors and swaptions. Derivatives that are more complex may have a combination of the characteristics of each category. 6

Derivatives may be used by entities for purposes such as: 7

- managing current or anticipated risks relating to operations and financial position; or
- taking open or speculative positions to benefit from anticipated market movements.

Some entities may be involved in derivatives not only from a corporate treasury perspective but also, or alternatively, in association with the production or use of a commodity.

While all financial instruments have certain risks, derivatives often possess particular features that leverage the risks, such as: 8

- little or no cash outflows/inflows are required until maturity of the transactions;
- no principal balance or other fixed amount is paid or received;
- potential risks and rewards can be substantially greater than the current outlays; and
- the value of an entity's asset or liability may exceed the amount, if any, of the derivative that is recognised in the financial statements, particularly in the UK and the Republic of Ireland, where the financial reporting framework does not currently require derivatives to be recorded at fair value in the financial statements.

The risks that attach to an entity's derivative activities will impact the auditors' assessment of audit risk. Auditors identify whether an entity has derivative activities and, if so, consider factors such as the knowledge and experience of management and those charged with governance in dealing with derivatives, the objectives for the entity's use of derivatives and the complexity of the derivatives. Related risks may be relatively low where derivatives are simple in nature. These factors, and others, are considered further in the sections below addressing 'knowledge of the business' and 'risk assessment and internal control'. 9

Responsibilities of management[3] and those charged with governance[4]

10 Management and those charged with governance are responsible for the preparation and presentation of the financial statements. As part of the process of preparing those financial statements, management and those charged with governance make specific assertions related to derivatives. Those assertions include that all derivatives recorded in the financial statements exist, that there are no unrecorded derivatives at the balance sheet date, that the derivatives recorded in the financial statements are properly valued and presented, and that all relevant disclosures are made in the financial statements.

11 Those charged with governance of an entity, through oversight of management, are responsible for:

- establishing an appropriate control environment, including clear rules on the extent to which those responsible for derivative activities are permitted to participate in the derivative markets[5] (see paragraph 38 below);
- the design and implementation of a system of internal control to:
  - monitor risk and financial control;
  - provide reasonable assurance that the entity's use of derivatives is within its risk management policies; and
  - ensure that the entity is in compliance with applicable laws and regulations; and
- the integrity of the entity's accounting and financial reporting systems to ensure the reliability of management's financial reporting of derivative activities.

12 The audit of the financial statements does not relieve management or those charged with governance of their responsibilities.

The auditors' responsibility

13 SAS 100 'Objective and General Principles Governing an Audit of Financial Statements' states that the objective of the audit is to enable auditors to give an opinion on the financial statements taken as a whole, and thereby to provide reasonable assurance that the financial statements give a true and fair view (where relevant) and have been prepared in accordance with relevant accounting and other requirements. The auditors' responsibility related to derivative financial instruments, in the context of the audit of the financial statements taken as a whole, is to consider whether management's assertions related to derivatives result in financial statements prepared in all material respects in accordance with relevant legislation, regulations and applicable accounting standards. Materiality may be difficult to assess in relation to derivative transactions, particularly given some of their characteristics. Materiality cannot be based on recorded balance sheet values alone, as derivatives may have little impact on the balance sheet even though significant risks may arise from them (see paragraph 71).

---

[3] *In the context of this Practice Note, 'management' includes directors, officers and others who perform senior managerial functions.*

[4] *'Those charged with governance' are those persons entrusted with the supervision, control and direction of an entity. They include the directors of a company or other body, the partners, proprietors, committee of management or trustees of other forms of entity, or equivalent persons responsible for directing the entity's affairs and preparing its financial statements.*

[5] *Such rules should have regard to any legal or regulatory restrictions on using derivatives. For example, UK public sector bodies may not have the power to conduct business using derivative financial instruments.*

Auditors establish an understanding with those charged with governance that the purpose of the audit work is to be able to express an opinion on the financial statements. The purpose of an audit of financial statements is not to provide assurance on the adequacy of the entity's risk management related to derivative activities, or the controls over those activities. To avoid any misunderstanding auditors may discuss with management and those charged with governance the nature and extent of the audit work related to derivative activities. SAS 140 'Engagement Letters' provides guidance on agreeing upon the terms of the engagement.

The need for special skill and knowledge

SAS 100 requires that auditors should comply with the ethical guidance issued by their relevant professional bodies. Among other things, SAS 100 states that the ethical principles which govern auditors' professional responsibilities include professional competence and due care. Also, SAS 240 'Quality Control for Audit Work (Revised)' requires that firms should assign staff with the competencies necessary to perform the work expected of them to individual engagements.

To comply with the requirements of SAS 100 and SAS 240, auditors may need special skills or knowledge to plan and perform auditing procedures for certain assertions about derivatives. Special skills and knowledge include obtaining an understanding of:

- the operating characteristics and risk profile of the industry in which an entity operates;
- the derivative financial instruments used by the entity, and their characteristics;
- the entity's information system for derivatives, including services provided by a service organisation. This may require auditors to have special skills or knowledge about computer applications when significant information about those derivatives is transmitted, processed, maintained or accessed electronically;
- the methods of valuation of the derivative; and
- the requirements of relevant legislation, regulations and applicable accounting standards for financial statement assertions related to derivatives. Derivatives may have complex features that require auditors to have special knowledge to evaluate their measurement, recognition and disclosure. For example, complex pricing structures may increase the complexity of the assumptions used in measuring the value of the instrument.

Where necessary the audit engagement team make use of the assistance of an expert, from within or external to the firm, with the necessary skills or knowledge to help plan and perform the auditing procedures, especially when the derivatives are very complex, or when simple derivatives are used in complex situations, the entity is engaged in active trading of derivatives, or the valuation of the derivatives are based on complex pricing models. SAS 240 provides guidance on the supervision of individuals who serve as members of the engagement team and assist in planning and performing auditing procedures. SAS 520 'Using the Work of an Expert' provides guidance on the use of an expert's work to obtain audit evidence.

Knowledge of the business

SAS 210 'Knowledge of the Business' requires auditors, in performing an audit of financial statements, to have or obtain a knowledge of the business sufficient to

19 enable them to identify and understand the events, transactions and practices that may have a significant effect on the financial statements, or the audit thereof. For example, auditors use such knowledge in assessing inherent and control risks and determining the nature, timing and extent of audit procedures.

19 Because derivative activities generally support the entity's business activities, factors affecting its day-to-day operations also will have implications for its derivative activities. For example, because of the economic conditions that affect the price of an entity's primary raw materials, an entity may enter into a futures contract to hedge the cost of its inventory. Similarly, derivative activities can have a major effect on the entity's operations and viability.

General economic factors

20 General economic factors are likely to have an influence on the nature and extent of an entity's derivative activities. For example, when interest rates appear likely to rise, an entity may try to fix the effective level of interest rates on its floating rate borrowings through the use of interest rate swaps, forward rate agreements or caps. General economic factors that may be relevant include:

- the general level of economic activity;
- interest rates, including the term structure of interest rates, and availability of financing;
- inflation and currency revaluation;
- foreign currency rates and controls; and
- the characteristics of the markets that are relevant to the derivatives used by the entity, including the liquidity or volatility of those markets.

The industry

21 Economic conditions in the entity's industry also are likely to influence the entity's derivative activities. If the industry is seasonal or cyclical, it may be inherently more difficult to accurately forecast interest rate, foreign exchange or liquidity exposures. A high growth rate or sharp rate of decline in an entity's business also may make it difficult to predict activity levels in general and, thus, its level of derivative activity. Economic conditions in a particular industry that may be relevant include:

- the price risk in the industry;
- the market and competition;
- cyclical or seasonal activity;
- declining or expanding operations;
- adverse conditions (for example, declining demand, excess capacity, serious price competition); and
- foreign currency transaction, translation or economic exposure.

The entity

22 To obtain a sufficient understanding of an entity's derivative activities, to be able to identify and understand the events, transactions and practices that, in the auditors' judgment, may have a significant effect on the financial statements or on the examination or auditors' report, auditors consider:

- *Knowledge and experience of management and those charged with governance.* Derivative activities can be complicated and often, only a few individuals within an entity fully understand these activities. In entities that engage in few derivative activities, management may lack experience with even relatively simple derivative transactions. Furthermore, the complexity of various contracts or agreements makes it possible for an entity to inadvertently enter into a derivative transaction particularly where such a derivative is embedded in another contract. Significant use of derivatives, particularly complex derivatives, without relevant expertise within the entity increases inherent risk. This may prompt auditors to question whether there is adequate management control, and may affect the auditors' risk assessment and the nature, extent and timing of audit testing considered necessary;

- *Availability of timely and reliable management information.* The control risk associated with derivative activities may increase with greater decentralisation of those activities. This especially may be true where an entity is based in different locations, some perhaps in other countries. Derivative activities may be run on either a centralised or a decentralised basis. Derivative activities and related decision making depend heavily on the flow of accurate, reliable, and timely management information. The difficulty of collecting and aggregating such information increases with the number of locations and businesses in which an entity is involved;
- *Objectives for the use of derivatives.* Derivative activities range from those whose primary objective is to reduce or eliminate risk (hedging) to those whose primary objective is to maximise profits (speculating). All other things being equal, risk increases as maximising profits becomes the focus of derivative activity. Auditors gain an understanding of the strategy behind the entity's use of derivatives and identify where the entity's derivative activities lie on the hedging-speculating continuum.

Key financial risks

Auditors obtain an understanding of the principal types of financial risk, related to derivative activities, to which entities may be exposed. Those key financial risks include:

(a) *Market risk*, which relates broadly to economic losses due to adverse changes in the value of the derivative. Related risks include:
- Price risk, which relates to changes in the level of prices due to changes in interest rates, foreign exchange rates, or other factors related to market volatilities of the underlying rate, index, or price. Price risk includes interest rate risk and foreign exchange risk;
- Liquidity risk, which relates to changes in the ability to sell or dispose of the derivative instrument. Derivative activities bear the additional risk that a lack of available contracts or counterparties may make it difficult to close out the derivative transaction, or enter into an offsetting contract. For example, liquidity risk may increase if an entity encounters difficulties obtaining the required security or commodity or other deliverable should the derivative call for physical delivery.

Economic losses also may occur if the entity makes inappropriate trades based on information obtained using poor valuation models.

Derivatives used in hedging transactions bear additional risk, known as basis risk. Basis is the difference between the price of the hedged item and the price of the related hedging instrument. Basis risk is the risk that the basis will change while the hedging contract is open, and thus, the price correlation between the hedged item and the hedging instrument will not be perfect. For example, basis risk may be affected by a lack of liquidity in either the hedged item, or the hedging instrument;

(b) *Credit risk*, which relates to the risk that a customer or counterparty will not settle an obligation for full value, either when due or at any time thereafter. For certain derivatives, market values are volatile, so the credit risk exposure also is volatile. Generally, a derivative has credit exposure only when the derivative has positive market value. That value represents an obligation of the counterparty and, therefore, an economic benefit that can be lost if the counterparty fails to fulfil its obligation. Furthermore, the market value of a derivative may fluctuate quickly, alternating between positive and negative values. The potential for rapid changes in prices, coupled with the structure of certain derivatives, also can affect credit risk exposure. For example, highly leveraged derivatives or derivatives with extended time periods can result in credit risk exposure increasing quickly after a derivative transaction has been undertaken.

Many derivatives are traded under uniform rules through an organised exchange (exchange-traded derivatives). Exchange traded derivatives generally remove individual counterparty risk and substitute the clearing organisation as the settling counterparty. Typically, the participants in an exchange-traded derivative settle changes in the value of their positions daily, which further mitigates credit risk. Other methods for minimising credit risk include requiring the counterparty to offer collateral, or assigning a credit limit to each counterparty based on its credit rating.

Settlement risk is the related risk that one side of a transaction will be settled without value being received from the customer or counterparty. One method for minimising settlement risk is to enter into a master netting agreement, which allows the parties to set off all their related payable and receivable positions at settlement;

(c) *Solvency risk*, which relates to the risk that the entity would not have the funds available to honour cash outflow commitments as they fall due. For example, an adverse price movement on a futures contract may result in a margin call that the entity may not have the liquidity to meet;

(d) *Legal risk*, which relates to losses resulting from a legal or regulatory action that invalidates or otherwise precludes performance by the end user or its counterparty under the terms of the contract or related netting arrangements. For example, legal risk could arise from insufficient documentation for the contract, an inability to enforce a netting arrangement in bankruptcy, adverse changes in tax laws, or statutes that prohibit entities from investing in certain types of derivatives.

Assertions to address

24 Financial statement assertions are the representations of management and those charged with governance that are embodied in the financial statements. By approving the financial statements, those charged with governance are making representations about the information therein. These representations or assertions may be described in general terms in number of ways, one of which is as follows:

- *Existence*: An asset or liability exists at a given date. For example, the derivatives recognised in the financial statements through measurement or disclosure exist at the date of the balance sheet;
- *Rights and obligations*: An asset or a liability pertains to the entity at a given date. For example, an entity has the rights and obligations associated with the derivatives reported in the financial statements;
- *Occurrence*: A transaction or event took place that pertains to the entity during the relevant period. For example, the transaction that gave rise to the derivative occurred within the financial reporting period;
- *Completeness*: There are no unrecorded assets, liabilities, transactions or events, or undisclosed items. For example, all of the entity's derivatives are reported in

the financial statements through measurement or disclosure and there are no derivatives 'off balance sheet' that should have been included;
- *Valuation*: An asset or liability is recorded at an appropriate carrying value. For example, the values of the derivatives reported in the financial statements through measurement or disclosure were determined in accordance with relevant legislation, regulations and applicable accounting standards;
- *Measurement*: A transaction or event is recorded at the proper amount and revenue or expense is allocated to the proper period. For example, the amounts associated with the derivatives reported in the financial statements through measurement or disclosure were determined in accordance with relevant legislation, regulations and applicable accounting standards, and the revenues or expenses associated with the derivatives reported in the financial statements were allocated to the correct financial reporting periods; and
- *Presentation and disclosure*: An item is disclosed, classified and described in accordance with relevant legislation, regulations and applicable accounting standards.

Risk assessment and internal control

Audit risk is the risk that auditors may give an inappropriate audit opinion on financial statements. Audit risk has three components: inherent risk, control risk and detection risk. Auditors consider knowledge obtained about the business and about the key financial risks in assessing the components of audit risk. 25

SAS 300 'Accounting and Internal Control Systems and Audit Risk Assessments' provides guidance on the auditors' consideration of audit risk and on the auditors' approach to obtaining an understanding of the accounting and internal control systems. The SAS requires that auditors use professional judgment to assess the components of audit risk and to design audit procedures to ensure that it is reduced to an acceptably low level. It also requires auditors to obtain an understanding of the accounting and internal control systems sufficient to plan the audit and develop an effective audit approach. 26

Inherent risk

Inherent risk is the susceptibility of an account balance or class of transactions to misstatement that could be material, individually or when aggregated with misstatements in other balances or classes, assuming that there were no related internal controls. 27

SAS 300 requires that, in developing their audit approach and detailed procedures, auditors should assess inherent risk in relation to financial statement assertions about material account balances and classes of transactions, taking account of factors relevant both to the entity as a whole and the specific assertions. In the absence of knowledge or information to enable auditors to make an assessment of inherent risk for a specific account balance or class of transactions they assume that inherent risk is high. 28

SAS 300 provides guidance to auditors in using professional judgment to evaluate numerous factors that may affect the assessment of inherent risk. Examples of factors that might affect the auditors' assessment of the inherent risk for assertions about derivatives include: 29

- *Economics and business purpose of the entity's derivative activities.* Auditors understand the nature of the entity's business and the economics and business purpose of its derivative activities, all of which may influence the entity's decision to buy, sell or hold derivatives;

  Derivative activities range from positions where the primary aim is to reduce or eliminate risk (hedging), to positions where the primary aim is to maximise profits (speculating). The inherent risks associated with risk management differ significantly from those associated with speculative investing;
- *The complexity of a derivative's features.* Generally, the more complex a derivative, the more difficult it is to determine its value. The values of certain derivatives, such as exchange-traded options, are available from independent pricing sources such as financial publications and broker-dealers not affiliated with the entity. Determining the value can be particularly difficult, however, if a transaction has been customised to meet individual user needs. When derivatives are not traded regularly, or are traded only in markets without published or quoted market prices, management may use a valuation model to determine value. Valuation risk is the risk that the value of the derivative is determined incorrectly. Model risk, which is a component of valuation risk, exists whenever models (as opposed to cost or quoted market prices) are used to determine the value of a derivative. Model risk is the risk associated with the imperfections and subjectivity of these models and their related assumptions. Both valuation risk and model risk contribute to the inherent risk for the valuation assertion about those derivatives;
- *Whether the transaction giving rise to the derivative involved the exchange of cash.* Many derivatives do not involve an exchange of cash at the inception of the transaction, or may involve contracts that have irregular or end of term cash flows. There is an increased risk that such contracts will not be identified, or will be only partially identified and recorded in the financial statements, increasing the inherent risk for the completeness assertion about those derivatives;
- *An entity's experience with the derivative.* Use of complex derivatives without relevant expertise within the entity increases inherent risk. Relevant expertise should reside with the personnel involved with the entity's derivative activities, including those charged with governance, those committing the entity to the derivative transactions (hereinafter referred to as 'dealers'), those involved with risk control and the accounting and operations personnel responsible for recording and settling the transactions. In addition, management may be more likely to overlook infrequent transactions for relevant accounting and disclosure issues;
- *Whether the derivative is an embedded feature of an agreement.* Management may be less likely to identify embedded derivatives, which increases the inherent risk for the completeness assertion about those derivatives;
- *Whether external factors affect the assertion.* For example, the increase in credit risk associated with entities operating in declining industries increases the inherent risk for the valuation assertion about those derivatives. In addition, significant changes in, or volatility of, interest rates increase the inherent risk for the valuation of derivatives whose value is significantly affected by interest rates;
- *Whether the derivative is traded on national exchanges or across borders.* Derivatives traded in cross-border exchanges may be subject to increased inherent risk because of differing laws and regulations, exchange rate risk, or differing economic conditions. These conditions may contribute to the inherent risk for the rights and obligations assertion or the valuation assertion.

30   Many derivatives have the associated risk that a loss might exceed the amount, if any, of the value of the derivative recognised on the balance sheet (off-balance-sheet risk). For example, a sudden fall in the market price of a commodity may force an entity to realise losses to close a forward position in that commodity. In some cases,

the potential losses may be enough to cast significant doubt on the entity's ability to continue as a going concern. SAS 130 'The Going Concern Basis in Financial Statements' establishes standards and provides guidance on the auditors' responsibility in the audit of financial statements with respect to the going concern assumption used in the preparation of the financial statements. The entity may perform sensitivity analyses or value-at-risk analyses to assess the hypothetical effects on derivative instruments subject to market risks. Auditors may consider these analyses in evaluating management's assessment of the entity's ability to continue as a going concern.

Accounting considerations

An entity's accounting method affects specific audit procedures and is, therefore, significant. A particular accounting issue for consideration is whether the entity adopts hedge accounting techniques and, if so, which hedge accounting techniques it adopts and whether the derivative involved has been designated as a hedge for hedge accounting purposes. 31

When a derivative is designated as a hedge, gains and losses on the derivative will usually be recognised in the profit and loss account in the same accounting period that the gains or losses on the hedged item are recognised. The nature and extent of audit evidence to determine whether management's designation of a derivative as a hedge is appropriate is considered in paragraph 87 below.

It is usually the case that entities adopting hedge accounting techniques require the hedging transaction, and the risks arising on the hedge and the hedged position, to meet certain criteria before hedge accounting can be adopted. It is possible that circumstances will change so that the transaction no longer meets those criteria. For example a derivative may be designated as a hedge of a future transaction (such as the future purchase of a fixed asset in a foreign currency). If that transaction is cancelled, then it will no longer be appropriate to designate the derivative as a hedge. The complexities of the accounting for derivatives increase the inherent risk for the presentation and disclosure assertion about those derivatives. 32

Accounting system considerations

SAS 300 requires that auditors obtain an understanding of the accounting system. To achieve this understanding, auditors obtain knowledge of the design of the accounting system, changes to that system and its operation. The extent of an entity's use of derivatives and the relative complexity of the instruments are important determinants of the necessary level of sophistication of both the entity's information systems (including the accounting system) and control procedures. 33

Certain instruments may require a large number of accounting entries. Although the accounting system used to post derivative transactions likely will need some manual intervention, ideally, the accounting system is able to post such entries accurately with minimal manual intervention. As the sophistication of the derivative activities increases, so should the sophistication of the accounting system. Because this is not always the case, auditors remain alert to the possible need to modify the audit approach if the quality of the accounting system, or aspects of it, appears weak. 34

Control environment

35 The control environment is influenced by the attitude towards corporate governance in an entity and affects the control consciousness of its people. It is the foundation for all other components of internal control, providing discipline and structure. The control environment has a pervasive influence on the way business activities are structured, objectives established and risks assessed.

36 SAS 300 requires auditors to obtain an understanding of the control environment sufficient to determine their audit approach.

37 Auditors consider the overall attitude toward, and awareness of, derivative activities on the part of both management and those charged with governance as a part of obtaining an understanding of the control environment, including any changes to it. It is the role of those charged with governance to determine an appropriate attitude towards the risks. It is management's role to monitor and manage the entity's exposures to those risks. Auditors obtain an understanding of how the control environment for derivatives responds to the risk assessment of management and those charged with governance. To effectively monitor and manage its exposure to risk, an entity implements a structure that:

- is appropriate and consistent with the entity's attitude toward risk as determined by those charged with governance;
- specifies the approval levels for the authorisation of different types of instruments and transactions that may be entered into and for what purposes. The permitted instruments and approval levels should reflect the expertise of those involved in derivative activities;
- sets appropriate limits for the maximum allowable exposure to each type of risk (including approved counterparties). Levels of allowable exposure may vary depending on the type of risk, or counterparty;
- provides for the independent and timely monitoring of the financial risks and control procedures; and
- provides for the independent and timely reporting of exposures, risks and the results of derivative activities in managing risk.

38 Management should establish suitable guidelines to ensure that derivative activities fulfil the entity's needs. In setting suitable guidelines, management should include clear rules on the extent to which those responsible for derivative activities are permitted to participate in the derivative markets. Once this has been done, management can implement suitable systems to manage and control those risks. Three elements of the control environment deserve special mention for their potential effect on controls over derivative activities:

- *Direction from management or those charged with governance.* Management is responsible for providing direction, through clearly stated policies, for the purchase, sale and holding of derivatives. These policies should begin with management clearly stating its objectives with regard to its risk management activities and an analysis of the investment and hedging alternatives available to meet those objectives. Policies and procedures should then be developed that consider the:
  - level of the entity's management expertise;
  - sophistication of the entity's internal control and monitoring systems;
  - entity's asset/liability structure;
  - entity's capacity to maintain liquidity and absorb losses of capital;
  - types of derivative financial instruments that management believes will meet its objectives;

- uses of derivative financial instruments that management believes will meet its objectives, for example, whether derivatives may be used for speculative purposes or only for hedging purposes.
An entity's policies for the purchase, sale and holding of derivatives should be appropriate and consistent with its attitude toward risk and the expertise of those involved in derivative activities.
- *Segregation of duties and the assignment of personnel.* Derivative activities may be categorised into three functions:
  - committing the entity to the transaction (dealing);
  - initiating cash payments and accepting cash receipts (settlements); and
  - recording of all transactions correctly in the accounting records, including the valuation of derivatives.

Segregation of duties should exist among these three functions. Where an entity is too small to achieve proper segregation of duties, management should take a more active role to monitor derivative activities.

Some entities have established a fourth function, *Risk Control,* which is responsible for reporting on and monitoring derivative activities. Examples of key responsibilities in this area may include:
  - setting and monitoring risk management policy (including analyses of the risks to which an entity may be exposed);
  - designing risk limit structures;
  - developing disaster scenarios and subjecting open position portfolios to sensitivity analysis, including reviews of unusual movements in positions; and
  - reviewing and analysing new derivative instrument products.

In entities that have not established a separate risk control function, reporting on and monitoring derivative activities may be a component of the accounting function's responsibility or management's overall responsibility.

- *Whether or not the general control environment has been extended to those responsible for derivative activities.* An entity may have a control culture that is generally focused on maintaining a high level of internal control. Because of the complexity of some treasury or derivative activities, this culture may not pervade the group responsible for derivative activities. Alternatively, because of the risks associated with derivative activities, management may enforce a more strict control environment than it does elsewhere within the entity. In groups without a treasury function, dealing in complex derivatives may be rare and management's knowledge and experience limited.

Some entities may operate an incentive compensation system for those involved in derivative transactions. In such situations, auditors consider the extent to which proper guidelines, limits and controls have been established to ascertain if the operation of that system could result in transactions that are inconsistent with the overall objectives of the entity's risk management strategy. **39**

When an entity uses electronic commerce for derivative transactions, it should address the security and control considerations relevant to the use of an electronic network. **40**

Control objectives and procedures

Internal controls over derivative transactions should prevent or detect problems that hinder an entity from achieving its objectives. These objectives may be either operational, financial reporting, or compliance in nature, and internal control is necessary to prevent or detect problems in each area. **41**

42   SAS 300 requires auditors to obtain an understanding of the internal control systems sufficient to plan the audit and develop an effective audit approach. Effective control procedures over derivatives generally will include adequate segregation of duties, risk management monitoring, management oversight, and other policies and procedures designed to ensure that the entity's control objectives are met. Those control objectives include:

- *Authorised execution.* Derivative transactions are executed in accordance with the entity's approved policies.
- *Complete and accurate information.* Information relating to derivatives, including valuation information, is recorded on a timely basis, is complete and accurate when entered into the accounting system, and has been properly classified, described and disclosed.
- *Prevention or detection of errors.* Misstatements in the processing of accounting information for derivatives are prevented or detected in a timely manner.
- *On-going monitoring.* Activities involving derivatives are monitored on an on-going basis to recognise and measure events affecting related financial statement assertions.
- *Valuation.* Changes in the value of derivatives are appropriately accounted for and disclosed to the right people from both an operational and a control viewpoint. Valuation may be a part of on-going monitoring activities.

In addition, internal controls should assure that those derivatives accounted for using hedge accounting meet criteria to justify hedge accounting, both at the inception of the hedge, and on an ongoing basis.

43   As it relates to the purchase, sale and holding of derivatives, the level of sophistication of an entity's internal control will vary according to:

- the complexity of the derivative and the related inherent risk - more complex derivative activities will require more sophisticated systems;
- the risk exposure of derivative transactions in relation to the capital employed by the entity; and
- the volume of transactions - entities that do not have a significant volume of derivative transactions will require less sophisticated accounting systems and internal control.

44   As the sophistication of derivative activity increases, so should internal control. In some instances, an entity may expand the types of financial activities it enters into without making corresponding adjustments to its internal control.

45   In larger entities, sophisticated computer information systems generally keep track of derivative activities, and to ensure that settlements occur when due. More complex computer systems may generate automatic postings to clearing accounts to monitor cash movements. Proper controls over processing will help to ensure that derivative activities are correctly reflected in the entity's records. Computer systems may be designed to produce exception reports to alert management to situations where derivatives have not been used within authorised limits or where transactions undertaken were not within the limits established for the chosen counterparties. However, even a sophisticated computer system may not ensure the completeness of derivative transactions.

46   Derivatives, by their very nature, can involve the transfer of sizable amounts of money both to and from the entity. Often, these transfers take place at maturity. In many instances, a bank is only provided with appropriate payment instructions or receipt notifications. Some entities may use electronic fund transfer systems. Such systems may involve complex password and verification controls, standard payment

templates and cash pooling/sweeping facilities. Auditors gain an understanding of the methods used to transfer funds, along with their strengths and weaknesses, as this will affect the risks the business is faced with and accordingly, the audit risk assessment.

Regular reconciliations are an important aspect of controlling derivative activities. Formal reconciliations should be performed on a regular, timely, basis to ensure that the financial records are properly controlled, all entries are promptly made and the dealers have adequate and accurate position information before formally committing the entity to a legally binding transaction. Reconciliations should be properly documented and independently reviewed. The following are some of the more significant types of reconciliation procedures associated with derivative activities: 47

- reconciliation of dealers' records to records used for the ongoing monitoring process and the position or profit and loss shown in the general ledger;
- reconciliation of subsidiary ledgers, including those maintained on computerised data bases, to the general ledger;
- reconciliation of all clearing and bank accounts and broker statements to ensure all outstanding items are promptly identified and cleared; and
- reconciliation of the entity's accounting records to records maintained by service organisations, where applicable.

An entity's deal initiation records should clearly identify the nature and purpose of individual transactions, and the rights and obligations arising under each derivative contract. In addition to the basic financial information, such as a notional amount, these records should include: 48

- the identity of the dealer;
- the identity of the person recording the transaction, if that person is not the dealer;
- the date and time of the transaction;
- the nature and purpose of the transaction, including whether or not it is intended to hedge an underlying commercial exposure; and
- information on compliance with accounting requirements related to hedging, such as:
  - designation as a hedge; and
  - identification of the hedged item in a hedging relationship.

Transaction records for derivatives may be maintained in a database, register or subsidiary ledger, which are then checked for accuracy with independent confirmations received from the counterparties to the transactions. Often, the transaction records will be used to provide accounting information, including information for disclosures in the financial statements, together with other information to manage risk, such as exposure reports against policy limits. Therefore, it is essential to have appropriate controls over input, processing and maintenance of the transaction records, whether they are in a database, a register or a subsidiary ledger. 49

The main control over the completeness of the derivative transaction records is the independent matching of counterparty confirmations against the entity's own records. Counterparties should be asked to send the confirmations back directly to employees of the entity that are independent from the dealers, to guard against dealers suppressing confirmations and 'hiding' transactions, and all details should be checked off against the entity's records. Employees independent of the dealer should resolve any exceptions contained in the confirmations, and fully investigate any confirmation that is not received. Dealers should only be allowed to deal with approved counterparties. 50

The role of internal audit

51 As part of the assessment of internal control, auditors consider the role of any internal audit. The knowledge and skills required to understand and audit an entity's use of derivatives are generally quite different from those needed in auditing other parts of the business. The external auditors consider the extent to which any internal audit function has the knowledge and skill to cover, and has in fact covered, the entity's derivatives activities.

52 In many entities, internal audit forms an essential part of the risk control function that enables senior management to review and evaluate the control procedures covering the use of derivatives. The work performed by internal audit may assist the external auditors in understanding the accounting systems and internal controls and therefore assessing control risk. Areas where the work performed by internal audit may be particularly relevant are:

- developing a general overview of the extent of derivative use;
- reviewing the appropriateness of policies and procedures and management's compliance with them;
- reviewing the effectiveness of control procedures;
- reviewing the accounting systems used to process derivative transactions;
- reviewing systems relevant to derivative activities;
- ensuring that objectives for derivative management are fully understood across the entity, particularly where there are operating divisions where the risk exposures are most likely to arise;
- assessing whether new risks relating to derivatives, are being identified, assessed and managed;
- evaluating whether the accounting for derivatives is in accordance with relevant legislation, regulations and applicable accounting standards and, if applicable, whether derivatives accounted for using hedge accounting meet criteria to justify hedge accounting; and
- conducting regular reviews to:
  - provide management with assurance that derivative activities are being properly controlled; and
  - ensure that new risks and the use of derivatives to manage these risks are being identified, assessed and managed.

53 Certain aspects of internal audit may be useful in determining the nature, timing and extent of external audit procedures. When it appears that this might be the case, the external auditors, during the course of planning the audit, obtain a sufficient understanding of internal audit activities and perform an assessment of the internal audit function. When the external auditors intend to use specific internal audit work, the external auditors evaluate that work to confirm its adequacy for the external auditors' purposes. SAS 500 'Considering the Work of Internal Audit' applies to external auditors in considering the work of internal audit.

Service organisations

54 Entities may use service organisations to initiate the purchase or sale of derivatives or maintain records of derivative transactions for the entity.

55 The use of service organisations may strengthen controls over derivatives. For example, a service organisation's personnel may have more experience with derivatives than the entity's management. The use of the service organisation also may allow for greater segregation of duties. On the other hand, the use of a service

organisation may increase risk because it may have a different control culture or process transactions at some distance from the entity.

SAS 480 "Service Organisations" establishes standards and provides guidance to auditors when the entity being audited uses a service organisation. SAS 480 requires auditors to determine whether activities undertaken by service organisations are relevant to the audit and determine the effect of relevant activities on their assessment of inherent risk and the user entity's control environment. SAS 480 provides further guidance in auditing entities using service organisations. When applying SAS 480 to a service organisation engaged in derivative transactions, auditors consider how a service organisation affects the entity's accounting and internal control systems. 56

Because service organisations often act as investment advisors, the auditor may consider risks associated with service organisations when acting as investment advisors, including: 57

- how their services are monitored;
- the procedures in place to protect the integrity and confidentiality of the information;
- contingency arrangements; and
- any related party issues that may arise because the service organisation can enter into its own derivative transactions with the entity while, at the same time, being a related party.

Control risk

Control risk is the risk that a misstatement that could occur in an account balance or class of transaction and that could be material, either individually or when aggregated with misstatements in other balances or classes, would not be prevented or detected and corrected on a timely basis, by the accounting and internal control systems. 58

SAS 300 requires that if auditors, after obtaining an understanding of the accounting system and control environment, expect to be able to rely on their assessment of control risk to reduce the extent of their substantive procedures, they should make a preliminary assessment of control risk for material financial statement assertions, and should plan and perform tests of control to support that assessment. SAS 300 states that if, as a result of their work on the accounting system and control environment, auditors decide it is likely to be inefficient or impossible to rely on any assessment of control risk to reduce their substantive procedures, no such assessment is necessary and control risk is assumed to be high. 59

When developing the audit approach, auditors consider the preliminary assessment of control risk (in conjunction with the assessment of inherent risk) to determine the nature, timing and extent of substantive procedures for the financial statement assertions. 60

Examples of considerations that might affect the auditors' assessment of control risk include: 61

- whether policies and procedures that govern derivative activities reflect management's objectives;
- how management informs its personnel of controls;
- how management captures information about derivatives; and

- how management assures itself that controls over derivatives are operating as designed.

62 SAS 300 requires that having undertaken tests of control, auditors should evaluate whether the preliminary assessment of control risk is supported. SAS 300 states that misstatements discovered in conducting substantive procedures may cause auditors to modify the previous assessment of control risk.

63 The assessment of control risk depends on the auditors' judgment as to the quality of the control environment and the control procedures in place. In reaching a decision on the nature, timing and extent of testing of controls, auditors consider factors such as:

- the importance of the derivative activities to the entity;
- the nature, frequency and volume of derivatives transactions;
- the potential effect of any identified weaknesses in control procedures;
- the types of controls being tested;
- the frequency of performance of these controls; and
- the evidence of performance.

Tests of controls

64 Where the assessment of control risk is less than high, auditors perform tests of controls to obtain evidence as to whether or not the preliminary assessment of control risk is supported. Notwithstanding the auditors' assessment of control risk, it may be that the entity undertakes only a limited number of derivative transactions, or that the magnitude of these instruments is especially significant to the entity as a whole. In such instances, a substantive approach, sometimes in combination with tests of control, may be more appropriate.

65 The population from which items are selected for detailed testing is not limited to the accounting records. Tested items may be drawn from other sources, for example counterparty confirmations and trader tickets, so that the possibility of overlooking transactions in the recording procedure can be tested.

66 Tests of controls are performed to obtain audit evidence about the effectiveness of the:
   (a) design of the accounting and internal control systems, that is, whether they are suitably designed to prevent or detect and correct material misstatements and
   (b) operation of the internal controls throughout the period. Key procedures may include evaluating, for a suitably sized sample of transactions, whether:
   - derivatives have been used in accordance with the agreed policies, guidelines and within authority limits;
   - appropriate decision-making processes have been applied and the reasons behind entering into selected transactions are clearly understandable;
   - the transactions undertaken were within the policies for derivative transactions, including terms and limits and transactions with foreign or related parties;
   - the transactions were undertaken with counterparties with appropriate credit risk;
   - derivatives are subject to appropriate timely measurement, and reporting of risk exposure, independent of the dealer;
   - counterparty confirmations have been sent;
   - incoming confirmations from counterparties have been properly matched and reconciled;

- early termination and extension of derivatives are subject to the same controls as new derivative transactions;
- designations, including any subsequent changes in designations, as hedging or speculative transactions, are properly authorised;
- transactions have been properly recorded and are entered completely and accurately in the accounting records, and correctly processed in any subsidiary ledger through to the financial statements; and
- adequate security has been maintained over passwords necessary for electronic fund transfers.

Examples of tests of controls to consider include: 67

- Reading minutes of meetings of those charged with governance of the entity (or, where the entity has established one, the Asset/Liability Risk Management Committee or Treasury Committee or similar group) for evidence of that body's periodic review of derivative activities, adherence to established policies, and periodic review of hedging effectiveness;
- Comparing derivative transactions, including those that have been settled to the entity's policies to determine whether the entity is following those policies. For example, auditors might:
  - test that transactions have been executed in accordance with authorisations specified in the entity's policy;
  - test that any pre-acquisition sensitivity analysis dictated by the investment policy is being performed;
  - test transactions to determine whether the entity obtained required approvals for the transactions and used only authorised brokers or counterparties;
  - inquire of management about whether derivatives and related transactions are being monitored and reported upon on a timely basis and read any supporting documentation;
  - test recorded purchases of derivatives, including their classification and prices, and the entries used to record related amounts;
  - test the reconciliation process. Auditors might test whether reconciling differences are investigated and resolved on a timely basis, and whether the reconciliations are reviewed and approved by supervisory personnel. For example, organisations that have a large number of derivative transactions may require reconciliation and review on a daily basis;
  - test the controls for unrecorded transactions. Auditors might examine the entity's third-party confirmations and the resolution of any exceptions contained in the confirmations;
  - test the controls over the adequate security and back-up of data to ensure adequate recovery in case of disaster. In addition, auditors may consider the procedures the entity adopts for annual testing and maintenance of the computerised records site.

Substantive procedures

SAS 300 requires auditors to consider the assessed levels of inherent and control risk in determining the nature, timing and extent of substantive procedures required to reduce audit risk to an acceptably low level. The higher the assessment of inherent and control risk, the more audit evidence auditors obtain from the performance of substantive procedures. 68

The assessed levels of inherent and control risk cannot be sufficiently low to eliminate the need for auditors to perform any substantive procedures. SAS 300 requires 69 that regardless of the assessed levels of inherent and control risks, auditors should perform some substantive procedures for financial statement assertions of material account balances and transaction classes. Nevertheless, auditors may not be able to obtain sufficient appropriate audit evidence to reduce detection risk, and therefore reduce audit risk to an acceptably low level by performing substantive tests alone. SAS 300 states that when auditors determine that detection risk regarding a material financial statement assertion cannot be reduced to an acceptably low level, they consider the implications for their report. Furthermore, SAS 610 (Revised) 'Communication of Audit Matters to Those Charged with Governance' requires auditors to communicate to those charged with governance material weaknesses in the accounting and internal control systems identified during the audit. Such communications should be on a sufficiently prompt basis to enable those charged with governance to take appropriate action.

Materiality

70 SAS 220 'Materiality and the Audit' states that auditors consider materiality at both the overall financial statement level and in relation to individual account balances, classes of transactions and disclosures. The auditors' judgment may include assessments of what constitutes materiality for significant captions in the balance sheet, income statement, and statement of cash flows both individually, and for the financial statements as a whole.

71 SAS 220 requires auditors to consider materiality when determining the nature, timing and extent of audit procedures. While planning the audit, materiality may be difficult to assess in relation to derivative transactions, particularly given some of their characteristics. Judgment will also be needed in considering materiality when evaluating audit evidence (see paragraph 78). Materiality cannot be based on recorded balance sheet values alone, as derivatives may have little effect on the balance sheet, even though significant risks may arise from them. Materiality is considered at both the overall financial statement level and in relation to individual account balances, classes of transactions and disclosures. A highly leveraged, or a more complex, derivative may be more likely to have a significant effect on the financial statements than a less highly leveraged or simpler derivative might. Greater potential for effect on the financial statements also exists when the exposure limits for entering into derivative transactions are high.

Types of substantive procedures

72 Substantive audit procedures are performed to obtain audit evidence to detect material misstatements in the financial statements, and are generally of two types:

(a) analytical procedures; and
(b) other substantive procedures, such as tests of details of transactions and balances, review of minutes of directors' meetings and enquiry.

73 In designing substantive tests, auditors consider:

- *Appropriateness of accounting.* A primary audit objective often addressed through substantive procedures is determining the appropriateness of an entity's accounting for derivatives;
- *Involvement of an outside organisation.* When planning the substantive procedures for derivatives, auditors consider whether another organisation holds, services or both holds and services the entity's derivatives;
- *Interim audit procedures.* When performing substantive procedures before the balance sheet date, auditors consider market movement in the period between

the interim testing date and year-end. The value of some derivatives can fluctuate greatly in a relatively short period. As the amount, relative significance, or composition of an account balance becomes less predictable, the value of testing at an interim date becomes less valuable;

- *Routine vs. non-routine transactions.* Many financial transactions are negotiated contracts between an entity and its counterparty. To the extent that derivative transactions are not routine and outside an entity's normal activities, a substantive audit approach may be the most effective means of achieving the planned audit objectives. In instances where derivative transactions are not undertaken routinely, auditors plan and perform their procedures having regard to the entity's possible lack of experience in this area;
- *Procedures performed in other audit areas.* Procedures performed in other financial statement areas may provide evidence about the completeness of derivative transactions. These procedures may include tests of subsequent cash receipts and payments, and the search for unrecorded liabilities.

Analytical procedures

SAS 410 'Analytical Procedures' requires auditors to apply analytical procedures at the planning and overall review stages of the audit. Analytical procedures also may be applied at other stages of the audit. Analytical procedures as a substantive procedure in the audit of derivative activities may give information about an entity's business but, by themselves, are generally unlikely to provide sufficient evidence with respect to assertions related to derivatives. The complex interplay of the factors from which the values of these instruments are derived often masks any unusual trends that might arise. 74

Some personnel responsible for derivative activities compile detailed analytical reviews of the results of all derivatives activity. They are able to capture the effect of derivatives trading volumes and market price movements on the financial results of the entity and compile such an analysis because of their detailed day-to-day involvement in the activities. Similarly, some entities may use analytical techniques in their reporting and monitoring activities. Where such analysis is available, auditors may use it to further understand the entity's derivative activity. In doing so, auditors seek satisfaction that the information is reliable and has been correctly extracted from the underlying accounting records by persons sufficiently objective to be confident that the information fairly reflects the entity's operations. When appropriate, auditors may use computer software for facilitating analytical procedures. 75

Analytical procedures may be useful in evaluating certain risk management policies over derivatives, for example, credit limits. Analytical procedures also may be useful in evaluating the effectiveness of hedging activities. For example, if an entity uses derivatives in a hedging strategy, and large gains or losses are noted as a result of analytical procedures, the effectiveness of the hedge may become questionable and accounting for the transaction as a hedge may not be appropriate. However, if analytical procedures are to be used in this way it is important that auditors have a clear understanding of the objectives of management for the use of derivatives. 76

Where no such analysis is compiled and auditors want to do one, the effectiveness of the analytical review often depends upon the degree to which management can provide detailed and disaggregated information about the activities undertaken. Where such information is available, auditors may be able to undertake a useful analytical review. If the information is not available, analytical procedures will be effective only as a means of identifying financial trends and relationships in simple, low volume, environments. This is because, as volume and complexity of operations 77 increase, unless detailed information is available, the factors affecting revenues and costs are such that meaningful analysis by auditors often proves difficult, and the value of analytical procedures as an audit tool decreases. In such situations, analytical procedures are not likely to identify inappropriate accounting treatments.

Evaluating audit evidence

78   Evaluating audit evidence for assertions about derivatives requires considerable judgment because the assertions, especially those about valuation, are based on highly subjective assumptions or are particularly sensitive to changes in the underlying assumptions. For example, valuation assertions may be based on assumptions about the occurrence of future events for which expectations are difficult to develop or about conditions expected to exist a long time. Accordingly, competent persons could reach different conclusions about valuation estimates or estimates of valuation ranges. Considerable judgment also may be required in evaluating audit evidence for assertions based on features of the derivative and applicable accounting principles, including underlying criteria, that are both extremely complex. SAS 420 'Audit of Accounting Estimates' provides guidance to auditors on obtaining and evaluating sufficient audit evidence to support significant accounting estimates contained in financial statements. SAS 520 provides guidance on the use of the work of an expert in performing substantive tests.

Substantive procedures related to assertions

Existence and occurrence

79   Substantive tests for existence and occurrence assertions about derivatives may include:

- confirmation with the holder of or the counterparty to the derivative;
- inspecting the underlying agreements and other forms of supporting documentation, including confirmations received by an entity, in paper or electronic form, for amounts reported;
- inspecting supporting documentation for subsequent realisation or settlement after the end of the reporting period; and
- inquiry and observation.

Rights and obligations

80   Substantive tests for rights and obligations assertions about derivatives may include:

- confirming significant terms with the holder of, or counterparty to, the derivative; and
- inspecting underlying agreements and other forms of supporting documentation, in paper or electronic form.

Completeness

81   Substantive tests for completeness assertions about derivatives may include:

- asking the holder of or counterparty to the derivative to provide details of all derivatives and transactions with the entity. In sending confirmations requests, auditors determine which part of the counterparty's organisation is responding,

- and whether the respondent is responding on behalf of all aspects of its operations;
- sending zero-balance confirmations to potential holders or counterparties to derivatives to test the completeness of derivatives recorded in the financial records;
- reviewing brokers' statements for the existence of derivative transactions and positions held;
- reviewing counterparty confirmations received but not matched to transaction records;
- reviewing unresolved reconciliation items;
- inspecting agreements, such as loan or equity agreements or sales contracts, for embedded derivatives;
- inspecting documentation for activity subsequent to the end of the reporting period; and
- reading other information, such as minutes of those charged with governance, and related papers and reports on derivative activities received by the governance body.

Valuation and Measurement

Tests of valuation assertions are designed according to the valuation method used for the measurement or disclosure. Substantive procedures to obtain evidence about the valuation of derivative financial instruments may include: 82

- inspecting documentation of the purchase price;
- confirming with the holder of or counterparty to the derivative;
- reviewing the creditworthiness of counterparties to the derivative transaction; and
- obtaining evidence corroborating the valuation of derivatives measured or disclosed.

Auditors obtain evidence corroborating the valuation of derivatives measured or disclosed. The method for determining value may vary depending on factors such as the consideration of price quotations from inactive markets and significant liquidity discounts, control premiums, and commissions and other costs that would be incurred when disposing of a derivative. The method for determining value also may vary depending on the type of asset or liability. SAS 420 provides guidance on the audit of accounting estimates contained in financial statements. 83

Quoted market prices for certain derivatives that are listed on exchanges or over-the-counter markets are available from sources such as financial publications, the exchanges or pricing services based on sources such as these. Quoted market prices for other derivatives may be obtained from broker-dealers who are market makers in those instruments. If quoted market prices are not available for a derivative, valuation estimates may be obtained from third-party sources based on proprietary models or from an entity's internally developed or acquired models. If information about the value is provided by a counterparty to the derivative, auditors consider whether such information is objective. In some instances, it may be necessary to obtain valuation estimates from additional independent sources. 84

Quoted market prices obtained from publications or from exchanges are generally considered to provide sufficient evidence of the value of derivative financial instruments. Nevertheless, using a price quote to test valuation assertions may require a special understanding of the circumstances in which the quote was developed. For example, quotations provided by the counterparty to an option to enter into a derivative financial instrument may not be based on recent trades and may be only 85

an indication of interest. In some situations, auditors may determine that it is necessary to obtain valuation estimates from broker-dealers or other third-party sources. Auditors also may determine that it is necessary to obtain estimates from more than one pricing source. This may be appropriate if the pricing source has a relationship with an entity that might impair its objectivity.

86   It is management's responsibility to estimate the value of the derivative instrument. If an entity values the derivative using a valuation model, the auditors' judgment is not substituted for that of the entity's management. Auditors may test assertions about the valuation determined using a model by procedures such as:

- assessing the reasonableness and appropriateness of the model. Auditors determine whether the market variables and assumptions used are reasonable and appropriately supported. Furthermore, auditors assess whether market variables and assumptions are used consistently, and whether new conditions justify a change in the market variables or assumptions used. The evaluation of the appropriateness of valuation models and each of the variables and assumptions used in the models may require considerable judgment and knowledge of valuation techniques, market factors that affect value, and market conditions, particularly in relation to similar financial instruments. Accordingly, auditors may consider it necessary to involve a specialist in assessing the model;
- calculating the value, for example, using a model developed by the auditors or by a specialist engaged by the auditors. The re-performance of valuations using the auditors own models and data enables auditors to develop an independent expectation to use in corroborating the reasonableness of the value calculated by the entity;
- comparing the valuation with recent transactions;
- considering the sensitivity of the valuation to changes in the variables and assumptions, including market conditions that may affect the value; and
- inspecting supporting documentation for subsequent realisation or settlement of the derivative transaction after the end of the reporting period to obtain further evidence about its valuation at the balance sheet date.

87   Where hedge accounting techniques are used, auditors gather audit evidence to determine whether management's designation of a derivative as a hedge is appropriate. The nature and extent of the evidence obtained by auditors will vary depending on the nature of the hedged items and the hedging instruments. Generally, auditors obtain evidence as to:

(a) whether the derivative was designated as a hedge at the inception of the transaction;
(b) the nature of the hedging relationship;
(c) the entity's risk management objective and strategy for undertaking the hedge;
(d) the entity's assessment of the effectiveness of the hedge; and
(e) where the derivative is hedging a future transaction, the entity's assessment of the certainty of that future transaction.

If sufficient audit evidence to support management's use of hedge accounting is not available, the auditors may have a scope limitation.

Presentation and disclosure

88   Management is responsible for preparing and presenting the financial statements in accordance with relevant legislation, regulations and applicable accounting standards, including fairly and completely presenting and disclosing the results of derivative transactions and relevant accounting policies.

89 Auditors assess whether the presentation and disclosure of derivatives is in conformity with relevant legislation, regulations and applicable accounting standards. The auditors' conclusion as to whether derivatives are presented in conformity with relevant legislation, regulations and applicable accounting standards is based on the auditors' judgment as to whether:
- the accounting principles selected and applied are in conformity with relevant legislation, regulations and applicable accounting standards;
- the accounting principles are appropriate in the circumstances;
- the financial statements, including the related notes, provide information on matters that may affect their use, understanding, and interpretation;
- disclosure is adequate to ensure that the entity is in full compliance with the current disclosure requirements of relevant legislation, regulations and applicable accounting standards (in particular FRS 13) under which the financial statements are being reported;
- the information presented in the financial statements is classified and summarised in an appropriate and meaningful manner; and
- the financial statements reflect the underlying transactions and events in a manner that presents the financial position, results of operations, and cash flows within a range of acceptable limits, that is, limits that are reasonable and practicable to attain in financial statements.

90 To comply with FRS 13, narrative disclosures must be provided concerning the role that financial instruments have had during the period in creating or changing the risks that an entity faces in its activities. Such disclosures should include an explanation of the objectives and policies for holding or issuing derivatives and the strategies for achieving those objectives that have been followed during the period.

91 As described in paragraph 22 of this Practice Note, in order to obtain a sufficient understanding of an entity's derivative activities, auditors consider management's objectives for the use of derivatives including gaining an understanding of the strategy behind the entity's use of derivatives. Auditors assess whether the disclosures made by management concerning objectives, policies and strategies in relation to derivatives are properly stated in accordance with the requirements of FRS 13, where applicable, and are consistent with their knowledge of the business and audit evidence obtained. As part of their tests of controls, auditors may include evaluating, for a suitably sized sample of transactions, whether derivatives have been used in accordance with the entity's policies and guidelines.

92 FRS 13, where applicable, also requires disclosure of the fair values of certain derivatives. Paragraphs 82 to 87 of this Practice Note provide guidance on auditing the valuation of derivatives.

93 Entities complying with FRS 13 are also encouraged, but not required, by the FRS to provide numerical disclosures that show the magnitude of market price risk arising over the period for all financial instruments including derivatives. Where an entity chooses to provide such information, auditors refer to paragraphs 101 to 115 of Practice Note 19 'Banks in the United Kingdom' which provides guidance on auditing such information on market risk.

Management representations

94 SAS 440 'Management Representations' requires auditors to obtain written confirmation of representations from management on matters material to the financial statements when those representations are critical to obtaining sufficient appropriate

audit evidence. Depending on the volume and complexity of derivative activities, management representations about derivative financial instruments may include representations about:

- management's objectives with respect to derivative financial instruments, for example, whether derivatives are used for hedging or speculative purposes;
- the financial statement disclosures required by FRS 13 concerning derivative financial instruments, for example:
  - the records reflect all derivative transactions;
  - all embedded derivative instruments have been identified;
  - the assumptions and methodologies used in the derivative valuation models are reasonable;
- whether all transactions have been conducted at arm's length and at market value;
- the terms of derivative transactions;
- whether there are any side agreements associated with any derivative instruments; and
- whether the entity has entered into any written options.

95 Sometimes, with respect to certain aspects of derivatives, management representations may be the only audit evidence that reasonably can be expected to be available; however, SAS 440 states that representations from management cannot be a substitute for other audit evidence that auditors expect to be available. If the audit evidence auditors expect to be available cannot be obtained, this may constitute a limitation on the scope of the audit and the auditors consider the implications for the auditors' report.

Communications with those charged with governance

96 As a result of obtaining an understanding of an entity's accounting and internal control systems and, if applicable, tests of controls, auditors may become aware of matters to be communicated to those charged with governance. SAS 610 (Revised) requires auditors to communicate to those charged with governance, on a sufficiently prompt basis to enable them to take appropriate action, material weaknesses in the accounting and internal control systems identified during the audit. With respect to derivatives, those matters may include:

- material weaknesses in the design or operation of the accounting and internal control systems;
- a lack of management understanding of the nature or extent of the derivative activities or the risks associated with such activities;
- a lack of comprehensive and clearly stated policies for the purchase, sale and holding of derivatives, including operational controls, procedures for designating derivatives as hedges, and monitoring exposures; or
- a lack of segregation of duties.

Glossary of terms

Asset/Liability Management – A planning and control process, the key concept of which is matching the mix and maturities of assets and liabilities.

Basis – The difference between the price of the hedged item and the price of the related hedging instrument.

Basis Risk – The risk that the basis will change while the hedging contract is open and, thus, the price correlation between the hedged item and hedging instrument will not be perfect.

Cap – A series of call options based on a notional amount. The strike price of these options defines an upper limit to interest rates.

Close Out – The consummation or settlement of a financial transaction.

Collateral – Assets pledged by a borrower to secure a loan or other credit; these are subject to seizure in the event of default.

Commodity – A physical substance, such as food, grains and metals that is interchangeable with other product of the same type.

Correlation – The degree to which contract prices of hedging instruments reflect price movements in the cash-market position. The correlation factor represents the potential effectiveness of hedging a cash-market instrument with a contract where the deliverable financial instrument differs from the cash-market instrument. Generally, the correlation factor is determined by regression analysis or some other method of technical analysis of market behaviour.

Counterparty – The other party to a derivative transaction.

Credit Risk – The risk that a customer or counterparty will not settle an obligation for full value, either when due or at any time thereafter.

Dealer – (for the purposes of this Practice Note) – The person who commits the entity to a derivative transaction.

Derivative – Financial Reporting Standard 13 'Derivatives and other financial instruments' defines a derivative financial instrument as a financial instrument that derives its value from the price or rate of some underlying item. Underlying items include equities, bonds, commodities, interest rates, exchange rates and stock market and other indices. Derivative financial instruments include futures, options, forward contracts, interest rate and currency swaps, interest rate caps, collars and floors, forward interest rate agreements, commitments to purchase shares or bonds, note issuance facilities and letters of credit.

Derivative financial instruments require no initial net investment or little net investment relative to other types of contracts that have a similar response to changes in market conditions. Derivative contracts are settled at future dates and can be linear or non-linear.

Embedded Derivative Instruments – Implicit or explicit terms in a contract or agreement that affect some or all of the cash flows or the value of other exchanges required by the contract in a manner similar to a derivative.

End User – An entity that enters into a financial transaction for the purpose of hedging, asset/liability management or speculating. End users consist primarily of corporations, government entities, institutional investors and financial institutions. The derivative activities of end users are often related the production or use of a commodity by the entity.

Exchange-traded Derivatives – Derivatives traded under uniform rules through an organised exchange.

Fair Value – The amount for which an asset could be exchanged, or a liability settled, between knowledgeable, willing parties in an arm's length transaction.

Floor – A series of put options based on a notional amount. The strike price of these options defines a lower limit to the interest rate.

Foreign Exchange Contracts – Contracts that provide an option for, or require a future exchange of foreign currency assets or liabilities.

Foreign Exchange Risk – The risk of losses arising through repricing of foreign currency instruments because of exchange rate fluctuations.

Forward Contracts – A contract negotiated between two parties to purchase and sell a specified quantity of a financial instrument, foreign currency, or commodity at a price specified at the origination of the contract, with delivery and settlement at a specified future date.

Forward Rate Agreements– An agreement between two parties to exchange an amount determined by an interest rate differential at a given future date based on the difference between an agreed interest rate and a reference rate (LIBOR, Treasury bills, etc.) on a notional principal amount.

Futures Contracts – Exchange-traded contracts to buy or sell a specified financial instrument, foreign currency or commodity at a specified future date or during a specified period at a specified price or yield.

Hedge – A strategy that protects an entity against the risk of an adverse price or interest-rate movements on certain of its assets, liabilities or anticipated transactions. A hedge is used to avoid or reduce net risks by creating a relationship by which losses on certain positions are expected to be counterbalanced in whole or in part by gains on separate positions in another market.

Hedging, (for accounting purposes) – Designating one or more hedging instruments so that their change in value or cash flows is offset, completely or in part, by the change in value or cash flows of a hedged item.

Hedged Item – An exposure that an entity has to the risk of changes in value or changes in future cash flows that, for hedge accounting purposes, is designated as being hedged.

Hedging Instrument, (for hedge accounting purposes) – An instrument – usually a derivative – that has been designated a hedge of a hedged item.

Hedge Effectiveness – The degree to which offsetting changes in value or cash flows attributable to a hedged risk are achieved by the hedging instrument.

Interest Rate Risk – The risk that a movement in interest rates would have an adverse effect on the value of assets and liabilities or would affect interest cash flows.

Interest Rate Swap – A contract between two parties to exchange periodic interest payments on a notional amount (referred to as the notional principal) for a specified period. In the most common instance, an interest rate swap involves the exchange of streams of variable and fixed-rate interest payments.

Legal Risk – The risk that a legal or regulatory action could invalidate or otherwise preclude performance by the end user or its counterparty under the terms of the contract.

LIBOR – (London Interbank Offered Rate) – An international interest rate benchmark. It is commonly used as a repricing benchmark for financial instruments such as interest rate swaps.

Linear Contracts – Contracts that involve obligatory cash flows at a future date.

Liquidity – The capability of a financial instrument to be readily convertible into cash.

Liquidity Risk – Changes in the ability to sell or dispose of a derivative. Derivatives bear the additional risk that a lack of sufficient contracts or willing counterparties may make it difficult to close out the derivative or enter into an offsetting contract.

Margin – An amount of money or securities deposited by both buyers and sellers of futures and options contracts to ensure performance of the terms of the contract.

Margin Call – A call from a broker to a customer or from a clearing house to a clearing member demanding the deposit of cash or marketable securities to maintain a requirement for the purchase or sale of futures or options or to cover an adverse price movement.

Market Risk – The risk of losses arising because of adverse changes in the value of derivatives due to changes in equity prices, interest rates, foreign exchange rates, commodity prices or other market factors. Interest rate risk and foreign exchange risk are sub-sets of market risk.

Model Risk – The risk associated with the imperfections and subjectivity of valuation models used to determine the value of a derivative.

Non-Linear Contracts – Contracts that have option features where one party has the right, but not the obligation to demand that another party deliver the underlying item to it.

Notional Amount – A number of currency units, shares, or other units specified in a derivative instrument.

Off-Balance-Sheet Instrument – A derivative financial instrument that is not recorded on the balance sheet, although it may be disclosed.

Off-Balance-Sheet Risk – The risk of loss to the entity in excess of the amount, if any, of the asset or liability that is recognised on the balance sheet.

Option – A contract that gives the holder (or purchaser) the right, but not the obligation to buy (call) or sell (put) a specific or standard commodity, or financial instrument, at a specified price during a specified period (the American option) or at a specified date (the European option).

Position – The status of the net of claims and obligations in financial instruments of an entity.

Price Risk – The risk of changes in the level of prices due to changes in interest rates, foreign exchange rates or other factors that relate to market volatility of the underlying rate, index or price.

Risk Management – Using derivatives and other financial instruments to mitigate the potential effect of risks associated with existing or anticipated transactions.

Sensitivity Analysis – A general class of models designed to assess the risk of loss in market-risk-sensitive instruments based upon hypothetical changes in market rates or prices.

Settlement Date – The date on which derivative transactions are to be settled by delivery or receipt of the underlying product or instrument in return for payment of cash.

Settlement Risk – The risk that one side of a transaction will be settled without value being received from the counterparty.

Solvency Risk – The risk that an entity would not have funds available to honour cash outflow commitments as they fall due.

Speculation – Entering into an exposed position to maximise profits, that is, assuming risk in exchange for the opportunity to profit on anticipate market movements.

Swaption – A combination of a swap and an option.

Term Structure of Interest Rates – The relationship between interest rates of different terms. When interest rates are plotted graphically according to the time periods to which they relate, this is called the 'yield curve'.

Trading – The buying and selling of financial instruments for short-term profit.

Underlying – A specified interest rate, security price, commodity price, foreign exchange rate, index of prices or rates, or other variable. An underlying may be a price or rate of an asset or liability, but it is not the asset or liability itself.

Valuation Risk – The risk that the value of the derivative is determined incorrectly.

Value at Risk – A general class of models that provides a probabilistic assessment of the risk of loss in market-risk-sensitive instruments over a period of time, with a selected likelihood of occurrences based upon selected confidence intervals.

Volatility – A measure of the variability of the price of an asset or index.

Written Option – The writing, or sale, of an option contract that obligates the writer to fulfil the contract should the holder choose to exercise the option.

[PN 24]
The audit of friendly societies in the United Kingdom (Revised)

(Issued January 2007)

Contents

	Paragraphs
Preface	
Introduction	4

The audit of financial statements

ISAs (UK and Ireland)		16
200	Objective and General Principles Governing the Audit of Financial Statements	16
210	Terms of Audit Engagement	17
220	Quality Control for Audits of Historical Financial Information	19
230	Audit Documentation (Revised)	20
240	The Auditor's Responsibility to Consider Fraud in an Audit of Financial Statements	21
250	Section A – Consideration of Laws and Regulations in an Audit of Financial Statements	25
	Section B – The Auditors' Right and Duty to Report to Regulators in the Financial Sector	
260	Communication of Audit Matters With Those Charged with Governance	37
300	Planning an Audit of Financial Statements	38
315	Obtaining an Understanding of the Entity and Its Environment and Assessing the Risks of Material Misstatement	41
320	Audit Materiality	50
330	The Auditor's Procedures in response to Assessed Risks	52
402	Audit Considerations Relating to Entities Using Service Organisations	55
500	Audit Evidence	57
505	External Confirmations	59
520	Analytical Procedures	61
540	Audit of Accounting Estimates	63
545	Auditing Fair Value Measurements and Disclosures	68
550	Related Parties	70
560	Subsequent Events	73
570	The Going Concern Basis in Financial Statements	74
580	Management Representation	76
600	Using the Work of Another Auditor	78
610	Considering the Work of Internal Audit	80
620	Using the Work of an Expert	81
700	The Auditors' Report on Financial Statements	83
720	Section A – Other Information in Documents Containing Audited Financial Statements (Revised)	86

Reporting on regulatory returns 88

Appendix 1   Illustrative examples of auditor's reports   101
              Reports to the members on financial statements
              1.1 Unqualified opinion: friendly society (no subsidiaries)
              1.2 Unqualified opinion: friendly society group (including an emphasis of matter concerning equalisation reserves)
              Reports on the regulatory returns to FSA
              1.3 Report by the Auditors: Directive society undertaking long term insurance business
              1.4 Report by the Auditors: Directive society undertaking general insurance business
              1.5 Report by the Auditors: Non – directive incorporated society
Appendix 2   The main parts of FSMA 2000 relevant to friendly societies   112
Appendix 3   The FSA Handbook   114
Appendix 4   Reporting direct to the FSA – statutory right and protection for disclosure under general law   117
Appendix 5   Definitions   119

Preface

This Practice Note contains guidance on the application of auditing standards issued by the Auditing Practices Board (the APB) to the audit of friendly societies in the United Kingdom. It also contains guidance on auditors' reports in connection with regulatory returns and the auditors' duty to report to the Financial Services Authority (FSA). This guidance applies to friendly societies carrying on insurance business.

The Practice Note is supplementary to, and should be read in conjunction with, International Standards on Auditing (ISAs) (UK and Ireland), which apply to all audits undertaken in the United Kingdom in respect of accounting periods commencing on or after 15 December 2004. This Practice Note sets out the special considerations relating to the audit of friendly societies which arise from individual ISAs (UK and Ireland) listed in the contents. It is not the intention of the Practice Note to provide step-by-step guidance to the audit of friendly societies, so where no special considerations arise from a particular ISA (UK and Ireland), no material is included.

This Practice Note has been prepared with advice and assistance from staff of the FSA and is based on legislation and regulations in effect as at 31 December 2006.

Introduction

The Practice Note applies both to those friendly societies incorporated under the Friendly Societies Act 1992 (the1992 Act) and those registered under the Friendly Societies Act 1974 (the 1974 Act). The Practice Note does not apply to other entities registered under the 1974 Act[1]. 1

This Practice Note addresses the auditor's reporting responsibilities under the 1992 Act and the Financial Services and Markets Act 2000 ('FSMA 2000'): 2

- to the members of the society as to whether the financial statements give a true and fair view,
- to the members of the society concerning the consistency of the financial statements with the Report of the Committee of Management and the Report's compliance with the 1992 Act and the regulations made under it,
- to the Committee of Management as required by Rule 5.11 of the IPRU (FSOC)(non directive friendly societies), and as required by rule 9.35 of IPRU(INS) (directive friendly societies) on the specified forms comprising the regulatory return, and
- to the FSA on an ad-hoc basis under the auditors' duty to report to the regulator in respect of matters which may be of material significance to the regulator.

Legislative and regulatory framework

Historically friendly societies were established as mutual institutions providing savings schemes and insurance plans designed to be affordable and accessible. Even today, their products require relatively low premium or contribution levels and are taken up by people on modest incomes, people without bank accounts, the elderly or 3

---

[1] *Societies other than friendly societies which are registered under the 1974 Act, are principally working men's clubs, benevolent societies, and specially authorised societies.*

on behalf of children. Friendly societies are often distinguished from other financial institutions in their commitment to mutuality. They may offer discretionary benefits or terms to which members are not contractually entitled.

4   Friendly societies vary by size and range of activity. Some societies have developed a single product niche. Others with subsidiaries offer a range of savings, insurance and banking services. Their focus remains individuals and families (the retail market) rather than commercial customers. In the present day, they compete with other insurance and banking groups in the financial services market.

5   The directing body of a society or branch is known as the Committee of Management. The Committee carries out equivalent functions to the Board of Directors of a company incorporated under the Companies Acts. It must have at least two members and must appoint one of its members to be Chairman. Members of the Committee of Management are generally elected to office in accordance with the rules of the society although individuals may be co-opted by the Committee itself.[2] The members of the Committee are subject to the FSA's 'Approved Persons' rules and have to be "fit and proper" to hold office. The Chief Executive Officer (CEO) is appointed by the Committee but need not necessarily be a member of it. However, the CEO is responsible under the immediate authority of the Committee for the conduct of the business of the society and would normally attend meetings.

The Friendly Societies Acts 1992 and 1974

6   The 1992 Act modified the 1974 Act and introduced a number of significant changes. Friendly societies existing at the time that the 1992 Act came into force have the option of either remaining registered[3] under the 1974 Act or incorporating[4] under the 1992 Act. Many of the larger friendly societies have now incorporated under the 1992 Act; however the majority by number of societies remain unincorporated[5]. Friendly societies which have commenced business since the 1992 Act came into force are required to be incorporated under it.

7   A summary of the legal forms of friendly society now existing and the main legislation applicable to each type is set out in the table below. Many of the provisions of the 1992 Act apply to both incorporated and registered societies; however the provisions set out in Part II of the 1992 Act (concerning constitutional matters) apply only to incorporated societies.

[2] A non-directive society is required to have a Committee of Management but the governing arrangements may be informal and flexible.

[3] A friendly society registered under the 1974 Act is an incorporated association of individuals. As such it does not have a separate legal 'personality'; it is not a body corporate. This has a number of consequences, including that the society's assets have to be held in the names of its trustees and that the society cannot form or acquire any subsidiaries.

[4] A friendly society incorporated under the 1992 Act is a body corporate, although it is not incorporated by shares in the way that companies are under the Companies Act 1985, and it remains a mutual institution. An incorporated friendly society's assets are held in its name (rather than by trustees), and as such a society is able to form or acquire subsidiaries or jointly controlled bodies.

[5] At the time of issue of this Practice Note there were 36 incorporated friendly societies and 166 societies remaining registered under the 1974 Act.

Legal form	Common designation	Applicable legislation
Established prior to the 1992 Act and re-registered under that Act	'Incorporated'	1992 Act
Established prior to the 1992 Act but not re-registered under it, i.e., remains registered under the 1974 Act	'Registered'	1992 Act and 1974 Act (as amended by Schedule 16 of 1992 Act)
Established after the 1992 Act	'Incorporated'	1992 Act

A small number of friendly societies registered under the 1974 Act have a central office and a network of separately registered branches (called an 'Order'). While the branches may provide services to relatively independent groups of members in different areas around the country, each branch will be subject to the overriding rules of the 'Order' and are subject to the control and direction of the central office. The central office may also undertake product development and marketing activities on behalf of the branches. 8

While the provisions relating to systems of business control are embodied in the FSA Handbook, there are also provisions relating to the maintenance of accounting records in section 68 of the 1992 Act. The requirement to prepare annual accounts appears in the 1992 Act. Only non directive societies are required to issue a controls exception report to the regulator. 9

Regulatory reporting

The nature of regulatory reporting depends on the status of friendly societies as 'directive' or 'non-directive' and, for non-directive societies, on whether they are 'incorporated' or 'registered.' 10

The rules for determining status as 'directive' or 'non-directive' are determined by the Friendly Societies (Solvency 1 Directive) Instrument 2003. The premium limit below which societies qualify as non-directive is 5m Euro. See Appendix 5 for the current definition of 'directive' and 'non-directive' for regulatory purposes. 11

There are distinct rules applicable to directive and non-directive societies respectively for regulatory reporting. The directive friendly societies are subject to IPRU(INS) in accordance with rule 5.1A of IPRU(FSOC) and GENPRU and INSPRU. Non – directive societies are subject to IPRU(FSOC). 12

Since the introduction of the Long Term Insurance Business Regulations 1987, and subsequently the 1992 Act, friendly societies may only commence new insurance business if authorised to do so. 13

Societies to which the EU Directives apply (directive societies) are in some respects subject to stronger regulatory controls than other societies. In addition the FSA has powers to establish specific requirements as well as to institute investigations into insurers, including friendly societies, and to suspend or remove authorisation to conduct insurance business where appropriate. 14

15 The FSA's general approach is to treat larger friendly societies consistently with insurance companies. It has therefore applied the regulatory financial reporting rules for insurers to the generally larger 'directive' societies. A fuller description of the requirements affecting directive and non-directive societies respectively appears under separate headings below.

Regulatory reporting deadlines

16 The regulatory reporting deadline for <u>directive</u> societies is 4 months for 2006 and 3 months for 2007 for electronic filing (or 3½ months and 2½ months respectively for submission on paper); representing progressive alignment with insurance companies. There are no rules at present accelerating reporting by non-directive societies from the requirement to report within 6 months of the year end.

DIRECTIVE SOCIETIES

17 Directive friendly societies are subject to GENPRU, INSPRU, IPRU(FSOC), and IPRU(INS).

18 GENPRU sets out the FSA's rules and guidance on the capital requirements and capital resources for these societies and risk assessment rules and guidance are included in INSPRU. However parts of IPRU(FSOC) remain applicable as it contains material derived from friendly societies legislation or where there is not yet an equivalent in GENPRU or INSPRU. Auditors have regard to the applicable rules of GENPRU, INSPRU and IPRU(FSOC) in planning the scope of their work.

19 In addition, directive friendly societies are subject to Chapter 9 and appendices 9.1 to 9.7 of the Interim Prudential Sourcebook for Insurers, IPRU (INS). This Chapter governs primarily the form and content of the regulatory return. In practical terms therefore, directive friendly societies prepare regulatory returns on Insurance Company forms.

20 The auditors of <u>directive societies</u> are aware of the following:
   Policyholder liabilities in respect of long-term business (including realistic value of liabilities where applicable) are within the scope of the auditors' report. (See IPRU(INS) rules 9.5 and 9.35 and Appendix 9.6 part II);
   For directive incorporated societies carrying on long term business, an Actuarial Function Holder is appointed by the society, and those having with-profits business require a With-profits Actuary (See SUP 4);
   In respect of any auditable element of the Regulatory Return that contains elements abstracted from the periodic actuarial investigation of a long-term insurer, the requirement for the auditor of the annual return to obtain and pay due regard to advice from a suitably qualified actuary who is independent of the insurer. This actuary is referred to in this Practice Note as the "Reviewing Actuary" consistent with the terminology introduced by the FSA. However, this terminology should not be taken to indicate that the work of the Reviewing Actuary is limited to "review" procedure; (See IPRU(INS) 9.35 (1A));
   An enhanced capital resources requirement (ECR) based on a so called "realistic balance sheet" is required for firms having with profit liabilities of over £500 million. Firms with smaller with – profit liabilities may also opt – in as a realistic basis life firm. The realistic balance is reported in the Regulatory Return on Form 19. The with-profit capital component is calculated on Form 18 and feeds through to the statement of solvency – long-term insurance business on Form 2 (See Appendices 9.1 and 9.2 of IPRU(INS)

and the corresponding rules and GENPRU 2.1.18R and GENPRU 2.1.19 R);
Rules concerning information on the actuary who has been appointed to perform the with-profit actuary function and material connected persons transactions (See IPRU(INS) rules 9.36 and 9.39) although this is not directly subject to audit.

21 The responsibilities for certification and reporting on the annual return rest with the Committee of Management and the auditors respectively.

22 There are no formal actuarial roles defined by the FSA for directive societies carrying on general insurance business. All societies are under an obligation to report material control failures to the FSA under Principle 11 of the Principles for Businesses.

NON-DIRECTIVE SOCIETIES

Non-directive incorporated friendly societies

23 In the case of non-directive incorporated friendly societies undertaking long term insurance business, equivalent rules to directive friendly societies apply in that there is a statutory requirement for societies to appoint an actuary (the 'Actuarial Function Holder') with responsibility, in particular, for conducting investigations into the financial condition of the society's long term business once in every period of twelve months and at any other time when there is to be a distribution of surplus from the long term fund. Those societies having with-profits business also require a 'With-profits Actuary.' An incorporated non-directive friendly society that carries on general insurance business must also appoint an 'Appropriate Actuary' to carry out a triennial actuarial investigation into the financial condition of the society in respect of its general insurance business.

24 All non-directive incorporated friendly societies are subject to IPRU(FSOC). As at the date of issue of this Practice Note these societies are not required to implement GENPRU and INSPRU.

25 These societies complete returns 'FSC 1' for long term business (an annual requirement) or 'FSC 3' for general business (a triennial requirement). In the latter case, a statement of 'no material changes' in interim years on return 'FSC 4' applies. Concerning FSC 1 returns, auditors are required to express an opinion as to whether the forms have been properly prepared and presented in accordance with FSA rules. As for directive societies this includes obtaining and paying due regard to advice from a suitably qualified actuary (the Reviewing Actuary). The annual return, FSC 1 is certified by specified officers of the society[6]. As from 31 December 2006 audit requirements in respect of the auditors' reliance on the Directors' certification will no longer apply. This brings IPRU (FSOC) requirements for non directive societies into line with IPRU (INS) requirements for directive friendly societies and insurers (IPRU (FSOC) rule 5.11(a)).

26 These societies file a report to the FSA under Rule 3.1(7) of IPRU(FSOC) concerning compliance with obligations for accounting records, systems of control and inspection and report.

---

[6] The specified officers are the Chief Executive, the Secretary and a member of the Committee of Management.

Non-directive unincorporated societies

27   The non–directive registered societies which have permission to carry on long term or general insurance business are required to be valued triennially through return 'FSC 2.' This requires an Appropriate Actuary. No audit requirement is specified by the FSA in connection with the return.

FINANCIAL STATEMENTS

The Accounts Regulations

28   The Friendly Societies (Accounts and Related Provisions) Regulations 1994[7], govern the preparation of the annual financial statements of societies subject to the 2004 regulations enabling societies to adopt International Financial Reporting Standards discussed below (collectively" the Accounts Regulations").

29   The Accounts Regulations apply to all societies, with reduced disclosure requirements for non-directive societies. Separately registered branches are considered non-directive for accounts purposes even if they are above the thresholds.

Supplementary financial information

30   Aside from the statutory reporting requirements, the rules of a friendly society may call for further or supplementary accounts to be prepared in a prescribed manner for designated funds.

Annual financial statements

31   The annual financial statements of all societies are required by Section 69 of the 1992 Act to show a true and fair view of the state of affairs of the society as at the end of the financial year and of its income and expenditure for the financial year. Friendly societies should therefore follow the Accounts Regulations and applicable accounting standards and related pronouncements issued by the Accounting Standards Board or the International Accounting Standards Board, as appropriate.

32   Legislation has been enacted to permit all friendly societies to choose whether to use International Financial Reporting Standards in the preparation of their accounts. The modifications are embodied in the Friendly Societies Act 1992 (International Accounting Standards and Other Accounting Amendments) Regulations 2004. They are designed to bring friendly societies into line with the regime applicable to companies in the UK and follow the European "IAS Directive" and "Modernisation Directive".

33   The Statement of Recommended Practice (SORP), 'Accounting for insurance business', issued by the Association of British Insurers, embodies recommended practice for the financial statements of friendly societies. The SORP has the objectives of narrowing the range of accounting practices within the overall framework of accounts legislation and accounting standards, and providing guidance on the application of accounts legislation where it is open to interpretation. Although the SORP is drafted in the context of the accounts legislation comprised in Schedule 9A

[7] *SI 1994 No.1983*

of the Companies Act 1985 there are few differences between Schedule 9A and the Accounts Regulations applicable to friendly societies[8].

Auditors of friendly societies which carry on insurance business refer as necessary to the full text of the SORP[9] and consider other accounting, reporting and regulatory developments that may impact insurance business since the SORP was last updated.

Financial Services and Markets Act 2000

FSMA 2000 sets out the high level regulatory framework for the financial sector more generally and not just friendly societies. Appendix 2 sets out the main parts of FSMA 2000 relevant to authorised firms[10] which are friendly societies.

The wide scope of FSMA 2000 reflects the FSA's extensive responsibilities. These are set out in FSMA 2000 as regulatory objectives covering:

- market confidence;
- public awareness;
- the protection of consumers; and
- the reduction of financial crime

FSMA 2000 covers not only the regulation and supervision of financial sector entities but also other issues such as official listing rules, business transfers, market abuse, compensation and ombudsman schemes, investment exchanges and clearing houses. FSMA 2000 is also supported by a large number of statutory instruments. Significant components of the definition and scope of the regulatory framework are contained in the main statutory instruments.

Under Part X FSMA 2000 the FSA has the power to make 'rules'. The legal effect of a rule varies depending on the power under which it is made and on the language used in the rule. Rules are mandatory unless a waiver has been agreed with the FSA. If an authorised firm contravenes a rule it may be subject to enforcement action and consequent disciplinary measures under Part XIV FSMA 2000. Furthermore, in certain circumstances an authorised firm may be subject to an action for damages under s150 FSMA 2000.

In contrast, guidance is generally issued to throw light on a particular aspect of regulatory requirements, and is not binding. However if an authorised firm acts in accordance with it in the circumstances contemplated by that guidance, the FSA will proceed on the basis that the authorised firm has complied with the rule to which the guidance relates.

---

[8] *Changes made to company law will not necessarily be mirrored in the corresponding legislation for friendly societies. For example, for 1997 financial reporting onwards, there has been no amending legislation in relation to directors' emoluments equivalent to The Company Accounts (Disclosure of Directors' Emoluments) Regulations 1997 (SI 1996 No.570). The emoluments disclosure requirements of friendly societies are set out in the Accounts Regulations (Schedule 4).*

The Accounts Regulations set out the requirements of group accounts for groups headed by a friendly society parent. Where consolidated accounts are produced, an income and expenditure account for the society is still required, as there is no exemption equivalent to that contained in Section 230 of the Companies Act 1985.

[9] *Copies of the SORP may be obtained from the ABI's website – www.abi.org.uk*

[10] *An entity which has been granted one of more Part IV permissions by the FSA and so is authorised under FSMA 2000 to undertake regulated activities.*

40 Rules made by the FSA and associated guidance are set out in the FSA Handbook of Rules and Guidance ('the FSA Handbook') (see Appendix 3). The main FSA systems and control requirements are set out in the Senior management arrangements, systems and controls element of the high level standards block of the FSA Handbook ('SYSC').

41 It is clearly unrealistic to expect all members of an audit engagement team to have detailed knowledge of the entire FSA Handbook; rather ISA (UK and Ireland) 250 Section B requires the level of knowledge to be commensurate with an individual's role and responsibilities in the audit process. ISA (UK and Ireland) 220 requires the auditor to establish procedures to facilitate consultation and, thereby, to draw on the collective expertise and specialist technical knowledge of those beyond the engagement team of the auditor.

Prudential requirements

42 Friendly societies carrying on insurance business are subject to certain prudential requirements which are detailed in IPRU(INS)[11], which sets out the reporting requirements, certain of the rules relating to long-term insurance business and various definitions, and GENPRU[12], INSPRU[13] and SYSC[14], which set out the rules and guidance on the assessment of risk, capital requirements and capital resources.

43 A significant part of the FSA's regulatory framework consists of provisions intended to maintain the solvency of insurers and so ensure their ability to meet future claims from policyholders. Friendly societies carrying on insurance business must maintain Capital Resources equal to or in excess of their Capital Resources Requirement at all times. In order to monitor solvency and assess other risks and exposures, insurers are required to submit returns to the FSA providing:

- information concerning the value and type of assets held, claims arising under policies written and other financial information (discussed separately under the headings 'Directive societies' and 'Non-directive societies' above);and
- the determination of the Individual Capital Assessment.

REPORTING DIRECT TO THE FSA – STATUTORY RIGHT AND DUTY

44 Under FSMA 2000 (Communications by Auditors) Regulations 2001 (SI 2001/2587) the auditor of an authorised firm or the auditor of an entity closely linked to an authorised firm who is also the auditor of that authorised firm has a statutory duty to communicate matters of material significance to the FSA. Under s.340 FSMA 2000 'the auditor' is defined as one required to be appointed under FSA 'rules' or appointed as a result of another enactment. In addition s.342 FSMA 2000 provides that no duty to which the auditor is subject shall be contravened by communicating in good faith to the FSA any information or opinion on a matter that the auditor reasonably believes is relevant to any functions of the FSA. These duties do not require auditors of friendly societies to undertake additional work directed at identifying matters to report over and above the work necessary to fulfil their obligations to report on financial statements and regulatory returns. Guidance on the

---

[11] *Interim Prudential Sourcebook for Insurers.*

[12] *General Prudential Sourcebook.*

[13] *Insurance Prudential Sourcebook.*

[14] *Senior management arrangements, systems and controls.*

identification of matters to be reported to the regulators is set out in the section dealing with ISA (UK and Ireland) 250 Section B.

COMMUNICATION BETWEEN THE FSA AND THE AUDITOR

45 Within the legal constraints that apply, the FSA may pass on to the auditor any information which it considers relevant to his function. Auditors are bound by the confidentiality provisions set out in Part XXIII of FSMA 2000 (Public record, disclosure of information and co-operation) Regulations in respect of confidential information received from the FSA. An auditor may not pass on such confidential information, even to the entity being audited, without lawful authority (for example, if an exception applies under FSMA 2000 (Disclosure of Confidential Information) Regulations 2001) or without the consent of the person from whom the information was received and, if different, to whom the information relates.

46 Before communicating to an authorised firm any information received from the FSA, the auditor considers carefully whether:

- the auditor has received the FSA's express permission to communicate a particular item of information;
- the information relates to any other party whose permission may need to be obtained before disclosure can be made;
- the information was received by FSA in a capacity other than discharging its functions under FSMA 2000 or from another regulator (in which case the auditor may either be prohibited from disclosure or may need permission of the party which provided the information to that regulator).

The auditors may however disclose to an authorised firm information they have communicated to the FSA except where to do so would have the effect of disclosing information communicated to them by the FSA. If there is any doubt the auditor considers the matters above.

47 Matters communicated by the FSA during any bilateral meeting may be conveyed by those representatives of the auditor who were present at the meeting (or otherwise received the communication directly) to other partners, directors and employees of the auditor who need to know the information in connection with the auditor's performance of its duties relating to that authorised firm and without the FSA's express permission. However, in the interests of prudence and transparency the auditors inform the FSA that they will be discussing the issues covered with colleagues.

48 Where the FSA passes to the auditors information which it considers is relevant to their function, they consider its implications in the context of their work and may need to amend their approach accordingly. However the fact that they may have been informed of such a matter by the regulator does not, of itself, require auditors to change the scope of the work, nor does it necessarily require them actively to search for evidence in support of the situation communicated by the regulator.

49 The auditor is required to cooperate with the FSA (SUP3.8.2R). This may involve attending meetings and providing the FSA with information about the authorised firm that the FSA may reasonably request in discharging its functions. For example this can arise in relation to FSA ARROW II risk assessments.

50 The auditor must notify the FSA without delay if the auditor is removed from office, resigns before the term of office expires or is not reappointed by the authorised firm. Notification to the FSA includes communicating any matters connected with this

event that the auditor considers ought to be drawn to the FSA's attention or a statement that there are no such matters (s.344 FSMA 2000 and SUP3.8.11R and 12R).

Responsibilities of the Committee of Management

51 ISAs (UK and Ireland) use the term 'those charged with governance' to describe the persons entrusted with the supervision, control and directions of an entity, who will normally be responsible for the quality of financial reporting, and the term "management" to describe those persons who perform senior managerial functions. The FSA Handbook of Rules and Guidance (FSA Handbook) uses the term "governing body" to describe collectively those charged with governance. In the context of this Practice Note, references to those charged with governance refer to members of the Committee of Management of a friendly society.

52 Friendly Societies Legislation requires the Committee of Management to prepare financial statements that comply with relevant legal and accounting requirements. In addition, it has significant responsibilities under the regulatory framework contained in FSMA 2000 and the FSA Handbook of Rules and Guidance (FSA Handbook) which places considerable emphasis upon senior management responsibilities. This includes a requirement to ensure that the friendly society:

- maintains a clear and appropriate apportionment of significant responsibilities among members of the Committee of Management and senior managers in such a way that it is clear who has which of those responsibilities and that the business and affairs of the friendly society can be adequately monitored and controlled by the members of the Committee of Management, relevant senior managers and the governing body of the society;
- establishes and maintains appropriate systems and controls (SYSC 3.1.1R); together with effective systems and controls for compliance with applicable requirements and standards under the regulatory system and for countering the risk that the firm might be used to further financial crime (SYSC 3.2.6R);
- maintains capital resources at all times at least equal to its capital resources requirement (GENPRU 2.1.9 R); and
- maintains overall financial resources which are adequate, both as to amount and quality to ensure that there is no significant risk that its liabilities cannot be met as they fall due, and carries out regular assessments of the adequacy of its financial resources, identifying the major sources of credit risk, liquidity risk, operational risk and market risk, including carrying out stress tests and scenario analysis.

In addition friendly societies have regard to 'The Combined Code on Corporate Governance – an annotated code for mutual insurers' (July 2005) published by the Association of Mutual Insurers (AMI) pursuant to the Myners' Review for HM Treasury.[15]

The audit of financial statements

ISAs (UK and Ireland) apply to the conduct of all audits in respect of accounting periods commencing on or after 15 December 2004. This includes audits of the financial statements of friendly societies. The purpose of the following paragraphs is to identify the special considerations arising from the application of certain 'bold letter'

---

[15] A copy of the annotated code can be found at the AMI website 'www.mutualinsurers.org'

requirements to the audit of friendly societies, and to suggest ways in which these can be addressed (extracts from ISAs (UK and Ireland) are indicated by grey-shaded boxes below). This Practice Note does not contain commentary on all of the bold letter requirements included in the ISAs (UK and Ireland) and reading it should not be seen as an alternative to reading the relevant ISAs (UK and Ireland) in their entirety. In addition, where no special considerations arise from a particular ISA (UK and Ireland), no material is included.

ISA (UK and IRELAND) 200: OBJECTIVE AND GENERAL PRINCIPLES GOVERNING THE AUDIT OF THE FINANCIAL STATEMENTS

Background note

The purpose of this ISA (UK and Ireland) is to establish standards and provide guidance on the objective and general principles governing an audit of financial statements.

The auditor should plan and perform an audit with an attitude of professional scepticism, recognising that circumstances may exist that cause the financial statements to be materially misstated. (paragraph 6)

53 Auditing standards include a requirement for auditors to comply with relevant ethical requirements relating to audit engagements. In the United Kingdom, the auditor should comply with the APB's Ethical Standards and relevant ethical guidance relating to the work of auditors issued by the auditor's professional body. A fundamental principle is that practitioners should not accept or perform work which they are not competent to undertake. The importance of technical competence is also underlined in the Auditor's Code[16], issued by the APB, which states that the necessary degree of professional skill demands an understanding of financial reporting and business. Practitioners should not undertake the audit of friendly societies unless they are satisfied that they have, or can obtain, the necessary level of competence.

Independence

54 Independence issues can be complex for the auditor of a friendly society because of insurance contracts that the auditor or its partners and staff may have with the friendly society. The auditor makes careful reference to the APB's Ethical Standard 2 – financial, business, employment and personal relationships.

ISA (UK and IRELAND) 210: TERMS OF AUDIT ENGAGEMENT

Background note

The purpose of this ISA (UK and Ireland) is to establish standards and provide guidance on agreeing the terms of the engagement with the client.

---

[16] This is appended to the APB's Scope and Authority of Pronouncements.

> The auditor and the client should agree on the terms of the engagement. (paragraph 2)
>
> The terms of the engagement should be recorded in writing. (paragraph 2-1)
>
> The auditor should ensure that the engagement letter documents and confirms the auditor's acceptance of the appointment, and includes a summary of the responsibilities of those charged with governance and of the auditor, the scope of the engagement and the form of any reports. (paragraph 5-1)

55 Auditors' engagement letters follow the principles of ISA (UK and Ireland) 210, referring to the 1992 Act and FSMA 2000 as being the relevant legislative framework within which the auditor is appointed.

56 The auditor may choose to combine into a single letter the terms of engagement in relation to the audit of the statutory accounts and regulatory returns. Matters which the auditor may decide to refer to in the engagement letter are as follows:

- the responsibility of the directors/senior management to comply with applicable FSMA 2000 legislation and FSA Handbook rules and guidance including the need to keep the FSA informed about the affairs of the entity;
- the statutory right and duty of the auditor to report direct to the FSA in certain circumstances (see the section of this Practice Note relating to ISA (UK and Ireland) 250 Section B);
- the requirement to cooperate with the auditor (SUP3.6.1R). This includes taking steps to ensure that, where applicable, each of its appointed representatives and material outsourcers gives the auditor the same right of access to records, information and explanations as the authorised firm itself is required to provide the auditor (s341 FSMA 2000 and SUP 3.6.2G to 3.6.8G). It a criminal offence for a society or its officers, controllers or managers to provide false or misleading information to the auditor (s.346 FSMA 2000);
- the need for the society to make the auditor aware when it appoints a third party (including another department or office of the same audit firm) to review, investigate or report on any aspects of its business activities that may be relevant to the audit of the financial statements and to provide the auditor with copies of reports by such a third party promptly after their receipt.

57 In this connection the auditor is aware that:

- the FSA does not need to approve the appointment of an auditor but may seek to satisfy itself that an auditor appointed by a firm is independent and has the necessary skills, resources and experience (SUP 3.4.4G, 3.4.7R and 3.4.8G);
- the auditor is required to cooperate with the FSA (SUP 3.8.2R); and
- the auditor must notify the FSA if the auditor ceases to be the auditor of an authorised firm.

ISA (UK and IRELAND) 220: QUALITY CONTROL FOR AUDITS OF HISTORICAL FINANCIAL INFORMATION

Background note

The purpose of this ISA (UK and Ireland) is to establish standards and provide guidance on specific responsibilities of firm personnel regarding quality control procedures for audits of historical financial information, including audits of financial statements.

Reference should also be made to ISQC 1 (UK and Ireland) – Quality Control for Firms that Perform Audits and Reviews of Historical Financial Information, and other Assurance and Related Services Engagements.

The engagement team should implement quality control procedures that are applicable to the individual audit engagement. (paragraph 2)

Quality control procedures cover the work of members of the engagement team with actuarial expertise or other specialist knowledge, and have regard to ISA (UK and Ireland) 620 'Using the work of an expert' in relation to the involvement of external actuarial or other expertise. 58

The engagement partner should be satisfied that the engagement team collectively has the appropriate capabilities, competence and time to perform the audit engagement in accordance with professional standards and regulatory and legal requirements, and to enable an auditor's report that is appropriate in the circumstances to be issued. (paragraph 19)

As well as ensuring that the engagement team has an appropriate level of knowledge of the industry and its corresponding products, the engagement partner also satisfies himself that the members of the engagement team have sufficient knowledge of the regulatory framework within which friendly societies operate commensurate with their roles on the engagement and that, where appropriate, the team includes members with actuarial expertise or has access to external actuarial expertise appropriate to the society's insurance business. 59

ISA (UK and IRELAND) 230 (Revised): AUDIT DOCUMENTATION

Background note

The purpose of this ISA (UK and Ireland) is to establish standards and provide guidance regarding documentation in the context of the audit of financial statements.

The auditor should document matters which are important in providing audit evidence to support the auditor's opinion and evidence that the audit was carried out in accordance with ISAs (UK and Ireland). (paragraph 2)

If the auditor uses in – house actuaries (employed by the audit firm) to assist in the audit process (including in the role of Reviewing Actuary described later in the section on reporting on regulatory returns), their working papers form part of the audit working papers. Where external actuaries are engaged by the auditors, the actuaries' report and notes of any meetings or discussions with them form part of the 60 audit working papers (see also ISA (UK and Ireland) 620 'Using the work of an expert').

ISA (UK and IRELAND) 240: THE AUDITOR'S RESPONSIBILITY TO CONSIDER FRAUD IN AN AUDIT OF FINANCIAL STATEMENTS

Background note

The purpose of this ISA(UK and Ireland) is to establish standards and provide guidance on the auditor's responsibility to consider fraud in an audit of financial statements and expand on how the standards and guidance in ISA (UK and Ireland) 315 and ISA (UK and Ireland) 330 are to be applied in relation to the risks of material misstatement due to fraud.

In planning and performing the audit to reduce audit risk to an acceptably low level, the auditor should consider the risks of material misstatements in the financial statements due to fraud. (paragraph 3)

The auditor should maintain an attitude of professional scepticism throughout the audit, recognizing the possibility that a material misstatement due to fraud could exist, notwithstanding the auditor's past experience with the entity about the honesty and integrity of management and those charged with governance. (paragraph 24)

61 The following are considered to be significant fraud risks which friendly societies conducting insurance business may be subject to:

(a) policyholder fraud;
(b) fraud by directors and employees; and
(c) fraud by agents, brokers or other related parties.

62 Responsibility for the prevention and detection of fraud and error lies with those charged with governance of a friendly society. In carrying out their responsibilities, the members of the Committee of Management have regard to the FSA Principles for Businesses (in particular with regard to the criteria for integrity, skill, care and diligence and management and control).

63 Principle 3 requires a friendly society to take reasonable care to organise and control its affairs responsibly and effectively with adequate risk management systems. SYSC 3.2.20R(1) requires a friendly society to make and retain adequate records of matters and dealings (including accounting records) which are the subject of requirements and standards under the regulatory system. Whilst the inherent risk of fraud may continue to exist, the establishment of accounting and internal controls systems sufficient to meet these requirements (particularly in the case of friendly societies that accept business involving a high volume of policies involving claims of comparatively low individual financial value) frequently reduces the likelihood of fraud giving rise to material misstatements in the financial statements. Guidance on the auditors' consideration of accounting systems and internal controls is provided in ISA (UK and Ireland) 315.

In many smaller friendly societies, segregation of duties is limited as the processing of receipts and payments vest in a few individuals; indeed there may be only one individual responsible for day to day management. Furthermore, as contributions received from an individual member will often only give rise to benefit payments to that individual over the longer term, there is a risk that amounts may be misappropriated in the interim and escape detection. There is also a risk that related party transactions will be entered into without appropriate review and approval, resulting in non-commercial terms which could be prejudicial to members' interests.

> The auditor should make inquiries of management, internal audit, and others within the entity as appropriate, to determine whether they have knowledge of any actual, suspected or alleged fraud affecting the entity. (paragraph 38)

> When obtaining an understanding of the entity and its environment, including its internal control, the auditor should consider whether the information obtained indicates that one or more fraud risk factors are present. (paragraph 48)

As with other entities, fraud on friendly societies, either fraudulent financial reporting (for example the manipulation of surpluses or the concealment of deficits) or misappropriation of assets, can occur through a combination of management fraud, employee fraud or fraud perpetrated by third parties. However, fraud risk factors particularly relevant to friendly societies may be due to the following:

- the commission driven nature of arrangements with many business introducers whose interests may be more focused on the volume of business and commission thereon rather than the ultimate profitability and sustainability of the business for the friendly society. This may increase the risk of fraud committed by agents and intermediaries;
- the existence of very large amounts of estimated liabilities which may not crystallise for many years and subject to judgmental estimates by management (see ISA (UK and Ireland) 540);
- the transfer of risk under a contract of insurance is not reflected in the passing of any physical asset which can make it difficult for insurers to ensure that all transactions are recorded completely and accurately.

The examples of weaknesses in control set out in the section on ISA (UK and Ireland) 315 below may be especially relevant when assessing fraud risk.

ISA (UK and Ireland) 240 requires auditors to give particular consideration to the likelihood of fraud in relation to the recognition of revenue. In the context of a friendly society, "revenue" for this purpose may reasonably be taken as premium income. However auditors will also consider the likelihood of fraud in relation to the recognition of other income or costs which may have a close relationship to premium income, including reinsurance costs and acquisition costs.

Friendly Societies might outsource insurance and accounting functions to service companies. Service companies are considered as agents of the friendly society and auditors will therefore consider the equivalent risk factors for service companies as they consider for all agents. Further guidance on this issue is contained in the section dealing with ISA (UK and Ireland) 402 'Audit Considerations Relating to Entities Using Service Organisations.'

> When obtaining an understanding of the entity and its environment, including its internal control, the auditor should consider whether other information obtained indicates risks of material misstatement due to fraud. (paragraph 55)

69 The auditor considers reports or information obtained from the society's compliance department, legal department, and money laundering reporting officer together with reviews undertaken by third parties such as skilled person's reports prepared under s166 FSMA 2000.

> If the auditor has identified a fraud or has obtained information that indicates that a fraud may exist, the auditor should communicate these matters as soon as practicable to the appropriate level of management. (paragraph 93)
>
> The auditor should document communications about fraud made to management, those charged with governance, regulators and others. (paragraph 109)

70 Reduction of financial crime is one of the FSA's statutory objectives. The FSA's rules require authorised firms to report 'significant' fraud, errors and other irregularities to the FSA (SUP 15.3.17R). The auditor is aware of the auditor's duty to report direct to the FSA in certain circumstances (see the section of this Practice Note relating to ISA (UK and Ireland) 250 Section B.

71 Instances of actual or suspected fraud may also involve breaches of specific statutory requirements relating to authorised friendly societies. Auditors assess suspected breaches to determine whether they have a duty to report the matter directly to the FSA. Any suspected fraud involving members of the Committee of Management or senior management is likely to give rise to such a duty.

ISA (UK and IRELAND) 250: SECTION A – CONSIDERATION OF LAWS AND REGULATIONS IN AN AUDIT OF FINANCIAL STATEMENTS

> **Background note**
>
> The purpose of this ISA (UK and Ireland) is to establish standards and provide guidance on the auditors responsibility to consider laws and regulations in the audit of financial statements.

> When designing and performing audit procedures and in evaluating and reporting the results thereof, the auditor should recognize that non compliance by the entity with laws and regulations may materially affect the financial statements. (paragraph 2)
>
> In accordance with ISA (UK and Ireland) 200, "Objective and General Principles Governing an Audit of Financial Statements" the auditor should plan and perform the audit with an attitude of professional scepticism recognising that the audit may reveal conditions or events that would lead to questioning whether an entity is complying with laws and regulations. (paragraph 13)

> In order to plan the audit, the auditor should obtain a general understanding of the legal and regulatory framework applicable to the entity and the industry and how the entity is complying with that framework. (paragraph 15)

In the context of friendly societies, laws and regulations are central to the conduct of business if breaches would have either of the following consequences:

(a) removal of authorisation to carry out insurance business;
(b) the imposition of fines or restrictions on business activities whose significance is such that, where relevant, the ability of the friendly society to continue as a going concern is threatened.

Non-compliance with laws and regulations that are central to a friendly society's activities is likely to give rise to a statutory duty to report to the FSA. Such reports are made in accordance with the requirements of ISA (UK and Ireland) 250 Section B, following the guidance set out in the relevant section of this Practice Note.

Friendly societies are affected by two types of regulation which are central to their activities and of which the auditor needs to obtain a general understanding:

(a) prudential supervision; and
(b) market conduct rules.

The principal purpose of prudential supervision is to ensure the protection of policyholders because of the promissory nature of transactions between insurers and the public. Much of the legislation for prudential supervision is based on European Directives.

Market conduct regulation relates to the sale of business and is primarily carried out by the FSA through its rules in respect of COB (designated investment business which includes long-term insurance investment business) and ICOB (general insurance and long-term pure protection business).

> After obtaining the general understanding, the auditor should perform further audit procedures to help identify instances of noncompliance with those laws and regulations where noncompliance should be considered when preparing financial statements, specifically:
>
> (a) Inquiring of management as to whether the entity is in compliance with such laws and regulations;
> (b) Inspecting correspondence with the relevant licensing or regulatory authorities; and
> (c) Enquiring of those charged with governance as to whether they are on notice of any such possible instances of non-compliance with law or regulations. (paragraph 18)
>
> In the UK and Ireland, the auditor's procedures should be designed to help identify possible or actual instances of non-compliance with those laws and regulations which provide a legal framework within which the entity conducts its business and which are central to the entity's ability to conduct its business and hence to its financial statements. (paragraph 18-1)

Specific areas that auditors' procedures may address include the following:

- obtaining a general understanding of the legal and regulatory framework applicable to the entity and industry, and of the procedures followed to ensure compliance with the framework;
- the friendly society's compliance with prudential capital requirements, the results of the friendly society's Individual Capital Assessment (ICA), and whether any Individual Capital Guidance has been given by the FSA;
- the friendly society's compliance with the scope of its permissions or any limits that may be specified in any Permission Notice issued by the FSA;
- reviewing correspondence with the FSA and other regulators (including that relating to any FSA supervisory visits, requests for information by FSA or progress concerning FSA ARROW II risk mitigation programmes);
- holding discussions with the friendly society's compliance officer and other personnel responsible for compliance;
- reviewing compliance reports prepared for the Committee of Management, audit committee and other committees;
- consideration of work on compliance matters performed by internal audit; and
- the results of the friendly society's complaints monitoring procedures and any trends that may indicate conduct of business issues.

78   Auditors are not themselves experts in the detailed standards, rules, guidance and practice a society would be expected to maintain. However, if the response of the society to their enquiries gives them cause for concern over the society's attitude and approach to compliance they will consider whether this gives rise to a duty to report to the FSA.

Taxation

79   The taxation of friendly societies is a particularly complex area, and auditors may wish to involve tax specialists. Some societies are exempt from tax in respect of business other than long-term insurance and others are not. The treatment of long-term insurance business itself follows that for mutual life insurance companies (a specialist area in itself) but with a number of added complications. The most important of these is a society may claim to treat part of its business as "tax exempt".

80   A unique feature of smaller friendly society policies is that the income and gains relating to them qualify for exemption. For policies taken out since 1995 this applies to life policies with an annual premium of up to £270 or £25 per month, and annuities of up to £156 per annum. The principles of life insurance taxation also require other classes of business to be separated and 'ring-fenced' one from the other. Societies may carry on taxable life, pensions, and permanent health business as well as tax-exempt life business. Each category has a different tax treatment. Societies also have onerous reporting responsibilities relating to the taxation of their policyholders, with severe penalties for errors.

Money laundering

> In the UK and Ireland, when carrying out procedures for the purpose of forming an opinion on the financial statements, the auditor should be alert for those instances of possible or actual non-compliance with laws and regulations that might incur obligations for partners and staff in audit firms to report money laundering offences. (paragraph 22-1)

Authorised firms including friendly societies are subject to the requirements of the Money Laundering Regulations 2003 (as amended) and the Proceeds of Crime Act 2002 as well as FSA rules. These laws and regulations require institutions to establish and maintain procedures to identify their customers, establish appropriate reporting and investigation procedures for suspicious transactions and maintain appropriate records. 81

Laws and regulations relating to money laundering are integral to the legal and regulatory framework within which insurers conduct their business. By the nature of their business, friendly societies are ready targets of those engaged in money laundering activities. The effect of this legislation is to make it an offence to provide assistance to those involved in money laundering and makes it an offence not to report suspicions of money laundering to the appropriate authorities, usually the Serious Organised Crime Agency ('SOCA').[17] FSA requirements are set out in SYSC 3.2.6AR – 3.2.6JG. In this context, FSA has due regard to compliance with the relevant provisions of guidance issued by the Joint Money Laundering Steering Group ('JMLSG')(SYSC 3.2.6EG). 82

In addition to considering whether a friendly society has complied with the money laundering laws and regulations, the auditor has reporting obligations under the Proceeds of Crime Act 2002 and the Money Laundering Regulations 2003 (as amended) to report knowledge or suspicion of money laundering offences, including those arising from fraud and theft, to SOCA. The auditor is aware of the prohibition on 'tipping off' when discussing money laundering matters with the friendly society. The auditor is aware of the short-form[18] of reporting to SOCA that can be used in appropriate circumstances to report minor and usually numerous items. Further guidance for auditors is provided in Practice Note 12 Money Laundering – Interim Guidance for Auditors in the United Kingdom (Revised). 83

The auditor, in the context of money laundering, is aware of the auditor's duty to report direct to FSA in certain circumstances (see the section of this Practice Note relating to ISA (UK and Ireland) 250 Section B). 84

ISA (UK and IRELAND) 250: SECTION B – THE AUDITOR'S RIGHT AND DUTY TO REPORT TO REGULATORS IN THE FINANCIAL SECTOR

> The auditor of a regulated entity should bring information of which the auditor has become aware in the ordinary course of performing work undertaken to fulfil the auditor's audit responsibilities to the attention of the appropriate regulator without delay when:
>
> (a) The auditor concludes that it is relevant to the regulator's functions having regard to such matters as may be specified in statute or any related regulations; and
>
> (b) In the auditor's opinion there is reasonable cause to believe it is or may be of material significance to the regulator. (paragraph 2)

---

[17] Previously National Criminal Intelligence Service ('NCIS').

[18] These are termed limited intelligence value reports.

> Where an apparent breach of statutory or regulatory requirements comes to the auditor's attention, the auditor should:
>
> (a) Obtain such evidence as is available to assess its implications for the auditor's reporting responsibilities;
> (b) Determine whether, in the auditor's opinion, there is reasonable cause to believe that the breach is of material significance to the regulator; and
> (c) Consider whether the apparent breach is criminal conduct that gives rise to criminal property and, as such, should be reported to the specified authorities. (paragraph 39)

Auditors' duty to report to the FSA

85 Under the FSMA 2000 (Communications by Auditors) Regulations 2001 (the 2001 Regulations), auditors have duties in certain circumstances to make reports to the FSA. **The 2001 Regulations do not require auditors to perform any additional audit work as a result of the statutory duty nor are auditors required specifically to seek out breaches of the requirements applicable to a particular authorised person.** Information and opinions to be communicated are those meeting the criteria set out below which relate to matters of which the auditor[19] of the authorised person (also referred to below as a 'regulated entity') has become aware:

in his capacity as auditor of the authorised person, and

if he is also the auditor of a person who has close links with the authorised person, in his capacity as auditor of that person.

86 The criteria for determining the matters to be reported are as follows:

the auditor reasonably believes that there is, or has been, or may be, or may have been a contravention of any 'relevant requirement' that applies to the person[20] concerned and that contravention may be of material significance to the FSA in determining whether to exercise, in relation to that person, any of its functions under FSMA 2000, or

the auditor reasonably believes that the information on, or his opinion on, those matters may be of material significance to the FSA in determining whether the person concerned satisfies and will continue to satisfy the 'Threshold Conditions[21]', or

the auditor reasonably believes that the person concerned is not, may not be, or may cease to be, a going concern, or

the auditor is precluded from stating in his report that the annual accounts have been prepared so as to conform with the Friendly Societies Act 1992 and the regulations made under it or, where applicable, give a true and fair view of the matters referred to in section 73(5) of that Act.

87 In relation to paragraph 86 (i) above, 'relevant requirement' is a requirement by or under FSMA 2000 which relates to authorisation under FSMA 2000 or to the carrying on of any regulated activity. This includes not only relevant statutory instruments but also the FSA's rules (other than the Listing Rules) including the

---

[19] An 'auditor' is defined for this purpose in the Regulations as a person who is, or has been, an auditor of an authorised person appointed under, or as a result of, a statutory provision including Section 340 of FSMA 2000.

[20] In this context the person is an 'Authorised Person'.

[21] The Threshold Conditions are set out in Schedule 6 to FSMA 2000 and represent the minimum conditions that a firm is required to satisfy and continue to satisfy to be given and to retain Part IV permission. The FSA's guidance on compliance with the Threshold Conditions is contained in the COND module of the FSA Handbook.

Principles for Businesses. The duty to report also covers any requirement imposed by or under any other Act[22] the contravention of which constitutes an offence which the FSA has the power to prosecute under FSMA 2000.

88 In relation to paragraph 86(ii) above the duty to report relates to either information or opinions held by the auditor which may be of significance to the FSA in determining whether the regulated entity satisfies and will continue to satisfy the Threshold Conditions. The duty to report opinions, as well as information, allows for circumstances where adequate information on a matter may not readily be forthcoming from the regulated entity, and where judgments need to be made.

Material significance

89 Determining whether a contravention of a relevant requirement or a Threshold Condition is reportable under the 2001 Regulations involves consideration both of whether the auditor 'reasonably believes' and that the matter in question 'is, or is likely to be, of material significance' to the regulator.

90 The 2001 Regulations do not require auditors to perform any additional audit work as a result of the statutory duty nor are auditors required specifically to seek out breaches of the requirements applicable to a particular regulated entity. However, in circumstances where auditors identify that a reportable matter may exist, they carry out such extra work, as they consider necessary, to determine whether the facts and circumstances cause them 'reasonably to believe' that the matter does in fact exist. It should be noted that the auditors' work does not need to prove that the reportable matter exists.

91 ISA (UK and Ireland) 250 Section B requires that, where an apparent breach of statutory or regulatory requirements comes to the auditors' attention, they obtain such evidence as is available to assess its implications for their reporting responsibilities and determine whether, in their opinion, there is reasonable cause to believe that the breach has occurred and that it relates to a matter that is of material significance to the regulator.

92 'Material significance' is defined by paragraph 14 of ISA (UK and Ireland) 250 Section B as follows:

"A matter or group of matters is normally of material significance to a regulator's function when, due either to its nature or its potential financial impact, it is likely of itself to require investigation by the regulator."

93 'Material significance' does not have the same meaning as materiality in the context of the audit of financial statements. Whilst a particular event may be trivial in terms of its possible effect on the financial statements of an entity, it may be of a nature or type that is likely to change the perception of the regulator. For example, a failure to reconcile client money accounts may not be significant in financial terms but would have a significant effect on the FSA's consideration of whether the regulated entity was satisfactorily controlled and was behaving properly towards its customers.

94 The determination of whether a matter is, or is likely to be, of material significance to the FSA inevitably requires auditors to exercise their judgment. In forming such judgments, auditors need to consider not simply the facts of the matter but also their

---

[22] *Examples include the Proceeds of Crime Act 2002 and prescribed regulations relating to money laundering.*

implications. In addition, it is possible that a matter, which is not materially significant in isolation, may become so when other possible breaches are considered.

95 The auditor of a regulated entity bases his judgment of 'material significance' to the FSA solely on his understanding of the facts of which he is aware without making any assumptions about the information available to the FSA in connection with any particular regulated entity.

96 Minor breaches of the FSA's rules that, for example, are unlikely to jeopardise the entity's assets or amount to misconduct or mismanagement would not normally be of 'material significance'. ISA (UK and Ireland) 250 Section B however requires auditors of regulated entities, when reporting on their financial statements, to review information obtained in the course of the audit and to assess whether the cumulative effect is of 'material significance' such as to give rise to a duty to report to the regulator. In circumstances where auditors are uncertain whether they may be required to make a report or not, they may wish to consider whether to take legal advice.

97 On completion of his investigations, the auditor ensures that the facts and circumstances, and the basis for his conclusion as to whether these are, or are likely to be of 'material significance' to the FSA, are adequately documented such that the reasons for his decision to report or not, as the case may be, may be clearly demonstrated.

98 Whilst confidentiality is an implied term of auditors' contracts with a regulated entity, section 342 FSMA 2000 states that an auditor does not contravene that duty if he reports to the FSA information or his opinion, if he is acting in good faith and he reasonably believes that the information or opinion is relevant to any function of the FSA. The protection afforded is given in respect of information obtained in his capacity as auditor.

Conduct of the audit

99 ISA (UK and Ireland) 250 Section B requires auditors to ensure that all staff involved in the audit of a regulated entity 'have an understanding of:

(a) The provisions of applicable legislation,
(b) The regulator's rules and any guidance issued by the regulator, and
(c) Any specific requirements which apply to the particular regulated entity,

appropriate to their role in the audit and sufficient (in the context of that role) to enable them to identify situations they encounter in the course of the audit which may give reasonable cause to believe that a matter should be reported to the regulator.'

100 Understanding, commensurate with the individual's role and responsibilities in the audit process, is required of:

- the provisions of the 2001 Regulations concerning the auditors' duty to report to the regulator,
- the standards and guidance in ISA (UK and Ireland) 250 Section B, and in this section of this Practice Note, and
- relevant sections of the FSA's Handbook including the Principles for Businesses and the Threshold Conditions.

101 The auditor includes procedures within his planning process to ensure that members of the audit team have such an understanding (in the context of their role) to enable

them to recognise potentially reportable matters, and that such matters are reported to the audit engagement partner without delay so that a decision may be made as to whether a duty to report arises.

An audit firm appointed as auditor of a regulated entity needs to have in place appropriate procedures to ensure that the audit engagement partner is made aware of any other relationship which exists between any department of the firm and the regulated entity when that relationship could affect the firm's work as auditors (this matter is covered in more detail in Appendix 2 of ISA (UK and Ireland) 250 Section B). The auditor also requests the regulated entity to advise him when it appoints a third party (including another department or office of the same firm) to review, investigate or report on any aspects of its business activities that may be relevant to the audit of the financial statements and to provide the auditor with copies of reports by such a third party promptly after their receipt. This matter may usefully be referred to in the engagement letter. 102

Closely linked entities

Where the auditor of a regulated entity is also auditor of a closely linked entity[23], a duty to report arises directly in relation to information relevant to the regulated entity of which he becomes aware in the course of his work as auditor of the closely linked entity. 103

The auditor establishes during audit planning whether the regulated entity has one or more closely linked entities of which the audit firm is also the auditor. If there are such entities the auditor considers the significance of the closely linked entities and the nature of the issues that might arise which may be of material significance to the regulator of the regulated entity. Such circumstances may involve: 104

- activities or uncertainties within the closely linked entity which might significantly impair the financial position of the regulated entity,
- money laundering and, if the closely linked entity is itself regulated,
- matters that the auditor of the closely linked entity is intending to report to its regulator.

Following the risk assessment referred to in paragraph 104, the auditor of the regulated entity identifies the closely related entities for which the procedures in this paragraph are necessary. The engagement team of the regulated entity communicates to the engagement team of the selected closely linked entities the audit firm's responsibilities to report to the FSA under the 2001 Regulations and notifies the engagement team of the circumstances that have been identified which, if they exist, might be of material significance to the FSA as regulator of the regulated entity. Prior to completion the auditor of the regulated entity obtains details from the auditor of the closely linked entity of such circumstances or confirmation, usually in writing, that such circumstances do not exist. Where the closely linked entities are part of the inter-auditor group reporting process these steps can be built into that process. 105

Whilst confidentiality is an implied term of auditors' contracts with a regulated entity, s.343 FSMA 2000 states that an auditor of an entity closely linked to an 106

---

[23] An entity has close links with an authorised person for this purpose if the entity is a:
(a) Parent undertaking of an authorised person;
(b) Subsidiary undertaking of an authorised person;
(c) Parent undertaking of a subsidiary undertaking of an authorised person; or
(d) Subsidiary undertaking of a parent undertaking of an authorised person.

authorised person who is also the auditor of that authorised person does not contravene that duty if he reports to the FSA information or his opinion, if he is acting in good faith and he reasonably believes that the information or opinion is relevant to any function of the FSA. The protection afforded is given in respect of information obtained in his capacity as auditor.

107 No duty to report is imposed on the auditor of an entity closely linked to a regulated entity who is not also auditor of the regulated entity.

108 In circumstances where he is not also the auditor of the closely linked entity, the auditor of the regulated entity decides whether there are any matters to be reported to the FSA relating to the affairs of the regulated entity in the light of the information that he receives about a closely linked entity for the purpose of auditing the financial statements of the regulated entity. If the auditor becomes aware of possible matters that may fall to be reported, he may wish to obtain further information from the management or auditor of the closely linked entity to ascertain whether the matter should be reported. To facilitate such possible discussions, at the planning stage of the audit, the auditor of the regulated entity will have considered whether arrangements need to be put in place to allow him to communicate with the management and the auditor of the closely linked entity. If the auditor of the regulated entity is unable to communicate with the management and auditor of the closely linked entity to obtain further information concerning the matters he has identified he reports the matters, and that he has been unable to obtain further information, direct to the FSA.

Information received in a capacity other than as auditor

109 There may be circumstances where it is not clear whether information about a regulated entity coming to the attention of the auditor is received in the capacity of auditor or in some other capacity, for example as a general adviser to the entity. Appendix 2 to ISA (UK and Ireland) 250 Section B provides guidance as to how information obtained in non-audit work may be relevant to the auditor in the planning and conduct of the audit and the steps that need to be taken to ensure the communication of information that is relevant to the audit.

Discussing matters of material significance with the Committee of Management

110 The Committee of Management are the persons principally responsible for the management of the society. The auditor will therefore normally bring a matter of material significance to the attention of the Committee subject to compliance with legislation relating to 'tipping off' and seek agreement on the facts and circumstances. However, ISA (UK and Ireland) 250 Section B emphasises that where the auditor concludes that a duty to report arises he should bring the matter to the attention of the regulator without undue delay. The Committee may wish to report the matters identified to the FSA themselves and detail the actions taken or to be taken. Whilst such a report from the Committee may provide valuable information, it does not relieve the auditor of the statutory duty to report directly to the FSA.

Timing of a report

111 The duty to report arises once the auditor has concluded that he reasonably believes that the matter is or is likely to be of material significance to the FSA's regulatory function. In reaching his conclusion the auditor may wish to take appropriate legal or other advice and consult with colleagues.

112 The report should be made without undue delay once a conclusion has been reached. Unless the matter casts doubt on the integrity of the Committee of Management this should not preclude discussion of the matter with the Committee and seeking such further advice as is necessary, so that a decision can be made on whether or not a duty to report exists. Such consultations and discussions are however undertaken on a timely basis to enable the auditor to conclude on the matter without undue delay.

Auditors' right to report to the FSA

113 Section 342 of FSMA 2000 provides that no duty to which an auditor of an authorised person is subject shall be contravened by communicating in good faith to the FSA information or an opinion on a matter that the auditor reasonably believes is relevant to any functions of the FSA.

114 The scope of the duty to report is wide particularly since, under the FSA's Principle for Businesses 11, an authorised firm must disclose to the FSA appropriately anything relating to the authorised firm of which the FSA would reasonably expect notice. However in circumstances where the auditor concludes that a matter does not give rise to a statutory duty to report but nevertheless should be brought to the attention of the regulator, in the first instance he advises the Committee of Management of his opinion. Where the auditor is unable to obtain, within a reasonable period, adequate evidence that the Committee has properly informed the FSA of the matter, then the auditor makes a report to the regulator without undue delay.

115 The auditor may wish to take legal advice before deciding whether, and in what form, to exercise his right to make a report direct to the regulator in order to ensure, for example, that only relevant information is disclosed and that the form and content of his report is such as to secure the protection of FSMA 2000. However, the auditor recognises that legal advice will take time and that speed of reporting is likely to be important in order to protect the interests of customers and/or to enable the FSA to meet its statutory objectives.

ISA (UK and IRELAND) 260: COMMUNICATION OF AUDIT MATTERS WITH THOSE CHARGED WITH GOVERNANCE

Background note

The purpose of this ISA (UK and Ireland) is to establish standards and provide guidance on communication of audit matters arising from the audit of financial statements between the auditor and those charged with governance of an entity. These communications relate to audit matters of governance interest as defined in this ISA (UK and Ireland). This ISA (UK and Ireland) does not provide guidance on communications by the auditor to parties outside the entity, for example, external regulatory or supervisory agencies.

The auditor should communicate audit matters of governance interest arising from the audit of financial statements with those charged with governance of an entity. (paragraph 2)

116 Auditors of friendly societies consider ISA (UK and Ireland) 260 in the context of

- the report on internal control exceptions prepared by management under Rule 3.1 (non-directive societies), and
- the possibility that the society may wish to provide a written communication to a third party such as the regulator.

> The auditor should determine the relevant persons who are charged with governance and with whom audit matters of governance interest are communicated. (paragraph 5)

117 ISA (UK and Ireland) 260 requires that auditors should communicate material weaknesses in the accounting and internal control systems identified during the audit to those charged with governance. A non-directive society's responsibility to prepare a Rule 3.1 report will be relevant to the timing of such communications.

118 Auditors have no specified reporting duty to the regulator in connection with the Rule 3.1 report. However, during the audit they enquire as to the society's progress with identifying and updating matters to be reported and discuss them with management in order to assess their impact, if any, on their audit of the financial statements. Auditors consider whether such weaknesses in internal control that have been identified by management have been communicated to those charged with governance.

ISA (UK and IRELAND) 300: PLANNING AN AUDIT OF FINANCIAL STATEMENTS

Background note

The purpose of this ISA (UK and Ireland) is to establish standards and provide guidance on the considerations and activities applicable to planning an audit of financial statements. This ISA (UK and Ireland) is framed in the context of recurring audits. In addition, matters the auditor considers in initial audit engagements are included in paragraphs 28 and 29.

> The auditor should plan the audit so that the engagement will be performed in an effective manner. (paragraph 2)
>
> The auditor should establish the overall audit strategy for the audit. (paragraph 8)
>
> The auditor should develop an audit plan for the audit in order to reduce audit risk to an acceptably low level. (paragraph 13)

119 In planning the audit of a society, the auditor obtains a detailed understanding of the particular types of insurance business undertaken. The planning process may include discussion with the management, in particular those with responsibility for:

- determining, implementing and monitoring underwriting policy;
- technical provisions;
- managing investments; and
- compliance and regulation.

Matters the auditor of a society may consider as part of the planning process for the audit of the financial statements include: 120
- the nature and scope of the friendly society's business;
- the society's relationships with the FSA and any other regulators;
- changes in applicable laws, regulations and accounting requirements; and
- issues relating to the auditor's statutory duty to report.

Guidance on the first three matters is included in the section on ISA (UK and Ireland) 315 and on the fourth matter in the section on ISA (UK and Ireland) 250 section B.

In addition, particular issues likely to require consideration in planning the audit of a society's financial statements are: 121

(a) the need to involve specialists. The nature and complexity of insurance businesses increases the likelihood that auditors may consider it necessary, in order to obtain sufficient appropriate evidence on which to base their report, to involve specialists in the audit process. For example, auditors may wish to rely on the work of an actuary or a statistician to assist their consideration of a society's technical provisions[24]. Similarly, the application of relevant tax legislation is likely to be complex, and hence auditors may wish to involve a tax specialist to assist the consideration of provisions for corporation and other taxes included in the financial statements. Other specialists the auditor may consider involving include regulatory, investment and systems specialists.
Consequently, auditors of a friendly society consider the need to involve such specialists at an early stage in planning their work. Where such specialists are to be used, they may take part in discussions with the society's management and staff, in order to assist in the development of knowledge and understanding relating to the friendly society's business. As part of the planning process the scope of work of the actuarial members of the audit team (or if applicable external actuarial advisors) and the form and content of their working papers and reports (in respect of external actuarial advisors) is agreed in advance.

(b) the effect of outsourcing of functions by the society, and the sources of evidence available to the auditors for transactions undertaken by service organisations. This may include the outsourcing of certain functions, such as investment management or the delegation of authority to underwrite and/or administer business, and to process and/or settle claims.
In certain cases, societies may be reliant upon third parties to provide financial and other information which may affect the financial statements and the audit thereof. Auditors consider the implications of such situations and plan their work accordingly.

In the case of a friendly society reporting under UK financial reporting standards undertaking long term insurance business, its Actuarial Function Holder plays a central role in the determination of the long term business technical provision disclosed in its financial statements. Auditors may discuss elements of their audit plan with the Actuarial Function Holder in order to ensure that their audit procedures are co-ordinated with the Actuary's work. Similarly for non-directive societies carrying on general business, the auditors would have reference to the work of the Appropriate Actuary. 122

It is normally advantageous for the Reviewing Actuary to be involved in the planning of the audit of the financial statements. In any case, the scope of the work to be 123

---

[24] For all societies undertaking long-term business, the auditors are **required** to refer to a 'Reviewing Actuary' in the context of the FSA return.

performed for the statutory audit and the audit of the regulatory return by the Reviewing Actuary is agreed and documented during the planning stages of the audit.

124 In view of their responsibilities to report on regulatory returns, auditors of friendly societies plan their work so as to carry out procedures necessary both to form an opinion on the financial statements and to report on matters included in the solvency return in an efficient and effective manner. Where the society appoints an external actuary to fulfil the duties of an Actuarial Function Holder or an Appropriate Actuary in relation to the friendly society's regulatory return, the auditors and their Reviewing Actuary also consider the need for liaison with that actuary.

ISA (UK and IRELAND) 315: OBTAINING AN UNDERSTANDING OF THE ENTITY AND ITS ENVIRONMENT AND ASSESSING THE RISKS OF MATERIAL MISSTATEMENT

Background note

The purpose of this ISA (UK and Ireland) is to establish standards and to provide guidance on obtaining an understanding of the entity and its environment, including its internal control, and on assessing the risks of material misstatement in a financial statement audit.

125 The auditor seeks to understand the business and the regulatory regime in which friendly societies operate. Generally, there is a close relationship between planning and obtaining an understanding of the business and the control environment, which is covered more fully below.

The auditor should obtain an understanding of relevant industry, regulatory, and other external factors including the applicable financial reporting framework. (paragraph 22)

The auditor should obtain an understanding of the nature of the entity. (paragraph 25)

126 The extent of knowledge required by the auditor in order to understand the friendly society's activities will vary according to the complexity of the business. This understanding addresses both external factors which affect the business and internal factors relating to the business itself.

127 When performing procedures to obtain an understanding of the society's activities, the auditor considers:

- the methods by which business is transacted;
- the characteristics of its insurance products, including those written in previous years where exposure remains;
- the introduction of new categories of products or customers or distribution channels;
- the reinsurance arrangements;
- the complexity of the friendly society's information systems;

- the legal and operational structure of the friendly society;
- the number and locations of branches;
- the regulatory capital position;
- a change in the market environment;
- relevant economic developments (for example, the impact on the level of savings of trends in interest rates and inflation);
- developments in relevant legislation and changes resulting from new judicial decisions (for example, new products promoted by government as incentives to save).

Insurance policies written in previous years may continue to have an impact upon friendly society's financial statements in subsequent years. For life assurance business guarantees and options and other policyholder promises made on the issue of policies in prior years will be one of the key factors in determining estimates for related technical provisions. 128

In obtaining an understanding of the regulatory factors the auditor considers: 129

- any formal communications between the FSA in its capacity as the regulator and the friendly society, including any new or interim risk assessments issued by the FSA and the results of any other supervisory visits conducted by the FSA;
- the contents of any recent reports prepared by 'skilled persons' under s.166 FSMA 2000 together with any correspondence, minutes or notes of meetings relevant to any recent skilled persons' report;
- any formal communications between the friendly society and other regulators;
- discussions with the friendly society's compliance officer together with others responsible for monitoring regulatory compliance.

> The auditor should obtain an understanding of the entity's selection and application of accounting policies and consider whether they are appropriate for its business and consistent with the applicable financial reporting framework and accounting policies used in the relevant industry. (paragraph 28)

Accounting policies of particular relevance may include those in relation to insurance and investment contracts, embedded derivatives in insurance contracts, deferred acquisition costs, classification of assets and liabilities (and thereby their measurement), revenue recognition (including investment management service contracts). The auditor undertakes procedures to consider whether the policies adopted are in compliance with applicable accounting standards and gains an understanding of the procedures, systems and controls applied to maintain compliance with them. 130

> The auditor should obtain an understanding of the entity's objectives and strategies, and the related business risks that may result in material misstatement of the financial statements. (paragraph 30)

It is important for the auditor to understand the multi-dimensional nature and extent of the financial and business risks integral to the environment, and how the friendly society's systems record and address these risks. Although they may apply to varying degrees, the risks include (but are not limited to): 131

- underwriting or insurance risk: which is inherent in any insurance business but will be influenced by, for example, the classes of business underwritten, new products or services introduced and guarantees given;

- credit risk: at its simplest, this is the risk that a third party will be unable to meet its obligations (for example, recoveries from reinsurers);
- liquidity risk: the risk that arises from the possibility that a friendly society has insufficient liquid funds to meet claims;
- interest rate risk: the risk that arises where there is a mismatch between the interest rate reset dates or bases used for asset and liability measurement;
- currency risk: the risk that arises from the mismatching of assets, liabilities and commitments denominated in different currencies;
- market risk: the risk that changes in the value of assets, liabilities and commitments will occur as a result of movements in relative prices (for example, as a result of changes in the market price of tradeable assets);
- operational risk: the risk of loss, arising from inadequate or failed internal processes, people or systems or from external events, including legal risk; and
- regulatory risk: the risk of public censure, fines (together with related compensation payments) and restriction or withdrawal of authorisation to conduct some or all of the friendly society's activities. In the UK this may arise from enforcement activity by the FSA.

Failure to manage the risks outlined above can also cause serious damage to a friendly society's reputation, potentially leading to loss of confidence in the friendly society's business (this is sometimes referred to as reputational risk).

> The auditor should obtain an understanding of the measurement and review of the entity's financial performance (paragraph 35).

132   The auditor obtains an understanding of the measures used by management to review the friendly society's performance. Further guidance is given in the section on ISA (UK and Ireland) 520.

> The auditor should obtain an understanding of internal control relevant to the audit. (paragraph 41)
>
> The auditor should obtain an understanding of the control environment. (paragraph 67)

133   The quality of the overall control environment is dependent upon management's attitude towards the operation of controls. A positive attitude may be evidenced by an organisational framework which enables proper segregation of duties and delegation of control functions and which encourages failings to be reported and corrected. Thus, where a lapse in the operation of a control is treated as a matter of concern, the control environment will be stronger and will contribute to effective control systems; whereas a weak control environment will undermine detailed controls, however well designed.

134   The systems of control need to have regard to the requirements of SYSC and PRIN as well as the provisions of IPRU (INS), INSPRU and GENPRU. Although the directors are required to certify they are satisfied that throughout the financial year the friendly society has complied in all material respects with these requirements, auditors of friendly societies do not have responsibility for reporting on whether systems of control meet regulatory requirements.

135 When third parties perform a significant role in a friendly society's business an important aspect of the control environment is how management exercise control over the use of such third parties.

136 The control environment within friendly societies may also be affected by the activities of voluntary staff. There is a risk that some staff may be performing duties without appropriate experience and training.

137 In the case of small friendly societies where the activities and products supplied may be relatively simple or uniform and the segregation of duties may be poor, the degree to which the auditors decide to test and rely on internal controls may be limited and audit evidence may be gained by use of analytical techniques and substantive tests. Further guidance on this matter is given in the section on ISA (UK and Ireland) 520.

138 The FSA requires authorised firms, including friendly societies, to maintain systems and controls appropriate for its business[25]. These include (but are not limited to):
- clear and appropriate reporting lines which are communicated within the society;
- appropriate controls to ensure compliance with laws and regulations (this may mean a separate Compliance function);
- appropriate risk assessment process;
- appropriate management information;
- controls to ensure suitability of staff;
- controls to manage tensions arising out of remuneration policies;
- documented and tested business continuity plans;
- documented business plans or strategies;
- an internal audit function (where appropriate);
- an audit committee (where appropriate); and
- appropriate record keeping arrangements.

139 Systems of internal control in a friendly society are important in ensuring orderly and prudent operations of the society and in assisting the Committee of Management to prepare financial statements which give a true and fair view. The following features of the business of larger societies may be relevant to the auditor's assessment of such internal controls:
- the substantial scale of transactions, both in terms of volume and relative value, makes it important that control systems are in place to ensure that transactions are recorded promptly, accurately and completely and are checked and approved, and that records are reconciled at appropriate intervals in order to identify and investigate differences promptly. Processing and accounting for complex transactions or high volumes of less complex transactions will almost inevitably involve the use of sophisticated technology. For example, transactions subject to 'straight through processing' involve little or no manual intervention after they have been initiated;
- proper segregation of duties between sales and underwriting and those responsible for establishing claims provisions, those responsible for claims handling, those responsible for claims settlement and those recording these transactions is particularly important;
- equally as important is the proper segregation of duties between and amongst those responsible for the purchase and sale of investments, those recording these transactions and those responsible for the physical security over the documents of title; and

---

[25] Most FSA systems and control requirements are set out in SYSC, but additional requirements relating to prudential matters also exist in GENPRU and INSPRU.

- the UK regulatory framework is both complex and evolving for friendly societies. This may give rise to significant liabilities for compensation to policyholders if not properly dealt with. Accordingly, an effective control system is essential to ensure that the requirements of the UK regulators are satisfied.

> The auditor should obtain an understanding of the entity's process for identifying business risks relevant to financial reporting objectives and deciding about actions to address those risks, and the results thereof. (paragraph 76)

140 Friendly societies should undertake appropriate risk assessment procedures as part of their risk management and internal control process under FSA rules. Friendly societies will normally be required to produce an individual capital assessment (ICA), which is designed to quantify risks specific to the entity and to generate and quantify an estimated capital requirement for the entity. The ICA includes an assessment of operational risk. Auditors will normally review such documentation in assessing the society's approach to addressing risks.

> The auditor should obtain a sufficient understanding of control activities to assess the risks of material misstatement at the assertion level and to design further audit procedures responsive to assessed risks (paragraph 90).

141 There is a wide variation between different friendly societies in terms of size, activity and organisation, so that there can be no standard approach to internal controls and risk. The auditor assesses the adequacy of controls in relation to the circumstances of each entity. Examples of weaknesses that may be relevant to the auditor's assessment of the risk of material misstatement are as follows:

- complex products or processes inadequately understood by management; this includes undue concentration of expertise concerning matters requiring the exercise of significant judgment or capable of manipulation such as valuations of financial instruments, insurance or reinsurance contracts;
- weaknesses in back office procedures undermining the completeness and accuracy of accounting records;
- backlogs in key reconciliations;
- inadequate maintenance of suspense or clearing accounts; and
- delays in the processing of premiums and claims.

Controls relating to outsourcing activities are considered in the ISA (UK and Ireland) 402 section.

> The auditor should obtain an understanding of how the entity has responded to risks arising from IT (paragraph 93).

142 As a result of the type and complexity of transactions undertaken, and records held, by friendly societies and the need for swift and accurate information processing and retrieval, many friendly societies are highly automated, including: the accounting function, the processing of premiums, reinsurance and claims, regulatory reporting and the supply of management information.

143 In addition to providing a basis for preparation of the financial statements and meeting requirements for maintenance of adequate accounting records, a key feature

of the information systems maintained by a friendly society is the importance of reliable and properly coded historical statistical data to operate the business. Historical statistical data is important, for example, in calculating technical provisions, and for providing analyses for regulatory returns.

An effective control system over the administration of insurance business will therefore seek to ensure the accurate collation, processing and storing of large volumes of data relating for example to: 144

- acceptance of risk;
- recording of policy details;
- collection of premiums;
- recording, investigation, evaluation and payment of claims;
- identification of classes of business required to be disclosed in the friendly society's regulatory returns, and
- transfer of data from the administration systems to systems used for calculating technical provisions.

The auditor assesses the extent, nature and impact of automation within the society and plans and performs work accordingly. In particular the auditor considers: 145

- the required level of IT knowledge and skills may be extensive and may require the auditor to obtain advice and assistance from staff with specialist skills;
- the extent of the application of audit software and related audit techniques;
- general controls relating to the environment within which IT based systems are developed, maintained and operated; and
- external interfaces susceptible to breaches of security.

A single computer system rarely covers all of the friendly society's requirements. It is common for friendly societies to employ a number of different systems and, in many cases use of PC-based applications, sometimes involving the use of complex spreadsheets, to generate important accounting and/or internal control information. 146

The auditor identifies and understands the communication between computer systems in order to assess whether appropriate controls are established and maintained to cover all critical systems and the links between them and to identify the most effective audit approach. 147

> The auditor should identify and assess the risks of material misstatement at the financial statement level, and at the assertion level for classes of transactions, account balances, and disclosures. (paragraph 100)
>
> As part of the risk assessment as described in paragraph 100, the auditor should determine which of the risks identified are, in the auditor's judgment, risks that require special audit consideration (such risks are defined as "significant risks"). (paragraph 108)
>
> For significant risks, to the extent the auditor has not already done so, the auditor should evaluate the design of the entity's related controls, including relevant control activities, and determine whether they have been implemented. (paragraph 113)

Significant risks are likely to arise in those areas that are subject to significant judgment by management or are complex and properly understood by comparatively few people within the friendly society. 148

149 Examples of significant risks for a friendly society requiring special audit consideration may include:

- the completeness and accuracy of processing of all insurance transactions (see section on ISA (UK and Ireland) 330);
- significant measurement uncertainty with respect to technical provisions (see section on ISA (UK and Ireland) 540);
- the structure of the reinsurance protection programme (see section on ISA (UK and Ireland) 330).

150 These are not the only risks – for example regulatory compliance, tax and IT are risk areas referred to elsewhere in this Practice Note.

151 Weaknesses in the control environment and in controls such as those described in paragraph 141 above could increase the risk of fraud.

152 The application of complex accounting standards such as IFRS 4 and IFRS 7 (for friendly societies using EU IFRS) and FRS 25, 26, 27 and 29 (for friendly societies using UK GAAP) may also give rise to significant risk. This arises from the classification, recognition and measurement of insurance and investment contracts, the classification and measurement of financial assets, hedge accounting, classification of assets/liabilities, and revenue/expense recognition. In addition significant risk may arise from the adequacy of financial statement disclosures, notably in respect of insurance and financial risk management.

ISA (UK and IRELAND) 320: AUDIT MATERIALITY

Background note

The purpose of this ISA (UK and Ireland) is to establish standards and provide guidance on the concept of materiality and its relationship with audit risk.

The auditor should consider materiality and its relationship with audit risk when conducting an audit. (paragraph 2)

Materiality should be considered by the auditor when:

(a) Determining the nature, timing and extent of audit procedures; and

(b) Evaluating the effect of misstatements. (paragraph 8)

153 The principles of assessing materiality in the audit of a society are the same as those applying to the audit of any other entity. In particular the auditor's consideration of materiality is a matter of professional judgment, and is affected by the auditor's perception of the common information needs of users as a group.

154 Factors that influence judgments as to materiality in relation to a society carrying on insurance business may include:

- transactions which have little or no direct effect on a society's technical account for the year. For example, an error on with-profits business written typically has a limited impact on surplus for the year as surplus is driven by the bonus distribution;

- reinsurance arrangements which are likely to affect the impact of claims on a society's funds. For example, any error in the gross estimate of a claim may have little or no effect on the net amount. The fact that the balance sheet of a society includes gross amounts of technical provisions within liabilities and any reinsurers' shares of technical provisions within assets needs to be considered.

In the case of many classes of insurance business, uncertainty relating to the ultimate cost of claims is an inherent feature of the business. As a result, whilst quantitative measures of materiality are of assistance in directing the focus of the auditors' work, qualitative factors relating to the extent and nature of disclosures in the financial statements will also be of importance. Where such uncertainty is considered to be significant, auditors consider the disclosures made in the financial statements, and the effect upon the auditors' report. This matter is dealt with in the section on ISA (UK and Ireland) 540 'Audit of Accounting Estimates' and under ISA (UK and Ireland) 700 'The auditors' report on financial statements'.

ISA (UK and IRELAND) 330: THE AUDITOR'S PROCEDURES IN RESPONSE TO ASSESSED RISKS

Background note

The purpose of this ISA (UK and Ireland) is to establish standards and provide guidance on determining overall responses and designing and performing further audit procedures to respond to the assessed risks of material misstatement at the financial statement and assertion levels in a financial statement audit.

When, in accordance with paragraph 115 of ISA (UK and Ireland) 315, the auditor has determined that it is not possible or practicable to reduce the risks of material misstatement at the assertion level to an acceptably low level with audit evidence obtained only from substantive procedures, the auditor should perform tests of relevant controls to obtain audit evidence about their operating effectiveness. (paragraph 25)

In practice the nature and volume of transactions relating to the operations of friendly societies often means that performing tests of relevant controls is the most efficient means of reducing audit risk to an acceptably low level.

When, in accordance with paragraph 108 of ISA (UK and Ireland) 315, the auditor has determined that an assessed risk of material misstatement at the assertion level is a significant risk, the auditor should perform substantive procedures that are specifically responsive to that risk. (paragraph 51)

Examples of significant risks for friendly societies requiring special audit consideration may include:

- the completeness and accuracy of processing of all insurance transactions;
- the structure of the reinsurance protection programme.

> The auditor should perform audit procedures to evaluate whether the overall presentation of the financial statements, including the related disclosures, are in accordance with the applicable financial reporting framework. (paragraph 65)

158 Specific financial reporting standards can require extensive narrative disclosures in the financial statements of friendly societies; for example, in relation to the nature and extent of risks arising from contracts. In designing and performing procedures to evaluate these disclosures the auditor obtains audit evidence regarding the assertions about presentation and disclosure described in paragraph 17 of ISA (UK and Ireland) 500 'Audit Evidence'.

Insurance transactions

159 When considering the completeness and accuracy of processing of insurance transactions, auditors have regard to the multiple purposes for which a friendly society will use data entered into its accounting records. Such data may be used not only for inclusion in the financial statements, but may also be included in the regulatory returns of the friendly society and be used as the basis for statistical analysis and extrapolation of past trends and transactions in assessing technical provisions. Errors in the data input may therefore have far reaching impact on the overall reported results. Data input required for such other purposes may therefore require additional detail or higher levels of accuracy of coding and allocation compared with those which might be required solely for the preparation of reliable financial statements.

160 For insurance transactions initiated by the friendly society, auditors consider the controls implemented for each material class of business and location, together with overall controls applied by the accounting function and management. Matters for consideration will include the procedures for the setting of and monitoring of compliance with underwriting guidelines, and controls over completeness of transactions and risks undertaken. Large friendly societies often transact very large volumes of transactions which are subject to extensive IT controls, and the use of computer-assisted audit techniques may be appropriate.

161 Auditors of a friendly society also have regard to the procedures implemented by the friendly society to ensure the completeness, accuracy and reliability of information provided by third parties, including intermediaries and agents. Procedures include reviewing the friendly society's procedures for the approval of such arrangements and the monitoring of the performance of business introduced through such contracts. These may include inspections by the friendly society or third parties of the agent's activities, records and reports to the friendly society.

162 Auditors review the contractual terms and assess the extent to which such agents are reporting transactions on a regular and prompt basis and whether the friendly society has completely and accurately recorded the reported transactions in the accounting records and statistical databases. Specific consideration will be paid to the terms of the agent's remuneration to ensure for example that all profit commission and expenses recovery entitlements have been recognised.

163 An important aspect of a friendly society's controls over completeness and accuracy of processing will often be its procedures for the reconciliation of balances with third parties, the settlement of transactions (including their correction where necessary) and the agreement and clearance of old items. Third parties will include

policyholders, brokers, underwriting agents and reinsurers, and procedures may vary for each category. Auditors review the friendly society's processes and monitoring procedures established to ascertain whether such reconciliations and settlements are up to date. Auditors pay particular attention to the use of suspense or similar accounts, and to whether they are reconciled and cleared regularly and promptly.

Reinsurance

When considering the impact of the friendly society's reinsurance arrangements on the financial statements auditors obtain a thorough understanding of the reinsurance programme. Auditors assess the procedures for the approval of reinsurance contracts, both in overall terms and in detail. 164

ISA (UK and IRELAND) 402: AUDIT CONSIDERATIONS RELATING TO ENTITIES USING SERVICE ORGANISATIONS

Background note

The purpose of this ISA (UK and Ireland) is to establish standards and provide guidance to an auditor where the entity uses a service organisation

In obtaining an understanding of the entity and its environment, the auditor should determine the significance of service organisation activities to the entity and the relevance to the audit. (paragraph 5)

Friendly societies are often of a size that outsourcing of one or more functions presents the most economical operating option. This can apply in even the largest friendly societies. Typically, functions such as investment management, custody of investments, and payroll will be outsourced to a service organisation. For premium collection, the relevant service organisation may be an employer around which membership of the society is based. 165

Based on the auditor's understanding of the aspects of the entity's accounting system and control environment relating to relevant activities, the auditor should:

(a) Assess whether sufficient appropriate audit evidence concerning the relevant financial statement assertions is available from records held at the entity; and if not,
(b) Determine effective procedures to obtain evidence necessary for the audit, either by direct access to records kept by service organisations or through information obtained from the service organisations or their auditor. (paragraph 9-18)

Of concern to the auditors will be the way that the Committee of Management of a society monitors the activities of a service organisation so as to ensure that it meets its legal and fiduciary responsibilities, particularly where this is relevant to the preparation of the financial statements. Where the Committee has established control and verification procedures over the information flows to and from a service 166 organisation, the auditors may be able to take assurance from this. The auditors will also need to assess whether the accounting records maintained by the society concerning the information processed and the system of control around the processing are sufficient to meet the requirements of Section 68 of the 1992 Act (in respect of accounting records) and Rule 3.1.

> If an auditor concludes that evidence from records held by a service organisation is necessary in order to form an opinion on the client's financial statements and the auditor is unable to obtain such evidence, the auditor should include a description of the factors leading to the lack of evidence in the basis of opinion section of their report and qualify their opinion or issue a disclaimer of opinion on the financial statements. (paragraph 18-1)

167 Given the limited resources available to many friendly societies it is possible that monitoring of the activities of service organisations is restricted. Auditors seek to identify any such circumstances at an early stage and explore ways to obtain sufficient appropriate audit evidence with the Committee of Management. The society is obliged to ensure that the auditor has appropriate access to records, information and explanations from material outsourced operations.

168 Whilst a friendly society may outsource functions to third parties the responsibility for these functions remains that of the society The society should have appropriate controls in place over these arrangements including:

- risk assessment prior to contracting with the service provider, which includes a proper due diligence and periodic review of the appropriateness of the arrangement;
- appropriate contractual agreements or service level agreements;
- contingency plans should the provider fail in delivery of services;
- appropriate management information and reporting from the outsourced provider;
- appropriate controls over customer information; and
- right of access of the society's internal audit to test the internal controls of the service provider.

169 If the auditor is unable to obtain sufficient appropriate audit evidence concerning outsourced operations the auditor considers whether it is necessary to report the matter direct to the FSA – see the section of this Practice Note relating to ISA (UK and Ireland) 250 Section B.

ISA (UK and IRELAND) 500: AUDIT EVIDENCE

> **Background note**
>
> The purpose of this ISA (UK and Ireland) is to establish standards and provide guidance on what constitutes audit evidence in an audit of financial statements, the quantity of audit evidence to be obtained, and the audit procedures that auditors use for obtaining that audit evidence.

> The auditor should obtain sufficient appropriate audit evidence to be able to draw reasonable conclusions on which to base the audit opinion. (paragraph 2)

> When information produced by the entity is used by the auditor to perform audit procedures, the auditor should obtain audit evidence about the accuracy and completeness of the information. (paragraph 11)

Audit evidence is particularly critical in material areas of the financial statements such as technical provisions.   170

In respect of technical provisions, auditors would enquire into the society's use of actuaries, and consider any report from the actuaries in assessing the provisions made and the related disclosures in the financial statements. This matter is considered further under ISA (UK and Ireland) 620.   171

In respect of long term business auditors will also consider: 172

- the consistency of recorded premium income with policies held on the policy master file; the master file being the basis for technical provisions. All recorded premium income should be supported by policy records on the policy master file and additions and deletions from the policy records should have the appropriate effect on recorded premium income;
- the consistency of recorded claims with policies extracted from the policy master file. If policies subject to claims are not removed from the master file there is a risk of double-counting the financial impact in 'claims paid' and in 'technical provisions';
- the methodology for determining and amortising new business acquisition costs. The amortisation period will be determined with reference to the expected development of profit margins from the new business written;
- the calculations, presentation and disclosure required under FRS 27 and the SORP.

In respect of general business auditors will also consider: 173

- the allocation of premium income earned to the period of risk covered; achieved by establishing unearned premium reserves,
- the nature and coverage of reinsurance and the operation of the reinsurance programme, and
- the need for, or adequacy of, any unexpired risk provision to recognise losses expected to arise on any business written.

Holloway societies are sometimes considered to be special cases. They typically issue policies that provide sickness benefits, death benefit and savings towards an eventual pension or lump sum. These policies are often considered to be long term business and accordingly require an actuarial valuation of liabilities. This may not always be the case, however, and auditors of such societies ensure that the classification of the business has been properly considered by the society and its actuarial advisers. The same basic principles as to integrity of accounting records and audit evidence otherwise apply to these societies as to other societies and insurers.   174

ISA (UK & Ireland) 505: EXTERNAL CONFIRMATIONS

Background note

The purpose of this ISA (UK and Ireland) is to establish standards and provide guidance on the auditor's use of external confirmations as a means of obtaining audit evidence.

> The auditor should determine whether the use of external confirmations is necessary to obtain sufficient appropriate audit evidence at the assertion level. In making this determination, the auditor should consider the assessed risk of material misstatement at the assertion level and how the audit evidence from other planned audit procedures will reduce the risk of material misstatement at the assertion level to an acceptably low level. (paragraph 2)

175 In general, external confirmation procedures may be useful as part of the audit of:

- cash and investments,
- amounts receivable from reinsurers in respect of claims paid or payable by the cedant, and
- premiums receivable from intermediaries.

However, external confirmations may not always provide useful audit evidence in relation to insurance balances due to the relative immateriality of individual policyholder balances or transactions.

176 Amounts receivable from reinsurers may comprise a friendly society's calculation of amounts that will be recoverable from reinsurers in respect of the friendly society's estimate of incurred claims. The relevant reinsurers are unlikely to be in a position to confirm amounts in relation to these claims until such time as the validity of these claims has been assessed, the amounts payable determined, and this has been communicated to and agreed by the relevant reinsurers. Therefore the relevant reinsurers may not be able to provide sufficient appropriate evidence in response to a confirmation request that includes such amounts. The auditor may though determine that confirmation would be an effective procedure in respect of individual material reinsurance recoveries where the reinsurer has agreed the amount involved but the balance has not yet been paid.

177 In deciding to what extent to use external confirmations in respect of premiums receivable from intermediaries the auditor considers the assessed risk of misstatement together with the characteristics of the environment in which the insurer operates and the practice of potential respondents in dealing with requests for direct confirmation. For example, where premiums receivable comprise a high volume of low value amounts which may be due from individuals or entities that do not have information systems that facilitate external confirmation, the auditor may decide that confirmation may not be an effective audit procedure and may seek to obtain sufficient appropriate evidence from other sources.

ISA (UK and IRELAND) 520: ANALYTICAL PROCEDURES

Background note

The purpose of this ISA (UK and Ireland) is to establish standards and provide guidance on the application of analytical procedures during an audit.

> The auditor should apply analytical procedures as risk assessment procedures to obtain an understanding of the entity and its environment and in the overall review at the end of the audit. (paragraph 2)

There are relationships between the movement in balance sheet items and specific income statement items (for example deferred acquisition costs, claims provisions and the long term business provision). 178

Friendly societies often offer a limited range of products with simple pricing and benefits structures. Audit evidence as to the completeness and accuracy of income received can be gained through analytical review. For example, there may be a single product with a uniform premium per month for all members. 179

If the society maintains accurate and up to date membership records, accounting for joiners and leavers, this information can be used to develop an expectation of premium income in the year, together with the standard terms of the policies, to be compared with the amount actually recorded. 180

Given the nature of insurance business non financial data plays a significant part in managing the pricing and reserving processes. The auditor may consider the usefulness of non financial data such as policy numbers, sums assured, retention levels and claim numbers and their interrelation with financial data in designing analytical review procedures. In addition the auditor may consider measures relating to regulatory compliance – e.g. complaints handling and breaches of conduct of business rules and operational risk measures – e.g. volumes of unreconciled items. 181

Auditors may also use software to interrogate a society's policy master file for unusual data items and exceptions, for example, to identify active policyholders who are over a specified age. 182

Evidence from the above techniques would be considered by auditors alongside systems and controls work and results from substantive testing. 183

Where non financial information or reports produced from systems or processes outside the financial statements accounting system are used in analytical procedures the auditor considers the reliability of that information or those reports. 184

ISA (UK and IRELAND) 540: AUDIT OF ACCOUNTING ESTIMATES

Background note

The purpose of this ISA (UK and Ireland) is to establish standards and provide guidance on the audit of accounting estimates contained within the financial statements.

The auditor should obtain sufficient appropriate audit evidence regarding accounting estimates (paragraph 2)

The auditor should adopt one or a combination of the following approaches in the audit of an accounting estimate:

(a) Review and test the process used by management to develop the estimate;
(b) Use an independent estimate for comparison with that prepared by management; or
(c) Review of subsequent events which provide audit evidence of the reasonableness of the estimate made. (paragraph 10)

185 For most friendly societies, the estimation of technical provisions will involve relatively high estimation uncertainty because it will involve significant assumptions about future conditions, transactions or events that are uncertain at the time of the estimation. Changes in estimation approach are likely to have a significant effect on the surplus figure in the financial statements.

186 Audit teams normally involve actuarial specialists in assessing technical provisions. Their level of involvement in the audit process will depend though on matters such as the level of expertise of other members of the audit team, the availability of independent actuarial advice to the friendly society, and the nature and complexity of the audit issues. They may be used in the initial assessment of the level of risk of each financial statement caption, in assessing the effectiveness of the control environment, in establishing the audit procedures to be adopted and in obtaining and assessing the audit evidence obtained. Further guidance on the use of an actuary is given in the section on ISA (UK and Ireland) 620 "Using the work of an expert".

187 When designing audit procedures to test the process used by management to develop the technical provisions, the auditor considers:

- the policies for setting such provisions;
- the complexity and nature of the models or measurement techniques used to estimate the technical provisions;
- the source data; and
- the assumptions used to develop those provisions.

188 The models used to estimate the technical provisions are dependent upon the accuracy and completeness of financial and non-financial data and accordingly the audit procedures will need to address the effectiveness of management's controls over the use and reliability of such data.

189 The assumptions made by management are intended to provide a reasonable basis for the setting of the technical provisions. The objective of the audit procedures performed for the purpose of evaluating these assumptions is not intended to obtain sufficient appropriate audit evidence to provide an opinion on the assumptions themselves. Furthermore, the auditor's consideration of management's assumptions is based only on information available to the auditor at the time of the audit. The auditor is not responsible for predicting future conditions, transactions or events that, if they had been known at the time of the audit, might have significantly affected management's actions or management's assumptions underlying the technical provisions and related disclosures.

190 For those friendly societies to which it applies, the realistic valuation of with-profits liabilities uses a range of estimation techniques. The provision will comprise both historic (most likely asset-share based) and projected (option and guarantee) information. Options and guarantees are often valued using stochastic modelling techniques. Auditors assess whether regulatory requirements have been met and whether sufficient scenarios have been run. Any assertions regarding future management and policyholder actions also require careful consideration, including the extent to which management actions are supported by the PPFM[26] or board resolution.

191 Pursuant to Regulation 10 to the Friendly Societies (Accounts and Related Provisions) Regulations 1994,Schedule 6 (Part VI para 37) provides that the computation

---

[26] A document intended to provide information to policyholders and others, in respect of the principles and practices in accordance with which a with-profits fund is managed. The prescribed scope and content of the document are set out in COB 6.10 in the FSA Handbook.

- whether management monitors the outcome of technical provisions made in the prior period, and whether management has appropriately responded to the outcome of that monitoring procedure.

195 The review of the outcome or re-estimation of prior period accounting estimates may assist the auditor in identifying circumstances or conditions that could increase the uncertainty of a technical provision. However, the review is not intended to call into question the auditor's judgments made in the prior year that were based on information available at the time.

196 Management bias, whether unintentional or intentional, can be difficult to detect in a particular technical provision. It may only be identified when there has been a change in the method for calculating technical provisions from the prior period based on a subjective assessment without evidence that there has been a change in circumstances when considered in the aggregate of groups of estimates or all estimates, or when observed over a number of accounting periods. Although some form of management bias is inherent in subjective decisions, management may have no intention of misleading the users of financial statements. If, however, there is intention to mislead through, for example, the intentional use of unreasonable estimates, management bias is fraudulent in nature. ISA 240, "The Auditor's Responsibility to Consider Fraud in an Audit of Financial Statements," provides standards and guidance on the auditor's responsibility to consider fraud in an audit of financial statements.

197 Insurance specific financial reporting standards, which form part of the applicable financial reporting frameworks applying to friendly societies, take into account the inherent uncertainty within the insurance industry and the needs of users of financial statements regarding disclosure of estimation uncertainty. The auditor considers the required disclosure of estimation uncertainty by the applicable financial reporting framework and whether the disclosure proposed by management is adequate. In making this determination, the auditor considers whether adequate disclosure is given regarding the sensitivities associated with the significant assumptions underlying the technical provisions, in light of the materiality level established for the engagement.

198 Insurance specific financial reporting standards can require extensive narrative disclosures in the financial statements of friendly societies; for example, in relation to the nature and extent of risks arising from insurance contracts. In designing and performing procedures to evaluate these disclosures the auditor obtains audit evidence regarding the assertions about presentation and disclosure described in paragraph 17 of ISA (UK and Ireland) 500 "Audit Evidence". Guidance on the types of audit procedures that can be used for obtaining audit evidence can be found in paragraphs 26 to 38 of ISA (UK and Ireland) 500.

199 Consideration of the adequacy of disclosure with regard to sensitivities of significant assumptions is of particular importance where the estimation uncertainty of technical provisions may cast significant doubt about the entity's ability to continue as a going concern. ISA (UK & Ireland) 570 "Going Concern" and ISA (UK and Ireland) 700 "The Auditor's Report on Financial Statements" establish standards and provide guidance in such circumstances.

200 Where the applicable financial reporting framework does not prescribe disclosure of estimation uncertainty, the auditor nevertheless considers management's description, in the notes to the financial statements, of the circumstances relating to the estimation uncertainty. ISA (UK & Ireland) 700, "The Auditor's Report on Financial Statements" provides guidance on the implications for the auditor's report when the auditor believes that management's disclosure of estimation uncertainty in the

of the long-term business provision[27] of a life insurer shall be made by a Fellow of the Institute or Faculty of Actuaries "on the basis of recognised actuarial methods, with due regard to the actuarial principles laid down in Council Directive 2002/83/EC of the European Parliament and of the Council of 5 November 2002 concerning life assurance". The actuary carrying out this statutory duty for the friendly society has been designated as the 'Reporting Actuary' by Guidance Note ("GN") 7 'The Role of Actuaries in Relation to Financial Statements of Insurers and Insurance Groups writing Long-term Business and their Relationship with Auditors' issued by the Institute and Faculty of Actuaries and now adopted by the Board for Actuarial Standards (BAS). The statutory duty of the Reporting Actuary[28] does not extend to any technical provisions other than the long-term business provision. The auditor understands the approach which the Reporting Actuary has adopted in calculating the long term business provision.

For any friendly societies carrying on general insurance business there will normally be a range of technical provisions that may be appropriate for inclusion in the financial statements. Guidance Note 12 'General Insurance Business: Actuarial Reports' issued by the Institute and Faculty of Actuaries and adopted by the BAS provides guidance to actuaries on the preparation of a formal report on, inter alia, technical provisions or on the financial soundness of a general insurance undertaking. If the actuary has prepared a formal report on the technical provisions or on the financial soundness of a general insurance undertaking the auditor reviews the report to gain a better understanding of the scope of the work performed and of any limitations on any opinions expressed. If such a report has not been prepared, it is necessary for auditors to understand the scope of the work carried out by the friendly society's actuary. 192

Given that the calculation of a friendly society's technical provisions is such a significant activity in the preparation of the friendly society's financial statements, once management has selected a specific estimation method, it is important that the friendly society consistently applies it. If management has changed the method for calculating technical provisions, the auditor considers whether the method to which it has been changed provides a more appropriate basis of measurement, or that the change is supported by a change in the applicable financial reporting framework, or a change in circumstances. 193

In obtaining an understanding of whether, and if so how, the friendly society has assessed the effect of estimation uncertainty on the technical provisions, the auditor considers matters such as: 194

- whether, and if so how, management has considered alternative assumptions or outcomes by, for example, performing a sensitivity analysis to determine the effect of changes in the assumptions on the level of technical provisions;
- how management determines the ultimate technical provisions when analysis indicates that there may be a number of outcome scenarios;

---

[27] *"Long-term business provision" is a term used in Schedule 9A to the Companies Act 1985 and under the Accounts Regulations for friendly societies. Insurers and friendly societies preparing financial statements under IFRS may use different designations for such items. In this Practice Note the term should be interpreted as meaning those items that would fall to be classified as long-term business provisions under the Accounts and Regulations regardless of how they are described in the financial statements. It may be noted that 'long-term business provision' in this context does not include provisions in respect of linked long-term contracts.*

[28] *The statutory duty of a Reporting Actuary arises in Schedule 9A to the Companies Act 1985 and so does not apply to long-term insurers preparing financial statements under IFRS; for those companies the term Reporting Actuary in the Practice Note should be taken to refer to any actuary given responsibility by management for the calculation of policyholder liabilities for the purpose of their inclusion in the financial statements.*

financial statements is inadequate or misleading.

> The auditor should make a final assessment of the reasonableness of the entity's accounting estimates based on the auditor's understanding of the entity and its environment and whether the estimates are consistent with other audit evidence obtained during the audit. (paragraph 24)

Based on the audit evidence obtained, the auditor may conclude that the evidence points to an estimate of the required technical provision that differs from management's estimate, and that the difference between the auditor's estimate or range and management's estimate constitutes a financial statement misstatement. In such cases, where the auditor has developed a range, a misstatement exists when management's estimate lies outside the auditor's range. The misstatement is measured as the difference between management's estimate and the nearest point of the auditor's range. **201**

ISA (UK and IRELAND) 545: AUDITING FAIR VALUE MEASUREMENTS AND DISCLOSURES

> **Background note**
>
> The purpose of this ISA (UK and Ireland) is to establish standards and provide guidance on auditing fair value measurements and disclosures contained in financial statements.

The auditor should obtain sufficient appropriate audit evidence that fair value measurements and disclosures are in accordance with the entity's applicable financial reporting framework. (paragraph 3)

As part of the understanding of the entity and its environment, including its internal control, the auditor should obtain an understanding of the entity's process for determining fair value measurements and disclosures and of the relevant control activities sufficient to identify and assess the risks of material misstatement at the assertion level and to design and perform further audit procedures. (paragraph 10)

The auditor should evaluate whether the fair value measurements and disclosures in the financial statements are in accordance with the entity's applicable financial reporting framework. (paragraph 17)

Guidance on the application of ISA (UK and Ireland) 545 given below is relevant to the financial statements of friendly societies that hold derivatives. **202**

The valuation of derivative and other financial instruments which are not traded in an active market and so for which valuation techniques are required is an activity that can give rise to significant audit risk. Such financial instruments are priced using valuation techniques such as discounted cashflow models, options pricing models or by reference to another instrument that is substantially the same as the financial instrument subject to valuation. The auditor reviews the controls, procedures and testing of the valuation techniques used by the friendly society. Controls and substantive testing could include focusing on: **203**

- valuation technique approval and testing procedures used by the friendly society;
- the independence of review, sourcing and reasonableness of observable market data and other parameters used in the valuation techniques;
- calibration procedures used by the friendly society to test the validity of valuation techniques applied by comparing outputs to observable market transactions;
- completeness and appropriate inclusion of all relevant observable market data;
- the observability in practice of data classified by the friendly society as observable market data;
- the appropriateness and validity of classification of instruments designated as being traded in a non active and in an active market;
- the appropriateness and validity of the particular valuation technique applied to particular financial instruments;
- the appropriateness and validity of the parameters used by the insurer to designate an instrument as substantially the same as the financial instrument being valued;
- mathematical integrity of the valuation models; and
- access controls over valuation models.

204 In the more subjective areas of valuation the auditor obtains an understanding of the assumptions used and undertakes a review of the estimates involved for reasonableness, consistency and conformity with generally accepted practices. In some cases, the auditor may use his own valuation techniques to assess the friendly society's valuations. Given the complexities involved and the subjective nature of the judgments inherent the auditor may involve an expert in elements of this work (see ISA (UK and Ireland) 620 section of this Practice Note).

ISA (UK and IRELAND) 550: RELATED PARTIES

Background note

The purpose of this ISA (UK and Ireland) is to establish standards and provide guidance on the auditor's responsibilities and audit procedures regarding related parties and transactions with such parties regardless of whether International Accounting Standard (IAS) 24, "Related Party Disclosures," or similar requirement, is part of the applicable financial reporting framework.

205 Both when applying IFRS or UK GAAP, under ISA (UK and Ireland) 550, the auditor is required to assess the risk that material undisclosed related party transactions may exist. It is in the nature of insurance business that transaction volumes are high but this factor will not, of itself, necessarily lead the auditor to conclude that the inherent risk of material undisclosed related party transactions is high.

206 There are annual reporting obligations to the FSA in respect of controllers and entities that are closely linked to the firm (SUP 16). As a result, it will therefore normally be the case that there are controls in place to ensure that this information is properly collated. However, the definition of 'controller and closely linked" for regulatory purposes is not congruent with the 'related party' definition in FRS 8/IAS 24 and the auditor therefore considers what controls have been put in place by management to capture information on those parties which fall within the accounting definition only.

In reviewing related party information for completeness, the auditor may compare the proposed disclosures in the financial statements to information prepared for regulatory reporting purposes (bearing in mind that the population may be different, as noted in the preceding paragraph).   207

> The auditor should perform audit procedures designed to obtain sufficient appropriate audit evidence regarding the identification and disclosure by management[29] of related parties and the effect of related party transactions that are material to the financial statements. (paragraph 102)

> Where there is any indication that such circumstances exist, the auditor should perform modified, extended or additional audit procedures as are appropriate in the circumstances. (paragraph 103)

Schedule 11 of the 1992 Act applies sections 62-69 of the Building Societies Act 1986 (the 1986 Act) concerning directors' loans and transactions to friendly societies. In the context of friendly societies, the term 'director' is applicable to members of the Committee of Management.   208

Section 65 of the 1986 Act[30] lists a number of such transactions which are either illegal or subject to strict limitations. Section 68 requires the maintenance of a Register by the society recording details of all permitted transactions with directors and connected persons. Extracts from this Register are required to be included in an unaudited annual statement, and to be made available to the members and to the FSA. Friendly societies are also required to disclose in their financial statements certain details of loans outstanding at the year end to Committee members and connected persons.   209

Section 69 requires societies to maintain a Register of certain specified details of business transactions with directors and with business associates of directors. There is no requirement for the Section 69 Register to be reported on by the auditors although annual extracts are required to be sent to the FSA and to be made available to the members.   210

> When planning the audit the auditor should assess the risk that material undisclosed related party transactions, or undisclosed outstanding balances between an entity and its related parties may exist. (paragraph 106-3)

In order to comply with statutory requirements, friendly societies should have appropriate systems to ensure that all such loans and transactions are identified, controlled and properly disclosed, both in the Registers and in the financial statements. In order to fulfil these requirements societies normally require each Committee member to confirm, in writing and on an annual basis, the existence and amount of any such matters: negative returns are usually required for completeness.   211

---

[29] In the UK and Ireland those charged with governance are responsible for the preparation of the financial statements.

[30] All section references in the immediately following paragraphs are to the 1986 Act.

212 Auditors consider whether loans and transactions recorded by the society in accordance with the requirements of Sections 65, 68 and 69 of the 1986 Act fall within the related parties criteria under accounting standards and legislation for disclosure in the financial statements.

213 If the auditors become aware of breaches of the statutory requirements relating to loans and other transactions by individual Committee members, including a failure to notify the society of any relevant matters, such a matter may be considered to trigger the statutory duty to report (see the ISA (UK and Ireland) 250 Section B section of this Practice Note).

ISA (UK and IRELAND) 560: SUBSEQUENT EVENTS

Background note

The purpose of this ISA (UK and Ireland) is to establish standards and provide guidance on the auditor's responsibility regarding subsequent events.

The auditor should perform audit procedures designed to obtain sufficient appropriate audit evidence that all events up to the date of the auditor's report that may require adjustment of, or disclosure in, the financial statements have been identified (paragraph 4).

214 Matters specific to friendly societies carrying on insurance business, which auditors may consider in their review of subsequent events in the context of reporting on the financial statements[31], include:

- an evaluation of the impact of any material subsequent events on the capital resources requirement for the society;
- an assessment of the influence of new information received relevant to claims provisions;
- an assessment of the impact of any regulatory developments since the balance sheet date; and
- a review of relevant correspondence with regulators and enquiries of management to determine whether any significant breaches of regulations or other significant regulatory concerns have come to light since the period end.

215 ISA (UK and Ireland) 560 provides guidance to auditors on facts discovered after the financial statements have been issued. If, in the course of their examination of the society's regulatory return, auditors become aware of subsequent events which, had they occurred or been known of at the date of their report on the financial statements, might have caused them to issue a different report, they and the Committee of Management consider whether the financial statements need to be revised. Where the auditors conclude that this step is appropriate, the matter concerned is likely to be of material significance to the FSA and so give rise to a duty to report to the FSA.

---

[31] *Subsequent events in the context of reporting on the solvency return are considered under 'Reporting on regulatory returns' below.*

ISA (UK and IRELAND) 570: THE GOING CONCERN BASIS IN FINANCIAL STATEMENTS

> **Background note**
>
> The purpose of this ISA (UK and Ireland) is to establish standards and provide guidance on the auditor's responsibility in the audit of financial statements with respect to the going concern assumption used in the preparation of the financial statements, including management's assessment of the entity's ability to continue as a going concern.

> When planning and performing audit procedures and in evaluating the results thereof, the auditor should consider the appropriateness of management's use of the going concern assumption in the preparation of the financial statements. (paragraph 2)
>
> The auditor should consider any relevant disclosures in the financial statements. (paragraph 2-1)

216 The Committee of Management is responsible for determining, on the basis of its own information and judgments, whether the going concern presumption is appropriate.

217 Factors that may alert auditors to potential solvency issues include:

- declining membership,
- poor volumes of new business,
- excessive strain of initial acquisition costs caused by high volumes of new business,
- significant departures from underlying pricing assumptions when business was written,
- adequacy of reserves,
- downward trend in the fund for future appropriations,
- large amounts of maturities or surrenders,
- poor investment performance, and
- a high expense ratio (the ratio of administration expenses to premiums earned in the year).

218 Where the solvency of a society writing long term business is subject to uncertainty the Committee of Management would be expected to consult closely with its actuarial advisers regarding:

- the level of bonuses it is able to pay out to members having with-profits policies, and
- whether it can realistically continue to write new business profitably or whether, in the interests of members, it should close to new business.

It is likely that poor performance by the society will result in the Actuarial Function Holder recommending that a higher proportion of the funds of the society be held in assets of lower risk and higher liquidity (cash and gilts rather than equities or property).

219 With reference to friendly societies, specific audit procedures may include:

- reviewing the means whereby the members of the Committee of Management of a friendly society satisfy themselves that the friendly society will have capital in excess of its capital resources requirement for the foreseeable future, including a review of the friendly society's Individual Capital Assessment prepared for regulatory purposes;
- considering whether the key assumptions underlying the budgets and/or forecasts appear appropriate in the circumstances. Key assumptions will normally include claims projections (numbers, cost and timing), the profitability of business written (especially for life business) and the level of provisions required;
- considering the liquidity of funds to enable the society to meet claims and other liabilities as they fall due;
- in the case of large friendly societies, reviewing any financial condition report produced by the holder of the actuarial function and other actuarial reports;
- reviewing correspondence with the regulators, and considering any action taken (or likely to be taken) by the regulators; and
- considering the potential costs of settling claims (for instance uncertainty resulting from judicial decisions) and additional provisions (for example product mis-selling).

220 If the auditor has any doubts as to the ability of a friendly society to continue as a going concern, the auditor considers whether he ought to make a report direct to the FSA on which guidance is set out in the section of this Practice Note relating to ISA (UK and Ireland) 250 Section B.

ISA (UK and IRELAND) 580: MANAGEMENT REPRESENTATIONS

Background note

The purpose of this ISA (UK and Ireland) is to establish standards and provide guidance on the use of management representations as audit evidence, the procedures to be applied in evaluating and documenting management representations and the action to be taken if management refuses to provide appropriate representations.

Written confirmation of appropriate representations from management, as required by paragraph 4 below, should be obtained before the audit report is issued. (paragraph 2-1)

The auditor should obtain written representations from management on matters material to the financial statements when other sufficient appropriate audit evidence cannot reasonably be expected to exist. (paragraph 4)

221 ISAs (UK and Ireland) 250 and 550 require auditors to obtain written confirmation in respect of completeness of disclosure to the auditors of:
- all known actual or possible non – compliance with laws and regulations (including breaches of FSMA 2000, FSA rules, the Money Laundering Regulations, other regulatory requirements or any other circumstance that could jeopardise the authorisation of the society under FSMA 2000) whose effects should be considered when preparing financial statements together with the actual or contingent consequences which may arise therefrom; and

- the completeness of information provided regarding the identification of related parties and the adequacy of related party disclosures in the financial statements.

ISA (UK and Ireland) 580 requires that auditors should obtain written confirmation of representations from management on matters material to the financial statements when these representations are critical to obtaining sufficient appropriate audit evidence. For friendly societies falling within FSA's realistic capital regime, representations in relation to the management actions assumed in the valuation of realistic liabilities are likely to be relevant. For other friendly societies, it may be appropriate to obtain a specific representation confirming the adequacy of the claims provisions and the IBNR. Auditors may also obtain written representations from those charged with governance regarding: 222

- the reasonableness of significant assumptions used by the entity in calculating technical provisions;
- all correspondence with regulators having been made available to the auditor.

Additionally, there may be a number of assumptions supporting the Committee of Management's evaluation of the friendly society's going concern status which reflect commercial judgments. It may be appropriate for the auditors to obtain written representation on such judgments. 223

ISA (UK and IRELAND) 600: USING THE WORK OF ANOTHER AUDITOR

Background note

The purpose of this ISA (UK and Ireland) is to establish standards and provide guidance when an auditor, reporting on the financial statements of an entity, uses the work of another auditor on the financial information of one or more components included in the financial statements of the entity. This ISA (UK and Ireland) does not deal with those instances where two or more auditors are appointed as joint auditors nor does it deal with the auditors' relationship with a predecessor auditor. Further, when the principal auditor concludes that the financial statements of a component are immaterial, the standards in this ISA (UK and Ireland) do not apply. When, however, several components, immaterial in themselves, are together material, the procedures outlined in this ISA (UK and Ireland) would need to be considered.

When the principal auditor uses the work of another auditor, the principal auditor should determine how the work of the other auditor will affect the audit. (paragraph 2)

In the UK and Ireland, when planning to use the work of another auditor, the principal auditors' consideration of the professional competence of the other auditor should include consideration of the professional qualifications, experience and resources of the other auditor in the context of the specific assignment. (paragraph 7-1)

ISA (UK and Ireland) 600 has particular relevance in the context of group audits where the subsidiary entity auditors are different from the auditors of the parent 224 friendly society. The principles equally apply where the auditors of registered branches of a society are different from those of the central office.

225 The principal auditor considers in particular the competence and capability of the other auditor having regard to the laws, regulation and industry practice relevant to the component to be reported on by the other auditor and, where relevant, whether the other auditor has access to actuarial or other expertise appropriate to the component's insurance business.

226 In certain circumstances a branch may be audited by another firm. In these circumstances the other auditor has a duty to report matters of material significance to the FSA rather than via the principal auditor. However, it is likely that any such matters would have a direct bearing on the work of the principal auditor and would be reported to the principal auditor. In such circumstances the principal auditor would consider also reporting such matters directly to the FSA. More detailed consideration of the auditors' duty to report to the FSA is set out in the section of this Practice Note dealing with ISA (UK and Ireland) 250.

227 In the case of a society having registered branches, the central office auditor will report on a consolidated statement of solvency or prudential return to the FSA following the actuarial investigation. There is no statutory requirement at present for consolidated financial statements in the case of a society comprising a central office and separately registered branches.

ISA (UK and IRELAND) 610: CONSIDERING THE WORK OF INTERNAL AUDIT

Background note

The purpose of this ISA (UK and Ireland) is to establish standards and provide guidance to external auditors in considering the work of internal auditing. This ISA (UK and Ireland) does not deal with instances when personnel from internal auditing assist the external auditor in carrying out external audit procedures. The audit procedures notes in this ISA (UK and Ireland) need only be applied to internal auditing activities which are relevant to the audit of the financial statements.

The external auditor should consider the activities of internal auditing and their effect, if any, on external audit procedures. (paragraph 2)

The external auditor should obtain a sufficient understanding of internal audit activities to identify and assess the risks of material misstatement of the financial statements and to design and perform further audit procedures. (paragraph 9)

When the external auditor intends to use specific work of internal auditing, the external auditor should evaluate and perform audit procedures on that work to confirm its adequacy for the external auditor's purposes. (paragraph 16)

228 The FSA specifies a 'system of inspection and report' to be undertaken by independent inspectors for non – directive friendly societies. Larger friendly societies can be expected to have their own dedicated internal audit departments. For small

societies, the approach may be very simple and the FSA considers that it is for the Committee of Management to determine how best to fulfil the requirements.

For the purposes of the audit of the society's annual financial statements the auditors consider whether there are some aspects of the programme of work carried out by internal audit, or others responsible for inspection and report, on which they may rely. The extent of such reliance will depend upon the auditors' opinion as to the scope and competence of the internal audit function. In assessing this, the auditors review the written record of the society's inspection policy and a selection of the working papers and reports produced by those responsible for inspection and report. 229

ISA (UK and IRELAND) 620: USING THE WORK OF AN EXPERT

> **Background note**
>
> The purpose of this ISA (UK and Ireland) is to establish standards and provide guidance on using the work of an expert as audit evidence.

> When using the work performed by an expert, the auditor should obtain sufficient appropriate audit evidence that such work is adequate for the purposes of the audit. (paragraph 2)

The preparation of the financial statements of a friendly society carrying on insurance business frequently involves the need for the Committee of Management to obtain advice from experts. Examples of experts and how they can be used by either the friendly society or the auditor include: 230

- actuaries and statisticians, in assessing the technical provisions required at the balance sheet date,
- property valuers and investment managers, in assessing the values of the society's investments at the balance sheet date,
- loss adjustors and legal advisers, in determining the outcome of particular individual claims or portfolios of claims,
- compliance specialists, in assessing compliance with laws and regulations, and
- taxation advisers, in assisting with the preparation of tax calculations.

As stated in the section on ISA (UK and Ireland) 540, given the nature and complexity of insurance business the auditor may involve an actuary in assessing technical provisions in the audit of the financial statements. The FSA requires the auditor of a life insurer to obtain and pay due regard to the advice of a reviewing actuary when reporting on regulatory returns (see 'Reporting on regulatory returns' section). Where the auditor uses an expert as part of the audit, the auditor remains solely responsible for the audit of the friendly society's financial statements and will not refer[32] to the work of the expert within the auditor's report. 231

Where the auditor decides to use an actuarial expert in relation to his audit of the friendly society's technical provisions, the auditor assesses the following: 232

---

[32] Although in the case of a report on regulatory returns, such a reference is required – see the 'Reporting on regulatory returns' section of this Practice Note.

(a) the professional competence of the actuary, taking into consideration his professional qualifications, experience and reputation in the market in which the friendly society operates;
(b) the objectivity of the actuary including whether the actuary is connected in some way to the friendly society e.g. being financially dependent on the friendly society or having a financial interest in the friendly society; and
(c) the scope of the work to be undertaken and degree of reliance that the auditor can place thereon.

An actuary involved in the audit process, although guided by his own profession's standards and guidance and by BAS standards, designs and performs his work to provide the auditor with the required level of audit comfort.

233 Where the actuary is employed by the audit firm, the auditor will be able to rely on his firm's quality control systems, recruitment and training to determine that the actuary's capabilities and competence, rather than having to evaluate them for each audit engagement.

234 Where the auditor plans to use an external actuary, the terms of his engagement are established formally in writing, which may include matters such as the following:

- the objectives and scope of the actuary's work;
- the specific matters that the actuary should report on;
- the extent of reliance to be placed by the auditor on the actuary's work;
- the auditor's access to the working papers produced by the actuary; and
- confidentiality of information arising from the client or the auditor.

235 The auditor does not have the same expertise as the actuary. Nevertheless, the auditor seeks to understand and assess the work performed by the actuarial expert and determines whether the actuary's findings are reasonable, based on the auditor's knowledge of the business and the results of other audit procedures. If the actuary's findings are not consistent with other audit evidence, the auditor attempts to resolve the differences by applying additional audit procedures. If the auditor is not satisfied that there is sufficient appropriate audit evidence to support the audit opinion and there is no satisfactory alternative source of audit evidence, the auditor considers the implications for the audit report.

ISA (UK and IRELAND) 700: THE AUDITOR'S REPORT ON FINANCIAL STATEMENTS

Background note

The purpose of this ISA (UK and Ireland) is to establish standards and provide guidance on the form and content of the auditor's report issued as a result of an audit performed by an independent auditor of the financial statements of an entity. Much of the guidance provided can be adapted to auditor reports on financial information other than financial statements.

The auditor's report should contain a clear written expression of opinion on the financial statements taken as a whole. (paragraph 4)

236 Auditors are required by Section 73 of the 1992 Act to report on the truth and fairness of the annual financial statements. They perform their work in accordance with ISAs (UK and Ireland) and report in accordance with ISA (UK and Ireland) 700.

237 An example of a suitable form of unqualified auditors' report for a friendly society without subsidiaries is given in Appendix 1, Example 1. Appendix 1, Example 2 provides a suitable form of unqualified auditors' report for a friendly society group having a subsidiary which carries on general insurance business. These forms of report set out, in the section 'Respective responsibilities of the Committee of Management and Auditors', the auditors' differing responsibilities with respect to the various elements of the financial statements and accompanying information.

238 Auditors' reports for friendly societies also include an opinion that is required to be published by Section 73(7) of the 1992 Act concerning the consistency of the financial statements with the Report of the Committee of Management and the latter's compliance with the 1992 Act and the regulations made under it.

> The auditor should consider modifying the auditor's report by adding a paragraph if there is a significant uncertainty (other than a going concern problem), the resolution of which is dependent on future events and which may affect the financial statements (paragraph 32)

239 The basis on which a friendly society's financial statements are prepared takes account of the extent of the inherent uncertainty in the types of insurance business it underwrites. Uncertainties arising from insurance contracts may include:

- general uncertainties arising where outcomes for provisiong are within a range which is not unusual for the nature of the business underwritten;
- specific uncertainties which are material and subject to an unusually wide range of outcomes; and
- uncertainties where financial reporting standards do not require a provision to be established but where a contingent liability disclosure may be appropriate.

240 If the auditor concludes that the technical provisions are materially misstated or that the disclosures relating to those provisions and the relevant uncertainties are inadequate or misleading and considers that the effect is material to the view given by the financial statements, he is required by ISA (UK and Ireland) 700 to qualify his opinion.

241 Determining technical provisions is subject to a high degree of inherent uncertainty and frequently involves statistical techniques. When reporting on a friendly society's financial statements, auditors assess whether such uncertainties fall within the category of significant, and so require to be disclosed in their report. In making this assessment, auditors take into account whether the financial statements provide a user with general information about the types of business written such that the overall level of inherent uncertainty likely to apply to those financial statements is apparent.

242 In rare circumstances the auditor may consider a matter disclosed in the financial statements to be of such importance to users' understanding of the financial statements as a whole that it is appropriate to draw their attention to it. The fact that an auditor of a friendly society has identified that the high estimation uncertainty associated with the calculation of technical provisions gives rise to a significant risk

does not automatically require the auditor to modify his report for the existence of a significant uncertainty.

243 Where high estimation uncertainties involve significant levels of concern about the validity of the going concern basis they will be regarded as significant and require the auditor to modify his report. In these circumstances the auditor takes account of the guidance in ISA (UK and Ireland) 570 'The going concern basis in the financial statements' and considers whether a duty to report to the regulator exists.

Reports to Committee of Management

244 Auditors' reports for friendly societies also include an opinion that is required to be published by Section 73(7) of the 1992 Act concerning the consistency of the financial statements with the Report of the Committee of Management and the latter's compliance with the 1992 Act and the regulations made under it.

245 In connection with their opinion on the Report of the Committee of Management, auditors consider whether all of the information called for by Section 71 of the 1992 Act and by Schedule 8 of the Accounts Regulations has been provided. In particular the regulations require the Committee of Management to present a fair review of the activities of the society during the financial year. The Report should give a balanced view of difficulties encountered and issues facing the society as well as achievements and ambitions.

246 As the auditors are required to confirm that the Report has been made in accordance with the regulations they need to consider whether it presents a fair review of the activities, taking into account the information and understanding that they have gained in the course of their work on the financial statements and returns and bearing in mind that these Reports can sometimes be used by management as a 'marketing tool' for the benefit of the society.

Non-directive societies and registered branches

247 Non-directive societies and registered branches are required to prepare accounts under the abbreviated format of Schedule 7 of the Accounts Regulations. Unlike the position for directive societies[33], this format contains no reference to technical provisions. However, this does not preclude the society or branch from providing additional analysis of the benefit funds to show the amount representing technical provisions. Indeed this disclosure will normally be required for the financial statements to show a true and fair view.

ISA (UK and IRELAND) 720 (Revised): Section A – OTHER INFORMATION IN DOCUMENTS CONTAINING AUDITED FINANCIAL STATEMENTS

Background note

The purpose of this ISA (UK and Ireland) is to establish standards and provide guidance on the auditor's consideration of other information, on which the auditor has no obligation to report, in documents containing audited financial

---

[33] The financial statements of directive societies follow the balance sheet format in Schedule 2 of the Accounts Regulations which requires the separate presentation of technical provisions.

> statements .This ISA (UK and Ireland) applies when an annual report is involved; however, it may also apply to other documents.

> The auditor should read the other information to identify material inconsistencies with the audited financial statements. (paragraph 2)
>
> If as a result of reading the other information, the auditor becomes aware of any apparent misstatement therein, or identifies any material inconsistencies with the audited financial statements the auditor should seek to resolve them. (paragraph 2-1)
>
> If, on reading the other information, the auditor identifies a material inconsistency, the auditor should determine whether the audited financial statements or the other information needs to be amended. (paragraph 11)

Friendly societies undertaking long term business may include supplementary financial statements prepared on an alternative basis to that used in drawing up the financial statements. Without adequate explanation, such supplementary statements may appear inconsistent with the audited financial statements. Auditors therefore consider whether an adequate explanation of the assumptions and different methodology has been provided in the annual report, and if not, they consider including an additional comment in their report on the financial statements. 248

Supplementary financial statements showing performance arising on long term business calculated on an alternative basis are prepared using different assumptions and methodologies from those applied in preparing the primary financial statements. There are many aspects of the supplementary statements not affected by the alternative assumptions and methodologies and where material the auditor considers whether they are treated consistently in both the primary financial statements and supplementary financial statements. For those material items where different assumptions and methodologies are applied to the same data to produce the supplementary statements the auditor considers whether consistent data has been used. 249

The auditor reads the supplementary financial statements in the light of knowledge acquired during the audit and considers whether there are any apparent misstatements therein. The auditor is not expected to verify or audit the information contained in the supplementary financial statements. 250

The work of the auditor in reporting to the Committee of Management on supplementary statements prepared on the alternative method of reporting long term business is outside the scope of this Practice Note. 251

REPORTING ON REGULATORY RETURNS

There are four distinct types of returns (referred to as solvency returns in this Practice Note), each designed for a specific type of friendly society as defined under the FSA Handbook. The solvency return comprises a package of forms to be completed by the society supported by supplementary notes. Guidance and instructions are contained in the relevant Interim Prudential Sourcebook (IPRU(INS) for directive societies and IPRU(FSOC) for other societies). 252

The returns are: 253

- The FSA Return for directive friendly societies (see detailed guidance in paragraphs 274-293 below).
- FSC 1 – designed for non-directive incorporated societies carrying on long term insurance business. This return must be prepared annually.
- FSC 2 – designed for non-directive unincorporated societies carrying on insurance business, long term or general. This return must be prepared once in every period of three years.
- FSC 3 – designed for non-directive incorporated societies carrying on general business including those societies that have long-term insurance business and prepare FSC 1 annually. This return on a society's general business must be prepared once in every period of three years.

All returns other than FSC2 are required to be audited.

For non directive friendly societies regulatory returns must be submitted within 6 months of the end of the financial year. The timetable for submission of returns by directive friendly societies is 4 months for financial year end 31 December 2006 and 3 months for financial year end 31 December 2007 and thereafter.

Contents of the return and comparison with financial statements

254 The returns primarily provide a statement of solvency for the society based on a valuation of its assets as at the year end and the actuary's calculation of its liabilities and commitments under the insurance business that it has written. The primary statement of solvency is supported by analyses of assets and liabilities; revenue account information; and the product data and assumptions used by the actuary in his calculations.

255 There are differences between the amounts reported in the return and the amounts reported in the financial statements prepared in accordance with the Accounts Regulations. The return has to be prepared with reference to IPRU(INS) or IPRU(FSOC); the auditors should have particular reference to this in performing their work.

256 The Sourcebook introduces additional prudence by defining asset admissibility criteria and limits. The return includes a reconciliation of the asset values it contains with those reported in the society's financial statements. In addition, although the valuation of long-term insurance business liabilities for solvency purposes may form the starting point for the amounts recorded in the financial statements, this is adjusted by segregating elements that do not qualify as liabilities for financial statement purposes. GENPRU 1.3 also requires that except where a rule in GENPRU or INSPRU provides for a different method of recognition or valuation, whenever a rule refers to an asset, liability, equity or income statement item, then the insurer for the purposes of that rule, recognises the item and measures its value in accordance with UK GAAP or, where IFRS has been adopted, in accordance with IFRS.

Types of return

Returns on subsidiary companies

257 It should be noted that the classes of long term and general insurance business which friendly societies may undertake are limited to those listed in Schedule 2 of the 1992 Act. For example, permitted general business is restricted to accident, sickness and personal financial loss categories. This does not preclude incorporated friendly

societies from undertaking other classes of business, such as household and motor insurance, through subsidiary companies. Banking is another activity that may be carried on by a subsidiary company, but is not a permitted activity of a friendly society itself.

Subsidiary companies carrying on regulated activities are currently subject to separate prudential rules and are accountable under these rules. This may include requirements to prepare separate prudential returns for the subsidiary companies under the Prudential Sourcebooks for insurers, banks or investment businesses as appropriate. The auditor's responsibility in connection with these returns is not considered in this Practice Note. Guidance is available elsewhere, for example, in Practice Note 19: 'The audit of banks and building societies in the United Kingdom (Revised)', PN 20 : 'The audit of insurers in the United Kingdom (Revised)' and PN 21: 'The audit of Investment Businesses in the United Kingdom'. 258

General audit considerations for directive and non–directive friendly societies

In most cases, an audit of the financial statements of the friendly society prepared under the Accounts Regulations will have already been completed in accordance with auditing standards to enable the report required by Section 73 of the 1992 Act to be given. The work that auditors perform on the return does not represent a second audit carried out in accordance with auditing standards, but represents a set of additional procedures which, in conjunction with the evidence drawn from their audit work on the financial statements, will enable them to form the required opinion on the return. Key areas in which auditors need to undertake procedures additional to those undertaken to report on the financial statements are: 259

- the application of the prescribed valuation and admissibility rules to assets and liabilities for which existence, title, etc. has already been considered as a part of the audit of the society's financial statements;
- the sub-division of revenue information into accounting classes, business categories and risk groups;
- presentation of the information in the prescribed forms; and
- the specific additional disclosures that fall within the scope of the auditors' report.

If an audit of financial statements in accordance with ISAs (UK and Ireland) has not been undertaken, the principal components of the solvency return will need to have been subjected to an audit in order to achieve an equivalent standard of evidence. Whilst this situation can be envisaged in respect of registered UK branches of overseas insurance companies, it is difficult to envisage circumstances in which this would apply to friendly societies under current legislation. 260

Work specific to the auditors' report on a friendly society's regulatory return may be undertaken concurrently with procedures designed to provide evidence for their report on its financial statements or at a later date. In either case, the auditors consider both aspects of their engagement when planning the audit of the financial statements. 261

Although IPRU(INS) does not require the regulatory return to be drawn up to show a true and fair view, rule 9.11 requires that the return: 262

'must fairly state the information provided on the basis required by the Accounts and Statements Rule'.

263 This is of a similar qualitative standard to the requirement of company law that financial statements prepared in accordance with UK financial reporting standards give a true and fair view of a company's state of affairs and profit or loss, hence equivalent considerations of materiality apply. In evaluating whether the requirements of rule 9.11 of IPRU (INS) have been met, auditors therefore apply materiality in relation to the business as a whole, rather than in relation to the particular business reporting category within which a particular item is reported. Following this approach, reliance on analytical review techniques is normally appropriate in relation to, for example, the segmental information provided within the regulatory return.

General Principles

264 The general principles applicable to reporting on regulatory returns are as follows:
- Auditors plan the work to be undertaken in relation to the regulatory return so as to perform that work in an effective manner, taking into account their other reporting responsibilities;
- Auditors familiarise themselves with the regulations governing the preparation of the regulatory return;
- Auditors comply, where relevant, with APB Ethical Standards for Auditors and with ethical guidance issued by their relevant professional bodies;
- Auditors agree the terms of the engagement with the society and record them in writing;
- Auditors consider materiality and its relationship with the risk of material misstatement in the regulatory return in planning their work and in determining the effect of their findings on their report;
- Auditors undertake their work with an attitude of professional scepticism and carry out procedures designed to obtain sufficient appropriate evidence on which to base their opinion on the regulatory return. In particular they:
  (a) perform procedures designed to obtain sufficient appropriate evidence that all material subsequent events up to the date of their report on the regulatory return which require adjustment of, or disclosure in, the regulatory return have been identified and properly reflected therein;
  (b) apply analytical procedures in forming an overall conclusion as to whether the regulatory return as a whole is consistent with their knowledge of the friendly society's business; and
  (c) obtain written confirmation of appropriate representations from management before their report is issued.
- Auditors record in their working papers:
  (a) details of the engagement planning;
  (b) the nature, timing and extent of the procedures performed in relation to their report on the regulatory return, and the conclusions drawn; and
  (c) their reasoning and conclusions on all significant matters which require the exercise of judgment.
- Auditors reporting on regulatory returns which include financial information on which other auditors have reported obtain sufficient appropriate evidence that the work of those other auditors is adequate for their purposes.
- Auditors issue a report containing a clear expression of their opinion on the regulatory return;
- Auditors consider the matters that have come to their attention while performing the procedures on the regulatory return and whether they should be included in a report to the Committee of Management;
- If the auditors become aware of matters of material significance to the FSA, they make a report direct to the FSA. In addition, when issuing their report on the regulatory return, auditors:

(a) consider whether there are consequential reporting issues affecting their opinion which arise from any report previously made direct to the FSA in the course of their appointment; and
(b) assess whether any matters encountered in the course of their work indicate a need for a further direct report.

Work specific to the auditors' report on a society's statement of solvency may be undertaken concurrently with procedures designed to provide evidence for their report on its financial statements or (more frequently) at a later date. In either case, considerations of efficiency require that the auditors consider both aspects of their engagement when planning the audit of the financial statements. **265**

Materiality

Although the relevant sourcebook does not require the regulatory return to be drawn up to show a true and fair view, materiality can be considered to apply in the same way as it applies to financial statements. Auditors therefore apply materiality in relation to the business as a whole, rather than in relation to the particular accounting class, business category or risk group within which a particular item is reported, except when considering figures which are required to be derived from a prescribed source elsewhere in the return, or to be calculated on a specified basis, when (other than rounding differences) no concept of materiality applies. **266**

Following this approach, reliance on analytical review techniques is normally appropriate in relation to the segmental information provided within the return. Where the return analyses the society's financial information into two or more funds, the auditors would not normally reduce the level of materiality applied in their work below that applied for the financial statements of the society as a whole. The auditors are not required by statute to report on the truth and fairness of each separate fund. However, they should discuss the extent of their work on the analysis in the return with the Committee of Management in advance and, if appropriate, refer to this in their engagement letter. **267**

Subsequent events

There may be a gap between the date on which a friendly society's statutory financial statements are approved and the date on which its regulatory return is signed. Auditors undertake a review of post-balance sheet events up to the date of their report on the regulatory return before signing that report. **268**

Qualifications or emphases of matter

When reporting on a society's returns auditors include an emphasis of matter or qualify their opinions as appropriate following the principles in ISA (UK and Ireland) 700 – *The Auditor's Report on Financial Statements*. It is possible for the auditors' opinion in their report on a society's financial statements to be qualified whilst that on its regulatory return is unqualified, and vice versa. This may occur where the grounds for qualification relate to the treatment of a particular item (for example, if an asset is included in the regulatory return at a value which does not take account of the specific requirements of the relevant sourcebook). Any qualification or emphasis of matter paragraph in respect of technical provisions would (in the absence of exceptional circumstances such as a Court judgement clarifying the liability after the signing of the financial statements) be expected to be reflected in both reports. **269**

270 When auditors include a qualification or emphasis of matter in their report on the solvency return, the guidance and instructions from the FSA requires them to state whether, in their opinion, the uncertainty is material to determining whether the society complied with its capital resources requirement.

271 Included in the regulatory return there is a description of the insurance business undertaken by the friendly society which is outside the scope of the audit and as such the auditor is not required to express an opinion on this statement. Therefore, despite the general requirement for auditors in ISA (UK and Ireland) 720 'Other information in documents containing audited financial statements' the auditor will not normally read The Committee of Management's Certificate for directive societies to identify any inconsistencies with the audited elements of the return. If, however, the auditor becomes aware of any apparent misstatements in The Committee of Management's Certificate for directive societies or identifies any material inconsistencies with the audited elements of the return, the auditor should seek to resolve them. This procedure should be extended to include any other form, statement, analysis or report required to be included in the return but not subject to audit.

Resubmitted returns

272 The FSA may require the friendly society to resubmit the regulatory return, or part thereof, where the original regulatory return is considered to be inaccurate or incomplete. The auditors are normally required to express an opinion on the amended or additional material. This can be done by either:

(a) withdrawing the original report and issuing a completely new report under rule 9.35 of IPRU(INS) or
(b) issuing a supplementary report on the amended material only, but including a reference to the original report.

273 The first option is preferable where the nature and volume of changes required gives rise to a resubmission of the complete return. The second option is preferable where the amendments are considered to be relatively minor or are few in number and only the amended forms, supplementary notes and/or statements are resubmitted.

Directive societies: Long-term Business

274 Part II of Appendix 9.6 to IPRU(INS) indicates the matters that must be included in the auditors' report. The basic elements prescribed are:

(a) an opinion as to whether Forms 1 to 3, 10 to 32, 34, 36 to 45, 48, 49, 56, 58 and 60 (including the supplementary notes thereto) and the statements, analyses and reports pursuant to rules 9.25 to 9.27, 9.29 and 9.31 of IPRU(INS) have been properly prepared in accordance with the provisions of the Accounts and Statements Rules (IPRU(INS) rules 9.1 to 9.36E and 9.39), GENPRU and INSPRU.
(b) an opinion as to whether the methods and assumptions determined by the friendly society and used to perform the actuarial valuation as set out in the valuation reports appropriately reflect the requirements of INSPRU 1.2 and 1.3.

The auditors of a friendly society carrying on long-term insurance business are also required to obtain, and state in their report that they have obtained and paid due regard to advice from a suitably qualified actuary independent of the friendly society in respect of any amounts or information abstracted from the actuarial investigation.

In addition, rule 9.35(2) of IPRU(INS) requires auditors to report by exception on the maintenance of adequate accounting records and other matters specified by section 237 of the Companies Act 1985.

The actuarial investigation includes:

"(a) a determination of the liabilities of the insurer attributable to its long-term insurance business;
(b) a valuation of any excess over those liabilities of the assets representing the long-term insurance fund or funds and, where any rights of any long-term policy-holders to participate in profits relate to particular parts of such a fund a valuation of any excess of assets over liabilities in respect of each of those parts; and
(c) for every long-term insurer which is a realistic basis life firm, a calculation of the with-profits insurance capital component."

The FSA Handbook does not set out the nature of the advice to be obtained from the reviewing actuary or provide guidance on the nature or extent of the work to be performed by the reviewing actuary in providing that advice. The responsibility for determining the nature of the advice and, consequently, the scope and extent of the reviewing actuary's work lies with the auditor, although the auditor discusses the proposed scope of work with the reviewing actuary and considers the views of the reviewing actuary before finalising the scope of work.

The auditor obtains advice from the reviewing actuary on those elements of the actuarial investigation that the auditor believes, for the purpose of the audit of the annual return, require expert actuarial input to assess. The areas of the actuarial investigation that the auditor will seek advice from a reviewing actuary on include:

- whether the methods and assumptions used to calculate the mathematical reserves appropriately reflect the requirements of INSPRU 1.2 ("Mathematical reserves");
- where applicable, whether the methods and assumptions used to calculate the "With-profits insurance capital components" ("WPICC") appropriately reflect the requirements of INSPRU 1.3 ("With-profits insurance capital components"); and
- whether the statement(s) made under rule 9.31 of IPRU(INS) ("Valuation reports on long-term insurance business") are made in accordance with the requirements of Appendix 9.4 and Appendix 9.4A of IPRU(INS).

In addition to obtaining advice on the matters set out in the paragraph above, the auditor obtains advice on all other elements of the actuarial investigation to the extent that they are relevant to the auditable parts of the return. The elements of the actuarial investigation, other than those detailed above, that the auditor may also seek to obtain advice from the reviewing actuary on include:

- whether the data underlying the calculation of the mathematical reserves and WPICC (where applicable) are reliable;
- whether the models used to apply the methods and assumptions underlying the mathematical reserves and WPICC (where applicable) are operating appropriately;
- whether the data contained in Forms 18, 19, 48, 49, 56, 58 and 60 have been correctly abstracted from the actuarial valuation;
- whether the data contained in line 51 of Form 11 has been correctly abstracted from the actuarial valuation (for friendly societies which transact health insurance).

280 Consideration of this guidance is likely to be of particular relevance to auditors where the auditable parts of the return include disclosure of data at the level of type of product or class of contract. Disclosures in this level of detail are included in the Valuation Reports required under IPRU (INS) 9.31.

281 The auditor engages the reviewing actuary to perform work to the scope the auditor, following discussion with the reviewing actuary, determines is appropriate. Whilst the formality of these arrangements may vary depending on whether the reviewing actuary is with a third party firm of actuaries or is an employee or partner of the auditor or his member firms, the auditor will agree in writing the scope of work and reporting by the reviewing actuary. It is expected that this will include, inter alia,

- the scope of work to be performed by the reviewing actuary including the areas of the actuarial valuation and auditable parts of the return on which the reviewing actuary will perform work and details of the nature and scope of the work to be performed;
- the form of the review that the auditor will carry out on the work of the reviewing actuary;
- the form of report to be issued to the auditor containing the advice from the reviewing actuary;
- a requirement that the reviewing actuary will perform their work having due regard to relevant guidance issued by the Faculty and Institute of Actuaries and the BAS and will notify the auditor immediately he becomes aware of any matters that may indicate non-compliance with the guidance;
- protocols for the timely reporting to the auditor of any issues arising in relation to the duty to report matters of material significance to the FSA;
- arrangements for the confirmation of the reviewing actuary's independence and qualifications (if not an employee or partner of the auditor or his member firms); and
- a requirement for the reviewing actuary to notify the auditor immediately of any significant facts and matters that bear upon the reviewing actuary's objectivity and independence.

Establishing the independence of the reviewing actuary

282 The auditor should be satisfied that any reviewing actuary will be independent and document the rationale for that conclusion. Guidance for the auditor on establishing the independence of the reviewing actuary is set out below.

283 When planning the audit of the regulatory return, the engagement partner obtains information from the reviewing actuary as to the existence of any connections that the reviewing actuary has with the client including:

- financial interests;
- business relationships (including the provision of services);
- employment (past, present and future); and
- family and other personal relationships.

284 The engagement partner assesses the threats to objectivity and independence that arise from any connections disclosed and considers whether the reviewing actuary has implemented safeguards to eliminate the threats or reduce them to an acceptable level.

285 When assessing the threats to objectivity and independence which arise from services provided to the client or its affiliates and the effectiveness of safeguards established by the actuarial firm, the engagement partner will consider the following factors:

- whether the reviewing actuary was the person responsible for the service provided;
- the materiality and the nature of the services to the actuarial firm;
- the extent to which the outcomes of services have been reviewed by another actuarial firm.

In certain circumstances, it is unlikely that any safeguards can eliminate the threat to objectivity and independence or reduce it to an acceptable level. Such circumstances are likely to include: **286**

- direct financial interests in the client or an affiliate held by the actuarial firm, the reviewing actuary, any member of the reviewing actuary's team, or immediate family members of such persons;
- material business relationships with the client or an affiliate entered into by the actuarial firm, the reviewing actuary, any member of the reviewing actuary's team, or immediate family members of such persons;
- any connection that enables the client to influence the affairs of the actuarial firm, or the performance of any actuarial review engagement undertaken by the firm;
- situations involving any employment[34] of the reviewing actuary or any member of the reviewing actuary's team, in the past two years, or their current or potential employment with the client;
- situations involving employment of immediate family members of the reviewing actuary, or any member of the reviewing actuary's team by the client in a key management position;
- in the case of listed companies, where the reviewing actuary has acted in this role for a continuous period longer than seven years;
- situations where more than 10% of the total fees of the actuarial firm are regularly receivable from the client and its subsidiaries;
- any contingent fee arrangements for services provided to the client and its affiliates by the actuarial firm where the fee is dependent on a future or contemporary actuarial judgment;
- any engagement in the current period of the actuarial firm to provide actuarial valuation or financial reporting services to the client[35] or services where the objectives of the engagement are inconsistent with the objectives of the work of the reviewing actuary.

The engagement partner requires the reviewing actuary to notify him immediately of changes in the circumstances on which information was obtained at the start of the engagement, or any others that might reasonably be considered a threat to their objectivity. **287**

Where the engagement partner identifies a significant threat to objectivity and independence which has not been eliminated or reduced to an acceptable level, he discusses with the FSA the circumstances that give rise to the threat and what course of action would be appropriate, including obtaining a rule waiver from the FSA. In circumstances where the matter cannot be resolved satisfactorily, the engagement partner considers making a reference to the independence of the reviewing actuary in the report made to the FSA. **288**

---

[34] Employment includes appointment to the committee of management of the audit client, any sub-committee of the board, or to such a position in an entity that holds, directly or indirectly, more than 20% of the voting rights in the audit client, or in which the audit client holds directly or indirectly more than 20% of the voting rights.

[35] This will include a service to act as Actuarial Function Holder or as With-Profits Actuary.

Reviewing the work of the reviewing actuary

289 When obtaining and paying due regard to the advice of a reviewing actuary auditors have regard to ISA (UK and Ireland) 620 "Using the Work of an Expert". In accordance with paragraph 5 of ISA (UK and Ireland) 620, when the auditor uses the work of an expert employed by the audit firm, the auditor will be able to rely on the firm's systems for recruitment and training that determine that expert's capabilities and competence, as explained in ISA (UK and Ireland) 220 "Quality control for audits of historical financial information" instead of needing to evaluate them for each audit engagement.

290 Consistent with the provisions of ISA (UK and Ireland) 620 the auditor assesses the appropriateness of the reviewing actuary's work as evidence regarding the elements of the annual return being considered. This involves assessment of whether the substance of the reviewing actuary's findings is properly reflected in the annual return, and includes consideration of:

- the source data used;
- the assumptions and methods used;
- when the reviewing actuary carried out the work;
- the reasons for any changes in assumptions and methods compared with those used in the prior period; and
- the results of the reviewing actuary's work in the light of the auditor's overall knowledge of the business and the results of other audit procedures.

291 When considering whether the reviewing actuary has used source data which is appropriate in the circumstances, the auditor may consider the following procedures:

(a) making enquiries regarding any procedures undertaken by the reviewing actuary to establish whether the source data is sufficient, relevant and reliable; and

(b) reviewing or testing the data used by the reviewing actuary.

292 The auditors do not have the same expertise as the reviewing actuary; however, they seek to obtain an understanding of the assumptions and methods used by the entity and consider whether they are reasonable, based on their knowledge of the business. If the results of the reviewing actuary's work are not consistent with other audit evidence, the auditor attempts to resolve the inconsistency by discussions with the reviewing actuary. Applying additional procedures, including possibly engaging another reviewing actuary, may also assist in resolving the inconsistency. If the auditors are not satisfied that the work of the reviewing actuary provides sufficient appropriate audit evidence to support their opinion on the regulatory returns and there is no satisfactory alternative source of audit evidence, they consider the implications for their audit report.

Auditors' reports on regulatory returns of directive societies

293 The requirements affecting directive societies, in particular the reference to IPRU(INS), GENPRU and INSPRU, and the associated reporting responsibilities are set out in Appendix 1 Examples 1.3 and 1.4 depending on whether the society undertakes long term or general insurance business.

Non-directive incorporated societies

294 As discussed in the Introduction to this Practice Note, all non-directive incorporated friendly societies are subject to IPRU(FSOC) as amended. These societies are not required to implement GENPRU and INSPRU at this stage. However certain

aspects of IPRU(FSOC) that previously only applied to directive friendly societies are now applied to non-directive incorporated societies. The requirements of the reviewing actuary in connection with long term business are consistent with those discussed above for directive friendly societies. These societies complete returns 'FSC 1' for long term business (an annual requirement) or 'FSC 3' for general business (a triennial requirement). The annual return, FSC 1 is certified by specified officers of the society[36]. As from 31 December 2006 audit requirements in respect of the auditor's reliance on the Directors' certification in IPRU (FSOC) will no longer apply. This brings IPRU (FSOC) requirements for non-directive societies into line with IPRU (INS) requirements for directive friendly societies and insurers.

IPRU(FSOC) provides that, where the auditors undertaking the central audit have relied on work done at branches by other firms of auditors, they should state that they have relied on other auditors for this work, appending a list of the firms and branches involved. If the auditors refer in their report to any uncertainty, the report shall state whether, in the auditors' opinion, that uncertainty is material to determining whether the society has available assets in excess of its required minimum margin. 295

A suitable form of unqualified report for a return by a non-directive incorporated society is shown in Appendix 1 example 1.5. This refers to return FSC 1 (long-term business), but may be adapted for other specific circumstances. 296

Appendix 1 – Illustrative examples of auditor's reports

This appendix contains the following example auditor's reports:

Reports to the members on financial statements

    1.1 Unqualified opinion: friendly society (no subsidiaries)

    1.2 Unqualified opinion: friendly society group (including an emphasis of matter concerning equalisation reserves)

Reports on the regulatory returns to FSA

    1.3 Report by the Auditors: Directive society undertaking long term insurance business

    1.4 Report by the Auditors: Directive society undertaking general insurance business

    1.5 Report by the Auditors: Non – directive incorporated society

---

[36] The specified officers are the Chief Executive, the Secretary and a member of the Committee of Management.

1.1 – Unqualified opinion: friendly society (no subsidiaries)

INDEPENDENT AUDITORS' REPORT TO THE MEMBERS OF XYZ FRIENDLY SOCIETY

We have audited the financial statements of (name of society) for the year ended .... which comprise (state primary financial statements such as the Income and Expenditure Account, the Balance Sheet) and the related notes[37]. These financial statements have been prepared under accounting policies set out therein. We are also required to report on the Report of the Committee of Management for the year ended .....

Respective responsibilities of the Committee of Management and auditors

The Committee of Management's responsibilities for preparing the Annual Report and the financial statements in accordance with applicable law and United Kingdom Accounting Standards are set out in the Statement of the Committee of Management's Responsibilities.

Our responsibility is to audit the financial statements in accordance with relevant legal and regulatory requirements and International Standards on Auditing (UK and Ireland).

We report to you our opinion as to whether the financial statements give a true and fair view and are properly prepared in accordance with the Friendly Societies Act 1992 and the regulations made under it. In addition we report to you if, in our opinion, the society has not kept proper accounting records, or if we have not received all the information, explanations and access to documents that we require for our audit.

We also report to you our opinion as to whether the Report of the Committee of Management has been prepared in accordance with the Friendly Societies Act 1992 and the regulations made under it, and as to whether the information given therein is consistent with the financial statements.

We read the other information contained in the Annual Report and consider whether it is consistent with the audited financial statements. This other information comprises only (the Report of the Committee of Management and the Chairman's Statement). We consider the implications for our report if we become aware of any apparent misstatements or material inconsistencies with the financial statements. Our responsibilities do not extend to any other information.

Basis of opinion

We conducted our audit in accordance with International Standards on Auditing (UK and Ireland) issued by the Auditing Practices Board. An audit includes examination, on a test basis, of evidence relevant to the amounts and disclosures in the financial statements. It also includes an assessment of the significant estimates and judgments made by the Committee of Management in the preparation of the financial statements, and of whether the accounting policies are appropriate to the Society's circumstances, consistently applied and adequately disclosed.

---

[37] *Auditors' reports on entities that do not publish their financial statements on a web site or publish them using 'PDF' format may continue to refer to the financial statements by reference to page numbers.*

We planned and performed our audit so as to obtain all the information and explanations which we considered necessary in order to provide us with sufficient evidence to give reasonable assurance that the financial statements are free from material misstatement, whether caused by fraud or other irregularity or error. In forming our opinion we also evaluated the overall adequacy of the presentation of information in the financial statements.

Opinion

In our opinion:

- the financial statements give a true and fair view, in accordance with UK Generally Accepted Accounting Practice, of the state of the society's affairs as at 31 December XXXX and of its income and expenditure for the year then ended, and have been properly prepared in accordance with the Friendly Societies Act 1992 and the regulations made under it.
- the Report of the Committee of Management has been prepared in accordance with the Friendly Societies Act 1992 and the regulations made under it, and the information given therein is consistent with the financial statements for the financial year.

Name of auditors

Registered Auditors

Date

1.2 – Unqualified opinion: friendly society group

(INCLUDING AN EMPHASIS OF MATTER CONCERNING EQUALISATION RESERVES)

INDEPENDENT AUDITORS' REPORT TO THE MEMBERS OF XYZ FRIENDLY SOCIETY

We have audited the financial statements of (name of society) for the year ended.... which comprise (state primary financial statements such as the Income and Expenditure Account, the Balance Sheet) and the related notes[38]. These financial statements have been prepared under accounting policies set out therein. We are also required to report on the Report of the Committee of Management for the year ended .....

Respective responsibilities of the Committee of Management and auditors

The Committee of Management's responsibilities for preparing the Annual Report and the financial statements in accordance with applicable law and United Kingdom Accounting Standards are set out in the Statement of the Committee of Management's Responsibilities.

Our responsibility is to audit the financial statements in accordance with relevant legal and regulatory requirements and International Standards on Auditing (UK and Ireland).

---

[38] *Auditors' reports of entities that do not publish their financial statements on a web site or publish them using 'PDF' format may continue to refer to the financial statements by reference to page numbers.*

We report to you our opinion as to whether the financial statements give a true and fair view and are properly prepared in accordance with the Friendly Societies Act 1992 and the regulations made under it. In addition we report to you if, in our opinion, the society has not kept proper accounting records, or if we have not received all the information, explanations and access to documents we require for our audit.

We also report to you our opinion as to whether the Report of the Committee of Management has been prepared in accordance with the Friendly Societies Act 1992 and the regulations made under it, and as to whether the information given therein is consistent with the financial statements.

We read the other information contained in the Annual Report and consider whether it is consistent with the audited financial statements. This other information comprises only (the Report of the Committee of Management and the Chairman's Statement). We consider the implications for our report if we become aware of any apparent misstatements or material inconsistencies with the financial statements. Our responsibilities do not extend to any other information.

Basis of opinion

We conducted our audit in accordance with International Standards on Auditing (UK and Ireland) issued by the Auditing Practices Board. An audit includes examination, on a test basis, of evidence relevant to the amounts and disclosures in the financial statements. It also includes an assessment of the significant estimates and judgments made by the Committee of Management in the preparation of the financial statements, and of whether the accounting policies are appropriate to the Society's circumstances, consistently applied and adequately disclosed.

We planned and performed our audit so as to obtain all the information and explanations which we considered necessary in order to provide us with sufficient evidence to give reasonable assurance that the financial statements are free from material misstatement, whether caused by fraud or other irregularity or error. In forming our opinion we also evaluated the overall adequacy of the presentation of information in the financial statements.

[*Equalisation reserves*

Our evaluation of the presentation of information in the group financial statements has had regard to the statutory requirement for certain subsidiary companies to maintain equalisation reserves in respect of general insurance business. The nature of equalisation reserves, the amounts set aside at 31 December XXXX, and the effect of the movement in those reserves during the year on the group technical account for general business are disclosed in notes x and x respectively.]*

Opinion

In our opinion:

- the financial statements give a true and fair view, in accordance with UK Generally Accepted Accounting Practice, of the state of the society's and the group's affairs as at 31 December XXXX and of the income and expenditure of the society and the group for the year then ended, and have been properly prepared in accordance with the Friendly Societies Act 1992 and the regulations made under it.

- the Report of the Committee of Management has been prepared in accordance with the Friendly Societies Act 1992 and the regulations made under it, and the information given therein is consistent with the financial statements for the financial year.

Name of auditors

Registered Auditors

Date

*Only applies if the friendly society group includes subsidiary companies undertaking general insurance business that are required to establish equalisation reserves under applicable legislation. Further guidance appears in APB Practice Note 20, 'The audit of insurers in the United Kingdom (Revised)'.

1.3 – Report by the auditors: directive society undertaking long term insurance business

..................*[FRIENDLY SOCIETY LIMITED]*

[Global business/UK branch business]

Financial year ended 31 December 200X

Report to the Committee of Management pursuant to Rule 9.35 of the Interim Prudential Sourcebook for Insurers

We have examined the following documents prepared by the society pursuant to the Accounts and Statements Rules set out in part I and part IV of chapter 9 to IPRU(INS) the Interim Prudential Sourcebook for Insurers, GENPRU the General Prudential Sourcebook and INSPRU Insurance Prudential Sourcebook ("the Rules") made by the Financial Services Authority under section 138 of the Financial Services and Markets Act 2000:

- Forms [2, 3, 10 to 19, 40 to 45, 48, 49, 56, 58 and 60], (including the supplementary notes) on pages [...] to [...] ("the Forms");
- the statement required by IPRU(INS) rule 9.29 on pages [...] to [...] ("the Statement");
- the statements, analysis and reports required by IPRU(INS) rules 9.31(a) (the valuation report) on pages [...] to [...] and 9.31 (b) (the realistic valuation report[39]) on pages [...] to [...].

We are not required to examine and do not express an opinion on:

- Forms [46 to 47, 50 to 55, 57 and 59A and 59B] (including the supplementary notes) on pages [...] to [...];
- the statements required by IPRU(INS) rules 9.30 and 9.36[40] on pages [...] to [...];
- the directors' certificate required by IPRU(INS) rule 9.34 on pages [...] to [...] ("the directors' certificate").

[39] *Required for 'Realistic Basis Life firms' only.*

[40] *Required where there is a With-Profits Actuary.*

Respective responsibilities of the society and its auditors

The society is responsible for the preparation of an annual return (including the Forms, the Statement, the valuation report,(and the realistic valuation report), the forms and statement not examined by us and the directors' certificate) under the provisions of the Rules. *[The requirements of the Rules have been modified by [a] waiver[s] issued under section 148 of the Financial Services and Markets Act 2000 on ....200X and ....200X.]* Under IPRU(INS) rule 9.11 the Forms, the Statement, the valuation report, (the realistic valuation report), the forms and statement not examined by us and the directors' certificate are required to be prepared in the manner specified by the Rules and to state fairly the information provided on the basis required by the Rules.

The methods and assumptions determined by the insurer and used to perform the actuarial investigation as set out in the valuation report (and realistic valuation report), prepared in accordance with IPRU (INS) rule 9.31 are required to reflect appropriately the requirements of INSPRU 1.2 (and[41] INSPRU 1.3).

It is our responsibility to form an independent opinion as to whether the Forms, the Statement, and the valuation report (and the realistic valuation report) meet these requirements, and to report our opinions to you. We also report to you if, in our opinion, the society has not kept proper accounting records or if we have not received all the information we require for our examination.

Basis of opinion

We conducted our work in accordance with Practice Note 24 'The audit of friendly societies in the United Kingdom (Revised)' issued by the Auditing Practices Board. Our work included examination, on a test basis, of evidence relevant to the amounts and disclosures in the Forms, the Statement and the valuation report (and the realistic valuation report). The evidence included that previously obtained by us relating to the audit of the financial statements of the society for the financial year. It also included an assessment of the significant estimates and judgments made by the society in the preparation of the Forms, the Statement and the valuation report (and realistic valuation report).

We planned and performed our work so as to obtain all the information and explanations which we considered necessary in order to provide us with sufficient evidence to give reasonable assurance that the Forms, the Statement and the valuation report (and the realistic valuation report) are free from material misstatement, whether caused by fraud or other irregularity or error and comply with IPRU (INS) rule 9.11.

In accordance with IPRU (INS) rule 9.35(1A), to the extent that any document, Form, Statement, analysis or report to be examined under IPRU (INS) rule 9.35(1) contains amounts or information abstracted from the actuarial investigation performed pursuant to IPRU (INS) rule 9.4, we have obtained and paid due regard to advice from a suitably qualified actuary who is independent of the society.

---

[41] *Required for 'Realistic Basis' firms only.*

Opinion

In our opinion:

(i) the Forms, the Statement and the valuation report (and realistic valuation report) fairly state the information provided on the basis required by the Rules *[as modified]* and have been properly prepared in accordance with the provisions of those Rules; and

(ii) the methods and assumptions determined by the society and used to perform the actuarial investigation as set out in the valuation report (and the realistic valuation report) prepared in accordance with IPRU(INS) rule 9.31 appropriately reflect the requirements of INSPRU1.2 (and INSPRU 1.3).

Name of auditors

Registered Auditors

Date

1.4 – REPORT BY THE AUDITORS: DIRECTIVE SOCIETY UNDERTAKING GENERAL INSURANCE BUSINESS

......................*[FRIENDLY SOCIETY LIMITED]*

[Global business/UK branch business]

Financial year ended 31 December 200X

Report to the Committee of Management pursuant to Rule 9.35 of the Interim Prudential Sourcebook for Insurers

We have examined the following documents prepared by the society pursuant to the Accounts and Statements Rules set out in part I and part IV of chapter 9 to IPRU(INS) the Interim Prudential Sourcebook for Insurers, GENPRU the General Prudential Sourcebook and INSPRU the Insurance Prudential Sourcebook ("the Rules") made by the Financial Services Authority under section 138 of the Financial Services and Markets Act 2000:

- Forms **[1,3,10 to 13, 15 to 17, 20 to 32, 34 and 36 to 39]**, (including the supplementary notes) on pages [...] to [...] ("the Forms"); and
- the statements required by IPRU(INS) rules 9.25, 9.26, 9.27 and 9.29 on pages [...] to [...] ("the Statements").

We are not required to examine and do not express an opinion on:

- the statements required by IPRU(INS) rules 9.30, 9.32 and 9.32(A) on pages [...] to [...] and
- the directors' certificate required by IPRU(INS) rule 9.34 on pages [...] to [...] ("the directors' certificate").

Respective responsibilities of the society and its auditors

The society is responsible for the preparation of an annual return (including the Forms, the Statements, the statements not examined by us and the directors' certificate) under the provisions of the Rules. **[The requirements of the Rules have been modified by [a] waiver(s) issued under section 148 of the Financial Services and Markets Act 2000 on ....200X and ....200X.]** Under IPRU(INS) rule 9.11 the Forms, the Statements, the statements not examined by us and the directors' certificate are required to be prepared in the manner specified by the Rules and to state fairly the information provided on the basis required by the Rules.

It is our responsibility to form an independent opinion as to whether the Forms, and the Statements meet these requirements, and to report our opinions to you. We also report to you if, in our opinion, the society has not kept proper accounting records or if we have not received all the information we require for our examination.

Basis of opinion

We conducted our work in accordance with Practice Note 24 'The audit of friendly societies in the United Kingdom (Revised)' issued by the Auditing Practices Board. Our work included examination, on a test basis, of evidence relevant to the amounts and disclosures in the Forms and the Statements. The evidence included that previously obtained by us relating to the audit of the financial statements of the society for the financial year. It also included an assessment of the significant estimates and judgments made by the society in the preparation of the Forms and statements.

We planned and performed our work so as to obtain all the information and explanations which we considered necessary in order to provide us with sufficient evidence to give reasonable assurance that the Forms and the Statements are free from material misstatement, whether caused by fraud or other irregularity or error and comply with IPRU(INS) rule 9.11.

Opinion

In our opinion the Forms and the Statements fairly state the information provided on the basis required by the Rules *[as modified]* and have been properly prepared in accordance with the provisions of those Rules.

Name of auditors

Registered Auditors

Date

1.5 – Report by the auditors: FSC 1 – non-directive incorporated society

......................[FRIENDLY SOCIETY LIMITED]

[Global business/UK branch business]

Financial year ended 31 December 200X

Report of the auditors to the Committee of Management pursuant to rule 5.11 of the Interim Prudential Sourcebook for Friendly Societies

We have examined Forms 9-17 and 40-45, 48, 49, 56, 58 and 60 (including the supplementary notes) ('the Forms') and the information relating thereto prepared by the society pursuant to the Prudential Reporting Rules set out in chapter 5 to the Interim Prudential Sourcebook for Friendly Societies ('the Rules') made by the Financial Services Authority (FSA) under section 138 of the Financial Services and Markets Act (FSMA) 2000.

Respective responsibilities of the society and its auditors

The society is responsible for the preparation of the annual return including the forms under the provisions of the Rules. The forms and statements are required to be prepared in the manner set out in the Rules and under rule 5.22 must state fairly the information provided on the basis required by the Rules.

It is our responsibility to form an independent opinion as to whether the Forms meet these requirements and to report our opinion to you. Our responsibilities as independent auditors are established in the United Kingdom by statute, by the Auditing Practices Board and by our profession's ethical guidance.

Basis of opinion

We conducted our work with reference to Practice Note 24, 'The audit of friendly societies in the United Kingdom (Revised)' issued by the Auditing Practices Board. Our work included examination, on a test basis, of evidence relevant to the amounts and disclosures in the Forms. The evidence included that previously obtained by us relating to the audit of the financial statements of the society for the financial year. It also included an assessment of the significant estimates and judgments made by the society in the preparation of the Forms.

We planned and performed our work so as to obtain all the information and explanations which we considered necessary in order to provide us with sufficient evidence to give reasonable assurance that the Forms are free from material misstatement, whether caused by fraud or other irregularity or error, and comply with the Rules.

Opinion

In our opinion the Forms have been properly prepared and presented in accordance with the Rules.

Name of auditors

Registered Auditors

Date

Appendix 2 – The main parts of fsma 2000 relevant to friendly societies

Part I (and Schedule 1) sets out matters concerning the structure and governance of the FSA including its regulatory objectives and the principles to be followed in meeting those objectives.

Part II (and Schedule 2) sets out the general prohibition on conducting regulated business unless a person (including in a corporate sense) is either authorised or exempt, including restrictions on financial promotions. Regulated activities are defined in a statutory instrument. (SI 2001/544)

Part III (and Schedules 3-5) sets out the requirements to become authorised either by receiving a specific permission from the FSA or through the EU single market rules. Exempt persons are listed in a separate statutory instrument. (SI 2001/1201).

Part IV (and Schedule 6) sets out the arrangements for application for a permission to undertake authorised business and the criteria (Threshold Conditions) that must be met. An applicant who is refused can apply to the Financial Services and Markets Tribunal (established under Part IX).

Part V sets out the provisions applying to individuals performing designated functions (controlled functions) in an authorised firm. The FSA can specify controlled functions and firms must take reasonable care to ensure that only persons approved by the FSA can undertake these functions. The FSA can specify qualification, training and competence requirements and approved persons must comply with the FSA's statement of principles and code of conduct for approved persons. Appeals can be made to the Tribunal.

Part X provides the FSA with general powers to make rules which apply to authorised persons, including rules on specific matters – e.g. client money, money laundering. Rules must be published in draft for consultation. Guidance may be provided individually or generally and may be published. The FSA may modify rules or waive particular rules for particular persons in certain situations.

Part XI allows the FSA to gather information from authorised persons, including use of skilled persons' reports under section 166, or to commission investigations into authorised persons.

Part XIV sets out the disciplinary measures available to the FSA which can include public censure, unlimited fines, withdrawal of authorisation.

Part XXII includes the provisions relating to auditors and their appointment.

Part XXVI brings together in one place the arrangements applying to warning notices and decision notices concerning possible breaches of various requirements imposed by FSMA 2000 or by FSA rules. A warning notice has to state the reasons for proposed actions and allow reasonable time for representations to be made. This will be followed by a decision notice with a right to appeal to the Tribunal.

Appendix 3 – The FSA handbook

297 Not all authorised firms are required to comply with all rules contained within the FSA Handbook. This varies with the type of permission – the regulated activity an

authorised firm is permitted to undertake is set out in the authorised firm's Scope of Permission. The following can be viewed on the FSA website:

- contents of the FSA Handbook – www.fsa.gov.uk/Pages/handbook
- FSA register which lists the regulated activities that each authorised firm has permission to undertake – www.fsa.gov.uk/Pages/register

In gaining an understanding of the FSA Handbook the auditor bears in mind the four statutory objectives of the FSA, set out in paragraph 36 above, which underpin the content of the FSA Handbook. To facilitate usage the FSA Handbook has been structured into a number of blocks and within each block the material has been subdivided into Sourcebooks, Manuals or Guides. There are Rules, evidential provisions[1] and guidance which are contained within all of the blocks[2]. Contravention of Rules (which includes Principles for Businesses) or evidential provisions can give rise to an obligation on the auditor to report the matter direct to the FSA – see the section of this Practice Note relating to ISA (UK and Ireland) 250 Section B. Outline details of certain elements of the FSA Handbook are set out below.

298

Principles for Businesses

The eleven Principles for Businesses, which are general statements that set out the fundamental obligations of firms under the regulatory system, are set out in the FSA Handbook. They derive their authority from the FSA's rule-making powers as set out in the Act and reflect the regulatory objectives. These Principles are as follows:

299

- an authorised firm must conduct its business with integrity;
- an authorised firm must conduct its business with due skill, care and diligence;
- an authorised firm must take reasonable care to organise and control its affairs responsibly and effectively with adequate risk management;
- an authorised firm must maintain adequate financial resources;
- an authorised firm must observe proper standards of market conduct;
- an authorised firm must pay due regard to the interests of its customers and treat them fairly;
- an authorised firm must pay due regard to the information needs of its clients, and communicate information to them in a way which is clear, fair and not misleading;
- an authorised firm must manage conflicts of interest fairly, both between itself and its customers and between a customer and another client;
- an authorised firm must take reasonable care to ensure the suitability of its advice and discretionary decisions for any customer who is entitled to rely on its judgement;
- an authorised firm must arrange adequate protection for clients' assets when it is responsible for them; and
- an authorised firm must deal with its regulators in an open and co-operative way, and must disclose to the FSA appropriately anything relating to the authorised firm of which the FSA would reasonably expect notice.

---

[1] *An evidential provision is not binding in its own right, but establishes a presumption of compliance or non-compliance with another rule. Guidance may be used to explain the implications of other provisions, to indicate possible means of compliance, or to recommend a particular course of action or arrangement.*

[2] *Rules are set out in emboldened type and are marked with the icon 'R', evidential provisions are marked 'E' and guidance 'G'. Further guidance on the status of the Handbook is set out in the General Provisions (GEN) Sourcebook Chapter 2.2 and Chapter 6 of the Reader's Guide.*

Senior management arrangements, systems and controls

300 SYSC amplifies Principle for Businesses 3, the requirement for a firm to take reasonable care to organise and control its affairs responsibly and effectively, with adequate risk management systems. The relevant chapters[3] are as follows;

- 2 – senior management arrangements
- 3 – systems and controls
- 4 – general organisational requirements
- 5 – employees, agents and other relevant persons
- 6 – compliance, internal audit and financial crime
- 7 – risk control
- 8 – outsourcing
- 9 – record keeping
- 10 – conflicts of interest
- 11 – liquidity risk systems and controls
- 12 – group risk systems and control requirements
- 13 – operational risk
- 14 – prudential risk management
- 15 – credit risk management
- 16 – market risk management
- 17 – insurance risk
- 18 – guidance on Public Disclosure Act – whistle blowing

Threshold Conditions

301 Under Section 41 and Schedule 6 FSMA 2000, the Threshold Conditions are the minimum requirements that must be met at authorisation and must continue to be met. The Threshold Conditions relevant to a friendly society are:

- Legal status – contracts of insurance can only be effected and carried out by a body corporate, or a registered friendly society,
- Location of offices – the head office of a body corporate must be in the same territory/member state as the registered office,
- Close links – close links must not prevent effective supervision. Entities are regarded as closely linked if there is a group relationship, i.e. parent/subsidiary/fellow subsidiary (but using the EC 7th Company Law Directive definition of subsidiary). They are also closely linked if one owns or controls 20% or more of the voting rights or capital of the other,
- Adequate resources – the entity must have adequate resources (financial and non financial) for the type of business conducted taking into account the impact of other group entities and having regard to provisions made against liabilities (including contingent and future liabilities) and the approach to risk management,
- Suitability – FSA will consider the fitness and propriety of individuals including whether business is conducted with integrity and in compliance with high standards and whether there is competent and prudent management and exercise of due skill, care and diligence. This will include consideration of whether those subject to the approved persons regime (i.e. those undertaking controlled functions) are, or will be, approved by FSA.

---

[3] *Chapters 13-17 apply only to insurers.*

Appendix 4 – Reporting direct to FSA – statutory right and protection for disclosure under general law

When the auditor concludes that a matter does not give rise to a statutory duty to report direct to the FSA, the auditor considers the right to report to FSA.   302

In cases of doubt, general law provides protection for disclosing certain matters to a proper authority in the public interest.   303

Audit firms are protected from the risk of liability from breach of confidence or defamation under general law even when carrying out work which is not clearly undertaken in the capacity of auditor provided that: 304

- in the case of breach of confidence:
  (i) disclosure is made in the public interest; and
  (ii) such disclosure is made to an appropriate body or person; and
  (iii) there is no malice motivating the disclosure; and
- in the case of defamation:
  (i) the information disclosed was obtained in a proper capacity; and
  (ii) there is no malice motivating the disclosure.

The same protection is given even if there is only a reasonable suspicion that non-compliance with law or regulations has occurred. Provided that it can be demonstrated that an audit firm, in disclosing a matter in the public interest, has acted reasonably and in good faith, it would not be held by the court to be in breach of duty to the institution even if, an investigation or prosecution having occurred, it were found that there had been no breach of law or regulation.   305

When reporting to proper authorities in the public interest, it is important that, in order to retain the protection of qualified privilege, auditors report only to one who has a proper interest to receive the information. The FSA is the proper authority in the case of an authorised institution.   306

'Public interest' is a concept which is not capable of general definition. Each situation must be considered individually. In general circumstances, matters to be taken into account when considering whether disclosure is justified in the public interest may include: 307

- the extent to which the suspected non-compliance with law or regulations is likely to affect members of the public;
- whether the directors (or equivalent) have rectified the matter or are taking, or are likely to take, effective corrective action;
- the extent to which non-disclosure is likely to enable the suspected non-compliance with law or regulations to recur with impunity;
- the gravity of the matter;
- whether there is a general management ethos within the entity of disregarding law or regulations;
- the weight of evidence and the degree of the auditors' suspicion that there has been an instance of non-compliance with law or regulations.

Determination of where the balance of public interest lies requires careful consideration. The auditor needs to weigh the public interest in maintaining confidential client relationships against the public interest of disclosure to a proper authority and to use their professional judgment to determine whether their misgivings justify them in carrying the matter further or are too insubstantial to deserve report.   308

309 In cases where it is uncertain whether the statutory duty requires or section 342 or section 343 FSMA 2000 permits an auditor to communicate a matter to the FSA, it is possible that the auditor may be able to rely on the defence of disclosure in the public interest if it communicates a matter to the FSA which could properly be regarded as having material significance in conformity with the guidance in ISA (UK and Ireland) 250 Section B and this Practice Note, although the auditor may wish to seek legal advice in such circumstances.

Appendix 5 – Definitions

Abbreviations and frequently used terms in this Practice Note are set out below:

ABI	Association of British Insurers.
Actuarial Function Holder	An actuary appointed to perform controlled function CF12, described more fully in SUP 4.3.13 and SUP10.7.17R.
Actuarial investigation	An investigation to which IPRU(INS) rule 9.4 applies.
Appropriate Actuary	If the society is under the duty imposed by section 340 of FSMA 2000 and SUP 4.4.1, the society's Appointed Actuary. If it is not under that duty, an actuary appointed to perform the function in question.
ARROW II	'Advanced Risk Responsive Operating frameWork'. The term used for FSA's risk assessment process – the application of risk based supervision. It is the mechanism through which the FSA evaluates the risk an authorised firm poses to its statutory objectives enabling it to allocate its resources appropriately and respond to the risks identified.
Authorised firm	An entity which has been granted one of more Part IV permissions by the FSA and so is authorised under FSMA 2000 to undertake regulated activities – an authorised person. Authorised firms include insurers.
Authorised person	Term used throughout FSMA 2000 and related statutory instruments to refer to an authorised firm – see above.
BAS	Board for Actuarial Standards
Closely linked entity	As defined in s343(8) FSMA 2000, an entity has close links with an authorised firm for this purpose if the entity is a: (a) Parent undertaking of an authorised firm; (b) Subsidiary undertaking of an authorised firm; (c) Parent undertaking of a subsidiary undertaking of an authorised firm; or (d) Subsidiary undertaking of a parent undertaking of an authorised firm.
COND	Threshold conditions element of the high level standards block of the FSA Handbook.
Directive friendly society	Thresholds contained in Section 37(2) and (3) of the 1992 Act mean that a society will be a directive society if: (a) its rules do not contain provisions for calling up additional contributions or for reducing benefits; or (b) its annual contribution income from long term business

	exceeds 500,000 Euros for three consecutive years; or (c) its annual contribution income from general business exceeds 1,000,000 Euros in any previous year. For regulatory purposes, it is a friendly society other than a non – directive friendly society.
EU IFRS	International Financial Reporting Standards adopted by the European Union.
FSA	The Financial Services Authority.
FSMA 2000	The Financial Services and Markets Act 2000.
GENPRU	General Prudential Sourcebook.
Holloway society	A society offering policies with sickness benefit and savings combined.
IBNR	"Incurred But Not Reported".
INSPRU	Insurance Prudential Sourcebook.
JMLSG	Joint Money Laundering Steering Group.
Material significance	A matter or group of matters is normally of material significance to a regulator's function when, due either to its nature or its potential financial impact, it is likely of itself to require investigation by the regulator.

Non-directive friendly society	For regulatory purposes:
	(a) a *friendly society* whose *insurance business* is restricted to the provision of benefits which vary according to the resources available and in which the contributions of the members are determined on a flat-rate basis;
	(b) a *friendly society* whose *long-term insurance business* is restricted to the provision of benefits for employed and self-employed *persons* belonging to an undertaking or group of undertakings, or a trade or group of trades, in the event of death or survival or of discontinuance or curtailment of activity (whether or not the commitments arising from such operations are fully covered at all times by mathematical reserves);
	(c) a *friendly society* which undertakes to provide benefits solely in the event of death where the amount of such benefits does not exceed the average funeral costs for a single death or where the benefits are provided in kind;
	(d) a *friendly society* (carrying on *long-term insurance business*):
	  (i) whose registered rules contain provisions for calling up additional contributions from members or reducing their benefits or claiming assistance from other *persons* who have undertaken to provide it; and
	  (ii) whose annual gross premium income (other than from contracts of reinsurance) has not exceeded 5 million Euro for each of the three preceding financial years;
	(e) a *friendly society* (carrying on *general insurance business*):
	  (i) whose registered rules contain provisions for calling up additional contributions from members or reducing their benefits;

        (ii) whose gross premium income (other than from contracts of reinsurance) for the preceding financial year did not exceed 5 million Euro; and

        (iii) whose members provided at least half of that *gross premium* income;

    (f)(i) a *friendly society* whose liabilities in respect of *general insurance contracts* are fully reinsured with or guaranteed by other *mutuals* (including *friendly societies*); and

        (ii) the *mutuals* providing the *reinsurance* or the *guarantee* are subject to the rules of the *First Non-Life Directive*;

and in each case whose *insurance business* is limited to that described in any of (a) to (f).

Part IV permission	A permission granted by FSA under Part IV FSMA 2000 permitting an authorised firm to carry on regulated activities as specified in the FSMA 2000 Regulated Activities Order SI 2001/544 as amended.
PPFM	Principles and Practices of Financial Management.
Principles for Businesses	FSA Handbook defined principles with which an authorised firm must comply. The 11 principles are included in a stand alone element of the high level Standards block of the FSA Handbook – PRIN.
Relevant requirement	In relation to the auditors' duty to report direct to the FSA – requirement by or under FSMA 2000 which relates to authorisation under FSMA 2000 or to the carrying on of any regulated activity. This includes not only relevant statutory instruments but also the FSA's rules (other than the Listing rules) including the Principles for Businesses. The duty to report also covers any requirement imposed by or under any other Act the contravention of which constitutes an offence which the FSA has the power to prosecute under FSMA 2000.
2001 Regulations	SI 2001/2587 – FSMA 2000 (Communications by Auditors) Regulations 2001.
SOCA	Serious Organised Crime Agency.
SUP	Supervision manual of the FSA Handbook.
SYSC	Senior management arrangements, systems and controls
The 1974 Act	The Friendly Societies Act 1974.
The 1992 Act	The Friendly Societies Act 1992.
The Insurance SORP	The Statement of Recommended Practice "Accounting for insurance business" issued in December 1998 by the Association of British Insurers (ABI).
Rule 3.1 Report	The report by management to the FSA on accounting records, systems of control of business and of inspection and report required under Rule 3.1 of the Sourcebook.
Those charged with governance	ISAs (UK and Ireland) use the term "those charged with governance" to describe the persons entrusted with the supervision, control and direction of an entity, who will normally be responsible for the quality of financial reporting, and

	the term "management" to describe those persons who perform senior managerial functions. The FSA Handbook of Rules and Guidance (FSA Handbook) uses the term "governing body" to describe collectively those charged with governance. In the context of this Practice Note, references to those charged with governance includes the Committee of Management.
Threshold Conditions	The minimum standards that an authorised firm needs to meet to become and remain authorised by the FSA. The 5 conditions are included in a stand alone element of the high level Standards block of the FSA Handbook – COND.
With-profits actuary	An actuary appointed to perform CF12A, described more fully in SUP 4.3.16AR and SUP 10.7.17AR.

PN 25
Attendance at stocktaking

(Issued January 2004)

Contents

	Paragraphs
Introduction	1 - 6
Assessment of risks and internal controls	7 - 9
Audit evidence	10 - 15
Procedures	
Before the stocktake	17 - 18
During the stocktake	19 - 25
After the stocktake	26 - 28
Work in progress	29
The use of expert valuers and stocktakers	30 - 31
Stocks held by third parties or in public warehouses	32

Introduction

Practice Note 25 contains guidance on how the requirements of Statement of Auditing Standards (SAS) 300: 'Accounting and Internal Control Systems and Audit Risk Assessments' and SAS 400: 'Audit Evidence' may be applied in relation to attendance at stocktaking. The Practice Note also comments briefly on the application of SAS 480: 'Service organisations' and SAS 520: 'Using the work of an expert'. The guidance is supplementary to, and should be read in conjunction with, the SASs which apply to all audits undertaken in the United Kingdom and the Republic of Ireland.

The main assertions[1] relating to stock and work in progress ('stocks') are existence, ownership, completeness and valuation. Practice Note 25 is primarily concerned with audit evidence relating to the existence assertion.

When stocks are material to an entity's financial statements, or where the risk of mis-statement of stocks is so great as to give rise to the risk of material mis-statement in the financial statements, it will normally be necessary for auditors to attend stocktakes to obtain evidence of the existence of stocks[2].

While the principal reason for attendance at a stocktake is to obtain evidence to substantiate the existence of the stocks, attendance can also enhance the auditors' understanding of the business by providing an opportunity to observe the production process and/or business locations at first hand and providing evidence in relation to the:

- completeness and valuation of stocks,
- 'cut-off' for recording stocks inwards and outwards, and the resultant impact on the measurement of revenues and costs, and
- design and operation of an entity's accounting and control systems.

It is the responsibility of the directors of an entity to ensure that the amount at which stocks are recorded in the financial statements represents stocks physically in existence and includes all stocks owned by the entity. To achieve this entities may maintain detailed stock records and check these by regular test counts. In some entities where the accounting records are less detailed, the amount of stock may be determined by way of a full physical count of all stocks held at a date close to the entity's balance sheet date.

In the case of a company incorporated under the Companies Acts, management also has responsibilities to maintain proper accounting records and to include any statements of stocktakings in those records[3].

---

[1] 'Assertions' are the representations of the directors that are embodied in the financial statements and are more fully described in SAS 400 'Audit evidence'.

[2] International Standard on Auditing 501 – 'Audit evidence-additional considerations for specific items' includes a 'bold letter' requirement which states – "When inventory is material to the financial statements, the auditor should obtain sufficient appropriate audit evidence regarding its existence and condition by attendance at physical inventory counting unless impracticable".

[3] In the United Kingdom – Section 221 of the Companies Act 1985; in the Republic of Ireland – Section 230.3(c) of the Companies Act 1990.

ASSESSMENT OF RISKS AND INTERNAL CONTROLS

7   **SAS 300: 'Accounting and Internal Control Systems and Audit Risk Assessments'** requires that auditors should obtain an understanding of the accounting and internal control systems sufficient to plan the audit and develop an effective audit approach. The SAS requires that auditors should use their professional judgment to assess the components of audit risk and to design audit procedures to reduce this to an acceptably low level.

8   In accordance with SAS 300 auditors should use professional judgment to assess the components of audit risk[4]. Risk factors relating to the 'existence assertion' in the context of the audit of stocks include the:

   - reliability of accounting and stock recording systems including, in relation to work in progress, the systems that track location, quantities and stages of completion;
   - timing of stocktakes relative to the year-end date, and the reliability of records used in any 'roll-forward' of balances;
   - location of stocks, including stocks on 'consignment' and those held at third-party warehouses;
   - physical controls over the stocks, and their susceptibility to theft or deterioration;
   - objectivity, experience and reliability of the stock counters and of those monitoring their work;
   - degree of fluctuation in stock levels;
   - nature of the stocks, for example whether specialist knowledge is needed to identify the quantity, quality and/or identity of stock items; and
   - difficulty in carrying out the assessment of quantity, for example whether a significant degree of estimation is involved.

9   When planning the audit, auditors also assess the risk that fraud may cause the financial statements to contain material mis-statements. Based on this risk assessment, the auditors design audit procedures so as to have a reasonable expectation of detecting material mis-statements arising from fraud. Fraudulent activities which can occur in relation to stocks include:

   - 'false sales' involving the movement of stocks still owned by the entity to a location not normally used for storing stocks;
   - movement of stocks between entity sites with stocktakes at different dates;
   - the appearance of stocks and work in progress being misrepresented so that they seem to be of a higher value/greater quantity;
   - the application of inappropriate estimation techniques;
   - stock count records prepared during stock counts deliberately being incorrectly completed or altered after the event; and
   - additional (false) stock count records being added to those prepared during the count.

AUDIT EVIDENCE

10   **SAS 400: 'Audit Evidence'** requires that auditors should obtain sufficient appropriate audit evidence to be able to draw reasonable conclusions on which to base their audit opinion. The SAS also requires that, in seeking to obtain audit evidence from substantive procedures, auditors should consider the extent to which that evidence

[4] *SAS 300.2.*

together with any evidence from tests of controls, supports the relevant financial statement assertions.

Where stocks are material to an entity's financial statements, or where the risk of mis-statement of stocks is so great as to give rise to the risk of material mis-statement in the financial statements, it will normally be necessary for auditors to attend a stocktake to obtain evidence of the existence of stocks. Such attendance might also provide evidence to the auditors in respect of completeness and valuation assertions (including consideration of possible obsolescence and deterioration). The extent and nature of evidence required will depend upon the auditors' assessment of risk.

11

The principal sources of evidence relating to the existence of stocks are:

12

- evidence from audit procedures which confirm the reliability of the accounting records upon which the amount in the financial statements is based;
- evidence from tests of the operation of internal controls over stocks, including the reliability of stock-counting procedures applied by the entity; and
- substantive evidence from the physical inspection tests undertaken by the auditors.

The nature of the auditors' procedures during their attendance at a stocktake will depend upon the results of the risk assessment carried out in accordance with SAS 300. In cases where the auditors decide to place reliance on accounting systems and internal controls, the auditors attend a stocktake primarily to obtain evidence regarding the design and operating effectiveness of management procedures for confirming stock quantities.

13

Where entities maintain detailed stock records and check these by regular test counts auditors perform tests designed to confirm whether management:

14

- maintains adequate stock records that are kept up-to-date;
- has satisfactory procedures for stocktaking and test-counting; and
- investigates and corrects all material differences between the book stock records and the physical counts.

Auditors attend a stocktake to gain assurance that the stock-checking as a whole is effective in confirming that accurate stock records are maintained. If the entity's stock records are not reliable the auditors may need to request management to perform alternative procedures which may include a full count at the year end.

In entities that do not maintain detailed stock records the quantification of stocks for financial statement purposes is likely to be based on a full physical count of all stocks held at a date close to the company's year end. In such circumstances auditors will consider the date of the stocktake recognising that the evidence of the existence of stocks provided by the stocktake is greater when the stocktake is carried out at the end of the financial year. Stocktaking carried out before or after the year end may also be acceptable for audit purposes provided the auditors are satisfied that the records of stock movements in the intervening period are reliable.

15

PROCEDURES

The following paragraphs set out the principal procedures which may be carried out by auditors when attending a stocktake, but are not intended to provide a comprehensive list of the audit procedures which the auditors may find it necessary to perform during their attendance.

16

Before the stocktake

17 The effectiveness of the auditors' attendance at stocktaking is increased by the use of audit staff who are familiar with the entity's business and where advance planning has been undertaken. Planning procedures include:
- performing analytical procedures, and discussing with management any significant changes in stocks over the year and any problems with stocks that have recently occurred, for example unexpected 'stock-out' reports and negative stock balances;
- discussing stocktaking arrangements and instructions with management;
- familiarising themselves with the nature and volume of the stocks, the identification of high value items, the method of accounting for stocks and the conditions giving rise to obsolescence;
- considering the location of the stock and assessing the implications of this for stock control and recording;
- considering the quantity and nature of work in progress, the quantity of stocks held by third parties, and whether expert valuers or stocktakers will be engaged (further guidance on these issues is set out in paragraphs 29-32 below);
- reviewing the systems of internal control and accounting relating to stocks, so as to identify potential areas of difficulty (for example cut-off);
- considering any internal audit involvement, with a view to deciding the reliance which can be placed on it;
- considering the results of previous stock counts made by the entity; and
- reviewing their working papers for the previous year.

18 The auditors examine the way the stocktake is organised and evaluate the adequacy of the client's stocktaking instructions. Such instructions, preferably in writing, should cover all phases of the stocktaking procedures, be issued in good time and be discussed with the person responsible for the stocktake to check that the procedures are understood and that potential difficulties are anticipated. If the instructions are found to be inadequate, the auditors seek improvements to them.

During the stocktake

19 During the stocktake, the auditors ascertain whether the client's staff are carrying out their instructions properly so as to provide reasonable assurance that the stocktake will be accurate. They make test counts to satisfy themselves that procedures and internal controls relating to the stocktake are working properly. If the manner of carrying out the stocktake or the results of the test-counts are not satisfactory, the auditors immediately draw the matter to the attention of the management supervising the stocktake and they may have to request a recount of part, or all of the stocks.

20 When carrying out test-counts, the auditors select items both from count records and from the physical stocks and check one to the other to gain assurance as to the completeness and accuracy of the count records. In this context, they give particular consideration to those stocks which they believe to have a high value either individually or as a category of stock. The auditors record in their working papers items for any subsequent testing considered necessary, such as copies of (or extracts from) stock count records and details of the sequence of those records, and any differences noted between the records and the physical stocks counted.

21 The auditors determine whether the procedures for identifying damaged, obsolete and slow moving stock operate properly. They obtain (from their observations and by discussion, for example with storekeepers and stock counters) information about

the stocks' condition, age, usage and, in the case of work in progress, its stage of completion. Further, they ascertain that stock held on behalf of third parties is separately identified and accounted for.

The auditors consider whether management has instituted adequate cut-off procedures, i.e. procedures intended to ensure that movements into, within and out of stocks are properly identified and reflected in the accounting records in the correct period. The auditors' procedures during the stocktake will depend on the manner in which the year end stock value is to be determined. For example, where stocks are determined by a full count and evaluation at the year end, the auditors test the arrangements made to identify stocks that correspond to sales made before the cut-off point and they identify goods movement documents for reconciliation with financial records of purchases and sales. Alternatively, where the full count and evaluation is at an interim date and year end stocks are determined by updating such an amount by the cost of subsequent purchases and sales, the auditors perform appropriate procedures during their attendance at the stocktaking and in addition they test the financial cut-off (involving the matching of costs with revenues) at the year end. 22

The auditors' working papers include details of their observations and tests (for example, of physical quantity, cut-off date and controls over stock count records), the manner in which points that are relevant and material to the stocks being counted or measured have been dealt with by the entity, instances where the entity's procedures have not been satisfactorily carried out and the auditors' conclusions. 23

Although the principal reason for attendance at a stocktake is usually to obtain evidence to substantiate the existence of the stocks, as noted in paragraph 4 above attendance can also enhance the auditors' understanding of the business by providing an opportunity to observe the production process and/or business locations at first hand and providing evidence regarding the completeness and valuation of stocks and the entity's accounting and control systems. Matters that the auditors may wish to observe whilst attending a stocktake include: 24

Understanding the business

- the production process;
- evidence of significant pollution and environmental damage;
- unused buildings and machinery.

Completeness and valuation of stocks

- physical controls;
- obsolete stock (for example goods beyond their sale date);
- scrap, and goods marked for re-work;
- returned goods.

Accounting and control systems

- exceptions identified by the production process (for example missing work tickets); and
- the operation of 'shop-floor' disciplines regarding the inputting of data such as stock movements into the computer systems.

Some entities use computer-assisted techniques to perform stocktakes; for example hand held scanners can be used to record stock items which update computerised records. In some situations there are no stock-sheets, no physical count records, and no paper records available at the time of the count. In these circumstances the 25 auditors consider the IT environment surrounding the stocktake and consider the need for specialist assistance when evaluating the techniques used and the controls over them. Relevant issues involve systems interfaces, and the controls over ensuring that the computerised stock records are properly updated for the stock count information.

The auditors consider the following aspects of the stock count:

- how the test counts (and double counts where two people are checking) are recorded,
- how differences are investigated before the computerised stock records are updated for the counts, and
- how the computerised stock records are updated, and how stocktake differences are recorded.

After the stocktake

26 After the stocktake, the matters recorded in the auditors' working papers at the time of the count or measurement, including apparent instances of obsolete or deteriorating stocks, are followed up. For example, details of the last serial numbers of goods inwards and outwards records and of movements during the stocktake may be used in order to check cut-off. Further, copies of (or extracts from) the stock count records and details of test counts, and of the sequence of stock count records may be used to check that the results of the count have been properly reflected in the accounting records of the entity.

27 The auditors review whether continuous stock records have been adjusted to the amounts physically counted or measured and that differences have been investigated. Where appropriate, they consider whether management has instituted procedures to ensure that all stock movements between the observed stock count and the period end have been adjusted in the accounting records, and they test these procedures to the extent considered necessary to address the assessed risk. In addition, they follow up queries and notify senior management of serious problems encountered during the stocktake.

28 In conclusion, the auditors consider whether attendance at the stocktake has provided sufficient reliable audit evidence in relation to relevant assertions (principally existence) and, if not, the other procedures that should be performed.

Work in progress

29 Management may place substantial reliance on accounting systems and internal controls designed to ensure the completeness and accuracy of records of work in progress. In such circumstances there may not be a stocktake which can be attended by the auditors. Nevertheless, inspection of the work in progress may assist the auditors in understanding the entity's control systems and processes. It will also assist them in planning their other audit procedures, and it may also help on such matters as the determination of the stage of completion of construction or engineering work in progress. For this purpose, auditors identify the accounting records that will be used by management to produce the work in progress figure in the year-end accounts and, where unfinished items are uniquely identifiable (for example by reference to work tickets or labels), they physically examine items to obtain evidence that supports the recorded stage of completion. In some cases, for example in connection with building projects, photographic evidence can also be useful evidence as

to the state of work in progress, particularly if provided by independent third parties or the auditors themselves.

The use of expert valuers and stocktakers

Prior to attending a stocktake, the auditors establish whether expert help, such as that provided by a quantity surveyor, needs to be obtained by management to substantiate quantities, or to identify the nature and condition of the stocks, where they are very specialised. In cases where the entity engages a third party expert auditors assess, in accordance with SAS 520: 'Using the work of an expert', the objectivity and professional qualifications, experience and resources of the expert engaged to carry out this work, and also the instructions given to the expert. 30

Management may from time to time appoint stocktakers from outside the entity, a practice common for stocks at, for example, farms, petrol stations and public houses. The use of independent stocktakers does not eliminate the need for auditors to obtain audit evidence as to the existence of stocks. In addition, as well as satisfying themselves as to the competence and objectivity of the independent stocktakers, the auditors consider how to obtain evidence as to the procedures followed by them to ensure that the stocktaking records have been properly prepared. In this connection, auditors have regard to the relevant guidance set out in SAS 480: 'Service organisations'. 31

Stocks held by third parties or in public warehouses

If stocks (including those on consignment) are located in public warehouses or with other third parties, the auditors normally obtain direct confirmation relating to quantities and ownership in writing from the custodian. If such stocks are material, auditors have regard to the relevant guidance set out in SAS 480 and consider one or more of the following procedures: 32

- testing the owner's procedures for investigating the custodian and evaluating the custodian's performance;
- obtaining an independent report on the custodian's control procedures relevant to custody of goods; and
- observing physical counts of the goods, or arranging for the third party's auditors to do so.

[PN 26]
Guidance on smaller entity audit documentation

(Issued September 2007)

Contents

		Paragraphs
1.	Introduction	1 – 6
2.	Purposes of audit documentation	7 – 10
3.	Special considerations in the documentation of a smaller entity audit	11 – 33
4.	Audit documentation requirements in ISAs (UK and Ireland)	34 – 39

Appendix – Illustrative examples of audit documentation

Introduction

1. This Practice Note provides guidance to auditors on the application of documentation requirements contained within International Standards on Auditing (ISAs) (UK and Ireland) to the audit of financial statements of smaller entities. It should be read in conjunction with the ISAs (UK and Ireland). It is not intended to be comprehensive guidance on the application of ISAs (UK and Ireland) to smaller audits.

2. The guidance in this Practice Note is directed to auditors of companies that are exempt from audit but choose nonetheless to have a voluntary audit and other smaller entities such as charities. However, a more detailed and rigorous approach may be necessary in small entities with complex operations.

3. The guidance may also be helpful to auditors of larger entities where:

- ownership of the entity is concentrated in a small number of individuals (sometimes a single individual) who are actively involved in managing the business; and
- the operations are uncomplicated with few sources of income and activities; and
- business processes and accounting systems are simple; and
- internal controls are relatively few and may be informal.

4. Initial feedback on the implementation of ISAs (UK and Ireland) during 2005 and 2006 suggests that increased documentation related to ISA (UK and Ireland) 315 is the primary area where additional cost has been incurred for audits of smaller entities. In particular, there is uncertainty about the extent of documentation required to evidence the auditor's understanding of the entity, especially with regard to internal control[1].

5. To comply with ISAs (UK and Ireland), it is not necessary to document the entirety of the auditor's understanding of the entity and matters related to it. Key elements of the understanding documented by the auditor include those on which the auditor has based the assessment of the risks of misstatement. For smaller entities the audit documentation may be simple in form and relatively brief.

6. There are many different ways in which audit documentation can be prepared to meet the requirements of ISAs (UK and Ireland). The examples which are included in the Appendix to this document are illustrative of some of the possible ways in which compliance with the documentation requirements related to ISA (UK and Ireland) 315 and other planning aspects can be achieved. The illustrative examples are not mandatory.

---

[1] *ISA (UK and Ireland) 315 requires the auditor to document key elements of understanding obtained regarding:*
- *Relevant industry, regulatory and other external factors including the applicable financial reporting framework;*
- *The nature of the entity;*
- *The entity's selection and application of accounting policies;*
- *The entity's objectives and strategies;*
- *The means by which the entity's financial performance is measured and reviewed; and*
- *Each of the internal control components (the control environment, the entity's risk assessment process, the information system, control activities, and monitoring controls).*

Purposes of audit documentation

7   ISA (UK and Ireland) 230 (Revised) requires that the auditor should prepare, on a timely basis, audit documentation that provides:

   (a) A sufficient and appropriate record of the basis for the auditor's report; and
   (b) Evidence that the audit was performed in accordance with ISAs (UK and Ireland) and applicable legal and regulatory requirements.

8   In relation to these objectives, ISA (UK and Ireland) 230 (Revised) explains that:

   - Preparing sufficient and appropriate audit documentation on a timely basis helps to enhance the quality of the audit and facilitates the effective review and evaluation of the audit evidence obtained and conclusions reached before the auditor's report is finalised. Documentation prepared at the time the work is performed is likely to be more accurate than documentation prepared subsequently.
   - Compliance with the requirements of ISA (UK and Ireland) 230 (Revised) together with the specific documentation requirements of other relevant ISAs (UK and Ireland) is ordinarily sufficient to achieve the objectives in paragraph 7.

9   In addition to the objectives in paragraph 7, audit documentation serves a number of purposes, including:

   - Assisting the audit team to plan and perform the audit;
   - Assisting members of the audit team responsible for supervision to direct and supervise the audit work, and to discharge their review responsibilities in accordance with ISA (UK and Ireland) 220, "Quality Control for Audits of Historical Financial Information;"
   - Enabling the audit team to be accountable for its work;
   - Retaining a record of matters of continuing significance to future audits;
   - Enabling an experienced auditor to conduct quality control reviews and inspections in accordance with International Standard on Quality Control (ISQC) (UK and Ireland) 1, "Quality Control for Firms that Perform Audits and Reviews of Historical Financial Information, and Other Assurance and Related Services Engagements;" and
   - Enabling an experienced auditor to conduct external inspections in accordance with applicable legal, regulatory or other requirements.

10 Complying with the documentation requirements of the ISAs (UK and Ireland) can also assist the auditor's consideration of the issues associated with significant matters arising during the audit. This often enhances the quality of the reasoning followed, the judgments made and the conclusions reached. In the UK and Ireland external monitoring of audits has consistently emphasised the need for high quality documentation of the rationale for the key audit judgments made in reaching the audit opinion.

Special considerations in the documentation of a smaller entity audit

11 The nature and extent of audit documentation that is appropriate for an audit of a smaller entity is influenced by special considerations which arise from:

   - the qualitative indicators of a simpler entity as set out in paragraph 3; and
   - the characteristics of a typical smaller entity audit team and the way in which they carry out the audit work, including:

- the provision of accounting and related business advice;
- relatively small team size;
- the use of proprietary audit systems.

Notwithstanding these special considerations, an audit of the financial statements for a smaller entity will still comply with ISAs (UK and Ireland) and all audit documentation must be prepared in sufficient detail to enable an experienced auditor, having no previous connection with the audit, to understand: 12

(a) The nature, timing, and extent of the audit procedures performed to comply with ISAs (UK and Ireland) and applicable legal and regulatory requirements;
(b) The results of the audit procedures and the audit evidence obtained; and
(c) Significant matters arising during the audit and the conclusions reached thereon.

Concentration of ownership and management

The ownership of a smaller entity is often concentrated in a small number of individuals, one or more of whom are actively involved in managing the business on a day-to-day basis. In these circumstances the auditor's documentation of the entity's ownership and governance arrangements is likely to be relatively brief. 13

Particular consideration and documentation may be needed of matters, such as family and other close relationships that may impact the auditor's risk assessments in relation to related parties. 14

Uncomplicated operations

Smaller entities often have a limited range of products or services and operate from a limited number of locations, with the consequence that their processes and structures are uncomplicated. In these circumstances, the documentation of the auditor's understanding of such an entity's operations and of the relevant industry, regulatory and other external factors required under ISA (UK and Ireland) 315 is likely to be simple in form and relatively brief. 15

This understanding may be documented using, for example, free-form narrative notes or by completing a structured form. The notes may be maintained separately or incorporated in the documentation of the overall audit strategy required by ISA (UK and Ireland) 300. 16

The key elements which are documented by the auditor include those that impact the auditor's assessment of the risks of material misstatement in the financial statements. 17

Simple accounting systems

Most smaller entities have a relatively uncomplicated accounting process. They are likely to employ few, if any, personnel solely engaged in record-keeping and there will be limited opportunities for segregation of duties. 18

Bookkeeping procedures and accounting records are often simple and there are usually no documented descriptions of accounting policies or procedures. Smaller entities are likely to use an off the shelf accounting package in producing their accounts. Understanding of the accounting package in question, including that gained from other audits, can help the auditor to identify and focus on areas of risk that arise from the accounting system. 19

20 The audit documentation associated with the accounting system is likely to be relatively simple, focussing on how the main transaction cycles operate (including how a transaction originates and gets recorded) and highlighting the risks of material misstatement that arise from the nature of the systems in place[2].

Relatively small number and informal nature of controls

21 In the audit of a smaller entity, the auditor may decide that most of the audit evidence will be obtained from substantive tests of detail. Notwithstanding this, as part of the process of assessing the risks of material misstatement, the auditor is required by ISA (UK and Ireland) 315 to obtain and document an understanding of the components of the entity's internal control relevant to the audit (including, for example, the control environment, information systems relevant to financial reporting, and control activities).

22 Size and economic considerations in smaller entities often reduce the opportunity for formal control activities, although some basic control activities are likely to exist for the main transaction cycles such as revenues, purchases and employment costs. Management's direct control over key decisions and the ability to intervene personally at any time to ensure an appropriate response to changing circumstances, are often important features of the management of any entrepreneurial venture. For example, management's sole authority for granting credit to customers and approving significant purchases can provide strong control over those important account balances and transactions, lessening or removing the need for more detailed control activities. Furthermore, management often has a personal interest in safeguarding the assets of the entity, measuring its performance and controlling its activities, and so they will apply their own controls and develop their own key indicators of performance.

23 However, the dominant position of management in a smaller entity may be abused and can result in the override of controls and inaccurate accounting records. Furthermore, personal and business objectives can be inextricably linked in the mind of the owner-manager, which increases audit risk. For example, personal tax planning considerations might be important and could provide management with the motivation to bias the financial statements.

24 The extent and nature of management's involvement in internal control in a smaller entity is likely to be a key aspect in the documentation of the auditor's understanding of the entity and assessment of risk, including for example:
- The evaluation of the control environment, including consideration of the attitude and motives of management based on prior year experience and the observation of management's actions during the audit.
- Specific control activities relevant to the audit. These are likely to be limited but may include management's direct involvement in, and/or supervision of, controls that mitigate risks of material misstatement.
- The key indicators used by management for evaluating financial performance.

---

[2] *Auditors of UK companies will be conscious of their responsibilities under Section 498 of the Companies Act 2006 to carry out such investigations as will enable them to form an opinion as to whether adequate accounting records have been kept by the company.*

Nature of the professional relationship between smaller entities and their auditors

25 Management of a smaller entity often need professional advice and assistance on a wide range of accounting and related financial and business issues which are not available 'in-house' and it is common for the audit firm to provide non-audit services, including accounting and taxation services. These services can enable the auditor to obtain useful information about the entity and about its objectives and strategies and the management style and ethos, as well as helping to keep the understanding of the entity up to date and so plan the audit efficiently.

26 In circumstances where the audit firm provides non-audit services, the auditor bears in mind the need to maintain objectivity when forming and expressing an opinion on the financial statements. When forming an opinion, but before issuing the report on the financial statements, the audit engagement partner reaches and documents an overall conclusion[3] that any threats to objectivity and independence have been properly addressed in accordance with APB Ethical Standards including, where appropriate, ES – Provisions Available for Small Entities[4].

27 The documentation considerations associated with providing non-audit services include the following:

- To achieve completeness of 'audit documentation', information, gained as a result of the provision of other services, which is used as audit evidence needs to be incorporated or cross-referenced into the audit documentation.
- The auditor's assessment of his or her objectivity and independence is documented, including a description of the threats identified and the safeguards applied to eliminate or reduce the threats to an acceptable level[5].
- The respective responsibilities of the directors (or equivalent) and the auditor are documented in an engagement letter. This is particularly important where the audit firm is involved in the preparation of the financial statements.

Relatively small audit team size

28 Audits of smaller entities may be conducted by small audit 'teams', possibly involving the audit engagement partner working with one audit assistant (or without any audit assistants).

29 In all circumstances, to meet the requirements of ISA (UK and Ireland) 230 (Revised), the audit documentation must, as a minimum, be sufficient to enable an experienced auditor, having no previous connection with the audit, to understand the audit approach adopted, the audit evidence obtained, and the significant matters arising during the audit and the conclusions reached thereon.

30 However, as the size of the engagement team increases, or where more inexperienced team members are introduced, more detailed documentation may assist the team in obtaining an appropriate understanding of the entity. There may also be more reviews performed in compliance with quality control policies and procedures,

---

[3] As required by paragraphs 43 and 54 of ES 1.

[4] ES – Provisions Available for Small Entities provides alternative provisions for auditors of Small Entities (size criteria for Small Entities are set out in paragraph 4) to apply in respect of certain threats arising from economic dependence and the provision of non-audit services and allows the option of exemptions from certain requirements in ES 1 to 5.

[5] As required by ES 1, paragraph 54, and ES 5, paragraph 37.

although the format of documentation for these reviews is not affected by the audit team size.

Use of proprietary audit systems

31 Where the auditor of a smaller entity operates in a small practice, it is likely that use will be made of an audit methodology and/or audit software provided by an external supplier (proprietary systems). Proprietary systems are usually comprehensive and are designed to deal with a wide variety of client situations. To be used efficiently and effectively, the auditor needs to think carefully about how the system should be applied to each individual client entity.

32 Documentation of the understanding of the entity including its controls is usually embedded into proprietary systems by use of optional check lists or 'white space' techniques. A risk exists that less experienced staff might think that it is compulsory to comply with all elements of these systems, without tailoring the approach to the needs of the particular entity, and thereby prepare excessive, and often irrelevant and costly audit documentation. Proper training and supervision of junior staff and communication within the engagement team can help to overcome this risk.

33 Even where a proprietary system is used, a free-form planning memorandum can be a good way of documenting the auditor's understanding of the business and the basis for the risk assessments made. Such a memorandum can then easily be updated from one year to the next.

Audit Documentation Requirements in ISAs (UK and Ireland)

34 In addition to ISA (UK and Ireland) 230 (Revised), several other ISAs (UK and Ireland) set out further specific audit requirements and guidance in relation to audit documentation. The Appendix to ISA (UK and Ireland) 230 (Revised) lists the main paragraphs that contain such specific requirements and guidance.

35 Taking these requirements and guidance into account, the content of the file(s) for an individual audit engagement includes the key matters to document summarised in the table below to the extent they apply in the context of the engagement. Where matters are not applicable, there is no need to include any references to them in the audit working papers.

Subject Matter	ISA/ISQC (UK and Ireland) main paragraphs setting out requirements and, in [ ], guidance	Key matters to document[6]
General		
– Departures, if any, from basic principles or essential procedures	ISA (UK and Ireland) 230 (Revised) "Audit Documentation" 21, [22]	How the alternative procedures performed achieve the objective of the audit and, unless otherwise clear, the reasons for the departure.[7]
– Audit procedures performed	ISA (UK and Ireland) 230 (Revised) 9	Sufficient detail to enable an experienced auditor, having no previous connection with the audit, to understand: (a) The nature, timing, and extent of the audit procedures performed to comply with ISAs (UK and Ireland) and applicable legal and regulatory requirements; (b) The results of the audit procedures and the audit evidence obtained; and (c) Significant matters arising during the audit and the conclusions reached thereon.
– Consideration of ethical requirements and, in particular, independence	ISA (UK and Ireland) 220 "Quality Control for Audits of Historical Financial Information" 12, [11, 13]	Conclusions on auditor independence (both actual and perceived) and any relevant discussions within the firm that support these conclusions. Including actions taken where threats to independence exist that safeguards may not be able to eliminate or reduce to an acceptable level. Any issues identified with respect to compliance with ethical requirements and how they were resolved, including identified threats and safeguards applied.

---

[6] *These matters are presented in the form of a summary combining both the bold text requirements and the supporting guidance that set out matters which the auditor documents. The footnotes include further guidance relating to matters such as the nature and form of documentation. It is necessary to refer to the relevant ISA/ISQC (UK and Ireland) paragraphs for the full detail of the specific documentation requirements and guidance. UK and Ireland "pluses" in the standards are highlighted by shading.*

[7] *The ISA (UK and Ireland) indicates that this documentation requirement does not apply to basic principles and essential procedures that are not relevant in the circumstances, e.g. those relating to internal audit where there is no such function (paragraph 22).*

Subject Matter	ISA/ISQC (UK and Ireland) main paragraphs setting out requirements and, in [ ], guidance	Key matters to document[6]
Engagement acceptance and continuation		
– Acceptance and continuance	ISQC (UK and Ireland) 1 "Quality Control for Firms that Perform Audits and Reviews of Historical Financial Information, and Other Assurance and Related Services Engagements" **28** ISA (UK and Ireland) 220 "Quality Control for Audits of Historical Financial Information" **14**, [16]	The quality control procedures performed regarding the acceptance/continuance of the engagement, conclusions reached from those procedures and how issues, if any, were resolved.
– Terms of the engagement	ISA (UK and Ireland) 210 "Terms of Audit Engagements" **5-1**, [2, 5, Appendix 2]	The terms of the engagement, including the auditor's acceptance of the appointment, the objective and scope of the audit, the extent of the auditor's responsibilities to the client and the form of any reports.[8]
		In the UK and Ireland, there is a requirement that the auditor should ensure that the engagement letter documents and confirms the auditor's acceptance of the appointment, and includes a summary of the responsibilities of those charged with governance and of the auditor, the scope of the engagement and the form of any reports.
		Appendix 2 to ISA (UK and Ireland) 210 (Revised) sets out illustrative wording to describe the responsibilities of the directors and the auditor and the scope of the audit, for a limited (non-listed) company client for an audit conducted in accordance with ISAs (UK and Ireland).

---

[8] *There is no specific requirement for an engagement letter, but the ISA (UK and Ireland) makes clear that one is in the interest of both client and auditor, and one is mandated by some professional accountancy bodies. Examples of matters that may be covered in an engagement letter are given in ISA (UK and Ireland) 210.*

Subject Matter	ISA/ISQC (UK and Ireland) main paragraphs setting out requirements and, in [ ], guidance	Key matters to document[6]
Planning the audit		
– Overall audit strategy	ISA (UK and Ireland) 300 "Planning an Audit of Financial Statements" **22**, [10, 12, 23, 25, 26]	The key decisions considered necessary to properly plan the audit and to communicate significant matters to the engagement team (e.g. regarding the overall scope, timing and conduct of the audit).[9] Any significant changes made during the audit, the reasons therefore, and the auditor's response to the events, conditions, or results of audit procedures that resulted in such changes.
– Audit plan, including procedures to respond to assessed risks	ISA (UK and Ireland) 300 **22**, [14, 15, 24, 25, 26]	The planned nature, timing and extent of risk assessment procedures, and further audit procedures at the assertion level for each material class of transaction, account balance, and disclosure in response to the assessed risks.[10] Any significant changes made during the audit, the reasons therefore, and the auditor's response to the events, conditions, or results of audit procedures that resulted in such changes.
– Understanding of the entity and its environment	ISA (UK and Ireland) 315 "Understanding the Entity and its Environment and Assessing the Risks of Material Misstatement" **122**, [20, 43, 123]	Key elements of the understanding obtained regarding: (a) Industry, regulatory, and other external factors, including the applicable financial reporting framework. (b) Nature of the entity, including the entity's selection and application of accounting policies. (c) Objectives and strategies and the related business risks that may result in a material misstatement of the financial statements. (d) Measurement and review of the entity's financial performance.[11]

[9] *The guidance in the ISA (UK and Ireland) indicates that a brief memorandum prepared at the completion of the previous audit, based on a review of the working papers and highlighting issues identified in the audit just completed, updated and changed in the current period based on discussions with the owner-manager, can serve as the basis for planning the current audit engagement (paragraph 12).*

[10] *The guidance in the ISA (UK and Ireland) indicates that the auditor may use standard audit programs or audit completion checklists appropriately tailored to reflect the particular engagement circumstances (paragraph 24).*

[11] *Smaller entities often do not have formal processes to measure and review financial performance. However, enquiries of management may reveal that they rely on certain key indicators for evaluating financial performance, for example, sales per day or week end bank balances.*

Subject Matter	ISA/ISQC (UK and Ireland) main paragraphs setting out requirements and, in [ ], guidance	Key matters to document[6]
		(e) Internal control, including: – The control environment. – The entity's risk assessment process. – The information system, including the related business processes, relevant to financial reporting, and communication. – Control activities. – Monitoring of controls. to assess the risks of material misstatement of the financial statements.
		The sources of information from which the understanding was obtained. The risk assessment procedures.[12]
– Use of a service Organisation	ISA (UK and Ireland) 402 "Audit Considerations Relating to Entities Using Service Organisations" 5-3, [5-4, 9-13]	The contractual terms which apply to relevant activities undertaken by the service organization and the way that the entity monitors those activities so as to ensure that it meets its fiduciary and other legal responsibilities.[13] For each relevant activity involving maintenance of material elements of the entity's accounting records by a service organisation – an understanding as to the way that the accounting records are maintained, including the way in which those charged with governance ensure that the entity's accounting records meet any relevant legal obligations.

---

[12] *The guidance in the ISA (UK and Ireland) indicates that the manner in which these matters are documented is for the auditor to determine using professional judgment. In particular, the results of the risk assessment may be documented separately, or may be documented as part of the auditor's documentation of further procedures (see below re paragraph 73 of ISA (UK and Ireland) 330). Examples of common techniques, used alone or in combination include narrative descriptions, questionnaires, check lists and flow charts (paragraph 123).*

[13] *Paragraph 5-4 of the ISA (UK and Ireland) gives examples of matters the auditor may consider.*

Subject Matter	ISA/ISQC (UK and Ireland) main paragraphs setting out requirements and, in [ ], guidance	Key matters to document[6]
– Assessment of the risks of material misstatement and, in particular, those risks related to fraud[14]	ISA (UK and Ireland) 315 **122**, [123] ISA (UK and Ireland) 240 "The Auditor's Responsibility to Consider Fraud in an Audit of Financial Statements" **107, 110** [60, 111]	The discussion among the engagement team regarding the susceptibility of the entity's financial statements to material misstatement due to error or fraud, and the significant decisions reached.[15] The identified and assessed risks of material misstatements, due to error or fraud, at the financial statement level and at the assertion level for classes of transactions, account balances and disclosure, including: Significant risks identified, and the related controls evaluated. The risks identified, and the related controls evaluated, where it is not possible or practicable to reduce the risks of material misstatement at the assertion level to an acceptably low level with audit evidence obtained only from substantive procedures. If the auditor has concluded that there is not a significant risk due to fraud related to revenue recognition, the reasons for that conclusion.
Procedures performed in response to assessed risks		
– Overall responses and specific procedures[10]	ISA (UK and Ireland) 330 "The Auditor's Procedures in Response to Assessed Risks" **73**, [73b] ISA (UK and Ireland) 240 **108**, [111]	The overall responses to the assessed risks of material misstatements due to error or fraud at the financial statement level. The nature, timing and extent of audit procedures, and the linkage of those procedures with the assessed risks of material misstatement due to error or fraud at the assertion level.
		If the auditor plans to use audit evidence about the operating effectiveness of controls obtained in prior audits, the auditor should document the conclusions reached with regard to relying on such controls that were tested in a prior audit.

---

[14] *ISA (UK and Ireland) 240 expands on the standards and guidance in ISAs (UK and Ireland) 315 and 330. Presenting ISA (UK Ireland) 240 separately, rather than embodying its content in ISAs (UK and Ireland) 315 and 330 emphasises the importance of the auditor's responsibility to consider fraud in an audit of financial statements. To comply with the requirements of ISA (UK and Ireland) 240, matters related to fraud need to be identifiable as such.*

[15] *This requirement would not apply where the audit is performed by a single individual.*

Subject Matter	ISA/ISQC (UK and Ireland) main paragraphs setting out requirements and, in [ ], guidance	Key matters to document[6]
– Identifying characteristics of the specific matters or items being tested	ISA (UK and Ireland) 230 (Revised) **12**, [13]	In documenting the nature, timing and extent of audit procedures performed – the identifying characteristics of the specific items or matters being tested.[16]
– Results	ISA (UK and Ireland) 330 "The Auditor's Procedures in Response to Assessed Risks" **73**, [73b] ISA (UK and Ireland) 240 **108**, [111]	Results and conclusions of audit procedures performed, including where applicable those designed to address the risk of management override of controls.
– Agreement of financial statements to accounting records	ISA (UK and Ireland) 330 "The Auditor's Procedures in Response to Assessed Risks" **73a**, [73b]	Demonstration that the financial statements agree or reconcile with the underlying accounting records.
– External confirmations	ISA (UK and Ireland) 505 "External Confirmations" [33]	Oral confirmations, if any, of responses received (e.g. where a response was received in electronic format and the auditor wishes to validate the source).[17]
– Discussion of significant matters with management or others	ISA (UK and Ireland) 230 (Revised) **16**, [17]	The significant matters discussed and when and with whom the discussions took place.[18]
– Information that contradicts or is inconsistent with the auditor's final conclusion regarding a significant matter.	ISA (UK and Ireland) 230 (Revised) **18**, [19]	How the auditor addressed the contradiction or inconsistency in forming the final conclusion.[19]

[16] *Identifying characteristics will vary with the nature of the audit procedure and the item or matter being tested. Paragraph 13 of the ISA (UK and Ireland) gives examples.*

[17] *The guidance in the ISA (UK and Ireland) states that if the information in the oral confirmations is significant, the auditor requests the parties involved to submit written confirmation of the specific information directly to the auditor (paragraph 33).*

[18] *The guidance in the ISA (UK and Ireland) indicates that the documentation may include records, such as agreed minutes, prepared by the entity. Others with whom the auditor may discuss significant matters include those charged with governance, other personnel within the entity, and external parties, such as persons providing professional advice to the entity (paragraph 17).*

[19] *The guidance in the ISA (UK and Ireland) indicates that the auditor does not need to retain documentation that is incorrect or superseded (paragraph 19).*

Subject Matter	ISA/ISQC (UK and Ireland) main paragraphs setting out requirements and, in [ ], guidance	Key matters to document[6]
– Consultation on difficult or contentious matters	ISA (UK and Ireland) 220 **30**, [31, 33]	Nature, scope and conclusions; in sufficient detail to enable an understanding of the issue; and the results of the consultation, including any decisions taken, the basis for those decisions and how they were implemented.
– Differences of opinion between members of the engagement team and/or others consulted	ISQC (UK and Ireland) 1 **57**	The conclusions reached and the implementation of them.
– Non compliance, if any, with laws and regulations	ISA (UK and Ireland) 250 "Consideration of Laws and Regulations in an Audit of Financial Statements" Section A: **28** [Section B: 46]	The findings, including copies of records and documents, and minutes of discussions with management about them, if appropriate. Where matters may be reportable to a regulator: the facts and the basis for the auditor's decision (whether to report or not), such that the reasons for that decision may be clearly demonstrated should the need to do so arise in future.
– Concerns, if any, about going concern	ISA (UK and Ireland) 570 "Going Concern" **30-1**	The extent of the auditor's concern.
– Management representations	ISA (UK and Ireland) 580 "Management Representations" [10]	A summary of oral discussions with management or written representations from management.
– Communications, if any, about fraud.	ISA (UK and Ireland) 240 **109**, [111]	Communications about fraud with management, those charged with governance, regulators and others.
– Communications with those charged with governance	ISA (UK and Ireland) 260 "Communication of Audit Matters With Those Charged With Governance" [16]	Matters of governance interest that are communicated orally and any responses to those matters.[20] [21]

---

[20] The guidance in the ISA (UK and Ireland) indicates that this documentation may take the form of a copy of the minutes of the auditor's discussion with those charged with governance (paragraph 16).

[21] Whilst not addressed by the ISA (UK and Ireland) it is reasonable to presume that the auditor will keep copies of written communications addressing audit matters of governance interest.

Subject Matter	ISA/ISQC (UK and Ireland) main paragraphs setting out requirements and, in [ ], guidance	Key matters to document[6]
– Directors' report	ISA (UK and Ireland) 720 "The auditor's statutory reporting responsibility in relation to directors' reports" Section B: **12**	Results of procedures performed to assess whether the information in the directors' report is consistent with the financial statements, including details of any material inconsistencies and how they were resolved. The conclusion reached as to whether the information in the directors' report is consistent with the financial statements.
Review of the audit		
– Engagement Quality Control Review[22]	ISQC (UK and Ireland) 1 **73**	Confirmation that: (a) The procedures required by the firm's policies on engagement quality control review have been performed. (b) The engagement quality control review has been completed before the report is issued. (c) The reviewer is not aware of any unresolved matters that would cause the reviewer to believe that the significant judgments the engagement team made and the conclusions they reached were not appropriate.
– Identification of preparer and reviewer	ISA (UK and Ireland) 220 [25, 27] ISA (UK and Ireland) 230 (Revised) **23**, [24]	Who performed the audit work and the date it was completed. Who reviewed the audit work and the date and extent of the review.[23]
The auditor's report		
	ISA (UK and Ireland) 700 "The Auditor's Report on Financial Statements"	Whilst not addressed by ISA (UK and Ireland) 700, it is reasonable to presume that the auditor will keep a copy of the auditor's report.

---

[22] *Engagement quality control reviews are not required for all audits. Further requirements on the nature and scope of these reviews are set out in paragraphs 60 to 73 of ISQC (UK and Ireland) 1 and paragraphs 36 to 40 of ISA (UK and Ireland) 220.*

[23] *The guidance in ISA (UK and Ireland) 230 indicates that the requirement to document who reviewed the audit work performed does not imply a need for each specific working paper to include evidence of review. The audit documentation, however, evidences who reviewed specified elements of the audit work performed and when (paragraph 24).*

Assembly of the Final Audit File

ISA (UK and Ireland) 230 (Revised) and ISQC (UK and Ireland) 1 also set out specific requirements and guidance in relation to the assembly of the final audit file and the confidentiality, safe custody, integrity, accessibility and retrievability and retention of engagement documentation. 36

With respect to individual engagements, ISA (UK and Ireland) 230 (Revised) requires that: 37

- The auditor should complete the assembly of the final audit file on a timely basis after the date of the auditor's report (paragraph 25).
- After the assembly of the final audit file has been completed, the auditor should not delete or discard audit documentation before the end of its retention period (paragraph 28).
- When the auditor finds it necessary to modify existing audit documentation or add new audit documentation after the assembly of the final audit file has been completed, the auditor should, regardless of the nature of the modifications or additions, document:
  (a) When and by whom they were made, and (where applicable) reviewed;
  (b) The specific reasons for making them; and
  (c) Their effect, if any, on the auditor's conclusions (paragraph 30).

Changes to Documentation after the Date of the Auditor's Report

ISA (UK and Ireland) 230 (Revised) recognises that in exceptional circumstances it may be necessary to change audit documentation after the date of the auditor's report. For example when the auditor subsequently discovers facts that existed at the date of the auditor's report that, had the auditor been aware of them at the time, might have affected the auditor's report. 38

When such exceptional circumstances arise, requiring the auditor to perform new or additional audit procedures or leading the auditor to reach new conclusions, the auditor is required to document: 39

(a) The circumstances encountered;
(b) The new or additional audit procedures performed, audit evidence obtained, and conclusions reached; and
(c) When and by whom the resulting changes to audit documentation were made, and (where applicable) reviewed (paragraph 31).

Appendix – Illustrative examples of audit documentation

This appendix includes a number of illustrative examples of audit documentation. The examples focus on aspects of ISAs (UK and Ireland) 315, 330 and 240. These represent the areas where most 'new' requirements were added as a result of the introduction of ISAs (UK and Ireland) in 2004 and initial feedback on the implementation of ISAs (UK and Ireland) suggests that this is the primary area where increased documentation has resulted in additional cost for audits of smaller entities.

Much of the information documented under the requirements of these ISAs (UK and Ireland) can be kept as 'permanent' information and reviewed and updated as necessary in subsequent years. Therefore, the documentation costs are likely to be highest in the first year of an audit following ISAs (UK and Ireland).

There are a number of different ways in which audit documentation requirements can be fulfilled. The following examples illustrate this by demonstrating more than one technique in a number of areas for the audit of one company, in some cases focussing on one particular sales cycle. They do not represent a comprehensive set of audit working papers and do not necessarily identify all the risks associated with a business of the nature described. They are not intended to set a minimum standard of documentation and other approaches can be used in practice with adaptations to the circumstances of the audit. For example, it would be possible to prepare one planning document that encompasses all the individual examples illustrated.

Area of documentation	Illustrative approach	Page
Understanding the entity	Example 1 – Free-form notes	21
	Example 2 – Based on a checklist	25
Audit team planning meeting	Example 3 – Excerpt from meeting using a pre-set agenda	30
Controls documentation	Example 4 – Free-form notes	33
	Example 5 – Based on a checklist and systems diagrams	38
Risk assessment	Example 6 - Based on risks	42
	Example 7 - Based on assertions	44

Example documentation: for illustrative purposes only

Example 1 – Free-form notes of Understanding the entity

(Documentation requirement at ISA (UK and Ireland) 315 paragraph 122(b))

Nature of the entity

Bulls Restaurant and Hotel Limited is a company that owns and operates a restaurant and hotel property in Manchester city centre. This property comprises a three storey building (wine bar on the ground floor, restaurant on the first floor and ballroom on the top floor) and an adjoining luxury hotel property of 10 en-suite rooms and 2 large family suites.

The company qualifies as a small company:

- Turnover is £2.5million.
- Balance sheet total is £1million.
- There are 25 permanent employees and a pool of approximately 15 casual staff who are used when special events are held.

The directors have chosen to have a voluntary audit for a number of reasons. However, if the property is reflected at its current value (about £3million) in the accounts, the audit exemption will not be available. Additionally, a non-executive (chartered accountant) director has suggested it would be valuable from a control viewpoint and in order that future expansion might be eased.

Revenue is generated from two sources – Food and Beverage (the wine bar, restaurant and function room) (70%) and Room revenue from the hotel (30%). A local brewer supplies all alcohol and soft drinks – long established relationship. The hotel business is reliant on travel agent and internet related bookings.

Industry factors

Regeneration of Manchester city centre brought in a large number of competitors a few years ago. Occupancy rates of 80% and average room rate were maintained during this time but this resulted in a squeeze on margins as costs of supply increased.

Customers are now demanding a higher quality dining experience. Bulls is set up to provide this, but past experience is keeping clientele away. The client base may change in the future as a result of the following two factors:

- Unlike other local bars and restaurants, Bulls do not plan to apply for a change in their licence in order to be able to open later (currently 11pm in the wine bar, 12midnight in the restaurant and 1am in the function suite);
- The forthcoming changes relating to a ban on smoking in public places may change the nature of the client base attracted to the wine bar on the ground floor which is the public face of the business.

The business is subject to seasonal variation. This is most pronounced during December, when Christmas events increase turnover by over 100% and casual staff are employed for a large proportion of the time during this month.

Example documentation: for illustrative purposes only

Regulatory factors

- Environmental health inspections continue to be thorough and turn up areas for improvement.
- National minimum wage legislation is relevant.
- Tax treatment of gratuity payments was under dispute, but now agreed by HMRC.
- Health and Safety at work and fire safety legislation is relevant – there are a number of hazardous environments, especially in kitchen areas.
- A premises licence is held for the sale and supply of alcohol and provision of entertainment.

Ownership and governance

Single company owned by two family shareholders with a number of other minority shareholders. The directors are as follows:

			Shareholding
Executive directors:	Fred Bull	Brother	40%
	Jo Giles	Sister	40%
Non-executive directors:	Mark Quinn	Qualified lawyer	5%
	Lisa Swann	Qualified accountant	5%
	Terry Bull	Father	10%

The executive directors are in a dominant position, but past experience indicates that the active involvement of non-executive directors prevents an abuse of their position.

Related parties

A number of large functions have been held at the hotel for family and friends of the directors in the past. These have typically been invoiced at reduced rates compared to other customers, but have not been material and payments have been received promptly. There has therefore been no requirement for disclosure under FRSSE.

Terry Bull runs a local meat distribution company – Melville Foods. Much of the fresh meat used in the restaurant and for functions are supplied by this company, representing approximately 20% of the food costs of the company.

Investments

No major investments, except for freehold property, which is continually refurbished in order to maintain its value.

Organisational structure and financing

Company originally set up with share finance and bank loans (now repaid). The company has an overdraft facility of £50,000. This facility is fully utilised once or twice during the year, but it typically runs at £25,000. Annual meetings are held with a bank representative at which time the overdraft and any other loan facilities required for the forthcoming year are agreed.

Example documentation: for illustrative purposes only

Accounting policies

The company follows the FRSSE. In the past the property has been valued at cost. The directors have confirmed that they will revalue the property this year, after which they will need to keep this valuation up to date.

Objectives and strategies and related business risks

Management want to raise the standard of the restaurant and gain higher quality ratings in hotel and restaurant listings. Directors are researching the possibility of a second (rural) location: they propose to fund such expansion largely through bank finance.

Measurement and review of financial performance

Management review monthly management accounts prepared by a part time bookkeeper, that include a comparison with budgets which are prepared by the directors. KPIs include occupancy, average room rate, covers served, turnover and rooms, food and beverage gross profit margins. Following a squeeze on margins in the late 1990s these have been steady for a number of years.

Originally prepared by *Sarah Cole*   Date *June 20XX*

Sources of information referred to:

- Discussion with Fred Bull and Jo Giles
- Share register
- Review of 20XW financial statements
- Management accounts for 20XX
- Review of debtor and creditor listings
- Company website

Risk assessment procedures performed in 20XY

Continuing relevance of the information above confirmed by discussion on 18th January with Fred Bull and Stacey Burrows, the bookkeeper.

Updated for 20XY audit by *Sarah Cole*   Date *January 20XY*

Impact on the audit – risks of material mis-statement relevant to audit for the year ended 31 January 20XY

At the Financial Statement Level

1. No pervasive risks of material misstatement have been identified. The assessment of risk at the financial statement level is "low".

At the Assertion Level

2. Family company means related party transactions likely to occur, but may not be classified as such. (R102)

Example documentation: for illustrative purposes only

3. Possible unrecorded liabilities resulting from fines and other liabilities arising from reviews by EHOs and HMRC – in the past few years there has been a potential liability relating to the tax treatment of gratuity payments. *(R101)*

4. The directors have confirmed that they will revalue the property this year for the first time. They have arranged for a valuation to be carried out by HBE Valuers. This will be a material change in accounting policy. **This constitutes a significant risk**.
(R103)

Example documentation: for illustrative purposes only

Example 2 – Understanding the entity based on a checklist

(Documentation requirement at ISA (UK and Ireland) 315 paragraph 122(b))

Objective:	To obtain an understanding of the entity and its environment sufficient to identify and assess the risks of material misstatement of the financial statements
Method:	Review notes from prior year audit, make enquiries of management, review recent industry press and management accounts.
Information sources:	Share register, management accounts for 20XX, debtor and creditor listings, company website

Factors to consider	Notes	Ref
Industry, regulatory and other external factors		
Industry conditions		
➤ Market and competition ➤ Cyclical/seasonal activity ➤ Product technology ➤ Energy supply and cost	The company owns and operates a restaurant and hotel. Regeneration in Manchester brought in a large number of competitors and it is still a competitive market. Occupancy rates of 80% and average room rates have been maintained, but margins are tight. Customers are demanding a higher quality dining experience. Bulls is set up to provide this but a poor reputation in the past is keeping people away. The business is subject to seasonal variation. This is most pronounced during December when Christmas events increase turnover by over 100% and casual staff are employed for a large part of the month.	

Example documentation: for illustrative purposes only

Factors to consider	Notes	Ref
Regulatory environment		
➢ Accounting principles and industry specific practices ➢ Legislation and regulation ➢ Taxation ➢ Government policies ➢ Environmental requirements	Environmental health inspections continue to be thorough and highlight areas for improvement. National minimum wage, fire safety and health and safety legislation are relevant. Tax treatment of gratuity payments was under dispute but is now agreed by HMRC. Premises licence held.	R101
Other factors affecting the business		
➢ General level of economic activity ➢ Interest rates ➢ Inflation	The company has maintained performance during the current year and draft accounts show a small profit for the year.	
Nature of the entity		
Business operations		
➢ Nature of revenue sources ➢ Products, services and markets ➢ Conduct of operations ➢ Alliances, joint ventures and outsourcing activities ➢ Involvement in e-commerce ➢ Geographic dispersion ➢ Industry segmentation ➢ Key customers ➢ Important suppliers ➢ Employment ➢ Research and development activities ➢ Related parties	Revenue is generated from two sources — the wine bar, restaurant and function room (70%) and rooms in the hotel (30%). A high proportion of these are cash transactions. A local brewer supplies all alcohol and soft drinks and this is a long established relationship. The hotel business is reliant on travel agent and internet related bookings. This is a family company so related party transactions are likely to occur but may not be classified as such. One non-executive director runs Melville Foods which supplies meat to Bulls, representing approximately 20% of the food costs of the company.	R102

Example documentation: for illustrative purposes only

Factors to consider	Notes	Ref
Investments		
➤ Acquisitions/mergers/ disposals ➤ Securities and loans ➤ Capital investment activities ➤ Investments in non-consolidated entities	No major investments other than the freehold property which is continually refurbished to maintain value.	
Financing		
➤ Group structure ➤ Debt structure ➤ Leasing ➤ Beneficial owners ➤ Related parties ➤ Use of derivative financial instruments	80% of the issued share capital is held by the executive directors (F Bull and J Giles) who are brother and sister. Three non executive directors each own 5-10% share capital and are effective in preventing management abusing their position. The company was originally set up with share finance and bank loans (now repaid) and now has an overdraft facility of £50K. The facility is fully utilised a couple of times a year but typically runs at £25K.	
Financial Reporting		
➤ Accounting principles and industry specific practices ➤ Revenue recognition practices ➤ Fair value accounting ➤ Inventories ➤ Foreign currency ➤ Industry specific categories ➤ Unusual or complex transactions ➤ Financial statement presentation and disclosure	The company follows the FRSSE. In the past the property has been valued at cost. The directors have confirmed that they will revalue it for the first time this year — after which it must be kept up to date.	R103

Example documentation: for illustrative purposes only

Factors to consider	Notes	Ref
Objective and strategies and related business risks		
How does the client address industry, regulatory and other external factors: ➤ Industry developments ➤ New products and services ➤ Expansion of the business ➤ New accounting requirements ➤ Regulatory requirements ➤ Current and prospective financing requirements ➤ Use of IT What effect will implementing this strategy have on the entity?	The management wish to raise the standard of the restaurant and gain higher quality ratings in hotel and restaurant listings. The board are researching the possibility of a second rural location.	
Measurement and review of the entity's financial performance		
➤ Key ratios and operating statistics ➤ Key performance indicators ➤ Employee performance measures and incentives ➤ Trends ➤ Use of forecasts, budgets and variance analysis ➤ Analyst and credit rating reports ➤ Competitor analysis ➤ Period on period financial performance	Management review monthly accounts prepared by a part time bookkeeper which include comparison with budgets. KPIs include occupancy, average room rate, turnover and gross profit margin. These have been steady for a number of years.	

Risks of material mis-statement arising from Understanding the Entity

No pervasive risks of material misstatement have been identified. The assessment of risk at the financial statement level is "low"

R101 – Possible unrecorded liabilities resulting from fines and other liabilities arising from reviews by EHOs and HMRC – in the past few years there has been a potential liability relating to the tax treatment of gratuity payments.

R102 – Family company means related party transactions likely to occur, but may not be classified as such.

R103 – The revaluation of property for the first time will be a material change in accounting policy. This constitutes a significant risk.

Example documentation: for illustrative purposes only

Example 3 – Excerpt from Audit Team Planning Meeting using pre-set agenda

(Documentation requirements at ISA (UK and Ireland) 315 paragraph 122(a), ISA (UK and Ireland) 240 paragraph 107(a))

Persons in attendance
Name: Paul Cox   Position: PARTNER

Sarah Cole   MANAGER

Richard Cannon   SENIOR

A. Susceptibility of the financial statements to material misstatements due to fraud

There are two types of fraud relevant to the auditor's considerations; fraudulent reporting and misappropriation of assets. For both types, the risk factors are further classified based on three conditions:

- Incentive or pressure for management or others to commit a fraud,
- Perceived or actual opportunity to commit a fraud, e.g. through management over-ride of controls, and
- Attitude, characters, culture, environment or set of ethical values that are consistent with a rationalisation by management or others to committing a fraud.

The auditor should maintain an attitude of professional scepticism throughout the audit, recognising the possibility that a material misstatement due to fraud could exist, notwithstanding the auditor's past experience with the entity and the auditor's belief about the honesty and integrity of management and those charged with governance.

1. **Notes of team discussion on consideration of any known external and internal factors that may result in fraud:**

(a) Due to the nature of the business there is a risk of cash and liquor stock theft (R104, R105)
(b) Generally culture/environment is good with internal controls in place.
(c) Segregation of duties in place over sales with responsibilities split between restaurant manager, receptionist and bookkeeper.
(d) While management are in a dominant position, two directors' signatures are required on all cheques and non-executive directors are actively involved in the business.
(e) Purchases from and sales to related parties (directors and Melville Foods) could be made not at arms length (R102)
(f) Fred Bull has complained about the amount of corporation tax and VAT the company is paying and has asked whether there are ways it could be

Example documentation: for illustrative purposes only

reduced. He indicated, however, that he would not want the company to mislead HMRC deliberately and risk penalties. (R106)

2. Team response to the assessed risks of material misstatement due to fraud including any additional work required

(a) Addressed in audit work on sales completeness
(b) Confirm control consciousness of management by observation during the audit
(c) Ensure that split of responsibilities is maintained by observation and walkthrough tests
(d) Review Board meeting minutes to confirm attendance of non-executive directors.
(e) Review invoicing for functions held for directors (unlikely to be material) and review invoices from Melville Foods
(f) Remain alert for mis-accounting particularly in relation to matters affecting tax, e.g. expenditure v capital.

B. Susceptibility of the financial statements to material misstatements due to error

The term 'error' refers to an unintentional misstatement in the financial statements, including the omission of an amount or a disclosure, such as:

- A mistake in gathering or processing data from which financial statements are prepared.
- An incorrect accounting estimate arising from oversight or misinterpretation of facts; or
- 0A mistake in the application of accounting principles relating to measurement, recognition, classification, presentation or disclosure.

1. Notes of team discussion on consideration of any known external and internal factors that may result in error

(a) Large number of small transactions so generally if errors arise should be small.
(b) Some manual processes e.g. transfer of till rolls to spreadsheet which could result in error but if material should be identified by sales review. (R201)
(c) Lack of preparation of debtors listing could lead to errors arising due to bad debts not being identified. (R202)

2. Team response to the assessed risks of material misstatement due to error together with additional testing required

Generally susceptibility to error is low, subject to items b) and c) identified above.
(b) Unlikely to result in material misstatement: ensure that bank reconciliation control is operating effectively.

Example documentation: for illustrative purposes only

(c) Request directors to compile a year end debtors listing and match invoices to cash received after year end.

OVERALL CONCLUSION
(subject to points carried forward in the final notes)

Generally susceptibility to fraud and error is low. Specific risks of material misstatement and responses are noted above. There is a limited risk of material misstatement at the financial statement level as there are few external users of the financial statements, the business is well-controlled and there are not many related parties.

Signed: P Cox .... Date: 10 April 20XY ....

Example documentation: for illustrative purposes only

Example 4 – Free-form notes of controls documentation

(Documentation requirement at ISA (UK and Ireland) 315 paragraph 122(b))

Control environment

Non-executive directors (including a professional accountant and lawyer) are personal friends or family of the two main directors, but are not involved in the business on a day-to-day basis. Directors' meetings are held on a bi-monthly basis, where management accounts are reviewed and business operational matters are discussed. A high level of reliance is placed on the part-time bookkeeper and the restaurant manager, who have been with the company for a number of years, and no significant problems with their work have been encountered in previous audits. The bookkeeper is a member of the Institute of Certified Bookkeepers.

Management's attitude to internal control is a very positive one. The two executive directors make a point of reviewing the records of the previous day's sales with key staff and holding regular staff meetings to emphasise the importance of maintaining both quality and control.

Risk assessment process

No formal process in place. Executive directors have an understanding of the key risks to the business:

Reputational risks:	o Possible failure of health and safety systems, resulting in poor reputation and possible fines or requirements for capital investment (R101)
	o Loss of customers resulting from poor reviews or experience of 'loutish behaviour' (R301)
Financial risks:	o Losses due to stock shrinkage (R105)
	o High level of cash transactions leading to potential loss through misappropriation (R104)
	o Poor cash flow management (R302)
	o Credit facilities given to corporate clients who are not credit-worthy (R303)

Information system

Food and beverage transactions are recorded on EPOS terminals in situ. Room revenue is generated from a separate hotel computer system. All revenues are totalled daily and input manually to the ACT accounting system. All systems have been in place for a number of years. ACT has been experienced on a number of other small clients in the firm.

Example documentation: for illustrative purposes only

Monitoring controls

Formal monitoring controls consist of:
- The executive directors review the monthly stock-take information and follow up any shrinkage with bar staff.
- The bank reconciliation is reviewed by one of the non-executive directors, who is a qualified accountant.

Originally prepared by Sarah Cole   Date June 20XX

Continuing relevance of the information above confirmed by discussion with Fred Bull and Stacey Burrows, the bookkeeper. These monitoring controls have been found by previous audits to have operated effectively in prior years. They will be tested again this year.

Internal control notes updated
   for 20XY audit by Sarah Cole   Date January 20XY

Impact on the audit – risks of material mis-statement relevant to audit for the year ended 31 January 20XY

A high volume of cash transactions (combined with manual transfers of information from till rolls to a spreadsheet summary and then to the accounting system) increases the risks of inaccuracies in the sales cycles for all sources of revenue.

Example documentation: for illustrative purposes only

Information system and control activities – extract from notes relevant to sales cycle

This is an extract of information from the permanent audit file, which is relevant only to liquor sales in the wine bar, restaurant and function room.

Liquor sales

Sources of income
Wine bar (40%), restaurant (35%), function room (25%)

Methods of recording orders
Alcoholic and soft drinks are all served from the bar areas in the wine bar, restaurant and function room. In the wine bar and function room these are dealt either:

- On a cash basis, where details of the drinks served are input to the EPOS system terminal and payment is made by the customer at the time of serving.

- On credit, where a tab is opened on the EPOS terminal and either a credit card is retained behind the bar for use in settling the account when the guests are leaving or an invoice is made up on the following day from the details recorded.

In the restaurant, the orders are input to a waiter's terminal by waiting staff and paid for by the guest at the end of the meal. Drinks are served from the bar area in accordance with what has been input to the system.

Method of ensuring all sales are recorded
At the end of each day (or shift), all EPOS terminal till rolls are printed. Beverage sales totals are input from the till rolls to a summary spreadsheet maintained by the restaurant manager, together with an analysis of credit card and cash takings and amounts to be invoiced.

Invoices are made up for credit sales in the function room by the restaurant manager or one of the directors, using the information recorded by the EPOS terminal. These are handwritten and are taken from a pad with pre-printed serial numbers.

Accounting records and method of use
Information on sales totals is taken from the spreadsheet maintained by the restaurant manager and input directly to the ACT accounting system on a weekly basis by the bookkeeper.

At the end of each month an independent stocktake is carried out on all bar stocks (excluding hotel mini-bar stock). Closing stock values are input to the general ledger and gross profit margins monitored by the directors. Any variations in stock shrinkage from the norm are followed up with bar staff.

Example documentation: for illustrative purposes only

> The bookkeeper reconciles the cash and credit card receipts with cash banked and receipts recorded on the bank statements. She also maintains a file of all unpaid invoices from the function room and where cash is received in the post, this is matched to these invoices. The file is reviewed on an ad hoc basis by one of the executive directors and clients are chased for payment where appropriate.
>
> ### Impact on the audit – risks of material mis-statement
>
> R104 There is a fraud risk arising from the possible misappropriation of cash when cash sales are not input to an EPOS terminal. **This is a significant risk.** In relation to this the independent monthly stocktake provides a mitigating control by highlighting stock shrinkages that are outside the norm (follow up of shrinkages has led to staff being dismissed in the past). **This control will be tested.**
>
> R201 A high volume of cash transactions (combined with manual transfers of information from till rolls to a spreadsheet summary and then to the accounting system) increases the risks of inaccuracies in the sales cycle.
>
> R202 No debtors listing is maintained and follow up of unpaid invoices is done on an ad hoc basis. This leads to a risk that bad debts are not provided for – past experience suggests a reluctance to accept that particular debts are 'bad'. Christmas and New Year functions are material and some debtors relating to this period are still outstanding two months after the year end.
>
> R203 Deposit invoices raised in advance of a function may be treated as sales at the time of invoicing rather than the date of the function, creating a possible cut-off error.

Originally prepared by Sarah Cole   Date June 20XX

Continuing relevance of the information above confirmed by discussion with Fred Bull and Stacey Burrows, the bookkeeper.

Updated for 20XY audit by Sarah Cole Date January 20XY

Example documentation: for illustrative purposes only

Example 5 – Controls documentation based on a checklist and systems diagrams

(Documentation requirement at ISA (UK and Ireland) 315 paragraph 122(b))

Objective: To obtain an understanding of internal control sufficient to identify and assess the risks of material misstatement of the financial statements

Method: Review notes from prior year audit, make enquiries of management and perform walk through tests on transaction cycles.

Factors to consider	Notes	Ref
Control environment		
➢ Communication and enforcement of integrity and ethical values ➢ Commitment to competence ➢ Participation by those charged with governance ➢ Management's philosophy and operating style ➢ Organisational structure ➢ Assignment of authority and responsibility ➢ Human resource policies and practices	Management's attitude to internal controls is a very positive one. Executive directors make a point of reviewing the records of the previous day's sales with key staff and holding regular staff meetings to emphasise the importance of maintaining both quality and control. Non executive directors are personal friends or family of the two main directors, but are not involved in the business on a day to day basis. Directors' meetings are held every two months where management accounts are reviewed and business operational matters are discussed. A high level of reliance is placed on the part time bookkeeper and the restaurant manager (both have been with the co. for a number of years and no significant problems encountered in previous audits) The bookkeeper is a member of the Institute of Certified Bookkeepers.	

Example documentation: for illustrative purposes only

Factors to consider	Notes	Ref
Entity's risk assessment process		
➤ Changes in operating environment ➤ New personnel ➤ New or revamped information systems ➤ Rapid growth ➤ New technology ➤ New business models, products or activities ➤ Corporate restructurings ➤ Expanded foreign operations ➤ New accounting pronouncements	No formal process is in place. Executive directors have an understanding of the key risks to the business: • reputational risk (due to the failure of H&S systems & loss of customers from poor reviews) • financial risks (due to stock shrinkage, misappropriation of cash, poor cash flow management and bad debts).	
Information system		
➤ Infrastructure and software ➤ Document individual transaction cycles ➤ Individual roles and responsibilities ➤ Financial and accounting manuals	Food and beverage transactions recorded on EPOS terminals in situ. Room revenue is generated from a separate hotel computer system. Sales totals are taken from each system daily and input manually to the ACT accounting system. ACT accounting system is used by bookkeeper to prepare trial balance information.	R201
Control activities		
➤ Performance reviews ➤ Information processing ➤ Physical controls ➤ Segregation of duties	See systems documentation on transaction cycles in Profit and Loss section: • Sales, Purchases, Payroll Segregation of duties in place over sales with responsibilities split between restaurant manager, receptionist and bookkeeper.	P20-23

Example documentation: for illustrative purposes only

Factors to consider	Notes	Ref
Monitoring of controls		
➤ Ongoing activities ➤ Separate evaluations ➤ Internal audit ➤ Use of external information	Executive directors review monthly stock takes and follow up any shrinkage with bar staff. The bank reconciliation is reviewed by one of the non executive directors – a qualified accountant. These monitoring controls have been found by previous audits to have operated effectively in prior years. They will be tested again this year.	

Risks of material mis-statement arising from Components of internal control

R201 – A high volume of transactions (combined with manual transfers of information from till rolls to a spreadsheet summary and then to the accounting system) increases the risks of inaccuracies in the sales cycle.

Arising from systems documentation of beverage sales at P20:

R104 – There is a fraud risk arising from the possible misappropriation of cash when cash sales are not input to an EPOS terminal. **This is a significant risk.** In relation to this the independent monthly stocktake provides a mitigating control by highlighting stock shrinkages that are outside the norm (follow up of shrinkages has led to staff being dismissed in the past). **This control will be tested.**

Example documentation: for illustrative purposes only

Beverage sales cycle – systems documentation Ref: P20

Transaction initiation and processing	Responsibility	Frequency	Controls in place over assertions	Risk
Details of F&B input to EPOS. Master price list held in system and applied to each item automatically.	Bar and restaurant staff	As F&B are ordered	C – No detailed control in place. Directors review daily sales totals and follow up where lower than expected. O, A, L – Customer would complain if not served with F&B ordered or charged more than expected.	
Payment made by customer and input to EPOS.	Bar and restaurant staff	When F&B ordered or customer leaves	C –Executive directors review gross margins and monthly stock take and follow up any shrinkages with bar staff. O, A – total for cash taken is reconciled to total charges at the end of each shift and followed up by restaurant manager	R104– Misappropriation of cash at point of sale
Function room invoices prepared for credit sales from customer and notes on pricing kept in function diary → Sales totals taken from till rolls and invoices and input to spreadsheet	Restaurant manager	At end of each shift	C, F – Manager logs till roll from each terminal and checks Z-totals. Directors review daily sales totals and follow up where lower than expected. Function room invoices pre-numbered O, A – Bank reconciliation performed monthly, reviewed by non executive director	R201– Manual posting errors
Spreadsheet information used to update ACT	Bookkeeper	Weekly	C, O, A – Bank reconciliation performed monthly, reviewed by non executive director	

Key to assertions: O = Occurrence, C = Completeness, A = Accuracy, F = Cutoff, L = Classification

Example documentation: for illustrative purposes only

Example 6 – Risk assessment based on risks

(Documentation requirements at ISA (UK and Ireland) 315 paragraph 122(c) and (d), ISA (UK and Ireland) 240 paragraph 107(b) and 108(a), ISA (UK and Ireland) 330 paragraph 73)

Beverage sales and debtors cycle
SALES and TRADE DEBTORS – SUMMARY of RISKS OF MATERIAL MISSTATEMENT and AUDIT RESPONSE

Risk of material misstatement identified	Significant risk?	Mitigating internal controls	Likelihood of risk resulting in material misstatement	Assertions impacted	Audit procedures	Audit program reference
					These procedures are specific to this example only. They are not exhaustive and will not necessarily be useful in relation to similar risks in other circumstances.	
R104 – Misappropriation of cash at point of sale	✓ (this is a fraud risk)	Independent monthly stocktake to identify abnormal stock shrinkages	High	**Sales:** Completeness **Debtors:** Completeness	Review records of monthly stocktakes. Ascertain follow up taken where margins out of line with expectation	
R201 – Manual posting errors from till rolls and invoices to ACT via spreadsheet		Monthly bank reconciliation will identify cash received but no sale posted	Med	**Sales:** Completeness, Accuracy, Classification **Debtors:** Valuation	Review monthly bank reconciliations and ensure outstanding items clear during following month. For sample of dates, check sales totals from till rolls and invoices to spreadsheets and accounting system	

Example documentation: for illustrative purposes only

Risk of material misstatement identified	Significant risk?	Mitigating internal controls	Likelihood of risk resulting in material misstatement	Assertions impacted	Audit procedures *These procedures are specific to this example only. They are not exhaustive and will not necessarily be useful in relation to similar risks in other circumstances.*	Audit program reference
R202 – Bad debts not provided for or written off			Med	Debtors: Valuation	From client debtor listing match invoices to cash received after year end or include in discussion of bad debts	
R203 – Sales not recorded or recorded in wrong period			Med	Sales: Completeness, Cutoff Debtors: Completeness	Check sample of function diary entries back to invoices to confirm sales recorded Check sample of invoices back to function diary to confirm sales recorded in the correct period	

Example documentation: for illustrative purposes only

Example 7 – Risk assessment based on assertions

(Documentation requirements at ISA (UK and Ireland) 315 paragraph 122(c) and (d), ISA (UK and Ireland) 240 paragraph 107(b) and 108(a), ISA (UK and Ireland) 330 paragraph 73)

Beverage sales and debtors cycle
SALES and TRADE DEBTORS – RISK ASSESSMENT and AUDIT APPROACH SUMMARY

As a result of the issues considered during the planning, note here the risks of material misstatement associated with the audit of this section:

R104 Due to the nature of the business there is a fraud risk of cash pilferage. Cash sales might not be input to EPOS at the point of sale and cash relating to these unrecorded sales stolen by bar and restaurant staff. This is a significant risk.

R201 Manual transfer of amounts from invoices, till rolls and spreadsheets could create errors.

R202 No debtors listing is maintained by the client with follow up of unpaid invoices not done systematically and bad debts not provided for.

R203 Sales recorded in wrong period

Assertion (and risk of material misstatement)	Risk factors	Control in operation	Tests of control (programme reference)	Substantive procedures (programme reference)
			These procedures are specific to this example only. They are not exhaustive and will not necessarily be useful in relation to similar risks in other circumstances.	
Sales				
Occurrence (Low)	None			
Completeness (High)	R104 – re. liquor sales	Monthly independent stocktake and review by directors will pick up significant amounts of pilferage	Review records of monthly stocktakes. Ascertain follow up taken where margins out of line with expectation (TC 3)	Check sample of function diary entries back to invoices to confirm sales recorded
	R201	Monthly bank reconciliation will identify cash received but no sale posted	Review monthly bank reconciliations and ensure outstanding items clear during following month. (TC 6)	For sample of dates, check sales totals from till rolls and invoices to spreadsheets and accounting system (ST4)

Example documentation: for illustrative purposes only

Assertion (and risk of material misstatement)	Risk factors	Control in operation	Tests of control (programme reference)	Substantive procedures (programme reference)
			These procedures are specific to this example only. They are not exhaustive and will not necessarily be useful in relation to similar risks in other circumstances.	
Accuracy (Medium)	R201	See above – monthly bank reconciliation	See above – review monthly bank reconciliations	See above – test postings from a sample of dates
Cut off (Medium)	R203	Pre-numbered function room invoices		Check sample of invoices back to function diary to confirm sales recorded in the correct period (ST 7)
Classification (Low)	R201	See above – monthly bank reconciliation	See above – review monthly bank reconciliations	See above – test postings from a sample of dates
Debtors				
Existence (Low)	None			
Rights and obligations (Low)	None			
Completeness (High)	R204, R201, R202	See above – independent stocktake and gross profit review, monthly bank reconciliation and pre-numbered invoices	See above – review records of monthly stocktakes and review monthly bank reconciliations	See above – test postings for a sample of dates and check sample of invoices back to function diary
Valuation and allocation (High)	R201	See above – monthly bank reconciliation	See above – review monthly bank reconciliations	See above – test postings for a sample of dates
	R202	None		From client debtor listing match invoices to cash received after year end or include in discussion of bad debts (DT 5)

[PN 27]
The audit of credit unions in the United Kingdom

(Issued January 2009)

	Page
Preface	3
Introduction	4
The Audit of Financial Statements	13
ISA (UK and Ireland) 200: Objective and General Principles Governing an Audit of Financial Statements	13
ISA (UK and Ireland) 210: Terms of Audit Engagements	15
ISA (UK and Ireland) 220: Quality Control for Audits of Historical Financial Information	17
ISA (UK and Ireland) 240: The Auditor's Responsibility to Consider Fraud in an Audit of Financial Statements	18
ISA (UK and Ireland) 250: Section A – Consideration of Law and Regulations in an Audit of Financial Statements	21
ISA (UK and Ireland) 250: Section B – The Auditors' Right and Duty to Report to Regulators in the Financial Sector	24
ISA (UK and Ireland) 260: Communication of Audit Matters to those Charged with Governance	30
ISA (UK and Ireland) 300: Planning an Audit of Financial Statements	32
ISA (UK and Ireland) 315: Obtaining an Understanding of the Entity and its Environment and Assessing the Risks of Material Misstatement	35
ISA (UK and Ireland) 330: The Auditors Procedures in Response to Assessed Risks	43
ISA (UK and Ireland) 402: Audit Considerations Relating to Entities using Service Organisations	45
ISA (UK and Ireland) 501: Audit Evidence – Additional Considerations for Specific Items	47
ISA (UK and Ireland) 505: External Confirmations	48
ISA (UK and Ireland) 520: Analytical Procedures	49
ISA (UK and Ireland) 540: Audit of Accounting Estimates	52
ISA (UK and Ireland) 545: Auditing fair value measurements and disclosures	54
ISA (UK and Ireland) 550: Related Parties	55
ISA (UK and Ireland) 560: Subsequent Events	56
ISA (UK and Ireland) 570: Going Concern	57
ISA (UK and Ireland) 580: Management Representations	59
ISA (UK and Ireland) 700: The Auditor's Report on Financial Statements	60
ISA (UK and Ireland) 720 (Revised): Other Information in Documents containing Audited Financial Statements	62
Reporting on regulatory returns	64

Appendix 1 – Illustrative Auditors' Reports for a Credit Union
Appendix 2 – The main parts of legislation relevant to credit unions in Great Britain
Appendix 3 – FSMA 2000 and related statutory instruments: Important provisions for auditors in Great Britain
Appendix 4 – The FSA Handbook
Appendix 5 – Possible factors that may indicate going concern issues

Appendix 6 – Reporting direct to the regulators– statutory right and protection for disclosure under general law
Appendix 7 – Trade associations in Northern Ireland
Appendix 8 – Definitions

Preface

This Practice Note contains guidance on the application of auditing standards issued by the Auditing Practices Board (APB) to the audit of credit unions in the United Kingdom (UK). In addition, it contains guidance intended to assist the auditors of credit unions in reporting on matters specified by the regulators, and guidance is also given on the auditors' right and duty to report to the regulators. For credit unions in Great Britain the regulator is the Financial Services Authority (FSA) and in Northern Ireland it is the Department of Enterprise, Trade and Investment (DETI).

The Practice Note is supplementary to, and should be read in conjunction with, International Standards on Auditing (ISAs) (UK and Ireland), which apply to all audits undertaken in the UK. This Practice Note sets out the special considerations relating to the audit of credit unions which arise from individual ISAs (UK and Ireland) listed in the contents. It is not the intention of the Practice Note to provide step-by-step guidance on the audit of credit unions, so where no special considerations arise from a particular ISA (UK and Ireland), no material is included.

This Practice Note has been prepared with advice and assistance from staff of the FSA (in so far as the obligations of credit unions and their auditors under the FSA Handbook are concerned) and with advice and assistance also from staff of DETI. It is based on the legislation and regulations which are in effect at 31 October 2008. The Practice Note does not constitute general guidance given by the FSA or Industry Guidance. It is not an exhaustive list of all the obligations that credit unions and their auditors may have under legislation and the FSA Handbook.

Introduction

1 Credit unions are mutual savings and loan organisations which are not-for-profit and which operate solely for the benefit of their members. Any surpluses which are not distributed to members by way of dividend, or otherwise, are retained within the organisation for its future expansion. The members save by investing in the credit union's shares. Like any other similar financial organisation, the savings and deposits which the credit union takes in, provide a fund from which loans are granted to members.

2 This Practice Note addresses the responsibilities and obligations of the auditor concerning:

- the audit of financial statements in accordance with the requirements of legislation; and
- the statutory duty to report directly to the regulators in certain circumstances.

3 Registered auditors are required to comply with ISAs (UK and Ireland) when conducting audits. This principle applies in the context of credit unions in the same way as to entities in any sector, but the way in which ISAs (UK and Ireland) are applied needs to be adapted to suit the particular characteristics of the entity audited.

4 Credit unions have as their basic aims:

- the promotion of thrift among their members through the accumulation of savings;
- the creation of sources of credit for the benefit of their members at fair and reasonable rates of interest;
- the use and control of members' savings for their mutual benefit; and

- the training and education of their members in the wise use of money and in the management of their financial affairs.

Members must be from the same locality, or be employed in the same industry or with the same employer or have some other "common bond". To become a member of a credit union each individual must hold at least one fully paid up share in the credit union and must qualify under the common bond set out in the credit union's rules. 5

The "Common Bond" between members of the credit union must be one of the following. Members must: 6

- follow a particular occupation; or
- reside in a particular locality; or
- be employed in a particular locality; or
- reside or be employed in a particular locality; or
- be employed by a particular employer; or
- be a member of a bona fide organisation or society which has been formed for purposes other than that of registration as a credit union; or
- have any other common bond approved by the regulators.

The Management and Operation of Credit Unions

The responsibility of directors

The primary responsibility for the conduct of the business of a credit union is vested in the board of directors, who have responsibility for the general control, direction, management of the affairs, funds and records of the credit union, and the management appointed by it. This responsibility includes: 7

- establishing adequate procedures and systems to ensure compliance with the law applicable to credit unions and guidance issued by the regulators;
- the preparation of financial statements that give a true and fair view of the credit union's affairs for the year and compliance with other aspects of credit union law; and
- providing information to the regulators.

Credit unions usually establish a committee, known either as a supervisory or audit committee, which normally consists of elected members who are all volunteers. This committee which is one of the most important from the internal governance perspective oversees the performance by the directors of their functions, and the observance of the credit union's own rules. Credit unions often also establish a credit committee to assess whether loans should be granted. 8

In both Great Britain and Northern Ireland there are a number of trade associations for credit unions. These issue rules and guidance for the benefit of their members, and credit unions normally take account of these when establishing their own rules. In Northern Ireland, the principal trade associations have a role in the oversight of credit unions, and a brief summary of such activities is set out in Appendix 7 of this Practice Note. 9

Financial Statements

10   FIPSA[1] and the NI Order[2] require the annual accounts of a credit union to give a true and fair view of its income and expenditure for the year, and of its state of affairs at the end of the year. The requirement for the accounts of credit unions to give a true and fair view is usually regarded as also requiring compliance with the requirements of the relevant accounting standards of the Accounting Standards Board (ASB) – in particular Statements of Standard Accounting Practice (SSAPs), Financial Reporting Standards (FRSs) and UITF Abstracts.

11   One FRS of particular relevance to credit unions is FRS 18 concerning estimation techniques. This FRS requires the selection of estimation techniques that enable the accounts to give a true and fair view, and that are judged to be the most appropriate in the particular circumstances for the purpose of a true and fair view (FRS 18, paragraph 51). An example of an estimation technique given in FRS 18 is the method of estimating the proportion of debts that will not be recovered (FRS 18, paragraph 4).

12   FRS 18 also requires disclosure of:
- each material accounting policy;
- a description of its significant estimation techniques; and
- the effects of changes in accounting policies or material effects of changes in estimation techniques (FRS 18, paragraph 55).

Legislative and regulatory framework

13   The legislative and regulatory framework within which credit unions operate in the UK is summarised in the following paragraphs.

Great Britain

Relevant Legislation

14   Credit unions are registered under relevant sections of the Industrial and Provident Societies Acts 1965-2002 (IPSA 65/02)[3], and comply with additional requirements set out in the Credit Unions Act 1979 (CU 79).

15   In Great Britain the principal legislation relevant to auditors of credit unions is the Friendly and Industrial and Provident Societies Act 1968 (FIPSA), and the Financial Services and Markets Act 2000 (FSMA 2000).

FIPSA

16   Credit unions are bound by the provisions of FIPSA which require them to produce audited annual accounts which will be put on the public file. An explanation of the requirements of FIPSA is set out in the FSA's Credit Unions Sourcebook (CRED) Chapter 14 annex 1, a part of the FSA Handbook. Auditors are bound by the duties

---

[1] *The Friendly and Industrial and Provident Societies Act 1968, Section 3.*

[2] *The Credit Unions (Northern Ireland) Order 1985, Article 42.*

[3] *For more details see Appendix 2 of this Practice Note.*

imposed by Section 9(4) of FIPSA. This requires them, in preparing their audit report to members, to carry out such investigations as will enable them to form an opinion on:

(a) whether the credit union has kept proper books of account in accordance with the requirements of section 1(1)(a) of FIPSA;
(b) whether the credit union has maintained a satisfactory system of control over its transactions in accordance with the requirements of section 1(1)(b) of FIPSA; and
(c) whether the revenue account or the other accounts (if any) to which the report relates and the balance sheet are in agreement with the books of account of the credit union.
(d) If the auditors are of the opinion that the credit union has failed to comply with any of the requirements of (a) to (c) above then they must state that fact in their report.

FSMA 2000

FSMA 2000 sets out the high level regulatory framework for the financial sector more generally and not just for credit unions. Appendix 2 sets out the main parts of FSMA 2000 relevant to authorised firms[4]. 17

The wide scope of FSMA 2000 reflects the FSA's extensive responsibilities. These are set out in FSMA 2000 as regulatory objectives covering: 18

- market confidence;
- public awareness;
- the protection of consumers; and
- the reduction of financial crime.

FSMA 2000 covers not only the regulation and supervision of financial sector entities but also other issues such as official listing rules, business transfers, market abuse, compensation and ombudsman schemes, investment exchanges and clearing houses. 19

FSMA 2000 is also supported by a large number of statutory instruments. Significant components of the definition and scope of the regulatory framework are contained in the main statutory instruments. A list of important provisions of FSMA 2000 and a list of statutory instruments relevant to the auditor is included in Appendix 3. 20

Under Part X FSMA 2000 the FSA has the power to make 'rules'. The legal effect of a rule varies depending on the power under which it is made and on the language used in the rule. Rules are mandatory unless a waiver has been agreed with the FSA. If an authorised firm contravenes a rule it may be subject to enforcement action and consequent disciplinary measures under Part XIV FSMA 2000. Furthermore, in certain circumstances an authorised firm may be subject to an action for damages under s150 FSMA 2000. In contrast, guidance is generally issued to throw light on a particular aspect of regulatory requirements, and is not binding. However if an authorised firm acts in accordance with it in the circumstances contemplated by that guidance, the FSA will proceed on the basis that the authorised firm has complied with the rule to which the guidance relates. 21

Rules made by the FSA and associated guidance are set out in the FSA Handbook of Rules and Guidance ('the FSA Handbook') (guidance on this, and in particular on 22

---

[4] *An entity which has been granted one of more Part IV permissions by the FSA and so is authorised under FSMA 2000 to undertake regulated activities.*

the FSA's Principles for Businesses and Threshold Conditions, is set out in Appendix 4 of this Practice Note). A summary of the high level requirements is set out in the 'Reader's Guide'. While the FSA's Handbook applies mainly to authorised firms, part of it also sets out Rules which impose duties on auditors. These can be found in the Supervision Manual and are referred to in CRED.

23   It is clearly unrealistic to expect all members of an audit engagement team to have detailed knowledge of the entire Handbook; rather ISA (UK and Ireland) 250 Section B requires the level of knowledge to be commensurate with an individual's role and responsibilities in the audit process. ISA (UK and Ireland) 220 requires the auditor to establish procedures to facilitate consultation and, thereby, to draw on the collective expertise and specialist technical knowledge of others within the audit firm.

Prudential requirements

24   Credit unions are subject to certain prudential requirements which are detailed in CRED. These include the main measures set out below and additional related aspects of systems and controls not covered in the Senior management arrangements, Systems and Controls section of the FSA Handbook (SYSC). There are also certain specific prudential measures applied by the FSA which credit unions are required to report to the FSA via prudential returns. The main measures include:

- capital adequacy – ensuring sufficient capital resources in relation to risk requirements to absorb losses;
- liquidity – ensuring sufficient liquid assets or maturing assets to meet liabilities as they fall due; and
- large exposures – avoiding undue credit risk concentrations.

The level of the prudential measures depends on whether a credit union is a version 1 or a version 2 credit union. A credit union has the choice of applying to be one or the other (the distinction being reflected in a requirement attached to its permission to accept deposits). A version 2 credit union has to satisfy higher requirements, but is able to lend larger amounts to members over longer periods. The differences between the two versions are set out in CRED.

Annual Returns to Regulator

25   The annual return (Form CY) that credit unions have to complete is a supervisory return and is not put on the public file and does not require to be audited. Instead it is required to contain a statement from the auditor as to whether the information contained in the balance sheet and revenue account of the annual return is consistent with the audited annual accounts of the credit union. The annual return is required to be submitted to the FSA no later than 7 months after the year end.

26   Credit unions are also required to submit unaudited quarterly returns to the FSA.

Reporting direct to the FSA

27   Under FSMA 2000 (Communications by Auditors) Regulations 2001 (SI 2001/2587) the auditor of an authorised firm or the auditor of an entity closely linked to an authorised firm who is also the auditor of that authorised firm has a statutory duty to communicate matters of material significance to the FSA. Under s340 FSMA 2000 'the auditor' is defined as one required to be appointed under FSA 'rules' or appointed as a result of another enactment. In addition s342 FSMA 2000 provides that no duty to which the auditor is subject shall be contravened by communicating

in good faith to the FSA any information or opinion on a matter that the auditor reasonably believes is relevant to any functions of the FSA.

Guidance on the identification of matters to be reported to the regulators is set out in the section of this Practice Note dealing with ISA (UK and Ireland) 250 Section B. In particular, auditors consider reporting to the FSA concerns they may have over apparent significant failures by the credit union to comply with the requirements of FIPSA set out above – for example the failure to maintain a satisfactory system of control over its transactions.   28

Communication between the FSA and the auditor

Within the legal constraints that apply, the FSA may pass on to the auditor any information which it considers relevant to his function. An auditor is bound by the confidentiality provisions set out in Part XXIII of FSMA 2000 (Public record, disclosure of information and co-operation) in respect of confidential information the auditor receives from the FSA. The auditor may not pass on such confidential information without lawful authority, for example if an exception applies under the FSMA 2000 (Disclosure of confidential information) Regulations 2001 or with the consent of the person from whom that information was received and, if different, to whom the information relates.   29

Before communicating to an authorised firm any information received from the FSA, the auditor considers carefully whether: 30

- the auditor has received the FSA's express permission to communicate a particular item of information;
- the information relates to any other party whose permission may need to be obtained before disclosure can be made;
- the information was received by FSA in a capacity other than discharging its functions under FSMA 2000 or from another regulator (in which case the auditor may either be prohibited from disclosure or may need permission of the party which provided the information to that regulator).

The auditor may however disclose to an authorised firm information they have communicated to the FSA except where to do so would have the effect of disclosing information communicated to them by the FSA.   31

Matters communicated by the FSA during any bilateral meeting may be conveyed by those representatives of the auditor who were present at the meeting (or otherwise received the communication directly) to other partners, directors and employees of the audit firm who need to know the information in connection with the auditor's performance of its duties relating to that authorised firm without FSA's express permission. However in the interests of prudence and transparency the auditor should inform the FSA that they will be discussing the issues covered with colleagues.   32

Where the FSA passes to the auditors information which it considers is relevant to their function, the auditors consider its implications in the context of their work and may need to amend their approach accordingly. However the fact that they may have been informed of such a matter by the regulator does not, of itself, require auditors to change the scope of the work, nor does it necessarily require them actively to search for evidence in support of the situation communicated by the regulator.   33

34 The auditor is required to co-operate with the FSA (SUP3.8.2R). This may involve attending meetings and providing the FSA with information about the authorised firm that the FSA may reasonably request in discharging its functions.

35 The auditor must notify the FSA without delay if the auditor is removed from office, resigns before the term of office expires or is not re-appointed by the authorised firm. Notification to the FSA includes communicating any matters connected with this event that the auditor considers ought to be drawn to the FSA's attention or a statement that there are no such matters (s344 FSMA 2000 and SUP3.8.11R and 12R).

Northern Ireland

Relevant Legislation

36 In Northern Ireland the principal legislation relevant to credit unions is the Credit Unions (Northern Ireland) Order 1985 (the NI Order).

The NI Order

37 Requirements relevant to auditors are set out in Articles 47 and 49 of the NI Order, relevant extracts from which are as follows:

- The auditors of a credit union shall make a report to the credit union on the accounts examined by them, and on the revenue account and the balance sheet of the credit union for the year of account in respect of which they are appointed.
- The report shall state whether the revenue account and the balance sheet for that year comply with the requirements of this Order and whether, in the opinion of the auditors –
  (a) the revenue account gives a true and fair view in accordance with Article 42 of the income and expenditure of the credit union for that year of account, and
  (b) the balance sheet gives a true and fair view in accordance with that Article of the state of the affairs of the credit union as at the end of that year of account.
- Without prejudice to the previous paragraph, where the report of the auditor relates to any accounts other than the revenue account for the year of account in respect of which they are appointed that report shall state whether those accounts give a true and fair view of any matter to which they relate.
- The auditors of a credit union, in preparing their report under this Article, shall carry out such investigations as will enable them to form an opinion as to the following matters, that is to say –
  (a) whether the credit union has kept proper books of account in accordance with the requirements of Article 40(1)(a);
  (b) whether the credit union has maintained a satisfactory system of control over its transactions in accordance with the requirements of Article 40(1)(b); and
  (c) whether the revenue account, the other accounts, if any, to which the report relates, and the balance sheet are in agreement with the books of account of the credit union,
  and if the auditors are of opinion that the credit union has failed to comply with Article 40(1)(a) or (b), or if the revenue account, the other accounts, if any, and the balance sheet are not in agreement with the books of account of the credit union, the auditors shall state that fact in their report.

- If the auditors fail to obtain all the information and explanations which, to the best of their knowledge and belief, are necessary for the purposes of their audit, they shall state that fact in their report.

Annual Returns to Regulator

Every credit union shall, not later than 31 March in each year, send to the Registry of credit unions (part of DETI) a return (Form AR 25) relating to its affairs for the period ended on the previous 30 September together with – 38

(a) a copy of the report of the auditor or auditors on the credit union's accounts for the period included in the return; and
(b) a copy of each balance sheet made during that period and of any report of the auditor or auditors on that balance sheet.

Annual Returns submitted to DETI do not therefore require to be audited, but a signed copy of the auditor's report on the accounts is to be appended.

Reporting direct to DETI

There is no statutory duty on auditors in Northern Ireland for whistleblowing to DETI. Auditors consider the guidance set out in the section on ISA (UK and Ireland) 250 B when deciding whether a report should be made to DETI in the public interest. 39

The Audit of Financial Statements

ISAs (UK and Ireland) apply to the conduct of all audits. This includes audits of financial statements of credit unions. The purpose of the following paragraphs is to identify the special considerations arising from the application of certain "bold letter" requirements (which are indicated by grey shaded boxes below) to the audit of credit unions and to suggest ways in which these can be addressed. This Practice Note does not contain commentary on all the bold letter requirements included in the ISAs (UK and Ireland) and reading it should not be seen as an alternative to reading the relevant ISAs (UK and Ireland) in their entirety. In addition, where no special considerations arise from a particular ISA (UK and Ireland) no material is included.

ISA (UK AND IRELAND) 200: OBJECTIVE AND GENERAL PRINCIPLES GOVERNING AN AUDIT OF FINANCIAL STATEMENTS

Background Note

The purpose of this ISA (UK and Ireland)) is to establish standards and provide guidance on the objective and general principles governing an audit of financial statements.

The objective of an audit of financial statements is to enable the auditor to express an opinion whether the financial statements are prepared, in all material respects, in accordance with an applicable financial reporting framework (paragraph 2)

> In the UK and Ireland the relevant ethical pronouncements with which the auditor should comply are the APB's Ethical Standards and the ethical pronouncements relating to the work of auditors issued by the auditor's relevant professional body. (paragraph 4-1)
>
> The auditor should plan and perform an audit with an attitude of professional scepticism recognizing that circumstances may exist that cause the financial statements to be materially misstated. (paragraph 6)
>
> The term "scope of an audit" refers to the audit procedures deemed necessary in the circumstances to achieve the objective of the audit. The audit procedures required to conduct an audit in accordance with ISAs (UK and Ireland) should be determined by the auditor having regard to the requirements of ISAs (UK and Ireland), relevant professional bodies, legislation, regulations and, where appropriate, the terms of the audit engagement and reporting requirements. (paragraph 7)

40   Auditing standards include a requirement for auditors to comply with relevant ethical requirements relating to audit engagements. In the UK, the auditor should comply with the APB Ethical Standards and relevant ethical guidance relating to the work of auditors issued by the auditor's professional body. A fundamental principle is that practitioners should not accept or perform work which they are not competent to undertake. The importance of technical competence is also underlined in the Auditors' Code[5], issued by the APB, which states that the necessary degree of professional skill demands an understanding of financial reporting and business. Practitioners should not undertake the audit of credit unions unless they are satisfied that they have, or can obtain, the necessary level of competence.

41   In connection with possible independence issues, auditors review any financial relationships that the firm or its partners and staff (and, separately, partners and staff assigned to that engagement) may have with a credit union to consider whether such relationships may affect independence.

ISA (UK AND IRELAND) 210: TERMS OF AUDIT ENGAGEMENTS

> **Background note**
>
> The purpose of this ISA (UK and Ireland) is to establish standards and provide guidance on:
> (a)   agreeing the terms of the engagement with the client; and
> (b)   the auditor's response to a request by a client to change the terms of an engagement to one that provides a lower level of assurance.

> The auditor and the client should agree on the terms of the engagement. (paragraph 2)
>
> The terms of the engagement should be recorded in writing. (paragraph 2-1)

---

[5] This is appended to the APB's Scope and Authority of Pronouncements.

> In the UK and Ireland, the auditor should ensure that the engagement letter documents and confirms the auditor's acceptance of the appointment, and includes a summary of the responsibilities of those charged with governance and of the auditor, the scope of the engagement and the form of any reports. (paragraph 5-1)

42 The same basic principles used in drafting engagement letters apply in relation to the audit of credit unions as to the audit of any entity. Practical considerations arising from the particular characteristics of credit unions are considered below.

43 Matters which the auditor may decide to refer to in the engagement letter are as follows:

- the responsibility of the directors/senior management to comply with applicable legislation (principally IPSA 65/02, CU 79 and FSMA 2000) and FSA Handbook rules and guidance, or relevant NI legislation, including the need to keep the regulators informed about the affairs of the entity;
- the statutory right and duty of the auditor to report direct to the FSA, or the right to report to DETI, in certain circumstances (see the section of this Practice Note relating to ISA (UK and Ireland) 250 Section B);
- the auditor's responsibility in respect of other information published with the financial statements in the annual report – see the section of this Practice Note on ISA (UK and Ireland) 720 (Revised);
- in Great Britain, the requirement to co-operate with the auditor (SUP 3.6.1R). This includes taking steps to ensure that, where applicable, each of its appointed representatives and material outsourcers gives the auditor the same right of access to records, information and explanations as the authorised firm itself is required to provide the auditor (s341 FSMA 2000 and SUP 3.6.2G to 3.6.8G). It a criminal offence for a credit union or its officers to provide false or misleading information to the auditor (s346 FSMA 2000);
- the need for the credit union to make the auditor aware when it appoints a third party (including another department or office of the same audit firm) to review, investigate or report on any aspects of its business activities that may be relevant to the audit of the financial statements and to provide the auditor with copies of reports by such a third party promptly after their receipt (see also paragraph 79 below).

44 The directors and supervisory committee are volunteers and are unlikely to be experts in financial and accounting matters. It may be appropriate for the engagement letter to specify the role and responsibilities of the directors regarding accounts preparation, selection of accounting polices and the role of the auditor.

ISA (UK AND IRELAND) 220: QUALITY CONTROL FOR AUDITS OF HISTORICAL FINANCIAL INFORMATION

> **Background Note**
>
> The purpose of this ISA (UK and Ireland) is to establish standards and provide guidance on specific responsibilities of firm personnel regarding quality control procedures for audits of historical financial information, including audits of financial statements.

> Reference should also be made to ISQC (UK and Ireland) 1 – Quality Control for Firms that Perform Audits and Reviews of Historical Financial Information and other Assurance and Related Services Engagements.

> The engagement partner should be satisfied that the engagement team collectively has the appropriate capabilities, competence and time to perform the audit engagement in accordance with professional standards and regulatory and legal requirements, and to enable an auditor's report that is appropriate in the circumstances to be issued. (paragraph 19)

45 The nature of financial services business is one of rapidly changing and evolving markets. Often credit unions and other financial services entities develop new products and practices which require specialised auditing and accounting responses. It is therefore important that the auditor is familiar with current practice.

46 As well as ensuring that the engagement team has an appropriate level of knowledge of the industry and its corresponding products, the engagement partner also satisfies himself that the members of the engagement team have sufficient knowledge of the regulatory framework within which credit unions operate commensurate with their roles on the engagement.

47 Given the public interest nature of a credit union, firms may establish policies to require an independent review in relation to credit union audits to be undertaken by a partner with sufficient experience and authority to fulfil that role. In the case of sole practitioners and small firms a suitably qualified external consultant may perform the role of independent partner and carry out the independent review. In such circumstances, appropriate arrangements are made to safeguard client confidentiality.

ISA (UK AND IRELAND) 240: THE AUDITOR'S RESPONSIBILITY TO CONSIDER FRAUD IN AN AUDIT OF FINANCIAL STATEMENTS

> **Background note**
>
> The purpose of this ISA (UK and Ireland) is to establish standards and provide guidance on the auditor's responsibility to consider fraud in an audit of financial statements[6] and expand on how the standards and guidance in ISA (UK and Ireland) 315, "Understanding the Entity and its Environment and Assessing the Risks of Material Misstatement" and ISA (UK and Ireland) 330, "The Auditor's Procedures in Response to Assessed Risks" are to be applied in relation to the risks of material misstatement due to fraud.

> The auditor should maintain an attitude of professional scepticism throughout the audit, recognising the possibility that a material misstatement due to fraud could exist, notwithstanding the auditor's past experience with the entity about the honesty and integrity of management and those charged with governance. (paragraph 24)

---

[6] *The auditor's responsibility to consider laws and regulations in an audit of financial statements is established in ISA (UK and Ireland) 250 "Consideration of Laws and Regulations".*

The auditor should make inquiries of management, internal audit and others within the entity as appropriate, to determine whether they have knowledge of any actual, suspected or alleged fraud affecting the entity. (paragraph 38)

When obtaining an understanding of the entity and its environment, including its internal control, the auditor should consider whether the information obtained indicates that one or more fraud risk factors are present. (paragraph 48)

When obtaining an understanding of the entity and its environment, including its internal control, the auditor should consider whether other information obtained indicates risks of material misstatement due to fraud.(paragraph 55)

The auditor should consider whether analytical procedures that are performed at or near the end of the audit when forming an overall conclusion as to whether the financial statement as a whole are consistent with the auditor's knowledge of the business indicate a previously unrecognised risk of material misstatement due to fraud (paragraph 85)

If the auditor has identified a fraud or has obtained information that indicates that a fraud may exist, the auditor should communicate these matters as soon as practicable to the appropriate level of management. (paragraph 93)

The auditor should document communications about fraud made to management, those charged with governance, regulators and others. (paragraph 109)

48 As outlined in paragraphs 13 to 16 of ISA (UK and Ireland) 240, it is the responsibility of those charged with governance of the entity and management, to take such steps as are reasonably open to then to prevent and detect fraud. It is the auditors' responsibility to plan, perform and evaluate their audit work in order to have a reasonable expectation of detecting material misstatements in the financial statements arising from error or fraud.

49 Credit unions have custody of valuable and fungible assets including money. As a result fraud is an inherent risk of undertaking credit union business. Frauds relating to most types of transactions can be facilitated by identity theft and so 'know your customer' procedures are an important component of the procedures taken by credit unions to mitigate the risk of fraud.

50 Every credit union is required by FIPSA[7] or the NI Order[8] to establish and maintain a system of control of its business and records. This would include the appropriate control procedure to minimise the risk of losses to the credit union from irregularities or fraud. The FSA's Principle 3 also requires a firm to take reasonable care to organise and control its affairs responsibly and effectively with adequate risk management systems. SYSC requires a firm to make and retain adequate records of matters and dealings (including accounting records) which are the subject of requirements and standards under the regulatory system. Whilst the inherent risk of fraud may continue to exist, the establishment of accounting and internal control systems sufficient to meet these requirements frequently reduces the likelihood of fraud giving rise to material misstatements in the financial statements. Guidance on the auditors' consideration of accounting systems and internal controls is provided in

---

[7] Section 1.1(b).

[8] Article 40.1(b).

ISA (UK and Ireland) 315. Examples of weaknesses in control that could give rise to fraud risk factors are also set out in that section.

51   Examples of conditions or events particularly relevant to credit unions which may increase the risk of fraud include:

- the non-participation in the running of the credit union on the part of some of the director or officers leading to a small number of their colleagues dominating the credit union's management;
- excessive influence of one or a few officers or employees;
- excessive influence on officers of a credit union by their extended family;
- inadequate segregation of duties between credit union staff;
- failure to document or follow the credit union's standard operating procedures;
- failure to control properly share withdrawals on dormant accounts;
- failure by the members of the supervisory committee to monitor the credit union's affairs on an ongoing basis during the year;
- loans granted in circumstances which do not appear to comply with the stated procedures of the credit union;
- failure to reconcile regularly funds received through payroll deductions particularly where the credit union's membership has an employment common bond;
- failure to prepare on a timely basis bank reconciliations and other control accounts in order to present periodic management accounts to the board of directors;
- funds disbursed, even if with board approval, in circumstances which do not appear to fall within the authorised activities of the credit union; or
- issuance of loans to, or failure to make appropriate bad debts provision in respect of, members already failing to meet the repayment schedule of existing loans.

52   The auditor considers reports or information obtained from the credit union's money laundering reporting officer together with any reviews undertaken by third parties.

53   Reduction of financial crime is one of the FSA's statutory objectives. The FSA's rules require authorised firms to report 'significant' fraud to the FSA (SUP 15.3.17R). The auditor of a credit union in Great Britain is aware of the auditor's duty to report direct to the FSA in certain circumstances (see the section of this Practice Note relating to ISA (UK and Ireland) 250 Section B).

ISA (UK AND IRELAND) 250: SECTION A – CONSIDERATION OF LAW AND REGULATIONS IN AN AUDIT OF FINANCIAL STATEMENTS

Background note

The purpose of this ISA (UK and Ireland) is to establish standards and provide guidance on the auditor's responsibility to consider laws and regulations in the audit of financial statements.

When designing and performing audit procedures and in evaluating and reporting the results thereof, the auditor should recognise that non-compliance by the entity with laws and regulations may materially affect the financial statements.(paragraph 2)

In accordance with ISA (UK and Ireland) 200, "Objective and General Principles Governing an Audit of Financial Statements" the auditor should plan and perform the audit with an attitude of professional scepticism recognising that the audit may reveal conditions or events that would lead to questioning whether an entity is complying with laws and regulations. (paragraph 13)

In order to plan the audit, the auditor should obtain a general understanding of the legal and regulatory framework applicable to the entity and the industry and how the entity is complying with that framework. (paragraph 15)

54 The directors of a credit union are responsible for ensuring that the necessary controls are in place to ensure compliance with applicable law and regulations, and to detect and correct any breaches that have occurred, even if they have delegated some of their executive functions to staff or professional advisors.

55 FSMA 2000 and related statutory instruments and, and in Northern Ireland the NI Order, contain sections that will normally be central to the ability of credit unions to conduct business. Detailed rules and guidance applicable to credit unions in Great Britain is set out in the FSA Handbook. In addition to accepting deposits, a credit union in Great Britain may also have one or more Part IV permissions from the FSA to undertake one or more types of other regulated activity. If this is the case, the auditor also considers the laws and regulations (which includes FSMA 2000 and the FSA Handbook) central to the credit union's ability to conduct these additional regulated activities.

56 The auditor is alert to any indication that a credit union is conducting business outside its objects or the scope of its permission or is failing to meet Threshold Conditions[9]. Such action may be a serious regulatory breach, which may result in fines, public censure, suspension or loss of authorisation. The auditor compares the current activities of the credit union with the permission granted by the regulators and considers as necessary the requirements of ISA (UK and Ireland) 250 Section A and where appropriate ISA (UK and Ireland) 250 Section B.

After obtaining the general understanding, the auditor should perform further audit procedures to help identify possible or actual instances of non-compliance with those laws and regulations where non-compliance should be considered when preparing financial statements, specifically:

(a) Inquiring of management as to whether the entity is in compliance with such laws and regulations;
(b) Inspecting correspondence with the relevant licensing or regulatory authorities;
(c) Enquiring of those charged with governance as to whether they are on notice of any such possible instances of non-compliance with laws or regulations. (paragraph 18)

In the UK and Ireland, the auditor's procedures should be designed to help identify possible or actual instances of non-compliance with those laws and regulations which provide a legal framework within which the entity conducts its business and which are central to the entity's ability to conduct its business and hence to its financial statements. (paragraph 18-1)

---

[9] *The minimum standards that a credit union in Great Britain needs to meet to become and remain authorised by the FSA – see Appendix 4.*

57   Specific areas that the auditor's procedures may address include the following:

- the adequacy of procedures to inform staff of the requirements of relevant legislation and the requirements of the regulator;
- the adequacy of procedures for authorisation of transactions;
- review of procedures for internal review of the entity's compliance with regulatory or other requirements;
- review of procedures to ensure that possible breaches of requirements are investigated by an appropriate person and are brought to the attention of senior management; and
- review of any compliance reports prepared for the directors or supervisory committee.

Money laundering

> In the UK and Ireland, when carrying out procedures for the purpose of forming an opinion on the financial statements, the auditor should be alert for those instances of possible or actual non compliance with laws and regulations that might incur obligations for partners and staff in audit firms to report money laundering offences. (paragraph 22-1)

58   Authorised firms including credit unions are subject to the requirements of the Money Laundering Regulations 2007 and the Proceeds of Crime Act 2002 as well, in Great Britain, to FSA rules. These laws and regulations require institutions to establish and maintain procedures to identify their customers, establish appropriate reporting and investigation procedures for suspicious transactions and maintain appropriate records.

59   Laws and regulations relating to money laundering are integral to the legal and regulatory framework within which credit unions conduct their business. By the nature of their business, credit unions are ready targets of those engaged in money laundering activities. The effect of this legislation is to make it an offence to provide assistance to those involved in money laundering and makes it an offence not to report suspicions of money laundering to the appropriate authorities, usually the Serious Organised Crime Agency ('SOCA')[10]. FSA requirements for credit unions in Great Britain are set out in SYSC 3.2.6AR.– 6.3.5G. In this context, FSA has due regard to compliance with the relevant provisions of guidance issued by the Joint Money Laundering Steering Group ('JMLSG')(SYSC 3.2.6EG).

60   In addition to considering whether a credit union has complied with the money laundering laws and regulations, the auditor has reporting obligations under the Proceeds of Crime Act, 2002 and the Money Laundering Regulations, 2007 to report knowledge or suspicion of money laundering offences, including those arising from fraud and theft, to SOCA. The auditor is aware of the prohibition on 'tipping off' when discussing money laundering matters with the credit union. Further guidance for auditors is provided in Practice Note 12 Money Laundering – Interim Guidance for Auditors in the United Kingdom (Revised).

---

[10] *Previously National Criminal Intelligence Service ('NCIS').*

ISA (UK AND IRELAND) 250: SECTION B – THE AUDITOR'S RIGHT AND DUTY TO REPORT TO REGULATORS IN THE FINANCIAL SECTOR

> The auditor of a regulated entity should bring information of which the auditor has become aware in the ordinary course of performing work undertaken to fulfil the auditor's audit responsibilities to the attention of the appropriate regulator without delay when:
>
> (a) The auditor concludes that it is relevant to the regulator's functions having regard to such matters as may be specified in statute or any related regulations; and
> (b) In the auditor's opinion there is reasonable cause to believe it is or may be of material significance to the regulator. (paragraph 2)
>
> Where an apparent breach of statutory or regulatory requirements comes to the auditor's attention, the auditor should:
>
> (a) Obtain such evidence as is available to assess its implications for the auditor's reporting responsibilities;
> (b) Determine whether, in the auditor's opinion, there is reasonable cause to believe that the breach is of material significance to the regulator; and
> (c) Consider whether the apparent breach is criminal conduct that gives rise to criminal property and, as such, should be reported to the specified authorities. (paragraph 39)

This section sets out the reporting requirements for auditors of credit unions in Great Britain. The guidance is however likely to be useful for auditors of credit unions in Northern Ireland when deciding whether to make a report to the regulator in the public interest. Auditors may need to take legal advice before making a decision on whether a matter should be reported in the public interest.

Auditor's duty to report to the FSA

Under FSMA 2000 (Communication by Auditors) Regulations 2001 ('the 2001 Regulations'), the auditor has duties in certain circumstances to make reports to the FSA. The 2001 Regulations do not require the auditor to perform any additional audit work as a result of the statutory duty nor is the auditor required specifically to seek out breaches of the requirements applicable to a particular authorised firm. Information and opinions to be communicated are those meeting the criteria set out below which relate to matters of which the auditor[11] of the authorised firm (also referred to below as a 'regulated entity') has become aware:

(i) in his capacity as auditor of the authorised firm, and
(ii) if he is also the auditor of an entity who has close links with the authorised firm, in his capacity as auditor of that authorised firm.

The criteria for determining the matters to be reported are as follows:

(i) the auditor reasonably believes that there is, or has been, or may be, or may have been a contravention of any 'relevant requirement' that applies to the authorised firm concerned and that contravention may be of material

---

[11] An 'auditor' is defined for this purpose in the Regulations as a person who is, or has been, an auditor of an authorised firm appointed under, or as a result of, a statutory provision including Section 340 of FSMA.

significance to the FSA in determining whether to exercise, in relation to that authorised firm, any of its functions under FSMA 2000, or

(ii) the auditor reasonably believes that the information on, or his opinion on, those matters may be of material significance to the FSA in determining whether the authorised firm concerned satisfies and will continue to satisfy the Threshold Conditions, or

(iii) the auditor reasonably believes that the authorised firm concerned is not, may not be, or may cease to be, a going concern, or

(iv) the auditor is precluded from stating in his report that the annual accounts have been properly prepared in accordance with FIPSA or, where applicable, give a true and fair view or have been prepared in accordance with relevant rules and legislation[12].

64 In relation to paragraph 63 (i) above, 'relevant requirement' is a requirement by or under FSMA 2000 which relates to authorisation under FSMA 2000 or to the carrying on of any regulated activity. This includes not only relevant statutory instruments but also the FSA's rules (other than the Listing rules) including the Principles for Businesses. The duty to report also covers any requirement imposed by or under any other Act[13] the contravention of which constitutes an offence which the FSA has the power to prosecute under FSMA 2000.

65 In relation to paragraph 63 (ii) above the duty to report relates to either information or opinions held by the auditor which may be of significance to the FSA in determining whether the regulated entity satisfies and will continue to satisfy the Threshold Conditions. The duty to report opinions, as well as information, allows for circumstances where adequate information on a matter may not readily be forthcoming from the regulated entity, and where judgments need to be made.

Material significance

66 Determining whether a contravention of a relevant requirement or a Threshold Condition is reportable under the 2001 Regulations involves consideration both of whether the auditor 'reasonably believes' and that the matter in question 'is, or is likely to be, of material significance' to the regulator.

67 The 2001 Regulations do not require the auditor to perform any additional audit work as a result of the statutory duty nor is the auditor required specifically to seek out breaches of the requirements applicable to a particular regulated entity. However, in circumstances where the auditor identifies that a reportable matter may exist, the auditor carries out such extra work, as he considers necessary, to determine whether the facts and circumstances cause them 'reasonably to believe' that the matter does in fact exist. It should be noted that the auditors' work does not need to prove that the reportable matter exists.

68 ISA (UK and Ireland) 250 Section B requires that, where an apparent breach of statutory or regulatory requirements comes to the auditors' attention, they should obtain such evidence as is available to assess its implications for their reporting responsibilities and determine whether, in their opinion, there is reasonable cause to believe that the breach has occurred and that it relates to a matter that is of material significance to the regulator.

[12] *Relevant rules and legislation comprise rules made by the FSA under Section 340 of FSMA 2000.*

[13] *Examples include The Proceeds of Crime Act 2002 and CU 79.*

'Material significance' is defined by ISA (UK and Ireland) 250 Section B as follows: 69

> *"A matter or group of matters is normally of material significance to a regulator's function when, due either to its nature or its potential financial impact, it is likely of itself to require investigation by the regulator."*

'Material significance' does not have the same meaning as materiality in the context 70
of the audit of financial statements. Whilst a particular event may be trivial in terms of its possible effect on the financial statements of an entity, it may be of a nature or type that is likely to change the perception of the regulator. For example, a failure to reconcile bank accounts may not be significant in financial terms but would have a significant effect on the FSA's consideration of whether the regulated entity was satisfactorily controlled and was behaving properly towards its members.

The determination of whether a matter is, or is likely to be, of material significance to 71
the FSA inevitably requires the auditor to exercise their judgment. In forming such judgments, the auditor needs to consider not simply the facts of the matter but also their implications. In addition, it is possible that a matter, which is not materially significant in isolation, may become so when other possible breaches are considered.

The auditor of a regulated entity bases his judgment of 'material significance' to the 72
FSA solely on their understanding of the facts of which they are aware without making any assumptions about the information available to the FSA in connection with any particular regulated entity.

Minor breaches of the FSA's rules that, for example, are unlikely to jeopardise the 73
entity's assets or amount to misconduct or mismanagement would not normally be of 'material significance'. ISA (UK and Ireland) 250 Section B however requires the auditor of the authorised firm when reporting on their financial statements, to review information obtained in the course of the audit and to assess whether the cumulative effect is of 'material significance' such as to give rise to a duty to report to the regulator. In circumstances where the auditor is uncertain whether he may be required to make a report or not, he may wish to consider whether to take legal advice.

On completion of their investigations, the auditor ensures that the facts and 74
circumstances, and the basis for his conclusion as to whether these are, or are likely to be, of 'material significance' to the FSA, are adequately documented such that the reasons for his decision to report or not, as the case may be, may be clearly demonstrated should the need to do so arise in future.

Whilst confidentiality is an implied term of auditors' contracts with a regulated 75
entity, s342 of FSMA 2000 states that an auditor does not contravene that duty if he reports to the FSA information or his opinion, if he is acting in good faith and he reasonably believes that the information or opinion is relevant to any function of the FSA. The protection afforded is given in respect of information obtained in his capacity as auditor.

Conduct of the audit

ISA (UK and Ireland) 250 Section B requires the auditor to ensure that all staff 76
involved in the audit of a regulated entity 'have an understanding of (a) the provisions of applicable legislation, (b) the regulator's rules and any guidance issued by the regulator, and (c) any specific requirements which apply to the particular regulated entity, appropriate to their role in the audit and sufficient (in the context of that role) to enable them to identify situations they encounter in the course of the

audit which may give reasonable cause to believe that a matter should be reported to the regulator.'

77   Understanding, commensurate with the individual's role and responsibilities in the audit process, is required of:

- the provisions of the Regulations concerning the auditors' duty to report to the regulator;
- the Standards and guidance in ISA (UK and Ireland) 250 Section B, and in this section of this Practice Note; and
- relevant sections of the FSA's Handbook including the Principles for Businesses and the Threshold Conditions.

78   The auditor includes procedures within his planning process to ensure that members of the audit team have such understanding (in the context of their role) as to enable them to recognise potentially reportable matters, and that such matters are reported to the audit engagement partner without delay so that a decision may be made as to whether a duty to report arises.

79   An audit firm appointed as auditor of an authorised firm needs to have in place appropriate procedures to ensure that the audit engagement partner is made aware of any other relationship which exists between any department of the audit firm and the regulated entity when that relationship could affect the audit firm's work as the auditor. (This matter is covered in more detail in Appendix 2 of ISA (UK and Ireland) 250 Section B). The auditor also requests the regulated entity to advise him when it appoints a third party (including another department or office of the same audit firm) to review, investigate or report on any aspects of its business activities that may be relevant to the audit of the financial statements and to provide the auditor with copies of reports by such a third party promptly after their receipt. This matter may usefully be referred to in the engagement letter.

Information received in a capacity other than as auditor

80   There may be circumstances where it is not clear whether information about an authorised firm coming to the attention of the auditor is received in the capacity of the auditor or in some other capacity, for example as a general adviser to the entity. Appendix 2 to ISA (UK and Ireland) 250 Section B provides guidance as to how information obtained in non-audit work may be relevant to the auditor in the planning and conduct of the audit and the steps that need to be taken to ensure the communication of information that is relevant to the audit.

Discussing matters of material significance with the directors

81   The directors are the persons principally responsible for the management of the authorised firm. The auditor will therefore normally bring a matter of material significance to the attention of the directors and seek agreement on the facts and circumstances. However, ISA (UK and Ireland) 250 Section B emphasises that where the auditor concludes that a duty to report arises, he should bring the matter to the attention of the regulator without undue delay. The directors may wish to report the matters identified to the FSA themselves and detail the actions taken or to be taken. Whilst such a report from the directors may provide valuable information, it does not relieve the auditor of the statutory duty to report directly to the FSA.

Timing of a report

82 The duty to report arises once the auditor has concluded that they reasonably believe that the matter is or is likely to be of material significance to the FSA's regulatory function. In reaching their conclusion the auditor may wish to take appropriate legal or other advice and consult with colleagues.

83 The report should be made without undue delay once a conclusion has been reached. Unless the matter casts doubt on the integrity of the directors this should not preclude discussion of the matter with the directors and seeking such further advice as is necessary, so that a decision can be made on whether or not a duty to report exists. Such consultations and discussions are however undertaken on a timely basis to enable the auditor to conclude on the matter without undue delay.

Auditors' right to report to the FSA

84 Section 342 of FSMA 2000 provides that no duty to which an auditor of an authorised firm is subject shall be contravened by communicating in good faith to the FSA information or an opinion on a matter that the auditor reasonably believes is relevant to any functions of the FSA.

85 The scope of the duty to report is wide particularly since, under the FSA's Principle for Businesses 11 (and corresponding application rules and guidance in SUP 15.3), an authorised firm must disclose to the FSA appropriately anything relating to the authorised firm of which the FSA would reasonably expect notice. However in circumstances where the auditor concludes that a matter does not give rise to a statutory duty to report but nevertheless should be brought to the attention of the regulator, in the first instance he advises the directors of his opinion. Where the auditors are unable to obtain, within a reasonable period, adequate evidence that the directors have properly informed the FSA of the matter, then the auditor makes a report themselves to the regulator without undue delay.

86 The auditor may wish to take legal advice before deciding whether, and in what form, to exercise their right to make a report direct to the regulator in order to ensure, for example, that only relevant information is disclosed and that the form and content of their report is such as to secure the protection of FSMA 2000. Appendix 6 provides additional guidance on disclosure in the public interest. This is relevant to both the auditor's consideration of the right to report and also where neither the right nor the duty to report exists. However, the auditor recognises that legal advice will take time and that speed of reporting is likely to be important in order to protect the interests of customers and/or to enable the FSA to meet its statutory objectives.

ISA (UK AND IRELAND) 260: COMMUNICATION OF AUDIT MATTERS TO THOSE CHARGED WITH GOVERNANCE

Background note

The purpose of this ISA (UK and Ireland) is to establish standards and provide guidance on communication of audit matters arising from the audit of financial statements between the auditor and those charged with governance of an entity.

> The auditor should communicate audit matters of governance interest arising from the audit of financial statements to those charged with governance of an entity. (paragraph 2)
>
> The auditor should determine the relevant persons who are charged with governance and with whom audit matters of governance interest are communicated. (paragraph 5)
>
> The auditor should communicate audit matters of governance interest on a timely basis. This enables those charged with governance to take appropriate action. (paragraph 13)
>
> The auditor should plan with those charged with governance the form and timing of communications to them. (paragraph 13-1)

87   As noted in the Introduction, a supervisory or audit committee usually plays an important role in the governance of credit unions. The auditors are required to communicate in writing with those charged with governance regarding the significant findings from their audit and, in the case of a credit union, will usually meet with the members of the supervisory committee.

88   The auditors' consideration of the system of internal control is undertaken both for the purpose of forming an opinion on the financial statements and so as to meet their statutory reporting requirements. Therefore, in the first instance their assessment is focused on controls designed to prevent or detect material misstatements in the financial statements arising from fraud, or other irregularity or error.

89   In addition, auditors obtain sufficient appropriate evidence that material weaknesses in control have not existed during the year. ISA (UK and Ireland) 260 defines a material weakness as " ...a condition which may result in a material misstatement in the financial statement".

90   ISA (UK and Ireland) 260 requires auditors to report any material weaknesses in the accounting and internal control system identified, during the audit procedures in paragraphs 88 and 89 above, to directors on a timely basis.

91   Where significant matters raised in previous reports to directors or management have not been dealt with effectively, the auditors enquire why appropriate action has not been taken. If the point is still significant, consideration is given to repeating the point in the current report, otherwise there is a risk that the auditors may give the impression that they are satisfied that the weakness has been corrected or is no longer significant.

ISA (UK AND IRELAND) 300: PLANNING AN AUDIT OF FINANCIAL STATEMENTS

Background note

The purpose of this ISA (UK and Ireland) is to establish standards and provide guidance on the considerations and activities applicable to planning an audit of financial statements. This ISA (UK and Ireland) is framed in the context of recurring audits. In addition, matters the auditor considers in initial engagements are included in paragraphs 28 and 29.

> The auditor should plan the audit so that the engagement will be performed in an effective manner. (paragraph 2)
>
> The auditor should establish the overall audit strategy for the audit. (paragraph 8)
>
> The overall audit strategy and the audit plan should be updated and changed as necessary during the course of the audit. (paragraph 16)
>
> The auditor should plan the nature, timing and extent of direction and supervision of engagement team members and review of their work. (paragraph 18)

92 Matters the auditors of a credit union may consider as part of the planning process for the audit of the financial statements include:

- the nature and scope of the credit union's activities;
- the complexity of the credit union's information systems;
- the credit union's relationship with the regulator;
- changes in applicable laws, regulations and accounting requirements;
- the need to involve specialists in the audit;
- the extent to which controls and procedures are outsourced to a third party provider;
- in Great Britain, issues relating to the auditor's statutory duty to report; and
- the appropriateness of the accounting policies adopted by the credit union.

93 Guidance on the first four of these matters is set out in the Section on ISA (UK and Ireland) 315 'Obtaining an Understanding of the Entity and its Environment and Assessing the Risk of Material Misstatement' below. Considerations in relation to other matters in planning the audit are:

- the auditor considers the need to involve specialists in the audit, for example in the valuation of complex investments and loans;
- the auditor considers the implications of the outsourcing of functions by the credit union and the sources of evidence available to the auditors for transactions undertaken by service organisations in planning their work. This may include the outsourcing of certain functions such as the management of investment funds;
- issues relating to the auditor's statutory duty to report include the adequacy of the audit team's understanding of the law; and
- the auditor considers the appropriateness and consistency of the application of the credit union's accounting policies particularly those applied to valuation of investments and loans.

94 When planning the work to be undertaken in respect of a credit union audit, it is important to identify those areas which are key to its operations as reflected in its financial statements. The key areas of credit unions' financial statements would include:

- shares held by members;
- loans to members and their recoverability;
- income recognition, including grants;
- cash;
- funds invested; and
- fixed assets.

95 When considering the key areas it is also important to identify other possible sources of information available to the credit union auditors that may assist in the planning process, including:

- correspondence between the credit union and the regulators;
- reports of the supervisory committees;
- minutes of board, and other relevant committee, meetings;
- the register of directors' interests;
- correspondence between the credit union and its solicitors;
- correspondence between the credit union and its investment advisors; and
- reports commissioned by the credit union or by the regulators from reporting accountants or other professional advisors.

ISA (UK AND IRELAND) 315: OBTAINING AN UNDERSTANDING OF THE ENTITY AND ITS ENVIRONMENT AND ASSESSING THE RISKS OF MATERIAL MISSTATEMENT

Background note

The purpose of this ISA (UK and Ireland) is to establish standards and to provide guidance on obtaining an understanding of the entity and its environment, including its internal control, and on assessing the risks of material misstatement in a financial statement audit.

96 The auditor seeks to understand the business activities and the regulatory regime in which credit unions operate. Generally, there is a close relationship between planning and obtaining an understanding of the business and the control environment, which is covered more fully below.

The auditor should obtain an understanding of relevant industry, regulatory, and other external factors including the applicable financial reporting framework. (paragraph 22)

The auditor should obtain an understanding of the nature of the entity. (paragraph 25)

97 When performing procedures to obtain an understanding of the credit union's business activities, the auditor considers:

- the relevant aspects of the credit union's risk management procedures;
- the complexity of the credit union's information systems;
- any changes in the market environment;
- the impact of recent legislation, government initiatives and changes to CRED;
- the consistency of products, methods and operations in different departments or locations;
- the legal and operational structure of the credit union;
- the role and competence of volunteers;
- the number and location of branches;
- the respective roles and responsibilities attributed to the finance, risk control, compliance and internal audit functions; and
- the recruitment, competence, and experience of management.

98 In obtaining an understanding of the regulatory factors the auditor considers:

- any formal communications between the regulators and trade associations and the credit union, including the results of any supervisory visits[14]; and
- the contents of any publications from the regulators and trade associations.

> The auditor should obtain an understanding of the entity's selection and application of accounting policies and consider whether they are appropriate for its business and consistent with the applicable financial reporting framework and accounting policies used in the relevant industry. (paragraph 28)

99 Accounting policies of particular relevance may include allowances for impairment, classification of assets and liabilities (and thereby their measurement), and revenue and expense recognition. The auditor undertakes procedures to consider whether the policies adopted are in compliance with applicable accounting standards, and gains an understanding of the procedures, systems and controls applied to maintain compliance with them.

> The auditor should obtain an understanding of the entity's objectives and strategies, and the related business risks that may result in material misstatement of the financial statements. (paragraph 30)

100 It is important for the auditor to understand the nature and extent of the financial and business risks which are integral to the environment, and how the credit union's systems record and address these risks. Although they may apply to varying degrees, the risks include (but are not limited to):

- credit risk: at its simplest, the risk that members will be unable to meet their obligations. Particular attention may be given to overreliance by the credit union on mechanistic approaches[15] to assessing doubtful loan provisions. Management and auditors exercise critical judgement in concluding on the adequacy of such provisions;
- liquidity risk: the risk that arises from the possibility that a credit union has insufficient liquid funds to meet the demands of members. Particular attention may be given to the nature of investments acquired by the credit union, in particular the maturity profile of investment bonds, and the appropriateness of acquisition control procedures and accounting policies in relation to such instruments;
- interest rate risk: the risk that arises where there is a mismatch between the interest rate contractual repricing dates or bases for assets and liabilities;
- operational risk: the risk of loss, arising from inadequate or failed internal processes, people and systems or from external events;
- investment risk: the risk of failure to comply with the regulator's rules regarding investments; and
- regulatory risk: the risk of public censure, fines (together with related compensation payments) and restriction or withdrawal of authorisation to conduct some or all of the credit union's activities. This could arise from enforcement activity by the regulators.

101 Failure to manage the risks outlined above can also cause serious damage to a credit union's reputation, potentially leading to a loss of confidence in the credit union,

---

[14] See Appendix 7 of this Practice Note for more details of trade associations in Northern Ireland.

[15] Including the application of the FSA's guidelines on minimum provisions.

withdrawal of shares and deposits or problems maintaining liquidity.

> The auditor should obtain an understanding of the measurement and review of the entity's financial performance. (paragraph 35)

102 The auditor obtains an understanding of the measures used by management to review the credit union's performance. Guidance on key performance indictors is included in the Section on ISA (UK and Ireland) 520 in this Practice Note.

> The auditor should obtain an understanding of internal control relevant to the audit. (paragraph 41)
>
> The auditor should obtain an understanding of the control environment. (paragraph 67)

103 The quality of the overall control environment is dependent upon management's attitude towards the operation of controls. A positive attitude may be evidenced by an organisational framework which enables proper segregation of duties and delegation of control functions and which encourages failings to be reported and corrected. Thus, where a lapse in the operation of a control is treated as a matter of concern, the control environment will be stronger and will contribute to effective control systems; whereas a weak control environment will undermine detailed controls, however well designed.

104 No internal control system can by itself guarantee effective administration and completeness and accuracy of the credit union's records. However, the attitude, role and actions of the directors are fundamental in shaping the control environment of a credit union. Factors to consider include:

- the amount of time committed by individual directors;
- the skills, experience and qualifications of individual directors;
- in the case of smaller credit unions, the number of members of the management and any restrictions on division of duties;
- the frequency and regularity of Board/Committee meetings; and
- the degree of supervision of the credit union's transactions by individual directors.

105 The FSA Handbook (SYSC 3.1.1R) requires an authorised firm, including a credit union in Great Britain, to maintain systems and controls that are appropriate to its business. CRED explains that this is a high level rule, going on to say: "What is appropriate for a particular credit union will depend upon such matters as the nature, scale, and complexity of its business, the volume and size of its transactions, and the level of risk associated with its operations". (CRED 4.3.2G). Issues for consideration include (but are not limited to):

- clear and appropriate reporting lines which are communicated within the credit union;
- appropriate controls to ensure compliance with laws and regulations;
- appropriate risk assessment process;
- appropriate management information;
- controls to ensure the suitability of staff;
- documented and tested business continuity plans;
- documented business plans and strategies;

- an internal audit function (where appropriate); and
- appropriate record keeping arrangements.

Requirements of auditors in relation to control systems

Legislation requires auditors of credit unions to state in their report on the financial statements if the credit union has failed to maintain a satisfactory system of internal control. In forming a view as to whether a system of internal control is satisfactory, the auditor obtains sufficient appropriate evidence that material weaknesses in control have not existed during the year. A material weakness is defined as 'a condition which may result in a material misstatement in the financial statements'. 106

The legislation does not establish the criteria by which auditors assess whether a system of control is satisfactory; this is a matter for the auditors' judgement. In forming a judgement, auditors consider, for example: 107

(a) evidence obtained in relation to compliance with ISAs (UK and Ireland); and
(b) their knowledge of the control procedures adopted by the entity, obtained in complying with paragraph 90 of ISA (UK and Ireland) 315.

> The auditor should obtain a sufficient understanding of control activities to assess the risks of material misstatement at the assertion level and to design further audit procedures responsive to assessed risks. (paragraph 90)

There is a wide variation between different credit unions in terms of size, activity and organisation, so that there can be no standard approach to internal controls and risk. In assessing whether there is a risk of material misstatement, the auditor may consider the factors outlined below: 108

(i) Control Environment
- inadequate segregation of duties;
- weaknesses in "know your customer" procedures;
- lack of an effective supervisory committee;
- inadequate definition of management responsibilities and supervision of staff and contractors;
- ineffective personnel practices;
- inadequate communication of information to management;
- voluntary nature of those charged with governance;
- controls over outsourced activities (see the section on ISA (UK and Ireland) 402 of this Practice Note);
- in Northern Ireland, reports issued by the main trade associations relating to internal controls;
- products or processes inadequately understood by management; this includes undue concentration of expertise concerning matters requiring the exercise of significant judgment or capable of manipulation such as valuations of financial instruments or allowances for impairments; and
- weaknesses in back office procedures contributing to completeness and accuracy of accounting records.

(ii) Loans:
- inadequate procedures relating to loan approvals;
- lack of proper documentation;
- failure to systematically validate security or guarantees given in respect of loans;
- failure to regularly review loan policies and related procedures;

- failure to consistently take into account the borrower's ability to repay the loan in accordance with the agreed terms and conditions;
- rescheduling loans to a member as a means of addressing repayment difficulties encountered in respect of original loan; and
- failure to monitor loan book on a regular basis to ensure that the specific statutory requirements governing loans in excess of stated amounts, or for longer than stated periods, are not breached.

(iii) Shares of members
- inadequate monitoring procedures relating to dormant accounts;
- failure to monitor deposit levels on a regular basis and develop appropriate cash flow forecasts to ensure that the credit union's lending activities will not give rise to significant bank borrowing;
- an individual member holding more than one share account;
- payment of appropriate dividend and where the credit union has allocated its depositors to differing categories, based on amounts deposited, confirmation that the appropriate rate has been paid to each category and the same rate to all members of a particular category; and
- where passbooks are not issued, failure to issue statements to members on a regular basis.

(iv) Distributions
- failure to distinguish correctly between realised and unrealised gains for the purpose of declaring a dividend; and
- desire to declare a dividend in line with members' expectations regardless of income and reserve levels.

(v) Investments
- non-compliance with any rules[16] issued by the regulators regarding investments.

> The auditor should obtain an understanding of how the entity has responded to risks arising from IT. (paragraph 93)

109 The auditor assesses the extent, nature and impact of automation within the credit union and plans and performs work accordingly. In particular the auditor considers:
- the required level of IT knowledge and skills may be extensive and may require the auditor to obtain advice and assistance from staff with specialist skills;
- the extent of the application of audit software and related audit techniques;
- general controls relating to the environment within which IT based systems are developed, maintained and operated; and
- external interfaces susceptible to breaches of security.

> The auditor should identify and assess the risks of material misstatement at the financial statement level, and at the assertion level for classes of transactions, account balances, and disclosures. (paragraph 100)
>
> As part of the risk assessment as described in paragraph 100, the auditor should determine which of the risks identified are, in the auditor's judgement, risks that require special audit consideration (such risks are defined as "significant risks"). (paragraph 108)

---

[16] *For credit unions in Great Britain see CRED chapter 7.*

> For significant risks, to the extent the auditor has not already done so, the auditor should evaluate the design of the entity's related controls, including relevant control activities, and determine whether they have been implemented. (paragraph 113)

110 Significant risks are likely to arise in those areas that are subject to significant judgment by management or are complex and are properly understood by comparatively few people in the credit union.

111 Examples of significant risks for credit unions requiring special audit consideration may include:

- allowances for loan impairment;
- (for the larger credit unions) valuation of investments; and
- assessment of going concern.

112 Weaknesses in the control environment and in controls such as those described above could increase the risk of fraud.

ISA (UK AND IRELAND) 330: THE AUDITOR'S PROCEDURES IN RESPONSE TO ASSESSED RISKS

> **Background note**
>
> The purpose of this ISA (UK and Ireland) is to establish standards and provide guidance on determining overall responses and designing and performing further audit procedures to respond to the assessed risks of material misstatement at the financial statement and assertion levels in a financial statement audit.

> When, in accordance with paragraph 115 of ISA (UK and Ireland) 315, the auditor has determined that it is not possible or practicable to reduce the risks of material misstatement at the assertion level to an acceptably low level with audit evidence obtained only from substantive procedures, the auditor should perform tests of relevant controls to obtain audit evidence about their operating effectiveness. (paragraph 25)

113 As in the audit of other entities, the auditor obtains and documents an understanding of the accounting system and control environment to assess whether they are adequate as a basis for drawing up the financial statements and to determine their audit approach. If, having carried out this task, the auditor expects to be able to rely on the assessment of risk to reduce the extent of the substantive procedures, the auditor makes a preliminary assessment of risk for material financial statement assertions and plans and performs tests of control to support that assessment.

114 Control procedures designed to address specified control objectives are subject to inherent limitations and accordingly, errors or irregularities may occur and not be detected. Such control procedures cannot guarantee protection against fraud or collusion especially on the part of those holding positions of authority or trust.

> When the auditor has determined that an assessed risk of material misstatement at the assertion level is a significant risk, the auditor should perform substantive procedures that are specifically responsive to that risk. (paragraph 51)

115 Examples of significant risks for credit unions requiring special audit consideration include allowances for loan impairment, and the valuation of investments and other financial instruments for which valuation techniques are required – see the Section on ISA (UK and Ireland) 540, and going concern – see the section on ISA (UK and Ireland) 570.

> The auditor should perform audit procedures to evaluate whether the overall presentation of the financial statements, including the related disclosures, are in accordance with the applicable financial reporting framework. (paragraph 65)

116 Specific financial reporting standards can require extensive narrative disclosures in the financial statements of some credit unions; for example, in relation to the nature and extent of risks arising from financial instruments. In designing and performing procedures to evaluate these disclosures the auditor obtains audit evidence regarding the assertions about presentation and disclosure described in paragraph 17 of ISA (UK and Ireland) 500: Audit Evidence.

ISA (UK AND IRELAND) 402: AUDIT CONSIDERATIONS RELATING TO ENTITIES USING SERVICE ORGANISATIONS

> **Background note**
>
> The purpose of this ISA (UK and Ireland) is to establish standards and provide guidance to an auditor where the entity uses a service organisation.

> In obtaining an understanding of the entity and its environment, the auditor should determine the significance of service organisation activities to the entity and the relevance to the audit. (paragraph 5)

117 The auditor gains an understanding of the extent of outsourced functions and their relevance to the financial statements. The credit union is obliged to ensure that the auditor has appropriate access to records, information and explanations from material outsourced operations.

118 In common with other industries the outsourcing of functions to third parties is becoming increasingly prevalent with credit unions albeit to a more limited degree for the smaller credit unions. Some of the more common areas may have a direct relevance to the audit such as IT services, investment management, payroll processing services and internal audit.

119 Whilst a credit union may outsource functions to third parties the responsibility for these functions remains that of the credit union. The credit union should have appropriate controls in place over these arrangements including:

- risk assessment prior to contracting with the service provider, which includes a proper due diligence and periodic review of the appropriateness of the arrangement;
- appropriate contractual agreements or service level agreements;
- contingency plans should the service provider fail in delivery of services;
- appropriate management information and reporting from the outsourced vendor;
- protection over member information; and
- right of access of the credit union's internal audit and external auditors to test the internal controls of the service provider.

If the auditor is unable to obtain sufficient appropriate audit evidence concerning outsourced operations the auditor considers whether it is necessary to report the matter direct to the regulator – see the section of this Practice Note relating to ISA (UK and Ireland) 250 Section B, and whether this represents a material weakness in internal control. 120

ISA (UK AND IRELAND) 501: AUDIT EVIDENCE – ADDITIONAL CONSIDERATIONS FOR SPECIFIC ITEMS

> **Background Note**
>
> The purpose of this ISA (UK and Ireland) is to establish standards and provide guidance additional to that contained in ISA (UK and Ireland) 500, "Audit Evidence" with respect to certain specific financial statement account balances and other disclosures.

> When long-term investments are material to the financial statements, the auditor should obtain sufficient appropriate audit evidence regarding their valuation and disclosure. (paragraph 38)

When investments, normally held only by the larger credit unions, are classified as long term, audit procedures ordinarily include obtaining audit evidence as to whether the entity has the authority to hold the investments on a long term basis and obtaining written representations from directors. 121

The auditor ordinarily considers information, such as market quotations and related financial statements, which provide an indication of value and compares such values to the carrying amount of the investments up to the date of the auditor's report. If such values do not exceed the carrying amounts, the auditor would consider whether a write-down is required. If there is an uncertainty as to whether the carrying amount will be recovered, the auditor would consider whether appropriate adjustments and/or disclosures have been made. 122

ISA (UK AND IRELAND) 505: EXTERNAL CONFIRMATIONS

> **Background note**
>
> The purpose of this ISA (UK and Ireland) is to establish standards and provide guidance on the auditor's use of external confirmations as a means of obtaining evidence.

> The auditor should determine whether the use of external confirmations is necessary to obtain sufficient appropriate evidence at the assertion level. In making this determination, the auditor should consider the assessed risk of material misstatement at the assertion level and how the audit evidence from other planned procedures will reduce the risk of material misstatement at the assertion level to an acceptably low level. (paragraph 2)

123 The following types of balances and transactions are worthy of particular consideration:

- members loans and shares; and
- investments held with investment managers and custodians.

124 The supervisory committee may decide to carry out a circularisation of a certain number of members' loans, in accordance with the credit union's own rules. In such circumstances the auditor is aware of the timing of that circularisation and any potential evidence available from it.

125 Members' loans and shares typically comprise high volumes of comparatively low value amounts. Members may not maintain independent records of their balances but rather depend on information provided to them by the credit union. Accordingly the auditor may consider the inherent reliability of such responses as comparatively low and will seek additional evidence from other audit procedures.

126 The credit union may obtain "certified" lists of investments held by custodians on a regular basis. Because these are sent directly to the credit union, they are not as conclusive as direct audit evidence. In the event that the auditor determines that a confirmation letter should be obtained from the investment custodians, arrangements should be made for such custodians to mail directly to the auditor a copy of such lists and confirmation of other matters the auditor deems appropriate.

ISA (UK AND IRELAND) 520: ANALYTICAL PROCEDURES

> **Background note**
>
> The purpose of this ISA (UK and Ireland) is to establish standards and provide guidance on the application of analytical procedures during an audit.

> The auditor should apply analytical procedures as risk assessment procedures to obtain an understanding of the entity and its environment and in the overall review at the end of the audit. (paragraph 2)
>
> When analytical procedures identify significant fluctuations or relationships that are inconsistent with other relevant information or that deviate from predicted amounts, the auditor should investigate and obtain adequate explanations and appropriate corroborative audit evidence. (paragraph 17)

127 Credit unions are required to submit annual returns to the regulators which contain a comprehensive range of information and data which may assist auditors by providing an indication of trends and current ratios. In addition, detailed internal

financial information produced for directors and management may provide a valuable source of evidence.

Examples of key ratios which auditors may wish to consider in carrying out analytical procedures on a credit union's results and balance sheet are as follows: **128**

- bad debt provisions to total loans;
- total arrears to total net liabilities;
- non-performing loans to total loans;
- earnings cover of loan losses;
- liquid assets to total assets;
- liquid assets to total relevant liabilities;
- cost to income ratio;
- loans to shares ratio;
- investment income received/dividend paid ratio;
- capital (general reserves) to total assets;
- total borrowing (by the credit union) to total shares;
- unattached shares/funds ratio;
- staff costs/gross income ratio;
- share withdrawal trends;
- average loan duration (months);
- value and number of re-scheduled loans;
- "weeks in arrears" value; and
- non-qualifying members to total members.

Key analytical procedures auditors may wish to perform include: **129**

- reviewing total loan interest earned from members' borrowings and comparing with the average monthly outstanding balance for the year taken at the prevailing interest rate;
- comparing the total dividends paid on members' shares with the credit union and testing against the dividend rate based on the average monthly share balance;
- comparing total payroll costs with previous years and obtaining explanations of variations;
- comparing the financial statements with budgets, forecasts, or management expectations;
- considering whether the financial statements adequately reflect any changes in the scope and nature of the credit union's activities of which the auditors are aware;
- enquiring into unexplained or unexpected features of the financial statements; and
- where industry information is available, this may be used to benchmark income, resources and expenditure against other credit unions.

Key performance indicators could also include measures relating to regulatory compliance and operational risk measures.

When performing their review of the financial statements as a whole for consistency with their knowledge of the entity's activities and the results of other audit procedures, the auditors consider transactions occurring either side of the year end, including: **130**

- loan repayments which are received shortly before the year end then re-advanced shortly afterwards; material sale and repurchase transactions or other financing or linked transactions. Experience and judgment are required to identify and assess the implications, if any, of these transactions; they may, for

example, be indicative of 'window dressing' of the balance sheet over the year end date;
- other transactions around the year end, apparently at rates which are significantly off market including those that appear or give rise to significant profits or losses;
- the reclassification of balances and transactions to achieve advantageous income recognition and balance sheet treatment/presentation.

131 Where non-financial information or reports produced from systems or processes outside the financial statements accounting system are used in analytical procedures, the auditor considers the reliability of that information or those reports.

ISA (UK AND IRELAND) 540: AUDIT OF ACCOUNTING ESTIMATES

Background note

The purpose of this ISA (UK and Ireland) is to establish standards and provide guidance on the audit of accounting estimates contained in the financial statements.

The auditor should obtain sufficient appropriate audit evidence regarding accounting estimates. (paragraph 2)

The auditor should adopt one or a combination of the following approaches in the audit of an accounting estimate:

(a) Review and test the process used by management to develop the estimate;
(b) Use an independent estimate for comparison with that prepared by management; or
(c) Review subsequent events which provide audit evidence of the reasonableness of the estimate made. (paragraph 10)

The auditor should make a final assessment of the reasonableness of the entity's accounting estimates based on the auditor's understanding of the entity and its environment and whether the estimates are consistent with other audit evidence obtained during the audit. (paragraph 24)

132 Accounting estimates are used for valuation purposes in a number of areas; the most common examples are for loan losses and valuation of investments not traded on an active market. Such estimates may represent significant risks.

133 The credit union will either calculate a bad debt provision or perform an impairment review of the loan book depending on whether fair value accounting is used. The auditor's review of a credit union's methods for making provisions and writing off bad loans includes consideration of their reasonableness, consistency with prior years and conformity with generally accepted practices.

134 In reviewing the reasonableness of loan loss provisions, both specific and general, credit union auditors ascertain that management have properly exercised their judgment, followed a consistently applied policy in determining the level of provisions and not merely followed a standard formula/matrix calculation. Auditors need to be mindful of practices such as re-scheduling, non-cash transfers

or top-up lending that can have the effect of understating provisions. In ascertaining the appropriateness of general provisions credit union auditors should take into consideration the level of risk inherent in the loan book and changes in the economic environment.

In reviewing the adequacy of loan impairment provisions the auditor assesses whether the assumptions made by management in arriving at their estimate of likely cash flows to be received from impaired loans have been made after due consideration and whether they are supported by relevant evidence, including evidence derived from backtesting and the issue of enforceability of contracts in relation to collateral. In the case of individual loan impairment calculations such evidence will be specific to the borrower but where impairment is estimated for a portfolio of similar loans the auditor considers observable data across a group of assets as a whole such as arrears statistics or economic conditions. **135**

Management bias, whether intentional or unintentional, can be difficult to detect in a particular estimate. It may only be identified when there has been a change in the method for calculating estimates from the prior period based on a subjective assessment without evidence that there has been a change in circumstances, when considered in the aggregate of groups of estimates, or when observed over a number of accounting periods. Although some form of management bias is inherent in subjective decisions, management may have no intention of misleading the users of financial statements. If however, there is intention to mislead through, for example, the intentional use of unreasonable estimates, or because of excessive pressure on management to recommend a distribution, management bias may be fraudulent in nature. ISA (UK & Ireland) 240 provides standards and guidance on the auditor's responsibility to consider fraud in an audit of financial statements. **136**

ISA (UK AND IRELAND) 545: AUDITING FAIR VALUE MEASUREMENTS AND DISCLOSURES

Background note

The purpose of this ISA (UK and Ireland) is to establish standards and provide guidance on auditing fair value measurements and disclosures contained in financial statements.

The auditor should obtain sufficient appropriate audit evidence that fair value measurements and disclosures are in accordance with the entity's applicable financial reporting framework. (paragraph 3)

As part of the understanding of the entity and its environment, including its internal control, the auditor should obtain an understanding of the entity's process for determining fair value measurements and disclosures and of the relevant control activities sufficient to identify and assess the risks of material misstatement at the assertion level and to design and perform further audit procedures. (paragraph 10)

The auditor should evaluate whether the fair value measurements and disclosures in the financial statements are in accordance with the entity's applicable financial reporting framework. (paragraph 17)

137 The valuation of derivative and other financial instruments[17] which are not traded in an active market and so for which valuation techniques are required is an activity that can give rise to significant audit risk. Auditors of larger credit unions which may hold such instruments consider the guidance on audit procedures set out in the ISA (UK and Ireland) 545 section in PN 19: The audit of Banks and Building Societies in the United Kingdom (Revised).

ISA (UK AND IRELAND) 550: RELATED PARTIES

> **Background note**
>
> The purpose of this ISA (UK and Ireland) is to establish standards and provide guidance on the auditor's responsibilities and audit procedures regarding related parties and transactions with such parties regardless of whether International Accounting Standard (IAS) 24, "Related Party Disclosures," or similar requirement, is part of the applicable financial reporting framework.

> When planning the audit the auditor should assess the risk that material undisclosed related party transactions or undisclosed outstanding balances between an entity and its related parties may exist. (paragraph 106-3)

138 The principles and procedures set out in ISA (UK and Ireland) 550 apply to the audit of credit unions as for other undertakings. However, the organisation of credit unions is such that the issue of a controlling shareholding of a credit union by any party will not arise. Related party transactions which are likely to arise include shares held by and/or loans to directors or members of the supervisory committee of the credit union.

139 Related party transactions are defined in FRS 8[18] 'Related party disclosures', and directors of the reporting entity are related parties of the reporting entity. The financial statements need to disclose material transactions with directors and these may be disclosed on an aggregated[19] basis. Paragraph 16 of FRS 8 states that the 'disclosure provisions do not apply where to comply with them conflicts with the reporting entity's duties of confidentiality arising by operation of law'. This is relevant in a credit union context: credit unions are usually under a strict duty of confidentiality (by operation of statute, contract or common law) regarding the affairs of their members.

140 Auditors will enquire as to the procedures, required under the rules of the individual credit union, governing the authorisation, recording and monitoring of any related party transactions. They will assess the operation of those procedures during the financial year and consider whether appropriate disclosure has been made in the financial statements.

---

[17] In Great Britain, credit unions' investment powers are limited by CRED chapter 7.2.

[18] As at the date of issue of this Practice Note, the ASB has amended FRS 8 to comply with changes to the law arising from the Companies Act 2006.

[19] Aggregate disclosures are allowed unless disclosure of an individual transaction, or connected transactions, is necessary for an understanding of the impact of the transactions.

ISA (UK AND IRELAND) 560: SUBSEQUENT EVENTS

Background note

The purpose of this ISA (UK and Ireland) is to establish standards and provide guidance on the auditor's responsibility regarding subsequent events.

The auditor should perform audit procedures designed to obtain sufficient appropriate audit evidence that all events up to the date of the auditor's report that may require adjustment of, or disclosure in, the financial statements have been identified. (paragraph 4)

Matters specific to credit unions which auditors may consider in their review of subsequent events include:

- an evaluation of material loans and other receivables identified as being in default or potential default at the period end to provide additional evidence concerning period end loan impairment provisions;
- the accounting treatment of dividends declared after the year end[20];
- an assessment of material loans and other receivables identified as (potential) defaults since the period end to consider whether any adjustment to the period end carrying value is required; and
- a review of correspondence with the regulators and enquiries of directors and management to determine whether any significant breaches of laws and regulations or other significant regulatory concerns have come to light since the period end.

ISA (UK AND IRELAND) 570: GOING CONCERN

Background note

The purpose of this ISA (UK and Ireland) is to establish standards and provide guidance on the auditor's responsibility on the audit of financial statements with respect to the going concern assumption used in the preparation of the financial statements, including considering management's[21] assessments of the entity's ability to continue as a going concern.

When planning and performing audit procedures and in evaluating the results thereof, the auditor should consider the appropriateness of management's[21] use of the going concern assumption in the preparation of the financial statements. (paragraph 2)

The auditor should consider any relevant disclosures in the financial statements. (paragraph 2-1).

---

[20] FRS 21 'Events after the Balance Sheet Date' (paragraph 12).

[21] In the UK and Ireland, those charged with governance are responsible for the preparation of the financial statements and the assessment of the entity's ability to continue as a going concern.

> In obtaining an understanding of the entity, the auditor should consider whether there are any events or conditions and related business risks which may cast significant doubt on the entity's ability to continue as a going concern.(paragraph 11)
>
> The auditor should remain alert for audit evidence of events or conditions and related business risks which may cast significant doubt on the entity's ability to continue as a going concern in performing audit procedures throughout the audit. If such events or conditions are identified, the auditor should, in addition to performing the procedures set out in paragraph 26, consider whether they affect the auditor's assessment of the risks of material misstatement. (paragraph 12)

142 When events or conditions have been identified which may cast significant doubt on a credit union's ability to continue as a going concern, the auditor should in accordance with ISA (UK and Ireland) 570, paragraph 26;

(a) review the directors' plans for future actions based on its going concern assessment;
(b) gather sufficient appropriate audit evidence to confirm or dispel whether or not a material uncertainty exists through carrying out audit procedures considered necessary, including considering the effect of any plans of directors and other mitigating factors; and
(c) seek written representations from directors regarding its plans for the future.

143 In reviewing going concern, the auditor may consider the following areas in addition to those set out in ISA (UK and Ireland) 570:

- capital adequacy ratios – review of management's analysis and rationale for ensuring that the credit union is capable of maintaining adequate financial resources in excess of the minimum;
- liquidity indicators – review of the credit union's liquidity management process for signs of undue deterioration; and
- reputational and other indicators – review of the financial press and other sources of market intelligence for evidence of deteriorating reputation; review of correspondence with regulators.

Further details of possible factors that may indicate going concern issues in these areas are set out in Appendix 5 to this Practice Note.

144 If the auditor has any doubts as to the ability of a credit union to continue as a going concern, the auditor considers whether he ought to make a report direct to the regulators on which guidance is set out in the section of this Practice Note relating to ISA (UK and Ireland) 250 Section B.

ISA (UK AND IRELAND) 580: MANAGEMENT REPRESENTATIONS

> **Background note**
>
> The purpose of this ISA (UK and Ireland) is to establish standards and provide guidance on the use of management representations as audit evidence, the procedures to be applied in evaluating and documenting management representations and the action to be taken if management refuses to provide appropriate representations.

> Written confirmation of appropriate representations from management, as required by paragraph 4 below, should be obtained before the audit report is issued.
> (paragraph 2-1)
>
> The auditor should obtain written representations from management on matters material to the financial statements when other sufficient appropriate audit evidence cannot reasonably be expected to exist. (paragraph 4)

ISA (UK and Ireland) 250 Section A and ISA (UK and Ireland) 550 require auditors to obtain written confirmation in respect of completeness of disclosure to the auditors of: **145**

- all known actual or possible non-compliance with laws and regulations (including, for credit unions in Great Britain, breaches of FSMA 2000, FSA rules, the Money Laundering Regulations, other regulatory requirements or any other circumstance that could jeopardise the authorisation of the credit union) whose effects should be considered when preparing financial statements together with the actual or contingent consequences which may arise therefrom; and
- the completeness of information provided regarding the identification of related parties and the adequacy of related party disclosures in the financial statements.

In addition to the examples of other representations given in ISA (UK and Ireland) 580, the auditor also considers obtaining confirmation: **146**

- as to the adequacy of provisions for loan impairment (including provisions relating to individual loans if material) and the appropriateness of other accounting estimates (such as investment valuations or adequate provisions for liabilities);
- that all contingent transactions or commitments have been adequately disclosed and/or included in the balance sheet as appropriate; and
- that all correspondence with regulators has been made available to the auditor.

ISA (UK AND IRELAND) 700: THE AUDITOR'S REPORT ON FINANCIAL STATEMENTS

> **Background note**
>
> The purpose of this ISA (UK and Ireland) is to establish standards and provide guidance on the form and content of the auditor's report issued as a result of an audit performed by an independent auditor of the financial statements of an entity. Much of the guidance provided can be adapted to auditor reports on financial information other than financial statements.

> The auditor should review and assess the conclusions drawn from the audit evidence obtained as the basis for the expression of an opinion on the financial statements. (paragraph 2)
>
> The auditor's report should contain a clear written expression of opinion on the financial statements taken as a whole. (paragraph 4)

> In the UK and Ireland, the auditor should not date the report earlier than the date on which all other information contained in a report of which the audited financial statements form a part have been approved by those charged with governance and the auditor has considered all necessary available evidence. (paragraph 24-1)

147 The form and content of auditors' reports on the financial statements of credit unions follow the basic principles and procedures established by ISA (UK and Ireland) 700. Illustrative auditor's reports for a credit union are included in Appendix 1 of this Practice Note.

148 ISA (UK and Ireland) 700 requires that Independent Auditors' reports on financial statements identify the financial reporting framework used to prepare the financial statements. The expression UK Generally Accepted Accounting Practice can be used to describe compliance with applicable law and accounting standards issued by the ASB.

149 As noted in the Introduction, auditors are bound by the duties imposed by FIPSA and the NI Order. These require them, in preparing their audit report, to carry out such investigations as will enable them to form an opinion on:

(a) whether the credit union has kept proper books of account in accordance with the requirements of the legislation;
(b) whether the credit union has maintained a satisfactory system of control over its transactions in accordance with the requirements of the legislation; and
(c) whether the revenue account or the other accounts (if any) to which the report relates and the balance sheet are in agreement with the books of account of the credit union.

If the auditors are of the opinion that the credit union has failed to comply with any of the requirements of (a) to (c) above then they must state that fact in their report.

150 If references to inadequate records or systems of internal control under the relevant legislation are included in the auditors' report, consideration is given by the auditors to a qualification on the grounds of limitation of the scope of the work the auditors were able to perform.

151 If any significant matters of concern have arisen during the audit of a credit union, the auditors consider whether they need to report the matter to the regulators (see the section on ISA (UK and Ireland) 250 B of this Practice Note).

ISA (UK AND IRELAND) 720 (REVISED): OTHER INFORMATION IN DOCUMENTS CONTAINING AUDITED FINANCIAL STATEMENTS

> **Background note**
>
> The purpose of this ISA (UK and Ireland) is to establish standards and provide guidance on the auditor's consideration of other information, on which the auditor has no obligation to report, in documents containing audited financial statements.

> The auditor should read the other information to identify material inconsistencies with the audited financial statements. (paragraph 2)
>
> If, as a result of reading the other information, the auditor becomes aware of any apparent misstatements therein, or identifies any material inconsistencies with the audited financial statements, the auditor should seek to resolve them. (paragraph 2-1)

152 Auditors are required to report on whether the information given in the report of the board of directors of a credit union is consistent with the financial statements. In addition, one of the fundamental principles set out in the Auditors' Code is that auditors do not allow their reports to be included in documents containing other information if they consider that the additional information is in conflict with the matters covered by the report or they have cause to believe it to be misleading.

153 The auditors are not responsible for auditing the additional information. ISA (UK and Ireland) 720 does not require auditors to undertake additional procedures to corroborate other information in documents containing audited financial statements but rather to read the other information in the context of the knowledge they have obtained during the audit.

154 It is important to ensure that the directors are made aware of the auditors' responsibilities in respect of the other information, as set out in ISA (UK and Ireland) 720, and the extent of those responsibilities is specifically dealt with in the engagement letter.

155 The information which may accompany the financial statements of a credit union include:

- directors' report;
- supervisory committee report;
- treasurer's report;
- credit committee report;
- credit control report;
- membership committee report; and
- financial highlights for previous years.

156 The directors may also distribute other documents with the financial statements such as newsletters, new rules booklets, statements of member's balances of loans and/or shares in the credit union. The auditors have no responsibility to consider these documents.

Reporting on regulatory returns

Great Britain

157 All credit unions in Great Britain are required[22] to submit an annual return (Form CY) to the FSA within seven months of each year-end. A copy of the audited annual financial statements of the credit union, together with the auditor's report, should also be submitted.

[22] *In accordance with SUP 16.3.6R – 16.3.13R.*

158 Auditors are required to complete a Statement included in Form CY on whether the information contained in the balance sheet and revenue account of the annual return is, or is not, consistent with the audited financial statements (with an attached statement detailing inconsistencies if there are any). Standard wording for the auditor's Statement is as follows:

> "In my opinion, the information contained in the balance sheet and revenue account of the Annual Return is/is not consistent with the audited accounts published in accordance with section 3A of the Friendly and Industrial and Provident Societies Act 1968".

159 The auditor is not required to form an opinion on whether the annual return gives a true and fair view. It is in any event unlikely that the annual return could give a true and fair view, as some of the detailed information in the financial statements is not included.

160 Matters which may give rise to an inconsistency include:

(a) information which has been inaccurately extracted from the annual financial statements (for example, incorrect extraction of amounts appearing in the balance sheet or revenue account);
(b) information which, in the auditor's opinion, has been presented in a manner which is not consistent with the annual financial statements and reports; and
(c) omission from the annual return of information which is necessary to ensure consistency with the annual financial statements and reports.

161 When the auditor identifies what he believes may be an inconsistency he discusses the matter with those charged with governance, so that they may eliminate the inconsistency, for example by including additional information in the annual return.

162 If discussion with those charged with governance does not result in the elimination of the inconsistency, the auditor attaches a description of the inconsistency to his Statement.

163 Credit unions in Great Britain are also required to submit quarterly returns (Form CQ) to the FSA within one month of each quarter end, but there is normally no involvement by auditors with this return.

Northern Ireland

164 As noted in the Introduction to this Practice Note, auditors of credit unions in Northern Ireland have no direct reporting responsibilities in respect of annual returns submitted to DETI, although a signed copy of their report on the annual financial statements is required to be included.

Appendix 1

1.1- Illustrative Auditor's Report for a Credit Union in Great Britain

Independent Auditor's Report to the Members of XYZ Credit Union

We have audited the financial statements of XYZ credit union for the year ended ....which comprise [specify the primary financial statements such as the income and expenditure account, appropriation account, the statement of general reserve, the balance sheet] and the related notes. These financial statements have been prepared under the accounting policies set out therein.

Respective responsibilities of directors and auditors

The directors' responsibilities for preparing the Annual Report and the financial statements in accordance with applicable law and United Kingdom Accounting Standards (UK Generally Accepted Accounting Practice), are set out in the Statement of Directors' Responsibilities. Our responsibility, as independent auditor, is to audit the financial statements in accordance with relevant legal and regulatory requirements and International Standards on Auditing (UK and Ireland).

We report to you our opinion as to whether the financial statements give a true and fair view and are properly prepared in accordance with UK Generally Accepted Accounting Practice, the Industrial and Provident Societies Acts 1965 to 2002 and the Credit Unions Act 1979. We also report to you if, in our opinion, a satisfactory system of control over transactions has not been maintained, or if proper books of account have not been kept by the credit union. In addition we state if we have not obtained all the information and explanations necessary for the purposes of our audit or if the credit union's balance sheet and its revenue account are not in agreement with the books of account.

We read other information contained in the Annual Report [e.g. Treasurer's Report, the Supervisory Committee Report and the Credit Committee Report] and consider whether it is consistent with the audited financial statements. We consider the implications for our report if we become aware of any apparent misstatements or material inconsistencies with the financial statements. Our responsibilities do not extend to any other information.

Basis of audit opinion

We conducted our audit in accordance with International Standards on Auditing (UK and Ireland) issued by the Auditing Practices Board. An audit includes examination, on a test basis, of evidence relevant to the amounts and disclosures in the financial statements. It also includes an assessment of the significant estimates and judgments made by the directors in the preparation of the financial statements and of whether the accounting policies are appropriate to the credit union's circumstances, consistently applied and adequately disclosed.

We planned and performed our audit so as to obtain all the information and explanations which we considered necessary in order to provide us with sufficient evidence to give reasonable assurance that the financial statements are free from material misstatement, whether caused by fraud or other irregularity or error. In forming our opinion we also evaluated the overall adequacy of the presentation of information in the financial statements.

Opinion

In our opinion the financial statements give a true and fair view of the state of the credit union's affairs as at .... and of its income and expenditure for the year then ended, and have been properly prepared in accordance with UK Generally Accepted Accounting Practice, and with the Industrial and Provident Societies Acts 1965 to 2002 and the Credit Unions Act 1979.

Registered Auditor   Address

Date

1.2- Illustrative Auditor's Report for a Credit Union in Northern Ireland

Independent auditor's report to the members of XYZ Credit Union Limited

We have audited the financial statements of XYZ Credit Union Limited for the year ended 30 September 200x, which comprise [specify the primary financial statements such as the income and expenditure account, appropriation account, the statement of general reserve, the balance sheet] and the related notes. These financial statements have been prepared under the accounting policies set out therein.

Respective responsibilities of directors and auditors

The directors' responsibilities for preparing the Annual Report and the financial statements in accordance with applicable law and United Kingdom Accounting Standards (UK Generally Accepted Accounting Practice), are set out in the Statement of Directors' Responsibilities. Our responsibility, as independent auditor, is to audit the financial statements in accordance with relevant legal and regulatory requirements and International Standards on Auditing (UK and Ireland).

We report to you our opinion as to whether the financial statements give a true and fair view, and are properly prepared in accordance with UK Generally Accepted Accounting Practice, and the Credit Unions (Northern Ireland) Order 1985. We also report to you if, in our opinion, a satisfactory system of control over transactions has not been maintained, or if proper books of account have not been kept by the credit union. In addition we state if we have not obtained all the information and explanations necessary for the purposes of our audit or if the credit union's balance sheet and its revenue account are not in agreement with the books of account.

We read the other information contained in the Annual Report and consider whether it is consistent with the audited financial statements. We consider the implications for our report if we become aware of any apparent misstatements or material inconsistencies with the financial statements. Our responsibilities do not extend to any other information.

Basis of audit opinion

We conducted our audit in accordance with International Standards on Auditing (UK and Ireland) issued by the Auditing Practices Board. An audit includes examination, on a test basis, of evidence relevant to the amounts and disclosures in the financial statements. It also includes an assessment of the significant estimates and judgments made by the directors in the preparation of the financial statements, and of whether the accounting policies are appropriate to the credit union's circumstances, consistently applied and adequately disclosed.

We planned and performed our audit so as to obtain all the information and explanations which we considered necessary in order to provide us with sufficient evidence to give reasonable assurance that the financial statements are free from material misstatement, whether caused by fraud or other irregularity or error. In forming our opinion we also evaluated the overall adequacy of the presentation of information in the financial statements.

Opinion

In our opinion the financial statements give a true and fair view of the state of the credit union's affairs as at 30 September 200x and of its income and expenditure for the year then ended, and have been properly prepared in accordance with UK Generally Accepted Accounting Practice, and with the Credit Unions (Northern Ireland) Order 1985.

Registered Auditor   Address

Date

Appendix 2 – The main parts of legislation relevant to credit unions in Great Britain

FSMA 2000

Part I (and Sch 1) sets out matters concerning structure and governance of the FSA including its regulatory objectives and the principles to be followed in meeting those objectives.

Part II (and Sch 2) sets out the general prohibition on conducting regulated business unless an entity is either authorised or exempt, including restrictions on financial promotions. Regulated activities are defined in SI 2001/544.

Part III (and Schs 3-5) sets out the requirements to become authorised either by receiving a specific permission from the FSA or through the exercise of EEA passport rights. Exempt persons are listed in SI 2001/1201.

Part IV (and Sch 6) sets out the arrangements for application for a permission to undertake authorised business and the criteria (Threshold Conditions) that must be met An applicant who is refused can apply to the Financial Services and Markets Tribunal (established under Part IX).

Part V sets out the provisions applying to individuals performing designated functions (controlled functions) in an authorised firm. The FSA can specify controlled functions and authorised firms must take reasonable care to ensure that only persons approved by the FSA can undertake these functions. The FSA can specify qualification, training and competence requirements and approved persons must comply with the FSA's statement of principles and code of conduct for approved persons. Appeals can be made to the Tribunal.

Part VIII gives the FSA powers to impose penalties for market abuse – using information not generally available; creating a false or misleading impression; or, failure to observe normal standards – abuse being judged from the point of view of a regular market user. The FSA's powers extend to all persons – not only authorised firms. The FSA is required to publish a code to provide guidance on behaviours that do and do not constitute market abuse. This forms part of the Market Conduct Sourcebook and is called the Code of Market Conduct.

Part X provides the FSA with general powers to make rules which apply to authorised firms, including rules on specific matters – e.g. client money, money laundering. Rules must be published in draft for consultation. Guidance may be provided individually or generally and may be published. The FSA may modify rules or waive particular rules for particular authorised firms in certain situations.

Part XI allows the FSA to gather information from authorised firms, including use of skilled persons' reports under s166, or to commission investigations into authorised firms.

Part XIV sets out the disciplinary measures available to the FSA which can include public censure, unlimited fines, withdrawal of authorisation.

Part XXII includes provisions relating to auditors and their appointment.

Part XXVI brings together in one place the arrangements applying to warning notices and decision notices concerning possible breaches of various requirements imposed by FSMA 2000 or by FSA rules. A warning notice has to state the reasons for proposed actions and allow reasonable time for representations to be made. This will be followed by a decision notice with a right to appeal to the Tribunal.

Industrial and Provident Societies Acts 1965-2002 and the Friendly and Industrial and Provident Societies Act 1968

1. The Industrial and Provident Societies Act 1965 (the 1965 Act) sets out important matters related to Industrial and Provident Societies. The 1965 Act sets out some basic requirements in relation to the audit of the accounts of an Industrial and Provident Society. In particular it requires that auditors should satisfy themselves that proper records have been kept of all transactions, assets and liabilities.
2. The Friendly and Industrial and Provident Societies Act 1968, which sets out the main accounting and audit requirements, requires proper financial records to be kept and that all financial statements agree with those records, that there is satisfactory internal control over transactions and that the financial statements show a true and fair view of the credit union's financial position. In particular, section 9(2) of FIPSA states that "The (auditor's) report shall state whether the revenue account or accounts and the balance sheet for that year comply with the requirements of this Act and the appropriate registration Act....."
3. The Industrial and Provident Societies Act 1978 altered Section 7(3) of the 1965 Act. More importantly, the 1978 Act sets out that the 1978 Act and the 1965 Act should be construed as one. The Industrial and Provident Societies Act 2002 gave power to the Treasury to modify the relevant statutory provisions in the 1965 Act for the purpose of assimilating the law relating to companies and the law relating to Industrial & Provident Societies. Because of this power it is necessary when referring to the 1965 Act also to refer to the 2002 Act. As a consequence, the accounts of an Industrial and Provident Society comply with the Industrial & Provident Societies Acts 1965 to 2002 and the audit report should cover those Acts.

Appendix 3 – FSMA 2000 and related statutory instruments: Important provisions for auditors in Great Britain

FSMA 2000 provisions and related statutory instruments relevant for the auditors of a credit union are set out below. Further details of the legislation can be found on The Stationery Office website- www.hmso.gov.uk.

FSMA 2000 and statutory instruments as amended:

Section/Sch	
19	General prohibition from undertaking regulated activity unless authorised
20	Authorised firms acting without permission
21	Restrictions on financial promotion
41	Threshold conditions
59	Approval by FSA of persons undertaking controlled functions
165	FSA's power to require information
166	Reports by skilled persons
167	Appointment of persons to carry out general investigations
168	Appointment of persons to carry out investigations in particular cases
178	Obligation to notify FSA concerning controllers of an authorised firm
340	Appointment of auditor or actuary by FSA
341	Access to books etc (by auditor or actuary)
342	Information given by auditor or actuary to the FSA
343	Information given by auditor or actuary to the FSA : entities with close links
344	Duty of auditor or actuary resigning etc to give notice
345	Disqualification (of auditor or actuary from acting by FSA)
346	Provision of false or misleading information to auditor or actuary
348	Restrictions on disclosure of confidential information by FSA etc
349	Exceptions from s348
351	Competition information (offence relating to the disclosure of competition information)
352	Offences (contravention of s348 to 350(5))
398	Misleading the FSA
Sch 6	Threshold Conditions
SI 2001	
544	Regulated Activities Order
1177	Carrying on Regulated Activities by Way of Business Order
1201	Exemption Order
1857	Disclosure of Information by Prescribed Persons
2188	Disclosure of Confidential Information
2587	Communications by Auditors

Appendix 4 – The FSA Handbook

Not all authorised firms are required to comply with all rules contained within the FSA Handbook. This varies with the type of permission – the regulated activity an authorised firm is permitted to undertake is set out in the authorised firm's Scope of Permission. The following can be viewed on the FSA website:

- contents of the FSA Handbook – www.fsa.gov.uk/Pages/handbook
- FSA register which lists the regulated activities that each authorised firm has permission to undertake – www.fsa.gov.uk/Pages/register.

2   In gaining an understanding of the Handbook the auditor bears in mind the four statutory objectives of the FSA, set out in the Introduction above, which underpin the content of the FSA Handbook. To facilitate usage the FSA Handbook has been structured into a number of blocks and within each block the material has been sub-divided into Sourcebooks, Manuals or Guides. There are Rules, evidential provisions[23] and guidance which are contained within all of the blocks[24]. Contravention of Rules (which includes Principles for businesses) or evidential provisions can give rise to an obligation on the auditor to report the matter direct to the FSA – see the section of this Practice Note relating to ISA (UK and Ireland) 250 Section B.

Principles for businesses

3   The eleven Principles for businesses, which are general statements that set out the fundamental obligations of firms under the regulatory system, are set out in the FSA Handbook (PRIN 2.1). They derive their authority from the FSA's rule-making powers as set out in the Act and reflect the regulatory objectives. These Principles are as follows:

- an authorised firm must conduct its business with integrity;
- an authorised firm must conduct its business with due skill, care and diligence;
- an authorised firm must take reasonable care to organise and control its affairs responsibly and effectively with adequate risk management;
- an authorised firm must maintain adequate financial resources;
- an authorised firm must observe proper standards of market conduct;
- an authorised firm must pay due regard to the interests of its customers and treat them fairly;
- an authorised firm must pay due regard to the information needs of its clients, and communicate information to them in a way which is clear, fair and not misleading;
- an authorised firm must manage conflicts of interest fairly, both between itself and its customers and between a customer and another client;
- an authorised firm must take reasonable care to ensure the suitability of its advice and discretionary decisions for any customer who is entitled to rely on its judgement;
- an authorised firm must arrange adequate protection for clients' assets when it is responsible for them; and
- an authorised firm must deal with its regulators in an open and co-operative way, and must disclose to the FSA appropriately anything relating to the authorised firm of which the FSA would reasonably expect notice (see SUP 15 – Notifications to the FSA).

---

[23] *An evidential provision is not binding in its own right, but establishes a presumption of compliance or non-compliance with another rule. Guidance may be used to explain the implications of other provisions, to indicate possible means of compliance, or to recommend a particular course of action or arrangement.*

[24] *Rules are set out in emboldened type and are marked with the icon 'R', evidential provisions are marked 'E' and guidance 'G'. Further guidance on the status of the Handbook text is set out in the General Provisions (GEN) Sourcebook Chapter 2.2 and Chapter 6 of the Reader' Guide.*

Senior management arrangements, systems and controls

SYSC amplifies Principle 3, the requirement for a firm to take reasonable care to organise and control its affairs responsibly and effectively, with adequate risk management systems. The relevant chapters are as follows;

- 2 – senior management arrangements
- 3 – systems and controls
- 4 – general organisational requirements
- 5 – employees, agents and other relevant persons
- 6 – compliance, internal audit and financial crime
- 7 – risk control
- 8 – outsourcing
- 9 – record keeping
- 10 – conflicts of interest
- 11 – liquidity risk systems and controls
- 12 – group risk systems and control requirements
- 18 – guidance on Public Disclosure Act – whistle blowing

Threshold Conditions

Under s41 and Schedule 6 of FSMA 2000 Threshold Conditions are the minimum requirements that must be met at authorisation and must continue to be met. The relevant statutory Threshold Conditions include:

- legal status: deposit taking business must be conducted through a body corporate or partnership – that is, individuals cannot undertake deposit taking business;
- location of offices: the head office of a body corporate must be in the same territory/member state as the registered office;
- adequate resources: the authorised firm must have adequate resources (financial and non-financial) for the type of business conducted taking into account the impact of other group entities and having regard to provisions made against liabilities (including contingent and future liabilities) and the approach to risk management; and
- suitability: the FSA will consider the fitness and propriety of authorised firms, including whether business is conducted with integrity and in compliance with high standards, and whether there is competent and prudent management and exercise of due skill, care and diligence. This will include consideration of whether those subject to the approved persons regime (i.e. those undertaking controlled functions) are, or will be, approved by the FSA.

Appendix 5 – Possible factors that may indicate going concern issues

Capital adequacy ratios

- the credit union operating at or near the limit of its individual capital guidance or limit otherwise set by management under the FSA's capital requirements, either on a group or solo basis;
- unjustified attempts to reduce the size of the buffer over and above the threshold solvency ratio that management has agreed to operate at;

Operations/profitability indicators

- marked decline in new lending/dealing volumes during the year or subsequently;
- marked decline in new business margins;
- severe overcapacity in markets leading to low pricing as well as low volumes;
- significant increase in loan defaults or seizure of collateral (e.g. house repossessions);
- overreliance on grants or government funding and inadequate planning as to how to refinance these when they expire;
- excessive exposures to troubled industry sectors;
- unusually aggressive dealing positions and/or regular breaches of dealing or lending limits;
- redundancies, layoffs or failure to replace natural wastage of personnel;

Liquidity indicators

- low ratio of liquid assets to total relevant liabilities;
- mismatch between loans being issued and shares in the credit union;
- anticipated defaults on loan repayments;
- expected cash flows;

Reputational and other indicators

- adverse publicity which could lead to loss of confidence or reputation, including fines or public censure by the regulator;
- urgent attempts to remove assets from the balance sheet, apparently involving material loss of profits or at significant expense;
- deferral of investment plans or capitalisation of expenditure.

Appendix 6 – Reporting direct to the regulators – statutory right and protection for disclosure under general law

1. When the auditor concludes that a matter does not give rise to a statutory duty to report direct to the regulators, the auditor considers the right to report to the regulators.

2. In cases of doubt, general law provides protection for disclosing certain matters to a proper authority in the public interest.

3. Audit firms are protected from the risk of liability from breach of confidence or defamation under general law even when carrying out work which is not clearly undertaken in the capacity of auditor provided that:

    - in the case of breach of confidence:
        (i) disclosure is made in the public interest; and
        (ii) such disclosure is made to an appropriate body or person; and
        (iii) there is no malice motivating the disclosure; and
    - in the case of defamation:
        (i) the information disclosed was obtained in a proper capacity; and
        (ii) there is no malice motivating the disclosure.

The same protection is given even if there is only a reasonable suspicion that non-compliance with law or regulations has occurred. Provided that it can be demonstrated that an audit firm, in disclosing a matter in the public interest, has acted reasonably and in good faith, it would not be held by the court to be in breach of duty to the institution even if, an investigation or prosecution having occurred, it were found that there had been no breach of law or regulation.

When reporting to proper authorities in the public interest, it is important that, in order to retain the protection of qualified privilege, auditors report only to one who has a proper interest to receive the information.

'Public interest' is a concept which is not capable of general definition. Each situation must be considered individually. In general circumstances, matters to be taken into account when considering whether disclosure is justified in the public interest may include:

- the extent to which the suspected non-compliance with law or regulations is likely to affect members of the public;
- whether the directors (or equivalent) have rectified the matter or are taking, or are likely to take, effective corrective action;
- the extent to which non-disclosure is likely to enable the suspected non-compliance with law or regulations to recur with impunity;
- the gravity of the matter;
- whether there is a general management ethos within the entity of disregarding law or regulations;
- the weight of evidence and the degree of the auditors' suspicion that there has been an instance of non-compliance with law or regulations.

Determination of where the balance of public interest lies requires careful consideration. The auditor needs to weigh the public interest in maintaining confidential client relationships against the public interest of disclosure to a proper authority and to use their professional judgment to determine whether their misgivings justify them in carrying the matter further or are too insubstantial to deserve report.

Appendix 7 – Trade Associations in Northern Ireland

In Northern Ireland, the principal trade associations have a role in the oversight of credit unions and the majority of credit unions are members of a trade association. The main trade associations are the Irish League of Credit Unions (ILCU) and the Ulster Federation of Credit Unions (UFCU). As at the date of issue of this Practice Note, of the 170 credit unions in Northern Ireland the approximate membership was:

- ILCU – 104,
- UFCU – 49.

The function of ILCU and UFCU is, broadly:

- to promote the credit union idea and ethos;
- to represent affiliated credit unions with Government, the EU and other agencies;
- to provide central services to credit unions.

The typical contact between a credit union and the trade associations is:

- submission of quarterly prudential returns;

- periodic visits from a field officer (by ILCU every 18 months). A report is issued after this visit to comment on aspects of internal control against the trade association's rulebook and requirements of the NI order. If there are any issues the field officer would report directly to DETI. The visit from the field officer is taken no less seriously then a monitoring officer visit (DETI) or auditor visit;
- payment of affiliation fees (deducted from member accounts);
- chapter meetings are held once a month between local credit unions and these meetings are attended by a liaison officer from the trade association;
- amendments to the trade association's rules are adopted at the annual AGM;
- credit unions are sent a copy of 'Credit Union year end requirements' each year; and
- credit unions contact the trade association on day to day enquiries on legal/secretarial/insurance matters.

4   Typical contact between the trade associations and auditors:
- ILCU also sends direct to auditors a copy of 'Credit Union year end requirements' each year. This includes specific guidance over accounting areas, for example bad debt provision, accounting for dividends, level of general reserves. It also includes guidance on AGM and election of officer procedures, pro-forma audit report, requirement to submit to them a copy of the annual return (AR25), audited accounts and management letter etc.;
- auditors review any report made by the trade association's field officers (treated the same as a monitoring officer report);
- auditors have a copy of the credit union rule book and have traditionally tested internal control procedures against the rule book in key areas such as work performed by the supervisory committee.

5   Auditors do not have an obligation to report to the trade associations, nor to report in line with their year end requirements. However the information available from the Standard Rules for credit unions is a useful tool in the assessment of the internal control framework, while the year end requirements sent directly to auditors provides focus for the year end audit and a consistent approach to accounting policies across credit unions.

Appendix 8 – Definitions

Abbreviations and frequently used terms in this Practice Note are set out below:

ARROW II	'Advanced Risk Responsive Operating frameWork'. The term used for FSA's risk assessment process – the application of risk based supervision. It is the mechanism through which the FSA evaluates the risk an authorised firm poses to its statutory objectives enabling it to allocate its resources appropriately and respond to the risks identified.
authorised firm	An entity which has been granted one or more Part IV permissions by the FSA and so is authorised under FSMA 2000 to undertake regulated activities – an authorised person. Authorised firms include deposit takers.
authorised person	Term used throughout FSMA 2000 and related statutory instruments to refer to an authorised firm – see above.
authorised by FSA	Same as authorised firm or authorised person – see above.

COND	Threshold conditions element of the high level standards block of the FSA Handbook.
CRD	Capital Requirements Directive
CRED	Credit Unions sourcebook
credit institution	An undertaking whose business is to receive deposits or other repayable funds from the public and to grant credits for its own account and to which the Banking Consolidation Directive applies.
Credit Union	A "credit union" in the context of this Practice Note is a society registered as a credit union under IPSA or the NI Order. A credit union is a body corporate with perpetual succession which is known by its registered name.
CU 79	Credit Unions Act 1979
deposit taker	Authorised firms which under FSMA 2000 have a Part IV permission to accept deposits.
DETI	Department of Enterprise, Trade and Investment in Northern Ireland
FIPSA	Friendly and Industrial and Provident Societies Act 1968
FRS	Financial Reporting Statements
FSA	The Financial Services Authority
FSMA 2000	Financial Services and Markets Act 2000
FRSSE	Financial Reporting Standard for Smaller Entities
IPSA 65/02	Industrial and Provident Societies Acts 1965-2002
JMLSG	Joint Money Laundering Steering Group
MiFID	Markets in Financial Instruments Directive
material significance	A matter or group of matters is normally of material significance to a regulator's function when, due either to its nature or its potential financial impact, it is likely of itself to require investigation by the regulator
NI Order	Credit Unions (Northern Ireland) Order 1985
Part IV permission	A permission granted by FSA under Part IV FSMA 2000 permitting an authorised firm to carry on regulated activities as specified in the FSMA 2000 Regulated Activities Order (SI 2001/544) as amended.
permission	Part IV permission under FSMA 2000 to undertake one or more regulated activities.
Principles for Businesses	FSA Handbook defined principles with which an authorised firm must comply. The 11 principles are included in a stand alone element of the high level Standards block of the FSA Handbook – PRIN.
regulated activities	Activities as defined in the Regulated Activities Order SI 2001/544 as amended

relevant requirement	In relation to the auditors' duty to report direct to the FSA – requirement by or under FSMA 2000 which relates to authorisation under FSMA 2000 or to the carrying on of any regulated activity. This includes not only relevant statutory instruments but also the FSA's rules (other than the Listing rules) including the Principles for businesses. The duty to report also covers any requirement imposed by or under any other Act the contravention of which constitutes an offence which the FSA has the power to prosecute under FSMA 2000.
SOCA	Serious Organised Crime Agency
SUP	Supervision manual of the FSA Handbook.
SYSC	Senior management arrangements, systems and controls element of the High Level Standards block of the FSA handbook.
The 2001 Regulations	SI 2001/2587 – FSMA 2000 (Communications by Auditors) Regulations 2001
Those charged with governance	ISAs (UK and Ireland) use the term "those charged with governance" to describe the persons entrusted with the supervision, control and direction of an entity, who will normally be responsible for the quality of financial reporting, and the term "management" to describe those persons who perform senior managerial functions. The FSA Handbook of Rules and Guidance (FSA Handbook) uses the term "governing body" to describe collectively those charged with governance. In the context of this Practice Note, references to those charged with governance include directors of credit unions.
Threshold Conditions	The minimum standards that an authorised firm needs to meet to become and remain authorised by the FSA. The 5 conditions are included in a stand alone element of the high level Standards block of the FSA Handbook – COND.

Part Seven

APB Bulletins

[Bulletin 2000/3]
Departure from Statements of Recommended Practice for the preparation of financial statements: Guidance for auditors

(Issued December 2000)

Contents

	Paragraphs
Introduction	1 - 4
Auditors' considerations when financial statements fall within the scope of, but depart from, a SORP	5 - 7

Appendix – Forming an opinion on the effect of a departure from a SORP

Departure from Statement of Recommenced Practice for the preparation of financial statements: guidance for auditors

Introduction

1 The purpose of this Bulletin is to provide guidance to auditors on the application of SAS 600 'Auditors' reports on financial statements' when reporting on financial statements for periods beginning on or after 24 December 2001[1] that fall within the scope of, but contain a departure from, a Statement of Recommended Practice (SORP), or on any financial statements for which paragraphs 58 to 60 of Financial Reporting Standard (FRS) 18 'Accounting Policies' have been applied before that date.

2 SORPs recommend particular accounting treatments with the aim of narrowing areas of difference between comparable entities. The Accounting Standards Board (ASB) does not issue SORPs but recognises other bodies who do so, subject to those bodies agreeing to abide by a code of practice for producing SORPs[2]. Paragraph 17 of FRS 18 requires that 'Where it is necessary to choose between accounting policies that satisfy the conditions in paragraph 14[3], an entity should select whichever of those accounting polices is judged by the entity to be most appropriate to its particular circumstances for the purpose of giving a true and fair view.' Paragraph 40 of FRS 18 indicates that 'In selecting accounting policies, an entity will assess whether accepted industry practices are appropriate to its particular circumstances. Such practices will be particularly persuasive if set out in a SORP that has been generally accepted by an industry or sector.'

3 Paragraph 58 of FRS 18 requires that 'Where an entity's financial statements fall within the scope of a SORP, the entity should state the title of the SORP and whether its financial statements have been prepared in accordance with those of the SORP's provisions currently in effect. In the event of a departure, the entity should give a brief description of how the financial statements depart from the recommended practice set out in the SORP, which should include:

(a) for any treatment that is not in accordance with the SORP, the reasons why the treatment adopted is judged more appropriate to the entity's particular circumstances, and
(b) details of any disclosures recommended by the SORP that have not been provided, and the reasons why they have not been provided.'

---

[1] This is the effective date for entities to comply with certain provisions set out in paragraphs 58 to 60 of FRS 18 'Accounting Policies', including relevant disclosure requirements in respect of compliance with, or departures from, SORPs. The ASB encourages earlier application of these provisions.

[2] SORPs issued by ASB recognised bodies include a statement by the ASB that outlines the limited nature of the review the ASB has undertaken; and confirms that the SORP does not appear to contain any fundamental points of principle that are unacceptable in the context of current accounting practice or to conflict with an accounting standard or the ASB's plans for future standards. A Summary of SORPs in issue or proposed is available on the ASB's website (www.asb.org.uk).

[3] The conditions set out in paragraph 14 of FRS 18 are that 'An entity should adopt accounting policies that enable its financial statements to give a true and fair view. Those accounting policies should be consistent with the requirements of accounting standards, Urgent Issues Task Force (UITF) Abstracts and companies legislation.'

Similar requirements to this are included in regulations applicable to certain industries[4].

Paragraph 59 of FRS 18 includes a statement that 'The effect of a departure from a SORP need not be quantified, except in those rare cases where such quantification is necessary for the entity's financial statements to give a true and fair view'[5]. 4

Auditors considerations when financial statements fall within the scope of, but depart from, a SORP

When an entity's financial statements fall within the scope of, but depart from, a SORP the auditors assess: 5

- whether the entity has adopted a reasonable position in concluding whether the treatment adopted is more appropriate to its particular circumstances for the purpose of giving a true and fair view[6]; and
- whether there is compliance with the requirements of FRS 18 to disclose how the financial statements[7] depart from the recommended practice set out in the SORP, including:
    - the reasons why the treatment adopted is judged more appropriate to the entity's particular circumstances; and
    - details of any disclosures recommended by the SORP that have not been provided, and the reasons why they have not been provided.

When assessing the treatment adopted by the entity, the auditors will have regard to: 6

- whether the treatment adopted is consistent with that used previously and, if not, the directors' justification for the change;
- the impact on the financial statements of the treatment adopted compared with compliance with the SORP;
- the extent to which other entities in that industry or sector comply with the SORP;
- compliance or otherwise of the treatment adopted with applicable accounting standards, UITF Abstracts, legislation and any industry specific rules and regulations[8];
- any other matters which might help them come to their opinion.

[4] For example, accounting regulations made under the Charities Act 1993 and the Pensions Act 1995.

[5] If auditors believe that compliance with a SORP is necessary for an entity's financial statements to show a true and fair view, quantification of a departure simply as a note to the financial statements will not be appropriate. Paragraph 18 of FRS 18 states that 'The provision of additional disclosures will not justify or remedy the adoption of an accounting policy other than that which is judged by the entity to be most appropriate to its particular circumstances for the purpose of giving a true and fair view.'

[6] If the entity adopts a treatment that is judged to be other than the most appropriate, that would be a departure from the requirements of FRS 18. FRS 18 includes guidance on the objectives and constraints to be considered when judging the appropriateness of accounting policies.

[7] Financial statements are defined in the APB's Glossary of terms as 'The balance sheet, profit and loss account (or other form of income statement), statements of cash flows and total recognised gains and losses, notes and other statements and explanatory material, all of which are identified in the auditors' report as being the financial statements.'

[8] For example, unincorporated charities in England and Wales that prepare their financial statements in accordance with accounting regulations made under the Charities Act 1993 are required by those regulations to determine the values of assets and liabilities in accordance with the principles set out in the Charities SORP.

7   If, as a result of their assessment, the auditors form the opinion that the financial statements do not show a true and fair view they issue a qualified or adverse opinion in their report on those financial statements. Non compliance with the disclosure requirements of FRS 18 will ordinarily result in a qualified opinion.

Appendix – Forming an opinion on the effect of a departure from a SORP

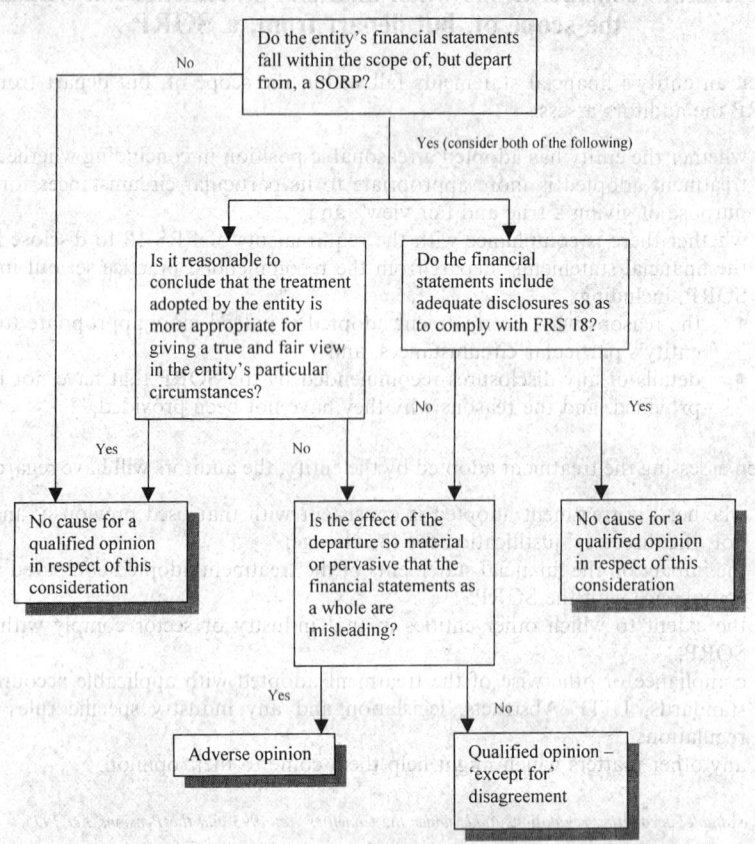

[Bulletin 2001/1]
The electronic publication of auditors' reports

(Issued January 2001)

Contents

	Paragraphs
Introduction	1 - 7
Responsibilities of the directors under Company Law	8 - 10
Best practice guidance for directors	11
Responsibilities of the auditors under Company Law	12
Auditors' considerations	
Checking information presented electronically	13 - 14
Prior period financial information	15
Auditors' report wording	16 - 25
Dating of the auditors' report	26
Directors' responsibility for controls to ensure that inappropriate changes are not made to audited financial statements	27 - 31
Engagement letters	32 - 34
Delivery to Registrar of Companies using electronic communication	35 - 36
Effective Date	37

Appendix 1 – Statutory requirements for the publication of financial information
Appendix 2 – Illustrative auditors' report for a listed company incorporated in Great Britain or Northern Ireland, for presentation on its web site
Appendix 3 – Extract from ICSA Guidance
Appendix 4 – Definitions

The electronic publication of auditors' reports

Introduction

1 The practice of communicating financial information by means of the internet is already well established. Various types of financial information can be found on web sites including information that has been audited (for example the annual financial statements), information which auditors may have reviewed (for example interim financial information) and information with which the auditors have had no direct involvement, such as financial highlights from a company's Annual Report or may never have seen, such as presentations for analysts. In addition, web sites typically contain a considerable amount of non-financial information.

2 In Great Britain The Companies Act 1985 (Electronic Communications) Order 2000 (the Electronic Communications Order) has recently been enacted, and this enables companies to meet, subject to certain conditions, their statutory reporting obligations to shareholders by distributing annual financial statements and certain other reports[1] electronically, or to post their financial statements on their web site and advise shareholders of this.

3 Notwithstanding the new legislation the APB is of the view that for a number of years many companies will continue to distribute hard copy financial statements to shareholders but will, in addition, post financial information on their web sites.

4 The purpose of this Bulletin is to provide guidance to auditors on their responsibilities not only if companies decide to take advantage of the Electronic Communications Order, but also in the more common current situation where the annual financial statements accompanied by the auditors' report are published on an entity's web site[2].

5 This Bulletin also applies when other auditors' reports are published electronically, such as the review report on interim financial information.

6 The dissemination of corporate information by electronic means is a relatively new phenomenon and the legal environment governing it has yet to be fully established. The APB has developed this Bulletin on the basis that the auditors' duty of care is not extended solely by virtue of their report being published in an electronic rather than in a hard copy form. However, uncertainty regarding legal requirements is compounded as information published on the internet is accessible in many countries with different legal requirements relating to the preparation and dissemination of financial statements. If the directors' responsibility statement does not refer to this, or if the auditors otherwise consider it appropriate, they add a note at the end of the electronic version of their report to the effect that 'Legislation in the United Kingdom[3] governing the preparation and dissemination of financial statements may differ from legislation in other jurisdictions'. Auditors with specific concerns may wish to take their own legal advice, particularly concerning their legal responsibility in jurisdictions in which the company is incorporated or its shares are listed.

---

[1] Other reports include Summary Financial Statements.

[2] The guidance in this Bulletin is therefore generally applicable both to auditors in Great Britain (where the Electronic Communications Order applies) and in Northern Ireland and the Republic of Ireland (where it does not).

[3] Or, if applicable, the Republic of Ireland.

Providing assurance on the maintenance and integrity of an entity's web site by reviewing, and perhaps testing, the entity's security and control arrangements, does not form part of the normal audit engagement but may be agreed with management as a separate engagement. This Bulletin does not provide guidance on such engagements.

Responsibilities of the directors under Company Law

The responsibilities of the directors under statute in the United Kingdom concerning the preparation, dissemination and signing[4] of the financial statements do not change simply because the financial statements are reproduced or distributed electronically.

In practice, to comply with the statutory requirements, the APB believes that paper based versions of the statutory accounts will continue to be needed. Paper based versions of the signed accounts are referred to in this Bulletin as the 'manually signed accounts'.

When statutory or non-statutory accounts are published on the web site, it is the directors' responsibility to have regard to the statutory provisions relating to the publication of financial information set out in section 240 of the Companies Act 1985[5], a summary of which is set out in Appendix 1.

Best practice guidance for directors

The Institute of Chartered Secretaries and Administrators (ICSA) has recently issued guidance for companies, their directors and certain other employees, on best practice in connection with information presented on corporate web sites[6]. This guidance was prepared at the request of the Department of Trade and Industry to accompany the publication of the Electronic Communications Order. Auditors enquire whether the directors have obtained a copy of this guidance and are following those recommendations that relate to the presentation of the Annual Report and Accounts on a web site. A relevant extract from the ICSA guidance is set out in Appendix 3.

Responsibilities of the auditors under Company Law

Section 235[7] of the Companies Act 1985 requires a company's auditors to make a report to the company's members on all annual accounts of the company of which copies are to be laid before the company in general meeting. Section 236[8] requires the

---

[4] Sections 242 and 233(4) of the Companies Act 1985 establish requirements for financial statements to be signed by the directors. The equivalent legislation in Northern Ireland is Articles 250 and 241 of the Companies (Northern Ireland) Order 1986, and sections 148, 156 and 159 of the Companies Act 1963 in the Republic of Ireland

[5] The equivalent legislation in Northern Ireland is in Article 248 of the Companies (Northern Ireland) Order 1986; in the Republic of Ireland it is set out in section 19 of the Companies (Amendment) Act 1986 and Regulation 40 of the European Communities (Companies: Group accounts) Regulations 1992: SI 201 (1992).

[6] 'Electronic Communications with Shareholders: A Guide to Recommended Best Practice'.

[7] The equivalent legislation in Northern Ireland is Article 243 of the Companies (Northern Ireland) Order 1986, and in the Republic of Ireland is set out in s.193 of the Companies Act 1990, s.15 of the Companies (Amendment) Act 1986 and Regulation 38 of the European Communities (Companies: Group Accounts) Regulations 1992.

[8] The equivalent legislation in Northern Ireland is Article 244 of the Companies (Northern Ireland) Order 1986.

auditors' report to be signed and also requires the copy of the auditors' report which is delivered to the Registrar to be signed.

Auditors' considerations

Checking information presented electronically

13 When companies include the annual financial statements and the auditors' report on their web site or, in Great Britain, decide to distribute annual financial statements to their shareholders electronically, auditors:

- review the process by which the financial statements to be published electronically are derived from the financial information contained in the manually signed accounts;
- check that the proposed electronic version is identical in content with the manually signed accounts; and
- check that the conversion of the manually signed accounts into an electronic format has not distorted the overall presentation of the financial information, for example, by highlighting certain information so as to give it greater prominence.

14 It is recommended that auditors retain a printout or disk of the final electronic version for future reference if necessary.

Prior period financial information[9]

15 A number of web sites already include audited and other financial information in respect of one or more previous years. Where applicable, auditors encourage the directors to present prior period financial information (including any related auditors' reports) clearly and appropriately or, alternatively, to delete it. The APB does not expect auditors to apply the procedures described in paragraph 13 to prior period financial information.

Auditors' report wording

16 The auditors consider whether the wording of their report is suitable for electronic distribution. Issues include:

- identifying the financial statements that have been audited and the information that has been reviewed, or read, by the auditors,
- identifying the nationality of the accounting and auditing standards applied, and
- limiting the auditors' association with any other information distributed with the Annual Report.

An example of an auditors' report for use if the audited financial information is to be posted to a company web site is set out in Appendix 2. Apart from the possible notes at the end, this is identical to that included as Appendix 1 to Bulletin 2001/2: 'Revisions to the wording of auditors' reports on financial statements and the interim review report.'

---

[9] *The term 'prior period financial information' denotes financial statements that have been posted to a web site before this Bulletin becomes effective. The guidance included in paragraph 15 does not apply to comparatives included in audited financial statements for financial periods commencing after 22 December 2000 posted to web sites.*

Identification of the financial statements that have been audited

In Annual Reports produced in a hard copy format, the auditors' report usually identifies the financial statements which have been audited by reference to page numbers. The use of page numbers is often[10] not a suitable method of identifying particular financial information presented on a web site. The auditors' report therefore needs to specify in another way the location and description of the information that has been audited. 17

The APB recommends that the auditors' report describes, by name, the primary statements that comprise the financial statements. The same technique can also be used to specify the information that has been reviewed or, because it is included in the Annual Report, read by the auditors. 18

Auditors ensure that their statutory report on the full financial statements is not associated with extracts from, or summaries of, those audited financial statements. 19

Identification of the nationality of the accounting and auditing standards applied

Auditors' reports on web sites will be accessible internationally, and it is therefore important that they indicate clearly the nationality of the accounting standards used in the preparation of the financial statements and the nationality of the auditing standards applied. For the same reason, auditors ensure that their report discloses sufficient of their address to enable readers to understand in which country the auditors are located. 20

Limitation of the auditors' association with any other information distributed with the Annual Report

In addition to the Annual Report many companies publish on their web sites a considerable volume of financial and non-financial information. This information could take the form of additional analyses or alternative presentations of audited financial information. Users of the web site are likely to find it difficult to distinguish financial information which the auditors have audited, or read, from other data. This issue is exacerbated when there are hyperlinks which allow users to move easily from one area of the web site to another. 21

Auditors give careful consideration to the use of hyperlinks between the audited financial statements and information contained on the web site that has not been subject to audit or 'reading' by the auditors ('other information'). To avoid possible misunderstandings concerning the scope of the audit, auditors request the directors to ensure that hyperlinks contain warnings that the linkage is from audited to unaudited information[11]. 22

---

[10] *The audited financial statements can be presented on the web site using a variety of webfile formats. As at the date of this Bulletin, examples of these are the Portable Document Format (PDF) or Hypertext Mark-up Language (HTML). Page numbers generally continue to be an effective referencing mechanism for PDF files but this is not always the case when data is represented in HTML.*

[11] *Sometimes audited information is not included in the financial statements themselves (e.g. certain information relating to directors' remuneration may be set out as part of a company's corporate governance disclosures). The APB is of the view that companies should be encouraged to make disclosures that are required to be audited, as part of the financial statements or included in the Annual Report in such a way that it is clear which elements of it have been audited. In other circumstances the auditors assess whether the scope of their audit will be capable of being clearly described. If this cannot be achieved to the satisfaction of the auditors it may be necessary to describe the particulars that have been audited within the auditors' report.*

23 Auditors are concerned to establish that the auditors' report on the financial statements is not inappropriately associated with other information. Auditors take steps to satisfy themselves that information that they have audited or, because it is included in the Annual Report, read, is distinguished from other information in a manner appropriate to the electronic format used by the entity[12].

24 During the course of the audit, the auditors discuss with the directors or, where appropriate, the audit committee how the financial statements and auditors' report will be presented on the entity's web site with a view to minimising the possibility that the auditors' report is inappropriately associated with other information. If the auditors are not satisfied with the proposed electronic presentation of the audited financial statements and auditors' report, they request that the presentation be amended. If the presentation is not amended the auditors will, in accordance with the terms of their engagement, not give consent for the electronic release of their audit opinion.

25 If the auditors' report is used without the auditors' consent, and the auditors have concerns about the electronic presentation of the audited financial statements or their report and appropriate action is not taken by the directors, the auditors seek legal advice as necessary. They also consider whether it would be appropriate to resign.

Dating of the auditors' report

26 The electronic version of the auditors' report is dated using the same date as the auditors' report on the manually signed accounts. If an auditors' report is amended at a later date, purely to reflect its electronic presentation[13], this does not constitute a new audit opinion and does not require a new date or consideration of subsequent events after the date of the manually signed accounts.

Directors' responsibility for controls to ensure that inappropriate changes are not made to audited financial statements

27 In the traditional reporting medium of hard copy reporting, information remains 'static', in that once published it can only be updated by replacing the printed copy with freshly published material. In contrast, electronic reporting occurs in a 'dynamic' environment which allows all or part of a report, once published, to be updated or replaced without it becoming apparent that a revision has occurred.

28 The dynamic environment on a web site makes it easier for inaccurate information to be included. Inaccurate information could potentially be added by:

---

[12] *Techniques that can be used to differentiate material within a web site include*

– *icons or watermarks,*
– *colour borders, and*
– *labels/banners such as 'annual report' or 'audited financial statements'.*

The appropriate mode of differentiation between audited and unaudited information will be dependent on the electronic format selected, and the nature and extent of other information presented on the web site. The method of differentiation would normally also be clearly stated in an introduction page within the web site.

[13] *Such amendments would be the minimum necessary to ensure that the wording of the auditors' report was relevant to the electronic medium: for example the substitution of narrative references for page numbers.*

- a company employee who is not fully aware of the consequences of amendments,
- a company employee who deliberately makes misleading and inaccurate amendments, or
- a person outside the company who is able to access the web site and alter the information presented.

In accordance with the ICSA guidance, directors establish a routine system of checking that statutory or audited information has not been tampered with. Auditors are not required to review such controls, nor to carry out ongoing reviews of the audited financial statements after they have been issued in electronic form. The APB recommends that auditors encourage the directors to state clearly their responsibility for the maintenance and integrity of the web site in their statement of directors' responsibilities. If the statement does not make this clear, or if the auditors otherwise consider it appropriate, they add a note at the end of the electronic version of the auditors' report to the effect that 'The maintenance and integrity of the (name of entity) web site is the responsibility of the directors; the work carried out by the auditors does not involve consideration of these matters and, accordingly, the auditors accept no responsibility for any changes that may have occurred to the financial statements since they were initially presented on the web site'. 29

However, if the auditors become aware that the audited financial statements have been altered, they notify the directors that the financial statements no longer correspond with the set that the directors have approved, and that they should therefore correct them immediately. 30

In addition, if the auditors become aware that their report is being used inappropriately on the entity's web site they request the directors to correct the situation. If the situation is not resolved satisfactorily, however, the auditors seek legal advice as necessary. They also consider whether it would be appropriate to resign. 31

Engagement letters

The electronic publication of an entity's financial statements gives rise to some difficult issues and the possibility exists that the directors of the entity may not fully understand their responsibilities and the auditors' role. The APB believes that it will be beneficial for auditors to clarify these in the engagement letter. 32

In particular, it is important that in the engagement letter the auditors establish that the directors should seek their consent to the electronic presentation of the auditors' report. This is done primarily to establish the auditors' right to request amendments to the electronic auditors' report if they are not satisfied with its proposed wording or its presentation in the context of the web site overall. 33

To clarify the situation engagement letters: 34

- acknowledge that the auditors recognise that the company may wish to publish its financial statements and the auditors' report on its web site or distribute them by means such as e-mail,
- note that it is the responsibility of the directors to ensure that any such publication properly presents the financial information and any auditors' report,
- establish that the company should advise the auditors of any intended electronic publication before it occurs,

- state that the auditors reserve the right to withold consent to the electronic publication of their report if the audited financial statements or the auditors' report are to be published in an inappropriate manner,
- note that the directors are responsible for the controls over, and the security of, the web site,
- state that the examination of the controls over the maintenance and integrity of the entity's web site is beyond the scope of the audit of the financial statements, and
- where applicable, state that the directors are responsible for establishing and controlling the process for electronically distributing Annual Reports and other financial information to shareholders and to the Registrar of Companies.

Delivery to Registrar of Companies using electronic communication

35 The Registrar of Companies is authorised to make its own rules regarding the filing of information at Companies House. As at the date of issue of this Bulletin, the rules relating to the electronic filing of audited financial statements have yet to be prepared. It is not yet known what arrangements will be established to control the authenticity of documents and what guidance, if any, will be established regarding manual, electronic or digital signatures.

36 In this connection, it should be noted that certain documents, such as the annual return and amendments to directors' details, are already being accepted in electronic form under the terms of section 707[14] of the Companies Act 1985.

Effective Date

37 Where companies in Great Britain decide to take advantage of the Electronic Communications Order to allow shareholders to elect to receive the annual accounts and reports electronically in place of hard copies, the guidance in Bulletin 2001/1 applies immediately. In other situations where the auditors' report is published in an electronic format, Bulletin 2001/1 is effective for audits of financial statements for financial periods commencing after 22 December 2000. Earlier implementation of the guidance set out in the Bulletin is, however, encouraged.

Appendix 1 – Statutory requirements for the publication of financial information

Companies Act 1985

At present there is legislation in place concerning the publication of both statutory and non-statutory financial statements. A company is deemed to have published financial statements, either statutory or non-statutory, under section 240(4)[15] of the Companies Act 1985 (CA 85) as follows:

---

[14] *The equivalent legislation in Northern Ireland is Article 656 of the Companies (Northern Ireland) Order 1986, and s.249 of the Companies Act 1990 in the Republic of Ireland.*

[15] *The equivalent legislation in Northern Ireland is Article 248(4) of the Companies (Northern Ireland) Order 1986 and in the Republic of Ireland it is s.19(4) of the Companies (Amendment) Act 1986 and Regulation 40(4) of the European Communities (Companies: Group Accounts) Regulations 1992.*

Review and the Corporate Governance Statement).[27] We consider the implications for our report if we become aware of any apparent misstatements or material inconsistencies with the financial statements. Our responsibilities do not extend to any other information.

Basis of audit opinion

We conducted our audit in accordance with United Kingdom Auditing Standards issued by the Auditing Practices Board. An audit includes examination, on a test basis, of evidence relevant to the amounts and disclosures in the financial statements. It also includes an assessment of the significant estimates and judgments made by the directors in the preparation of the financial statements, and of whether the accounting policies are appropriate to the company's circumstances, consistently applied and adequately disclosed.

We planned and performed our audit so as to obtain all the information and explanations which we considered necessary in order to provide us with sufficient evidence to give reasonable assurance that the financial statements are free from material misstatement, whether caused by fraud or other irregularity or error. In forming our opinion we also evaluated the overall adequacy of the presentation of information in the financial statements.

Opinion

In our opinion the financial statements give a true and fair view of the state of the [group's and the] company's affairs as at .... and of [the group's] [its] profit [loss] for the year then ended and have been properly prepared in accordance with the [Companies Act 1985] [Companies (Northern Ireland) Order 1986].

Registered auditors   *Address*
Date

Possible Notes:

1. The maintenance and integrity of the [name of entity] web site is the responsibility of the directors; the work carried out by the auditors does not involve consideration of these matters and, accordingly, the auditors accept no responsibility for any changes that may have occurred to the financial statements since they were initially presented on the web site.
2. Legislation in the United Kingdom governing the preparation and dissemination of financial statements may differ from legislation in other jurisdictions.

---

[27] *The other information that is 'read' is the content of the printed Annual Report other than the financial statements. The description of the information that has been read is tailored to reflect the terms used in the Annual Report.*

Appendix 2 – Illustrative auditors' report for a listed company incorporated in Great Britain or Northern Ireland[23], for presentation on its web site

INDEPENDENT AUDITORS' REPORT TO THE SHAREHOLDERS OF XYZ PLC

We have audited the financial statements of (name of entity) for the year ended ... which comprise (state the primary financial statements such as the Profit and Loss Account, the Balance Sheet, the Cash Flow Statement, the Statement of Total Recognised Gains and Losses) and the related notes [24],[25]. These financial statements have been prepared under the historical cost convention [as modified by the revaluation of certain fixed assets] and the accounting policies set out therein.

Respective responsibilities of directors and auditors

The directors' responsibilities for preparing the Annual Report and the financial statements in accordance with applicable law and United Kingdom Accounting Standards are set out in the Statement of Directors' Responsibilities.

Our responsibility is to audit the financial statements in accordance with relevant legal and regulatory requirements, United Kingdom Auditing Standards and the Listing Rules of the Financial Services Authority.[26]

We report to you our opinion as to whether the financial statements give a true and fair view and are properly prepared in accordance with the [Companies Act 1985] [Companies (Northern Ireland) Order 1986]. We also report to you if, in our opinion, the Directors' Report is not consistent with the financial statements, if the company has not kept proper accounting records, if we have not received all the information and explanations we require for our audit, or if information specified by law or the Listing Rules regarding directors' remuneration and transactions with the company [and other members of the group] is not disclosed.

We review whether the Corporate Governance Statement reflects the company's compliance with the seven provisions of the Combined Code specified for our review by the Listing Rules, and we report if it does not. We are not required to consider whether the board's statements on internal control cover all risks and controls, or form an opinion on the effectiveness of the [company's] [group's] corporate governance procedures or its risk and control procedures.

We read other information contained in the Annual Report and consider whether it is consistent with the audited financial statements. This other information comprises only (the Directors' Report, the Chairman's Statement, the Operating and Financial

---

[23] Bulletin 2001/2 includes an example of an audit report for a listed company incorporated in the Republic of Ireland.

[24] Auditors' reports of entities that publish their financial statements using 'PDF' format may continue to refer to them by reference to page numbers.

[25] Consider the need for additional references to those directors' remuneration disclosures that have been audited and included in the Board's report to shareholders on directors' remuneration without cross-reference in the financial statements.

[26] The expression 'the Listing Rules of the United Kingdom Listing Authority' may also be used.

'For the purposes of this section a company shall be regarded as publishing a document if it publishes, issues or circulates it or otherwise makes it available for public inspection in a manner calculated to invite members of the public generally, or any class of members of the public, to read it'.

The practice of putting statutory or non-statutory financial statements onto a web site constitutes the publication of the information in a different medium. Section 240, therefore, governs the display of the company's Annual Report and annual information contained in non-statutory financial statements such as preliminary announcements and summary financial statements on company web sites.

Statutory Financial Statements

Section 240 (5)[16] defines statutory financial statements[17] for the purposes of that section as comprising individual or group financial statements prepared under sections 226[18] or 227[19] of CA 85 which are required to be delivered to the Registrar of Companies. Where statutory financial statements are published, they must be accompanied by the relevant auditors' report (or a report by a reporting accountant in the case of small charitable companies).

Non-Statutory Financial Statements

Non-statutory financial statements comprise any profit or loss account or balance sheet of a company or group which relate to, or purport to deal with, a financial year of that entity otherwise than as part of the company's statutory financial statements. Where non-statutory financial statements are published, they should not be accompanied by the auditors' (or reporting accountants') report relating to the statutory financial statements.

In most instances non-statutory financial statements are summaries of, or extracts from, the statutory financial statements, and section 240 of CA 85 requires a statement indicating their status to be published with them. Illustrative wording for such a statement, which company directors could consider, may be as follows:

'The financial information presented on this web site does not comprise the statutory financial statements of XYZ plc for the financial year ended 30 June 20XX issued on [date], but represents extracts from them. These extracts cannot be expected to provide as full an understanding of the financial performance, financial position and financing and investing activities of the company as a reading of the complete Annual Report.

---

[16] *The equivalent legislation in Northern Ireland is Article 248(5) and in the Republic of Ireland is s.19(4) of the Companies (Amendment) Act 1986 and Regulation 40(4) of the European Communities (Companies: Group Accounts) Regulations 1992.*

[17] *The equivalent Republic of Ireland legal terms for 'statutory' and 'non-statutory' financial statements are 'full' and 'abbreviated' respectively.*

[18] *The equivalent legislation in Northern Ireland is Article 234, and in the Republic of Ireland it is ss.148 and 149 of the Companies Act 1963 and s.3 of the Companies (Amendment) Act 1986.*

[19] *The equivalent legislation in Northern Ireland is Article 235 and in the Republic of Ireland it is ss.150(1), 151 and 152 of the Companies Act 1963 and Regulation 5 of the European Communities (Companies: Group Accounts) Regulations 1992.*

The statutory financial statements have been delivered to the Registrar of Companies and the auditors have reported on them; their report was unqualified and did not contain statements under section 237(2) or (3)[20] of the Companies Act 1985. The complete Annual Report, including the auditors' report, can be obtained, free of charge, on request to the company at (address) or: [registrar@XYZemail.address]'.

The principal examples of non-statutory financial statements are:

- Preliminary Announcements

    Preliminary announcements constitute non-statutory financial statements under section 240 (5) of the CA 85, as they comprise financial information relating to a company's financial year.

- Summary Financial Statements

    Under section 251 of CA 85 fully listed companies may prepare summary financial statements and send these to shareholders instead of the full financial statements. Section 251(7)[21] exempts summary financial statements from the publication requirements of section 240 in relation to the provision of such statements to entitled persons[22]. The inclusion, however, of summary financial statements on a company's web site may render them accessible to an audience wider than entitled persons. In these circumstances the requirements of section 240 concerning the publication of a statement indicating the status of the financial statements become applicable.

The Electronic Communications Order

The Companies Act 1985 (Electronic Communications) Order 2000 became effective in December 2000, and applies to companies incorporated in Great Britain.

The Order modifies various provisions of the CA 85 for the purpose of authorising or facilitating the use of electronic communications between companies and their members and debenture holders, and between companies and the Registrar of Companies.

In particular, Article 12 modifies section 238 of the CA 85 (persons entitled to receive copies of accounts and reports) to enable copies of the annual accounts and reports to be sent electronically to those entitled to receive them. Either the accounts and reports can be sent directly to an electronic address supplied for the purpose by the recipient, or they can be published on a web site or sites and the recipient notified of their availability in a manner agreed with him. In the latter case, the accounts and reports must be published on the web site for at least 21 days before the annual general meeting before which they are to be laid. Articles 14, 32(2) and schedule 2 make equivalent modifications to section 251 concerning the sending of summary financial statements in place of the full accounts.

---

[20] *The equivalent legislation in Northern Ireland is Articles 245(2) and (3) of the Companies (Northern Ireland) Order 1986 and in the Republic of Ireland is section 193(4) Companies Act 1990.*

[21] *The equivalent legislation in Northern Ireland is Article 259(6) of the Companies (Northern Ireland) Order 1986.*

[22] *Persons normally entitled to receive copies of a company's report and accounts are:*

- *every member of the company,*
- *every debenture holder of the company, and*
- *every person entitled to receive notice of general meetings.*

Appendix 3 – Extract from ICSA guidance

Electronic Communications with Shareholders: A Guide to Recommended Best Practice

15. Identification of Statutory and Audited information.

In a paper copy of the Annual Report and Accounts it is relatively easy, simply by referring to the relevant pages, to identify 'statutory' information or that which has been subjected to audit and is, therefore, covered by the Auditors' Report. When similar information is placed on a website however things are not quite so simple. For one thing, pages tend not to be numbered and visitors to the site can flit about from page to page without necessarily being aware of the status of the information on each individual page. Also instead of having to turn to the back of the accounts for the notes these can be provided with hyperlink connections or brought up in windows and read alongside the basic information as can any other information the company might want to highlight in relation to a specific item. There is also the problem of pages being downloaded or printed off in isolation. How is the reader to know whether the particular information being read forms part of the audited accounts or not?

Several different organisations (including the IASC) are looking at the subject of reporting on the internet and it is not ICSA's place to prejudge what these organisations might say. The current view is that reporting can best be done by having a 'watermark' on, or a 'banner' down one side of each relevant page clearly indicating that the information on that page is statutory or audited information. In addition, a warning page should appear each time a visitor enters or leaves the 'statutory' part of the website.

It is recommended that the home page of the company's website provides a direct link to the 'statutory' section of the website and that audited and non-audited information should not be mixed on the same page.

In ICSA's opinion it is the company's responsibility to and ***it is Recommended Best Practice that the company should clearly identify 'statutory' information on its website and to indicate when the information being viewed forms part of the audited accounts.***

The Auditing Practices Board is publishing a Bulletin[28] which encourages auditors to tailor their report to the electronic medium. It is, therefore, recommended that the auditors should be asked at an early stage to provide clearance for audited information to be placed on the website and to confirm that they are satisfied with the way it is being presented including, in particular, the exact format of the Auditors' Report as it will appear on the website. Early consultation with the auditors should help to minimise any additional costs that might be associated with the auditors' review of statutory financial information posted on the website.

It is Recommended Best Practice that the company liaises closely with and obtains clearance from its auditors prior to the display of audited information and the Audit Report on a company website.

Directors should be aware that they have ultimate responsibility for the display of information on the company's website and it is important that procedures are in

---

[28] 'The Electronic Publication of Auditors' Reports'.

place to ensure that the information provided is accurate and properly authorised for publication. Care should be taken (in particular by listed companies) to ensure that no price sensitive information is released on a website until the appropriate authorities have been notified. Companies should also heed the provisions of s.240 of the Act which establishes that: 'if a company publishes any of its statutory accounts, they must be accompanied by the relevant auditors' report è if a company publishes non-statutory accounts it shall publish with them a statement indicating è that they are not the company's statutory accounts'.

It is Recommended Best Practice that the company establishes a routine system of checking that statutory or audited information made available via a website has not been tampered with and that the home page of the statutory section of the website contains a message indicating the time and date when the contents of that section of the site were last verified. Companies might wish to consider extending any such verification system to include other non-statutory, but equally vulnerable and potentially damaging, information.

Appendix 4 – Definitions

Definitions of information technology terms can vary significantly. For the purpose of this Bulletin the following definitions have been adopted.

'Digital signatures' – a combination of technologies and processes that can make electronic documents admissible as evidence in legal jurisdictions that have relevant legislation in place. The key components of digital signatures are often collectively described as a Public Key Infrastructure (PKI). In summary, a PKI usually includes: encryption software, message hashing software (like check digits), a process to register identities and processes to issue and store pairs of electronic keys (one secret key like a password, and one public key for distribution to a wide audience).

A feature of digital signatures is that they can enable a user of information to obtain comfort as to the identity of the information's originator and that the information itself is complete and genuine.

'Electronic signatures' are scanned versions of manual signatures.

'HTML' (hypertext markup language) – a set of tags and rules used in developing hypertext documents. HTML is an example of one of the languages which may be used in hypertext documents, to describe the relationship between a document's content and its structure.

'Hyperlink' – a reference (link) from some point in one hypertext document to (some point in) another document or another place in the same document. A browser usually displays a hyperlink in some distinguishing way, for example by using a different colour, font or style. When the user activates the link (e.g. by clicking on it with the mouse) the browser will display the target of the link.

'Icon' – a graphic symbol (usually a simple picture) that denotes a program or a command or a data file.

'Internet' – the worldwide network of computer networks.

'PDF' (Portable Document Format) – the file format for Adobe Systems' Acrobat. PDF is the file format for representing documents in a manner that is independent of the original application software, hardware, and operating system used to create those documents. A PDF file can describe documents containing any combination of text, graphics, and images in a device-independent and resolution-independent format. These documents can be one page or thousands of pages, very simple or extremely complex with an extensive use of fonts, graphics, colour and images.

'URL' (Uniform Resource Locator) – specifies the location of an object on the Internet, such as a file or a newsgroup. URLs are used extensively on the World Wide Web. They are used in HTML documents to specify the target of a hyperlink which is often another HTML document (possibly stored on another computer).

'Web site' – any computer on the internet running a World Wide Web server process. A particular web site is identified by the hostname part of a URL.

[Bulletin 2001/3]
E-business: identifying financial statement risks

(Issued April 2001)

Contents

	Paragraphs
Introduction	1 - 4
Implications for auditors	5 - 7
Knowledge of the business	8 - 15
Risk identification and assessment	16 - 22
Specialist skills and knowledge	23 - 25

Appendix – Examples of e-business risks that may affect the financial statements

Introduction

1 The objective of this Bulletin is to provide guidance for auditors on identifying financial statement risks when performing the audit of an entity that undertakes e-business. It covers the areas of: knowledge of the business; risk identification and assessment; and specialist skills and knowledge.

2 The use of electronic media for commercial and other business activities is commonly referred to as 'e-commerce' or 'e-business'. There are no standard definitions of these terms and both are, on occasion, used interchangeably[1]. Throughout this Bulletin the term 'e-business' is used to refer to any commercial or business activity with third parties that takes place by means of connected computers, including over the internet, or other electronic devices which remotely communicate with computers.

3 The use of computer networks to conduct e-business is not a new development. Methods such as electronic data interchange (EDI) have been in existence for many years primarily for business to business applications. Historically, EDI systems were relatively expensive to implement, required specialist knowledge to operate and were generally developed by larger companies that possessed in-house IT expertise. The evolution of the internet and associated systems has enabled e-business applications to be developed that are affordable to entities of all sizes. It is possible to supplement in-house IT expertise by using IT consultants and external service or application providers.

4 Internet technologies are continuing to evolve, especially for sales applications, but full integration with accounting systems is still rare. Integration is likely to increase over the coming years as businesses implement new technologies within the boundaries of their own businesses and as they establish real time trading links with customers and suppliers. Business strategies, organisation structures, management processes and control procedures are also likely to change as real time trading and processing is implemented.

Implications for auditors

5 The basic principles and essential procedures underlying the audit of an entity conducting e-business will be no different to those that apply to the audit of any other type of entity. However, e-business can have a significant impact on:

- the accounting and internal control systems (including possible reliance on automation of processing and on third parties such as payment collection businesses);
- the volume, velocity and nature of transactions processed;
- the taxation, legal and regulatory requirements the entity needs to comply with, including those of any foreign jurisdictions in which the entity, either intentionally or unintentionally, undertakes e-business;
- the accounting policies in respect of e-business related revenue and cost recognition and the capitalisation of certain types of expenditure; and
- consideration of whether the entity is a going concern.

Examples of e-business risks affecting financial statements are given in the appendix.

---

[1] Typically, where a distinction is made, 'e-commerce' is used to refer solely to commercial activities (e.g. buying and selling goods and services) and 'e-business' is used to refer to all business activities, both commercial and non-commercial such as customer relations and communications (i.e. it encompasses but goes wider than e-commerce).

6 Auditors will wish to obtain a knowledge of the entity's business which is sufficient to allow them to be able to identify risks arising from e-business operations that could lead to material misstatements in the audited financial statements. Auditors will need to understand the relationship between e-business and the entity's accounting system. Auditors may require specialist skills and knowledge to make appropriate enquiries and understand the implications of the responses obtained, identify the risks associated with e-business and to evaluate the internal controls that the entity has established. In some cases auditors may need to make use of an IT expert with appropriate e-business knowledge[2].

7 In addition to the risks which may have a direct impact on the financial statements, directors need to be aware of other e-business related risks such as the unauthorised disclosure of confidential information[3] or the use of the entity for criminal activities such as money laundering[4]. Auditors ordinarily are not required to plan and perform procedures to identify issues that are outside the scope of the audit of financial statements[5]. However, where possible non-compliance with laws and regulations comes to their attention they consider the implications in accordance with the standards and guidance set out in SAS 120 'Consideration of law and regulations'.

Knowledge of the business

8 In developing their knowledge of the business, auditors may consider the matters set out below.

Understanding the e-business strategy

9 In order to obtain or update their knowledge of the entity's e-business activity, auditors make appropriate enquiries to understand the entity's e-business strategy and how it fits in with the overall business strategy. As part of this process, auditors obtain an understanding of: whether e-business supports a new activity for the entity, or whether it is intended to add value to an existing activity or make it more efficient; sources of revenue for the entity and how these are changing (e.g. whether the entity will be acting as a principal or agent for goods and services sold, or enter into barter transactions); the directors' evaluation of how e-business affects the earnings of the entity and its funding requirements; and the directors' attitude to risk and how this may affect the risk profile of the entity.

Understanding what e-business operations are undertaken and how e-business applications are likely to evolve

10 Some entities' e-business operations are simple, others are more complex. Auditors obtain knowledge of where the entity is conducting e-business transactions (such as for sales or purchasing), the nature of any such transactions and the nature of relationships with e-business trading partners.

[2] SAS 520 'Using the work of an expert' sets out relevant standards and guidance.

[3] For example, entities must take positive measures to comply with the Data Protection Act 1998 (In Ireland, the Data Protection Act 1988).

[4] Information about legislation concerning money laundering and guidance as to its relationship with auditors' responsibilities is set out in Practice Note 12 'Money Laundering'.

[5] For some sectors, such as the public sector, the auditors' duties may be wider than for the audit of a company's financial statements.

The use of e-business within an entity will often evolve in response to market conditions and changes in technology. Over time simple e-business operations can be expected to become more complex. Auditors obtain an understanding of changes in the e-business operations and consider the impact that such changes may have on the audit.

11

Understanding how the e-business operations may be supported by third parties

Many entities do not have the technical expertise to establish and operate in-house the systems needed to undertake e-business. These entities may rely either in part, or wholly, on third parties such as Internet Service Providers[6] (ISPs), Application Service Providers[7] (ASPs) and data hosting companies to provide many or all of the IT requirements of e-business. The entity may also outsource various other functions in relation to e-business such as order fulfilment, delivery of goods, payment collection, operation of call centres or certain accounting functions. Auditors consider the outsourcing arrangements, having regard to the standards and guidance in SAS 480 'Service organisations'. Auditors also obtain an understanding of the contractual terms of any alliances or joint ventures with third parties.

12

Understanding how e-business systems interact with the entity's accounting and management information systems

Auditors determine: whether the e-business systems are based on use of the internet, private communications networks, third party systems or combinations of these and/or other software; the level of automation of decision taking and information processing; and the level of integration between different systems (including management information systems such as those from which key performance indicators are derived).

13

Auditors obtain an understanding of how the entity ensures the completeness, accuracy and reliability of the information recorded in the entity's financial records. The nature and level of sophistication of the entity's use of IT for e-business influences the nature of the risks related to the recording and processing of transactions. In some systems the origination of a transaction (e.g. a customer order) will automatically trigger all other steps in processing the transaction (e.g. selection and shipping of goods, raising and issuing the sales invoice etc.). This means that the integrity of the original transaction is fundamental to the integrity of subsequent entries in the e-business system and, in particular, in the accounting records.

14

Auditors obtain an understanding of: the way in which transactions are captured and transferred to the entity's accounting systems (including how it is ensured that transactions processed by an ISP or ASP are included in the correct accounting period by the entity); how the entity ensures that captured transactions are accurate, valid (including authentication of origin) and complete; and how unauthorised changes to transaction data are prevented.

15

---

[6] Entities that provide access to the internet. Additional services also may be provided such as e-mail.

[7] Entities that offer on-line real-time access to standard software packages on a bureau basis. Packages may include accounting and payroll and access to e-business tools and facilities.

Risk identification and assessment

16 When an entity engages in e-business there may be many new risks that confront the entity deriving from new, and sometimes unproven, business strategies. Auditors apply their knowledge of the business in order to identify and assess risks arising from e-business operations that could lead to material misstatements in the audited financial statements. At an early stage auditors ascertain the directors' and management's views regarding such risks and how they seek to mitigate them.

17 The complexity of the entity's e-business operations is likely to affect the auditors' assessment of financial statement risk. For example, if the entity uses a web site simply to provide information, and the site is not connected to the core operating and accounting systems, the related risks would be remote. Higher levels of risk will attach to e-business systems which are linked to the entity's operating and accounting systems, especially if they are used to enable transactions with third parties. Also, higher levels of risk may attach to e-business conducted through a public network than e-business conducted through a private network.

18 Many established businesses set up e-business operations to support existing activities. In these circumstances directors and management will have the benefit of their existing business knowledge and accumulated management skills and experience to help them identify risks associated with e-business and develop controls to mitigate those risks. However, e-business may introduce new risks which may require new business skills.

19 There are also new (start-up) entities that have been formed that conduct their business as e-business. Some of these entities have received external funding on the basis of aggressive growth targets, and are often valued on multiples of turnover. In start-up entities, directors and management may have ambitious plans for the business, that may increase risk, but be lacking in general business experience. Relevant expert advice may or may not have been obtained from third parties. Auditors reflect this when considering matters such as: the control environment; the motivation for aggressive earnings management; the directors' awareness of relevant accounting standards and laws and regulations; whether the resources of the entity are being over stretched (e.g. in an attempt to meet plans that may be over ambitious or to make acquisitions); and the ability of the entity to remain a going concern.

Going concern

20 The risk of the entity not being able to continue as a going concern can be a particular issue both for established 'traditional' businesses that have made significant investment in e-business and for entities that conduct all their business as e-business.

21 Auditors have regard to the standards and guidance set out in SAS 130 'The going concern basis in financial statements' when considering an entity's ability to continue as a going concern. For many entities undertaking e-business, the primary risk consideration will be whether they have sufficient funding. Where the excess is marginal, or the rate at which cash is spent compared to how it is earned indicates that it may become so within the foreseeable future, the auditors pay particular attention to the directors' plans for maintaining adequate financing.

E-business performance indicators published with the financial statements

22 Financing from third parties is often obtained on the basis of non financial measures and projections such as the number of registered or unique users and the number of 'hits' on their internet web site over a specified period of time. Entities may choose to publish these indicators with the financial statements. Such non financial performance indicators should be considered cautiously by those who read them as there may be uncertainties as to the accuracy or meaning of the data. The auditors' responsibilities with respect to the consideration of other information in documents containing audited financial statements are limited and are set out in SAS 160 'Other information in documents containing audited financial statements'. Auditors can help make readers of the auditors' report aware of the scope of their work by using the wording in the example reports included in Bulletin 2001/2 'Revisions to the wording of auditors' reports on financial statements and the interim review report'.

Specialist skills and knowledge

23 When e-business has a significant impact on the entity's business, the auditors consider whether the entity has the necessary skills and knowledge in-house or, if not, is being advised or supported by third party experts. The auditors may require special skills and knowledge to be able to make appropriate enquires and understand the implications of the responses obtained[8] in order to identify financial statement risks.

24 The nature of the e-business strategy adopted by the entity will affect the special skills and knowledge that auditors require. Depending on the circumstances, auditors may need an appropriate knowledge of:

- IT issues related to e-business:
    - understanding of e-business software and systems;
    - systems reliability and integrity;
    - unauthorised access to data and/or systems;
    - security techniques;
    - back up techniques and disaster recovery.
- Tax and legal issues:
    - knowledge of the taxation requirements in the different jurisdictions in which the entity is trading;
    - a general understanding of the legal and regulatory framework applicable to the entity's e-business activities[9];
    - the legal enforceability of electronic contracts and signatures;
    - privacy issues which are governed by varying data protection legislation.

    The global nature of e-business, particularly that conducted through the internet, means that knowledge of relevant legal and regulatory requirements in the different overseas jurisdictions in which the entity may do business can be important.

- Accounting issues:
    - revenue and cost recognition in respect of complex arrangements;
    - recognition of liabilities in different countries.

---

[8] SAS 240 'Quality control for audit work (revised)' sets out standards and guidance in respect of the competencies of audit firms and their staff.

[9] SAS 120 'Consideration of laws and regulations' sets out relevant standards and guidance.

25 Where auditors do not have the necessary expertise within their firm they may need to consult external experts.

Appendix – Examples of e-business risks that may affect the financial statements

The table below is not intended to be an exhaustive checklist; there may be many other types of risk that could affect the financial statements depending on factors such as the e-business strategy, the nature of the IT systems and the experience of directors and management. Auditors consider the risks relating to different entities having regard to the specific circumstances pertaining to each of them.

Accounting systems and internal control	
Loss of reliability of the information recorded in the entity's financial records	The reliability of information in the financial records relating to e-business transactions will be affected by the way in which e-business transactions are captured and transferred to the accounting records. Manual or poor interfaces between e-business and accounting systems may lead to incomplete or inaccurate capture or transfer of data. Risks relating to transaction execution include: • transactions recorded in the wrong period; • duplication or omission of transactions; • incomplete processing (e.g. not recording all steps such as order accepted, payment received, goods despatched and financial records updated); • records not properly entered or retained, resulting in accounts not balancing before and after each transaction; • disputed transactions not recognised; and • customer browsing being incorrectly treated as an order placed.
Unauthorised access to accounting systems	The nature of e-business systems, with a wide range of computer connections, increases the risk that accounting systems and data may be accessed by unauthorised individuals both within and outside the entity. This affects the risk of fraud on the entity and other actions (intentional or unintentional) that may cause transaction information to be incomplete or inaccurate.
Lack of direct control over transaction processing at a service organisation	Depending on the nature of the e-business operations that are outsourced, financial statement risks may include those related to maintenance of accounting records, completeness of income, credit risk and understatement of liabilities.

Systems failure	Similar risks exist as for the failure of any computerised financial system. These include incomplete or inaccurate accounting records and loss of audit trail.
Velocity, volume and nature of transactions	
Inadequate checks of the authenticity and integrity of trading partners	The nature of e-business may cause entities to conduct business over the internet with relatively few, if any, effective checks on the authenticity and integrity of the parties they are trading with. A particular risk is that retail customers are not who they claim to be and use stolen credit card details to order goods or services. This introduces a credit risk as banks may force retailers that do not make adequate credit card checks to pay the full cost of fraudulent transactions. Another risk is that of repudiation of a transaction by a party who denies placing an order and refuses to pay for the goods or services supplied.
Returns of goods sold electronically	There is typically a higher level of returns of goods that are purchased from remote locations by customers that have not had a chance to see and handle the goods before placing their order. This affects the risks relating to revenue recognition, provisions for returned goods and provisions against stock.
Unauthorised purchases	Use of e-business systems to make purchases may increase the risk that unauthorised purchases will be made in the name of the entity and that there will be unrecognised liabilities.
Compliance with tax and legal requirements	Internet web sites are accessible on a global basis. The legal registration of an entity, its base of operations, the country where goods or services are supplied from and where its customers are located may all be in different countries. This may give rise to risks such as: • taxes due on cross border transactions not correctly recognised and accounted for; • breaches of laws and regulations that affect trading in overseas jurisdictions. This may result in risks such as fines for wrongful trading, an inability to enforce contracts or inability to collect debts.
Electronic contracts not legally binding	Failure to ensure that electronic contracts are legally binding (e.g. by not ensuring that all terms and conditions are brought to the third party's attention or by not ensuring the authenticity of the third party entering into the contract) introduces the risk of repudiation which affects credit risk and the risk of goods being returned. If the entity is ordering goods or services there is a risk that payments may be made for goods or

	services that will not be received and disputes that cannot be satisfactorily resolved because the contract is not legally binding.
Inappropriate accounting policies	New business strategies associated with e-business may introduce a number of issues related to accounting practices and policies related to matters such as revenue and cost recognition and capitalisation of certain types of expenditure[10]. Revenue recognition issues include: • whether the entity is acting as principal or agent and whether gross sales or commission only should be recognised; • whether other entities are given advertising space on the web site and, if so, how revenues will be determined and settled (e.g. by the use of barter transactions); • the treatment of introductory offers and volume discounts (e.g. a percentage off the sales price or free goods worth a certain amount); and • cut-off (e.g. whether sales are only recognised when goods or services have been supplied).
Going concern considerations	E-business operations can be expensive to implement and support, particularly with regard to the amount that needs to be spent on marketing. The ability of the entity to remain a going concern may be an issue where cash is spent at a higher rate than it is earned and there are insufficient cash reserves or financing facilities available to support the business.

---

[10] The Accounting Standards Board's Urgent Issues Task Force has issued relevant guidance, including: Abstract 24 'Accounting for start-up costs', Abstract 26 'Barter transactions for advertising' and Abstract 29 'Website development costs'.

[Bulletin 2002/2]*
The United Kingdom directors' remuneration report regulations 2002

(Issued October 2002)

Contents

	Paragraphs
Introduction	1
The Directors' Remuneration Report	2 - 3
Requirements of Schedule 6 to the Companies Act 1985	4 - 6
Requirements of auditors	7 - 9
Reporting on the Directors' Remuneration Report	10 - 16
Difference between the disclosures required by Schedule 6 and Schedule 7A	17 - 18
Disclosure requirements in the Listing Rules	19 - 20
The auditors' responsibilities with respect to the unaudited part of the Directors' Remuneration Report	21
Issuing the Directors' Remuneration Report as a separate document	22 - 23
The auditors' statement on the Summary Financial Statement	24 - 28
Superseded guidance	29

Appendices

1. Illustrative auditors' report for a quoted company incorporated in Great Britain
2. Illustrative terms of engagement for a quoted company
3. Illustrative statement on the Summary Financial Statement for a quoted company incorporated in Great Britain

---

* *Editor's note:* The examples in the Bulletin have been superseded by examples in Bulletin 2006/6 Auditor's Reports on Financial Statements in the United Kingdom *and Bulletin 2007/1* Example Reports by Auditors under Company Legislation in Great Britain.

Introduction

1 With effect from 1 August 2002 the United Kingdom Government brought into force 'The Directors' Remuneration Report Regulations 2002'[1] (the Regulations) which will be effective for financial years ending on or after 31 December 2002[2]. These Regulations require 'quoted companies' to prepare a Directors' Remuneration Report, for each financial year, that contains specified information, some of which is required to be audited.

The Directors' Remuneration Report

2 The directors of a 'quoted company' are required to produce for each financial year a Directors' Remuneration Report which is required to be approved by the board of directors and signed on behalf of the directors by a director or the secretary of the company. The required content of the Directors' Remuneration Report is set out in Schedule 7A to the Companies Act 1985 (the Act).

3 A 'quoted company' is defined as a company incorporated under the Act:
- whose equity share capital has been included in the official list; or which
- is officially listed in an EEA[3] State; or which
- is admitted to dealing on either the New York Stock Exchange or the exchange known as Nasdaq.

The definition does not include companies that have been admitted to trading on the Alternative Investment Market (AIM).

Requirements of Schedule 6 to the Companies Act 1985

4 Schedule 6 to the Act requires a company to produce certain information concerning directors' remuneration by way of notes to the company's financial statements. The Regulations exempt a quoted company from disclosing the information specified in paragraphs 2 to 14 in Part I of Schedule 6. A quoted company is, however, required to disclose the information specified in paragraph 1 in Part I of Schedule 6 in the notes to the company's financial statements.

5 Part I of Schedule 6 will continue to apply in its entirety to companies which are not quoted and Parts II and III of that Schedule will apply to both quoted and unquoted companies.

6 The table set out below shows which of the requirements of Schedules 6 and 7A apply to quoted and unquoted companies respectively and the requirements with respect to audit.

---

[1] These Regulations are set out in Statutory Instrument 2002 No. 1986 which can be downloaded from http://www.legislation.hmso.gov.uk/si/si2002/20021986.htm.

[2] SI 2002/1986 applies to companies incorporated in Great Britain. Northern Ireland is responsible for its own companies legislation and it is expected that in due course the Companies (Northern Ireland) Order 1986 will be amended to introduce the same requirements as those set out in the Regulations.

[3] EEA is the European Economic Area.

Requirement	Quoted companies	Unquoted companies	Required to be audited
Schedule 6 to the Companies Act 1985 Disclosure of Information: Emoluments and other Benefits of Directors and others (These disclosures are required to be made in the notes to the financial statements)			
Part I, paragraph 1	✓	✓	✓
Part I, paragraphs 2-14		✓	✓
Part II	✓	✓	✓
Part III	✓	✓	✓
Schedule 7A to the Companies Act 1985 Directors' Remuneration Report (These disclosures are required to be made in the Directors' Remuneration Report)			
Part 2 (relating to information about remuneration committees, performance related remuneration and liabilities in respect of directors' contracts)	✓		
Part 3 (relating to detailed information about directors' remuneration)	✓		✓

Requirements of auditors

In addition to reporting on the financial statements, the company's auditors are required, through an amendment to Section 235 of the Act, to report to the company's members as to whether the 'auditable part' of the Directors' Remuneration Report has been properly prepared in accordance with the Companies Act 1985. The 'auditable part' of the Directors' Remuneration Report is the part which contains the information required by Part 3 of Schedule 7A.

The auditors are also required to carry out such investigations as will enable them to form an opinion as to whether the auditable part of the Directors' Remuneration Report is in agreement with the accounting records and returns.

To the extent that the requirements of Schedule 6 or Part 3 of Schedule 7A are not complied with, the auditors are required to include in their report, so far as they are reasonably able to do so, a statement giving the required particulars.

Reporting on the Directors' Remuneration Report

The auditors have to report on the Directors' Remuneration Report within their report on the financial statements. To communicate the opinion required of the auditors in the most effective way the APB recommends that the opinion paragraph of the auditors' report for quoted companies be drafted along the following lines:

> In our opinion:
> - the financial statements give a true and fair view of the state of the [group's and the] company's affairs as at ... and of [the group's] [its] profit [loss] for the year then ended; and
> - the financial statements and the part of the Directors' Remuneration Report to be audited have been properly prepared in accordance with the Companies Act 1985.

11 An illustration of an auditors' report for a quoted company incorporated in Great Britain is set out in Appendix 1. In Appendix 1 the changes that need to be made to the example auditors' report illustrated in Appendix 1 to Bulletin 2001/2 are shown as marked up text.

12 As the auditors are not required to audit all of the information contained in the Directors' Remuneration Report they will need, in their report, to describe accurately which elements of the Directors' Remuneration Report they have audited.

13 Companies, therefore, need to make the disclosures that are required to be audited in such a way that it is clear which elements have been audited. One way of doing this would be for the audited disclosures to be set out in a discrete section under a suitable heading such as 'audited information'.

14 It would be unsatisfactory for auditors, in their report, to describe what they have audited in an uninformative manner such as 'the disclosures required by Part 3 of Schedule 7A to the Companies Act' as this would require readers of the auditors' report to have a detailed knowledge of the requirements.

15 The auditors assess whether the scope of their audit will be capable of being clearly described. If this cannot be achieved to their satisfaction by cross-reference, they set out the particulars that have been audited within the auditors' report.

16 The auditors make arrangements with the directors, well in advance of the year end, to ensure that the audited disclosures will be clearly distinguished from those that have not been audited. Illustrative terms of engagement are set out in Appendix 2 to this Bulletin.

Difference between the disclosures required by Schedule 6 and Schedule 7A

17 As described above, the Regulations will continue to apply paragraph 1 of Schedule 6 to the Act to quoted companies. The consequence of this will be that the financial statements of quoted companies will disclose aggregate directors' emoluments that may differ from the aggregate directors' remuneration disclosed in the Directors' Remuneration Report. This arises because the Act's definition of 'emoluments' differs from its definition of 'remuneration'.

18 Both of these disclosures will be reported on by the auditors. Where both disclosures have been prepared in accordance with the relevant requirements of the Act any difference between the disclosures is not an 'inconsistency'[4] between the financial

---

[4] SAS 160 'Other information in documents containing audited financial statements (Revised) at SAS 160.1 requires: *Auditors should read the other information. If as a result they ... identify any material inconsistency with the audited financial statements, they should seek to resolve them'.*

statements and the information in the Directors' Remuneration Report. Where the difference between the disclosures of directors' emoluments and remuneration are material the auditors encourage the directors to provide an explanation of the difference.

Disclosure requirements in the Listing Rules

19 Following the introduction of the Regulations the APB understands that the United Kingdom Listing Authority (the UKLA) is aware that a certain level of duplication exists between the requirements of the Regulations and the requirements of Listing Rule 12.43A (c) relating to directors' remuneration. The UKLA is currently considering the most appropriate way of addressing this issue.

20 In the meantime additional care will need to be taken when auditing the disclosure of directors' remuneration. This is because not all of the requirements of Listing Rule 12.43A (c) are duplicated in the Regulations.

The auditors' responsibilities with respect to the unaudited part of the Directors' Remuneration Report

21 Although the Regulations do not require the Directors' Remuneration Report to be included in the Annual Report it is likely that many quoted companies will continue their practice of including directors' remuneration disclosures in the Annual Report. As the information given in Part 2 of the Directors' Remuneration Report is neither required to be audited nor reviewed by the auditors it constitutes 'other information'. Statement of Auditing Standards 160 'Other information in documents containing audited financial statements' requires auditors to read such 'other information' and if they become aware of any apparent misstatements or identify material inconsistencies with the financial statements to seek to resolve them.

Issuing the Directors' Remuneration Report as a separate document

22 If a quoted company issues its Directors' Remuneration Report as a separate document the scope of the auditors' report included in the Annual Report will, nevertheless, be required to encompass the auditable part of the Directors' Remuneration Report. For this reason, the requirements of SAS 160 apply to the content of a separate Directors' Remuneration Report, notwithstanding the fact that the Report is not included in a document containing audited financial statements.

23 When the Directors' Remuneration Report is issued as a separate document, although not required by the Act, the auditors:

- when their report is unqualified, encourage the directors to indicate within the Directors' Remuneration Report where the auditors' report, prepared in accordance with Section 235 of the Act, may be found; or
- when their report expresses either a qualified or adverse opinion or disclaims an opinion, which is relevant to the Directors' Remuneration Report, require the directors to reproduce the relevant parts of the auditors' report as part of the Directors' Remuneration Report. In the event that the directors do not agree to do so, the auditors consider whether to resign.

The auditors' statement on the Summary Financial Statement

24 Following the introduction of the Regulations the Government has amended the Companies (Summary Financial Statement) Regulations 1995[5] to expand the disclosure required in a Summary Financial Statement in relation to directors' remuneration.

25 Certain of the companies which are permitted under section 251 of the Act to produce a Summary Financial Statement will fall within the category of companies required to produce a Directors' Remuneration Report (ie quoted companies). Such companies that prepare summarised financial statements will be required to include either the whole, or a summary, of certain information concerning directors' remuneration contained in the notes to the financial statements and in the Directors' Remuneration Report.

26 The relevant information is the aggregate amount of directors' emoluments (from the notes to the company's financial statements)[6], a statement of the company's policy on directors' remuneration for the next following financial year and the performance graph (the last two items are required by the Regulations but are not required to be audited).

27 These requirements apply to companies and groups, whether or not they are banking or insurance companies and groups.

28 A revised illustrative example of the 'Auditors' Statement on the Summary Financial Statement' reflecting the requirements of the amended Companies (Summary Financial Statement) Regulations is set out as Appendix 3 to this Bulletin. In Appendix 3 the changes that need to be made to the example Statement on the summary financial statement illustrated in Appendix 5 to Bulletin 2001/2 are shown as marked up text.

Superseded guidance

29 With the publication of this Bulletin the following guidance issued by the APB is withdrawn:
- Bulletin 1999/5 – Appendix 3
- Bulletin 2001/2 – Appendices 1 and 5

---

[5] These amendments are set out in Statutory Instrument 2002 No. 1780 which can be downloaded from http/www.legislation.hmso.gov.uk/si/si2002/20021780.htm.

[6] This is a summary of all the information required by paragraph 1(1) of Part I to Schedule 6 to the Act.

[Bulletin 2002/3]
Guidance for reporting accountants of stakeholder pension schemes in the United Kingdom

(Issued November 2002)

Contents

	Paragraphs
Introduction	1 - 12
Trustees' or managers' declarations	13
Reporting Accountants' procedures	14 - 23
Reporting Accountants' reports	24 - 25
Reporting to the regulators	26 - 29
Letters of comment	30 - 35

Appendix 1: Example report of the Reporting Accountants to the Trustees or Managers of a stakeholder pension scheme

Appendix 2: Example paragraphs for a Letter of Engagement

Appendix 3: Regulation 12 of the Stakeholder Pension Schemes Regulations 2000 (As amended)

Introduction

1 The introduction of Stakeholder pensions was first announced in 1999. Registered stakeholder schemes were permitted to collect premiums from new members from April 2001.

2 Stakeholder pension schemes can be set up by trustees (trust schemes) or can be established by managers (contract schemes). The Occupational Pensions Regulatory Authority (Opra) has responsibility for maintaining the register of stakeholder pension schemes, and for the governance of schemes. Under the regulations Opra cannot register, and must de-register, stakeholder schemes if they fail to meet the conditions for being a stakeholder scheme set out in legislation. The Financial Services Authority (FSA) has responsibility for regulating the sales and marketing of stakeholder pensions, and is also responsible for authorising and supervising the firms acting as stakeholder managers as well as firms involved in managing the funds invested in stakeholder schemes.

3 Bulletin 2002/3 has been issued by the APB to provide guidance for reporting accountants in relation to the requirements placed upon them in connection with stakeholder pension schemes. It does not constitute guidance from Opra or the FSA; however the APB acknowledges the advice and assistance provided by Opra and the FSA during the development of the Bulletin.

4 The principal legislation regulating Stakeholder pensions is The Welfare Reform and Pensions Act 1999 ('the Act') and The Stakeholder Pension Schemes Regulations 2000[1] (as amended) ('the Regulations'). The relevant parts of the Regulations came into force on 1 October 2000 but have been subject to amending regulations issued in 2001 and 2002.

5 Regulation 12(2)(a) requires the trustees or manager to make an annual declaration[2]; containing various statements. Regulation 12(5)(a) requires a statement that in the opinion of the trustees or manager there are systems and controls in place which provide reasonable assurance that:

   (i) Regulations 13 and 14[3] of the regulations have been complied with in relation to the scheme;
   (ii) transactions for the purposes of the scheme in securities, property or other assets have occurred at a fair market value;
   (iii) the value of members' rights has been determined in accordance with the provisions in the instruments establishing the scheme; and
   (iv) adequate records have been maintained for the purposes of providing to members the statement required by Regulation 18(2)[4] of the regulations.

6 Regulation 12(5)(b) requires the trustees or manager to provide a statement describing the process that has been undertaken in order to arrive at the opinion expressed in the statement required by Regulation 12(5)(a).

---

[1] *SI 2000 no.1403.*

[2] *Regulation 12 of The Stakeholder Pension Schemes Regulations 2000, as amended by Regulation 4 of the Stakeholder Pension Schemes (Amendment No. 2) Regulations 2002, is reproduced in full in Appendix 3 of this Bulletin.*

[3] *These regulations impose limits on the amount of charges and deductions which may be made by a stakeholder pension scheme and on the manner in which charges may be made by such a scheme.*

[4] *This regulation requires a stakeholder pension scheme to provide an annual benefit statement to each member.*

Regulations 12(5)(c) and (d) require the trustees or manager also to provide statements concerning compliance with the conditions in section 1(1) of the Act, and explaining the requirements of Regulations 13,14 and 18(2). Reporting accountants are not required to review these statements.

Regulation 12(6) requires the trustees or manager to provide the reporting accountant with documentation to demonstrate that the process described in the statement in accordance with Regulation 12(5)(b) has taken place.

Regulation 12(2)(b) requires that the trustees or manager shall obtain from a reporting accountant[5] statements made in accordance with Regulation 12(7) that

(i) the reporting accountant has been provided with documentation as required by Regulation 12(6); and
(ii) nothing has come to the attention of the reporting accountant that is inconsistent with the statement made in accordance with Regulation 12(5)(b), or

so far as the reporting accountant is unable to provide such statements, an explanation as to why he is unable to do so.

In this connection, reporting accountants are required to consider whether the documentation supports the trustees' or managers' description of the process made in accordance with Regulation 12(5)(b), and whether anything is inconsistent with that description. However, the reporting accountants are not required to consider whether the trustees' or managers' description of the process covers all relevant risks and controls, or to reach a conclusion on the adequacy of the process or on the effectiveness of the controls.

The trustees or managers are required by the Regulations to annex the reporting accountants' report to their declaration, and shall make the whole document available to members and beneficiaries of the scheme on request.

It is a condition of a scheme being a stakeholder pension scheme that the requirements of the Regulations are complied with. Opra, as the relevant regulator, expects to receive copies of the annual declarations made by the trustees or managers, together with the reporting accountants' report. As discussed in paragraph 30 of this Bulletin, Opra also expects to receive from scheme trustees or managers copies of reporting accountants' letters of comment (or, where appropriate, written confirmations that no letters of comment are to be issued) which have been submitted to them. This information will assist Opra in meeting its regulatory responsibilities, and it has indicated that it is likely to pay particular attention to a scheme where the declaration or report is qualified or where material weaknesses in internal control come to its attention.

Under normal circumstances both the declarations by the trustees or managers and the reporting accountants' reports are due 6 months after the end of the scheme accounting period. In respect of scheme accounting periods ending on or before 30

---

[5] *Regulation 11 defines a reporting accountant as follows:*
"A person is eligible for appointment as a reporting accountant only if he is eligible (but subject to paragraph 10) under section 25 of the Companies Act 1989 for appointment as a company auditor" (Paragraph 10 states that a person is not eligible for appointment as a company auditor if section 34 of the 1989 Act applies to him (individuals retaining only authorisation granted by the Board of Trade to audit an unquoted company)). Before accepting appointment, reporting accountants of stakeholder pension schemes also consider the ethical guidance issued by the accountancy bodies.

September 2002, however, there is a transitional provision[6] to the effect that the declarations and reports do not need to be completed until 31 December 2002.

Trustees' or managers' declarations

13 As described above, the trustees or managers are required to make statements to the effect that systems and controls provide reasonable assurance that specified aspects of the Regulations have been complied with and to describe the process that has been undertaken to make such statements. Guidance for trustees and managers to assist them in fulfilling these responsibilities has been issued by the Pensions Research Accountants Group (PRAG)[7]. The guidance has been prepared in consultation with both Opra and the Association of British Insurers (ABI).

Reporting Accountants' procedures

14 Regulation 11 sets out the process to be followed for the appointment and resignation of the reporting accountant. The Regulation requires in particular that reporting accountants acknowledge in writing within one month their receipt of the notice of appointment, and confirm that they will notify the trustees or managers of any conflict of interest to which they are subject in relation to the scheme immediately they become aware of its existence. Reporting accountants are also required, on resignation, to serve on the trustees or managers a written notice containing a statement specifying any circumstances connected with the resignation which in their opinion significantly affect the interests of the members or beneficiaries of the scheme, or a declaration that they know of no such circumstances.

15 The objective of the reporting accountants' review in accordance with Regulation 12 is to obtain evidence to support an assessment of whether the trustees' or managers' description of the process, undertaken to support the statements required by Regulation 12(5)(a), is supported by the documentation prepared by or for them and appropriately reflects that process. Before commencing their review procedures, reporting accountants:

(a) plan the work to be undertaken in relation to the declaration by the trustees or managers so as to perform that work in an effective manner;
(b) familiarise themselves with the Stakeholder Pensions Regulations, particularly those sections governing the preparation of the trustees' or managers' declaration;
(c) understand the structure and management of the scheme and its processing arrangements, including those that are outsourced;
(d) ensure that they comply with the independence guidance issued by their relevant professional bodies and discuss, where appropriate, with the trustees or managers any relationships which may affect the reporting accountants' independence or their objectivity and any related safeguards that are in place; and
(e) agree the terms of the engagement with the trustees or managers and record them in writing. Example paragraphs for a letter of engagement are set out in Appendix 2 of this Bulletin.

[6] *SI 2002 no. 1480.*

[7] *"Making the Annual Declaration – A Guide for Trustees and Managers of Stakeholder Pension Schemes". Copies of this guidance may be obtained from PRAG's website:www.prag.org.uk.*

Appropriate evidence to support the reporting accountants' assessment will usually be obtained by performing the following procedures: 16

(a) obtaining through enquiry of appropriate individuals an understanding both of the framework of controls relevant to the legislation referred to in Regulation 12(5)(a), and the process established by the trustees or managers for the review of the effectiveness of those controls, to enable them to arrive at their opinion and sign the declaration;
(b) enquiring of the trustees or managers whether they are familiar with, and have considered the applicability to their scheme of relevant guidance issued to trustees and managers by PRAG[8] and Opra[9] and, if necessary, recommending that they should so consider it;
(c) reviewing relevant minutes of the meetings of the trustees or managers, and of other committees (for example audit and risk management committees) together with supporting papers presented at those meetings;
(d) enquiring of the trustees or managers whether they are aware of any instances of non-compliance with the legislation referred to in Regulation 12(5)(a);
(e) reviewing any relevant correspondence with regulators, particularly Opra and the FSA;
(f) reviewing the documentation prepared by, or for, the trustees or managers, including any documentation relating to functions outsourced to a third party, to ascertain that it demonstrates that the process described in the statement, made in accordance with Regulation 12(5)(b), has taken place;
(g) enquiring of the audit engagement partner whether any relevant matters have come to his attention during the audit work (see paragraph 19 below); and
(h) attending meetings at which the declaration, including the statement concerning the review process, is considered and approved for signature.

Reporting accountants also: 17

(a) record in their working papers
   – details of the engagement planning,
   – the nature, timing and extent of the procedures performed in relation to their report, and the conclusions drawn; and
   – their reasoning and conclusions on all significant matters which require the exercise of judgment;
(b) consider the matters which have come to their attention while performing the procedures on the declaration and whether they should result in a qualification to their statement or be included in a letter of comment to the trustees or managers; and
(c) take steps to ensure that any delegated work is directed, supervised and reviewed in a manner which provides reasonable assurance that such work is performed competently.

The reporting accountants may request the trustees or managers to provide written confirmation of oral representations made during the course of the review. 18

In most cases reporting accountants of stakeholder pension schemes will also be the appointed auditors of the managing entity (in the case of contract schemes), or of the 19

---

[8] In addition to the PRAG guidance referred to in paragraph 13, PRAG has also issued non-binding guidance on possible control procedures entitled "Stakeholder pension schemes – a controls checklist". This is also available on PRAG's website.

[9] As at the date of issue of this Bulletin, Opra has published an exposure draft of ON 11 – "Stakeholder pension scheme charges". Copies may be obtained from Opra's website – www.opra.gov.uk. ON 6 – "The right to report problems to Opra" and ON 8 – "Direct payment arrangements by employers", may also be relevant to a stakeholder pension scheme.

schemes managed by the trustees (in the case of trust schemes). Whilst the reporting accountants' assignment is entirely separate from the audit engagement, the partner in charge of the reporting accountants' work nevertheless requests the audit engagement partner to advise him of any breaches of the requirements specified in Regulation 12(5)(a) of which the audit engagement partner has become aware as a result of the audit.

20　Reporting accountants are not required to consider whether the trustees' or managers' description of the process made in accordance with Regulation 12(5)(b) covers all relevant risks and controls, or to reach a conclusion on the adequacy of the process or on the effectiveness of the controls. However they do consider:

- whether they have been provided with documentation which supports the trustees' or managers' description of the process, and
- whether they have become aware of matters which are inconsistent with the description of the process,

and, if necessary, they qualify their statement.

21　Reporting accountants are not required to obtain evidence concerning the specific requirements underlying Regulation 12(5)(a) – for example that the value of members' rights has been determined in accordance with the provisions establishing the scheme. However, if during their review of the trustees' or managers' documentation reporting accountants identify facts or circumstances which suggest that:

- the trustees or managers may not be justified in their belief that their systems and controls provide reasonable assurance to enable them to make the statement required by Regulation 12(5)(a), or
- because of apparent breaches of the legislation or other matters, the proposed statement required by Regulation 12(5)(a) is not supportable,

they discuss their concerns with the trustees or managers as soon as is practicable.

22　If as a result of the discussion the reporting accountants remain of the view that significant internal control weaknesses or other matters exist which, in their opinion, call into question the credibility of the statement made by the trustees or managers in accordance with Regulation 12(5)(a), they consider qualifying the statement in their report in respect of these matters.

23　Under normal circumstances reporting accountants qualify their report in respect of apparent undisclosed breaches of the legislation referred to in Regulation 12(5)(a) of which they become aware. In deciding whether to qualify their report in respect of such breaches, reporting accountants consider their significance. The materiality of the breach in monetary terms would not be relevant to a consideration of its significance. However, where breaches have occurred which were identified by the scheme's own control systems, which were not indicative of a systemic problem, and which were corrected subsequently such that there was no monetary impact on any member or beneficiary of the scheme, then they are unlikely to be significant.

Reporting Accountants' reports

24　Reporting accountants' reports on declarations normally include the following matters:

- a title identifying the persons to whom the report is addressed (which will normally be the trustees or managers of the scheme);

- an introductory paragraph identifying the Regulations which are covered by the report;
- separate sections, appropriately headed, dealing with
    - respective responsibilities of the trustees or managers and the reporting accountants, and
    - the basis of the reporting accountants' statement, including (where appropriate) a reference to compliance with the guidance in this Bulletin;
- the reporting accountants' statement on the matters required by the Regulations;
- the signature of the reporting accountants; and
- the date of the reporting accountants' report.

In addition, reporting accountants consider including in their report wording to the effect that they owe no duty of care to individual beneficiaries of the scheme. Appendix 1 of this Bulletin sets out an illustrative example of a reporting accountants' report on the declaration. This example wording may need to be tailored to reflect particular circumstances.

As indicated in paragraphs 20-23 above, reporting accountants qualify the statement in their report if: 25

- they have not been provided with documentation that supports the trustees' or managers' description of the process, or
- they are aware of matters that are inconsistent with the trustees' or managers' description of the process, made in accordance with Regulation 12(5)(b), or
- they are aware of matters which call into question the credibility of the statement made by the trustees or managers in accordance with Regulation 12(5)(a). These matters are likely to be connected with significant internal control weaknesses, or with breaches of the legislation referred to in Regulation 12(5)(a).

Reporting to the regulators

Reporting accountants of trust schemes have a right to report to Opra[10] as described in Opra Note (ON) 6 : 'Pensions Act 1995 – the right to report problems to Opra'. ON 6 emphasises that reporting to Opra on a voluntary basis does not breach any normal duties of confidentiality, providing that the person or firm has been appropriately appointed by the trustees and there is reasonable cause to believe that a breach of regulations has occurred which is likely to be of material significance to Opra. Reporting accountants bear in mind that, if they or their firm are also the scheme auditors of a scheme established under trust, they have a legal duty under Section 48(1) of the Pensions Act 1995 to report to Opra when they have reasonable cause to believe that a breach of the regulations has occurred which is likely to be of material significance to the regulator.   26

In the case of contract schemes, reporting accountants do not have a similar right to report matters of which they become aware to Opra. Where, in the course of their work, reporting accountants become aware of matters which appear to be of material significance to the regulator, they discuss these with the managers with a view to the managers making a report to Opra. If, following these discussions the managers do not make an appropriate report to Opra in circumstances where it appears that they should, the reporting accountants consider taking legal advice.   27

---

[10] Further guidance on reporting to Opra is set out in Bulletin 2000/2 – Supplementary guidance for auditors of occupational pension schemes in the United Kingdom.

28 Reporting accountants of contract schemes who are also the auditors of the managing entity consider whether they have a duty to report matters of material significance, of which they become aware in their capacity of auditors of the managing entity, to the FSA[11] under the FSMA[12] 2000 (Communications by Auditors) Regulations 2001. This is because there may be situations where it is not clear whether information coming to the attention of the reporting accountants is received in that capacity or in their other role as auditors. Appendix 2 to SAS 620 provides guidance as to how information obtained in non-audit work may be relevant to the auditors in the planning and conduct of the audit and the steps that need to be taken to ensure the communication of information that is relevant to the audit.

29 In general, if reporting accountants are in any doubt as to whether a report should be made to the regulator or not, they consider taking legal advice.

Letters of comment

30 Opra expects trustees or managers to include a copy of any letter of comment from the reporting accountants with their annual declaration and the reporting accountants' report when these are submitted to it.

31 As indicated in paragraph 25 above, if the reporting accountants consider that significant weaknesses in internal control or other matters exist which call into question whether the trustees' or managers' statements made in accordance with Regulations 12(5)(a) and (b) are justified, they qualify the statement in their report.

32 If, however, the reporting accountants are of the opinion that control weaknesses or other matters exist, but these do not affect the credibility of the statement made by the trustees or managers in accordance with Regulation 12(5)(a), they report them in a letter of comment to the trustees or managers.

33 Where no significant weaknesses in the scheme's internal control systems come to their attention during the review, the reporting accountants advise the trustees or managers in writing that no letter of comment is to be issued.

34 Because letters of comment issued by reporting accountants will be submitted to Opra, trustees or managers will normally wish to have the opportunity of responding in writing to the comments made. Reporting accountants agree with the trustees or managers the way in which their responses are to be presented. These discussions should not, however, be allowed to cause an unreasonable delay in submitting the letter of comment.

35 Reporting accountants of contract schemes bear in mind that they have no right to report directly to Opra as they have a duty of confidentiality to the scheme managers. Should Opra wish to discuss the contents of a letter of comment it should communicate with the managers in the first instance. In some circumstances Opra may also wish to discuss the letter of comment with the reporting accountants: in this case Opra agrees with the managers and the reporting accountants beforehand the basis upon which these discussions are to be held.

---

[11] *Further guidance on reporting to the FSA is set out in Bulletin 2001/6 – Supplementary guidance for auditors of insurers in the United Kingdom following 'N2'.*

[12] *The Financial Services and Markets Act.*

Appendix 1 – Example report of the reporting accountants to the trustees or managers of a stakeholder pension scheme

The Trustees/Managers of the XYZ pension scheme,
Address.

XYZ STAKEHOLDER PENSION SCHEME

We report in accordance with the requirements of Regulation 12(7) of the Stakeholder Pension Schemes Regulations 2000 (as amended) (the Regulations), concerning the annual declaration by the trustees/managers of the XYZ pension scheme. The declaration is made in respect of the period of 12 months ended on xxxx.

Respective responsibilities of the trustees/managers and the reporting accountant

In accordance with Regulation 12(2)(a) the trustees/managers are responsible for the preparation of a declaration, which contains a statement describing the process that the trustees/ managers have undertaken, in order to arrive at their opinion as to whether systems and controls are in place which provide reasonable assurance that specified regulations in relation to stakeholder pensions have been complied with.

It is our responsibility to consider whether documentation has been provided to us to support the trustees'/managers' description of the process and to report if this is not the case. We also report if anything has come to our attention that is inconsistent with the description of the process.

We are not required to consider whether the trustees'/managers' description of the process made in accordance with Regulation 12(5)(b) covers all relevant risks and controls, or to reach a conclusion on the adequacy of the process or on the effectiveness of the controls or to undertake any work in this regard.

(Reporting accountants consider including wording to the effect that they owe no duty of care to individual beneficiaries of the scheme)

Basis of reporting accountant's statement

We conducted our work in accordance with Bulletin 2002/3 'Guidance for reporting accountants of stakeholder pension schemes in the United Kingdom' issued by the Auditing Practices Board. The work performed involved making enquiries of management and staff and examination of the documentary evidence supporting the existence of the process.

Statement

(Other than the Exception set out below)[13] In accordance with Regulation 12(7) we report that in our opinion:

- we have been provided by the trustees/managers with documentation, which is required by Regulation 12(6) to demonstrate that the process described in the trustees'/managers' statement has taken place; and

[13] *In cases where there are no exceptions, the wording in italics would be omitted.*

- nothing has come to our attention that is inconsistent with the trustees'/ managers' description of the process.

(Exception

The trustees'/managers' description concerning ... does not appropriately reflect our understanding of the process undertaken by you because......")

Reporting accountants   Address
Date

Appendix 2 – Example paragraphs for a letter of engagement

The purpose of this letter is to set out the basis on which, in accordance with the requirements of Regulation 12(7) of the Stakeholder Pension Schemes Regulations 2000 (as amended), we are to act as the Reporting Accountant of the [scheme] ("the Scheme") and the respective areas of responsibility of the trustees/managers and of ourselves.

Duties of trustees/managers

As the trustees/managers of [stakeholder provider] you are responsible for the design, implementation and maintenance of control procedures that provide adequate levels of protection for Members' assets and records and to ensure that the Scheme has complied with the provisions of the Stakeholder Pension Schemes Regulations 2000 as amended ("the Regulations").

Under Regulation 12(2) of the Regulations you are required to make a declaration in writing containing the statements set out in Regulation 12(5), to provide us with documentation to demonstrate the process you have described, and obtain from us the statements specified in Regulation 12(7). It is our responsibility to examine the documentation supporting the statements required in the declaration and report our conclusion to you.

Scope of work

In accordance with Regulation 12(7) we are required to report to you that:

(i) we have been provided with documentation as required by Regulation 12(6); and
(ii) nothing has come to our attention that is inconsistent with the statement made by you in accordance with Regulation 12(5)(b), or

so far as we are unable to provide such statements, an explanation as to why we are unable to do so.

The work we shall perform will be conducted in accordance with the framework set out in the Bulletin 2002/3 – 'Guidance for reporting accountants of stakeholder pension schemes in the United Kingdom', issued by the Auditing Practices Board. Our work will include enquiries of management and staff and examination of the documentary evidence supporting the existence of the processes. Our work will be planned in advance. In developing our plan we shall liaise with you to ensure that our work is properly coordinated.

We are not required to consider whether the trustees'/managers' description of the process made in accordance with Regulation 12 (5)(b) covers all relevant risks and controls, or to reach a conclusion on the adequacy of the process or the effectiveness of the controls.

Use of our report

Our report will be addressed to you as trustees/managers of [stakeholder provider]. We consent to the disclosure of a copy of the report to the Occupational Pensions Regulatory Authority ("Opra") and to the members and beneficiaries of the Scheme on request on the basis that we will not accept any liability/responsibility to those parties or to any other party to whom our report is shown or into whose hands it may come.

You agree not to use our report, or make references to it, in material disseminated to the general public without our express written permission. In any cases where marketing literature is prepared and where you may wish to refer either to us or our report, you will seek our consent to those references in advance. We reserve the right to refuse in either of the above cases.

Limitations of work

Control procedures are subject to inherent limitations and, accordingly, errors or irregularities may occur and not be detected. Such procedures cannot guarantee protection against fraudulent collusion, especially on the part of those holding positions of authority or trust. Furthermore, our statements will be based on historical information, and the projection of any information or conclusions contained in our statements or your declaration to any future periods is subject to the risk that changes in procedures or circumstances may alter their validity.

Reports to management

Our work is restricted to an examination of the documents provided and the statements describing the process undertaken by management in order to give them reasonable assurance that the rules identified under Regulation 12(5)(a) had been complied with. Therefore our work is not designed to identify significant weaknesses in the Scheme's system of internal controls. However, we shall report to management in writing in a letter of comment any significant weaknesses in the Scheme's system of internal controls which come to our notice during the course of our work, and that we consider should be brought to management's attention. Where no such matters have come to our attention we shall confirm this to you in writing.

Our examination is only performed to the extent required to express an opinion on these statements, and therefore our comments on these systems will not necessarily address all possible improvements which might be suggested as a result of a more extensive special examination.

We consent to you making such reports available to Opra on the basis that we will not accept any liability/responsibility to that party or to any other parties.

No such report may be provided to any other third parties without our prior written consent. Such consent will be granted only on the basis that such reports are not prepared with the interests of anyone other than the trustees/managers in mind and that we accept no duty or responsibility to any other party. We reserve the right to withhold our consent.

Appendix 3 – Regulation 12 of the stakeholder pension schemes regulations 2000 (as amended by the stakeholder pension schemes (amendment no.2) regulations 2002)

Requirement for declaration by trustees or manager

12.—(1) For the purposes of section 1(1)(b), it shall be a condition of a scheme being a stakeholder pension scheme that the requirements of this regulation are complied with.

(2) Subject to paragraph (11), the trustees or manager of the scheme shall, no later than the end of 6 months beginning with each reporting date—

(a) make a declaration in writing signed by the trustees or manager containing the statements set out in paragraph (5) in relation to the reporting period or, in so far as they are unable to make those statements containing a statement explaining why they are unable to do so; and

(b) obtain from the reporting accountant appointed by virtue of regulation 11 the statement specified in paragraph (7) or, in so far as the reporting accountant is unable to make that statement, a statement from the reporting accountant explaining why he is unable to do so.

(3) Subject to paragraph (10), in this regulation reporting date means—

(a) in the case of the first reporting date, a date chosen by the trustees or manager that is no later than the last day of the period of 12 months beginning with the date on which the scheme is registered under section 2 of the Act; and

(b) in the case of each subsequent reporting date, a date chosen by the trustees or manager that is no later than the last day of the period of 12 months beginning with the date immediately following the previous reporting date.

(4) Subject to paragraph (10), in this regulation reporting period means—

(a) in the case of the first reporting period, the period beginning with the date of registration of the scheme under section 2 of the Act and ending on and including the first reporting date;

(b) in the case of subsequent reporting periods, the period beginning on the date immediately following the previous reporting date and ending on and including the reporting date.

(5) The statements specified in paragraph (2)(a) shall be—

(a) a statement that in the opinion of the trustees or manager there are systems and controls in place which provide reasonable assurance that —
 (i) regulations 13 and 14 have been complied with in relation to the scheme;
 (ii) transactions for the purposes of the scheme in securities, property or other assets have occurred at a fair market value;
 (iii) the value of members' rights has been determined in accordance with the provisions in the instruments establishing the scheme; and

(iv) adequate records have been maintained for the purposes of providing to members the statement required by regulation 18(2);
(b) a statement describing the process that the trustees or manager have or has undertaken in order to arrive at the opinion expressed in the statement described in paragraph (5)(a);
(c) a statement that in the opinion of the trustees or manager there are systems and controls in place which provide reasonable assurance that the scheme has complied with the conditions in section 1(1) of the Act, apart from those conditions that are covered by the statement in paragraph (5)(a); and
(d) a statement which explains that—
  (i) regulations 13 and 14 impose limits on the amount of charges and deductions which may be made by a stakeholder pension scheme and on the manner in which charges may be made by such a scheme; and
  (ii) regulation 18(2) requires a stakeholder pension scheme to provide an annual benefit statement to each member.

(6) The trustees or manager shall provide the reporting accountant with documentation to demonstrate that the process described in the statement in paragraph (5)(b) has taken place.

(7) The statement specified in paragraph (2)(b) shall be a statement that—

(a) the reporting accountant has been provided with documentation as required by paragraph (6); and
(b) nothing has come to the attention of the reporting accountant that is inconsistent with the statement made in paragraph (5)(b).

(8) The trustees or manager shall make available to members and beneficiaries of the scheme on request the declaration made by the trustees or manager and the statement obtained from the reporting accountant in accordance with paragraph (2).

(9) If the statement to be obtained by the trustees or manager under paragraph (2)(b) is obtained from the reporting accountant acting as such while ineligible in contravention of regulation 11(7A)(a)—

(a) the trustees or manager shall not be regarded as having complied with paragraph (2)(b); and
(b) for the purposes of paragraph (8), the statement from the reporting accountant shall not be regarded as obtained in accordance with paragraph (2)(b).

(10) Where a scheme is registered under section 2 of the Act on or before 6th April 2001—

(a) the first reporting date shall be 5th April 2002; and
(b) the first reporting period shall be the period commencing on and including 6th April 2001 and ending on and including 5th April 2002.

(11) Where the reporting date is on or before 30th September 2002 the trustees or manager of the scheme shall make the declaration specified in paragraph (2)(a) and obtain the statement specified in paragraph (2)(b) from the reporting accountant—

(a) on or before 31st December 2002; or
(b) by the end of 6 months beginning with the reporting date,

whichever is later.

[Bulletin 2003/1]
Corporate governance: requirements of public sector auditors (central government)

(Issued November 2003)

Contents

	Paragraphs
Section 1: Introduction	1 - 2
Purpose of this Bulletin	3 - 4
Structure of this Bulletin	5 - 7
Section 2: Corporate Governance Framework	
The Main Types of Central Government Body	8
Application of Corporate Governance Principles	9 - 14
Statement on Internal Control	15 - 19
Audit Committees	20 - 21
Section 3: Auditors' Responsibilities	
Statements of Auditors' Responsibilities	22 - 26
The Auditors' Review of the Statement on Internal Control	27 - 38
Significant Internal Control Issues	39 - 44
Failure to Conduct a Review	45
Coverage of Effectiveness Review	46
Reporting by Exception	47 - 49
Audit Committees	50 - 52

Appendix 1: Respective Responsibilities of the Accounting Officer and the Auditor

Appendix 2: Example Draft Paragraphs for Inclusion in a Letter of Understanding/ Engagement

Glossary of Terms

List of References

Section 1: Introduction

The corporate governance framework that applies to listed companies in the private sector is well developed. The structures and processes for decision making and accountability, control systems and behaviour at the top of organisations are equally important issues for public sector organisations. Not surprisingly, therefore, over the last decade corporate governance has also become an increasingly significant issue for the public sector.

Unlike listed companies, which are subject to the same broad framework of company law, public sector bodies do not operate within a common legislative framework. Consequently different models of governance have evolved within the public sector in response to different sets of accountabilities. Hence the need for more than one Bulletin covering the requirements of external auditors in the public sector.

Purpose of this Bulletin

The APB has produced this Bulletin to:

- set out the corporate governance arrangements that apply in the central government sector; and
- provide guidance to central government auditors on their review and reporting responsibilities in relation to the corporate governance disclosures central government bodies are required to make.

Notwithstanding the differences in accountabilities, central government has followed the general principle that best practice in the private sector should be reflected to the extent that it is meaningful and appropriate in the central government context. The corporate governance requirements placed on central government entities therefore reflect the Treasury's[1] consideration of how the Combined Code[2] and the Turnbull Report[3] can be adapted to the sector.

Structure of this Bulletin

As the corporate governance framework within the public sector evolves, the APB is issuing guidance to cover other areas of the sector. Bulletin 2003/2 "Corporate Governance: Requirements of Public Sector Auditors (National Health Service Bodies)" was issued in November 2003. Guidance for other major public sector areas will be considered in due course.

The principles outlined in each part of this Bulletin apply equally in all parts of the United Kingdom. Differences in organisational structure, governance requirements

---

[1] In Scotland similar requirements are set by the Scottish Executive, and by the Department of Finance and Personnel in Northern Ireland.

[2] The corporate governance requirements placed on listed companies are set out in the 'Combined Code' which was published by the Committee on Corporate Governance in June 1998. The Combined Code has been appended to the Listing Rules of the Financial Services Authority and consolidates the recommendations of the earlier Cadbury, Greenbury and Hampel reports on private sector corporate governance issues. The Financial Reporting Council has recently issued a revised Code which comes into effect for reporting years beginning on or after 1 November 2003.

[3] The report of the Internal Control Working Party of the ICAEW (commonly referred to as The Turnbull Report) was published in September 1999.

and terminology applying in Scotland, Wales and Northern Ireland are noted where appropriate.

7 Section 2 of this Bulletin covers the corporate governance framework applying to central government bodies in the UK. Section 3 sets out the auditors' responsibilities in relation to the corporate governance disclosures central government bodies are required to make.

Section 2: Corporate governance framework

The Main Types of Central Government Body

8 The central government sector consists of the following main types of entity:

- government departments;
- executive agencies;
- trading funds;
- bodies not administered as government departments but which are subject to Ministerial and department control, for example non-departmental public bodies (NDPBs)[4]; and
- the Scottish Executive, the National Assembly for Wales, the Northern Ireland Executive, their executive agencies and sponsored / related public bodies.

Certain other bodies, while not formally classified as non-departmental bodies, are dependent upon grant or grant-in-aid. In general such bodies are treated as analogous to non-departmental public bodies.

Application of Corporate Governance Principles to the Central Government Sector

9 Whilst aspects of the Combined Code and the general thrust of the Turnbull recommendations are wholly relevant to central government, the environment in which central government operates is significantly different in some key respects from that of listed companies to which the recommendations were addressed. Most significantly, such differences include the legislative role of Parliaments/devolved government authorities and the personal responsibilities of Accounting Officers[5] and their relationship with Ministers.

10 Accounting Officers for government departments and the National Assembly for Wales are appointed by the Treasury. In Northern Ireland, departmental Accounting Officers are appointed by the Department of Finance and Personnel. In Scotland departmental Accountable Officers are appointed by the senior full time official of the Scottish Executive who is designated under statute as the Principal Accountable Officer. The role and duties of a departmental Accounting Officer are set out in the Treasury Memorandum *The Responsibilities of an Accounting Officer*, which is sent

---

[4] *Assembly Sponsored Public Bodies in Wales (ASPBs)*.

[5] *In Scotland the Public Finance and Accountability (Scotland) Act 2000 uses the term 'Accountable Officer' as an equivalent of the Accounting Officer.*

to every new Accounting Officer on appointment[6]. The text of this Memorandum is reproduced in Government Accounting (Chapter 4, Annex 1)[7]. Accounting Officers have a personal responsibility for, amongst other things, signing the financial statements, ensuring that proper financial procedures are followed and accounting records maintained, ensuring that public funds and assets are properly managed and safeguarded, and making provision for internal audit.

Accounting Officers for executive agencies are either appointed by the Treasury[8], where the agency is not funded as part of a government department, or by the Accounting Officer of the parent department where the agency is funded as part of a government department. In Scotland Accountable Officers for executive agencies are appointed by the Principal Accountable Officer of the Scottish Executive. The Chief Executive of an NDPB is normally designated as the Accounting Officer by the Accounting Officer of the sponsoring department. In Wales the National Assembly's Principal Accounting Officer designates the Chief Executives of Assembly Sponsored Public Bodies (ASPBs) as Accounting Officers. In these circumstances the departmental Accounting Officer should write to the senior official making clear their responsibilities and referring to the separate version of the Accounting Officer Memorandum dealing with the responsibilities of the Accounting Officer of an NDPB (chapter 8 of Government Accounting refers). The responsibilities of executive agency and NDPB Accounting Officers for the stewardship of public funds are similar to those of a departmental Accounting Officer.

11

Accounting Officers are responsible for the overall organisation, management and staffing of their departments. To assist in the discharge of these duties they should appoint a Principal Finance Officer (PFO)[9]. The PFO is a senior individual who is directly responsible to the Accounting Officer for financial and related matters. In most executive agencies and NDPBs a similar function is carried out by the Finance Director, where the Finance Director is responsible to the Chief Executive.

12

The private sector unitary Board model that combines both non-executive (who have a strategic and monitoring function) and executive directors (who have management functions) is not generally found in the central government sector. In the central government sector powers are separated between the legislature (Parliament) and the Crown (Ministers and civil servants). The Accounting Officer has a unique position in central government. Directors of a company have collective responsibility, but in contrast, in central government departments and agencies, the Accounting Officer has full responsibility, under the Minister, for the organisation and management of the entity. In the case of executive NDPBs, the Chief Executive, whilst responsible to the Board for the day to day management of the body, also has personal

13

---

[6] In Scotland the responsibilities of Accountable Officers are set out in a "Memorandum to Accountable Officers from the Principal Accountable Officer" or a "Memorandum to Accountable Officers of Other Public Bodies" both of which are published in the Scottish Public Finance Manual. In Northern Ireland the roles and duties of a departmental Accounting Officer are set out in the Department of Finance and Personnel Memorandum The Responsibilities of an Accounting Officer. For Wales the Treasury have prepared a National Assembly for Wales Accounting Officer's Memorandum.

[7] Government Accounting is issued by the Treasury and is available from the Stationery Office. Its starting point is the arrangements for accounting to Parliament for public funds and the requirements for Parliamentary and Treasury approval for expenditure. Whilst it also provides some guidance on accounting systems and procedures, guidance on accounting principles is provided elsewhere, most notably in the Treasury's Resource Accounting Manual.

[8] In Northern Ireland, by the Department of Finance and Personnel.

[9] From December 2003 the Treasury have decided that PFOs will be referred to as Departmental Finance Directors.

responsibility as Accounting Officer for ensuring compliance with Parliamentary requirements in the control of expenditure and any requirements imposed by the sponsor department.

14 An overview of the key corporate governance requirements placed on central government entities, including the well established governance framework as embodied in the personal responsibilities of an Accounting Officer, is set out in the table below. The table also highlights the related requirements of the auditors and the paragraphs of this Bulletin dealing with the particular requirements.

Subject	Key Requirements	Auditors' Responsibilities	Relevant paragraphs in this Bulletin
Corporate governance framework	Embodied in Accounting Officer's personal responsibilities (as set out in Government Accounting Chapter 4 and Government Accounting Northern Ireland Chapter 6) for: • ensuring that effective management systems appropriate for the achievement of the organisation's objectives including financial monitoring and control systems have been put in place. • keeping proper accounts. • ensuring internal audit is established and organised in accordance with the Government Internal Audit Standards. • Ensuring the regularity and propriety of public finances.	Required to report to Parliament or the relevant Devolved Government Authority if the Accounting Officer has not kept proper accounting records. Audit opinion required to include specific attestation relating to regularity of the transactions included within the financial statements.	Guidance on the audit of regularity included within APB Practice Note 10: Audit of Financial Statements of Public Sector Entities in the United Kingdom (Revised).

Statement on Internal Control	Required for all central government entities from 2001-02 onwards. Requirements set out in Government Accounting, Chapter 21 'Risk Management and the Statement on Internal Control'. Guidance on developing a strategic approach to risk management contained in 'The Orange Book' – published by HM Treasury January 2001 as 'Management of Risk – A Strategic Overview'.	Review the Statement on Internal Control for the entity's compliance with Treasury requirements. Auditor will report if: • disclosure requirements specified by the Treasury are not met; or • the Statement is misleading or inconsistent with other information that the auditor is aware of.	15-19, 27-49
Audit Committees	Audit committees are not mandatory in central government. However, the Treasury 'strongly encourages' audit committees as best practice in all central government bodies. Guidance on central government audit committees is set out in DAO(Gen) 13/00 and in 'Guidance on Codes of Practice for Board Members' – see List of References for full details. As at the date of issue of this Bulletin, the Treasury has issued an Audit Committee Handbook in draft form	No specific reporting responsibilities. However, the auditor will attend relevant audit committee meetings as a means of gaining evidence for the review of the Statement on Internal Control	20-21, 50-52

Statement on Internal Control

Following their consideration of the Combined Code and the Turnbull Report the Treasury widened the scope of the existing corporate governance disclosures by introducing the requirement for central government entities to:

- maintain a system of internal control, with emphasis on risk management;
- review at least annually the effectiveness of the system; and

- include a Statement on Internal Control (SIC) in the accounts.

16 Central government entities were required to include a SIC in their accounts of the first financial period beginning on or after 1 January 2001. However, the Treasury acknowledged that some entities would take longer to develop all the necessary underpinning risk management and review processes. In these cases the Treasury has set a deadline of 31 March 2004 for implementation of the underpinning processes.

17 The Treasury therefore requires that SICs for the financial year 2003/04 for all central government entities should reflect the establishment of all the required risk management and review processes by the year end at the latest, and SICs for 2004/05 and subsequent years should reflect the operation of all the required processes throughout the year.

18 SICs are required to include the following disclosures:
- acknowledgement of the Accounting Officer's responsibility for ensuring that a sound system of internal control is maintained;
- an explanation that the system of internal control is designed to manage rather than eliminate risk of failure to achieve policies, aims and objectives; it can therefore only provide reasonable and not absolute assurance of effectiveness;
- reference to an ongoing process designed to identify the principal risks to achievement of the entity's policies, aims and objectives, evaluate and manage them and confirmation that the process accords with Treasury guidance (and with guidance issued by devolved government authorities where applicable). A comment is also included on the staff's capacity to manage the risk process;
- confirmation that the above process was in place for the duration of the financial year and remained so up until the date of the approval of the annual report and accounts;
- acknowledgement of the Accounting Officer's responsibility for reviewing the effectiveness of the system of internal control, and describing the process for review;
- for 2003/04 and subsequently, confirmation that the results of the Accounting Officer's review of the effectiveness of internal control has been discussed with the Board, the Audit Committee and, if applicable, the Risk Committee; and
- where appropriate, set out details of actions taken, or proposed, to deal with significant internal control issues.

19 The Treasury's requirements in relation to the corporate governance disclosure requirements, as summarised in paragraphs 14 to 18 above, are set out in Government Accounting, Chapter 21 'Risk Management and the Statement on Internal Control'[10][11].

Audit Committees

20 The purpose of an Audit Committee in the central government sector is to give advice to the Accounting Officer on the adequacy of audit arrangements (internal and external) and on the implications of assurances provided in respect of risk and

---

[10] At the time of issue of this Bulletin Chapter 21 of Government Accounting was scheduled for publication in November 2003. Until this date the requirements were set out in DAO (Gen) 13/00 'Corporate Governance: Statement on Internal Control' issued on 22 December 2000 as revised by DAO (Gen) 09/03 'Statement on Internal Control' issued 29 May 2003.

[11] In Scotland and Northern Ireland the requirements are set out in the Scottish Public Finance Manual and DAO (DFP)s 05/01 and 25/03 respectively.

control in an organisation. The Treasury has set out a number of 'Policy Principles' relating to central government Audit Committees which cover, along with other matters, their composition, membership, meeting frequency and terms of reference[12]. In addition, the Cabinet Office produced earlier guidance on NDPB Audit Committees which covers the same issues as the Treasury's subsequent 'Policy Principles' guidance[13].

Audit Committees are not mandatory in the central government sector. However, the Treasury 'strongly encourages' the establishment of Audit Committees in all central government bodies[14]. Where a body elects not to have an Audit Committee the Treasury expects the circumstances justifying the decision to be clearly identified. For NDPBs the Cabinet Office recommends that all such bodies, unless otherwise agreed with their sponsor department, should set up an Audit Committee as a committee of the board.

Section 3: Auditors' responsibilities

Statements of Auditors' Responsibilities

Auditors have different responsibilities with respect to the various component parts of the annual report and accounts. They are required to 'audit' the financial statements, 'review' the entity's SIC and 'read' all the information in the annual report that is not subject to any other requirement. Auditors read such 'other information' because the credibility of the financial statements and the related auditors' certificate may be undermined by material inconsistencies between the financial statements and the 'other information', or by apparent misstatements within the other information.

In some instances auditors have to report positively the results of their work whereas in other instances the auditors only have to report by exception. The APB is of the view that users of financial statements will find it difficult to understand the scope of the auditors' involvement in the absence of a clear statement of their responsibilities towards the financial statements and the information presented with them.

The key elements of a statement of the auditors' responsibilities relate to the requirements of:

- statute and Auditing Standards (with guidance on the application of Auditing Standards provided by APB Practice Note 10[15]) with respect to the audit of the financial statements;
- the agreement between the Comptroller and Auditor General and the Treasury to review the Statement of Internal Control for compliance with Treasury

---

[12] *Policy Principles for Audit Committees in Central Government – included as Annex C to DAO(Gen) 13/00: Corporate Governance: Statement on Internal Control. As at the date of issue of this Bulletin, the Treasury has also issued an Audit Committee Handbook in draft form. When published this handbook will update and expand on the 'Policy Principles' with the aim of helping Accounting Officers and Boards work out the best audit committee arrangements as well as helping audit committee members reflect on their role and the ways in which they function.*

[13] *Published as Appendix 2 to Guidance on Codes of Practice for Board Members of Public Bodies – Cabinet Office January 1997.*

[14] *The Scottish Executive and the Department of Finance and Personnel in Northern Ireland similarly encourage the establishment of audit committees.*

[15] *APB Practice Note 10: Audit of Financial Statements of Public Sector Entities in the United Kingdom (Revised April 2001).*

disclosure requirements and inconsistencies between the information of which the auditors are aware from their audit work on the financial statements[16]; and
- Statement of Auditing Standards 160 'Other information in documents containing audited financial statements' to read the 'other information' presented with the financial statements.

25 In accordance with SAS 600 'Auditors reports on financial statements' (and the guidance on the application of Auditing Standards in the public sector provided by APB Practice Note 10), a description of the auditors' responsibilities, covering the key elements set out in the above paragraph, should be included within the auditors' certificate on the financial statements. The examples in Appendix 1 illustrate the wording that may be used to explain the auditors' responsibilities. The APB is of the view that a statement of auditors' responsibilities as further described in paragraphs 27 to 29, avoids the need for a separate auditors' report dealing with their review of corporate governance matters.

26 The auditors' responsibilities in relation to their review of the SIC are not designed to provide 'positive assurance'. In view of the limited nature of the review, and in order to avoid the possibility of misunderstandings arising the APB recommends that:

- the auditors' letter of understanding/engagement explains the scope of the auditors' review. Example paragraphs to put in place the content of this Bulletin are set out in Appendix 2; and
- prior to the release of the annual report and accounts the auditors communicate, and discuss, with senior management the findings of their review.

The Auditors' Review of the Statement on Internal Control

27 In accordance with the agreement between the Treasury and the Comptroller and Auditor General the auditors are required to review the SIC[17]. As summarised in Annex 21.2 of Government Accounting (DAO (DFP) 5/01 in Northern Ireland) the nature of the auditors' review of the SIC will follow a similar approach to that set out in the APB's Bulletin 1999/5 dealing with the requirements of auditors under the listing rules of the United Kingdom Listing Authority [18]. The auditor's review will be directed at:

- considering the completeness of the disclosures in meeting Treasury requirements; and
- identifying any inconsistencies between the disclosures and the information that the auditor is aware of from their work on the financial statements and other work.

28 The reference to 'other work' in the last bullet of paragraph 27 above is significant in the central government sector. Parliament and the relevant devolved government authorities might reasonably expect the auditors to draw upon knowledge gained from all their audit work in performing their review of the SIC. Thus, in concluding their review of the statement, they will wish to have taken into account not only the

---

[16] *In Scotland the review requirement is set out in the Scottish Public Finance Manual. The Auditor General for Wales and the Comptroller and Auditor General for Northern Ireland follows the practice adopted by the Comptroller and Auditor General.*

[17] *In Scotland the review requirement is set out in the Scottish Public Finance Manual.*

[18] *At the time of writing this guidance was set out in APB Bulletin 1999/5.*

> **Opinion**
>
> In my opinion:
>
> - The financial statements give a true and fair view of the state of affairs of .... at 31 March 20xx and of the net resource outturn, resources applied to objectives, recognised gains and losses and cash flows for the year then ended, and have been properly prepared in accordance with the Government Resources and Accounts Act 2000 and directions made thereunder by the Treasury and;
>
> - In all material respects the expenditure and income have been applied to the purposes intended by Parliament and the financial transactions conform to the authorities which govern them.
>
> **Other Matter**
>
> I have reviewed the Accounting Officer's description of his/her processes for reviewing the effectiveness of internal control set out on page x of the annual report. In my opinion the Accounting Officer's comments concerning... do not appropriately reflect our understanding of the process undertaken by the Accounting Officer because....

49 In addition, the Comptroller and Auditor General may choose to use his wide ranging powers to issue separate reports to Parliament under the Government Resources and Accounts Act 2000 and the statutes governing particular audits to report on corporate governance matters[22]. The guiding principle is that the power to report should be used to draw Parliament's attention to matters which are necessary to the understanding of the financial statements or the entity's stewardship of public funds.

Audit Committees

50 Unlike the private sector where companies are required by the listing rules to require their auditors to review their compliance with Combined Code provision D.3.1 relating to Audit Committees[23], the central government auditor has no specific reporting responsibilities in relation to the establishment (or otherwise) and workings of the Audit Committee.

51 However, as set out in paragraph 30 above, the auditor will attend Audit Committee meetings at which corporate governance, internal control and risk management matters are discussed in order to obtain the required assurance regarding the disclosures made by the Accounting Officer in the SIC.

52 Where a body elects not to establish an Audit Committee, the auditors confirm that the body has complied with the Treasury expectation to identify clearly the circumstances justifying this decision. Where no justification is provided, or where in

---

[22] The Auditor General for Scotland has similar powers under s22 and s23 of the Public Finance and Accountability (Scotland) Act 2000. The Auditor General for Wales has similar powers to report under the Government of Wales Act 1998. The Comptroller and Auditor General for Northern Ireland has similar powers to report under the Government Resources and Accounts Act (Northern Ireland) 2001.

[23] Combined Code provision D.3.1: 'The Board should establish an Audit Committee of at least three directors, all non-executive, with written terms of reference which deal clearly with its authority and duties. The members of the committee, a majority of whom should be independent non-executive directors, should be named in the report and accounts'.

the auditor's view it is inadequate, the auditor raises the matter with senior management of the body concerned.

Appendix 1 – Respective responsibilities of the accounting officer and the auditor

ILLUSTRATIVE EXTRACTS FROM CENTRAL GOVERNMENT AUDIT CERTIFICATES

1. Department Preparing a Resource Account

Respective responsibilities of the Accounting Officer and Auditor

As described on pages ... the Accounting Officer is responsible for the preparation of the financial statements in accordance with the Government Resources and Accounts Act 2000 and Treasury directions made thereunder and for ensuring the regularity of financial transactions. The Accounting Officer is also responsible for the preparation of the other contents of the Accounts. My responsibilities as independent auditor are established by statute and I have regard to the standards and guidance issued by the Auditing Practices Board and the ethical guidance applicable to the auditing profession.

I report my opinion as to whether the financial statements give a true and fair view and are properly prepared in accordance with the Government Resources and Accounts Act 2000 and Treasury directions made thereunder and whether in all material respects the expenditure and income have been applied to the purposes intended by Parliament and the financial transactions conform to the authorities which govern them. I also report if in my opinion the Foreword is not consistent with the financial statements, if the Department has not kept proper accounting records or if I have not received all the information and explanations I require for my audit.

I read the other information contained in the Accounts and consider whether it is consistent with the audited financial statements. I consider the implications for my certificate if I become aware of any apparent misstatements or material inconsistencies with the financial statements.

I review whether the statement on page ... reflects the Department's compliance with Treasury's guidance 'Corporate Governance: Statement on Internal Control'. I report if it does not meet the requirements specified by Treasury or if the statement is misleading or inconsistent with other information I am aware of from my audit of the financial statements. I am not required to consider, nor have I considered whether the Accounting Officer's statements on internal control cover all risks and controls. I am also not required to form an opinion on the effectiveness of the Department's corporate governance procedures or its risk and control procedures.

2. Executive Agency Preparing an Accruals Account

Respective responsibilities of the Agency, the Chief Executive and Auditor

As described on page ... the Agency and Chief Executive are responsible for the preparation of the financial statements in accordance with the Government Resources and Accounts Act 2000 and Treasury directions made thereunder and for ensuring the regularity of financial transactions. The Agency and Chief Executive are also responsible for the preparation of other contents of the Annual Report. My responsibilities as independent auditor are established by statute and I have regard to the standards and guidance issued by the Auditing Practices Board and the ethical guidance applicable to the auditing profession.

I report my opinion as to whether the financial statements give a true and fair view and are properly prepared in accordance with the Government Resources and Accounts Act 2000 and Treasury directions made thereunder and whether in all material respects the expenditure and income have been applied to the purposes intended by Parliament and the financial transactions conform to the authorities which govern them. I also report if in my opinion the Foreword is not consistent with the financial statements, if the Agency has not kept proper accounting records or if I have not received all the information and explanations I require for my audit.

I read the other information contained in the Annual Report and consider whether it is consistent with the audited financial statements. I consider the implications for my certificate if I become aware of any apparent misstatements or material inconsistencies with the financial statements.

I review whether the statement on page ... reflects the Agency's compliance with Treasury's guidance 'Corporate Governance: Statement on Internal Control'. I report if it does not meet the requirements specified by Treasury or if the statement is misleading or inconsistent with other information I am aware of from my audit of the financial statements. I am not required to consider, nor have I considered whether the Accounting Officer's statements on internal control cover all risks and controls. I am also not required to form an opinion on the effectiveness of the Agency's corporate governance procedures or its risk and control procedures.

3. Executive NDPB Preparing an Accruals Account

Respective responsibilities of the ...[1] .the Chief Executive[2] and Auditor

As described on page ... the ...[1] and Chief Executive[2] are responsible for the preparation of the financial statements in accordance with the ... Act. [3] and Treasury[4] directions made thereunder and for ensuring the regularity of financial transactions. The ... and Chief Executive[2] are also responsible for the preparation of the Foreword/other contents of the Annual Report. [5] My responsibilities as independent auditor are [established by statute and][6] I have regard to the standards and guidance issued by the Auditing Practices Board and the ethical guidance applicable to the auditing profession.

I report my opinion as to whether the financial statements give a true and fair view and are properly prepared in accordance with the ... Act[3] and Treasury[4] directions made thereunder and whether in all material respects the expenditure and income have been applied to the purposes intended by Parliament and the financial transactions conform to the authorities which govern them. I also report if in my opinion the Foreword is not consistent with the financial statements, if the ... [7] has not kept proper accounting records or if I have not received all the information and explanations I require for my audit.

I read the other information contained in the Annual Report and consider whether it is consistent with the audited financial statements. I consider the implications for my certificate if I become aware of any apparent misstatements or material inconsistencies with the financial statements.

I review whether the statement on page ... reflects the ...[7] compliance with Treasury's guidance 'Corporate Governance: Statement on Internal Control'. I report if it does not meet the requirements specified by Treasury or if the statement is misleading or inconsistent with other information I am aware of from my audit of the financial statements. I am not required to consider, nor have I considered whether the Accounting Officer's statements on internal control cover all risks and controls. I am also not required to form an opinion on the effectiveness of the entity's corporate governance procedures or its risk and control procedures.[8]

Notes

1. The title used should reflect who is responsible for the preparation of the financial statements and be consistent with the statement of responsibilities. For example it may be a 'Board' or it may be the audited entity.
2. Or other title given in the statement of responsibilities.
3. Refer to relevant legislative authority.
4. Or other authority as appropriate.
5. If the financial statements are laid separately from the annual Report (ie as 'white paper' accounts) the reference here should be to 'the Foreword'. If the financial statements are laid as part of an annual report and accounts the reference should be to 'other contents of the Annual Report'.
6. For those agreement audits where there is no legislative requirement for an audit the words 'established by statute and' should be deleted.
7. Short name of the audited entity eg Council/Commission.
8. The two paragraphs here ('I read the other information...' and 'I review whether the statement') should be used when the financial statements are laid as part of an annual report and accounts. If this is not the case (ie 'white paper accounts') then the first paragraph should be deleted ('I read the other information...'etc).

Appendix 2 – Example draft paragraphs for inclusion in letter of understanding/engagement

The following is an illustrative example of paragraphs that may be included in the auditors' engagement letter dealing with their responsibilities with respect to the entity's Statement on Internal Control. In practice auditors tailor their engagement letter to the specific circumstances of the engagement.

REVIEW OF THE ACCOUNTING OFFICER'S STATEMENT ON INTERNAL CONTROL

Responsibilities

As Accounting Officer of the Authority you are responsible for ensuring that the *[name of entity]* complies with the guidance issued by HM Treasury entitled "Corporate Governance: statement on internal control". This requires you to include alongside the accounts a statement on internal control. The guidance requires the external auditors to review the statement.

Scope of Review

Our review of the statement will be conducted in compliance with the relevant recommendations of Bulletins issued by the Auditing Practices Board, which, among other things, set out the scope of our review. For this purpose you will provide us with such information and explanations as we consider necessary. We may request you to provide written confirmation of oral representations which you make to us during the course of our review. We shall request sight of all documents or statements which are due to be issued with the statement on internal control and all documentation prepared in support of the statement.

Our work will be restricted to a consideration of whether your statement:

- provides the disclosures required by the Treasury guidance; and
- is not inconsistent with the information of which we have become aware from our audit of the financial statements.

As our work is not designed to consider whether your statement on internal control covers all risks and controls, or form an opinion on the effectiveness of *[name of entity]'s* risk and control procedures, our work on internal control will not be sufficient to enable us to express any assurance as to whether or not your internal controls are effective. In addition our financial statement audit should not be relied upon to draw to your attention matters that may be relevant to your consideration as to whether or not your system of internal control is effective.

Glossary of terms

Accounting Officer (Accountable Officer in Scotland) – usually the permanent head or senior full-time official of a central government entity, appointed or designated as the Accounting Officer for that entity and with a personal responsibility for, amongst other things, signing of the financial statements, ensuring that proper financial procedures are followed and accounting records are maintained, and ensuring that public funds and assets are properly managed and safeguarded. See also **Agency Accounting Officer** and **Principal Accounting Officer**.

Agency Accounting Officer – the senior full-time official, usually the Chief Executive, of an executive agency who is designated by the appropriate Accounting Officer of the parent department to assume personal responsibility for the management of the entity's activities.

Auditor General for Scotland – is appointed by the Crown and is independent of the Scottish Executive. He plays a key role in holding the Scottish Executive and most other public spending bodies in Scotland (with the exception of local authorities and fire and police boards which are the responsibility of the Accounts Commission) to account for the proper, efficient and effective use of public money. He is a member of the board of Audit Scotland. He is responsible for the appointment of auditors to NHS Scotland bodies.

Central government (sector) auditors – any external auditors or audit firm, from the public or private sectors, responsible for the external audit of an entity in central government.

Central government entities – defined as government departments and their executive agencies, any entity which operates as a trading fund (a government department, part of a department or an executive agency) and non-departmental public bodies. For the purposes of this Bulletin, central government does not include National Heath Service bodies, local authorities, public corporations or nationalised industries.

Chief executive – the title applied to the senior official of an executive agency or non-departmental public body accountable to the Secretary of State of the parent or sponsor department for the management and operations of that agency.

Comptroller and Auditor General – the Comptroller and Auditor General's full title is 'Comptroller General of the Receipts and Issue of Her Majesty's Exchequer and Auditor General of Public Accounts'. As Comptroller General he authorises the issue of public funds to government departments and other public sector bodies. As Auditor General his statutory duties are to certify and report to Parliament on the accounts of all government departments and a wide range of public bodies. The Comptroller and Auditor General is head of the National Audit Office.

Entity – the generic term used in this Bulletin for any government department, executive agency, trading fund, non-departmental public body, company or other body or organisation which produces audited financial statements.

Executive Agency – an entity established to carry out the executive functions of government as distinct from providing policy advice.

Government Accounting – the manual published by HM Treasury through the Stationery Office, which sets out the overall rules and requirements for accountability in central government.

Government Departments – these represent the top tier of central government. Parliament provides money annually to each department. Each government department is headed by an Accounting Officer who is responsible to Parliament for the application and expenditure of the funds provided.

Non-departmental public body – an entity that has a role in the process of government but is neither a government department nor forms part of a department. It is established at arm's length from departments and may carry out executive, regulatory, administrative or commercial functions.

Parent department – used in the context of executive agencies, in contrast with the term 'sponsor department' as used for non-departmental public bodies, to refer to the government department which any individual executive agency remains a part of, both in terms of Parliamentary funding and accountability.

Resource Accounting Manual – the manual published by the Treasury which sets out the principles applicable to the accounting and disclosure requirements for the presentation of resource accounts by central government entities.

Scottish Public Finance Manual – the manual published by the Scottish Ministers which sets out the overall rules and requirements for accountability in central government in Scotland.

Sponsor department – normally the department through which Parliamentary funding and accountability is made for non-departmental public bodies.

List of references

- Government Accounting – The Stationery Office
- Resource Accounting Manual – HM Treasury
- Management of Risk – A Strategic Overview – HM Treasury, January 2001

- Guidance on Codes of Practice for Board Members of Public Bodies – Cabinet Office, January 1997
- DAO(Gen) 13/00: Corporate Governance – Statement on Internal Control – HM Treasury, 22 December 2000
- DAO(Gen) 09/03: Statement on Internal Control – HM Treasury, 29 May 2003
- APB Practice Note 10: Audit of Financial Statements of Public Sector Entities in the United Kingdom (Revised), April 2001
- DAO(Gen) 4/97: Board members' Pensions and Compensation Guidance Notes – HM Treasury, 11 June 1997
- DAO(Gen) 3/00: Salary and Pension Disclosures – HM Treasury, 6 March 2000
- Code of Audit Practice – Audit Scotland, July 2001
- Scottish Public Finance Manual – Audit Scotland
- Government Accounting Northern Ireland – Department of Finance and Personnel
- Northern Ireland Resource Accounting Manual – Department of Finance and Personnel

[Bulletin 2003/2]
Corporate governance: requirements of public sector auditors (National Health Service bodies)

(Issued November 2003)

Contents

	Paragraphs
Section 1: Introduction	1 - 2
Purpose of this Bulletin	3 - 4
Structure of this Bulletin	5 - 7
Composition of the NHS Sector	8
Section 2: Corporate Governance framework	
Background	9 - 12
Statement on Internal Control	13 - 16
Audit Committees	17 - 19
Section 3: Auditors' Responsibilities	
Statements of Auditors' Responsibilities	20 - 25
The Auditors' Review of the Statement on Internal Control	26 - 36
Significant internal control issues	37 - 42
Failure to Conduct a Review	43
Reporting by Exception	44 - 46
Audit Committees	47 - 48

Appendix 1

Respective Responsibilities of the Directors and Auditors

Glossary of Terms

List of References

Section 1: Introduction

The corporate governance framework that applies to listed companies in the private sector[1] is well developed. The structures and processes for decision making and accountability, control systems and behaviour at the top of organisations are equally important issues for public sector organisations. Not surprisingly, therefore, over the last decade corporate governance has also become an increasingly significant issue for the public sector.

1

Unlike listed companies, which are subject to the same broad framework of company law, public sector bodies do not operate within a common legislative framework. Consequently different models of governance have evolved within the public sector in response to different sets of accountabilities. Hence the need for more than one Bulletin covering the requirements of external auditors in the public sector.

2

Purpose of this Bulletin

The APB has produced this Bulletin to:

3

- set out the corporate governance arrangements that apply in the NHS sector; and
- provide guidance to NHS auditors on their review and reporting responsibilities in relation to the corporate governance disclosures NHS bodies are required to make.

The Department of Health and the Welsh Assembly Government have asked the Audit Commission in England and Wales to make arrangements for its appointed auditors to review audited bodies' corporate governance disclosures. In Scotland, appointed auditors are required by the Code of Audit Practice to review audited bodies' corporate governance disclosures. In Northern Ireland, the Department of Health, Social Services and Public Safety expects appointed auditors to review Health and Social Services (HSS) bodies' corporate governance disclosures.

4

Structure of this Bulletin

As the corporate governance framework within the public sector evolves, the APB is issuing guidance to cover other areas of the sector. Bulletin 2003/1 "Corporate Governance: Requirements of Public Sector Auditors (Central Government)" was issued in November 2003. Guidance for other major public sector areas will be considered in due course.

5

The principles outlined in each part of this Bulletin apply equally in all parts of the UK. Differences in organisational structure, governance requirements and terminology applying in Scotland, Wales and Northern Ireland are noted where appropriate.

6

---

[1] *The corporate governance requirements placed on listed companies are set out in the 'Combined Code' which was published by the Committee on Corporate Governance in June 1998. The Combined Code has been appended to the Listing Rules of the Financial Services Authority and consolidates the recommendations of the earlier Cadbury, Greenbury and Hampel reports on private sector corporate governance issues. The Financial Reporting Council has recently issued a revised Code which comes into effect for reporting years beginning on or after 1 November 2003. Also relevant is the report of the Internal Control Working Party of the ICAEW (commonly referred to as The Turnbull Report) which was published in September 1999.*

7   Section 2 of this Bulletin covers the corporate governance frameworks applying to NHS bodies in the United Kingdom. Section 3 sets out the auditors' responsibilities in relation to the corporate governance disclosure NHS bodies are required to make.

Composition of the NHS Sector

8   For the purposes of this Bulletin, the NHS sector is taken to comprise National Health Service bodies, including strategic health authorities, special health authorities, NHS trusts, and primary care trusts in England, (local) health boards and NHS trusts in Wales and Scotland, and HPSS bodies in Northern Ireland, including health and social service boards, trusts and agencies.

Section 2: Corporate governance framework

Background

9   Chief Executives of NHS bodies are appointed locally but designated by the Department of Health (DoH)[2] as the Accountable Officer. The role and duties of an Accountable Officer are set out in the *Accountable Officer Memorandum* which is sent to every new Accountable Officer on appointment. Accountable Officers have a personal responsibility for, amongst other things, ensuring that effective management systems are in place which safeguard public funds, achieving value for money from the resources available to the organisation, ensuring that assets are properly safeguarded, and for ensuring that expenditure complies with Parliamentary requirements.

10 NHS bodies operate on a unitary Board model, similar to that of private sector listed companies. The Board consists of executive members and part-time non-executive members, and is chaired by a non-executive member. All non-executive members are appointed by the NHS Appointments Commission[3]. The roles and responsibilities of NHS boards are set out in the Codes of Conduct and Accountability issued by the DoH in 1994[4]. The Chief Executive is responsible to the Board for day to day management of the organisation but, as Accountable Officer, is also responsible to the DoH[5] for the proper stewardship of public money and assets. In addition to the Board, primary care trusts also have professional executive committees.

11 Corporate governance developments in the NHS have included the following measures:
- designation of Chief Executives as Accountable Officers;
- the establishment of remuneration committees and audit committees (mandatory), and risk management committees (optional);
- adoption of measures recommended by Greenbury relating to disclosure of directors' remuneration; and
- the introduction of a statement on internal control.

[2] *NHS Wales Department for Welsh bodies, Principal Accountable Officer for Scottish bodies and DHSSPS (or the body itself) for Northern Ireland bodies.*

[3] *Assembly Minister for Health & Social Services for Welsh bodies, Scottish Ministers for Scottish bodies and the Minister for Health, Social Services and Public Safety for Northern Ireland HSS bodies.*

[4] *In Northern Ireland separate Codes of Conduct and Accountability were issued by the DHSS in 1994.*

[5] *NHS Wales Department for Welsh bodies, Scottish Parliament for Scottish bodies and DHSSPS for Northern Ireland bodies.*

An overview of the key corporate governance requirements for NHS bodies, the auditors' responsibilities, and the relevant paragraphs in this Bulletin are set out in the table below:

Subject	Key Requirements	Auditors' Responsibilities	Relevant paragraphs in this Bulletin
Corporate governance framework	Personal responsibility of Accountable Officers as set out in the Accountable Officer Memorandum for: • ensuring that the body operates effective management systems • achieving value for money from the available resources • keeping proper accounts • ensuring the regularity and propriety of expenditure	Required to report if the Accountable Officer has not kept proper accounting records. Audit opinions on certain NHS bodies are required to include specific attestation relating to the regularity of transactions included within the financial statements.[6]	9 Covered by APB Practice Note 10: Audit of financial statements of public sector entities in the United Kingdom (Revised)
Statement on Internal Control	Required by NHS bodies with effect from financial year 2001/02 as part of the financial statements. Requirements set out in guidance issued by the Department of Health, NHS Wales Department, Scottish Executive Health Department and the Department of Finance and Personnel in Northern Ireland.	Review the statement to: • consider the completeness of the disclosures in meeting the specified requirements, and • identify any known inconsistencies in the disclosures made by the Accountable Officer.	13-16, 26-46
Audit Committees	Audit committees are mandatory for NHS bodies as specified in the Codes of Conduct and Accountability (1994). Best practice guidance is set out in the Audit Committee Handbook.	No specific reporting responsibilities. However auditors will attend audit committee meetings at which corporate governance, internal control, and risk management matters	17-19, 47-48

[6] Applicable to Primary Care Trusts and Strategic Health Authorities in England, Local Health Boards in Wales, Health and Social Services Boards and Trusts in Northern Ireland and all NHS bodies in Scotland.

		are considered as a means of gaining evidence for the review of the Statement on Internal Control (SIC).	

Statement on Internal Control

13   In line with HM Treasury guidance for central government, all NHS bodies in England, Wales, Scotland and Northern Ireland[7] are required to submit a SIC as part of their annual accounts. The Treasury's requirements are set out in Government Accounting[8], Chapter 21 'Risk Management and the Statement on Internal Control'[9]

14   Specific guidance on the requirements for SICs is issued by the Department of Health, NHS Wales Department, the Scottish Executive Health Department and the Department of Health, Social Services and Public Safety in Northern Ireland. The extant guidance for the financial year ending 31 March 2004 is:

- England – The Statement on Internal Control 2003/04 – Department of Health, September 2003;
- Northern Ireland – HSS(FAU) 19/2003 Statement of Internal Control: Transitional Statement 2002/3 – Department of Health, Social Services and Public Safety;
- Wales – WHC (2002)74 Statement on Internal Control 2001/02 – National Assembly for Wales, June 2002 (to be read in conjunction with guidance issued in April 2003 for Trusts and in March 2003 for Local Health Boards) plus supplementary guidance for 2003/04 issued in September 2003;
- Scotland – Health Department Letter (2002) 11 (Corporate Governance: Statement on Internal Control) – Scottish Executive Health Department.

15   The Chief Executive, as Accountable Officer, is required to sign, on behalf of the board, a SIC providing a brief but comprehensive summary of the actual processes in place in their organisations, including a description of how current initiatives are being taken forward. It was, however, recognised that some bodies would take time to develop all the necessary underpinning risk management and review processes. In these cases a deadline of 31 March 2004 has been set for implementation of the underpinning processes[10]. SICs for the financial year 2003/04 should therefore reflect the establishment of all the required risk management and review processes by the

---

[7] *A transitional Statement on Internal Control is required in Northern Ireland until the financial year ending 31 March 2004.*

[8] *At the time of issue of this Bulletin, Chapter 21 of Government Accounting was scheduled for publication in November 2003. Until this date the requirements were set out in DAO (GEN) 13/00 'Corporate Governance: Statement on Internal Control' issued on 22 December 2000 as revised by DAO (GEN) 09/03 'Statement on Internal Control' issued on 29 May 2003.*

[9] *In Scotland and Northern Ireland the requirements are set out in the Scottish Public Finance Manual and DAO (DFP) 05/01.*

[10] *In Wales Local Health Boards are not expected to have a fully operational risk management system until 2004-05.*

year end at the latest and SICs for 2004/05 and subsequent years should reflect the operation of all the required processes throughout the year[11].

SICs are required to include the following disclosures: 16

- acknowledgement of the Accountable Officer's responsibility for ensuring that a sound system of internal control is maintained;
- an explanation that the system of internal control is designed to manage risk to a reasonable level rather than to eliminate all risk of failure to achieve the organisation's policies, aims and objectives; it can therefore only provide reasonable and not absolute assurance of effectiveness;
- reference to an ongoing risk management process designed to identify and prioritise the risks to the achievement of the organisation's policies, aims and objectives, to evaluate the likelihood of those risks being realised, and to manage them efficiently, effectively and economically;
- confirmation that the above process was in place for the duration of the financial year and remained so up until the date of the approval of the annual report and accounts;
- a description of the capacity of the staff to manage the risk process;
- a description of the key elements of the risk and control framework;
- acknowledgement of the Accountable Officer's responsibility for reviewing the effectiveness of the system of internal control, and a description of the review process undertaken;
- for 2003/04 and subsequently, confirmation that the results of the Accountable Officer's review of the effectiveness of internal control has been discussed with the Board, the Audit Committee and other relevant committees where applicable; and
- where appropriate, set out details of actions taken, or proposed, to deal with significant internal control issues.
  Additional requirements
- **for Northern Ireland** – confirmation that the system of internal control is underpinned by compliance with the requirements of the HPSS core controls assurance standards[12] of governance, financial management, and risk management; and
- **for Wales** – reference to performance against the Welsh Risk Management Standards[13] (WRMS), and in particular those deemed core to the management of risk within NHS organisations: risk management policy and strategy; risk profile; incident and hazard reporting, governance and financial management.

Audit Committees

The Codes of Conduct and Accountability issued by the DoH in 1994 set down the basic principles of corporate governance that should be followed by every NHS body, and included the requirement for the establishment of an audit committee. Practical guidance and best practice for audit committees in the NHS is set down in the relevant Audit Committee Handbook. 17

Every NHS body is required to establish a non-executive committee of the board to be known as the audit committee. The main objective of the audit committee is to 18

---

[11] These timescales are not applicable in Scotland, where full internal control statements are required from 1 April 2003.

[12] See glossary.

[13] See glossary.

contribute independently to the board's overall process for ensuring that an effective internal control and risk management system is maintained. The Audit Committee Handbook sets out the duties of audit committees under four main headings:

- Internal control and risk management;
- Internal audit;
- External audit;
- Financial reporting.

The Handbook also covers matters such as membership, authority, frequency of meetings and reporting, and provides specimen terms of reference.

19 Audit committees should comprise not less than three non-executive directors[14], with a quorum of two. The Chairman of the board should not be a member of the audit committee, although he/she could be invited to attend meetings that discuss issues pertinent to the whole board. Attendees should include representatives from internal and external audit, the Director of Finance, and other executive directors as required. The external auditor may request a meeting of the audit committee if considered necessary, and may meet with the committee without the presence of any executive directors.

Section 3: Auditors' responsibilities

Statements of Auditors' Responsibilities

20 Auditors of NHS bodies are appointed by the Audit Commission (England and Wales) and the Auditor General for Scotland. The responsibilities of the auditors are set out in the respective Code of Audit Practice[15], and also in the Statement of Responsibilities of Auditors and Audited Bodies (Audit Commission and Audit Scotland) provided to each audited body. The structure of Health Services audit in Northern Ireland has been reorganised with effect from 1 April 2003. Whereas previously auditors had been appointed to HSS bodies by the Department of Health, Social Services and Public Safety, the Audit and Accountability Order (Northern Ireland) 2003 transferred responsibility for the statutory audit of HSS bodies from the DHSSPS to the Comptroller and Auditor General for Northern Ireland.

21 Auditors of NHS bodies have different responsibilities with respect to the various component parts of the financial statements and the information presented with the financial statements. They are required to 'audit' the financial statements, 'review' the body's Statement on Internal Control, and 'read' the information contained in the annual report[16]. Auditors read such 'other information' because the credibility of the financial statements and the related auditors' report may be undermined by material inconsistencies between the financial statements and the 'other information', or by apparent misstatements within the 'other information'.

22 In some instances auditors have to report positively the results of their work whereas in other instances the auditors only have to report by exception. The APB is of the

---

[14] *In the case of Local Health Boards, non-officer/co-opted members are appointed to the audit committee and not non-executive directors, although their function remains the same.*

[15] *Code of Audit Practice approved by Parliament and issued by the Audit Commission, Code of Audit Practice approved by the Auditor General and issued by Audit Scotland and Code of Practice issued by DHSSPS in Northern Ireland.*

[16] *In Scotland the auditors should 'read the other information published with the financial statements.'*

view that users of financial statements will find it difficult to understand the scope of the auditors' involvement in the absence of a clear statement of their responsibilities towards the financial statements and the information presented with them.

23 The key elements of a statement of the auditors' responsibilities relate to the requirements of:

- Statute, Auditing Standards (with guidance on the application of Auditing Standards provided by APB Practice Note 10[17]) and the respective Code of Audit Practice with respect to the audit of the financial statements;
- the agreements between the relevant audit regulators and the DoH, Welsh Assembly Government and DHSSPS[18] to review the Statement on Internal Control for compliance with the relevant disclosure requirements and inconsistencies between the information of which the auditors are aware from their audit work; and
- Statement of Auditing Standards 160 'Other information in documents containing audited financial statements' to read the 'other information' presented with the financial statements.

24 In accordance with SAS 600 'Auditors' reports on financial statements' (and the guidance on the application of auditing standards in the public sector provided by APB Practice Note 10), a description of the auditors' responsibilities should be included within the auditors' report on the financial statements. The extract examples in Appendix 1 illustrate the wording that may be used by auditors of NHS bodies to explain the auditor's responsibilities. The APB is of the view that a statement of auditors' responsibilities as further described in paragraphs 26 to 29, avoids the need for a separate auditors' report dealing with their review of corporate governance matters.

25 The auditors' responsibilities in relation to their review of the SIC are not designed to provide 'positive assurance'. In view of the limited nature of the review, and in order to avoid the possibility of misunderstandings arising, the APB recommends that prior to the release of the annual report and accounts the auditors communicate, and discuss, with both management and those charged with governance the findings of their review.

The Auditors' Review of the Statement on Internal Control

26 The nature of the auditors' review of the SIC will follow a similar approach to that set out in the APB's Bulletin 1999/5 dealing with the requirements of auditors under the listing rules of the United Kingdom Listing Authority. The auditor's review will be directed at:

- considering the completeness of the disclosures in meeting the relevant Departmental requirements; and
- identifying any inconsistencies between the disclosures and the information that the auditors are aware of from their work on the financial statements and other work.

27 In Wales and Northern Ireland the auditors' review will specifically consider the arrangements put in place by the body to ensure compliance with the five core

---

[17] APB Practice Note 10: *Audit of Financial Statements of Public Sector Entities in the United Kingdom* (Revised April 2001).

[18] In Scotland, appointed auditors are required by the Code of Audit Practice to review the SIC.

WRMS (Wales) and the three HPSS core controls assurance standards (Northern Ireland).

28   The reference to 'other work' in the second bullet of paragraph 26 above is significant in the NHS sector. The relevant Code of Audit Practice requires auditors to review the financial statements, aspects of corporate governance arrangements, and aspects of performance management arrangements. Work in relation to one element of the audit informs and is complementary to work in relation to the others. Thus, in concluding their review of the statement, they will have taken into account not only the results of their work on the financial statements, but also their work on the other elements required by the Code.

29   The extent of the auditors' review procedures will therefore vary according to the nature and content of their other work. However, such review procedures will always include consideration of the disclosures set out in paragraph 16 above. In particular, they will assess whether the Accountable Officer's summary of the process he/she has adopted in reviewing the effectiveness of the system of internal control, is both supported by the documentation prepared for the Accountable Officer, board and audit committee, and appropriately reflects that process.

30   Appropriate evidence regarding the disclosures will usually be obtained by:
- considering whether the disclosures are consistent with the auditors' review of board, audit committee and other relevant committee minutes;
- reviewing supporting documents prepared for the board, Accountable Officer and audit committee that are relevant to disclosures made in the SIC. In doing this the auditors will pay particular attention to the documentation prepared for Accountable Officers to support their statement made in connection with their effectiveness review and assess whether or not it provides sound support for that statement;
- gaining an understanding of the process defined by the Accountable Officer for his/her review of the effectiveness of internal control through enquiry of appropriate board members and executive directors, and comparing their understanding to the statement made by the Accountable Officer in the SIC;
- attending audit committee meetings at which corporate governance, internal control, and risk management matters are considered;
- reviewing the Head of Internal Audit's formal annual report to the Accountable Officer and audit committee which includes the opinion of the overall adequacy and effectiveness of the organisation's risk management, control and governance processes; and
- relating the statement made by the Accountable Officer to the auditors' knowledge of the body obtained during the audit of the financial statements and other work required by the respective Code of Audit Practice. As explained in paragraph 33, the scope of the Accountable Officer's review will be considerably broader in its scope than the knowledge the auditors can be expected to have obtained during their audit.

31   Where auditors feel it is appropriate, they may request written confirmation of oral representations made during the course of the review.

32   The SIC covers the year under review and the period to the date of approval of the annual report and accounts. The auditors, therefore, consider whether the statement covers the year under review and whether there are any material developments between the balance sheet date and the date the accounts are signed which should properly be included in the statement.

In carrying out their review, the auditors will have regard to the knowledge of the body they have obtained from their audit work. To enable them to perform their audit and express an opinion on the financial statements, auditors are required by Auditing Standards to understand the body's control environment and to assess the components of audit risk. Such an assessment encompasses control risk to the extent that the auditors expect to be able to rely on such an assessment in order to reduce the extent of their substantive audit procedures. Consequently, the auditor's assessment required by Auditing Standards will be considerably narrower in scope than the review performed by the Accountable Officer. 33

Auditors are not therefore expected to assess whether all risks and controls have been addressed by the Accountable Officer and the board, or that risks are satisfactorily addressed by internal controls. In order to communicate this fact to users of the financial statements the following sentence is included in the auditors' report on the financial statements: 34

> *I am not required to consider, nor have I considered whether the directors' statements on internal control cover all risks and controls. I am also not required to form an opinion on the effectiveness of the entity's corporate governance procedures or its risk and control procedures.*

Statement of Auditing Standards 610.5 requires: 35

> *'Auditors should communicate to those charged with governance:....c) material weaknesses in the accounting and internal control systems identified during the audit.'*

The APB recommends that any material weakness in internal control identified by the auditors be reported on as soon as practicable. The auditors do not wait until the financial statement audit has been completed before reporting any such weakness[19]. In this way the Accountable Officer and audit committee will be aware of any material weakness that the auditors have identified and be able to take account of them in the Statement on Internal Control. 36

Significant Internal Control Issues

Where appropriate, the Accountable Officer is required to set out details of actions taken, or proposed, to deal with significant internal control issues. The purpose of this disclosure is to deliver assurance that significant internal control issues have been, or are being, addressed and that the SIC is a balanced reflection of the actual position. 37

This may be a difficult requirement for Accountable Officers to satisfy, and for auditors to review, because a 'significant internal control issue' cannot be defined to suit all contexts; the same issue may or may not be significant depending on the circumstances. 38

Whilst the term 'significant internal control issue' cannot be absolutely defined, the following indicators (which are not exhaustive) may be useful in considering whether or not an issue is significant enough to be reported in the SIC: 39

- it seriously prejudices or prevents achievement of a principal objective;

---

[19] *The requirements and guidance for auditors on this subject are set out in SAS 610: Communication of audit matters to those charged with governance.*

- It has resulted in the need to seek additional funding to allow it to be resolved, or has resulted in significant diversion of resources from another aspect of the business;
- the external auditor would regard it as having a material impact on the accounts;
- the Audit Committee advises it should be considered significant for this purpose;
- the Head of Internal Audit reports on it as significant for this purpose in his annual opinion on the whole of risk, control and governance;
- the issue, or its impact has attracted significant public interest or has seriously damaged the reputation of the organisation.

40 The auditor's review responsibility consists of assessing whether the disclosures made by the Accountable Officer of the processes he/she has applied to address any significant internal control issues appropriately reflect those processes.

41 The auditors are not required to assess whether the processes described in the SIC will, in fact, remedy any underlying weakness associated with the significant internal control issue.

42 If the auditors are aware of a significant internal control issue which the Accountable Officer has not disclosed they discuss the position with senior management and those charged with governance in the organisation. At the time of preparing the SIC for a particular year, disclosure of information about a significant internal control issue might prejudice the outcome of a special investigation (possibly preventing successful prosecution of a case of fraud or inhibiting a disciplinary case against members of staff). In such circumstances the Treasury require that the SIC should record that there are issues which cannot be disclosed because to do so would prejudice the outcome of an investigation. However, if the auditors are not able to agree with the Accountable Officer and those charged with governance as to how the matter should be resolved they consider the need to report by exception.

Failure to Conduct a Review

43 Where the Accountable Officer does not undertake a review of the effectiveness of the system of internal control, this departure from the specified requirements should be disclosed and explained by the Accountable Officer in the SIC. The auditors consider whether this requirement is met and whether the explanation is consistent with the auditors' understanding. If the auditors decide that it is not, they consider the need to report by exception.

Reporting by Exception

44 If the auditors conclude:

- that the Accountable Officer's summary of the process applied in reviewing the effectiveness of the internal control system is either not supported by or does not appropriately reflect the auditor's understanding of the process undertaken (paragraphs 26-36);
- that the processes disclosed to deal with significant internal control issues do not appropriately reflect the auditors' understanding of the process undertaken (paragraphs 37 to 42);
- that no disclosure has been made by the Accountable Officer that he/she failed to conduct a review of the effectiveness of the internal control system (paragraph 43); or

- where the Accountable Officer discloses that he/she has not reviewed the effectiveness of the internal control system, but that his/her explanation is not consistent with the auditor's understanding (paragraph 43)

they report this in the opinion section of their report on the financial statements.

However, as this does not give rise to a qualified opinion on the financial statements, the APB recommends that the auditors' comments be included under the heading 'Other Matter' as illustrated in the example opinion for a NHS trust below:

Opinion

In my/our opinion:

- the financial statements give a true and fair view of the state of affairs of xx NHS Trust at 31 March 20xx and of its income and expenditure for the year then ended......;

Other Matter

I/we have reviewed the Accountable Officer's description of the processes undertaken for reviewing the effectiveness of the system of internal control as set out on page xx. In my/our opinion the Accountable Officer's comments concerning.... do not appropriately reflect my/our understanding of the processes undertaken because.....

In addition, in England and Wales, the auditor considers whether any matters arising from the review of the SIC are significant enough to warrant a report in the public interest under section 8 of the Audit Commission Act 1998 and/or a referral to the Secretary of State for Health under section 19[20]. A report in the public interest will only be made where the auditor considers a matter sufficiently important to be brought to the notice of the audited body and the public. Copies of all reports in the public interest in respect of NHS bodies are submitted to the DoH, or the National Assembly for Wales, or Scottish Ministers. A section 19 referral is required where a NHS body makes or is about to make decisions involving potentially unlawful expenditure, or takes or is about to take potentially unlawful action likely to cause a loss or deficiency.

Audit Committees

Unlike the private sector where companies are required by the Listing Rules to require their auditors to review their compliance with Combined Code provisions relating to Audit Committees, auditors of NHS bodies have no specific reporting responsibilities in relation to the establishment and workings of the audit committee.

---

[20] *The Auditor General for Scotland has powers to report to the Scottish Parliament under s22 and s23 of the Public Finance and Accountability Act 2000. The Comptroller and Auditor General for Northern Ireland will have similar powers to report to the Northern Ireland Assembly under the Audit and Accountability Order (Northern Ireland) 2003. These powers apply to financial statements for accounting periods beginning on or after 1 April 2003. For earlier accounting periods auditors appointed by DHSSPS are required, under Article 92 A(4) of the Health and Personal Social Services Order (NI) 1972, to consider whether, in the public interest, a report should be made on any matter which comes to their attention in the course of an audit in order that it may be considered by the body concerned and brought to the attention of the Department. In addition, under Article 92A(5) if the auditor has reason to believe that the body or any officer makes or is about to make a decision involving potentially unlawful expenditure, or takes or is about to take potentially unlawful action likely to cause a loss or deficit, then the matter must be referred to the Department immediately.*

48 However, as set out in paragraph 30 above, the auditors will attend audit committee meetings at which corporate governance, internal control, and risk management matters are discussed in order to obtain the required assurance regarding the disclosures made by the Accountable Officer in the SIC.

Appendix 1 – Respective responsibilities of the directors and auditors

ILLUSTRATIVE EXTRACTS FROM NHS AUDIT REPORTS

1. NHS Trusts (England)

Respective Responsibilities of Directors and Auditors

As described on page x the Directors are responsible for the preparation of the financial statements in accordance with directions issued by the Secretary of State. My/Our responsibilities as independent auditor are established by statute, and by the Code of Audit Practice issued by the Audit Commission, which requires adherence to the auditing standards issued by the Auditing Practices Board (APB) and relevant ethical standards. It also requires me/us to have regard to other guidance and advice issued by the APB.

I/we report to you my/our opinion as to whether the financial statements give a true and fair view of the state of affairs of the Trust and its income and expenditure for the year, in accordance with the accounting policies directed by the Secretary of State as being relevant to the National Health Service in England.

I/We review whether the directors' statement on internal control reflects compliance with the Department of Health's guidance 'The Statement on Internal Control 2003/04'. I/we report if it does not meet the requirements specified by the Department of Health or if the statement is misleading or inconsistent with other information I/we am/are aware of from my/our audit of the financial statements. I/We am/are not required to consider, nor have I/We considered whether the directors' statements on internal control cover all risks and controls. I/We are also not required to form an opinion on the effectiveness of the Trust's corporate governance procedures or its risk and control procedures. My/Our review was not performed for any purpose connected with any specific transaction and should not be relied upon for any such purpose.

I/We read the information contained in the Annual Report and consider the implications for
my/our report if I/we become aware of any apparent misstatements or material inconsistencies with the statement of accounts.

2. NHS Trusts (Wales)

Respective Responsibilities of Directors and Auditors[21]

As described on page x the Directors are responsible for the preparation of the financial statements in accordance with directions issued by the National Assembly for Wales. My/Our responsibilities as independent auditor are established by statute,

---

[21] *These roles and responsibilities also apply to Local Health Boards for 2003-04 and to Health Authorities for 2002-03.*

and by the Code of Audit Practice issued by the Audit Commission, which requires adherence to the auditing standards issued by the Auditing Practices Board (APB) and relevant ethical standards. It also requires me/us to have regard to other guidance and advice issued by the APB.

I/we report to you my/our opinion as to whether the financial statements give a true and fair view of the state of affairs of the Trust and its income and expenditure for the year, in accordance with the accounting policies directed by the National Assembly for Wales as being relevant to the National Health Service in Wales.

I/We review whether the Chief Executive's statement on internal control reflects compliance with WHC(2002)74 *Statement on Internal Control 2001-02* and with supplementary guidance issued for 2003/04. I/We report if it does not meet the requirements specified in the Circular or if the statement is misleading or inconsistent with other information I/we am/are aware of from my/our audit of the financial statements. I/We am/are not required to consider, nor have I/We considered whether the directors' statements on internal control cover all risks and controls.
I/We are also not required to form an opinion on the effectiveness of the Trust's corporate governance procedures or its risk and control procedures. My/Our review was not performed for any purpose connected with any specific transaction and should not be relied upon for any such purpose.

I/We read the information contained in the Annual Report and consider the implications for my/our report if I/we become aware of any apparent misstatements or material inconsistencies with the statement of accounts.

3. NHS Boards (Scotland)

Respective responsibilities of the Board Members, Accountable Officer and Auditors

As described on page x the Board and the Accountable Officer of the NHS Board are responsible for the preparation of the financial statements in accordance with the National Health Service (Scotland) Act 1978 and directions made thereunder. The Accountable Officer is also responsible for ensuring the regularity of expenditure and income. The Board and Accountable Officer are also responsible for the preparation of the [Directors' Report/Foreword]. My/our responsibilities, as independent auditor(s), are established by the Public Finance and Accountability (Scotland) Act 2000 and the Code of Audit Practice approved by the Auditor General for Scotland, which requires adherence to the auditing standards issued by the Auditing Practices Board (APB) and relevant ethical standards. It also requires me/us to have regard to other guidance and advice issued by the APB.

I/we report my/our opinion as to whether the financial statements give a true and fair view and are properly prepared in accordance with the National Health Service (Scotland) Act 1978 and directions made thereunder and whether, in all material respects, the expenditure and income shown in the financial statements have been incurred or applied in accordance with any applicable enactments and guidance issued by the Scottish Ministers. I/we also report if, in my/our opinion, the NHS Board has not kept proper accounting records, or if I/we have not received all the information and explanations I/we require for my/our audit.

I/we review whether the statement on page....... complies with the guidance issued by the Scottish Executive Health Department 'Corporate Governance: Statement on Internal Control'. I/we report if the statement does not comply with the guidance or if it is misleading or inconsistent with other information I/we am/are aware of from my/our audit. I/We am/are not required to consider, nor have I/We considered whether the statement covers all risks and controls. I/We are also not required to form an opinion on the effectiveness of the NHS Board's corporate governance procedures or its risk and control processes.

I/we read the other information published with the financial statements and consider the implications for my/our report if I/we become aware of any apparent misstatements or material inconsistencies with the financial statements.

4. HSS Trusts (Northern Ireland)

Respective responsibilities of Trust and Auditors

As described in the Statement of Trust Responsibilities, the Trust is required to prepare financial statements for each year in the form and on the basis determined by the Department of Health, Social Services and Public Safety. My responsibilities as independent auditor are established by statute, the auditing standards issued by the Auditing Practices Board (APB) and relevant ethical standards. I also have regard to other guidance and advice issued by the APB. This opinion has been prepared for and only for the Department of Health, Social Services and Public Safety in accordance with Article 90(2)(a) of The Health and Personal Social Services (Northern Ireland) Order 1972 and for no other purpose.

I report to you my opinion as to whether the financial statements present fairly the state of affairs of the Trust and are properly prepared in accordance with the Health and Personal Social Services (Northern Ireland) Order 1972 and directions made thereafter by the Department of Health, Social Services and Public Safety. I also report to you if in my opinion the Trust has not kept proper accounting records, or if I have not received all the information and explanations I require for my audit.

I review whether the statement on pages x to x reflects the Trust's compliance with the Department of Health, Social Services and Public Safety's guidance "Statement of Internal Control - transitional statement 200x/x". I report if it does not meet the requirements specified by the Department of Health, Social Services and Public Safety, or if the statement is misleading or inconsistent with other information I am aware of from my audit of the financial statements. I am not required to consider, nor have I considered, whether the chief executive's statement on internal control covers all risks and controls. I am also not required to form an opinion on the effectiveness of the Trust's system of internal control.

Glossary of terms

Accountable Officer – the designated officer (Chief Executive) responsible for the propriety and regularity of the public finances of NHS bodies, and for the keeping of proper records, as set out in the Accountable Officers' Memorandum.

Audit Commission – the independent body with statutory responsibilities to regulate the audit of local government and health bodies in England and Wales, and to promote improvements in the economy, efficiency and effectiveness of local government services. In relation to
the audit of financial statements, the Commission is responsible for the appointment of auditors, setting the required standards for its appointed auditors, and regulating the quality of audits.

Auditor General for Scotland – is appointed by the Crown and is independent of the Scottish Executive. He plays a key role in holding the Scottish Executive and most other public spending bodies in Scotland (with the exception of local authorities and fire and police boards which are the responsibility of the Accounts Commission) to account for the proper, efficient and effective use of public money. He is a member of the board of Audit Scotland. He is responsible for the appointment of auditors to NHS Scotland bodies.

Audit Scotland – is a corporate body, established under Section 10, Public Finance and Accountability Act 2000 to provide assistance and support to the Auditor General and the Accounts Commission in the exercise of their respective functions.

The Comptroller and Auditor General for Northern Ireland – heads the Northern Ireland Audit Office and is responsible to the Northern Ireland Assembly for the audit of central government departments and most of their sponsored bodies.

HSS bodies – defined for the purposes of this paper as HSS Boards, HSS Trusts, HSS Special Agencies and the Central Services Agency.

HPSS controls assurance standards – developed by the Department of Health, Social Services and Public Safety to assist HSS bodies in identifying and managing risk. For financial year 2003/04 there are 6 controls assurance standards, of which three are deemed to be 'core': governance; financial management; and risk management.

National Assembly for Wales – the parliamentary body for Wales established by the Government of Wales Act 1998.

NHS Appointments Commission – an independent body within the NHS, established in April 2001, responsible for the appointment of all chairmen and non-executive directors to NHS bodies in England.

NHS bodies – defined for the purposes of this Bulletin as strategic health authorities, special health authorities, NHS trusts, primary care trusts, and care trusts (England), NHS trusts and local health boards (Wales), unified NHS boards, island health boards, special health boards, acute NHS trusts, primary care NHS trusts and local health councils (Scotland).

Scottish Public Finance Manual – the manual published by the Scottish Ministers which sets out the overall rules and requirements for accountability in central government in Scotland.

Welsh Assembly Government – the executive body of the National Assembly for Wales. Led by the First Minister with a Cabinet comprised of Assembly Ministers with responsibility for specific areas of policy, e.g. Health & Social Services, Economic Development.

Welsh Risk Management Standards (WRMS) – developed by the National Assembly for Wales and the Welsh Risk Pool with the objective being to support NHS bodies in Wales in developing effective systems of risk management and control. For financial year 2002/03 there are thirty-eight WRMS, of which five are deemed to be core to the management of risk: risk management policy and strategy; risk profile; incident and hazard reporting, governance and financial management.

List of references

- The Statement on Internal Control 2003/04 – Department of Health, August 2003
- WHC (2002)74 Statement on Internal Control 2001-02 – National Assembly for Wales, June 2002
- Health Department Letter (2002) 11 (Corporate Governance: Statement on Internal Control) – Scottish Executive Health Department
- MISC (95)9 Accountable Officer Memorandum for Chief Executives – Department of Health 1995
- Codes of Conduct and Accountability for NHS Boards – Department of Health 1994
- APB Practice Note 10: Audit of Financial Statements of Public Sector Entities in the United Kingdom (Revised), April 2001
- Code of Audit Practice – Audit Commission, March 2002
- Statement of Responsibilities of Auditors and Audited Bodies – Audit Commission
- Audit Committee Handbook – Department of Health, April 2001
- Corporate Governance Framework for NHS Wales – 1998
- Code of Conduct, Code of Accountability for NHS Boards – Scottish Office Home and Health Department, April 1994
- Management Executive Letter (1996)42 NHS Internal Audit Standards and Audit Committee Handbook – the Scottish Office Deparment of Health, May 1996
- Scottish Public Finance Manual
- Code of Audit Practice – Audit Scotland, July 2001
- Statement of Responsibilities of Auditors and Audited Bodies – Audit Scotland, July 2001
- Circular HSS (F) 24/2001 – Corporate Governance: Statement on Internal Control Department of Health, Social Services and Public Safety, May 2001
- Circular HSS(FAU) 19/2003 – Statement on Internal Control:Transitional Statement 2002/03 – Department of Health, Social Services and Public Safety, May 2003
- Circular HSS (PDD) 8/94 – Corporate Governance in the HPSS: Codes of Conduct and Accountability – Department of Health and Social Services 1994

[Bulletin 2004/2]
Corporate governance: requirements of public sector auditors (local government bodies)

(Issued June 2004)

Contents

	Paragraphs
Section 1: Introduction	1 - 2
Applicability of this Bulletin	3 - 4
Purpose of this Bulletin	5 - 6
Structure of this Bulletin	7 - 8
Composition of the local government sector	9
Section 2: Corporate Governance Framework	
Background	10 - 12
Statement on Internal Control	13 - 16
Audit Committees	17 - 18
Section 3: Auditors' Responsibilities	
Statements of Auditors' Responsibilities	19 - 24
The Auditors' Review of the Statement on Internal Control	25 - 35
Significant Internal Control Issues	36 - 41
Failure to Conduct a Review	42
Reporting by Exception	43 - 45
Audit Committees	46 - 47

Appendix 1: Respective Responsibilities of the Chief Financial Officer and Auditors

Glossary of Terms

List of References

Section 1: Introduction

1 The corporate governance framework that applies to listed companies in the private sector[1] is well developed. The structures and processes for decision making and accountability, control systems and behaviour at the top of organisations are equally important issues for public sector organisations. Not surprisingly, therefore, over the last decade corporate governance has also become an increasingly significant issue for the public sector.

2 Unlike listed companies, which are subject to the same broad framework of company law, public sector bodies do not operate within a common legislative framework. Consequently different models of governance have evolved within the public sector in response to different sets of accountabilities. Hence the need for more than one Bulletin covering the requirements of external auditors in the public sector.

Applicability of this Bulletin

3 This Bulletin provides guidance to auditors of local government bodies that publish a statement on internal control (SIC). At the time of publication the requirement to produce a SIC only applies to local government bodies in England where there is a statutory requirement to prepare and publish a SIC under the Accounts and Audit Regulations 2003[2].

4 In Scotland, Wales and Northern Ireland, local government bodies are required by the Local Authority SORP[3] to include in their financial statements, as a minimum, a statement on the system of internal financial control but may voluntarily decide to include a SIC or a wider statement on corporate governance arrangements. Appointed auditors are required through the respective Code of Audit Practice to review any such statement. The APB expects that the guidance in this Bulletin, adapted as necessary, will assist auditors with such reviews.

Purpose of this Bulletin

5 The APB has produced this Bulletin to:
- set out the corporate governance arrangements that apply in the local government sector; and
- provide guidance to local government auditors on their review and reporting responsibilities in relation to the corporate governance disclosures local government bodies are required to make.

---

[1] The corporate governance requirements placed on listed companies are set out in the 'Combined Code' which was published by the Committee on Corporate Governance in June 1998. The Combined Code has been appended to the Listing Rules of the Financial Services Authority and consolidates the recommendations of the earlier Cadbury, Greenbury and Hampel reports on private sector corporate governance issues. The Financial Reporting Council has issued a revised Code which came into effect for reporting years beginning on or after 1 November 2003. Also relevant is the report of the Internal Control Working Party of the ICAEW (commonly referred to as The Turnbull Report) which was published in September 1999.

[2] A similar requirement is likely to be introduced for local government bodies in Wales from 1 April 2005 by the proposed Accounts and Audit Regulations (Wales) 2004.

[3] The Code of Practice on Local Authority Accounting in the United Kingdom: A Statement of Recommended Practice (CIPFA/LASAAC).

The bodies responsible for the appointment of auditors[4] require auditors, as part of their statutory audit of the financial statements, to review audited bodies' corporate governance disclosures.

Structure of this Bulletin

As the corporate governance framework within the public sector has evolved, the APB has issued guidance to cover other areas of the sector. Bulletin 2003/1 "Corporate Governance: Requirements of Public Sector Auditors (Central Government)" and Bulletin 2003/2 "Corporate Governance: Requirements of Public Sector Auditors (National Health Service Bodies)" were issued in November 2003.

Section 2 covers the corporate governance framework applying to local government bodies. Section 3 sets out the auditors' responsibilities in relation to the corporate governance disclosures local government bodies are required to make.

Composition of the Local Government Sector

For the purposes of this Bulletin, the local government sector is taken to comprise those local government bodies subject to the Local Authority SORP. In England, Wales and Scotland this is local authorities, police authorities, fire authorities, joint committees and joint boards of principal authorities, and (in England and Wales) relevant parish, town and community councils. In Northern Ireland the SORP applies to all district councils.

Section 2: Corporate governance framework

Background

Local government bodies are governed by democratically elected or appointed members who are supported by professional officers. It is the responsibility of the body to ensure that sound systems of financial management and internal control are in place. However, local authorities also have three designated statutory officers each of whom has a specific role in relation to accountability and control:

- Head of Paid Service[5] – usually the Chief Executive, responsible to the full council for the corporate and overall strategic management of the authority;
- Monitoring Officer[6] – responsible for reporting to the authority any actual or potential breaches of the law or any maladministration, and for ensuring that procedures for recording and reporting key decisions are operating effectively;

---

[4] Audit Commission for England and Wales, Accounts Commission in Scotland, and Department of the Environment in Northern Ireland. From 1 April 2005, the functions of the Audit Commission in Wales and the National Audit Office are being brought together to form the Wales Audit Office. The Public Audit Bill (Wales) will, if enacted, extend the role of the Auditor General for Wales to include the Audit Commission's current functions in relation to the audit and inspection of local government bodies in Wales.

[5] England and Wales only.

[6] England and Wales only.

- Chief Financial Officer[7] – local authorities are required to appoint an officer with responsibility for the proper administration of their financial affairs.

11 Corporate governance developments in local government have included the following measures:

- new ethical frameworks including codes of conduct for elected members and employees;
- improved accountability through new political management structures[8]; and
- the introduction of a statement on internal control (SIC)[9].

12 An overview of the key corporate governance requirements for local government bodies, the auditors' responsibilities, and the relevant paragraphs in this Bulletin are set out in the table below:

Subject	Key Requirements	Auditors' Responsibilities	Relevant paragraphs in this Bulletin
Corporate governance framework	It is the responsibility of the corporate body to ensure that sound systems of financial management and internal control are in place. Personal responsibility for the overall corporate governance framework is therefore not allocated to any one officer. The three statutory officers referred to in paragraph 10 above all have some responsibility for elements of the framework. The Chief Financial Officer is charged with personal responsibility for the proper administration of an authority's financial affairs.	Auditors are required to be satisfied that proper practices have been observed in compiling the accounts, and that proper arrangements have been made for securing economy, efficiency and effectiveness in the use of resources.	10

[7] In England and Wales, this postholder is designated the 'Responsible Financial Officer' under section 151 of the Local Government Act 1972; in Scotland, the 'proper officer' under section 95 of the Local Government (Scotland) Act 1973; and, in Northern Ireland, the 'Chief Financial Officer' under section 54 of the Local Government Act (Northern Ireland) 1972.

[8] Introduced in England and Wales by the Local Government Act 2000, and in Scotland following the recommendations of the McIntosh Commission.

[9] Introduced in England by the Accounts and Audit Regulations 2003.

Subject	Key Requirements	Auditors' Responsibilities	Relevant paragraphs in this Bulletin
Statement on Internal Control	Required by the Accounts and Audit Regulations 2003 for local government bodies in England. With effect from financial year 2003/04 a SIC is required to be prepared in accordance with proper practice, as defined by CIPFA, and published with the statement of accounts.	Review the statement to: consider the completeness of the disclosures in meeting the specified requirements, and identify any known inconsistencies in the disclosures made.	13-16, 25-45
Audit Committees	Audit committees are not mandatory for local government bodies with the exception of police authorities in England and Wales.	No specific reporting responsibilities. However, auditors will attend committee meetings at which corporate governance, internal control, and risk management matters are considered as a means of gaining evidence for the review of the SIC.	17-18, 46-47

Statement on Internal Control

In line with developments in other areas of the public sector, the Accounts and Audit Regulations 2003 (A&A Regulations) introduced, for local government bodies in England, the requirement for a SIC to be published with the statement of accounts.

13

The A&A Regulations specify that the SIC must be 'prepared in accordance with proper practices'. The Chartered Institute of Public Finance and Accountancy (CIPFA)'s publication 'The Statement on Internal Control in Local Government: Meeting the requirements of the Accounts and Audit Regulations 2003' (April 2004), defines proper practice on the form and content of the SIC and provides guidance on the process for preparing it. It advises that the SIC should be signed by the most senior officer and the most senior member of council.

14

The requirement for a SIC to be published commences from financial year 2003/04. However, the CIPFA guidance recognises that not all authorities will be in a position to obtain the necessary assurances to support a full SIC for the first year, although it encourages those authorities with strong internal control and risk management processes already embedded to adopt the full requirements. For those authorities still developing their internal control and risk management processes, the guidance allows for an interim statement to be produced for 2003/04 with an action plan to ensure full compliance for 2004/05.

15

SICs are required to include the following disclosures:

16

- acknowledgement of the authority's responsibility for ensuring that a sound system of internal control is maintained;
- an explanation that the system of internal control is designed to manage risk to a reasonable level rather than to eliminate all risk of failure to achieve the organisation's policies, aims and objectives; it can therefore only provide reasonable and not absolute assurance of effectiveness;
- reference to an ongoing risk management process designed to identify and prioritise the risks to the achievement of the organisation's policies, aims and objectives, to evaluate the likelihood of those risks being realised, and to manage them efficiently, effectively and economically;
- confirmation that the system of internal control was in place for the duration of the financial year and remained so up until the date of approval of the annual accounts;
- a description of the key elements of the internal control environment;
- acknowledgement of the authority's responsibility for reviewing the effectiveness of the system of internal control, and a description of the review process undertaken;
- confirmation that the results of the review of effectiveness of internal control have been discussed by the authority and the relevant committee; and
- where appropriate, details of actions taken, or proposed, to deal with significant internal control issues.

Audit Committees

17   Audit committees are not mandatory for local government bodies with the exception of police authorities in England and Wales[10]. However, bodies are expected to establish an appropriate process to allow elected members to discuss audit matters with both internal and external auditors.

18   The above functions in relation to audit matters are discharged by local government bodies in a variety of ways, for example through an audit committee, the full council/authority, the cabinet executive, or overview and scrutiny committee[11].

Section 3: Auditors' responsibilities

Statements of Auditors' Responsibilities

19   Auditors of local government bodies are appointed by the Audit Commission (England and Wales)[12], the Accounts Commission (Scotland), and the Department of the Environment (Northern Ireland). The responsibilities of the auditor are set out in the respective 'Code of Audit Practice'[13] and the 'Statement of Responsibilities of Auditors and Audited Bodies'[14] which are provided to each audited body.

[10] *Required by the Code of Practice on Financial Management issued under section 39 of the Police Act 1996*

[11] *Introduced for local authorities in England and Wales by the Local Government Act 2000.*

[12] *In Wales, the Wales Audit Office from 1 April 2005. See footnote 2.*

[13] *A 'Code of Audit Practice' is issued by the Audit Commission (England and Wales), Audit Scotland with the approval of the Accounts Commission (Scotland), and the Local Government Audit Office (Northern Ireland).*

[14] *Audit Commission and Accounts Commission only.*

Auditors of local government bodies have different responsibilities with respect to the various component parts of the statement of accounts and the information presented with the statement of accounts. They are required to 'audit' the statement of accounts, 'review' the body's SIC, and 'read' the other information published with the statement of accounts. Auditors read such 'other information' because the credibility of the statement of accounts and the related auditors' report may be undermined by material inconsistencies between the statement of accounts and the 'other information', or by apparent misstatements within the 'other information'.

In some instances auditors have to report positively the results of their work whereas in other instances the auditors only have to report by exception. The APB is of the view that users of financial statements will find it difficult to understand the scope of the auditors' involvement in the absence of a clear statement of their responsibilities towards the financial statements and the information presented with them.

The key elements of a statement of the auditors' responsibilities relate to the requirements of:

- statute, the respective Code of Audit Practice with respect to the audit of the financial statements, and Auditing Standards (with guidance on the application of Auditing Standards provided by APB Practice Note 10[15]); and
- Statement of Auditing Standards 160 'Other information in documents containing audited financial statements' to read the 'other information' presented with the financial statements.

In accordance with SAS 600 'Auditors reports on financial statements' (and the guidance on the application of auditing standards in the public sector provided by APB Practice Note 10), a description of the auditors' responsibilities, covering the key elements set out in the above paragraph, should be included within the auditors' report on the financial statements. The extract example in Appendix 1 illustrates the wording that may be used to explain the auditors' responsibilities. The APB is of the view that a statement of auditors' responsibilities as further described in paragraphs 25 to 27, avoids the need for a separate auditors' report dealing with their review of corporate governance matters.

The auditors' responsibilities in relation to their review of the SIC are not designed to provide 'positive assurance'. In view of the limited nature of the review, and in order to avoid the possibility of misunderstandings arising, the APB recommends that prior to the release of the annual accounts the auditors communicate, and discuss, with both management and those charged with governance the findings of their review.

The Auditors' Review of the Statement on Internal Control

The nature of the auditors' review of the SIC will follow a similar approach to that set out in the APB's Bulletin 1999/5 dealing with the requirements of auditors under the listing rules of the United Kingdom Listing Authority. The auditors' review will be directed at:

- considering the completeness of the disclosures in meeting the requirements of proper practices as specified by CIPFA; and

---

[15] APB Practice Note 10: Audit of Financial Statements of Public Sector Entities in the United Kingdom (Revised April 2001).

- identifying any inconsistencies between the disclosures and the information that the auditors are aware of from their work on the financial statements and other work.

26 The reference to 'other work' in the second bullet of paragraph 25 above is significant in the local government sector. The relevant Code of Audit Practice requires auditors to review the financial statements, aspects of corporate governance arrangements, and aspects of performance management arrangements. Work in relation to one element of the audit informs and is complementary to work in relation to the others. Thus, in concluding their review of the statement, they will have taken into account not only the results of their work on the financial statements, but also their work on the other elements required by the Code.

27 The extent of the auditors' review procedures will therefore vary according to the nature and content of their other work. However, such review procedures will always include consideration of the disclosures set out in paragraph 16 above. In particular, they will assess whether the summary of the process adopted by the authority in reviewing the effectiveness of the system of internal control, is both supported by relevant documentation, and appropriately reflects that process.

28 Appropriate evidence regarding the disclosures will usually be obtained by:
- considering whether the disclosures are consistent with the auditors' review of the minutes of meetings of the authority and of relevant committees (for example cabinet executive, audit committee, overview and scrutiny committee, standards committee);
- reviewing supporting documents prepared for the authority and relevant committees that are relevant to disclosures made in the SIC. In doing this the auditors will pay particular attention to the documentation prepared for the authority to support the statement made in connection with the effectiveness review and assess whether or not it provides sound support for that statement;
- gaining an understanding of the process defined for the review of the effectiveness of internal control through enquiry of appropriate members and officers, and comparing their understanding to the statement made in the SIC;
- attending committee meetings at which corporate governance, internal control, and risk management matters are considered;
- reviewing the Head of Internal Audit's formal annual report to those charged with governance which includes an opinion on the overall adequacy and effectiveness of the organisation's internal control environment[16]; and
- relating the statement made by the authority to the auditors' knowledge of the body obtained during the audit of the statement of accounts and other work required by the respective Code of Audit Practice. (As explained in paragraph 32, the scope of the authority's review will be considerably broader in its scope than the knowledge the auditors can be expected to have obtained during their audit.)

29 Where auditors feel it is appropriate, they may request written confirmation of oral representations made during the course of the review.

30 When reviewing the authority's disclosures relating to the process for reviewing the effectiveness of the system of internal control, the auditor recognises that the authority does not need to review the effectiveness of every internal control, such as those designed to manage immaterial risks. The review process, however, includes all

---

[16] Required by the CIPFA Code of Practice for Internal Audit in Local Government in the United Kingdom 2003.

types of controls including those of an operational and compliance nature, as well as internal financial controls.

The SIC covers the year under review and the period to the date of approval of the annual accounts. The auditors, therefore, consider whether the statement covers the year under review and whether there are any material developments between the balance sheet date and the date the accounts are signed which should properly be included in the statement.

In carrying out their review, the auditors will have regard to the knowledge of the body they have obtained from their audit work. To enable them to perform their audit and express an opinion on the financial statements, auditors are required by Auditing Standards to understand the body's control environment and to assess the components of audit risk. Such an assessment encompasses control risk to the extent that the auditors expect to be able to rely on such an assessment in order to reduce the extent of their substantive audit procedures. Consequently, the auditor's assessment required by Auditing Standards will be considerably narrower in scope than the review performed by the authority.

Auditors are not, therefore, expected to assess whether all risks and controls have been addressed by the authority, or whether all risks are satisfactorily addressed by internal controls. In order to communicate this fact to users of the financial statements the following sentence is included in the auditors' report on the financial statements:

> *I/We am/are not required to consider, nor have I/we considered, whether the authority's statement on internal control covers all risks and controls. I/We am/are also not required to form an opinion on the effectiveness of the authority's corporate governance procedures or its risk and control procedures.*

Statement of Auditing Standards 610.5 requires:

> *'Auditors should communicate to those charged with governance:...c) material weaknesses in the accounting and internal control systems identified during the audit.'*

The APB recommends that any material weakness in internal control identified by the auditors be reported on as soon as practicable. The auditors do not wait until the financial statement audit has been completed before reporting any such weakness[17]. In this way those charged with governance will be aware of any material weakness that the auditors have identified and be able to take account of it in the SIC.

Significant Internal Control Issues

Where appropriate, the authority is required to set out details of actions taken, or proposed, to deal with significant internal control issues. The purpose of this disclosure is to deliver assurance that significant internal control issues have been, or are being, addressed and that the SIC is a balanced reflection of the actual position.

---

[17] The requirements and guidance for auditors on this subject are set out in SAS 610: Communication of audit matters to those charged with governance.

37 This may be a difficult requirement for authorities to satisfy, and for auditors to review, because a 'significant internal control issue' cannot be defined to suit all contexts; the same issue may or may not be significant depending on the circumstances.

38 Whilst the term 'significant internal control issue' cannot be absolutely defined, the following indicators (which are not exhaustive) may be useful in considering whether or not an issue is significant enough to be reported in the SIC:

- it seriously prejudices or prevents achievement of a principal objective of the authority;
- it has resulted in the need to seek additional funding to allow it to be resolved, or has resulted in significant diversion of resources from another aspect of the business;
- it has led to a material impact on the accounts;
- the audit committee, or equivalent, advises it should be considered significant for this purpose;
- the Head of Internal Audit reports on it as significant, for this purpose, in the annual opinion on the internal control environment;
- the issue, or its impact, has attracted significant public interest or has seriously damaged the reputation of the organisation;
- the issue has resulted in formal action being undertaken by the Chief Financial Officer and/or the Monitoring Officer.

39 The auditor's review responsibility consists of assessing whether the disclosures made by the authority of the actions applied to address any significant internal control issues appropriately reflect those actions.

40 The auditors are not required to assess whether the actions described in the SIC will, in fact, remedy any underlying weakness associated with the significant internal control issue.

41 If the auditors are aware of a significant internal control issue which the authority has not disclosed they discuss the position with senior management and those charged with governance of the authority. At the time of preparing the SIC for a particular year, disclosure of information about a significant internal control issue might prejudice the outcome of a special investigation (possibly preventing successful prosecution of a case of fraud or inhibiting a disciplinary case against members of staff). In such circumstances, it would be advisable for the SIC to record that there are issues which cannot be disclosed because to do so would prejudice the outcome of an investigation. However, if the auditors are not able to agree with senior management and those charged with governance as to how the matter should be resolved they consider the need to report by exception.

Failure to Conduct a Review

42 Where the authority has failed to undertake a review of the effectiveness of internal control, this departure from specified statutory requirements should be disclosed and explained by the authority in the SIC. The auditors consider whether this requirement is met and whether the explanation is consistent with the auditors' understanding. If the auditors decide that it is not, they consider the need to report by exception.

Reporting by Exception

If the auditors conclude: 43

- that the summary of the process applied in reviewing the effectiveness of the internal control system is either not supported by or does not appropriately reflect the auditors' understanding of the process undertaken (paragraphs 25-35);
- that the actions disclosed to deal with significant internal control issues do not appropriately reflect the auditors' understanding of the action undertaken (paragraphs 36-41);
- that no disclosure has been made by the authority that it failed to conduct a review of the effectiveness of the internal control system (paragraph 42);
- where the authority discloses that a review of effectiveness has not been undertaken, but the explanation is not consistent with the auditors' understanding (paragraph 42)

they report this in the opinion section of their report on the financial statements.

However, as this does not give rise to a qualified opinion on the financial statements, the APB recommends that the auditors' comments be included under the heading 'Other Matter' as illustrated in the example opinion below: 44

Opinion

In my/our opinion the statement of accounts presents fairly the financial transactions of xx Authority at 31 March 20xx and its income and expenditure for the year then ended.

Other Matter

I/we have reviewed the authority's description of the processes undertaken for reviewing the effectiveness of the system of internal control as set out on page xx. In my/our opinion the authority's comments concerning.... do not appropriately reflect my/our understanding of the processes undertaken because....

In addition, the auditor considers whether any matters arising from the review of the statement are significant enough to warrant a report in the public interest under section 8 of the Audit Commission Act 1998 or a written recommendation under section 11[18]. A report in the public interest should only be made where the auditor considers a matter sufficiently important to be brought to the notice of the audited body and the public. In Scotland, the Controller of Audit may report to the Accounts Commission on any matter arising from the audit of an authority's accounts which the Controller considers should be brought to the attention of the authority or the public[19]. In Northern Ireland, a local government auditor reports to the Department of the Environment at the completion of the audit[20]. 45

---

[18] *England and Wales.*

[19] *Section 102 Local Government (Scotland) Act 1973 as amended by the Local Government in Scotland Act 2003.*

[20] *Section 80 of the Local Government Act (Northern Ireland) 1972.*

Audit Committees

46   Auditors of local government bodies have no specific reporting responsibilities in relation to the establishment and workings of audit committees or their equivalent.

47   However, as set out in paragraph 28 above, the auditors will attend committee meetings at which corporate governance, internal control, and risk management matters are considered in order to obtain the required assurance regarding the disclosures made by the authority in the SIC.

Appendix 1 – Respective responsibilities of the chief financial officer and auditors

Illustrative extract from local authority Audit Report (England)

Respective Responsibilities of Chief Financial Officer and Auditors

As described on page x, the Chief Financial Officer is responsible for the preparation of the statement of accounts in accordance with the Statement of Recommended Practice on Local Authority Accounting in the United Kingdom. My/Our responsibilities as independent auditor/auditors are established by statute, and by the Code of Audit Practice issued by the Audit Commission, which requires adherence to the auditing standards issued by the Auditing Practices Board (APB) and relevant ethical standards. It also requires me/us to to have regard to other guidance and advice issued by the APB.

I/We report to you my/our opinion as to whether the statement of accounts present fairly the financial position of the Council and its income and expenditure for the year.

I/We review whether the statement on internal control on page x reflects compliance with CIPFA's guidance 'The Statement on Internal Control in Local Government: Meeting the Requirements of the Accounts and Audit Regulations 2003'. I/We report if it does not comply with proper practices specified by CIPFA or if the statement is misleading or inconsistent with other information I/we are aware of from my/our audit of the financial statements. I/We are not required to consider, nor have I/we considered, whether the statement on internal control covers all risks and controls. I/We are also not required to form an opinion on the effectiveness of the authority's corporate governance procedures or its risk and control procedures. My/Our review was not performed for any purpose connected with any specific transaction and should not be relied upon for any such purpose.

I/we read the other information published with the statement of accounts and consider the implications for my/our report if I/we become aware of any apparent misstatements or material inconsistencies with the statement of accounts.

Glossary of terms

Audit Commission – the independent body with statutory responsibilities to regulate the audit of local government and health bodies in England and Wales, and to promote improvements in the economy, efficiency and effectiveness of local government services. In relation to the audit of financial statements, the Commission is responsible for the appointment of auditors, setting the required standards for its appointed auditors, and regulating the quality of audits.

Accounts Commission – equivalent body in Scotland to Audit Commission in respect of local government.

Chief Financial Officer – generic title applied to a local government body's Director of Finance who is responsible for the proper administration of the authority's financial affairs.

Head of Paid Service – statutory title applied to the senior official of a local authority, usually the Chief Executive, responsible to the authority for corporate and overall strategic management.

Local Government bodies – defined for the purposes of this paper as principally local authorities, police authorities, and fire authorities.

Monitoring Officer – statutory title applied to the local authority officer responsible for reporting to the authority any actual or potential breaches of the law or any maladministration.

Statement on Internal Control (SIC) – statement required by the Accounts and Audit Regulations 2003 to be included with the statement of accounts for local government in England. The SIC confirms that the body has a sound system of internal control which facilitates the effective exercise of the body's functions and which includes arrangements for the management of risk. It also confirms that a review of the effectiveness of the system of internal control has been conducted.

List of references

- Local Government Act 2000 – The Stationery Office
- Local Government Act 1972 – The Stationery Office
- Accounts and Audit Regulations 2003 – The Stationery Office
- Local Government in Scotland Act 2003 – The Stationery Office
- Local Government (Scotland) Act 1973 – The Stationery Office
- Code of Audit Practice – Audit Commission, March 2002
- Code of Audit Practice – Audit Scotland (with the approval of the Accounts Commission), July 2001
- Code of Audit Practice – Local Government Audit Office (Northern Ireland)
- The Statement on Internal Control in Local Government: Meeting the Requirements of the Accounts and Audit Regulations 2003 – CIPFA, April 2004
- Police Act 1996 – The Stationery Office
- APB Practice Note 10: Audit of Financial Statements of Public Sector Entities in the United Kingdom (Revised), April 2001
- Code of Practice for Internal Audit in Local Government in the United Kingdom – CIPFA, 2003

[Bulletin 2005/3]
Guidance for auditors on first-time application of IFRSs in the United Kingdom and the Republic of Ireland

Contents

	Paragraphs
Introduction	1 - 12
Objective	1 - 7
Limitations of the Bulletin	8
Responsibilities of the directors	9 - 12
Summary of significant issues covered in the Bulletin	13
Application of ISAs (UK and Ireland): specific issues	14 - 132

ISQC 1	Quality Control for Firms that Perform Audits and Reviews of Historical Financial Information, and other Assurance and Related Services Engagements	15 - 16
200	Objective and General Principles Governing an Audit of Financial Statements	17 - 19
210	Terms of Audit Engagements	20 - 21
220	Quality Control for Audits of Historical Financial Information	22 - 23
240	The Auditor's Responsibility to Consider Fraud in an Audit of Financial Statements	24 - 25
250	Section A – Consideration of Laws and Regulations in an Audit of Financial Statements	26 - 54
250	Section B – The Auditor's Right and Duty to Report to Regulators in the Financial Sector	55
260	Communication of Audit Matters With Those Charged With Governance	56 - 59
300	Planning an Audit of Financial Statements	60 - 66
315	Obtaining an Understanding of the Entity and Its Environment and Assessing the Risks of Material Misstatement, and 330 The Auditor's Procedures in Response to Assessed Risks	67 - 70
320	Audit Materiality	71 - 74
510	Initial Engagements-Opening Balances and Continuing Engagements-Opening Balances, and 710 Comparatives	75 - 83
520	Analytical Procedures	84 - 89
540	Audit of Accounting Estimates	90 - 94
545	Auditing Fair Value Measurements and Disclosures	95 - 97
550	Related Parties	98 - 99
560	Subsequent Events	100 - 101
570	Going Concern	102 - 109
580	Management Representations	110 - 112
600	Using the Work of Another Auditor	113 - 114
620	Using the Work of an Expert	115 - 116
700	The Auditor's Report on Financial Statements	117 - 128

720 Other Information in Documents Containing Audited Financial Statements	129 - 132
Review of interim financial information under IFRSs	133 - 155

Appendices

1: Equivalent Legislative References for Northern Ireland and Comparative Legislative References for the Republic of Ireland
2: Example review report

Introduction

Objective

1 This Bulletin provides auditors with guidance on issues that may arise when companies (and other entities that are subject to audit) undertake the transition from United Kingdom, or Republic of Ireland, Generally Accepted Accounting Practice (UK/ROI GAAP) to International Financial Reporting Standards (IFRSs)[1].

2 Regulation EC 1606/2002[2] (IAS Regulation) requires European Union companies with securities that are admitted to trading on a regulated market of any Member State to prepare their consolidated financial statements in conformity with IFRSs as adopted for use in the European Union.

3 At the same time as IFRSs take effect in 2005, changes to legal accounting requirements also enter into force in UK and ROI law, arising mainly from the Fair Value Directive and the Modernisation Directive. Consequently, there is substantial complexity in the interaction of legal issues, accounting standards, and auditing requirements.

4 As this Bulletin reflects the requirements of the Companies Act 1985 (CA 1985) it is of direct application to audits of entities that are incorporated in Great Britain. The UK DTI has published 'Guidance for British Companies on Changes to the Accounting and Reporting Provisions of the Companies Act 1985' ("DTI Guidance")[3], which describes the main changes to the CA 1985, as well as highlighting certain practical issues. Appendix 1 of this Bulletin sets out a table of the equivalent legislative references for Northern Ireland and of comparative legislative references for the Republic of Ireland.

5 IFRS 1 'First-time adoption of International Financial Reporting Standards' has been issued to enable preparers to ensure that an entity's first IFRS financial statements, and its interim reports for part of the period covered by those financial statements, contain high quality information that:

(a) is transparent for users and comparable over all periods presented;
(b) provides a suitable starting point for accounting under IFRSs; and
(c) can be generated at a cost that does not exceed the benefits to users.

Appended to IFRS 1 is 'Guidance on Implementing IFRS 1', which explains how the requirements of IFRS 1 interact with the requirements of those IFRSs that are most likely to involve questions that are specific to first time adopters. The guidance also includes an illustrative example of how a first time adopter might disclose how the transition to IFRSs affected its reported financial position, financial performance and cash flows as required by IFRS 1.

[1] *IFRSs is a defined term which incorporates all International Financial Reporting Standards, International Accounting Standards (IASs) and Interpretations originated by the International Financial Reporting Interpretations Committee (IFRIC) or the former Standards Interpretation Committee of the IASC. Details of all IFRSs can be found at the IASB website at www.iasb.org; IASB publications include helpful executive summaries of the standards. Unless otherwise stated, references in this Bulletin to IFRSs encompass both the IFRSs as issued by the IASB and IFRSs as adopted for use in the European Union (which may not be the same).*

[2] *EC 1606/2002 can be found on the Europa website at http://europa.eu.int/eur-lex/pri/en/oj/dat/2002/l_243/l_24320020911en00010004.pdf. Subsequent EC Regulations adopt specific IFRSs.*

[3] *This can be found on the DTI website at http://www.dti.gov.uk/cld/guidance.doc*

APB published two earlier drafts of this Bulletin in August 2004 and April 2005 to provide auditors with interim guidance. Since then, a number of uncertainties have been resolved and there have been various developments in auditing and financial reporting that are reflected in this Bulletin. In particular:

- The European Commission has adopted the majority of the extant IFRSs and Interpretations, apart from certain parts of IAS 39 on financial instruments and various very recent pronouncements from the IASB.[4]
- Further implementing legislation in the UK and the ROI has been passed,[5] as well as other guidance issued, for example on IFRS and distributable profits.
- Consensus has emerged in Europe about the specific wording to be used in auditor's reports when describing the financial reporting framework.

In spite of the progress made in resolving many of the legal and regulatory issues, there are some remaining uncertainties that are relevant to auditors. The APB will therefore continue to keep the situation under review.

Limitations of the Bulletin

The Bulletin does not give guidance on every aspect of the introduction of IFRSs in the UK and ROI. Specifically, it does not deal with the following:

(a) *Reporting on the opening IFRS balance sheet and/or the 2004 comparatives:* These represent non-statutory assurance engagements that are beyond the scope of this Bulletin.[6]
(b) *Identification of key differences between UK/ROI GAAP and IFRSs:* While the Bulletin refers to some differences between UK/ROI GAAP and IFRSs as examples, it does not provide a comprehensive list of differences.
(c) *Identification of those company law requirements that still apply to accounts prepared under IFRSs:* In the case of the CA 1985, this is provided in the DTI Guidance.
(d) *The Companies Act 1985 (Operating and Financial Review and Directors' Report) Regulations 2005.*

Responsibilities of the directors

General responsibilities of the directors

Under company law, the directors are responsible for preparing financial statements. Implicitly, this requires them to take reasonable steps to ensure that the entity will cope with the introduction of IFRSs, where applicable. The directors, through the entity's management, need to consider the specific impacts of IFRSs on the financial statements and whether proper accounting records will be maintained. The auditor considers whether management has put in place procedures with subsidiaries and branches such that the relevant accounting information will be received by the parent company on a timely basis to enable the group accounts to be properly prepared under IFRSs.

---

[4] Information about adopted IFRSs can be found on the Europa website at http://europa.eu.int/comm/internal_market/accounting/ias_en.htm#comments.

[5] See the DTI website at http://www.dti.gov.uk/cld/ for further details.

[6] The International Auditing and Assurance Standards Board (IAASB) has issued a non-authoritative paper on the subject 'First Time Adoption of International Financial Reporting Standards – Guidance for Auditors on Reporting Issues', in the form of a series of questions and answers.

Analysing the impact on the business

10 When preparing an "impact analysis" the entity will need to consider the effect of the introduction of IFRSs on:

   (a) computer and other data systems, internal controls and systems for preparing financial statements, for example systems capable of capturing all requisite information on financial instrument fair values, hedging arrangements and embedded derivatives;
   (b) the financial statements themselves, including interim results in the year of change. For example, how the financial statements should communicate the effect of the introduction of IFRSs to the users of the entity's financial statements;
   (c) business-critical issues that arise from the financial statements, for example the calculation of debt covenants and borrowing powers limitations in the entity's constitutional documents, or the impact on distributable profits where IFRSs are adopted in individual entity financial statements; and
   (d) other regulatory concerns, for example changes to the measurement of regulatory capital as a result of changes in the financial statements.

Management plans that address the issues identified

11 Given the likely pervasiveness of the changes introduced by IFRSs, it is unlikely that any company, group or other entity moving to IFRSs will have financial statements and/or a business so straightforward that no formal plan is necessary. Matters likely to be included in a plan, depending on the size and complexity of the organisation, are:

   • Creating an appropriate overall project steering structure.
   • Defining the individual projects (for critical accounting policies or line items).
   • Planning to resource these projects, including estimates for costs, time, external resources, (eg for input from specialists), staffing levels for the changeover period, hardware capacity and new software.
   • Developing a testing and implementation strategy.
   • Identifying constraints such as staff availability and the realistic ability to secure further resources.
   • Developing a high-level milestone plan to co-ordinate the overall programme of projects.
   • Reviewing and updating the plan to reflect actual progress.
   • Identifying alternative actions for systems issues which will not be addressed in time (contingency or damage limitation plans).

12 The auditor considers how the impact analysis and management plans affect its risk assessment for the audit during the period of transition from UK/ROI GAAP to IFRSs.

Summary of significant issues covered in the bulletin

13 In relation to the audit of IFRS information for the first time, certain issues are likely to be of particular importance. The Bulletin discusses the issues by relevant ISAs (UK and Ireland). The main features of the guidance are as follows:

   (a) There are major implications for audit risk (Paragraph 67)

(b) Auditors are likely to need to perform additional procedures on comparatives and opening balances for both full year financial statements (Paragraph 75) and interim reports (Paragraph 149)
(c) The need for audit staff to have appropriate knowledge and understanding of IFRSs (Paragraph 16) and the increased likelihood for the need for consultation with those responsible for technical financial reporting issues (Paragraph 22)
(d) There are implications for the auditor's consideration of laws and regulations, including:
  (i) The need to consider whether companies have complied with the legal requirement to prepare group accounts in accordance with IFRSs as adopted for use in the EU (Paragraph 28)
  (ii) The requirement for auditors of parent companies to consider whether directors have secured that the individual accounts of subsidiary undertakings prepare their statutory accounts following the same financial reporting framework, unless in their opinion there is a good reason for not doing so (Paragraph 39)
(e) Going concern issues may arise in relation to the impact of IFRSs on debt covenants (Paragraphs 105 – 109)
(f) The introduction of IFRSs will give rise to complexities regarding taxation (Paragraphs 51 – 52) and the distribution of profits (Paragraphs 49 – 50)
(g) Uncertainties for interim reports caused by the possible need for companies to anticipate the adoption of some IFRSs for use in the EU (Paragraphs 152 – 154)
(h) Careful consideration will need to be given to the tailoring of auditor's reports especially with respect to:
  (i) The need to refer to the applicable financial reporting framework (Paragraphs 119 – 122).
  (ii) Parent companies adopting IFRSs but also taking advantage of the Section 230 exemption (Paragraphs 42 – 43 and 123 – 124)
  (iii) The use of different financial reporting frameworks for group and parent company financial statements gives rise to separate auditor's reports for these if they are presented in separate sections of the Annual Report (Paragraph 44).
(i) The disclosures required in the year of transition to IFRSs, including:
  (i) Reconciliations of IFRS information to previous GAAP (Paragraph 16)
  (ii) More extensive disclosure of estimation uncertainty (Paragraphs 93 – 94)
(j) Potential difficulties relating to the audit of fair value information (Paragraphs 95 – 97)

Application of ISAS (UK and Ireland): specific issues

This section highlights some of the specific issues raised by the introduction of IFRSs in the application of ISAs (UK and Ireland).

International Standard on Quality Control (UK and Ireland)

ISQC 1 'Quality Control for Firms that Perform Audits and Reviews of Historical Financial Information, and other Assurance and Related Services Engagements'

ISQC 1 requires a firm of auditors to establish policies and procedures designed to provide reasonable assurance that it has sufficient personnel with the capabilities, competence, and commitment to ethical principles necessary to perform its engagements in accordance with professional standards and regulatory and legal requirements, and to enable the firm or engagement partners to issue reports that are appropriate in the circumstances. ISQC 1 requires firms to assign appropriate staff with the necessary capabilities, competence and time to perform engagements in accordance with professional standards and regulatory and legal requirements, and to enable the firm or engagement partners to issue reports that are appropriate in the circumstances.

16 Audit staff require knowledge and understanding of IFRSs. In the year of transition it will be particularly important for audit staff to have sufficient knowledge of both UK/ROI GAAP and IFRSs in order to audit the reconciliations between the two required by IFRS 1. Without such knowledge and understanding they may fail to

(a) detect improper or incorrect reconciling items such as changes in previous estimates or correction of errors;
(b) consider an omission from the reconciling items or items which have been incorrectly included within other reconciliation amounts; or
(c) identify incorrect IFRS figures (where UK/ROI GAAP figures have been left unchanged) which may result in no reconciling item being shown at all.

International Standards on Auditing (UK and Ireland)

ISA (UK & Ireland) 200 'Objective and General Principles Governing an Audit of Financial Statements'

Ethical Standards for Auditors

17 If the auditor is asked to assist the directors with their preparations for the introduction of IFRSs, careful consideration will need to be given to the implications of this for the auditor's independence and objectivity.

18 APB Ethical Standard 5 (ES 5) states that for listed companies, or significant affiliates of such an entity, the threats to the auditor's objectivity and independence that would be created are too high to allow the audit firm to undertake an engagement to provide any accounting services save in certain exceptional circumstances[7]. ES 5 also prohibits audit firms from accepting an engagement to provide a valuation to an audit client where the valuation would both involve a significant degree of subjective judgment, and is material to the financial statements.

19 These prohibitions do not extend to separate engagements to provide assurance to those charged with governance on the application of IFRSs, or to provide advice on accounting policies, or train management in IFRS-related matters. In order to help ensure that engagements of this nature are not confused with the statutory audit, it is advisable for auditors to clarify responsibilities for each engagement in separate engagement letters.

ISA (UK & Ireland) 210 'Terms of Audit Engagements'

Clarifying with directors their responsibilities

20 To avoid confusion as to the respective responsibilities of directors and auditors, concerning the introduction of IFRSs, the auditors communicate formally with the directors to avoid any misunderstandings. The directors are responsible for ensuring

---

[7] 'Accounting services' are defined as the provision of services that involve the maintenance of accounting records or the preparation of financial statements that are then subject to audit.

that the entity is prepared for the introduction of IFRSs and the auditors will wish to state explicitly in writing that the issue will be considered by them only in so far as it affects their audit responsibilities under statute and ISAs (UK and Ireland). This could be done by updating the audit engagement letter.

Particular matters that auditors may wish to clarify in the engagement letter are that the directors are responsible for: 21

(a) analysing the impact of the introduction of IFRSs on the business;
(b) developing plans to mitigate the effects identified by this analysis;
(c) assessing any impact of the introduction of IFRSs on the appropriateness of adopting the going concern basis in preparing the financial statements; and
(d) the preparation of financial statements as required under IFRSs, including comparative figures, and the disclosures needed to give a fair presentation and hence give a true and fair view.[8]

ISA (UK & Ireland) 220 'Quality Control for Audits of Historical Financial Information'

ISA (UK and Ireland) 220 addresses consultation, both within the audit team and with others within and outside the audit firm. The auditor considers the need for consultation on those matters deemed critical for an entity in its IFRS financial statements in the year of transition. Consultations are more likely at this time with those responsible for technical financial reporting issues within the audit firm and externally in cases where internal technical expertise is not available. 22

It will also be important at this time to ensure differences of opinion, particularly those on financial reporting issues relating to the application of IFRSs, are dealt with properly. Similarly, the engagement quality control review is likely to focus on the significant judgments made by the engagement team relating to the application of IFRSs. 23

ISA (UK & Ireland) 240 'The Auditor's Responsibility to Consider Fraud in an Audit of Financial Statements'

The introduction of IFRSs may lead to significant changes in financial reporting for many entities. Substantial changes to accounting systems may give greater opportunity for aggressive earnings management and, in extreme cases, fraud. Auditors consider the increased risk of fraud in planning and designing the audit procedures to be performed in the year an entity converts to IFRSs. 24

ISA (UK and Ireland) 240 requires the members of the engagement team to discuss the susceptibility of the entity's financial statements to material misstatements due to fraud. In the year of transition to IFRSs, this discussion will encompass the increased risk of fraud and its non-detection arising from the transition in the context of the specific circumstances of the entity. 25

ISA (UK & Ireland) 250, Section A 'Consideration of Laws and Regulations in an Audit of Financial Statements'

ISA (UK & Ireland) 250, Section A states that the auditor should obtain sufficient appropriate audit evidence about compliance with those laws and regulations 26

---

[8] *The Financial Reporting Council (FRC) has issued a paper "The Implications of New Accounting and Auditing Standards for the "True and Fair View" and Auditors' Responsibilities" which can be found on the FRC website at www.frc.org.uk.*

generally recognized by the auditor to have an effect on the determination of material amounts and disclosures in financial statements. The auditor should have a sufficient understanding of these laws and regulations in order to consider them when auditing the assertions related to the determination of the amounts to be recorded and the disclosures to be made.

27 Some of the relevant sources of law and regulation identified in the footnotes to paragraphs 20 and 20-1 of ISA (UK & Ireland) 250, Section A, are disapplied (or at least partially so) by the requirements of the IAS Regulation, for example the statutory formats in Schedule 4A CA 1985 for group accounts.[9]

28 The auditor considers whether an entity falls within the mandatory requirement to prepare its consolidated financial statements in accordance with IFRSs adopted for use in the European Union. This is important because, should any entity fail to follow IFRSs when *required* to do so, auditors would be required to qualify their audit report on the grounds of non-compliance with company law.

The IAS Regulation

29 The IAS Regulation requires certain companies[10] to prepare their consolidated financial statements in accordance with IFRSs adopted for use in the European Union, for accounting periods beginning on or after 1 January 2005. This requirement applies to companies:

(a) that are subject to the law of a Member State; and
(b) whose securities are admitted (as at the balance sheet date) to trading on a regulated market (publicly traded companies); and
(c) that are required by Member State law to prepare group accounts.

30 The IAS Regulation also contains Member State options[11], one of which is to permit or require adopted IFRSs to be used by:

(a) publicly traded companies, in their individual company accounts; and
(b) non publicly traded companies, in both, or either of, their group and individual company accounts.

The UK and ROI have introduced a permissive regime in relation to this Member State option. This means that, from 2005 and until such time as ASB's standards become the same as IASB's, there will be two regimes of Generally Accepted Accounting Practice in the UK and ROI: IFRSs as adopted for use in the EU and UK/ROI GAAP[12].

[9] *The DTI Guidance lists at paragraph 4.21, those provisions in Part VII (Accounts and Audit) of the Companies Act 1985 that still apply.*

[10] *In the EC IAS Regulation 'company' has the same meaning as in Article 48 of the Treaty of Rome (DTI Guidance, paragraph 4.8).*

[11] *One Member State option allows deferral to 2007 of the mandatory requirement to follow IFRS for companies that already follow an internationally accepted GAAP or those that only have listed debt securities. The DTI has stated that the UK will not take up this Member State option. However, the 2005 ROI Regulations provide for deferral of the obligation to prepare IFRS accounts to 2007 in respect of debt listed securities in the ROI.*

[12] *ASB has begun to effect UK convergence to IFRSs by issuing its first 'convergence standards', namely FRSs 20-26, to bring certain aspects of UK accounting standards more into line with IFRSs in 2005. It has also issued (in March 2005) an Exposure Draft on the future role of the Board, including its approach to convergence with IFRS. See www.frc.org.uk/asb.*

Subject to the law of a Member State

For companies to be subject to the law of a Member State, they have to be incorporated in a Member State. From 1 May 2004, Member States include the Accession States (i.e. those that joined the EU in May 2004)[13].

The corollary to this is that companies incorporated in a jurisdiction outside the EU, e.g. the USA, and hence not subject to any EU Member State's law, will not be subject to the mandatory requirement to follow IFRSs even if they have securities admitted to trading on a regulated market in an EU Member State.

Securities traded on a regulated market

There are several regulated markets in the UK and ROI. It should be noted that not all markets on which listed securities are traded are necessarily "regulated markets" as defined by the Prospectus Directive. An example is the Professional Securities Market, which is operated and regulated by the London Stock Exchange. Issuers listed on such non regulated markets are not required to adopt IFRSs.

Required to prepare group accounts

As stated in the DTI Guidance, the test as to whether a company is required to prepare group accounts, for the purpose of the EC Regulation, is by reference to the European Seventh Directive, as adopted into the CA 1985. The relevant Sections are 227 for companies and 255A for banks and insurance companies.

The CA 1985 has recently been amended (as outlined in Section 5 of the DTI Guidance), to implement parts of the Modernisation Directive and take up some options in the existing Seventh Directive. In particular, there will no longer be a requirement for a company to have a "participating interest" in its investee for a parent/subsidiary relationship to exist.[14]

Voluntary adoption of IFRSs

The new legislation allows publicly traded companies to prepare their individual accounts in accordance with adopted IFRSs. The individual accounts of other group companies may also be prepared in accordance with adopted IFRSs, subject to the consistency requirements discussed in paragraphs 38 to 41. Non-publicly traded companies are also able to apply IFRSs as adopted for use in the EU, in:

(a) their group accounts; or
(b) their individual company accounts; or
(c) both their group and individual company accounts.

There are no specific formalities required in order to make a voluntary move to IFRSs; however, the CA 1985 has a number of restrictions that are discussed in the following paragraphs.

---

[13] The complete list of Member States at any time can be found at http://www.europa.eu.int?abc/index_en.htm

[14] This amendment is permitted by Article 2.1 of the Modernisation Directive, although the amendment to the 1985 Act does not extend to removing the parallel requirement to have a participating interest in an associate undertaking. The Accounting Standards Board has in turn issued amendments to FRS 2 to bring it into line with the revised parts of the 1985 Act. The requirements in FRS 5 to consolidate quasi-subsidiaries are not relevant to the legal requirement to consolidate.

All companies within a group to report using the same accounting framework

38 Those entities that adopt IFRSs for their group financial statements will prepare those group financial statements under IFRSs regardless of which financial reporting framework is used in the preparation and presentation of the individual statutory accounts of the parent and its subsidiaries. Consequently, the directors of the parent company will need to ensure that management has put systems in place to ensure that all necessary information is available from subsidiaries, on a timely basis, in order to permit proper preparation of IFRS group accounts.

39 The CA 1985 states (in Section 227C(1)) that the directors of a *parent* company must secure that the individual accounts of the parent and each of its subsidiary undertakings are all prepared using the same financial reporting framework "except to the extent that in their opinion there are good reasons for not doing so"[15]. This provision is intended to provide a degree of flexibility where there are genuine grounds for using different accounting frameworks within a group. Paragraph 4.16 of the DTI Guidance gives some examples of what might constitute 'good reasons'. These examples relate to very specific circumstances and the Guidance notes that the key point is that "the directors of the parent company must be able to justify any inconsistency, to shareholders, regulators or other interested parties."

40 Auditors enquire as to whether the directors have considered the question and documented their reasons and the auditors consider the acceptability of such reasons, including any advice the directors have taken. If the auditors doubt whether the directors are correct in their opinion that there is a 'good reason', the auditors discuss their concerns with those charged with governance. If, having considered the reason given, the auditors continue to have doubts as to whether there is a justification, they may consider seeking legal advice and consider the implications for their audit report.

41 The requirement to have a "good reason" where all companies in a group do not use the same accounting framework is a parent company responsibility; it is not an issue for the directors or auditors of any individual subsidiary as long as the subsidiary has properly followed a legally acceptable GAAP which has been clearly disclosed.

Parent company individual financial statements

42 Under Section 230 of the CA 1985, a parent company need not present its individual profit and loss account, nor certain related notes, where it has presented group financial statements[16]. The DTI Guidance states that taking the Section 230 exemption (which it describes as a publication exemption) should not affect the ability of a parent company to be treated as a "first time adopter" and hence to take advantage of exemptions for first time use under the provisions of IFRS 1.

---

[15] *There are various exemptions to this as laid out in Paragraph 4.14 of the DTI Guidance. The 2004 Regulations also provide a partial exemption (in new Section 227C(5) of the 1985 Act), such that if a parent company prepares both its consolidated and its individual accounts under IFRS, it is not required to ensure that all its subsidiary undertakings also use IFRSs, although it must still ensure that all its GB subsidiary undertakings use the same GAAP as each other, again unless there are good reasons for not doing so.*

[16] *The Section 230 exemption relates only to the profit and loss account and, by virtue of Section 261(2), the notes to the profit and loss account. The parent individual IFRS financial statements will, however, still need to include the other primary statements and note disclosures required by IFRS, including a cash flow statement and a statement of changes in shareholders' equity.*

IAS 1 and IFRS 1 both require an "explicit and unreserved statement of compliance with IFRSs" in order to be a first-time adopter. In view of the fact that Paragraph 8 of IAS 1 'Presentation of Financial Statements' requires a profit and loss account to be presented in a set of IFRS financial statements, and in order for the statement of compliance with IFRSs not to be misleading, it will be important for an IFRS parent company (particularly one taking advantage of the IFRS 1 exemptions) to indicate that the compliance statement is based on its full IFRS financial statements, of which those presented are an extract (excluding the profit and loss account and related notes). This impacts the auditor's description of the financial reporting framework in the auditor's report as discussed in the ISA (UK and Ireland) 700 section of this Bulletin. 43

If the group financial statements are prepared under IFRSs but the parent company does not adopt IFRSs in its individual financial statements, the parent and group will present information on different bases. Section 240(2) of the CA 1985 requires group and individual accounts to be published but does not specify whether these accounts should be presented in separate sections of the annual report or combined into a single set of primary statements and notes. Where different financial reporting frameworks are applied, the DTI Guidance notes that using separate sections of the annual report is likely to lead to clearer presentation. The approach taken to the presentation of the parent company financial information will affect the auditor's report (as discussed under ISA (UK and Ireland) 700). 44

The decision to move is irreversible

The CA 1985 makes a company's decision to switch to IFRSs irreversible, except under certain limited circumstances. The exceptions are laid out in new Sections 226(5) and 227(6) to the CA 1985 and relate to where, for example, companies and groups cease to be publicly traded and when a company becomes a subsidiary of an undertaking that does not prepare its accounts in accordance with IFRSs. 45

Applicable law: remaining elements of the Companies Act 1985 and related regulation

Entities that switch to IFRSs still have to follow aspects of UK company accounting and reporting law, as indicated by the European Commission[17] and by the DTI Guidance (at Paragraphs 4.18-4.21). The auditors need to be aware of which elements of the accounting and reporting provisions of the CA 1985 are still applicable and which are not.[18] 46

Duty to maintain proper accounting records

Auditors are required by Section 237(1) (a) of CA 1985 to investigate whether proper accounting records have been kept by the company and proper returns adequate for their audit have been received from branches not visited by them. That requirement is in relation to the accounting records of individual companies, not the group. Where individual companies within a group have adopted IFRSs, the auditors will need to consider whether the legal responsibility to maintain proper accounting records has been satisfied by appropriate changes in accounting systems and records. 47

---

[17] *The guidance from the European Commission on which elements of the accounting directives will continue to apply to IFRS companies can be found at http://europa.eu.int/comm/internal_market/accounting/docs/ias/200311-comments/ias-200311-comments_en.pdf.*

[18] *The DTI Guidance provides useful guidance to small companies in relation to publication exemptions and abbreviated accounts in Paragraphs 4.25-4.31.*

48   If a group's consolidated accounts are prepared under IFRSs, but the individual accounts of all (or most of) the companies within the group remain on UK/ROI or other local GAAP(s), the primary accounting records from which the IFRS consolidated accounts are created may still be based on local GAAP. There is no legal requirement for management to change or adapt accounting systems at the individual company level to capture the new or different accounting information required for IFRS consolidated accounts. The responsibility for ensuring that the necessary information and records are available lies with the parent company's management. In these circumstances, where the requisite adjustments to apply IFRSs to subsidiary financial information is made by way of consolidation adjustments, the group auditor considers whether it is possible to obtain sufficient appropriate audit evidence. If not there may be a limitation on the scope of the auditor's work. (See comments on limitations of scope in the ISA (UK and Ireland) 700 section of the Bulletin).

Distributable profits

49   ISA (UK & Ireland) 250 Section A refers to the laws relating to distributions under Section 263 CA 1985. Group accounts are not relevant to determining the ability of a parent company to make a distribution. However, companies choosing to switch to IFRSs in their individual accounts may produce 'relevant accounts' that result in a different amount of distributable profits from the amount that would have been determined under UK/ROI accounting standards[19].

50   The amount of profits a company has available for distribution may change as a result of the transition to IFRSs. When a distribution is being considered, the last set of audited financial statements, which are the relevant accounts for the purpose of Section 270 of the CA 1985, may be under UK/ROI GAAP. Nevertheless, the directors may know that, in the following accounting period (which will already have begun), the changes introduced by IFRSs may have a significant detrimental impact on distributable reserves, thus potentially affecting the directors' assessment of their common law duty not to make a distribution out of capital, as well as their general fiduciary duties.

Taxes Acts

51   Compliance with the Taxes Acts is addressed in ISA (UK & Ireland) 250 Section A. The Chancellor of the Exchequer announced in 2003 that the law would be amended to allow IFRS accounts to be used as the basis of corporation tax assessments for companies (as with distributable profits, only individual financial statements of companies are relevant; group accounts are not used to assess UK corporation tax liabilities). The 2004 Finance Act reflects this move for accounting periods beginning on or after 1 January 2005 and the overall stated aim of Her Majesty's Revenue and Customs (HMRC) is to achieve broadly equivalent tax treatment whether UK/ROI GAAP or IFRS accounts comprise the starting point for corporation tax computations, even where there are material differences in accounting treatment.

---

[19] *Auditors will be aware of the guidance on this subject issued in 2003 by the Institutes of Chartered Accountants in England and Wales and of Scotland, which has been supplemented by guidance on the impact on distributable profits of new pension accounting standards and of new standards (UITF Abstracts) on share-based payment and the presentation of shares in ESOP trusts. Draft guidance has been published on IFRSs and distributable profits, which will also be relevant to the application of converged UK standards. See www.icaew.co.uk or www.icas.org.uk.*

In the Chancellor's 2004 Pre-Budget Report, the government considered the transitional adjustments arising from certain changes in accounting for financial instruments and decided to defer any tax effects from the transition, in this respect, until the impact could be determined and managed. For most companies, this deferral will operate until accounting periods beginning on or after 1 January 2006 (i.e. for their 2005 accounting periods). In July 2005 it was announced that for tax purposes most transitional adjustments relating to financial instruments will be spread over 10 years from 2006. The position will be reviewed again in 2006 when more information is available and further transitional measures may be introduced. Transactions occurring following transition will be taxed in accordance with IFRSs. Measures were introduced in the Finance Act 2005 to enable securitisation vehicles to continue applying existing UK/ROI accounting standards for tax purposes for accounting periods ending before 1 January 2007 and to address specific technical issues.[20]

Listing Rules

Companies subject to the mandatory application of IFRSs under the IAS Regulation will also be subject to the requirements of the regulated market on which their securities are traded. Where the authorities over such markets make pronouncements in relation to the introduction of IFRSs, regard to these may be relevant in order for the company to maintain its listing.[21]

In September 2003 the FSA wrote to the Company Secretaries of all Listed Issuers and amongst other things noted "That a consequence of not being in a position to adopt IFRSs will be that issuers are unable to meet the reporting requirements and deadlines of the Listing Rules. Failure by issuers to submit preliminary or interim results within the required timescale is likely to result in the suspension of the issuer's securities". However, the FSA has subsequently allowed, by concession, that companies' first set of interim accounts under IFRSs may be presented up to 120 days after the relevant period end, rather than the usual 90 days.[22] Companies must inform the market that they are taking advantage of this concession before the end of the half-year period to which the interim accounts relate in order to be claimed. In April 2005 the FSA wrote to the Chief Executives of all Listed Issuers regarding IFRS readiness, reminding them, among other things, that a failure to submit interim results within the required timescale is likely to result in the suspension of the issuer's securities.

---

[20] *HMRC has published guidance on tax and IFRS, with links to legislation and commentary, which can be accessed at http://www.hmrc.gov.uk/practitioners/int_accounting.htm#note15*

[21] *Auditors will be aware that the regime for regulated markets changed in the UK from 1 July 2005 as a result, inter alia, of the implementation of the requirements of the EU Prospectus Directive.*

[22] *The text of the FSA's letter to Chief Executives of listed companies can be found at http://www.fsa.gov.uk/pubs/ceo/ceo_letter_25oct04.pdf.*

ISA (UK & Ireland) 250, Section B 'The Auditor's Right and Duty to Report to Regulators in the Financial Sector'

55   Entities that are required to maintain a certain level of regulatory capital may be affected by the introduction of IFRSs. Auditors consider whether the introduction of IFRSs impacts on their assessment of going concern and on their responsibility to report matters of material significance to a regulator.[23]

ISA (UK & Ireland) 260 'Communication of Audit Matters With Those Charged With Governance'

56   Auditors may identify issues related to the introduction of IFRSs which they consider they should report to those charged with governance. These may be matters which need to be formally communicated because they represent material weaknesses in internal control. However, in addition, they may report other matters which have come to light as a result of the enquiries made about the introduction of IFRSs. For example, where, after making enquiries, the auditors conclude that management has not sufficiently considered all the potential impacts of the introduction of IFRSs, or that management do not have a "good reason" for individual companies in the group not preparing their individual accounts using the same accounting framework (paragraph 39).

57   The auditors also consider all relevant aspects of the financial reporting framework, covering not only IFRSs but also those statutory and regulatory requirements which still apply. Auditors consider whether the accounting policies adopted by an entity in its first IFRS financial statements comply with the requirements of IAS 8, which includes a hierarchy of sources of guidance where no IFRS or Interpretation is available. Where IFRSs are silent on a subject it would be permissible for entities to continue to follow existing practice as long as it did not run counter to similar standards or the IASB's 'Framework for the Preparation and Presentation of Financial Statements'.

58   Auditors consider the qualitative aspects of financial reporting in the context of IFRSs and in particular the selection of accounting policies. When auditors identify that an entity has adopted an accounting policy that was not available to it under UK/ROI GAAP, where it could have continued to apply its existing policy, they draw such circumstances to the attention of those charged with governance.

59   The disclosure requirements in respect of the transition to IFRSs, as required by paragraphs 38-43 of IFRS 1, are substantial. As well as auditing the disclosures given by the entity for compliance with the standard, auditors consider whether the entity's approach to disclosure leads to information that is as clear as possible, given the complexity of the exercise. The overall requirement for fair presentation will be of particular importance in the transition period.

ISA (UK & Ireland) 300 'Planning an Audit of Financial Statements'

60   The introduction of IFRSs is likely to be a major factor in the planning of the audit for the year of implementation. Auditors consider how their audit plan is likely to be

---

[23] *The FSA announced in April 2005 the changes in its regulatory accounting rules in the light of new accounting standards. The changes are published in (Policy Statement) PS 05/5 entitled "Implications of a changing accounting framework" and reflect the introduction of IFRSs. The document can be downloaded from http://www.fsa.gov.uk/pubs/policy/ps05_05.pdf.*

affected by the change and how to ensure that all members of the audit team are fully briefed and have sufficient knowledge of IFRSs.

Initial risk assessment at the planning stage

Audit risk is likely to be increased in the year of transition to IFRSs. As part of their risk assessment process, auditors ascertain by enquiry of management: 61

- The major changes likely to the entity's financial statements due to the introduction of IFRSs.
- The impact of the introduction of IFRSs on key systems which generate specific accounting information.
- The extent to which fair value accounting has been adopted for certain items, including financial instruments.

Auditors also direct their enquiries more specifically in order to understand management's views on: 62

- Any increased risk of error in accounting information or other information supporting items in the financial statements.
- The potential impact, if any, on the going concern basis.
- The possible impact on specific financial statement amounts or disclosures.

The auditor's conclusions from these initial inquiries may be that no particular procedures need to be performed, that is, where the entity's management considers that the effect on the financial statements is minimal and the auditor's judgment is that, based on its knowledge of the business and its systems, the conclusion is reasonable. In the far more likely situation where management identifies the introduction of IFRSs as being of potential financial statement significance, the auditors obtain an understanding of management's impact analysis and detailed plans to deal with the introduction of IFRSs.   63

In considering the entity's 'impact analysis', the auditors might, for example, enquire about factors such as: 64

- Whether the impact analysis was carried out systematically and the quality of records documenting that process.
- Whether all significant business units were involved in the process.
- The skills, knowledge and experience of the staff involved in the impact analysis.

In considering management's statements about plans and implementation progress, auditors might, for example, consider whether: 65

- Financial reporting and systems replacement/modification projects are being led by staff with experience of such projects (whether internal or provided by external advisors).
- Resources have been committed to the projects identified, whether relating to systems changes or financial reporting issues.
- Information or test results are available, whether generated internally or obtained from external IT suppliers, on relevant accounting systems.
- Timescales have been allocated to the projects identified.
- Progress against plans is being monitored rigorously and regularly.
- Slippage against the plan has resulted in positive action or reprioritisation

Lack of any of the above may indicate a higher risk that plans or progress reports are unreliable.

Comparatives and opening balances

66 At the planning stage auditors consider the work required on opening balances and comparatives. (See the discussion on ISA (UK and Ireland) 510 and ISA (UK and Ireland) 710 below.)

ISA (UK & Ireland) 315 'Obtaining an Understanding of the Entity and Its Environment and Assessing the Risks of Material Misstatement' and ISA (UK & Ireland) 330 'The Auditor's Procedures in Response to Assessed Risks'

67 The increase in overall audit risk in the year of transition of an entity to IFRSs is likely to be substantial (and some increase is also possible in the periods leading up to the change). Some of the main factors leading to the increase in audit risk are as follows:

- In 2005/6 companies will have limited practical experience of working with IFRSs. The application in the UK and ROI of existing accounting standards is based on experience that has built up over many years; this accumulated knowledge base does not exist for IFRSs.
- One of the major difficulties faced by both preparers and auditors is the identification of all differences between the old and new accounting frameworks. Although UK and ROI accounting standards are, in some ways, similar to IFRSs, there are some major differences, for example in relation to accounting for business combinations, and a large number of smaller differences that are less immediately obvious (so that some may assume some old and new standards are the same when in fact they are not). Moreover, the interaction between different IFRSs, for example IFRS 1 and the other IFRSs, is complex.
- Major changes may be necessary to financial reporting systems and the controls over them, in order to produce the necessary information for IFRS financial statements. As well as increasing the risk of error, this also increases the opportunity for fraud.
- There may be opportunities for aggressive earnings management by companies. For example, management may wish to set an advantageous starting figure for earnings under IFRSs in the year of transition, conscious of the implications for future years. This could involve setting the figure as *low* as possible in a year of such a major change, while attention is focussed on the changeover itself, so giving leeway for flattering increases in earnings in future years.
- Recent changes to IFRSs, some of which are being introduced into UK/ROI GAAP as well, bring new challenges for auditors and preparers. In particular, the valuation of certain items, such as employee share options and non-traded financial instruments, are subject to many variables and can be subjective.
- Entities applying IFRSs for the first time are required by IFRS 1 (paragraph 41) to distinguish between GAAP changes and the correction of prior period errors when describing the changes to their financial statements. There is a risk that past errors may not be disclosed as such.
- There are a number of possible consequences of implementing IFRSs, including changes to a company's tax base and charge, restrictions on or reductions to distributable profits and breaches of accounts-based debt or similar covenants. All these could have substantial implications for the financial statements and even, perhaps, for the ability of the company to remain a going concern.

68 As noted above under ISA (UK and Ireland) 240 and below under ISA (UK and Ireland) 540, directors and managers will need to be aware of the greater risk of error and opportunities for fraud that could arise where an entity has to make major adaptations to its systems or where the systems are functioning incorrectly. The

extent of change and the urgency may cause a relaxation of formal testing and program change control procedures.

Auditors use the entity's impact analysis and detailed plans for the implementation of IFRSs to aid identification of risks of misstatement in the IFRS financial statements. 69

Auditors consider extending their risk assessment procedures as a result of the introduction of IFRSs and in particular consider: 70

(a) making enquiries of any consultants used by the company, (whether internal teams or external consultants), about the success or otherwise of the IFRS conversion process, the problems identified and how they were remedied and the areas of main concern for the business; and
(a) investigating changes in systems and controls that have been implemented as part of the IFRS conversion project.

ISA (UK & Ireland) 320 'Audit Materiality'[24]

The definition of 'material' in IAS 1 'Presentation of Financial Statements' (which is in line with the IASB's 'Framework for the Preparation and Presentation of Financial Statements') is: 71

> "Omissions or misstatements of items are material if they could, individually or collectively, influence the economic decisions of users taken on the basis of the financial statements. Materiality depends on the size and nature of the omission or misstatement judged in the surrounding circumstances. The size or nature of the item, or a combination of both, could be the determining factor."

UK and ROI accounting standards do not define 'materiality' or 'material'. However, the discussion of materiality in the ASB's Statement of Principles (paragraphs 3.28 – 3.32) includes the following: 72

> "An item of information is material to the financial statements if its misstatement or omission might reasonably be expected to influence the economic decisions of users of those financial statements, including their assessment of management's stewardship.
>
> Whether information is material will depend on the size and nature of the item in question judged in the particular circumstances of the case..."

As these definitions of 'material' are not inconsistent with each other auditors adopt the same approach to determining materiality for an audit of IFRS financial statements as for an audit of UK/ROI GAAP financial statements[25]. However, the application of IFRSs may impact the benchmark upon which materiality has been calculated (eg profit before tax may be reduced) giving rise to a potential need to adjust the recording of uncorrected misstatements of prior periods (see section on ISA (UK and Ireland) 520) 73

One aspect to be considered in light of possible pressure on management to achieve a particular result is highlighted by Paragraph 8 of IAS 8 (December 2003), in the context of the application of accounting policies: 74

---

[24] In January 2005 the APB published an exposure draft of a revised version of ISA (UK and Ireland) 320. See www.frc.org.uk/apb for details.

[25] An exception to this is related parties: see paragraph 99 for details.

"IFRSs set out accounting policies that the IASB has concluded result in financial statements containing relevant and reliable information about the transactions, other events and conditions to which they apply. Those policies need not be applied when the effect of applying them is immaterial. However, it is inappropriate to make, or leave uncorrected, immaterial departures from IFRSs to achieve a particular presentation of an entity's financial position, financial performance or cash flows."

ISA (UK & Ireland) 510 'Initial Engagements – Opening Balances and Continuing Engagements – Opening Balances' and ISA (UK & Ireland) 710 'Comparatives'

Opening balances and comparatives under IFRSs and the impact on the audit

75   The issues of comparatives and opening balances for any particular year's audit are closely linked. It is unlikely to be possible to audit the first financial statements under IFRSs without performing procedures on the opening IFRS balance sheet[26] and then rolling these forward to the 2005 comparative figures and ultimately the 2005 figures themselves. For a 31 December preparer, the opening IFRS balance sheet will be as at 1 January 2004 (ie. the 31 December 2003 balance sheet as previously published under UK/ROI GAAP, but converted to IFRSs).

76   In this context, however, it is important to note that Section 235 of CA 1985 does not bring the comparative figures of the previous year, presented alongside the current period financial statements, within the scope of the auditor's report, nor does the auditor's report make direct reference to the comparative figures. Nevertheless, IAS 1 requires comparative figures to be presented (as they are by UK and Irish company law under UK/ROI GAAP) and auditors have specific responsibilities with regard to opening balances to the extent they affect and determine current period figures in the financial statements.

77   Overall, it is unlikely that the usual level of audit work for continuing engagements, as outlined in ISAs UK & Ireland) 510 and 710, will be sufficient to ensure that opening balances in the year of transition to IFRSs are not materially misstated. The additional work required to be carried out will depend on the nature and complexity of the changes on a case-by-case basis. ISA (UK and Ireland) 510 and ISA (UK and Ireland) 710, which deal with the audit of opening balances and comparatives for incoming auditors, provide useful guidance on additional procedures.

78   In light of the expected pressure on time and resources in the 2005 reporting season, auditors are encouraged to carry out relevant procedures on the IFRS opening balance sheet and 2005 comparatives, to the extent these are necessary for completion of the audit on the 2005 financial statements, as early as possible. Companies may wish their auditors to give some level of private or public assurance on 2004 figures. This work will constitute an engagement separate from the statutory audit; however, auditors can use any such work, updated and amended as necessary, for the purposes of the procedures required by ISAs (UK & Ireland) 510 and 710.

The application of IFRS 1

79   Auditors refer to the requirements of IFRS 1 in order to assess whether the directors of the audited entity have dealt with the opening position correctly. Companies that

---

[26] *It is important to distinguish between ISA (UK and Ireland) 510 opening balances, which refers to the current period opening balance sheet, and the opening IFRS balance sheet as required by IFRS 1, which refers to the opening balance sheet, as described here.*

are classed as 'first-time adopters' of IFRSs are those making an explicit and unreserved statement of compliance with IFRSs when presenting their first annual financial statements under IFRSs. Broadly, IFRS 1 requires first-time adopters to prepare an opening balance sheet under IFRSs at the date of transition, which is the beginning of the earliest period for which an entity presents full comparative information under IFRSs in its first IFRS financial statements.[27]

The opening IFRS balance sheet should be prepared in accordance with IFRSs that are in force as at the reporting date[28] (IFRSs which are not yet mandatory can also be adopted if early adoption is permitted by the IFRS in question). IFRS 1 therefore requires IFRSs to be applied as if they always had been. The exceptions to this rule are that: 80

(a) the transitional arrangements in each IFRS should not be followed;
(b) IFRS 1 gives specific exemptions to the general rule on retrospective adjustment for all standards; and
(c) IFRS 1 also prohibits retrospective application of certain IFRSs.

Broadly speaking, entities have a choice in applying some, all, or none of the exemptions to retrospective restatement given in IFRS 1 but must disclose which exemptions have been taken. Auditors consider the completeness and accuracy of the disclosure of the exemptions in the financial statements and consider whether the consequential implications for the opening balance sheet and restated comparatives have been taken into account (for example, if past business combinations have not been restated as permitted by IFRS 1, there may be consequential requirements to amend the opening balance sheet figures for assets and liabilities recognised in the business combination, including goodwill). This will be necessary in order for the auditors to assess whether the closing balance sheet at the reporting date has been properly prepared, not merely to assess whether comparative information has been properly presented.[29] 81

Auditors consider whether only differences between UK requirements and IFRSs are included as reconciling items in the opening balance sheet and comparatives. In particular, corrections of errors and revisions of estimates in past results should not be included as reconciling items from UK/ROI GAAP to IFRSs, but should be accounted for as required by IAS 8. 82

Different first-time adoption dates

In the light of implementation difficulties regarding, for example, distributable profits, it is highly likely that many UK listed groups may choose not to move their parent and subsidiary individual financial statements to IFRSs at the same time as their consolidated financial statements. Similarly, where there is a "good reason"[30] some subsidiaries may remain under UK GAAP while the rest of the group's subsidiaries move over to IFRSs. IFRS 1 gives guidance (at paragraphs 24-25) on situations where parents and subsidiaries become first-time adopters at different times. 83

---

[27] Hence, for a 2005 first-time adopter that is a 31 December preparer, the date of transition will be 1 January 2003.

[28] So for 2005 first-time adopters that are 31 December preparers, the reporting date is 31 December 2005.

[29] IFRS 1 was published with application guidance which will be useful to both preparers and auditors in applying IFRS 1 in practice.

[30] See paragraph 41.

ISA (UK & Ireland) 520 'Analytical Procedures'

Analytical procedures as risk assessment and substantive procedures

84   Whilst analytical procedures are still likely to be important to the auditor, the lack of historical information in relation to a particular entity arising through the wholesale change in its accounting basis means that additional care will be required in the auditor's use of analytical techniques. As well as a lack of historical data for a particular company or group, industry figures and information may not be available other than on a UK/ROI GAAP basis. A related issue is that some IFRSs require prospective application, so there will be no restated comparative figures for analytical review purposes. Analytical procedures might therefore be of reduced effectiveness throughout the audit.

85   Auditors consider whether they need to perform additional, alternative, substantive procedures in order to compensate for the inability to carry out certain analytical procedures that have been used as substantive procedures in the past. The usefulness of analytical procedures in the overall review of the financial statements may also be weakened and lead the auditors to conclude that additional alternative procedures are necessary.

Analytical procedures in the overall review at the end of the audit

Uncorrected misstatements

86   One of the principal considerations when carrying out the overall review of the financial statements is "The potential impact on the financial statements of the aggregate of uncorrected misstatements (including those arising from bias in making accounting estimates) identified during the course of the audit and the preceding period's audit, if any". Where the adoption of IFRSs gives rise to a lower level of materiality than that used under UK/ROI GAAP the auditors consider whether their evaluation of misstatements identified in the prior year audit needs to be revised.

87   The reference to the uncorrected misstatements of previous periods is of particular relevance in the context of paragraph 41 of IAS 8:

> "Financial statements do not comply with IFRSs if they contain either material errors or immaterial errors made intentionally to achieve a particular presentation of an entity's financial position, financial performance or cash flows. Potential current period errors discovered in that period are corrected before the financial statements are authorised for issue. However, material errors are sometimes not discovered until a subsequent period, and these prior period errors are corrected in the comparative information presented in the financial statements for that subsequent period."

88   The decision to leave errors uncorrected in the prior period will have been based on an assessment of materiality in the context of UK/ROI GAAP. That assessment will now be made in the context of IFRS figures. Auditors, therefore, examine the schedule of unadjusted differences from the prior period audit and consider whether retrospective restatement is necessary because of a combination of the requirements of IAS 8 in this respect and the reassessment of materiality in the context of the IFRS figures. As well as quantitative aspects, auditors also consider qualitative factors in forming their judgment.

89   One point of difference between IFRSs and UK/ROI GAAP is in relation to how errors are corrected. IAS 8 (revised December 2003) requires all errors to be

corrected by prior period adjustment. Accounting standards only relate to material items, so by definition IAS 8 is referring to all material errors. The UK standard, FRS 3 'Reporting Financial Performance', requires only 'fundamental errors' to be corrected in this way, all others being corrected through the profit and loss account in the period in which they are discovered.[31] Auditors consider whether any errors discovered during the course of the audit of the first IFRS accounts, which relate to prior periods, should be corrected by prior period adjustment. As required by IFRS 1, any restatement of errors made under previous GAAP should be clearly differentiated (in the entity's explanation of the transition to IFRSs) from items relating to the restatement of prior year comparatives to comply with IFRSs.

ISA (UK & Ireland) 540 'Audit of Accounting Estimates'[32]

Errors vs. changes in estimate

Accounting estimates are dealt with in IAS 1 and IAS 8 'Accounting Policies, Changes in Accounting Estimates and Errors'. The IAS 8 definitions of 'changes in accounting estimates' and 'prior period errors' are fundamental to the decisions that management have to make when differentiating between circumstances giving rise to either a retrospective restatement of an error, or prospective application of a change in an accounting estimate. 90

Care should be taken that management does not use hindsight when assessing the calculation of estimates for comparative information as IFRS 1 specifically prohibits the restatement of estimates at the date of transition to IFRSs or in comparative figures, unless objective evidence is available to show that the estimates were in error. The principle set out in IFRS 1 is that an entity's estimates under IFRSs at the date of transition to IFRSs shall be consistent with estimates made for the same date under previous GAAP (after adjustments to reflect any differences in accounting policies), unless there is objective evidence that those estimates were in error. 91

Where IFRSs require estimates to be made that were not required under UK/ROI GAAP, the lack of track record and management experience in making such estimates will lead to greater risk of misstatement. Auditors consider whether additional audit procedures are required with regard to such estimates. 92

Disclosure of estimation uncertainty

IAS 1, at paragraph 116, requires disclosure in the financial statements of information about the key assumptions concerning the future and other key sources of estimation uncertainty at the balance sheet date that have a significant risk of causing a material adjustment to the carrying amounts of assets and liabilities within the next financial year.[33] These disclosures relate to the estimates that require management's most difficult, subjective or complex judgments. The disclosures required by IAS 1 are different to, and may be more extensive than, those required by paragraph 55(b) of FRS 18. The Basis for Conclusions to IAS 1 indicates the IASB's expectation that 93

---

[31] *The previous version of IAS 1 made a distinction between fundamental errors and other material prior period errors. The distinction has been eliminated because the definition of fundamental error was difficult to interpret consistently.*

[32] *In January 2005 the APB published an exposure draft of a revised version of ISA (UK and Ireland) 540. See www.frc.org.uk/apb for details.*

[33] *This disclosure requirement does not apply to assets and liabilities measured at fair value based on recently observed market prices.*

disclosure in accordance with this requirement would be made in respect of relatively few assets or liabilities (or classes of them).

94 IAS 1, at paragraph 113, also requires an entity to disclose in its financial statements the judgments, apart from those involving estimations, management has made in applying the entity's accounting policies that have the most significant effect on the amounts recognised in the financial statements, for example whether the substance of the relationship between the entity and a special purpose entity indicates that the special purpose entity is controlled by the entity. Auditors consider extending their evaluations of these types of disclosure, bearing in mind they go beyond the requirements of FRS 18.

ISA (UK and Ireland) 545 'Auditing Fair Value Measurements and Disclosures'

95 IFRSs require certain assets and liabilities to be recognised at fair value rather than historical cost. Incorporating more fair values in financial statements (also reflected in recent changes to ASB standards), may give rise to difficulties for auditors, particularly on transition to IFRSs, for example:

- Paragraphs 16-19 of IFRS 1 permit companies to elect to use fair value at transition as deemed cost for some assets, such amounts will not previously have been audited.
- IFRS 2 'Share-based Payment' does not prescribe particular techniques for valuing employee (and other) share options, but sets out general requirements for valuation, which require management and possibly external expert judgment in selecting a model and adapting it to the particular circumstances. This is in the context of several complicating factors, such as the fact that established models are not necessarily suited to non-traded options, a lack of established techniques and standards against which the auditors can judge an expert's work and the difficulty in obtaining and assessing some of the inputs to any valuation model, such as share price volatility.
- IFRS 3 'Business Combinations' and IAS 38 'Intangible Assets' require many more intangibles to be fair-valued separately from goodwill than is currently the case under FRS 10. Auditing valuations of unique intangibles is likely to be particularly difficult due to subjective assumptions and the potential to use different techniques which might give different answers.
- Fair value information is required for leases of land and buildings under IAS 17 'Leases' (Paragraphs 14-19). On first-time adoption, entities may need to look back many years to obtain the information, in turn raising potential audit issues.

96 Even though the EC has "carved out" some aspects of fair values from IAS 39 'Financial Instruments: Recognition and Measurement', fair value measurements are still required for many financial instruments.[34] Application guidance has been issued

---

[34] In June 2005 the IASB published an amendment to the fair value option in IAS 39. In July 2005, the European Commission's Accounting Regulatory Committee supported the Commission's proposal to endorse the "IAS 39 Fair Value Option", which should lead to a removal of one part of the carve-out, but (as at November 2005) the difference with respect to hedge accounting remains.

by the IASB on IAS 39; guidance has also been issued by the ASB on whether and to what extent the full version of IAS 39 can be applied in Europe.[35] Given the complexity of the issue, auditors consider whether an entity has made full and clear disclosure of the extent to which it has applied IAS 39.[36]

Guidance on the audit of fair values in financial statements has been introduced for the first time in the UK and Ireland by ISA (UK and Ireland) 545. The standard anticipates the types of difficulties noted above and attention is drawn, in particular, to the following paragraphs of the standard.

- Paragraph 10 requires the auditors to assess the management process for determining fair values and the controls over it, recognising management's primary responsibility for producing the relevant fair value information.
- Paragraphs 17 and 56 require consideration by auditors of the entity's use and disclosure of fair value information according to the relevant financial reporting framework. The issue of disclosure is particularly important as several of the standards discussed above have substantial disclosure requirements.
- Paragraph 24 deals with situations where alternative valuation methodologies are permitted by accounting standards, requiring auditors to consider the suitability of those used.
- The importance of the work of an expert in the context of fair values is highlighted in Paragraphs 29-32.
- Paragraph 39 addresses the auditor's evaluation of the significant assumptions used by management.

ISA (UK & Ireland) 550 'Related Parties'

Auditing standards on related parties are closely linked to the underlying accounting framework. From 2005 two accounting frameworks will be in use in the UK and Ireland – IFRS (including IAS 24 "Related party disclosures") and UK/ROI GAAP (including FRS 8 "Related party disclosures"). To accommodate the differences between the two frameworks, ISA (UK and Ireland) 550 has separate parts for use where the financial statements being audited are intended to comply with IAS 24 and FRS 8 respectively.

Although the requirements of IAS 24 and FRS 8 are broadly similar, there are a number of differences that may have an impact on the auditor's evaluation of the adequacy of the disclosure of related party transactions. These differences include:

- The use of different, but similar, definitions of terms such as related party transaction.
- IAS 24 requires disclosure of an outstanding balance between an entity and its related parties even if there have been no transactions between those parties within the reporting period. FRS 8 does not require such disclosure.
- IAS 24 requires the disclosure of related party transactions and outstanding balances in separate financial statements of a parent, investor or venturer. FRS 8 provides an exemption for such disclosure.
- IAS 24 does not reflect that aspect of the FRS 8 definition of materiality which, uniquely, requires assessment of materiality from the point of view of the related party as well as the point of view of the reporting entity.

[35] This guidance is available on the ASB website at http://www.asb.org.uk/images/uploaded/documents/ASB%20Guidance%20on%20Applic%20of%20IAS%2039%20-%20attach%20to%20262.pdf.

[36] The FSA wrote to listed companies in October 2004 warning them on clarity of disclosure on this issue. The letter is at http://www.fsa.gov.uk/pubs/ceo/ceo_letter_25oct04.pdf.

- Both standards require disclosures of controlling parties. IAS 24 does not contemplate the situation where an entity does not know the identity of its ultimate controlling party and, therefore, does not have the requirement, which is included in FRS 8, to disclose that fact.

ISA (UK & Ireland) 560 'Subsequent Events'

100 IAS 10 'Events After the Balance Sheet Date' and the recent UK/ROI standard FRS 21 of the same title are substantially the same as SSAP 17 'Post-Balance Sheet Events'. The main difference, which has been facilitated by a change in company law, relates to the treatment of dividends declared after the end of an accounting period but before the accounts are approved. Under UK/ROI GAAP, until now, these have been treated as a liability in the accounts of the period just passed, but in future they will only be disclosed as they do not meet the recognition criteria of a liability at the period end.

101 FRS 21 (along with enabling changes to UK legislation) will change UK accounting practice to bring it into line with IAS 10. This will affect single entity accounts and so may affect a parent company in a group which relies on the receipt of dividends from subsidiaries to distribute on to its own shareholders. The change in treatment of dividends paid may affect the period in which the receipt of the dividend can be recorded in the parent's 'relevant accounts'. This may be relevant to the assessment of compliance with laws and regulations under ISA (UK and Ireland) 250 Section A as discussed above.

ISA (UK & Ireland) 570 'Going Concern'

Foreseeable future

102 IAS 1 requires that management make an assessment of the entity's ability to continue as a going concern. IAS 1 addresses going concern on a similar but not identical basis to FRS 18 'Accounting Policies', the relevant UK/ROI standard. Guidance regarding 'the future period to which the directors have paid particular attention in assessing going concern' differs slightly between IAS 1 and FRS 18, as do the detailed disclosure requirements.

103 It is technically possible for management to meet the requirements of IAS 1 by looking forward 12 months from the balance sheet date rather than 12 months from the date of approval of the financial statements. However, this is only possible in circumstances where there is no other information available about the future. If, in such circumstances, the directors do not disclose the length of the future period to which they have paid particular attention, ISA (UK and Ireland) 570 requires the auditors to disclose the length of the period considered in an emphasis of matter paragraph within their report.

104 For UK listed companies, Listing Rule 9.8.6R(3) requires the annual report and accounts to include a statement by the directors that the business is a going concern with supporting assumptions or qualifications as necessary. The rule refers to guidance on the interpretation of this point issued by ICAEW[37]. This guidance is closely aligned to the requirements of ISA (UK and Ireland) 570. It is unlikely that any reason will arise for management to change their approach to the assessment of going concern due to the switch from FRS 18 to IAS 1.

---

[37] *Guidance on Going Concern and Financial Reporting for directors of listed companies in the United Kingdom*, ICAEW November 1994. http://www.icaew.co.uk/index.cfm?AUB=TB21_67522.MNXI_67522

Borrowing powers and debt covenants

105 Listed companies may have limits, in their Articles of Association or other constitutional documents, on the extent to which they can borrow funds without obtaining specific shareholder consent. These provisions are usually expressed by reference to the consolidated financial statements, generally an adjusted net assets position. The legal drafting usually uses, as the starting point before adjustments, balances on share capital and reserves as a proxy for net assets.

106 Similar, but more extensive, financial covenants are often found in debt instruments and borrowing agreements, including those for straightforward bank loans and overdrafts. As well as limiting borrowing, these will often include limits on ratios between interest and earnings and even absolute minimum levels for tangible net assets.

107 Both of these types of arrangement may be affected by the introduction of IFRSs through:
(a) increases in the type and extent of liabilities recognised, for example in relation to financial instruments measured at fair value; and
(b) changes in the value of net assets, again through the recognition of new assets or liabilities or the use of new measurement bases.

108 Where applicable, the auditors consider whether the directors have made provision to obtain approval for an increase in the company's borrowing powers from the shareholders in general meeting in sufficient time for the introduction of IFRSs. In the case of financial covenants in debt agreements, auditors consider whether clauses exist that allow the use of 'frozen GAAP' (i.e. GAAP that was being used when the agreement was signed is continued for the life of the agreement for covenant purposes, ignoring new accounting requirements); where there is no clause allowing the use of 'frozen GAAP', the auditors consider, in their review of going concern, whether any necessary renegotiation of covenants has taken place in good time and any risk of default by the borrower or termination by the lender as a result of the change in the financial statements caused by the introduction of IFRSs.

109 Where any breach of an undertaking to a lender has taken place before the year end, the auditors consider whether the liability to which it relates has been treated correctly as current or non-current in the balance sheet, depending on the requirements of Paragraphs 65-67 of IAS 1.

ISA (UK & Ireland) 580 'Management Representations'

110 In the periods leading up to the period of transition, auditors may in many cases require, as part of their audit evidence, management assurances on matters such as the potential impact of the introduction of IFRSs on the business. The auditors consider obtaining written representation on these points.

111 In the year of transition, auditors may wish to use the management representation letter to clarify the responsibilities of the directors in relation to the transition to IFRSs. Specific representations are likely to be required by auditors that the directors have obtained all necessary information from subsidiaries that have not adopted IFRSs, to enable adjustments to be made to their financial statements for the purposes of consolidation into the group accounts.

112 Auditors consider the need to obtain representations on management's intentions for future actions, where these will have a direct impact on the accounting treatment of

certain items. For example, the treatment of non-current assets held for sale arises from management intention to sell the assets.

ISA (UK & Ireland) 600 'Using the Work of Another Auditor'

113 Co-operation between the principal auditors and the other auditors will be vital in the year of transition to IFRSs. This is particularly the case where the subsidiaries (and parent) are following UK/ROI or another national GAAP in their financial statements, but the group financial statements are prepared under IFRSs. While this is no different, in theory, from those existing situations where a UK/ROI parent owns foreign subsidiaries that report locally under other accounting frameworks, in 2005 there may be substantially more group companies than in the past preparing their statutory accounts under one accounting framework, but reporting for consolidation purposes to the parent under another.

114 Principal auditors consider the extent to which they will need to instruct the other auditors about the need to perform additional procedures and provide information relevant to the transition. The principal auditors also consider whether they will need to perform further procedures in relation to the other auditors' work, which may require additional visits to the other auditors. The principal auditors may wish to ascertain whether other auditors have made enquiries about the introduction of IFRSs in relation to the entities they are auditing, particularly in those subsidiaries which comprise major parts of the group's business. This will be relevant whether or not the subsidiary entities in question are required to follow IFRSs; their results will still be required to be included in the group accounts of a parent following IFRSs.

ISA (UK & Ireland) 620 'Using the Work of an Expert'

115 There is likely to be a wider range of circumstances in which auditors consider the need to use the work of an expert because of the increased use of valuations in IFRSs as noted under ISA (UK and Ireland) 545 above.

116 Auditors consider the need to use the work of an expert as early as possible in the planning process in the year of transition, to ensure that expert advice can be obtained in a timely fashion. However specialised the work of an expert, auditors assess it and consider the impact of this assessment on the audit report in the context of ISA (UK and Ireland) 620.

ISA (UK & Ireland) 700 'The Auditor's Report on Financial Statements'

'True and fair'/'present fairly'

117 IAS 1 requires management to prepare financial statements that 'present fairly' the financial position, performance and cash flows of the company. However, the CA 1985 continues to require the auditors to report whether the financial statements give a true and fair view. (A company following UK/ROI GAAP will still be required to prepare financial statements that present a true and fair view.) New Section 262(2A) of the CA 1985 makes clear that the terms "present fairly" and "true and fair view" should be read as having the same meaning. There is, therefore, no discrepancy between the standard management brings to bear in its preparation of IFRS financial statements and the auditor's opinion on them.[38]

---

[38] *A view supported by the Financial Reporting Council (FRC) in its paper "The Implications of New Accounting and Auditing Standards for the "True and Fair View" and Auditors' Responsibilities".*

Section 235 of CA 1985 includes a new requirement (Section 235(1A)) for the auditor's report to identify the financial reporting framework applied in the preparation of the financial statements. It is important to appreciate the context in which this reference is made, the DTI Guidance notes that "The requirement that an audit opinion states whether the annual or consolidated accounts give a true and fair view in accordance with the relevant financial reporting framework clarifies the context in which the audit opinion was given, it does not represent a restriction of the scope of that opinion". 118

Reference to the financial reporting framework

The requirement for IFRSs to be adopted for use in the EU gives rise to a potential for differences to exist between IFRSs as issued by the IASB and IFRSs as adopted for use in the European Union. While there has been considerable attention given to IAS 39 'Financial Instruments: Recognition and Measurement' (where the EC has adopted a so-called 'carved-out' version), the difference between the effective date of a standard established by IASB and when that standard is adopted into EU law, for the purposes of the IAS Regulation, may also give rise to further differences in the future. 119

Differences between IFRSs as issued by the IASB and IFRSs adopted for use in the European Union raise an issue concerning the description of the financial reporting framework a company is following in both the financial statements and the auditor's report thereon. The APB's view is for auditors to express an opinion in the terms 'true and fair view, in accordance with IFRSs as adopted for use in the European Union'.[39] 120

Many companies will be in a position of complying with both IFRSs as issued by the IASB and IFRSs as adopted for use in the European Union[40]. Consequently, the entity may also wish the auditors to express an opinion in terms of 'true and fair view, in accordance with IFRSs'. In these circumstances, it is preferable to state separately a second opinion with regard to full IFRSs to avoid confusing readers of the auditor's report and to leave intact the opinion required by law on compliance with IFRSs as adopted by the EU. The example auditors' reports set out in Bulletin 2005/4 'Auditor's Reports on Financial Statements' illustrate this point (see for example Appendix 1, Example 7). 121

For a minority of companies compliance with IFRSs as issued by the IASB may not ensure compliance with IFRSs as adopted for use in the European Union. Such situations will require auditors to consider carefully how to refer to the financial reporting framework in their audit reports. Auditors may need to take legal advice depending on the precise circumstances. However, the overriding requirement, in all circumstances, is for the *company* to provide full and clear disclosure of the accounting policies that have been adopted, so that users of financial statements can 122

---

[39] *This is also the consensus view that has emerged across Europe following a consultation paper issued by FEE (the Fédération des Experts Comptables Européens). More details can be found at www.fee.be.*

[40] *In relation to IAS 39 the ASB has produced guidance on what it believes to be the correct approach to the situation in the UK and Ireland. It is assumed, for the purposes of this Bulletin, that most companies:*
(a) *will follow the more restrictive hedge accounting rules in the IASB's IAS 39, as recommended by the ASB; and*
(b) *will not use the 'full fair value' option in the IASB's IAS 39 (although the European Commission may be about to endorse a revised version of the full fair value option which will remove this particular difference). Consequently, the majority of companies are expected to be in compliance with both full IFRSs and the EU carved-out version.*

make an informed assessment about what the company has done and how its results are affected by the decisions it has made. Consequently, auditors consider carefully the disclosure made and, where it is in their view deficient:

(a) discuss the relevant disclosures with those charged with governance; and
(b) consider the implications for their report.

Group accounts and the parent's own individual financial statements

123   As described in the ISA (UK and Ireland) 250 section of this Bulletin, the introduction of IFRSs may give rise to issues regarding the presentation of the parent company financial statements where different accounting frameworks are applied and/or the Section 230 exemption is applied. To address this, companies may decide to present the financial statements in separate sections of the annual report.

124   Where companies adopt the separate sections approach, separate audit reports will be prepared for the group and parent company financial statements and, as recommended by the DTI Guidance, where advantage has been taken of the Section 230 exemption, the reference to the framework used in the auditor's report needs to make clear that it is "IFRSs as adopted for use in the European Union *and as applied in accordance with the provisions of the 1985 Act*".[41] An illustrative example of an auditor's report on parent company accounts prepared under IFRSs and using the Section 230 exemption is set out in Appendix 1, Example 11 of Bulletin 2005/4.

Statements of compliance with and departures from IFRSs

125   An unqualified opinion may be expressed only when the auditors are able to conclude that the financial statements give a true and fair view in accordance with the identified financial reporting framework. In all other circumstances the auditors are required to disclaim an opinion or to issue a qualified or adverse opinion. Accordingly, the auditors do not express an unqualified opinion that financial statements have been prepared in accordance with IFRSs if the financial statements contain any departure from IFRSs and the departure has a material effect on the financial statements.

126   When the auditors report on whether the financial statements have been prepared in accordance with IFRSs and those financial statements contain a material departure from IFRSs, such a departure results in a disagreement with management regarding the acceptability of the accounting policies selected, the method of their application, or the adequacy of disclosures in the financial statements[42]. In the light of paragraph 41 of IAS 8, auditors consider whether failure to correct misstatements produces financial statements that are so seriously misleading that an adverse opinion is required, rather than a qualified opinion.

---

[41] *See Paragraph 43 regarding the need to explain the company's approach.*

[42] *Paragraph 17 of IAS 1 (revised December 2003) allows an entity to depart from the requirements of a standard in the rare circumstances that management concludes that compliance with the requirement would be so misleading that it would conflict with the objective of fair presentation. A departure from the requirements of a particular IFRS made under the provisions of paragraph 17 of IAS 1 does not constitute a departure from IFRSs for this purpose.*

Limitations of scope

As noted in the section on ISA (UK and Ireland) 250 individual companies within the group may continue to prepare their financial statements under UK/ROI GAAP and adjustments required to bring the group financial statements into line with IFRSs may be made only as consolidation adjustments. In such circumstances, the auditors pay particular attention to whether this approach is adequate in order to permit the auditors to form an opinion on the consolidated financial statements. 127

Given the pervasive nature of the change to the basis of accounting, it may be the case that the auditors will be subject to a limitation of scope if the entity simply adjusts the information provided in consolidation schedules by accounting systems based on UK/ROI GAAP. Auditors, therefore, assess whether the company has put in place new or adapted accounting systems to record the information required for consolidated financial statements to be prepared under IFRSs to the necessary level of detail and accuracy for the auditors to obtain sufficient audit evidence. Where this is not the case, the auditors consider the implications for their audit report. 128

ISA (UK & Ireland) 720 "Other Information in Documents Containing Audited Financial Statements"

Companies that are subject to the mandatory application of adopted IFRSs are unlikely to wish to wait for the first period of application (accounting periods beginning on or after 1 January 2005) to communicate with users of their financial statements about the likely impact of the change. The Committee of European Securities Regulators (CESR) has issued a Recommendation to regulators to give guidance for listed companies on this point.[43] The FSA has drawn the attention of publicly traded companies to the Recommendation in an article in its publication LIST!, and in its letter to Chief Executives dated 15 April 2005. 129

Commentary following the publication of the CESR recommendation has indicated that there are likely to be variations in practice in the periods leading up to 2005: 130

(a) some companies may provide disclosures about the transition to IFRSs at the same time and alongside their 2004 published interim and annual financial statements; whereas
(b) other companies may provide such information separately and at different times.

Where such information is issued in conjunction with the financial statements, the auditors have regard to the requirements of ISA (UK and Ireland) 720. Where companies disclose such information in the notes to the financial statements, the auditors consider the implications for their report.[44] 131

Paragraph 36 of IFRS 1 requires one year of comparatives to be given under IFRSs, paragraph 37 considers the situation where older comparative financial information is also presented under the previous GAAP of the entity. Such presentation is permitted, but the standard requires it to be clearly labelled as not being prepared under 132

---

[43] The recommendation can be downloaded from the CESR website at www.cesr-eu.org.
Broadly, the CESR guidance suggests various "milestones" of disclosure leading up to 2005. The milestones coincide with the publication of the 2003 annual financial statements, the 2004 annual financial statements, the 2005 interim financial statements and the 2005 annual financial statements. At each milestone, publicly traded companies are encouraged to provide investors with certain specified information.

[44] IAPS 1014, published by the IAASB, provides guidance on this matter.

IFRSs as well as a description to be given of the main adjustments that would be required for the information to be compliant with IFRSs (such adjustments do not need to be quantified).

Review of interim financial information under IFRSs

133 This section sets out guidance for auditors undertaking an engagement to review interim financial information in accordance with Bulletin 1999/4 "Review of Interim Financial Information" on interim financial information published before a company's full annual financial statements are published under IFRSs for the first time.

Listing Rules[45]

134 The Listing Rules require that the accounting policies and presentation applied to interim figures must be consistent with those in the latest published annual accounts, save where they are to be changed in the subsequent annual financial statements, in which case the new accounting policies and presentation should be followed, and the changes and reasons therefore should be disclosed in the interim report. Accordingly, for listed companies that are adopting IFRSs in their annual financial statements, interim financial information for the accounting period must also be prepared using the new accounting policies and presentation that follows from the adoption of those standards.

135 The Listing Rules also require that the interim financial information must contain enough information to enable a comparison to be made with the corresponding period of the preceding financial year.

Accounting Standards[45]

136 Under UK/ROI GAAP, the guidance in the ASB's Statement "Interim Reports" is persuasive rather than mandatory. Under IFRSs, however, there are specific requirements governing the content and presentation of interim reports, which may result in significant changes for some companies.

137 The FSA has indicated[46] that, in line with the recommendation of the Committee of European Securities Regulators (CESR), issuers should prepare 2005 interims on the basis of the IFRS measurement and recognition principles that are expected to apply at the year end and comparatives should be restated. The FSA reiterated this view in June 2005[47], stating that this should include IFRSs not yet adopted for use in the EU but which are expected to be adopted in time to be applied to the full 2005 financial statements.

138 IAS 34 "Interim Financial Reporting" has been adopted for use in the EU. However, as the IAS Regulation applies only to annual financial statements, and given the FSA's statement described above, the standard is not considered mandatory in respect of interim financial statements.

---

[45] Reference should be made to the Listing Rules, IFRS 1 and IAS 34 for full details of the specific requirements in relation to interim financial reports.

[46] December 2004 edition of List!

[47] June 2005 edition of List!

146 The illustrative procedures set out in Appendix 2 of Bulletin 1999/4 include:

> "(q) considering whether the classification and presentation of disclosures is appropriate and in accordance with Stock Exchange requirements, including consideration of the proper presentation of comparative figures, changes thereto and disclosure thereof."

147 When performing a review of interim financial information for which IFRSs have been adopted for the first time, the auditor considers whether the relevant requirements of paragraphs 38 to 46 of IFRS 1 have been complied with, reviewing the adjustments and disclosures made in accordance therewith. These requirements include disclosure of details of changes to the comparative figures.

148 Guidance for the auditor in relation to opening balances and comparatives and the impact on the audit of the annual financial statements is given in the section of this draft bulletin dealing with ISA (UK and Ireland) 510 and ISA (UK and Ireland) 710. This guidance indicates that overall, it is unlikely that the usual level of audit work for continuing engagements, as outlined in ISAs (UK and Ireland) 510 and 710, will be sufficient to ensure that opening balances in the year of transition to IFRSs are not materially misstated and additional procedures, such as those for incoming auditors (for which guidance is given in ISAs (UK and Ireland) 510 and 710) will be required.

149 Paragraph 75 includes the statement that "It is unlikely to be possible to audit the first financial statements under IFRSs without performing procedures on the opening IFRS balance sheet and then rolling these forward to the 2005 comparative figures and ultimately the 2005 figures themselves." The auditor is unlikely to be able to issue a review conclusion on interim financial information until these procedures have been performed and the auditor has considered the results.

New systems, or changes to existing systems, that give rise to financial information needed to reflect IFRSs

150 In addition to the guidance in paragraph 20 of Bulletin 1999/4, the illustrative procedures set out in Appendix 2 of Bulletin 1999/4 include:

> "(i) enquiring about changes in the company's procedures for recording, classifying and summarising transactions, accumulating information for disclosure, and preparing the financial information;"

The adoption of IFRSs will require some companies to change, or introduce new, accounting systems (e.g. to record the information necessary for compliance with IAS 39 "Financial Instruments: Recognition and Measurement" or IFRS 2 "Share-based Payment"). As noted above, where this is the case, the considerations for the auditor are similar to those where the auditor did not audit the previous financial statements. In particular, the auditor needs to obtain an understanding of, and where appropriate test, accounting and internal control systems to determine whether those systems provide the necessary information to enable the preparation of financial statements in accordance with the new accounting policies.

Reference to financial reporting framework in the auditor's review report

151 In the section on "Directors' responsibilities" in the review report the auditor adds a paragraph emphasising the fact that IFRSs as adopted in the EU have been followed for the first time. The precise wording adopted by the auditor will depend on the

IAS 34 requires that if an entity's interim financial report is in compliance with it, that fact shall be stated. IAS 34 also states (in paragraph 19) that an interim financial report shall not be described as complying with International Financial Reporting Standards unless it complies with all IFRSs. Thus, the choice of following only endorsed standards or anticipating unendorsed standards in the interim financial statements will mean that care will be required as to what a company claims to be compliant with. The overriding consideration should be for full and clear disclosure of both the standards followed and any uncertainties about the likely adoption of any new or revised IFRSs that are followed before their adoption by the EU. **139**

For companies that adopt IAS 34 "Interim Financial Reporting" for their interim report, that standard prescribes the minimum content of an interim financial report and the principles for recognition and measurement in complete or condensed financial statements for an interim period. **140**

IFRS 1 requires that, if an entity presents an interim financial report under IAS 34, the interim financial report include reconciliations of the figures reported under previous GAAP to the IFRS figures, giving sufficient detail to enable users to understand the material adjustments to the balance sheet, income statement and cash flow statement. Even where an entity is not reporting under IAS 34, this information is likely to be necessary in order to give a clear picture to the market about the impact of IFRSs. **141**

Guidance for auditors

The review procedures outlined in Bulletin 1999/4 assume that the auditor has audited the latest annual financial statements and has reviewed the corresponding financial information for the preceding year. The adoption of IFRSs gives rise to some particular issues in relation to the auditor's review of the interim financial information in the year of adoption. These include the extent to which the auditor needs to perform procedures on: **142**

(a) adjustments made to the opening balance sheet and comparative information to reflect the adoption of IFRSs; and
(b) new systems, or changes to existing systems, that generate financial information needed to reflect IFRSs.

Members of the engagement team need to have obtained an understanding of IFRSs commensurate with their responsibilities and sufficient as a whole to perform the engagement competently. When assessing the risks of material misstatements the auditors consider the possible effect of management's lack of experience of accounting under IFRSs (see paragraph 67). **143**

Paragraph 20 of Bulletin 1999/4 addresses the situation when the auditor did not audit the previous financial statements. It notes that Auditing Standards require the auditors to obtain sufficient appropriate evidence that opening balances do not contain errors or misstatements which materially affect the current period's financial statements and obtain an understanding of, and where appropriate test, accounting and internal control systems. **144**

Similarly, paragraph 38 of Bulletin 1999/4 addresses changes in accounting policy. It states that: **145**

> "Auditors review the adjustments and disclosures made. If the auditors do not consider that accounting policy changes have been properly reflected in the financial information, they consider the implications for their review report."

nature and level of disclosure made by the directors in the interim financial report. Example wording of an interim review report is set out in Appendix 2.

As noted in Paragraph 139 above differences may exist between the effective date of a standard established by IASB and when that standard is adopted by the European Union, for the purposes of the IAS Regulation. In such circumstances companies may face a situation, when preparing interim information, where an IFRS that has been issued by the IASB has yet to be formally adopted for use in the EU. The company may wish to anticipate the standard's adoption in its interim report, in the expectation that the EC will have adopted the standard in time for its application in the company's annual financial statements. **152**

As it is possible that any standard may not be formally adopted within the relevant timescale, this approach carries certain risks, and the auditors discuss the decision with those charged with governance to ensure they are aware of those risks. The position of the particular pronouncement in the adoption process (including existence or otherwise of adoption advice by EFRAG (the European Financial Reporting Advisory Group)) will be relevant in assessing these risks. Again, disclosure by the company on this point should be very clear, to ensure that readers of the interim review understand which standards the company is complying with. **153**

Where a company anticipates the adoption of a new or revised IFRS by the EC which has a significant impact on the company's results, the auditors consider the disclosures made by the company and may conclude that it is appropriate to highlight the uncertainty in their report. Illustrative wording of this nature is given in the example interim review report in Appendix 2. **154**

Reporting timetable

As noted in paragraph 54 the FSA has given companies a concession relating to the timing of the publication of their first set of half yearly accounts under IFRSs. **155**

Appendix 1 – Equivalent Legislative References for Northern Ireland and Comparative Legislative References for the Republic of Ireland.

Legislative references in Northern Ireland

The legal requirements in Northern Ireland are very similar to those in Great Britain. The following table shows the corresponding references to those contained in the Bulletin in relation to Great Britain.

Legislative references in the Republic of Ireland

The principal legislation relating to the form and content of group accounts is contained in the Companies (Amendment) Act 1986 and the European Communities (Companies: Group Accounts) Regulations 1992 (SI 201of 1992), which implement the EU Seventh Directive and amend certain provisions of the Companies Acts 1963 to (then) 1990 relating to group accounts.

Implementation of the IAS Regulation in the Republic of Ireland follows a broadly equivalent approach to that in the United Kingdom, with the exception that application of the requirement to prepare accounts following IFRS has been deferred until 2007 in the case of listed debt securities. The following table shows the comparative legislative references to those contained in this Bulletin in relation to Great Britain.

Bulletin Paragraph Reference	GB Legislation Reference (all references to Companies Act 1985)	Equivalent NI Legislative Reference	Comparative ROI Legislative Reference
4	The Companies Act 1985 (International Accounting Standards and Other Accounting Amendments) Regulations 2004 (Statutory Instrument 2004/2947) – *Implement the IAS Regulation, the Accounts Modernisation and Fair Value Directives.*	The Companies (1986 Order) (International Accounting Standards and Other Accounting Amendments) Regulations (Northern Ireland) 2004 (Statutory Rule 2004/496)	European Communities (International Financial Reporting Standards and Miscellaneous Amendments) Regulations 2005, SI 116 of 2005. European Communities (Fair Value Accounting) Regulation 2004, SI 765 of 2004
8(c)	The Companies Act 1985	The Companies (Northern Ireland) Order 1986	The Companies Acts 1963 to 2003.
27	Schedule 4A CA 1985	Schedule 4A of the Companies (Northern Ireland) Order 1986	Schedule Part 1, Companies (Amendment) Act 1986

Bulletin Paragraph Reference	GB Legislation Reference (all references to Companies Act 1985)	Equivalent NI Legislative Reference	Comparative ROI Legislative Reference
34	S 227 – requirement to produce consolidated accounts companies	Article 235	S 150 Companies Act 1963
34	S 255A – requirement to produce consolidated accounts banks and insurance companies	Article 263A	S 150 Companies Act 1963
39	S 227C(1) requirement that the directors of a parent company should ensure that all the individual companies (including the parent) within a group follow the same accounting framework "except to the extent that in their opinion there are good reasons for not doing so".	Article 235C (1)	S 150 Companies Act 1963
39 (footnote 15)	S 227C (5) – provision of partial exemption re. S 227C(1)	Article 235C (5)	S 150(C) (1) Companies Act 1963, as amended by European Communities (International Financial Reporting Standards and Miscellaneous Amendments) Regulations 2005
42	S 230 – publication exemption for Profit and Loss account.	Article 238	S 3(2) Companies (Amendment) Act 1986
42 (footnote 16)	S 261 (2) – publication exemption – notes to Profit and Loss	Article 269 (2)	Schedule Part IV 23 Companies (Amendment) Act 1986
44	S 240 (2) – requirement for consolidated and individual accounts to be published together	Article 248 (2)	S 150 Companies Act 1963

Bulletin Paragraph Reference	GB Legislation Reference (all references to Companies Act 1985)	Equivalent NI Legislative Reference	Comparative ROI Legislative Reference
45	S 226(5) decision to switch to IFRS irreversible except where companies and groups cease to be publicly traded.	Article 234 (5)	S 148 (5) (b) and (c) Companies Act 1963, as amended by European Communities (International Financial Reporting Standards and Miscellaneous Amendments) Regulations 2005
45	S 227(6) – decision to switch to IFRS irreversible except where company becomes a subsidiary of an undertaking that does not prepare its accounts in accordance with IFRS.	Article 234 (5) and Article 235 (6)	S 148 (5) (a) Companies Act 1963, as amended by European Communities (International Financial Reporting Standards and Miscellaneous Amendments) Regulations 2005
47	S 237 (1) – auditors required to investigate whether proper accounting records kept	Article 245(1)	S 194 Companies Act 1990
49	S 263 – laws relating to distributions	Article 271	Part IV Companies Act 1983
76	S 235 – comparatives not within scope of auditor's report	Article 243	S 193 Companies Act 1990
117	S 262 (2A) – terms – "present fairly" and "true and fair view" read as having the same meaning.	Article 270 (2A)	Schedule 1, 1(B) – European Communities (International Financial Reporting Standards and Miscellaneous Amendments) Regulations 2005
118	S 235 (1A) – auditor's report to identify financial reporting framework applied in the preparation of the financial statements	Article 243 (1A)	S 8 (4) Companies Act 1990, as amended by European Communities (International Financial Reporting Standards and Miscellaneous Amendments) Regulations 2005

Appendix 2 – Example Review Report

INDEPENDENT REVIEW REPORT TO XYZ PLC

Introduction

We have been instructed by the company to review the financial information for the [three months] [six months] [nine months] ended ... which comprises [specify primary financial statements and the related notes that have been reviewed].[48] We have read the other information contained in the interim report and considered whether it contains any apparent misstatements or material inconsistencies with the financial information.

Directors' responsibilities

The interim report, including the financial information contained therein, is the responsibility of, and has been approved by the directors. The directors are responsible for preparing the interim report in accordance with the Listing Rules of the Financial Services Authority.

As disclosed in note X, the next annual financial statements of the [group/company] will be prepared in accordance with IFRSs as adopted for use in the European Union***. [This interim report has been prepared in accordance with International Accounting Standard 34, "Interim Financial Reporting" and the requirements of IFRS 1, "First Time Adoption of International Financial Reporting Standards" relevant to interim reports.][49]

The accounting policies are consistent with those that the directors intend to use in the next annual financial statements. [There is, however, a possibility that the directors may determine that some changes to these policies are necessary when preparing the full annual financial statements for the first time in accordance with IFRSs as adopted for use in the European Union. This is because, as disclosed in note Y, the directors have anticipated that [new] [revised] IFRS X, which has yet to be formally adopted for use in the EU will be so adopted in time to be applicable to the next annual financial statements.][50]

Review work performed

We conducted our review in accordance with guidance contained in Bulletin 1999/4 issued by the Auditing Practices Board for use in the United Kingdom. A review consists principally of making enquiries of [group] management and applying analytical procedures to the financial information and underlying financial data and based thereon, assessing whether the disclosed accounting policies have been consistently applied unless otherwise disclosed. A review excludes audit procedures such as tests of controls and verification of assets, liabilities and transactions. It is substantially less in scope than an audit and, therefore, provides a lower level of

---

[48] Review reports of entities that do not publish their interim reports on a web site or publish them using 'PDF' format may continue to refer to the pages of the interim report.

[49] This wording should be tailored accordingly to reflect the approach adopted by the directors (see Paragraphs 138 – 141).

[50] This wording should be tailored accordingly to reflect the approach adopted by the directors and the disclosures given in the interim report (see Paragraphs 139 and 153).

assurance. Accordingly, we do not express an audit opinion on the financial information.

Review conclusion

On the basis of our review we are not aware of any material modifications that should be made to the financial information as presented for the [three] [six] [nine] months ended ....

ABC & Company   *Designation*
Date   *Address*

> *** Subsequent to this Bulletin being printed the Accounting Regulatory Committee (ARC) of the European Commission indicated that it was supportive of the following standard formulation for use in the notes to the accounts and in the auditor's report "...in accordance with International Financial Reporting Standards as adopted by the EU" or (abbreviated version) "in accordance with IFRSs as adopted by the EU". The ARC wording differs slightly from that used in the Appendix and auditors may wish to use the ARC's wording in their reports. *(See APB Press Notice No. 25 of 21 December 2005)*

[Bulletin 2006/1]
Auditor's reports on financial statements in the Republic of Ireland

Contents

	Paragraphs
Introduction	1 - 5
Changes to the reporting and accounting provisions of the Companies Acts 1963 to 2005	6 - 7
International Financial Reporting Standards	8 - 15
Corporate governance	16 - 18
Other matters required to be expressly stated in the auditor's report	19 - 26
Example modified auditor's reports in ISA 700	27 - 28
Statement of directors' responsibilities	29

Appendix 1 – Unmodified auditor's reports on financial statements

   Explanatory note regarding the Appendix

Navigation aid to the 13 examples of unmodified auditor's reports on financial statements

   13 examples of unmodified auditor's reports

Appendix 2 – Modified auditor's reports on financial statements (excluding going concern issues)

   Explanatory note regarding the Appendix

Navigation aid to the 7 examples of modified auditor's reports (excluding going concern issues)

   7 examples of modified auditor's reports (excluding going concern issues)

Appendix 3 – Modified auditor's reports on financial statements arising from going concern issues

   Explanatory note regarding the Appendix

Navigation aid to the 8 examples of modified auditor's reports arising from going concern issues

   8 examples of modified auditor's reports arising from going concern issues

Appendix 4 – Illustrative statement of directors' responsibilities

> Note: Readers are advised to use the navigation aids (shaded above) to assist in locating particular example auditor's reports.

Introduction

1   The purpose of this Bulletin is to provide illustrative examples of:

   a) unmodified auditor's reports for audits of financial statements of companies incorporated in the Republic of Ireland:
      i) performed in accordance with International Standards on Auditing (UK and Ireland) (ISAs (UK and Ireland)) issued by the Auditing Practices Board; and
      ii) for periods commencing on or after 15 December 2004 (see Appendix 1);
   b) modified auditor's reports (excluding going concern issues) (see Appendix 2); and
   c) modified auditor's reports arising from going concern issues (see Appendix 3).

2   For the purposes of this Bulletin companies incorporated in the Republic of Ireland are either:

   a) 'publicly traded companies' – defined as 'those whose securities are admitted to trading on a regulated market in any Member State in the European Union'; or
   b) 'non-publicly traded companies' – defined as 'those who do not have any securities that are admitted to trading on a regulated market in any Member State in the European Union (EU)'.

3   This Bulletin updates the example auditor's reports on financial statements that were originally published by the APB in SAS 600 'The auditor's report on financial statements' and which were updated in subsequent Bulletins[1]. This is the first edition of the Bulletin referred to in various paragraphs of ISA (UK and Ireland) 700 'The auditor's report on financial statements'.

4   The example auditor's reports included in the Bulletin take account of the following matters:

   a) changes to the reporting and accounting provisions of the Companies Acts 1963 to 2005 (see paragraphs 6 and 7);
   b) the adoption by the EU of International Financial Reporting Standards ('IFRSs') for the consolidated financial statements of publicly traded companies (see paragraphs 8 to 15); and
   c) changes to the corporate governance reporting requirements following the publication of the 2003 FRC Combined Code (see paragraphs 16 to 18).

APB Bulletin 2005/3 'Guidance for Auditors on First-time Application of IFRSs in the United Kingdom and the Republic of Ireland' provides the background to the changes described in (a) and (b).

5   The Bulletin does not address the changes to the structure of the auditor's report contemplated by ISA 700 (Revised). The APB has exposed a revision to ISA 700 (UK and Ireland) based on ISA 700 (revised) but has decided to defer its implementation.

Changes to the reporting and accounting provisions of the Companies Acts, 1963 to 2005

6   In February 2005, S.I. No. 116 of 2005, 'European Communities (International Financial Reporting Standards and Miscellaneous Amendments) Regulations 2005'

---
[1] *Bulletin 1997/3 – paragraph 19, Bulletin 2001/2 – Appendices 6 to 9, and Bulletin 2004/4 – Appendix 2.*

('S.I. No. 116') implemented a number of changes to the Companies Acts 1963 to 2005. These regulations apply to financial years beginning on or after 1 January 2005.

This Bulletin addresses the effect that these changes will have on the wording of the auditor's report. Regulation 8 of S.I. No. 116 amends subsection 4 of section 193 of the Companies Act, 1990 by substituting the text shown in the table below. The principal changes are:

a) In relation to section 193(4)(a) below, the first paragraph of the auditor's report identifies the financial statements that are subject to audit. The section of the auditor's report that describes directors' and auditor's responsibilities includes wording describing the accounting framework;

b) By virtue of section 193(4A)(a) audit opinions are required to state whether the annual accounts have been properly prepared in accordance with the requirements of the Companies Acts (and, where applicable, Article 4 of the IAS Regulation); and

c) To take account of the requirement in section 193(4)(C)(i) below, where applicable:
   i) the words 'in accordance with IFRSs as adopted for use in the European Union'; or
   ii) the words 'in accordance with Generally Accepted Accounting Practice in Ireland'
   have been added to the example auditor's reports.

7

---

(4) The auditors'[2] report shall include –
  (a) an introduction identifying the individual accounts, and where appropriate, the group accounts, that are the subject of the audit and the financial reporting framework that has been applied in their preparation, and
  (b) a description of the scope of the audit identifying the auditing standards in accordance with which the audit was conducted.

(4A) (a) Except in the case of a company that has taken advantage of any of the provisions of Part III of the Sixth Schedule to the Principal Act, the auditors' report shall state clearly whether in the auditors' opinion the annual accounts have been properly prepared in accordance with the requirements of the Companies Acts (and, where applicable, Article 4 of the IAS Regulation).
  (b) In the case of a company that has taken advantage of any of the provisions of Part III of the Sixth Schedule to the Principal Act, the auditors' report shall state whether, in their opinion, the annual accounts and, where it is a holding company submitting group accounts, the group accounts have been properly prepared in accordance with the Companies Acts (and, where applicable, Article 4 of the IAS Regulation) and give a true and fair view of the matters referred to in subsection (4B)(e)(i) and (ii) and, where appropriate, subsection (4B)(e)(iii) subject to the non-disclosure of any matters (to be indicated in the report) which by virtue of the said Part III are not required to be disclosed.

(4B) The auditors' report shall also state –
  (a) whether they have obtained all the information and explanations which, to the best of their knowledge and belief, are necessary for the purposes of their audit,

---

[2] In its documents the APB ordinarily uses the singular when referring to auditors. Frequently, however, laws and regulations describe auditors in the plural. With respect to quotations from such laws and regulations, and in other appropriate contexts, the plural is used in this Bulletin.

> (b) whether, in their opinion, proper books of account have been kept by the company,
> (c) whether, in their opinion, proper returns adequate for their audit have been received from branches of the company not visited by them, and
> (d) whether the company's balance sheet and (unless it is framed as a consolidated profit and loss account) profit and loss account are in agreement with the books of account and returns.
>
> (4C) The auditor's report shall state, in particular –
> (i) whether the annual accounts give a true and fair view in accordance with the relevant financial reporting framework–
> (I) in the case of an individual balance sheet, of the state of affairs of the company as at the end of the financial year,
> (II) in the case of an individual profit and loss account, of the profit or loss of the company for the financial year,
> (III) in the case of group accounts, of the state of affairs as at the end of the financial year and of the profit or loss for the financial year of the undertakings included in the consolidation as a whole, so far as concerns members of the company,
> and
> (ii) whether, in their opinion, there existed at the balance sheet date a financial situation which under section 40(1) of the Companies (Amendment) Act 1983 would require the convening of an extraordinary general meeting of the company.
>
> (4D) The auditors' report –
> (a) shall be signed and dated by the statutory auditors,
> (b) shall, in relation to each matter referred to in subsections (4A), (4B) and (4C) contain a statement or opinion, as the case may be, which shall be either –
> (i) unqualified, or
> (ii) qualified,
> and
> (c) shall include a reference to any matters to which the auditors wish to draw attention by way of emphasis without qualifying the report.
>
> (4E) For the purposes of subsection (4D)(b)(ii), a statement or opinion may be qualified, including to the extent of an adverse opinion or a disclaimer of opinion, where there is a disagreement or limitation in scope of work.
>
> (4F) Where the individual accounts of a parent undertaking are attached to the group accounts, the auditors' report on the group accounts may be combined with the report on the individual accounts.

International Financial Reporting Standards

Reference to the accounting framework in the auditor's report

8   Bulletin 2005/3 notes APB's view that the accounting framework used by companies adopting IFRSs as adopted for use in the EU be referred to in the auditor's opinion in the following terms:

> 'true and fair view, in accordance with IFRSs as adopted for use in the European Union',

The example auditor's reports included in the Appendices have been prepared on this basis[3].

Many companies will be in a position of complying with both IFRSs as issued by the IASB and 'IFRSs as adopted for use in the European Union', and may request the auditor to express an opinion in terms of 'true and fair view, in accordance with IFRSs'. In these circumstances the APB believes that it is preferable for the auditor to state a second separate opinion with regards to IFRSs as issued by the IASB in order to avoid confusing readers of the auditor's report, and to leave intact the opinion required by law on compliance with IFRSs as adopted for use in the European Union. Where applicable, the example auditor's reports set out in Appendix 1 illustrate this point.

Different financial reporting frameworks used for group and parent company financial statements

Bulletin 2005/3 notes that a significant development arising from the adoption of IFRSs as adopted by the EU, as the financial reporting framework for group financial statements, is that group and parent company financial statements may be prepared in accordance with different financial reporting frameworks.

The example unmodified reports in Appendix 1 illustrate, among others, the following scenarios for auditor's reports on the group and parent company financial statements of publicly traded companies incorporated in the Republic of Ireland:

> EU adopted IFRSs used for group financial statements (required for publicly traded companies) and either:
> i) EU adopted IFRSs used for parent company financial statements; or
> ii) Irish GAAP[4] used for parent company financial statements.

In such instances, companies may choose to present the financial statements of the group and the parent company in separate sections of the annual report and in such circumstances separate auditor's reports would be provided. Appendix 1 includes example auditor's reports for situations where the group and parent company financial statements are presented separately or together (see also paragraph 14 below).

Where separate auditor's reports are provided on the group and parent company financial statements the illustrative examples describe the auditor's responsibilities with respect to the Corporate Governance Statement in the auditor's report on the group financial statements[5].

---

[3] *Subsequent to the issuance of Bulletin 2005/3 the Accounting Regulatory Committee (ARC) of the European Commission indicated that it was supportive of the following standard formulation for use in the notes to the accounts and in the auditor's report. '...in accordance with International Financial Reporting Standards as adopted by the EU' or (abbreviated version) 'in accordance with IFRSs as adopted by the EU'. Auditors may wish to use the ARC's wording in their reports.*

[4] *For the purposes of this Bulletin, Irish GAAP means the generally accepted accounting practices employed to prepare accounts of Irish entities intended to give a true and fair view and includes relevant Irish company law and the accounting standards issued by the Accounting Standards Board and promulgated by the Institute of Chartered Accountants in Ireland.*

[5] *A number of references in the Combined Code are to the 'group' rather than to 'the company'. In particular paragraph 14 of the Turnbull Guidance states that 'where reference is made to 'company' it should be taken, where applicable, as referring to the group of which the reporting company is the parent company.*

Exemption for presentation of parent company profit and loss account

13   Bulletin 2005/3 discusses the exemption in Section 148(8) – Companies Act, 1963, which allows a parent company not to publish its profit and loss account and certain related information. Where advantage has been taken of the Section 148(8) exemption and the parent company financial statements have been prepared in accordance with 'IFRSs as adopted for use in the European Union' the financial reporting framework is described in the auditor's report as:

> 'true and fair view, in accordance with IFRSs as adopted for use in the European Union *and as applied in accordance with the provisions of the Companies Act 1963 to 2005*'.

14   Where the group and parent company financial statements are both prepared in accordance with 'IFRSs as adopted for use in the European Union' it is likely that issuers may wish to present those financial statements separately so that the Section 148(8) exemption can be utilised without giving rise to, what might be considered to be, a modified auditor's report on the group financial statements. This is illustrated in example reports 11 and 12 in Appendix 1.

15   The example unmodified reports in Appendix 1 to this Bulletin illustrate the impact of the Section 148(8) exemption and the company's decision whether or not to present the group and parent company financial statements and auditor's reports separately in the annual report. The example reports cover the following scenarios for auditor's reports on the group and parent company financial statements of publicly traded companies incorporated in the Republic of Ireland:

	Scenario
a)	Section 148(8) exemption taken and either:
i)	The group and parent company financial statements are presented separately with two separate auditor's report; or
ii)	The group and parent company financial statements are NOT presented separately and one auditor's report is issued covering both the group and parent company financial statements.
b)	Section 148(8) exemption NOT taken and either:
i)	The group and parent company financial statements are presented separately with two separate auditor's report; or
ii)	The group and parent company financial statements are NOT presented separately and one auditor's report is issued covering both the group and parent company financial statements.

Corporate governance

16   In July 2003, the Combined Code issued by the Hampel Committee on Corporate Governance in June 1998 (the 'Hampel Code') was superseded and replaced by a new Code, 'The Combined Code on Corporate Governance', issued by the Financial Reporting Council (the '2003 FRC Combined Code'). The 2003 FRC Combined Code applies for reporting years beginning on or after 1 November 2003.

Chapter 6 of the Listing Rules of the Irish Stock Exchange[6] deals with Continuing Obligations and rules 6.8.9 to 6.8.11 set out certain requirements in respect of auditor's reports of listed companies incorporated in Ireland as follows:-

"**Auditors' report**

6.8.9 A listed company must ensure that the auditors review each of the following before the annual report is published:

(1) LR 6.8.6 (3) (statement by the directors that the business is a going concern); and

(2) the parts of the statement required by LR 6.8.6 (7) (corporate governance) that relate to the following provisions of the Combined Code:

(a) C1.1;

(b) C.2.1; and

(c) C3.1 – C3.7.

6.8.10 A listed company must ensure that the auditors review the following disclosures:

(1) LR 6.8.8 (2) (amount of each element in the remuneration package & information on share options);

(2) LR 6.8.8 (3), (4) and (5) (details of long term incentive schemes for directors);

(3) LR 6.8.8 (11) (defined contribution schemes);

(4) LR 6.8.8 (12) (defined benefit schemes);

6.8.11 If, in the opinion of the auditors the listed company has not complied with any of the requirements set out in LR 6.8.10, the listed company must ensure that the auditors report includes, to the extent possible, a statement giving details of the non-compliance."

LR 6.8.9 (2) above sets out nine provisions of the 2003 FRC Combined Code for the auditor's review.

APB Bulletin 2004/4, 'The Combined Code on Corporate Governance: Requirements of auditors under the Listing Rules of the Irish Stock Exchange' issued in December 2004 provides guidance for auditors when reviewing a company's statement made under the 2003 FRC Combined Code. The example reports included in Appendix 1 to this Bulletin have been updated to refer to the nine provisions of the 2003 FRC Combined Code as follows:

> 'We review whether the Corporate Governance Statement reflects the company's compliance with the nine provisions of the FRC Combined Code issued in 2003 specified for our review by the Listing Rules of the Irish Stock Exchange, and we report if it does not. We are not required to consider whether the board's statements on internal control cover all risks and controls, or form an opinion on the effectiveness of the [company's] [group's] corporate governance procedures or its risk and control procedures.'

---

[6] The Listing Rules of the Irish Stock Exchange effective from 1 July 2005 are available on the Exchange's website (http://www.ise.ie/?locID=444&docID=382).

Other matters required to be expressly stated in the auditor's report

19 Company legislation in the Republic of Ireland requires the following matters to be expressly stated in the auditors' report:-

  (i) whether, in their opinion, proper books of account have been kept by the company,
  (ii) whether, in their opinion, proper returns adequate for their audit have been received from branches of the company not visited by them;
  (iii) whether, in their opinion, there existed at the balance sheet date a financial situation which under section 40(1) of the Companies (Amendment) Act 1983 ('the 1983 Act') would require the convening of an extraordinary general meeting of the company (see paragraphs 20 to 22 below);
  (iv) whether, in their opinion, the information given in the directors' report is consistent with the financial statements (see paragraphs 23 and 24 below);
  (v) whether the company's balance sheet and (unless it is framed as a consolidated profit and loss account) profit and loss account are in agreement with the books of account and returns; and
  (vi) whether the auditors have obtained all the information and explanations which, to the best of their knowledge and belief, are necessary for the purposes of their audit (see paragraph 25 below).

Section 40 of the 1983 Act

20 Paragraph 19(iii) above outlines the requirement for the auditors to express an opinion as to whether or not a particular financial situation existed at the balance sheet date. Section 40 of the 1983 Act refers to the financial situation where net assets are 'half or less of the company's called-up share capital' which in certain circumstances requires the convening of an extraordinary general meeting (EGM). Matters to be considered by the auditors in this context include:

  a) the auditors base their opinion, as to whether a financial situation exists, solely on the amounts of the assets (whether at cost or valuation) and liabilities included in the balance sheet on which the auditors are reporting. Reporting on the financial situation shown in the balance sheet means that the auditors ignore disclosure of the market values of property and investments that is made merely by way of note to the balance sheet. Furthermore, post-balance sheet events that are defined by *FRS 21 (IAS10) Events after the balance sheet date* are not taken into account;
  b) Section 40 of the 1983 Act does not apply to situations which existed and were known by the directors to exist before 13 October 1983, the day on which the Act came into force. In such situations, there is no obligation on the auditors to report as to whether or not a financial situation existed;
  c) even though the balance sheet shows that a financial situation exists, there may be additional circumstances which avoid the need to convene an EGM. The auditors' responsibility is confined to reporting on the existence of the financial situation regardless of whether an EGM has been or will be held. The auditors need not comment in the auditors' report on such additional circumstances.

21 Where the auditors have added an emphasis of matter paragraph to an unqualified auditors' report referring to a significant uncertainty it will be possible to express the separate 'financial situation' opinion.

22 Where the auditors cannot report without qualification to the effect that in their opinion the financial statements give a true and fair view, this may have an impact on

the further 'financial situation' opinion referred to above at paragraph 19(iii), since that further opinion is based on the amounts shown in the balance sheet.

The impact of audit qualifications in this context may be summarized as follows:-

a) Where the auditors have qualified their opinion because of the effect of a limitation on the scope of their work, the auditors consider whether the adjustments which might be required, had there been no limitation of scope, could result in the net assets of the company altering from more than half of the called-up share capital to half or less (or vice versa). Except where the adjustments could result in the financial situation being affected in this way, it is possible to express the separate 'financial situation' opinion.

b) Where the auditors have disclaimed an opinion because the possible effect of a limitation on the scope of their work is so material or pervasive that the auditors have not been able to obtain sufficient evidence to support, and accordingly is unable to express, an opinion on the financial statements, it will be necessary for the auditors to give a disclaimer of opinion in relation to the separate 'financial situation'.

c) Finally, where the auditors have qualified their opinion due to disagreement affecting balance sheet amounts, the auditors express the further special opinion based on the assumption that the balance sheet is adjusted for the amounts in disagreement.

Consistency of director's report with financial statements

Section 15 of the Companies (Amendment) Act 1986 requires the auditors to state whether, in their opinion, the information given in the report of the directors relating to the financial year concerned is consistent with the accounts prepared by the company for that year. A similar obligation for group accounts is imposed by Regulation 38 of the European Communities (Companies: Group Accounts) Regulations 1992 (1992 Regulations). The auditors are not required to form an opinion on the directors' report itself. 23

The auditors have no statutory responsibilities in respect of items in the directors' report which, in its opinion, are misleading but not inconsistent with the financial statements. However, if the auditors believe that the other information is misleading, and the auditors are unable to resolve the matter with management and those charged with governance, the auditors consider the implication for the auditors' report and what further actions may be appropriate. The Exposure Draft ISA (UK & Ireland) 720 'Other Information in Documents Containing Audited Financial Statements' (Revised) also addresses this area. 24

Obtaining all necessary information and explanations

As noted in paragraph 19(vi) above, the auditors must state whether they have obtained all the information and explanations necessary for the purpose of their audit. In particular circumstances, for example where there has been a limitation of the scope of the audit giving rise to a qualification of the auditors' report, the auditors consider whether they can make that statement. 25

Other requirements of the Companies Acts

In the following two circumstances the auditors are required to set out the required particulars in the auditors' report, so far as the auditors are reasonably able to do so. 26

i) **Section 191(8) of the 1983 Act.** If the financial statements do not comply with the requirements of Section 191 which deals with 'Particulars of directors' salaries and payments to be given in accounts'

ii) **Section 46 of the 1990 Act.** If the financial statements do not comply with the requirements of Section 41 or 43 which deal with particulars of substantial contracts, loans and other transactions with directors, together with particulars of related amounts outstanding at the balance sheet date.

Example modified auditor's reports in ISA 700

27   ISA 700 contains illustrative modified auditor's opinions within the standard and although these address similar issues to the illustrative modified reports previously published by the APB the situations described and wording used are slightly different. The APB has concluded that, where the illustrative opinions used in the ISA are relevant to the Republic of Ireland, the situation described in the ISA and the wording used for the modified auditor's report in the ISA should be tailored for use in the Republic of Ireland and published in this Bulletin. The same approach was adopted for modified auditor's reports included in ISAs 510, 570 and 710. Where the APB considers that the modified reports previously published by the APB are more relevant than the ISA wording the APB wording has been updated and included instead of the equivalent ISA report.

28   Example 6 in Appendix 2 is included to illustrate the issue of multiple uncertainties which is described in paragraph 34 of ISA 700 (UK and Ireland).

Statement of directors' responsibilities

29   Appendix 4 is an illustrative example of a statement of directors' responsibilities for a non-publicly traded company preparing its parent company financial statements under Irish GAAP. In more complicated company and group situations where the financial statements may be prepared under 'IFRSs as adopted for use in the European Union' the directors may need to take legal advice on what is included in the statement of directors' responsibilities.

Appendix 1 – Unmodified auditor's reports on financial statements

This Appendix contains updated examples of unmodified reports for:
- Non-publicly traded companies incorporated in the Republic of Ireland (example reports 1-4); and
- Publicly traded companies incorporated in the Republic of Ireland (example reports 5-13)

The example reports take into account the following factors illustrated in the navigation aid on page 16:
- Whether the company is a parent company preparing group financial statements;
- Whether the group financial statements are prepared using 'IFRSs as adopted for use in the European Union';
- Whether the group financial statements comply with both 'IFRSs as adopted for use in the European Union' and IFRSs as issued by the International Accounting Standards Board;
- Whether the parent company financial statements are prepared using 'IFRSs as adopted for use in the European Union';
- Whether the Section 148(8) Companies Act, 1963 exemption ('Section 148(8) exemption') from presenting the parent company profit and loss account or income statement has been taken;
- Whether the group and parent company financial statements are presented separately (i.e. two separate auditor's reports)

Navigation aid to the examples of unmodified auditor's reports on financial statements

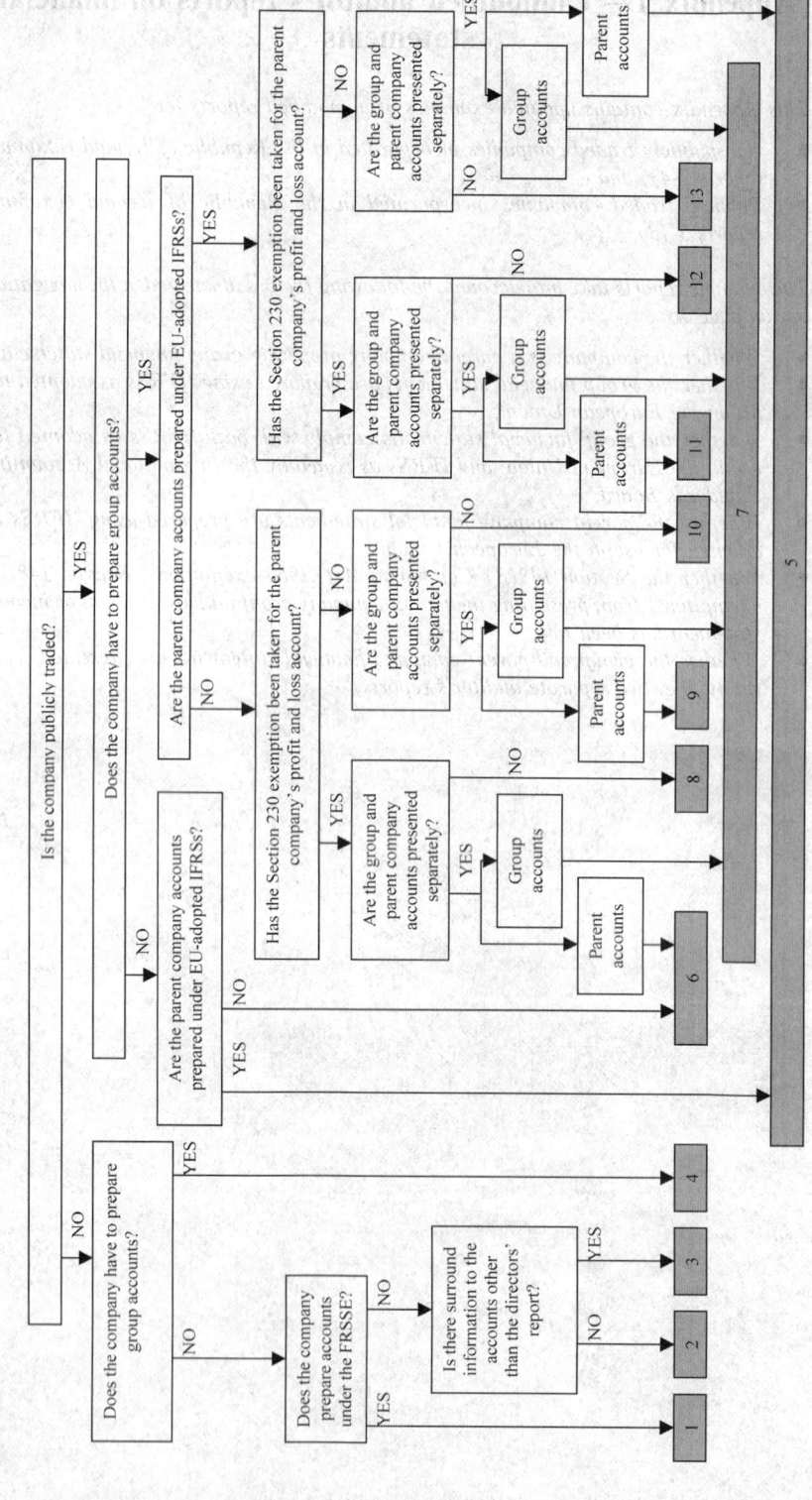

Example 1 – Non-publicly traded company incorporated in the Republic of Ireland preparing financial statements under the FRSSE

- Company qualifies as a small company.
- Company DOES NOT prepare group financial statements.
- Financial statements contain NO surround information other than the directors' report.
- Auditor does not take advantage of ES PASE.

INDEPENDENT AUDITOR'S REPORT TO THE SHAREHOLDERS OF XYZ LIMITED

We have audited the financial statements of (name of entity) for the year ended ... which comprise [state the primary financial statements such as the Profit and Loss Account, the Balance Sheet, [the Cash Flow Statement,] the Statement of Total Recognised Gains and Losses] and the related notes[7]. These financial statements have been prepared under the accounting policies set out therein and the requirements of the Financial Reporting Standard for Smaller Entities.

Respective responsibilities of directors and auditors

As described in the Statement of Directors' Responsibilities the company's directors are responsible for the preparation of the financial statements in accordance with applicable law and the accounting standards issued by the Accounting Standards Board and promulgated by the Institute of Chartered Accountants in Ireland (Generally Accepted Accounting Practice in Ireland).

Our responsibility is to audit the financial statements in accordance with relevant legal and regulatory requirements and International Standards on Auditing (UK and Ireland).

We report to you our opinion as to whether the financial statements give a true and fair view, in accordance with Generally Accepted Accounting Practice in Ireland applicable to Smaller Entities, and are properly prepared in accordance with the Companies Acts, 1963 to 2005. We also report to you whether in our opinion: proper books of account have been kept by the company; whether at the balance sheet date, there exists a financial situation requiring the convening of an extraordinary general meeting of the company; and whether the information given in the directors' report is consistent with the financial statements. In addition, we state whether we have obtained all the information and explanations necessary for the purposes of our audit, and whether the financial statements are in agreement with the books of account.

We also report to you if, in our opinion, any information specified by law regarding directors' remuneration and directors' transactions is not disclosed and, where practicable, include such information in our report.

We read the directors' report and consider the implications for our report if we become aware of any apparent misstatements within it.

---

[7] *Auditor's reports of entities that do not publish their financial statements on a web site or publish them using 'PDF' format may continue to refer to the financial statements by reference to page numbers.*

Basis of audit opinion

We conducted our audit in accordance with International Standards on Auditing (UK and Ireland) issued by the Auditing Practices Board. An audit includes examination, on a test basis, of evidence relevant to the amounts and disclosures in the financial statements. It also includes an assessment of the significant estimates and judgments made by the directors in the preparation of the financial statements, and of whether the accounting policies are appropriate to the company's circumstances, consistently applied and adequately disclosed.

We planned and performed our audit so as to obtain all the information and explanations which we considered necessary in order to provide us with sufficient evidence to give reasonable assurance that the financial statements are free from material misstatement, whether caused by fraud or other irregularity or error. In forming our opinion we also evaluated the overall adequacy of the presentation of information in the financial statements.

Opinion

In our opinion the financial statements:

- give a true and fair view, in accordance with Generally Accepted Accounting Practice in Ireland applicable to Smaller Entities, of the state of the company's affairs as at ... and of its profit [loss] for the year then ended; and
- have been properly prepared in accordance with the Companies Acts, 1963 to 2005.

We have obtained all the information and explanations which we consider necessary for the purposes of our audit. In our opinion proper books of account have been kept by the company. The financial statements are in agreement with the books of account.

In our opinion the information given in the directors' report is consistent with the financial statements.

The net assets of the company, as stated in the balance sheet are more than half of the amount of its called-up share capital and, in our opinion, on that basis there did not exist at ... a financial situation which under Section 40 (1) of the Companies (Amendment) Act, 1983 would require the convening of an extraordinary general meeting of the company.

Registered auditors　　　　　　　　　　　　　　　　　　　　　　　　　　　　　　　*Address*
Date

Example 2 – Non-publicly traded company incorporated in the Republic of Ireland – Auditor's report on individual company financial statements

- Company DOES NOT prepare group financial statements.
- Irish GAAP used to prepare individual company financial statements.
- Financial statements contain NO surround information other than the directors' report.

INDEPENDENT AUDITOR'S REPORT TO THE SHAREHOLDERS OF XYZ LIMITED

We have audited the financial statements of (name of entity) for the year ended ... which comprise [state the primary financial statements such as the Profit and Loss Account, the Balance Sheet, the Cash Flow Statement, the Statement of Total Recognised Gains and Losses] and the related notes[8]. These financial statements have been prepared under the accounting policies set out therein.

Respective responsibilities of directors and auditors

As described in the Statement of Directors' Responsibilities the company's directors are responsible for the preparation of the financial statements in accordance with applicable law and the accounting standards issued by the Accounting Standards Board and promulgated by the Institute of Chartered Accountants in Ireland (Generally Accepted Accounting Practice in Ireland).

Our responsibility is to audit the financial statements in accordance with relevant legal and regulatory requirements and International Standards on Auditing (UK and Ireland).

We report to you our opinion as to whether the financial statements give a true and fair view, in accordance with Generally Accepted Accounting Practice in Ireland, and are properly prepared in accordance with the Companies Acts, 1963 to 2005. We also report to you whether in our opinion: proper books of account have been kept by the company; whether at the balance sheet date, there exists a financial situation requiring the convening of an extraordinary general meeting of the company; and whether the information given in the directors' report is consistent with the financial statements. In addition, we state whether we have obtained all the information and explanations necessary for the purposes of our audit, and whether the financial statements are in agreement with the books of account.

We also report to you if, in our opinion, any information specified by law regarding directors' remuneration and directors' transactions is not disclosed and, where practicable, include such information in our report.

We read the directors' report and consider the implications for our report if we become aware of any apparent misstatements within it.

---

[8] *Auditor's reports of entities that do not publish their financial statements on a web site or publish them using 'PDF' format may continue to refer to the financial statements by reference to page numbers*

Basis of audit opinion

We conducted our audit in accordance with International Standards on Auditing (UK and Ireland) issued by the Auditing Practices Board. An audit includes examination, on a test basis, of evidence relevant to the amounts and disclosures in the financial statements. It also includes an assessment of the significant estimates and judgments made by the directors in the preparation of the financial statements, and of whether the accounting policies are appropriate to the company's circumstances, consistently applied and adequately disclosed.

We planned and performed our audit so as to obtain all the information and explanations which we considered necessary in order to provide us with sufficient evidence to give reasonable assurance that the financial statements are free from material misstatement, whether caused by fraud or other irregularity or error. In forming our opinion we also evaluated the overall adequacy of the presentation of information in the financial statements.

Opinion

In our opinion the financial statements:

- give a true and fair view, in accordance with Generally Accepted Accounting Practice in Ireland, of the state of the company's affairs as at ... and of its profit [loss] for the year then ended; and
- have been properly prepared in accordance with the requirements of the Companies Acts, 1963 to 2005.

We have obtained all the information and explanations which we consider necessary for the purposes of our audit. In our opinion proper books of account have been kept by the company. The financial statements are in agreement with the books of account.

In our opinion the information given in the directors' report is consistent with the financial statements.

The net assets of the company, as stated in the balance sheet are more than half of the amount of its called-up share capital and, in our opinion, on that basis there did not exist at ... a financial situation which under Section 40 (1) of the Companies (Amendment) Act, 1983 would require the convening of an extraordinary general meeting of the company.

Registered auditors *Address*
Date

Example 3 – Non-publicly traded company incorporated in the Republic of Ireland – Auditor's report on individual company financial statements:

- Company DOES NOT prepare group financial statements.
- Irish GAAP used to prepare individual company financial statements.
- Financial statements contain surround information other than the directors' report.

INDEPENDENT AUDITOR'S REPORT TO THE SHAREHOLDERS OF XYZ LIMITED

We have audited the financial statements of (name of entity) for the year ended ... which comprise [state the primary financial statements such as the Profit and Loss Account, the Balance Sheet, the Cash Flow Statement, the Statement of Total Recognised Gains and Losses] and the related notes[9]. These financial statements have been prepared under the accounting policies set out therein.

Respective responsibilities of directors and auditors

The directors' responsibilities for preparing the Annual Report and the financial statements in accordance with applicable law and the accounting standards issued by the Accounting Standards Board and promulgated by the Institute of Chartered Accountants in Ireland (Generally Accepted Accounting Practice in Ireland) are set out in the Statement of Directors' Responsibilities.

Our responsibility is to audit the financial statements in accordance with relevant legal and regulatory requirements and International Standards on Auditing (UK and Ireland).

We report to you our opinion as to whether the financial statements give a true and fair view, in accordance with Generally Accepted Accounting Practice in Ireland, and are properly prepared in accordance with the Companies Acts, 1963 to 2005. We also report to you whether in our opinion: proper books of account have been kept by the company; whether at the balance sheet date, there exists a financial situation requiring the convening of an extraordinary general meeting of the company; and whether the information given in the directors' report is consistent with the financial statements. In addition, we state whether we have obtained all the information and explanations necessary for the purposes of our audit, and whether the financial statements are in agreement with the books of account.

We also report to you if, in our opinion, any information specified by law regarding directors' remuneration and directors' transactions is not disclosed and, where practicable, include such information in our report.

We read the other information contained in the Annual Report, and consider whether it is consistent with the audited financial statements. This other information comprises only [the Directors' Report and the Chairman's Statement and the Operating and Financial Review][10]. We consider the implications for our report if we

---

[9] *Auditor's reports of entities that do not publish their financial statements on a web site or publish them using 'PDF' format may continue to refer to the financial statements by reference to page numbers*

[10] *The other information that is 'read' is the content of the printed Annual Report other than the financial statements. The description of the information that has been read is tailored to reflect the terms used in the Annual Report.*

become aware of any apparent misstatements or material inconsistencies with the financial statements. Our responsibilities do not extend to any other information.

Basis of audit opinion

We conducted our audit in accordance with International Standards on Auditing (UK and Ireland) issued by the Auditing Practices Board. An audit includes examination, on a test basis, of evidence relevant to the amounts and disclosures in the financial statements. It also includes an assessment of the significant estimates and judgments made by the directors in the preparation of the financial statements, and of whether the accounting policies are appropriate to the company's circumstances, consistently applied and adequately disclosed.

We planned and performed our audit so as to obtain all the information and explanations which we considered necessary in order to provide us with sufficient evidence to give reasonable assurance that the financial statements are free from material misstatement, whether caused by fraud or other irregularity or error. In forming our opinion we also evaluated the overall adequacy of the presentation of information in the financial statements.

Opinion

In our opinion the financial statements:

- give a true and fair view, in accordance with Generally Accepted Accounting Practice in Ireland, of the state of the company's affairs as at ... and of its profit [loss] for the year then ended; and
- have been properly prepared in accordance with the Companies Acts, 1963 to 2005.

We have obtained all the information and explanations which we consider necessary for the purposes of our audit. In our opinion proper books of account have been kept by the company. The financial statements are in agreement with the books of account.

In our opinion the information given in the directors' report is consistent with the financial statements.

The net assets of the company, as stated in the balance sheet are more than half of the amount of its called-up share capital and, in our opinion, on that basis there did not exist at ... a financial situation which under Section 40 (1) of the Companies (Amendment) Act, 1983 would require the convening of an extraordinary general meeting of the company.

Registered auditors   *Address*
Date

Example 4 – Non-publicly traded company incorporated in the Republic of Ireland – Auditor's report on group and parent company financial statements:

- Group and parent company financial statements NOT presented separately.
- Company prepares group financial statements.
- Irish GAAP used for group and parent company financial statements.
- Section 148(8) Companies Act, 1963 exemption taken for parent company's own profit and loss account.

INDEPENDENT AUDITOR'S REPORT TO THE SHAREHOLDERS OF XYZ LIMITED

We have audited the group and parent company financial statements (the 'financial statements') of (name of entity) for the year ended ... which comprise [state the primary financial statements such as the Group Profit and Loss Account, the Group and Company Balance Sheets, the Group Cash Flow Statement, the Group Statement of Total Recognised Gains and Losses] and the related notes[11]. These financial statements have been prepared under the accounting policies set out therein.

Respective responsibilities of directors and auditors

The directors' responsibilities for preparing the Annual Report and the financial statements in accordance with applicable law and the accounting standards issued by the Accounting Standards Board and promulgated by the Institute of Chartered Accountants in Ireland (Generally Accepted Accounting Practice in Ireland) are set out in the Statement of Directors' Responsibilities.

Our responsibility is to audit the financial statements in accordance with relevant legal and regulatory requirements and International Standards on Auditing (UK and Ireland).

We report to you our opinion as to whether the financial statements give a true and fair view, in accordance with Generally Accepted Accounting Practice in Ireland, and are properly prepared in accordance with the Companies Acts, 1963 to 2005, and the European Communities (Companies: Group Accounts) Regulations, 1992[12]. We also report to you whether in our opinion: proper books of account have been kept by the company; whether at the balance sheet date, there exists a financial situation requiring the convening of an extraordinary general meeting of the company; and whether the information given in the Directors' Report is consistent with the financial statements. In addition, we state whether we have obtained all the information and explanations necessary for the purposes of our audit, and whether the company's balance sheet is in agreement with the books of account.

We also report to you if, in our opinion, any information specified by law regarding directors' remuneration and directors' transactions is not disclosed and, where practicable, include such information in our report.

---

[11] *Auditor's reports of entities that do not publish their financial statements on a web site or publish them using 'PDF' format may continue to refer to the financial statements by reference to page numbers*

[12] *Regulation 6 of SI 116 amends regulation 2 of the European Communities (Companies; Group accounts) Regulations, 1992 such that it now applies to 'Companies Acts group accounts'. Consequently, auditor's reports on group financial statements, where IFRSs as adopted for use in the EU is the financial reporting framework, do not refer to these regulations.*

We read the other information contained in the Annual Report, and consider whether it is consistent with the audited financial statements. This other information comprises only [the Directors' Report, the Chairman's Statement and the Operating and Financial Review][13]. We consider the implications for our report if we become aware of any apparent misstatements or material inconsistencies with the financial statements. Our responsibilities do not extend to any other information.

Basis of audit opinion

We conducted our audit in accordance with International Standards on Auditing (UK and Ireland) issued by the Auditing Practices Board. An audit includes examination, on a test basis, of evidence relevant to the amounts and disclosures in the financial statements. It also includes an assessment of the significant estimates and judgments made by the directors in the preparation of the financial statements, and of whether the accounting policies are appropriate to the group's and company's circumstances, consistently applied and adequately disclosed.

We planned and performed our audit so as to obtain all the information and explanations which we considered necessary in order to provide us with sufficient evidence to give reasonable assurance that the financial statements are free from material misstatement, whether caused by fraud or other irregularity or error. In forming our opinion we also evaluated the overall adequacy of the presentation of information in the financial statements.

Opinion

In our opinion the financial statements:

- give a true and fair view, in accordance with Generally Accepted Accounting Practice in Ireland, of the state of the group's and the company's affairs as at .... and of the group's profit [loss] for the year then ended; and
- have been properly prepared in accordance with the requirements of the Companies Acts, 1963 to 2005 and the European Communities (Companies: Group Accounts) Regulations, 1992.

We have obtained all the information and explanations which we consider necessary for the purposes of our audit. In our opinion proper books of account have been kept by the company. The company's balance sheet is in agreement with the books of account.

In our opinion the information given in the directors' report is consistent with the financial statements.

The net assets of the company, as stated in the company's balance sheet are more than half of the amount of its called-up share capital and, in our opinion, on that basis there did not exist at ... a financial situation which under Section 40 (1) of the Companies (Amendment) Act, 1983 would require the convening of an extraordinary general meeting of the company.

Registered auditors   Address
Date

---

[13] *The other information that is 'read' is the content of the printed Annual Report other than the financial statements. The description of the information that has been read is tailored to reflect the terms used in the Annual Report.*

Example 5 – Publicly traded company incorporated in the Republic of Ireland – Auditor's report on parent company financial statements:

- Group and parent company financial statements presented separately.
- IFRSs as adopted for use in the European Union used for group and parent company financial statements.
- Section 148(8) Companies Act, 1963 exemption NOT taken for parent company's own income statement.
- Corporate governance statement reported on in the report on the group financial statements.

INDEPENDENT AUDITOR'S REPORT TO THE SHAREHOLDERS OF XYZ PLC

We have audited the parent company financial statements of (name of entity) for the year ended ... which comprise [state the primary financial statements such as the Income Statement, the Balance Sheet, the Cash Flow Statement, the Statement of Change in Shareholders' Equity] and the related notes[14]. These parent company financial statements have been prepared under the accounting policies set out therein.

We have reported separately on the group financial statements of (name of entity) for the year ended ...

Respective responsibilities of directors and auditors

The directors' responsibilities for preparing the Annual Report and the parent company financial statements in accordance with applicable law and International Financial Reporting Standards (IFRSs) as adopted for use in the European Union are set out in the Statement of Directors' Responsibilities.

Our responsibility is to audit the financial statements in accordance with relevant legal and regulatory requirements and International Standards on Auditing (UK and Ireland).

We report to you our opinion as to whether the parent company financial statements give a true and fair view, in accordance with IFRSs as adopted for use in the European Union, and have been properly prepared in accordance with the Companies Acts, 1963 to 2005. We also report to you whether, in our opinion: proper books of account have been kept by the parent company; whether at the balance sheet date, there exists a financial situation requiring the convening of an extraordinary general meeting of the company; and whether the information given in the directors' report is consistent with the financial statements. In addition, we state whether we have obtained all the information and explanations necessary for the purposes of our audit, and whether the parent company financial statements are in agreement with the books of account.

We also report to you if, in our opinion, any information specified by law regarding directors' remuneration and directors' transactions is not disclosed and, where practicable, include such information in our report.

---

[14] *Auditor's reports of entities that do not publish their financial statements on a web site or publish them using 'PDF' format may continue to refer to the financial statements by reference to page numbers.*

We read the other information contained in the Annual Report and consider whether it is consistent with the audited parent company financial statements. The other information comprises only [the Directors' Report, the Chairman's Statement and the Operating and Financial Review][15]. We consider the implications for our report if we become aware of any apparent misstatements or material inconsistencies with the parent company financial statements. Our responsibilities do not extend to any other information.

Basis of audit opinion

We conducted our audit in accordance with International Standards on Auditing (UK and Ireland) issued by the Auditing Practices Board. An audit includes examination, on a test basis, of evidence relevant to the amounts and disclosures in the parent company financial statements. It also includes an assessment of the significant estimates and judgments made by the directors in the preparation of the parent company financial statements, and of whether the accounting policies are appropriate to the company's circumstances, consistently applied and adequately disclosed.

We planned and performed our audit so as to obtain all the information and explanations which we considered necessary in order to provide us with sufficient evidence to give reasonable assurance that the parent company financial statements are free from material misstatement, whether caused by fraud or other irregularity or error. In forming our opinion we also evaluated the overall adequacy of the presentation of information in the parent company financial statements.

Opinion

In our opinion the parent company financial statements:

- give a true and fair view, in accordance with IFRSs as adopted for use in the European Union, of the state of the company's affairs as at .... and of its profit [loss] for the year then ended; and
- have been properly prepared in accordance with the Companies Acts, 1963 to 2005.

We have obtained all the information and explanations which we consider necessary for the purposes of our audit. In our opinion proper books of account have been kept by the company. The financial statements are in agreement with the books of account.

In our opinion the information given in the directors' report is consistent with the financial statements.

The net assets of the company, as stated in the balance sheet are more than half of the amount of its called-up share capital and, in our opinion, on that basis there did not exist at ... a financial situation which under Section 40 (1) of the Companies (Amendment) Act, 1983 would require the convening of an extraordinary general meeting of the company.

Registered auditors   *Address*
Date

---

[15] *The other information that is 'read' is the content of the printed Annual Report other than the financial statements. The description of the information that has been read is tailored to reflect the terms used in the Annual Report.*

Example 6 – Publicly traded company incorporated in the Republic of Ireland – Auditor's report on parent company financial statements:

- Group and parent company financial statements presented separately.
- IFRSs as adopted for use in the European Union used for group financial statements.
- Irish GAAP used to prepare parent company financial statements.
- Section 148(8) Companies Act, 1963 exemption taken for parent company's own profit and loss account.
- Corporate governance statement reported on in the report on the group financial statements.

INDEPENDENT AUDITOR'S REPORT TO THE SHAREHOLDERS OF XYZ PLC

We have audited the parent company financial statements of (name of entity) for the year ended ... which comprise [state the primary financial statements such as the Balance Sheet] and the related notes[16]. These parent company financial statements have been prepared under the accounting policies set out therein.

We have reported separately on the group financial statements of (name of entity) for the year ended...

Respective responsibilities of directors and auditors

The directors' responsibilities for preparing the Annual Report and the parent company financial statements in accordance with applicable law and the accounting standards issued by the Accounting Standards Board and promulgated by the Institute of Chartered Accountants in Ireland (Generally Accepted Accounting Practice in Ireland) are set out in the Statement of Directors' Responsibilities.

Our responsibility is to audit the financial statements in accordance with relevant legal and regulatory requirements and International Standards on Auditing (UK and Ireland).

We report to you our opinion as to whether the parent company financial statements give a true and fair view, in accordance with Generally Accepted Accounting Practice in Ireland, and have been properly prepared in accordance with the Companies Acts, 1963 to 2005. We also report to you whether, in our opinion: proper books of account have been kept by the parent company; whether at the balance sheet date, there exists a financial situation requiring the convening of an extraordinary general meeting of the company; and whether the information given in the Directors' Report is consistent with the financial statements. In addition, we state whether we have obtained all the information and explanations necessary for the purposes of our audit, and whether the parent company financial statements are in agreement with the books of account.

We also report to you if, in our opinion, any information specified by law regarding directors' remuneration and directors' transactions is not disclosed and, where practicable, include such information in our report.

---

[16] *Auditor's reports of entities that do not publish their financial statements on a web site or publish them using 'PDF' format may continue to refer to the financial statements by reference to page numbers*

We read the other information contained in the Annual Report and consider whether it is consistent with the audited parent company financial statements. The other information comprises only [the Directors' Report, the Chairman's Statement and the Operating and Financial Review][17]. We consider the implications for our report if we become aware of any apparent misstatements or material inconsistencies with the parent company financial statements. Our responsibilities do not extend to any other information.

Basis of audit opinion

We conducted our audit in accordance with International Standards on Auditing (UK and Ireland) issued by the Auditing Practices Board. An audit includes examination, on a test basis, of evidence relevant to the amounts and disclosures in the parent company financial statements. It also includes an assessment of the significant estimates and judgments made by the directors in the preparation of the parent company financial statements, and of whether the accounting policies are appropriate to the company's circumstances, consistently applied and adequately disclosed.

We planned and performed our audit so as to obtain all the information and explanations which we considered necessary in order to provide us with sufficient evidence to give reasonable assurance that the parent company financial statements are free from material misstatement, whether caused by fraud or other irregularity or error. In forming our opinion we also evaluated the overall adequacy of the presentation of information in the parent company financial statements.

Opinion

In our opinion the parent company financial statements:

- give a true and fair view, in accordance with Generally Accepted Accounting Practice in Ireland, of the state of the company's affairs of the as at .... ; and
- have been properly prepared in accordance with the Companies Acts, 1963 to 2005.

We have obtained all the information and explanations which we consider necessary for the purposes of our audit. In our opinion proper books of account have been kept by the company. The financial statements are in agreement with the books of account.

In our opinion the information given in the directors' report is consistent with the financial statements.

The net assets of the company, as stated in the balance sheet are more than half of the amount of its called-up share capital and, in our opinion, on that basis there did not exist at ... a financial situation which under Section 40 (1) of the Companies (Amendment) Act, 1983 would require the convening of an extraordinary general meeting of the company.

Registered auditors   Address
Date

---

[17] The other information that is 'read' is the content of the printed Annual Report other than the financial statements. The description of the information that has been read is tailored to reflect the terms used in the Annual Report.

Example 7 – Publicly traded company incorporated in the Republic of Ireland – Auditor's report on group (not including parent company) financial statements:

- Group and parent company financial statements presented separately.
- IFRSs as adopted for use in the European Union used for both group and parent company financial statements.
- Reporting obligations in relation to proper books, the agreement of the company balance sheet to the books of account and the section 40 opinion on the company balance sheet apply to the parent company alone and accordingly are not included in the example separate audit report on the group below. The opinions relating to these reporting obligations are included in the separate report on the parent company financial statements – see example 5 or 6 in this regard.
- Section 148(8) - Companies Act, 1963 exemption taken for parent company's own income statement.
- Corporate governance statement reported on in the report on the group financial statements.

This example report may also be used for the auditor's report on the group financial statements (ie not including the parent company) where IFRSs as adopted for use in the European Union are used for the group financial statements, the group and parent company financial statements are presented separately and either:

- IFRSs as adopted for use in the European Union used for parent company accounts and Section 148(8) Companies Act, 1963 exemption NOT taken;
- Irish GAAP is used for parent company financial statements and Section 148(8) exemption taken; or
- Irish GAAP is used for prepare parent company financial statements and Section 148(8) exemption NOT taken.

INDEPENDENT AUDITOR'S REPORT TO THE SHAREHOLDERS OF XYZ PLC

We have audited the group financial statements of (name of entity) for the year ended ... which comprise [state the primary financial statements such as the Group Income Statement, the Group Balance Sheet, the Group Cash Flow Statement, the Group Statement of Change in Shareholders' Equity] and the related notes[18]. These group financial statements have been prepared under the accounting policies set out therein.

We have reported separately on the parent company financial statements of (name of entity) for the year ended ...

Respective responsibilities of directors and auditors

The directors' responsibilities for preparing the Annual Report and the group financial statements in accordance with applicable law and International Financial Reporting Standards (IFRSs) as adopted for use in the European Union are set out in the Statement of Directors' Responsibilities.

---

[18] *Auditor's reports of entities that do not publish their financial statements on a web site or publish them using 'PDF' format may continue to refer to the financial statements by reference to page numbers*

Our responsibility is to audit the financial statements in accordance with relevant legal and regulatory requirements and International Standards on Auditing (UK and Ireland).

We report to you our opinion as to whether the group financial statements give a true and fair view, in accordance with IFRSs as adopted for use in the European Union, and whether the group financial statements have been properly prepared in accordance with the Companies Acts, 1963 to 2005 and Article 4 of the IAS Regulation. We also report to you whether the information given in the Directors' Report is consistent with the financial statements. In addition, we state whether we have obtained all the information and explanations necessary for the purposes of our audit.

We also report to you if, in our opinion, any information specified by law or the Listing Rules of the Irish Stock Exchange regarding directors' remuneration and directors' transactions is not disclosed and, where practicable, include such information in our report.

We review whether the Corporate Governance Statement reflects the company's compliance with the nine provisions of the 2003 FRC Combined Code specified for our review by the Listing Rules of the Irish Stock Exchange, and we report if it does not. We are not required to consider whether the board's statements on internal control cover all risks and controls, or form an opinion on the effectiveness of the group's corporate governance procedures or its risk and control procedures.

We read the other information contained in the Annual Report and consider whether it is consistent with the audited group financial statements. The other information comprises only [the Directors' Report, the Chairman's Statement, the Operating and Financial Review and the Corporate Governance Statement][19]. We consider the implications for our report if we become aware of any apparent misstatements or material inconsistencies with the group financial statements. Our responsibilities do not extend to any other information.

Basis of audit opinion

We conducted our audit in accordance with International Standards on Auditing (UK and Ireland) issued by the Auditing Practices Board and generally accepted in Ireland. An audit includes examination, on a test basis, of evidence relevant to the amounts and disclosures in the group financial statements. It also includes an assessment of the significant estimates and judgments made by the directors in the preparation of the group financial statements, and of whether the accounting policies are appropriate to the group's circumstances, consistently applied and adequately disclosed.

We planned and performed our audit so as to obtain all the information and explanations which we considered necessary in order to provide us with sufficient evidence to give reasonable assurance that the group financial statements are free from material misstatement, whether caused by fraud or other irregularity or error. In forming our opinion we also evaluated the overall adequacy of the presentation of information in the group financial statements.

---

[19] *The other information that is 'read' is the content of the printed Annual Report other than the financial statements. The description of the information that has been read is tailored to reflect the terms used in the Annual Report.*

Opinion

In our opinion the group financial statements:

- give a true and fair view, in accordance with IFRSs as adopted for use in the European Union, of the state of the group's affairs as at ... and of the profit [loss] of the group for the year then ended; and
- have been properly prepared in accordance with the Companies Acts, 1963 to 2005 and Article 4 of the IAS Regulation.

We have obtained all the information and explanations which we consider necessary for the purposes of our audit.

In our opinion the information given in the directors' report is consistent with the financial statements.

[Separate opinion in relation to IFRSs

As explained in Note X to the group financial statements, the group in addition to complying with its legal obligation to comply with IFRSs as adopted for use in the European Union, has also complied with the IFRSs as issued by the International Accounting Standards Board.

In our opinion the group financial statements give a true and fair view, in accordance with IFRSs, of the state of the group's affairs as at ...and of its profit [loss] for the year then ended.]

Registered auditors *Address*
Date

Example 8 – Publicly traded company incorporated in the Republic of Ireland – Auditor's report on group and parent company financial statements:

- Group and parent company financial statements NOT presented separately.
- IFRSs as adopted for use in the European Union used for group financial statements.
- Irish GAAP used for parent company financial statements.
- Section 148(8) Companies Act, 1963 exemption taken for parent company's own profit and loss account.

INDEPENDENT AUDITOR'S REPORT TO THE SHAREHOLDERS OF XYZ PLC

We have audited the group and parent company financial statements of (name of entity) for the year ended ... which comprise [state the primary financial statements such as the Group Income Statement, the Group and Parent Company Balance Sheets, the Group Cash Flow Statement, the Group Statement of Change in Shareholders' Equity] and the related notes[20]. These financial statements have been prepared under the accounting policies set out therein.

Respective responsibilities of directors and auditors

The directors' responsibilities for preparing the Annual Report and the group financial statements in accordance with applicable law and International Financial Reporting Standards (IFRSs) as adopted for use in the European Union, and for preparing the parent company financial statements in accordance with applicable law and the accounting standards issued by the Accounting Standards Board and promulgated by the Institute of Chartered Accountants in Ireland (Generally Accepted Accounting Practice in Ireland), are set out in the Statement of Directors' Responsibilities.

Our responsibility is to audit the financial statements in accordance with relevant legal and regulatory requirements and International Standards on Auditing (UK and Ireland).

We report to you our opinion as to whether the group financial statements give a true and fair view, in accordance with IFRSs as adopted for use in the European Union, and have been properly prepared in accordance with the requirements of the Companies Acts, 1963 to 2005 and Article 4 of the IAS Regulation. We report to you our opinion as to whether the parent company financial statements give a true and fair view, in accordance with Generally Accepted Accounting Practice in Ireland, and have been properly prepared in accordance with the requirements of the Companies Acts, 1963 to 2005. We also report to you whether, in our opinion: proper books of account have been kept by the company; whether at the balance sheet date, there exists a financial situation requiring the convening of an extraordinary general meeting of the company; and whether the information given in the directors' report is consistent with the financial statements. In addition, we state whether we have obtained all the information and explanations necessary for the purposes of our audit, and whether the parent company balance sheet is in agreement with the books of account.

---

[20] *Auditor's reports of entities that do not publish their financial statements on a web site or publish them using 'PDF' format may continue to refer to the financial statements by reference to page numbers*

We also report to you if, in our opinion, any information specified by law or the Listing Rules of the Irish Stock Exchange regarding directors' remuneration and directors' transactions is not disclosed and, where practicable, include such information in our report.

We review whether the Corporate Governance Statement reflects the company's compliance with the nine provisions of the 2003 FRC Combined Code specified for our review by the Listing Rules of the Irish Stock Exchange, and we report if it does not. We are not required to consider whether the board's statements on internal control cover all risks and controls, or form an opinion on the effectiveness of the group's corporate governance procedures or its risk and control procedures.

We read the other information contained in the Annual Report and consider whether it is consistent with the audited financial statements. The other information comprises only [the Directors' Report, the Chairman's Statement, the Operating and Financial Review, and the Corporate Governance Statement][21]. We consider the implications for our report if we become aware of any apparent misstatements or material inconsistencies with the financial statements. Our responsibilities do not extend to any other information.

Basis of audit opinion

We conducted our audit in accordance with International Standards on Auditing (UK and Ireland) issued by the Auditing Practices Board. An audit includes examination, on a test basis, of evidence relevant to the amounts and disclosures in the financial statements. It also includes an assessment of the significant estimates and judgments made by the directors in the preparation of the financial statements, and of whether the accounting policies are appropriate to the group's and company's circumstances, consistently applied and adequately disclosed.

We planned and performed our audit so as to obtain all the information and explanations which we considered necessary in order to provide us with sufficient evidence to give reasonable assurance that the financial statements are free from material misstatement, whether caused by fraud or other irregularity or error. In forming our opinion we also evaluated the overall adequacy of the presentation of information in the financial statements.

Opinion

In our opinion

- the group financial statements give a true and fair view, in accordance with IFRSs as adopted for use in the European Union, of the state of the group's affairs as at ... and of its profit [loss] for the year then ended;
- the group financial statements have been properly prepared in accordance with the Companies Acts, 1963 to 2005 and Article 4 of the IAS Regulation;
- the parent company financial statements give a true and fair view, in accordance with Generally Accepted Accounting Practice in Ireland, of the state of the parent company's affairs as at ...;
- the parent company financial statements have been properly prepared in accordance with the Companies Acts, 1963 to 2005.

---

[21] The other information that is 'read' is the content of the printed Annual Report other than the financial statements. The description of the information that has been read is tailored to reflect the terms used in the Annual Report.

We have obtained all the information and explanations which we consider necessary for the purposes of our audit. In our opinion proper books of account have been kept by the company. The company balance sheet is in agreement with the books of account.

In our opinion the information given in the directors' report is consistent with the financial statements.

The net assets of the company, as stated in the company balance sheet are more than half of the amount of its called-up share capital and, in our opinion, on that basis there did not exist at ... a financial situation which under Section 40 (1) of the Companies (Amendment) Act, 1983 would require the convening of an extraordinary general meeting of the company.

[Separate opinion in relation to IFRSs

As explained in Note x to the group financial statements, the group in addition to complying with its legal obligation to comply with IFRSs as adopted for use in the European Union, has also complied with the IFRSs as issued by the International Accounting Standards Board.

In our opinion the group financial statements give a true and fair view, in accordance with IFRSs, of the state of the group's affairs as at ...and of its profit [loss] for the year then ended.]

Registered auditors *Address*
Date

Example 9 – Publicly traded company incorporated in the Republic of Ireland – Auditor's report on parent company financial statements:

- Group and parent company financial statements presented separately.
- IFRSs as adopted for use in the European Union used for group financial statements.
- Irish GAAP used for parent company financial statements.
- Section 148(8) – Companies Act, 1963 exemption NOT taken for parent company's own profit and loss account.
- Corporate governance statement reported on in the report on the group financial statements.

This example report may also be used for the report on the parent company financial statements prepared under Irish GAAP of a publicly traded company incorporated in the Republic of Ireland that does not prepare group financial statements.

- In such cases a reference to the Cash Flow Statement would be included in the first paragraph of the report.
- the second paragraph 'We have reported separately on the group financial statements of (name of entity) for the year ended...' would need to be deleted.
- a corporate governance paragraph such as the fourth paragraph in the respective responsibilities section of Example 8 would need to be added.

INDEPENDENT AUDITOR'S REPORT TO THE SHAREHOLDERS OF XYZ PLC

We have audited the parent company financial statements of (name of entity) for the year ended ... which comprise [state the primary financial statements such as the Profit and Loss Account, the Balance Sheet, the Statement of Total Recognised Gains and Losses] and the related notes[22]. These parent company financial statements have been prepared under the the accounting policies set out therein.

We have reported separately on the group financial statements of (name of entity) for the year ended ...

Respective responsibilities of directors and auditors

The directors' responsibilities for preparing the Annual Report and the parent company financial statements in accordance with applicable law and the accounting standards issued by the Accounting Standards Board and promulgated by the Institute of Chartered Accountants in Ireland (Generally Accepted Accounting Practice in Ireland) are set out in the Statement of Directors' Responsibilities.

Our responsibility is to audit the financial statements in accordance with relevant legal and regulatory requirements and International Standards on Auditing (UK and Ireland).

We report to you our opinion as to whether the parent company financial statements give a true and fair view, in accordance with Generally Accepted Accounting Practice in Ireland, and have been properly prepared in accordance with the Companies Acts, 1963 to 2005. We also report to you whether, in our opinion: proper books of

---

[22] Auditor's reports of entities that do not publish their financial statements on a web site or publish them using 'PDF' format may continue to refer to the financial statements by reference to page numbers

account have been kept by the parent company; whether at the balance sheet date, there exists a financial situation requiring the convening of an extraordinary general meeting of the company; and whether the information given in the directors' report is consistent with the financial statements. In addition, we state whether we have obtained all the information and explanations necessary for the purposes of our audit, and whether the parent company financial statements are in agreement with the books of account.

We also report to you if, in our opinion, any information specified by law regarding directors' remuneration and directors' transactions is not disclosed and, where practicable, include such information in our report.

We read the other information contained in the Annual Report and consider whether it is consistent with the audited parent company financial statements. The other information comprises only [the Directors' Report, the Chairman's Statement and the Operating and Financial Review][23]. We consider the implications for our report if we become aware of any apparent misstatements or material inconsistencies with the parent company financial statements. Our responsibilities do not extend to any other information.

Basis of audit opinion

We conducted our audit in accordance with International Standards on Auditing (UK and Ireland) issued by the Auditing Practices Board. An audit includes examination, on a test basis, of evidence relevant to the amounts and disclosures in the parent company financial statements. It also includes an assessment of the significant estimates and judgments made by the directors in the preparation of the parent company financial statements, and of whether the accounting policies are appropriate to the company's circumstances, consistently applied and adequately disclosed.

We planned and performed our audit so as to obtain all the information and explanations which we considered necessary in order to provide us with sufficient evidence to give reasonable assurance that the parent company financial statements are free from material misstatement, whether caused by fraud or other irregularity or error. In forming our opinion we also evaluated the overall adequacy of the presentation of information in the parent company financial statements.

Opinion

In our opinion the parent company financial statements:

- give a true and fair view, in accordance with Generally Accepted Accounting Practice in Ireland, of the state of the company's affairs as at .... and of the profit [loss] for the year then ended; and
- have been properly prepared in accordance with the Companies Acts, 1963 to 2005.

We have obtained all the information and explanations which we consider necessary for the purposes of our audit. In our opinion proper books of account have been

---

[23] *The other information that is 'read' is the content of the printed Annual Report other than the financial statements. The description of the information that has been read is tailored to reflect the terms used in the Annual Report.*

kept by the company. The financial statements are in agreement with the books of account.

In our opinion the information given in the directors' report is consistent with the financial statements.

The net assets of the company, as stated in the balance sheet are more than half of the amount of its called-up share capital and, in our opinion, on that basis there did not exist at ... a financial situation which under Section 40 (1) of the Companies (Amendment) Act, 1983 would require the convening of an extraordinary general meeting of the company.

Registered auditors   *Address*
Date

Example 10 – Publicly traded company incorporated in the Republic of Ireland – Auditor's report on group and parent company financial statements:

- Group and parent company financial statements NOT presented separately.
- IFRSs as adopted for use in the European Union used for group financial statements.
- Irish GAAP used for prepare parent company financial statements.
- Section 148(8) Companies Act, 1963 exemption NOT taken for parent company's own profit and loss account.

INDEPENDENT AUDITOR'S REPORT TO THE SHAREHOLDERS OF XYZ PLC

We have audited the group and parent company financial statements of (name of entity) for the year ended ... which comprise [state the primary financial statements such as the Group Income Statement, the Parent Company Profit and Loss Account, the Group and Parent Company Balance Sheets, the Group Cash Flow Statement, the Group Statement of Change in Shareholders' Equity, the Parent Company Statement of Total Recognised Gains and Losses] and the related notes[24]. These financial statements have been prepared under the accounting policies set out therein.

Respective responsibilities of directors and auditors

The directors' responsibilities for preparing the Annual Report and the group financial statements in accordance with applicable law and International Financial Reporting Standards (IFRSs) as adopted for use in the European Union, and for preparing the parent company financial statements in accordance with applicable law and the accounting standards issued by the Accounting Standards Board and promulgated by the Institute of Chartered Accountants in Ireland (Generally Accepted Accounting Practice in Ireland) are set out in the Statement of Directors' Responsibilities.

Our responsibility is to audit the financial statements in accordance with relevant legal and regulatory requirements and International Standards on Auditing (UK and Ireland).

We report to you our opinion as to whether the group financial statements give a true and fair view, in accordance with International Financial Reporting Standards (IFRSs) as adopted for use in the European Union, and have been properly prepared in accordance with the requirements of the Companies Acts, 1963 to 2005 and Article 4 of the IAS Regulation. We report to you our opinion as to whether the parent company financial statements give a true and fair view, in accordance with Generally Accepted Accounting Practice in Ireland, and have been properly prepared in accordance with the Companies Acts, 1963 to 2005. We also report to you whether, in our opinion: proper books of account have been kept by the company; whether at the balance sheet date, there exists a financial situation requiring the convening of an extraordinary general meeting of the company; and whether the information given in the Directors' Report is consistent with the financial statements. In addition, we state whether we have obtained all the information and explanations necessary for the

---

[24] Auditor's reports of entities that do not publish their financial statements on a web site or publish them using 'PDF' format may continue to refer to the financial statements by reference to page numbers

purposes of our audit, and whether the parent company financial statements are in agreement with the books of account.

We also report to you if, in our opinion, any information specified by law or the Listing Rules of the Irish Stock Exchange regarding directors' remuneration and directors' transactions is not disclosed and, where practicable, include such information in our report.

We review whether the Corporate Governance Statement reflects the company's compliance with the nine provisions of the 2003 FRC Combined Code specified for our review by the Listing Rules of the Irish Stock Exchange, and we report if it does not. We are not required to consider whether the board's statements on internal control cover all risks and controls, or form an opinion on the effectiveness of the group's corporate governance procedures or its risk and control procedures.

We read the other information contained in the Annual Report and consider whether it is consistent with the audited financial statements. The other information comprises only [the Directors' Report, the Chairman's Statement, the Operating and financial Review, and the Corporate Governance Statement][25]. We consider the implications for our report if we become aware of any apparent misstatements or material inconsistencies with the financial statements. Our responsibilities do not extend to any other information.

Basis of audit opinion

We conducted our audit in accordance with International Standards on Auditing (UK and Ireland) issued by the Auditing Practices Board. An audit includes examination, on a test basis, of evidence relevant to the amounts and disclosures in the financial statements. It also includes an assessment of the significant estimates and judgments made by the directors in the preparation of the financial statements, and of whether the accounting policies are appropriate to the group's and company's circumstances, consistently applied and adequately disclosed.

We planned and performed our audit so as to obtain all the information and explanations which we considered necessary in order to provide us with sufficient evidence to give reasonable assurance that the financial statements are free from material misstatement, whether caused by fraud or other irregularity or error. In forming our opinion we also evaluated the overall adequacy of the presentation of information in the financial statements.

Opinion

In our opinion,

- the group financial statements give a true and fair view, in accordance with IFRSs as adopted for use in the European Union, of the state of the group's affairs as at ... and of its profit [loss] for the year then ended;
- the group financial statements have been properly prepared in accordance with the Companies Acts, 1963 to 2005 and Article 4 of the IAS Regulation;
- the parent company financial statements give a true and fair view, in accordance with Generally Accepted Accounting Practice in Ireland, of the state of the

---

[25] The other information that is 'read' is the content of the printed Annual Report other than the financial statements. The description of the information that has been read is tailored to reflect the terms used in the Annual Report.

parent company's affairs as at ... and of its profit [loss] for the year then ended; and
- the parent company financial statements have been properly prepared in accordance with the Companies Acts, 1963 to 2005.

We have obtained all the information and explanations which we consider necessary for the purposes of our audit. In our opinion proper books of account have been kept by the company. The parent company financial statements are in agreement with the books of account.

In our opinion the information given in the directors' report is consistent with the financial statements.

The net assets of the company, as stated in the company balance sheet are more than half of the amount of its called-up share capital and, in our opinion, on that basis there did not exist at ... a financial situation which under Section 40 (1) of the Companies (Amendment) Act, 1983 would require the convening of an extraordinary general meeting of the company.

[Separate opinion in relation to IFRSs

As explained in Note x to the group financial statements, the group, in addition to complying with its legal obligation to comply with IFRSs as adopted for use in the European Union, has also complied with the IFRSs as issued by the International Accounting Standards Board.

In our opinion the group financial statements give a true and fair view, in accordance with IFRSs, of the state of the group's affairs as at ...and of its profit [loss] for the year then ended.]

Registered auditors *Address*
Date

Example 11 – Publicly traded company incorporated in the Republic of Ireland – Auditor's report on parent company financial statements:

- Group and parent company financial statements presented separately.
- IFRSs as adopted for use in the European Union used for both group and parent company financial statements.
- Section 148(8) Companies Act, 1963 exemption taken for parent company's own income statement.
- Corporate governance statement reported on in the report on the group financial statements.

INDEPENDENT AUDITOR'S REPORT TO SHAREHOLDERS OF XYZ PLC

We have audited the parent company financial statements of (name of entity) for the year ended ... which comprise [state the primary financial statements such as the Balance Sheet, the Cash Flow Statement, the Statement of Change in Shareholders' Equity] and the related notes[26]. These parent company financial statements have been prepared under the accounting policies set out therein.

We have reported separately on the group financial statements of (name of entity) for the year ended ...

Respective responsibilities of directors and auditors

The directors' responsibilities for preparing the Annual Report and the parent company financial statements in accordance with applicable law and International Financial Reporting Standards (IFRSs) as adopted for use in the European Union are set out in the Statement of Directors' Responsibilities.

Our responsibility is to audit the parent company financial statements in accordance with relevant legal and regulatory requirements and International Standards on Auditing (UK and Ireland).

We report to you our opinion as to whether the parent company financial statements give a true and fair view, in accordance with International Financial Reporting Standards (IFRSs) as adopted for use in the European Union as applied in accordance with the provisions of the Companies Acts, 1963 to 2005, and have been properly prepared in accordance with the Companies Acts, 1963 to 2005. We also report to you whether, in our opinion: proper books of account have been kept by the company; whether at the balance sheet date, there exists a financial situation requiring the convening of an extraordinary general meeting of the company; and whether the information given in the directors' report is consistent with the financial statements. In addition, we state whether we have obtained all the information and explanations necessary for the purposes of our audit, and whether the parent company financial statements are in agreement with the books of account.

We also report to you if, in our opinion, any information specified by law or the Listing Rules of the Irish Stock Exchange regarding directors' remuneration and

---

[26] *Auditor's reports of entities that do not publish their financial statements on a web site or publish them using 'PDF' format may continue to refer to the financial statements by reference to page numbers*

directors' transactions is not disclosed and, where practicable, include such information in our report.

We read the other information contained in the Annual Report and consider whether it is consistent with the audited parent company financial statements. The other information comprises only [the Directors' Report, the Chairman's Statement and the Operating and Financial Review][27]. We consider the implications for our report if we become aware of any apparent misstatements or material inconsistencies with the parent company financial statements. Our responsibilities do not extend to any other information.

Basis of audit opinion

We conducted our audit in accordance with International Standards on Auditing (UK and Ireland) issued by the Auditing Practices Board. An audit includes examination, on a test basis, of evidence relevant to the amounts and disclosures in the parent company financial statements. It also includes an assessment of the significant estimates and judgments made by the directors in the preparation of the parent company financial statements, and of whether the accounting policies are appropriate to the company's circumstances, consistently applied and adequately disclosed.

We planned and performed our audit so as to obtain all the information and explanations which we considered necessary in order to provide us with sufficient evidence to give reasonable assurance that the parent company financial statements are free from material misstatement, whether caused by fraud or other irregularity or error. In forming our opinion we also evaluated the overall adequacy of the presentation of information in the parent company financial statements.

Opinion

In our opinion:

- the parent company financial statements give a true and fair view, in accordance with IFRSs as adopted for use in the European Union as applied in accordance with the provisions of the Companies Acts, 1963 to 2005, of the state of the company's affairs as at …; and
- have been properly prepared in accordance with the Companies Acts, 1963 to 2005.

We have obtained all the information and explanations which we consider necessary for the purposes of our audit. In our opinion proper books of account have been kept by the company. The financial statements are in agreement with the books of account.

In our opinion the information given in the directors' report is consistent with the financial statements.

The net assets of the company, as stated in the balance sheet are more than half of the amount of its called-up share capital and, in our opinion, on that basis there did not exist at … a financial situation which under Section 40 (1) of the Companies

---

[27] *The other information that is 'read' is the content of the printed Annual Report other than the financial statements. The description of the information that has been read is tailored to reflect the terms used in the Annual Report.*

(Amendment) Act, 1983 would require the convening of an extraordinary general meeting of the company.

Registered auditors   Address
Date

Example 12 – Publicly traded company incorporated in the Republic of Ireland – Auditor's report on group and parent company financial statements:

- Group and parent company financial statements NOT presented separately.
- IFRSs as adopted for use in the European Union used for both group and parent company financial statements.
- Section 148(8) Companies Act, 1963 exemption taken for parent company's own income statement.

INDEPENDENT AUDITOR'S REPORT TO THE SHAREHOLDERS OF XYZ PLC

We have audited the group and parent company financial statements (the 'financial statements') of (name of entity) for the year ended ... which comprise [state the primary financial statements such as the Group Income Statement, the Group and Parent Company Balance Sheets, the Group and Parent Company Cash Flow Statements, the Group and Parent Company Statement of Change in Shareholders' Equity] and the related notes[28]. These financial statements have been prepared under the accounting policies set out therein.

Respective responsibilities of directors and auditors

The directors' responsibilities for preparing the Annual Report and the financial statements, in accordance with applicable law and International Financial Reporting Standards (IFRSs) as adopted for use in the European Union, are set out in the Statement of Directors' Responsibilities.

Our responsibility is to audit the financial statements in accordance with relevant legal and regulatory requirements and International Standards on Auditing (UK and Ireland).

We report to you our opinion as to whether the group financial statements give a true and fair view, in accordance with IFRSs as adopted for use in the European Union. We report to you our opinion as to whether the parent financial statements give a true and fair view, in accordance with IFRSs as adopted for use in the European Union as applied in accordance with the provisions of the Companies Acts 1963 to 2005. We also report to you whether the financial statements have been properly prepared in accordance with the Companies Acts, 1963 to 2005 and Article 4 of the IAS Regulation. We also report to you whether, in our opinion: proper books of account have been kept by the company; whether at the balance sheet date, there exists a financial situation requiring the convening of an extraordinary general meeting of the company; and whether the information given in the directors' report is consistent with the financial statements. In addition, we state whether we have obtained all the information and explanations necessary for the purposes of our audit, and whether the financial statements are in agreement with the books of account.

We also report to you if, in our opinion, any information specified by law or the Listing Rules of the Irish Stock Exchange regarding directors' remuneration and

---

[28] *Auditor's reports of entities that do not publish their financial statements on a web site or publish them using 'PDF' format may continue to refer to the financial statements by reference to page numbers*

kept by the company. The company balance sheet is in agreement with the books of account.

In our opinion the information given in the directors' report is consistent with the financial statements.

The net assets of the company, as stated in the company balance sheet are more than half of the amount of its called-up share capital and, in our opinion, on that basis there did not exist at ... a financial situation which under Section 40 (1) of the Companies (Amendment) Act, 1983 would require the convening of an extraordinary general meeting of the company.

[Separate opinion in relation to IFRSs

As explained in Note x to the group financial statements, the company and the group in addition to complying with its legal obligation to comply with IFRSs as adopted for use in the European Union, have also complied with the IFRSs as issued by the International Accounting Standards Board.

In our opinion the group financial statements give a true and fair view, in accordance with IFRSs, of the state of the group's affairs as at ...and of the profit [loss] of the group for the year then ended.]

Registered auditors   *Address*
Date

directors' transactions is not disclosed and, where practicable, include such information in our report.

We review whether the Corporate Governance Statement reflects the company's compliance with the nine provisions of the 2003 FRC Combined Code specified for our review by the Listing Rules of the Irish Stock Exchange, and we report if it does not. We are not required to consider whether the board's statements on internal control cover all risks and controls, or form an opinion on the effectiveness of the group's corporate governance procedures or its risk and control procedures.

We read the other information contained in the Annual Report and consider whether it is consistent with the audited financial statements. The other information comprises only [the Directors' Report, the Chairman's Statement, the Operating and Financial Review and the Corporate Governance Statement][29]. We consider the implications for our report if we become aware of any apparent misstatements or material inconsistencies with the financial statements. Our responsibilities do not extend to any other information.

Basis of audit opinion

We conducted our audit in accordance with International Standards on Auditing (UK and Ireland) issued by the Auditing Practices Board. An audit includes examination, on a test basis, of evidence relevant to the amounts and disclosures in the financial statements. It also includes an assessment of the significant estimates and judgments made by the directors in the preparation of the financial statements, and of whether the accounting policies are appropriate to the group's and company's circumstances, consistently applied and adequately disclosed.

We planned and performed our audit so as to obtain all the information and explanations which we considered necessary in order to provide us with sufficient evidence to give reasonable assurance that the financial statements are free from material misstatement, whether caused by fraud or other irregularity or error. In forming our opinion we also evaluated the overall adequacy of the presentation of information in the financial statements.

Opinion

In our opinion:

- the group financial statements give a true and fair view, in accordance with IFRSs as adopted for use in the European Union, of the state of the group's affairs as at ... and of its profit [loss] for the year then ended;
- the parent company financial statements give a true and fair view, in accordance with IFRSs as adopted for use in the European Union as applied in accordance with the provisions of the Companies Acts 1963 to 2005, of the state of the parent company's affairs as at ...;
- the financial statements have been properly prepared in accordance with the Companies Acts, 1963 to 2005 and Article 4 of the IAS Regulation.

We have obtained all the information and explanations which we consider necessary for the purposes of our audit. In our opinion proper books of account have been

---

[29] *The other information that is 'read' is the content of the printed Annual Report other than the financial statements. The description of the information that has been read is tailored to reflect the terms used in the Annual Report.*

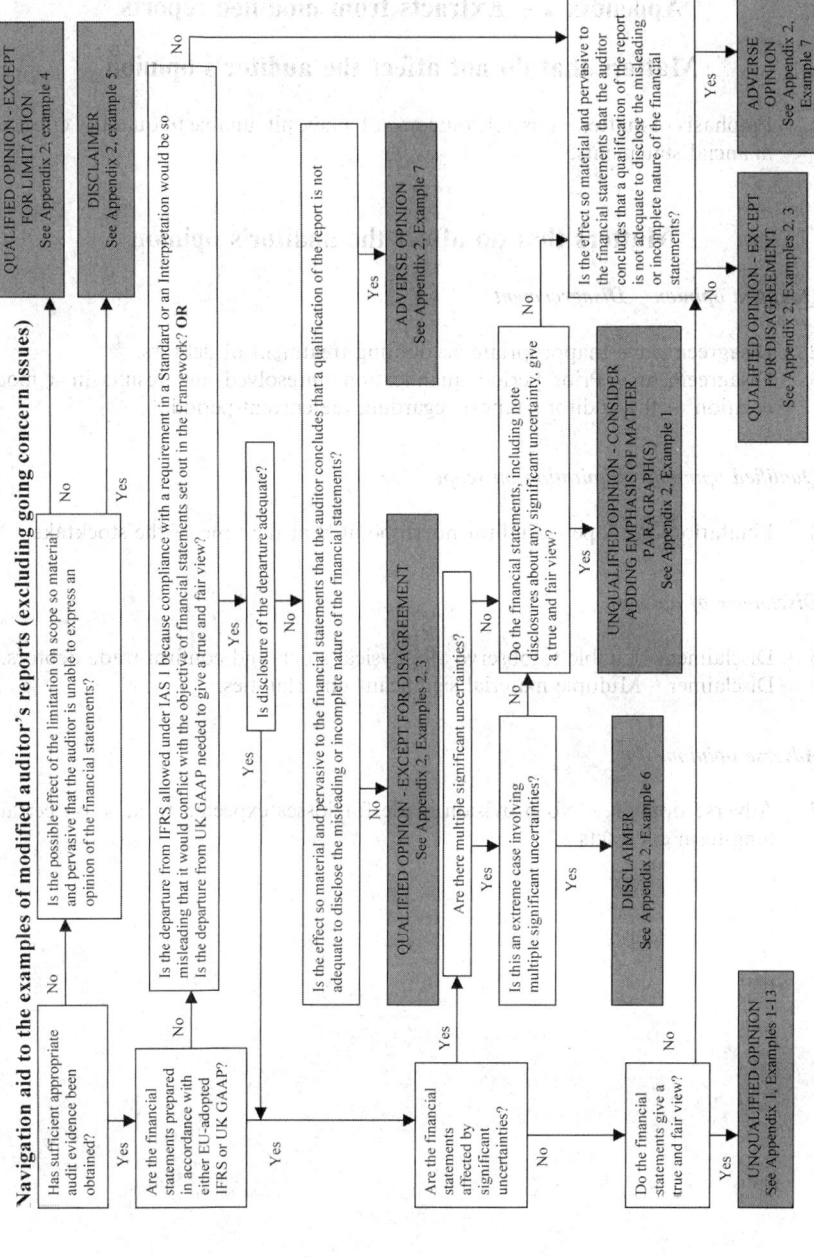

Appendix 2 – Extracts from modified reports

Matters that do not affect the auditor's opinion

1 Emphasis of matter – Possible outcome of a lawsuit, unable to quantify effect on financial statements.

Matters that do affect the auditor's opinion

Qualified opinion – Disagreement

2 Disagreement – Inappropriate accounting treatment of debtors.
3 Disagreement – Prior period qualification unresolved and results in a modification of the auditor's report regarding the current period.

Qualified opinion – Limitation on scope

4 Limitation on scope – Auditor not appointed at the time of the stocktake.

Disclaimer of opinion

5 Disclaimer – Unable to observe all physical stock and confirm trade debtors.
6 Disclaimer – Multiple material/significant uncertainties.

Adverse opinion

7 Adverse opinion – No provision made for losses expected to arise on certain long-term contracts.

Example 1 – Unqualified opinion – Emphasis of matter. Possible outcome of a lawsuit, unable to quantify effect on financial statements.

- *Irish non-publicly traded company prepares Irish GAAP financial statements.*
- *A lawsuit alleges that the company has infringed certain patent rights and claims royalties and punitive damages. The company has filed a counter action, and preliminary hearings and discovery proceedings on both actions are in progress.*
- *The ultimate outcome of the matter cannot presently be determined, and no provision for any liability that may result has been made in the financial statements.*
- *The company makes relevant disclosures in the financial statements.*
- *The auditor issues an unqualified auditor's report with an emphasis of matter paragraph describing the situation giving rise to the emphasis of matter and its possible effects on the financial statements, including that the effect on the financial statements of the resolution of the uncertainty cannot be quantified.*

Basis of audit opinion

We conducted our audit in accordance with International Standards on Auditing (UK and Ireland) issued by the Auditing Practices Board. An audit includes examination, on a test basis, of evidence relevant to the amounts and disclosures in the financial statements. It also includes an assessment of the significant estimates and judgments made by the directors in the preparation of the financial statements, and of whether the accounting policies are appropriate to the company's circumstances, consistently applied and adequately disclosed.

We planned and performed our audit so as to obtain all the information and explanations which we considered necessary in order to provide us with sufficient evidence to give reasonable assurance that the financial statements are free from material misstatement, whether caused by fraud or other irregularity or error. In forming our opinion we also evaluated the overall adequacy of the presentation of information in the financial statements.

Opinion

In our opinion the financial statements:

- give a true and fair view, in accordance with Generally Accepted Accounting Practice in Ireland, of the state of the company's affairs as at .... and of its profit[loss] for the year then ended; and
- have been properly prepared in accordance with the Companies Acts, 1963 to 2005.

We have obtained all the information and explanations which we consider necessary for the purposes of our audit. In our opinion proper books of account have been kept by the company. The financial statements are in agreement with the books of account.

In our opinion the information given in the directors' report is consistent with the financial statements.

The net assets of the company, as stated in the balance sheet are more than half of the amount of its called-up share capital and, in our opinion, on that basis there did not exist at ... a financial situation which under Section 40 (1) of the Companies

(Amendment) Act, 1983 would require the convening of an extraordinary general meeting of the company.

Emphasis of matter – possible outcome of a lawsuit
In forming our opinion, which is not qualified, we have considered the adequacy of the disclosures made in note x to the financial statements concerning the possible outcome of a lawsuit, alleging infringement of certain patent rights and claiming royalties and punitive damages, where the company is the defendant. The company has filed a counter action, and preliminary hearings and discovery proceedings on both actions are in progress. The ultimate outcome of the matter cannot presently be determined, and no provision for any liability that may result has been made in the financial statements.

Registered auditors   *Address*
Date

Example 2 – Qualified opinion – Disagreement. Inappropriate accounting treatment of debtors.

- *XYZ Limited, an Irish non-publicly traded company, prepares Irish GAAP financial statements.*
- *The debtors shown on the balance sheet include an amount of €Y due from a company which has ceased trading. XYZ Limited has no security for this debt.*
- *The auditor's opinion is that the company is unlikely to receive any payment and full provision of €Y should have been made.*
- *The auditor does not believe that the effect of the disagreement is so material and pervasive that the financial statements as a whole are misleading and issues a qualified opinion – except for disagreement about the accounting treatment of debtors.*
- *The auditor concludes that it is still possible to express the 'financial situation' opinion*

Qualified opinion arising from disagreement about accounting treatment

Included in the debtors shown on the balance sheet is an amount of €Y due from a company which has ceased trading. XYZ Limited has no security for this debt. In our opinion the company is unlikely to receive any payment and full provision of €Y should have been made. Accordingly, debtors should be reduced by €Y, deferred taxes should be reduced by €X and profit for the year and retained earnings should be reduced by €Z.

Except for the financial effect of not making the provision referred to in the preceding paragraph, in our opinion the financial statements:

- give a true and fair view, in accordance with Generally Accepted Accounting Practice in Ireland, of the state of the company's affairs as at . . . . . and of its profit[loss] for the year then ended; and
- have been properly prepared in accordance with the Companies Acts, 1963 to 2005.

We have obtained all the information and explanations which we consider necessary for the purposes of our audit. In our opinion proper books of account have been kept by the company. The financial statements are in agreement with the books of account.

In our opinion the information given in the directors' report is consistent with the financial statements.

The net assets of the company, as stated in the balance sheet are more than half of the amount of its called-up share capital and, in our opinion, on that basis there did not exist at ... a financial situation which under Section 40 (1) of the Companies (Amendment) Act, 1983 would require the convening of an extraordinary general meeting of the company.

Registered auditors   *Address*
Date

Example 3 – Qualified opinion – Disagreement. Prior period qualification unresolved and results in a modification of the auditor's report regarding the current period figures.

- *Irish non-publicly traded company prepares Irish GAAP financial statements.*
- *Included in the debtors shown on the balance sheet of 31 December 20X4 and 31 December 20X5 is an amount of €Y* which is the subject of litigation and against which no provision has been made. The auditor considers that a full provision of €Y should have been made in the year ended 31 December 20X4.
- *The auditor concludes that it is still possible to express the 'financial situation' opinion*

Qualified opinion arising from disagreement over accounting treatment

Included in the debtors shown on the balance sheets of 31 December 20X4 and 31 December 20X5 is an amount of €Y which is the subject of litigation and against which no provision has been made. In our opinion, full provision of €Y should have been made in the year ended 31 December 20X4. Accordingly, debtors at 31 December 20X4 and 20X5 should be reduced by €Y, deferred income taxes at 31 December 20X4 and 20X5 should be reduced by €X, and profit for the year ended 31 December 20X4 and retained earnings at 31 December 20X4 and 20X5 should be reduced by €Z.

In our opinion:

- the financial statements give a true and fair view, in accordance with Generally Accepted Accounting Practice in Ireland, of the company's profit [loss] for the year ended 31 December 20X5.

Except for the financial effect of not making the provision referred to in the preceding paragraph, in our opinion the financial statements:

- give a true and fair view, in accordance with Generally Accepted Accounting Practice in Ireland, of the state of the company's affairs as at 31 December 20X5 and of its profit [loss] for the year then ended; and
- have been properly prepared in accordance with the Companies Acts, 1963 to 2005.

We have obtained all the information and explanations which we consider necessary for the purposes of our audit. In our opinion proper books of account have been kept by the company. The financial statements are in agreement with the books of account.

In our opinion the information given in the directors' report is consistent with the financial statements.

The net assets of the company, as stated in the balance sheet are more than half of the amount of its called-up share capital and, in our opinion, on that basis there did not exist at 31 December 20X5 a financial situation which under Section 40 (1) of the Companies (Amendment) Act, 1983 would require the convening of an extraordinary general meeting of the company.

Registered auditor   *Address*
Date

Example 4 – Qualified opinion – Limitation on scope. Auditor not appointed at the time of the stocktake.

- Irish non-publicly traded company prepares Irish GAAP financial statements.
- The evidence available to the auditor was limited because they did not observe the counting of the physical stock as of 31 December 20X1, since that date was prior to the time the auditor was initially engaged as auditor for the company. Owing to the nature of the company's records, the auditor was unable to satisfy themselves as to stock quantities by other audit procedures.
- The limitation in audit scope causes the auditor to issue a qualified opinion except for any adjustments that might have been found to be necessary had they been able to obtain sufficient evidence concerning stock.

Basis of audit opinion

We conducted our audit in accordance with International Standards on Auditing (UK and Ireland) issued by the Auditing Practices Board, except that the scope of our work was limited as explained below.

An audit includes examination, on a test basis, of evidence relevant to the amounts and disclosures in the financial statements. It also includes an assessment of the significant estimates and judgments made by the directors in the preparation of the financial statements, and of whether the accounting policies are appropriate to the company's circumstances, consistently applied and adequately disclosed.

We planned and performed our audit so as to obtain all the information and explanations which we considered necessary in order to provide us with sufficient evidence to give reasonable assurance that the financial statements are free from material misstatement, whether caused by fraud or other irregularity or error. However, with respect to stock having a carrying amount of €X the evidence available to us was limited because we did not observe the counting of the physical stock as of 31 December 20X1, since that date was prior to our appointment as auditors of the company. Owing to the nature of the company's records, we were unable to obtain sufficient appropriate audit evidence regarding the stock quantities by using other audit procedures.

In forming our opinion we also evaluated the overall adequacy of the presentation of information in the financial statements.

Qualified opinion arising from limitation in audit scope

Except for the financial effects of such adjustments, if any, as might have been determined to be necessary had we been able to satisfy ourselves as to physical stock quantities, in our opinion the financial statements:

- give a true and fair view, in accordance with Generally Accepted Accounting Practice in Ireland, of the state of the company's affairs as at 31 December 20X1 and of its profit [loss] for the year then ended; and
- have been properly prepared in accordance with the Companies Acts, 1963 to 2005.

In respect solely of the limitation on our work relating to stocks:

- we have not obtained all the information and explanations that we considered necessary for the purposes of our audit; and

- we were unable to determine whether proper accounting records had been maintained.

The financial statements are in agreement with the books of account.

In our opinion the information given in the directors' report is consistent with the financial statements.

The net assets of the company, as stated in the balance sheet are more than half of the amount of its called-up share capital and, in our opinion, on that basis there did not exist at 31 December 20X1 a financial situation which under Section 40 (1) of the Companies (Amendment) Act, 1983 would require the convening of an extraordinary general meeting of the company.

Registered auditors   *Address*
Date

Example 5 – Disclaimer of opinion. Unable to observe all physical stock and confirm trade debtors.

- *Irish non-publicly traded company prepares Irish GAAP financial statements.*
- *The evidence available to the auditor was limited because the auditor was not able to observe all physical stock and confirm trade debtors due to limitations placed on the scope of the auditor's work by the company.*
- *As a result, the auditor has been unable to form a view on the financial statements and issues a modified opinion disclaiming the view given by the financial statements.*

Basis of audit opinion

We conducted our audit in accordance with International Standards on Auditing (UK and Ireland) issued by the Auditing Practices Board, except that the scope of our work was limited as explained below.

An audit includes examination, on a test basis, of evidence relevant to the amounts and disclosures in the financial statements. It also includes an assessment of the significant estimates and judgments made by the directors in the preparation of the financial statements, and of whether the accounting policies are appropriate to the company's circumstances, consistently applied and adequately disclosed

We planned ~~and performed~~ our audit so as to obtain all the information and explanations which we considered necessary in order to provide us with sufficient evidence to give reasonable assurance that the financial statements are free from material misstatement, whether caused by fraud or other irregularity or error. However, the evidence available to us was limited because we were unable to observe the counting of physical stock having a carrying amount of €X and send confirmation letters to trade debtors having a carrying amount of €Y due to limiatations placed on the scope of our work by the company. As a result of this we have been unable to obtain sufficient appropriate audit evidence concerning both stock and trade debtors. Because of the significance of these items, we have been unable to form a view on the financial statements.

In forming our opinion we also evaluated the overall adequacy of the presentation of information in the financial statements.

Opinion: disclaimer on view given by financial statements

Because of the possible effect of the limitation in evidence available to us, we are unable to form an opinion as to whether the financial statements:

- give a true and fair view, in accordance with Generally Accepted Accounting Practice in Ireland, of the state of the company's affairs as at ... and of its profit [loss] for the year then ended; and
- have been properly prepared in accordance with the Companies Acts, 1963 to 2005; or

whether there did or did not exist at ... a financial situation which under Section 40(1) of the Companies (Amendment) Act, 1983 would require the convening of an extraordinary general meeting of the company.

In respect solely of the limitation of our work referred to above:

- we have not obtained all the information and explanations that we consider necessary for the purpose of our audit; and
- we were unable to determine whether proper books of account have been kept by the company

The financial statements are in agreement with the books of account.

In our opinion the information given in the directors' report is consistent with the financial statements.

~~The net assets of the company, as stated in the balance sheet are more than half of the amount of its called-up share capital and, in our opinion, on that basis there did not exist at 31 December 20X1 a financial situation which under Section 40 (1) of the Companies (Amendment) Act, 1983 would require the convening of an extraordinary general meeting of the company.~~

Registered auditors   *Address*
Date

Example 6 – Disclaimer of opinion. Multiple material/significant uncertainties.

As discussed in ISA (UK and Ireland) 700 paragraph 34 the addition of a paragraph emphasising a going concern problem or significant uncertainty is ordinarily adequate to meet the auditor's reporting responsibilities regarding such matters. However, in extreme cases, such as situations involving multiple uncertainties that are significant to the financial statements, the auditor may consider it appropriate to express a disclaimer of opinion instead of adding an emphasis of matter paragraph.

This example does not include a description of the multiple material/significant uncertainties that might lead to a disclaimer of opinion because circumstances will vary and auditors will have to use their judgment when deciding whether it is an extreme case involving multiple uncertainties that are significant to the financial statements. Often, if such matters were considered individually, because the company makes relevant disclosures in the financial statements, the auditor would normally issue an unqualified auditor's report with an emphasis of matter paragraph setting out the basis of the auditor's opinion, describing the situation giving rise to the emphasis of matter and its possible effects on the financial statements, including (where practicable) quantification but the audit opinion would be unqualified.

Opinion: disclaimer on view given by financial statements

In forming our opinion, we have considered the adequacy of the disclosures made in the financial statements concerning the following matters:

- [Significant uncertainty 1]
- [Significant uncertainty 2]
- [Significant uncertainty 3]

Because of the potential significance, to the financial statements, of the combined effect of the three matters referred to in the paragraph above, we are unable to form an opinion as to whether the financial statements:

- give a true and fair view, in accordance with Generally Accepted Accounting Practice in Ireland, of the state of the company's affairs as at ... and of its profit [loss] for the year then ended; and
- have been properly prepared in accordance with the Companies Acts, 1963 to 2005; or

whether there did or did not exist at ... a financial situation which under Section 40(1) of the Companies (Amendment) Act, 1983 would require the convening of an extraordinary general meeting of the company.

We have obtained all the information and explanations which we consider necessary for the purposes of our audit. In our opinion proper books of account have been kept by the company. The financial statements are in agreement with the books of account.

In our opinion the information given in the directors' report is consistent with the financial statements.

The net assets of the company, as stated in the balance sheet are more than half of the amount of its called-up share capital and, in our opinion, on that basis there did not exist at 31 December 20X1 a financial situation which under Section 40 (1) of the Companies (Amendment) Act, 1983 would require the convening of an extraordinary general meeting of the company.

Registered auditors   *Address*
Date

Example 7 – Adverse opinion. No provision made for losses expected to arise on certain long-term contracts

- Irish non-publicly traded company prepares Irish GAAP financial statements.
- No provision has been made for losses expected to arise on certain long-term contracts currently in progress, as the directors consider that such losses should be off-set against amounts recoverable on other long-term contracts.
- In the auditor's opinion, provision should be made for foreseeable losses on individual contracts as required by [specify accounting standards].
- The auditor issues an adverse opinion due to the failure to provide for the losses and quantifies the impact on the profit for the year, the contract work in progres, and deferred taxes payable at the year end.
- The auditor concludes that it is still possible to express the 'financial situation' opinion

Adverse opinion

As more fully explained in note x to the financial statements no provision has been made for losses expected to arise on certain long-term contracts currently in progress, as the directors consider that such losses should be off-set against amounts recoverable on other long-term contracts. In our opinion, provision should be made for foreseeable losses on individual contracts as required by [specify accounting standards]......... If losses had been so recognised the effect would have been to reduce the carrying amount of contract work in progress by €X, deferred taxes payable by €Y, and the profit for the year and the retained earnings at 31 December 20X1 by €Z.

In view of the effect of the failure to provide for the losses referred to above, in our opinion the financial statements do not give a true and fair view, in accordance with Generally Accepted Accounting Practice in Ireland, of the state of the company's affairs as at 31 December 20X1 and of its profit [loss] for the year then ended.

In all other respects, in our opinion the financial statements have been properly prepared in accordance with the Companies Acts, 1963 to 2005.

We have obtained all the information and explanations which we consider necessary for the purposes of our audit. In our opinion proper books of account have been kept by the company. The financial statements are in agreement with the books of account.

In our opinion the information given in the directors' report is consistent with the financial statements.

The net assets of the company, as stated in the balance sheet are more than half of the amount of its called-up share capital and, in our opinion, on that basis there did not exist at ... a financial situation which under Section 40 (1) of the Companies (Amendment) Act, 1983 would require the convening of an extraordinary general meeting of the company.

Registered auditors   Address
Date

Appendix 3 – Modified auditor's reports arising from going concern issues – Extracts from modified reports

Note: Example reports addressing issues other than going concern are included in Appendix 2.

The example reports included in Appendix 3 are only illustrative examples and it has not been possible to describe all of the facts that the auditors would have to consider when forming their opinion. Auditors use their professional judgment when deciding what form of modified report to give, taking into account the particular circumstances of the reporting entity.

The Appendix gives illustrative examples of modified auditor's reports on financial statements arising from the going concern issues illustrated in the navigation aid on page 72.

Preceding each example report is a description of the background to the particular modification. The full text of the example unmodified auditor's reports are included in Appendix 1 but for the purpose of illustrating the modification, only those sections of the auditor's report affected by the modification are included. Additions and deletions to the examples in Appendix 1, arising from the modification, are shown as shaded and struck out text respectively.

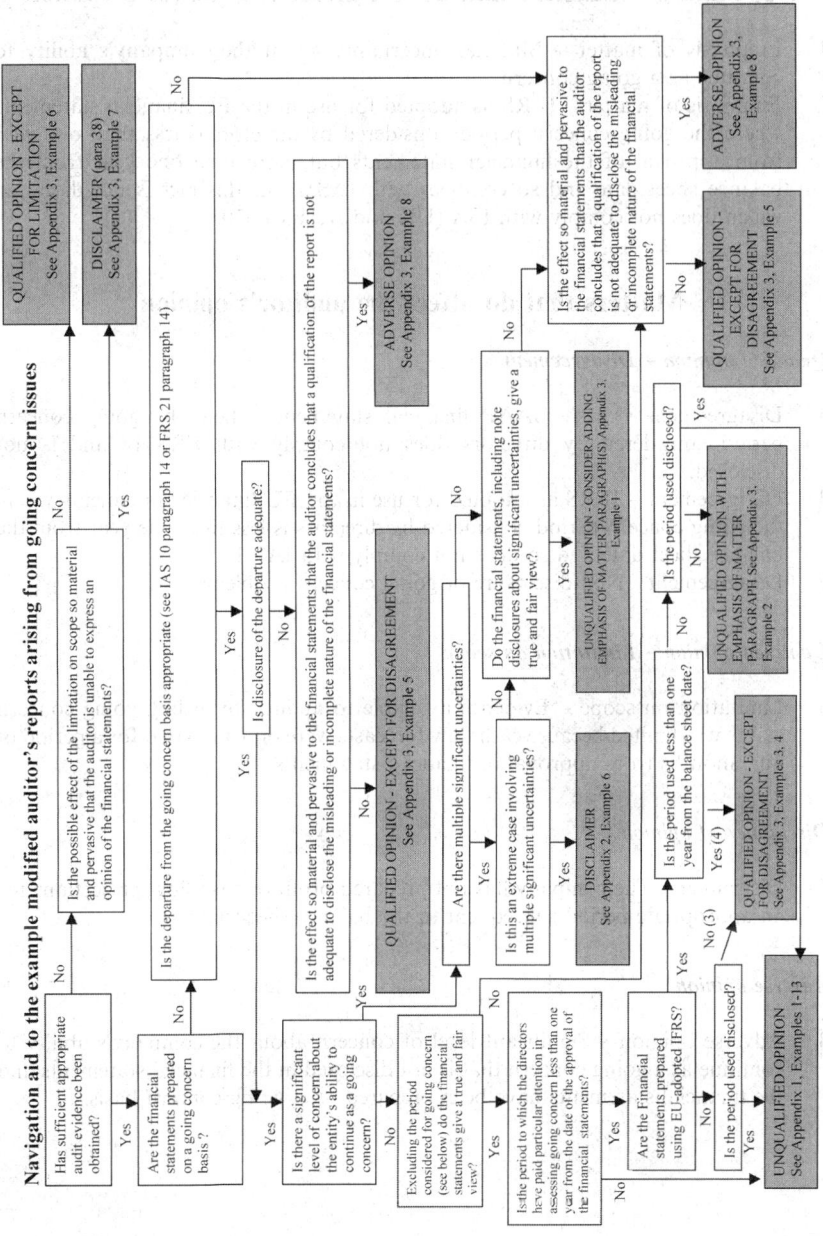

Appendix 3 – Matters that do not affect the auditor's opinion

1. Emphasis of matter – Material uncertainty about the Company's ability to continue as a going concern.
2. Emphasis of matter – IFRS as adopted for use in the EU financial statements where the going concern period considered by directors is less than one year from approval of the financial statements but more than one year from the balance sheet date and so complies with IAS 1 but this fact is not disclosed which does not comply with ISA (UK and Ireland) 570.

Matters that do affect the auditor's opinion

Qualified opinion – Disagreement

3. Disagreement – Irish GAAP financial statements where the going concern period considered by directors does not comply with FRS 18 and is not disclosed.
4. Disagreement – IFRS as adopted for use in the EU financial statements where the going concern period considered by directors is less than one year from the balance sheet date and so does not comply with IAS 1.
5. Disagreement - Non-disclosure of going concern problems.

Qualified opinion – Limitation on scope

6. Limitation on scope – Evidence available to auditor regarding going concern status was limited because cash flow forecasts were only prepared for a period of nine months from approval of financial statements

Disclaimer of opinion

7. Disclaimer – The company has not prepared profit or cash flow projections for an appropriate period subsequent to the balance sheet date.

Adverse opinion

8. Adverse opinion – Significant level of concern about the company's ability to continue as a going concern that is not disclosed in the financial statements and the financial statements have been prepared on a going concern basis.

Example 1 – Unqualified opinion – Emphasis of matter. Material uncertainty about the Company's ability to continue as a going concern.

- Irish non-publicly traded company prepares Irish GAAP financial statements.
- The company incurred a net loss of €X during the year ended 31 December 20X1 and, as of that date, the company's current liabilities exceeded its total assets by €Y.
- These conditions, along with other matters set forth in the notes to the financial statements, indicate the existence of a material uncertainty, which may cast significant doubt about the company's ability to continue as a going concern.
- The company makes relevant disclosures in the financial statements.
- The auditor issues an unqualified auditor's report with an emphasis of matter paragraph setting out the basis of the auditor's opinion, describing the situation giving rise to the emphasis of matter and its possible effects on the financial statements, including (where practicable) quantification

Basis of audit opinion

We conducted our audit in accordance with International Standards on Auditing (UK and Ireland) issued by the Auditing Practices Board. An audit includes examination, on a test basis, of evidence relevant to the amounts and disclosures in the financial statements. It also includes an assessment of the significant estimates and judgments made by the directors in the preparation of the financial statements, and of whether the accounting policies are appropriate to the company's circumstances, consistently applied and adequately disclosed

We planned and performed our audit so as to obtain all the information and explanations which we considered necessary in order to provide us with sufficient evidence to give reasonable assurance that the financial statements are free from material misstatement, whether caused by fraud or other irregularity or error. In forming our opinion we also evaluated the overall adequacy of the presentation of information in the financial statements.

Opinion

In our opinion the financial statements:

- give a true and fair view, in accordance with Generally Accepted Accounting Practice in Ireland, of the state of the company's affairs as at 31 December 20X1 and of its profit [loss] for the year then ended; and
- have been properly prepared in accordance with the Companies Acts, 1963 to 2005.

We have obtained all the information and explanations which we consider necessary for the purposes of our audit. In our opinion proper books of account have been kept by the company. The financial statements are in agreement with the books of account.

In our opinion the information given in the directors' report is consistent with the financial statements.

The net assets of the company, as stated in the balance sheet are more than half of the amount of its called-up share capital and, in our opinion, on that basis there did not exist at 31 December 20X1 a financial situation which under Section 40 (1) of the

Companies (Amendment) Act, 1983 would require the convening of an extraordinary general meeting of the company.

Emphasis of matter – Going concern
In forming our opinion, which is not qualified, we have considered the adequacy of the disclosures made in note x to the financial statements concerning the company's ability to continue as a going concern. The company incurred a net loss of €X during the year ended 31 December 20X1 and, at that date, the company's current liabilities exceeded its total assets by €Y. These conditions, along with the other matters explained in note x to the financial statements, indicate the existence of a material uncertainty which may cast significant doubt about the company's ability to continue as a going concern. The financial statements do not include the adjustments that would result if the company was unable to continue as a going concern.

Registered auditors   *Address*
Date

Example 2 – Unqualified opinion – Emphasis of matter. IFRS Financial statements where the going concern period considered by directors complies with IAS 1 but not ISA (UK and Ireland) 570 and is not disclosed.

- Irish publicly traded company uses IFRSs as adopted for use in the European Union for financial statements.
- The balance sheet date being audited is 31 December 20X1.
- The date of approval of the financial statements was 31 May 20X2.
- In assessing whether the going concern assumption is appropriate the directors have taken into account the period up to 31 March 20X3 which is:
  - 15 months from the balance sheet date ie more than the 12 months from the balance sheet date required by IAS 1 but only
  - 10 months from the date of approval of the financial statements ie less than the 12 months from the date of approval of the financial statements required by ISA (UK and Ireland)570.
- The directors have refused to either extend their assessment period to twelve months from the date of approval of the financial statements or to disclose the fact that the period they have used for their assessment is less than twelve months from the date of approval of the financial statements.
- The auditor issues an unqualified auditor's report with an emphasis of matter paragraph disclosing the fact that the going concern period considered by the directors is less than one year from the date of approval of the financial statements and that this fact has not been disclosed.

Basis of audit opinion

We conducted our audit in accordance with International Standards on Auditing (UK and Ireland) issued by the Auditing Practices Board. An audit includes examination, on a test basis, of evidence relevant to the amounts and disclosures in the financial statements. It also includes an assessment of the significant estimates and judgments made by the directors in the preparation of the financial statements, and of whether the accounting policies are appropriate to the company's circumstances, consistently applied and adequately disclosed

We planned and performed our audit so as to obtain all the information and explanations which we considered necessary in order to provide us with sufficient evidence to give reasonable assurance that the financial statements are free from material misstatement, whether caused by fraud or other irregularity or error. In forming our opinion we also evaluated the overall adequacy of the presentation of information in the financial statements.

Opinion

In our opinion the financial statements:

- give a true and fair view, in accordance with IFRSs as adopted for use in the European Union, of the state of the company's affairs as at 31 December 20X1 and of its profit [loss] for the year then ended; and
- have been properly prepared in accordance with the Companies Acts, 1963 to 2005, and Article 4 of the IAS Regulation.

We have obtained all the information and explanations which we consider necessary for the purposes of our audit. In our opinion proper books of account have been kept by the company. The financial statements are in agreement with the books of account.

In our opinion the information given in the directors' report is consistent with the financial statements.

The net assets of the company, as stated in the balance sheet are more than half of the amount of its called-up share capital and, in our opinion, on that basis there did not exist at 31 December 20X1 a financial situation which under Section 40 (1) of the Companies (Amendment) Act, 1983 would require the convening of an extraordinary general meeting of the company.

Emphasis of matter – Going concern
In forming our opinion, which is not qualified, we have considered the adequacy of the disclosures made in note x to the financial statements concerning the period used by the directors in assessing whether the going concern assumption is appropriate. In making their assessment the directors have considered the period up to 31 March 20X3 which is less than twelve months from the date of approval of the financial statements and the directors have not disclosed this fact. International Standards on Auditing (UK and Ireland) require the auditors to draw this fact to the attention of readers of the financial statements.

Registered auditors *Address*
31 May 20X2

Example 3 – Qualified opinion – Disagreement. Irish GAAP financial statements where the going concern period considered by directors does not comply with FRS 18 but is disclosed.

- Irish non-publicly traded company prepares Irish GAAP financial statements.
- In assessing whether it is appropriate to prepare the financial statements on a going concern basis, the directors have paid particular attention to a period ending on 30 September 20X3 which is less than one year from the date of approval of the financial statements on 31 October 20X2.
- The directors have not disclosed this fact in the financial statements breaching the requirements of paragraph 61(b) of Financial Reporting Standard 18 'Accounting policies'. FRS 18 requires the disclosure of the fact that ' the foreseeable future considered by the directors has been limited to a period of less than one year from the date of approval of the financial statements'.
- Although the auditors have concluded that there is no significant level of concern about going concern, the failure to disclose the fact that the foreseeable future considered by the directors has been limited to a period of less than one year from the date of approval of the financial statements is a breach of FRS 18 and the auditors issue a qualified 'except for' opinion describing the disagreement over the departure from FRS 18.

Qualified opinion arising from departure from FRS 18 'Accounting policies'

In assessing whether it is appropriate to prepare the financial statements on a going concern basis the directors have paid particular attention to a period ending on 30 September 20X3 which is less than twelve months from the date of approval of the financial statements. This fact has not been disclosed in the financial statements, contrary to the requirements of Financial Reporting Standard 18 'Accounting policies'.

Except for the absence of the disclosure referred to above in our opinion the financial statements:

- give a true and fair view, in accordance with Generally Accepted Accounting Practice in Ireland, of the state of the company's affairs as at 31 December 20X1 and of its profit [loss] for the year then ended; and
- have been properly prepared in accordance with the Companies Acts, 1963 to 2005.

We have obtained all the information and explanations which we consider necessary for the purposes of our audit. In our opinion proper books of account have been kept by the company. The financial statements are in agreement with the books of account.

In our opinion the information given in the directors' report is consistent with the financial statements.

The net assets of the company, as stated in the balance sheet are more than half of the amount of its called-up share capital and, in our opinion, on that basis there did not exist at 31 December 20X1 a financial situation which under Section 40 (1) of the Companies (Amendment) Act, 1983 would require the convening of an extraordinary general meeting of the company.

Registered auditors   *Address*
31 October 20X2

Example 4 – Qualified opinion – Disagreement. IFRS Financial statements where the going concern period considered by directors does not comply with IAS 1.

- Irish publicly traded company uses IFRSs as adopted for use in the European Union for financial statements.
- The balance sheet date being audited is 31 December 20X1.
- The date of approval of the financial statements was 31 May 20X2.
- In assessing whether the going concern assumption is appropriate the directors have taken into account the period up to 30 November 20X2 which is:
  - only 11 months from the balance sheet date ie less than the 12 months from the balance sheet date required by IAS 1 and
  - only 6 months from the date of approval of the financial statements ie less than the 12 months from the date of approval of the financial statements required by ISA (UK and Ireland) 570.
- The directors have refused to either extend their assessment period to a period of more than twelve months from the balance sheet date (to comply with IAS 1) or twelve months from the date of approval of the financial statements (to comply with ISA (UK and Ireland) 570) or to disclose the fact that the period they have used for their assessment is less than twelve months from the date of approval of the financial statements (to comply with ISA (UK and Ireland) 570).
- The auditor:
  - Includes an emphasis of matter paragraph explaining that in making their going concern assessment the directors have considered a period which is less than twelve months from the date of approval of the financial statements and the directors have not disclosed this fact
  - issues a qualified 'except for' opinion describing the disagreement over the disclosing the fact that the going concern period considered by the directors is less than the twelve months from the balance sheet date required by IAS 1.

Qualified opinion arising from departure from IAS 1 'Presentation of financial statements'

In assessing whether it is appropriate to prepare the financial statements on a going concern basis the directors have paid particular attention to a period ending on 30 November 20X2 which is less than twelve months from the balance sheet date. This is contrary to the requirements of International Accounting Standard 1 'Presentation of financial statements'.

Except for the non-compliance with IAS 1 referred to above in our opinion the financial statements:

- give a true and fair view, in accordance with the IFRSs as adopted for use in the European Union, of the state of the company's affairs as at 31 December 20X1 and of the profit[loss] for the year then ended; and
- have been properly prepared in accordance with the Companies Acts, 1963 to 2005, and Article 4 of the IAS Regulation.

We have obtained all the information and explanations which we consider necessary for the purposes of our audit. In our opinion proper books of account have been kept by the company. The financial statements are in agreement with the books of account.

In our opinion the information given in the directors' report is consistent with the financial statements.

The net assets of the company, as stated in the balance sheet are more than half of the amount of its called-up share capital and, in our opinion, on that basis there did not exist at 31 December 20X1 a financial situation which under Section 40 (1) of the Companies (Amendment) Act, 1983 would require the convening of an extraordinary general meeting of the company.

Emphasis of matter – Going concern
In forming our opinion, we have considered the adequacy of the disclosures made in note x to the financial statements concerning the period used by the directors in assessing whether the going concern assumption is appropriate. In making their assessment the directors have considered the period up to 30 November 20X2 which is less than twelve months from the date of approval of the financial statements and the directors have not disclosed this fact. International Standards on Auditing (UK and Ireland) require the auditors to draw this fact to the attention of readers of the financial statements. Our opinion is not further qualified in respect of this matter.

Registered auditors   *Address*
30 May 20X2

Example 5 – Qualified opinion – Disagreement. Non-disclosure of going concern problems.

- *Irish non-publicly traded company prepares Irish GAAP financial statements.*
- *The financial statements do not disclose that the Company's financing arrangements expire and amounts outstanding are payable on 19 July 20X2 and that the Company has been unable to re-negotiate or obtain replacement financing.*
- *This situation indicates the existence of a material uncertainty which may cast significant doubt on the Company's ability to continue as a going concern and therefore it may be unable to realize its assets and discharge its liabilities in the normal course of business.*
- *The auditor concludes that there is a significant level of concern about going concern and disagrees with the failure to disclose this information in the financial statements. The auditors issue a qualified except for opinion describing the disagreement.*

Qualified opinion arising from omission of information concerning going concern

The company's financing arrangements expire and amounts outstanding are payable on 19 July 20X2. The company has been unable to re-negotiate or obtain replacement financing. This situation indicates the existence of a material uncertainty which may cast significant doubt on the company's ability to continue as a going concern and therefore it may be unable to realise its assets and discharge its liabilities in the normal course of business. The financial statements (and notes thereto) do not disclose this fact.

Except for the omission of the information included in the preceding paragraph, in our opinion the financial statements:

- give a true and fair view, in accordance with Generally Accepted Accounting Practice in Ireland, of the state of the company's affairs as at 31 December 20X1 and of its profit [loss] for the year then ended; and
- have been properly prepared in accordance with the Companies Acts, 1963 to 2005.

We have obtained all the information and explanations which we consider necessary for the purposes of our audit. In our opinion proper books of account have been kept by the company. The financial statements are in agreement with the books of account.

In our opinion the information given in the directors' report is consistent with the financial statements.

The net assets of the company, as stated in the balance sheet are more than half of the amount of its called-up share capital and, in our opinion, on that basis there did not exist at 31 December 20X1 a financial situation which under Section 40 (1) of the Companies (Amendment) Act, 1983 would require the convening of an extraordinary general meeting of the company.

Registered auditors   *Address*
Date

Example 6 – Qualified opinion – Limitation of scope. Evidence available to auditor regarding going concern status was limited because cash flow forecasts were only prepared for a period of nine months from approval of financial statements.

- Irish non-publicly traded company prepares Irish GAAP financial statements.
- The evidence available to the auditor was limited because the company had prepared cash flow forecasts and other information needed for the assessment of the appropriateness of the going concern basis of preparation of the financial statements only for a period of nine months from the date of approval of the financial statements.
- Although this fact is disclosed in the financial statements had the information been available the auditor might have formed a different opinion. The auditor considers that those charged with governance have not taken adequate steps to satisfy themselves that it is appropriate for them to adopt the going concern basis.
- The auditor does not consider that the future period to which those charged with governance have paid particular attention in assessing going concern is reasonable in the entity's circumstances. The auditor considers that the particular circumstances of the company and the nature of the company's business require that such information be prepared, and reviewed by the directors and auditor for a period of at least twelve months from the date of approval of the financial statements.
- The auditor issues an 'except for' qualified opinion referring to the adjustments that might have been found to be necessary had they obtained sufficient evidence concerning the appropriateness of the going concern basis of preparation of the financial statements.

Basis of audit opinion

We conducted our audit in accordance with International Standards on Auditing (UK and Ireland) issued by the Auditing Practices Board, except that the scope of our work was limited as explained below.

An audit includes examination, on a test basis, of evidence relevant to the amounts and disclosures in the financial statements. It also includes an assessment of the significant estimates and judgments made by the directors in the preparation of the financial statements, and of whether the accounting policies are appropriate to the company's circumstances, consistently applied and adequately disclosed

We planned ~~and performed~~ our audit so as to obtain all the information and explanations which we considered necessary in order to provide us with sufficient evidence to give reasonable assurance that the financial statements are free from material misstatement, whether caused by fraud or other irregularity or error. However, the evidence available to us was limited because the company has prepared cash flow forecasts and other information needed for the assessment of the appropriateness of the going concern basis of preparation of the financial statements for a period of only nine months from the date of approval of these financial statements. We consider that the directors have not taken adequate steps to satisfy themselves that it is appropriate for them to adopt the going concern basis because the circumstances of the company and the nature of the business require that such information be prepared, and reviewed by the directors and ourselves, for a period of at least twelve months from the date of approval of the financial statements. Had this information been available to us we might have formed a different opinion.

In forming our opinion we also evaluated the overall adequacy of the presentation of information in the financial statements.

Qualified opinion arising from limitation in audit scope

Except for any adjustments that might have been found to be necessary had we been able to obtain sufficient evidence concerning the appropriateness of the going concern basis of preparation of the financial statements, in our opinion the financial statements:

- give a true and fair view, in accordance with Generally Accepted Accounting Practice in Ireland, of the state of the company's affairs as at 31 December 20X1 and of its profit [loss] for the year then ended; and
- have been properly prepared in accordance with the Companies Acts, 1963 to 2005.

In respect solely of the limitation on our work relating to the assessment of the appropriateness of the going concern basis of preparation of the financial statements we have not obtained all the information and explanations that we considered necessary for the purpose of our audit.

In our opinion proper books of account have been kept by the company. The financial statements are in agreement with the books of account.

In our opinion the information given in the directors' report is consistent with the financial statements.

The net assets of the company, as stated in the balance sheet are more than half of the amount of its called-up share capital and, in our opinion, on that basis there did not exist at 31 December 20X1 a financial situation which under Section 40 (1) of the Companies (Amendment) Act, 1983 would require the convening of an extraordinary general meeting of the company.

Registered auditors   *Address*
Date

Example 7 – Disclaimer of opinion. Going concern – company has not prepared profit or cash flow projections for an appropriate period subsequent to the balance sheet date.

- *Irish non-publicly traded company prepares Irish GAAP financial statements.*
- *The evidence available to the auditor to confirm the appropriateness of preparing the financial statements on the going concern basis was limited because the company has not prepared profit or cash flow projections for an appropriate period subsequent to the balance sheet date.*
- *The auditor considers that the circumstances of the company and the nature of the company's business requires that such information be prepared, and reviewed by the directors and the auditor, for a period of at least twelve months from the date of approval of the financial statements.*
- *The auditor concludes that the possible effect of this limitation on scope is so material and pervasive that the auditor has been unable to obtain sufficient appropriate audit evidence and accordingly is unable to form an opinion on whether or not it is appropriate to prepare the financial statements on a going concern basis. As a result, the auditor issues an opinion disclaiming the view given by the financial statements.*

Basis of audit opinion

We conducted our audit in accordance with International Standards on Auditing (UK and Ireland) issued by the Auditing Practices Board, except that the scope of our work was limited as explained below.

An audit includes examination, on a test basis, of evidence relevant to the amounts and disclosures in the financial statements. It also includes an assessment of the significant estimates and judgments made by the directors in the preparation of the financial statements, and of whether the accounting policies are appropriate to the company's circumstances, consistently applied and adequately disclosed

We planned ~~and performed~~ our audit so as to obtain all the information and explanations which we considered necessary in order to provide us with sufficient evidence to give reasonable assurance that the financial statements are free from material misstatement, whether caused by fraud or other irregularity or error. However, the evidence available to us to confirm the appropriateness of preparing the financial statements on the going concern basis was limited because the company has not prepared any profit or cash flow projections for an appropriate period subsequent to the balance sheet date. As a result, and in the absence of any alternative evidence available to us, we have been unable to form a view as to the applicability of the going concern basis, the circumstances of which, together with the effect on the financial statements should this basis be inappropriate, are set out in note x to the financial statements.

In forming our opinion we also evaluated the overall adequacy of the presentation of information in the financial statements.

Opinion: disclaimer on view given by financial statements

Because of the possible effect of the limitation in evidence available to us, we are unable to form an opinion as to whether the financial statements:

- give a true and fair view, in accordance with Generally Accepted Accounting Practice in Ireland, of the state of the company's affairs as at 31 December 20X1 and of its profit [loss] for the year then ended; and
- have been properly prepared in accordance with the Companies Acts, 1963 to 2005.

In respect solely of the limitation of our work referred to above we have not obtained all the information and explanations that we considered necessary for the purpose of our audit.

In our opinion proper books of account have been kept by the company. The financial statements are in agreement with the books of account.

In our opinion the information given in the directors' report is consistent with the financial statements.

The net assets of the company, as stated in the balance sheet are more than half of the amount of its called-up share capital and, in our opinion, on that basis there did not exist at 31 December 20X1 a financial situation which under Section 40 (1) of the Companies (Amendment) Act, 1983 would require the convening of an extra-ordinary general meeting of the company.

Registered auditors   *Address*
Date

Example 8 – Adverse opinion. Significant level of concern about the company's ability to continue as a going concern that is not disclosed in the financial statements.

- Irish non-publicly traded company prepares Irish GAAP financial statements.
- Although there is a significant level of concern about the company's ability to continue as a going concern the financial statements and notes do not disclose this fact and the directors have prepared the financial statements on the going concern basis.
- The auditor considers that the financial statements should disclose that there is a material uncertainty, which may cast significant doubt on the company's ability to continue as a going concern.
- The effect of this disagreement is so material and pervasive to the amounts included within the financial statements that the auditor concludes that a qualification of the report is not adequate to disclose the misleading or incomplete nature of the financial statements.
- The auditor issues an adverse audit opinion stating that, because the material uncertainty regarding going concern is not disclosed, the financial statements do not give a true and fair view.

Adverse opinion

As explained in note x to the financial statements the company's financing arrangements expired and the amount outstanding was payable on 31 December 20X1. The company has been unable to re-negotiate or obtain replacement financing and is considering entering insolvency proceedings. These events indicate a material uncertainty which may cast significant doubt on the company's ability to continue as a going concern and therefore it may be unable to realise its assets and discharge its liabilities in the normal course of business. The financial statements (and notes thereto) do not disclose this fact and have been prepared on the going concern basis.

In our opinion, because of the omission of the information mentioned above, the financial statements do not give a true and fair view, in accordance with Generally Accepted Accounting Practice in Ireland, of the state of the company's affairs as at 31 December 20X1 and of its profit [loss] for the year then ended.

In all other respects, in our opinion the financial statements have been properly prepared in accordance with the Companies Acts, 1963 to 2005.

We have obtained all the information and explanations which we consider necessary for the purposes of our audit. In our opinion proper books of account have been kept by the company. The financial statements are in agreement with the books of account.

In our opinion the information given in the directors' report is consistent with the financial statements.

The net assets of the company, as stated in the balance sheet are more than half of the amount of its called-up share capital and, in our opinion, on that basis there did not exist at 31 December 20X1 a financial situation which under Section 40 (1) of the Companies (Amendment) Act, 1983 would require the convening of an extraordinary general meeting of the company.

Registered auditors *Address*
Date

Appendix 4 – Illustrative statement of directors' responsibilities

Example wording of a description of the directors' responsibilities for inclusion in the annual report of a non-publicly traded company incorporated in the Republic of Ireland

Statement of directors' responsibilities

The directors are responsible for preparing the Annual Report and the financial statements in accordance with applicable law and Generally Accepted Accounting Practice in Ireland including the accounting standards issued by the Accounting Standards Board and promulgated by the Institute of Chartered Accountants in Ireland.

Company law requires the directors to prepare financial statements for each financial year which give a true and fair view of the state of affairs of the company and of the profit or loss of the company for that period. In preparing these financial statements, the directors are required to:

- select suitable accounting policies and then apply them consistently;
- make judgments and estimates that are reasonable and prudent;
- prepare the financial statements on the going concern basis unless it is inappropriate to presume that the company will continue in business.[32]

The directors are responsible for keeping proper books of account that disclose with reasonable accuracy at any time the financial position of the company and enable them to ensure that the financial statements comply with the Companies Acts 1963 to 2005. They are also responsible for safeguarding the assets of the company and hence for taking reasonable steps for the prevention and detection of fraud and other irregularities.

The directors are responsible for the maintenance and integrity of the corporate and financial information included on the company's website. Legislation in the Republic of Ireland governing the preparation and dissemination of financial statements may differ from legislation in other jurisdictions.[33]

> The APB has not prepared an illustrative example of a statement of directors' resonsibilities for a publicly traded company as their responsibilities, which are in part dependent on the particular regulatory environment, will vary dependent on the rules of the market on which its securities are admitted to trading.

---

[32] *Included where no separate statement on going concern is made by the directors.*

[33] *Included where the financial statements are published on the internet.*

[Bulletin 2006/4]
Regulatory and legislative background to the application of standards for investment reporting in the Republic of Ireland

Contents

	Paragraphs
Introduction	1 - 9
Application of the SIRs in the Republic of Ireland	10
Ethical Standard for Reporting Accountants	11 - 12
Principal Legislation and the Prospectus Directive	13 - 25
Rules of the Irish Stock Exchange	26 - 32

Appendices

1. Glossary of terms
2. Mapping from SIRs to equivalent Irish references
    (1) SIR 1000 'Investment Reporting Standards Applicable To All Engagements In Connection With An Investment Circular'
    (2) SIR 2000 'Investment Reporting Standards Applicable To Public Reporting Engagements On Historical Financial Information'
    (3) SIR 3000 'Investment Reporting Standards Applicable To Public Reporting Engagements On Profit Forecasts'
    (4) SIR 4000 'Investment Reporting Standards Applicable To Public Reporting Engagements on Pro Forma Financial Information'

Introduction

1. The Auditing Practices Board (APB) has recently issued four Standards for Investment Reporting (SIRs):

    (a) SIR 1000 'Investment Reporting Standards Applicable To All Engagements In Connection With An Investment Circular' ('SIR 1000');
    (b) SIR 2000 'Investment Reporting Standards Applicable To Public Reporting Engagements on Historical Financial Information' ('SIR 2000');
    (c) SIR 3000 'Investment Reporting Standards Applicable to Public Reporting Engagements on Profit Forecasts' ('SIR 3000'); and
    (d) SIR 4000 'Investment Reporting Standards Applicable to Public Reporting Engagements on Pro Forma Financial Information' (SIR 4000).

2. The SIRs reflect the requirements of the EU Prospectus Directive, the implementing EU Regulation 809/2004 that provides the detailed rules concerning Prospectuses and their contents (Referred to in the SIRs as the PD Regulation and in 'Irish Prospectus Law[1]' as the Prospectus Regulation[2]), and other related regulations that came into force on 1 July 2005.

3. The SIRs contain basic principles and essential procedures (Investment Reporting Standards), indicated by paragraphs in bold type, with which a reporting accountant is required to comply in the conduct of all engagements in connection with an investment circular.

SIRs 1000 and 2000

4. Under the new regulations issuers, rather than reporting accountants, are responsible for preparing and presenting historical financial information in an investment circular and the reporting accountant's role is to express an opinion as to whether that financial information gives a true and fair view.

5. SIR 1000 provides Investment Reporting Standards applicable to all engagements involving investment circulars. SIR 2000 establishes additional Investment Reporting Standards for reporting accountants when examining historical financial information which is intended to give a true and fair view.

6. SIRs 1000 and 2000 apply to reports signed by reporting accountants after 31 August 2005. SIRs 100 and 200 (which were issued in 1997) were withdrawn with effect from the same date.

SIRs 3000 and 4000

7. Under the Prospectus Regulation a reporting accountant has to express an opinion as to whether or not a profit forecast and pro forma financial information has been 'properly compiled' on the basis stated by the issuer.

8. SIRs 3000 and 4000 establish Investment Reporting Standards for reporting accountants when reporting on profit forecasts and pro forma financial information respectively. These are additional to the requirements of SIR 1000. Among other

---

[1] See Appendix 1 for definition of this term.

[2] In this Bulletin the term 'the Prospectus Regulation' refers to EU Regulation 809/2004. The equivalent term used in the published SIRs is 'PD Regulation'.

things the SIRs require the reporting accountant to obtain sufficient appropriate evidence that the directors have applied the criteria provided by the Prospectus Regulation and the CESR recommendations that affect the 'proper compilation' of the profit forecast or pro forma financial information.

SIRs 3000 and 4000 apply to reports signed after 31 March 2006. With effect from the same date Bulletin 1998/08 'Reporting on Pro forma Financial Information Pursuant to the Listing Rules' was withdrawn.

Application of the SIRs in the Republic of Ireland

The SIRs have been drafted with reference to legislation and regulations implementing the Prospectus Directive in the United Kingdom. The provisions and the principles contained within the SIRs are applicable to the Irish legislative and regulatory environment. The purpose of this Bulletin, therefore, is to provide an explanation of the background to the legislative and regulatory environment in Ireland and to provide a mapping of legislative and technical references within the SIRs, as published, to the Irish equivalent.

Ethical Standard for Reporting Accountants (ESRA)

Bulletin 2005/7 'Integrity, Objectivity and Independence – Guidance for reporting Accountants Undertaking Engagements in Connection with an Investment Circular' provides interim guidance to reporting accountants as to how to apply Ethical Standards ES1 to 5 to assist them in complying with the requirement of SIR 1000 to 'comply with the applicable ethical standards issued by the Auditing Practices Board'.

In January 2006 the APB issued an Exposure Draft of an Ethical Standard for Reporting Accountants (ESRA) which in due course will supersede Bulletin 2005/7.

Principal Legislation and the Prospectus Directive

(1) Principal Legislation

The principal legislation governing the regulation of companies and the publication of financial information in Ireland are the Companies Acts, 1963 – 2005 (the 'Companies Acts').

The Companies Acts 1963 -2005 include the 'Investment Funds, Companies and Miscellaneous Provisions Act, 2005' enacted on 29 June 2005 as Act Number 12 of 2005.

(2) Prospectus (Directive 2003/71/EC) Regulations, 2005 ('the Regulation[3]')

The Regulation made by the Minister for Enterprise, Trade and Employment, came into operation on 1 July 2005. This Regulation transposed the EU Prospectus Directive into Irish law by statutory instrument.

[3] These regulations are referred to as 'The Regulation' in the definition of Irish Prospectus Law. See Appendix 1 and also item 1.2 of the 'Prospectus Rules'

16 Upon implementation of the Prospectus Directive, the existing regime regarding the issue of listing particulars in connection with an application for listing or prospectuses in connection with a public offer of securities in Ireland, pursuant to Council Directive 80/390/EEC or Council Directive 89/298EEC, respectively, was repealed.

17 The Regulation along with Part 5 of the Investment Funds, Companies and Miscellaneous Provisions Act 2005 (the Act of 2005) give effect to the Prospectus Directive in Ireland on prospectuses to be published when securities are offered to the public or admitted to trading on a regulated market. The annexes to the Prospectus Regulation provide detailed rules on prospectuses and, in particular, the content requirements of prospectuses.

(3) Market Abuse (Directive2003/6/EC) Regulations, 2005 (the 'Market Abuse Directive')

18 The Market Abuse Regulations made by the Minister for Enterprise, Trade and Employment, came substantially into operation on 6 July 2005, these regulations transposed the EU Market Abuse Directive into Irish law by statutory instrument, remaining provisions of the Market Abuse Directive (insider lists, manager transactions) came into effect on 1 October 2005.

19 The Market Abuse (Directive 2003/6/EC) Regulations 2005 along with Part 4 of the Investment Funds, Companies and Miscellaneous Provisions Act 2005 give effect to the Market Abuse Directive in Ireland, as well as implementing Directives 2003/124/EC, 2003/125/EC and 2004/72/EC on insider dealing and market manipulation.

(4) Role of the Financial Regulator, Prospectus Rules, Market Abuse Rules and CESR

Role of the Financial Regulator
20 Under the Prospectus Directive and the Market Abuse Directive, the Financial Regulator (previously titled the Irish Financial Services Regulatory Authority) ('the Financial Regulator') is the competent authority.

Prospectus Rules
21 The Financial Regulator, in exercising its functions as competent authority under the Prospectus Directive, has published finalised 'Prospectus Rules Issued Under Section 51 of the Investment Funds, Companies and Miscellaneous Provisions Act, 2005' (the 'Prospectus Rules'). The Prospectus Rules will replace the Interim Rules and Guidance Note that have been in place since the Prospectus Regulations came into operation in July 2005. The Prospectus Rules set out procedural and administrative requirements and guidance in respect of the Directives.

22 The Prospectus Rules indicate that in determining whether Commission Regulation (EC) No 809/2004 has been complied with, the Financial Regulator will take into account whether an issuer has complied with 'CESR's[4] recommendations for the consistent implementation of the European Commission's Regulation on

---

[4] *The Committee of European Securities Regulators ('CESR') is an independent committee of European Securities Regulators, the Financial Regulator is a member of CESR.*
The role of CESR is to:
  (i)   Improve co-ordination among securities regulators;
  (ii) Act as an advisory group to assist the EU Commission; and
  (iii) Work to ensure more consistent and timely day-today implementation of community legislation in Member States.
Further information about CESR can be found on its web-site: www.cesr-eu.org

Prospectuses no. 809/2004 (CESR/05-054b)' to be followed when preparing a prospectus.

Market Abuse Rules
The Financial Regulator, in exercising its functions as competent authority under the Market Abuse Directive, has issued 'Rules Issued Under Section 34 of the Investment Funds, Companies and Miscellaneous Provisions Act 2005' (the 'Market Abuse Rules'). The Rules set out procedural and administrative requirements and guidance in respect of the Directives.

The Market Abuse Rules make it clear that in determining whether Commission Regulation (EC) No 809/2004 has been complied with, the Financial Regulator will take into account whether an issuer has complied with 'CESR's Guidance and Information on the Common Operation of the Market Abuse Directive (CESR/04-505b)' to be followed when preparing a prospectus.

Copies of the Prospectus Rules and the Market Abuse Rules are available from www.financialregulator.ie.

Rules of the Irish Stock Exchange

(1) Irish Stock Exchange Listing Rules

In relation to the Listing Rules, the Irish Stock Exchange is performing its functions as the competent authority under Regulation 7 of the European Communities (Stock Exchange) Regulations, 1984.

Given the new regulatory environment following implementation of the Prospectus Directive and Market Abuse Directive, the Irish Stock Exchange no longer adopts the Listing Rules of the Financial Services Authority (FSA) in the UK, and instead has developed its own stand alone listing rule book. To facilitate the dual listing of securities on the Irish and London stock exchanges, the Irish Stock Exchange has retained its policy of maintaining parity of listing standards with the FSA.

From 1 July 2005 the Exchange's Listing Rules cover *inter alia*:

- conditions for listing.
- listing applications procedures.
- listing principles.
- continuing obligation requirements, including super-equivalent requirements.
- requirements for sponsors.

The Listing Rules are available on the Exchange's website at the following address: www.ise.ie

(2) Alternative Securities Market ('ASM') Rules

From 1 July 2005, issuers seeking a listing of asset backed, debt or derivative securities on the Irish Stock Exchange may choose to have those securities admitted to trading on the Alternative Securities Market (ASM), rather than the 'regulated market' (as defined by Article 1(13) of Directive 93/22/EEC). Issuers seeking a listing on the ASM must prepare a listing particulars document which is reviewed, and subject to approval, by the Exchange. Certain third country issuers are not required to report historical financial information under IFRSs or an EU approved equivalent standard either in listing particulars or as a continuing obligation requirement.

(3) Irish Enterprise Exchange ('IEX') Rules

31 Under the Irish Enterprise Exchange ('IEX') Rules of the Irish Stock Exchange, companies seeking admission to IEX must publish an IEX admission document. This is the case whether or not they are required by Prospectus Law to prepare a prospectus (because they are also making an offer of securities to the public which is not exempt from the requirement to produce a prospectus).

32 The IEX Rules provide that the content of an admission document should be based on the disclosure requirements that apply to issuers of shares in the Prospectus Regulation, modified as set out in the IEX Rules, as well as certain additional IEX disclosure requirements.

Appendix 1 – Glossary of terms

Alternative Securities Market – A market for debt and derivative securities which is operated and regulated by the Irish Stock Exchange. This is not a 'regulated market' as defined by Article 1(13) of Directive 93/22/EEC.

ASM – The Alternative Securities Market

CESR – The Committee of European Securities Regulators

CESR Recommendations – 'CESR's recommendations for the consistent implementation of the European Commission's Regulation on Prospectuses no. 809/2004 (CESR/05-054b)'

Circular – A circular issued by any company to its shareholders and/or holders of its debt securities in connection with a transaction, which does not constitute a prospectus, listing particulars or IEX admission document.

City Code – Takeover Rules and Substantial Acquisition Rules. The application of these rules is monitored by the Irish Takeover Panel.

Class 1 transaction – A transaction where one or more of a number of specified percentage ratios exceed a predetermined level as specified in Chapter 7 of the Listing Rules.

Financial Regulator – Irish Financial Services Authority of Ireland (IFSRA).

IEX - The Irish Enterprise Exchange.

IEX Admission Document – The document prepared in connection with an application for admission of an issuer's securities to IEX.

IEX adviser – An adviser whose name appears on the Irish Stock Exchange's most recently published register of IEX advisers.

IEX Rules – The Rules of the Irish Enterprise Exchange.

IFSRA – The Irish Financial Services Regulatory Authority (Financial Regulator)

Irish Enterprise Exchange – A market for small to mid-sized companies which is operated and regulated by the Irish Stock Exchange.

Irish Stock Exchange – The Irish Stock Exchange Limited.

Issuer – For the purposes of Prospectus Law 'A body corporate or other legal entity which issues or proposes to issue securities'. For the purposes of the Listing Rules 'Any company or other legal person or undertaking (including a public sector issuer), any class of whose securities has been admitted to listing or is the subject of an application for admission to listing'.

Listing Rules – The Listing Rules of the Irish Stock Exchange.

Official List – Official List of the Irish Stock Exchange.

Prospectus Law – Any or all of the following as the context so requires:

(1) Part 5 of the Investment Funds, Companies and Miscellaneous Provisions Act 2005 (the Act of 2005);
(2) The Regulation;
(3) The Prospectus Regulation;
(4) CESR Recommendations; and
(5) Prospectus Rules.

Prospectus Rules – Rules issued under Section 51 of the Investment Funds, Companies and Miscellaneous Provisions Act, 2005.[5]

(The) Prospectus Regulation Commission Regulation (EC) No 809/2004 of 29 April 2004[6]. (The equivalent term used in the published SIRs is PD Regulation).

(The) Regulation – Prospectus (Directive 2003/71/EC) Regulations 2005.

Sponsor – A person approved by the Irish Stock Exchange as a registered sponsor.

---

[5] Readers are cautioned that in the UK, and in the SIRs as published, the expression 'Prospectus Rules' has a different meaning. For the purposes of this Bulletin the equivalent Irish term to the UK 'Prospectus Rules' is 'Prospectus Law'.

[6] Readers are cautioned that in the UK, and in the SIRs as published, the expression 'Prospectus Regulations' has a different meaning. For the purposes of this Bulletin the equivalent Irish term to the UK 'Prospectus Regulations' is 'Prospectus Law'.

Appendix 2 – Mapping from SIRS to Equivalent Irish References

(1) SIR 1000 'Investment Reporting Standards Applicable To All Engagements In Connection With An Investment Circular'

SIR 1000 – Paragraph Reference	UK Reference	Irish Equivalent
Main Document		
5, 61, 65, 68(a), Appendix 1	Prospectus Rules	Prospectus Law
68(a), 68(b), 68(c)	Listing Rules	Listing Rules of the Irish Stock Exchange
68(a), 68(b)	Item 23.1 of Annex I of the Prospectus Rules	Item 23.1 of Annex I of the Prospectus Regulation
68(c)	Paragraph 13.4.1(6) of the Listing Rules	Paragraph 10.4.1(6) of the Listing Rules of the Irish Stock Exchange
68(d), 74	City Code	Takeover Rules and Substantial Acquisition Rules.
68(d)	Rule 28.4 City Code	Rule 28.4 – Takeover Rules
68(d), 73	Rule 28.5 City Code	Rule 28.5 – Takeover Rules
68(e), Appendix 2	Alternative Investment Market (AIM) Rules	IEX Rules
68(e)	Item 23.1 of Annex I of the Prospectus Rules	Item 23.1 of Annex I of The Prospectus Regulation
Appendix 2	**Principal Legal and Regulatory Requirements**	
Paragraphs 1 to 6	FSA Handbook	Listing Rules of the Irish Stock Exchange and the Prospectus Regulation.
7	Annexes to the Prospectus Rules	Annexes to the Prospectus Regulation
8	Listing Rule 13.5	Section 10.5 of the Listing Rules of the Irish Stock Exchange
9(a)	Item 13.1 of Annex I to the Prospectus Directive	Item 13.1 of Annex I of the Prospectus Regulation
11	Annex I item 20.2 and Annex II of the Prospectus Rules	Annex I item 20.2 and Annex II of the Prospectus Regulation

SIR 1000 – Paragraph Reference	UK Reference	Irish Equivalent
15	Admission to Main Market of the London Stock Exchange	Admission to a regulated market of the Irish Stock Exchange
18	Professional Securities Market	Alternative Securities Market
19	City Code Rule 28.3	Rule 28.3 – Takeover Rules
19	City Code Rule 19.1	Rule 19.1 – Takeover Rules
19	City Code Rule 28.6(c)	Rule 28.6 (d) – Takeover Rules
20	S. 240 Companies Act 1985, ('non-statutory accounts')	S. 19 Companies Amendment Act 1986 ('abbreviated accounts')
20	S. 240 (3) Companies Act 1985	S. 19 (2) Companies Amendment Act 1986 ('abbreviated accounts')
Paragraphs 21 to 26	Financial Services and Markets Act 2000	'the Regulation'
Appendix 3	**Example of Consent Letter**	
Paragraph 2	Prospectus Rule 5.5.3R(2)(f)	Paragraph 2(2)(f) of Schedule 1 to 'the Regulation'
Paragraph 2	Prospectus Rule 5.5.4R(2)(f)	Paragraph 3(2)(f) of Schedule 1 to 'the Regulation'
Paragraph 2	Regulation 6(1)(e) of The Financial Services and Markets Act 2000 (Official Listing of Securities) Regulations 2001	Chapter 16 of the Listing Rules of the Irish Stock Exchange
Paragraph 2	Schedule Two to the AIM Rules	Schedule Two to the IEX Rules

(2) SIR 2000 'Investment Reporting Standards Applicable To Public Reporting Engagements on Historical Financial Information'

SIR 2000 – Paragraph Reference	UK Reference	Irish Equivalent
Main Document		
3(b), 4	PD Regulation	The Prospectus Regulation
3(b), 21, Annex I	Listing Rules	Listing Rules of the Irish Stock Exchange
4, 19, Appendix 3	Prospectus Rules	Prospectus Law
4	Annex I of the PD Regulation	Annex I of the Prospectus Regulation
5, Appendix 2	Chapter 13 of the Listing Rules	Chapter 10 of the Listing Rules of the Irish Stock Exchange
17	Companies Act 1985	Companies Acts 1963 to 2005
63	Chapter 3 of the Prospectus Rules	Regulations 51 and 52 of 'the Regulation'
63	FSA	The Financial Regulator
Appendix 2	**Examples of Engagement Letter Clauses**	
For a Prospectus Paragraph 1	Annex I item 20.1 of the Prospectus Rules	Annex I item 20.1 of the Prospectus Regulation
For a Class 1 circular Paragraph 1	Chapter 13 of the Listing Rules	Chapter 10 of the Listing Rules of the Irish Stock Exchange
Appendix 3	**Example of an Accountant's Report on Historical Financial Information**	
Footnote 1	AIM admission document	IEX admission document
Declaration	Prospectus Rule 5.5.3R(2)(f)	Paragraph 2(2)(f) of Schedule 1 to 'the Regulation'
Declaration	Prospectus Rule 5.5.4R(2)(f)	Paragraph 3(2)(f) of Schedule 1 to 'the Regulation'
Declaration	Item 1.2 of Annex I of the PD Regulation	Item 1.2 of Annex I of Prospectus Regulation
Declaration	Item 1.2 of Annex III of the PD Regulation	Item 1.2 of Annex III of Prospectus Regulation
Declaration	Schedule 2 of the AIM Rules	Schedule 2 of the IEX Rules

SIR 2000 – Paragraph Reference	UK Reference	Irish Equivalent
Footnote 3	AIM admission document under Schedule Two of the AIM Rules	IEX admission document under Schedule Two of the IEX Rules
Annexure		
8	PD Regulation (subject to certain transitional provisions in Article 35 of the PD Regulation)	The Prospectus Regulation (subject to certain transitional provisions in Article 35 of the Prospectus Regulation)
51	Chapter 13 of the Listing Rules	Chapter 10 of the Listing Rules of the Irish Stock Exchange
52	Listing Rule 13.3	Listing Rule 10.3 of the Irish Stock Exchange
55, 62	UK Listing Authority	Irish Stock Exchange

(3) SIR 3000 'Investment Reporting Standards Applicable To Public Reporting Engagements On Profit Forecasts'

(i) Main Body of Document

SIR 3000 – Paragraph Reference	UK Reference	Irish Equivalent
1, 2(b), 3, 22, 24, 39	PD Regulation	The Prospectus Regulation
1	Listing Rules	Listing Rules of the Irish Stock Exchange
1, 22, 39, 76	City Code	Takeover Rules and Substantial Acquisition Rules
1	AIM Admission Document	Irish Enterprise Exchange ('IEX') Admission Document
10	Prospective Financial Information – Guidance for UK directors – ICAEW[7] Guidance	Prospective Financial Information – Guidance for UK directors – ICAEW Guidance (for information)
81	Sections 81 and 87G of the FSMA, Prospectus Rule 3.4, and Listing Rule 4.4.1, preparation.	Regulation 51 of 'the Regulation' and Irish Stock Exchange Listing Rule 16.4.
Appendix 1	Notes 1(c) and (d) to Rule 28.2 of the City Code	Notes 1(c) and (d) to Rule 28.2 of the Takeover Rules

[7] Institute of Chartered Accountants in England & Wales

(ii) Appendix 2 – Reporting Accountant's Criteria

	Prospectus Regulation	Annex I[8] Prospectus Regulation	CESR Recommendations
A statement setting out the principal assumptions upon which the issuer has based its forecast or estimate.		13.1	
There must be a clear distinction between assumptions about factors which the members of the administrative, management or supervisory bodies can influence and assumptions about factors which are exclusively outside the influence of the members of the administrative, management or supervisory bodies; the assumptions must be readily understandable by investors, be specific and precise and not relate to the general accuracy of the estimates underlying the forecast.		13.1	
The profit forecast or estimate must be prepared on a basis comparable with the historical financial information.		13.3	
The following principles should be taken into consideration when profit forecasts or estimates are being compiled. Profit forecasts or estimates should be • **Understandable**, ie Profit forecasts or estimates should contain disclosure that is not too complex or extensive for investors to understand; • **Reliable**, ie Profit forecasts should be supported by a thorough analysis of the issuer's business and should represent factual and not hypothetical strategies, plans and risk analysis; • **Comparable**, ie Profit forecasts or estimates should be capable of justification by comparison with outcomes in the form of historical financial information;			para 41

8 The column illustrates Annex I as an example. Other annexes to the Prospectus Regulation contain identical requirements with respect to profit forecasts. See Appendix 1 of SIR 1000.

(iii) *Appendix 3 – Other Regulatory Provisions Relevant to the Preparers of Profit Forecasts*

	Prospectus Regulation	Annex 1 of Prospectus Regulation	CESR Recommendations
(8) Voluntary disclosure of profit forecasts in a share registration document should be presented in a consistent and comparable manner and accompanied by a statement prepared by independent accountants or auditors. This information should not be confused with the disclosure of known trends or other factual data with material impact on the issuer's prospects. Moreover, they should provide an explanation of any changes in disclosure policy relating to profit forecasts when supplementing a prospectus or drafting a new prospectus.	Recital 8		
Profit forecast means a form of words which expressly states or by implication indicates a figure or a minimum or maximum figure for the likely level of profits or losses for the current financial period and/or financial periods subsequent to that period, or contains data from which a calculation of such a figure for future profits or losses may be made, even if no particular figure is mentioned and the word "profit" is not used.	Article 2		
Profit estimate means a profit forecast for a financial period which has expired and for which results have not yet been published	Article 2		
If an issuer chooses to include a profit forecast or profit estimate the registration document must contain the information set out in items 13.1 and 13.2		13	

Prospectus Regulation	Annex I of Prospectus Regulation	CESR Recommendations
A report prepared by independent accountants or auditors stating that in the opinion of the independent accountants or auditors the forecast or estimate has been properly compiled on the basis stated and that the basis of accounting used for the profit forecast or estimate is consistent with the accounting policies of the issuer	13.2	
If a profit forecast in a prospectus has been published which is still outstanding, then provide a statement setting out whether or not that forecast is still correct as at the time of the registration document, and an explanation of why such forecast is no longer valid if that is the case.	13.4	
The inclusion of a profit forecast or estimate in a prospectus is the responsibility of the issuer and persons responsible for the prospectus and due care and diligence must be taken to ensure that profit forecasts or estimates are not misleading to investors		para 40
The following principles should be taken into consideration when profit forecasts or estimates are being compiled. Profit forecasts or estimates should be • **Relevant**, ie profit forecasts and estimates must have an ability to influence economic decisions of investors and provided on a timely basis so as to influence such decisions and assist in confirming or correcting past evaluations or assessments		para 41

Prospectus Regulation	Annex I of Prospectus Regulation	CESR Recommendations
Where an issuer provides a profit forecast or estimate in a registration document, if the related schedules so requires, it must be reported on by independent accountants or auditors in the registration document (as described in item 13.2 of Annex I of the Regulation) Where the issuer does not produce a single prospectus, upon the issuance of the securities note and summary at a later time, the issuer should either: • Confirm the profit estimates or forecasts; or • State that the profit forecasts or estimates are no longer valid or correct; or Make appropriate alteration of profit forecasts or estimates. In this case they must be reported upon as described in item 13.2 of Annex I of the Regulation.		para 42
If an issuer has made a statement other than in a previous prospectus that would constitute a profit forecast or estimate if made in a prospectus, for instance, in a regulatory announcement, and that statement is still outstanding at the time of publication of the prospectus, the issuer should consider whether the forecasts or estimates are still material and valid and choose whether or not to include them in the prospectus. CESR considers that there is a presumption that an outstanding forecast made other than in a previous prospectus will be material in the case of share issues (especially in the context of an IPO). This is not necessarily the presumption in case of non-equity securities.		paras 43 & 44
When there is an outstanding profit forecast or estimate in relation to a material undertaking which the issuer has acquired, the issuer should consider whether it is appropriate to make a statement as to whether or not the profit forecast or estimate is still valid or correct. The issuer should also evaluate the effects of the acquisition and the profit forecast made by that undertaking on its own financial position and report on it as it would have done if the profit forecast or estimate had been made by the issuer.		paras 45 & 46

	Prospectus Regulation	Annex I of Prospectus Regulation	CESR Recommendations
The forecast or estimate should normally be of profit before tax (disclosing separately any non-recurrent items and tax charges if they are expected to be abnormally high or low). If the forecast or estimate is not of profit before tax, the reasons for presenting another figure from the profit and loss account must be disclosed and clearly explained. Furthermore the tax effect should be clearly explained. When the results are published relating to a period covered by a forecast or estimate, the published financial statements must disclose the relevant figure so as to enable the forecast and actual results to be directly compared.			paras 47 & 48
CESR recognises that often in practice, there is a fine line between what constitutes a profit forecast and what constitutes trend information as detailed in item 12 of Annex I of the Regulation. A general discussion about the future or prospects of the issuer under trend information will not normally constitute a profit forecast or estimate as defined in Articles 2.10 and 2.11 of the Regulation. Whether or not a statement constitutes a profit forecast is a question of fact and will depend upon the circumstances of the particular issuer.			para 49
This is a non-exhaustive list of factors that an issuer is expected to take into consideration when preparing forecasts: • Past results, market analysis, strategic evolutions, market share and position of the issuer • Financial position and possible changes therein • Description of the impact of an acquisition or disposal, change in strategy or any major change in environmental matters and technology • Changes in legal and tax environment • Commitments towards third parties			para 50

(4) SIR 4000 'Investment Reporting Standards Applicable To Public Reporting Engagements on Pro Forma Financial Information'

(i) Main Body of Document

SIR 4000 – Paragraph Reference	UK Reference	Irish Equivalent
1, 4, 5(a), 10, 12, 27, 58, 62, 63,	PD Regulation	The Prospectus Regulation
1, 10	Listing Rules of the FSA	Listing Rules of the Irish Stock Exchange
1	City Code	Takeover Rules and Substantial Acquisition Rules
1	AIM Admission Document	Irish Enterprise Exchange ('IEX') Admission Document
3	Item 1 of Annex II of the PD Regulation	Item 1 of Annex II of the Prospectus Regulation
4	Prospective Financial Information – Guidance for UK directors – ICAEW Guidance	Prospective Financial Information – Guidance for UK directors – ICAEW Guidance (for information)
26	Item 5 of Annex II of the PD Regulation	Item 5 of Annex II of the Prospectus Regulation
30, 39, 40	Item 6 of Annex II to the PD Regulation	Item 6 of Annex II to the Prospectus Regulation
44	Item 4 of Annex II of the PD Regulation	Item 4 of Annex II of the Prospectus Regulation
47 (a)	Item 1 of Annex II of the PD Regulation	Item 1 of Annex II of the Prospectus Regulation
47 (b)	Item 3 of Annex II of the PD Regulation	Item 3 of Annex II of the Prospectus Regulation
66	Section 81 and 87G of the FSMA, Prospectus Rule 3.4 and Listing Rule 4.4.1	Regulation 51 of 'the Regulation' and Irish Stock Exchange Listing Rule 16.4.

(ii) Appendix 1 – Reporting Accountant's Criteria

Reporting Accountant's Criteria	Annex I of Prospectus Regulation	Annex II of Prospectus Regulation	CESR Recommendations
In the case of a significant gross change, a description of how the transaction might have affected the assets and liabilities and earnings of the issuer, had the transaction been undertaken at the commencement of the period being reported on or at the date reported. This requirement will normally be satisfied by the inclusion of pro forma financial information.	20.2		
The pro forma information must normally be presented in columnar format composed of: a) the historical unadjusted information; b) the pro forma adjustments; and c) the resulting pro forma financial information in the final column		3	
The sources of the pro forma financial information have to be stated.		3	
The pro forma information must be prepared in a manner consistent with the accounting policies adopted by the issuer in its last or next financial statements and shall identify the following: a) the basis upon which it is prepared; b) the source of each item of information and adjustment.		4	
Pro forma adjustments related to the pro forma financial information must be: a) clearly shown and explained.		6	

	Annex I of Prospectus Regulation	Annex II of Prospectus Regulation	CESR Recommendations
Pro forma adjustments related to the pro forma financial information must be: b) directly attributable to the transaction.		6	
'*Directly attributable to transactions*'. Pro forma information should only reflect matters that are an integral part of the transactions which are described in the prospectus. In particular, pro forma financial information should not include adjustments which are dependent on actions to be taken once the current transaction has been completed, even where such actions are central to the issuer's purpose in entering into the transactions			Para 88
Pro forma adjustments related to the pro forma financial information must be: c) factually supportable.		6	
'*Factually supportable*'. The nature of the facts supporting an adjustment will vary according to the circumstances. Nevertheless, facts are expected to be capable of some reasonable degree of objective determination. Support might typically be provided by published accounts, management accounts, other financial information and valuations contained in the document, purchase and sale agreements and other agreements to the transaction covered by the prospectus. For instance in relation to management accounts, the interim figures for an undertaking being acquired may be derived from the consolidation schedules underlying that undertaking's interim statements			Para 87
In respect of a pro forma profit and loss or cash flow statement, the adjustments must be clearly identified as to those expected to have a continuing impact on the issuer and those which are not.		6	

Annex I of Prospectus Regulation	Annex II of Prospectus Regulation	CESR Recommendations
The accounting treatment applied to adjustments should be presented and prepared in a form consistent with the policy the issuer would adopt in its last or next published financial statements.		Para 89[9]

9 Paragraph 89 of the CESR guidance also provides guidance that although not constituting a criterion is useful guidance to this criterion.

(iii) *Appendix 2 – Other Regulatory Provisions Relevant to the Preparers of Pro Forma Financial Information*

	Prospectus Regulation	Annex I & II of Prospectus Regulation	CESR Recommendations
(9) Pro forma financial information is needed in case of significant gross change, i.e. a variation of more than 25% relative to one or more indicators of the size of the issuers business, in the situation of an issuer due to a particular transaction, with the exception of those situations where merger accounting is required.	Recital 9		
For these purposes, 'Significant gross change' is described in recital 9 of the PD Regulation. Thus, in order to assess whether the variation to an issuer's business as a result of a transaction is more than 25%, the size of the transaction should be assessed relative to the size of the issuer by using appropriate indicators of size prior to the relevant transaction. A transaction will constitute a significant gross change where at least one of the indicators of size is more than 25%. A non-exhaustive list of indicators is provided below: – Total assets – Revenue – Profit or loss Other indicators of size can be applied by the issuer especially where the stated indicators of size produce an anomalous result or are inappropriate to the specific industry of the issuer, in these cases the issuers should address these anomalies by agreement of the competent authority. The appropriate indicators of size should refer to figures from the issuer's last or next published annual financial statements.			Paras 90 to 94
Pro forma financial information should be preceded by an introductory explanatory paragraph that states in clear terms the purpose of including this information in the prospectus		Article 5	

	Prospectus Regulation	Annex I & II of Prospectus Regulation	CESR Recommendations
This pro forma financial information is to be presented as set out in Annex II and must include the information indicated therein. Pro forma financial information must be accompanied by a report prepared by independent accountants or auditors.		20.2 (I)	
The pro forma information must include a description of the transaction, the business involved and the period to which it refers.		1 (II)	
The pro forma information must clearly state the purpose to which it has been prepared		1 (II)	
The pro forma information must clearly state that it has been prepared for illustrative purposes only		1 (II)	
The pro forma information must clearly state that it addresses a hypothetical situation and, therefore, does not represent the company's actual financial position or results.		1 (II)	
In order to present pro forma financial information, a balance sheet and profit and loss account, and accompanying explanatory notes, depending on the circumstances may be included		2 (II)	
Where applicable the financial statements of the acquired businesses or entities must be included in the prospectus.		3 (II)	

	Prospectus Regulation	Annex I & II of Prospectus Regulation	CESR Recommendations
Pro forma information may only be published in respect of: a) the current financial period; b) the most recently completed financial period; c) the most recent interim period for which relevant unadjusted information has been or will be published or is being published in the same document		5 (II)	

[Bulletin 2006/5]
The combined code on corporate governance: requirements of auditors under the listing rules of the Financial Services Authority and the Irish Stock Exchange

Contents

	Paragraphs
Introduction	1 - 4
Requirements of the Listing Rules relating to corporate governance matters	5 - 10
The auditor's review of the statement of compliance	11 - 13
Combined Code provisions that the auditor is required to review	14
General procedures	15 - 22
Specific procedures	23 - 67
Directors' statement on going concern	68 - 72
Reporting requirements derived from other Auditing Standards	73

Appendices

1. Extracts from the FSA Listing Rules
2. Equivalent Irish Stock Exchange Listing Rules
3. Example terms of engagement paragraphs

Introduction

This Bulletin provides guidance for auditors when reviewing a company's statement made in relation to "The Combined Code on Corporate Governance" ("Combined Code") in accordance with Listing Rule ("LR") 9.8.10R of the Financial Services Authority ("FSA") or LR 6.8.9 of the Irish Stock Exchange ("ISE"). It replaces the guidance in:

- APB Bulletin 2004/3, "The Combined Code on Corporate Governance: Requirements of Auditors under the Listing Rules of the Financial Services Authority" published in November 2004; and
- APB Bulletin 2004/4"The Combined Code on Corporate Governance: Requirements of Auditors under the Listing Rules of the Irish Stock Exchange" published in December 2004.

This Bulletin reflects the following:

(a) The issuance of "Internal Control: Revised Guidance for Directors on the Combined Code" ("Turnbull Guidance") by the Financial Reporting Council in October 2005. The Turnbull Review Group made only a small number of changes to the Turnbull Guidance as first issued in 1999. One of these changes is that the board's statement on internal control should confirm that necessary actions have been, or are being, taken to remedy any significant failings or weaknesses identified from its review of the effectiveness of the system of internal control. This development is set out in paragraph 36 of the revised Turnbull Guidance and is discussed in paragraphs 40 to 44 in this Bulletin.

(b) The issuance of revised Listing Rules in July 2005. Although there has been no change to the substance of the requirements of the Listing Rules in this regard the text of the rules differs from the previous rules.

This Bulletin provides guidance for auditors of both:

(a) companies listed on the Official List maintained by the FSA that are incorporated in the United Kingdom; and
(b) companies listed on the Official List maintained by the ISE that are incorporated in Ireland.

The text of the applicable revised Listing Rules issued by the FSA is set out in Appendix 1. Appendix 2 sets out the references to the equivalent Listing Rules of the ISE. In the remainder of this Bulletin reference is made to the "Listing Rules" and footnotes provide the specific references to the Listing Rules issued by the FSA and the ISE.

This Bulletin does not address the report to shareholders on executive directors' remuneration that is required by the Listing Rules[1].

---

[1] FSA LR 9.8.6R(7) and LR 9.8.8R; ISE LR 6.8.6(8) and LR 6.8.8.

Requirements of the Listing Rules relating to corporate governance matters

Requirement for companies to "comply or explain"

5 The FSA Listing Rules require listed companies[2] that are incorporated in the United Kingdom to include in their annual report and accounts a two-part disclosure statement in relation to the Combined Code. The Listing Rules of the ISE have a similar requirement with respect to listed companies that are incorporated in the Republic of Ireland. The first part of the disclosure statement is to explain how the company has applied the principles set out in Section 1 of the Combined Code, in a manner that would enable shareholders to evaluate how the principles have been applied[3].

6 The second part of the disclosure statement requires the company to either[4]:

(a) Comply - include "*a statement as to whether the listed company has complied throughout the accounting period with all relevant provisions set out in Section 1 of the Combined Code*"; or

(b) Explain – include "*a statement as to whether the listed company has not complied throughout the accounting period with all relevant provisions set out in Section 1 of the Combined Code and if so, setting out:*
   (i) those provisions, if any, it has not complied with;
   (ii) in the case of provisions whose requirements are of a continuing nature, the period within which, if any, it did not comply with some or all of those provisions; and
   (iii) the company's reasons for non-compliance".

7 It is expected that listed companies will comply with the provisions of the Combined Code most of the time. However, it is recognised that departures from the provisions of the Code may be justified in particular circumstances. The auditor has no responsibility to review or otherwise assess and comment upon a company's decision to depart from the provisions of the Code. It is for shareholders and others to evaluate any such departure and the company's explanation for it.

8 The Listing Rules[5] requires an overseas company with a primary listing to disclose in its annual report and accounts certain matters relating to its corporate governance. There are no requirements relating to auditors in respect of these Listing Rules.

Review of the company's disclosure statement by the auditor

9 The Listing Rules[6] require that "*A listed company must ensure that the auditors review the parts of the statement that relate to the following provisions of the Combined Code C1.1, C2.1, and C3.1 to C3.7.*" They require the auditor to review nine of the ten objectively verifiable Combined Code provisions relating to accountability and audit.

---

[2] *A listed company is defined by the FSA and the Irish Stock Exchange as "a company that has any class of its securities listed".*

[3] *FSA LR 9.8.6R(5); ISE LR 6.8.6(6)*

[4] *FSA LR 9.8.6R(6); ISE LR 6.8.6(7)*

[5] *FSA LR 9.8.7R; ISE LR 6.8.7*

[6] *FSA LR 9.8.10R(2); ISE LR 6.8.9(2)*

The tenth accountability and audit Combined Code provision (C.1.2 on going concern) is addressed by different Listing Rules[7]. These Listing Rules require the directors to make a statement that the business is a going concern, together with supporting assumptions or qualifications as necessary. This statement is required to be included in the annual report and accounts and to be reviewed by the auditor before publication.

The auditor's review of the statement of compliance

The scope of the auditor's review required by the Listing Rules[8], in comparison to the totality of the Combined Code, is narrow. The auditor is not required to review the directors' narrative statement of how they have applied the Code principles and is required only to review the directors' compliance statement in relation to nine of the forty-eight Code provisions applicable to companies. Nevertheless, because the directors' narrative statement comprises other information included in a document containing audited financial statements there is a broader requirement under Auditing Standards[9] for the auditor to read such "other information" and if the auditor becomes aware of any apparent misstatements therein, or identifies any material inconsistencies with the audited financial statements, to seek to resolve them.

The Listing Rules are silent as to whether the auditor should report on the auditor's review of the directors' compliance statement and whether any such report should be published or referred to in the annual report. The APB is of the view that if the auditor's report itself contains a description of the auditor's responsibilities (including the auditor's responsibilities under the Listing Rules), as discussed in paragraphs 24 to 29, there is no necessity for a separate auditor's report dealing with the auditor's review of corporate governance matters.

Because of the limited nature of the auditor's review and in order to avoid the possibility of misunderstandings arising the APB recommends that:

(a) the auditor's engagement letter explains the scope of the auditor's review. Example paragraphs are set out in Appendix 3; and
(b) prior to the release of the annual report and accounts the auditor communicates, and discusses, with those charged with governance the factual findings of the auditor's review.

Combined Code provisions that the auditor is required to review

The provisions of the Combined Code that the auditor is required to review are set out below, together with a reference to the specific procedures recommended by the APB:

---

[7] FSA LR 9.8.6R(3) and LR 9.8.10R(1); ISE LR 6.8.6(3) and LR 6.8.9(1)

[8] FSA LR 9.8.10R; ISE LR 6.8.9

[9] ISA (UK and Ireland) 720 (Revised) Section A, "Other information in documents containing audited financial statements".

Provision	Detailed recommendation	Specific procedures
C.1.1	The directors should explain in the annual report their responsibility for preparing the accounts and there should be a statement by the auditors about their reporting responsibilities.	23-29
C.2.1	The board should, at least annually, conduct a review of the effectiveness of the group's system of internal controls and should report to shareholders that they have done so. The review should cover all material controls, including financial, operational and compliance controls and risk management systems.	30-55
C.3.1	The board should establish an audit committee of at least three, or in the case of smaller companies[10] two, members, who should all be independent non-executive directors. The board should satisfy itself that at least one member of the audit committee has recent and relevant financial experience.	56-59
C.3.2	The main role and responsibilities of the audit committee should be set out in written terms of reference and should include: • to monitor the integrity of the financial statements of the company, and any formal announcements relating to the company's financial performance, reviewing significant financial reporting judgements contained in them; • to review the company's internal financial controls and, unless expressly addressed by a separate board risk committee composed of independent directors, or by the board itself, to review the company's internal control and risk management systems; • to monitor and review the effectiveness of the company's internal audit function; • to make recommendations to the board, for it to put to the shareholders for their approval in general meeting, in relation to the appointment, re-appointment and removal of the external auditor and to approve the remuneration and terms of engagement of the external auditor; • to review and monitor the external auditor's independence and objectivity and the effectiveness of the audit process, taking into consideration relevant UK professional and regulatory requirements; • to develop and implement policy on the engagement of the external auditor to supply non-audit services, taking into account relevant ethical guidance regarding the provision of non-audit services by the	60

[10] In the UK, a smaller company is one that is below the FTSE 350 throughout the year immediately prior to the reporting year. The Irish Stock Exchange considers a smaller company to be one that is included in the ISEQ Small Cap Index throughout the year immediately prior to the reporting year.

	external audit firm; and to report to the board, identifying any matters in respect of which it considers that action or improvement is needed and making recommendations as to the steps to be taken.	
C.3.3	The terms of reference of the audit committee, including its role and the authority delegated to it by the board, should be made available. A separate section of the annual report should describe the work of the committee in discharging those responsibilities.	61
C.3.4	The audit committee should review arrangements by which staff of the company may, in confidence, raise concerns about possible improprieties in matters of financial reporting or other matters. The audit committee's objective should be to ensure that arrangements are in place for the proportionate and independent investigation of such matters and for appropriate follow-up action.	62
C.3.5	The audit committee should monitor and review the effectiveness of the internal audit activities. Where there is no internal audit function, the audit committee should consider annually whether there is a need for an internal audit function and make a recommendation to the board, and the reasons for the absence of such a function should be explained in the relevant section of the annual report.	63
C.3.6	The audit committee should have primary responsibility for making a recommendation on the appointment, reappointment and removal of the external auditors. If the board does not accept the audit committee's recommendation, it should include in the annual report, and in any papers recommending appointment or re-appointment, a statement from the audit committee explaining the recommendation and should set out reasons why the board has taken a different position.	64
C.3.7	The annual report should explain to shareholders how, if the auditor provides non-audit services, auditor objectivity and independence is safeguarded.	65-67

General procedures

Paragraphs 16 to 22 set out general procedures relating to the auditor's review of the statement of compliance. These general procedures are applicable to all of the nine provisions of the Combined Code that the auditor is required to review. 15

In relation to all elements of the corporate governance disclosures relating to the provisions of the Combined Code that are within the scope of the auditor's review, the auditor obtains appropriate evidence to support the compliance statement made by the company. The type of procedures usually performed include: 16

(a) reviewing the minutes of the meetings of the board of directors, and of relevant board committees;
(a) reviewing supporting documents prepared for the board of directors or board committees that are relevant to those matters specified for review by the auditor;
(a) making enquiries of certain directors (such as the chairman of the board of directors and the chairmen of relevant board committees) and the company

secretary to satisfy themselves on matters relevant to those provisions of the Combined Code specified for review by the auditor; and

(a) attending meetings of the audit committee (or the full board if there is no audit committee) at which the annual report and accounts, including the statement of compliance, are considered and approved for submission to the board of directors.

17 The auditor may request the directors to provide written confirmation of oral representations made during the course of the review.

Non-compliance with provisions of the Combined Code

18 Where the auditor becomes aware of any provision of the Combined Code that is within the scope of the auditor's review and with which the company has not complied, the auditor establishes that the departure is described in the directors' statement of compliance. However, the auditor is not required to, and does not, perform additional procedures to investigate the appropriateness of reasons given for non-compliance with the provision.

19 Where there is a departure from a provision specified for the auditor's review but there is proper disclosure of this fact and of the reasons for the departure, as envisaged by the Listing Rules[11], the auditor does not refer to this in its report on the financial statements.

20 However, where the auditor considers that there is not proper disclosure of a departure from a provision of the Combined Code specified for the auditor's review the auditor reports this in the auditor's report on the financial statements. Paragraph 55 describes the way in which such a matter (which does not give rise to a qualified opinion on the financial statements) is reported and provides an example of such an opinion.

Auditor's association with company's corporate governance disclosures

21 The auditor would not wish to be associated with either the statement of compliance or the company's narrative statement of how it has applied the Code principles if the auditor has reason to believe that they may be misleading. The auditor, therefore, reads both of these statements and considers whether any information in either of them is apparently misstated or materially inconsistent with other information of which the auditor has become aware in the course of either the review of the company's compliance statement (insofar as it relates to the nine provisions of the Combined Code that the auditor is required to review under the Listing Rules) or the audit of the financial statements.

22 The auditor is not expected actively to search for misstatements or inconsistencies. However, if the auditor becomes aware of such a matter the auditor discusses it with the directors in order to establish the significance of the lack of proper disclosure. If such lack of proper disclosure is considered significant by the auditor and the directors cannot be persuaded to amend the disclosure to the auditor's satisfaction, the auditor considers the implications for the auditor's reporting responsibilities and the auditor may need to take legal advice.

[11] *FSA LR 9.8.10R; ISE LR 6.8.9*

Specific procedures

Responsibilities of the directors and the auditor

> **C.1.1** The directors should explain in the annual report their responsibility for preparing the accounts and there should be a statement by the auditors about their reporting responsibilities.

Directors' responsibilities

While the content of the statement of the directors' responsibilities is determined by the directors, the auditor establishes that the directors' responsibility for preparing the accounts is explained in the annual report. 23

Auditor's responsibilities

The auditor has different responsibilities with respect to the various component parts of the annual report. For example, the auditor is required to "audit" the financial statements, "review" the company's compliance with certain aspects of the Combined Code and "read" all information in the annual report that is not subject to any other requirement. The auditor reads such "other information" because the credibility of the financial statements and the related auditor's report may be undermined by material inconsistencies between the financial statements and the "other information", or by apparent misstatements within the other information. 24

In some instances the auditor has to report positively the results of the work whereas in other instances the auditor only has to report by exception. The APB is of the view that users of annual reports will find it difficult to understand the scope of the auditor's involvement in the absence of a clear statement of the auditor's responsibilities towards the whole annual report. 25

The key elements of a statement of the auditor's responsibilities relate to the requirements of: 26

(a) statute and Auditing Standards with respect to the audit of the financial statements;
(b) statute with respect to the auditor's opinion as to whether the information given in the directors report for the financial year for which the financial statements are prepared is consistent with those financial statements;
(c) statute and the Listing Rules where the auditor is only required to report by exception;
(d) the Listing Rules for the auditor to review the statement concerning the company's compliance with certain provisions of the Combined Code; and
(e) Auditing Standards to read the "other information" in the annual report.

A description of the auditor's responsibilities may either be included as a separate section of the auditor's report on the financial statements or set out as a separate statement within the annual report. The APB encourages auditors to include a description of the auditor's responsibilities within the auditor's report on the financial statements. Illustrative examples of auditor's reports containing descriptions of the auditor's responsibilities are given in the most recent version of the APB Bulletin "Auditor's Reports on Financial Statements"[12]. 27

---

[12] At the date of publication of this Bulletin the most recent version was Bulletin 2005/4

28 The content of the statement of the auditor's responsibilities ought to be determined by the auditor regardless of whether it is published as a separate statement, or incorporated into the auditor's report on the financial statements.

29 Appendix 3 to this Bulletin includes illustrative paragraphs that may be included in the auditor's engagement letter to describe the auditor's responsibilities with respect to the company's compliance with the Listing Rules[13]. In practice the auditor tailors the engagement letter to the specific circumstances of the engagement.

Internal control

> C.2.1 **The board should, at least annually, conduct a review of the effectiveness of the group's system of internal controls and should report to shareholders that they have done so. The review should cover all material controls, including financial, operational and compliance controls and risk management systems.**

The auditor's responsibilities with respect to the directors' narrative statement

30 The annual report will contain a narrative statement of how the company has applied Code principle C.2. The Turnbull Guidance recommends that, "In its narrative statement of how the company has applied Code Principle C.2, the board should, as a minimum, disclose that there is an ongoing process for identifying, evaluating and managing the significant risks faced by the company, that it has been in place for the year under review and up to the date of approval of the annual report and accounts, that is regularly reviewed by the board...".[14] The Turnbull Guidance also states that "The annual report and accounts should include such meaningful, high-level information as the board considers necessary to assist shareholders' understanding of the main features of the company's risk management processes and system of internal control, and should not give a misleading impression"[15]. The content of such narrative statements is likely, therefore, to vary widely from company to company.

31 Although the Listing Rules do not require the auditor to review the narrative statement, there are requirements under Auditing Standards for the auditor to read the other information (of which the company's narrative statement forms a part) issued with the audited financial statements and to seek to resolve any apparent misstatements or material inconsistencies with the audited financial statements.

Auditor's review of compliance

32 The Turnbull Guidance[16], recommends that the company discloses a summary of the process the board (and where applicable, its committees) has adopted in reviewing

---

[13] FSA LR 9.8.10R; ISE LR 6.8.9

[14] Paragraph 34 of the Turnbull Guidance.

[15] Paragraph 33 of the Turnbull Guidance

[16] Paragraphs 26-32 and 36 of the Turnbull Guidance.

the effectiveness of the system of internal control. The Turnbull Guidance[17] describes the directors' process for reviewing effectiveness and in particular states[18]: "*The board should define the process to be adopted for its review of the effectiveness of internal control. This should encompass both the scope and frequency of the reports it receives and reviews during the year, and also the process for its annual assessment, such that it will be provided with sound, appropriately documented, support for its statement on internal control in the company's annual report and accounts*".

The objective of the auditor's review of compliance is to assess whether the company's summary of the process the board (and where applicable its committees) has adopted in reviewing the effectiveness of the system of internal control, is both supported by the documentation prepared by or for the directors and appropriately reflects that process. 33

To achieve this objective the auditor, in addition to the procedures outlined in paragraph 16; 34

(a) obtains an understanding, through enquiry of the directors, of the process defined by the board for its review of the effectiveness of all material internal controls and compares that understanding to the statement made by the board in the annual report and accounts;
(b) reviews the documentation prepared by or for the directors to support their statement made in connection with Code provision C.2.1 and assesses whether or not it provides sound support for that statement; and
(c) relates the statement made by the directors to the auditor's knowledge of the company obtained during the audit of the financial statements. As explained in paragraph 36, the scope of the directors' review will be considerably broader in its scope than the knowledge the auditor can be expected to have based on their audit.

The auditor considers whether the directors' statement covers the year under review and the period to the date of approval of the annual report and accounts, as recommended by the Turnbull Guidance[19]. 35

In carrying out the review, the auditor will have regard to the knowledge of the company the auditor has obtained from the audit work. To enable the auditor to perform the audit and express an opinion on the financial statements, the auditor is required by Auditing Standards[20] to obtain an understanding of the entity and its environment, including its internal control, sufficient to identify and assess the risks of material misstatement of the financial statements. Consequently, the auditor's assessment required by Auditing Standards will be considerably narrower in scope than the review performed by the directors for the purpose of reporting on compliance with Code provision C.2.1. 36

The auditor, therefore, is not expected to assess whether all risks and controls have been addressed by the directors or that risks are satisfactorily addressed by internal controls. In order to communicate this fact to users of the annual report, the following sentence is included in the auditor's report on the financial statements. 37

---

[17] *Paragraphs 26-32 of the Turnbull Guidance.*

[18] *Paragraph 27 of the Turnbull Guidance.*

[19] *Paragraph 26 of the Turnbull Guidance.*

[20] *ISA (UK and Ireland) 315, "Obtaining an understanding of the entity and its environment and assessing the risks of material misstatement".*

> "We are not required to consider whether the board's statements on internal control cover all risks and controls, or form an opinion on the effectiveness of the company's corporate governance procedures or its risk and control procedures."

38 However, ISA (UK and Ireland) 260 "Communication of audit matters with those charged with governance" requires, among other things, that the auditor communicates, on a timely basis, to those charged with governance material weaknesses in internal control identified during the audit. A material weakness in internal control is a deficiency in design or operation which could adversely affect the entity's ability to record, process, summarize and report financial and other relevant data so as to result in a material misstatement in the financial statements. A material weakness in control identified by the auditor will be considered by the directors, in the context of the reports they receive and review during the year as part of their overall process for undertaking an annual assessment of the effectiveness of the company's internal control procedures, and it may be considered by them to be a significant failing or weakness as described in the Turnbull Guidance.

39 In view of the obligations placed on directors by the Turnbull Guidance the APB recommends that any material weaknesses in internal control identified by the auditor be reported to those charged with governance as soon as is practicable. The auditor does not wait until the financial statement audit has been completed before reporting such weaknesses. In this way, the directors will be aware of the weaknesses that the auditor has identified and be able to take account of them in making their statements on internal control[21].

Actions taken by the directors to remedy significant failings or weaknesses

40 A revision made to the Turnbull Guidance in October 2005 was to expand the existing recommendation regarding the board's statement on internal control in the annual report in relation to Code provision C2.1. The recommendation was expanded to say that the board should in its statement on internal control, *"confirm that necessary actions have been or are being taken to remedy any significant failings or weaknesses identified from that review"*[22] (The reference to "that review" relates to the board's annual review of the effectiveness of the system of internal control).

41 The auditor's review responsibility with respect to this recommendation includes:
(a) reviewing the documentation prepared by or for the directors supporting their statement made in connection with Code provision C2.1 that discusses those failings or weaknesses, if any, in internal control that they have assessed as "significant" and assessing whether or not it provides sound support for that statement;
(b) discussing with the directors the actions they have already taken, or consider necessary to take, with respect to the identified significant failings or weaknesses; and
(c) relating the statement made by the directors to the auditor's knowledge of the company obtained during the audit of the financial statements.

---

[21] *The auditor has a responsibility under ISA (UK and Ireland) 260 to consider whether there is adequate two-way communication between the auditor and those charged with governance, such that an effective audit can take place. As part of this responsibility, amongst other things, the auditor will need to consider the appropriateness and timeliness of actions taken by those charged with governance in response to the recommendations made by the auditor including those regarding material weaknesses in internal control.*

[22] *Paragraph 36 of the Turnbull Guidance*

42 With respect to 41(c) above, the auditor assesses whether the directors, in making their statement, have taken into consideration the material weaknesses in internal control reported to those charged with governance by the auditor in accordance with ISA (UK and Ireland) 260 (See paragraph 38 above).

43 However, the auditor is not required to assess either the directors' decision as to what constitutes a significant failing or weakness, or whether the actions, taken or to be taken by the directors, will in fact remedy the significant failings or weaknesses identified by the directors. The APB recommends that a statement to this effect be included in the engagement letter (see Appendix 3).

44 If the auditor:

(a) considers that the documentation and discussions do not support the directors' confirmation that necessary actions have been, or are being, taken or
(b) based on its audit findings is aware of material weaknesses in internal control that have not been considered by the directors

it discusses the position with the directors. If the auditor is not satisfied with the directors' explanations it considers the consequences for its opinion (see paragraph 54).

Internal control aspects of problems disclosed in the annual report

45 The Turnbull Guidance[23] also recommends that the board discloses *"the process it has applied to deal with material internal control aspects of any significant problems disclosed in the annual report and accounts"*.

46 This may be a difficult recommendation for directors to satisfy, and for the auditor to review, because what is meant by "significant problems" is not defined and the word "problem" encompasses more than financial matters. A directors' description, for example, of difficulties obtaining raw materials at a remote overseas location may be seen as a significant problem by directors of some companies but not the directors of others. Even when the directors have identified a problem it may not always be clear whether the problem has material internal control aspects. A significant loss-making contract, for example, will necessitate an assessment of whether the problem is attributable to changes in circumstances that could not reasonably have been foreseen as opposed to weaknesses in internal control.

47 The auditor's review responsibility with respect to this recommendation includes:

(a) discussing with the directors the steps the directors have taken to determine what "significant problems" are disclosed in the annual report and accounts; and
(b) assessing whether disclosures made by the board of the processes it has applied to deal with material internal control aspects of any significant problems disclosed in the annual report and accounts appropriately reflect those processes.

48 The auditor is not required to assess whether the processes described by the directors will, in fact, remedy the problem described in the annual report and accounts.

49 If the auditor is aware of a significant problem that is disclosed in the annual report and accounts for which the board has not disclosed the material internal control aspects it discusses the position with the directors of the company.

---

[23] *Paragraph 36 of the Turnbull Guidance.*

50   If the auditor is not able to agree with the directors as to how the matter should be resolved it considers the consequences for its opinion (see paragraph 54).

Failure to conduct a review

51   The Listing Rules[24] require the company to disclose if the board has failed to conduct a review of the effectiveness of internal control. The Turnbull Guidance[25] recommends that where it has not made the required disclosures the board should state that fact and provide an explanation. The auditor considers whether this recommendation is met and whether the explanation is consistent with the auditor's understanding.

Groups of companies

52   The Turnbull Guidance establishes that, for groups of companies, the review of effectiveness should be from the perspective of the group as a whole[26]. Accordingly, the auditor's consideration of the board's description of its process for reviewing the effectiveness of internal control encompasses the group as a whole.

53   Where material joint ventures and associated companies have not been dealt with as part of the group for the purposes of applying the Turnbull Guidance, this fact should be disclosed by the board[27]. The auditor assesses, based on the auditor's knowledge of the group obtained during the audit of the financial statements, whether any material joint ventures or associated companies have not been dealt with and, therefore, if such a disclosure is necessary.

Reporting by exception

54   If the auditor concludes:

(a) that the board's summary of the process it has applied in reviewing the effectiveness of internal control is either not supported by or does not appropriately reflect the auditor's understanding of the process undertaken (paragraphs 32 to 39);
(b) that the documentation and discussions do not support the directors' confirmation that necessary actions have been, or are being taken; (paragraphs 40 to 44);
(c) that the processes disclosed to deal with material internal control aspects of significant problems disclosed in the annual report and accounts do not appropriately reflect the auditor's understanding of the process undertaken (paragraphs 45 to 50);
(d) that no disclosure has been made by the board that it has failed to conduct a review of the effectiveness of internal control (paragraph 51);
(e) where the board discloses that it has not reviewed the effectiveness of internal control, that its explanation is not consistent with the auditor's understanding (paragraph 51); or

[24] *FSA LR 9.8.6R(6)(b); ISE LR 6.8.6(7)(b)*

[25] *Paragraph 37 of the Turnbull Guidance*

[26] *Paragraph 13 of the Turnbull Guidance*

[27] *Paragraph 38 of the Turnbull Guidance*

(f) that no disclosure has been made by the board that a material joint venture or associated company has not been dealt with as part of the group (paragraphs 52 to 53),

they report this in their report on the financial statements.

However, as this does not give rise to a qualified audit opinion on the financial statements the APB recommends that the auditor's comments be included under the heading "Other matter" which would be included in the auditor's report below the auditor's opinion and any emphasis of matter related to the auditor's report on the financial statements as illustrated below:

55

Opinion
[Standard opinion wording for an auditor's report on group (not including parent company) financial statements of a publicly traded company incorporated in Great Britain[28]]

Emphasis of matter
Where applicable any emphasis of matter paragraph relating to the auditor's report on the financial statements.

Other matter
We have reviewed the board's description of its process for reviewing the effectiveness of internal control set out on page x of the annual report. In our opinion the board's comments concerning ... do not appropriately reflect our understanding of the process undertaken by the board because.....

An audit committee of independent non-executive directors

C.3.1 The board should establish an audit committee of at least three, or in the case of smaller companies[29] two, members, who should all be independent non-executive directors. The board should satisfy itself that at least one member of the audit committee has recent and relevant financial experience.

Auditor's review of compliance

When reviewing the company's compliance with this provision of the Combined Code the APB recommends that the auditor performs the following procedures:

56

(a) Checking that the audit committee comprises at least three, or in the case of smaller companies two, members.
(b) Obtaining an understanding of the process adopted by the board for determining whether:
 (i) the members of the audit committee are all independent non-executive directors (see paragraphs 57 to 58); and
 (ii) at least one member of the audit committee has recent and relevant financial experience (see paragraph 59).

---

[28] See Example 7 in Bulletin 2005/4

[29] In the UK a smaller company is one that is below the FTSE 350 throughout the year immediately prior to the reporting year. The Irish Stock Exchange considers a smaller company to be one that is included in the ISEQ Small Cap Index throughout the year immediately prior to the reporting year.

(c) Reviewing evidence such as minutes and other documentation supporting the board's view that the non-executive directors on the audit committee are independent and, where appropriate, have recent and relevant financial experience.

57 Provision A.3.1 of the Combined Code, requires the board to identify in the annual report each non-executive director it considers to be independent. This provision includes guidance on how independence might be interpreted by listing a number of relationships or circumstances that may indicate that a director is not independent[30]. The Code makes clear, however, that notwithstanding such relationships or circumstances the company is entitled to explain why a director is considered independent.

58 It is not the auditor's responsibility to satisfy itself whether directors are properly described as being "independent" non-executives. Nor does the auditor lay down more precise criteria with respect to the meaning of the term "independent" than those set out in the Combined Code. When reviewing the company's compliance with this provision of the Combined Code the APB recommends that the review procedures be limited to establishing that the audit committee is comprised of non-executive directors who are identified in the annual report as being, in the opinion of the board, independent. However, if the auditor doubts whether the directors are properly described as being "independent" non-executives the auditor communicates those concerns to the audit committee and the board of directors.

59 Similarly, it is not the auditor's responsibility to satisfy itself whether the company is correct in concluding that a particular audit committee member has "recent and relevant financial experience". Nor should the auditor lay down more precise criteria with respect to the meaning of the term "recent and relevant financial experience". When reviewing the company's compliance with this provision of the Combined Code the APB recommends that the review procedures be limited to considering the process adopted by the board for determining that at least one member of the audit committee has "recent and relevant financial experience". However, if the auditor doubts whether the company is correct in concluding that a particular audit committee member has "recent and relevant financial experience" the auditor communicates those concerns to the audit committee and the board of directors.[31]

Role and responsibilities of the audit committee[32]

> **C.3.2 The main role and responsibilities of the audit committee should be set out in written terms of reference and should include:**
> - **to monitor the integrity of the financial statements of the company, and any formal announcements relating to the company's financial performance, reviewing significant financial reporting judgements contained in them;**
> - **to review the company's internal financial controls and, unless expressly**

---

[30] *A footnote to A.3.1 explains 'A.2.2 states that the chairman should on appointment meet the independence criteria set out in this provision, but thereafter the test of independence is not appropriate in relation to the chairman'.*

[31] *The Combined Code recommends that the board should satisfy itself that at least one member of the audit committee has recent and relevant financial experience. Where this is not the case there is a need for an explanation such as the board has concluded that the audit committee "collectively" has recent and relevant financial experience.*

[32] *In Ireland Section 42(2) of the Companies (Auditing and Accounting) Act 2003 requires the board of directors to establish an audit committee and sets out its responsibilities.*

> - addressed by a separate board risk committee composed of independent directors, or by the board itself, to review the company's internal control and risk management systems;
> - to monitor and review the effectiveness of the company's internal audit function;
> - to make recommendations to the board, for it to put to the shareholders for their approval in general meeting, in relation to the appointment, re-appointment and removal of the external auditor and to approve the remuneration and terms of engagement of the external auditor;
> - to review and monitor the external auditor's independence and objectivity and the effectiveness of the audit process, taking into consideration relevant UK professional and regulatory requirements;
> - to develop and implement policy on the engagement of the external auditor to supply non-audit services, taking into account relevant ethical guidance regarding the provision of non-audit services by the external audit firm; and to report to the board, identifying any matters in respect of which it considers that action or improvement is needed and making recommendations as to the steps to be taken.

Auditor's review of compliance

60 When reviewing the company's compliance with this provision of the Combined Code the APB recommends that the auditor obtains a copy of the terms of reference of the audit committee and reviews whether the roles and responsibilities of the audit committee described in the terms of reference reflect the recommendations of Code provision C.3.2. It is not the auditor's responsibility to consider whether the audit committee has fulfilled its roles and responsibilities.

Terms of reference of the audit committee

> C.3.3 The terms of reference of the audit committee, including its role and the authority delegated to it by the board, should be made available[23]. A separate section of the annual report should describe the work of the committee in discharging those responsibilities.

Auditor's review of compliance

61 When reviewing the company's compliance with this provision of the Combined Code the APB recommends that the auditor performs the following procedures:

(a) Reviewing whether the terms of reference of the audit committee are included on the company's website or that the terms of reference have been reasonably made available or communicated by another method.
(b) Reviewing whether a description of the work performed by the audit committee in discharging its responsibilities, is included in a separate section of the annual report, and is not materially inconsistent with the information that the auditor has obtained in the course of the audit work on the financial statements.

Arrangements by which company's staff may raise concerns

> C.3.4 The audit committee should review arrangements by which staff of the company may, in confidence, raise concerns about possible improprieties in matters of financial reporting or other matters. The audit committee's

> objective should be to ensure that arrangements are in place for the proportionate and independent investigation of such matters and for appropriate follow-up action.

Auditor's review of compliance

62 When reviewing the company's compliance with this provision of the Combined Code the APB recommends that the auditor performs the following procedures:

(a) Reviewing supporting documentation to determine whether there is evidence that the audit committee has reviewed the arrangements and, if necessary, discussing with members of the audit committee what review procedures they performed.
(b) Reviewing documentation supporting the company's arrangements for the proportionate and independent investigation of concerns raised in confidence by staff relating to possible improprieties in matters of financial reporting or other matters and for appropriate follow-up action. It is not the responsibility of the auditor to consider whether such arrangements will facilitate "proportionate and independent" investigation or "appropriate" follow-up action but the auditor reviews the process by which the audit committee satisfies itself that the recommendation of the Combined Code has been satisfied.

Monitoring and review of the effectiveness of the internal audit activities

> **C.3.5** The audit committee should monitor and review the effectiveness of the internal audit activities. Where there is no internal audit function, the audit committee should consider annually whether there is a need for an internal audit function and make a recommendation to the board, and the reasons for the absence of such a function should be explained in the relevant section of the annual report.

Auditor's review of compliance

63 When reviewing the company's compliance with this provision of the Combined Code the APB recommends that the auditor performs the following procedures:

(a) Where there is an internal audit function discussing with the audit committee chairman and reviewing the supporting documentation to establish that the audit committee has monitored and reviewed the effectiveness of the internal audit activities. It is not the auditor's responsibility to consider whether the internal audit activities are effective.
(b) Where there is no internal audit function, reviewing whether:
  (i) the audit committee has considered whether there is a need for an internal audit function;
  (ii) there is documentation that evidences the audit committee's recommendation to the board;
  (iii) the reasons for the absence of such a function are explained in the relevant section of the annual report. It is not the auditor's responsibility to consider whether the reasons given are appropriate.

Appointment, reappointment and removal of the external auditor

> **C.3.6** The audit committee should have primary responsibility for making a recommendation on the appointment, reappointment and removal of the external auditors. If the board does not accept the audit committee's recommendation, it should include in the annual report, and in any papers recommending appointment or re-appointment, a statement from the audit committee explaining the recommendation and should set out reasons why the board has taken a different position.

Auditor's review of compliance

When reviewing the company's compliance with this provision of the Combined Code the APB recommends that the auditor performs the following procedures: 64

(a) Reviewing documentation, for example inclusion in the terms of reference of the audit committee, which explains that the audit committee has primary responsibility for making a recommendation on the appointment, reappointment and removal of the external auditors.
(b) Reviewing documentation that evidences the audit committee's recommendation to the board.
(c) Where the board has not accepted the audit committee's recommendation, reviewing whether there is included in the annual report and in any papers recommending appointment or re-appointment of the auditors:
   (i) a statement from the audit committee explaining its recommendation; and
   (ii) a statement from the board setting out reasons why the board has taken a different position from that recommended by the audit committee.

Non-audit activities

> **C.3.7** The annual report should explain to shareholders how, if the auditor provides non-audit services, auditor objectivity and independence is safeguarded.

Auditor's review of compliance

When reviewing the company's compliance with this provision of the Combined Code the APB recommends that the auditor establishes whether the annual report includes a statement explaining to shareholders how, if the auditor provides non-audit services, auditor objectivity and independence is safeguarded. 65

The auditor considers the explanation of how auditor objectivity and independence is safeguarded in the context of the information of which they are aware. While it is not the auditor's responsibility to establish that the audit committee has fulfilled its responsibilities as set out in the terms of reference recommended by the Combined Code (to review and monitor the independence and objectivity of the external auditor and to develop and implement policy on the engagement of the external auditor to supply non-audit services taking into account relevant ethical guidance regarding the provision of non-audit services by the external auditor[24]) the auditor will be aware of whether the audit committee has undertaken these responsibilities and: 66

(a) notifies the audit committee and the board of directors if they believe these responsibilities have not been undertaken; and

(b) considers the requirements of Auditing Standards in relation to other information issued with audited financial statements if they believe the explanation is misleading.

67 APB Ethical Standards ("ESs") 1 to 5 set out the integrity, objectivity and independence requirements for auditors in the audit of financial statements. ES1[33] requires the audit engagement partner to ensure that those charged with governance of the audit client are appropriately informed on a timely basis of all significant facts and matters that bear upon the auditors "objectivity and independence". In relation to non-audit services, ES5[34] requires the audit engagement partner to ensure that those charged with governance are informed of any inconsistencies between APB Ethical Standards and the company's policy for the supply of non-audit services by the audit firm and any apparent breach of that policy.

Directors' statement on going concern

> C.1.2 The directors should report that the business is a going concern, with supporting assumptions or qualifications as necessary.

Auditor's review of compliance

68 The Listing Rules[35] require the directors of certain listed companies[36] to include in the annual report and accounts a statement that:

> "the business is a going concern, together with supporting assumptions or qualification as necessary, that has been prepared in accordance with "Going Concern and Financial Reporting: Guidance for directors of listed companies registered in the United Kingdom, published in November 1994[37]".

69 The Listing Rules[38] require a listed company to ensure that the auditor reviews the directors' going concern statement. In order for the auditor to meet the review requirements of this rule the auditor:

(a) assesses the consistency of the directors' going concern statement with the knowledge obtained in the course of the audit of the financial statements. This knowledge will primarily have been obtained in meeting Auditing Standards[39] relating to going concern; and

---

[33] *Paragraph 49*

[34] *Paragraph 35*

[35] *FSA LR 9.8.6R(3); ISE LR 6.8.6R(3)*

[36] *In the case of the FSA the Listing Rule applies to companies incorporated in the United Kingdom and in the case of the ISE the Listing Rule applies to companies incorporated in the Republic of Ireland.*

[37] *Going Concern and Financial Reporting: Guidance for directors of listed companies registered in the UK, ICAEW, November 1994. This guidance can be downloaded from the ICAEW web-site.*

[38] *FSA LR 9.8.10R(1); ISE LR 6.8.9(1)*

[39] *ISA (UK and Ireland) 570, 'The going concern basis in financial statements".*

(b) assesses whether the directors' statement meets the disclosure requirements of the guidance for directors referred to in the Listing Rules[40]. Illustrative suggested disclosures for directors are set out in paragraphs 47 to 54 of that guidance.

The auditor does not assess or report on whether the directors have complied with any other detailed requirements of the guidance for directors. In particular, as the auditor does not express an opinion on the ability of the company to continue in operational existence they do not undertake additional procedures that would support such an opinion.

Paragraph 49 of the guidance for directors (dealing with going concern) provides the following illustrative example of the basic disclosure that directors make when the going concern presumption is appropriate:

> "After making enquiries, the directors have a reasonable expectation that the company has adequate resources to continue in operational existence for the foreseeable future. For this reason, they continue to adopt the going concern basis in preparing the accounts".

It is particularly important that the directors' statement on going concern is not inconsistent with any disclosures regarding going concern in either the financial statements or the auditor's report thereon. Where going concern matters are discussed in the financial statements one method of achieving consistency is for the directors' statement to include a cross reference to the relevant note to the financial statements.

Reporting requirements derived from other Auditing Standards

Auditing Standards set out the auditor's responsibilities in relation to other information in documents containing audited financial statements. These responsibilities extend to the Combined Code disclosures where there is either a material misstatement of fact or a material inconsistency with the audited financial statements. Application of these Standards requires that:

(a) Where the auditor identifies a material inconsistency between the audited financial statements and the Combined Code disclosures the auditor determines whether the audited financial statements or the Combined Code disclosures need to be amended and seeks to resolve the matter through discussion with those charged with governance:
   (i) If an amendment is necessary in the audited financial statements and the entity refuses to make the amendment, the auditor expresses a qualified or adverse opinion on the financial statements.
   (ii) If an amendment is necessary in the Combined Code disclosures and the entity refuses to make the amendment, the auditor considers including in the auditor's report an emphasis of matter paragraph describing the material inconsistency[41] or taking other actions.
(b) Where the auditor identifies a material misstatement of fact in the Combined Code disclosures the auditor discusses the matter with those charged with governance. Where, after discussion, the auditor still considers that there is an apparent misstatement of fact, the auditor requests those charged with

---

[40] FSA 9.8.6R(3); ISE LR 6.8.6(3)

[41] As explained in paragraph 55, the APB recommends that the auditor's comments be included under the heading 'other matter' which would be included in the auditor's report below the auditor's opinion.

governance to consult with a qualified third party, such as the entity's legal counsel, and considers the advice received.

If the auditor concludes that an amendment is necessary in the Combined Code disclosures, which the entity refuses to correct, the auditor considers taking further appropriate action and considers including in the auditor's report an emphasis of matter paragraph describing the material misstatement.

(1) LR 9.8.6R (3) (statement by the directors that the business is a going concern); and

(2) the parts of the statement required by LR9.8.6R (6) (corporate governance) that relate to the following provisions of the *Combined Code:*
   a. C1.1;
   b. C.2.1; and
   c. C3.1 to C3.7

Appendix 1 – Extracts from the FSA Listing Rules[42]

Additional information

LR 9.8.6R   In the case of a *listed company* incorporated in the *United Kingdom*, the following additional items must be included in its annual report and accounts:

(3) a statement made by the *directors* that the business is a going concern, together with supporting assumptions or qualifications as necessary, that has been prepared in accordance with "Going Concern and Financial Reporting: Guidance for Directors of listed companies registered in the United Kingdom", published in November 1994;

(5) a statement of how the *listed company* has applied the principles set out in Section 1 of the *Combined Code*, in a manner that would enable shareholders to evaluate how the principles have been applied;

(6) a statement as to whether the *listed company* has;
  (a) complied throughout the accounting period with all relevant provisions set out in Section 1 of the *Combined Code*; or
  (b) not complied throughout the accounting period with all relevant provisions set out in Section 1 of the *Combined Code* and if so, setting out:
      i. those provisions, if any, it has not complied with;
      ii. in the case of provisions whose requirements are of a continuing nature, the period within which, if any, it did not comply with some or all of those provisions; and
      iii. the *company's* reasons for non-compliance; ...

LR 9.8.7R   An *overseas company* with a *primary listing* must disclose in its annual report and accounts:

(1) whether or not it complies with the corporate governance regime of its country of incorporation;

(2) the significant ways in which its actual corporate governance practices differ from those set out in the *Combined Code*; and

(3) the unexpired term of the service contract of any *director* proposed for election or re-election at the forthcoming annual general meeting and, if any *director* for election or re-election does not have a service contract, a statement to that effect.

Auditors report

LR 9.8.10R   A *listed company* must ensure that the auditors review each of the following before the annual report is published:

---

[42] See Appendix 2 for references to equivalent Irish Stock Exchange Listing Rules

As we have agreed we will attend the meeting of the audit committee [full board] at which the annual report and accounts, including the going concern statement and the statement of compliance, are considered and approved for submission to the board of directors.

Internal control

With respect to Code Provision C.2.1, our work will be restricted to:

(a) assessing, based on enquiry of the directors, the supporting documentation prepared by or for the directors and our knowledge obtained during the audit of the financial statements, whether the company's summary of the process the board (and where applicable its committees) has adopted in reviewing the effectiveness of internal control appropriately reflects that process; and
(b) assessing whether the company's disclosures of the processes it has applied to deal with material internal control aspects of any significant problems disclosed in the annual report and accounts appropriately reflects those processes.

As our work is not designed to:

(a) consider whether the board's statements on internal control cover all risks and controls; or
(b) form an opinion on the effectiveness of the company's risk and control procedures; or
(c) assess either the directors' decision as to what constitutes a significant failing or weakness, or whether the actions, taken or to be taken, will in fact remedy the significant failings or weaknesses identified by the directors,

our work on internal control will not be sufficient to enable us to express any assurance as to whether or not your internal controls are effective. In addition our financial statement audit should not be relied upon to draw to your attention matters that may be relevant to your consideration as to whether or not your system of internal control is effective.

Going concern

With respect to the company's going concern statement our work will be restricted to a consideration of whether the statement provides the disclosures required by [LR 9.8.6R (3)] [LR 6.8.6 (3)] and is not inconsistent with the information of which we are aware from our audit work on the financial statements. We will not carry out the additional work necessary to give an opinion that the company has adequate resources to continue in operational existence.

Statement of auditor's responsibilities

Code provision C.1.1 recommends, among other things, that there should be a statement in the annual report about the auditor's reporting responsibilities. As we have agreed we will incorporate a description of our reporting responsibilities in our audit report on the financial statements.

[Bulletin 2006/6]
Auditor's reports on Financial Statements in the United Kingdom

Contents

	Page
Introduction	2
Change to the Companies Act 1985	3
International Financial Reporting Standards	3
Statement of directors' responsibilities	5
Additional example auditor's reports	5

Appendix 1 – Unmodified auditor's reports on financial statements
Explanatory note regarding the Appendix 7
Navigation aids to the 15 examples of unmodified auditor's reports on financial statements .... 8 – 9
15 examples of unmodified auditor's reports .... 10 – 50

Appendix 2 – Modified auditor's reports on financial statements (excluding going concern issues)
Explanatory note regarding the Appendix 51
Navigation aid to the 7 examples of modified auditor's reports (excluding going concern issues) 52
7 examples of modified auditor's reports (excluding going concern issues)
.... 53 – 63

Appendix 3 – Modified auditor's reports on financial statements arising from going concern issues
Explanatory note regarding the Appendix 64
Navigation aid to the 8 examples of modified auditor's reports arising from going concern issues 65
8 examples of modified auditor's reports arising from going concern issues
.... 66 – 79

Appendix 4 – Extracts from an auditor's report with a modified opinion on the directors' report 80

Appendix 5 – Illustrative statement of directors' responsibilities 81

Note: Readers are advised to use the navigation aids (shaded above) to assist in locating particular example auditor's reports.

Editor's note: This Bulletin should only be used for periods commenced before 6 April 2008.

Introduction

The purpose of this Bulletin is to provide illustrative examples of: 1

(a) unmodified auditor's reports for audits of financial statements of companies incorporated in Great Britain or Northern Ireland for periods commencing on or after 1 April 2005 (see Appendix 1);
(b) modified auditor's reports (excluding going concern issues) (see Appendices 2 and 4); and
(c) modified auditor's reports arising from going concern issues (see Appendix 3).

For the purposes of this Bulletin companies are classified as either: 2

(a) "publicly traded companies" – defined as "those whose securities are admitted to trading on a regulated market in any Member State in the European Union"; or
(b) "non-publicly traded companies" – defined as "those who do not have any securities that are admitted to trading on a regulated market in any Member State in the European Union" (EU).

This is the second edition of the Bulletin referred to in various paragraphs of ISA (UK and Ireland) 700 "The auditor's report on financial statements". It supersedes Bulletin 2005/4. 3

The example auditor's reports included in the Bulletin take account of: 4

(a) changes made to the Companies Act 1985 (CA 1985) and the Companies (Northern Ireland) Order 1986 to require the auditor to give a positive opinion as to the consistency of the directors' report with the financial statements[1] (see paragraphs 6 and 7);
(b) the revised standard formulation for expressing compliance with the financial reporting framework applicable to companies subject to Regulation 1606/2002/ EC ("IAS Regulation"). This formulation was proposed by the European Commission to the meeting of The Accounting Regulatory Committee (ARC) held on 30 November 2005. As the revised formulation was determined after the publication of Bulletin 2005/4 the wording differs slightly from that used in the example auditor's reports in that Bulletin (see paragraphs 8 and 9); and
(c) changes made to certain of the example auditor's reports in order to conform with the presentation of the other reports.

The Bulletin does not address: 5

(a) the changes to the auditor's report and the directors' responsibility statement that may be necessary when the Companies Bill is enacted;
(b) the changes to the structure of the auditor's report contemplated by ISA 700 (Revised). The APB has concluded that the revision of ISA (UK and Ireland) 700 should be deferred until progress has been made in resolving the following issues:
 • the finalisation of the Companies Bill which will impact the responsibilities of auditors and directors.
 • whether the revised ISA 700 will be approved for adoption in the EU.
 • finalisation of the exposure drafts of ISAs 705 and 706 that address modifications to the auditor's report.

---

[1] This subject is dealt with in International Standard on Auditing (ISA) (UK and Ireland) 720 (Revised) Section B – "The auditor's statutory reporting responsibility in relation to directors' reports.

Change to the Companies Act 1985

6   In 2005 Statutory Instrument 2005 No. 1011 "The Companies Act 1985 (Operating and Financial Review and Directors' Report etc)) Regulations 2005" amended the CA 1985 so that the auditor must give a positive opinion as to the consistency of the directors' report with the financial statements. This regulation applies to financial years beginning on or after 1 April 2005.

7   A similar change has been made with respect to companies incorporated in Northern Ireland by Statutory Rule 2005 No. 61 "The Companies (1986 Order) (Operating and Financial Review and Directors' Report etc) Regulations (Northern Ireland) 2005. This regulation similarly applies to financial years beginning on or after 1 April 2005.

International Financial Reporting Standards

Reference to the accounting framework in the auditor's report

8   As the APB supports the ARC formulation discussed in paragraph 4(b) it takes the view that the accounting framework used by companies adopting IFRSs as adopted by the EU should be referred to in the auditor's opinion in the following terms:

> *"true and fair view, in accordance with IFRSs as adopted by the European Union".*

The example auditor's reports included in the Appendices have been prepared on this basis. As explained in paragraph 4(b) this wording differs slightly from that used in Bulletin 2005/4.

9   Many companies will be in a position of complying with both IFRSs as issued by the IASB and "IFRSs as adopted by the European Union", and may request the auditor to express an opinion in terms of "true and fair view, in accordance with IFRSs". In these circumstances the APB believes that it is preferable for the auditor to state a second separate opinion with regards to IFRSs as issued by the IASB in order to avoid confusing readers of the auditor's report, and to leave intact the opinion required by law on compliance with IFRSs as adopted by the European Union. To accomplish this the second opinion is clearly separated from the opinion required by CA 1985 by use of an appropriate heading. Where applicable, the example auditor's reports set out in Appendix 1 illustrate this point.

Different financial reporting frameworks used for group and parent company financial statements

10   A significant development arising from the use of IFRSs as adopted by the EU, as the financial reporting framework for group financial statements, is that group and parent company financial statements may be prepared in accordance with different financial reporting frameworks.

11   The example unmodified reports in Appendix 1 illustrate, among other things, the following scenarios for auditor's reports on the group and parent company financial statements of publicly traded companies:

> IFRSs as adopted by the EU used for group financial statements (required for publicly traded companies) and either:
> i) IFRSs as adopted by the EU used for parent company financial statements; or
> ii) UK GAAP used for parent company financial statements.

In such instances, companies may choose to present the financial statements of the group and the parent company in separate sections of the annual report and in such circumstances separate auditor's reports might be provided[2]. Appendix 1 includes example auditor's reports for situations where the group and parent company financial statements are presented separately or together (see also paragraph 14 below).

Where separate auditor's reports are provided on the group and parent company financial statements the illustrative examples assume that: 12

(a) the auditor's responsibilities with respect to the Corporate Governance Statement are described in the auditor's report on the group financial statements; and
(b) the Directors Remuneration Report is reported on in the auditor's report on the parent company financial statements[3]

However, other approaches may be adopted.

Exemption for presentation of parent company profit and loss account

Bulletin 2005/3 discusses the exemption in Section 230 CA 1985,[4] which allows a parent company not to publish its profit and loss account and certain related information. Where advantage has been taken of the Section 230 exemption and the parent company financial statements have been prepared in accordance with "IFRSs as adopted by the European Union" the financial reporting framework is described in the auditor's report as: 13

> "true and fair view, in accordance with IFRSs as adopted by the European Union and as applied in accordance with the provisions of the Companies Act 1985".

14

Where the group and parent company financial statements are both prepared in accordance with "IFRSs as adopted by the European Union" it is likely that issuers may wish to present those financial statements separately so that the Section 230 exemption can be utilised without giving rise to, what might be considered to be, a modified auditor's report on the group financial statements. This is illustrated in example reports 11 and 12 in Appendix 1.

The example unmodified reports in Appendix 1 illustrate the impact of the Section 230 exemption and the company's decision whether or not to present the group and parent company financial statements and auditor's reports separately in the annual report. 15

[2] *The Companies Act 1985 does not require the directors to sign the group balance sheet and thereby evidence their approval of it. Where separate financial statements are presented the auditor obtains evidence of the directors' approval of the group financial statements before signing the auditor's report on those financial statements.*

[3] *In the Directors' Remuneration Report the information subject to audit relates to each person who has served as a director of the company.*

[4] *Article 238 of the Companies (Northern Ireland) Order 1986.*

Statement of directors' responsibilities

16 Appendix 5 is an illustrative example of a statement of directors' responsibilities for a non-publicly traded company preparing its parent company financial statements under UK GAAP. The APB has not prepared an illustrative example of a statement of directors' responsibilities for a publicly traded company as the directors' responsibilities, which are in part dependent on the particular regulatory environment, will vary dependent on the rules of the market on which its securities are admitted to trading.

Additional example auditor's reports

17 Three additional example auditor's reports have been included in this edition of the Bulletin. These examples are:

(a) An unmodified auditor's report for a publicly traded company that does not prepare group accounts and prepares financial statements in accordance with IFRSs as adopted by the European Union (ie a publicly traded company having no subsidiaries). (Example 14 in Appendix 1)

(b) An unmodified auditor's report for a publicly traded company that does not prepare group accounts and prepares financial statements in accordance with UK GAAP (ie a publicly traded company having no subsidiaries). (Example 15 in Appendix 1)

(c) An extract from an auditor's report with a modified opinion on the directors' report. (Appendix 4)

18 The numbering of examples provided in Appendices to the previous edition of this Bulletin has been retained.

Appendix 1 – Unmodified auditor's reports on financial statements

This Appendix contains updated examples of unmodified auditor's reports for:

- *Non-publicly traded companies incorporated in Great Britain (example reports 1 - 4); and*
- *Publicly traded companies incorporated in Great Britain (example reports 5 - 15)*

The example auditor's reports take into account the following factors illustrated in the navigation aids on pages 8 and 9:

- *Whether the company prepares group financial statements;*
- *Whether the financial statements are prepared using "IFRSs as adopted by the European Union";*
- *Whether the group financial statements comply with both "IFRSs as adopted by the European Union" and IFRSs as issued by the International Accounting Standards Board;*
- *Whether the parent company financial statements are prepared using "IFRSs as adopted by the European Union";*
- *Whether the Section 230 exemption from presenting the parent company profit and loss account or income statement has been taken;*
- *Whether group and parent company financial statements are presented separately (i.e. two separate auditor's reports).*

Application to Northern Ireland

The example auditor's reports can be used with respect to companies incorporated in Northern Ireland subject to changing references to the "Companies Act 1985" to references to the "Companies (Northern Ireland) Order 1986".

In Northern Ireland, the requirement for a Directors' Remuneration Report was introduced in 2005 by Statutory Rule 2005 No. 56 "The Directors' Remuneration Report Regulations (Northern Ireland) 2005". This statutory rule came into operation on 30th March 2005 and is, therefore, effective for financial years commencing on or after 1 April 2005.

Directors' Remuneration Report

The provisions of CA 1985, and the Companies (Northern Ireland) Order 1986, relating to the Directors Remuneration Report apply to "quoted companies". The definition of a quoted company differs from that of a publicly traded company. For the purposes of the examples it is assumed that non-publicly traded companies are not quoted companies and that publicly traded companies are quoted companies.

Navigation aid (1) to the examples of unmodified auditor's reports on financial statements where the company does not prepare group accounts

```
Is the company publicly traded?
    │
    ├── YES ──► Are the accounts prepared under IFRSs as adopted by the EU?
    │                   │
    │                   ├── YES ──► [15]
    │                   │
    │                   └── NO ───► [14]
    │
    └── NO ───► Are the accounts prepared under UK GAAP?
                        │
                        ├── NO ───► Example reports not provided
                        │
                        └── YES ──► Does the company prepare accounts under the FRSSE?
                                            │
                                            ├── NO ───► Is there surround information to the accounts other than the directors' report?
                                            │                   │
                                            │                   ├── YES ──► [3]
                                            │                   │
                                            │                   └── NO ───► [2]
                                            │
                                            └── YES ──► [1]
```

Navigation aid (2) to the examples of unmodified auditor's reports on financial statements where the company prepares group accounts

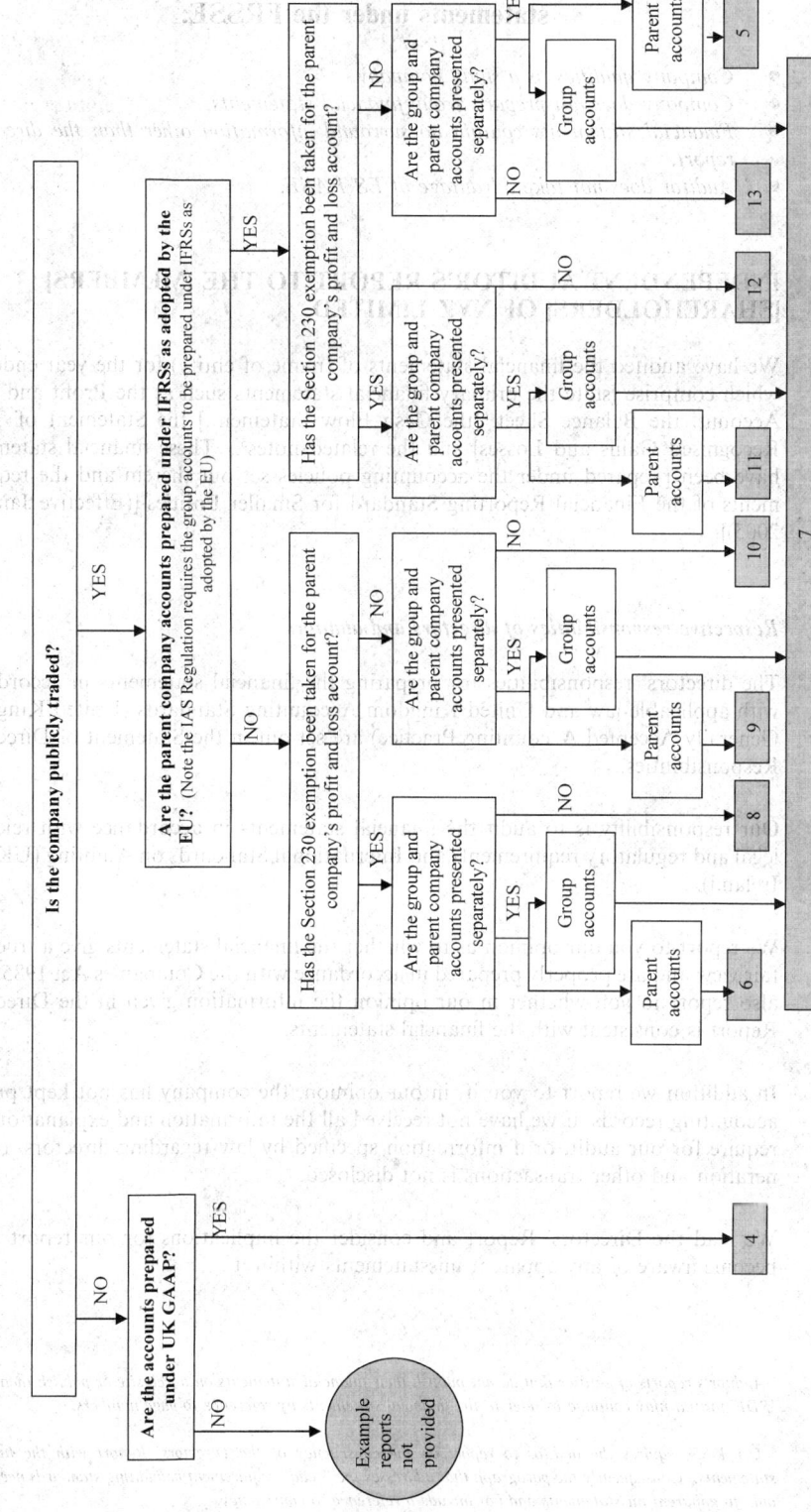

Example 1 – Non-publicly traded company preparing financial statements under the FRSSE:

- Company qualifies as a small company.
- Company does not prepare group financial statements.
- Financial statements contain no surround information other than the directors' report.
- Auditor does not take advantage of ES PASE.

INDEPENDENT AUDITOR'S REPORT TO THE [MEMBERS] [SHAREHOLDERS] OF XYZ LIMITED

We have audited the financial statements of (name of entity) for the year ended ... which comprise [state the primary financial statements such as the Profit and Loss Account, the Balance Sheet, [the Cash Flow Statement,] the Statement of Total Recognised Gains and Losses] and the related notes[5]. These financial statements have been prepared under the accounting policies set out therein and the requirements of the Financial Reporting Standard for Smaller Entities [(Effective January 2005)].

Respective responsibilities of directors and auditors

The directors' responsibilities for preparing the financial statements in accordance with applicable law and United Kingdom Accounting Standards (United Kingdom Generally Accepted Accounting Practice) are set out in the Statement of Directors' Responsibilities.

Our responsibility is to audit the financial statements in accordance with relevant legal and regulatory requirements and International Standards on Auditing (UK and Ireland).

We report to you our opinion as to whether the financial statements give a true and fair view and are properly prepared in accordance with the Companies Act 1985. We also report to you whether in our opinion the information given in the Directors' Report is consistent with the financial statements.

In addition we report to you if, in our opinion, the company has not kept proper accounting records, if we have not received all the information and explanations we require for our audit, or if information specified by law regarding directors' remuneration and other transactions is not disclosed.

We read the Directors' Report and consider the implications for our report if we become aware of any apparent misstatements within it[6].

---

[5] Auditor's reports of entities that do not publish their financial statements on a web site or publish them using 'PDF' format may continue to refer to the financial statements by reference to page numbers.

[6] CA 1985 requires the auditor to report on the consistency of the Directors' Report with the financial statements. Consequently the paragraph that addresses the "read" requirement in auditing standards need refer only to apparent misstatements and not include a reference to consistency.

Basis of audit opinion

We conducted our audit in accordance with International Standards on Auditing (UK and Ireland) issued by the Auditing Practices Board. An audit includes examination, on a test basis, of evidence relevant to the amounts and disclosures in the financial statements. It also includes an assessment of the significant estimates and judgments made by the directors in the preparation of the financial statements, and of whether the accounting policies are appropriate to the company's circumstances, consistently applied and adequately disclosed.

We planned and performed our audit so as to obtain all the information and explanations which we considered necessary in order to provide us with sufficient evidence to give reasonable assurance that the financial statements are free from material misstatement, whether caused by fraud or other irregularity or error. In forming our opinion we also evaluated the overall adequacy of the presentation of information in the financial statements.

Opinion

In our opinion:

- the financial statements give a true and fair view, in accordance with United Kingdom Generally Accepted Accounting Practice applicable to Smaller Entities, of the state of the company's affairs as at .... and of its profit [loss] for the year then ended;
- the financial statements have been properly prepared in accordance with the Companies Act 1985; and
- the information given in the Directors' Report is consistent with the financial statements.

Registered auditors   *Address*
Date

Example 2 – Non-publicly traded company – Auditor's report on individual company financial statements:

- Company does not prepare group financial statements.
- Company does not meet the Companies Act definition of a quoted company.
- UK GAAP used for individual company financial statements.
- Financial statements contain no surround information other than the directors' report.

INDEPENDENT AUDITOR'S REPORT TO THE [MEMBERS] [SHAREHOLDERS] OF XYZ LIMITED

We have audited the financial statements of (name of entity) for the year ended ... which comprise [state the primary financial statements such as the Profit and Loss Account, the Balance Sheet, the Cash Flow Statement, the Statement of Total Recognised Gains and Losses] and the related notes[7]. These financial statements have been prepared under the accounting policies set out therein.

Respective responsibilities of directors and auditors

The directors' responsibilities for preparing the financial statements in accordance with applicable law and United Kingdom Accounting Standards (United Kingdom Generally Accepted Accounting Practice) are set out in the Statement of Directors' Responsibilities.

Our responsibility is to audit the financial statements in accordance with relevant legal and regulatory requirements and International Standards on Auditing (UK and Ireland).

We report to you our opinion as to whether the financial statements give a true and fair view and are properly prepared in accordance with the Companies Act 1985. We also report to you whether in our opinion the information given in the Directors' Report is consistent with the financial statements.

In addition we report to you if, in our opinion, the company has not kept proper accounting records, if we have not received all the information and explanations we require for our audit, or if information specified by law regarding directors' remuneration and other transactions is not disclosed.

We read the Directors' Report and consider the implications for our report if we become aware of any apparent misstatements within it[8].

Basis of audit opinion

We conducted our audit in accordance with International Standards on Auditing (UK and Ireland) issued by the Auditing Practices Board. An audit includes examination, on a test basis, of evidence relevant to the amounts and disclosures in

---

[7] Auditor's reports of entities that do not publish their financial statements on a web site or publish them using 'PDF' format may continue to refer to the financial statements by reference to page numbers.

[8] CA 1985 requires the auditor to report on the consistency of the Directors' Report with the financial statements. Consequently the paragraph that addresses the "read" requirement in auditing standards need refer only to apparent misstatements and not include a reference to consistency.

the financial statements. It also includes an assessment of the significant estimates and judgments made by the directors in the preparation of the financial statements, and of whether the accounting policies are appropriate to the company's circumstances, consistently applied and adequately disclosed.

We planned and performed our audit so as to obtain all the information and explanations which we considered necessary in order to provide us with sufficient evidence to give reasonable assurance that the financial statements are free from material misstatement, whether caused by fraud or other irregularity or error. In forming our opinion we also evaluated the overall adequacy of the presentation of information in the financial statements.

Opinion

In our opinion:
- the financial statements give a true and fair view, in accordance with United Kingdom Generally Accepted Accounting Practice, of the state of the company's affairs as at .... and of its profit [loss] for the year then ended;
- the financial statements have been properly prepared in accordance with the Companies Act 1985; and
- the information given in the Directors' Report is consistent with the financial statements.

Registered auditors *Address*
Date

Example 3 – Non-publicly traded company – Auditor's report on individual company financial statements:

- Company does not prepare group financial statements.
- Company does not meet the Companies Act definition of a quoted company.
- UK GAAP used for individual company financial statements.
- Financial statements contain surround information other than the directors' report.

INDEPENDENT AUDITOR'S REPORT TO THE [MEMBERS] [SHAREHOLDERS] OF XYZ LIMITED

We have audited the financial statements of (name of entity) for the year ended ... which comprise [state the primary financial statements such as the Profit and Loss Account, the Balance Sheet, the Cash Flow Statement, the Statement of Total Recognised Gains and Losses] and the related notes[9]. These financial statements have been prepared under the accounting policies set out therein.

Respective responsibilities of directors and auditors

The directors' responsibilities for preparing the Annual Report and the financial statements in accordance with applicable law and United Kingdom Accounting Standards (United Kingdom Generally Accepted Accounting Practice) are set out in the Statement of Directors' Responsibilities.

Our responsibility is to audit the financial statements in accordance with relevant legal and regulatory requirements and International Standards on Auditing (UK and Ireland).

We report to you our opinion as to whether the financial statements give a true and fair view and are properly prepared in accordance with the Companies Act 1985. We also report to you whether in our opinion the information given in the Directors' Report is consistent with the financial statements. [The information given in the Directors' Report includes that specific information presented in the Operating and Financial Review that is cross referred from the Business Review section of the Directors' Report.][10]

In addition we report to you if, in our opinion, the company has not kept proper accounting records, if we have not received all the information and explanations we require for our audit, or if information specified by law regarding directors' remuneration and other transactions is not disclosed.

We read other information contained in the Annual Report, and consider whether it is consistent with the audited financial statements. This other information comprises only [the Directors' Report, the Chairman's Statement and the Operating and Financial Review][11]. We consider the implications for our report if we become aware

---

[9] *Auditor's reports of entities that do not publish their financial statements on a web site or publish them using 'PDF' format may continue to refer to the financial statements by reference to page numbers.*

[10] *Include and tailor as necessary to clarify the information covered by the auditor's opinion.*

[11] *The other information that is 'read' is the content of the printed Annual Report other than the financial statements. The description of the information that has been read is tailored to reflect the terms used in the Annual Report.*

of any apparent misstatements or material inconsistencies with the financial statements. Our responsibilities do not extend to any other information.

Basis of audit opinion

We conducted our audit in accordance with International Standards on Auditing (UK and Ireland) issued by the Auditing Practices Board. An audit includes examination, on a test basis, of evidence relevant to the amounts and disclosures in the financial statements. It also includes an assessment of the significant estimates and judgments made by the directors in the preparation of the financial statements, and of whether the accounting policies are appropriate to the company's circumstances, consistently applied and adequately disclosed.

We planned and performed our audit so as to obtain all the information and explanations which we considered necessary in order to provide us with sufficient evidence to give reasonable assurance that the financial statements are free from material misstatement, whether caused by fraud or other irregularity or error. In forming our opinion we also evaluated the overall adequacy of the presentation of information in the financial statements.

Opinion

In our opinion:
- the financial statements give a true and fair view, in accordance with United Kingdom Generally Accepted Accounting Practice, of the state of the company's affairs as at .... and of its profit [loss] for the year then ended;
- the financial statements have been properly prepared in accordance with the Companies Act 1985; and
- the information given in the Directors' Report is consistent with the financial statements.

Registered auditors   *Address*
Date

Example 4 – Non-publicly traded company – Auditor's report on group and parent company financial statements:

- Group and parent company financial statements not presented separately.
- Company prepares group financial statements.
- Company does not meet the Companies Act definition of a quoted company.
- UK GAAP used for group and parent company financial statements.
- Section 230 exemption taken for parent company's own profit and loss account.

INDEPENDENT AUDITOR'S REPORT TO THE [MEMBERS] [SHAREHOLDERS] OF XYZ LIMITED

We have audited the group and parent company financial statements (the "financial statements") of (name of entity) for the year ended ... which comprise [state the primary financial statements such as the Group Profit and Loss Account, the Group and Company Balance Sheets, the Group Cash Flow Statement, the Group Statement of Total Recognised Gains and Losses] and the related notes[12]. These financial statements have been prepared under the accounting policies set out therein.

Respective responsibilities of directors and auditors

The directors' responsibilities for preparing the Annual Report and the financial statements in accordance with applicable law and United Kingdom Accounting Standards (United Kingdom Generally Accepted Accounting Practice) are set out in the Statement of Directors' Responsibilities.

Our responsibility is to audit the financial statements in accordance with relevant legal and regulatory requirements and International Standards on Auditing (UK and Ireland).

We report to you our opinion as to whether the financial statements give a true and fair view and are properly prepared in accordance with the Companies Act 1985. We also report to you whether in our opinion the information given in the Directors' Report is consistent with the financial statements. [The information given in the Directors' Report includes that specific information presented in the Operating and Financial Review that is cross referred from the Business Review section of the Directors' Report.][13]

In addition we report to you if, in our opinion, the company has not kept proper accounting records, if we have not received all the information and explanations we require for our audit, or if information specified by law regarding directors' remuneration and other transactions is not disclosed.

We read other information contained in the Annual Report, and consider whether it is consistent with the audited financial statements. This other information comprises only [the Directors' Report, the Chairman's Statement and the Operating and

---

[12] Auditor's reports of entities that do not publish their financial statements on a web site or publish them using 'PDF' format may continue to refer to the financial statements by reference to page numbers.

[13] Include and tailor as necessary to clarify the information covered by the auditor's opinion.

Financial Review]¹⁴. We consider the implications for our report if we become aware of any apparent misstatements or material inconsistencies with the financial statements. Our responsibilities do not extend to any other information.

Basis of audit opinion

We conducted our audit in accordance with International Standards on Auditing (UK and Ireland) issued by the Auditing Practices Board. An audit includes examination, on a test basis, of evidence relevant to the amounts and disclosures in the financial statements. It also includes an assessment of the significant estimates and judgments made by the directors in the preparation of the financial statements, and of whether the accounting policies are appropriate to the group's and company's circumstances, consistently applied and adequately disclosed.

We planned and performed our audit so as to obtain all the information and explanations which we considered necessary in order to provide us with sufficient evidence to give reasonable assurance that the financial statements are free from material misstatement, whether caused by fraud or other irregularity or error. In forming our opinion we also evaluated the overall adequacy of the presentation of information in the financial statements.

Opinion

In our opinion:

- the financial statements give a true and fair view, in accordance with United Kingdom Generally Accepted Accounting Practice, of the state of the group's and the parent company's affairs as at .... and of the group's profit[loss] for the year then ended;
- the financial statements have been properly prepared in accordance with the Companies Act 1985; and
- the information given in the Directors' Report is consistent with the financial statements.

Registered auditors   *Address*
Date

---

[14] *The other information that is 'read' is the content of the printed Annual Report other than the financial statements. The description of the information that has been read is tailored to reflect the terms used in the Annual Report.*

Example 5 – Publicly traded company – Auditor's report on parent company financial statements:

- Group and parent company financial statements presented separately.
- IFRSs as adopted by the European Union used for group and parent company financial statements.
- Company does meet the Companies Act definition of a quoted company.
- Section 230 exemption not taken for parent company's own income statement.
- Corporate governance statement reported on in the report on the group financial statements.
- Directors' Remuneration Report reported on in the report on the parent company financial statements.

INDEPENDENT AUDITOR'S REPORT TO THE [MEMBERS] [SHAREHOLDERS] OF XYZ PLC

We have audited the parent company financial statements of (name of entity) for the year ended ... which comprise [state the primary financial statements such as the Income Statement, the Balance Sheet, the Cash Flow Statement, the Statement of Changes in Equity/Statement of Recognised Income and Expense] and the related notes[15]. These parent company financial statements have been prepared under the accounting policies set out therein. We have also audited the information in the Directors' Remuneration Report that is described as having been audited.[16]

We have reported separately on the group financial statements of (name of entity) for the year ended .... [That report is modified by the inclusion of an emphasis of matter] [The opinion in that report is (qualified)/(an adverse opinion)/(a disclaimer of opinion)].

Respective responsibilities of directors and auditors

The directors' responsibilities for preparing the Annual Report, the Directors' Remuneration Report and the parent company financial statements in accordance with applicable law and International Financial Reporting Standards (IFRSs) as adopted by the European Union are set out in the Statement of Directors' Responsibilities.

Our responsibility is to audit the parent company financial statements and the part of the Directors' Remuneration Report to be audited in accordance with relevant legal and regulatory requirements and International Standards on Auditing (UK and Ireland).

We report to you our opinion as to whether the parent company financial statements give a true and fair view and whether the parent company financial statements and the part of the Directors' Remuneration Report to be audited have been properly prepared in accordance with the Companies Act 1985. We also report to you whether in our opinion the information given in the Directors' Report is consistent with the parent company financial statements. [The information given in the

---

[15] Auditor's reports of entities that do not publish their financial statements on a web site or publish them using 'PDF' format may continue to refer to the financial statements by reference to page numbers.

[16] Part 3 of Schedule 7A to the Companies Act 1985 sets out the information in the Directors' Remuneration Report that is subject to audit. Companies should describe clearly which disclosures within the Directors' Report have been audited.

Directors' Report includes that specific information presented in the Operating and Financial Review that is cross referred from the Business Review section of the Directors' Report.][17]

In addition we report to you if, in our opinion, the company has not kept proper accounting records, if we have not received all the information and explanations we require for our audit, or if information specified by law regarding directors' remuneration and other transactions is not disclosed.

We read other information contained in the Annual Report and consider whether it is consistent with the audited parent company financial statements. The other information comprises only [the Directors' Report, the unaudited part of the Directors' Remuneration Report, the Chairman's Statement and the Operating and Financial Review][18]. We consider the implications for our report if we become aware of any apparent misstatements or material inconsistencies with the parent company financial statements. Our responsibilities do not extend to any other information.

Basis of audit opinion

We conducted our audit in accordance with International Standards on Auditing (UK and Ireland) issued by the Auditing Practices Board. An audit includes examination, on a test basis, of evidence relevant to the amounts and disclosures in the parent company financial statements and the part of the Directors' Remuneration Report to be audited. It also includes an assessment of the significant estimates and judgments made by the directors in the preparation of the parent company financial statements, and of whether the accounting policies are appropriate to the company's circumstances, consistently applied and adequately disclosed.

We planned and performed our audit so as to obtain all the information and explanations which we considered necessary in order to provide us with sufficient evidence to give reasonable assurance that the parent company financial statements and the part of the Directors' Remuneration Report to be audited are free from material misstatement, whether caused by fraud or other irregularity or error. In forming our opinion we also evaluated the overall adequacy of the presentation of information in the parent company financial statements and the part of the Directors' Remuneration Report to be audited.

Opinion

In our opinion:
- the parent company financial statements give a true and fair view, in accordance with IFRSs as adopted by the European Union, of the state of the company's affairs as at .... and of its profit[loss] for the year then ended;
- the parent company financial statements and the part of the Directors' Remuneration Report to be audited have been properly prepared in accordance with the Companies Act 1985; and

[17] *Include and tailor as necessary to clarify the information covered by the auditor's opinion.*

[18] *The other information that is 'read' is the content of the printed Annual Report other than the financial statements. The description of the information that has been read is tailored to reflect the terms used in the Annual Report.*

- the information given in the Directors' Report is consistent with the parent company financial statements.

Registered auditors   *Address*
Date

Example 6 – Publicly traded company – Auditor's report on parent company financial statements:

- Group and parent company financial statements presented separately.
- IFRSs as adopted by the European Union used for group financial statements.
- UK GAAP used for parent company financial statements.
- Company does meet the Companies Act definition of a quoted company.
- Section 230 exemption taken for parent company's own profit and loss account.
- Corporate governance statement reported on in the report on the group financial statements.
- Directors' Remuneration Report reported on in the report on the parent company financial statements.

INDEPENDENT AUDITOR'S REPORT TO THE [MEMBERS] [SHAREHOLDERS] OF XYZ PLC

We have audited the parent company financial statements of (name of entity) for the year ended ... which comprise [state the primary financial statements such as the Balance Sheet] and the related notes[19]. These parent company financial statements have been prepared under the accounting policies set out therein. We have also audited the information in the Directors' Remuneration Report that is described as having been audited[20].

We have reported separately on the group financial statements of (name of entity) for the year ended .... [That report is modified by the inclusion of an emphasis of matter] [The opinion in that report is (qualified)/(an adverse opinion)/(a disclaimer of opinion)].

Respective responsibilities of directors and auditors

The directors' responsibilities for preparing the Annual Report, the Directors' Remuneration Report and the parent company financial statements in accordance with applicable law and United Kingdom Accounting Standards (United Kingdom Generally Accepted Accounting Practice) are set out in the Statement of Directors' Responsibilities.

Our responsibility is to audit the parent company financial statements and the part of the Directors' Remuneration Report to be audited in accordance with relevant legal and regulatory requirements and International Standards on Auditing (UK and Ireland).

We report to you our opinion as to whether the parent company financial statements give a true and fair view and whether the parent company financial statements and the part of the Directors' Remuneration Report to be audited have been properly prepared in accordance with the Companies Act 1985. We also report to you whether in our opinion the Directors' Report is consistent with the parent company financial statements. [The information given in the Directors' Report includes that

---

[19] Auditor's reports of entities that do not publish their financial statements on a web site or publish them using 'PDF' format may continue to refer to the financial statements by reference to page numbers.

[20] Part 3 of Schedule 7A to the Companies Act 1985 sets out the information in the Directors' Remuneration Report that is subject to audit. Companies should describe clearly which disclosures within the Directors' Report have been audited.

specific information presented in the Operating and Financial Review that is cross referred from the Business Review section of the Directors' Report.][21]

In addition we report to you if, in our opinion, the company has not kept proper accounting records, if we have not received all the information and explanations we require for our audit, or if information specified by law regarding directors' remuneration and other transactions is not disclosed.

We read other information contained in the Annual Report and consider whether it is consistent with the audited parent company financial statements. The other information comprises only [the Directors' Report, the unaudited part of the Directors' Remuneration Report, the Chairman's Statement and the Operating and Financial Review][22]. We consider the implications for our report if we become aware of any apparent misstatements or material inconsistencies with the parent company financial statements. Our responsibilities do not extend to any other information.

Basis of audit opinion

We conducted our audit in accordance with International Standards on Auditing (UK and Ireland) issued by the Auditing Practices Board. An audit includes examination, on a test basis, of evidence relevant to the amounts and disclosures in the parent company financial statements and the part of the Directors' Remuneration Report to be audited. It also includes an assessment of the significant estimates and judgments made by the directors in the preparation of the parent company financial statements, and of whether the accounting policies are appropriate to the company's circumstances, consistently applied and adequately disclosed.

We planned and performed our audit so as to obtain all the information and explanations which we considered necessary in order to provide us with sufficient evidence to give reasonable assurance that the parent company financial statements and the part of the Directors' Remuneration Report to be audited are free from material misstatement, whether caused by fraud or other irregularity or error. In forming our opinion we also evaluated the overall adequacy of the presentation of information in the parent company financial statements and the part of the Directors' Remuneration Report to be audited.

Opinion

In our opinion:

- the parent company financial statements give a true and fair view, in accordance with United Kingdom Generally Accepted Accounting Practice, of the state of the company's affairs as at ....;
- the parent company financial statements and the part of the Directors' Remuneration Report to be audited have been properly prepared in accordance with the Companies Act 1985; and
- the information given in the Directors' Report is consistent with the parent company financial statements.

Registered auditors   *Address*
Date#

---

[21] *Include and tailor as necessary to clarify the information covered by the auditor's opinion.*

[22] *The other information that is 'read' is the content of the printed Annual Report other than the financial statements. The description of the information that has been read is tailored to reflect the terms used in the Annual Report.*

Example 7 – Publicly traded company – Auditor's report on group (not including parent company) financial statements:

- Group and parent company financial statements presented separately.
- IFRSs as adopted by the European Union used for group financial statements.
- Company does meet the Companies Act definition of a quoted company.
- Corporate governance statement reported on in the report on the group financial statements.
- Directors' Remuneration Report reported on in the report on the parent company financial statements.

INDEPENDENT AUDITOR'S REPORT TO THE [MEMBERS] [SHAREHOLDERS] OF XYZ PLC

We have audited the group financial statements of (name of entity) for the year ended ... which comprise [state the primary financial statements such as the Group Income Statement, the Group Balance Sheet, the Group Cash Flow Statement, the Group Statement of Changes in Equity/Statement of Recognised Income and Expense] and the related notes[23]. These group financial statements have been prepared under the accounting policies set out therein.

We have reported separately on the parent company financial statements of (name of entity) for the year ended and on the information in the Directors' Remuneration Report that is described as having been audited. [That report is modified by the inclusion of an emphasis of matter] [The opinion in that report is (qualified)/(an adverse opinion)/(a disclaimer of opinion)].

Respective responsibilities of directors and auditors

The directors' responsibilities for preparing the Annual Report and the group financial statements in accordance with applicable law and International Financial Reporting Standards (IFRSs) as adopted by the European Union are set out in the Statement of Directors' Responsibilities.

Our responsibility is to audit the group financial statements in accordance with relevant legal and regulatory requirements and International Standards on Auditing (UK and Ireland).

We report to you our opinion as to whether the group financial statements give a true and fair view and whether the group financial statements have been properly prepared in accordance with the Companies Act 1985 and Article 4 of the IAS Regulation. We also report to you whether in our opinion the information given in the Directors' Report is consistent with the group financial statements. [The information given in the Directors' Report includes that specific information presented in the Operating and Financial Review that is cross referred from the Business Review section of the Directors' Report.][24]

In addition we report to you if, in our opinion, we have not received all the information and explanations we require for our audit, or if information specified by law regarding director's remuneration and other transactions is not disclosed.

---

[23] *Auditor's reports of entities that do not publish their financial statements on a web site or publish them using 'PDF' format may continue to refer to the financial statements by reference to page numbers.*

[24] *Include and tailor as necessary to clarify the information covered by the auditor's opinion.*

We review whether the Corporate Governance Statement reflects the company's compliance with the nine provisions of the [2003[25]] Combined Code specified for our review by the Listing Rules of the Financial Services Authority, and we report if it does not. We are not required to consider whether the board's statements on internal control cover all risks and controls, or form an opinion on the effectiveness of the group's corporate governance procedures or its risk and control procedures.

We read other information contained in the Annual Report and consider whether it is consistent with the audited group financial statements. The other information comprises only [the Directors' Report, the Chairman's Statement, the Operating and Financial Review and the Corporate Governance Statement][26]. We consider the implications for our report if we become aware of any apparent misstatements or material inconsistencies with the group financial statements. Our responsibilities do not extend to any other information.

Basis of audit opinion

We conducted our audit in accordance with International Standards on Auditing (UK and Ireland) issued by the Auditing Practices Board. An audit includes examination, on a test basis, of evidence relevant to the amounts and disclosures in the group financial statements. It also includes an assessment of the significant estimates and judgments made by the directors in the preparation of the group financial statements, and of whether the accounting policies are appropriate to the group's circumstances, consistently applied and adequately disclosed.

We planned and performed our audit so as to obtain all the information and explanations which we considered necessary in order to provide us with sufficient evidence to give reasonable assurance that the group financial statements are free from material misstatement, whether caused by fraud or other irregularity or error. In forming our opinion we also evaluated the overall adequacy of the presentation of information in the group financial statements.

Opinion

In our opinion:

- the group financial statements give a true and fair view, in accordance with IFRSs as adopted by the European Union, of the state of the group's affairs as at .... and of its profit[loss] for the year then ended;
- the group financial statements have been properly prepared in accordance with the Companies Act 1985 and Article 4 of the IAS Regulation; and
- the information given in the Directors' Report is consistent with the group financial statements.

[25] *In June 2006 the Financial Reporting Council issued a revised version of the Combined Code. An announcement is expected from the Financial Services Authority regarding the period from which the reference to 2003 should be changed to 2006.*

[26] *The other information that is 'read' is the content of the printed Annual Report other than the financial statements. The description of the information that has been read is tailored to reflect the terms used in the Annual Report.*

[Separate opinion in relation to IFRSs

As explained in Note x to the group financial statements, the group in addition to complying with its legal obligation to comply with IFRSs as adopted by the European Union, has also complied with the IFRSs as issued by the International Accounting Standards Board.

In our opinion the group financial statements give a true and fair view, in accordance with IFRSs, of the state of the group's affairs as at ...and of its profit [loss] for the year then ended.]

Registered auditors   *Address*
Date

Example 8 – Publicly traded company – Auditor's report on group and parent company financial statements:

- Group and parent company financial statements not presented separately.
- IFRSs as adopted by the European Union used for group financial statements.
- UK GAAP used for parent company financial statements.
- Company does meet the Companies Act definition of a quoted company.
- Section 230 exemption taken for parent company's own profit and loss account.

INDEPENDENT AUDITOR'S REPORT TO THE [MEMBERS] [SHAREHOLDERS] OF XYZ PLC

We have audited the group and parent company financial statements (the "financial statements") of (name of entity) for the year ended ... which comprise [state the primary financial statements such as the Group Income Statement, the Group and Parent Company Balance Sheets, the Group Cash Flow Statement, the Group Statement of Changes in Equity/Statement of Recognised Income and Expense] and the related notes[27]. These financial statements have been prepared under the accounting policies set out therein. We have also audited the information in the Directors' Remuneration Report that is described as having been audited[28].

Respective responsibilities of directors and auditors

The directors' responsibilities for preparing the Annual Report and the group financial statements in accordance with applicable law and International Financial Reporting Standards (IFRSs) as adopted by the European Union, and for preparing the parent company financial statements and the Directors' Remuneration Report in accordance with applicable law and United Kingdom Accounting Standards (United Kingdom Generally Accepted Accounting Practice) are set out in the Statement of Directors' Responsibilities.

Our responsibility is to audit the financial statements and the part of the Directors' Remuneration Report to be audited in accordance with relevant legal and regulatory requirements and International Standards on Auditing (UK and Ireland).

We report to you our opinion as to whether the financial statements give a true and fair view and whether the financial statements and the part of the Directors' Remuneration Report to be audited have been properly prepared in accordance with the Companies Act 1985 and whether, in addition, the group financial statements have been properly prepared in accordance with Article 4 of the IAS Regulation. We also report to you whether in our opinion the information given in the Directors' Report is consistent with the financial statements. [The information given in the Directors' Report includes that specific information presented in the Operating and Financial Review that is cross referred from the Business Review section of the Directors' Report.][29]

---

[27] Auditor's reports of entities that do not publish their financial statements on a web site or publish them using 'PDF' format may continue to refer to the financial statements by reference to page numbers.

[28] Part 3 of Schedule 7A to the Companies Act 1985 sets out the information in the Directors' Remuneration Report that is subject to audit. Companies should describe clearly which disclosures within the Directors' Report have been audited.

[29] Include and tailor as necessary to clarify the information covered by the auditor's opinion.

In addition we report to you if, in our opinion, the company has not kept proper accounting records, if we have not received all the information and explanations we require for our audit, or if information specified by law regarding directors' remuneration and other transactions is not disclosed.

We review whether the Corporate Governance Statement reflects the company's compliance with the nine provisions of the [2003[30]] Combined Code specified for our review by the Listing Rules of the Financial Services Authority, and we report if it does not. We are not required to consider whether the board's statements on internal control cover all risks and controls, or form an opinion on the effectiveness of the group's corporate governance procedures or its risk and control procedures.

We read other information contained in the Annual Report and consider whether it is consistent with the audited financial statements. The other information comprises only [the Directors' Report, the unaudited part of the Directors' Remuneration Report, the Chairman's Statement, the Operating and Financial Review and the Corporate Governance Statement][31]. We consider the implications for our report if we become aware of any apparent misstatements or material inconsistencies with the financial statements. Our responsibilities do not extend to any other information.

Basis of audit opinion

We conducted our audit in accordance with International Standards on Auditing (UK and Ireland) issued by the Auditing Practices Board. An audit includes examination, on a test basis, of evidence relevant to the amounts and disclosures in the financial statements and the part of the Directors' Remuneration Report to be audited. It also includes an assessment of the significant estimates and judgments made by the directors in the preparation of the financial statements, and of whether the accounting policies are appropriate to the group's and company's circumstances, consistently applied and adequately disclosed.

We planned and performed our audit so as to obtain all the information and explanations which we considered necessary in order to provide us with sufficient evidence to give reasonable assurance that the financial statements and the part of the Directors' Remuneration Report to be audited are free from material misstatement, whether caused by fraud or other irregularity or error. In forming our opinion we also evaluated the overall adequacy of the presentation of information in the financial statements and the part of the Directors' Remuneration Report to be audited.

Opinion

In our opinion.

- the group financial statements give a true and fair view, in accordance with IFRSs as adopted by the European Union, of the state of the group's affairs as at .... and of its profit[loss] for the year then ended;

---

[30] *In June 2006 the Financial Reporting Council issued a revised version of the Combined Code. An announcement is expected from the Financial Services Authority regarding the period from which the reference to 2003 should be changed to 2006.*

[31] *The other information that is 'read' is the content of the printed Annual Report other than the financial statements. The description of the information that has been read is tailored to reflect the terms used in the Annual Report.*

- the group financial statements have been properly prepared in accordance with the Companies Act 1985 and Article 4 of the IAS Regulation;
- the parent company financial statements give a true and fair view, in accordance with United Kingdom Generally Accepted Accounting Practice, of the state of the parent company's affairs as at ....;
- the parent company financial statements and the part of the Directors' Remuneration Report to be audited have been properly prepared in accordance with the Companies Act 1985; and
- the information given in the Directors' Report is consistent with the financial statements.

[Separate opinion in relation to IFRSs

As explained in Note x to the group financial statements, the group in addition to complying with its legal obligation to comply with IFRSs as adopted by the European Union, has also complied with the IFRSs as issued by the International Accounting Standards Board.

In our opinion the group financial statements give a true and fair view, in accordance with IFRSs, of the state of the group's affairs as at ...and of its profit [loss] for the year then ended.]

Registered auditors   *Address*
Date

Example 9 – Publicly traded company – Auditor's report on parent company financial statements:

- Group and parent company financial statements presented separately.
- IFRSs as adopted by the European Union used for group financial statements.
- UK GAAP used for parent company financial statements.
- Company does meet the Companies Act definition of a quoted company.
- Section 230 exemption not taken for parent company's own profit and loss account.
- Corporate governance statement reported on in the report on the group financial statements.
- Directors' Remuneration Report reported on in the report on the parent company financial statements.

INDEPENDENT AUDITOR'S REPORT TO THE [MEMBERS] [SHAREHOLDERS] OF XYZ PLC

We have audited the parent company financial statements of (name of entity) for the year ended ... which comprise [state the primary financial statements such as the Profit and Loss Account, the Balance Sheet, the Statement of Total Recognised Gains and Losses] and the related notes[32]. These parent company financial statements have been prepared under the accounting policies set out therein. We have also audited the information in the Directors' Remuneration Report that is described as having been audited[33].

We have reported separately on the group financial statements of (name of entity) for the year ended .... [That report is modified by the inclusion of an emphasis of matter] [The opinion in that report is (qualified)/(an adverse opinion)/(a disclaimer of opinion).]

Respective responsibilities of directors and auditors

The directors' responsibilities for preparing the Annual Report, the Directors' Remuneration Report and the parent company financial statements in accordance with applicable law and United Kingdom Accounting Standards (United Kingdom Generally Accepted Accounting Practice) are set out in the Statement of Directors' Responsibilities.

Our responsibility is to audit the parent company financial statements and the part of the Directors' Remuneration Report to be audited in accordance with relevant legal and regulatory requirements and International Standards on Auditing (UK and Ireland).

We report to you our opinion as to whether the parent company financial statements give a true and fair view and whether the parent company financial statements and the part of the Directors' Remuneration Report to be audited have been properly prepared in accordance with the Companies Act 1985. We also report to you whether in our opinion the information given in the Directors' Report is consistent with the parent company financial statements. [The information given in the

---

[32] Auditor's reports of entities that do not publish their financial statements on a web site or publish them using 'PDF' format may continue to refer to the financial statements by reference to page numbers.

[33] Part 3 of Schedule 7A to the Companies Act 1985 sets out the information in the Directors' Remuneration Report that is subject to audit. Companies should describe clearly which disclosures within the Directors' Report have been audited.

Directors' Report includes that specific information presented in the Operating and Financial Review that is cross referred from the Business Review section of the Directors' Report.][34]

In addition we report to you if, in our opinion, the company has not kept proper accounting records, if we have not received all the information and explanations we require for our audit, or if information specified by law regarding directors' remuneration and other transactions is not disclosed.

We read other information contained in the Annual Report and consider whether it is consistent with the audited parent company financial statements. The other information comprises only [the Directors' Report, the unaudited part of the Directors' Remuneration Report, the Chairman's Statement and the Operating and Financial Review][35]. We consider the implications for our report if we become aware of any apparent misstatements or material inconsistencies with the parent company financial statements. Our responsibilities do not extend to any other information.

Basis of audit opinion

We conducted our audit in accordance with International Standards on Auditing (UK and Ireland) issued by the Auditing Practices Board. An audit includes examination, on a test basis, of evidence relevant to the amounts and disclosures in the parent company financial statements and the part of the Directors' Remuneration Report to be audited. It also includes an assessment of the significant estimates and judgments made by the directors in the preparation of the parent company financial statements, and of whether the accounting policies are appropriate to the company's circumstances, consistently applied and adequately disclosed.

We planned and performed our audit so as to obtain all the information and explanations which we considered necessary in order to provide us with sufficient evidence to give reasonable assurance that the parent company financial statements and the part of the Directors' Remuneration Report to be audited are free from material misstatement, whether caused by fraud or other irregularity or error. In forming our opinion we also evaluated the overall adequacy of the presentation of information in the parent company financial statements and the part of the Directors' Remuneration Report to be audited.

Opinion

In our opinion:

- the parent company financial statements give a true and fair view, in accordance with United Kingdom Generally Accepted Accounting Practice, of the state of the company's affairs as at ……. and of its profit[loss] for the year then ended;
- the parent company financial statements and the part of the Directors' Remuneration Report to be audited have been properly prepared in accordance with the Companies Act 1985; and
- the information given in the Directors' Report is consistent with the parent company financial statements.

Registered auditors   *Address*
Date

---

[34] *Include and tailor as necessary to clarify the information covered by the auditor's opinion.*

[35] *The other information that is 'read' is the content of the printed Annual Report other than the financial statements. The description of the information that has been read is tailored to reflect the terms used in the Annual Report.*

Example 10 – Publicly traded company – Auditor's report on group and parent company financial statements:

- Group and parent company financial statements not presented separately.
- IFRSs as adopted by the European Union used for group financial statements.
- UK GAAP used for parent company financial statements.
- Company does meet the Companies Act definition of a quoted company.
- Section 230 exemption not taken for parent company's own profit and loss account.

INDEPENDENT AUDITOR'S REPORT TO THE [MEMBERS] [SHAREHOLDERS] OF XYZ PLC

We have audited the group and parent company financial statements (the "financial statements") of (name of entity) for the year ended ... which comprise [state the primary financial statements such as the Group Income Statement, the Parent Company Profit and Loss Account, the Group and Parent Company Balance Sheets, the Group Cash Flow Statement, the Group Statement of Changes in Equity/Statement of Recognised Income and Expense, the Parent Company Statement of Total Recognised Gains and Losses] and the related notes[36]. These financial statements have been prepared under the accounting policies set out therein. We have also audited the information in the Directors' Remuneration Report that is described as having been audited[37].

Respective responsibilities of directors and auditors

The directors' responsibilities for preparing the Annual Report and the group financial statements in accordance with applicable law and International Financial Reporting Standards (IFRSs) as adopted by the European Union, and for preparing the parent company financial statements and the Directors' Remuneration Report in accordance with applicable law and United Kingdom Accounting Standards (United Kingdom Generally Accepted Accounting Practice) are set out in the Statement of Directors' Responsibilities.

Our responsibility is to audit the financial statements and the part of the Directors' Remuneration Report to be audited in accordance with relevant legal and regulatory requirements and International Standards on Auditing (UK and Ireland).

We report to you our opinion as to whether the financial statements give a true and fair view and whether the financial statements and the part of the Directors' Remuneration Report to be audited have been properly prepared in accordance with the Companies Act 1985 and whether, in addition, the group financial statements have been properly prepared in accordance with Article 4 of the IAS Regulation. We also report to you whether in our opinion the information given in the Directors' Report is consistent with the financial statements. [The information given in the Directors' Report includes that specific information presented in the Operating and

---

[36] Auditor's reports of entities that do not publish their financial statements on a web site or publish them using 'PDF' format may continue to refer to the financial statements by reference to page numbers.

[37] Part 3 of Schedule 7A to the Companies Act 1985 sets out the information in the Directors' Remuneration Report that is subject to audit. Companies should describe clearly which disclosures within the Directors' Report have been audited.

Financial Review that is cross referred from the Business Review section of the Directors' Report.][38]

In addition we report to you if, in our opinion, the company has not kept proper accounting records, if we have not received all the information and explanations we require for our audit, or if information specified by law regarding directors' remuneration and other transactions is not disclosed.

We review whether the Corporate Governance Statement reflects the company's compliance with the nine provisions of the [2003[39]] Combined Code specified for our review by the Listing Rules of the Financial Services Authority, and we report if it does not. We are not required to consider whether the board's statements on internal control cover all risks and controls, or form an opinion on the effectiveness of the group's corporate governance procedures or its risk and control procedures.

We read other information contained in the Annual Report and consider whether it is consistent with the audited financial statements. The other information comprises only [the Directors' Report, the unaudited part of the Directors' Remuneration Report, the Chairman's Statement, the Operating and Financial Review and the Corporate Governance Statement][40]. We consider the implications for our report if we become aware of any apparent misstatements or material inconsistencies with the financial statements. Our responsibilities do not extend to any other information.

Basis of audit opinion

We conducted our audit in accordance with International Standards on Auditing (UK and Ireland) issued by the Auditing Practices Board. An audit includes examination, on a test basis, of evidence relevant to the amounts and disclosures in the financial statements and the part of the Directors' Remuneration Report to be audited. It also includes an assessment of the significant estimates and judgments made by the directors in the preparation of the financial statements, and of whether the accounting policies are appropriate to the group's and company's circumstances, consistently applied and adequately disclosed.

We planned and performed our audit so as to obtain all the information and explanations which we considered necessary in order to provide us with sufficient evidence to give reasonable assurance that the financial statements and the part of the Directors' Remuneration Report to be audited are free from material misstatement, whether caused by fraud or other irregularity or error. In forming our opinion we also evaluated the overall adequacy of the presentation of information in the financial statements and the part of the Directors' Remuneration Report to be audited.

---

[38] *Include and tailor as necessary to clarify the information covered by the auditor's opinion.*

[39] *In June 2006 the Financial Reporting Council issued a revised version of the Combined Code. An announcement is expected from the Financial Services Authority regarding the period from which the reference to 2003 should be changed to 2006.*

[40] *The other information that is 'read' is the content of the printed Annual Report other than the financial statements. The description of the information that has been read is tailored to reflect the terms used in the Annual Report.*

Opinion

In our opinion:

- the group financial statements give a true and fair view, in accordance with IFRSs as adopted by the European Union, of the state of the group's affairs as at .... and of its profit[loss] for the year then ended;
- the group financial statements have been properly prepared in accordance with the Companies Act 1985 and Article 4 of the IAS Regulation;
- the parent company financial statements give a true and fair view, in accordance with United Kingdom Generally Accepted Accounting Practice, of the state of the parent company's affairs as at .... and of its profit [loss] for the year then ended;
- the parent company financial statements and the part of the Directors' Remuneration Report to be audited have been properly prepared in accordance with the Companies Act 1985; and
- the information given in the Directors' Report is consistent with the financial statements.

[Separate opinion in relation to IFRSs

As explained in Note x to the group financial statements, the group in addition to complying with its legal obligation to comply with IFRSs as adopted by the European Union, has also complied with the IFRSs as issued by the International Accounting Standards Board.

In our opinion the group financial statements give a true and fair view, in accordance with IFRSs, of the state of the group's affairs as at ...and of its profit [loss] for the year then ended.]

Registered auditors   *Address*
Date

Example 11 – Publicly traded company – Auditor's report on parent company financial statements:

- Group and parent company financial statements presented separately.
- IFRSs as adopted by the European Union used for both group and parent company financial statements.
- Company does meet the Companies Act definition of a quoted company.
- Section 230 exemption taken for parent company's own income statement.
- Corporate governance statement reported on in the report on the group financial statements.
- Directors' Remuneration Report reported on in the report on the parent company financial statements.

INDEPENDENT AUDITOR'S REPORT TO THE [MEMBERS] [SHAREHOLDERS] OF XYZ PLC

We have audited the parent company financial statements of (name of entity) for the year ended ... which comprise [state the primary financial statements such as the Balance Sheet, the Cash Flow Statement, the Statement of Changes in Equity/ Statement of Recognised Income and Expense] and the related notes[41]. These parent company financial statements have been prepared under the accounting policies set out therein. We have also audited the information in the Directors' Remuneration Report that is described as having been audited[42].

We have reported separately on the group financial statements of (name of entity) for the year ended .... [That report is modified by the inclusion of an emphasis of matter] [The opinion in that report is (qualified)/(an adverse opinion)/(a disclaimer of opinion).]

Respective responsibilities of directors and auditors

The directors' responsibilities for preparing the Annual Report, the Directors' Remuneration Report and the parent company financial statements in accordance with applicable law and International Financial Reporting Standards (IFRSs) as adopted by the European Union are set out in the Statement of Directors' Responsibilities.

Our responsibility is to audit the parent company financial statements and the part of the Directors' Remuneration Report to be audited in accordance with relevant legal and regulatory requirements and International Standards on Auditing (UK and Ireland).

We report to you our opinion as to whether the parent company financial statements give a true and fair view and whether the parent company financial statements and the part of the Directors' Remuneration Report to be audited have been properly prepared in accordance with the Companies Act 1985. We also report to you whether in our opinion the information given in the Directors' Report is consistent with the parent company financial statements. [The information given in the Directors' Report includes that specific information presented in the Operating and

---

[41] Auditor's reports of entities that do not publish their financial statements on a web site or publish them using 'PDF' format may continue to refer to the financial statements by reference to page numbers.

[42] Part 3 of Schedule 7A to the Companies Act 1985 sets out the information in the Directors' Remuneration Report that is subject to audit. Companies should describe clearly which disclosures within the Directors' Report have been audited.

Financial Review that is cross referred from the Business Review section of the Directors' Report.][43]

In addition we report to you if, in our opinion, the company has not kept proper accounting records, if we have not received all the information and explanations we require for our audit, or if information specified by law regarding directors' remuneration and other transactions is not disclosed.

We read other information contained in the Annual Report and consider whether it is consistent with the audited parent company financial statements. The other information comprises only [the Directors' Report, the unaudited part of the Directors' Remuneration Report, the Chairman's Statement and the Operating and Financial Review][44]. We consider the implications for our report if we become aware of any apparent misstatements or material inconsistencies with the parent company financial statements. Our responsibilities do not extend to any other information.

Basis of audit opinion

We conducted our audit in accordance with International Standards on Auditing (UK and Ireland) issued by the Auditing Practices Board. An audit includes examination, on a test basis, of evidence relevant to the amounts and disclosures in the parent company financial statements and the part of the Directors' Remuneration Report to be audited. It also includes an assessment of the significant estimates and judgments made by the directors in the preparation of the parent company financial statements, and of whether the accounting policies are appropriate to the company's circumstances, consistently applied and adequately disclosed.

We planned and performed our audit so as to obtain all the information and explanations which we considered necessary in order to provide us with sufficient evidence to give reasonable assurance that the parent company financial statements and the part of the Directors' Remuneration Report to be audited are free from material misstatement, whether caused by fraud or other irregularity or error. In forming our opinion we also evaluated the overall adequacy of the presentation of information in the parent company financial statements and the part of the Directors' Remuneration Report to be audited.

Opinion

In our opinion:
- the parent company financial statements give a true and fair view, in accordance with IFRSs as adopted by the European Union as applied in accordance with the provisions of the Companies Act 1985, of the state of the company's affairs as at ....;
- the parent company financial statements and the part of the Directors' Remuneration Report to be audited have been properly prepared in accordance with the Companies Act 1985; and
- the information given in the Directors' Report is consistent with the parent company financial statements.

Registered auditors   *Address*
Date

---

[43] Include and tailor as necessary to clarify the information covered by the auditor's opinion.

[44] The other information that is 'read' is the content of the printed Annual Report other than the financial statements. The description of the information that has been read is tailored to reflect the terms used in the Annual Report.

Example 12 – Publicly traded company – Auditor's report on group and parent company financial statements:

- Group and parent company financial statements not presented separately.
- IFRSs as adopted by the European Union used for both group and parent company financial statements.
- Company does meet the Companies Act definition of a quoted company.
- Section 230 exemption taken for parent company's own income statement.

INDEPENDENT AUDITOR'S REPORT TO THE [MEMBERS] [SHAREHOLDERS] OF XYZ PLC

We have audited the group and parent company financial statements (the "financial statements") of (name of entity) for the year ended ... which comprise [state the primary financial statements such as the Group Income Statement, the Group and Parent Company Balance Sheets, the Group and Parent Company Cash Flow Statements, the Group and Parent Company Statements of Changes in Equity/ Statements of Recognised Income and Expense] and the related notes[45]. These financial statements have been prepared under the accounting policies set out therein. We have also audited the information in the Directors' Remuneration Report that is described as having been audited[46].

Respective responsibilities of directors and auditors

The directors' responsibilities for preparing the Annual Report, the Directors' Remuneration Report and the financial statements in accordance with applicable law and International Financial Reporting Standards (IFRSs) as adopted by the European Union are set out in the Statement of Directors' Responsibilities.

Our responsibility is to audit the financial statements and the part of the Directors' Remuneration Report to be audited in accordance with relevant legal and regulatory requirements and International Standards on Auditing (UK and Ireland).

We report to you our opinion as to whether the financial statements give a true and fair view and whether the financial statements and the part of the Directors' Remuneration Report to be audited have been properly prepared in accordance with the Companies Act 1985 and, as regards the group financial statements, Article 4 of the IAS Regulation. We also report to you whether in our opinion the information given in the Directors' Report is consistent with the financial statements. [The information given in the Directors' Report includes that specific information presented in the Operating and Financial Review that is cross referred from the Business Review section of the Directors' Report.][47]

In addition we report to you if, in our opinion, the company has not kept proper accounting records, if we have not received all the information and explanations we

---

[45] Auditor's reports of entities that do not publish their financial statements on a web site or publish them using 'PDF' format may continue to refer to the financial statements by reference to page numbers.

[46] Part 3 of Schedule 7A to the Companies Act 1985 sets out the information in the Directors' Remuneration Report that is subject to audit. Companies should describe clearly which disclosures withinh the Directors' Report have been audited.

[47] Include and tailor as necessary to clarify the information covered by the auditor's opinion.

require for our audit, or if information specified by law regarding directors' remuneration and other transactions is not disclosed.

We review whether the Corporate Governance Statement reflects the company's compliance with the nine provisions of the [2003[48]] Combined Code specified for our review by the Listing Rules of the Financial Services Authority, and we report if it does not. We are not required to consider whether the board's statements on internal control cover all risks and controls, or form an opinion on the effectiveness of the group's corporate governance procedures or its risk and control procedures.

We read other information contained in the Annual Report and consider whether it is consistent with the audited financial statements. The other information comprises only [the Directors' Report, the unaudited part of the Directors' Remuneration Report, the Chairman's Statement, the Operating and Financial Review and the Corporate Governance Statement][49]. We consider the implications for our report if we become aware of any apparent misstatements or material inconsistencies with the financial statements. Our responsibilities do not extend to any other information.

Basis of audit opinion

We conducted our audit in accordance with International Standards on Auditing (UK and Ireland) issued by the Auditing Practices Board. An audit includes examination, on a test basis, of evidence relevant to the amounts and disclosures in the financial statements and the part of the Directors' Remuneration Report to be audited. It also includes an assessment of the significant estimates and judgments made by the directors in the preparation of the financial statements, and of whether the accounting policies are appropriate to the group's and company's circumstances, consistently applied and adequately disclosed.

We planned and performed our audit so as to obtain all the information and explanations which we considered necessary in order to provide us with sufficient evidence to give reasonable assurance that the financial statements and the part of the Directors' Remuneration Report to be audited are free from material misstatement, whether caused by fraud or other irregularity or error. In forming our opinion we also evaluated the overall adequacy of the presentation of information in the financial statements and the part of the Directors' Remuneration Report to be audited.

Opinion

In our opinion:
- the group financial statements give a true and fair view, in accordance with IFRSs as adopted by the European Union, of the state of the group's affairs as at .... and of its profit[loss] for the year then ended;
- the parent company financial statements give a true and fair view, in accordance with IFRSs as adopted by the European Union as applied in accordance with

---

[48] In June 2006 the Financial Reporting Council issued a revised version of the Combined Code. An announcement is expected from the Financial Services Authority regarding the period from which the reference to 2003 should be changed to 2006.

[49] The other information that is 'read' is the content of the printed Annual Report other than the financial statements. The description of the information that has been read is tailored to reflect the terms used in the Annual Report.

the provisions of the Companies Act 1985, of the state of the parent company's affairs as at ....;
- the financial statements and the part of the Directors' Remuneration Report to be audited have been properly prepared in accordance with the Companies Act 1985 and, as regards the group financial statements, Article 4 of the IAS Regulation; and
- the information given in the Directors' Report is consistent with the financial statements.

[Separate opinion in relation to IFRSs

As explained in Note x to the group financial statements, the group in addition to complying with its legal obligation to comply with IFRSs as adopted by the European Union, has also complied with the IFRSs as issued by the International Accounting Standards Board.

In our opinion the group financial statements give a true and fair view, in accordance with IFRSs, of the state of the group's affairs as at ...and of its profit [loss] for the year then ended.]

Registered auditors   *Address*
Date

Example 13 – Publicly traded company – Auditor's report on group and parent company financial statements:

- Group and parent company financial statements not presented separately.
- IFRSs as adopted by the European Union used for both group and parent company financial statements.
- Company does meet the Companies Act definition of a quoted company.
- Section 230 exemption not taken for parent company's own income statement.

INDEPENDENT AUDITOR'S REPORT TO THE [MEMBERS] [SHAREHOLDERS] OF XYZ PLC

We have audited the group and parent company financial statements (the "financial statements") of (name of entity) for the year ended ... which comprise [state the primary financial statements such as the Group and Parent Company Income Statements, the Group and Parent Company Balance Sheets, the Group and Parent Company Cash Flow Statements, the Group and Parent Company Statements of Changes in Equity/Statement of Recognised Income and Expense] and the related notes[50]. These financial statements have been prepared under the accounting policies set out therein. We have also audited the information in the Directors' Remuneration Report that is described as having been audited[51].

Respective responsibilities of directors and auditors

The directors' responsibilities for preparing the Annual Report, the Directors' Remuneration Report and the financial statements in accordance with applicable law and International Financial Reporting Standards (IFRSs) as adopted by the European Union are set out in the Statement of Directors' Responsibilities.

Our responsibility is to audit the financial statements and the part of the Directors' Remuneration Report to be audited in accordance with relevant legal and regulatory requirements and International Standards on Auditing (UK and Ireland).

We report to you our opinion as to whether the financial statements give a true and fair view and whether the financial statements and the part of the Directors' Remuneration Report to be audited have been properly prepared in accordance with the Companies Act 1985 and, as regards the group financial statements, Article 4 of the IAS Regulation. We also report to you whether in our opinion the information given in the Directors' Report is consistent with the financial statements. [The information given in the Directors' Report includes that specific information presented in the Operating and Financial Review that is cross referred from the Business Review section of the Directors' Report.][52]

In addition we report to you if, in our opinion, the company has not kept proper accounting records, if we have not received all the information and explanations we

---

[50] Auditor's reports of entities that do not publish their financial statements on a web site or publish them using 'PDF' format may continue to refer to the financial statements by reference to page numbers.

[51] Part 3 of Schedule 7A to the Companies Act 1985 sets out the information in the Directors' Remuneration Report that is subject to audit. Companies should describe clearly which disclosures within the Directors' Report have been audited.

[52] Include and tailor as necessary to clarify the information covered by the auditor's opinion.

require for our audit, or if information specified by law regarding directors' remuneration and other transactions is not disclosed.

We review whether the Corporate Governance Statement reflects the company's compliance with the nine provisions of the [2003[53]] Combined Code specified for our review by the Listing Rules of the Financial Services Authority, and we report if it does not. We are not required to consider whether the board's statements on internal control cover all risks and controls, or form an opinion on the effectiveness of the group's corporate governance procedures or its risk and control procedures.

We read other information contained in the Annual Report and consider whether it is consistent with the audited financial statements. The other information comprises only [the Directors' Report, the unaudited part of the Directors' Remuneration Report, the Chairman's Statement, the Operating and Financial Review and the Corporate Governance Statement][54]. We consider the implications for our report if we become aware of any apparent misstatements or material inconsistencies with the financial statements. Our responsibilities do not extend to any other information.

Basis of audit opinion

We conducted our audit in accordance with International Standards on Auditing (UK and Ireland) issued by the Auditing Practices Board. An audit includes examination, on a test basis, of evidence relevant to the amounts and disclosures in the financial statements and the part of the Directors' Remuneration Report to be audited. It also includes an assessment of the significant estimates and judgments made by the directors in the preparation of the financial statements, and of whether the accounting policies are appropriate to the group's and company's circumstances, consistently applied and adequately disclosed.

We planned and performed our audit so as to obtain all the information and explanations which we considered necessary in order to provide us with sufficient evidence to give reasonable assurance that the financial statements and the part of the Directors' Remuneration Report to be audited are free from material misstatement, whether caused by fraud or other irregularity or error. In forming our opinion we also evaluated the overall adequacy of the presentation of information in the financial statements and the part of the Directors' Remuneration Report to be audited.

Opinion

In our opinion:

- the financial statements give a true and fair view, in accordance with IFRSs as adopted by the European Union, of the state of the group's and the parent company's affairs as at ……. and of the group's and the parent company's profit[loss] for the year then ended;
- the financial statements and the part of the Directors' Remuneration Report to be audited have been properly prepared in accordance with the Companies Act

---

[53] In June 2006 the Financial Reporting Council issued a revised version of the Combined Code. An announcement is expected from the Financial Services Authority regarding the period from which the reference to 2003 should be changed to 2006.

[54] The other information that is 'read' is the content of the printed Annual Report other than the financial statements. The description of the information that has been read is tailored to reflect the terms used in the Annual Report.

- 1985 and, as regards the group financial statements, Article 4 of the IAS Regulation; and
- the information given in the Directors' Report is consistent with the financial statements.

[Separate opinion in relation to IFRSs

As explained in Note x to the group financial statements, the group in addition to complying with its legal obligations to comply with IFRSs as adopted by the European Union, has also complied with the IFRSs as issued by the International Accounting Standards Board.

In our opinion the group financial statements give a true and fair view, in accordance with IFRSs, of the state of the group's affairs as at ...and of its profit [loss] for the year then ended.]

Registered auditors   *Address*
Date

Example 14 – Publicly traded company that does not prepare group accounts:

- IFRSs as adopted by the European Union used for financial statements.
- Company does meet the Companies Act definition of a quoted company.

INDEPENDENT AUDITOR'S REPORT TO THE [MEMBERS] [SHAREHOLDERS] OF XYZ PLC

We have audited the financial statements of (name of entity) for the year ended ... which comprise [state the primary financial statements such as the Income Statement, the Balance Sheet, the Cash Flow Statement, the Statement of Changes in Equity/ Statement of Recognised Income and Expense] and the related notes[55]. These financial statements have been prepared under the accounting policies set out therein. We have also audited the information in the Directors' Remuneration Report that is described as having been audited.[56]

Respective responsibilities of directors and auditors

The directors' responsibilities for preparing the Annual Report, the Directors' Remuneration Report and the financial statements in accordance with applicable law and International Financial Reporting Standards (IFRSs) as adopted by the European Union are set out in the Statement of Directors' Responsibilities.

Our responsibility is to audit the financial statements and the part of the Directors' Remuneration Report to be audited in accordance with relevant legal and regulatory requirements and International Standards on Auditing (UK and Ireland).

We report to you our opinion as to whether the financial statements give a true and fair view and whether the financial statements and the part of the Directors' Remuneration Report to be audited have been properly prepared in accordance with the Companies Act 1985. We also report to you whether in our opinion the information given in the Directors' Report is consistent with the financial statements. [The information given in the Directors' Report includes that specific information presented in the Operating and Financial Review that is cross referred from the Business Review section of the Directors' Report.][57]

In addition we report to you if, in our opinion, the company has not kept proper accounting records, if we have not received all the information and explanations we require for our audit, or if information specified by law regarding directors' remuneration and other transactions is not disclosed.

---

[55] Auditor's reports of entities that do not publish their financial statements on a web site or publish them using 'PDF' format may continue to refer to the financial statements by reference to page numbers.

[56] Part 3 of Schedule 7A to the Companies Act 1985 sets out the information in the Directors' Remuneration Report that is subject to audit. Companies should describe clearly which disclosures within the Directors' Report have been audited.

[57] Include and tailor as necessary to clarify the information covered by the auditor's opinion.

We review whether the Corporate Governance Statement reflects the company's compliance with the nine provisions of the [2003[58]] Combined Code specified for our review by the Listing Rules of the Financial Services Authority, and we report if it does not. We are not required to consider whether the board's statements on internal control cover all risks and controls, or form an opinion on the effectiveness of the company's corporate governance procedures or its risk and control procedures.

We read other information contained in the Annual Report and consider whether it is consistent with the audited financial statements. The other information comprises only [the Directors' Report, the unaudited part of the Directors' Remuneration Report, the Chairman's Statement and the Operating and Financial Review][59]. We consider the implications for our report if we become aware of any apparent misstatements or material inconsistencies with the financial statements. Our responsibilities do not extend to any other information.

Basis of audit opinion

We conducted our audit in accordance with International Standards on Auditing (UK and Ireland) issued by the Auditing Practices Board. An audit includes examination, on a test basis, of evidence relevant to the amounts and disclosures in the financial statements and the part of the Directors' Remuneration Report to be audited. It also includes an assessment of the significant estimates and judgments made by the directors in the preparation of the financial statements, and of whether the accounting policies are appropriate to the company's circumstances, consistently applied and adequately disclosed.

We planned and performed our audit so as to obtain all the information and explanations which we considered necessary in order to provide us with sufficient evidence to give reasonable assurance that the financial statements and the part of the Directors' Remuneration Report to be audited are free from material misstatement, whether caused by fraud or other irregularity or error. In forming our opinion we also evaluated the overall adequacy of the presentation of information in the financial statements and the part of the Directors' Remuneration Report to be audited.

Opinion

In our opinion:
- the financial statements give a true and fair view, in accordance with IFRSs as adopted by the European Union, of the state of the company's affairs as at .... and of its profit[loss] for the year then ended;
- the financial statements and the part of the Directors' Remuneration Report to be audited have been properly prepared in accordance with the Companies Act 1985; and
- the information given in the Directors' Report is consistent with the financial statements.

[58] *In June 2006 the Financial Reporting Council issued a revised version of the Combined Code. An announcement is expected from the Financial Services Authority regarding the period from which the reference to 2003 should be changed to 2006.*

[59] *The other information that is 'read' is the content of the printed Annual Report other than the financial statements. The description of the information that has been read is tailored to reflect the terms used in the Annual Report.*

[Separate opinion in relation to IFRSs

As explained in Note x to the financial statements, the company in addition to complying with IFRSs as adopted by the European Union, has also complied with the IFRSs as issued by the International Accounting Standards Board.

In our opinion the financial statements give a true and fair view, in accordance with IFRSs, of the state of the company's affairs as at ... and of its profit [loss] for the year then ended.]

Registered auditors   *Address*
Date

Example 15 – Publicly traded company that does not prepare group accounts:

- UK GAAP used for financial statements.
- Company does meet the Companies Act definition of a quoted company.

INDEPENDENT AUDITOR'S REPORT TO THE [MEMBERS] [SHAREHOLDERS] OF XYZ PLC

We have audited the financial statements of (name of entity) for the year ended ... which comprise [state the primary financial statements such as the Profit and Loss Account, the Balance Sheet, the Cash Flow Statement, the Statement of Total Recognised Gains and Losses] and the related notes[60]. These financial statements have been prepared under the accounting policies set out therein. We have also audited the information in the Directors' Remuneration Report that is described as having been audited[61].

Respective responsibilities of directors and auditors

The directors' responsibilities for preparing the Annual Report, the Directors' Remuneration Report and the financial statements in accordance with applicable law and United Kingdom Accounting Standards (United Kingdom Generally Accepted Accounting Practice) are set out in the Statement of Directors' Responsibilities.

Our responsibility is to audit the financial statements and the part of the Directors' Remuneration Report to be audited in accordance with relevant legal and regulatory requirements and International Standards on Auditing (UK and Ireland).

We report to you our opinion as to whether the financial statements give a true and fair view and whether the financial statements and the part of the Directors' Remuneration Report to be audited have been properly prepared in accordance with the Companies Act 1985. We also report to you whether in our opinion the information given in the Directors' Report is consistent with the financial statements. [The information given in the Directors' Report includes that specific information presented in the Operating and Financial Review that is cross referred from the Business Review section of the Directors' Report.][62]

In addition we report to you if, in our opinion, the company has not kept proper accounting records, if we have not received all the information and explanations we require for our audit, or if information specified by law regarding directors' remuneration and other transactions is not disclosed.

---

[60] Auditor's reports of entities that do not publish their financial statements on a web site or publish them using 'PDF' format may continue to refer to the financial statements by reference to page numbers.

[61] Part 3 of Schedule 7A to the Companies Act 1985 sets out the information in the Directors' Remuneration Report that is subject to audit. Companies should describe clearly which disclosures within the Directors' Report have been audited.

[62] Include and tailor as necessary to clarify the information covered by the auditor's opinion.

We review whether the Corporate Governance Statement reflects the company's compliance with the nine provisions of the [2003[63]] Combined Code specified for our review by the Listing Rules of the Financial Services Authority, and we report if it does not. We are not required to consider whether the board's statements on internal control cover all risks and controls, or form an opinion on the effectiveness of the company's corporate governance procedures or its risk and control procedures.

We read other information contained in the Annual Report and consider whether it is consistent with the audited financial statements. The other information comprises only [the Directors' Report, the unaudited part of the Directors' Remuneration Report, the Chairman's Statement and the Operating and Financial Review][64]. We consider the implications for our report if we become aware of any apparent misstatements or material inconsistencies with the financial statements. Our responsibilities do not extend to any other information.

Basis of audit opinion

We conducted our audit in accordance with International Standards on Auditing (UK and Ireland) issued by the Auditing Practices Board. An audit includes examination, on a test basis, of evidence relevant to the amounts and disclosures in the financial statements and the part of the Directors' Remuneration Report to be audited. It also includes an assessment of the significant estimates and judgments made by the directors in the preparation of the financial statements, and of whether the accounting policies are appropriate to the company's circumstances, consistently applied and adequately disclosed.

We planned and performed our audit so as to obtain all the information and explanations which we considered necessary in order to provide us with sufficient evidence to give reasonable assurance that the financial statements and the part of the Directors' Remuneration Report to be audited are free from material misstatement, whether caused by fraud or other irregularity or error. In forming our opinion we also evaluated the overall adequacy of the presentation of information in the financial statements and the part of the Directors' Remuneration Report to be audited.

Opinion

In our opinion:

- the financial statements give a true and fair view, in accordance with United Kingdom Generally Accepted Accounting Practice, of the state of the company's affairs as at .... and of its profit[loss] for the year then ended;
- the financial statements and the part of the Directors' Remuneration Report to be audited have been properly prepared in accordance with the Companies Act 1985; and
- the information given in the Directors' Report is consistent with the financial statements.

Registered auditors   *Address*
Date

---

[63] *In June 2006 the Financial Reporting Council issued a revised version of the Combined Code. An announcement is expected from the Financial Services Authority regarding the period from which the reference to 2003 should be changed to 2006.*

[64] *The other information that is 'read' is the content of the printed Annual Report other than the financial statements. The description of the information that has been read is tailored to reflect the terms used in the Annual Report.*

Appendix 2 – Modified auditor's reports on financial statements (excluding going concern issues)

Note: Example auditor's reports addressing going concern issues are included in Appendix 3. Illustrative wording for an auditor's report with a modified opinion on the consistency of the directors' report with the financial statements is provided by Appendix 4.

This Appendix gives illustrative examples of modified auditor's reports on financial statements and includes:

- Examples of auditor's reports where the matter does not affect the auditor's opinion for example, emphasis of matter paragraphs; and
- Examples of auditor's reports where the matter does affect the auditor's opinion for example:
  - Qualified opinions;
  - Disclaimers of opinion; or
  - Adverse opinions.

The example auditor's reports are designed to illustrate the modified auditor's reports that might be issued for the different reporting situations illustrated in the navigation aid on page 52 and do not depend on the accounting framework adopted. In most cases the examples have been based on Example 2 in Appendix 1 (ie a non-publicly traded company incorporated in Great Britain that does not prepare group financial statements and prepares its parent company financial statements under United Kingdom Generally Accepted Acounting Practice). There are some exceptions where the example illustrates an issue relating to compliance with IFRSs as adopted by the European Union.

Tailoring of the examples will be required if they are to be used in other circumstances. Preceding each example is a description of the background to the particular modification. The full text of the example unmodified auditor's reports are included in Appendix 1 but for the purpose of illustrating the modification only those sections of the auditor's report affected by the modification are included. Deletions to the examples in Appendix 1, arising from the modification, are shown as struck out text.

Navigation aid to the examples of modified auditor's reports (excluding going concern issues)

```
Has sufficient appropriate audit evidence been obtained?
  │
  ├── No ──► Is the possible effect of the limitation on scope so material and pervasive that the auditor is unable to express an opinion of the financial statements?
  │              ├── No ──► QUALIFIED OPINION - EXCEPT FOR LIMITATION
  │              │          See Appendix 2, Example 4
  │              └── Yes ─► DISCLAIMER
  │                         See Appendix 2, Example 5
  │
  └── Yes ──► Are the financial statements prepared in accordance with either EU-adopted IFRSs or UK GAAP?
                  │
                  ├── No ──► Is the departure from IFRS allowed under IAS 1 because compliance with a requirement in a Standard or an Interpretation would be so misleading that it would conflict with the objective of financial statements set out in the Framework? OR
                  │          Is the departure from UK GAAP needed to give a true and fair view?
                  │              ├── Yes ──► Is disclosure of the departure adequate?
                  │              │              ├── Yes ──► UNQUALIFIED OPINION - CONSIDER ADDING EMPHASIS OF MATTER PARAGRAPH(S)
                  │              │              │           See Appendix 2, Example 1
                  │              │              └── No
                  │              └── No
                  │          ──► Is the effect so material and pervasive to the financial statements that the auditor concludes that a qualification of the report is not adequate to disclose the misleading or incomplete nature of the financial statements?
                  │              ├── No ──► QUALIFIED OPINION - EXCEPT FOR DISAGREEMENT
                  │              │          See Appendix 2, Examples 2, 3
                  │              └── Yes ─► ADVERSE OPINION
                  │                         See Appendix 2, Example 7
                  │
                  └── Yes ──► Are the financial statements affected by significant uncertainties?
                                 │
                                 ├── Yes ──► Are there multiple significant uncertainties?
                                 │              ├── No ──► Do the financial statements, including note disclosures about any significant uncertainty, give a true and fair view?
                                 │              │              ├── Yes ──► UNQUALIFIED OPINION - CONSIDER ADDING EMPHASIS OF MATTER PARAGRAPH(S)
                                 │              │              │           See Appendix 2, Example 1
                                 │              │              └── No ──► Is the effect so material and pervasive to the financial statements that the auditor concludes that a qualification of the report is not adequate to disclose the misleading or incomplete nature of the financial statements?
                                 │              │                              ├── No ──► QUALIFIED OPINION - EXCEPT FOR DISAGREEMENT
                                 │              │                              │          See Appendix 2, Examples 2, 3
                                 │              │                              └── Yes ─► ADVERSE OPINION
                                 │              │                                         See Appendix 2, Example 7
                                 │              └── Yes ─► Is this an extreme case involving multiple significant uncertainties?
                                 │                             └── Yes ─► DISCLAIMER
                                 │                                        See Appendix 2, Example 6
                                 └── No ──► Do the financial statements give a true and fair view?
                                                ├── Yes ──► UNQUALIFIED OPINION
                                                │           See Appendix 1, Examples 1-15
                                                └── No
```

Appendix 2 – Extracts from modified auditor's reports

MATTERS THAT DO NOT AFFECT THE AUDITOR'S OPINION

1. Emphasis of matter – Possible outcome of a lawsuit, unable to quantify effect on financial statements.

MATTERS THAT DO AFFECT THE AUDITOR'S OPINION

Qualified opinion – Disagreement

2. Disagreement – Inappropriate accounting treatment of debtors.
3. Disagreement – Prior period qualification unresolved and results in a modification of the auditor's report regarding the current period.

Qualified opinion – Limitation on scope

4. Limitation on scope – Auditor not appointed at the time of the stocktake.

Disclaimer of opinion

5. Disclaimer – Unable to observe all physical stock and confirm trade debtors.
6. Disclaimer – Multiple material/significant uncertainties.

Adverse opinion

7. Adverse opinion – No provision made for losses expected to arise on certain long-term contracts.

Example 1 – Unqualified opinion – Emphasis of matter. Possible outcome of a lawsuit, unable to quantify effect on financial statements.

- UK non-publicly traded company prepares UK GAAP financial statements.
- A lawsuit alleges that the company has infringed certain patent rights and claims royalties and punitive damages. The company has filed a counter action, and preliminary hearings and discovery proceedings on both actions are in progress.
- The ultimate outcome of the matter cannot presently be determined, and no provision for any liability that may result has been made in the financial statements.
- The company makes relevant disclosures in the financial statements.
- The auditor issues an unqualified auditor's report with an emphasis of matter paragraph describing the situation giving rise to the emphasis of matter and its possible effects on the financial statements, including that the effect on the financial statements of the resolution of the uncertainty cannot be quantified.

Basis of audit opinion

We conducted our audit in accordance with International Standards on Auditing (UK and Ireland) issued by the Auditing Practices Board. An audit includes examination, on a test basis, of evidence relevant to the amounts and disclosures in the financial statements. It also includes an assessment of the significant estimates and judgments made by the directors in the preparation of the financial statements, and of whether the accounting policies are appropriate to the company's circumstances, consistently applied and adequately disclosed.

We planned and performed our audit so as to obtain all the information and explanations which we considered necessary in order to provide us with sufficient evidence to give reasonable assurance that the financial statements are free from material misstatement, whether caused by fraud or other irregularity or error. In forming our opinion we also evaluated the overall adequacy of the presentation of information in the financial statements.

Opinion

In our opinion:

- the financial statements give a true and fair view, in accordance with United Kingdom Generally Accepted Accounting Practice, of the state of the company's affairs as at ... and of its profit [loss]for the year then ended;
- the financial statements have been properly prepared in accordance with the Companies Act 1985; and
- the information given in the Directors' Report is consistent with the financial statements.

Emphasis of matter – possible outcome of a lawsuit

In forming our opinion on the financial statements, which is not qualified, we have considered the adequacy of the disclosures made in note x to the financial statements concerning the possible outcome of a lawsuit, alleging infringement of certain patent rights and claiming royalties and punitive damages, where the company is the defendant. The company has filed a counter action, and preliminary hearings and discovery proceedings on both actions are in progress. The ultimate outcome of the matter cannot presently be determined, and no provision for any liability that may result has been made in the financial statements.

Registered auditors *Address*
Date

Example 2 – Qualified opinion – Disagreement. Inappropriate accounting treatment of debtors.

- UK non-publicly traded company prepares UK GAAP financial statements.
- The debtors shown on the balance sheet include an amount of £Y due from a company which has ceased trading. XYZ plc has no security for this debt.
- The auditor's opinion is that the company is unlikely to receive any payment and full provision of £Y should have been made.
- The auditor does not believe that the effect of the disagreement is so material and pervasive that the financial statements as a whole are misleading and issues a qualified opinion – except for disagreement about the accounting treatment of debtors.

Qualified opinion arising from disagreement about accounting treatment

Included in the debtors shown on the balance sheet is an amount of £Y due from a company which has ceased trading. XYZ plc has no security for this debt. In our opinion the company is unlikely to receive any payment and full provision of £Y should have been made. Accordingly, debtors should be reduced by £Y, deferred taxes should be reduced by £X and profit for the year and retained earnings should be reduced by £Z.

Except for the financial effect of not making the provision referred to in the preceding paragraph, in our opinion the financial statements:

- give a true and fair view, in accordance with United Kingdom Generally Accepted Accounting Practice, of the state of the company's affairs as at ... and of its profit [loss]for the year then ended; and
- have been properly prepared in accordance with the Companies Act 1985.

In our opinion the information given in the Directors' Report is consistent with the financial statements.

Registered auditors *Address*
Date

Example 3 – Qualified opinion – Disagreement. Prior period qualification unresolved and results in a modification of the auditor's report regarding the current period figures.

- *UK non-publicly traded company prepares UK GAAP financial statements.*
- *Included in the debtors shown on the balance sheet of 31 December 20X4 and 31 December 20X5 is an amount of £Y which is the subject of litigation and against which no provision has been made. The auditor considers that a full provision of £Y should have been made in the year ended 31 December 20X4.*

Qualified opinion arising from disagreement over accounting treatment

Included in the debtors shown on the balance sheets of 31 December 20X4 and 31 December 20X5 is an amount of £Y which is the subject of litigation and against which no provision has been made. In our opinion, full provision of £Y should have been made in the year ended 31 December 20X4. Accordingly, debtors at 31 December 20X4 and 20X5 should be reduced by £Y, deferred taxes at 31 December 20X4 and 20X5 should be reduced by £X, and profit for the year ended 31 December 20X4 and retained earnings at 31 December 20X4 and 20X5 should be reduced by £Z.

In our opinion the financial statements give a true and fair view, in accordance with United Kingdom Generally Accepted Accounting Practice, of the company's profit [loss] for the year ended 31 December 20X5.

Except for the financial effect of not making the provision referred to in the preceding paragraph, in our opinion the financial statements:

- give a true and fair view, in accordance with United Kingdom Generally Accepted Accounting Practice, of the state of the company's affairs as at 31 December 20X5 ~~and of its profit [loss]for the year then ended~~; and
- have been properly prepared in accordance with the Companies Act 1985.

In our opinion the information given in the Directors' Report is consistent with the financial statements.

Registered auditor   *Address*
Date

Example 4 – Qualified opinion – Limitation on scope. Auditor not appointed at the time of the stocktake.

- UK non-publicly traded company prepares UK GAAP financial statements.
- The evidence available to the auditor was limited because they did not observe the counting of the physical stock as of 31 December 20X1, since that date was prior to the time the auditor was initially engaged as auditor for the company. Owing to the nature of the company's records, the auditor was unable to satisfy themselves as to stock quantities by other audit procedures.
- The limitation in audit scope causes the auditor to issue a qualified opinion – except for any adjustments that might have been found to be necessary had they been able to obtain sufficient evidence concerning stock.
- The limitation of scope was determined by the auditor not to be so material and pervasive as to require a disclaimer of opinion.

Basis of audit opinion

We conducted our audit in accordance with International Standards on Auditing (UK and Ireland) issued by the Auditing Practices Board, except that the scope of our work was limited as explained below.

An audit includes examination, on a test basis, of evidence relevant to the amounts and disclosures in the financial statements. It also includes an assessment of the significant estimates and judgments made by the directors in the preparation of the financial statements, and of whether the accounting policies are appropriate to the company's circumstances, consistently applied and adequately disclosed.

We planned and performed our audit so as to obtain all the information and explanations which we considered necessary in order to provide us with sufficient evidence to give reasonable assurance that the financial statements are free from material misstatement, whether caused by fraud or other irregularity or error. However, with respect to stock having a carrying amount of £X the evidence available to us was limited because we did not observe the counting of the physical stock as of 31 December 20X1, since that date was prior to our appointment as auditor of the company. Owing to the nature of the company's records, we were unable to obtain sufficient appropriate audit evidence regarding the stock quantities by using other audit procedures.

In forming our opinion we also evaluated the overall adequacy of the presentation of information in the financial statements.

Qualified opinion arising from limitation in audit scope

Except for the financial effects of such adjustments, if any, as might have been determined to be necessary had we been able to satisfy ourselves as to physical stock quantities, in our opinion the financial statements:

- give a true and fair view, in accordance with United Kingdom Generally Accepted Accounting Practice, of the state of the company's affairs as at 31 December 20X1 and of its profit [loss] for the year then ended; and
- have been properly prepared in accordance with the Companies Act 1985.

In respect solely of the limitation on our work relating to stocks:

- we have not obtained all the information and explanations that we considered necessary for the purpose of our audit; and
- we were unable to determine whether proper accounting records had been maintained.

In our opinion the information given in the Directors' Report is consistent with the financial statements.

Registered auditors *Address*
Date

Example 5 – Disclaimer of opinion. Unable to observe all physical stock and confirm trade debtors.

- UK non-publicly traded company prepares UK GAAP financial statements.
- The evidence available to the auditor was limited because the auditor was not able to observe all physical stock and confirm trade debtors due to limitations placed on the scope of the auditor's work by the directors of the Company.
- As a result, the auditor has been unable to form a view on the financial statements and issues a modified opinion disclaiming the view given by the financial statements.

Basis of audit opinion

We conducted our audit in accordance with International Standards on Auditing (UK and Ireland) issued by the Auditing Practices Board, except that the scope of our work was limited as explained below.

An audit includes examination, on a test basis, of evidence relevant to the amounts and disclosures in the financial statements. It also includes an assessment of the significant estimates and judgments made by the directors in the preparation of the financial statements, and of whether the accounting policies are appropriate to the company's circumstances, consistently applied and adequately disclosed

We planned ~~and performed~~ our audit so as to obtain all the information and explanations which we considered necessary in order to provide us with sufficient evidence to give reasonable assurance that the financial statements are free from material misstatement, whether caused by fraud or other irregularity or error. However, the evidence available to us was limited because we were unable to observe the counting of physical stock having a carrying amount of £X and send confirmation letters to trade debtors having a carrying amount of £Y due to limitations placed on the scope of our work by the directors of the company. As a result of this we have been unable to obtain sufficient appropriate audit evidence concerning both stock and trade debtors. Because of the significance of these items, we have been unable to form a view on the financial statements.

In forming our opinion we also evaluated the overall adequacy of the presentation of information in the financial statements.

Opinion: disclaimer on view given by the financial statements

Because of the possible effect of the limitation in evidence available to us, we are unable to form an opinion as to whether the financial statements:

- give a true and fair view, in accordance with United Kingdom Generally Accepted Accounting Practice, of the state of the company's affairs as at ... and of its profit [loss]for the year then ended; and
- have been properly prepared in accordance with the Companies Act 1985.

In respect solely of the limitation of our work referred to above:

- we have not obtained all the information and explanations that we considered necessary for the purpose of our audit; and
- we were unable to determine whether proper accounting records have been maintained.

Notwithstanding our disclaimer on the view given by the financial statements, in our opinion the information given in the Directors' Report is consistent with the financial statements.

Registered auditors *Address*
Date

Example 6 – Disclaimer of opinion. Multiple material/significant uncertainties.

As discussed in ISA (UK and Ireland) 700 paragraph 34 the addition of a paragraph emphasising a going concern problem or significant uncertainty is ordinarily adequate to meet the auditor's reporting responsibilities regarding such matters. However, in extreme cases, such as situations involving multiple uncertainties that are significant to the financial statements, the auditor may consider it appropriate to express a disclaimer of opinion instead of adding an emphasis of matter paragraph.

This example does not include a description of the multiple material/significant uncertainties that might lead to a disclaimer of opinion because circumstances will vary and auditors will have to use their judgment when deciding whether it is an extreme case involving multiple uncertainties that are significant to the financial statements. Often, if such matters were considered individually, because the company makes relevant disclosures in the financial statements, the auditor would normally issue an unqualified auditor's report with an emphasis of matter paragraph setting out the basis of the auditor's opinion, describing the situation giving rise to the emphasis of matter and its possible effects on the financial statements, including (where practicable) quantification but the audit opinion would be unqualified.

Opinion: disclaimer on view given by the financial statements

In forming our opinion on the financial statements, we have considered the adequacy of the disclosures made in the financial statements concerning the following matters:

- [Significant uncertainty 1]
- [Significant uncertainty 2]
- [Significant uncertainty 3]

Because of the potential significance, to the financial statements, of the combined effect of the three matters referred to in the paragraph above, we are unable to form an opinion as to whether the financial statements:

- give a true and fair view, in accordance with United Kingdom Generally Accepted Accounting Practice, of the state of the company's affairs as at ... and of its profit [loss]for the year then ended; and
- have been properly prepared in accordance with the Companies Act 1985.

Notwithstanding our disclaimer on the view given by the financial statements, in our opinion the information given in the Directors' Report is consistent with the financial statements.

Registered auditors   Address
Date

Example 7 – Adverse opinion. No provision made for losses expected to arise on certain long-term contracts.

- UK non-publicly traded company prepares UK GAAP financial statements.
- No provision has been made for losses expected to arise on certain long-term contracts currently in progress, as the directors consider that such losses should be off-set against amounts recoverable on other long-term contracts.
- In the auditor's opinion, provision should be made for foreseeable losses on individual contracts as required by [specify accounting standards].
- The auditor issues an adverse opinion due to the failure to provide for the losses and quantifies the impact on the profit for the year the contract work in progress and deferred taxes payable at the year end.

Adverse opinion on the financial statements

As more fully explained in note x to the financial statements no provision has been made for losses expected to arise on certain long-term contracts currently in progress, as the directors consider that such losses should be off-set against amounts recoverable on other long-term contracts. In our opinion, provision should be made for foreseeable losses on individual contracts as required by [specify accounting standards]......... If losses had been so recognised the effect would have been to reduce the carrying amount of contract work in progress by £X, deferred taxes payable by £Y, and the profit for the year and retained earnings at 31 December 20X1 by £Z.

In view of the effect of the failure to provide for the losses referred to above, in our opinion the financial statements do not give a true and fair view, in accordance with United Kingdom Generally Accepted Accounting Practice, of the state of the company's affairs as at 31 December 20X1 and of its profit [loss]for the year then ended.

In all other respects, in our opinion the financial statements have been properly prepared in accordance with the Companies Act 1985.

Notwithstanding our adverse opinion on the financial statements, in our opinion the information given in the Directors' Report is consistent with the financial statements.

Registered auditors *Address*
Date

Appendix 3 – Modified auditor's reports arising from going concern issues – Extracts from modified reports

Note: Example auditor's reports addressing issues other than going concern are included in Appendix 2.

The auditor's reports included in Appendix 3 are illustrative examples only and it has not been possible to describe all of the facts that the auditors would have to consider when forming their opinion. Auditors use their professional judgment when deciding what form of modified auditor's report to give, taking into account the particular circumstances of the reporting entity.

The Appendix gives illustrative examples of modified auditor's reports on financial statements arising from the going concern issues illustrated in the navigation aid on page 65.

Preceding each example auditor's report is a description of the background to the particular modification. The full text of the example unmodified auditor's reports is included in Appendix 1 but for the purpose of illustrating the modification, only those sections of the auditor's report affected by the modification are included. Deletions to the examples in Appendix 1, arising from the modification, are shown as struck out text.

Navigation aid to the example modified auditor's reports arising from going concern issues

- **Has sufficient appropriate audit evidence been obtained?**
  - No → **Is the possible effect of the limitation on scope so material and pervasive that the auditor is unable to express an opinion of the financial statements?**
    - No → QUALIFIED OPINION - EXCEPT FOR LIMITATION See Appendix 3, Example 6
    - Yes → DISCLAIMER (para 38) See Appendix 3, Example 7
  - Yes → **Are the financial statements prepared on a going concern basis?**
    - No → **Is the departure from the going concern basis appropriate (see IAS 10 paragraph 14 or FRS 21 paragraph 14)**
      - No → **Is disclosure of the departure adequate?**
        - Yes → **Is the effect so material and pervasive to the financial statements that the auditor concludes that a qualification of the nature of the financial statements?**
          - No → QUALIFIED OPINION - EXCEPT FOR DISAGREEMENT See Appendix 3, Example 5
          - Yes → ADVERSE OPINION See Appendix 3, Example 8
        - No → (to adverse path)
      - Yes → (continue)
    - Yes → **Is there a significant level of concern about the entity's ability to continue as a going concern?**
      - No → **Excluding the period considered for going concern (see below) do the financial statements give a true and fair view?**
        - Yes → **Is the period to which the directors have paid particular attention in assessing going concern less than one year from the date of the approval of the financial statements?**
          - No → **Are the Financial statements prepared using EU-adopted IFRS?**
            - Yes → **Is the period used disclosed?**
              - Yes → UNQUALIFIED OPINION See Appendix 1, Examples 1-15
              - No (3) → QUALIFIED OPINION - EXCEPT FOR DISAGREEMENT See Appendix 3, Examples 3, 4
          - Yes (4) → (to qualified path)
      - Yes → **Is the effect so material and pervasive to the financial statements that the auditor concludes that a qualification of the report is not adequate to disclose the misleading or incomplete nature of the financial statements?**
        - Yes → ADVERSE OPINION See Appendix 3, Example 8
        - No → **Is the effect so material and pervasive to the financial statements that the auditor concludes that a qualification of the report is not adequate to disclose the misleading or incomplete nature of the financial statements?**
          - Yes → QUALIFIED OPINION - EXCEPT FOR DISAGREEMENT See Appendix 3, Example 5
          - No → **Do the financial statements, including note disclosures about significant uncertainties, give a true and fair view?**
            - Yes → UNQUALIFIED OPINION - CONSIDER ADDING EMPHASIS OF MATTER PARAGRAPH(S) Appendix 3, Example 1
              - **Is the period used disclosed?**
                - Yes → UNQUALIFIED OPINION WITH EMPHASIS OF MATTER PARAGRAPH See Appendix 3, Example 2
                - No → **Is the period used less than one year from the balance sheet date?**
                  - Yes → (to qualified)
                  - No → (back)
            - No → **Are there multiple significant uncertainties?**
              - No → (see disagreement path)
              - Yes → **Is this an extreme case involving multiple significant uncertainties?**
                - Yes → DISCLAIMER See Appendix 2, Example 6
                - No → (continue)

Appendix 3 – Extracts from modified auditor's reports arising from going concern issues

MATTERS THAT DO NOT AFFECT THE AUDITOR'S OPINION

1. Emphasis of matter – Material uncertainty about the company's ability to continue as a going concern.
2. Emphasis of matter – IFRSs as adopted by the European Union financial statements where the going concern period considered by directors complies with IAS 1 but not ISA (UK and Ireland) 570 and this fact is not disclosed.

MATTERS THAT DO AFFECT THE AUDITOR'S OPINION

Qualified opinion – Disagreement

3. Disagreement – UK GAAP financial statements where the going concern period considered by directors does not comply with FRS 18 and this fact is not disclosed.
4. Disagreement – IFRSs as adopted by the European Union financial statements where the going concern period considered by directors is less than one year from the balance sheet date and so does not comply with IAS 1.
5. Disagreement – Non-disclosure of going concern problems.

Qualified opinion – Limitation on scope

6. Limitation on scope – Evidence available to auditor regarding going concern status was limited because cash flow forecasts were only prepared for a period of nine months from approval of financial statements

Disclaimer of opinion

7. Disclaimer – The company has not prepared profit or cash flow projections for an appropriate period subsequent to the balance sheet date.

Adverse opinion

8. Adverse opinion – Significant level of concern about the company's ability to continue as a going concern that is not disclosed in the financial statements and the financial statements have been prepared on a going concern basis.

Example 1 – Unqualified opinion – Emphasis of matter. Material uncertainty about the company's ability to continue as a going concern.

- UK non-publicly traded company prepares UK GAAP financial statements.
- The Company incurred a net loss of £X during the year ended 31 December 20X1 and, as of that date, the Company's current liabilities exceeded its total assets by £Y.
- These conditions, along with other matters set forth in the notes to the financial statements, indicate the existence of a material uncertainty, which may cast significant doubt about the Company's ability to continue as a going concern.
- The Company makes relevant disclosures in the financial statements including that referred to in paragraphs 32 and 33 of ISA (UK and Ireland) 570 "Going Concern".
- The auditor issues an unqualified auditor's report with an emphasis of matter paragraph describing the situation giving rise to the emphasis of matter and its possible effects on the financial statements, including (where practicable) quantification.

Basis of audit opinion

We conducted our audit in accordance with International Standards on Auditing (UK and Ireland) issued by the Auditing Practices Board. An audit includes examination, on a test basis, of evidence relevant to the amounts and disclosures in the financial statements. It also includes an assessment of the significant estimates and judgments made by the directors in the preparation of the financial statements, and of whether the accounting policies are appropriate to the company's circumstances, consistently applied and adequately disclosed

We planned and performed our audit so as to obtain all the information and explanations which we considered necessary in order to provide us with sufficient evidence to give reasonable assurance that the financial statements are free from material misstatement, whether caused by fraud or other irregularity or error. In forming our opinion we also evaluated the overall adequacy of the presentation of information in the financial statements.

Opinion

In our opinion:

- the financial statements give a true and fair view, in accordance with United Kingdom Generally Accepted Accounting Practice, of the state of the company's affairs as at 31 December 20X1 and of its profit [loss]for the year then ended;
- the financial statements have been properly prepared in accordance with the Companies Act 1985; and
- the information given in the Directors' Report is consistent with the financial statements.

Emphasis of matter – Going concern

In forming our opinion on the financial statements, which is not qualified, we have considered the adequacy of the disclosure made in note x to the financial statements concerning the company's ability to continue as a going concern. The company incurred a net loss of £X during the year ended 31 December 20X1 and, at that date, the company's current liabilities exceeded its total assets by £Y. These conditions, along with the other matters explained in note x to the financial statements, indicate the existence of a material uncertainty which may cast significant doubt about the company's ability to continue as a going concern. The financial statements do not include the adjustments that would result if the company was unable to continue as a going concern.

Registered auditors   *Address*
Date

Example 2 – Unqualified opinion – Emphasis of matter. Financial statements where the going concern period considered by directors complies with IAS 1 but not ISA (UK and Ireland) 570 and this fact is not disclosed.

- UK publicly traded company uses IFRSs as adopted by the European Union for financial statements.
- The balance sheet date being audited is 31 December 20X1.
- The date of approval of the financial statements was 31 May 20X2.
- In assessing whether the going concern assumption is appropriate the directors have taken into account the period up to 31 March 20X3 which is:
  - 15 months from the balance sheet date ie more than the 12 months from the balance sheet date required by IAS 1; but only
  - 10 months from the date of approval of the financial statements ie less than the 12 months from the date of approval of the financial statements required by ISA (UK and Ireland) 570.
- The directors have refused to either extend their assessment period to twelve months from the date of approval of the financial statements or to disclose the fact that the period they have used for their assessment is less than twelve months from the date of approval of the financial statements.
- The auditor issues an unqualified auditor's report with an emphasis of matter paragraph disclosing the fact that the going concern period considered by the directors is less than one year from the date of approval of the financial statements and that this fact has not been disclosed.

Basis of audit opinion

We conducted our audit in accordance with International Standards on Auditing (UK and Ireland) issued by the Auditing Practices Board. An audit includes examination, on a test basis, of evidence relevant to the amounts and disclosures in the financial statements and the part of the Directors' Remuneration Report to be audited. It also includes an assessment of the significant estimates and judgments made by the directors in the preparation of the financial statements, and of whether the accounting policies are appropriate to the company's circumstances, consistently applied and adequately disclosed.

We planned and performed our audit so as to obtain all the information and explanations which we considered necessary in order to provide us with sufficient evidence to give reasonable assurance that the financial statements and the part of the Directors' Remuneration Report to be audited are free from material misstatement, whether caused by fraud or other irregularity or error. In forming our opinion we also evaluated the overall adequacy of the presentation of information in the financial statements and the part of the Directors' Remuneration Report to be audited.

Opinion

In our opinion:

- the financial statements give a true and fair view, in accordance with IFRSs as adopted by the European Union, of the state of the company's affairs as at 31 December 20X1 and of its profit [loss]for the year then ended;

- the financial statements and the part of the Directors' Remuneration Report to be audited have been properly prepared in accordance with the Companies Act 1985 and Article 4 of the IAS Regulation; and
- the information given in the Directors' Report is consistent with the financial statements.

Emphasis of matter – Going concern

In forming our opinion on the financial statements, which is not qualified, we have considered the adequacy of the disclosures made in note x to the financial statements concerning the period used by the directors in assessing whether the going concern assumption is appropriate. In making their assessment the directors have considered the period up to 31 March 20X3 which is less than twelve months from the date of approval of the financial statements and the directors have not disclosed this fact. International Standards on Auditing (UK and Ireland) require the auditor to draw this fact to the attention of readers of the financial statements.

Registered auditors   *Address*
31 May 20X2

Example 3 – Qualified opinion – Disagreement. Financial statements where the going concern period considered by directors does not comply with FRS 18 and this fact is not disclosed.

- UK non-publicly traded company prepares UK GAAP financial statements.
- In assessing whether it is appropriate to prepare the financial statements on a going concern basis, the directors have paid particular attention to a period ending on 30 September 20X3 which is less than one year from the date of approval of the financial statements on 31 October 20X2.
- The directors have not disclosed this fact in the financial statements breaching the requirements of paragraph 61(b) of Financial Reporting Standard 18 "Accounting policies". FRS 18 requires the disclosure of the fact that " the foreseeable future considered by the directors has been limited to a period of less than one year from the date of approval of the financial statements".
- Although the auditor has concluded that there is no significant level of concern about going concern, the failure to disclose the fact that the foreseeable future considered by the directors has been limited to a period of less than one year from the date of approval of the financial statements is a breach of FRS 18 and the auditor issues a qualified "except for" opinion describing the disagreement over the departure from FRS 18.

Qualified opinion arising from departure from FRS 18 'Accounting policies'

In assessing whether it is appropriate to prepare the financial statements on a going concern basis the directors have paid particular attention to a period ending on 30 September 20X3 which is less than twelve months from the date of approval of the financial statements. This fact has not been disclosed in the financial statements, contrary to the requirements of Financial Reporting Standard 18 'Accounting policies'.

Except for the absence of the disclosure referred to above in our opinion the financial statements:

- give a true and fair view, in accordance with United Kingdom Generally Accepted Accounting Practice, of the state of the company's affairs as at 31 December 20X1 and of its profit [loss]for the year then ended; and
- have been properly prepared in accordance with the Companies Act 1985.

In our opinion the information given in the Directors' Report is consistent with the financial statements.

Registered auditors *Address*
31 October 20X2

Example 4 – Qualified opinion – Disagreement. Financial statements where the going concern period considered by directors does not comply with IAS 1.

- UK publicly traded company uses IFRSs as adopted by the European Union for financial statements.
- The balance sheet date being audited is 31 December 20X1.
- The date of approval of the financial statements was 31 May 20X2.
- In assessing whether the going concern assumption is appropriate the directors have taken into account the period up to 30 November 20X2 which is:
  - only 11 months from the balance sheet date ie less than the 12 months from the balance sheet date required by IAS 1; and
  - only 6 months from the date of approval of the financial statements ie less than the 12 months from the date of approval of the financial statements required by ISA (UK and Ireland) 570.
- The directors have refused to either extend their assessment period to a period of more than twelve months from the balance sheet date (to comply with IAS 1) or twelve months from the date of approval of the financial statements (to comply with ISA (UK and Ireland) 570) or to disclose the fact that the period they have used for their assessment is less than twelve months from the date of approval of the financial statements (to comply with ISA (UK and Ireland) 570).
- The auditor:
  - includes an emphasis of matter paragraph explaining that in making their going concern assessment the directors have considered a period which is less than twelve months from the date of approval of the financial statements and the directors have not disclosed this fact; and
  - issues a qualified "except for" opinion describing the disagreement over the disclosing the fact that the going concern period considered by the directors is less than the twelve months from the balance sheet date required by IAS 1.

Qualified opinion arising from departure from IAS 1 'Presentation of financial statements'

In assessing whether it is appropriate to prepare the financial statements on a going concern basis the directors have paid particular attention to a period ending on 30 November 20X2 which is less than twelve months from the balance sheet date. This is contrary to the requirements of International Accounting Standard 1 'Presentation of financial statements'.

Except for the non-compliance with IAS 1 referred to above in our opinion:

- the financial statements give a true and fair view, in accordance with IFRSs as adopted by the European Union, of the state of the company's affairs as at 31 December 20X1 and of its profit [loss]for the year then ended; and
- the financial statements and the part of the Directors' Remuneration Report to be audited have been properly prepared in accordance with the Companies Act 1985 and, as regards the group financial statements, Article 4 of the IAS Regulation

In our opinion the information given in the Directors' Report is consistent with the financial statements.

Emphasis of matter – Going concern

In forming our opinion on the financial statements, we have considered the adequacy of the disclosures made in note x to the financial statements concerning the period used by the directors in assessing whether the going concern assumption is appropriate. In making their assessment the directors have considered the period up to 30 November 20X2 which is less than twelve months from the date of approval of the financial statements and the directors have not disclosed this fact. International Standards on Auditing (UK and Ireland) require the auditor to draw this fact to the attention of readers of the financial statements. Our opinion is not further qualified in respect of this matter.

Registered auditors *Address*
31 May 20X2

Example 5 – Qualified opinion – Disagreement. Non-disclosure of going concern problems.

- UK non-publicly traded company prepares UK GAAP financial statements.
- Neither the financial statements nor the directors' report disclose that the Company's financing arrangements expire and amounts outstanding are payable on 19 July 20X2 and that the Company has been unable to re-negotiate or obtain replacement financing.
- This situation indicates the existence of a material uncertainty which may cast significant doubt on the Company's ability to continue as a going concern and therefore it may be unable to realise its assets and discharge its liabilities in the normal course of business.
- The auditor concludes that there is a significant level of concern about going concern and disagrees with the failure to disclose this information in the financial statements. The auditor issues a qualified except for opinion describing the disagreement.

Qualified opinion arising from omission of information concerning going concern

The company's financing arrangements expire and amounts outstanding are payable on 19 July 20X2. The company has been unable to re-negotiate or obtain replacement financing. This situation indicates the existence of a material uncertainty which may cast significant doubt on the company's ability to continue as a going concern and therefore it may be unable to realise its assets and discharge its liabilities in the normal course of business. The financial statements (and notes thereto) do not disclose this fact.

Except for the omission of the information included in the preceding paragraph, in our opinion the financial statements:

- give a true and fair view, in accordance with United Kingdom Generally Accepted Accounting Practice, of the state of the company's affairs as at 31 December 20X1 and of its profit [loss]for the year then ended; and
- have been properly prepared in accordance with the Companies Act 1985.

In our opinion the information given in the Directors' Report is consistent with the financial statements.

Registered auditors *Address*
Date

Example 6 – Qualified opinion – Limitation of scope. Evidence available to auditor regarding going concern status was limited because cash flow forecasts were only prepared for a period of nine months from approval of financial statements.

- UK non-publicly traded company prepares UK GAAP financial statements.
- The evidence available to the auditor was limited because the company had prepared cash flow forecasts and other information needed for the assessment of the appropriateness of the going concern basis of preparation of the financial statements only for a period of nine months from the date of approval of the financial statements.
- Although this fact is disclosed in the financial statements had the information been available the auditor might have formed a different opinion. The auditor considers that those charged with governance have not taken adequate steps to satisfy themselves that it is appropriate for them to adopt the going concern basis.
- The auditor does not consider that the future period to which those charged with governance have paid particular attention in assessing going concern is reasonable in the entity's circumstances. The auditor considers that the particular circumstances of the company and the nature of the company's business require that such information be prepared, and reviewed by the directors and auditor for a period of at least twelve months from the date of approval of the financial statements.
- The auditor issues an 'except for' qualified opinion referring to the adjustments that might have been found to be necessary had they obtained sufficient evidence concerning the appropriateness of the going concern basis of preparation of the financial statements.

Basis of audit opinion

We conducted our audit in accordance with International Standards on Auditing (UK and Ireland) issued by the Auditing Practices Board, except that the scope of our work was limited as explained below.

An audit includes examination, on a test basis, of evidence relevant to the amounts and disclosures in the financial statements. It also includes an assessment of the significant estimates and judgments made by the directors in the preparation of the financial statements, and of whether the accounting policies are appropriate to the company's circumstances, consistently applied and adequately disclosed

We planned ~~and performed~~ our audit so as to obtain all the information and explanations which we considered necessary in order to provide us with sufficient evidence to give reasonable assurance that the financial statements are free from material misstatement, whether caused by fraud or other irregularity or error. However, the evidence available to us was limited because the company has prepared cash flow forecasts and other information needed for the assessment of the appropriateness of the going concern basis of preparation of the financial statements for a period of only nine months from the date of approval of these financial statements. We consider that the directors have not taken adequate steps to satisfy themselves that it is appropriate for them to adopt the going concern basis because the circumstances of the company and the nature of the business require that such information be prepared, and reviewed by the directors and ourselves, for a period of at least twelve months from the date of approval of the financial statements. Had this information been available to us we might have formed a different opinion.

In forming our opinion we also evaluated the overall adequacy of the presentation of information in the financial statements.

Qualified opinion arising from limitation in audit scope

Except for any adjustments that might have been found to be necessary had we been able to obtain sufficient evidence concerning the appropriateness of the going concern basis of preparation of the financial statements, in our opinion the financial statements:

- give a true and fair view, in accordance with United Kingdom Generally Accepted Accounting Practice, of the state of the company's affairs as at 31 December 20X1 and of its profit [loss] for the year then ended; and
- have been properly prepared in accordance with the Companies Act 1985.

In respect solely of the limitation on our work relating to the assessment of the appropriateness of the going concern basis of preparation of the financial statements we have not obtained all the information and explanations that we considered necessary for the purpose of our audit.

In our opinion the information given in the Directors' Report is consistent with the financial statements.

Registered auditors   *Address*
Date

Example 7 – Disclaimer of opinion. Going concern – company has not prepared profit or cash flow projections for an appropriate period subsequent to the balance sheet date.

- UK non-publicly traded company prepares UK GAAP financial statements.
- The evidence available to the auditor to confirm the appropriateness of preparing the financial statements on the going concern basis was limited because the company has not prepared profit or cash flow projections for an appropriate period subsequent to the balance sheet date.
- The auditor considers that the circumstances of the company and the nature of the company's business requires that such information be prepared, and reviewed by the directors and the auditor, for a period of at least twelve months from the date of approval of the financial statements.
- The auditor concludes that the possible effect of this limitation on scope is so material and pervasive that the auditor has been unable to obtain sufficient appropriate audit evidence and accordingly is unable to form an opinion on whether or not it is appropriate to prepare the financial statements on a going concern basis. As a result, the auditor issues an opinion disclaiming the view given by the financial statements.

Basis of audit opinion

We conducted our audit in accordance with International Standards on Auditing (UK and Ireland) issued by the Auditing Practices Board, except that the scope of our work was limited as explained below.

An audit includes examination, on a test basis, of evidence relevant to the amounts and disclosures in the financial statements. It also includes an assessment of the significant estimates and judgments made by the directors in the preparation of the financial statements, and of whether the accounting policies are appropriate to the company's circumstances, consistently applied and adequately disclosed

We planned ~~and performed~~ our audit so as to obtain all the information and explanations which we considered necessary in order to provide us with sufficient evidence to give reasonable assurance that the financial statements are free from material misstatement, whether caused by fraud or other irregularity or error. However, the evidence available to us to confirm the appropriateness of preparing the financial statements on the going concern basis was limited because the company has not prepared any profit or cash flow projections for an appropriate period subsequent to the balance sheet date. As a result, and in the absence of any alternative evidence available to us, we have been unable to form a view as to the applicability of the going concern basis, the circumstances of which, together with the effect on the financial statements should this basis be inappropriate, are set out in note x to the financial statements.

In forming our opinion we also evaluated the overall adequacy of the presentation of information in the financial statements.

Opinion: disclaimer on view given by the financial statements

Because of the possible effect of the limitation in evidence available to us, we are unable to form an opinion as to whether the financial statements:

- give a true and fair view, in accordance with United Kingdom Generally Accepted Accounting Practice, of the state of the company's affairs as at 31 December 20.. and of its profit [loss]for the year then ended; and
- have been properly prepared in accordance with the Companies Act 1985.

In respect solely of the limitation of our work referred to above we have not obtained all the information and explanations that we considered necessary for the purpose of our audit.

Notwithstanding our disclaimer on the view given by the financial statements, in our opinion the information given in the Directors' Report is consistent with the financial statements.

Registered auditors   *Address*
Date

Example 8 – Adverse opinion. Significant level of concern about the company's ability to continue as a going concern that is not disclosed in the financial statements.

- UK non-publicly traded company prepares UK GAAP financial statements.
- Although there is a significant level of concern about the company's ability to continue as a going concern the financial statements and notes do not disclose this fact and the directors have prepared the financial statements on the going concern basis.
- The auditor considers that the financial statements should disclose that there is a material uncertainty, which may cast significant doubt on the company's ability to continue as a going concern.
- The effect of this disagreement is so material and pervasive to the amounts included within the financial statements that the auditor concludes that a qualification of the report is not adequate to disclose the misleading or incomplete nature of the financial statements.
- The auditor issues an adverse audit opinion stating that, because the material uncertainty regarding going concern is not disclosed, the financial statements do not give a true and fair view.

Adverse opinion on financial statements

As explained in note x to the financial statements the company's financing arrangements expired and the amount outstanding was payable on 31 December 20X1. The company has been unable to re-negotiate or obtain replacement financing and is considering entering insolvency proceedings. These events indicate a material uncertainty which may cast significant doubt on the company's ability to continue as a going concern and therefore it may be unable to realise its assets and discharge its liabilities in the normal course of business. The financial statements (and notes thereto) do not disclose this fact and have been prepared on the going concern basis.

In our opinion, because of the omission of the information referred to above, the financial statements do not give a true and fair view, in accordance with United Kingdom Generally Accepted Accounting Practice, of the state of the company's affairs as at 31 December 20X1 and of its profit [loss]for the year then ended.

In all other respects, in our opinion the financial statements have been properly prepared in accordance with the Companies Act 1985.

Notwithstanding our adverse opinion on the financial statements, in our opinion the information given in the Directors' Report is consistent with the financial statements.

Registered auditors *Address*
Date

Appendix 4 – Extract from an auditor's report with a modified opinion on the directors' report (financial statements prepared under UK GAAP)[65]

Respective responsibilities of directors and auditors

[Details of directors' and the auditor's other responsibilities as are applicable – for examples see Appendix 1]

We also report to you whether in our opinion the information given in the Directors' Report is consistent with the financial statements. [The information given in the Directors' Report includes that specific information presented in the Operating and Financial Review that is cross referred from the Business Review section of the Directors' Report.][66]

Basis of audit opinion

...

Opinion

In our opinion:

- *[Opinion on the financial statements and other opinions, if any, that are required.]*

Emphasis of matter – ...[include if applicable]

Material inconsistency between the financial statements and the directors' report

In our opinion, the information given in the seventh paragraph of the Business Review in the Directors' Report is not consistent with the financial statements. That paragraph states without amplification that "the company's trading for the period resulted in a 10% increase in profit over the previous period's profit". The profit and loss account, however, shows that the company's profit for the period includes a profit of £Z which did not arise from trading but arose from the disposal of assets of a discontinued operation. Without this profit on the disposal of assets the company would have reported a profit for the year of £Y, representing a reduction in profit of 25% over the previous period's profit on a like for like basis. Except for this matter, in our opinion the information given in the Directors' Report is consistent with the financial statements.

Registered auditors *Address*
Date

---

[65] This example is also included as Example B in the Appendix to ISA (UK and Ireland) 720 (Revised) "Section B – The auditor's statutory reporting responsibility in relation to Directors' Reports"

[66] Include and tailor as necessary to clarify the information covered by the auditor's opinion.

Appendix 5 – Illustrative statement of directors' responsibilities

Example wording of a description of the directors' responsibilities for inclusion in the annual report of a non-publicly traded company incorporated in the United Kingdom preparing its financial statements under UK GAAP

Statement of directors' responsibilities

The directors are responsible for preparing the Annual Report and the financial statements in accordance with applicable law and regulations.

Company law requires the directors to prepare financial statements for each financial year. Under that law the directors have elected to prepare the financial statements in accordance with United Kingdom Generally Accepted Accounting Practice (United Kingdom Accounting Standards and applicable law). The financial statements are required by law to give a true and fair view of the state of affairs of the company and of the profit or loss of the company for that period. In preparing these financial statements, the directors are required to:

- select suitable accounting policies and then apply them consistently;
- make judgments and estimates that are reasonable and prudent[67];
- state whether applicable UK Accounting Standards have been followed, subject to any material departures disclosed and explained in the financial statements;[68]
- prepare the financial statements on the going concern basis unless it is inappropriate to presume that the company will continue in business.[69]

The directors are responsible for keeping proper accounting records that disclose with reasonable accuracy at any time the financial position of the company and enable them to ensure that the financial statements comply with the [Companies Act 1985] [Companies (Northern Ireland) Order 1986]. They are also responsible for safeguarding the assets of the company and hence for taking reasonable steps for the prevention and detection of fraud and other irregularities.

The directors are responsible for the maintenance and integrity of the corporate and financial information included on the company's website. Legislation in the United Kingdom governing the preparation and dissemination of financial statements may differ from legislation in other jurisdictions.[70]

The APB has not prepared an illustrative example of a statement of directors' responsibilities for a publicly traded company as the directors' responsibilities, which are in part dependent on the particular regulatory environment, will vary dependent on the rules of the market on which its securities are admitted to trading.

---

[67] Paragraph 12 of Part II of Schedule 4 to CA 1985 requires that the amount of any item "shall be determined on a prudent basis".

[68] This bullet does not apply to small and medium sized companies as defined by CA 1985.

[69] Included where no separate statement on going concern is made by the directors.

[70] Where the financial statements are published on the internet.

[Bulletin 2007/1]
Example reports by auditors under company legislation in Great Britain

Contents

Page

Introduction

Example 1: Auditor's report on revised financial statements: revision by replacement.
Example 2: Auditor's report on revised financial statements: revision by supplementary note.
Example 3: Auditor's report on revised directors' report.
Example 4: Report on abbreviated accounts. **(SEE BULLETIN 2006/3)**
Example 5: Auditor's statement on a summary financial statement.
Example 6: Report on entitlement to exemption from preparing group financial statements. **(WITHDRAWN)**
Example 7: Statement on a company's ability to make a distribution.
Example 8: Statement when a private company wishes to re-register as a public company.
Example 9: Report on balance sheet prepared other than in respect of an accounting reference period for the purpose of a private company re-registering as a public company.
Example 10: Report when a private company wishes to redeem or purchase its own shares out of capital.
Example 11: Report when a private company wishes to provide financial assistance for the purchase of its own shares or those of its holding company.
Example 12: Report when a public company wishes to allot shares otherwise than for cash.
Example 13: Report when non-cash assets are transferred to a public company by certain of its members.
Example 14: Report on initial accounts when a public company wishes to make a distribution.
Example 15: Report on ceasing to hold office.

Introduction

The purpose of this Bulletin is to provide updated illustrative examples of reports by auditors under the Companies Act 1985 (CA 1985) originally published in Appendix 1 of Practice Note 8 'Reports by auditors under company legislation in the United Kingdom'. Illustrative examples of auditor's reports on financial statements are provided in Bulletin 2006/6 'Auditor's Reports on Financial Statements in the United Kingdom'.

In order to understand the legislative background giving rise to the need for these reports this Bulletin should be read in conjunction with Practice Note 8 which was issued in October 1994, and Bulletin 1999/6 'The auditor's statement on the summary financial statement'. Both of these documents can be downloaded from the Auditing Practices Board's web site www.frc.org.uk/apb.

The wording of the example reports by auditors is based on current legislative requirements and, in some cases, on ISA (UK and Ireland) 700 'The Auditor's Report on Financial Statements' issued by the APB in December 2004. Changes to these example reports may be needed when the Companies Act 2006 (CA 2006) comes into force.

During the period between the issuance of this Bulletin and CA 2006 coming into force, the APB will consider whether to update the whole of Practice Note 8 to reflect the requirements of CA 2006.

Examples of two of the fifteen reports by auditors included in Appendix 1 to Practice Note 8 are not included in this Bulletin. With respect to Example 6 the report is no longer required by CA 1985 and with respect to Example 4 updated examples are included in APB Bulletin 2006/3 'The Special Auditor's Report on Abbreviated Accounts in the United Kingdom'. However, to assist users of the Bulletin the numbering of the examples used in Practice Note 8 has been retained.

With respect to Example 5 'Auditor's statement on a summary financial statement' the example in Practice Note 8 was superseded by the examples in Appendix 1 to Bulletin 1999/6 and Appendix 3 to Bulletin 2002/2. Example 5 in this Bulletin supersedes all of these examples.

Unless otherwise indicated in a footnote, these example reports are effective immediately upon publication.

Example 1 – Auditor's report on revised financial statements: revision by replacement[1]

This example is based on the following assumptions:
- Non-publicly traded company that does not prepare group accounts.
- UK GAAP used for individual company accounts.
- Financial statements contain no surround information other than the directors' report.

REPORT OF THE INDEPENDENT AUDITOR TO THE [MEMBERS] [SHAREHOLDERS] OF XYZ LIMITED

We have audited the revised financial statements of XYZ Limited for the year ended ... which comprise [state the primary financial statements such as the Profit and Loss Account, the Balance Sheet, the Cash Flow Statement, the Statement of Total Recognised Gains and Losses] and the related notes[2]. These revised financial statements have been prepared under the accounting policies set out therein and replace the original financial statements approved by the directors on....

The revised financial statements have been prepared under the Companies (Revision of Defective Accounts and Report) Regulations 1990 and accordingly do not take account of events which have taken place after the date on which the original financial statements were approved.

Respective responsibilities of directors and auditors

As described in the Statement of Directors' Responsibilities the company's directors are responsible for the preparation of revised financial statements in accordance with applicable law and United Kingdom Accounting Standards (United Kingdom Generally Accepted Accounting Practice).[3]

Our responsibility is to audit the revised financial statements in accordance with relevant legal and regulatory requirements and International Standards on Auditing (UK and Ireland).

We report to you our opinion as to whether the revised financial statements give a true and fair view and are properly prepared in accordance with the Companies Act 1985 as they have effect under the Companies (Revision of Defective Accounts and

---

[1] This example report is effective for accounting periods commencing on or after 1 April 2005.

[2] Auditor's reports of entities that do not publish their financial statements on a web site or publish them using 'PDF' format may continue to refer to the financial statements by reference to page numbers.

[3] If the directors' responsibilities with respect to revised financial statements are not set out in a separate statement, the auditors will include a description in their report, for example:
'Under section 245 (or section 245B) of the Companies Act 1985 the directors have the authority to revise financial statements or a directors' report if they do not comply with the Act[, or, where applicable, Article 4 of the IAS Regulation]. The revised financial statements must be amended in accordance with the Companies (Revision of Defective Accounts and Report) Regulations 1990. These require that the revised financial statements show a true and fair view as if they were prepared and approved by the directors as at the date of the original financial statements and accordingly do not take account of events which have taken place after the date on which the original financial statements were approved.' (This example does not make reference to Article 4 of the IAS Regulation as such a reference is only included when the entity is required to prepare consolidated financial statements in accordance with IFRSs as adopted by the EU and the restatement is in respect of such consolidated financial statements.)

Report) Regulations 1990. We also report to you whether in our opinion the information given in the [revised][4] Directors' Report is consistent with the revised financial statements.

In addition we report to you if, in our opinion, the company has not kept proper accounting records, if we have not received all the information and explanations we require for our audit, or if information specified by law regarding directors' remuneration and other transactions is not disclosed.

We read the [revised][4] Directors' Report and consider the implications for our report if we become aware of any apparent misstatements within it.

We are also required to report whether in our opinion the original financial statements failed to comply with the requirements of the Companies Act 1985 in the respects identified by the directors.

Basis of audit opinion

We conducted our audit in accordance with International Standards on Auditing (UK and Ireland) issued by the Auditing Practices Board. An audit includes examination, on a test basis, of evidence relevant to the amounts and disclosures in the revised financial statements. It also includes an assessment of the significant estimates and judgments made by the directors in the preparation of the revised financial statements, and of whether the accounting policies are appropriate to the company's circumstances, consistently applied and adequately disclosed.

The audit of revised financial statements includes the performance of additional procedures to assess whether the revisions made by the directors are appropriate and have been properly made.

We planned and performed our audit so as to obtain all the information and explanations which we considered necessary in order to provide us with sufficient evidence to give reasonable assurance that the revised financial statements are free from material misstatement, whether caused by fraud or other irregularity or error. In forming our opinion we also evaluated the overall adequacy of the presentation of information in the revised financial statements.

Opinion

In our opinion:

- the revised financial statements give a true and fair view, in accordance with United Kingdom Generally Accepted Accounting Practice, seen as at the date the original financial statements were approved, of the state of the company's affairs as at .... and of its profit [loss] for the year then ended;
- the revised financial statements have been properly prepared in accordance with the provisions of the Companies Act 1985 as they have effect under the Companies (Revision of Defective Accounts and Report) Regulations 1990;
- the original financial statements for the year ended... failed to comply with the requirements of the Companies Act 1985 in the respects identified by the directors in the statement contained in note [x] to these revised financial statements; and

---

[4] The word 'revised' will be needed if the Directors' Report has also been revised.

- the information given in the [revised]⁴ Directors' Report is consistent with the revised financial statements.

Registered auditors   *Address*
Date

Example 2 – Auditor's report on revised financial statements: revision by supplementary note[5]

This example is based on the following assumptions:
- *Non-publicly traded company that does not prepare group accounts.*
- *UK GAAP used for individual company accounts.*
- *Financial statements contain no surround information other than the directors' report.*

REPORT OF THE INDEPENDENT AUDITOR TO THE [MEMBERS] [SHAREHOLDERS] OF XYZ LIMITED

We have audited the revised financial statements of XYZ Limited for the year ended.... which comprise [state the primary financial statements such as the Profit and Loss Account, the Balance Sheet, the Cash Flow Statement, the Statement of Total Recognised Gains and Losses] and the related notes.[6] The revised financial statements replace the original financial statements approved by the directors on... and consist of the attached supplementary note together with the original financial statements which were circulated to [members] [shareholders] on....

The revised financial statements have been prepared under the Companies (Revision of Defective Accounts and Report) Regulations 1990 and accordingly do not take account of events which have taken place after the date on which the original financial statements were approved.

Respective responsibilities of directors and auditors

As described in the Statement of Directors' Responsibilities the company's directors are responsible for the preparation of revised financial statements in accordance with applicable law and United Kingdom Accounting Standards (United Kingdom Generally Accepted Accounting Practice).[7]

Our responsibility is to audit the revised financial statements in accordance with relevant legal and regulatory requirements and International Standards on Auditing (UK and Ireland).

We report to you our opinion as to whether the revised financial statements give a true and fair view and are properly prepared in accordance with the Companies Act 1985 as they have effect under the Companies (Revision of Defective Accounts and Report) Regulations 1990. We also report to you whether in our opinion the

---

[5] *This example report is effective for accounting periods commencing on or after 1 April 2005.*

[6] *Auditor's reports of entities that do not publish their financial statements on a web site or publish them using 'PDF' format may continue to refer to the financial statements by reference to page numbers.*

[7] *If the directors' responsibilities with respect to revised financial statements are not set out in a separate statement, the auditors will include a description in their report, for example:*
'Under section 245 (or section 245B) of the Companies Act 1985 the directors have the authority to revise financial statements or a directors' report if they do not comply with the Act [, or, where applicable, Article 4 of the IAS Regulation]. The revised financial statements must be amended in accordance with the Companies (Revisions of Defective Accounts and Report) Regulations 1990. These require that the revised financial statements show a true and fair view as if they were prepared and approved by the directors as at the date of the original financial statements and accordingly do not take account of events which have taken place after the date on which the original financial statements were approved.' (This example does not make reference to Article 4 of the IAS Regulation as such a reference is only included when the entity is required to prepare consolidated financial statements in accordance with IFRSs as adopted by the EU and the restatement is in respect of such consolidated financial statements.)

information given in the [revised][8] Directors' Report is consistent with the financial statements.

In addition we report to you if, in our opinion, the company has not kept proper accounting records, if we have not received all the information and explanations we require for our audit, or if information specified by law regarding directors' remuneration and transactions is not disclosed.

We read the [revised][8] Directors' Report and consider the implications for our report if we become aware of any apparent misstatements within it.

We are also required to report whether in our opinion the original financial statements failed to comply with the requirements of the Companies Act 1985 in the respects identified by the directors.

Basis of audit opinion

We conducted our audit in accordance with International Standards on Auditing (UK and Ireland) issued by the Auditing Practices Board. An audit includes examination, on a test basis, of evidence relevant to the amounts and disclosures in the revised financial statements. It also includes an assessment of the significant estimates and judgments made by the directors in the preparation of the revised financial statements, and of whether the accounting policies are appropriate to the company's circumstances, consistently applied and adequately disclosed.

The audit of revised financial statements includes the performance of additional procedures to assess whether the revisions made by the directors are appropriate and have been properly made.

We planned and performed our audit so as to obtain all the information and explanations which we considered necessary in order to provide us with sufficient evidence to give reasonable assurance that the revised financial statements are free from material misstatement, whether caused by fraud or other irregularity or error. In forming our opinion we also evaluated the overall adequacy of the presentation of information in the revised financial statements.

Opinion

In our opinion:
- the revised financial statements give a true and fair view, in accordance with United Kingdom Generally Accepted Accounting Practice, seen as at the date the original financial statements were approved, of the state of the company's affairs as at .... and of its profit [loss] for the year then ended;
- the revised financial statements have been properly prepared in accordance with the provisions of the Companies Act 1985 as they have effect under the Companies (Revision of Defective Accounts and Report) Regulations 1990;
- the original financial statements for the year ended .... failed to comply with the requirements of the Companies Act 1985 in the respects identified by the directors in the statement contained in the supplementary note; and
- the information given in the [revised][8] Directors' Report is consistent with the revised financial statements.

Registered auditors   *Address*
Date

---

[8] *The word 'revised' will be needed if the Directors' Report has also been revised.*

Example 3 – Auditor's report on revised directors' report

REPORT OF THE INDEPENDENT AUDITOR TO THE [MEMBERS] [SHAREHOLDERS] OF XYZ LIMITED

We have considered the information given in the revised directors' report for the year ended.... The revised directors' report replaces the original directors' report approved by the directors on... [and consists of the attached supplementary note together with the original report which was circulated to [members] [shareholders] on...][9]. The revised directors' report has been prepared under the Companies (Revision of Defective Accounts and Report) Regulations 1990 and accordingly does not take account of events which have taken place after the date on which the original directors' report was approved.

Respective responsibilities of directors and auditors

The directors are responsible for the preparation of the revised directors' report.

Our responsibility is to report to you whether the revised directors' report is consistent with the annual financial statements.

Basis of opinion

Our consideration has been directed towards matters of consistency alone and not to whether the revised directors' report complies with the requirements of the Companies Act 1985.

Opinion

In our opinion the information given in the revised directors' report is consistent with the annual financial statements for the year ended... which were circulated to [members] [shareholders] on....

Registered auditors   Address
Date

---

[9] Omit the words in brackets when the revision is by way of a full replacement.

Example 4 – Report on abbreviated accounts

Updated guidance on reporting on abbreviated accounts, including example reports, is provided by Bulletin 2006/3 'The Special Auditor's Report on Abbreviated Accounts in the United Kingdom'.

Example 5 – Auditor's statement on a summary financial statement[10]

The following example supersedes the examples provided in Bulletin 1999/6 'The auditors' statement on the summary financial statement' and Bulletin 2002/2 'The United Kingdom Directors' Remuneration Report Regulations 2002', and is for entities that prepare UK GAAP consolidated financial statements.

INDEPENDENT AUDITOR'S STATEMENT TO THE [MEMBERS] [SHAREHOLDERS] OF XYZ PLC

We have examined the summary financial statement [which comprises the Summary Consolidated Profit and Loss Account, Summary Consolidated Balance Sheet, Summary Consolidated Statement of Total Recognised Gains and Losses, [Summary Consolidated Cash Flow Statement][11] [and the Summary Directors' Remuneration Report][12] [set out on pages....][13].

Respective responsibilities of directors and auditors

The directors are responsible for preparing the [*summarised annual report*] in accordance with United Kingdom law.

Our responsibility is to report to you our opinion on the consistency of the summary financial statement within the [*summarised annual report*] with the full annual financial statements [, the Directors' Report][14] [and the Directors' Remuneration Report][12], and its compliance with the relevant requirements of section 251 of the Companies Act 1985 and the regulations made thereunder.

We also read the other information contained in the [*summarised annual report*] and consider the implications for our report if we become aware of any apparent misstatements or material inconsistencies with the summary financial statement.

Basis of opinion

We conducted our work in accordance with Bulletin 1999/6 'The auditor's statement on the summary financial statement' issued by the Auditing Practices Board. Our report on the company's full annual financial statements describes the basis of our

---

[10] This example report is effective for accounting periods commencing on or after 1 January 2005.

[11] The wording in the example is for entities preparing UK GAAP consolidated financial statements. For entities preparing consolidated financial statements under IFRSs as adopted by the EU the equivalent wording would be 'Summary Consolidated Income Statement, Summary Consolidated Balance Sheet, Summary Consolidated Statement of [Changes in Equity]/[Recognised Income and Expense], Summary Consolidated Cash Flow Statement'.

[12] A Summary Directors' Remuneration Report is needed only when a summary financial statement is prepared by a quoted company.

[13] Reports of entities that do not publish their summary financial statement on a web site or publish it using 'PDF' format may continue to refer to the summary financial statement by reference to page numbers.

[14] There is no requirement for an entity to include a Summary Directors' Report. If the directors include information in the summary financial statement that is derived from the Directors' Report the auditor is required to report that such information is consistent with the Directors' Report.

audit opinion[s] on those financial statements [and the Directors' Remuneration Report][12].

Opinion

In our opinion the summary financial statement is consistent with the full annual financial statements [, the Directors' Report][14] [and the Directors' Remuneration Report][12] of XYZ plc for the year ended ... and complies with the applicable requirements of section 251 of the Companies Act 1985, and the regulations made thereunder. [We have not considered the effects of any events between the date on which we signed our report on the full annual financial statements (insert date) and the date of this statement.][15]

Registered auditors   *Address*
Date

---

[15] Include this sentence where the date of this statement is after the date of the auditor's report on the full annual financial statements.

Example 6 – Report on entitlement to exemption from preparing group financial statements

Subsections (3) and (4) of section 248 of CA 1985 (auditors' report on entitlement to claim exemption from preparation of group accounts) were repealed by Statutory Instrument 1996 No. 189 'The Companies Act 1985 (Miscellaneous Accounting Amendments) Regulations 1996'.

Example 7 – Statement on a company's ability to make a distribution[16]

This example is based on the assumption that the financial statements have been prepared in accordance with UK GAAP.

STATEMENT OF THE INDEPENDENT AUDITOR TO THE [MEMBERS] [SHAREHOLDERS] OF XYZ LIMITED PURSUANT TO SECTION 271(4) OF THE COMPANIES ACT 1985

We have audited the financial statements of XYZ Limited for the year ended... in accordance with International Standards on Auditing (UK and Ireland) issued by the Auditing Practices Board and have expressed a qualified opinion thereon in our report dated....

Respective responsibilities of directors and auditors

As set out in the Statement of Directors' Responsibilities in the financial statements for the year ended [date], the directors are responsible for the preparation of the financial statements in accordance with applicable law and United Kingdom Accounting Standards. They are also responsible for considering whether the company, subsequent to the balance sheet date, has sufficient distributable profits to make a distribution at the time the distribution is made.

Our responsibility is to report whether, in our opinion, the subject matter of our qualification of our auditor's report on the financial statements for the year ended ... is material for determining, by reference to those financial statements, whether the distribution proposed by the company is permitted under section 263[17] [section 264/265] of the Companies Act 1985. We are not responsible for giving an opinion on whether the company has sufficient distributable reserves to make the distribution proposed at the time it is made.

Basis of opinion

We have carried out such procedures as we considered necessary to evaluate the effect of the qualified opinion for the determination of profits available for distribution.

Opinion

In our opinion the subject matter of the qualification is not material for determining, by reference to those financial statements, whether [the distribution of £...]/[the interim/final dividend for the year ended... of £...]/[any distribution] proposed by the company is permitted under section 263[17] [section 264/265] of the Companies Act 1985.

Registered auditors   Address
Date

---

[16] *This example report is effective for accounting periods commencing on or after 15 December 2004.*

[17] *The reference in all cases to section 263 in this example is extended to cover also section 264 in the case of a public company and also sections 264 and 265 if the public company is also an 'investment company'.*

Notes:

1 As an alternative the auditor's statement might be expressed in terms of the company's ability to make potential distributions up to a specific level. This may be particularly appropriate where the amount of the dividend has not yet been determined. In such circumstances the opinion paragraph would be worded as follows:

'In our opinion the subject matter of the qualification is not material for determining, by reference to those financial statements, whether a distribution of not more than £... by the company is permitted under section 263[17] [section 264/265] of the Companies Act 1985'.

2 Where the auditor concludes that the subject matter of the qualification is material to either a specific distribution which is proposed or to any distribution, then an adverse opinion is given. In such circumstances the opinion paragraph would be worded as follows:

'**Adverse opinion**
In our opinion the subject matter of the qualification is material for determining, by reference to those financial statements, whether [the distribution of £...]/[the interim/final dividend for the year ended ... of £...]/[any distribution] proposed by the company is permitted under section 263[17] [section 264/265] of the Companies Act 1985.'

3 In this example it is assumed that a separate report is given regarding the company's ability to make a distribution. However, as an alternative, this matter is sometimes addressed in the auditor's report on the financial statements by adding a separate statement after the audit opinion paragraph. That statement might be worded as follows:

'Statement of the independent auditors to the members of XYZ Limited pursuant to section 271(4) of the Companies Act 1985

Basis of opinion
We have carried out such procedures as we considered necessary to evaluate the effect of the qualified opinion for the determination of profits available for distribution.

Opinion
In our opinion the subject matter of the above qualification is not material for determining, by reference to those financial statements, whether [the distribution of £...]/ [the interim/final dividend for the year ended .... of £....]/[any distribution] proposed by the company is permitted under section 263[17] [section 264/ 265] of the Companies Act 1985.'

Example 8 – Statement when a private company wishes to re-register as a public company[18]

This example is used when the company's financial statements were prepared within seven months before its application to re-register as a public company.

If the company's financial statements were not prepared within seven months then this statement must be made in respect of a specially prepared balance sheet which must be audited by the auditor. This statement is made in addition to a separate report made by the auditor on such a specially prepared balance sheet (see Example 9).

STATEMENT OF THE INDEPENDENT AUDITOR TO XYZ LIMITED FOR THE PURPOSE OF SECTION 43(3)(B) OF THE COMPANIES ACT 1985

We have examined the balance sheet and related notes of XYZ Limited as at... [which formed part of the financial statements for the year then ended]/[which were prepared for the purpose of the proposed re-registration of XYZ Limited as a public company] and audited by [us]/[ABC LLP].

Respective responsibilities of directors and auditors

As described on page... the company's directors are responsible for the preparation of the balance sheet and related notes. It is our responsibility to form an independent opinion, based on our examination, and to report our opinion to you.

Basis of opinion

The scope of our work, for the purpose of this statement, was limited to an examination of the relationship between the company's net assets and its called-up share capital and undistributable reserves as stated in the audited balance sheet.

Opinion

Where opinion on [financial statements]/[specially prepared balance sheet] is unqualified

[In our opinion the audited balance sheet at... shows that the amount of the company's net assets (within the meaning given to that expression by section 264(2) of the Companies Act 1985) was not less than the aggregate of its called-up share capital and undistributable reserves.]

Where opinion on financial statements is qualified but the qualification is not 'material' for the purposes of this statement

[We audited the financial statements of XYZ Limited for the year ended ...in accordance with International Standards on Auditing (UK and Ireland) issued by the Auditing Practices Board and expressed a qualified opinion thereon.

[Description of qualified opinion.]

---

[18] *This example report is effective for accounting periods commencing on or after 15 December 2004.*

In our opinion the matter giving rise to our qualification is not material for determining by reference to the balance sheet at ... whether, at that date, the amount of the company's net assets (within the meaning given to that expression by section 264(2) of the Companies Act 1985) was not less than the aggregate of its called-up share capital and undistributable reserves.]

Registered auditors   *Address*
Date

Example 9 – Report on balance sheet prepared other than in respect of an accounting reference period for the purpose of a private company re-registering as a public company[19]

This example is used when the latest financial statements are not eligible for use as they were prepared more than seven months before the company's application to re-register as a public company, or because at the time they were prepared the balance sheet did not meet the test in s43(3)(b) of CA 1985. In these circumstances it is necessary for the company to prepare a balance sheet which is required to be audited. In such circumstances the statement in Example 8 is also made in respect of the prepared balance sheet.

This example is based on the assumption that the balance sheet has been prepared in accordance with UK GAAP.

REPORT OF THE INDEPENDENT AUDITOR TO XYZ LIMITED FOR THE PURPOSE OF SECTION 43(3)(C) OF THE COMPANIES ACT 1985

We have audited the balance sheet and related notes of (name of entity) as at...set out on pages... to...., which have been prepared under the accounting policies set out therein.

Respective responsibilities of directors and auditors

As described on page... the company's directors are responsible for the preparation of the balance sheet in accordance with applicable law and United Kingdom Accounting Standards.

Our responsibility is to audit the balance sheet in accordance with relevant legal and regulatory requirements and International Standards on Auditing (UK and Ireland).

Basis of audit opinion

We conducted our audit in accordance with International Standards on Auditing (UK and Ireland) issued by the Auditing Practices Board. An audit includes examination, on a test basis, of evidence relevant to the amounts and disclosures. It also includes an assessment of the significant estimates and judgments made by the directors in the preparation of the balance sheet and related notes, and of whether the accounting policies are appropriate to the company's circumstances, consistently applied and adequately disclosed.

We planned and performed our audit so as to obtain all the information and explanations which we considered necessary in order to provide us with sufficient evidence to give reasonable assurance that the balance sheet is free from material misstatement, whether caused by fraud or other irregularity or error. In forming our opinion we also evaluated the overall adequacy of the presentation of information in the balance sheet.

---

[19] *This example report is effective for accounting periods commencing on or after 15 December 2004.*

Opinion

Unqualified[20]

In our opinion the balance sheet as at ... has been properly prepared in accordance with the provisions of the Companies Act 1985, which would have applied had the balance sheet been prepared for a financial year of the company.

Qualified

[Description of qualified opinion]

Except for the financial effect of the matter referred to in the preceding paragraph, in our opinion the balance sheet has been properly prepared in accordance with the provisions of the Companies Act 1985, which would have applied had the balance sheet been prepared for a financial year of the company.

In our opinion, the matter giving rise to our qualification is not material for determining by reference to the balance sheet at .... whether, at that date, the amount of the company's net assets was less than the aggregate of its called-up share capital and undistributable reserves.

Registered auditors   Address
Date

---

[20] *The meaning of unqualified report is set out in section 46 of CA 1985.*

Example 10 – Report when a private company wishes to redeem or purchase its own shares out of capital

REPORT OF THE INDEPENDENT AUDITOR TO THE DIRECTORS OF XYZ LIMITED PURSUANT TO SECTION 173(5) OF THE COMPANIES ACT 1985

We report on the attached statutory declaration of the directors dated..., prepared pursuant to the Companies Act 1985, in connection with the company's proposed [purchase]/[redemption] of... (number) [ordinary]/[preferred] shares by a payment out of capital.

Basis of opinion

We have inquired into the company's state of affairs in order to review the bases for the statutory declaration.

Opinion

In our opinion the amount of £... specified in the statutory declaration as the permissible capital payment for the shares to be [purchased]/[redeemed] is properly determined in accordance with sections 171 and 172 of the Companies Act 1985.

We are not aware of anything to indicate that the opinion expressed by the directors in their statutory declaration as to any of the matters mentioned in section 173(3) of the Companies Act 1985 is unreasonable in all the circumstances.

Registered auditors   *Address*
Date

Example 11 – Report when a private company wishes to provide financial assistance for the purchase of its own shares or those of its holding company[21]

REPORT OF THE INDEPENDENT AUDITOR TO THE DIRECTORS OF XYZ LIMITED PURSUANT TO SECTION 156(4) OF THE COMPANIES ACT 1985

We report on the attached [statutory declaration]/[statement] of the directors dated ..., prepared pursuant to the Companies Act 1985, in connection with the proposal that the company should give financial assistance for the purchase of ... (number) of the company's [ordinary]/[preferred] shares.

Basis of opinion

We have enquired into the state of the company's affairs in order to review the bases for the [statutory declaration]/[statement].

Opinion

We are not aware of anything to indicate that the opinion expressed by the directors in their [statutory declaration]/[statement] as to any of the matters mentioned in section 156(2) of the Companies Act 1985 is unreasonable in all the circumstances.

Registered auditors   *Address*
Date

---

[21] When CA 2006 comes into force this report will no longer be required.

Example 12 – Report when a public company wishes to allot shares otherwise than for cash

REPORT OF THE INDEPENDENT [PERSON] [AUDITOR][22] TO XYZ PLC FOR THE PURPOSES OF SECTION 103(1) OF THE COMPANIES ACT 1985

We report on the value of the consideration for the allotment to... [name of allottee] of... [number] shares, having a nominal value of [...] each, to be issued at a premium of... pence per share. The shares and share premium are to be treated as fully paid up.

The consideration for the allotment to [name of allottee] is the freehold building situated at... [address] and... [number] shares, having a nominal value of [...] each, in LMN PLC.

Basis of valuation

The freehold building was valued on the basis of its open market value by [name of specialist], a Fellow of the Royal Institution of Chartered Surveyors, on... and in our opinion it is reasonable to accept such a valuation.

The shares in LMN PLC were valued by us on... on the basis of the price shown in the Stock Exchange Daily Official List at....

Opinion

In our opinion, the methods of valuation of the freehold building and the shares in LMN PLC were reasonable in all the circumstances. There appears to have been no material change in the value of either part of the consideration since the date(s) at which the valuations were made.

On the basis of the valuations, in our opinion, the value of the total consideration is not less than £... (being the total amount to be treated as paid up on the shares allotted together with the share premium).

Registered auditors   Address
Date

---

[22] Section 108 of CA 1985 requires the valuation and report required by section 103 to be made by an independent person, that is to say a person qualified at the time of the report to be appointed, or continue to be, an auditor of the Company. In circumstances where the auditor is designated by legislation as being eligible to carry out a valuation, paragraph 56 of ES 5 'Non-Audit services provided to audit clients' disapplies the general prohibition in paragraph 54 of ES5 on audit firms undertaking an engagement to provide any valuation to an audit client where the valuation involves a significant degree of subjective judgment and has a material effect on the financial statements. In such circumstances the audit engagement partner considers the threats to the auditor's objectivity and independence and applies relevant safeguards.

Example 13 - Report when non-cash assets are transferred to a public company by certain of its members

REPORT OF THE INDEPENDENT [PERSON] [AUDITOR][23] TO XYZ PLC FOR THE PURPOSES OF SECTION 104(4) OF THE COMPANIES ACT 1985

We report on the transfer of non-cash assets to XYZ PLC ('the Company') by subscribers to the Company's memorandum of association.

The consideration to be received by the Company is a freehold building situated at... [address] ('the consideration to be received').

The consideration to be given by the Company is... [number] shares, having a nominal value of £1 each, in LMN PLC ('the consideration to be given').

Basis of valuation

The freehold building was valued on the basis of its open market value by [name of specialist], a Fellow of the Royal Institution of Chartered Surveyors, on... and in our opinion it is reasonable to accept such a valuation.

The shares in LMN PLC were valued by us on... on the basis of the price shown in the Stock Exchange Daily Official List at....

Opinion

In our opinion, the methods of valuation of the freehold building and the shares in LMN PLC were reasonable in all the circumstances. There appears to have been no material change in the value of the consideration to be received or the consideration to be given since the date(s) at which the valuations were made.

On the basis of the valuations, in our opinion, the value of the consideration to be received by the Company is not less than the value of the consideration to be given by the Company.

Registered auditors   *Address*
Date

---

[23] Section 109 (via section 108) of CA 1985 requires the valuation and report required by Section 104(4) to be made by an independent person, that is to say a person qualified at the time of the report to be appointed, or continue to be, an auditor of the Company. In circumstances where the auditor is designated by legislation as being eligible to carry out a valuation, paragraph 56 of ES 5 'Non-Audit services provided to audit clients' disapplies the general prohibition in paragraph 54 of ES5 on audit firms undertaking an engagement to provide any valuation to an audit client where the valuation involves a significant degree of subjective judgment and has a material effect on the financial statements. In such circumstances the audit engagement partner considers the threats to the auditor's objectivity and independence and applies relevant safeguards.

Example 14 – Report on initial accounts when a public company wishes to make a distribution[24]

This example is based on the assumption that the initial accounts have been prepared in accordance with UK GAAP.

REPORT OF THE INDEPENDENT AUDITOR TO THE DIRECTORS OF XYZ PLC UNDER SECTION 273(4) OF THE COMPANIES ACT 1985

We have audited the initial accounts of XYZ PLC for the period from .... to ... which comprise [state the primary financial statements such as the Profit and Loss Account, the Balance Sheet, the Cash Flow Statement, the Statement of Total Recognised Gains and Losses] and the related notes. The initial accounts have been prepared under the accounting policies set out therein.

Respective responsibilities of directors and auditors

As described on page ... the directors are responsible for the preparation of the initial accounts in accordance with applicable law and United Kingdom Accounting Standards.

Our responsibility is to audit the initial accounts in accordance with relevant legal and regulatory requirements and International Standards on Auditing (UK and Ireland). We report to you our opinion as to whether the initial accounts have been properly prepared within the meaning of section 273 of the Companies Act 1985.

Basis of audit opinion

We conducted our audit in accordance with International Standards on Auditing (UK and Ireland) issued by the Auditing Practices Board. An audit includes examination, on a test basis, of evidence relevant to the amounts and disclosures in the initial accounts. It also includes an assessment of the significant estimates and judgments made by the directors in the preparation of the initial accounts, and of whether the accounting policies are appropriate to the company's circumstances, consistently applied and adequately disclosed.

We planned and performed our audit so as to obtain all the information and explanations which we considered necessary in order to provide us with sufficient evidence to give reasonable assurance that the initial accounts are free from material misstatement, whether caused by fraud or other irregularity or error. In forming our opinion we also evaluated the overall adequacy of the presentation of information in the initial accounts.

Opinion

In our opinion the initial accounts for the period from... to... have been properly prepared within the meaning of section 273 of the Companies Act 1985.

Registered auditors   Address
Date

---

[24] *This example report is effective for accounting periods commencing on or after 15 December 2004.*

Example 15 – Report on ceasing to hold office

No circumstances connected with ceasing to hold office as auditor

STATEMENT TO THE DIRECTORS OF XYZ LIMITED ON CEASING TO HOLD OFFICE AS AUDITOR

In accordance with section 394 of the Companies Act 1985, we confirm that there are no circumstances connected with our ceasing to hold office that we consider should be brought to the attention of the company's [members] [shareholders] or creditors.

Registered auditors   Address
Date

Circumstances connected with ceasing to hold office that the auditor considers should be brought to the attention of the members or creditors of the company

STATEMENT OF CIRCUMSTANCES RELATING TO:
- [THE INTENTION OF PQR NOT TO SEEK RE-APPOINTMENT AS AUDITORS OF XYZ LIMITED AT THE CONCLUSION OF OUR TERM OF OFFICE];or
- [THE RESIGNATION OF PQR AS AUDITORS OF XYZ LIMITED]; or
- [THE REMOVAL OF PQR AS AUDITORS OF XYZ LIMITED]

In accordance with section 394 of the Companies Act 1985, we consider that the following circumstances connected with our ceasing to hold office should be brought to the attention of the [members] [shareholders] and creditors:

[Set out circumstances]

Unless the company applies to the court, this statement of circumstances, which we consider should be brought to the attention of [members] [shareholders] and creditors of the company, must be sent within 14 days to every person entitled under section 238 of the Companies Act 1985 to be sent copies of the company's accounts. This is a requirement of section 394(3) of that Act.

Registered auditors   Address
Date

[Bulletin 2007/2]
The duty of auditors in the Republic of Ireland to report to the Director of Corporate Enforcement

Contents

Section		Page
1.0	Introduction	
2.0	Section 194 (as amended) of the Companies Act, 1990	
3.0	Auditing Standards	
4.0	Non-Audit Assignments	
5.0	Reportable Information	
6.0	Legal or Other Professional Advice	
7.0	Reportable Persons	
8.0	Standard of Certainty	
9.0	Indictable Offences	
10.0	Timing of Formation and Notification of Opinion	
11.0	Details of the Grounds	
12.0	Provision of Further Information by Auditors to the Director	
13.0	Protection Against Liability	
14.0	Reporting of Suspected Offences Beyond the Scope of Section 194(5) in the Public Interest	
15.0	The Director's Response to Auditors' Reports	
Appendix 1	Section 194 of the Companies Act 1990 as amended by Section 74 of the 2001 Act, Section 37 of the 2003 Act and Section 73 of the 2005 Act	
Appendix 2	Legal Professional Privilege	

Introduction 1.0

Under the Companies Acts and other legislation, the primary responsibility for a company's compliance with legal and regulatory requirements rests with its directors. This responsibility includes reporting to the company's shareholders, keeping proper books of account, safeguarding the assets of the company and taking appropriate steps to prevent fraud and other irregularities. 1.1

The corporate governance structure established in the Companies Acts also provides that, subject to the exemption introduced by Part III of the Companies (Amendment) (No. 2) Act 1999 (as amended), shareholders are entitled to receive a report from an independent auditor as to whether, in that auditor's opinion, the financial statements presented by the directors give a true and fair view of the state of affairs of the company and of its profits (or losses) for the period under review and have been properly prepared in accordance with the accounting provisions of the Companies Acts and on certain other aspects of the directors' responsibilities for financial reporting. 1.2

While auditors perform these duties in the interests of a company's primary stakeholders, namely its shareholders, they also have to have regard to the public interest. Accordingly, in addition to requiring an auditor to report to shareholders, the Companies Acts and other legislation also impose certain duties on auditors to make disclosures to regulatory authorities in the public interest. 1.3

In 2001, the Oireachtas decided that auditors should be required to report to the Director of Corporate Enforcement ("the Director") instances of the suspected commission of indictable offences under the Companies Acts by a company, its officers or agents. Section 74 of the Company Law Enforcement Act 2001 ("the 2001 Act") accordingly introduced this new duty by amending the existing duties of auditors in section 194 of the Companies Act 1990 ("the 1990 Act"). Section 74 was brought into effect on 28 November 2001[1]. 1.4

In 2003, section 37 of the Companies (Auditing and Accounting) Act 2003 ("the 2003 Act") made a number of further changes to section 194 of the 1990 Act. These changes sought to provide inter alia that the failure to comply with certain obligations to file annual returns would be exempted from the obligation to report to the Director and that auditors would be required to give additional assistance to the Director in his investigation of reported suspected indictable offences under the Companies Acts. 1.5

Sections 73(2)(d) and (3) of the Investment Funds, Companies and Miscellaneous Provisions Act 2005 ("the 2005 Act") made a further amendment to section 194 which clarified the provision in the 2003 Act relating to the exemption of auditors from the requirement to report filing defaults to the Director. This exemption provision was commenced with effect from 1 September 2005[2]. 1.6

The guidance set out in this Bulletin cannot be construed as a definitive legal interpretation of the relevant provisions. However, this guidance discusses the scope of section 194(5), (5A) and (5B) of the 1990 Act (as amended) and takes into account and applies the terms of relevant auditing standards to that provision. It has been 1.7

---

[1] Commencement was achieved in the Investment Funds, Companies and Miscellaneous Provisions Act 2005 (Commencement) Order 2005 (S.I. No. 323 of 2005).

[2] Commencement was achieved in the Investment Funds, Companies and Miscellaneous Provisions Act 2005 (Commencement) Order 2005 (S.I. No.323 of 2005).

developed in conjunction with the Office of the Director of Corporate Enforcement and the Consultative Committee of Accountancy Bodies – Ireland.

2.0   **Section 194 (as amended) of the Companies Act, 1990**

2.1   The original section 194 of the 1990 Act sets out the duties of auditors where they form the opinion that proper books of account are not being kept by a company and its directors. The amendments to section 194 made by the 2001, 2003 and the 2005 Acts prescribe new or amended reporting requirements for auditors. A copy of section 194 of the 1990 Act, following amendment by section 74 of the 2001 Act, section 37 of the 2003 Act and section 73 of the 2005 Act, is attached at Appendix 1 to this Bulletin.

2.2   The purpose of this Bulletin is to outline the scope of the duties which arise for auditors in this context and to address certain issues arising within each part of section 194(5), (5A) and 5(B) of the 1990 Act as amended. The requirement under section 194(5) provides as follows:

> "Where, in the course of, and by virtue of, their carrying out an audit of the accounts of the company, information comes into the possession of the auditors of a company that leads them to form the opinion that there are reasonable grounds for believing that the company or an officer or an agent of it has committed an indictable offence under the Companies Acts (other than an indictable offence under section 125(2) or 127(12) of the Principal Act), the auditors shall, forthwith after having formed it, notify that opinion to the Director and provide the Director with details of the grounds on which they have formed that opinion."[3].

2.3   Section 37(e) of the 2003 Act introduced sections 194(5A) and (5B) as follows:

> "(5A) Where the auditors of a company notify the Director of any matter pursuant to subsection (5), they shall, in addition to performing their obligations under that subsection, if requested by the Director—
>
> (a) furnish the Director with such further information in their possession or control relating to the matter as the Director may require, including further information relating to the details of the grounds on which they formed the opinion referred to in that subsection,
>
> (b) give the Director such access to books and documents in their possession or control relating to the matter as the Director may require, and
>
> (c) give the Director such access to facilities for the taking of copies of or extracts from those books and documents as the Director may require.
>
> (5B) Nothing in this section compels the disclosure by any person of any information that the person would be entitled to refuse to produce on the grounds of legal professional privilege or authorises the inspection or copying of any document containing such information that is in the person's possession."

---

[3] As amended by Section 73(2)(d) of the Investment Funds, Companies and Miscellaneous Provisions Act 2005.

The reporting obligation applies to all persons practising as Responsible Individuals / Registered Auditors[4] of companies to which the provision applies. This includes auditors resident outside the State who are legally permitted under the Companies Acts to audit the accounts of such companies.	2.4
Auditing standards[5] also require auditors to exercise adequate control and supervision over their staff conducting audit work. Consequently, as indicated in ISA (UK and Ireland) 250(B), "The Auditor's Right and Duty to Report to Regulators in the Financial Sector", (paragraph 35), in planning and conducting the audit of a company, auditors need to ensure that staff are alert to the possibility that a report may be required. Auditors should also refer to ISA (UK and Ireland) 220 "Quality Control for Audits of Historical Financial Information" for further guidance on this matter. ISA (UK and Ireland) 250(B) also states that auditing firms need to establish adequate procedures to ensure that any matters which are discovered in the course of, or as a result of, audit work which may give rise to a report are brought to the attention of the engagement partner on a timely basis (ISA (UK and Ireland) 250(B) paragraph 36).	2.5

Auditing Standards 3.0

A number of standards are of relevance to this subject. These include, primarily, ISA (UK and Ireland) 250(A) "Consideration of Law and Regulations in an Audit of Financial Statements" and ISA (UK and Ireland) 250(B) "The Auditor's Right and Duty to Report to Regulators in the Financial Sector". Paragraph 38-3 of ISA (UK and Ireland) 250(A) indicates that the procedures and guidance set out in ISA (UK and Ireland) 250(B) can be adapted to other circumstances in which the auditor becomes aware of a suspected instance of non-compliance with laws or regulations which the auditor is under a statutory duty to report. Where applicable, reference is made to these Standards in the text of this guidance.	3.1

Non-Audit Assignments 4.0

"Where in the course of, and by virtue of, their carrying out an audit of the accounts of a company..."

The subsection indicates that the obligation on auditors to report a suspected indictable offence under the Companies Acts to the Director of Corporate Enforcement arises where auditors are undertaking an audit of the financial statements of a company. Therefore, the reporting obligation does not apply to persons providing non-audit services to a company. Similarly, the subsection does not impose a legal obligation on persons undertaking non-audit services to inform the auditors within their firm of the information which has come into their possession.	4.1

[4] *The Institutes of Chartered Accountants in Ireland (ICAI), England & Wales (ICAEW) and Scotland (ICAS) register firms for audit. The Institute of Certified Public Accountants in Ireland (ICPAI) also registers firms. Persons within those firms who are entitled to sign audit reports are known as Responsible Individuals. The Association of Chartered Certified Accountants (ACCA) registers both firms and individuals for audit while the Institute of Incorporated Public Accountants Ltd. (IIPA) registers individuals for audit. Individuals registered by these bodies are known as Registered Auditors.*

[5] *International Standards on Auditing (UK and Ireland) may be accessed through the APB website at www.frc.org.uk/apb.*

4.2 However, where a person performs, or has performed, non-audit work for a company for whom s/he also acts, or subsequently accepts appointment, as auditor, that auditor, acting as such, has certain responsibilities in relation to any information suggesting the commission of an indictable offence which came to attention during the course of the non-audit work.

4.3 The statutory duty to report to a regulator applies to information which comes to the attention of auditors in their capacity as such. In determining whether information is obtained in that capacity, ISA (UK and Ireland) 250(B) identifies two criteria in particular which need to be considered, namely:

(i) whether the person who obtained the information also undertook the audit work and, if so,
(ii) whether it was obtained in the course of, or as a result of, undertaking the audit work (ISA (UK and Ireland) 250(B) Appendix 2 - paragraph 6).

4.4 Where partners or staff, involved in the audit of an entity, carry out work other than the audit (i.e. non-audit work), information about the entity will be known to them as individuals. In circumstances which suggest that a matter would otherwise give rise to a statutory duty to report if obtained in the capacity of auditor, it will be prudent for them to make enquiries in the course of their audit work in order to establish whether this is the case from information obtained in that capacity (ISA (UK and Ireland) 250(B) Appendix 2 - paragraph 8).

4.5 Where non-audit work is carried out by other partners or staff, neither of the aforementioned criteria (at (i) and (ii) above) are satisfied in respect of the information that becomes known to them. Nevertheless, in such circumstances, ISA (UK and Ireland) 250(B) states that the firm in question should take proper account of such information when it could affect the audit so that it is treated in a responsible manner, particularly since in partnership law the knowledge obtained by one partner in the course of partnership business may be imputed to the entire partnership (ISA (UK and Ireland) 250(B) Appendix 2 - paragraph 9).

4.6 A firm appointed as auditor of an entity needs to have in place appropriate procedures to ensure that the partner responsible for the audit function is made aware of any relationship which exists between any department of the firm and the regulated entity when that relationship could affect the firm's work as auditor (ISA (UK and Ireland) 250(B) Appendix 2 - paragraph 10).

4.7 The ISA goes on to state that, *prima facie*, information obtained in the course of non-audit work is not covered by the duty to report. However, the firm appointed as auditor needs to consider whether the results of other work undertaken for the entity in question needs to be assessed as part of the audit process. In principle this is no different to seeking to review a report prepared by outside consultants on the entity's accounting systems so as to ensure that the auditor makes a proper assessment of the risks of misstatement in the financial statements and of the work needed to form an opinion. Consequently, the partner responsible for the audit needs to make appropriate enquiries in the process of planning (see below) and completing the audit. Such enquiries would be directed to those aspects of the non-audit work which might reasonably be expected to be relevant to the audit (ISA (UK and Ireland) 250(B) Appendix 2 - paragraph 11).

4.8 In the context of the foregoing, the provisions of ISA (UK and Ireland) 300 "Planning an Audit of Financial Statements", ISA (UK and Ireland) 210 "Terms of Audit Engagements", and ISA (UK and Ireland) 315 "Understanding the Entity and its Environment and Assessing the Risks of Material Misstatement" are also of particular relevance. Auditors are required by these standards to:

- plan the audit (ISA (UK and Ireland) 300),
- agree the terms of engagement with the client (ISA (UK and Ireland) 210), and
- obtain an understanding of the entity and its environment (ISA (UK and Ireland) 315).

In planning the audit, agreeing the terms of engagement, and obtaining a knowledge of the business, the auditor is expected to consider all material relevant to the audit including: **4.9**

- internal control relevant to the audit (ISA (UK and Ireland) 315 paragraph 41),
- relevant industry, regulatory and other external factors (ISA (UK and Ireland) 315 paragraph 22),
- scope of the audit, including reference to applicable legislation (ISA (UK and Ireland) 210 paragraph 6), and
- where relevant, information about the entity and its environment obtained in prior periods (ISA (UK and Ireland) 315 paragraph 12).

ISA (UK and Ireland) 300 is framed in the context of recurring audits. However, it draws auditors' attention (in paragraph 29) to the fact that *"for an initial audit, the auditor may need to expand the planning activities because the auditor does not ordinarily have the previous experience with the entity that is considered when planning recurring engagements"*. **4.10**

Compliance with the provisions of ISAs (UK and Ireland) 250, 300 and 315 respectively may result in auditors successfully identifying any matters arising from non-audit work that may require them to make a report to the Director pursuant to their obligations under section 194(5) of the 1990 Act. **4.11**

With regard to the point in time at which auditors' reporting obligations arise in respect of matters first identified in the course of providing non-audit services: **4.12**

- where a person providing non-audit services to a company becomes aware of an indictable offence and s/he also acts as the auditor of that company, the obligation to report the suspected indictable offence will arise when the auditor comes into possession of the information in question as part of the undertaking of the audit, and
- where a person providing non-audit services to a company becomes aware of an indictable offence and s/he is subsequently appointed to act as the auditor of that company, the obligation to report the suspected indictable offence will arise when the auditor comes into possession of the information in question as part of the undertaking of the audit.

Reportable Information 5.0

"...information comes into the possession of the auditors of a company..."

The provision indicates that the obligation on auditors to report to the Director of Corporate Enforcement arises when information comes into their possession as part of the undertaking of the audit. Without prejudice to the above guidance on the need for proper audit planning and associated requirements, the Director does not regard the obligation as requiring auditors to seek out possible indictable offences as part of **5.1** the audit process. However, auditors react to information coming into their possession which suggests that a possible indictable offence has occurred and to make the necessary enquiries to enable them to form a considered opinion on the question.

5.2 ISA (UK and Ireland) 250(A) sets out standards and guidance for auditors on the consideration of law and regulations. It requires that *"the auditor should plan and perform the audit with an attitude of professional scepticism, recognising that the audit may reveal conditions or events that could lead to questioning whether an entity is complying with law and regulations."* (ISA (UK and Ireland) 250(A) paragraph 13).

5.3 ISA (UK and Ireland) 250(A) requires that *"in order to plan the audit, the auditor should obtain a general understanding of the legal and regulatory framework applicable to the entity and the industry and how the entity is complying with that framework."* (ISA (UK and Ireland) 250(A) paragraph 15).

5.4 The ISA also indicates that in obtaining a general understanding of the legal and regulatory framework applicable to an entity and procedures followed to ensure compliance with this framework, auditors would particularly recognise that non-compliance with some laws and regulations may give rise to business risks that have a fundamental effect on the operations of the entity. That is, non-compliance with certain laws and regulations may cause the entity to cease operations, or call into question the entity's continuance as a going concern. For example, non-compliance with the requirements of the entity's license or other title to perform its operations could have such an impact (for example, for a bank, non-compliance with capital or investment requirements) (ISA (UK and Ireland) 250(A) paragraph 16).

5.5 The ISA goes on to state that *"To obtain the general understanding of laws and regulations, the auditor would ordinarily:*

- *Use the existing understanding of the entity's industry, regulatory and other external factors;*
- *Inquire of management concerning the entity's policies and procedures regarding compliance with laws and regulations;*
- *Inquire of management as to the laws or regulations that may be expected to have a fundamental effect on the operations of the entity;*
- *Discuss with management the policies or procedures adopted for identifying, evaluating and accounting for litigation claims and assessments; and*
- *Discuss the legal and regulatory framework with auditors of subsidiaries in other countries (for example, if the subsidiary is required to adhere to the securities regulations of the parent company)."* (ISA (UK and Ireland) 250(A) paragraph 17).

5.6 The auditor should then perform further audit procedures to help identify instances of non-compliance with those laws and regulations where non-compliance should be considered when preparing financial statements, specifically:

- Inquiring of management as to whether the entity is in compliance with such laws and regulations;
- Inspecting correspondence with the relevant licensing or regulatory authorities; and
- Enquiring of those charged with governance as to whether they are on notice of any such possible instances of non-compliance with law or regulations. (ISA (UK and Ireland) 250(A) paragraph 18).

5.7 The auditor's procedures should be designed to help identify possible or actual instances of non-compliance with those laws and regulations which provide a legal framework within which the entity conducts its business and which are central to the entity's ability to conduct its business and hence to its financial statements (ISA (UK and Ireland) 250(A) paragraph 18-1).

5.8 On discovery of a possible instance of non-compliance, the ISA provides the following direction to auditors: "*when the auditor becomes aware of information concerning a possible instance of non-compliance, the auditor should obtain an understanding of the nature of the act and the circumstances in which it has occurred and sufficient other information to evaluate the possible effect on the financial statements*" (ISA (UK and Ireland) 250(A) paragraph 26).

5.9 The ISA goes on to state that when evaluating the possible effect on the financial statements, the auditor considers, *inter alia*, "*the potential financial consequences, such as fines, penalties, damages, threat of expropriation of assets, enforced discontinuation of operations and litigation*" (ISA (UK and Ireland) 250(A) paragraph 27).

5.10 It is clear, therefore, that where auditors detect the suspected commission of an indictable offence under the Companies Acts, they are required by professional standards to carry out such further investigations into the matter as to provide them with an understanding of the nature of the act and to allow them to properly evaluate the possible effects on the financial statements, including the potential consequences of any fines or other sanctions (imposed on the company, its directors or officers) which might result from that non-compliance.

5.11 In general the maximum penalty on conviction on indictment (see [section 10.0] – Indictable Offences) of an indictable offence under the Companies Acts is €12,700 and/or 5 years' imprisonment. However, the Companies Acts also provide for considerably higher sanctions in respect of certain offences, e.g. fraudulent trading (€63,000 and/or 7 years imprisonment) and insider dealing/market abuse (€10,000,000 and/or 10 years' imprisonment). Moreover, persons convicted on indictment of an indictable offence involving fraud or dishonesty are automatically disqualified from acting as company directors/officers. The Director of Corporate Enforcement can also apply to the Courts seeking the disqualification of any person:

- guilty of two or more offences of failing to maintain proper books and records, or,
- guilty of three or more defaults under the Companies Acts.

5.12 Accordingly, the conviction on indictment of a company or any of its officers under the Companies Acts and any consequential claims arising can have potentially very serious consequences for the company and its continuing operations, and by extension on its financial statements.

5.13 In the context of their investigations, section 193(3) of the Companies Act 1990 entitles auditors, *inter alia*, to require from the officers of the company such information as they think necessary for the performance of their duties. If an auditor is unable, as part of the audit, to obtain information regarding a potential breach due to the non co-operation of one of the company's officers or agents, this in itself constitutes a suspected indictable offence under section 197[6] of the 1990 Act. Naturally, any such non co-operation will also have to be taken into account by an auditor when:

---

[6] Section 197(3) Companies Act, 1990 states: "An officer of a company who fails to provide to the auditors of the company or of the holding company of the company, within two days of the making of the relevant request, any information or explanations that the auditors require as auditors of the company or of the holding company of the company and that is within the knowledge of or can be procured by the officer shall be guilty of an offence".

- forming his or her audit opinion,
- drafting the audit report under section 193(4) of the Companies Act 1990,
- deciding whether to continue in office or to decline re-appointment.

5.14 In the event that an auditor was to resign or to decline re-appointment in such circumstances, s/he would be obliged under section 185 of the 1990 Act to:

- serve a notice of resignation on the company (subsection (1)),
- provide in the notice a statement of the circumstances which should be brought to the attention of the members or creditors of the company (subsection (2)), and
- copy the notice to the Registrar of Companies within 14 days (subsection (3)).

6.0 Legal or Other Professional Advice

"...that leads them to form the opinion that there are reasonable grounds for believing..."

6.1 Section 194(5) requires auditors to exercise their professional judgement in determining if the information and evidence in their possession leads to the formation of the opinion that the matter is reportable to the Director of Corporate Enforcement by virtue of providing reasonable grounds for a belief that an indictable offence has been committed. A collective judgement may be made in the case of an auditing firm. While there is no obligation on auditors to obtain legal or other professional advice before forming that opinion, the Director recognises that auditors may wish to seek such independent advice as part of the process of forming their opinion.

6.2 Where legal or other professional advice is obtained by the company in relation to the matter(s) about which the auditor has concerns, the auditor is similarly required to exercise professional judgement in determining if the information is reportable to the Director of Corporate Enforcement. While in many cases, auditors could expect to be satisfied with legal advice emanating from a reputable source, auditors would not be entitled to rely on such advice if, having taken it into account, they formed the opinion that the advice was in error, incomplete or otherwise inadequate by reference to the information in their possession.

7.0 Reportable Persons

"...that the company or an officer or an agent of it..."

7.1 In the subsection, *"the company"* is the company which is being audited by the auditor ("Company A"). Subject to what follows, the reporting obligation does not therefore extend to another company ("Company B"), which the auditor of Company A may believe has committed a reportable offence.

7.2 In addition, the term *"company"* must comply with the general definition of company in the Companies Act 1963 which is *"a company formed and registered under this Act, or an existing company"*.

indictable offence. This guidance is supported by ISA (UK and Ireland) 250(B) which requires, *inter alia*, "*the auditor should bring the matter to the attention of the regulator...in a form and manner which will facilitate appropriate action by the regulator*" (ISA (UK and Ireland) 250(B) paragraph 50).

The information provided by auditors as part of their reports to the Director of Corporate Enforcement should include: **11.2**

- auditor details;
- statutory authority under which the report is being made;
- details of the company/person(s) who are the subject of the report;
- whether the matter has been discussed with the directors and/or relevant officer(s) and/or agent(s) of the company;
- details of the suspected indictable offence(s);
- details of the grounds on which the auditor has formed the opinion that an indictable offence has been committed. Auditors should ensure that this description is of sufficient detail to facilitate appropriate action by the Director;
- the context in which the report is being made. ISA (UK and Ireland) 250(B) offers guidance to auditors as to the type of information that might be included in this regard e.g.
  - the extent to which the auditor has investigated the circumstances giving rise to the matter reported, and
  - whether steps to rectify the matter have been taken (ISA (UK and Ireland) 250(B) paragraph 63).
- any other information considered relevant by the auditor;
- auditor's signature;
- date of report.

The ODCE publication 'A Guide to Transactions Involving Directors' sets out information that, if known to the auditor as a result of audit work, the Director considers useful to include as part of the report to his Office where the subject matter of the report is a suspected offence under section 40 of the Companies Act 1990 indicating a loan to a director(s) exceeding 10% of the company's relevant assets. Such information includes, if possible: **11.3**

- the date(s) on which the loan(s) was/were advanced;
- the identity of each individual to whom the loan(s) was/were given;
- the value of the loan(s);
- whether the company's relevant assets were calculated by reference to the company's net assets as shown in the last preceding financial statements laid before an AGM or by reference to the company's called up share capital; and
- the extent to which 10% of the company's relevant assets were exceeded by the loan(s)[8].

Where such information is not readily available to the auditor (Ie from information contained in the audit working papers), the auditor refers the Director to the company and its directors.

Auditors may afford the company's officer(s) or agent(s), as appropriate, the opportunity to compile a statement for submission to the Director of Corporate Enforcement together with the auditor's report. Issues that the officer(s) or agent(s) may wish to address if they choose to prepare such a statement might include, for example, their views on the report's subject matter and details of any corrective or remedial action taken or proposed. **11.4**

---

[8] *Section 8.2, Contents of Auditors' Reports*, excerpt from '*A Guide to Transactions Involving Directors*', published by the ODCE in November 2003.

11.5 However, where the officer(s) or agent(s) elect to submit a statement to the Director, auditors should ensure that their reports are not delayed. Accordingly, it is recommended that in such circumstances, auditors should allow a period of two days for the furnishing of statements by the officer(s) or agent(s), after which time auditors should submit their report. Naturally, the officer(s) or agent(s) can, if they so wish, subsequently furnish a statement to the Director.

12.0 Provision of Further Information by Auditors to the Director

12.1 Section 37(e) of the Companies (Auditing and Accounting) Act 2003 extends the responsibilities of auditors in situations where they make a report to the Director under Section 194(5) of the Companies Act 1990. In particular, it provides in a new subsection (5A) that if requested by the Director, auditors shall:

> "(a) furnish the Director with such further information in their possession or control relating to the matter as the Director may require, including further information relating to the details of the grounds on which they formed the opinion referred to in that subsection,
> (b) give the Director such access to books and documents in their possession or control relating to the matter as the Director may require, and
> (c) give the Director such access to facilities for the taking of copies of or extracts from those books and documents as the Director may require."

12.2 The purpose of this additional provision is to enable the Director to acquire on an efficient and effective basis the quality of information and evidence which initially led the auditor to report the suspected offence and thereby to facilitate the Director in reaching an informed decision as to what enforcement action (if any) is warranted by him as a result of the indicated circumstances.

12.3 The decision of the Director as to whether he will close the case without further action, recommend administrative resolution of the case perhaps by way of letter, or commence the preparation of a case for legal proceedings, depends on him having access to the fullest possible information concerning the incident or incidents that gave rise to the auditor's report. Every report made to the Office is dealt with in this manner so it is to the benefit of all parties that this information be gathered as efficiently as possible.

12.4 The information or books and documents to be made available is limited only to that which is actually in the possession of the auditor or under his control. The term "books and documents" is defined in section 3(1) of the 1990 Act as including "accounts, deeds, writings and records made in any other manner". Accordingly, the information, books and documents to be made available comprise both electronic and physical material. It should be noted that the auditor is not required to provide original documentation and there is no requirement to seek out additional information beyond that which is in the auditor's possession or control as a result of a request under this section.

12.5 Section 194(5B) of the 1990 Act makes clear that the Director's right to the information, books and documents referred to in section 194(5A) does not extend to material which is covered by legal professional privilege. An auditor can accordingly properly refuse to provide such material. Appendix 2 provides commentary on legal professional privilege.

12.6 The meaning of the phrase "relating to the matter" will depend on the particular circumstances of each report and the nature and amount of information in the

good faith in informing an authority of a breach of law or regulations which they think has been committed would not be held by the court to have been in breach of duty to the client even if, an investigation or prosecution having occurred, it were to be found that there had been no offence.

The ISA goes on to state that: **14.7**

- the auditor needs to remember that the auditor's decision as to whether to report, and if so to whom, may be called into question at a future date, for example on the basis of:
  - what the auditor knew at the time;
  - what the auditor ought to have known in the course of the audit;
  - what the auditor ought to have concluded, and;
  - what the auditor ought to have done (ISA (UK and Ireland) 250(A) paragraph 38-11).
- the auditor may also wish to consider the possible consequences if financial loss is occasioned by non-compliance with law or regulations which they suspect (or ought to suspect) has occurred but decide not to report (ISA (UK and Ireland) 250(A) paragraph 38-11).

Where, having considered any views expressed on behalf of the entity and in the light of any legal advice obtained, the auditor concludes that the matter ought to be reported to an appropriate authority in the public interest, the auditor notifies those charged with governance in writing of their view and, if the entity does not voluntarily do so itself or is unable to provide evidence that the matter has been reported, the auditor reports it (ISA (UK and Ireland) 250(A) paragraph 38-5). The auditor reports a matter to the proper authority in the public interest and without discussing the matter with the entity if the auditor concludes that the suspected or actual instance of non-compliance has caused the auditor no longer to have confidence in the integrity of those charged with governance (ISA (UK and Ireland) 250(A) paragraph 38-6). **14.8**

The Director's Response to Auditors' Reports 15

Every auditor's report received will be examined by the Office of the Director of Corporate Enforcement and an acknowledgement issued. Where considered necessary, clarification or further information will be sought from the directors, auditor or other persons as required for example under the provisions of Section 194(5A) and (5B). Assuming that a *prima facie* breach of the Companies Acts is disclosed, the Director and his officers will consider various matters before determining the next step. These include: **15.1**

- whether the offence is proper to the Director's Office. It may be, for instance, that the offence is better handled by another authority,
- what additional evidence may be required by way of documentation or oral statements from the company, its officers, agents or third parties to address the indicated breach and the manner in which such evidence should be obtained,
- the seriousness of the suspected offence,
- whether the offence has been remedied and the extent to which the remedy in itself is a sufficient outcome,
- the urgency of the case, and
- the extent to which viable options are available to the Director to remedy or sanction the suspected offence.

15.2 Where action is appropriate by his Office, the Director will endeavour to respond in a manner which is likely to be both effective and proportionate in relation to the indicated offence.

Appendix 1 – Section 194 of the Companies Act 1990 as amended by Section 74 of the 2001 Act, Section 37 of the 2003 Act and Section 73 of the 2005 Act

(Please note that the text as amended by the 2003 and 2005 Acts is underlined)

Duty of auditors if proper books of account are not being kept

194.—(1) If, at any time, the auditors of a company form the opinion that the company is contravening, or has contravened, *section 202* by failing to cause to be kept proper books of account (within the meaning of that section) in relation to the matters specified in *subsections (1)* and *(2)* of that section, the auditors shall—

(a) as soon as may be, by recorded delivery, serve a notice in writing on the company stating their opinion, and
(b) not later than 7 days after the service of such notice on the company, notify the registrar of companies in the prescribed form of the notice and the registrar shall forthwith forward a copy of the notice to the Director.

(2) Where the auditors form the opinion that the company has contravened *section 202* but that, following such contravention, the directors of the company have taken the necessary steps to ensure that proper books of account are kept as required by that section, *subsection (1)(b)* shall not apply.

(3) This section shall not require the auditors to make the notifications referred to in *subsection (1)* if they are of opinion that the contraventions concerned are minor or otherwise immaterial in nature.

(3A) Where the auditors of a company file a notice pursuant to *subsection (1)(b)*, they shall, if requested by the Director-

(a) furnish to the Director such information, including an explanation of the reasons for their opinion that the company has contravened section 202, and
(b) give to the Director such access to books and documents, including facilities for inspecting and taking copies, being information, books or documents in their possession or control and relating to the matter the subject of the notice, as the Director may require.

(3B) Any written information given in response to a request of the Director under *subsection (3A)* shall in all legal proceedings be admissible without further proof, until the contrary is shown, as evidence of the facts stated therein.

(4) A person who contravenes *subsection (1), (3A), (5)* or *(5A)* shall be guilty of an offence.

(5) Where, in the course of, and by virtue of, their carrying out an audit of the accounts of the company, information comes into the possession of the auditors of a company that leads them to form the opinion that there are reasonable grounds for believing that the company or an officer or an agent of it has committed an indictable offence under the Companies Acts (other than an indictable offence under section

125(2) or 127(12) of the Principal Act), the auditors shall, forthwith after having formed it, notify that opinion to the Director and provide the Director with details of the grounds on which they have formed that opinion.

(5A) Where the auditors of a company notify the Director of any matter pursuant to subsection (5), they shall, in addition to performing their obligations under that subsection, if requested by the Director—

(a) furnish the Director with such further information in their possession or control relating to the matter as the Director may require, including further information relating to the details of the grounds on which they formed the opinion referred to in that subsection,
(b) give the Director such access to books and documents in their possession or control relating to the matter as the Director may require, and
(c) give the Director such access to facilities for the taking of copies of or extracts from those books and documents as the Director may require.

(5B) Nothing in this section compels the disclosure by any person of any information that the person would be entitled to refuse to produce on the grounds of legal professional privilege or authorises the inspection or copying of any document containing such information that is in the person's possession.

(6) No professional or legal duty to which an auditor is subject by virtue of his appointment as an auditor of a company shall be regarded as contravened by, and no liability to the company, its shareholders, creditors or other interested parties shall attach to, an auditor, by reason of his compliance with an obligation imposed on him by or under this section.

Appendix 2 – Legal Professional Privilege (The commentary below relates to the Republic of Ireland only)

Section 194(5B) of the 1990 Act states:

> 'Nothing in this section compels the disclosure by any person of any information that the person would be entitled to refuse to produce on the grounds of legal professional privilege or authorises the inspection or copying of any document containing such information that is in the person's possession.'

The issue of whether information or documents attract legal professional privilege will need to be considered carefully. The question is one of law which, in appropriate circumstances, may fall to be determined by the Courts. *Accordingly, auditors seeking to limit disclosure on the basis of legal professional privilege are advised to consider taking legal advice.*

A brief explanation of legal privilege and the circumstances in which it may apply are set out below. Such situations are likely to be rare. For example, it is unlikely that the audit work carried out and documented by the auditor which resulted in the identification of a reportable matter will be privileged. This is because such audit work would not have been in contemplation of litigation; identification of a reportable matter is incidental to the audit. Nor will it apply to other non-audit documentation prepared by the audit firm in advance of the formation of an opinion that a report should be made to the Director and which relates to the subject matter of that report.

Legal professional privilege exists in two forms – legal advice privilege and litigation privilege.

Legal advice privilege

Legal advice privilege prevents the disclosure of communications between a lawyer and a client where such communications are made for the purpose of obtaining legal advice. It is not necessary for litigation to be pending or contemplated for this to apply. However, for legal advice privilege to apply, the advice must come from a professionally-qualified lawyer (solicitor or barrister). Advice from an auditor or tax advisor to a client is not subject to privilege.

The subject matter of the document must be legal advice rather than legal assistance (eg company secretarial services).

As noted above, the circumstances in which this form of legal professional privilege will apply to an auditor are likely to be rare.

Litigation privilege

Litigation privilege prevents the disclosure of communications between the client and his lawyer or either the client or his lawyer and a third party, such as, in this case, the auditor.

For litigation privilege to apply, the Courts have set out certain criteria:

- litigation must be pending, contemplated, or reasonably apprehended[9];
- the dominant purpose for the creation of the document must have been that of pending/contemplated or reasonably apprehended litigation; there may be more than one purpose behind the preparation of the document;
- documents in existence prior to litigation being contemplated will not be privileged.

It is important to note that legal professional privilege "belongs" to the client who has sought the legal advice, or is party to the relevant litigation. It is for that client to decide whether to assert the privilege or, alternatively, whether he/she wishes to waive it.

Where the auditor or his/her firm has sought legal advice (including from the audit firm's professionally-qualified in-house lawyers) such advice clearly attracts legal professional privilege and it is for the auditor to decide whether or not to assert the privilege. The same situation applies where the auditor or his/her firm is a party to pending or contemplated litigation and documents have been created for the dominant purpose of that litigation.

Where an auditor or his/her firm is in possession of information or documents over which the audit client enjoys legal professional privilege the situation is somewhat more complicated. Legal professional privilege is concerned with protecting confidential communications and, accordingly, if a client has opted to substantially publicise those communications the privilege may be lost or may be taken to have been waived. However it is thought that confidential disclosure by a company to its statutory auditors of material over which it (the company) enjoys legal professional privilege will not ordinarily give rise to a loss or waiver of the company's privilege – certainly in cases where the auditor, as such, shares a common interest in the communications with the company.

---

[9] These terms have received judicial consideration and should be read in light of the relevant case law.

[Bulletin 2008/1]
Audit issues when financial market conditions are difficult and credit facilities may be restricted

(Issued January 2008)

Contents

	Paragraphs
Introduction	1 - 5
Risk assessment, quality control and communication with those charged with governance.	6 - 7
Going concern	8 - 11
Valuation and disclosure of financial instruments	12 - 18
Disclosure of risk in Directors' Report	19 - 22
Implications for the auditor's report	23 - 25
Ethical issues	26 - 27

Appendix – Risk Factors

Introduction

1. This Bulletin provides guidance on matters that auditors may need to consider when conducting audits in the economic environment following recent developments in the financial markets commonly termed "the credit crunch."

2. In recent months financial market conditions have been characterised by significant trading difficulties compounded by a reduction in liquidity. Although the primary market shock arose due to defaults on sub-prime mortgages in the United States, the effect has been felt globally due to widespread use of structured securities and leveraged funding. Entities with exposure to the financial markets through debt, equity, derivative and leveraged finance activities may experience significant difficulty in trading in and thus valuing certain investments, with a consequential increase in the risk of material misstatement of financial statements. More generally, entities may find it difficult to finance their operations as a result of restricted credit facilities.

3. While the credit crunch is likely to have a particular effect on the audit of financial institutions such as banks, insurance companies and investment businesses, many entities operating outside the financial services sector could also be affected by current market conditions, especially if those entities are dependent on refinancing their operations over the coming months, or may be at risk of having current facilities withdrawn, or have significant investments that have reduced significantly in value or are difficult to value in the absence of an active market.

4. While this Bulletin may be of assistance to the auditors of financial institutions it has been written to apply more generally and focuses on the risks and uncertainties associated with:

    - Reduced liquidity in the financial markets and in particular the reduced availability of finance for those who require it. As financing arrangements expire, replacement may prove expensive or impossible, with potentially serious consequences in relation to the "going concern" assumption; and
    - Valuation of investments. For some investments there may be a severe curtailment or cessation of market trading, introducing particular difficulties for valuation measurements. Investment in such financial instruments may not be limited to financial institutions. It is possible that other entities, such as those with developed treasury activities and pension funds, may have invested in financial instruments that are currently experiencing severely curtailed/ceased trading which will make their valuation for balance sheet purposes difficult.

5. This Bulletin draws on existing material within APB's standards and guidance and should be read in conjunction with them. It does not establish any new requirements. Not all of the issues addressed will be relevant to all audits, and there may be other issues that auditors need also to consider that are not addressed in this Bulletin.

Risk assessment, quality control and communication with those charged with governance

6. While the credit crunch is most likely to be relevant to the audit of financial institutions, it may also affect audits of entities operating outside the financial services sector. Auditors, as part of their planning and risk assessment process of all entities, consider whether current market conditions could give rise to the risk of material misstatement of the financial statements and respond accordingly. The appendix to this Bulletin identifies some factors that may increase the risk of material

misstatement in financial statements when financial market conditions are difficult and credit facilities may be restricted.

If the audited entity is at risk of material misstatement of the financial statements due to current market conditions, the audit engagement partner will have particular regard to:

- his/her own involvement in the direction, supervision and performance of the audit when complying with the requirements of ISA (UK and Ireland) 220, paragraph 21,
- the capabilities and competence of the engagement team (especially if the audit involves evaluation of the fair value of financial instruments) when complying with the requirements of ISA (UK and Ireland) 220, paragraph 19,
- consultation with other professionals on difficult and contentious matters when complying with the requirements of ISA (UK and Ireland) 220, paragraph 30, and
- the nature and timing of communications with those charged with governance when complying with the requirements of ISA (UK and Ireland) 260.

Going concern

One impact of the 'credit crunch' may be to limit finance available to companies and other entities, with, in extreme cases, potentially serious consequences in relation to the "going concern" assumption. Past experience of obtaining necessary financing cannot be relied on alone to provide sufficient evidence of an entity's ability to obtain financing in the future. Lenders may be more risk averse when considering whether to provide or renew finance facilities and may establish new criteria and/or may increase interest rates.

Against that background, auditors will have regard to ISA (UK and Ireland) 570, which establishes standards and provides guidance on the auditor's responsibility with respect to consideration of the going concern assumption used in the preparation of the financial statements. In particular, the guidance on the auditor's examination of borrowing facilities in paragraphs 21-2 and 21-3 may assist.

- Paragraph 21-2 states: 'The auditor might be more likely to decide that it is necessary to obtain confirmations of the existence and terms of bank facilities, and to make an independent assessment of the intentions of the bankers relating thereto, in cases where, for example there is a low margin of financial resources available to the entity', and
- Paragraph 21-3 states: 'The auditor considers whether any inability to obtain sufficient appropriate audit evidence regarding the existence and terms of borrowing facilities and the intentions of the lender relating thereto, and/or the factors giving rise to this inability, need to be:
  - Disclosed in the financial statements in order that they give a true and fair view; and/or
  - Referred to in the auditor's report (by way of an explanatory paragraph, or a qualified opinion if the auditor believes that the disclosures in the financial statements are not adequate).

Standards and guidance on explanatory paragraphs (e.g. to highlight a material matter that is disclosed in the financial statements regarding a going concern problem) or qualified opinions (e.g. where there is inadequate disclosure in the financial statements of a going concern problem) in the auditor's report are provided in ISAs (UK and Ireland) 570 and 700.

11 Additional considerations apply to the audit of listed companies. Directors of listed companies are required by the Listing Rules[1] to make a statement in the annual financial report that the business is a going concern, together with supporting assumptions or qualifications as necessary, that has been prepared in accordance with "Going Concern and Financial Reporting: Guidance for directors of listed companies registered in the United Kingdom," published November 1994[2]. APB Bulletin 2006/5[3] emphasises the importance of ensuring that the directors' statement on going concern is not inconsistent with any disclosures regarding going concern in either the financial statements or the auditor's report thereon.

Valuation and disclosure of financial instruments

12 A second impact of the 'credit crunch' may be to impair the value of some investments or, especially when they are required to be measured at 'fair value', make their valuation for balance sheet purposes difficult (e.g. when trading in a particular investment has been severely curtailed and current market values are difficult to establish). Against this background, auditors will have regard to ISA (UK and Ireland) 545, which establishes standards and provides guidance on auditing fair value measurements and disclosures contained in financial statements. The use of experts with particular knowledge of the valuation of complex financial instruments may be appropriate and, in such cases, the standards and guidance in ISA (UK and Ireland) 620 will be relevant.

13 When the auditor determines there is a significant risk related to fair value, the auditor should evaluate whether the significant assumptions used by management in measuring fair values, taken individually and as a whole, provide a reasonable basis for the fair value measurements and disclosures (ISA (UK and Ireland) 545, paragraph 39). This evaluation includes consideration of whether these assumptions reflect current market conditions and information.

14 Particular difficulties may arise where there is a severe curtailment or even cessation of market trading in certain investments. For example, in these circumstances, investments that have previously been marked to market may need to be valued using a model. If management has changed the valuation method, the auditor considers whether management can adequately demonstrate that the valuation method to which it has changed provides a more appropriate basis of measurement.

15 Auditors also need to evaluate whether the disclosures about fair values made by the entity are in accordance with the financial reporting framework (ISA (UK and Ireland) 545, paragraph 56). In the current environment, it will be important that disclosures of material risks and uncertainties related to fair value measurements are appropriate to the entity.

16 For entities applying International Accounting Standards, IAS 1, "Presentation of Financial Statements," disclosure requirements include:
- The judgments, apart from those involving estimations (see the next bullet), that management has made in the process of applying the entity's accounting policies

---

[1] Listing Rule 9.8.6R (3)

[2] This guidance was a publication of the Cadbury Committee and can be accessed at http://www.icaew.com/index.cfm?route=117590

[3] Bulletin 2006/5 "The Combined Code on Corporate Governance: Requirements of Auditors under the Listing Rules of the Financial Services Authority and the Irish Stock Exchange".

and that have the most significant effect on the amounts recognised in the financial statements.
- Information about the key assumptions concerning the future, and other key sources of estimation uncertainty at the balance sheet date, that have a significant risk of causing a material adjustment in the carrying amount of assets and liabilities within the next financial year.

In addition, recent developments in accounting standards will affect the extent and nature of disclosures relating to some financial instruments for audits of financial statements for periods commencing on or after 1 January 2007[4]. The disclosures required are extensive and potentially complex including:

- Qualitative disclosures such as the exposures to risk arising from the financial instruments,
- Quantitative disclosures such as summary data about the exposures at the reporting date, and
- Market risk information such as a sensitivity analysis for each type of market risk to which the entity is exposed at the reporting date, showing how profit or loss and equity would have been affected by changes in the relevant risk variable that were reasonably possible at that date.

APB Practice Note 19 'The Audit of Banks and Building Societies in the United Kingdom' provides guidance, in paragraphs 113 to 125, on auditing the disclosure of market risk information under IFRS 7 and FRS 29, and whether the risk measurement method adopted has been applied reasonably[5].

Disclosure of risk in Directors' Report

Section 234ZZB of the Companies Act 1985[6] requires that the Directors' Report for all companies (except small companies) contain a business review that includes:

(a) a fair review of the business of the company, and
(b) a description of the principal risks and uncertainties facing the company.

The review is required to be a balanced and comprehensive analysis of the development and performance of the business of the company during the financial year, and the position of the company at the end of that year, consistent with the size and complexity of the business.

It is likely that companies affected by the credit crunch will decide to make some reference to the risks and uncertainties facing the company in the business review, such as those relating to the availability of financing and the valuation of financial instruments where relevant. ISA (UK and Ireland) 720, which establishes standards and provides guidance on the auditor's consideration of other information in documents containing audited financial statements, will be particularly relevant in these circumstances.

---

[4] FRS 29 'Financial Instruments: Disclosures' and IFRS 7 'Financial Instruments: Disclosures' contain substantially the same requirements. Reporting entities applying the Financial Reporting Standard for Smaller Entities (FRSSE) currently applicable are exempt from FRS 29.

[5] The same guidance is in the current Exposure Draft of Practice Note 19(I) 'Banks in the Republic of Ireland' (paragraphs 101 to 113).

[6] The requirements of Section 234ZZB have been carried over to section 417 of the Companies Act 2006. Section 417 has some additional requirements for quoted companies and relief when disclosures could be seriously prejudicial to the interests of the company or certain persons.

21 ISA (UK and Ireland) 720 has two sections. Section A applies to all other information in documents containing audited financial statements. Section B contains additional standards and guidance in relation to the auditor's statutory reporting responsibility in relation to Directors' Reports.

22 In the UK and the Republic of Ireland, legislation requires the auditor of a company to state in the auditor's report whether, in the auditor's opinion, the information given in the Directors' Report is consistent with the financial statements. Omission of information from the Directors' Report is not classed as an 'inconsistency' in ISA (UK and Ireland) 720 but Section B, paragraph 4, states 'The auditor is not required to verify, or report on, the completeness of the information in the directors' report. If, however, the auditor becomes aware that information that is required by law or regulations to be in the directors' report has been omitted the auditor communicates the matter to those charged with governance'.

Implications for the auditor's report

23 If the financial statements include a note that discusses a material matter regarding a going concern problem, the auditor is required to highlight that matter by adding an emphasis of matter paragraph to the auditor's report (ISA (UK and Ireland) 700, paragraph 31). If there is a significant uncertainty[7] (other than a going concern problem) disclosed in the financial statements, the resolution of which is dependent upon future events and which may affect the financial statements, the auditor is required to consider adding an emphasis of matter paragraph to highlight that uncertainty (ISA (UK and Ireland) 700, paragraph 32). Significant uncertainties relating to the valuation of financial instruments may be matters that exist and give rise to such an emphasis of matter.

24 In determining whether an uncertainty is significant, the auditor considers:

(a) the risk that the estimate included in financial statements may be subject to change;
(b) the range of possible outcomes; and
(c) the consequences of those outcomes on the view shown in the financial statements.

25 The inclusion of an emphasis of matter paragraph in the auditor's report does not affect the auditor's opinion and is not a substitute for either:

(a) a qualified opinion or an adverse opinion, or disclaiming an opinion, when required by the circumstances of a specific audit engagement; or
(b) disclosures in the financial statements that are required by the applicable financial reporting framework.

Ethical issues

26 The APB's Ethical Standards (ESs) are based on a 'threats and safeguards approach' whereby auditors identify and assess the circumstances, which could adversely affect the auditor's objectivity ('threats'), including any perceived loss of independence, and apply procedures ('safeguards'), which will either eliminate the threat or reduce it to an acceptable level, that is a level at which it is not probable that a reasonable and

---

[7] An uncertainty is a matter whose outcome depends upon future actions or events not under the direct control of the entity but that may affect the financial statements.

informed third party would conclude that the auditor's objectivity is impaired or is likely to be impaired.

In the current circumstances, where financial market conditions are difficult and credit facilities may be restricted, auditors need to be alert to the possibility of a "management threat" arising that might jeopardise their objectivity and independence. There is a danger that, if asked to provide advice or assistance that could result in them undertaking work that involves making judgments and taking decisions which are the responsibility of the entity's management, the audit firm may become closely aligned with the views and interests of management and the auditor's objectivity and independence may be impaired, or may be perceived to be, impaired (ES 1, paragraph 28[8]).

---

[8] In October 2007 the APB issued a draft of revised Ethical Standards for Auditors. The intention is that the revised standards will apply to audits for accounting periods commencing on or after 6 April 2008. These include the proposal, to meet the requirements of the Statutory Audit Directive, to add a specific requirement in ES 1 for the audit firm to establish policies and procedures to require partners and employees of the firm to take no decisions taking that is that are the responsibility of management of the audited entity.

Appendix – Risk Factors

This appendix identifies some factors that may increase the risk of material misstatement in financial statements, especially when financial market conditions are difficult and credit facilities may be restricted. There are many ways in which the current market conditions could impact the financial statements of an entity and its ability to continue as a going concern and other risk factors may exist in the particular circumstances of each entity.

These risk factors may also be relevant in connection with an auditor's review of interim financial information in accordance with ISRE (UK and Ireland) 2410.

Going concern

- Obtaining external financing
  - Entity has experienced difficulties in the past in obtaining external finance facilities and/or complying with the related terms and covenants
  - Finance facilities are due for renewal in the next year but have not yet been agreed
  - Management have no plans for alternative arrangements should current facilities not be extended
  - Borrowing agreements or executory contracts include clauses relating to debt covenants or subjective clauses (e.g. a "material adverse change clause") that may trigger repayment
  - Entity has breached some of the terms or covenants giving rise to the risk that the facilities may be withdrawn or not renewed
  - Terms or covenants of renewed financing are changed and more difficult to comply with (e.g. increased interest rates or charges)
  - Finance facility is secured on assets (e.g. properties) that have decreased in value below the amount of the facility
  - For financial institutions, reduced deposits from retail customers or reduced availability of funding from wholesale financial markets
- Management plans to overcome financing difficulties include disposal of assets
  - Plans developed prior to current market conditions have not been updated
  - Lack of evidence that management can sell the assets at the values included in the plans
- Entity provides significant loans or guarantees
  - Guarantees may be called in
  - Borrowers may be unable to make payments
- Entity dependent on guarantees provided by another party
  - Guarantor no longer able/prepared to provide the guarantee
- Future cash flows
  - Uncertain or volatile
  - Customers taking longer/unable to pay
- Entity dependent on key suppliers
  - Suppliers facing financial difficulties not able to provide essential goods/services
  - Entity unable to find alternative suppliers

Fair Values

- Fair values are affected by current market conditions
  - Entity needs to change valuation model and/or management's assumptions to reflect current market conditions

- Active market no longer exists, requiring use of a model for valuation purposes
- Inputs to a model are not based on observable market inputs but rather are based on the entity's own data
- Impairment of non-financial assets held at fair value (e.g. properties)
- Suspension of external valuation indices triggering a need for alternative valuation approaches
- Entity uses an external pricing service for fair value measurements that needs to change its valuation model and/or assumptions to reflect current market conditions
- Entity does not have necessary expertise to undertake valuations

Other Risk Factors

- Impairments of assets other than those held at fair value (e.g. need for increased doubtful debts provisions)
- Impairment of the carrying value of purchased goodwill
- Pension obligations of an entity increased by reduction in values of assets in a related defined benefits pension scheme
- Hedging arrangements no longer effective
- Effects on accounting for Special Purpose Entities and other off balance sheet arrangements

[Bulletin 2008/2]
The auditor's association with preliminary announcements made in accordance with the requirements of the UK and Irish listing rules

(Issued February 2008)

Contents

	Paragraphs
Introduction	1 - 9
Listing Rule requirements	10 - 11
Companies Act requirements	12
Terms of engagement	13 - 16
Procedures	17 - 32
Communication of agreement	33 - 35

Appendices

1 Illustrative example letter to directors indicating auditor's agreement with preliminary announcement
2 Illustrative example terms of engagement; audit completed
3 Illustrative example terms of engagement; audit not completed
4 United Kingdom Listing Authority's summary of the Committee of European Securities Regulators "Recommendation on the use of alternative performance measures"

Introduction

This Bulletin provides updated guidance for the auditor concerning its responsibilities with regard to preliminary announcements[1]. The updated Bulletin:

(a) reflects the change in the Listing Rules to move from a mandatory to a permissive regime for the publication of preliminary announcements;

(b) reflects the change in the Listing Rules to require preliminary announcements to give details of any likely modification (rather than qualification) of the auditor's report required to be included with the annual financial report;

(c) reflects the introduction of International Standards on Auditing (ISAs) (UK and Ireland); and

(d) continues to emphasise the need for the auditor to consider the way in which alternative performance measures and management commentary are presented in preliminary announcements before agreeing to their release.

In this Bulletin the term "Preliminary Announcement" encompasses:

(a) the disclosures required to be made by United Kingdom Listing Authority (UKLA) Listing Rule 9.7A.1R and Irish Stock Exchange (ISE) Listing Rule 6.7.1; and

(b) other additional information (highlights, Chairman's Statement, narrative disclosures, management commentary, press release etc) that is released to a Regulatory Information Service[2] as part of a preliminary announcement.

Any presentation to analysts, trading statement, interim management statement or half-yearly financial report is not included within the definition of preliminary announcement.

If a company decides to make a preliminary announcement it will be the first public communication of that company's full year results and year-end financial position. Preliminary announcements form one of the focal points for investor interest, primarily because they confirm or update market expectations. Because of this the auditor of a listed company has an important role to play in the process leading to the orderly release of preliminary announcements.

Both the content and the preparation of any preliminary announcement are the responsibility of the company's directors. The directors of companies having equities on the Official List are required by the Listing Rules to have agreed the preliminary announcement with the auditor prior to publication (UKLA Listing Rule 9.7A.1R (2); ISE Listing Rule 6.7.1 (2)).

The Listing Rules do not indicate what form the agreement with the auditor should take, or the extent of work expected of the auditor before the auditor gives its agreement. This Bulletin provides guidance on the procedures that would normally be carried out by the auditor and on communicating the outcome of such procedures to the directors.

Many companies provide more information in their preliminary announcement than the minimum requirements of the Listing Rules. In the opinion of the APB it is

---

[1] In the Listing Rules preliminary announcements are described as "preliminary statements of annual results".

[2] Regulatory Information Service is the term used for any organisation through which the Listing Rules require listed companies to disseminate price sensitive information. In the Republic of Ireland all price sensitive information must be sent to the Company Announcements Office of the ISE.

neither practical nor desirable for the auditor to agree to anything less than the entire content of the preliminary announcement.

7   There is an expectation that the information in a preliminary announcement will be consistent with that in the audited financial statements. The risk of later changes to the figures in the preliminary announcement is not completely extinguished unless the preliminary announcement is issued at the same time that the full financial statements are approved by the directors and the auditor has signed the auditor's report on them. However, it has also been the accepted practice of some companies to issue the preliminary announcement, with their auditor's agreement, when the audit is at an "advanced stage" but before the auditor's report on the financial statements has been signed. This Bulletin provides guidance on interpreting the expression "advanced stage".

8   Although the APB would not wish to prevent the auditor from agreeing to the release of preliminary announcements before the auditor's report has been signed there is, in such circumstances, an unavoidable risk that the company may wish to revise its preliminary announcement in the light of audit findings or other developments arising between the preliminary announcement being issued and the completion of the audit.

9   There is no requirement for a preliminary announcement to include an auditor's report. In the view of the APB this is appropriate, as it is unlikely that a communication, that contains both a clear expression of opinion and sets out the information necessary for a proper understanding of that opinion, can be developed without producing a report of excessive length and complexity; which would be out of place in the context of the preliminary announcement as a whole. However, to avoid possible misunderstanding and to make explicit their agreement to the preliminary announcement the auditor issues a letter to the company signifying its agreement (see Appendix 1).

Listing Rule requirements

10 Under UKLA Listing Rule 9.7A.1R (1): ISE Listing Rule 6.7.1 (1) a company that prepares a preliminary announcement must publish it as soon as possible after it has been approved by the Board. The preliminary announcement must:

(a) be agreed with the company's auditor prior to publication;
(b) show the figures in the form of a table, including the items required for a half-yearly report, consistent with the presentation to be adopted in the annual accounts for that financial year;
(c) give details of the nature of any likely modification that may be contained in the auditor's report required to be included with the annual financial report; and
(d) include any significant additional information necessary for the purpose of assessing the results being announced.

11 In accordance with UKLA Listing Rule 9.7A.3 G: ISE Listing Rule 6.7.2 the Listing Authority[3] may authorise the omission from any preliminary announcement of information required by UKLA Listing Rule 9.7A.1 R: ISE Listing Rule 6.7.1 if it

---

[3] *In the UK the term "Listing Authority" refers to the United Kingdom Listing Authority of the Financial Services Authority ("FSA") acting in its capacity as the competent authority for the purposes of Part VI of the Financial Services and Markets Act 2000. In the Republic of Ireland, the ISE is the competent authority for the purposes of the European Communities (Admission to Listing and Miscellaneous Provisions) Regulations 2007 (S.I. No.286 of 2007).*

considers that disclosure of such information would be contrary to the public interest or seriously detrimental to the listed company, provided that such omission would not be likely to mislead the public with regard to facts and circumstances, knowledge of which is essential for the assessment of the shares.

Companies Act requirements

In the United Kingdom, preliminary announcements[4] constitute non-statutory accounts under section 435 of the Companies Act 2006[5] (CA 2006) and must include a statement indicating:

(a) that they are not the company's statutory accounts;
(b) whether statutory accounts dealing with any financial year with which the non-statutory accounts purport to deal have been delivered to the registrar of companies;
(c) whether the auditor has reported on the statutory accounts for any such year; and
(d) if so whether the auditor's report:
  (i) was qualified or unqualified or included a reference to any matters to which the auditor drew attention by way of emphasis without qualifying its report; or
  (ii) contained a statement under section 498(2) (accounting records or returns inadequate or accounts or directors' remuneration report not agreeing with records and returns), or section 498(3) (failure to obtain necessary information and explanations)[6].

Terms of engagement

It is in the interests of both the auditor and the company that the auditor's role in respect of the preliminary announcement is set out in writing; typically by including relevant paragraphs in the audit engagement letter. To avoid misunderstandings the engagement letter describes the auditor's understanding of the process of "agreeing" the preliminary announcement.

In circumstances where the auditor is to agree to a preliminary announcement based on financial statements on which its audit is not complete the engagement letter includes cautionary language to the effect that there is an unavoidable risk that the

---

[4] In the Republic of Ireland, a preliminary announcement made by a single entity constitutes abbreviated accounts under section 19 of the Companies (Amendment) Act, 1986. A preliminary announcement made by a group constitutes abbreviated group accounts under Regulation 40 of the European Communities (Companies: Group Accounts) Regulations, 1992. This states that where a parent undertaking publishes abbreviated group accounts relating to any financial year, it shall also publish a statement indicating:
  (a) that the abbreviated group accounts are not the group accounts, copies of which are required by law to be annexed to the annual return;
  (b) whether the copies of the group accounts so required to be annexed have in fact been so annexed;
  (c) whether the auditors have made a report under section 193 of the Companies Act, 1990 in respect of the group accounts which relate to any financial year with which the abbreviated group accounts purport to deal; and
  (d) whether the report of the auditors contained any qualifications.
Where a company publishes abbreviated accounts, it shall not publish with those accounts any such report of the auditors as is mentioned in (c) above. The statement required for a single entity is similar.

[5] The equivalent section in the Companies Act 1985 is section 240.

[6] The equivalent sections in the Companies Act 1985 are sections 237(2) and 237(3).

company may wish to revise its preliminary announcement in the light of audit findings or other developments occurring before the completion of the audit.

15 Matters that may be dealt with in the engagement letter include:

(a) the responsibility of the directors for the preparation of any preliminary announcement;
(b) the fact that the auditor will conduct its work in accordance with this Bulletin;
(c) a statement as to whether the auditor believes it is management's intention that the preliminary announcement will be based on audited financial statements or on draft financial statements upon which the auditor has not issued a report;
(d) a statement that the auditor will issue a letter confirming its agreement to the preliminary announcement; and
(e) a statement explaining the inherent limitations of the auditor's work.

16 Examples of suitable paragraphs for inclusion in a letter of engagement are given in Appendix 2 for circumstances where the preliminary announcement is to be based on audited financial statements and in Appendix 3 for circumstances where the preliminary announcement is to be based on draft financial statements.

Procedures

Planning

17 Where the preliminary announcement is to be based on draft financial statements the company's timetable should allow the auditor to have completed the audit other than for those matters set out in paragraph 21 below.

Preliminary announcements based on audited financial statements

18 There is an expectation on the part of users that the information in a preliminary announcement will be consistent with that in the audited financial statements. The only way of achieving absolute certainty of this is for the audit of the financial statements to have been completed and the contents of the preliminary announcement to have been extracted from audited financial statements that had been approved and signed by the directors and upon which the auditor has signed the auditor's report.

Preliminary announcements based on draft financial statements

19 Companies may wish to issue their preliminary announcement before the audit is complete. There are additional risks for directors in these circumstances if further information comes to light as a result of the auditor's procedures that the directors decide should be reflected in the financial statements and gives rise to the need for a revised announcement by the company. Before agreeing to the release of the preliminary announcement, therefore, the directors will need to ensure they are satisfied that the information it contains will be consistent with the information that will be contained in the audited financial statements.

20 The auditor will need to be satisfied that any matters outstanding with respect to the audit will be unlikely to result in changes to the information contained in the preliminary announcement. This means that the audit of the financial statements must be at an advanced stage and that, subject only to unforeseen events, the auditor expects to be in a position to issue the auditor's report on the financial statements

incorporating the amounts upon which the preliminary announcement is based, and know what that auditor's report will state.

This means completing the audit, including the engagement quality control review as described in paragraphs 38 to 40 of ISA (UK and Ireland) 220 "Quality control for audits of historical financial information", subject only to the following:

(a) clearing outstanding audit matters which the auditor is satisfied are unlikely to have a material impact on the financial statements or disclosures insofar as they affect the preliminary announcement;
(b) completing audit procedures on the detail of note disclosures to the financial statements that will not have a material impact on the primary financial statements and completing the auditor's reading of "other information" in the annual report, in accordance with ISA (UK and Ireland) 720 "Other information in documents containing audited financial statements";
(c) updating the subsequent events review to cover the period between the issue of the preliminary announcement and the date of the auditor's report on the financial statements; and
(d) obtaining final signed written representations from management and establishing that the financial statements have been reviewed and approved by the directors.

In advance of the preliminary announcement the auditor discusses with management the representations that the auditor will be likely to require in order to issue its report on the financial statements. If management expresses reservations about its ability or willingness to make such representations the auditor does not agree to the preliminary announcement.

All preliminary announcements

The following procedures will normally be carried out by the auditor in relation to the preliminary announcement itself regardless of whether it is based on draft financial statements or extracted from audited financial statements:

(a) checking that the figures in the preliminary announcement covering the full year have been accurately extracted from the audited or draft financial statements; and reflect the presentation to be adopted in the audited financial statements. For example, any summarisation should not change the order in which items are presented where this is specified by law or accounting standards;
(b) considering whether the information (including the management commentary) is consistent with other expected contents of the annual report of which the auditor is aware; and
(c) considering whether the financial information in the preliminary announcement is misstated. A misstatement exists when the information is stated incorrectly or presented in a misleading manner. A misstatement may arise, for example, as a result of an omission of a significant change of accounting policy disclosed, or due to be disclosed, in the audited financial statements.

The auditor considers whether the preliminary announcement includes a statement by directors as required by section 435[7] of CA 2006[8] (see paragraph 12) and whether the preliminary announcement includes the minimum information required by UKLA Listing Rule 9.7A.1: ISE Listing Rule 6.7.1 (see paragraph 10).

---

[7] *The equivalent section in the Companies Act 1985 is section 240.*

[8] *See footnote 4 for the equivalent legislation in the Republic of Ireland.*

Alternative performance measures

25 Regulators recognise that in some circumstances the presentation of alternative performance measures (APMs)[9] and associated narrative explanations with the statutory results may help shareholders understand better the financial performance of a company. However, regulators are concerned that in other instances such APMs have the potential to be misleading[10] and shareholders may sometimes be misinformed by the manner in which APMs are included in preliminary announcements with which the auditor is associated. In those circumstances the APB believes that the potential for APMs to be misleading is considerable when:

   (a) inappropriate prominence is given to the APMs;
   (b) there is no description of the APMs;
   (c) APMs resemble defined performance measures but do not actually have the characteristics of the defined measures; and
   (d) where relevant, the APMs are not reconciled to the statutory financial information.

Appendix 4 is the UKLA's summary of a recommendation published by the Committee of European Securities Regulators (CESR) on the use of APMs.

26 In this context where the preliminary announcement includes APMs, before agreeing to its release, the auditor considers whether:

   (a) appropriate prominence is given to statutory financial information and related narrative explanations compared to the prominence given to APMs and their related narrative explanations;
   (b) APMs are reconciled, where appropriate, to the statutory financial information and sufficient prominence is given to that reconciliation;
   (c) APMs are clearly and accurately described; and
   (d) APMs are not otherwise misleading in the form and context in which they appear.

If the auditor does not believe that the preliminary announcement satisfies these conditions, it seeks to resolve the issues arising with the directors. If it is unable to resolve the issues the auditor considers whether to withhold its consent to the release of the announcement.

Management commentary

27 An important feature of preliminary announcements is a management commentary on the company's performance during the year and its position at the year-end. Such management commentary may include comments on the final interim period in the preliminary announcement and separate presentation of the final interim period figures to the extent this is necessary to support the management commentary. The extent of information on the final interim period will vary from company to company

---

[9] *Alternative performance measures include the adjustment of statutory financial information to, for example:*
   - *Exclude certain items to give alternative earnings numbers eg earnings before interest, tax, depreciation and amortisation (EBITDA).*
   - *Exclude certain business segments or activities.*
   - *Reflect significant non-adjusting post balance sheet events eg disposals or acquisitions.*

[10] *UKLA Listing Rule 1.3.3R and ISE Listing Rule 1.3.3 require that "An issuer must take all reasonable care to ensure that any information it notifies to a Regulatory Information Service or makes available through the FSA/ISE is not misleading, false or deceptive and does not omit anything likely to affect the import of the information."*

and in some cases this may only consist of a reference to the key figures in the management commentary.

28 The auditor reads the management commentary, any other narrative disclosures and any final interim period figures and considers whether they are in conflict with the information that it has obtained in the course of the audit. If the auditor becomes aware of any apparent inconsistencies with information obtained during the audit or with the draft financial statements, it seeks to resolve them with the directors. If it is unable to resolve the matters the auditor withholds its consent to the publication of the preliminary announcement.

29 In the case of a preliminary announcement based on audited financial statements, the auditor will read the text of any Chairman's Statement, business review or similar document to be included in the annual report from which the management commentary in the preliminary announcement will usually be derived. For a preliminary announcement based on draft financial statements, this will be done on the latest draft of such documents that are available.

Directors' approval of the preliminary announcement

30 The auditor does not agree to the preliminary announcement until its entire content has been formally approved by the board or by a duly authorised committee[11] of the board.

Modification of the auditor's report

31 The Listing Rules require that, if the auditor's report (on the financial statements) is likely to be modified, the preliminary announcement should give details of the nature of the modification. In doing this, care should be taken to ensure compliance with section 435[12] of CA 2006[13] which states that an auditor's report on the statutory accounts may not be published with non-statutory accounts.

32 Where reference is made in a preliminary announcement to an actual or possible qualified opinion or emphasis of matter, the directors should give adequate prominence to that information in the announcement and the auditor should be satisfied in this regard. If the auditor has concerns about the appropriateness of the wording of a statement referring to a modified report it is encouraged to seek legal advice.

Communication of agreement

33 The APB encourages the auditor to make explicit its agreement to the issue of the preliminary announcement by sending a letter to the directors. An example of such a letter is given in Appendix 1. Similarly, if the auditor is not in agreement with the content of the preliminary announcement, it communicates this to the directors by

---

[11] *The Combined Code states that one of the main roles and responsibilities of the audit committee is "to monitor the integrity of the financial statements of the company, and any formal announcements relating to the company's financial performance, reviewing significant financial reporting judgements contained in them" (Combined Code provision C.3.2).*

[12] *The equivalent section in the Companies Act 1985 is section 240.*

[13] *See footnote 4 for the equivalent legislation in the Republic of Ireland.*

sending them a letter setting out the reasons for its disagreement, advising the directors that the preliminary announcement should not be published.

34 The auditor may become aware that a company has released a preliminary announcement without first obtaining its agreement. There may be a number of reasons for this ranging from innocent oversight on the part of the directors to the directors knowingly releasing a preliminary announcement with which the auditor disagrees. The action that the auditor takes depends on the particular circumstances. In circumstances where a preliminary announcement is inadvertently released without the auditor's knowledge, but with which the auditor does in fact agree, the auditor may wish to remind the directors of their obligation under the Listing Rules to have obtained the auditor's agreement.

35 However, at the other end of the spectrum, where the auditor becomes aware that the directors have released an announcement with which it disagrees, it takes legal advice with a view to notifying the Listing Authority of the fact that it had not agreed to the announcement.

Appendix 1 – Illustrative example letter to directors indicating auditor's agreement with preliminary announcement

Dear Sirs

XYZ plc: preliminary announcement of results for year ended [...]

In accordance with the terms of our engagement letter dated [ ], we have reviewed the attached proposed preliminary announcement of XYZ plc for the year ended [ ]. Our work was conducted having regard to Bulletin 2008/2 "The auditor's association with preliminary announcements made in accordance with the requirements of the UK and Irish listing rules" issued by the Auditing Practices Board. As directors you have accepted responsibility for preparing and issuing the preliminary announcement.

Our responsibility is solely to give our agreement to the preliminary announcement having carried out the procedures specified in the Bulletin as providing a basis for such agreement. In this regard we agree to the preliminary announcement being notified to [a Regulatory Information Service] [and/or the Company Announcements Office of the Irish Stock Exchange, as appropriate].

[As you are aware we are not in a position to sign our auditor's report on the annual financial statements as they have not yet been approved by the directors and we have not yet ... [insert significant procedures that are yet to be completed, for example completing the subsequent events review and obtaining final signed written representations from directors ...]. Consequently there can be no absolute certainty that we will be in a position to issue an unmodified audit report on financial statements consistent with the results and financial position reported in the preliminary announcement. However, at the present time, we are not aware of any matters that may give rise to a modification to our report. In the event that such matters do come to our attention we will inform you immediately.]

Yours faithfully

Appendix 2 – Illustrative example terms of engagement; audit completed

Extract from Letter of Engagement

The Listing Rules require that "a preliminary statement[1] of annual results .... must be agreed with the company's auditor prior to publication". As directors of the company, you are responsible for preparing and issuing any preliminary announcement and ensuring that we agree to its release.

We undertake to review the preliminary announcement having regard to Bulletin 2008/2 "The auditor's association with preliminary announcements made in accordance with the requirements of the UK and Irish listing rules" issued by the Auditing Practices Board. Accordingly, our review will be limited to checking the accuracy of extraction of the financial information in the preliminary announcement from the audited financial statements of the company for that year, considering whether any "alternative performance measures" and associated narrative explanations may be misleading and reading the management commentary, including any comments on, or separate presentation of, the final interim period figures, and considering whether it is in conflict with the information that we obtained in the course of our audit.

You will provide us with such information and explanations as we consider necessary for the purposes of our work. We shall request sight of the preliminary announcement in sufficient time to enable us to complete our work. The Board/committee of the Board will formally approve the preliminary announcement before we agree to it.

Appendix 3 – Illustrative example terms of engagement; audit not completed

Extract from Letter of Engagement

The Listing Rules require that "a preliminary statement[1] of annual results ...... must be agreed with the company's auditor prior to publication". As directors of the company, you are responsible for preparing and issuing any preliminary announcement and ensuring that we agree to its release.

We undertake to review the preliminary announcement having regard to Bulletin 2008/2 "The auditor's association with preliminary announcements made in accordance with the requirements of the UK and Irish listing rules" issued by the Auditing Practices Board. Accordingly, our review will be limited to checking the accuracy of extraction of the financial information in the preliminary announcement from the latest available draft financial statements of the company for that year, considering whether any "alternative performance measures" and associated narrative explanations may be misleading and reading the management commentary, including any comments on, or separate presentation of, the final interim period figures, and considering whether it is in conflict with the information that we have obtained in the course of our audit.

You will provide us with such information and explanations as we consider necessary for the purposes of our work. We shall request sight of the preliminary announcement in sufficient time to enable us to complete our work. The Board/committee of the Board will formally approve the preliminary announcement before we agree to it. You will also make available to us the proposed text of the company's annual report.

We will not agree to the release of the preliminary announcement until the audit is complete subject only to the following:

(a) clearing outstanding audit matters which we are satisfied are unlikely to have a material impact on the financial statements or disclosures insofar as they affect the preliminary announcement;
(b) completing audit procedures on the detail of note disclosures to the financial statements that will not have a material impact on the primary financial statements and completing our reading of other information in the annual report, in accordance with ISA (UK and Ireland) 720 "Other information in documents containing audited financial statements";
(c) updating the subsequent events review to cover the period between the date of the preliminary announcement and the date of our auditor's report on the financial statements; and
(d) obtaining final signed written representations from management and establishing that the financial statements have been reviewed and approved by the directors.

The scope of our work will be necessarily limited in that, we will only be able to check the consistency of the preliminary announcement with draft financial statements on which our audit is incomplete. Accordingly, we shall not, at that stage, know whether further adjustments may be required to those draft financial statements. Consequently, there is an unavoidable risk that the company may wish to revise its preliminary announcement in the light of audit findings or other developments occurring between the preliminary announcement being notified to [a Regulatory Information Service] [and/or the Company Announcements Office of the Irish Stock Exchange, as appropriate] and the completion of the audit.

In the event that we disagree with the release of the preliminary announcement we will send you a letter setting out the reasons why.

Appendix 4 – United Kingdom listing authority's summary of the CESR "recommendation on the use of alternative performance measures"

In List! 12 of February 2006 the UKLA summarised the key points of a recommendation on the use of APMs issued by CESR as follows:

1. Under the IAS Framework, there are four qualitative characteristics that make the information provided in financial statements useful to users: understandability, relevance, reliability and comparability. CESR believes that issuers should follow these principles when preparing APMs.
2. Issuers should define the terminology used and the basis of calculation adopted (ie defining the components included in an APM). Clear disclosure is key to the understandability.
3. Where possible issuers should present APMs only in combination with defined measures (ie GAAP measures). Furthermore, issuers should explain the differences between both measures.
4. Comparatives should be provided for any APM presented.
5. APMs should be presented consistently over time.
6. To ensure that investors are not misled, CESR recommends that APMs should not be presented with greater prominence than defined GAAP measures. Where APMs are derived from audited financial statements and resemble defined performance measures but do not actually have the characteristics of the defined

measures, CESR recommends that defined measures should have greater prominence than the APMs.

In our (ie the UKLA) view the CESR recommendation represents best practice for the disclosure of APMs and we would encourage issuers to follow the recommendation.

[Bulletin 2008/3]
The auditor's statement on the summary financial statement in the United Kingdom

(Issued April 2008)

Contents

	Paragraphs
Introduction	1 – 3
Summary financial statement	1 – 2
Summary annual report	3
Legislative changes since publication of previous guidance	4
Requirements of sections 427 and 428 of the Companies Act 2006	5 – 7
Requirements of the SI 374 Regulations and the Listing Rules	8 – 12
The auditor's procedures	13 – 22
Consistency	17 – 21
Other requirements of sections 427 and 428 of CA 2006	22
Auditor's report on the annual accounts [directors' remuneration report] and directors' report	23 – 26
Modified auditor's report or statement	27 – 30
Qualified report or statement	27 – 28
Emphasis of matter or other matter	29 – 30
Considering the possibility of misstatements in summarised information derived from the directors' report and the directors' remuneration report included in the summary financial statement	31 – 32
Other information included in the summarised annual report	33 – 35
The auditor's statement	36 – 39

Appendices illustrating the auditor's statement on a summary financial statement of:

1. A quoted company which includes a summary directors' report, summary directors' remuneration report and other surround information.
2. An unquoted company which does not include either a summary directors' report or any other surround information.
3. An unquoted company which includes a summary directors' report but no other surround information.
4. An unquoted company which includes both a summary directors' report and other surround information.

Introduction

Summary financial statement

Under section 426(1) of the Companies Act 2006 (CA 2006) and "The Companies (Summary Financial Statement) Regulations 2008"[1] (the SI 374 Regulations) a company has the option, if the recipient is willing, to send a summary financial statement, in place of copies of its full accounts and reports, to:

(a) every member of a company;
(b) every holder of a company's debentures;
(c) every person who is entitled to receive notice of general meetings of a company; and
(d) a person nominated to enjoy information rights under section 146 of CA 2006.

The purpose of this Bulletin is to clarify the auditor's responsibilities in connection with such summary financial statements. A summary financial statement is required to be in such form, and contain such information, as may be specified by CA 2006 and the SI 374 Regulations. The mandatory and optional content of a summary financial statement differs for quoted and unquoted companies as illustrated in the following table:

The required and permitted content of a summary financial statement:

Information derived from:	Unquoted company	Quoted company
Required		
Annual accounts, as prescribed by the SI 374 Regulations	✓	✓
Directors' remuneration report, as prescribed by the SI 374 Regulations	n/a	✓
Permitted at directors' option		
Annual accounts, additional to that prescribed by the SI 374 Regulations	✓	✓
Directors' remuneration report, additional to that prescribed by the SI 374 Regulations	n/a	✓
Directors' report	✓	✓

Summary annual report

Some companies may include their summary financial statement within a summarised annual report containing other information. Other information may include, for example, a chairman's or chief executive's statement or a corporate governance

---

[1] *Statutory Instrument, SI 2008 No. 374*

report. Such summarised annual reports are often described as an "annual review", or an "annual review and summary financial statement".

Legislative changes since publication of previous guidance

4   Guidance for auditors on reporting on summary financial statements was previously provided in Bulletin 1999/6. Effective 1 October 2005, the Companies (Summary Financial Statement) (Amendment) Regulations 2005[2] had come into force which, among other things, had:

(a) extended to all companies the ability to send out summary financial statements instead of the full annual accounts and reports, subject to certain conditions being satisfied. Previously only listed public companies had that ability. One of the conditions that is required to be satisfied is that the full annual accounts and reports for the year in question must have been audited;

(b) specified the form and content of the Summary Financial Statement of companies and groups that prepare their accounts in accordance with International Financial Reporting Standards as adopted by the EU; and

(c) dispensed with the requirement for the Summary Financial Statement to contain a summary of the directors' report. Companies are able, however, to include such a summary if they wish.

Requirements of sections 427 and 428 of the Companies Act 2006

5   Sections 427 and 428 of CA 2006 address the form and content of summary financial statements for unquoted and quoted companies respectively. Both sections require that the summary financial statement be derived from the company's annual accounts[3] and be prepared in accordance with the respective section of CA 2006 and the SI 374 Regulations. Section 428 additionally requires the summary financial statement of a quoted company to include certain information derived from the directors' remuneration report. Both sections state that the SI 374 Regulations may require the statement to include information derived from the directors' report. However, at the time of writing the SI 374 Regulations do not include such requirements.

6   Neither CA 2006 nor the SI 374 Regulations prevent a company from including in a summary financial statement additional information derived from the company's annual accounts, the directors' report and, in the case of quoted companies, the directors' remuneration report.

7   Sections 427(4) and 428(4) of CA 2006 state that the summary financial statement must:

(a) state that it is only a summary of information derived from the company's annual accounts [and the directors' remuneration report][4];

(b) state whether it contains additional information derived from the directors' report and, if so, that it does not contain the full text of that report;

---

[2] *Statutory Instrument SI 2005 No. 2281*

[3] *In the illustrative auditor's statements in the appendices to this Bulletin, rather than the term "annual accounts" which is used in the Act and this Bulletin, the more conventional term "full annual financial statements" is used.*

[4] *Throughout this Bulletin references to the directors' remuneration report apply to quoted companies only. Section 385 of CA 2006 provides a definition of the term "quoted company".*

(c) state how a person entitled to them can obtain a full copy of the company's annual accounts, [the directors' remuneration report][4] or the directors' report;
(d) contain a statement by the company's auditor of its opinion as to whether the summary financial statement –
  (i) is consistent with the company's annual accounts [and the directors' remuneration report][4] and, where information derived from the directors' report is included in the statement with that report, and
  (ii) complies with the requirements of this section (ie either section 428 or 427) and regulations made under it;
(e) state whether the auditor's report on the annual accounts [and the auditable part of directors' remuneration report][4] was unqualified or qualified, and, if it was qualified, set out the report in full together with any further material needed to understand the qualification;
(f) state whether, that auditor's report, contained a statement under –
  (i) section 498(2) of CA 2006 (accounting records or returns inadequate or accounts [or directors' remuneration report][4] not agreeing with the records and returns), or
  (ii) section 498(3) of CA 2006 (failure to obtain necessary information and explanations),
  and if so, set out the statement in full;
(g) state whether, in that report, the auditor's statement under section 496 of CA 2006 (whether directors' report consistent with accounts) was qualified or unqualified and, if it was qualified, set out the qualified statement in full together with any further material needed to understand the qualification.

(The above is based on section 428(4) of CA 2006. The requirements of section 427(4) vary slightly from this).

Requirements of the SI 374 Regulations and the Listing Rules

Schedules to the SI 374 Regulations set out the requirements for the form and content of summary financial statements for eight different circumstances. These are:

8

No.	Description
1	Form and content of summary financial statement of company preparing Companies Act individual accounts (other than a banking or insurance company)
2	Form and content of summary financial statement of banking company preparing Companies Act individual accounts
3	Form and content of summary financial statement of insurance company preparing Companies Act individual accounts
4	Form and content of summary financial statement of company preparing Companies Act group accounts (other than banking or insurance group accounts)
5	Form and content of summary financial statement of parent company of banking group preparing Companies Act group accounts
6	Form and content of summary financial statement of parent company of insurance group preparing Companies Act group accounts
7	Form and content of summary financial statement of company preparing IAS individual accounts
8	Form and content of summary financial statement of company preparing IAS group accounts

9   In overview, summary financial statements of all companies are required to comprise:

   (a) a summary profit and loss account/summary income statement;
   (b) information concerning recognised and proposed dividends included in the annual accounts and reports;
   (c) a summary balance sheet;
   (d) corresponding amounts for the immediately preceding financial year in respect of every item shown in the summary profit and loss account/summary income statement, and in the summary balance sheet; and
   (e) information relating to directors' remuneration that is required by paragraph 1 of Schedule 3 to the Small Companies and Groups (Accounts and Directors' Report) Regulations 2008[5] (the SI 409 Regulations) or paragraph 1 of Schedule 5 to the Large and Medium-sized Companies and Groups (Accounts and Reports) Regulations 2008[6] (the SI 410 Regulations).

   It is beyond the scope of this Bulletin to describe the requirements of the SI 374 Regulations in more detail. Although not explicitly required by CA 2006 or the SI 374 Regulations, many summary financial statements include a summary cash flow statement and a summary statement of total recognised gains and losses (or the equivalent under IFRSs as adopted by the EU).

10 The summary financial statement of a quoted company must contain the whole of, or a summary of, those portions of the directors' remuneration report that set out the matters required by paragraph 3 (statement of company's policy on directors' remuneration) and 4 (performance graph) of Schedule 8 to the SI 410 Regulations.

11 The summary financial statement of a company having certain securities publicly traded as specified in paragraph 13 of Schedule 7 to the SI 410 Regulations (disclosure required by certain publicly-traded companies) must:

   (a) include in the summary financial statement the explanatory material required to be included in the directors' report by paragraph 14 of Schedule 7; or
   (b) send that material to the person receiving the summary financial statement at the same time as the company sends the summary financial statement.

12 Under the Listing Rules of the Financial Services Authority any summary financial statement issued by a listed company must additionally disclose earnings per share. (LR 9.8.13R)

The auditor's procedures

13 When planning the audit of the annual accounts of a company, the auditor ascertains whether a summary financial statement will be prepared and whether it is to be included in a summarised annual report. The audit engagement letter, or a separate engagement letter, records the scope of the examination of the summary financial statement, the respective responsibilities of directors and the auditor and the expected wording of the auditor's statement.

14 The auditor normally carries out its work on the summary financial statement at the same time as completing the audit, rather than after its completion. In this way the auditor's statement under section 427(4)(d) or 428(4)(d) of CA 2006 and the auditor's

---

[5] *Statutory Instrument SI 2008 No. 409.*

[6] *Statutory Instrument SI 2008 No. 410.*

report on the annual accounts can be issued at the same time. The auditor, therefore, encourages the directors to take this into account when planning the year end timetable.

The auditor's procedures in relation to the summary financial statement are directed towards consideration of the matters on which it is required, by section 427(4)(d) or 428(4)(d) of CA 2006, to express an opinion, namely:

(a) whether the summary financial statement is consistent with the annual accounts, [the directors' remuneration report][4] and where information derived from the directors' report is included in the statement, with that report; and
(b) whether the summary financial statement complies with the requirements of section 427 or 428 of CA 2006 and the (SI 374) Regulations made under it.

These opinions are not independent of each other as the SI 374 Regulations require that the summary financial statement must contain any other information necessary to ensure that the statement is consistent with the full accounts and reports for the financial year in question. The requirement for consistency is considered in the following paragraphs.

Consistency

The auditor states whether in its opinion the summary financial statement is consistent with the company's annual accounts [, the directors' report] [and the Directors' Remuneration Report][4]. The auditor is not required to form an opinion on whether the summary financial statement gives a true and fair view. It is in any event most unlikely that the summary financial statement could give a true and fair view in any practical situation, as much of the detailed information from which it has been extracted is not presented. There is no basis, therefore, for shareholders and other users to have the same expectations of summary financial statements as they do of the annual accounts and reports.

Matters which may give rise to an inconsistency include:

(a) information which has been inaccurately extracted from the annual accounts and reports (for example, incorrect extraction of amounts appearing in the summary balance sheet or summary profit and loss account/summary income statement);
(b) the use of headings in the summary profit and loss account/summary income statement or summary balance sheet that are incompatible with the headings in the annual accounts from which they are derived (for example, the description of fixed assets as 'current assets');
(c) information which, in the auditor's opinion has been summarised in a manner which is not consistent with the annual accounts and reports (for example, unduly selective summarisation of the directors' remuneration disclosures); and
(d) omission from the summary financial statement of information which although not specifically prescribed by the SI 374 Regulations, in the auditor's opinion, is necessary to ensure consistency with the annual accounts and reports (for example, omission of information relating to a non-adjusting subsequent event which the auditor considers fundamental to a shareholder's understanding of the company's results or financial position or information about going concern)[7].

---

[7] *Regulation 9(8) of the SI 374 Regulations requires that "The summary financial statement must contain any other information necessary to ensure that the statement is consistent with the full accounts and reports for the financial year in question".*

19 When the auditor identifies what it believes may be an inconsistency it discusses the matter with those charged with governance, so that they may eliminate the inconsistency, for example by including additional information in the summary financial statement.

20 If discussion with those charged with governance does not result in the elimination of the inconsistency, the auditor modifies its statement under section 427(4)(d) or 428(4)(d) of CA 2006 to include a description of the inconsistency.

21 An inconsistency between the summary financial statement and the annual accounts and reports means that the summary financial statement is not properly derived from them and does not comply with the SI 374 Regulations. Such an inconsistency, therefore, leads to a qualification of the auditor's statement both on the grounds of non-compliance with section 427 or 428 of CA 2006 and the SI 374 Regulations as well as on the grounds of the inconsistency.

Other requirements of sections 427 and 428 of CA 2006

22 The auditor satisfies itself that the information prescribed by sections 427 or 428 of CA 2006 and by the SI 374 Regulations (such as the statements referred to in paragraph 7 above) is included in the summary financial statement.

Auditor's report on the annual accounts [directors' remuneration report] and directors' report

23 Sections 427(4)(e) and 428(4)(e) of CA 2006 require the summary financial statement to state whether the auditor's report on the annual accounts (required under section 495 of CA 2006) [and the auditable part of the directors' remuneration report (required under section 497 of CA 2006)][4] was unqualified or qualified and if it was qualified set out the report in full together with any further material needed to understand the qualification.

24 Sections 427(4)(f) and 428(4)g) of CA 2006 require the summary financial statement to state whether the auditor's statement under section 496 of CA 2006 (whether directors' report consistent with accounts) was qualified or unqualified and if it was qualified set out the qualified statement in full together with any further material needed to understand the qualification.

25 Sections 427(4)(g) and 428(4)(f) of CA 2006 require the summary financial statement to state whether the auditor's report contained a statement regarding:

   (a) accounting records or returns inadequate; or
   (b) accounts [or directors' remuneration report][4] not agreeing with records and returns; or
   (c) failure to obtain necessary information and explanations,

and if so, set out that statement in full.

26 When the auditor's report and statements described in paragraphs 23 to 25 are unqualified it is usual for the directors to include a statement to that effect immediately following the auditor's statement (see Appendices).

Opinion

In our opinion the summary financial statement is consistent with the full annual financial statements of XYZ Limited for the year ended ... and complies with the applicable requirements of section 427 of the Companies Act 2006, and the regulations made thereunder.

[We have not considered the effects of any events between the date on which we signed our report on the full annual financial statements (insert date) and the date of this statement.][10]

Statutory auditor
Date
Address

> **DIRECTORS' STATEMENT**
> The auditor has issued unqualified reports on the full annual financial statements and on the consistency of the directors' report with those financial statements. Their report on the full annual financial statements contained no statement under sections 498(2)(a), 498(2)(b) or 498(3) of the Companies Act 2006[11].

Appendix 3 – Illustrative auditor's statement on a summary financial statement of an unquoted company which includes a summary directors' report but no other surround information

INDEPENDENT AUDITOR'S STATEMENT TO THE [MEMBERS] [SHAREHOLDERS] OF XYZ LIMITED

We have examined the summary financial statement for the year ended .....

Respective responsibilities of the directors and the auditor

The directors are responsible for preparing the summarised financial statement in accordance with applicable United Kingdom law. Our responsibility is to report to you our opinion on the consistency of the summary financial statement with the full annual financial statements and the Directors' Report, and its compliance with the relevant requirements of section 427 of the Companies Act 2006 and the regulations made thereunder.

We conducted our work in accordance with Bulletin 2008/3 issued by the Auditing Practices Board. Our report on the company's full annual financial statements describes the basis of our opinion[s] on those financial statements and on the Directors' Report.

---

[10] Include this sentence where the date of this statement is after the date of the auditor's report on the full annual financial statements.

[11] This statement is a requirement of sections 427(4)(e), 427(4)(f) and 427(4)(g) of CA 2006.

Opinion

In our opinion the summary financial statement is consistent with the full annual financial statements and the Directors' Report of XYZ Limited for the year ended ... and complies with the applicable requirements of section 427 of the Companies Act 2006, and the regulations made thereunder.

[We have not considered the effects of any events between the date on which we signed our report on the full annual financial statements (insert date) and the date of this statement.][12]

Statutory auditor   *Address*
Date

DIRECTORS' STATEMENT

The auditor has issued unqualified reports on the full annual financial statements and on the consistency of the directors' report with those financial statements. Their report on the full annual financial statements contained no statement under sections 498(2)(a), 498(2)(b) or 498(3) of the Companies Act 2006[13].

Appendix 4 – Illustrative auditor's statement on a summary financial statement of an unquoted company which includes both a summary directors' report and other surround information

INDEPENDENT AUDITOR'S STATEMENT TO THE [MEMBERS] [SHAREHOLDERS] OF XYZ LIMITED

We have examined the summary financial statement [for the year ended ...] [set out on pages....].

Respective responsibilities of the directors and the auditor

The directors are responsible for preparing the [*summarised annual report*] in accordance with applicable United Kingdom law.

Our responsibility is to report to you our opinion on the consistency of the summary financial statement within the [*summarised annual report*] with the full annual financial statements and the Directors' Report, and its compliance with the relevant requirements of section 427 of the Companies Act 2006 and the regulations made thereunder.

We also read the other information contained in the [*summarised annual report*] and consider the implications for our report if we become aware of any apparent misstatements or material inconsistencies with the summary financial statement. The

---

[12] *Include this sentence where the date of this statement is after the date of the auditor's report on the full annual financial statements.*

[13] *This statement is a requirement of sections 427(4)(e), 427(4)(f) and 427(4)(g) of CA 2006.*

other information comprises only [the Chairman's Statement and the Corporate Governance Statement].

We conducted our work in accordance with Bulletin 2008/3 issued by the Auditing Practices Board. Our report on the company's full annual financial statements describes the basis of our opinion[s] on those financial statements and on the Directors' Report.

Opinion

In our opinion the summary financial statement is consistent with the full annual financial statements and the Directors' Report of XYZ Limited for the year ended ... and complies with the applicable requirements of section 427 of the Companies Act 2006, and the regulations made thereunder.

[We have not considered the effects of any events between the date on which we signed our report on the full annual financial statements (insert date) and the date of this statement.][14]

Statutory auditor *Address*
Date

DIRECTORS' STATEMENT
The auditor has issued unqualified reports on the full annual financial statements and on the consistency of the directors' report with those financial statements. Their report on the full annual financial statements contained no statement under sections 498(2)(a), 498(2)(b) or 498(3) of the Companies Act 2006[15].

---

[14] Include this sentence where the date of this statement is after the date of the auditor's report on the full annual financial statements.

[15] This statement is a requirement of sections 427(4)(e), 427(4)(f) and 427(4)(g) of CA 2006.

[Bulletin 2008/4]
The special auditor's report on abbreviated accounts in the United Kingdom

(Issued April 2008)

Contents

	Paragraphs
Introduction	1
Companies subject to the small companies regime	2 - 14
Accounts sent to members	4 - 6
Accounts placed on the public record	7 - 9
Delivering accounts subject to the small companies regime other than abbreviated accounts	10 - 12
Delivering abbreviated accounts	13 - 14
Medium-sized companies	15 - 22
Accounts sent to members	16 - 17
Accounts placed on the public record	18 - 20
Delivering abbreviated accounts	21 - 22
Abbreviated accounts of small and medium-sized companies	23 – 26
Auditor's procedures when reporting on abbreviated accounts	27
Special report of the auditor on abbreviated accounts	28 – 46
Title and addressee	31
Introductory paragraph	32
Respective responsibilities	33 – 34
Opinion	35 – 40
Other information required in the Auditor's Special Report	41 – 44
Signature	45
Date	46
Change of auditor	47

Appendices

1. Filing options available to small companies which are exempt from audit
2. The two filing options available to medium-sized companies
3. Illustrative example of a special report on the abbreviated accounts of a small company
4. Illustrative example of a special report on the abbreviated accounts of a medium-sized company
5. Illustrative example of a special report on the abbreviated accounts of a small company including other information – emphasis of matter paragraph regarding a material uncertainty (going concern)
6. Illustrative example of a special report on the abbreviated accounts of a medium-sized company including a paragraph regarding a material inconsistency between the full annual accounts and the directors' report

Introduction

This Bulletin provides guidance for auditors regarding the filing obligations of small and medium-sized companies, under the United Kingdom Companies Act 2006 (CA 2006). In particular, it provides guidance concerning the "Special Auditor's Report on Abbreviated Accounts". 1

Companies subject to the small companies regime

Section 381 of CA 2006 states that the small companies regime for accounts and reports applies to a company for a financial year in relation to which the company: 2

(a) qualifies as small (see sections 382 and 383 of CA 2006); and
(b) is not excluded from the regime (see section 384 of CA 2006).

With respect to companies preparing accounts under UK GAAP[1] (described in CA 2006 as Companies Act accounts), section 396 (3) of CA 2006 provides for the Secretary of State to make regulations as to: 3

(a) the form and content of the balance sheet and profit and loss account; and
(b) additional information to be provided by way of notes to the accounts.

The Small Companies and Groups (Accounts and Directors' Report) Regulations 2008[2] (the SI 409 Regulations) provide the regulations that are applicable to companies subject to the small companies regime.

Accounts sent to members

A small company that prepares accounts under UK GAAP is required to prepare and send to its members its "full" annual accounts and a directors' report prepared in accordance with the relevant requirements of CA 2006, the SI 409 Regulations and either: 4

(a) the Financial Reporting Standard for Smaller Entities (FRSSE)[3]; or
(b) UK Financial Reporting Standards.

A small company that prepares IAS accounts is required to prepare and send to its members its "full" annual accounts and a directors' report prepared in accordance with the relevant requirements of CA 2006, the SI 409 Regulations and International Financial Reporting Standards as adopted by the European Union. 5

All small companies are required to send to their members an auditor's report prepared in accordance with sections 495 and 496 of CA 2006, except where the company is exempt from audit and the directors have taken advantage of that exemption[4]. 6

---

[1] *Generally accepted accounting practice.*

[2] *Statutory Instrument, SI 2008 No. 409.*

[3] *Example 1 of Appendix 1 of Bulletin 2006/6 "Auditor's Reports on Financial Statements in the United Kingdom" provides an illustrative example of an auditor's report of a non-publicly traded company preparing financial statements under the FRSSE.*

[4] *This Bulletin provides guidance with respect to small companies that are either not exempt from audit; or, where exempt have not taken advantage of that exemption.*

Accounts placed on the public record

7   With respect to the accounts that a small company is required to place on the public record, by delivering them to the Registrar of Companies[5], it has the following three choices. These are, delivering to the Registrar:

(a) a copy of the balance sheet as sent to its members; or
(b) a copy of the balance sheet and the profit and loss account as sent to its members; or
(c) where its accounts are prepared using UK GAAP, abbreviated accounts prepared in accordance with Regulation 6 and Schedule 4 of the SI 409 Regulations.

In the case of (a) and (b) the company is required to deliver to the Registrar a copy of the auditor's report prepared in accordance with section 495 of CA 2006. In the case of (c) the company is required to deliver the "special auditor's report" prepared in accordance with section 449 of CA 2006.

8   A small company is not required to deliver to the Registrar a copy of the directors' report. However, where it chooses to deliver a copy of the directors' report, the auditor's report prepared in connection with section 496 of CA 2006 on the directors' report must also be delivered to the Registrar[6].

9   These requirements are discussed further in the following paragraphs and are summarised in the table in Appendix 1.

Delivering accounts subject to the small companies regime other than abbreviated accounts

10   Where a small company delivers to the Registrar IAS accounts or UK GAAP accounts that are not abbreviated accounts and does not deliver a copy of the company's profit and loss account or a copy of the directors' report, the copy of the balance sheet delivered to the Registrar is required to contain in a prominent position a statement that the company's accounts and reports have been delivered in accordance with the provisions applicable to companies subject to the small companies regime[7].

11   The company is also required to deliver to the Registrar a copy of the auditor's report prepared in accordance with section 495 [and section 496 if a Directors' Report is filed] of CA 2006 notwithstanding that the auditor's opinion is expressed on the full accounts and report rather than being restricted in scope to the balance sheet [and directors' report] that has been filed. As the auditor's report that is filed has to be a copy of the report prepared in accordance with section 495 [and, if applicable, 496] of CA 2006 the auditor is not permitted to amend the report to refer to only those items that are delivered.

12   However, the auditor is not precluded from adding a preface to the copy report explaining that the auditor's report had been prepared in connection with the audit of the full annual accounts and directors' report and that certain primary statements

---

[5] *In CA 2006 the expressions "the registrar of companies" and "the registrar" mean the registrar of companies for England & Wales, Scotland or Northern Ireland, as the case may require (section 1060(3) CA 2006).*

[6] *Section 444(2) CA 2006.*

[7] *Section 444(5) CA 2006.*

and the directors' report originally reported on are not included within the filing. Illustrative wording for such a preface is as follows:

> Although the company is only required to file a balance sheet, the Companies Act 2006 requires the accompanying auditor's report to be a copy of our report to the members on the company's full annual accounts and directors' report. Readers are cautioned that the profit and loss account and certain other primary statements and the directors' report, referred to in the copy of our auditor's report, are not required to be filed with the Registrar of Companies.

Delivering abbreviated accounts

Abbreviated accounts for small companies: 13

(a) comprise a balance sheet and prescribed notes (including the disclosure of accounting policies) drawn up in accordance with Schedule 4 of the SI 409 Regulations, and
(b) if a profit and loss account is filed it may omit those items specified by the SI 409 Regulations[8].

If abbreviated accounts are delivered to the Registrar and an audit has been undertaken the obligation to deliver a copy of the auditor's report is to deliver a copy of the special auditor's report required by section 449 of CA 2006[9]. 14

Medium-sized companies

The criteria for a company to qualify as medium-sized are set out in sections 465 to 467 of CA 2006. The Large and Medium-sized Companies and Groups (Accounts and Reports) Regulations 2008[10] (the SI 410 Regulations) provide the regulations that are applicable to medium sized companies that prepare accounts under UK GAAP. 15

Accounts sent to members

A medium-sized company that prepares accounts under UK GAAP is required to prepare and send to its members its "full" annual accounts prepared in accordance with the relevant requirements of CA 2006, the SI 410 Regulations and UK Financial Reporting Standards. 16

A medium-sized company that prepares IAS accounts is required to prepare and send to its members its "full" annual accounts prepared in accordance with the relevant requirements of CA 2006 and International Financial Reporting Standards as adopted by the European Union. 17

---

[8] *Section 444(3) CA 2006.*

[9] *Section 444(4) CA 2006.*

[10] *Statutory Instrument, SI 2008 No. 410.*

Accounts placed on the public record

18 The directors of a company that qualifies as a medium-sized company in relation to a financial year must deliver to the Registrar a copy of:

(a) the company's annual accounts; and
(b) the directors' report[11].

The directors are also required to deliver to the Registrar a copy of the auditor's report on the accounts and on the directors' report prepared in accordance with sections 495 and 496 of CA 2006[12] respectively.

19 However, where the company prepares UK GAAP accounts the directors may deliver to the Registrar abbreviated accounts rather than the company's full annual accounts and directors' report as described in paragraph 18[13].

20 The filing obligations of medium-sized companies, described above, are discussed further in the following paragraphs and summarised in tabular form in Appendix 2.

Delivering abbreviated accounts

21 Abbreviated accounts for medium-sized companies comprise:

(a) a balance sheet; and
(b) a profit and loss account in which items are combined in accordance with the SI 410 Regulations[14] and that does not contain items whose omission is authorised by those Regulations[15] (See paragraphs 4, 5 and 6 of the SI 410 Regulations).

22 If abbreviated accounts are delivered to the Registrar and an audit has been undertaken[16] the obligation to deliver a copy of the auditor's report is to deliver a copy of the special auditor's report required by section 449 of CA 2006.

Abbreviated accounts of small and medium-sized companies

23 As described above, companies which are small companies or medium-sized companies in relation to a financial year and that are preparing "full" UK GAAP individual accounts are entitled to deliver "abbreviated accounts" to the Registrar. These provisions are only available to companies preparing UK GAAP accounts, as the format of accounts on which abbreviated accounts are based does not apply to companies preparing IAS accounts.

---

[11] Section 445(1) CA 2006.

[12] Section 445(2) CA 2006.

[13] Section 445(3) CA 2006.

[14] For companies that are not banking or insurance companies these regulations are set out in Schedule 1 of the SI 410 Regulations. (Schedules 2 and 3 of the SI 410 Regulations set out the requirements for banking and insurance companies).

[15] Section 445 (3) CA 2006.

[16] An audit exemption may arise with respect to non-profit making companies subject to public sector audit.

Section 384 (for small companies) and 467 (for medium-sized companies) of CA 2006 specify cases in which the provisions permitting the delivery of abbreviated accounts do not apply.

Section 450(3) of CA 2006 requires, with respect to abbreviated accounts that the balance sheet include a statement, in a prominent position above the director's signature, that the accounts are prepared in accordance with the special provisions of CA 2006 relating (as the case may be) to companies subject to the small companies regime or to medium-sized companies.

CA 2006 provides for abbreviated accounts to be prepared in respect of an individual company only. CA 2006 does not provide for "abbreviated group accounts".

Auditor's procedures when reporting on abbreviated accounts

Before issuing the special auditor's report on abbreviated accounts the auditor:

(a) assesses by reference to section 444 (small companies) or section 445 (medium-sized companies) of CA 2006 whether the company is entitled to deliver abbreviated accounts;
(b) compares the abbreviated accounts to the underlying audited annual accounts from which they have been derived and assesses whether the abbreviated accounts are consistent with the audited annual accounts;
(c) checks whether the content of the abbreviated accounts complies with the requirements of the SI 409 Regulations with respect to small companies and the SI 410 Regulations with respect to medium-sized companies; and
(d) considers whether the omission of information, other than through compliance with the relevant regulations, results in the abbreviated accounts being misleading.

Special report of the auditor on abbreviated accounts

If abbreviated accounts prepared in accordance with the relevant provision are delivered to the Registrar, sections 444(4), 445(4) and 449(2) of CA 2006 require that they be accompanied by a copy of a special report of the auditor.

By virtue of section 449(4) of CA 2006, the provisions of sections 503 to 506 (signature of auditor's report) and sections 507 to 509 (offences in connection with auditor's report) apply to the special report of the auditor as they apply to an auditor's report on the company's annual accounts prepared under Part 16 of CA 2006.

The elements of the special report of the auditor are set out in the following paragraphs and illustrated in appendices 3 to 6 of this Bulletin.

Title and addressee

CA 2006 does not state to whom the special report of the auditor should be addressed. In the absence of any requirement the auditor addresses the report to the company. It is appropriate to use the term "Independent Auditor" in the title.

Introductory paragraph

32 The auditor identifies the abbreviated accounts examined.

Respective responsibilities

33 The auditor includes a description of its responsibilities and also states that the directors are responsible for preparing the abbreviated accounts in accordance with the relevant section of CA 2006.

34 The auditor indicates that its work was conducted in accordance with this Bulletin and was limited to determining whether the company is entitled to deliver abbreviated accounts to the Registrar and whether the abbreviated accounts to be delivered are properly prepared in accordance with the relevant provisions.

Opinion

35 Although abbreviated accounts must be properly prepared in accordance with the relevant provisions, they are not required to give a true and fair view (in practice, they will not do so).

36 Section 449(2) of CA 2006 requires the auditor to state that in its opinion:
   (a) the company is entitled to deliver abbreviated accounts prepared in accordance with the section in question[17]; and
   (b) the abbreviated accounts to be delivered are properly prepared in accordance with regulations under that section.

37 The fact that the auditor's report under section 495 of CA 2006 on the "full" accounts was modified (e.g. qualified or contained an emphasis of matter paragraph), does not prevent the abbreviated accounts from being prepared in accordance with the relevant section of CA 2006.

38 The matter in question may, however, affect the company's eligibility as "small" or "medium-sized". The auditor therefore considers whether the maximum effect of the matter giving rise to the modification would cause two or more of the criteria for determining eligibility (that is, the turnover, employee or balance sheet totals) to exceed the relevant limits. An auditor may be unable to assess properly the criteria for small or medium sized eligibility where an adverse opinion or disclaimer of opinion has been given under section 495 of CA 2006.

39 Where either:
   (a) the criteria exceed the relevant limits; or
   (b) the auditor is unable to assess the criteria,

the auditor will be unable to express an opinion that the company is entitled to deliver abbreviated accounts.

40 CA 2006 does not envisage a qualified opinion being expressed on the abbreviated accounts. An auditor unable to make the positive statements required, reports this fact to the directors. In such circumstances, the directors cannot deliver the abbreviated accounts to the Registrar.

---

[17] Section 444(3) of CA 2006 for a small company and section 445(3) of CA 2006 for a medium-sized company.

Other information required in the Auditor's Special Report

Under section 449(3) of CA 2006, if the auditor's report under section 495 of CA 2006 on the "full" annual accounts: 41

(a) was qualified, the special report must set out that report in full (together with any further material necessary to understand the qualification); or
(b) contained a statement under section 498(2)(a) or (b) (accounts, records or returns inadequate or accounts not agreeing with records or returns), or section 498(3) (failure to obtain necessary information and explanations) of CA 2006, the special report is required to set out the statement in full.

These are, however, minimum requirements and do not preclude the inclusion in the special auditor's report of other information which the auditor considers important to a proper understanding of that report. In particular, when the auditor's report under section 495 of CA 2006 is unqualified but contains an emphasis of matter paragraph, the APB considers that it is necessary for the auditor to include such a paragraph (together with any further material necessary to understand it) in the special auditor's report (see Appendix 5). 42

When a qualified report or an emphasis of matter paragraph includes a reference to a note to the "full" annual accounts, without stating explicitly all the relevant information contained in that note, the auditor includes the necessary information in their report on the abbreviated accounts, immediately following the reproduction of the text of its report on the "full" annual accounts. Alternatively the auditor could request the company to include such information in the notes to the abbreviated accounts. 43

For a medium-sized company, where the auditor's report under sections 495 and 496 of CA 2006 draws attention to an inconsistency between the directors' report and the "full" financial statements (as described in Example B to Section B of ISA (UK and Ireland) 720 (Revised)) the paragraph describing the inconsistency is likely to be included in the special report of the auditor as illustrated in Appendix 6[18]. 44

Signature

Where the auditor is an individual the special report is signed by the individual. Where the auditor is a firm, the report must be signed by the senior statutory auditor in his own name for and on behalf of the auditor (See Bulletin 2008/6 "The 'Senior Statutory Auditor' under the United Kingdom Companies Act 2006". 45

Date

The auditor dates the special report with the date on which it is signed. The auditor does not sign the special report until the directors have approved and signed the abbreviated accounts. It is desirable that the auditor complete and sign its special report on the date that they complete and sign their report on the "full" annual accounts to avoid the impression that the special report in any way 'updates' the auditor's report on the "full" annual accounts. Where the auditor dates its special report after the date of their report on the "full" annual accounts, the special report 46

---

[18] For a small company the abbreviated accounts may exclude the directors' report and therefore the paragraph describing the inconsistency is unlikely to be included in the special report of the auditor as it does not affect the reader's understanding of the information in the abbreviated accounts.

states that the auditor has not considered the effects of any events between the two dates.

Change of auditor

47 Where there is to be a change of auditor, it is preferable for the auditor who reported on the "full" annual accounts to report on the abbreviated accounts for that financial year. Where this is not possible, the new auditor performing the latter function may decide to accept the "full" annual accounts audited by its predecessor as a basis for its work, unless it has grounds to doubt the company's eligibility to deliver abbreviated accounts (for example, because a qualified opinion affects the criteria for determining eligibility). If there is a need to refer in the special report to the predecessor auditor's report on the "full" annual accounts, the new auditor indicates in its report by whom the audit of the "full" annual accounts was carried out.

Appendix 1 – Filing options available to small companies which are exempt from audit

Option	1 Full Accounts	2 Full Balance Sheet only	3 Full Abbreviated Accounts	4 Abbreviated Balance Sheet only
Applicability	UK GAAP and IAS companies	UK GAAP and IAS companies	UK GAAP companies only	UK GAAP companies only
Copy full Balance Sheet	✓	✓		
Balance sheet to include statement that the company's annual accounts and reports have been delivered in accordance with the provisions applicable to companies subject to the small companies regime	✗	✓		
Copy full Profit and Loss Account	✓	✗		
Copy Directors' Report	✓	✗		
Auditor's report required by section 495 of CA 2006	✓	✓		
Auditor's report required by section 496 of CA 2006	✓	✗		
Abbreviated balance sheet drawn up in accordance with the SI 409 Regulations			✓	✓
Abbreviated profit and loss account drawn up in accordance with the SI 409 Regulations			✓	✗

Copy Directors' Report		✓	✗
Special auditor's report required by section 449 of CA 2006		✓	✓

NOTE: It is a small company's choice as to whether it files its profit and loss account or director's report. Options 1 and 3 illustrate the filing of both. Options 2 and 4 illustrate the filing of neither. Small companies may also file one but not the other. For simplicity these other alternatives are not illustrated.

Appendix 2 – The two filing options available to medium-sized companies

Option	1: Full Accounts	2: Abbreviated Accounts
Applicability	UK GAAP and IAS companies	UK GAAP companies only
Copy Annual Accounts	✓	
Copy Abbreviated Accounts drawn up in accordance with the SI 410 Regulations		✓
Copy Directors' Report	✓	✓
Auditors' report required by sections 495 and 496 of CA 2006	✓	
Special auditor's report required by section 449 of CA 2006		✓

Appendix 3 – Illustrative example of a special report on the abbreviated accounts of a small company

INDEPENDENT AUDITOR'S REPORT TO XYZ LIMITED UNDER SECTION 449 OF THE COMPANIES ACT 2006

We have examined the abbreviated accounts set out on pages ... to ...[19], together with the financial statements of XYZ Limited for the year ended ... prepared under section 396 of the Companies Act 2006.

Respective responsibilities of directors and auditors

The directors are responsible for preparing the abbreviated accounts in accordance with section 444 of the Companies Act 2006. It is our responsibility to form an independent opinion as to whether the company is entitled to deliver abbreviated accounts to the Registrar of Companies and whether the abbreviated accounts have

---

[19] *If the profit and loss account and/or directors' report are included (as is permitted but not required) they are included within these page numbers.*

been properly prepared in accordance with the regulations made under that section and to report our opinion to you.

We conducted our work in accordance with Bulletin 2008/4 issued by the Auditing Practices Board. In accordance with that Bulletin we have carried out the procedures we consider necessary to confirm, by reference to the financial statements, that the company is entitled to deliver abbreviated accounts and that the abbreviated accounts are properly prepared[20].

Opinion

In our opinion the company is entitled to deliver abbreviated accounts prepared in accordance with section 444(3) of the Companies Act 2006, and the abbreviated accounts have been properly prepared in accordance with the regulations made under that section.

[Other information[21]]

[Signature]   *Address*
John Smith (senior statutory auditor)   *Date*
for and on behalf of ABC LLP, Statutory Auditors

Appendix 4 – Illustrative example of a special report on the abbreviated accounts of a medium-sized company

INDEPENDENT AUDITOR'S REPORT TO XYZ LIMITED UNDER SECTION 449 OF THE COMPANIES ACT 2006

We have examined the abbreviated accounts set out on pages ... to ...,[22] together with the financial statements of XYZ Limited for the year ended ... prepared under section 396 of the Companies Act 2006.

Respective responsibilities of directors and auditors

The directors are responsible for preparing the abbreviated accounts in accordance with section 445 of the Companies Act 2006. It is our responsibility to form an independent opinion as to whether the company is entitled to deliver abbreviated accounts to the Registrar of Companies and whether the abbreviated accounts have been properly prepared in accordance with the regulations made under that section and to report our opinion to you.

We conducted our work in accordance with Bulletin 2008/4 issued by the Auditing Practices Board. In accordance with that Bulletin we have carried out the procedures we consider necessary to confirm, by reference to the financial statements, that the

---

[20] Add appropriate wording such as "The scope of our work for the purposes of this report does not include examining events occurring after the date of our auditor's report on the full financial statements" where special report is dated after the signing of the auditor's report on the full annual accounts (see paragraph 46).

[21] This section is included only in the circumstances described in paragraphs 41 to 44 (see Appendices 5 and 6).

[22] The directors' report is included within these page numbers.

company is entitled to deliver abbreviated accounts and that the abbreviated accounts are properly prepared[23].

Opinion

In our opinion the company is entitled to deliver abbreviated accounts prepared in accordance with section 445(3) of the Companies Act 2006, and the abbreviated accounts have been properly prepared in accordance with the regulations made under that section.

[Other information[24]]

[Signature]   Address
John Smith (senior statutory auditor)   Date
for and on behalf of ABC LLP, Statutory Auditors

Appendix 5 – Illustrative example of a special report on the abbreviated accounts of a small company including other information – emphasis of matter paragraph regarding a material uncertainty (going concern)

INDEPENDENT AUDITOR'S REPORT TO XYZ LIMITED UNDER SECTION 449 OF THE COMPANIES ACT 2006

We have examined the abbreviated accounts set out on pages ... to ...,[25] together with the financial statements of XYZ Limited for the year ended ... prepared under section 396 of the Companies Act 2006.

Respective responsibilities of directors and auditors

The directors are responsible for preparing the abbreviated accounts in accordance with section 444 of the Companies Act 2006. It is our responsibility to form an independent opinion as to whether the company is entitled to deliver abbreviated accounts to the Registrar of Companies and whether the abbreviated accounts have been properly prepared in accordance with the regulations made under that section and to report our opinion to you.

Basis of opinion

We conducted our work in accordance with Bulletin 2008/4 issued by the Auditing Practices Board. In accordance with that Bulletin we have carried out the procedures we consider necessary to confirm, by reference to the financial statements, that the

---

[23] Add appropriate wording such as "The scope of our work for the purposes of this report does not include examining events occurring after the date of our auditor's report on the full financial statements" where special report is dated after the signing of the auditor's report on the full annual accounts (see paragraph 46).

[24] This section is included only in the circumstances described in paragraphs 41 to 44 (see Appendices 5 and 6).

[25] If the profit and loss account and/or directors' report are included (as is permitted but not required) they are included within these page numbers.

company is entitled to deliver abbreviated accounts and that the abbreviated accounts are properly prepared[26].

Opinion

In our opinion the company is entitled to deliver abbreviated accounts prepared in accordance with section 444 of the Companies Act 2006, and the abbreviated accounts have been properly prepared in accordance with the regulations made under that section.

Other information

On ...[27] we reported as auditor to the members of the company on the financial statements prepared under section 396 of the Companies Act 2006 and our report [included the following paragraph][28] *[was as follows]*[29]

Emphasis of matter - Going concern

In forming our opinion on the financial statements, which is not qualified, we have considered the adequacy of the disclosure made in note x to the financial statements concerning the company's ability to continue as a going concern. The company incurred a net loss of £X during the year ended 31 December 20X1 and, at that date, the company's current liabilities exceeded its total assets by £Y. These conditions, along with the other matters explained in note x to the financial statements, indicate the existence of a material uncertainty which may cast significant doubt about the company's ability to continue as a going concern. The financial statements do not include the adjustments that would result if the company was unable to continue as a going concern.'[30]

[Signature]   *Address*
John Smith (senior statutory auditor)   *Date*
for and on behalf of ABC LLP, Statutory Auditors

---

[26] *Add appropriate wording such as "The scope of our work for the purposes of this report does not include examining events occurring after the date of our auditor's report on the full annual accounts" where special report is dated after the signing of the auditor's report on the full annual accounts (see paragraph 46).*

[27] *The date of the auditor's report on the annual accounts.*

[28] *In this example, the "other information" section of the report on the abbreviated accounts reproduces an emphasis of matter paragraph from the auditors' report on the annual accounts and consequently the words "included the following paragraph" are used (see paragraph 42).*

[29] *Where the auditor's opinion is qualified the words "was as follows" are used.*

[30] *Further material necessary to understand the explanatory paragraph may be added (see paragraph 43).*

Appendix 6 – Illustrative example of a special report on the abbreviated accounts of a medium-sized company including a paragraph regarding a material inconsistency between the full annual accounts and the directors' report

INDEPENDENT AUDITOR'S REPORT TO XYZ LIMITED UNDER SECTION 449 OF THE COMPANIES ACT 2006

We have examined the abbreviated accounts set out on pages ... to ...,[31] together with the financial statements of XYZ Limited for the year ended ... prepared under section 396 of the Companies Act 2006.

Respective responsibilities of directors and auditors

The directors are responsible for preparing the abbreviated accounts in accordance with section 445 of the Companies Act 2006. It is our responsibility to form an independent opinion as to whether the company is entitled to deliver abbreviated accounts to the Registrar of Companies and whether the abbreviated accounts have been properly prepared in accordance with the regulations made under that section and to report our opinion to you.

We conducted our work in accordance with Bulletin 2008/4 issued by the Auditing Practices Board. In accordance with that Bulletin we have carried out the procedures we consider necessary to confirm, by reference to the financial statements, that the company is entitled to deliver abbreviated accounts and that the abbreviated accounts are properly prepared[32].

Opinion

In our opinion the company is entitled to deliver abbreviated accounts prepared in accordance with section 445(3) of the Companies Act 2006, and the abbreviated accounts have been properly prepared in accordance with the regulations made under that section.

Other information

On ...[33] we reported as auditor to the members of the company on the full financial statements prepared under section 396 of the Companies Act 2006 and our report included the following paragraph:[34]

---

[31] *The directors' report is included within these page numbers.*

[32] *Add appropriate wording such as "The scope of our work for the purposes of this report does not include examining events occurring after the date of our auditor's report on the full annual accounts" where special report is dated after the signing of the auditor's report on the full financial statements (see paragraph 46).*

[33] *The date of the auditor's report on the financial statements.*

[34] *In this example, the "other information" section of the report on the abbreviated accounts reproduces a paragraph from the auditor's report on the financial statements drawing attention to an inconsistency between the directors' report and the full financial statements (see paragraph 44).*

Material inconsistency between the full financial statements and the directors' report

In our opinion, the information given in the seventh paragraph of the Business Review in the directors' report is not consistent with the full financial statements. That paragraph states without amplification that "the company's trading for the period resulted in a 10% increase in profit over the previous period's profit. The income statement, however, shows that the company's profit for the period includes a profit of £Z which did not arise from trading but from the disposal of assets of a discontinued operation. Without this profit on the disposal of assets the company would have reported a profit for the year of £Y, representing a reduction in profit of 25% over the previous period's profit on a like for like basis. Except for this matter, in our opinion the information given in the directors' report is consistent with the full financial statements on which we separately reported on [insert date][35].

[Signature]   *Address*
John Smith *(senior statutory auditor)*   *Date*
for and on behalf of ABC LLP, Statutory Auditors

---

[35] *Further material necessary to understand the explanatory paragraph may be added (see paragraph 43).*

[Bulletin 2008/5]
Auditor's reports on revised accounts and reports, in the United Kingdom

(Issued April 2008)

Contents

	Paragraphs
Introduction	1 – 10
Voluntary revision of accounts or reports	1 – 3
Application to court in respect of defective accounts or reports	4 – 6
Avenues available to an auditor on becoming aware that accounts or reports are defective	7 – 8
Limitation as to extent of revisions permitted by law	9
Applicable requirements and guidance of ISAs (UK and Ireland)	10
Revision by replacement or by supplementary note	11 – 13
Dating the auditor's revised report	14
Auditor's procedures when reporting on revised accounts, directors' reports and directors' remuneration reports	15 – 16
Requirements of the SI 373 Regulations that establish requirements with respect to auditor's reports	17 – 32
Revised annual accounts	18 – 24
Auditor's report where company ceases to be exempt from audit	25
Revised reports	26 – 30
Abbreviated accounts	31
Summary financial statement	32

Appendices
1. Summarisation of requirements of the Companies (Revision of Defective Accounts and Reports) Regulations 2008 (the SI 373 Regulations)
2. Illustrative example of an auditor's report on revised annual accounts: revision by replacement
3. Illustrative example of an auditor's report on revised annual accounts: revision by supplementary note
4. Illustrative auditor's report on revised directors' report: revision by replacement
5. Illustrative auditor's report on revised directors' remuneration report: revision by replacement
6. Illustrative example of a special report on the revised abbreviated accounts of a small company when full financial statements are revised
7. Illustrative auditor's statement on a revised summary financial statement of a quoted company: revision by replacement

Introduction

Voluntary revision of accounts or reports

1 Section 454 of the Companies Act 2006 (CA 2006) grants company directors the authority to revise annual accounts[1], directors' remuneration reports, directors' reports and summary financial statements which do not comply with CA 2006 (or, where applicable, Article 4 of the IAS Regulation).

2 Section 454(3) of CA 2006 enables the Secretary of State to make provision by regulations as to the application of the provisions of CA 2006 in relation to:

   (a) revised annual accounts;
   (b) revised directors' remuneration reports;
   (c) revised directors' reports; and
   (d) revised summary financial statements.

3 Section 454(4) of CA 2006 states that, the regulations may in particular "make provision with respect to the functions of the company's auditor in relation to the revised accounts, report or statement". The regulations referred to in section 454 of CA 2006 are set out in the "Companies (Revision of Defective Accounts and Reports) Regulations 2008"[2] (the SI 373 Regulations).

Application to court in respect of defective accounts or reports

4 Sections 455 and 456 of CA 2006 give the Secretary of State, or a person authorised by him, power to apply to the court for a declaration that the annual accounts of a company do not comply, or a directors' report does not comply, with the requirements of CA 2006 (or, where applicable, Article 4 of the IAS Regulation) and for an order requiring the directors to prepare revised accounts or a revised report.

5 If the court orders the preparation of revised accounts it may give directions as to:

   (a) the auditing of the accounts;
   (b) the revision of any directors' remuneration report, directors' report or summary financial statement;
   (c) the taking of steps by the directors to bring the making of the order to the notice of persons likely to rely on the previous accounts; and
   (d) such other matters as the court thinks fit.

6 Similarly, if the court orders the preparation of a revised directors' report it may give directions as to:

   (a) the review of the report by the auditors;
   (b) the revision of any summary financial statement;
   (c) the taking of steps by the directors to bring the making of the order to the notice of persons likely to rely on the previous report; and
   (d) such other matters as the court thinks fit.

---

[1] *Including abbreviated accounts*

[2] *Statutory Instrument, SI 2008 No.373*

Avenues available to an auditor on becoming aware that accounts or reports are defective

7 If the auditor becomes aware of a fact relevant to the audited accounts or reports, of which it was unaware at the date of the auditor's report, which indicates that the annual accounts or reports were defective there are no statutory provisions that require the accounts, or the report, to be revised.

8 Therefore, in such circumstances, the auditor discusses with those charged with governance whether they wish to withdraw the accounts or the report and revise them voluntarily in accordance with the provisions of section 454 of CA 2006. If those charged with governance decide not to do so the auditor may wish to take legal advice. Possible courses of action include the making of a statement by those charged with governance, or the auditor, at the annual general meeting[3].

Limitation as to extent of revisions permitted by law

9 When accounts are revised care needs to be taken that the extent of the revisions does not exceed those permitted by CA 2006. In particular section 454 (2) of CA 2006 requires that "the revisions must be confined to:

(a) the correction of those respects in which the previous accounts or report did not comply with the requirements of this Act (or, where applicable, of Article 4 of the IAS Regulation), and
(b) the making of any necessary consequential alterations".

Applicable requirements and guidance of ISAs (UK and Ireland)

10 With respect to revised annual accounts ISA (UK and Ireland) 560 "Subsequent Events" at paragraph 16 requires that "The new auditor's report should include an emphasis of matter paragraph referring to a note to the financial statements[4] that more extensively discusses the reason for the revision of the previously issued financial statements and to the earlier report issued by the auditor". Subsequent guidance in that paragraph states "Local regulations of some countries permit the auditor to restrict the audit procedures regarding the revised financial statements to the effects of the subsequent event that necessitated the revision. In such cases, the new auditor's report would contain a statement to that effect". The application of this requirement and guidance is illustrated in the example auditor's reports set out in Appendices 2 and 3.

Revision by replacement or by supplementary note

11 Under the SI 373 Regulations annual accounts (including abbreviated accounts), directors' reports, directors' remuneration reports and summary financial statements may be revised either:

(a) by replacement; or
(b) by the issue of a supplementary note.

---

[3] These paragraphs are derived from paragraph 14-1 of ISA (UK and Ireland) 560 "Subsequent events", additional guidance is provided in paragraphs 15 to 18 of that ISA (UK and Ireland).

[4] In this Bulletin, other than where necessary in context, the term "annual accounts", which is used in CA 2006, is used rather than "financial statements".

12 Revision by replacement means revision by the preparation of a replacement set of accounts, directors' report or directors' remuneration report, in substitution for the original defective accounts or reports. Revision by supplementary note means revision by the preparation of a note indicating corrections to be made to the original defective accounts or reports.

13 The SI 373 Regulations contain no conditions which require one form or the other to be used and, therefore, the directors may use whichever approach appears more appropriate to the circumstances. In both instances, the accounts or report are to be prepared as if prepared and approved by the directors as at the date of the original annual accounts or report.

Dating the auditor's revised report

14 The auditor's report on the revised annual accounts (or report) is dated the actual date on which it is signed. From that date it becomes the date of the auditor's report in place of the auditor's report on the original audited accounts (or report). However, this does not imply that the auditor has undertaken a subsequent events review between that date and the previous date.

Auditor's procedures when reporting on revised accounts, directors' reports and directors' remuneration reports

15 The basis of the auditor's opinion on revised annual accounts states: "The audit of revised financial statements includes the performance of procedures to assess whether the revisions made by the directors are appropriate and have been properly made".

16 Therefore, before issuing a report on revised annual accounts, directors' reports or directors' remuneration reports the auditor:
 (a) through discussion with those charged with governance, determines the reasons for the revision and forms a view from available evidence as to whether the reasons are legitimate;
 (b) reviews those working papers relating to the audit of the original accounts or report that will enable the auditor to ascertain whether the issue giving rise to the revision had been considered during the audit and if so how they were resolved. The purpose of this review is to enable the auditor to properly assess the context in which the revision is being made;
 (c) considers the integrity of management and those charged with governance. In particular, the auditor re-assesses earlier representations made by management and those charged with governance;
 (d) obtains sufficient appropriate audit evidence to support the changes being made to the original accounts or report; and
 (e) considers whether the auditor has become aware of events that have occurred since it signed the original auditor's report which are of such significance that the auditor may be unwilling to sign a report on the revised accounts or report.

Requirements of the SI 373 Regulations that establish requirements with respect to auditor's reports

17 The following paragraphs provide a summary of certain of the requirements of the SI 373 Regulations insofar as they establish requirements with respect to the various

auditor's reports set out in Appendices 2 to 7. Appendix 1 provides a summary of those requirements of the SI 373 Regulations that establish requirements with respect to various statements that the directors are required to make with respect to revised accounts and reports. This Bulletin is not intended to be an authoritative guide to all of the requirements of CA 2006 and the SI 373 Regulations with respect to revising annual accounts and reports. For complete and authoritative guidance reference should always be made to CA 2006 and the SI 373 Regulations themselves.

Revised annual accounts

A company's current auditor is required to make a report to the company's members on any revised annual accounts prepared under section 454 of CA 2006. However, where the auditor's report on the original defective accounts was not made by the company's current auditor, the directors of the company may resolve that the report is to be made by the auditor that made the original report provided that, that auditor agrees to do so and remains qualified for appointment as auditor of the company. 18

Where the company requests the current auditor to report to the company's members on revised annual accounts, on which the current auditor has not previously reported, the responsibility of the current auditor is to express its opinion on the revised accounts as a whole. Consequently it informs the company of the need for it to both: 19

(a) audit the proposed revisions; and
(b) obtain sufficient appropriate audit evidence as to the truth and fairness of the annual accounts in question. Such evidence is likely to be obtained from performing a review of the audit working papers of the auditor that made the original report.

An auditor's report on revised annual accounts is required to state whether in the auditor's opinion the revised annual accounts have been properly prepared in accordance with the requirements of CA 2006 and, where applicable, Article 4 of the IAS Regulation, as they have effect under the Regulations. In particular the auditor is required to state whether a true and fair view, seen as at the date the original defective annual accounts were approved, is given by the revised annual accounts with respect to the matters set out in section 495(3)(a) to (c) of CA 2006. 20

The report is also required to state whether in the auditor's opinion the original defective annual accounts failed to comply with the requirements of CA 2006 and, where applicable, Article 4 of the IAS Regulation in the respects identified by the directors: 21

(a) (in the case of revision by replacement) in the statement required by Regulation 4(2)(a)(iv);
(b) or (in the case of revision by supplementary note) in the supplementary note.

The auditor is also required to state whether the information contained in the directors' report for the financial year for which the annual accounts are prepared (or the revised report if the directors' report has been revised under the Regulations) is consistent with those financial statements. 22

Sections 503 (signature of auditor's report)[5] and 505 (names to be stated in published copies of auditor's reports) of CA 2006 apply to an auditor's report made under the 23

---

[5] See Bulletin 2008/6 "The Senior Statutory Auditor" under the United Kingdom Companies Act 2006.

SI 373 Regulations as they apply to an auditor's report under section 495(1) of CA 2006, with any necessary modifications.

24 Appendix 2 is an illustrative example of an auditor's report on annual accounts that have been revised by replacement showing changes from a standard auditor's report as shaded text. Appendix 3 is an illustrative example of an auditor's report on annual accounts that have been revised by supplementary note.[6]

Auditor's report where company ceases to be exempt from audit

25 Where, as a result of revisions to the accounts, the company is no longer entitled to exemption from audit, Regulation 8 of the SI 373 Regulations requires the company to cause an auditor's report on the revised accounts to be prepared. The auditor's report is required to be delivered to the Registrar within 28 days after the date of revision of the accounts.

Revised reports

26 A company's current auditor is required to make a report (or further report) to the company's members on any revised directors' report or directors' remuneration report prepared under section 454 of CA 2006 if the relevant annual financial statements have not been revised at the same time. However, where the auditor's report on the annual accounts for the financial year covered by the revised report was not made by the company's current auditor, the directors of the company may resolve that the report is to be made by the auditor that made the original report provided that auditor remains qualified for appointment as auditor of the company.

27 Where the company requests the current auditor to report to the company's members on a revised directors' remuneration report on which the current auditor has not previously reported, the responsibility of the current auditor is to express its opinion on the whole of the auditable part of the directors' remuneration report. Consequently it informs the company of the need for it to both:

(a) audit the proposed revisions; and
(b) obtain sufficient appropriate audit evidence as to the proper preparation of the Directors Remuneration Report. Such evidence is likely to be obtained from performing a review of the audit working papers of the auditor that made the original report.

28 Where a revised directors' report is prepared the auditor's report is required to state whether in the auditor's opinion the information given in that revised report is consistent with the annual financial statements for the relevant year.

---

[6] *The illustrative reports are based on the examples provided in Bulletin 2006/6 "Auditor's reports on financial statements in the United Kingdom". Certain aspects of the illustrative reports will likely need to be revised when Bulletin 2006/6 is revised to reflect the requirements of the Companies Act 2006, and any other changes that may arise from the APB's December 2007 Discussion Paper "The Auditor's Report: A Time for Change?"*

Where a revised directors' remuneration report is prepared the auditor's report is required to state whether in the auditor's opinion any auditable part[7] of that revised report has been properly prepared[8]. 29

Appendix 4 is an illustrative example of an auditor's report on a directors' report revised by replacement. Appendix 5 is an illustrative auditor's report on a directors' remuneration report revised by replacement. 30

Abbreviated accounts

The SI 373 Regulations require revised abbreviated accounts to be drawn up in accordance with various sections of CA 2006 including sections 444(4) and 445(4) which are the sections that require the directors to deliver a copy of the special auditor's report required by section 449 of CA 2006. An illustrative example of a special report on the revised abbreviated accounts of a small company is provided in Appendix 6. 31

Summary financial statement

Regulation 17(2) of the SI 373 Regulations requires a revised summary financial statement to contain the statement from the auditor required by sections 427(d) and 428(d) of CA 2006. (This arises from the fact that the directors are required to prepare a further summary financial statement under section 426 and it in turn requires a summary financial statement to comply with either section 427 or 428). An illustrative example of an auditor's statement on a revised summary financial statement of a quoted company is provided in Appendix 7. 32

Appendix 1 – Summarisation of requirements of the Companies (Revision of Defective Accounts and Reports) Regulations 2008 (the SI 373 Regulations)

This Appendix summarises certain of the requirements of the SI 373 Regulations. Neither this Appendix nor the Bulletin is intended to be an authoritative guide to all of the requirements of CA 2006 and the SI 373 Regulations with respect to revising annual accounts and reports. For complete and authoritative guidance reference should always be made to CA 2006 and the SI 373 Regulations themselves. 1

Directors' statement relating to revised annual accounts: revision by replacement

The directors must include a statement concerning the revision in a prominent position in the revised financial statements. In the case of a revision by replacement, Regulation 4(2)(a) requires this to state: 2

(a) "that the revised accounts replace the original annual accounts for the financial year (specifying it);
(b) that they are now the statutory accounts of the company for that financial year;

---

[7] *The "auditable part" is defined in Part 3 of Schedule 8 to the Large and Medium-sized Companies and Groups (Accounts and Reports) Regulations 2008 (the SI 410 Regulations).*

[8] *The SI 373 Regulations require the auditor always to report when the directors' remuneration report has been revised. There is no derogation from this requirement for the auditor in those circumstances where the revision affects only the part of the report that is not required to be audited.*

(c) that they have been prepared as at the date of the original annual accounts and not as at the date of revision and accordingly do not deal with events between those dates;
(d) the respects in which the original annual accounts did not comply with the requirements of CA 2006; and
(e) any significant amendments made consequential upon the remedying of those defects."

Directors' statement relating to revised annual accounts: revision by supplementary note

3   When revision is effected by supplementary note, the note itself should provide adequate information concerning the defect in the original financial statements and any consequential amendments, and is required by Regulation 4(2)(b) to include a statement:

(a) "that the note revises in certain respects the original annual accounts of the company and is to be treated as forming part of those accounts; and
(b) that the annual accounts have been revised as at the date of the original annual accounts and not as at the date of revision and accordingly do not deal with events between those dates."

Directors' statement relating to a revised directors' report or a revised directors' remuneration report: revision by replacement

4   Where a directors' report or a directors' remuneration report is to be revised by replacement the directors are required, before approving the revised report, to cause statements as to the following matters to be made in a prominent position in the revised directors' report [or directors' remuneration report]:

(a) that the revised directors' report [or directors' remuneration report] replaces the original directors' report [or directors' remuneration report] for the financial year (specifying it);
(b) that it has been prepared as at the date of the original directors' report [or directors' remuneration report] and not as at the date of revision and accordingly does not deal with any events between those dates;
(c) the respects in which the original directors' report [or directors' remuneration report] did not comply with CA 2006; and
(d) any significant amendments made consequential upon the remedying of those defects.

Directors' statement relating to a revised directors' report or a revised directors' remuneration report: revision by supplementary note

5   Where a directors' report or a directors' remuneration report is to be revised by supplementary note the directors are required, before approving the supplementary note, to cause statements as to the following matters to be made in a prominent position in the supplementary note:

(a) that the note revises in certain respects the original directors' report [or directors' remuneration report] and is to be treated as forming part of that report; and
(b) that the directors' report [or directors' remuneration report] has been revised as at the date of the original report and not as at the date of the revision and accordingly does not deal with events between those dates.

Abbreviated accounts

Regulations 15 and 16 of the SI 373 Regulations apply to abbreviated accounts filed by small and medium sized companies (See Bulletin 2008/4 "The special auditor's report on abbreviated accounts in the United Kingdom"). Regulation 15 addresses the implications for the abbreviated accounts where revised annual financial statements are required to be prepared and the company has, prior to the date of revision, delivered abbreviated accounts to the Registrar. Regulation 16 addresses the revision of abbreviated accounts that may arise in other circumstances. 6

Regulation 15(2) addresses circumstances where the abbreviated accounts delivered to the registrar would, if they had been prepared by reference to the revised financial statements, not comply with the requirements of CA 2006. This may be because the company would not have qualified as a small or medium-sized company in the light of the revised financial statements or because the financial statements have been revised in a manner which affects the content of the abbreviated accounts. 7

In such cases the directors of the company are required to cause the company either: 8

(a) to deliver to the registrar a copy of the revised annual accounts, together with a copy of the directors' report and the auditor's report on the revised annual accounts; or
(b) if on the basis of the revised annual accounts they are entitled to do so to prepare further abbreviated accounts and to deliver them to the registrar together with a statement as to the effect of the revisions made.

Where the abbreviated accounts would, if they had been prepared by reference to the revised annual accounts, remain the same as those originally filed the company is required to deliver to the registrar 9

(a) a note stating that the annual accounts of the company have been revised in a respect which has no bearing on the abbreviated accounts delivered for that year, together with;
(b) a copy of the auditor's report on the revised annual accounts.

Where the directors have delivered to the registrar abbreviated accounts which do not comply with the requirements of CA 2006 for reasons other than those specified in Regulation 15(2) the directors of the company shall cause the company: 10

(a) to prepare revised abbreviated accounts; and
(b) to deliver those accounts to the registrar within 28 days after the date of the revision together with a statement as to the effect of the revisions made.

Summary financial statement: revision by replacement

Where a summary financial statement does not comply with the requirements of section 426 of CA 2006 or if it had been prepared by reference to revised annual financial statements or a revised report would not have complied with those requirements the directors are required to cause the company to prepare a revised summary financial statement and to send that statement to: 11

(a) any person who received a copy of the original summary financial statement; and
(b) any person to whom the company would be entitled, as at the date the revised summary financial statement is prepared, to send a summary financial statement for the current financial year.

12 Sections 426(1) to (4) (Option to provide summary financial statement), 434(6) (Requirements in connection with publication of statutory accounts) and 435(7) (Requirements in connection with publication of non-statutory accounts) of CA 2006 apply with necessary modifications to a revised summary financial statement.

13 A revised summary financial statement is required to contain a short statement of the revisions made and their effect.

Summary financial statement: revision by supplementary note

14 As an alternative to preparing a revised summary financial statement the company may prepare and send to the persons mentioned in paragraph 11 above a supplementary note indicating the corrections to be made to the original defective summary financial statement. Such a supplementary note is required to contain a statement that it revises the original defective summary financial statement in certain respects and is to be treated as forming part of that statement.

Revision of annual financial statements that has no effect on the summary financial statement

15 Regulation 17(6) of the Regulations contemplates the situation where the directors revise the annual financial statements or reports but that this has no effect on the summary financial statement as issued. In such circumstances the Regulations require the directors to cause the company to send to the persons mentioned in paragraph 11 above a note stating that annual accounts for a specified financial year or the directors' report or directors' remuneration report for that year have or has been revised in a respect which has no bearing on the summary financial statement for that year.

16 If the auditor's report on the revised annual accounts or report is qualified, a copy of that report is required to be attached to the note described in the preceding paragraph.

Companies that are exempt from audit

17 Where a company is exempt from audit:

(a) by virtue of section 477(1) (small companies: conditions for exemption from audit) or
(b) by virtue of section 480 (dormant companies: conditions for exemption from audit),

of CA 2006 the Regulations have effect as if any reference to an auditor's report, or the making of such a report were omitted. In other words the audit exemptions apply to the revised accounts and reports.

Modifications of Companies Act 2006

18 Where the requirements of CA 2006 as to the matters to be included in the annual accounts of a company, abbreviated accounts, a directors' report, a directors' remuneration report or a summary financial statement have been amended after the date of the original defective accounts, report or statement references in the Regulations to the requirements of CA 2006 shall be construed as references to the

provisions of CA 2006 as in force as at the date of the original defective accounts, report or statement.

Appendix 2 – Illustrative example of an auditor's report on revised annual accounts: revision by replacement

This example is based on the following assumptions:
- *Non-publicly traded company that does not prepare group accounts.*
- *UK GAAP used for individual company accounts.*
- *Financial statements contain no surround information other than the directors' report.*

REPORT OF THE INDEPENDENT AUDITOR TO THE [MEMBERS] [SHAREHOLDERS] OF XYZ LIMITED

We have audited the revised financial statements of XYZ Limited for the year ended ... which comprise [state the primary financial statements such as the Profit and Loss Account, the Balance Sheet, the Cash Flow Statement, the Statement of Total Recognised Gains and Losses] and the related notes[9]. These revised financial statements have been prepared under the accounting policies set out therein and replace the original financial statements approved by the directors on....

The revised financial statements have been prepared under The Companies (Revision of Defective Accounts and Reports) Regulations 2008 and accordingly do not take account of events which have taken place after the date on which the original financial statements were approved.

Respective responsibilities of directors and auditors

The directors' responsibilities for preparing revised financial statements in accordance with applicable law and United Kingdom Accounting Standards (United Kingdom Generally Accepted Accounting Practice) and for being satisfied that they give a true and fair view are set out in the Statement of Directors' Responsibilities.[10]

Our responsibility is to audit the revised financial statements in accordance with relevant legal and regulatory requirements and International Standards on Auditing (UK and Ireland).

We report to you our opinion as to whether the revised financial statements give a true and fair view, have been properly prepared in accordance with United Kingdom Generally Accepted Accounting Practice and are prepared in accordance with the requirements of the Companies Act 2006 as they have effect under the Companies (Revision of Defective Accounts and Reports) Regulations 2008. We also report to you whether in our opinion the information given in the [revised][11] Directors' Report is consistent with the revised financial statements.

---

[9] *Auditor's reports of entities that do not publish their financial statements on a web site or publish them using 'PDF' format may continue to refer to the financial statements by reference to page numbers.*

[10] *If the directors' responsibilities with respect to revised financial statements are not set out in a separate statement, the auditors will include a description in their report.*

[11] *The term 'revised' will be needed if the Directors' Report has also been revised.*

In addition we report to you if, in our opinion, the company has not kept adequate accounting records or if we have not received all the information and explanations we require for our audit or if disclosures of directors' benefits, remuneration, pensions and compensation for loss of office specified by law are not made.

We read the [revised][9] Directors' Report and consider the implications for our report if we become aware of any apparent misstatements within it.

We are also required to report whether in our opinion the original financial statements failed to comply with the requirements of the Companies Act 2006 in the respects identified by the directors.

Basis of audit opinion

We conducted our audit in accordance with International Standards on Auditing (UK and Ireland) issued by the Auditing Practices Board. An audit includes examination, on a test basis, of evidence relevant to the amounts and disclosures in the revised financial statements. It also includes an assessment of the significant estimates and judgments made by the directors in the preparation of the revised financial statements, and of whether the accounting policies are appropriate to the company's circumstances, consistently applied and adequately disclosed.

The audit of revised financial statements includes the performance of procedures to assess whether the revisions made by the directors are appropriate and have been properly made.

We planned and performed our audit so as to obtain all the information and explanations which we considered necessary in order to provide us with sufficient evidence to give reasonable assurance that the revised financial statements are free from material misstatement, whether caused by fraud or other irregularity or error. In forming our opinion we also evaluated the overall adequacy of the presentation of information in the revised financial statements.

Opinion

In our opinion:

- the revised financial statements give a true and fair view, seen as at the date the original financial statements were approved, of the state of the company's affairs as at .... and of its profit [loss] for the year then ended;
- the revised financial statements have been properly prepared in accordance with United Kingdom Generally Accepted Accounting Practice seen as at the date the original financial statements were approved;
- the revised financial statements have been properly prepared in accordance with the provisions of the Companies Act 2006 as they have effect under the Companies (Revision of Defective Accounts and Reports) Regulations 2008;
- the original financial statements for the year ended... failed to comply with the requirements of the Companies Act 2006 in the respects identified by the directors in the statement contained in note [x] to these revised financial statements; and
- the information given in the [revised][9] Directors' Report is consistent with the revised financial statements.

Emphasis of matter – revision of...
In forming our opinion on the revised financial statements, which is not qualified, we have considered the adequacy of the disclosures made in note [x] to these revised financial statements concerning the need to revise the .... The original financial statements were approved on ...and our previous report was signed on that date. We have not performed a subsequent events review for the period from the date of our previous report to the date of this report.

[Signature]   Address
John Smith (senior statutory auditor)   Date
For and on behalf of ABC LLP, Statutory auditor

Note: Changes from a standard auditor's report are shown as shaded text.

Appendix 3 – Illustrative example of an auditor's report on revised annual accounts: revision by supplementary note

This example is based on the following assumptions:

- Non-publicly traded company that does not prepare group accounts.
- UK GAAP used for individual company accounts.
- Financial statements contain no surround information other than the directors' report.

REPORT OF THE INDEPENDENT AUDITOR TO THE [MEMBERS] [SHAREHOLDERS] OF XYZ LIMITED

We have audited the revised financial statements of XYZ Limited for the year ended.... which comprise [state the primary financial statements such as the Profit and Loss Account, the Balance Sheet, the Cash Flow Statement, the Statement of Total Recognised Gains and Losses] and the related notes.[12] The revised financial statements replace the original financial statements approved by the directors on... and consist of the attached supplementary note together with the original financial statements which were circulated to [members] [shareholders] on....

The revised financial statements have been prepared under The Companies (Revision of Defective Accounts and Reports) Regulations 2008 and accordingly do not take account of events which have taken place after the date on which the original financial statements were approved.

Respective responsibilities of directors and auditors

The directors' responsibilities for preparing revised financial statements in accordance with applicable law and United Kingdom Accounting Standards (United Kingdom Generally Accepted Accounting Practice) and for being satisfied that they give a true and fair view are set out in the Statement of Directors' Responsibilities.[13]

---

[12] Auditor's reports of entities that do not publish their financial statements on a web site or publish them using 'PDF' format may continue to refer to the financial statements by reference to page numbers.

[13] If the directors' responsibilities with respect to revised financial statements are not set out in a separate statement, the auditors will include a description in their report.

Our responsibility is to audit the revised financial statements in accordance with relevant legal and regulatory requirements and International Standards on Auditing (UK and Ireland).

We report to you our opinion as to whether the revised financial statements give a true and fair view, have been properly prepared in accordance with United Kingdom Generally Accepted Accounting Practice and are prepared in accordance with the requirements of the Companies Act 2006 as they have effect under the Companies (Revision of Defective Accounts and Reports) Regulations 2008. We also report to you whether in our opinion the information given in the [revised][14] Directors' Report is consistent with the financial statements.

In addition we report to you if, in our opinion, the company has not kept adequate accounting records or if we have not received all the information and explanations we require for our audit or if disclosures of directors' benefits, remuneration, pensions and compensation for loss of office specified by law are not made.

We read the [revised][12] Directors' Report and consider the implications for our report if we become aware of any apparent misstatements within it.

We are also required to report whether in our opinion the original financial statements failed to comply with the requirements of the Companies Act 2006 in the respects identified by the directors.

Basis of audit opinion

We conducted our audit in accordance with International Standards on Auditing (UK and Ireland) issued by the Auditing Practices Board. An audit includes examination, on a test basis, of evidence relevant to the amounts and disclosures in the revised financial statements. It also includes an assessment of the significant estimates and judgments made by the directors in the preparation of the revised financial statements, and of whether the accounting policies are appropriate to the company's circumstances, consistently applied and adequately disclosed.

The audit of revised financial statements includes the performance of procedures to assess whether the revisions made by the directors are appropriate and have been properly made.

We planned and performed our audit so as to obtain all the information and explanations which we considered necessary in order to provide us with sufficient evidence to give reasonable assurance that the revised financial statements are free from material misstatement, whether caused by fraud or other irregularity or error. In forming our opinion we also evaluated the overall adequacy of the presentation of information in the revised financial statements.

Opinion

In our opinion:

- the revised financial statements give a true and fair view, seen as at the date the original financial statements were approved, of the state of the company's affairs as at .... and of its profit [loss] for the year then ended;

---

[14] The term 'revised' will be needed if the Directors' Report has also been revised.

- the revised financial statements have been properly prepared in accordance with United Kingdom Generally Accepted Accounting Practice seen as at the date the original financial statements were approved;
- the revised financial statements have been properly prepared in accordance with the provisions of the Companies Act 2006 as they have effect under the Companies (Revision of Defective Accounts and Reports) Regulations 2008;
- the original financial statements for the year ended .... failed to comply with the requirements of the Companies Act 2006 in the respects identified by the directors in the statement contained in the supplementary note; and
- the information given in the [revised][12] Directors' Report is consistent with the revised financial statements.

Emphasis of matter – revision of ...
In forming our opinion on the revised financial statements, which is not qualified, we have considered the adequacy of the disclosures made in the supplementary note concerning the need to revise the .... The original financial statements were approved on ...and our previous report was signed on that date. We have not performed a subsequent events review for the period from the date of our previous report to the date of this report.

[Signature]   *Address*
John Smith (senior statutory auditor)   *Date*
For and on behalf of ABC LLP, Statutory auditor

Appendix 4 – Illustrative auditor's report on revised directors' report: revision by replacement

REPORT OF THE INDEPENDENT AUDITOR TO THE [MEMBERS] [SHAREHOLDERS] OF XYZ LIMITED

We have considered the information given in the revised directors' report for the year ended.... The revised directors' report replaces the original directors' report approved by the directors on... [and consists of the attached supplementary note together with the original report which was circulated to [members] [shareholders] on...][15]. The revised directors' report has been prepared under the Companies (Revision of Defective Accounts and Reports) Regulations 2008 and accordingly does not take account of events which have taken place after the date on which the original directors' report was approved.

Respective responsibilities of directors and auditors

The directors are responsible for the preparation of the revised directors' report.

Our responsibility is to report to you whether the revised directors' report is consistent with the annual financial statements.

Basis of opinion

Our consideration has been directed towards matters of consistency alone and not to whether the revised directors' report complies with the requirements of the Companies Act 2006.

---

[15] Omit the words in brackets when the revision is by way of a full replacement.

Opinion

In our opinion the information given in the revised directors' report is consistent with the annual financial statements for the year ended... which were circulated to [members] [shareholders] on....

[Signature]   Address
John Smith (senior statutory auditor)   Date
For and on behalf of ABC LLP, Statutory auditor

Appendix 5 – Illustrative auditor's report on revised directors' remuneration report: revision by replacement

REPORT OF THE INDEPENDENT AUDITOR TO THE [MEMBERS] [SHAREHOLDERS] OF XYZ LIMITED

We have considered the revised directors' remuneration report for the year ended.... The revised directors' remuneration report replaces the original directors' remuneration report approved by the directors on... [and consists of the attached supplementary note together with the original report which was circulated to [members] [shareholders] on...][16]. The revised directors' remuneration report has been prepared under the Companies (Revision of Defective Accounts and Reports) Regulations 2008 and accordingly does not take account of events which have taken place after the date on which the original directors' remuneration report was approved.

Respective responsibilities of directors and auditors

The directors are responsible for the preparation of the revised directors' remuneration report.

Our responsibility is to report to you whether the part of the revised directors' remuneration report to be audited has been properly prepared.

Basis of opinion

Our consideration has been directed towards forming an opinion as to whether the part of the revised directors' remuneration report to be audited has been properly prepared in accordance with the requirements of Part 3 of Schedule 8 to the Large and Medium-sized Companies and Groups (Accounts and Reports) Regulations 2008.

Opinion

In our opinion the part of the revised directors' remuneration report to be audited has been properly prepared in accordance with the Companies Act 2006.

[Signature]   Address
John Smith (senior statutory auditor)   Date
For and on behalf of ABC LLP, Statutory auditor

---

[16] Omit the words in brackets when the revision is by way of a full replacement.

Appendix 6 – Illustrative example of a special report on the revised abbreviated accounts of a small company when full financial statements are revised

INDEPENDENT AUDITOR'S REPORT TO XYZ LIMITED UNDER SECTION 449 OF THE COMPANIES ACT 2006

We have examined the revised abbreviated accounts set out on pages ... to ... , together with the revised financial statements of XYZ Limited for the year ended...prepared under section 396 of the Companies Act 2006.

Respective responsibilities of directors and auditors

The directors are responsible for preparing the revised abbreviated accounts in accordance with section 444 of the Companies Act 2006. It is our responsibility to form an independent opinion as to whether the company is entitled to deliver abbreviated accounts prepared in accordance with section 444(3) of the Act to the Registrar of Companies and whether the revised abbreviated accounts have been properly prepared in accordance with the regulations made under that section and to report our opinion to you.

We conducted our work in accordance with Bulletin 2008/4 issued by the Auditing Practices Board. In accordance with that Bulletin we have carried out the procedures we consider necessary to confirm, by reference to the revised financial statements, that the company is entitled to deliver abbreviated accounts and that the revised abbreviated accounts to be delivered are properly prepared[17].

Opinion

In our opinion the company is entitled to deliver abbreviated accounts prepared in accordance with section 444(3) of the Companies Act 2006 and the revised abbreviated accounts have been properly prepared in accordance with the regulations made under that section.

[Other information[18]]

[Signature]   Address
John Smith (senior statutory auditor)   Date
For and on behalf of ABC LLP, Statutory Auditor

---

[17] Add appropriate wording such as "The scope of our work for the purposes of this report does not include examining events occurring after the date of our auditor's report on the full revised financial statements" where special report is dated after the signing of the auditor's report on the full revised financial statements (see paragraph 46 of Bulletin 2008/4).

[18] This section is only included in the circumstances described in paragraphs 41 to 44 of Bulletin 2008/4.

Appendix 7 – Illustrative auditor's statement on a revised summary financial statement of a quoted company: revision by replacement

INDEPENDENT AUDITOR'S STATEMENT TO THE [MEMBERS] [SHAREHOLDERS] OF XYZ PLC

We have examined the revised summary financial statement [for the year ended....] [set out on pages....].

Respective responsibilities of the directors and the auditor

The directors are responsible for preparing the [*revised summarised annual report*] in accordance with applicable United Kingdom law.

Our responsibility is to report to you our opinion on the consistency of the revised summary financial statement within the [*revised summarised annual report*] with the revised full annual financial statements [, the [revised][19] Directors' Report][20] and the [revised][21] Directors' Remuneration Report, and its compliance with the relevant requirements of section 428 of the Companies Act 2006 and the regulations made thereunder.

We also read the other information contained in the [*revised summarised annual report*] and consider the implications for our report if we become aware of any apparent misstatements or material inconsistencies with the revised summary financial statement. The other information comprises only [the Chairman's Statement and the Corporate Governance Statement].

We conducted our work in accordance with Bulletin 2008/3 issued by the Auditing Practices Board. Our report on the company's full annual financial statements describes the basis of our opinion[s] on those revised financial statements, the [revised][19] Directors' Report][20] and the [revised][21] Directors' Remuneration Report.

Opinion

In our opinion the revised summary financial statement is consistent with the revised full annual financial statements [, the [revised][19] Directors' Report][20] and the [revised][21] Directors' Remuneration Report of XYZ plc for the year ended ... and complies with the applicable requirements of section 428 of the Companies Act 2006, and the regulations made thereunder.

---

[19] The word "revised" is inserted where the Directors' Report has also been revised

[20] There is no requirement for an entity to include a Summary Directors' Report. However, if the directors include information in the summary financial statement that is derived from the Directors' Report the auditor is required to report that such information is consistent with the Directors' Report.

[21] The word "revised" is inserted where the Directors' Remuneration Report has also been revised

[We have not considered the effects of any events between the date on which we signed our report on the revised full annual financial statements and the [revised Directors' Remuneration Report] (insert date) and the date of this statement.][22]

Statutory auditor Address
Date

DIRECTORS' STATEMENT
The auditor has issued unqualified reports on the revised full annual financial statements, the auditable part of the [revised][21] directors' remuneration report and on the consistency of the [revised][19] directors' report with those annual financial statements. Their report on the full annual financial statements and the auditable part of the directors' remuneration report contained no statement under sections 498(2) or 498(3) of the Companies Act 2006.[23]

---

[22] *Include this sentence where the date of this statement is after the date of the auditor's report on the revised full annual financial statements and the [revised] Directors' Remuneration Report.*

[23] *This statement is a requirement of sections 428(4)(e), 428(4)(f) and 428(4)(g) of CA 2006.*

[Bulletin 2008/6]
The "senior statutory auditor" under the United Kingdom Companies Act 2006

(Issued April 2008)

Contents

	Paragraphs
Introduction	1 - 3
Eligibility for appointment as "senior statutory auditor"	4
Meaning of "senior statutory auditor"	5 - 6
Involvement of more than one partner in an audit engagement	7
Meaning of "signing" the auditor's report	8 - 10
Changing the senior statutory auditor during the reporting period	11
Senior statutory auditor unable to be present to sign the auditor's report	12 - 17
Joint Audits	18

Appendices:

1 Sections 503 and 504 of the Companies Act 2006
2 Illustrative example of presentation of signature of senior statutory auditor on the auditor's report where the auditor is a firm

Introduction

Section 503(3) of the Companies Act 2006 (CA 2006) requires, where the auditor is a firm, that the auditor's report must be signed by the "senior statutory auditor in his own name for and on behalf of the auditor". This is a new requirement and the Secretary of State has appointed the Auditing Practices Board[1] (APB) to issue guidance with respect to the meaning of the term "senior statutory auditor". This Bulletin constitutes that guidance.

Sections 503 and 504 of CA 2006 address the signature of the auditor's report and are reproduced in Appendix 1. The requirement for the senior statutory auditor to sign in his own name applies to auditor's reports:
 (a) prepared in accordance with the requirements of sections 495, 496 and 497 of CA 2006;
 (b) in respect of voluntary revisions of annual accounts and reports made in accordance with section 454 of CA 2006; and
 (c) on the special auditor's report where abbreviated accounts are delivered to the Registrar[2] (section 449 CA 2006),

for financial years beginning on or after 6 April 2008.

CA 2006 sets out a number of requirements regarding the appointment of auditors. However, other than as described in paragraph 4, there are no legal requirements concerning eligibility for appointment as the senior statutory auditor. This is an internal matter for the audit firm as under section 504(1) of CA 2006 it is the firm which is required to identify which individual is the senior statutory auditor.

Eligibility for appointment as "Senior Statutory Auditor"

Section 504(2) of CA 2006 requires that the person identified as senior statutory auditor of a company must be eligible for appointment as auditor of the company in question. Eligibility for appointment is dealt with in sections 1212 to 1225 of CA 2006.

Meaning of "Senior Statutory Auditor"

Subject to meeting the CA 2006 requirement described in paragraph 4, the term "senior statutory auditor" has the same meaning as the term "engagement partner" when used in International Standards on Auditing (ISAs) (UK and Ireland).

ISA (UK and Ireland) 220 "Quality Control for Audits of Historical Financial Information" contains the following definition of "engagement partner":

> The partner or other person in the firm who is responsible for the audit engagement and its performance, and for the auditor's report that is issued on behalf of the firm, and who, where required, has the appropriate authority from a professional, legal or regulatory body.

---

[1] The Auditing Practices Board is appointed by virtue of Article 11 of the "Statutory Auditors (Delegation of Functions etc) Order 2008. SI 2008 No. 496

[2] In CA 2006 the expressions "the Registrar of Companies" and "the Registrar" mean the registrar of companies for England & Wales, Scotland or Northern Ireland, as the case may require. (section 1060 (3) CA 2006)

Involvement of more than one partner in an audit engagement

7   Where more than one partner is involved in the conduct of an audit engagement, it is important that the responsibilities of the respective partners are clearly defined and understood by the engagement team[3]. In particular, it is necessary for it to be clearly understood which partner is designated as the engagement partner and is, therefore, the senior statutory auditor identified by the firm in accordance with section 504(1) of CA 2006.

Meaning of "signing" the auditor's report

8   Section 503 of CA 2006 requires that where the auditor is a firm, the auditor's report must be signed by the senior statutory auditor in his own name, for and on behalf of the auditor (i.e. the firm). The signature of the senior statutory auditor is also required to be dated. An illustration of the presentation of these requirements in an auditor's report is shown in Appendix 2. Section 505(1) further requires that the name of the senior statutory auditor must be stated in copies of the auditor's report published by, or on behalf of, the company.

9   In paragraph 8 references to the auditor's report is to the auditor's report provided to the company by the auditor upon completion of the audit. Such references do not refer to the authentication of the copy auditor's reports required to be delivered to the Registrar.

10 Paragraphs 6 to 10 of Schedule 1 of "The Companies Act 2006 (Commencement No.5, Transitional Provisions and Savings) Order 2007"[4] address the authentication of accounts and reports filed with the Registrar. With effect from 6 April 2008 this order requires the copies of auditor's reports delivered to the Registrar to:

   (a) state the name of the auditor and (where the auditor is a firm) the name of the person who signed it as senior statutory auditor; and
   (b) be signed by the auditor or (where the auditor is a firm) in the name of the firm by a person authorised to sign on its behalf.

The senior statutory auditor, therefore, does not necessarily need to sign copy auditor's reports that are required to be delivered to the Registrar.[5]

Changing the senior statutory auditor during the reporting period

11 Where the audit firm changes the senior statutory auditor (i.e. the engagement partner) during the engagement the new senior statutory auditor reviews the audit work performed to the date of the change. The review procedures are sufficient to satisfy the new senior statutory auditor that the audit work performed to the date of the review had been planned and performed in accordance with professional standards and regulatory and legal requirements[6].

---

[3] ISA (UK and Ireland) 220 "Quality control for audits of historical financial information" paragraph 29

[4] SI 2007 No. 3495.

[5] Paragraph 10 describes transitional arrangements that came into force on 6 April 2008. Readers are cautioned that these arrangements are subject to change subsequent to the publication of this Bulletin.

[6] ISA (UK and Ireland) 220 paragraph 28.

Senior statutory auditor unable to be present to sign the auditor's report

Under section 503(3) of CA 2006, the senior statutory auditor must sign the auditor's report. Another partner, or responsible individual, is <u>not</u> able to sign for and on behalf of the senior statutory auditor.

12

In circumstances where the senior statutory auditor is unable to continue to take responsibility for the direction, supervision and performance of the audit the audit firm appoints a replacement senior statutory auditor and the circumstances are treated in the same way as a change of senior statutory auditor described in paragraph 11.

13

In circumstances where the senior statutory auditor is absent but is still able to, and does, take responsibility for the direction, supervision and performance of the audit the senior statutory auditor may sign the auditor's report using electronic means (e.g. e-mail or fax).

14

In circumstances where the auditor's report needs to be signed by a certain date (e.g. listed entities and other public interest entities) it would be pragmatic for the audit firm to have a contingency plan as to who would succeed as senior statutory auditor in the event that the audit is at an advanced stage[7] but the senior statutory auditor is unable to sign the auditor's report. If another audit partner is actively involved in the audit engagement, a suitable contingency plan may be for that other partner to work in parallel with the senior statutory auditor and be able to take over as senior statutory auditor if the need arises. An efficient contingency plan would be one that was developed in conjunction with the firm's plans for partner rotation in accordance with the requirements of Ethical Standard 3 "Long association with the audit engagement".

15

The APB recognises that circumstances may arise where another partner has not worked in parallel with the senior statutory auditor. The APB is of the view that in such exceptional circumstances it is permissible for the engagement quality control reviewer[8] to be appointed as the replacement senior statutory auditor[9] where:

16

(a) the engagement quality control reviewer has completed his or her review; and
(b) the audit is at an "advanced stage".

---

[7] Bulletin 2008/2 "The auditor's association with preliminary announcements made in accordance with the requirements of the UK and Irish Listing Rules" describes an audit as being at an "advanced stage" when it is complete subject only to the following:
    (a) clearing outstanding matters which are unlikely to have a material impact on the financial statements;
    (b) completing audit procedures on the detail of note disclosures on the financial statements that will not have a material impact on the primary financial statements and completing the auditor's reading of "other information" in the annual report, in accordance with ISA (UK and Ireland) 720 "Other information in documents containing audited financial statements";
    (c) updating the subsequent events review covering the period to the date of the auditor's report on the financial statements; and
    (d) obtaining final written representations from management and establishing that the financial statements have been reviewed and approved by the directors.

[8] This is on the assumption that the engagement quality control reviewer is eligible to be appointed as the senior statutory auditor (see paragraph 4 for eligibility criterion).

[9] ISA (UK and Ireland) 220 "Quality control for audits of historical financial information" requires an engagement quality control reviewer to be appointed in respect of all listed entities.

17 However, once an engagement quality reviewer has been appointed as a replacement senior statutory auditor he or she can no longer act as the engagement quality control reviewer because his or her objectivity may have been impaired through assuming the role of senior statutory auditor.

Joint Audits

18 The Companies Act 2006 permits companies to appoint an auditor or auditors. Where a company appoints joint auditors each of the auditing firms appoints a senior statutory auditor both of which are required to sign the auditors' report in accordance with the requirements of section 503 of CA 2006.

Appendix 1 – Sections 503 and 504 of the Companies Act 2006

503 Signature of auditor's report

(1) The auditor's report must state the name of the auditor and be signed and dated.
(2) Where the auditor is an individual, the report must be signed by him.
(3) Where the auditor is a firm, the report must be signed by the senior statutory auditor in his own name, for and on behalf of the auditor.

504 Senior statutory auditor

(1) The senior statutory auditor means the individual identified by the firm as senior statutory auditor in relation to the audit in accordance with –
   (a) standards issued by the European Commission, or
   (b) if there is no applicable standard so issued, any relevant guidance issued by –
      (i) the Secretary of State, or
      (ii) a body appointed by order of the Secretary of State.
(2) The person identified as senior statutory auditor must be eligible for appointment as auditor of the company in question (see Chapter 2 of Part 42 of this Act).
(3) The senior statutory auditor is not, by reason of being named or identified as senior statutory auditor or by reason of his having signed the auditor's report, subject to any civil liability to which he would not otherwise be subject.
(4) An order appointing a body for the purpose of subsection (1)(b)(ii) is subject to negative resolution procedure.

Appendix 2 – Illustrative example of presentation of signature of senior statutory auditor on the auditor's report where the auditor is a firm

...

Opinion

In our opinion:
- the financial statements give a true and fair view of the state of the company's affairs as at ... and of its profit[loss] for the year then ended;
- the financial statements have been properly prepared in accordance with United Kingdom Generally Accepted Accounting Practice;
- the financial statements have been prepared in accordance with the Companies Act 2006; and
- the information given in the Directors' Report is consistent with the financial statements.

[Signature]   *Address*
John Smith (Senior Statutory Auditor)   *Date*
for and on behalf of ABC LLP, Statutory Auditor

[Bulletin 2008/7]
Illustrative auditor's reports on public sector financial statements in the United Kingdom

(Issued May 2008)

Contents

	Page
Introduction	3
Example 1: Audit Certificate and Report for a Department preparing a Resource Account	4
Resource Accounts: Table of modifications required to the Auditor's Certificate and Report in Wales, Scotland and Northern Ireland	7
Example 2: Audit Certificate and Report for an NDPB or Trading Fund preparing an accruals account	9
NDPB Accounts: Table of modifications required to the Auditor's Certificate and Report in Wales, Scotland and Northern Ireland.	12
Example 3: Audit Report for a local government body in England that does not administer a pension fund	14
Example 4: Audit Report for a local government body in Wales that does not administer a pension fund	16
Example 5: Audit Report for a local government body in Scotland that does not administer a pension fund	18
Example 6: Audit Report for a local government body in Northern Ireland that does not administer a pension fund	20
Example 7: Audit Report for a local government body in England that administers a pension fund	22
Example 8: Audit Report for an NHS Trust in England	25
Example 9: Audit Report for a NHS Primary Care Trust/Strategic Health Authority in England	28
Health Accounts: Table of modifications required to the Auditor's Certificate and Report in Wales, Scotland and Northern Ireland	31
Example 10: Audit Report for a Probation Board in England and Wales	33

Illustrations of Qualifications and other Modifications to the Auditor's Reports Arising from the Consideration of Regularity

Example 11: Qualified opinion on the regularity of expenditure and unqualified opinion on the truth and fairness of the accounts	36
Example 12: Qualified opinion for limitation of scope on regularity in England and unqualified opinion on the truth and fairness of the accounts	37
Example 13: Qualified opinions arising from expenditure in excess of amounts authorized	39
Example 14: Wording for a Primary Care Trust's/ Strategic Health Authority's regularity opinion where the Revenue Resource Limit or the Capital Resource Limit has been breached	41

Introduction

This Bulletin should be read in conjunction with Practice Note 10 "Audit of financial statements of public sector bodies in the United Kingdom (Revised)" which was issued in January 2006. Paragraph 4 of Practice Note 10 explains what the public sector comprises for the purposes of this Bulletin.

The purpose of this Bulletin is to provide illustrative examples of:

- Unmodified auditor's reports for audits of financial statements of public sector bodies in the United Kingdom for audits performed in accordance with International Standards on Auditing (UK and Ireland).
- Auditor's reports modified for regularity issues.

Pages 36-41 provide examples of regularity qualifications. Examples of other types of modifications to the auditor's report have not been provided in this Bulletin as they would follow the format provided for companies in APB Bulletin 2006/6.

Statutory Instrument 2005 No 1011 "The Companies Act 1985 (Operating and Financial Review and Directors' Report etc) Regulations 1985" amended the Companies Act 1985 so that the auditors must give a positive opinion as to the consistency of the directors' report with the financial statements. The heads of the national audit agencies have decided to adopt this as best practice where relevant in public sector audit reports. Current reporting frameworks mean that local government auditors do not give a consistency opinion. The main change to this Bulletin is to incorporate this consistency opinion in the auditor's report for the public sector where relevant.

The variations in public sector auditor's reports largely reflect the differing statutory frameworks and financial reporting requirements that exist across the administrations and sectors.

For NHS bodies, the Bulletin contains illustrative auditor's reports for NHS Trusts and English Strategic Health Authorities/Primary Care Trusts, and an example of a qualified opinion arising from non-compliance with governing authorities at an English SHA/PCT. Modifications necessary to adapt the illustrative auditor's certificate and report for Wales, Scotland and Northern Ireland are presented in a table.

This Bulletin does not contain an example of an illustrative audit report for an NHS Foundation Trust. Auditors of NHS Foundation Trusts are required to prepare an audit report in accordance with ISA (UK and Ireland) 700, as set out in Monitor's Code of Audit Practice for NHS Foundation Trusts.

Example 1: Audit Certificate and Report for a Department preparing a Resource Account[1]

THE CERTIFICATE AND REPORT[2] OF THE COMPTROLLER AND AUDITOR GENERAL TO THE HOUSE OF COMMONS

I certify that I have audited the financial statements of (name of department) for the year ended *[insert date]* under the Government Resources and Accounts Act 2000. These comprise the Statement of Parliamentary Supply, the Operating Cost Statement and Statement of Recognised Gains and Losses, the Balance Sheet, the Cash Flow Statement and the Statement of Operating Costs by Departmental Aim and Objectives and the related notes. These financial statements have been prepared under the accounting policies set out within them. I have also audited the information in the Remuneration Report that is described in that report as having been audited.

Respective responsibilities of the Accounting Officer and auditor

The Accounting Officer is responsible for preparing the Annual Report, which includes the Remuneration Report, and the financial statements in accordance with the Government Resources and Accounts Act 2000 and HM Treasury directions made thereunder and for ensuring the regularity of financial transactions. These responsibilities are set out in the Statement of Accounting Officer's Responsibilities.

My responsibility is to audit the financial statements and the part of the remuneration report to be audited in accordance with relevant legal and regulatory requirements, and with International Standards on Auditing (UK and Ireland).

I report to you my opinion as to whether the financial statements give a true and fair view and whether the financial statements and the part of the Remuneration Report to be audited have been properly prepared in accordance with HM Treasury directions issued under the Government Resources and Accounts Act 2000. I report to you whether, in my opinion, the information which comprises the management commentary[3] [and...(list other elements if appropriate)], included in the Annual Report, is consistent with the financial statements. I also report whether in all material respects the expenditure and income have been applied to the purposes intended by Parliament and the financial transactions conform to the authorities which govern them.

In addition, I report to you if in my opinion the Department has not kept proper accounting records, if I have not received all the information and explanations I require for my audit, or if information specified by HM Treasury regarding remuneration and other transactions is not disclosed.

I review whether the Statement on Internal Control reflects the Department's compliance with HM Treasury's guidance, and I report if it does not. I am not required

---

[1] The audit certificate and report of an Executive Agency will generally follow the same form as that of a Department.

[2] Where there is a separate C&AG's report, the words 'AND REPORT' should be deleted from the title.

[3] The references within the certificate should reflect the naming conventions applied by the audited Department, and must cover the material in paragraphs 7.2.5 to 7.2.19 of the FReM, of which the main element is the management commentary. Where this cross refers to information in other sections of the published document, the consistency opinion must be extended to cover this other information.

to consider whether this statement covers all risks and controls, or to form an opinion on the effectiveness of the Department's corporate governance procedures or its risk and control procedures.

I read the other information contained in the Annual Report and consider whether it is consistent with the audited financial statements. This other information comprises [the Foreword, the unaudited part of the Remuneration Report and the Chairman's Statement (list other elements if appropriate)].[4] I consider the implications for my certificate if I become aware of any apparent misstatements or material inconsistencies with the financial statements. My responsibilities do not extend to any other information.

Basis of audit opinions

I conducted my audit in accordance with International Standards on Auditing (UK and Ireland) issued by the Auditing Practices Board. My audit includes examination, on a test basis, of evidence relevant to the amounts, disclosures and regularity of financial transactions included in the financial statements and the part of the Remuneration Report to be audited. It also includes an assessment of the significant estimates and judgments made by the Accounting Officer in the preparation of the financial statements, and of whether the accounting policies are most appropriate to the Department's circumstances, consistently applied and adequately disclosed.

I planned and performed my audit so as to obtain all the information and explanations which I considered necessary in order to provide me with sufficient evidence to give reasonable assurance that the financial statements and the part of the Remuneration Report to be audited are free from material misstatement, whether caused by fraud or error, and that in all material respects the expenditure and income have been applied to the purposes intended by Parliament and the financial transactions conform to the authorities which govern them. In forming my opinion I also evaluated the overall adequacy of the presentation of information in the financial statements and the part of the Remuneration Report to be audited.

Opinions

In my opinion:

- the financial statements give a true and fair view, in accordance with the Government Resources and Accounts Act 2000 and directions made thereunder by HM Treasury, of the state of the Department's affairs as at *[insert date]*, and the net cash requirement, net resource outturn, net operating cost, operating costs applied to objectives, recognised gains and losses and cash flows for the year then ended;
- the financial statements and the part of the Remuneration Report to be audited have been properly prepared in accordance with HM Treasury directions issued under the Government Resources and Accounts Act 2000; and
- information which comprises the management commentary[5] included within the Annual Report, is consistent with the financial statements.

---

[4] *The description of the other information that is read should be tailored to reflect the naming conventions adopted.*

[5] *The references within the certificate should reflect the naming conventions applied by the audited Department, and must cover the material in paragraphs 7.2.5 to 7.2.19 of the FReM.*

Opinion on Regularity

In my opinion, in all material respects, the expenditure and income have been applied to the purposes intended by Parliament and the financial transactions conform to the authorities which govern them.

Report[6]

I have no observations to make on these financial statements.

Name

Comptroller and Auditor General

National Audit Office

Address

Date

Resource Accounts: Table of modifications required to the Auditor's Certificate and Report in Wales, Scotland and Northern Ireland.

	Wales	Scotland	Northern Ireland
Addressee	The Certificate and Report of the Auditor General for Wales to the National Assembly for Wales	The Independent Auditor's report to the [audited body], the Auditor General for Scotland and the Scottish Parliament	The Certificate and Report of the Comptroller and Auditor General to the Northern Ireland Assembly
Legislation – references to the Government Resources and Accounts Act 2000 to be replaced with:	Government of Wales Act 1998 or 2006.	Public Finance and Accountability (Scotland) Act 2000	Government Resources and Accounts Act (Northern Ireland) 2001
Parliament – references to Parliament to be replaced with:	National Assembly for Wales	Scottish Parliament	Northern Ireland Assembly
HM Treasury directions – references to HM Treasury directions to be replaced with:	HM Treasury directions	Directions issued by the Scottish Ministers	Department of Finance and Personnel directions
Reference to the Department's compliance with HM Treasury guidance on the SIC should be replaced with:	HM Treasury guidance applies in Wales, no amendment required	"compliance with the Scottish Government's guidance on the Statement on Internal Control"...	"compliance with the Department of Finance and Personnel's guidance on the Statement on Internal Control"...

[6] *Heading to be used where there is no separate C&AG's report.*

	Wales	Scotland	Northern Ireland
Signature of the audit report – the audit report is signed by:	(name) Auditor General for Wales Wales Audit Office Address Date	Various – such as a member of Audit Scotland staff or a firm	(name) Comptroller and Auditor General Northern Ireland Audit Office Address Date

In Wales, the audited body is referred to by name throughout the certificate rather than being referred to as "the Department".

In Scotland "I certify that" would not be used in the first paragraph.

Central Government bodies in Scotland have Accountable Officers, not Accounting Officers.

In Scotland, the report paragraph "I have no observations to make on these financial statements" would not be used.

In Scotland, "My responsibility is to audit the financial statements in accordance with relevant legal and regulatory requirements, and with International Standards on Auditing (UK and Ireland), which I have chosen to adopt as the basis of my approach to the audit of financial statements" is replaced with "My responsibility is to audit the financial statements in accordance with relevant legal and regulatory requirements and with International Standards on Auditing (UK and Ireland) as required by the Code of Audit Practice approved by the Auditor General for Scotland".

In Scotland, the description of the regularity assertion in the Respective Responsibilities, Basis of opinion and Opinion sections would need to change to "whether, in all material respects, the expenditure and receipts shown in the financial statements were incurred or applied in accordance with any applicable enactments and guidance issued by the Scottish Ministers, the Budget Act(s) covering the financial year and sections 4 to 7 of the Public Finance and Accountability (Scotland) Act 2000; and the sums paid out of the Scottish Consolidated Fund for the purpose of meeting the expenditure shown in the financial statements were applied in accordance with section 65 of the Scotland Act 1998."

Example 2: Audit Certificate and Report for an NDPB or Trading Fund preparing an accruals account

THE CERTIFICATE[7] [AND REPORT][8] OF THE COMPTROLLER AND AUDITOR GENERAL TO THE HOUSE OF COMMONS / HOUSES OF PARLIAMENT / ADDRESSEE OF THE AUDIT CERTIFICATE

I [certify that I][9] have audited the financial statements of [name of entity] for the year ended *[insert date]* under the ....Act [year]. These comprise the Income and Expenditure Account, the Balance Sheet, the Cash Flow Statement and Statement of [Total] Recognised Gains and Losses and the related notes. These financial statements have been prepared under the accounting policies set out within them. I have also audited the information in the Remuneration Report that is described in that report as having being audited.

Respective responsibilities of the ....[10], Chief Executive/ Accounting Officer[11] and auditor

The ....[10] and Chief Executive as Accounting Officer[11] are responsible for preparing the Annual Report, the Remuneration Report and the financial statements in accordance with the .... Act [year] and [insert appropriate authority] directions made thereunder and for ensuring the regularity of financial transactions. These responsibilities are set out in the Statement of ....[10] and Chief Executive's/Accounting Officer's[11] Responsibilities.

My responsibility is to audit the financial statements and the part of the remuneration report to be audited in accordance with relevant legal and regulatory requirements, and with International Standards on Auditing (UK and Ireland).

I report to you my opinion as to whether the financial statements give a true and fair view and whether the financial statements and the part of the Remuneration Report to be audited have been properly prepared in accordance with the .... Act [year] and [insert appropriate authority] directions made thereunder. I report to you whether, in my opinion, the information which comprises....[12], given in the Annual Report, is consistent with the financial statements. I also report whether in all material respects the expenditure and income have been applied to the purposes intended by Parliament and the financial transactions conform to the authorities which govern them.

---

[7] *The word 'CERTIFICATE' should only be used where the C&AG is required to certify the account by Statute. Otherwise the title should be 'INDEPENDENT AUDITOR'S REPORT TO...'*

[8] *These words should only be included where the C&AG is required to Report by Statute. Where there is a separate report, the words 'AND REPORT' should be deleted from the title.*

[9] *The words 'I certify' should only be included if the C&AG is required 'to certify' the accounts by Statute.*

[10] *The title used should reflect who is responsible for the preparation of the financial statements and be consistent with the statement of responsibilities. For example, it may be a "board" or it may be the audited entity.*

[11] *Or other title given in the statement of responsibilities.*

[12] *The Financial Reporting Manual, Section 7.2.2 describes the elements of an annual report. The references within the certificate should reflect the naming conventions applied, and must cover the material on paragraphs 7.2.2 to 7.2.8 of the FReM. Where this cross refers to information in other sections of the published accounts, the consistency opinion must be extended to cover this other information.*

In addition, I report to you if in my opinion [the entity] has not kept proper accounting records, if I have not received all the information and explanations I require for my audit, or if information specified by HM Treasury regarding remuneration and other transactions is not disclosed.

I review whether the Statement on Internal control reflects [the entity's] compliance with HM Treasury's guidance, and I report if it does not. I am not required to consider whether this statement covers all risks and controls, or form an opinion on the effectiveness of [the entity's] corporate governance procedures or its risk and control procedures.

I read the other information contained in the Annual Report and consider whether it is consistent with the audited financial statements. This other information comprises [the Foreword, the unaudited part of the Remuneration Report and the Chairman's Statement (list other elements if appropriate)].[13] I consider the implications for my report if I become aware of any apparent misstatements or material inconsistencies with the financial statements. My responsibilities do not extend to any other information.

Basis of audit opinions

I conducted my audit in accordance with International Standards on Auditing (UK and Ireland) issued by the Auditing Practices Board. My audit includes examination, on a test basis, of evidence relevant to the amounts, disclosures and regularity of financial transactions included in the financial statements and the part of the Remuneration Report to be audited. It also includes an assessment of the significant estimates and judgments made by the ......[10] and Accounting Officer in the preparation of the financial statements, and of whether the accounting policies are most appropriate to the [entity's] circumstances, consistently applied and adequately disclosed.

I planned and performed my audit so as to obtain all the information and explanations which I considered necessary in order to provide me with sufficient evidence to give reasonable assurance that the financial statements and the part of the Remuneration Report to be audited are free from material misstatement, whether caused by fraud or error, and that in all material respects the expenditure and income have been applied to the purposes intended by Parliament and the financial transactions conform to the authorities which govern them. In forming my opinion I also evaluated the overall adequacy of the presentation of information in the financial statements and the part of the Remuneration Report to be audited.

Opinions

In my opinion:

- the financial statements give a true and fair view, in accordance with the .... Act [year] and directions made thereunder by [insert appropriate authority], of the state of [the entity's] affairs as at *[insert date]* and of its surplus [deficit], recognised gains and losses and cash flows for the year then ended;
- the financial statements and the part of the Remuneration Report to be audited have been properly prepared in accordance with the .... Act [year] and [insert appropriate authority] directions made thereunder; and

---

[13] The description of the other information that is read should be tailored to reflect the naming conventions adopted.

- information which comprises....[14], given within the Annual Report, is consistent with the financial statements.

Opinion on Regularity

In my opinion, in all material respects the expenditure and income have been applied to the purposes intended by Parliament and the financial transactions conform to the authorities which govern them.

Report[15]

I have no observations to make on these financial statements.

Name

Comptroller and Auditor General

National Audit Office

Address

Date

NDPB Accounts: Table of modifications required to the Auditor's Certificate and Report in Wales, Scotland and Northern Ireland.

	Wales	Scotland	Northern Ireland
Addressee	The Certificate and Report of the Auditor General for Wales to the National Assembly for Wales	The Independent Auditor's report to the [audited body], the Auditor General for Scotland and the Scottish Parliament	The Certificate [and Report] of the Comptroller and Auditor General to the Northern Ireland Assembly. Use the reference to "the Report" as per the above only where a report is required. Refer to the relevant legislation.
Parliament – references to Parliament to be replaced with:	National Assembly for Wales	Scottish Parliament	Northern Ireland Assembly
Reference to the Department's compliance with HM Treasury guidance on the SIC should be replaced with:	HM Treasury guidance applies in Wales, no amendment required	"compliance with the Scottish Government's guidance on the Statement on Internal Control"...	"compliance with the Department of Finance and Personnel's guidance on the Statement on Internal Control"...

[14] *The Financial Reporting Manual, section 7.2.2 describes the elements of an annual report. The references within the certificate should reflect the naming conventions applied by the audited body, and must cover the material in paragraphs 7.2.2 to 7.2.8 of the FReM.*

[15] *Heading to be used where there is no separate C&AG's report, and the C&AG is required to report by Statute.*

	Wales	Scotland	Northern Ireland
Signature of the audit report – the audit report is signed by:	(name) Auditor General for Wales Wales Audit Office Address Date	Various – such as a member of Audit Scotland staff or a firm	(name) Comptroller and Auditor General Northern Ireland Audit Office Address Date

In Wales, NDPBs are Assembly Government Sponsored Bodies (AGSBs).

In Scotland "I certify that" would not be used in the first paragraph.

Central Government and NHS bodies in Scotland have Accountable Officers, not Accounting Officers.

In Scotland, the report paragraph "I have no observations to make on these financial statements" would not be used. In Northern Ireland, the auditor should refer to the relevant legislation to see whether a report is required.

In Scotland, "My responsibility is to audit the financial statements in accordance with relevant legal and regulatory requirements, and with International Standards on Auditing (UK and Ireland)" is replaced with "My responsibility is to audit the financial statements in accordance with relevant legal and regulatory requirements, and with International Standards on Auditing (UK and Ireland) as required by the Code of Audit Practice approved by the Auditor General for Scotland".

In Scotland, the description of the regularity assertion in the Respective Responsibilities, Basis of opinion and Opinion sections would need to change to "whether, in all material respects, the expenditure and receipts shown in the financial statements were incurred or applied in accordance with any applicable enactments and guidance issued by the Scottish Ministers."

In Northern Ireland, the legislation quoted in the certificate may be an Order rather than an Act.

Example 3: Audit Report for a local government body in England that does not administer a pension fund

INDEPENDENT AUDITOR'S REPORT TO THE MEMBERS OF [NAME OF LOCAL GOVERNMENT BODY IN ENGLAND]

Opinion on the accounting statements

I/We have audited the accounting statements and related notes of (name of local government body) [and its Group] for the year ended *[insert date]* under the Audit Commission Act 1998. The accounting statements comprise the Income and Expenditure Account, Statement of Movement on General Fund Balance, Statement of Total Recognised Gains and Losses, Balance Sheet, Cash Flow Statement, Housing Revenue Account Income and Expenditure Account, Statement of Movement on Housing Revenue Account Balance and Collection Fund [together with the Group Accounts]. The accounting statements have been prepared under the accounting policies set out in the Statement of Accounting Policies.

This report is made solely to the Members of (name of local government body) in accordance with Part II of the Audit Commission Act 1998 and for no other purpose, as set out in paragraph 36 of the Statement of Responsibilities of Auditors and of Audited Bodies prepared by the Audit Commission.

Respective responsibilities of the Responsible Financial Officer and the independent auditor

The Responsible Financial Officer's responsibilities for preparing the statement of accounts in accordance with relevant legal and regulatory requirements and the Statement of Recommended Practice on Local Authority Accounting in the United Kingdom 2007 are set out in the Statement of Responsibilities for the Statement of Accounts.

My/Our responsibility is to audit the accounting statements and related notes in accordance with relevant legal and regulatory requirements and International Standards on Auditing (UK and Ireland).

I/We report to you my/our opinion as to whether the accounting statements and related notes present fairly, in accordance with relevant legal and regulatory requirements and the Statement of Recommended Practice on Local Authority Accounting in the United Kingdom 2007, the financial position of the local government body and its income and expenditure for the year.

I/We review whether the Governance Statement reflects compliance with 'Delivering Good Governance in Local Government: Framework' published by CIPFA/SOLACE in June 2007. I/We report if it does not comply with proper practices specified by CIPFA/SOLACE or if the statement is misleading or inconsistent with other information I/we are aware of from my/our audit. I am/We are not required to consider, nor have I/we considered, whether the Governance Statement covers all risks and controls. Neither am I/are we required to form an opinion on the effectiveness of the local government body's corporate governance procedures or its risk and control procedures.

I/We read other information published with the accounting statements and related notes and consider whether it is consistent with the audited accounting statements and related notes. This other information comprises [only] the Explanatory Foreword [and specify]. I/We consider the implications for my/our report if I/we become aware of any apparent misstatements or material inconsistencies with the accounting statements and related notes. My/Our responsibilities do not extend to any other information.

Basis of audit opinion

I/We conducted my/our audit in accordance with the Audit Commission Act 1998, the Code of Audit Practice issued by the Audit Commission, and International Standards on Auditing (UK and Ireland) issued by the Auditing Practices Board. An audit includes examination, on a test basis, of evidence relevant to the amounts and disclosures in the accounting statements and related notes. It also includes an assessment of the significant estimates and judgments made by the [local government body] in the preparation of the accounting statements, and of whether the accounting policies are appropriate to the local government body's circumstances, consistently applied and adequately disclosed.

I/We planned and performed my/our audit so as to obtain all the information and explanations which I/we considered necessary in order to provide me/us with sufficient evidence to give reasonable assurance that the accounting statements and related notes are free from material misstatement, whether caused by fraud or other irregularity or error. In forming my/our opinion I/we also evaluated the overall adequacy of the presentation of information in the accounting statements and related notes.

Opinion

In my/our opinion the accounting statements and related notes present fairly, in accordance with relevant legal and regulatory requirements and the Statement of Recommended Practice on Local Authority Accounting in the United Kingdom 2007, the financial position of (name of the local government body) [and its Group] as at *[insert date]* and its income and expenditure for the year then ended.

Certificate

I/We certify that I/we have completed the audit of the accounts of (name of local government body) in accordance with the requirements of the Audit Commission Act 1998 and the Code of Audit Practice issued by the Audit Commission.

Appointed Auditor
Address
Date

Example 4: Audit Report for a local government body in Wales that does not administer a pension fund

INDEPENDENT AUDITOR'S REPORT TO THE MEMBERS OF [NAME OF LOCAL GOVERNMENT BODY IN WALES]

I/We have audited the accounting statements and the related notes of (name of local government body) [and its Group] for the year ended *[insert date]* under the Public Audit (Wales) Act 2004. The accounting statements comprise the Income and Expenditure Account, Statement of Movement on Council Fund Balance, Statement of Total Recognised Gains and Losses, Balance Sheet, Cash Flow Statement, Housing Revenue Account Income and Expenditure Account and Statement of Movement on Housing Revenue Account Balance [together with the Group Accounts]. The accounting statements have been prepared under the accounting policies set out in the Statement of Accounting Policies.

This report is made solely to the Members of (name of local government body) in accordance with Part 2 of the Public Audit (Wales) Act 2004 and for no other purpose, as set out in paragraph 42 of the Statement of Responsibilities of Appointed Auditors, and Inspectors and of Audited and Inspected Bodies (2005) prepared by the Auditor General for Wales.

Respective responsibilities of the Responsible Financial Officer and the independent auditor

The Responsible Financial Officer's responsibilities for preparing the statement of accounts in accordance with relevant legal and regulatory requirements and the Statement of Recommended Practice on Local Authority Accounting in the United Kingdom 2007 are set out in the Statement of Responsibilities for the Statement of Accounts.

My/Our responsibility is to audit the accounting statements and related notes in accordance with relevant legal and regulatory requirements and International Standards on Auditing (UK and Ireland).

I/We report to you my/our opinion as to whether the accounting statements and related notes present fairly, in accordance with relevant legal and regulatory requirements and the Statement of Recommended Practice on Local Authority Accounting in the United Kingdom 2007, the financial position of the local government body and its income and expenditure for the year.

I/We review whether the Statement on Internal Control [Governance Statement] reflects compliance with 'The statement on internal control in local government: meeting the requirements of the Accounts and Audit Regulations 2003' published by CIPFA in April 2004 ['Delivering Good Governance in Local Government: Framework' published by CIPFA/SOLACE in June 2007]. I/We report if it does not comply with proper practices specified by CIPFA [CIPFA/SOLACE] or if the statement is misleading or inconsistent with other information I/we are aware of from my/our audit. I am/We are not required to consider, nor have I/we considered, whether the Statement on Internal Control [Governance Statement] covers all risks and controls. Neither am I/are we required to form an opinion on the effectiveness of the local government body's corporate governance procedures or its risk and control procedures.

I/We read other information published with the accounting statements and related notes and consider whether it is consistent with the audited accounting statements and related notes. This other information comprises only the Explanatory Foreword [and specify]. I/We consider the implications for my/our report if I/we become aware of any apparent misstatements or material inconsistencies with the accounting statements and related notes. My/Our responsibilities do not extend to any other information.

Basis of audit opinion

I/We conducted my/our audit in accordance with the Public Audit (Wales) Act 2004, the Code of Audit and Inspection Practice issued by the Auditor General for Wales, and International Standards on Auditing (UK and Ireland) issued by the Auditing Practices Board. An audit includes examination, on a test basis, of evidence relevant to the amounts and disclosures in the accounting statements and related notes. It also includes an assessment of the significant estimates and judgments made by the [local government body] in the preparation of the accounting statements, and of whether the accounting policies are appropriate to the local government body's circumstances, consistently applied and adequately disclosed.

I/We planned and performed my/our audit so as to obtain all the information and explanations which I/we considered necessary in order to provide me/us with sufficient evidence to give reasonable assurance that the accounting statements and related notes are free from material misstatement, whether caused by fraud or other irregularity or error. In forming my/our opinion I/we also evaluated the overall adequacy of the presentation of information in the accounting statements and related notes.

Opinion

In my/our opinion the accounting statements and related notes present fairly, in accordance with relevant legal and regulatory requirements and the Statement of Recommended Practice on Local Authority Accounting in the United Kingdom 2007, the financial position of (name of the local government body) [and its Group] as at *[insert date]* and its income and expenditure for the year then ended.

Certificate

I/We certify that I/we have completed the audit of the accounts of (name of local government body) in accordance with the requirements of the Public Audit (Wales) Act 2004 and the Code of Audit and Inspection Practice issued by the Auditor General for Wales.

Appointed Auditor

Address

Date

Example 5: Audit Report for a local government body in Scotland that does not administer a pension fund

INDEPENDENT AUDITOR'S REPORT TO THE MEMBERS OF [NAME OF LOCAL GOVERNMENT BODY IN SCOTLAND]

I/We certify that I/we have audited the financial statements of (name of local government body) [and its Group] for the year ended *[insert date]* under the Local Government (Scotland) Act 1973. The financial statements comprise the Income and Expenditure Account, Statement of Movement on Council Fund Balance, Statement of Total Recognised Gains and Losses, Balance Sheet, Cash Flow Statement, Housing Revenue Account Income and Expenditure Account and Statement of Movement on Housing Revenue Account Balance, Council Tax Income Account, Non-Domestic Rate Income Accounts and the related notes and the Statement of Accounting Policies [together with the Group Accounts]. The financial statements have been prepared under the accounting policies set out therein.

This report is made solely to the members of (name of local government body) in accordance with Part VII of the Local Government (Scotland) Act 1973 and for no other purpose. In accordance with paragraph 123 of the Code of Audit Practice approved by the Accounts Commission for Scotland, I do not undertake to have responsibilities to members or officers, in their individual capacities, or to third parties.

Respective responsibilities of the Responsible Financial Officer and the auditor

The Responsible Financial Officer's responsibilities for preparing the financial statements in accordance with relevant legal and regulatory requirements and the

Statement of Recommended Practice on Local Authority Accounting in the United Kingdom 2007 are set out in the Statement of Responsibilities for the financial statements.

My/Our responsibility is to audit the financial statements in accordance with relevant legal and regulatory requirements and International Standards on Auditing (UK and Ireland).

I/We report to you my/our opinion as to whether the financial statements present fairly, in accordance with relevant legal and regulatory requirements and the Statement of Recommended Practice on Local Authority Accounting in the United Kingdom 2007 the financial position of the local government body and its income and expenditure for the year.

I/We review whether the Statement on Internal Financial Control reflects compliance with Statement of Recommended Practice on Local Authority Accounting in the United Kingdom 2007. I/We report if it does not comply with proper practices specified by the SoRP or if the statement is misleading or inconsistent with other information I/we are aware of from my/our audit. I am not required to consider, nor have I considered, whether the statement on internal financial control covers all risks and controls. Neither am I/are we required to form an opinion on the effectiveness of the local government body's corporate governance procedures or its risk and control procedures.

I/We read other information published with the financial statements and consider whether it is consistent with the audited financial statements. This other information comprises [only] the Explanatory Foreword [and specify]. I/We consider the implications for my/our report if I/we become aware of any apparent misstatements or material inconsistencies with the financial statements. My/Our responsibilities do not extend to any other information.

Basis of audit opinion

I/We conducted my/our audit in accordance with Part VII of the Local Government (Scotland) Act 1973, the Code of Audit Practice approved by the Accounts Commission, and International Standards on Auditing (UK and Ireland) issued by the Auditing Practices Board. An audit includes examination, on a test basis, of evidence relevant to the amounts and disclosures in the financial statements. It also includes an assessment of the significant estimates and judgments made by the [local government body] in the preparation of the financial statements and of whether the accounting policies are appropriate to the local government body's circumstances, consistently applied and adequately disclosed.

I/We planned and performed my/our audit so as to obtain all the information and explanations which I/we considered necessary in order to provide me/us with sufficient evidence to give reasonable assurance that the financial statements are free from material misstatement, whether caused by fraud or other irregularity or error. In forming my/our opinion I/we also evaluated the overall adequacy of the presentation of information in the financial statements.

Opinion

In my/our opinion the financial statements:

- present fairly, in accordance with relevant legal and regulatory requirements and the Statement of Recommended Practice on Local Authority Accounting in the United Kingdom 2007, the financial position of (name of the local government body) [and its Group] as at *[insert date]* and its income and expenditure for the year then ended; and
- have been properly prepared in accordance with the Local Government (Scotland) Act 1973.

Auditor

Address

Date

Example 6: Auditor's Report for a local government body in Northern Ireland that does not administer a pension fund

INDEPENDENT AUDITOR'S REPORT TO THE MEMBERS OF [NAME OF LOCAL GOVERNMENT BODY IN NORTHERN IRELAND]

I have audited the statement of accounts of (name of local government body) [and its Group] for the year ended 31 March 2008 under the Local Government (Northern Ireland) Order 2005. The statement of accounts comprises the Income and Expenditure Account, Statement of Movement on General Fund Balance, Statement of Total Recognised Gains and Losses, Balance Sheet, Cash Flow Statement and the Loans Pool Account [together with the Group Accounts]. The statement of accounts has been prepared under the accounting policies set out within them.

[This report is made solely to the Members of [name of local government body] in accordance with [Local Government (Northern Ireland) Order 2005] and for no other purpose, as specified in the Local Government Code of Audit Practice issued by the Chief Local Government Auditor.]

Respective responsibilities of the Chief Financial Officer and the independent auditor

The Chief Financial Officer's responsibilities for preparing the statement of accounts in accordance with relevant legal and regulatory requirements and the Statement of Recommended Practice on Local Authority Accounting in the United Kingdom 2007 are set out in the Statement of Responsibilities for the Statement of Accounts.

My responsibility is to audit the statement of accounts in accordance with relevant legal and regulatory requirements and International Standards on Auditing (UK and Ireland).

I report to you my opinion as to whether the statement of accounts present fairly, in accordance with relevant legal and regulatory requirements and the Statement of Recommended Practice on Local Authority Accounting in the United Kingdom 2007, the financial position of the local government body and its income and expenditure for the year.

I review whether the Statement on Internal Control reflects compliance with Statement of Recommended Practice on Local Authority Accounting in the United Kingdom 2007. I report if it does not comply with proper practices specified by the Statement of Recommended Practice on Local Authority Accounting in the United Kingdom 2007 or if the statement is misleading or inconsistent with other information I am aware of from my audit. I am not required to consider, nor have I considered, whether the statement on internal control covers all risks and controls. Neither am I required to form an opinion on the effectiveness of the local government body's corporate governance procedures or its risk and control procedures.

[I read other information published with the statement of accounts] and consider whether it is consistent with the audited statement of accounts. This other information comprises [only] the Explanatory Foreword [and specify]. I consider the implications for my report if I become aware of any apparent misstatements or material inconsistencies with the statement of accounts. My responsibilities do not extend to any other information.]

Basis of audit opinion

I conducted my audit in accordance with the Local Government (Northern Ireland) Order 2005, the Local Government Code of Audit Practice issued by the Chief Local Government Auditor and International Standards on Auditing (UK and Ireland) issued by the Auditing Practices Board. An audit includes examination, on a test basis, of evidence relevant to the amounts and disclosures in the statement of accounts. It also includes an assessment of the significant estimates and judgments made by the local government body in the preparation of the statement of accounts, and of whether the accounting policies are appropriate to the local government body's circumstances, consistently applied and adequately disclosed.

I planned and performed my audit so as to obtain all the information and explanations which I considered necessary in order to provide me with sufficient evidence to give reasonable assurance that the statement of accounts is free from material misstatement, whether caused by fraud or other irregularity or error. In forming my opinion I also evaluated the overall adequacy of the presentation of information in the statement of accounts.

Opinion

In my opinion the statement of accounts presents fairly, in accordance with relevant legal and regulatory requirements and the Statement of Recommended Practice on Local Authority Accounting in the United Kingdom 2007, the financial position of (name of the local government body) [and its Group] as at *[insert date]* and its income and expenditure for the year then ended.

Certificate

I certify that I have completed the audit of the accounts of (name of local government body) in accordance with the requirements of the Local Government (Northern Ireland) Order 2005 and the Local Government Code of Audit Practice issued by the Chief Local Government Auditor.

Local Government Auditor

Address

Date

Example 7: Audit Report for a local government body in England that does administer a pension fund[16]

INDEPENDENT AUDITOR'S REPORT TO THE MEMBERS OF [NAME OF LOCAL GOVERNMENT BODY IN ENGLAND]

Opinion on the accounting statements

I/We have audited the accounting statements, pension fund accounts and related notes of (name of local government body) [and its Group] for the year ended *[insert date]* under the Audit Commission Act 1998. The accounting statements comprise the Income and Expenditure Account, Statement of Movement on General Fund Balance, Statement of Total Recognised Gains and Losses, Balance Sheet, Cash Flow Statement, Housing Revenue Account Income and Expenditure Account, Statement of Movement on Housing Revenue Account Balance and Collection Fund [together with the Group Accounts]. The pension fund accounts comprise the Fund Account and the Net Assets Statement. The accounting statements and pension fund accounts have been prepared under the accounting policies set out in the Statement of Accounting Policies.

This report is made solely to the Members of (name of local government body) in accordance with Part II of the Audit Commission Act 1998 and for no other purpose, as set out in paragraph 36 of the Statement of Responsibilities of Auditors and of Audited Bodies prepared by the Audit Commission.

Respective responsibilities of the Responsible Finance Officer and the independent auditor

The Responsible Financial Officer's responsibilities for preparing the statement of accounts, including the pension fund accounts, in accordance with relevant legal and regulatory requirements and the Statement of Recommended Practice on Local Authority Accounting in the United Kingdom 2007 are set out in the Statement of Responsibilities for the Statement of Accounts.

My/Our responsibility is to audit the accounting statements, pension fund accounts and related notes in accordance with relevant legal and regulatory requirements and International Standards on Auditing (UK and Ireland).

I/We report to you my/our opinion as to whether the accounting statements, pension fund accounts and related notes present fairly, in accordance with relevant legal and regulatory requirements and the Statement of Recommended Practice on Local Authority Accounting in the United Kingdom 2007 the financial position of the local government body and its income and expenditure for the year; and the financial transactions of the pension fund during the year and the amount and disposition of the fund's assets and liabilities, other than liabilities to pay pensions and benefits after the end of the scheme year.

I/We review whether the Governance Statement reflects compliance with 'Delivering Good Governance in Local Government: Framework' published by CIPFA/SOLACE in June 2007. I/We report if it does not comply with proper practices specified by CIPFA/SOLACE or if the statement is misleading or inconsistent with

---

[16] *There are regional variations to this format for the other administrations and this illustrative example will need to be amended to reflect these.*

other information I/we are aware of from my/our audit. I am/We are not required to consider, nor have I/we considered, whether the Governance Statement covers all risks and controls. Neither am I/are we required to form an opinion on the effectiveness of the local government body's corporate governance procedures or its risk and control procedures.

I/We read other information published with the accounting statements, pension fund accounts and related notes and consider whether it is consistent with the audited accounting statements, pension fund accounts and related notes. This other information comprises [only] the Explanatory Foreword [and specify]. I/We consider the implications for my/our report if I/we become aware of any apparent misstatements or material inconsistencies with the accounting statements, pension fund accounts and related notes. My/Our responsibilities do not extend to any other information.

Basis of audit opinion

I/We conducted my/our audit in accordance with the Audit Commission Act 1998 , the Code of Audit Practice issued by the Audit Commission, and International Standards on Auditing (UK and Ireland) issued by the Auditing Practices Board. An audit includes examination, on a test basis, of evidence relevant to the amounts and disclosures in the accounting statements, pension fund accounts and related notes. It also includes an assessment of the significant estimates and judgments made by the local government body in the preparation of the accounting statements and pension fund accounts and related notes, and of whether the accounting policies are appropriate to the local government body's and pension fund's circumstances, consistently applied and adequately disclosed.

I/We planned and performed my/our audit so as to obtain all the information and explanations which I/we considered necessary in order to provide me/us with sufficient evidence to give reasonable assurance that the accounting statements, pension fund accounts and related notes are free from material misstatement, whether caused by fraud or other irregularity or error. In forming my/our opinion I/we also evaluated the overall adequacy of the presentation of information in the accounting statements pension fund accounts and related notes.

Opinion

In my/our opinion:

- The accounting statements and related notes present fairly, in accordance with relevant legal and regulatory requirements and the Statement of Recommended Practice on Local Authority Accounting in the United Kingdom 2007, the financial position of (name of the local government body) [and its Group] as at *[insert date]* and its income and expenditure for the year then ended; and
- The pension fund accounts and related notes present fairly, in accordance with the Statement of Recommended Practice on Local Authority Accounting in the United Kingdom 2007, the financial transactions of (name of) Pension Fund during the year ended *[insert date]* and the amount and disposition of the fund's assets and liabilities, other than liabilities to pay pensions and benefits after the end of the scheme year.

Certificate

I/We certify that I/we have completed the audit of the accounts of (name of local government body) in accordance with the requirements of the Audit Commission Act 1998 and the Code of Audit Practice issued by the Audit Commission.

Appointed Auditor

Address

Date

Example 8: Audit Report for an NHS Trust in England

INDEPENDENT AUDITOR'S REPORT TO THE DIRECTORS OF (NAME OF TRUST)

Opinion on the financial statements

I/We have audited the financial statements of (*name of Trust*) for the year ended [*insert date*] under the Audit Commission Act 1998. The financial statements comprise the Income and Expenditure Account, the Balance Sheet, the Cash Flow Statement, the Statement of Total Recognised Gains and Losses and the related notes. These financial statements have been prepared in accordance with the accounting policies directed by the Secretary of State with the consent of the Treasury as relevant to the National Health Service set out within them. I/We have also audited the information in the Remuneration Report that is described as having been audited.

Respective responsibilities of directors and auditor(s)

The directors' responsibilities for preparing the financial statements in accordance with directions made by the Secretary of State are set out in the Statement of Directors' Responsibilities.

My/Our responsibility is to audit the financial statements in accordance with relevant legal and regulatory requirements and International Standards on Auditing (UK and Ireland).

I/We report to you my/our opinion as to whether the financial statements give a true and fair view, in accordance with the accounting policies directed by the Secretary of State as being relevant to the National Health Service in England. I/We report whether the financial statements and the part of the Remuneration Report to be audited have been properly prepared in accordance with the accounting policies directed by the Secretary of State as being relevant to the National Health Service in England. I/We report to you whether, in my opinion, the information which comprises the commentary on the financial performance included within the Operating and Financial Review[17] [and...(list other elements if appropriate)], included in the Annual Report, is consistent with the financial statements

I/We review whether the directors' Statement on Internal Control reflects compliance with the Department of Health's requirements, set out in 'The Statement on Internal Control 2003/04' issued on 15 September 2003 and the further guidance relating to

---

[17] This reference should be amended to reflect the naming conventions used by the audited body in its annual report.

that Statement issued on 7 April 2006 and 2 April 2007. I/We report if it does not meet the requirements specified by the Department of Health or if the statement is misleading or inconsistent with other information I/we am/are aware of from my/our audit of the financial statements. I/We am/are not required to consider, nor have I/we considered, whether the directors' Statement on Internal Control covers all risks and controls. Neither am I/are we required to form an opinion on the effectiveness of the Trust's corporate governance procedures or its risk and control procedures.

I read the other information contained in the Annual Report and consider whether it is consistent with the audited financial statements. This other information comprises [the Foreword, the unaudited part of the Remuneration Report, the Chairman's Statement and the remaining elements of the Operating and Financial Review (list other elements if appropriate)].[18] I/We consider the implications for my/our report if I/we become aware of any apparent misstatements or material inconsistencies with the financial statements. My/Our responsibilities do not extend to any other information.

Basis of audit opinion

I/We conducted my/our audit in accordance with the Audit Commission Act 1998, the Code of Audit Practice issued by the Audit Commission and International Standards on Auditing (UK and Ireland) issued by the Auditing Practices Board. An audit includes examination, on a test basis, of evidence relevant to the amounts and disclosures in the financial statements and the part of the Remuneration Report to be audited. It also includes an assessment of the significant estimates and judgments made by the directors in the preparation of the financial statements, and of whether the accounting policies are appropriate to the Trust's circumstances, consistently applied and adequately disclosed.

I/We planned and performed my/our audit so as to obtain all the information and explanations which I/we considered necessary in order to provide me/us with sufficient evidence to give reasonable assurance that the financial statements are free from material misstatement, whether caused by fraud or other irregularity or error; and the financial statements and the part of the Remuneration Report to be audited have been properly prepared. In forming my/our opinion I/we also evaluated the overall adequacy of the presentation of information in the financial statements and the part of the Remuneration Report to be audited.

Opinion

In my/our opinion:

- the financial statements give a true and fair view, in accordance with the accounting policies directed by the Secretary of State as being relevant to the National Health Service in England, of the state of the Trust's affairs as at *[insert date]* and of its income and expenditure for the year then ended;
- the financial statements and the part of the Remuneration Report to be audited has been properly prepared in accordance with the accounting policies directed by the Secretary of State as being relevant to the National Health Service in England; and

---

[18] *The description of the other information that is read should be tailored to reflect the naming conventions adopted.*

- information which comprises commentary on the financial performance included within the Operating and Financial Review, included within the Annual Report, is consistent with the financial statements.

Certificate[19]

I/We certify that I/we have completed the audit of the accounts in accordance with the requirements of the Audit Commission Act 1998 and the Code of Audit Practice issued by the Audit Commission.

Auditor

Address

Date

Example 9: Audit Report for a NHS Primary Care Trust/Strategic Health Authority in England

INDEPENDENT AUDITOR'S REPORT TO THE DIRECTORS OF (NAME OF BODY)

Opinion on the financial statements

I/We have audited the financial statements of (*name of body*) for the year ended *[insert date]* under the Audit Commission Act 1998. The financial statements comprise the Operating Cost Statement, the Balance Sheet, the Cash Flow Statement, the Statement of Total Recognised Gains and Losses and the related notes. These financial statements have been prepared in accordance with the accounting policies directed by the Secretary of State with the consent of the Treasury as relevant to the National Health Service set out within them. I/We have also audited the information in the Remuneration Report that is described as having been audited.

Respective responsibilities of directors and auditor(s)

The directors' responsibilities for preparing the financial statements in accordance with directions made by the Secretary of State are set out in the Statement of Directors' Responsibilities. The Chief Executive's responsibility, as Accountable Officer, for ensuring the regularity of financial transactions is set out in the Statement of the Chief Executive's Responsibilities.

My/Our responsibility is to audit the financial statements in accordance with relevant legal and regulatory requirements and International Standards on Auditing (UK and Ireland).

I/We report to you my/our opinion as to whether the financial statements give a true and fair view, in accordance with the accounting policies directed by the Secretary of State as being relevant to the National Health Service in England. I/We report whether the financial statements and the part of the Remuneration Report to be audited have been properly prepared in accordance with the accounting policies directed by the Secretary of State as being relevant to the National Health Service in

---

[19] *The full Audit Commission auditor's report would also include a conclusion on the use of resources (the VFM conclusion).*

England. I/We report to you whether, in my/our opinion, the information which comprises the commentary on the financial performance included within the Operating and Financial Review[20] [and...(list other elements if appropriate)], included in the Annual Report, is consistent with the financial statements. I/we also report whether in all material respects the expenditure and income have been applied to the purposes intended by Parliament and the financial transactions conform to the authorities which govern them.

I/We review whether the directors' Statement on Internal Control reflects compliance with the Department of Health's requirements, set out in 'The Statement on Internal Control 2003/04' issued on 15 September 2003 and the further guidance relating to that Statement issued on 7 April 2006 and 2 April 2007. I/We report if it does not meet the requirements specified by the Department of Health or if the statement is misleading or inconsistent with other information I/we am/are aware of from my/our audit of the financial statements. I/We am/are not required to consider, nor have I/we considered, whether the directors' Statement on Internal Control covers all risks and controls. Neither am I/are we required to form an opinion on the effectiveness of the Authority's/Trust's corporate governance procedures or its risk and control procedures.

I/We read the other information contained in the Annual Report and consider whether it is consistent with the audited financial statements. This other information comprises [the Foreword, the unaudited part of the Remuneration Report, the Chairman's Statement and the remaining elements of the Operating and Financial Review (list other elements if appropriate)].[21] I/We consider the implications for my/our report if I/we become aware of any apparent misstatements or material inconsistencies with the financial statements. My/Our responsibilities do not extend to any other information.

Basis of audit opinion

I/We conducted my/our audit in accordance with the Audit Commission Act 1998, the Code of Audit Practice issued by the Audit Commission and International Standards on Auditing (UK and Ireland) issued by the Auditing Practices Board. An audit includes examination, on a test basis, of evidence relevant to the amounts and disclosures in the financial statements and the part of the Remuneration Report to be audited. It also includes an assessment of the significant estimates and judgments made by the directors in the preparation of the financial statements, and of whether the accounting policies are appropriate to the Authority's/Trust's circumstances, consistently applied and adequately disclosed.

I/We planned and performed my/our audit so as to obtain all the information and explanations which I/we considered necessary in order to provide me/us with sufficient evidence to give reasonable assurance that the financial statements are free from material misstatement, whether caused by fraud or other irregularity or error; the financial statements and the part of the Remuneration Report to be audited have been properly prepared; and in all material respects the expenditure and income have been applied to the purposes intended by Parliament and the financial transactions conform to the authorities which govern them. In forming my/our opinion I/we also

---

[20] This reference should be amended to reflect the naming conventions used by the audited body in its annual report.

[21] The description of the other information that is read should be tailored to reflect the naming conventions adopted.

evaluated the overall adequacy of the presentation of information in the financial statements and the part of the Remuneration Report to be audited.

Opinion

In my/our opinion:
- the financial statements give a true and fair view, in accordance with the accounting policies directed by the Secretary of State as being relevant to the National Health Service in England, of the state of the Authority's/Trust's affairs as at *[insert date]* and of its net operating costs for the year then ended;
- the financial statements and the part of the Remuneration Report to be audited has been properly prepared in accordance with the accounting policies directed by the Secretary of State as being relevant to the National Health Service in England;
- in all material respects the expenditure and income have been applied to the purposes intended by Parliament and the financial transactions conform to the authorities which govern them; and
- information which comprises commentary on the financial performance included within the Operating and Financial Review, included within the Annual Report, is consistent with the financial statements.

Certificate[22]

I/We certify that I/we have completed the audit of the accounts in accordance with the requirements of the Audit Commission Act 1998 and the Code of Audit Practice issued by the Audit Commission.

Auditor

Address

Date

Health Accounts: Table of modifications required to the Auditor's Certificate and Report in Wales, Scotland and Northern Ireland

Wales

NHS Trusts and Local Health Boards

The NDPB certificate is used as the basis of the certificate for NHS trusts and Local Health Boards in Wales. The financial statements are audited under Section 61 of the Public Audit (Wales) Act 2004. The directors and Chief Executive are responsible for preparing the financial statements in accordance with paragraph 3 of schedule 9 to the NHS (Wales) Act 2006 and Welsh Ministers' directions made thereunder and for ensuring the regularity of financial transactions.

The auditor reports whether the financial statements give a true and fair view and whether the financial statements and the part of the remuneration report to be audited have been properly prepared in accordance with paragraph 3 of schedule 9 to the NHS (Wales) Act 2006 and Welsh Ministers' directions made thereunder and

---

[22] *The full Audit Commission auditor's report would also include a conclusion on the use of resources (the VFM conclusion).*

whether in all material respects the expenditure and income have been applied to the purposes intended by the National Assembly for Wales and the financial transactions conform to the authorities that govern them.

Currently no opinion is given on the consistency of the annual report with the financial statements. The auditor reports where the Foreword the unaudited part of the Remuneration Report, the Chairman's Statement and the remaining elements of the Operating and Financial Review is not consistent with the financial statements, if the Board/Trust has not kept proper accounting records, if he/she has not received all the information and explanations required for the audit, or if information specified by relevant authorities regarding remuneration and other transactions is not disclosed.

The Treasury and Welsh Ministers set the requirements for the Statement on Internal Control.

Scotland

In Scotland, the NDPB certificate is used as the basis of the certificate for health boards and special health boards. The Act under which the accounts are prepared is the National Health Service (Scotland) Act 1978 and the authority for the Statement on Internal Control is guidance issued by the Scottish Government Health Directorates. The responsibility for NHS audits in Scotland lies with the Auditor General for Scotland. Other amendments to the NDPB certificate are as per the differences for Scotland outlined on page 12 of the Bulletin.

Northern Ireland

In Northern Ireland the NDPB certificate and report is used as the basis for Northern Ireland health boards preparing accruals accounts. The legislation under which the accounts are prepared and audited is the Health and Personal Social Services (Northern Ireland) Order 1972 as amended. Directions are made thereunder by the Department of Health, Social Services and Public Safety. Expenditure and income should be applied for the purposes intended by the Northern Ireland Assembly. The authority for the Statement on Internal Control is guidance issued by the Department of Health, Social Services and Public Safety.

The addressee of the audit certificate and report is the Northern Ireland Assembly. The audit certificate and report is signed by the C&AG, Northern Ireland Audit Office.

Example 10: Audit Report for a Probation Board in England and Wales[23]

INDEPENDENT AUDITOR'S REPORT TO THE MEMBERS OF (NAME OF BOARD) PROBATION BOARD

I/We have audited the financial statements of (name of board) for the year ended *[insert date]* under the Audit Commission Act 1998[24]. The financial statements

---

[23] In Northern Ireland a probation board is an NDPB. In Scotland, the probation service is undertaken by the social services departments of local authorities.

[24] In Wales, the financial statements are audited under the Public Audit (Wales) Act 2004.

comprise the Operating Cost Statement, the Balance Sheet, the Cash Flow Statement, the Statement of Total Recognised Gains and Losses and the related notes. These financial statements have been prepared under the accounting policies set out within them. I/We have also audited the information in the Remuneration report that is described as having been audited.

Respective responsibilities of the Accountable Officer and auditor

The Accountable Officer's responsibilities for preparing the financial statements in accordance with the Criminal Justice and Court Services Act 2000 and directions made thereunder by the Secretary of State and for ensuring the regularity of financial transactions are set out in the Statement of Accountable Officer's Responsibilities.

My/Our responsibility is to audit the financial statements in accordance with relevant legal and regulatory requirements and International Standards on Auditing (UK and Ireland).

I/We report to you my/our opinion as to whether the financial statements give a true and fair view, in accordance with the accounting policies directed by the Criminal Justice and Courts Services Act 2000 and directions made thereunder by the Secretary of State. I/We report whether the financial statements and the part of the Remuneration Report to be audited have been properly prepared in accordance with the accounting policies directed by the Criminal Justice and Courts Services Act 2000 and directions made thereunder by the Secretary of State. I/We report to you whether, in my/our opinion, the information which comprises the Financial Review[25] [and...(list other elements if appropriate)], included in the Annual Report, is consistent with the financial statements. I/We also report whether in all material respects the expenditure and income have been applied to the purposes intended by Parliament and the financial transactions conform to the authorities which govern them.

I/We review whether the Accountable Officer's statement on internal control reflects the Probation Board's compliance with the HM Treasury's guidance on the Statement on Internal Control. I/We report if it does not meet the requirements specified by the HM Treasury or if the statement is misleading or inconsistent with other information I/we are aware of from my/our audit of the financial statements. I/We are not required to consider, nor have I/we considered, whether the Accountable Officer's statement on internal control covers all risks and controls. Neither am I/ are we required to form an opinion on the effectiveness of the Probation Board's corporate governance procedures or its risk and control procedures.

I/we read the other information contained in the Annual Report and consider whether it is consistent with the audited financial statements. This other information comprises [the Foreword, the unaudited part of the Remuneration Report, the Chairman's Statement and the remaining elements of the Operating and Financial Review (list other elements if appropriate)].[26] I/We consider the implications for my/our report if I/we become aware of any apparent misstatements or material inconsistencies with the financial statements. My/Our responsibilities do not extend to any other information.

---

[25] This reference should be amended to reflect the naming conventions used by the audited body in its annual report.

[26] The description of the other information that is read should be tailored to reflect the naming conventions adopted by the audited body in its Annual Report.

Basis of audit opinion

I/We conducted my/our audit in accordance with the Audit Commission Act 1998, the Code of Audit Practice issued by the Audit Commission[26] and International Standards on Auditing (UK and Ireland) issued by the Auditing Practices Board. An audit includes examination, on a test basis, of evidence relevant to the amounts and disclosures in the financial statements and the part of the Remuneration Report to be audited. It also includes an assessment of the significant estimates and judgments made by the Accountable Officer in the preparation of the financial statements, and of whether the accounting policies are appropriate to the Probation Board's circumstances, consistently applied and adequately disclosed.

I/We planned and performed my/our audit so as to obtain all the information and explanations which I/we considered necessary in order to provide me/us with sufficient evidence to give reasonable assurance that the financial statements are free from material misstatement, whether caused by fraud or other irregularity or error; the financial statements and the part of the Remuneration Report to be audited have been properly prepared; and in all material respects the expenditure and income have been applied to the purposes intended by Parliament and the financial transactions conform to the authorities which govern them. In forming my/our opinion I/we also evaluated the overall adequacy of the presentation of information in the financial statements and the part of the Remuneration Report to be audited.

Opinion

In my/our opinion:

- the financial statements give a true and fair view, in accordance with the accounting policies directed by the Criminal Justice and Courts Services Act 2000 and directions made thereunder by the Secretary of State, of the state of the Probation Board's affairs as at *[insert date]* and of its net operating costs, recognised gains and losses and cash flows for the year then ended;
- the financial statements and the part of the Remuneration Report to be audited has been properly prepared in accordance with the accounting policies directed by the Criminal Justice and Courts Services Act 2000 and directions made thereunder by the Secretary of State;
- in all material respects the expenditure and income have been applied to the purposes intended by Parliament and the financial transactions conform to the authorities which govern them; and
- information which comprises commentary on the financial performance included within the Operating and Financial Review, included within the Annual Report, is consistent with the financial statements.

Certificate

I/We certify that I/we have completed the audit of the accounts in accordance with the requirements of the Audit Commission Act 1998 and the Code of Audit Practice issued by the Audit Commission.[27]

Auditor

Address

Date

---

[27] *In Wales, the audit is completed in accordance with the requirements of the Public Audit (Wales) Act 2004 and the Code of Audit and Inspection Practice issued by the Auditor General for Wales.*

Example 11 – Qualified opinion on the regularity of expenditure and unqualified opinion on the truth and fairness of the accounts

This example reflects the situation where there has been non-compliance with a regularity requirement but this has been adequately disclosed in the financial statements.

Opinions

In my opinion:

- the financial statements give a true and fair view, in accordance with the ...... Act [year] and directions made thereunder by HM Treasury (or other appropriate authority), of the state of the (entity's) affairs as at .... and of its surplus [deficit], recognised gains and losses and cash flows for the year then ended;
- the financial statements and the part of the Remuneration Report to be audited have been properly prepared[28] in accordance with the .... Act [year] and HM Treasury (or other appropriate authority) directions made thereunder; and
- information which comprises the management commentary included within the Annual Report[29], is consistent with the financial statements.

Qualified Opinion on Regularity arising because of irregular payments to overseas manufacturers

As disclosed in the Notes to the accounts, grant expenditure includes payments totalling £5 million, made by the ...[30] during the year ended 31 March 20XX, to assist an overseas manufacturer to carry out research and development into new technology.

Under the ...[31] Act 19XX, which sets out the scope, nature and extent of the ... operations, the ... has no power to make grants to overseas manufacturers. Accordingly I have concluded that this expenditure has not been applied to the purposes intended by Parliament and is not in conformity with the authorities which govern it.

In my opinion, except for the expenditure to assist an overseas manufacturer referred to above, in all material respects the expenditure and income have been applied to the purposes intended by Parliament and conform to the authorities which govern them.

---

[28] *Properly prepared is only used where required by legislation. If the legislation does not require the auditor to report in whether the accounts have been properly prepared in accordance with the Act, this part of the opinion is deleted.*

[29] *The Financial Reporting Manual, section 7.2.2 describes the elements of an annual report. The references within the certificate should reflect the naming conventions applied by the audited body, and must cover the material in paragraphs 7.2.2 to 7.2.8 of the FReM.*

[30] *Name of audited entity.*

[31] *Refer to relevant legislation.*

Example 12 – Qualified opinion for limitation of scope on regularity in England and unqualified opinion on the truth and fairness of the accounts

Basis of audit opinions

I conducted my audit in accordance with International Standards on Auditing (UK and Ireland) issued by the Auditing Practices Board, except that the scope of our work was limited as explained below. My audit includes examination, on a test basis, of evidence relevant to the amounts, disclosures and regularity of financial transactions included in the financial statements. It also includes an assessment of the significant estimates and judgments made by the Accounting Officer in the preparation of the financial statements, and of whether the accounting policies are appropriate to the Department's circumstances, consistently applied and adequately disclosed.

I planned my audit so as to obtain all the information and explanations which I considered necessary in order to provide me with sufficient evidence to give reasonable assurance that the financial statements are free from material misstatement, whether caused by fraud or other irregularity or error and that in all material respects the expenditure and income have been applied to the purposes intended by Parliament and the financial transactions conform to the authorities which govern them. However, the evidence available to me was limited because ...... was unable to provide me with sufficient evidence to demonstrate that £5m of payments made to overseas manufacturers during the year ended 31 March 20XX were paid out in accordance with the ....Act 19XX. There were no other satisfactory procedures that I could adopt to confirm that payments to overseas manufacturers had been applied to the purposes intended by Parliament.

In forming my opinion I also evaluated the overall adequacy of the presentation of information in the financial statements.

Opinions

In my opinion:

- the financial statements give a true and fair view, in accordance with the .... Act [year] and directions made thereunder by HM Treasury (or other appropriate authority), of the state of the (entity's) affairs as at .... and of its surplus [deficit], recognised gains and losses and cash flows for the year then ended;
- the financial statements have been properly prepared[32] in accordance with the .... Act [year] and HM Treasury (or other appropriate authority) directions made thereunder; and
- information which comprises the management commentary included within the Annual Report[33], is consistent with the financial statements.

---

[32] *Properly prepared is only used where required by legislation. If the legislation does not require the auditor to report in whether the accounts have been properly prepared in accordance with the Act, this part of the opinion is deleted.*

[33] *The Financial Reporting Manual, section 7.2.2 describes the elements of an annual report. The references within the certificate should reflect the naming conventions applied by the audited body, and must cover the material in paragraphs 7.2.2 to 7.2.8 of the FReM.*

Qualified Opinion on Regularity arising from limitation in audit scope

Because of the limitation described above on the evidence available to me, I am unable to form an opinion whether the expenditure relating to overseas manufacturers has been applied to the purposes intended by Parliament and the financial transactions conform to the authorities that govern them. Except for the expenditure relating to overseas manufacturers, in my opinion, in all material respects the expenditure and income have been applied to the purposes intended by Parliament and the financial transactions conform to the authorities which govern them.

In respect alone of the limitation on my work relating to payments made to overseas manufacturers I have not obtained all the information and explanations that I considered necessary for the purposes of our audit and I was unable to determine whether proper accounting records had been maintained[34].

Example 13 – Qualified opinions arising from expenditure in excess of amounts authorised

The certificate will include a qualification of the "Opinion on regularity" section of the certificate and will include a paragraph explaining the nature of the excess vote qualification. This explanatory paragraph and qualified opinion will be under the heading "Qualified opinion on regularity arising from expenditure in excess of amounts authorised".

For a resource excess:

The explanatory paragraph and qualified opinion on regularity is to be expressed, as appropriate, as follows:

"As explained more fully in the attached report, Parliament authorised Request(s) for Resources for the {department} in the Appropriation Act(s) 200X (and 200Y). Net resources of £X were authorised for Request for Resources A. Against this authorised limit, the department incurred net resource expenditure of X as shown in Summary of Resource Outturn in the Resource Accounts for 200X-0Y and have thus exceeded the authorised limit.

Except for net resource expenditure of £X in excess of the amount authorised for Request for Resources A, referred to in paragraphs .. to .. of my report, in all material respects the expenditure and income have been applied for the purposes intended by Parliament and the financial transactions conform to the authorities which govern them."

Drafting note - if an excess arises on more than one request for resource, each excess should be separately expressed.

For a cash excess:

The explanatory paragraph and qualified opinion on regularity is to be expressed, as appropriate, as follows

---

[34] Depending on the nature of the limitation on regularity, it may not be appropriate to include this sentence.

"As explained more fully in the attached report, Parliament authorised a Net Cash Requirement for the {department} of £X in the Appropriation Act(s) 200X (and 200Y). Against this authorised limit, the department incurred an actual Net Cash Requirement of £X as shown in Statement of Parliamentary Supply in the Resource Accounts for 200X-0Y and have thus exceeded the authorised limit.

Except for net cash expenditure of £X in excess of the authorised Net Cash Requirement, referred to in paragraphs .. to .. of my report, in all material respects the expenditure and income have been applied for the purposes intended by Parliament and the financial transactions conform to the authorities which govern them."

For an excess of resource and cash:

The explanatory paragraph and qualified opinion on regularity is to be expressed, as appropriate, as follows:

"As explained more fully in the attached report, Parliament authorised Request(s) for Resources and a net cash requirement for the {department} in the Appropriation Act(s) 200X (and 200Y). Net resources of £X where authorised for Request for Resources A and £X authorised for the Net Cash Requirement. Against these authorised limits, the department incurred net resource expenditure of £X and an actual Net Cash Requirement of £X as shown in the Statement of Parliamentary Supply in the Resource Accounts for 200X-0Y, and have thus exceeded both authorised limits.

Except for net resource expenditure of £X in excess of the amount authorised for Request for Resource A and net cash expenditure of £X in excess of the authorised Net Cash Requirement, referred to in paragraphs .. to .. of my report, in all material respects the expenditure and income have been applied for the purposes intended by Parliament and the financial transactions conform to the authorities which govern them."

Drafting note – if an excess arises on more than one request for resource, each excess should be separately expressed.

For a breach of Administration Costs Limit:

The explanatory paragraph and qualified opinion on regularity is to be expressed, as appropriate, as follows:

"As explained more fully in the attached report, the HM Treasury set an Administration Cost Limit of £X for the {department}. Against this limit, the department incurred resource expenditure of £X as shown in Note A to the Resource Accounts for 200X-0Y and have thus exceeded the limit.

Except for resource expenditure on Administration of £X in excess of the Administration Costs Limit(s), referred to in paragraphs .. to .. of my report, in all material respects the expenditure and income have been applied for the purposes intended by Parliament and the financial transactions conform to the authorities which govern them."

Illustrative auditor's reports on public sector financial statements Bulletin 2008/7 2381

In all cases the opinion is to be followed by:

"My report on these financial statements is at pages .. to .."

Example 14 – Wording for a Primary Care Trust's/ Strategic Health Authority's regularity opinion where the Revenue Resource Limit or the Capital Resource Limit has been breached

Example of a qualified opinion arising from non-compliance with governing authorities at an English PCT/SHA

Qualified opinion arising from non-compliance with governing authorities

As disclosed in Note x on page y, the PCT/SHA exceeded the revenue/capital (delete as applicable) resource limit specified by the Secretary of State under section 226/229 (delete as applicable) of the National Health Service Act 2006 by £xx,000.

In my/our opinion:

- the financial statements give a true and fair view, in accordance with the accounting policies directed by the Secretary of State as being relevant to the National Health Service in England of the state of the Authority's/Trust's affairs as at (insert date) and of its net operating costs for the year then ended;
- the part of the Remuneration Report to be audited has been properly prepared in accordance with the accounting policies directed by the Secretary of State as being relevant to the National Health Service in England;
- except for the incurrence of expenditure in excess of the specified revenue/capital resource limit, in all material respects, the expenditure and income have been applied to the purposes intended by Parliament and the financial transactions conform to the authorities which govern them; and
- information which comprises commentary on the financial performance included within the Operating and Financial Review included within the Annual Report, is consistent with the financial statements.

[Bulletin 2008/8]
Auditor's reports for short accounting periods in compliance with the United Kingdom Companies Act 2006

(Issued September 2008)

Contents

	Paragraphs
Introduction	1 - 3
Short accounting periods to which the Companies Act 2006 is applicable	4
Marked-up examples from Bulletin 2006/6	5 - 6
Plans for future revision of Bulletin 2006/6	7
Other APB Bulletins providing guidance on the requirements of the Companies Act 2006	8

Appendices:
1. Example 4 – Non-publicly traded company – Auditor's report on group and parent company financial statements
2. Example 8 – Publicly traded company – Auditor's report on group and parent company financial statements. (Different financial reporting frameworks used for group and parent company financial statements.)
3. Example 12 – Publicly traded company – Auditor's report on group and parent company financial statements (IFRSs as adopted by the EU used for both group and parent company financial statements)

Introduction

The APB has decided to revise ISA (UK and Ireland) 700 in response to comments received on its Discussion Paper "The Auditor's Report: A time for change?" which was issued in December 2007. During the latter part of 2008, the APB will be consulting on the proposed ISA (UK and Ireland) 700 (Revised) which it intends will be effective for accounting periods ending on or after 5 April 2009.

1

Financial statements for accounting periods commencing on or after 6 April 2008[1] need to comply with the requirements of the Companies Act 2006 (CA 2006) rather than with the requirements of the Companies Act 1985, or, for Northern Ireland, the 1986 Order.

2

The purpose of this Bulletin is to illustrate how the illustrative example auditor's reports set out in Appendix 1 to Bulletin 2006/6 "Auditor's reports on financial statements in the United Kingdom" may be amended to reflect the requirements of CA 2006 for accounting periods that begin on or after 6 April 2008 and end before 5 April 2009 (i.e. short accounting periods).

3

Short accounting periods to which the Companies Act 2006 is applicable

There are a number of circumstances where entities may be required to prepare financial statements for a short accounting period. For example, where, part way through a year, a group seeks admission to trading on a regulated market using a structure involving a "NewCo" as the holding company. If the group retains its original accounting reference date then the accounts of "NewCo" will be for less than a year.

4

Marked-up examples from Bulletin 2006/6

Appendix 1 of APB's Bulletin 2006/6 comprises fifteen example auditor's reports that comply with the requirements of the Companies Act 1985, or the 1986 Order. In the appendices to this Bulletin three of these fifteen example auditor's reports are reproduced and marked up to illustrate the changes that are appropriate to reflect the requirements of CA 2006. The three updated examples are numbers 4, 8, and 12. For convenience the numbering of the examples used in Bulletin 2006/6 has been retained in this Bulletin. These examples are intended to be used when reporting on short accounting periods beginning on or after 6 April 2008 and ending before 5 April 2009.

5

By illustrating the required changes to the examples in mark up, users of this Bulletin may deduce the changes required to be made to the other twelve example auditor's reports illustrated in Bulletin 2006/6.

6

---

[1] Most of the accounting and reporting provisions of CA 2006 came into effect for financial years beginning on or after 6 April 2008. They include the provisions relating to the auditor's report in sections 495 to 509 of CA 2006. The Companies Act 1985 and the 1986 Order (which is applicable to companies incorporated in Northern Ireland) continue to apply to financial years beginning before 6 April 2008.

Plans for future revision of Bulletin 2006/6

7   The APB intends to issue a complete revision of Bulletin 2006/6, including each of the illustrative examples therein, when ISA (UK and Ireland) 700 (Revised) has been finalised and in time to guide auditors when issuing auditor's reports for periods ending on or after 5 April 2009 (this will include accounting periods of a full year beginning on or after 6 April 2008).

Other APB Bulletins providing guidance on the requirements of the Companies Act 2006

8   The APB has published the following four Bulletins that provide guidance on other aspects of the requirements of CA 2006:

- 2008/3 "The auditor's statement on the summary financial statement in the United Kingdom".
- 2008/4 "The special auditor's report on abbreviated accounts in the United Kingdom".
- 2008/5 "Auditor's reports on revised accounts and reports, in the United Kingdom".
- 2008/6 "The Senior Statutory Auditor" under the United Kingdom Companies Act 2006".

Appendix 1
Example 4 – Non-publicly traded company – Auditor's report on group and parent company financial statements:

- *Group and parent company financial statements not presented separately.*
- *Company prepares group financial statements.*
- *Company does not meet the Companies Act definition of a quoted company.*
- *UK GAAP used for group and parent company financial statements.*
- *Section 230408 exemption taken for parent company's own profit and loss account.*

INDEPENDENT AUDITOR'S REPORT TO THE [MEMBERS] [SHAREHOLDERS] OF XYZ LIMITED

We have audited the group and parent company financial statements (the "financial statements") of (name of entity) for the period year ended ... which comprise [state the primary financial statements such as the Group Profit and Loss Account, the Group and Company Balance Sheets, the Group Cash Flow Statement, the Group Statement of Total Recognised Gains and Losses] and the related notes[2]. These financial statements have been prepared under the accounting policies set out therein.

Respective responsibilities of directors and auditors

The directors' responsibilities for preparing the Annual Report and the financial statements in accordance with applicable law and United Kingdom Accounting Standards (United Kingdom Generally Accepted Accounting Practice) and for being

---

[2] *Auditor's reports of entities that do not publish their financial statements on a web site or publish them using 'PDF' format may continue to refer to the financial statements by reference to page numbers.*

satisfied that the financial statements give a true and fair view are set out in the Statement of Directors' Responsibilities.

Our responsibility is to audit the financial statements in accordance with relevant legal and regulatory requirements and International Standards on Auditing (UK and Ireland).

We report to you our opinion as to whether the financial statements give a true and fair view have been properly prepared in accordance with United Kingdom Generally Accepted Accounting Practice, and are properly have been prepared in accordance with the Companies Act 2006, and give a true and fair view 1985. We also report to you whether in our opinion the information given in the Directors' Report is consistent with the financial statements. [The information given in the Directors' Report includes that specific information presented in the Operating and Financial Review that is cross referred from the Business Review section of the Directors' Report.][3]

In addition we report to you if, in our opinion, the company has not kept proper adequate accounting records, if we have not received all the information and explanations we require for our audit, or if certain disclosures of directors' remuneration specified by law are not made information specified by law regarding directors' remuneration and other transactions is not disclosed.

We read other information contained in the Annual Report, and consider whether it is consistent with the audited financial statements. This other information comprises only [the Directors' Report, the Chairman's Statement and the Operating and Financial Review][4]. We consider the implications for our report if we become aware of any apparent misstatements or material inconsistencies with the financial statements. Our responsibilities do not extend to any other information.

Basis of audit opinion

We conducted our audit in accordance with International Standards on Auditing (UK and Ireland) issued by the Auditing Practices Board. An audit includes examination, on a test basis, of evidence relevant to the amounts and disclosures in the financial statements. It also includes an assessment of the significant estimates and judgments made by the directors in the preparation of the financial statements, and of whether the accounting policies are appropriate to the group's and company's circumstances, consistently applied and adequately disclosed.

We planned and performed our audit so as to obtain all the information and explanations which we considered necessary in order to provide us with sufficient evidence to give reasonable assurance that the financial statements are free from material misstatement, whether caused by fraud or other irregularity or error. In forming our opinion we also evaluated the overall adequacy of the presentation of information in the financial statements.

---

[3] *Include and tailor as necessary to clarify the information covered by the auditor's opinion.*

[4] *The other information that is 'read' is the content of the printed Annual Report other than the financial statements. The description of the information that has been read is tailored to reflect the terms used in the Annual Report.*

Opinion

In our opinion:

- ~~the financial statements give a true and fair view, in accordance with United Kingdom Generally Accepted Accounting Practice, of the state of the group's and the parent company's affairs as at .... and of the group's profit[loss] for the year then ended;~~
- <u>the financial statements have been properly prepared in accordance with United Kingdom Generally Accepted Accounting Practice;</u>
- the financial statements have been ~~properly~~ prepared in accordance with the Companies Act 2006<s>1985</s>; <s>and</s>
- <u>the financial statements give a true and fair view of the state of the group's and the parent company's affairs as at .... and of the group's profit[loss] for the period then ended; and</u>
- the information given in the Directors' Report is consistent with the financial statements.

~~Registered auditors~~   ~~Address~~
~~Date~~
[Signature]   *Address*
John Smith (Senior Statutory Auditor)   *Date*
for and on behalf of ABC LLP, Statutory Auditor

Appendix 2
Example 8 – Publicly traded company – Auditor's report on group and parent company financial statements:

- Group and parent company financial statements not presented separately.
- IFRSs as adopted by the European Union used for group financial statements.
- UK GAAP used for parent company financial statements.
- Company does meet the Companies Act definition of a quoted company.
- Section <u>408</u><s>230</s> exemption taken for parent company's own profit and loss account.

INDEPENDENT AUDITOR'S REPORT TO THE [MEMBERS] [SHAREHOLDERS] OF XYZ PLC

We have audited the group and parent company financial statements (the "financial statements") of (name of entity) for the <u>period</u><s>year</s> ended ... which comprise [state the primary financial statements such as the Group Income Statement, the Group and Parent Company Balance Sheets, the Group Cash Flow Statement, the Group Statement of Changes in Equity/Statement of Recognised Income and Expense] and the related notes[5]. These financial statements have been prepared under the accounting policies set out therein. We have also audited the information in the Directors' Remuneration Report that is described as having been audited[6].

---

[5] Auditor's reports of entities that do not publish their financial statements on a web site or publish them using 'PDF' format may continue to refer to the financial statements by reference to page numbers.

[6] Schedule 8 of "The Large and Medium-sized Companies and Groups (Accounts and Reports) Regulations 2008 (SI 2008 No. 410) ~~Part 3 of Schedule 7A to the Companies Act 1985~~ sets out the information in the Directors' Remuneration Report that is subject to audit. Companies should describe clearly which disclosures within the Directors' <u>Remuneration</u> Report have been audited.

European Union, has also complied with the IFRSs as issued by the International Accounting Standards Board (IASB).

In our opinion the group financial statements comply with IFRSs as issued by the IASBgive a true and fair view, in accordance with IFRSs, of the state of the group's affairs as at ...and of its profit [loss] for the year then ended.]

Registered auditors   Address
Date
[Signature]   Address
John Smith (Senior Statutory Auditor)   Date
for and on behalf of ABC LLP, Statutory Auditor

we become aware of any apparent misstatements or material inconsistencies with the financial statements. Our responsibilities do not extend to any other information.

Basis of audit opinion

We conducted our audit in accordance with International Standards on Auditing (UK and Ireland) issued by the Auditing Practices Board. An audit includes examination, on a test basis, of evidence relevant to the amounts and disclosures in the financial statements and the part of the Directors' Remuneration Report to be audited. It also includes an assessment of the significant estimates and judgments made by the directors in the preparation of the financial statements, and of whether the accounting policies are appropriate to the group's and company's circumstances, consistently applied and adequately disclosed.

We planned and performed our audit so as to obtain all the information and explanations which we considered necessary in order to provide us with sufficient evidence to give reasonable assurance that the financial statements and the part of the Directors' Remuneration Report to be audited are free from material misstatement, whether caused by fraud or other irregularity or error. In forming our opinion we also evaluated the overall adequacy of the presentation of information in the financial statements and the part of the Directors' Remuneration Report to be audited.

Opinion

In our opinion:

- ~~the group financial statements give a true and fair view, in accordance with IFRSs as adopted by the European Union, of the state of the group's affairs as at .... and of its profit[loss] for the year then ended;~~
- ~~the parent company financial statements give a true and fair view, in accordance with IFRSs as adopted by the European Union as applied in accordance with the provisions of the Companies Act 1985, of the state of the parent company's affairs as at ....;~~
- the group financial statements have been properly prepared in accordance with IFRSs as adopted by the European Union;
- the parent company financial statements have been properly prepared in accordance with IFRSs as adopted by the European Union as applied in accordance with the provisions of the Companies Act 2006;
- the financial statements ~~and the part of the Directors' Remuneration Report to be audited~~ have been ~~properly~~ prepared in accordance with the Companies Act 2006~~1985~~ and, as regards the group financial statements, Article 4 of the IAS Regulation;
- the financial statements give a true and fair view of the state of the group's and the parent company's affairs as at ...., and of the group's profit[loss] for the period then ended;
- the part of the Directors' Remuneration Report to be audited has been properly prepared in accordance with the Companies Act 2006; and
- the information given in the Directors' Report is consistent with the financial statements.

[Separate opinion in relation to IFRSs as issued by the IASB

As explained in Note x to the group financial statements, the group in addition to complying with its legal obligation to comply with IFRSs as adopted by the

Respective responsibilities of directors and auditors

The directors' responsibilities for preparing the Annual Report, the Directors' Remuneration Report and the financial statements in accordance with applicable law and International Financial Reporting Standards (IFRSs) as adopted by the European Union and for being satisfied that the financial statements give a true and fair view are set out in the Statement of Directors' Responsibilities.

Our responsibility is to audit the financial statements and the part of the Directors' Remuneration Report to be audited in accordance with relevant legal and regulatory requirements and International Standards on Auditing (UK and Ireland).

We report to you our opinion as to whether the financial statements ~~give a true and fair view~~ have been properly prepared in accordance with the relevant financial reporting framework, ~~and whether the financial statements and the part of the Directors' Remuneration Report to be audited~~ have been ~~properly~~ prepared in accordance with the Companies Act 2006~~1985~~ and, as regards the group financial statements, Article 4 of the IAS Regulation, and give a true and fair view. We also report to you whether in our opinion the part of the Directors' Remuneration Report to be audited has been properly prepared in accordance with the Companies Act 2006, and whether the information given in the Directors' Report is consistent with the financial statements. [The information given in the Directors' Report includes that specific information presented in the Operating and Financial Review that is cross referred from the Business Review section of the Directors' Report.][13]

In addition we report to you if, in our opinion, the company has not kept adequate~~proper~~ accounting records, if we have not received all the information and explanations we require for our audit, or if certain disclosures of directors' remuneration specified by law are not made~~information specified by law regarding directors' remuneration and other transactions is not disclosed~~.

We review whether the Corporate Governance Statement reflects the company's compliance with the nine provisions of the ~~[2003[14]]~~ [2006]/[June 2008][15] Combined Code specified for our review by the Listing Rules of the Financial Services Authority, and we report if it does not. We are not required to consider whether the board's statements on internal control cover all risks and controls, or form an opinion on the effectiveness of the group's corporate governance procedures or its risk and control procedures.

We read other information contained in the Annual Report and consider whether it is consistent with the audited financial statements. The other information comprises only [the Directors' Report, the unaudited part of the Directors' Remuneration Report, the Chairman's Statement, the Operating and Financial Review and the Corporate Governance Statement][16]. We consider the implications for our report if

---

[13] Include and tailor as necessary to clarify the information covered by the auditor's opinion.

[14] ~~In June 2006 the Financial Reporting Council issued a revised version of the Combined Code. An announcement is expected from the Financial Service Authority regarding the period from which the reference to 2003 should be changed to 2006.~~

[15] The June 2008 Combined Code applies to accounting periods beginning on or after 29 June 2008; the 2006 Combined Code applies before that date.

[16] The other information that is 'read' is the content of the printed Annual Report other than the financial statements. The description of the information that has been read is tailored to reflect the terms used in the Annual Report.

- the part of the Directors' Remuneration Report to be audited has been properly prepared in accordance with the Companies Act 2006; and
- the information given in the Directors' Report is consistent with the financial statements.

[Separate opinion in relation to IFRSs as issued by the IASB

As explained in Note x to the group financial statements, the group in addition to complying with its legal obligation to comply with IFRSs as adopted by the European Union, has also complied with the IFRSs as issued by the International Accounting Standards Board (IASB).

In our opinion the group financial statements comply with IFRSs as issued by the IASB give a true and fair view, in accordance with IFRSs, of the state of the group's affairs as at ...and of its profit [loss] for the year then ended.]

Registered auditors   Address
Date
[Signature]   Address
John Smith (Senior Statutory Auditor)   Date
for and on behalf of ABC LLP, Statutory Auditor

Appendix 3
Example 12 – Publicly traded company – Auditor's report on group and parent company financial statements:

- Group and parent company financial statements not presented separately.
- IFRSs as adopted by the European Union used for both group and parent company financial statements.
- Company does meet the Companies Act definition of a quoted company.
- Section 408 230 exemption taken for parent company's own income statement.

INDEPENDENT AUDITOR'S REPORT TO THE [MEMBERS] [SHAREHOLDERS] OF XYZ PLC

We have audited the group and parent company financial statements (the "financial statements") of (name of entity) for the period year ended ... which comprise [state the primary financial statements such as the Group Income Statement, the Group and Parent Company Balance Sheets, the Group and Parent Company Cash Flow Statements, the Group and Parent Company Statements of Changes in Equity/ Statements of Recognised Income and Expense] and the related notes[11]. These financial statements have been prepared under the accounting policies set out therein. We have also audited the information in the Directors' Remuneration Report that is described as having been audited[12].

---

[11] Auditor's reports of entities that do not publish their financial statements on a web site or publish them using 'PDF' format may continue to refer to the financial statements by reference to page numbers.

[12] Schedule 8 of "The Large and Medium-sized Companies and Groups (Accounts and Reports) Regulations 2008 (SI 2008 No. 410) Part 3 of Schedule 7A to the Companies Act 1985 sets out the information in the Directors' Remuneration Report that is subject to audit. Companies should describe clearly which disclosures within the Directors' Remuneration Report have been audited.

Introduction

1 The purpose of this Bulletin is to provide guidance with respect to those reports and statements required to be made by an auditor under the Companies Act 2006 (CA 2006), that are not dealt with in other Bulletins published by the APB.

2 Other Bulletins published by the APB that address reports and statements required to be made by an auditor under CA 2006 are:

(a) The auditor's statement on the summary financial statement in the United Kingdom (Bulletin 2008/3);
(b) The special auditor's report on abbreviated accounts in the United Kingdom (Bulletin 2008/4);
(c) Auditor's reports on revised accounts and reports, in the United Kingdom (Bulletin 2008/5); and
(d) Auditor's reports for short accounting periods in compliance with the United Kingdom Companies Act 2006 (Bulletin 2008/8).

3 The table in the Appendix lists the example reports in Bulletin 2007/1[1] indicating within which APB Bulletin the equivalent example, revised to reflect the requirements of CA 2006, can be found.

4 The guidance in this Bulletin takes account of the law as at 6 April 2008. Readers are cautioned that the provisions of CA 2006 on which the guidance and examples on pages 21 to 42 are based do not come into effect until 1 October 2009, and may be subject to transitional provisions under the final "Commencement Order" which at the date of this Bulletin is still in draft. Until the provisions of CA 2006 apply, the equivalent illustrative reports in Bulletin 2007/1 "Example reports by auditors under company legislation in Great Britain" remain in effect[2].

5 Readers are cautioned that the references within CA 2006 may change subsequent to publication of this Bulletin.

Distributions: Justification of distribution by reference to relevant accounts (sections 836 to 839 of CA 2006) *Effective where distribution made on or after 6 April 2008*

6 Section 830(1) of CA 2006 prohibits companies from making a distribution otherwise than out of profits available for the purpose.

7 Whether a distribution may be made by a company is determined by reference to the items described in section 836(1) of CA 2006 as stated in the "relevant accounts". The items are:

(a) profits, losses, assets and liabilities;
(b) provisions of the following kinds;
  (i) where the relevant accounts are Companies Act accounts, provisions of a kind specified by paragraph 7 of Schedule 9 to The Large and Medium-sized Companies and Groups (Accounts and Reports) Regulations 2008[3] or

---

[1] *Bulletin 2007/1 updated example reports originally issued by the APB in Practice Note 8.*

[2] *However, see footnote 32 on page 43 for description of transitional provisions.*

[3] *SI 2008 No. 410.*

by paragraph 5 of Schedule 7 to The Small Companies and Groups (Accounts and Directors' Report) Regulations 2008[4];

(ii) where the relevant accounts are IAS accounts, provisions of any kind;

(c) share capital and reserves (including undistributable reserves).

8   The relevant accounts are the company's last annual accounts (as defined in section 837 of CA 2006), except that:

(a) where the distribution would be found to contravene the requirements of Part 23 of CA 2006 by reference to the company's last annual accounts[5], the distribution may be justified by reference to interim accounts; and

(b) where the distribution is proposed to be declared during the company's first accounting reference period, or before any accounts have been circulated in respect of that period, the distribution may be justified by reference to initial accounts.

Requirements where the auditor has issued a qualified report on the last annual accounts

9   Where the auditor has issued a "qualified report"[6] on the last annual accounts, the company's ability to make a distribution, by reference to those accounts, could be in doubt. In such circumstances, the company may not proceed to make the distribution unless the auditor has made a statement under section 837(4) of CA 2006 as to whether, in the auditor's opinion, the matters in respect of which the auditor's report is qualified are material for determining whether a distribution would contravene the requirements of Part 23 of CA 2006.

10   The auditor's statement under section 837(4) of CA 2006 must be in writing and can be:

(a) made in a separate statement which would be addressed to the members (See Example 1 on page 7); or

(b) included as a separate paragraph at the end of the auditor's report to the members on the financial statements (See Example 2 on page 9).

11   The auditor is required to state whether in its opinion the subject matter of the qualification is material for determining whether proposed distributions are permitted[7]. A qualification is not material for this purpose if the financial effect of the matters giving rise to the qualification could not be such as to reduce the distributable profits below the levels required for the purpose of such distributions

12   The level of the proposed or potential distribution will normally be quantified in the opinion. Where the maximum effect of a qualification cannot be quantified, it would normally be material for distribution purposes unless the auditor can conclude that

---

[4] SI 2008 No. 409.

[5] For transitional provisions see paragraph 35 of Schedule 4 of The Companies Act 2006 (Commencement No. 5, Transitional Provisions and Savings) Order 2007 (SI 2007 No. 3495 (C. 150). Amongst other things these provisions permit the relevant accounts to be accounts for financial years beginning before 6 April 2008 to which the provisions of the Companies Act 1985 apply.

[6] A report that expresses an unqualified opinion but includes an emphasis of matter or "other matter" paragraph is not regarded as being qualified.

[7] Section 837(5) of CA 2006 states that "An auditor's statement is sufficient for the purposes of a distribution if it relates to distributions of a description that includes the distribution in question, even if at the time of the statement it had not been proposed."

the qualification either does not impact distributable profits or that its effect could only be favourable.

A disclaimer of opinion on the financial statements as a whole would be material as the auditor would be unable to form an opinion on the amount at which the company's distributable profits are stated. 13

If a separate statement is made, the date used is that on which the statement is completed. The statement will need to have been completed by the date of the distribution, at the latest. 14

On a change of auditor the report under section 837(4) of the Companies Act 2006 can only be made by the statutory auditor who reported on the last annual financial statements. 15

Requirements where interim accounts used

Section 838 of CA 2006 establishes the requirements for making a distribution where interim accounts are used. In this circumstance there are no requirements made of the company's auditor. 16

Requirements where initial accounts used

Section 839 of CA 2006 establishes the requirements for making a distribution where initial accounts are used. Where initial accounts are used by a public company to justify a distribution the company's auditor is required to have made a report stating whether, in its opinion, the initial accounts have been "properly prepared". 17

The "properly prepared report" is discussed in more detail in connection with Example 3, on pages 10 and 11. 18

Example 1 – Separate statement on a company's ability to make a distribution where auditor's report was qualified *Effective where distribution made on or after 6 April 2008*

STATEMENT OF THE INDEPENDENT AUDITOR TO THE [MEMBERS] [SHAREHOLDERS] OF XYZ LIMITED PURSUANT TO SECTION 837(4)[8] OF THE COMPANIES ACT 2006

We have audited the financial statements of XYZ Limited for the year ended... in accordance with International Standards on Auditing (UK and Ireland) issued by the Auditing Practices Board and have expressed a qualified opinion thereon in our report dated....

Respective responsibilities of directors and auditor

[S*ummarisation of directors' responsibilities with respect to the financial statements referred to in the introductory paragraph*]. They are also responsible for considering whether the company, subsequent to the balance sheet date, has sufficient distributable profits to make a distribution at the time the distribution is made.

---

[8] *Section 837(4) applies where the last annual accounts are used. Where initial accounts are used a similar report is prepared based on the report in Example 3 on page 11.*

Our responsibility is to report whether, in our opinion, the subject matter of our qualification of our auditor's report on the financial statements for the year ended ... is material for determining, by reference to those financial statements, whether the distribution proposed by the company is permitted under section 830[9] [section 831/832] of the Companies Act 2006. We are not required to form an opinion on whether the company has sufficient distributable reserves to make the distribution proposed at the time it is made.

Opinion

In our opinion the subject matter of the qualification is not material for determining, by reference to those financial statements, whether [the distribution of £...]/[the interim/final dividend for the year ended... of £...] proposed by the company is permitted under section 830[9] [section 831/832] of the Companies Act 2006.

Statutory auditor   *Address*
Date

Notes:

1 As an alternative the auditor's statement might be expressed in terms of the company's ability to make potential distributions up to a specific level. This may be particularly appropriate where the amount of the dividend has not yet been determined. In such circumstances the opinion paragraph would be worded as follows:

"*In our opinion the subject matter of the qualification is not material for determining, by reference to those financial statements, whether a distribution of not more than £... by the company is permitted under section 830[9] [section 831/832] of the Companies Act 2006*".

2 As a further alternative the auditor's statement might be expressed in terms of the company's ability to make "any distribution". In such circumstances the opinion paragraph would be worded as follows:

"*In our opinion the subject matter of the qualification is not material for determining by reference to those financial statements, whether any distribution proposed by the company is permitted under section 830[9] [section 831/832] of the Companies Act 2006*".

3 Where the auditor concludes that the subject matter of the qualification is material to either a specific distribution which is proposed or to any distribution, then an adverse opinion is given. In such circumstances the opinion paragraph would be worded as follows:

"**Adverse opinion**

In our opinion the subject matter of the qualification is material for determining, by reference to those financial statements, whether [the distribution of £...]/[the interim/final dividend for the year ended ... of £...]/[any distribution] proposed by the company is permitted under section 830[9] [section 831/832] of the Companies Act 2006."

[9] The reference in all cases to section 830 in this example is extended to cover also section 831 in the case of a public company and also sections 831 and 832 if the public company is also an "investment company".

Example 2 – "Other matter" paragraph included in auditor's report on financial statements on a company's ability to make a distribution where auditor's report was qualified *Effective where distribution made on or after 6 April 2008*

The following statement is added to the end of the auditor's report following either the opinion paragraph or, where there is one, the emphasis of matter paragraph.

"**Statement pursuant to section [837(4)][10] [839(6)][11] of the Companies Act 2006**

Respective responsibilities of directors and the auditor

In addition to their responsibilities described above, the directors are also responsible for considering whether the company, subsequent to the balance sheet date, has sufficient distributable profits to make a distribution at the time the distribution is made.

Our responsibility is to report whether, in our opinion, the subject matter of our qualification of our auditor's report on the financial statements for the year ended .... is material for determining, by reference to those financial statements, whether the distribution proposed by the company is permitted under section 830[12] [section 831/ 832] of the Companies Act 2006. We are not required to form an opinion on whether the company has sufficient distributable reserves to make the distribution proposed at the time it is made.

Opinion

In our opinion the subject matter of the above qualification is not material for determining whether [the distribution of £...]/[the interim/final dividend for the year ended .... of £....] proposed by the company is permitted under section 830[12] [sections 831/ 832] of the Companies Act 2006."

Notes:

The notes to Example 1 also apply to this Example

Distributions: the use of initial accounts (section 839(5) of CA 2006) *Effective where distribution made on or after 6 April 2008*

A company may wish to make a distribution during its first accounting reference period or after the end of that period but before the accounts for that period have been circulated.

---

[10] *Section 837(4) applies where the last annual accounts are used.*

[11] *Section 839(6) applies to Example 3 on page 11 where the report on the initial accounts is qualified.*

[12] *The reference in all cases to section 830 in this example is extended to cover also section 831 in the case of a public company and also sections 831 and 832 if the public company is also an "investment company".*

20 In such instances section 839(1) of CA 2006 requires "initial accounts" to be accounts that enable a reasonable judgment to be made as to the amounts of the items mentioned in section 836(1) of CA 2006.

21 Initial accounts of a public company are required to have been "properly prepared" or have been so prepared except for matters that are not material for determining (by reference to the items mentioned in section 836(1) of CA 2006) whether the distribution would contravene Part 23 of CA 2006 (Distributions).

22 "Properly prepared" means prepared in accordance with sections 395 to 397, and the regulations made thereunder, of CA 2006 (requirements for company individual accounts), applying those requirements with such modifications as are necessary because the accounts are prepared otherwise than in respect of an accounting reference period.

23 With respect to a public company, the company's auditor is required, by section 839(5) of CA 2006 to make a report stating whether, in its opinion, the accounts have been properly prepared. (Such a report is illustrated in Example 3 on page 11).

24 If the auditor's opinion is qualified, the auditor must state, in writing (either at the time of the report or subsequently), whether in its opinion the matters giving rise to the qualification are material for determining whether the distribution is permitted. These requirements are discussed further in paragraphs 9 to 15.

25 CA 2006 does not state to whom the report should be addressed. However, it is implicit from CA 2006 that it be addressed to the directors.

26 The same principles apply for the dating of initial accounts as apply to the dating of annual accounts.

Example 3 – Report on initial accounts when a public company wishes to make a distribution *Effective where distribution made on or after 6 April 2008*

This example is based on the assumption that the initial accounts have been prepared in accordance with UK GAAP. (Initial accounts may also be prepared in accordance with IFRSs as adopted by the European Union.)

REPORT OF THE INDEPENDENT AUDITOR TO THE DIRECTORS OF XYZ PLC UNDER SECTION 839(5) OF THE COMPANIES ACT 2006

We have examined the initial accounts of XYZ PLC for the period from .... to ...which comprise [state the primary financial statements such as the Profit and Loss Account, the Balance Sheet, the Cash Flow Statement, the Statement of Total Recognised Gains and Losses] and the related notes. The initial accounts have been prepared under the accounting policies set out therein.

Respective responsibilities of directors and auditors

As described ... the directors are responsible for the preparation of the initial accounts in accordance with applicable law and United Kingdom Accounting Standards (United Kingdom Generally Accepted Accounting Practice).

Our responsibility is to report to you our opinion as to whether the initial accounts have been properly prepared within the meaning of section 839(4) of the Companies Act 2006.

Opinion

In our opinion the initial accounts for the period from... to... have been properly prepared within the meaning of section 839(4) of the Companies Act 2006.

[Signature]   Address
John Smith *(Senior Statutory Auditor)*   Date
for and on behalf of ABC LLP, *Statutory Auditor*

Statement by auditor on ceasing to hold office (section 519 of CA 2006) *Effective when auditor ceases to hold office on or after 6 April 2008*

Unquoted companies

Where an auditor of an unquoted company ceases for any reason to hold office, it must deposit at the company's registered office either: 27

(a) a statement of the circumstances connected with it ceasing to hold office (see Example 4 on page 16); or
(b) where it considers that there are no circumstances in connection with it ceasing to hold office that need to be brought to the attention of members or creditors of the company, a statement to that effect (see Example 5 on page 17).

Quoted companies[13]

Where an auditor of a quoted company ceases for any reason to hold office, it must deposit at the company's registered office a statement of the circumstances connected with its ceasing to hold office. The auditor of a quoted company is not able to deposit a statement stating that there are no circumstances connected with it ceasing to hold office.   28

Deadlines for filing the statement

The auditor's statement is required to be deposited –   29

(a) in the case of resignation along with the notice of resignation;
(b) in the case of failure to seek re-appointment, not less than 14 days before the end of the time allowed for next appointing an auditor;
(c) in any other case, not later than the end of the period of 14 days beginning with the date on which the auditor ceases to hold office.

---

[13] *The definition of "quoted company" set out in sections 385 and 531 of CA 2006 do not strictly apply to the section of CA 2006 that deals with auditor resignation statements. The Institute of Chartered Accountants in England & Wales (ICAEW) suggests, in its note entitled "Auditor cessation statements (Version 2 July 2008), www.icaew.com/auditnews? that "quoted company" should be taken to mean a company whose equity share capital on the day of the audit cessation:*

(a) *has been included in the official list in accordance with the provisions of Part 6 of the Financial Services and Markets Act 2000, or*
(b) *is officially listed in an EEA State, or*
(c) *is admitted to dealing on either the New York Stock Exchange or the exchange known as Nasdaq.*

Company's duties in relation to statement (section 520 of CA 2006)

30 Where the statement deposited by the auditor sets out the circumstances connected with the auditor ceasing to hold office (ie is not a statement of no circumstances) the company must, within 14 days, either:

(a) send a copy of it to every person who under section 423 of CA 2006 is entitled to be sent copies of the accounts, or
(b) apply to the court (in which case it must notify the auditor of the application) to direct that copies need not be sent out where the auditor is using the provisions of section 519 of CA 2006 to secure needless publicity for defamatory matter.

Obligation to send copy of statement to the Registrar of Companies

31 Unless within 21 days beginning with the day on which the auditor deposited the statement under section 519 of CA 2006 the auditor receives notice of an application to the court under section 520 of CA 2006 it must within a further seven days send a copy of the statement to the Registrar of Companies. There are criminal offences for failure to comply with these provisions.

32 If an application to the court has been made under section 520 and the auditor subsequently receives notice that the court is not going to direct that copies of the statement not be sent out, the auditor must within seven days of receiving the notice send a copy of the statement to the Registrar of Companies.

Duty of auditor to notify appropriate audit authority (section 522 of CA 2006)

33 Where in the case of:

(a) a "major audit" (see paragraph 38), an auditor ceases for any reason to hold office, or
(b) an audit that is not a major audit, an auditor ceases to hold office before the end of its term of office[14],

the auditor must notify the "appropriate audit authority" (see paragraph 37).

34 The notice must:
(a) inform the appropriate audit authority that the auditor has ceased to hold office, and
(b) be accompanied by a copy of the statement deposited by the auditor at the company's registered office in accordance with section 519 of CA 2006.

35 If the statement deposited is to the effect that the auditor considers that there are no circumstances in connection with the auditor ceasing to hold office that need to be brought to the attention of members or creditors of the company, the notice must also be accompanied by a statement of the reasons for the auditor ceasing to hold office.

36 The auditor must notify the appropriate audit authority;

---

[14] The question of when an auditor's term of office ends is more complicated under the provisions of CA 2006 (compared to the provisions of the Companies Act 1985) whereby the auditor of a private company is deemed to be re-appointed automatically. The ICAEW's note referred to in footnote 13 provides helpful guidance in this area.

IMPORTANT NOTE:

READERS ARE CAUTIONED THAT THE GUIDANCE (AND THE EXAMPLES) SET OUT ON THE FOLLOWING PAGES DOES NOT COME INTO EFFECT UNTIL 1 OCTOBER 2009 AND MAY BE SUBJECT TO TRANSITIONAL PROVISIONS UNDER THE FINAL "COMMENCEMENT ORDER" WHICH AT THE DATE OF THIS BULLETIN IS STILL IN DRAFT.

Readers should consult the table in the Appendix which sets out where example reports that are effective for the period up to 1 October 2009 may be found.

Auditor's statement with respect to net assets when a private company re-registers as a public company (section 92 of CA 2006)
Effective 1 October 2009

42 Under CA 2006 a private company may re-register as a public company if, among other things, it meets certain requirements regarding its net assets. The company's auditor is required to:

(a) make a written statement regarding the net assets; and
(b) to have issued a report on a balance sheet that is prepared at a date no more than seven months before application for re-registration is made to the Registrar of Companies, that is either:
  (i) unqualified; or
  (ii) qualified and the auditor expresses an opinion that the qualification is not material for determining the net assets of the company.

Requirements as to net assets

43 Section 92 of CA 2006 requires a private company applying to re-register as a public company to obtain:

(a) a balance sheet of the company prepared as at a date not more than seven months before the date on which the application is delivered to the Registrar of Companies;
(b) an "unqualified report" by the company's auditor on that balance sheet (see paragraph 46 for discussion of the meaning of "unqualified report"),
(c) a written statement by the company's auditor that in its opinion at the balance sheet date the amount of the company's net assets was not less than the aggregate of its called-up share capital and undistributable reserves[19]. (The terms "net assets" and "undistributable reserves" have the same meaning as in section 831 of CA 2006).

44 Between the balance sheet date and the date on which the application for re-registration is delivered to the Registrar of Companies, there must be no change in the company's financial position that results in the amount of its net assets becoming less than the aggregate of its called-up share capital and undistributable reserves[20]. As the auditor's statement is required to be made as at the balance sheet date, the auditor has no responsibility for the period between the balance sheet date and the date the application is delivered to the Registrar of Companies by the company.

45 The balance sheet included with the company's latest financial statements is eligible for the purpose of section 92(1)(a) of CA 2006 if :

(a) it was prepared less than seven months before the company's application to re-register as a public company; and
(b) at the time it was prepared the balance sheet met the net assets test in section 92(1)(c) of CA 2006.

---

[19] Section 92 CA 2006

[20] Section 92(2) CA 2006.

Meaning of unqualified report

In paragraph 43(b) above an unqualified report means[21]: 46

(a) if the balance sheet was prepared for a financial year of the company, a report stating without material qualification the auditor's opinion that the balance sheet has been properly prepared in accordance with the requirements of CA 2006;

(b) if the balance sheet was not prepared for a financial year of the company, a report stating without material qualification the auditor's opinion that the balance sheet has been properly prepared in accordance with the provisions of CA 2006 which would have applied if it had been prepared for a financial year of the company[22].

A qualification is material unless the auditor states in its report that the matter giving rise to the qualification is not material for the purpose of determining (by reference to the company's balance sheet) whether at the balance sheet date the amount of the company's net assets was not less than the aggregate of its called up share capital and undistributable reserves[23]. 47

The auditor's statement on net assets

Section 92(1) of CA 2006 makes reference to a company applying to re-register as a public company. Therefore, the auditor's statement required by section 92(1)(c) is addressed to the company. 48

With respect to the auditor's responsibility the auditor's statement states that it is limited to an examination of the relationship between the company's net assets and its called up share capital and undistributable reserves as stated in the audited balance sheet, so that it is clear that no further audit procedures have been carried out. 49

The statement by the auditor is dated when it is signed, which cannot be earlier than the date of the auditor's report on the balance sheet. 50

Auditor's report on the balance sheet

Section 92 of CA 2006 requires that, for it to be "unqualified", the auditor's report on the balance sheet must state without material qualification the auditor's opinion that the balance sheet has been properly prepared in accordance with the requirements of CA 2006. For a qualified report to be acceptable, the auditors are required to state in their report that the matter giving rise to the qualification is not material for determining (by reference to the balance sheet) whether at the balance sheet date the amount of the net assets of the company were not less than the aggregate of its called-up share capital and undistributable reserves. 51

If there has been a change of auditor, the new auditor can accept the balance sheet audited by the previous auditor, as a basis for the work referred to in paragraph 49 above, unless the auditor's report thereon contains a material qualification regarding 52

---

[21] Section 92(3) CA 2006.

[22] Under section 92(4) of CA 2006 "For the purposes of an auditor's report on a balance sheet that was not prepared for a financial year of the company, the provisions of this Act apply with such modifications as are necessary by reason of that fact".

[23] Section 92(5) CA 2006.

the proper preparation of the balance sheet in accordance with CA 2006. The new auditor indicates in its report by whom the audit of the balance sheet was carried out.

53 If the balance sheet included with the company's latest financial statements is not eligible for use, it will be necessary for the company to prepare a balance sheet. A balance sheet may not be eligible for use if:

(a) it was prepared more than seven months before the company's application to re-register as a public company; or
(b) at the time it was prepared it did not meet the net assets test in section 92(1)(c) of CA 2006.

54 With respect to a balance sheet that has been specially prepared and has not been included with the company's annual financial statements the auditor is required to report without material qualification the auditor's opinion that the balance sheet has been properly prepared in accordance with the provisions of CA 2006 which would have applied had it been prepared for a financial year of a company.

Reporting

55 CA 2006 does not require the auditor's report on the balance sheet and the auditor's statement on the net assets to be included within a combined report. However, as a practical matter this will often be the most effective way for the auditor to report on these matters.

56 The following examples of such combined reports are provided:

(a) Example 6 Balance Sheet in annual financial statements reported on without qualification (see page 25)
(b) Example 7 Balance sheet in annual financial statements reported on with a qualification in respect of proper preparation in accordance with CA 2006, but the qualification is not material (see page 26)
(c) Example 8 Specially prepared balance sheet reported on without qualification (see page 28)
(d) Example 9 Specially prepared balance sheet reported on with a qualification in respect or proper preparation in accordance with the Companies Act 2006, but the qualification is not material (see page 29)

Example 6 – Statement when a private company wishes to re-register as a public company where the auditor's opinion on the balance sheet is unqualified *Effective 1 October 2009*

This example is used when the company's annual financial statements were prepared within seven months before its application to re-register as a public company.

STATEMENT OF THE INDEPENDENT AUDITOR TO XYZ LIMITED FOR THE PURPOSE OF SECTION 92(1)(b) and (c) OF THE COMPANIES ACT 2006

We have examined the balance sheet and related notes of XYZ Limited as at... which formed part of the financial statements for the year then ended which were audited by [us]/[ABC LLP].

Respective responsibilities of directors and auditors

The company's directors are responsible for the preparation of the balance sheet and related notes.

It is our responsibility to:

(a) report on whether the balance sheet has been properly prepared in accordance with the requirements of the Companies Act 2006; and
(b) form an independent opinion, based on our examination, concerning the relationship between the company's net assets and its called-up share capital and undistributable reserves at the balance sheet date.

Opinion concerning proper preparation of balance sheet

In our opinion the audited balance sheet at... has been properly prepared in accordance with the requirements of the Companies Act 2006.

Statement on net assets

In our opinion, at ... the amount of the company's net assets (within the meaning given to that expression by section 831(2) of the Companies Act 2006) was not less than the aggregate of its called-up share capital and undistributable reserves.

Statutory auditor   Address
Date

Example 7 – Statement when a private company wishes to re-register as a public company where the auditor's opinion on the balance sheet is qualified with respect to proper preparation in accordance with the Companies Act 2006, but the qualification is not material *Effective 1 October 2009*

This example is used when the company's annual financial statements were prepared within seven months before its application to re-register as a public company

STATEMENT OF THE INDEPENDENT AUDITOR TO XYZ LIMITED FOR THE PURPOSE OF SECTION 92(1)(b) and (c) OF THE COMPANIES ACT 2006

We have examined the balance sheet and related notes of XYZ Limited as at... which formed part of the financial statements for the year then ended which were audited by [us]/[ABC LLP].

Respective responsibilities of directors and auditors

The company's directors are responsible for the preparation of the balance sheet and related notes.

It is our responsibility to:

(a) report on whether the balance sheet has been properly prepared in accordance with the requirements of the Companies Act 2006; and

(b) form an independent opinion, based on our examination, concerning the relationship between the company's net assets and its called-up share capital and undistributable reserves at the balance sheet date.

Qualified opinion concerning proper preparation of balance sheet

[We] / [ABC LLP] audited the financial statements for the year ended...and expressed a qualified opinion regarding the proper preparation of the balance sheet in accordance with the requirements of the Companies Act 2006.

The matter giving rise to [our] / [the] qualification is not material for determining by reference to the balance sheet at ... whether, at that date, the amount of the company's net assets (within the meaning given to that expression by section 831(2) of the Companies Act 2006) was not less than the aggregate of its called-up share capital and undistributable reserves.

Statement on net assets

In our opinion at... the amount of the company's net assets (within the meaning given to that expression by section 831(2) of the Companies Act 2006) was not less than the aggregate of its called-up share capital and undistributable reserves.

Statutory auditor   Address
Date

Example 8 – Statement when a private company wishes to re-register as a public company based on a specially prepared balance sheet that is unqualified *Effective 1 October 2009*

This example is used when the latest financial statements are not eligible for use as they were prepared more than seven months before the company's application to re-register as a public company, or because at the time they were prepared the balance sheet did not meet the test in section 92(1)(c) of CA 2006. In these circumstances it is necessary for the company to prepare a balance sheet which is required to be audited.

REPORT OF THE INDEPENDENT AUDITOR TO XYZ LIMITED FOR THE PURPOSE OF SECTIONS 92(1)(b) and (c) OF THE COMPANIES ACT 2006

We have audited the balance sheet and related notes of XYZ Limited as at...set out on pages... to.... which have been prepared under the accounting policies set out therein.

Respective responsibilities of directors and auditors

The company's directors are responsible for the preparation of the balance sheet and related notes.

It is our responsibility to:

(a) report on whether the balance sheet has been properly prepared in accordance with the provisions of the Companies Act 2006 that would have applied if it had been prepared for a financial year of the company with such modifications as are necessary by reason of that fact; and having made full inquiry into the affairs and prospects of the company, the directors have formed the opinion:

(a) as regards its initial situation immediately following the date on which the payment out of capital is proposed to be made, that there will be no grounds on which the company could then be found unable to pay its debts, and
(b) as regards its prospects for the year immediately following that date, that having regard to –
   (i) their intentions with respect to the management of the company's business during that year, and
   (ii) the amount and character of the financial resources that will in their view be available to the company during that year,
   (iii) the company will be able to continue to carry on business as a going concern (and will accordingly be able to pay its debts as they fall due) throughout that year.

In forming their opinion, in respect of paragraph 58(a) above, the directors are required to take into account all of the company's liabilities (including any contingent or prospective liabilities).   59

The permissible capital payment (section 710 of CA 2006)

The payment that may be made out of capital is described as the "permissible capital payment" and is such amount as, after applying: 60

(a) any available profits of the company; and
(b) the proceeds of any fresh issue of shares made for the purposes of the redemption or purchase

is required to meet the price of redemption or purchase.

Determination of available profits (sections 711 and 712 of CA 2006)

The available profits of the company are determined as follows: 61

> 1. First, determine the profits of the company by reference to the following items as stated in the relevant accounts (see paragraph 62):
>   (a) profits, losses, assets and liabilities;
>   (b) provisions of the following kinds:
>   (i) where the relevant accounts are Companies Act accounts, provisions of a kind specified for the purposes of this subsection by paragraph 4 of Schedule 9 to The Large and Medium-sized Companies and Groups (Accounts and Reports) Regulations 2008[26] or by paragraph 4 of Schedule 7 to The Small Companies and Groups (Accounts and Directors' Report) Regulations 2008[27] by regulations under section 396 of CA 2006;
>   (ii) where the relevant accounts are IAS accounts, provisions of any kind.
>   (c) share capital and reserves (including undistributable reserves).
> 2. Second, reduce the amount so determined by the amount of

---

[26] SI 2008 No. 410.

[27] SI 2008 No. 409.

> (a) any distribution lawfully made by the company, and
> (b) any other relevant payment lawfully made[28] by the company out of distributable profits,
> after the date of the relevant accounts and before the end of the relevant period (see paragraph 62).
> 3. The resulting figure is the amount of available profits.

62 The "relevant accounts" are any accounts that:

(a) are prepared as at a date within the relevant period, and
(b) are such as to enable a reasonable judgment to be made as to the amounts of the items mentioned under "1" in the above table.

The "relevant period" means the period of three months ending with the date on which the directors' statement is made in accordance with section 714 of CA 2006.

Report by the company's auditor

63 The directors' statement is required by section 714(6) to have annexed to it a report addressed to the directors by the company's auditor (see Example 10 on page 34) stating that:

(a) it has inquired into the company's state of affairs,
(b) the amount specified in the statement as the permissible capital payment for the shares in question is in its view properly determined in accordance with sections 710 to 712 of CA 2006, and
(c) it is not aware of anything to indicate that the opinion expressed by the directors in their statement as to any of the matters mentioned in subsection (3) of section 714 of CA 2006 is unreasonable in all the circumstances.

64 The directors' statement and therefore the annexed auditor's report are required to be made in the week before the resolution is passed specifying the amount of the permissible capital payment for the shares in question. The auditor's report cannot be dated earlier than the date of the director's statement to which it relates. The date of the auditor's report is the date on which the auditor signs its report expressing its opinion.

65 There is no provision for the auditor's report to be other than unqualified. Unless the opinion is unqualified the auditor does not issue a report.

Example 10 – Report when a private company wishes to redeem or purchase its own shares out of capital *Effective 1 October 2009*

REPORT OF THE INDEPENDENT AUDITOR TO THE DIRECTORS OF XYZ LIMITED PURSUANT TO SECTION 714(6) OF THE COMPANIES ACT 2006

We report on the attached statement of the directors dated..., prepared pursuant to the Companies Act 2006, in connection with the company's proposed [purchase]/[redemption] of... (number) [ordinary]/[preferred] shares by a payment out of capital.

---

[28] *See section 712(4) of CA 2006 for definition of "other payments lawfully made".*

Basis of opinion

We have inquired into the company's state of affairs in order to review the bases for the directors' statement.

Opinion

In our opinion the amount of £... specified in the directors' statement as the permissible capital payment for the shares to be [purchased]/[redeemed] is properly determined in accordance with sections 710 to 712 of the Companies Act 2006.

We are not aware of anything to indicate that the opinion expressed by the directors in their statement as to any of the matters mentioned in section 714(3) of the Companies Act 2006 is unreasonable in all the circumstances.

Statutory auditor   *Address*
Date

Report when a public company wishes to allot shares otherwise than for cash (section 593 of CA 2006) *Effective 1 October 2009*

66   Section 593 of CA 2006 addresses the valuation of non-cash consideration for shares in a public company. Where a public company proposes to allot shares for such non-cash consideration it must, subject to certain exceptions, obtain during the six months before the date of the allotment a report on the value of the assets to be received in payment for the shares. Sections 594 and 595 of CA 2006 set out exceptions to the valuation requirement with respect to mergers and certain "arrangements" with other companies.

67   Section 596 of CA 2006 sets out the requirements as to the valuation and the report and in particular provides that the provisions of sections 1150 to 1153 of CA 2006 should apply to the valuation and report required by section 593. Under section 1150 of CA 2006 the valuation and the report must be made by a person who:

(a) is eligible for appointment as a statutory auditor (see section 1212 of CA 2006), and
(b) meets the independence requirement in section 1151 of CA 2006.

68   However, where it appears to the valuer to be reasonable for the valuation of the consideration, or part of it, to be made by another person (an expert) the valuer may arrange for or accept such a valuation, together with a report which will enable him to make his own report.

69   If the company's own statutory auditor is requested to undertake a valuation in accordance with section 593 of CA 2006 the standards and guidance in APB Ethical Standard 5 (Revised) "Non-audit services provided to audited entities" are applied[29].

70   Guidance on the work to be carried out when relying on an expert is contained in ISA (UK and Ireland) 620 "Using the work of an expert". The expert must report to the valuer so as to enable the valuer to make its report.

---

[29] *Section 1150 of CA 2006 requires the valuation and report required by section 593 to be made by a person who is eligible for appointment as a statutory auditor and meets the independence requirements in Section 1151 of CA 2006. By virtue of section 1151(2) of CA 2006 the auditor of the company meets the independence requirements in section 1151.*

71 The valuer's report will incorporate the following elements (see Example 11 on page 38):
   (a) *Addressee* – the report is made to the company itself and sent to the company secretary for circulation to the proposed allottees.
   (b) *Introductory paragraph/s* – in addition to expressing the opinion set out in (d) below, the report must include the following information:
      (i) the nominal value of the shares to be wholly or partly paid for by the consideration in question;
      (ii) the amount of any premium payable on the shares;
      (iii) a description of the consideration;
      (iv) a description of the part of the consideration valued by the valuer, the method used to value it and the date of the valuation; and
      (v) the extent to which the nominal value of the shares and any premium are to be treated as paid up –
         - by the consideration;
         - in cash
   (c) *Basis of valuation* – the report indicates the basis of valuation of the consideration. If the valuation has been made by another person (ie an expert) the expert's name and relevant qualifications are stated in the basis of valuation. The basis of valuation also describes the part of the consideration valued by the expert, the method used to value it and specifies the date of the valuation.
   (d) *Opinion* – section 596(3) of CA 2006 requires that the valuer's report must contain, or be accompanied by, a note from the valuer, stating:
      (i) if the valuation has been made by an expert, it appears to be reasonable to arrange for it to be so made or to accept a valuation so made;
      (ii) the method of valuation of the consideration was reasonable in all the circumstances.
      (iii) there appears to have been no material change in the value of the consideration since the date at which the valuation was made; and
      (iv) on the basis of the valuation, the value of the consideration, together with any cash by which the nominal value of the shares or any premium payable on them is to be paid up, is not less than so much of the aggregate of the nominal value and the whole of any such premium as is treated as paid up by the consideration and any such cash.
   (e) *Date* – the date used is the date on which the report is signed.

72 There is no provision for the report to be qualified. Unless the opinion is unqualified the valuer does not issue a report.

73 In certain circumstances the allotment of shares may represent only a part of the consideration for the transfer of a non-cash asset to the allotting company (e.g. cash may also be paid). In such cases, the valuer's report must cover the proportion of the value of the non-cash assets which apples to the full value of shares issued (ie nominal value and any premium). The report must also state:
   (a) what valuations have been made in order to determine that proportion of the consideration;
   (b) the reason for those valuations;
   (c) the method and date of any such valuation; and
   (d) any other matters which may be relevant to that determination.

74 Before the valuer can make a statement that there appears to have been no material change in the value of the asset since the valuation, it may have to perform additional work. If the period of time between the making of the valuation and the date of the report is such that there may have been a change in the value, the valuer will need to reconsider the valuation. If the auditor made arrangements for an expert to perform

the valuation the auditor obtains written confirmation from that expert as to whether there has been a change in value.

Example 11 – Report when a public company wishes to allot shares otherwise than for cash *Effective 1 October 2009*

REPORT OF THE INDEPENDENT [VALUER] [AUDITOR] TO XYZ PLC FOR THE PURPOSES OF SECTION 593(1) OF THE COMPANIES ACT 2006

We report on the value of the consideration for the allotment to... [name of allottee] of... [number] shares, having a nominal value of [...] each, to be issued at a premium of... pence per share. The shares and share premium are to be treated as fully paid up.

The consideration for the allotment to[name of allottee] is the [freehold building situated at... address] and... [number] shares, having a nominal value of [...] each, in LMN PLC.

Basis of valuation

The freehold building was valued on the basis of its open market value by [name of expert], a Fellow of the Royal Institution of Chartered Surveyors.

The shares in LMN PLC were valued by us on... on the basis of the price shown in the Stock Exchange Daily Official List at....

Opinion

In our opinion:

- it is reasonable to accept the valuation made by (name of expert);
- the methods of valuation of the freehold building and the shares in LMN PLC were reasonable in all the circumstances; and
- there appears to have been no material change in the value of either part of the consideration since the date(s) at which the valuations were made.

On the basis of the valuations, in our opinion, the value of the total consideration is not less than the aggregate of the nominal value and share premium to be treated as paid up by the consideration.

Qualified independent person   *Address*
Date

Report when non-cash assets are transferred to a public company by certain of its members (section 599 of CA 2006) *Effective 1 October 2009*

Section 598 of CA 2006 requires, amongst other things, that during the first two years following receipt of its trading certificate[30] a public company may not lawfully

---

[30] *A trading certificate is conclusive evidence that the company is entitled to do business and exercise any borrowing powers.*

acquire from certain of its members a non-cash asset for a consideration worth one tenth or more of the company's issued share capital unless:

(a) the terms of the transfer have been approved by an ordinary resolution of the company (see section 601 of CA 2006); and
(b) a valuer's report has been made to the company within six months immediately preceding the date of the agreement to transfer the non-cash assets (see section 599 of CA 2006).

76 Under section 1150 of CA 2006 the valuation and the report must be made by a person who:

(a) is eligible for appointment as a statutory auditor (see section 1212 of CA 2006), and
(b) meets the independence requirement in section 1151 of CA 2006.

77 However, where it appears to the valuer to be reasonable for the valuation of the consideration to be made by another person (an expert) the valuer may arrange for or accept such a valuation, together with a report which will enable him to make his own report.

78 If the company's own statutory auditor is requested to undertake a valuation in accordance with section 599 of CA 2006 the standards and guidance in APB Ethical Standard 5 (Revised) "Non-audit services provided to audited entities" are applied[31].

79 Guidance on the work to be carried out when relying on an expert is contained in ISA (UK and Ireland) 620 "Using the work of an expert". The expert must report to the valuer so as to enable the valuer to make its own report.

80 Section 600 (2) of CA 2006 requires that the valuer's report must state:

(a) the consideration to be received by the company, describing the asset in question (specifying the amount to be received in cash) and the consideration to be given by the company (specifying the amount to be given in cash), and
(b) the method and date of valuation.

81 Section 600 (3) further requires that the valuer's report must contain or be accompanied by a note from the valuer stating:

(a) in the case of a valuation made by an expert that it appeared reasonable to arrange for it to be so made or to accept a valuation so made,
(b) that the method of valuation was reasonable in all the circumstances (whoever made the valuation),
(c) that it appears to the valuer that there has been no material change in the value of the consideration since the valuation, and
(d) that, on the basis of the valuation, the value of the consideration to be received by the company is not less than the value of the consideration to be given by it.

82 Sections 600(4) and (5), of CA 2006, set out the requirements where the consideration is given partly for the transfer of the asset.

83 Where the consideration, or part of it, is valued by an expert rather than the valuer the valuer's report must state that fact and also:

---

[31] *Section 1150 CA 2006 requires the valuation and report required by Section 599 to be made by a person ("the valuer") who is eligible for appointment as a statutory auditor and meets the independence requirements in section 1151 of CA 2006. By virtue of section 1151(2) of CA 2006 the auditor of the company meets the independence requirements in section 1151.*

(a) state the expert's name and what knowledge and experience the expert has to carry out the valuation, and
(b) describe the asset valued by the expert and the method used to value it specifying the date of the valuation.

The report which is illustrated in example 12 on page 42 incorporates the following elements: **84**

(a) *Addressee* – the report is made to the company itself and sent to the company secretary for circulation to the members of the company and to the person selling the asset.
(b) *Introductory Paragraphs* – in addition to expressing the opinion set out in (d) below, the report must contain the following information:
    (i) the consideration to be received by the company, describing the asset in question, and the consideration to be given by the company and specifying any amounts to be received or given in cash, and
    (ii) the method and date of valuation.
(c) *Basis of valuation* – the report indicates the basis of valuation of the consideration. If the valuation has been made by another person (ie an expert) the expert's name is stated in the basis of opinion as well as the knowledge and experience the expert has to carry out the valuation. The basis of opinion also describes the part of the consideration valued by the expert, the method used to value it and specifies the date of the valuation.
(d) *Opinion* – the valuer must state that in its opinion:
    (i) if the valuation has been made by an expert, it appears to be reasonable to accept or arrange for such a valuation;
    (ii) the method of valuation was reasonable in all the circumstances;
    (iii) there appears to have been no material change in the values of the asset in question since the date at which the valuation was made, and
    (iv) on the basis of the valuation used, the value of the consideration to be received by the company is not less than the value of the consideration to be given by the company.
(e) *Date* – the date used is that on which the report is signed.

There is no provision for the report to be qualified. Unless the opinion is unqualified the valuer does not issue a report. **85**

Before the valuer can make a statement that there appears to have been no material change in the value of the asset since the valuation, it may have to perform additional work. If the period of time between the making of the valuation and the date of the report is such that there may have been a change in the value, the valuer will need to reconsider the valuation. If the auditor made arrangements for an expert to perform the valuation the auditor obtains written confirmation from that expert as to whether there has been a change in value. **86**

Example 12 – Report when non-cash assets are transferred to a public company by certain of its members *Effective 1 October 2009*

REPORT OF THE INDEPENDENT [VALUER] [AUDITOR] TO XYZ PLC FOR THE PURPOSES OF SECTION 599 OF THE COMPANIES ACT 2006

We report on the transfer of non-cash assets to XYZ PLC ('the Company') by subscribers to the Company's memorandum of association.

The consideration to be received by the Company is a [freehold building situated at... address] ('the consideration to be received').

The consideration to be given by the Company is... [number] shares, having a nominal value of £1 each, in LMN PLC ('the consideration to be given').

Basis of valuation

The freehold building was valued on the basis of its open market value by [name of expert], a Fellow of the Royal Institution of Chartered Surveyors.

The shares in LMN PLC were valued by us on... on the basis of the price shown in the Stock Exchange Daily Official List at....

Opinion

In our opinion:

- it is reasonable to accept the valuation made by (name of expert);
- the methods of valuation of the freehold building and the shares in LMN PLC were reasonable in all the circumstances; and
- there appears to have been no material change in the value of the consideration to be received or the consideration to be given since the date(s) at which the valuations were made.

On the basis of the valuations, in our opinion, the value of the consideration to be received by the Company is not less than the value of the consideration to be given by the Company.

Qualified Independent Person   *Address*
Date

Appendix – Checklist of example reports in Bulletin 2007/1 indicating which Bulletin, or example report in this Bulletin, reflects the requirements of the Companies Act 2006

Example Report in Bulletin 2007/1 (reflecting the requirements of CA 1985)	Location of equivalent example report reflecting the requirements of CA 2006	Commencement date of report under CA 2006
1 Auditor's report on revised financial statements: revision by replacement.	Bulletin 2008/5 (Appendix 2)	Periods beginning on or after 6 April 2008
2 Auditor's report on revised financial statements: revision by supplementary note.	Bulletin 2008/5 (Appendix 3)	Periods beginning on or after 6 April 2008

Example Report in Bulletin 2007/1 (reflecting the requirements of CA 1985)	Location of equivalent example report reflecting the requirements of CA 2006	Commencement date of report under CA 2006
3 Auditor's report on revised directors' report.	Bulletin 2008/5 (Appendix 4)	Periods beginning on or after 6 April 2008
4 Report on abbreviated accounts.	Bulletin 2008/4	Periods beginning on or after 6 April 2008
5 Auditor's statement on a summary financial statement.	Bulletin 2008/3	Periods beginning on or after 6 April 2008
6 Report on entitlement to exemption from preparing group financial statements.	Requirement withdrawn in 1996	n/a
7 Statement on a company's ability to make a distribution.	Examples 1 and 2 of this Bulletin	6 April 2008
8 Statement when a private company wishes to re-register as a public company[32].	Examples 6, 7, 8 and 9 of this Bulletin	1 October 2009
9 Report on balance sheet prepared other than in respect of an accounting reference period for the purpose of a private company re-registering as a public company.	Now combined with the statement when a private company wishes to re-register as a private company (see Examples 8 and 9)	1 October 2009
10 Report when a private company wishes to redeem or purchase its own shares out of capital	Example 10 of this Bulletin	1 October 2009
11 Report when a private company wishes to provide financial assistance for the purchase of its own shares or those of its holding company.	Report no longer required under CA 2006. (Provisions under CA 1985 repealed as from 1 October 2008 in relation to financial assistance given on or after that date[33])	n/a
12 Report when a public company wishes to allot shares otherwise than for cash.	Example 11 of this Bulletin	1 October 2009

---

[32] For private companies re-registering as public companies after 6 April 2008 but before 1 October 2009, paragraph 58 of Schedule 1 to The Companies Act 2006 (Consequential Amendments etc) Order 2008 (SI No. 2008 No 948) will require references to section 264(2) of the Companies Act 1985, in Example 8 of Bulletin 2007/1, to be replaced by references to section 831 of CA 2006.

[33] The Companies Act 2006 (Commencement No. 5, Transitional Provisions and Savings) Order 2007 (SI 2007 No. 3495 (C. 150)), Schedule 4 paragraph 51.

Example Report in Bulletin 2007/1 (reflecting the requirements of CA 1985)	Location of equivalent example report reflecting the requirements of CA 2006	Commencement date of report under CA 2006
13 Report when non-cash assets are transferred to a public company by certain of its members.	Example 12 of this Bulletin	1 October 2009
14 Report on initial accounts when a public company wishes to make a distribution.	Example 3 of this Bulletin	6 April 2008
15 Report on ceasing to hold office.	Examples 4 and 5 of this Bulletin	6 April 2008

[Bulletin 2008/10]
Going concern issues during the current economic conditions

(Issued December 2008)

Contents

	Paragraphs
Introduction	1 – 7
The potential impact of the economic outlook on the directors' approach to going concern	8 – 11
Developments in corporate reporting	12 – 13
Planning	14 – 15
Considering the directors' assessment of going concern	16
Evaluating how the directors have satisfied themselves that it is appropriate to adopt the going concern basis	17 – 22
Concluding whether or not to concur with the directors' view	23 – 25
Adequacy of disclosures	26 – 28
Determining the implications for the auditor's report	29 – 40
Documentation	41
Preliminary announcements	42 – 45
Reviewing interim financial information	46 – 48
Ethical Issues	49 – 54

Appendices
1. FRC Publication: "An update for directors of listed companies: going concern and liquidity risk" *(page 17)*
2. Events or conditions that may affect going concern *(page 38)*
3. Risk factors arising from current economic conditions *(page 40)*
4. Examples of conclusions the auditor might draw *(page 42)*

Introduction

1 Current economic conditions provide particular challenges to all involved with annual reports and accounts. One consequence is expected to be an increase in the disclosures in annual reports and accounts about going concern and liquidity risk. As a result, the current conditions will present challenges for:

   (a) directors – who will need to ensure that they prepare thoroughly for their assessment of going concern and make appropriate disclosures; and
   (b) auditors – who will need to ensure that they fully consider going concern assessments and only refer to going concern in their auditor's reports when appropriate.

2 In January 2008 the Auditing Practices Board (APB) issued Bulletin 2008/1[1] to provide guidance on matters that auditors needed to consider when conducting audits in the economic environment that was, at that time, characterised as the "credit crunch".

3 Since then the economic environment has worsened and the UK and Irish economies are entering a period of recession. This economic environment leads to added uncertainty regarding:

   (a) bank lending intentions and the availability of finance more generally;
   (b) the impact of the recession on a company's own business; and
   (c) the impact of the recession on counterparties, including customers and suppliers.

These conditions will create a number of challenges for the preparers of financial statements and their auditors.

4 The effect of the current market conditions on any particular entity requires careful evaluation. However, the general economic situation at the present time does not, of itself, necessarily mean that a material uncertainty exists about an entity's ability to continue as a going concern or justify auditors modifying their auditor's reports to draw attention to going concern. The auditor makes a judgment on the need, or otherwise, to draw attention to going concern on the basis of the facts and circumstances of the entity at the time of signing the auditor's report. This Bulletin gives guidance on relevant factors to be considered and highlights certain requirements and guidance in the ISAs (UK and Ireland).

5 This Bulletin supplements Bulletin 2008/1 and in particular:

   (a) updates the list of risk factors included in that Bulletin (see appendices 2 and 3); and
   (b) provides guidance on a number of going concern issues that auditors are likely to encounter during the forthcoming reporting cycle.

This guidance draws on ISA (UK and Ireland) 570 "Going concern" and does not establish any new requirements.

6 To assist directors, the Financial Reporting Council (FRC), has published guidance entitled "An update for directors of listed companies: going concern and liquidity risk" (Update for Directors). Its purpose is to bring together existing guidance in the context of recent developments relating to going concern and liquidity risk

---

[1] *Bulletin 2008/1 "Audit Issues when Financial Market Conditions are Difficult and Credit Facilities may be Restricted".*

disclosures to assist directors, audit committees and finance teams of listed companies during the forthcoming reporting season. It is expected that this Update for Directors will also be useful to directors of unlisted companies and other entities who have similar responsibilities to assess going concern and make appropriate disclosures. This Update for Directors is attached as Appendix 1 to this Bulletin.

As with Bulletin 2008/1, this Bulletin has been written by reference to the challenges arising in relation to audits of all entities. The challenges arising in relation to audits of financial institutions such as banks, insurance companies and investment businesses give rise to additional specialist considerations that are not addressed in this Bulletin. 7

The potential impact of the economic outlook on the directors' approach to assessing going concern

Accounting standards (both IFRS and UK GAAP) require directors to: 8

(a) make an assessment of a company's ability to continue as a going concern when preparing financial statements, and
(b) disclose the uncertainties that the directors are aware of in making their assessment of going concern where those uncertainties may cast significant doubt on the company's ability to continue as a going concern.

The APB believes that the FRC's publication of the Update for Directors will assist auditors as it emphasises the need for directors to apply an appropriate degree of rigour and formality when making their judgments and suggests that directors will need to plan their assessment of going concern as early as practicable, including deciding on the information that will need to be produced (such as board papers) and the processes and procedures that will be undertaken. The Update for Directors further suggests that the directors should address the evidence to be obtained to support their conclusion and develop, where necessary, any remedial action plan. 9

To help minimise the risk of last minute surprises, the Update for Directors recommends companies have early discussions with their auditor about their plans. It also suggests that it may be useful for a draft of the relevant disclosures about going concern and liquidity risk to be prepared and discussed with the auditor before the end of the financial year. Such discussions may help the auditor plan its audit procedures and minimise the risk of the auditor qualifying its opinion on the grounds of a scope limitation or of a disagreement due to inadequate disclosure. It may also encourage the directors to develop a realistic remedial action plan where one is needed. 10

Notwithstanding early discussions between the company and its auditors both directors and auditors need to take account of subsequent developments as final assessments of going concern need to be made at the date that the directors approve the annual report and accounts taking into account the relevant facts and circumstances at that date. 11

Developments in corporate reporting

The Update for Directors describes recent developments in corporate reporting relating to: 12

(a) the disclosure of the principal risks and uncertainties facing the company in the Business Review to be included in Director's Reports; and
(b) additional disclosures relating to going concern and liquidity risk arising from changes to IFRS and UK GAAP.

13 The current squeeze on corporate cash-flows means that liquidity risk is likely to be a material risk this year for many more entities. As a consequence a greater number of companies are likely to need to present relevant disclosures concerning liquidity risk[2]. Examining the directors' processes underlying the preparation of these disclosures is likely to provide useful audit evidence for auditors with respect to the validity of the going concern assumption.

Planning

14 Risks arising from current economic circumstances are likely to impact a number of different aspects of the financial statements, for example the economic conditions may impact matters such as inventory obsolescence, goodwill impairments and cash flows, which may in turn affect whether the company is a going concern. It is important that auditor judgments on such matters are based on consistent underlying information and views.

15 Because of the significance and pervasive nature of the current economic circumstances auditors need to take account of them at all stages of forthcoming audits and in particular when:

(a) making risk assessments during the planning process and re-assessing those risks as the audit progresses;
(b) performing audit procedures to respond to assessed risks;
(c) evaluating the results of audit procedures (including as part of any engagement quality control review); and
(d) forming an opinion on the financial statements.

Considering the directors' assessment of going concern

16 ISA (UK and Ireland) 570 requires the auditor to consider the appropriateness of the directors' use of the going concern assumption in the preparation of the financial statements, and consider whether there are material uncertainties about the entity's ability to continue as a going concern that need to be disclosed in the financial statements[3]. In order to meet this requirement the auditor's procedures will comprise:

(a) evaluating the means by which the directors have satisfied themselves it is appropriate for them to adopt the going concern basis in preparing the financial statements, (see paragraphs 17 to 22);
(b) concluding whether or not they concur with the directors' view, (see paragraphs 23 to 25);
(c) assessing whether the financial statements contain adequate disclosures relating to going concern, (see paragraphs 26 to 28);
(d) determining the implications for the auditor's report on the financial statements (see paragraphs 29 to 40); and
(e) preparing appropriate documentation (see paragraph 41).

---

[2] *For IFRS, disclosures concerning liquidity risk are required by IFRS 7, IAS 1 and IAS 7. For UK GAAP, disclosures are required by FRS 18 and, where applicable, FRS 13 and FRS 29.*

[3] *Paragraphs 2 and 9 of ISA (UK and Ireland) 570.*

Evaluating how the directors have satisfied themselves that it is appropriate to adopt the going concern basis

Audit procedures that are likely to be relevant when evaluating the adequacy of the means by which the directors have satisfied themselves whether it is appropriate for them to adopt the going concern basis in preparing the financial statements include: 17

- Analysing and discussing cash flow, profit and other relevant forecasts with management.
- Reviewing the terms of loan agreements and determining whether any may have been breached.
- Reading minutes of the meetings of shareholders, those charged with governance and relevant committees for references to financing difficulties.
- Reviewing events after period end to identify those that may mitigate or otherwise affect the entity's ability to continue as a going concern[4].

When analysis of cash flow is a significant factor in considering the future outcome of future events or conditions the auditor considers: 18

(a) the reliability of the entity's information system for generating such information; and
(b) whether there is adequate support for the assumptions underlying the forecast[5].

The Update for Directors notes that one impact of current conditions may be to limit finance available from trading counterparties (including suppliers and customers) and providers of finance. Furthermore, lenders may be more risk averse when considering whether to provide or renew finance facilities and may establish new conditions and these conditions may affect the company and its trading counterparties. 19

The Update for Directors indicates that directors will need to consider carefully the position in the light of the information available to them and the assumptions as to the future availability of finance. It: 20

(a) notes that in the present economic environment, bankers may be reluctant to provide positive confirmations to the directors that facilities will continue to be available;
(b) provides a number of examples of understandable reasons for this (see paragraph 37); and
(c) concludes that the absence of bank confirmation of bank facilities does not, of itself, necessarily cast significant doubt upon the ability of an entity to continue as a going concern.

ISA (UK and Ireland) 570 requires that when events or conditions have been identified which may cast significant doubt on the entity's ability to continue as a going concern, the auditor should: 21

(a) review the directors' plans for future action based on their going concern assessment;
(b) gather sufficient appropriate audit evidence to confirm or dispel whether or not a material uncertainty exists through carrying out audit procedures considered

---

[4] Additional procedures are described in paragraph 28 of ISA (UK and Ireland) 570.

[5] Paragraph 29 of ISA (UK and Ireland) 570.

necessary, including considering the effect of any plans of the directors and other mitigating factors; and

(c) seek written representations from the directors regarding their plans for future action[6].

In general terms, the greater the risks arising from current economic circumstances the more audit evidence will be required.

22 The auditor's procedures necessarily involve a consideration of the entity's ability to continue in operational existence for the foreseeable future. In turn, that necessitates consideration both of the current and the likely future circumstances of the business and the environment in which it operates[7]. The auditor may conclude that it will be appropriate to request from the directors written representations on specific matters relating to their assumptions and plans. Such representations may usefully include confirmation as to the completeness of the information provided to the auditor regarding events and conditions relating to going concern at the date of approval of the financial statements.

Concluding whether or not to concur with the directors' view

23 Assessing the going concern assumption involves making a judgment, at a particular point in time, about the future outcome of events or conditions which are inherently uncertain. Generally, the degree of uncertainty associated with the outcome of an event or condition increases the further into the future a judgment is being made about the outcome of an event or condition. Any judgment about the future is based on available evidence and reasonable assumptions about the outcome of the future events made at the time at which the judgment is made.

24 The basis for the auditor's conclusion is the information upon which the directors have based their assessment and their reasoning[8], including, where applicable, advice obtained from external advisers including lawyers. In evaluating the assessment of the directors, the auditor considers the process they followed to make their assessment, the assumptions on which the assessment is based and their plans for future action. The auditor considers whether the assessment has taken into account all relevant information of which the auditor is aware as a result of the audit[9].

25 Where there are events or conditions that cast significant doubt on the ability of the entity to continue as a going concern, the auditor assesses the directors' plans for future action, including plans to liquidate assets, borrow money or restructure debt, reduce or delay expenditures, or increase capital.

Adequacy of disclosures

26 Developments in accounting standards, including those relating to liquidity risk, together with the current economic conditions can be expected to give rise to a

---

[6] Paragraph 26 of ISA (UK and Ireland) 570.

[7] Paragraph 9-2 of ISA (UK and Ireland) 570.

[8] Paragraph 18-3 of ISA (UK and Ireland) 570.

[9] Paragraph 20 of ISA (UK and Ireland) 570.

greater number of company annual reports and accounts containing liquidity and going-concern related disclosures.

The Update for Directors emphasises the importance, in the current economic conditions, of appropriate disclosures regarding liquidity risk and uncertainties. In its Appendix[10] it provides three illustrative examples of how directors might explain their going concern conclusion in a manner that would facilitate an understanding by readers of annual reports and accounts.

The IASB Framework notes that an essential quality of the information provided in financial statements is that it is readily understandable by users[11]. In reviewing the presentation of the disclosures the auditor considers whether the notes to the financial statements taken together with the primary financial statements present a true and fair view. The understandability of the disclosures is an important factor in determining whether the financial statements give a true and fair view.

Determining the implications for the auditor's report

ISAs (UK and Ireland) provide for a number of different auditor reports depending upon the specific facts and circumstances[12]. For example, if auditors conclude that the disclosures regarding going concern are not adequate to meet the requirements of accounting standards, including the need for financial statements to give a true and fair view, they are required either to express a qualified or adverse opinion, as appropriate. The report is also required to include specific reference to the fact that there is a material uncertainty that may cast significant doubt about the entity's ability to continue as a going concern[13].

If the auditor concludes that a material uncertainty exists that leads to significant doubt about the ability of the entity to continue as a going concern, and those uncertainties have been adequately disclosed in the financial statements, it is required to modify its report by including an emphasis of matter paragraph[14].

The current economic circumstances are likely to increase the level of uncertainty existing when the directors make their judgment about the outcome of future events or conditions. However, whilst the effect of current market conditions on individual entities requires careful evaluation, it should not be assumed that the general economic situation at the present time in itself means that a material uncertainty, which casts significant doubt on the ability of the entity to continue as a going concern, exists. Nor are extensive disclosures necessarily indicative of the existence of a

---

[10] *See page 35 of this Bulletin.*

[11] *In UK GAAP, Chapter 1 of the Statement of Principles for financial reporting states that "the objective of financial statements is to provide information about the reporting entity's financial performance and position that is useful to a wide range of users for assessing the stewardship of the entity's management and for making economic decisions".*

[12] *See Appendix 4.*

[13] *Paragraph 34 of ISA (UK and Ireland) 570.*

[14] *Paragraph 31 of ISA (UK and Ireland) 700 requires "The auditor should modify the auditor's report by adding a paragraph to highlight a material matter regarding a going concern problem". Whereas, ISA (UK and Ireland) 570 uses the term "material uncertainty relating to the event or condition that may cast significant doubt on the entity's ability to continue as a going concern". The term used in ISA (UK and Ireland) 570 is equivalent to the term "material matter regarding a going concern problem" used in ISA (UK and Ireland) 700.*

significant doubt on the entity's ability to continue as a going concern. Indeed an objective of the disclosures may be to explain why the going concern issues that affect the company do not give rise to a significant doubt.

32   What constitutes a material uncertainty that may cast significant doubt on the entity's ability to continue as a going concern is a judgment involving not only

(a) the nature and materiality of the events or conditions giving rise to uncertainty; but also:
(b) the ability of the entity to adopt strategies that mitigate the uncertainty.

Nature and materiality of the events or conditions

33   Accounting standards do not define what constitutes a "material uncertainty". However, determining whether a "material uncertainty" exists involves assessing:

(a) the likelihood of events or conditions occurring; and
(b) their impact.

Assessment of these elements may require a high degree of judgment both by the directors and subsequently by the auditors depending upon the individual circumstances of the company and/or group.

34   Examples of possible events or conditions which may give rise to business risks, that individually or collectively may cast significant doubt about the going concern assumption are set out in ISA (UK and Ireland) 570 paragraph 8[15], these include:

- A net liability or current liability position.
- Negative operating cash flows.
- Fixed-term borrowings approaching maturity without realistic prospects of renewal or repayment, or excessive reliance on short-term borrowings to finance long-term assets.
- Major debt repayment falling due where refinancing is necessary to the entity's continued existence.
- Inability to comply with the terms of loan agreements or to pay creditors on due dates.
- Loss of a major market, franchise, license or principal supplier.

A list of other possible events and conditions that may affect the auditor's assessment of going concern are set out in Appendix 2.

35   A factor listed in ISA (UK and Ireland) 570 is that necessary borrowing facilities have not been agreed. In examining borrowing facilities the auditor could decide, for example, that it is necessary:

(a) to obtain confirmations of the existence and terms of bank facilities; and
(b) to make its own assessment of the intentions of the bankers relating thereto.

This latter assessment could involve the auditor examining written evidence or making notes of meetings which it would hold with the directors and, where appropriate, with the directors and the entity's bankers.

36   As discussed in paragraph 20(a), in the present economic environment bankers may be reluctant to confirm to entities or their auditors that facilities will be renewed.

---

[15] *That paragraph also notes that the existence of one or more of the factors does not always signify that a material uncertainty that casts significant doubt on the entity's ability to continue as a going concern exists.*

This reluctance may extend to companies with a profitable business and relatively small borrowing requirements. The lack of a positive confirmation from a bank does not of itself provide evidence of a material uncertainty that casts significant doubt on the entity's ability to continue as a going concern. Auditors seek to differentiate between circumstances where the lack of a confirmation reflects the existence of a material matter regarding going concern (which, therefore, falls to be emphasised in the auditor's report) and increased caution on the part of bankers that is not indicative of a material matter regarding going concern (and which, therefore, does not fall to be emphasised in the auditor's report).

There may be a number of reasons why a bank may be reluctant to confirm that a facility will be available in the future, which would not be a material matter regarding going concern, including: 37

- The bank responding that in the current economic environment, as a matter of policy, it is not providing such confirmations to its customers or their auditors.
- The entity and its bankers are engaged in negotiations about the terms of a facility (e.g. the interest rate), and where there is no evidence that the bank is reluctant to lend to the company.
- The bank renewed a rolling facility immediately prior to the date of the issuance of the annual report and accounts and is reluctant to go through the administrative burden to confirm that the facility will be renewed on expiry.

However, if the auditor concludes that an entity's bankers may be refusing to confirm facilities for reasons that are specific to the entity the auditor considers the significance of this and, where appropriate, discusses with the directors whether there are alternative strategies or sources of financing that would enable the financial statements to be prepared on the going concern basis. 38

Ability to adopt alternative strategies that mitigate an uncertainty

The adverse factors described in paragraph 34 may be mitigated by other favourable factors. For example, the effect of an entity being unable to make its debt repayments from operating cash flows may be counterbalanced by management's plans to maintain adequate cash flows by alternative means, such as by disposal of assets, rescheduling of loan repayments, or obtaining additional capital. Similarly the loss of a principal supplier may be mitigated by the availability of another suitable source of supply. Where an entity contends that it has alternative strategies to overcome any adverse factors the auditor assesses the effectiveness of such strategies and the ability of management to execute them. 39

If the auditor, in assessing the alternative strategies, considers that they: 40

(a) are realistic;
(b) have a reasonable expectation of resolving any problems foreseen; and
(c) that the directors are likely to put the strategies into place effectively[16],

the auditor may decide that it is unnecessary to include an emphasis of matter paragraph in the auditor's report[17].

[16] Paragraph 20-1 of ISA (UK and Ireland) 570.

[17] Paragraph 26(b) of ISA (UK and Ireland) 570.

Documentation

41 ISA (UK and Ireland) 230 (Revised) "Audit Documentation" requires the auditor to prepare audit documentation so as to enable an experienced auditor, having no previous connection with the audit, to understand significant matters arising during the audit and the conclusions reached thereon. Significant matters include, amongst other things, findings that could result in a modification to the auditor's report. With respect to going concern, it is important, therefore, that the auditor documents its knowledge of conditions and events at the date of the auditor's report, and its reasoning with respect to the conclusions it has drawn.

Preliminary announcements

42 While preliminary announcements are no longer mandatory for listed companies, where a preliminary announcement is issued the directors are required by the Listing Rules to have agreed it with the auditor prior to publication.

43 The Listing Rules require that preliminary announcements "include any significant additional information necessary for the purposes of assessing the results being announced". An example of such information may be the disclosures that the directors propose to make in the annual report and accounts explaining their rationale for adopting the going concern basis in the annual accounts and setting out the uncertainties that they have considered in making their assessment.

44 Under both the UK and Irish Listing Rules a preliminary announcement is required to give details of the nature of any likely modification that may be contained in the auditor's report on the full financial statements. Under the Listing Rules modified auditor's reports encompass auditor's reports that contain an emphasis of matter paragraph. This would include a paragraph highlighting a material uncertainty relating to an event or condition that may cast significant doubt on the entity's ability to continue as a going concern.

45 Before agreeing to a preliminary announcement, therefore, the auditor assesses
   (a) whether the directors have given adequate prominence to significant additional information concerning going concern[18]; and
   (b) the adequacy of the directors' disclosure, within the announcement, of any likely modification relating to going concern that may be contained in the auditor's report.

Reviewing interim financial information

46 International Standard on Review Engagements (ISRE) (UK and Ireland) 2410 "Review of Interim Financial Information Performed by the Independent Auditor of the Entity", establishes standards and provides guidance on the auditor's professional responsibilities when the auditor undertakes an engagement to review interim financial information of an audit client and on the form and content of the report.

47 If, as a result of enquiries or other review procedures, a material uncertainty relating to an event or condition comes to the auditor's attention that may cast significant doubt on the entity's ability to continue as a going concern, and adequate disclosure

---

[18] *Guidance for auditors on preliminary announcements is set out in Bulletin 2008/2 "The auditor's association with preliminary announcements made in accordance with the requirements of the UK and Irish Listing Rules".*

is made in the interim financial information the auditor modifies its review report by adding an emphasis of matter paragraph.

However, if a material uncertainty that casts significant doubt about the entity's ability to continue as a going concern is not adequately disclosed in the interim financial information, the auditor is required by ISRE 2410 to express a qualified or adverse conclusion as appropriate. In such circumstances the report is required to include specific reference to the fact that there is such a material uncertainty.

Ethical issues

The APB's Ethical Standards (ESs) are based on a "threats and safeguards approach" whereby auditors identify and assess the circumstances which could adversely affect the auditor's objectivity ("threats"), including any perceived loss of independence, and apply procedures ("safeguards"), which will either eliminate the threat or reduce it to an acceptable level, that is a level at which it is not probable that a reasonable and informed third party would conclude that the auditor's objectivity is impaired or is likely to be impaired.

In the current circumstances, where financial market conditions are difficult and credit facilities may be restricted, auditors need to be particularly alert to the possibility of self-review, management or advocacy threats arising from the provision of non-audit services in relation to a refinancing or restructuring that might jeopardise their objectivity and independence.

Examples of engagements that the audit firm may be requested to undertake in the current economic environment and which may give rise to threats to the auditor's independence and objectivity include:

- Undertaking a review of the business with a view to advising the audited entity on restructuring options.
- Advising on forecasts or projections, for presentation to lenders and other stakeholders, including assumptions.
- Advising the audited entity on how to fund its financing requirements, including debt restructuring programmes.

When such work is undertaken a threat arises from the risk that the audit team may not review objectively the work undertaken in relation to going concern for audit purposes. Accordingly, where audit firms (and, in particular, members of the audit team) do undertake such engagements, consideration should be given to safeguards such as:

- A review of the going concern assessment and the conclusion reached by a partner or other senior staff member with appropriate expertise who is not a member of the audit team.
- Additional procedures undertaken as part of an Engagement Quality Control Review.

ES 5 (Revised) states that it is unlikely that safeguards can eliminate a threat or reduce it to an acceptable level:

(a) in the absence of 'informed management' (paragraph 27 of ES 5 (Revised)) and
(b) when the non-audit service would require the auditors to act as advocates for the entity in relation to matters that are material to the Financial Statements (paragraph 30 of ES 5 (Revised)).

54 Consequently, where an audit firm is engaged to provide advice to assist an entity it audits to demonstrate that it is a going concern, the audit firm ensures that the entity has "informed management"[19] capable of taking responsibility for the decisions to be made, thereby reducing the risk that the audit firm may be regarded as taking management decisions for the entity concerned. If the audit firm attends meetings with the entity's bank or other interested parties it takes particular care to avoid assuming responsibility for the entity's proposals or being regarded as negotiating on behalf of the entity or advocating the appropriateness of the proposals such that its independence is compromised.

---

[19] *'ES – Provisions Available for Small Entities'* provides exemptions relating to informed management for auditors of small entities.

APPENDIX 1

FINANCIAL REPORTING COUNCIL

AN UPDATE FOR DIRECTORS OF LISTED COMPANIES:
GOING CONCERN AND LIQUIDITY RISK

NOVEMBER 2008

Contents

		Page
One	Introduction	19
Two	Accounting requirements with respect to going concern	22
Three	Going concern review period	27
Four	Insolvency	28
Five	Disclosures relevant to going concern and liquidity risk	29
Six	Preliminary announcements	34
Appendix – Examples of going concern disclosures		35

One – Introduction

1. Current economic conditions provide particular challenges to all involved with annual reports and accounts. One consequence is expected to be an increase in the disclosures in annual reports and accounts about going concern and liquidity risk. As a result the current conditions will present challenges for all of the parties involved:

    - directors will need to ensure that they prepare thoroughly for their assessment of going concern and make appropriate disclosures;
    - auditors will need to ensure that they fully consider going concern assessments and only refer to going concern in their audit reports when appropriate; and
    - investors and lenders will need to be prepared to read all of the relevant information in annual reports and accounts before making decisions.

2. The purpose of this document is to bring together existing guidance in the context of recent developments relating to going concern and liquidity risk disclosures to assist directors, audit committees and finance teams of listed companies during the forthcoming reporting season. It does not establish any new requirements but it does highlight the importance of clear disclosure about going concern and liquidity risk in current economic conditions. This update may also be useful for directors of unlisted companies who have similar responsibilities to assess going concern and make appropriate disclosures.

3. Going concern is a fundamental accounting concept that underlies the preparation of the annual report and accounts of all UK companies. Under both International Financial Reporting Standards (IFRS) and UK Generally Accepted Accounting Principles (UK GAAP) directors are required to satisfy themselves that it is reasonable for them to conclude that it is appropriate to prepare financial statements on a going concern basis. These requirements are not intended to, and do not, guarantee that a company will remain a going concern until the next annual report and accounts is issued.

4. Both IFRS and UK GAAP require disclosure of the uncertainties that the directors are aware of in making their assessment of going concern where those uncertainties may cast significant doubt on the group's and company's ability to continue as a going concern.

5. The economic conditions being faced by many companies will necessitate careful consideration by directors when assessing whether it is reasonable for them to use the going concern basis of accounting, and whether adequate disclosure has been given of going concern risks and other uncertainties. Addressing these challenges well before the preparation of annual reports and accounts may help avoid a last minute problem that might unsettle investors and lenders unnecessarily.

6. Directors will need to plan their assessment of going concern as early as practicable including deciding on the information and analysis that will need to be produced (such as board papers) and the processes and procedures that will be undertaken. These plans should also address the evidence to be

obtained to support their conclusion and develop, where necessary, any remedial action plan.

7. Early discussions with company auditors about these plans may help minimise the risk of last minute surprises, and it may be helpful for a draft of the relevant disclosures about going concern and liquidity risk to be prepared and discussed with the auditors before the end of the financial year.

8. The Financial Reporting Council (FRC) published a consultation document on "Going concern and financial reporting: proposals to revise the guidance for directors of listed companies" (the 2008 Consultation) at the beginning of September 2008. Responses to the 2008 Consultation were due on 24 November 2008. The FRC anticipates that an exposure draft will be issued towards the end of the first quarter next year and will not become effective before mid 2009.

9. The FRC would welcome further feedback on the practical challenges of applying the existing guidance "Going concern and financial reporting: guidance for directors of listed companies registered in the United Kingdom" (the 1994 Guidance), before the end of February 2009.

10. In the meantime the FRC believes that the existing guidance contained in the 1994 Guidance is fit for purpose even in these times of significant economic stress. This guidance can be found on the FRC website at: *http://www.frc.org.uk/corporate/goingconcern.cfm*.

11. The 1994 Guidance indicates that directors may seek confirmation from their bankers regarding the existence and status of their finance arrangements. In the present economic environment bankers may be reluctant to provide positive confirmation that facilities will continue to be available. The absence of confirmations of bank facilities does not of itself necessarily cast significant doubt upon the ability of an entity to continue as a going concern nor necessarily require auditors to refer to going concern in their reports.

12. The effect of current market conditions on individual entities requires careful evaluation. The general economic situation at the present time does not of itself necessarily mean that a material uncertainty exists about a company's ability to continue as a going concern. However, it is important that annual accounts contain appropriate disclosure of liquidity risk and uncertainties such as are necessary in order to give a true and fair view.

13. Examples illustrating how directors might explain their going concern conclusion taking account of current economic conditions which would facilitate an understanding by readers of annual reports and accounts are included in the appendix to this update.

14. The FRC has recently conducted a study of going concern and liquidity risk disclosures made by companies applying IFRS 7 (Financial instruments: Disclosures) in December 2007 and March 2008 year end annual reports and accounts. The study concluded that there are significant opportunities for improvement by way of better, rather than more, disclosure. In particular, it noted that there was often a significant lack of clarity about how liquidity

risk is managed in practice and that much of the relevant information was distributed amongst different parts of annual reports, making it difficult for users to appreciate the full picture.

Two – Accounting requirements with respect to going concern

15. Going concern is a fundamental accounting concept that underlies the preparation of financial statements of all UK companies.

16. Preparing financial statements on a going concern basis is not compatible with the intention or the necessity of a company:

    - entering into a scheme of arrangement with the company's creditors;
    - making an application for an administration order; or
    - being placed into administrative receivership or liquidation.

Assessment of going concern

17. International Accounting Standard (IAS) 1 (Presentation of financial statements) and UK Financial Reporting Standard (FRS) 18 (Accounting policies) require management/directors to make an assessment of an entity's ability to continue as a going concern when preparing financial statements. IAS 1.25 states:

    > "When preparing financial statements, management shall make an assessment of an entity's ability to continue as a going concern. An entity shall prepare financial statements on a going concern basis unless management either intends to liquidate the entity or to cease trading, or has no realistic alternative but to do so. When management is aware, in making its assessment, of material uncertainties related to events or conditions that may cast significant doubt upon the entity's ability to continue as a going concern, the entity shall disclose those uncertainties."[20]

21. For financial reporting purposes, the assessment of going concern is made at the date that the directors approve the annual report and accounts and takes into account the relevant facts and circumstances at that date. IAS 1.26 also notes that the degree of consideration that may need to be given to the going concern assessment will depend upon the facts of each case.

22. The Listing Rules of the Financial Services Authority also require that the annual reports of listed companies include a statement by the directors that the business is a going concern, together with supporting assumptions or qualifications as necessary, that has been prepared in accordance with the 1994 Guidance.

23. The Directors statement on going concern is required to be prepared in accordance with the 1994 Guidance which outlines procedures that the directors may wish to adopt in making their assessment. The 1994 Guidance addresses both annual and interim accounts. In relation to the latter directors of listed companies will also need to consider the requirements of IAS 34 (Interim financial reporting).

24. The procedures that are necessary for the directors to comply with the requirements of IAS 1 or FRS 18 are likely to be similar to those adopted to

---

[20] *Similar provision is made by FRS 18 paragraphs 21-25.*

meet their obligations under the Listing Rules. The 1994 Guidance places particular emphasis on the importance of the processes and procedures that directors carry out and highlights some major areas in which procedures are likely to be appropriate, including:

- forecasts and budgets;
- borrowing requirements;
- liability management;
- contingent liabilities;
- products and markets;
- financial risk management;
- other factors; and
- financial adaptability.

25. The 1994 Guidance notes that this list is not exhaustive and the significance of factors will vary from company to company. In the current economic climate many of these factors will have increased in significance which will require directors to consider them with more rigour and formality.

26. In forming their conclusion on going concern directors will need to evaluate which of three potential outcomes is appropriate to the specific circumstances of the group and company. The directors may conclude:

- there are no material uncertainties that lead to significant doubt upon the entity's ability to continue as a going concern;
- there are material uncertainties that lead to significant doubt upon the entity's ability to continue as a going concern; or
- the use of the going concern basis is not appropriate.

27. In addition to the assessment that must be made by directors, auditors are required by auditing standards to determine if, in the auditors' judgment, a material uncertainty exists that may cast significant doubt on the entity's ability to continue as a going concern.

28. Auditing standards provide for a number of different audit reports depending upon the specific facts and circumstances. Auditors may conclude that it is necessary to qualify their opinion, disclaim an opinion, issue an adverse opinion or modify their report by including an emphasis of matter paragraph.

29. Auditors are required to consider the disclosures about going concern and liquidity risk made in the financial statements. If auditors conclude that the disclosures are not adequate to meet the requirements of accounting standards, including the need for financial statements to give a true and fair view, they are required to qualify their opinion and to provide their reasons for doing so. If auditors conclude that a material uncertainty exists that leads to significant doubt about the ability of the entity to continue as a going concern, and those uncertainties have been adequately disclosed in the

financial statements, they are required to modify their report by including an emphasis of matter paragraph.

30. The combination of these requirements will generally result in one of the following three outcomes:

Outcome	Consequence for the directors' statement on going concern	Consequence for the auditors' report
No material uncertainties leading to significant doubt about going concern have been identified by the directors.	Disclosure explaining the conclusion on going concern and how that has been reached. Examples 1 and 2 in the attached appendix illustrate this outcome.	Unmodified report (clean) – provided the auditors concur with the directors' assessment and supporting disclosures.
Material uncertainties leading to significant doubt about going concern have been identified by the directors.	Disclosures explaining the specific nature of the material uncertainties and explaining why the going concern basis has still been adopted. Example 3 in the attached appendix illustrates this outcome.	Modified report including an emphasis of matter paragraph highlighting the existence of material uncertainties – provided auditors concur with the directors' assessment and supporting disclosures.
The directors conclude that the going concern basis is not appropriate.	Disclosures explaining the basis of the conclusion and the accounting policies applied in drawing up financial statements on a non-going concern basis.	Unmodified report (clean) – provided that the accounts contain the necessary disclosures and the auditors consider the basis to be appropriate to the specific facts and circumstances.

31. The 1994 Guidance also provides for disclosure when directors conclude that the going concern basis should be used despite having identified factors which cast doubt on the ability of the company to continue in existence for the foreseeable future. Significant changes to disclosure requirements about risks and uncertainties in IFRS, UK GAAP and the Companies Act 2006 (the Act) since 1994 may mean that sufficient disclosure of the factors giving rise to the problem will have been provided through these disclosures (see paragraphs 40 to 49).

32. One impact of current conditions may be to limit finance available from trading counterparties including suppliers, customers and providers of finance. Furthermore, lenders may be more risk averse when considering whether to provide or renew finance facilities and may establish new conditions and these conditions may affect the company and the group and their trading counterparties.

33. In relation to bank and other facilities, paragraphs 30 to 32 of the 1994 Guidance may assist:

> 30. The facilities available to the company should be reviewed and compared to the detailed cash flow forecasts for the period to the next balance sheet date, as a minimum. Sensitivity analyses on the critical assumptions should also be used in the comparison. The directors should seek to ensure that there are no anticipated:
>
> - shortfalls in facilities against requirements;
> - arrears of interest; or
> - breaches of covenants.
>
> 31. The directors have responsibility to manage borrowing requirements actively. Any potential deficits, arrears or breaches should be discussed with the company's bankers in order to determine whether any action is appropriate. This may prevent potential problems crystallising. The onus is on the directors to be satisfied that there are likely to be appropriate and committed financing arrangements in place.
>
> 32. The directors may seek confirmation from their bankers regarding the existence and status of any finance arrangements which the company has entered into.

34. Directors will need to consider carefully the position in the light of the information available to them and the assumptions as to the future availability of finance. Accounting standards do not define what constitutes a 'material uncertainty that may cast significant doubt upon the entity's ability to continue as a going concern'. This involves assessing both the probability of an event occurring and the impact it will have if it does occur. Assessment of these elements may require a high degree of judgment both by the directors, and subsequently by the auditors depending upon individual company and group circumstances.

35. In the present economic environment bankers may be reluctant to provide positive confirmations to the directors that facilities will continue to be available. This reluctance may extend to companies with a profitable business and relatively small borrowing requirements. There may be a number of understandable reasons why a bank may be reluctant to confirm that a facility will be available in the future including:

    - the bank responding that in the current economic environment, as a matter of policy, it is not providing such confirmations to its customers;
    - the entity and its bankers are engaged in negotiations about the terms of a facility (e.g. the interest rate), however there is no evidence that the bank is reluctant to lend to the company; and
    - the bank renewed a rolling facility immediately prior to the date of the issuance of the annual report and accounts and is reluctant to go through the administrative burden to confirm that the facility will be renewed again in a year's time.

36. The absence of confirmations of bank facilities does not of itself necessarily cast significant doubt upon the ability of an entity to continue as a going concern nor require necessarily auditors to refer to going concern in their reports.

Three – Going concern review period

37. IFRS contains specific requirements about the period which directors are required to review when assessing going concern. IAS 1.26 provides that management should take into account all available information about the future, which is at least, but not limited to, twelve months from the end of the reporting period.

38. FRS 18 requires disclosure if the period considered by the directors is less than twelve months from the date of approval of the financial statements.

39. Directors should consider the 1994 Guidance which provides that budgets and forecasts should be prepared to cover the period to the next balance sheet date as a minimum and notes that further periods are generally covered by medium or long-term plans which give an indication in general terms of how the directors expect the company to fare. The guidance also notes that the assessment is based on what is known to the directors at the date on which they approve the annual report and accounts which includes events or circumstances of which they are aware that arise after the end of the review period.

40. Where the period considered by the directors has been limited, for example, to a period of less than twelve months from the date of the approval of the annual report and accounts, the directors need to consider whether additional disclosures are necessary to explain adequately the assumptions that underlie the adoption of the going concern basis.

41. Auditing standards also address going concern and the period of the review by the directors. Auditors have an explicit obligation to include an extra paragraph in their audit report if the period covered by the directors' review is less than twelve months from the date of approval of the annual report and accounts and this fact is not disclosed by the directors.

Four – Insolvency

42. Doubts upon the ability of a company to remain a going concern do not necessarily mean that the company is, or is likely to become, insolvent. The solvency of a company is determined by reference to a comparison of its assets and liabilities and by its ability to meet liabilities as they fall due. Where the directors are unable to state that the going concern basis is appropriate, they should consider taking professional advice.

Five – Disclosures relevant to going concern and liquidity risk

Disclosure requirements of the Listing Rules about going concern

43. The Listing Rules require that the annual reports of listed companies include a statement by the directors that the business is a going concern, together with supporting assumptions or qualifications as necessary.

44. The 1994 Guidance notes that if there are doubts as to the appropriateness of the going concern presumption then the annual accounts may need to reflect any relevant factors in greater detail if they are to show a true and fair view. The guidance also notes that when there are factors which, in the event of an unfavourable outcome, cast doubt on the appropriateness of the going concern presumption, the directors should explain the circumstances so as to identify the factors which give rise to the problems (including any external factors outside their control which may affect the outcome) and an explanation of how they intend to deal with the problem so as to resolve it.

Disclosure requirements of IFRS and UK GAAP about going concern and liquidity risk

45. IAS 1 and FRS 18 have explicit disclosure requirements in the event that the directors conclude that there are material uncertainties that may cast significant doubt upon the entity's ability to continue as a going concern. In addition, in recent years there have also been significant changes to specific accounting standards that are relevant to disclosures about liquidity risk and other risks and uncertainties including:

Requirement	IFRS Reference (2008)	UK GAAP (2007/8)
Disclosures relating to risks arising from financial instruments, including liquidity risk where it is material.	IFRS 7 paragraphs 31 to 42	FRS 29 paragraphs 31 to 42
Estimating future cash flows (in connection with impairment of intangible assets).	IAS 36 paragraphs 33 to 54	FRS 11 paragraphs 36 to 40
Disclosure of undrawn borrowing facilities and any restrictions such as covenant requirements, where relevant.	IAS 7 paragraph 50 (a)	No explicit requirement
Disclosure of defaults and covenant breaches and potential reclassification of loans in default as current liabilities.	IAS 1 paragraphs 74 to 76	No explicit requirement
Disclosure of key sources of estimation uncertainty about the carrying amounts of assets and liabilities.	IAS 1 paragraphs 125 to 133	FRS 18 paragraphs 50 to 55

IFRS liquidity risk disclosures

46. Liquidity risk is the risk that an entity will encounter difficulty in meeting its obligations associated with financial liabilities. IFRS 7 (FRS 29) requires an

entity to make both qualitative and quantitative disclosures concerning liquidity risk, where it is a material financial risk.

47. Where liquidity risk is material, IFRS 7 (FRS 29) requires:

    - disclosure of information that enables users to evaluate the nature and extent of the entity's exposure to liquidity risk;
    - narrative disclosures explaining how liquidity risk arises in the business and how it is managed in practice;
    - summary numerical data about liquidity risk based on the information that is provided to key management personnel, often the Board of Directors; and
    - certain mandatory disclosures such as a maturity analysis of financial liabilities.

48. The disclosures required by IFRS 7 are supplemented by disclosures required by other IFRS standards. For example, IAS 7 (Statement of cash flows) requires disclosure of undrawn borrowing facilities where relevant to users understanding of the financial position and liquidity of the entity, whilst IAS 1 requires disclosure of defaults and breaches of loan terms and conditions.

49. The current squeeze on corporate cash flows means that liquidity risk is likely to be a material risk this year for many more entities. As a consequence, a greater number of companies are likely to need to present relevant disclosures as required by IFRS 7 (FRS 29), IAS 1, IAS 7 and FRS 18.

Disclosure requirements of the Companies Act 2006 related to Directors' Reports

50. The Act requires the Directors' Report of all companies (except companies subject to the small companies' regime) to include a Business Review.

51. The Business Review is required to be a balanced and comprehensive analysis of the development and performance of the business of the company during the financial year and the position of the company at the end of that year, consistent with the size and complexity of the business. In particular it should include a description of the principal risks and uncertainties facing the company.

52. In the case of a quoted company, the Business Review is also required to provide information on a number of other matters including:

    - the main trends and factors likely to affect the future development, performance or position of the company's business; and
    - information about persons with whom the company has contractual or other arrangements which are essential to the business of the company.

53. Directors will need to explain in the Business Review the principal risks and uncertainties facing the company arising from the current difficult economic conditions. One of the purposes of the Business Review is to help the members assess how the directors have performed their duties so it is

reasonable to expect that it will also contain an account of how the directors intend to respond to these risks and uncertainties. Issues which may require disclosure depend upon individual facts and circumstances and may include:

- uncertainties about current financing arrangements (whether committed or uncommitted);
- potential changes in financing arrangements such as critical covenants and any need to increase borrowing levels ;
- risks arising from current credit arrangements (including the availability of insurance where relevant) with either customers or suppliers;
- a dependency on key suppliers and customers ; and
- uncertainties posed by the potential impact of the economic outlook on business activities.

54. The Act also requires auditors to review the Directors' Report and to state in their report whether the information given in the Directors' Report is consistent with the financial statements. Auditing standards provide guidance for auditors on how they should carry out this work.

FRC review of going concern and liquidity risk disclosures

55. The FRC has published a study into going concern and liquidity risk disclosures in the financial statements of listed companies that have adopted IFRS 7. The study can be obtained from the FRC http://www.frc.org.uk/corporate/goingconcern.cfm. The study notes that information about going concern and liquidity risk was distributed amongst a number of different parts of the annual report and accounts reviewed, thus making it difficult for users to determine and evaluate the extent to which liquidity concerns were relevant to the business and how liquidity risk was being managed in practice.

56. The study concluded that it would be particularly helpful if all of these disclosures could be brought together into a single section of a company's annual reports and accounts.

57. If it is not practical to provide the information in a single section, the study recommends that the key disclosures be brought together by way of a note including cross references to help readers of annual reports and accounts to find all of the relevant pieces of information.

58. It would be useful if such a note included the following components:

- Paragraph 1 explaining cash and borrowing positions and how liquidity risk is managed in practice.
- Paragraph 2 explaining whether confirmation of the renewal of banking and other facilities has been sought and if so whether those confirmations have been obtained[21].

---

[21] See paragraphs 29 to 33.

- Paragraph 3 stating that the use of the going concern basis of accounting is appropriate and explaining the basis of that conclusion.

22. Examples illustrating these disclosures are included in the appendix to this update.

23. The FRC study also concluded that, while in general information about cash balances, borrowings and facilities was provided on a comprehensive basis, the level of detail about how liquidity risk was managed in practice and the information used by key management to monitor liquidity risk varied greatly. In particular:

- For many companies, the disclosures were generic rather than specific in nature. Only a minority of companies provided information that shed light on how the business managed its day to day cash flow and borrowing levels.

- A conclusion could not be reached on whether appropriate disclosure had been made of summarised data about liquidity risk as provided to key management personnel (generally the directors). Reaching such a conclusion would have required access to internal company documentation.

Six – Preliminary announcements

24. Preliminary announcements of annual results form one of the focal points for investor interest, primarily because they confirm or update market expectations. Under the Listing Rules such announcements are voluntary, although if made their contents are subject to minimum requirements. Where a company chooses to publish a preliminary announcement the directors are required by the Listing Rules to have agreed the preliminary announcement with their auditor prior to publication.

25. The Listing Rules provide that, if a preliminary announcement is made, it should give details of the nature of any likely modification that may be contained in the auditor's report required to be included with the annual report and accounts. Modified audit reports encompass audit reports that:

    - are qualified;
    - express an adverse opinion;
    - express a disclaimer of opinion; or
    - contain an emphasis of matter paragraph (including a paragraph highlighting a material matter regarding a going concern problem).

Appendix – examples of going concern disclosures

The purpose of this appendix is merely to illustrate the principles in paragraph 55 in bringing together going concern and liquidity risk disclosures. In practice such disclosures should be specific to the individual circumstances of each company.

> **Example 1** – A group with significant positive bank balances, uncomplicated circumstances and little or no exposure to uncertainties in the current economic environment which may impact the going concern assumption.
>
> The group's business activities, together with the factors likely to affect its future development, performance and position are set out in the Business Review on pages X to Y. The financial position of the group, its cash flows, liquidity position and borrowing facilities are described in the Chief Financial Officer's Review on pages P to Q. In addition note A to the financial statements includes the group's objectives, policies and processes for managing its capital; its financial risk management objectives; details of its financial instruments and hedging activities; and its exposures to credit risk and liquidity risk.
>
> The group has considerable financial resources together with long-term contracts with a number of customers and suppliers across different geographic areas and industries. As a consequence, the directors believe that the group is well placed to manage its business risks successfully despite the current uncertain economic outlook.
>
> After making enquiries, the directors have a reasonable expectation that the company and the group have adequate resources to continue in operational existence for the foreseeable future. Accordingly, they continue to adopt the going concern basis in preparing the annual report and accounts.

Example 2 – A group with uncomplicated circumstances, some exposure to the current economic uncertainties and either a current material bank overdraft or loan and a need to renew this facility in the foreseeable future albeit not imminently.

Paragraph similar to example 1, paragraph 1.

As highlighted in note B to the financial statements, the group meets its day to day working capital requirements through an overdraft facility which is due for renewal on [date]. The current economic conditions create uncertainty particularly over (a) the level of demand for the group's products; (b) the exchange rate between sterling and currency X and thus the consequence for the cost of the group's raw materials; and (c) the availability of bank finance in the foreseeable future.

The group's forecasts and projections, taking account of reasonably possible changes in trading performance, show that the group should be able to operate within the level of its current facility. The group will open renewal negotiations with the bank in due course and has at this stage not sought any written commitment that the facility will be renewed. However, the group has held discussion with its bankers about its future borrowing needs and no matters have been drawn to its attention to suggest that renewal may not be forthcoming on acceptable terms.

Paragraph as per example 1, paragraph 3.

Example 3 – A group with complicated circumstances, considerable exposure to the current economic uncertainties and either a current material bank overdraft or loan which requires renewal and perhaps an increase in the year ahead.

Paragraph as example 1, paragraph 1.

As described in the directors' report on page X the current economic environment is challenging and the group has reported an operating loss for the year. The directors' consider that the outlook presents significant challenges in terms of sales volume and pricing as well as input costs. Whilst the directors have instituted measures to preserve cash and secure additional finance, these circumstances create material uncertainties over future trading results and cash flows.

As explained on page X, the directors are seeking to sell a property to provide additional working capital. The group is in negotiations with a potential purchaser but there can be no certainty that a sale will proceed. Based on negotiations conducted to date the directors have a reasonable expectation that it will proceed successfully, but if not the group will need to secure additional finance facilities.

As explained in the Business Review on Page Y, the group's has commenced discussions with its bankers about an additional facility that may prove to be necessary should the sale of the property not proceed or should material adverse changes in sales volumes or margins occur. It is likely that these discussions will not be completed for some time. The directors are also pursuing alternative sources of funding in case an additional facility is not forthcoming, but have not yet secured a commitment.

The directors have concluded that the combination of these circumstances represent a material uncertainty that casts significant doubt upon the group's and the company's ability to continue as a going concern. Nevertheless after making enquiries, and considering the uncertainties described above, the directors have a reasonable expectation that the group and the company have adequate resources to continue in operational existence for the foreseeable future. For these reasons, they continue to adopt the going concern basis in preparing the annual report and accounts.

Appendix 2 – Events or Conditions That May Affect Going Concern

Possible events and conditions that may affect the auditor's assessment of going concern are listed below:

- Obtaining external finance:
  - Entity has experienced difficulties in the past in obtaining external finance facilities and/or complying with the related terms and covenants.
  - Borrowing agreements or executory contracts include clauses relating to debt covenants or subjective clauses (e.g. a "material adverse change clause") that trigger repayment.
  - Entity has breached some of the terms or covenants giving rise to the risk that the facilities may be withdrawn or not renewed.
  - Finance facilities are due for renewal in the next year.
  - Management have no plans for alternative arrangements should current facilities not be extended.
  - Finance facility is secured on assets (e.g. properties) that have decreased in value below the amount of the facility.
  - There are significant doubts about the financial strength of the entity's bankers.
  - Financing is provided by a syndicate of banks and other financial institutions and there are concerns about the viability of one or more of the members of the syndicate.
- Management plans to overcome financing difficulties include disposal of assets or possible rights issues:
  - Plans developed prior to current market conditions have not been updated or stress tested.
  - Lack of evidence that management can realise the assets at the values arising from planned disposals or obtain the support of shareholders in relation to a rights issue.
- Entity provides significant loans or guarantees:
  - Guarantees that may be called in.
  - Borrowers who may be unable to make payments.
- Entity dependent on guarantees provided by another party:
  - Guarantor no longer able/prepared to provide the guarantee.
- Future cash flows:
  - Reduction in cash flows resulting from unfavourable economic conditions.
  - Customers taking longer/unable to pay.
  - Terms or covenants of renewed financing are changed and become more difficult to comply with (e.g. increased interest rates or charges).
  - Entity is subject to margin calls as a result of a decrease in fair market value of financial instruments that it holds.
  - Entities have issued loans (or received borrowings) having an introductory period during which favourable terms are in force which revert to normal market rates in the forthcoming year.
- Entity heavily dependent on counterparties such as suppliers and customers:
  - Suppliers facing financial difficulties provide essential goods/services.
  - Entity unable to find alternative suppliers.

Appendix 3 – Risk Factors Arising From Current Economic Conditions

This Appendix identifies some factors that may increase the risk of material misstatement in financial statements during the current economic conditions, other than in relation to going concern.

Fair Values:

- Entity needs to change valuation model and/or management's assumptions to reflect current market conditions.
- Active market no longer exists, requiring use of a model for valuation purposes.
- Inputs to a model are not based on observable market inputs but rather are based on the entity's own data.
- Impairment of non-financial assets held at fair value (e.g. properties).
- Suspension of external valuation indices triggering a need for alternative valuation approaches.
- Entity uses an external pricing service for fair value measurements that needs to change its valuation model and/or assumptions to reflect current market conditions.
- Entity does not have necessary expertise to undertake valuations.
- Recent amendments to GAAP (IAS 39, IFRS 7, FRS 26 and FRS 29) may require or permit the reclassification of certain financial assets.

Impairments:

- Impairments of assets other than those held at fair value (e.g. need for increased doubtful debt provisions because previously reliable customers may not be able to pay their debts when due).
- Stock obsolescence resulting from significant decreases in demand for certain types of product.
- Impairment of the carrying amount of purchased goodwill.
- Increasing discount rates used in impairment calculations because capital has become more expensive.
- Effect on impairment calculations of subsequent events, in particular those relating to counterparties.
- Current credit market conditions may lead to the triggering of acceleration clauses which may lead to the impairment of financial assets.

Current versus non-current classification:

- Current market conditions may bring into question the classification of assets and liabilities as current or non-current. (For example the re-classification of liabilities as a result of a breach of loan covenants).

Revenue Recognition:

- Current credit market conditions may make it more difficult to demonstrate that the revenue recognition criteria, in (IAS 18/FRS 5) have been met.

Pensions:

- Pension obligations of an entity increased by reduction in value of assets in a related defined benefits pension scheme.
- Effect of illiquid investments and decreases in expected rates of return on investments.

Hedging:

- Hedging arrangements no longer effective when a derivative counterparty is experiencing financial difficulty or, more generally due to widening credit spreads on the derivative counterparty.
- In current market conditions, hedge effectiveness may have failed for the current period either because it is no longer probable that a derivative counterparty will meet its obligations, or because counterparty credit spreads have increased substantially, or because of the effect of changes in inter-bank lending rates on fair value interest rate hedges.

Insurance:

- The ability of an insurance company providing credit insurance to meet claims.

Deferred income taxes:

- If a company is reporting losses or is exposed to future losses there may be a need for a valuation allowance for deferred tax assets.

Appendix 4 – Examples of conclusions the auditor might draw

Auditor's report	Circumstances	Example modified audit reports[22]
	Auditor agrees with the directors' assessment	
Clean	Preparing the financial statements on the going concern basis is appropriate, the going concern and liquidity disclosures are adequate and there are no material uncertainties that cast significant doubt on the entity's ability to continue as a going concern. (See examples 1 and 2 in the appendix to the Update for Directors)	n/a

[22] *References are to the examples in Appendix 3 to Bulletin 2006/6 'Auditor's Reports on Financial Statements in the United Kingdom'*

Auditor's report	Circumstances	Example modified audit reports
Modified by inclusion of emphasis of matter paragraph[23]	Preparing the financial statements on the going concern basis is appropriate but there are material uncertainties described in the financial statements that cast significant doubt on the entity's ability to continue as a going concern. (See example 3 in the appendix to the Update for Directors)	Example 1
	Auditor disagrees with the directors' assessment	
Qualified opinion	Preparing the financial statements on the going concern basis is appropriate but there are material uncertainties that cast significant doubt on the entity's ability to continue as a going concern that are not adequately described in the financial statements	Example 5
Adverse opinion	The financial statements have been prepared on the going concern basis but the auditor has concluded that using the going concern basis is inappropriate.	–
	The directors refuse to undertake, or extend, an assessment of going concern	
Disclaimer of opinion	Where the directors' refusal either to undertake or to extend an assessment of going concern results in the auditor being unable to form an opinion on whether the financial statements give a true and fair view as the scope of the audit has been limited because the directors' consideration of going concern is completely inadequate.	Example 7

In all cases, if the period used by the directors in making their assessment of going concern is less than one year from the date of approval of the financial statements, and they have not disclosed that fact in the financial statements, the auditor is required by paragraph 31 4 of ISA (UK and Ireland) 570 to do so within the auditor's report.

---

[23] *ISA (UK and Ireland) 700 Paragraph 34 notes that in extreme cases, such as situations involving multiple uncertainties that are significant to the financial statements, the auditor may consider it appropriate to express a disclaimer of opinion.*

[Bulletin 2009/1]
Auditor's Reports – Supplementary guidance for auditors of charities with 31 March 2009 year ends

(Issued March 2009)

Contents

	Paragraphs
Introduction	*1 - 17*

Illustrative examples of auditor's reports on charities' financial statements

Example 1 – charitable company registered only in England and Wales, audited under the Companies Act 1985

Example 2 – small charitable company registered only in England and Wales, audited under the Charities Act 1993

Example 3 – charitable company registered in Scotland (can also be used for cross-border charitable companies registered in Scotland and England and Wales)

Example 4 – non-company charity registered only in England and Wales

Example 5 – non-company charity registered only in Scotland

Example 6 – charitable company group registered in Scotland, whose consolidated financial statements are required to be prepared and audited under the Companies Act 1985 (can also be used for large cross border charity groups audited under the Companies Act 1985)

- make no reference to the Trustees' Annual Report in the scope of the true and fair view opinion,
- do not include in the opinion a positive statement that the Trustees' Annual Report is consistent with the financial statements. However for these charities auditors will comment in their report where they are aware of inconsistencies.

Illustrative examples

Illustrative examples 1 to 5 address charitable companies and non-company charities. Particular features of these examples are set out in the table below.

	Audit requirement				Accounts drawn up under			Address to members or trustees?
	Companies Act 1985	Charities Act 1993 S43	Charities and Trustee Investment (Scotland) Act 2005 S44 (1) (c)	Companies Act 1985	Charities Act 1993 S42	Charities and Trustee Investment (Scotland) Act 2005 S44(1)(b)	
England & Wales only							
Charitable company. (unless Trustees of small charitable company elect not to be audited under the Companies Act 1985) (Example 1)	✓			✓			Members
Small charitable company audited under the Charities Act 1993. (Example 2)		✓		✓			Trustees
Non-company charity (Example 4)		✓			✓		Trustees
Scotland only							
Charitable company (unless Trustees of small charitable company elect not to be audited under the Companies Act 1985) (Example 3)	✓		✓	✓		✓	Members & Trustees

	Audit requirement			Accounts drawn up under			Address to members or trustees?
	Companies Act 1985	Charities Act 1993 S43	Charities and Trustee Investment (Scotland) Act 2005 S44 (1) (c)	Companies Act 1985	Charities Act 1993 S42	Charities and Trustee Investment (Scotland) Act 2005 S44(1)(b)	
Small charitable company audited under the Charities and Trustee Investment (Scotland) Act 2005 (Example 3)			✓			✓	Trustees
Non-company charity (Example 5)			✓			✓	Trustees
Dual registered England & Wales and Scotland							
Charitable company (unless Trustees of small charitable company elect not to be audited under the Companies Act 1985) (Example 3)	✓		✓	✓		✓	Members & Trustees
Small company where Trustees elect not to be audited under the Companies Act 1985 (Example 3)		✓	✓	✓		✓	Trustees
Non-company charity		✓	✓		✓	✓	Trustees

14 In order to avoid excessive length, the differing requirements under each type of legislation are set out in the footnotes to the illustrative auditor's reports. The auditor will need to select the appropriate disclosures for the charity using the table above and the footnotes to the individual examples.

15 APB hopes that the examples included in this Bulletin will address the most usual situations encountered, however the inter-relationship between company and charity law is complex and for some types of charity other legal requirements may apply.

16 In particular the examples do not deal with the special features of the auditor's report associated with:

- Charities adopting the FRSSE
- Charities preparing their accounts on a receipts and payments basis
- Industrial and Provident Societies
- Friendly Societies
- Audit reports by auditors appointed by the Charity Commission
- National Health Service Charities
- Exempt charities

17 Charitable company groups add further complexities. Example 6 illustrates an auditor's report for a larger charitable company group registered in Scotland audited under the Companies Act 1985. However there can be further issues related to the audit of small and medium sized groups headed by a charitable company. For example in England and Wales, the Charities Act 2006 (Charitable Companies Audit and Group Accounts Provisions) Order 2008, which requires parent charitable companies of small and medium sized groups to prepare consolidated financial statements, also requires the audit of these consolidated financial statements to be conducted under the Charities Act 1993. Therefore, unless the charitable parent company elects for exemption from audit under the Companies Act 1985, then the group accounts will be audited under both the Companies Act 1985 and the Charities Act 1993.

Illustrative examples of auditor's reports on charities' financial statements

Example 1: Charitable company registered only in England and Wales, audited under the Companies Act 1985

INDEPENDENT AUDITOR'S REPORT TO THE MEMBERS OF XYZ CHARITY LIMITED

We have audited the financial statements of (name of charity) for the year ended 31 March 2009 which comprise [state primary financial statements such as the Statement of Financial Activities, the Summary Income and Expenditure Account, the Balance Sheet, the Cash Flow Statement] and the related notes. The financial statements have been prepared under the accounting policies set out therein.

Respective responsibilities of trustees and auditors

The trustees' (who are also the directors of the company for the purposes of company law) responsibilities for preparing the Trustees' Annual Report[6] and the financial statements in accordance with applicable law and United Kingdom Accounting Standards (United Kingdom Generally Accepted Accounting Practice) are set out in the Statement of Trustees' Responsibilities.

Our responsibility is to audit the financial statements in accordance with relevant legal and regulatory requirements and International Standards on Auditing (UK and Ireland).

We report to you our opinion as to whether the financial statements give a true and fair view and are properly prepared in accordance with the Companies Act 1985 and whether the information given in the Trustees' Annual Report is consistent with those financial statements.

We also report to you if, in our opinion, the charity has not kept proper accounting records, if we have not received all the information and explanations we require for our audit, or if information specified by law regarding trustees' remuneration and transactions with the charity is not disclosed.

[We read other information contained in the Annual Report[7], and consider whether it is consistent with the audited financial statements. The other information comprises only [list all documents published with the financial statements such as the Chairman's Statement and the Trustees' Annual Report]. We consider the implications for our report if we become aware of any apparent misstatements or material inconsistencies with the financial statements. Our responsibilities do not extend to other information[8].]

OR

---

[6] Use the actual title of the document which in some cases may be referred to as the Directors' Report.

[7] Use the title of the document issued by the charity containing the audited financial statements.

[8] This paragraph is used where the financial statements are published with surround information in addition to the Trustees' Annual Report.

[We read the Trustees' Annual Report and consider the implications for our report if we become aware of any apparent misstatements within it[9].]

Basis of audit opinion

We conducted our audit in accordance with International Standards on Auditing (UK and Ireland) issued by the Auditing Practices Board. An audit includes examination, on a test basis, of evidence relevant to the amounts and disclosures in the financial statements. It also includes an assessment of the significant estimates and judgements made by the trustees in the preparation of the financial statements, and of whether the accounting policies are appropriate to the charity's circumstances, consistently applied and adequately disclosed.

We planned and performed our audit so as to obtain all the information and explanations which we considered necessary in order to provide us with sufficient evidence to give reasonable assurance that the financial statements are free from material misstatement, whether caused by fraud or other irregularity or error. In forming our opinion we also evaluated the overall adequacy of the presentation of information in the financial statements.

Opinion

In our opinion

- the financial statements give a true and fair view, in accordance with United Kingdom Generally Accepted Accounting Practice, of the state of affairs of the charity as at 31 March 2009, and of its incoming resources and application of resources, including its income and expenditure, for the year then ended;
- the financial statements have been properly prepared in accordance with the Companies Act 1985; and
- the information given in the Trustees' Annual Report is consistent with the financial statements.

[Name of firm]
Registered Auditors
[Town/City]
Date:

---

[9] *This paragraph is used where the financial statements are not published with surround information other than the Trustees' Annual Report.*

Example 2: Small charitable company registered only in England and Wales, audited under the Charities Act 1993

INDEPENDENT AUDITOR'S REPORT TO THE TRUSTEES OF XYZ CHARITY LIMITED

We have audited the financial statements of (name of charity) for the year ended 31 March 2009 which comprise the [state primary financial statements such as the Statement of Financial Activities, the Summary Income and Expenditure Account, the Balance Sheet, the Cash Flow Statement] and the related notes. The financial statements have been prepared under the accounting policies set out therein.

Respective responsibilities of trustees and auditors

The trustees' (who are also the directors of the company for the purposes of company law) responsibilities for preparing the Trustees' Annual Report[10] and the financial statements in accordance with applicable law and United Kingdom Accounting Standards (United Kingdom Generally Accepted Accounting Practice) are set out in the Statement of Trustees' Responsibilities.

The trustees have elected for the financial statements not to be audited in accordance with the Companies Act 1985. Accordingly we have been appointed as auditors under section 43 of the Charities Act 1993 and report in accordance with regulations made under section 44 of that Act.

Our responsibility is to audit the financial statements in accordance with relevant legal and regulatory requirements and International Standards on Auditing (UK and Ireland).

We report to you our opinion as to whether the financial statements give a true and fair view and are properly prepared in accordance with the Companies Act 1985. We also report to you if, in our opinion, the information given in the Trustees' Annual Report is not consistent with those financial statements, if the charity has not kept proper accounting records, if the charity's financial statements are not in agreement with these accounting records or if we have not received all the information and explanations we require for our audit.

[We read other information contained in the Annual Report[11], and consider whether it is consistent with the audited financial statements. The other information comprises only [list all documents published with the financial statements such as the Chairman's Statement and the Trustees' Annual Report]. We consider the implications for our report if we become aware of any apparent misstatements or material inconsistencies with the financial statements. Our responsibilities do not extend to other information[12].]

OR

---

[10] Use the actual title of the document which in some cases may be referred to as the Directors' Report.

[11] Use the title of the document issued by the charity containing the audited financial statements.

[12] This paragraph is used where the financial statements are published with surround information in addition to the Trustees' Annual Report.

[We read the Trustees' Annual Report and consider the implications for our report if we become aware of any apparent misstatements within it[13].]

Basis of audit opinion

We conducted our audit in accordance with International Standards on Auditing (UK and Ireland) issued by the Auditing Practices Board. An audit includes examination, on a test basis, of evidence relevant to the amounts and disclosures in the financial statements. It also includes an assessment of the significant estimates and judgements made by the trustees in the preparation of the financial statements, and of whether the accounting policies are appropriate to the charity's circumstances, consistently applied and adequately disclosed.

We planned and performed our audit so as to obtain all the information and explanations which we considered necessary in order to provide us with sufficient evidence to give reasonable assurance that the financial statements are free from material misstatement, whether caused by fraud or other irregularity or error. In forming our opinion we also evaluated the overall adequacy of the presentation of information in the financial statements.

Opinion

In our opinion:

- the financial statements give a true and fair view, in accordance with United Kingdom Generally Accepted Accounting Practice, of the state of affairs of the charity as at 31 March 2009, and of its incoming resources and application of resources, including its income and expenditure, for the year then ended; and
- the financial statements have been properly prepared in accordance with the Companies Act 1985.

[Name of firm]
Registered Auditors
[Town/City]
Date:

---

[13] *This paragraph is used where the financial statements are not published with surround information other than the Trustees' Annual Report.*

Example 3: Charitable company registered in Scotland (can also be used for cross border charitable companies registered in Scotland and England and Wales)

INDEPENDENT AUDITOR'S REPORT TO THE TRUSTEES AND MEMBERS[14] OF XYZ CHARITY LIMITED

We have audited the financial statements of (name of charity) for the year ended 31 March 2009 which comprise [state primary financial statements such as the Statement of Financial Activities, the Summary Income and Expenditure Account, the Balance Sheet, the Cash Flow Statement] and the related notes. The financial statements have been prepared under the accounting policies set out therein.

Respective responsibilities of trustees and auditors

The trustees' (who are also the directors of the company for the purposes of company law) responsibilities for preparing the Trustees' Annual Report[15] and the financial statements in accordance with applicable law and United Kingdom Accounting Standards (United Kingdom Generally Accepted Accounting Practice) are set out in the Statement of Trustees' Responsibilities.

Option 1: This paragraph to be used for charitable companies audited under the Companies Act 1985

We have been appointed auditors under section 44(1)(c) of the Charities and Trustee Investment (Scotland) Act 2005 and under the Companies Act 1985 and report to you in accordance with those Acts.

Option 2: This paragraph to be used for charitable companies electing for audit exemption under the Companies Act 1985

The trustees have elected for the financial statements not to be audited in accordance with the Companies Act 1985. Accordingly we have been appointed auditors under section 44(1)(c) of the Charities and Trustee Investment (Scotland) Act 2005 [and under the Charities Act 1993][16] and report to you in accordance with that/those Act(s).

Our responsibility is to audit the financial statements in accordance with relevant legal and regulatory requirements and International Standards on Auditing (UK and Ireland).

We report to you our opinion as to whether the financial statements give a true and fair view and are properly prepared in accordance with the Companies Act 1985, the Charities and Trustee Investment (Scotland) Act 2005 and Regulation 8 of the

---

[14] Refer to members and trustees unless the charity has elected for audit exemption under the Companies Act 1985, then refer to just the trustees.

[15] Use the actual title of the document which in some cases may be referred to as the Directors' Report.

[16] This should only be included for cross border charitable companies registered in Scotland and England and Wales.

Charities Accounts (Scotland) Regulations 2006 [and whether the information given in the Trustees' Annual Report is consistent with those financial statements][17].

We also report to you if, in our opinion, [the information given in the Trustees Annual Report is not consistent with those financial statements, if][18] the charity has not kept proper accounting records, if the charity's financial statements are not in agreement with these accounting records, if we have not received all the information and explanations we require for our audit, [or if information specified by law regarding trustees' remuneration and transactions with the charity is not disclosed][19].

[We read other information contained in the Annual Report[20], and consider whether it is consistent with the audited financial statements. The other information comprises only [list all documents published with the financial statements such as the Chairman's Statement and the Trustees' Annual Report]. We consider the implications for our report if we become aware of any apparent misstatements or material inconsistencies with the financial statements. Our responsibilities do not extend to other information[21].]

OR

[We read the Trustees' Annual Report and consider the implications for our report if we become aware of any apparent misstatements within it[22].]

Basis of audit opinion

We conducted our audit in accordance with International Standards on Auditing (UK and Ireland) issued by the Auditing Practices Board. An audit includes examination, on a test basis, of evidence relevant to the amounts and disclosures in the financial statements. It also includes an assessment of the significant estimates and judgements made by the trustees in the preparation of the financial statements, and of whether the accounting policies are appropriate to the charity's circumstances, consistently applied and adequately disclosed.

We planned and performed our audit so as to obtain all the information and explanations which we considered necessary in order to provide us with sufficient evidence to give reasonable assurance that the financial statements are free from material misstatement, whether caused by fraud or other irregularity or error. In forming our opinion we also evaluated the overall adequacy of the presentation of information in the financial statements.

[17] *This should be included where the charity has not elected for exemption from audit under the Companies Act 1985.*

[18] *This should only be included where the charity has elected for exemption from audit under the Companies Act 1985.*

[19] *This should only be included where the charity has not elected for exemption from audit under the Companies Act 1985.*

[20] *Use the title of the document issued by the charity containing the audited financial statements.*

[21] *This paragraph is used where the financial statements are published with surround information in addition to the Directors'/Trustees' Annual Report.*

[22] *This paragraph is used where the financial statements are not published with surround information other than the Directors'/Trustees' Annual Report.*

Opinion

In our opinion

- the financial statements give a true and fair view, in accordance with United Kingdom Generally Accepted Accounting Practice, of the state of affairs of the charity as at 31 March 2009, and of its incoming resources and application of resources, including its income and expenditure, for the year then ended;
- the financial statements have been properly prepared in accordance with the Companies Act 1985, the Charities and Trustee Investment (Scotland) Act 2005 and regulation 8 of the Charities Accounts (Scotland) Regulations 2006; and
- [the information given in the Trustees' Annual Report is consistent with the financial statements.[23]]

[Name of firm]
Eligible to act as an auditor in terms of section 25 of the Companies Act 1989
Registered Auditors [Town/City]
Date:

---

[23] *Not required for audits conducted solely under charity law.*

Example 4: Non-company charity registered only in England and Wales

INDEPENDENT AUDITOR'S REPORT TO THE TRUSTEES OF XYZ CHARITY

We have audited the financial statements of (name of charity) for the year ended 31 March 2009 which comprise [state primary financial statements such as the Statement of Financial Activities, the Balance Sheet, the Cash Flow Statement] and the related notes. The financial statements have been prepared under the accounting policies set out therein.

Respective responsibilities of trustees and auditors

The trustees' responsibilities for preparing the Trustees' Annual Report and the financial statements in accordance with applicable law and United Kingdom Accounting Standards (United Kingdom Generally Accepted Accounting Practice) are set out in the Statement of Trustees' Responsibilities.

We have been appointed as auditors under section 43 of the Charities Act 1993 and report in accordance with regulations made under that Act. Our responsibility is to audit the financial statements in accordance with relevant legal and regulatory requirements and International Standards on Auditing (UK and Ireland).

We report to you our opinion as to whether the financial statements give a true and fair view and are properly prepared in accordance with the Charities Act 1993. We also report to you if, in our opinion, the information given in the Trustees' Annual Report is not consistent with those financial statements, if the charity has not kept sufficient accounting records, if the charity's financial statements are not in agreement with these accounting records or if we have not received all the information and explanations we require for our audit.

[We read the other information contained in the Annual Report[24], and consider whether it is consistent with the audited financial statements. The other information comprises only [list all documents published with the financial statements such as the Chairman's Statement and the Trustees' Annual Report]. We consider the implications for our report if we become aware of any apparent misstatements or material inconsistencies with the financial statements. Our responsibilities do not extend to other information[25].]

OR

[We read the Trustees' Annual Report and consider the implications for our report if we become aware of any apparent misstatements within it[26].]

---

[24] Use title of the document issued by the charity containing the audited financial statements.

[25] This paragraph is used where the financial statements are published with surround information in addition to the Trustees' Annual Report.

[26] This paragraph is used where the financial statements are not published with surround information other than the Trustees' Annual Report.

Basis of audit opinion

We conducted our audit in accordance with International Standards on Auditing (UK and Ireland) issued by the Auditing Practices Board. An audit includes examination, on a test basis, of evidence relevant to the amounts and disclosures in the financial statements. It also includes an assessment of the significant estimates and judgements made by the trustees in the preparation of the financial statements, and of whether the accounting policies are appropriate to the charity's circumstances, consistently applied and adequately disclosed.

We planned and performed our audit so as to obtain all the information and explanations which we considered necessary in order to provide us with sufficient evidence to give reasonable assurance that the financial statements are free from material misstatement, whether caused by fraud or other irregularity or error. In forming our opinion we also evaluated the overall adequacy of the presentation of information in the financial statements.

Opinion

In our opinion
- the financial statements give a true and fair view, in accordance with United Kingdom Generally Accepted Accounting Practice, of the state of affairs of the charity as at 31 March 2009, and of its incoming resources and application of resources, for the year then ended; and
- the financial statements have been properly prepared in accordance with the Charities Act 1993.

[Name of firm]
Registered Auditors
[Town/City]
Date:

Example 5: Non-company charity registered only in Scotland

INDEPENDENT AUDITOR'S REPORT TO THE TRUSTEES OF XYZ CHARITY

We have audited the financial statements of (name of charity) for the year ended 31 March 2009 which comprise [state primary financial statements such as the Statement of Financial Activities, the Balance Sheet, Cash Flow Statement] and the related notes. These financial statements have been prepared under the accounting policies set out therein.

Respective responsibilities of trustees and auditors

The trustees' responsibilities for preparing the Trustees' Annual Report and the financial statements in accordance with applicable law and United Kingdom Accounting Standards (United Kingdom Generally Accepted Accounting Practice) are set out in the Statement of Trustees' Responsibilities.

We have been appointed as auditors under section 44(1)(c) of the Charities and Trustee Investment (Scotland) Act 2005 and report in accordance with regulations made under that Act. Our responsibility is to audit the financial statements in accordance with relevant legal and regulatory requirements and International Standards on Auditing (UK and Ireland).

We report to you our opinion as to whether the financial statements give a true and fair view and are properly prepared in accordance with the Charities and Trustee Investment (Scotland) Act 2005 and regulation 8 of the Charities Accounts (Scotland) Regulations 2006.

We also report to you if, in our opinion the information given in the Trustees' Annual Report is not consistent with the financial statements, if the charity has not kept proper accounting records, if the charity's financial statements are not in agreement with these accounting records or if we have not received all the information and explanations we require for our audit.

[We read the other information contained in the Annual Report[27], and consider whether it is consistent with the audited financial statements. The other information contains only [list all documents published with the financial statements such as the Chairman's Statement and the Trustees' Annual Report]. We consider the implications for our report if we become aware of any apparent misstatements or material inconsistencies with the financial statements. Our responsibilities do not extend to other information[28].]

OR

[We read the Trustees' Annual Report and consider the implications for our report if we become aware of any apparent misstatements within it[29].]

---

[27] Use title of the document issued by the charity containing the audited financial statements.

[28] This paragraph is used where the financial statements are published with surround information in addition to the Trustees' Annual Report.

[29] This paragraph is used when the financial statements are not published with surround information other than the Trustees' Annual Report.

Basis of audit opinion

We conducted our audit in accordance with International Standards on Auditing (UK and Ireland) issued by the Auditing Practices Board. An audit includes examination, on a test basis, of evidence relevant to the amounts and disclosures in the financial statements. It also includes an assessment of the significant estimates and judgments made by the trustees in the preparation of the financial statements, and of whether the accounting policies are appropriate to the charity's circumstances, consistently applied and adequately disclosed.

We planned and performed our audit so as to obtain all the information and explanations which we considered necessary in order to provide us with sufficient evidence to give reasonable assurance that the financial statements are free from material misstatement, whether caused by fraud or other irregularity or error. In forming our opinion we also evaluated the overall adequacy of the presentation of information in the financial statements.

Opinion

In our opinion:
- the financial statements give a true and fair view, in accordance with United Kingdom Generally Accepted Accounting Practice, of the state of affairs of the charity as at 31 March 2009 and of its incoming resources and application of resources, for the year then ended; and
- the financial statements have been properly prepared in accordance with the Charities and Trustee Investment (Scotland) Act 2005 and regulation 8 of the Charities Accounts (Scotland) Regulations 2006.

[Name of firm]
Registered Auditors
Eligible to act as an auditor in terms of section 25 of the Companies Act 1989
[Town/City]
Date:

Example 6: Charitable company group registered in Scotland, whose consolidated financial statements are required to be prepared and audited under the Companies Act 1985 (can also be used for large cross-border charity groups audited under the Companies Act 1985)

INDEPENDENT AUDITOR'S REPORT TO THE MEMBERS AND TRUSTEES OF XYZ CHARITY LIMITED

We have audited the group and parent company financial statements of (name of charity) for the year ended 31 March 2009 which comprise [state primary financial statements such as the Consolidated Statement of Financial Activities, the Consolidated Summary Income and Expenditure Account, the Consolidated and parent company Balance Sheets, the Consolidated Cash Flow Statement] and the related notes. These financial statements have been prepared under the accounting policies set out therein.

Respective responsibilities of trustees and auditors

The trustees' (who are also the directors of the company for the purposes of company law) responsibilities for preparing the Trustees' Annual Report[30] and the financial statements in accordance with applicable law and United Kingdom Accounting Standards (United Kingdom Generally Accepted Accounting Practice) are set out in the Statement of Trustees' Responsibilities.

We have been appointed auditors under the Companies Act 1985 and under section 44(1)(c) of the Charities and Trustee Investment (Scotland) Act 2005 and report to you in accordance with those Acts.

Our responsibility is to audit the financial statements in accordance with relevant legal and regulatory requirements and International Standards on Auditing (UK and Ireland).

We report to you our opinion as to whether the financial statements give a true and fair view and are properly prepared in accordance with the Companies Act 1985, the Charities and Trustee Investment (Scotland) Act 2005 and regulations 6 and 8 of the Charities Accounts (Scotland) Regulations 2006. We also report to you whether in our opinion the information given in the Trustees' Annual Report is consistent with the financial statements.

In addition we report to you if, in our opinion, the charity has not kept proper accounting records, if the charity's financial statements are not in agreement with these accounting records, if we have not received all the information and explanations we require for our audit, or if information specified by law regarding trustees' remuneration and transactions with the charity and other members of the group is not disclosed.

[We read the other information contained in the Annual Report[31], and consider whether it is consistent with the audited financial statements. The other information comprises only [list all documents published with the financial statements such as the Chairman's Statement and the Trustees' Annual Report]. We consider the implications for our report if we become aware of any apparent misstatements or material

---

[30] *Use the actual title of the document which in some cases may be referred to as the Directors' Report.*

[31] *Use the title of the document issued by the charity containing the audited financial statements.*

inconsistencies with the financial statements. Our responsibilities do not extend to other information[32].]

OR

[We read the Trustees' Annual Report and consider the implications for our report if we become aware of any apparent misstatements within it[33].]

Basis of audit opinion

We conducted our audit in accordance with International Standards on Auditing (UK and Ireland) issued by the Auditing Practices Board. An audit includes examination, on a test basis, of evidence relevant to the amounts and disclosures in the financial statements. It also includes an assessment of the significant estimates and judgments made by the trustees in the preparation of the financial statements, and of whether the accounting policies are appropriate to the group's and the charitable parent company's circumstances, consistently applied and adequately disclosed.

We planned and performed our audit so as to obtain all the information and explanations which we considered necessary in order to provide us with sufficient evidence to give reasonable assurance that the financial statements are free from material misstatement, whether caused by fraud or other irregularity or error. In forming our opinion we also evaluated the overall adequacy of the presentation of information in the financial statements.

Opinion

In our opinion:
- the group financial statements give a true and fair view, in accordance with United Kingdom Generally Accepted Accounting Practice, of the state of the group's affairs as at 31 March 2009 and of the group's incoming resources and application of resources, including its income and expenditure, for the year then ended;
- the parent charitable company financial statements give a true and fair view, in accordance with United Kingdom Generally Accepted Accounting Practice, of the state of the parent charitable company's affairs as at 31 March 2009;
- the financial statements have been properly prepared in accordance with the Companies Act 1985, the Charities and Trustee Investment (Scotland) Act 2005 and regulations 6 and 8 of the Charities Accounts (Scotland) Regulations 2006; and
- the information given in the Trustees' Annual Report is consistent with the financial statements.

[Name of firm]
Registered Auditors
Eligible to act as an auditor in terms of section 25 of the Companies Act 1989
[Town/City]
Date:

---

[32] This paragraph is used where the financial statements are published with surround information in addition to the Trustees' Annual Report.

[33] This paragraph is used where the financial statements are not published with surround information other than the Trustees' Annual Report.

[Bulletin 2009/2]
Auditor's reports on financial statements in the United Kingdom

(Issued April 2009)

Contents

Introduction

Description of the "Scope of an Audit"

Alternative presentation options of the financial statements of a group

Omitting the Parent Company Profit and Loss Account

Opinion in respect of an additional financial reporting framework

Modifying the auditor's report on the financial statements

Modifying the auditor's opinion on the Directors' Report

Illustrative Directors' Responsibilities Statement

Appendix 1 *Unmodified auditor's reports where company does not prepare group financial statements*
1. Non-publicly traded company preparing financial statements under the FRSSE
2. Non-publicly traded company preparing financial statements under UK GAAP
3. Publicly traded company preparing financial statements under UK GAAP
4. Publicly traded company preparing financial statements under IFRSs as adopted by the European Union

Appendix 2 *Unmodified auditor's reports where group and parent company financial statements reported on in a single auditor's report*
5. Non-publicly traded group preparing financial statements under UK GAAP
6. Publicly traded group – Parent company financial statements prepared under UK GAAP
7. Publicly traded group – Parent company financial statements prepared under IFRSs as adopted by the European Union

Appendix 3 *Unmodified auditor's report on group financial statements reported on separately from the parent company financial statements*
8. Publicly traded group – Auditor's report on group financial statements prepared under IFRSs as adopted by the European Union

Appendix 4 *Unmodified auditor's reports on parent company financial statements reported on separately from the group financial statements*
9. Publicly traded group – Auditor's report on parent company financial statements prepared under UK GAAP
10. Publicly traded group – Auditor's report on parent company financial statements prepared under IFRSs as adopted by the European Union

Appendix 5 *Modified auditor's reports – Emphasis of matter paragraphs*

11. Emphasis of matter: Material uncertainty that may cast significant doubt about the company's ability to continue as a going concern
12. Emphasis of matter: Possible outcome of a lawsuit

Appendix 6   Modified auditor's reports – Qualified opinion on financial statements
13. Qualified opinion: Disagreement – Inappropriate accounting treatment of debtors
14. Qualified opinion: Disagreement – Non-disclosure of a going concern problem
15. Qualified opinion: Scope Limitation – Auditor not appointed at the time of the stocktake
16. Qualified opinion: Scope Limitation – Directors did not prepare cash flow forecasts sufficiently far into the future to be able to assess the going concern status of the company

Appendix 7   Modified auditor's reports – Adverse opinion on financial statements
17. Adverse opinion: No provision made for losses expected to arise on long term contracts
18. Adverse opinion: Significant level of concern about going concern status that is not disclosed in the financial statements

Appendix 8   Modified auditor's reports – Disclaimer of opinion on financial statements
19. Disclaimer of opinion: Auditor unable to attend stocktake and confirm trade debtors
20. Disclaimer of opinion: Multiple uncertainties

Appendix 9   Descriptions of the "Scope of an Audit" that may be cross referenced from auditor's reports
- UK Publicly Traded Company (issued 26 March 2009)
- UK Non-Publicly Traded Company (issued 26 March 2009)

Appendix 10   Modified auditor's report – Modified opinion on the directors' report

Appendix 11   Illustrative Directors' Responsibilities Statement for a non-publicly traded company preparing its financial statements under UK GAAP

Introduction

1 Auditor's reports of companies incorporated in the United Kingdom (UK), for accounting periods commencing on or after 6 April 2008, need to comply with the requirements of the Companies Act 2006 (CA 2006) rather than with the requirements of the Companies Act 1985 or, for Northern Ireland, the 1986 Order.

2 In March 2009 the Auditing Practices Board revised ISA (UK and Ireland) 700 "The auditor's report on financial statements". With respect to UK companies, except for those that are charities, ISA (UK and Ireland) 700 (Revised) is effective for periods beginning on or after 6 April 2008 and ending on or after 5 April 2009[1].

3 To support the requirements of ISA (UK and Ireland) 700 (Revised) and the requirements of CA 2006 with respect to the auditor's report, this Bulletin provides illustrative examples of:

(a) unmodified auditor's reports (see Appendices 1 to 4);
(b) modified auditor's reports where the matter does not affect the auditor's opinion on the financial statements (see Appendix 5);
(c) modified auditor's reports where the auditor's opinion on the financial statements is qualified (see Appendix 6);
(d) modified auditor's reports where the auditor's opinion on the financial statements is adverse (see Appendix 7);
(e) modified auditor's reports where the auditor disclaims an opinion on the financial statements (see Appendix 8);
(f) auditor's report with a modified opinion on the directors' report (see Appendix 10); and
(g) a statement of directors' responsibilities for a non-publicly traded company (see Appendix 11).

4 For the purposes of this Bulletin companies are classified as either:

(a) "publicly traded companies" – defined as "those whose securities are admitted to trading on a regulated market in any Member State in the European Union"; or
(b) "non-publicly traded companies" – defined as "those who do not have any securities that are admitted to trading on a regulated market in any Member State in the European Union".

5 The provisions of CA 2006 relating to the Directors' Remuneration Report apply to "quoted companies". The definition of a quoted company differs from that of a publicly traded company. However, for the purposes of the examples in this Bulletin it is assumed that non-publicly traded companies are not quoted companies and that publicly traded companies are quoted companies. The definition of "quoted company" for the purposes of the Directors' Remuneration Report is set out in section 385(2) of CA 2006.

Description of the "scope of an audit"

6 Paragraph 14 of ISA (UK and Ireland) 700 (Revised) requires:

An auditor's report should either:

---

[1] The illustrative examples in this Bulletin do not apply to those accounting periods of longer than one year that ended on or after 5 April 2009 but commenced prior to 6 April 2008. The illustrative examples in Bulletin 2006/6 apply to such long accounting periods.

(a) cross refer to a "Statement of the Scope of an Audit" that is maintained on the APB's web-site; or
(b) cross refer to a "Statement of the Scope of an Audit" that is included elsewhere within the Annual Report; or
(c) include the following description of the scope of an audit.

"An audit involves obtaining evidence about the amounts and disclosures in the financial statements sufficient to give reasonable assurance that the financial statements are free from material misstatement, whether caused by fraud or error. This includes an assessment of: whether the accounting policies are appropriate to the *[describe nature of entity]* circumstances and have been consistently applied and adequately disclosed; the reasonableness of significant accounting estimates made by *[describe those charged with governance]*; and the overall presentation of the financial statements"

7 In the illustrative auditor's reports in Appendices 1 to 4 of this Bulletin these alternatives are shown by means of two text boxes. The alternative shown by the first text box is the wording that is used when the auditor's report cross refers to a Statement of the Scope of an Audit maintained on the APB's web site, or included elsewhere within the Annual Report. The alternative shown by the second text box is the wording that must be used if the description of the Scope of an Audit is included within the auditor's report.

8 Appendix 9 sets out the text of the two "Statements of the Scope of an Audit" posted to the APB's web site on 26 March 2009. One applies to publicly traded companies and the other applies to non-publicly traded companies.

Alternative presentation options of the financial statements of a group

9 When United Kingdom Generally Accepted Accounting Practice (UK GAAP) was the sole financial reporting framework permitted by company law it was common practice for the group and parent company financial statements to be presented as if they were a single set of financial statements, typically using separate columns for the group and parent company financial statements respectively.

10 A significant development arising from the adoption of International Financial Reporting Standards (IFRSs) as adopted by the European Union, as the financial reporting framework for the group financial statements of publicly traded companies, is that group and parent company financial statements may be prepared in accordance with different financial reporting frameworks (for example IFRSs as adopted by the European Union used for the group financial statements and UK GAAP used for the parent company financial statements).

11 Where the financial statements of the group and the parent company are presented in accordance with different financial reporting frameworks the financial statements might be presented separately within the Annual Report and in such circumstances separate auditor's reports might be provided[2].

12 The examples in Appendix 2 of this Bulletin illustrate auditor's reports where the report on the group financial statements and the report on the parent company financial statements are presented as a single auditor's report.

---

[2] CA 2006 does not require the directors to sign the group balance sheet and thereby evidence their approval of it. Where separate financial statements are presented the auditor obtains evidence of the directors' approval of the group financial statements before signing the auditor's report on those group financial statements.

13   The examples in Appendices 3 and 4 illustrate auditor's reports where the group and the parent company financial statements are presented separately. In such cases the auditor might provide separate auditor's reports on the group financial statements (See Appendix 3) and on the parent company financial statements (See Appendix 4).

14   Where separate auditor's reports are provided on the group and parent company financial statements the illustrative examples assume that:

   (a) the auditor's responsibilities with respect to the Corporate Governance Statement are described in the auditor's report on the group financial statements; and
   (b) the Directors' Remuneration Report is reported on in the auditor's report on the parent company financial statements.

   However, other approaches may be adopted.

Omitting the parent company profit and loss account

15   Section 408 CA 2006 allows a company that prepares group accounts to omit the parent company's profit and loss account from the company's annual accounts provided that:

   (a) the notes to the parent company's balance sheet show the company's profit or loss for the financial year determined in accordance with CA 2006; and
   (b) it is disclosed in the company's annual accounts that the exemption applies.

16   Where advantage has been taken of the section 408 exemption and the parent company financial statements have been prepared in accordance with "IFRSs as adopted by the European Union" the financial reporting framework is described in the auditor's report as:

> "have been properly prepared in accordance with IFRSs as adopted by the European Union *as applied in accordance with the provisions of the Companies Act 2006*"[3].

17   The example unmodified reports in Appendices 2 and 4 illustrate (by way of shaded text) the wording that is required to be inserted in the auditor's report when the company does not take advantage of the section 408 exemption (i.e. a parent company profit and loss account is included). They illustrate by way of struck out text, wording that should be deleted when the shaded text is included (i.e. the struck out text is included in the auditor's report when the company excludes the profit and loss account from the parent company financial statements).

Opinion in respect of an additional financial reporting framework

18   The financial statements of some companies may comply with two financial reporting frameworks (for example IFRSs as adopted by the European Union and IFRSs as issued by the IASB) and those charged with governance may engage the auditor to express an opinion in respect of both frameworks.

---

[3] See paragraph 9.24 of "Guidance for UK Companies on Accounting and Reporting: Requirements under the Companies Act 2006 and the application of the IAS regulation" Department for Business Enterprise & Regulatory Reform. June 2008. (*www.berr.gov.uk/files/file46791.pdf*)

ISA (UK and Ireland) 700 (Revised) requires that the second opinion should be clearly separated from the first opinion on the financial statements by use of an appropriate heading. This is illustrated in examples 4, 6, 7 and 8[4].

Modifying the auditor's report on the financial statements

An auditor's report on financial statements is considered to be modified in the following situations.

Matters that do not affect the auditor's opinion

(a) Emphasis of matter (Illustrative examples set out in Appendix 5);

Matters that do affect the auditor's opinion

(b) Qualified opinion arising from either a disagreement or a scope limitation (Illustrative examples set out in Appendix 6);

(c) Adverse opinion (Illustrative examples set out in Appendix 7); and

(d) Disclaimer of opinion (Illustrative examples set out in Appendix 8).

Modifying the auditor's opinion on the directors' report

Section 496 of CA 2006 requires the auditor to state in its report on the company's annual accounts whether in its opinion the information given in the directors' report for the financial year for which the accounts are prepared is consistent with those accounts. The example report in Appendix 10 illustrates a modified opinion on the consistency of the directors' report with the annual accounts.

Illustrative directors' responsibilities statement

Appendix 11 is an illustrative example of a Directors' Responsibilities Statement for a non-publicly traded company preparing its parent company financial statements under UK GAAP. The APB has not prepared an illustrative example of a Directors' Responsibilities Statement for a publicly traded company as the directors' responsibilities, which are in part dependent on the particular regulatory environment, will vary dependent on the rules of the market on which its securities are admitted to trading.

---

[4] *The wording used in these examples is illustrative to reflect the requirement of the Securities and Exchange Commission of the USA whose Final Rule "Acceptance From Foreign Private Issuers of Financial Statements Prepared in Accordance With International Financial Reporting Standards Without Reconciliation to US GAAP (4 January 2008) states "...the independent auditor must opine in its report on whether those financial statements comply with IFRS as issued by the IASB. ...the auditor's report can include this language in addition to any opinion relating to compliance with standards required by the home country".*

ns where
Appendix 1 – Unmodified auditor's reports where company does not prepare group financial statements

1. Non-publicly traded company preparing financial statements under the FRSSE
2. Non-publicly traded company preparing financial statements under UK GAAP
3. Publicly traded company preparing financial statements under UK GAAP
4. Publicly traded company preparing financial statements under IFRSs as adopted by the European Union

Example 1 – Non-publicly traded company preparing financial statements under the FRSSE

- Company qualifies as a small company.
- Company does not prepare group financial statements.

INDEPENDENT AUDITOR'S REPORT TO THE MEMBERS OF XYZ LIMITED

We have audited the financial statements of (name of entity) for the year ended ... which comprise [specify the titles of the primary statements such as the Profit and Loss Account, the Balance Sheet, the Cash Flow Statement, the Statement of Total Recognised Gains and Losses, the Reconciliation of Movements in Shareholders' Funds] and the related notes[5]. The financial reporting framework that has been applied in their preparation is applicable law and the Financial Reporting Standard for Smaller Entities [(Effective April 2008)][6] (United Kingdom Generally Accepted Accounting Practice applicable to Smaller Entities).

Respective responsibilities of directors and auditors

As explained more fully in the Directors' Responsibilities Statement [set out [on page ...]], the directors are responsible for the preparation of the financial statements and for being satisfied that they give a true and fair view. Our responsibility is to audit the financial statements in accordance with applicable law and International Standards on Auditing (UK and Ireland). Those standards require us to comply with the Auditing Practices Board's [(APB's)] Ethical Standards for Auditors[, including "APB Ethical Standard – Provisions Available for Small Entities (Revised)", in the circumstances set out in note [x] to the financial statements][7].

Scope of the audit of the financial statements

Either:

> A description of the scope of an audit of financial statements is [provided on the APB's web-site at www.frc.org.uk/apb/scope/UKNP] / [set out [on page ...] of the Annual Report].

Or:

> An audit involves obtaining evidence about the amounts and disclosures in the financial statements sufficient to give reasonable assurance that the financial statements are free from material misstatement, whether caused by fraud or error. This includes an assessment of: whether the accounting policies are appropriate

---

[5] *Auditor's reports of entities that do not publish their financial statements on a web site or publish them using 'PDF' format may continue to refer to the financial statements by reference to page numbers.*

[6] *Specify the version of The Financial Reporting Standard for Smaller Entities.*

[7] *Delete the words in square brackets if the relief and exemptions provided by ES PASE are not utilised. Paragraph 22 of ES PASE requires disclosure in the auditor's report where the audit firm has taken advantage of an exemption provided by ES PASE. The Appendix to ES PASE provides illustrative disclosures of relevant circumstances where the audit firm has taken advantage of an exemption provided by ES PASE.*

> to the company's circumstances and have been consistently applied and adequately disclosed; the reasonableness of significant accounting estimates made by the directors; and the overall presentation of the financial statements.

Opinion on financial statements

In our opinion the financial statements:

- give a true and fair view of the state of the company's affairs as at .... and of its profit [loss] for the year then ended[8];
- have been properly prepared in accordance with United Kingdom Generally Accepted Accounting Practice applicable to Smaller Entities; and
- have been prepared in accordance with the requirements of the Companies Act 2006.

Opinion on other matter prescribed by the Companies Act 2006

In our opinion the information given in the Directors' Report for the financial year for which the financial statements are prepared is consistent with the financial statements.[8]

Matters on which we are required to report by exception

We have nothing to report in respect of the following matters where the Companies Act 2006 requires us to report to you if, in our opinion:

- adequate accounting records have not been kept, or returns adequate for our audit have not been received from branches not visited by us; or
- the financial statements are not in agreement with the accounting records and returns; or
- certain disclosures of directors' remuneration specified by law are not made; or
- we have not received all the information and explanations we require for our audit; or
- the directors were not entitled to prepare the financial statements and the directors' report in accordance with the small companies regime.

[Signature]   *Address*
John Smith (Senior statutory auditor)   *Date*
for and on behalf of ABC LLP, Statutory Auditor

---

[8] *Guidance for auditors when a company takes advantage of the option in section 444(1) of CA 2006 not to file the profit and loss account or the directors' report is set out in paragraph 12 of APB Bulletin 2008/4 "The Special Auditor's Report on Abbreviated Accounts in the United Kingdom".*

Example 2 – Non-publicly traded company preparing financial statements under UK GAAP

- Company is not a quoted company.
- Company does not qualify as a small company.
- Company does not prepare group financial statements.

INDEPENDENT AUDITOR'S REPORT TO THE MEMBERS OF XYZ LIMITED

We have audited the financial statements of (name of entity) for the year ended ... which comprise [specify the titles of the primary statements such as the Profit and Loss Account, the Balance Sheet, the Cash Flow Statement, the Statement of Total Recognised Gains and Losses, the Reconciliation of Movements in Shareholders' Funds] and the related notes[9]. The financial reporting framework that has been applied in their preparation is applicable law and United Kingdom Accounting Standards (United Kingdom Generally Accepted Accounting Practice).

Respective responsibilities of directors and auditors

As explained more fully in the Directors' Responsibilities Statement [set out [on page ...]], the directors are responsible for the preparation of the financial statements and for being satisfied that they give a true and fair view. Our responsibility is to audit the financial statements in accordance with applicable law and International Standards on Auditing (UK and Ireland). Those standards require us to comply with the Auditing Practices Board's [(APB's)] Ethical Standards for Auditors.

Scope of the audit of the financial statements

Either:

> A description of the scope of an audit of financial statements is [provided on the APB's web-site at www.frc.org.uk/apb/scope/UKNP] / [set out [on page ...] of the Annual Report].

Or:

> An audit involves obtaining evidence about the amounts and disclosures in the financial statements sufficient to give reasonable assurance that the financial statements are free from material misstatement, whether caused by fraud or error. This includes an assessment of: whether the accounting policies are appropriate to the company's circumstances and have been consistently applied and adequately disclosed; the reasonableness of significant accounting estimates made by the directors; and the overall presentation of the financial statements.

---

[9] Auditor's reports of entities that do not publish their financial statements on a web site or publish them using 'PDF' format may continue to refer to the financial statements by reference to page numbers.

Opinion on financial statements

In our opinion the financial statements:

- give a true and fair view of the state of the company's affairs as at .... and of its profit [loss] for the year then ended;
- have been properly prepared in accordance with United Kingdom Generally Accepted Accounting Practice; and
- have been prepared in accordance with the requirements of the Companies Act 2006.

Opinion on other matter prescribed by the Companies Act 2006

In our opinion the information given in the Directors' Report for the financial year for which the financial statements are prepared is consistent with the financial statements.

Matters on which we are required to report by exception

We have nothing to report in respect of the following matters where the Companies Act 2006 requires us to report to you if, in our opinion:

- adequate accounting records have not been kept, or returns adequate for our audit have not been received from branches not visited by us; or
- the financial statements are not in agreement with the accounting records and returns; or
- certain disclosures of directors' remuneration specified by law are not made; or
- we have not received all the information and explanations we require for our audit.

[Signature]   *Address*
John Smith (Senior statutory auditor)   *Date*
for and on behalf of ABC LLP, Statutory Auditor

Example 3 – Publicly traded company preparing financial statements under UK GAAP

- Company is a quoted company.
- Company does not prepare group financial statements.

INDEPENDENT AUDITOR'S REPORT TO THE MEMBERS OF XYZ PLC

We have audited the financial statements of (name of entity) for the year ended ... which comprise [specify the titles of the primary statements such as the Profit and Loss Account, the Balance Sheet, the Cash Flow Statement, the Statement of Total Recognised Gains and Losses, the Reconciliation of Movements in Shareholders' Funds] and the related notes[10]. The financial reporting framework that has been applied in their preparation is applicable law and United Kingdom Accounting Standards (United Kingdom Generally Accepted Accounting Practice).

Respective responsibilities of directors and auditors

As explained more fully in the Directors' Responsibilities Statement [set out [on page ...]], the directors are responsible for the preparation of the financial statements and for being satisfied that they give a true and fair view. Our responsibility is to audit the financial statements in accordance with applicable law and International Standards on Auditing (UK and Ireland). Those standards require us to comply with the Auditing Practices Board's [(APB's)] Ethical Standards for Auditors.

Scope of the audit of the financial statements

Either:

> A description of the scope of an audit of financial statements is [provided on the APB's web-site at www.frc.org.uk/apb/scope/UKP] / [set out [on page ...] of the Annual Report].

Or:

> An audit involves obtaining evidence about the amounts and disclosures in the financial statements sufficient to give reasonable assurance that the financial statements are free from material misstatement, whether caused by fraud or error. This includes an assessment of: whether the accounting policies are appropriate to the company's circumstances and have been consistently applied and adequately disclosed; the reasonableness of significant accounting estimates made by the directors; and the overall presentation of the financial statements.

Opinion on financial statements

In our opinion the financial statements:

---

[10] *Auditor's reports of entities that do not publish their financial statements on a web site or publish them using 'PDF' format may continue to refer to the financial statements by reference to page numbers.*

- give a true and fair view of the state of the company's affairs as at .... and of its profit [loss] for the year then ended;
- have been properly prepared in accordance with United Kingdom Generally Accepted Accounting Practice; and
- have been prepared in accordance with the requirements of the Companies Act 2006.

Opinion on other matters prescribed by the Companies Act 2006

In our opinion:
- the part of the Directors' Remuneration Report to be audited has been properly prepared in accordance with the Companies Act 2006[11]; and
- the information given in the Directors' Report for the financial year for which the financial statements are prepared is consistent with the financial statements.

Matters on which we are required to report by exception

We have nothing to report in respect of the following:

Under the Companies Act 2006 we are required to report to you if, in our opinion:
- adequate accounting records have not been kept, or returns adequate for our audit have not been received from branches not visited by us; or
- the financial statements and the part of the Directors' Remuneration Report to be audited are not in agreement with the accounting records and returns; or
- certain disclosures of directors' remuneration specified by law are not made; or
- we have not received all the information and explanations we require for our audit.

Under the Listing Rules we are required to review:
- the directors' statement, [set out [on page...]], in relation to going concern; and
- the part of the Corporate Governance Statement relating to the company's compliance with the nine provisions of the [2006] [June 2008][12] Combined Code specified for our review.

[Signature]   Address
John Smith (Senior statutory auditor)   Date
for and on behalf of ABC LLP, Statutory Auditor

---

[11] *Part 3 of Schedule 8 to the Large and Medium-sized Companies and Groups (Accounts and Reports) Regulations 2008 (SI 2008 No. 410) sets out the information in the Directors' Remuneration Report that is subject to audit. Companies should describe clearly which disclosures within the Directors' Remuneration Report have been audited.*

[12] *The June 2008 Combined Code applies to accounting periods beginning on or after 29 June 2008. The 2006 Combined Code applies before that date.*

Example 4 – Publicly traded company preparing financial statements under IFRSs as adopted by the European Union

- Company is a quoted company.
- Company does not prepare group financial statements.

INDEPENDENT AUDITOR'S REPORT TO THE MEMBERS OF XYZ PLC

We have audited the financial statements of (name of entity) for the year ended ... which comprise [specify the titles of the primary statements such as the Statement of Financial Position, the Statement of Comprehensive Income, the Statement of Cash Flow, the Statement of Changes in Equity[13]] and the related notes[14]. The financial reporting framework that has been applied in their preparation is applicable law and International Financial Reporting Standards (IFRSs) as adopted by the European Union.

Respective responsibilities of directors and auditors

As explained more fully in the Directors' Responsibilities Statement [set out [on page ...]], the directors are responsible for the preparation of the financial statements and for being satisfied that they give a true and fair view. Our responsibility is to audit the financial statements in accordance with applicable law and International Standards on Auditing (UK and Ireland). Those standards require us to comply with the Auditing Practices Board's [(APB's)] Ethical Standards for Auditors.

Scope of the audit of the financial statements

Either:

> A description of the scope of an audit of financial statements is [provided on the APB's web-site at www.frc.org.uk/apb/scope/UKP] / [set out [on page ...] of the Annual Report].

Or:

> An audit involves obtaining evidence about the amounts and disclosures in the financial statements sufficient to give reasonable assurance that the financial statements are free from material misstatement, whether caused by fraud or error. This includes an assessment of: whether the accounting policies are appropriate to the company's circumstances and have been consistently applied and adequately disclosed; the reasonableness of significant accounting estimates made by the directors; and the overall presentation of the financial statements.

---

[13] *The names of the primary statements given in this illustration are those terms used in IAS 1 (2007) which applies for accounting periods beginning on or after 1 January 2009 (although early adoption is permitted). The names used for the primary statements in the auditor's report should reflect the precise titles used by the company for them.*

[14] *Auditor's reports of entities that do not publish their financial statements on a web site or publish them using 'PDF' format may continue to refer to the financial statements by reference to page numbers.*

Opinion on financial statements

In our opinion the financial statements:

- give a true and fair view of the state of the company's affairs as at .... and of its profit [loss] for the year then ended;
- have been properly prepared in accordance with IFRSs as adopted by the European Union; and
- have been prepared in accordance with the requirements of the Companies Act 2006.

[*Separate opinion in relation to IFRSs as issued by the IASB*

As explained in note [x] to the financial statements, the company in addition to applying IFRSs as adopted by the European Union, has also applied IFRSs as issued by the International Accounting Standards Board (IASB).

In our opinion the financial statements comply with IFRSs as issued by the IASB.][15]

Opinion on other matters prescribed by the Companies Act 2006

In our opinion:

- the part of the Directors' Remuneration Report to be audited has been properly prepared in accordance with the Companies Act 2006[16]; and
- the information given in the Directors' Report for the financial year for which the financial statements are prepared is consistent with the financial statements.

Matters on which we are required to report by exception

We have nothing to report in respect of the following:

Under the Companies Act 2006 we are required to report to you if, in our opinion:

- adequate accounting records have not been kept, or returns adequate for our audit have not been received from branches not visited by us; or
- the financial statements and the part of the Directors' Remuneration Report to be audited are not in agreement with the accounting records and returns; or
- certain disclosures of directors' remuneration specified by law are not made; or
- we have not received all the information and explanations we require for our audit.

Under the Listing Rules we are required to review:

- the directors' statement, [set out [on page...]], in relation to going concern; and

---

[15] *See footnote 4 on page 6*

[16] *Part 3 of Schedule 8 to the Large and Medium-sized Companies and Groups (Accounts and Reports) Regulations 2008 (SI 2008 No. 410) sets out the information in the Directors' Remuneration Report that is subject to audit. Companies should describe clearly which disclosures within the Directors' Remuneration Report have been audited.*

- the part of the Corporate Governance Statement relating to the company's compliance with the nine provisions of the [2006] [June 2008][17] Combined Code specified for our review.

[Signature]   *Address*
John Smith (Senior statutory auditor)   *Date*
for and on behalf of ABC LLP, Statutory Auditor

---

[17] *The June 2008 Combined Code applies to accounting periods beginning on or after 29 June 2008. The 2006 Combined Code applies before that date.*

Appendix 2 – Unmodified auditor's reports where group and parent company financial statements reported on in a single auditor's report

5. Non-publicly traded group preparing financial statements under UK GAAP
6. Publicly traded group – Parent company financial statement prepared under UK GAAP
7. Publicly traded group – Parent company financial statements prepared under IFRSs as adopted by the European Union

Example 5 – Non-publicly traded group preparing financial statements under UK GAAP

- Company is not a quoted company.
- Company does not qualify as a "small group".
- Section 408 exemption taken for parent company's own profit and loss account.
- Company does prepare group financial statements.

INDEPENDENT AUDITOR'S REPORT TO THE MEMBERS OF XYZ LIMITED

We have audited the financial statements of (name of entity) for the year ended ... which comprise [specify the titles of the primary statements such as the Group Profit and Loss Account, the Group and Parent Company Balance Sheets, the Group Cash Flow Statement, the Group Statement of Total Recognised Gains and Losses, the Group and Parent Company Reconciliation of Movements in Shareholders' Funds] and the related notes[18]. The financial reporting framework that has been applied in their preparation is applicable law and United Kingdom Accounting Standards (United Kingdom Generally Accepted Accounting Practice).

Respective responsibilities of directors and auditors

As explained more fully in the Directors' Responsibilities Statement [set out [on page ...]], the directors are responsible for the preparation of the financial statements and for being satisfied that they give a true and fair view. Our responsibility is to audit the financial statements in accordance with applicable law and International Standards on Auditing (UK and Ireland). Those standards require us to comply with the Auditing Practices Board's [(APB's)] Ethical Standards for Auditors.

Scope of the audit of the financial statements

Either:

> A description of the scope of an audit of financial statements is [provided on the APB's web-site at www.frc.org.uk/apb/scope/UKNP] / [set out [on page ...] of the Annual Report].

Or:

> An audit involves obtaining evidence about the amounts and disclosures in the financial statements sufficient to give reasonable assurance that the financial statements are free from material misstatement, whether caused by fraud or error. This includes an assessment of: whether the accounting policies are appropriate to the group's and the parent company's circumstances and have been consistently applied and adequately disclosed; the reasonableness of significant accounting estimates made by the directors; and the overall presentation of the financial statements.

[18] *Auditor's reports of entities that do not publish their financial statements on a web site or publish them using 'PDF' format may continue to refer to the financial statements by reference to page numbers.*

Opinion on financial statements

In our opinion the financial statements:

- give a true and fair view of the state of the group's and the parent company's affairs as at ……. and of the group's profit [loss] for the year then ended;
- have been properly prepared in accordance with United Kingdom Generally Accepted Accounting Practice; and
- have been prepared in accordance with the requirements of the Companies Act 2006.

Opinion on other matter prescribed by the Companies Act 2006

In our opinion the information given in the Directors' Report for the financial year for which the financial statements are prepared is consistent with the financial statements.

Matters on which we are required to report by exception

We have nothing to report in respect of the following matters where the Companies Act 2006 requires us to report to you if, in our opinion:

- adequate accounting records have not been kept by the parent company, or returns adequate for our audit have not been received from branches not visited by us; or
- the parent company financial statements are not in agreement with the accounting records and returns; or
- certain disclosures of directors' remuneration specified by law are not made; or
- we have not received all the information and explanations we require for our audit.

[Signature]   *Address*
John Smith (Senior statutory auditor)   *Date*
for and on behalf of ABC LLP, Statutory Auditor

Example 6 – Publicly traded group – Parent company financial statements prepared under UK GAAP

- Company is a quoted company.
- Shaded text to be included only where section 408 exemption <u>not</u> taken in respect of parent company's own profit and loss account.
- Company does prepare group financial statements.

INDEPENDENT AUDITOR'S REPORT TO THE MEMBERS OF XYZ PLC

We have audited the financial statements of (name of entity) for the year ended ... which comprise [specify the titles of the primary statements such as the Group Statement of Financial Position and Parent Company Balance Sheet, the Group Statement of Comprehensive Income, the Parent Company Profit and Loss Account, the Group Statement of Cash Flow, the Group Statement of Changes in Equity, the Parent Company Statement of Total Recognised Gains and Losses, the Parent Company Reconciliation of Movements in Shareholders' Funds] and the related notes[19]. The financial reporting framework that has been applied in the preparation of the group financial statements is applicable law and International Financial Reporting Standards (IFRSs) as adopted by the European Union. The financial reporting framework that has been applied in the preparation of the parent company financial statements is applicable law and United Kingdom Accounting Standards (United Kingdom Generally Accepted Accounting Practice).

Respective responsibilities of directors and auditors

As explained more fully in the Directors' Responsibilities Statement [set out [on page ...]], the directors are responsible for the preparation of the financial statements and for being satisfied that they give a true and fair view. Our responsibility is to audit the financial statements in accordance with applicable law and International Standards on Auditing (UK and Ireland). Those standards require us to comply with the Auditing Practices Board's [(APB's)] Ethical Standards for Auditors.

Scope of the audit of the financial statements

Either:

> A description of the scope of an audit of financial statements is [provided on the APB's web-site at www.frc.org.uk/apb/scope/UKP] / [set out [on page ...] of the Annual Report].

Or:

> An audit involves obtaining evidence about the amounts and disclosures in the financial statements sufficient to give reasonable assurance that the financial statements are free from material misstatement, whether caused by fraud or error. This includes an assessment of: whether the accounting policies are appropriate to the group's and the parent company's circumstances and have been

---

[19] *Auditor's reports of entities that do not publish their financial statements on a web site or publish them using 'PDF' format may continue to refer to the financial statements by reference to page numbers.*

> consistently applied and adequately disclosed; the reasonableness of significant accounting estimates made by the directors; and the overall presentation of the financial statements.

Opinion on financial statements

In our opinion:

- the financial statements give a true and fair view of the state of the group's and of the parent company's affairs as at .... and of the group's and the parent company's profit [loss] for the year then ended;
- the group financial statements have been properly prepared in accordance with IFRSs as adopted by the European Union;
- the parent company financial statements have been properly prepared in accordance with United Kingdom Generally Accepted Accounting Practice;
- the financial statements have been prepared in accordance with the requirements of the Companies Act 2006; and, as regards the group financial statements, Article 4 of the IAS Regulation.

[*Separate opinion in relation to IFRSs as issued by the IASB*

As explained in note [x] to the group financial statements, the group in addition to complying with its legal obligation to apply IFRSs as adopted by the European Union, has also applied IFRSs as issued by the International Accounting Standards Board (IASB).

In our opinion the group financial statements comply with IFRSs as issued by the IASB.][20]

Opinion on other matters prescribed by the Companies Act 2006

In our opinion:

- the part of the Directors' Remuneration Report to be audited has been properly prepared in accordance with the Companies Act 2006[21]; and
- the information given in the Directors' Report for the financial year for which the financial statements are prepared is consistent with the financial statements.

Matters on which we are required to report by exception

We have nothing to report in respect of the following:

Under the Companies Act 2006 we are required to report to you if, in our opinion:

- adequate accounting records have not been kept by the parent company, or returns adequate for our audit have not been received from branches not visited by us; or

---

[20] See footnote 4 on page 6

[21] Part 3 of Schedule 8 to the Large and Medium-sized Companies and Groups (Accounts and Reports) Regulations 2008 (SI 2008 No. 410) sets out the information in the Directors' Remuneration Report that is subject to audit. Companies should describe clearly which disclosures within the Directors' Remuneration Report have been audited.

- the parent company financial statements and the part of the Directors' Remuneration Report to be audited are not in agreement with the accounting records and returns; or
- certain disclosures of directors' remuneration specified by law are not made; or
- we have not received all the information and explanations we require for our audit.

Under the Listing Rules we are required to review:

- the directors' statement, [set out [on page...]], in relation to going concern; and
- the part of the Corporate Governance Statement relating to the company's compliance with the nine provisions of the [2006] [June 2008][22] Combined Code specified for our review.

[Signature]   *Address*
John Smith (Senior statutory auditor)   *Date*
for and on behalf of ABC LLP, Statutory Auditor

---

[22] *The June 2008 Combined Code applies to accounting periods beginning on or after 29 June 2008. The 2006 Combined Code applies before that date.*

Example 7 – Publicly traded group – Parent company financial statements prepared under IFRSs as adopted by the European Union

- Company is a quoted company.
- Shaded text to be included, and struck through text omitted, where section 408 exemption <u>not</u> taken in respect of parent company's own profit and loss account.
- Company does prepare group financial statements.

INDEPENDENT AUDITOR'S REPORT TO THE MEMBERS OF XYZ PLC

We have audited the financial statements of (name of entity) for the year ended ... which comprise [specify the titles of the primary statements such as, the Group and Parent Company Statements of Financial Position, the Group and Parent Company Statements of Comprehensive Income, the Group and Parent Company Cash Flow Statements, the Group and Parent Company Statements of Changes in Equity][23] and the related notes[24]. The financial reporting framework that has been applied in their preparation is applicable law and International Financial Reporting Standards (IFRSs) as adopted by the European Union ~~and, as regards the parent company financial statements, as applied in accordance with the provisions of the Companies Act 2006~~.

Respective responsibilities of directors and auditors

As explained more fully in the Directors' Responsibilities Statement [set out [on page ...]], the directors are responsible for the preparation of the financial statements and for being satisfied that they give a true and fair view. Our responsibility is to audit the financial statements in accordance with applicable law and International Standards on Auditing (UK and Ireland). Those standards require us to comply with the Auditing Practices Board's [(APB's)] Ethical Standards for Auditors.

Scope of the audit of the financial statements

Either:

> A description of the scope of an audit of financial statements is [provided on the APB's web-site at www.frc.org.uk/apb/scope/UKP] / [set out [on page ...] of the Annual Report].

Or:

> An audit involves obtaining evidence about the amounts and disclosures in the financial statements sufficient to give reasonable assurance that the financial statements are free from material misstatement, whether caused by fraud or error.

---

[23] *The names of the primary statements given in this illustration are those terms used in IAS 1 (2007) which applies for accounting periods beginning on or after 1 January 2009 (although early adoption is permitted). The names used for the primary statements in the auditor's report should reflect the precise titles used by the company for them.*

[24] *Auditor's reports of entities that do not publish their financial statements on a web site or publish them using 'PDF' format may continue to refer to the financial statements by reference to page numbers.*

> This includes an assessment of: whether the accounting policies are appropriate to the group's and the parent company's circumstances and have been consistently applied and adequately disclosed; the reasonableness of significant accounting estimates made by the directors; and the overall presentation of the financial statements.

Opinion on financial statements

In our opinion:

- the financial statements give a true and fair view of the state of the group's and of the parent company's affairs as at .... and of the group's and the parent company's profit [loss] for the year then ended;
- the ~~group~~ financial statements have been properly prepared in accordance with IFRSs as adopted by the European Union; and
- ~~the parent company financial statements have been properly prepared in accordance with IFRSs as adopted by the European Union and as applied in accordance with the provisions of the Companies Act 2006; and~~
- the financial statements have been prepared in accordance with the requirements of the Companies Act 2006 and, as regards the group financial statements, Article 4 of the IAS Regulation.

[*Separate opinion in relation to IFRSs as issued by the IASB*

As explained in note [x] to the group financial statements, the group in addition to complying with its legal obligation to apply IFRSs as adopted by the European Union, has also applied IFRSs as issued by the International Accounting Standards Board (IASB).

In our opinion the group financial statements comply with IFRSs as issued by the IASB.][25]

Opinion on other matters prescribed by the Companies Act 2006

In our opinion:

- the part of the Directors' Remuneration Report to be audited has been properly prepared in accordance with the Companies Act 2006[26]; and
- the information given in the Directors' Report for the financial year for which the financial statements are prepared is consistent with the financial statements.

Matters on which we are required to report by exception

We have nothing to report in respect of the following:

Under the Companies Act 2006 we are required to report to you if, in our opinion:

---

[25] See footnote 4 on page 6

[26] Part 3 of Schedule 8 to the Large and Medium-sized Companies and Groups (Accounts and Reports) Regulations 2008 (SI 2008 No. 410) sets out the information in the Directors' Remuneration Report that is subject to audit. Companies should describe clearly which disclosures within the Directors' Remuneration Report have been audited.

- adequate accounting records have not been kept by the parent company, or returns adequate for our audit have not been received from branches not visited by us; or
- the parent company financial statements and the part of the Directors' Remuneration Report to be audited are not in agreement with the accounting records and returns; or
- certain disclosures of directors' remuneration specified by law are not made; or
- we have not received all the information and explanations we require for our audit.

Under the Listing Rules we are required to review:

- the directors' statement, [set out [on page...]]; in relation to going concern; and
- the part of the Corporate Governance Statement relating to the company's compliance with the nine provisions of the [2006] [June 2008][27] Combined Code specified for our review.

[Signature]   Address
John Smith (Senior statutory auditor)   Date
for and on behalf of ABC LLP, Statutory Auditor

---

[27] The June 2008 Combined Code applies to accounting periods beginning on or after 29 June 2008. The 2006 Combined Code applies before that date.

Appendix 3 – Unmodified auditor's report on group financial statements reported on separately from the parent company financial statements

8. Publicly traded group – Auditor's report on group financial statements prepared under IFRSs as adopted by the European Union

Example 8 – Publicly traded group – Auditor's report on group financial statements prepared under IFRSs as adopted by the European Union

- Company is a quoted company.
- Corporate governance statement reported on in the report on the group financial statements.
- Directors' Remuneration Report reported on in the report on the parent company financial statements.
- Company does prepare group financial statements.

INDEPENDENT AUDITOR'S REPORT TO THE MEMBERS OF XYZ PLC

We have audited the group financial statements of (name of entity) for the year ended ... which comprise [specify the titles of the primary statements such as the Group Statement of Financial Position, the Group Statement of Comprehensive Income, the Group Statement of Cash Flows, the Group Statement of Changes in Equity][28] and the related notes[29]. The financial reporting framework that has been applied in their preparation is applicable law and International Financial Reporting Standards (IFRSs) as adopted by the European Union.

Respective responsibilities of directors and auditors

As explained more fully in the Directors' Responsibilities Statement [set out [on page ...]], the directors are responsible for the preparation of the group financial statements and for being satisfied that they give a true and fair view. Our responsibility is to audit the group financial statements in accordance with applicable law and International Standards on Auditing (UK and Ireland). Those standards require us to comply with the Auditing Practices Board's [(APB's)] Ethical Standards for Auditors.

Scope of the audit of the financial statements

Either:

> A description of the scope of an audit of financial statements is [provided on the APB's web-site at www.frc.org.uk/apb/scope/UKP] / [set out [on page ...] of the Annual Report].

Or:

> An audit involves obtaining evidence about the amounts and disclosures in the financial statements sufficient to give reasonable assurance that the financial

---

[28] The names of the primary statements given in this illustration are those terms used in IAS 1 (2007) which applies for accounting periods beginning on or after 1 January 2009 (although early adoption is permitted). The names used for the primary statements in the auditor's report should reflect the precise titles used by the company for them.

[29] Auditor's reports of entities that do not publish their financial statements on a web site or publish them using 'PDF' format may continue to refer to the financial statements by reference to page numbers.

statements are free from material misstatement, whether caused by fraud or error. This includes an assessment of: whether the accounting policies are appropriate to the group's circumstances and have been consistently applied and adequately disclosed; the reasonableness of significant accounting estimates made by the directors; and the overall presentation of the financial statements.

Opinion on financial statements

In our opinion the group financial statements:

- give a true and fair view of the state of the group's affairs as at .... and of its profit [loss] for the year then ended;
- have been properly prepared in accordance with IFRSs as adopted by the European Union; and
- have been prepared in accordance with the requirements of the Companies Act 2006 and Article 4 of the IAS Regulation.

[Separate opinion in relation to IFRSs as issued by the IASB

As explained in note [x] to the group financial statements, the group in addition to complying with its legal obligation to apply IFRSs as adopted by the European Union, has also applied IFRSs as issued by the International Accounting Standards Board (IASB).

In our opinion the group financial statements comply with IFRSs as issued by the IASB.][30]

Opinion on other matter prescribed by the Companies Act 2006

In our opinion the information given in the Directors' Report for the financial year for which the group financial statements are prepared is consistent with the group financial statements.

Matters on which we are required to report by exception

We have nothing to report in respect of the following:

Under the Companies Act 2006 we are required to report to you if, in our opinion:

- certain disclosures of directors' remuneration specified by law are not made; or
- we have not received all the information and explanations we require for our audit.

Under the Listing Rules we are required to review:

- the directors' statement, [set out [on page...]], in relation to going concern; and
- the part of the Corporate Governance Statement relating to the company's compliance with the nine provisions of the [2006] [June 2008][31] Combined Code specified for our review.

---

[30] See footnote 4 on page 6

[31] The June 2008 Combined Code applies to accounting periods beginning on or after 29 June 2008. The 2006 Combined Code applies before that date.

Other matter

We have reported separately on the parent company financial statements of (name of entity) for the year ended ... and on the information in the Directors' Remuneration Report that is described as having been audited. [That report is modified by the inclusion of an emphasis of matter] [The opinion in that report is (qualified)/(an adverse opinion)/(a disclaimer of opinion)].

[Signature]
John Smith (Senior statutory auditor)
for and on behalf of ABC LLP, Statutory Auditor

Address
Date

Appendix 4 – Unmodified auditor's reports on parent company financial statements reported on separately from the group financial statements

9. Publicly traded group – Auditor's report on parent company financial statements prepared under UK GAAP
10. Publicly traded group – Auditor's report on parent company financial statements prepared under IFRSs as adopted by the European Union

Example 9 – Publicly traded group – Auditor's report on parent company financial statements prepared under UK GAAP

- Company is a quoted company.
- Shaded text to be included only where section 408 exemption <u>not</u> taken in respect of parent company's own profit and loss account.
- Corporate governance statement reported on in the report on the group financial statements.
- Directors' Remuneration Report reported on in the report on the parent company financial statements.
- Company does prepare group financial statements.

INDEPENDENT AUDITOR'S REPORT TO THE MEMBERS OF XYZ PLC

We have audited the parent company financial statements of (name of entity) for the year ended ... which comprise [specify the titles of the primary statements such as the Parent Company Balance Sheet, the Parent Company Profit and Loss Account the Parent Company Statement of Total Recognised Gains and Losses, the Parent Company Reconciliation of Movements in Shareholders' Funds] and the related notes[32]. The financial reporting framework that has been applied in their preparation is applicable law and United Kingdom Accounting Standards (United Kingdom Generally Accepted Accounting Practice).

Respective responsibilities of directors and auditors

As explained more fully in the Directors' Responsibilities Statement [set out [on page ...]], the directors are responsible for the preparation of the parent company financial statements and for being satisfied that they give a true and fair view. Our responsibility is to audit the parent company financial statements in accordance with applicable law and International Standards on Auditing (UK and Ireland). Those standards require us to comply with the Auditing Practices Board's [(APB's)] Ethical Standards for Auditors.

Scope of the audit of the financial statements

Either:

> A description of the scope of an audit of financial statements is [provided on the APB's web-site at www.frc.org.uk/apb/scope/UKP] / [set out [on page ...] of the Annual Report].

Or:

> An audit involves obtaining evidence about the amounts and disclosures in the financial statements sufficient to give reasonable assurance that the financial statements are free from material misstatement, whether caused by fraud or error. This includes an assessment of: whether the accounting policies are appropriate to the parent company's circumstances and have been consistently applied and

---

[32] *Auditor's reports of entities that do not publish their financial statements on a web site or publish them using 'PDF' format may continue to refer to the financial statements by reference to page numbers.*

adequately disclosed; the reasonableness of significant accounting estimates made by the directors; and the overall presentation of the financial statements.

Opinion on financial statements

In our opinion the parent company financial statements:

- give a true and fair view of the state of the company's affairs as at .... and of its profit [loss] for the year then ended;
- have been properly prepared in accordance with United Kingdom Generally Accepted Accounting Practice; and
- have been prepared in accordance with the requirements of the Companies Act 2006.

Opinion on other matters prescribed by the Companies Act 2006

In our opinion:

- the part of the Directors' Remuneration Report to be audited has been properly prepared in accordance with the Companies Act 2006[33]; and
- the information given in the Directors' Report for the financial year for which the financial statements are prepared is consistent with the parent company financial statements.

Matters on which we are required to report by exception

We have nothing to report in respect of the following matters where the Companies Act 2006 requires us to report to you if, in our opinion:

- adequate accounting records have not been kept by the parent company, or returns adequate for our audit have not been received from branches not visited by us; or
- the parent company financial statements and the part of the Directors' Remuneration Report to be audited are not in agreement with the accounting records and returns; or
- certain disclosures of directors' remuneration specified by law are not made; or
- we have not received all the information and explanations we require for our audit.

Other matter

We have reported separately on the group financial statements of (name of entity) for the year ended .... [That report is modified by the inclusion of an emphasis of matter] [The opinion in that report is (qualified)/(an adverse opinion)/(a disclaimer of opinion)].

[Signature]   Address
John Smith (Senior statutory auditor)   Date
for and on behalf of ABC LLP, Statutory Auditor

---

[33] Part 3 of Schedule 8 to the Large and Medium-sized Companies and Groups (Accounts and Reports) Regulations 2008 (SI 2008 No. 410) sets out the information in the Directors' Remuneration Report that is subject to audit. Companies should describe clearly which disclosures within the Directors' Remuneration Report have been audited.

Example 10 – Publicly traded group – Auditor's report on parent company financial statements prepared under IFRSs as adopted by the European Union

- Company is a quoted company.
- Shaded text to be included, and struck through text omitted, where section 408 exemption <u>not</u> taken in respect of parent company's own profit and loss account.
- Corporate governance statement reported on in the report on the group financial statements.
- Directors' Remuneration Report reported on in the report on the parent company financial statements.
- Company does prepare group financial statements.

INDEPENDENT AUDITOR'S REPORT TO THE MEMBERS OF XYZ PLC

We have audited the parent company financial statements of (name of entity) for the year ended ... which comprise [specify the titles of the primary statements such as the Statement of Financial Position, the Statement of Comprehensive Income, the Statement of Cash Flow, the Statement of Changes in Equity][34] and the related notes[35]. The financial reporting framework that has been applied in their preparation is applicable law and International Financial Reporting Standards (IFRSs) as adopted by the European Union ~~and as applied in accordance with the provisions of the Companies Act 2006~~.

Respective responsibilities of directors and auditors

As explained more fully in the Directors' Responsibilities Statement [set out [on page ...]], the directors are responsible for the preparation of the parent company financial statements and for being satisfied that they give a true and fair view. Our responsibility is to audit the parent company financial statements in accordance with applicable law and International Standards on Auditing (UK and Ireland). Those standards require us to comply with the Auditing Practices Board's [(APB's)] Ethical Standards for Auditors.

Scope of the audit of the financial statements

Either:

> A description of the scope of an audit of financial statements is [provided on the APB's web-site at www.frc.org.uk/apb/scope/UKP] / [set out [on page ...] of the Annual Report].

Or:

---

[34] The names of the primary statements given in this illustration are those terms used in IAS 1 (2007) which applies for accounting periods beginning on or after 1 January 2009 (although early adoption is permitted). The names used for the primary statements in the auditor's report should reflect the precise titles used by the company for them.

[35] Auditor's reports of entities that do not publish their financial statements on a web site or publish them using 'PDF' format may continue to refer to the financial statements by reference to page numbers.

> An audit involves obtaining evidence about the amounts and disclosures in the financial statements sufficient to give reasonable assurance that the financial statements are free from material misstatement, whether caused by fraud or error. This includes an assessment of: whether the accounting policies are appropriate to the parent company's circumstances and have been consistently applied and adequately disclosed; the reasonableness of significant accounting estimates made by the directors; and the overall presentation of the financial statements.

Opinion on financial statements

In our opinion the parent company financial statements:

- give a true and fair view of the state of the company's affairs as at .... and of its profit [loss] for the year then ended;
- have been properly prepared in accordance with IFRSs as adopted by the European Union and as applied in accordance with the provisions of the Companies Act 2006; and
- have been prepared in accordance with the requirements of the Companies Act 2006.

Opinion on other matters prescribed by the Companies Act 2006

In our opinion:

- the part of the Directors' Remuneration Report to be audited has been properly prepared in accordance with the Companies Act 2006[36]; and
- the information given in the Directors' Report for the financial year for which the financial statements are prepared is consistent with the parent company financial statements.

Matters on which we are required to report by exception

We have nothing to report in respect of the following matters where the Companies Act 2006 requires us to report to you if, in our opinion:

- adequate accounting records have not been kept by the parent company, or returns adequate for our audit have not been received from branches not visited by us; or
- the parent company financial statements and the part of the Directors' Remuneration Report to be audited are not in agreement with the accounting records and returns; or
- certain disclosures of directors' remuneration specified by law are not made; or
- we have not received all the information and explanations we require for our audit.

Other matter

We have reported separately on the group financial statements of (name of entity) for the year ended .... [That report is modified by the inclusion of an emphasis of matter]

---

[36] *Part 3 of Schedule 8 to the Large and Medium-sized Companies and Groups (Accounts and Reports) Regulations 2008 (SI 2008 No. 410) sets out the information in the Directors' Remuneration Report that is subject to audit. Companies should describe clearly which disclosures within the Directors' Remuneration Report have been audited.*

[The opinion in that report is (qualified)/(an adverse opinion)/(a disclaimer of opinion).]

[Signature]
John Smith (Senior statutory auditor)
for and on behalf of ABC LLP, Statutory Auditor

Address
Date

Appendix 5 – Modified auditor's reports – Emphasis of matter paragraphs

11. Emphasis of matter: Material uncertainty that may cast significant doubt about the company's ability to continue as a going concern
12. Emphasis of matter: Possible outcome of a lawsuit

Example 11 – Emphasis of matter: Material uncertainty that may cast significant doubt about the company's ability to continue as a going concern

- *UK non-publicly traded company prepares UK GAAP financial statements (Example 2).*
- *The company incurred a net loss of £X during the year ended 31 December 20X1 and, as of that date, the company's current liabilities exceeded its total assets by £Y.*
- *These conditions, along with other matters set forth in the notes to the financial statements, indicate the existence of a material uncertainty, which may cast significant doubt about the Company's ability to continue as a going concern.*
- *The company makes relevant disclosures in the financial statements including those referred to in paragraphs 32, 33 and 33-2 of ISA (UK and Ireland) 570 "Going Concern".*
- *The auditor issues an unqualified auditor's report with an emphasis of matter paragraph describing the situation giving rise to the emphasis of matter and its possible effects on the financial statements, including (where practicable) quantification.*

Extract from auditor's report

...

Opinion on financial statements

In our opinion the financial statements:

- give a true and fair view of the state of the company's affairs as at 31 December 20X1 and of its loss for the year then ended;
- have been properly prepared in accordance with United Kingdom Generally Accepted Accounting Practice; and
- have been prepared in accordance with the requirements of the Companies Act 2006.

Emphasis of matter – Going concern

In forming our opinion on the financial statements, which is not qualified, we have considered the adequacy of the disclosure made in note [x] to the financial statements concerning the company's ability to continue as a going concern. The company incurred a net loss of £X during the year ended 31 December 20X1 and, at that date, the company's current liabilities exceeded its total assets by £Y. These conditions, along with the other matters explained in note [x] to the financial statements, indicate the existence of a material uncertainty which may cast significant doubt about the company's ability to continue as a going concern. The financial statements do not include the adjustments that would result if the company was unable to continue as a going concern.

Opinion on other matter prescribed by the Companies Act 2006

...

Example 12 – Emphasis of matter: Possible outcome of a lawsuit

- UK non-publicly traded company prepares UK GAAP financial statements (Example 2).
- A lawsuit alleges that the company has infringed certain patent rights and claims royalties and punitive damages. The company has filed a counter action, and preliminary hearings and discovery proceedings on both actions are in progress.
- The ultimate outcome of the matter cannot presently be determined, and no provision for any liability that may result has been made in the financial statements.
- The company makes relevant disclosures in the financial statements.
- The auditor issues an unqualified auditor's report with an emphasis of matter paragraph describing the situation giving rise to the emphasis of matter and its possible effects on the financial statements, including that the effect on the financial statements of the resolution of the uncertainty cannot be quantified.

Extract from auditor's report

...

Opinion on financial statements

In our opinion the financial statements:

- give a true and fair view of the state of the company's affairs as at ... and of its profit [loss] for the year then ended;
- have been properly prepared in accordance with United Kingdom Generally Accepted Accounting Practice; and
- have been prepared in accordance with the requirements of the Companies Act 2006.

Emphasis of matter – possible outcome of a lawsuit

In forming our opinion on the financial statements, which is not qualified, we have considered the adequacy of the disclosures made in note [x] to the financial statements concerning the possible outcome of a lawsuit, alleging infringement of certain patent rights and claiming royalties and punitive damages, where the company is the defendant. The company has filed a counter action, and preliminary hearings and discovery proceedings on both actions are in progress. The ultimate outcome of the matter cannot presently be determined, and no provision for any liability that may result has been made in the financial statements.

Opinion on other matter prescribed by the Companies Act 2006

...

Appendix 6 – Modified auditor's reports – Qualified opinion on financial statements

13. Qualified opinion: Disagreement – Inappropriate accounting treatment of debtors
14. Qualified opinion: Disagreement – Non-disclosure of a going concern problem
15. Qualified opinion: Scope Limitation – Auditor not appointed at the time of the stocktake
16. Qualified opinion: Scope Limitation – Directors did not prepare cash flow forecasts sufficiently far into the future to be able to assess the going concern status of the company

Example 13 – Qualified opinion: Disagreement – Inappropriate accounting treatment of debtors

- UK non-publicly traded company prepares UK GAAP financial statements (Example 2).
- The debtors shown on the balance sheet include an amount of £Y due from a company which has ceased trading. XYZ Limited has no security for this debt.
- The auditor's opinion is that the company is unlikely to receive any payment and full provision of £Y should have been made.
- The auditor does not believe that the effect of the disagreement is so material / pervasive that the financial statements as a whole are misleading and issues a qualified opinion – except for disagreement about the accounting treatment of debtors.

Extract from auditor's report

...

Qualified opinion on financial statements arising from disagreement about accounting treatment

Included in the debtors shown on the balance sheet is an amount of £Y due from a company which has ceased trading. XYZ Limited has no security for this debt. In our opinion the company is unlikely to receive any payment and full provision of £Y should have been made. Accordingly, debtors should be reduced by £Y, the deferred tax liability should be reduced by £X and profit for the year and retained earnings should be reduced by £Z.

Except for the financial effect of not making the provision referred to in the preceding paragraph, in our opinion the financial statements:

- give a true and fair view of the state of the company's affairs as at ... and of its profit [loss] for the year then ended;
- have been properly prepared in accordance with United Kingdom Generally Accepted Accounting Practice; and
- have been prepared in accordance with the requirements of the Companies Act 2006.

Opinion on other matter prescribed by the Companies Act 2006

In our opinion the information given in the Directors' Report for the financial year for which the financial statements are prepared is consistent with the financial statements.

Matters on which we are required to report by exception[37]

We have nothing to report in respect of the following matters where the Companies Act 2006 requires us to report to you if, in our opinion:

- adequate accounting records have not been kept, or returns adequate for our audit have not been received from branches not visited by us; or

---

[37] The auditor needs to consider whether the circumstances leading to the disagreement about the accounting treatment affect the matters on which the auditor is required to report by exception.

- the financial statements are not in agreement with the accounting records and returns; or
- certain disclosures of directors' remuneration specified by law are not made; or
- we have not received all the information and explanations we require for our audit.

Example 14 – Qualified opinion: Disagreement – Non-disclosure of a going concern problem

- UK non-publicly traded company prepares UK GAAP financial statements (Example 2).
- The company's year-end is 31 December 20X1 and neither the financial statements nor the directors' report disclose that the Company's financing arrangements expire and amounts outstanding are payable on 19 July 20X2 and that the Company has been unable to re-negotiate or obtain replacement financing. The directors continue to talk to potential alternative providers of finance.
- This situation indicates the existence of a material uncertainty which may cast significant doubt on the company's ability to continue as a going concern and therefore it may be unable to realise its assets and discharge its liabilities in the normal course of business.
- The auditor concludes that there is a significant level of concern about going concern and disagrees with the failure to disclose this information in the financial statements. The auditor issues a qualified except for opinion describing the disagreement.

Extract from auditor's report

...

Qualified opinion on financial statements arising from omission of information concerning going concern

The company's financing arrangements expire and amounts outstanding are payable on 19 July 20X2. While the directors continue to investigate alternative sources of finance, the company has so far been unable to re-negotiate or obtain replacement financing. This situation indicates the existence of a material uncertainty which may cast significant doubt on the company's ability to continue as a going concern and therefore it may be unable to realise its assets and discharge its liabilities in the normal course of business. The financial statements (and notes thereto) do not disclose this fact.

Except for the omission of the information included in the preceding paragraph, in our opinion the financial statements:

- give a true and fair view of the state of the company's affairs as at 31 December 20X1 and of its profit [loss] for the year then ended;
- have been properly prepared in accordance with United Kingdom Generally Accepted Accounting Practice; and
- have been prepared in accordance with the requirements of the Companies Act 2006.

Opinion on other matter prescribed by the Companies Act 2006

...

Example 15 – Qualified opinion: Limitation on scope – Auditor not appointed at the time of the stocktake

- UK non-publicly traded company prepares UK GAAP financial statements (Example 2).
- The evidence available to the auditor was limited because they did not observe the counting of the physical stock as at 31 December 20X1, since that date was prior to the time the auditor was initially engaged as auditor for the company. Owing to the nature of the company's records, the auditor was unable to satisfy themselves as to stock quantities using other audit procedures.
- The limitation in audit scope causes the auditor to issue a qualified opinion "except for" any adjustments that might have been found to be necessary had they been able to obtain sufficient evidence concerning stock.
- The limitation of scope was determined by the auditor not to be so material / pervasive as to require a disclaimer of opinion.

Extract from auditor's report

...

Qualified opinion on financial statements arising from limitation in audit scope

With respect to stock having a carrying amount of £X the audit evidence available to us was limited because we did not observe the counting of the physical stock as at 31 December 20X1, since that date was prior to our appointment as auditor of the company. Owing to the nature of the company's records, we were unable to obtain sufficient appropriate audit evidence regarding the stock quantities by using other audit procedures.

Except for the financial effects of such adjustments, if any, as might have been determined to be necessary had we been able to satisfy ourselves as to physical stock quantities, in our opinion the financial statements:

- give a true and fair view of the state of the company's affairs as at 31 December 20X1 and of its profit [loss]for the year then ended;
- have been properly prepared in accordance with United Kingdom Generally Accepted Accounting Practice; and
- have been prepared in accordance with the requirements of the Companies Act 2006.

Opinion on other matter prescribed by the Companies Act 2006

In our opinion the information given in the Directors' Report for the financial year for which the financial statements are prepared is consistent with the financial statements.

Matters on which we are required to report by exception

In respect solely of the limitation on our work relating to stock, described above:

- we have not obtained all the information and explanations that we considered necessary for the purpose of our audit; and
- we were unable to determine whether adequate accounting records had been kept.

We have nothing to report in respect of the following matters where the Companies Act 2006 requires us to report to you if, in our opinion:

- returns adequate for our audit have not been received from branches not visited by us; or
- the financial statements are not in agreement with the accounting records and returns; or
- certain disclosures of directors' remuneration specified by law are not made.

[Signature]   Address
John Smith (Senior statutory auditor)   Date
for and on behalf of ABC LLP, Statutory Auditor

Example 16 – Qualified opinion: Limitation of scope – Directors did not prepare cash flow forecasts sufficiently far into the future to be able to assess the going concern status of the company

- UK non-publicly traded company prepares UK GAAP financial statements (Example 2).
- The evidence available to the auditor was limited because the company had prepared cash flow forecasts and other information needed for the assessment of the appropriateness of the going concern basis of preparation of the financial statements only for a period of nine months from the date of approval of the financial statements and there were no sufficient alternative procedures that the auditor could perform.
- Although this fact is disclosed in the financial statements had the information been available the auditor might have formed a different opinion. The auditor considers that the directors have not taken adequate steps to satisfy themselves that it is appropriate for them to adopt the going concern basis.
- The auditor does not consider that the future period to which the directors have paid particular attention in assessing going concern is reasonable in the company's circumstances. The auditor considers that the particular circumstances of the company and the nature of the company's business require that such information be prepared, and reviewed by the directors and auditor for a period of at least twelve months from the date of approval of the financial statements.
- The auditor considers that the possible effect of the limitation of scope is not so material / pervasive that they are unable to form an opinion on the financial statements.
- The auditor issues an "except for" qualified opinion referring to the adjustments that might have been found to be necessary had they obtained sufficient evidence concerning the appropriateness of the going concern basis of preparation of the financial statements.

Extract from auditor's report

...

Qualified opinion on financial statements arising from limitation in audit scope

The audit evidence available to us was limited because the directors of the company have prepared cash flow forecasts and other information needed for the assessment of the appropriateness of the going concern basis of preparation of the financial statements for a period of only nine months from the date of approval of these financial statements. We consider that the directors have not taken adequate steps to satisfy themselves that it is appropriate for them to adopt the going concern basis because the circumstances of the company and the nature of the business require that such information be prepared, and reviewed by the directors and ourselves, for a period of at least twelve months from the date of approval of the financial statements. Had this information been available to us we might have formed a different opinion on the financial statements.

Except for the financial effects of any adjustments that might have been found to be necessary had we been able to obtain sufficient evidence concerning the appropriateness of the going concern basis of preparation of the financial statements, in our opinion the financial statements:

- give a true and fair view of the state of the company's affairs as at ... and of its profit [loss] for the year then ended;

- have been properly prepared in accordance with United Kingdom Generally Accepted Accounting Practice; and
- have been prepared in accordance with the requirements of the Companies Act 2006.

Opinion on other matter prescribed by the Companies Act 2006

In our opinion the information given in the Directors' Report for the financial year for which the financial statements are prepared is consistent with the financial statements.

Matters on which we are required to report by exception

In respect solely of the limitation on our work relating to the assessment of the appropriateness of the going concern basis of preparation of the financial statements, described above, we have not obtained all the information and explanations that we considered necessary for the purpose of our audit.

We have nothing to report in respect of the following matters where the Companies Act 2006 requires us to report to you if, in our opinion:

- adequate accounting records have not been kept, or returns adequate for our audit have not been received from branches not visited by us; or
- the financial statements are not in agreement with the accounting records and returns; or
- certain disclosures of directors' remuneration specified by law are not made.

[Signature]
John Smith (Senior statutory auditor)
for and on behalf of ABC LLP, Statutory Auditor

Address
Date

Appendix 7 – Modified auditor's reports – Adverse opinion on financial statements

17. Adverse opinion: No provision made for losses expected to arise on long term contracts
18. Adverse opinion: Significant level of concern about going concern status that is not disclosed in the financial statements

Example 17 – Adverse opinion: No provision made for losses expected to arise on long-term contracts

- UK non-publicly traded company prepares UK GAAP financial statements (Example 2).
- No provision has been made for losses expected to arise on certain long-term contracts currently in progress, as the directors consider that such losses should be off-set against amounts recoverable on other long-term contracts.
- In the auditor's opinion, provision should be made for foreseeable losses on individual contracts as required by SSAP 9.
- In the auditor's view, the financial effect of this disagreement in accounting treatment is so material / pervasive to the financial statements that an "except for" qualification of the auditor's report would not be sufficient to disclose the misleading nature of the financial statements.
- The auditor issues an adverse opinion due to the failure to provide for the losses and quantifies the impact on the profit for the year, the contract work in progress and the deferred tax liability at the year end.
- The auditor considers that notwithstanding its adverse opinion on the financial statements that adequate accounting records had been kept by the company and that it had received all the information and explanations it required for the audit.

Extract from auditor's report

...

Adverse opinion on financial statements

As more fully explained in note [x] to the financial statements no provision has been made for losses expected to arise on certain long-term contracts currently in progress, as the directors consider that such losses should be off-set against amounts recoverable on other long-term contracts. In our opinion, provision should be made for foreseeable losses on individual contracts as required by Statement of Standard Accounting Practice 9: *Stocks and long-term contracts*. If losses had been so recognised the effect would have been to reduce the carrying amount of contract work in progress by £X, the deferred tax liability by £Y and the profit for the year and retained earnings at 31 December 20X1 by £Z.

In view of the effect of the failure to provide for the losses referred to above, in our opinion the financial statements:

- do not give a true and fair view of the state of the company's affairs as at 31 December 20X1 and of its profit [loss] for the year then ended; and
- have not been properly prepared in accordance with United Kingdom Generally Accepted Accounting Practice.

In all other respects, in our opinion the financial statements have been prepared in accordance with the requirements of the Companies Act 2006.

Opinion on other matter prescribed by the Companies Act 2006

Notwithstanding our adverse opinion on the financial statements, in our opinion the information given in the Directors' Report for the financial year for which the financial statements are prepared is consistent with the financial statements.

Matters on which we are required to report by exception[38]

We have nothing to report in respect of the following matters where the Companies Act 2006 requires us to report to you if, in our opinion:

- adequate accounting records have not been kept, or returns adequate for our audit have not been received from branches not visited by us; or
- the financial statements are not in agreement with the accounting records and returns; or
- certain disclosures of directors' remuneration specified by law are not made; or
- we have not received all the information and explanations we require for our audit.

[Signature]   *Address*
John Smith (Senior statutory auditor)   *Date*
for and on behalf of ABC LLP, Statutory Auditor

---

[38] *The auditor needs to consider whether the circumstances leading to the adverse opinion on the financial statements affect the matters on which the auditor is required to report by exception.*

Example 18 – Adverse opinion: Significant level of concern about going concern status that is not disclosed in the financial statements

- UK non-publicly traded company prepares UK GAAP financial statements (Example 2).
- Although there is a significant level of concern about the company's ability to continue as a going concern the financial statements and notes do not disclose this fact and the directors have prepared the financial statements on the going concern basis.
- The auditor considers that the financial statements should disclose that there is a material uncertainty, which may cast significant doubt on the company's ability to continue as a going concern.
- The effect of this disagreement is so material / pervasive to the amounts included within the financial statements that the auditor concludes that a qualification of the report is not adequate to disclose the misleading or incomplete nature of the financial statements.
- The auditor issues an adverse audit opinion stating that, because the material uncertainty regarding going concern is not disclosed, the financial statements do not give a true and fair view.

Extract from auditor's report

...

Adverse opinion on financial statements

As explained in note [x] to the financial statements the company's financing arrangements expired and the amount outstanding was payable on [a past date]. The company has been unable to re-negotiate or obtain replacement financing and the directors of the company are considering whether the company should enter insolvency proceedings [but are continuing to investigate alternative sources of finance]. These events indicate a material uncertainty which may cast significant doubt on the company's ability to continue as a going concern and, therefore, it may be unable to realise its assets and discharge its liabilities in the normal course of business. The financial statements (and notes thereto) do not disclose this fact and have been prepared on the going concern basis.

In our opinion, because of the omission of the information referred to above:

- the financial statements do not give a true and fair view of the state of the company's affairs as at ... and of its profit [loss] for the year then ended; and
- have not been properly prepared in accordance with United Kingdom Generally Accepted Accounting Practice.

In all other respects, in our opinion the financial statements have been prepared in accordance with the requirements of the Companies Act 2006.

Opinion on other matter prescribed by the Companies Act 2006

Notwithstanding our adverse opinion on the financial statements, in our opinion the information given in the Directors' Report for the financial year for which the financial statements are prepared is consistent with the financial statements.

Matters on which we are required to report by exception

We have nothing to report in respect of the following matters where the Companies Act 2006 requires us to report to you if, in our opinion:

- adequate accounting records have not been kept, or returns adequate for our audit have not been received from branches not visited by us; or
- the financial statements are not in agreement with the accounting records and returns; or
- certain disclosures of directors' remuneration specified by law are not made; or
- we have not received all the information and explanations we require for our audit.

[Signature] Address
John Smith (Senior statutory auditor) Date
for and on behalf of ABC LLP, Statutory Auditor

Appendix 8 – Modified auditor's reports – Disclaimer of opinion on financial statements

19. Disclaimer of opinion: Auditor unable to attend stocktake and confirm trade debtors
20. Disclaimer of opinion: Multiple uncertainties

Example 19 – Disclaimer of opinion: Auditor unable to attend stocktake and confirm trade debtors

- UK non-publicly traded company prepares UK GAAP financial statements (Example 2).
- The evidence available to the auditor was limited because the auditor was not able to observe all physical stock and confirm trade debtors due to limitations placed on the scope of the auditor's work by the directors of the company.
- The limitation in scope is considered by the auditor to be so material / pervasive that it is unable to form an opinion on the financial statements.
- As a result, the auditor issues a modified opinion disclaiming an opinion on the financial statements.

Extract from auditor's report

...

Opinion: disclaimer on view given by the financial statements

The audit evidence available to us was limited because we were unable to observe the counting of physical stock having a carrying amount of £X and send confirmation letters to trade debtors having a carrying amount of £Y due to limitations placed on the scope of our work by the directors of the company. As a result of this we have been unable to obtain sufficient appropriate audit evidence concerning both stock and trade debtors.

Because of the possible effect of the limitation in evidence available to us, we are unable to form an opinion as to whether the financial statements:

- give a true and fair view of the state of the company's affairs as at ... and of its profit [loss] for the year then ended;
- have been properly prepared in accordance with United Kingdom Generally Accepted Accounting Practice; and
- have been prepared in accordance with the requirements of the Companies Act 2006.

Opinion on other matter prescribed by the Companies Act 2006

Notwithstanding our disclaimer of an opinion on the view given by the financial statements, in our opinion the information given in the Directors' Report for the financial year for which the financial statements are prepared is consistent with the financial statements.

Matters on which we are required to report by exception

In respect solely of the limitation of our work referred to above:

- we have not obtained all the information and explanations that we considered necessary for the purpose of our audit; and
- we were unable to determine whether adequate accounting records have been kept.

We have nothing to report in respect of the following matters where the Companies Act 2006 requires us to report to you if, in our opinion:

- returns adequate for our audit have not been received from branches not visited by us; or
- the financial statements are not in agreement with the accounting records and returns; or
- certain disclosures of directors' remuneration specified by law are not made.

[Signature]   *Address*
John Smith (Senior statutory auditor)   *Date*
for and on behalf of ABC LLP, Statutory Auditor

Example 20 – Disclaimer of opinion: Multiple uncertainties

- *As discussed in ISA (UK and Ireland) 700(Revised) paragraph 54 the addition of a paragraph emphasising a going concern problem or significant uncertainty is ordinarily adequate to meet the auditor's reporting responsibilities regarding such matters. However, in extreme cases, such as situations involving multiple uncertainties that are significant to the financial statements, the auditor may consider it appropriate to express a disclaimer of opinion instead of adding an emphasis of matter paragraph.*
- *This example does not include a description of the multiple material/significant uncertainties that might lead to a disclaimer of opinion because circumstances will vary and auditors will have to use their judgment when deciding whether it is an extreme case involving multiple uncertainties that are significant to the financial statements. Often, if such matters were considered individually, because the company makes relevant disclosures in the financial statements, the auditor would normally issue an unqualified auditor's report with an emphasis of matter paragraph describing the situation giving rise to the emphasis of matter and its possible effects on the financial statements, including (where practicable) quantification but the audit opinion would be unqualified.*

Extract from auditor's report

...

Opinion: disclaimer on view given by the financial statements

In forming our opinion on the financial statements, we have considered the adequacy of the disclosures made in the financial statements concerning the following matters:

- [Significant uncertainty 1]
- [Significant uncertainty 2]
- [Significant uncertainty 3]

Because of the potential significance, to the financial statements, of the combined effect of the three matters referred to in the paragraph above, we are unable to form an opinion as to whether the financial statements:

- give a true and fair view of the state of the company's affairs as at ... and of its profit [loss] for the year then ended;
- have been properly prepared in accordance with United Kingdom Generally Accepted Practice; and
- have been prepared in accordance with the requirements of the Companies Act 2006.

Opinion on other matter prescribed by the Companies Act 2006

Notwithstanding our disclaimer of an opinion on the view given by the financial statements, in our opinion the information given in the Directors' Report for the financial year for which the financial statements are prepared is consistent with the financial statements.

Matters on which we are required to report by exception[39]

We have nothing to report in respect of the following matters where the Companies Act 2006 requires us to report to you if, in our opinion:

- adequate accounting records have not been kept, or returns adequate for our audit have not been received from branches not visited by us; or
- the financial statements are not in agreement with the accounting records and returns; or
- certain disclosures of directors' remuneration specified by law are not made; or
- we have not received all the information and explanations we require for our audit.

[Signature] Address
John Smith (Senior statutory auditor) Date
for and on behalf of ABC LLP, Statutory Auditor

---

[39] The auditor needs to consider whether the circumstances leading to the disclaimer of opinion on the financial statements affects the matters on which the auditor is required to report by exception.

Appendix 9 – Descriptions of the "Scope of an Audit" that may be cross referenced from auditor's reports

- UK Publicly Traded Company (issued 26 March 2009)
- UK Non-Publicly Traded Company (issued 26 March 2009)

Scope of an audit of the financial statements of a United Kingdom publicly traded company or group (issued 26 March 2009)[40]

> This statement may be cross referred to from auditor's reports that are effective for accounting periods commencing on or after 6 April 2008 and ending on or after 5 April 2009. If the auditor's report is required to be read out, only the shaded paragraph is to be regarded as forming part of the auditor's report for that purpose.

1. THE SCOPE OF AN AUDIT OF FINANCIAL STATEMENTS ARISING FROM THE REQUIREMENTS OF COMPANY LAW

The Companies Act 2006 (CA 2006) requires the auditor to make a report to the company's members that must state clearly whether, in the auditor's opinion, the financial statements:

- give a true and fair view-
  - in the case of an individual balance sheet, of the state of affairs of the company as at the end of the financial year;
  - in the case of an individual profit and loss account, of the profit or loss of the company for the financial year; and
  - in the case of group accounts, of the state of affairs as at the end of the financial year and of the profit or loss for the financial year of the undertakings included in the consolidation as a whole, so far as concerns members of the company;
- have been properly prepared in accordance with the relevant financial reporting framework[41];
- have been prepared in accordance with the requirements of CA 2006 and, in the case of the consolidated accounts of publicly traded companies, the requirements of Article 4 of the IAS Regulation[42].

CA 2006 further requires the auditor's report on the financial statements to be either unqualified or qualified and to include a reference to any matters to which the auditor wishes to draw attention by way of emphasis without qualifying the report. Requirements of International Standards on Auditing (ISAs) (UK and Ireland) regarding qualified reports, unqualified reports and "emphasis of matter paragraphs" are discussed further in the next part of this statement.

2. THE SCOPE OF AN AUDIT OF FINANCIAL STATEMENTS ARISING FROM THE REQUIREMENTS OF ISAS (UK AND IRELAND)

Overall objective

In conducting an audit of financial statements, the overall objectives of the auditor are to:

---

[40] The web reference is www.frc.org.uk/apb/scope/UKP.

[41] The report will identify the relevant financial reporting framework.

[42] Regulation (EC) No 1606/2002 of the European Parliament and of the Council of 19 July 2002 on the application of international accounting standards.

(a) obtain reasonable assurance about whether the financial statements as a whole are free from material misstatement, whether due to fraud or error; and
(b) report on the financial statements and communicate, as required by ISAs (UK and Ireland), the auditor's findings.

Compliance with ISAs (UK and Ireland) and APB's Ethical Standards for Auditors

The auditor is required to comply with:

(a) all ISAs (UK and Ireland) that are relevant to the audit; and
(b) APB's Ethical Standards for Auditors.

ISAs (UK and Ireland) require the auditor to plan and perform an audit with professional scepticism recognizing that circumstances may exist that cause the financial statements to be materially misstated.

ISAs (UK and Ireland) and the Ethical Standards for Auditors contain basic principles and essential procedures together with related guidance. The nature of these Standards requires an auditor to exercise professional judgment in applying them.

Some ISAs (UK and Ireland) address the core aspects of the audit process such as:

- Planning.
- Understanding the company and its environment (including internal controls).
- Assessing the risks of material misstatement.
- Responding to assessed risks.

Other ISAs (UK and Ireland) establish requirements in relation to those areas of the auditor's work where it is particularly important that the views of auditors and users of financial statements, regarding the nature and extent of work to be performed, are aligned. Such areas include:

- Going concern.
- The auditor's responsibility to consider fraud in an audit of financial statements.
- Consideration of laws and regulations in an audit of financial statements.

Scope of an audit of financial statements

> An audit involves obtaining evidence about the amounts and disclosures in the financial statements sufficient to give reasonable assurance that the financial statements are free from material misstatement, whether caused by fraud or error. This includes an assessment of: whether the accounting policies are appropriate to the [group's and the parent] company's circumstances and have been consistently applied and adequately disclosed; the reasonableness of significant accounting estimates made by the directors; and the overall presentation of the financial statements.

Other information in the Annual Report

An auditor is required to read all financial and non-financial information included in the Annual Report and consider whether such "other information" is consistent with the audited financial statements. The auditor considers the implications for its report if it becomes aware of any material inconsistencies with the financial statements or any apparent material misstatements in the other information.

Communicating with those charged with governance

The auditor is required to communicate its significant findings arising from the audit with those charged with governance. Those charged with governance are the persons (usually the directors) with responsibility for overseeing the strategic direction of the company and obligations relating to the accountability of the company.

Significant findings from the audit include:

(a) the auditor's view about significant qualitative aspects of the entity's accounting practices, including accounting policies, accounting estimates and financial statement disclosures;
(b) significant difficulties encountered during the audit; and
(c) material weaknesses in internal control identified during the audit.

Reporting on the financial statements

The auditor's report is required to contain a clear expression of opinion on the financial statements taken as a whole.

To form an opinion on the financial statements the auditor concludes as to whether:

(a) sufficient appropriate audit evidence has been obtained;
(b) uncorrected misstatements are material, individually or in aggregate;
(c) the financial statements, including the related notes, give a true and fair view; and
(d) the financial statements are prepared, in all material respects, in accordance with the requirements of the relevant financial reporting framework, including the requirements of applicable law.

In particular an audit involves evaluating whether:

(a) the financial statements adequately refer to or describe the relevant financial reporting framework;
(b) the financial statements adequately disclose the significant accounting policies selected and applied;
(c) the accounting policies selected and applied are consistent with the applicable financial reporting framework, and are appropriate in the circumstances;
(d) accounting estimates are reasonable;
(e) the information presented in the financial statements is relevant, reliable comparable and understandable;
(f) the financial statements provide adequate disclosures to enable the intended users to understand the effect of material transactions and events on the information conveyed in the financial statements; and
(g) the terminology used in the financial statements, including the title of each financial statement, is appropriate.

Expressing an unqualified opinion

An unqualified opinion is expressed when the auditor is able to conclude that the financial statements comply with the applicable financial reporting framework (including applicable law) and give a true and fair view.

Qualifying the auditor's opinion

An auditor expresses a qualified opinion when either of the following circumstances exists and, in the auditor's judgment, the effect of the matter is or may be material to the financial statements:

(a) there is a limitation on the scope of the auditor's work that has prevented the auditor from obtaining sufficient appropriate audit evidence; or
(b) there is a disagreement regarding the acceptability of the accounting policies selected, the method of their application or the adequacy of financial statement disclosures.

The circumstances in (a) could lead to either a qualified opinion or a disclaimer of opinion whereas those in (b) could lead to either a qualified opinion or an adverse opinion.

Emphasising certain matters without qualifying the opinion

In certain circumstances an auditor's report includes an emphasis of matter paragraph to highlight a matter affecting the financial statements. An emphasis of matter paragraph does not affect the auditor's opinion. The auditor is required to consider adding an emphasis of matter paragraph where there is a significant uncertainty the resolution of which is dependent upon future events and which may affect the financial statements. However, the auditor is required to add an emphasis of matter paragraph to highlight a material uncertainty relating to an event or condition that may cast significant doubt on the entity's ability to continue as a going concern.

Communicating "other matters"

If the auditor considers it necessary to communicate a matter other than those that are presented or disclosed in the financial statements that, in the auditor's judgment is relevant to users' understanding of the audit, the auditor's responsibility or the auditor's report, the auditor does so in a paragraph in the auditor's report with the heading "Other Matter" or other appropriate heading.

3. OTHER LEGAL AND REGULATORY REQUIREMENTS

Requirements of ISA (UK and Ireland) 700 (Revised)

The auditor is required to address other legal and regulatory requirements relating to the auditor's report in a separate section of the auditor's report following the opinion on the financial statements. If the auditor is required to report on certain matters by exception the auditor should describe its responsibilities under the heading "Matters on which we are required to report by exception" and to incorporate a suitable conclusion in respect of such matters.

Requirements of CA 2006

CA 2006 establishes the following duties for auditors to which reference is, or may be, required in the auditor's report.

Directors' report

The auditor is required to report its opinion as to whether the information given in the directors' report (including the business review) for the financial year for which the financial statements are prepared is consistent with those financial statements.

Directors' remuneration report (Applies to those publicly traded companies that also meet the definition of quoted company in the Companies Act 2006)

If the company is a quoted company[43] the auditor is required to report whether the part of the Directors' Remuneration Report to be audited has been properly prepared in accordance with the requirements of CA 2006.

Duty to report on certain matters by exception

If the auditor is of the opinion:

(a) that adequate accounting records have not been kept, or that returns adequate for the audit have not been received from branches not visited by the auditor; or
(b) that the company's individual accounts are not in agreement with the accounting records and returns; or
(c) in the case of a quoted company, that the part of the Directors' Remuneration Report to be audited is not in agreement with the accounting records and returns, or
(d) certain disclosures of directors' remuneration specified by law are not made

the auditor is required to state that fact in the auditor's report.

If the auditor fails to obtain all the information and explanations which, to the best of the auditor's knowledge and belief, are necessary for the purposes of the audit, the auditor is required to state that fact in its report.

Duty of the auditor to include certain particulars, which have been omitted from the financial statements, in the auditor's report

The auditor is required to include in the auditor's report, so far as it is reasonably able to do so, a statement giving the required particulars, if:

(a) the requirements concerning the disclosure of directors' benefits: remuneration, pensions and compensation for loss of office are not complied with in the accounts; or
(b) in the case of a quoted company, the requirements as to information forming the part of the Directors' Remuneration Report to be audited are not complied with in that report,

---

[43] A quoted company is a company whose equity share capital –
  (a) has been included in the official list in accordance with the provisions of Part 6 of the Financial Services and Markets Act 200 (c. 8), or
  (b) is officially listed in an EEA state, or
  (c) is admitted to dealing on either the New York Stock Exchange or the exchange known as NASDAQ.

Corporate Governance (Applies to listed companies only)

The Listing Rules of the Financial Services Authority (the FSA) require listed companies[44] to ensure that their auditor reviews each of the following statements required by the Listing Rules, before the annual report is published:

(a) the directors' statement in relation to going concern;
(b) the parts of the statement by the directors that relate to the following provisions of the Combined Code:
- C1.1 (The directors should explain their responsibility for preparing the financial statements and there should be a statement about their reporting responsibilities;
- C2.1 (The Board should conduct a review of the effectiveness of the group's system of internal controls); and
- C3.1 to C3.7 (Various matters relating to Audit Committees and Auditors)

If, based on its review, the auditor disagrees with the statement by the directors on going concern or concludes that the Corporate Governance Statement does not appropriately reflect the company's compliance with the nine provisions of the Combined Code the auditor reports that under the heading "Other matter" in its report.

However, the auditor is not required to consider whether the directors' statements on internal control cover all risks and controls, or form an opinion on the effectiveness of the group's corporate governance procedures or its risk and control procedures.

---

[44] A listed company is a company that has any class of its securities admitted to the Official List maintained by the FSA in accordance with section 74 of the Financial Services and Markets Act 2000.

Scope of an audit of the financial statements of a United Kingdom non-publicly traded company or group (issued 26 March 2009)[45]

This statement may be cross referred to from auditor's reports that are effective for accounting periods commencing on or after 6 April 2008 and ending on or after 5 April 2009. If the auditor's report is required to be read out, only the shaded paragraph is to be regarded as forming part of the auditor's report for that purpose.

1. THE SCOPE OF AN AUDIT OF FINANCIAL STATEMENTS ARISING FROM THE REQUIREMENTS OF COMPANY LAW

The Companies Act 2006 (CA 2006) requires the auditor to make a report to the company's members that must state clearly whether, in the auditor's opinion, the financial statements:

- give a true and fair view-
    - in the case of an individual balance sheet, of the state of affairs of the company as at the end of the financial year;
    - in the case of an individual profit and loss account, of the profit or loss of the company for the financial year; and
    - in the case of group accounts, of the state of affairs as at the end of the financial year and of the profit or loss for the financial year of the undertakings included in the consolidation as a whole, so far as concerns members of the company;
- have been properly prepared in accordance with the relevant financial reporting framework[46];
- have been prepared in accordance with the requirements of CA 2006.

CA 2006 further requires the auditor's report on the financial statements to be either unqualified or qualified and to include a reference to any matters to which the auditor wishes to draw attention by way of emphasis without qualifying the report. Requirements of International Standards on Auditing (ISAs) (UK and Ireland) regarding qualified reports, unqualified reports and "emphasis of matter paragraphs" are discussed further in the next part of this statement.

2. THE SCOPE OF AN AUDIT OF FINANCIAL STATEMENTS ARISING FROM THE REQUIREMENTS OF ISAS (UK AND IRELAND)

Overall objective

In conducting an audit of financial statements, the overall objectives of the auditor are to:

(a) obtain reasonable assurance about whether the financial statements as a whole are free from material misstatement, whether due to fraud or error; and
(b) report on the financial statements and communicate, as required by ISAs (UK and Ireland), the auditor's findings.

---

[45] *The web reference is www.frc.org.uk/apb/scope/UKNP.*

[46] *The report will identify the relevant financial reporting framework.*

Compliance with ISAs (UK and Ireland) and APB's Ethical Standards for Auditors

The auditor is required to comply with:

(a) all ISAs (UK and Ireland) that are relevant to the audit; and
(b) APB's Ethical Standards for Auditors.

ISAs (UK and Ireland) require the auditor to plan and perform an audit with professional scepticism recognizing that circumstances may exist that cause the financial statements to be materially misstated.

ISAs (UK and Ireland) and the Ethical Standards for Auditors contain basic principles and essential procedures together with related guidance. The nature of these Standards requires an auditor to exercise professional judgment in applying them.

Some ISAs (UK and Ireland) address the core aspects of the audit process such as:

- Planning.
- Understanding the company and its environment (including internal controls).
- Assessing the risks of material misstatement.
- Responding to assessed risks.

Other ISAs (UK and Ireland) establish requirements in relation to those areas of the auditor's work where it is particularly important that the views of auditors and users of financial statements, regarding the nature and extent of work to be performed, are aligned. Such areas include:

- Going concern.
- The auditor's responsibility to consider fraud in an audit of financial statements.
- Consideration of laws and regulations in an audit of financial statements.

Scope of an audit of financial statements

> An audit involves obtaining evidence about the amounts and disclosures in the financial statements sufficient to give reasonable assurance that the financial statements are free from material misstatement, whether caused by fraud or error. This includes an assessment of: whether the accounting policies are appropriate to the [group's and the parent] company's circumstances and have been consistently applied and adequately disclosed; the reasonableness of significant accounting estimates made by the directors; and the overall presentation of the financial statements.

Other information in the Annual Report

If the financial statements are included in a document (such as an Annual Report) that contains surround information, other than the Directors' Report, an auditor is required to read all financial and non-financial information included in the document and consider whether such "other information" is consistent with the audited financial statements. The auditor considers the implications for its report if it becomes aware of any material inconsistencies with the financial statements or any apparent material misstatements in the other information.

Communicating with those charged with governance

The auditor is required to communicate its significant findings arising from the audit with those charged with governance. Those charged with governance are the persons (usually the directors) with responsibility for overseeing the strategic direction of the company and obligations relating to the accountability of the company.

Significant findings from the audit include:

(a) the auditor's view about significant qualitative aspects of the entity's accounting practices, including accounting policies, accounting estimates and financial statement disclosures;
(b) significant difficulties encountered during the audit; and
(c) material weaknesses in internal control identified during the audit.

Reporting on the financial statements

The auditor's report is required to contain a clear expression of opinion on the financial statements taken as a whole.

To form an opinion on the financial statements the auditor concludes as to whether:

(a) sufficient appropriate audit evidence has been obtained;
(b) uncorrected misstatements are material, individually or in aggregate;
(c) the financial statements, including the related notes, give a true and fair view; and
(d) the financial statements are prepared, in all material respects, in accordance with the requirements of the relevant financial reporting framework, including the requirements of applicable law.

In particular an audit involves evaluating whether:

(a) the financial statements adequately refer to or describe the relevant financial reporting framework;
(b) the financial statements adequately disclose the significant accounting policies selected and applied;
(c) the accounting policies selected and applied are consistent with the applicable financial reporting framework, and are appropriate in the circumstances;
(d) accounting estimates are reasonable;
(e) the information presented in the financial statements is relevant, reliable comparable and understandable;
(f) the financial statements provide adequate disclosures to enable the intended users to understand the effect of material transactions and events on the information conveyed in the financial statements; and
(g) the terminology used in the financial statements, including the title of each financial statement, is appropriate.

Expressing an unqualified opinion

An unqualified opinion is expressed when the auditor is able to conclude that the financial statements comply with the applicable financial reporting framework (including applicable law) and give a true and fair view.

Qualifying the auditor's opinion

An auditor expresses a qualified opinion when either of the following circumstances exists and, in the auditor's judgment, the effect of the matter is or may be material to the financial statements:

(a) there is a limitation on the scope of the auditor's work that has prevented the auditor from obtaining sufficient appropriate audit evidence; or
(b) there is a disagreement regarding the acceptability of the accounting policies selected, the method of their application or the adequacy of financial statement disclosures.

The circumstances in (a) could lead to either a qualified opinion or a disclaimer of opinion whereas those in (b) could lead to either a qualified opinion or an adverse opinion.

Emphasising certain matters without qualifying the opinion

In certain circumstances an auditor's report includes an emphasis of matter paragraph to highlight a matter affecting the financial statements. An emphasis of matter paragraph does not affect the auditor's opinion. The auditor is required to consider adding an emphasis of matter paragraph where there is a significant uncertainty the resolution of which is dependent upon future events and which may affect the financial statements. However, the auditor is required to add an emphasis of matter paragraph to highlight a material uncertainty relating to an event or condition that may cast significant doubt on the entity's ability to continue as a going concern.

Communicating "other matters"

If the auditor considers it necessary to communicate a matter other than those that are presented or disclosed in the financial statements that, in the auditor's judgment is relevant to users' understanding of the audit, the auditor's responsibility or the auditor's report, the auditor does so in a paragraph in the auditor's report with the heading "Other Matter" or other appropriate heading.

3. OTHER LEGAL AND REGULATORY REQUIREMENTS

Requirements of ISA (UK and Ireland) 700 (Revised)

The auditor is required to address other legal and regulatory requirements relating to the auditor's report in a separate section of the auditor's report following the opinion on the financial statements. If the auditor is required to report on certain matters by exception the auditor should describe its responsibilities under the heading "Matters on which we are required to report by exception" and to incorporate a suitable conclusion in respect of such matters.

Requirements of CA 2006

CA 2006 establishes the following duties for auditors of non-publicly traded companies to which reference is, or may be, required in the auditor's report.

Directors' report

The auditor is required to report its opinion as to whether the information given in the directors' report (including, where required, the business review) for the financial year for which the financial statements are prepared is consistent with those financial statements.

Duty to report on certain matters by exception

If the auditor is of the opinion:

(a) that adequate accounting records have not been kept, or that returns adequate for the audit have not been received from branches not visited by the auditor; or
(b) that the company's individual accounts are not in agreement with the accounting records and returns, , or
(c) certain disclosures of directors' remuneration specified by law are not made.

the auditor is required to state that fact in the auditor's report.

If the auditor fails to obtain all the information and explanations which, to the best of the auditor's knowledge and belief, are necessary for the purposes of the audit, the auditor is required to state that fact in its report.

If the directors of the company have prepared accounts and report in accordance with the small companies regime and in the auditor's opinion they were not entitled so to do, the auditor is required to state that fact in the auditor's report.

Duty of the auditor to include certain particulars, which have been omitted from the financial statements, in the auditor's report

The auditor is required to include in the auditor's report, so far as it is reasonably able to do so, a statement giving the required particulars, if the requirements concerning the disclosure of directors' benefits: remuneration, pensions and compensation for loss of office are not complied with in the accounts.

Appendix 10 – Modified auditor's report – Modified opinion on the directors' report

- UK non-publicly traded company prepares UK GAAP financial statements (Example 2).
- Auditor gives an unqualified opinion on the financial statements.
- There is an unresolved inconsistency between the directors' report and the financial statements.

Extract from auditor's report

...

Opinion on financial statements

In our opinion the financial statements:

- give a true and fair view of the state of the company's affairs as at .... and of its profit [loss] for the year then ended;
- have been properly prepared in accordance with United Kingdom Generally Accepted Accounting Practice; and
- have been prepared in accordance with the requirements of the Companies Act 2006.

Material inconsistency between the financial statements and the Directors' Report

In our opinion, the information given in the seventh paragraph of the Business Review in the Directors' Report is not consistent with the financial statements. That paragraph states without amplification that "the company's trading for the period resulted in a 10% increase in profit over the previous period's profit". The profit and loss account, however, shows that the company's profit for the period includes a profit of £Z which did not arise from trading but arose from the disposal of assets of a discontinued operation. Without this profit on the disposal of assets the company would have reported a profit for the year of £Y, representing a reduction in profit of 25% over the previous period's profit on a like for like basis. Except for this matter, in our opinion the information given in the Directors' Report is consistent with the financial statements.

Matters on which we are required to report by exception

We have nothing to report in respect of the following matters where the Companies Act 2006 requires us to report to you if, in our opinion:

- adequate accounting records have not been kept, or returns adequate for our audit have not been received from branches not visited by us; or
- the financial statements are not in agreement with the accounting records and returns; or
- certain disclosures of directors' remuneration specified by law are not made; or
- we have not received all the information and explanations we require for our audit.

[Signature]
John Smith (Senior statutory auditor)
for and on behalf of ABC LLP, Statutory Auditor

Address
Date

Appendix 11 – Illustrative Directors' Responsibilities Statement for a non-publicly traded company preparing its financial statements under UK GAAP

Statement of directors' responsibilities

The directors are responsible for preparing the Directors' Report and the financial statements in accordance with applicable law and regulations.

Company law requires the directors to prepare financial statements for each financial year. Under that law the directors have elected to prepare the financial statements in accordance with United Kingdom Generally Accepted Accounting Practice (United Kingdom Accounting Standards and applicable law). Under company law the directors must not approve the financial statements unless they are satisfied that they give a true and fair view of the state of affairs of the company and of the profit or loss of the company for that period. In preparing these financial statements, the directors are required to:

- select suitable accounting policies and then apply them consistently;
- make judgments and accounting estimates that are reasonable and prudent[47];
- state whether applicable UK Accounting Standards have been followed, subject to any material departures disclosed and explained in the financial statements;[48]
- prepare the financial statements on the going concern basis unless it is inappropriate to presume that the company will continue in business[49].

The directors are responsible for keeping adequate accounting records that are sufficient to show and explain the company's transactions and disclose with reasonable accuracy at any time the financial position of the company and enable them to ensure that the financial statements comply with the Companies Act 2006. They are also responsible for safeguarding the assets of the company and hence for taking reasonable steps for the prevention and detection of fraud and other irregularities.

> The APB has not prepared an illustrative example of a Directors' Responsibilities Statement for a publicly traded company as the directors' responsibilities, which are in part dependent on the particular regulatory environment, will vary dependent on the rules of the market on which its securities are admitted to trading.

---

[47] Paragraph 13 of Part II of Schedule 2 to each of "The Small Companies and Groups (Accounts and Reports) Regulations 2008" (SI 2008 No. 409) and "The Large and Medium-sized Companies and Groups (Accounts and Reports) Regulations 2008" (SI 2008 No. 410) require that the amount of any item "must be determined on a prudent basis".

[48] This bullet does not apply to companies subject to the small companies regime and medium-sized companies as defined by CA 2006.

[49] Included where no separate statement on going concern is made by the directors.

Part Eight

Statement of Standards for Reporting Accountants

APB Statement of Standards for Reporting Accountants applicable to small (charitable) companies

Since the Statement of Standards was issued, the legislation has been amended so that the provisions set out below are now only applicable to small charitable companies. The Statement is, however, reproduced in its original form without amendments to reflect either the change of legislation or to make it specific to charitable companies.

Certain smaller charitable companies are exempt from the requirement for an audit under the provisions of the Companies Act 1985. Reporting Accountants engaged to report on the financial statements of such charities follow the procedures for making audit exemption reports contained in the Statement of Standards set out below.

Audit exemption reports

This statement sets out the basic principles and essential procedures, indicated by paragraphs in bold type, to be observed by reporting accountants engaged to prepare a report for the purposes of section 249A (2) of the Companies Act 1985 ('the Act') on the accounts of a small company; it also includes explanatory and other material which, rather than being prescriptive, is designed to assist reporting accountants. The limited nature of such a report derives from the relevant legislation and this statement has been prepared in consultation with the DTI. In this statement, the word 'report' is used to refer to the report for the purposes of section 249A (2). A summary of some of the key points of the legislative background to such reports is given in Appendix 1. For a proper understanding of the statutory requirements, however, reference should be made to the Act.

Accountancy work performed by reporting accountants
The directors of small companies usually engage an accounting firm to assist them to comply with the statutory responsibility to prepare annual accounts. Often the same accounting firm is engaged both to assist with accounts preparation (and related accountancy work) and to act as reporting accountants.

The procedures performed by the accounting firm in the preparation of the accounts will often be directly relevant to the report, but will not necessarily be sufficient to enable them to express all of the opinions which the Act requires in the report. However, where the accounting firm has prepared the accounts from the accounting records, and is satisfied that its procedures comply with paragraphs 1 to 17 of this statement, no additional work will be required in order to express the opinions which are to be provided in the report.

Objective of the engagement

1   The reporting accountants should perform such procedures as are necessary to provide a reasonable basis on which to express the opinions which are to be provided in the report.

1.1 The report requires opinions to be expressed on three specific matters and provides assurance only on those matters (see Appendix 1). The reporting accountants' work is designed to provide a reasonable basis for these opinions. As the scope of the opinions is narrow, the reporting accountants' procedures are limited and much less extensive than, for example, in an audit.

1.2 In particular, the reporting accountants do not consider the completeness, accuracy and validity of the accounting records; nor do they consider whether the accounts give a true and fair view, the company's compliance with applicable accounting standards, the treatment of events after the balance sheet date, the appropriateness of the going concern basis, or the company's compliance with other laws and regulations.

Agreeing the terms of the engagement

2   The reporting accountants and the directors should set out in writing and agree on the terms of the engagement.

2.1 To qualify for the exemption it is necessary for the directors to cause a report to be prepared. It is therefore in the interests of both the reporting accountants and the company that the reporting accountants send a letter confirming their acceptance of the appointment and documenting the key terms of the engagement.

2.2 If the reporting accountants already have an appointment as auditors of the company, under terms specified in an existing audit engagement letter, a new engagement letter will need to be agreed. There is no requirement to resign from the appointment as auditors. However, if it appears likely that the company will not require an audit of its accounts for the foreseeable future, then, in order to avoid any possible confusion, the accounting firm may wish to resign as auditors (and to make the statement required by section 394). In such circumstances the reporting accountants and the directors may agree terms of engagement on a continuing rather than an annual basis.

2.3 Matters dealt with in the engagement letter will normally include:

(a) the respective responsibilities of the directors and of the reporting accountants;
(b) the scope of the reporting accountants' work;
(c) the circumstances in which, and the form in which, a report can be issued; and
(d) the terms of any non-statutory professional services to be provided by the reporting accountants (for example, to assist the directors in preparing the accounts).

2.4 The reporting accountants can agree with the directors a limit on any liability arising out of the work. Section 310, which would make void any such agreement made by an auditor, does not apply to this or any other non-audit engagement. Legal advice may be required regarding the terms of any such agreement and on the form of words to be included in the engagement letter.

2.5 An illustrative example of an annual engagement letter for this type of engagement is given in Appendix 2.

The report should include the following matters: 13

(a) a title identifying the shareholders of the company as the persons to whom the report is addressed;
(b) an introductory paragraph identifying the accounts reported on;
(c) a statement that the directors are responsible for the preparation of the accounts;
(d) a description of the basis of the reporting accountants' opinion;
(e) the reporting accountants' opinion;
(f) the name and signature of the reporting accountants;
(g) the date of the report.

Addressee

The report is to be made to the members of the company, who are normally the shareholders (section 249A(2)). 13.1

Directors' responsibilities

A company is not entitled to the exemption unless the balance sheet includes a statement by the directors acknowledging their responsibilities for ensuring that the company keeps accounting records which comply with section 221 and for preparing accounts which give a true and fair view and which otherwise comply with the requirements of the Act (section 249B(4)(c)). It is sufficient for the report to include a reference to that statement rather than reproducing it in full. 13.2

Basis of opinion

This section of the report describes the scope of the engagement, to enable the reader to understand the nature of the procedures performed and the assurance expressed. 13.3

Name and signature of the reporting accountants

The copy of the report which is delivered to the registrar of companies is required to state the name of, and to be signed by, the reporting accountants. Copies of the report laid before the company in general meeting, or which are otherwise circulated, published or issued, need only state the name of the reporting accountants. 13.4

The report is signed in the name of the accounting firm, indicating their capacity as reporting accountants. 13.5

Date of the report

The date of the report is the date on which the reporting accountants sign the report. The reporting accountants do not date the report earlier than the date on which the accounts are approved by the directors. 13.6

Modification of the report

Disagreement

If the reporting accountants conclude that in respect of a particular matter either: 14

(a) the accounts are not in agreement with the accounting records kept by the company under section 221; or
(b) the accounts have not been drawn up in a manner consistent with the accounting requirements specified in section 249C(6):

they should issue a report including a negative opinion in respect of the relevant part of the opinion section.

14.1 The negative opinion indicates that, in the opinion of the reporting accountants, because of the matter in question, the relevant requirement has not been met. An illustrative example of a report containing a negative opinion is given in Appendix 4.

14.2 If the reporting accountants express a negative opinion in respect of one of the matters specified by the Act, they may need to consider the implications for the other opinions. For example, if the reporting accountants conclude that the accounts do not agree with the accounting records, it will be necessary to consider whether that particular matter raises doubts about the company's entitlement to the exemption from an audit of the accounts.

14.3 However, the fact that the reporting accountants identify a matter giving rise to a negative opinion does not of itself give rise to a need to perform additional or more extensive procedures in relation to other aspects of the accounts or of the accounting records.

Limitation on scope

15 If a limitation on the scope of the reporting accountants' procedure prevents them from obtaining a reasonable basis for an opinion as to whether either:

(a) the accounts are in agreement with the accounting records kept by the company under section 221; or
(b) the accounts have been drawn up in a manner consistent with the accounting requirements specified in section 249C(6):

they should issue a report including a qualified opinion in respect of the relevant part of the opinion section.

15.1 A limitation on scope may be:

(a) imposed by the directors (for example, where they refuse to provide information or explanations requested by the reporting accountants); or
(b) imposed by circumstances (for example, where parts of the accounting records have been lost or destroyed).

15.2 If there is a limitation on scope due to the absence of part of the accounting records, the reporting accountants may nevertheless be able, by comparing the accounts with the remaining accounting records (including any source documents which may be available), to conclude that the company satisfied the report conditions and that a report can be issued (see paragraph 11.1). In such circumstances, the opinion as to whether the accounts are in agreement with the accounting records will be qualified; the reporting accountants will need to consider whether the limitation on scope prevents them from forming an opinion as to whether the accounts have been drawn up in a manner consistent with the specified accounting requirements.

The qualified opinion indicates that it is expressed 'except for' the matter in question. An illustrative example of a report where there has been a limitation on scope is given in Appendix 5. 15.3

The use of an explanatory paragraph

If the reporting accountants have become aware of information which indicates to them that the accounts may be misleading, and their concern cannot be resolved by procedures which are within the scope of the examination, they should add an explanatory paragraph to the 'basis of opinion' section of the report, referring to the matter. It should be clearly stated that no opinion is expressed on the matter referred to. 16

If the reporting accountants' concerns have not been resolved by discussion with the directors, a negative or qualified opinion will be inappropriate if the matter in question is one that is outside the scope of the opinions required by the Act. In such cases the matter is highlighted by means of an additional explanatory paragraph in the 'basis of opinion' section of the report, to provide readers with a proper understanding of the basis of the opinion. An illustrative example of a report including an explanatory paragraph is given in Appendix 6. 16.1

The inclusion of an explanatory paragraph indicates only that the reporting accountants have become aware of that matter in the course of carrying out their procedures. When no explanatory paragraph is included this does not signify that the reporting accountants have satisfied themselves that the accounts are not misleading, but only that no matters have come to their attention to suggest otherwise. 16.2

Circumstances which may lead to resignation

If the reporting accountants either: 17
(a) have become aware of information which indicates to them that the accounts may be misleading, and they conclude that the matter cannot be adequately dealt with by means of modification of their report; or
(b) have serious doubts about the integrity of the directors,

the reporting accountants should resign from the engagement, notifying the directors in writing of the reason without undue delay.

Where the reporting accountants identify several different matters, each giving rise to a separate reason to modify the report, it will be necessary to consider the nature of the matters in question, and whether their combined effect is such as to raise doubts as to whether the reporting accountants can be associated with the accounts. 17.1

The reporting accountants may need to take legal advice on the wording of any letter of resignation relating to the integrity of the directors. 17.2

Appendix 1 – Legislative background

This appendix summarises some of the key points of the legislative background. For a proper understanding of the statutory requirements, however, reference should be made to the Act.

Exemptions from audit

1 The Act confers exemptions from audit for certain categories of small company: under section 249A(1) those companies which meet the 'total exemption conditions' (section 249A(3)) in respect of a financial year are exempt from the obligation to have their annual accounts audited, whilst under section 249A(2) those meeting the 'report conditions' (section 249A(4)) are similarly exempt if the directors cause a report to be prepared in accordance with section 249C and made to the company's members by suitably qualified reporting accountants.

2 No statutory report is required in the case of a company which meets the total exemption conditions.

3 The report conditions specified in section 249A(4) are that:
   (a) the company qualifies as a small company in relation to that year for the purposes of section 246;
   (b) its turnover for that year is more than £90,000 but not more than £350,000 (The turnover threshold was increased in 2000 to £1,000,000 for small companies other than charitable companies);
   (c) its balance sheet total for the year is not more than £1.4 million.

For a company which is a charity, the report conditions are modified by section 249A(5): the reference to turnover is replaced by gross income, on which the limit is £250,000.

The report

4 Section 249C specifies that the report for the purposes of section 249A(2) is required to state whether in the opinion of the reporting accountants making it:
   (a) the accounts of the company for the financial year in question are in agreement with the accounting records kept by the company under section 221, and
   (b) having regard only to, and on the basis of, the information contained in those accounting records, those accounts have been drawn up in a manner consistent with the provisions of the Act (i.e. accounting requirements) specified in section 249C(6), so far as they are applicable to the company.

5 The report also states that in the opinion of the reporting accountants, having regard only to, and on the basis of, the information contained in the accounting records kept by the company under section 221, the company satisfied the requirements of section 249A(4), modified by section 249A(5) where the company is a charity, for the financial year in question, and did not fall within the categories of company not entitled to the exemption specified in section 249B(1)(a) to (f) at any time within that financial year.

6 The provisions specified in section 249C(6) are:
   (a) section 226(3) and Schedule 4 ('Form and content of company accounts')

(b) section 231 and paragraphs 7 to 9A and 13(1), (3) and (4) of Schedule 5 ('Disclosure of information: related undertakings')
(c) section 232 and Schedule 6 ('Disclosure of information: emoluments and other benefits of directors and others') where appropriate as modified by section 246(1)(a) and (1A) and section A of Part I of Schedule 8.

Cases where exemptions are not available

Section 249B(1) specifies that a company is not entitled to exemption in respect of a financial year if at any time within that year it was: 7

(a) a public company;
(b) a banking or insurance company;
(c) enrolled in a list maintained by the Insurance Brokers Registration Council under section 4 of the Insurance Brokers (Registration) Act 1977;
(d) an authorised person or appointed representative under the Financial Services Act 1986;
(e) a special register body as defined in section 117(1) of the Trade Union and Labour Relations (Consolidation) Act 1992 or an employers' association as defined by section 122 of that Act; or a parent company or subsidiary undertaking

Section 249B(4) specifies that a company shall not be entitled to exemption unless the balance sheet includes a statement by the directors acknowledging their responsibilities, *inter alia*, for: 8

(a) ensuring that the company keeps accounting records which comply with section 221; and
(b) preparing accounts which give a true and fair view and which otherwise comply with the requirements of the Act.

Abbreviated accounts

If the directors of a company which satisfies the report conditions propose to take advantage of the exemptions conferred by Part III of Schedule 8 (exemptions with respect to delivery of accounts) and to deliver to the registrar of companies 'abbreviated accounts', a copy of the report for the purposes of section 249A(2) is also to be delivered to the registrar of companies. 9

No special report by the reporting accountants on the abbreviated accounts is required. 10

To avoid any possible confusion, however, the directors may choose to append to the copy of the report that is to be delivered some explanatory words, such as follows: 11

'The following reproduces the text of the report prepared for the purposes of section 249A(2) Companies Act 1985 in respect of the company's annual accounts, from which the abbreviated accounts (set out on pages . . . to . . .) have been prepared.'

Appendix 2 – Illustrative example of an engagement letter

This example is intended to illustrate the principles set out and the guidance given in the statement. In any particular engagement the letter will need to be tailored to the specific circumstances. The reporting accountants' professional body may specify other matters which are to be included in an engagement letter.

To the directors of . . .
The purpose of this letter is to set out the basis on which we are engaged:

(a) to act as reporting accountants to prepare a report for the purposes of section 249A(2) Companies Act 1985 (the Act), in respect of the company's accounts for the year ended . . ., in accordance with section 249C of the Act; and
(b) to provide other professional services to the company. and the respective responsibilities of the directors and of ourselves.

1 Responsibilities of the directors

1.1 As directors of the company, you are responsible for ensuring that the company maintains proper accounting records and for preparing accounts which give a true and fair view and which have been prepared in accordance with the Act.

1.2 You are also responsible for determining whether, in respect of the year, the company needs the conditions for exemption from an audit of the accounts set out in section 249A of the Act, and for determining whether, in respect of the year, the exemption is not available for any of the reasons set out in section 249B.

1.3 If, in respect of the year, the availability of the exemption from an audit of the accounts is conditional upon your causing a report in respect of these accounts to be prepared for the purposes of section 249A(2), you are responsible for deciding whether that report shall be made and for appointing us as reporting accountants to make that report to the shareholders of the company.

2 Responsibilities of the reporting accountants

2.1 We shall plan our work on the basis that a report for the purposes of section 249A(2) is required for the year, unless you inform us in writing that either:

(a) the company requires an audit of the accounts; or
(b) the company requires neither an audit nor such a report.

2.2 Should you instruct us to carry out an audit, then a separate letter of engagement will be required.

2.3 Should you inform us that the company requires neither an audit nor a report, then we shall have no responsibilities to the company, except those specifically agreed upon between us in respect of other professional services.

2.4 As reporting accountants, we have a statutory responsibility to report to the shareholders of the company whether in our opinion:

(a) the accounts are in agreement with the accounting records kept by the company under section 221 of the Act; and
(b) having regard only to, and on the basis of, the information contained in those accounting records, the accounts have been drawn up in a manner consistent

with the accounting requirements specified in section 249C(6) of the Act, so far as they are applicable to the company.

2.5 We also have a statutory responsibility to state that, having regard only to, and on the basis of, the information contained in the accounting records kept by the company under section 221, in our opinion the company satisfied the conditions for exemption from an audit of the accounts specified in section 249A(4) of the Act and did not, at any time within the year, fall within any of the categories, specified in section 249B(1), of companies not entitled to the exemption.

2.6 We do not have any responsibility to report whether any shareholder of the company has notified the company that he or she requires an audit, consequently we have no responsibility to carry out any work in respect of this matter.

2.7 Should our work lead us to conclude that the company is not entitled to exemption from an audit of the accounts, or should we be unable to reach a conclusion on this matter, then we will not issue any report and will notify you in writing of the reasons. In these circumstances, if appropriate, we will discuss with you the need to appoint an auditor.

Scope of the reporting accountants' work   3

3.1 Our engagement will be conducted in accordance with the Statement of Standards for Reporting Accountants issued by the Auditing Practices Board. Our procedures will consist of comparing the accounts with the accounting records kept by the company, and making such limited enquiries of the officers of the company as we may consider necessary for the purposes of our report.

3.2 Our work as reporting accountants will not be an audit of the accounts in accordance with Auditing Standards. Accordingly, we will not seek any independent evidence to support the entries in the accounting records, the existence, ownership or value of assets, or the completeness of income, liabilities and disclosures in the accounts. Nor will we make any assessment of the estimates and judgements made by you in your preparation of the accounts. Consequently our work as reporting accountants will not provide any assurance that the accounting records or the accounts are free from material misstatement, whether caused by fraud, other irregularities or error.

3.3 We have a professional responsibility not to allow our name to be associated with accounts which we consider may be misleading. Therefore, although we are not required to search for such matters, should we become aware, for any reason, that the accounts may be misleading, and the matter cannot be adequately dealt with by means of modification of our report, we will not issue any report and will withdraw from the engagement, and will notify you in writing of the reasons.

3.4 As part of our normal procedures, we may request you to provide written confirmation of any information or explanations given by you orally during the course of our work.

3.5 We attach to this letter a specimen of the form of report, setting out, in the manner specified by the professional standards, the opinions required by the Act.

Accounting and other services   4

4.1 You have asked us to assist you in the maintenance of the accounting records and in the preparation of the accounts, as follows:

(*describe the work to be performed or refer to a separate letter of engagement*)

4.2 You have asked us to provide other professional services, in respect of . . .

(*describe the other services*)

4.3 Our engagement with the company as reporting accountants for the purpose of preparing the report is a statutory responsibility and is distinct, and entirely separate, from any obligations or responsibilities arising out of the contractual arrangements agreed between us under which we are to provide the professional services described in [4.1] to [4.2] above.

5 Limitation of liability

5.1 (*The reporting accountants can agree with the directors a limit on any liability arising out of the work. In such circumstances, legal advice may be required regarding the form of words to be included in the engagement letter.*)

6 Fees

6.1 Our fees are computed on the basis of time spent on the company's affairs by the partners and our staff, and on the level of skills and responsibility involved. Our fees will be charged separately for each of the main classes of work described above, will be billed at appropriate intervals during the year and will be due on presentation.

6.2 If, in the circumstances described in [2.7], we do not issue any report, or if, in the circumstances described in [3.3], or for any other reason, it becomes necessary for us to withdraw from the engagement, our fees for work performed will be payable by the company.

7 Agreement of terms

7.1 We shall be grateful if you could confirm in writing your agreement to the terms of this letter, or let us know if they are not in accordance with your understanding. Yours faithfully ....

Appendix 3 – Illustrative example of report

ACCOUNTANTS' REPORT TO THE SHAREHOLDERS ON THE UNAUDITED ACCOUNTS OF XYZ LIMITED

We report on the accounts for the year ended . . . set out on pages . . . to . . .

Respective responsibilities of directors and reporting accountants

As described on page . . . the company's directors are responsible for the preparation of the accounts, and they consider that the company is exempt from an audit. It is our responsibility to carry out procedures designed to enable us to report our opinion.

Basis of opinion

Our work was conducted in accordance with the Statement of Standards for Reporting Accountants, and so our procedures consisted of comparing the accounts with the accounting records kept by the company, and making such limited enquiries of the officers of the company as we considered necessary for the purposes of this report. These procedures provide only the assurance expressed in our opinion.

Opinion

In our opinion:
(a) the accounts are in agreement with the accounting records kept by the company under section 221 of the Companies Act 1985;
(b) having regard only to, and on the basis of, the information contained in those accounting records:
(i) the accounts have been drawn up in a manner consistent with the accounting requirements specified in section 249C(6) of the Act; and
(ii) the company satisfied the conditions for exemption from an audit of the accounts for the year specified in section 249A(4) of the Act as modified by section 249A(5) and did not, at any time within that year, fall within any of the categories of companies not entitled to the exemption specified in section 249B(1).

[*Signature*]
Reporting accountants
Date   [*Address*]

Appendix 4 – Illustrative example of report: opinion including disagreement

ACCOUNTANTS' REPORT TO THE SHAREHOLDERS ON THE UNAUDITED ACCOUNTS OF XYZ LIMITED

We report on the accounts for the year ended . . . set out on pages . . . to . . .

Respective responsibilities of directors and reporting accountants

. . .

Basis of opinion

. . .

Opinion - including disagreement

As stated in note . . ., the directors have made no provision in the accounts for the depreciation of plant and machinery shown in the balance sheet at £. . . . Paragraph 18 of Schedule 4 to the Companies Act 1985 requires that any fixed asset which has a limited useful economic life be depreciated. In our opinion:

(a) the accounts are in agreement with the accounting records kept by the company under section 221 of the Companies Act 1985;
(b) having regard only to, and on the basis of, the information contained in those accounting records:
   (i) because of the absence of the provision for depreciation referred to above, the accounts have not been drawn up in a manner consistent with the accounting requirements specified in section 249C(6) of the Act; and
(ii) the company satisfied the conditions for exemption from an audit of the accounts for the year specified in section 249A(4) of the Act and did not, at any time within that year, fall within any of the categories of companies not entitled to the exemption specified in section 249B(1).

[Signature]
Reporting accountants
Date   Address

Appendix 5 – Illustrative example of report: opinion including limitation on scope

ACCOUNTANTS' REPORT TO THE SHAREHOLDERS ON THE UNAUDITED ACCOUNTS OF XYZ LIMITED

We report on the accounts for the year ended . . . set out on pages . . . to . . .

Respective responsibilities of directors and reporting accountants

Basis of opinion

Our work was conducted in accordance with the Statement of Standards for Reporting Accountants, and so our procedures consisted of comparing the accounts with the accounting records kept by the company, and making such limited enquiries of the officers of the company as we considered necessary for the purpose of this report, except that the scope of our work was limited as explained below. These procedures provide only the assurance expressed in our opinion. Owing to flood damage, certain accounting records relating to sales for the first month of the year have been destroyed, and so we have been unable to compare the sales shown in the accounts with those accounting records.

Opinion – including limitation on scope

In our opinion:

(a) except for the uncertainty relating to sales, which arises from the limitation on the scope of our work described above, the accounts are in agreement with the accounting records kept by the company under section 221 of the Companies Act 1985.

(b) having regard only to, and on the basis of, the information contained in those accounting records:
    (i) the accounts have been drawn up in a manner consistent with the accounting requirements specified in section 249C(6) of the Act; and
    (ii) the company satisfied the conditions for exemption from an audit of the accounts for the year specified in section 249A(4) of the Act and did not, at any time within the year, fall within any of the categories of companies not entitled to the exemption specified in section 249B(1).

[*Signature*]
Reporting accountants
Date   *Address*

Note: In this example the reporting accountants have been able to conclude that the company satisfied the report conditions and that the limitation of scope did not prevent them from forming an opinion as to whether the accounts been drawn up in manner consistent with the specified accounting requirements.

Appendix 6 – Illustrative example of report: including explanatory paragraph

ACCOUNTANTS' REPORT TO THE SHAREHOLDERS ON THE UNAUDITED ACCOUNTS OF XYZ LIMITED

We report on the accounts for the year ended . . . set out on pages . . . to . . .

Respective responsibilities of directors and reporting accountants

. . .

Basis of opinion

. . .

Trade debtors

In carrying out our procedures it has come to our attention that the balance sheet total of debtors includes a debt of £. . . which has been outstanding for in excess of one year. XYZ Limited has no security for this debt. The directors have made no provision against the debt being irrecoverable and they have informed us that they are satisfied that it will be recovered in full. We are not required to and have not performed any procedures to corroborate the directors' views, and we therefore express no opinion on this matter.

Opinion

. . .

[*Signature*]
Reporting accountants
Date

International Standard on Review Engagements (UK and Ireland) 2410
Review of interim financial information performed by the independent auditor of the entity

(Effective for reviews of interim financial information for periods ending on or after 20 September 2007. Early adoption is permitted.)

Contents

	Paragraph
Introduction	1 - 3-1
General Principles of a Review of Interim Financial Information	4 - 6
Objective of an Engagement to Review Interim Financial Information	7 - 9
Agreeing the Terms of the Engagement	10 - 11
Procedures for a Review of Interim Financial Information	12 - 29-1
Evaluation of Misstatements	30 - 33-1
Management Representations	34 - 35
Auditor's Responsibility for Accompanying Information	36 - 37
Communication	38 - 42
Reporting the Nature, Extent and Results of the Review of Interim Financial Information	43 - 63
Documentation	64
Effective Date	65

Appendix 1: Example of an Engagement Letter for a Review of Interim Financial Information

Appendix 2: Analytical Procedures the Auditor May Consider When Performing a Review of Interim Financial Information

Appendix 3: Example of a Management Representation Letter

Appendix 4: Examples of Review Reports on Interim Financial Information

Appendix 5: Examples of Review Reports with a Qualified Conclusion for a Departure from the Applicable Financial Reporting Framework

Appendix 6: Examples of Review Reports with a Qualified Conclusion for a Limitation on Scope Not Imposed by Management

Appendix 7: Examples of Review Reports with an Adverse Conclusion for a Departure from the Applicable Financial Reporting Framework

Appendix 8: Example Review Report for a UK or Irish Company Listed in the UK or Ireland Preparing a Half-Yearly Financial Report in Compliance with IAS 34 as Adopted by the European Union

Appendix 9: Summary of Particular Requirements of Half-Yearly Financial Reports Prepared by Listed Companies in the UK and Ireland

International Standard on Review Engagements (UK and Ireland) (ISRE (UK and Ireland)) 2410, "Review of Interim Financial Information Performed by the Independent Auditor of the Entity" should be read in the context of the Auditing Practices Board's Statement "The Auditing Practices Board - Scope and Authority of Pronouncements (Revised)" which sets out the application and authority of APB pronouncements.

ISRE (UK and Ireland) 2410 adopts the text of ISRE 2410 as issued by the International Auditing and Assurance Standards Board (IAASB) in July 2005. Supplementary material added by the APB is differentiated by the use of grey shading.

Introduction

The purpose of this International Standard on Review Engagements (UK and Ireland) (ISRE (UK and Ireland)) is to establish standards and provide guidance on the auditor's professional responsibilities when the auditor undertakes an engagement to review interim financial information of an audit client, and on the form and content of the report. The term "auditor" is used throughout this ISRE (UK and Ireland), not because the auditor is performing an audit function but because the scope of this ISRE (UK and Ireland) is limited to a review of interim financial information performed by the independent auditor of the financial statements of the entity. 1

This ISRE (UK and Ireland) uses the terms 'those charged with governance' and 'management'. The term 'governance' describes the role of persons entrusted with the supervision, control and direction of an entity. Ordinarily, those charged with governance are accountable for ensuring that the entity achieves its objectives, and for the quality of its financial reporting and reporting to interested parties. Those charged with governance include management only when they perform such functions. 1-1

In the UK and Ireland, those charged with governance include the directors (executive and non-executive) of a company or other body, the members of an audit committee where one exists, the partners, proprietors, committee of management or trustees of other forms of entity, or equivalent persons responsible for directing the entity's affairs and preparing its financial statements. 1-2

'Management' comprises those persons who perform senior managerial functions. 1-3

In the UK and Ireland, depending on the nature and circumstances of the entity, management may include some or all of those charged with governance (e.g. executive directors). Management will not normally include non-executive directors. 1-4

For purposes of this ISRE (UK and Ireland), interim financial information is financial information that is prepared and presented in accordance with an applicable financial reporting framework[1] and comprises either a complete or a condensed set of financial statements for a period that is shorter than the entity's financial year. 2

In the UK and Ireland, interim financial information usually comprises condensed financial information prepared for the first six months of the financial year. For entities listed on the London Stock Exchange the applicable financial reporting framework is established by the Disclosure and Transparency Rules of the Financial Services Authority (FSA)[1a]. For entities listed on the Irish Stock Exchange the applicable financial reporting framework is established by the 2-1

---

[1] *For example, International Financial Reporting Standards as issued by the International Accounting Standards Board.*

[1a] *Disclosure and Transparency Rule (DTR) 4.2 "Half-yearly financial reports" applies to all issuers whose shares or debt securities are admitted to trading and whose home state is the UK, subject to the exemptions set out in DTR 4.4.*

Transparency (Directive 2004/109/EC) Regulations 2007 and the Transparency Rules of the Financial Regulator[1b].

2-2 For entities listed on the London or Irish Stock Exchanges, issuers that are required to prepare consolidated annual accounts using International Financial Reporting Standards (IFRS) are required to prepare half-yearly financial reports that include a condensed set of financial statements that comply with International Accounting Standard (IAS) 34, "Interim Financial Reporting," as adopted by the European Union. The relatively few issuers that do not prepare consolidated accounts are required to comply with the minimum disclosure requirements set out in the relevant rules of the UK FSA and the Irish Transparency Regulations and rules of the Irish Financial Regulator as applicable. These rules and regulations also make clear that the persons making the required responsibility statements can satisfy the requirement to confirm that the condensed set of financial statements give a true and fair view by giving a statement that they have been prepared in accordance with IAS 34 as adopted by the European Union or, for UK or Irish issuers not using IFRS, pronouncements on interim reporting issued by the Accounting Standards Board[1c], provided always that such persons have reasonable grounds to be satisfied that the condensed set of financial statements is not misleading. Further information on the rules and regulations applicable to issuers is given in Appendix 9.

2-3 In the context of a review of consolidated interim financial information "the entity," as referred to in this ISRE (UK and Ireland), is the group.

3 **The auditor who is engaged to perform a review of interim financial information should perform the review in accordance with this ISRE (UK and Ireland).** Through performing the audit of the annual financial statements, the auditor obtains an understanding of the entity and its environment, including its internal control. When the auditor is engaged to review the interim financial information, this understanding is updated through inquiries made in the course of the review, and assists the auditor in focusing the inquiries to be made and the analytical and other review procedures to be applied. A practitioner who is engaged to perform a review of interim financial information, and who is not the auditor of the entity, performs the review in accordance with ISRE 2400, "Engagements to Review Financial Statements."[1d] As the practitioner does not ordinarily have the same understanding of the entity and its environment, including its internal control, as the auditor of the entity, the practitioner needs to carry out different inquiries and procedures to meet the objective of the review.

[1b] *Requirements for half yearly financial reports are set out in regulations 6 to 8 of Part 2 of the Transparency (Directive 2004/109/EC) Regulations 2007, subject to the exemptions set out in Part 3. Further requirements applicable to half-yearly financial reports are set out in the Transparency Rules issued by The Financial Regulator in Ireland.*

[1c] *For half-yearly periods ending on or after 20 September 2007, the relevant ASB pronouncement is the Statement "Half-Yearly Financial Reports".*

[1d] *ISRE 2400 has not been promulgated by the APB for application in the UK and Ireland.*

In some cases the auditor may be asked to carry out specific agreed-upon procedures as an alternative to a review, or the auditor may be approached for advice and guidance on specific accounting and financial reporting issues such as the policies relating to asset impairment or the useful life of an intangible asset. In such circumstances the auditor first agrees the procedures to be carried out, and then reports within that context. Such engagements are outside the scope of this ISRE (UK and Ireland) and, in such circumstances, the auditor requests the entity to describe interim financial information as 'neither audited nor reviewed'[1e].

3-1

General Principles of a Review of Interim Financial Information

The auditor should comply with the ethical requirements relevant to the audit of the annual financial statements of the entity[1f]. These ethical requirements govern the auditor's professional responsibilities in the following areas: independence, integrity, objectivity, professional competence and due care, confidentiality, professional behavior, and technical standards.

4

The auditor should implement quality control procedures that are applicable to the individual engagement. The elements of quality control that are relevant to an individual engagement include leadership responsibilities for quality on the engagement, ethical requirements, acceptance and continuance of client relationships and specific engagements, assignment of engagement teams, engagement performance, and monitoring.

5

The auditor should plan and perform the review with an attitude of professional skepticism, recognizing that circumstances may exist that cause the interim financial information to require a material adjustment for it to be prepared, in all material respects, in accordance with the applicable financial reporting framework. An attitude of professional skepticism means that the auditor makes a critical assessment, with a questioning mind, of the validity of evidence obtained and is alert to evidence that contradicts or brings into question the reliability of documents or representations by management of the entity.

6

Objective of an Engagement to Review Interim Financial Information

The objective of an engagement to review interim financial information is to enable the auditor to express a conclusion whether, on the basis of the review, anything has come to the auditor's attention that causes the auditor to believe that the interim financial information is not prepared, in all material respects, in accordance with an

7

[1e] *The FSA's Disclosure and Transparency Rule 4.2.9(1), and the Irish Regulation 8(4)(a), requires that if the half-yearly financial report has been audited or reviewed by auditors pursuant to the Auditing Practices Board guidance on Review of Interim Financial Information, the audit report or review report must be reproduced in full.*
The FSA's Disclosure and Transparency Rule 4.2.9(2), and the Irish Regulation 8(4)(b), requires that if the half-yearly financial report has not been audited or reviewed by auditors pursuant to the Auditing Practices Board guidance on Review of Interim Financial Information, an issuer must make a statement to this effect in its report.

[1f] *In the UK and Ireland the relevant ethical pronouncements with which the auditor complies are the APB's Ethical Standards for Auditors and the ethical pronouncements relating to the work of auditors issued by the auditor's relevant professional body.*

applicable financial reporting framework. The auditor makes inquiries, and performs analytical and other review procedures in order to reduce to a moderate level the risk of expressing an inappropriate conclusion when the interim financial information is materially misstated.

8 The objective of a review of interim financial information differs significantly from that of an audit conducted in accordance with International Standards on Auditing (UK and Ireland) (ISAs (UK and Ireland)). A review of interim financial information does not provide a basis for expressing an opinion whether the financial information gives a true and fair view, or is presented fairly, in all material respects, in accordance with an applicable financial reporting framework.

9 A review, in contrast to an audit, is not designed to obtain reasonable assurance that the interim financial information is free from material misstatement. A review consists of making inquiries, primarily of persons responsible for financial and accounting matters, and applying analytical and other review procedures. A review may bring significant matters affecting the interim financial information to the auditor's attention, but it does not provide all of the evidence that would be required in an audit.

Agreeing the Terms of the Engagement

10 **The auditor and the client should agree on the terms of the engagement.**

11 The agreed terms of the engagement are ordinarily recorded in an engagement letter. Such a communication helps to avoid misunderstandings regarding the nature of the engagement and, in particular, the objective and scope of the review, management's responsibilities, the extent of the auditor's responsibilities, the assurance obtained, and the nature and form of the report. The communication ordinarily covers the following matters:

- The objective of a review of interim financial information.
- The scope of the review.
- Management's responsibility for the interim financial information.
- The applicable financial reporting framework (e.g. IAS 34 as adopted by the European Union and/or, where applicable, rules and regulations of a listing/regulatory authority relating to the form and content of interim financial information).
- Management's responsibility for establishing and maintaining effective internal control relevant to the preparation of interim financial information.
- Management's responsibility for making all financial records and related information available to the auditor.
- Management's agreement to provide written representations to the auditor to confirm representations made orally during the review, as well as representations that are implicit in the entity's records.
- The anticipated form and content of the report to be issued, including the identity of the addressee of the report.
- Management's agreement that where any document containing interim financial information indicates that the interim financial information has been reviewed by the entity's auditor, the review report will also be included in the document.

An illustrative engagement letter is set out in Appendix 1 to this ISRE (UK and Ireland). The terms of engagement to review interim financial information can also be combined with the terms of engagement to audit the annual financial statements.

Procedures for a Review of Interim Financial Information

Understanding the Entity and its Environment, Including its Internal Control

The auditor should have an understanding of the entity and its environment, including its internal control, as it relates to the preparation of both annual and interim financial information, sufficient to plan and conduct the engagement so as to be able to: 12

(a) **Identify the types of potential material misstatement and consider the likelihood of their occurrence; and**
(b) **Select the inquiries, analytical and other review procedures that will provide the auditor with a basis for reporting whether anything has come to the auditor's attention that causes the auditor to believe that the interim financial information is not prepared, in all material respects, in accordance with the applicable financial reporting framework.**

As required by ISA (UK and Ireland) 315, "Understanding the Entity and its Environment and Assessing the Risks of Material Misstatement," the auditor who has audited the entity's financial statements for one or more annual periods has obtained an understanding of the entity and its environment, including its internal control, as it relates to the preparation of annual financial information that was sufficient to conduct the audit. In planning a review of interim financial information, the auditor updates this understanding. The auditor also obtains a sufficient understanding of internal control as it relates to the preparation of interim financial information as it may differ from internal control as it relates to annual financial information. 13

The auditor uses the understanding of the entity and its environment, including its internal control, to determine the inquiries to be made and the analytical and other review procedures to be applied, and to identify the particular events, transactions or assertions to which inquiries may be directed or analytical or other review procedures applied. 14

The procedures performed by the auditor to update the understanding of the entity and its environment, including its internal control, ordinarily include the following: 15

- Reading the documentation, to the extent necessary, of the preceding year's audit and reviews of prior interim period(s) of the current year and corresponding interim period(s) of the prior year, to enable the auditor to identify matters that may affect the current-period interim financial information.
- Considering any significant risks, including the risk of management override of controls, that were identified in the audit of the prior year's financial statements.
- Reading the most recent annual and comparable prior period interim financial information.
- Considering materiality with reference to the applicable financial reporting framework as it relates to interim financial information to assist in determining the nature and extent of the procedures to be performed and evaluating the effect of misstatements.
- Considering the nature of any corrected material misstatements and any identified uncorrected immaterial misstatements in the prior year's financial statements.

- Considering significant financial accounting and reporting matters that may be of continuing significance such as material weaknesses in internal control.
- Considering the results of any audit procedures performed with respect to the current year's financial statements.
- Considering the results of any internal audit performed and the subsequent actions taken by management.
- Reading management accounts and commentaries for the period.
- Considering any findings from prior periods relating to the quality and reliability of management accounts.
- Inquiring of management about the results of management's assessment of the risk that the interim financial information may be materially misstated as a result of fraud.
- Inquiring of management about the effect of changes in the entity's business activities.
- Inquiring of management about any significant changes in internal control and the potential effect of any such changes on the preparation of interim financial information.
- Inquiring of management of the process by which the interim financial information has been prepared and the reliability of the underlying accounting records to which the interim financial information is agreed or reconciled.

16 The auditor determines the nature of the review procedures, if any, to be performed for components and, where applicable, communicates these matters to other auditors involved in the review. Factors to be considered include the materiality of, and risk of misstatement in, the interim financial information of components, and the auditor's understanding of the extent to which internal control over the preparation of such information is centralized or decentralized.

17 **In order to plan and conduct a review of interim financial information, a recently appointed auditor, who has not yet performed an audit of the annual financial statements in accordance with ISAs (UK and Ireland), should obtain an understanding of the entity and its environment, including its internal control, as it relates to the preparation of both annual and interim financial information.**

18 This understanding enables the auditor to focus the inquiries made, and the analytical and other review procedures applied in performing a review of interim financial information in accordance with this ISRE (UK and Ireland). As part of obtaining this understanding, the auditor ordinarily makes inquiries of the predecessor auditor and, where practicable, reviews the predecessor auditor's documentation for the preceding annual audit, and for any prior interim periods in the current year that have been reviewed by the predecessor auditor. In doing so, the auditor considers the nature of any corrected misstatements, and any uncorrected misstatements aggregated by the predecessor auditor, any significant risks, including the risk of management override of controls, and significant accounting and any reporting matters that may be of continuing significance, such as material weaknesses in internal control.

Inquiries, Analytical and Other Review Procedures

19 **The auditor should make inquiries, primarily of persons responsible for financial and accounting matters, and perform analytical and other review procedures to enable the**

auditor to conclude whether, on the basis of the procedures performed, anything has come to the auditor's attention that causes the auditor to believe that the interim financial information is not prepared, in all material respects, in accordance with the applicable financial reporting framework.

A review ordinarily does not require tests of the accounting records through inspection, observation or confirmation. Procedures for performing a review of interim financial information are ordinarily limited to making inquiries, primarily of persons responsible for financial and accounting matters, and applying analytical and other review procedures, rather than corroborating information obtained concerning significant accounting matters relating to the interim financial information. The auditor's understanding of the entity and its environment, including its internal control, the results of the risk assessments relating to the preceding audit and the auditor's consideration of materiality as it relates to the interim financial information, affects the nature and extent of the inquiries made, and analytical and other review procedures applied. 20

The auditor ordinarily performs the following procedures: 21

- Reading the minutes of the meetings of shareholders, those charged with governance, and other appropriate committees to identify matters that may affect the interim financial information, and inquiring about matters dealt with at meetings for which minutes are not available that may affect the interim financial information.
- Considering the effect, if any, of matters giving rise to a modification of the audit or review report, accounting adjustments or unadjusted misstatements, at the time of the previous audit or reviews.
- Communicating, where appropriate, with other auditors who are performing a review of the interim financial information of the reporting entity's significant components.
- Inquiring of members of management responsible for financial and accounting matters, and others as appropriate about the following:
  - Whether the interim financial information has been prepared and presented in accordance with the applicable financial reporting framework.
  - Whether there have been any changes in accounting principles or in the methods of applying them.
  - Whether any new transactions have necessitated the application of a new accounting principle.
  - Whether the interim financial information contains any known uncorrected misstatements.
  - Unusual or complex situations that may have affected the interim financial information, such as a business combination or disposal of a segment of the business.
  - Significant assumptions that are relevant to the fair value measurement or disclosures and management's intention and ability to carry out specific courses of action on behalf of the entity.
  - Whether related party transactions have been appropriately accounted for and disclosed in the interim financial information.
  - Significant changes in commitments and contractual obligations.
  - Significant changes in contingent liabilities including litigation or claims.
  - Compliance with debt covenants.
  - Matters about which questions have arisen in the course of applying the review procedures.
  - Significant transactions occurring in the last several days of the interim period or the first several days of the next interim period.
  - Knowledge of any fraud or suspected fraud affecting the entity involving:

- Management;
- Employees who have significant roles in internal control; or
- Others where the fraud could have a material effect on the interim financial information.
- Knowledge of any allegations of fraud, or suspected fraud, affecting the entity's interim financial information communicated by employees, former employees, analysts, regulators, or others.
- Knowledge of any actual or possible noncompliance with laws and regulations that could have a material effect on the interim financial information.
- For group interim financial information, reviewing consolidation adjustments for consistency with the preceding annual financial statements and enquiring into large or unusual adjustments, and into adjustments made in the preceding annual financial statements but not made in the financial information in the interim report.
- Reviewing correspondence with regulators where applicable.
- Applying analytical procedures to the interim financial information designed to identify relationships and individual items that appear to be unusual and that may reflect a material misstatement in the interim financial information. Analytical procedures may include ratio analysis and statistical techniques such as trend analysis or regression analysis and may be performed manually or with the use of computer-assisted techniques. Appendix 2 to this ISRE (UK and Ireland) contains examples of analytical procedures the auditor may consider when performing a review of interim financial information.
- Reading the interim financial information, and considering whether anything has come to the auditor's attention that causes the auditor to believe that the interim financial information is not prepared, in all material respects, in accordance with the applicable financial reporting framework.

22 The auditor may perform many of the review procedures before or simultaneously with the entity's preparation of the interim financial information. For example, it may be practicable to update the understanding of the entity and its environment, including its internal control, and begin reading applicable minutes before the end of the interim period. Performing some of the review procedures earlier in the interim period also permits early identification and consideration of significant accounting matters affecting the interim financial information.

23 The auditor performing the review of interim financial information is also engaged to perform an audit of the annual financial statements of the entity. For convenience and efficiency, the auditor may decide to perform certain audit procedures concurrently with the review of interim financial information. For example, information gained from reading the minutes of meetings of the board of directors in connection with the review of the interim financial information also may be used for the annual audit. The auditor may also decide to perform, at the time of the interim review, auditing procedures that would need to be performed for the purpose of the audit of the annual financial statements, for example, performing audit procedures on significant or unusual transactions that occurred during the period, such as business combinations, restructurings, or significant revenue transactions.

24 A review of interim financial information ordinarily does not require corroborating the inquiries about litigation or claims. It is, therefore, ordinarily not necessary to send an inquiry letter to the entity's lawyer. Direct communication with the entity's

lawyer with respect to litigation or claims may, however, be appropriate if a matter comes to the auditor's attention that causes the auditor to question whether the interim financial information is not prepared, in all material respects, in accordance with the applicable financial reporting framework, and the auditor believes the entity's lawyer may have pertinent information.

The auditor should obtain evidence that the interim financial information agrees or reconciles with the underlying accounting records. The auditor may obtain evidence that the interim financial information agrees or reconciles with the underlying accounting records by tracing the interim financial information to: 25

(a) The accounting records, such as the general ledger, or a consolidating schedule that agrees or reconciles with the accounting records; and
(b) Other supporting data in the entity's records as necessary.

> For a review of consolidated group interim financial information, the auditor traces the financial information of group components to the consolidation schedules and records of significant consolidation journals and adjustments. The auditor is not required to check the financial information back to the accounting records of individual group components. 25-1

The auditor should inquire whether management has identified all events up to the date of the review report that may require adjustment to or disclosure in the interim financial information. It is not necessary for the auditor to perform other procedures to identify events occurring after the date of the review report. 26

The auditor should inquire whether management has changed its assessment of the entity's ability to continue as a going concern. When, as a result of this inquiry or other review procedures, the auditor becomes aware of events or conditions that may cast significant doubt on the entity's ability to continue as a going concern, the auditor should: 27

(a) Inquire of management as to its plans for future actions based on its going concern assessment, the feasibility of these plans, and whether management believes that the outcome of these plans will improve the situation; and
(b) Consider the adequacy of the disclosure about such matters in the interim financial information.

> The guidance in "Going concern and financial reporting - guidance for directors of listed companies registered in the UK" issued in 1994 states "Directors cannot be expected to consider going concern as fully at the interim, but they should undertake a review of their previous work." Paragraph 57 of that guidance also states: "They should look at the position at the previous year-end to see whether any of the significant factors which they had identified at that time have changed in the interim to such an extent as to affect the appropriateness of the going concern assumption." 27-1

Events or conditions which may cast significant doubt on the entity's ability to continue as a going concern may have existed at the date of the annual financial statements or may be identified as a result of inquiries of management or in the course of performing other review procedures. When such events or conditions come to the auditor's attention, the auditor inquires of management as to its plans for future action, such as its plans to liquidate assets, borrow money or restructure debt, 28 reduce or delay expenditures, or increase capital. The auditor also inquires as to the feasibility of management's plans and whether management believes that the outcome of these plans will improve the situation. However, it is not ordinarily necessary for the auditor to corroborate the feasibility of management's plans and whether the outcome of these plans will improve the situation.

29 When a matter comes to the auditor's attention that leads the auditor to question whether a material adjustment should be made for the interim financial information to be prepared, in all material respects, in accordance with the applicable financial reporting framework, the auditor should make additional inquiries or perform other procedures to enable the auditor to express a conclusion in the review report. For example, if the auditor's review procedures lead the auditor to question whether a significant sales transaction is recorded in accordance with the applicable financial reporting framework, the auditor performs additional procedures sufficient to resolve the auditor's questions, such as discussing the terms of the transaction with senior marketing and accounting personnel, or reading the sales contract.

Comparative Interim Financial Information

29-1 When comparative interim financial information is presented, the auditor should consider whether:

(a) The accounting policies used for the comparative financial information are consistent with those of the current period and appropriate adjustments and disclosures have been made where this is not the case; and
(b) The comparative amounts agree with the amounts and other disclosures presented in the preceding interim financial report for the corresponding period or whether appropriate disclosures and adjustments have been made where this is not the case.

Evaluation of Misstatements

30 The auditor should evaluate, individually and in the aggregate, whether uncorrected misstatements that have come to the auditor's attention are material to the interim financial information.

31 A review of interim financial information, in contrast to an audit engagement, is not designed to obtain reasonable assurance that the interim financial information is free from material misstatement. However, misstatements which come to the auditor's attention, including inadequate disclosures, are evaluated individually and in the aggregate to determine whether a material adjustment is required to be made to the interim financial information for it to be prepared, in all material respects, in accordance with the applicable financial reporting framework.

32 The auditor exercises professional judgment in evaluating the materiality of any misstatements that the entity has not corrected. The auditor considers matters such as the nature, cause and amount of the misstatements, whether the misstatements originated in the preceding year or interim period of the current year, and the potential effect of the misstatements on future interim or annual periods.

33 The auditor may designate an amount below which misstatements need not be aggregated, because the auditor expects that the aggregation of such amounts clearly would not have a material effect on the interim financial information. In so doing, the auditor considers the fact that the determination of materiality involves

quantitative as well as qualitative considerations, and that misstatements of a relatively small amount could nevertheless have a material effect on the interim financial information.

> The amount designated by the auditor, below which misstatements that have come to the auditors attention need not be aggregated, is the amount below which the auditor believes misstatements are clearly trivial[1g].   33-1

Management Representations

The auditor should obtain written representation from management that: 34

(a) It acknowledges its responsibility for the design and implementation of internal control to prevent and detect fraud and error;
(b) The interim financial information is prepared and presented in accordance with the applicable financial reporting framework;
(c) It believes the effect of those uncorrected misstatements aggregated by the auditor during the review are immaterial, both individually and in the aggregate, to the interim financial information taken as a whole. A summary of such items is included in or attached to the written representations;
(d) It has disclosed to the auditor all significant facts relating to any frauds or suspected frauds known to management that may have affected the entity;
(e) It has disclosed to the auditor the results of its assessment of the risks that the interim financial information may be materially misstated as a result of fraud;[2]
(f) It has disclosed to the auditor all known actual or possible noncompliance with laws and regulations whose effects are to be considered when preparing the interim financial information; and
(g) It has disclosed to the auditor all significant events that have occurred subsequent to the balance sheet date and through to the date of the review report that may require adjustment to or disclosure in the interim financial information.

The auditor obtains additional representations as are appropriate related to matters specific to the entity's business or industry. An illustrative management representation letter is set out in Appendix 3 to this ISRE (UK and Ireland).   35

Auditor's Responsibility for Accompanying Information[2a]

The auditor should read the other information that accompanies the interim financial information to consider whether any such information is materially inconsistent with the   36

[1g] *This is not another expression for 'immaterial'. Matters which are 'clearly trivial' will be of an wholly different (smaller) order of magnitude than the materiality thresholds used in the review, and will be matters that are clearly inconsequential, whether taken individually or in aggregate and whether judged by any quantitative and/ or qualitative criteria. Further, whenever there is any uncertainty about whether one or more items are 'clearly trivial' (in accordance with this definition), the presumption should be that the matter is not 'clearly trivial'.*

[2] *Paragraph 35 of ISA (UK and Ireland) 240, "The Auditor's Responsibility to Consider Fraud in an Audit of Financial Statements" explains that the nature, extent and frequency of such an assessment vary from entity to entity and that management may make a detailed assessment on an annual basis or as part of continuous monitoring. Accordingly, this representation, insofar as it relates to the interim financial information, is tailored to the entity's specific circumstances.*

[2a] *Other information in the half-yearly financial report of a listed entity includes the interim management report and the responsibility statements required by the rules and regulations of the listing/regulatory authorities. It may also include, for example, performance summaries, prospective information and a chairman's statement.*

interim financial information. If the auditor identifies a material inconsistency, the auditor considers whether the interim financial information or the other information needs to be amended. If an amendment is necessary in the interim financial information and management refuses to make the amendment, the auditor considers the implications for the review report. If an amendment is necessary in the other information and management refuses to make the amendment, the auditor considers including in the review report an additional paragraph describing the material inconsistency, or taking other actions, such as withholding the issuance of the review report or withdrawing from the engagement. For example, management may present alternative measures of earnings that more positively portray financial performance than the interim financial information, and such alternative measures are given excessive prominence, are not clearly defined, or not clearly reconciled to the interim financial information such that they are confusing and potentially misleading[2b].

37 **If a matter comes to the auditor's attention that causes the auditor to believe that the other information appears to include a material misstatement of fact, the auditor should discuss the matter with the entity's management.** While reading the other information for the purpose of identifying material inconsistencies, an apparent material misstatement of fact may come to the auditor's attention (i.e., information, not related to matters appearing in the interim financial information, that is incorrectly stated or presented). When discussing the matter with the entity's management, the auditor considers the validity of the other information and management's responses to the auditor's inquiries, whether valid differences of judgment or opinion exist and whether to request management to consult with a qualified third party to resolve the apparent misstatement of fact. If an amendment is necessary to correct a material misstatement of fact and management refuses to make the amendment, the auditor considers taking further action as appropriate, such as notifying those charged with governance and obtaining legal advice.

Communication

38 **When, as a result of performing the review of interim financial information, a matter comes to the auditor's attention that causes the auditor to believe that it is necessary to make a material adjustment to the interim financial information for it to be prepared, in all material respects, in accordance with the applicable financial reporting framework, the auditor should communicate this matter as soon as practicable to the appropriate level of management.**

[2b] *The APB recognises that in some circumstances the presentation of alternative performance measures and associated narrative explanations may help shareholders understand better the financial performance of a company. However, the APB is concerned that in other circumstances such alternative performance measures have the potential to be misleading and shareholders may sometimes be misinformed by the manner in which alternative performance measures are presented. The APB believes that the potential for alternative performance measures to be misleading is considerable when they are given undue and inappropriate prominence, when there is no description of the basis on which the information was produced and, where appropriate, the adjusted numbers are not reconciled to the financial information that is presented in accordance with the applicable financial reporting framework.*

The APB's concerns are shared by the UK Listing Authority (UKLA). In its September 2005 newsletter, List!, the UKLA reminded issuers that they were free to disclose additional non-GAAP numbers in their interim accounts but, where they did, the UKLA said they should make clear the basis on which the numbers are calculated in order to avoid misleading investors. The UKLA also explained that it would not expect non-GAAP figures to be given greater prominence in interim announcements than any GAAP numbers. On 3 November 2005, the Committee of European Securities Regulators (CESR) published a recommendation on the use of alternative performance measures. In the February 2006 edition of List! the UKLA indicated that in its view the CESR recommendation represents best practice for the disclosure of alternative performance measures and encouraged issuers to follow the recommendation.

When, in the auditor's judgment, management does not respond appropriately within a reasonable period of time, the auditor should inform those charged with governance. The communication is made as soon as practicable, either orally or in writing. The auditor's decision whether to communicate orally or in writing is affected by factors such as the nature, sensitivity and significance of the matter to be communicated and the timing of such communications. If the information is communicated orally, the auditor documents the communication. 39

When, in the auditor's judgment, those charged with governance do not respond appropriately within a reasonable period of time, the auditor should consider: 40

(a) Whether to modify the report; or
(b) The possibility of withdrawing from the engagement; and
(c) The possibility of resigning from the appointment to audit the annual financial statements.

When, as a result of performing the review of interim financial information, a matter comes to the auditor's attention that causes the auditor to believe in the existence of fraud or noncompliance by the entity with laws and regulations the auditor should communicate the matter as soon as practicable to the appropriate level of management. The determination of which level of management is the appropriate one is affected by the likelihood of collusion or the involvement of a member of management. The auditor also considers the need to report such matters to those charged with governance and considers the implication for the review. 41

The auditor should communicate relevant matters of governance interest arising from the review of interim financial information to those charged with governance. As a result of performing the review of the interim financial information, the auditor may become aware of matters that in the opinion of the auditor are both important and relevant to those charged with governance in overseeing the financial reporting and disclosure process. The auditor communicates such matters to those charged with governance. 42

Reporting the Nature, Extent and Results of the Review of Interim Financial Information

The auditor should issue a written report that contains the following: 43

(a) An appropriate title.
(b) An addressee, as required by the circumstances of the engagement.
(c) Identification of the interim financial information reviewed, including identification of the title of each of the statements contained in the complete or condensed set of financial statements and the date and period covered by the interim financial information.
(d) If the interim financial information comprises a complete set of general purpose financial statements prepared in accordance with a financial reporting framework designed to achieve fair presentation, a statement that management is responsible for the preparation and fair presentation of the interim financial information in accordance with the applicable financial reporting framework.
(e) In other circumstances, a statement that management is responsible for the preparation and presentation of the interim financial information in accordance with the applicable financial reporting framework.
(f) A statement that the auditor is responsible for expressing a conclusion on the interim financial information based on the review.

(g) A statement that the review of the interim financial information was conducted in accordance with International Standard on Review Engagements (UK and Ireland) (ISRE (UK and Ireland)) 2410, "Review of Interim Financial Information Performed by the Independent Auditor of the Entity," and a statement that that such a review consists of making inquiries, primarily of persons responsible for financial and accounting matters, and applying analytical and other review procedures.

(h) A statement that a review is substantially less in scope than an audit conducted in accordance with International Standards on Auditing (UK and Ireland) and consequently does not enable the auditor to obtain assurance that the auditor would become aware of all significant matters that might be identified in an audit and that accordingly no audit opinion is expressed.

(i) If the interim financial information comprises a complete set of general purpose financial statements prepared in accordance with a financial reporting framework designed to achieve fair presentation, a conclusion as to whether anything has come to the auditor's attention that causes the auditor to believe that the interim financial information does not give a true and fair view, or does not present fairly, in all material respects, in accordance with the applicable financial reporting framework (including a reference to the jurisdiction or country of origin of the financial reporting framework when the financial reporting framework used is not International Financial Reporting Standards); or

(j) In other circumstances, a conclusion as to whether anything has come to the auditor's attention that causes the auditor to believe that the interim financial information is not prepared, in all material respects, in accordance with the applicable financial reporting framework (including a reference to the jurisdiction or country of origin of the financial reporting framework when the financial reporting framework used is not International Financial Reporting Standards).

(k) The date of the report.

(l) The location in the country or jurisdiction where the auditor practices.

(m) The auditor's signature.

Illustrative review reports are set out in Appendix 4 to this ISRE (UK and Ireland).

43-1 An illustrative review report for a UK or Irish Company listed in the UK or Ireland and complying with IAS 34 as adopted by the European Union is set out in Appendix 8 to this ISRE (UK and Ireland).

44 In some jurisdictions, law or regulation governing the review of interim financial information may prescribe wording for the auditor's conclusion that is different from the wording described in paragraph 43(i) or (j). Although the auditor may be obliged to use the prescribed wording, the auditor's responsibilities as described in this ISRE (UK and Ireland) for coming to the conclusion remain the same.

Date of the Review Report

44-1 The date of the review report on an entity's financial information is the date on which the auditor signs the review report. The auditor should not date the review report earlier than the date on which the financial information is approved by management and those charged with governance.

Departure from the Applicable Financial Reporting Framework

The auditor should express a qualified or adverse conclusion when a matter has come to the auditor's attention that causes the auditor to believe that a material adjustment should be made to the interim financial information for it to be prepared, in all material respects, in accordance with the applicable financial reporting framework. 45

If matters have come to the auditor's attention that cause the auditor to believe that the interim financial information is or may be materially affected by a departure from the applicable financial reporting framework, and management does not correct the interim financial information, the auditor modifies the review report. The modification describes the nature of the departure and, if practicable, states the effects on the interim financial information. If the information that the auditor believes is necessary for adequate disclosure is not included in the interim financial information, the auditor modifies the review report and, if practicable, includes the necessary information in the review report. The modification to the review report is ordinarily accomplished by adding an explanatory paragraph to the review report, and qualifying the conclusion. Illustrative review reports with a qualified conclusion are set out in Appendix 5 to this ISRE (UK and Ireland). 46

When the effect of the departure is so material and pervasive to the interim financial information that the auditor concludes a qualified conclusion is not adequate to disclose the misleading or incomplete nature of the interim financial information, the auditor expresses an adverse conclusion. Illustrative review reports with an adverse conclusion are set out in Appendix 7 to this ISRE (UK and Ireland). 47

Limitation on Scope

A limitation on scope ordinarily prevents the auditor from completing the review. 48

When the auditor is unable to complete the review, the auditor should communicate, in writing, to the appropriate level of management and to those charged with governance the reason why the review cannot be completed, and consider whether it is appropriate to issue a report. 49

Limitation on Scope Imposed by Management

The auditor does not accept an engagement to review the interim financial information if the auditor's preliminary knowledge of the engagement circumstances indicates that the auditor would be unable to complete the review because there will be a limitation on the scope of the auditor's review imposed by management of the entity. 50

If, after accepting the engagement, management imposes a limitation on the scope of the review, the auditor requests the removal of that limitation. If management refuses to do so, the auditor is unable to complete the review and express a conclusion. In such cases, the auditor communicates, in writing, to the appropriate level of management and those charged with governance the reason why the review cannot be completed. Nevertheless, if a matter comes to the auditor's attention that causes the auditor to believe that a material adjustment to the interim financial information is necessary for it to be prepared, in all material respects, in accordance with the applicable financial reporting framework, the auditor communicates such matters in accordance with the guidance in paragraphs 38-40. 51

52 The auditor also considers the legal and regulatory responsibilities, including whether there is a requirement for the auditor to issue a report. If there is such a requirement, the auditor disclaims a conclusion, and provides in the review report the reason why the review cannot be completed. However, if a matter comes to the auditor's attention that causes the auditor to believe that a material adjustment to the interim financial information is necessary for it to be prepared, in all material respects, in accordance with the applicable financial reporting framework, the auditor also communicates such a matter in the report.

Other Limitations on Scope

53 A limitation on scope may occur due to circumstances other than a limitation on scope imposed by management. In such circumstances, the auditor is ordinarily unable to complete the review and express a conclusion and is guided by paragraphs 51-52. There may be, however, some rare circumstances where the limitation on the scope of the auditor's work is clearly confined to one or more specific matters that, while material, are not in the auditor's judgment pervasive to the interim financial information. In such circumstances, the auditor modifies the review report by indicating that, except for the matter which is described in an explanatory paragraph to the review report, the review was conducted in accordance with this ISRE (UK and Ireland), and by qualifying the conclusion. Illustrative review reports with a qualified conclusion are set out in Appendix 6 to this ISRE (UK and Ireland).

54 The auditor may have expressed a qualified opinion on the audit of the latest annual financial statements because of a limitation on the scope of that audit. The auditor considers whether that limitation on scope still exists and, if so, the implications for the review report.

Going Concern and Significant Uncertainties

55 In certain circumstances, an emphasis of matter paragraph may be added to a review report, without affecting the auditor's conclusion, to highlight a matter that is included in a note to the interim financial information that more extensively discusses the matter. The paragraph would preferably be included after the conclusion paragraph and ordinarily refers to the fact that the conclusion is not qualified in this respect.

56 **If adequate disclosure is made in the interim financial information, the auditor should add an emphasis of matter paragraph to the review report to highlight a material uncertainty relating to an event or condition that may cast significant doubt on the entity's ability to continue as a going concern.**

57 The auditor may have modified a prior audit or review report by adding an emphasis of matter paragraph to highlight a material uncertainty relating to an event or condition that may cast significant doubt on the entity's ability to continue as a going concern. If the material uncertainty still exists and adequate disclosure is made in the interim financial information, the auditor modifies the review report on the current interim financial information by adding a paragraph to highlight the continued material uncertainty.

58 If, as a result of inquiries or other review procedures, a material uncertainty relating to an event or condition comes to the auditor's attention that may cast significant doubt on the entity's ability to continue as a going concern, and adequate disclosure is made in the interim financial information the auditor modifies the review report by adding an emphasis of matter paragraph.

If a material uncertainty that casts significant doubt about the entity's ability to continue as a going concern is not adequately disclosed in the interim financial information, the auditor should express a qualified or adverse conclusion, as appropriate. The report should include specific reference to the fact that there is such a material uncertainty.   59

The auditor should consider modifying the review report by adding a paragraph to highlight a significant uncertainty (other than a going concern problem) that came to the auditor's attention, the resolution of which is dependent upon future events and which may affect the interim financial information.   60

Requests to Discontinue an Interim Review Engagement

There may be rare circumstances in which the auditor indicates in advance to management and those charged with governance that the review report may be modified for one or more of the reasons set out in paragraphs 45 to 60 above. In these cases the auditor may be requested to discontinue the review engagement rather than include a modified review report with the interim financial information.   60-1

The auditor informs the audit committee, where one exists, of this situation as soon as practicable. If information is communicated orally, the auditor subsequently documents the communication as appropriate. For a listed entity, if, in the auditor's judgment, the entity does not take appropriate action to address the auditor's concerns regarding the financial information to be published, the auditor considers requesting those charged with governance to discuss the matter with the entity's brokers, including whether the matter should be reported to the relevant regulatory authority. The auditor also evaluates whether to resign as the entity's auditor and include the auditor's reasons for resigning in a statement of circumstances as required by the Companies Act. The auditor may wish to take legal advice when considering resignation.   60-2

Other Considerations

The terms of the engagement include management's agreement that where any document containing interim financial information indicates that such information has been reviewed by the entity's auditor, the review report will also be included in the document. If management has not included the review report in the document, the auditor considers seeking legal advice to assist in determining the appropriate course of action in the circumstances.   61

If the auditor has issued a modified review report and management issues the interim financial information without including the modified review report in the document containing the interim financial information, the auditor considers seeking legal advice to assist in determining the appropriate course of action in the circumstances, and the possibility of resigning from the appointment to audit the annual financial statements.   62

Interim financial information consisting of a condensed set of financial statements does not necessarily include all the information that would be included in a complete set of financial statements, but may rather present an explanation of the events and changes that are significant to an understanding of the changes in the financial position and performance of the entity since the annual reporting date. This is because it is presumed that the users of the interim financial information will have access to the latest audited financial statements, such as is the case with listed entities.   63

In other circumstances, the auditor discusses with management the need for such interim financial information to include a statement that it is to be read in conjunction with the latest audited financial statements. In the absence of such a statement, the auditor considers whether, without a reference to the latest audited financial statements, the interim financial information is misleading in the circumstances, and the implications for the review report.

Documentation

64 **The auditor should prepare review documentation that is sufficient and appropriate to provide a basis for the auditor's conclusion and to provide evidence that the review was performed in accordance with this ISRE (UK and Ireland) and applicable legal and regulatory requirements.** The documentation enables an experienced auditor having no previous connection with the engagement to understand the nature, timing and extent of the inquiries made, and analytical and other review procedures applied, information obtained, and any significant matters considered during the performance of the review, including the disposition of such matters.

Effective Date

65 This ISRE (UK and Ireland) is effective for reviews of interim financial information for periods ending on or after 20 September 2007. Early adoption is permitted.

Public Sector Perspective

1 *Paragraph 10 requires that the auditor and the client agree on the terms of engagement. Paragraph 11 explains that an engagement letter helps to avoid misunderstandings regarding the nature of the engagement and, in particular, the objective and scope of the review, management's responsibilities, the extent of the auditor's responsibilities, the assurance obtained, and the nature and form of the report. Law or regulation governing review engagements in the public sector ordinarily mandates the appointment of the auditor. Consequently, engagement letters may not be a widespread practice in the public sector. Nevertheless, an engagement letter setting out the matters referred to in paragraph 11 may be useful to both the public sector auditor and the client. Public sector auditors, therefore, consider agreeing with the client the terms of a review engagement by way of an engagement letter.*

2 *In the public sector, the auditor's statutory audit obligation may extend to other work, such as a review of interim financial information. Where this is the case, the public sector auditor cannot avoid such an obligation and, consequently, may not be in a position not to accept (see paragraph 50) or to withdraw from a review engagement (see paragraphs 36 and 40(b)). The public sector auditor also may not be in the position to resign from the appointment to audit the annual financial statements (see paragraphs 40(c)) and 62).*

3 *Paragraph 41 discusses the auditor's responsibility when a matter comes to the auditor's attention that causes the auditor to believe in the existence of fraud or noncompliance by the entity with laws and regulations. In the public sector, the auditor may be subject to statutory or other regulatory requirements to report such a matter to regulatory or other public authorities.*

Appendix 1 – Example of an Engagement Letter for a Review of Interim Financial Information

The following letter is to be used as a guide in conjunction with the consideration outlined in paragraph 10 of this ISRE (UK and Ireland) and will need to be adapted according to individual requirements and circumstances.

> For an engagement to review interim financial information prepared by a listed company in the UK or Ireland, the letter would ordinarily include paragraphs such as:
>
> "As directors of XYZ PLC you are responsible under the [Companies Act 1985] [Companies Act 1990] for keeping proper accounting records. You are also responsible for presenting the half-yearly financial report in accordance with [International Accounting Standard 34, "Interim Financial Reporting," as adopted by the European Union] [the Accounting Standards Board Statement "Half-Yearly Financial Reports"] and the requirements of the [Disclosure and Transparency Rules of the Financial Services Authority] [Transparency (Directive 2004/109/EC) Regulations 2007 and the Transparency Rules of the Financial Regulator]." [*The second sentence identifies the applicable financial reporting framework for the entity and should be amended as necessary.*]
>
> "For the purpose of our review you will make available to us all of the company's accounting records and all other related information, including minutes of directors' shareholders', and audit committee meetings and of all relevant management meetings, that we consider necessary."

To the Board of Directors (or the appropriate representative of senior management)

We are providing this letter to confirm our understanding of the terms and objectives of our engagement to review the entity's interim balance sheet as at June 30, 20X1 and the related statements of income, changes in equity and cash flows for the six-month period then ended.

Our review will be conducted in accordance with International Standard on Review Engagements (UK and Ireland) 2410, "Review of Interim Financial Information Performed by the Independent Auditor of the Entity" issued by the Auditing Practices Board with the objective of providing us with a basis for reporting whether anything has come to our attention that causes us to believe that the interim financial information is not prepared, in all material respects, in accordance with the [indicate applicable financial reporting framework, including a reference to the jurisdiction or country of origin of the financial reporting when the financial reporting framework used is not International Financial Reporting Standards]. Such a review consists of making inquiries, primarily of persons responsible for financial and accounting matters, and applying analytical and other review procedures and does not, ordinarily, require corroboration of the information obtained. The scope of a review of interim financial information is substantially less than the scope of an audit conducted in accordance with International Standards on Auditing (UK and Ireland) whose objective is the expression of an opinion regarding the financial statements and, accordingly, we shall express no such opinion.

We expect to report on the interim financial information as follows:

[Include text of sample report]

Responsibility for the interim financial information, including adequate disclosure, is that of management of the entity. This includes designing, implementing and maintaining internal control relevant to the preparation and presentation of interim financial information that is free from material misstatement, whether due to fraud or error; selecting and applying appropriate accounting policies; and making accounting estimates that are reasonable in the circumstances. As part of our review, we will request written representations from management concerning assertions made in connection with the review. We will also request that where any document containing interim financial information indicates that the interim financial information has been reviewed, our report will also be included in the document.

A review of interim financial information does not provide assurance that we will become aware of all significant matters that might be identified in an audit. Further, our engagement cannot be relied upon to disclose whether fraud or errors, or illegal acts exist. However, we will inform you of any material matters that come to our attention.

We look forward to full cooperation with your staff ~~and we trust that they will make available to us whatever records, documentation and other information are requested in connection with our review.~~[2c]

[Insert additional information here regarding fee arrangements and billings, as appropriate.]

This letter will be effective for future years unless it is terminated, amended or superseded (if applicable).

Please sign and return the attached copy of this letter to indicate that it is in accordance with your understanding of the arrangements for our review of the financial statements.

Acknowledged on behalf of ABC Entity by
(signed)
Name and Title
Date

Appendix 2 – Analytical Procedures the Auditor May Consider When Performing a Review of Interim Financial Information

Examples of analytical procedures the auditor may consider when performing a review of interim financial information include the following:

- Comparing the interim financial information with the interim financial information of the immediately preceding interim period, with the interim financial information of the corresponding interim period of the preceding financial year, with the interim financial information that was expected by management for the current period, and with the most recent audited annual financial statements.
- Comparing current interim financial information with anticipated results, such as budgets or forecasts (for example, comparing tax balances and the

---

[2c] *Rendered unnecessary by the alternative text presented in the shaded note immediately before this example letter.*

relationship between the provision for income taxes to pretax income in the current interim financial information with corresponding information in (a) budgets, using expected rates, and (b) financial information for prior periods).
- Comparing current interim financial information with relevant non-financial information.
- Comparing the recorded amounts, or ratios developed from recorded amounts, to expectations developed by the auditor. The auditor develops such expectations by identifying and applying relationships that are reasonably expected to exist based on the auditor's understanding of the entity and of the industry in which the entity operates.
- Comparing ratios and indicators for the current interim period with those of entities in the same industry.
- Comparing relationships among elements in the current interim financial information with corresponding relationships in the interim financial information of prior periods, for example, expense by type as a percentage of sales, assets by type as a percentage of total assets, and percentage of change in sales to percentage of change in receivables.
- Comparing disaggregated data. The following are examples of how data may be disaggregated:
  - By period, for example, revenue or expense items disaggregated into quarterly, monthly, or weekly amounts.
  - By product line or source of revenue.
  - By location, for example, by component.
  - By attributes of the transaction, for example, revenue generated by designers, architects, or craftsmen.
  - By several attributes of the transaction, for example, sales by product and month.

Appendix 3 – Example of a Management Representation Letter

The following letter is not intended to be a standard letter. Representations by management will vary from entity to entity and from one interim period to the next.

(Entity Letterhead)

(To Auditor) (Date)

Opening paragraphs if interim financial information comprises condensed financial statements:

This representation letter is provided in connection with your review of the condensed balance sheet of ABC Entity as of March 31, 20X1 and the related condensed statements of income, changes in equity and cash flows for the three-month period then ended for the purposes of expressing a conclusion whether anything has come to your attention that causes you to believe that the interim financial information is not prepared, in all material respects, in accordance with [indicate applicable financial reporting framework, including a reference to the jurisdiction or country of origin of the financial reporting framework when the financial reporting framework used is not International Financial Reporting Standards].

We acknowledge our responsibility for the preparation and presentation of the interim financial information in accordance with [indicate applicable financial reporting framework].

Opening paragraphs if interim financial information comprises a complete set of general purpose financial statements prepared in accordance with a financial reporting framework designed to achieve fair presentation:

This representation letter is provided in connection with your review of the balance sheet of ABC Entity as of March 31, 20X1 and the related statements of income, changes in equity and cash flows for the three-month period then ended and a summary of the significant accounting policies and other explanatory notes for the purposes of expressing a conclusion whether anything has come to your attention that causes you to believe that the interim financial information does not give a true and fair view of *(or "does not present fairly, in all material respects,")* the financial position of ABC Entity as at March 31, 20X1, and of its financial performance and its cash flows in accordance with [indicate applicable financial reporting framework, including a reference to the jurisdiction or country of origin of the financial reporting framework when the financial reporting framework used is not International Financial Reporting Standards].

We acknowledge our responsibility for the fair presentation of the interim financial information in accordance with [indicate applicable financial reporting framework].

We confirm, to the best of our knowledge and belief, the following representations:

- The interim financial information referred to above has been prepared and presented in accordance with [indicate applicable financial reporting framework].
- We have made available to you all books of account and supporting documentation, and all minutes of meetings of shareholders and the board of directors (namely those held on [insert applicable dates]).
- There are no material transactions that have not been properly recorded in the accounting records underlying the interim financial information.
- There has been no known actual or possible noncompliance with laws and regulations that could have a material effect on the interim financial information in the event of noncompliance.
- We acknowledge responsibility for the design and implementation of internal control to prevent and detect fraud and error.
- We have disclosed to you all significant facts relating to any known frauds or suspected frauds that may have affected the entity.
- We have disclosed to you the results of our assessment of the risk that the interim financial information may be materially misstated as the result of fraud.
- We believe the effects of uncorrected misstatements summarized in the accompanying schedule are immaterial, both individually and in the aggregate, to the interim financial information taken as a whole.
- We confirm the completeness of the information provided to you regarding the identification of related parties.
- The following have been properly recorded and, when appropriate, adequately disclosed in the interim financial information:
    - Related party transactions, including sales, purchases, loans, transfers, leasing arrangements and guarantees, and amounts receivable from or payable to related parties;
    - Guarantees, whether written or oral, under which the entity is contingently liable; and
    - Agreements and options to buy back assets previously sold.
- The presentation and disclosure of the fair value measurements of assets and liabilities are in accordance with [indicate applicable financial reporting framework]. The assumptions used reflect our intent and ability to carry specific

courses of action on behalf of the entity, where relevant to the fair value measurements or disclosure.
- We have no plans or intentions that may materially affect the carrying value or classification of assets and liabilities reflected in the interim financial information.
- We have no plans to abandon lines of product or other plans or intentions that will result in any excess or obsolete inventory, and no inventory is stated at an amount in excess of realizable value.
- The entity has satisfactory title to all assets and there are no liens or encumbrances on the entity's assets.
- We have recorded or disclosed, as appropriate, all liabilities, both actual and contingent.
- [Add any additional representations related to new accounting standards that are being implemented for the first time and consider any additional representations required by a new International Standard on Auditing (UK and Ireland) that are relevant to interim financial information.]

To the best of our knowledge and belief, no events have occurred subsequent to the balance sheet date and through the date of this letter that may require adjustment to or disclosure in the aforementioned interim financial information.

_____
(Senior Executive Officer)

_____
(Senior Financial Officer)

Appendix 4 – Examples of Review Reports on Interim Financial Information

An example review report for a UK or Irish company listed in the UK or Ireland is set out in Appendix 8.

Complete Set of General Purpose Financial Statements Prepared in Accordance with a Financial Reporting Framework Designed to Achieve Fair Presentation (see paragraph 43(i))

Report on Review of Interim Financial Information

(Appropriate addressee)

Introduction

We have reviewed the accompanying balance sheet of ABC Entity as of March 31, 20X1 and the related statements of income, changes in equity and cash flows for the three-month period then ended, and a summary of significant accounting policies and other explanatory notes.[3] Management is responsible for the preparation and fair presentation of this interim financial information in accordance with [indicate applicable financial reporting framework]. Our responsibility is to express a conclusion on this interim financial information based on our review.

Scope of Review

We conducted our review in accordance with International Standard on Review Engagements 2410, "Review of Interim Financial Information Performed by the Independent Auditor of the Entity." A review of interim financial information consists of making inquiries, primarily of persons responsible for financial and accounting matters, and applying analytical and other review procedures. A review is substantially less in scope than an audit conducted in accordance with International Standards on Auditing and consequently does not enable us to obtain assurance that we would become aware of all significant matters that might be identified in an audit. Accordingly, we do not express an audit opinion.

Conclusion

Based on our review, nothing has come to our attention that causes us to believe that the accompanying interim financial information does not give a true and fair view of (or "does not present fairly, in all material respects,") the financial position of the entity as at March 31, 20X1, and of its financial performance and its cash flows for the three-month period then ended in accordance with [applicable financial reporting framework, including a reference to the jurisdiction or country of origin of the financial reporting framework when the financial reporting framework used is not International Financial Reporting Standards].

---

[3] *The auditor may wish to specify the regulatory authority or equivalent with whom the interim financial information is filed.*

AUDITOR

Date

Address

Other Interim Financial Information (see paragraph 43(j))

Report on Review of Interim Financial Information

(Appropriate addressee)

Introduction

We have reviewed the accompanying [condensed] balance sheet of ABC Entity as of March 31, 20X1 and the related [condensed] statements of income, changes in equity and cash flows for the three-month period then ended.[4] Management is responsible for the preparation and presentation of this interim financial information in accordance with [indicate applicable financial reporting framework]. Our responsibility is to express a conclusion on this interim financial information based on our review.

Scope of Review

We conducted our review in accordance with International Standard on Review Engagements 2410, "Review of Interim Financial Information Performed by the Independent Auditor of the Entity." A review of interim financial information consists of making inquiries, primarily of persons responsible for financial and accounting matters, and applying analytical and other review procedures. A review is substantially less in scope than an audit conducted in accordance with International Standards on Auditing and consequently does not enable us to obtain assurance that we would become aware of all significant matters that might be identified in an audit. Accordingly, we do not express an audit opinion.

Conclusion

Based on our review, nothing has come to our attention that causes us to believe that the accompanying interim financial information is not prepared, in all material respects, in accordance with [applicable financial reporting framework, including a reference to the jurisdiction or country of origin of the financial reporting framework when the financial reporting framework used is not International Financial Reporting Standards].

AUDITOR

Date

Address

---

[4] The auditor may wish to specify the regulatory authority or equivalent with whom the interim financial information is filed.

Appendix 5 – Examples of Review Reports with a Qualified Conclusion for a Departure from the Applicable Financial Reporting Framework

> An example unqualified review report for a UK or Irish company listed in the UK or Ireland is set out in Appendix 8 and can be tailored to give a report with a qualified conclusion when appropriate.

Complete Set of General Purpose Financial Statements Prepared in Accordance with a Financial Reporting Framework Designed to Achieve Fair Presentation (see paragraph 43(i))

Report on Review of Interim Financial Information

(Appropriate addressee)

Introduction

We have reviewed the accompanying balance sheet of ABC Entity as of March 31, 20X1 and the related statements of income, changes in equity and cash flows for the three-month period then ended, and a summary of significant accounting policies and other explanatory notes.[5] Management is responsible for the preparation and fair presentation of this interim financial information in accordance with [indicate applicable financial reporting framework]. Our responsibility is to express a conclusion on this interim financial information based on our review.

Scope of Review

We conducted our review in accordance with International Standard on Review Engagements 2410, "Review of Interim Financial Information Performed by the Independent Auditor of the Entity." A review of interim financial information consists of making inquiries, primarily of persons responsible for financial and accounting matters, and applying analytical and other review procedures. A review is substantially less in scope than an audit conducted in accordance with International Standards on Auditing and consequently does not enable us to obtain assurance that we would become aware of all significant matters that might be identified in an audit. Accordingly, we do not express an audit opinion.

Basis for Qualified Conclusion

Based on information provided to us by management, ABC Entity has excluded from property and long-term debt certain lease obligations that we believe should be capitalized to conform with [indicate applicable financial reporting framework]. This information indicates that if these lease obligations were capitalized at March 31, 20X1, property would be increased by $_____, long-term debt by $_____, and net income and earnings per share would be increased (decreased) by $_____, $_____, $_____, and $_____, respectively for the three-month period then ended.

---

[5] The auditor may wish to specify the regulatory authority or equivalent with whom the interim financial information is filed.

Qualified Conclusion

Based on our review, with the exception of the matter described in the preceding paragraph, nothing has come to our attention that causes us to believe that the accompanying interim financial information does not give a true and fair view of (or "does not present fairly, in all material respects,") the financial position of the entity as at March 31, 20X1, and of its financial performance and its cash flows for the three-month period then ended in accordance with [indicate applicable financial reporting framework, including the reference to the jurisdiction or country of origin of the financial reporting framework when the financial reporting framework used is not International Financial Reporting Standards].

AUDITOR

Date

Address

Other Interim Financial Information (see paragraph 43(j))

Report on Review of Interim Financial Information

(Appropriate addressee)

Introduction

We have reviewed the accompanying [condensed] balance sheet of ABC Entity as of March 31, 20X1 and the related [condensed] statements of income, changes in equity and cash flows for the three-month period then ended.[6] Management is responsible for the preparation and presentation of this interim financial information in accordance with [indicate applicable financial reporting framework]. Our responsibility is to express a conclusion on this interim financial information based on our review.

Scope of Review

We conducted our review in accordance with International Standard on Review Engagements 2410, "Review of Interim Financial Information Performed by the Independent Auditor of the Entity." A review of interim financial information consists of making inquiries, primarily of persons responsible for financial and accounting matters, and applying analytical and other review procedures. A review is substantially less in scope than an audit conducted in accordance with International Standards on Auditing and consequently does not enable us to obtain assurance that we would become aware of all significant matters that might be identified in an audit. Accordingly, we do not express an audit opinion.

Basis for Qualified Conclusion

Based on information provided to us by management, ABC Entity has excluded from property and long-term debt certain lease obligations that we believe should be capitalized to conform with [indicate applicable financial reporting framework]. This information indicates that if these lease obligations were capitalized at March 31, 20X1, property would be increased by $_____, long-term debt by $_____, and net

---

[6] The auditor may wish to specify the regulatory authority or equivalent with whom the interim financial information is filed.

income and earnings per share would be increased (decreased) by $_____, $_____, $_____, and $_____, respectively for the three-month period then ended.

Qualified Conclusion

Based on our review, with the exception of the matter described in the preceding paragraph, nothing has come to our attention that causes us to believe that the accompanying interim financial information is not prepared, in all material respects, in accordance with [indicate applicable financial reporting framework, including a reference to the jurisdiction or country of origin of the financial reporting framework when the financial reporting framework used is not International Financial Reporting Standards].

AUDITOR

Date

Address

Appendix 6 – Examples of Review Reports with a Qualified Conclusion for a Limitation on Scope Not Imposed By Management

An example unqualified review report for a UK or Irish company listed in the UK or Ireland is set out in Appendix 8 and can be tailored to give a report with a qualified conclusion when appropriate.

Complete Set of General Purpose Financial Statements Prepared in Accordance with a Financial Reporting Framework Designed to Achieve Fair Presentation (see paragraph 43(i))

Report on Review of Interim Financial Information

(Appropriate addressee)

Introduction

We have reviewed the accompanying balance sheet of ABC Entity as of March 31, 20X1 and the related statements of income, changes in equity and cash flows for the three-month period then ended, and a summary of significant accounting policies and other explanatory notes.[7] Management is responsible for the preparation and fair presentation of this interim financial information in accordance with [indicate applicable financial reporting framework]. Our responsibility is to express a conclusion on this interim financial information based on our review.

---

[7] The auditor may wish to specify the regulatory authority or equivalent with whom the interim financial information is filed.

Scope of Review

Except as explained in the following paragraph, we conducted our review in accordance with International Standard on Review Engagements 2410, "Review of Interim Financial Information Performed by the Independent Auditor of the Entity." A review of interim financial information consists of making inquiries, primarily of persons responsible for financial and accounting matters, and applying analytical and other review procedures. A review is substantially less in scope than an audit conducted in accordance with International Standards on Auditing and consequently does not enable us to obtain assurance that we would become aware of all significant matters that might be identified in an audit. Accordingly, we do not express an audit opinion.

Basis for Qualified Conclusion

As a result of a fire in a branch office on (date) that destroyed its accounts receivable records, we were unable to complete our review of accounts receivable totaling $_____ included in the interim financial information. The entity is in the process of reconstructing these records and is uncertain as to whether these records will support the amount shown above and the related allowance for uncollectible accounts. Had we been able to complete our review of accounts receivable, matters might have come to our attention indicating that adjustments might be necessary to the interim financial information.

Qualified Conclusion

Except for the adjustments to the interim financial information that we might have become aware of had it not been for the situation described above, based on our review, nothing has come to our attention that causes us to believe that the accompanying interim financial information does not give a true and fair view of (or "does not present fairly, in all material respects,") the financial position of the entity as at March 31, 20X1, and of its financial performance and its cash flows for the three-month period then ended in accordance with [indicate applicable financial reporting framework, including a reference to the jurisdiction or country of origin of the financial reporting framework when the financial reporting framework used is not International Financial Reporting Standards].

AUDITOR

Date

Address

Other Interim Financial Information (see paragraph 43(j))

Report on Review of Interim Financial Information

(Appropriate addressee)

Introduction

We have reviewed the accompanying [condensed] balance sheet of ABC Entity as of March 31, 20X1 and the related [condensed] statements of income, changes in equity and cash flows for the three-month period then ended.[8] Management is responsible for

---

[8] The auditor may wish to specify the regulatory authority or equivalent with whom the interim financial information is filed.

the preparation and presentation of this interim financial information in accordance with [indicate applicable financial reporting framework]. Our responsibility is to express a conclusion on this interim financial information based on our review.

Scope of Review

Except as explained in the following paragraph, we conducted our review in accordance with International Standards on Review Engagements 2410, "Review of Interim Financial Information Performed by the Auditor of the Entity." A review of interim financial information consists of making inquiries, primarily of persons responsible for financial and accounting matters, and applying analytical and other review procedures. A review is substantially less in scope than an audit conducted in accordance with International Standards on Auditing and consequently does not enable us to obtain assurance that we would become aware of all significant matters that might be identified in an audit. Accordingly, we do not express an audit opinion.

Basis for Qualified Conclusion

As a result of a fire in a branch office on (date) that destroyed its accounts receivable records, we were unable to complete our review of accounts receivable totaling $_____ included in the interim financial information. The entity is in the process of reconstructing these records and is uncertain as to whether these records will support the amount shown above and the related allowance for uncollectible accounts. Had we been able to complete our review of accounts receivable, matters might have come to our attention indicating that adjustments might be necessary to the interim financial information.

Qualified Conclusion

Except for the adjustments to the interim financial information that we might have become aware of had it not been for the situation described above, based on our review, nothing has come to our attention that causes us to believe that the accompanying interim financial information is not prepared, in all material respects, in accordance with [indicate applicable financial reporting framework, including a reference to the jurisdiction or country of origin of the financial reporting framework when the financial reporting framework used is not International Financial Reporting Standards].

AUDITOR

Date

Address

Appendix 7 – Examples of Review Reports with an Adverse Conclusion for a Departure from the Applicable Financial Reporting Framework

An example unqualified review report for a UK or Irish company listed in the UK or Ireland is set out in Appendix 8 and can be tailored to give a report with an adverse conclusion when appropriate.

Complete Set of General Purpose Financial Statements Prepared in Accordance with a Financial Reporting Framework Designed to Achieve Fair Presentation (see paragraph 43(i))

Report on Review of Interim Financial Information

(Appropriate addressee)

Introduction

We have reviewed the accompanying balance sheet of ABC Entity as of March 31, 20X1 and the related statements of income, changes in equity and cash flows for the three-month period then ended, and a summary of significant accounting policies and other explanatory notes.[9] Management is responsible for the preparation and fair presentation of this interim financial information in accordance with [indicate applicable financial reporting framework]. Our responsibility is to express a conclusion on this interim financial information based on our review.

Scope of Review

We conducted our review in accordance with International Standard on Review Engagements 2410, "Review of Interim Financial Information Performed by the Auditor of the Entity." A review of interim financial information consists of making inquiries, primarily of persons responsible for financial and accounting matters, and applying analytical and other review procedures. A review is substantially less in scope than an audit conducted in accordance with International Standards on Auditing and consequently does not enable us to obtain assurance that we would become aware of all significant matters that might be identified in an audit. Accordingly, we do not express an audit opinion.

Basis for Adverse Conclusion

Commencing this period, management of the entity ceased to consolidate the financial statements of its subsidiary companies since management considers consolidation to be inappropriate because of the existence of new substantial non-controlling interests. This is not in accordance with [indicate applicable financial reporting framework, including a reference to the jurisdiction or country of origin of the financial reporting framework when the financial reporting framework used is not International Financial Reporting Standards]. Had consolidated financial statements been prepared, virtually every account in the interim financial information would have been materially different.

---

[9] The auditor may wish to specify the regulatory authority or equivalent with whom the interim financial information is filed.

Adverse Conclusion

Our review indicates that, because the entity's investment in subsidiary companies is not accounted for on a consolidated basis, as described in the preceding paragraph, this interim financial information does not give a true and fair view of (or "does not present fairly, in all material respects,") the financial position of the entity as at March 31, 20X1, and of its financial performance and its cash flows for the three-month period then ended in accordance with [indicate applicable financial reporting framework, including a reference to the jurisdiction or country of origin of the financial reporting framework when the financial reporting framework used is not International Financial Reporting Standards].

AUDITOR

Date

Address

Other Interim Financial Information (see paragraph 43(j))

Report on Review of Interim Financial Information

(Appropriate addressee)

Introduction

We have reviewed the accompanying [condensed] balance sheet of ABC Entity as of March 31, 20X1 and the related [condensed] statements of income, changes in equity and cash flows for the three-month period then ended.[10] Management is responsible for the preparation and presentation of this interim financial information in accordance with [indicate applicable financial reporting framework]. Our responsibility is to express a conclusion on this interim financial information based on our review.

Scope of Review

We conducted our review in accordance with International Standard on Review Engagements 2410, "Review of Interim Financial Information Performed by the Independence Auditor of the Entity." A review of interim financial information consists of making inquiries, primarily of persons responsible for financial and accounting matters, and applying analytical and other review procedures. A review is substantially less in scope than an audit conducted in accordance with International Standards on Auditing and consequently does not enable us to obtain assurance that we would become aware of all significant matters that might be identified in an audit. Accordingly, we do not express an audit opinion.

Basis for Adverse Conclusion

Commencing this period, management of the entity ceased to consolidate the financial statements of its subsidiary companies since management considers consolidation to be inappropriate because of the existence of new substantial non-controlling interests. This is not in accordance with [indicate applicable financial reporting framework, including the reference to the jurisdiction or country of origin of the financial reporting

---

[10] *The auditor may wish to specify the regulatory authority or equivalent with whom the interim financial information is filed.*

framework when the financial reporting framework used is not International Financial Reporting Standards]. Had consolidated financial statements been prepared, virtually every account in the interim financial information would have been materially different.

Adverse Conclusion

Our review indicates that, because the entity's investment in subsidiary companies is not accounted for on a consolidated basis, as described in the preceding paragraph, this interim financial information is not prepared, in all material respects, in accordance with [indicate applicable financial reporting framework, including a reference to the jurisdiction or country of origin of the financial reporting framework when the financial reporting framework used is not International Financial Reporting Standards].

AUDITOR

Date

Address

Appendix 8 – Example Review Report for a UK or Irish Company Listed in the UK or Ireland Preparing a Half-Yearly Financial Report in Compliance with IAS 34 as Adopted by the European Union

INDEPENDENT REVIEW REPORT TO XYZ PLC

Introduction

We have been engaged by the company to review the condensed set of financial statements in the half-yearly financial report for the six months ended ... which comprises [specify the primary financial statements and the related explanatory notes that have been reviewed].[10a] We have read the other information contained in the half-yearly financial report and considered whether it contains any apparent misstatements or material inconsistencies with the information in the condensed set of financial statements.

Directors' Responsibilities

The half-yearly financial report is the responsibility of, and has been approved by, the directors. The directors are responsible for preparing the half-yearly financial report in accordance with the [Disclosure and Transparency Rules of the United Kingdom's Financial Services Authority] [Transparency (Directive 2004/109/EC) Regulations 2007 and the Transparency Rules of the Republic of Ireland's Financial Regulator].

[10a] *Review reports of entities that do not publish their half-yearly reports on a web site or publish them using 'PDF' format may continue to refer to the pages of the half-yearly report.*

As disclosed in note X, the annual financial statements of the [group/company] are prepared in accordance with IFRSs as adopted by the European Union. The condensed set of financial statements included in this half-yearly financial report has been prepared in accordance with International Accounting Standard 34, "Interim Financial Reporting," as adopted by the European Union.

Our Responsibility

Our responsibility is to express to the Company a conclusion on the condensed set of financial statements in the half-yearly financial report based on our review.

Scope of Review

We conducted our review in accordance with International Standard on Review Engagements (UK and Ireland) 2410, "Review of Interim Financial Information Performed by the Independent Auditor of the Entity" issued by the Auditing Practices Board for use in [the United Kingdom] [Ireland]. A review of interim financial information consists of making enquiries, primarily of persons responsible for financial and accounting matters, and applying analytical and other review procedures. A review is substantially less in scope than an audit conducted in accordance with International Standards on Auditing (UK and Ireland) and consequently does not enable us to obtain assurance that we would become aware of all significant matters that might be identified in an audit. Accordingly, we do not express an audit opinion.

Conclusion

Based on our review, nothing has come to our attention that causes us to believe that the condensed set of financial statements in the half-yearly financial report for the six months ended .... is not prepared, in all material respects, in accordance with International Accounting Standard 34 as adopted by the European Union and [the Disclosure and Transparency Rules of the United Kingdom's Financial Services Authority] [the Transparency (Directive 2004/109/EC) Regulations 2007 and the Transparency Rules of the Republic of Ireland's Financial Regulator].

AUDITOR

Date

Address

Appendix 9 – Summary of Particular Requirements of Half-Yearly Reports Prepared by Listed Companies in the UK and Ireland

This Appendix sets out a summary of particular requirements of the FSA's Disclosure and Transparency Rules (DTRs) applicable to half-yearly financial reports prepared by an 'issuer' whose shares or debt securities are admitted to trading and whose home state is the United Kingdom, subject to the exemptions in DTR 4.4. Equivalent requirements are included in the Irish Transparency (Directive 2004/109/EC) Regulations 2007 (specifically Regulations 6 – 8 in Part 2, subject to the exemptions in Part 3) and Transparency Rules of the Financial Regulator in the Republic of Ireland (specifically Rule 6.2). It also gives a summary of Companies Act requirements relevant to the publication of non-statutory accounts. It does not set out in full all the applicable requirements and, therefore, is not intended to provide a substitute for the auditor reading the applicable Rules, Regulations and legislation to obtain an understanding of them.

FSA Disclosure and Transparency Rules

Rule 4.2.3 requires that an issuer publish a half-yearly financial report, containing:

(1) a condensed set of financial statements;
(2) an interim management report; and
(3) responsibility statements.

Rule 4.2.4 requires that if an issuer is required to prepare consolidated accounts, the condensed set of financial statements must be prepared in accordance with International Accounting Standard 34 "Interim Financial Reporting". (Under the FSA's definitions of "International Accounting Standards" this will be IAS 34 as adopted by the European Union.)

If an issuer is not required to prepare consolidated accounts, the condensed set of financial information must contain, as a minimum, the following:

(a) a condensed balance sheet;
(b) a condensed profit and loss account; and
(c) explanatory notes on these accounts.

Rule 4.2.5 requires that the condensed balance sheet and condensed profit and loss account referred to in (a) and (b) above must:

- follow the same principles for recognising and measuring as when preparing annual financial reports,
- show each of the headings and subtotals included in the most recent annual financial statements of the issuer. Additional line items must be included if, as a result of their omission, the half-yearly financial statements would give a misleading view of the assets, liabilities, financial position and profit or loss of the issuer.

For issuers not required to prepare consolidated accounts the Rules also set out further specific requirements in relation to comparative information and the content of the explanatory notes.

Rule 4.2.6 requires that the accounting policies and presentation applied to the half-yearly figures must be consistent with those applied in the latest published annual accounts except where:

(1) the accounting policies and presentation are to be changed in the subsequent annual financial statements, in which case the new accounting policies and presentation should be followed, and the changes and the reasons for the changes should be disclosed in the half-yearly report; or
(2) the FSA otherwise agrees.

Companies may choose to have the half-yearly financial report reviewed or audited by an auditor. Rule 4.2.9 requires that "if the half-yearly financial report has been audited or reviewed by auditors pursuant to the Auditing Practices Board guidance on Review of Interim Financial Information, the audit report or review report must be reproduced in full."

Responsibility Statements

Rule 4.2.10 requires that for each person making a responsibility statement, the statement must confirm that to the best of his or her knowledge, inter alia:

> "the condensed set of financial statements, which has been prepared in accordance with the applicable set of accounting standards, gives a true and fair view of the assets, liabilities, financial position and profit or loss of the issuer, or the undertakings included in the consolidation as a whole ..."

However, Rule 4.2.10 also provides that:

> "A person making a responsibility statement will satisfy the requirement ... to confirm that the condensed set of financial statements gives a true and fair view ... by including a statement that the condensed set of financial statements have been prepared in accordance with:
>
> (a) IAS 34; or
> (b) for UK issuers not using IFRS, pronouncements on interim reporting issued by the Accounting Standards Board[10b]; or
> (c) for all other issuers not using IFRS, a national accounting standard relating to interim reporting,
>
> provided always that a person making such a statement has reasonable grounds to be satisfied that the condensed set of financial statements prepared in accordance with such a standard is not misleading."

Companies Act Requirements

United Kingdom

Financial statements included in half-yearly financial reports constitute non-statutory accounts under the provisions of the Companies Act[10c] and therefore must include a statement indicating:

(a) that they are not the statutory accounts;

[10b] For half-yearly periods ending on or after 20 September 2007, the relevant ASB pronouncement is the Statement "Half-Yearly Financial Reports".

[10c] Relevant references are: for the Companies Act 1985 – section 240 (the equivalent legislation in Northern Ireland is Article 243(3) of the Companies (Northern Ireland) Order, 1986); for the Companies Act 2006 – section 435 (this also applies in Northern Ireland).

(b) whether statutory accounts for any relevant financial year have been delivered to the registrar of companies;
(c) whether the auditors reported on the statutory accounts for any such year; and
(d) if so, whether it was qualified or unqualified, or included an emphasis of matter, or contained a statement by the auditor required under the Companies Act[10d] (accounting records or returns inadequate or accounts or directors' remuneration report not agreeing with records and returns, or failure to obtain necessary information and explanations).

Republic of Ireland

In the Republic of Ireland, financial statements included in a half-yearly report made by a single entity constitute abbreviated accounts under section 19 of the Companies (Amendment) Act, 1986. Financial statements included in a half-yearly report made by a group constitute abbreviated group accounts under regulation 40 of the European Communities (Companies: Group Accounts) Regulations, 1992. This states that where a parent undertaking publishes abbreviated group accounts relating to any financial year, it shall also publish a statement indicating:

(a) that the abbreviated group accounts are not the group accounts, copies of which are required by law to be annexed to the annual return,
(b) whether the copies of the group accounts so required to be annexed have in fact been so annexed,
(c) whether the auditors have made a report under section 193 of the Companies Act, 1990 in respect of the group accounts which relate to any financial year with which the abbreviated group accounts purport to deal, and
(d) whether the report of the auditors contained any qualifications.

The statement required for a single entity is similar.

[10d] *Relevant references are: for the Companies Act 1985 – section 237(2) and (3); for the Companies Act 2006 – section 498(2) and (3).*

[Audit Briefing Paper]
Providing assurance on the effectiveness of internal control

(Issued July 2001)

Contents

	Paragraphs
Introduction	
Concepts underlying the provision of assurance on internal control	
Background	1 - 16
The interrelationship between business objectives, risk identification, control design and control operation	17 - 39
The elements of providing assurance on internal control	40 - 62
Inherent limitations of internal control	62 - 67
Illustration of a narrative report providing assurance on the effectiveness of internal control	
Appendix I Conclusions of the APB's 1998 consultation	1 - 22
Appendix II Internal control requirements of the Combined Code, the Listing Rules and associated APB guidance	

Providing assurance on the effectiveness of internal control

Introduction

During the 1990's there was much debate surrounding the desirability of public statements by directors of listed companies concerning the effectiveness of internal control, and the extent to which auditors should express assurance on such statements. Publication of the report of the Turnbull Committee *'Internal Control: Guidance for Directors on the Combined Code'* (Turnbull report) and associated APB Bulletins[1] has brought that debate to a conclusion.

The Turnbull report provides guidance for directors on the implementation of the internal control provisions of the Combined Code[2]. Its guidance is intended to reflect sound business practice whereby internal controls are embedded in the business processes by which an entity pursues its objectives.

Under the Listing Rules and the associated APB Bulletins the auditors review whether the company's published summary of the process it has adopted in reviewing the effectiveness of its system of internal control is both supported by the documentation prepared by, or for, the directors and appropriately reflects that process. The auditors are not required to provide assurance on internal control.

The procedures to support the review required by the Listing Rules are considerably narrower in scope than those that would be required for an engagement to provide assurance on internal control. This paper does not deal with the narrow requirements of auditors under the Listing Rules but with the much broader concepts of providing assurance on the effectiveness of internal control.

Interest in the effectiveness of internal control has not been restricted to the capital markets. Regulators in the financial services sector have shown considerable interest in the internal control of the entities they regulate. In the public sector there are specific requirements for auditors to consider aspects of the internal control of many bodies

The APB has issued two discussion papers on the subject of providing assurance on internal control[3]. These papers explained the issues associated with providing assurance on internal control, especially in reports that are made public, and explored different approaches. Responses to these discussion papers indicate that there is still some way to go before a consensus is reached on how engagements to provide assurance on internal control should be performed and how conclusions should be reported.

If a demand for either external or internal auditors to provide assurance on internal control develops, then the conceptual and practical difficulties that have been identified will need to be overcome.

---

[1] *Guidance for auditors in meeting the requirements of the Listing Rules are dealt with in APB Bulletins 1999/5 (United Kingdom) and 2000/1 (Republic of Ireland). See Appendix 2 of this paper.*

[2] *See Appendix 2 of this paper*

[3] *'Internal financial control effectiveness' in April 1995, and 'Providing assurance on internal control' in March 1998.*

The APB hopes this Briefing Paper will contribute to developing a model of how practitioners might be able to express assurance on the reliability of systems of internal control. This paper will also assist directors, regulators and others, better appreciate the challenges associated with reporting on the effectiveness of internal control and, in particular, the advantages of providing assurance through a narrative, rather than a standardised, report.

Following the concepts described in this Briefing Paper will, almost invariably, give rise to a lengthy narrative report. A lengthy narrative report is necessary in order to communicate the various judgments made by the practitioners, the reasoning underpinning those judgments, and the context in which the opinion is given. Owing to the lack of generally accepted suitable criteria available to practitioners in carrying out such engagements, and the difficulties of communicating conclusions relating to internal control, a standardised short-form report is likely to lead to misunderstandings and unfulfilled expectations.

The illustrative narrative report set out in Section 3 of the paper is nine pages long and relates to only the revenue of the subject entity. Furthermore, it does not include a full description of the design of the system of internal control for revenue. It is not difficult to imagine, therefore, that a narrative report dealing with all aspects of an entity's system of internal control, and including a full description of the system, could be a substantial document.

It is likely to be impractical to circulate widely reports of such length and, therefore, it seems most likely that reports providing assurance on the effectiveness of internal control will usually be provided by practitioners to those who have instructed them, and not be published.

Concepts underlying the provision of assurance on internal control

Background

1 In 1998 the APB published a consultation paper entitled *'Providing Assurance on Internal Control'*. It set out preliminary proposals for a Framework of Principles applicable to engagements intended to provide assurance on internal control.

2 The proposed Framework of Principles drew heavily on the exposure draft *'Reporting on the credibility of information'* which had been published by the International Auditing Practices Committee (IAPC) in August 1997.

3 Thirty eight detailed and helpful responses to the consultation paper were received. A summary of the conclusions that the APB has drawn from the comment letters is set out as Appendix I to this paper.

4 The adoption of a common reporting framework will be in the public interest if it results in more consistent practice, and avoids the development of expectation gaps between practitioners and the users of their reports. If the demand for either external or internal auditors to provide assurance reports on internal control increases, the accountancy profession will need to overcome the conceptual and practical difficulties that currently exist.

Publication of Turnbull Report

In September 1999 the Institute of Chartered Accountants in England & Wales, with the support of the UK Listing Authority, published *'Internal Control: Guidance for Directors on the Combined Code'* (the Turnbull report). The Turnbull report places a much greater emphasis on objective setting, risk identification and risk assessment than earlier guidance for directors. It requires, for example, the board's deliberations to 'include consideration of the following factors:

- the nature and extent of the risks facing the company;
- the extent and categories of risk which it regards as acceptable for the company to bear;
- the likelihood of the risks concerned materialising;
- the company's ability to reduce the incidence and impact on the business risks that do materialise; and
- the costs of operating particular controls relative to the benefit thereby obtained in managing the related risks'.

Although the Turnbull report is directed at the boards of listed companies it has been adopted in many other sectors. As can be seen from Appendix I a number of commentators considered that the APB's 1998 proposals should have placed a greater emphasis on risk identification and assessment.

Finalisation of IAPC Assurance Framework

In July 2000 the IAPC published an International Standard on Assurance Engagements (ISAE) that describes the objectives and elements of assurance engagements intended to provide either a high or moderate level of assurance. The ISAE has evolved from the IAPC's proposal *'Reporting on the credibility of information'* which is referred to above.

One of the more significant differences between the original proposal of the IAPC and the ISAE is that the ISAE does not require a standardised format for reporting on assurance engagements but rather identifies the minimum information required to be included in the report. The ISAE envisages that, for certain assurance engagements, practitioners may choose to adopt a flexible approach using a narrative, long-form, style of reporting, rather than a standardised short-form format.

This more flexible approach to reporting accommodates the views of many commentators on our 1998 proposals, that reports intended to provide assurance on internal control should be narrative rather than standardised.

The ISAE explains the importance in assurance engagements of 'criteria' that establish and inform the intended user of the basis against which the subject matter has been evaluated or measured in forming the conclusion. An evaluation of internal controls is however very judgmental – generally accepted criteria do not exist. In this briefing paper the APB seeks to explore how to compensate, through narrative reporting, for the absence of generally accepted criteria.

Further development of APB's thinking

In considering the comments received on the 1998 paper and in light of the developments since 1998, described above, the APB has developed its thinking regarding the interrelationship between business objectives, risk identification and assessment, internal control design, and the operation of internal controls.

12　This has reconfirmed the importance of clearly distinguishing between:

(a) providing assurance on internal control design; and
(b) providing assurance on the operation of a system of internal controls in accordance with its design.

The scope of each of these engagements would be quite different.

13　As established suitable criteria are typically not available to practitioners the APB has further concluded that practitioners need to explain their conclusions in the context of:

(a) the significant 'applicable risks' identified by the client;
(b) how these risks were identified by the client;
(c) the aspects of the system design that are intended to mitigate these risks; and
(d) a description of the system of internal control[4].

Consequently reports intended to provide assurance on internal control will typically be narrative rather than standardised..

14　All systems of internal control have inherent limitations. It is important that any assurance report should draw attention to those limitations and the consequence that performance of the engagement may not detect that unintended events or results could have occurred.

15　These further developments in APB's thinking are explained more fully in the text that follows and are illustrated by the assurance report on the effectiveness of a system of internal control set out in Section 3.

16　The narrative report in Section 3 is included for the sole purpose of illustrating the application of the concepts described in this section of the paper. The illustration is not intended to be used as an authoritative model of how such reports ought to be presented.

The interrelationship between business objectives, risk identification, control design and control operation

17　Internal controls exist to mitigate the risks that threaten the achievement of an entity's business objectives. In order to have effective internal control, the entity needs, once its business objectives have been established, to:

(a) have identified and assessed the risks that threaten achievement of those objectives;
(b) have designed internal controls that will manage those risks; and
(c) operate the internal controls in accordance with their design specification.

18　The framework depicted on page 10 shows the interrelationship between these activities together with illustrative considerations that apply to the judgments involved in reaching an overall conclusion about the effectiveness of internal control.

19　The framework depicts three of the processes that management will typically undertake when reviewing the effectiveness of internal control.

---

[4] Inclusion of a description of the system of internal control may not be necessary in those circumstances where the practitioner is aware that the user of the report is fully conversant with the system in place. For example, a regulator may mandate many aspects of the system design and consequently not need to have the design description included in the practitioners' report.

The first process is risk identification and assessment which is based on understanding the entity's business objectives. The output of the process is an understanding of the 'applicable risks' that need to be addressed in the design of the system of internal control.

The second process is designing the system of internal control, based on a knowledge of the applicable risks. The output of this process would be a record of the system of internal control, typically in the form of a systems manual.

The third process is evaluating whether the system actually operates in accordance with the system description. The output of all of the processes taken together would be a conclusion on internal control effectiveness.

For each process there are a number of important and quite different considerations that management will take into account. On the diagram illustrative examples of these considerations are listed against each process.

Although the diagram is intended to illustrate management's processes it will be these processes that practitioners will need to assess when engaged to provide assurance on the effectiveness of internal control.

The diagram, therefore, serves to illustrate:

(a) the separate elements of an engagement to provide assurance on internal control;
(b) that practitioners could be engaged to provide assurance on individual processes or on a combination of the three processes;
(c) the range of 'considerations' that apply to each process; and consequently
(d) the inherent complexity of an engagement to provide assurance about the effectiveness of internal control.

Business objectives

All entities have business objectives; they are the goals that an entity sets for itself. At an overall level business objectives may be general statements, (such as a mission or vision statement) but will usually be specified in more detail as they are incorporated into business plans.

Clear business objectives need to be identified before an effective system of control can be established. Without clear objectives, management will be unable to identify and evaluate the risks that threaten the achievement of their objectives and design and operate a system of internal control to manage those risks.

Many internal control frameworks such as COCO[5], COSO[6] and that of the Basel Committee on Banking Supervision divide business objectives into three categories. The Turnbull report uses the same three categories to describe what an internal control system encompasses:

---

[5] *Criteria of Control Board of the Canadian Institute of Chartered Accountants*

[6] *Committee of Sponsoring Organizations of the Treadway Commission (a USA organisation)*

Framework for forming an opinion on the effectiveness of internal control

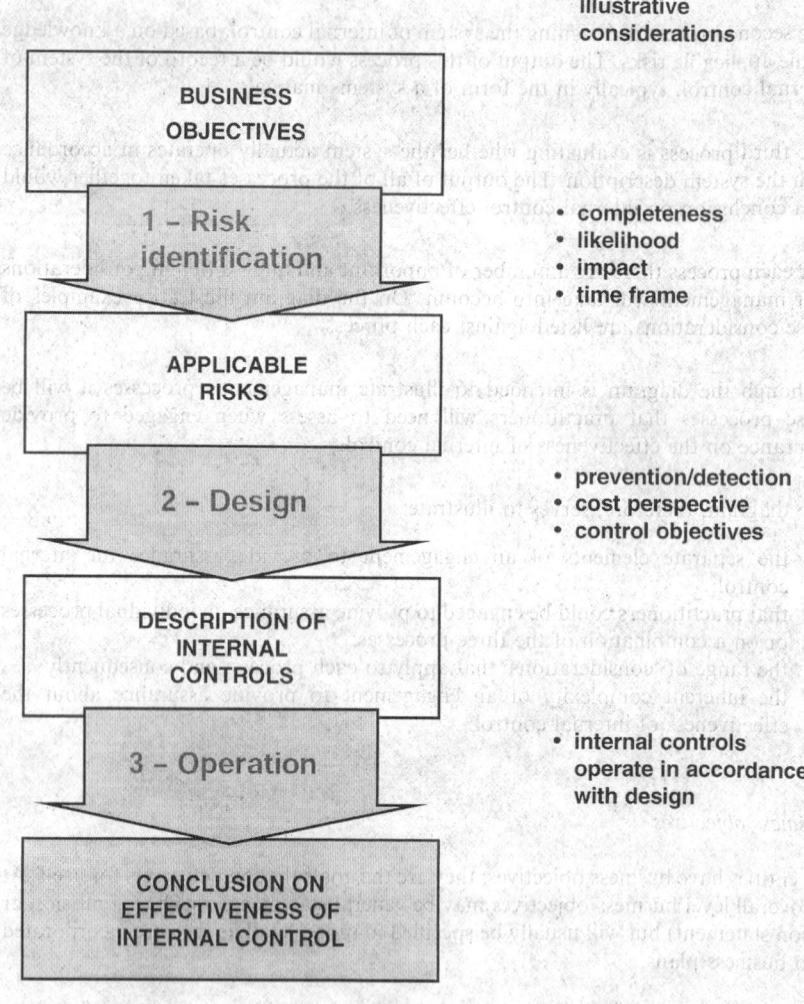

> (a) **Effectiveness and efficiency of operations** includes objectives related to an entity's goals, such as customer service, the safeguarding and efficient use of resources, profitability and meeting social obligations.
> (b) **Reliability of internal and external reporting** (sometimes referred to as internal financial control).
> (c) **Compliance with applicable laws and regulations and internal policies with respect to the conduct of the business.**

29 Objective setting is the responsibility of the directors and senior management. Although practitioners engaged to provide assurance on internal control need to be aware of the entity's objectives, it is not appropriate for them, as part of an assurance engagement on the effectiveness of internal control, to be involved in the entity's objective setting processes.

Applicable risks

30 A risk is a threat that circumstances, events or actions will adversely affect an entity's ability to achieve its business objectives. Risks, therefore, affect an entity's ability to survive, successfully compete within its industry and maintain the overall quality of its products, services and people. An entity's objectives, its internal organisation and the environment in which it operates are continually changing. An effective system of internal control therefore depends on a thorough and regular evaluation of the nature and extent of the risks to which the entity is exposed.

31 Risk identification involves identifying the risks that may potentially threaten achievement of an entity's business objectives. Completeness is the key consideration; all significant risks need to be considered.

32 Once identified, risks can then be assessed in terms of their likelihood (probability), imminence (timing) and potential impact (materiality). Risk assessment is the process of prioritising the 'potential risks' into those 'applicable risks' that need to be actively managed.

33 There is no single process through which management identifies and assesses risks. Although a number of useful mechanisms have been developed none of them eliminates the need for a great deal of judgment, not least in assessing the likelihood and potential impact of risks.

34 The following discussion is provided purely as an example of one possible mechanism:

> **Illustration of a process of risk identification and assessment**
> A typical risk identification and assessment exercise, when carried out for the first time, is likely to consist of brainstorming sessions involving directors, management and employees[7]. Such sessions may be facilitated by those with an expertise in risk management.

---

[7] *Each director and manager in an entity is likely to have a different viewpoint regarding the risks an entity faces and consequently the most comprehensive identification of potential risks is likely to be the result of a risk identification process that involves directors and managers from all departments within an entity. Informed outsiders such as auditors, actuaries, suppliers and bankers are also likely to provide useful input in identifying potential risks.*

To maximise the effectiveness of brainstorming sessions the entity should have defined its business objectives in detail in advance. However, such brainstorming is likely to generate more detailed business objectives as well as a more comprehensive understanding of potential risks.

The perceptions of individual directors and managers as to what constitutes a risk, its likelihood and potential impact may differ. Consequently, the more directors and managers that are involved the more useful the exercise is likely to be.

Potential risks are then evaluated through a 'risk screening' process that involves locating each identified risk on a map such as that depicted overleaf[8]:

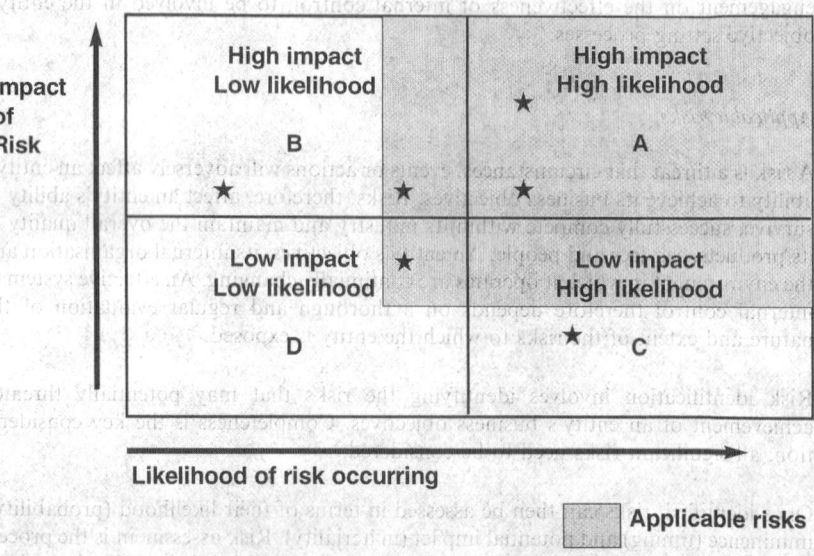

Management will designate an area on the map within which risks are deemed to be 'applicable risks'. This is depicted by the shaded area in the diagram above. The identification of the risks and the determination of the shaded area is likely to be an iterative process during which particular attention will be paid to those risks that initially fall either just outside or just inside the area of the risk map designated to contain the applicable risks.

Risks falling outside the shaded area are not disregarded by management and internal controls may be developed to control these risks. The significance of the risks within the shaded area is that these are the risks that management has determined need to be addressed in order for them to be satisfied that internal control is effective.

---

[8] *Techniques, often using information technology tools, have been developed that enable participants' assessments, both individually and in aggregate, to be depicted on a risk map. The same techniques may enable a group of managers or directors to analyse their individual and collective views on specific risks and facilitate discussion among participants with differing views on a particular risk.*

Internal control design

Active management of 'applicable risks' may involve: 35

(a) acceptance of the risk (with appropriate monitoring);
(b) transfer of the risk (eg through insurance);
(c) terminating the risk generating activity; or
(d) mitigating the risk through internal control.

With respect to 35 (d), the Turnbull report states that a system of internal control should: 36

- 'be embedded in the operations of the company and form part of its culture;
- be capable of responding quickly to evolving risks to the business arising from factors within the company and to changes in the business environment; and
- include procedures for reporting immediately to appropriate levels of management any significant control failings or weaknesses that are identified together with details of corrective action being undertaken'.

In designing internal controls to manage 'applicable risks', management consider: 37

(a) **The desired balance between prevention and detection controls.** Prevention controls are controls designed to avoid an unintended event or result from occurring (for example a control built into a computer system to raise purchase orders once stock levels become so low that there is a risk to an entity's production activities). Detection controls, by contrast, are designed to discover an unintended event or result that has occurred (for example analysing the effluent from a chemical plant to measure whether the pollution controls within the plant have been effective). While most systems will involve both prevention and detection controls the nature and extent of each will be influenced by factors such as:
   - the degree of risk;
   - the quality of staff, especially those that undertake prevention controls; and
   - the reliability of information processing systems.
(b) **The cost perspective of the entity.** The extent and nature of internal control will be influenced by cost considerations. These considerations may not always lead to the lowest cost solution being implemented. For example, an oil and gas refiner may be required to control the amount of sulphur emitted into the atmosphere from its refinery. Operational management may initially recommend that state of the art monitoring equipment (that is integrated into the production processes of the refinery) should not be installed on the basis that the cost per barrel is too high in the context of the then prevailing world oil price. The directors may, however, overrule a recommendation based on short term considerations in circumstances where they have made the minimisation of sulphur emissions as one of their primary business objectives regardless of short term fluctuations in world oil prices.
(c) **Specific control objectives.** Applicable risks' may need further analysis to focus the design of discrete actions. For example the risk that cash is not collected from credit sales may need to be split into control objectives involving:
   - ensuring a customer's credit rating is checked before shipments are made;
   - preparing monthly ageing analysis of receivables; and
   - sending follow up notices to overdue debtors.

Internal control operation

An entity's objectives, policies and procedures with respect to internal control are usually embedded into the operations of the entity by being documented in its 38 systems manuals or software. Such manuals provide criteria for management, and practitioners, to measure whether internal control has operated in accordance with its design.

39 However, even with a well-documented system design, judgment will be required in determining whether controls have operated as designed. A key consideration is likely to be the extent to which deficiencies in the operation of controls are tolerated before the achievement of objectives is considered to be threatened.

The elements of providing assurance on internal control

40 The framework depicted on page 10 illustrates that providing assurance on the effectiveness of internal control consists (at least conceptually) of up to three areas of judgment. These being consideration of:

(a) risk identification and assessment;
(b) the design of the internal controls; and
(c) whether the internal controls operated in accordance with the design.

41 Practitioners will need to have a knowledge of the business of the entity that is sufficient to enable them to identify and understand the events, transactions and practices that may, or ought to, have a significant effect on the entity's system of internal control. The extent of knowledge required will depend on the scope of each individual engagement.

42 Depending on the needs of the engaging party, the starting point (other than the requisite knowledge of the business) of a particular internal control assurance engagement may be:

(a) the description of the system of internal control (in which case consideration of management's risk identification process and internal control design is not within the scope of the engagement);
(b) the 'applicable risks' (in which case management's risk identification process is not within the scope of the engagement); or
(c) the entity's business objectives.

Providing assurance that a system operated in accordance with the description of internal control

43 In undertaking an engagement to provide assurance on the operation of internal control practitioners will wish to clarify, when agreeing the terms of engagement, whether the assurance relates to a point of time or to a period. The date (or period covered) will be set out in the narrative assurance report.

44 Provided that the entity's description of its system of internal control is sufficiently detailed practitioners are likely to be able to gather sufficient appropriate evidence to express a high level of assurance that internal controls have operated as designed.

45 If the engagement involves providing assurance on the operation of a known system of internal controls practitioners may be able to issue a relatively concise report. This is because it will be unnecessary to include in the report a detailed description of the design of the system of internal control. The report is, nevertheless, likely to be narrative in nature as there may be a number of issues that practitioners wish to describe including, for example:

- isolated control failures;

- observations concerning the abilities of staff involved; and
- potential weaknesses identified by the practitioners not contemplated within the systems description.

Responses to the APB's 1998 consultation paper suggest that an engagement to provide assurance that a system operated in accordance with the description of internal controls may be of limited value. Many believe that practitioners should address the more judgmental areas of systems design and risk identification and assessment.

Providing assurance on the effectiveness of the design and operation of the system of internal control.

In such an engagement the practitioners seek to provide assurance concerning both the design of the system of controls to address a defined set of 'applicable risks' and the operation of those controls. (Assurance concerning the operation of controls is dealt with in paragraphs 43-46 above). The practitioner does not consider whether the applicable risks are complete.

In undertaking such an engagement the practitioner will need to obtain and evaluate management's views on various important considerations concerning the design of the internal controls including, for example:

- the desired balance between prevention and detection controls;
- the balance between cost and benefits; and
- the importance of specific control objectives.

As the practitioners' judgment regarding the effectiveness of the systems design will be based on their evaluation of the considerations identified by management they will need to describe management's considerations in their narrative report in order to provide an adequate context for their conclusions.

The narrative report will also set out:

- the applicable risks;
- any framework for design or benchmarking exercise used by either the directors or the practitioners; and
- a description of the design of the system of internal control.

Such narrative reports will be much longer than the auditors' report on annual financial statements. It will, however, be appreciated that the context for the auditors' report on financial statements is provided by the financial statements themselves which include the balance sheet, profit and loss account, the accounting policies and a reference to the accounting framework. Without these 'criteria' the auditors' report would have little meaning. In a narrative report on internal control the applicable risks and the systems description can be likened to the primary financial statements and the key considerations to the accounting policies.

If sufficient contextual information is provided in the report regarding the systems design and the key considerations, then practitioners may determine that they are able to express a high level of assurance that the design of the internal controls is effective to mitigate specified applicable risks. However, as the design of any system of internal control is highly judgmental practitioners may take the view that they are unable to express a high level of assurance on the effectiveness of the design of the system.

53 The level of assurance provided by practitioners will be a function of many factors, including:

- the nature of the entity;
- the extent of the practitioners' knowledge; and
- the scope of the engagement.

Providing assurance on the applicable risks, effectiveness of the design and operation of the system of internal control.

54 In such an engagement the practitioners seek to provide assurance concerning the identification and evaluation of 'applicable risks' as well as the design of the system of controls and the operation of those controls. In other words all three processes depicted in the framework on page 10.

55 The APB is not aware of the existence of any universally accepted criteria suitable for evaluating the effectiveness of an entity's risk identification and assessment activities. A great deal of judgment is needed, not least in assessing likelihood and potential impact. In most circumstances it is likely to be impossible for practitioners to determine, with any degree of certainty, that all potentially significant risks that threaten the achievement of business objectives have, in fact, been identified and have been properly evaluated.

56 As the risk identification and assessment process is highly judgmental, practitioners are unlikely to be able to obtain sufficient evidence to be able to express a high level of assurance regarding the completeness of an entity's 'applicable risks' or the effectiveness of the process that was used to determine them. However, practitioners may be able to obtain sufficient evidence to provide moderate assurance and conclude that nothing has come to their attention indicating that there are any other risks, apart from the identified applicable risks, that should have been assessed as both likely to arise and having high impact.

57 When determining what constitutes sufficient appropriate evidence of the effectiveness of the entity's risk identification and assessment processes, practitioners will need to consider whether they need to observe some or all of the meetings at which management and directors carry out the risk identification and assessment processes. Attending such meetings is likely to provide the most persuasive evidence regarding the risk identification and assessment processes.

58 In an engagement that involves providing assurance on the applicable risks, the practitioners' starting point is the entity's business objectives. The key considerations relating to the risk identification and assessment process include:

- the completeness of the applicable identified risks;
- the probability of an applicable risk actually crystallising;
- the materiality of the likely impact of the risk; and
- the time period over which the risk is expected to materialise.

59 There are no established criteria for risk identification. As the risks facing each entity are unique to it, the process is inherently judgmental. Consequently, the practitioners need to set out in their report:

- the business objectives;
- a description of the risk identification and assessment process, including the key considerations; and
- the applicable risks.

Narrative reports

It can be seen, therefore, that the more extensive the scope of a controls assurance engagement, the more information needs to be included in the practitioners' report. Only if this information is provided to the user, can the user understand the judgments that support the practitioners' conclusions.

A formalised short-form opinion to the effect that internal control is 'effective' or 'adequate' would be insufficient as it would not enable users to understand the context in which the opinion is given or the judgments that have had to be made in reaching the conclusion, and the reasoning underpinning those judgments. Consequently, short-form reports expressing assurance regarding internal controls are likely to lead to misunderstandings and unfulfilled expectations.

Section 3 of this paper provides an illustration of a narrative assurance report. It is based on an imaginary engagement to provide assurance on the effectiveness of the system of internal control relating to the recording of advertising revenue by a newspaper publishing company. The example is included for the sole purpose of illustrating the concepts described above. It is not intended to be used as an authoritative model of how such reports ought to be presented.

Inherent limitations of internal control

Those who commission reports on internal control from practitioners may be looking for absolute assurance and, as a consequence, have unrealistic expectations. They may, for example, believe that internal control:

(a) can ensure an entity's success, that is will ensure achievement of basic business objectives, or at least the entity's survival; and
(b) can ensure the reliability of financial reporting and compliance with laws and regulations.

Decisions made in designing internal control inevitably involve the acceptance of some degree of risk. As the outcome of the operation of internal control cannot be predicted with absolute assurance any assessment of internal control is very judgmental.

Consequently, when accepting an engagement to provide assurance on internal control it will be necessary for practitioners to explain what internal control cannot do. The Turnbull report provides the following useful summary:

'A sound system of internal control reduces, but cannot eliminate, the possibility of poor judgment in decision-making, human error, control processes being deliberately circumvented by employees and others, management overriding controls and the occurrence of unforeseeable circumstances.

A sound system of internal control therefore provides reasonable, but not absolute assurance that a company will not be hindered in achieving its business objectives, or in the orderly and legitimate conduct of its business, by circumstances which may reasonably be foreseen. A system of internal control cannot, however, provide protection with certainty against a company failing to meet its business objectives or all material errors, losses, fraud or breaches of laws and regulations.'

66 Entities and their internal control needs differ by industry, size, culture and management philosophy. When designing a system of internal control there are many options as to the nature and extent of controls that may be implemented. Internal controls, for example, may be preventive or detective in nature and may be performed by people or by information technology systems. There is a balance to be achieved between the cost of implementation of controls and the identified benefits derived from the controls. Consequently one entity's internal control system may be very different from another's in relation to similar business processes.

67 To avoid the development of an unnecessary expectation gap, narrative assurance reports should caution the reader that any projection of the evaluation of the risks and control procedures to future periods is subject to risk. For example, the business risks facing the entity may change and the control procedures may become inadequate because of changes in conditions. In addition the degree of compliance with the control procedures may deteriorate.

Illustration of a narrative report providing assurance on the effectiveness of internal control

> Cautionary note: This example has been developed for the sole purpose of illustrating what a narrative report on the effectiveness of internal control might look like following the concepts described in Section 2 of this Briefing Paper. As such reports could be presented in many ways, and will usually be tailored to reflect the requirements of the engaging party, it is not intended to be authoritative. Consequently, the example is not intended to provide a model of how such reports ought to be presented or to reflect the APB's views as to the ideal content of such reports.

15 April 2001
The Audit Committee
PQR Group Limited

Dear Sirs

Effectiveness of internal controls relating to the advertising revenues of PQR Limited

In accordance with the arrangements set out in our letter dated 3 March 2000, we are writing to summarise the outcome of our work in assessing the effectiveness of the internal controls relating to the advertising revenues of PQR Limited during the period 30 September 2000 to 28 February 2001. A separate report submitted to senior management contains a full description of the design of the system of internal control which, in the interests of brevity, has been excluded from this report.

Scope of Engagement

Included in the scope of our engagement were the processes relating to:

- maintaining PQR's competitiveness by keeping current with the advertisement presentation styles of its competitors;
- the booking in and recording of advertisements;
- the accuracy and timeliness of the inclusion of advertisement in the newspapers published by PQR Limited;

- adherence of the advertisements to PQR's 'Code of publication values';
- the processing of the related advertising revenues to the general ledger and the management accounts; and
- the collection and banking of cash and the recording of cash receipts.

As agreed we have not assessed the systems that control bank payments or the onward reporting and summarisation of general ledger information into either the management or statutory accounts.

Inherent Limitations of the Engagement

There are inherent limitations as to what can be achieved by internal control and consequently limitations to the conclusions that can be drawn from this engagement. These limitations include the possibility of faulty judgment in decision making, of breakdowns because of human error, of control activities being circumvented by the collusion of two or more people and of management overriding controls. Also there is no certainty that internal controls will continue to operate effectively in future periods or that the controls will be adequate to mitigate all significant risks which may arise in future. Accordingly we express no opinion about the adequacy of the system of internal control to mitigate future risk.

Companies and their internal control needs differ by industry, size, culture and management philosophy. When designing a system of internal control there are many options as to the nature and extent of controls that may be implemented. Internal controls, for example, may be preventive or detective in nature and may be performed by people or by information technology systems. There is a balance to be achieved between the cost of implementation of controls and the identified benefits derived from the controls. Consequently one company's internal control system may be very different from another's in relation to similar business processes. Decisions made in designing internal controls inevitably involve the acceptance of some degree of risk. As the outcome of the operation of internal controls cannot be predicted with absolute assurance any assessment of internal control is very judgmental.

Business Objectives

We discussed the business and control objectives of PQR Limited relating to advertising revenues with the executive directors and senior management and understand them to be:

- To maximise revenues from advertisements placed in PQR Limited newspapers by ensuring that the presentation of advertisements keeps pace with developments at its competitors but without incurring the expense of being the brand leader.
- To ensure that all advertisements booked by customers are published accurately in accordance with each advertiser's requirements.
- To ensure that all advertisements placed in newspapers are invoiced in accordance with the appropriate rate card.
- To accept that a proportion of revenues may not be collectible as a result of credit risk, but given the low marginal cost of advertisements being published, to accept a level of uncollectible revenue of up to 2.5% of total revenue as a feature of the business.
- To ensure that the textual and pictorial content of advertisements adhere to PQR's 'Code of publication values'.
- To ensure that PQR Limited is able to receive and process advertisements even when its computer systems are unavailable.

Work Performed

We performed our work during the period from 15 June 2000 to 31 March 2001.

Our assessment of the effectiveness of internal controls was divided into four phases:

- Understanding the business and management's business objectives in controlling advertising revenues.
- Reviewing management's embedded risk identification processes and observing management's risk screening process that is intended to identify those risks (the 'applicable risks') that represent both a significant and likely risk to the business.
- Assessing the effectiveness of the design of controls intended to control the applicable risks.
- Testing the effectiveness of the operation of those controls during the period 30 September 2000 to 28 February 2001.

Understanding the business

To provide the necessary background information to carry out the engagement we obtained an understanding of the following:

- The trends in the financial results of the business, and the key performance measures used by management, together with comparisons to similar businesses.
- The systems used to process transactions and produce management information.

We also obtained an understanding of the background to the business, including its people, customers, suppliers and competitors, the key business processes and the current business environment.

Risk Identification

We assessed both the effectiveness and results of management's on-going processes for identifying and managing risks. This included obtaining an understanding of the overall control environment, the key performance measures used by management and management's processes designed to identify emerging risks.

Using these assessments and this background information about the business we reviewed the adequacy of the listing of potential risks identified by management. The potential risks identified are set out in the annexe to this letter.

Risk Screening

Risk screening is a process whereby all of the potential risks are evaluated by management, based on their assessment of the likelihood of the risk occurring and the potential impact of the risk. Risks meeting certain criteria are deemed to be applicable risks. The screening process was organised and facilitated by consultants skilled in this field from LMN. We observed and participated in risk screening meetings held at each division.

The process of risk screening involves a significant degree of judgment and the culmination of the process was the final screening meeting with the executive directors, which the audit committee also attended, on 15 July 2000. This meeting considered:

ANNEXE

Risk Description	Risk screened from further consideration	Reasons
Risk of loss of revenue through one or all of • Failure of the business to invest in its titles and keep its product up to date. • New media products developed by competitors. • Attractiveness of competitor publications	No	PQR has adopted a strategy of following developments at its competitors rather than setting the pace for the industry. It is, therefore, crucial for its business success to have controls to ensure that it is fully aware of the activities of its competitors on a timely basis. Failure to respond to competitor innovation is the major business threat to revenue.
Risk that advertisements may be published that do not meet PQR's 'Code of publication values'	No	Although the company maintains comprehensive insurance cover which effectively mitigates the financial cost of the company being sued for advertising illegal services such as prostitution, the risk to the company's reputation is regarded as high. There is a high turnover of staff who process advertisements and consequently a need for strong controls over their work to ensure that the company's guidelines in this area are adhered to.
Risk that not all advertisements published are invoiced. This risk can be focussed more specifically to the risk that the transfer of data between the editorial system and the billing system is incomplete or inaccurate	No	Judged to be likely and potentially significant.
Inaccurate production of the advertisement in the newspaper	Yes	Individual advertisements are not significant to the business and there is no evidence of any systemic problems in this area.

The charges for advertisements placed, are not in line with the approved rates – either in error or as a result of deliberate collusion with advertisers	Yes	Individual advertisements are not significant to the business. Actual yields achieved are very closely monitored and there is no evidence of yields being out of line with expectations.
Cheques received are not deposited at the bank on a timely basis or are misappropriated	No	Judged to be likely and potentially significant.
Inappropriate credit limits are set resulting in acceptance of business from uncreditworthy customers.	Yes	The business objectives recognise that a proportion of revenue will not prove collectible but this is accepted given the low cost of publishing an advertisement. Monitoring of bad debts expense is ongoing and is a relatively static proportion of turnover. Given the large number of customers, management accept this ongoing cost and do not believe that additional controls in this area would be cost effective.
Cash receipts at the front desk are not passed to the cashiers or are misappropriated	No	Cash receipts are significant and this is judged to be a likely and potentially significant risk.
Transfer of accounting information to the nominal ledger from the billing system is not complete or accurate	Yes	Although potentially significant to the reported results failure of the transfer system is not judged to be likely as this process is computerised and there are strong integrity controls over the computer system.
The risk of unauthorised access to the editorial and billing systems	Yes	The potential for either deliberate or unintentional error arising from unrestricted or unauthorised access to these systems was not judged to be a significant and likely risk.
The risk that the editorial and billing systems are not available	No	Systems unavailability were judged both significant and likely.

Appendix I – Conclusions of the APB's 1998 consultation

Purpose of the 1998 consultation

In 1998 the APB published a consultation paper entitled *'Providing Assurance on Internal Control'*. It set out the APB's preliminary proposals for a Framework of Principles applicable to engagements intended to provide assurance on internal control. In the paper the APB expressed the view that a Framework of Principles would avoid expectation gaps developing between practitioners and users of their reports and result in more consistent practices. In publishing the consultation paper, therefore, the APB had hoped to stimulate debate and develop further the role of reporting accountants in providing assurance about the operation of internal controls.

Comments received

Thirty eight responses to the consultation paper were received[9]. In addition to answering the specific questions posed, a number of additional issues were raised. The comment letters were thought provoking and have been of considerable assistance to the APB in progressing its thinking.

Overview of the comments

The conclusions that the APB has drawn from the consultation, are set out below under the following headings:

- Framework of principles
- More emphasis on risk assessment
- Narrative reporting
- Difficulties with 'suitable criteria'
- Scope of the proposals
- Private or public reporting
- Scepticism
- Application to internal auditors

Framework of principles

There was strong support among commentators for the development of a Framework of Principles. Twenty one commentators stated that such a Framework would be worthwhile.

The thirteen proposed 'Principles' were generally supported although many found the proposed distinction between 'basic' and 'additional' Principles confusing. Some commentators suggested other Principles that are applicable to such engagements.

More emphasis on risk assessment

A number of commentators considered that a greater emphasis should have been placed on risk identification and assessment. In many models of internal control,

---

[9] *Copies of the comment letters have been placed on public record in the libraries of the six accountancy bodies that constitute the CCAB*

business objective setting and risk identification and assessment are considered to be pre-requisites for designing a system of internal control.

7   In response to this concern the content of this Briefing Paper addresses risk identification and assessment and business objective setting. This has the benefit of more closely aligning the APB's thinking with the Turnbull report.

Narrative reporting

8   The consultation paper set out specimen reports for a number of example engagements. Many commentators thought that these reports were:

(a) overly formalised (boiler plate);
(b) unnecessarily caveated;
(c) defensive; and
(d) unhelpful.

9   These commentators suggested that reports on internal control should be 'discursive' but acknowledged the difficulties that could exist in publishing 'discursive' reports.

10 Arising from these comments, the APB has developed an illustration of a narrative report. It is included as Section 3 of this Briefing Paper.

Difficulties with 'suitable criteria'

11 The consultation paper emphasised the importance of 'suitable criteria', and suggested that before being in a position to express an opinion on the adequacy or effectiveness of internal controls the reporting accountant would need either generally accepted criteria or a detailed list of control objectives.

12 Commentators expressed many reservations on the need for suitable criteria. As such criteria are typically not available to assurance providers, the proposals were seen, in effect, to require detailed control objectives to be provided to practitioners before they would be in a position to provide assurance on internal control.

13 This was interpreted, by some commentators, as reducing the practitioners' role to one of 'certificate provider' rather than 'useful adviser'. Many commentators, including regulators, thought this was unhelpful and expressed the view that the value that they were seeking from practitioners might involve the reporting accountants contributing to the identification and assessment of risks or providing advice on the design of the system of internal control.

14 In the absence of generally accepted criteria commentators recognised that the reporting accountants' report would need to provide sufficient information to allow users to put the reporting accountants' judgments into an appropriate context. This seems to provide further support for narrative, rather than standardised short-form, reporting.

Scope of the proposals

15 A number of commentators seemed to misinterpret what the APB meant by the expression 'assurance engagement'. As a result they were concerned that the APB was trying to prohibit both reporting accountants and internal auditors from undertaking a wide range of engagements that they have traditionally, and quite properly, performed. This was not the intent of the APB.

The objective of an assurance engagement is for a professional accountant to evaluate a subject matter that is the responsibility of another party against identified suitable criteria and to express a conclusion that provides the intended user with a level of assurance about that subject matter.

16

It follows that an assurance engagement does not encompass engagements such as 'agreed-upon procedures' compilation of financial or other information, management consulting or other advisory services such as comparing or benchmarking internal control systems. This is not to say that practitioners or others should not undertake such engagements only that such engagements are not assurance engagements.

17

Private or public reporting

Commentators were uncertain whether the Framework proposed in the consultation paper was intended to support public or private reporting. Many commentators thought that private reporting should be encouraged but thought that the proposed reporting style was more appropriate for public reporting.

18

In order for the reader to fully appreciate the context in which the reporting accountants have drawn their conclusions the illustrative report in this Briefing Paper sets out, in some detail, key considerations concerning an entity's business objectives, applicable risks and design characteristics of the internal control system. The illustrative narrative report developed for this Briefing Paper is quite lengthy and, consequently, APB envisages that such reports will have a limited circulation.

19

Scepticism

Concern was expressed by a number of commentators with respect to the proposed Principle that reporting accountants should plan and conduct an engagement to provide assurance on internal control with an attitude of professional scepticism. Some commentators interpreted 'scepticism' as meaning 'disbelieving' and thought that the concept of 'objectivity' would be preferable to scepticism

20

The APB remains strongly of the view that practitioners should be sceptical in the sense that they should neither assume that the responsible party is dishonest nor assume unquestioned honesty. In this regard the APB is entirely consistent with the International Standard on Assurance Engagements.

21

Application to internal auditors

Many internal auditors interpreted the proposals as restricting the scope of work that they should undertake and consequently objected to the notion that the proposals should apply to them.

22

Appendix 2 – Internal control requirements of the Combined Code, the Listing Rules and associated APB guidance

Internal control requirements of the Combined Code

Principle D.2 of the Code states that 'The Board should maintain a sound system of internal control to safeguard shareholders' investment and the company's assets'.

Provision D.2.1 states that 'The directors should, at least annually, conduct a review of the effectiveness of the group's system of internal control and should report to shareholders that they have done so. The review should cover all controls, including financial, operational and compliance controls and risk management'.

Provision D.2.2 states that 'Companies which do not have an internal audit function should from time to time review the need for one'.

Requirements of the Listing Rules

Paragraph 12.43A of the Listing Rules of both the UK and Irish Listing Authorities require the following to be included in a company's annual report and accounts:

(a) a narrative statement of how it has applied the principles set out in Section 1 of the Combined Code, providing explanation which enables its shareholders to evaluate how the principles have been applied;

(b) a statement as to whether or not it has complied throughout the accounting period with the Code provisions set out in section 1 of the Combined Code. A company that has not complied with the Code provisions, or complied with only some of the Code provisions or (in the case of provisions whose requirements are of a continuing nature) complied for only part of an accounting period, must specify the Code provisions with which it has not complied, and (where relevant) for what part of the period such non-compliance continued, and give reasons for any non compliance.

Requirements of auditors
A company's statement under 12.43A(b) must be reviewed by the auditors before publication only insofar as it relates to Code provisions A.1.2, A.1.3, A.6.1, A.6.2, D.1.1, D.2.1, and D.3.1 of the Combined Code.

Extracts from APB Bulletin 1999/5 'The Combined Code: Requirements of Auditors under the Listing Rules of the London Stock Exchange'.

17   In relation to all elements of the corporate governance disclosures relating to the Code provisions that are within the scope of their review, the auditors obtain appropriate evidence to support the compliance statement made by the company. Appropriate evidence will usually be obtained by performing the following procedures:

(a) reviewing the minutes of the meetings of the board of directors, and of relevant board committees (for example audit, nomination and risk management committees);
(b) reviewing supporting documents prepared for the board of directors or board committees that are relevant to those matters specified for review by the auditors;
(c) making enquiries of certain directors (such as the chairman of the board of directors and the chairmen of relevant board committees) and the company secretary, regarding procedure and its implementation, to satisfy themselves on matters relevant to those Code provisions specified for review by the auditors; and
(d) attending meetings of the audit committee (or the full board if there is no audit committee) at which the annual report and accounts, including the statement of compliance, are considered and approved for submission to the board of directors.

Auditors review of compliance with Code provision D.2.1
Although the Turnbull guidance addresses all of the internal control requirements of the Combined Code, Listing Rule 12.43A requires the auditors to review only the disclosures made with respect to Code provision D.2.1. 32

The objective of the auditors' review is to assess whether the company's summary of the process the board (and where applicable its committees) has adopted in reviewing the effectiveness of the system of internal control, is both supported by the documentation prepared by or for the directors and appropriately reflects that process. 35

To achieve this objective the auditors, in addition to the procedures outlined in paragraph 17: 36

(a) through enquiry of the directors obtain an understanding of the process defined by the board for its review of the effectiveness of internal control and compare their understanding to the statement made by the board in the annual report and accounts;
(b) review the documentation prepared by or for the directors to support their statement made in connection with Code provision D.2.1 and assess whether or not it provides sound support for that statement; and
(c) relate the statement made by the directors to the auditors' knowledge of the company obtained during the audit of the financial statements. As explained in paragraph 39, the scope of the directors review will be considerably broader in its scope than the knowledge the auditors can be expected to have based on their audit.

The Stock Exchange considers this approach to be consistent with its Listing Rules' requirement.

Auditors, therefore, are not expected to assess whether all risks and controls have been addressed by the directors or that risks are satisfactorily addressed by internal controls. In order to communicate this fact to users of the annual report the following sentence is included in the auditors' report on the financial statements. 40

We are not required to consider whether the board's statements on internal control cover all risks and controls, or form an opinion on the effectiveness of the company's corporate governance procedures or its risk and control procedures.

Part Nine

Other APB Papers

Part Nine

Other APB Papers

[Briefing Paper]
Effective communication between audit committees and external auditors

(Issued September 2002)

Contents

	Paragraphs
Preface	1.1 - 1.4
Introduction	1 - 2
Executive summary	3 - 7
Role of the audit committee	8 - 11
Role of the auditors	12
Benefits of working together	13 - 14
Matters to communicate with the auditors	
Establish expectations	15 - 21
The scope of the audit	22 - 25
Findings from the audit	26 - 44
The independence of the auditors	45 - 49
Form and timing of communication	
Form	50 - 51
Timing	52 - 54
Private meetings	55

Appendix 1: Requirements of the Combined Code relating to accountability and audit

Appendix 2: Combined Code provisions that auditors are required to review

Preface

1.1 This Briefing Paper builds on and supersedes the Briefing Paper 'Communication between external auditors and audit committees' which was published by the Auditing Practices Board (APB) in June 1998.

1.2 Since the publication of the original Briefing Paper the APB has revised the Statement of Auditing Standards (SAS) 610 which establishes standards for auditors on 'Communication of audit matters to those charged with governance'[1]. Auditors are required to comply with the new standards in respect of audits of financial statements for periods *commencing* on or after 23 December 2001.

1.3 The APB has produced this Paper to provide guidance for audit committees on the communications they might expect to have with their external auditors, having regard to the new standards in SAS 610 published last year. The APB hopes the Paper will assist effective communication between audit committees and auditors and, in so doing, help both groups fulfil their responsibilities which are important ingredients in helping ensure the integrity and high quality of financial reporting and thereby maintaining the confidence of users of financial statements.

1.4 At the time of publishing this Paper active consideration is being given to the role and effectiveness of non-executive directors and the remit of audit committees[2]. This paper does not take account of any of the numerous recommendations currently being considered for possible changes to the responsibilities of non-executive directors and audit committees. Nor does it reflect the APB's own views on how those responsibilities might evolve which will be discussed with the Financial Reporting Council. The APB will update, or add to, its guidance in the light of developments including changes to the Combined Code.

Introduction

1 This Briefing Paper is intended to assist audit committees review the scope and results of the audit of the financial statements, assist them in asking questions of the auditors and in assessing whether they have received information from the auditors that meets their needs.

2 Following the executive summary below are brief overviews of the respective roles of the audit committee and the auditors and the benefits of good communication between them.

Executive Summary

3 The main part of the Paper describes the matters that will typically be addressed in communications between the audit committee and the auditors, and focuses on:

---

[1] SAS 610 can be obtained from the APB's web site (www.apb.org.uk) or purchased from Croner.CCH Group Ltd (telephone 020 8247 1287).

[2] Reviews in progress include Mr D Higgs' 'Review of the role and effectiveness of non-executive directors' which was commissioned by the Government. A consultation paper was published by Mr Higgs in June 2002 and a final report is expected around the end of 2002. In July 2002, the Co-ordinating Group on Auditing and Accounting Issues released their interim report. In this report it was announced that the Financial Reporting Council, which is the custodian of the Combined Code, is to set up a small group to develop the existing Code provisions. This work will be taken forward in tandem with that of Mr Higgs and a report is also expected at the end of 2002.

- ***Establishing expectations*** (paragraphs 15 to 21)
  In order to maximise the benefits to the audit committee and to the auditors of communications between them, it is essential that they both have a clear understanding of each other's expectations.
- ***The scope of the audit*** (paragraphs 22 to 25)
  This section identifies information that can help the audit committee to understand, and help keep under review, the scope and focus of the audit.
- ***Findings from the audit*** (paragraphs 26 to 44)
  This section addresses matters that the audit committee may expect to receive feedback on from the auditors at or near completion of the audit.
  - *unadjusted misstatements* (paragraphs 30 to 35)
    An understanding of the reasons why misstatements identified by the auditors have not been adjusted, and the implications for the auditors' report, may assist the audit committee to appraise the actions and judgments of management and the adequacy of the audit. Relatively small misstatements should not be ignored without consideration of whether they may be indicative of larger problems, such as aggressive earnings management.
  - *material weaknesses in the accounting and internal control systems* (paragraphs 36 to 39)
    Information from the auditors about material weaknesses in the accounting and internal control systems can help the audit committee monitor management's commitment to the establishment and maintenance of a satisfactory control environment and a sound system of internal control, review the effectiveness of the company's system of internal control pursuant to the Combined Code[3], and review the scope and results of the audit and its cost effectiveness.
  - *the auditors' views on the quality of the company's accounting practices and financial reporting* (paragraphs 40 to 42)
    The auditors' observations regarding the quality of the company's financial reporting may assist the audit committee consider whether the board has met the requirement of the Combined Code to present a balanced and understandable assessment of the company's position and prospects, and appraise the actions and judgements of management as they relate to the financial reporting process.
  - *expected modifications to the auditors' report and differences of view* (paragraphs 43 to 44)
    In order to review the financial reporting process and the audit, the audit committee will wish to discuss any proposed qualifications of the auditors' opinion on the financial statements or any fundamental uncertainties that the auditors intend to refer to in their report, as well as any significant disagreements between the auditors and the management arising from the audit.
- ***The independence of the auditors*** (paragraphs 45 to 49)
  This section explains the disclosures that auditing standards now specifically require auditors to make to the audit committee. These disclosures will assist the audit committee to comply with the requirements of the Combined Code to keep under review the independence and objectivity of the auditors. It also considers the actions that the audit committee may itself take to help safeguard the auditors' independence.

---

[3] *The Combined Code was published in June 1998 and has been appended to the Listing Rules of the FSA and the Irish Stock Exchange. The Listing Rules require companies to include a narrative statement in their annual report and accounts of how they have applied the 'Code principles' that are set out in Section 1 'Companies' of the Code and also give a statement as to their compliance with the Code provisions.*

4   The last part of the Paper addresses the form and timing of communications between the audit committee and auditors.

5   The guidance in this Paper has been written primarily with regard to the audit committees of listed companies but is also of relevance to the audit committees, and those persons who perform a similar role, of other types of entity, including public sector bodies. Much of the guidance could apply to communications by the auditors with the full board, especially if there is no audit committee.

6   In this Paper the APB is not seeking to set out specific requirements applicable to all circumstances. The precise nature of communication between a company's auditors and its audit committee is determined by the particular remit given to the committee by the company's board. This will vary, reflecting the size and activities of the company, the responsibilities of the audit committee and manner in which it operates.

7   Audit committees will also have important communications with internal auditors, where such a function exists, but those communications are outside the scope of this Paper.

Role of the audit committee

8   The audit committee plays an important role in underpinning the integrity of financial reporting by listed companies and other entities, as well as making a significant contribution to the control environment and the governance arrangements for which, as directors, its members share responsibility with other directors. The quality of oversight exercised by the audit committee is likely to be an important factor taken into account by auditors in their assessment of the company's overall control environment and the way in which this may affect audit risk[4].

9   Principle D.3 'Audit Committee and Auditors' of the Combined Code states that 'The board should establish formal and transparent arrangements for considering how they should apply the financial reporting and internal control principles and for maintaining an appropriate relationship with the company's auditors.' To this end, the provisions of the Combined Code indicate that the board should establish an audit committee, and that 'the duties of the audit committee should include keeping under review the scope and results of the audit and its cost effectiveness and the independence and objectivity of the auditors.'

10 The audit committee's specific responsibilities are determined by the terms of reference set by the company's board. In order to discharge its responsibilities, the audit committee might be expected, inter alia, to:

- appraise and, where appropriate, challenge the actions and judgments of management as they relate to the financial reporting process. As well as considering the general quality of the financial reporting process, the audit committee may wish to satisfy itself that management's attitude to financial reporting has not been unduly influenced by commercial pressures such as:
    - adverse market reactions affecting the share price of a listed company should results fail to meet the market's expectations;
    - management's incomes being highly geared to results and/or heavily supplemented by stock options and other possibilities for capital gains;
    - the need to meet targets to ensure protection of the jobs of management and other employees;

[4] 'Audit risk' is the risk that auditors may give an inappropriate audit opinion on financial statements.

- legal or regulatory requirements to meet specific financial thresholds or ratios; and
- the desire to demonstrate compliance with loan covenants or other requirements or expectations of lenders.

There may be benefit in the audit committee discussing with the auditors the pressures on management that could affect their attitude to financial reporting; and for the audit committee to discuss with management what safeguards exist to ensure that, notwithstanding those pressures, the financial statements show a true and fair view and that the annual report presents a balanced and understandable assessment of the company's position.

- monitor management's commitment to the establishment and maintenance of a satisfactory control environment and a sound system of internal control (including any arrangements for internal audit);
- consider the scope and results of the external audit and the cost effectiveness of the auditors by:
  - understanding the scope of the audit and reviewing the audit fee;
  - facilitating discussion of audit findings;
  - helping to resolve any differences of view between management and the auditors;
  - reviewing the risks and, where relevant, safeguards relating to the independence and objectivity of the auditors;
  - reviewing the nature and extent of any other services provided by the auditors, together with the fees for such services; and
  - making recommendations in respect of the appointment of auditors.

In addition to communications with the external auditors, the audit committee may establish arrangements for regular reporting from management and, where appropriate, internal audit in order to obtain assurance that key issues with which the audit committee ought to be concerned are properly identified and addressed.

The audit committee should be prepared to ask relevant and challenging questions of those involved in the financial reporting process to satisfy the committee of the integrity of the process. The audit committee cannot simply rely on management and the auditors to bring to its attention matters with which it should be concerned but should take responsibility for ensuring it is informed and should request information where appropriate. **11**

Role of the auditors

Auditors have different responsibilities with respect to the various component parts of the annual report. They are required to: **12**

- *audit* the financial statements in accordance with relevant legal and regulatory requirements and Auditing Standards;
- *review* whether the corporate governance statement included in the annual report reflects the company's compliance with the provisions of the Combined Code specified for their review[5]; and
- *read* the other information contained in the annual report and consider whether it is consistent with the audited financial statements. If, as a result, they become aware of any inconsistencies, or apparent misstatements, they seek to resolve them and, if they are unable to, they consider the implications for their report on the financial statements. Where the financial statements are published on the

---

[5] There are 45 provisions in Section 1 of the Combined Code, which are required to be covered by the company's statement of compliance (see footnote 3), of which The Listing Rules specify seven provisions for review by the auditors (see Appendix 2).

internet, the auditors will be concerned to establish that the auditors' report is not inappropriately associated with any other information published on the web site.

Benefits of working together

13 Good communication between the audit committee and the auditors will:
   - ensure that there is a mutual understanding of the scope of the audit and the respective responsibilities of the auditors, management and the audit committee;
   - share information that will assist both the audit committee and the auditors fulfil their respective responsibilities; and
   - provide the audit committee with constructive observations arising from the audit process.

14 Effective communication requires a two-way process. The audit committee should expect the auditors to provide them with relevant information in a way that helps committee members understand the issues concerned. Equally, auditors will expect to receive from the audit committee both specific feedback on the matters they raise and information about the committee's views on the company's corporate governance and its control environment, so that they can take account of any concerns felt by the audit committee.

Matters to communicate with the auditors

Establish expectations

15 In order to maximise the benefits to the audit committee and to the auditors of communications between them, it is essential that they both have a clear understanding of each other's expectations.

16 The auditors will wish to obtain an understanding of how the audit committee operates, including its role in relation to identification and management of business risks. This understanding enables them both to plan their work and to evaluate the effectiveness of the audit committee's contribution to the overall control environment.

17 Auditors normally discuss with the audit committee the extent, form and frequency of the communications they will make (see paragraphs 50 to 55). These will vary, reflecting the size and activities of the company, the responsibilities of the audit committee and manner in which it operates, and any legal or regulatory requirements, as well as the auditors' views of the importance of the relevant matters relating to the audit. Auditors also consider whether the audit committee is in a position to provide the information and explanations they need for the purpose of their audit and whether there may be a need to repeat their communications to the whole board. Irrespective of what may be agreed, auditors may judge it necessary to communicate directly to the board when a matter is sufficiently important.

18 Issues identified by auditors in the course of their work are normally initially reported to senior management and the executive directors so that appropriate action can be taken. Reports to the audit committee are likely to be of greatest value if they permit the committee's members to form a view on the overall adequacy of the management's response to matters identified by the audit process.

Auditors are required to communicate to the audit committee only such matters arising from the audit of financial statements as the auditors believe to be both relevant and important to the audit committee. Auditors are not required, for the purpose of their audit of the financial statements, to design procedures for the specific purpose of identifying matters of relevance to the audit committee. Minor matters noted by the auditors will usually not be reported separately, except where in combination they are indicative of patterns or trends that the auditors believe to be significant.   19

In order to ensure that effective two way communication is established, the expectations both of the audit committee and the auditors regarding the form, level of detail and timing of communications are best established at an early stage in the audit process.   20

Early discussions may also consider the terms of the audit engagement, as set out in the engagement letter, and whether the audit committee wishes the auditors to undertake other work in addition to the audit to meet the committee's particular needs[6].   21

The scope of the audit

Auditors are required by Auditing Standards to communicate an outline of the nature and scope, including, where relevant, any limitations thereon, of the work they propose to undertake and the form of the reports they expect to make.   22

Information that can help the audit committee to understand, and help keep under review, the scope of the audit may include: 23

- the views of management of the nature and extent of significant internal and external operational, financial, compliance and other risks facing the company which might affect the financial statements, including the likelihood of those risks materialising and how they are managed;
- the way the auditors propose to address the risk of material misstatements, with particular reference to areas of higher risk;
- the application of materiality to the audit approach;
- whether there is a process for keeping under review the effectiveness of the system of internal control and, where a review of the effectiveness of internal control has been carried out, the results of that review;
- the auditors' approach to the assessment of, and reliance on, internal controls;
- the auditors' views on the control environment within the company, including the attitude of management to controls;
- the extent, if any, to which reliance will be placed on the work of internal audit and on the way in which the external and internal auditors plan to work together on a constructive and complementary basis;
- where relevant, the work to be undertaken by any other firms of auditors and how the principal auditors intend to obtain assurance as to the adequacy of the other auditors' procedures in so far as it relates to their role as principal auditors;
- to the extent that it is relevant, developments in law, accounting standards, corporate governance reporting, Listing Rules, and other developments relevant to the company's financial statements and annual report;
- whether the auditors will review or audit interim financial information.

[6] *Such work normally would be performed as a separate engagement to the audit.*

24 Any limitation of the audit scope may have significant implications for the auditors' report and, in some circumstances, their willingness to continue in office[7].

25 Notwithstanding any discussions between the audit committee and the auditors, ultimate responsibility for determining the nature and scope of work necessary to express an opinion on the company's financial statements and meet other statutory obligations rests with the auditors.

Findings from the audit

26 At or near completion of the audit, the auditors give feedback on the conduct of the audit work and matters arising from it.

27 The information provided by the auditors may assist the audit committee to:
- appraise the actions and judgements of management as they relate to the financial reporting process;
- monitor management's commitment to a satisfactory control environment and a sound system of internal control;
- consider the adequacy and cost effectiveness of the external audit; and
- assess whether the directors have discharged their responsibilities for the financial statements.

28 The information provided by the auditors will take into account the scope and form of the explanations and commentary already provided by management to the audit committee, of which the auditors are aware. The auditors usually discuss their proposed report with management (including executive directors as appropriate) and take account of their views before presenting their report to the audit committee. However, the auditors report openly and fully to the audit committee and do not allow themselves to be swayed by any desire on the part of management to play down sensitive issues.

29 Matters that Auditing Standards require auditors to communicate include:
- misstatements identified by the audit that have not been adjusted by management;
- material weaknesses in the accounting and internal control systems;
- their views on the quality of the company's financial reporting; and
- expected modifications to the auditors' report.

Unadjusted misstatements

30 Auditing Standards indicate that auditors bring to the attention of management all unadjusted misstatements they have identified, other than those that they believe are clearly trifling, and request them to make the adjustments. Should management refuse to make some or all of the adjustments the auditors consider the appropriateness of their reasons for not making those adjustments, having regard to qualitative as well as quantitative considerations[8].

---

[7] *Auditing Standards require that auditors should not accept an engagement where they are aware that the directors, or those who appoint the auditors, will impose a limitation which is likely to result in the need to issue a disclaimer of opinion. If such a limitation is imposed after accepting the engagement, auditors will consider whether they should resign.*

[8] *SAS 610 requires that auditors should seek to obtain a written representation from those charged with governance that explains their reasons for not adjusting misstatements brought to their attention by the auditors.*

When considering the implications for the auditors' report, of the effect of misstatements that remain unadjusted, auditors will form a view on the materiality of the unadjusted misstatements in the context of their duties under the Companies Act 1985, and in particular whether they cause the financial statements not to give a true and fair view. Auditors also need to consider whether they have received all the information and explanations which, to the best of their knowledge and belief, are necessary for the purpose of their audit – if they have not, they are required by the Companies Act to state that fact in their report. 31

An understanding of the reasons why misstatements identified by the auditors have not been adjusted, and the implications for the auditors' report, may assist the audit committee to appraise the actions and judgments of management and the adequacy of the audit. 32

Misstatements can arise from errors or may relate to differences of opinion between the auditors and management over the appropriateness of the assumptions and/or methods of calculation applied in arriving at accounting estimates such as provisions. For some accounting estimates, no single set of assumptions or single method of calculation may be clearly the most appropriate, and the auditors may on the basis of the available audit evidence conclude that there is a range of acceptable amounts at which the item(s) concerned could fairly be recognised in the financial statements. Normally, if an amount intended to be included in the financial statements is outside this range, the auditors will regard it as a misstatement. 33

Misstatements, whether arising from errors or differences in opinion over the appropriateness of assumptions and/or methods of calculation applied in arriving at accounting estimates, should not be ignored simply because, on the face of it, they appear to be immaterial. Relatively small misstatements can be indicative of a larger problem, such as aggressive earnings management (see paragraph 41 below). 34

The audit committee may also discuss with the auditors details of significant misstatements identified by the auditors that have been adjusted as a result of the audit process. This may assist the committee in appraising the actions and judgments of management as they relate to the financial reporting process; in monitoring management's commitment to the establishment and maintenance of a satisfactory control environment and a sound system of internal control; and in considering the effectiveness of the audit. 35

Material weaknesses in the accounting and internal control systems

For the purposes of an audit, a material weakness in the accounting and internal control systems is a deficiency in design or operation which could adversely affect the company's ability to record, process, summarise and report financial and other relevant data so as to result in a material misstatement in the financial statements. 36

Information from the auditors about material weaknesses in the accounting and internal control systems can help the audit committee perform aspects of the role it may have such as monitoring management's commitment to the establishment and maintenance of a satisfactory control environment and a sound system of internal control, reviewing the effectiveness of the company's system of internal control pursuant to Provision D.2.1 of the Combined Code (see Appendix 1), and reviewing the scope and results of the audit and its cost effectiveness. 37

38 Auditors are not required by Auditing Standards, or by the Listing Rules, to conclude as to the effectiveness of internal controls[9]. Auditing Standards require auditors to plan and perform tests of internal control only to the extent they expect to be able to rely on those controls, and consider it to be efficient to do so, to help them form an opinion on the truth and fairness of the financial statements. Any work the auditors may do on internal control will tend to be focused on those controls that relate to amounts included in the financial statements. When reporting to management and the audit committee, therefore, the auditors can only address those matters which have come to their attention as a result of the audit procedures performed to enable them to report on the financial statements, and cannot provide a comprehensive statement of all weaknesses which may exist in the accounting and internal control systems.

39 With respect to the directors' statement in the annual report summarising the process the board has applied in reviewing the effectiveness of the system of internal control, as required by the Turnbull guidance[10] (pursuant to provision D.2.1 of the Combined Code), the auditors:

(a) through enquiry of the directors, obtain an understanding of the process defined by the board for its review of the effectiveness of internal control and compare their understanding to the statement made by the board in the annual report and accounts;
(b) review the documentation prepared by or for the directors to support their statement and assess whether it provides sound support for that statement; and
(c) relate the statement made by the directors to the auditors' knowledge of the company obtained during the audit of the financial statements.

Since the directors' review is required to cover all controls, including financial, operational and compliance controls and risk management, the directors' review will be considerably broader in its scope than the knowledge the auditors can be expected to have based on their audit.

The auditors' views on the quality of the company's accounting practices and financial reporting

40 The auditors' observations regarding the quality of the company's financial reporting may help the audit committee appraise the actions and judgements of management as they relate to the financial reporting process. The benefit is maximised when the auditors' observations are discussed with the committee face to face in an open and frank manner, rather than being confined to written comments that could lead to the use of 'boiler plate' wording. Management normally should be included in the discussions as they have responsibility for the preparation of the financial statements and are most familiar with the transactions and the environment in which the company operates. Such discussions may include:

- the appropriateness of the accounting policies, and any changes thereto, to the particular circumstances of the company (accounting standards require that where it is necessary to choose between accounting policies, an entity should select whichever of those accounting policies is judged by the entity to be the

---

[9] *Assurance on internal control may be provided by a separate engagement to the audit. The APB has published a Briefing Paper 'Providing assurance on the effectiveness of internal control' that outlines the concepts involved in such an engagement. The Briefing Paper may assist directors, and others, to better understand the challenges associated with reporting on the effectiveness of internal control.*

[10] *'Internal Control: Guidance for Directors on the Combined Code' published by the Institute of Chartered Accountants in England and Wales, September 1999.*

most appropriate to its particular circumstances for the purpose of giving a true and fair view);
- the timing of transactions and the period in which they are recorded, with particular relevance to the recognition of revenue and costs;
- the appropriateness of accounting estimates and judgments, for example in relation to provisions, including the consistency of assumptions and degree of prudence reflected in the recorded amounts.

The audit committee may benefit from understanding the issues and assumptions involved in formulating particularly sensitive accounting estimates. To the extent that estimates and judgments involve a range of possible outcomes, the discussion could include how the amount recorded in the financial statements relates to the range and how other selections from within the range would affect the financial reporting;

- the extent to which the financial statements are affected by any unusual transactions including non-recurring profits and losses recognised during the period and the extent to which such transactions are separately disclosed in the financial statements;
- the potential effect on the financial statements of any uncertainties including significant risks and exposures, such as those relating to guarantees, other financial commitment and pending litigation, that are required to be disclosed in the financial statements;
- material uncertainties related to events and conditions that may cast significant doubt on the company's ability to continue as a going concern.

It is particularly important for a listed company that the directors' statement[11] on going concern is not inconsistent with any disclosures regarding going concern in either the financial statements or the auditors' report thereon;

- apparent misstatements in the other information in the document containing the audited financial statements or material inconsistencies between it and the audited financial statements;
- the overall balance and clarity of the information contained in the annual report.

The presentation of other information, including pro forma amounts and non financial information, is increasingly important for many companies. Such information should comply with Principle D1 of the Combined Code that 'The board should present a balanced and understandable assessment of the company's position and prospects.'

The auditors may want to discuss with the audit committee any concerns regarding the company's accounting policies or practices, or the manner in which the company's financial performance is presented and the possible implications thereof. For example the auditors may be concerned that as a result of commercial pressures (see paragraph 10), management are seeking to adopt aggressive accounting practices that present the financial performance of the company in a favourable light that does not reflect fairly the underlying reality. Alternatively, there may be a concern that management is seeking to understate earnings in the current period, (e.g. by

---

[11] The Listing Rules, in both the UK and the Republic of Ireland, require the directors to include in the annual report and accounts a statement that the business is a going concern with supporting assumptions or qualification as necessary, as interpreted by the guidance for directors in 'Going concern and Financial Reporting: Guidance for directors of listed companies registered in the UK' (published by the Institute of Chartered Accountants in England and Wales, in November 1994).

overstating provisions or accruals) in order to be able to enhance future reported financial performance.

42 The auditors may also want to discuss with the audit committee any difficulties encountered in performing the audit, such as unreasonable delays in the provision of information to the auditors, or significant shortcomings in the quality of the information provided.

Expected modifications to the auditors' report and differences of view

43 The audit committee should discuss with the auditors any proposed modifications to the auditors' report on the financial statements before it is finalised, such as a qualification of the auditors' opinion or a description of a fundamental uncertainty. An understanding of the reasons for the modification may assist with any appraisal of the actions and judgment of management and of the adequacy of the audit.

44 In order to review the financial reporting process and the audit, the audit committee needs to be aware of and understand any disagreements between the auditors and management that have arisen about matters which, individually or in aggregate, could be significant to the company's financial statements (for example in relation to the company's accounting practices). Discussions should include consideration of the significance of the matters concerned and whether the disagreements have, or have not, been resolved. The audit committee may, where appropriate, be able to assist with the resolution of any matters of disagreement.

The independence of the auditors

45 Duties of audit committees complying with the Combined Code include keeping under review the independence and objectivity of the auditors. To assist with this, Auditing Standards require that at least annually, for all audit engagements where the audited entity is a listed company, auditors should:

(a) disclose in writing to the audit committee, and discuss as appropriate:
- all relationships between the audit firm and its related entities and the client entity and its related entities that may reasonably be thought to bear on the firm's independence and the objectivity of the audit engagement partner and the audit staff; and
- the related safeguards that are in place; and

(b) where this is the case, confirm in writing to the audit committee that, in their professional judgment, the firm is independent within the meaning of regulatory and professional requirements and the objectivity of the audit engagement partner and audit staff is not impaired.

46 Auditing Standards also encourage auditors to discuss these matters with the audit committees of other types of entity where they consider it would be beneficial to do so.

47 In determining which relationships and related safeguards to report to the audit committee, the auditors would consider relevant professional, legal and regulatory requirements and guidance.

48 It is appropriate for the audit committee to be informed of any possible impairment to the auditors' independence and objectivity before the appointment or reappointment of auditors is proposed, and for it to be informed of any relevant changes in circumstances as and when they occur. Examples of circumstances that may give

rise to possible impairments include undue financial dependence on an audit client, providing services to the client in a way that would result in the auditors having to audit their own numbers and judgments, over familiarity with management (e.g. where a senior employee of the audit firm has joined the client or vice versa), loans or other financial interests.

The audit committee may wish to establish its own safeguards in addition to those maintained by the auditors. Actions the audit committee may take to help safeguard the auditors' independence include: 49

- ensuring the committee has received the auditors' confirmation of independence, understands the implications of any disclosed relationships and is satisfied with the related safeguards;
- monitoring the quality and nature of relationships between the auditors and management and, where possible, assisting with the resolution of disagreements;
- considering whether the audit fee is reasonable for a high quality audit. The audit should be cost effective and the audit committee should be concerned if the audit fees appear to be either unrealistically low or excessive having regard to the nature and extent of the risks facing the company, its scale and complexity, and the scope of work required to carry out an effective and efficient audit of the company's financial statements. The audit committee should understand the process by which the fees have been or are to be agreed with management. They may wish to inquire of the auditors about issues such as the adequacy of the audit staffing levels, the experience of the audit staff and the amount of time to be spent on the audit by the senior members of the audit team;
- considering the appropriateness of the company obtaining other services from the audit firm. The audit committee may wish to be assured, for example, that:
  - the services will not result in the auditors having to audit judgments made by their firm or place reliance on systems or controls that have been designed or recommended by their firm;
  - the audit firm will not perform a management role or make management decisions for the audit client; and
  - the total fees paid by the company to the audit firm are not significant in relation to the total revenues of the audit firm.

Form and timing of communication

Form

Auditing Standards permit the auditors to communicate with the audit committee orally or in writing. The auditors' decision whether to communicate orally or in writing is affected by factors such as: 50

- the size, operating structure, legal structure and communication process of the company being audited;
- the nature, sensitivity and significance of the matters being communicated;
- statutory and regulatory requirements; and
- the arrangements made with respect to periodic meetings or reporting of significant matters.

The audit committee may expect auditors to: 51

- provide frank and unambiguous information both in response to any concerns expressed by the committee and on matters arising out of the audit which are relevant to the committee's terms of reference; and

- communicate to the audit committee in a way that takes account of the information made available to the committee by management, whilst ensuring that all relevant matters arising from the audit are fully and openly discussed.

Timing

52 Auditing Standards require that auditors communicate relevant matters relating to the audit of financial statements to management and the audit committee on a sufficiently prompt basis to enable them to take appropriate action, recognising that in certain circumstances the auditors may identify matters of such significance that they may need to be communicated without delay. Findings from the audit that are relevant to the financial statements, including the auditors' views about the qualitative aspects of the company's accounting and financial reporting, will usually be communicated before the financial statements are approved.

53 The timing of communication to the audit committee is usually linked to the timing of the audit committee's meetings, although this should not preclude communication at any time when requested by the auditors or by the audit committee. However, in most circumstances communication would be expected to occur:

- when the auditors are determining the plans for conducting the audit;
- when assessing findings from the audit, preferably before the directors give approval for publication of financial information which has been subject to audit or review by the auditors – for example, issue of a preliminary announcement; and
- with respect to consideration of the auditors' independence and objectivity, before the appointment or reappointment of auditors is proposed. The audit committee should expect the auditors to inform it of any relevant changes in circumstances.

54 If matters arise during the year that require immediate contact, this should be initiated by either the audit committee or auditors, as appropriate.

Private meetings

55 A private meeting between the audit committee and the auditors allows discussion of sensitive issues. It will normally be appropriate for the audit committee (or the chairman of the audit committee on behalf of the committee) to hold at least one private meeting each year with the auditors. Matters discussed in the private meeting will be specific to the particular circumstances of the company but are likely to include:

- observations on the overall control consciousness and operating style of management;
- the state of relationships between the auditors and management; and
- observations on the extent to which the spirit of good corporate governance is followed within the company.

Appendix 1 – Requirements of the combined code relating to accountability and audit

D.1 FINANCIAL REPORTING

Principle

The board should present a balanced and understandable assessment of the company's position and prospects.

Code Provisions

D.1.1 The directors should explain their responsibility for preparing the accounts and there should be a statement by the auditors about their reporting responsibilities.

D.1.2 The board's responsibility to present a balanced and understandable assessment extends to interim and other price-sensitive public reports and reports to regulators as well as to information required to be presented by statutory requirements.

D.1.3 The directors should report that the business is a going concern, with supporting assumptions or qualifications as necessary.

D.2 INTERNAL CONTROL

Principle

The board should maintain a sound system of internal control to safeguard shareholders' investment and the company's assets.

Code Provisions

D.2.1 The directors should, at least annually, conduct a review of the effectiveness of the group's system of internal controls and should report to shareholders that they have done so. The review should cover all controls, including financial, operational and compliance controls and risk management.

D.2.2 Companies which do not have an internal audit function should from time to time review the need for one.

D.3 AUDIT COMMITTEE AND AUDITORS

Principle

The board should establish formal and transparent arrangements for considering how they should apply the financial reporting and internal control principles and for maintaining an appropriate relationship with the company's auditors.

Code Provisions

D.3.1 The board should establish an audit committee of at least three directors, all non-executive, with written terms of reference which deal clearly with its authority and duties. The members of the committee, a majority of whom should be independent non-executive directors, should be named in the report and accounts.

D.3.2 The duties of the audit committee should include keeping under review the scope and the results of the audit and its cost effectiveness and the independence and objectivity of the auditors. Where the auditors also supply a substantial volume of non-audit services to the company, the committee should keep the nature and extent of such services under review, seeking to balance the maintenance of objectivity and value for money.

Appendix 2 – Combined code provisions that auditors are required to review

D.1.1, D.2.1, D.3.1 (see Appendix 1) and:

A.1.2 The board should have a formal schedule of matters specifically reserved to it for decision.

A.1.3 There should be a procedure agreed by the board for directors in the furtherance of their duties to take independent professional advice if necessary, at the company's expense.

A.6.1 Non-executive directors should be appointed for specified terms subject to re-election and to Companies Act provisions relating to the removal of a director, and re-appointment should not be automatic.

A.6.2 All directors should be subject to election by shareholders at the first opportunity after their appointment, and to re-election thereafter at intervals of no more than three years. The names of directors submitted for election or re-election should be accompanied by sufficient biographical details to enable shareholders to take an informed decision on their election.

Part Ten

ICAEW Guidance on Auditing and Reporting

[Statement 903]
The ascertainment and confirmation of contingent liabilities arising from pending legal matters

(Issued August 1970)

The Council of The Institute of Chartered Accountants in England and Wales issues the following Statement of the guidance of members. It has been prepared after discussions with the Council of the Law Society and consideration of the Statement published by it entitled 'Information by solicitors for company audit purposes'.

1. It is the duty of directors to ensure that proper account is taken of all liabilities, including contingent liabilities, in the preparation of company financial statements. From the audit viewpoint, pending lawsuits and other actions against the company may present problems both of ascertainment and appraisal.

2. The following audit procedures are suggested for the verification of the existence of such claims though they will not necessarily provide the auditor with adequate information of the likely amounts for which the company may ultimately be responsible:
   (a) reviewing the client's system of recording claims and the procedure for bringing these to the attention of the management or board;
   (b) discussing the arrangements for instructing solicitors with the official(s) responsible for legal matters (for example, the head of the legal department (if any) or the company secretary);
   (c) examining the minutes of the board of directors and/or executive or other relevant committee for references to, or indications of, possible claims;
   (d) examining bills rendered by solicitors and correspondence with them, in which connection the solicitors should be requested to furnish bills or estimates of charges to date, or to confirm that they have no unbilled charges;
   (e) obtaining a list of matters referred to solicitors from the appropriate director or official with estimates of the possible ultimate liabilities;
   (f) obtaining a written assurance from the appropriate director or official that he is not aware of any matters referred to solicitors other than those disclosed.

3. In appropriate circumstances, auditors may decide to obtain written confirmations from third parties of certain representations made by directors; for example, the identification and appraisal of contingent liabilities. In the field of legal actions the normal and proper source of such confirmations is the company's legal advisers.

4. Requests for such confirmations should be kept within the solicitor–client relationship and should thus be issued by the client with a request that a copy of the reply should be sent direct to the auditors.

5. In order to ascertain whether the information provided by the directors is complete, auditors (especially in certain overseas countries) may decide to arrange for solicitors to be requested to advise whether they have matters in hand which are not listed in the letter of request, and to provide information as to the likely amounts involved.

When considering such a non-specific enquiry, auditors should note that the Council of the Law Society has advised solicitors that it is unable to recommend them to comply with requests for information which are more widely drawn than the specimen form of wording set out in paragraph 6 below.

6 In these circumstances, the enquiry should normally list matters identified as having been referred to the company's legal advisers in accordance with paragraph 2(e) above. The following form of wording, appropriate to specific enquiries, has been agreed between the Councils of the Law Society and The Institute of Chartered Accountants in England and Wales as one which may be properly addressed to, and answered by, solicitors:

> 'In connection with the preparation and audit of our accounts for the year ended ... the directors have made estimates of the amounts of the ultimate liabilities (including costs) which might be incurred, and are regarded as material, in relation to the following matters on which you have been consulted. We should be obliged if you would confirm that in your opinion these estimates are reasonable.
>
> Matter   Estimated liability including costs.

7 The Council of The Institute of Chartered Accountants in England and Wales understands the reasons for the view of the Council of the Law Society regarding non-specific enquiries, but nevertheless believes that there may be circumstances in which it is necessary as an audit procedure for an enquiry of a general nature to be addressed to the solicitors in order to confirm that the information provided by the directors is complete in all material particulars.

8 If the outcome of the enquiries set out in paragraphs 2 and 5 above appears satisfactory, auditors would not normally regard the absence of a corroboration of the completeness of a list of legal matters as a reason in itself for qualifying their report. If the enquiries lead to the discovery of significant matters not previously identified, the auditors will wish to extend their enquiries and to request their clients to address further enquiries to, or arrange a meeting with, the solicitors, at which the auditors will wish to be present. If, however, having regard to all the circumstances, the auditors are unable to satisfy themselves that they have received all the information they require for the purpose of their audit, they must qualify their report.

Legal and practical considerations

Reservation of title depends on the terms of each contract between purchaser and supplier and difficulty may be experienced in interpreting the contractual relationship between the parties. There is at present no clear legal view as to the effect of contracts containing Romalpa-type reservation of title, for example, as applied to goods which may have been mixed with other materials or used in the manufacture of new products and to the sale proceeds of such new products. However, the following matters, *inter alia*, would appear to be relevant:

(a) *The contractual relationship.* The form of contractual relationship between the parties may not be clear. Where the wording of the documents indicates that the purchaser is acting as agent or bailee or custodian, the purchaser may be accountable to the supplier of goods or proceeds of sale; if, on the other hand, the purchaser is acting as principal which may well be the majority of cases, it would appear that in England and Ireland a security may arise which may need to be registered under Section 95 Companies Act 1948, or Section 93 Companies Act (Northern Ireland) 1960, or Section 99 Companies Act 1963 (Republic of Ireland) before it is effective. Under the law of Scotland it is not, however, possible in the case of corporeal moveables for any valid right of security to be created in favour of the supplier under a reservation of title condition.

(b) Have the supplier's terms of trade been adequately brought to the purchaser's notice?

(c) Has the purchaser explicitly or impliedly – for example, by not refuting them – agreed to the supplier's terms?

(d) Has the purchaser specifically excluded reservations of title, for example, by a clause in his purchase order?

(e) Has the supplier reinstated his terms by means of a new offer expressed in an 'order-acknowledgement'?

If there is doubt about the legal effectiveness of terms of trade which purport to reserve title, consider whether any legal opinion obtained by the directors supports the manner in which the assets and liabilities have been treated. Where material amounts are subject to doubt in this respect, the directors should be encouraged to obtain a legal opinion. Exceptionally, if they decline to do so, the auditor may need to consider obtaining legal advice himself.

Where the contractual relationship or the amounts involved cannot be determined so as to enable the directors to disclose the position in the accounts, the auditor should ensure that a note adequately explains the situation.

In considering the practical effects of reservation of title it will be necessary to establish the extent to which the supplier can trace or identify his interest in the goods. The following points, *inter alia*, appear to be relevant:

(a) Are the goods separately identifiable in the form in which they were delivered from other identical goods already supplied and paid for by the purchaser?

(b) Where the goods have been subject to processing, are they still identifiable, for example, as partly completed or finished stocks?

(c) Can the goods be traced to, or identified with, particular debts?

(d) Can the cash proceeds of debts be traced or distinguished so as to enable them to be adopted by the supplier; for example, paid into a bank account opened for the purpose of the transaction or paid into a general bank account in credit at the time the proceeds were deposited?

(e) Where cash identifiable as in (d) above has been applied in the acquisition of other assets, can those assets be traced or identified?

Other circumstances

8   Where an opinion other than an audit opinion is requested, for example, an opinion for debenture deed or loan purposes, the implications of goods sold subject to reservation of title will need to be assessed having regard to the purpose of the opinion required.

[Statement 909]
Paid cheques (FRAG 27/93)

(Issued December 1993)

Contents

	Paragraphs
Introduction	1 - 4
Audit evidence	5 - 7
Internal controls	8
The implications for auditors of the Cheques Act 1992	9 - 10
Use of other payment methods	11
Means of obtaining paid cheques	12 - 18
Truncation	19 - 20

Appendix 1 – Preferred methods for providing paid cheques

Appendix 2 – Suggested form of authority where paid cheques are to be sent to an auditor direct

Paid cheques

Introduction

1 Traditionally, clearing banks returned paid cheques to their customers with their statements. In recent years, however, this practice has diminished as banks have sought to reduce their costs. The provision of paid cheques to auditors was previously addressed in a guidance note issued in 1982 (TR472) by the Consultative Committee of Accountancy Bodies, following consultation with the then Committee of London Clearing Bankers.

2 This guidance note, which replaces TR472, returns to the subject of paid cheques in the light of recent changes in auditing and banking practice, and the additional security afforded by the Cheques Act 1992. Its principal objectives are as follows:

(a) to encourage auditors to consider using alternative, more cost-effective ways of obtaining audit evidence (where possible) rather than examining paid cheques;
(b) to encourage auditors to advise clients to adopt rigorous controls over cheque payments; and
(c) where it is considered necessary to examine paid cheques, to encourage auditors to do so in a cost-effective manner that accords, as far as possible, with the banks' preferred methods for providing paid cheques.

However, this guidance note does not seek to give detailed procedural guidance.

3 The contents of this guidance note have been agreed between the Institute of Chartered Accountants in England and Wales and the British Bankers' Association. Banks which have issued guidelines to their branches based on this guidance note are listed in an appendix, which also indicates their preferred methods for providing paid cheques. However, this listing is merely indicative of what is available; it is not prescriptive, and the facilities offered by individual branches of the same bank may vary. Nevertheless, auditors should normally be able to obtain paid cheques even where they cannot use the preferred method.

4 The charges levied by a bank are the subject of a contractual agreement between the bank and the customer. Where an auditor does not require to examine a paid cheque for audit purposes the resulting charge must be borne by the bank's customer and not the auditor.

Audit evidence

5 In many circumstances, such as when controls over purchasing and payments are adequate, it is not necessary to examine paid cheques. However, where, for example, controls are weak or there are concerns about the authorisation of cheque payments or the identity of payees, auditors may want to examine paid cheques in order to obtain assurance that business funds have been disbursed as accounted for, and that liabilities are not understated or expenses overstated. Particular risks are fraudulent endorsement (but see paragraphs 9 and 10 below on the Cheques Act 1992), and falsification of the cheque payee and cash book. The auditor may seek to examine a paid cheque for the following purposes:

(a) to identify unusual circumstances, such as alterations or endorsements, or cheques made payable to cash of bearer: in such circumstances, the auditor will need to examine supporting documentation;

(b) to confirm that the payee and amount match the details in the client's accounting records;
(c) to confirm that it has been signed by an authorised signatory; and
(d) when the auditor judges it to be necessary, to check other details such as the date, and the name and location of the bank which cleared the cheque.

With regard to purchase ledger items, it will often be possible to perform substantive tests on balances (such as examining third party evidence of receipt and reconciling suppliers' statements) which will make a physical examination of paid cheques unnecessary. Nominal ledger items may be more problematical, and in the absence of other evidence it may be desirable to examine the relevant paid cheques. Other evidence may be obtained from an analytical review of the profit and loss account, examination of supporting evidence or from a review of internal controls. 6

In deciding whether to make a physical examination of paid cheques, an auditor should consider the potential cost to his client of such an exercise and whether other, more cost-effective, audit techniques could be employed. 7

Internal controls

Good internal controls over cheque payments are designed to prevent the fraudulent or irregular diversion of funds and to ensure that creditors and expenses are not materially under or over stated. An adequate system of internal controls is likely to include the following procedures: 8

(a) rigorous controls over the custody of cheque books, and the issue and completion of cheques;
(b) the listing of authorised signatories, together with details of their authorisation limits. Such records should also clearly set out where a payment needs to be authorised by more than one person;
(c) a requirement for independent documentation to support all cheque payments. Once a payment has been made, this should be clearly shown on the related documents in order to ensure that no payment is duplicated;
(d) segregation of duties to ensure that responsibilities (for authorising cheque payments, preparing cheques, recording and signing) do not overlap; and
(e) regular bank reconciliations and independent review.

The implications for auditors of the Cheques Act 1992

Further control is afforded by the Cheques Act 1992. The Act gives statutory recognition to the 'account payee' crossing, in that a cheque so crossed is not transferable, and is only valid as between the drawer of a cheque and the payee. By definition, therefore, such cheques cannot be transferred by way of endorsement. 9

Most banks are now pre-printing their cheques 'account payee' since this will protect their customers from the danger of fraudulent endorsements. Where a client's cheques are pre-printed 'account payee', this should greatly reduce the risk of fraudulent endorsement, and auditors may wish to take this into account in deciding whether there is a need to examine paid cheques. If such an examination is considered necessary, photo-copies (if available – see paragraph 17(c) below) may well be sufficient. Equally, if a client does not use 'account payee' cheques, auditors may wish to consider recommending a change of policy. 10

Use of other payment methods

11 Auditors may also wish to consider whether a particular client could curtail the use of cheques through adopting other methods of payment. Alternatives include CHAPS, BACS, standing orders and direct debits. Other electronic methods of payment may also be available, and details should be available from the account-holding branch. The audit implications of alternative methods of payment will need to be taken into account when planning and carrying out an audit.

Means of obtaining paid cheques

12 Banks keep paid cheques – where they have not already been returned to the customer or his agent – for varying periods. However, the Money Laundering Regulations 1993 require that supporting evidence and records of transactions (which include paid cheques) must be retained for a period of at least five years after the date on which the relevant transaction or series of transactions is completed. Such records must be the original documents or copies admissible in court proceedings. Where paid cheques are not returned to the customer or his agent they should be kept, in their original form, for at least one year. Thereafter, paid cheques will be available – if not in their original form then in the form of legally admissible copies – for the remainder of the five year period mentioned above. The banks appreciate that original paid cheques may be required for audit purposes for up to 10 months (or longer in exceptional circumstances) after the end of the relevant accounting period. Many banks retain paid cheques in their original form for more than the one year provided for in the Money Laundering Guidance Notes (which supplement the Money Laundering Regulations 1993), and banks have agreed to take account of audit requirements in any future review of their retention policy for original paid cheques.

13 While a bank can normally provide paid cheques if a customer asks for them, finding the cheques may well take time. Typically, paid cheques are stored at bank branches, and are filed in batches according to their date of payment. Within each batch, the cheques may be sorted into account number order, although not all banks do this.

14 Alternatively, some banks operate centralised clearing systems, in which case paid cheques are unlikely to be returned to an account holding branch, but will probably be stored centrally.

15 Even in a medium-sized branch, a single day's batch of paid cheques may number up to 2,000 items. Retrieving paid cheques will almost certainly involve a significant amount of manual work, and this will increase in proportion to the number of batches examined. A bank will usually charge its customer for providing him – or his auditor – with paid cheques, and the charge is likely to increase significantly as the number of items to be retrieved increases.

16 If it is decided that an examination of paid cheques is to be carried out, the auditor's client (that is, the account holder) should consult the account-holding branch to determine how the auditor's needs may best be met. Alternatively, the auditor may approach the branch direct if the account holder has given appropriate authority.

17 The account-holding bank may have a preference for one of the following options:

  (a) to return all paid cheques to the customer concerned.
   Although most banks no longer return all paid cheques to their customers, in some cases this may be the most cost-effective way of providing paid cheques.

4   Other listed options may also be available. Refer to the account holding branch for further details.
5   Prior notification required for this option (see paragraph 17(d)).
3   For small business customers, upon request.
4   Other listed options may also be available. Refer to the account holding branch for further details.
5   Prior notification required for this option (see paragraph 17(d)).
6   Other listed options are available in the following order of preference: (d), (e), (c) and (a).
7   If requested by the customer.
8   Options (a), (c) and (d) are also possible: option (e) is likely to be expensive.

Appendix 2 – Suggested form of authority where paid cheques are to be sent to an auditor direct

To: [name and address of account holding   date
    bank branch]

Dear Sirs

[NAME OF CUSTOMER AND ACCOUNT NUMBER(S)]

I should be grateful if you would provide our auditors (name and address given below) with such paid cheques or other vouchers as they may request in respect of the above account(s).

It is understood that a charge may be made for providing these items.

This authority is to remain in force until (date)/further notice*.

The name and address of our auditors are as follows:

Messrs A B & C
1 XYZ Street
Anytown
AB1 2CD

Yours faithfully

Authorised signature**

* *Delete as appropriate*

** *This form of authority must be signed in accordance with the current mandate held by the bank.*

[Statement 910]
Reading of auditors' reports at annual general meetings (FRAG 1/94)

(Issued January 1994)

In some larger companies the audit partner attends the annual general meeting and reads out in full the auditors' report on the annual accounts. In the past this has been a straightforward task but under SAS 600 it is a lengthy process which may not be appreciated.

Under the Companies Act an auditor is not obliged to read out the audit report at all. It is enough (and indeed it is required) that the auditors' report and the annual accounts are laid before the members. This is achieved by including the auditors' report in the annual report and accounts document provided to the members for the purposes of the meeting. This does not mean that the auditor is prevented from reading out the report in full or the highlights of the report. However, if the auditor decides to read out the highlights of the report he or she should make sure that:

(a) what is read out cannot be construed as the full report; and
(b) where there is a need to modify the normal wording of the auditors' report the modifications are made clear.

Given the unattractiveness of reading out the full SAS 600 report, some auditors may wish to adopt the 'highlights' route. A suitable wording for a group would normally be as follows:

> 'Ladies and gentlemen
>
> [The firm's] report on the financial statements is set out on page x of the annual report and accounts. This includes confirmation that we have performed our audit in accordance with Auditing Standards and that in our opinion the financial statements give a true and fair view of the state of affairs of the company and the group as at [date] and of the profit of the group for the year then ended and have been properly prepared in accordance with the Companies Act 1985.'
>
> Also include where appropriate – ['I would also draw your attention to page y which sets out [the firm's] report on the directors' statement of compliance with the Cadbury Committee's Code of Best Practice. This includes confirmation that we have reviewed the statement insofar as it relates to the paragraphs of the Code which the London Stock Exchange has specified for our review, and that it appropriately reflects the company's compliance with the specified paragraphs of the Code.']

[Statement 912]
Reports on internal controls of investment custodians made available to third parties (FRAG 21/94 Revised; now AUDIT 4/97)

(Issued September 1997)

Contents

	Paragraphs
Introduction	1 - 6
Elements of the reporting package	7 - 11
Engagement letters	12 - 13
Preparation of directors' report	14 - 16
The reporting accountants' review	17 - 23
Material weaknesses	24 - 28

Appendix 1 – Example of a report by the directors

Appendix 2 – Example of a report by the reporting accountants, with attachment describing tests performed

Appendix 3 – Example of an engagement letter

Reports on internal controls of investment custodians made available to third parties

Foreword

In the period which has elapsed since the Institute first issued guidance on reporting on internal controls of investment custodians (FRAG 21/94), requests for such reports have gradually increased. Recipients of the reports have found them useful and are increasingly requesting that they cover other areas of activity.

The increased usage of reports on internal controls have resulted in the recipients identifying more precisely the information they need. At the same time reporting accountants have gained experience in assessing the risks to them of issuing reports that relate to what are often very significant levels of customer assets. No report should provide assurance that nothing can possibly go wrong at the custodian. In drawing conclusions on what assurance can reasonably be provided, reporting accountants should consider how their risk can be effectively managed, particularly through clear terms of engagement and explicit opinions.

The Auditing Practices Board has recently issued a draft Practice Note on the audit of pension schemes which, amongst other things, suggests that pension scheme auditors may need to consider trustees' arrangements with custodians/investment managers. This may involve consideration of controls operated by investment custodians. One way of responding to these suggestions is for the auditors of pension schemes to request the pension scheme trustees to obtain access to reports by the reporting accountants to the investment custodians.

These factors and comments on the use made of reports by the investment custodians have led the Audit Faculty of the Institute to revise FRAG 21/94. The new guidance puts more emphasis on the matters which should be referred to in the reporting package and engagement letter. Although primarily intended for the reporting accountants of investment custodians, it may also assist reporting accountants involved in reporting on related activities.

Introduction

1 Certain customers of investment custodians are expected to report to their shareholders, as well as regulators, that they have reviewed relevant internal control systems in their organisations. The Pensions Act 1995 emphasises the responsibilities of management and trustees to review such controls. Where control of assets has been outsourced to a custodian, those responsible will be concerned to ensure that the control procedures at the custodian complement those operated by their organisation and that there is adequate security of assets held physically or in a dematerialised form. Using an external custodian does not diminish the responsibility to ensure that the overall integrity of data and safeguarding of assets is maintained.

2 As a result customers and their auditors are seeking additional comfort relating to controls operated by custodians. Auditors, as part of their work on assets held by custodians, may find it relevant and useful to obtain evidence of the operation of specific internal controls by the custodian. The quality of the evidence is enhanced by the presence of a report by reporting accountants.

It is now common practice for custodians to receive requests to provide information on specified internal controls to their customers and their customers' auditors. This information often includes a report by reporting accountants. The purpose of this guidance is to provide assistance to the reporting accountants. It focuses on custodial activities relating to investment business but it may also be followed, to the extent appropriate, by accountants reporting on custodial activities in other contexts or on procedures and controls operated by investment managers and administrators.

Reports by directors for the use of the customers should focus on the operations which are likely to be relevant from the point of view of customers, namely safeguarding their money and other assets and recording of transactions. It is therefore appropriate that any generic report provided by the custodian should include these areas.

It is for the directors of the custodian to decide whether to prepare a report on their internal controls and whether to have their report reviewed by reporting accountants. In certain circumstances, directors may, for example, consider it more appropriate to provide a report on a full asset reconciliation at a certain date or to allow appropriate access to customers and/or their auditors. It is not the intention of this guidance to compel directors to report on internal controls in the manner described here. However, if they decide to provide a report other than in accordance with this guidance, they should not make any reference to this document in their report.

Where the directors decide to prepare an internal controls report, it would be of greater benefit to customers and their auditors if it covered control procedures in operation throughout a given period. However, reports on internal controls at a single point in time may be a cost effective alternative. The guidance that follows generally assumes that the report will cover a period.

Elements of the reporting package

The reporting package should comprise a report by the directors of the custodian concerning the internal controls of the custodian and a report by the accountants explaining the scope of work carried out and giving their opinion on relevant parts of the directors' report.

Report by the directors

A report prepared by the directors of the custodian should set out:

- a statement of responsibility;
- the custodian's control objectives in relation to the safeguarding of customers' assets and the recording of transactions;
- details of each of the specific control procedures designed to achieve the control objectives;
- details of any significant changes to the objectives and procedures during the period;
- details of any exception to the above objectives and procedures during the period;
- an assertion by the directors that they have reviewed the control objectives and the control procedures in operation.

Report by the reporting accountants

9 The report by the reporting accountants should be addressed to the directors of the custodian rather than the customer or the auditors of the customer.

10 The report by the reporting accountants will depend on the specific terms and conditions agreed with the customer. But such reports would normally be expected to contain:

- a statement that the report is intended for the use of the directors. It may be helpful to acknowledge that they may wish to make it available to customers and the auditors of the customers. In those circumstances it will generally be appropriate to attach to the report a copy of the engagement letter which, *inter alia*, limits the liability of the reporting accountants;
- a statement as to the scope of the report and the reporting accountants' responsibilities;
- if not included in the directors' report, a statement that it is the responsibility of the directors to design, implement and maintain the control procedures of the custodian;
- a statement that the reporting accountants have performed tests on specified control procedures to determine whether they have operated as described. The scope of the accountants' work will not include those control procedures identified in the directors' report which are not capable of objective testing. Specific mention should be made of the fact that the reporting accountants have not performed an assessment of the adequacy or completeness of the control objectives identified by the directors nor whether the control procedures achieve the control objectives which were set;
- a statement that transactions in relation to any particular customer's assets may not have been tested;
- a statement that the testing carried out related to the control procedures of the custodian and that their relevance to any customer is dependent on their interaction with the control procedures in place at the customer;
- a statement that all control systems have inherent limitations and accordingly errors and irregularities may occur and not be detected. Also they cannot guarantee protection against fraudulent collusion especially on the part of those holding positions of authority or trust;
- a statement (if relevant) that the report refers to procedures in place during a historical period and that there is a risk that changes may alter the validity of any conclusions;
- an opinion that the directors' report describes fairly the control procedures in place; and
- an opinion in relation to the specific control procedures tested.

A list of the control procedures that have been tested, together with the tests performed and results should be given. This may be attached as an appendix. An example of a report by the reporting accountants is shown in Appendix 2.

11 If the report by management includes any opinion or assertion in relation to the design or operating effectiveness of the control objectives or procedures, the reporting accountant should specifically exclude these matters from their reporting on policies and procedures in place (unless the reporting accountants have accepted an engagement, to report in relation to the design or operation of the procedures. This will normally require considerably more work.)

The reporting accountants will not be responsible for carrying out a review of disclosed systems changes subsequent to the specified date or for the identification of changes not disclosed by management.

Material weaknesses

In order that the statement by directors is fairly described, the directors should include in their report a description of any material weaknesses identified which have, in their view, affected whether control procedures are in place, or reduced the effectiveness or have prevented the operation of control procedures, if those weaknesses were not themselves identified and rectified within an appropriate time. It would also be helpful for the status of any corrective action taken by the directors in relation to any reported weakness to be included in their report.

Where the reporting accountants have become aware of material weaknesses which are inadequately described in the directors' report, they should qualify their report and provide such a description in their report or a reference to such a description in the directors' report. The reporting accountants should also refer to any inaccurate or inadequate description of the custodian's control procedures in the directors' report of which they have become aware.

On occasions directors may seek to alter control objectives in order to prevent a qualification in the report by the reporting accountants. Reporting accountants should assess carefully the appropriateness of any changes proposed to the directors' report and the risks arising from this and consider their opinion in the light of that assessment.

The directors may express their intention to rectify a weakness at some future time. No opinion should be given by the reporting accountants in relation to such an expressed intention and the report by the reporting accountants should specifically state that fact. Reporting accountants may, at the request of the directors, test and report on any corrective action taken in respect of a weakness.

Reporting accountants should consider whether weaknesses should be reported to any applicable regulator or other body either as part of normal regulatory reporting or in accordance with the duty to report under Auditing Standards.

Appendix 1 – Report by the directors

As the directors of XYZ we are responsible for:
(a) the identification of control objectives relating to the protection of customer assets and to ensure that all transactions are properly recorded;
(b) the design, implementation and maintenance of control procedures to ensure with reasonable assurance on an ongoing basis that the control objectives are achieved.

In carrying out these responsibilities we have regard not only to the interest of customers but also to those of the owners of the business and the general effectiveness and efficiency of the relevant operations.

We have reviewed the control objectives and procedures in operation.

We set out in this report the relevant control objectives together with the specific control procedures which were operating as described during the period [ ] to [ ] to meet each of these objectives.

Extract from a sample report (starts at section B of the report)

References in brackets are to procedures tested by the reporting accountants as set out in the attachment to their report.

B. Physical controls and reconciliation procedures

We seek to ensure safe custody of customers' assets through physical and reconciliation controls to prevent loss from error or fraud

Access to the premises is restricted solely to authorised personnel by the use of swipe cards, security guards and photo passes, with further restrictions on access to the Custody Department. These access rights are reviewed by management.

All title documents are held in locked fireproof safes. Access to title documents is restricted to authorised personnel.

Title documents are released only to the customer, to an eligible custodian or a recognised depository in accordance with the terms of the customer agreement. Physical securities are released only on receipt of a customer authorised instruction validated against a customer signatory list. (B1)

All customers are contacted annually to verify the accuracy of the authorised signatory list. (B2)

Six monthly physical counts of all securities are undertaken by staff independent of those responsible for the authentication and recording of transactions. (B3)

Six monthly reconciliations of the count of all physical securities held to the books and records is undertaken by individuals not responsible for the day to day physical custody or the authentication and recording of customer instructions. The reconciliations are reviewed by management on a timely basis to ensure that any differences are adequately resolved or appropriate action is being taken. (B4)

Through segregation of duties, persons involved in the reconciliation function are only allowed appropriate and supervised access to the title documents during the security counts. Persons involved in transaction processing are not permitted access to title documents at any time.

The securities' compliance department, independent of custody operations, reviews and scrutinises the results of the securities' counts and stock reconciliations. (B5)

C. Sub-custodians appointment and reconciliation procedures

We seek to ensure that sub-custodians are of a high standard and customers' assets held are duly protected and reconciled to our accounting records

All sub-custodian appointments are approved by the Head of Securities. Selection is based upon an assessment of individual performance, track record and standing in the market.

Sub-custodians and the level of risk associated with them are monitored. The sub-custodians are retained based on an annual review by management in terms of their effectiveness at providing all of the services agreed.

Arrangements with independent sub-custodians are documented and subject to review by the compliance department. (C1)

Sub-custodians are required to provide written confirmation that customer assets are held in segregated accounts to afford maximum possible protection in the event of any default. (C2)

Monthly reconciliations of securities held at sub-custodians to the books and records are undertaken by individuals not responsible for the day to day physical custody or the authentication and recording of customer instructions. The reconciliations are reviewed by management on a timely basis to ensure that any differences are adequately resolved or appropriate action is being taken. (C3)

Appendix 2 – An illustrative report by the reporting accountants to the directors of XYZ plc

Use of this report

This report is intended solely for the use of the directors of XYZ plc and, without giving rise to any liability or duty to them on our part, for the information of its customers and their auditors. The attention of customers of XYZ plc and their auditors is drawn to the engagement letter dated [ ] which includes the limitations of liability [set out below], a copy of which is attached.

[Include here more detail on engagement terms if the engagement letter is not attached].

Scope

This report covers solely the custodial operations of XYZ plc carried out by business units of the company located at [ ] as described in your report of [ ] and does not extend to any other custodial business of XYZ plc.

Respective responsibilities of directors and reporting accountants

Your responsibilities as directors are set out in the attached engagement letter and on page X of the accompanying report. It is our responsibility to form an independent opinion, based on the work we have carried out, and to report our opinion to you as directors of XYZ plc.

[Include here directors' responsibilities if not in directors' report].

Basis of opinion

Our review was conducted in accordance with the framework for reporting set out in FRAG 21/94 (revised) issued by the Institute of Chartered Accountants in England and Wales. Our work was based upon obtaining an understanding of the control procedures in operation by enquiry of management and review of documents supplied to us. Our work included tests of certain specific control procedures, as set out in the appendix to our report, to determine whether they operated as described.

We have not performed an assessment of the adequacy or completeness of the control objectives in relation to the risks they are designed to address nor have we assessed whether the control procedures achieve the control objectives which were set. Our opinion relates solely to the control procedures which we tested and not to any others.

Our tests did not include tests of transactions in respect of any particular customer. They were restricted to the procedures of XYZ plc's custodial function carried out at the specified business units and their relevance to any individual customer is dependent on their interaction with the particular procedures and other circumstances of that customer.

Control procedures designed to address specified control objectives are subject to inherent limitations and, accordingly, errors or irregularities may occur and not be detected. Such procedures cannot guarantee protection against fraudulent collusion especially on the part of those holding positions of authority or trust. Furthermore, this opinion is based on historical information and the projection of any information or conclusions in the attached report to any future periods would be inappropriate.

Opinion

Based on the above, in our opinion:

1. the accompanying report by the directors[1] describes fairly the control procedures in place as at [ ]
2. the specific control procedures that we tested as set out in the attachment to this report operated as described as at [ ] / in the period from [ ] to [ ].

Signature   **Address**

Chartered Accountants

Date of Signature

Attachments:

Tests performed by the reporting accountants

Engagement letter covering, *inter alia*, the limitation of liability of [Firm].

ATTACHMENT TO THE REPORTING ACCOUNTANTS' REPORT

This is not intended to be a specimen work programme and should not be used as such.

Where the period of testing is different from that set out in the reporting accountants' report, it should be specified as such.

[1] *Insert except for (reference to opinion on effectiveness)* if part of the directors' report.

Tests performed by the Reporting Accountants

Section B – Physical controls and reconciliation procedures

B1. Physical securities are released only on receipt of a customer authorised instruction validated against a customer signatory list.

- Inspected a sample of authorised customer instructions and tested for evidence of validation against the customer signatory list for a sample of sales and withdrawals of securities extracted from the records: *No exceptions*

B2. All customers are contacted annually to verify the accuracy of the authorised signatory list.

- Reviewed recent correspondence with a sample of customers, verifying that there is evidence of the check having been carried out by management: *Specify exceptions....*

B3. Six monthly physical counts of all securities are undertaken by staff independent of those responsible for the authentication and recording of transactions.

- Attended physical count at [date] and reperformed physical count for a small sample of securities: *No exceptions*

B4. Six monthly reconciliations of the count of all physical securities held to the books and records is undertaken by individuals not responsible for the day to day physical custody or the authentication and recording of customer instructions. The reconciliations are reviewed by management on a timely basis to ensure that any differences are adequately resolved or appropriate action is being taken.

- Inspected a small sample of reconciliation documentation and observed the presence of an appropriate signature and: *Specify exceptions....*

B5. The securities' compliance department, independent of custody operations, reviews and scrutinises the results of the securities' counts and stock reconciliations.

- Inspected a small sample of work programmes and reports confirming that procedures were carried out: *No exceptions*

Section C – Sub-custodian appointment and reconciliation procedures

C1. Arrangements with independent sub-custodians are documented and subject to review by the Compliance Department.

- Inspected a small sample of sub-custodian agreements and verified evidence of review and approval by the Compliance Department for sub-custodians in use during the period: *No exceptions*

C2. Sub-custodians are required to provide written confirmation that customer assets are held in segregated accounts to afford maximum possible protection in the event of any default.

- Inspected written confirmations for a small sample of sub-custodians in use during the period: *No exceptions*

C3. Monthly reconciliations of securities held at sub-custodians to the books and records are undertaken by individuals not responsible for the day to day physical custody or the authentication and recording of customer instructions. The reconciliations are reviewed by management on a timely basis to ensure that any differences are adequately resolved or appropriate action is being taken.

- Inspected a sample of reconciliations to ensure that they bear evidence of having been performed by independent personnel, cover all sub-custodians and that they are completed monthly: *No exceptions*

- Inspected reconciliation documentation for evidence of management review and sign off on a timely basis: *No exceptions*

Appendix 3 – Engagement letter

The Directors
XYZ plc

Dear Sirs

Following our recent meeting when you invited us to report on your report on the custodial operations of XYZ plc carried out by business units of the company located at [ ] for the period [ ] to [ ], we are writing to set out our proposed responsibilities, our understanding of the work to be performed and the terms and conditions upon which we offer to perform such work.

Respective responsibilities of directors and reporting accountants

As the directors of XYZ plc you are responsible for the design, implementation and maintenance of control procedures that provide adequate levels of protection of customers' assets and records to ensure that all transactions are properly recorded. You are also responsible for the definition of adequate levels of protection in terms of control objectives and for ensuring that these objectives are achieved by the control procedures in place. You will describe the control objectives and the related control procedures in a report. It is our responsibility [as applicable] to form an independent opinion on whether you have fairly described the control procedures and whether the specific control procedures which we tested operated as described, and to report to you. We shall not report on any opinions or assertion by you on the effectiveness of objectives, policies and procedures.

Scope of work

The work we shall perform will be conducted in accordance with the framework set out in technical release, FRAG 21/94 (revised), issued by the Institute of Chartered Accountants in England and Wales. Our work will [if applicable] include enquiries of management together with tests of certain specific control procedures which will be set out in the attachment to our report. Our work will be planned in advance. [In developing our plan we shall liaise with your Internal Audit Department to ensure that our work is properly co-ordinated with theirs.]

We shall not be responsible for a review of changes to control procedures beyond the period reported upon or for the identification of changes not disclosed by management.

Use of report

Our report will be addressed to you as directors of the company, although we understand that you may wish to make the report available to customers using the company's custodial services or their auditors, and we consent to the report being

Access to working papers by investigating accountants

Introduction

1. During certain investment and lending transactions such as flotations, often the potential purchasers, investors or lenders (called 'purchasers') or their agents instruct investigating accountants to review aspects of the affairs of the 'target' company on their behalf. Access to the audit working papers of the auditors of the target company will frequently assist the investigating accountants in doing a more efficient job than if they had to redo this work themselves. In the past few years, however, it has become increasingly difficult for investigating accountants to gain such access.

2. The auditors of the target company have been reluctant to permit access as there are problems of confidentiality and the auditors may be alleged to have accepted an additional duty of care. Their audit would not have been planned and performed in contemplation of any particular commercial transaction. The onus is on the purchasers and their agents to arrange for appropriate due diligence work to be performed.

3. The working papers of auditors are their legal property and they have the right to restrict or decline access to them. However, not permitting access is unhelpful to their clients who are normally willing participants in the transaction, nor is it economical for the purchasers; gaining access to the auditors' working papers would enable work to proceed more efficiently. An alternative way forward is for firms to have a developed policy regarding access to working papers, providing certain conditions are met.

Facilitating access

4. The reluctance to permit access can be largely overcome by the use of client authorisation and 'release' letters. The purpose of these letters is to deal with any confidentiality issues and to provide a framework within which auditors can make their papers available and provide explanations while limiting as far as possible any additional risks.

5. Auditors are recommended not to provide access to their audit working papers or to provide explanations until they have obtained from the prospective purchasers and their investigating accountants signed release letters which agree that the auditors do not assume any duties, liabilities or obligations as a result of permitting access and may provide for an indemnity against any claims from third parties arising out of permitting access. Occasionally the request will extend to papers concerning dealings with the Inland Revenue (taxation papers). In this case, the release letters should also specifically cover these papers.

6. Auditors should also obtain from their clients or relevant parties letters authorising them to permit access to the audit working papers and to provide explanations of them. An example of an authorisation letter is given in Appendix 1.

Explanations

7. In providing explanations of the working papers, auditors should take care to restrict their explanations to the working papers and should avoid giving oral

[Statement 913]
Access to working papers by investigating accountants (AUDIT 3/95)

(Issued October 1995)

Contents

	Paragraphs
Introduction	1 - 3
Facilitating access	4 - 6
Explanations	7
Content of release letters	8 - 9
Consideration	10
Acceptance of release letters	11
Conclusion	12

Appendix 1 – Example authorisation letter

Appendix 2 – Example release letter

representations, or warranties about any matters arising after the date of the audit report. Also auditors should recognise an obligation to make it known to the investigating accountants if the audit working papers are, or may not be, all the relevant papers that exist.

Content of the release letters

Appendix 2 gives an example of a release letter. The terms of the release letter require the potential purchaser to agree that the auditors do not assume any duty or liability as a result of providing access or explanations and that the purchaser will hold harmless and will indemnify the auditors against any claim arising from the access. The investigating accountants are also required to sign the letter agreeing to the terms and conditions. The terms and conditions must satisfy the requirements for reasonableness under the Unfair Contract Terms Act 1977. 8

Release letters should not include a requirement for the investigating accountant to bring to the auditors' attention points which they intend to pass orally or in a written report arising from a review of the working papers. This term does not give the auditor any added protection and may serve to confuse the auditors' role in the transaction. 9

Consideration

Normally no charge would be levied by the auditor upon the purchaser for grant of access to the working papers. Should consideration be received by the auditor this may affect the perceived 'reasonableness' of the exclusion clause in the release letter. A real risk exists that if an auditor charges on a profit basis for access, the exclusion clause would be declared unreasonable if challenged in court under the Unfair Contract Terms Act 1977. (Note that nominal costs for copying charges are unlikely to invalidate the clause). 10

Acceptance of release letters

Potential purchasers may try to resist release letters but experience has shown that frequently the greatest resistance arises in situations in which the auditors are most at risk. The auditors should explain that the use of such letters is standard and has been endorsed by the Institute. The wording in the examples has been approved by leading Counsel. Their use is not unreasonable in any acquisition situation or when accountants are reporting for the purpose of prospectus type documents. Auditors are not being uncooperative in insisting that they will provide access to their files and give explanations only on the receipt of signed release and authorisation letters. 11

Conclusion

Auditors have the right to decide whether they should give access to their working papers or not and also on what terms access should be given. Their decision has to be made on consideration of the various interests represented. This paper, however, will give them a framework for alleviating the risk of allowing access to their working papers. 12

Appendix 1 – Specimen client authorisation letter to allow access to client confidential information

Finance Director
Client Plc
(Address)

Dear

Thank you for your telephone call today alerting me to the proposed [describe transaction: e.g., 'sale of the ordinary shares of your subsidiary, Subsidiary Company Limited, to Purchaser plc'] in which you requested me to allow Purchaser plc and/or Investigating Accountants & Co access to our working papers for the statutory audits of Subsidiary's accounts for the year(s) ended 31 December 19XX, and to the taxation computations together with access to copies of the correspondence and related formalities between us and the Inland Revenue in respect of the computations, and to provide them with whatever explanations are necessary. [Note 1].

My firm's policy does not normally allow me to disclose working papers to third parties. In exceptional circumstances I am authorised to agree to this providing certain conditions are met. I am now writing to confirm the terms on which my firm will allow access to be given in this instance and to confirm your authorisation for us to allow such access and to provide explanations.

Prior to making the working papers available to Purchaser plc and/or Investigating Accountants & Co, we need Subsidiary's consent. In addition, we require from Purchaser plc and/or Investigating Accountants & Co an agreement that Purchaser plc [or the other parties to whom the release letter may be addressed] will not acquire any rights against Registered Auditor & Co as a result of such access, an indemnity from Purchaser plc against claims from third parties arising out of such access and an acknowledgement from Purchaser plc and/or Investigating Accountants & Co that they recognise the basis on which access is provided.

As you will appreciate, our working papers were created for the particular purpose of our audit(s) of Subsidiary's statutory financial statements and not for the purpose of the proposed sale of Subsidiary, or indeed for any other purpose. Consequently, the working papers and the information in them may not be suitable for the purposes of the proposed transaction. However, Client and Subsidiary will accept the risk, and not hold Registered Auditor & Co responsible, if Purchaser plc and/or Investigating Accountants & Co's review of our working papers or our explanations or representations made orally to them results in the termination of, or alteration to, the proposed transaction or in any action at any time against Client or Subsidiary respectively, if Purchaser plc, Investigating Accountants & Co or any of the other parties involved with this proposed transaction, misuse any confidential information obtained from a review of our working papers or by way of explanation from us.

Please confirm that you agree to our disclosing the working papers on the terms described above by signing the enclosed copy of this letter, arranging for the signature of the Finance or Managing Director of Subsidiary to consent to the access on Subsidiary's behalf and returning it to me.

I hope the proposed transaction proceeds smoothly and look forward to working with you over the next few weeks.

Yours sincerely,

A Partner

ACKNOWLEDGEMENT

Acknowledged and agreed.

_____ Finance Director _____
                        Position   Date

I hereby consent to the disclosure of the working papers referred to above on the terms described above.

For and on behalf of Subsidiary Company Limited:

Signed

_____ Director   _____
                        Position   Date

Notes:

1) If access is to be granted to audit papers on an incomplete audit, the following paragraph should be added:

    'However, we have not yet completed this year's statutory audit of Subsidiary's financial statements, and therefore, our audit papers are incomplete. Consequently, I am not able to give any opinion on those financial statements. Nevertheless, Purchaser plc and/or Investigating Accountants & Co believe it would be helpful if they were to review our working papers prepared to date. We agreed that it would be time consuming, and not without cost, if I have to inform them of any changes that may be made to our audit papers during the course of completing our audit. Accordingly, you concurred that I should refuse to accept any responsibility to them to keep them informed as the audit progresses.'

2) The client (that is the company) may not always be the only party to whom the letter is addressed as, in certain circumstances such as a management buy-out, this may not be appropriate. In such cases, probably the owner of the company or, perhaps a non-executive director, would be relevant parties.

Appendix 2 – Release letter to prospective purchaser/investor/lender and investigating accountants

(The Release Letter assumes a proposed purchase of a company. It must be amended as appropriate for the circumstances of each transaction).

PRIVATE AND CONFIDENTIAL

Purchaser plc
Address

Investigating Accountants & Co
Address

Dear Sirs

PROPOSED [ACQUISITION] OF SUBSIDIARY COMPANY LIMITED

1. In connection with the proposed [acquisition] of Subsidiary Company Limited ('the Company') by Purchaser plc the Company has requested us to allow Investigating Accountants & Co. access to our working papers relating to our audit(s) [currently in progress] of the accounts of the Company for the year(s) ended 31 December 19XX ('the Audit Papers') and the taxation computations as submitted to and/or agreed with the Inland Revenue for each of the last [ ] years and copies of the correspondence and related documents between us and the Inland Revenue in respect of those computations ('the Taxation Papers'), in connection with the proposed [acquisition]. The Company has further authorised us at our discretion to give explanations in relation to the Audit Papers and the Taxation Papers (together referred to as 'the Working Papers') where we consider it appropriate to do so.

2. We point out that the Audit Papers were prepared solely for the purpose of our forming an opinion, in accordance with the statutory (or regulatory) requirement for audit, on whether the financial statements, which are the responsibility of the directors of the Company, give a true and fair view of the state of affairs as at the end of the financial year and of the profit and loss for the period then ended. [see Note 1].

3. Our audit(s) of the Company's financial statements, and the Audit Papers prepared or obtained in connection therewith, was [were] not planned or conducted in contemplation, or for the purpose, of the proposed [acquisition]. Further, the scope of an audit is normally substantially narrower than an investigation on behalf of a [purchaser]. Therefore, items of possible interest to Purchaser plc may not have been specifically addressed for the purposes of the audit.

4. Moreover, there are a number of inherent limitations in audited financial statements (see for example Practice Note 4 issued by the Auditing Practices Committee). Our use of professional judgment and the assessment of materiality for the purpose of our audit means that matters may have existed that would have been assessed differently by Purchaser plc or Investigating Accountants & Co. for the purposes of the proposed [acquisition]. We do not warrant or represent that the information in our Working Papers is sufficient or even appropriate for your purposes. That is a matter for your judgment. Nor have we expressed an opinion or other form of assurance on individual account balances, financial amounts, financial information or the adequacy of financial, accounting or management systems.

5. You should further note that we have not reported on the Company's financial statements for any period subsequent to [31 December 19XX] and significant events may well have occurred since that date.

6. It must also be understood that the Taxation Papers were prepared solely for the purpose of calculating and/or agreeing the Company's tax liability for the years in question. The comments made in relation to the Audit Papers in paragraph 3 above apply with equal force in relation to the Taxation Papers.

7. For the foregoing reasons, the Working Papers cannot in any way serve as a substitute for other enquiries and procedures that [Purchaser plc] and Investigating Accountants & Co would (or should) otherwise undertake for the purpose of satisfying themselves regarding the Company's financial condition or for any other purpose in connection with the [acquisition].

8. In view of the purposes for which the Working Papers were prepared, we are prepared to grant Investigating Accountants & Co access to the Working Papers, and at our discretion give explanations in relation thereto in response to requests for information from Investigating Accountants & Co, on condition that Purchaser plc and Investigating Accountants & Co agree to the following Conditions upon which access to the Working Papers is granted and the explanations in relation thereto are made:

    (1) Purchaser plc and Investigating Accountants acknowledge that:

    (a) No-one is authorised by Registered Auditor & Co. whether expressly or ostensibly to make representations or reach an agreement in relation to the Conditions upon which access to the Working Papers is granted to Investigating Accountants & Co and representations in relation thereto are made which is inconsistent with or varies or adds to the terms and conditions set out in this Release Letter.

    (b) Registered Auditor & Co, its partners, employees and agents (collectively referred to as 'Registered Auditor & Co' hereinafter) neither warrant nor represent that the information in the Working Papers is sufficient or appropriate for the purposes of considering the proposed [acquisition].

    (c) All explanations made to Purchaser plc or Investigating Accountants & Co by Registered Auditor & Co in relation to the Working Papers are no more than explanations of matters contained in the Working Papers and to the extent that any such explanation may be construed as relating to the affairs of the Company, the onus shall be upon Purchaser plc or Investigating Accountant & Co to verify the statement with the Company before relying upon it for the purpose of any decision relating to the proposed [acquisition].

    (d) This letter sets out the entire understanding of the parties in relation to the conditions upon which access to the Working Papers is granted to Investigating Accountants & Co and upon which representations in relation thereto are made and supplants all prior representations, if any, made by Registered Auditor & Co in relation to the said Conditions.

    (2) Purchaser plc and Investigating Accountants agree that Registered Auditor & Co its partners and staff neither owe nor accept any duty to Purchaser plc or Investigating Accountants & Co, whether in contract or in tort (including without limitation, negligence and breach of statutory duty) or howsoever otherwise arising, and shall not be liable, in respect of any loss damage or expense of whatsoever nature which is caused by Purchaser plc's or Investigating Accountants & Co's reliance upon the Working Papers or representations made in relation thereto or which is otherwise consequent upon [Purchaser plc's] or Investigating Accountants & Co's access to Working Papers or receipt of such representations. Provided that this clause shall not exclude liability (if it would otherwise but for this clause have arisen) for death or personal injury caused by the negligence (as defined in Section 1 of the Unfair Contracts Terms Act 1977) of Registered Auditor & Co its partners and staff and loss or damage caused by their fraud. In the premises, if Purchaser plc and Investigating Accountant wish

to rely upon the Working Papers and representations made by Registered Auditor & Co in relation thereto, they do so entirely at their own risk.

(3) Purchaser plc shall indemnify and hold harmless Registered Auditor & Co its partners and staff against all actions, proceedings and claims brought or threatened against Registered Auditor & Co (whether by Purchaser plc, the Company, another Purchaser party or any other third party), and all loss damage and expense (including legal expenses) relating thereto, in any way arising out of or in connection with the grant of access to the Working Papers to Investigating Accountants including, without limitation, all actions, proceedings, and claims brought or threatened by the Company and the loss, damage and expense (including legal expenses) relating thereto concerning matters disclosed as a result of the grant of access to the Working Papers to Investigating Accountants & Co and representations made in relation thereto (but with the exception of actions, proceedings, and claims which are successfully brought by Purchaser plc against Registered Auditor & Co in relation to death or personal injury caused by the negligence (within the meaning of section 1 of the Unfair Contract Terms Act 1977) of Registered Auditor & Co or in relation to fraud perpetrated by Registered Auditor & Co, and the loss damage and expense relating thereto).

(4) Purchaser plc and Investigating Accountant & Co shall not use the Working papers or any information provided by Registered Auditor & Co for any purpose other than the proposed [acquisition].

(5) Purchaser plc and Investigating Accountant & Co shall not allow access to the Working Papers, or give information obtained from the Working Papers or from representations made by Registered Accountant in relation thereto, to any other party except their professional advisers.

(6) Purchaser plc shall show this letter to its professional advisers who are involved in the transaction and hereby undertakes to take all reasonable steps to secure their compliance with the Conditions (4) and (5) of this letter as if the obligations stated therein extended to the professional advisers.

9. Please confirm your agreement to the foregoing Conditions by signing, dating and returning to us a copy of this letter. Registered Auditor & Co acts as agent for its partners and staff as well as for itself as to clauses 8(2) and (3) above.

Yours faithfully

Registered Auditor & Co

Purchaser plc hereby acknowledges that it understands and agrees to the conditions upon which access to the Working Papers is granted and explanations in relation thereto are made.

....
Signature   Position   Date

Investigating Accountants hereby acknowledges that it understands and agrees to the conditions upon which access to the Working Papers is granted and explanations in relation thereto are made.

....
Investigating Accountants & Co   Date

Notes:

1) If access is to be granted to audit papers on an incomplete audit, the following paragraph should be added:

'However, we have not yet completed the statutory audit of the financial statements of Subsidiary Company Limited for the year ending ... Accordingly we are unable to, and do not express at this time any opinion on those financial statements. Further, we have no responsibility to inform you, or any other of the Purchaser parties of any changes that may be made to such audit papers during the course of completing our audit.'

[Statement 916]
Derivatives in a corporate environment: a guide for auditors (AUDIT 1/97)

(Issued January 1997)

Contents

	Paragraphs
Introduction	1.1 - 1.11
Knowledge of the business	2.1 - 2.22
Accounting and internal control systems	3.1 - 3.25
Audit procedures	4.1 - 4.21
Audit completion considerations	5.1 - 5.4

Appendix 1 – Suggestions for detailed audit tests

Appendix 2 – Aide memoire

Appendix 3 – Accounting for derivatives and audit considerations

Appendix 4 – Relevant sources of accounting and other guidance

Derivatives in a corporate environment: a guide for auditors

1 Introduction

PURPOSE OF THE TECHNICAL RELEASE

This Technical Release gives guidance to auditors on special features which may need to be considered in the audit of non-financial sector entities which use derivatives. This will include entities which use commodity derivatives to manage their commodity risk. This technical release does not cover the use of derivatives in banks and other financial sector entities. Banks will often use derivatives as part of their proprietary trading. This gives rise to control issues on a different scale to that of the average corporate. Further information can be obtained from the various statements of recommended practice which have been issued by the British Bankers Association ('BBA'). 1.1

The application of this guidance is not mandatory. What this guidance cannot achieve, and indeed does not purport to do, is to replace the judgement required of auditors in determining the nature and extent of work required. Such decisions can only be made in the context of the specific business operations and the level and nature of derivative activity, through a consideration of risk and materiality factors. If auditors are in any doubt as to the extent or nature of testing that is required, it may be helpful to seek guidance from specialists in derivatives. 1.2

BACKGROUND

All entities are concerned with treasury management to a greater or lesser extent, whether they have a formal 'Treasurer' or not. At its simplest level, treasury management might entail an entity deciding where to place surplus cash and/or from whom to borrow or, at the next level, deciding whether to take fixed or floating rate borrowings. A fixed rate loan will enable the entity to predict future cash flows while a floating rate loan will enable it to take advantage of falls in interest rates, but expose it to the risk of interest rates rising. 1.3

At its most complex, treasury management involves active participation in the global financial markets. This may consist of an array of inter-connecting decisions on currency rates, interest rates, liquidity and credit management and the use of financial instruments to manage the associated risks and, sometimes, to take speculative positions unrelated to the underlying risks of the business. The financial markets have developed a proliferation of financial instruments available for the use of the corporate treasurer over the last 10 to 20 years to protect entities against such fundamentals as foreign exchange risk, interest risk and commodity risk. These have been mainly in the form of **derivative contracts**. Derivatives have become important management tools for many entities. 1.4

Derivatives can be used by entities to: 1.5

- manage the risks relating to day to day operations;
- manage the balance sheet and results; and
- take open or speculative positions to benefit from anticipated market movements.

Some entities may be involved in derivatives not only from a corporate treasury perspective but also, or alternatively, in association with the production or use by their business of a commodity. An example would be an oil producer which hedges output prices using an energy derivative such as an oil swap.

1.6 It is worth highlighting at the outset that the nature of the risks attached to derivatives is not fundamentally different from those attached to transactions in other markets such as cash, currency, bonds, equities and commodities. What distinguishes derivatives, however, is the potentially large effect they could have on the liquidity of the entity due to the use of options and the ability to make margin payments which can result in greater gearing and complexity compared with other instruments. If derivative contracts are misused, whether deliberately or in error, they can cause an entity to suffer significant losses which may threaten its financial stability. The complexity of some derivatives can increase the risk that an entity may enter into transactions without fully understanding the risks involved. This combination of complexity and gearing can result in losses from derivatives' activity developing very quickly.

DEFINITIONS OF A DERIVATIVE

1.7 A derivative is a generic term used to categorise a wide variety of financial instruments whose value 'depends on' or is 'derived from' an underlying rate or price, such as interest rates, exchange rates, equity prices, or commodity prices. Simpler derivative contracts generally have the characteristics of one of two principal categories. Either, they are contracts involving obligatory cash flows at a future date, or they have option features where one party has the right but not the obligation to require another party to deliver the underlying item (eg cash, security, commodity) to them. The most common types of contract in each of these two categories respectively are:

- forward and futures contracts, forward rate agreements and swaps;
- caps, floors and swaptions.

More complex derivatives may have a combination of the characteristics of each category.

1.8 For the purposes of this guidance, the term derivatives covers futures, forwards, swaps and option contracts, and other financial instruments with similar characteristics, including the more complex instruments essentially constructed from those more basic instruments and products possessing similar characteristics whose value is determined in relation to the prices of commodities and equities. For ease of use the remainder of this guidance refers primarily to corporate treasury activities. However, the principles discussed would apply equally to a commodity producer/user dealing in commodity derivatives.

1.9 Financial and commodity futures and some options are traded primarily on exchanges while other derivatives are traded primarily 'over the counter' (OTC) (ie directly between the participants). Exchange traded contracts have pre-agreed terms (amount, settlement, etc) and are effectively uniform, whereas OTC contracts are not necessarily uniform. The terms of each transaction are agreed between two or more parties.

1.10 Further guidance on derivatives and their use can be obtained from relevant accounting and other guidance which is available. Appendix 4 outlines some of the literature.

ENGAGEMENT LETTERS

Auditors determine the nature and extent of their work on derivatives solely for the purpose of providing an audit opinion on an entity. It is important that management fully understands the scope of work being undertaken in this area and that, unless an extension of scope beyond the statutory audit has been agreed, they are not expecting the auditors to perform more work than is necessary for them to express an opinion on the truth and fairness of the accounts. If the auditors consider that an 'expectation gap' exists with respect to the work on derivatives, they consider whether this should be addressed in discussions with management and/or whether the audit engagement letter should draw management's attention to the scope of work being undertaken in relation to the corporate treasury.   1.11

2 Knowledge of the business

Auditors reviewing corporate treasury operations assess the entity's attitude to risk and its control as this can have a major impact on the business. They need to develop their own understanding of the risks so that they can objectively make a judgement on management's attitude towards them. As the corporate treasury activity generally supports the business activities of the entity, factors impacting the day to day operations of the business will also have implications for corporate treasury. Similarly corporate treasury activities can have a major impact on the operations and viability of the business. These factors are discussed below.   2.1

GENERAL ECONOMIC FACTORS

General economic factors are likely to have implications and so auditors consider how they are likely to have influenced treasury activities during the period under review. For example, when there are fears of interest rates rising, an entity may seek to fix the effective level of interest rates on its floating rate borrowings through the use of interest rate swaps.   2.2

THE INDUSTRY – CONDITIONS AFFECTING THE ENTITY'S BUSINESS

Auditors also consider how economic conditions in the industry in which the entity operates are likely to have influenced treasury activities. If the industry is seasonal or cyclical, it may be inherently more difficult for the treasurer to forecast accurately interest rate, foreign exchange or liquidity exposures. For example, a holiday company whose activities involve pre-purchasing hotel rooms, the charges for which are denominated in foreign currency, has a currency exposure which may be difficult to forecast. The extent of this exposure (and the extent, if any, to which the entity determines that it should cover this through hedging) may depend upon demand for holidays in general, whether the rooms it has pre-purchased are likely to be taken up and management's ability to flex the price of holidays in response to exchange rate movements. A high growth rate or sharp rate of decline in a business may also make it difficult to predict activity levels in general and thus its treasury exposures.   2.3

THE ENTITY

Structure of operations

2.4 The audit risk profile of the corporate treasury may increase with greater distribution of the treasury operations around the entity's other operations and where the entity is based at different locations, some perhaps overseas. The treasury function may be run on either a centralised or a decentralised basis. Corporate treasury operations depend heavily upon the flow of accurate management information for derivative activity assessments and decisions to be made. The difficulty of collecting and aggregating such information on a timely basis increases with the number of locations and businesses in which an entity is involved.

2.5 Auditors identify at the outset whether the treasury function is more in the nature of a profit or a cost centre. A cost centre's primary aim is to reduce or eliminate risk and all derivative transactions are undertaken for hedging purposes while a profit centre treasury may be allowed to take positions which need not directly relate to underlying commercial exposures. This is obviously a riskier strategy. These are the two extremes. In most corporate environments, the treasury will operate as a 'service centre' providing services to the operating divisions of the business and adding value to the business by actively managing risk but without necessarily undertaking purely speculative transactions.

General standards of control

2.6 Corporate treasuries are generally characterised by low transaction volumes, although the range of derivatives used can be as broad as that in small to medium sized banks. Depending on the size of the entity, the treasury function is often delegated to an individual such as the 'treasurer' or 'finance director' or to a treasury department. Often there is not sufficient staff to implement a complete range of controls and to ensure a high level of segregation of duties. One approach is to use the general finance and administrative functions to handle certain procedures, such as receipt and checking of counterparty confirmations.

Management's attitude to risk

2.7 The Board has ultimate responsibility and it should approve clear policies and guidelines on the manner in which risk is to be identified, monitored and managed. Treasury's role is to implement the Board's policies and to make decisions to reduce the overall level of risk within an agreed limit.

2.8 Management should identify the key treasury risks facing the entity before they decide on the strategy to manage those risks. This will include identifying:
- the macro-economic risks faced by the entity;
- the translational risk due to net assets being held in overseas locations;
- the foreign exchange and interest rate risks arising from the activities of the entity and from the transactions entered into;
- the amount of net debt and cash in each major currency, analysed between fixed and floating rate; and
- the maturity profile of its cash/debt and committed credit lines.

The types of treasury risk faced by each entity will be different, as will be the attitude of each entity's management towards managing those risks. Using derivatives to hedge the risks is only one approach.

2.9 Whilst all financial instruments have certain risks, derivatives often possess particular features which leverage the risks such as the following:

- little or no cash outflows/inflows are required until maturity of the transaction;
- no principal balance or other fixed amount is paid or received; and
- potential risks and rewards can be substantially greater than the current outlays especially where the derivative is speculative.

2.10 The value of derivatives can be more volatile than those of other financial instruments, potentially alternating between positive and negative values over a short period of time because of movements in, for example, interest rates, exchange rates or commodity prices. Also, they may not be symmetrical in their impact. For example, the possible loss for the buyer of some types of options is limited to the premium paid, yet the upside is effectively unlimited. Conversely, the writer of an option has unlimited downside risk yet the upside is limited to the premium received. Furthermore, the impact of derivatives can rarely be considered in isolation, since they usually interact (and may do so in a complex manner) with other transactions and activities of the entity. These characteristics usually make the consideration of risk in relation to derivatives complex.

Key risks of derivatives

2.11 It is clearly important for management to have an understanding of the nature and extent of the key risks associated with derivatives. There is no complete list of risk characteristics that covers all the possible interactions, but they can be broadly categorised into **financial** and **operational** risks and this can give some structure to the risk analysis. There are five principal types of **financial** risk to which entities may be exposed. Although other classifications of risk exist, they are normally combinations of the principal risks.

FOREIGN EXCHANGE RISK	Where the entity's assets are denominated in one currency but its liabilities are denominated in a different currency, the entity will be exposed to any change in the exchange rate between the two currencies (translation exposure). Until they have been realised and the proceeds converted to the base currency, transactions denominated in foreign currency also present foreign exchange risk (transaction exposure). Exchange rate movements may also result in other indirect impacts on future cash flows of the entity (economic exposure);
INTEREST RATE RISK	Where the interest rate profile of the entity exposes it to movements in interest rates (e.g. if funds are borrowed on a floating rate basis, the entity is exposed to any rise in rates);
CREDIT RISK	The risk of default by a customer, a counterparty or an issuer of security held by the entity;
LIQUIDITY RISK	The risk that the entity cannot meet its liabilities as, and when, they fall due; and
LEGAL RISK	The risk that a legal or regulatory action could invalidate a derivative contract.

There is also a further risk for commodities that the quality may not be as expected.

2.12 It is increasingly common for organisations involved in derivatives to try to mitigate some of the credit and liquidity risks that they face by entering into netting agreements. These agreements enable the treasury to offset amounts owed to and from the same counterparty to give a net amount receivable or payable. Netting can take place on cashflows within a transaction (for example, the payable and receivable legs of a swap) or across transactions and products. Auditors will need sufficient understanding of the extent to which the treasury is capable of netting its exposures and whether the netting that is adopted meets current accounting or regulatory criteria laid down to enable amounts to be shown net in the financial statements of the entity.

2.13 It is also important for management to recognise that derivatives can complicate the entity's tax arrangements – for example, the tax treatment of a hedge may not be symmetrical with the tax treatment of the underlying exposure – and it is therefore necessary to consider the tax consequences of derivatives activity and the impact of any related risks.

2.14 **Operational** (or control) risk represents the broad category of risks which may expose an entity to a financial loss in the event of a failure of systems of internal controls to:

- authorise, confirm, record, process, settle, reconcile and account for derivative transactions;
- safeguard the entity's assets from fraud, theft or conversion; and
- control the activities of those involved in derivatives.

2.15 In addition to the above, management will need to assess the entity's exposure to 'reputational' risk. This is the risk that an entity's reputation suffers adverse publicity as a result of activities in which it is involved. Publicity disclosing that an entity has, say, transacted in derivatives totally unsuited to it could cause the reputation of the entity to be damaged. This in turn could make funding harder to obtain from banks because they might question management's competence.

THE BOARD'S ROLE

2.16 It is the Board's role to determine an appropriate attitude towards the principal risks described above and management's role to monitor and manage the entity's exposures to these risks. To do so effectively requires a framework which:

- is appropriate and consistent with the entity's attitude towards risk as determined by the Board;
- specifies the types of instruments and transactions that may be entered into and for what purposes – the permitted instruments should reflect the expertise of those involved in the treasury function;
- sets limits for the maximum allowable exposure to each type of risk (including approved counterparties);
- provides for the monitoring of the financial risks and control procedures; and
- provides for the reporting of exposures, risks and the results of the actions taken by the treasury function in managing risk.

Management has to establish suitable guidelines to ensure that the treasury function fulfils the entity's needs. In setting suitable guidelines, management should include clear rules on the extent to which the corporate treasury is permitted to participate in the derivative markets. Management may document these rules. Once this has been done management can implement suitable systems to manage and control those risks.

MANAGEMENT EXPERIENCE

2.17 Treasury activities have in the past led to significant losses to both financial and non-financial entities alike. Auditors need to assess the Board's attitude to risk and how management operates as a consequence of the Board's instructions. One common reason for these losses has been the failure of senior management either to identify risks or to monitor exposures properly once risks have been identified. Auditors need to assess the experience senior management has of corporate treasury activities. Since corporate treasury activities can be complicated, it is often the case that only a very few individuals within the entity fully understand these activities. This may cause auditors to question whether there is adequate management control and may impact the auditors' risk assessment and the extent and scope of audit testing considered necessary.

2.18 It is important that senior management fully understand the contents of the management reports they receive in order to properly discharge their responsibilities. Management information systems relating to treasury products usually involve comparisons of actual trading positions and stop loss positions (see paragraph 2.21) against the limits established by the Board. Any breaches of limits should be explained and appropriate action taken. The reporting of treasury activities should provide senior management and the Board with sufficient information to enable them to measure the performance of the treasury function in managing risk and to monitor compliance with policies, strategies, procedures and controls.

2.19 Auditors should be familiar with the limits to which the corporate treasury should adhere and the mechanisms by which the entity measures its compliance with those limits. Clearly if these limits are being breached then this may indicate that the entity is being exposed to a greater level of risk than that which senior management are willing to accept.

2.20 Some corporate treasuries operate a bonus system for treasury staff based on the value added to the services provided by the treasury. However, in a 'service centre' (see paragraph 2.5) treasury such a bonus scheme should not operate in such a way as to encourage the wrong behaviour by staff. Auditors consider the extent to which proper guidelines, limits and controls have been established to ascertain if the operation of any bonus system could result in transactions which are inconsistent with the overall objectives of the treasury function.

2.21 To safeguard against sudden falls in market values of derivative instruments, many entities use 'stop loss' limits. These limits require all speculative positions to be closed out immediately if the unrealised loss on those positions reaches a certain level. Equally, if the unrealised loss on the unhedged portion of the balance sheet reaches a certain level, they may require that the treasury department enter into hedging contracts to close the unhedged gap to an acceptable level. Clearly if these limits are being breached then this may indicate that the entity is being exposed to a greater level of risk than that which senior management are willing to accept.

2.22 Auditors undertaking a review of corporate treasury operations assess the above matters to help them in reaching a judgement as to the entity's attitude towards risk. This will impact on the audit approach adopted. To take an extreme example, it may be that the auditors conclude that management does not have a comprehensive understanding of the risks involved, that there are unclear policies or guidelines and that the corporate treasury is viewed as a potential profit enhancer. In this example, the auditors are likely to conclude, in the absence of any mitigating factors, that the corporate treasury is of high risk and would plan audit procedures accordingly.

3 Accounting and internal control systems

ACCOUNTING CONSIDERATIONS

3.1 The method of accounting used by an entity will impact specific audit procedures and is, therefore, of critical importance. Accounting for derivatives is usually driven by the purpose for which the transaction is entered into, specifically whether the transaction is for hedging or speculative purposes. The auditor therefore seeks to understand fully the purpose of the transaction when assessing the appropriateness of the accounting treatment adopted and its disclosure. Appendix 3 includes further consideration of accounting for derivatives in the light of current practice and auditing considerations in relation to the accounting treatment. The accounting treatment of derivatives is currently being considered by the Accounting Standards Board and if this results in changes in current practice, Appendix 3 may require updating.

ACCOUNTING SYSTEMS

3.2 The extent of an entity's use of derivatives and the relative complexity of the instruments are important determinants of the necessary level of sophistication of both the entity's accounting systems and internal control systems.

3.3 Certain instruments may require a large number of accounting entries. Ideally the accounting system should be able to post such entries accurately with only minimal manual intervention. When a corporate treasury expands the types of derivative transactions it enters into, however, its existing accounting systems may not be able to account properly for the new products. A separate accounting system focused specifically around the new product may be established. This could result in a complex corporate treasury running an accounting system using a wide variety of systems all developed or purchased at different times, which are not inter-linked, and which require a high degree of manual intervention.

3.4 Auditors obtain a clear overview of the strengths and weaknesses of the accounting systems. As sophistication within the corporate treasury increases then so should the sophistication of the accounting system. Because this is not always the case, auditors should be alert to the possible need to adapt their audit approach if they believe the quality of the accounting system, or aspects of it, is weak.

INTERNAL CONTROL SYSTEM

3.5 Auditors assess management's overall attitude towards and awareness of the corporate treasury activities in assessing the control environment. This was considered in the previous chapter.

3.6 A particular question which auditors face in reviewing corporate treasury activities is whether the general control environment extends to the corporate treasury. An entity may have a control culture which is generally very focused upon maintaining a high level of internal control. However, this culture may not pervade into the corporate treasury operation because management are unclear or uncertain about the activities of the treasury. Alternatively, because of the perception of the risks associated with the corporate treasury, it may be that management enforce a harsher control environment than they do elsewhere within the organisation.

CONTROL PROCEDURES

Effective internal control procedures over derivatives will generally include adequate segregation of duties, risk management monitoring, management oversight and other policies and procedures designed to ensure that: 3.7

- derivative transactions are executed in accordance with the entity's written policies as approved by the Board or its delegated sub-committee;
- information relating to derivatives is complete and accurate when entered into the accounting system;
- derivatives accounted for as hedges meet the applicable criteria for hedge accounting;
- changes in the value of derivatives are appropriately accounted for and disclosed to the right people both from an operational and a control viewpoint;
- misstatements in the processing of accounting information for derivatives are prevented or detected in a timely manner;
- derivative activities are monitored on an ongoing basis to recognise and measure events affecting related financial statement assertions; and
- information about derivatives in the financial statements is accurate and complete, and has been properly classified, described and disclosed.

The key risks arising from weaknesses in internal systems within the treasury activities include: 3.8

- limit systems and risk reporting procedures fail to monitor and control all exposures adequately;
- treasury dealers breach Board guidelines and expose the entity to unacceptable risks;
- treasury exposures and transactions are not completely and accurately captured by the reporting systems, resulting in 'hidden' exposures. The entity can be committed to sizable transactions over the telephone with no immediate cash flow impact;
- unauthorised payments are made, either in error or through deliberate act;
- deals are contracted at off-market rates, (other than controlled OTC contracts) either due to error or through fraudulent trading;
- disputes arise with counterparties over the existence, nature or terms of contracts;
- the accounting treatment of transactions is inconsistent with generally accepted accounting principles and the underlying substance of the transaction; and
- operational failures result in a failure to safeguard assets or claims against the entity.

The key components of control procedures that may be expected to be observed in a corporate treasury are discussed below. 3.9

ACCOUNTING AND PROCESSING CONTROLS

The dealing and transaction related activities of a corporate treasury can be compartmentalised into three categories: 3.10

- Dealing: responsible for committing the entity to the transaction;
- Settlements: responsible for initiating cash payments and receiving cash receipts; and
- Accounting: responsible for the correct recording of all transactions in the accounting records (including valuation).

3.11 It is important that there is adequate segregation of duties between these functions in order to avoid the potential for manipulation. For example, dealers or accounting staff should not also be responsible for both initiating settlements and checking confirmations. In some large treasuries adequate segregation is achieved but often, because of the small size of a treasury, it is not possible to achieve full segregation, although the finance and administrative functions can provide some segregation by undertaking certain tasks. Some of the key areas where segregation is very important are discussed below.

3.12 Before entering into transactions, dealers need to ensure that the transaction will not exceed the entity's exposure limits. For very large entities this normally requires systems with on-line access to real-time information as there will be transactions occurring constantly throughout the entity that are affecting its risk profile. Having established that the transaction is within limits, proper authorisation and initiation procedures normally provide for:

- dealers to carry out only transactions which have been approved by the treasurer or finance director unless they are small transactions within prescribed limits. Large 'one-off' transactions may require the approval of the Board;
- transactions to be initiated within the accounting system by a sequential deal ticket. The details on the deal tickets should be completed by the dealer who should input the deals into the system immediately upon execution;
- obtaining comparative prices from at least two counterparties to ensure that best execution procedures have been compiled with; and
- the taping of all phone calls and the time and date stamping of all deal tickets prior to them being transferred to the settlements area for checking and counterparty confirmation.

3.13 The deal initiation records maintained by any entity should be sufficient to identify the nature and purpose of individual transactions. This should include:

- the identity of the dealer;
- the time of the transaction;
- the nature and purpose of the transaction – whether it relates to an underlying commercial exposure or is speculative; and
- evidence that best execution procedures have been compiled with.

3.14 Ensuring that all transactions are accurately recorded is a key objective in controlling treasury activities. To achieve this, the entity needs to ensure that all transactions are recorded by the dealers and that all transactions recorded by the dealers are accurately reflected in the records of the entity.

3.15 The main control on the completeness of the dealers' records is the independent matching of counterparty confirmations against the entity's own records. Confirmations should be received directly by persons independent from the dealers, to guard against dealers suppressing confirmations and 'hiding' transactions, and all details should be checked off against the entity's records.

3.16 For larger entities, treasury operations often involve sophisticated IT systems to keep track of treasury activities and to ensure that settlements occur when due. The more complex IT systems may automatically generate postings to clearing accounts to monitor cash movements (e.g. on maturity of a forward foreign exchange deal the computer automatically posts entries to clearing accounts in the relevant currencies; these are then cleared by corresponding entries when the cash is posted to the bank accounts). Proper controls over processing will help to ensure that treasury activities are correctly reflected in the entity's records.

3.17 Derivatives by their very nature can involve the transfer of sizeable amounts of money both to and from the treasury. In many instances the system used will simply involve providing the bank with appropriate payment instructions or receipt notifications. Complex treasury operations that are heavily involved in derivatives may well, however, operate sophisticated electronic fund transfer systems. Such systems may involve complex password and verification controls, standard payment templates and cash pooling/sweeping facilities. The auditors will need to be aware of the methods used to transfer funds and their strengths and weaknesses as this will impact the risks the business is faced with and accordingly the audit risk assessment.

3.18 Regular reconciliations are an important aspect of controlling treasury systems. Formal reconciliations should be performed on a regular basis to ensure that the financial records are properly controlled, all entries are being promptly made, and the dealers (or treasurer) have adequate and accurate position information prior to formally committing the entity to a legally binding transaction. Reconciliations should be properly documented and independently reviewed. These should include:

- reconciliation of dealers' position sheets to the positions shown in the general ledger. Dealers should formally sign off their position report and review the reconciliations with their own records to ensure that they are properly recorded in the accounting system;
- reconciliation of subsidiary ledgers to the general ledger, for example, where subsidiary ledgers are maintained in different currencies or where treasury operations are on a separate system; and
- reconciliation of clearing and all bank accounts and broker statements to ensure all outstanding items are promptly identified and cleared.

THE ROLE OF INTERNAL AUDIT

3.19 As part of the assessment of the accounting system and control environment, auditors consider the role, if any, played by internal audit. The knowledge and skills required to understand and audit an entity's use of derivatives are generally quite different from those needed in auditing other parts of the business. Therefore, the internal audit function may not be sufficiently experienced in the use of derivatives to be able to perform its function effectively in this area. External auditors consider the extent to which the internal audit function has the skill and experience to cover, and has in fact covered, the treasury and derivative activities of the business.

3.20 The internal audit function should be an integral part of the internal controls operated by management in the treasury area. In many entities, it forms an essential part of the risk management function to enable senior management to review and evaluate the control processes over an entity's use of derivatives. The work performed by internal audit should be capable of providing assistance to the external auditors in assessing the control environment and control risk of the audit. Areas where the work performed by internal audit may be particularly relevant are:

- undertaking a general overview of treasury operations and the extent of their use of derivatives;
- reviewing the appropriateness of policies and procedures and management's compliance with them;
- reviewing the effectiveness of internal controls;
- reviewing treasury systems;
- ensuring that objectives for treasury management are fully understood across the entity, particularly where there are operating divisions where the risk exposures are most likely to arise; and
- conducting regular reviews to:

- provide senior management with an assurance that treasury operations are being properly controlled;
- ensure that new risks and the use of derivatives to manage these risks are being identified, assessed and managed;
- provide assurance that the accounting for derivatives is reliable.

CONTROL RISK

3.21 Having obtained an understanding of the accounting systems and control environment auditors consider whether they expect to rely on their assessment of control risk to reduce the level of substantive testing for this aspect of the entity's operations. Where this is the case, they first make a preliminary assessment of that control risk and document and assess those control procedures on which they expect to rely. Then they plan and perform tests of control to support that assessment. It may be the case in a smaller treasury operation that the auditors are unable to rely upon their assessment of control risk and a substantive approach may need to be adopted.

3.22 The auditors' assessment of control risk is highly subjective and will depend on their judgement as to the quality of the control procedures and of the risk management framework in place. In reaching a decision on the extent of testing the auditors consider factors such as:

- the importance of the derivative function to their overall opinion;
- materiality;
- the potential impact of any identified weaknesses in control procedures;
- the types of control being tested;
- the frequency of performance of these controls; and
- the evidence of performance.

3.23 One of the most critical aspects of an assessment of whether the control procedures can be relied upon in a corporate treasury transacting derivatives is whether there is adequate segregation of duties combined with the extent of management oversight. In more developed corporate treasury operations the level of segregation is often satisfactory. However, in smaller entities segregation is often inadequate and this may lead the auditors to question whether any of the control procedures over derivatives can be relied upon to reduce control risk.

3.24 Ultimately, a control system can only be an effective measure in addressing the risks inherent in derivative operations if it is maintained by individuals with appropriate knowledge and experience of derivative instruments. The auditors therefore seek assurance that the knowledge and experience of those involved in the treasury function is commensurate with the risks which the use of derivatives attracts.

3.25 In reaching a conclusion as to the likely effectiveness of the control procedures the auditors consider whether controls exist to ensure that all transactions entered into are appropriately captured and that the accounting records represent a complete picture of the entity's exposure.

4 Audit procedures

MATERIALITY

4.1 Materiality may be difficult to assess in relation to derivative transactions, particularly given some of their characteristics. Materiality cannot be based on balance sheet values as derivatives may have little impact on the balance sheet, even though significant risks may arise from them. Otherwise the application of materiality should follow the same principles as those applied to other transactions and balances.

USING THE WORK OF AN EXPERT

It is possible that the auditors may seek guidance or assistance from an expert in auditing a corporate treasury activity. This is more probable where the corporate treasury is involved in very sophisticated derivatives and the auditors may, for example, not have sufficient knowledge or capabilities to audit the value of these derivatives. Such an expert may be drawn from within the audit firm. In certain circumstances the auditors may request such an internal expert to undertake the audit of the whole of the corporate treasury activity. 4.2

In other circumstances (e.g., in relation to the valuation of certain complex instruments) the auditors may seek assistance from an external expert. Where the auditors determine that it will be necessary to rely on the work of an external expert then reference would be made to SAS 520 'Using the work of an expert', in determining the extent to which reliance may be placed on their work. 4.3

GOING CONCERN

When considering the directors' assessment of going concern, the auditors would be aware that derivatives could have a significant impact. The directors consider (among other factors) both the 'availability' risks (that the expected sources of funding for the business will not be available to meet the maximum expected funding requirements) and the 'financing' risks underlying the expected funding requirements (that the actual funding requirements are greater than expected). A key availability risk is that the facilities expected to be available as sources of funding are recalled due to a breach of financial or other covenants. The impact of derivatives trading on the likelihood of a breach of the covenants is therefore considered. 4.4

Key financing risks include the impact of movements in interest rates, foreign exchange rates and commodity prices on the derivatives held. The impact of margining on hedges may result in the cash-flows on hedges not matching the cash-flows on the underlying instrument as the margins require payment immediately whereas payment on the underlying instrument will only occur on maturity. This mismatch of cash flows could, in extreme circumstances, impact the entity's ability to continue as a going concern. If the entity uses esoteric instruments it is particularly important for the directors to understand the potential cash-flows. 4.5

ANALYTICAL PROCEDURES

The degree of reliance that auditors place on analytical procedures in the audit of derivatives is largely driven by the volume, complexity and diversity of derivatives used. To the extent that analytical procedures can be used in obtaining an understanding of the nature of operations and the source of revenues or costs, then it is a useful audit tool. In particular, review of non-financial data (e.g., trading volumes, numbers of unconfirmed transactions, etc.) can be beneficial. 4.6

It is often the case that personnel within a complex corporate treasury function compile a detailed analytical review of the results of the corporate treasury operations incorporating all derivative activity. They are able to capture the impact of derivative trading volumes and market price movements on the financial results of 4.7

the entity and compile such an analysis because of their detailed day to day involvement in the activities. This degree of involvement can obviously rarely be obtained by the auditors. Where such analysis is available, the auditors may seek to use it to further their understanding of the derivative activity undertaken by the entity. However, in doing so the auditors seek to satisfy themselves that the information has been correctly extracted from the underlying accounting records by persons sufficiently independent such that it represents a fair reflection of the operations.

4.8 Where no such analysis is compiled and the auditors wish to do so themselves the effectiveness of the analytical review often depends upon the degree to which management can provide detailed and desegregated information about the activities undertaken. Where such information is available, the auditors may be able to undertake a useful analytical review. If no such information is available then analytical review will only be effective as a means of explaining financial trends and relationships in simple, low volume environments.

4.9 This is because as volume and complexity of operations increase, unless detailed information is available, the factors impacting revenues and costs are such that meaningful analysis by the auditors often proves difficult and the value of analytical review as an audit tool decreases. Analytical review is not likely to identify incorrect accounting treatments and the complex interplay of the factors from which the values of these instruments are derived often masks any unusual trends which might arise. For example, if the value of an instrument is derived from an interplay of exchange rates (both spot and forward), interest rates or interest rate differentials or a combination of them and is further complicated by a degree of leveraging, then attempting to explain trends may not prove to be an efficient and effective audit procedure.

4.10 The role of analytical procedures as a substantive procedure in the audit of a corporate treasury function dealing in derivatives is limited. Analytical procedures will give information on the business but, by themselves, they are generally unlikely to provide sufficient evidence.

ASSERTIONS TO BE ADDRESSED

4.11 In performing detailed audit procedures, auditors seek to ensure that the following financial statement assertions are addressed by the tests which have been selected:

- **Existence**: the derivative transaction exists at a given date;
- **Rights and obligations**: the derivative transaction pertains to the entity at a given date;
- **Occurrence**: the derivative transaction was entered into by the entity during the relevant period, or that the reason for any change in status of the transaction (e.g., from a hedge to trading) is reasonable;
- **Completeness**: there are no unrecorded derivative transactions;
- **Valuation**: the derivative transaction is recorded as an appropriate carrying value;
- **Measurement**: the derivative transaction is recorded at the proper amount and revenue or expense is allocated to the proper period; and
- **Presentation and disclosure**: the derivative transaction is disclosed, classified and described in accordance with the applicable reporting framework (for example, relevant legislation and applicable accounting standards).

TESTS OF CONTROL

Where the auditors determine that they expect to place reliance on the accounting and internal control systems for derivatives they carry out tests to obtain evidence as to whether their assessment of control risk is supported. As noted above it is more likely that a sophisticated corporate treasury operation will lend itself to such an audit approach. Notwithstanding the auditors' assessment of the control environment, it may be the case that the entity only undertakes a limited number of derivatives transactions, or that the magnitude of these instruments is significant to the entity as a whole. In such instances a more substantive approach may be more appropriate. **4.12**

Tests of control seek to confirm that the controls, as described in the policies, procedures and guidelines or as discussed with senior management, are operating satisfactorily. Key procedures may include confirming, for a suitably sized sample of transactions, that: **4.13**

- derivatives have been used in line with the agreed policies, guidelines and within authority limits;
- the correct decision-making processes have been applied and the logic behind entering into selected transactions is clearly understandable;
- the transactions undertaken were bona fide within the terms of treasury limits and the mandates for undertaking business with the chosen counterparties;
- properly authorised confirmations have been sent;
- incoming confirmations from counterparties have been properly matched and reconciled;
- early termination of derivatives is controlled;
- switches between the hedging and trading portfolios are properly authorised;
- transactions have been completely and accurately recorded in the accounting records – correctly processed in any subledger through to the management accounts and financial statements;
- valuations have been correctly carried out. Checking that reconciliations are performed and reviewed on a regular basis is a key control in this regard.

The sample of items selected for detailed testing would not be limited to, say, the accounting records (which could comprise a PC spreadsheet program or simply manual records). At least part of the sample would be drawn from other sources so that the possibility of overlooking transactions in the recording procedure can be tested.

Appendix 1 sets out further examples of specific audit procedures that may be undertaken in testing the controls operated for each of the assertions in paragraph 4.11 above. The tests are not exhaustive, nor will they be relevant in all cases, and a significant degree of professional judgement will be required in determining which are relevant. Furthermore, the procedures specifically cover derivative operations and exclude general controls (for example, appropriate computer security and password access controls) which may exist in any operating environment. The auditors may also need to obtain evidence that general controls are operating satisfactorily. **4.14**

SUBSTANTIVE PROCEDURES

Substantive audit procedures would cover tests to confirm that the appropriate accounting treatments have been applied to derivative transactions undertaken (and matured) during the year and to those transactions that are still unmatured at the balance sheet date. **4.15**

4.16 To the extent that the treasury has entered into derivative transactions not directly related to the entity's underlying exposures, the auditors may wish to confirm that mark to market accounting has been correctly applied and that any resulting gains or losses have been correctly recorded in the profit and loss account. To the extent that treasury has entered into transactions as hedges and is applying hedge accounting, the auditors may wish to confirm that the transactions are indeed hedges. In such cases, the accounting treatment for the hedge will be in accordance with the accounting treatment of the underlying exposure.

4.17 Where auditors, for example, during their interim visit, discover that treasury has entered into or is planning to enter into derivatives or new instruments they may make enquiries to confirm that:

- it is logical for treasury to enter into such instruments;
- the treasurer, finance director and the board of directors appreciate all the risks associated with the instruments;
- in so far as the instruments impact the entity's banking covenants (and credit capacity), the covenant monitoring properly reflects the impact of the new instruments;
- proper limits have been put in place to keep the risks arising from using the instruments within acceptable levels;
- appropriate consideration has been given to the tax implications;
- the entity's accounting system can full reflect the substance of the transaction; and
- management reporting provides sufficient information to allow the use of and risk associated with the instruments to be fully understood.

4.18 If the auditors identify that the entity is not fully competent in the use of derivatives or that their use is not properly controlled, these matters should be brought to the attention of the Board.

4.19 Examples of substantive procedures that may be used in auditing derivatives activity are set out in Appendix 1. As noted earlier, substantive audit procedures are likely to be more important where transactions volumes are low or limited segregation of duties exists.

REVIEW OF DISCLOSURES

4.20 Management should aim to ensure that the disclosure of derivatives in the financial statements provides users with information to enhance their understanding of the significance of and treatment adopted in respect of derivative transactions.

4.21 The auditors therefore assess, inter alia:

- the completeness, accuracy and clarity of the disclosure of accounting policies for derivatives in the nates to the financial statements;
- the adequacy of disclosure to ensure that it is in full compliance with current disclosure requirements.

5 Audit completion considerations

5.1 Where management have made representations to the auditors in connection with derivative activities, these should be confirmed in writing to the auditors. Such representations might include:

- all trades have been recorded in the accounting records;
- the terms of all trades have not been amended by any side agreements;
- the value at which a transaction is recorded in the financial statements is, in the opinion of the directors, a fair value;
- all trades in derivatives are intra vires.

In undertaking normal subsequent event procedures, auditors may identify matters relating to derivatives activity, for which the potential impact on the financial statements should be considered. For example: 5.2

- open positions at the balance sheet date have deteriorated significantly and the contracts may soon require settlement resulting in material losses;
- the market value of, say, over-the-counter derivatives, has changed in a way which calls into question the validity of their earlier market value;
- information comes to light which indicates the situation on an underlying position, which was hedged, has changed, calling into question whether the derivative should be treated as a hedge in the changed circumstances.

There may be instances where information on the entity's derivative policies, procedures or activities is included in documents containing audited financial statements. Examples include: details of treasury policies disclosed in complying with the Cadbury Code; details of the impact on the financial results of losses resulting from derivative contracts; disclosures about treasury activities in the Operating and Financial Review or directors' report. Where such disclosures are made, auditors should review them for misstatements and/or inconsistencies. There is often a desire for brevity in such documents and auditors should assess, particularly given the complexity of derivatives, whether this has resulted in the relevant statements being diluted to a level where misstatements and/or inconsistencies arise. 5.3

The auditors consider deficiencies in internal control and/or errors identified (including those relating to derivatives) and, where appropriate report these to senior management. In the event that appropriate action is not taken by management, and in the case of matters of sufficient importance, the auditors should bring them to the attention of the Board. 5.4

Appendix 1 – Possible detailed audit tests

This appendix sets out a number of suggested tests. In practice alternative tests may be used providing they address relevant audit assertions.

For 'assertions addressed', see paragraph 4.11 of this Release.

COMPLIANCE TESTING

	Assertions addressed						
	a	b	c	d	e	f	g

Controls that may be relevant to determining the integrity of the operating systems that may be tested include:

- Adequate segregation of duties exists between:
  - deal initiation
  - processing and validation
  - valuation of open positions
  - accounting and management reporting
- Deal tickets are only processed where evidenced by authorised employees, within individual authority limits and within other limits defined by senior management.
- Access to deal making system and related records is restricted.
- Confirmations are issued for all contracts entered into.
- Incoming confirmations are received by an independent department and agreed to internal records. Discrepancies are resolved promptly.
- Dealing records are reconciled periodically to external records such as bank and broker statements as well as general ledger accounts and discrepancies promptly resolved.
- All transactions are promptly and accurately processed.
- Appropriate cut-off procedures exist to ensure complete and accurate processing in the proper period.
- All excesses over authorised positions are reported and approved or actioned by senior management.
- Trading limits are regularly reviewed by management for adequacy.

Payment and receipt

- Access to settlement systems and related records is restricted.
- Disbursement of funds is only effected after suitable authorisation procedures have been effected.
- Receipts of funds are properly identified and listed immediately upon receipt and matched to operating records or queried.
- Bank account reconciliations are promptly performed and reviewed and reconciling items followed up. Management review is undertaken.

	Assertions addressed						
	a	b	c	d	e	f	g

Positions

- Management review of reconciliations between dealing records and general ledger accounts is regularly performed.
- Appropriate review and reconciliation of suspense and clearing account balances is undertaken.
- Dealer sign off of profit and loss and position records is performed regularly.
- Open positions are regularly independently valued and reviewed by management.
- Valuation models are independently reviewed and approved by management.
- Inputs to valuation models are independently verified.
- Accounting treatment is formally considered and approved by management.

SUBSTANTIVE TESTING

- For selected derivative contracts made during the year, obtain deal slips and ensure:
    - deal was approved by trader
    - deal was within bank customer and trading limits (or excess approved)
    - deal slip agrees with general ledger
    - details agree with outward and inward confirmations
    - purpose of deal is appropriately documented (e.g., trading or hedging)
    - legal contract and support (if appropriate) are obtained subsequently.
- Obtain a listing of outstanding derivative contracts at period end and:
    - agree to general ledger and dealers' position records
    - review rates used in valuing positions in light of market rates
    - recalculate contract valuations
    - check profit and loss calculation
    - ensure valuations are only applied to relevant contracts (e.g., hedge contracts should be valued on the same basis as the underlying asset or liability being hedged)
    - trace recording of gains and losses to the general ledger.

| | Assertions addressed |
	a	b	c	d	e	f	g

- Obtain reconciliation of dealers' records to the general ledger and:
    - test mathematical accuracy
    - trace amounts to appropriate sources
    - investigate large or unusual reconciling items
- Obtain dealers records and:
    - test mathematical accuracy
    - trace amounts to appropriate sources e.g., inward confirmations, sub systems
    - investigate large or unusual reconciling items.
- Circularise counterparties and perform appropriate follow up procedures.
- Review reconciliations to brokers statements and follow up any reconciling items.
- Review year end bank account reconciliations and consider need for cut-off adjustments.
- Review sequence of deal tickets to ensure correct cut-off adjustments.
- Review sequence of deal tickets to ensure correct cut-off respected.
- Analyse significant suspense accounts.

Analytical procedures

- Explain movements and investigate any unexpected or unusual relationships between current year, prior year and budgeted amounts for open contracts by:
    - type of contract
    - purpose
    - notional principal
    - nature of counterparties
- Analyse occurrence, ageing and volume of reconciling items.
- Review volume and value of transactions comprising suspense and exception accounts.
- Analyse profit and loss by product type. Consider success of hedging strategy.

Appendix 2 – Aide memoire

This aide memoire incorporates a number of pertinent questions relating to derivative activities which may assist the auditor in planning and undertaking the audit of a business which engages in such activities. It needs to be recognised that in practice alternative questions may be used. It is not necessarily a complete list of factors and questions to consider – the auditor needs to apply his judgment in addressing factors which may be relevant in the circumstances.

RISK IDENTIFICATION

Inherent risks

Are there any factors relating to the business which indicate higher than normal audit risk, such as: 1

- unexpected or rapid growth in an entity's use of derivatives;
- significant use of derivatives with no relevant expertise: or dependence on one individual for all organisational expertise on derivatives activities;
- large one-off transactions where the purpose of the derivative is unclear or ill defined;
- little involvement by senior management or the Board in authorising, monitoring and controlling derivative activities;
- failure to segregate adequately duties involving the execution of derivative transactions;
- high volatility in interest rates, currencies or other factors affecting the value of derivatives;
- inclusion of embedded options or other complex (and volatile) contractual terms;
- uncertainty regarding the financial stability of a counterparty;
- concentrations of credit risk with one counterparty; and
- inadequate information to monitor effectively derivatives transactions, (including inadequate or untimely information about the market value of derivative instruments)?

a. What procedures has management implemented to identify, monitor and report all the key derivative risks faced by the entity? Who is primarily responsible for this function? 2
b. What are the entity's key exposures to the following risks:
   - foreign exchange risk;
   - interest rate risk;
   - credit risk;
   - liquidity risk; and
   - legal risk?
c. Does senior management understand the effect of significant market movements on the entity's financial position?

Operational (or control) risk

a. What is the entity's philosophy / objectives in relation to treasury activities, including the attitude towards speculation. Is the treasury activity regarded as a profit centre? How does the treasury department fit into the entity's overall operations? 3
b. What are the entity's guidelines for the use of treasury products? Are these clearly documented and circulated to personnel?
c. Who is responsible for reviewing treasury guidelines? Do amendments require approval from the Board?
d. How does senior management ensure that adequate procedures are in place to:
   - capture;
   - record;
   - settle;
   - account for; and
   - report and monitor?
e. Are dealing limits established independently from the treasury department and approved by the Board?

f. What trading limits are established for:
    - exposure to any one individual, entity, financial institution or group of entities;
    - exposure to particular countries;
    - the total open foreign exchange position allowed during the day and overnight for:
        - each currency; and
        - all currencies;
    - total interest mismatch which is permitted (e.g. between fixed and floating or between different interest bases);
    - forward gaps between expected available funds/rates and contracted commitments for:
        - liquidity;
        - interest rates; and
        - exchange rates;
    - amounts and instruments with which each trader is authorised to deal?
g. What codes of conduct exist in relation to matters such as personal trading on their own behalf through the entity's approved counterparties? Are these codes approved by the Board and clearly documented?

CONTROL ENVIRONMENT

4   a. Has the Board established a clear and internally consistent risk management policy, including risk limits (as appropriate)?
    b. Are management's strategies and implementation policies consistent with the Board's authorisation?
    c. Do key controls exist to ensure that only authorised transactions take place and that unauthorised transactions are quickly detected and appropriate action is taken?
    d. What are the entity's risk exposures and are they commensurate with the entity's objectives?
    e. Are personnel with authority to engage in and monitor derivative transactions well qualified and appropriately trained?
    f. Do the right people have the right information to make the right decisions?

MANAGEMENT INFORMATION

5   a. What are the reporting mechanisms to ensure that executive management and the Board are kept informed of treasury activities and adherence to Board guidelines?
    b. Are summary reports produced for:
        - liquidity (maturity gap / mismatch position);
        - interest rate gap;
        - dealing positions (currency and interest rate management);
        - exposure to counterparties?
    c. Are open positions regularly 'marked to market' (MtM)?
        Points to consider in relation to the MtM valuation of open positions:
        i) What procedures exist to ensure that all treasury positions are marked to market at regular intervals? Are these valuations:
            - sufficiently frequent;
            - performed by persons independent from the dealing function; and
            - accurately compiled, based on prevailing market rates?
        ii) What are the established procedures for obtaining rates for valuations? If the rates are obtained from the dealing room, are they independently checked?

iii) Is the MtM valuation formally reviewed and approved by senior management? What procedures are used to ensure that the valuations are properly compiled?
iv) Outline the stop loss limits established by senior management in relation to treasury exposures. How does management monitor adherence to these limits?
v) Does the entity account for hedging transactions separately from trading transactions? Where some hedging transactions are not revalued, how does executive management ensure that only the relevant transactions are revalued?
vi) Are complex derivative transactions properly analysed and an accurate valuation procedure put in place before being deemed appropriate for the entity?

d. Is the information presented to management / the Board in an easily understandable format, highlighting major exposures and any breaches of Board guidelines? Is this information presented on a timely basis?
e. How does management ensure that the information contained in reports it receives is accurate and complete?
f. How are transactions in excess of established limits promptly identified? Is this task performed and approved by senior management independent from the treasury function?
g. What action is initiated as a result of identifying breaches of limits? For example:
- how are breaches advised to the Board;
- are records kept of which traders are responsible for breaches;
- is suitable disciplinary action initiated if warranted; and
- do breaches require post-fact approval by the Board, together with an action plan for rectifying the position?

TRANSACTION AUTHORISATION PROCEDURES

a. Prior to committing the entity to a transaction how does the dealer ensure that exposure limits will not be exceeded?
b. How are treasury transactions authorised (e.g. through dealers initialling deal slips)?
c. What independent review of treasury transactions is carried out to ensure that they appear bona fide (e.g. independent review of deal slips for reasonableness / proximity to prevailing market rates)?
d. How are alterations to deal slips authorised (e.g. are dealers required to countersign all copies of the deal slip)?
e. How does the entity confirm and formally evidence trades with third parties? For instance:
- are standard confirmation letters and, where necessary, pro-forma contracts, used for all standard deals;
- what procedures are established for authorising contracts for non-standard deals; and
- are confirmation letters raised and sent to all counterparties by staff independent from the dealing room?
f. What procedures exist to safeguard the entity against disputes or third parties falsely claiming to have entered into deals?

OVERALL ACCOUNTING AND PROCESSING CONTROLS

a. What is the structure of the treasury department, including accounting and settlement responsibilities?

b. Are the following duties performed by separate departments:
   - trading;
   - operations / settlements; and
   - accounting / reconciliations?
c. How does the entity ensure that all treasury transactions entered into are properly recorded? For instance:
   - use of sequentially numbered deal slips;
   - regular monitoring of the issuance of deal slips; and/or
   - daily check on the sequence of deal slips completed against IT records by a person independent of the dealers to ensure that all deals have been processed.
d. What procedures exist to check confirmation letters received from counterparties to the entity's own records? Is this task performed by persons independent from the dealing function? How are discrepancies resolved?
e. What procedures exist to monitor non-receipt of counterparty confirmations by persons independent from the dealing function? How are non-receipts followed up?
f. Where telephone confirmations are received is this appropriately evidenced?
g. What systems exist to clearly distinguish between hedging trades and speculative trades (i.e. is the nature of the deal identified on the deal slip at the time of the trade)?

COMPUTER INPUT PROCESSING

8   a. What controls exist to ensure that all transactions are properly entered into the IT system? For example:
   - are deal slips checked on a one for one basis against daily transaction reports; and
   - are dealers' own position sheets reconciled on a regular basis to the accounting records?
b. Where clearing accounts are used to match receipts and payments, what procedures exist to ensure that these accounts are adequately monitored and that outstanding items are properly investigated and cleared on a timely basis? For example:
   - are outstanding items identified and appropriately investigated by persons independent from the dealing and settlement functions; and
   - do senior management regularly review the clearing account to ensure all outstanding items are being properly identified and cleared?
c. Where treasury activities are recorded in subsidiary ledgers, are these ledgers reconciled to the general ledger on a regular basis? Are the persons performing these reconciliations independent from the persons responsible for the original postings to the general ledger?

INTERNAL AUDIT

9   Does the internal audit function:

a. perform reviews of the derivative operations with appropriate frequency?
b. have personnel with sufficient skill and experience?
c. have special procedures for reviewing new products and activities?

10   Based on the above considerations, what is the impact of the work performed by internal audit and can certain parts of the work be relied upon in determining the nature, extent and timing of audit testing in the derivatives area?

ANALYTICAL REVIEW

Auditors might consider some of the following procedures in their analytical review of the financial exposures, both firm and anticipated, for current and future periods together with the level of cover (ie hedging) in place. 11

a. In respect of foreign exchange exposures:
   - comparison of the level of cover with the total firm and anticipated exposures;
   - review the extent to which hedging activity is carried out on a gross or net basis. The effect could be that only one side of an exposure is hedged and thus the total exposures could be increased rather than decreased by hedging actions. For example, hedging of only one side of the exposure could leave a larger exposure than the original net position;
   - comparison of the average exchange rate cover in each of the relevant years to budgeted rates, the rates at the previous year end and the rate at which the underlying exposure is profitable;
   - reviewing the foreign exchange losses and gains arising on the maturity of contracts;
   - reviewing the extent to which contracts are rolled over to future accounting periods and the rate at which contracts are rolled over. This may provide evidence on any use of 'cherry picking' (see Appendix 3);
   - comparison of the mark to market position on the exposures on a monthly and yearly basis.
b. For interest rate exposures:
   - comparison of fixed and floating rate percentages;
   - review of actual and forecast positions, by currency and by underlying interest rate exposures and the impact of interest rate swaps, collars and caps in place;
   - review of maturity analysis of debt and investments and the extent to which the year end positions are sensitive to interest rate movements.
c. Comparison of any trading/speculative positions and stop loss positions against the limits established by senior management and the extent to which any have been breached during the period under review.

Appendix 3 – Accounting for derivatives and audit considerations

HEDGING TRANSACTIONS

Hedging transactions are entered into to reduce, match or eliminate a substantial portion of the risk exposures which may affect: 1

- the value of assets and liabilities recorded in the balance sheet;
- the revenue or expenses arising from existing assets and liabilities;
- the value of commitments or contingent assets or liabilities at the balance sheet date;
- the proceeds or cost of future transactions which can be anticipated with reasonable certainty;
- the value of other cashflows anticipated (eg intragroup dividends).

The accounting treatment adopted for derivatives should reflect the substance of the transaction rather than its legal form. Accordingly, it is appropriate to account for the underlying item being hedged together with the hedge transactions as a whole, rather than to reflect the legal form of the hedge transaction in isolation. For 2 example, an entity may, instead of borrowing a fixed rate loan, achieve the same effect through a floating rate loan with an interest rate swap. Incorporating the terms of the interest rate swap into those of the floating rate loan will result in appropriate consistency of revenue recognition. Simple examples of hedging foreign exchange, interest rate and commodity exposures using forwards, options, swaps and futures are set out below for illustrative purposes.

3   To the extent they are involved in options at all, corporate treasuries are normally buyers of put options, although some large participants may sell options as part of their foreign exchange management strategies. It is important to appreciate the difference between buying options and selling options. If an entity buys, say, a put option then the maximum amount it can lose is the premium it has paid. If, instead, it writes a put option, it gives the other party the right to sell the underlying asset to it in the future at a fixed rate specified in the option. Consequently the amount of loss that can be suffered is potentially unlimited. If a corporate treasury is a seller of options then its risk profile is likely to be higher than one that is not, because the potential for loss by the entity is greater.

> *Example 1: Foreign exchange hedging*
>
> A UK exporter to the US expects to receive payment for goods (US$10 million) in a year's time. The built-in profit margin of the underlying contract has been evaluated at a rate of $1.55 = £1. The current spot rate is $1.52 and the one year forward rate is $1.50. This transaction can be hedged using a wide range of strategies, the simpler ones of which include:
>
> - sell the US$ forward (using a foreign exchange contract) for delivery in one year when the cash is received from the customer;
> - buy a put option (currency option) to sell the US$ in one year's time at the current forward rate; or
> - do not hedge, sell the US$ for the spot rate one year from now.
>
> With a forward deal, the entity is committed to buying or selling foreign currency in the future at a rate which is fixed now and the profit margin in the underlying commercial contract may therefore be 'locked in'. There is no up front payment required when the deal is entered into. At inception, the transaction is recorded 'off balance sheet' as a commitment to sell $10m for £6.67m in a year's time. On receipt of the $10m in a year's time, the money is converted into sterling at $1.50 and the total profit on the underlying contract (including the foreign exchange effects) is accounted for at that date.
>
> Forward deals may be more suitable when the exposure to be hedged is a firm commitment. Options are more often used as a way of hedging contingent exposures where there is a large amount of uncertainty. For example, if the above exposure represented an export order which did not materialise and the exchange rate in a year's time was in fact, $1.35 = £1, the bank would pay the entity £6.67m ($10m at $1.50). The entity, however, does not have any dollars to sell, so it has to buy them in the spot market for £7.41m ($10m at $1.35). The entity has therefore made a loss of £740,000 and hedging, which was supposed to reduce risk, has in fact increased it.
>
> Options can be regarded as an insurance policy which cap the downside risk and enable the entity to benefit from favourable exchange rate movements since there is no obligation to deal at the guaranteed rate (of $1.50). As with any insurance policy, there is a premium cost which is paid as an up front payment at inception.

This premium is commonly deferred and brought to account when the underlying exposure (ie $10m) is received.

If the rate is above $1.50 when the US$10m is received, the entity will exercise the option to sell the dollars at $1.50; on the other hand, if the rate is below $1.50, the entity will allow the option to lapse and deal at the spot rate.

Hedging using options can be expensive in terms of premiums and in recent years various types of options (cylinder, barrier, knock-out options, to name but a few) have emerged to hedge future exposures but which are not as expensive in premium cost but limit the upside benefit from favourable rate movements.

Example 2: Interest rate hedging

A small entity, which does not have the financial standing to access the fixed rate markets, currently has long term floating rate debt priced at LIBOR + 0.25%. It wishes to swap into fixed rate as it wants to eliminate its exposure to interest rate volatility. It believes that now would be a good time to arrange the swap as its expectation is that interest rates will rise during the remaining life of the debt. Its bank offers a swap on the following terms:

- the entity pays a fixed rate of 9% through the swap; and
- it receives floating rate interest at LIBOR.

When interest on the existing long term is included, the entity's interest flows are as follows:

- pays   (9.0%)
- receives   LIBOR
- pays   (LIBOR + 0.25%)
- net effect: pays fixed   (9.25%)

On the other hand, a large plc has a fixed rate debt priced at 8% which it wishes to swap to a floating rate basis. The bank offers the entity a swap on the following basis:

- the entity receives 9%
- the entity pays LIBOR + 0.25%

When interest on the entity's existing debt is included, the entity's interest flows are as follows:

- pays   (8.0%)
- receives   9.0%
- pays   (LIBOR + 0.25%)
- net effect: pays floating   LIBOR 2 0.75%

Through the swap mechanism, the entity has both achieved floating rate status for the funding and achieved an overall interest rate which is lower than that which it would have had to pay if it had funded itself directly with the floating rate debt.

An interest rate swap has a mark to market value that can be determined at any time based on prevailing market interest rates. However, in practice, at an intervening balance sheet date the accounting treatment of a swap reflects the accounting treatment of the underlying borrowing to which it relates. In so far as it is not normal to revalue borrowings to a market valuation, it is not normal to revalue an associated interest rate swap either.

Swaps are generally used to fix interest rates for the medium to long term while forward rate agreements (FRA's) are used to fix a rate for one specific period in the future. For example, they could be used to fix the LIBOR fr a loan rollover starting in three months' time. Caps and floors are used when borrowers/investors want some protection but, at the same time, want to retain flexibility to take advantage of movements in interest rates. Unlike swaps and FRA's, caps and floors have a cost which is normally payable up-front. Collars are used to protect borrowers and investors from rate movements over a predetermined range of rates.

Example 3: Commodity hedging in the futures market

A producer of oil is exposed to movements in the price of oil. By selling some of the expected oil production in future months, at times when the prices in the futures market are acceptable, the entity can lock in margins at acceptable levels. Of course, if oil prices rise further the entity would make an opportunity 'loss' on these future derivative trades. Alternatively, the entity may decide to leave its oil revenue exposed to oil price movements on the spot market.

Similar considerations apply to the hedging of raw material prices and entities with large exposures to commodity prices. For example, a gold mining entity can use a wide variety of future and option instruments to hedge its exposures and reduce the impact of fluctuations in gold prices on its profitability and cash flow. Realised and unrealised gains and losses on commodity futures contracts and options are normally deferred and recorded as stock/income in the period in which the purchase or sale occurs.

4   It is important to note that many hedges are imperfect. The identification of whether a transaction constitutes a hedge, and should therefore be accounted for on a consistent basis to the underlying exposure, is a matter of judgement, which auditors assess by considering factors such as:

- the motivation for the transaction and evidence to support the classification from the time of inception of the transaction;
- the degree of certainty, including the nature, pattern, volume and frequency of the entity's hedging transactions;
- the correlation between the 'hedge' and the underlying exposure.

5   The classification of derivative transactions as hedges or speculative should be adopted on a consistent basis between periods and across the range of transactions entered into by the entity. Where the transaction is considered to be for hedging purposes, auditors assess for each financial period being reported on the continued appropriateness of classification of the derivative transaction as a hedge. This involves a review of changes in the underlying exposure, of the new hedge transactions undertaken during the period and of the continued effectiveness of the derivative in reducing the risk exposure.

6   Where the hedged amounts exceed the underlying exposures then the excess should be accounted for as a speculative transaction. Difficulty can arise when the hedge in place and the underlying exposure do not relate to the same accounting period. Many entities adopt a portfolio approach and treat the hedge as a book providing

cover for a period of years and will roll over the hedge as and when required. The auditors are alerted to the possibility of 'cherry picking' by management in reviewing the effectiveness of the hedging transactions in place at the year end. The concept of cherry picking is best explained by using an example.

> **Example 4: Cherry picking**
>
> Assume that an entity has entered into a series of currency hedges and that approaching the entity's financial year end some of these hedges are standing at a profit and some are standing at a loss. If the entity is seeking to report higher profits in the current period, it might close the hedges that are standing at a profit and replace them with new hedges before the year end. The new hedges will be at rates which reduce the future profits locked in. The entity might then argue that the profits realised on closing out the hedges should be brought to account in the current period's profit and loss account while the new hedges ('less profitable' in the future) and the 'loss making' hedges (not 'cherry picked' for realisation before the year end) will be deferred until the underlying positions reach maturity. The correct treatment for any profits or losses realised on closing out a hedge prior to maturity of the underlying transaction should, however, be to defer them and to recognise them in line with the profits or losses on the underlying transactions.
>
> The position may be even more complex where the hedges were taken against a basket of exposures maturing beyond the year end and where the true exposures are now believed to be lower than the level of such exposures originally hedged. The realisation of some of the hedges (to reduce the hedge cover to an appropriately lower level) may result in the realisation of profitable hedges whilst unprofitable hedges (taken out at a different time in relation to the same basket of exposures) are not realised. Again, it would not be appropriate to recognise the profits while deferring the losses and some 'portfolio' approach which recognises the 'fungible' nature of the hedge contracts (both realised and unrealised) might be more appropriate.

If cherry picking has been identified, perhaps the key questions are: why has the entity resorted to the technique; is it indicative of more fundamental problems; and what are the accounting implications – for example, recognising realised profits up front (rather than over a period) while deferring realised losses to the future? This is a very difficult matter. The auditor considers whether proper documentation was established by an entity when it entered into each hedge transaction. This would support the intent of management at the time that the trades were entered into and would make later cherry picking much harder. 7

SPECULATIVE TRANSACTIONS

Transactions may be entered into for speculative purposes or may become speculative, due to changes either in the underlying exposures or in the effectiveness of the derivative transactions in eliminating a substantial proportion of the risk (see Example 1 above). Consideration may need to be given to whether such transactions are permitted by the entity's constitution. 8

Where transactions are speculative or no longer provide an effective hedge, hedge accounting will not be appropriate and the accounts should reflect any diminution in value of the derivative transactions. Where the alternative accounting rules permitted under the Companies Act (Sch 4) have been applied then entities may recognise both profits and losses arising on marking transactions to market. 9

10 Where transactions are classified as speculative the auditor will assess the appropriateness of the market value. Market value testing may not be required if all derivatives are accounted for using hedge accounting.

VALUATIONS

11 Derivatives are unlike many other types of asset or liability in the extent to which their value can fluctuate significantly in a very short space of time. Further, because of the nature of some types of derivative instruments, very significant gains or losses can result from a relatively modest initial outlay (for example, where trading in certain options or futures occurs). Where an entity is exposed to treasury risks it is therefore essential that this exposure is monitored through valuing positions to reflect prevailing market conditions; this procedure is known either as 'marking to market' or, increasingly, as determining the 'fair value' of a transaction. Fair value is the amount at which the instrument underlying the transaction would be exchanged in an arm's length transaction between a willing buyer and seller (i.e., quoted market prices where available).

12 Determining fair value is an essential early warning system to compare exposures against limits and to consider whether hedges are badly constructed and/or if the risks are misunderstood. Some entities argue that, in respect of hedged transactions, they do not need to calculate fair value on the basis that the resulting profit or loss is not relevant or it is negligible. Experience has, however, shown that many losses incurred in derivatives have resulted from positions which were supposedly hedged, yet imperfections in the hedge were not detected because of the use of hedge accounting for management reporting. Determining fair value is generally regarded as the appropriate method of monitoring derivatives instruments for internal reporting purposes, regardless of the method used by the entity to report in its external financial statements.

13 The G30 Report (see also Appendix 4) on derivatives recommended that end-users (including entities) should determine the fair value of their derivative portfolios on a regular basis for risk management purposes and should measure the performance and effectiveness of the hedge. Depending on the size of the entity and the complexity of the treasury department, this may be daily, weekly or monthly.

14 For certain derivative products reliable market prices might not be available, in which case alternative means of valuing the products are commonly used (e.g. through computer modelling, or through obtaining quotes from market specialists). Management should ensure that reliable and consistent market sources are used as the basis for the valuation of open positions.

15 An entity will have to undertake different procedures depending upon whether it is hedge accounting or using fair value to record its derivative transactions. Auditors seek not only to ensure that the appropriate method of accounting is being applied but also to apply different audit tests depending upon the method adopted.

Appendix 4 – Relevant sources of accounting and other guidance

Set out below is a list of the authoritative sources that contains guidance on internal controls, accounting and disclosure for derivative transactions. Some of the guidance is not written for non-financial users of derivatives but the principles set out may provide useful information to the auditor in performing his work.

ACCOUNTING TREATMENT AND DISCLOSURE

Accounting Standards

FRS 4   Capital Instruments – addresses accounting treatments and disclosures for the issuers of capital instruments.

FRS 5   Reporting the Substance of Transactions – whilst most derivative contracts are excluded from the scope, the standard provides guidance on the fundamental principles when determining the substance of transactions and the appropriate disclosures.

SSAP 20   Foreign Currency Translation provides guidance on translation of foreign currencies but does not address the treatment of currency dealing profits.

Discussion Paper   Derivatives and other financial instruments

STATEMENTS OF RECOMMENDED PRACTICE

The following SORPs are issued by the British Bankers' Association and provide guidance as to how accounting standards can best be interpreted in the circumstances of a bank. They may however provide relevant guidance in other environments.

The SORP on 'Derivatives' and 'Contingent Liabilities and Commitments' provides guidance on valuation, and income recognition as well as disclosure for derivative contracts.

The SORP on 'Securities', whilst not specifically relating to derivatives provides useful guidance on valuation considerations and the distinction between investment assets carried at cost and trading assets which are carried at market value.

INTERNATIONAL ACCOUNTING STANDARDS

IAS 25   Accounting for Investments lays down guidance on the classification, accounting treatment and disclosure in respect of current and fixed asset investments.

IAS 32   Financial instruments and Disclosure lays down guidance on the presentation and disclosure of on and off balance sheet instruments and the related risks and controls.

OTHER GUIDANCE

The Group of Thirty: Derivatives Practices and Principles ('The G30 Report').

This report was published in July 1993 and made 20 recommendations to help dealers and end-users manage derivatives. It also contains an overview of derivatives activities that explains what derivatives are, the needs they serve, their risks and their relationship to traditional financial instruments. The G30 report, whilst primarily aimed at market professionals, is the most authoritative statement issued to date on best practice in the derivatives area.

The Future and Options Association: Managing Derivatives Risk – guidelines for end-users.

The guidance was published in December 1995 and provides guidance to end-users on risk management for derivatives. It sets out six core principles which the FOA consider important for end-users to consider and embrace in relation to risk management for derivatives.

'Banks – an accounting and auditing guide' – ICAEW

'The Business of Finance' guides published by the Association of Corporate Treasurers, including:

- Derivatives for Directors (published in association with the Institute of Chartered Accountants of Scotland)
- Risk Management and Control of Derivatives
- Financial Risk and Internal Control: Guidance for non-financial corporations

COSO report on 'Internal control issues in derivatives and usage; an information tool for considering the COSO Internal control-integrated framework in derivatives applications' report'.

[Statement 917]
Receipt of information in confidence by auditors (AUDIT 2/99)

(Issued November 1999)

Introduction

It is in the interest of auditors and their clients as well as the entire financial community for accurate, timely and honest information to be available to auditors, from whatever source. It is therefore in the public interest for there to be a general business climate which encourages the open disclosure of financial information to auditors, whether in response to auditors enquiries or on an unsolicited basis. Chartered Accountants should encourage the development of such a climate, both by their reactions as auditors in the receipt of such information and as management, in setting the corporate tone of organisations.

Current professional guidance on the ethics of the disclosure and use of confidential information is contained in the Guide to Professional Ethics and in particular in Handbook Statement **1.205**. This Guidance has been developed to provide additional assistance in the resolution of ethical problems that may arise where auditors receive information from any source, with a request or the implication that the information or its source should be kept confidential. Such circumstances may arise in relation to information received from regulators, from employees or from third parties such as trading partners. Auditors may show this Guidance to clients' management or staff, where this would assist in clarifying the auditors' position, or to any person indicating that they wish to pass on sensitive information.

There is a certain minimum standard of behaviour that should be adhered to by auditors at all times. This may be summarised as follows:

- Auditors should at all times act with integrity;
- Auditors should take into account relevant guidance and any obligations they have under the law;
- Auditors should use their best endeavours to protect the identity of informants;
- Auditors should assess the information received, taking into account any steps taken by the informant; and
- Auditors should consider significant issues raised by informants, in relation to their audit.

Auditors are not obliged to follow up matters if they are satisfied, on the basis of the information available to them, that they are not relevant to their role as auditors. Relevant law and guidance may include that applying in the country where the client or informant is based, as well as in the UK.

Where information is given to the auditors by an employee of the client (including a director), this may be particularly sensitive since the informant's future employment prospects may be affected, though the position of employees has been strengthened by the bringing into force of the Public Interest Disclosure Act 1998. Employees should be advised to report their concerns through their firm's usual procedures, where they can do so without fear of victimisation or concealment of evidence, and where they have not yet done so. They may also be advised as to the appropriate external authority to which a report might be made.

5 The Act enables employees to claim unlimited compensation if they are dismissed or otherwise disadvantaged following a disclosure which comes within certain defined categories, known as protected disclosures. Although the Act does not specifically cover the particular case of disclosure to an external auditor, qualifying disclosures will include those made to auditors in accordance with the employer's laid down procedures and in those circumstances where disclosure to any appropriate third party is protected. These will cover most significant unauthorised disclosures to auditors. Further information on the terms of the Public Interest Disclosure Act and its implications for employers is contained in Technical Release 17/99.

Investigation

6 The receipt of any substantive information by auditors will put them on notice. As a minimum, careful consideration will need to be given to the implications of the disclosure for the audit. If additional tests and enquiries are necessary, they should be carried out with discretion. Auditors should, wherever possible, conduct their enquiries in a way that does not reveal the source of their information. Tests which do so should be used only as a last resort. This will not only help protect the informant, but will also increase the chances of auditors being able to perform their tests without action being taken to conceal or obscure the true position.

7 It will also be remembered that:

- auditors may also be required to report their findings or suspicions to third parties such as regulators (under the duty to report matters of material significance to regulators in the financial sector) or the criminal authorities (where money laundering is suspected); and
- in the case of suspected money laundering, any action which may result in 'tipping off' the perpetrator is a criminal offence.

8 Two Statements of Auditing Standards, numbers 110 – *Fraud and Error* and 120 – *Consideration of Law and Regulation* (SAS 110 and SAS 120), lay down requirements for the discussion of suspected non-compliance with law and regulation, error or fraudulent conduct with an appropriate level of management and its communication to the Board or other appropriate body. These requirements do not indicate that the procedures used or information obtained by the auditors in forming their suspicions need be disclosed to management. So far as is possible, it will be in the interests both of an effective audit and of informants that details of tests and procedures are not made known to management as well as the fact that confidential information has been received. The source of information given in good faith should not be revealed without the agreement of the informant.

9 In some cases, information given to auditors will be vague or imprecise, making it difficult to act upon. So far as is possible, the auditors should seek to persuade the informant to clarify the details of their concern. The fact that little practical benefit will result if the auditors are given inadequate information to enable them to follow up disclosures should be explained, and it made clear to informants that whatever their motives for making the disclosure, the desired outcome is unlikely to be achieved if details are withheld.

Auditors should receive all disclosures in a proper spirit of professional scepticism. In some cases information may be received which the auditor judges to be unfounded or irrelevant to the audit.

Duty to informant

Auditors should use their best endeavours to protect the identity of informants. They should also ensure, from the outset, that they do not mislead informants on the extent to which they can maintain confidentiality, or obscure the fact that the information will be used by the auditors in assessing the need for further investigations. Though these investigations should be carried out as discreetly as possible, in some cases management may be able to deduce that information has been given and occasionally its source. No unrealistic undertakings as to confidentiality should be given.

Many informants will find themselves in a difficult ethical and practical position, and be making disclosure only after reaching a carefully considered decision as to the appropriate action and the balance of public interest. It will be appropriate for auditors to discuss with informants the implications of the disclosure, including internal actions or other reporting procedures that could be used by the informant. Ethical guidance on when disclosure of information to third parties in the public interest is appropriate is included in Handbook Statement **1.402** (Professional Conduct in Relation to Defaults or Unlawful Acts by or on behalf of a Member's Employer). Informants who are members may also be referred to the Institute's ethical advisory service for members in business (known as IMACE, Industrial Members Advisory Committee on Ethics – telephone number 01908 248 008).

In their dealings with informants, as in any other aspect of their professional lives, members of the Institute are bound by the fundamental principle of integrity. This principle would be breached where an auditor (or any other member) allowed or encouraged the disclosure of confidential information with an assurance or implication that confidentiality would be maintained and then disclosed the circumstances surrounding the disclosure to the client's management. Fair dealing applies to bona fide informants as well as to clients.

Where information on the source of information has been withheld from management, a member of the client's staff may be erroneously assumed to be the provider of such information, to their disadvantage. Auditors should be aware of this possibility in designing their tests but cannot be expected to have a duty of care to such third parties.

Auditors need not consider that they have any responsibilities towards an anonymous informant, whether of good or bad faith.

False information, given maliciously, might be subject to a report to management. Where false and malicious information has been received from a member of the Institute, consideration should be given to the need to make a report under the Duty to Report Misconduct (Handbook Statement **1.113**).

[Statement 918]
Pension scheme auditors' liaison with employers' auditors (AUDIT 1/99)

(Issued November 1999)

Memorandum prepared in November 1999 by the Pensions Committee on communication between the auditor of a pension scheme and the auditor of the scheme's employer.

Introduction

1 The Pensions Act 1995 ushered in a number of regulatory changes that affect arrangements for pension scheme auditors and employers' auditors to cooperate in the collection of information and audit evidence to support the scheme auditors' statutory audit. The Pensions Committee of the ICAEW believes it would be helpful to issue practical guidance on liaison between scheme auditors and employers' auditors. The guidance is intended to minimise the risk of unproductive debate where new arrangements are being established or existing arrangements are being revised rather than to unsettle existing arrangements which are operating satisfactorily.

The scheme auditors' objectives

2 The scheme auditors are responsible for the opinions on the financial statements of the scheme and on the payment of contributions to the scheme. The scheme auditors therefore need to understand the accounting and internal control systems relating to the scheme that are either maintained by employers or are dependent upon information supplied by employers.

3 The scheme auditors may also require audit evidence in relation to the matters set out below where in their view it is needed to enable them to form the opinions referred to in paragraph 2 above:

- the payment of contributions to the scheme;
- the payment of benefits by the scheme, where these are made by employers on behalf of the scheme;
- expenses borne by the employer and recharged to the scheme;
- the handling of cash accounts and financial instruments on behalf of the scheme;
- property managed by the employer.

When does this guidance apply?

4 This guidance applies where the scheme auditors decide to seek the assistance of the employers' auditors in obtaining the audit evidence they need. It does not address the question whether it is indeed appropriate that the work should be carried out other than by the scheme auditors themselves. Where the audit of components of the financial statements is carried out by other auditors, SAS 510.2 requires principal auditors to consider whether their own participation is sufficient to enable them to act as principal auditors.

The guidance deals with liaison between the scheme auditors and the employer's external rather than internal auditors.

Issues

Who should give the instructions?

Under the Scheme Administration Regulations[1], it is the duty of the employer and the employer's auditors to disclose on request to the trustees such information as is reasonably required for the performance of the duties of the trustees or professional advisers. The trustees in turn have a duty to disclose to the scheme's professional advisers such information as may reasonably be required for the performance of their duties. This includes information required for the scheme audit.

Hence, if any work is to be performed by the employer's auditors, the initial request to them is made both through the trustees and the employer. This gives the initial request some statutory backing. It also provides the trustees with the opportunity to ensure that the request addresses any needs for information that the trustees themselves may have: for example, for information about the controls over contributions, benefits and related records. The report on the factual findings of the work and response to the information request will be addressed to the employer, through whom the request was channelled. However, after the preliminary communications have been established, the two firms of auditors would generally communicate directly regarding the work programme. A recommended approach is set out in Appendix 1.

Responsibilities

The scheme auditors are responsible for the opinions on the scheme financial statements and on the payment of contributions. The scheme auditors consider the findings of the employer's auditors reported in response to the request for information and may decide that further supplementary tests are necessary.

The employer's auditors are responsible for performing the agreed procedures and responding to the request for information with due care and within the agreed timetable. They check that they understand their brief and inform the trustees and the scheme auditors if they are unable to carry out any aspect of the work as requested.

If in the course of performing the work and responding to the request for information, the employer's auditors identify any matter which they consider likely to be relevant to the scheme auditors' work, they bring it to the attention of the scheme auditors (having first obtained permission to do so from the employer if necessary).

Scope and timing of the work and costs

In most cases the employer's auditors will find that it is not possible to meet the request for information entirely from work done for the purposes of the statutory company audit. The scheme and the employer will frequently have non-coterminous financial years. The scope of work on the employers' audit (for example deciding which sites are to be visited) may be dictated by considerations that are of no

---

[1] *The Occupational Pension Schemes (Scheme Administration) Regulations 1996 (SI 1996/1715).*

particular relevance to the scheme audit. The employer's auditors will typically therefore have to carry out additional work in order to carry out the agreed procedures. It is important therefore that the trustees and employer should recognise that there are likely to be costs incurred by the employer's auditors in responding to the request.

Materiality

12 It is for the scheme auditors to set the scope of the tests that they require the employers' auditors to carry out. The scheme auditors provide the employer's auditors with an assessment of the monetary amount of materiality to be used. Similarly, the scheme auditors either specify the nature of the errors that they wish to have reported by the employer's auditors or request that all errors are to be reported.

Report on completion by employer's auditors

13 On completion of their work the employer's auditors report their findings. The report by the employer's auditors will be addressed to the employer. It will report findings against the specified tests performed and questions answered in accordance with the instructions issued by the scheme auditors.

Reporting to OPRA

14 The statutory duty to report to OPRA is imposed on the scheme auditors and not the employer's auditors. The employer's auditors, therefore, do not have a duty to ensure that staff involved in performing the work and responding to the request for information have an understanding of the regulatory requirements applicable to pension schemes sufficient to enable them to identify situations that might give rise to a report to OPRA. Accordingly, the employer's auditors cannot be expected to respond to a general enquiry as to whether or not they are aware of circumstances that might give rise to a report to OPRA.

15 The scheme auditors therefore include in the detailed work programme clear instructions on any specific matters or events that they wish to have reported to them. For example, if the trustees require the scheme auditors to provide specific confirmation that employee contributions are being paid to the scheme within 19 days of the end of the month of deduction, the scheme auditors will include a corresponding specific request for confirmation of the matter in the detailed work programme provided to the employer's auditors.

16 If the employer's auditors come across a matter which is not covered by the scheme auditors' instructions, then they should bring it to the attention of the employer's management and advise that they should bring it to the attention of the scheme trustees, who in turn should disclose this to the scheme auditors.

Appendix 1 – suggested procedures

- The scheme auditors ask the trustees to make a request to the employer for the employer's auditors to carry out agreed procedures and make the results available to the scheme auditors.
- The scheme auditors obtain and document an understanding of the relevant accounting systems and internal control systems through enquiry of and

discussion with the trustees, employer and employer's auditors sufficient to enable the scheme auditors to plan the audit approach.
- The scheme auditors discuss and agree an outline programme of work with the trustees, employer and employer's auditors (see note below).
- The scheme auditors make it clear to the employer's auditors that the scheme auditors have sole responsibility for their opinions on contributions and the scheme financial statements.
- The employer's auditors agree terms of engagement with the employer under which they will perform the necessary work.
- The scheme auditors agree a timetable with employer and employer's auditors for completion of the work, including a method and deadline by which outstanding queries are to be resolved (including intermediate deadlines where the work is done in stages).
- The scheme auditors specify in detail the programme of work that they wish the employer's auditors to perform and the information they wish the employer's auditors to provide.
- The employer's auditors perform the work and report their factual findings to the employer. This report will be made available to the scheme auditors and should be in sufficient detail to enable the scheme auditors to be satisfied that the work has been properly carried out and to understand the findings.

Note: There may need to be an iterative process where the results of work on internal control need to be assessed before the planned scope of substantive tests is determined.

[Statement 919]
Firms' reports and duties to lenders in connection with loans and other facilities to clients and related covenants
(AUDIT 4/00)

Contents

Preface

	Paragraphs
Introduction	1 - 6
Duties of care for the statutory audit report	7 - 13
Draft accounts	14
Disclaimer of responsibility	15 - 16
The Contracts (Rights of Third Parties) Act 1999	17 - 18
Members in practice in Scotland	19
Separate engagements to provide specific assurances to lenders	20 - 22
Duties of care for non-statutory audits or reviews	23 - 26
Covenants in agreements for loans and other facilities	27 - 32
The requirements for the acceptance of engagements to report on covenant compliance	
The lenders's requirement for evidence of covenant compliance	33 - 38
The firm's duty of care when reporting on the directors' statement of covenant compliance	39 - 41
The firm's consideration of acceptance of the engagement	42 - 46
Client confidentiality	47
Engagement letter	48
Scope of the work and the report	
Scope of the work	49 - 53
The report	54
Liability protection	55

Appendices

1 – Example disclaimer of responsibility
2 – Example letter to lender setting out basis of report
3 – Example engagement letter
4 – Example representation letter
5 – Example report
6 – Common covenant restrictions and ratios

[Statement 919]
Firms' reports and duties to lenders in connection with loans and other facilities to clients and related covenants
(AUDIT 4/00)

Preface

This statement is issued by the Audit Faculty of the Institute of Chartered Accountants in England and Wales and replaces Practice Note 4 *Reliance by Banks on Audited Financial Statements* which was issued by the Auditing Practices Committee of CCAB Limited in March 1991 and has now been withdrawn by the Auditing Practices Board.

The accounting bodies consider that APC Practice Note 4 contained important guidance for firms and that, following its withdrawal, replacement guidance should be available. Accordingly a CCAB working party was appointed to revise the Practice Note so as to reflect experience and developments in market practice since 1991. The guidance has been extended to cover reporting in connection with financial covenants in loan agreements and other facilities. The guidance is generally applicable to review as well as to audit engagements and refers to 'firms' rather than 'auditors' unless the context requires otherwise.

The guidance in this statement is based on the present law governing duties of care. A major review of company law is currently in progress and as and when the proposals arising from this Review are enacted into law, this statement may need substantial revision. However until such time as the law changes, the statement gives guidance on the matters that should be considered by firms regarding the extent of their duty of care in respect of audit and review reports and ancillary reporting services in connection with loans and other facilities made available to their clients.

The guidance provides an authoritative summary of the relevant considerations but should not be regarded as a substitute for the specific legal and professional advice which firms may need to take on particular matters or engagements.

Introduction

The responsibilities of auditors to third parties in respect of the statutory audit report are established in case law. The House of Lords in its judgment in *Caparo Industries Plc v Dickman (1990) 2 WLR 353* set out the essential ingredients by which the existence of a duty of care is to be recognised. 1

In his judgment, Lord Bridge described the salient features of earlier cases, stating that for a duty of care to a third party to arise in respect of the advice or information given, the person who it is alleged owes that duty of care must be fully aware: 2

- of the nature of the transaction contemplated by the third party;
- that the advice or information given would be passed to the third party, directly or indirectly; and

- that it was very likely that the third party intended to rely on that advice or information in deciding whether or not to engage in the transaction in contemplation.

3 In these circumstances, Lord Bridge considered that, subject to the effect of any disclaimer of responsibility, the person giving advice or information would be expected specifically to anticipate that the third party would rely on the advice or information given in deciding whether or not to engage in the transaction in contemplation.

4 Since the issue of the Caparo judgment, banks and other lenders have sought ways to document a direct and sufficient relationship between themselves and their customers' auditors so as to be able to rely on audit reports contained in financial statements prepared for statutory purposes.

5 This statement gives guidance on the implications of such practices by lenders and the matters that should be taken into consideration by firms regarding the extent of their duty of care in respect of audit, review and other reports on financial statements which they may provide.

6 It also provides guidance on reports which firms may be requested to provide to lenders in connection with their clients' compliance with covenants and other conditions included in agreements for loans and other facilities.

Duties of care for the statutory audit report

7 Auditors would not normally expect to owe duties of care in respect of their audit report to anyone other than their audit client. However, the general trend of authorities since Caparo makes it clear that, unless there is an effective disclaimer, an auditor may owe a duty of care to a lender or other third party. The test is whether the auditor, in making the statements in the audit report, assumed a responsibility to a lender who may have been provided with those statements. This test is an objective one: it is not whether the particular auditor intended to assume such a responsibility, but whether a reasonable auditor in those circumstances would have assumed such a responsibility.

8 Whether a duty of care to a lender exists will depend upon all the circumstances. The following factors will, however, be relevant:

- The precise relationship between the auditor and the lender;
- The precise circumstances in which the audit report came into existence;
- The precise circumstances in which the audit report was communicated to the lender, and for what purpose(s), and whether the communication was made by the auditor or a third party (such as the client);
- The presence or absence of other advisers on whom the lender would or could rely;
- The opportunity, if any, given to the auditor to issue a disclaimer.

9 Accordingly, auditors need to be alert to the possibility that circumstances may be such that, unless steps are taken to limit their exposure, they may, however inadvertently, have assumed responsibility and, therefore, a duty of care, to a lender for the statements in their audit report. This may result from events contemporaneous with the audit, such as the client's discussions with the lender, or from events subsequent to the audit, such as a request for sight of the most recent audited accounts. For this reason, the auditors' relationship with lenders needs to be managed

carefully, using established risk management techniques, and clear statements defining the auditors' duties, if any.

In seeking to document a sufficient relationship so as to enable them to rely on the audited financial statements of their customers, certain banks have included a clause in the conditions precedent to the granting of loan facilities which seeks to require the auditor of the borrower to provide written acknowledgement to the bank that, in connection with the facilities offered, the bank may rely on the audited financial statements of the borrower. An example of such a clause is as follows: 10

> 'The bank shall have received written acknowledgement from the borrower's auditor that in connection with the facilities or any increase or extension thereof the bank may, with the auditor's knowledge and consent, rely on the audited financial statements of the borrower (and the group) from time to time made available to the bank, directly or indirectly, in connection with the bank's assessment and monitoring of the financial condition of the borrower (and the group) and compliance with the terms and conditions of the agreement.'

Whether a duty of care to a bank arises in fact will depend upon whether the criteria set out in paragraph 2 above are met. Nevertheless, auditors in receipt or aware of a request to provide acknowledgement of their responsibility to their client's bankers or other lenders should not allow it to go unanswered. 11

In addition to, or as part of, a notification which seeks to establish an ongoing duty of care, a duty in respect of a lending decision might also be established if the lenders write to a firm expressing their intention to rely on audited or reviewed financial statements in connection with a proposed transaction. The presumption in such a situation would be that the firm had accepted that it had a duty of care to the lender unless it had robustly denied it. Should the firm wish to disclaim responsibility to the lender, as would normally be the case, it should state this expressly in writing. An example of a response which might be appropriate and can be customised to the circumstances of the lender's notification is provided in Appendix 1. 12

Where a firm is contemplating signing a statement containing a specific undertaking or form of words provided by the lender (rather than responding along the lines of Appendix 1), it should consider obtaining legal advice regarding the consequences for its legal responsibilities to the lender of complying with such a request and discuss its proposed response with its client. 13

Draft accounts

Care needs to be taken in relation to the provision and circulation of draft audited or reviewed accounts to lenders prior to the report being signed. Whilst the courts have held that reliance upon draft audited accounts was not actionable because a reasonable auditor would not intend such reliance, nevertheless there may be circumstances in which a duty of care could arise based on statements in draft accounts. Accordingly, the status of the accounts needs to be stressed, and representations and assurances as to the reliability of the accounts, or whether the final position is likely to differ materially from that shown in the draft accounts, should be avoided. 14

Disclaimer of responsibility

Disclaimers of responsibility will be subject to a test of reasonableness set out in section 2 of the Unfair Contract Terms Act 1977. It is for a person seeking to rely 15 upon the disclaimer to show it is reasonable, failing which it will be void. Disclaimers of responsibility to lenders (and other third parties) who seek to claim reliance on a report, and disclaimers made for the avoidance of doubt to confirm that a firm does not accept a duty to a lender or other third party to whom a report is shown or reference to a report is otherwise made, should be capable of being worded so as to pass the reasonableness test. Consequently they are an effective method of excluding or limiting a firm's liability to a lender or other third party.

16 Issuing a disclaimer of responsibility does not remove a firm's obligation to carry out the audit or review of the financial statements in accordance with Auditing Standards (or other applicable standards) and it should therefore plan, control and record its work appropriately.

The Contracts (Rights of Third Parties) Act 1999

17 The Contracts (Rights of Third Parties) Act 1999 came into force on 11 November 1999 and applies to all contracts entered into after 10 May 2000. Under the Act, third parties have the right to enforce a term of a contract if that is the intention of the parties, which intention shall be determined from the contract. An intention will be found if, upon proper construction, the contract purports to confer a benefit or an express term grants the right.

18 Accordingly, if under the engagement between the firm and the client reference is made to the provision of the accounts to a lender, or to a lender requiring the accounts for specific purposes, it is conceivable that a benefit will have been conferred upon that lender. Furthermore, in considering the reasonableness of any exclusion of liability to that lender, any such provisions will be taken into account, which has the potential of defeating any such exclusion in its entirety. It is therefore important that the engagement letter between the firm and the client makes clear that it does not confer any rights on any third party and that, for the avoidance of doubt, any rights conferred on third parties pursuant to the Contracts (Rights of Third Parties) Act 1999 shall be excluded.

Members in practice in Scotland

19 Though the Contracts (Rights of Third Parties) Act 1999 does not apply to Scotland, Scots law has long recognised the principle at common law of *ius quaesitum tertio* (a right vested in and secured to a third party in and by a contract between two parties). Accordingly a third party has the right to enforce a contract between two parties if the intention to confer a benefit on that third party can be gathered from the terms of the document. Members must therefore consider whether there is an express or implied intention that the third party acquires a right to enforce the contract. However, it should be borne in mind that each case depends upon its own circumstances and a member who is in doubt should seek independent legal advice.

Separate engagements to provide specific assurances to lenders

20 If a firm decides that it is able and prepared to provide specific assurances to a lender regarding, for example:

- financial statements where the audit or review report has been signed or will be signed in the near future;
- the design and/or operation of the client's systems of internal control or the financial reporting procedures; or
- other matters of primary interest to a lender,

they should be the subject of an engagement between the firm, the client and the lender which is entirely separate from the work on the financial statements and is the subject of a separate engagement letter and separate fee arrangements as agreed between the parties for whom the engagement is carried out.

Before a firm enters into such an engagement to provide specific assurances to a lender to a client, it should consider its position carefully in the light of the Accountancy Bodies' ethical statements since its responsibilities to the client and the lender could, in certain circumstances, present it with a conflict of interest. The same consideration applies when a loan agreement purports to appoint the firm as agent for, or financial advisers to, the lenders for the purpose of providing services and reports in connection with a loan agreement, facility or drawdown. 21

The firm should also consider professional guidance (e.g. the ICAEW Statement on 'Managing the Professional Liability of Accountants') in deciding the scope and terms of business of any engagement to provide specific assurances to a client's lenders. 22

Duties of care for non-statutory audits or reviews

Companies which take advantage of the exemption from the statutory audit requirement available to them by virtue of their small size may nevertheless decide to have their financial statements independently audited or reviewed for other purposes. Such reports will not be on the public record and the firm will generally include a restriction on use in its report, requiring its prior written consent before the report can be made available to any third party. However, if a 'small' company chooses not to take advantage of the exemption and continues to have a statutory audit, the audit report will be filed at Companies House with the statutory accounts and the duties of care of the firm which undertakes the audit will be the same as those discussed in paragraphs 7 to 13 above. 23

If a firm undertakes an audit or review engagement of financial statements other than on express terms that the purpose of the engagement is to provide a report which will be made available to and relied upon by a lender to the client, the firm will wish to avoid subsequently incurring a duty of care to the lender in respect of the report. Accordingly, the firm will usually only consent to its report on the financial statements being made available to the lender if the lender acknowledges in writing that the report is provided for information purposes only and does not give rise to any responsibility, liability, duty or obligation whatsoever from the firm to the lender. Similar considerations apply and an acknowledgement from the lender in equivalent terms will usually be required by a firm which, while not providing an audit or review report, has assisted a client with the compilation of financial information which is to be made available to a lender. 24

If a firm decides to accept an audit or review engagement of financial statements on the express understanding with the client and a lender that its report will be made available to and relied upon by the lender, the firm is unlikely subsequently to be able to avoid assuming a duty of care to the lender in respect of the report. It is a commercial and risk management decision for the firm as to whether to accept such an engagement and it may wish to take legal advice before doing so. 25

Where an engagement likely to result in a duty of care to a lender is accepted, the firm will wish to put the limitations of that duty into context by obtaining the lender's written acknowledgement of an engagement letter which sets out (inter alia): 26

(a) the objective of the firm's work (e.g. to provide a report to the company giving a specified form of assurance as to whether in the firm's opinion the financial statements give a true and fair view in accordance with Financial Reporting Standards as set out in the Financial Reporting Standard for Smaller Entities or other relevant accounting standards);
(b) that users of financial statements should be aware that there are inherent limitations in any set of financial statements. The limitations of audited financial statements include the matters listed below; similar limitations are broadly applicable to reviewed financial statements but the illustrative wording below may need modification or amplification to reflect the circumstances of the review:
- financial statements present a company's state of affairs only at the balance sheet date and an historical view of the company's results for the period then ended;
- financial statements must be interpreted having careful regard to the underlying accounting policies;
- financial statements may not reflect items which are considered to be immaterial;
- certain revenues, costs, assets and liabilities, for which no precise means of measurement exist, may be included in the financial statements on the basis of the directors' best estimates;
- events that have occurred between the balance sheet date and the date of the audit or review report will only be reflected in the financial statements in so far as they relate to the period being reported on;
- although financial statements are normally prepared on a going concern basis, they do not give any indication of the level of future profitability or cash flows of the business or guarantee that the business will remain financially viable;
(c) that the extent to which a lender may rely on a company's financial statements in connection with its assessment and monitoring of the financial condition of that company may depend on the effect of the inherent limitations set out above and whether:
- the accounting policies adopted by the directors as a basis for preparing the financial statements are appropriate for the lender's purposes;
- the lender's assessment of the financial condition of the company is being undertaken sufficiently near to the balance sheet date for reliance on the financial statements to be meaningful;
- it is necessary to obtain more up to date financial information from the company's directors regarding current trading and future projections of results and cash flows;
- additional information is required from the company's directors in order to assess whether the company has complied with the terms and conditions of a lending agreement;
- there are any other matters in which the lender may be primarily interested as a lender;
(d) that accordingly, the decision as to whether to enter into or continue with a lending transaction is solely that of the lender and a firm's audit or review work does not in any way constitute a recommendation as to what decision the lender should take or supplant the enquiries and procedures that the lender should undertake in its consideration of that decision.

Covenants in agreements for loans and other facilities

The agreements documenting certain financial instruments, including for example facility agreements supporting bank lending, often contain a number of covenants with which the borrower is expected to comply. These are more common in term loans and other committed facilities which are not repayable on demand. Compliance with such covenants is intended to help assure the lender of the continuing security for the advance. Failure to comply would be regarded as a breach of covenant and would normally be dealt with as an event of default under the loan facility agreement. 27

Covenant clauses are most commonly encountered in loan facility agreements and debentures, but similar clauses are often included in the terms of other types of financial instruments. The precise nature of the financial instrument does not affect the applicability of this guidance to a firm's responsibilities or reports in connection therewith. The principles underlying the guidance are relevant to any report in connection with the assessment of compliance with covenants or conditions contained in a commercial agreement. They are also relevant to reports relating to audited financial statements required by regulatory bodies, trade associations and other third parties. 28

Covenants contained in loan agreements can pertain to a variety of financial and non-financial information relating to the borrower's financial condition and actions. These covenants normally comprise a series of general covenants together with a number of detailed clauses tailored to the specific circumstances of the borrower. Typically, the directors of the borrower are required to prepare a periodic statement, report or representation to the lender confirming compliance with the terms of the loan agreement. Such statements, reports or representations are hereinafter referred to in this statement as 'Statements of Covenant Compliance'. 29

The more routine non-financial covenants in such agreements record commitments by the borrower as to its future actions. For example: 30

- to provide information to the lender (for example monthly management accounts, audited accounts etc.), within a specified period;
- to continue to insure assets, maintain and develop the business, to comply with laws and regulations; and
- not to sell or charge substantial assets or dispose of parts of the business, without the lender's consent.

In addition to these non-financial covenants, the lender often will require the borrower to maintain certain financial statement ratios (e.g. gearing, interest cover, etc). The imposition of these financial covenants is intended to provide the lender with some assurance as to the continuing financial condition of the business and its progress in accordance with the information provided to the lender at the time of initial advance. 31

Examples of the subject matter of the more common financial and non-financial covenants for borrowings are set out in Appendix 6. In specialised industries, the scope of such covenants may be extended to the maintenance of key operating statistics or key performance indicators ('KPIs') which are derived from management information outside the audited financial statements. 32

The requirement for and acceptance of engagements to report on covenant compliance

The lender's requirement for evidence of covenant compliance

33   The borrower's commitment to comply with the covenants at all times is evidenced in the loan agreement which will normally also provide for specified financial covenants to be tested at intervals (e.g. quarterly, six monthly or annually). Typically the lender will require a written confirmation from the directors that they have complied with the covenants for the period under review. This is usually contained in or supported by a Statement of Covenant Compliance prepared by the directors at each period end confirming and setting out the computation of the relevant financial covenants for the applicable date and period.

34   The lender will seek to obtain some assurance that these calculations are reliable. Simple calculations of gearing and interest cover based upon audited or management accounts are usually self evident and the lender can recalculate the financial ratios itself. However, the basis of calculation of compliance with KPI based covenants may not be self evident from the accounts, as the underlying information may be drawn from sources within the company concerned.

35   It is customary for the lender to include in the loan agreement a provision for a report to be received from the borrower's auditors relating to the directors' Statement of Covenant Compliance. The requirement for this report and its subject matter is normally negotiated directly between the lender and borrower as part of the facility terms and set out in the loan agreement itself. Typically this requirement is expressed only in general terms; the nature of the report often is not clearly specified in the agreement but firms may expect it to extend to the calculation or extraction of the financial information which form the basis of the covenant compliance calculations and to the accuracy of the calculations themselves.

36   Firms are not obliged to accept an engagement to report in connection with a client's borrowing facilities, whatever the express provisions of the loan agreement, since they cannot be bound to comply with the terms of an agreement to which they were not party. However, situations where firms find themselves unable to report in the required terms are obviously best avoided if possible. Consequently, if a firm becomes aware that a client is involved in a loan or other facility negotiation, it is good practice for it to enquire into whether the draft loan agreement seeks to place any duties or reporting obligations on it and to advise whether the covenants are capable of subsequently being reported upon.

37   Representatives of The City of London Law Society, whose members are regularly engaged in the drafting of loan agreements, have confirmed (1) that they recognise that it is important that covenants in lending documentation relating to auditors' reports should subsequently be able to be complied with, and (2) that a well-advised borrower would therefore only agree to requirements for reports by its auditors if this was cleared with the firm or if the borrower was otherwise sure that the firm would be able to provide the relevant report and in full knowledge of the costs which may be incurred.

38   When a firm becomes aware of references in loan agreements to reports required of it in relation to covenant compliance (and particularly if it receives direct communications from the lender seeking to assert the basis on which it intends to rely on such reports), it should, for the avoidance of doubt, consider responding to the

lender setting out the basis on which it will be prepared to report. An example of such a letter where a firm acts as auditor is in Appendix 2.

The firm's duty of care when reporting on the directors' statement of covenant compliance

In accepting an engagement to report to lenders on the extraction and compilation of the financial covenants, a firm acknowledges a duty of care to the lender in relation to the subject matter of its report on the directors' Statement of Covenant Compliance. 39

Firms use established risk management techniques to control the duties of care in relation to the subject matter of their report, for example by entering into an engagement letter with the addressees of the intended report, which restricts the use of the report to them, specifies liability limitations and includes a disclaimer of responsibility to any other person. 40

However, it is possible that in the specific circumstances of an engagement, for example to report upon information to be extracted from the audited or reviewed financial statements, firms might be found to have (perhaps unintentionally) assumed responsibility to the lenders for an audit or review report (a duty of care which, but for the report in connection with covenant compliance, would not otherwise have existed). Consequently, and for the avoidance of doubt, firms will normally include in their terms of engagement for reporting on the directors' Statement of Covenant Compliance an express disclaimer of any duty of care to the lenders in respect of their audit or review report. 41

The firm's consideration of acceptance of the engagement

Reports by firms on a directors' Statement of Covenant Compliance are normally provided as an ancillary service to the audit or review of the borrower's financial statements and are conducted under a separate engagement letter and fee arrangements. The engagement could take the form of an assignment to report to the directors to provide them with assurance in connection with the discharge of their responsibilities. Such a report might be relevant where there is no requirement from the lender for an independent report. More commonly, however, the engagement would require a report to the lender on the extraction and compilation of the financial information in the Statement of Covenant Compliance. 42

In deciding whether to accept the engagement, firms need to ensure that the reporting structure reflects an appropriate delineation between the clients' responsibilities to provide financial information to the lender and the firm's responsibility to report upon it. It is the directors' responsibility to prepare the financial information supporting their assertion that they have complied with the terms of the loan agreement. The firm's responsibility should be to report upon that information to the extent that it relates to financial and accounting matters. 43

The directors will prepare their Statement of Covenant Compliance in accordance with their responsibilities under the loan agreement. The Statement would normally set out the calculations of financial ratios etc. as provided for in the loan agreement. The Statement may deal separately with the non-financial covenants often in terms of a negative statement (e.g. that there have been no breaches of the covenants set out in Clauses [ ] to [ ]). Alternatively the Statement may recite each such covenant individually. 44

45 The loan agreement will usually require the borrower to comply with the covenants at all times. The firm's report will relate to financial covenants by reference to financial information as of specified dates and periods. Firms will not normally accept an engagement in which they are to provide wide-ranging assurance that the borrower has complied or is in compliance with the covenants contained in the agreements or that, based on prospective financial information, the borrower will be in compliance with the covenants for a future period. The scope of their engagement will usually be confined to reporting the results of applying specified procedures to financial information in the Statement of Covenant Compliance, where such information is objectively ascertainable.

46 Before accepting the engagement the firm needs to be sure that the matters on which it is asked to report are clear, unambiguous and appropriate in the circumstances. Firms should consider carefully the implications of accepting an engagement to report on a Statement of Covenant Compliance based on financial covenants whose terms are imprecise, require subjective interpretation beyond the scope of recognised accounting expertise or are based upon data extracted from records outside the borrowers' system of internal financial control. Examples of such difficulties are where a firm is required to report on a Statement of Covenant Compliance 'after making such adjustments as they consider necessary' or 'immediately after' the occurrence of an event or transaction which may not coincide with a date at which accounts are prepared. Where ambiguity, imprecision or subjectivity is capable of being resolved by agreement between the parties, the firm should seek the joint written instructions of its client and the lender as to how the financial covenant concerned is to be interpreted before undertaking the engagement.

Client confidentiality

47 Firms will need to ensure that the client authorises them to comply with the request. Notwithstanding the terms of any loan agreement, they have a duty of confidentiality to their client. Consequently, they cannot agree to report on client confidential information without the prior agreement of their client, which should be obtained in writing.

Engagement letter

48 Firms will need to consider whether the request is a separate engagement, whether directly between the lender and themselves or a further engagement between the client and themselves. A separate engagement letter normally will be required unless the provision of the report was specifically contemplated in another such engagement letter addressed to the relevant parties. (An example engagement letter where a firm acts as auditor is in Appendix 3).

Scope of the work and the report

Scope of the work

49 The precise scope of work will need to be agreed with the client and the lender to reflect the specific circumstances. Typically the firm would:

(1) read the relevant clauses of the loan agreement and understand the operation of the relevant covenants to the extent they pertain to accounting matters;
(2) read the directors' Statement of Covenant Compliance;

(3) agree the financial information in the Statement to the sources from which it has been extracted;
(4) recompute the calculations and ratios set out in the directors' Statement with the objective of confirming their arithmetical accuracy;
(5) obtain representation from the client to the completeness of disclosure in the Statement. An example representation letter is provided in Appendix 4.

The firm will report on accounting, financial and quantitative matters which are within the scope of its professional expertise. It does not provide comment on matters to which its skill or experience has little or no relevance or application. 50

Normally firms do not undertake procedures to confirm the reliability of financial information in the Statement nor of the sources from which the data has been extracted. Equally, they do not report on non-financial information or on matters primarily involving the exercise of the directors' business judgement, for example explanations of operating trends (to the extent that the directors are required by a covenant to provide such explanations) since these may depend on factors beyond their expertise. Consequently, the firm's report in connection with covenant compliance will normally be confined to the accuracy of the extraction and computation of those financial matters which are the subject of covenants within the facility and only to the extent they are capable of clear definition, relate to accounting matters and are extracted from records within the borrower's system of internal financial control. 51

In view of the limited nature of these procedures, firms would not be expected to provide assurance as to judgemental matters, such as fair presentation in accordance with the loan agreement or to report on the extraction of, or underlying procedures relating to, non-financial information, without undertaking a substantive engagement designed for that purpose which is beyond the scope of this statement. 52

As noted in paragraph 41 above, when a firm reports on a directors' Statement of Covenant Compliance it will normally disclaim any duty of care to the lender in respect of any audit or review report it has given on the borrower's financial statements. In any event, the period to which a Statement of Covenant Compliance relates will not necessarily correspond with a period for which an audit or review has been performed. If the periods do coincide, and the firm's report on the financial statements has been modified or qualified in respect of matters which could have a material effect on the Statement of Covenant Compliance, the firm will consider its position accordingly. 53

The report

The firm's report should be prepared in accordance with the engagement letter. The report will normally: 54

(1) identify the addressees who can rely on it;
(2) contain a statement as to the scope of the report and the respective responsibilities of the directors and the firm;
(3) refer to the Statement of Covenant Compliance prepared by the directors in accordance with the loan agreement;
(4) set out the basis for the report;
(5) provide a description of the procedures undertaken, either in the body of the report or in an appendix;
(6) report as to the arithmetical accuracy of the extraction and calculation of the financial information contained in the Statement; and

(7) where the elements and composition of the financial information contained in the Statement are the subject of objective accounting definition in the loan agreement or have been subsequently agreed by the parties, report whether the financial information is presented in compliance with the relevant definitions and agreement.

An illustrative form of report is provided in Appendix 5.

Liability protection

55 Firms would expect to exclude liability in respect of any loss or damage caused by, or arising from, fraudulent acts, misrepresentation or concealment on the part of the client entity, its directors, employees or agents. They would also exclude liability to third parties. They would expect to agree a limitation of their liability to the lender and the client which was appropriate to the limited scope of the engagement. References to such clauses are contained in the example engagement letter at Appendix 3.

Appendix 1 (Guidance reference: paragraph 12)

EXAMPLE DISCLAIMER OF RESPONSIBILITY TO LENDERS FOR AUDIT OR REVIEW REPORTS

[Lender plc]

Dear Sirs,

[Client plc] – [Loan Agreement/Transaction Reference]

We acknowledge receipt of your letter of [...date...] in which you state your intention to rely on the financial statements of Client plc for the year ended [...date...] and our audit [or review] report thereon [in connection with the above mentioned loan agreement].

Our audit [or review] of the financial statements [was/is] neither planned nor conducted for the purpose of (or in contemplation of) the loan agreement (and transaction) referred to above. In particular, the scope of our work [was/is] set and judgments made by reference to our assessment of materiality in the context of the financial statements taken as a whole, rather than in the context of your needs. For this reason, our work would not necessarily [have addressed/address] or reflect[ed] matters in which you may be primarily interested as lenders. Therefore, we cannot accept any responsibility to you in relation to our report and disclaim all liability to you in connection therewith (and your lending decision in relation to the proposed transaction and any other actions you may take).

Should you require any specific assurances from us regarding any matters in which you may be primarily interested as a lender, we should be happy to discuss them with you in the context of an engagement between ourselves, Lender plc and Client plc which would be entirely separate from our audit [or review] of Client plc's financial statements.

Yours faithfully,

cc Client plc

Appendix 2 (Guidance reference: paragraph 38)

EXAMPLE LETTER TO LENDER SETTING OUT BASIS ON WHICH REPORTS UNDER LOAN AGREEMENTS WILL BE PROVIDED

[Lender plc]

Dear Sirs

[Client plc] – [Loan Agreement Reference]

Client plc has provided us with a copy of [and you have written to us in connection with], the Loan Agreement referred to above, Clause X of which contemplates that reports will periodically be provided to you by the auditors of Client plc in connection with Client plc's compliance with certain covenants.

As auditors of Client plc, we confirm that, provided that Client plc authorises us to do so and you sign an engagement letter with us substantially in the attached form, we will report to you on the following matters:

1) whether the financial information contained in the Statement of Covenant Compliance prepared by the directors of Client plc has been accurately extracted from the sources identified therein and, where applicable, agrees with the underlying accounting records;
2) whether the calculations shown in the Statement made in accordance with Clause [●] of the Loan Agreement are arithmetically accurate; and
3) where the elements and composition of the financial information contained in the Statement are the subject of objective accounting definition in the Loan Agreement, or have subsequently been agreed by Lender plc and Client plc, whether the financial information is presented in compliance with the relevant definitions and agreement.

As regards our audit work on Client plc's financial statements for future periods, our work will be carried out in accordance with our statutory and professional obligations and will not be planned or conducted in contemplation of your requirements or any matters which might be set out in the Loan Agreement. In particular, the scope of our audit works will be set and judgments made by reference to our assessment of materiality in the context of the audited accounts taken as a whole, rather than in the context of your needs. For this reason, our work will not necessarily address or reflect matters in which you may be primarily interested as lenders. Therefore, we cannot accept any responsibility to you in relation to our audit opinions and disclaim all liability to you in connection therewith.

Yours faithfully

cc Client plc

Attachment: Form of engagement letter

Appendix 3 (Guidance reference: paragraph 48)

EXAMPLE ENGAGEMENT LETTER

[Lender plc]
[Other addressees as provided for in the second paragraph of the letter]

Dear Sirs

[Client plc] – [Loan Agreement reference]

Under the terms of Clause [●] of the agreement dated [●] between Client plc and Lender plc (the 'Loan Agreement'), the Directors of Client plc are required to procure that their auditors report to you in connection with the Directors' Statement of Covenant Compliance, (the 'Statement'), prepared in accordance with Clause [●] of the Loan Agreement. At the request of the Directors of Client plc, we are writing to set out our understanding of the work you wish us to perform and the terms and conditions upon which we are prepared to provide such a report for your use. A copy of this letter is being sent to the Directors of Client plc to confirm their authorisation and understanding of the basis on which we will report to you.

[This engagement letter is addressed to Lender plc, as lead manager/arranger of the facility/syndication agreement, and to each of the other lenders participating in the facility/syndication agreement whose names, as set out in Attachment 1, have been notified to us by Lender plc as having validly authorised it to accept this engagement letter on their behalf. By signing and accepting the terms of this engagement letter, Lender plc confirms that it will ensure that it receives prima facie authority from each other lender identified in Attachment 1 as participating in the facility/syndication agreement authorising it to enter into this engagement letter on the relevant lender's behalf.]

Respective responsibilities of directors and auditors

The directors of Client plc are responsible for ensuring that Client plc complies with all of the terms and conditions of the Loan Agreement including each of the Covenants set out in Clauses [●] to [●] thereof. Under Clause [●] thereof, the Directors are responsible for preparing their Statement of Covenant Compliance. Our responsibility is to prepare a report to you on the computation of those financial covenants which pertain to accounting matters as identified below.

We are auditors of Client plc and have audited the annual accounts of Client plc (the 'audited accounts'), and reported to its members in accordance with our responsibilities to them under the Companies Acts on [●] 200Y. Our audit of the accounts of Client plc was not intended to address compliance with financial covenants or other matters in which the addressees of this letter may be primarily interested. In particular, the scope of our audit work was set and our judgments made by reference to our assessment of materiality in the context of the audited accounts taken as a whole, rather than in the context of the report contemplated in this letter. Accordingly, we do not acknowledge any responsibility, and deny any liability, to the addressees of this letter in relation to the audited accounts.

Basis of report

[Our work will be conducted in accordance with the framework for reporting in connection with loan covenants set out in [Practice Note X] issued by the Institute of

Chartered Accountants in England and Wales.] We will read the Statement prepared by the Directors. Our work will be based on obtaining an understanding of the compilation of the Statement by enquiry of management, reference to the Loan Agreement, comparison of the financial information in the Statement to the sources from which it was obtained and recomputation of the calculations in the Statement. [The specific procedures which we have agreed to conduct are set out in the Appendix to this letter.] Other than as set out herein, we will not carry out any work by way of audit, review or verification of the financial information nor of the management accounts, accounting records or other sources from which that information is to be extracted for the purpose of providing you with our report.

Use of report

Our report will be provided solely for your use in connection with the Loan Agreement and should not be made available to any other party without our written consent. The report is confidential to you and will be provided only for the purpose of your assessment of Client plc's compliance with the terms of Clause [●] of the Loan Agreement. We accept no liability to any other party who is shown or gains access to our report.

Obligations and Liabilities

We undertake that we will exercise reasonable professional skill and care in the performance of our work as set out in this letter in accordance with applicable professional standards. This engagement is undertaken subject to certain terms excluding liability where information is or has been misrepresented to us, or withheld or concealed from us, and providing for our aggregate liability to the addressees of this letter and Client plc to be limited to a maximum aggregate amount of £[●] and subject to that cap, to the part of any loss suffered which is proportional to our responsibility. These detailed terms are set out in the attached Terms of Business which shall apply as if set out in full herein.

Acknowledgement and acceptance

We will be grateful if, having considered the provisions of this letter together with the attachments and having concluded that they are reasonable in the context of all the factors relating to our proposed engagement, you will indicate your agreement to these arrangements by signing and returning to us the enclosed copy of this letter.

Yours faithfully

The terms and conditions contained in this letter and the attached Terms of Business are agreed and accepted on behalf of Lender plc by:

....
Signature of Authorised Person

Authorised and accepted on behalf of Client plc by:

....
Signature of Authorised Person

Appendix 4 (Guidance reference: paragraph 49)

EXAMPLE REPRESENTATION LETTER FROM CLIENT

[Auditors]

Dear Sirs

[Loan Agreement Reference]

In connection with your proposed report in accordance with the arrangements set out in your letter of [ ], we are writing to confirm to the best of our knowledge and belief the following representations we have made to you and on which you need to rely in providing your report on the Statement of Covenant Compliance (the 'Statement'), to Lender plc.

1   We are responsible for preparing the Statement accurately reflecting the matters contained therein at the relevant dates.
2   The Statement is complete and accurate and reflects all matters of significance relating to Lender plc's assessment of Client plc's compliance with the Covenants set out therein as at the relevant dates and all significant matters relevant to that assessment have been brought to your attention.
3   Throughout the period since [ ] the Company has at all times been in compliance with the terms of the Loan Agreement or, if not, all such instances of non-compliance have been notified to the Lender plc in accordance with the terms of the Loan Agreement. Copies of such notifications have been made available to you.
[4   No events have occurred subsequent to [date of last audited financial statements] that would have required adjustment to, or disclosure in, the audited financial statements had their approval by the Board been deferred until the date of this letter.]

Yours faithfully

....

Signature of Authorised Person on behalf of Client plc

Appendix 5 (Guidance reference: paragraph 54)

EXAMPLE REPORT

[Lender plc]
[Other addressees as provided for in engagement letter]

Dear Sirs

[Client plc] – [Loan Agreement reference]

We refer to the above mentioned agreement (the 'Loan Agreement'). Under the terms of Clause [●] thereof, Client plc is required to comply with specified financial covenants and to supply the addressees of this letter with information in connection therewith reported upon by its auditors.

The directors of Client plc have prepared a Statement of Covenant Compliance (the 'Statement'), a copy of which is appended to this letter.

This report letter is provided pursuant to, and must be read in conjunction with, our engagement letter dated [200Y] and is subject to the terms and limitations set out therein.

Basis of report

Our work was conducted in accordance with the framework for reporting in connection with loan covenants set out in guidance issued by the Consultative Committee of Accountancy Bodies [and published as audit technical Release [xx] by the Institute of Chartered Accountants in England and Wales]. We have read the attached Statement prepared by the Directors. Our work was based on obtaining an understanding of the compilation of the Statement by enquiry of management, reference to the Loan Agreement, comparison of the financial information in the Statement to the sources from which it was obtained and recomputation of the calculations in the Statement. [The specific procedures we performed are set out in the Appendix to this letter.] For the purpose of providing you with this letter, other than as set out herein, we have not carried out any work by way of audit, review or verification of the financial information nor of the management accounts, accounting records or other sources from which that information has been extracted.

Report

Based solely on the procedures described above, we confirm that:

1) the financial information contained in the accompanying Statement has been accurately extracted from the sources identified therein and, where applicable, agrees with the underlying accounting records;
2) the calculations shown in the Statement made in accordance with Clause [●] of the Loan Agreement are arithmetically accurate; and
3) the financial information in the Statement is presented in compliance with the relevant accounting definitions as to its elements and composition set out in Clause [●] of the Loan Agreement [and as agreed between Lender plc and Client plc and confirmed to us in a letter dated ● 200Y].

Our report as set out herein is confidential to the addressees of this letter and should not be made available to any other party without our written consent. It is provided solely for the purpose of your assessment of Client plc's compliance with the terms of [Clause [●] of] the Loan Agreement. We accept no liability to any other party who is shown or gains access to this letter.

Yours faithfully

cc Client plc

Appendix 6 (Guidance reference: paragraph 32)

COMMON COVENANT RESTRICTIONS AND RATIOS

Examples of the subject matter of more common financial and non-financial covenants for borrowings are set out below.

Accounting-based
Cash flow to total debt service
Dividend cover
Minimum share capital and reserves
PBIT-based interest cover
Gearing
Cash flow-based interest cover
Other interest cover
Net current assets/borrowings
Proportion of debtors below certain days outstanding
Current ratio
Quick asset ratio
EBITDA
Gross profit margin
Rent roll ratios

Non-accounting based
First charge over specified assets
Audited annual accounts within specified period
Cross default clauses
Monthly management accounts within specified period
Restrictions on changes to ownership
Restrictions on additional borrowings (from other sources)
Maintenance of adequate fire, theft and other insurances
Restrictions in mergers/acquisitions
Restrictions on asset disposals
No capital expenditure beyond certain limits without approval
Compliance with environmental laws and regulations
Compliance with other laws and regulations
No redemption of preference shares while loans outstanding
Charges over keyman insurance
Keyman critical illness policy
Limits on director's remuneration

[Statement 920]
Reporting to third parties
(AUDIT 1/01)

(Issued September 2001)

This guidance is issued by the Audit and Assurance Faculty of the Institute of Chartered Accountants in England and Wales in September 2001 to assist reporting accountants when asked to provide reports that have been requested by third parties. The guidance does not constitute an auditing standard. Professional judgement should be used in its application.

Contents

	Paragraphs
Introduction	1 - 7
Determine who will rely on the accountants' work and for what purpose	8 - 11
Consider the form of report requested by the third party	12 - 14
Agree the work to be performed and the form of report to be given	15 - 24
Agree appropriate terms of engagement	25 - 28
Perform the work	29 - 30
Report	31 - 33

Appendix 1 – Flowchart illustrating the process accountants follow in response to requests for reports from third parties

Appendix 2 – Examples of types of wording or opinions that are unacceptable to accountants providing special reports

Appendix 3 – Example extracts from an engagement letter for an agreed upon procedures engagement

Appendix 4 – Illustrative contents of a report of factual findings for an agreed upon procedures engagement

Appendix 5 – Example of a Disclaimer Notice for an Accountants' Report

Appendix 6 – Example of a Liability Cap for the accountants' reporting engagement

Reporting to third parties

Introduction

1 Accountants are often asked by their clients to sign reports that have been requested by trade bodies, regulators and other third parties with whom the client has a relationship ('third parties').

2 Accountants are not bound by arrangements between clients and third parties to which they were not party and so have no obligation to sign such reports. However, accountants wish to assist their clients if possible and endeavour to become familiar with clients' reporting requirements at an early stage in their relationship with their clients and negotiate appropriate engagement terms for providing such reports sufficiently far in advance of the reports becoming due. This helps to avoid any disagreements with the client or the third party regarding the form of the report that is needed.

3 In the past there has been limited guidance available to assist accountants with such requests and accountants often signed reports for third parties without considering the potential liability to which they were exposed. The Institute, through the Audit and Assurance Faculty, has developed the practical guidance in this Technical Release to assist accountants in deciding whether to accept these engagements and, if they do, the key points they consider when determining the process to follow (see paragraph 7).

4 This Technical Release provides general guidance for accountants seeking to manage their risks effectively. The Institute's Audit & Assurance Faculty is also active in helping with specific problematic reporting engagements and communicates with a number of third parties in order to agree appropriate forms of report and engagement terms. Where appropriate, specific guidance is issued relating to such reports.

5 Additional guidance on reporting to third parties can be found in the Technical Release Audit 4/00 *'Firms' reports and duties to lenders in connection with loans and other facilities to clients and related covenants'*. Audit 4/00 is based on the law governing the duty of care and gives guidance on the matters that should be taken into consideration by accountants regarding the extent of their duty of care in respect of audit, review reports and ancillary reporting services.

6 This Technical Release does not cover:

- corporate finance engagements;
- reports required under UK company legislation (in this case accountants follow the guidance in the Auditing Practices Board's Practice Note 8, *'Reports by auditors under company legislation in the United Kingdom'*);
- reports in respect of and/or to public sector[1] entities (the Institute's Audit and Assurance Faculty is proposing to set up a Working Group to consider the issues relating to these reports);
- simple requests for references on clients' financial status and their ability to service loans (guidance on these requests is provided in Audit 2/01, *'Requests for references on clients' financial status and their ability to service loans'*).

---

[1] *'Public sector'* is defined in the Auditing Practices Board's Practice Note 10, *'Audit of financial statements of public sector entities in the United Kingdom'*.

However, many of the principles of risk management in this Technical Release will still apply.

The guidance in this Technical Release is set out under the following headings that describe the process accountants follow in response to requests for reports from third parties:

(a) Determine who will rely on the accountants' work and for what purpose.
(b) Consider the form of report requested by the third party.
(c) Agree the work to be performed and the form of report to be given.
(d) Agree appropriate terms of engagement.
(e) Perform the work.
(f) Report.

The process is illustrated by the flowchart in Appendix 1.

Determine who will rely on the accountants' work and for what purpose

When accountants know that their report has been requested by a third party and that the third party will rely on the report, there is a risk, in the absence of an effective disclaimer[2], that the accountants owe the third party a duty to take reasonable care in preparing and providing the report. If the accountants do owe the third party such a duty, they could be liable to that third party if they were negligent and the third party suffered loss in reliance on the report.

It is vital, therefore, for accountants to understand who the third party is, why it requires the report and the extent of loss which the third party could suffer in reliance on the report. If, for example, the third party runs a scheme for compensating the client's customers in the event of the client's insolvency, the accountants' risk is much greater than if, for example, the third party's only role is to perform marketing for a particular service sector.

The accountants' understanding of the risks involved in providing a report underpins the decisions they make about whether to accept the engagement and on what terms. Depending upon the circumstances accountants either:—

(a) accept that they owe a duty of care to the third party and enter into an engagement contract with the third party, including provisions limiting liability if appropriate; or
(b) proceed with an engagement for their client but before allowing the third party access to their report, require the third party to acknowledge in writing that the accountants owe the third party no duty of care; or
(c) proceed with an engagement for their client but disclaim or limit any liability or duty to the third party by notice in their report; or
(d) do not accept the engagement.

If accountants regard a report as high risk, they agree to provide the report *only* if the third party is a party to the engagement contract or the third party has acknowledged in writing that the accountants owe no duty of care to the third party. If accountants regard a report as low risk, typically because the third party could suffer little or no loss in reliance on the report, then they may decide to provide the report without contracting with the third party. In this case a notice can be included in the report disclaiming or limiting the accountants' liability to the third party. In addition to

---

[2] Accountants consider the legal effectiveness of disclaiming liability and of the proposed disclaimer in the particular circumstances of their engagement.

that notice, it may be appropriate for the accountants to write to the third party, in advance of the third party receiving the report, notifying the third party of the basis on which the report will be provided. Also, if a third party writes to the accountants in an attempt to indicate reliance on a report, the accountants consider whether it is reasonable to accept such reliance. Where it is not, a disclaimer is given in writing.

11 Accountants are advised not to allow their reports to be provided to a third party unless the basis and extent of their liability to the third party is clear and agreed. Accountants refer to the guidance in Statement 1.311 of the Institute's Members' Handbook, '*Managing the professional liability of accountants*' and consider the consequences of The Contracts (Rights of Third Parties) Act 1999 – see the guidance in Audit 4/00.

Consider the form of report requested by the third party

12 As stated in paragraph 2, accountants maintain a dialogue with their clients to enable requests for reports to be highlighted at the earliest possible stage, so that difficulties may be addressed. Accountants are not bound by any form of report agreed between the client and the third party without the accountants' consent. The requested form of report (which can – but might not – take the form of a 'standard' report on a pre-printed form), will often be inappropriate because the considerations in this guidance are not met. In such circumstances, accountants do not accept third parties' arguments that such reports cannot be changed. If a third party refuses to accept the principles in this guidance, it may be beneficial for the accountants to consult the Audit and Assurance Faculty of the Institute. Examples of wording in requested reports that are unacceptable to accountants following this guidance are given in Appendix 2 (NB: this is not intended to be an exhaustive list).

13 Accountants only sign reports if they have performed sufficient work and obtained sufficient evidence to support the statement they are asked to make in the report. Sometimes third parties ask accountants to sign statements concerning such matters as the future solvency or performance of the client, which cannot be supported by any amount of work performed by the accountants. By signing such reports misunderstandings may arise that accountants may become the equivalent to insurers or guarantors of the clients' obligations to third parties. Accountants do not accept this responsibility and refuse to sign such reports, but they may propose alternative forms of report which are capable of being supported by work performed by them. Accountants may determine that an agreed upon procedures form of report is the most appropriate (see paragraph 21). If third parties require a guarantee regarding the future solvency of a client, it is usually most appropriate for them to introduce their own procedures to monitor clients' financial solvency, or to require the clients to obtain bank guarantees, or to take out their own separate insurance to cover their potential exposure – an accountants' report can never be a substitute for any of these options and it is no part of the accountants' function to act as an insurer. The Audit and Assurance Faculty of the Institute expects to issue further guidance on requests from third parties for solvency statements or similar reports.

14 Accountants do not agree to forms of report, used by third parties, which place reliance on the statutory audit of the client, for example, wording such as that under the fourth heading in Appendix 2. To avoid the risk of this reliance being established, accountants also take into account the guidance in Audit 4/00 on duties of care for the statutory audit. Accountants avoid circumstances that may result in a duty of care for the statutory audit report becoming established with a third party. They exercise caution if asked to send audited accounts direct to a third party. For example, they avoid sending the audited accounts direct to the third party unless this

is accompanied by an effective disclaimer and they respond in writing to attempts by a third party to establish a duty of care in respect of the statutory audit report by disclaiming all liability to the third party (see Appendix 1 of Audit 4/00).

Agree the work to be performed and the form of report to be given

Accountants make clear to clients and third parties that engagements to provide reports to a third party are separate engagements from the statutory audit engagement. The work performed in order to provide the report for the third party will be separate work and subject to a separate fee from the work performed on the statutory audit, and liability will be limited as appropriate (see paragraph 27).   15

Accountants agree with the client and the third party a form of report that is appropriate taking into account the purpose of the report, the amount of work to be performed and the cost of the work. The timescale for providing the report is agreed at this stage. This timescale should provide sufficient time for the work to be completed and the report to be given – accountants do not agree to timescales for providing reports where it is not possible to plan and complete all the necessary work within the timescale requested.   16

Generally, the higher the level of assurance sought in a report, the more work is necessary and the greater the cost to the client. A common problem is that the third party requests a demanding report but expects the client to pay for the necessary work. If the client is not prepared to pay for the work needed to provide the level of assurance sought then the accountants decline to act.   17

There are no UK auditing standards on the forms of reporting envisaged by this guidance, although there are international standards which give some guidance[3]. However, it should be noted that these standards do not apply directly in the UK. In general terms, there are four options for these reporting engagements: 18

- High level of assurance.
- Moderate level of assurance.
- Agreed upon procedures.
- Compilation engagements.

High level assurance is usually regarded as providing a conclusion expressed in positive terms. It can only be provided where the subject matter reported on and/or the scope of work are/is such as to enable the accountants to give a high level of assurance. According to ISA 100, an assurance engagement exhibits *all* of the following elements: 19

(a) a three party relationship involving:
 – a professional accountant;
 – a responsible party; and
 – an intended user;
(b) a subject matter;
(c) suitable criteria;
(d) an engagement process; and
(e) a conclusion.

---

[3] At present, the most relevant international standards in issue are ISA 920 'Engagements to Perform Agreed-Upon Procedures Regarding Financial Information' and the International Standard on 'Assurance Engagements' (ISA 100)

ISA 100 provides guidance on each of these elements and establishes basic principles and essential procedures for the performance of engagements intended to provide a high level of assurance.

20 An assurance engagement which provides a moderate level of assurance involves performing more limited procedures and may involve providing a negative assurance in the style of *'nothing has come to our attention ...'*. It may also be appropriate to situations where the subject matter reported upon is not capable of being reported on in high level of assurance terms. Reports with a moderate level of assurance are currently the subject of research on behalf of the International Auditing Practices Committee.

21 An agreed upon procedures engagement involves performing certain specified procedures on factual information and reporting the findings without giving any form of opinion on the implications of the work performed. Example extracts from an engagement letter for an agreed upon procedures engagement are given in Appendix 3 and illustrative contents of a report of factual findings are given in Appendix 4. Accountants tailor the engagement letter and report to reflect the specific circumstances of the engagement. They attach to the engagement letter a draft of the type of report of factual findings that will be issued.

22 A compilation engagement involves preparing financial information on behalf of clients. Guidance on such engagements is given in the Technical Release Audit 1/95 *'Reports on accounts compiled (prepared) by accountants'*.

23 In most situations where accountants are asked to provide a report to a third party, an agreed upon procedures engagement will best meet the expectations of the third party and the client regarding the work the accountants perform and the fees the accountants charge. These engagements (see paragraph 21 above) have the advantage that there is less scope for misunderstanding about the work to be performed and the nature of the results.

24 When determining the appropriate level of work to perform and the appropriate fee, accountants consider risks relating to who the client is and the purpose of the report. In some circumstances, however, the risks, even after appropriate limitation of liability, are so great that they cannot be adequately compensated by any reward and if this is the case, the accountants decline to do the work.

Agree appropriate terms of engagement

25 When accountants are requested by a client to provide a report for the purposes of a third party, accountants manage their relationship with not only the client but also with the third party.

26 Accountants usually manage their relationships by agreeing engagement terms in writing with the client and the third party. If the third party refuses to engage with the accountants, then accountants either refuse to provide the report or only do so subject to a disclaimer of liability to the third party (see paragraphs 10 and 11). In deciding to issue a disclaimer, accountants consider whether the disclaimer will be reasonable and therefore likely to be effective. Accountants need to be aware that disclaimers might not always be effective. An example disclaimer notice is provided in Appendix 5.

27 Engagement contracts include the following:

- a clear unambiguous description of the scope of work to be performed and the form of report to be provided using defined terms where appropriate to avoid misunderstandings;
- a description of the client's obligations and the client's responsibility for the information on which the accountants report;
- clarification that the engagement is separate from the statutory audit and that the accountants have no duty of care to the third party in relation to the statutory audit;
- an appropriate liability cap[4], agreed having regard to the nature of the work being performed, the level of fee charged and other relevant factors. Any limitation of liability must be negotiated and agreed with the client, and must be fair and reasonable in compliance with the Unfair Contract Terms Act 1977[5];
- details of the addressee for the report, limitations as to the purpose for which the report is prepared and restrictions on who is entitled to see and rely upon the report and on the distribution of it;
- a copy of the form of report to be provided.

An example of a liability cap is provided in Appendix 6.

In deciding the appropriate engagement terms, accountants also refer to the guidance in Statement 1.311 of the Institute's Members' Handbook, 'Managing the professional liability of accountants', in particular the sections on limiting or excluding liability. 28

Perform the work

The work for a third party report is separate from the work involved in the statutory audit and the accountants plan and document the work, retaining separate working papers for each reporting engagement. 29

Accountants perform work on a third party reporting engagement in the same professional manner as any other engagement and in accordance with the scope agreed and recorded in the engagement letter. If it is necessary to depart from the terms of the engagement letter, an amended scope of work is agreed, in writing with the client and with the third party. 30

Report

Accountants provide a report that reflects the agreement set out in the engagement letter and is supported by the work carried out by them (see paragraph 13). The report makes clear: 31

- for whom it is prepared and who is entitled to rely upon it and for what purpose;
- that the engagement was undertaken in accordance with the engagement terms;
- the work performed and the findings.

Where considered appropriate, they also provide a statement that by delivering this report the accountants accept no additional duties in relation to the statutory audit.

---

[4] Accountants consider whether the liability cap is reasonable given the specific circumstances of the engagement.

[5] See the guidance in Statement 1.311 of the Institute's Members' Handbook, 'Managing the professional liability of accountants'

32 Accountants' reports do not include either undefined terms such as *'review'*, without specifying what the terms mean, or open-ended wording, without indicating the scope of the work which has been performed by reference to an engagement letter or relevant standards or guidance. Examples of inappropriate wording are given under the fifth heading in Appendix 2.

33 Accountants do not modify the form of their report in response to comments from the client or the third party that it does not meet their needs unless such modification is both appropriate and they have the opportunity to perform the necessary/additional work. If it subsequently transpires that a different form of report is now being requested to that agreed in the engagement terms, the accountants either agree a new engagement or decline to issue the requested report, giving the reasons in writing.

Appendix 1 – Flowchart illustrating the process accountants follow in response to requests for reports from third parties

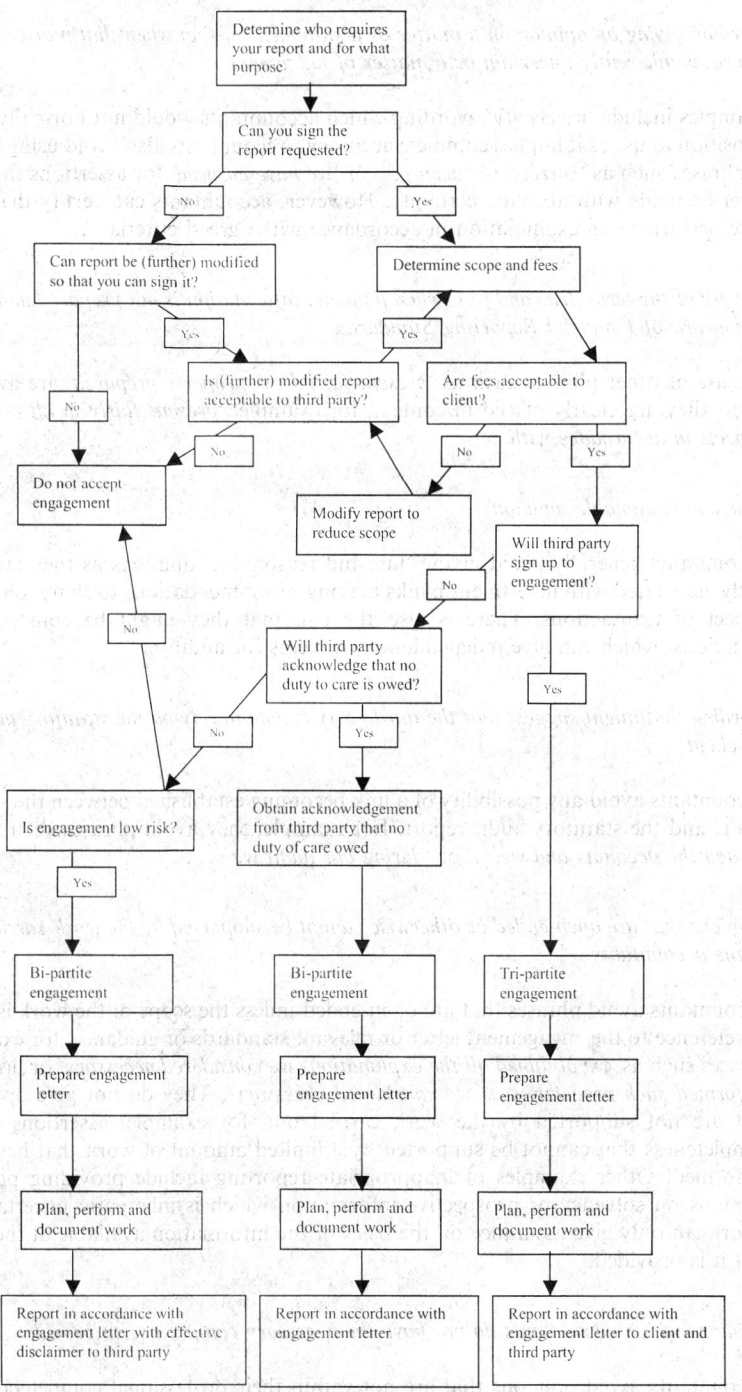

Appendix 2 – Examples of types of wording or opinions that are unacceptable to accountants providing special reports

Wording giving an opinion on a matter as a statement of fact when that matter, by its nature, is inherently uncertain or a matter of judgement

1   Examples include '*we certify*', wording which accountants would not normally be in a position to use as it implies complete accuracy. Accountants also avoid using words or phrases such as '*correct*' or '*accurate*' or '*we have ensured*' for assertions that can never be made with absolute certainty. However, accountants can certify that they have performed an examination in accordance with agreed criteria.

The use of the term 'true and fair' when financial information is not prepared under the framework of Financial Reporting Standards

2   The use of other phrases such as '*present fairly*' or '*properly prepared*' are avoided unless they are clearly placed in context, for example, '*present fairly in all material respects in accordance with. . .*'.

'Fair and reasonable' opinions

3   Accountants generally avoid giving 'fair and reasonable' opinions as they are normally associated with investment banks making recommendations to shareholders in respect of transactions. There is also the risk that they might be construed as valuations, which can give independence problems for auditors.

Wording that might suggest that the third party is able to rely on the statutory audit of the client

4   Accountants avoid any possibility of a link becoming established between the special report and the statutory audit report. For example, they avoid phrases such as '*we audited the accounts and we. . .*' or '*during our audit we . . .*'.

Opinions that are open-ended or otherwise cannot be supported by the work carried out by the accountants

5   Accountants avoid phrases that are open-ended unless the scope of the work is clear by reference to the engagement letter or relevant standards or guidance, for example phrases such as '*we obtained all the explanations we considered necessary*' or '*we have performed such procedures as we considered necessary*'. They do not give opinions that are not supported by the work carried out, for example, assertions about completeness that cannot be supported by a limited amount of work that has been performed. Other examples of inappropriate reporting include providing positive opinions on solvency or prospective information which is inherently uncertain. A report can only give assurance on the basis of the information available at the time that it is provided.

Opinions which accountants do not have the necessary competence to provide

6   Accountants avoid opinions that are not within their professional competence, for example an opinion of an actuarial nature or a property valuation, where there has

been no input from a relevant expert. Another example of this would be the appropriateness of insurance cover.

Opinions on matters beyond the accountants' knowledge and experience

Accountants avoid giving any opinion about how *'appropriate'* operational information or records being held or maintained by the client are, where the information or records relate to matters concerning the specific operational circumstances of the client which are beyond the scope of the accountants' professional knowledge and experience. 7

Wording that is open to interpretation

Certain words or phrases might be open to interpretation and these are only appropriate to use in clearly defined circumstances where the meaning is well established and understood. The word *'review'* is best avoided as it can be unclear what has been reviewed and the extent of the work. Words to avoid can also include accounting terms, for example, *'net current assets'* in sectors where specific adjusting items might be recognised when assessing liquidity. Accountants always define terms if the meaning might be unclear and do not otherwise use such terms. The word *'material'* is avoided unless this can be referenced to a clear definition. 8

Reports on internal controls

Reports on internal controls are only possible in well defined and well established circumstances, where the reporting arrangements have been agreed in a clear manner. Reports on systems and controls are avoided where there are inadequate criteria specified. Reports include an indication of the limitations of a system and are related to a point in time or period. Guidance is given in the APB Briefing Paper *'Providing assurance on the effectiveness of internal control'*. It is also useful to clarify in writing the responsibilities of management and in particular, to indicate that they are responsible for identifying, evaluating and managing new and changing risks on an ongoing basis. 9

Reports without addressees

Accountants do not provide reports where it is unclear to whom the report is being provided. 10

Reports on financial information which is not explicitly approved by the client

The client has responsibility for the financial information being provided and it is, therefore, not appropriate for the accountants to report on financial information unless it is clear that it has first been approved by the client. 11

Qualifications in the covering letter only

Accountants do not provide qualifications in their covering letter. Such qualifications are included in the main body of the report, so that they cannot be detached. 12

Opinions which would impair the auditors' independence

13 Accountants do not provide opinions that would impair their independence as auditors. For example, where the client is an SEC registrant, certain forms of valuation opinion are not permitted from auditors.

Appendix 3 – Example extracts from an engagement letter for an agreed upon procedures engagement

Services to be provided

We will complete the specified limited scope procedures set out below:

(describe the nature, timing and extent of the procedures to be performed, including specific reference, where applicable, to the identity of documents and records to be read, individuals to be contacted and parties from whom confirmations will be obtained.)

The above procedures will be performed solely for your purposes. You are responsible for determining whether the scope of our work specified above is sufficient for your purposes.

Upon completion of the procedures we will provide you with a report of our findings in the form of that attached to this letter, solely for your information *(attach proforma of report)*. Our report is not to be used for any other purpose or disclosed to any other person without our consent. [We consent to the report being released to [name of third party] provided that [name of third party] acknowledges in writing that we owe no duty of care to [name of third party] and we will not be liable to [name of third party] for any reliance it chooses to place on the report.]

We have agreed that, under this engagement, we will not perform an audit or any verification procedures other than those which are specified in the scope section above. [If we were to perform additional procedures or if we were to perform an audit or any more limited review, other matters might come to our attention that would be reported to you.] Our report will not extend to any financial statements of the Company taken as a whole.

Audit work

Our audit work on the financial statements of the Company is carried out in accordance with our statutory obligations and is subject to a separate engagement letter. Our audit report is intended for the sole benefit of the Company's shareholders as a body, to whom it is addressed, to enable them to exercise their rights in general meeting. Our audits of the Company's financial statements are not planned or conducted to address or reflect matters in which anyone other than such shareholders as a body may be interested.

We do not and will not, by virtue of this report or otherwise, assume any responsibility whether in contract, negligence or otherwise in relation to our audits of the Company's financial statements; we and our employees shall have no liability whether in contract, negligence or otherwise to [name of third party addressee (if applicable), or to] any [other] third parties in relation to our audits of the Company's financial statements.

Requests for references on clients' financial status and their ability to service loans

Introduction

1   Banks, building societies, insurance companies, letting agents and others may seek references from accountants regarding the financial status of intending borrowers or of those undertaking other obligations. The request may be to report on a borrower's present financial position, on ability to pay debts as they fall due, or on ability to service or repay a loan.

2   In many circumstances, the type of reference by accountants as to the financial status of their client, as outlined in this statement, will meet a lender or other third party's needs. Such a reference may be particularly appropriate in relation to individuals or small businesses where lenders would not normally wish borrowers to be obliged to incur the time and expense of an investigation. However, such references might also be needed for larger businesses and the principles in this statement will be equally applicable in these situations.

3   This statement provides guidance to reporting accountants seeking to manage their risks effectively, when they receive requests for references. The type of reference covered by this statement is only appropriate where there is no need for the accountants to perform any work, research or investigation to produce the reference. Where this is not the case, accountants agree a specific formal engagement, following the guidance in Audit 1/01 *'Reporting to Third Parties'* (see paragraphs 10 and 11 below). In these situations, they are also aware of the duty of care implications of entering into such engagements and take account of the guidance in Audit 4/00 *'Firms' reports and duties to lenders in connection with loans and other facilities to clients and related covenants'*.

4   This statement replaces the Institute statements TR 698 'Requests for confirmation of clients' ability to service loans' (issued in May 1988) and TR 846 'Accountants' references on clients' financial status' (issued in October 1991).

The principal considerations involved

5   Future income and expenditure is inherently uncertain. No amount of enquiry can provide accountants with the assurance needed to enable them to confirm that a client will have sufficient income to service a loan or other obligation. Accountants are, therefore, unable to report in positive terms on future income or future solvency. The Audit and Assurance Faculty of the Institute expects to issue further guidance on requests from third parties for solvency statements or similar reports.

6   Reporting on the present solvency of a client presents difficulties for accountants unless they are engaged (in accordance with full and proper terms reflecting the limits in the scope of the engagement, see paragraphs 10 and 11 below) to report on accounts, computations and projections as at a stated date. It is likely that in many cases the time and expense of such an exercise would be out of proportion to the nature of the assurance being sought.

[Statement 921]
Requests for references on clients' financial status and their ability to service loans (AUDIT 2/01)

(Issued September 2001)

This guidance is issued by the Audit and Assurance Faculty of the Institute of Chartered Accountants in England and Wales in September 2001 to assist reporting accountants when asked to provide reports that have been requested by third parties. The guidance does not constitute an auditing standard. Professional judgement should be used in its application.

Contents

	Paragraphs
Introduction	1 - 4
The principal considerations involved	5 - 12
Meeting lenders' needs for individuals and other small borrowers	13 - 17
Forms of reporting	18 - 22
Example of accountants' reference	23

Appendix Example of an accountants' reference in connection with a lending application made by an individual or other small borrower

Lenders and other third parties may use audited accounts to assess a client's 7
approach to the fulfilment of past obligations, but the audited accounts do not give
any certainty in relation to going concern (see paragraphs 11 and 12 of SAS 130[1]).

Auditors would not normally expect to owe duties of care in respect of their audit 8
report to anyone other than the members of the client company as a body, to whom
the audit report is addressed, to enable them to exercise their rights in general
meeting. For the avoidance of doubt, auditors issue a disclaimer of responsibility to
third parties where a request for reference or confirmation is received, particularly in
situations where they send the audited accounts direct to the third party. Generally,
auditors do *not* send audited accounts direct to third parties. Accountants refer to the
guidance on this subject in Audit 4/00 *'Firms' reports and duties to lenders in connection with loans and other facilities to clients and related covenants'*.

Accountants do not carry out any specific procedures in order to make the type of 9
reference covered in this statement and this is made clear in the reference. To avoid
the possibility of an implied contract, accountants do not charge any additional fees
for the reference and they disclaim, in writing, any liability for providing the reference. It should be noted that it is legitimate for accountants to decline to provide a
reference if the risks of so doing are judged to be unreasonably high. For example,
this could occur if the amounts involved are judged by the accountants to be too
large.

Where no specific assurance is to be provided but third parties still request specific 10
procedures to be carried out, accountants usually negotiate an agreed upon procedures engagement in accordance with Audit 1/01 *'Reporting to Third Parties'*.

In the specific circumstances where lenders are seeking assurance beyond that given 11
by the type of reference considered in this statement, a specific engagement is agreed
between the accountants, the borrower and the lender. The terms of such an
engagement set out the precise scope of the work to be carried out, the type of report
that will be produced and a reasonable limitation of liability. Accountants refer to
the guidance on this in Audit 4/00 *'Firms' reports and duties to lenders in connection
with loans and other facilities to clients and related covenants'*.

Any reference made in accordance with this statement should be made in writing so 12
as to avoid any misunderstanding.

Meeting lenders' needs for individuals and other small borrowers

When lenders consider lending applications from individuals or other small bor- 13
rowers, they are likely to seek assurance on the potential borrower's financial status.
However, there is unlikely to be financial data of the kind that may exist in the case,
for example, of a borrower that is incorporated.

Nevertheless, for individuals and other small borrowers there is likely to be infor- 14
mation that accountants can supply that might be useful to a lender. Examples are:
a) the length of time during which the accountants have acted on behalf of the client;
b) the net income or profits of the client as declared by the client to the Inland
Revenue in the latest tax return; c) based on the reporting accountants' experience
and having exercised judgement, a statement that the accountants have no reason to

---

[1] *Paragraph 12 of SAS 130 concludes that any judgement made on going concern, although reasonable at the
time, can be valid only at that time and can be overturned by subsequent events.*

suppose that the client would be likely to enter into a commitment, such as that proposed, that the client did not expect to be able to fulfil.

15 A combination of paragraphs 14a) and b) above will often provide the lender with the sort of information required. However, sometimes the lender will receive additional benefit from the accountants' judgement that is provided in connection with 14c). That judgement is formed in the light of the accountants' professional experience of the client's attitude to the assumption of obligations. Any view formed by the accountants is based on their experience of the client's attitude towards commercial obligations generally. It is limited in line with their experience of the client and in recognition that they can only act in relation to information which they have the client's authority to disclose. In some cases accountants decline to express a view due to their limited amount of experience, for example, if they have insufficient information or if they have only recently started acting for the client. They also decline to comment where there is any doubt regarding a judgement, or where the client asks the accountants to give overly selective information merely provided by the client. It should be noted that accountants are not obliged to express a view.

16 The accountants' knowledge of the client is often not up to date and this fact is stated in the written report.

17 The considerations outlined in this section are also relevant when dealing with requests for references from other third parties, for example, requests from letting agents seeking to arrange a rental agreement involving the accountants' client.

Forms of reporting

18 Accountants report in a way that is appropriate to the particular circumstances. Any limitation in the view being given is clearly stated, for example, in relation to future income and expenditure.

19 Lenders and other third parties may prescribe their own forms of report as a matter of administrative convenience to cater for the more usual types of loan or arrangement. However, such prescribed forms may not always reflect the considerations referred to in this statement. If necessary, accountants amend the wording of the report to be given or provide explanatory wording so as to reflect the limited view that they are in a position to provide. In particular, this may be necessary if the accountants are invited to comment in indefinite terms which they are unable to do. For example, the accountants may be asked for general comments on the proposed transaction in relation to the client or for any information which the accountants consider should be brought to the third party's attention.

20 It will sometimes be necessary to refer the third party to information more appropriately provided direct by the client. An example would be a question about what part of the funding is coming from the client's business where, without the expense of an investigation, the accountants can only rely on the representations of their client.

21 Accountants avoid the possibility of misinterpretation, particularly regarding any technical terms used. For example, a reference to *income* might be interpreted as either *net income* or *gross income*. Accountants therefore define any terms used. These terms are normally interpreted as follows: *gross income* means sales, turnover or other revenues *before* costs are deducted; *net income* is the amount *after* costs have been deducted.

22 In circumstances where accountants are uncertain about whether they are able to provide either the requested report or a modified version of it, they do not do so.

Example of accountants' reference

23 An example of an accountants' reference for a lender is provided in the attached Appendix. It should be regarded as illustrative only but may assist accountants in assessing the form in which it may be appropriate to communicate to a third party *(NB: whilst the example is for a lender, the form of report may also be used for any reference provided to a third party covered by this statement)*. The example is designed to cater for the more usual cases and is amended by accountants, as appropriate, to reflect the particular circumstances of the client. In certain cases accountants may be able to provide alternative or additional information to assist a third party, but in doing so they take into account the considerations set out in this statement.

Appendix – Example of an accountant's reference in connection with a lending application made by an individual or other small borrower

Without responsibility

To *[Name and address of lender]*

Dear Sirs

REFERENCE IN CONNECTION WITH THE LENDING APPLICATION MADE BY *[Name of client and application reference, as appropriate]*

Our above named client has approached us for a reference in connection with the proposed loan by you of £... *[repayable by monthly instalments of £... over ... years]*.

We have acted in connection with our client's *[personal / business / corporate tax]* affairs since . . . However, it should be noted that our knowledge of our client's affairs may not be fully up to date. In addition, we have not carried out any specific work with regard to this statement.

Our client's net income[2] declared by our client to the Inland Revenue as at 5 April 20.. amounted to £... *[To be adapted as appropriate for borrowers who are not individuals]*.

[Income / profits for previous years and identification of those agreed with the Inland Revenue may be added].

Whilst we have no reason to believe that our client would enter into a commitment such as that proposed which our client did not expect to be able to fulfil, we can make no assessment of our client's continuing income or future outgoings.

Whilst the information provided above is believed to be true, it is provided without acceptance by *[name of firm / signatory]* of any responsibility whatsoever, and any use you wish to make of the information is, therefore, entirely at your own risk.

---

[2] Define 'net income' – see paragraph 21.

Yours faithfully

Signed ....

Dated ....

cc *[Client name]*

[Statement 922]
Practical points for auditors in connection with the implementation of FRS 17 'Retirement Benefits' – defined benefit schemes (AUDIT 1/02)

(Issued February 2002)

This guidance does not constitute an auditing standard. Professional judgement should be used in applying it. No responsibility for loss occasioned to any person acting or refraining from action as a result of any material in this guidance can be accepted by the Institute.

Contents

	Paragraphs
Introduction	
Approach to the audit and any problems encountered	1 - 5
Others issues	
Faculty monitoring of the progress of implementing FRS 17	
Appendix Company processes for gathering FRS 17 disclosure information	

Practical points for auditors in connection with the implementation of FRS 17 'Retirement Benefits' – defined benefit schemes

Introduction

The Auditing Practices Board issued Practice Note 22[1] (PN 22) in November 2001 on *'The Auditors' Consideration of FRS 17 'Retirement Benefits' – Defined Benefit Schemes'*. PN 22 provides guidance for auditors when auditing entities with defined benefit schemes following the introduction of Financial Reporting Standard 17 (FRS 17) *'Retirement Benefits'*. This guidance is being issued by the Institute's Audit and Assurance Faculty to supplement PN 22 in certain areas and to assist auditors in dealing with specific practical audit issues that they may encounter.

Whilst the FRS only comes fully into effect for periods ending on or after 22 June 2003[2], certain disclosures are required for all periods ending on or after 22 June 2001[3]. This guidance provides illustrative practical help for dealing with situations arising from the minimum disclosures required in the first transitional year of the implementation of FRS 17. It is not intended to be comprehensive or to deal with all situations that might be encountered, i.e. it is supplementary to and not a substitute for PN 22, which should be regarded as the primary source of guidance for auditors.

Approach to the audit and any problems encountered

As emphasised in PN 22, it is the responsibility of the directors to obtain all of the information necessary to make the disclosures required by FRS 17. Auditors might use the attached Appendix, which lists planning points, and the process and specific tasks expected of directors, to identify, at as early a stage as possible, any difficulties that there might be. Where issues are identified early, it may be possible to suggest ways to assist the company to rectify the situation, without the company's reporting timetable being affected.

In practice, whilst every effort should be made to ensure that a full and proper process is in place, there will be a need for auditors to exercise judgement regarding the materiality of the issues involved. The five sections below highlight particular scenarios that auditors might encounter and suggest possible approaches:

Information required for FRS 17 disclosure not available

1   It is possible that auditors will encounter situations where they are informed that the company has not obtained, and will not be able to obtain, the information that is needed to make the disclosures required by FRS 17 in the first year of its operation. Exceptionally, this could be because of a reluctance to implement any part of FRS 17 before the FRS comes fully into effect or because of a concern that the costs that would be incurred, e.g. for the actuarial valuation information, would outweigh benefits from providing the disclosure. More commonly, this situation might arise where the company has not requested and therefore has not obtained the necessary information on time from the actuaries or insurers or pension scheme fund

---

[1] PN 22 is available (price £4.00, post free) from Wolters Kluwer (UK) Limited (telephone 0870 777 2906).

[2] For entities applying the FRSSE, 22 June 2004.

[3] Entities applying the FRSSE are exempt until 22 June 2002.

managers. It is therefore important for directors to make sure the necessary requests are sent out on a timely basis.

In practice where this situation is encountered by auditors, it would be useful to discuss with the directors whether there are ways of overcoming the difficulty. It is very unlikely that the difficulty would be truly insurmountable. For example, if the company's or pension scheme actuaries are unable to respond to a request for information at short notice other actuaries might be used to obtain the necessary information. It is quite likely that the company will not have fully appreciated the consequences of not making the disclosure and the auditors should therefore explain what the consequences might be.

If in respect of a scheme material to the company's financial statements the disclosures required by FRS 17 are still not made, auditors consider qualifying their opinion on the grounds of disagreement (also see section on distributable profits on page 8).

Failing in the process for providing and obtaining information

There is the possibility that a failing in the process for the company to provide relevant information on a timely basis to the reporting actuaries could, unless it is improved, give rise to a limitation of scope qualification of opinion.

The consequences of a failing in the process include:

(a) a large range (see section 3b), which covers the possible impact of this on the audit report); or
(b) failure to take account of major changes.

The best way of overcoming b) above is to consider before the year end (or as soon as possible thereafter) whether the process enables the actuaries to take account of all major changes since the latest full actuarial valuation was carried out, which would, according to the latest actuarial guidance, include:

- salary growth or pension increases which are materially different from those assumed;
- settlements, curtailments (including redundancies) and other material scheme changes; and
- other material events including benefit improvements, bulk transfers or constructive obligations.

In many instances the actuaries performing the FRS 17 valuations will be the scheme actuaries and the trustees will have formally agreed to inform them of any events expected to have a significant impact on the funding of the scheme. This does not however, remove the obligation from the directors to ensure that the actuaries are informed of all relevant information.

Response to ranges around a 'best estimate' of a scheme surplus or deficit

FRS 17 requires disclosures about retirement benefits, including the surplus or deficit, to be based on 'best estimates'. Actuarial calculations involve a number of assumptions about events and circumstances in the future. Some of these assumptions are normal and relate to external factors, such as rates of return on investments and interest rates. However, others will be scheme specific and relate to internal matters, such as rates of salary increase, and rates at which staff join, leave or retire from the scheme. In practice the result of actuarial calculations may be affected by uncertainties that mean that a best estimate will lie within a range of possible values. These uncertainties may arise because:

- different sets of actuarial assumptions could be adopted;
- the company's process is inadequate, e.g. there are concerns about the reliability of information on internal matters; or
- events have occurred whose impact on the actuarial liability cannot be determined with certainty.

As explained below the auditors' response to uncertainty depends on its source and materiality. It is therefore likely to be important for auditors who are presented with a range for a scheme surplus/deficit to be able to distinguish between the effects of the different possible causes. This is likely to require close liaison between the auditors, the directors and the actuaries.

Where the figures in the quoted range are not material, the existence of the range will not (in isolation) impact on the auditors' ability to express an opinion on the financial statements, nor will there be a need for specific disclosure in the financial statements of the range or the factors affecting its size. However, where the figures in the range are large, the following problems may arise:

(a) Large range arising from 'flexing' normal actuarial assumptions

In practice, actuaries who are engaged to carry out actuarial calculations will suggest a set of self-consistent assumptions, in consultation with their client, but to demonstrate the sensitivity of the results to changes in key assumptions the actuaries may re-run the calculations using different sets of assumptions and provide their client with a range of assessments of the scheme surplus or deficit. The directors have to be satisfied, after taking advice, which assumptions are most appropriate.

Where the range of reasonable monetary amounts is so large that the use of a different amount from within that range could materially affect the view shown by the entity's financial statements, directors should consider whether FRS 18 'Accounting Policies' requires disclosures to be made in the financial statements of the estimation techniques adopted, including details of those underlying assumptions to which the monetary amount is particularly sensitive. The disclosure of key assumptions is also required by FRS 17.

At least in relation to the first year of the FRS 17 disclosures, under the transitional provisions, where appropriate disclosures are included in the notes to the financial statements the financial effects of applying alternative sets of actuarial assumptions will not normally require a modification to the audit report, even if potentially large.

(b) Large range arising from inadequacy in the company's process

As described in section 2 above, the company should set up an adequate process for providing the necessary information to the actuaries on a timely basis.

In contrast to a full actuarial valuation, when actuaries are requested to carry out a more limited exercise to update a previous full valuation as permitted by paragraph 35 of FRS 17, they may need to make assumptions about the following:

- the manner and extent to which the membership data has changed in the intervening period, for example because they have been provided by the employer with summarised, rather than detailed, current information; and
- the impact of significant business events that occurred after the latest full actuarial valuation.

As a result of such factors, the actuaries may express their 'best estimate' arising from the calculations as a point in a range of values that typically will be affected by the actuaries' degree of confidence about the matter.

Where the figures in the quoted range are material to the financial statements the auditors consider taking the following steps:

- by discussion with the actuaries, establish which factor or factors have the greatest impact on the size of the range and whether there is scope within the employer's reporting timetable for the employer to provide data that is more up to date or more finely analysed.
- where the range is not capable of being reduced below the auditors' assessment of materiality, consider whether the range primarily arises from:
  - constraints in relation to the quality of the information which is supplied for the purposes of the updated valuation; or
  - events or circumstances between the last full valuation and the balance sheet date which give rise to changes in scheme liabilities that cannot be calculated precisely because their effect on the scheme is inherently uncertain – see (c) below.

In the case of a constraint in relation to the quality of the information supplied to the actuaries, the range may mask a lack of good process for deriving the FRS 17 disclosures and represents a limitation of the evidence available to the auditors to support the FRS 17 disclosures in the accounts. The auditors therefore consider issuing a report which is qualified on the grounds of a limitation of the scope of the evidence available to them in respect of the disclosures made about retirement benefits.

(c) Large range arising from an unusual event

Examples of unusual events are as follows:

- a voluntary redundancy programme where the characteristics of the staff who will be made redundant in due course will not be known at the date of approval of the employer's financial statements and, as a result, the actuaries are unable to be certain about the effects of the redundancy programme on the future benefit liabilities of the scheme
- the outcome of a recent court case or other change in the law whose possible impact on the scheme could be fundamental, but cannot be established with certainty as at the date of approval of the employer's financial statements.

Where factors such as those above result in a large range of possible figures around the best estimate, the auditors respond by checking that the notes to the financial statements contain sufficient disclosures about the assumptions. Where they do, there will normally be no impact on the report issued by the auditors.

In very exceptional circumstances, where the uncertainty caused by the range is unusually great because of the unusual event(s), auditors might consider its effect on the meaningfulness of the 'best estimates' disclosed under FRS 17. In these circumstances, auditors consider including a fundamental uncertainty, explanatory paragraph in the audit report.

Group schemes treated as defined contribution schemes

4   Group schemes are a type of multi-employer[4] scheme and companies may seek to claim the exemption given in FRS 17 to account for the scheme as if it were a defined contribution scheme. It should be noted that FRS 17 does require the use of defined benefit accounting for group schemes where it is structurally possible. The type of evidence that may suggest to the auditors that defined benefit accounting is possible includes the following:

- different contribution rates apply to different group companies;
- substantially all of the contributions to the scheme relate to one group company (indicating that that group company can apply defined benefit accounting, whereas the other group companies may be permitted to apply defined contribution accounting);
- most of the assets and liabilities can be related to active members who can be identified with individual group companies;
- a group scheme that is unfunded with no assets; and
- the scheme's trust deed and rules specify what would happen on the sale of a group company, e.g. the basis for calculating a share of fund.

It should also be noted that the method adopted historically under SSAP 24 could in some circumstances be relevant to determining whether an allocation of assets and liabilities can be made for the purposes of FRS 17.

Paragraph 39 of Practice Note 22 states that where the multi-employer exemption is being claimed, auditors make enquiries of the directors regarding the basis for their conclusion that the entity's share of the scheme assets and liabilities cannot be identified. The auditors also consider any relevant professional advice (for example, actuarial or legal advice) that the directors may have obtained on this issue. It would be useful for auditors to document the rationale for the conclusion reached by the directors and the audit evidence that has enabled the auditors to concur with the treatment in the accounts.

Issues arising from overseas schemes

5   FRS 17 applies to all types of benefits that an employer is committed to providing after employees have completed their service, whether the commitment is statutory, contractual or implicit in the employer's actions. Paragraph 4 makes it clear that FRS 17 applies to retirement benefits arising overseas, not just those in the UK and the Republic of Ireland. Unlike SSAP 24, there is no concession to multinational groups in respect of overseas schemes that have been accounted for under a different accounting standard. Although in principle SSAP 24 required that adjustments should be made to account for the costs of foreign schemes in accordance with the UK standard, it recognised that in some situations it may be impractical and costly to obtain the necessary actuarial information. In such circumstances, compliance was encouraged but was not mandatory provided disclosure was made. Under FRS 17, however, **all** schemes, subject to materiality considerations, must be accounted for consistently in compliance with FRS 17 and so adjustments are required, where necessary, to convert retirement benefits accounting from local GAAP to a measurement and recognition basis that complies with the FRS.

This requirement introduces several issues that must be considered by preparers and auditors of group accounts. These include:

---

[4] *See paragraphs 8–12 of FRS 17.*

- how the principles of FRS 17 apply to schemes in the group's overseas locations: this may not be a straightforward question. For example, in certain countries, pension schemes are run by the state whilst in others there may be difficulty in identifying scheme assets;
- whether the year end reporting timetable includes sufficient time to obtain the necessary information;
- whether accounts staff in overseas locations are familiar with the measurement and recognition requirements of FRS 17;
- whether it is possible to communicate with overseas actuaries so as to check that assumptions and valuation bases are appropriate; and
- whether there are material schemes within overseas (or UK) joint ventures and associates.

Other issues

Preliminary announcements

In the case of listed companies auditors need to give consent to the issue of the preliminary announcement. Where FRS 17 issues arise and there is the potential for a qualified or modified audit report, consideration will need to be given to the content of preliminary announcements. In these situations auditors refer to the Auditing Practices Board's Bulletin 1998/7 *'The auditors' association with preliminary announcements'*.

Consideration of going concern

FRS 17 will not, of itself, impact on the cash flows of a sponsoring company into a defined benefit scheme. The contributions required by an employer will be arrived at through negotiations with trustees or through statutory requirements (or both), either of which may involve measuring surpluses or deficits on a different basis to that required by FRS 17. Given this, it may seem unlikely that the introduction of FRS 17 in itself would have any particular impact on the appropriateness, or otherwise, of the going concern concept. However, the disclosure (and, in due course, accounting) requirements of the new standard will certainly focus attention on the health of company pension schemes. This in turn may influence the stance taken by various parties with whom sponsoring companies transact.

When considering the appropriateness of the going concern concept, directors consider whether an FRS 17 deficit, either on or off balance sheet, will prejudice the ability of the employer to raise or renew necessary finance (either because of expectations of a cash drain, doubts about the ability of the employer to maintain dividend payments or otherwise). The directors will also need to consider the impact of deficits on existing borrowing arrangements.

Where there is a substantial deficit on the FRS 17 valuation basis, auditors make enquiries as to whether there is a problem on a funding basis. In such circumstances, further consideration is given to the appropriateness of the going concern basis and auditors follow SAS 130 *'The going concern basis in financial statements'*.

Distributable profits

Whether or not it is lawful to make dividend distributions depends both on statute and common law. FRS 17 transitional disclosures are not relevant to the determination of dividend distributions under the Companies Act, nor are they directly relevant to the common law position. However, in the latter case, where there is a substantial FRS 17 pensions deficit, the auditors make enquiries as to how the directors have satisfied themselves concerning whether, under the relevant funding basis, the pension scheme obligations of the employer company could create solvency problems for the company and whether there are any implications arising from loan covenant conditions.

If the auditors qualify their report due to matters regarding FRS 17 transitional disclosures, this is not, in itself, grounds for indicating in any Section 271(4) statement that the matter is material for the purpose of determining whether the proposed dividend contravenes Sections 263 to 265 of the Companies Act.

Further guidance on FRS 17 transitional disclosures and distributions by companies will be given in a Technical Release to be issued shortly.

Post balance sheet events

Where significant events occur after the balance sheet date e.g. constructive obligations arising from the announcement of a major redundancy programme just after the year end, they should be dealt with in accordance with SSAP 17 '*Accounting for post balance sheet events*'.

Faculty monitoring of the progress of implementing FRS 17

The ICAEW's Audit and Assurance Faculty will continue to monitor the situation and communicate with members as appropriate. Should you encounter situations of likely interest, please contact Chris Cantwell at the Faculty, e-mail chris.cantwell@icaew.co.uk

Appendix – Company processes for gathering FRS 17 disclosure information

Implementing FRS 17 requires the practical application of a disciplined process. Companies need to focus on the key issues that will enable them to deliver reliable disclosures.

The following is designed to help audit teams assess company processes. It does not deal with the practicalities such as arranging for permission from the trustees for company auditors to contact scheme administrators, bankers or managers; these and other practicalities can only be addressed by auditors once they understand the company's process.

The process for first year implementation of FRS 17 is analysed below into five sub-processes. Asking whether directors have taken all the steps included in the five sub-processes will help identify:

- client steps to prepare for the drafting of the relevant disclosures;
- urgent client action points and potential improvements in the company's process;
- specific risks of financial statement error to be addressed by audit work[5]; and

---

[5] Examples of risks of material misstatement in relation to FRS 17 are provided in Appendix 2 of the Auditing Practices Board's Practice Note 22.

- issues relating to potential limitations of audit scope or disagreement that might impact the auditors' report.

(1) **To identify and aggregate schemes**, directors should:

   (a) identify defined benefit schemes, excluding relevant multi-employer schemes but including overseas, medical benefit and unfunded schemes;
   (b) understand the reasons for any change from the schemes covered by SSAP 24 *'Accounting for pension costs'*;
   (c) appropriately aggregate schemes with similar attributes for disclosure purposes; and
   (d) decide which schemes are immaterial and do not require further consideration, and be able to explain the basis for that determination.

(2) **To measure and analyse scheme assets**, directors should:

   (a) identify the types of assets held within material identified schemes;
   (b) find out what information is already available (e.g. from scheme accounts and from trustees, administrators, investment managers and custodians);
   (c) consider whether existing information reports assets at values appropriate for FRS 17, for example insurance policies that secure particular members' benefits and which for the purpose of reporting by the pension scheme will have been left out of the accounts; and
   (d) consider how and on what timescale the information in the scheme accounts will be updated to the end of the year.

(3) **To determine asset assumptions**, directors should:

   (a) appreciate the significance of the new concept of expected rates of return;
   (b) identify all asset categories for which rates will be required;
   (c) agree respective responsibilities of the company and the actuaries;
   (d) seek advice as to likely ranges of normal rates; and
   (e) consider the impact of expected rates on future profit and loss account charges.

(4) **To report liabilities and related assumptions**, directors should:

   (a) consider what information is already available, such as the most recent funding or SSAP 24 valuation of the liabilities;
   (b) satisfy themselves that appropriately qualified actuaries are in place for each scheme or group of schemes;
   (c) see whether the actuaries need to change the valuation method and/or discount rate to comply with FRS 17;
   (d) consider how the most recent valuation of liabilities will be updated for significant business events other than normal service costs and pension payments;
   (e) identify when, how and from whom information for any updates will be sourced; and
   (f) review a summary of the assumptions that are likely to be disclosed.

(5) **To summarise and finalise disclosures**, directors should:

   (a) identify sources of contribution rates (e.g. last year's and next year's contribution schedules for UK defined benefit schemes);
   (b) consider the need to disclose any restriction on the use of any surplus;

(c) identify the need to warn about the effect of an ageing population (e.g. for schemes that are closed to new entrants);
(d) consider the potential impact of any substantial deficit (on the funding basis) on their distribution policy and take advice as appropriate; and
(e) consider the potential reaction to the disclosures of key users of the financial statements.

[Statement 923]
New arrangements for reporting to the Association of British Travel Agents Limited (ABTA) (AUDIT 2/02)

This guidance is issued by the Audit and Assurance Faculty of the Institute of Chartered Accountants in England and Wales in March 2002 to explain new reporting arrangements being introduced by the Association of British Travel Agents Limited (ABTA) and to endorse these new arrangements to Institute members. The guidance does not constitute an auditing standard. Professional judgement should be used in its application.

Contents

	Paragraphs
Introduction	1 - 2
Explanation of the reporting 'package'	3 - 5
a) The model tripartite agreement	6 - 9
b) Guidance notes for reporting accountants	10
c) Reports/confirmations to ABTA	11
Endorsement of 'package' to Institute members	12
Ongoing monitoring of arrangements	13

Appendices

1. Association of British Travel Agents Limited (ABTA) returns – the model tripartite agreement
2. Guidance notes for the use of accountants reporting on information required of members of the Association of British Travel Agents Limited (ABTA)

[Statement 923]
New arrangements for reporting to the Association of British Travel Agents Limited (ABTA) (AUDIT 2/02)

Introduction

1 Following discussions between the Institute's Audit and Assurance Faculty and the Association of British Travel Agents Limited (ABTA), ABTA has agreed a new reporting regime or 'package' for special reports provided by accountants in respect of ABTA members.

2 This Technical Release explains the elements of that 'package' and endorses it to Institute members.

Explanation of the reporting 'package'

3 The reporting 'package' is based on the reporting framework outlined in Technical Release Audit 1/01 *'Reporting to Third Parties'*. It is recommended that accountants refer to Audit 1/01 when establishing their ABTA reporting engagements in addition to the individual elements of the 'package' (as outlined below).

4 The 'package' comprises of three elements:

(a) a model tripartite agreement;
(b) guidance notes for reporting accountants; and
(c) reports/confirmations to ABTA. Each of these elements is covered in the following sections.

5 When reporting accountants embark on an ABTA reporting engagement they do not deal with any element of the reporting 'package' in isolation from the others as each element is dependent on the others. For example, the accountants' report is made in accordance with the tripartite agreement and the guidance notes are referred to in order to understand the purpose of the report that has been requested and the issues that are likely to be relevant.

a) The model tripartite agreement

6 The model agreement, which is reproduced in Appendix 1, follows Audit 1/01 and ABTA has agreed that it will accept any engagement letter that follows this model. However, it does not apply to ABTA's Audit001 series of forms. *The Institute's recommendation to accountants is that they do not sign these reports since it is unlikely that work of sufficient depth and breadth to support a signed report will be possible.*

7 The one agreement will apply for all reports made and once in place should not need to be amended in subsequent periods (practical matters, including charges, will be dealt with separately).

8 The model agreement highlights that the responsibility for producing financial information rests with the ABTA member and the accountants report on the information provided by the member. The duty to ABTA is limited to delivery of the reports/confirmations in the agreed form.

These engagements are entirely separate from the audit which is carried out for a different purpose. ABTA requires audits of all ABTA members, irrespective of size or legal status. 9

b) Guidance notes for reporting accountants

These guidance notes, reproduced in Appendix 2, have been issued so that accountants appreciate the purpose of each return, including the context and what ABTA is seeking in requesting the report. The notes group the reports into five different types and outline various issues that accountants need to consider with respect to each of these. 10

c) Reports/confirmations to ABTA

Accountants provide their reports/confirmations to ABTA on standard forms issued by ABTA and agreed with the Institute. These forms are available on ABTA's website – www.abtamembers.org/accforms. 11

Endorsement of 'package' to Institute members

The Institute is endorsing the reporting 'package' to its members as it follows the framework laid down in Audit 1/01 and has been developed jointly by ABTA and the Institute. 12

Ongoing monitoring of arrangements

The Institute's Audit and Assurance Faculty intends to monitor the reporting arrangements outlined in this document and to deal with any issues emerging as necessary. 13

Appendix 1 – Association of British Travel Agents Limited (ABTA) returns – the model tripartite agreement[1]

(this model agreement issued in March 2002)

Addressee details:

(i) The ABTA member

(ii) ABTA

Dear Sirs

ABTA reports/confirmations

We are writing to confirm the terms and conditions on which you have engaged [name of firm] to provide reports/confirmations in connection with [ABTA

---

[1] This model does not cover any reports requested by ABTA in connection with the release of bonds (covered by the Audit 001 series of forms).

member]'s membership of the Association of British Travel Agents ('ABTA'). These terms and conditions will apply to the reports/confirmations to be supplied for the period [ended / ending ...] and for subsequent periods unless otherwise agreed in writing. We will write separately regarding practical matters such as the timing of our work, staffing and our charges. Our invoice will be addressed to [ABTA member], who will be solely responsible for payment in full.

Scope of our work

In respect of the information contained in the reports/confirmations, we will carry out procedures solely to be able to report on whether the information has been accurately extracted from the underlying records of [ABTA member].

Preparation of any document that [ABTA member] may be required to submit to ABTA in connection with our work will be the responsibility of [ABTA member]'s Directors[2], who will also be responsible for ensuring that [ABTA member] maintains proper accounting records and such other records as may be required by ABTA. [ABTA member]'s Directors will on request supply us with confirmation of matters affecting our work which are dependent on the Directors' judgement.

Save as set out above, we will not seek to establish the accuracy, completeness or reliability of any of the information or documentation made available to us. Our work will not amount to an audit of financial statements and will not give the same level of assurance as an audit.

Our audit work on the financial statements of [ABTA member] is carried out in accordance with our statutory obligations and is subject to separate terms and conditions. This engagement will not be treated as having any effect on our duties and responsibilities as [ABTA member]'s auditors. Our audit report is intended for the sole benefit of [ABTA member]'s shareholders, to whom it is addressed, to enable them to exercise their rights as a body in general meeting. Our audits of [ABTA member]'s financial statements are not planned or conducted to address or reflect matters in which anyone other than such shareholders as a body may be interested for such purpose.

To the fullest extent permitted by law we do not and will not, by virtue of our reports/confirmations or otherwise, assume or accept any responsibility or liability under this engagement to [ABTA member] or to ABTA or to any other party, whether in contract, negligence or otherwise in relation to our audits of [ABTA member]'s financial statements.

Having carried out our work we will issue reports/confirmations addressed to ABTA in the form determined from time to time by ABTA following consultation with the Institute of Chartered Accountants in England & Wales, if our findings support this. We will deliver copies to [ABTA member] at the same time. This letter will be identified in our reports/confirmations as the 'tripartite agreement' under which our reports/confirmations have been issued. Our reports/confirmations will be released on the basis that they are not to be copied, referred to or disclosed, in whole or in part, to any other party without our prior written consent, which may be conditional. We will not issue any qualified reports and if we are unable to report in the agreed form, we will let you know.

---

[2] All references to Directors in this model mean either Directors, Partners, Proprietors, Company Secretary, or other Authorised Signatory, as appropriate.

Other matters

Our duties and liabilities in connection with this engagement owed to [ABTA member] and to ABTA will differ.

[Detail any exclusions and limitations on the firm's liability to the ABTA member and any relevant qualifications required to satisfy statutory reasonableness criteria. Consider the guidance in the ICAEW's Audit 1/01, *'Reporting to third parties'*.]

Our duty to ABTA will be limited to delivery of reports/confirmations in the agreed form. Delivery of such reports/confirmations (or the supply of confirmation that we are unable to do so in the agreed form) at any time will discharge that obligation in full. We will not owe ABTA any other duty, in contract, negligence or otherwise, in connection with our reports/confirmations or their preparation. In particular, we will not owe ABTA a duty to exercise any care or skill in our work and ABTA will not acquire any right in contract or negligence or on any other basis to bring any action against us in connection with our work.

This agreement shall be subject to and governed by English law and all disputes arising from, or under, it shall be subject to the exclusive jurisdiction of the English courts.

[Detail or append any other terms and conditions to apply to this work.]

Please confirm, by signing below, your agreement to this letter. Once you have done so, this letter will form a tripartite contract between us in respect of the matters covered. If you wish to discuss any aspects of this letter, please contact [name and telephone number].

Yours faithfully

[Name of accountancy firm]

[ABTA member]

[ABTA]

Appendix 2 – Guidance notes for the use of accountants reporting on information required of members of the Association of British Travel Agents Limited ('ABTA')

Issued March 2002

Introduction

These notes have been drafted as guidance for those accountants whose clients ('client' or 'ABTA member') are members of ABTA and are required from time to time to report on information submitted to ABTA (the 'Reports') in their role as a 'regulator'. As a result of discussions between ABTA and the Institute of Chartered Accountants in England & Wales ('ICAEW') concerning the general issue of duty of care in respect of the work performed, a working party was set up to review the terms of engagement and the format of Reports required of the accounting and auditing professions. A revised set of Reports and guidance notes have been issued by ABTA and these guidance notes have been issued for reporting accountants to assist them in providing their Reports on the information supplied by their client to ABTA. This guidance has been based upon the ICAEW Audit and Assurance Faculty Technical Release Audit 1/01 *'Reporting to Third Parties'* (available from the ICAEW Audit and Assurance Faculty website – www.icaew.co.uk/auditassfac).

These notes should therefore be read in conjunction with the:

- Revised Reports from reporting accountants required by ABTA, the latest versions of which are available from the ABTA website – www.abta-members.org/accforms.
- Guidance notes from ABTA concerning the completion of the 'Turnover Return and Analysis (Audit003N)', which gives definitions necessary for its appropriate completion (also available from the ABTA website).
- Model tripartite agreement developed by ABTA and the ICAEW for these specific engagements (available from both the ABTA and ICAEW websites).

Letters of engagement

All the revised Reports make reference to a tripartite agreement between ABTA, the ABTA member and the reporting accountants, and it is suggested that the model tripartite agreement developed by ABTA and the ICAEW is used as a basis for specific terms of engagement in each case. The terms of the model tripartite agreement address the issues of the respective responsibilities of the Directors, Partners, Proprietors, Company Secretary, or other Authorised Signatory; and the reporting accountants, and in particular explain duty of care and limitation of liability as they relate to this specific work.

For the avoidance of doubt, the terms 'reporting accountants', 'accountants' and 'auditors' used throughout these guidance notes, the Reports and ABTA's 'Notes To The Turnover Return And Analysis' refer to the firm that conducted the statutory audit of the ABTA member and not to that firm's role as statutory auditors.

It is recommended that you agree the terms of engagement with your client(s) using this model as a basis and where you do so, ABTA will sign up to the tripartite agreement.

Reports

ABTA may request Reports on the following:

(i) turnover;
(ii) adjusted net current assets (as defined by ABTA);
(iii) certain other financial matters;
(iv) reports concerning the release of bonds; and
(v) audit reports in respect of ABTA members.

Each of these is dealt with in turn below.

(i) Turnover

There is one all encompassing report on turnover entitled 'Turnover Return and Analysis (AUDIT003)' and three subsidiary reports on turnover namely:

- Gross Principal Turnover (Non-Licensable) (Audit009(M)) and Audit009(S));

- Confirmation of Credit Turnover (Audit010);
- Confirmation of BSP Turnover (Audit011); and
- Quarterly Return of Gross Principal Turnover (FM002(SN) and FM002(MN)).

Definitions of the terminology used in the Reports are contained in the 'Notes to the Turnover Return and Analysis (Audit003N)' issued by ABTA. All reports are annual with the exception of the quarterly returns.

Each of these reports has a specific purpose, as follows:

Turnover Return and Analysis (Audit003) - The information collected on this return provides a detailed analysis of gross turnover (sales) and is used *inter alia* to calculate:

- the level of security (e.g. bonding) required by ABTA which in turn is based upon all categories of turnover, except licensable turnover which is normally covered by the ATOL scheme and bonding; and
- the amount of annual subscriptions and any contributions that may be required to the ABTA Retail Fund and/or ABTA Principals Fund, which are turnover based.

Gross Principal Turnover (Non-Licensable) (Audit009 (M) and Audit009 (S)) – This report provides confirmation of the four quarterly turnover returns that a member conducting business of a non-licensable nature is required to provide. This information is used by ABTA to determine the level of security (e.g. bonding) required by the member. The turnover should be on a cash receipts basis to match the projected turnover given at the beginning of the bonding year and also to match the risk faced by the customer – i.e. the customer is not at risk if they have taken credit from the agent, not settled and the agent then goes out of business.

Confirmation of Credit Turnover (Audit010) – An ABTA member can claim for an allowance against the retail turnover conducted on credit with a Principal on which the level of security (e.g. bonding) has been calculated. An allowance is only granted where the Principals themselves have also confirmed to ABTA that they are granting credit to the member. The reason for giving an allowance is that ABTA does not want to bear the credit risk that the Principal should be covering. If the agent taking credit from the Principal goes out of business, the tour operator will be asked to honour their contract with the customer and bear the cost of poor credit control. This return provides confirmation of the value of the member's turnover that has been conducted on a credit basis and where the member wishes to claim an allowance against the retail turnover on which the level of security has been calculated.

Confirmation of BSP Turnover (Audit011) – This provides confirmation of the value of member's transactions through the IATA BSP payments system where the member wishes to claim 100% allowance against the retail turnover on which the level of security has been calculated. This allowance is given because IATA scheduled air tickets are issued at the time of payment creating a contract between the airline and the customer. As with credit turnover, ABTA does not want to cover the airlines' risk - if the agent fails to pay the airline, the airline still needs to honour its contract with the customer.

Quarterly Return of Gross Principal Turnover (FM002(MN) and FM002(SN)) – For a new member conducting non-licensable principal turnover, the quarterly returns of actual turnover in the bonding year (either to 31 March or to 30 September) require a report from the reporting accountant. The turnover should be compiled on a cash receipts basis to match the projected turnover given at the beginning of the bonding year.

The information being collected in the above returns is used by ABTA to assess the security requirements of the member (which is based upon the turnover of the member) and therefore the accountants are requested to confirm its accurate extraction from the books and records.

To complete this work, you are advised to make reference to Technical Release Audit 1/01, *'Reporting to Third Parties'*, issued by the Audit and Assurance Faculty of the ICAEW, available on the ICAEW website (see above).

(ii) Adjusted Net Current Assets (Audit008)

Where required, this annual report is normally completed and submitted to ABTA by ABTA members at the same time as the audited financial statements and the 'Turnover Return and Analysis' (Audit 003). ABTA uses this document to help it assess whether the liquidity of members conducting 'non-licensable business as a Principal' meets the minimum liquidity requirement, which allows continued membership without the provision of additional security. The information in the report should be extracted from the books and records of the member, which should have been subject to an annual audit under UK GAAS (as required by the ABTA Articles of Association). The accountants are asked to confirm that the figures have been accurately extracted from the books and records of the ABTA member.

Most categories of adjustment have definitions included within the report or are self-evident. However your notice is drawn to the following when reviewing this form:

a) *Net current assets/(liabilities) per balance sheet* – this figure should agree to the audited balance sheet contained in the audited financial statements that should be submitted to ABTA by the ABTA member.
b) *Amounts not demonstrably recoverable* – the figures extracted from the books and records and included within this document should have been the subject of an audit under UK GAAS. Accordingly it should not be necessary to adjust the Net Current Assets/(Liabilities) by any such amount since a provision should have been made for any doubtful recoveries.
c) *Other* – consideration needs to be given to the items that should be adjusted for in the context of ABTA's intended use of the return, as explained above.

(iii) Confirmation of certain matters

There are two such reports, **Audit005** and **Audit007**, both entitled 'Report To The Association Of British Travel Agents' which are to be completed for agents and principals respectively who joined ABTA six months ago. A new member is required to provide management accounts made up to a date six months after entry into membership as a check on progress against the forecasts submitted in support of their membership application. The information provided may affect the level of security(e.g. bonding) required of the member. The reports require that the accountants confirm certain matters of a factual nature by reference to the books and records of the ABTA member. It is recommended that the directors formally approve the management accounts that are reported on by the accountants. The directors separately confirm to ABTA the accuracy of the other information being confirmed by the accountants and consequently there is no director sign off on Audit005 and Audit007. No issues are expected to arise from this.

(iv) The release of bonds

ABTA holds bonds for ABTA members for a period of 18 months and the bonds run to their full term even where an ABTA member has ceased to operate a business as a principal or agent. In order for the ABTA member to secure an early return of their bond the accountants are required to confirm that there are no outstanding or future liabilities relating to the discontinued operations of the business. These reports are the series **Audit001**.

It is likely that circumstances that give rise to the need to issue these reports will be extremely rare. Accountants need to be sure beyond reasonable doubt that there are no outstanding or future liabilities before signing this report. *The recommendation to accountants is that this report is not signed since it is unlikely that work of sufficient depth and breadth to support a signed report will be possible.* Specifically the agreement developed by ABTA and ICAEW does not cover the reporting on these returns and therefore does not remove the duty of care from accountants signing these reports. In the event that there is a claim arising after the early release of the bond, ABTA will look to the accountants for settlement of the claim. You may wish to discuss this with ABTA before signing any of the Audit001 series of reports.

In any event, the bond will be returned to the bond provider at the end of the 18-month bonding period assuming it is not called upon, so this must be the minimum period of time that accountants would require to have elapsed before considering the issue of such a report.

(v) Audit reports in respect of ABTA members

Under ABTA's Articles of Association, each ABTA member irrespective of its legal status (unincorporated, partnership, sole trader, exempt small company) must have accounts that give a true and fair view under the Companies Act and have an annual audit carried out under UK GAAS.

It has been the previous experience of ABTA that some audit reports issued for unincorporated ABTA members do not conform with the Statement of Auditing Standard ('SAS') 600 *'Auditors' reports on financial statements'*. Consequently Form **Audit002** was introduced.

Where a UK GAAS audit is carried out, an audit report in accordance with SAS 600 should be issued in respect of the financial statements that have been audited. Where this is the case and your client forwards the audited financial statements to ABTA, then this form should not be completed.

[Statement 924]
Bank reports for audit purposes
(AUDIT 3/02)

This guidance does not constitute an auditing standard. Professional judgement should be used in applying it. No responsibility for loss occasioned to any person acting or refraining from action as a result of any material in this guidance can be accepted by the Institute.

Contents

Paragraphs

Introduction	1 - 3
Considerations for auditors and banks – bank acknowledgement of auditor	4
Considerations for auditors	5 - 6
Considerations for banks	7
Acknowledgements	8
Responses to requests	9
Minor omissions or discrepancies	10
Debit and credit balances	11
Guarantees and other third party securities	12
Accrued interest and charges	13

Bank acknowledgement of auditor request

Bank reports for audit purposes (AUDIT 3/02)

Introduction

UK auditors confirm information about their clients' banking facilities by means of bank reports for audit purposes (bank reports). Bank reports are an important part of the independent audit process. The provision of such reports is an integral part of the lending process and constitutes a service to customers for which banks charge. The format of the bank report is agreed by the British Bankers' Association (BBA) and the Auditing Practices Board (APB). Formats for bank reports are included in BBA instructions to banks regarding the receipt of requests for information for audit purposes, and in APB Practice Note 16 'Bank reports for audit purposes'.

The completion of bank reports has become increasingly complicated for several reasons:

- many companies operate through complex group structures;
- even relatively small entities are making use of a broader range of financial services;
- statutory accounting and auditing requirements are becoming increasingly stringent. Greater emphasis has been placed in recent years on, for example, information concerning going concern assumptions, related party transactions and the risks associated with financial instruments;
- the expanding range of facilities generally made available by banks has necessitated the involvement of an increasing number of specialist divisions in the provision of services to individual customers.

Moreover, entities and their auditors are coming under increasing pressure to prepare the accounts and complete the audit process within shorter time periods than were previously necessary.

Considerations for auditors and banks – bank acknowledgement of auditor requests

In order to expedite the provision of responses to requests for bank reports, auditors and banks should use the example 'Bank Acknowledgement of Auditor Request' (acknowledgement) detailed below. The purpose of the acknowledgement is to provide auditors with assurance that the request for the bank report has been received, and with a point of contact within the bank to whom enquiries can be addressed. The named contact may be an account relationship manager, an assistant to the account relationship manager or a contact within a national or regional service centre, depending on the bank's internal arrangements.

Considerations for auditors

APB Practice Note 16 describes the procedures auditors follow and includes the agreed format of the bank report. Auditors indicate whether they wish the bank to provide standard information comprising the more mainstream facilities that are likely to have been extended to any entity, or whether they also require supplementary information to cover other specialist facilities, such as trade finance, derivatives and custodian services.

The following aspects of the bank audit confirmation process are important in improving the efficiency with which standard bank reports are submitted and processed:

- requests for bank reports must be submitted, accompanied where necessary with the customer's authority to disclose information, no less than 14 days in advance of the audit confirmation date. Delays in submitting requests for bank reports lead to delays in responses, particularly at busy times of the year. Auditors draw attention to any ongoing standing authority that continues to apply or enclose a new authority where necessary (where they are undertaking an audit for a client for the first time, for example);
- requests for bank reports should be accompanied by the acknowledgement referred to above and detailed below;
- envelopes should be headed 'Bank report for audit purposes' and addressed to the account relationship manager at the branch or division maintaining the main banking relationship with the customer. Heading the envelope in this way will ensure that processing starts without delay in the event that the relationship manager is away from the office.

Considerations for banks

7 Requests for bank reports do not provide account numbers and sort codes because auditors are seeking to ascertain if there are any bank accounts or facilities of which they are unaware. Much of the usefulness of the bank report as audit evidence is lost if account numbers and sort codes are provided in requests for bank reports. In responding to requests for bank reports, banks may need to consult a number of business divisions internally, including those responsible for:

- current account balances;
- sterling account balances;
- money market deposits;
- securities;
- contingent liabilities (including acceptances, endorsements, guarantees, irrevocable letters of credit and assets pledged as collateral security);
- commitments (including documentary credits and short-term trade related facilities, forward asset purchases and forward deposits placed, undrawn note issuance and revolving underwriting facilities and undrawn formal standby facilities, credit lines and other commitments to lend);
- derivatives (including futures and forwards, forward rate agreements, swaps, options, caps, collars and floors);
- leasing;
- factoring and invoice discounting.

Acknowledgements

8 Where auditors include the acknowledgement, referred to above and detailed below, with a request for a bank report, the acknowledgement should be returned to the auditor as soon as possible. Auditors should be aware that some several hundred thousand bank reports need to be completed every year and accordingly appreciate that it takes time for individual requests to be processed.

Responses to requests

9 In collating responses banks should bear in mind that the bank report is an essential element of the audit process for many entities and the information it contains is required within two months of the audit confirmation date. For listed companies and other entities subject to tight reporting deadlines the period may be significantly shorter. Failure to submit or complete bank reports within a reasonable time can have a significant effect on customers and may result in the need for a qualified audit

report or in an investigation by relevant regulatory bodies. It also means that the bank has not provided the customer with a service integral to the lending relationship and may create difficulties for the bank when it comes to reviewing facilities provided.

Minor omissions or discrepancies

Minor omissions or discrepancies in the information provided by the bank may be dealt with informally by telephone or e-mail, although auditors may request written confirmation of changes to the information provided.   10

Debit and credit balances

A borrowing customer may maintain several accounts with a bank, some in debit and others in credit, perhaps at different branches of the bank. These balances should not be netted off in the bank report. The standard and supplementary requests for information agreed by the BBA and the APB request details of all bank accounts. Auditors are obliged to form their own independent opinion as to whether debit and credit balances should be aggregated into a single net item.   11

Guarantees and other third party securities

The provision of information about guarantees and other third party securities has, on occasion, resulted in significant delays in the completion of bank reports because banks have been unable to release the information sought without specific customer consent. When banks do not have sufficient authority to provide full disclosure of the information requested, they should advise the auditor of that fact and indicate, where that is the case, that such guarantees or third party securities exist. The auditor can then obtain details of the arrangement from the client, by asking to see the relevant facility letter or loan agreement, for example. In some cases, these procedures will suffice. In other cases, auditors will require further independent evidence, and in such cases they can ask banks for the specific information to be provided once consent from the guarantor or third party has been received.   12

Accrued interest and charges

Banks frequently receive requests for information about accrued interest and charges on a daily basis. This information is not within the guidance agreed by the BBA and the APB and any such request may be declined if the bank cannot generate the data from its computerised records.   13

This Explanatory Note has been prepared and issued by the British Bankers' Association and the Consultative Committee of Accountancy Bodies (the CCAB). It does not form part of APB Practice Note 16 'Bank reports for audit purposes'. It has been forwarded to the Review Panel of the Small Business Banking Code for consideration of whether the Code should in future include a commitment on the part of the industry concerning the completion of bank reports for audit purposes.

It has been proposed within the context of the Company Law Review that certain companies with a turnover of up to £4.8m should be exempt from audit. It is likely, however, that many companies will forego their statutory right to audit exemption on the grounds that they consider the audit to be relevant to their circumstances or because of a current or future dependency on external financing.

BANK ACKNOWLEDGEMENT OF AUDITOR REQUEST

PART A – This Part To Be Completed By The Auditor

This acknowledgement should be returned to:

Name _____

Position _____

Firm _____

Address _____

_____

_____

Tel. No _____

E-mail* _____ * If available.

PART B – This Part To Be Completed By The Bank

Thank you for your request for a bank report for audit purposes in respect of
_____ (customer's name)

The request was received on:
_____ (day/month/year)

Your request is being processed and the letter will be completed once we have gathered the information sought. In the event of your needing to contact us, please address any enquiries to:

Name _____

Position _____

Bank _____

Address _____

_____

_____

Tel. No _____

E-mail* _____ * If available.

[Statement 925]
Management representation letters – explanatory notes (AUDIT 4/02)

(Issued November 2002)

This guidance does not constitute an auditing standard. Professional judgement should be used in applying it. No responsibility for loss occasioned to any person acting or refraining from action as a result of any material in this guidance can be accepted by the Institute.

Contents

Management representation letters

Background

SAS 440 'Management representations'

Increasing the usefulness of management representation as audit evidence

Future developments

Management representation letters

The purpose of this Technical Release is to help auditors to increase the usefulness of management representations as audit evidence. This guidance draws attention to specific explanatory paragraphs in Statement of Auditing Standards 440, 'Management Representations' (SAS 440), in order to underline the importance of ensuring that such representations are reliable. The guidance is not intended to be comprehensive and is not a substitute for the procedures or related material contained in SAS 440, or for specific measures that may be appropriate to particular matters or engagements.

Background

Barings Futures Singapore v Deloitte & Touche Singapore

A recent High Court decision in a preliminary hearing concerning the audit by Deloitte & Touche (D&T) of Barings Futures (Singapore) Pte Ltd. (BFS) has identified some key points in relation to management representations, and the protection they afford to auditors.

It was noted in the course of the Barings hearing that the BFS director who signed the representation letters in question had little knowledge or understanding of Nick Leeson's activities, despite being nominally his boss. However, the director made written statements to the effect that there had been no irregularities involving management or having a material effect on the financial systems, and that the financial statements were free of material errors and omissions.

On this basis, D&T claimed that the representations by the BFS director were recklessly fraudulent, and therefore gave them an absolute defence of circuity against the claim in damages which they faced. D&T's claim failed, however, because they did not establish to the judge's satisfaction that the BFS director signed the representation letters:

(i) knowing that the statements in the letters were untrue, without an honest belief in their truth, or indifferent as to whether or not they were true;
(ii) knowing that he had no reasonable grounds for making the statements, without an honest belief that he had such grounds, or indifferent as to whether he had or not.

The judge did, however, address the issue of the result if D&T had proved that, in signing the representation letters, the director was reckless of their truth or falsity. He concluded that, had such a case for fraudulent misrepresentation been established, he would have held that BFS was vicariously liable for the director's action, and thus D&T would have succeeded in their claim.

SAS 440 'Management Representations'

SAS 440 requires auditors to obtain written confirmation of appropriate representations from management before their report is issued. In particular, auditors should obtain evidence that the directors acknowledge their collective responsibility for the preparation of the financial statements and that they have approved them. The SAS also requires that auditors should obtain written confirmation of representations from management on matters material to the financial statements, when those representations are critical to gathering sufficient audit evidence.

Paragraph 10 of SAS 440 states that, 'In addition to obtaining representations from the directors as to their responsibility for the financial statements, auditors often rely on representations by management as part of their audit evidence.' However, as paragraph 15 points out, 'Representations by management cannot be a substitute for other evidence that auditors expect to be available.' Unsupported representations by management do not normally constitute sufficient audit evidence. The only situations where corroborative evidence may not be available are those where the subject of the representations are management judgment or intentions.

Whatever their function in the body of evidence collected by an auditor to support the audit opinion, management representation letters are not a mere formality. This is why the final part of SAS 440 states that, 'If management refuses to provide written confirmation of a representation that the auditors consider necessary, the auditors should consider the implications of this scope limitation for their report' (SAS 440.5).

Barings Futures Singapore v Deloitte & Touche Singapore [2002] All ER (D) Mar

Increasing the usefulness of management representations as audit evidence

The Barings judgment does not contradict the basic procedures or principles contained in SAS 440. What it does do, however, is emphasise the need for auditors to have regard to the 'grey lettering' material in the SAS in relation to obtaining comfort from representation letters.

Paragraph 12 suggests that auditors discuss such matters with those responsible for giving the written confirmation before they sign it to ensure that they understand what it is they are being asked to confirm. Paragraph 14 invites auditors to '...consider whether the individuals making the representations can be expected to be well-informed on the particular matters'.

In order to assist this process, and in particular to focus directors' attention on whether proper enquiries have been made, auditors may find it helpful to request management to add a sentence to the representation letter along the following lines:

We confirm that the above/following representations are made on the basis of enquiries of management and staff with relevant knowledge and experience (and, where appropriate, of inspection of supporting documentation) sufficient to satisfy ourselves that we can properly make each of the above/following representations to you.

This wording is suggested for illustration only, and is not mandatory. It could help to reduce the impression given to directors that phrases such as 'to the best of our knowledge and belief' may enable them not to make proper enquiries. Auditors would further be well advised to ask the signatory(ies) what steps they took to obtain comfort that such an assertion had substance. In circumstances where the representations are being made by those distanced from the activities involved, for example the use of complex financial instruments, auditors could suggest that the relevant member of management responsible provide specialised representations to the board. In this case it may be useful for the directors' own letter of representation to attach and refer to the specialist memorandum, to ensure that they retained overall responsibility.

It is already a criminal offence, under section 389A of the 1985 Companies Act, for an officer of a company knowingly or recklessly to make a misleading or false statement to the company's auditors. Auditors may, therefore, take the opportunity when discussing representations with the directors (and other staff, if applicable), to remind them of the statutory provisions relating to false or misleading statements.

Future developments

It is generally considered that section 389A of the 1985 Companies Act has not had much impact to date. The importance of written representations by management, and their reliability as audit evidence, may be increased if draft clauses 107 and 108 in Part 6 of the recently published Companies Bill are enacted. These clauses require directors of companies and certain subsidiaries, and people connected with a company and its subsidiaries in Great Britain, to provide information or explanations in answer to the company auditor's questions. Failure to answer the questions, or the knowing or reckless provision of a misleading, false or materially deceptive statement, is a criminal offence, punishable by a fine of up to £5,000 and/or imprisonment.

[Statement 926]
The audit report and auditors' duty of care to third parties (AUDIT 1/03)

This guidance is issued by the Audit and Assurance Faculty of the Institute of Chartered Accountants in England and Wales in January 2003 to assist auditors in managing the risk of inadvertently assuming a duty of care to third parties in relation to their audit reports. This guidance does not constitute an auditing standard. Professional judgement should be used in its application. No responsibility for loss occasioned to any person acting or refraining from action as a result of any material in this guidance can be accepted by the Institute.

Contents

	Paragraphs
Preface	
Background	1 - 2
Responsibilities of auditors	3
Wording to include in the audit report	4 - 5
Purpose of the recommended wording	6
Wording for the engagement letter	7
Other points to communicate to clients	8
Alternative and/or additional actions	9 - 10
Legal considerations	11
Scope	12

Appendices

1. Extract from November 2002 True & Fair article
2. Example audit report with an unqualified opinion
3. Extract from Audit 4/00
4. Questions and answers

The audit report and auditors' duty of care to third parties

Preface

In recent years auditors have become increasingly aware of the risk of taking on responsibilities to third parties with regard to their audit reports. Sometimes a duty of care to a third party might be assumed inadvertently as a result of action or inaction by the auditors. The Institute has already issued a number of guidance documents to cover these risks and the guidance in these documents, for example in Audit 4/00 and Audit 1/01, remains relevant – see paragraph 1 below.

As the result of a legal judgment in the Scottish Court of Session auditors have considered whether they should include additional wording in their audit reports to protect against exposure to third party claims. The Institute believes that it is important to issue guidance that provides practical guidance for appropriate action which members may take.

The various options which firms may take in response to this judgment have been considered and the Institute has also taken the advice of Leading Counsel in this respect. The guidance in this Technical Release is based on the advice the Institute has received.

It should be noted that the court decision in the Scottish case in question was a preliminary order only on a legal point and is the subject of an appeal. Whilst the judgment might be overturned on appeal, the Institute recommends that members act now in accordance with this guidance. Even if this judgment is overturned on the basis of the particular facts of the case, the legal principle is not new and the initial finding may represent a trend in judicial thinking that may be followed by English courts and may encourage third parties to pursue claims. It should also be emphasised that the best risk management policy is for firms to take the steps that are necessary to carry out quality audits. The Audit and Assurance Faculty has recently provided guidance on this in its publication *'Audit Quality'* – this makes it clear that the Institute actively promotes audit quality with a view to the production of audit reports that are independent, reliable and supported by adequate audit evidence. Nothing in this Technical Release in any way diminishes the messages provided in that publication.

The Questions and Answers in Appendix 4 have been included to assist members in dealing with possible misunderstandings that they might encounter.

Background

1   A recent Scottish judgment in *Royal Bank of Scotland* v *Bannerman Johnstone Maclay and others ('Bannerman')* has highlighted the potential exposure of auditors to parties, other than the members of a company as a body, who assert that they rely on audit reports, in circumstances where the auditors have failed expressly to disclaim responsibility to those third parties. The Institute is issuing this guidance to assist members in managing the risk of inadvertently assuming a duty of care in relation to their audit reports to third parties and to remind members of the guidance on these matters already given in the Institute Statements 919 (Audit 4/00 *'Firms' reports and duties to lenders in connection with loans and other facilities to clients and related covenants'*) and 920 (Audit 1/01 *'Reporting to third parties'*). Paragraphs 1–22

of Audit 4/00 are highly relevant to the matters considered in this Technical Release and so are reproduced in Appendix 3 to this guidance.

The facts of the *Bannerman* case were summarised in an article in the Audit and Assurance Faculty's newsletter *'True & Fair'* – an extract from this is reproduced in Appendix 1 to this Technical Release. The full text of the judgment can be found at www.scotcourts.gov.uk/opinionsv/mcf1807c.html.

Responsibilities of auditors

Auditors have a responsibility to carry out their audits in accordance with auditing standards. These responsibilities are unchanged as a result of the guidance in this Technical Release. The guidance is instead concerned with the question of to whom responsibilities are owed.

Wording to include in the audit report

It is clear that an auditor assumes responsibility for the audit report to the shareholders as a body. The decision in *Bannerman* indicates that the absence of a disclaimer may (depending on the other circumstances in the particular case) enable an inference to be drawn that the auditor has assumed responsibility for the audit report to a third party. Having taken advice from Leading Counsel, the Institute recommends that auditors who wish to manage the risk of liability to third parties use a disclaimer. The Institute would regard the following wording as appropriate (although other wording may also be appropriate, and auditors will have regard to any legal advice they may take), and as suitably placed in the first or second paragraph of the audit report:

> 'This report is made solely to the company's members, as a body, in accordance with Section 235 of the Companies Act 1985. Our audit work has been undertaken so that we might state to the company's members those matters we are required to state to them in an auditor's report and for no other purpose. To the fullest extent permitted by law, we do not accept or assume responsibility to anyone other than the company and the company's members as a body, for our audit work, for this report, or for the opinions we have formed.'

An example unqualified audit report (based on the example in Appendix 3 of Bulletin 2001/2 *'Revisions to the wording of auditors' reports'*), with this wording included, is attached as Appendix 2 to this guidance. In the event that the text of the audit report differs from the example attached, a check should be made (with the assistance of legal advice where appropriate) to ensure that the language suggested above remains suitable without amendment.

Purpose of the recommended wording

Auditors' responsibilities to their clients remain unaltered and as stated in paragraph 3 above, they are still required to carry out the audit in accordance with auditing standards[1]. The purpose of this clarification language is to reduce the scope for the assumption of responsibilities to third parties.

Wording for the engagement letter

The form of an audit report is a matter for the discretion of the auditors (see SAS 600 *'Auditors' reports on financial statements'*), provided that the opinion meets

Companies Act requirements and is in accordance with auditing standards. It is not necessary to amend engagement letters to make provision for the clarification wording in the audit report outlined in paragraph 4. However, if auditors wish to inform their clients in this way, it might be helpful to include the following language in the engagement letter:

> 'As noted above, our report will be made solely to the company's members, as a body, in accordance with Section 235 of the Companies Act 1985. Our audit work will be undertaken so that we might state to the company's members those matters we are required to state to them in an auditor's report and for no other purpose. In those circumstances, to the fullest extent permitted by law, we will not accept or assume responsibility to anyone other than the company and the company's members as a body, for our audit work, for the audit report, or for the opinions we form.'

Other points to communicate to clients

8 When auditors include the recommended wording, it may be helpful to explain the following important points to their clients:

(a) The inclusion of the new wording does not affect the auditors' obligations to their clients. In fact it clarifies that the audit is for the benefit of the company's members in accordance with section 235 of the Companies Act 1985. Auditors will have the same duties and liabilities to their clients as they have always had.

(b) The new wording does not mean that auditors will never agree to take on responsibilities to third parties such as lenders. All it does is make clear that auditors will only accept duties that are expressly agreed. Auditors maintain that if parties want to rely on their work then they should approach the auditors to agree expressly the scope and nature of work auditors can do for them that meets their purposes[2].

Alternative and/or additional actions

9 Auditors may take alternative or additional steps to communicate with third parties which are intended to have the same effect as the words in the audit report recommended above. However, if auditors consider taking these alternative or additional measures, they judge them on their practicality and efficiency, as well as their effectiveness. In doing this they consider both the completeness and the timing of the measures they propose to take.

10 If the wording recommended in paragraph 4 above is included in audit reports, auditors nevertheless remain vigilant to avoid the words being overridden by actions (contemporaneous or subsequent) which are inconsistent. In particular, auditors are aware of circumstances that might give rise to a duty of care to a third party. Where auditors wish to disclaim responsibility to the third party in these circumstances, as would normally be the case, they state this expressly in writing through the issue of a letter to the particular third party. Appendix 1 of Audit 4/00, tailored to the specific circumstances, can be used for this purpose.

Legal considerations

11 This guidance provides a summary of what the Institute believes to be the most relevant considerations, based on the law at the time of issue and advice from Leading Counsel, but should not be regarded as a substitute for the specific legal and

professional advice which firms may need to take on particular matters or engagements.

Scope

This guidance applies to all Section 235 audit reports issued by firms. Auditors may also consider the application of the guidance to other public reporting engagements, such as interim reviews, regulatory reports and reports issued under other statutes.

12

Appendix 1 – Extract from the article in the November 2002 issue of *'True & Fair'*

The Scottish Court of Session held that a company's auditors could owe a duty of care to a lending bank if they knew (or ought to have known) that the bank would rely on their client's audited accounts and they did not disclaim liability.

The background

Royal Bank of Scotland ('RBS') provided overdraft facilities to APC Limited and Bannerman Johnstone Maclay ('Bannerman') were APC's auditors. The relevant facility letters between RBS and APC contained a clause requiring APC to send to RBS, each year, a copy of the annual audited financial statements.

In 1998 APC was put into receivership with approximately £13,250,000 owing to RBS. RBS claimed that, due to a fraud, APC's financial statements for the previous years had misstated the financial position of APC and Bannerman had been negligent in not detecting the fraud. RBS contended that it had continued to provide the overdraft facilities in reliance on Bannerman's unqualified opinions.

Bannerman applied to the court for an order striking out the claim on the grounds that, even if all the facts alleged by RBS were true, the claim could not succeed in law because Bannerman owed no duty of care to RBS.

The decision

The judge held that the facts pleaded by RBS were sufficient in law to give rise to a duty of care and so the case can now proceed to trial.

This article does not deal in detail with the reasons behind the judgement or contrast it with previous cases such as the House of Lords' decision in *Caparo v Dickman*. This area of law is highly fact-dependent with situations examined on a case by case basis. However, one of the key reasons behind the decision highlights a significant potential exposure for auditors to third parties. The judge held that, although there was no direct contact between Bannerman and RBS, knowledge gained by Bannerman in the course of their ordinary audit work was sufficient, in the absence of any disclaimer, to create a duty of care owed by Bannerman to RBS. In order to consider APC's ability to continue as a going concern, Bannerman would have reviewed the facility letters and so would have become aware that the audited financial statements would be provided to RBS for the purpose of RBS making lending decisions. Having acquired this knowledge, Bannerman could have disclaimed liability to RBS but did not do so. The absence of such a disclaimer was an important circumstance supporting the finding of a duty of care.

Risk management lessons

It has long been and remains a risk that in dealing with third parties a duty of care may be inadvertently assumed by auditors in relation to their opinions. A key feature of this case is that there were no direct dealings between the auditors and the third party. In spite of this, the auditors were found to owe a duty to a third party based on knowledge of the use to which the bank could be expected to put the accounts acquired as part of their ordinary audit work (required by Auditing Standards), and without having done anything else to suggest a relationship of proximity with, or assumption of responsibility to, the third party. It was then the omission to send a disclaimer to the third party, rather than any positive action by the auditors, that supported the existence of the duty of care.

In the current economic environment, the consideration of the going concern basis in financial statements in accordance with SAS 130 is a key part of the audit process. This is likely to involve the review of loan agreements or facility letters. Given that many such agreements will contain a requirement that the borrower provide a copy of its accounts to the lender, auditors should consider what steps they should take to protect themselves by disclaiming liability to their clients' lenders.

Appendix 2 – Example audit report with an unqualified opinion (based on the example in Appendix 3 of Bulletin 2001/2 'Revisions to the wording of auditors' reports')

Independent Auditors' Report to the Shareholders of XYZ Ltd

We have audited the financial statements of (name of entity) for the year ended ... which comprise [state the primary financial statements such as the Profit and Loss Account, the Balance Sheet, the Cash Flow Statement, the Statement of Total Recognised Gains and Losses] and the related notes. These financial statements have been prepared under the historical cost convention [as modified by the revaluation of certain fixed assets] and the accounting policies set out therein.

This report is made solely to the company's members, as a body, in accordance with Section 235 of the Companies Act 1985. Our audit work has been undertaken so that we might state to the company's members those matters we are required to state to them in an auditor's report and for no other purpose. To the fullest extent permitted by law, we do not accept or assume responsibility to anyone other than the company and the company's members as a body, for our audit work, for this report, or for the opinions we have formed.

Respective responsibilities of directors and auditors

As described in the Statement of Directors' Responsibilities the company's directors are responsible for the preparation of financial statements in accordance with applicable law and United Kingdom Accounting Standards.

Our responsibility is to audit the financial statements in accordance with relevant legal and regulatory requirements and United Kingdom Auditing Standards.

[1] *This example is for an unlisted company. For a listed company additional wording will be required on directors' remuneration disclosures to reflect APB Bulletin 2002/2.*

We report to you our opinion as to whether the financial statements give a true and fair view and are properly prepared in accordance with the Companies Act 1985. We also report to you if, in our opinion, the Directors' Report is not consistent with the financial statements, if the company has not kept proper accounting records, if we have not received all the information and explanations we require for our audit, or if information specified by law regarding directors' remuneration and transactions with the company is not disclosed.

We read the Directors' Report and consider the implications for our report if we become aware of any apparent misstatement within it.

Basis of audit opinion

We conducted our audit in accordance with United Kingdom Auditing Standards issued by the Auditing Practices Board. An audit includes examination, on a test basis, of evidence relevant to the amounts and disclosures in the financial statements. It also includes an assessment of the significant estimates and judgments made by the directors in the preparation of the financial statements, and of whether the accounting policies are appropriate to the company's circumstances, consistently applied and adequately disclosed.

We planned and performed our audit so as to obtain all the information and explanations which we considered necessary in order to provide us with sufficient evidence to give reasonable assurance that the financial statements are free from material misstatement, whether caused by fraud or other irregularity or error. In forming our opinion we also evaluated the overall adequacy of the presentation of information in the financial statements.

Opinion

In our opinion the financial statements give a true and fair view of the state of the company's affairs as at ... and of its profit [loss] for the year then ended and have been properly prepared in accordance with the Companies Act 1985.

Registered auditors

Address
Date

Appendix 3 – Extract from Institute Statement 919 'Firms' reports and duties to lenders in connection with loans and other facilities to clients and related covenants' (Audit 4/00)

Introduction

The responsibilities of auditors to third parties in respect of the statutory audit report are established in case law. The House of Lords in its judgment in *Caparo Industries Plc* v *Dickman (1990) 2 WLR 353* set out the essential ingredients by which the existence of a duty of care is to be recognised.

2 In his judgment, Lord Bridge described the salient features of earlier cases, stating that for a duty of care to a third party to arise in respect of the advice or information given, the person who it is alleged owes that duty of care must be fully aware:

- of the nature of the transaction contemplated by the third party;
- that the advice or information given would be passed to the third party, directly or indirectly; and
- that it was very likely that the third party intended to rely on that advice or information in deciding whether or not to engage in the transaction in contemplation.

3 In these circumstances, Lord Bridge considered that, subject to the effect of any disclaimer of responsibility, the person giving advice or information would be expected specifically to anticipate that the third party would rely on the advice or information given in deciding whether or not to engage in the transaction in contemplation.

4 Since the issue of the *Caparo* judgment, banks and other lenders have sought ways to document a direct and sufficient relationship between themselves and their customers' auditors so as to be able to rely on audit reports contained in financial statements prepared for statutory purposes.

5 This Statement gives guidance on the implications of such practices by lenders and the matters that should be taken into consideration by firms regarding the extent of their duty of care in respect of audit, review and other reports on financial statements which they may provide.

6 It also provides guidance on reports which firms may be requested to provide to lenders in connection with their clients' compliance with covenants and other conditions included in agreements for loans and other facilities.

Duties of Care for the Statutory Audit Report

7 Auditors would not normally expect to owe duties of care in respect of their audit report to anyone other than their audit client. However, the general trend of authorities since *Caparo* makes it clear that, unless there is an effective disclaimer, an auditor may owe a duty of care to a lender or other third party. The test is whether the auditor, in making the statements in the audit report, assumed a responsibility to a lender who may have been provided with those statements. This test is an objective one: it is not whether the particular auditor intended to assume such a responsibility, but whether a reasonable auditor in those circumstances would have assumed such a responsibility.

8 Whether a duty of care to a lender exists will depend upon all the circumstances. The following factors will, however, be relevant:

- the precise relationship between the auditor and the lender;
- the precise circumstances in which the audit report came into existence;
- the precise circumstances in which the audit report was communicated to the lender, and for what purpose(s), and whether the communication was made by the auditor or a third party (such as the client);
- the presence or absence of other advisers on whom the lender would or could rely;
- the opportunity, if any, given to the auditor to issue a disclaimer.

9   Accordingly, auditors need to be alert to the possibility that circumstances may be such that, unless steps are taken to limit their exposure, they may, however inadvertently, have assumed responsibility and, therefore, a duty of care, to a lender for the statements in their audit report. This may result from events contemporaneous with the audit, such as the client's discussions with the lender, or from events subsequent to the audit, such as a request for sight of the most recent audited accounts. For this reason, the auditors' relationship with lenders needs to be managed carefully, using established risk management techniques, and clear statements defining the auditors' duties, if any.

10 In seeking to document a sufficient relationship so as to enable them to rely on the audited financial statements of their customers, certain banks have included a clause in the conditions precedent to the granting of loan facilities which seeks to require the auditor of the borrower to provide written acknowledgement to the bank that, in connection with the facilities offered, the bank may rely on the audited financial statements of the borrower. An example of such a clause is as follows:

> 'The bank shall have received written acknowledgement from the borrower's auditor that in connection with the facilities or any increase or extension thereof the bank may, with the auditor's knowledge and consent, rely on the audited financial statements of the borrower (and the group) from time to time made available to the bank, directly or indirectly, in connection with the bank's assessment and monitoring of the financial condition of the borrower (and the group) and compliance with the terms and conditions of the agreement.'

11 Whether a duty of care to a bank arises in fact will depend upon whether the criteria set out in paragraph 2 above are met. Nevertheless, auditors in receipt or aware of a request to provide acknowledgement of their responsibility to their client's bankers or other lenders should not allow it to go unanswered.

12 In addition to, or as part of, a notification which seeks to establish an ongoing duty of care, a duty in respect of a lending decision might also be established if the lenders write to a firm expressing their intention to rely on audited or reviewed financial statements in connection with a proposed transaction. The presumption in such a situation would be that the firm had accepted that it had a duty of care to the lender unless it had robustly denied it. Should the firm wish to disclaim responsibility to the lender, as would normally be the case, it should state this expressly in writing. An example of a response which might be appropriate and can be customised to the circumstances of the lender's notification is provided in Appendix 1 of Audit 4/00.

13 Where a firm is contemplating signing a statement containing a specific undertaking or form of words provided by the lender (rather than responding along the lines of Appendix 1 of Audit 4/00), it should consider obtaining legal advice regarding the consequences for its legal responsibilities to the lender of complying with such a request and discuss its proposed response with its client.

Draft accounts

14 Care needs to be taken in relation to the provision and circulation of draft audited or reviewed accounts to lenders prior to the report being signed. Whilst the courts have held that reliance upon draft audited accounts was not actionable because a reasonable auditor would not intend such reliance, nevertheless there may be circumstances in which a duty of care could arise based on statements in draft accounts. Accordingly, the status of the accounts needs to be stressed, and representations and assurances as to the reliability of the accounts, or whether the final

position is likely to differ materially from that shown in the draft accounts, should be avoided.

Disclaimer of responsibility

15 Disclaimers of responsibility will be subject to a test of reasonableness set out in section 2 of the Unfair Contract Terms Act 1977. It is for a person seeking to rely upon the disclaimer to show it is reasonable, failing which it will be void. Disclaimers of responsibility to lenders (and other third parties) who seek to claim reliance on a report, and disclaimers made for the avoidance of doubt to confirm that a firm does not accept a duty to a lender or other third party to whom a report is shown or reference to a report is otherwise made, should be capable of being worded so as to pass the reasonableness test. Consequently they are an effective method of excluding or limiting a firm's liability to a lender or other third party.

16 Issuing a disclaimer of responsibility does not remove a firm's obligation to carry out the audit or review of the financial statements in accordance with Auditing Standards (or other applicable standards) and it should therefore plan, control and record its work appropriately.

The Contracts (Rights of Third Parties) Act 1999

17 The Contracts (Rights of Third Parties) Act 1999 came into force on 11 November 1999 and applies to all contracts entered into after 10 May 2000. Under the Act, third parties have the right to enforce a term of a contract if that is the intention of the parties, which intention shall be determined from the contract. An intention will be found if, upon proper construction, the contract purports to confer a benefit or an express term grants the right.

18 Accordingly, if under the engagement between the firm and the client reference is made to the provision of the accounts to a lender, or to a lender requiring the accounts for specific purposes, it is conceivable that a benefit will have been conferred upon that lender. Furthermore, in considering the reasonableness of any exclusion of liability to that lender, any such provisions will be taken into account, which has the potential of defeating any such exclusion in its entirety. It is therefore important that the engagement letter between the firm and the client makes clear that it does not confer any rights on any third party and that, for the avoidance of doubt, any rights conferred on third parties pursuant to the Contracts (Rights of Third Parties) Act 1999 shall be excluded.

Members in practice in Scotland

19 Though the Contracts (Rights of Third Parties) Act 1999 does not apply to Scotland, Scots law has long recognised the principle at common law of *ius quaesitum tertio* (a right vested in and secured to a third party in and by a contract between two parties). Accordingly a third party has the right to enforce a contract between two parties if the intention to confer a benefit on that third party can be gathered from the terms of the document. Members must therefore consider whether there is an express or implied intention that the third party acquires a right to enforce the contract. However, it should be borne in mind that each case depends upon its own circumstances and a member who is in doubt should seek independent legal advice.

Separate engagements to provide specific assurances to lenders

If a firm decides that it is able and prepared to provide specific assurances to a lender regarding, for example: 20
- financial statements where the audit or review report has been signed or will be signed in the near future;
- the design and/or operation of the client's systems of internal control or the financial reporting procedures; or
- other matters of primary interest to a lender,

they should be the subject of an engagement between the firm, the client and the lender which is entirely separate from the work on the financial statements and is the subject of a separate engagement letter and separate fee arrangements as agreed between the parties for whom the engagement is carried out.

Before a firm enters into such an engagement to provide specific assurances to a   21
lender to a client, it should consider its position carefully in the light of the Accountancy Bodies' ethical statements since its responsibilities to the client and the lender could, in certain circumstances, present it with a conflict of interest. The same consideration applies when a loan agreement purports to appoint the firm as agent for, or financial advisers to, the lenders for the purpose of providing services and reports in connection with a loan agreement, facility or drawdown.

The firm should also consider professional guidance (e.g. the ICAEW Statement on   22
'Managing the Professional Liability of Accountants') in deciding the scope and terms of business of any engagement to provide specific assurances to a client's lenders.

Appendix 4 – Questions and Answers intended to be of practical help for members in applying the guidance and in countering possible misunderstandings about it

References are to this guidance unless stated otherwise.

Q1: Does the inclusion of the recommended language devalue the audit?

A1: No, the purpose and value of the audit remains the same. It is still carried out in accordance with auditing standards and firms should be doing all they can to achieve the highest audit quality (see comments about this in the fifth paragraph of the Preface). However, other than the addressees of the audit report, readers of the audit opinion rely on the report entirely at their own risk and the auditors do not accept any duty or responsibility to them. The recommended language does no more than clarify to whom the auditors owe duties.

Q2: Aren't auditors paid to take on these risks?

A2: No, auditors are paid to carry out an audit to provide a report for, and only for, the members of the company as a body in accordance with Section 235 of the Companies Act 1985.

Q3: Is the legal position of auditors altered as a result of this guidance?

A3: No, the recommended language in the audit report simply clarifies to whom auditors owe duties as established by the case *Caparo Industries plc* v *Dickman* – see paragraph 6. Auditors are not restricting their liability to the members of the company as a body.

Q4: If my firm includes the wording as recommended in the audit report, does this guarantee that we will not owe any duty of care to third parties?

A4: No. Auditors should remain vigilant and take or avoid any additional actions as appropriate to prevent such duties being created – see paragraph 10 of this guidance and paragraph 15 of Audit 4/00.

Q5: My firm is considering the alternative option of writing to all banks expressly disclaiming any responsibility to them. Isn't this a suitable alternative to the wording for the audit report provided in this Technical Release?

A5: There are serious practical shortcomings. Banks are not the only third parties who may claim that the absence of a disclaimer is a circumstance enabling the inference of an assumption of responsibility by the auditors. Even as regards banks, there would be a risk that not all banks reading the audit report would have received the letter.

Q6: What do we do when a third party seeks our agreement in writing that they can rely on the audited accounts? In these situations there might be some client pressure to comply with this request.

A6: In these situations auditors clarify the purpose of the audit and their responsibilities with regard to it as set out in the audit report – see Appendix 2. The audit is for a specific purpose and is not carried out with the interests of third parties in mind. If lenders or other third parties seek assurance on certain matters auditors discuss the possibility of separate engagements to provide specific assurances to them – see paragraphs 20-22 of Audit 4/00.

[Statement 927]
New arrangements for reporting to the Civil Aviation Authority (CAA) in connection with the Civil Aviation (Air Travel Organisers' Licensing) Regulations 1995 (AUDIT 02/03)

This guidance is issued by the Audit and Assurance Faculty of the Institute of Chartered Accountants in England & Wales in August 2003 to outline to Institute members new reporting arrangements being introduced after discussion with the Civil Aviation Authority (CAA) in connection with the Civil Aviation (Air Travel Organisers' Licensing) Regulations 1995. The guidance does not constitute an auditing standard. Professional judgement should be used in its application.

Contents

	Paragraphs
Introduction	1 - 2
Explanation of the reporting arrangements	3 - 14

   a) Guidance notes for Reporting Accountants
   b) The model engagement terms
   c) Work programmes adn reports to CAA

Effective date	15
Ongoing monitoring of arrangments	16

Appendices
1. Guidance notes for the use of Accountants reporting on information that is required to support Air Travel Organisers' Licence (ATOL) applications to grant, vary or renew licences
2. Civil Aviation Authority (CAA) reports – the model engagement terms
3. Example letter confirming terms of engagement
4. Suggested work procedures:
   - Annual Turnover
   - Factual Confirmations
   - Ring Fencing Confirmations
5. Recommended wording for reports:
   - Annual Licensable Turnover Report and Ticket Provider Report
   - Proforma Factual Confirmations Report
   - Proforma Ring Fencing Confirmations Report
6. Letter from CAA to Organiser and Accountants requesting additional work procedures

Introduction

1 Following discussions between the Institute's Audit and Assurance Faculty and the Civil Aviation Authority (CAA), with the CAA acting on its own behalf and as agent for the Trustees of the Air Travel Trust (ATT), new arrangements have been agreed for reports provided by Accountants in connection with the Civil Aviation (Air Travel Organisers' Licensing) Regulations 1995.

2 This Technical Release explains the main elements of these arrangements.

Explanation of the reporting arrangements

3 The reporting arrangements are based on the reporting framework outlined in Technical Release Audit 1/01 *'Reporting to Third Parties'*. It is recommended that Accountants refer to Audit 1/01 when establishing their CAA reporting engagements in addition to the individual elements as outlined below.

4 This Technical Release provides guidance on the following:
   a) guidance notes for the use of Accountants reporting on information that is required to support Air Travel Organisers' Licence applications/renewals;
   b) model engagement terms and example confirmation of terms of engagement letter to be used;
   c) suggested work procedures covering the Accountants' work on Annual Licensable Turnover, Ticket Providers, Factual Confirmations and Ring Fencing Confirmations; and
   d) recommended wording for the Accountants' reports on Annual Licensable Turnover, Ticket Providers and on Factual and Ring Fencing Confirmations.

Each of these is covered in the following sections.

5 When Accountants embark on a CAA reporting engagement they make use of all the relevant elements included in this guidance. For example, the Accountants' report is made in accordance with an agreement including the model engagement terms and the guidance notes are referred to in order to understand the purpose of the report that has been requested and the issues that are likely to be relevant.

a) Guidance notes for Reporting Accountants

6 Guidance notes, which are reproduced in Appendix 1, have been issued so that Accountants can understand the CAA's purpose in seeking each report. The notes outline the various issues that Accountants need to consider with respect to each of these and the work approach which is therefore likely to be most appropriate for the Accountants. The guidance notes should be read in conjunction with the suggested work programmes (see (c) below).

b) The model engagement terms

7 The model engagement terms, reproduced in Appendix 2, follow the principles of the Technical Release Audit 1/01 referred to in paragraph 3 above. The CAA has agreed that the CAA and the Air Travel Trust will contract with Accountants on these terms. However, these terms do not apply to CAA's lapsed licence and release of bonds, sub-ordinated loans, guarantees and redemption of preference shares reports where the CAA requests Accountants to confirm that there are no outstanding or

future liabilities relating to the applicable licensable operations of the business. *The Institute's recommendation to Accountants is that they do not sign these latter reports since it is unlikely that work of sufficient depth and breadth to support a signed report will be possible and there would be no contractual limit to the duty of care arising from Accountants signing these reports (see Appendix 1 (v)).*

8 As a practical matter the CAA will not need to sign each individual engagement letter. The CAA has published these model engagement terms in its Official Record Series 3 '*Guide to ATOL*', available on the CAA's website www.atol.org.uk, and by so doing the CAA and the Air Travel Trust offer to contract on these terms. Once the offer is accepted by the Organiser[1] and the Accountants upon signature and submission of a Report to the CAA, the necessary contract is formed.

9 The contract will usually apply to all reports made by Accountants for each Organiser and once in place should not normally require amendment in subsequent periods. Where other specific work is requested, e.g. because of a CAA investigation, the CAA may propose either separate engagement terms or that the model engagement terms will apply. In the latter case, the standard letter which the CAA will use for this purpose is included as Appendix 6.

10 Practical matters between the Accountants and their client, including confirmation of the terms of engagement and charges, are dealt with separately – an example letter confirming terms of engagement is included as Appendix 3.

11 The CAA has offered to agree to a cap on the Accountants' liability in accordance with their capping formula which is set out in their Guidance Note 10. An extract from this Guidance Note is included in Box 1. Individual firms of Accountants need to consider whether or not to accept the CAA's capping formula or negotiate a liability cap by separate agreement. Such consideration will take into account, inter alia, whether the limitation is appropriate to the scope of the engagement, the fees generated, their assessment of the risks in undertaking the work, their internal risk management policies and the level of professional indemnity insurance. Where firms consider that they are unable to accept the formula, they may wish to negotiate their own individual capping arrangements with the CAA. While the Institute has approved and recommends to its members the model engagement terms reproduced at Appendix 2, it has not approved the CAA's capping formula and does not, by including the extract below in this Technical Release, intend to endorse the formula. Firms of Accountants must form their own view on whether to accept the CAA's capping formula or negotiate a different limitation with the CAA. Under clause 5.1.3 of the model terms, the absence of separate agreement results automatically in the application of the CAA's capping formula.

Box 1: Extract from CAA Guidance Note 10 [Annex 2] dated 15 August 2003 CAA's capping formula

The total aggregate liability of the Accountants whether in contract, tort (including negligence) or otherwise, to the CAA, the ATT and the Organiser, arising from or in connection with the work which is the subject of these terms (including any addition or variation to the work), shall not exceed an amount as determined by the following formula ('the Liability Cap'). Where the ATOL bond (as at the date of the Accountants' Report) is:

- less than or equal to £500,000 then the Liability Cap shall be £500,000;

---

[1] *All references to the 'Organiser', 'ATOL holder' or 'client' in this Technical Release are to the ATOL holder applying for, varying or renewing a licence.*

- more than £500,000 but less than or equal to £5 million then the Liability Cap shall be the amount of the ATOL bond;
- more than £5 million but less than or equal to £15 million then the Liability Cap shall be £5 million plus 50% of any proportion of the ATOL bond that exceeds £5million;
- more than £15 million but less than or equal to £100 million then the Liability Cap shall be £10 million;
- greater than £100 million then the Liability Cap shall be £20 million.

The reference to ATOL bond in the above capping formula relates to the total bonds held by a licence holder or where the licence holder is part of a group the aggregate bond amount held by all licence holders within that group.

12 The model engagement terms highlight that the responsibility for producing financial information rests with the Organiser and that the Accountants' responsibility is to report on the information provided by the Organiser. Where applicable, the CAA's standard reports have been amended to require a signature from a responsible officer of the Organiser confirming that they take responsibility for the confirmations made.

13 These engagements are separate from and unrelated to the Accountants' audit work on the financial statements of the Organiser for the purposes of the Companies Act 1985 and do not create any obligations or liabilities regarding the Accountants' statutory audit work, which would not otherwise exist.

c) Work programmes and reports to the CAA

14 For the Accountants' work on Annual Licensable Turnover, Ticket Provider Sales, Factual Confirmations and Ring Fencing Confirmations, suggested work procedures have been developed with the CAA and are provided in Appendix 4. The opinion in respect of Licensable Turnover is 'fairly presented in accordance with CAA regulations', whereas all other reports are factual confirmations using agreed upon procedures. Recommended wordings for the various reports are given in Appendix 5. These wordings have been compiled taking account of the guidance in Appendix 2 of Audit 1/01. If alternative wordings are suggested, Accountants refer to Appendix 2 of Audit 1/01 to determine whether the suggested wording would be appropriate.

Effective date

15 The CAA has stated in writing to all Organisers that the new reporting arrangements (with the exception of the work in relation to passenger numbers for Small Firm ATOLs) will apply to all reports signed in connection with the September 2003 ATOL renewals.

Ongoing monitoring of arrangements

16 The Institute's Audit and Assurance Faculty intends to monitor the reporting arrangements outlined in this document.

Appendix 1 – Guidance notes for the use of Accountants reporting on information that is required to support Air Travel Organisers' Licence (ATOL) applications to grant, vary or renew licences

Issued 15 August 2003

Introduction

These notes have been drafted as guidance for those Accountants whose clients ('Organiser', 'ATOL holder' or 'client') are required to submit Reports to the CAA on an annual basis in support of ATOL applications/renewals. There are a number of confirmations required solely from Organisers ('Organiser' refers to the ATOL holder or air travel organiser that is required to submit Reports to the CAA). For those confirmations where Reports from Accountants are requested, discussions have been held between the CAA and the Institute of Chartered Accountants in England & Wales ('ICAEW') concerning the general issue of duty of care in respect of the work performed. A working party was set up to review the terms of engagement and the format of Reports required of Accountants. Revised wordings of the key Reports have been agreed (see Appendix 5 of Audit 2/03) and these guidance notes are issued for Accountants to assist them in providing their Reports on the information supplied by their client to the CAA. Suggested work procedures for the key Reports are given in Appendix 4 of Audit 2/03 and these guidance notes should be read in conjunction with that Appendix.

These notes do not cover other Reports (in addition to the key Reports referred to above) which may be required. In situations not covered here where a Report is requested from the Accountants, it will be for the Accountants to determine the specific procedures appropriate for these based on the principles in Audit 1/01 (see below) and this guidance. Where other such Reports are provided, the existing model engagement terms might be used to cover this work. In that case, the standard letter which the CAA will use for this purpose is included as Appendix 6 of Audit 2/03.

This guidance has been based upon the ICAEW Audit and Assurance Faculty Technical Release Audit 1/01 *'Reporting to Third Parties'* (available from the ICAEW Audit and Assurance Faculty website – www.icaew.co.uk/auditassfac). Advice for Accountants on ATOL and ATOL requirements including the Reports needed is provided in the CAA's revised Guidance Note 10, dated 15 August 2003, available on the CAA's website, **www.atol.org.uk**.

These notes should be read in conjunction with the model engagement terms provided in Appendix 2 of Audit 2/03.

Terms of engagement

It is recommended that Reports make reference to the agreement between CAA, the Air Travel Trust ('ATT'), the Organiser and the Reporting Accountants, and it is suggested that the model engagement terms developed by CAA and the ICAEW may be used as a basis for specific terms of engagement in each case. The model engagement terms address the issues of the respective responsibilities of the Organiser and the Reporting Accountants, and in particular explain duty of care and limitation of liability as they relate to this specific work.

For the avoidance of doubt, the terms 'Reporting Accountants', 'Accountants' and 'Auditors' used throughout these guidance notes do not refer to a firm's role as statutory auditor.

It is recommended that Accountants agree the terms of engagement with their client(s) using the model engagement terms as a basis and where they do so, the CAA and the ATT will become parties to the agreement[2]. If clients do not agree, Accountants revert to the CAA and consider whether to undertake the engagement. When the model terms are used, the only issue that may require separate negotiation with the CAA is the level of the liability cap.

Reports

The CAA requests Reports on the following[3]:

(i) annual licensable turnover;
(ii) non-licensable turnover;
(iii) specific factual confirmations;
(iv) ring fencing confirmations; and
(v) lapsed licence report for the release of bonds, subordinated loans, guarantees and redemption of preference shares.

Each of these is dealt with in turn below.

(i) Annual Licensable Turnover Report

Background

ATOL is a statutory scheme which provides financial protection for holidaymakers and air travellers from the UK and with few exceptions, all travel firms advertising or selling air travel in the UK must hold an ATOL[4]. The CAA obtains a financial 'bond' from every Organiser. This is a mechanism that provides finance in the event that an Organiser ceases to trade and has customers overseas who require repatriating or where refunds need to be made to customers that have not yet travelled. As a consequence, the size of the bond required to be posted by the Organiser will depend upon (i) the value/number of customers to whom holidays will be sold in the coming period of the bond ('bonded turnover'); and (ii) the risk of the Organiser going out of business as assessed by the CAA[5].

In addition to the above arrangements, the Air Travel Trust Fund has been established as part of the ATOL system. The purpose of the Air Travel Trust Fund is to act as a back-up to individual bonds which prove to be insufficient to meet all the customers' claims made upon them.

[2] *This is achieved by the CAA and ATT making an offer to contract on these terms without the need for any additional signatures on their behalf – see paragraph 8 of Audit 2/03.*

[3] *The specific circumstances of each Organiser will determine which reports need to be provided.*

[4] *One significant exception to the scheme is where the customer is sold (knowingly or otherwise) the flight and accommodation elements separately. This 'split contracting' as it is known can leave the customer unprotected in the event of a failure. Further guidance will be forthcoming from the CAA in due course.*

[5] *The CAA sets out in its 'Guide to ATOL' (available from www.atol.org.uk) the broad basis for calculating bond levels.*

One of the key tools used to assess the estimated value of prospective holidays that are to be bonded is the reporting of actual licensable turnover on a quarterly basis by the Organiser. Organisers are required to report on each of the categories of turnover, whether or not they attract a bond. The CAA requires that all categories of licensable turnover are reported on annually by the Accountants.

This requirement gives rise to the annual Turnover Report. In all instances the bonded turnover can be extracted from the books and records of the Organiser, typically the reservation system.

Licensable turnover falls into the following categories:
- **Fully bonded business:** scheduled or charter packages, and seat only charters
- **Scheduled bonded business:** scheduled seat-only tickets covered by a bond
- **Agency business:** scheduled seat-only tickets covered by airline Deed(s) of Undertaking
- **Other facilities:** sold in conjunction with tickets covered by airline Deed(s) of Undertaking
- **ATOL to ATOL business:** licensable products sold to other Organisers for resale under the buyer's licences.

All these categories of business attract a bond rate except for ATOL to ATOL. Agency turnover only attracts a minimal bond. In granting the licence and determining the level of bond, the CAA is primarily concerned about the split of turnover both between separate categories under the licence and between licensed and non-licensed turnover and takes into account all categories of business. The CAA may also reflect the risk profile of the business through the bond percentage rates applied to each category of licence. Accountants should therefore concentrate on checking whether turnover has been properly apportioned between the different categories.

Whilst the bond amount is not intended to cover the exposure in the peak season, the CAA will adjust the rates where there is a very marked unevenness in the licensed programme over the year as would be the case, for example with a ski operator, or sports firm specialising in specific sporting events. The CAA may also require higher bonds where repatriation costs would be high or the Organiser has decided not to provide directors guarantees. The CAA considers it important that Organisers trade within their quarterly turnover authorisations and Accountants need to focus on the split of turnover between calendar quarters.

The Accountants are required to confirm that the turnover which arose from the licensable operation in the category and in the calendar quarters indicated in the annual Turnover Report have been tested in accordance with a prescribed schedule of work and is fairly presented in accordance with the CAA regulations.

Substantive and/or Control testing

As with any testing, the Accountants have the choice of substantive testing or a combination of substantive and controls based testing.

Controls based testing of the reservation system used to generate the turnover figures reported in the Turnover Report will only be adopted when the Accountants have assessed that the control environment surrounding the reservation system in the Organiser is adequate for the purpose (see below).

Whilst the Accountants' assessment will be focussed on the specific controls over turnover, it is necessary to gain an understanding of whether the Organiser has a strong overall control environment and this will depend upon a host of factors that influence the effectiveness of the policies and procedures intended to provide reasonable assurance that the Organiser's business objectives will be achieved. Some factors will be more important than others. The more critical factors are likely to be the quality of senior management and the manner in which they monitor and control the performance of the business.

The following factors are likely to be relevant to Accountants acquiring an understanding of the overall control environment including IT controls, but there might be others in addition to those listed:

- Management's methods for controlling and monitoring performance.
- The entity's organisational structure
- The functioning of the Board of Directors and its committees
- Methods of delegation
- Personnel practices.

Where the control environment is strong the risk of misstatement will be reduced through:

- the constraint of review by senior management
- supervisory procedures that provide some assurance that material misstatements in the accounting records will be prevented or detected
- the operation of an effective budgeting or management reporting system which allows senior management to plan, control and monitor the performance of operations.

Where the Accountants have identified that the control environment is strong then the most likely method of testing is through re-performance of the extraction of the licensable turnover based either on the bookings database of the Organiser or the use of dummy data. Accountants test controls to ensure they have been in operation throughout the year.

For Organisers where the control environment is assessed as being not sufficiently strong to rely upon the controls, the Accountants will obtain the necessary assurance to be able to sign the Turnover Report through detailed substantive testing (i.e. a sample of bookings from the reservation system traced through to the Turnover Report).

Where substantive testing is adopted, the Accountants use their judgement to assess the sample size required to give the necessary evidence on which to base their opinion.

The Accountants would however still be expected to review the systems and controls applied to those systems by the Organiser to capture and identify its turnover into the correct categories as defined by the CAA (see above).

A combination of controls based testing and substantive testing may also be appropriate.

The suggested work procedures issued along with this guidance note (Appendix 4a of Audit 2/03) provide more detail as to some of the expected methods of testing and the level of materiality.

The Accountants either sign the CAA's standard Report (provided as Appendix 5a of Audit 2/03), or, where they are not in a position to do so, no Report is provided. In such circumstances, the Accountants would normally contact the CAA by telephone, or send a letter with an unsigned report outlining why an opinion could not be issued.

Small Firm's ATOL (this confirmation in respect of passenger numbers is not required for the September 2003 renewals)

Licences granted to Organisers who sell only a small number (up to 500 per year) of flights and packages will be subject to a 500 seat limit on the total number of passengers carried across all categories of the licence. The CAA has to satisfy itself as required by the Regulations as to the applicant's fitness to hold a licence, but it does not apply any financial tests or require a minimum capitalisation. It requires a bond to be provided in accordance with normal requirements, and personal guarantees to protect against overtrading.

The CAA asks that in addition to the checks on licensable turnover the Accountants report on the number of passengers carried in each of the calendar quarters.

(ii) Non-licensable turnover

Ticket Provider Sales

The CAA asks Organisers to provide details of Ticket Provider Sales to confirm that turnover is being transacted correctly. Tickets for air travel should be issued to customers either immediately upon payment or within 24 hours where a booking has been made remotely. The CAA needs to be satisfied that the reported turnover of tickets sold on a ticket provider basis, are actually sold on this basis. This confirmation can be obtained by checking the reservation or ticketing system to bookings made by customers in person or remotely.

(iii) Specific factual confirmations

A number of the confirmations set out below are requested by the CAA to help it gain a level of comfort on an Organiser's solvency (principally to meet CAA's 'free asset' test). For guidance on any specific request outside the scope of these arrangements regarding solvency, Accountants refer to paragraph 13 of Audit 1/01.

The suggested work procedures to be performed are set out in Appendix 4b) and the specific format of reporting of factual confirmations is provided in Appendix 5b) of Audit 2/03 or exceptionally, other agreed formats. Receipt of these confirmations is only a part of the CAA's licensing process.

Subordinated Loans

- The CAA seeks the Accountants' written Report on the Organiser's confirmation that since [Date] £[X] of new cash has been injected into [Organiser] in the form of a subordinated loan, and the subordinated loans within the company now total £[Y].

The CAA wants confirmation that the cash injections that the CAA has been informed of by the management of the Organiser have actually been received into the Organiser's bank account and that the Organiser has completed the appropriate CAA subordinated loan documentation for the same amount. The Organiser will need to determine the appropriate disclosure in the statutory accounts in accordance with generally accepted accounting principles.

Cash gift (Sole Traders and Partnerships)

- The CAA seeks the Accountants' written Report on the Organiser's confirmation that since [Date] £[X] of new cash has been donated into [Organiser] in the form of a cash gift.

The CAA wants confirmation that the cash injections that the CAA has been informed of by the management of the Organiser have actually been received into the Organiser's bank account and that the Organiser has completed the appropriate CAA memorandum of cash gift documentation for the same amount. This means of donating new funds is only applicable to sole traders and partnerships. The Organiser will need to determine the appropriate disclosure in the statutory (or other annual) accounts in accordance with generally accepted accounting principles.

Guarantees

- The CAA seeks written confirmation from the Accountants that the completed Deed of guarantee has been drawn to the Accountants' attention.

In giving this guarantee the provider of the guarantee acknowledges that it will meet all actual and potential liabilities of the Organiser (occasionally the parent group). The CAA asks the Accountants to acknowledge the existence of the guarantee. The Accountants are not required to consider scope of the guarantee or its legal enforceability as this is primarily a matter for lawyers. The Organiser will need to determine the appropriate disclosure in the statutory accounts in accordance with generally accepted accounting principles.

New share capital/rights issue

- The CAA seeks written confirmation from the Accountants that £[X] new cash has been injected into [Organiser] in the form of Paid Up Capital and/or that £[Y] of the profit and loss account or existing subordinated loan has been capitalised as fully Paid Up Share Capital.

The CAA requests the above confirmations to obtain comfort that funds have actually flowed into the bank account of the Organiser and that share capital has been issued for the consideration received by the Organiser. For the capitalisation of a subordinated loan, the Accountants can confirm the existence of an agreement with the lender converting the subordinated loan into paid up share capital and that shares have been issued. The Accountants are not required to consider the scope of the agreement or its legal enforceability as this is primarily a matter for lawyers. The capitalisation of profit and loss reserves is executed by way of a bonus issue of shares, which can be confirmed by reference to the relevant Companies House filings for an issue of shares.

Bank loan funding

- The CAA seeks confirmation that an amount of £[X] has been injected into [Organiser] in the form of a bank loan.

The CAA monitors whether the Organiser has adequate working capital to support normal operational or capital expenditure in order to facilitate the renewal or the retention of a licence. Where this was dependent on a loan, then the CAA needs to obtain comfort that this has now been provided. As this is purely a factual confirmation relating to the receipt of funds; the Accountants are not expected to review any business plan or budget.

The CAA wants confirmation that the cash it has been told will be introduced has indeed been received into the Organiser's bank account, and that the facility terms and conditions are as previously indicated to the CAA.

Repayment of item post year end

- *The CAA seeks confirmation that since [Date] the sum of £[X] has been received from [Named debtor] in respect of the [named debt].*

If the balance sheet of the Organiser includes certain current assets, in particular other debtors, then the CAA may seek to establish if these assets have been recovered. Part of this assessment is to ascertain if the debt has been settled since the year-end – in which case the CAA seeks confirmation of the cash amount received. This may include capital items sold since the year-end, associate debt, deposit refunds, etc.

The CAA wants the Accountants to confirm the receipt of the item or items in question, such that £[X] has been received since the year-end into the Organiser's bank account.

Change of ownership

- *The CAA seeks confirmation of the shareholders and their shareholdings following a restructure or change of ownership.*

The CAA wishes to identify the individuals or companies who are controlling the business. It should be noted that the CAA has a statutory duty to consider the fitness of those that control (or appear to control) an Organiser/applicant.

The CAA wants the Accountants to check the share register to confirm who now owns the shares in the company that already holds an ATOL at a given date or is applying for a licence. The CAA uses this as part of its work to establish ownership and control of companies.

(iv) Ring fencing confirmations

The reasons for the **financial** and **structural** ring fence confirmations in essence relate to circumstances where Organisers are part of a wider group and would be unable to satisfy the CAA's financial criteria on a group basis. A primary function of both the financial and structural ring fence confirmations is to satisfy the CAA that the Organiser is operating independently and would have at least a chance of survival in the event of the failure of the group that operates outside of the ring fence. Further guidance on financial ring fence confirmations is set out in the CAA's Guidance Note 18, which is available from the CAA's website at **www.atol.org.uk**.

Financial ring fencing

When reaching a decision on the financial position of an Organiser the CAA normally assesses that Organiser on the basis of the finances of the largest organisation in which it operates (in most cases the group at the Ultimate Holding Company level). Some Organisers are however unable to meet the financial criteria set by the CAA at this level and request that the CAA considers the Organiser on an individual or sub-group basis for solvency purposes. In such cases the CAA will consider whether it is realistic to assess the Organiser (or sub-group) on a 'ring fence' basis: an essential test to the CAA is whether or not the Organiser is operating independently and could survive financially the failure of the rest of the wider group outside the ring fence. The CAA takes a similar view when an Organiser has a very close relationship with associate firms or groups under similar (common) control. CAA defines 'associate' as a company which has a link with the Organiser through common shareholders, directors, partners, significant levels of trading or with whom there are financial links. Financial links include inter-firm loans and cross guarantees. (see Guidance Note 18). In order to obtain some comfort over the financial independence of the Organiser, when it forms part of a group of companies for the year in question, the CAA is concerned that:

- No guarantees, loans or letters of support have been given by the Organiser in favour of any group companies;
- The Organiser maintains its own separate bank, account(s) and it's cash is not managed centrally with other group companies;
- All trading with group or associated companies is transacted on normal commercial terms, with balances settled at least monthly; and
- The Organiser has its own merchant agreement with a credit card company.

Accordingly the CAA requires Accountants to perform the suggested work procedures set out in Appendix 4(c) and report the results. The specific format of reporting of ring fencing confirmation is provided in Appendix 5c of Audit 2/03.

The confirmations above may also be required on associated companies as defined in Guidance Note 18.

Structural ring fencing

Structural separation confirmations are required in conjunction with the CAA's financial confirmations, however the CAA has introduced new procedures regarding these which do not involve the Accountants. It is considered that Accountants do not usually have the knowledge and experience of such matters and they are therefore unable to add any effective comfort to the confirmations made by the Organiser direct to the CAA. Accountants are not expected simply to report to the CAA representations they have received from management which are incapable of practical independent testing.

The rationale behind the **structural** separation confirmations is also connected with the ability of the Organiser to survive operationally in the event of the failure of the wider group outside the ring fence. If a company was financially ring fenced from a group in terms of inter group trading, but relied on group facilities such as computer networks or shared office premises for example, the CAA would consider that its chances of surviving the failure of the group would be small. This is because at the very least, it would not have been used to paying commercial rates for such services and may therefore be unable to bear the additional overhead. The same applies to companies which are associated in the CAA's terms, sharing common Directors.

It is also important for the CAA to ensure that the Organiser directly employs both staff and management and have their own separate trading contracts with suppliers. The CAA's view is that companies that contract these services on a group basis would be unable to re-negotiate such services quickly if the group outside of the ring fence were to fail. In some cases suppliers would not wish to deal directly with the subsidiary or, would require substantial increases in the rates charged.

The CAA would look for comfort from Organisers in respect of higher bonds and/or asset base requirements in cases where a company, which is subject to financial ring fence undertaking, is not able to provide the CAA with the full list of confirmations in respect of its structural separation. In some cases the CAA may not be able to renew a licence in the absence of the structural separation confirmations.

(v) Lapsed licences and the release of bonds, sub-ordinated loans, guarantees and redemption of preference shares

Unless called, Bonds will normally expire six months after the licence is due to expire. In the event of a lapsed licence the Organiser may request the early return of their bond from the CAA. However the CAA would first need to be satisfied that there are no outstanding or future liabilities relating to the applicable licensable operations of the business. As part of the process of obtaining this assurance the CAA would require the Accountants to confirm that there are no outstanding or future liabilities relating to the applicable licensable operations of the business.

Accountants need to be sure beyond reasonable doubt that there are no outstanding or future liabilities before signing this type of report. **The recommendation to Accountants is that this report is not signed since it is unlikely that work of sufficient depth and breadth to support a signed report will be possible.** Specifically the model engagement terms in Appendix 2 of Audit 2/03 do not cover the reporting on these returns and therefore does not remove or limit the duty of care from Accountants signing these reports.

Additionally where the licence has lapsed without a call on the bond, the CAA requires an undertaking before it will release guarantees, subordinated loan agreements or preference share undertakings. This will mean a confirmation that all claims of other creditors in respect of liabilities incurred by the Organiser in the period during which it held an Air Travel Organisers' Licence, have been satisfied. *Once again, the recommendation to Accountants is that these reports are not signed since it is unlikely that work of sufficient depth and breadth to support a signed report will be possible.*

Appendix 2 – Civil Aviation Authority (CAA) reports – the model engagement terms[6] (these model terms were issued on 15 August 2003)

The following are the terms of engagement on which the CAA agrees to engage Accountants to report in connection with the Civil Aviation (Air Travel Organisers' Licensing) Regulations 1995.

A contract between an air travel organiser, its Reporting Accountants, the CAA on its own behalf and as agent for the Trustees of the Air Travel Trust on these terms is formed when the air travel organiser and the Accountants sign and submit to the CAA a Report as set out in Clause 3 herein.

In these terms of engagement:

---

[6] *These model terms do not cover any reports requested by CAA in connection with lapsed licences and the release of bonds, sub-ordinated loans, guarantees and redemption of preference shares (see Section v of Appendix 1 to the ICAEW Technical Release Audit 2/03).*

'CAA' refers to the Civil Aviation Authority;

'ATT' refers to the Air Travel Trust;

'the Organiser' refers to the air travel organiser that is required to submit the Report to the CAA;

'the Accountants' refers to the Organiser's Reporting Accountants

1 Introduction

The Organiser is required to submit to the CAA Reports as set out in Clause 3 below that are signed by their Accountants to provide independent assurance on the information provided. These terms of engagement set out the basis on which the Accountants will sign the Report.

2 The Organiser's responsibilities

2.1 The Organiser is responsible for producing the information set out in the Reports, maintaining proper records complying with the terms of the CAA's Licensing Regulations and providing relevant financial information to the CAA on a quarterly and annual basis in accordance with the requirements of the Licensing Regulations. The Organiser is responsible for ensuring that the non-financial records are reconcilable to the financial records.

2.2 The management of the Organiser will make available to the Accountants all records, correspondence, information and explanations that the Accountants consider necessary to enable the Accountants to perform the Accountants' work.

2.3 The Organiser, the CAA and the ATT accept that the ability of the Accountants to perform their work effectively depends upon the Organiser providing full and free access to the financial and other records and the Organiser shall procure that any such records held by a third party are made available to the Accountants.

2.4 The Accountants accept that, whether or not the Organiser meets its obligations, the Accountants remain under an obligation to the CAA and the ATT to perform their work with reasonable care. The failure by the Organiser to meet its obligations may cause the Accountants to qualify their report or be unable to provide a report.

3 Scope of the Accountants' Work

3.1 The Organiser will provide the Accountants with such information, explanations and documentation that the Accountants consider necessary to carry out their responsibilities. The Accountants will seek written representations from management in relation to matters for which independent corroboration is not available. The Accountants will also seek confirmation that any significant matters of which the Accountants should be aware have been brought to the Accountants' attention.

3.2 The Accountants will perform the following work in relation to Reports required by the CAA:

3.2.1 Turnover Report: The Accountants will perform the suggested work procedures set out in appendix 4(a) of Technical Release Audit 2/03 issued by the Institute of Chartered Accountants in England and Wales ('the Release') annually and subject to any adverse findings will produce a Turnover report in the form set out in Appendix 5(a) of the Release;

3.2.2 Ring Fencing Report: The Accountants will perform the suggested work procedures set out in Appendix 4(c) of the Release on request by the CAA and subject to any adverse findings will produce a Ring Fencing report in the form set out in Appendix 5(c) of the Release;

3.2.3 Factual Confirmations Report: The Accountants will perform the suggested procedures set out in Appendix 4(b) of the Release on request by the CAA and subject to any adverse findings will produce a Factual Confirmations report in the form set out in Appendix 5(b) of the Release.

3.3 The Accountants will not subject the information provided by the Organiser to checking or verification except to the extent expressly stated. While the Accountants will perform their work with reasonable skill and care and will report any misstatements, frauds or errors that are revealed by enquiries within the scope of the engagement, the Accountants' work should not be relied upon to disclose all misstatements, fraud or errors that might exist.

4 Form of the Accountants' Report

4.1 The Accountants' Reports are prepared on the following bases:

4.1.1 the Accountants' Reports are prepared solely for the confidential use of the Organiser and the CAA and solely for the purpose of submission to the CAA in connection with the CAA's requirements in connection with the Organiser's Air Travel Organisers' Licence. They may not be relied upon by the Organiser or the CAA for any other purpose except as provided in 4.1.2 below;

4.1.2 the CAA may disclose the Reports to the ATT in connection with any actual or potential liability to the ATT that may arise out of the business conducted by the Organiser, and the ATT will be entitled to rely on them subject to the terms of this agreement.

4.1.3 neither the Organiser, the CAA nor the ATT may rely on any oral or draft reports the Accountants provide. The Accountants accept responsibility to the Organiser, the CAA and the ATT for the Accountants' final signed reports only;

4.1.4 the Accountants' Reports must not be recited or referred to in whole or in part in any other document (including, without limitation, any publication issued by the CAA);

4.1.5 except to the extent required by court order, law or regulation or to assist in the resolution of any court proceedings, the Accountants' Reports must not be made available, copied or recited to any other person (including, without limitation, any person who may use or refer to any of the CAA's publications);

4.1.6 except as provided by 4.1.2 herein, the Accountants, their partners and staff neither owe nor accept any duty to any other person (including, without limitation, any person who may use or refer to any of the CAA's Publications) and shall not be liable for any loss, damage or expense of whatsoever nature which is caused by their reliance on representations in the Accountants' Reports.

5 Liability Provisions

5.1 The Accountants will perform the engagement with reasonable skill and care and acknowledge that they will be liable to the Organiser, the CAA and the ATT for losses, damages, costs or expenses ('losses') caused by their breach of contract, negligence or wilful default, subject to the following provisions:

5.1.1 The Accountants will not be so liable if such losses are due to the provision of false, misleading or incomplete information or documentation or due to the acts or omissions of any person other than the Accountants, except where, on the basis of the enquiries normally undertaken by Accountants within the scope set out in these terms of engagement, it would have been reasonable for the Accountants to discover such defects.

5.1.2 The Accountants accept liability without limit for the consequences of their own fraud and for any other liability which it is not permitted by law to limit or exclude.

5.1.3 Subject to the previous paragraph (5.1.2), the total aggregate liability of the Accountants whether in contract, tort (including negligence) or otherwise, to the CAA, the ATT and the Organiser, arising from or in connection with the work which is the subject of these terms (including any addition or variation to the work), shall not exceed an amount to be agreed between the parties by separate written agreement or, in the absence of such agreement, calculated in accordance with the CAA's capping formula published in CAA's Guidance Note 10 dated 15 August 2003, ('the Liability Cap').[7]

In the event of successful claims against the Accountants by more than one of the CAA, the ATT and the Organiser, the CAA and the ATT shall be entitled to recover their loss in priority to the Organiser subject always to the maximum Liability Cap. The Accountants shall notify the CAA if a claim is commenced by the Organiser against the Accountants.

5.2 The CAA and the ATT agree that neither the CAA nor the ATT will bring any legal proceedings against the Accountants arising out of or in connection with the services provided under this contract unless they have been unable to recover the loss suffered out of the ATOL bond or have taken reasonable steps to recover any remaining loss from the Organiser and any guarantees provided to the CAA by the principals of the Organiser.

---

[7] *The CAA's Guidance Note 10, issued 15 August 2003, is available on the CAA's website www.atol.org.uk. Individual firms of accountants need to consider whether or not to accept the CAA's offered capping formula or negotiate a liability cap with the CAA by separate agreement. Such consideration will take into account, inter alia, whether the limitation is appropriate to the scope of the engagement, the fees generated, their assessment of the risks in undertaking the work, their internal risk management policies and the level of professional indemnity insurance. Where firms consider that they are unable to accept the formula, they may wish to negotiate their own individual capping arrangements with the CAA.*

The Organiser, the CAA and the ATT agree that they will not bring any claims or proceedings against any individual partners, members, directors or employees of the Accountants. This clause is intended to benefit such partners, members, directors and employees who may enforce this clause pursuant to the Contracts (Rights of Third Parties) Act 1999 (the 'Act'). Notwithstanding any benefits or rights conferred by this agreement on any third party by virtue of the Act, the parties to this agreement may agree to vary or rescind this agreement without any third party's consent. Other than as expressly provided in these terms, the Act is excluded. 5.3

Any claims, whether in contract, negligence or otherwise, must be formally commenced within two years after the party bringing the claim becomes aware (or ought reasonably to have become aware) of the facts which give rise to the action and in any event no later than four years after any alleged breach of contract, negligence or other cause of action. This expressly overrides any statutory provision which would otherwise apply. In the event that the CAA and/or the ATT delay commencing a claim against the Accountants in order to comply with their obligations under clause 5.2 to take reasonable steps to recover loss from the Organiser and any guarantors, time will be deemed to have stopped running for the purposes of this clause 5.4 for the period that the CAA and/or the ATT are taking such reasonable steps. 5.4

This engagement is separate from and unrelated to the Accountants' audit work on the financial statements of the Organiser for the purposes of the Companies Act 1985 and nothing herein creates obligations or liabilities regarding the Accountants' statutory audit work, which would not otherwise exist. 5.5

6 Fees

The Accountants' fees, together with VAT and out of pocket expenses, will be agreed with and billed to the Organiser. Neither the CAA nor the ATT is liable to pay the Accountants' fees.

7 Quality of Service

The Accountants will investigate all complaints. The CAA, the ATT and the Organiser have the right to take any complaint up with the Institute of Chartered Accountants in England and Wales ('the ICAEW'). The CAA, the ATT and the Organiser may obtain an explanation of the mechanisms that operate in respect of a complaint to the ICAEW at www.icaew.co.uk/complaints or by writing to the ICAEW. To contact the ICAEW write to the Professional Standards Office, Silbury Court, 412-416 Silbury Boulevard, Central Milton Keynes, MK9 2AF.

8 Providing Services to Other Parties

The Accountants will not be prevented or restricted by virtue of the Accountants' relationship with the Organiser, the CAA and the ATT, including anything in these terms of engagement, from providing services to other clients. The Accountants' standard internal procedures are designed to ensure that confidential information communicated to the Accountants during the course of an assignment will be maintained confidentially.

9 Applicable law and jurisdiction

9.1 This agreement shall be governed by, and interpreted and construed in accordance with, English law.

9.2 The Organiser, the CAA, the ATT and the Accountants irrevocably agree that the courts of England shall have exclusive jurisdiction to settle any dispute (including claims for set-off and counterclaims) which may arise in connection with the validity, effect, interpretation or performance of, or the legal relationship established by this agreement or otherwise arising in connection with this agreement.

10 Alteration to Terms

All additions, amendments and variations to these terms of engagement shall be binding only if in writing and signed by the duly authorised representatives of the parties. These terms supersede any previous agreements and representations between the parties in respect of the scope of the Accountants' work and the Accountants' Report or the obligations of any of the parties relating thereto (whether oral or written) and, together with the matters included in the letter confirming terms of engagement, represent the entire understanding between the parties.

Appendix 3 – Example letter confirming terms of engagement

The Board of Directors
[XYZ Plc
Address]

[Date]

Our Ref:

Dear Sirs

CAA reporting

We are writing to confirm our terms of engagement for performing procedures and reporting in respect of [XYZ Plc] [and of the other specified companies listed in Attachment 1] in connection with the Civil Aviation (Air Travel Organisers' Licensing) Regulations 1995.

Under the arrangements agreed between the Civil Aviation Authority (the 'CAA') and the Institute of Chartered Accountants in England and Wales which are set out in Technical Release Audit 2/03, model engagement terms governing this reporting were published. A copy of those engagement terms are attached as Attachment 2. Subject to your acceptance of this letter, a contract between you, this firm and the CAA and the Air Travel Trust on those terms is formed when you and we sign and submit to the CAA a report as set out in Clause 3 therein.

Personnel

It is our intention that X will act as the engagement partner. [A second partner, Y, will work with *him/her*, and will be available to substitute for X in his/her absence.] XX will be the manager.

Fees

Our fees for this reporting engagement will be payable by XYZ Plc.

[*Fixed fee*. Assuming no undue complications and provided we do not agree to undertake additional work, the fee for our reporting to the CAA (excluding disbursements and VAT) will be £X.]

[Or *variable fee*. Our fees will be charged on the basis of time spent on your affairs according to the level of seniority of the personnel involved. Unless the engagement has to be extended for reasons beyond our control, we estimate that the fee for our reporting to the CAA (excluding disbursements and VAT) will be approximately £X.]

Timetable

We understand that you require our opinion to be given by [date].

Liability

Please note that under the model contract, our aggregate liability to you, the CAA and the ATT is capped at the amount of [£XX] as agreed by letter dated [date]/ in accordance with the CAA's capping arrangements set out in the CAA Guidance Note 10 dated 15 August 2003. [delete as appropriate].

We should be grateful if you would confirm acceptance of the terms of engagement on behalf of [XYZ Plc] [and the subsidiary companies listed in Attachment 1] by signing below [arranging for an authorised signatory to sign below on behalf of each company] and returning a copy of this letter and the appendices by [date].

Yours faithfully

[Name of firm]

Confirmed on behalf of [XYZ Plc/Ltd][and the subsidiary companies listed in Attachment 1]

_____
[signature]

_____
[name], Director

_____
Date

Or if separate signatures are required on behalf of each company

Accepted on behalf of	Signature	[name], Director	Date
XYZ Plc			
Sub 1			
Sub 2 etc			

Attachment 1

LIST OF OTHER SPECIFIED COMPANIES FALLING WITHIN THE SCOPE OF THE TERMS OF ENGAGEMENT

Attachment 2

[Attach model engagement terms from Appendix 2 of Technical Release Audit 2/03]

Appendix 4 – Suggested Work procedures

a) Annual Turnover

(Accountants should use their professional judgement when applying these procedures)

(i) Licensable Turnover	
1. Read the Guidance Note 10 for Accountants issued by the CAA dated 15 August 2003.	
2. Enquire and document the basis and methodology used by the management of the Organiser to compile its quarterly turnover returns to the CAA and also how it recognises all turnover in its accounting records. Identify and perform walkthrough tests on the controls utilised in producing these returns and recording turnover. The Accountants will then determine whether to take a substantive or control based approach to the detailed testing of the bookings included in the returns/turnover.	
3. Obtain a copy of the ATOL Licence, the renewal decision letter and any variation decision and grant letter(s) filed during the year.	
4. Obtain from the Organiser reconciliations for: • The four quarterly returns for each category of licensable turnover to the Annual Return. Obtain supporting documentation and explanations from management for any reconciling items • The Annual Return to statutory turnover for the closest accounting reference period (this will be more complex where turnover is not recognised on a departure date basis or where the bonding period is different to the Organiser's financial year). Although statutory turnover is not reported to the CAA, it is necessary for the Accountants to understand how statutory turnover compares with all turnover reported to the CAA to safeguard against any errors of omission of licensable turnover in the Annual Return • Agree the quarterly returns for each category of turnover to the Organiser's General Ledger or reservation system	
DETAILED TESTING For detailed testing it has been agreed with the CAA that the Reporting Accountants use a materiality level equivalent to 5% of licensable turnover	
For controls based testing:	
5. Test check the controls, including relevant IT controls, surrounding the reservation system to provide assurance that bookings are: • classified into the correct category of turnover (eg fully bonded) by reference to the booking details and definitions of turnover • included in the correct quarterly return by reference to the departure date	

• that the reservation was not cancelled before departure confirmed by reference to initial deposit and subsequent payment of balance of booking • and for ticket provider sales only, the date the ticket is issued is properly recorded in the reservation/ticketing system	
AND/OR For substantive testing of turnover:	
6. Obtain a sample (the size of the sample will be determined by the Accountants' assessment of risk) of bookings from the reservation system. (The sample to include bookings for all categories of turnover applicable to the Organiser) 7. For the sample selected test that each booking is: • classified into the correct category of turnover (e.g. fully bonded) by reference to the booking details and CAA definitions of turnover • included in the correct quarterly return by reference to the departure date • confirmed by reference to initial deposit and subsequent payment of balance of booking 8. Analytical review to be undertaken and documented detailing how the returns and respective categories of turnover are in accordance with the Accountants' understanding of the business and how it has performed in the period and its performance in comparison with its sector of the wider travel industry.	
Small Firm's ATOL	
For small firm's selling less than 500 Seats per year: 9. Follow all steps as above for checking turnover as for a full licence. 10. Agree the total number of licensed passengers shown in the return to the Organiser's reservation system. (***This work procedure in respect of passenger numbers does not need to be applied for the September 2003 renewals***)	
(ii) Non-licensable turnover	
Ticket Provider Sales: For a sample of bookings, check the reservation or ticketing system to establish whether the ticket is recorded as having been issued to the customer either promptly at the point when the payment is made or within 24 hours where the booking is made remotely (where the customer is not present). The size of the sample will be determined by the Accountants' assessment of controls over the recording of the issue date of the ticket.	

b) Factual Confirmations

The following is a full list of potential confirmations that may be requested by the CAA. Accordingly the suggested work procedures listed should be undertaken only in respect of the particular confirmations requested. **In each case, in order to support their procedures, Accountants should obtain a direct confirmation from the directors of the Organiser regarding the requested matter in the form set out in the proforma report in Appendix 5b.**

1.	**Confirmation of Subordinated loans**	
a)	*Confirmation of new subordinated loans*	
	Obtain copy of the subordinated loan agreement.	
	Agree the receipt of cash is from the parties identified in the loan agreement.	
	Agree the receipt of cash to the bank statement of an account in the name of the Organiser.	
b)	*Confirmation of total subordinated loans at the balance sheet date*	
	Obtain confirmation from each lender of the subordinated loans owed to them at the balance sheet date.	
2.	**Confirmation of receipt of a memorandum of cash gift**	
	Obtain a copy of the 'memorandum of a cash gift' form.	
	Agree the receipt of cash is from the parties identified in the form.	
	Agree the receipt of cash to the bank statement of an account in the name of the Organiser.	
3.	**Guarantees**	
	Obtain copy of deed of guarantee and any other guarantees (usually from the parent or Ultimate Holding Company) given in favour of the Organiser (occasionally to the parent group).	
	Confirm that the guarantee has been brought to your attention.	
4.	**Confirmation of new share capital/rights issue**	
	Obtain copy of the stamped Form 88(2) submitted to Companies House.	
	Obtain minutes and shareholder agreements (if applicable) in respect of the new share issue and confirm that the share register records that the new shares have been issued in accordance with the minutes and agreements.	
	For shares issued for cash:	
	Agree the receipt of consideration for the shares and any premium thereon to the bank statement of a bank account of the Organiser.	
	Agree the receipt of cash is from the parties identified on the Form 88(2).	
	Agree to receipt of cash into a bank account of the Organiser.	
	If cash is initially placed in an escrow account, agree the amount to the bank statement and enquire of the directors as to when it is intended that the money will be transferred from escrow to a bank account of the Organiser.	

Where a subordinated loan has been waived and additional share capital has been issued as consideration:	
Confirm the existence of an agreement between the lender and company to this end signed by both parties.	
5.	**Confirmation of bank loan funding**
Obtain a copy of the bank loan agreement.	
Agree the receipt of cash is from the parties identified in the loan agreement.	
Agree receipt of loan monies to the bank statement of a bank account of the Organiser.	
6.	**Confirmation of repayment of item post year end**
Obtain detail of asset being queried by the CAA.	
Agree receipt of cash post year end to supporting documentation and the bank statement of a bank account of the Organiser.	
7.	**Confirmation of change of ownership**
Obtain copies of share transfer/issue forms.	
Obtain a copy of the new ownership structure provided by the directors of the Organiser to the CAA.	
Confirm that the share register held by the Organiser correctly reflects these changes.	

c) Ring Fencing Confirmations

These suggested work procedures only cover the areas Accountants might be able to provide the CAA with the confirmations they are looking for. The CAA has revised its procedures for obtaining certain confirmations from Organisers as the Accountants are unlikely to be able to provide meaningful assurance on the Organiser's confirmations – see the CAA's Guidance Note 18 available on the CAA's website. These confirmations include the following:

- Sharing of any premises with other group companies
- Sharing of any administrative functions with other group companies
- Confirmation that staff and management are directly employed
- Whether supplier contracts are separate from other group undertakings.

The confirmations below may also be required on associated companies as defined in Guidance Note 18.

The following is a full list of potential confirmations over which the CAA may request Accountants to perform the suggested work procedures. Accordingly the relevant work procedures listed should be undertaken only in respect of the particular confirmations requested. **In each case, in order to support their work procedures, the Accountants should obtain a direct confirmation from the directors of the Organiser regarding the requested matter in the form set out in the proforma report in Appendix 5c.**

1.	Read the CAA's Guidance Note 18 dated 15 August 2003, for Organisers about licensing requirements for firms that are part of a group or have associates.

2.	Obtain copy of ATOL Licence decision letters and any variation decision and grant letter(s) filed during the year to understand the agreed ring fence criteria stated as being met by the Organiser in their application. **WHERE IT IS UNREALISTIC TO OBTAIN THE EVIDENCE TO GIVE THE CONFIRMATION DO NOT GIVE IT BUT STATE WHY IN YOUR LETTER TO THE CAA.**
3.	**Guarantees, loans and letters of support**
	Obtain and read board minutes of all group companies for the financial year defined by the CAA in their letter to the Organiser and note whether any guarantees, loans or letters of support have been provided by the Organiser. Also enquire of the directors whether any Guarantees, loans or letters of support have been provided by the Organiser.
4.	**Inter-company debtors**
	Enquire of the directors as to the nature of all inter-company debtors to the Organiser and whether they all arise from trading and are repaid on normal commercial terms. (For normal commercial terms the CAA would expect the balances to be settled at least monthly). Test that the inter-company balance has been settled at least monthly. Test a sample of entries for each inter-company account to backing invoices to agree that they are trading in nature. Where the debtor relates to funding of the group undertaking this is to be separately identified to the CAA.
5.	**Inter-company creditors**
	Enquire of the directors as to the nature of all inter-company creditors to the Organiser and whether they all arise from trading. Test a sample of entries for each inter-company account to backing invoices to agree that they are trading in nature. Test that the inter-company balance has been settled at least monthly. Where the creditor relates to funding by the group undertaking this is to be separately identified to the CAA.
6.	**Merchant agreements with credit card companies**
	Obtain from management all merchant agreements with credit card companies in the Organiser's name and agree whether they are solely for the Organiser.
7.	**Banking arrangements**
	Check the Organiser's bank accounts to ensure that they are in the sole name of the Organiser. Obtain from management copies of the current banking agreements to which the Organiser is a party and check that the Organiser's bank accounts are not subject to rights of set-off against the accounts of other entities.

Appendix 5 – Recommended Wording for Reports

Appendix 5a (i) and (ii) sets out the CAA standard form for the Annual Licensable Turnover Report and Ticket Provider Report respectively. Recommended wordings for factual confirmation reports and ring fencing confirmation reports are set out in Appendices 5b and 5c respectively.

5a) (i) Annual Licensable Turnover Report

ATOL Holder	ATOL Number

Twelve months From	to

This report relates to the licensable turnover earned by the ATOL Holder during the four calendar quarters immediately prior to its latest financial year end.

The turnover in this report should relate to only one of the following categories of business. If the ATOL Holder does more than one of these categories of business, please complete a separate form for each category. Please refer to the Guide to ATOL or Guidance Note 10 for an explanation of the different categories of licensable turnover.

Please indicate by ticking one box below which category of business this report covers:

- ***Fully bonded business:*** scheduled or charter packages, and seat-only charters ☐
- ***Scheduled bonded business:*** scheduled seat-only tickets covered by a bond ☐
- ***Agency business:*** scheduled seat-only tickets covered by airline Deed(s) of Undertaking ☐
- ***Other facilities:*** sold in conjunction with tickets covered by airline Deed(s) of Undertaking ☐
- ***ATOL to ATOL business:*** licensable products sold to other Organisers for resale under the buyers' licences ☐

Calendar Quarter		Turnover
From	To	(£)

Tick one of the statements below: if the second applies, please indicate the number of other reports submitted.

- This report covers all of the turnover which arose from licensable operations of the ATOL Holder during the quarters indicated ☐

- I supply herewith _____ (number) other reports, relating to other categories of licensable business undertaken during the same periods ☐

Confirmation by the ATOL Holder

I have read the relevant guidance notes and confirm that the analysis of turnover shown above is in accordance therewith, and with the Civil Aviation (Air Travel Organisers' Licensing) Regulations 1995 relevant to the operation of an Air Travel Organisers' Licence.

Signed   Date

Print Name
(BLOCK CAPITALS)

Position

Report of the Accountants

Licensable Turnover

In accordance with the model engagement terms dated 15 August 2003 set out in the CAA Guidance Note 10, we confirm that the turnover which arose from the licensable operation in the category and in the calendar quarters indicated above have been tested in accordance with the schedule of work set out in appendix 4(a) of Technical Release Audit 2/03 issued by the Institute of Chartered Accountants in England and Wales and in our opinion is fairly presented in accordance with CAA Regulations and guidance.

Our report is prepared solely for the confidential use of the ATOL Holder, the CAA and the Air Travel Trust, and solely for the purpose of reporting to the CAA on the company's licensable turnover. Our report must not be recited or referred to in whole or in part in any other document. Our report must not be made available, copied or recited to any other party without our express written permission.

We neither owe nor accept any duty to any other party and shall not be liable for any loss, damage or expense of whatsoever nature, which is caused by other parties' reliance on our report.

Signed   Date

Name of firm
(BLOCK CAPITALS)

Address
(BLOCK CAPITALS)

5a) (ii) Ticket Provider Report

Licence Holder	ATOL Number

Twelve months	
From	to

This report relates to the turnover earned by the licence holder as a 'ticket provider' during the latest financial year. Please refer to the Civil Aviation (Air Travel Organisers' Licensing) Regulations 1995, a Guide to ATOL and Guidance Note 10 for an explanation of sales that may be classified as 'ticket provider'.

Confirmation by the ATOL Holder

I, the undersigned, have read the relevant Regulations and guidance issued by the CAA and confirm that in the twelve month period stated above, sales made by this firm as a 'ticket provider' were

£____

Signed   Date

Print Name
(BLOCK CAPITALS)

Position

Report of the Accountants

Ticket Provider Turnover

In accordance with the model engagement terms dated 15 August 2003 set out in CAA Guidance Note 10, we confirm that the turnover which arose from the licence holder acting as a ticket provider over the period stated above has been tested in accordance with the schedule of work set out in appendix 4(a) of Technical Release Audit 2/03 issued by the Institute of Chartered Accountants in England and Wales. Accordingly, for a sample of bookings, we checked the reservation or ticketing system and noted in each case that the ticket was recorded as having been issued to the customer either promptly at the point when the payment was made or within 24 hours where the booking was not made in the presence of the customer.

Our report is prepared solely for the confidential use of the ATOL holder, the CAA and the Air Travel Trust, and solely for the purpose of reporting to the CAA on the company's licensable turnover. Our report must not be recited or referred to in whole or in part in any other document. Our report must not be made available, copied or recited to any other party without our express written permission.

We neither owe nor accept any duty to any other party and shall not be liable for any loss, damage or expense of whatsoever nature which is caused by other parties' reliance on our report.

Signed	Date
Name of firm (BLOCK CAPITALS)	
Address (BLOCK CAPITALS)	

5b) Proforma Factual Confirmation Report

To: The Civil Aviation Authority

CAA House
45-59 Kingsway
London
WC2B 6TE

Factual Confirmations Report

We have performed the work procedures agreed with you and XYZ Limited ATOL Number [...] ('the Organiser') with respect to XYZ Limited. The confirmations made by XYZ Limited are attached (*to be attached*) and are repeated below. Our engagement was undertaken in accordance with Technical Release Audit 2/03 issued by the Institute of Chartered Accountants in England and Wales ('the Technical Release') and under the model engagement terms dated 15 August 2003 set out in CAA Guidance Note 10. The work procedures were performed solely to assist you in your process for licensing the Organiser under the Civil Aviation (Air Travel Organisers' Licensing) Regulations 1995 and our findings are summarised as follows:

[Note: The following is a full list of potential confirmations. Delete those confirmations not requested by the CAA]

[*Delete the inapplicable option where indicated below.]

Confirmation of Subordinated loans

a) confirmation of new subordinated loans

The directors of the Organiser confirmed to us that since **[date] £[XX]** of new cash has been injected into the bank account of **[company name]** in the form of a subordinated loan (as issued to the Organiser in the CAA's approved form of words) from **[the parties from whom the cash was received]**.

In respect of the confirmation above, we performed the work procedures set out in section 1(a) of Appendix 4b to the Technical Release [without exception.]/[and noted the following exceptions: *List exceptions.*]*

b) confirmation of total subordinated loans at the balance sheet date

The directors of the Organiser confirmed to us that the total subordinated loans held within **[company name]** at **[date]** is **[£XX]**.

In respect of the confirmation above, we performed the work procedures set out in section 1(b) of Appendix 4b to the Technical Release [without exception.]/[and noted the following exceptions: *List exceptions.*]*

Confirmation of cash gift (Sole Traders and Partnerships)

The directors of the Organiser confirmed to us that since [date] £[XXX] of new cash has been donated into the bank account of the [company name] by [the parties] in the form of a cash gift.

In respect of the confirmation above, we performed the work procedures set out in section 2 of Appendix 4b to the Technical Release [without exception.]/[and noted the following exceptions: *List exceptions.*]*

Guarantees

We confirm that the completed deed of guarantee dated [date] provided in favour of [Organiser]/[Parent Group] by [issuer of guarantee] has been drawn to our attention.

Confirmation of new share capital/rights issue

Either – The directors of the Organiser confirmed to us that at [date] £[XXXX] new cash has been injected into the bank account of [company name] in the form of [specify share capital type] paid up share capital.

Or – The directors of the Organiser confirmed to us that at [date] £[YYYY] of the [profit and loss account]/[existing subordinated loan] has been capitalised as fully paid up [specify share capital type] share capital.

In respect of the confirmation above, we performed the procedures set out in section 4 of Appendix 4b to the Technical Release [without exception.]/[and noted the following exceptions: *List exceptions including, if cash is initially placed in an escrow account, the date the directors intend that the money will be transferred from escrow to a bank account of the Organiser.*]*

Confirmation of bank loan funding

The directors of the Organiser confirmed to us that an amount of **£[XXX]** was injected on [date] into the bank account of [company name] in the form of a bank loan from [lender].

In respect of the confirmation above, we performed the work procedures set out in section 5 of Appendix 4b to the Technical Release [without exception.]/[and noted the following exceptions: *List exceptions.*]*

Confirmation of repayment of item post year end

The directors of the Organiser confirmed to us that since [date] the sum of **£[XXX]** has been received into the bank account of [company name] from [named debtor] in respect of the [named debt].

In respect of the confirmation above, we performed the work procedures set out in section 6 of Appendix 4b to the Technical Release [without exception.]/[and noted the following exceptions: *List exceptions.*]*

Confirmation of change of ownership

The directors of the Organiser confirmed to us that the ownership structure at **[date]** is as follows **[List all shareholders and their shareholdings]**.

In respect of the confirmation above, we performed the work procedures set out in section 7 of Appendix 4b to the Technical Release [without exception.]/[and noted the following exceptions: *List exceptions.*]*

The work procedures we have performed do not constitute either an audit or a review made in accordance with United Kingdom auditing standards and bulletins issued by the Auditing Practices Board. Had we performed additional work procedures or had we performed an audit or review in accordance with such auditing standards and bulletins, other matters might have come to our attention that would have been reported to you.

Our report is prepared solely for the confidential use of the Organiser, the CAA and the Air Travel Trust, and solely for the purpose of reporting to the CAA under its licensing procedures. Our report must not be recited or referred to in whole or in part in any other document. Our report must not be made available, copied or recited to any other party without our express written permission. [*insert name of Accountants*] neither owes nor accepts any duty to any other party and shall not be liable for any loss, damage or expense of whatsoever nature which is caused by other parties' reliance on our report.

Date   Chartered Accountants

Address

5c) Proforma Ring Fencing Confirmations Report

To: The Civil Aviation Authority

CAA House
45-59 Kingsway
London
WC2B 6TE

Ring Fencing Confirmations Report

We have performed the work procedures agreed with you and XYZ Limited ATOL Number [...] ('the Organiser') with respect to XYZ Limited. The confirmations made by XYZ Limited are attached (*to be attached*) and repeated below. Our engagement was undertaken in accordance with Technical Release Audit 2/03 issued by the Institute of Chartered Accountants in England and Wales ('the Technical Release') and under the model engagement terms dated 15 August 2003 set out in CAA Guidance Note 10. The work procedures were performed solely to assist you in your process for licensing the Organiser under the Civil Aviation (Air Travel Organisers' Licensing) Regulations 1995 and our findings are summarised as follows:

[Notes: The following is a full list of potential confirmations. Delete those confirmations not requested by the CAA. Where it is unrealistic to obtain the evidence to give a confirmation do not give it but state why below.

Where there are associates, similarly worded confirmations will be required.]

[*Delete the inapplicable option where indicated below.]

Licensing requirements

We have read the CAA's Guidance Note 18, dated 15 August 2003, for ATOL holders about licensing requirements for firms that are part of a group or have associates.

Ring fencing criteria

We obtained a copy of the Organiser's ATOL Licence decision letter dated **[date]** and the variation decision and grant letter(s) dated **[dates]** filed during the year to understand the agreed ring fence criteria stated as being met by the Organiser in their application.

Guarantees, loans and letters of support

The directors of the Organiser confirmed to us that during the financial year to **[date]** no guarantees, loans or letters of support were given by **[company name]** in favour of any group companies.

In respect of the confirmation above, we performed the work procedures set out in section 3 of Appendix 4c to the Technical Release [without exception.]/[and noted the following exceptions: *List exceptions including any guarantees, loans or letters of support.*]*

Inter-company balances or balances with associated companies

The directors of the Organiser confirmed to us that during the financial year to **[date]** all trading with group companies was transacted on normal commercial terms, with balances settled at least monthly.

In respect of the confirmation above, we performed the work procedures set out in sections 4 and 5 of Appendix 4c to the Technical Release [without exception.]/[and noted the following exceptions: *List exceptions including any inter-company debtors not settled on a monthly basis and/or any inter-company debtors or creditors not of a trading nature including funding by group undertakings.*]*

Merchant agreements with credit card companies

The directors of the Organiser confirmed to us that during the financial year to **[date]** **[Company name]** had its own merchant agreements with credit card companies.

In respect of the confirmation above, we performed the work procedures set out in section 6 of Appendix 4c to the Technical Release [without exception.]/[and noted the following exceptions: *List exceptions including any merchant agreements with credit card companies not in the Organiser's name nor solely for the Organiser.*]*

Banking arrangements

The directors of the Organiser confirmed to us that during the financial year to [date] [Company name] maintained its own separate bank accounts and its cash is not managed centrally with other group companies.

In respect of the confirmation above, we performed the work procedures set out in section 7 of Appendix 4c to the Technical Release [without exception.]/[and noted the following exceptions: *List exceptions including any bank accounts not in the sole name of the Organiser or any accounts that are subject to rights of set-off against the accounts of other entities.*]*

The work procedures we have performed do not constitute either an audit or a review made in accordance with United Kingdom auditing standards and bulletins issued by the Auditing Practices Board. Had we performed additional work procedures or had we performed an audit or review in accordance with such auditing standards and bulletins, other matters might have come to our attention that would have been reported to you.

Our report is prepared solely for the confidential use of the Organiser, the CAA and the Air Travel Trust, and solely for the purpose of reporting to the CAA under its licensing procedures. Our report must not be recited or referred to in whole or in part in any other document. Our report must not be made available, copied or recited to any other party without our express written permission. [*insert name of Accountants*] neither owes nor accepts any duty to any other party and shall not be liable for any loss, damage or expense of whatsoever nature which is caused by other parties' reliance on our report.

Date   Chartered Accountants

Address

Appendix 6 – Letter from CAA to Organiser and Accountants requesting additional work procedures

We refer to [name of Organiser]'s ('the Organiser') application for an Air Travel Operator's Licence and the reports we have received from the Organiser's Accountants, [name of Accountants].

We request that the Organiser's Accountants perform the additional procedures listed in the appendix to this letter and report their findings to us.

The work performed in accordance with this letter is an extension of the scope of work set out in section 3 of the model engagement terms dated 15 August 2003 set out in CAA Guidance Note 10 and will be performed subject to the model engagement terms.

[Statement 928]
Public Sector Special Reporting Engagements – Grant Claims (AUDIT 3/03)

(Issued September 2003)

Contents

Paragraphs

Glossary of Terms

1 Introduction	1 - 16
2 To whom does an accountant report?	17 - 27
3 Engagement terms	28 - 67
4 Access to an accountant's working papers	68 - 72

Appendices

1. Roles and responsibilities
2. Example of a tri-partite engagement letter
3. Example of standardised terms of engagement (agreed as part of the grant conditions instead of a tri-partite engagement)
4. Illustrative contents of a report
5. Examples of types of wording or opinions that are unacceptable to accountants providing special reports
6. Example of a disclaimer notice for an accountant's report
7. Example of a liability cap for an accountant's reporting engagement
8. Authorisation letter (to be signed by the grant recipient) allowing the accountant to give access to his working papers and report on the grant claim
9. Release letter (to be signed by the body requiring access) confirming that the accountant does not owe it a duty of care or responsibility

Glossary of Terms

Terms Meaning

Accountant(s) The term *Accountant* refers to an individual accountant, firm of accountants, partner, director, or engagement leader who is the individual responsible for the reporting engagement. The *Accountant* provides the requested reports separately from the audit of the annual financial statements of the client. The term *Accountant* is therefore also used to differentiate from auditors who audit the annual financial statements.

Clients The grant recipients.

Committee of Public Accounts (PAC) The Committee of Public Accounts is a Select Committee of the House of Commons. Historically, the primary purpose of the PAC's enquiries was to satisfy itself on the accounting for and regularity and propriety of public expenditure. The PAC retains its interest in these matters, but it also explores matters related to economy, efficiency and effectiveness of government business. The Committee consists of sixteen members, in party proportions similar to those in the House of Commons. The Audit Committee of the National Assembly for Wales performs the Committee of Public Accounts function within its devolved context.

Grant In this guidance, reference to grant monies is in relation to payments made by the grant paying body to other bodies where the grant is to be used for a specific purpose and the grant paying body seeks to impose detailed control over the expenditure.

Grant in aid Grant in aid is where a government department (sponsoring body) finances all or part of the costs of an organisation through paying grant in aid, but the body operates at arm's length and the sponsoring body does not seek to impose detailed controls over the expenditure.

Grant paying bodies These are the bodies that are providing the funding directly to grant recipients. **Grant recipients** These organisations receive the funding from the grant paying bodies.

The Panel The Public Sector Special Reports of Accountants Panel set up by the Audit and Assurance Faculty of the Institute of Chartered Accountants in England and Wales.

Private arrangements These are the arrangements under which the reporting accountant contracts with his client or both the client and the grant paying body through an engagement letter to provide a report on those grants outside of the arrangements agreed by the Audit Commission.

Propriety Linked to regularity, it is the requirement that expenditure and receipts should be dealt with in accordance with Parliament's intentions and the principles of parliamentary control, including the convention agreed with Parliament (and in particular the Committee of Public Accounts).

Public sector For the purpose of this guidance only, the public sector is defined as:

- government departments and their executive agencies;
- the National Assembly for Wales and their sponsored bodies;

- trading funds;
- bodies not administered as government departments but which are subject to Ministerial and departmental control, for example NDPBs;
- local authorities and other local government bodies; and
- National Health Service bodies. This definition does not include public corporations (except where they are NDPBs) or the nationalised industries. The first four parts of the definition are collectively referred to as Central Government. Additionally, it applies to bodies that receive government grants for specific purposes although they are not public sector bodies:
- Higher education institutions; and
- Further education colleges.

Regularity Linked to propriety, it is the requirement for all expenditure and receipts to be dealt with in accordance with the legislation authorising them, any applicable delegated authority and the rules of *Government Accounting 2000*.

Special reports In the context of this guidance, these are specific reports provided by an accountant to grant recipients and/or other parties in relation to work performed on grant claims or returns. The work carried out under these special reports is under a separate arrangement from the statutory audit.

Sponsoring bodies These are the bodies that provide the initial allocation of funding to a grant paying body to distribute the funds to grant recipients.

Statutory arrangements Some reports to public sector bodies are put in place through requirements of legislation.

Section 1 Introduction

The Audit and Assurance Faculty of the Institute of Chartered Accountants in England and Wales issued Technical Release Audit 1/01, *Reporting to Third Parties*, in September 2001. As the scope of that Technical Release excluded reports to public sector entities, a separate panel the Public Sector Special Reports of Accountants Panel ('the Panel'), was set up by the Faculty, to consider the issues relating to reporting to such bodies and the application of the principles outlined in Audit 1/01 to such reporting.

In conducting its work, the Panel has involved representatives from:

- the accountancy profession, including the ACCA, CIPFA, ICAEW, ICAS;
- audit agencies, including the National Audit Office, the Audit Commission, and Audit Scotland;
- Government departments: Department for Education and Skills, Department for Environment, Food and Rural Affairs, Department of Trade and Industry, Department for Works and Pensions, HM Treasury, Office of the Deputy Prime Minister; and
- National Assembly for Wales.

Accountants and grant paying bodies both recognise the need to achieve consistency in the principles adopted in reporting on grant claims and returns in the public sector. There is a need for guidance in respect of the reports that accountants provide and also a need to take account of the statutory, regulatory or propriety requirements that grant paying bodies have to observe when requiring such reports. This guidance is therefore intended to help both those involved in providing special reports on grants and returns to the public sector and those public sector bodies that receive such reports.

Background

4   The public sector is responsible for the provision of public services and for the proper use of public funds. Government departments are accountable to Parliament for ensuring that public business is conducted in accordance with the law, and meets the requirements of propriety and regularity.

5   Many organisations, both in the private and public sectors, receive grant in aid and grants from a number of government departments and other funding agencies (grant paying bodies). Grant schemes are administered by grant paying bodies in different ways and often with differing reporting requirements, which in some cases may be laid down in statute. When an organisation receives grant in aid, it is effectively being financed for all or a major part of its costs by the grant paying body. A typical example of this is the framework set up by the Learning Skills Council (LSC), whereby it may fund a large proportion of the total costs of a college. The college remains at arm's length from the LSC which does not impose detailed controls over the expenditure. Instead it requires a regularity assertion to be given on the specific use of the grant in aid as part of the overall audit opinion on the financial statements. This requirement is built into the financial memorandum with which each college is required to comply.

6   In contrast, other grants are provided to organisations for specific purposes and the grant paying body, when allocating the grant monies, seeks to attach detailed conditions to the expenditure. In this case, it requires a separate report on the eligibility and/or use of the grant monies.

7   The guidance contained within this document does not apply to situations where a grant paying body has awarded grant in aid or grants and requires a regularity opinion on the use of these funds. It refers only to situations where a grant paying body has awarded a grant for specific purposes and it has requested that a special accountant's report be provided.

8   Guidelines covering eligibility and/or use of such grants are usually outlined in the terms and conditions of the particular grant schemes under which the monies are received. Recipients are responsible for ensuring that they meet the eligibility criteria and that funds received are used in accordance with the terms and conditions attaching to the grants.

9   A grant recipient often asks an accountant to provide assurance on the eligibility of amounts claimed and/or on the use of grant money and to sign special reports that have been requested by the grant paying body from which the grant recipient receives a grant. However, before requesting an accountant's report, the grant paying body may wish to consider whether obtaining an accountant's report is the most appropriate form of gaining the assurance they require, and particularly whether the expected cost and relative administrative burden of obtaining an accountant's report is disproportionate to the level of grant. Whilst the grant paying body may still need to have some assurance in these instances, in some cases self certification by the grant recipient may provide sufficient assurance. The grant paying body may still wish to reserve the right either to seek an accountant's report or to carry out its own investigations on a sample basis of smaller claims or when it has concerns about

whether the grant monies have been spent in accordance with the terms and conditions of the grant.

Where special reports are requested, the accountant wishes to assist the grant recipient, if possible, in providing these reports. In many cases, the accountant is also the external auditor of the grant recipient's financial statements. However, the grant recipient may also ask another accountant for such special reports. The grant recipient should ensure that sufficient notice is given to the accountant to allow this work to be planned into his work programme. Where the grant recipient chooses to use another accountant the external auditor should be informed. 10

These special reports fall within a range of frameworks (depending on legislation), the nature of the grant paying body, the grant recipient, and the audit regime for the grant recipient. In some parts of the public sector, this assurance is obtained using statutory arrangements. In local government and the National Health Service in England and Wales these statutory arrangements currently fall within the remit of the Audit Commission. Outside of this framework, private arrangements exist between the grant recipient and the accountant. Appendix 1 outlines the various roles and responsibilities of the bodies and individuals that are involved in the public sector special reporting process. 11

Good practice suggests that the grant paying body may wish to consider its requirements in the following areas in relation to grant claims and returns: 12

- the level of assurance and when it is required;
- the form of report; and
- levels of materiality.

It is important that the accountant, the grant recipient and the grant paying body discuss and clarify expectations about the scope of work, the form of report, level of assurance required and the timing of the work before the accountant agrees to take on the engagement. It is essential for the accountant to have an understanding of the requirements of the grant paying body at an early stage in his relationship so that he can consider whether or not he wishes to take on the engagement. Otherwise, there is a risk that the accountant may not be able to provide the assurance required with the result that the grant paying body may decide that it cannot pay the grant or where the grant has already been paid, require repayment of part or all of it. 13

This guidance concentrates on how the terms of these special reporting engagements and the forms of report can be discussed and agreed with all parties that enter into the engagement. It is not intended to provide guidance on how these engagements should be carried out in practice. Building on the principles outlined in Audit 1/01, *Reporting to Third Parties*, this guidance seeks to establish a framework for reporting on the eligibility and/or use of specific grant monies to grant paying bodies in the public sector. It aims to provide consistency for those requesting and receiving such reports and for those providing the reports. 14

The guidance is not intended to apply to those arrangements that are governed by a statutory framework other than the wording of the reports where they should be applied as consistently as possible throughout the public sector subject to legislative requirements. In addition this guidance does not cover: 15

- statutory audit engagements (audit of financial statements which are governed by the APB's Statements of Auditing Standards);
- corporate finance engagements;
- reports required under UK company legislation (APB Practice Note 8, *Reports by auditors under company legislation in the UK*, should be referred to);

- simple requests for references on clients' financial status and their ability to service loans (guidance on these requests is provided in Audit 2/01, *Requests for references on clients' financial status and their ability to service loans*);
- requests for reports in connection with loans and other facilities to clients and related covenants (guidance on these requests is provided in Audit 4/00, *Firm's reports and duties to lenders in connection with loans and other facilities to clients and related covenants*;
- reports to non public sector organisations (guidance on these requests is provided in Audit 1/01, *Reporting to Third Parties*); and
- areas covered by other APB Practice Notes e.g. reports on landlords service charges within Practice Note 14.

Effective Date

16 The reporting arrangements outlined within this guidance will apply from September 2003. The Treasury will alert government departments about the publication of Audit 3/03, *Public Sector Special Reporting Engagements – Grant Claims* through a Dear Accounting Officer (DAO) letter and will also include a cross-reference to it in its guidance *Government Accounting 2000*.

Section 2 To whom does an accountant report?

Who uses an accountant's report and for what purpose?

17 The first step in providing a reporting framework within the public sector is to understand why reports are requested, to whom an accountant reports and what use the report is put to. This will then help in determining how best to apply the normal principles of reporting to these special reports.

18 In arriving at this understanding, there are three distinct categories that an accountant will need to consider when he is reporting. These are those that:
- receive and are entitled to rely on the reports, (and could therefore suffer a direct loss);
- have a need to see the reports to make judgements, are entitled to place reliance on them for monitoring purposes, but may not suffer a direct loss (e.g. National Audit Office); and
- have access to reports through legislation but may not make judgements or are not entitled to place reliance on the reports.

Recipients of reports who are entitled to rely on them and may suffer a direct loss

19 A grant paying body usually requires assurance that:
- the grant recipient meets the eligibility criteria for receipt of grant monies (which could mean that monies have not yet been fully received); and/or
- the grant monies have been spent in accordance with the terms and conditions of the grant.

20 An accountant is therefore asked to provide such assurances in a report, not only to the grant recipient, but also to the grant paying body, which may then seek to place reliance on it. Even when the accountant is not providing that report directly to the

grant paying body, nevertheless that body may place reliance on the report. In either case there is an expectation that the accountant may have a duty to take reasonable care in preparing and providing the report on the eligibility and/or use of grant monies.

Good practice therefore suggests that the accountant enter into an engagement with both the grant recipient and the grant paying body, acknowledging the duty of care to both parties. Appendices 2 and 3 are examples of possible engagement terms.   21

In addition to his duty to the grant recipient and the grant paying body, an accountant may also owe a duty of care to a sponsoring body which has a particular need to satisfy itself of the regularity and propriety of grants distributed by the grant paying body for which it is ultimately accountable. It is likely therefore that the sponsoring body specifies that an accountant's report is required.   22

If the sponsoring body has indicated that it will seek to rely directly on the accountant's report, it should also be bound into the engagement separately. However, realistically, due to its remoteness from the grant recipient, the sponsoring body is unlikely to want a direct relationship with the accountant and will instead seek to rely on the grant paying body to provide it with the required assurances that the grants have been spent for the purposes intended.   23

Recipients of reports who may use them, are entitled to place reliance on them, but will not suffer a direct loss

In the public sector, these might typically be: 24

- audit agencies connected with any of the above parties, including the National Audit Office and, possibly European Commission Auditors;
- Parliament, in particular the PAC; and
- sponsoring bodies (where they have made clear that the grant paying body is accountable to them and have therefore not entered into an engagement with the accountant).

Other bodies may want to have access to the accountant's report or may have a statutory right of access. However, the extent to which these other bodies may be placing reliance on the report is not always clear and the impact that this reliance could have on the accountant providing the report. Reasons for requiring access will vary between bodies. Some bodies may want to place direct reliance on the report by acting on the information contained within it. Others will require access to the report as part of an overview process and for the purpose of discharging their statutory duties, and may need to place reliance on it.   25

The accountant may stipulate in his report that it must not be disclosed to any other person (except to those who may have a statutory right of access) and so the grant recipient or the grant paying body would need to seek the accountant's consent to release the report to another person. The accountant should establish at the outset with the grant recipient and the grant paying body which other parties may have statutory rights of access to his report. This may avoid unenforceable stipulations on disclosure/release of reports being included within the accountant's report.   26

General access to reports through legislation where no entitlement for reliance may be placed

27 It is unreasonable to consider that an accountant should accept a duty of care to anyone who may see a report where that report is freely available. The wider availability of these reports is a requirement of government rather than the choice of the accountant and availability will be through the grant paying body. If another body writes to the accountant in an attempt to indicate reliance on a report, the accountant should consider whether it is reasonable to accept that such reliance should exist. Where it is not, a disclaimer should be sent to that body in writing. Access to an accountant's report may be based in statute, but the accountant is able to limit his liability to other third parties through appropriate engagement arrangements. This matter is dealt with in more detail in Section 3.

Section 3 Engagement terms

Duty of care and liability

To whom does an accountant owe a duty of care?

28 As established earlier (paragraphs 17 to 23), the accountant may owe a duty of care to those who receive and subsequently are entitled to rely on a report. Since the expectations and/or scope of the work will be determined by parties to the engagement (although, in some cases, it will be prescribed by the grant paying body), it may be considered unreasonable for the accountant to accept a duty of care to third parties whose interest in the work may not have been known at the time that the work was accepted and performed.

29 The accountant's understanding of the risks involved in providing a report underpins the decisions he makes about whether to accept the engagement and on what terms. The flowchart overleaf provides a route map of the decision making process. Depending on the circumstances, an accountant can either:

a) accepts that he may owe a duty of care to the grant paying body and enters into an engagement with both the grant recipient and the grant paying body, including provisions limiting liability if appropriate; or

b) proceeds with an engagement with the grant recipient but, before allowing the grant paying body access to his report, requires the grant paying body to acknowledge in writing that the accountant owes the grant paying body no duty of care; or

c) proceeds with an engagement with the grant recipient but disclaims or limits any liability or duty to the grant paying body by notice in his report; or

d) refuses to accept the engagement.

30 If the duty of care is expected to be extended further to others such as the sponsoring body which is allowed access to the accountant's report, these other parties may need to be brought into the discussions about the wording of the report. The accountant needs to distinguish clearly between those who are permitted access and to whom a duty is owed, and others who may see the report but to whom there is no responsibility.

31 Some grant paying bodies limit their requirement to sight of the report and are willing to accept in writing that the accountant does not owe them a duty of care. In other cases, the accountant might regard the report as low risk because the grant

paying body could suffer little or no loss. In both scenarios, there might not be a formal engagement between the accountant and the grant paying body. The accountant may wish to notify the grant paying body of the proposed scope of work and the wording of the report and the basis on which it will be provided prior to performing the work.

Agreeing the terms of the engagement

Once it is clear which parties are entering into the engagement, the terms can then be discussed and agreed. Agreeing engagement terms in writing should ensure that all parties understand the nature of the relationship and their respective responsibilities. 32

The grant recipient has the ultimate responsibility for meeting the eligibility criteria of the grant, for expenditure financed by the grant funding and for being able to demonstrate that it has used the grant for its designated purpose. The grant paying body has responsibility for ensuring that its eligibility criteria, terms and conditions of the grant and the expectations of the reporting accountant are clear and not open to misinterpretation and that it can be satisfied that the grant was used for the agreed purposes. The accountant has the responsibility for giving an opinion on the eligibility and/or use of grant, through the processes agreed. 33

Appendix 2 is an example of a model tri-partite engagement letter which accountants, grant recipients and grant paying bodies may use to agree engagement terms separately on individual grant claims. This is the preferred option as all parties have the opportunity to enter into the dialogue to clarify expectations, scope of work and the agreed form of report. 34

However, where there are likely to be a large number of grant recipients for a particular grant scheme, the grant paying body may feel unable to negotiate and agree individual engagement letters with individual accountants. It may therefore choose to issue standardised terms of engagement under which it is willing to engage. Appendix 3 sets out a suggested format for standardised terms of engagement. Under this type of engagement, the grant paying body agrees to enter into an engagement with the grant recipient and the accountant on the basis set out in its standard terms of engagement. The grant recipient and the accountant consider the standard terms set by the grant paying body. If both agree that the terms are reasonable and acceptable, they enter into the engagement as set out by the grant paying body. In some cases, it may be necessary to tailor the terms outlined within the grant paying body's standard engagement to accommodate individual circumstances and, if this is the case, the grant recipient and the accountant will need to discuss the revised terms with the grant paying body prior to the accountant accepting the engagement and carrying out the work. 35

If the grant paying body refuses to engage with the accountant through either the tri-partite engagement letter or a standardised terms of engagement, or the accountant feels unable to enter into the standardised terms laid out by the grant paying body and the grant paying body is not willing to discuss or negotiate revised terms, then the accountant may choose not to accept the engagement. 36

An engagement letter should include the following: 37

- a clear unambiguous description of the expectations of the engagement agreed by the grant recipient and, where party to the engagement letter, the grant paying body, the level of assurance, and/or the scope of work to be performed (where the grant paying body agrees the procedures);

2854 ICAEW Guidance on Auditing and Reporting

Flowchart illustrating the process an accountant reporting to the public sector follows in response to requests for reports from a grant paying body

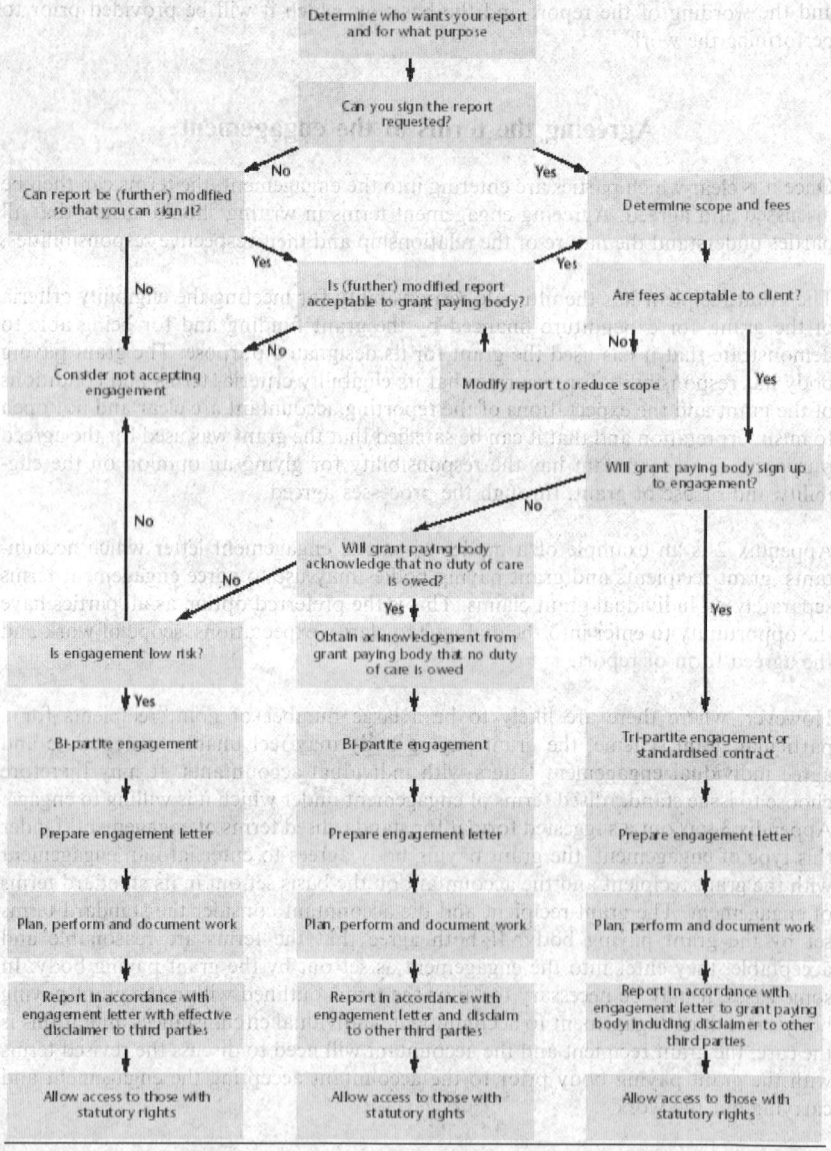

- the form of report to be provided (the words of which have been agreed in advance) using defined terms where appropriate to avoid misunderstanding;
- a description of all parties' obligations and their responsibility for the information (in accordance with the requirement of the scheme) on which the accountant reports;
- clarification that the engagement is separate from the audit of the annual financial statements and that the accountant has no duty of care to any third party in relation to their audit of the financial statements (if they are also auditors of the grant recipient);
- an appropriate liability cap, agreed having regard to the nature and scope of the work being performed, the level of the grant, the fees charged and other relevant factors. Any limitation of liability must be negotiated and agreed with the grant recipient and, where party to the engagement letter, the grant paying body, (and, in both cases, in England and Wales, must be fair and reasonable in compliance with the Unfair Contract Terms Act 1977); and
- details of the addressee for the report, limitations as to the purpose for which the report is prepared and restrictions on who is entitled to see and rely upon the report and the distribution of it.

If, after work has commenced, it is necessary to depart from the terms of the engagement letter, an amended scope of work should be agreed, in writing, with all parties to the engagement letter. 38

Liability

Accountants in England and Wales are advised to address their reports to grant paying bodies only when the basis and extent of their liability to the grant paying body is clear and agreed within an engagement letter. In deciding and agreeing appropriate engagement terms in England and Wales, accountants should refer to the guidance in Statement 1.311 of the Institute's Members' Handbook, 'Managing the professional liability of accountants' and consider the consequences of the Contracts (Rights of Third Parties) Act 1999. They should also refer to Technical Release Audit 4/00, 'Firms' reports and duties to lenders in connection with loans and other facilities to clients and related covenants.' 39

If a disclaimer is used, accountants will need to consider whether it is reasonable and therefore likely to be effective taking account of the requirements of the Unfair Contract Terms Act 1977. It should be noted that disclaimers are not always effective. Accountants are advised to seek their own independent legal advice on the effectiveness of any disclaimers that they intend to include within their reports. 40

Possible ways of arriving at a liability limit are: 41
- to limit the liability to the amount of the grant or cap it at a fixed monetary amount; or
- by separate negotiation.

In most cases, the grant paying body will seek to recover losses from the grant recipient directly and may only seek to recover losses from the accountant where it believes that the accountant has been negligent in carrying out his work, and/or in providing the report and/or where the grant paying body has suffered a direct loss by relying on the report. 42

It is becoming common practice now to limit liability to that proportion of the loss or damage suffered by the grant paying body for which the accountant has 43 contributed to the overall cause for such loss or damage, as agreed between the parties or, in the absence of agreement, as finally determined by the courts (subject to an upper limit).

Clarification of expectations

44 There are currently no UK auditing standards on the types of engagements covered by this guidance. There are international standards in place, which cover levels of assurance and agreed upon procedures.[1] However, these do not apply in the UK. In agreeing public sector reporting engagements, these are the options:

- agreed upon procedures; and
- assurance engagements:
  - high level assurance; and
  - moderate assurance.

45 In agreeing the expectations of the reporting assignment, there may be a conflict between the level of assurance required by the grant paying body and the amount of work required of the accountant to support such assurances. A grant paying body may seek a high level of assurance although the accountant prefers an agreed upon procedures assignment as this seeks to minimise risk by providing more clarity about the work to be carried out.

46 The level of testing carried out depends on the type of engagement required and agreed with the grant recipient and/or the grant paying body at the outset of the engagement. The grant paying body should also consider whether everything that it wants a report on is capable of verification e.g. whether or not receipt of a grant has positively resulted in certain events occurring such as the number of jobs created or safeguarded. The higher the level of assurance required, the more detailed will be the testing. The more testing that is carried out, the more likelihood there is of any errors being detected. It is worth noting that, however detailed the testing, not all errors will necessarily be detected.

47 The amount of grant involved is also a key factor in determining the level of assurance. The grant paying body should consider the amount of grant that it requires a report on and clarify within the terms and conditions a materiality level that determines the level of error and/or risk that they are prepared to accept. In some cases, the total expenditure on the project will equal the total amount of grant received and the grant paying body may require a report on the total expenditure. In other cases, the actual grant given may only be a percentage of the total expenditure and the grant paying body may have set conditions about the expenditure reaching a certain level before grant is given e.g. the grant recipient may be required to spend at least £10 million before a £5million grant is allocated. Therefore, it may only want a report to confirm that at least £10 million has been spent on the specific project. The accountant should ensure that assignments are scoped in relation to the level of assurance, the amount of grant and the materiality level that is specified and required.

48 An accountant is willing and generally able to provide the level of assurance required by the grant recipient and the grant paying body, but the level of assurance impacts

---

[1] *ISA 100 'Assurance Engagements'* provide guidance on levels of assurance and ISA 920 *'Engagements to perform agreed upon procedures on factual information'* provides some guidance on agreed upon procedures. Both will be reviewed by the International Audit & Assurance Standards Board with its review of all International Standards of Auditing.

upon the cost of such work. Generally, the higher the level of assurance required the higher the level of testing performed and the higher the cost and administrative burden for the recipient incurred. This factor should be taken into consideration when determining what is absolutely necessary to confirm that the grant recipient is eligible to receive the funds and/or that funds have been spent in accordance with the terms and conditions of the grant scheme.

Agreed upon procedures

An 'agreed upon procedures' assignment involves performing certain specified procedures, the results of which the grant paying body uses to derive its assurance. The procedures to be performed are agreed in advance and set out in the engagement letter. The accountant tailors the engagement letter and report to reflect the specific requirements of the grant paying body and the circumstances of the engagement. He also attaches to the engagement letter a draft of the type of report that will be issued. 49

Audit 1/01, *Reporting to Third Parties*, suggested that, in most situations where an accountant is asked to provide a report to a third party, an agreed upon procedures engagement will best meet the expectations of the third party and the client regarding the work the accountant performs. These engagements serve to lessen the scope for misunderstanding about the work to be performed, the nature of the results and the assurance provided within the report. However, grant paying bodies have expressed concern that they may not have sufficiently trained staff with the requisite knowledge and/or expertise to agree procedures with the accountants and are therefore reluctant to agree procedures with individual firms of accountants. Instead, they expect to rely on the accountant's professional judgement in determining the appropriate procedures to provide the level of assurance required. 50

Where a grant paying body feels unable to agree procedures with the accountant, it may be possible to carry out a high or medium level of assurance engagement which will still require the grant paying body to meet certain criteria, clarify its expectations and agree the form of report. 51

Assurance engagements

For an engagement to provide a specific level assurance it needs to exhibit all of the following elements: 52

(a) a three party relationship involving:
- a professional accountant;
- a responsible party; and
- an intended user.

(b) a subject matter;
(c) suitable criteria;
(d) an engagement process; and
(e) a conclusion.

For an accountant to provide a level of assurance, the grant paying body has to identify suitable criteria against which the accountant can make his judgement. If a grant paying body requires an assurance engagement, it needs to ensure that its staff are able to identify suitable criteria, clearly interpret and properly define the terms and conditions of the grant and define and agree the form of words required on reports. When considering the level of assurance required, the grant paying body will have regard to the likely number of transactions. If the grant paying body is unable 53 to meet all the requirements of an assurance engagement, the accountant should not agree to carry out this type of engagement.

High levels of assurance

54 Many grant paying bodies require a high level of assurance. A high level of assurance is usually regarded as providing a conclusion expressed in positive terms such that, in the opinion of the accountant, the grant eligibility criteria has been met and/or grant monies been spent for the intended purpose. To express a positive opinion an accountant might have to perform a significant amount of detailed testing in order to satisfy himself that all of the grant monies have been expended as intended. In some cases, under a high level assurance engagement, it may be necessary for the accountant to carry out 100% testing. For example, a requirement to ensure that a grant had been used in a particular way, e.g. towards a particular fixed asset could mean a low number of transactions (even as little as one invoice) and therefore it would be relatively easy to provide a high level assurance.

Moderate assurance

55 Agreeing a moderate assurance engagement is a potential solution to any concerns from either party over the balance between assurance and other factors. A moderate level of assurance requires all of the above elements of an assurance engagement to be met, but a limited amount of detailed testing. This type of engagement would provide a negative assurance opinion in the style of *'having carried out the procedures stated, nothing has come to our attention to suggest that the grant has not been spent for the intended purpose...'*. This opinion would reflect that the accountant has performed limited procedures and has not carried out the level of detailed testing that is required by a high level of assurance.

Audit of the financial statements

56 An accountant may also be the auditor of the grant recipient's annual financial statements. If he agrees to provide an accountant's report on a grant claim or return, he will need to clarify with both the grant recipient and the grant paying body that this engagement is separate from the audit of the annual financial statements.[2] This clarification may be provided within the engagement letter if the grant paying body is a party to the engagement letter and/or by including appropriate wording in the form of the report to this effect.

57 The auditing standards that need to be complied with in order to sign off an audit opinion on a set of annual financial statements / statutory accounts are not fully applicable to these types of special reporting engagements. Accordingly it is not appropriate for the terms of the engagement or the resulting accountant's report on a grant claim to make a reference to the standards used for the purpose of the audit of the financial statements.

---

[2] *The audit of the financial statements is carried out under a separate engagement for specific statutory purposes and work is performed for specific objectives using the Auditing Practices Board's Statement of Auditing Standards that are specifically designed for the purpose of the audit of the annual financial statements.*

Form of report

Agreeing the words and form of report at the outset helps to avoid disagreements with the grant recipient or the grant paying body at a later stage. An accountant's report should reflect the agreement set out in the engagement letter and be supported by the work he has carried out. The report should make clear: 58

- for whom it is prepared, who is entitled to rely upon it and for what purpose;
- that the engagement was undertaken in accordance with the agreed engagement terms;
- the work performed and the findings; and
- who is permitted to have access to the report.

Appendix 4 includes illustrative contents of a report.

The grant paying body, when determining the terms and conditions of the schemes and the level of assurance that it may require from an accountant's report, needs to consider carefully the form of words that it may require. In doing so, it should bear in mind the responsibilities of the various parties in the process and consider whether the assurances it requires are those that would be the responsibility of the grant recipient rather than the accountant. For example, responsibility for using a grant for its intended purpose lies with the grant recipient and hence assurance may be most appropriately obtained from them on this. 59

In considering the form of words that it may require, a grant paying body will need to bear in mind that the accountant is not bound to sign any form of report (pre-printed or otherwise) that has not been discussed with the accountant. Nor does any form of report that has been endorsed as being acceptable by the accountant's professional body bind an accountant but the accountant should carefully consider the reasons behind the agreement by the professional body before deciding not to agree to the requested form of words. 60

Good practice suggests that all parties including the reporting accountant should be involved in the process of agreeing the wording on the report rather than having standard forms of words that may not be justified by any level of work carried out. The form of report requested should take into account the terms and conditions of the grant, the level of assurance required, the amount of work to be performed to provide the form of report, the risk attaching to the work and the cost and relative administrative burden of the work. 61

It is important that, before commencing work, the accountant discusses with both the grant recipient and the grant paying body the form of report that the grant paying body has requested and whether he believes he will be able to provide this. If the grant paying body wishes the accountant to exercise his professional judgement in carrying out procedures to provide a level of assurance that they require, then it must also be appropriate for the accountant to exercise his professional judgement in considering the forms of words that he uses in the opinion he gives, based on the work performed. 62

An accountant's report should not include undefined terms such as *'review'* or *'reasonable'* without specifying clearly what the terms mean. Similarly, he should not use open-ended wording, without indicating the scope of the work that has been performed by reference to an engagement letter or relevant guidance. This is crucial when providing high or moderate levels of assurance. Such wording may lead to confusion as to the precise extent of work, and therefore the assurance that can be 63 taken from their reports. Examples of wording that an accountant is advised not to accept or use when providing special reports are shown in Appendix 5.

64 An accountant signs reports when he has performed sufficient work and obtained sufficient evidence to support the opinions and/or conclusions that he is asked to give in the report. It can be difficult for an accountant to sign opinions in relation to *'the reasonableness of a body's value for money arrangements'*, or *'satisfaction that the systems of internal control are appropriate'* as these could be interpreted as the accountant confirming that the grant recipient is actually achieving value for money or that systems of internal control are adequate. By signing such reports misunderstandings may arise in relation to the meaning of opinions made by the accountant and so care should be taken to ensure the meaning of the opinion sought is clear before accepting such assignments.

65 An accountant might however be able to provide an opinion on whether the grant recipient has actively put arrangements in place, to seek value for money if the grant paying body has provided clear criteria against which such a judgement can be made. An opinion such as this might take the following form, *'as at [date], we have carried out procedures as set out by the [grant paying body] to gain evidence that the [grant recipient] has taken steps to seek value for money in line with the guidance provided to it by the [grant paying body].'*

66 An accountant should bear in mind that some wording included within prescribed forms of report might be wording that is enshrined in legislation. If this is the case, the grant paying body should define clearly these words to avoid any misunderstandings later. In all cases, the accountant has a right not to accept any engagement if he feels that the required wording is too onerous or where it has not been properly defined. Where he does not feel able to accept such responsibility he should decline this work.

67 Sometimes, the grant paying body may amend its terms and conditions for the grant or require a higher level of assurance than previously agreed. This may require a different form of words for the report. If the wording in a form of report is to be changed at the request of the grant paying body or the grant recipient, then the accountant needs to:

- consider whether he can sign the new form of report, based on the work already performed;
- consider what additional work needs to be performed, if the new form of report cannot be signed; and
- discuss and agree a revised engagement letter (with the grant recipient and, where party to the engagement letter, the grant paying body), if appropriate.

Section 4 Access to an accountant's working papers

68 Some government departments or audit agencies may require access to the accountant's working papers to either clarify or confirm the processes put in place by the grant paying body to allocate and verify the use of grant monies or because they have a statutory duty to report to Parliament matters of significance which arise out of their review.

69 The accountant's working papers are his legal property, and he has a right to restrict or decline access to them. The working papers may contain confidential information about the grant recipient and, by permitting access to them, an accountant could be acquiring a significant legal risk. However, refusing access could be unhelpful to the

grant recipient and those requiring access. An accountant is usually prepared to permit access to the working papers, provided the issues below have been addressed. Before permitting access to others, such as a government department or audit agency, to review these papers, an accountant needs to establish the reasons for the access and agree a protocol with the government department or audit agency on how access to working papers may be obtained so that the interests of all parties can be protected.

Prior to allowing access to the working papers, an accountant will consider such issues as ownership and confidentiality of the working papers as well as whether or not such access creates an additional duty of care. The accountant should not provide access to his working papers or provide explanations until he has obtained: 70

- an authorisation letter signed by the grant recipient giving authorisation for the accountant to permit access to the working papers and provide explanations of the working papers where appropriate as well as agreeing that the accountant has no liability to the grant recipient or other parties as a result of providing this access (Appendix 8); and
- a release letter signed by the body requiring access, stating the purpose of the access and agreeing that the accountant does not assume any duties, liabilities, or obligations as a result of allowing access (Appendix 9).

The accountant should take care to restrict explanations to the working papers and should avoid giving oral representations or warranties about any matters arising after the date of their report. 71

Access to the accountant's reports and working papers is granted on receipt of a suitable letter from the grant paying body acknowledging that this does not extend a duty of care or responsibility to them. To this end, it is the responsibility of the person requiring access to determine the extent to which he relies on the accountant's report or working papers. The accountant should not accept any responsibility for any reliance that the person chooses to place on the judgements and conclusions formed by the accountant. It should be a condition of access that the person does not disclose to any other party, any findings that do not relate to the grant and which might arise from their review of the report and working papers. 72

Appendix 1 – Roles and responsibilities

This Appendix outlines the various roles and responsibilities of the bodies and individuals that are involved in the public sector special reporting process:

- Sponsoring bodies;
- Grant paying bodies;
- Grant recipients;
- Accountants;
- Comptroller and Auditor General and the National Audit Office;
- Auditor General for Wales;
- Audit Commission;
- H M Treasury; and
- National Assembly for Wales.

Sponsoring bodies

Sponsoring bodies are the ultimate funders of an activity. However, they may pass the funding through a single grant paying body or a chain of grant paying bodies rather than directly to the grant recipient. Examples are where a government department funnels grant through non-departmental public bodies to the private sector, or where Government Offices for the Regions are a focal point in the region for schemes funded by different departments. Sponsoring bodies have a duty to ensure that all monies paid out in grants to grant recipients are fully accounted for and are utilised in line with grant conditions. As they need to be satisfied that the grant paying body has properly disbursed public funds, they often set a framework and terms and conditions that grant paying bodies must abide by in order to receive this overall funding. This may specify that an independent accountant's report is required or may leave grant paying bodies' discretion to establish the most appropriate assurance arrangements. Sponsoring bodies may review grant paying bodies systems to see if the grant paying body is properly implementing and monitoring the allocation and use of funds. Sponsoring bodies can be European Union bodies, Government departments or agencies.

Grant paying bodies

Grant paying bodies have a duty to ensure that all monies paid out in grants to grant recipients are fully accounted for and are utilised in line with the grant conditions. The grant paying body dealing directly with the grant recipient is accountable to and may owe a duty of care to the sponsoring body for ensuring that it has disbursed the grant according to central criteria, whilst looking to the grant recipient to provide assurance of eligibility to receive grant and to confirm that it has been used for designated purposes. To assist them in meeting these responsibilities many grant paying bodies require grant recipients to provide an independent accountant's reports providing assurance on the eligibility of the grant recipient to receive the grant and/or that grant monies have been spent in accordance with the terms and conditions of the grant scheme. Grant paying bodies have a responsibility to ensure that the terms and conditions are specified, reasonable, practicable, robust and achievable.

Grant recipients

Grant recipients are responsible for ensuring that they meet the eligibility criteria for the grant and that funds received from grant paying bodies have been used appropriately, in accordance with the terms and conditions of the grant. They are also responsible for establishing and maintaining effective administrative and financial systems to support and record the transactions in relation to these funds and for preparing the claims or returns accurately.

Accountants

An accountant reviews the information contained within the claim or return in accordance with the appropriate procedures for such special reports and provide an accountant's report. For local government and the National Health Service grant recipients in England and Wales, the accountant will carry out this work under the statutory arrangement as separate engagements, as agents of the Audit Commission.

Comptroller and Auditor General and the National Audit Office (NAO)

The Comptroller & Auditor General (C&AG) is the statutory auditor of all government departments and agencies. Most of the work to support him in this responsibility is carried out by the NAO, which performs both financial audit and value for money audit work. The C&AG reports to Parliament, and in practice the Public Accounts Committee, on the results of his audit work. In so doing, he will draw to the attention of Parliament any significant matters arising from his work.

In completing his financial audit work, the C&AG will consider the arrangements put in place by departments to meet their responsibilities for the regularity of public expenditure. It is likely that this consideration will include examination of the arrangements in place for departments to satisfy themselves that grants are distributed and consumed for their designated purposes, especially where a department provides substantial grant funding to external bodies. As auditor to a range of government bodies, including non-departmental public bodies, the C&AG is also requested in certain instances to report to third parties on specific engagements.

Auditor General for Wales

The Auditor General for Wales (AGW) is the statutory auditor for National Assembly for Wales and all Assembly sponsored public bodies and considers the arrangements in place by the Assembly and its sponsored public bodies to meet their responsibilities for the regularity of public expenditure. The AGW reports to the National Assembly for Wales on the results of his audit work.

Audit Commission

Under section 28 of the Audit Commission Act 1998 (the Act), the Audit Commission shall, if required by bodies subject to audit under the Act, make arrangements for certifying claims and returns in respect of grants or subsidies made or paid by any Minister of the Crown or public authorities to any body subject to audit under the Act.

The responsibilities of grant paying bodies, other bodies subject to audit under the Act, the Audit Commission and the auditors it appoints to undertake claims and returns work are set out in the Audit Commission publication '*Statement of responsibilities of grant-paying bodies, authorities, the Audit Commission and appointed auditors in relation to grant claims and returns*' (February 2002) (www.audit-commission.gov.uk). Under these arrangements it is not necessary for auditors to have a separate engagement letter as the Statement of responsibilities acts as a memorandum of understanding between all parties. As part of the arrangements the Audit Commission develops certification instructions after discussion and agreement with grant paying bodies. These confirm the nature and scope of individual grant claims, the form and wording of the report, the format that a qualification letter might take and the circumstances under which one might be issued.

H M Treasury

The Treasury has set out the over arching accountability requirements for English government departments in Government Accounting 2000 (www.government-accounting.gov.uk), by stating that, 'Government Departments are responsible for ensuring that grants are spent for the purposes for which they were provided.'

In particular, Government Accounting 2000 also requires Accounting Officers[3] in England to be responsible for ensuring that the grant is consumed by the recipient on the specific services for which it is authorised. It follows that the Accounting Officer has to be satisfied that systems are in place within the department to ensure this principle is adhered to.

National Assembly for Wales

In Wales, Government Accounting 2000 is adhered to as a model of best practice. The Treasury has appointed the Permanent Secretary of the National Assembly for Wales as its Principal Accounting Officer (PAO) and his responsibilities are laid down in his letter of appointment. The PAO in turn appoints the Chief Executives of the Assembly sponsored public bodies as Accounting Officers.

Appendix 2 – Example of a tri-partite engagement letter

Where a sponsoring body is to be bound into the engagement process, then all references to the grant paying body should also include references to the sponsoring body.

Government Grant Claim/returns – the model tri-partite agreement

Addressee details:

(i) The [grant paying body]
(ii) Grant Recipient

Dear Sirs

Government Grant reports/confirmations

We are writing to confirm the terms and conditions on which you have engaged [name of firm] to provide reports/confirmations in connection with [description or name of grant] paid by [grant paying body] to [grant recipient]. These terms and conditions will apply to the reports/confirmations to be supplied for the period [ended/ ending ...] and for subsequent periods unless otherwise agreed in writing. We will write separately to the grant recipient regarding practical matters such as the timing of our work, staffing and our charges. Our invoice will be addressed to [Grant Recipient], who will be solely responsible for payment in full.

Scope of our work

We will complete the relevant work specified below on the schedule (as defined in the offer letter). The schedule is to be prepared by, and is the sole responsibility of [grant recipient].

Our work will comprise the following:

---

[3] *An Accounting Officer is the senior official, normally the permanent head of a government department, who is personally accountable to Parliament for expenditure incurred by his or her department.*

[Details of planned work relevant to the nature of the claim or grant, level of assurance and form and content of report required]

[*High level assurance*] On the basis of the detailed tests carried out, we will report whether, in our opinion, we have obtained sufficient appropriate evidence that the amounts shown in the schedule are [*presented fairly in all material respects in the context of reporting upon this grant claim and in accordance with the terms and conditions set by the grant paying body*].

[*Moderate assurance*] We will report whether anything has come to our attention arising from the limited tests carried out (as specified in the schedule) to suggest that the amounts shown in the schedule have not been spent in accordance with the terms and conditions set by the grant paying body.

[*Agreed upon procedures*] We will complete the specified limited scope procedures set out below on the attached schedule. Upon completion of the procedures, we will provide you with a report of our findings. You have both agreed that the scope of our work, as specified below, is sufficient for your purposes.

[Preparation of any document that [Grant recipient] may be required to submit to [grant paying body] in connection with our work will be the responsibility of [Grant recipient]'s Directors,[4] who will also be responsible for ensuring that [Grant recipient] maintains proper accounting records and such other records as may be required by [grant paying body]. [Grant recipient]'s Directors will on request supply us with confirmation of matters affecting our work which are dependent on the Directors' judgement.]

Save as set out above, we will not seek to establish the accuracy, completeness or reliability of any of the information or documentation made available to us. Our work will not amount to an audit of financial statements and will not give the same level of assurance as an audit.

Our audit work on the financial statements of [Grant recipient] is carried out in accordance with our statutory obligations and is subject to separate terms and conditions. This engagement will not be treated as having any effect on our separate duties and responsibilities as [Grant recipient]'s external auditors. Our audit report on the financial statements is intended for the sole benefit of [Grant recipient]'s shareholders as a body, to whom it is addressed, to enable them to exercise their rights as a body in a general meeting. Our audits of [Grant recipient]'s financial statements are not planned or conducted to address or reflect matters in which anyone other than such shareholders as a body may be interested for such purpose.[5]

To the fullest extent permitted by law we do not and will not, by virtue of our reports/confirmations or otherwise, assume or accept any duty of care or liability under this engagement to [Grant recipient] or to [grant paying body] or to any other party, whether in contract, negligence or otherwise in relation to our audits of [Grant recipient]'s financial statements.

Having carried out our work we will issue reports/confirmations addressed to [grant recipient] and [grant paying body] in the form set out in the appendix to this

---

[4] All references to Directors in this model mean either Directors, Partners, Proprietors, Board Members, Trustees, Company Secretary, or other Authorised Signatory, as appropriate.

[5] This paragraph is necessary in those situations where the accountants are also the auditors of the grant recipient.

engagement letter, if our findings support this. In determining the form of our report we will take into account, (though without being bound by it) any form of reporting that the [grant paying body] has suggested or agreed with the Institute of Chartered Accountants in England and Wales following consultation with them. We will deliver copies to [Grant recipient] at the same time. This letter will be identified in our reports/ confirmations as the 'tri-partite agreement' under which our reports/confirmations have been issued. Our reports/ confirmations will be released on the basis that they are not to be copied, referred to or disclosed, in whole or in part, to any other party without our prior written consent, which may be conditional. If we need to qualify our opinion,
we will issue a qualified report but will continue to use the agreed form of report for all aspects that are not qualified.

Other matters

Our duties and liabilities in connection with this engagement owed to [Grant recipient] and to [grant paying body] will differ.

[Detail any exclusions and limitations on the firm's liability to both the grant paying body and the grant recipient and any relevant qualifications required to satisfy statutory reasonableness criteria. Consider the guidance in the ICAEW's guidance in Technical Release Audit 3/03 on *Public Sector Special Reporting Engagements – Grant Claims*.]. [See suggested wording in Appendix 7.]

Our duty to [grant paying body] will be limited to delivery of reports/confirmations in the agreed form to enable it to meet its statutory obligations. Delivery of such reports/confirmations (or the supply of confirmation that we are unable to do so in the agreed form) at any time will discharge that obligation in full. We will not owe [grant paying body] any other duty, in contract, negligence or otherwise, in connection with our reports/confirmations or their preparation. [See alternative wording in Appendix 6.]

This agreement shall be subject to and governed by English law and all disputes arising from, or under, it shall be subject to the exclusive jurisdiction of the English courts.

[Detail or append any other terms and conditions to apply to this work.]

Please confirm, by signing below, your agreement to this letter. Once you have done so, this letter will form a tri-partite contract between us in respect of the matters covered. If you wish to discuss any aspects of this letter, please contact
[name and telephone number].

Yours faithfully

[Name of accountant]

[grant recipient]

[grant paying body]

Appendix 3 – Example of a standardised terms of engagement (offered as part of the grant conditions instead of a tri-partite engagement)

Where a sponsoring body is to be bound into the engagement process, then all references to the grant paying body should also include references to the sponsoring body.

The following are the terms of engagement on which the [grant paying body] agrees to engage accountants to perform [a high or medium level of assurance or agreed upon procedures] engagement and report in connection with the [name of grant claim]

An agreement between [grant recipient], its reporting accountants and the [grant paying body] on these terms is formed [grant recipient] and the accountant signs and submits to the [grant paying body] a report as set out in Clause 3 herein. *[NB: The [grant paying body] will not need to sign anything. By publishing this document the [grant paying body] makes an offer to engage on these terms. Once the offer is accepted by the [grant recipient] and the accountants then an agreement is formed.* If the terms of the standardised engagement letter are to be revised, the [grant paying body] will need to confirm its acceptance of the new terms before an agreement is formed.]

In these terms of engagement:

'[grant paying body]' refers to the body that is providing the grant funding;

'the [grant recipient]' refers to the organisation that is required to submit the report to the [grant paying body];

'the accountant' refers to the [grant recipient]'s reporting accountants.

1 Introduction

The [grant recipient] is required to submit to the [grant paying body] reports as set out in Clause 3 below that are also signed by an accountant to provide independent assurance. These terms of engagement set out the basis on which the accountant will sign the report.

2 The [grant recipient]'s responsibilities

2.1 The [grant recipient] is responsible for producing the [information], maintaining proper records complying with the terms of any legislation or regulatory requirements and the [grant paying body]'s terms and conditions of grant ('the grant conditions') and providing relevant information to the [grant paying body] on a basis in accordance with the requirements of the grant conditions. The [grant recipient] is responsible for ensuring that the non-financial records can be reconciled to the financial records.

2.2 The management of the [grant recipient] will make available to the accountant all records, correspondence, information and explanations that the accountant considers necessary to enable the accountant to perform the accountant's work.

2.3 The [grant recipient] and the [grant paying body] accept that the ability of the accountant to perform his work effectively depends upon the grant recipient providing full and free access to the financial and other records and the [grant recipient] shall procure that any such records held by a third party are made available to the accountant.

2.4 The accountant accepts that, whether or not the [grant recipient] meets its obligations, the accountant remains under an obligation to the [grant paying body] to perform his work with reasonable care. The failure by the [grant recipient] to meet its obligations may cause the accountant to qualify his report or be unable to provide a report.

3 Scope of the accountant's work

3.1 The [grant recipient] will provide the accountant with such information, explanations and documentation that the accountant considers necessary to carry out his responsibilities. The accountant will seek written representations from management in relation to matters for which independent corroboration is not available. The accountant will also seek confirmation that any significant matters of which the accountant should be aware have been brought to the accountant's attention.

3.2 The accountant will perform the following work in relation to reports required by the [grant paying body]:

3.2.1 Grant return: The accountant will [carry out a high/medium level of assurance assignment or perform agreed tests] [as set out in the terms and conditions of the grant] and subject to any adverse findings will produce a report in the form set out in the attached Appendix (these should be in line with ICAEW guidance Audit 3/03 on Public Sector Special Reporting Engagements – Grant Claims);

3.2.2 Where a [high/medium] level of assurance is required by the [grant paying body], the criteria is identified as per the Appendix to this letter.

3.2.3 For an agreed upon procedures engagement, the tests are laid out in the Appendix to this letter.

3.3 The accountant will not subject the information provided by the [grant recipient] to checking or verification except to the extent expressly stated. While, the accountant will perform the accountant's work with reasonable skill and care, the accountant's work should not be relied upon to disclose all misstatements, fraud or errors that might exist.

4 Form of the accountant's report

4.1 The accountant's reports are prepared on the following basis:

4.1.1 The accountant's reports are prepared solely for the confidential use of the [grant recipient] and the [grant paying body] and solely for the purpose of submission to the [grant paying body] in connection with the [grant paying body]'s requirements in connection with [name of grant]. They may not be relied upon by the [grant recipient], or the [grant paying body] for any other purpose except as provided in 4.1.2 below;

4.1.2 The [grant paying body] may only disclose the reports to others who may have statutory rights of access to the report. There may be an actual or potential liability to [other bodies] that may arise out of the eligibility and/or use of monies by the [grant recipient], and [the others] who will be entitled to rely on the report;

4.1.3 Neither the [grant recipient], nor the [grant paying body] [nor others] may rely on any oral or draft reports the accountant provides. The accountant accepts responsibility to the [grant recipient], the [grant paying body] for the accountant's final signed reports only;

4.1.4 The accountant's reports must not be recited or referred to in whole or in part in any other document (including, without limitation, any publication issued by the [grant paying body]) without the prior written approval of the accountant;

4.1.5 Except to the extent required by court order, law or regulation or to assist in the resolution of any court proceedings the accountant's reports must not be made available, copied or recited to any other person (including, without limitation, any person who may use or refer to any of the [grant paying body]'s publications);

4.1.6 Except as provided by 4.1.2 herein, the firm of accountants, its partners and staff neither owe nor accept any duty to any other person (including, without limitation, any person who may use or refer to any of the [grant paying body]'s publications) and shall not be liable for any loss, damage or expense of whatsoever nature which is caused by their reliance on representations in the accountant's reports.

5 Liability Provisions

5.1 The accountant will perform the engagement with reasonable skill and care and acknowledges that it will be liable to the [grant recipient], the [grant paying body] for losses, damages, costs or expenses ('losses') caused by its breach of contract, negligence or wilful default, subject to the following provisions:

5.1.1 The accountant will not be so liable if such losses are due to the provision of false, misleading or incomplete information or documentation or due to the acts or omissions of any person other than the accountant, except where, on the basis of the enquiries normally undertaken by accountants within the scope set out in these terms of engagement, it would have been reasonable for the accountant to discover such defects;

5.1.2 The accountant accepts liability without limit for the consequences of its own fraud and for any other liability which it is not permitted by law to limit or exclude;

5.1.3 Subject to the previous paragraph (5.1.2), the total aggregate liability of the accountant whether in contract, tort (including negligence) or otherwise, to the [grant paying body] and the sponsoring body, arising from or in connection with the work which is the subject of these terms (including any addition or variation to the work), shall not exceed the amount of *[To be discussed and negotiated]*;

5.2 The [grant recipient] and the [grant paying body] agree that they will not bring any claims or proceedings against any individual partners, members, directors or employees of the accountant. This clause is intended to benefit such partners, members, directors and employees who may enforce this clause pursuant to the Contracts (Rights of Third Parties) Act 1999 ('the Act'). Notwithstanding any benefits or rights conferred by this agreement on any third party by virtue of the Act, the parties to this agreement may agree to vary or rescind this agreement without any third party's consent. Other than as expressly provided in these terms, the provisions of the Act is excluded;

5.3 Any claims, whether in contract, negligence or otherwise, must be formally commenced within [years] after the party bringing the claim becomes aware (or ought reasonably to have become aware) of the facts which give rise to the action and in any event no later than [years] after any alleged breach of contract, negligence or other cause of action. This expressly overrides any statutory provision which would otherwise apply;

5.4 This engagement is separate from, and unrelated to, the accountant's audit work on the financial statements of the [grant recipient] for the purposes of the Companies Act 1985 (or its successor) or other legislation and nothing herein creates obligations or liabilities regarding the accountant's statutory audit work, which would not otherwise exist. [equivalent paragraphs where grant recipient is other than a Companies Act entity].

6 Fees

The accountant's fees, together with VAT and out of pocket expenses, will be agreed with and billed to the [grant recipient]. The [grant paying body] is not liable to pay the accountant's fees.

7 Quality of Service

The accountant will investigate all complaints. The [grant paying body] or the [grant recipient] have the right to take any complaint to the Institute of Chartered Accountants in England and Wales ('the ICAEW'). The [grant paying body] or the [grant recipient] may obtain an explanation of the mechanisms that operate in respect of a complaint to the ICAEW at www.icaew.co.uk/complaints or by writing to the ICAEW. To contact the ICAEW write to the Professional Standards Office, Silbury Court, 412-416 Silbury Boulevard, Central Milton Keynes, MK9 2AF.

8 Providing Services to Other Parties

The accountant will not be prevented or restricted by virtue of the accountant's relationship with the [grant recipient] and the [grant paying body], including anything in these terms of engagement, from providing services to other clients. The accountant's standard internal procedures are designed to ensure that confidential information communicated to the accountant during the course of an assignment will be maintained confidentially.

9 Applicable law and jurisdiction

9.1 This agreement shall be governed by, and interpreted and construed in accordance with, English law.

9.2 The [grant recipient], the [grant paying body] and the accountant irrevocably agree that the courts of England shall have exclusive jurisdiction to settle any dispute (including claims for set-off and counterclaims) which may arise in connection with the validity, effect, interpretation or performance of, or the legal relationship established by this agreement or otherwise arising in connection with this agreement.

10 Alteration to Terms

All additions, amendments and variations to these terms of engagement shall be binding only if in writing and signed by the duly authorised representatives of the parties. These terms supersede any previous agreements and representations between the parties in respect of the scope of the accountant's work and the accountant's report or the obligations of any of the parties relating thereto (whether oral or written) and represents the entire understanding between the parties.

Appendix 4 – Illustrative contents of a report

These include:

- Addressee(s);
- Identification of the applicable engagement letter and specific information on which the work has been performed and tests have been applied;
- Under an agreed upon procedures engagement, a statement that the procedures/tests performed were those agreed with the grant recipient (*and grant paying body*);
- Under an agreed upon procedures engagement, a statement that, had the accountants performed additional procedures, an audit or a review, other matters may have come to light that would have been reported;
- Under a high or moderate assurance engagement, a statement of the procedures necessary to provide the agreed level of assurance;
- Identification of the purpose for which the procedures/tests were performed;
- Listing of the specific procedures/tests performed (*procedures may include: inquiry and analysis; recomputation; comparison and other clerical accuracy checks; observation; inspection; and obtaining confirmations*); and
- Description of the accountants' findings, including sufficient details of errors and exceptions found;
- Statement that the procedures/tests performed do not constitute either an audit or a review;
- Statement that the report is restricted to those parties that are bound by the terms of the engagement letter;
- Statement that this engagement is separate from the audit of the annual financial statements and that the report relates only to the matters specified and that it does not extend to the grant recipient's annual financial statements taken as a whole;
- Name and signature of reporting accountants; and
- Date of the report.

Appendix 5 – Examples of types of wording or opinions that are unacceptable to accountants providing special reports

1. Wording giving an opinion on a matter as a statement of fact when that matter, by its nature, is inherently uncertain or a matter of judgement

Examples include '*we certify*', wording which accountants would not normally (except where required to by legislation) be in a position to use as it implies complete accuracy. Accountants also avoid using words or phrases such as '*correct*' or '*accurate*' or ' *we have ensured*' for assertions that can never be made with absolute certainty. However, accountants can certify that they have performed an examination in accordance with agreed criteria.

2. The use of the term 'true and fair' when financial information is not prepared under the framework of Financial Reporting Standards

The use of other phrases such as ' *present fairly*' or '*properly prepared*' are avoided unless they are clearly placed in context, for example, '*present fairly in all material respects in the context of reporting upon this grant claim in accordance with...*'.

3. 'Fair and reasonable' opinions

Accountants generally avoid giving '*fair and reasonable*' opinions as they are normally associated with investment banks making recommendations to shareholders in respect of transactions. There is also the risk that they might be construed as valuations, which can give independence problems for accountants.

4. Wording that might suggest that the grant paying body is able to rely on the statutory audit of the grant recipient

Accountants avoid any possibility of a link becoming established between the special report and the statutory audit report. For example, they avoid phrases such as '*we audited the accounts and we...*' or '*during our audit we ...*'.

5. Opinions that are open-ended or otherwise cannot be supported by the work carried out by the accountants

Accountants avoid phrases that are open-ended unless the scope of the work is clear by reference to the engagement letter or relevant standards or guidance, for example phrases such as '*we obtained all the explanations we considered necessary*' or '*we have carried out such tests/performed such procedures as we considered necessary*' are not acceptable. Accountants do not give opinions that are not supported by the work carried out. For example, assertions about completeness that cannot be supported by a limited amount of work that has been performed. Accountants could use, '*we have performed the tests laid out in the schedule/work programme which is attached to the engagement letter*'. These words would link the report back to the scope of work. Other examples of inappropriate reporting include providing positive opinions on solvency or prospective information which is inherently uncertain. In the same way, it is impossible for accountants to be able positively to state whether receipt of a grant has created or safeguarded '*value for money*' can never be given as VFM is an intangible concept. However, it is reasonable to determine whether or not a client has sought VFM by reference to specific criteria set by the grant paying body. A report can only give assurance on the basis of the information available at the time that it is provided.

6. Opinions which accountants do not have the necessary competence to provide

Accountants avoid opinions that are not within their professional competence, for example an opinion of an actuarial nature or a property valuation, where there has been no input from a relevant expert. Another example of this would be the appropriateness of insurance cover.

7. Opinions on matters beyond the accountants' knowledge and experience

Accountants avoid giving any opinion about how '*appropriate*' operational information or records being held or maintained by the grant recipient are, where the information or records relate to matters concerning the specific operational circumstances of the grant recipient which are beyond the scope of the accountants' professional knowledge and experience.

8. Wording that is open to interpretation

Certain words or phrases might be open to interpretation and these are only appropriate to use in clearly defined circumstances where the meaning is well established and understood. The word '*review*' is best avoided as it can be unclear what has been reviewed and the extent of the work. Words to avoid can also include accounting terms, for example, *net current assets* in sectors where specific adjusting items might be recognised when assessing liquidity. Accountants always define terms if the meaning might be unclear and do not otherwise use such terms. The word *material* is avoided unless this can be referenced to a clear definition.

9. Reports on internal controls

Reports on internal controls are only possible in well defined and well established circumstances, where the reporting arrangements have been agreed in a clear manner. Reports on systems and controls are avoided where there are inadequate criteria specified. Reports include an indication of the limitations of a system and are related to a point in time or period. Guidance is given in the APB Briefing Paper *Providing assurance on the effectiveness of internal control*. It is also useful to clarify in writing the responsibilities of management and in particular, to indicate that they are responsible for identifying, evaluating and managing new and changing risks on an ongoing basis.

10. Reports without addressees

Accountants do not provide reports where it is unclear to whom the report is being provided.

11. Reports on financial information which is not explicitly approved by the grant recipient

The grant recipient has responsibility for the financial information being provided and it is, therefore, not appropriate for the accountants to report on financial information unless it is clear that this has first been approved by the grant recipient.

12. Qualifications in the covering letter only

Accountants provide qualifications in their covering letter where a pre-printed report (with wording that is acceptable) is requested. In this case, a clear reference to the report and qualification is included in the covering letter. Otherwise, such qualifications are included in the main body of the report, so that they cannot be detached. Hence accountants should include any reservations about the claim or qualifications on the claim in the main body of the report. In a similar vein all explanations of respective responsibilities of the grant recipient, grant giving body and reporting accountants or limits being placed on circulation of the report or disclaiming of liability by the reporting accountant should be included in the main body of the report. Covering letters should normally be used to explain to the recipients of the letter that a report is being enclosed.

13. Opinions which would impair the auditors' independence

Accountants do not provide opinions that would impair their independence as auditors. For example, where the grant recipient is an SEC registrant, certain forms of valuation opinion are not permitted from auditors.

Appendix 6 – Example of a disclaimer notice for an accountant's report

Where the grant paying body signs the engagement letter

Our Report is prepared solely for the confidential use of [grant recipient] [and [grant paying body]], and solely for the purpose of [describe the purpose]. It may not be relied upon by [grant recipient] [or [grant paying body]] for any other purpose whatsoever. Our Report must not be recited or referred to in whole or in part in any other published document without the written permission of the accountant. (Please see comments in Appendix 3 item 4.1.4) Our Report must not be made available, copied or recited to any other party without our express written permission in every case except for [grant paying body] may disclose the report where it has a statutory obligation to do so. Other than to [grant recipient] [and [grant paying body]], [accountant] neither owes nor accepts any duty to any other party to whom his Report may be disclosed.

Where the grant paying body does not sign the engagement letter

Our Report is prepared solely for the confidential use of [grant recipient] and solely for the purpose of [describe the purpose]. It may not be relied upon by [grant recipient] for any other purpose whatsoever. Our Report must not be recited or referred to in whole or in part in any other external document without the written permission of the accountants. Our Report must not be made available, copied or recited without our express written permission in every case to any other party, except for [grant paying body], to whom we owe no duty of care. [Accountant] neither owes nor accepts any duty of care to any other party who may receive our Report and specifically disclaims any liability for any loss, damage or expense of whatsoever nature, which is caused by their reliance on our Report.

Appendix 7 – Example of a liability cap for an accountant's reporting engagement[6]

The total aggregate liability, whether to [grant recipient] or [grant paying body] or any other party, of whatever nature, whether in contract, tort (including negligence) or otherwise, of [accountant] for any losses whatsoever and howsoever caused arising from or in any way connected with this engagement [and this transaction] shall not exceed [insert amount] (including interest) [insert proportionality clause].

Where there is more than one addressee of the engagement, the limit of the liability specified will have to be allocated between these addressees. Such allocation will be entirely a matter for the addressees, and the addressees will be under no obligation to inform [accountant] of it; if (for whatever reason) no such allocation is agreed, the addressees will not dispute the validity, enforceability or operation of the limit of liability on the grounds that no such allocation was agreed.

---

[6] *This is an example of a liability cap only, which will be one of a number of provisions relating to the accountant's liability and any limitations thereon. For example, the liability provisions will need to make it clear that the accountant is not seeking to exclude those liabilities (such as liability for his own fraud) which cannot be excluded by law.*

Possible words for a proportionality clause

Insert these words in liability paragraph:

'we limit liability to that proportion of the loss or damage suffered by the [grant paying body] for which the [accountant] has contributed to the overall cause for such loss or damage, as agreed between the parties, or in the absence of the an agreement, as finally determined by the courts (subject to an upper limit)'

Appendix 8 – Authorisation letter (to be signed by the grant recipient) allowing the accountant to give access to his working papers and report on the grant claim

I understand that the [body requesting access] believes that it would be helpful if they were to review our working papers and report on [grant claim].

Our policy does not normally allow me to disclose our working papers to any third party. In accordance with the guidance contained within Technical Release Audit 3/03 Public Sector Special Reporting Engagements – Grant Claims issued by the ICAEW, this firm is content to allow such access to the working papers and report providing certain conditions are met. I am now writing to confirm your agreement to the terms set out in this letter and to secure the authorisation of the grant recipient for that access.

As a condition of providing access and responding to any request for information or explanations in relation to the working papers in the course of or in connection with the review of the papers, this firm requires the [body requiring access] to agree to the terms of the letter.

Prior to making the working papers and reports on [grant claim] available, we need the consent of [grant recipient]. In addition, we will require from [body requiring access] an agreement (in the form of a release letter) that they will not acquire any rights against [name of firm] as a result of such access, and an acknowledgement from [body requiring access] that they recognise the basis on which such access is provided.

As you will appreciate, our working papers were created for the sole particular purpose of providing assurance on [grant claim] in line with [procedures/expectations] agreed with yourselves [and [body requiring access]]. They were not created for any other purpose. Furthermore, it is not this firm's function or responsibility to provide to the [body requesting access] any papers that come into existence or information that may come to the firm's attention after the date of this letter. Consequently, the working papers, report and any subsequent information and explanations provided in relation to the working papers and report are subject to the following conditions:

1) the [grant paying body] or any other parties involved, do not misuse any confidential information obtained from their review of the working papers and reports or from any explanations provided by the firm; and
2) the [grant paying body] accept that, to the fullest extent permitted by law, [firm] owes them no duty of care or other obligation and will incur no liability whatsoever to them in relation to or in connection with their review as a result of granting them access or providing explanations.

Please, therefore, confirm that you agree to our disclosing the working papers, reports and providing explanations in relation to the working papers and reports on [grant claim] on the terms described above by signing and dating and returning to us the enclosed copy of this letter on behalf of the [grant recipient] and returning it to me.

Yours faithfully

Name of firm

(BLOCK CAPITALS)

Acknowledged and agreed, for and on behalf of [grant paying body] and its directors

Director Date

Appendix 9 – Release letter (to be signed by the body requiring access) confirming that the accountant does not owe it a duty of care or responsibility

In connection with [grant claim], the [grant recipient] has requested us to allow [body requiring access] access to our working papers, reports and provision of explanations in relation to the working papers and reports as necessary.

The procedures and working papers were designed and prepared solely for the purpose of forming our opinion, in accordance with the form of report agreed in the engagement letter with [the grant recipient] and the [grant paying body]. Accordingly, we have not expressed any opinion or other form of assurance on other issues related to [grant recipient].

You should note that we have only reported on transactions related to [grant claim] in accordance with the agreed procedures/expectations for the period from [date] and to [date] and significant events may well have occurred since that date.

Neither the working papers, reports and explanations provided, can in any way serve to substitute enquiries that you may need to make for the purpose of satisfying yourself in relation to the review that you are carrying out.

Notwithstanding the purposes for which the working papers and reports were prepared, we are prepared to grant [body requiring access] access to them on the condition that the [body requiring access] acknowledges and accepts the previous paragraphs and agree to the following conditions upon which access will be granted:

1) [body requiring access] agrees and acknowledges that:
   - to the extent that any of the working papers or reports may be construed as relating to the state of affairs of the [grant recipient] the onus will be on the [body requiring access] to verify the information directly with the [grant recipient] before relying upon it for the purpose of their review;
   - to the fullest extent permitted by law, the [grant paying body] accept that the [name of firm] owes no duty of care to it whether in contract or tort or under statute or otherwise and will not bring any actions, proceedings or claims against the [name of firm] with respect to or in connection with the working papers [or report] on [grant claim]; and

- agrees that, to the fullest extent permitted by law, [name of firm] has no liability to it for any loss or damage suffered or costs incurred by it, arising out of or in connection with the provision of access to the working papers [or reports], however such loss or damage is caused, including as a result of negligence.

Please confirm your agreement to the foregoing terms and conditions and your acceptance of the rest of this letter by signing, dating and returning to us a copy of this letter.

Yours faithfully

Name of firm

(BLOCK CAPITALS)

The [body requiring access] acknowledges and agrees to the provisions of this letter.

For and on behalf of [body requiring access]

Date

[Statement 929]
Access to working papers by investigating accountants (AUDIT 04/03)

(Issued October 2003)

Contents

	Paragraphs
Preface	
Introduction	1 - 2
Background	3 - 4
Facilitating access	5 - 6
Managing duty of care	7 - 11
Information or explanations additional to the working papers	12 - 15
Content of the authorisation letters	16 - 17
Content of the release letters	18 - 22
Other parties who will have access to information derived from the audit working papers	23 - 43
Investigating accountants from the same firm as the auditors	44 - 45
Consideration	46 - 48
Conclusion	49

Appendices

1) Specimen client authorisation letter
2) Specimen release letter To Prospective Purchaser and Investigating Accountants

Preface

The Institute first issued guidance on access to working papers by investigating accountants (Audit 3/95) in October 1995. That guidance and its example letters provided a useful and effective framework under which auditors could manage the potential risks of assuming duties of care to third parties whilst facilitating corporate transactions.

However, the complexity of transaction funding, coupled with the emergence of different approaches such as vendor due diligence, has resulted in an increase in the number and diversity of parties that may seek to gain access to audit working papers. The variety of such situations can lead to considerable practical difficulties for all parties in applying the guidance. As a result, a number of different approaches have developed and there is market inconsistency in the implementation of the guidance.

Accordingly the Institute has reviewed and updated the original Technical Release. This new guidance provides more emphasis on and explanation of the risks associated with the variety of situations which auditors may come across when requested to provide access to working papers.

The basic principles in relation to providing access to auditors working papers are still the same. The working papers are the auditors' legal property and they can restrict or decline access to them. Where access is permitted, it is not provided until:

- an authorisation letter is obtained from the vendor and target company authorising the auditors to provide such access; and
- a release letter is signed by the prospective purchaser and its investigating accountants agreeing, amongst other things, that auditors do not assume any duty or liabilities as a result of permitting the access.

The main area of change in the release letter is in relation to the indemnity sought by the auditors, which is now an indemnity against loss caused by the breach by the purchasers or the investigating accountants of the terms of the letter.

In addition, it is now recommended that auditors include a disclaimer notice with the working papers and require such a notice to be attached to the investigating accountants' due diligence report.

Although the example letters envisage a simple transaction where one corporate entity purchases another, the guidance also provides more emphasis on the risks associated with the variety of situations that exist in the current market place which auditors may come across when requested to provide access to working papers.

The Institute has also taken the advice of Leading Counsel. The guidance in this Technical Release is based on the advice the Institute has received. The approach laid out in the Technical Release has been reviewed by the British Venture Capital Association (BVCA) which makes the following comment:

> 'In connection with the preparation of this Technical Release, the Institute received and considered representations made on behalf of the BVCA concerning Appendix 2 of Technical Release 3/95. A number of amendments to Appendix 2 of Technical Release 3/95 contained in this Technical Release reflect certain of those representations'.

The review of the Technical Release was initiated by the Institute's Corporate Finance Faculty which makes the following comments:

'The Corporate Finance Faculty was keen to initiate a review of the guidance set out in Technical Release 3/95. The Faculty's purpose was to deterimine whether the guidance could be expanded to address a broader range of transactional activities and whether any amendments might enhance the efficiency of transactions whilst continuing to afford appropriate protection to auditors. The Faculty is pleased to have been involved in the review and has made representations on the guidance to the Audit & Assurance Faculty during the course of the review.'

For the guidance to be useful and effective, it is essential that all practitioners involved in the process apply it consistently and with minimal change.

Auditors are also reminded to take account of the separate guidance already issued by the Institute which covers the risks of taking on responsibilities to third parties with regard to their audit reports, for example in Audit 4/00 ('Firms' reports and duties to lenders in connection with loans and other facilities to clients and related covenants'), Audit 1/01 ('Reporting to third parties') and Audit 01/03 ('The audit report and auditors' duty of care to third parties').

Introduction

1   During certain investment and lending transactions, potential purchasers, investors and lenders (referred to below as 'purchasers') or their agents instruct investigating accountants to investigate and report on aspects of the affairs of the 'target' company. As part of this investigation, investigating accountants may request access to the audit working papers of the target company's auditors.

2   Prior to allowing access to the audit working papers, the auditors of the target company will want to consider such issues as ownership of the audit working papers and confidentiality as well as whether such access might create an additional duty of care. This guidance note is intended to assist auditors in relation to the issues they must consider when deciding if and how any audit working papers are released.

Background

3   The working papers of auditors are their legal property and they have the right to restrict or decline access to them. Furthermore, by permitting investigating accountants to review the auditors' working papers, the auditors risk creating a duty of care to the purchaser and the investigating accountants in relation to those working papers. In addition, the working papers may contain confidential information.

4   However, refusing access is unhelpful to the auditors' clients, vendors and purchasers. If the auditors are prepared to permit access to their working papers, the issues referred to below will have to be addressed to the auditors' satisfaction.

Facilitating access

5   Auditors do not expect to provide access to their audit working papers or provide information or explanations in relation to those papers until they have obtained:

(a) An authorisation letter signed by the vendor and the target company authorising the auditors to permit access to the audit working papers and provide explanations of them where appropriate as well as agreeing that the auditors will have no liability to the vendor, the target company or their respective directors as a result of providing access to the audit working papers or providing information or explanations. An example of an authorisation letter is given in Appendix 1; and

(b) A release letter signed by the prospective purchaser and its investigating accountants in which the purchaser and the investigating accountants agree that the auditors do not assume any duties or liabilities as a result of permitting access or providing information or explanations and the purchaser agrees to indemnify the auditors against claims arising out of breach of the release letter by the purchaser or the investigating accountants. The release letter will also require the purchaser and the investigating accountants to include a standard notice on the due diligence report bringing out the point that the auditors do not accept any liability in relation to the grant of access or provision of information or explanations. An example of a release letter is given in Appendix 2.

The request may also extend to papers concerning dealings with the Inland Revenue (taxation papers). In this case, the authorisation and release letters should also specifically cover these papers. Firms will need to consider whether access is also provided to working papers relating to returns and computations. Accordingly, the guidance which follows applies equally to the tax working papers. In addition, where the audit was conducted for purposes other than normal statutory requirements under the Companies Acts, the letters should be appropriately tailored.

Managing duty of care

In managing the risks associated with giving access to working papers, this guidance proposes three cumulative risk management steps:

1) Limiting the circumstances in which a duty of care by the auditors may be said to arise;
2) Excluding any duty that might otherwise arise; and
3) Seeking an indemnity to protect against any claims that are made against the auditors arising from failure to comply with the release letter.

These are expanded upon in turn below.

A significant protection for the auditors is achieved by obtaining a written acknowledgement that no duty of care is owed. In addition it is important to explain in summary the more important characteristics of the audit working papers. In very broad terms such characteristics include: what the working papers are (and what they are not), what an audit is, and that the working papers were not created for the purpose of the transaction and should not be treated as suitable for that purpose. They are detailed in paragraphs 1 to 6 of the release letter.

To reinforce the importance of the characteristics and to assist in excluding any duty that might otherwise arise, this guidance suggests two actions:

1) attaching a 'Notice' to the working papers when access is provided which summarises the characteristics and records the exclusion of liability (an example of such a Notice is included as Attachment 1 of the example release letter in Appendix 2); and
2) obtaining an undertaking from the purchaser and investigating accountants to include such a standard Notice in the text of their due diligence report (see paragraph 7(3) and Attachment 1 of the example release letter in Appendix 2).

10   The above protections are built upon an additional undertaking provided by the purchaser and investigating accountants that they will not (save in defined cases, as set out in paragraph 7(1)(g) of Appendix 2) provide information obtained from their review to any other parties without the written consent of the auditors. The auditors will need to consider whether to grant such written consent based upon the relevant circumstances, including whether the release letter has been or is to be accepted by or on behalf of the new proposed recipient.

11   The release letter provides that the purchaser indemnifies the auditors for all loss, damage and costs (including legal costs) incurred by the auditors arising in the event that the purchaser or investigating accountants fail to comply with their obligations under the release letter and, as a result, a claim is made against the auditors. It is considered reasonable to require the protection of an indemnity in addition to a damages claim for breach of contract because the auditors are not performing any work for the parties to the transaction but are merely allowing access to papers (and related information and explanations) from separate audit work performed for a different purpose. In the circumstances the reinforcement, and the simplification of remedy, provided by an indemnity are considered justified.

Information or explanations additional to the working papers

12   In providing information or explanations in relation to the working papers, auditors should be aware that extending explanations beyond those matters documented in the working papers increases the risk of assuming a duty of care to the recipient of such information. In particular the auditors should avoid giving oral representations, or warranties, especially about any matters arising after the date of the audit report.

13   Accordingly, in addition to considering carefully the nature of oral information or explanations they are willing to provide, auditors should re-emphasise at the beginning of such meetings the nature of the audit working papers, the purpose for and date on which they were prepared and that the auditors do not assume any duties, liabilities or obligations as a result of permitting access or providing information or explanations. This could be achieved by reading out or circulating the Notice contained in Attachment 1 to Appendix 2 at the start of the meeting.

14   Where potential purchasers wish to discuss matters outside of the auditors' working papers, auditors request (preferably written) clarification of the detailed matters which the purchaser and/or investigating accountants wish to discuss and consider whether they are willing to do so. If they conclude that the risks can be properly managed then they seek informed consent from the target and vendor, and consider structuring such an arrangement as a separate engagement for the purchaser with appropriate liability protection. In all such cases auditors record the basis on which such discussions are held. The above considerations apply equally to explanations of tax matters and working papers.

15   Auditors would usually give access to all working papers recording the audit work performed. If auditors decide not to provide certain papers to the investigating accountants then they inform the investigating accountants and the purchaser that certain papers have been omitted (see footnote vii to the example release letter in Appendix 2).

Content of the authorisation letters

The example authorisation letter in Appendix 1 is intended to be signed on behalf of the vendor and the target company whose working papers are to be made available. The purpose of the authorisation letter is to: **16**

- obtain authorisation from the target company to disclose confidential information to the purchaser and the investigating accountants; and
- obtain the agreement of the vendor, the target company and their directors that the auditors will not be held responsible for the consequences of giving access to the working papers and the disclosure of confidential information.

In circumstances where the vendor is not a single corporate body but a number of individual shareholders, it may not be practicable or appropriate for the auditors to obtain the signature of all the shareholders in addition to the directors of the target company. In such situations the auditors will need to determine whether or not to give access without obtaining the shareholders' signatures to the authorisation letter. A relevant factor will be whether the shareholder has any involvement in the sale process. Such would be unlikely to be the case, for example, where shareholders in a public company are passive investors in receipt of an offer for their shares, rather than being personally involved in initiating the sale of their company. In the latter case, regulatory issues will be of particular relevance in determining whether it is appropriate or necessary for the auditors to seek the signature of the shareholders to an authorisation letter. Where the auditors determine that it is appropriate to seek an authorisation letter, but there is a practical constraint in their ability to obtain signature by all the shareholders, the auditors might be willing to proceed to release the papers on the basis of an authorisation letter signed by a majority of the shareholders. In so doing, the auditors would need to consider the risk that an individual shareholder may claim that such an approach did not carry his authority. Obtaining an indemnity from a majority of the shareholders might be possible in order to minimise this risk. **17**

Content of the release letters

Appendix 2 gives an example of a release letter. The terms of the example release letter: **18**

(1) require the purchaser and the investigating accountants to acknowledge that the auditors owe no duty of care to them as a result of permitting access;
(2) restrict the purchaser and the investigating accountants from passing information obtained from the review to other parties;
(3) require the purchaser and the investigating accountants to agree that the auditors have no liability to them and accordingly that they will not bring any claims against the auditors;
(4) require the investigating accountants to include within any[1] report that they issue a brief Notice (see Attachment 1 to the release letter) explaining the characteristics of the working papers and disclaiming any duty of care by the auditors as a result of providing access to the working papers; and
(5) provide for the purchaser to agree to indemnify the auditors against any claims arising from any breach of the release letter by the purchaser or the investigating accountants.

[1] Refer to paragraph 32 with respect to an accountants' report in an investment circular.

19 The indemnity in the example release letter in Appendix 2 is not as widely drafted as the indemnity in the previous example of the release letter that was attached to the guidance note issued in October 1995. This included an indemnity for any claim arising from the access to the working papers, whereas the indemnity in the example release letter in Appendix 2 is restricted to any claims arising from any breach of the release letter by the purchaser or the investigating accountants.

20 Following representations with member firms and groups representing purchasers and after taking legal advice, the Institute has concluded that the new form of indemnity, when used with the new release letter and Notice and in conjunction with the new authorisation letter, should expedite the process of providing access to working papers, while at the same time providing reasonable protection to auditors.

21 Member firms must decide whether, in a particular case, the new form of indemnity provides adequate protection or whether the auditors should insist on a more widely drafted indemnity. If disclosure of the working papers, or a report prepared from the papers, is to be made to a wider group, not all of whom are prepared to provide an indemnity in respect of their own breach of the terms of the release letter, the auditors may alternatively seek an indemnity from one of the principal parties to the transaction who is prepared to indemnify the auditors generally against claims arising from the release of the working papers. (See footnote xi to the example release letter in Appendix 2).

22 Auditors are recommended not to agree to any request by the investigating accountants to review or approve their due diligence report. Such requests do not give auditors any added protection and may serve to confuse auditors' roles in transactions.

Other parties who will have access to information derived from the audit working papers

23 The example release letter in Appendix 2 is drafted envisaging a simple investment transaction where an existing corporate entity purchases a subsidiary of the vendor. Where there are investment and lending transactions which do not fall easily into this category (management buy outs and flotations are examples), the auditors will need to consider whether or not the release letter needs to be amended and further guidance is provided below.

24 In general, the auditors need to consider which entities might wish to have access to their working papers and any report which includes information derived from the audit working papers.

25 In particular, auditors should note the impact of paragraph 7(1)(g) of the release letter in Appendix 2. This restricts the addressees of the release letter from passing on information derived from the audit working papers to third parties without the prior written consent of the auditors. If the addressees fail to obtain such a consent and pass on the information to a third party, the addressees will, subject to the exceptions set out in that paragraph, be in breach of the release letter and the indemnity will apply to the extent that any loss arises as a result of such a breach.

(A) Syndicated financings

26 In certain situations, for example in connection with syndicated financings, the investigating accountants may be requested to provide copies of their investigation

report, incorporating information derived from their examination of the audit working papers, to other parties who may be considering participating in the proposed transaction, for example as co-investors or lenders. Typically such parties will not be signatories to the auditors' release letter because they could not be identified at the time the release letter was originally executed. Disclosure of the report in these circumstances and without consent would be in breach of paragraph 7(1)(g) of the example release letter.

In these circumstances, the investigating accountants would need to seek the consent of the auditors to release the report to actual or potential investing or lending syndicates. In considering whether to give consent, the auditors will need to be assured that an appropriate mechanism is to be put in place to obtain the protections of the release letter in respect of all members of the syndicate. Depending on the size of the syndicate, it might be appropriate for the example release letter to be modified for signature by the lead bank or equity provider for itself and on behalf of all members of the syndicate, for example by inclusion of the following paragraph: 27

> 'This letter is addressed to [Lead Bank/Lead Equity Provider] for itself and on behalf of all [banks/equity providers] listed in the [Loan/Equity Agreement] (together "the [Banks/Equity Providers]"). By signing and accepting the terms of this letter, [Lead Bank/Lead Equity Provider] warrants and represents that it has authority to accept the same on its own behalf and as agent for the [Banks/Equity Providers]'

The auditors might be asked to consider modifying the form of indemnity at paragraph 7(2) of the letter in these circumstances, for example to provide that the Lead Bank/Lead Equity Provider provides an indemnity in respect of its own breach only and that other syndicate banks are not required to provide an indemnity. In these circumstances the auditors would, for example, not have the benefit of an indemnity where a person has without permission received information from the working paper review from a syndicate bank other than the Lead Bank. Accordingly the auditors will need to understand the basis of any such requests for amendment before deciding whether to accept such requests. The fact that there may be less proximity (and hence a lower risk of a duty of care being established) between the auditors and a recipient who has not had direct access to the working papers and who gains access to information without permission might be a relevant consideration. 28

Where syndication agreements have not yet been drawn up providing for a Lead Bank/Equity Provider to act as agent for other members of the syndicate, it is normally appropriate to require potential members of the syndicate to sign a release letter in their own right. In some cases there may be practical problems with this approach, for example where a large number of potential syndicate members are involved. It is not uncommon for the investigating accountants' report to be distributed, typically in draft form, to assist potential finance parties to consider whether they wish to proceed to provide equity or loan finance. In seeking consent from the auditors to distribute the report in these situations, the investigating accountants will need to explain to the auditors the arrangements which are being made for the circulation of the report (containing the appropriate Notice – see Attachment 1 to the release letter), in order to determine whether the auditors can benefit from appropriate protections which the investigating accountants will themselves be obtaining from such parties prior to and as a condition of distribution of their report. These might for example take the form of an acknowledgement by the receiving party that no rights are acquired against the investigating accountants. This acknowledgement might be extended to the auditors, for example drawing attention to the Notice reproduced within the report. 29

30 In the event that the receiving party does proceed to join the syndicate, the auditors would normally expect the investigating accountants to include the signing of a modified release letter, as discussed in paragraph 27 above, as one of the completion processes required prior to the finalisation of its due diligence report.

31 These arrangements may, for example, be anticipated in the following illustrative form in the investigating accountants' own release letter for their [draft] report to a prospective lender or investor:

'a. It is a condition of the receipt of our [draft] report by you as a prospective [lender]/[investor] that you accept that:
- we have no responsibility or liability whatsoever to you in connection with our report;
- [auditors] have no responsibility or liability whatsoever to you in connection with their audit or any information or explanations sought by us in the course of our review of the audit working papers [and the tax papers]. We draw your attention to the Notice included on page [ ] of the report.

b. If you do lend to or invest in [Company], we agree to consider acceding to a request from you, if made in advance of your lending or investing, to recognise you as an addressee of the report, on the following conditions:
- that you will be bound by and will accept all the provisions of our engagement letter (and will bind yourself to the auditors and accept all the provisions of a letter in the terms of the release letter of the auditors dated [ ] (but adjusted to refer to you) setting out the terms under which access to the audit working papers [and tax papers] and any information and explanations in relation to them have been provided);
- [other conditions required by the Investigating Accountants].'

(B) Flotations

32 Where access is to be provided in connection with the flotation of the target company, (a situation envisaged, for example, by paragraph 76 of Statement of Investment Circular Reporting Standard 200) the auditors are advised to obtain a release letter from the firm acting as reporting accountants (assuming that the audit firm and the reporting accountants are not the same entity). Where a new company is to be incorporated for the purpose of the float, that company would also be expected to sign the release letter, including the indemnity (being for this purpose similar to the purchaser in an acquisition situation). The sponsor would also be expected to sign the release letter in its role as professional adviser to the company being floated. Where there is no new company being formed and the auditors wish to seek the protection of an indemnity before releasing the audit papers, the auditors may wish to seek legal advice as to whether an indemnity is legally available from the audit client in the particular circumstances. The auditors will normally expect the audit client and, where applicable, its shareholders (refer to paragraph 17) to sign an authorisation letter. Where the reporting accountants are preparing an accountants' report (short form report), it would be appropriate to tailor paragraph 7(3) of Appendix 2 to make clear that there is no requirement to attach or refer to the Notice within the published accountants' report.

33 If the firm acting as reporting accountants has previously also acted as auditors, the firm may wish to explain in its reporting accountants engagement letter the basis on which any audit work was previously undertaken and how audit opinions were previously given.

(C) Vendor due diligence ('VDD')

Where a vendor has instructed a firm of accountants to prepare a due diligence report which eventually will be addressed to a purchaser (the 'vendor due diligence report'), the auditors will need to consider how they will manage their risk if the investigating accountants preparing the vendor due diligence report wish to review the auditors' working papers. The principles of protecting the auditors from risk arising from granting access to working papers apply equally in a vendor due diligence situation as in an ordinary acquisition due diligence situation.

Authorisation letter for VDD

The auditors will require the vendor and the target company to sign an authorisation letter as the first stage prior to any access being given to the audit working papers. Further, given that the vendor instructs the investigating accountants to undertake the vendor due diligence, the auditors will extend the wording of the authorisation letter to include a duty of confidentiality in respect of the working papers and any information derived from them or provided in relation to them and will consider requesting the vendor to provide an indemnity in respect of any claims against the auditors that arise as a result of a breach of the vendor's or investigating accountants' obligations under the authorisation letter. The rationale for requesting such an indemnity from the vendor rests on the fact that the vendor (rather than the purchaser) controls distribution of the vendor due diligence report. Auditors assess the risks associated with the vendor's and investigating accountants' control of the report in deciding whether such an indemnity is required.

Release letters for VDD

Assuming that the investigating accountants are not from the same firm as the auditors, the auditors will require a release letter signed by the investigating accountants engaged by the vendor (at that stage potential purchasers will not have been identified). This release letter will be adapted from but substantially in the form of Appendix 2, without the indemnity paragraph (7(2)). In the normal course of events, paragraph 7(1)(g) in the release letter manages the risk to the auditors by including a prohibition on the investigating accountants releasing their report to the purchaser without the prior consent of the auditors which would only be given on the condition that such purchaser has agreed to its own release letter as set out in the following paragraph (although an alternative to this consent mechanism is included in paragraph 38).

The auditors manage their risks to potential purchasers and the eventual purchaser in broadly the same way as they manage their risks to potential members of banking syndicates (see paragraphs 29 to 31 above). Before consenting to the distribution to potential purchasers of a vendor due diligence report, the investigating accountants will need to explain to the auditors the arrangements which are being made for the circulation of the report (containing the appropriate Notice – see Attachment 1 to the release letter). Such arrangements will normally involve the investigating accountants agreeing their own release letter with the potential purchasers, including an acknowledgement by the receiving party that no rights are acquired against the investigating accountants. As envisaged for banking syndicates, the auditors would normally expect the investigating accountants to modify their release letter to reflect the conditions imposed by the auditors. The auditors would not consent to the due diligence report being addressed to the eventual purchaser until the eventual purchaser has signed a release letter in the standard form attached as Appendix 2.

38 Alternatively, however, the auditors might be prepared to recognise from the outset that the investigating accountants will require permission to circulate their report to prospective purchasers and ultimately address their report to the successful purchaser. Illustrative language which the auditors might be prepared to incorporate in the release letter to permit this arrangement is set out below.

Replace final sentence of paragraph 7(1)(g) and the whole of paragraph 7(2) with the following:

> 'The Investigating Accountants may allow access to the Information or any part thereof, in the form of a report of Investigating Accountants incorporating or referring to any part of the Information, to any prospective purchaser of the Company ("Prospective Purchaser") provided that the Investigating Accountants obtain the express prior agreement and acknowledgement of each Prospective Purchaser, addressed to this firm, that (a) this firm has, to the fullest extent permitted by law, no duty or liability and assumes no responsibility to Prospective Purchaser or its professional advisers, whether in contract or tort or under statute or otherwise (including in negligence), with respect to or in connection with the Information or any part thereof or the report and that (b) Prospective Purchaser will not disclose (including by reference or by copy, in whole or in part) any Information, including without limitation the report, to any other person or entity. Prior to the Investigating Accountants addressing to any party acquiring interests in the Company ('Purchaser') any report incorporating or referring to any part of the Information, the Investigating Accountants shall procure that Purchaser binds itself to this firm and accepts all the provisions of a letter in the terms of this letter (but adjusted to refer to Purchaser), together with an obligation in the following terms:
> To the fullest extent permitted by law, Purchaser agrees to indemnify and hold harmless this firm against all actions, proceedings and claims brought or threatened against this firm and all loss, damage and expense (including legal expenses) relating thereto, where such action, proceedings or claim has arisen out of or results from or is connected with the failure of Purchaser, or any of its professional advisers or Investigating Accountants to comply with the terms of this letter.'

VDD performed by the same firm as the auditors

39 If the vendor due diligence report is prepared by the same firm as the auditors, the manner in which the auditors manage their risk to the purchaser (including prospective purchasers) in relation to their audit working papers might be linked to the management of their risk (as investigating accountants) to such parties in relation to the vendor due diligence report.

40 The firm could require the purchaser to agree to the terms of the release letter before agreeing to address the vendor due diligence report to the purchaser. The release letter would then not be signed until the purchaser has been identified and the vendor due diligence report is about to be addressed to the purchaser.

41 Alternatively, the firm could place an obligation on the vendor to procure the purchaser's agreement with the firm to the release letter prior to releasing the vendor due diligence report to the purchaser or as a further alternative the accountants' engagement letter with the purchaser could include the appropriate protection.

42 In all situations, the auditors will also wish to address the circumstances where the report, or a draft of the report, is to be circulated to prospective purchasers. The auditors might obtain at the same time a release of liability from any prospective

purchaser both in respect of their capacity as auditors and investigating accountants as contemplated in paragraph 37 above.

(D) Business refinancing where there is no acquisition

A firm of accountants may be instructed to report to funders in respect of a proposed refinancing of an entity. The accountants may, as part of their work, wish to review the audit working papers of that entity's auditors. In such circumstances, the risks to auditors are, in principle, the same as when investigating accountants review auditors' working papers in connection with the preparation of a report for a purchaser. Accordingly, it is recommended that auditors obtain a signed release letter from funders and investigating accountants prior to releasing the audit working papers. 43

Investigating accountants from the same firm as the auditors

If with the consent of the vendor, the target and the purchaser and assuming that appropriate measures have been implemented (including to protect each party's confidential information), the investigating accountants are from the same firm as the auditors, this does not decrease the risk to the auditors and so the auditors require the same protections in this situation as when the investigating accountants are from a different firm. 44

In such cases, practices will vary from auditor to auditor (for example, the release letter may be altered because the auditors do not see the need for the investigating accountants to be an addressee or signatory to the release letter). In addition, auditors may be prepared to restrict the indemnity to breaches of the release letter by the purchaser only. 45

Consideration

Normally no charge in addition to a charge for the actual cost of copying certain working papers would be levied by the auditors (whether upon the purchaser, vendor or target) for grant of access to the working papers. Should consideration be received by the auditors, this may affect the perceived 'reasonableness' of the exclusion paragraph in the release letter and could increase the prospect of the auditors being taken to have assumed a duty of care. 46

If parts of the working papers are copied (at the sole discretion of the auditors) then a charge equal to the actual cost of copying may be made although it is highly desirable that there is a clear explanation that the charge is simply for the cost of copying. Where administrative costs in connection with the disclosure of the working papers are incurred and charged, it is normally more advantageous for them to be borne by the vendor. 47

In addition, any decision to charge a material fee to the target will require assessment in each case to ensure that the payment by the target does not amount to unlawful financial assistance in the purchase of its own shares. 48

Conclusion

Auditors have the right to decide whether they should give access to their working papers or not and also on what terms access should be given. Their decision has to be 49 made on consideration of the various interests represented. This paper, however, will give them a framework for alleviating the risk if they decide to allow access to their working papers.

Appendix 1 – Specimen client authorisation letter

PRIVATE AND CONFIDENTIAL

The Directors [Vendor]

[Address]

The Directors [The Company] [Address]

[Date]

Dear Sirs

Proposed sale of [Company Limited] ('the Company') by [XYZ plc] ('the Vendor') to [ABC plc] ('the Purchaser')

Thank you for your telephone call [today] alerting me to the proposed sale by the Vendor [of the ordinary shares of the Company] to the Purchaser ('the Proposed Transaction') in which you requested this firm to allow [the Purchaser and/or][2] the Purchaser's accountants, [PQR & Co] ('the Investigating Accountants') access to this firm's working papers relating to the statutory audit[s] of the Company's [and its subsidiaries'] financial statements for the year ended 31 December 20XX ('the Audit Working Papers').

[As you are aware, this firm has not yet completed this year's statutory audit[s] of the Company's [and its subsidiaries'] financial statements, and therefore, the Audit Working Papers for this year are incomplete. Further this firm is not able to give any opinion on those financial statements and has not done so. Nevertheless, I understand that the Purchaser and the Investigating Accountants still wish the Investigating Accountants to review such Audit Working Papers as are available to date.]

[In addition, you requested this firm to allow the Investigating Accountants to review the taxation returns and computations of the Company [and its subsidiaries], so far as in the possession of this firm, as submitted to and/or agreed with the UK Inland Revenue for each of the last *[insert number]* years[, working papers relating to those returns and computations] and copies of the correspondence and related documents passing between this firm and the UK Inland Revenue in respect of those returns and computations (together, 'the Tax Papers').]

This firm's general policy is not to allow third parties to have access to the working papers in the possession of this firm. However, this firm is content to allow such access to the Audit Working Papers [and the Tax Papers] ([together,] 'the Papers'), but only on the basis of the guidance contained in Technical Release Audit 04/03

---

[2] *The auditors will expect to provide access only to persons knowledgeable as to the audit process i.e. typically the Investigating Accountants only.*

issued by the Institute of Chartered Accountants in England & Wales. In accordance with that guidance I am now writing to confirm your agreement to the terms set out in this letter and to secure the authorisation of the Company [and its subsidiaries] for that access.

As a condition of providing access to the Investigating Accountants and responding to any requests for information and explanations in relation to the Papers in the course of or in connection with their review of the Papers, this firm requires that the Purchaser and the Investigating Accountants agree to the terms of the letter enclosed.

As you will appreciate, the Audit Working Papers were created for the sole purpose of the statutory audit[s] of the Company's [and its subsidiaries'] financial statements [and the Tax Papers were prepared and/or obtained for the purpose of calculating and agreeing the Company's [and its subsidiaries'] UK tax liabilities]. The Papers were not created for the purpose of the Proposed Transaction. Consequently, the information in the Papers should not be treated as suitable for the purposes of the Proposed Transaction. Furthermore, it is not this firm's function or responsibility to provide to the Purchaser or the Investigating Accountants any Papers that may come into existence, or information that may come to this firm's attention, after *[insert date]*.

Accordingly, this firm requires the Vendor and its directors and the Company [(and its subsidiaries)] and [its] [their] directors to agree to the following conditions:

(a) They each accept the risk, and do not and will not hold this firm responsible, if the Investigating Accountants' review of the Papers or any information or explanations that this firm gives to them in relation to the Papers or in connection with their review of the Papers:
    (i) results in or contributes to the termination or reduction of the interest of the Purchaser in, or to the alteration to the proposed terms of, the Proposed Transaction, or otherwise affects the Proposed Transaction or the prospects of its maturing into a binding transaction; or
    (ii) causes an action or proceeding to be brought at any time against the Vendor or its directors or the Company [(or any of its subsidiaries)] or [its] [their] directors [respectively]; or
    (iii) results in the Purchaser, the Investigating Accountants or any other person or entity using or misusing any confidential information obtained from a review of the Papers or from any information or explanations given by this firm.

(b) They each accept that, to the fullest extent permitted by law, this firm owes them no duty of care or other obligation and has no liability to them, in relation to or in connection with the Proposed Transaction as a result of granting the Investigating Accountants access to the Papers or any information or explanations that this firm gives in relation to the Papers or in connection with the review by the Investigating Accountants of the Papers.

The audit of the financial statements of the [Company/Companies] was undertaken by and is the sole responsibility of this firm, that is [*insert full, exact name of UK firm carrying out the audit*]. In paragraph (a) and (b) above references to 'this firm', where appropriate in the context, shall have an extended meaning so that they include, in addition to [*insert full, exact name of the UK firm carrying out the audit*], [partners/ directors/ members], employees and agents of this firm [and any person or organisation associated with this firm through membership of the international association of professional service firms to which this firm belongs and their [partners/ directors/

members], employees and agents].[3] This letter is for the benefit of all those included within the reference to this firm and each of them may enforce in their own right all of the terms of this letter.

Please confirm that the Company [and its subsidiaries] authorise[s] this firm to allow access to the Papers and to give information or explanations on the terms described above by signing the enclosed copy of this letter on behalf of the Vendor and its directors and the Company and its directors [and its subsidiaries and their directors] and returning it to this firm marked for my attention.

I hope the Proposed Transaction proceeds smoothly.

Yours faithfully

ACKNOWLEDGEMENT

Acknowledged and agreed, for and on behalf of [Vendor] and the directors of [Vendor].

Director

Date

Acknowledged and agreed, for and on behalf of [the Company] and the directors of [the Company]

Director

Date

[Acknowledged and agreed, for and on behalf of [subsidiaries] and the directors of [subsidiaries]

Director

Date]

Appendix 2 – Specimen release letter to prospective purchaser and investigating accountants

(The Release Letter assumes a proposed purchase of a company and that both Audit Working Papers and Tax Papers are to be made available. It must be amended as appropriate for the circumstances of each transaction.)

PRIVATE AND CONFIDENTIAL [Purchaser]

[Address]

[Investigating Accountants] [Address]

---

[3] *The clause in square brackets is intended to be used where the audit firm is a member of an international group and wishes to seek to extend material protections of the letter to all members of the group for example, where the UK audit firm's working papers contain information derived from an overseas audit firm within the same international group.*

[Date]

Dear Sirs

PROPOSED ACQUISITION OF [COMPANY] LIMITED

In connection with the proposed acquisition by [ABC plc] ('the Purchaser')[4] of [Company] Limited ('the Company') ('the Proposed Transaction') the Company [(and the subsidiary undertakings identified in Attachment 2[5]) (together 'the Companies')] [has/have] requested this firm to allow [the Purchaser and/or] [Firm of Accountants] ('the Investigating Accountants') access to this firm's working papers relating to the statutory audit[s] [(including the audit[s] currently in progress)[6]] of the financial statements of the [Company/Companies] for the year[s] ended [*date*] ('the Audit Working Papers') [and the taxation returns and computations of the [Company/ Companies], so far as in this firm's possession, as submitted to and/or agreed with the UK Inland Revenue for each of the last [*insert number*] years[, working papers relating to those returns and computations] and copies of the correspondence and related documents passing between this firm and the UK Inland Revenue in respect of those returns and computations (together 'the Tax Papers')[7]]. [[The Company/Companies] [has/have] authorised this firm at this firm's discretion to give information or explanations in relation to the Audit Working Papers [and the Tax Papers] or in connection with the review by the Investigating Accountants of the Audit Working Papers [and the Tax Papers]]. The Audit Working Papers [and the Tax Papers together] are also referred to below as 'the Papers'.

1

The Purchaser and the Investigating Accountants should note that this firm has not reported on [the Company's/ the Companies'] financial statements for any period subsequent to [*date*] [nor have any tax liabilities of the Company/Companies] been agreed for any period subsequent to [*date*]] and significant events may well have occurred since [that date/ those dates]. It is not this firm's function or responsibility

2

---

[4] *If there is an identified investor or acquisition lender consideration should be given to addressing the letter to them as well and adapting the contents accordingly.*

[5] *Where access is to be given to the Papers for a group of companies, the names of the companies should be listed in an Attachment 2.*

[6] *If access is to be granted to the Audit Working Papers on an incomplete audit, the following wording should be added to the end of paragraph 2:*
   'This firm has not yet completed this year's statutory audit[s] of the Company's [the Companies'] financial statements, and therefore, Audit Working Papers for this year are incomplete. For the avoidance of any doubt the audit will not be completed in order that or with the intention that the Purchaser or the Investigating Accountants should rely on it.'

[7] *If the tax information to be provided includes any relating to pre self-assessment periods for which the return and computations have not been finally agreed by the Inland Revenue, the following wording might be added:*
   'The corporation tax return[s] and computations for the accounting period ended [date] have not yet been agreed finally with the Inland Revenue. Accordingly, you will appreciate that the figures and tax liabilities shown in the Tax Papers may change.'
Where tax information to be provided includes any company tax returns relating to self-assessment accounting periods, the appropriate wording might be added from the following:
   'The company tax return[s] for [identify relevant company or companies] for the accounting period[s] ended [date] have not been subject to a formal Inland Revenue enquiry.'
   'The company tax return[s] for [identify relevant company or companies] for the accounting period[s] ended [date] [has/have] been subject to a formal Inland Revenue enquiry which [has/have] been completed [and the return[s] amended accordingly].'
   'The company tax return[s] for [identify relevant company or companies] for the accounting period[s] ended [date] [is/are] currently the subject of a formal Inland Revenue enquiry and accordingly you will appreciate that the return[s] and the figures and liabilities shown in the Tax Papers may change.'

to provide to the Purchaser or the Investigating Accountants any Audit Working Papers [or Tax Papers] that may come into existence, or information that may come to this firm's attention, at any point after [*insert date*].[8]

3   This firm does not accept or assume responsibility to anyone other than the [Company/Companies] and the [Company's/Companies' respective] members as a body, for its audit work, for its audit report(s) or for the opinions it has formed. The statutory audit is undertaken in order that this firm might report to the [Company's/Companies' respective] members, as a body, in accordance with Section 235 of the Companies Act 1985. The audit procedures and the Audit Working Papers were designed and created solely for the purpose of enabling this firm to form and state an opinion to the [Company's/Companies' respective] members as a body, in accordance with the statutory requirements for audit, on whether the financial statements of [the Company/the Companies], which are the responsibility of the directors of [the Company/the Companies], give a true and fair view of the state of affairs of [the Company/the Companies] as at the end of the relevant financial year and of the profit and loss for the period then ended. This firm's auditing procedures were designed to enable this firm to express an opinion on [the Company's/the Companies' respective] financial statements as a whole and not, for example and save where otherwise expressly stated, on individual account balances, financial amounts, financial information or the adequacy of financial, accounting or management systems. [The Tax Papers were prepared and/or obtained solely for the purpose of calculating and/or agreeing [the Company's/the Companies'] tax liabilities.]

4   This firm's audit(s) of [the Company's/the Companies'] financial statements, and the Audit Working Papers prepared or obtained in connection therewith, [was/were] not planned or conducted in contemplation, or for the purpose, of the Proposed Transaction. [Nor were the Tax Papers.] Further, the scope of an audit is normally substantially narrower than an investigation on behalf of a potential purchaser. Moreover, there are a number of inherent limitations in audited financial statements [and the calculation or agreement of tax liabilities] as the Investigating Accountants will be able to advise.

5   Therefore, items of possible interest to the Purchaser may not have been specifically addressed for the purposes of the audit [or of calculating and agreeing [the Company's/the Companies'] tax liabilities]. The use of professional judgement and the assessment of materiality for the purpose of this firm's audit [or of calculating and agreeing [the Company's/the Companies'] tax liabilities] means that matters may have existed that would have been assessed differently by the Purchaser or the Investigating Accountants for the purposes of the Proposed Transaction. This firm does not warrant or represent that the information in the Papers, or that information or explanations given by this firm in relation to the Papers or in connection with the review by the Investigating Accountants of the Papers, is appropriate for the purposes of the Purchaser or the Investigating Accountants. The Audit Working Papers were not created for, and should not be treated as suitable for, any purpose other than the Statutory Audit. [The Tax Papers were not created for, and should not be treated as suitable for, any purpose other than [calculating and agreeing [the Company's/the Companies'] tax liabilities]].

6   For the foregoing reasons, neither the Papers nor information or explanations given by this firm in relation to the Papers or in connection with the review by the Investigating Accountants of the Papers can in any way serve as a substitute for

---

[8] *It would normally be expected that the firm would give access to all Audit Working Papers. If certain Audit Working Papers are not to be made available that fact should be stated. Arrangements for access to electronic working papers could also be confirmed here.*

other enquiries and procedures that the Purchaser and the Investigating Accountants would (or should) otherwise undertake and judgements they must make for the purpose of satisfying themselves regarding [the Company's/ the Companies' respective] financial condition or for any other purpose in connection with the Proposed Transaction. No one should rely for any purpose whatsoever upon the Papers or any information or explanations that this firm may give in relation to them or in connection with the review by the Investigating Accountants of them.

This firm is prepared to grant the [Purchaser and/or the][9] Investigating Accountants access to the Papers and at this firm's discretion to give information and explanations in relation to the Papers or in connection with the review by the Investigating Accountants of the Papers, on condition that the Purchaser and the Investigating Accountants acknowledge and accept the foregoing paragraphs (including that the position in respect of this firm's audit reports on the [Company's/Companies'] financial statements will remain as stated at paragraph 3 above following the grant of access to the Papers and the giving of information and explanations in relation to the Papers) and agree to the following conditions upon which access to the Papers is granted and the explanations and information referred to are given: 7

(1) The Purchaser and the Investigating Accountants accept, agree and acknowledge that:
(a) for the purposes of this letter, the expression 'the Information' shall mean the Papers and any information and explanations given by this firm in relation to the Papers or in connection with the review by the Investigating Accountants of the Papers.
(b) where any information or explanation is given by this firm the onus shall be upon the Purchaser and the Investigating Accountants to verify any such information or explanation direct with [the Company/the Companies] rather than seek to rely on this firm.
(c) to the fullest extent permitted by law, this firm owes no duty to them, whether in contract or in tort or under statute or otherwise (including in negligence) with respect to or in connection with the Information or its provision or in relation to the audit reports on the [Company's/Companies'] financial statements.
(d) if, notwithstanding the terms of this letter, they do rely upon any of the Information or the audit reports on the [Company's/Companies'] financial statements for any purpose, they will do so entirely at their own risk
(e) they will not bring any actions, proceedings or claims against this firm where the action, proceeding or claim in any way relates to or concerns or is connected with the use of or reliance on the Information or the audit reports on the [Company's/Companies'] financial statements.
(f) to the fullest extent permitted by law, this firm has no liability to them for any loss or damage suffered or costs incurred by them, arising out of or in connection with the Information or its use or the audit reports on the [Company's/Companies'] financial statements, however such loss or damage is caused.
(g) they will not refer to the Information nor allow access to it or any report derived therefrom to any person or entity without this firm's prior written consent. (However the Investigating Accountants will not need to obtain such consent in order to disclose and discuss the same (i) with [the Company/the Companies] for the purpose of obtaining information or verification from [the Company/the Companies] in respect of any report to be prepared by the Investigating Accountants in connection with the

[9] *The auditors will expect to provide access only to persons knowledgeable as to the audit process i.e. typically the Investigating Accountants only.*

Proposed Transaction; (ii) with the Purchaser's legal advisers but then only on the basis that this firm will have no duty or liability to them; or (iii) otherwise as required by a Court or by statute.) Where this firm is willing to give written consent, this firm will require as a condition of such consent that the other person or entity agrees in writing to be bound by and to observe the terms set out in this letter, as if references to the Purchaser were a reference to the other person or entity.[10],[11]

(2) To the fullest extent permitted by law, the Purchaser agrees to indemnify and hold harmless this firm against all actions, proceedings and claims brought or threatened against this firm, and all loss, damage and expense (including legal expenses) relating thereto where such action, proceeding or claim has arisen out of or results from or is connected with the failure of the Purchaser, or any of its professional advisers or the Investigating Accountants to comply with the terms of this letter.[12]

(3) Without limiting the obligation in paragraph 7(1)(g) above, the Purchaser and the Investigating Accountants agree to ensure that the notice attached as Attachment 1 to this letter is attached to any document obtained as a result of the Investigating Accountants' access to the Papers and is included in any note or report or other document in which they make reference to the Information.

---

[10] *The following words, adapted as appropriate, could be used by the auditors to provide such consent if subsequently requested under paragraph 7(1)(g): 'We will consent to allowing [other person/entity] access to [information obtained from the provision of access to our audit working papers] to [purchaser] and [investigating accountants] subject to and upon [other person/entity] agreeing in writing that they will be bound by and observe the terms of our release letter dated [date], as if references to the Purchaser were a reference to [other person/entity]'.*

[11] *In certain transactions, a newly incorporated company will be the purchasing vehicle of a target company (a 'Newco'). A management team and other parties will be equity investors in the Newco. Frequently, a Newco will not have been incorporated at the time the investigating accountants seek access to the audit working papers and the equity investors will therefore be addressees and signatories to the auditors' release letter. However, if a Newco wishes to see and rely on the investigating accountants' report (and assuming it contains information covered by the auditors' release letter), then consideration must be given by the auditors as to how it will manage its risk to a Newco.*

It is not necessary for a Newco to be an addressee and signatory of the original release letter because paragraph 7(1)(g) allows the auditors to provide subsequent consent. It will therefore in practice be incumbent upon the signatories to the release letter to ensure that the Newco agrees to be bound by the terms of the release letter. In relation to the indemnity sought in the release letter, although there is always a commercial risk that the party providing the indemnity may not be able to meet such an obligation, it has been suggested that there is an increased risk in relation to the indemnity given by a Newco because the most likely scenario where an auditor will want to enforce an indemnity is when a target and, in all likelihood, the Newco has failed. In order to minimise this risk, auditors may wish to consider extending the indemnity given by Newco's equity investors to cover any breach by a Newco. Certain equity investors in Newcos are reluctant to provide an enduring indemnity themselves beyond the completion of the transaction and request that it be transferred to Newco once it has been incorporated. For the reasons stated above concerning the financial viability of an indemnity from a Newco, it is recommended that firms give careful consideration to the risks described above before agreeing to such an amendment.

Example wording anticipating a novation of the indemnity to a Newco is as follows: 'This firm agrees that it is prepared to consider releasing [X] from the indemnity contained in paragraph 7(2) (the Indemnity) provided always that (1) [X] procures that a new indemnifier, acceptable to this firm, assumes towards this firm all the obligations of [X] under the Indemnity; and (2) the new indemnifier signs a release letter in similar terms to this letter.'

[12] *The scope of the indemnity included here is limited to the situation where there has been a breach by the Purchaser, its professional advisers or the Investigating Accountants of the terms of the letter. An alternative and wider form of indemnity might extend to any claims in connection with the use of or reliance on the information. For example the wording 'where such action, proceedings or claim has arisen out of or results from or is connected with the failure of the Purchaser, or any of its professional advisers or the Investigating Accountants to comply with the terms of this letter' could be replaced by 'where the action, proceeding or claim in any way relates to or concerns or is connected with the use of or reliance on the Information'*

The audit of the financial statements of the [Company/Companies] was undertaken by and is the sole responsibility of this firm, that is [*insert full, exact name of UK firm carrying out the audit*]. In paragraph 7(1)(c) to (g) and 7(2) of this letter all references to 'this firm' (except for the first and the last two references in the paragraph 7(1)(g)) shall have an extended meaning so that they include, in addition to [*insert full, exact name of the UK firm carrying out the audit*], [partners/ directors/ members], employees and agents of this firm [and any person or organisation associated with this firm through membership of the international association of professional service firms to which this firm belongs and their [partners/ directors/ members], employees and agents][13] This letter is for the benefit of all of those referred to in the previous sentence and each of them may enforce in their own right all of the terms of this letter.   8

This letter sets out the entire agreement as between the Purchaser and the Investigating Accountants and this firm in relation to the conditions upon which access to the Papers is given by this firm and upon which information or explanations in relation to the Papers or in connection with the review by the Investigating Accountants are given by this firm to the Purchaser and the Investigating Accountants. It replaces all prior agreements or understandings (if any) between or amongst the Purchaser, the Investigating Accountants and this firm in that regard.   9

The terms of the agreement shall be governed solely by English law, and the Courts of England and Wales shall have exclusive jurisdiction in respect of any dispute arising out of it or in connection with it. [The Purchaser, the Investigating Accountants and this firm irrevocably waive any right to object to proceedings being brought in those Courts, to claim that the proceedings have been brought in an inappropriate forum, or to claim that those Courts do not have jurisdiction.][14]   10

Please confirm the agreement of the Purchaser and the Investigating Accountants to and acceptance of the provisions of this letter by signing, dating and returning to us a copy of this letter.   11

Yours faithfully

[Firm]

The Purchaser hereby acknowledges that it agrees to and accepts the provisions of this letter.

Director

Date

The Investigating Accountants hereby acknowledge that they agree to and accept the provisions of this letter.

Director

Date

---

[13] *The clause in square brackets is intended to be used where the audit firm is a member of an international group and wishes to seek to extend material protections of the letter to all members of the group, for example, where the UK audit firm's working papers contain information derived from an overseas audit firm within the same international group.*

[14] *This sentence might be used where the purchaser is not a UK based entity to help to mitigate the risk that an overseas purchaser decides to sue in its own court.*

ATTACHMENT 1 TO RELEASE LETTER

Notice of the Auditor[15]

1. [] ('the Auditor'), the auditor of [] ('the Company'), has, on certain conditions, allowed [] ('the Investigating Accountants') to have access to the Auditor's working papers relating to the statutory audit of the Company's financial statements for the [year/period] ended [] ('the Audit Working Papers').

2. The Auditor does not accept or assume responsibility to anyone other than the Company and the Company's members as a body, for its audit work, for its audit report or for the opinions it has formed. To the fullest extent permitted by law, the Auditor does not accept or assume responsibility to anyone as a result of the access given to the Audit Working Papers or for any information or explanation given to the Investigating Accountants in relation to the Audit Working Papers or in connection with the review by the Investigating Accountants of the Audit Working Papers.

3. The Audit Working Papers were not created for, and should not be treated as suitable for, any purpose other than the statutory audit. The statutory audit is undertaken in order that the Auditor might report to the Company's members, as a body, in accordance with Section 235 of the Companies Act 1985. The audit work of the Auditor is undertaken so that the Auditor might state to the Company's members those matters it is required to state to them in an auditor's report and for no other purpose.

ATTACHMENT 2 TO RELEASE LETTER

List of companies referred to in paragraph 1 for which access to the Audit Working Papers [and the Tax Papers] is to be provided

---

[15] *The Notice as drafted is confined to situations where access is confined to the Audit Working Papers of a single company. It should be tailored where access covers a group of companies and/or Tax Papers.*

[Statement 930]
Reporting to regulators of regulated entities (AUDIT 05/03)

This guidance is issued by the Audit and Assurance Faculty of the Institute of Chartered Accountants in England & Wales in October 2003 to outline to Institute members new reporting arrangements being introduced after discussions with the Regulators and Regulated Entities. This guidance does not constitute an auditing standard. Professional judgement should be used in its application.

Contents

	Paragraphs
Glossary of Terms	
1 Introduction	1 - 7
2 Duty of Care and Engagement Contracts	8 - 23
3 Form of Report	24 - 34
4 Materiality	35 - 44
5 Working with Independent Experts	45 - 53

Appendices

A Regulatory Accounts
B Example of an unqualified audit report for regulatory accounts
C Example tri partite engagement contract
D Example bi-partite engagement contract
E Example written notice from the Independent Accountants to the Regulator for bi-partite engagement arrangements

Glossary of Terms

Terms	Meaning
Cross-Regulatory Group	An inter-regulatory Regulatory Accounts working group set up by the Regulators to consider the issues surrounding Regulatory Accounts.
Cross-Regulatory Paper	The paper 'The role of regulatory accounts in regulated industries – A final proposals paper' issued by the Cross-Regulatory Group in April 2001.
RAGs	Regulatory Accounting Guidelines issued by, or agreed with, the Regulators which specify how Regulatory Accounts are to be prepared by the Regulated Entities. In certain industries, RAGS may be supplemented by more detailed framework documentation which is not prepared by, nor agreed with, the Regulator.
Regulators/Regulating	Government appointed regulatory bodies that oversee the activities of Regulated Bodies Entities. For the purposes of this document, these are: Ofgem (The Office of Gas and Electricity Markets) Ofwat (Office of Water Services) Oftel (Office of Telecommunications) Postcomm (Postal Services Commission) CAA (Civil Aviation Authority) ORR (Office of the Rail Regulator) Ofreg (Office for the Regulation of Electricity and Gas in Northern Ireland) OfCom (Office of Communications).
Regulatory Accounts	Accounts prepared under bases and principles and incorporating information specified by, or agreed with, the Regulators.
Regulated Activities	Those activities of the Regulated Entities covered by the powers of the Regulators, usually defined in the Regulated Entities' regulatory licence.
Regulated Entities	Those entities whose activities are covered by the powers of the Regulators (as defined above) and who are required to provide Regulatory Accounts and/or Regulatory Information that is required to be reported upon by Independent Accountants.
Regulatory Information	Information provided to the Regulators by the Regulated Entities in connection with their regulated operations.
Regulatory Licence	The instrument of appointment of the Regulated Entity.

Regulatory Reports/Reporting	Reports made by Regulated Entities and/or accountants to Regulators.
Regulatory Return	A return of Regulatory Information (which can include Regulatory Accounts) provided to the Regulator by the Regulated Entities. Certain items within the Return are required to be reported upon by Independent Accountants as part of their regulatory rep
The Working Group	The sub-group of the 'Reporting to Third Parties' group set up by the ICAEW to consider Regulatory Reporting to Regulators of Regulated Entities.
Third Party	Any party, other than the Regulator, who has access to Regulatory Accounts, Regulatory Returns or Regulatory Information.
UK GAAP	Generally Accepted Accounting Principles in the United Kingdom.

Section 1 Introduction

The Audit and Assurance Faculty of the ICAEW issued Technical Release Audit 1/01, 'Reporting to Third Parties' in September 2001. A separate working group ('the Working Group') was set up to consider the issues relating to reporting to Regulators of Regulated Entities and the application of Audit 1/01 to this reporting. The Working Group's scope of work specifically excluded reporting to other regulatory bodies, for example the Financial Services Authority. [1]

The Working Group comprised representatives from the accountancy profession and the ICAEW, and consulted with the Regulators. The Regulated Entities were included in the consultation process. The Working Group took advice from Leading Counsel in respect of the wording of the second paragraph of the example Independent Accountants' report in Appendix B. [2]

It is recognised that there is a need to achieve consistency in the practices adopted in respect of Regulatory Reporting by Independent Accountants. There is a need for guidance in respect of Regulatory Reporting and a need also to take account of issues raised by the Regulators in such reporting. This guidance is intended to help those involved in Regulatory Reporting. [3]

Background

Regulated Entities are required to submit a large volume of information to their Regulating Bodies/Regulators, much of which is financial in nature. [4]

The exact reporting requirements can vary significantly between industries and are determined and set out in the holders' regulatory operating licences and in related guidance and instructions issued by the Regulators. In some cases, elements of this information are required to be reported upon by Independent Accountants, often being the Regulated Entities' statutory auditors. It is this form of reporting by Independent Accountants which is the subject of this guidance. [5]

6   The information required by the Regulators has evolved and generally extended since the time of privatisation. At the outset, the financial information required by the Regulators was centred around 'Regulatory Accounts' (see Appendix A for an overview of what these contained), sometimes drawn up under Current Cost Accounting principles. Developments in the level of data required to be submitted and independently reported upon have changed as a result of:

- changes in the boundaries of the Regulated Activities, with previously Regulated Activities dropping out of the regulatory environment as competition develops;
- developments in the information requirements of Regulators as the relevant regulatory regime has developed;
- the desire of the Regulators to establish greater consistency in the form of Regulatory Reporting by Regulated Entities and in the form of independent reporting by accountants and others on such information. In this context, an inter-regulatory Regulatory Accounts working group comprising representatives from Ofgem, Ofwat, Oftel, Postcomm, CAA and ORR ('the Cross-Regulatory Group') has been established.

This Group has issued a paper 'The role of regulatory accounts in regulated industries – A final proposals paper' dated April 2001 ('the Cross-Regulatory Paper'). In this paper, the Regulators agreed to adopt a set of common regulatory accounting principles, including the use of Regulatory Accounting Guidelines (RAGs) to provide guidance and instruction on the preparation and content of Regulatory Accounts;

- the Regulators' desire to find reliable bases of measuring output performance of the Regulated Entities against their regulatory contract and the use of the Regulatory Accounts to assist in measurement; and
- the development of new Regulatory Information requirements designed to promote competition in certain markets.

7   In the light of these developments, this guidance is for the use of Independent Accountants to assist them where they are conducting work which involves reporting on Regulatory Information which is addressed to Regulators and is required to be produced by the Regulated Entity under its Licence or Instrument of Appointment or otherwise by the Regulator. However, this guidance should not be regarded as a substitute for the specific legal and professional advice which firms may need to take on particular matters or engagements.

Section 2 Duty of care and engagement contracts

8   This section considers the issue of reliance by the Regulators on the work of Independent Accountants reporting on Regulatory Information and provides guidance on this matter. It also considers the question of the potential for reliance by others on Regulatory Reports, and the steps which may be taken to clarify the scope of the Independent Accountants' work and responsibility to such third parties.

Who might rely on the accountants' work

9   The ICAEW's Technical Release Audit 1/01, 'Reporting to Third Parties' provides the guidance laid out in the following box:

Extract from Technical Release Audit 1/01

- When accountants know that their report has been requested by a third party and that the third party will rely on the report, there is a risk, in the absence of an effective disclaimer, that the accountants owe the third party a duty to take reasonable care in preparing and providing the report. If the accountants do owe the third party such a duty, they could be liable to that third party if they were negligent and the third party suffered loss in reliance on the report.
  Accountants consider the legal effectiveness of disclaiming liability and of the proposed disclaimer in the particular circumstances of their engagement.
- It is vital, therefore, for accountants to understand who the third party is, why it requires the report and the extent of loss which the third party could suffer in reliance on the report. If, for example, the third party runs a scheme for compensating the client's customers in the event of the client's insolvency, the accountants' risk is much greater than if, for example, the third party's only role is to perform marketing for a particular service sector.
- The accountants' understanding of the risks involved in providing a report underpins the decisions they make about whether to accept the engagement and on what terms. Depending upon the circumstances accountants either:
  (a) accept that they owe a duty of care to the third party and enter into an engagement contract with the third party, including provisions limiting liability if appropriate; or
  (b) proceed with an engagement for their client but before allowing the third party access to their report, require the third party to acknowledge in writing that the accountants owe the third party no duty of care; or
  (c) proceed with an engagement for their client but disclaim or limit any liability or duty to the third party by notice in their report; or
  (d) do not accept the engagement.
- If accountants regard a report as high risk, they agree to provide the report only if the third party is a party to the engagement contract or the third party has acknowledged in writing that the accountants owe no duty of care to the third party. If accountants regard a report as low risk, typically because the third party could suffer little or no loss in reliance on the report, then they may decide to provide the report without contracting with the third party. In this case a notice can be included in the report disclaiming or limiting the accountants' liability to the third party. In addition to that notice, it may be appropriate for the accountants to write to the third party, in advance of the third party receiving the report, notifying the third party of the basis on which the report will be provided. Also, if a third party writes to the accountants in an attempt to indicate reliance on a report, the accountants consider whether it is reasonable to accept such reliance. Where it is not, a disclaimer is given in writing.

Accountants are advised not to allow their reports to be provided to a third party unless the basis and extent of their liability to the third party is clear and agreed. Accountants refer to the guidance in Statement 1.311 of the Institute's Members' Handbook, 'Managing the professional liability of accountants' and consider the consequences of The Contracts (Rights of Third Parties) Act 1999 – see the guidance in Audit 4/00.

10 There are a number of parties who might be interested in the contents of information published or otherwise supplied by Regulated Entities to their Regulatory Bodies. As well as the Regulatory Body itself, these might include others in the same industry,

potential entrants to the market, academics, journalists, analysts, consumer bodies and consumers/members of the public at large. Independent Accountants do not accept that they owe a duty of care or have any other legal responsibility to any person in respect of their report on Regulatory Information except those who have engaged the Independent Accountants to perform services under a written engagement contract or with whom the Independent Accountants have otherwise agreed in writing to accept such a responsibility.

11 Regulatory Accounts and Regulatory Returns are required by an individual Regulator, who specifies or agrees what they should contain and who uses that information as part of its overall role in regulating the regulated business. In these circumstances, Independent Accountants only accept that they owe a responsibility/duty of care to the Regulated Entity and the Regulator if either:

i) both the Regulated Entity and the Regulator are parties to the written engagement contract with the Independent Accountants ('a tri-partite engagement contract'). The tri-partite engagement contract contains appropriate terms clarifying and limiting the scope and extent of the Independent Accountants' responsibilities and liability; or

ii) the Regulated Entity alone is a party to a written engagement contract with the Independent Accountants ('a bi-partite engagement contract') which makes provision for the Independent Accountants to accept separately a responsibility also to the Regulator, provided that the Regulator and the Independent Accountants can agree in writing the basis of this responsibility ('written notice') AND the Regulator and the Independent Accountants actually agree, in writing, the basis on which this responsibility/duty of care is extended to the Regulator.

The bi-partite engagement contract contains appropriate terms clarifying and limiting the scope and extent of the Independent Accountants' responsibilities and liability, and includes a mechanism enabling Independent Accountants to extend their responsibilities to the Regulator through the written notice on the basis that the Independent Accountants' liability is capped, in aggregate, at a level no greater than the amount which would have been payable by them to the Regulated Entity under the bi-partite engagement contract. It will be a matter for the Regulator and the Regulated Entity to agree how the aggregate liability will be shared and recorded in the bi-partite engagement contract and the written notice. Should such an agreement not be reached, the Independent Accountants will consider capping their liability in aggregate.

The written notice between the Independent Accountants and the Regulator will confirm that the Independent Accountants accept a responsibility to the Regulator for the Independent Accountants' report (even though the Regulator is a not an addressee of the bi-partite engagement contract) provided that the Regulator agrees, in writing, that this will be on the same terms as the bi-partite engagement contract, a copy of which will be attached to the written notice, as if the Regulator had been an original addressee of the bi-partite engagement contract. An example of a written notice between the Independent Accountants and the Regulator is set out as Appendix E.

12 If the Regulator will not agree the basis on which the Independent Accountants are willing to accept a duty of care to the Regulator, either through (a) a tri-partite engagement contract, or (b) a bi-partite engagement contract supplemented by the written notice, the Independent Accountants do not accept a duty of care to the Regulator and will make that clear in their report. In these circumstances the Independent Accountants disapply in their bi-partite engagement letter any rights

that the Regulator might otherwise have acquired under the Contracts (Rights of Third Parties) Act 1999 and send a copy of the bi-partite engagement contract to the Regulator.

Independent Accountants do not accept a responsibility/duty of care to other parties who may have an interest in, or who may ultimately use, the Regulatory Accounts, Regulatory Returns or other Regulatory Information reported upon by the Independent Accountants unless the Independent Accountants have identified the other party and agreed with the other party, in writing, the basis on which they accept this duty of care. Where a report is made by Independent Accountants to a Regulated Entity and a Regulator under a tri-partite engagement contract, that report will include a specific disclaimer of any liability or duty to any Third Party. Where a report is made by the Independent Accountants to a Regulated Entity and/or a Regulator under a bi-partite engagement contract, whether or not supplemented by written notice, that report will include a specific disclaimer of any liability or duty to any other person other than those to whom the Independent Accountants have addressed their report. The report is addressed to the Regulator as well as to the Company without any disclaimer of responsibility to the Regulator only where the Regulator has signed a tri-partite engagement contract or there is a bi-partite engagement contract supplemented by written notice signed by the Regulator. In other cases the report may be addressed to the Company and the Regulator (to meet the requirements of the Regulatory Licence) but includes a disclaimer under which responsibility is accepted to the Company only and co-addressing to the Regulator is expressed to be only to meet the requirements of the Regulatory Licence. 13

Where the Regulator has indicated to the Independent Accountants that they would like a Third Party to be able to rely on the Independent Accountants' report and the Independent Accountants are in agreement with this, the Independent Accountants include in their report a clear statement that the Third Party can only rely on the report after becoming a party to the engagement contract for that report or agree with the Third Party a written notice specifying the basis on which the Independent Accountants extend their duty of care to the Third Party. 14

It has not previously been common practice for Regulators to sign engagement contracts commissioning the Independent Accountants' reports. These contracts have tended to be bilateral between the Independent Accountants and the Regulated Entity or its parent company. 15

In the Cross-Regulatory Paper, the members of the Cross-Regulatory Group proposed that the Regulators would be a party to a tri-partite engagement contract with the Independent Accountants and the Regulated Entities. That proposal is recognised in this guidance. 16

Certain Regulators have subsequently expressed a preference not to enter into a tri-partite engagement contract for certain engagements but rather, in these cases, to agree engagement terms with the Independent Accountants through the written notice procedure supplementing a bi-partite engagement contract agreed by the Independent Accountants and the Regulated Entity. That preference is also recognised in this guidance. 17

Guidance on the content of engagement contracts

18   Technical Release Audit 1/01 includes the following guidance on engagement contracts:

> **Extract from Technical Release Audit 1/01**
>
> Engagement contracts include the following:
>
> - a clear unambiguous description of the scope of work to be performed and the form of report to be provided using defined terms where appropriate to avoid misunderstandings;
> - a description of the client's obligations and the client's responsibility for the information on which the accountants report;
> - clarification that the engagement is separate from the statutory audit and that the accountants have no duty of care to the third party in relation to the statutory audit;
> - an appropriate liability cap,[1] agreed having regard to the nature of the work being performed, the level of fee charged and other relevant factors. Any limitation of liability must be negotiated and agreed with the client, and must be fair and reasonable in compliance with the Unfair Contract Terms Act 1977[2]
> - details of the addressee for the report, limitations as to the purpose for which the report is prepared and restrictions on who is entitled to see and rely upon the report and on the distribution of it;
> - a copy of the form of report to be provided.

Tri-partite engagement contracts

19   The above guidance from Technical Release Audit 1/01 is incorporated into the tri-partite engagement contract, and is applied to both the Regulator and the Regulated Entity. In addition, in the circumstances covered by this guidance, engagement contracts signed by the Regulator, the Regulated Entity and the Independent Accountants include the following:

i)   an acknowledgement of a duty of care by the Independent Accountants both to the Regulated Entity and to the Regulator;

ii) an explicit denial of liability by the Independent Accountants to any other party other than the Regulator and the Regulated Entity whose information is being reported on. This denial should also be incorporated into the Independent Accountants' report (see paragraph 30 v);

iii) an acknowledgement from the Regulator and the Regulated Entity that;

   a) wherever the complete Regulatory Accounts or other Regulatory Information covered by the Independent Accountants' report is published or otherwise made available, the Independent Accountants' report will also be published or otherwise made available; and

   b) wherever substantial extracts[3] from the Regulatory Accounts or other Regulatory Information covered by the Independent Accountants' report are published or otherwise made available, and reference is made to the fact

---

[1] *Accountants consider whether the liability cap is reasonable given the specific circumstances of the engagement.*

[2] *See the guidance in Statement 1.311 of the Institute's Members' Handbook, 'Managing the professional liability of accountants'.*

[3] *For example, reproduction of primary statements as a whole.*

that they are audited or otherwise examined by Independent Accountants, there will be explicit statements: a) that the information published is only an extract; and b) about the limitation of scope of the Independent Accountants' report and the duty of care owed by the Independent Accountants; and c) referring to where the full set of Regulatory Accounts or Regulatory Information can be found or otherwise obtained;

c) wherever any other information is referenced from the Regulatory Accounts or other Regulatory Information covered by the Independent Accountants' report, there will be an explicit reference by the Regulator to the source of that information and the limitation of scope of the Independent Accountants' report and the duty of care owed by the Independent Accountants;

iv) clarification that the Independent Accountants' opinion on the Regulatory Accounts is separate from their opinion on the statutory accounts of the Company, which are prepared for a different purpose;

v) clarification, where relevant, that the Regulatory Accounts are/other Regulatory Information is prepared by disaggregating balances recorded in the general ledgers and other accounting records of the Company maintained in accordance with the Companies Act 1985 and used, in accordance with that Act, for the preparation of the Company's statutory financial statements;

vi) a statement, where appropriate, that no additional tests will be performed of the transactions and balances which are recorded in the general ledgers of the Regulated Entity other than those carried out in performing the audit of the statutory financial statements that include the Regulated Entity;

vii) a statement, where appropriate, clarifying what work is done in respect of any other information accompanying the Regulatory Accounts or other Regulatory Information, and confirmation if no audit opinion is expressed on this;

viii) clarification about the obligations, if any, of the Independent Accountants to attend tri-partite meetings with the Regulator, including frequency and timing, subject matter, arrangements for minutes and if appropriate the form of hold harmless letters to precede such meetings;

ix) clarification of how any liability cap will be split between the Regulated Entity and the Regulator;

x) a statement that the nature and format of the Regulatory Accounts or other Regulatory Information, RAGs and Regulatory Returns are determined by the individual Regulators, and that it is not appropriate for the Independent Accountants to assess whether the information being reported upon is suitable or appropriate for the Regulator's purpose. Independent Accountants do not agree to provide any implicit or explicit affirmation that the information being reported upon is suitable for the Regulator's purpose;

xi) confirmation that there are differences between UK GAAP and the basis of any information supplied to the Regulators. The engagement contract and the Independent Accountants' report will include a statement that financial information other than that prepared on the basis of UK GAAP does not necessarily represent a true and fair view of the financial performance or financial position of a company as shown in financial statements prepared in accordance with the Companies Act 1985;

xii) an example of the type of audit report/opinion that the Independent Accountants would expect to provide if the results of the audit work are satisfactory. This will be based on the example report set out in Appendix B, amended as appropriate for the particular circumstances of the engagement; and

xiii) a statement that nothing in the tri-partite engagement contract is intended to, nor should it, affect or in any way alter the relationship or the rights and obligations between the Regulated Entity and the Regulator as set out in the Regulatory Licence.

20 An example of a tri-partite engagement contract is shown at Appendix C. This should be tailored as necessary for the circumstances of each particular engagement.

Bi-partite engagement contracts supplemented by a written notice

21 The guidance from Technical Release Audit 1/01 is also incorporated into bi-partite engagement contracts where the Regulator has agreed to sign a written notice, and is applied to both the Regulator and the Regulated Entity. In addition, in the circumstances covered by this guidance, bi-partite engagement contracts signed by the Regulated Entity and the Independent Accountants include the following:

i) an acknowledgement of a duty of care by the Independent Accountants to the Regulated Entity and an agreement to extend the duty of care to the Regulator provided that it agrees appropriate terms with the Independent Accountants in the form of a written notice;

ii) an explicit denial of liability by the Independent Accountants to any persons to whom they have not agreed, in writing, to accept responsibility. This denial should also be incorporated into the Independent Accountants' report (see paragraph 30 v);

iii) an acknowledgement from the Regulated Entity (and from the Regulator where the Regulator has agreed to sign a written notice[4]) that;
    a) wherever the complete Regulatory Information covered by the Independent Accountants' report is published or otherwise made available, the Independent Accountant's report will also be published or otherwise made available; and
    b) wherever substantial extracts[5] from the Regulatory Accounts or other Regulatory Information covered by the Independent Accountants' report are published or otherwise made available, and reference is made to the fact that they are audited or otherwise examined by Independent Accountants, there will be explicit statements: a) that the information published is only an extract; and b) about the limitation of scope of the Independent Accountants' report and the duty of care owed by the Independent Accountants; and c) referring to where the full set of Regulatory Accounts or Regulatory Information can be found or otherwise obtained;
    c) wherever any other information is referenced from the Regulatory Accounts or other Regulatory Information covered by the Independent Accountants' report, there will be an explicit reference by the Regulator to the source of that information and the limitation of scope of the Independent Accountants' report and the duty of care owed by the Independent Accountants';

iv) clarification that the Independent Accountants' opinion on the Regulatory Accounts is separate from their opinion on the statutory accounts of the Company, which are prepared for a different purpose;

v) clarification, where relevant, that the Regulatory Accounts are/other Regulatory Information is prepared by disaggregating balances recorded in the general ledgers and other accounting records of the Company maintained in accordance with the Companies Act 1985 and used, in accordance with that Act, for the preparation of the Company's statutory financial statements;

vi) a statement, where appropriate, that no additional tests will be performed of the transactions and balances which are recorded in the general ledgers of the Regulated Entity other than those carried out in performing the audit of the statutory financial statements that include the Regulated Entity;

---

[4] See Appendix E, example of a written notice.

[5] For example, reproduction of primary statements as a whole.

vii) a statement, where appropriate, clarifying what work is done in respect of any other information accompanying the Regulatory Accounts or other Regulatory Information, and confirmation if no audit opinion is expressed on this;
viii) clarification about the obligations, if any, of the Independent Accountants to attend tri-partite meetings with the Regulator, including frequency and timing, subject matter, arrangements for minutes and if appropriate the form of hold harmless letters to precede such meetings;
ix) clarification of how any liability cap will be split between the Regulated Entity and the Regulator;
x) a statement that the nature and format of the Regulatory Accounts or other Regulatory Information, RAGs and Regulatory Returns are determined by the individual Regulators, and that it is not appropriate for the Independent Accountants to assess whether the information being reported upon is suitable or appropriate for the Regulator's purpose. Independent Accountants do not agree to provide any implicit or explicit affirmation that the information being reported upon is suitable for the Regulator's purpose;
xi) confirmation that there are differences between UK GAAP and the basis of any information supplied to the Regulators. The engagement contract and the Independent Accountants' report will include a statement that financial information other than that prepared on the basis of UK GAAP does not necessarily represent a true and fair view of the financial performance or financial position of a company as shown in financial statements prepared in accordance with the Companies Act 1985;
xii) an example of the type of audit report/opinion that the Independent Accountants would expect to provide if the results of the audit work are satisfactory. This will be based on the example report set out in Appendix B, amended as appropriate for the particular circumstances of the engagement; and
xiii) a statement that nothing in the bi-partite engagement contract is intended to, nor should it, affect or in any way alter the relationship or the rights and obligations between the Regulated Entity and the Regulator as set out in the Regulatory Licence.

An example of a bi-partite engagement contract is shown at Appendix D. This should be tailored as necessary for the circumstances of each particular engagement.

Bi-partite engagement contracts not supplemented by a written notice

If the Regulator will not agree engagement terms, either on a tri-partite basis or on a bi-partite basis supplemented by written notice, the Independent Accountants will agree a bi-partite engagement contract with the Regulated Entity incorporating the relevant aspects of paragraph 21 (that is excluding irrelevant aspects, such as items (viii), (ix) and (x), and will expressly deny any duty of care to the Regulator in the engagement contract and their report.

Section 3 Form of report

This section provides guidance on the form of report that is issued by Independent Accountants reporting on Regulatory Accounts and other Regulatory Information.

The Regulatory Licence

As noted in Section 1 of this guidance, the Regulatory Licence prescribes the Regulatory Information that it requires the Regulated Entity to report to the Regulator.

26 The Regulated Entity is usually required, under the terms of its Regulatory Licence, to procure an Independent Accountants' report, addressed to the Regulated Entity and/or the Regulator, supporting certain of the Regulatory Information submitted by the Regulated Entity to the Regulator.

27 Where a report on Regulatory Information is to be addressed to the Regulator and a duty of care is acknowledged to the Regulator, Independent Accountants agree either a tri-partite engagement contract with the Regulator and the Regulated Entity or a bi-partite engagement contract with the Regulated Entity supplemented by written notice with the Regulator, in accordance with the guidance set out in Section 2 (Duty of care and engagement contracts) of this paper.

Regulatory Accounts

28 SAS 600 (Auditors Reports on Financial Statements) states that 'much of the guidance provided can be adapted to auditors' reports on financial information other than financial statements' [SAS 600, paragraph 1]. Regulatory Accounts are not prepared in accordance with the Companies Act nor necessarily in accordance with UK GAAP. Nevertheless, the guidance contained in SAS 600 can be applied equally to opinions expressed by Independent Accountants on Regulatory Accounts.

29 Applying SAS 600 to reports issued by Independent Accountants:

- Independent Accountants' reports on financial statements should include the following matters:
  (a) a title identifying the person or persons to whom the report is addressed;
  (b) an introductory paragraph identifying the financial statements audited;
  (c) separate sections, appropriately headed, dealing with
    (i) respective responsibilities of directors (or equivalent persons) and the Independent Accountants;
    (ii) the basis of the Independent Accountants' opinion;
    (iii) the Independent Accountants' opinion on the financial statements;
  (d) the manuscript or printed signature of the Independent Accountants; and
  (e) the date of the Independent Accountants' report. (SAS 600.2).
    - The use of a standard format for Independent Accountants' reports on financial statements assists the reader to follow the report's contents. The section headings indicate to the reader the nature of the matters contained in the section concerned: for example, where a qualified opinion is expressed, the heading 'Qualified opinion' may be used.
    - Independent Accountants draft each section of their report on financial statements to reflect the requirements which apply to the particular engagement. However, the use of common language in Independent Accountants' reports assists the reader's understanding.

30 The above guidance drawn from SAS 600 is incorporated into the form of report issued by Independent Accountants. In addition, opinions expressed by Independent Accountants on Regulatory Accounts include the following:

  i) a paragraph setting out the basis of the preparation of the Regulatory Accounts, for example in accordance with the RAGs;
  ii) a statement that the Regulatory Accounts are separate from the statutory financial statements of the Company and have not been prepared on the basis of UK GAAP, and that financial information other than that prepared on the basis of UK GAAP does not necessarily represent a true and fair view of the financial position of a company;

iii) a statement that the nature, form and content of Regulatory Accounts are determined by the Regulator, and that it is not appropriate for the auditors/ Independent Accountants or the directors to assess whether the nature of the information being reported upon is suitable or appropriate for the Regulator's purposes.

iv) a statement that the audit of the Regulatory Accounts has been conducted in accordance with Auditing Standards issued by the Auditing Practices Board except that, as the nature, form and content of Regulatory Accounts are determined by the Regulator, the Independent Accountants' did not evaluate the overall adequacy of the presentation of the information, which would have been required if they were to express an audit opinion under Auditing Standards.

v) a statement clarifying to whom the Independent Accountants accept a responsibility, and to whom they do not;[6] and

vi) a statement that the Independent Accountants' opinion on the Regulatory Accounts is separate from their opinion on the statutory accounts of the Company, which are prepared for a different purpose.

31 Independent Accountants make clear, in their report, the Regulatory Information on which they are providing assurance, and that on which they are not. Where the Regulatory Information is part of a wider report or Regulatory Return, those additional matters being considered in connection with the Independent Accountants' report are clearly identified.

32 The Independent Accountants' report on Regulatory Accounts will be based on the example unqualified report set out at Appendix B, modified as appropriate for the particular circumstances of the engagement. Where such modifications are made, Independent Accountants will use existing guidance (for example Technical Release Audit 1/01 and SAS 600) in making those modifications. Where such modifications result in a departure from auditing standards, this will be reflected in the Independent Accountants' Report on the Regulatory Accounts.

33 An example of such a departure would arise if the Regulatory Accounts are an integral part of a broader Regulatory Return. If the Independent Accountants did not read the other information contained in the Regulatory Return for apparent misstatements therein, or any material inconsistency with the audited Regulatory Accounts (as required under SAS 160 (Other information in documents containing audited financial statements (Revised)), then noncompliance with SAS 160 will be referred to in the 'basis of audit opinion' and 'opinion' paragraphs of the report on the Regulatory Accounts.

Other Regulatory Information/Regulatory Returns

34 When reporting on other Regulatory Information, Independent Accountants follow the guidance set out in Technical Release Audit 1/01, SAS 600 and this paper.

---

[6] *The Working Group has taken the advice of Leading Counsel in respect of appropriate wording to do this. The suggested wording is that in the second paragraph of the example Independent Accountants' report in Appendix B.*

Section 4 Materiality

35 This section considers the assessment of materiality in respect of work performed, and reports issued, by Independent Accountants reporting on Regulatory Accounts and other Regulatory Information, and provides guidance on this matter.

General guidance

36 Materiality, as defined in SAS 220 (Materiality and the Audit) and the Glossary of Terms published alongside APB Auditing Standards, is

'An expression of the relative significance or importance of a particular matter in the context of financial statements as a whole. A matter is material if its omission or mis-statement would reasonably influence the decisions of an addressee of the auditors' report. Materiality may also be considered in the context of any individual primary statement within the financial statements or of individual items included in them. Materiality is not capable of general mathematical definition as it has both qualitative and quantitative aspects.'

37 Materiality is a matter of professional judgement for the Independent Accountants/auditors, based on their understanding of the circumstances of the engagement and communications with the addressees of their report, and cannot be expressed purely as a numerical value. Accordingly, Independent Accountants do not quantify a level of materiality applied in their reports on Regulatory Information, nor do they express an opinion which is 'certified' to be within a numerical materiality value. This recognises that the concept of materiality is not capable of expression in such manner.

Regulatory Accounts

38 There is a growing trend, amongst Regulators, to draft licence conditions that require the Regulated Entity to include a number of different analyses of their business segments and/or operations within the Regulatory Accounts. In providing their report, Independent Accountants assess materiality in the context of the Regulatory Accounts as a whole, taking together the component analyses/disclosures in the Regulatory Accounts, rather than each component analysis/disclosure separately.

39 Where the Regulator is an addressee to the Independent Accountants' report, the Regulator may specify, with supporting reasons, particular factors that it considers to be material in the context of the Regulatory Accounts and the Independent Accountants' report. These factors are specified in the engagement contract, discussed in Section 2 of this guidance, and incorporated into the Independent Accountants' assessment of materiality. Independent Accountants plan their work to gain reasonable assurance that the Regulatory Accounts are free from material error, whether caused by fraud or other mis-statement. Where, as a consequence of considering the Regulator's specified matters/factors, the Independent Accountants are required to perform additional procedures to provide the level of assurance required, they assess and agree with the parties to the engagement contract the scope of their work and the likely impact on audit fees for performing this work.

40 Although Independent Accountants consider the individual factors that the Regulator has asked them to consider in assessing materiality for the Regulatory Accounts, they only express an opinion on the Regulatory Accounts as a whole, and not on those individual factors.

Where the Regulator requires specific factors to be reported upon by the Independent Accountants, the Independent Accountants agree a list of procedures ('Agreed Upon Procedures') that they will perform for the Regulator. These procedures are specified within the engagement contract with the Regulator. The Independent Accountants report the findings of the procedures separately from the Regulatory Accounts opinion, by way of a factual report to the Regulator. The Independent Accountants do not express an opinion on the results of the Agreed Upon Procedures, nor the appropriateness of these procedures for the purposes of the Regulator. The engagement contract and report for the 'Agreed Upon Procedures' include a statement that the Regulator needs to make its own assessment of the appropriateness of the Agreed Upon Procedures and the reported findings. 41

Where Agreed Upon Procedures are required in addition to an opinion on the Regulatory Accounts, Independent Accountants may choose not to complete their work nor express their opinion on the Regulatory Accounts until: 42

i) the Agreed Upon Procedures that have been specified by the Regulator have been completed and reported upon; and
ii) the Regulator has provided assurance to the Independent Accountants that nothing has come to the attention of the Regulator from that report (or otherwise) that indicates that there are any matters that the Regulator believes the Independent Accountants should take into account in arriving at their opinion on the Regulatory Accounts. If such matters do exist, the Independent Accountants will consider, in arriving at their opinion on the Regulatory Accounts, the matters noted by the Regulator and/or agree additional Agreed Upon Procedures with the Regulator.

Other Regulatory Information/Regulatory Returns

The principles of SAS 220 can be applied to any form of reporting which is performed in accordance with Generally Accepted Auditing Standards in the UK. 43

When reporting on other Regulatory Information, the Independent Accountants follow the principles set out in SAS 220, as appropriate. 44

Section 5 Working with independent experts

This section considers the use of other experts in respect of work performed, and reports issued, by Independent Accountants reporting on Regulatory Accounts and other Regulatory Information, and provides guidance on this matter. 45

Background

The provision of opinions on Regulatory Information may involve work with, or reliance upon, other independent experts, for example there may be reliance upon technical/engineering experts to determine whether the cost of projects should be capitalised or expensed. In addition, other independent experts may work with, or place reliance upon the Independent Accountants' work or report in discharging their own reporting responsibilities. 46

Independent Accountants rely on other independent experts

47   Guidance in respect of the use of experts is contained within SAS 520 (Using the work of an expert), which states that 'Auditors have sole responsibility for their opinion, but may use the work of an expert' [para 1] and 'When using the work performed by an expert, the auditors should obtain sufficient appropriate audit evidence that such work is adequate for the purposes of the audit' [para 2].

48   Where the Independent Accountants have performed audit procedures and expressed an audit opinion, it is not expected that the use and/or findings of the expert would be referred to in that report, unless such reference is required to explain the report given. For example, if a qualified/modified audit report is given it may refer to the expert if reference would facilitate an understanding of the reason for the modification/qualification.

49   Where the Independent Accountants have performed Agreed Upon Procedures and the report provided does not include an audit opinion, it is expected that the use and/or findings of the expert would be referred to in that report, unless such reference is clearly not required. Such Agreed Upon Procedures and report would include, for example, Agreed Upon Procedures that the Independent Accountants may agree with the Regulator in relation to the Regulated Entity's compliance with Regulatory Accounting Guidelines which may include steps such as obtaining the opinion of the Regulated Entity's appointed technical consultants (sometimes referred to as the reporter) for example, as to the appropriateness of capital expenditure outlay and tendering procedures.

50   The Independent Accountants would need the consent of the expert prior to making reference to, and/or including extracts from the expert's report in the Independent Accountants' report.

Independent experts rely on work performed by the Independent Accountants

51   The Independent Accountants may be requested by a Third Party to perform certain procedures in connection with that Third Party's own regulatory reporting. For example, the Third Party (who may itself be an independent expert) may ask the Independent Accountants to verify that certain financial information is correctly extracted from a company's accounting records when reporting on information to be included in Regulatory Returns.

52   In such circumstances, the Independent Accountants obtain permission from the Regulated Entity prior to agreeing to do the work, and agree a tri-partite engagement contract with the Regulated Entity and the independent expert in accordance with the guidance set out in Technical Release Audit 1/01 and Section 2 of this paper.

53   The form of report issued to the independent expert should be prepared in accordance with the guidance set out in SAS 600 and Section 3 of this guidance.

Appendix A – Regulatory accounts

There is no precise definition of Regulatory Accounts, either in law or in practice, although they are commonly referred to by Regulatory Bodies, Regulated Entities and accountants and within RAGs and the Regulated Entities' licence arrangements.

Regulatory Accounts are analogous to financial statements prepared under the Companies Act, but are usually prepared under some variation of, or other basis to, UK GAAP[7] and therefore a 'fairly presents in accordance with' opinion is more appropriate in the circumstances of Regulatory Accounts. Financial information other than that prepared on the basis of UK GAAP does not necessarily represent a true and fair view of the financial performance or financial position of a company as shown in financial statements prepared in accordance with the Companies Act 1985.

Regulatory Accounts typically include:

- a profit and loss account;
- a balance sheet or statement of mean capital employed;
- detailed/segmental analyses of operations, costs and income, as defined in the Regulatory licence; and
- a reconciliation between the results and net assets reported within the Regulatory Accounts and those reported within the statutory financial statements prepared in accordance with the Companies Act 1985.

Regulatory Returns usually incorporate Regulatory Accounts but may also include other financial information required by the Regulator. Independent Accountants are usually expected to report upon certain identified elements of the additional information contained within the Regulatory Return only.

Regulatory Accounts do not include other items included within Regulatory Returns, such as:

- the reports of other experts;
- management commentary on the accounting informationl; or
- other types of Regulatory Information required to comply with the Regulatory Licence.

Appendix B – Example of an unqualified audit report for regulatory accounts

(to be tailored as appropriate for the particular circumstances of each engagement)

Independent Accountants' report to the Director General, [Regulator] ('the Regulator') and ABC Limited[8]

We have audited the Regulatory Accounts of ABC Limited ('the Company') on pages x to x which comprise the profit and loss account, the statement of total recognised gains and losses, the balance sheet, [the cashflow statement] and the related notes to the Regulatory Accounts.

---

[7] Except as specified in the RAGs.

[8] Any modification to this form of report should be made in accordance with SAS 600 – see Section 3. The report is addressed to the Regulator as well as to the Company without any disclaimer of responsibility to the Regulator only where the Regulator has signed a tri-partite engagement contract or there is a bi-partite engagement contract supplemented by written notice signed by the Regulator. In other cases the report may be addressed to the Company and the Regulator (to meet the requirements of the Regulatory Licence) but includes a disclaimer under which responsibility is accepted to the Company only and co-addressing to the Regulator is expressed to be only to meet the requirements of the Regulatory Licence. Refer to paragraph 13 for further guidance.

This report is made, on terms that have been agreed,[9] solely to the Company and the Regulator in order to meet [the requirements of the Regulatory Licence[10]]. Our audit work has been undertaken so that we might state to the Company and the Regulator those matters that we have agreed to state to them in our report, in order (a) to assist the Company to [meet its obligation under the Regulatory Licence to procure such a report] and (b) to facilitate the carrying out by the Regulator of its regulatory functions, and for no other purpose. To the fullest extent permitted by law, we do not accept or assume responsibility to anyone other than the Company and the Regulator, for our audit work, for this report or for the opinions we have formed.

Basis of preparation

The Regulatory Accounts have been prepared under the historical cost convention (as modified by the revaluation of certain fixed assets) and in accordance with conditions [ ], [ ] and [ ] of the Company's Regulatory Licence, Regulatory Accounting Guidelines [ ], [ ] and [ ] ('the RAGs') issued by the Regulator and the accounting policies set out in the statement of accounting policies.

The Regulatory Accounts are separate from the statutory financial statements of the Company and have not been prepared under the basis of Generally Accepted Accounting Principles in the United Kingdom ('UK GAAP'). Financial information other than that prepared on the basis of UK GAAP does not necessarily represent a true and fair view of the financial performance or financial position of a company as shown in financial statements prepared in accordance with the Companies Act 1985.

Respective responsibilities of the Regulator, the Directors and Auditors

The nature, form and content of Regulatory Accounts are determined by the Regulator. It is not appropriate for us to assess whether the nature of the information being reported upon is suitable or appropriate for the Regulator's purposes. Accordingly we make no such assessment.

The directors' responsibilities for preparing the Regulatory Accounts in accordance with conditions [ ], [ ] and [ ] of the Regulatory Licence are set out in the statement of directors' responsibilities on page x.

Our responsibility is to audit the Regulatory Accounts in accordance with United Kingdom Auditing Standards issued by the Auditing Practices Board, except as stated in the 'Basis of audit opinion', below and having regard to the guidance contained in Audit 05/03 'Reporting to Regulators of Regulated Entities'.

We report our opinion as to whether the Regulatory Accounts present fairly, in accordance with conditions [ ], [ ] and [ ] of the Company's Regulatory Licence, the RAGs [ ], [ ] and [ ], and the accounting policies set out on page x, the results and financial position of the company. We also report to you if, in our opinion, the Company has not kept proper accounting records or if we have not received all the information and explanations we require for our audit.

[We read the other information contained within the Regulatory Accounts, including any supplementary schedules on which we do not express an audit opinion, and

---

[9] This requires an engagement letter in a satisfactory form to be in place.

[10] Or other reference. If the appropriate reference is to a Regulatory Licence that licence will require to be defined appropriately in the reference or in some other suitable place.

consider the implications for our report if we become aware of any apparent mis-statements or material inconsistencies with the Regulatory Accounts.]

Basis of audit opinion

We conducted our audit in accordance with Statement of Auditing Standards issued by the Auditing Practices Board except as noted below. An audit includes examination, on a test basis, of evidence relevant to the amounts and disclosures in the Regulatory Accounts. It also includes an assessment of the significant estimates and judgements made by the Directors in the preparation of the Regulatory Accounts, and of whether the accounting policies are consistently applied and adequately disclosed.

We planned and performed our audit so as to obtain all the information and explanations which we considered necessary in order to provide us with sufficient evidence to give reasonable assurance that the Regulatory Accounts are free from material mis-statement, whether caused by fraud or other irregularity or error. However, as the nature, form and content of Regulatory Accounts are determined by the Regulator, we did not evaluate the overall adequacy of the presentation of the information, which would have been required if we were to express an audit opinion under Auditing Standards.

Our opinion on the Regulatory Accounts is separate from our opinion on the statutory accounts of the Company on which we reported on [date], which are prepared for a different purpose. Our audit report in relation to the statutory accounts of the Company (our 'Statutory' audit) was made solely to the Company's members, as a body, in accordance with section 235 of the Companies Act 1985. Our Statutory audit work was undertaken so that we might state to the Company's members those matters we are required to state to them in a Statutory auditor's report and for no other purpose. In these circumstances, to the fullest extent permitted by law, we do not accept or assume any responsibility to anyone other than the Company and the Company's members as a body, for our Statutory audit work, for our Statutory audit report, or for the opinions we have formed in respect of that Statutory audit.

Opinion

In our opinion the Regulatory Accounts fairly present in accordance with conditions [ ], [ ] and [ ] of the Company's Regulatory Licence, Regulatory Accounting Guidelines [ ], [ ] and [ ], and the accounting policies set out on page x, the state of the Company's affairs at [date] and of its profit (or loss) [and cashflow] for the year then ended, and have been properly prepared in accordance with those conditions, guidelines and accounting policies.

[Name of auditor]

[Chartered Accountants and Registered Auditors]

[Address]

[Date]

The maintenance and integrity of the [name of entity] web site is the responsibility of the Directors and the maintenance and integrity of the [name of Regulator] web site is the responsibility of the Regulator; the work carried out by the auditors does not involve consideration of these matters and, accordingly, the auditors accept no responsibility for any changes that may have occurred to the Regulatory Accounts since they were initially presented on the web sites.

2 Legislation in the United Kingdom governing the preparation and dissemination of financial statements and Regulatory Accounts may differ from legislation in other jurisdictions.

Appendix C – Example tri-partite engagement contract

(to be tailored as appropriate for the particular circumstances of each engagement)

Private and Confidential

The Directors

[Name and address of Regulated Entity]

For the attention of [   ]

The Director General

[Name and address of Regulator]

For the attention of [   ]

[Date]

[Name of Regulated Entity] ('the Company') Audit of the regulatory financial statements for the year ended [DATE]

Dear Sirs,

Introduction

This letter (including the attached Appendices and the Terms and Conditions) sets out our understanding of the basis on which we act as auditors reporting on the regulatory financial statements ('the Regulatory Accounts') as specified in [LICENCE CONDITION OR OTHER REFERENCE] of the Instrument of Appointment of the Company as a [TYPE OF BUSINESS] under the [APPLICABLE LEGISLATION] ('the Regulatory Licence') and the Regulatory Accounting Guidelines ('RAGs') [agreed with/]issued by the Director General of [IDENTITY OF REGULATOR], [NAME OF REGULATOR] ('the Regulator'). We also set out the respective areas of responsibility of the directors of the Company ('the Directors'), the Regulator and ourselves, in respect of the audit of the Regulatory Accounts (the 'Services'). This letter (with all its attachments) applies only to the audit report on the Regulatory Accounts and the scope of our work will be limited accordingly. If any additional work or report is required, separate engagement terms and conditions will need to be agreed.

This letter and the attached terms and conditions together comprise the entire contract ('the Contract') for the provision of the Services [to the exclusion of any other express or implied terms, whether expressed orally or in writing, including any conditions, warranties and representations unless made fraudulently] and shall supersede all previous contracts, letters of engagement, undertakings, agreements and correspondence regarding the Services.

Responsibilities of the Directors and the Auditors

The Directors are required to ensure that the Company complies with all of the terms of its Regulatory Licence [or other reference].

The Directors are required to prepare Regulatory Accounts in accordance with the Company's Regulatory Licence [or other reference] and the RAGs [agreed with/] issued by the Regulator, a copy of which are attached as Appendix [ ]. The Directors are also required to:

- [OTHER LICENCE CONDITIONS ON WHICH THE DIRECTORS ARE REQUIRED TO GIVE A FINANCE-BASED REPORT PER THE REGULATORY LICENCE, for example]:
- [Confirm that, in their opinion, the Company has sufficient financial and management resources for the next twelve months];
- [Confirm that, in their opinion, the Company has sufficient rights and assets which would enable a special administrator to manage the affairs, business and property of the Company];
- [Report to the Director General of [NAME OF REGULATOR] changes in the Company's activities which may be material in relation to the Company's ability to finance its regulated activities];
- [Undertake the transactions entered into by the business consisting of the carrying out of the regulated activity ('the appointed business'), with or for the benefit of any group companies or related companies ('associated companies') or activities of the appointed business, at arms length]; and
- [Keep proper accounting records which comply with [LICENCE CONDITION OR OTHER REFERENCE].

We refer to the above as 'the Specific Obligations'.

Other than reporting on whether or not proper accounting records have been kept by the Company as required by Condition [ ] of the Regulatory Licence [or other reference], it is not our responsibility in providing the Services to report on the Specific Obligations or on any other obligations of the Company or the Directors under the Regulatory Licence [or other reference].

The Directors are also responsible for ensuring that the Company maintains accounting records which disclose with reasonable accuracy, at any time, the financial position of the Company, and for preparing Regulatory Accounts which present the results of the Company fairly in accordance with the Regulatory Licence. They are also responsible for making available to us, as and when required, all of the Company's accounting records, all other relevant records, including minutes of all directors', management and shareholders' meetings, and such information and explanations which we consider necessary for the performance of our duties as auditors.

It is our responsibility to form an independent opinion, based on our audit, on the Regulatory Accounts and to report our opinion to the Company and the Regulator.

Our report will be addressed to the Company and the Regulator and will state whether, in our opinion, the Regulatory Accounts present fairly in accordance with conditions [ ], [ ] and [ ] of the Regulatory Licence [or other reference] the state of the Company's affairs at [DATE] and of its profit (or loss) for the year then ended, and have been properly prepared in accordance with conditions [ ], [ ] and [ ] of that Licence [or other reference].

Our report will be made in accordance with the Contract, solely to the Company and the Regulator in order to meet the requirements of the Regulatory Licence [or other reference]. Our audit work will be undertaken so that we might state to the Company and the Regulator those matters we have agreed in the Contract to state to them in our report in order to (a) assist the Company to [meet its obligations under the Regulatory Licence to procure such a report] and (b) to facilitate the carrying out by the Regulator of its regulatory functions, and for no other purpose. To the fullest extent permitted by law, we will not accept or assume responsibility to anyone other than the Company and the Regulator for our audit work, for our report, or for the opinions we will form. Our report will contain a disclaimer of liability to other parties to this effect.

The Contract does not confer benefits on any parties who are not parties to it and the application of the Contracts (Rights of Third Parties) Act 1999 is excluded.

In arriving at our opinion, and in accordance with the Regulatory Licence (condition [REFERENCE]) [or other reference], we will consider the following matters, and report on any in respect of which we are not satisfied:

- whether appropriate accounting records have been kept by the Company and proper returns adequate for our audit have been received from operating locations not visited by us;
- whether the Regulatory Accounts are in agreement with the accounting records and returns retained for the purpose of preparing the Regulatory Accounts; and
- whether we have obtained all the information and explanations which we consider necessary for the purposes of our audit.

Our responsibilities also include:

- Providing in our report a description of the Directors' responsibilities for the Regulatory Accounts where the Regulatory Accounts or accompanying information do not include such a description; and
- Considering whether other information in documents containing the Regulatory Accounts is consistent with those Regulatory Accounts.

The Regulator and the Company acknowledge and agree that:

- wherever the Regulatory Accounts or other Regulatory Information covered by the Independent Accountants' report are published or otherwise made available in full, our audit report will also be published or otherwise made available in full as part of that communication;
- wherever substantial extracts[11] from the Regulatory Accounts or other Regulatory Information covered by the Independent Accountants' report are published or otherwise made available, and reference is made to the fact that they are audited or otherwise examined by an Independent Accountants, there will be explicit statements by the Regulator: a) that the information published is only an extract; and b) about the limitation of scope of the Independent Accountants' report and the duty of care owed by the Independent Accountants; and c) referring to where the full set of Regulatory Accounts can be found or otherwise obtained; and

---

[11] For example, reproduction of primary statements as a whole.

- wherever any other information is referenced from the Regulatory Accounts or other Regulatory Information covered by the Independent Accountants' report, there will be an explicit reference by the Regulator to the source of that information and the limitation of scope of the Independent Accountants' report and the duty of care owed by the Independent Accountant

Relationship between the Regulator and the Company

For the avoidance of doubt, nothing in this Contract is intended to nor does it affect or in any way alter the relationship or the rights and obligations between the Company and the Regulator as set out in the Regulatory Licence [and all relevant legislation].

Scope of our audit

Our audit will be performed with regard to the guidance contained in 'Audit 05/03: Reporting to Regulators of Regulated Entities' issued by the Institute of Chartered Accountants in England & Wales.

Our audit will be conducted in accordance with Statements of Auditing Standards issued by the Auditing Practices Board except that, as the nature, form and content of Regulatory Accounts are determined by the Regulator, we will not evaluate the overall adequacy of the presentation of the information, which would have been required if we were to express an audit opinion under Auditing Standards. Our audit will include such tests of transactions and of the existence, ownership and valuation of assets and liabilities as we consider necessary. We shall obtain an understanding of the accounting and internal financial control systems to the extent necessary in order to assess their adequacy as a basis for the preparation of the Regulatory Accounts and to establish whether appropriate accounting records have been maintained by the Company.

We shall expect to obtain such appropriate evidence as we consider sufficient to enable us to draw reasonable conclusions therefrom. The nature and extent of our procedures will vary according to our assessment of the Company's accounting system and, where we wish to place reliance on it, the internal financial control system and may cover any aspect of the business operations.

[The Regulatory Accounts are prepared by disaggregating balances recorded in the general ledgers and other accounting records of the [NAME OF STATUTORY ENTITY] maintained in accordance with the Companies Act 1985 and used, in accordance with that Act, for the preparation of [NAME OF STATUTORY ENTITY]'s statutory financial statements.]

[No additional tests will be performed of the transactions and balances which are recorded in the general ledgers of [NAME OF STATUTORY ENTITY] other than those carried out in performing the audit of the statutory financial statements that include the Company.]

Our audit includes assessing the significant estimates and judgements made by the Directors in the preparation of the Regulatory Accounts and whether the accounting policies are appropriate to the Company's circumstances, consistently applied and adequately disclosed.

[We will read the [SPECIFY INFORMATION] ('Other Information') contained within the Regulatory Accounts, including any supplementary schedules on which we do not express an audit opinion, and consider the implications for our report if we become aware of any apparent mis-statements or material inconsistencies with the Regulatory Accounts. We will not perform any audit procedures nor provide any other assurance on the Other Information.]

We will plan our work to gain reasonable assurance that the Regulatory Accounts are free from material error, whether caused by fraud or other mis-statement.

The concept of materiality affects our audit planning and our consideration of matters arising from our audit. We take into account both qualitative and quantitative factors when assessing materiality. We will only express an opinion on the Regulatory Accounts as a whole and not on individual factors/components within Regulatory Accounts.

Where the Regulator requires specific factors to be reported upon by us, this should be addressed through the powers vested in the Regulator through the Regulatory Licence [or other reference]. For such reporting, we will agree a list of procedures ('Agreed Upon Procedures') that we will perform for the Regulator. These procedures will be specified in a separate engagement contract between us and the Regulator [and will be shown to the Company]. We will report the findings of the Agreed Upon Procedures separately from the Regulatory Accounts opinion, by way of a factual report to the Regulator, in which we will not express an opinion on the results of the Agreed Upon Procedures, nor the appropriateness of those procedures for the purposes of the Regulator. As with the form and content of Regulatory Accounts, the Regulator will need to make its own assessment of the appropriateness of the Agreed Upon Procedures and the reported findings.

Where Agreed Upon Procedures are required in addition to an opinion on the Regulatory Accounts, we may choose not to complete our work nor express an opinion on the Regulatory Accounts until:

i) the Agreed Upon Procedures that have been specified by the Regulator have been completed and reported upon; and
ii) the Regulator has provided a written notice to us confirming that nothing has come to the attention of the Regulator from that report (or otherwise) that indicates that there are any matters which the Regulator believes that we should take into account in arriving at our opinion on the Regulatory Accounts. If such matters do exist we will consider, in arriving at our opinion on the Regulatory Accounts, the matters noted by the Regulator and/or agree additional Agreed Upon Procedures with the Regulator.

The Services are separate from our audit work on the statutory financial statements of the Company which is carried out in accordance with our statutory obligations under the Companies Act 1985. Our audit report on those statutory financial statements is intended for the sole benefit of the Company's shareholders as a group, to whom it is addressed, and not for any other purpose. Our audit of the Company's statutory financial statements are not planned or conducted in contemplation of the requirements of anyone other than such shareholders and, consequently, our audit work is not intended to address or reflect matters in which anyone other than such shareholders may be interested.

We do not and will not, by virtue of this report or otherwise in connection with this engagement, assume any responsibility whether in contract, negligence or otherwise in relation to our audits of the Company's statutory financial statements required by the Companies Act 1985; we and our employees shall have no liability whether in contract, tort (including negligence) or otherwise to any parties other than the

Company and its members in relation to our audit of the Company's statutory financial statements.

The nature and format of the Regulatory Accounts are determined by the requirements of the Regulator. It is not appropriate for us to assess, and accordingly we will not make any assessment on, whether the nature of the information being reported upon is suitable or appropriate for the Regulator's purpose. It is a matter for the Regulator to consider whether the information being reported upon is appropriate for its own purposes and we will not give any implicit or explicit affirmation that the information being reported upon is suitable for the Regulator's purpose.

The Regulator and the Company accept that there [may be/are] differences between United Kingdom Generally Accepted Accounting Principles ('UK GAAP') and the basis of information provided in the Regulatory Accounts. Financial information, other than that prepared on the basis of UK GAAP, does not necessarily represent a true and fair view of the financial performance or financial position of a Company.

Internal audit

In developing our audit plan, we will liaise with the Company's internal auditors to ensure that our work is properly co-ordinated with theirs. It is our policy to rely upon internal audit work whenever possible, whilst ensuring that adequate audit coverage is achieved of all significant areas.

Meetings with the Regulator

We are willing to attend meetings with the Regulator to discuss the Services, if requested to do so, provided that we can agree appropriate terms on which such meetings are held. For the avoidance of doubt appropriate terms will include meeting only on a tri-partite basis in the absence of specific consent of the Company allowing us to meet with the Regulator [and its advisors].

Management representations

The information used by the Directors in preparing the Regulatory Accounts will invariably include facts or judgements which are not themselves recorded in the accounting records. As part of our normal audit procedures, we shall request appropriate directors or senior officials/management of the Company to provide written confirmation each year of such facts or judgements and any other oral representations which we have received during the course of the audit on matters having a material effect on the Regulatory Accounts. We will also ask the Directors to confirm in that letter that all important and relevant information has been brought to our attention. In connection with representations and the supply of information to us generally, we draw your attention to section 389A of the Companies Act 1985 under which it is an offence for an officer of the company to mislead the auditors.

Detection of fraud, error and non-compliance with laws and regulations

The responsibility for safeguarding the assets of the Company and for the prevention and detection of fraud, error and non-compliance with law or regulations rests with the Directors. However, we shall endeavour to plan our audit so that we have a reasonable expectation of detecting material mis-statements in the Regulatory Accounts or accounting records (including any material mis-statements resulting from fraud, error or non-compliance with law or regulations), but our examination should not be relied upon to disclose all such material mis-statements or frauds, errors or instances of non-compliance as may exist.

Timetable

We expect to commence our work on [DATE] and would normally expect to issue our report by [DATE].

Completion of our work will depend upon receiving, without undue delay, full co-operation from all relevant officials of the Company and their disclosure to us of all the accounting records of the Company and all other records and related information (including certain representations) that we may need for the purpose of our work.

Other requirements

In order to assist us with the examination of the Regulatory Accounts, we shall request early sight of all documents or statements which are due to be issued with those Regulatory Accounts.

Once we have issued our report we have no further direct responsibility in relation to the Regulatory Accounts for that financial year.

Preparation of Regulatory Accounts

Assistance with the preparation of Regulatory Accounts does not form a part of the audit function, but we shall discuss the Company's accounting principles with the management and/or the Directors and we may propose adjusting entries for their consideration.

Other services

We shall not be treated as having notice, for the purposes of our regulatory audit responsibilities, of information provided to members of our firm other than those engaged on the audit (for example information provided in connection with accounting, taxation and other services).

Fiduciary responsibilities

Because our audit work under the terms of this engagement is directed at forming an opinion on the Company's Regulatory Accounts our audit procedures will not normally extend to assets or documents of title in respect of assets that are in the Company's possession but owned by others.

Terms and conditions

The attached Terms and Conditions set out the duties of all parties in respect of the Services. The Terms and Conditions amongst other things:

i) limit our liability to a maximum aggregate amount of £[X]. This limitation shall be allocated between the Company and the Regulator. [It is agreed that such allocation will be entirely a matter for the addressees of this letter, who shall be under no obligation to inform [Name of Auditor] of it, provided always that if (for whatever reason) no such allocation is agreed, neither the Company nor the Regulator shall dispute the validity, enforceability or operation of the limit of liability on the grounds that no such allocation was agreed];[12] and

ii) limit the period within which a claim may be brought.

[NAME OF AUDITOR] alone will be responsible for the performance of the engagement contract formed by this letter. You therefore agree that you will not bring any claim in respect of or in connection with this engagement whether in contract, tort (including negligence), breach of statutory duty or otherwise against any partner or employee of [NAME OF AUDITOR]. The foregoing exclusion does not apply to any liability that cannot be excluded under the laws of England and Wales.

Fees

[Details]

The fee for the work covered by this engagement letter will be agreed with, and paid by, the Company.

Safeguarding service

It is our desire to provide you at all times with a high quality service to meet your needs. If at any time you would like to discuss with us how our service to you could be improved or if you are dissatisfied with any aspect of our services, please raise the matter immediately with the partner responsible for that aspect of our services to you. If, for any reason, you would prefer to discuss these matters with someone other than that partner, please contact [ ] at [ ]. In this way we are able to ensure that your concerns are dealt with carefully and promptly. We undertake to look into any complaint carefully and promptly and to do all we can to explain the position to you. This will not affect your right to complain to the Institute of Chartered Accountants in England and Wales.

Acknowledgement and acceptance

Please acknowledge your acceptance of the terms of our engagement under the Contract by signing the confirmation below and returning a copy of this letter and the attached Terms and Conditions to us at the above address, whereupon the Contract will take effect from the date of the commencement by us of the Services.

Once it has been agreed, this letter will remain effective, from one audit appointment to another, until it is replaced.

If you have any questions regarding this Contract, please do not hesitate to contact us.

Yours faithfully,

[Name of Auditor]

---

[12] This paragraph may be replaced by a specific allocation of the aggregate liability between the Company and the Regulator where the Company and the Regulator have reached such agreement, independently of the Independent Accountants, and wish to incorporate this into the engagement contract.

I have read the above letter and accept the terms and conditions set out therein.

Signed:

(Name and position) (Date) for and on behalf of [Name of Company]

(Name and position) (Date) for and on behalf of [Name of Regulator]

Appendix D – Example bi-partite engagement contract

(to be tailored for the particular circumstances of each engagement)

Private and Confidential

The Directors

[Name and address of Regulated Entity]

For the attention of [   ]

[Date]

[Name of Regulated Entity] ('the Company') Audit of the regulatory financial statements for the year ended [DATE]

Dear Sirs,

Introduction

This letter (including the attached Appendices and the Terms and Conditions) sets out our understanding of the basis on which we act as auditors reporting on the regulatory financial statements ('the Regulatory Accounts') as specified in [LICENCE CONDITION OR OTHER REFERENCE] of the Instrument of Appointment of the Company as a [TYPE OF BUSINESS] under the [APPLICABLE LEGISLATION] ('the Regulatory Licence') and the Regulatory Accounting Guidelines ('RAGs') [agreed with/]issued by the Director General of [IDENTITY OF REGULATOR], [NAME OF REGULATOR] ('the Regulator'). We also set out the respective areas of responsibility of the directors of the Company ('the Directors') and ourselves, in respect of the audit of the Regulatory Accounts (the 'Services'). This letter (with all its attachments) applies only to the audit report on the Regulatory Accounts and the scope of our work will be limited accordingly.

If any additional work or report is required, separate engagement terms and conditions will need to be agreed.

This letter and the attached Terms and Conditions together comprise the entire contract ('the Contract') for the provision of the Services [to the exclusion of any other express or implied terms, whether expressed orally or in writing, including any conditions, warranties and representations unless made fraudulently] and shall supersede all previous contracts, letters of engagement, undertakings, agreements and correspondence regarding the Services.

The Regulator is not a party to the Contract. On condition that the Regulator accepts in writing a notice in the form appended ('the Regulator's Contract'), we will accept duties and responsibilities to the Regulator in respect of our audit work, our audit report and our audit opinion on the Regulatory Accounts. Any such agreement will be on the basis that, amongst other things, the Company and the Regulator agree that our aggregate liability to the Company and the Regulator is limited to the maximum amount which would have been payable to the Company alone in respect of any breach of our obligations to the Company. References to rights and obligations between the Regulator and the auditors in relation to the Services and the Agreed upon Procedures are included in the Contract for the purpose only of the Regulator's Contract and are not intended to create rights or obligations between the Regulator and the Company.

Responsibilities of the Directors and the Auditors

The Directors are required to ensure that the Company complies with all of the terms of its Regulatory Licence [or other reference].

The Directors are required to prepare Regulatory Accounts in accordance with the Company's Regulatory Licence [or other reference] and the RAGs [agreed with/] issued by the Regulator, a copy of which are attached as Appendix [   ]. The Directors are also required to:

- [OTHER LICENCE CONDITIONS ON WHICH THE DIRECTORS ARE REQUIRED TO GIVE A FINANCE-BASED REPORT PER THE REGULATORY LICENCE, for example]:
- [Confirm that, in their opinion, the Company has sufficient financial and management resources for the next twelve months];
- [Confirm that, in their opinion, the Company has sufficient rights and assets which would enable a special administrator to manage the affairs, business and property of the Company];
- [Report to the Director General of [NAME OF REGULATOR] changes in the Company's activities which may be material in relation to the Company's ability to finance its regulated activities];
- [Undertake the transactions entered into by the business consisting of the carrying out of the regulated activity ('the appointed business'), with or for the benefit of any group companies or related companies ('associated companies') or activities of the appointed business, at arms length]; and
- [Keep proper accounting records which comply with [LICENCE CONDITION OR OTHER REFERENCE].

We refer to the above as 'the Specific Obligations'.

Other than reporting on whether or not proper accounting records have been kept by the Company as required by Condition [   ] of the Regulatory Licence [or other reference], it is not our responsibility in providing the Services to report on the Specific Obligations or on any other obligations of the Company or the Directors under the Regulatory Licence [or other reference].

The Directors are also responsible for ensuring that the Company maintains accounting records which disclose with reasonable accuracy, at any time, the financial position of the Company, and for preparing Regulatory Accounts which present the results of the Company fairly in accordance with the Regulatory Licence. They are also responsible for making available to us, as and when required, all of the Company's accounting records, all other relevant records, including minutes of all directors', management and shareholders' meetings, and such information and explanations which we consider necessary for the performance of our duties as auditors.

It is our responsibility to form an independent opinion, based on our audit, on the Regulatory Accounts and to report our opinion to the Company and (in order to meet the requirements of the Regulatory Licence) to the Regulator.

Our report will be made in accordance with the Contract, solely to the Company and the Regulator in accordance with the Regulatory Licence [or other reference]. Our audit work will be undertaken so that we might state to the Company and the Regulator those matters we have agreed in the Contract to state to them in our report in order to (a) assist the Company to [meet its obligations under the Regulatory Licence to procure such a report] and (b) to facilitate the carrying out by the Regulator of its regulatory functions, and for no other purpose. To the fullest extent permitted by law, we will not accept or assume responsibility to anyone other than the Company for our audit work, for our report, or for the opinions we will form. Our report will contain a disclaimer of liability to all other parties but we will confirm acceptance in our report of responsibility in respect of our audit work to the Regulator also if the Regulator has agreed to the Regulator's Contract by signing the written notice appended.

Our report will be addressed to the Company and the Regulator to meet the requirements of the Regulatory Licence and will state whether, in our opinion, the Regulatory Accounts present fairly in accordance with conditions [ ], [ ] and [ ] of the Company's Regulatory Licence [or other reference] the state of the Company's affairs at [DATE] and of its profit (or loss) for the year then ended, and have been properly prepared in accordance with conditions [ ], [ ] and [ ] of that licence [or other reference].

The Contract does not confer benefits on any parties who are not parties to it and the application of the Contracts (Rights of Third Parties) Act 1999 is excluded.

In arriving at our opinion, and in accordance with the Regulatory Licence (condition [REFERENCE]) [or other reference], we will consider the following matters, and report on any in respect of which we are not satisfied:

- whether appropriate accounting records have been kept by the Company and proper returns adequate for our audit have been received from operating locations not visited by us;
- whether the Regulatory Accounts are in agreement with the accounting records and returns retained for the purpose of preparing the Regulatory Accounts; and
- whether we have obtained all the information and explanations which we consider necessary for the purposes of our audit.

Our responsibilities also include:

- providing in our report a description of the Directors' responsibilities for the Regulatory Accounts where the Regulatory Accounts or accompanying information do not include such a description; and
- considering whether other information in documents containing the Regulatory Accounts is consistent with those Regulatory Accounts.

The Company and (where the Regulator signs the written notice appended) the Regulator acknowledge and agree that:

- wherever the Regulatory Accounts or other Regulatory Information covered by the Independent Accountants' report are published or otherwise made available in full, our audit report will also be published or otherwise made available in full as part of that communication;

- wherever substantial extracts[13] from the Regulatory Accounts or other Regulatory Information covered by the Independent Accountants' report are published or otherwise made available, and reference is made to the fact that they are audited or otherwise examined by an Independent Accountant, there will be explicit statements by the Regulator: a) that the information published is only an extract; and b) about the limitation of scope of the Independent Accountants' report and the duty of care owed by the Independent Accountants; and c) referring to where the full set of Regulatory Accounts can be found or otherwise obtained; and
- wherever any other information is referenced from the Regulatory Accounts or other Regulatory Information covered by the Independent Accountants' report, there will be an explicit reference by the Regulator to the source of that information and the limitation of scope of the Independent Accountants' report and the duty of care owed by the Independent Accountant.

Where the Regulator does not sign a written notice in the form appended, the Company will procure that these events take place in the circumstances identified.

Relationship between the Regulator and the Company

For the avoidance of doubt, nothing in this Contract is intended to nor does it affect or in any way alter the relationship or the rights and obligations between the Company and the Regulator as set out in the Regulatory Licence [and all relevant legislation].

Scope of our audit

Our audit will be performed with regard to the guidance contained in 'Audit 05/03: Reporting to Regulators of Regulated Entities' issued by the Institute of Chartered Accountants in England & Wales.

Our audit will be conducted in accordance with Statements of Auditing Standards issued by the Auditing Practices Board except that, as the nature, form and content of Regulatory Accounts are determined by the Regulator, we will not evaluate the overall adequacy of the presentation of the information, which would have been required if we were to express an audit opinion under Auditing Standards. Our audit will include such tests of transactions and of the existence, ownership and valuation of assets and liabilities as we consider necessary. We shall obtain an understanding of the accounting and internal financial control systems to the extent necessary in order to assess their adequacy as a basis for the preparation of the Regulatory Accounts and to establish whether appropriate accounting records have been maintained by the Company.

We shall expect to obtain such appropriate evidence as we consider sufficient to enable us to draw reasonable conclusions therefrom. The nature and extent of our procedures will vary according to our assessment of the Company's accounting system and, where we wish to place reliance on it, the internal financial control system and may cover any aspect of the business operations.

[The Regulatory Accounts are prepared by disaggregating balances recorded in the general ledgers and other accounting records of the [NAME OF STATUTORY ENTITY] maintained in accordance with the Companies Act 1985 and used, in

---

[13] For example, reproduction of primary statements as a whole.

accordance with that Act, for the preparation of [NAME OF STATUTORY ENTITY]'s statutory financial statements.]

[No additional tests will be performed of the transactions and balances which are recorded in the general ledgers of [NAME OF STATUTORY ENTITY] other than those carried out in performing the audit of the statutory financial statements that include the Company.]

Our audit includes assessing the significant estimates and judgements made by the Directors in the preparation of the Regulatory Accounts and whether the accounting policies are appropriate to the Company's circumstances, consistently applied and adequately disclosed.

[We will read the [SPECIFY INFORMATION] ('Other Information') contained within the Regulatory Accounts, including any supplementary schedules on which we do not express an audit opinion, and consider the implications for our report if we become aware of any apparent mis-statements or material inconsistencies with the Regulatory Accounts. We will not perform any audit procedures nor provide any other assurance on the Other Information.]

We will plan our work to gain reasonable assurance that the Regulatory Accounts are free from material error, whether caused by fraud or other mis-statement.

The concept of materiality affects our audit planning and our consideration of matters arising from our audit. We take into account both qualitative and quantitative factors when assessing materiality. We will only express an opinion on the Regulatory Accounts as a whole and not on individual factors within Regulatory Accounts.

Where the Regulator requires specific factors to be reported upon by us, this should be addressed through the powers vested in the Regulator through the Regulatory Licence [or other reference]. For such reporting, we will agree a list of procedures ('Agreed Upon Procedures') that we will perform for the Regulator. These procedures will be specified in a separate engagement contract between us [and] the Regulator and [will be shown to] the Company. We will report the findings of the Agreed Upon Procedures separately from the Regulatory Accounts opinion, by way of a factual report to the Regulator, in which we will not express an opinion on the results of the Agreed Upon Procedures, nor the appropriateness of those procedures for the purposes of the Regulator. As with the form and content of Regulatory Accounts, the Regulator will need to make its own assessment of the appropriateness of the Agreed Upon Procedures and the reported findings.

Where Agreed Upon Procedures are required in addition to an opinion on the Regulatory Accounts, we may choose not to complete our work nor express an opinion on the Regulatory Accounts until:

i) the Agreed Upon Procedures that have been specified by the Regulator have been completed and reported upon; and
ii) the Regulator has provided a written notice to us confirming that nothing has come to the attention of the Regulator from that report (or otherwise) that indicates that there are any matters which the Regulator believes that we should take into account in arriving at our opinion on the Regulatory Accounts. If such matters do exist we will consider, in arriving at our opinion on the Regulatory Accounts, the matters noted by the Regulator and/or agree additional Agreed Upon Procedures with the Regulator.]

The Services are separate from our audit work on the statutory financial statements of the Company which is carried out in accordance with our statutory obligations under the Companies Act 1985. Our audit report on those statutory financial statements is intended for the sole benefit of the Company's shareholders as a group, to whom it is addressed, and not for any other purpose. Our audits of the Company's statutory financial statements are not planned or conducted in contemplation of the requirements of anyone other than such shareholders and, consequently, our audit work is not intended to address or reflect matters in which anyone other than such shareholders may be interested.

We do not and will not, by virtue of this report or otherwise in connection with this engagement, assume any responsibility whether in contract, tort (including negligence) or otherwise in relation to our audits of the Company's statutory financial statements required by the Companies Act 1985; we and our employees shall have no liability whether in contract, tort (including negligence) or otherwise to any parties other than the Company and its members in relation to our audits of the Company's statutory financial statements.

The nature and format of the Regulatory Accounts are determined by the requirements of the Regulator. It is not appropriate for us to assess, and accordingly we will not make any assessment on, whether the nature of the information being reported upon is suitable or appropriate for the Regulator's purpose, whether or not the Regulator signs the written notice in the form appended. It is a matter for the Regulator to consider whether the information being reported upon is appropriate for its own purposes and we will not give any implicit or explicit affirmation that the information being reported upon is suitable for the Regulator's purpose.

There [may be/are] differences between United Kingdom Generally Accepted Accounting Principles ('UK GAAP') and the basis of information provided in the Regulatory Accounts. Financial information, other than that prepared on the basis of UK GAAP, does not necessarily represent a true and fair view of the financial performance or financial position of a Company.

Internal audit

In developing our audit plan, we will liaise with the Company's internal auditors to ensure that our work is properly co-ordinated with theirs. It is our policy to rely upon internal audit work whenever possible, whilst ensuring that adequate audit coverage is achieved of all significant areas.

Meetings with the Regulator

We are willing to attend meetings with the Regulator to discuss the Services, if requested to do so, provided that we can agree appropriate terms on which such meetings are held. For the avoidance of doubt appropriate terms will include meeting only on a tri-partite basis in the absence of specific consent of the Company allowing us to meet with the Regulator [and its advisors].

Management representations

The information used by the Directors in preparing the Regulatory Accounts will invariably include facts or judgements which are not themselves recorded in the accounting records. As part of our normal audit procedures, we shall request appropriate directors or senior officials/management of the Company to provide written confirmation each year of such facts or judgements and any other oral representations which we have received during the course of the audit on matters having a material effect on the Regulatory Accounts. We will also ask the Directors to confirm in that letter that all important and relevant information has been brought to our attention. In connection with representations and the supply of information to us generally, we draw your attention to section 389A of the Companies Act 1985 under which it is an offence for an officer of the Company to mislead the auditors.

Detection of fraud, error and non-compliance with laws and regulations

The responsibility for safeguarding the assets of the Company and for the prevention and detection of fraud, error and non-compliance with law or regulations rests with the Directors. However, we shall endeavour to plan our audit so that we have a reasonable expectation of detecting material mis-statements in the Regulatory Accounts or accounting records (including any material mis-statements resulting from fraud, error or non-compliance with law or regulations), but our examination should not be relied upon to disclose all such material mis-statements or frauds, errors or instances of non-compliance as may exist.

Timetable

We expect to commence our work on [DATE] and would normally expect to issue our report by [DATE].

Completion of our work will depend upon receiving, without undue delay, full co-operation from all relevant officials of the Company and their disclosure to us of all the accounting records of the Company and all other records and related information (including certain representations) that we may need for the purpose of our work.

Other requirements

In order to assist us with the examination of the Regulatory Accounts, we shall request early sight of all documents or statements which are due to be issued with those Regulatory Accounts.

Once we have issued our report we have no further direct responsibility in relation to the Regulatory Accounts for that financial year.

Preparation of Regulatory Accounts

Assistance with the preparation of Regulatory Accounts does not form a part of the audit function, but we shall discuss the Company's accounting principles with the management and/or the Directors and we may propose adjusting entries for their consideration.

Other services

We shall not be treated as having notice, for the purposes of our regulatory audit responsibilities, of information provided to members of our firm other than those engaged on the audit (for example information provided in connection with accounting, taxation and other services).

Fiduciary responsibilities

Because our audit work under the terms of this engagement is directed at forming an opinion on the Company's Regulatory Accounts our audit procedures will not normally extend to assets or documents of title in respect of assets that are in the Company's possession but owned by others.

Terms and conditions

The attached Terms and Conditions set out the duties of all parties in respect of the Services. The Terms and Conditions amongst other things:

i) limit our liability to a maximum aggregate amount of £[X]. Where the Regulator accepts in writing a notice in the form appended (and on that basis we accept duties and responsibilities to the Regulator), this limitation shall be allocated between the Company and the Regulator. [In such circumstances such allocation will be entirely a matter for the Company and the Regulator, who shall be under no obligation to inform [Name of Auditor] of it, provided always that if (for whatever reason) no such allocation is agreed, neither the Company nor the Regulator shall dispute the validity, enforceability or operation of the limit of liability on the grounds that no such allocation was agreed];[14] and

ii) limit the period within which a claim may be brought.

[NAME OF AUDITOR] alone will be responsible for the performance of the engagement contract formed by this letter. You therefore agree that you will not bring any claim in respect of or in connection with this engagement whether in contract, tort (including negligence), breach of statutory duty or otherwise against any partner or employee of [NAME OF AUDITOR]. The foregoing exclusion does not apply to any liability that cannot be excluded under the laws of England and Wales.

Fees

[Details]

The fee for the work covered by this engagement letter will be agreed with, and paid by, the Company.

Safeguarding service

It is our desire to provide you at all times with a high quality service to meet your needs. If at any time you would like to discuss with us how our service to you could be improved or if you are dissatisfied with any aspect of our services, please raise the matter immediately with the partner responsible for that aspect of our services to you. If, for any reason, you would prefer to discuss these matters with someone other than that partner, please contact [ ] at [ ]. In this way we are able to ensure that your concerns are dealt with carefully and promptly. We undertake to look into any complaint carefully and promptly and to do all we can to explain the position to you. This will not affect your right to complain to the Institute of Chartered Accountants in England and Wales.

---

[14] *This paragraph may be replaced by a specific allocation of the aggregate liability between the Company and the Regulator where the Company and the Regulator have reached such agreement, independently of the Independent Accountants, and wish to incorporate this into the engagement contract.*

Acknowledgement and acceptance

Please acknowledge your acceptance of the terms of our engagement under the Contract by signing the confirmation below and returning a copy of this letter and the attached Terms and Conditions to us at the above address, whereupon the Contract will take effect from the date of the commencement by us of the Services.

Once it has been agreed, this letter will remain effective, from one audit appointment to another, until it is replaced.

If you have any questions regarding this Contract, please do not hesitate to contact us.

Yours faithfully,

[Name of Auditor]

I have read the above letter and accept the terms and conditions set out therein.

(Name and position) (Date) for and on behalf of [Name of Company]

Appendix E – Example written notice from the independent accountants to the regulator for bi-partite engagement arrangements

(to be tailored for the particular circumstances of each engagement)

Private and Confidential

The Director General

[Name and address of Regulator]

For the attention of [   ]

[Date]

[Name of Regulated Entity] ('the Company') Audit of the regulatory financial statements for the year ended [DATE]

Dear Sirs,

We refer to our engagement letter with the Company dated [DATE] ('the Contract') relating to our audit of the Company's regulatory financial statements for the year ended [DATE] ('the Regulatory Accounts'). A copy of the Contract is attached as Appendix 1 to this letter.

In the Contract we set out the basis on which we will act as auditors reporting on the Regulatory Accounts of the Company, together with the respective areas of responsibility of the directors of the Company and ourselves in respect of that audit and the scope of our audit. We also set out in the Contract the agreed extent of our liability to the Company in respect of our work. We confirm in the Contract that we will address our report on the Regulatory Accounts to the Company and, in order to meet the requirements of the Regulatory Licence, to you as well but we clarify that in our report we will deny liability in respect of our audit work and our report to any party other than the Company.

You have confirmed your interest in our audit of the Regulatory Accounts in your capacity as the Company's Regulator and your interest in the scope of our engagement agreed with the Company. You have asked us to accept responsibility for our audit work and our report to you as well as to the Company so that there is no denial of responsibility to you

in our report. This letter ('the Regulator's Contract') sets out the basis on which we are willing to accept such a responsibility, in return for your agreement to the terms of this letter including the following:

Our duties and responsibilities to you and your obligations to us will be those set out in the Contract as if incorporated into this letter. This sets out, amongst other things, terms relating to the disclosure of the Regulatory Accounts and other Regulatory Information covered by the Independent Accountants' Report.   1

Our aggregate liability to you will be strictly limited to £[   ][15] in the event of any breach of our obligations to you under the Regulator's Contract.   2

You do not wish to acquire rights against us in respect of use of the audit report for any purposes other than as the Company's Regulator and accept the disclaimer of liability to any Third Party (being a person other than the Company or the Regulator) as set out in the Contract.   3

You accept that the nature and format of the Regulatory Accounts are determined by your requirements and that it will be for you to consider whether the information on which we report as auditors is suitable or appropriate for your needs and purposes.   4

You will not be bound by any amendment to the Contract, whether written, oral or arising from the Contract, which is not formally accepted by you in writing.   5

Please acknowledge your acceptance of the terms and conditions of this letter by signing the confirmation below and returning a copy of it and the Contract to us at the above address.

Yours faithfully,

[Independent Accountants]

I have read the above letter and confirm acceptance of its terms and conditions on behalf of [NAME OF REGULATOR]

Signed

Name and position

[Cc: The Directors, [Name of Company]]

Enclosure: Copy of the Contract.

---

[15] *Independent Accountants will agree a figure by which their maximum aggregate liability to the Company and the Regulator is no greater than the amount which would have been payable by them to the Company under the Contract. For further guidance, see paragraph 11(ii).*

[Statement 931]
Reporting to the Audit Bureau of Circulations Limited (ABC) (AUDIT 01/04)

This guidance is issued by the Audit and Assurance Faculty of the Institute of Chartered Accountants in England & Wales in April 2004 to outline to Institute members new reporting arrangements being introduced after discussions with the Audit Bureau of Circulations Limited (ABC). The guidance does not constitute an auditing standard. Professional judgement should be used in its application.

Contents

	Paragraphs
Introduction	1 - 2
Explanation of the reporting arrangements	3 - 5
(a) The model tripartite agreement	6 - 13
(b) Reports to ABC 14 The ABC/ICAEW Circulation Audits Forum (ABC Forum)	15 - 17

Appendices

I. Audit Bureau of Circulations Limited (ABC) Returns – the model tripartite agreement
II. Training and communications

Reporting to the Audit Bureau of Circulations Ltd (ABC) Statement 931

Introduction

Following discussions between the Institute's Audit and Assurance Faculty and the Audit Bureau of Circulations Limited (ABC), arrangements have been agreed for reports provided by accountants in respect of returns made to ABC by ABC members. 1

This Technical Release explains the main elements of these arrangements. 2

Explanation of the reporting arrangements

The reporting arrangements are based on the reporting framework outlined in Technical Release Audit 1/01, *'Reporting to Third Parties'*. 3

ABC has agreed that accountants' reports on ABC returns be provided in accordance with a tripartite agreement between (1) the accountants, (2) ABC and (3) the ABC member. ABC has agreed a model tripartite agreement for this purpose. 4

This Technical Release provides guidance on the following: 5

(a) the model tripartite agreement; and
(b) reports to ABC.

(a) The model tripartite agreement

The model tripartite agreement, reproduced in Appendix I, follows the principles of Audit 1/01 referred in paragraph 3 above. ABC has agreed that it will contract with accountants on these terms. Once the letter is signed by all relevant parties (ie. the accountants, ABC and the ABC member), the necessary contract is formed. 6

The contract will apply to all reports made by the accountants for the ABC member in respect of all of that member's publications. From time to time the list of publications (attached as an appendix to the tripartite agreement) may need updating, and the tripartite agreement contains provisions for such updating. Once the tripartite agreement is in place, it will continue until either it is terminated or amended by written agreement between the parties to it. 7

The model tripartite agreement highlights the responsibilities of the ABC member. These include responsibility for: 8

- producing circulation data and maintaining proper records for that purpose;
- preventing and detecting fraud and irregularities;
- preparing the ABC returns for which the member owes a duty of care to ABC; and
- cooperating with the accountants in providing information, documentation and letters of representation to enable the accountants to perform their work.

The model tripartite agreement sets out the scope of the work that accountants are required to perform and clarifies the limitations on that work. Accountants interpret the ABC Rules as necessary. ABC recognises that accountants will report on the basis of their (the accountants') understanding of the Rules, but that accountants are not giving legal advice to ABC or the member on that interpretation. If accountants are uncertain as to the interpretation of the Rules, they consider either seeking clarification from ABC, or requesting that the member reach agreement with ABC as 9 to the interpretation. The work performed by accountants is often described as a 'circulation audit'.

10 The model tripartite agreement includes provisions relating to accountants' liability to ABC and the ABC member for the accountants' reports. ABC has agreed that accountants may cap their liability on an annual basis for all reports provided within each year (running from the date the tripartite agreement is signed). Accountants must agree the amount of any such liability cap with both the ABC and the ABC member.

11 Whereas the model tripartite agreement uses the word 'circulation', it is also used in connection with publications that are 'distributed' i.e. given away free.

12 These reporting engagements to ABC are entirely separate from, and unrelated to, the accountants' audit of the financial statements of the ABC member for the purposes of the Companies Act 1985 and do not create any obligations or liabilities with respect to the statutory audit which would otherwise not exist.

13 Accountants enter into separate agreements with the ABC member regarding matters such as fees, timing of the work, and staffing arrangements. ABC is not a party to these separate agreements.

(b) Reports to ABC

14 Accountants provide their reports on the ABC member's circulation return on standard forms that are completed by the ABC member. Accountants are required to complete an 'audit programme' and submit the completed programme to ABC, together with the forms. ABC supplies the return form, the 'audit programme' and any changes to the Rules to publishers prior to the end date of each audit period. Additional copies of these documents are available from ABC (contact details on www.abc.org.uk).

The ABC/ICAEW Circulation Audits Forum (ABC Forum)

15 A joint ABC/ICAEW Circulation Audits Forum was set up in 2001 following meetings between senior representatives of ABC and the ICAEW. Since its establishment, the ABC Forum has been a vehicle to resolve issues and improve communication between ABC and accountants. The ABC Forum encourages and champions the highest quality of circulation auditing. Accountants performing circulation audits have appropriate skills, knowledge of ABC rules and apply sufficient rigour and consistency to their work in relation to ABC.

16 Accountants performing circulation audits ensure that their staff receive appropriate training. Information about training offered by ABC is given in Appendix II.

17 Various communication channels exist between ABC and accountants. Further information is also provided in Appendix II.

Appendix I – Audit Bureau of Circulation Limited (ABC) returns – the model tripartite agreement

(NB: in this model tripartite agreement, the term 'Publishers' is used to refer to an ABC member)

The Board of Directors
CLIENT
[Address]

Audit Bureau of Circulations Limited
[Address]

Ref: [DD/MM/YY]

Dear Sirs

ABC CIRCULATION AUDITS OF MEMBER PUBLICATIONS

1. Introduction

1.1 We are writing to confirm the terms on which you have engaged [name of firm] to provide a report[s] on Certificates of Average Net Circulation ('ABC Returns'), which CLIENT ('the Publishers') is required to submit to the Audit Bureau of Circulations Limited ('ABC') in respect of the publications listed in the attached appendix ('the Publications'). The Publishers may add or remove publications from this list from time to time by giving us and ABC notice in writing of the proposed changes at least 28 days before the ABC Returns are due.

1.2 These terms will apply to our report(s) to be supplied for the period ending [...] and for subsequent periods unless otherwise agreed in writing by all the parties hereto. We will write separately to the Publishers regarding practical matters such as the timing of our work, staffing and our charges. Our invoice will be addressed to the Publishers, who will be solely responsible for payment of the same in full.

2. The Publishers' Responsibilities

2.1 The Publishers are responsible for producing the circulation data, maintaining proper records and completing the ABC Return in accordance with the Audit Bureau of Circulation Rules ('the ABC Rules'). The Publishers are further responsible for ensuring that the non-financial records are reconcilable to the financial records.

2.2 The Publishers will make available to us all records, correspondence, information and explanations that we consider necessary to enable us to perform our work.

2.3 The Publishers and ABC accept that any work performed by us under this letter cannot be accepted as being complete, unless we have been given full and free access to the financial and other records in connection with the distribution of the Publications under consideration, and the Publishers shall procure that any such records held by a third party are made available to us.

2.4 The Publishers will supply to ABC such information as ABC may reasonably require as relevant to the Publications under consideration and other Publications published by the Publishers.

2.5 The responsibility for the prevention and detection of fraud and irregularities rests with the management of the Publishers.

2.6 The Publishers owe a duty of care to ABC in relation to their obligations to prepare the ABC Return.

3. Scope of our Work

3.1 We will prepare a report in respect of the ABC Return for each of the Publications (each a 'Report' and together 'our Reports') which will be addressed to ABC. In order to prepare each Report we will perform the following procedures. We will:

3.1.1 perform the work set out in the Audit Programme as laid down by ABC in accordance with the instructions contained in the ABC Rules, as updated and in force at the time our work is conducted;

3.1.2 subject to the prior consent of the Publishers, answer ABC's reasonable questions arising from our work. However, all working papers and documentation generated by us as auditors are our property and will only be made available to ABC at our discretion, by prior agreement in writing and subject to any terms and conditions we may deem necessary;

3.1.3 report to ABC if there have been any limitations or restrictions to the scope of our work and/or the completed ABC Return does not comply with the ABC Rules and instructions prepared by ABC.

3.2 We will not subject the circulation data or related systems including those systems used by the Publishers for compiling the circulation data and complying with the ABC Rules to checking or verification procedures, except to the extent expressly stated.

3.3 The nature of the work we will undertake is not designed to detect significant weaknesses in any of the Publishers' systems, including circulation systems, and consequently we (i) may not detect such weaknesses; and (ii) do not accept any liability whatsoever for not detecting any such weaknesses. The responsibility for the Publishers' circulation and other systems rests entirely with the Publishers. However, in the event that we do detect any such weaknesses, we will bring these to the attention of the Publishers.

3.4 The Publishers and ABC accept that our work will be based on internal management information and will be carried out on the assumption that information provided to us by the management of the Publishers is reliable and, in all material respects, accurate and complete. We shall seek written representations from management in relation to matters for which independent corroboration is not available. We shall also seek confirmation that any significant matters of which we should be aware have been brought to our attention.

3.5 This is normal practice when carrying out work of this type, but contrasts significantly with, for example, a statutory audit. Even statutory audit work, with a significant level of detailed testing of transactions and balances, provides no guarantee that fraud will be detected. You will therefore understand that the work we undertake is not designed to and is not likely to reveal fraud or misrepresentation by the Publishers or their management. Accordingly, we cannot accept responsibility for detecting fraud (whether by management or by external parties) or for misrepresentation by the Publishers or their management. The responsibility for the prevention and detection of fraud, irregularity, error and/or non-compliance with law or regulation therefore rests with the management of the Publishers.

3.6 Our work will be based on our understanding of the ABC Rules. We will not give legal advice to the Publishers or ABC on the interpretation of the ABC Rules and, to the fullest extent permitted by law, we do not accept any liability in contract, tort (including negligence) or otherwise for any loss suffered by the Publishers or ABC or any other person as a result of incorrect interpretation of the ABC Rules by us or any other person.

4. Form and use of Report

4.1 Our Report will be addressed and issued to ABC and, subject to any adverse findings, will be in the form determined from time to time by ABC following consultation with the Institute of Chartered Accountants of England and Wales. So that the Publishers are aware of the contents of our Report, we will deliver copies to the Publishers at the same time. However, our Report is delivered to the Publishers for their information only and they should not use our Report for any other purpose. This letter will be identified in our Reports as the 'tripartite agreement' under which our Reports have been issued. Our Reports will be issued to the ABC and delivered to the Publishers on the basis that they are not to be copied, referred to or disclosed in whole or in part, to any other person without our prior written consent, which may be conditional.

4.2 Neither the Publishers nor ABC may rely on any oral or draft reports we provide. We accept responsibility to the Publishers and ABC for our final, signed Reports only.

4.3 During the engagement we may wish to communicate electronically with each other and ABC may request that we report in electronic form. However, the electronic transmission of information cannot be guaranteed to be secure or virus or error free and consequently such information could be intercepted, corrupted, lost, destroyed, arrive late or incomplete or otherwise be adversely affected or unsafe to use. We each recognise that systems and procedures cannot be a guarantee that transmissions will be unaffected by such hazards, but we each agree to use commercially reasonable procedures to check for the then most commonly known viruses before sending information electronically.

4.4 We confirm that we each accept these risks and authorise electronic communications between us. We will each be responsible for protecting our own systems and interests in relation to electronic communications and, to the fullest extent permitted by law, neither we, the Publishers, nor ABC (in each case including our respective members, partners, employees, sub-contractors or agents) will have any liability to each other on any basis, whether in contract, tort (including negligence) or otherwise in respect of any error, damage, loss or omission arising from or in connection with the electronic communication of information between us and our reliance on such information.

5. Liability Provisions

5.1 We will perform the services set out in this letter with reasonable skill and care.

5.2 We shall accept liability to ABC and the Publishers to pay damages for losses caused by breach of contract or negligence on our part in respect of services provided in connection with or arising out of the engagement set out in this letter (or any variation or addition thereto) but, to the fullest extent permitted by law, our liability to ABC, Publishers or any other party (whether in contract, negligence or otherwise) shall in no circumstances exceed [....]in the aggregate per year (running from the date of this letter and from each anniversary thereafter) in respect of all such services provided in that year.

5.3 This engagement is completely separate from and unrelated to the audit of the Publishers' financial statements for the purposes of the Companies Act 1985 and performed in accordance with separate engagement terms. We do not, and will not, by virtue of providing a report under this letter or otherwise, assume any responsibility whether in contract, negligence or otherwise in relation to the audits of the Publishers' financial statements; we and our partners and employees shall have no liability whether in contract, negligence or otherwise to any other party, including ABC, in relation to the audits of the Publishers' financial statements.

5.4 We do not owe nor accept any duty to any person other than you for the services set out in this letter. We shall not be liable for any losses suffered by any other person caused by that or any other person's use of or reliance on our Reports/confirmations or our advice. You agree that none of our partners or employees will have any liability to you and you will not bring any claim or proceedings of any nature howsoever arising (whether in contract, tort, breach of statutory duty or otherwise and including, but not limited to, a claim for negligence) in respect of or in connection with this engagement against any of our partners, employees or any subcontractors that we may use to provide the services.

5.5 The foregoing exclusions do not apply to any liability for fraud or other liability that cannot lawfully be excluded under the laws of England and Wales.

5.6 No person who is not a party to this agreement other than us and our subcontractors, if any, shall have any rights under the Contracts (Rights of Third Parties) Act 1999 to enforce any of its terms. This agreement can be varied without any third party's consent.

6. Safeguarding Service

It is our desire to provide you at all times with a professional service to meet your needs. If at any time you would like to discuss with us how our service to you could be improved or if you are dissatisfied with any aspect of our services, please raise the matter immediately with the engagement leader responsible for that aspect of our services to you. If, for any reason, you would prefer to discuss these matters with someone other than the engagement leader, please contact [...........]. We undertake to look into any complaint carefully and promptly and to do allwe can to explain the position to you. This will not affect your right to complain to the Institute of Chartered Accountants in England and Wales or other relevant professional body. You may obtain an explanation of the mechanisms that operate in respect of a complaint to the ICAEW at **www.icaew.co.uk/complaints** or by writing to the ICAEW. To contact the ICAEW write to the Professional Standards Office, Silbury Court, 412-416 Silbury Boulevard, Milton Keynes, MK9 2AF.

7. Other matters

7.1 Any party may terminate this engagement letter by giving the other parties hereto 30 days notice in writing.

7.2 We may agree additional terms with the Publishers in a separate letter.

7.3 This agreement shall be governed by English law and all disputes arising from or under it shall be subject to the exclusive jurisdiction of the English courts.

8. Acceptance of Terms

Please confirm that you agree to the terms of this letter [including the attached terms of business][1] by signing and returning to us the enclosed copy of this letter.

Yours faithfully

[name of firm]

Countersigned on behalf of the Publishers_____

PRINT NAME_____

Countersigned on behalf of ABC_____

PRINT NAME_____

Attachment:

Appendix – member publications

Appendix II – Training and communications

Background to ABC

The Audit Bureau of Circulations was founded in 1931, initially to provide an independent verification of circulation/ data figures to facilitate the buying and selling of advertising space within national newspapers. The various publisher associations became involved and ABC has developed into the organisation we know today, providing independent verification of data for print, lists/databases, exhibitions and electronic media.

ABC is a non profit organisation governed by a council of permanent and elected representatives from advertisers, advertising agencies, media owners and their representative trade bodies.

Training

ABC offers training for external accountancy firms to encourage best practice when carrying out circulation audits and to ensure compliance with ABC rules. Details of the training are available from the ABC website (**www.abc.org.uk** – click on 'about ABC' tab – click on 'Training' tab).

---

[1] *Firms may consider whether there are additional terms which it would be appropriate to incorporate with the engagement letter by agreement between the three parties. It will be important to ensure that any such additional terms are consistent with those in the model tripartite agreement.*

Communications

The ABC Forum facilitates two-way communication between ABC and accountants. The ICAEW, ABC and accounting firms are represented on the ABC Forum. A list of Forum members can be obtained from the Forum secretary (contact Chris Cantwell, **chris.cantwell@icaew.co.uk**). Details of who to contact at ABC are available from its web site (address above).

The ABC website also provides access to the current rulebooks. The website can be accessed without restriction, and the rulebooks can be downloaded as PDF files.

Scope

1. This Technical Release is intended to give general guidance to members when they compile financial statements for their clients[1]. The guidance applies to the compilation of financial statements of incorporated entities i.e. financial statements prepared in accordance with the Companies Act 1985. Limited Liability Partnerships are included in the scope of this guidance[2]. This guidance supersedes Audit 1/95, *Reports on Accounts Compiled (Prepared) by Accountants* in relation to the financial statements of incorporated entities only.

2. The general principles included in this guidance may also be applied, in appropriate circumstances, to other entities that prepare financial statements in accordance with legislation other than the Companies Act 1985 or in accordance with other comprehensive financial reporting frameworks such as International Financial Reporting Standards.

3. This Technical Release does not provide guidance on 'audit exemption reports' that may be required for certain charitable companies.

Professional ethics

4. In carrying out financial statements compilation engagements, members of the Institute are subject to the ethical and other guidance laid down by the Institute, including the Fundamental Principles of the *Guide to Professional Ethics* (the Guide), as set out in Statement 1.200 and the relevant sections of the *Guide* that deal with objectivity and, where appropriate, independence in relation to preparation of financial statements.

5. The Fundamental Principles are:

   Fundamental Principle 1 – Integrity: A member should behave with integrity in all professional and business relationships. Integrity implies not merely honesty but fair dealing and truthfulness. A member's advice and work must be uncorrupted by self-interest and not be influenced by the interests of other parties.

   Fundamental Principle 2 – Objectivity: A member should strive for objectivity in all professional and business judgements. Objectivity is the state of mind which has regard to all considerations relevant to the task in hand but no other.

   Fundamental Principle 3 – Competence: A member should undertake professional work only where he has the necessary competence required to carry out that work, supplemented where necessary by appropriate assistance or consultation.

   Fundamental Principle 4 – Performance: A member should carry out his professional work with due skill, care, diligence and expedition and with proper regard for the technical and professional standards expected of him as a member.

   Fundamental Principle 5 – Courtesy: A member should conduct himself with courtesy and consideration towards all with whom he comes into contact during the course of performing his work.

---

[1] The term 'compile' is defined as 'to make or compose from other sources'.

[2] References to companies and directors throughout this Technical Release should therefore be substituted with the words Limited Liability Partnerships and designated members accordingly.

[AUDIT 02/04]
Chartered Accountants' Reports on the Compilation of Financial Statements of Incorporated Entities

This guidance is issued by the Audit and Assurance Faculty of the Institute of Chartered Accountants in England & Wales in April 2004. The guidance does not constitute an auditing standard. Professional judgement should be used in its application.

Contents

	Paragraphs
Scope	1 - 3
Professional ethics	4 - 9
Compilation of financial statements	10
Terms of engagement	11 - 13
Content of financial statements	14
Responsibilities of directors	15 - 17
Planning	18
Procedures	19 - 21
Documentation	22
Management representations	23
Misleading financial statements	24 - 27
Approval of financial statements	28
Accountants' reports	29 - 32

Appendices

A Example extracts to insert into an engagement letter 6

B Example reports 8

No responsibilities for loss occasioned to any person acting or refraining from action as a result of any material in this Technical Release can be accepted by the Institute.

Members should not, therefore, compile financial statements or permit their names to be associated with financial statements that they consider may be misleading. 6

The part of the *Guide* dealing with objectivity and independence in relation to the preparation of financial statements indicates that independence, in the sense in which it is sometimes applied to audit assignments, is not essential to engagements to prepare financial statements, provided that objectivity is not impaired. It highlights that there are certain factors, which by their nature are a threat to objectivity in any professional role and considers appropriate safeguards. These areas of risk include: 7

- family and other relationships;
- loans;
- goods and services: hospitality or other benefits;
- beneficial interests in shares and other investments; and
- acting as a business adviser and investing in or sponsoring or promoting shares.

The relevant section (Statement 1.201, Section C) advises against, inter-alia: 8

- receiving a loan from a client (unless from financial institutions in the normal course of business, under normal commercial terms and where the significance of the loan does not cast doubt on objectivity);
- accepting hospitality, goods or services unless the value of any benefits are modest;
- acting for clients where the value of an investment in the client is material to the financial circumstances of the investing member or firm.

This section also makes reference to conflicts of interest. The relevant Statement, 1.205, considers possible safeguards, including disclosure of conflicts of interest to all relevant parties. 9

Compilation of financial statements

When compiling financial statements, the accountants use their accounting expertise to collect, classify and present accounting information from the sources made available to them. This normally entails summarising detailed data into a manageable and understandable form. There is no requirement for the accountants to test the assertions underlying the information. This guidance is not designed and does not enable the accountants to express any assurance on the financial statements. Nevertheless, users of the financial statements derive benefit because Chartered Accountants are required to carry out work with professional competence and due care and are subject to the ethical and other guidance of the Institute. 10

Terms of engagement

There needs to be a clear understanding between the client and the accountants regarding the terms of the engagement. The client needs to understand from the outset the responsibility which the accountants accept in relation to the financial statements. This is best dealt with by a discussion followed by an engagement letter. The engagement letter includes matters such as: 11

- the Board of Directors as addressees;
- the directors will be responsible for the reliability, accuracy and completeness of the accounting records and for the truth and fairness of the financial statements themselves, as specified in the Companies Act 1985;

- the information to be supplied by the client to the accountants and a confirmation that any other information that the accountants consider necessary for the performance of the engagement will be supplied[3];
- the nature of the engagement;
- the accountants will make enquiries of management and undertake any procedures that they judge appropriate but are under no obligation to perform procedures that may be required for assurance engagements such as audits or reviews;
- the engagement cannot be relied on to disclose errors, fraud, weaknesses in internal controls or other irregularities;
- an audit will not be carried out and so no opinion will be given and no assurance either implied or expressed;
- the accounting bases on which the financial statements will be prepared and the fact that any known departures will be disclosed;
- the accountants' obligation not to allow their name to be associated with misleading financial statements;
- written management representations may be required prior to the completion of the engagement and the issuing of the accountants' report;
- the form of report to be issued.

12 In addition, after discussions with the client, it may be appropriate to include a section on the limitation of the accountants' liability.

13 Appendix A sets out example extracts (including a limitation of liability clause) which can be inserted into an engagement letter, alongside the accountants' standardised engagement terms.

Content of financial statements

14 Financial statements prepared under the Companies Act 1985 are required to give a true and fair view. They are subject to the accounting and disclosure requirements of that Act and applicable accounting standards including, where relevant, the Financial Reporting Standard for Smaller Entities (FRSSE).

Responsibilities of directors

15 The directors are responsible for ensuring that the company maintains proper accounting records and for preparing financial statements which give a true and fair view and have been prepared in accordance with the Companies Act 1985.

16 The directors are required to:

- select suitable accounting policies and then apply them consistently;
- make judgements and estimates that are reasonable and prudent; and
- prepare financial statements on a going concern basis unless it is inappropriate to presume that the company will continue in business.

The directors are also responsible for safeguarding the assets of the company and for taking steps for the prevention and detection of fraud and other irregularities.

---

[3] *Paragraph 3 of Statement 1.306* Professional conduct *in relation to defaults or illegal acts states that where a member is engaged to prepare or audit accounts, he should always make it clear that he can only do so on the basis of full disclosure of all information relevant to the work in question. If the client will not agree, the member should not act for him.*

The engagement to compile the financial statements cannot be regarded as providing assurance on the adequacy of the company's systems or on the incidence of fraud, non-compliance with laws and regulations or weaknesses in internal controls. Engaging external accountants to compile the financial statements does not relieve the directors of their responsibilities in this respect.   17

Planning

The accountants plan engagements to compile financial statements. The level of planning may vary according to the complexity of the company's accounting records and the accountants' experience of the business.   18

Procedures

The accountants obtain a general understanding of the business and operations of the company. They need to be familiar with the accounting principles and practices of the sector in which the company operates and with the form and content of the accounting information that is appropriate in the circumstances. The accountants' understanding of the business is usually obtained through experience of the company or enquiry of the company's management and staff.   19

The accountants consider whether the financial statements are consistent with their understanding of the business and whether the financial statements are misleading. In so doing, the accountants make such enquiries of management and undertake such procedures as they judge appropriate but are under no obligation to perform procedures that may be required for assurance engagements such as audits or reviews.   20

The accountants consider methods available, such as disclosure checklists or software packages, to check that relevant disclosures have been made on the basis of information available.   21

Documentation

There is no mandatory requirement to document the work that has been carried out. However, where the quality of the accountants' work is subsequently challenged, documentation may help the accountants demonstrate the adequacy of the work performed and that the engagement was carried out in accordance with the terms of engagement. The level of documentation may vary according to the complexity of the company's accounting records and accounting procedures, according to the accountants' experience with the business and whether any matters have arisen during the course of the engagement.   22

Management representations

In compiling financial statements, the accountants are normally reliant on representations by management, particularly in relation to estimates and the reliability, accuracy and completeness of information provided. The accountants therefore consider obtaining written management representations on these matters.   23

Misleading financial statements

24 Financial statements prepared under the Companies Act 1985 are required to give a true and fair view. Without carrying out an assurance service, the accountants cannot form an opinion as to the truth and fairness of the view given by financial statements. During the course of the engagement, however, matters may come to light which appear to indicate that the financial statements may be misleading. In such cases the accountants discuss the matter with the directors with a view to agreeing appropriate adjustments and/or disclosures to be made in the financial statements. Where there are departures from accounting standards and appropriate disclosures are made in the financial statements, the accountants may wish to highlight these disclosures in their report by way of an explanatory paragraph (see Appendix B for example wording for such a report).

25 In certain circumstances, adjustments and/or disclosures that the accountants consider appropriate may not be made in the financial statements, or appropriate information may not be provided to the satisfaction of the accountants. If the accountants consider that the financial statements are therefore misleading then they should withdraw from the engagement and should not permit their name to be associated with the financial statements.

26 In considering whether financial statements are misleading, the accountants consider whether the financial statements appear to be appropriate in form and free from material misstatements that appear obvious to them as a result of, for example:
- misclassifications in the financial statements;
- mistakes in the application of, or non-disclosure of known departures from, any relevant statutory, regulatory or other reporting requirements, including applicable accounting standards and non-disclosure of significant changes in accounting policies;
- other significant matters of which the accountants are aware.

27 When the accountants withdraw from an engagement, they should normally explain to their client their reasons for withdrawing, unless this would constitute a breach of legal or other regulatory requirement (such as the 'tipping off' provisions of the money laundering legislation).

Approval of financial statements

28 Financial statements should be approved and signed by the directors before the accountants' report is signed. The directors are statutorily responsible for the financial statements. The Companies Act 1985 requires that directors approve the financial statements and that the balance sheet states the name of the director signing the financial statements on behalf of the Board. The directors of companies that are audit exempt are required to acknowledge, on the face of the balance sheet, their responsibilities for keeping proper accounting records and for preparing true and fair financial statements as well as entitlement of the company to exemption from audit.

Accountants' reports

29 The accountants' report helps users derive comfort from the involvement of Chartered Accountants who are subject to the ethical and other guidance issued by the Institute in relation to the preparation of the financial statements. It also helps prevent users from deriving unwarranted assurance from the financial statements

where no audit has been performed and no opinion is being expressed by the accountants.

The accountants' report on the financial statements of a company includes: 30

- a title identifying the persons to whom the report is addressed (usually the Board of Directors) and including the words 'Chartered Accountant's / Accountants' Report to...'[4];
- a statement that, in accordance with the engagement letter, the accountants have compiled the financial statements which comprise [state the primary financial statements such as the Profit and Loss Account, the Balance Sheet, the Cash Flow Statement, the Statement of Total Recognised Gains and Losses] and the related notes from the accounting records and information and explanations supplied by the client;
- a statement that the report is made to the Company's Board of Directors as a body in accordance with the terms of engagement. An explanation as to the work involved and the purpose of the work and that, to the fullest extent permitted by law, no responsibility will be accepted for the work or the report to anyone other than the Company and the Company's Board of Directors, as a body.
- a statement that the accountants have carried out the engagement in accordance with technical guidance issued by the Institute and that they have complied with the ethical guidance laid down by the Institute relating to members undertaking the compilation of financial statements;
- a statement that the directors have acknowledged their responsibility to prepare financial statements that give a true and fair view under the Companies Act 1985;
- a statement that the accountants have not carried out an audit of the financial statements, verified the accuracy or completeness of the accounting records or information and explanations supplied, and that the accountants do not express any opinion on the financial statements;
- the name and signature of the accountant and any appropriate designation (but not 'Registered Auditor');
- the date of the report.

The financial statements contain a reference to the fact that they are unaudited either on the front cover or on each page of the financial statements. 31

Examples of accountants' reports are set out in Appendix B. The second example is of an accountants' report with an explanatory paragraph, as discussed in paragraph 24. 32

---

[4] *Members should have regard to the Institute's Regulations relating to the use of the description 'Chartered Accountants'. Generally, a member may use the description if signing reports in a personal capacity. A firm may only use the description if it complies with the relevant Regulations concerning the control of firms and general affiliates of the Institute. Where a firm is not permitted to use the term Chartered Accountant(s), the title 'Accountants' Report to...' should be used, rather than 'Chartered Accountants' Report to....'.*

Appendix A – Example extracts to insert into an engagement letter for the compilation of the unaudited financial statements of a limited company

Responsibilities of directors

1   As directors of the company, you are responsible for maintaining proper accounting records and for preparing financial statements which give a true and fair view and which have been prepared in accordance with the Companies Act 1985 (*the Act*).

2   In preparing the financial statements, you are required to:
    - select suitable accounting policies and then apply them consistently;
    - make judgements and estimates that are reasonable and prudent; and
    - prepare the financial statements on the going concern basis unless it is inappropriate to presume that the company will continue in business.

3   You are responsible for keeping proper accounting records which disclose with reasonable accuracy at any time the financial position of the company and for ensuring that the financial statements comply with *the Act*. You are also responsible for safeguarding the assets of the company and hence for taking reasonable steps for the prevention and detection of fraud and other irregularities.

4   You are also responsible for determining whether, in respect of each financial year, the company meets the conditions for exemption from audit, as set out in Section 249A [or 249AA] of *the Act* and for determining whether, in respect of that year, the exemption is not available for any of the reasons set out in Section 249B.

5   You have undertaken to make available to us, as and when required, all the company's accounting records and related financial information, including minutes of management and shareholders' meetings, necessary to carry out our work. You will make full disclosure to us of all relevant information.

Scope of the accountants' work

6   You have asked us to assist you in the preparation of the financial statements. We will compile the annual financial statements for your approval based on the accounting records maintained by you and the information and explanations given to us by you. We shall plan our work on the basis that no report is required by statute or regulation for the year, unless you inform us in writing to the contrary. In carrying out our engagement we will make enquiries of management and undertake any procedures that we judge appropriate but are under no obligation to perform procedures that may be required for assurance engagements such as audits or reviews.

7   You have advised us that the company is exempt from an audit of the financial statements. We will not carry out any work to determine whether or not the company is entitled to audit exemption. However, should our work indicate that the company is not entitled to the exemption, we will inform you of this.

8   Our work will not be an audit of the financial statements in accordance with Auditing Standards. Consequently, our work will not provide any assurance that the accounting records or the financial statements are free from material misstatement,

whether caused by fraud, other irregularities or error and cannot be relied on to identify weaknesses in internal controls.

Since we have not carried out an audit, nor confirmed in any way the accuracy or reasonableness of the accounting records maintained by the company, we are unable to provide any assurance as to whether the financial statements that we prepare from those records present a true and fair view.

We have a professional duty to compile financial statements that conform with generally accepted accounting principles from the accounting records and information and explanations given to us. Furthermore, as directors, you have a duty to prepare financial statements that comply with *the Act* and applicable accounting standards. Where we identify that the financial statements do not conform to accepted accounting principles or if the accounting policies adopted are not immediately apparent this will need to be disclosed in the financial statements.

We have a professional responsibility not to allow our name to be associated with financial statements which may be misleading. Therefore, although we are not required to search for such matters, should we become aware, for any reason, that the financial statements may be misleading, we will discuss the matter with you with a view to agreeing appropriate adjustments and/or disclosures in the financial statements. In circumstances where adjustments and/or disclosures that we consider appropriate are not made or where we are not provided with appropriate information, and as a result we consider that the financial statements are misleading, we will withdraw from the engagement.

As part of our normal procedures, we may request you to provide written confirmation of any information or explanations given by you orally during the course of our work.

Form of the accountants' report

We shall report to the Board of Directors, with any modifications that we consider may be necessary, that in accordance with this engagement letter and in order to assist you to fulfil your responsibilities, we have compiled, without carrying out an audit, the financial statements from the accounting records of the company and from the information and explanations supplied to us.

Liability provisions

We will perform the engagement with reasonable skill and care. The total aggregate liability to the Company and the Board of Directors, as a body, of whatever nature, whether in contract, tort or otherwise, of *[insert name of accountants]* for any losses whatsoever and howsoever caused arising from or in any way connected with this engagement shall not exceed *[insert amount]*[5].

Members may also wish to consider guidance issued in Statement 1.311 of the *Guide to Professional Ethics* on Managing the professional liability of accountants.

---

[5] *This is an example of a liability cap only, which will be one of a number of provisions relating to the accountants' liability and any limitations thereon. For example, the liability provisions will need to make it clear that the accountants are not seeking to exclude those liabilities (such as liability for their own fraud) which cannot be excluded by law.*

Appendix B – Example report chartered accountant's/accountants' report to the board of directors on the unaudited financial statements of XYZ Ltd

In accordance with the engagement letter dated x.x.y, and in order to assist you to fulfil your duties under the Companies Act 1985, we have compiled the financial statements of the company which comprise [state the primary financial statements such as the Profit and Loss Account, the Balance Sheet, the Cash Flow Statement, the Statement of Total Recognised Gains and Losses] and the related notes from the accounting records and information and explanations you have given to us.

This report is made to the Company's Board of Directors, as a body, in accordance with the terms of our engagement. Our work has been undertaken so that we might compile the financial statements that we have been engaged to compile, report to the Company's Board of Directors that we have done so, and state those matters that we have agreed to state to them in this report and for no other purpose. To the fullest extent permitted by law, we do not accept or assume responsibility to anyone other than the Company and the Company's Board of Directors, as a body, for our work or for this report.

We have carried out this engagement in accordance with technical guidance issued by the Institute of Chartered Accountants in England and Wales and have complied with the ethical guidance laid down by the Institute relating to members undertaking the compilation of financial statements.

You have acknowledged on the balance sheet for the year ended ... your duty to ensure that the company has kept proper accounting records and to prepare financial statements that give a true and fair view under the Companies Act 1985. You consider that the company is exempt from the statutory requirement for an audit for the year.

We have not been instructed to carry out an audit of the financial statements. For this reason, we have not verified the accuracy or completeness of the accounting records or information and explanations you have given to us and we do not, therefore, express any opinion on the financial statements.

Signature

PQR LLP

[Description of accountant(s)]

Address

Date

EXAMPLE REPORT – EXPLANATORY PARAGRAPH CHARTERED ACCOUNTANT'S/ACCOUNTANTS' REPORT TO THE BOARD OF DIRECTORS ON THE UNAUDITED FINANCIAL STATEMENTS OF XYZ LTD

In accordance with the engagement letter dated x.x.y, and in order to assist you to fulfil your duties under the Companies Act 1985, we have compiled the financial statements of the company which comprise [state the primary financial statements such as the Profit and Loss Account, the Balance Sheet, the Cash Flow Statement, the Statement of Total Recognised Gains and Losses] and the related notes from the accounting records and information and explanations you have given to us.

This report is made to the Company's Board of Directors, as a body, in accordance with the terms of our engagement. Our work has been undertaken so that we might compile the financial statements that we have been engaged to compile, report to the Company's Board of Directors that we have done so, and state those matters that we have agreed to state to them in this report and for no other purpose. To the fullest extent permitted by law, we do not accept or assume responsibility to anyone other than the Company and the Company's Board of Directors, as a body, for our work or for this report.

We have carried out this engagement in accordance with technical guidance issued by the Institute of Chartered Accountants in England and Wales and have complied with the ethical guidance laid down by the Institute relating to members undertaking the compilation of financial statements.

You have acknowledged on the balance sheet for the year ended ... your duty to ensure that the company has kept proper accounting records and to prepare financial statements that give a true and fair view under the Companies Act 1985. You consider that the company is exempt from the statutory requirement for an audit for the year.

We have not been instructed to carry out an audit of the financial statements. For this reason, we have not verified the accuracy or completeness of the accounting records or information and explanations you have given to us and we do not, therefore, express any opinion on the financial statements.

We draw your attention to note x in the financial statements which discloses and explains a departure from applicable accounting standards. The company has not depreciated its goodwill held in the financial statements in the year and this is a departure from the Financial Reporting Standard for Smaller Entities (Effective June 2002) and from the Companies Act 1985.

Signature

PQR LLP

[Description of accountant(s)]

Address

Date

[AUDIT 03/04]
Auditing Implications of IFRS Transition

This guidance is issued by the Audit and Assurance Faculty of the Institute of Chartered Accountants in England and Wales in July 2004 to assist auditors to assess and comment on the state of their clients' readiness for the transition to International Financial Reporting Standards and prepare for the auditing implications. This guidance does not constitute an auditing standard. Professional judgement should be used in its application.

Contents

1 Background

2 Purpose of technical release

3 What auditors should expect management to be doing

4 What auditors should expect audit committees to be doing

5 What auditors themselves should be doing

6 Potential effects on 2005 financial statements

No responsibility for loss occasioned to any person acting or refraining from action as a result of any material in this Technical Release can be accepted by the Institute.

Summary

Listed companies in the UK must prepare their financial statements for the year ending 31 December 2005 in compliance with International Financial Reporting Standards (IFRS). The conversion to IFRS will be complex and detailed for many companies and recent research and surveys on the state of preparedness for this important change are not encouraging. The combination of this complexity and the apparent lack of preparation results in an increase in risk for auditors as they prepare to audit financial statements prepared under IFRS.

This technical release (TR), gives guidance on what auditors should expect the management and the audit committees at their clients to be doing as they manage the transition to financial reporting in accordance with IFRS. It also sets out good practice on what auditors themselves should be doing in the period up to the first audit under IFRS.

Most importantly, auditors should be actively assessing the quality of their clients' transition processes and the judgements that are being made to enable the change to IFRS. If they believe that these are not adequate or could potentially not meet the standards they will require in their 2005 audit, they should discuss those issues with their clients as soon as possible to alert them to the potential effect on the reporting timetable or the audit report.

Section 1 Background

1. Listed companies in the UK have to prepare their consolidated financial statements in compliance with European Union (EU) approved International Financial Reporting Standards (IFRS) for financial years beginning on or after 1 January 2005. The first time that companies will present a full set of IFRS accounts will be for the year ending 31 December 2005. In March 2003, the Department of Trade and Industry (DTI) issued proposals that would allow all other UK companies to adopt IFRS voluntarily from 2005 if they wish. Requirements for companies listed on the Alternative Investment Markets (AIM) are subject to consultation.

2. At the end of March 2004, the International Accounting Standards Board (IASB) published the finalised standards that companies will need to comply with in 2005. However, the Regulation (EC) No.1606 2002 requires that, in preparing their consolidated accounts companies only apply those standards that are endorsed by the EU. Two standards have not yet been endorsed by the EU: IAS 32, *Financial instruments: Disclosure and Presentation*, and IAS 39, *Financial Instruments: Recognition and Measurement*, but this should not be a barrier to preparing for the 2005 transition. The International Financial Reporting Interpretation Committee (IFRIC) also publishes interpretations which will be mandatory for the first set of IFRS statements. Prior to the creation of the IFRIC, interpretations were issued by the Standing Interpretations Committee (SIC) and some of their interpretations remain in force.

First-time adoption issues

3. In June 2003, the IASB published IFRS 1, *First-time adoption of international financial reporting standards*. As new standards are published, and existing financial standards improved, there have been, and there are likely to be, continuing amendments to this standard. IFRS 1 sets out how companies should apply IFRS for the first time, requiring one full year of comparative financial information. For 2005

financial statements, this will be the year ending 31 December 2004. The key date of transition at the beginning of this period, 1 January 2004, has already passed. IFRS 1 requires the preparation of an opening balance sheet as at this date. The first set of IFRS compliant statements will also need to include extensive disclosures to explain the transition to IFRS from UKGAAP. If IAS 39 is not adopted, then it is possible that the risk profile and complexity of the statements will change.

The current state of preparedness

4　Research carried out by academics[1] (due to be published later in the year) indicates that:

- although there is strong support for the principle of common accounting standards throughout Europe, realisation among practitioners in companies and in audit firms about the scale and complexity of the project is still growing;
- the delay in adoption of all standards by the EU is undermining preparations for change;
- education is a major issue; there is a shortage of knowledgeable practitioners. Company boards and audit committees may not understand the changes and there are also concerns about how much key users of financial statements, such as banks and analysts, will be aware of the specific impact on individual company results;
- accountants are accustomed to incremental change, and initially some may find that such major conceptual shifts are difficult to absorb and apply correctly to complex accounting issues. This is likely to increase the risks of mistakes being made in preparation of financial statements and of auditors failing to pick them up;
- there are concerns that some companies may view the transition as an opportunity to bury bad news; and
- there is a growing expectation among audit firms that more audit reports will be qualified because companies have not managed the transition process properly and therefore will not be in a position to prepare IFRS compliant financial statements.

5　This research is supported by the findings of recent surveys:

- a survey by PricewaterhouseCoopers[2] of listed companies in Europe indicated that one in ten companies had not begun their IFRS project, with less than a third of companies having IFRS transition projects fully set up and running.
- another survey carried out by ATOS KPMG Consulting[3] revealed that 26% of all UK companies have said that they will not be ready for the 2005 deadline.
- a survey carried out by Accountancy Age in May 2004 highlighted that finance staff in UK listed companies were less prepared for the impact of IFRS than they were three months earlier because companies had previously underestimated the impact of the transition to IFRS. The survey revealed that nearly a third of FTSE 350 companies were still unsure of how to rate the readiness of their staff.

---

[1] *Stella Fearnley, Tony Hines, Annette Gillies and Caroline Willett from Portsmouth Business School are carrying out a study of attitudes and beliefs in the UK about IFRS with company directors, auditors and regulators. The same individuals have been re-interviewed after a two-year gap.*

[2] *The results of the PwC survey can be found in its publication,* International Financial Reporting Standards, Ready to take the plunge *(May 2004)*

[3] *The results of the ATOS KPMG Consulting survey are published in its publication,* International Financial Reporting Standards, the challenge facing businesses *(June 2004)*

- most recently, in July 2004, a survey carried out by the ICAEW[4] indicated that while 77% of listed companies state that they are prepared for IAS, most of these (61%) report that they are only 'fairly well prepared', suggesting that there is still some work to do.

Analysts and investors are also starting to engage with companies on the transition to IFRS, as they will soon have to work with revised financial information. The way that such information is presented will influence investors' views of companies' transparency and preparedness. Some feel that transition to IFRS may have a substantial effect the way company performance is viewed, For example a report published by Fitch Ratings[5] states that, *"it cannot rule out the possibility that the additional disclosure and information contained in the accounts could lead to rating changes due to an improved perception of risk based on the enhanced information available."* Almost certainly, more enquiries are likely to emanate from the markets in the near future.

IFRS are different

It is easy to make a high-level comparison of UK GAAP and IFRS and conclude that there are few major differences; however there are many important detailed differences, many of which will be discovered only by a thorough analysis of a company's transactions and exposures. Matters that need to be considered include:

- changes brought by the move to IFRS will mean a major change in the actual format of the accounts;
- differences in definitions may mean that items previously classified in one way will need to be classified differently;
- some items that are not recognised under UK GAAP are recognised as assets or liabilities under IFRS, whilst others may cease to be recognised;
- some items may have to be measured differently in the accounts of an individual subsidiary and in the consolidated accounts;
- more extensive disclosure requirements will result in greater data capture needs; and
- some changes in accounting policies may require accounting systems to give different information.

The transition to IFRS is also made more difficult by the changes to company law. A number of the regulations supersede parts of the Companies Act, resulting in some complex reporting and disclosure requirements.

However, it is not the purpose of this TR to give a comprehensive description of the differences between IFRS and UK GAAP. Readers requiring such information are referred to the ICAEW's publication, *The Convergence Handbook* which will be revised and updated later this year.

Section 2 Purpose of Technical Release

With the technical complexity of IFRS, the tight transition timescales and the apparent lack of current preparedness, there will be an increase in risk for the review of interim information and the audit of 2005 financial statements of listed companies. The adoption of IFRS brings new challenges for management and auditors. The

---

[4] *The results of the ICAEW survey are published in a document,* Closing the GAAP *(July 2004)*

[5] *The Fitch Ratings research results are published in its special report entitled,* Mind the GAAP *(May 2004)*

review of interims typically places greater reliance on techniques which will be difficult to apply in an environment where there is limited history and where other material, such as management accounts, may be prepared on a different accounting basis. With the adoption of new accounting policies and accounting estimates, there is an increased risk of error. In this context it should be noted that IAS 8 *Accounting Policies, Changes in Accounting Estimates and Errors* requires entities to correct all material prior period errors by restating the relevant amounts in the prior period financial statements. This will potentially result in more restatements of financial statements than we have been accustomed to in the UK as FRS 3 *Reporting financial performance* requires restatements for material adjustments only where they arise from the correction of fundamental errors, a subtle but potentially significant difference in wording. The APB, with whom the Faculty has liaised in preparing this TR is currently drafting guidance on the effect of the introduction of IFRS and the requirements of auditing standards. It expects to issue a Bulletin in August 2004.

11 The guidance in this TR aims to help auditors to both assess and comment on their clients' transition process and their state of IFRS preparedness. Accordingly it provides auditors with guidance in three key areas:

- what auditors should expect management to be doing;
- what auditors should expect audit committees to be doing; and
- what the auditors themselves need to consider.

Each section includes key questions that auditors might wish to consider.

12 Although primarily directed at auditors, management and audit committees may also find parts of this guidance useful.

Section 3 What auditors should expect management to be doing

Clarification of directors' responsibilities

13 The directors' responsibility for running a company implicitly requires them to take reasonable steps to ensure that the company implements IFRS successfully without material impact on the business. The directors will need to review the impact on the business and ensure that there are appropriate plans to train the staff, update the accounting systems, and implement changes in reporting encompassing all significant business units.

Communication Requirements

14 There is increasing pressure on companies to demonstrate their IFRS preparedness. The Committee of European Securities Regulators (CESR) recommended in the *European Regulation on the application of IFRS in 2005* (issued in December 2003) that:

- companies explain, in their 2003 Annual Report, how they intend to carry out the transition to IFRS, with listed companies being encouraged to explain in a narrative format the key differences between their present accounting policies and the ones that they know with sufficient certainty that they will have to apply under IFRS;
- once a company is able to quantify the impact of the change on its 2004 financial statements in a sufficiently reliable manner, it is encouraged to disclose the relevant quantified information;

- companies start to apply the IFRS recognition and measurement principles for interim financial reports in 2005, including the comparative information from the corresponding previous period; and
- the first complete set of 2005 financial statements be prepared and presented under IFRS by listed companies in Europe, should have at least one year of comparatives.

The Financial Services Authority has agreed to the CESR recommendations by virtue of its membership and has drawn attention to them in its monthly newsletter, LIST! (November 2003) outlining them as best practice for companies.

Assess the need for resource and identify training requirements at an early date

The need for resources depends on the complexity of the accounting and system issues. At the beginning of the process it is essential that companies carefully assess and plan for the number and skills of staff required for a timely and effective transition. The business will need to assess the training required by the employees, which should extend beyond the finance function. This assessment should include the needs of the company's subsidiaries, which will differ depending on the degree of centralisation or devolution of the group's accounting functions. Overseas businesses may present particular challenges. Needs will differ between EU and non-EU operations, depending on the extent to which a jurisdiction has already adopted IFRS.

Identify gaps between current accounting policies and IFRS

It is important that the transition process starts with a comprehensive comparison between the business' current accounting policies and the requirements of IFRS. Some policies will need to change and new policies will need to be set. Management will have a choice in the selection of some policies. Companies should also assess the financial impact of the accounting policy changes so that informed decisions can be made.

Identify changes in financial data and additional information to meet the revised disclosure requirements

Once the accounting issues have been identified, the impact on systems and processes can be assessed. Any changes will need to be implemented in a sustainable way. If a company assembles information in a less than rigorous and structured way for 2005 (planning more changes later) risk will be increased. The areas that companies should consider include:

- the need to revise and rollout updated IFRS group accounting manuals;
- the need for changes in the capture of data which may be more complex than companies realise;
- alignment with current system projects as amendments to existing accounting systems may be required to cope with the new data needs;
- the format of group reporting packs and preparation of consolidated accounts, for instance capturing segmental information;
- whether individual business units will report in accordance with IFRS for group reporting purposes or whether the business units will provide information to the central team who will then convert this to IFRS;
- whether the central project team has sufficient knowledge of the local accounting practices of the group's subsidiaries, to plan for the transition;

- whether the company has resources with the appropriate level of skills and expertise to generate all the financial data required under IFRS; and
- whether assistance will be required from external advisors.

Identify the impact on business issues and manage these

19   The company's other business needs should be considered, including:

- review of bank covenant arrangements and negotiating amendments as required;
- review deal structures;
- communication plan to discuss the impact of transition to IFRS with analysts and shareholders;
- prepare 2004 and 2005 budgets on an IFRS basis and explain the differences from UK GAAP;
- establish the impact on reserves and dividend policy;
- re-assess impact on taxation and current structures;
- the impact on remuneration and incentive schemes; and
- the particular consequences for regulated business and their capital adequacy.

Planning the transition process

20   In planning their transition process, companies should bear the following in mind:

- getting commitment throughout the organisation (including the board, audit committee, business units, IT, human resources, investor relations);
- training relevant staff in IFRS;
- identifying the data needed to generate the IFRS statements;
- building pro formas for financial statements, budgets, and reporting packages;
- converting systems or developing pragmatic solutions as necessary;
- testing the systems;
- parallel running the new systems; and
- reporting "live" IFRS information.

Implementation

21   The actual transition process should include:

- preparation of opening balance sheet under IFRS (as at 1 January 2004);
- preparation of the comparative figures for December 2004 under IFRS (closing balance sheet and income statement);
- preparation of the interims in 2005, with comparatives;
- live IFRS reporting for the 2005 accounts; and
- running the business under IFRS.

22   The appendix sets out a fuller timetable on how this might proceed.

Operating and Financial Review (OFR)

23   In May 2004, the DTI published a consultative document on the draft regulations on the OFR and the Directors' Report. The draft regulations would require companies to publish an account of its business, objectives and strategy, a review of developments over the past year and a description of the main risks with their annual financial statements. It would also need to cover prospects for the future. It is also proposed that in addition to their current duties in respect of directors' reports,

auditors should report whether, in their opinion, the directors have prepared the OFR after due and careful enquiry. The implications of these requirements are likely to coincide with the first set of IFRS financial statements in 2005. This will therefore place further additional burden on companies and auditors as the financial commentary in the OFR will need to be based on IFRS data.

Additional Considerations for US registrants

There are additional specific considerations for US registrants which need to be considered:

- the introduction of IFRS will coincide with the first year of application of Section 404 of the Sarbanes-Oxley Act to foreign private issuers. This requires management to report on the effectiveness of their systems of internal control over financial reporting and auditors to attest to that assessment. Auditing Standard 2, issued by the Public Company Accounting Oversight Board in the US, sets a high standard for the quality of companies' processes and procedures, their documentation and management testing. Achievement of this benchmark may be challenging for the IFRS transition processes, in particular where companies are working with limited resources to tight reporting timetables.
- companies will be converting their UK GAAP accounts to IFRS for 2005. Historically those not producing full US financial statements will have included in their 20F filings a bridging reconciliation of their key financial data from UK GAAP to US GAAP. From 2005 onwards, this bridging statement will need to reconcile the IFRS data and comparatives to US GAAP basis. This further reconciliation will provide additional challenges. This reconciliation should be considered as part of the transition project so that unexpected anomalies do not arise later in the project, closer to the date of first IFRS reporting.

Subsidiaries

The consolidated accounts of listed groups must be prepared in accordance with IFRS. Although companies that comprise the group do not have the same requirement, they will have the option of doing so. In the long term, this will help to simplify the consolidation process.

Where all of a company's subsidiaries are based in the UK, management will need to ensure that the transition issues are properly managed by the whole group. There are choices in IFRS, as with UK GAAP, and management should be making policy decisions for the consolidation. Auditors will need to confirm whether or not similar policies are being applied in respect of each subsidiary.

Overseas subsidiaries may present some problems depending on whether IFRS are allowed, required or prohibited in the countries in which the subsidiaries operate. Where IFRS are allowed or required, subject to timing issues, the situation will be similar to that of a UK subsidiary. Where IFRS are not allowed, then there are two potential problems. Firstly, there will be a need for additional accounting to allow the financial statements to be restated for consolidation purposes. Secondly, consideration will need to be given to whether or not the local management have IFRS expertise to be able to prepare the restated figures.

Internal audit

Management will need to consider what role the internal audit function may be able to fulfil in the transition process. Internal audit may be well placed to assist with the project management of the transition process and, in particular with the planning and design of the project plan, its execution, monitoring, evaluation and completion.

29 The box on the following page outlines some key questions that auditors might wish to consider asking of management.

What auditors might wish to ask their clients' management

- Have they properly estimated the degree of resource with the necessary skill and knowledge required to manage the transition process?

- Do they have sufficient access to the specialist expertise that will be required, valuations, for example?

- Have they properly estimated the magnitude of change inherent in the transition process?

- Are they fully aware of the timetables and deliverables?

- Have they started the transition process?

- Is there effective project management with senior management commitment and sponsorship?

- Are they undertaking a thorough diagnostic exercise to understand the accounting policy changes necessary before moving into the detail of restatement processes?

- Is the entire group of companies (not just the head office) sufficiently involved in the process?

- Where IFRS are being adopted by individual companies, do they understand that there are other implications of IFRS transition including reviewing deal structures, analysing the impact on reserves and dividends, and re-assessing impact on taxation?

- Are they considering how to build their data collection architecture and process for the future? Spreadsheets are not a long-term option.

- Are they communicating to third party stakeholders as soon as they have an understanding of the impact of the IFRS transition?

- Is a realistic view being taken of the 2005 reporting timetable, given the challenge of the IFRS transition to the company?

- Has management put into place robust mechanisms to prevent and detect anyone taking advantage of the IFRS transition to deliberately misstate financial reports?

- If the company is a US registrant, are they planning for the additional challenges that they will have to meet?

Section 4 What auditors should expect audit committees to be doing

30 The board has overall responsibility for the preparation of the financial statements. These are existing responsibilities set out in company law and the Combined Code. In practice, the board usually delegates this responsibility to the audit committee who then has an oversight responsibility for the preparation of the accounts. This framework is confirmed and established through detailed terms of reference by the board. Auditors should engage early with the audit committee at their client in relation to the transition to IFRS to discuss the quality and progress of the transition project.

new standards by the IASB for which early adoption will be encouraged. Auditors need to keep abreast of these developments and ensure that clients are preparing their first IFRS financial statements on the appropriate IFRS basis.

Audit documentation needs to provide a clear audit trail of the judgements and conclusions reached

Firms will need to consider whether their approach and audit work programmes need to be amended and updated for an IFRS environment. 41

The transition to IFRS will require auditors to place more reliance on the work of experts in more complex areas such as valuations of employee share options or non-traded financial instruments. They will therefore need to obtain sufficient appropriate audit evidence of the work that has been carried out by the experts and how they have arrived at their judgements. Auditors will need to assess the adequacy of the judgement made by the experts for the purposes of an audit. The impact of this assessment will need to be recorded clearly. Auditors should refer to the requirements of SAS 520[6] *Using the work of an expert*. 42

Communication responsibilities

The auditor needs to have continuing communication with management, the board and its audit committee to ensure that they are all fully aware of their responsibilities and the scope and progress of their company's transition project. In particular the auditor needs to consider: 43

- whether the transition project is capable of ensuring complete and accurate quantification of the accounting policy differences at the date of transition;
- how embedded is the transition process within the company's business; and
- the principles of SAS 610[7] *Communication of audit matters to those charged with governance (revised)* suggest that the auditors should provide the board or audit committee with their appraisal of the quality of the company's IFRS transition project and IFRS readiness, highlighting those issues that may impact the audit of the first IFRS financial statements.

These matters will ordinarily be discussed initially with management in order to clarify facts and issues, and to provide management with the opportunity to provide further information and explanation. 44

Planning

When planning their work, auditors need to: 45

- agree with management the nature of, and timetable for, auditor involvement, assistance and reporting throughout the transition process;
- determine the nature, extent and quality of audit evidence they will need to support the judgements made and conclusions reached by management in the transition to IFRS and in their preparation of the first set of IFRS financial statements. They should communicate their information needs to management;
- consider the particular issues affecting the audit of restated comparative figures; and

---

[6] to be superseded by ISA 620 Using the work of an expert

[7] to be superseded by ISA 260 Communication of audit matters to those charged with governance

- consider to what extent unadjusted audit differences, arising on UK GAAP audits at the transition balance sheet date and for the comparative period, that do not eliminate on transition to IFRS, impact on the audit opinion on the first IFRS financial statements. In so doing, the auditor will need to consider the level of audit materiality in respect of IFRS financial statements in accordance with SAS 220[8] *Materiality and the audit*.

Meeting the challenge of fraud

46 In recent years there has been increasing concern amongst investors about the problem of aggressive earnings management which has changed the focus of thinking around fraud. Whilst misappropriation of assets is still an issue, the potential for aggressive earnings management fraud is often more likely to be a material risk of misstatement in the financial statements. Auditors will need to be alert to increased opportunities for the manipulation of the first set of accounts on the transition to IFRS. Specific risk areas include:

- the restatement of the opening balances;
- increased pressure on management to deliver results;
- some aspects of IFRS which introduce more choices; and
- increased use of fair values.

Assistance with IFRS transition

47 Auditors may be asked by management to give assistance with their IFRS transition project as a separate engagement to the audit. There are many areas where auditors can valuably assist their clients' transition to IFRS, using their wider knowledge of developments and their particular knowledge of their clients' circumstances. Such assistance could include:

- providing training on IFRS;
- commenting on areas where changes in accounting policy or disclosure are likely;
- assisting with preliminary diagnosis of the impact on financial reporting and accounting systems;
- reviewing accounting issue papers prepared by the client;
- providing technical guidance on IFRS standards and advising on the interpretation of IFRS;
- reviewing and discussing transition project scope, and governance, including roles and responsibilities; and
- reviewing early draft IFRS financial statements.

48 However, auditors will need to consider carefully what work they agree to do to ensure their independence and objectivity is not compromised. It is possible that work done in the transition to IFRS will form part of the evidence on which the audit opinion will rely. Most importantly the final decision on the appropriateness of accounting policies to be adopted must be that of the directors.

Early assurance

49 Auditors may also be called upon by management to give early assurance on the company's state of readiness or on IFRS information that is produced prior to the

---

[8] *to be superseded by ISA 320,* Materiality and the audit

company's first IFRS financial statements. There may also be requests for public reporting. Areas where management may ask for such early assurance could include:

- confirmation of appropriateness of accounting policies and interpretation of IFRS;
- confirmation of appropriateness of additional disclosures in 2004 financial statements relating to their company's IFRS transition; and
- audit or review of the transition balance sheet, 2004 full year or interim IFRS information.

Auditors will need to consider to what extent clients' requests for early assurance or private reports can be met through the auditors continuing technical advice in the context of the statutory audit, or whether a separate audit or review engagement, an agreed upon procedures engagement or an assurance engagement is appropriate in the circumstances. There are limited procedures for review engagements, and on their own, they may not be sufficient to provide evidence that management has selected and appropriately applied IFRS policies in its IFRS balance sheet.

In considering the nature and timing of such engagements, auditors should be conscious of the fact that there are inherent difficulties in giving such early assurances and care is needed:

- it may be difficult to report at an early stage because of the impact of continuing IFRS interpretation prior to the company's first IFRS reporting date;
- auditors need to have regard to the quality of the base data from which the IFRS information has been prepared, and whether this has been audited;
- auditors will need to consider the scope, rigour and completeness of the company's transition to IFRS at the time of the assignment;
- the absence of comparative data will limit the effectiveness of analytical review that the auditors are able to do as part of their work;
- the opening balance sheet is prepared using its best knowledge of the expected standards, interpretations, facts and circumstances that will be applied when the company prepares its first full time financial statements. The possibility cannot be excluded that the accompanying preliminary/initial balance sheet may have to be adjusted; and
- only a complete set of financial statements can give a true and fair view or fairly present the financial information, results and cash flow.

The International Federation of Accountants (IFAC) is currently developing guidance on such reports, which will shortly be available on their web site (www.ifac.org). The IAASB also has this matter under review.

The box on the following page outlines some key considerations for auditors.

Considerations for auditors

- Have you and your audit staff received sufficient IFRS training and do you have an adequate knowledge base to perform IFRS assignments?
- Have you agreed the timing of your involvement with your client's IFRS project with management?
- Have you considered the type of engagement that is appropriate depending on the involvement that the client has requested?
- Can you confirm and evidence that your independence and objectivity has not been compromised?

- Have you agreed the terms of the engagement and the form of any early reporting with management?
- Have you communicated your information needs to the company?
- Have you considered the implication of the IFRS transition for the preparation of the OFR?
- Have you considered whether the company has mechanisms in place to prevent or detect fraud particularly in the following areas: restatement of comparative data, the choices made on accounting treatments and the use of fair value?
- Do your working papers record properly and accurately your judgements and conclusions?
- Have you considered whether you need additional management representations on the IFRS financial statements, especially where management assumptions are key to valuations of assets and liabilities?
- Have you considered any concerns you may have on the timeliness and quality of the transition process and the potential consequences to the company? In particular, are you satisfied that your client's conversion project is capable of complete and accurate quantification of GAAP differences?
- Do you have a communication plan to enable you to discuss issues with the board, audit committee and management?

Section 6 Potential effects on 2005 financial statements

54 Auditors will need to assess carefully the degree of complexity of the transition to IFRS for each of their clients. They will also carefully assess the adequacy of their clients' process to make that transition. Research and surveys, referred to earlier, suggest that it cannot be taken for granted that all companies will complete their IFRS transition for 2005 in a timely and rigorous manner.

55 Where auditors believe that their client's IFRS transition will fall short of the standard they will require for their audit, they need to consider the possible consequences.

56 The company may need to extend the timetable for the production of its 2005 financial statements to give additional time for further work to be performed by themselves or by their auditors. This could have an effect on the timing of their preliminary announcement to the Stock Exchange and the timing of the annual general meeting.

57 The auditors may decide that it is necessary to qualify their audit report on the 2005 financial statements where they believe that IFRS has not been correctly applied. In practice it is to be hoped that any such disagreement between the auditor and the client could be resolved. It is more likely that any such qualification will be in the nature of a limitation of scope because auditors believe that the transition process has been insufficiently robust to enable them to carry out their audit to their satisfaction.

58 If auditors believe that there is a likelihood that either the reporting timetable needs to be extended or that their report could be qualified, they should discuss this with management and the audit committee of their client, as soon as possible.

[AUDIT 01/05]
Chartered Accountants' Reports on the Compilation of Historical Financial Information of Unincorporated Entities

This guidance is issued by the Audit and Assurance Faculty of the Institute of Chartered Accountants in England & Wales in February 2005. The guidance does not constitute an auditing or assurance standard. Professional judgement should be used in its application.

Contents

	Paragraphs
Scope	1 - 6
Professional ethics	7 - 9
Compilation of financial information	10
Accounting basis and format	11 - 13
Terms of engagement	14 - 16
Content of financial information	17
Client responsibilities	18 - 19
Planning	20 - 21
Procedures	22 - 24
Documentation	25
Management representations	26
Misleading financial information	27 - 30
Approval of financial information	31 - 32
Accountants' reports	33 - 36

Appendices

A: Example paragraphs to insert into an engagement letter
B: Example wording for approval of financial information
C: Example report

No responsibility for loss occasioned to any person acting or refraining from action as a result of any material in this Technical Release can be accepted by the Institute.

Scope

1 This Technical Release is intended to give general guidance to members when they compile historical financial information for their clients[1].

2 This guidance covers the compilation of historical financial information of unincorporated entities for a specific purpose or purposes, for example financial information compiled for tax purposes, partnership accounts or the compilation of financial information (without providing any form of assurance) for grant claims.

3 Where, however, accountants are asked to compile a set of financial statements in full compliance with the provisions of UK GAAP for an unincorporated entity then accountants should follow the general principles in Audit 02/04, *Chartered Accountants' Reports on the Compilation of Financial Statements of Incorporated Entities*.

4 Financial information on unincorporated entities may be compiled by accountants for a number of different purposes. Unincorporated entities may not require full financial statements, which give a true and fair view and comply with all applicable accounting standards. This guidance is designed to reflect this and to help ensure that Chartered Accountants are able to provide such services where there is an appropriate framework established for the compilation and presentation of the financial information and that relevant and appropriate disclosures of the accounting basis of compilation are made.

5 This guidance supersedes Audit 1/95, *Reports on Accounts Compiled (Prepared) by Accountants* in relation to the compilation of financial information of unincorporated entities[2].

6 This guidance may also be relevant to the compilation of financial information, other than financial statements[3], of incorporated entities[4].

Professional ethics

7 In carrying out a compilation engagement for an unincorporated entity, members of the Institute are subject to the ethical and other guidance laid down by the Institute, including the Fundamental Principles of the *Guide to Professional Ethics (the Guide)*, as set out in Statement 1.200.

8 The Fundamental Principles are:

Fundamental Principle 1 – Integrity: A member should behave with integrity in all professional and business relationships. Integrity implies not merely honesty but fair dealing and truthfulness. A member's advice and work must be uncorrupted by self-interest and not be influenced by the interests of other parties.

---

[1] The term 'compile' is defined as 'to make or compose from other sources'.

[2] Audit 1/95 has therefore been replaced in its entirety by Audit 02/04 and Audit 01/05.

[3] Guidance on the compilation of financial statements of incorporated entities is set out in Audit 02/04, Chartered Accountants' Reports on the Compilation of Financial Statements of Incorporated Entities.

[4] Attention is drawn to S240 of the Companies Act 1985. Where a company publishes non-statutory accounts (any balance sheet or profit and loss account relating to or purporting to deal with a financial year of the company) it needs to publish a statement with them that they are not the statutory accounts.

Fundamental Principle 2 – Objectivity: a member should strive for objectivity in all professional and business judgements. Objectivity is the state of mind which has regard to all considerations relevant to the task in hand but no other.

Fundamental Principle 3 – Competence: A member should undertake professional work only where he has the necessary competence required to carry out that work, supplemented where necessary by appropriate assistance or consultation.

Fundamental Principle 4 – Performance: A member should carry out his professional work with due skill, care, diligence and expedition and with proper regard for the technical and professional standards expected of him as a member.

Fundamental Principle 5 – Courtesy: A member should conduct himself with courtesy and consideration towards all with whom he comes into contact during the course of performing his work.

Members should not, therefore, compile financial information or permit their names to be associated with financial information that they consider may be misleading for the purpose(s) for which it is being compiled. 9

Compilation of financial information

When compiling financial information, the accountants use their accounting expertise to collect, classify and present accounting information from the sources made available to them. This normally entails summarising detailed data into a manageable and understandable form. There is no requirement for the accountants to test the assertions underlying the information. This guidance is not designed and does not enable the accountants to express any assurance on the financial information being compiled. Nevertheless, users of the financial information compiled derive benefit because Chartered Accountants are required to carry out work with professional competence and due care and are subject to the ethical and other guidance of the Institute. 10

Accounting basis and format

Unlike for the statutory financial statements of companies, there is no statutory requirement for the financial information of unincorporated entities to give a true and fair view. Where financial information is compiled for a specific purpose which is clearly identifiable then it is acceptable to compile the information on an accounting basis other than full UK GAAP. 11

The accountants discuss with clients the purpose and use of the financial information to be compiled and agree an appropriate accounting basis and format for the compilation of the financial information. The accounting basis needs to be clearly defined in order that accountants can compile the information presented. For example, an agreed accounting basis may be financial information compiled on a basis: 12

- enabling profits to be calculated such as to meet the requirements of Section 42 of the Finance Act 1998, as amended by the Finance Act 2002; and
- which provides sufficient and relevant information to enable the completion of a tax return.

Where an appropriate accounting basis and/or format cannot be agreed then the accountants should not accept the engagement. 13

Terms of engagement

14 There needs to be a clear understanding between the client and the accountants of the terms of the engagement.

The client needs to understand from the outset the responsibility which the accountants accept in relation to the financial information being compiled. This is best dealt with by a discussion followed by an engagement letter. The engagement letter includes matters such as:

- the client as addressee;
- the client is responsible for the reliability, accuracy and completeness of the accounting records;
- the client will provide the accountants with all information and explanations relevant to the purpose and compilation of the financial information[5];
- the nature of the engagement, including the purpose and accounting basis of compilation of the financial information;
- the accountants will make enquiries of management and undertake any procedures that they judge appropriate but are under no obligation to perform procedures that may be required for assurance engagements such as audits or reviews;
- the engagement cannot be relied on to disclose errors, fraud, weaknesses in internal controls or other irregularities;
- neither an audit nor a review will be carried out and so no opinion will be given and no assurance either implied or expressed;
- the accounting basis on which the information has been compiled, its purpose and limitations will be disclosed in an accounting policy note to the financial information and referred to in the accountants' report;
- the accountants' obligation not to allow their name to be associated with misleading financial information;
- written management representations may be required prior to the completion of the engagement and the issuing of the accountants' report;
- the client will approve and sign the financial information which includes a statement acknowledging responsibility for the financial information, including the appropriateness of the accounting basis, and for having provided all information and explanations necessary to the accountants for its compilation.
- the form of report to be issued.

15 In addition, it may be appropriate to include a section on the limitation of the accountants' liability.

16 Appendix A sets out example paragraphs (including a limitation of liability clause) which can be inserted into an engagement letter, alongside the accountants' standardised engagement terms.

Content of financial information

17 Financial information is compiled on an appropriate accounting basis and format which is agreed with the client.

---

[5] *Paragraph 3 of Statement 1.306* Professional conduct in relation to defaults or illegal acts *states that where a member is engaged to prepare or audit accounts, he should always make it clear that he can only do so on the basis of full disclosure of all information relevant to the work in question. If the client will not agree, the member should not act for him.*

The accounting basis, purpose and limitations of the information presented should be fully disclosed in an accounting policy note to the financial information and referred to in the accountants' report that accompanies it, so that the financial information is not misleading.

Client responsibilities

Under the terms of the engagement the client is responsible for the reliability, accuracy and completeness of the accounting records of the entity and for the provision and disclosure to the accountants of all information relevant to the purpose and compilation of the financial information. 18

The engagement to compile the financial information cannot be regarded as providing any assurance on the adequacy of the entity's systems or on the incidence of fraud, non-compliance with laws and regulations or weaknesses in internal controls. 19

Planning

The accountants plan engagements to compile financial information. The accountants discuss and agree with the client an appropriate accounting basis and format for compiling the financial information. In considering the appropriateness of the accounting basis, accountants consider the purpose for which the information is being compiled. If the accountants are not satisfied as to the appropriateness of the accounting basis and/or format they should refuse to continue with the engagement. 20

The level of planning will vary according to the complexity and completeness of the entity's accounting records and system and the accountants' experience of the business. 21

Procedures

The accountants obtain a general understanding of the business and operations of the entity. They need to be familiar with the accounting principles and practices of the sector in which the entity operates and with the form and content of the accounting information that is appropriate in the circumstances and is appropriate for the purpose for which the information is being compiled. The accountants' understanding of the business is usually obtained through experience of the entity or enquiry of the entity's management and staff. 22

The accountants consider the underlying financial records of the entity and make such enquiries of management and undertake such procedures as they judge appropriate. They consider whether the financial information is consistent with their understanding of the business, appropriate for the purpose for which it is required and whether it is misleading. Where appropriate, the accountants consider using checklists or software packages, to check that relevant disclosures have been made. 23

The accountants are under no obligation to perform procedures that may be required for assurance engagements such as audits or reviews. 24

Documentation

There is no mandatory requirement to document the work that has been carried out. However, where the quality of the accountants' work is subsequently challenged, documentation may help the accountants demonstrate the adequacy of the work 25 performed and that the engagement was carried out in accordance with the terms of engagement. The level of documentation may vary according to the complexity of the entity's accounting records and accounting procedures, according to the accountants' experience with the business and whether any matters have arisen during the course of the engagement.

Management representations

26 In compiling financial information, the accountants are normally reliant on representations by management, particularly in relation to estimates and the reliability, accuracy and completeness of information provided. They therefore consider obtaining written management representations on these matters.

Misleading financial information

27 During the course of the engagement matters may come to light which appear to indicate that the financial information may be misleading. In such cases the accountants discuss the matter with the client with a view to agreeing appropriate adjustments and/or disclosures to be made in the financial information.

28 In certain circumstances, adjustments and/or disclosures that the accountants consider appropriate may not be made in the financial information, or appropriate information may not be provided to the satisfaction of the accountants. If the accountants consider that the financial information presented is misleading then they should withdraw from the engagement and should not permit their name to be associated with the financial information.

29 In considering whether financial information is misleading, the accountants consider whether the financial information appears to be appropriate for the purpose for which it is compiled, appropriate in respect of the accounting basis agreed and free from material misstatements that appear obvious to them as a result of, for example, misclassifications in the financial information or mistakes in the application of the accounting basis.

30 When the accountants withdraw from an engagement, they should normally explain to their clients their reasons for withdrawing, unless this would constitute a breach of legal or other regulatory requirement (such as the 'tipping off' provisions of the money laundering legislation).

Approval of financial information

31 Although there is no statutory requirement for the financial information of unincorporated entities to be signed or approved by the client it is recommended that the client does approve and sign the financial information.

In so doing, the client acknowledges responsibility for the financial information, including the appropriateness of the accounting basis on which it has been compiled, and for having provided all information and explanations necessary to the accountants for its compilation.

32 Example wording is included at Appendix B.

Accountants' reports

33 The accountants' report helps users derive comfort from the involvement of Chartered Accountants who are subject to the ethical and other guidance issued by the Institute in relation to the preparation of the financial information. It also helps prevent users from deriving unwarranted assurance from the financial information compiled where no audit has been performed and no opinion is being expressed by the accountants.

34 The accountants' report on the financial information of an unincorporated entity includes:

- a title identifying the persons to whom the report is addressed and including the words 'Chartered Accountants'/Accountants' Report to...'[6];
- a statement that, in accordance with the engagement letter, the accountants have compiled the financial information which comprises *[state the primary financial statements that have been compiled, such as the Profit and Loss Account, the Balance Sheet and the Cash Flow Statement and, where relevant, related notes]* from the accounting records and information and explanations supplied by the client;
- a reference to the accounting policy note which sets out the accounting basis of compilation and the purpose and limitations of the financial information;
- a statement that the report is made to the client in accordance with the terms of engagement. An explanation as to the work involved and the purpose of the work and that, to the fullest extent permitted by law, no responsibility will be accepted for the work or the report to anyone other than the client;
- a statement that the accountants have carried out the engagement in accordance with technical guidance issued by the Institute and that they have complied with the ethical guidance laid down by the Institute;
- a statement that the client has acknowledged his responsibility for the financial information;
- a statement that the accountants have not verified the accuracy or completeness of the accounting records or information and explanations supplied, and that the accountants do not express any opinion on the financial information;
- the name and signature of the accountant and any appropriate designation (but not 'Registered Auditor');
- the date of the report.

35 The financial information contains a reference to the fact that it is unaudited either on the front cover or on each page of the financial information.

36 An example of an accountants' report is set out in Appendix C.

---

[6] *Members should have regard to the Institute's Regulations relating to the use of the description 'Chartered Accountants'. Generally, a member may use the description if signing reports in a personal capacity. A firm may only use the description if it complies with the relevant Regulations concerning the control of firms and general affiliates of the Institute. Where a firm is not permitted to use the term Chartered Accountant(s), the title 'Accountants' Report to...' should be used, rather than 'Chartered Accountants' Report to...'.*

Appendix A – Example paragraphs to insert into an engagement letter for the compilation of the unaudited financial information of an unincorporated entity client's responsibilities

1   You will be responsible for the reliability, accuracy and completeness of the accounting records.

2   You have undertaken to make available to us, as and when required, all your accounting records and related financial information, including any minutes of management meetings, necessary to carry out our work. You will provide us with all information and explanations relevant to the purpose and compilation of the financial information.

Scope of the accountants' work

3   You have asked us to assist you in the preparation of *[insert type of financial information required e.g. a profit and loss account and balance sheet and relevant notes]* for *[insert purpose e.g. to enable profits to be calculated such as to meet the requirements of Section 42 of the Finance Act 1998, as amended by the Finance Act 2002 and which provides sufficient and relevant information to enable the completion of a tax return]*. We will compile the financial information for your approval based on the accounting records maintained by you and the information and explanations you give us.

4   We shall plan our work on the basis that no report is required by statute or regulation, unless you inform us in writing to the contrary. In carrying out our engagement we will make enquiries of *[management]* and undertake any procedures that we judge appropriate but are under no obligation to perform procedures that may be required for assurance engagements such as audits or reviews.

5   Our work will not be an audit of the financial information in accordance with Auditing Standards. Consequently, our work will not provide any assurance that the accounting records or the financial information are free from material misstatement, whether caused by fraud, other irregularities or error and cannot be relied on to identify weaknesses in internal controls.

6   Since we have not carried out an audit, nor confirmed in any way the accuracy or reasonableness of the accounting records maintained by the entity, we are unable to provide any assurance as to whether the financial information that we prepare from those records presents a true and fair view.

7   We have a professional duty to compile financial information that conforms with the generally accepted accounting principles selected by management as being appropriate for the purpose for which the information is prepared. The accounting basis on which the information has been compiled, its purpose and limitations will be disclosed in an accounting policy note to the financial information and will be referred to in our accountants' report.

8   We also have a professional responsibility not to allow our name to be associated with financial information which we believe may be misleading. Therefore, although we are not required to search for such matters, should we become aware, for any reason, that the financial information may be misleading, we will discuss the matter

with you with a view to agreeing appropriate adjustments and/or disclosures in the financial information. In circumstances where adjustments and/or disclosures that we consider appropriate are not made or where we are not provided with appropriate information, and as a result we consider that the financial information is misleading, we will withdraw from the engagement.

As part of our normal procedures, we may request you to provide written confirmation of any information or explanations given by you orally during the course of our work. 9

You will approve and sign the financial information thereby acknowledging responsibility for it, including the appropriateness of the accounting basis on which it has been compiled, and for providing us with all information and explanations necessary for its compilation. 10

Form of the accountants' report

We shall report to you that in accordance with this engagement letter we have compiled, without carrying out an audit, the financial information from the accounting records of the entity and from the information and explanations supplied to us. The report should not be used for any purpose other than as set out in this engagement letter. 11

Liability provisions

We will perform the engagement with reasonable skill and care. The total aggregate liability to you, of whatever nature, whether in contract, tort or otherwise, of *[insert name of accountants]* for any losses whatsoever and howsoever caused arising from or in any way connected with this engagement shall not exceed *[insert amount]*[7]. 12

Members may also wish to consider guidance issued in Statement 1.311 of the *Guide to Professional Ethics* on Managing the professional liability of accountants.

Appendix B – Example Wording For Approval Of Financial Information

In accordance with the engagement letter dated *[date]*, I/we approve the financial information which comprises *[state the financial information compiled]*. I/we acknowledge my/our responsibility for the financial information, including the appropriateness of the accounting basis as set out in note x, and for providing *[the accountants]* with all information and explanations necessary for its compilation.

Appendix C – Example Report

Chartered Accountants'/Accountants' Report to *[Entity]* on the Unaudited Financial Information of XYZ

---

[7] This is an example of a liability cap only, which will be one of a number of provisions relating to the accountants' liability and any limitations thereon. For example, the liability provisions will need to make it clear that the accountants are not seeking to exclude those liabilities (such as liability for their own fraud) which cannot be excluded by law.

In accordance with the engagement letter dated [date] we have compiled the financial information of [the entity] which comprises [state the financial information compiled, e.g. Profit and Loss Account, the Balance Sheet, the Cash Flow Statement and, where relevant, the related notes] from the accounting records and information and explanations you have given to us.

The [financial information] has been compiled on the accounting basis set out in note [x] to the [financial information]. The financial information is not intended to achieve full compliance with the provisions of UK Generally Accepted Accounting Principles.

This report is made to you, in accordance with the terms of our engagement. Our work has been undertaken so that we might compile the [financial information] that we have been engaged to compile, report to you that we have done so, and state those matters that we have agreed to state to you in this report and for no other purpose. To the fullest extent permitted by law, we do not accept or assume responsibility to anyone other than the [addressee of this report], for our work, or for this report.

We have carried out this engagement in accordance with technical guidance issued by the Institute of Chartered Accountants in England & Wales and have complied with the ethical guidance laid down by the Institute.

You have approved the [financial information] [where appropriate, insert period to which the financial information relates] and have acknowledged your responsibility for it, for the appropriateness of the accounting basis and for providing all information and explanations necessary for its compilation.

We have not verified the accuracy or completeness of the accounting records or information and explanations you have given to us and we do not, therefore, express any opinion on the financial information.

Signature

PQR LLP

[Description of accountant(s)]

Address

Date

[Statement 935]
Guidance on the implications of the Freedom of Information Act 2000 (AUDIT 02/05)

This guidance has been issued by the Audit and Assurance Faculty of the Institute of Chartered Accountants in England and Wales in July 2005 to assist members in considering the implications of the Freedom of Information Act 2000 to information held by them or provided to public authorities.

Contents

	Paragraphs
Summary of key issues	1 - 11
Background and purpose	12 - 36
Potential impact of the Act for firms	37 - 58
Practical implications on specific areas	59 – 84
What should firms do now?	85

Summary of key issues

1 This technical release is intended to give general guidance to members on the impact of the Freedom of Information Act 2000 (the Act). The Act may affect members in a number of ways, including where members carry out work for public authorities or where reports, issued by members on private sector entities, are held by a public authority. Members who deal with public authorities need to consider the impact, if any, of the Act on them. The extent of the applicability of the Act to information held by or provided to public authorities by firms will depend on the nature of the services provided.

Who and what does the Act apply to (paragraphs 12 to 36)

2 The Act applies to all information held by a public authority, in respect of its public function or service. A request for information can be made by anyone, regardless of age, location, and nationality. It also allows for retrospective application. Therefore, a request can be made for information dating back over a number of years. If a public body still has the information in its possession, it is required to make this available. It requires public authorities, to not only disclose information that they hold, but also to disclose information that they themselves did not generate; including information that might have been provided to them in confidence without any contemplation of future possible disclosure.

3 A number of exemptions are available. The Act distinguishes between two types of exemption: absolute and qualified. Absolute exemptions apply as of right and could include situations where another statute prohibits the disclosure of information. For qualified exemptions, the public authority must consider whether the public interest in not disclosing the information outweighs the public interest in disclosure. Determining whether an exemption applies or not can be a time consuming process, as it applies to information contained within a document, rather than the document itself.

4 There are appeals processes available to applicants if they are not satisfied with the response to their request for information. The rights of appeal range from using the public authority's own complaints process first to the Information Commissioner, Information Tribunal and finally to the High Court.

Impact of the Act on accountancy firms (paragraphs 37 to 58)

5 The Act impacts on firms of accountants in a number of ways. It does not, currently apply to firms carrying out audits of public authorities. It does, however, apply in the following ways to firms:

- acting in their capacity as auditors contacted to the National Audit Office;
- in their capacity as appointed auditors carrying out work for the Audit Commission as their agentsor contractors and in discharge of the Commission's own functions;
- providing other services directly to or in partnership with public authorities through separate engagements or contracts e.g. provision of an internal audit service; and
- who may have provided reports to public authorities in relation to a client and in order to discharge a statutory or regulatory duty.

Information held by firms in relation to engagements (paragraphs 59 to 69)

During an engagement, firms will gather information about their clients, management, staff, clients' systems and processes. Documentation may contain information that has been provided confidentially or about control weaknesses in relation to specific systems and the investigation processes that the firms may use to carry out their work. If such information were available more widely, it could seriously undermine the authority's key systems and subject them to potential future abuse, infiltration and/or sabotage.

Firms are reminded that their working papers remain their own and are not, save in exceptional circumstances, made available to anyone else. Clients would not normally gain access to firms' working papers (unless the work involves auditing in an agency role and the working papers are part of the product of work which will be passed onto the client because the client owns them).

Contracts (paragraphs 70 to 84)

The Act applies to information which is held (not owned) by a public authority (otherwise than on behalf of another person) or held by another person on behalf of the public authority. Firms will therefore need to be very clear when entering into contracts with public authorities as to what information is held by whom. In some cases, contracts give ownership of working papers created, to the public authority, who could demand copies and then disclose them under the provisions of the Act; in others, ownership rests with the firm. Where information is owned by the firm, and not held by the public authority, this information currently falls outside the scope of the Act. If it is clear that the papers are owned by the public authority, then the nature of the engagement or the provisions in the contract will not be relevant.

Confidentiality will be a key factor to consider and may be a factor which outweighs the public interest in disclosure. The law of confidence itself includes a public interest test. The Act, however, avoids clauses that claim to create an exemption in relation to information that should not properly be confidential as when the public interest overrides the obligation of confidence, which means that there could be no actionable breach of confidence.

It is therefore important that contracts clearly identify the clauses that are and are not confidential and firms will need to distinguish between specific confidentiality clauses which may be enforceable, and general ones, which may not.

Public authorities are unlikely to accept clauses that will restrict their ability to disclose information; however, it is encouraged by the Information Commissioner to consult with the contractor and/or third parties before disclosing information. The decision to disclose information is for the public authority to make, regardless of whether or not it has consulted with the firm.

Background and purpose

This technical release is intended to give general guidance to members on the impact of the Freedom of Information Act 2000 (the Act), which came into full force from 1 January 2005. The Act may affect members in a number of ways, including where members carry out work for public authorities or where reports issued by members on private sector entities are held by a public authority. The definition of 'public authority' is very wide, ranging from Parliament and central government departments down to individual schools and GPs, covering approximately 140,000 bodies in total.

13 The Act requires public authorities that have functions in England, Wales and/or Northern Ireland to:

- adopt a publication scheme setting out the information which they publish or intend to publish, how the information is published and whether the information is free or charged for; and
- respond to requests for information from applicants who have the right:
  - to be told whether or not the public authority holds the information; and
  - to have that information communicated to them.

14 There is similar legislation in Scotland. In addition, the Environmental Information Regulations (which also came into effect from 1 January 2005) establish a similar regime allowing people to request environmental information from public authorities and those bodies carrying out a public function.

15 The Government's aim for the Act is to promote a culture of openness and accountability amongst public sector bodies by providing rights of access to the information held by them, facilitating better public understanding of how public authorities carry out their duties, why they make the decisions they do and how they spend public money.

16 Members who have dealings with public authorities need to consider the impact, if any, of the Act on them. Where firms of accountants (the firm(s)) are providing (or have provided) services to public authorities, the extent of the applicability of the Act to information held by or provided to such public authorities by firms is likely to depend on the nature of the services provided. Members should also be aware of the impact of the Act on information relating to services provided to private sector clients being held by public authorities e.g. regulatory returns and on information contained in statutory reports made to regulators.

Who does the Act apply to?

17 The Act applies initially to bodies designated as public authorities listed in Schedule 1 of the Act. This is a very wide-ranging list which includes:

- central government departments, Parliament, the Northern Ireland Assembly and National Assembly for Wales;
- local authorities and similar bodies;
- NHS entities ranging from NHS trusts down to individual GPs and dentists;
- maintained schools and other educational institutions;
- the police; and
- other public bodies and offices including Non Departmental Public Bodies (NDPBs).

A current listing of these bodies covered may be found at http://www.dca.gov.uk/foi/coverage.htm. In addition the Act also applies to companies that are owned by the Crown or another public authority. The listing will change as designation for various bodies occurs over time. Therefore, the website should be consulted for an up to date list of public authorities that fall under the provisions of the Act.

18 The Secretary of State also has the power to designate other bodies as public authorities if it appears to him that they 'exercise functions of a public nature' or 'provide, under a contract made with a public authority, any service which is a

function of that authority'. Such bodies need not be part of the public sector itself. The Department for Constitutional Affairs is due to consult later in 2005 on potential designation of additional bodies, which may include some firms who act as appointed auditors of public authorities and those regulating the profession. Further guidance will be provided if such designation does occur.

What information does the Act apply to?

The Act applies to information which is held by a public authority in respect of their public functions or services[1] (otherwise than on behalf of another person) or held by another person on behalf of the authority. Where information is owned by the public authority and either held by the public authority or held by firms providing services to the public on behalf of the public authority, the information will fall within the scope of the Act. However, the request needs to be made to the public authority, because the firms currently have no obligation under the Act. Therefore, a firm receiving a request in relation to information it holds on behalf of a public authority does not need to respond. The request has to come via the public authority to which the information relates. Subject to any applicable exemptions available under the Act or restrictions in other legislation by the public authority, any information provided to and held by public authorities may be available upon request to members of the public. Information may also be available as a matter of course under the publication scheme (e.g. annual audit letters). 19

The Act applies to all information, not just information generated or received after the Act came into force. It refers to information held at the time of the request and is applicable to retrospective information. It applies to information, not documents. A document may contain information covered by exemptions or for which disclosure is prohibited. In this case, a summary of the non-exempt information, or a copy of the document with the exempt information blanked out would need to be provided. The Act applies to any correspondence (not just reports) between firms and public authorities including email correspondence. 20

Who can request information?

Anybody, regardless of age, location, or nationality, can apply for information from a public authority. They do not have to be resident in this country. They are required to provide an address for correspondence, although this can take the form of an email address. Those requesting information are not required to disclose the purpose of their request and the purpose of the request is not a factor that the public authority may take into account when considering the request and the applicability of the relevant exemptions. 21

Responding to requests for information

Where information is held by or on behalf of a public authority, that public authority is responsible for compliance with the Act. Therefore, it will need to have a robust information handling system in place which records all the information that it holds and will need to ensure that it is maintained and kept up to date. Under section 1 of the Act, a person making a request for information to a public authority has a right 22

---

[1] A body is seen to be performing a public function or service when it seeks to achieve some collective benefit for the public or section of the public e.g. when it provides 'public goods or services' such as defence, healthcare, education, adjudicatory services, regulation of commercial or professional activities. All these functions need not be the exclusive domain of the state.

to be told whether the information requested is held by that authority (the duty to confirm or deny) and, if it is held, to have it communicated to him/her. There may be circumstances where the public authority itself requires further information in order to identify or locate the requested information from the applicant. Under these circumstances, it does not need to comply with the request until such time as it has all the relevant information it needs. The public authority will, however, need to work with the person requesting the information to help make the request more clearly.

23 Once the public authority has received all the information that it needs to comply with the request, the information needs to be provided to the applicant within 20 days. The information that is provided also needs to be up to date at the time of request. The public authority is also going to need a system to log and track each request for information and ensure that, as each request is dealt with, an audit trail is maintained which records the outcome of the decision and the reasons for disclosure or non-disclosure.

24 In most cases, the public authority will consider the request and where appropriate, provide the information. However, it is possible that where the requested information relates to a service or function that another entity is providing to or on behalf of the public authority under a contractual arrangement, the public authority may request that entity to respond on its behalf.

25 Under section 21, *Information readily accessible by other means*, if information is reasonably accessible and readily available to the public by other means (e.g. if available under a publication scheme), then the public authority does not need to provide that information. However, in a recent ruling, the Scottish Information Commissioner has ruled that placing on a website may not be enough as not everyone has internet access.

26 Each public authority will need to have designated key people in place to deal with all requests. These people will need to be fully trained in all provisions of the Act, the available exemptions and how they apply, the public interest and prejudice tests, and the complaints and the appeals process.

Exemptions

27 The Act operates on a presumption that the public interest is best served by disclosure. However, it does acknowledge that there are areas where the public interest may be better served by non-disclosure. This includes obvious areas such as national security and others that are less obvious, including the conduct of an effective audit.

28 The Act distinguishes between two types of exemption – absolute and qualified. Absolute exemptions apply as of right, and include situations such as where information is subject to Parliamentary privilege, where it is already available via another route (e.g. the publication scheme) or where another statute prohibits the disclosure of the information.

29 Where an absolute exemption applies, a public authority need not confirm or deny that it holds the information, nor communicate the information if held. For qualified exemptions, the public authority must consider whether the public interest in not disclosing the information (or in not confirming or denying that they hold the information) outweighs the public interest in disclosure.

30 The holder of the information will need to consider whether they wish to take advantage of an exemption and where a qualified exemption applies, taking account

of all circumstances of the case. The exemptions apply to information, not documents, so the public authority will need to spend time filtering out the exempt information.

The exemptions available are:

Section	Exemption	A = Absolute Q = Qualified
21	Information accessible to applicant by other means.	A
22	Information intended for future publication.	Q
23	Information supplied by, or relating to, bodies dealing with security matters.	A
24	National security.	Q
26	Defence.	Q
27	International relations.	Q
28	Relations within the United Kingdom.	Q
29	The economy.	Q
30	Investigations and proceedings conducted by public authorities.	Q
31	Law enforcement.	Q
32	Court records, etc.	A
33	Audit functions.	Q
34	Parliamentary privilege.	A
35	Formulation of government policy, etc.	Q
36	Prejudice to effective conduct of public affairs.	A/Q
37	Communications with Her Majesty, etc. and honours.	Q
38	Health and safety.	Q
39	Environmental information.	Q
40	Personal information.	A/Q
41	Information provided in confidence.	A
42	Legal professional privilege.	Q
43	Commercial interests.	Q
44	Prohibitions on disclosure.	A

The Act provides an absolute exemption for information where disclosure is prohibited by another statutory provision. This includes:

- The Data Protection Act 1998 (DPA 1998) – This prohibits the disclosure of personal data but contains various exemptions. The DPA 1998 falls under Section 40 of the Act which contains a specific exemption for personal data. Tech 7/04 on the ICAEW website www.icaew.co.uk/technicalpolicy provides more information on the application of the DPA 1998.
- Section 348 Financial Services and Markets Act 2000 – Confidential information passed to the Financial Services Authority may only be disclosed to other regulatory bodies as provided in this section, and accordingly is exempt from disclosure under the Freedom of Information Act. This will include the majority of members' regulatory reporting on financial services clients, as well as information on investment business carried out by members who are themselves regulated by the FSA.
- Section 49A of the Audit Commission Act 1998 (ACA 1998)- public authorities may disclose information that has been collected in the course of undertaking audits under the ACA 1998 except where doing so would harm the performance of their statutory functions. This will apply to auditors when they act as agents of the Audit Commission in discharging its functions.

- Reporting to the National Criminal Intelligence Services, through firms' money laundering reporting officers.

33 In general, the DCA is trying to remove statutory bars on disclosure hence the enactment of Section 49A of the ACA 1998. Section 44 contains a further exemption from disclosure if disclosure is incompatible with a European Community Objective or would constitute or be punishable as a contempt of court.

Enforcement and appeal

The Information Commissioner and Information Tribunal

34 The Information Commissioner is an independent officer of the Crown appointed to oversee and enforce compliance with the Act and the DPA 1998.

35 Part IV of the Act enables an applicant who is not satisfied with the response by a public authority to a request for information to apply to the Information Commissioner for a decision on whether the public authority has acted in accordance with the provisions of the Act. The Information Commissioner then has a duty to reach a decision which will be communicated in a Decision Notice. In the course of his investigation he may issue Information Notices which require the public authority to provide him with such information as he may require, to make his decision. It should be noted that, even though a public authority may have invoked a public interest test and withheld information, the Information Commissioner still has the right to see all the information in order to assess whether the information has been legitimately withheld.

36 There is a right of appeal to the Information Tribunal (the same body which deals with appeals under the DPA 1998), and thereafter to the High Court. Once a decision or Information Notice has been issued and any appeals exhausted, a public authority must comply with its terms. Failure to comply with a decision or Information Notice, or to knowingly or recklessly make a false statement in response to an Information Notice, will leave the public authority open to contempt of court proceedings.

Potential impact of the act for accountancy firms

37 The Act may affect firms in a number of ways. This guidance identifies and considers a number of scenarios that illustrates the impact for firms:
- reports to regulators, grant-paying bodies and contract counterparties, whether relating to private or public sector entities;
- as auditors contracted to the NAO;
- as appointed auditors under the Audit Commission regime and suppliers of related services to the Audit Commission; and
- as contractors to or in partnership with public bodies listed under Schedule I.

The Act is far reaching and this is not a definitive list and there may be other situations which require further consideration.

Reports to regulators, grant-paying bodies and contract counterparties

38 Currently private sector entities are exempt from the Act, although in due course those performing public functions (either in their own right or under contract to a public authority) may be designated. However, the vast majority of regulators of

both private and public sector entities are public authorities, and therefore any reports issued by accountants on those entities that are sent to a regulator are potentially discloseable under the Act. For example reports to economic regulators such as OFGEM and OFWAT and other regulators such as the Charity Commission. Firms may also have a statutory duty to report to certain regulators, for example auditors of charities and pension funds are required to 'whistleblow' to the Charity Commissioners and Pensions Regulator.

Firms, in carrying out their work, discharge a number of statutory or regulatory duties. These duties include reporting suspicions of criminal activity. The specific legislation imposing this duty prohibits disclosure of information by the auditors to anyone other than a designated body (the National Criminal Intelligence Service through the firm's Money Laundering Reporting Officer). This is covered by section 44 of the Act (Disclosure otherwise prohibited) and accordingly exempt from both disclosure and from the duty to confirm whether or not the information is held. 39

Accountants in business and in practice may also be required to provide whistle blowing reports to regulators, and some of these regulatory bodies have been designated, for example, the Financial Services Authority and the Pensions Regulator. Designated regulatory bodies may also have powers to require documents from members, for example, the Pensions Regulator has the power to require documentation relevant to the financial position of employers from the employer and those holding relevant papers (which could include the employer's auditors). Such statutory reports or information otherwise required by regulators may therefore potentially be discloseable, although some regulatory regimes prohibit this 40

Similarly there are a number of public authorities that pay grants for specific purposes to, or enter into contracts with, private sector entities and require reports from accountants as a condition of the grant payment or contract to confirm that grant or monies have been used for the purposes intended. For example, a company researching a new project may obtain a grant from the DTI or a local charity may be paid a fixed amount in respect of the number of homeless people it feeds. These reports, provided by firms in relation to private sector entities, may therefore potentially be discloseable. 41

In addition, where firms report to a public authority itself, their reports may be held by several other public authorities. For example, an auditor of a university issues a management letter to the governing body of the university. A copy of this letter is required to be sent to the Higher Education Funding Council for England (HEFCE). A request under the Act could be made to both the university's governing body and HEFCE for the letter. Each would have to consider the request separately; it is not possible to decline a request simply because another more appropriate body also holds the information. 42

As auditors contracted to the NAO

The NAO is listed as a public authority under Schedule 1 of the Act. As a result, information is covered by the Act if it is either held by: 43

- the NAO;
- another person on the NAO's behalf (such as a firm employed by the NAO); or
- any person designated as a public body by the Secretary of State pursuant to section 5(1)(b) of the Act[2].

---

[2] To fall within this category a person must be providing, under a contract made with the NAO, services whose provision is a function of the NAO.

In some cases, audit exemptions, along with other exemptions may be relevant to information held by the NAO.

Under the Public Audit (Wales) Act 2004, ownership of documents held by the NAO for the Auditor General for Wales passed to the Wales Audit Office.

44 A proportion of the NAO's work is contracted out to firms. Many contracts between the NAO and firms bring papers created or used by firms within the 'held on behalf of' provision of the Act. This is the case for all firms undertaking financial audits of public bodies under contract to the NAO and is also the case with a number of other contracts. In such cases, information held by firms working for the NAO may be potentially discloseable under the Act. Papers possessed by firms which are not held on behalf of the NAO are not within the scope of the Act unless that firm has been designated a public authority by the Secretary of State, although copies of such papers held by the NAO (or any other public authority) are. The NAO has set up its own arrangements for dealing with requests for information and firms that are affected should use the dedicated Freedom of Information email address: foi@-nao.gsi.gov.uk for queries in relation to the Act.

As appointed auditors under the Audit Commission regime and suppliers of related services to the Audit Commission

45 The ACA 1998 sets out the framework for the audit of local authorities and NHS bodies in England and Wales. It sets out some functions which are carried out by appointed auditors (whether a firm or an officer of the Commission) and others that are carried out by the Commission itself. The Act currently covers the Commission but not individual appointed auditors. The position of appointed auditors is, therefore, different to that of audit suppliers to the NAO. This means that, currently, information held by appointed auditors (e.g. audit working papers) is not covered by the Act.

46 Appointed auditors are often engaged to carry out other work for the Audit Commission as their agents or contractors and in discharge of the Commission's functions. For example, they may be asked to certify grant claims as agents for the Commission, or carry out fieldwork for national studies on value for money. In these circumstances any information generated falls within the scope of the Act as it is held on behalf of the Commission which is a public authority and therefore will be subject to the provisions of the Act.

47 The distinction between the functions of the Commission and the functions of the appointed auditor sometimes becomes blurred when appointed auditors also perform the Commission's functions. An example is where an appointed auditor is also the relationship manager for a particular body. In these situations, the auditor would need to decide whether he/she holds information solely in his/her capacity on the 'appointed auditor' (in which case, the Act would not apply) or whether the information was also relevant to his/her functions as a relationship manager or as agents for the Commission (in which case, it would be deemed to be held by the Commission and subject to the Act.) The Commission has issued guidance to its staff on this issue.

48 The DCA has indicated that it intends to consult on the designation of appointed auditors of public authorities in their capacity as such. Whilst this may clarify the position it may also bring a number of individuals and firms within the scope of the Act itself for the first time.

The Audit Commission is working with its appointed auditors to develop guidance for dealing with requests.   49

As contractors to or in partnership with public bodies listed under Schedule I

Firms providing non-audit services to public authorities are likely to be affected by the Act. There is a very wide range of services including: 50

- Contracted out functions such as outsourcing of debt recovery or internal audit.
- Provision of advisory services, e.g. value for money and strategic consulting.

Whatever the nature of the service, it is likely that the public authority will hold information relating to the services. Examples include reports, proposals and contracts. Requests for such information may be made to the public authority that will have to consider them.   51

There may be wider impact where the work of firms can be disclosed under the Act: 52

- A firm may hold information on behalf of the public authority. It may be asked by the public authority to respond to requests under the Act. In this instance, the firm is advised not to provide information directly to the member of the public, but to send it to the public authority who has received the original request to provide the information as it is the obligation of the public authority to respond even if it does not have physical possession of the information.
- The Secretary of State may, in due course, consider designation of firms in their own capacity when carrying out a public function under contract with a public authority. If this does happen then firms will need to comply with the Act themselves.

In the case of consultancy and advisory engagements it is unlikely that the services provided by the contractor will be a public function. Examples of consultancy services that would not appear to be public functions include benchmarking, business modelling, feasibility studies, financial management advice, options reviews, policy development and strategy development. As a result, in respect of such services, only information held by the public authority (or by the firm on behalf of the public authority) in connection with the engagement is likely to be subject to the Act. This will include final reports and other information such as proposals, interim reports and detailed analyses.   53

In the case of outsourcing though it is less clear. Where public authorities have contracted out support functions not directly related to service delivery, it is less likely that these activities would be classified as public functions. Whilst in some cases (such as outsourcing of the core functions of a public authority) it will be clear whether something is a public function, in others the line may be difficult to draw. For example, some public bodies are required by law to have an internal audit function, others are not.   54

Impact of future possible designation

Firms in practice are regulated under statutory powers in three main areas of business – audit, insolvency and investment business. Of the bodies regulating firms, currently only the Financial Services Authority is covered by the Act.   55

However, we understand that the DCA may propose designating the other bodies involved in regulating accountants in these areas including the relevant professional bodies (ICAEW, ICAS, ICAI and ACCA) and the various bodies under the   56

Financial Reporting Council (Accountants Investigation and Discipline Board and Public Oversight Board for Accountancy (including the Audit Inspection Unit)).

57 It is also understood that the DCA is proposing to designate the Financial Reporting Review Panel, which can require information and documentation from company directors, employees and auditors and therefore this may have an impact on members in business, and indirectly on members in practice.

58 The DCA has been asked to highlight which bodies it is actually considering designating and the reasons for their inclusion. Once the DCA has decided which bodies will be designated, the ICAEW will ask it to provide guidance on the functions of those bodies (and the areas that those bodies regulate) that it thinks will be open to the public because they are 'functions of a public nature'. Accountants will need to be aware of the impact of designation on the information provided to these bodies about themselves and/or their clients and their clients' employees and suppliers/customers. The ICAEW plans to discuss with the DCA the designation of such bodies as part of its consultation exercise. If these bodies are designated, the ICAEW will issue more guidance in due course.

Practical implications in specific areas

59 Firms should be aware of the potential impact of the Act whenever they are carrying out work for, or preparing information which may be provided to, a public authority including bodies regulating the member or their clients. Firms subject to the Act themselves will need to understand when they may apply an exemption themselves. Where a public authority consults a firm relating to information generated by it, they will also wish to consider suggesting to the public authority which particular information they think that an exemption should be invoked for. The final decision to release or exempt will rest with the public authority.

Evidence gathering by firms

60 During an engagement, the staff of the client often provide information to firms in confidence, including their personal views on a matter. If an individual believes that their confidentiality may be compromised and that their views may not be anonymous, this could seriously prejudice the willingness of people to openly discuss issues, to openly voice their concerns and to disclose all relevant information. This would undermine a fundamental aspect of any investigative process, its effectiveness and its rigour.

61 A number of qualified exemptions may apply in such circumstances including:

- section 33 – *Audit Exemption*: Information need not be disclosed where, subject to the public interest test, it may prejudice the conduct of an audit of the financial statements or of the arrangements to secure economy, efficiency and effectiveness. The exemption is, however, narrowly drawn in that it only covers audits required by statute. Whilst this covers the majority of public authorities, there are a number where the requirement for an audit stems from a funding memorandum instead, and accordingly the exemption will not apply. In applying the public interest test it will be necessary to argue why non-disclosure is favoured, for example because disclosure might reveal the detailed operation of the audit and allow someone to circumvent future audit procedures to conceal fraud or error.

66 Disclosure may be exempt under section 36 Prejudice to the effective conduct of public affairs as the public interest in disclosing the weakness (e.g. informing local electors that a council is badly run) is outweighed by the public interest in concealing the weakness (e.g. allowing the council to fix the weakness before further frauds are committed). However, the Information Commissioner has suggested that once a weakness in a system has been corrected, then the reason for non-disclosure may fall away. It should also be noted that the use of the section 36 exemption requires a senior officer of the public authority to authorise its use.

Anything subject to legal action/investigation

67 Accountants' work can sometimes be subject to pending legal action and/or further investigation (e.g. disciplinary action against accountants by regulatory bodies). Wider availability of these working papers may prejudice any investigation or subsequent action. Accountants will need to take their own legal advice.

Firms review of commercially confidential information (e.g. contracts/contract rates)

68 There are documents and information that firms review which would be considered as commercially confidential. Examples of this include contracts, letters of intent, bank facility agreements and the amounts charged by suppliers to a specific entity for the provision of goods and/or services. Disclosure of commercially sensitive business information could seriously undermine the client's business and give its competitors an unfair advantage. Such situations appear to be covered by section 43 *Commercial Interests*.

69 Contractors may wish to keep confidential the price at which they are carrying out a contract for a public body, or the details of performance related or penalty clauses. Whilst there is a general acceptance that these may be confidential during negotiation and operation of a contract, not least because they encourage clear competitive tendering, many public authorities have indicated that once a performance period is complete they believe the private interest in disclosing such information and demonstrating whether they have achieved value for money outweighs the public interest in withholding the information. Members may wish to consider such attitudes when deciding whether to tender for engagements with the public sector and the possibility of imposing time limits beyond which confidentiality may be relaxed. Further information is available from the Office of Government Commerce.

Contracts with public authorities

70 In deciding whether to carry out services for a public authority, members will wish to consider the potential impact of the Act. Confidentiality will be a key factor to consider. Under Section 41 of the Act confidentiality may be a factor outweighing the public interest in disclosure. The law of confidence itself includes a public interest test, so the absolute nature of the confidentiality exemption may not be watertight. What the Act does, however, is override clauses that purport to create an obligation of confidence in relation to information that is not properly confidential or where the public interest overrides the obligation of confidence, meaning that there could be no actionable breach of confidence. It is therefore important that confidentiality restrictions are set out clearly and in terms that are actionable if breached. Ideally, confidentiality restrictions should, for the purposes of the Act, include flexibility in relation to distinguishing between what is and is not confidential in the same document (to avoid blanket confidentiality restrictions, which are not likely to be supported by the Information Commissioner as blankets have no regard to what is

- section 22 – *Information intended for publication*: During the conduct of an engagement, firms often form initial views on matters and then change these views after discussion with the client or after carrying out further tests. Firms' working papers should clarify the status of their work e.g. where there are draft points, there should be evidence of how these have been dealt with and actioned. The various stages of reports need to be identified e.g. preliminary findings, draft report (not final views) etc. Firms need to be aware that once a report is final and is requested, even draft reports may have to be provided, if requested.

There are number of key areas inherent in the work that firms carry out where it would be inappropriate for them to disclose information as it could undermine the integrity and quality of the their work. These key areas are set out below.

Incomplete engagements

Firms' working papers normally remain the property of the firm and are not, save in exceptional circumstances, made available to anyone else. Clients would not normally gain access to working papers (unless the work involves auditing in an agency role and the working papers are part of the product of work which will be passed onto the client as the client owns them). The working papers normally contain audit methodology, risk analysis, judgements and assessments, of one form or another, and therefore remain incomplete until the end of the engagement when the final opinion/conclusion is reached. This could include information provided by the client, its management or audit staff in relation to how the work will be carried out, the areas to be tested, the sample test sizes to be applied, what aspects of what systems are to be concentrated on to be made available. Firms' methodologies are fully embedded into their working papers, through the use of work programmes; therefore, it is not easy to separate out information that does not include elements of their approach, planning and methodology.

It would therefore be inappropriate to make such information available before the end of the engagement, as further work may be undertaken during the period that could change the initial judgements. It could also result in initial 'gut feelings' or judgements not being recorded properly where firms' staff themselves believe that their work may be under scrutiny prior to their making their final conclusions on aspects of the engagement. In addition, e.g. when carrying out the statutory audit, firms discharge their statutory duties in the form of the final audit report (or similar) and making preliminary judgements available for scrutiny could undermine the value of the final audit report and the assurance that it provides. Firms will therefore need to manage the risks where the audit or engagement has not been completed. Firms will also need to ensure that their staff are properly trained to record all (and only) vital information to evidence their judgements and decisions on engagement.

Details of clients' internal systems of control

Accountants (both internal and external) often review and document in detail a client's systems of internal control (including financial systems). The documentation may include information about controls weaknesses in the systems which have been identified by accountants. For example, discussions of a system weakness at a local authority relating to housing benefit which may leave it vulnerable to fraud. Information about investigation processes could make it easier for individuals who are being investigated to circumvent procedures which could result in errors and/or fraud going undetected during the engagement. If such information were available more widely, it could seriously undermine the authority's key systems and subject them to potential future abuse, infiltration and/ or sabotage.

truly confidential and merits protection, and what has been described as confidential but which does not, on examination have the quality of confidence).

Information which firms have provided to public authorities will most likely be information provided pursuant to the contract with them and accordingly is likely to be subject to a confidentiality obligation on the public authority not to disclose to third parties. Public authorities are also required to have regard to the Code of Practice issued under section 45 of the Act by the Lord Chancellor. Amongst the guidance included in this Code is a statement that when entering into contracts, public authorities should not accept confidentiality clauses that restrict their ability to comply with the Act. In practice, although public authorities may not accept contract terms that purport to fetter this discretion in the application of exemptions, it is recognised there may be a fine line between fettering a discretion and requiring active consultation.

Whilst it is unlikely that a public authority will accept clauses that will restrict its ability to disclose information under the Act, it is perfectly possible, and indeed encouraged by the Information Commissioner, that it should consult with affected third parties before disclosing information. There may be confidentiality clauses contained within pre-existing contracts which may still be effective. These will need to be considered carefully by the public authority before disclosing information in relation to the contract.

Firms will need to distinguish between specific confidentiality clauses (which may be enforceable and will help the Act to function properly) and general ones (which may not). Some pre-existing confidentiality clauses may still be effective in certain circumstances, although it is likely that the public interest in disclosure under the Act requirements may well override the duty of confidentiality. Firms will also need to note that they will be unable to use certain confidentiality clauses in future engagements.

Members may wish to include wording in contracts along the lines of:

> In the event that, pursuant to a request which the Client has received under the Freedom of Information Act 2000, it is required to disclose any information provided to them by the Contractor (including but not limited to any Deliverables), it will notify the Contractor promptly and consult with the Contractor prior to disclosing such information. The Client agrees to pay due regard to any representations which the Contractor may make in connection with such disclosure and to apply any relevant exemptions which may exist under the Act to such information. If, following consultation with the Contractor, the Client discloses any such information, it shall ensure that any disclaimer which the Contractor has included or may subsequently wish to include in such information is reproduced in full in any copies disclosed.

The wording above does not refer to any confidentiality restriction, but is related to the fact that such restrictions are actionable or that disclosure in breach will prejudice the firm's commercial interests. It is therefore important to remind the authority that the information/deliverables are confidential and that there are disclosure restrictions and that these restrictions are actionable.

Firms will need to be aware that the decision is for the public authority to make and if the public authority does choose to disclose information which could be subject to exemption, regardless of whether or not it has consulted with the firm, it will be the public authority that will breach the confidence of the information in relation to the firm's client and the firm. Therefore, there may well be others that the public authority needs to consult with and firms are advised to inform public authorities of this potential breach if they are consulted.

Ownership of material

77   Contracts between firms and public authorities should usually specify ownership of materials and information provided pursuant to or generated in connection with the contract. This will often be closely linked to the nature of the services provided, with firms tending to own information relating to a consultancy engagement, whilst public authorities would tend to own information relating to contracted out services, although this is not always the case.

78   The Act applies to information which is held (not owned) by a public authority (otherwise than on behalf of another person) or held by another person on behalf of the public authority. Firms will therefore need to be very clear when contracting with public authorities as to what information will be held by whom. In some cases contracts give ownership of working papers created, to the public authority, who could demand copies and then disclose them under the Act; in others ownership rests with the firm. Where information is owned by the firm and not held by the public authority, this information currently falls outside of the scope of the Act. The nature of the engagement and contract will not be relevant where the papers are owned by the public authority.

Separation of information

79   Often members may be generating documents that contain a mixture of information that is likely to be exempt and not exempt. In such cases it may be easier to clearly split documents so that these two classes of information are easily separable. For example, in a proposal a member may wish to put information about their firm etc. that is unlikely to be confidential in one part and their fee proposal (which is likely to be confidential, at least during the life of the contract) in another part.

Duty of care

80   Some information that the firm has provided to the public authority may already be in the public domain. However, there may be other information that is not and which the firm may be requested to provide. At this stage, requests to firms from members of the public are likely to be rare and most requests will be directed towards the public body. Providing information to members of the public may open up several areas of concern in respect of establishing a potential duty of care to the third party recipient of the information. This matter is not covered by the Act, but is clearly an important area for firms to consider. Possible actions to manage this risk might include:

- Inclusion within contracts of a provision that any information created under the contract that is disclosed under the Act will be accompanied by a clear disclaimer setting out the fact that the information was not created in contemplation of the needs of someone requesting it under the Act, and accordingly that they rely on it at their own risk;
- Inclusion of a similar disclaimer in any report issued. This is particularly relevant where members are aware that a report on a non-public body will be passed to a public authority, for example regulatory returns and grant claims.

This guidance is issued by the Audit and Assurance Faculty of the Institute of Chartered Accountants in England & Wales in June 2006 to provide guidance to reporting accountants on undertaking an assurance engagement and providing a report in relation to internal controls of a service organisation. This guidance does not constitute an auditing standard. Professional judgement should be used in its application, and where appropriate, professional legal assistance should be sought.

(c) The Institute of Chartered Accountants in England & Wales

No responsibility for loss occasioned to any person acting or refraining from action as a result of any material in this Technical Release can be accepted by the Institute.

Introduction

Importance of outsourcing activities

1. Many entities use outside service organisations to accomplish tasks that affect the entity's internal controls. These services range from performing a specific task under the direction of the entity to replacing entire business units as functions of an entity. In recent years, there has been a significant increase in the use of service organisations, and because many of the functions performed are integral to the entity's business operations, the entity's management is concerned to ensure the control procedures at the service organisation complement those operated by their own organisation. In addition, because many of the functions performed by service organisations affect an entity's financial statements, auditors may also seek information about the control procedures surrounding those services.

2. The provision of outsourced services is particularly prevalent within financial service activities. The service organisations include custodians that hold and service assets, investment managers for securities and property, and organisations that provide software applications and a technology environment for the processing of transactions or accounting for pension schemes and investment funds. Accordingly, reporting accountants may be engaged by a service organisation to issue a report on specific control procedures undertaken by the service organisation which it may wish to make available to its customers ("customers") and the auditors of those customers. Reporting accountants are the accountants that perform an engagement for the service organisation. Customers are the clients of the service organisation using its services.

Need for new guidance

3. Since the original issue of FRAG 21/94, interest in reporting on internal controls among the investment communities has increased as a direct response to changes in the corporate governance environment and specific government initiated projects such as Paul Myners' report on investment practices. In order to provide information to these investment communities, third party reporting using frameworks such as FRAG 21/94 has been widely applied as a means to increase external scrutiny of internal control processes.

4. Meanwhile, customers of service organisations have begun to focus on the need to replace the existing reporting framework that was last reviewed in 1997. Customers are increasingly seeking assurance on both the design and operating effectiveness of service organisations' control procedures. They are also seeking greater consistency between service organisations as to the scope and contents of their reports and greater transparency as to the extent of testing undertaken by reporting accountants.

5. These factors and comments on the use made of such reports on internal controls have led the Audit and Assurance Faculty of the Institute of Chartered Accountants in England & Wales ("the Institute") to issue new reporting guidance[1]. This guidance sets out the conditions service organisations meet in providing information on internal controls, control procedures and the framework within which reporting accountants deliver assurance reporting.

---

[1] In conducting its work, the working group has included representatives from the Institute of Chartered Accountants in England & Wales, the National Association of Pension Funds, the Investment Management Association and service organisations.

This guidance is specifically developed for a range of financial service activities, including:

- Custody;
- Investment management;
- Pension administration;
- Property management;
- Fund accounting; and
- Transfer agency.

To apply this guidance to other engagement circumstances involving activities such as payroll processing, additional considerations may be required.

The Audit and Assurance Faculty of the Institute will keep the guidance under regular review to accommodate industry developments in relation to the control objectives set out in Appendix 1 and the range of activities set out in paragraph 6. Industry groups and other representative bodies or service organisations who wish to propose further service activities for inclusion within the guidance or to comment on the control objectives currently contained within Appendix 1 are encouraged to submit any such proposals in writing to the Audit and Assurance Faculty at tdaf@icaew.co.uk.

Within the financial service activities listed above, it is anticipated that the control objectives include appropriate references to information technology.

It is for the directors of the service organisation to decide whether to prepare a report on their organisation's control procedures and whether to have this reported on by reporting accountants. In certain circumstances, directors may, for example, consider it more appropriate to allow access to customers and their auditors or provide a report on a specific aspect of its operations as this impacts an individual customer. It is not the intention of the guidance to oblige service organisations to report on control procedures in the manner described in this guidance. However, if the directors decide to provide a report other than in accordance with this guidance, they may not make any reference to this guidance in their report.

Where the directors decide to prepare a report on internal controls, it is of greater benefit to customers and their auditors if it covers control procedures in operation throughout a given period. However, a report on control procedures at a single point in time may be an alternative where a service organisation is preparing its report on internal controls for the first time[2]. The guidance that follows generally assumes that the report covers a period.

A service organisation may have more than one type of financial service activity. In such a case, the directors explain to the reporting accountants the types of financial services the service organisation carries out at the outset of the engagement. The directors may prepare either a combined report or a separate report on each area of financial service activity as they deem appropriate. The reporting accountants report accordingly.

---

[2] Where the directors and reporting accountants are reporting only on controls in place and not on their operating effectiveness during the specified period, this fact is clearly stated in the reports. The accountants modify their conclusions so as not to conclude on the operating effectiveness of control procedures during the specified period.

Scope

12 This Technical Release provides guidance to reporting accountants on undertaking an assurance engagement and providing a report ("assurance report") in relation to the internal controls of a service organisation.

13 It is also expected to assist customers in understanding the scope and type of assurance conveyed in the assurance report. The guidance is also aimed at providing assistance to the directors of service organisations who prepare a report on their internal controls by clarifying their expected responsibilities.

14 This guidance replaces the Institute's guidance AUDIT 4/97 *Reports on internal controls of investment custodians made available to third parties, FRAG 21/94 (Revised)*.

Transition from FRAG 21/94 (Revised)

15 The Technical Release is effective for periods ending on or after 31 March 2007. However, service organisations and reporting accountants are encouraged to apply this guidance before that date as best practice.

Assurance engagements

International developments

16 In 2004, the International Auditing and Assurance Standards Board published the *International Framework for Assurance Engagements* (the Framework) and the first International Standard on Assurance Engagements (ISAE) 3000, *Assurance Engagements Other Than Audits or Reviews of Historical Financial Information*. These pronouncements provide high level principles for assurance engagements other than audits and reviews of historical financial statements.

17 The Framework defines the elements of assurance engagements and describes objectives for such engagements.

ISAE 3000 provides generic guidance on the principal aspects of assurance engagements and refers to an assurance engagement involving three separate parties. Together these two international pronouncements provide the appropriate framework within which to develop specific guidance covering subject areas and topics such as internal control where, hitherto, no specific guidance has existed.

The types of assurance

18 There are two types of assurance engagements and associated objectives specified in the Framework: reasonable assurance engagements and limited assurance engagements.

19 In a reasonable assurance engagement, reporting accountants seek to obtain sufficient appropriate evidence that enables them to express a positive conclusion on the directors' report prepared for customers. In a limited assurance engagement, reporting accountants seek to gather evidence sufficient to obtain a meaningful level of assurance as the basis for a negative form of expression. This guidance is prepared for reporting accountants performing a reasonable assurance engagement.

Nature of engagement

The service organisation is responsible for providing information on specific control procedures ("control procedures") to meet the control objectives described in this guidance. The reporting accountants perform the engagement in accordance with this guidance. As discussed below the directors' and assurance reports may be made available to others, e.g. pension scheme trustees or auditors.

The directors of the service organisation are responsible for preparing a report concerning the control procedures in place. The report is for the information of customers and their auditors and focuses on the operations which are likely to be relevant to them. It is therefore appropriate that any report provided by service organisations has regard to these relevant operations as well as those specified in this guidance.

The reporting package comprises a report by the directors of the service organisation concerning the control procedures of the service organisation and a reasonable assurance report by the reporting accountants, explaining the scope of work carried out and giving their conclusion on relevant parts of the directors' report. The conclusion is in the form of a qualitative judgment. The judgment and the report relate to historic matters.

Control objectives as criteria

Assurance engagements require reporting accountants to express an overall conclusion on the information assessed relative to certain criteria. Criteria also help the directors of a service organisation and their customers to understand how the reporting accountants have evaluated internal controls to reach their conclusion. In an assurance report on internal controls, the criteria are the control objectives around which the service organisation has designed its control procedures. The criteria need to be relevant, complete, reliable, neutral and understandable so as to communicate the basis of the evaluation.

The control objectives collectively reflect the level of control over customers' assets[3] and related transactions set by the service organisation.

Appendix 1 sets out detailed control objectives for the financial service activities referred to in paragraph 6.

These control objectives are guidance only and not intended to be exhaustive and it remains the responsibility of the directors to ensure that the described control objectives are sufficient to meet the expectations of customers. A service organisation may therefore consider the need to add further objectives and supporting control procedures where appropriate. If certain criteria do not apply to a service organisation, for example because the relevant activities are outsourced, the service organisation explains the omission of the criteria in the directors' report.

Reporting accountants consider the control objectives and observe supporting control procedures specified by the service organisation to form an overall opinion in the specific engagement circumstances at the time the work was undertaken. Reporting accountants also consider the linkage of the control procedures to the stated objectives and obtain sufficient appropriate evidence to reach their opinion. Through tests of control procedures, reporting accountants obtain sufficient

---

[3] Reference may need to be made for liabilities, for instance for pension administration.

appropriate evidence to conclude whether the relevant specified control objectives are met.

Responsibilities of a service organisation

The role of a service organisation

27 The role of a service organisation in relation to the customers is likely to involve some combination of initiation, recording, processing, safeguarding or reporting the customers' assets and related transactions.

The responsibility of the directors

28 To meet the customers' expectations in terms of the level of control over customers' assets and related transactions, the directors of the service organisation identify control objectives together with the control procedures which they consider appropriate to enable these control objectives to be met. The key responsibilities of the directors in relation to these are summarised as:

    a. Acceptance of responsibility for internal controls;
    b. Evaluation of the effectiveness of the service organisation's control procedures using suitable criteria;
    c. Supporting their evaluation with sufficient evidence, including documentation; and
    d. Providing a written report of the effectiveness of the service organisation's control procedures for the relevant period.

a. Acceptance of responsibility for internal controls

29 The directors are responsible for the design, implementation and operation of the control procedures of the service organisation. This is acknowledged in their report. It is also the responsibility of the directors to take reasonable steps to prevent and detect fraud.

30 Suitably designed control procedures, when complied with individually or in combination with other control procedures, are expected to operate so as to prevent or detect errors that could result in the failure to achieve specified control objectives. The directors also evaluate the design and operation of control procedures during the relevant reporting period. In this regard, the reporting accountants' tests are separate from the service organisation's own procedures for evaluating the effectiveness of the control procedures. The work of the reporting accountants cannot be used as part of the basis for the service organisation's assessment of whether control procedures are suitably designed or the operation of the control procedures is effective.

b. Evaluation of the effectiveness of the service organisation's control procedures using suitable criteria

31 In order to evaluate the effectiveness of control procedures the directors refer to suitable criteria.

32 The control objectives in Appendix 1 are considered to be suitable criteria for the financial service activities specified in paragraph 6 of this guidance. The directors make a statement in their report that they have referred to the control objectives in

this guidance. Most service organisations depend on computer processing to perform commissioned services and the service organisations' description of control procedures also includes a description of the computer environment and the related general computer control procedures. Suitable criteria relating to such information technology are also provided in Appendix 1.

c. Supporting their evaluation with sufficient evidence, including documentation

The directors support their assertions with respect to the design, implementation and operating effectiveness of the service organisation's control procedures with sufficient evidence. The nature of the directors' evaluation activities depends largely on the circumstances of the entity and the significance of particular controls but evaluation procedures include review and testing by internal audit, business risk and compliance review, direct testing by others under the direction of management or review by means of a self assessment process. The directors consider the sufficiency of this evidence and whether any additional evaluation of specific areas or locations may be appropriate to enable them to provide a written assessment of the effectiveness of the internal controls.

The process that the directors undertake includes considering:

- evidence available from on-going monitoring of control procedures;
- whether further control procedures are to be tested by them, including consideration of the locations or business units to include in the evaluation for an entity with multiple locations or business units;
- any deficiencies in control procedures that have come to their attention, for example, through management testing, internal audit reports and reports by regulators; and
- evaluation as to the likelihood that the failure of certain control procedures could result in a control objective not being met, the extent to which it might not be met and the degree to which other control procedures, if effective, achieve the same control objective.

Documentation of control procedures in place is in itself evidence of control procedures being identifiable, capable of being monitored and communicable to those responsible for their performance. Inadequate documentation may indicate a deficiency in the service organisation's control procedures and is subject to evaluation by the reporting accountants as to its significance (e.g. it could be merely a deficiency, a material weakness or in extreme cases a limitation on the scope of the engagement).

Documentation of control procedures may take various forms depending on the nature and the type of the relevant information. For instance, policy manuals, process models, flowcharts and job descriptions could be used for recording the control procedure design, while documents and forms could be the record of operating and monitoring of control procedures.

The directors evaluate whether the documentation includes:

- the design of control procedures over all relevant control objectives;
- information about how significant transactions are initiated, authorised, recorded, processed and reported; and
- the results of management's testing and evaluation.

Where the service organisation has introduced significant changes to its control procedures within the past 12 months, the control procedures before and after the change and the implications are documented. The judgement as to the significance of the change is based on its impact on the risk assessment of the customers and their auditors.

d. Providing a written report of the effectiveness of the service organisation's control procedures for the relevant period

37   Through evaluation and documentation, the directors accumulate sufficient information to come to an overall conclusion as to the effectiveness of the service organisation's control procedures during a specified period. Their conclusion is based on the specified criteria, and includes an assessment of the impact of exceptions and deficiencies. The directors communicate the conclusion and the details of significant deficiencies to customers in their report. The following key matters are to be included in the report of the directors:

Contents of the directors' report
(a) A statement of the directors' responsibilities.
(b) The service organisation's control objectives, and a reference to the control objectives specified in this guidance, with details of any omitted or additional control objectives considered appropriate by the directors with explanations for such omissions and additions.
(c) Aspects of the service organisation's control environment, risk assessment, management information, communication and monitoring process that may be relevant to the services provided.
(d) Details of each of the specific control procedures designed to achieve the control objectives.
(e) Reference to the use of this guidance.
(f) Details of any significant changes to the control objectives and procedures during the period.
(g) Details of any significant deficiencies and exceptions and their impact on the control objectives during the period.
(h) The assertions by the directors that they have assessed the effectiveness of the control procedures and their opinion that:
   (i) their report describes fairly the control procedures that relate to the control objectives referred to in (b) above which were in place as at [date];
   (ii) the control procedures described are suitably designed such that there is reasonable assurance that the specified control objectives would be achieved if the described control procedures were complied with satisfactorily [and customers applied the control procedures contemplated]; and
   (iii) the control procedures described were operating with sufficient effectiveness to provide reasonable assurance that the related control objectives were achieved during the specified period.
(i) The name and signature of the director signing on behalf of the Board of Directors.
(j) The directors' report date.

Example paragraphs from an illustrative directors' report on matters referred to at (a), (e), (h), and (i) above are set out at Appendix 2.

38   In applying the framework presented above, it is not necessary to list the control procedures and related control objectives in both the directors' report and in the assurance report.

39   The directors are responsible for the completeness, accuracy, validity and method of presentation of the description of control objectives and procedures. The description sets out information about the service organisation's control objectives and

management or employees that may affect its customers and the entity's whistleblowing arrangements;
- disclosing to the reporting accountants any relevant design deficiencies in control procedures of which it is aware, including those for which the directors believe the cost of corrective action may exceed the benefits;
- disclosing to the reporting accountants all significant instances of which it is aware when control procedures have not operated with sufficient effectiveness to achieve the specified control objectives; and
- providing the reporting accountants with a letter of representation.

Service organisations that use other service organisations

45   Additional considerations are required where a service organisation uses another service organisation (a sub-service organisation) to perform certain aspects of the processing performed for the customers.

46   In addition to describing its control objectives and procedures, a service organisation that uses a sub-service organisation describes the functions and nature of the processing performed by the sub-service organisation in sufficient detail for the customers and their auditors to understand the significance of the sub-service organisation's operations to the processing of the customers' transactions.

47   The purpose of the description of the functions and nature of the processing performed by the sub-service organisation is to alert the customers and their auditors to the fact that another entity is involved in the processing of the customers' transactions and to summarise the functions the sub-service organisation performs.

48   The service organisation determines whether its description of control procedures includes the relevant control procedures of the sub-service organisation. The two alternative methods of dealing with sub-service organisations are as follows:
- **The exclusive method:** The sub-service organisation's relevant control objectives and procedures are excluded from the description and from the scope of the reporting accountants' engagement. The service organisation states in the description that the sub-service organisation's control objectives and related procedures are omitted from the description and that the control objectives in the report include only the objectives which the service organisation's control procedures are intended to achieve.
- **The inclusive method:** The sub-service organisation's relevant control procedures are included in the description and in the scope of the engagement. The description clearly differentiates between control procedures of the service organisation and control procedures of the sub-service organisation. The set of control objectives includes all of the control objectives which both the service organisation and the sub-service organisation are expected to achieve. To accomplish this, the service organisation co-ordinates the preparation and presentation of the description of control procedures with the sub-service organisation.

Other information provided by the service organisation

49   A service organisation may wish to present other information that is not a part of the description of internal controls in its report: for example, background information on the entities involved and the services they provide. Where information of this nature is presented, it is presented in a separate section of the report and made clear

procedures that may be relevant to the customers. The reporting accountants may assist the service organisation in preparing the description; however, the representations in the description are the responsibility of the service organisation's directors.

The directors, where appropriate, seek to describe control procedures in a manner which permits verification and is understandable to customers. To achieve this and to promote consistency in approach, the directors may find it helpful to differentiate between the different components of the overall system which are being described in their report. The principal components are in general likely to include control objectives, control policies, process descriptions and control procedures. Process and control procedure descriptions in particular are factual and precise wherever possible in order to avoid the possibility of different interpretations being placed on these by different customers. 40

The description of control objectives and procedures does not necessarily address every service provided by the service organisation but presents a level of detail that provides sufficient information for customers to assess control risk and for the auditors of the customers to plan an audit of the customers' financial statements, as if a service organisation were not used. 41

Significant deficiencies

A control procedure deficiency (or a combination of control procedure deficiencies) is classified as a significant deficiency where, by itself or in combination with other control procedure deficiencies, it results in more than a remote likelihood that a control objective may not be met. Where such significant deficiencies are corrected during the year, customers may find it helpful to be informed of this in the directors' report. 42

Complementary control procedures of customers

The activities of the service organisation may be described with the assumption that customers have control procedures in place, with respect to such general matters as the authorisation of transactions, the written notification of changes, the timely review of reports provided by the service organisation, and appropriate restrictions on access to on-line terminals. If this is the case, the description of the control procedures at the service organisation refers to such required complementary control procedures of the customers. 43

Other responsibilities of the service organisation

Other responsibilities of the service organisation include: 44
- providing the reporting accountants with access to appropriate service organisation resources, such as service organisation personnel, systems documentation, contracts and minutes of management/audit committee meetings;
- disclosing to the reporting accountants any significant changes in control procedures that have occurred since the service organisation's last examination or within the last 12 months if the service organisation has not previously engaged reporting accountants to issue an assurance report;
- disclosing to the reporting accountants and the affected customers any illegal acts, fraud, or uncorrected errors attributable to the service organisation's

that it does not constitute a part of the service organisation's description of control objectives and control procedures.

Guidance for reporting accountants

Accepting an engagement

It is important that there is a clear understanding and agreement concerning the scope and purpose of the engagement between the reporting accountants and the service organisation and, if applicable, the customers that are party to the engagement (see paragraph 55). 50

Reporting accountants consider whether the engagement team collectively possesses the necessary professional competencies having regard to the nature of the assignment. As part of the engagement acceptance process reporting accountants also consider relevant ethical requirements. 51

In carrying out an assurance engagement, Chartered Accountants are subject to ethical guidance as laid down by the Institute in its ethical code. The requirements in the ethical code include, among other things, adherence to the Fundamental Principles in all of their professional and business activities as set out in the introduction. When conducting an assurance engagement, there are additional requirements in *Independence for Assurance Engagements* within the code. This applies to all assurance engagements outside the scope of audit and is in compliance with the Code of Ethics established by the International Federation of Accountants (IFAC). 52

The reporting accountants' adherence to the independence requirements involves an assessment of likely threats to independence and, where necessary, the application of safeguards. For example, the provision of assistance to a service organisation in preparing its report may result in a self-review threat if the impact of the assistance on the matter being reported on is highly subjective and material. The subjectivity of the report proposed to be issued will also be relevant. If other than insignificant threats are identified, safeguards need to be considered. These might include: 53

- the use of independent teams, where appropriate; or
- an independent review of the key judgements on the engagement

The assurance report may be received by a range of persons who are not party to the engagement. Reporting accountants do not intend to assume responsibility to persons who are not party to the engagement, but legal actions from such persons may nonetheless occur. Reporting accountants therefore need to apply appropriate engagement acceptance procedures in order to assess the risks associated with taking on a particular engagement and accordingly whether to do so and, if so, on what terms. Where the reporting accountants do accept such an engagement, suitably rigorous internal risk management policies are applied to manage any increased level of risk. Relevant steps for managing professional liability are covered in the following section[4]. 54

Managing professional liability

Depending on the engagement circumstances reporting accountants enter into one or a combination of the following arrangements: 55

---

[4] *Further guidance may be found in Statement 1.311, Managing the professional liability of accountants in the Institute's Members Handbook.*

(a) A tri-partite or multi-partite engagement contract with the service organisation and the customers, accepting that they owe a duty of care not only to the service organisation but also to those customers, including provisions limiting liability if appropriate (recognising that such a contract may not be achievable where the customers are numerous).

(b) An engagement with the service organisation with the facility for customers to enjoy a duty of care from the reporting accountants if they accept the relevant terms of the engagement letter previously agreed with the service organisation as if they had signed that letter when originally issued, including the same provisions limiting liability[5].

(c) An engagement with the service organisation alone but before allowing the customers access to the assurance report, require the customers (i) to acknowledge in writing that the reporting accountants owe the customers no duty of care and (ii) to agree in writing that no claims may be brought against the reporting accountants by the customers in relation to the assurance report[6].

(d) An engagement with the service organisation alone disclaiming any liability or duty to others (including customers) by notice in the assurance report. Reporting accountants also consider supporting this disclaimer with an indemnity from the service organisation to apply where a third party claim is made (recognising that such an indemnity may not be attractive commercially, may not be effective if the service organisation is not financially stable, and may not operate to prevent a claim: see further paragraph 63 below)[7].

It is also open to reporting accountants to consider with their legal advisers the use of the Contract (Rights of Third Parties) Act 1999 to manage the risk of liability to third parties. The above arrangements do not prevent customers taking legal action against the service organisation.

56 Reporting accountants will describe carefully in their report the work that they do, including the description of the tests. In the latter context, close definition of what is meant by enquiry, inspection, observation and re-performance is desirable. Some illustrative definitions are set out at Appendix 7.

57 Reporting accountants disclaim responsibility and liability to customers' auditors, having regard to the responsibility of customers' auditors for their own audit reports and for determining to what extent (if any) the assurance report amounts to sufficient appropriate audit evidence for the purposes of their audit of a relevant customer's financial statements.

58 Reporting accountants may become aware of other third parties that are not customers of the service organisation, such as banks and other lenders or prospective purchasers of the service organisation, who may also request the assurance report. The service organisation or the third party may approach the reporting accountants for consent to make the assurance report available to such third parties, as the engagement contract agreed with the service organisation contains disclosure and use

---

[5] *This will require the consent of the service organisation/original addressees, ideally in the engagement letter. Also see footnotes 18 and 20, page 29.*

[6] *Reporting accountants may wish to have regard to the principles outlined in Audit 04/03 Access to working papers by investigating accountants, bearing in mind that Audit 04/03 addresses different circumstances relating to third party issues, when developing a written form of such acknowledgment and agreement.*

[7] *Reporting accountants consider the legal effectiveness of disclaiming liability and of the proposed disclaimer in light of the particular circumstances of their engagement (see for example, the guidance in Statement 1.311 on Managing the professional liability of accountants).* Reporting accountants are advised to seek their own independent legal advice.

restrictions. The assurance report is not prepared for third parties or with their interests or needs in mind, and the reporting accountants may decline this request. The reporting accountants will have set out the purpose of their report in the assurance report, and will have included a disclaimer of liability to third parties in line with paragraph 55(d) above in that report. If the request is not declined, the reporting accountants will advise the third party that the assurance report was not prepared for the third party or the third party's benefit, that consent to their report being made available to a third party will only be given if the third party agrees that the third party should not rely on the report and acknowledges in writing that the reporting accountants owe the third party no duty of care and agrees that no claims may be brought against the reporting accountants by the third party in relation to the report.

Reporting accountants may also receive requests from the service organisation for consent to the release of the assurance report to potential customers with whom the service organisation may be exploring the possibility of a relationship, or reporting accountants may become aware that contrary to disclosure and use restrictions agreed with the service organisation in the engagement contract, such potential customers are gaining access to the assurance report. The reporting accountants may decline any such request. If the request is not declined, the written acknowledgement and agreement described above in relation to other third parties may be a practical solution to the management of risk in relation to potential customers. Where that is not practical, the reporting accountants require the service organisation (as a condition for giving consent, where requested) to send all such potential customers a written statement, to accompany the assurance report, pointing out that the reporting accountants did not undertake the work for potential customers and do not accept any responsibility to potential customers and deny liability to them. Reporting accountants may wish to provide the service organisation with a pro-forma statement and may wish to include reference to this in their engagement letter. 59

If correspondence between reporting accountants and customers, potential customers or third parties results from a disclaimer notice or otherwise, the reporting accountants decide (with independent legal advice if appropriate) how to bring such correspondence to a satisfactory close before it becomes protracted or undermines the original objective. 60

Agreeing on the terms of engagement

Prior to accepting the engagement, reporting accountants establish that the directors of the service organisation acknowledge in writing their responsibility on behalf of the organisation for the design and operation of effective internal controls over its activities to achieve control objectives. 61

Reporting accountants agree on the terms of engagement with the parties to the engagement in accordance with the contractual relationship as discussed in paragraph 55. To avoid misunderstandings, the agreed terms are recorded in writing in an engagement letter. Example extracts from an engagement letter for an assurance report on internal controls of a service organisation are given in Appendix 5 for illustrative purposes. Reporting accountants apply their own judgement to develop suitable wording for their engagement letters to reflect the guidance in this Technical Release and their own particular circumstances. Where the engaging parties include customers, the nature and the content of an engagement letter may differ from the example extracts. 62

The written terms of the reporting accountants' engagement include: 63

- the agreed use of the report and the extent to which, the context in which, and the basis on which, the report may be made available by the directors to customers and their auditors;
- the directors' and the reporting accountants' respective responsibilities for the different elements of the report;
- the scope of the work to be performed by the reporting accountants;
- a reference to the likely need for management representations;
- an explanation of the inherent limitations of the work, and for whom the work is being undertaken;
- limitations to the liability of the reporting accountants, including an appropriate liability cap; and
- provisions for an indemnity if considered appropriate[8].

64 In particular, reporting accountants exclude liability in respect of any loss or damage caused by, or arising from fraudulent acts, misrepresentation, concealment of information or deliberate default on the part of the service organisation, its directors, employees or agents.

65 If, before the completion of the engagement, reporting accountants receive a request from the service organisation, to change an assurance engagement to a non-assurance or limited assurance engagement or to change, for instance, the scope of the engagement, the reporting accountants consider whether this has reasonable justification. Engagement parties' misunderstanding concerning the nature of the engagement or a change in circumstances that affects the customers' requirements is likely to justify such a request from the service organisation. Where accepting a request for a change, the reporting accountants do not disregard evidence that was already obtained prior to the change, and the details of the change should be documented and agreed in writing with the parties to the engagement letter.

Planning

66 Where reports are referred to as being prepared in accordance with the framework for reporting set out in this Technical Release, reporting accountants plan and perform their work so as to provide a reasonable basis for their conclusion. Professional judgement is needed to determine the required nature, timing and extent of the tests to be carried out and the reliance, if applicable, on the service organisation's internal audit department.

67 The reporting accountants' work is planned so as to have a reasonable expectation of detecting, at the time the work is undertaken, significant deficiencies in respect of the control procedures described by the directors and tested in accordance with the terms of the engagement. However, the work cannot be expected to detect problems which may be considered significant from the point of view of a particular customer and the scope of the work may mean that all control procedures relevant to an individual customer may not have been tested.

68 Reporting accountants are not expected to assess the adequacy of the evaluation of controls performed by the directors as part of an engagement to report on the entity's control procedures.

---

[8] It may be appropriate to obtain an indemnity from the service organisation in respect of claims from third parties arising from the contents of the assurance report. It must be remembered that an indemnity does not prevent a claim from being brought against the indemnified party. It merely gives him a right to pass on the liability to the indemnifier. It follows, therefore, that if the indemnity is in some way ineffective or the indemnifier does not have adequate resources to meet the liability, the indemnified party may be left unprotected.

Reporting accountants' procedures Fairness of the description

69 Reporting accountants read the description of control procedures to gain an understanding of the representations made by the directors in the description. After reading the description, the reporting accountants perform procedures to determine whether the description presents fairly, in all material respects, the service organisation's control procedures that relate to the control objectives referred to by the directors which were in place as at the end of the relevant period.

70 To determine whether the description is fairly presented, the reporting accountants gain an understanding of the services provided by the service organisation. Procedures to gain this understanding may include:

- discussing aspects of the control framework and relevant control procedures with management and other personnel of the service organisation;
- determining who the customers are and how the services provided by the service organisation are likely to affect the customers, for example, the predominant type of customers;
- reviewing standard terms of contracts with the customers to gain an understanding of the service organisation's contractual obligations;
- observing the procedures performed by the service organisation's personnel;
- reviewing the service organisation's policy and procedure manuals and other systems documentation, for example, flowcharts and narratives; and
- performing walk-throughs of selected transactions and control procedures.

71 Reporting accountants compare their understanding of the services provided to the customers by the service organisation with the directors' representations made in their report to determine the fairness of the description. Fairly described control procedures do not omit or distort significant information that may affect the customers' assessments of control risk.

72 Fairly described control procedures include a complete set of associated control objectives that are developed based on the criteria in Appendix 1. If there are omissions or misstatements with regard to the control objectives, the reporting accountants ask the directors to amend the description. If it is not amended the reporting accountants consider the need to state that fact in their report.

Design of control procedures

73 As a part of their work, reporting accountants determine whether the control procedures are suitably designed.

A control procedure is suitably designed if individually, or in combination with other control procedures, it is likely to prevent or detect errors that could result in the non-achievement of specified control objectives when the described control procedures are complied with satisfactorily.

74 The reporting accountants' assessment of the suitability of control procedure design may include:

- considering the linkage between the control procedures and the associated control objectives;
- considering the ability of the control procedures to prevent or detect errors related to the control objectives;
- performing walk-throughs of selected transactions and control procedures; and

- performing further procedures, such as enquiry of appropriate entity personnel, inspection of documents and reports and observation of the application of specific control procedures, to determine whether they are suitably designed to achieve the specified control objectives and if they are operated as prescribed, by appropriately qualified or experienced persons.

75 Where certain control procedures of the service organisation are reliant on generic control procedures executed by the customers in order to achieve control objectives, reporting accountants consider whether such complementary control procedures are described in the directors' report. If they are not and the directors fail or refuse to amend the description, the reporting accountants consider adding an explanatory paragraph to describe the required complementary control procedures and consider the implication for the reporting accountants' conclusion on the fairness of the description (see paragraphs 85-90).

Operating effectiveness

76 Reporting accountants perform tests of the relevant control procedures to obtain evidence about the operating effectiveness of the control procedures during a specified reporting period. Operating effectiveness is concerned with how a control procedure is applied, the consistency with which it is applied, and by whom it is applied. Reporting accountants determine the nature, timing and extent of the tests to be performed to form their conclusion on the operating effectiveness of the control procedures. Reporting accountants may wish to provide the customers with a further explanation of the tests that they have performed in an appendix to their report.

77 Where reporting accountants are unable to test a described control procedure because, for example, it has not operated during the year, they state the fact that no tests have been carried out and the reason in their description of tests.

Nature, timing and extent of tests

78 Tests of control procedures over operating effectiveness might include a combination of enquiry of the appropriate personnel, observation of the application of the control procedure, inspection of relevant documentation and re-performance of the control procedure. Enquiry alone does not generally provide sufficient evidence to support a conclusion about the operating effectiveness of a specific control procedure.

79 The period of time over which reporting accountants perform tests of control procedures varies with the nature of the control procedures being tested and with the frequency of specific control procedures. Tests of operating effectiveness provide evidence that enables the reporting accountants to report on the entire period covered by the report. Certain control procedures may not have evidence of their operation that can be tested at a later date and accordingly, reporting accountants test the operating effectiveness of such control procedures at various times throughout the reporting period.

80 Where the service organisation implemented changes to its control procedures to improve them or to address deficiencies during the period covered, the reporting accountants evaluate the impact which the superseded control procedures had on the control objectives over the period covered. Where a change of control procedures occurs during the period, the reporting accountants agree with the directors whether it is possible for the control procedures to be tested before and after the change. The description of their tests clearly states which control procedures have been tested.

The number of control operations selected as a sample for testing depends on the frequency of performance (for example, quarterly, monthly, daily or multiple times a day), the nature (for example, manual or automated) of control procedures, and the reporting accountants' assessment of the system (including the risk of failure of the control procedure that is being tested). An example table for setting sample sizes is given in Appendix 6. 81

Describing tests of operating effectiveness and exception reporting

Reporting accountants describe the control procedures that were tested, the control objectives they were intended to achieve, the tests carried out and the results of the tests in the assurance report. This information is typically incorporated within the service organisation's description of control procedures or contained within an attachment to the assurance report. The reporting accountants describe tests of operating effectiveness that provide sufficient information to support their conclusion as to whether the service organisation has achieved the relevant control objectives during the period. 82

In describing the results of the tests, reporting accountants include details and other information where relevant to the customers and their auditors. Test results are also described whether or not the reporting accountants have concluded that the results constitute an exception (see paragraph 89). 83

Reporting accountants describe the nature, timing and extent of tests applied. In describing the nature of tests, the reporting accountants define the types of tests performed. Illustrative definitions of tests such as enquiry, inspection, observation and re-performance are provided in Appendix 7. In describing the extent of tests, the reporting accountants indicate whether the items tested represent a sample or all the items in the population. If sampling was used, it may be helpful to provide information on the sample size. 84

Reporting on description misstatements, design deficiencies or when control procedures are not operating effectively

Reporting accountants discuss with the directors when they become aware that the control objectives are incomplete or inappropriate in light of the criteria in this guidance so that the directors may amend the description to include the recommended control objective(s). If the directors refuse or fail to do so the reporting accountants add an explanation in the criteria and scope paragraph of the assurance report identifying the omitted or inappropriate control objective(s) to draw the attention of the customers and their auditors. In addition, the wording of the conclusion paragraph may also be modified. An example paragraph illustrating an exception to the fair description is provided in Appendix 4 (a). 85

Although reporting accountants may qualify their conclusion on the fairness of the description of control procedures, this does not necessarily affect the suitability of design or operating effectiveness of the control procedures because the reporting accountants' conclusion relates only to the control objectives that are included in the service organisation's description. Reporting accountants note that it is the responsibility of the directors and not the reporting accountants to ensure the completeness and the reasonableness of control procedures over the activities of the service organisation. 86

Where control procedures associated with stated control objectives are incomplete or inappropriate, reporting accountants also discuss this with the directors so that the 87 directors may amend the description to include the associated control procedures. If the directors refuse or fail to amend the description, the reporting accountants add an explanatory paragraph preceding the conclusion to the report identifying the omitted or inappropriate control procedures to draw the attention of the customers and their auditors. In addition, the wording of the conclusion paragraph may be modified. An example paragraph illustrating an exception to the fair description is provided in Appendix 4 (a).

88 Where reporting accountants conclude that a set of control procedures are not suitably designed in relation to a specified control objective, they consider the design deficiencies in their overall assessment of the control procedures. If the reporting accountants determine that control procedures are not suitably designed to achieve a specified control objective, they add an explanatory paragraph preceding the conclusion to the report identifying the design deficiencies and modify the conclusion. An example paragraph illustrating an exception to the suitability of design is provided in Appendix 4 (b).

89 Where the reporting accountants' tests identify exceptions to the operating effectiveness of the control procedures, the reporting accountants consider whether this exception means that a control objective has not been achieved. In some cases deficiencies may be so pervasive that the reporting accountants modify their conclusion on the achievement of one or more control objective or issue an adverse opinion. An example paragraph illustrating an exception to the operating effectiveness is provided in Appendix 4 (c).

90 Where significant changes are introduced during the period covered in the report, the directors report this fact.

If reporting accountants become aware that the description on changes is missing, they request the directors to amend the description. However, the omission of information related to changes in the service organisation's control procedure does not warrant a qualification of the conclusion on the fairness of the description, provided that the directors' description of control procedures is fair as at the date of the description.

Elements of the service organisation report that are not covered by the assurance report

91 As discussed in paragraph 49 where the service organisation has included information other than that which constitutes a part of the description of control procedures, in its report, this is outside the scope of the assurance report. The reporting accountants read such information for consistency with their understanding of the entity.

Assurance report

92 The reporting accountants' conclusion is expressed in a written report attached to the directors' report. The title of the report includes the term 'assurance' to distinguish it from non assurance engagements, for instance, agreed upon procedures engagements. The report draws the attention of the readers to the basis of the reporting accountants' work, i.e. ISAE 3000 and this guidance.

93 The report by the reporting accountants reflects the agreement set out in the engagement letter. The report makes clear for whom it is prepared and who is entitled to rely upon it and for what purpose as established in paragraphs 55 to 60.

Reporting accountants conclude on the fairness of the description and the design and operating effectiveness of control procedures in relation to a specified reporting period.

Control procedures have inherent limitations and accordingly errors and irregularities may occur and not be detected. Also control procedures cannot guarantee protection against fraudulent collusion especially on the part of those holding positions of authority or trust. Reporting accountants refer to such inherent limitations in their report.

Key elements of the assurance report are shown in the table below. Pro forma reports on the internal controls over custodial operations are available in Appendix 3 (i) and (ii).

Elements of reporting accountants' assurance report

(a) A title indicating that the report is an assurance report.
(b) An addressee identifying the engaging parties to whom the assurance report is directed.
(c) Identification of the applicable engagement letter.
(d) Use of the report by the directors.
(e) Restrictions on the use of the assurance report to the directors [and customers party to the engagement] and the replication of the report in whole or in part.
(f) Limitation of the liability of the reporting accountants to the directors [and customers party to the engagement].
(g) An identification and description of the subject matter information.
(h) The identification of the directors as the responsible party and the respective responsibilities of the directors and the reporting accountants.
(i) Reference to ISAE 3000.
(j) Criteria against which control procedures were evaluated.
(k) A summary of the work performed.
(l) Inherent limitations associated with the evaluation/measurement of the subject matter against the criteria.
(m) The reporting accountants' conclusion with the description of the reporting accountants' findings including sufficient details of errors and exceptions found.
(n) The name and signature of the firm/reporting accountants and the location of the office performing the engagement.
(o) The assurance report date.

The engagement letter confirms that the assurance report is not to be recited or referred to in whole or in part in any other published document. This may also be stated in the report.

Using the work of internal auditors

A service organisation may have an internal audit department that performs tests of control procedures as part of its audit plan. The reporting accountants may determine that it might be effective and efficient to use the results of testing performed by internal auditors to alter the nature, timing or extent of the work they might otherwise have performed in forming their conclusion. Where using the work of internal auditors, however, the reporting accountants perform sufficient testing themselves which provides the principal evidence for their conclusion.

The reporting accountants also make reference to the work of internal auditors in their report and attribute the performance of the tests and the results of tests to them where appropriate.

Considerations for uncorrected errors, fraud or illegal acts

99   In the course of performing procedures at a service organisation, reporting accountants may become aware of uncorrected errors, fraud or illegal acts attributable to the service organisation's systems, management or employees that may affect one or more customers.

100 Unless clearly inconsequential, reporting accountants determine from the directors of the service organisation whether this information has been communicated to the affected customers. If the directors of the service organisation have not communicated this information and are unwilling to do so, the reporting accountants inform the service organisation's audit committee or other group of directors with equivalent authority. If the audit committee does not respond appropriately, the reporting accountants consider whether to resign from the engagement. The reporting accountants are generally not required to confirm with the customers that the service organisation has communicated such information.

Management representation letter

101 In all engagements, reporting accountants obtain written representations signed by the directors of the service organisation who the reporting accountants believe are responsible for and knowledgeable, directly or through others in the service organisation, about the matters covered in the representations. The refusal by the directors of the service organisation to provide the written representations considered necessary by the reporting accountants constitutes a limitation on the scope of the engagement and may be considered in forming the reporting accountants' conclusion. The representation letter is normally dated on the day the directors' report is dated.

Appendices

1. CONTROL OBJECTIVES

This section sets out detailed control objectives for the financial service activities referred to in paragraph 6. These control objectives are for guidance only and are not intended to be exhaustive, and it remains the responsibility of the directors to ensure that the described control objectives are sufficient to meet the expectations of customers.

(a) Custody

Accepting clients

- Accounts are set up and administered in accordance with client agreements and applicable regulations
- Complete and authorised client agreements are operative prior to initiating custody activity
- Investment holdings transferred from prior custodians are received and recorded completely, accurately and on a timely basis
- Client take-ons are monitored, documented and accurately reported to clients

Authorising and processing transactions

- Investment and related cash and foreign exchange transactions are authorised and recorded completely, accurately and on a timely basis
- Investment and related cash and foreign exchange transactions are settled and failures are resolved in a timely manner
- Corporate actions and voting instructions are identified, processed and recorded on a timely basis
- Cash receipts and payments are authorised, processed and recorded completely, accurately and on a timely basis
- Lender and borrower participation in lending programs is authorised and loan initiation, maintenance and termination are accurate and timely
- Loans are fully collateralised and the collateral together with its related income is recorded completely, accurately and on a timely basis

Maintaining financial and other records

- Investment income and related tax reclaims are collected and recorded accurately and on a timely basis
- Investments are valued using current prices obtained from independent external pricing sources and portfolio valuations are complete and distributed on a timely basis
- Asset positions for securities held by third parties such as sub custodians and depositories are accurately recorded and regularly reconciled

Safeguarding assets

- Physically held securities are safeguarded from loss, misappropriation and unauthorised use

Monitoring compliance

- Sub-custodians are approved and performance standards are monitored on a timely basis
- Outsourced activities are properly managed and monitored
- Transaction errors are rectified promptly and clients treated fairly

Reporting

- Client reporting in respect of client asset holdings is complete and accurate and provided within required timescales
- Asset positions and details of securities lent are reported to interested parties accurately and within the required time scale, including those responsible for initiating voting instructions, accurately and within required timescales

Information technology

See Appendix 1 (g)

(b) Investment management

Accepting clients

- Accounts are set up and administered in accordance with client agreements and applicable regulations
- Complete and authorised client agreements are operative prior to initiating investment activity
- Client take-ons are monitored, documented and accurately reported to clients

- Investment guidelines and restrictions are established
- Responsibility for generating proxy voting instructions is clearly established
- Pooled fund unitholder activity is recorded completely, accurately and in a timely manner

Authorising and processing transactions

- Investment strategy is set and implemented in a timely manner
- Investment transactions are properly authorised, executed and allocated in a timely, cost effective and accurate manner
- Transactions are undertaken only with approved counterparties
- Commission levels and transaction costs are monitored
- Investment and related cash transactions are completely and accurately recorded and settled in a timely manner
- Corporate actions and proxy voting instructions are identified and generated, respectively, and then processed and recorded accurately and in a timely manner
- Client new monies and withdrawals are authorised, processed and recorded completely and accurately

Maintaining financial and other records

- Investment income is accurately recorded in the proper period
- Investments are valued using current prices obtained from independent external pricing sources
- Cash and securities positions are completely and accurately recorded and reconciled to third party data
- Investment management fees and other account expenses are accurately calculated and recorded
- Pooled funds are priced and administered accurately and in a timely manner

Safeguarding assets

- Uninvested cash is managed with due regard to diversification of risk and security of funds
- Investments are properly registered and client money is segregated

Monitoring compliance

- Client portfolios are managed in accordance with investment objectives, monitored for compliance with investment guidelines and restrictions and performance is measured
- Outsourced activities are properly managed and monitored
- Transaction errors (including guideline breaches) are rectified promptly and clients treated fairly
- The effective transmission of proxy voting instructions is assessed regularly on a sample basis

Reporting to clients

- Client reporting in respect of portfolio transactions, holdings and performance, commission and voting is complete and accurate and provided within required timescales

Information technology

See Appendix 1 (g)

(c) Pension administration

Accepting clients

- Accounts are set up and administered in accordance with client agreements and applicable regulations
- Complete and authorised client agreements are operative prior to initiating administration activity
- Pension schemes taken on are properly established in the system in accordance with the scheme rules and individual elections

Authorising and processing transactions

- Contributions to defined contribution plans, defined benefit schemes, or both, and transfers of members' funds between investment options are processed accurately and in a timely manner
- Benefits payable and transfer values are calculated in accordance with scheme rules and relevant legislation and are paid on a timely basis

Maintaining financial and other records

- Member records consist of up to date and accurate information and are updated and reconciled regularly
- Contributions and benefit payments are completely and accurately recorded in the proper period
- Investment transactions, balances and related income are completely and accurately recorded in the proper period
- Scheme documents (deeds, policies, contracts, booklets etc) are complete, up to date and securely held

Safeguarding assets

- Member and scheme data is appropriately stored to ensure security and protection from unauthorised use
- Cash is safeguarded and payments are suitably authorised and controlled

Monitoring compliance

- Contributions are received in accordance with scheme rules and relevant legislation
- Services provided to pension schemes are in line with service level agreements
- Transaction errors are rectified promptly and clients treated fairly

Reporting to clients

- Periodic reports to participants and scheme sponsors are accurate and complete and provided within required timescales
- Annual reports and accounts are prepared in accordance with applicable law and regulations
- Regulatory reports are made if necessary

Information technology

See Appendix 1 (g)

(d) Property management

Accepting clients

- Accounts are set up and administered in accordance with client agreements and applicable regulations
- Complete and authorised client agreements are operative prior to initiating investment activity
- Client take-ons are monitored, documented and accurately reported to clients
- Investment guidelines and restrictions are established
- Pooled fund unitholder activity is recorded completely, accurately and in a timely manner

Authorising and processing transactions

- Investment decisions are properly formulated in accordance with investment guidelines, authorised, implemented and reviewed on a timely basis
- Property developments are only undertaken in accordance with acceptable risk criteria
- Costs associated with buying and selling properties are authorised and recorded accurately
- Tenants' covenants and lease conditions are assessed and authorised on a timely basis
- Property and related cash transactions are completely and accurately recorded and settled in a timely manner
- Rental income and service charges are accurately calculated and recorded on a timely basis
- Client new monies and withdrawals are authorised, processed and recorded completely and accurately

Maintaining financial and other records

- Complete and accurate records of each property are maintained
- Valuations are obtained at regular intervals from independent external valuers
- Income entitlements are received in full, wherever possible, and expenses, both recoverable and irrecoverable, are controlled
- Property management fees and other account expenses are accurately calculated and recorded
- Rents are monitored and rent reviews are recorded promptly and accurately
- Pooled funds are priced and administered accurately and in a timely manner

Safeguarding assets

- Properties purchased are of good and marketable title
- Title deeds are safeguarded from loss, misappropriation and unauthorised use
- Uninvested cash is managed with due regard to diversification of risk and security of funds
- Risks arising from investing in property are insured where this is economic to the interests of owners (for example consider claims etc arising from the public where large shopping malls are owned)

Monitoring compliance

- Client portfolios are managed in accordance with investment objectives, monitored for compliance with investment guidelines and restrictions and performance is measured
- Outsourced activities are properly managed and monitored

- Transaction errors (including guideline breaches) are rectified promptly and clients treated fairly

Reporting to clients

- Client reporting in respect of property transactions, holdings and performance is complete and accurate and provided within required timescales

Information technology

See Appendix 1 (g)

(e) Fund accounting

Accepting clients

- Accounts are set up and administered in accordance with client agreements and applicable regulations
- Complete and authorised client agreements are operative prior to initiating accounting activity
- Client take-ons are monitored, documented and accurately reported to clients

Authorising and processing transactions

- Portfolio transactions are recorded completely, accurately and on a timely basis
- Corporate actions are processed and recorded accurately and on a timely basis
- Expenses are accurately calculated and recorded in accordance with the requirements of the fund and on a timely basis
- Distribution rates are accurately calculated and authorised and distribution amounts are recorded in a timely manner

Maintaining financial and other records

- Investment income and related tax are accurately calculated and recorded on a timely basis
- Investments are valued using current prices obtained from independent external pricing sources
- Share/unit activity is recorded completely, accurately and positions are regularly reconciled
- Fund pricing is accurate and timely and box positions are reported accurately and monitored
- Cash and securities positions are completely and accurately recorded and reconciled to third party data

Monitoring compliance

- Services provided to clients are in line with service level agreements

Reporting to clients

- Net asset value is accurately calculated and reported in a timely manner
- Periodic reports to unitholders and fund sponsors are accurate and complete and distributed on a timely basis
- Annual reports and accounts are prepared in accordance with applicable law and regulations

Information technology

See Appendix 1 (g)

(f) Transfer agency

Accepting clients

- Accounts are set up and administered in accordance with client agreements and applicable regulations
- Adherence to subscription limits is checked and recording of client information required by legislation is accurate
- Complete and authorised client agreements are operative prior to initiating accounting activity
- Client take-ons are monitored, documented and accurately reported to clients

Authorising and processing transactions

- Documents received are checked, sorted and distributed for processing in a timely manner
- Investor transactions and adjustments are authorised, processed accurately, completely and in a timely manner
- Cash receipts are processed accurately and banked promptly
- Cheques and certificates issued are accurately generated, matched and authorised prior to despatch
- Fund distributions and related tax withholdings are accurately calculated and authorised and distributed in a timely manner

Maintaining financial and other records

- Transfer agent records accurately reflect securities and cash held by third parties
- Share/unit activity is recorded completely, accurately and positions are regularly reconciled

Safeguarding assets

- Lost and stolen certificates are recorded in a timely manner

Monitoring compliance

- Transaction errors are rectified promptly and clients treated fairly

Reporting to clients

- Compensation payments are authorised, calculated and reviewed by management
- Client reporting is complete and accurate and processed within required timescales

Information technology

See Appendix 1 (g)

(g) Information technology

Restricting access to systems and data

- Physical access to computer networks, equipment, storage media and program documentation is restricted to authorised individuals
- Logical access to computer systems, programs, master data, transaction data and parameters, including access by administrators to applications, databases, systems and networks, is restricted to authorised individuals via information security tools and techniques
- Segregation of incompatible duties is defined, implemented and enforced by logical security controls in accordance with job roles

Providing integrity and resilience to the information processing environment, commensurate with the value of the information held, information processing performed and external threats

- IT processing is authorised and scheduled appropriately and exceptions are identified and resolved in a timely manner
- Data transmissions between the service organisation and its counterparties are complete, accurate, timely and secure
- Appropriate measures are implemented to counter the threat from malicious electronic attack (e.g. firewalls, anti-virus etc.)
- The physical IT equipment is maintained in a controlled environment

Maintaining and developing systems hardware and software

- Development and implementation of new systems, applications and software, and changes to existing systems, applications and software, are authorised, tested, approved and implemented
- Data migration or modification is authorised, tested and, once performed, reconciled back to the source data

Recovering from processing interruptions

- Data and systems are backed up regularly, retained offsite and regularly tested for recoverability
- IT hardware and software issues are monitored and resolved in a timely manner
- Business and information systems recovery plans are documented, approved, tested and maintained

Monitoring compliance

- Outsourced activities are properly managed and monitored

2. EXAMPLE PARAGRAPHS FROM THE REPORT BY THE DIRECTORS

As directors we are responsible for the identification of control objectives relating to customers' assets[9] and related transactions in the provision of [financial services[10]] and the design, implementation and operation of the control procedures of [name of entity] to provide reasonable assurance that the control objectives are achieved.

In carrying out those responsibilities we have regard not only to the interests of customers but also to those of the owners of the business and the general effectiveness and efficiency of the relevant operations.

We have evaluated the effectiveness of the [name of entity]'s control procedures having regard to the Institute of Chartered Accountants in England & Wales Technical Release AAF 01/06 and the criteria for [financial services] set out therein.

We set out in this report a description of the relevant control procedures together with the related control objectives which operated during the period [x] to [y] and confirm that

(i) the report describes fairly the control procedures that relate to the control objectives referred to above which were in place as at [date];
(ii) the control procedures described are suitably designed such that there is reasonable assurance that the specified control objectives would be achieved if the described control procedures were complied with satisfactorily [and customers applied the control procedures contemplated[11]]; and
(iii) the control procedures described were operating with sufficient effectiveness to provide reasonable assurance that the related control objectives were achieved during the specified period.

Director

Date

Signed on behalf of the Board of Directors

---

[9] *The reference to "assets" may need to be expanded here and elsewhere in the report: see footnote 3, page 4.*

[10] *Refer to relevant financial services as per paragraph 6, page 1.*

[11] *This additional wording may be considered appropriate in circumstances described in paragraph 43, page 8.*

3. PRO FORMA REPORTING ACCOUNTANTS' ASSURANCE REPORTS (I) AND (II)

(i) Engagement formed between the reporting accountant and the service organisation and to which customers of the service organisation are party

---

Reporting accountants' assurance report on internal controls of service organisations[12]

To the directors of [name of entity] and [customers party to the engagement]

Use of report[13]

This report is made solely for the use of the directors, as a body, of [name of entity] and [customers party to the engagement], and solely for the purpose of reporting on the internal controls of [name of entity], in accordance with the terms of our engagement letter dated [date][and attached[14] as appendix [...............]].

Our work has been undertaken so that we might report to the directors and [customers party to the engagement] those matters that we have agreed to state to them in this report and for no other purpose. Our report must not be recited or referred to in whole or in part in any other document nor made available, copied or recited to any other party, in any circumstances, without our express prior written permission.

To the fullest extent permitted by law, we do not accept or assume responsibility to anyone other than the directors as a body, [name of entity] and [customers party to the engagement] for our work, for this report or for the opinions we have formed.

Subject matter

This report covers solely the internal controls of [name of entity] as described in your report as at [date]. Internal controls are processes designed to provide reasonable assurance regarding the level of control over customers' assets[15] and related transactions achieved by [name of entity] in the provision of [outsourced activities] by [name of entity].

Respective responsibilities

The directors' responsibilities and assertions are set out on page [...............] of your report. Our responsibility is to form an independent conclusion, based on

---

[12] Reporting accountants consider a suitable form of report in accordance with the specific engagement as described in paragraph 55. This report provides an example for an engagement to which customers of the service organisation are party (see paragraph 55(a)).

[13] The two last paragraphs in "Use of report" provide example wording, disclaiming reporting accountants' liability or duty to the customers that are not party to the engagement. Reporting accountants consider the legal effectiveness of disclaiming liability in the particular circumstances of their engagement.

[14] Reporting accountants that do not attach the engagement letter consider including relevant extracts.

[15] The reference to "assets" may need to be expanded here and elsewhere in the report: see footnote 3, page 4.

the work carried out in relation to the control procedures of [name of entity]'s [................] function carried out at the specified business units of [name of entity] [located at [................]] as described in the directors' report and report this to the directors of [name of entity] and [customers party to the engagement].

Criteria and scope

We conducted our engagement in accordance with International Standard on Assurance Engagements (ISAE) 3000 and the Institute of Chartered Accountants in England & Wales Technical Release AAF 01/06. The criteria against which the control procedures were evaluated are the internal control objectives developed for service organisations as set out within the Technical Release AAF 01/06 and identified by the directors as relevant control objectives relating to the level of control over customers' assets and related transactions in the provision of [outsourced activities]. Our work was based upon obtaining an understanding of the control procedures as described on page [................] to [................] in the report by the directors, and evaluating the directors' assertions as described on page [................] to [................] in the same report to obtain reasonable assurance so as to form our conclusion. Our work also included tests of specific control procedures, to obtain evidence about their effectiveness in meeting the related control objectives. The nature, timing and extent of the tests we applied are detailed on pages [................] to [................].

Our tests are related to [name of entity] as a whole rather than performed to meet the needs of any particular customer.

Inherent limitations

Control procedures designed to address specified control objectives are subject to inherent limitations and, accordingly, errors or irregularities may occur and not be detected. Such control procedures cannot guarantee protection against (among other things) fraudulent collusion especially on the part of those holding positions of authority or trust. Furthermore, our conclusion is based on historical information and the projection of any information or conclusions in the attached report to any future periods would be inappropriate.

Conclusion

In our opinion, in all material respects:

1. the accompanying report by the directors describes fairly the control procedures that relate to the control objectives referred to above which were in place as at [date];
2. the control procedures described on pages [................] to [................] were suitably designed such that there is reasonable, but not absolute, assurance that the specified control objectives would have been achieved if the described control procedures were complied with satisfactorily [and customers applied the control procedures contemplated[16]]; and
3. the control procedures that were tested, as set out in the attachment to this report, were operating with sufficient effectiveness for us to obtain reasonable, but not absolute, assurance that the related control objectives were achieved in the period [x] to [y].

---

[16] See footnote 11, page 26.

Name of firm
Chartered Accountants
Location
Date

(ii) Engagement formed between the reporting accountant and the service organisation only

Reporting accountants' assurance report on internal controls of service organisations[17]
To the directors of [name of entity]
Use of report[18]
This report is made solely for the use of the directors, as a body, of [name of entity], and solely for the purpose of reporting on the internal controls of [name of entity], in accordance with the terms of our engagement letter dated [date] [and attached[19] as appendix [..............]].
Our work has been undertaken so that we might report to the directors those matters that we have agreed to state to them in this report and for no other purpose. Our report must not be recited or referred to in whole or in part in any other document nor made available, copied or recited to any other party, in any circumstances, without our express prior written permission.
We permit the disclosure of this report, in full only, by the directors at their discretion to customers [of [name of entity] using [name of entity]'s [financial services[20]] ("customers"),] and to the auditors of such customers, to enable customers and their auditors to verify that a report by reporting accountants has been commissioned by the directors of [name of entity] and issued in connection with the internal controls of [name of entity], and without assuming or accepting any responsibility or liability to customers or their auditors on our part.

---

[17] *Reporting accountants consider a suitable form of report in accordance with the specific engagement as described in paragraph 55. This report provides an example for an engagement formed between the reporting accountants and the service organisation only, applicable to arrangements (c) and (d) as described in paragraph 55, page 10-11. The sentence beginning "we permit" is adapted where paragraph 55(c) is applied.*

[18] *The three last paragraphs in "Use of report" provide example wording, disclaiming reporting accountants' liability or duty to the customers that are not party to the engagement. Reporting accountants consider the legal effectiveness of disclaiming liability in the particular circumstances of their engagement.*

[19] *Reporting accountants that do not attach the engagement letter consider including relevant extracts.*

[20] *See footnote 10, page 26.*

To the fullest extent permitted by law, we do not accept or assume responsibility to anyone other than the directors as a body and [name of entity] for our work, for this report or for the conclusions we have formed.[21]

Subject matter

This report covers solely the internal controls of [name of entity] as described in your report as at [date]. Internal controls are processes designed to provide reasonable assurance regarding the level of control over customers' assets[22] and related transactions achieved by [name of entity] in the provision of [outsourced activities] by [name of entity].

Respective responsibilities

The directors' responsibilities and assertions are set out on page [................] of your report. Our responsibility is to form an independent conclusion, based on the work carried out in relation to the control procedures of [name of entity]'s [................] function carried out at the specified business units of [name of entity] [located at [................]] as described in your report and report this to you as the directors of [name of entity].

Criteria and scope

We conducted our engagement in accordance with International Standard on Assurance Engagement (ISAE) 3000 and the Institute of Chartered Accountants in England & Wales Technical Release AAF 01/06. The criteria against which the control procedures were evaluated are the internal control objectives developed for service organisations as set out within the Technical Release AAF 01/06 and identified by the directors as relevant control objectives relating to the level of control over customers' assets and related transactions in the provision of [outsourced activities]. Our work was based upon obtaining an understanding of the control procedures as described on page [................] to [................] in the report by the directors, and evaluating the directors' assertions as described on page [................] to [................] in the same report to obtain reasonable assurance so as to form our conclusion. Our work also included tests of specific control procedures, to obtain evidence about their effectiveness in meeting the related control objectives. The nature, timing and extent of the tests we applied are detailed on pages [................] to [................].

---

[21] *If arrangement (b) as described in paragraph 55 is considered appropriate then accountants consider including reference to the facility for customers meeting a firm's client acceptance criteria to enjoy a duty of care from the accountants if they accept the relevant terms of the engagement letter agreed previously with the service organisation. Wording that might be used (in particular in place of the paragraphs shown above and beginning "We permit" and "To the fullest extent" is as follows: "Subject as follows, we are prepared to extend our assumption of responsibility to those customers who first accept in writing (in a form provided to us and confirmed by us to be acceptable to us) the relevant terms of the engagement letter agreed previously with [name of entity] as if the customer had signed that letter when originally issued, and including the provisions limiting liability contained in that letter. This extension will not apply to a customer where we inform that customer, whether before or after the customer accepts the relevant terms of the engagement letter, that they do not meet our client acceptance criteria. To the fullest extent permitted by law, we do not accept or assume responsibility to anyone other than the directors as a body, the organisation and any customer to whom the extension does apply, for our work, for this report or for the conclusions we have formed."*

[22] *The reference to "assets" may need to be expanded here and elsewhere in the report: see footnote 3, page 4.*

> *Except for the matter referred to above concerning the operating effectiveness of the control procedures, in our opinion, ...*

Where the results of the reporting accountants' tests of operational effectiveness and the deficiency have been integrated and fully explained into the report by the directors the reporting accountants may alternatively consider cross-referring their qualification to where these details may be found. For example:

> *Except for the matter explained on page [z] concerning the follow up of reconciling items on physical security reconciliations, the control procedures tested, as set out [on pages [x] to [y] of the report by the directors/ in the attachment to this report], in our opinion, ...*

5. EXAMPLE EXTRACTS FROM AN ENGAGEMENT LETTER

These extracts are provided for illustrative purposes only. Reporting accountants apply their own judgement to develop suitable wording for their engagement letters to reflect the guidance in this Technical Release and their own particular circumstances.[24]

Responsibilities of directors

> The board of directors ("the Directors") of [name of entity] in relation to which the reporting accountants' assurance report is to be provided ("the Organisation") are and shall be responsible for the design, implementation and operation of control procedures that provide adequate level of control over customers' assets[25] and related transactions. The Directors' responsibilities are and shall include:
>
> - acceptance of responsibility for internal controls;
> - evaluation of the effectiveness of the service organisation's control procedures using suitable criteria;
> - supporting their evaluation with sufficient evidence, including documentation; and
> - providing a written report ("Directors' Report") of the effectiveness of the service organisation's internal controls for the relevant financial period.
>
> In drafting this report the Directors have regard to, as a minimum, the criteria specified within the Technical Release AAF 01/06 issued by the Institute of Chartered Accountants in England & Wales ("the Institute") but they may add to these to the extent that this is considered appropriate in order to meet customers' expectations.

[24] The above extracts may be appropriate illustrations only for an engagement formed between the reporting accountants and the service organisation. Where a multi-party engagement is formed in line with para 55(a), wording should be revised and additional clauses should be inserted as appropriate. Where a customer agrees to sign up to the engagement terms at a later date, additional wording may be inserted in line with para 55(b) to clarify the basis on which the customer signs up and to secure the consent of the service organisation/original addressees. The wording will include adjustment of the section on "Use of Report" and the addition of wording in the section on Liability Provisions to refer to the provisions applying to "the Directors as a body, the Organisation (and customers who are or become, by signature, a party to the engagement letter)" and to losses suffered by, and aggregate liability to, "the Directors as a body, the Organisation (and any customers who are or become, by signature, a party to the engagement letter)".

[25] The reference to "assets" may need to be expanded here and elsewhere in the report: see footnote 3, page 4.

Responsibilities of reporting accountants

> It is our responsibility to form an independent conclusion, based on the work carried out in relation to the control procedures of the Organisation's [...............] function carried out at the specified business units of the Organisation [located at [...............]] as described in the Directors' report and report this to the Directors.

Scope of the reporting accountants' work

> We conduct our work in accordance with the procedures set out in AAF 01/06, issued by the Institute. Our work will include enquiries of management, together with tests of certain specific control procedures which will be set out in an appendix to our report.
>
> In reaching our conclusion, the criteria against which the control procedures are to be evaluated are the internal control objectives developed for service organisations as set out within the AAF 01/06 issued by the Institute.
>
> Any work already performed in connection with this engagement before the date of this letter will also be governed by the terms and conditions of this letter.
>
> We may seek written representations from the Directors in relation to matters on which independent corroboration is not available. We shall seek confirmation from the Directors that any significant matters of which we should be aware have been brought to our attention.

Inherent limitations

> The Directors acknowledge that control procedures designed to address specified control objectives are subject to inherent limitations and, accordingly, errors or irregularities may occur and not be detected. Such procedures cannot guarantee protection against fraudulent collusion especially on the part of those holding positions of authority or trust. Furthermore, the opinion set out in our report will be based on historical information and the projection of any information or conclusions in our report to any future periods will be inappropriate.

Use of our report

> Our report will, subject to the permitted disclosures set out in this letter, be made solely for the use of the Directors of the Organisation, and solely for the purpose of reporting on the internal controls of the Organisation, in accordance with these terms of our engagement.
>
> Our work will be undertaken so that we might report to the Directors those matters that we have agreed to state to them in our report and for no other purpose.

Our report will be issued on the basis that it must not be recited or referred to or disclosed, in whole or in part, in any other document or to any other party, without the express prior written permission of the reporting accountants. We permit the disclosure of our report, in full only, to customers [of the Organisation using the Organisation's [financial services[26]] ("customers")] [(as defined in appendix [...............] to this letter),] and to the auditors of such customers, to enable customers and their auditors to verify that a report by reporting accountants has been commissioned by the Directors of the Organisation and issued in connection with the internal controls of the Organisation without assuming or accepting any responsibility or liability to them on our part.

To the fullest extent permitted by law, we do not and will not accept or assume responsibility to anyone other than the Directors as a body and the Organisation for our work, for our report or for the opinions we will have formed[27].

Liability provisions[28]

We will perform the engagement with reasonable skill and care and acknowledge that we will be liable to the Directors as a body and the Organisation for losses, damages, costs or expenses ("losses") suffered by the Directors as a body and the Organisation as a result of our breach of contract, negligence, fraud or other deliberate breach of duty. Our liability shall be subject to the following provisions:

- We will not be so liable if such losses are due to the provision of false, misleading or incomplete information or documentation or due to the acts or omissions of any person other than us, except where, on the basis of the enquiries normally undertaken by us within the scope set out in these terms of engagement, it would have been reasonable for us to discover such defects;
- We accept liability without limit for the consequences of our own fraud or other deliberate breach of duty and for any other liability which it is not permitted by law to limit or exclude;
- Subject to the previous provisions of this Liability paragraph, our total aggregate liability whether in contract, tort (including negligence) or otherwise, to the Directors as a body and the Organisation, arising from or in connection with the work which is the subject of these terms (including any addition or variation to the work), shall not exceed the amount of *[To be discussed and negotiated]*;

To the fullest extent permitted by law, the Organisation agrees to indemnify and hold harmless [name of reporting accountants] and its partners and staff against all actions, proceedings and claims brought or threatened against [name of reporting accountants] or against any of its partners and staff by any persons other than the Directors as a body and the Organisation, and all loss, damage and expense (including legal expenses) relating thereto, where any such action,

---

[26] See footnote 10, page 26.

[27] See footnote 20, page 29.

[28] Reporting accountants may wish to seek independent legal advice on language that addresses both the matters covered in the illustrative wording set out in this Liability section together with any related matters such as provisions indicating that liability does not extend to consequential losses. Accountants may also consider any applicable independence requirements.

proceeding or claim in any way relates to or concerns or is connected with any of [name of reporting accountants]'s work under this engagement letter.

The Directors as a body and the Organisation agree that they will not bring any claims or proceedings against any of our individual partners, members, directors or employees. This clause is intended to benefit such partners, members, directors and employees who may enforce this clause pursuant to the Contracts (Rights of Third Parties) Act 1999 ("the Act"). Notwithstanding any benefits or rights conferred by this agreement on such partners, members, directors or employees by virtue of the Act, we and the Directors as a body may together agree in writing to vary or rescind the agreement set out in this letter without the consent of any such partners, members, directors or employees. Other than as expressly provided in this paragraph, the provisions of the Act are excluded;

Any claims, whether in contract, negligence or otherwise, must be formally commenced within [years] after the party bringing the claim becomes aware (or ought reasonably to have become aware) of the facts which give rise to the action and in any event no later than [years] after any alleged breach of contract, negligence or other cause of action. This expressly overrides any statutory provision which would otherwise apply.

This engagement is separate from, and unrelated to, our audit work on the financial statements of the Organisation for the purposes of the Companies Act 1985 (or its successor) or other legislation and nothing herein creates obligations or liabilities regarding our statutory audit work, which would not otherwise exist. [Equivalent paragraphs where the Organisation is other than a Companies Act entity].

[Appendix

The list of customers to whom the assurance report may be made available[29].]

6. EXAMPLE SAMPLE SIZE TABLE

In determining the number of items to be tested the reporting accountants need to consider the factors referred to in paragraph 81. Although the extent of testing is a matter of judgement on the part of the reporting accountants the table set out below illustrates a range of possible sample sizes which may assist in making such judgements.

Frequency of Control	Number of items tested
Annual	1
Quarterly	1, 2, 3
Monthly	2, 3, 4, 5
Weekly	5, 10, 15
Daily	15, 20, 30, 40
Multiple times per day	25, 30, 45, 60

[29] *A list of customers may not be practical where they are multiple.*

7. ILLUSTRATIVE DEFINITION OF ENQUIRY, INSPECTION, OBSERVATION AND RE-PERFORMANCE

In describing the nature of tests carried out, it is desirable for the reporting accountants to define in their report what is meant by such procedures as enquiry, inspection, observation and re-performance (see paragraph 84). Illustrative definitions which may assist reporting accountants in this regard are set out below.

Enquiry:

> Enquired of appropriate [name of entity] personnel. Enquiries seeking relevant information or representation from personnel were performed to obtain, among other things:
> - knowledge, additional information and affirmation regarding the control of procedures; and
> - corroborating evidence of the control procedures.

Inspection:

> Inspected documents and records indicating performance of the control procedures. This included, among other things:
> - inspection of reconciliations and management reports that age and/or quantify reconciling items to assess whether balances and reconciling items appear to be properly monitored, controlled and resolved on a timely basis, as required by the related control;
> - examination of source documentation and authorisations related to selected transactions processed;
> - examination of documents or records for evidence of performance such as the existence of initials or signatures; and
> - inspection of [name of entity]'s systems documentation, such as operations, manuals, flow charts and job descriptions.

Observation:

> Observed the application or existence of specific control procedures as represented.

Re-performance

> Re-performed the control or processing application of the control procedures to check the accuracy of their operation. This included, among other things:
> - obtaining evidence of the arithmetical accuracy and correct processing of transactions by performing independent calculations; and
> - re-performing the matching of various system records by independently matching the same records and comparing reconciling items to reconciliations prepared by the service organisation.

AAF 02/06
Identifying and managing certain risks arising from the inclusion of reports from auditors and accountants in prospectuses (and certain other investment circulars)

Contents

	Paragraphs
Background	1
Third party risk and existing practice	3
Third party risk	6
Prospectuses	11
Inclusion of a statutory audit report in an investment circular	15
Reporting accountant's special purpose reports intended for inclusion in an investment circular	22
Reference, by notice under s240 Companies Act 1985 only, to a statutory audit report in an investment circular	25
Addressing a report	29
Status and effect of guidance	33

Appendices

1. Relevant regulatory provisions
2. Illustrative consent wording, applicable for consent letters required in connection with the inclusion of audit reports
3. Illustrative clarifying language for insertion in reporting accountant's separate, special purpose reports

This guidance is issued by the Audit and Assurance Faculty of the Institute of Chartered Accountants in England and Wales in April 2006 to assist auditors and accountants in identifying and managing the risks of being found to have assumed a duty of care to third parties in connection with the inclusion of their reports in prospectuses (and certain other investment circulars). This guidance does not constitute an auditing standard. Professional judgment should be used in its application and, where appropriate, professional legal assistance should be sought.

© Institute of Chartered Accountants in England and Wales

No responsibility for loss occasioned to any person acting or refraining from action as a result of any material in this Technical Release can be accepted by the Institute.

Prospectuses

The Prospectus Rules include, by Rules 5.5.3 and 5.5.4, among the persons responsible for a prospectus "each person who accepts, and is stated in the prospectus as accepting responsibility for the prospectus" and "each person (not falling within any of the previous paragraphs) who has authorised the contents of the prospectus". By Rule 5.5.8 a person who accepts responsibility for a prospectus may state that they do so only in relation to specified parts of the prospectus, or only in specified respects.

Reporting accountants accept responsibility (where required) in relation to specified parts of a prospectus only or in specified respects only and take care to identify with precision those parts or respects in relation to which they accept responsibility and to see that their acceptance of responsibility is accurately stated in the prospectus.

Reporting accountants accepting responsibility in relation to specified parts of the prospectus or for the prospectus in specified respects further take care to see that their acceptance of responsibility is limited to responsibility to those to whom the Prospectus Rules contemplated that they would be responsible, and not to third parties.

In order not to extend their responsibility, reporting accountants may decline to address any report to any person other than the issuer. Further general guidance on addressing a report is given below.

Inclusion of a statutory audit report in an investment circular

In some situations the entity responsible for an investment circular may need to include in it an audit report made under section 235 of the Companies Act 1985. Under section 240 of the Companies Act 1985, the entity is required to accompany any publication of its statutory accounts with the auditors' report under section 235.

There are situations in which the entity may not need to obtain the auditors' consent, depending on the circumstances in which the audit report is proposed to be reproduced and the applicable regulatory requirements. If consent is given it could affect the responsibility assumed by the auditors and for that reason auditors will ordinarily not give consent where it is not needed. Auditors are not required by the Prospectus Directive Regulation to consent to the inclusion of previously issued audit reports in the investment circular. The paragraphs below deal only with the situation where consent is needed and for that reason is requested.

The section 235 audit report addresses an entity's state of affairs at a particular point in time. It contains an opinion from the entity's auditors on historical financial information. Language clarifying to whom the auditors will accept responsibility, inserted in accordance with Audit 1/03, demonstrates to whom the auditors have reported, on what they have reported, what they have reported and for what purpose they have reported.

The provision of consent to the inclusion of the audit report in an investment circular may in some situations be argued to extend the compass of the auditors' responsibility beyond that reflected by language inserted in accordance with Audit 1/03 and inserted at the time of the audit. The question therefore arises as to whether, in an effort to manage the risk of third party claims, auditors should, where their consent is required, insist on the insertion of additional clarification language in the investment circular over and above that already in the section 235 audit report itself, as a condition for giving that consent.

19 In the light of advice obtained from Leading Counsel, the Institute's guidance to audit firms is that additional clarification language is not desirable, provided that the auditors (i) limit their consent to the inclusion of the audit report, (ii) clarify when consenting the specific purpose for which the consent is given, and (iii) consider and follow SIR 1000 in connection with the form and context in which the audit report appears in the investment circular. Attempts by auditors to clarify their responsibilities further could simply have the effect of undermining or confusing the auditors' position as stated in the historical section 235 audit report. Auditors will not however consent to the inclusion of anything other than their full section 235 audit report.[4]

20 Illustrative consent wording, applicable for consent letters required in connection with the inclusion of audit reports in investment circulars, can be found in Appendix 2.

21 Auditors may, when considering whether to accede to a request for consent to the inclusion of a statutory audit report in an investment circular, become aware that there are defects in the statutory accounts that the entity proposes to publish. In such cases the auditors discuss with those charged with governance at the entity the provisions of section 245 of the Companies Act 1985 relating to the revision of statutory accounts, and in appropriate circumstances may refuse to give the consent requested.

Reporting accountant's special purpose reports intended for inclusion in an investment circular

22 Reporting accountants may be engaged to prepare reports intended specifically for inclusion in an investment circular[5]. Where required by regulation, the entity responsible for the investment circular, and requesting the preparation of the report, will need to obtain the reporting accountant's consent to inclusion of their report in the investment circular[6].

23 Unlike the position in respect of the section 235 audit report, separate special purpose reports prepared by reporting accountants for inclusion in investment circulars are not historical documents but are prepared in the context of the particular investment offering. Reporting accountants therefore use language in their reports to clarify the particular, special purpose for which their report is prepared and avoid giving consent for the inclusion of their report in the investment circular in a manner, context or circumstance which undermines or is inconsistent with their report's clarifying language.

24 Illustrative clarifying language for insertion in reporting accountant's separate, special purpose reports, can be found at Appendix 3. The illustration of consent wording found at Appendix 2 can be adapted as appropriate.

[4] *This paragraph applies equally to audit reports on non-statutory accounts of an entity issuing an investment circular, on the basis (see also footnote 1 above) that such audit reports will include clarification language reflecting Audit 1/03.*

[5] *Such reports may include reporting accountant's reports on historical financial information, profit forecasts or estimates, or proforma financial information. A list of published reports is included in Appendix 1 of SIR 1000.*

[6] *For example under item 23.1 of Annex I to the Prospectus Directive Regulation.*

Reference, by notice under s240 Companies Act 1985 only, to a statutory audit report in an investment circular

25 The entity responsible for an investment circular may be subject to a requirement, under the rules applicable to the proposed investment offering, that relevant financial information must be included in the investment circular. In certain circumstances, for example under Rule 24 of the City Code on Takeovers and Mergers, the entity responsible for the investment circular is able to meet that requirement by including historical financial information in tabular form.

26 Financial information included in this way should not comprise the inclusion of the statutory accounts of the entity and the audit report is not reproduced within or alongside such a table. Issues of acceptance of responsibility by auditors for the prospectus (in respect of specified parts or in specified respects), and a statement of acceptance of responsibility, of the type discussed elsewhere in this Technical Release should not therefore arise. Similarly the provision by the auditors of consent in connection with inclusion of their audit report in the investment circular in such circumstances should not arise. Consistently, the only reference to the audit report will be in the form of a notice by the entity addressing the requirements of section 240(3) of the Companies Act 1985.

27 The requirements for such a notice are set out in section 240(3) of the Companies Act 1985. The notice must in summary state (a) that the accounts are not the entity's statutory accounts (b) whether statutory accounts dealing with the relevant financial year have been delivered to the registrar of companies (c) whether the entity's auditors have made a report under section 235 for the relevant financial year and (d) whether any auditors' report so made was qualified or contained a statement as to inadequacy of records or failures to obtain necessary information.

28 Any other reference will require individual consideration by the reporting accountants. If additional work for the entity is undertaken by accountants, it is desirable that in any document issued by the accountants it is made clear for whom the work is undertaken and that limitations in the scope of the additional work undertaken and restrictions on the use to which the additional work may be put are clearly stated. The management of risk in relation to additional work that is to receive wider or public circulation requires particularly careful individual consideration.

Addressing a report

29 The inclusion of a person as an addressee of a report may affect the responsibility that is assumed by the reporting accountant. Terms of engagement should be agreed between reporting accountants and proposed addressees in an engagement letter, and will affect the responsibility that the reporting accountants assume towards the addressee.

30 Where an accountant is asked to assume responsibility to a person by addressing a report to that person, before doing so, and in order to evaluate the risks, the accountant should bring into consideration, among other things, why the person has asked for the report to be addressed to it, and the role that that person will undertake in relation to the transaction and the investment circular (including whether (and how, and to what extent, and to whom) that person has or has not assumed responsibility in respect of the transaction or the investment circular).

31 In this connection, in the case of a prospectus to which the requirements of the Prospectus Rules apply, reporting accountants note whether the proposed addressee is a person who is responsible for the prospectus under Rules 5.5.3 and 5.5.4 and the terms of any statement of responsibility including one made under Rule 5.5.8.

32 Where reporting accountants do agree to address a report to a person, they will wish the engagement letter to make clear (as appropriate) that the responsibility assumed to the addressee is in respect of the addressee's own responsibility to others arising from the contents of the report included in the prospectus or investment circular and not in respect of any profit the addressee may claim to have lost or expense that the addressee may have incurred.

Status and effect of this guidance

33 The illustrative wording appended to this Technical Release has been endorsed by Leading Counsel as likely to make a valuable and appropriate contribution to the management of risk. The UK Listing Authority has been approached by the Institute and has been made aware of this guidance and the illustrative wording that the Institute suggests to auditors and reporting accountants.

34 The Technical Release is effective from the date of issue.

Appendix – 1 Relevant regulatory provisions EU Prospectus Directive Regulation (809/2004/EC)

Annex I 1. Persons Responsible

1.2 A declaration by those responsible for the registration document that, having taken all reasonable care to ensure that such is the case, the information contained in the registration document is, to the best of their knowledge, in accordance with the facts and contains no omission likely to affect its import. As the case may be, a declaration by those responsible for certain parts of the registration document that, having taken all reasonable care to ensure that such is the case, the information contained in the part of the registration document for which they are responsible is, to the best of their knowledge, in accordance with the facts and contains no omission likely to affect its import.

23. Third Party Information and Statement by Experts and Declarations of any Interest

23.1 Where a statement or report attributed to a person as an expert is included in the Registration Document, provide such person's name, business address, qualifications and material interest if any in the issuer. If the report has been produced at the issuer's request a statement to the effect that such statement or report is included, in the form and context in which it is included, with the consent of the person who has authorised the contents of that part of the Registration Document.

The language above is set out in materially identical terms in other annexes in respect of registration documents, securities notes and prospectuses[7].

Prospectus Rules

Chapter 5: Other provisions

5.5 Persons responsible for a prospectus

Persons responsible for a prospectus

5.5.1R The *rules* in this section specify in accordance with section 84(1)(d) of the *Act* and for the purposes of Part 6 of the *Act*, the *persons* responsible for a *prospectus*.

Note: In accordance with PR 1.1.9R a reference in this section to a *prospectus* includes a *supplementary prospectus*.

Rules only apply if UK is home State

5.5.2R The *rules* in this section only apply in respect of a *prospectus* if the *United Kingdom* is the *Home State* for the *issuer* in relation to the *transferable securities* to which the *prospectus* relates.

Equity shares

5.5.3R (1) This *rule* applies to a *prospectus* relating to:

(a) *equity shares*;
(b) warrants or options to subscribe for *equity shares*, that are issued by the *issuer* of the *equity shares*; and
(c) other *transferable securities* that have similar characteristics to *transferable securities* referred to in paragraphs (a) or (b).

(2) Each of the following *persons* are responsible for the *prospectus*:

(a) the *issuer* of the *transferable securities*;
(b) if the *issuer* is a *body corporate*:
   (i) each *person* who is a *director* of that *body corporate* when the *prospectus* is published; and
   (ii) each *person* who has authorised himself to be named, and is named, in the *prospectus* as a *director* or as having agreed to become a *director* of that *body corporate* either immediately or at a future time;
(c) each *person* who accepts, and is stated in the *prospectus* as accepting, responsibility for the *prospectus*;
(d) in relation to an *offer*:
   (i) the *offeror*, if this is not the *issuer*; and
   (ii) if the *offeror* is a *body corporate* and is not the *issuer*, each *person* who is a *director* of the *body corporate* when the *prospectus* is published;
(e) in relation to a request for the *admission to trading* of *transferable securities*:
   (i) the *person* requesting admission, if this is not the *issuer*; and

---

[7] *See for example Annex III, paragraph 10.3 (securities note); Annex IV, paragraph 16.1 (registration document); Annex V, paragraph 7.3 (securities note); Annex VII, paragraph 9.1 (registration document); Annex IX, paragraph 13.1 (registration document); Annex X, paragraph 23.1 (prospectus); Annex XI, paragraph 13.1 (registration document); Annex XII, paragraph 7.3 (securities note); Annex XIII, paragraph 7.3 (securities note); Annex XVI, paragraph 7. (registration document); and Annex XVII, paragraph 6. (registration document).*

(ii) if the *person* requesting admission is a *body corporate* and is not the *issuer*, each *person* who is a *director* of the *body corporate* when the *prospectus* is published; and
(f) each *person* not falling within any of the previous paragraphs who has authorised the contents of the *prospectus*.

All other securities

5.5.4R (1) This *rule* applies to a *prospectus* relating to *transferable securities* other than those to which PR 5.5.3R applies.

(2) Each of the following *persons* are responsible for the *prospectus*:

(a) the *issuer* of the *transferable securities*;
(b) each *person* who accepts, and is stated in the *prospectus* as accepting, responsibility for the *prospectus*;
(c) in relation to an *offer*, the *offeror* of the *transferable securities*, if this is not the *issuer*;
(d) in relation to a request for an *admission to trading* of *transferable securities*, the *person* requesting admission, if this is not the *issuer*;
(e) if there is a *guarantor* for the issue, the *guarantor* in relation to information in the *prospectus* that relates to the *guarantor* and the *guarantee*; and
(f) each *person* not falling within any of the previous paragraphs who has authorised the contents of the *prospectus*.

Issuer not responsible if it has not authorised offer or admission to trading

5.5.5R A *person* is not responsible for a prospectus under PR 5.5.3R (2)(a) or (b) or PR 5.5.4R (2)(a) if the *issuer* has not made or authorised the *offer* or the request for *admission to trading* in relation to which the *prospectus* was published.

Publication without directors consent

5.5.6R A *person* is not responsible for a *prospectus* under PR 5.5.3R (2)(b)(i) if it is published without his knowledge or consent and on becoming aware of its publication he, as soon as practicable, gives reasonable public notice that it was published without his knowledge or consent.

Offeror not responsible in certain circumstances

5.5.7R A *person* is not responsible for a *prospectus* under PR 5.5.3R (2)(d) or PR 5.5.4 (2)(c) if:

(1) the *issuer* is responsible for the *prospectus* in accordance with the *rules* in this section;
(2) the *prospectus* was drawn up primarily by the *issuer*, or by one or more *persons* acting on behalf of the *issuer*; and
(3) the *offeror* is making the *offer* in association with the *issuer*.

Person may accept responsibility for, or authorise, part of contents

5.5.8R A *person* who accepts responsibility for a *prospectus* under PR 5.5.3R (2)(c) or PR 5.5.4R (2)(b) or authorises the contents of a *prospectus* under PR 5.5.3R (2)(f) or PR 5.5.4R (2)(f), may state that they do so only in relation to specified parts of the *prospectus*, or only in specified respects, and in that case the *person* is responsible under those paragraphs:

(1) only to the extent specified; and
(2) only if the material in question is included in (or substantially in) the form and context to which the *person* has agreed.

Advice in a professional capacity

5.5.9R Nothing in the *rules* in this section is to be construed as making a *person* responsible for any *prospectus* by reason only of the *person* giving advice about its contents in a professional capacity.

Section 90 of the Financial Services and Markets Act 2000

Compensation for false or misleading particulars

(1) Any person responsible for listing particulars is liable to pay compensation to a person who has –
  (a) acquired securities to which the particulars apply; and
  (b) suffered loss in respect of them as a result of –
    (i) any untrue or misleading statement in the particulars; or
    (ii) the omission from the particulars of any matter required to be included by section 80 or 81.
(2) Subsection (1) is subject to exemptions provided by Schedule 10.
(3) If listing particulars are required to include information about the absence of a particular matter, the omission from the particulars of that information is to be treated as a statement in the listing particulars that there is no such matter.
(4) Any person who fails to comply with section 81 is liable to pay compensation to any person who has –
  (a) acquired securities of the kind in question; and
  (b) suffered loss in respect of them as a result of the failure.
(5) Subsection (4) is subject to exemptions provided by Schedule 10.
(6) This section does not affect any liability which may be incurred apart from this section.
(7) References in this section to the acquisition by a person of securities include references to his contracting to acquire them or any interest in them.
(8) No person shall, by reason of being a promoter of a company or otherwise, incur any liability for failing to disclose information which he would not be required to disclose in listing particulars in respect of a company's securities –
  (a) if he were responsible for those particulars; or
  (b) if he is responsible for them, which he is entitled to omit by virtue of section 82.
(9) The reference in subsection (8) to a person incurring liability includes a reference to any other person being entitled as against that person to be granted any civil remedy or to rescind or repudiate an agreement.
(10) "Listing particulars", in subsection (1) and Schedule 10, includes supplementary listing particulars.

The Prospectus Regulations 2005

Schedule 1: Amendments to the Act

6 (1) Section 90 (compensation for false or misleading particulars) is amended as follows.
  (2) After subsection (10) insert –

    "(11) This section applies in relation to a prospectus as it applies to listing particulars, with the following modifications –

(a) references in this section or in Schedule 10 to listing particulars, supplementary listing particulars or sections 80, 81 or 82 are to be read, respectively, as references to a prospectus, supplementary prospectus and sections 87A, 87G and 87B;
(b) references in Schedule 10 to admission to the official list are to be read as references to admission to trading on a regulated market;
(c) in relation to a prospectus, "securities" means "transferable securities".

(12) A person is not to be subject to civil liability solely on the basis of a summary in a prospectus unless the summary is misleading, inaccurate or inconsistent when read with the rest of the prospectus; and, in this subsection, a summary includes any translation of it."

(3) For the title substitute "Compensation for false or misleading statements or omissions".

Appendix 2 – Illustrative consent wording, applicable for consent letters required in connection with the inclusion of audit reports

> We hereby give our consent to the inclusion in the [document] dated [date] issued by [issuer] of our [report] dated [date] in the form and context in which it is included, as shown in the enclosed proof of the [document] which we have signed for identification.
>
> Our consent is required by [provision requiring consent[8]] and is given for the purpose of complying with that provision and for no other purpose.
>
> [We also hereby authorise the contents of the [report] which is included in the [document] for the purposes of [relevant provision[9]].][10]

---

[8] For example item 23.1 of Annex I to the Prospectus Directive Regulation in respect of a Share Registration Document.

[9] For example Prospectus Rule 5.5.3R (2)(f), 5.5.4R (2)(f) or Regulation 6(1)(e) of the Financial Services and Markets Act 2000 (Official Listing of Securities) Regulations 2001.

[10] This paragraph is only included where authorisation of the report is required by regulation.

Appendix 3 – Illustrative clarifying language for insertion in reporting accountant's separate, special purpose reports

Where rule or regulation provides for the preparation of the special purpose report, and the report takes the form contemplated by the rule or regulation:

> "This report is required by [insert reference to applicable rule or regulation[11]] and is given for the purpose of complying with that regulation and for no other purpose.
>
> Save for any responsibility arising under [insert reference to applicable rule or regulation] to any person as and to the extent there provided [, and save for any responsibility that we have expressly agreed in writing to assume[12]], to the fullest extent permitted by law we do not assume any responsibility and will not accept any liability to any other person for any loss suffered by any such other person as a result of, arising out of, or in connection with this report [or our statement, required by and given solely for the purposes of complying with [insert reference to rule or regulation[13]], consenting to its inclusion in [describe document]]."

---

[11] *For example item 20.1 of Annex I to the Prospectus Directive Regulation in respect of a an accountant's report on historical financial information included in a Share Registration Document.*

[12] *Where the special purpose report has been prepared pursuant to instructions requiring the report to take a bespoke form differing from or going beyond the form contemplated by rule or regulation, reporting accountants consider making specific reference to the source of the agreement, for example the engagement letter governing the provision of the report.*

[13] *For example item 23.1 of Annex I to the Prospectus Directive Regulation in respect of a Share Registration Document.*

AAF 03/06
The ICAEW Assurance Service on Unaudited Financial Statements

Interim Technical Release

Contents

	Paragraphs
Preface	1
International Framework	2 – 6
Scope	7 – 8
Types of assurance	9 – 13
Nature of engagement	14
Directors' responsibilities	15 -18
Reporting criteria	19
Professional ethics	20
Compliance with Data Protection Act 1998	21
Accepting an engagement	22 – 25
Managing professional liability	26 – 30
Planning	31 – 33
Materiality and consideration of risk	34 – 36
Procedures	37 – 39
Documentation	40 – 41
Events after the balance sheet	42 – 43
Reporting	
a. Management representations	44 – 46
b. Approval of financial statements	47 – 49
c. Accountants' reports	50 – 60

Appendices

A. Classification of assurance and non-assurance services
B. Illustrative contents and extracts of an engagement letter

i. Illustrative contents
ii. Example extracts of an engagement letter
C. Illustrative management representation letter
D. Example directors' statement
E. Example reports
  a. i Reporting to the directors
  a. ii Reporting to the directors with an explanatory paragraph
  b. i Reporting to the directors and other parties
  b. ii Reporting to the directors and members
F. Work procedures for the engagement   23 – 25

AAF 03/06 is issued by the Audit and Assurance Faculty of the Institute of Chartered Accountants in England & Wales (ICAEW) in August 2006. AAF 03/06 is best practice guidance and professional judgement should be used in its application. No responsibilities for loss occasioned to any person acting or refraining from action as a result of any material in AAF 03/06 can be accepted by the ICAEW.

© Institute of Chartered Accountants in England & Wales

Preface

1   Following the increase in the audit exemption threshold, many companies with a turnover below £5.6 million are no longer required to have a statutory audit of their financial statements although some still choose to do so. As an alternative, directors may however wish to obtain an independent assurance report on their financial statements from chartered accountants ('accountants'). The purpose of this report may be to enhance the credibility of historical financial information with third parties to whom the accountants may agree to provide an assurance report, or to give directors themselves additional comfort about financial statements for which they are responsible.

International Framework

2   In January 2004, the International Auditing and Assurance Standards Board (IAASB) issued the International Framework for Assurance Engagements ('the International Framework') that sets out principles for assurance engagements. The International Framework is applicable to a wide range of assurance services, including services related to historical financial information.

3   The International Framework has been the primary source of reference in the development of AAF 03/06 which helps accountants to perform assurance engagements other than audit. AAF 03/06 also has regard to existing guidance and standards on similar types of assurance engagements.

4   In an assurance engagement, accountants[1] 'express a conclusion designed to enhance the degree of confidence of intended users about the outcome of the evaluation or measurement of a subject matter against criteria'. In other words, assurance is a conclusion drawn by accountants where sufficient appropriate evidence has been gathered and evaluated against criteria suitable for the subject.

5   The expression of a conclusion separates assurance engagements from engagements to compile financial statements or to perform agreed-upon procedures. With compilation engagements, accountants are involved in the compilation of financial information, but express no conclusion upon that information[2]. When accountants perform agreed-upon procedures, they report on findings of fact rather than giving an overall conclusion derived from their work[3].

6   Statutory and non-statutory audits[4] are types of assurance engagements, but are outside the scope of AAF 03/06. In these engagements accountants give a positive

---

[1] The term *Accountant(s)* refers to an individual accountant, firm of accountants, partner, director, or engagement leader who is responsible for an assurance engagement as distinct from auditors who audit financial statements.

[2] The Faculty has issued specific publications on the compilation of financial information: AUDIT 01/05, *Chartered Accountants' Reports on the Compilation of Historical Financial Information of Unincorporated Entities* and AUDIT 02/04, *Chartered Accountants' Reports on the Compilation of Financial Statements of Incorporated Entities*.

[3] Additional information on reporting on agreed-upon procedures is available in AUDIT 1/01, *Reporting to Third Parties*.

[4] There are different types of audits for companies that are exempt from a statutory audit. Details are available from the Audit and Assurance Faculty publication: *£5.6 million – threat or opportunity? – A guide for practitioners on the audit exemption threshold increase (2004)*.

conclusion in the form of an audit opinion on financial statements. By contrast, in the engagements illustrated in AAF 03/06, accountants give a negative form of conclusion on unaudited financial statements. Accountants performing statutory and non-statutory audits comply with International Standards on Auditing (ISAs) (UK and Ireland) as adopted in the UK by the Auditing Practices Board (APB). A summary structure of assurance and non-assurance engagements is shown in Appendix A[5].

Scope

AAF 03/06 gives guidance to members of the Institute of Chartered Accountants in England & Wales ('the ICAEW') when they perform an assurance engagement, but not a statutory or non-statutory audit, to provide a conclusion on unaudited financial statements of incorporated entities based on limited work procedures.

AAF 03/06 principally applies to financial statements prepared in accordance with the Companies Act 1985[6]. Accountants may also find the general principles that follow useful when they perform similar engagements on historical financial statements prepared for limited liability partnerships, or under legislation other than the Companies Act 1985. Financial statements prepared under Schedule 8A 'Form and Content of Abbreviated Accounts of Small Companies Delivered to Registrar' of the Companies Act 1985 are excluded from the scope, because the basis of preparing the abbreviated financial statements is different from that of full financial statements and separate guidance on the special auditors' report is given in the APB Bulletin 2006/3, *The special auditors' report on abbreviated accounts in the United Kingdom*.

Types of assurance

The International Framework sets out two types of assurance engagements and associated objectives. These are reasonable and limited assurance engagements. The extent of work required differs based on the type of assurance. AAF 03/06 deals with limited assurance engagements. Existing auditing standards deal with reasonable assurance engagements performed on financial statements.

In reasonable assurance engagements, accountants seek to obtain sufficient appropriate evidence that enable them to express a positive opinion on the report prepared for users. For instance in an audit, accountants express their opinion that '... *in our opinion the financial statements give a true and fair view, ...*' Accountants perform sufficient work procedures to reduce the risk of a material misstatement so as to support a positive form of conclusion.

In limited assurance engagements, accountants seek to gather evidence sufficient to obtain a level of assurance which provides the basis for a negative form of conclusion on unaudited financial statements, that is '... *nothing has come to our attention to refute the directors' confirmation that ... the financial statements give a true and fair view* ...'.

---

[5] *AAF 03/06 is consistent with, but does not implement, the International Standard on Review Engagements (ISRE) 2400 Engagements to review financial statements.* This guidance is specifically developed for unaudited small entities and is distinct from, for instance, ISRE 2410, *Review of Interim Financial Information Performed by the Independent Auditor of the Entity*, that is issued in relation to interim review engagements where accountants have accumulated audit knowledge based on audits of annual financial statements.

[6] *The term 'company' refers to a legal entity, formed and registered under the Companies Act 1985. A company is responsible for keeping accounting records under section 221 of the same Act.*

12   A limited assurance engagement consists principally of making enquiries of management and directors, applying analytical procedures to the financial statements and assessing whether the applied accounting policies are appropriate to the circumstances and adequately disclosed. It may include some examination of evidence relevant to certain balances and disclosures in the financial statements. This is, however, limited to situations where, after performing analytical procedures, enquiring of management and assessing the accounting policies, accountants have become aware of matters that might indicate a risk of material misstatement in the financial statements.

13   In contrast to an audit, a limited assurance engagement does not include a comprehensive assessment of the risks of material misstatement, a consideration of fraud or of laws and regulations or the gaining of an understanding of, or the testing of, internal control performed in accordance with ISAs (UK and Ireland). It also does not include the gathering of evidence in relation to all material areas of the financial statements and in respect of all relevant assertions. It is therefore substantially less in scope and provides a lower level of assurance than an audit performed in accordance with ISAs (UK and Ireland). Accountants clarify this in their engagement letter and in their report.

Nature of engagement

14   An assurance engagement involves three separate parties: the accountants, the directors who are responsible for the preparation of the company's financial statements and the users of the accountants' report. The members of the company can also be the users of the accountants' report when the assurance report is addressed to them. This guidance assumes that the directors, and in some cases other parties who are users, will each engage the accountants to provide the assurance service.

Directors' responsibilities

15   In accordance with the Companies Act 1985, the directors are responsible for ensuring that the company maintains proper accounting records and for preparing financial statements which give a true and fair view and have been prepared in accordance with Generally Accepted Accounting Practice in the UK ('UK GAAP')[7].

16   The directors' responsibilities include but are not limited to:

- selecting and applying appropriate accounting policies; and
- making accounting estimates that are reasonable in the circumstances.

The directors are also responsible for safeguarding the assets of the company and for taking steps for the prevention and detection of errors, fraud and other irregularities. The directors' responsibilities are unaffected whether there is a requirement for a statutory audit or not.

---

[7] *The components of UK GAAP may vary according to the type of company or entity. In general, UK GAAP can be considered in terms of two elements: mandatory and non-mandatory (in law or in practice). The mandatory elements are: the Companies Act 1985 (for incorporated entities), accounting standards issued by the Accounting Standards Board (ASB), e.g. Statements of Standard Accounting Practice (SSAPs) and Financial Reporting Standards (FRSs) (or Financial Reporting Standard for Smaller Entities (FRSSE)), abstracts issued by the ASB's Urgent Issues Task Force and the Listing Rules (for listed companies). Other elements of UK GAAP may be authoritative but non-mandatory: the ASB's Statement of principles for financial reporting and other statements, statements and recommendations from the professional bodies and established practice.*

17 The accountants' conclusion on unaudited financial statements cannot be regarded as expressing assurance on the adequacy of the company's systems or on the incidence of fraud, non-compliance with laws and regulations or weaknesses in internal controls. Engaging accountants to perform an assurance engagement on unaudited financial statements does not relieve directors of their responsibilities in these respects.

18 So that it is clear where the boundaries between the duties of directors and accountants lie, directors add a brief statement on their responsibilities and Appendix D provides an example. This complements the accountants' report examples of which are set out in Appendix E. The directors' statement is positioned immediately before the accountants' report.

Reporting criteria

19 Any assurance engagement requires accountants to express an overall conclusion on the information, assessed relative to certain *criteria*. For engagements performed in accordance with AAF 03/06 the applicable criteria would be accounting policies selected by the directors within the framework of UK GAAP (see paragraphs 15-16). The criteria also help users to understand how the accountants have come to their conclusion and to obtain comfort from it, if appropriate.

Professional ethics

20 In carrying out an assurance engagement, accountants who are members of the ICAEW are subject to ethical guidance as laid down by the ICAEW's Code of Ethics. The requirements in the Code include, amongst other things, adherence to the Fundamental Principles in all of their professional and business activities as set out in the introduction. When conducting an assurance engagement, there are additional requirements in *Independence for Assurance Engagements* within the Code. This applies to all assurance engagements outside the scope of audit and is in compliance with the Code of Ethics established by the International Federation of Accountants (IFAC).

Compliance with Data Protection Act 1998[8]

21 The accountants and the company are required to comply with the Data Protection Act 1998 ('DPA'). Accountants carrying out assurance engagements can clarify these respective responsibilities in their engagement letters[9].

Accepting an engagement

22 Accountants discuss the terms of the engagement with the directors and obtain a clear understanding and agreement on the scope and purpose of the engagement, including their respective responsibilities. Where the accountants' report will be addressed to users, the users also become party to the engagement (see paragraph 26).

---

[8] For more information, the ICAEW's Technical Release TECH 7-04 *Data Protection Act 1998 and its Application to the Major Practice Streams of Accountancy Practices* is available to members from the ICAEW's website.

[9] Example wording is included in Appendix B. ii.

23 Accountants agree the terms of engagement with the parties to the engagement. To avoid misunderstandings, the agreed terms are recorded in an engagement letter. The illustrative contents of an example engagement letter are set out in Appendix B. Accountants may wish to consider this illustration as a basis for their letter.

24 Accountants consider the appropriateness of a request, made before the completion of the engagement, to change this type of engagement to a non-assurance engagement and do not agree to a change without reasonable justification. A change in circumstances that affects the users' requirements or misunderstanding concerning the nature of the engagement ordinarily justifies a request for a change in the engagement. If such a change is made, the accountants do not disregard evidence that was obtained prior to the change.

25 The assurance report may be received by a range of persons who are not party to the engagement. Accountants do not intend to assume responsibility to persons who are not party to the engagement, but legal actions from such persons may nonetheless occur. The accountants therefore need to apply appropriate engagement acceptance procedures in order to assess the risks associated with taking on a particular engagement and accordingly whether to do so and, if so, on what terms. Where accountants do accept such an engagement, suitably rigorous internal risk management policies are applied to manage any increased level of risk. Relevant steps for managing professional liability are covered in the following section.

Managing professional liability

26 Where accountants are planning to perform an engagement in accordance with AAF 03/06 and intend to issue a report on unaudited financial statements, they consider whether there are any parties other than the addressees of the report who may seek to obtain a copy of the report and place reliance on and, if so, for what purposes. The existence, nature and interest of such third parties affect the accountants' risk assessment and their consideration of whether or not to accept the engagement and, if so, on what terms[10]. Depending on the engagement circumstances accountants may:

(a) accept that they owe a duty of care to the third parties and enter into a tri-partite or multi-partite engagement contract with the board of directors and the third parties, including provisions limiting liability if appropriate;

(b) proceed with an engagement for the board of directors alone (disclaiming any duty or liability to third parties by notice in the assurance report) and before allowing third parties access to the assurance report, require the third parties to (i) acknowledge in writing that the accountants owe them no duty of care and (ii) agree that they will assert no rights against accountants in connection with the assurance report;

(c) engage with the board of directors alone disclaiming any duty or liability to third parties by notice in the assurance report[11]. Accountants also consider supporting this disclaimer with an indemnity from the client to apply where a third party claim is made (recognising that such an indemnity may not be

---

[10] For further guidance on managing risk in the light of third party reporting, see *AUDIT 1/01*.

[11] If a disclaimer is used, accountants consider whether it is reasonable and therefore likely to be effective taking account of the requirements of the Unfair Contract Terms Act 1977.

attractive commercially, may not be effective if the client is not financially stable, and may not operate to prevent a claim[12]; or
(d) decline to accept the engagement.

In all cases, accountants (i) clarify in their engagement letter that the assurance report will be for the use and benefit of the addressees of the engagement letter and that the assurance report will disclaim any duty or liability to any other party and (ii) include a notice in the assurance report disclaiming any duty or liability to any party other than those parties with whom the accountants are engaged under the terms of the engagement letter. Illustrative contents and example wording of an engagement letter are available in Appendix B i and ii. If during the course of the engagement (or at any time thereafter) the accountants' risk assessment of the engagement changes, they consider varying the engagement letter or obtaining an acknowledgement of no duty or liability, in the manner envisaged in (b) above.

27 Accountants may, during the performance of the engagement or after issuing their report, become aware of third parties, such as banks and other lenders or prospective purchasers of the client, who may request sight of the assurance report[13]. The client or the third party may approach the accountants for consent to make the assurance report available to such third parties, as the engagement contract agreed with the client contains disclosure and use restrictions. Since the assurance report has not been prepared for third parties or with their interests or needs in mind the accountants may decline this request. The accountants will have set out the purpose of their engagement in the assurance report, and will have included a disclaimer of liability to third parties in line with paragraph 26 (c) above in that report. If the request is not declined, the accountants will advise the third party that the assurance report will not be and was not prepared nor will it be completed for the third party or the third party's benefit, that consent to their report being made available to a third party will only be given if the third party agrees that the third party should not rely on the report and acknowledges in writing that the accountants owe the third party no duty of care; and agrees that no claims may be brought against the accountants by the third party in relation to the report.

28 Accountants may also receive requests from the client for consent to the release of the assurance report to potential third parties with whom the client may be exploring the possibility of a relationship. The accountants may decline any such request. If the request is not declined, the written acknowledgement and agreement described above in relation to other third parties may be a practical solution to the management of risk in relation to such recipients. Where that is not practical, the accountants require the clients (as a condition for giving consent, where requested) to send all such potential recipients a written statement, to accompany the assurance report, pointing out that the accountants did not undertake the work for potential recipients and do not accept any responsibility to potential recipients and deny liability to them. Accountants may wish to provide the client with a pro-forma statement for this purpose and may wish to include reference to this in their engagement letter.

[12] *It may be appropriate to obtain an indemnity from the client in respect of claims from third parties arising from the contents of the assurance report. The risk of such claims may arise, for example, where the accountants' report is widely circulated, in breach of confidentiality and disclosure restrictions that have been agreed or where, with the accountants' consent, the report is attached to the financial statements filed with Companies House. However, it must be remembered that an indemnity does not prevent a claim from being brought against the indemnified party. It merely gives him a right to pass on the liability to the indemnifier. It follows, therefore, that if the indemnity is in some way ineffective or the indemnifier does not have adequate resources to meet the liability, the indemnified party may be left unprotected.*

[13] *Further guidance may be found in the Audit and Assurance Faculty's guidance AUDIT 4/00, Firms' Reports and Duties to Lenders in Connection with Loans and Other Facilities to Clients and Related Covenants.*

29 Accountants may also become aware that a third party has (despite disclosure restrictions) obtained a copy of the assurance report and may place reliance on it. In such circumstances, the accountants consider writing to the third party informing the third party that the accountants did not undertake the work for third parties and do not accept any responsibility to third parties and deny liability to them. Accountants might also suggest to the third party that, if there are specific matters of interest regarding the client, the third party should let the accountants know, so that the accountants might consider performing a separate engagement for this third party with a separate engagement letter to meet the interests/needs of this third party[14]. This would be regardless of whether the new engagement would be an assurance or an agreed-upon procedures engagement with this third party.

30 To guard against potential liability, accountants may also wish to consider the guidance provided in the ICAEW's Statement 1.311 *Managing the Professional Liability of Accountants* of Members' Handbook. This includes:

- defining the scope and responsibilities of the engagement;
- defining the purpose of the accountants' report;
- restricting the use of the accountants' name;
- identifying the authorised recipients of report;
- limiting (or excluding) liability;
- obtaining an indemnity[15]; and
- defining the scope of professional competence.

Planning

31 Accountants plan the engagement and in doing so they obtain and update their knowledge of the business and consider the company's organisation, the type of accounting records maintained, operating characteristics, accounting principles and practices and the nature of its assets, liabilities, revenues and expenses. The accountants need to be alert to areas where potential risk of material misstatement may exist and plan their further enquiries in order to be able to assess the extent of that risk. However, they are not expected to carry out a comprehensive risk assessment. The level of planning may vary according to the complexity of the company's accounting records and the accountants' experience of the business.

32 To obtain a general understanding of the business and operations of the company, accountants familiarise themselves with the accounting principles and practices of the sector in which the company operates and with the form and content of the accounting information that is appropriate in the circumstances. The accountants' understanding of the business is usually obtained through experience of the company and enquiry of the company's management and staff. The accountants may also

---

[14] All the usual client acceptance procedures, including independence considerations, will need to be undertaken but these are outside the scope of AAF 03/06.

[15] It may be appropriate to obtain an indemnity from the client in respect of claims from third parties arising from the contents of the assurance report. The risk of such claims may arise, for example, where the accountants' report is widely circulated, in breach of confidentiality and disclosure restrictions that have been agreed or where, with the accountants' consent, the report is attached to the financial statements filed with Companies House. However, it must be remembered that an indemnity does not prevent a claim from being brought against the indemnified party. It merely gives him a right to pass on the liability to the indemnifier. It follows, therefore, that if the indemnity is in some way ineffective or the indemnifier does not have adequate resources to meet the liability, the indemnified party may be left unprotected.

perform walk-throughs[16] on the accounting records where considered necessary to support their understanding of the business and operations of the company and plan their further procedures.

The purpose of the planning process is to establish the nature, extent and timing of the further work to be performed. Further guidance on the work procedures for limited assurance engagements is set out in Appendix F. Factors that accountants take into account include, but are not limited to, their assessment of the risk of misstatement in the financial information and the strength of the accounting and reporting processes.

Materiality and consideration of risk

The definition of materiality is provided in the International Accounting Standards Board's 'Framework for the Preparation and Presentation of Financial Statements' and incorporated in ISA (UK and Ireland) 320 *Audit Materiality*:

> *'Information is material if its omission or misstatement could influence the economic decisions of users taken on the basis of the financial statements. Materiality depends on the size of the item or error judged in the particular circumstances of its omission or misstatement. Thus, materiality provides a threshold or cut-off point rather than being a primary qualitative characteristic which information must have if it is to be useful.'*

Accountants apply the same principles when considering materiality as would be applied to an audit of the financial statements. The objective is to be able to judge whether, in the event of their enquiries and other procedures identifying a misstatement, it will be necessary to adjust the financial statements. Although there is a greater risk that misstatements will not be detected from limited work procedures, the judgement as to what is material is made by reference to the information on which the accountants are reporting and the needs of those relying on that information, not on the type of assurance provided. Because the accountants are not expected to plan and perform significant substantive procedures when undertaking this type of engagement, ordinarily it will be unnecessary for the accountants to consider the impact of materiality at the account balance or classes of transaction level. Individual misstatements are considered against the materiality applied to the overall financial statements.

Matters to consider in relation to the risk of material misstatement include:

- the current financial position and trading environment in which the company operates;
- accumulated knowledge acquired in carrying out such engagements in prior periods;
- the knowledge of the business, including accounting policies and practices of the industry in which the company operates;
- the knowledge of the company's accounting;
- the extent to which a particular item is potentially affected by management judgement;
- management's own assessment of the risks underlying the financial information and the monitoring and other controls established to manage those risks;

---

[16] *Walk-throughs are performed to trace one or more transactions through the accounting system to obtain an understanding of how the accounting system works. The procedure is not performed to observe the application of the internal control system.*

- management's own assessment of the company's ability to continue as a going concern and the impact of post balance sheet events; and
- the accountants' assessment of the materiality of transactions and account balances and the impact of any individually significant transactions.

Procedures

37 As explained in paragraphs 12-13, accountants obtain evidence principally through enquiry of management and analytical procedures when performing work in accordance with AAF 03/06.

38 Where, after performing the above procedures, accountants consider that a significant risk of material misstatement has come to their attention, they discuss with management whether further work is required by management to establish if an adjustment is needed. In the event that there is insufficient information on which to base a request to management they may carry out additional work including substantive procedures as they consider necessary to support their conclusion. If management does not make any necessary adjustment, the accountants will consider the impact on their report or for other reporting requirements (e.g. submission of corporation tax returns), including whether to withdraw from the engagement (see paragraphs 57-60). This contrasts with an audit where auditors obtain sufficient appropriate evidence in respect of all material financial statement assertions, following a comprehensive risk assessment.

39 Accountants also consider methods available, such as disclosure checklists or software packages, to check whether relevant disclosures have been made on the basis of the information available. Guidance on work procedures is available in Appendix F.

Documentation

40 Accountants document matters that, in their professional judgement, are important to support the content of the report. Matters documented usually include:

- the planning and performance of the engagement;
- the nature, timing and extent of the procedures performed in relation to the financial information, and the conclusions reached;
- the evidence resulting from the procedures carried out; and
- the accountants' reasoning and conclusions on all significant matters which require the exercise of judgement.

41 The level of documentation may vary according to the complexity of the company's accounting records and accounting procedures, according to the accountants' experience with the business and whether any other matters have arisen during the course of the engagement.

Events after the balance sheet date

42 Accountants enquire about events, subsequent to the date of the financial statements and up to the date that the accountants sign their report, which may require adjustment to, or disclosure in, the financial statements. Examples of specific enquiries which may be made of management include:

- the current status of items involving subjective judgement or which were accounted for on the basis of preliminary data; and

- whether any events have occurred which might bring into question the appropriateness of accounting policies used in the financial statements.

Accountants do not have any responsibility to perform procedures to identify events occurring after the date of their report. Accountants may wish to clarify this in their engagement letter.

Reporting

a. Management representations

In the course of the engagement, accountants may make enquiries of directors and management to obtain information and explanations concerning specific matters. The possibility of misunderstandings arising from oral responses to such enquiries may be reduced by obtaining confirmations in writing. Accountants may also wish to confirm in writing more general matters such as the completeness of relevant information made available to them for the purpose of their work. Accountants obtain from the directors such written representations as they consider necessary in the circumstances. Such representations by the directors normally include:

- acknowledgment of the directors' responsibility for the financial statements;
- acknowledgment of the directors' responsibility for the completeness of the financial records and of the minutes of meetings and summaries of any meetings for which minutes have not been prepared that were made available to the accountants for the purposes of the engagement;
- confirmation that the directors are not aware of any material amounts, transactions, agreements or contingencies not properly reflected in the accounting records underlying the financial information;
- notification of any subsequent events that would require adjustment to, or disclosure in, the financial statements; and
- other matters, if any, for which the accountants consider written representations are appropriate in the circumstances. Such matters might include the substance of significant assertions, estimates or judgements or interpretations of facts by the directors that have a significant effect on the financial information.

A management representation letter is normally dated on the day the unaudited financial statements are approved and signed by the directors.

An illustrative management representation letter is given in Appendix C. Accountants request a representation letter to meet the specific circumstances of the engagement.

b. Approval of financial statements

The directors are legally responsible for the financial statements. The Companies Act 1985 requires that directors approve the financial statements and that the balance sheet states the name of the director signing the financial statements on behalf of the Board. The directors of companies that are exempt from statutory audit are required to acknowledge, on the face of the balance sheet, their responsibilities for keeping proper accounting records and for preparing true and fair financial statements as well as entitlement of the company to exemption from audit.

The financial statements contain a reference to the fact that they are unaudited either on the front cover or on each page of the financial statements.

49 Financial statements are approved and signed by the directors before the accountants' report is signed. The directors also sign the directors' statement to confirm that they have met their duty in accordance with the Companies Act 1985. An example directors' statement is given in Appendix D.

c. Accountants' reports

50 Accountants' reports help addressees derive comfort from the involvement of accountants who are subject to the ethical and other professional guidance issued by the ICAEW in relation to the engagement. It will also assist addressees in clarifying the scope of the engagement and the difference in the level of comfort obtained from an audit and an engagement envisaged in this guidance. Example reports are available in Appendix E.

51 Accountants' reports are headed up as 'independent'. This is because they have followed the ICAEW's ethical guidance (see paragraph 20).

52 Accountants' reports on the unaudited historical financial statements of a company include:

- a title stating that it is an assurance report, identifying the persons to whom the report is addressed and including the words 'Independent chartered accountants'/accountants'[17] report to...';
- an introductory paragraph identifying the unaudited financial information on which the accountants' conclusion is given;
- a statement that the report is made in accordance with the terms of engagement;
- restrictions on the use of the assurance report to the addressees in accordance with the terms of the engagement letter and identification of the purpose for which the engagement is performed;
- a statement that the directors have acknowledged their responsibility to prepare financial statements that give a true and fair view in accordance with the Companies Act 1985;
- identification of the purpose for which the engagement was performed;
- a statement that the work was carried out in accordance with AAF 03/06;
- a description of the work performed in undertaking the engagement;
- a negative form of conclusion;
- the name and signature of the accountants and any appropriate designation (but not 'Registered Auditor');
- the date of the report; and
- the details of the accountants (the name of the firm/accountants and the location of the office performing the engagement).

53 Accountants' reports are addressed to the parties to the engagement letter and include a disclaimer of any duty or liability to any parties who are not addressees of the report. In a tri-partite or multi-partite engagement, the addressees of the report include others, such as the company's members or identified third parties, who have agreed to be bound by the engagement and to whom the accountants have agreed to report and have accepted a duty of care (Appendix E. b. i). In a bi-partite engagement, the addressees of the report will be the directors alone (Appendix E. a. i)[18].

---

[17] The title "Accountants' report to..." should be used rather than "Chartered accountants' report to..." where a firm is not permitted to use the term chartered accountant(s). For further details, see footnote 4 in AUDIT 02/04.

[18] Further guidance may be found in the Audit and Assurance Faculty's guidance AUDIT 4/00, Firms' Reports and Duties to Lenders in Connection with Loans and Other Facilities to Clients and Related Covenants.

If the accountants provide their prior written consent, copies of the accountants' assurance reports may be laid before the members at the annual general meeting (AGM) and attached to the copy of the company's unaudited financial statements and the directors' report for that year to be delivered to the Registrar of Companies. A specific example assurance report is available in Appendix E. b. ii.

Where inherent uncertainties about the outcome of future events exist and accountants are unable to obtain sufficient evidence to support their conclusion, they consider the impact of such uncertainties on the financial statements as a whole. If the impact of such uncertainties is considered to be material, and these uncertainties are adequately disclosed in the financial statements, accountants consider modifying the report by adding an explanatory paragraph to emphasise the uncertainties and separate the accountants' conclusion from the uncertainties paragraph(s).

The addition of such uncertainties paragraph(s) does not affect the accountants' conclusion. Example wording for such a report is suggested in Appendix E. a. ii.

There are no provisions for the report to be qualified within this guidance. If accountants have any doubt over the validity of the financial statements on which the report is to be given or identify a material limitation of scope, they consider declining to issue any report and resign from the engagement and not permitting their name to be associated with the financial statements.

In certain circumstances, adjustments or disclosures that accountants consider appropriate may not be made in the financial statements, or information provided in the financial statements may not be satisfactory. If the accountants consider that the financial statements are misleading as a result, then they decline to issue any report and resign from the engagement and do not permit their name to be associated with the financial statements.

In considering whether financial statements are misleading, accountants consider whether the financial statements appear to be appropriate in form and free from material misstatements that appear evident to them as a result of, for example:

- misclassifications in the financial statements;
- mistakes in the application of, or non-disclosure of known departures from, any relevant statutory, regulatory or other reporting requirements, including applicable accounting standards and non-disclosure of significant changes in accounting policies; and
- other significant matters of which the accountants are aware.

When accountants resign from an engagement, they normally explain to the parties to the engagement their reasons for resigning, unless this would constitute a breach of legal or other regulatory requirements (such as the 'tipping off' provisions of the money laundering legislation).

Appendix A – Classification of assurance and non-assurance services

Type of engagement			
ASSURANCE Accountants express a conclusion.			**NON-ASSURANCE** No provision of a conclusion but a report on factual findings (agreed-upon procedures) or a report on collecting, classifying and summarising financial information (e.g. compilation engagement under Audit 02/04, *Chartered Accountants' Reports on the compilation of financial statements of incorporated entities*).
Type of information			
Historical financial information		Other information*	
Type of assurance		e.g. Reporting on internal controls Reporting on profit forecast	
Reasonable assurance e.g. Statutory audits	Limited assurance e.g. Assurance Service under AAF 03/06 Independent examination on charities		

* Both reasonable and limited assurance engagements are performed on information other than historical financial information. Technical Release AAF 01/06, *Assurance reports on internal controls of service organisations made available to third parties* is based on reasonable assurance.

Appendix B – Illustrative contents and extracts of an engagement letter

i. Illustrative contents

The engagement letter includes matters such as:

- the identity of the addressees;
- the accountants who will conduct the engagement in accordance with AAF 03/06;
- the directors' responsibilities for the accounting records and the financial statements as specified in the Companies Act 1985;
- the information to be supplied by the directors to the accountants and confirmation that any other information that the accountants consider necessary for the performance of the engagement will be supplied;
- the accounting bases on which the financial statements will be prepared and the fact that any known departures will be disclosed;
- written management representations may be required prior to the completion of the engagement and the issuing of the accountants' report;
- the nature of the engagement;
- the accountants will enquire, perform analytical procedures and engage in discussions with management to obtain limited assurance over the information supplied to the accountants. In order to obtain limited assurance over the financial statements, the accountants will perform sufficient additional procedures as required to pursue any material matters that have come to their attention;

- the form of report to be provided, using defined terms appropriate for a limited assurance engagement to avoid misunderstanding, and any restrictions on its use;
- that the engagement cannot be relied on to prevent or detect errors, fraud and weaknesses in internal controls;
- an audit is not being carried out and no audit opinion is being given;
- the accountants' obligation not to be associated with false or misleading financial statements;
- if the accountants' association with the information being reported on is to be communicated to third parties, the accountants' prior written consent will be required, which may (if given) be conditional;
- the addressees of the report, limitations as to the purpose for which the report is prepared and restrictions on who is entitled to see and rely upon the report and on its distribution;
- the limitation of the accountants' liability including any liability cap as negotiated and agreed with the addressees of the engagement letter having regard to the nature and scope of the work being performed (and being fair and reasonable in compliance with the Unfair Contract Terms Act 1977);
- fee arrangement to cover situations where the accountants are unable to issue an assurance report; and
- respective responsibilities under the Data Protection Act 1998.

ii. Example extracts of an engagement letter

This engagement letter relates to a bi-partite engagement as envisaged in paragraph 26 (b); the engagement is formed by two parties, i.e. the accountants and the board of directors. Accountants are advised to use appropriate wording where the engagement involves others, such as members. The extracts are provided as illustrative guidance only.

> **Scope of our work**
>
> You have asked us to report to you on a limited assurance basis on the unaudited financial statements of the company. We shall plan our work on the basis that the company is not required by statute or regulation to have an audit of its financial statements for the year [/period] ended [date], unless you inform us in writing to the contrary. In carrying out this engagement we will make enquiries, perform analytical procedures and assess the consistency of application of your accounting policies in accordance with Generally Accepted Accounting Practice in the United Kingdom ('UK GAAP').
>
> We will perform limited examination of evidence relevant to certain balances and disclosures in the financial statements where, after performing the above work, we become aware of matters that might indicate material misstatements in the financial statements.
>
> Our work will be undertaken and our report will be made in accordance with AAF 03/06 issued by the Institute of Chartered Accountants in England & Wales.
>
> Our conclusion on the unaudited financial statements cannot be regarded as providing assurance on the adequacy of the company's systems or on the incidence of fraud, non-compliance with laws and regulations or weaknesses in internal controls. Engaging us to perform this assurance engagement on the

unaudited financial statements does not relieve the directors of their responsibilities in these respects.

You have advised us that the company is exempt from an audit of the financial statements. We will not carry out any work to determine whether or not the company is entitled to audit exemption. However, should our work indicate that the company is not entitled to the exemption, we will inform you of this.

Our work will not be an audit of the financial statements in accordance with International Standards on Auditing (UK and Ireland). Consequently, it does not include a comprehensive assessment of the risks of material misstatement, a consideration of fraud or of laws and regulations, or the gaining of an understanding of, or the testing of, internal control in accordance with International Standards on Auditing (UK and Ireland). It also does not include the gathering of evidence in relation to all material areas of the financial statements and in respect of all relevant assertions.

Since we will not carry out an audit, nor confirm the accuracy or reasonableness of the accounting records maintained by the company, we can only provide a limited assurance report as to whether the financial statements present a true and fair view.

Furthermore, as the Board of Directors, you have a duty to prepare financial statements that comply with the Companies Act 1985 and applicable accounting standards. Where we identify that the financial statements do not conform to UK GAAP or if the accounting policies adopted are not immediately apparent this will need to be disclosed in the financial statements.

We have a professional responsibility not to be associated with financial statements which may be false or misleading. Therefore, although we are not required to search for such matters, should we become aware, for any reason, that the financial statements may be misleading, we will discuss the matter with you with a view to agreeing appropriate adjustments and/or disclosures in the financial statements. In circumstances where adjustments and/or disclosures that we consider appropriate are not made or where we are not provided with appropriate information, and as a result we consider that the financial statements are misleading, we will withdraw from the engagement.

Basis of the accountants' report

Our report is prepared on the following basis:

- our report is prepared solely for your confidential use. It may not be relied upon by anyone else; and
- except to the extent required by court order, law or regulation, or where required in any court proceedings in which you may be involved, our report must not be made available, copied, referred to or recited to any other person, or included in any other document, nor may you make reference to us or the services, without our prior written permission.

Data Protection Act

In the conduct of our professional services we may need to collect and use personal information about you, your partners, your company, your trustees, your clients or customers and your or their employees, agents or contractors, which we will hold as data controllers under the Data Protection Act 1998 (DPA). You confirm that you have complied with the requirements of the DPA when providing us with such personal information.

Liability provisions[19]

We (that is, [name of firm],) will perform the engagement with reasonable skill and care and we acknowledge that in respect of liability (if any) on our part to the Company for losses, damages, costs or expenses ('losses') caused by our breach of contract, negligence, fraud or other deliberate breach of duty, the following provisions will apply:

- we will not be liable if such losses are due to the provision of false, misleading or incomplete information or documentation or due to the acts or omissions of any person other than us, except where, on the basis of the work normally undertaken by us within the scope set out in these terms of engagement, it would have been reasonable for us to discover such defects;
- we will accept liability without limit for the consequences of our own fraud or other deliberate breach of duty and for any other liability which it is not permitted by law to limit or exclude; and
- subject to the previous provisions of this liability paragraph, our total aggregate liability whether in contract, tort (including negligence) or otherwise, to the Company, for losses arising from or in connection with the work which is the subject of these terms (including any addition or variation to the work), shall not exceed in aggregate the amount of [*To be discussed and negotiated*][20].

The Company and the directors of the Company will not bring any claims or proceedings against any of our individual partners, members, directors or employees. This clause is intended to benefit such partners, members, directors and employees who may enforce this clause pursuant to the Contracts (Rights of Third Parties) Act 1999 ('the Act'). Notwithstanding any benefits or rights conferred by this agreement on such partners, members, directors or employees by virtue of the Act, we and the directors of the Company may together agree in writing to vary or rescind the agreement set out in this letter without the consent of any such partners, members, directors or employees. Other than as expressly provided in this paragraph, the provisions of the Act are excluded.

Any claims, whether in contract, negligence or otherwise, must be formally commenced within [years] after the party bringing the claim becomes aware (or ought reasonably to have become aware) of the facts which give rise to the action and in any event no later than [years] after any alleged breach of contract, negligence or other cause of action. This expressly overrides any statutory provision which would otherwise apply.

---

[19] Accountants may wish to seek independent legal advice on language that addresses the matters covered in the illustrative wording set out in this liability section.

[20] Audit Liability: Claims by Third Parties *published by the Audit and Assurance Faculty in 2005 provides information on third party claims. Appendix 2 of the publication reproduces an article from October 2004 issue of* True & Fair *on liability caps which is relevant to assurance engagements.*

Appendix C – Illustrative management representation letter

A Company Limited

[Address]

[Address]

A Firm of Accountants

[Address]

[Address]

Date..................................

Dear Sirs,

Letter of Representation

We confirm that the following representations are made on the basis of enquiries of management and staff with relevant knowledge and experience (and, where appropriate, of inspection of the supporting documentation) sufficient to satisfy ourselves that we can properly make each of the following representations to you in connection with your report on the financial statements of the company for the year ended [date]:

1. We acknowledge that the work performed by you is substantially less in scope than an audit performed in accordance with Auditing Standards and that you do not express an audit opinion.
2. We confirm that the company was entitled to exemption under section 249A (1) of the Companies Act 1985 from the requirement to have its financial statements for the financial year ended [date] audited. We also confirm that the members have not required the company to obtain an audit of its financial statements for the financial year in accordance with Section 249B, (2) of the Companies Act 1985.
3. We acknowledge as directors our responsibility for the financial statements which give a true and fair view of the state of affairs of the company as at the end of the financial year and of its profit or loss for the financial year in accordance with the requirements of section 226 of the Companies Act 1985, and which otherwise comply with the requirements of that Act relating to financial statements, so far as applicable to the company. All the accounting records have been made available to you and all transactions undertaken by the company have been properly reflected in those accounting records. All records and related information, including the minutes of the directors' and shareholders' meetings have been made available to you.
4. We confirm that we have maintained proper accounting records, as required by the Companies Act 1985.
5. We confirm, to the best of our knowledge and belief that there have been no instances of non-compliance or breaches of any laws or regulations which are essential to the activities of the company's business.
6. We are not aware of any pending litigation which may result in a significant loss to the company.
7. There were no contingent liabilities at the balance sheet date.

8. As directors, we have considered the financial position of the company. We are not aware of any material uncertainties or doubts about the ability of the company to continue as a 'going concern' for the foreseeable future.
9. We confirm that there were no transactions with related parties of the company or amounts due to or from related parties at the balance sheet date which are required to be disclosed in the financial statements other than those which are detailed in the notes to the financial statements.
10. There have been no events since the balance sheet date which necessitate revision of the figures included in the financial statements or disclosure in the notes to the financial statements.

Signatures

A Company Limited Date

Appendix D – Example directors' statement

The purpose of the directors' statement is to make clear that responsibility for preparing the financial statements rests with the board of directors and to remove any misconception that the accountants are responsible for the financial statements. The directors' statements should be placed immediately before the accountants' report.

We confirm that as directors we have met our duty in accordance with the Companies Act 1985 to:

- ensure that the company has kept proper accounting records;
- prepare financial statements which give a true and fair view of the state of affairs of the company as at [date] and of profit and loss for that period in accordance with Generally Accepted Accounting Practice in the UK [or Financial Reporting Standard for Smaller Entities]; and
- follow the applicable accounting policies, subject to any material departures disclosed and explained in the notes to the financial statements.

Signatures

A Company Limited

Date

Appendix E – Example reports

E. a. i Reporting to the directors

Chartered accountants' independent assurance report on the unaudited financial statements of [name of entity]

To the Board of Directors of [name of entity] ('the Company')

We have performed certain procedures in respect of the Company's unaudited financial statements for the year [/period] ended [date] as set out on pages [ ] to [ ], made enquiries of the Company's directors and assessed accounting policies adopted by the directors, in order to gather sufficient evidence for our conclusion in this report.

This report is made solely to the Company's directors, as a body, in accordance with the terms of our engagement letter dated [date]. It has been released to the directors on the basis that this report shall not be copied, referred to or disclosed, in whole (save for the directors' own internal purposes or as may be required by law or by a competent regulator) or in part, without our prior written consent. Our work has been undertaken so that we might state to the directors those matters that we have agreed to state to them in this report and for no other purpose. To the fullest extent permitted by law, we do not accept or assume responsibility to anyone other than the Company and the Company's directors as a body for our work, for this report or the conclusions we have formed.

Respective responsibilities

You have confirmed that you have met your duty as set out in the directors' statement on page [ ]. You consider that the Company is exempt from the statutory requirement for an audit for the year [/period]. Our responsibility is to form and express an independent conclusion, based on the work carried out, to you on the financial statements.

Scope

We conducted our engagement in accordance with the Institute of Chartered Accountants in England & Wales Interim Technical Release AAF 03/06. Our work was based primarily upon enquiry, analytical procedures and assessing accounting policies in accordance with Generally Accepted Accounting Practice in the UK [/the Financial Reporting Standard for Smaller Entities]. If we considered it to be necessary, we also performed limited examination of evidence relevant to certain balances and disclosures in the financial statements where we became aware of matters that might indicate a risk of material misstatement in the financial statements.

The terms of our engagement exclude any requirement to carry out a comprehensive assessment of the risks of material misstatement, a consideration of fraud, laws, regulations and internal controls, and we have not done so. We are not required to, and we do not, express an audit opinion on these financial statements.

Conclusion

Based on our work, nothing has come to our attention to refute the directors' confirmation that in accordance with the Companies Act 1985 the financial statements give a true and fair view of the state of the Company's affairs as at [date] and of its profit [/loss] for the year [/period] then ended and have been properly prepared in accordance with Generally Accepted Accounting Practice in the UK [/the Financial Reporting Standard for Smaller Entities].

Name of firm

Chartered accountants

Location

Date

E. a. ii Reporting to the directors with an explanatory paragraph

Chartered accountants' independent assurance report on the unaudited financial statements of [name of entity]

To the Board of Directors of [name of entity] ('the Company')

We have performed certain procedures in respect of the Company's unaudited financial statements for the year [/period] ended [date] as set out on pages [ ] to [ ], made enquiries of the Company's directors and assessed accounting policies adopted by the directors, in order to gather sufficient evidence for our conclusion in this report.

This report is made solely to the Company's directors, as a body, in accordance with the terms of our engagement letter dated [date]. It has been released to the directors on the basis that this report shall not be copied, referred to or disclosed, in whole (save for the directors' own internal purposes or as may be required by law or by a competent regulator) or in part, without our prior written consent. Our work has been undertaken so that we might state to the directors those matters that we have agreed to state to them in this report and for no other purpose. To the fullest extent permitted by law, we do not accept or assume responsibility to anyone other than the Company and the Company's directors as a body for our work, for this report or the conclusions we have formed.

Respective responsibilities

You have confirmed that you have met your duty as set out in the directors' statement on page [ ]. You consider that the Company is exempt from the statutory requirement for an audit for the year [/period]. Our responsibility is to form and express an independent conclusion, based on the work carried out, to you on the financial statements.

Scope

We conducted our engagement in accordance with the Institute of Chartered Accountants in England & Wales Interim Technical Release AAF 03/06. Our work was based primarily upon enquiry, analytical procedures and assessing accounting policies in accordance with Generally Accepted Accounting Practice in the UK [/the Financial Reporting Standard for Smaller Entities]. If we considered it to be necessary, we also performed limited examination of evidence relevant to certain balances and disclosures in the financial statements where we became aware of matters that might indicate a risk of material misstatement in the financial statements.

The terms of our engagement exclude any requirement to carry out a comprehensive assessment of the risks of material misstatement, a consideration of fraud, laws, regulations or internal controls, and we have not done so. We are not required to, and we do not, express an audit opinion on these financial statements.

Significant uncertainty

Without qualifying our opinion, we draw attention to Note [X] to the financial statements. The Company is the defendant in a lawsuit alleging infringement of certain patent rights and claiming royalties and punitive damages. The Company has filed a counter action, and preliminary hearings and discovery proceedings on both actions are in progress. The ultimate outcome of the matter cannot presently be determined, and no provision for any liability that may result has been made in the financial statements.

Conclusion

Based on our work, nothing has come to our attention to refute the directors' confirmation that in accordance with the Companies Act 1985 the financial statements give a true and fair view of the state of the Company's affairs as at [date] and of its profit [/loss] for the year [/period] then ended and have been properly prepared in accordance with Generally Accepted Accounting Practice in the UK [/the Financial Reporting Standard for Smaller Entities].

Name of firm

Chartered accountants

Location

Date

E. b. i. Reporting to the directors and other parties

> Chartered accountants' independent assurance report on the unaudited financial statements of [name of entity]
>
> **To the Board of Directors of [name of entity] ('the Company') and [X]**
>
> We have performed certain procedures in respect of the Company's unaudited financial statements for the year [/period] ended [date] as set out on pages [ ] to [ ], made enquiries of the Company's directors and assessed accounting policies adopted by the directors, in order to gather sufficient evidence for our conclusion in this report.
>
> This report is made solely to the Company's directors, as a body, and to [X], [as a body][21], in accordance with the terms of our engagement letter dated [date]. It has been released to the directors and [X] on the basis that this report shall not be copied, referred to or disclosed, in whole (save for the directors' own internal purposes or amongst the directors and [X] or as may be required by law or by a competent regulator) or in part, without our prior written consent.[22] Our work has been undertaken so that we might state to the directors and [X] those matters that we have agreed to state to them in this report and for no other purpose. To the fullest extent permitted by law, we do not accept or assume responsibility to anyone other than the Company and the Company's directors as a body and [X] [as a body], for our work, for this report or the conclusions we have formed.
>
> **Respective responsibilities**
>
> The Company's directors have confirmed that they have met their duty as set out in the directors' statement on page [ ]. They consider that the Company is exempt

---

[21] The "other parties" ([X]) are described "as a body" on the assumption that they are more than one.

[22] This assumes that, if [X] is more than a single party, the relevant parties comprising [X] are few in number and have all signed the engagement letter.

from the statutory requirement for an audit for the year [/period]. Our responsibility is to form and express an independent conclusion, based on the work carried out, to the Company's directors and [X] on the financial statements.

Scope

We conducted our engagement in accordance with the Institute of Chartered Accountants in England & Wales Interim Technical Release AAF 03/06. Our work was based primarily upon enquiry, analytical procedures and assessing accounting policies in accordance with Generally Accepted Accounting Practice in the UK [/the Financial Reporting Standard for Smaller Entities]. If we considered it to be necessary, we also performed limited examination of evidence relevant to certain balances and disclosures in the financial statements where we became aware of matters that might indicate a risk of material misstatement in the financial statements.

The terms of our engagement exclude any requirement to carry out a comprehensive assessment of the risks of material misstatement, a consideration of fraud, laws, regulations or internal controls, and we have not done so. We are not required to, and we do not, express an audit opinion on these financial statements.

Conclusion

Based on our work, nothing has come to our attention to refute the directors' confirmation that in accordance with the Companies Act 1985 the financial statements give a true and fair view of the state of the Company's affairs as at [date] and of its profit [/loss] for the year [/period] then ended and have been properly prepared in accordance with Generally Accepted Accounting Practice in the UK [/the Financial Reporting Standard for Smaller Entities].

Name of firm

Chartered accountants

Location

Date

E. b. ii. Reporting to the directors and members

Chartered accountants' independent assurance report on the unaudited financial statements of [name of entity]

To the Board of Directors and the members of [name of entity] ('the Company')

We have performed certain procedures in respect of the Company's unaudited financial statements for the year [/period] ended [date] as set out on pages [ ] to [ ], made enquiries of the Company's directors and assessed accounting policies adopted by the directors, in order to gather sufficient evidence for our conclusion in this report.

This report is made solely to the Company's directors and the Company's members, in each case as a body, in accordance with the terms of our engagement letter dated [date]. It has been released to the directors and the members on the basis that this report shall not be copied, referred to or disclosed, in whole (save for the directors' own internal purposes or amongst the directors and members or as may be required by law or by a competent regulator) or in part, without our prior written consent.[23] Our work has been undertaken so that we might state to the directors and the members those matters that we have agreed to state to them in this report and for no other purpose. To the fullest extent permitted by law, we do not accept or assume responsibility to anyone other than the Company and the Company's directors as a body and the Company's members as a body, for our work, for this report or the conclusions we have formed.

Respective responsibilities

The Company's directors have confirmed that they have met their duty as set out in the directors' statement on page [ ]. They consider that the Company is exempt from the statutory requirement for an audit for the year [/period]. Our responsibility is to form and express an independent conclusion, based on the work carried out, to the Company's directors and the Company's members on the financial statements.

Scope

We conducted our engagement in accordance with the Institute of Chartered Accountants in England & Wales Interim Technical Release AAF 03/06. Our work was based primarily upon enquiry, analytical procedures and assessing accounting policies in accordance with Generally Accepted Accounting Practice in the UK [/the Financial Reporting Standard for Smaller Entities]. If we considered it to be necessary, we also performed limited examination of evidence relevant to certain balances and disclosures in the financial statements where we became aware of matters that might indicate a risk of material misstatement in the financial statements.

The terms of our engagement exclude any requirement to carry out a comprehensive assessment of the risks of material misstatement, a consideration of fraud, laws, regulations or internal controls, and we have not done so. We are not required to, and we do not, express an audit opinion on these financial statements.

Conclusion

Based on our work, nothing has come to our attention to refute the directors' confirmation that in accordance with the Companies Act 1985 the financial statements give a true and fair view of the state of the Company's affairs as at [date] and of its profit [/loss] for the year [/period] then ended and have been properly prepared in accordance with Generally Accepted Accounting Practice in the UK [/the Financial Reporting Standard for Smaller Entities].

Name of firm

Chartered accountants

Location

Date

---

[23] *This assumes that the members are few in number and have all signed the engagement letter.*

Appendix F – Work procedures for the engagement

This guidance is intended for accountants who carry out the ICAEW Assurance Service on unaudited financial statements.

As discussed in paragraphs 11 to 13, the engagement procedures consist primarily of making enquiries of management and the directors, applying analytical procedures to the financial statements and assessing whether the applicable accounting policies are appropriate to the circumstances, and adequately disclosed. It may also include some examination of evidence relevant to certain balances and disclosures in the financial statements where, after performing the above work, accountants have become aware of matters that might indicate a risk of material misstatement in the financial statements. The engagement procedures will fall short of those of a full audit performed under ISAs (UK and Ireland), which include a comprehensive assessment of the risks of material misstatement, including a consideration of the risk of fraud and of non-compliance with relevant of laws and regulations, the gaining of an understanding of, and where relevant the testing of, internal control, and the gathering of evidence in respect of all material areas of the financial statements and for all relevant assertions.

The objectives stated below are to assist the thought process of accountants in designing and performing engagement procedures. The engagement procedures need not necessarily follow the described order in all respects and the process may be iterative to respond to the findings. The accountants use their professional judgement in establishing the work programme for individual engagements.

Planning

1. Ethical requirements

Accountants ensure that the ICAEW's Code of Ethics, including the Fundamental Principles and the requirements in *Independence for Assurance Engagements* is followed. Accountants check that suitable safeguards are in place if a threat to independence is perceived, for instance, if the accountants have been involved in the compilation of the financial statements.

2. Understanding the entity

Accountants ensure that their understanding of the entity is sufficient to plan appropriate work procedures to issue an assurance report. The objective of gaining the knowledge of the entity is primarily to enable the accountants to establish the accounting principles applied, consider materiality and plan their further enquiries. This knowledge is in particular used to form expectations for and to design appropriate analytical procedures. Understanding the entity may involve:

- discussions with management and, where appropriate, members of staff;
- reviewing minutes of board meetings to ascertain details of major events, plans and decisions;
- obtaining details of accounting records maintained and methods of recording financial transactions;
- understanding areas in which accounting estimates need to be made; and
- walk-throughs of the accounting records.

3. Establishing accounting principles adopted

Accountants establish the accounting principles adopted by the entity and consider if these are appropriate to the circumstances. Considerations include the effect of recent accounting pronouncements and changes in accounting policies because these could affect the work procedures. Accountants also identify areas where accounting estimates are made or management has exercised their judgement.

Accountants stay alert to inconsistencies during the performance of analytical procedures and management enquiry. If matters come to their attention that indicate that the accounting policies may be inappropriate they discuss what action is necessary with management. In certain circumstances in order to obtain further information accountants may perform substantive procedures (see below).

Work procedures may involve:

- reviewing accounting policies;
- discussions with management and where appropriate members of staff; and
- analytical procedures.

4. Establishing materiality

Accountants consider materiality in reference to the information on which they are reporting and the needs of the users of the financial statements. The purpose of establishing materiality is to help accountants to judge whether, having found any misstatements, there is a need to make adjustments; the purpose is not to judge the nature, extent and timing of substantive work in relation to all material assertions.

To establish materiality, accountants may wish to consider the following:

- the entity's size, trading environment, industry and accounting process;
- discussion with management on their assessment of the risks to the financial information and controls in place; and
- the entity's ability to continue in business as a going concern.

Performance

5. Performing analytical procedures

Accountants perform analytical procedures to see if the financial statements are consistent and make sense. Analytical procedures involve identifying unusual items or disclosures in the financial statements. Inconsistencies arising from the analytical procedures may indicate the risk of material misstatement. Accountants seek to address these inconsistencies by discussing them with management. Where further information is needed before agreeing with management what action needs to be taken, substantive procedures may need to be performed (see below).

Analytical procedures may include:

- comparison with expectations based on prior year's figures, budgets and industry statistics; and
- consideration of interrelationships between changes in balances and other fluctuations and significant events during the period.

6. Enquiry of management

Accountants obtain management explanations to understand events and reasoning that underpin the reported financial results. Such explanations may also address any inconsistencies identified from the performance of analytical procedures. Accountants may also wish to view supporting documentation for management explanations, such as reading minutes of board meetings and correspondence with third parties.

7. Performing substantive procedures

As stated in paragraphs 37 to 39, accountants perform substantive procedures to verify balances and transactions where significant risk of material misstatement exists as a result of enquiry of management and performing analytical procedures as described above in 5 and 6. Accountants are not expected to apply substantive procedures to every material balance and relevant financial statement assertion as expected in an audit.

Accountants exercise professional judgement in deciding the extent of substantive procedures to support their conclusions.

Where accountants have decided that substantive procedures may be necessary, these may include:

- comparing the financial statements with underlying accounting records;
- physical inspection of fixed assets/stock;
- verification of title to or the price of an asset;
- inspection of third party documents;
- third party certification of debit/credit balances;
- examination of post year end receipts/payments to confirm recoverability of a debt/the quantum of a liability; and
- checking cut-off.

8. Considering events subsequent to the year end

Accountants enquire of management whether there have been any material events subsequent to the year end to identify items that require adjustment to or disclosure in the financial statements. Accountants may request sight of the supporting documentation.

9. Reviewing the form and content of the financial statements

Accountants may wish to ensure the form and content of the financial statements are in compliance with the adopted accounting principles. This may be assisted by using a disclosure checklist.

AAF 04/06
Assurance Engagements: Management of Risk and Liability

Interim Technical Release

This guidance is issued by the Audit and Assurance Faculty of the Institute of Chartered Accountants in England & Wales (ICAEW) in November 2006 to assist accountants in managing their risk and liability when undertaking assurance engagements. This guidance does not constitute an auditing standard. AAF 04/06 is best practice guidance and professional judgement should be used in its application.

Contents

	Paragraphs
Introduction	1 – 3
Types of assurance	4 – 7
Related guidance	8 – 10
Scope of this guidance	11 – 14
Accepting an engagement	15 – 18
Managing professional liability	19 – 24
Agreeing on the terms of the engagement	25 – 30

Form of report 31

© Institute of Chartered Accountants in England & Wales

Introduction

In 2004, the International Auditing and Assurance Standards Board published the *International Framework for Assurance Engagements* (the Framework) and the first International Standard on Assurance Engagements (ISAE) 3000, *Assurance Engagements Other Than Audits or Reviews of Historical Financial Information*. These pronouncements provide high level principles for assurance engagements other than audits and reviews of historical financial statements.

1

The Framework defines the elements of assurance engagements and describes objectives for such engagements. ISAE 3000 provides generic guidance on the principal aspects of assurance engagements and refers to an assurance engagement involving three separate parties. Together these two international pronouncements provide the appropriate framework within which to develop specific guidance covering subject areas and topics such as internal control where, before now, no specific guidance has existed.

2

This technical release provides some principles for reporting accountants to consider around managing their risk and liability when agreeing to undertake assurance engagements and providing assurance reports to third parties. The scope of the guidance is laid out in paragraphs 11 and 12.

3

Types of assurance

Clients are increasingly asking accountants to provide assurance reports on specific operations/functions within their organisation or on information prepared by the client, in order to enable the client to provide comfort to other parties who have an interest in the client's operations/functions or information (for example a customer of the client). A convenient way of facilitating this provision of client comfort to others may be for clients to seek to engage the accountants to issue an assurance report. In an assurance report, the accountants express their conclusions, based on the outcome of their evaluation or measurement over the operations/functions or information against criteria, designed to enhance the degree of confidence of the intended users. An assurance engagement involves three separate parties: the accountants, the client (who is responsible for the operations/ functions or information) and the other parties or intended users[1] (for whom the accountants are preparing the assurance report).

4

In an assurance engagement, reporting accountants are asked to express an opinion or conclusion where sufficient and appropriate evidence has been gathered and evaluated against criteria specific to that function. This assurance is provided through either reasonable assurance engagements or limited assurance engagements. The extent of work required differs based on the type of assurance that the client requires.

5

In a reasonable assurance engagement, reporting accountants seek to obtain sufficient appropriate evidence that enables them to express a positive conclusion. In a limited assurance engagement, reporting accountants seek to gather evidence sufficient to obtain a meaningful level of assurance as the basis for a negative form of expression.

6

---

[1] *The intended users are those for whom the accountants prepare the assurance report. The client may be one of the intended users, but not the only one.*

7   When providing these reports, reporting accountants will need to be clear about why the report has been requested, the purpose for which it will be used, and who may obtain access to the report and assert rights against the accountants. This guidance considers the steps that reporting accountants may take to manage the risks associated with such reporting.

Related guidance

8   The Institute of Chartered Accountants in England and Wales (ICAEW) has issued general guidance as part of its Members Handbook, Statement 1.311[2] on *Managing the professional liability of accountants*. This includes:

> Defining the scope and responsibilities of the engagement;
> Defining the purpose of the accountants' report;
> Restricting the use of the accountants' name;
> Identifying the authorised recipients of report;
> Limiting (or excluding) liability;
> Obtaining an indemnity[3]; and
> Defining the scope of professional competence.

9   The Audit and Assurance Faculty (the Faculty) has over recent years also provided general guidance to assist accountants who have had requests for reports from third parties to manage the resulting risks. General guidance on reporting to third parties can be found in the following publications;

> Technical Release Audit 4/00 *"Firms reports and duties to lenders in connection with loans and other facilities to clients and related convents"*;
> Technical Release Audit 1/01 *"Reporting to third parties"*; and
> Technical Release Audit 1/03 *"The audit report and the auditors duty of care to third parties"*.

10 In addition, the Faculty has also recently developed specific guidance with relevant stakeholders, which includes model engagement terms and addresses specific risk issues including limitations of liability. These are:

> Technical Release AAF 01/06, *Assurance reports on internal controls of service organisations made available to third parties*.
> Technical Release AAF 03/06, *The ICAEW Assurance Service on Unaudited Financial Statements*.

Scope of this guidance

11 This guidance does not seek to provide detailed advice or practical steps on the planning and conduct of the work, nor on how to manage risk and liability in particular circumstances because much will depend on the purpose of the request for

---

[2] *Statement 1.311 will be renamed Statement 9.1 in the rewrite of the Members Handbook.*

[3] *It may be appropriate to obtain an indemnity from the client in respect of claims from third parties arising from the contents of the assurance report. The risk of such claims may arise, for example, where the accountants' report is widely circulated, in breach of confidentiality and disclosure restrictions that have been agreed or where, with the accountants' consent, the report is attached to the financial statements filed with Companies House. However, it must be remembered that an indemnity does not prevent a claim from being brought against the indemnified party. It merely gives him/her the right to pass on the liability to the indemnifier. It follows, therefore, that if the indemnity is in some way ineffective or the indemnifier does not have adequate resources to meet the liability, the indemnified party may be left unprotected.*

the report and the likely users of the report. The intention is that this guidance will provide the over arching principles, whilst the practical steps will be considered in the development of separate technical releases for specific topics and areas. Where appropriate, new assurance technical releases will cross-refer to this guidance and suggest how this guidance can be applied to the particular circumstance.

This guidance is also not intended as a substitute for independent legal advice. Reporting accountants will need to exercise judgement in assessing the risks for each particular engagement having regard to any relevant commercial considerations, their own appetite for risk, their internal quality control procedures and risk management policies, and the level of professional indemnity insurance that they have in place. This guidance also does not replace, rather supplements, firms' usual client and engagement acceptance procedures, so reporting accountants need to satisfy themselves that the client and work sought are suitable and that they can provide that service. 12

This guidance does not consider the independence considerations, ethical standards or any other regulatory considerations that may apply to assurance engagements. 12

The guidance in this technical release is set out under the following headings that describe the process accountants take when considering requests for assurance reports:

> Accepting an engagement;
> Managing professional liability;
> Agreeing on the terms of the engagement; and
> Form of report.

Accepting an Engagement

When requested to provide any services, the reporting accountant needs to clarify the purpose for which the work is being sought, the party/parties seeking to benefit from the work, and the use that will be made of the work. It is important that there is a clear understanding and agreement concerning the scope and purpose of the engagement between the reporting accountants and the client and, if applicable, the other parties or users that may also be party to the engagement. 15

Reporting accountants consider whether the engagement team collectively possesses the necessary professional competencies having regard to the nature of the assignment. As part of the engagement acceptance process reporting accountants also consider relevant ethical requirements.[4] 16

Where an assurance report may be received by a range of persons who are not party to the engagement, and whilst the reporting accountants may not intend to assume responsibility to others who are not party to the engagement, legal actions from such other parties may nonetheless occur. The following are examples of circumstances that may arise: 17

a. the third party requires a report to be prepared (e.g. in accordance with obligations between the client and the third party) and the third party intends to rely

---

[4] Section 210 Professional Appointments of the Code of Ethics specifically deals with changes in a professional appointment. Consideration may also be given, where relevant, to section 290, Independence – Assurance Engagements and section 220, Conflicts of Interest. Reporting accountants may also refer to the APB Ethical Standards (ES), in particular ES2 (Financial, business, employment and personal relationships) and ES5 (Non audit services provided to audit clients).

on it because it has an interest in the work that is aligned to the client's or a common interest; or
b. the reporting accountants and client have already entered into an engagement contract which allows for a third party to have sight of and rely on the report at a later date; or
c. the third party requires sight of the report but is not willing to or it is unsuitable for them to sign up to an engagement contract; or
d. an engagement with the client alone restricting the client from making the report available to any others.

18 The reporting accountants will therefore need to apply appropriate engagement acceptance procedures in order to assess the risks associated with taking on a particular engagement. They will then determine whether in the light of those risks, it is appropriate to take on the engagement and, if so, on what terms. Where the reporting accountants do accept an engagement, they need to apply suitably rigorous internal risk management policies to manage any increased level of risk. Relevant steps for managing professional liability are covered in the following section.

Managing professional liability

19 Depending on the engagement circumstances, reporting accountants enter into one or a combination of the following arrangements.

a. A tri-partite or multi-partite engagement contract with the client and the third parties, accepting that they owe a duty of care not only to the client but also to those third parties, including provisions limiting liability if appropriate (recognising that such a contract may not be achievable where there are numerous third parties).
b. An engagement with the client, with the facility for other third parties to enjoy a duty of care from the reporting accountants if they accept the relevant terms of the engagement letter previously agreed with the client as if they had signed that letter when originally issued, including the same provisions limiting liability[5].
c. An engagement with the client alone but before allowing the third parties access to the assurance report, requiring the third parties:
   (i) to acknowledge in writing that the reporting accountants owe the third parties no duty of care; and
   (ii) to agree in writing that no claims shall be brought against the reporting accountants by the third party in relation to the assurance report[6].
d. An engagement with the client alone disclaiming any liability or duty to others (including third parties) by notice in the assurance report. Reporting accountants also consider supporting this disclaimer with an indemnity from the client to apply where a third party claim is made (recognising that such an indemnity may not be attractive commercially, may not be effective if the client is not

[5] This will require the consent of the client/original addressees which should be obtained in the engagement letter.

[6] *Reporting accountants may wish to have regard to the principles outlined in Audit 04/03 Access to working papers by investigating accountants*, when developing a written form of such acknowledgment and agreement, bearing in mind that Audit 04/03 addresses different circumstances and the third party issues are also different.

financially stable, and may not operate to prevent a claim see further paragraph 30 below)[7].

e. If the risks are considered to be too high e.g. because the engagement itself is very complex or the reporting accountant is unable to agree acceptable terms with the client (and/or the third party), then the reporting accountants decline to accept the engagement.

It is also open to reporting accountants to consider with their legal advisers the use of the Contract (Rights of Third Parties) Act 1999 to manage the risk of liability to third parties. 20

Reporting accountants disclaim responsibility and liability to third party auditors, having regard to responsibility of the third party auditors for their own audit reports and for determining to what extent (if any) the assurance report amounts to sufficient appropriate audit evidence for the purposes of their audit of relevant third parties' financial statements. 21

Reporting accountants may become aware of other third parties that are not customers of the client, such as banks and other lenders or prospective purchasers of the client, who may also request access to the assurance report. The client or one of the third parties may approach the reporting accountants for consent to make the assurance report available to such other third parties, as the engagement contract agreed with the client contains disclosure and use restrictions. The assurance report is not prepared for third parties or with their interests or needs in mind, and the reporting accountants may decline this request. The reporting accountants will have set out the purpose of their report in the assurance report, and will have included a disclaimer of liability to third parties in line with paragraph 19 (d) above in that report. If the request is not declined, the reporting accountants will advise the third party that the assurance report was not prepared for the third party or the third party's benefit, that consent to their report being made available to a third party will only be given if the third party agrees that the third party should not rely on the report and acknowledges in writing that the reporting accountants do not owe it a duty of care and agrees that no claims may be brought against the reporting accountants by the third party in relation to the report[8]. 22

Reporting accountants may also receive requests from the client for consent to the release of the assurance report to other potential third parties with whom the client may be exploring the possibility of a relationship or reporting accountants may become aware that contrary to disclosure and use restrictions agreed with the client in the engagement contract, such potential third parties are gaining access to the assurance report. The reporting accountants may decline any such request. If the request is not declined, the written acknowledgement and agreement described in paragraph 22 above in relation to these third parties may be a practical solution to the management of risk in relation to these other third parties. Where that is not practical, the reporting accountants require the client (as a condition for giving consent, where requested) to send all such potential third parties a written statement, to accompany the assurance report, pointing out that the reporting accountants did not undertake the work for them and do not accept any responsibility to them and deny liability to them. Reporting accountants may wish to provide the client with a 23

---

[7] Reporting accountants consider the legal effectiveness of disclaiming liability and of the proposed disclaimer in light of the particular circumstances of their engagement (see for example, the guidance in Statement 1.311 on Managing the professional liability of accountants). Reporting accountants may need to seek their own independent legal advice.

[8] See Paragraph 19.b.

pro-forma statement and may wish to include reference to this in their engagement letter.

24 If correspondence between the reporting accountants and other third parties results from a disclaimer notice or otherwise, the reporting accountants decide (with independent legal advice if appropriate) how to bring such correspondence to a satisfactory close before it becomes protracted or undermines the original objective.

Agreeing on the terms of engagement

25 Right at the outset, accountants will need to manage their relationship for assurance engagements with the client and any third parties. They will also need to make clear to clients and third parties that engagements to provide such assurance reports are separate from statutory audit engagements.

26 Prior to accepting the engagement, the reporting accountants will also need to establish that the directors of the client will acknowledge in writing their responsibilities on behalf of the organisation for the subject matter of the report (e.g. for the design and operation of effective internal controls over its activities to achieve control objectives).

27 The reporting accountants will need to agree on the terms of engagement with all the parties to the engagement in accordance with the contractual relationship that is decided upon from paragraph 19. The agreed terms are recorded in writing in an engagement letter.

28 The reporting accountants consider the following for inclusion in their engagement letter:
> the purpose of the report and its agreed use, with accompanying disclosure restrictions setting out the extent to which, the context in which, and the basis on which, the report may be made available by the client to third parties;
> the directors' and the reporting accountants' respective responsibilities;
> the nature of the engagement and the type of assurance required (i.e. reasonable or limited assurance);
> scope of the work to be performed by the reporting accountants;
> the timescales within which the report will be provided (allowing the accountant sufficient time to plan and complete all the necessary work);
> a reference to any likely need for management representations;
> an explanation of the inherent limitations of the work, and for whom the work is being undertaken;
> limitations to the liability of the reporting accountants, including an appropriate liability cap;
> provisions for an indemnity if considered appropriate[9];
> the criteria used for the evaluation and measurement of the operations/functions or information (and how this information has been prepared);
> reference to the appropriate guidance, if any, that the accountants are using to perform the engagement; and

[9] *It may be appropriate to obtain an indemnity from the client in respect of claims from third parties arising from the contents of the assurance report. It must be remembered that an indemnity does not prevent a claim from being brought against the indemnified party. It merely gives him a right to pass on the liability to the indemnifier. It follows, therefore, that if the indemnity is in some way ineffective or the indemnifier does not have adequate resources to meet the liability, the indemnified party may be left unprotected.*

> once the engagement has already been entered into, the scope of work or terms of engagement are only varied after reasonable justification.

In particular, the reporting accountants exclude liability in respect of any loss or damage caused by, or arising from fraudulent acts, misrepresentation, and concealment of information or deliberate default on the part of the client, its directors, employees or agents. 29

If, before the completion of the engagement, the reporting accountants receive a request from the client, to change an assurance engagement to a non-assurance engagement or to change, for instance, the scope of the engagement, the reporting accountants will consider whether this has reasonable justification. They consider also whether the change will undermine any risk protections in place or add new risks. The engagement parties' misunderstanding in relation to the nature of the engagement or a change in circumstances that affects the third parties' requirements may justify a change to be requested by the client. Where accepting a request for a change, the reporting accountants will not disregard evidence that was already obtained prior to the change, and the details of the change should be documented and agreed in writing with all the parties to the engagement letter. 30

Form of report

The report by the reporting accountants reflects the agreement set out in the engagement. Reporting accountants will describe in their report for whom their work was done, the procedures performed, including the description of the tests and the purpose for which the work was done. Reporting accountants should take care to use clear and precise language to describe any specific terms used (such as 'enquiry' or 'inspection'). 31

AAF 01/07
Independent Accountants Report on Packaging Waste

Interim Technical Release

This interim guidance is designed to aid accountants approached by their clients to report under the Producer Responsibility Obligations (Packaging Waste) Regulations 2005 for the year ended 31 December 2006. Revised regulations for future years are expected in early 2007 following which final guidance will be issued. This guidance does not constitute an Auditing Standard and professional judgement should be used in its application.

Contents

	Paragraphs
Introduction	1
Explanation of the Reporting Arrangements	2 – 10
Effective Date	11
Appendices	
1. Guidance notes for the use of Accountants reporting on the PRNs/PERNS	3 – 8
2. Illustrative engagement terms	9 – 12
3. Suggested work programme	13 – 15
4. Example format and wording of Accountants' report.	16 – 18

AAF 03/06 is issued by the Audit and Assurance Faculty of the Institute of Chartered Accountants in England & Wales (ICAEW) in August 2006. AAF 03/06 is best practice guidance and professional judgement should be used in its application. No responsibilities for loss occasioned to any person acting or refraining from action as a result of any material in AAF 03/06 can be accepted by the ICAEW.

© Institute of Chartered Accountants in England & Wales

Introduction

1 The guidance has been drafted following discussions between the Institute of Chartered Accountants in England and Wales (ICAEW), the Institute of Chartered Accountants of Scotland (ICAS), the Environment Agency (EA) and the Scottish Environment Protection Agency (SEPA). For the purpose of this guidance, the EA and SEPA will be referred to as either the Agencies or the Agency.

Explanation of the reporting arrangements

2 The reporting arrangements are based on the reporting framework outlined in Technical Releases Audit 1/01 *Reporting to third parties* and Audit 3/03 *Public Sector Special Reporting Engagements – Grant Claim"*. Accountants may wish to refer to these technical releases. It is also recommended that Accountants refer to AAF 04/06, *Managing Risk and Liability*, which provides some principles that Accountants may wish to be aware of when considering these engagements[1].

3 This Technical Release provides guidance on the following:

a. background for Accountants on the Agencies' reporting requirements to support the accreditation process for Exporters and Reprocessors of UK packaging waste;
b. illustrative engagement terms and example confirmation of terms of engagement letter to be used;
c. suggested work procedures covering the Accountants work demonstrating[2] that the Packaging Waste Recovery Notes (PRNs) or Packaging Waste Exporter Recovery Notes (PERNs) issued by the Reprocessor or Exporter in the previous year are consistent with the records of the tonnage of packaging waste received or exported for reprocessing that year; and
d. recommended wording for the Accountants' report.

Each of these is covered in the following sections.

4 When Accountants embark on this reporting engagement they make use of all the relevant elements included in this guidance. For example, the Accountants' report is made in accordance with an agreement including the illustrative engagement terms and the guidance notes are referred to in order to understand the purpose of the report that has been requested and the issues that are likely to be relevant.

Guidance notes for Reporting Accountants

5 Guidance notes, which are included at Appendix 1, have been issued so that Accountants can understand the Agencies' purpose in seeking each report. The notes outline the various issues that Accountants need to be aware of when carrying out this work. The guidance notes should be read in conjunction with the suggested work programme.

---

[1] *AAF 04/06 is only applicable to members of the ICAEW.*

[2] *The wording in the Regulations in relation to the requirement are likely to change for reports relating to 2007, however this wording will still apply for reports relating to 2006.*

Illustrative engagement terms

6 The illustrative engagement terms, reproduced in Appendix 2, follow the principles of Technical Release Audit 1/01 referred to in paragraph 2 above. They take the form of a bi-partite engagement with the Exporter/Reprocessor. The guidance within this technical release assumes that an agreed upon procedures engagement will be agreed. However, Accountants are at liberty to agree another form of engagement with their client if both parties consider it to be more appropriate. Whatever form that the engagement takes, Accountants are reminded to manage their risk and liability appropriately (considering the steps outlined in AAF 4/06[3]), including the use of appropriate wording disclaiming liability to all other third parties.

7 Accountants need to be mindful of entering into any dialogue with any third party in relation to the engagement. Should it become necessary to enter into such dialogue, Accountants may wish to consider whether the third party should sign up to the engagement letter.

8 These engagements are separate from and unrelated to the Accountants' audit work on the financial statements of the Exporter/Reprocessor for the purposes of the Companies Act 1985 and do not create any obligations or liabilities regarding the Accountants' statutory audit work, which would not otherwise exist.

Work programme and reports to the Agencies

9 For the Accountants' work on PRNs/PERNs, suggested work procedures have been developed with the Agencies and are provided in Appendix 3. All reports arising from the completion of this work programme will be factual findings arising from the performance of agreed upon procedures. Recommended language for such a report is given in Appendix 4. These words have been compiled taking account of the guidance provided in Appendix 2 of Audit 1/01. If alternative words are suggested, Accountants refer to Appendix 2 of Audit 1/01 to determine whether the suggested text would be appropriate.

Fraud

10 Accountants are reminded of the need to comply with their duties in relation to serious and organised crime and consider other guidance in this area. Where they suspect proceeds have arisen from criminal activities they are mindful of the 'tipping off' provisions under the relevant legislation.

Effective date

11 This guidance is effective from the date of publication, but for reports issued in 2007 only.

Appendices

Appendix 1 – Guidance notes for the use of Accountants reporting on PRNs/PERNs

Appendix 2 – Illustrative engagement terms

Appendix 3 – Suggested work programme

Appendix 4 – Example format and wording of Accountants' report

---

[3] See Note 1.

Appendix 1 – Guidance notes for the use of accountants reporting on PRNS/PERNS

Background

The EC Directive on Packaging and Packaging Waste 94/62/EC came into force in 1994 and it is implemented in Great Britain by (i) The Producer Responsibility Obligations (Packaging Waste) Regulations 2005 (the "Regulations"); and (ii) the Packaging (Essential Requirements) Regulations 2003 (as amended). The Regulations set targets for recovery and recycling of packaging waste to be met by obligated businesses each year so that the Great Britain can meet Directive targets by the specified deadline. The Government is required to submit packaging data to the European Commission on a yearly basis and needs to be confident that the data it supplies is accurate. 1

Packaging Waste Recovery Notes (PRNs) and Packaging Waste Export Recovery Notes (PERNs) are issued by reprocessors and exporters of packaging waste. Under the Regulations, all business (producers) with turnovers exceeding £2m and handling more than 50 tonnes of obligated packaging per year are required to recover and recycle a specified amount of packaging waste determined by the amount of packaging that they handle, the activity carried out on the packaging and the packaging targets. Producers demonstrate compliance with their recovery and recycling obligations themselves or by joining a scheme that will discharge their obligations on their behalf. Producers and schemes demonstrate such compliance by obtaining PRNs and/or PERNs from Reprocessors/Exporters. 2

The form of the PRN/PERN is determined by the Agencies. Currently they issue a book of individually and uniquely numbered PRN/PERNs to each Reprocessor/Exporter to be completed. PRN/PERNs can only be issued by accredited Reprocessors/Exporters. These PRNs and PERNs are issued in relation to tonnages of UK packaging waste delivered or exported for reprocessing in the UK and overseasThe National Packaging Waste Database has been designed to to provide an online system for accredited Reprocessors/Exporters to provide their quarterly returns. During 2006, accredited Reprocessors and Exporters were able to submit quarterly returns to the relevant agency. By early 2007, it is intended that this system will provide a method for accredited Reprocessors and Exporters to issue electronic PRNs/PERNs. 3

To be accredited, a Reprocessor/Exporter needs to apply to the relevant agency. Accreditation is granted upon a number of conditions which are primarily concerned with how PRNs/PERNs are issued and the maintenance of underlying records. Accreditation lasts up to the end of the calendar year in which it is granted. 4

In relation to exports, materials moving within the UK (Scotland, England, Wales and Northern Ireland) are not classed as exports. Materials moving between the UK and the Republic of Ireland, or any other country, are classed as exports. 5

Since the original regulations were first published in 1997, a government investigation revealed that some exporters and reprocessors of plastic packaging waste were failing to meet government requirements on recycling. The investigation indicated that Exporters/Reprocessors were incorrectly issuing compliance documentation which made it appear as if they were recycling more plastic packaging waste than they actually were and issued PERNs more than the tonnage of packaging waste that has actually been exported. Similar investigations were carried out for wood and 6 paper. As a result of this investigation, the Regulations were amended in 2003 to include a requirement for exporters and reprocessors to have an Accountants' report by an Independent Auditor.

7 Reprocessors and Exporters issuing more than 400 tonnes of PRNs and/or PERNs in a calendar year are required to provide an Accountants' Report by an Independent Auditor to the Agency by 28 February each year (see Appendix 2 – 4).

8 An Independent Auditor[4] is defined in the Regulations as *"an auditor who would be eligible for appointment as company auditor of the reprocessor or exporter under Part II of the Companies Act 1989"*. For the avoidance of doubt, the terms "Reporting Accountants", "Accountants" and "Auditors" used throughout these guidance notes do not refer to a firm's role as statutory auditor. For ease of reference, the guidance within this technical release uses Independent Accountant as this term is understood by the profession for this type of work.

Guidance for Accountants

9 These notes have been issued as guidance for those Accountants whose clients, the Exporters and Reprocessors, are required to submit reports to the relevant Agency which "*demonstrate that the PRNs or PERNS issued by the reprocessor or exporter in the previous year are consistent with the tonnage of packaging waste received or exported for reprocessing that year*". Where reports from Accountants are required, discussions have been held between the Agencies, ICAEW and ICAS concerning the general duty of care in respect of the work performed. The Agencies have confirmed that they do not wish to enter into a tri-partite engagement with Accountants and do not envisage a situation whereby Accountants would owe them a duty of care. However, Accountants should be aware that anyone who furnishes any information to the appropriate Agency in connection with its functions under the Regulations may be guilty of an offence if, in furnishing the information, they know the information to be false or misleading in a material particular; or furnish such information recklessly and it is false or misleading in a material particular.

10 These guidance notes are issued for Accountants to assist them in providing their reports on the information supplied by their client to the relevant Agency. Suggested work procedures for the reports are given in Appendix 3 and these guidance notes should be read in conjunction with that Appendix. Accountants are reminded to consider and manage their risk and liability appropriately, particularly given the Agencies' position in relation to these engagements.

Terms of engagement

11 It is recommended that Accountants' reports make reference to the agreement between the Exporter/Reprocessor and the Accountants and it is suggested that the illustrative engagement terms developed by the Institutes may be used as a basis for specific terms of engagement in each case. These illustrative engagement terms address the issues of the respective responsibilities of the Exporter/Reprocessor and the Accountants, and in particular explains the duty of care and limitation of liability as they relate to this specific work. The terms also state that the work is not carried

---

[4] As part of its change to the Regulations, DEFRA is considering changing this to include environmental auditors provided they are independent.

out in contemplation of others' needs or requirements and Accountants do not accept a duty to secondary users of PRN/PERNs.

It is recommended that Accountants agree the terms of engagement with their client(s) using the illustrative engagement terms as a basis[5]. This technical release has been drafted on the assumption that an agreed upon procedures engagement will be carried out. However, Accountants are free to discuss and agree other forms of engagements with their clients.

PRN/PERN reports

The following information is provided as information for Accountants so that they can come to an understanding about how the Exporters/Reprocessors' systems work and where the Accountant's report fits into the process. This information is provided to enable Accountants to put the work into context so that they can determine whether or not to take on the work.

Reprocessors

To apply for accreditation, Reprocessors will need to provide suitable evidence to confirm that UK packaging waste been reprocessed. As a minimum, they will need to provide information to the Agency to confirm:

a. The material type (e.g. paper, aluminium, steel);
b. the source of the UK packaging waste;
c. the weight of the UK packaging waste received and reprocessed;
d. compliance with requirements of relevant environmental legislation [this includes waste management licenses, complying with the terms of an exemption from waste management licensing and a permit issued under the Pollution Prevention and Control Regulations.];
e. the efficiency of the reprocessing plan and that they meet the appropriate operating standards (appendix X); and
f. the final use of the recovered material.

Exporters

To apply for accreditation, Exporters will need to provide evidence to confirm that UK packaging waste has been exported for reprocessing. As a minimum, they will need to confirm:

a. The material type (e.g. paper, aluminium, steel);
b. the source of the UK packaging waste;
c. that they are the last owner of the waste prior to it leaving the UK;
d. the weight of the UK packaging waste exported by load/container etc.;
e. the overseas order and specification for the packaging waste;
f. acceptance of the waste load for transport to the overseas port;
g. the point of export from the UK;
h. whether the waste shipment has cleared customs in the destination country;

---

[5] In deciding and agreeing appropriate engagement terms in England and Wales, accountants should refer to the guidance in Statement 9.1 of the Institute's Members' Handbook, "Managing the professional liability of accountants" and Technical Release Audit 1/01. In Scotland, accountants should refer to Technical Release Audit 1/01.

i. that the packaging waste has been received for reprocessing by the named Reprocessor; and
j. that any Reprocessors located outside the European Community operate to broadly equivalent environmental standards to those within the EC.

16 Exporters must submit information relating to each overseas Reprocessor that they intend to use through the period of accreditation. Evidence may only be issued against material exported to those that have been notified to and approved by the Agency. For SEPA and the Environment Agency, these sites and the effective date of accreditation will be listed in the Notice of Accreditation.

Sampling and Inspection Plan

17 As part of the application, Reprocessors and Exporters must submit a Sampling and Inspection Plan. The aim of this plan is to ensure that any waste received or exported against which PRN/PERNs are to be issued is UK packaging waste. As a minimum the plan must include details of:

> checks with waste suppliers to ensure that the waste has originated in the UK and that it is packaging waste
> periodic sampling of loads to verify the quantities of packaging waste received or exported for reprocessing
> delivery documentation (such as weighbridge tickets or goods received notes) to verify the quantities of the packaging waste received or exported for reprocessing
> inspection and audit of other documentary evidence, for example delivery notes, invoices, etc.
> procedures implemented by Reprocessors/Exporters over the receipt of deliveries and accurate recording of delivery details
> the use of material protocols acknowledged by the Agencies (see below) to determine the proportion of packaging waste that is contained in waste loads.
> Reprocessors/Exporters rationale for the proportion of packaging waste that is contained in mixed waste loads that are not subject to a protocol acknowledged by the Agencies. The rationale should include:
>   – Description of packaging waste loads received by the site
>   – Percentage of packaging waste content claimed by the site
>   – Sampling procedure used to develop protocol

18 Material protocols have been developed for certain grades of steel, aluminium and paper. This allows Reprocessors and Exporters handling these grades to apply a set percentage to the tonnages instead of developing a protocol for themselves. The application of protocols should be covered in the Sampling and Inspection Plan prepared by the Reprocessors or Exporters.

Information held

19 Once accredited, a business can issue the PRNs/PERNs against the tonnage of packaging waste received or exported from the date of accreditation to 31 December. Most Reprocessors/Exporters are likely to be accredited on 1 January in any year. If accreditation is not granted until after that date, then the Reprocessor/Exporter is only entitled to issue PRN/PERNs for packaging waste received after the date of accreditation. These PRNs/PERNs should then be issued by the following 31 January (e.g. for the year ending 31 December 2006, all PRNs/PERNs should be issued by 31 January 2007).

Any PRN/PERN issued in the following January can only be used as a "carry over" PRN/PERN if it relates to packaging waste received/exported in the December period. 20

Where PRN/PERNs have not been issued to a producer, scheme or their representative by 31 January, a final (surplus) PRN/PERN for the un-issued balance must be submitted to the Agency by 15 February. 21

Status of PRN/PERN books

PRN/PERN books are provided free of charge to accredited businesses. If a business is accredited to reprocess or export more than one material type, it will have a separate accreditation number and PRN/PERN book for each material type. Each book can only be used for one material type. The accredited business must keep the counterfoil copy of all PRNs/PERNs issued. 22

Whole tonnes

The tonnage shown on a PRN/PERN should be a whole number. Any balance of packaging waste accepted for reprocessing at the year end that is less than one tonne should be rounded up or down by the Reprocessor or Exporter to the nearest tonne. 23

Substitutes

A substitute PRN/PERN replaces the original document, provided that the original is returned by the scheme or producer to the Agencies. Accredited businesses may issue substitute PRNs/PERNs for the original when requested by a producer, scheme or their representative. This most commonly occurs when a mistake is made when completing the original. A substitute may also be issued when a producer or scheme requests that the original PRN/PERN is replaced with several PRNs/PERNs of smaller denominations, e.g. to replace a 100 tonne PRN with two PRNs for 50 tonnes. The substitutes must be for the same total tonnage and the same year as the original and all substitutes must be issued at the same time i.e. a balance cannot be held in credit against part of the original. No substitution can be made after the 31 January for PRNs/PERNs issued on waste received for reprocessing in the previous year. A replacement PRN/PERN cannot be issued for one that has been lost and accredited businesses need to have measures in place to address situations which may lead to the loss of a PRN/PERN. 24

Management and records

PRNs/PERNs are only issued to producers or operators of compliance schemes or to their representatives. Where a representative is supplied with evidence, the accredited business should complete the PRN/PERN with only the name of the producer or scheme and not the name of the representative. 25

The accredited business needs to retain records as specified on the reporting form provided by the Agency. The records are required, by the Agencies be maintained on a quarterly basis and kept for at least four years after the record is made. 26

27 The accredited business will provide the Agency with quarterly reports with the following information:

> the tonnage of UK packaging waste received or exported for reprocessing in that quarter;
> the tonnage of UK packaging waste sent to another Reprocessor or Exporter (the evidence relating to this tonnage will be issued by the other Reprocessor or Exporter);
> the tonnage of packaging waste reprocessed in that quarter;
> the quantity of PRN/PERNs (in tonnes) issued in that quarter, together with the PRN/PERN summary sheet from the PRN/PERN book; and
> tonnage to another Exporter and Reprocessor for the purpose of issuing PRN/PERNs.

28 Accredited Reprocessors and Exporters will also submit an annual report by 28 February detailing:

> an annual summary of information provided in the quarterly reports;
> the amount of revenue received in the previous year from the sale of PRNs or PERNs; and
> a statement of what it has been spent on.

In addition, they must obtain an Accountant's Report by an Independent Accountant if the PRN/PERN's issued in a calendar year exceeds 400 tonnes covering each accredited site.

29 Accredited Reprocessors that have a number of sites may centralise their administration of PRNs, however, separate records, returns and PRN books must still be used for each accredited site. The Independent Accountants' Report must be site specific. If carrying out this work on a group of companies, it is acceptable to provide a general report on the work carried out with a detailed report on the findings for each individual site in the group.

30 PRNs/PERNs are not necessarily issued against individual loads. Tonnages may be aggregated together and evidence issued for the total amount. At no time must the tonnage of evidence issued exceed the tonnage of material accepted or exported for reprocessing. Although exporters can issue PERNs when the load is exported, it is recommended that acceptance of the load at the overseas site is obtained first in case the load is rejected or downgraded. Any subsequent deductions in tonnage, for example to take account of a high moisture content, must be reflected in the tonnages of evidence available

31 There is no restriction to the amount of overall annual tonnage of material accepted or exported for reprocessing. Exporters can export as much waste as they like, (subject to other regulatory controls) and Reprocessors may accept as much waste as they like. However, the PRN/PERNs must not exceed the total amount of packaging waste received/exported.

Appendix 2 – Illustrative engagement terms

The following are illustrative terms of engagement on which the [Exporter/Reprocessor] agrees to engage Accountants to report in connection with the Producer Responsibility Obligations (Packaging Waste) Regulations 2005 SI 2005/3468 ("the Regulations"). Accountants are free to use this as a basis for agreement with their client i.e. they can be changed and negotiated.

A contract between the [Exporter/Reprocessor] and the Accountants is formed when the [Exporter/Reprocessor] and the Accountants agree and sign up to these terms of engagement.

In these terms of engagement:

"the Agency" refers to the [Environment Agency/ Scottish Environment Protection Agency]

"the [Exporter/Reprocessor]" refers to [name of Exporter/Reprocessor] which is required to submit the report to the Agency;

"the Accountants" refers to the [Exporter/Reprocessor]'s reporting accountants;

"the Regulations" refers to the Producer Responsibility Obligations (Packaging Waste) Regulations 2005 SI 3468.

Example Letter

[Addressee details for Exporter/Reprocessor]

We are writing to confirm the terms and conditions on which you have engaged [name of firm] to provide you with reports which you are required to submit to the Agency, as set out in clause 4 below. These terms of engagement set out the basis on which the Accountants will issue the reports. — 1

The [Exporter/Reprocessor]'s responsibilities — 2

The [Exporter/Reprocessor] is responsible for producing the information set out in the reports, maintaining proper records complying with the terms of the Regulations and providing information to the Agency on a quarterly and annual basis in accordance with the requirements of the Agency's guidance notes. — 2.1

The management of the [Exporter/Reprocessor] will make available to the Accountants all records, correspondence, information and explanations that the Accountants consider necessary to enable them to perform their work. — 2.2

The [Exporter/Reprocessor] accepts that the ability of the Accountants to perform the work effectively depends upon the [Exporter/Reprocessor] providing full and free access to the financial and other records and the [Exporter/Reprocessor] shall procure that any such records held by a third party are made available to the Accountants. — 2.3

The failure by the [Exporter/Reprocessor] to meet its obligations may cause the Accountants to qualify their report or be unable to provide a report or issue a report containing exceptions discovered as a result of carrying out the agreed procedures. — 2.4

Scope of the Accountants' work — 3

The [Exporter/Reprocessor] will provide the Accountants with such information, explanations and documentation that the Accountants will consider necessary to carry out their responsibilities. The Accountants will seek written representations from management of the [Exporter/Reprocessor] in relation to matters for which — 3.1

independent corroboration is not available. The Accountants will seek confirmation that any significant matters of which the Accountants should be aware have been brought to the Accountants' attention.

3.2 The Accountants will perform the procedures listed in Appendix [X] on the reports prepared by the [Exporter/ Reprocessor]. The [Exporter/Reprocessor] is responsible for determining whether the scope of work specified in that Appendix is sufficient for its purpose.

3.3 The Accountants will not subject the information provided by the [Exporter/ Reprocessor] to checking or verification except to the extent expressly stated. While the Accountants will perform their work with reasonable skill and care and will report any misstatement or errors that are revealed by enquiries within the scope of the engagement, the Accountants work should not be relied upon to disclose all misstatements or errors that might exist.

4 Form of the Accountants report

4.1 The Accountants' report ("Report"), an example of which is included as an appendix to this letter, will be prepared on the following basis:

4.1.1 The Report will be addressed to and prepared for the confidential use of the Exporter/Reprocessor for the purpose of assisting the management of the [Exporter/ Reprocessor] in meeting the requirements of paragraph 1(p) of Schedule 5 of the Regulations. They may not be relied upon by the [Exporter/Reprocessor] or any other party for any other purpose.

4.1.2 We agree that a copy of our Report may be provided to the Agency for their information in connection with this purpose but only on the basis that we accept no duty, liability or responsibility, whatsoever, to the Agency in relation to our Report. The Report is not to be used for any other purpose, recited or referred to in any document, copied or made available (in whole or in part) to any other person without our prior written express consent, except to the extent required by court order, law or regulation. We accept no duty, responsibility or liability to any party, other than the [Exporter/Reprocessor] in connection with the Report or this engagement.

4.1.3 The [Exporter/Reprocessor] may not rely on any oral or draft reports that the Accountants provides. The Accountant only accepts responsibility to the [Exporter/ Reprocessor] for the Accountants' final signed reports only.

4.1.4 Except as provided by clause 4.1.1 herein, the firm of Accountants, its partners members, directors and employees neither owe nor accept any duty to any other person (including, without limitation, any person who may use or refer to any of the [Exporter/Reprocessor]'s publications) and shall not be liable for any loss, damage or expense of whatsoever nature which is caused by their reliance or representations in the Accountants' reports.

5 Liability provisions

5.1 The Accountants will perform the engagement with reasonable skill and care and acknowledge that they will be liable to the [Exporter/Reprocessor] for losses, damages, costs or expenses ("losses") caused by their breach of contract, negligence or wilful default, subject to the following provisions:

The Accountants will not be liable if such losses are due to the provision of false, misleading or incomplete information or documentation or due to the acts or missions of any other person other than the Accountants.	5.1.1
The Accountants accept liability without limitation for the consequences of their own fraud and for any other liability which it is not permitted by law to limit or exclude.	5.1.2
Subject to the previous paragraph 5.1.2, the total aggregate liability of the Accountants whether in contract, tort (including negligence) or otherwise, to the Agency, arising from or in connection with the work which is the subject of these terms (including any addition or variation to the work), shall not exceed [to be discussed and negotiated⁶].	5.1.3
The [Exporter/Reprocessor] agrees that it will not bring any claim or proceedings against individual partners, members, directors or employees of the Accountants. [This clause is intended to benefit such partners, members, directors and employees who may enforce this clause pursuant to the Contracts (Rights of Third Parties) Act 1999. Notwithstanding any benefits or rights conferred by this agreement on any third party by virtue of the Act, the parties to this agreement may agree to vary or rescind this agreement without any third party's consent. Other than as expressly provided in these terms, the provisions of the Act are excluded.]⁷	5.2
Any claims whether in contract, negligence or otherwise must be formally commenced within 3 years after the party bringing the claim becomes aware (or ought reasonably to have become aware) of the facts which give rise to the action and in any event no later than 6 years after any alleged breach of contract, negligence or other cause of action. This expressly over rides any statutory provision, which would otherwise apply.	5.3
Where the Accountants are also the appointed auditors of the [Exporter/Reprocessor]'s financial statements, this engagement is separate from, and unrelated to, the Accountants' audit work on the financial statements of the [Exporter/Reprocessor] for the purposes of the Companies Act 1985 (or its successor) or other legislation and nothing herein creates obligations or liabilities regarding the Accountants' statutory audit work, which would not otherwise exist.	5.4

Fees   6

The Accountants' fees, together with VAT and out of pocket expenses, will be agreed with and billed to the [Exporter/Reprocessor].	6.1

Quality of service   7

The Accountants will investigate all complaints concerning the Accountants' work. The [Exporter/Reprocessor] has the right to make any complaint to [ICAEW/ICAS] as appropriate.	7.1

---

⁶ *There are a number of possible ways of arriving at the most appropriate liability wording e.g. it could be fixed at a monetary amount or liability could be limited to the proportion of the loss and damage suffered by the [Exporter/Reprocessor] for which the accountants have contributed (as agreed between the parties or in the absence of an agreement, as finally determined by the courts). Accountants should consider other guidance previously issued by their respective Institutes for the most appropriate wording and discuss with their clients.*

⁷ *This paragraph should be deleted if Scots law applies.*

8 Providing services to other parties

8.1 The Accountants will not be prevented or restricted by virtue of the Accountants' relationship with the [Exporter/Reprocessor], including anything in these terms of engagement, from providing services to other clients. The Accountants' standard internal procedures are designed to ensure that confidential information communicated to the Accountants during the course of an assignment will be maintained confidentially.

9 Applicable law and jurisdiction

9.1 This agreement shall be governed by, and interpreted and construed in accordance with the laws of [England and Wales/Scotland].

9.2 The [Exporter/Reprocessor], and the Accountants irrevocably agree that the courts of [England/Scotland] shall have exclusive jurisdiction to settle any dispute (including claims for set-off and counterclaims) which may arise in connection with the validity, effect, interpretation or performance of, or the legal relationship established by this agreement or otherwise arising in connection with this agreement.

10 Alteration to terms

10.1 All additions, amendments and variations to these terms of engagement shall be binding only if in writing and signed by the duly authorised representatives of the parties. These terms supersede any previous agreements and representations between the parties in respect of the scope of the Accountants' work and the Accountants' reports or the obligations of any of the parties relating thereto (whether oral or written) and represents the entire understanding between the parties.

Please confirm by signing below, your agreement to this letter. Once you have done so, this letter will form a contract between us in respect of the matters covered. If you wish to discuss any aspect of this letter, please contact [name and telephone number].

Yours faithfully

[Name of Reporting Accountants]

[Exporter/Reprocessor]

Appendix 3 – Suggested work programme

Reprocessor accreditation

For accredited Reprocessors, PRNs can only be issued on the tonnage of UK packaging waste received in the calendar year that the business is accredited from the date of accreditation. Once the waste has been received, a PRN can be issued against that tonnage but only on the basis that the material goes on to be reprocessed. Accountants will need to perform procedures to check that the Reprocessor has underlying records (evidence) which verify:

   a. the source of the UK packaging waste using information contained within delivery notes and/or a representation from management;

b. the weight of the UK packaging waste received using information from delivery notes and weighbridge tickets; and
c. the PRNs issued are equal or less than the tonnage of packaging waste received on site (based on management's records of deliveries received and PRN's issued).

Exporter accreditation

For accredited Exporters, PERNs can only be issued on the tonnage of UK packaging waste exported to approved sites in the calendar year that the business is accredited from the date of accreditation. Once the waste has been exported from the UK, a PERN can be issued against that tonnage but only on the basis that the material goes on to be reprocessed at an overseas reprocessing site. Accountants will need to perform procedures to check that the exporter has underlying records (evidence) which verify:

a. the material type e.g. glass, plastic etc;
b. the source of the UK packaging waste using information contained within delivery notes and/or a representation from management;
c. the weight of the UK packaging waste exported by load/container etc using information from delivery notes and weighbridge tickets;
d. whether or not the packaging waste has been received for reprocessing by the named reprocessor;
e. that PERNs are only issued against material exported to sites that have been notified to and approved by the Agency;
f. evidence of receipt of material at destination; and
g. PERNs issued do not exceed the exported tonnage.

Accountants need to check that the amount of packaging waste included in PRN/PERNs issued during the year to 31 December and the 'carry over' PRN/PERN issued in the following January, does not exceed the tonnage of UK packaging waste received for reprocessing or exported during that year. The accuracy of the 'carry over' PRN/PERN requires specific verification to documentation of deliveries received in December to check that it is not overstated.

Where PRN/PERNs remain unissued as of 31 January for waste received in the previous year to 31 December, a final (surplus) PRN/PERN can be issued up to 15 February, with specific disclosure to the Agency. Accountants need to check that no further PRN/PERNs are issued after 31 January except for this final (surplus) PRN/PERN.

Sampling and Inspection Plan

The procedures to be conducted in respect of the Sampling and Inspection Plan prepared by the Reprocessor/Exporter are as follows:

1) Obtain a copy of the Reprocessor/Exporter's year end return submitted to the Agency in accordance with the Regulations and identify whether there are procedures in place at the Reprocessor/Exporter to record:
   > The receipt of material for reprocessing or exporting
   > The issue of PRN/PERNs.
2) Agree the tonnages of waste in the annual return of PRNs/PERNS prepared under paragraph 1(o) of Schedule 5 of the Regulations to the total of the duplicate PRNs/PERNs held by the Reprocessor/Exporter.

Reprocessors only

3) For a sample of PRNs issued by the Reprocessor for each of the four quarters during the year in respect of waste received:
   > Obtain a representation from the senior management of the Reprocessor/Exporter that they intend to reprocess the waste and will not transfer the waste on to another reprocessor;
   > Agree that the tonnage of waste on the PRN was, to the nearest 0.5 tonne, supported by the tonnage of waste received on purchase invoice(s) and/or weighbridge ticket(s);
   > Agree that the description of the waste on the purchase invoice(s) met the definition of packaging waste set out in the Regulations; and
   > Check that documentation from the supplier(s) is held confirming it became waste within the UK.

Exporters only

4) For a sample of PERNs issued by the Exporter during the year in respect of waste exported:
   > Agree that the description of the waste on the purchase invoice(s) meets the definition of packaging waste set out in the Regulations;
   > Agree to confirmation from the supplier(s) of the waste that it has become waste within the UK; and
   > Agree that the tonnage of waste on the PERN is, to the nearest 0.5 tonne, supported by the tonnage of waste on shipping manifests and proof of delivery showing a destination outside the UK.
5) For a sample of UK package waste deliveries received for reprocessing which was in turn received from another reprocessor (other than other sites operated by the Reprocessor), check that the Reprocessor has received an undertaking from that other reprocessor that they have not already issued a PRN/PERN in respect of that waste.
6) For a sample of waste deliveries received for reprocessing which was in turn received from another site operated by the Reprocessor, if it is possible, check via the PRN/PERN book that the Reprocessor has not already issued a PRN/PERN in respect of that waste.
7) For a sample of waste deliveries received for reprocessing or export, subsequently sold on to another reprocessor, check via the PRN/PERN book that no PRN/PERN has been issued by the Reprocessor in respect of that waste.
8) Check that the tonnages on the annual return are equal to the four quarterly returns.
9) Check that the tonnage included in PRNs/PERNs, in respect of UK packaging waste received/exported in December 2006, issued to producers or schemes (up to 31 January 2007) and to the appropriate agency (after 31 January 2007) is not greater than the tonnage of waste received in 2006.

In the Accountants' Report, the Accountant may wish to provide an explanation of the samples selected for each test in the above agreed upon procedures, as appropriate.

Appendix 4 – Example format and wording of accountants' reports

This is an example of a report for an Accountant's report for a Reprocessor. Accountants will need to tailor this accordingly when carrying out such work at an Exporter.

Example of an Independent Accountant's report [with exceptions] to the directors of XYZ Limited in respect of the issue of PRNs/PERNs for the year ended 31 December XXX.

Introduction

Paragraph 1(p) of Schedule 5 to the Producer Responsibility Obligations (Packaging Waste) Regulations 2005 (SI 2005/3468) ("the Regulations") requires that a report by an independent auditor is provided to the [exporter/ reprocessor] which demonstrates that the packaging waste recovery notes ("PRNs") or packaging waste export recovery notes ("PERNs") issued by an accredited reprocessor or exporter in a year are consistent with the tonnage of packaging waste received or exported for reprocessing that year.

Our report ("Report") is prepared solely for the confidential use of the directors of XYZ Limited [("the reprocessor")/ ("the exporter")] and solely for the purpose of assisting the directors of the [reprocessor/exporter] to meet the requirements of paragraph 1(p) of Schedule 5 of the Regulations. However, we understand that this report will be submitted to the [Environment Agency/Scottish Environment Protection Agency] ("the Agency") for the purpose of assisting the directors to meet the requirements of the Regulations. We agree that a copy of our Report may be provided to the Agency for their information in connection with this purpose but only on the basis that we accept no duty, liability or responsibility whatsoever to the Agency in relation to our Report. Our Report is not to be used for any other purpose, recited or referred to in any document, copied or made available (in whole or in part) to any other person without our prior written express consent, except to the extent required by court order, law or regulation. We accept no duty, responsibility or liability to any party, other than the [reprocessor/exporter] in connection with the Report or this engagement.

Basis of Report

Our work was carried out in accordance with the Interim Technical Release AAF 01/07 *"Independent Accountants Report on Packaging Waste"*.

The scope of our work in preparing this Report was limited solely to those procedures set out below. Accordingly, we do not express any opinion or overall conclusion on the procedures we have performed. You are responsible for determining whether the scope of our work specified is sufficient for your purposes and we make no representation regarding the sufficiency of these procedures for your purposes. If we were to perform additional procedures, other matters might come to our attention that would be reported to you.

Our Report should not be taken to supplant any other enquiries and procedures that may be necessary to satisfy the requirements of the recipients of the Report.

The procedures we have performed did not constitute a review or an audit of any kind. We did not subject the information contained in our Report or given to us by the senior management to checking or verification procedures except to the extent expressly stated above. This is normal practice when carrying out such limited scope procedures, but contrasts significantly with, for example, an audit. The procedures we performed were not designed to and are not likely to reveal fraud.

Sampling

Give sampling method/basis (i.e. how you determined what sampling method to use (e.g. haphazard), how sample size was chosen, the period and percentage of total population (tonnage/number of transactions)) Testing was carried on x number of deliveries, which included [y] tonnage ([x]% of total tonnage of [XX]). This was [z]% of total entries on the logs.

Tests performed

We have performed the procedures agreed with you as set out below:

> We agreed the source of the UK packaging waste to underlying records.
> We agreed the tonnages of UK packaging waste in the annual return prepared under paragraph 1 (o) of Schedule 5 of the Regulations to the total of the duplicate PRNs held by the reprocessor;
> For each quarterly return for the year ended 31 December XXXX, in respect of [x] deliveries of UK packaging waste received for reprocessing we:
>   – Agreed the tonnage of packaging waste for each delivery as per the goods inward report was, to the nearest 0.5 tonne, was supported by the tonnage of packaging waste received on purchase invoice(s) and weighbridge ticket(s);
>   – Agreed that the description of the waste on the purchase invoice(s) met the definition of packaging waste set out in the Regulations;
>   – Checked that the reprocessor held confirmation from the supplier(s) of the waste that it had become packaging waste within the UK;
>   – Obtained from the directors/senior management of the Reprocessor, a representation that either:
> The waste has been reprocessed already; or
> The directors/senior management intended to reprocess the waste and would not transfer the waste on to another reprocessor.
> For a sample of X deliveries of UK packaging waste received for reprocessing which was in turn received from another reprocessor we checked whether the reprocessor had received an undertaking from that other reprocessor that they had not already issued a PRN/PERN in respect of that waste.
> [For a sample of X deliveries of waste received for reprocessing and subsequently sold on to another reprocessor we checked that no PRN/PERN has been issued by the reprocessor in respect of that waste.][8]
> We checked that the tonnages on the annual return were equal to the four quarterly returns.
> We checked that the tonnage of PRNs/PERNs in respect of UK packaging waste received/exported in 2006 issued to producers or schemes (up to 31 January 2007) and to the appropriate agency (after 31 January 2007) is not greater than the tonnage of waste received in 2006.

[8] *Where it has not been possible to carry out this test, accountants may wish to report this as an exception.*

Our work was limited to the procedures set out above. In particular we did not perform procedures on any of the following issues for the reasons given:

> All deliveries received at the site have a declared percentage of packaging waste which is applied to the total weight of the delivery, and it is this percentage that is subsequently used to calculate the amount at which the PRN/PERN is issued. As we were not present to observe and check the deliveries when received, it is not possible for us to verify these percentages, or the amount of packaging waste material received which PRNs/PERNs have been subsequently issued.
> [The senior management of the reprocessor have represented that no packaging waste is sold on to other reprocessors; as such we have performed no work in respect of this procedure.][9]
> We could only agree tonnages received to records rather than to actual tonnages as we were not there to observe the receipt of waste.
> For packaging waste which the reprocessor received for reprocessing and stated had already been reprocessed we were not able to test whether the stated outputs of the reprocessing activity were consistent with the recycling methodology employed as this judgement is outside the expertise of an Accountant.
> For packaging waste which the reprocessor had received for reprocessing on which the PRNs had been issued but which had not yet been reprocessed our work was limited to obtaining the senior managements' representation that they would reprocess the packaging waste in due course and would not in due course transfer it to another reprocessor.

Findings

[No exceptions/The following exceptions] were noted as a result of our testing [which are shown in the attached table]:

a. [No confirmation was held that the waste received had become packaging waste in the UK, however all deliveries of waste were received from UK suppliers although we cannot verify that their waste became packaging waste in the UK.
b. In respect of packaging waste received from other reprocessors, no confirmation was obtained with each delivery that the supplier had not issued a PRN on the waste, however this is confirmed annually and management represented to us that they only receive waste from registered environment agency suppliers]

[Name of Reporting Accountants]

Chartered Accountants

[Address]

[Date]

---

[9] *This wording would not be appropriate where some waste has been sold on, when alternative procedures may be necessary.*

AAF 02/07
Technical release: a framework for assurance reports on third party operations

(Issued November 2007)

Contents

Introduction

   Preface
   Assurance on third party operations
   Scope
   International framework

Characteristic of third party operations

   Third party operations

Types and elements of assurance engagements over third party operations

Types of Assurance engagements Elements of assurance engagements

Guidance for practitioners

   Accepting an engagement
   Professional ethics and independence
   Quality control
   Agreeing the terms of engagement
   Planning and performing the engagement
   Nature, timing and extent of tests
   Responsible parties that use other organisations
   Considering subsequent events
   Documentation
   Assurance reporting
   Other reporting responsibilities
   Using the work of internal auditors
   Consideration of uncorrected errors, fraud or illegal acts
   Management representation letter

Appendices

1. Characteristics of third party operations and assurance engagements
2. Assurance report
   (i) Illustrative contents of an assurance report
   (ii) Example assurance reports on third party operations
3. Criteria
4. References

Introduction

Preface

AAF 02/07 *A framework for assurance reports* on third party operations sets out a framework for performing assurance engagements on various aspects of business relations that are undertaken between organisations[1]. AAF 02/07 provides definitions and objectives of this type of assurance engagement and sets out engagement procedures to promote consistency in the performance of an assurance engagement in line with pronouncements published by the International Auditing and Assurance Standards Board (IAASB) of which the ICAEW is a member.

Assurance on third party operations

Many user organisations rely on services provided by, or have relationships with, other parties (each such third party is referred to as 'a responsible party')[2]. User organisations may:

- outsource functions or parts of their business operations;
- contract with suppliers, customers and service providers for specific activities, use of intellectual property or other items; or
- undertake joint ventures, licensing or other shared arrangements
- in often complex arrangements usually governed by contractual commitments.

User organisations and responsible parties are increasingly seeking assurance on various aspects of the operations performed by responsible parties for user organisations. User organisations may wish to be confident, for example, that they are receiving the service as agreed or paying the appropriate fee for the rights received. In contrast, responsible parties may wish to demonstrate that they are performing tasks as agreed with user organisations. This technical release refers to the aspects of operations that responsible parties provide and may be subject to external examinations as third party operations.

Professional accountants in public practice (practitioners) can help increase the confidence of either responsible party or user organisations in their relationships by performing a number of professional services; namely assurance engagements, agreed-upon procedures and investigative work. Agreed-upon procedures and investigative work generally do not result in an independent conclusion conveying assurance. Such engagements may bear similarities to assurance engagements, but their purpose, scope and form of reporting are different: in particular, non-assurance reports typically provide factual findings rather than an independent conclusion conveying assurance.

Scope

AAF 02/07 provides generic guidance to practitioners undertaking an assurance engagement on aspects of third party operations such as transactions, operations, or

---

[1] Where reporting on regulated entities, the practitioner may wish to refer to the guidance given in the Audit and Assurance Faculty AUDIT 05/03 Reporting to Regulators of Regulated Entities.

[2] The specific terminology used in AAF 02/07, such as "the responsible party" and "the subject matter", is based on the pronouncements published by the IAASB: International Framework for Assurance Engagements ('the IAASB Assurance Framework') and ISAE 3000, Assurance Engagements Other Than Audits or Reviews of Historical Financial Information. The term 'user organisations' is used in place of 'intended users' in this guidance. See paragraph 10 for further information on the IAASB pronouncements.

arrangements (the 'subject matter', see also paragraphs 33–36). It is intended to provide high-level guidance for practitioners who provide assurance services on third party operations where other detailed guidance does not exist[3]. It is based on the principles set out in the IAASB's pronouncements on assurance engagements as they relate to third party operations (see paragraph 10).

6   AAF 02/07 is also expected to assist user organisations in understanding the scope and type of assurance conveyed in the assurance report. It is also aimed at providing assistance to the directors of the responsible party (or their equivalent in other types of organisation) who prepare a report on the subject matter by clarifying their expected responsibilities.

7   In an assurance engagement, practitioners express a conclusion designed to enhance the degree of confidence of the intended users of the report (usually other than, but possibly including, the responsible party) over the outcome of the evaluation or measurement of a specific aspect of the operations performed by a responsible party against certain criteria.

8   In an agreed-upon procedures engagement, practitioners carry out specific procedures as agreed with the client and other relevant parties as necessary. The report describes the purpose and the agreed-upon procedures of the engagement in sufficient detail to communicate to the addressees the nature and the extent of the work performed. The report lists the specific procedures performed and describes the practitioners' factual findings including description of errors and exceptions found. The report clearly states that the procedures performed do not constitute an assurance engagement and that the report conveys no assurance.

9   In other investigative work, practitioners typically carry out such procedures as are proposed by the practitioners and agreed with the client with the objective of proving or disproving a hypothesis, obtaining specified information or providing what facts the practitioners have found during their enquiries. The report describes the objective and results of the work. It may have a conclusion but also it clearly states that the procedures performed do not constitute an assurance engagement and that the report conveys no assurance.

International framework

10   This guidance follows the framework for assurance engagements set out in the IAASB Assurance Framework and ISAE 3000, published by the IAASB. The IAASB Assurance Framework defines the elements of assurance engagements and describes objectives for such engagements. ISAE 3000 provides generic guidance on the principal aspects of assurance engagements. Together these pronouncements provide high-level principles for assurance engagements other than audits and reviews of historical financial statements.

---

[3] *Practitioners follow other detailed guidance in relation to the provision of specific third party operations where available. For instance, AAF 01/06 Assurance reports on internal controls of service organisations made available to third parties provides guidance to practitioners undertaking an assurance engagement and providing a report in relation to the internal controls of financial services organisations. Similarly ITF 01/07 Assurance reports on the outsourced provision of information services and information processing services provides guidance to practitioners undertaking an assurance engagement on internal controls of outsourced IT services and IT processing services. Also see Appendix 2 for example reports.*

Characteristics of third party operations

11 The third party operations discussed in this guidance may take a number of different forms. This section describes how assurance engagements over the operations performed by third parties may be structured.

12 Relationships between the responsible party and user organisations are usually contractual, but other non-contractual arrangements may exist. Third party operations will typically arise from the outsourcing of user organisations' own activities and the procurement of external services. User organisations may also rely on contractual arrangements with third parties, for example, for the sale of the user organisations' products and services. Other circumstances can also exist, such as joint venture arrangements for the development of a new product for a user organisation or an investor/investee relationship. The nature of the assurance engagement varies accordingly.

Third party operations

13 Assurance engagements over the operations performed by third parties usually take one of two forms (illustrated in figures (a) and (b)).

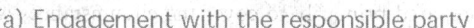
(a) Engagement with the responsible party

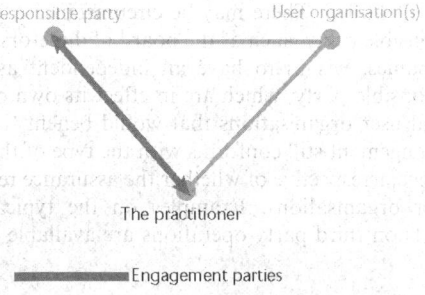

14 Figure (a) illustrates a form of engagement where the responsible party engages the practitioner. The practitioner performs an engagement to provide an assurance report over the operations performed by the responsible party. This will typically be with the objective of increasing the confidence of current and possibly prospective user organisations in the responsible party's activities (see paragraph 15). The responsible party usually has contractual obligations to current user organisations and may also be expected to comply with industry or other standards. It also has responsibilities to the practitioner in relation to the performance of the assurance engagement. Examples of these responsibilities and the potential consequences for the practitioner arising from them are set out in paragraph 58.

15 In this type of engagement, user organisations may be identified or unidentified, existing or prospective, or combinations of these. Where user organisations are unidentified, the practitioner accepts an assurance engagement only where a typical user organisation is identifiable in the context. This is because, without a reasonably defined user organisation, the practitioner may not be able to specify suitable criteria against which to assess the subject matter. As discussed in paragraph 14, the practitioner considers the issues related to the duty of care as discussed in paragraph and 57.

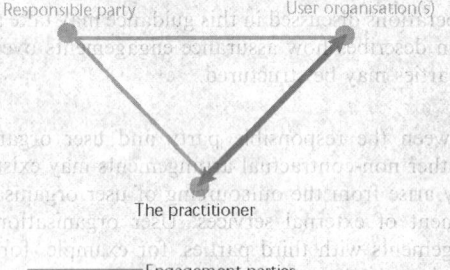

(b) Engagement with user organisations

16 Figure (b) shows an engagement where one or more user organisations (user organisations) contracts with the practitioner to assess the operations of the responsible party with the objective of increasing the user organisations' confidence over the activities of the responsible party. In this type of engagement, the responsible party has contractual (or other) obligations to the user organisations, and the user organisations have responsibilities to the practitioner in relation to the assurance engagement. Examples of these responsibilities and the potential consequences for the practitioner arising from them are set out in paragraph 63.

17 This guidance is prepared primarily to cover the circumstances where external user organisations that benefit from an assurance engagement on the subject matter exist or can be reasonably identified. There may be circumstances, for instance, where a body within the responsible party, such as the board of directors, or a member of the same group of companies, wishes to have an independent assessment of certain activities of that responsible party, which are in effect its own operations. Provided that there are external user organisations that would benefit from such an engagement, this type of arrangement still conforms with the type of third party operations covered in this guidance, irrespective of whether the assurance report would be made available to the user organisations. Examples on the typical characteristics of assurance engagements on third party operations are available in Appendix 1.

Types and elements of assurance engagements over third party operations

Types of Assurance engagements

18 An assurance engagement is carried out by the practitioner with the objective of conveying assurance either in a positive or negative form. The type of report is agreed at the start of the engagement between the practitioner and the client based on the expected evidence available to form such a conclusion and the requirements of the client.

19 Where the practitioner is able to reduce the assurance engagement risk to an acceptably low level in the specific engagement circumstances to issue a positive conclusion, the engagement is referred to as a reasonable assurance engagement.

20 Where the practitioner is able to reduce the assurance engagement risk to an acceptably low level but where the risk is nevertheless greater than that of a reasonable assurance engagement, the engagement is referred to as a limited assurance

engagement. A limited assurance conclusion is typically expressed in a negative form in contrast to a reasonable assurance conclusion.

Elements of assurance engagements

The IAASB Assurance Framework discusses elements of an assurance engagement. This section expands upon certain aspects of these elements which are likely to require specific consideration where the assurance report is provided on third party operations. These elements are:

(a) Three party relationship
(b) An appropriate subject matter
(c) Suitable criteria
(d) Sufficient appropriate evidence; and
(e) A written assurance report in the form appropriate to the type of assurance engagement.

(a) Three party relationship

Assurance engagements envisaged in this technical release involve three parties: the responsible party, user organisations, and the practitioner. The responsible party performs operations or provides information for the benefit of user organisations and hence is responsible for the subject matter over which assurance is sought. User organisations are typically the recipients of services, assets or information of the responsible party, although in some cases the relationship between a user organisation and a responsible party may not be simply one way[4].

Where such a relationship exists, the practitioner may be engaged to perform an assurance engagement in relation to the operations of the responsible party or in relation to the information prepared about those operations. Specific definitions of the responsible party, user organisations and practitioner are given below.

Either the responsible party or user organisations, or in some circumstances both, may become a client.

The responsible party

The responsible party typically performs operations or provides information for user organisations in a manner usually governed by a written contract.

The responsible party may also prepare its own report on the subject matter on which the practitioner performs the assurance engagement.

User organisations

User organisations are the parties that contract with the responsible party to perform specific activities for their benefit. Where appropriate, user organisations may also receive information in relation to the operations of the responsible party. Depending on the type of the operation performed or information provided by the responsible

---

[4] For third party operations, the responsible party will typically be the party that provides services or assets to user organisations. However, this guidance also refers to a party that performs or shares activities as agreed with a business partner, for instance in a joint venture or as a customer who agrees to comply with certain conditions as a responsible party.

party, the number of user organisations and type of relevant criteria may vary. The assurance engagement may be performed in relation to all user organisations or may be restricted to specific user organisations. Where an assurance report is intended for specific user organisations, the assurance report clearly indicates that fact.

28 In some cases, there may be user organisations that are unidentified at the start of the engagement. This may happen where the responsible party intends to enable its prospective user organisations to view the report. Where this is the case, the risk of the assurance report being received by those who are not party to the engagement increases. The practitioner's duty of care needs be clearly reflected in the engagement letter, in the assurance report and throughout the conduct of the engagement. See paragraph 56 for further guidance.

The practitioner

29 The practitioner performs the assurance engagement on the operations performed or information provided on such operations by the responsible party. The practitioner is governed by ethical and quality control requirements as set out in paragraphs 51–56.

30 The practitioner agrees with the client the scope of the engagement, the reporting requirements and ensures that there is secure appropriate access to the personnel and information of the responsible party and, if applicable, the user organisation(s).

31 The practitioner's responsibilities will vary depending on the client and their needs. To a large degree, those responsibilities and needs will be driven by whether the client is the responsible party, the user organisations or both. The practitioner considers whether the responsibilities have been defined to an appropriate level for the assignment including the nature of the deliverables when accepting an engagement.

32 In an assurance engagement, the practitioner is responsible for determining the nature, timing and extent of procedures. The practitioner also pursues, to the extent possible, any matter of which the practitioner becomes aware and which leads the practitioner to question whether a material modification should be made by the responsible party to the subject matter where possible or the subject matter information and to consider the effect on the assurance report if no modification is made.

(b) An appropriate subject matter

33 The subject matter includes transactions, operations, or arrangements performed or provided by the responsible party on which the user organisations seek assurance. The responsible party may prepare a written representation about the subject matter (the subject matter information), for instance about its compliance with the agreed contract with the customer. The practitioner may be engaged to report either directly on the subject matter or on the subject matter information.

34 A written contract between the responsible party and the user organisations need to sufficiently describe the aspect of third party operations on which the practitioner performs an assurance engagement. When this does not exist, the practitioner may risk performing an assurance engagement on an inappropriate subject matter, which could lead to the practitioner issuing an inappropriate conclusion or one which is subject to misinterpretation by its recipient. Therefore the practitioner considers their responsibilities in relation to the assurance engagement and whether the subject matter has been defined to an appropriate level when accepting an engagement.

In assurance engagements over third party operations, the subject matter may take a number of different forms depending on what those operations are. It may comprise:

- Systems and processes (for example, an entity's internal controls or IT system) for which the subject matter information may be an assertion about effectiveness.
- Compliance with agreed contracts or other standards (for example, carrying out certain actions, providing certain information or meeting objective standards; for example, legal and regulatory requirements, ISO standards or industry regulation) for which the subject matter information may be an assertion about compliance therewith.
- Financial performance or conditions (for example, historical or prospective financial position, financial performance and cash flows) for which the subject matter information may be the recognition, measurement, presentation and disclosure in a financial statement or statements.
- Non-financial performance or conditions (for example, performance of a particular function) for which the subject matter information may be key indicators of performance, quantity, condition, efficiency or effectiveness.
- Physical characteristics (for example, capacity of a facility) for which the subject matter information may be a specifications document.
- Behaviour (for example, corporate governance, compliance with regulation, human resource practices) for which the subject matter information may be a statement of compliance or a statement of effectiveness.

The practitioner will consider whether he possesses the relevant skills and competence before agreeing to take on reporting against the subject matter, in particular non-financial performance, physical characteristics and behaviour.

Subject matters have different characteristics, including the degree to which information about them is qualitative versus quantitative, objective versus subjective, historical versus prospective and relates to a point in time or covers a period. Such characteristics affect:

- whether the subject matter is identifiable and capable of being consistently evaluated or measured against criteria; and

- the availability and the persuasiveness of evidence.

The practitioner considers whether the characteristics of the subject matter affect the type of assurance when accepting the engagement as this affects the criteria for assessing the information, evidence gathering and ultimately the assurance report. The assurance report notes any characteristics of particular relevance to the intended users of the report, if appropriate.

(c) Suitable criteria

Assurance engagements require the practitioner to express an overall conclusion on the subject matter assessed in reference to certain criteria. Criteria also help the client and agreed recipients to understand how the practitioner has evaluated the subject matter to reach the conclusion. Criteria are dependent on the subject matter and may be already established or developed for a specific engagement.

The practitioner assesses the suitability of criteria for the purpose of a specific assurance engagement. Suitable criteria as set out in the IAASB Assurance Framework exhibit the following characteristics:

- Relevance: relevant criteria contribute to conclusions that assist decision-making by the intended users of the assurance report.
- Completeness: criteria are sufficiently complete when relevant factors that could affect the conclusions in the context of the engagement circumstances are not omitted. Complete criteria include, where relevant, benchmarks for presentation and disclosure.
- Reliability: reliable criteria allow reasonably consistent evaluation or measurement of the subject matter including, where relevant, presentation and disclosure, when used in similar circumstances by similarly qualified practitioners.
- Neutrality: neutral criteria contribute to conclusions that are free from bias.
- Understandability: understandable criteria contribute to conclusions that are clear, comprehensive, and not subject to significantly different interpretations.

39 Established criteria tend to be formal in nature, but the degree of formality depends on the subject matter. Criteria in areas such as compliance with legal or regulatory requirements may be widely recognised, either because they are available to the public or because there is an established standard, for example, BS7799 (information security management) and the COSO framework (internal control). Performance criteria may be set out in contractual arrangements as agreed with the user organisation. The practitioner considers the suitability of the criteria, in particular where established standards are used to ensure their relevance to the needs of the intended users of the assurance report.

40 Criteria may be developed specifically for the engagement where there are no suitable established criteria. Where criteria are developed for a specific engagement, the practitioner considers whether specifically developed criteria are suitable for the purpose of the engagement and considers obtaining a formal acknowledgement from the client and if appropriate also the responsible party or user organisation(s).

41 Criteria need to be available to all the addressees identified in the report. Established criteria are often publicly available and examples are given in Appendix 3. Where criteria are available only to specific parties, for instance in the terms of a contract, the use of the assurance report may need to be restricted to these parties.

(d) Sufficient appropriate evidence

42 The practitioner plans and performs an assurance engagement with an attitude of professional scepticism to obtain sufficient appropriate evidence about whether the subject matter satisfies the criteria or the subject matter information is free of material misstatement. The practitioner considers materiality, assurance engagement risk, and the quantity and quality of available evidence when planning and performing the engagement, in particular when determining the nature, timing and extent of evidence-gathering procedures. Assurance engagement risk is the risk that the practitioner expresses an inappropriate conclusion when the subject matter information is materially misstated.

(e) A written assurance report

43 The practitioner provides a written report containing a conclusion that conveys the assurance obtained about the subject matter or subject matter information. In the context of assurance engagements over third party operations, ISAE 3000 provides basic elements for assurance reports as included in Appendix 2(i). In addition, the practitioner considers other reporting responsibilities, including communicating with those charged with governance where it is appropriate.

Where the subject matter information is made up of a number of aspects, separate conclusions may be provided on each aspect. While not all such conclusions need to relate to the same extent of evidence-gathering procedures, each conclusion is expressed in the form that is appropriate to either a reasonable assurance or a limited assurance engagement.

44

The IAASB Assurance Framework states that the practitioner expresses a qualified or adverse conclusion or a disclaimer of conclusion where:

45

- the practitioner concludes that there is not sufficient appropriate evidence to support an assurance conclusion due to the limitation on the scope of the practitioner's work;
- the responsible party's assertion or the report on the subject matter is materially misstated; or
- after accepting the engagement, the criteria or subject matter turns out to be inappropriate for an assurance engagement.

The practitioner may need to consider withdrawing from the engagement when necessary.

Guidance for practitioners

Accepting an engagement

The practitioner accepts an assurance engagement only where the practitioner's preliminary knowledge of the engagement circumstances indicates that:

46

- Relevant ethical requirements, such as independence, will be satisfied (see paragraphs 51–53); and
- The engagement exhibits all of the following characteristics:
    - The subject matter is appropriate;
    - The criteria to be used are suitable and will be available to the intended users of the assurance report;
    - The practitioner will have access to sufficient appropriate evidence to support the conclusion;
    - The practitioner's conclusion, in the form appropriate to either a reasonable assurance engagement or a limited assurance engagement, is to be contained in a written report;
    - The practitioner is satisfied that there is a rational purpose for the engagement. If there is a significant limitation on the scope of the practitioner's work, it is unlikely that the engagement has a rational purpose; and
    - The practitioner believes that the client has no intention to associate the practitioner's name with the subject matter or subject matter information in an inappropriate manner.
- The engagement team collectively possesses the necessary professional competencies, having regard to the nature of the assignment. Where the required knowledge and skills are so specialised that the fundamental principle of competence is not expected to be met, the practitioner considers whether to accept the engagement.

The ability of the practitioner to perform the engagement and to report on the findings depends upon information and access being provided by the responsible party. The nature of the information and access required will be agreed where possible, formally and in writing, between the practitioner, the client, and where

47

appropriate, other parties to the engagement. This requirement for information and access will be referred to in the engagement letter.

48   The practitioner ensures that there is sufficient clarity about the criteria that are to be applied during the engagement and in the assurance report by including appropriate references to the criteria in the engagement letter, particularly where the engagement requires the practitioner to examine the support for management assertions, for example concerning compliance with contractual terms or service standards.

49   The practitioner reads the terms of the contract agreed between the responsible party and the user organisations and consider the impact on the assurance engagement. For instance, unless specifically agreed in writing, the practitioner is not bound by any form of report or the terms of contract agreed between the client and any other party. Where the practitioner becomes aware that there is such an agreement and has identified that the form of report expected from the practitioner is inappropriate because the guidance in this technical release would not be met, the practitioner considers the implications of this for the engagement, which may ultimately result in the practitioner declining the engagement.

50   The assurance report may be received by a range of persons who are not party to the engagement. The practitioner does not normally intend to assume responsibility to persons who are not party to the engagement, but legal actions from such persons may nonetheless occur. The practitioner therefore needs to apply appropriate engagement acceptance procedures in order to assess the risks associated with taking on a particular engagement and accordingly whether to do so and, if so, on what terms. Where the practitioner accepts such an engagement, suitably rigorous internal risk management policies are applied to manage any increased level of risk. Guidance is available in AAF 04/06 *Assurance engagements: Management of risk and liability*.

Professional ethics and independence

51   Before accepting any professional engagement, the practitioner considers whether there are any ethical factors which should lead the practitioner to decline the appointment. Chartered accountants are subject to the ethical and other guidance laid down by the Institute, including the Fundamental Principles of the Code of Ethics, as set out in Statement 1.100 *Introduction and Fundamental Principles* in performing any professional services, to maintain the standard of their conduct. The ICAEW Code of Ethics is in compliance with the Code of Ethics established by the International Federation of Accountants.

52   When performing non-audit assurance engagements, the practitioner needs to consider applicable independence requirements set out in Statement 1.290 *Independence – Assurance Engagements*. Statement 1.290 is based on a conceptual approach that takes into account threats to independence, accepted safeguards and the public interest. Under this approach, firms and members of assurance teams have an obligation to identify and evaluate circumstances and relationships that create threats to independence and, where necessary, to take appropriate action to eliminate these threats or to reduce them to an acceptable level by the application of safeguards. In particular, appropriate consideration should also be given to independence of mind and in appearance in respect of the responsible party and user organisations. For example, the provision of assistance to a responsible party in preparing its report may result in a self-review threat if the impact of the assistance on the matter being reported on is subjective and material. The subjectivity of the report to be issued will also be relevant. If the practitioner identifies threats other than insignificant, safeguards need to be considered. These might include:

- The use of independent teams where appropriate; and
- An independent review of the key judgements on the engagement.

The practitioner considers the existing relationships between the responsible party and the user organisation in this type of engagement. The practitioner considers the objectivity requirements in Statements 1.280 *Objectivity – all services* which is applicable to all services. Furthermore, a threat to the practitioner's objectivity or confidentiality may also be created when the practitioner performs services for clients whose interests are in conflict or the clients are in dispute with each other in relation to the matter or transaction in question. Statement 1.220 *Conflict of interest* sets out guidance on threats to objectivity or confidentiality when the practitioner provides services to multiple clients whose interests may be in conflict.

Quality control

The practitioner performs the assurance engagement in the same professional manner as any other engagement and in accordance with the scope agreed and recorded in the engagement letter. If it is necessary to depart from the terms of the engagement letter, the practitioner agrees an amended scope of work in writing with the client and with the other parties to the engagement. See paragraph 95 for further information on the circumstances where the practitioner is unable to obtain sufficient evidence.

When performing an assurance engagement under ISAE3000, the practitioner is subject to International Standard on Quality Control (ISQC) 1 *Quality control for firms that perform audits and reviews of historical financial information, other assurance and related services engagements*[5]. ISQC 1 requires that a firm of professional accountants has an obligation to establish a system of quality control designed to provide it with reasonable assurance that the firm and its personnel comply with relevant professional standards and regulatory and legal requirements and that the assurance reports issued by the firm or engagement partners are appropriate in the circumstances.

The elements of such a system of quality control which are relevant to an individual engagement include leadership responsibilities for quality on the engagement, ethical requirements, acceptance and continuance of client relationships and specific engagements, assignment of engagement teams, engagement performance (in particular supervision, consultation, review and documentation) and monitoring.

Agreeing the terms of engagement

When the practitioner is requested to provide an assurance report on third party operations, it is important that there is a clear understanding and agreement concerning the scope and purpose of the engagement between the practitioner, the client and, where appropriate, other parties that are party to the engagement. To help avoid possible misunderstandings the agreed terms are recorded in writing. AAF 04/06 sets out detailed matters to note in relation to the terms of engagement and how the overall risks of the engagement may be managed by the practitioner. However, these will need to be carefully applied to the particular engagement circumstances because AAF 04/06 primarily focuses on situations where the responsible party is the

---

[5] In the UK, the Auditing Practices Board has issued ISQC 1 (UK and Ireland) for audits and other engagements where APB standards apply. ISQC 1 (UK and Ireland) is virtually identical to ISQC1 issued by International Federation of Accountants (IFAC).

client (see paragraphs 58–61 below). Paragraphs 62–65 below highlight some of the considerations which arise when the user organisation(s) is the client.

Where the responsible party is the client

58 The responsible party may engage the practitioner to perform an assurance engagement to increase its own and user organisations' comfort over its operations performed in relation to user organisations. Where the responsible party engages the practitioner to perform an assurance engagement, it becomes responsible for enabling the practitioner to perform the necessary procedures to form the assurance conclusion. These include:

- providing sufficient access for the practitioner to allow performance of the necessary procedures. This should include access to personnel within the responsible party, as well as to premises and relevant operational and other records. The responsible party should also be made responsible for the completeness and accuracy of information supplied to the practitioner during the course of the engagement. If the responsible party (or any other party to the engagement) restricts the practitioner from obtaining the evidence required to reach the assurance conclusion, this may be considered a material limitation on the scope of the practitioner's work and may affect the assurance conclusion. See paragraph 77 for further guidance on dealing with circumstances where the responsible party restricts the practitioner's access to obtaining necessary evidence;
- disclosing to the practitioner any significant changes or events that have occurred or are expected to occur that could reasonably be expected to have an effect on the assurance conclusion;
- disclosing to the practitioner, and where appropriate, affected user organisation(s) any illegal acts, fraud, or uncorrected errors attributable to the responsible party's management or employees that may affect the user organisation(s), and the responsible party's whistle-blowing arrangements;
- disclosing to the practitioner at the start of the engagement all other significant matters of which it is aware that affect the operations performed for the user organisation(s) as well as disclosing facts to the practitioner that may significantly impact or change the nature of the report or conclusion to be issued by the practitioner;
- disclosing sufficient information to the practitioner to fully understand the requirements of the assignment. Failure to do so may mean that the requirements are not met by the procedures performed by the practitioner or relevant facts are not disclosed within the report of the practitioner;
- disclosing significant issues within, and with, the user organisations that may have an impact on the scope of the engagement and the practitioner's conclusion; and
- providing the practitioner with a letter of representation that includes the confirmation of the responsible party's responsibilities for the provision of information to the practitioner, and, where appropriate, that the responsible party has complied with the contractual requirements with user organisations and other relevant standards and obligation.

59 Where the responsible party reports on the subject matter, this may contain descriptions of the operations performed, the evaluation or assessment of the actual performance, any other relevant information (e.g. internal controls exercised over the operations) and any significant matters that the responsible party considers need to be brought to the attention of the user organisations. If the report constitutes the subject matter information, the practitioner assesses whether the responsible party's assertion that it has performed the operations as agreed with the user organisations

based on suitable criteria and includes an assessment of the impact of exceptions and deficiencies disclosed in the report.

The responsible party is responsible for the completeness, accuracy, validity and method of presentation of the information within the responsible party's report. The assertions made in the report are also the responsibility of the responsible party and the practitioner obtains representations to that effect.

The practitioner considers the duty of care to its client. AAF 04/06 provides principles-based best practice guidance on the process that the practitioner undertakes when considering requests from the responsible party for assurance reports.

When the user organisations are the client

User organisations may engage the practitioner to assess aspects of the operations performed, or information provided, by the responsible party with a view to increasing their confidence in these aspects. The practitioner considers the increased assurance engagement risk when accepting an engagement assigned by the user organisations because the responsible party may not be part of the engagement which affects the practitioner's knowledge of the subject matter and evidence gathering process. In this type of engagement, the responsible party has a contractual obligation only to the user organisations and not to the practitioner.

Where the user organisations engage the practitioner to perform an assurance engagement, it is expected to fulfil its responsibilities, such as:

- providing sufficient access to the practitioner to perform necessary procedures. This should include access to personnel within the user organisation, as well as premises and relevant operational and other records. The user organisations are also responsible for the completeness and accuracy of information they supply to the practitioner during the course of the engagement.
- arranging access for the practitioner to the responsible party's personnel, information and documentation. The user organisations and the responsible party will need to contract or agree other arrangements that are suitable for the practitioner to obtain sufficient information and evidence to support conclusions. If the responsible party (or any other party to the engagement) restricts the practitioner from obtaining the evidence required to reach the assurance conclusion, this may be considered a material limitation on the scope of the practitioner's work and may affect the assurance conclusion. See paragraph 76 for further guidance on dealing with circumstances when the responsible party restricts the practitioner's access to obtaining the necessary evidence;
- disclosing to the practitioner any significant changes or event that have occurred or are expected to occur that could reasonably be expected to have an effect on the assurance conclusion;
- disclosing sufficient information to enable the practitioner to fully understand the requirements of the assignment. Failure to do so may mean that the needs of the user organisations are not met by the procedures performed by the practitioner or relevant facts are not disclosed within the report of the practitioner;
- disclosing significant issues within, and with, the responsible party, including illegal acts, fraud or uncorrected errors attributable to the responsible party's management or employees that may affect user organisations, and may have an impact on the scope of the engagement and the practitioner's conclusion to the extent that the user organisations are aware of such issues; and
- disclosing to the practitioner all significant matters of which user organisations are aware that affect the operations performed for user organisations as well as

disclosing facts to the practitioner that may significantly impact or change the nature of the report prepared by the practitioner, at the start of the engagement.

64 Although a management representation letter from the responsible party may not be obtainable for this type of engagement, the practitioner may find it useful to obtain a written confirmation from the responsible party on the factual findings and its responsibilities in relation to the subject matter (e.g. the terms of the contract) before releasing the draft report to the client. The practitioner may need to contract separately with the responsible party to ensure rights of access and agree information agreement protocols. The practitioner ensures that reporting protocols regarding who has access to draft or final reports and the rights and obligations (for example to confirm factual accuracy of findings) of the responsible party to comment on, or require the practitioner to reflect comments in, the report, are agreed with the responsible party and where appropriate with the user organisations. The basis of such provision is agreed in writing and does not establish any additional duty of care outside the terms of the engagement.

65 The practitioner considers the duty of care to its client. While AAF 04/06 provides principles-based best practice guidance on process the practitioner takes when considering requests for assurance reports, it is designed for circumstances where the responsible party is the client. The practitioner may wish to seek independent legal advice where appropriate.

Planning and performing the engagement

66 The practitioner agrees with the client (and any other party to the engagement letter) the form of report that is appropriate for the purpose of the assurance engagement and the work to be performed. In an assurance engagement, the nature, timing, and extent of evidence-gathering procedures to be performed are planned in accordance with the type of assurance report to be issued.

67 The practitioner obtains an understanding of the subject matter and other engagement circumstances, sufficient to identify and assess the risks of the subject matter information or the assurance report on the subject matter being materially misstated and sufficient to design and perform evidence-gathering procedures.

68 Obtaining an understanding of the subject matter and other engagement circumstances such as whether the assurance report is to be made available to specific addressees only or for unidentified recipients is an essential part of planning and performing an assurance engagement. This understanding provides the practitioner with a frame of reference for exercising professional judgement throughout the engagement, for example, when considering the characteristics of the subject matter, assessing the suitability of criteria or determining the nature, timing and extent of procedures for gathering evidence.

69 As part of the engagement, the practitioner assesses the appropriateness of the subject matter based on the characteristics listed in paragraph 36. The practitioner also assesses the suitability of the criteria to evaluate or measure the subject matter. Suitable criteria have the characteristics listed in paragraph 38. As indicated in paragraph 46, the practitioner does not accept an assurance engagement unless the practitioner's preliminary knowledge of the engagement circumstances indicates that the subject matter is appropriate and criteria are suitable.

The scope and approach to be followed are communicated to the client and documented, normally in the form of an engagement plan or work programme and communicated to the engagement team.

The practitioner considers materiality when planning and performing an assurance engagement. The consideration of materiality is relevant when the practitioner determines the nature, timing and extent of evidence-gathering procedures and when evaluating whether the subject matter information is free of misstatement. Materiality is considered in the context of quantitative and qualitative factors, such as relative magnitude, the nature and extent of the effect of these factors on the evaluation or measurement of the subject matter and the interest of the user organisations. The practitioner uses professional judgement when assessing materiality and the relative importance of quantitative and qualitative factors in a particular engagement.

The practitioner applies procedures to reduce assurance engagement risk to an acceptably low level in the circumstances of the engagement in order to express the agreed type of assurance conclusion which might be either reasonable or limited assurance.

After accepting the engagement, if the practitioner concludes that the subject matter or criteria is not appropriate, the practitioner expresses a qualified or adverse conclusion or a disclaimer of conclusion. In some cases, the practitioner may consider withdrawing from the engagement.

Nature, timing and extent of tests

The practitioner obtains sufficient and appropriate evidence on which to base the practitioner's conclusion. The nature, timing and extent of work may differ according to the type of assurance engagement. Sufficiency is the measure of the quantity of evidence while appropriateness is the measure of the quality of evidence; that is, its relevance and its reliability. The practitioner uses professional judgement and exercises professional scepticism in evaluating the quantity and quality of evidence, and thus its sufficiency and appropriateness to support the assurance conclusion. The practitioner describes the tests performed to provide sufficient information to support the assurance conclusion.

The practitioner therefore plans the nature, timing and extent of work depending on the subject matter and criteria for the specific engagement. Whereas there is no guidance on evidence gathering when performing assurance engagements specifically over the operations performed by third parties, some of the existing standards or guidance on specific subject matters may provide useful information. Such sources are shown in Appendix 3.

In particular, depending on the nature of the subject matter, the practitioner may perform tests over a period of time or at a point in time. The decision affects whether the practitioner is able to report on the entire period covered in the assurance report. The practitioner describes the timing of tests and considers the impact on the assurance conclusion.

The practitioner may be prevented by the responsible party from access to personnel, premises or operational information during the course of the assignment, in particular when the client is user organisations. Similarly, there may be circumstances beyond the control of the client, regardless of whether the client is the responsible party or the user organisation, where sufficient appropriate evidence may not be available. The practitioner considers whether these restrictions have an impact on the assurance report. Where the practitioner's work is affected by restricted access, the practitioner may need to consider whether to issue a qualified or adverse conclusion, issue a disclaimer of a conclusion, or where appropriate, withdraw from the engagement.

Responsible parties that use other organisations

78 The practitioner may become aware that the responsible party contracts out part of the functions that significantly affect the operations it performs for the user organisation. The responsible party may also have arrangements with another organisation to provide services that significantly affect the overall operations of the responsible party, affecting the functions that the responsible party performs for user organisations. The entity to whom the responsible party contracts out a significant part of its operations is referred to in this guidance as a significant external service provider. For example, a payroll outsourcing organisation may in turn outsource aspects of its information processing to a third party. A pharmaceutical company may have its distribution organised by a service provider that subcontracts logistics in a particular jurisdiction (where it does not have a suitable presence itself) to another organisation that does.

79 The practitioner considers the extent to which subject matter is provided by a significant external service provider to the responsible party and whether the scope of the engagement needs to include consideration of the part of operations provided by the significant external service provider and whether such access is available. If such access is not available and this restricts the practitioner from obtaining the evidence required in reaching the assurance conclusion, the practitioner considers whether this may result in a material limitation on the scope of the practitioner's work the requirement to issue a qualified or adverse conclusion, issue a disclaimer of a conclusion, or where appropriate, withdraw from the engagement.

80 Where the involvement of a significant external service provider is known prior to the engagement, the practitioner discusses with the client, regardless of whether it is the responsible party or user organisations, whether the scope of the engagement includes the assessment of functions provided by the significant external service provider. If such involvement is identified during the engagement a similar discussion is undertaken and any amendments to engagement terms and scope are agreed in writing.

81 Depending on the discussion, the practitioner and the client agree in writing how the functions performed by the significant external service provider should be dealt with.

- In the case where the practitioner and the client agree that the scope of the practitioner's work excludes externally provided functions, the report on the functions performed by the responsible party describes the functions performed by the significant external service provider in sufficient detail for the user to understand the scope of the practitioner's work and the limitation thereon.
- Where the scope of the engagement includes externally provided functions, the practitioner performs procedures that may include, but are not limited to:
  - describing the functions performed by the significant external service provider, differentiating the role of the responsible party and the significant external service provider. To accomplish this, the practitioner may request the responsible party to co-ordinate with the significant external service provider;
  - reviewing the qualification of the significant external service provider to establish whether any further work would be required;

- reviewing the contract between the responsible party and the significant external service provider to establish to what extent the practitioner may rely on reports from the significant external service provider, including an assurance report on the services provided by the service provider if available. Where the practitioner plans to use the reports received from the significant external service provider, the practitioner considers the professional competence of the preparer of the report including professional qualifications and experience. The practitioner perform procedures to obtain sufficient appropriate evidence that the externally prepared report is adequate for the practitioners purposes in the context of the engagement covered in this guidance;
- performing procedures directly on the functions provided by the significant external service provider, if appropriate.

If no suitable approach can be determined, the practitioner discusses this limitation with the client and concludes, in the light of the available information, whether to issue a qualified or adverse conclusion, issue a disclaimer of a conclusion, or where appropriate, withdraw from the engagement. 82

Considering subsequent events

The practitioner considers the effect on the subject matter information and on the assurance report of events up to the date of the assurance report. The extent of consideration of subsequent events depends on the extent such events may affect the subject matter information and the appropriateness of the practitioner's conclusion. For example, when the engagement requires a conclusion about the accuracy of historical information at a point in time, events occurring between that point in time and the date of the assurance report may not affect the conclusion or require disclosure. 83

Documentation

The practitioner documents matters that are significant and relevant to support the assurance report and that the engagement was performed as agreed with the client and as set out in the engagement letter. The documentation may include the description of the extent, nature and results of tests, sampling, evidence to support the practitioner's conclusion and a record of the practitioner's reasoning on significant matters that require the exercise of judgement and relevant facts[6]. 84

Assurance reporting

The practitioner prepares a written report expressing the assurance conclusion and refers to the key elements of the assurance report shown in the table in Appendix 2(ii)(a). The practitioner tailors these elements for the specific engagement depending on the subject matter and, where appropriate, adapts for a qualified conclusion. Illustrative assurance reports on third party operations, derived from existing guidance, are available in Appendix 2(ii)(b)[7]. 85

[6] *Additional guidance on documentation can be found in paragraph 42–44 of ISAE 3000 which sets out high level principles. The IAASB is currently drafting ISAE 3402* Assurance reports on a service organization's controls *at the time of publication of this technical release and*
practitioners have regard to further guidance set out in ISAE 3402 as it progresses towards finalisation.

[7] *The illustrative reports in Appendix 2(ii) are examples of reasonable assurance conclusions. The guidance does not preclude a limited assurance report where the practitioner and the client agree on the form of the report.*

86 The title of the report includes the term 'assurance' to distinguish it from non assurance engagements, for instance agreed-upon procedures engagements. The report draws the attention of the addressees to the basis of the practitioner's work, e.g. ISAE 3000 and this technical release.

87 The assurance report reflects the agreement set out in the engagement letter and is supported by the work carried out by the practitioner. The report makes clear for whom it is prepared, who may have access to it, and who is entitled to rely upon it and for what purpose, in accordance with the engagement terms. The practitioner also refers to the guidance in AAF 04/06.

88 Where relevant, the practitioner considers a form of report to be issued by the practitioner, agreed between the responsible party and user organisation but without the practitioner's consent. The form of report requested by the responsible party or user organisation(s) may be inappropriate because the considerations in this guidance are not met. In such circumstances, the practitioner does not agree to issue such a report.

89 Where the practitioner is also the auditor of the responsible party, the practitioner may include a statement that by delivering the assurance report the practitioner accepts no additional duties in relation to the statutory audit.

90 The practitioner describes any significant, inherent limitation associated with the evaluation or measurement of the subject matter against the criteria in the assurance report.

91 Where the responsible party decides the scope of engagement or, in particular, provides the subject matter information, the practitioner communicates the fact, including how the scope of the report is defined and how the criteria have been selected, in the assurance report.

92 In order for the assurance conclusion not to be misleading, the practitioner needs to consider whether subject matter information provided by the responsible party is complete. The practitioner does not provide an unqualified conclusion where the practitioner becomes aware that the responsible party's set of assertions is incomplete in any material respect.

93 The assurance report states the restrictions on its replication in whole or in part in other published documents. The practitioner also refers to the guidance in AAF 04/06.

94 Based on the relevant evidence obtained during the engagement, the practitioner concludes whether the assurance objective has been met. The objective would be for either a positive or negative assurance conclusion to be issued in accordance with the type of assurance as agreed at the start of the engagement.

95 The practitioner may become aware that the evidence is insufficient to issue the agreed type of assurance conclusion. Insufficient evidence does not however constitute a valid reason for making a change in the agreed type of engagement, for instance, from a reasonable assurance engagement to a limited assurance engagement or from an assurance engagement to non-assurance engagement. The practitioner, however, considers whether to issue a qualified or adverse conclusion, issue a disclaimer of a conclusion, or where appropriate, withdraw from the engagement.

96 As discussed in paragraph 64, the practitioner may wish, or be required, to provide the draft findings to the responsible party before releasing it to the user organisations

for confirmation of the factual accuracy of the details, so that any misunderstandings or unintended limitations of the documentation provided to the practitioner may be addressed or rectified before the report is released to the client where, in particular, it is the user organisations. The basis of such provision is agreed in writing and does not establish any additional duty of care outside the terms of the engagement.

Other reporting responsibilities

The practitioner considers other information supplied by the responsible party or user organisations. If such other information is inconsistent with the assurance conclusion or with other matters that the practitioner is or has become aware of, the practitioner discusses this with the client and may wish to draw attention to the fact in the assurance report. 97

The practitioner only signs the assurance report as agreed in the engagement letter if sufficient and appropriate evidence to support the assurance conclusion is obtained. Where either the responsible party or user organisations subsequently asks the practitioner to provide reports on related matters which are not directly covered by the scope of the engagement, the practitioner is unlikely to be able to issue such reports. The practitioner may, however, be able to issue an alternative form of report which is capable of being supported by work performed as part of the engagement, such as a report of the factual findings of agreed-upon procedures. The practitioner agrees a separate engagement for such assignment with the party that requests an additional report. 98

Using the work of internal auditors

A responsible party may have an internal audit department that as part of its audit plan performs tests of some aspects of the operations which are also the subject of the assurance report. The practitioner may wish to consider whether it might be effective and efficient to use the results of testing performed by internal auditors to alter the nature, timing or extent of the work the practitioner otherwise might have performed in forming the assurance conclusion. Where using the work of internal auditors, the practitioner performs sufficient testing which provides the principal evidence for the assurance conclusion and assesses the independence and competence of the internal auditors where changing the nature, timing or extent of the practitioner's testing. The practitioner also makes reference to the internal auditors in the assurance report and clarifies the extent of use of internal auditors' work. 99

Consideration of uncorrected errors, fraud or illegal acts

While performing procedures on the operations performed by third parties, the practitioner may become aware of uncorrected errors, fraud or illegal acts attributable to the responsible party's systems, management or employees that may affect the functions that interact with the user organisation. 100

Unless clearly inconsequential, the practitioner determines from the responsible party whether this information has been communicated to the affected user organisations. If the responsible party has not communicated this information to the user organisations and is unwilling to do so, then the practitioner considers the implications for the engagement. Where the engagement is with the responsible party, the practitioner informs the responsible party's audit committee or other management with equivalent authority. If the audit committee or equivalent authority does not respond appropriately, the practitioner considers whether to resign from the 101 engagement and whether any other action or reporting is appropriate such as to report in the public interest.

102 The practitioner is generally not required to confirm with the user organisations whether the responsible party has communicated such information. However, if the client is user organisations, the practitioner considers the materiality of the matter and whether the matter has been brought to the attention of the responsible party and promptly corrected. Depending on the outcome, the practitioner may consider communicating the matter to the user organisations.

Management representation letter

103 The practitioner normally obtains written representations or a form of written confirmation as referred to in paragraph 64 signed by the directors of the responsible party who are responsible for and knowledgeable, directly or through others within the responsible party, about the subject matter. The refusal by the directors of the responsible party to provide written representations considered necessary by the practitioner may constitute a limitation on the scope of the engagement. The representation letter and the assurance report are both dated as of the completion of the engagement.

104 Management representations cannot replace other evidence that the practitioner could reasonably be able to obtain. Where the practitioner is unable to obtain sufficient appropriate evidence regarding a matter that has, or may have, a material effect on the evaluation or measurement of the subject matter, when such evidence would ordinarily be expected to be available, the practitioner considers if it would constitute a limitation on the scope of the engagement even if management representations are available.

105 The practitioner is associated with a subject matter when the practitioner reports on information about that subject matter or consents to the use of the practitioner's name in a professional connection with respect to that subject matter. If the practitioner learns that the client (or any other party) is inappropriately using the practitioner's name in association with a subject matter, the practitioner requires the client to cease doing so. The practitioner may also consider what other steps may be needed, such as informing any known parties that may have received the report that inappropriately uses the practitioner's name and seeking legal advice.

Appendix 1 – Characteristics of third party operations and assurance engagements

A number of characteristics of the relationship between the responsible party and user organisations may affect the nature of the engagement, as well as the requirements of the clients. The characteristics set out below are often important when considering the risk profile of an engagement. These characteristics are illustrative only and neither mutually exclusive nor exhaustive. Other relevant characteristics also need to be considered for their impact on the specific engagement as appropriate.The characteristics discussed in this appendix are:

(a) Whether the engagement is initiated by the responsible party or by user organisations;
(b) Whether outsourced services or functions form part of the user organisations' internal control/operational environment or whether the subject matter relates to a procurement or other business activity which does not; and

(c) Whether the evaluation of the subject matter against the selected criteria is performed and reported to user organisations by the responsible party or the practitioners.

(a) Engagements initiated by the responsible party or by user organisations

An assurance engagement may be initiated by the responsible party or user organisations, and may be performed to cover overall aspects of performance or to address specific risks or concerns.

An engagement covering wider aspects of a subject matter is typically performed where a responsible party intends to demonstrate to existing and potential user organisations that it performs the relevant services or functions as agreed or to meet a desired standard. The responsible party is likely to be the client and hence defines the scope of the engagement. Some user organisations may be involved in discussions with the responsible party over setting the scope of the engagement. Where user organisations are unidentified or many, it may be difficult to reasonably understand their expectations or needs when identifying suitable criteria. This may affect the practitioner's decision on who may receive the report and to whom the practitioner owes a duty of care.

The responsible party may find the need to defend itself against repeated reviews by user organisations, or respond to the general scrutiny over the provision of particular types of service in the market place. The responsible party, who typically would be the client in this situation, may specify at the start of the engagement which user organisations may have access to the assurance report. The practitioner may wish to refer to AAF 04/06 for guidance in this regard.

User organisations may commission an engagement to have the responsible party's services or functions assessed with specific concerns in mind. This may mean that the practitioner will assess the responsible party's operations to establish if the responsible party's activities for mitigating or managing the user organisation's concerns are appropriate and sufficient.

Alternatively, user organisations may contract with the practitioner to perform an assurance engagement on specific aspects of operations performed by, or reported by, the responsible party; for instance to confirm the accuracy of the fee charged for the service provided by the responsible party. In this case, the practitioner is likely to be engaged to directly report on the operations the responsible party performs as the subject matter and the client may be the only addressee of the report.

(b) Outsourced services or functions that form part of the user organisation's internal control/operational environment

Some organisations outsource parts of their operations. Outsourcing may be regular and continuous, ad-hoc or possibly one-off. The process of outsourcing to a responsible party does not take away a user organisation's need to maintain its oversight, its overall responsibility and, in some cases, a level of management of the outsourced activities and functions. An assurance conclusion from the practitioner may be helpful for the user organisation in demonstrating that it is meeting aspects of its responsibility over the outsourced activity and could form, for instance, part of information requested within the scope of statutory audit of the user organisation.

Typically, the requirement for assurance is over the ongoing performance of the outsourced activities to contractually agreed (and other) standards, which may include reference to specific criteria and service level agreements about, for example, internal control standards or key performance indicators.

In procurement, a user organisation may have pre-requisites for contractual standards that a successful tenderer is expected to meet. In these cases, the practitioner may be engaged by the user organisation to assess whether the tenderer (prospective responsible party) satisfies the requirements or by a tenderer to strengthen its bid.

On an on-going basis, a business may wish to obtain assurance that its suppliers (responsible parties) are continuously compliant with contractually agreed standards. Alternatively, a supplier may wish to be able to demonstrate to its customer (user) organisations that it is in compliance with particular standards.

There are other similar relationships that arise from other business activities. Relationships with agents and distributors, such as sales agents, may give rise to circumstances where one party needs to increase the confidence of the other party about its performance. Similar situations arise under licence agreements. In practice, the form of assurance sought in such cases is likely to be specific to particular risks or concerns and is more likely to originate from the beneficiary (user organisation) rather than the agent or licensee (responsible party). An assurance engagement may be commissioned, for instance, on regularly reported information that forms the basis for the calculation of payments by the beneficiary.

(c) Reporting of subject matter information by the responsible party or the practitioners

Evaluation of the subject matter against the selected criteria may be carried out by the responsible party, the user organisation, or the practitioner.

Where the practitioner gives a conclusion on the outcome of the evaluation or measurement (subject matter information) performed either by the responsible party or by a user organisation, it is referred to as an 'assertion-based engagement' as the preparer of the report on the information will make a statement or assertion about its view of the subject matter. Assertions may be about the effectiveness of operations or controls, about the accuracy of performance statistics or about compliance with a contract or with relevant standards. The report may set out facts about the operations of the responsible party and the outcome of its own evaluation and assessment of the operations measured against, for instance, the terms of the contract or relevant standards. The practitioner may be engaged to form a view on the assertions made in the report. In this case, the practitioner is likely to use the criteria used in the report for conducting the engagement, having assessed the suitability of the criteria.

Where the practitioner directly evaluates or measures the subject matter and issues an assurance conclusion, it is referred to as a 'direct reporting engagement'. The practitioner's report describes the operations of the responsible party, how the practitioner assessed the subject matter and the criteria used to communicate the basis of the conclusion. The criteria used are typically determined by the practitioner for direct reporting engagements, but may be discussed for suitability with the client.

Appendix 2 – Assurance report

(i) Illustrative contents of an assurance report

The contents that are consistent with ISAE 3000 are shown in bold below. The remainder are not covered in ISAE 3000 but have been discussed in this guidance.

(a) A title indicating that the report is an assurance report.
(b) An addressee identifying the parties to whom the assurance report is directed.
(c) Identification of the applicable engagement letter.
(d) Restrictions on the use of the assurance report to the client [and other parties to the engagement letter] and on the replication of the report in whole or in part.
(e) Limitation of the liability of the practitioner to the client [and other parties to the engagement letter].
(f) An identification and description of the subject matter information and when appropriate, the subject matter.
(g) The identification of the responsible party, [user organisation(s)] and the respective responsibilities of the client and the practitioner.
(h) Reference to applicable standard and guidance, including this technical release.
(i) Identification of the criteria against which the subject matter is evaluated or measured.
(j) A summary of the work performed including the period covered and frequency of tests, if appropriate.
(k) Inherent limitations associated with the evaluation or measurement of the subject matter against the criteria and any limitations on scope incurred during the work.
(l) Where the criteria used to evaluate or measure the subject matter are available only to specific recipient of the assurance report, or are relevant only to a specific purpose, a statement restricting the use of the assurance report to those intended recipients or that purpose and wording setting out matters related to the practitioner's duty of care.
(m) The practitioner's conclusion in the agreed form (with or without 'except for's), adverse conclusion or disclaimer of a conclusion - with the description of the practitioner's findings including sufficient details of errors and exceptions found. Where appropriate, the conclusion should inform the intended users of the context in which the practitioner's conclusion is to be read.
(n) The name and signature of the firm/ practitioner and the location of the office performing the engagement.
(o) The assurance report date.

(ii) Example assurance reports on third party operations

The following extracts are taken from (a) AAF 01/06 *Assurance reports on internal controls of service organisations made available to third parties*[8] and (b) FIT 01/07

---

[8] AAF 01/06 was issued by the ICAEW in June 2006 to provide guidance to reporting accountants on undertaking an assurance engagement and providing a report in relation to internal controls of a service organisation. AAF 01/06 does not constitute an auditing standard. Professional judgement should be used in its application, and where appropriate, legal assistance should be sought. No responsibility for loss occasioned to any person acting or refraining from acting as a result of any material in AAF 01/06 can be accepted by the ICAEW. The full report is available to download at www.icaew.co.uk/assurance.

Assurance reports on the outsourced provision of information services and information processing services by service organisations made available to third parties.

(a) Reporting accountants' assurance report on internal controls of service organisations[9]

To the directors of [name of entity] and [customers party to the engagement]

Use of report[10]

This report is made solely for the use of the directors, as a body, of [name of entity] and [customers party to the engagement], and solely for the purpose of reporting on the internal controls of [name of entity], in accordance with the terms of our engagement letter dated [date] [and attached[11] as appendix []].

Our work has been undertaken so that we might report to the directors and [customers party to the engagement] those matters that we have agreed to state to them in this report and for no other purpose. Our report must not be recited or referred to in whole or in part in any other document nor made available, copied or recited to any other party, in any circumstances, without our express prior written permission.

To the fullest extent permitted by law, we do not accept or assume responsibility to anyone other than the directors as a body, [name of entity] and [customers party to the engagement] for our work, for this report or for the opinions we have formed.

Subject matter

This report covers solely the internal controls of [name of entity] as described in your report as at [date]. Internal controls are processes designed to provide reasonable assurance regarding the level of control over customers' assets and related transactions achieved by [name of entity] in the provision of [outsourced activities] by [name of entity].

Respective responsibilities

The directors' responsibilities and assertions are set out on page [ ] of your report. Our responsibility is to form an independent conclusion, based on the work carried out in relation to the control procedures of [name of entity]'s [ ] function carried out at the specified business units of [name of entity] [located at [ ]] as described in the directors' report and report this to the directors of [name of entity] and [customers party to the engagement].

Criteria and scope

We conducted our engagement in accordance with International Standard on Assurance Engagements (ISAE) 3000 and the Institute of Chartered Accountants in

---

[9] Reporting accountants consider a suitable form of report in accordance with the specific engagement. This report provides an example for an engagement to which the service organisation and the customers of the service organisation are party.

[10] The two last paragraphs in "Use of report" provide example wording, disclaiming reporting accountants' liability or duty to the customers that are not party to the engagement. Reporting accountants consider the legal effectiveness of disclaiming liability in the particular circumstances of their engagement.

[11] Reporting accountants that do not attach the engagement letter consider including relevant extracts.

England and Wales Technical Release AAF 01/06. The criteria against which the control procedures were evaluated are the internal control objectives developed for service organisations as set out within the Technical Release AAF 01/06 and identified by the directors as relevant control objectives relating to the level of control over customers' assets and related transactions in the provision of [outsourced activities].

Our work was based upon obtaining an understanding of the control procedures as described on page [ ] to [ ] in the report by the directors, and evaluating the directors' assertions as described on page [ ] to [ ] in the same report to obtain reasonable assurance so as to form our conclusion. Our work also included tests of specific control procedures, to obtain evidence about their effectiveness in meeting the related control objectives. The nature, timing and extent of the tests we applied are detailed on pages [ ] to [ ].

Our tests are related to [name of entity] as a whole rather than performed to meet the needs of any particular customer.

Inherent limitations

Control procedures designed to address specified control objectives are subject to inherent limitations and, accordingly, errors or irregularities may occur and not be detected. Such control procedures cannot guarantee protection against (among other things) fraudulent collusion especially on the part of those holding positions of authority or trust.

Furthermore, our conclusion is based on historical information and the projection of any information or conclusions in the attached report to any future periods would be inappropriate.

Conclusion

In our opinion, in all material respects:

1. the accompanying report by the directors describes fairly the control procedures that relate to the control objectives referred to above which were in place as at [date];
2. the control procedures described on pages [ ] to [ ] were suitably designed such that there is reasonable, but not absolute, assurance that the specified control objectives would have been achieved if the described control procedures were complied with satisfactorily [and customers applied the control procedures contemplated]; and
3. the control procedures that were tested, as set out in the attachment to this report, were operating with sufficient effectiveness for us to obtain reasonable, but not absolute, assurance that the related control objectives were achieved in the period [x] to [y].

Name of firm

Chartered Accountants

Location

Date

(b) Assurance reports on the outsourced provision of information services and information processing services[12]

Reporting accountants' assurance report, made available to third parties, on control procedures of service organisations[13] providing information services [/ information processing services]

To the directors of [name of entity] and [customers party to the engagement]

Use of report[14]

This report is made solely for the use of the directors, as a body, of [name of entity] and [customers party to the engagement], and solely for the purpose of reporting on the control procedures of [name of entity], in accordance with the terms of our engagement letter dated [date] [and attached[15] as appendix [ ]].

Our work has been undertaken so that we might report to the directors and [customers party to the engagement] those matters that we have agreed to state to them in this report and for no other purpose. Our report must not be recited or referred to in whole or in part in any other document nor made available, copied or recited to any other party, in any circumstances, without our express prior written permission.

To the fullest extent permitted by law, we do not accept or assume responsibility to anyone other than the directors as a body, [name of entity] and [customers party to the engagement] for our work, for this report or for the conclusions we have formed.

Subject matter

This report covers solely the control procedures of [name of entity] as described in the directors' report as at [date]. Control procedures are designed to provide reasonable assurance regarding the level of control over the information services [/ information processing services] provided by [name of entity].

Respective responsibilities

The directors' responsibilities and assertions are set out on page [ ] of the directors' report. Our responsibility is to form an independent conclusion, based on the work carried out in relation to the control procedures of [name of entity]'s information services [/information processing services] carried out at the specified business units of [name of entity] [located at [ ]] as described in the directors' report and report this to the directors of [name of entity] and [customers party to the engagement].

---

[12] *This guidance is jointly issued by the Information Technology Faculty and Audit and Assurance Faculty of the Institute of Chartered Accountants in England and Wales in April 2007. The technical release does not constitute an auditing standard. Professional judgement should be used in its application, and where appropriate, professional legal assistance should be sought.*

[13] *Reporting accountants consider a suitable form of report in accordance with the specific engagement. This report provides an example for an engagement to which the service organisation and the customers of the service organisation are party.*

[14] *The two last paragraphs in 'Use of report' provide example wording, disclaiming reporting accountants' liability or duty to the customers that are not party to the engagement. Reporting accountants consider the legal effectiveness of disclaiming liability in the particular circumstances of their engagement.*

[15] *Reporting accountants that do not attach the engagement letter consider including relevant extracts.*

Appendix 3 – Criteria

As stated in paragraphs 37 to 41, assurance engagements require the practitioner to express an overall conclusion on the information assessed relative to certain criteria.

While criteria may be specifically developed for an engagement where there are no suitable established criteria, there is a number of standards and guidance that may be relevant to the assurance engagements over different types of third party operations. Such standards and guidance provide a suitable basis for criteria which the responsible party may use to develop its criteria. The directors of responsible party ensure that these criteria meet the characteristics listed in paragraph 39 and consider if these are sufficient to meet the expectations of the user organisation.

These suggestions are set out for guidance only and are not intended to be exhaustive. Directors should describe, as an integral and essential part of their report, a complete set of criteria. It remains the responsibility of the directors to ensure that the described criteria are sufficient to meet the expectations of the user organisation.

Internal controls

- AAF 01/06 *Guidance on Assurance reports on internal controls of service organisations made available to third parties*, published by the Audit and Assurance Faculty in 2006 and replacing FRAG 21/94 (revised) (AUDIT 4/97) *Reports of Internal Controls of Investment Custodians Made Available to Third Parties* provides internal control objectives for financial services.
- The report from the Committee of Sponsoring Organizations of the Treadway Commission (COSO): *Enterprise Risk Management — Integrated Framework* (September 2004). www.coso.org

IT Risk management

- Guidance from the International Federation of Accountants (IFAC): *E-Business and the Accountant: Risk Management for Accounting Systems in an E-Business Environment*, a discussion paper including comments on E-business assurance and advisory services. www.ifac.org/store
- International Auditing and Assurance Standards Board (IAASB):
  - IAPS 1013 "*Electronic Commerce: Effect on the Audit of Financial Statements*"
  - IAPS 1008 "*Risk Assessments and Internal Control–CIS Characteristics and Considerations*"
  - IAPS 1002 "*CIS Environments–Online Computer Systems*"
  - IAPS 1003 "*CIS Environments–Database Systems*",
- British Standards Institution: BS ISO/IEC 27001:2005 (BS 7799-2:2005) BS ISO/IEC 17799:2005: international/British standards on information security management. (Part of ISO 9000:2000 series: international standards on quality management.) www.bsi-global.com
- ISACA (formerly Information Systems Audit & Control Association): *Control Objectives for Information and related Technology* (CobiT). www.isaca.org
- The IT Governance Institute (ITGI; part of ISACA): a reference guide, entitled *IT Control Objectives for Sarbanes-Oxley*, which maps many of the CobiT control objectives to the COSO framework for internal control. www.itgi.org
- *Directive 2006/43/EC of the European Parliament and of the Council of 17 May 2006 on statutory audits of annual accounts and consolidated accounts, amending Council Directives 78/660/EEC and 83/349/EEC and repealing Council Directive 84/253/EEC.*

Criteria and scope

We conducted our engagement in accordance with International Standard on Assurance Engagement 3000 and the Institute of Chartered Accountants in England and Wales Technical Release ITF 01/07. The criteria against which the control procedures were evaluated are the control objectives developed for the service organisation in reference to the control objectives as set out within ITF 01/07 and identified by the directors as relevant control objectives relating to the level of control over the information services [/information processing services] provided by [name of entity] [as outsourced activities]. Our work was based upon obtaining an understanding of the control procedures as described on page [ ] to [ ] in the report by the directors, and evaluating the directors' assertions as described on page [ ] to [ ] in the same report to obtain reasonable assurance so as to form our conclusion. [Our work also included tests of specific control procedures, to obtain evidence about their effectiveness in meeting the related control objectives. The nature, timing and extent of the tests we applied are detailed on pages [ ] to [ ].]

Our tests are related to [name of entity] as a whole rather than performed to meet the needs of any particular user.

Inherent limitations

Control procedures designed to address specified control objectives are subject to inherent limitations and, accordingly, errors or irregularities may occur and not be detected. Such control procedures cannot guarantee protection against (among other things) fraudulent collusion especially on the part of those holding positions of authority or trust. Furthermore, our conclusion is based on historical information and the projection of any information or conclusions in the attached report to any future periods would be inappropriate.

Conclusion

In our opinion, in all material respects:

1. the accompanying report by the directors describes fairly the control procedures that relate to the control objectives referred to above which were in place as at [date];
2. the control procedures described on pages [ ] to [ ] were suitably designed such that there is reasonable, but not absolute, assurance that the specified control objectives would have been achieved if the described control procedures were complied with satisfactorily [and customers applied the control procedures contemplated]; and
[3. the control procedures that were tested, as set out in the attachment to this report, were operating with sufficient effectiveness for us to obtain reasonable, but not absolute, assurance that the related control objectives were achieved in the period [x] to [y].]

Name of firm

Chartered Accountants

Location

Date

- The ITIL (*IT Infrastructure Library*), forming the basis of the BS ISO/IEC 20000 (formerly BS 15000) standard. ITIL has been widely adopted across Europe as the standard for best practice in the provision of IT Service. Although the ITIL covers a number of areas, its main focus is on IT Service Management (ITSM). ITSM itself is divided into two main areas: Service Support and Service Delivery. www.itil.org.uk

Appendix 4 – References

The ICAEW

AAF 01/06 *Assurance reports on internal controls of service organisations made available to third parties*, 2006

AAF 04/06 *Assurance engagements: Management of risk and liability*, 2006

Code of Ethics (UK and Ireland), 2006

ITF 01/07 *Assurance reports on the outsourced provision of information services and information processing services*, 2007

Other

The Auditing Practices Board

International Standard on Quality Control (ISQC) (UK and Ireland) 1 *Quality control for firms that perform audits and reviews of historical financial information, other assurance and related services engagements*, amended by conforming amendments introduced by ISA (UK and Ireland) 230 (Revised), 2006

The International Auditing and Assurance Standards Board

The International Framework for Assurance Engagements, 2004

ISAE 3000 *Assurance Engagements Other Than Audits or Reviews of Historical Financial Information*, 2004

International Federation of Accountants

International Standard on Quality Control (ISQC) 1 *Quality control for firms that perform audits and reviews of historical financial information, other assurance and related services engagements*, 2006

AAF 01/08
Technical release: access to information by successor auditors

(Issued August 2008)

Contents

1. **Background**
   Statutory Audit Directive
   Companies Act
   Audit Regulation
   Audit Choice Market Participants Group
   Mandatory framework

2. **Guidance to the audit regulation**

3. **Application**
   Auditors of UK entities
   Auditors where there is a group of companies
      Irish Entities

4. **Relevant auditing standards**
   ISA (UK and Ireland) 300, Planning an audit of financial statements
   ISA (UK and Ireland) 510, Initial engagements – opening balances
   ISA (UK and Ireland) 710, Comparatives

5. **Access and risk**
   Information or explanations additional to the working papers

6. **Relevant information**
   Legal professional privilege

7. **Practicalities of access**
   Format
   Timing and period of access
   Location
   Cost

8. **Confidentiality issues**
   Duty of confidentiality
   Data protection
   Money laundering
   Tipping off

Appendices

Appendix A: Extracts from legislation
Appendix B: Specimen letter from the successor requesting access
Appendix C: Specimen letter from predecessor responding to the successor's request for access
Appendix D: Money laundering – Interim guidance for auditors in the United Kingdom
   Extract from Practice Note 12 Resignation and communication with successor auditors

Technical release: access to information by successor auditors AAF 01/08

1 Background

For accounting periods starting on or after 6 April 2008, following a change in the law, when there is a change in an audit appointment, the registered auditor ceasing to hold office ("the predecessor") will be required to provide access to relevant information where the newly appointed registered auditor ("the successor") makes a written request for such access. This guidance is intended to provide a helpful and effective framework to assist auditors in managing the process in relation to such access.

Statutory Audit Directive

This requirement arose out of the European Union's (EU) Statutory Audit Directive (2006/43/EC). Article 23 (3) states that: *"where a statutory auditor or audit firm is replaced by another statutory auditor or audit firm, the former statutory auditor or audit firm shall provide the incoming statutory auditor or audit firm with access to all relevant information concerning the audited entity."*

Companies Act

To bring the EU requirement into UK law, schedule 10 of the Companies Act 2006 (the '2006 Act') was amended to require that this requirement is provided for under the rules of the Recognised Supervisory Bodies. This clause[1] states *"the Body must have adequate rules and practices designed to ensure that… a person ceasing to hold office as a statutory auditor makes available to his successor in that office all relevant information which he holds in relation to that office."* Therefore, as with many other aspects of the 2006 Act's (and the underlying Statutory Audit Directive's) requirements in respect of registered auditors, the obligation on registered auditors is to comply with the Audit Regulations which implement the law.

Audit Regulation

Audit Regulation 3.09[2] provides as follows:

> *When a **Registered Auditor** (the 'predecessor') ceases to hold an audit appointment and another **Registered Auditor** (the 'successor') is appointed the predecessor must, if requested in **writing** by the successor, allow the successor access to all relevant information held by the predecessor in respect of its **audit work**. If relevant information is to be sought by the successor, it should be sought and provided in accordance with the following guidance. Any information obtained by the successor is for the purposes of its **audit** and must not be disclosed to a third party unless the successor is required to do so by a legal or professional obligation.*

The guidance referred to in the Audit Regulation is set out in Section 2[3]. Terms shown in bold above are defined terms in the Audit Regulations.

---

[1] Sub-Paragraph 3 of Paragraph 9 of Schedule 10 to the Companies Act 2006 (extract at Appendix A).

[2] Joint Audit Regulations are issued by the three Institutes: the Institute of Chartered Accountants in England and Wales, the Institute of Chartered Accountants of Scotland and the Institute of Chartered Accountants in Ireland.

[3] The Institutes have taken leading counsel's advice in the drafting of Audit Regulation 3.09 and the associated Guidance. Leading counsel has confirmed that in his opinion they have complied with the obligation to make adequate rules and practices designed as provided by Schedule 10 of the Companies Act 2006.

5   The guidance to the Audit Regulation states that *"the purpose of this regulation is to assist in maintaining the effectiveness (including cost effectiveness) and the efficiency of the audit process in the context of a change of auditor…."* and *"is intended to reduce the (actual or perceived) risk of changing auditors."*

Audit Choice Market Participants Group

6   The Financial Reporting Council's Audit Choice Market Participants Group ('MPG') published a final report in October 2007 which addressed (amongst other things) the subject of establishing mechanisms to improve access by incoming auditors to information relevant to the audit held by the outgoing auditor. The MPG's report informed the drafting of the guidance to the Audit Regulation.

Mandatory framework

7   The combination of the Directive, legislation and Audit Regulation creates a mandatory framework for the provision of access to relevant information in respect of the predecessor's audit work. Responsibility for the implementation of the Directive rests with BERR which has chosen to discharge this responsibility through the 2006 Act (paragraph 3 above). The faculty provides practical guidance on the application of the Audit Regulation as it is this that auditors must comply with.

8   As the Audit Regulation provides, *"If relevant information is to be sought by the successor, it should be sought and provided in accordance with the….guidance".*

2   Guidance to the audit regulation

The following text is the guidance that sits underneath Audit Regulation 3.09 ("the Guidance").

Origin and purpose

This audit regulation ("the Regulation") gives effect to the obligation in the 2006 Act that RSBs must have adequate rules and practices designed to ensure that a person ceasing to hold office as a statutory auditor makes available to his successor in that office all relevant information which he holds in relation to that office. The requirement derives from Article 23(3) of the EU Statutory Audit Directive. The Department for Business, Enterprise and Regulatory Reform has stated that the Regulation should provide "the most appropriate minimum requirement in relation to access to relevant information".

The purpose of the Regulation is to assist in maintaining the effectiveness (including cost effectiveness) and the efficiency of the audit process in the context of a change of auditor. The Regulation is intended to reduce the (actual or perceived) risk of changing auditors.

It takes time for a successor to develop a comprehensive understanding of the business of an audit client. A wide variety of different arrangements have existed to facilitate an effective handover between successor and predecessor, including exchanges of letters, discussion, exchange of audit committee papers and minutes, and shadowing of the predecessor at key meetings such as the final audit committee meeting. Before the Regulation it was however unusual for a predecessor to share audit working papers. This was due mainly to liability concerns.

Liability concerns formerly arose in the context of access to audit working papers being allowed voluntarily, but any access will now be compulsory. Further it is no part of the purpose or object of the Regulation to involve one auditor in liability for another's audit. Also the Department for Business, Enterprise and Regulatory Reform has confirmed its view that Article 23(3) and the 2006 Act provision implementing it do not alter the existing liability of each auditor in relation to its respective audit.

Provision is already made separately by statute for the making of representations, for the attendance and hearing at meetings, and for the making of a statement of circumstances, where the predecessor has been removed as auditor, where there has been a failure to re-appoint the predecessor as auditor, where the predecessor has resigned as auditor, and where the predecessor has ceased to hold office. The Regulation and guidance do not seek to duplicate that framework, and are framed in recognition of the fact that that framework already exists.

This guidance is separate from and additional to the Institute's Code of Ethics which sets out procedures to be followed before accepting a professional appointment.

Timing

A request for relevant information may be made by a successor once the successor has been formally appointed to the audit client. In all cases the provision of information should be on a timely basis.

"Audit"

It should be borne in mind that the 2006 Act sets out a number of functions that are required of the registered auditor in specific circumstances. These are within the definition of an audit (and so fall within the definitions of audit report and audit work). The situations in which they arise currently include the following:

- section 92   a company applying to re-register as a public company;
- section 428   statement on summary financial statements issued by a quoted company;
- section 449   abbreviated accounts;
- section 714   when a private company makes a payment out of capital for the redemption or purchase of its own shares;
- section 837   when a distribution is to be made by a company and the audit report was qualified; or
- section 838   when initial accounts are prepared for a proposed distribution by a public company.

(Where the registered auditor is appointed to an entity that is not a company similar reporting requirements may apply.)

Procedure

Before making a request for relevant information the successor should as part of its planning consider the need to make a request to the predecessor under the Regulation, and the extent of that request. This will involve judgement by the successor in each case, so as to ensure that necessary request is made and an unnecessary request is not. It is also important to assess what information will be relevant in each case and what will not.

It does not follow that a successor is required or expected to request information in every case, or to request extensive information in a case in which only limited information is necessary. The successor's consideration will include consideration of what work it would do with any information provided to it pursuant to a request. There are specific references to reviewing the predecessor's audit work in ISA 510 (opening balances), ISA 710 (comparatives) and ISA 300 (planning). Accordingly, information is likely to be necessary in particular for such purposes.

The provision of information under this regulation will be achieved more efficiently where the successor auditor is as specific as possible as to the nature of the information being sought. The successor should therefore, wherever possible, avoid a request framed simply as a request for "all relevant information held by the predecessor and concerning the audited entity" or "all relevant information held by the predecessor in relation to the office of auditor". Thus the successor should strive to identify the information required, or the type of information required, as precisely as possible.

For example, where relevant information is requested by the successor, the information will normally be that contained in the working papers produced by the predecessor, and the appropriate request may therefore be for some or all of those working papers. In some audits there will be Institute or APB guidance indicating the working papers expected for such an audit. For example in the case of a financial statement audit, ISAs will indicate the audit working papers to be prepared. In other cases, where there is no guidance, the predecessor will have determined the working papers to be prepared.

Where the information related to audit work is requested by the successor but is not filed on the current audit file but, for example, on a 'permanent' or 'systems' file, or there is a reference to a prior audit file, access should be provided by the predecessor to this information.

The predecessor should be prepared to assist the successor by providing oral or written explanations on a timely basis to assist the latter's understanding of the audit working papers.

Period

Normally the period for which relevant information is requested would be in respect of any audit report relating to a period falling between the beginning of the last financial statements on which the predecessor reported and the date of cessation of the predecessor's audit appointment. The request would include any subsequent review conducted by the predecessor in accordance with guidance published by the APB in relation to published interim reports.

A successor may consider that it needs to have information in addition to that within the period mentioned above. In the normal case, in the interests of cost and efficiency, the successor should first review the information already provided. If after that review a judgment is made that additional information is needed, the additional information sought should be described in writing, as precisely as possible. The successor should be prepared to provide reasons which demonstrate that the additional information is "relevant" information and therefore within the Regulation. Here as elsewhere the successor should be prepared to confirm that the information is needed to aid its audit work for the audit client and not for some other purpose.

Other points

The request for information may be made of the immediate predecessor only.

Because (as indicated above) it is no part of the purpose or object of the Regulation to involve one auditor in liability for another's audit, it would be usual for the basis on which the information is to be provided to be documented in writing by an exchange of letters between the two registered auditors, copied to the audited entity. Guidance on suitable letters is available on each Institute's website as part of a technical release.

There is no obligation to allow the copying of working papers but it would be usual to allow copying of extracts of the books and records of the audit client that are contained in the audit working papers. Generally speaking, where access to relevant information is necessary, the practical arrangements to allow that access to be provided in a cost effective and efficient way should be discussed and agreed between the successor and the predecessor.

A request for information under the Regulation should not be made other than in connection with the successor's audit. The successor should refuse to accept an additional engagement, such as to act as an expert witness or to review the quality of the predecessor's audit work, where the engagement would involve the use of the information obtained by it under the Regulation. In any event, the successor should not comment on the quality of the predecessor's audit work unless required to do so by a legal or professional obligation.

The reference in the Regulation to the information not being disclosed to a third party includes to the audit client. This does not prevent the successor discussing the information with the client where to do so is a necessary part of its audit work. Nor does it prevent the provision of this information to any third party if that is required of the successor by a legal or professional obligation.

Section 1210 of the 2006 Act sets out a list of appointments to which this Regulation and guidance apply. Section 1210(h) allows additional types of appointments to be added to the list. Registered auditors are not required to allow access to their working papers in respect of other appointments.

This regulation only applies in respect appointments for the audits of financial years starting on or after 6 April 2008.

3 Application

The new requirement applies to all statutory audits. Statutory audits are defined by section 1210 of the 2006 Act, (reproduced in Appendix A). 10

Statutory audits include audits of the following types of entity: 11

- Companies;
- Building societies;
- Various categories of insurer and insurance undertaking; and
- Banks.

Section 1210(h) allows other audits to be added to the new requirement. At the time of publication of this technical release, additional audits included:

- Qualifying partnerships (each partner being a company or a Scottish partnership in which each partner is a limited company); and
- Limited Liability Partnerships (from October 2008).

Where an 'audit exempt' company has an audit, for example because shareholders have required one, this is a statutory audit and the new requirement applies.

12 The new requirement (and hence this technical release) only applies to the statutory audits listed in section 1210. Thus, for example, the requirement does not apply to:

- Unincorporated charities;
- Pension schemes; and
- General partnerships which are not qualifying partnerships (see paragraph 11).

13 In circumstances where, although the requirement and this technical release do not apply, predecessors are prepared to consider granting access, it is important that they bear in mind that the range of matters requiring consideration may extend beyond those addressed in this technical release.

Auditors of UK entities

14 The requirement only applies between auditors of UK entities which are subject to the 2006 Act.

Auditors where there is a group of companies

15 If the predecessor was the principal auditor[4] of a group of companies and a successor is appointed principal auditor, then the requirement applies only to relevant information in respect of the audit of the parent's single entity and consolidated accounts. Accordingly, the successor auditor will have access to that relevant information whether held by the predecessor on a consolidation audit file or elsewhere in accordance with the ISAs. A successor will not have access to information if it is held by a predecessor who, although the principal auditor, holds that information only in his capacity as statutory auditor of the UK subsidiary, unless the successor is also appointed as the statutory auditor of that subsidiary.

16 Access to relevant information held only in the capacity as statutory auditor of UK subsidiaries will be covered to the extent that the audit appointments change at the individual subsidiary level.

Irish Entities

17 Irish audit firms can audit UK entities and (subject to certain restrictions) vice versa. Implementation of the Statutory Audit Directive in the Republic of Ireland will be at a later date than in the UK. Therefore, at the time of publication, there is no legal obligation on the predecessor to allow the successor access to relevant information in respect of an Irish entity audit. This position will change when the Irish law is amended to implement the Directive and it is understood that auditors of Irish entities will be informed of the requirements when this becomes clearer.

18 Audit Regulation 3.09 and this technical release therefore have no application in respect of Irish entity audits. In circumstances where, although the requirement and this technical release do not apply, auditors of Irish entities are nonetheless prepared to consider granting access, it is important that they bear in mind that the range of matters requiring consideration may extend beyond those addressed in this technical release.

---

[4] *Principal auditor is defined in ISA (UK and Ireland) 600.*

4 Relevant auditing standards

The Guidance under the Audit Regulation states: *"where relevant information is requested by the successor, the information will normally be that contained in the working papers produced by the predecessor, and the appropriate request may therefore be for some or all of those working papers. In some audits there will be Institute or APB guidance indicating the working papers expected for such an audit. For example in the case of a financial statement audit, ISAs will indicate the audit working papers to be prepared. In other cases, where there is no guidance, the predecessor will have determined the working papers to be prepared.... There are specific references to reviewing the predecessor's audit work is made in ISA 510 (opening balances), ISA 710 (comparatives) and ISA 300 (planning). Accordingly, information is likely to be necessary in particular, for such purposes."* 19

The three standards[5] referred to in this technical release make reference to initial engagements and underpin the work that the successor needs to carry out to develop the overall audit strategy and audit plan and to obtain sufficient appropriate evidence about the opening balances and consistency of accounting policies. 20

ISA (UK and Ireland) 300, Planning an audit of financial statements

Paragraphs 28 and 29 of this ISA are relevant when carrying out an audit of a client for the first time. 21

Paragraph 28 states: *"The auditor should perform the following activities prior to starting an initial audit....* 22

...(b) communicate with the previous auditor, where there has been a change of auditors...".

Paragraph 29 states: *"The purpose and objective of planning are the same whether the audit is an initial or recurring engagement. However, for an initial audit, the auditor may need to expand the planning activities because the auditor does not ordinarily have the previous experience with the entity that is considered when planning recurring engagements. For initial audits, additional matters the auditor may consider in developing the overall audit strategy and audit plan include the following:* 23

- *"Unless, prohibited by law or regulation, arrangements to be made with the previous auditor, for example, to review the previous auditor's working papers;... and*
- *The planned audit procedures to obtain sufficient appropriate audit evidence regarding opening balances (see paragraph 2 of ISA (UK and Ireland) 510, "Initial Engagements – Opening Balances")".*

ISA (UK and Ireland) 510, Initial engagements – opening balances

This ISA would be relevant when an auditor is carrying out an audit of a client for the first time. As part of the work under this ISA, auditors need to obtain sufficient appropriate audit evidence that: 24

"(a) the opening balances do not contain misstatements that materially affect the current period's financial statements;

---

[5] These are correct at the time of going to press but the outcome and future implementation of the International Auditing and Assurance Standards Board's (IAASB's) clarity project may have an impact on these standards.

(b) the prior period's closing balances have been correctly brought forward to the current period or, when appropriate, have been restated; and
(c) appropriate accounting policies are consistently applied or changes in accounting policies have been properly accounted for and adequately presented and disclosed."

25 One of the audit procedures that is available to the successor to meet this objective is the review of the predecessor's working papers.

ISA (UK and Ireland) 710, Comparatives

26 Under this ISA, auditors need to obtain sufficient appropriate audit evidence that:

"(a) the accounting policies used for the corresponding amounts are consistent with those of the current period and appropriate adjustments and disclosures have been made where this is not the case;
(b) the corresponding amounts agree with the amounts and other disclosures presented in the preceding period and are free from errors in the context of the financial statements of the current period; and
(c) where corresponding amounts have been adjusted as required by relevant legislation and accounting standards, appropriate disclosures have been made."

5 Access and risk

27 As the Audit Regulation states, a request for relevant information should be made in writing.

28 An example of a proforma request from the successor is attached at Appendix B. An example of a proforma letter from the predecessor (which should be copied to the client) setting out the basis on which the information is to be provided is attached at Appendix C. These proformas do not contemplate countersignature; where a predecessor and a successor proceed in accordance with the basis described in them, their effectiveness is not dependent on countersignature.

29 The Guidance further states: *"It is no part of the purpose or object of the Regulation to involve one auditor in liability for another's audit"*.

30 The requesting and granting of access to relevant information can carry risk. In managing the associated risks a risk management strategy would include:

- (in the case of the predecessor) limiting the circumstances in which a duty of care to the successor or the client may be said to arise;
- (in the case of the successor) limiting the circumstances in which a duty of care other than any accepted in its audit report[6] may be said to arise;
- (in the case of the predecessor and the successor) excluding any duty that might otherwise be said to arise;
- (in the case of the predecessor and the successor) limiting the circumstances in which a duty of care (if any) may be said to be breached.

31 The risk management procedures adopted will generally include:

- the exchange of letters referred to above;

---

[6] Refer also to the guidance contained within Technical Release Audit 01/03, The Audit Report and Auditors' Duty of Care to Third Parties.

- compliance with available guidance on audit reporting;
- the approach to information or explanations referred to below; and
- focusing on information that is relevant.

Mindful of the cost and resource involved in a successor looking at information provided (as well as in a predecessor providing that information), whilst a successor will look to make a necessary request for information it will also guard against making an unnecessary request for information. Of course in some cases a request will be unnecessary because the information requested is irrelevant rather than relevant information: in such a case the predecessor may challenge the successor's entitlement to make the request.

Information or explanations additional to the working papers

The Guidance states: *"The predecessor should be prepared to assist the successor by providing oral or written explanations on a timely basis to assist the latter's understanding of the audit working papers."* 32

The predecessor can provide explanations orally or in writing and can request that any questions be put in writing by the successor, whilst recognising the need for as smooth a process as possible. Questions should be directed to clarification or explanation about the audit working papers that have been accessed. 33

In providing explanations in relation to the audit working papers in response to a request by the successor, the predecessor should keep in mind: 34

- that its obligation does not extend beyond relevant information;
- that explanations should be given a factual or evidential reference point; and
- the desirability of an internal written note or record of the request made and explanation given.

The predecessor may re-emphasise at the beginning of any such discussion with the successor that any statements made by the predecessor are made in accordance with the terms of the letter (Appendix C). 35

6 Relevant information

The Guidance reproduced in Section 2 sets out the procedures, period and other points relevant to what constitutes 'relevant information'. The Guidance provides: 36

> *"The successor should therefore, wherever possible, avoid a request framed simply as a request for "all relevant information held by the predecessor and concerning the audited entity" or "all relevant information held by the predecessor in relation to the office of auditor thus the successor should strive to identify the information required, or the type of information required, as precisely as possible.*
>
> *For example, where relevant information is requested by the successor, the information will normally be that contained in the working papers produced by the predecessor, and the appropriate request may therefore be for some or all of those working papers. In some audits there will be Institute or APB guidance indicating the working papers expected for such an audit. For example in the case of a financial statement audit, the ISAs (UK and Ireland) will indicate the audit working papers to be prepared. In other cases, where there is no guidance, the predecessor will have determined the working papers to be prepared....*

...Period Normally the period for which relevant information is requested would be in respect of any audit report relating to a period falling between the beginning of the last financial statements on which the predecessor reported and the date of cessation of the predecessor's audit appointment. The request would include any subsequent review conducted by the predecessor in accordance with guidance published by the APB in relation to published interim reports."

37 Audit Regulation 3.09 and its associated Guidance have been drafted to comply with the statutory obligation to have adequate rules and practices designed to ensure that all relevant information is made available by a predecessor to his successor[7].

38 Auditors are required to comply with the Audit Regulation under which the predecessor allows access to all relevant information held by him in respect of his "audit work". This technical release is intended to provide practical guidance on the application of the Audit Regulation. This section provides guidance as to what might constitute relevant information. The Guidance provided with the Audit Regulation indicates that 'relevant information' will normally be that contained in the audit working papers of the predecessor. It is not possible for the faculty to list or prescribe what will constitute relevant information in each case. Ultimately, it is a question for auditors to use their professional judgement as to what to request.

39 ISA (UK and Ireland) 230, *Documentation* states that *"The auditor should document matters which are important to providing audit evidence to support the auditor's opinion and evidence that the audit was carried out in accordance with ISAs (UK and Ireland).* "Documentation" *means the material (working papers) prepared by and for, or obtained and retained by the auditor in connection with the performance of the audit. Working papers include papers prepared to:*

   (a) assist in the planning and performance of the audit;
   (b) assist in the supervision and review of the audit work; and
   (c) record the audit evidence resulting from the audit work performed to support the auditors opinion."[8]

40 The information in the audit working papers can be in any form, including as data, text, image or sound and may be stored in any type of information system as hard copy documents or as electronic communication in any data storage device. Where access may involve access to integrated proprietary software, the predecessor may need to consider how it provides appropriate means of access to relevant audit documentation. The provision of access to any intellectual property of the predecessor or any material in which the predecessor has copyright does not amount to permission to the successor to use or exploit that intellectual property or copyright in any way.

41 Files may contain papers relating to the client that are not held by the predecessor in respect of its audit work. In a particular case, for example, tax papers held by the predecessor in respect of tax rather than audit work may be on the same file as the audit working papers. The obligation to provide access in this situation will not extend to those tax papers.

42 The successor may separately request access to the tax papers where they belong to the client. It may, however, be appropriate to facilitate access to such papers directly

---

[7] See footnote 3.

[8] This is correct at the time of going to press but the outcome and future implementation of the IAASB's clarity project may have an impact on this standard.

particular circumstances and the predecessor should consider obtaining legal advice on their disclosure obligations.

7 Practicalities of access

49 The written request for access to relevant information needs to be sent to the immediate predecessor registered auditor. The request will be made to the firm as the registered auditor marked for the attention of the audit partner designated as the Senior Statutory Auditor for that audit. Both the requests for access and the granting of access need to be timely with a view to minimising the costs/burden on the predecessor, the successor or the client. There needs to be a clear understanding about which papers will be provided, by what method and when.

Format

50 In the case of access to audit working papers, it will be for the predecessor to determine the format in which they are willing to provide access. This may either be in hard copy or in electronic form. However, it will wish to do so in a manner that does not put at risk the confidentiality of its firm's audit methodologies or of the confidential information of other clients.

51 It is reasonable for the successor to make notes of its review in support of its own documentation requirements under ISA (UK & Ireland) 230.

52 The predecessor is under no obligation to allow copying of its audit working papers, but it would be reasonable to allow, as a minimum, the copying of extracts of the books and records of the client. It would also be reasonable and indeed helpful to allow copying of papers such as: breakdown of analyses of financial statement figures and documentation of the client's systems and processes.

53 Whilst there is no obligation to allow copying of papers that show judgements or the nature, scope and results of tests conducted to form an audit opinion and to which access has been provided, it would be for the predecessor and the successor to discuss and arrive at an agreement between them of what it is reasonable to copy.

54 Ultimately, the predecessor will maintain control of which audit working papers can be and are copied. It would be sensible to check through any documents that the successor asks to copy and keep a record of all the copied items.

Timing and period of access

55 Access can only be requested after the appointment of the successor to the entity has been completed. In the normal course, requests for access will be made soon after the appointment of the successor at the planning stage of its first audit. Correspondingly, the predecessor should grant access within a reasonable amount of time of receipt of the request. The timing of access should have regard to the following:
- the point at which the audit file will be complete (ISA (UK and Ireland) 230 allows the predecessor up to 60 days after the date of the audit report to complete the assembly of its final audit file); and
- the successor's reporting timetable.

56 Requests for access need to be reasonable without causing either the predecessor or the successor undue resourcing or timing difficulties.

via the client. If the successor wishes to have access to tax papers held by the predecessor, then the predecessor should consider adapting the guidance contained within Audit 04/03, *Access to Working Papers by Investigating Accountants*. Similar considerations apply to accounts preparation papers held by the predecessor.

43 Typically information that will not constitute relevant information and that will not (save possibly in exceptional cases, where relevance will have to be demonstrated by the successor) be disclosable, will be:

- the internal budgeting documents concerning costing and billing for the audit assignment;
- information relating to staffing for the engagement and any incidental personnel records or information about the engagement team; and
- certain information that is subject to legal professional privilege (see further below).

Special considerations apply to any documents that form part of a disclosure to the Serious Organised Crime Agency ("SOCA"). This is referred to in paragraphs 67 to 69 below.

44 "Relevant information" includes information that comes to the knowledge of, or into the possession of the predecessor between the completion of the latest audit or interim review and the date on which their appointment as auditor ceases. Although a successor may enquire about this information, it recognises that the predecessor may not have been made aware of all matters that might be relevant to the successor's first audit.

Legal professional privilege

45 "Relevant information" may be subject to legal professional privilege. Whether or not legally privileged information is disclosed to the successor will depend on the circumstances in which legal privilege arises in respect of that information.

46 Information may have legally privileged status because the client has asserted, when providing the information originally to the predecessor, that such "client information" was legally privileged and that the privilege was not being waived on disclosure to the predecessor. An example might include legal advice concerning the merits of litigation against the client by a third party. In any such case, or where the predecessor is uncertain about the legally privileged status of client information, the predecessor will make enquiries of the client to ascertain whether it objects to disclosure of that information to the successor, or whether the client wishes to impose any terms regulating disclosure to the successor.

47 If the client does not authorise the disclosure to the successor of client information held by the predecessor on the basis that it is legally privileged, the predecessor considers informing the successor that certain information is being withheld (without disclosing any details regarding that information) because the client asserts legal privilege. The matter should then be addressed between the client and the successor. If the client does not object to client privileged information being disclosed to the successor, the predecessor should disclose it.

48 Information may also be relevant but subject to legal professional privilege because legal privilege is asserted by the predecessor. This may arise where information has been generated by the predecessor who has, for example, sought legal advice on matters relating to the client and the audit. Whether or not such information needs to be disclosed to the successor will be dependent on the legal position applicable to the

There will need to be cooperation between the predecessor and the successor regarding the period of time during which the successor can have access to the audit working papers. The period needs to be reasonable.

Location

The location where access is to be provided will be for the predecessor to determine. Access will normally be at the predecessor's premises in the UK.

Whatever location is chosen, firms will need to be mindful of the confidentiality of other clients' information.

Cost

The legislation is silent on the question of the predecessor charging, either the client or the successor, for providing access. A significant level of charging could be seen as a barrier to competition and choice and could potentially introduce an unnecessary burden on the process of changing auditors, which is not the intention of the legislation. On the other hand, some recovery of actual costs may be considered reasonable.

Actual costs may be incurred in retrieving the information, gathering it together, extracting what is not relevant, and then making it available to the successor. Payment for these actual costs can be justified on the basis that without payment, disclosure could impose an unnecessary and unreasonable burden on the predecessor, who would otherwise incur a financial loss through its compliance with its statutory obligations. Thus, it may be reasonable to charge for the cost of:

- copying documents;
- paying someone to make the copies;
- retrieving documents from archive sources; and
- paying someone to attend to such retrieval and to provide documents for inspection by the successor.

It is, however, unlikely to be reasonable to include in any charge any element for profit, or to charge on any footing that a service was being provided. If a charge is made that goes beyond "actual costs" of the type described above, there is a risk that payment for such wider costs may affect the reasonableness of the denial of any responsibility in connection with the provision of information and its use. Any payment for such wider costs could therefore increase the prospect of the predecessor being taken to have assumed a duty of care to the paying party in relation to the provision of that information and its use.

In practice, it is unlikely that the successor will be willing to bear responsibility for any payment, whether or not limited to the actual costs incurred by the predecessor. Accordingly, the predecessor is likely to be able to look only to the client for any payment. The client may recognise that, to avoid the transfer process becoming an unnecessary and unreasonable burden on the predecessor, a payment limited to actual costs incurred with no element for profit or services might be made. It may be considered appropriate as a matter of policy to provide for the recovery of costs of providing access to an eventual successor in the audit engagement letter, thereby making it a contractual obligation with the client. Even though some recovery of actual costs may be considered reasonable, the predecessor cannot use a failure to be reimbursed for costs as a reason for failing to meet the obligation to allow access.

8 Confidentiality issues

Duty of confidentiality

64 The predecessor providing the successor with access to relevant information is complying with a mandatory requirement and therefore access will not breach professional confidentiality. Nonetheless before providing access to relevant information a letter from the predecessor to the successor (in the form set out in Appendix C) will be copied to the client as a matter of courtesy.

65 The Audit Regulation and Guidance provides expressly:

- *"Any information obtained by the successor is for the purposes of its* **audit** *and must not be disclosed to a third party unless the successor is required to do so by a legal or professional obligation."*
- *"A request for information under the Regulation should not be made other than in connection with the successor's audit. The successor should refuse to accept an additional engagement, such as to act as an expert witness or to review the quality of the predecessor's audit work, where the engagement would involve the use of the information obtained by it under the Regulation. In any event, the successor should not comment on the quality of the predecessor's audit work unless required to do so by a legal or professional obligation."*
- *"The reference in the Regulation to the information not being disclosed to a third party includes to the audit client. This does not prevent the successor discussing the information with the client where to do so is a necessary part of its audit work. Nor does it prevent the provision of this information to any third party if that is required of the successor by a legal or professional obligation."*

Data protection

66 Data protection laws apply to the personal data of individuals. Relevant information may contain personal data (for example about employees or about sole traders with whom the client does business). However, the predecessor is obliged to provide access to relevant information by legislation. Therefore, where personal data is disclosed as a result of providing access to the relevant information, as long as the information being provided is necessary to discharge that legal obligation there are no data protection risks for the predecessor in complying with the Audit Regulation.

Money laundering

67 All auditors are subject to the Money Laundering Regulations 2007 and relevant underlying legislation (including the Proceeds of Crime Act 2002 and Terrorism Act 2000). The reporting requirements of the money laundering legislation are beyond the scope of this guidance. Full information is available from the Anti-Money Laundering Guidance for the Accountancy Sector, issued by the CCAB (available from www.icaew.com/moneylaundering). Reference should also be made to APB Practice Note 12, in particular paragraphs 56 to 60 (attached at Appendix D) which deals with the predecessor's communication with the successor.

Tipping off

68 There are various tipping off offences which can be committed if there is disclosure of knowledge or suspicion that a report has been made to an MLRO, SOCA or, in

some cases, anyone authorised to receive a disclosure. Details of the offences and the elements which give rise to them are beyond the scope of this guidance.

Full information is available from the Anti-Money Laundering Guidance for the Accountancy Sector, issued by the CCAB (available from www.icaew.com/money-laundering). Subject to the full terms of that guidance:

- Any money laundering report and papers recording the predecessor's related consideration of apparently suspicious activities should not be provided by the predecessor to any person (including the successor) unless the predecessor has clear advice that to do so would be lawful. Accordingly it is recommended that such advice is sought from the MLRO or externally.
- So far as concerns the successor, if any relevant information provided to the successor causes the successor to conclude that there are circumstances that require a report to the money laundering authorities, the successor should make that report whether or not it believes that a report might already have been made by the predecessor.

Appendix A – Extracts from legislation

Statutory Audit Directive Article 23 (3)

Where a statutory auditor or audit firm is replaced by another statutory auditor or audit firm, the former statutory auditor or audit firm shall provide the incoming statutory auditor or audit firm with access to all relevant information concerning the audited entity.

Paragraph 9 of Schedule 10 to the Companies Act 2006

Sub-paragraph (3)

The body must also have adequate rules and practices designed to ensure that—

....

(c) a person ceasing to hold office as statutory auditor makes available to his successor in that office all relevant information which he holds in relation to that office."

Section 1210 of the Companies Act 2006 (as amended by SI 2008/565)

Meaning of "statutory auditor" etc

(1) In this Part "statutory auditor" means–
 (a) a person appointed as auditor under Part 16 of this Act,
 (b) a person appointed as auditor under section 77 of or Schedule 11 to the Building Societies Act 1986 (c. 53),
 (c) a person appointed as auditor of an insurer that is a friendly society under section 72 of or Schedule 14 to the Friendly Societies Act 1992 (c. 40),
 [(d) *a person appointed as auditor of an insurer that is an industrial and provident society under section 4 of the Friendly and Industrial and Provident Societies*

Act 1968 (c. 55) or under section 38 of the Industrial and Provident Societies Act (Northern Ireland) 1969 (c. 24 (N.I.))]⁹,

(e) a person appointed as auditor for the purposes of regulation 3 of the Insurance Accounts Directive (Lloyd's Syndicate and Aggregate Accounts) Regulations 2004 (S.I. 2004/3219) or appointed to report on the "aggregate accounts" within the meaning of those Regulations,

(f) a person appointed as auditor of an insurance undertaking for the purposes of the Insurance Accounts Directive (Miscellaneous Insurance Undertakings) Regulations 2008,

(g) a person appointed as auditor of a bank for the purposes of regulation 4 of the Bank Accounts Directive (Miscellaneous Banks) Regulations 1991 (S.I. 1991/2704), and

(h) a person appointed as auditor of a prescribed person under a prescribed enactment authorising or requiring the appointment;

and the expressions "statutory audit" and "statutory audit work" are to be construed accordingly.

Appendix B – Specimen letter from the successor requesting access

[Predecessor firm]
[Address]

For the attention of: [Name of Senior Statutory Auditor]

Dear Sirs,

Provision of Information pursuant to audit regulation 3.09 relating to the audit of [audit client]

This firm was duly appointed statutory auditor (as defined by section 1210 of the Companies Act 2006 ("the Act")) on [date] to [company] ("the Company") [and its UK subsidiaries as listed in the schedule to this letter (together "the Companies")].

Pursuant to paragraph 9(3) of Schedule 10 to the Companies Act 2006 and Audit Regulation 3.09, and in accordance with Technical Release AAF 01/08 issued by the Institute of Chartered Accountants in England and Wales, we request for the purposes of our audit work, access to the following information:

[*Set out information necessary at this stage, noting the guidance under Audit Regulation 3.09 that wherever possible a request framed simply as a request for "all relevant information held by the predecessor and concerning the audited entity" or "all relevant information held by the predecessor in relation to the office of auditor" should be avoided. The successor should strive to identify the information required, or the type of information required, as precisely as possible.*]

[*Where the request is for access to audit working papers and subsequent interim review working papers, insert where applicable*:

[The working papers in respect of your audit report on the financial statements of the [Company/Companies] relating to [*insert period between the beginning of*

---

⁹ *Subsection (1)(d) was omitted by SI 2008 No 565.*

the last financial statements on which the predecessor reported and the date of cessation of the predecessor's appointment].

[Where in your capacity as auditor you conducted a review of interim financial information subsequent to the audit report referred to above, this request includes a request for access to the working papers relating to that review also.]

We may also request explanations from you in connection with our consideration of the above information, and on the same basis.

[We/ the Company will meet reasonable costs that you will incur in giving access/ providing copies, provided that a maximum amount is agreed first.]

We look forward to receiving your confirmation letter in response to this request, which should be addressed for the attention of [name of successor engagement partner].

Yours faithfully

[Successor]

[Schedule of UK subsidiaries to which this letter applies in addition to the Company

Company 2 Limited

Company 3 Limited

............]

Appendix C – Specimen letter from predecessor responding to the successor's request for access

[Successor firm]
[address]

Dear Sirs,

Provision of Information pursuant to audit regulation 3.09 relating to the audit of [audit client]

We refer to your letter dated [] following your appointment as statutory auditors of [company] ("the Company") [and its UK subsidiaries listed in the schedule to your letter (together "the Companies")].

We confirm we will provide access to the information requested, namely:

[*This should reflect the information set out in the successor's request letter which is necessary at this stage, noting the guidance under Audit Regulation 3.09 that wherever possible a request framed simply as a request for "all relevant information held by the predecessor and concerning the audited entity" or "all relevant information held by the predecessor in relation to the office of auditor" should be avoided. The successor should have identified the information required, or the type of information required, as precisely as possible.*]

[*Where the request is for access to audit working papers and subsequent interim review working papers if applicable, the following language reflects that set out in the proforma request letter in Appendix B*:

[The working papers in respect of our audit report on the financial statements of the [Company/Companies] relating to [*insert period specified by the successor, such as the period between the beginning of the last financial statements on which the predecessor reported and the date of cessation of the predecessor's appointment*].

[The working papers relating to our review of interim financial information for the period ended [insert period subsequent to the audit report referred to above, as specified by the successor].]

We understand that you may also request explanations from us in connection with your consideration of the above information, and on the same basis.

In accordance with the guidance under Audit Regulation 3.09 and Technical Release AAF 01/08 issued by the Institute of Chartered Accountants in England and Wales this letter sets out the basis on which the information and explanations (if any) are to be provided. Should you request or we provide any supplementary information to that set out above, such provision will be made on the same basis.

The access is provided to you:

(a) solely in your capacity as duly appointed statutory auditor (as defined by section 1210 of the Companies Act 2006 ("the Act")) of the [Company/Companies];
(b) solely because we are required to give you access to information pursuant to paragraph 9(3) of Schedule 10 to the Act and Audit Regulation 3.09.

The provision of access does not and will not alter any responsibility that we may have accepted or assumed to the [Company/Companies] or the [Company's/ respective Companies'] members as a body, in accordance with the statutory requirements for audit, for our audit work, for our audit report or for the opinions we have formed in the course of our work as auditors.

To the fullest extent permitted by law we do not accept or assume responsibility to you or to anyone else:

(a) as a result of the access given;
(b) for the information to which we provide access;
(c) for any explanation given to you;
(d) in respect of any audit work you may undertake, any audit you may complete, and audit report you may issue, or any audit opinion you may give.

Where access is provided to audit [and interim review] working papers, those papers were not created or prepared for, and should not be treated as suitable for, any purpose other than the statutory audit that was the subject of our audit report [and respectively the interim review we carried out]. The statutory audit was planned and undertaken solely for the purpose of forming and giving the audit opinion required by the relevant statutory provision to the persons contemplated by that statutory provision. [The interim review was planned and undertaken solely for the purpose of meeting the requirements of the relevant standard.] The statutory audit [and the interim review] [was/were] not planned or undertaken, and the working papers were not created prepared, in contemplation of your appointment as statutory auditor or for the purpose of assisting you in carrying out your appointment as statutory auditor.

Neither you nor anyone else should rely on the information to which access is provided, or any explanations given in relation to that information. The information cannot in any way serve as a substitute for the enquiries and procedures that you should undertake and the judgments that you must make for any purpose in connection with the audit for which you are solely responsible as the auditor.

If notwithstanding this letter you rely on the information for any purpose and to any degree, you will do so entirely at your own risk.

[Insert where applicable:]

[We will remove/ have removed from the audit working papers all material in respect of which legal professional privilege is asserted.][10]

[Thank you for your confirmation that you/ the Company will meet the reasonable costs that we will incur in giving access. [As already agreed] these will not exceed £*.]

In accordance with the guidance issued under Audit Regulation 3.09:

(a) you should refuse to accept an additional engagement, such as to act as an expert witness or to review the quality of our audit work, where the engagement would involve the use of the information obtained by you under the Regulation;
(b) you should not comment on the quality of our audit work unless required to do so by a legal or professional obligation;
(c) the information should not be disclosed beyond persons who have a need to access the information where to do so is a necessary part of your audit work, nor should the information be disclosed to a third party including the [Company/ Companies] (although this does not prevent you discussing the information with the [Company/ Companies] where to do so is a necessary part of your audit work, or providing information to any third party if that is required of you by a legal or professional obligation).

In the event that access to information involves your having access to any intellectual property of ours or any material in which we have copyright, we do not grant permission to you to use or exploit that intellectual property or copyright and you must respect the same at all times.

When in this letter we refer to ourselves, we include [any person or organisation associated with this firm through membership of the international association of professional service firms to which this firm belongs], our [and their] partners, directors, members, employees and agents. This letter is for the benefit of all those referred to in the previous sentence and each of them may rely on and enforce in their own right all of the terms of this letter.

Yours faithfully

[Predecessor]

cc The Company/Companies

---

[10] See Section 6, paragraphs 45 to 48 on Legal Professional Privilege.

Appendix D – Money laundering – interim guidance for auditors in the united kingdom

Extract from Practice Note 12 Resignation and communication with successor auditors

56 The auditor may wish to resign from the position as auditor if the auditor believes that the client or an employee is engaged in money laundering or any other illegal act, particularly where a normal relationship of trust can no longer be maintained. Where the auditor intends to cease to hold office there may be a conflict between the requirements under section 519 of the Companies Act 2006 for the auditor to deposit a statement at a company's registered office of any circumstances that the auditor believes need to be brought to the attention of members or creditors and the risk of 'tipping off'. This may arise if, for example, the circumstances connected with the resignation of the auditor include knowledge or suspicion of money laundering and an internal or external disclosure being made. See section 9 of CCAB Guidance for guidance on cessation of work and resignation.

57 Where such disclosure of circumstances may amount to 'tipping off', the auditor seeks to agree the wording of the section 519 disclosure with the relevant law enforcement agency and, failing that, seeks legal advice. The auditor seeks advice from the MLRO who acts as the main source of guidance and if necessary is the liaison point for communication with lawyers, SOCA and the relevant law enforcement agency. The auditor may as a last resort need to apply to the court for direction as to what is included in the section 519 statement.

58 The offence of 'tipping off' may also cause a conflict with the need to communicate with the prospective successor auditor in accordance with legal and ethical requirements relating to changes in professional appointment. For example, the existing auditor might feel obliged to mention knowledge or suspicion regarding suspected money laundering and any external disclosure made to SOCA. Under section 333C of POCA this would not constitute 'tipping off' if it was done to prevent the incoming auditor from committing a money laundering offence. However, as an audit opinion is rarely used for money laundering purposes, this is unlikely to apply in an audit situation.

59 If information about internal and external reports made by the auditor is considered relevant information for the purposes of paragraph 9 of Schedule 10 of the Companies Act 2006[11], the auditor considers whether the disclosure of that information would constitute a 'tipping off' offence under section 333A, because it may prejudice an investigation. If the auditor considers a 'tipping off' offence might be committed, the auditor speaks to SOCA to see if they are content that disclosure in those circumstances would not prejudice any investigation. The auditor may, as a last resort, need to apply to the Court for directions as to what is disclosed to the incoming auditor.

60 Where the only information which needs to be disclosed is the underlying circumstances which gave rise to the disclosure, there are two scenarios to consider:

- Where the auditor only wishes to disclose the suspicions about the underlying criminal conduct and the basis for those suspicions, the auditor will not commit

---

[11] SI 2007/3494 "The Statutory Auditors and Third Country Auditors Regulation 2007" comes into force on 6th April 2008 and requires the auditor to make available all relevant information held in relation to hold the office as auditor to a successor auditor.

an offence under POCA if that information only is disclosed. For example, if audit files are made available to the incoming auditor containing working papers that detail circumstances which have lead the audit team to suspect the management of a fraud and this suspicion is noted on the file, this will not constitute a 'tipping off' offence.
- If the auditor wishes to disclose any suspicions specifically about money laundering (for example, if the working papers in the example above indicated that the suspected fraud also constituted a suspicion of money laundering), then as a matter of prudence, the approach adopted follows that described in paragraphs 56 and 57 in relation to the section 519 statement.

[AAF 01/09]
Technical Release: Paid cheques

AAF 01/09 is issued by the Audit and Assurance Faculty of the Institute of Chartered Accountants in England and Wales (ICAEW) in February 2009. It gives guidance for practitioners who need to examine paid cheques for the purposes of an engagement, being designed to give practical help on streamlining the procedures for obtaining paid cheques to make the exercise as cost effective as possible.

AAF 01/09 does not constitute an auditing or assurance standard. Professional judgement should be used in its application and procedures adapted to the circumstances of the engagement.

Introduction

This guidance is designed for practitioners who need to examine paid cheques for the purposes of an engagement. It is intended to give practical help on streamlining the procedures for obtaining paid cheques to make the exercise as cost effective as possible.

It is many years since banks returned paid cheques to their customers with their bank statements, and it is no longer a standard audit procedure to check a sample of paid cheques for evidence that a payment recorded in the audit entity's accounts was made to the person named in the record and in the amount shown. Many companies now make payments electronically and the proportion of payments made by cheque has decreased; this, coupled with improvements in practice relating to cheques paid to "a/c payee only" means that the inspection of paid cheques as an audit technique has become the exception rather than the rule. However, there may be occasions when the auditors' assessment of internal control and risk causes them to decide to review paid cheques.

In addition, the Solicitors' Accounts Rules (SAR) still require testing of paid cheques (or digital images of the front and back). Although the number of cheques being used by solicitors is declining, there is still a significant volume, particularly where there are large numbers of private individuals as clients rather than companies.

The Audit and Assurance Faculty has therefore decided to update the guidance on obtaining paid cheques, which was last revised in 1993 (FRAG 27/93), to bring the material into line with current banking practice.

This guidance has been agreed between the Institute of Chartered Accountants in England and Wales and the British Bankers' Association. However, the banks do not have a standard, common procedure for storing, retrieving or returning paid cheques to customers. If paid cheques are needed, therefore, auditors and reporting accountants will need to discuss with their client and/or the bank on a case by case basis how paid cheques are to be obtained and request that their client make appropriate arrangements with the account holder.

The charges levied by a bank for returning paid cheques are the subject of a contractual agreement between the bank and the client (customer), which therefore normally bears the cost of the service.

Solicitors' Accounts Rules

Rule 32(10) of the SAR requires the solicitor to retain all original paid cheques for the withdrawal of money from a client account (or digital images of the front and back of all original paid cheques) for at least two years, unless there is a written arrangement with the bank that it will retain the original cheques on the solicitor's behalf for that period. Alternatively, in the event of destruction of any original cheques, the bank, building society or other financial institution will retain digital images of the front and back of those cheques on the solicitor's behalf for that period and will, on demand by the solicitor, the solicitor's reporting accountant or the Solicitors Regulation Authority, produce copies of the digital images accompanied, when requested, by a certificate of verification signed by an authorised officer. It is now common practice for reporting accountants to obtain digital images rather than original paid cheques, as this is the format in which the documents are generally stored.

Means of obtaining paid cheques

8   Banks keep paid cheques – where they have not already been returned to the customer or the customer's agent – for varying periods. However, the Money Laundering Regulations 2007 require that supporting evidence and records (which include paid cheques) must be retained for a period of at least five years after the date on which the relevant transaction or series of transactions is completed. Such records must be the original documents or copies admissible in court proceedings. Where paid cheques are not returned to the customer or the customer's agent they should be kept, in their original form, for at least one year. Thereafter, paid cheques will be available, if not in their original form, then in the form of legally admissible copies, for the remainder of the five year period mentioned above.

9   While a bank can usually provide paid cheques if a customer asks for them, finding the cheques may well take some time. Some banks hold cheques centrally, others at individual branches. The cheques are normally filed in batches according to their date of payment: within each batch, the cheques may be sorted into account number order, but not all banks do this. Retrieving paid cheques will, therefore, almost certainly involve a significant amount of manual work, and this will increase in proportion to the number of batches that have to be searched. This means that, if the sample is drawn from cheques that will have cleared on different dates, the larger the sample, the greater is likely to be the cost to the client unless all paid cheques are returned to the client as a matter of course.

10 If it is decided that an examination of paid cheques is to be carried out, the auditor/reporting accountant can ask the client (that is, the account holder) to agree with the account-holding branch how, and in what format, paid cheques should be retrieved. Alternatively, the auditor/reporting accountant may approach the branch direct if the account holder has given appropriate authority. It may be possible to instruct the bank before the start of the year in question to collect and send cheques on a regular basis, rather than locating paid cheques after the year end. Such advance arrangements will be particularly useful for work in connection with SAR for which examination of paid cheques (or legally admissible copies) is a standard procedure. However, advance arrangements will often not be practical, for example where the sample selection of paid cheques is linked to the sample testing of payments from client accounts, so that the sample cannot be selected until after the period has ended. Practitioners may also wish to retain control of the sample selection itself, rather than leaving this to the bank.

11 So far as procedures for providing paid cheques are concerned, the account-holding bank may have a preference for one of the following options:

(a) to return all paid cheques to the customer concerned. Although most banks no longer return all paid cheques to their customers, in some cases this may be the most cost-effective way of providing paid cheques. Auditors/reporting accountants will need to consider whether they are content for paid cheques to be made available in this way, and the possible cost to their client;

(b) to provide a pre-arranged number of paid cheques direct to the auditor/reporting accountant, the selection to be left to the account-holding branch (but see the comments in the last paragraph in this subsection).
Where the auditor/reporting accountant only needs to see a random selection of their client's paid cheques, this may be the most cost-effective method. The auditor/reporting accountant will need to obtain an appropriate form of authority from the customer (see the appendix) in order that the bank can send the paid cheques direct to the auditor/reporting accountant. The auditor/reporting accountant may wish to consider obtaining such an authority before

the assignment is undertaken, particularly if such a measure is seen as acting as a deterrent to fraud.

The auditor/reporting accountant tells the account-holding branch how many paid cheques to provide unless the auditor/reporting accountant is content to leave this to the discretion of the branch concerned. The selection process should make due allowance for the need to guard against fraud; for example, it would normally be inadvisable to make the selection from cheques paid during the course of a few days only.

This option may not be appropriate for SAR reporting engagements, where the selection of a sample is often part of a risk assessment, and may be linked to other procedures such as the selection of client payments for testing. In addition, SAR rule 42(1)(c) requires the sample of payments from client account to be selected from the bank and building society statements and reporting accountants are likely to want to keep control of the sample selection;

(c) to provide photocopies or digital scans of paid cheques.

In some cases, it may be easier for the account-holding bank – and therefore less costly for the customer – to provide photocopies of paid cheques, or copies of comparable authenticity created by other image-retrieval procedures. Such copes should nevertheless permit an auditor/reporting accountant to check payee names, payment authorisations, the date of a cheque, and the cheque amount. If it is agreed that copies or digital images will be provided by the bank, reporting accountants are reminded that images of the backs as well as the fronts of cheques are required for SAR purposes. Checking the reverse of paid cheques may also be necessary where the auditor suspects fraud, although fraudulent endorsement should only be possible where the cheque is not pre-printed crossed 'account payee';

(d) to extract paid cheques before they are stored, for despatch to the auditor/reporting accountant direct.

It may be possible for a bank to extract paid cheques, and send them direct to the auditor/reporting accountant, as part of the sorting process and before they are stored. In this case, the account-holding branch will need adequate prior notification from its customer – not less than, say, one month. In addition, the branch will need an appropriate form of authority from its customer before paid cheques can be despatched to the auditor/reporting accountant (see the appendix). This option may not be used very often, however, as there could be a very large number of paid cheques if they were all sent to the auditor/reporting accountant. The cheques would have to be kept safely in accordance with the Money Laundering Regulations referred to in paragraph 8 above, unless the auditor/reporting accountant arranged to return them to the bank or the client; or

(e) providing specific paid cheques at the auditor's/reporting accountant's request.

An auditor may, from time to time, need to examine a particular cheque or cheques. As explained in paragraph 9 above, this may be expensive, and such requests should not be made lightly. If such a request is to be made, the following details should be provided to the account-holding branch:

the date the cheque was paid;
the amount;
the cheque number; and
the payee name.

It should be possible to obtain this information from the customer's own records and/or from the bank statements.

The methods set out above will generally be useful when seeking a sample of paid cheques throughout an audit period. However, if the audit approach only requires examining cheques in unusual circumstances, these methods may not always be appropriate.

Truncation

13 Truncation (the process whereby cheques can be retained at a processing centre rather than at the individual branch) does not preclude the provision of documentary evidence such as cheques. Even where the movement of paper between bank branches is restricted, cheques can still be provided in the manner outlined in paragraphs 8 to 11 above.

Appendix: suggested form of authority where paid cheques are to be sent to an auditor/reporting accountant direct

To: [name and address of account-holding Date
    Bank branch]

Dear Sirs

[NAME OF CUSTOMER AND ACCOUNT NUMBER(S) AND SORT CODES(S)]

We should be grateful if you would provide our auditors (name and address given below) with such paid cheques or other vouchers as they may request in respect of the above account(s).

It is understood that a charge may be made for providing these items.

This authority is to remain in force until [date]/further notice*.

The name and address of our auditors are as follows:

[Firm name
and address]

Yours faithfully

Authorised signature**

*   *Delete as appropriate*

** *This form of authority must be signed in accordance with the current mandate held by the bank*

Audit Regulations and Guidance 2008

Abbreviations

The following abbreviations are used in this booklet:

ICAEW	The Institute of Chartered Accountants in England and Wales
ICAI	The Institute of Chartered Accountants in Ireland
ICAS	The Institute of Chartered Accountants of Scotland
APB	Auditing Practices Board
ACCA	Association of Chartered Certified Accountants
CPD	Continuing professional development
ISA	International Standards on Auditing (UK and Ireland)
ISQC1	International Standard on Quality Control (UK and Ireland) 1
PII	Professional indemnity insurance
RSB	Recognised Supervisory Body

Preface

Changes to the audit regulations

The Audit Regulations were first issued in 1991, revised in 1995 and this is the second major revision. The following gives a brief outline of the contents of each chapter.

Chapter 1 – General

This chapter contains interpretative, transitional regulations and details of how documents may be served on the Institute and by the Institute on firms.

Schedule – Definitions and interpretation

This section contains all the definitions used in the regulations. When used in the regulations the defined terms are shown in *italics*.

Chapter 2 – Eligibility, application for registration, continuing obligations and cessation of registration

Chapter 2 contains key regulations on eligibility requirements. These are set out as what a sole practitioner must do, and then extra requirements are added for firms. Then there are regulations about the application process and regulations covering a registered auditor's obligations to:

- comply with the regulations (some of which extend beyond the cessation of a firm's registration);
- cooperate with the Institute;
- notify changes to the Institute; and
- pay registration fees.

Where a registered auditor has other audit firms as principals, then that firm must be represented at meetings by some one with an audit qualification.

Registered auditors who are part of a network or who have affiliates have to make details of these available to the public.

There are also regulations which deal with situations when a registered auditor cannot, for some reason, comply with the regulations. Finally there are regulations about how registration may cease and the consequences that may follow.

Chapter 3 – Conduct of audit work

This chapter deals with the conduct of audit work. It requires registered auditors to act with independence and integrity, and comply with ethical and auditing (including quality control) standards and legal requirements.

A 'predecessor' auditor must allow the 'successor' auditor access to 'all relevant information' connected with holding the office of auditor on a change of audit appointment and there is a requirement to keep audit working papers for at least six years.

If a registered auditor has any of its audit work undertaken by another firm, or part of a group is audited by another auditor, then the registered auditor must make arrangements concerning access to the audit working papers. There are also notification requirements when a registered auditor takes on a 'major' audit client and an audit appointment ceases.

Other regulations cover requirements about:

- signing audit reports;
- maintaining competence, at the level of the firm and individual principals and staff;
- monitoring the registered auditor's compliance with the audit regulations; and
- appointing an audit compliance principal.

Additional guidance is given in part 2 of this booklet.

Chapter 4 – Appropriate qualifications and responsible individuals

These are key concepts in the regulations. An 'appropriate qualification' is the qualification (or an EEA equivalent) that is needed if individuals are to be counted towards the control percentage. A responsible individual is the holder of an appropriate qualification who has been designated to undertake audit work on the firm's behalf. Such designation must be confirmed by the Institute that registers the firm. Schedule 1 to chapter 4 sets out the relationships between the appropriate qualification (and its EEA equivalent) and responsible individual status. Under UK company law, responsible individuals are statutory auditors in their own right but can only accept audit appointments in accordance with the rules of a Recognised Supervisory Body, which the Institutes are. There is also a regulation about how responsible individual status may cease.

Chapter 5 – Audit affiliates

A principal in a registered audit firm who is not a member of an Institute, the ACCA or a registered auditor, must become an affiliate of the Institute that registers the firm. This chapter deals with how that status is obtained, continued if an affiliate moves between two firms which are registered auditors or if a firm is taken over, or how affiliate status can end.

Chapter 6 – The committees

This chapter deals with the powers and duties of the various committees involved in audit regulation.

Chapter 7 – Regulatory action

The first part of this chapter sets out the regulatory action that can be taken against registered auditors. This includes imposing conditions or restrictions on how a firm operates and suspending or withdrawing registration. It also deals with how orders come into effect. The second part of this chapter allows ICAS and ICAI to offer regulatory penalties to registered auditors.

Chapter 8 – Representation before committees, review and appeal

This chapter sets out the ways in which a registered auditor (or an applicant for registered auditor status) can seek a review and appeal against a decision of a committee.

Chapter 9 – Disciplinary arrangements

This chapter applies disciplinary arrangements to registered auditors.

Guidance chapter 1 – Guidance on fit and proper status

The guidance in this chapter is to assist firms in deciding whether or not the firm, its principals and employees are fit and proper.

Guidance chapter 2 – Guidance on monitoring compliance with the audit regulations

This chapter is to assist firms in complying with the requirements to monitor its compliance with the audit regulations.

Contents

Introduction

Part 1 – Audit Regulations

Chapter 1 – General

Scope and status
Definitions and interpretation
Transitional arrangements
Notifications
Guidance

Schedule 1 – Definition and interpretation

Definitions
Interpretation

Chapter 2 – Eligibility, application for registration, continuing obligations and cessation of registration.

Eligibility
Application for registration
Continuing obligations
Changes in circumstances
Fees
Dispensation
Cessation of registration

Chapter 3 – Conduct of audit work

Independence and integrity
Technical standards
Audit report
Maintaining competence
Monitoring
Schedule 1 – Independence

Chapter 4 – Appropriate qualifications and responsible individuals

Appropriate qualification
Responsible individual
Cessation of responsible individual status
Schedule 1 – Relationship between appropriate (audit) qualification and responsible individual status

Chapter 5 – Audit affiliates

General
Granting of audit affiliate status
Withdrawal of audit affiliate status
Cessation of audit affiliate status
Changes in circumstances
Review of regulatory decisions
Implementation of decisions
Fees

Disciplinary arrangements

Chapter 6 – The committees

Registration Committee
Notification to committees
Review Committee and Panel
Appeal Committee
Procedures of the committees

Chapter 7 – Regulatory action

Section 7A – Firms registered by the Institute of Chartered Accountants in England and Wales, the Institute of Chartered Accountants of Scotland and the Institute of Chartered Accountants in Ireland
    Restrictions and conditions
    Withdrawal of registration
    Suspension
    Urgent orders
    Implementation of committee decisions and orders
Section 7B – Firms registered by the Institute of Chartered Accountants of Scotland and the Institute of Chartered Accountants in Ireland
    Regulatory penalties

Chapter 8 – Representation before committees, review and appeal

Section 8A – Firms registered by the Institute of Chartered Accountants in England and Wales and the Institute of Chartered Accountants in Ireland
    Representation before committees
    Review of regulatory decisions
    Appeal
Section 8B – Firms registered by the Institute of Chartered Accountants of Scotland
    Procedures
    Appeal

Chapter 9 – Disciplinary arrangements

Section 9A – Firms registered by the Institute of Chartered Accountants in England and Wales, the Institute of Chartered Accountants of Scotland and the Institute of Chartered Accountants in Ireland
    Application of disciplinary arrangements
Section 9B – Firms registered by the Institute of Chartered Accountants in England and Wales
    Regulatory penalties

Part 2 – Guidance

Chapter 1 – Guidance on fit and proper status

Background
Principals and employees
Partnerships and corporate practices
Procedures
Cause for concern or notification to the Institute
Appendix A – Fit for proper form for a Registered Auditor
Appendix B – Example of a 'fit and proper' form for individuals

Chapter 2 – Guidance on monitoring compliance with the audit regulations

Introduction
Why is an audit compliance review required?
What is an audit compliance review?
What is involved in an audit compliance review?
Who might carry out the audit compliance review?
When should the audit compliance review be carried out?
What should be the scope of the audit compliance review?
What should happen after the audit compliance review?
Conclusion

Introduction

The Institutes are all Recognised Supervisory Bodies in the UK and Recognised Bodies in the RoI for the purposes of regulating auditors. They must have rules setting out how auditors are regulated, which this booklet contains, with guidance on how they should be followed.

The Institutes are also Recognised Qualifying Bodies in the UK. This means that membership of an Institute, provided it is accompanied by practical audit experience, would qualify a member as the holder of an 'appropriate qualification' (see chapter 4). This in turn allows a member to apply to become a registered auditor. There are other routes to obtaining the appropriate qualification and these are set out in chapter 4.

The objectives of the Institutes in issuing these audit regulations are to make sure:

- registered auditors maintain high standards of audit work;
- the reputation of registered auditors with the public is maintained;
- the application of the regulations is fair but firm;
- the regulations are clear; and
- the regulations apply to all sizes of firm.

Registered auditors must comply with the regulations, which require them to:

- carry out audit work with integrity;
- be and be seen to be independent;
- comply with auditing standards;
- make sure that all principals and employees are fit and proper persons; and
- make sure that all principals and employees are competent and continue to be competent to carry out audit work.

Guidance is given to help firms apply the regulations. This is printed in light type and the regulations are in **bold** type. Where the guidance is too long to be included with the regulations, it has been put into part 2 of this booklet in separate guidance chapters.

As each firm is different, no guidance can be sufficiently comprehensive to cover all firms. Firms may develop other procedures to comply with these regulations but it is compliance with the regulations that is important.

The regulations should be read in conjunction with:

- the Institutes' Code of Ethics (including the fundamental principles);
- publications issued by the Auditing Practices Board:
- International Standards on Auditing (UK and Ireland);
- International Standards on Quality Control (UK and Ireland);
- Ethical Standards;
- Financial Reporting Standards issued by the Accounting Standards Board;
- relevant parts of company legislation in the United Kingdom and the Republic of Ireland; and
- the Professional Indemnity Insurance Regulations.

Each Institute issues a magazine which often has new material on audit related matters. The ICAEW publishes Accountancy, ICAS the CA Magazine and ICAI Accountancy Ireland. One of these should also be read. In addition, Audit News is issued by the Institutes and contains information for registered auditors, including changes to the regulations.

9   Schedule 1 to chapter 1 contains definitions and interpretation of these regulations which apply both to the regulations and the related guidance. A word or phrase which is defined in schedule 1 is printed in *italics* when used in the regulations.

How to become and continue to be a Registered Auditor

To help firms, a brief step-by-step guide follows. This is a summary, and firms need to pay particular attention to the regulations and guidance provided in this booklet. Firms should also refer to material listed in paragraphs 7 and 8 above.

Becoming a Registered Auditor

Obtain an application form from one of the Institutes.	See the list of telephone numbers at the end of this introduction.
Make sure that the firm meets the eligibility criteria.	See regulations 2.02 and 2.03.
Make sure that the firm, all principals and employees are fit and proper.	See the guidance on fit and proper status (part 2, guidance chapter 1).
Check that the firm has adequate professional indemnity insurance (PII).	See regulation 2.02(b) and the separate PII regulations of your registering Institute.
Make sure that all principals and employees who will deal with audit work are competent to do so.	See regulation 3.17.
Are all the principals members of one of the Institutes or the ACCA or a registered auditor?	If they are not, non-members need to become audit affiliates of the registering Institute (chapter 5).

Fill in and return the application form with a cheque for the registration fees.

Remaining a Registered Auditor

At least once a year check that:

• principals and employees are fit and proper persons;	See regulation 3.06 and the guidance on fit and proper status (part 2, guidance chapter 1).
• principals and employees who carry out audit work are competent and complying with CPD guidelines;	See regulation 3.17 and the guidance from your registering Institute on continuing professional development.
• the firm is competent in the conduct of audits;	See regulation 3.18.
• principals and employees are independent;	See regulation 3.02 and 3.03.
• PII is in place and adequate;	See regulation 2.02 (b).
• the firm's quality control procedures are being complied with;	See regulation 3.20 and the guidance on monitoring compliance with the audit regulations (part 2, guidance chapter 2).
• each audit reappointment has been properly considered;	See regulation 3.05.

- the annual registration fee is paid promptly; See regulation 2.13.

When necessary make sure that:
- all changes are notified within ten business days; See regulations 2.11 and 5.09.
- details of a firm's network and members and affiliates of the network are kept up to date; See regulation 2.12.
- new principals and employees are independent, fit and proper, and competent; See regulations 3.02, 3.05 and 3.20.
- the firm properly considers each audit appointment to new clients; See regulations 3.03 and 3.05.
- if you cease to hold an audit appointment, then the notifications to the oversight body or the Institute may be needed; See guidance under regulation 3.08.
- changes in 'major audit' appointments are notified within 21 business days. See regulation 3.15.

Help and advice

While registered auditors must comply with the regulations and the related pronouncements and guidelines, help and advice is available. The Institutes and other organisations (such as training consortia) can offer advice and give practical help.

Telephone numbers

Institute of Chartered Accountants in England and Wales:
- Professional Conduct Department (Audit Regulation): +44 (0)1908 546 302
  - application forms +44 (0)1908 546 336
  - queries on audit regulations +44 (0)1908 546 336
  - professional indemnity insurance
- Technical enquiries +44 (0)1908 248 025
- Ethical enquiries +44 (0)1908 248 258
- Advice on practice matters +44 (0)1908 248 186
- Support members helpline +44 (0)800 917 3526
- Audit and Assurance Faculty +44 (0)20 7920 8526
- Audit related courses +44 (0)20 8247 1646
- Audit related books and manuals +44 (0)87 0777 2906
- Learning and Professional Development Department:
  - queries on appropriate qualifications +44 (0)1908 248 028

Application forms and other information, including the audit regulations can be found at www.icaew.com/auditnews. Information about PII is at www.icaew.com/pii.

Institute of Chartered Accountants of Scotland:

- Professional Authorisation Department: +44 (0)131 347 0282
  - application forms   +44 (0)131 347 0282
  - queries on audit regulations   +44 (0)131 347 0286
  - professional indemnity insurance   +44 (0)131 347 0282
  - queries on appropriate qualifications   +44 (0)131 347 0241
- Technical enquiries   +44 (0)131 347 0280
- Ethical enquiries   +44 (0)131 347 0232
- Audit related courses   +44 (0)131 347 0138
- Audit related books and manuals

Application forms and other information, including the audit regulations can be found at www.icas.org.uk. Information about PII is at www.icas.org.uk.

Institute of Chartered Accountants in Ireland:

If you are telephoning within the Republic of Ireland, telephone 01 6680400 for all enquiries. From the United Kingdom, use the following numbers:

- Chartered Accountants Regulatory Board: +44 (0)28 9023 1541
  - application forms   +44 (0)28 9023 1541
  - queries on audit regulations   +44 (0)28 9023 1541
  - professional indemnity insurance   00 353 1637 7200
- Technical enquiries   +44 (0)28 9023 1541
- Ethical enquiries   +44 (0)28 9032 1600
- Audit related courses   +44 (0)28 9032 1600
- Audit related books and manuals
- Education and Training Department:
  - queries on appropriate qualifications   00 353 1637 7200

Application forms and other information, including the audit regulations can be found at www.carb.ie. Information about PII is at www.carb.ie.

Audit Regulations

Chapter 1

General

This chapter deals with the scope and interpretation of the regulations, transitional arrangements and how notifications should be made between the Institute and firms.

The regulations apply to all firms regardless of the registering Institute, unless stated otherwise.

The regulations are printed in **bold** type and guidance in light type. Where defined terms (see schedule 1) are used in the regulations they are printed in *italics*. This does not apply to the guidance.

Guidance is provided to help registered auditors to comply with the regulations. However, each firm is different and no guidance can be sufficiently comprehensive to deal with all firms. Firms may develop their own procedures to comply with these regulations, but it is compliance with the regulations that is essential. It should be noted that in some instances, for example regulation 3.09, the guidance is prescriptive and should be followed.

A copy of any changes or amendments to these regulations will be sent to the audit compliance principal.

Scope and status

These *regulations* apply to *firms* seeking registration and to *firms* registered by the Institute as eligible for appointment as a registered auditor under the *Act*. The *regulations* also apply to *principals* and *responsible individuals* of the *firm*. In certain instances the *regulations* continue to apply notwithstanding that registration has ceased. 1.01

Each Institute is a Recognised Supervisory Body under the legislation of the United Kingdom, and a Recognised Body under legislation in the Republic of Ireland. Each Institute can register auditors in each country. Unless a Registration Committee decides otherwise, this usually means that a firm registered by an Institute can carry out audits of companies incorporated in the other jurisdiction.

There are exceptions as follows.

- Sole practitioners whose audit qualification derives from Section 161(1)(b) of the Companies Act 1948 (adequate knowledge and experience or pre-1947 practice) cannot be registered in Northern Ireland because this qualification is not recognised there. This exception also applies to partnerships if all the partners only have this qualification.
- A similar situation exists for firms registered under the laws of Northern Ireland. They cannot be registered in Great Britain if they are sole practitioners whose audit qualification derives from Section 155 of the Companies Act (Northern Ireland) 1960 (adequate knowledge and experience or pre-1960 practice). This exception also applies to partnerships if all the partners only have this qualification.

These *regulations* are issued by authority of *Council*. 1.02

Definitions and interpretation

The definitions of terms used in the *regulations* and the rules of interpretation are in schedule 1 to this chapter. Section headings are not part of the *regulations* and are for guidance only. 1.03

Transitional arrangements

These *regulations* come into force on 6 April 2008 subject to regulation 1.05. From this date the Audit Regulations (December 1995 edition, as amended) are no longer in force, subject to regulations 1.05 and 1.06. 1.04

Regulations 3.09, 3.13, 3.14 and 3.16 come into effect as specified in those *regulations*. 1.05

The liability of a *principal*, *audit affiliate* or *registered auditor* to regulatory or disciplinary action is to be determined in accordance with the regulations in force at the time that the matter now the subject of regulatory or disciplinary action occurred, but the regulatory or disciplinary proceedings shall be conducted in accordance with these regulations (including any subsequent amendments). 1.06

The above means that whether or not there has been an 'offence' under these regulations is determined by the regulations in force at the time the 'offence' took place, but the process of dealing with the matter will be as set out in these regulations (together with any subsequent amendments).

1.07 **The Audit Regulations (December 1995 edition, as amended) remain in effect and must be followed in respect of an *audit* of an entity incorporated in the Republic of Ireland.**

Until the EU's Statutory Audit Directive is transposed into RoI law, any firm that undertakes an audit of an entity incorporated in the Republic of Ireland must comply with the 1995 audit regulations (as amended) in respect of that audit. The effect of this is that, for example, a firm with RoI audits cannot take advantage of the new provisions in chapter 2 of these regulations regarding control of an audit firm and a corporate practice cannot undertake RoI audits. Also, audit work in respect of a RoI audit should be conducted in accordance with chapter 3 of the 1995 regulations, not chapter 3 of these regulations.

Notifications

1.08 **Any notice or document may be served on the relevant registering *Institute* by sending it to the appropriate address as follows:**

> **The Institute of Chartered Accountants in England and Wales: Professional Conduct Department, Metropolitan House, 321 Avebury Boulevard, Milton Keynes, MK9 2FZ.**
>
> **The Institute of Chartered Accountants of Scotland:**
> **CA House, 21 Haymarket Yards, Edinburgh, EH12 5BH.**
>
> **The Institute of Chartered Accountants in Ireland:**
> **Chartered Accountants Regulatory Board, The Linenhall, 32-38 Linenhall Street, Belfast, BT1 8BG.**
>
> **or as otherwise notified to *firms*.**

1.09 **Any notice, decision, order or other document which needs to be served on a *firm* or other person under these *regulations* will be delivered by hand, or sent by fax or post:**

   a   **if it is delivered by hand to the addressee service will take effect immediately;**
   b   **if sent by fax, it will be sent to the latest fax number given by the addressee and service will take effect immediately; or**
   c   **if sent by post, it will be sent to the latest address given by the addressee and service will take effect two business days after posting.**

Guidance

Guidance is provided to help with the application of the regulations. It is distinguished from the regulations by being in light type. In a few cases there is too much guidance to include it with the regulations and so it is included in a separate section after the regulations and cross-referenced.

The guidance is merely that. It is impractical to provide guidance for every situation that may arise and the regulations may be complied with in different but equally valid ways. However, registered auditors must always comply with the regulations, which take precedence over the guidance.

Schedule 1
Definitions and interpretation

Definitions

If a term has more than one meaning defined, the one to use will depend on the country of the registering Institute, or the country of the client being audited as appropriate.

ICAEW   The Institute of Chartered Accountants in England and Wales
ICAI   The Institute of Chartered Accountants in Ireland
ICAS   The Institute of Chartered Accountants of Scotland

In the regulations the following words have the following meanings.

the Act	The Companies Act 2006 of the United Kingdom or the Companies Act 1990 of the Republic of Ireland.
the 2006 Act	The Companies Act 2006.
the RI 1990 Act	The Companies Act 1990 of the Republic of Ireland.
Appeal Committee	The committee of the registering *Institute* appointed under the *Institute's Bye-laws*, regulations or *Rules* with responsibility for hearing appeals against a decision of the *Review Committee* under these *regulations*. When a committee discharges these functions its members are to be treated as officers of the *Institute* for the purpose of regulation 2.04e.
appropriate qualification	A qualification as defined by section 1219 of the 2006 Act or section 187 of the RI 1990 Act.
associate	In relation to an entity, another entity in which it holds an interest on a long-term basis for the purpose of securing a contribution to its own activities by the exercise of control or influence arising from or related to that interest, or which holds such an interest in it. A holding of 20% or more is presumed to create an associate relationship.
associated undertaking	In relation to a *body corporate*: a parent undertaking or subsidiary undertaking of the *body corporate* referred to; or a subsidiary undertaking of a parent undertaking of the *body corporate*.
audit	a) (i) any function in respect of a company incorporated in the United Kingdom or the Republic of Ireland which is required to be performed by a *Registered Auditor* as auditor of that company; (ii) any function in respect of any of the following entities constituted in the United Kingdom or the Republic of Ireland which is required to be performed by a *Registered Auditor* as auditor of that entity: • a building society; • a credit union; • a charity; • an industrial and provident society;

- a friendly society;
- a pension scheme;
- a limited liability partnership;
- a partnership;
- an open ended investment company;
- a unit trust;
- a Lloyds' syndicate;
- a mutual life office; and
- a person authorised under legislation relating to the conduct of investment, insurance or mortgage business;

where such function is expressly required to be discharged either by or under United Kingdom or Republic of Ireland legislation.

b) any function in respect of a company incorporated in the United Kingdom or the Republic of Ireland which is included on the official list which is performed by a *Registered Auditor* following appointment as auditor of that company in relation to its financial statements or extracts of financial statements as required by a listing authority or a recognised company stock exchange in either of those jurisdictions.

The reference above to an 'official list' is to the official list as defined in the Financial Services and Markets Act 2000, Part 6 or to the official list of the Irish Stock Exchange in the Republic of Ireland. It therefore does not include companies whose shares are publicly traded but that are not included in the official list.

The reference above to a 'listing authority' is to the Financial Services Authority in the UK and the Irish Financial Services Regulatory Authority in the Republic of Ireland.

The reference above to a partnership is to a partnership where all the partners are companies or Scottish partnerships and in the latter case, each partner in the partnership is a limited company.

The definition does not extend to reports relating to entities other than those specified.

The definition only embraces those circumstances where a report is required to be provided by a registered auditor in respect of any of the entities specified and the requirement is express and emanates from legislation (whether primary or secondary) or the rules of a recognised stock exchange (in connection with a company admitted to the official list). The definition does not encompass situations where a report is required by a registered auditor but where the firm does not have to be appointed as auditor to the entity (for example, a report about non-cash consideration under section 593 of the Companies Act 2006).

The report must be required by legislation that is applicable solely to one of the entities listed above. Reports commissioned, for example by a grant making organisation, where the grant could have been made to any person, to ensure that beneficiaries of funds have used them appropriately would not fall within the definition (even where the requirement for the body to commission such a report itself emanates from statute).

	Persons authorised under legislation relating to the conduct of investment, insurance or mortgage business are those who can undertake investment advice etc. In the UK these would be entities with permission under Part IV of the Financial Services and Markets Act 2000 (or regulations made under that Act) or equivalent legislation in the RoI
	This definition of 'audit' does not include an independent examination for charities. Nor does it include any report required as part of a public offer of securities (prospectus) required by investment business legislation or any report on a circular to shareholders, required by a stock exchange, to authorise a transaction.
audit affiliate	a) a person granted affiliate status by the ICAEW under clause 12A of the Supplemental Royal Charter of 21 December 1948 for the purposes of these *regulations*; b) a person granted status as an affiliate by the ICAI under Bye-law 41 for the purposes of these *regulations*; or c) a person granted regulated non-member status by the ICAS under chapter XX of the Rules for the purposes of these *regulations*.
audit client	Any person whose accounts are being audited under these *regulations* by a *Registered Auditor*.
audit compliance principal	A *responsible individual* who is either a *principal* of the *Registered Auditor* (or a sole practitioner where the *Registered Auditor* is a sole practice) or a member of its *management board* who is responsible for monitoring that the *Registered Auditor* has complied, and is likely to continue to comply, with these *regulations*, and whose identity is notified in writing to the *Institute* and who is the first point of contact with the *Institute* in connection with these *regulations*.
	The role of the audit compliance principal is to be responsible for ensuring that the firm complies with the audit regulations. A major part of the responsibilities is to make sure the monitoring required by these regulations is carried out. The audit compliance principal need not carry out the reviews personally but should make sure that they are carried out satisfactorily and any appropriate action taken.
audit report	A report by a *Registered Auditor* which relates to an audit.
auditing standards	The basic principles and essential procedures (shown in bold type) in the International Standards on Auditing (UK and Ireland) which are to be construed and applied having regard to the explanatory text and other material in those standards; issued by the Auditing Practices Board.
audit work	Any work done by or on behalf of the *Registered Auditor* in respect of an *audit*.
body corporate	An entity that has a legal personality (including a limited liability partnership) and a similar body constituted under the laws of a country or territory outside the United Kingdom or Republic of Ireland.
business day	A day excluding weekends and public holidays.

Bye-laws	The bye-laws of the ICAEW, the ICAS or the ICAI.
Controller	A person who, alone or with any *associate* or *associates*, is entitled to exercise or control 15% or more of the rights to vote on all or substantially all matters at general meetings of a *body corporate*, or of another *body corporate* of which it is a subsidiary undertaking.
corporate practice	A *body corporate*, excluding a limited liability partnership.
Council	a) the Council of the ICAEW under Clause 2 of the Supplemental Royal Charter of 21 December 1948; b) the Council of the ICAS under Rule 45; or c) the Council of the ICAI under paragraph 3 of the Charter Amendment Acts.
director	Any person occupying the position of director (called by whatever name) in a *corporate practice*. Also any person under whose directions or instructions the directors of the *corporate practice* are used to acting.
Disciplinary Committee	The committee of the registering *Institute* appointed under the *Institute's Bye-laws*, regulations or *Rules* with responsibility for disciplining members, firms and others in accordance with the *Bye-laws*, regulations or *Rules*. When a committee discharges these functions its member are to be treated as officers of the *Institute* for the purpose of *regulation* 2.04e.
Disciplinary Scheme	Any investigation and discipline scheme in which the Institute participates for the purposes of the independent investigation of matters concerning members and firms.
employee	Anyone who carries out audit work for a *Registered Auditor*, including a sub-contractor or a consultant. A sub-contractor or consultant cannot become a responsible individual.
ethical standards	The basic principles and essential procedures (shown in bold type) in the Ethical Standards issued by the Auditing Practices Board which are to be construed and applied having regard to the explanatory text and other material in those standards.
EEA auditor	An individual who holds a qualification to audit accounts under the law of an *EEA member state* other than the UK and the RoI. While an EEA auditor can be counted towards those who control a registered auditor, unless any required aptitude test is taken, an EEA auditor cannot be a responsible individual and so in charge of audit work, see chapter 4.
EEA audit firm	A *firm* eligible for appointment as an auditor under the law of an *EEA member state*.
EEA member state	Any country that is a signatory to the European Union and European Community Treaties (ie EU member states) and Iceland, Liechtenstein, Norway. Gibraltar is also treated as an EEA member state by the 2006 Act.
firm	a) an individual who engages in the profession of accountancy as a sole practitioner; b) a partnership which engages in the profession of accountancy;

	c) a limited liability partnership which engages in the profession of accountancy; or
	d) a *corporate practice* which engages in the profession of accountancy.
Group	A *corporate practice*, any parent or subsidiary undertakings and any parent or subsidiary undertakings of any of them.
Institute	a) the Institute of Chartered Accountants in England and Wales (ICAEW); b) the Institute of Chartered Accountants of Scotland (ICAS); or c) the Institute of Chartered Accountants in Ireland (ICAI).
Investigation Committee	The committee of the registering *Institute* appointed under the *Institute's Bye-laws*, regulations or *Rules* with responsibility for considering complaints against members, firms and others as specified in the *Byelaws*, regulations or *Rules*. When a committee discharges these functions its members are to be treated as officers of the *Institute* for the purpose of *regulation* 2.04e.
management board	Any committee, board or other management body that is responsible for setting and directing the implementation of the *firm*'s policies.
monitoring unit	The *Institute* or any body undertaking monitoring in accordance with paragraph 12 or paragraph 23 of schedule 10 of the 2006 Act.
oversight body	A body which pursuant to the Act is responsible for the regulation and/or supervision of Recognised Supervisory Bodies. In the UK the oversight body is the Professional Oversight Board (www.frc-pob.org.uk) and in the RoI it is the Irish Auditing and Accounting Supervisory Authority (www.iaasa.ie).
Panel	A sub-committee of the Registration Committee of the ICAS.
PII regulations	a) the Professional Indemnity Insurance Regulations of the ICAEW; b) the Professional Indemnity Insurance Regulations of the ICAI; or c) the Professional Indemnity Insurance Bye-laws of the ICAS.
practising certificate	A certificate issued to a member by an *Institute* authorising the member to engage in public practice.
practice notes	Practice notes and bulletins issued by, or with the authority of, the Auditing Practices Board. These give guidance on how auditing standards can be applied and on new or emerging issues.
principal	An individual in sole practice, (where the *firm* is a sole practice), a person who is a partner (including both salaried and equity partners) (where the *firm* is a partnership), a member of a limited liability partnership (where the *firm* is a limited liability partnership) a *director* (where the *firm* is a company) or any individual who is held out as being a company director, partner or member. Corporate practices or limited liability partnerships may be principals, where these regulations allow.
quality control standards	The basic principles and essential procedures (shown in bold type) in the International Standards on Quality Control (UK and Ireland) which are to be construed and applied having regard to the

	explanatory text and other material in those standards, as issued by the Auditing Practices Board.
Recognised Supervisory Body	A body recognised under the *2006 Act* or the *RI 1990 Act* for the purposes of the registration and supervision of *Registered Auditors*.
Register	The register of auditors compiled under section 1239 of the *2006 Act* or section 198 of the *RI 1990 Act*.
Registered Auditor	A *firm* entered on the *register* as eligible for appointment as a statutory auditor under section 1239 of the *2006 Act* or section 198 of the *RI 1990 Act*.
registering Institute	The *Institute* to which the *firm* is applying for or from which it has obtained registration.
Registration Committee	The committee of the registering *Institute* appointed under the *Institute's* Bye-laws, regulations or *Rules* with responsibility for discharging the functions set out in Chapter 6 or any sub-committee of that committee. When a committee discharges these functions its members are to be treated as officers of the *Institute* for the purpose of regulation 2.04e.
regulations	These regulations as modified or amended.
regulatory penalty	An amount imposed with the consent of a *Registered Auditor* as a penalty for breaches of these *regulations* which the *Registered Auditor* agrees have been committed.
responsible individual	A *principal* or employee responsible for *audit work* and designated as such under *regulation 4.01*. The 2006 Act uses the term "senior statutory auditor" for the individual identified by a registered auditor in relation to a specific audit who signs the audit report in his own name on behalf of the registered auditor. This individual must be a responsible individual.
Review Committee	Any committee appointed under an Institute's Bye-laws, regulations or *Rules* with responsibility for reviewing decisions made by the *Registration Committee* as specified in these *regulations*. When a committee discharges these functions its members are to be treated as officers of the *Institute* for the purpose of regulation 2.04e.
Rules	The rules of the ICAS.
voting rights	The rights to vote on all or substantially all matters at meetings of principals or shareholders of the body in question. In deciding what voting rights are to be taken into account, paragraphs 5 to 11 of schedule 7 to the *2006 Act* apply to *corporate practices* and limited liability partnerships, and paragraphs 5 to 7 and 11 of that schedule apply to partnerships.

Interpretation

Words and expressions have the meanings given by the Act and the Interpretation Act 1978 unless defined in these regulations. The definitions in these regulations take precedence.

In these regulations words importing the singular number include the plural number and vice versa. Words importing the masculine gender include the feminine.

Headings do not affect the interpretation of these regulations. These regulations will be governed by, and interpreted according to, the law of the country of the registering Institute.

Any references to legislation, regulations, bye-laws, rules, standards or other documents, will apply to any re-enactment, re-issue or amendment.

Chapter 2

Eligibility, application for registration, continuing obligations and cessation of registration

This chapter sets out the eligibility criteria for becoming a registered auditor and how to make an application. It then sets out the continuing obligations once registered and how registration can end. Chapter 4 has the regulations concerning responsible individuals and chapter 5 has the regulations covering audit affiliates.

A firm registered under these regulations is eligible to carry out audits under the laws of the United Kingdom and the Republic of Ireland. No separate registration is necessary. However, there are some different eligibility requirements which relate to individuals qualified by experience or overseas qualifications and to the composition of a firm. The guidance after regulation 1.01 and in chapter 4 gives further details.

There is no requirement in the regulations for a firm's notepaper to carry a legend stating that it is a registered or statutory auditor. If a firm wishes to use a legend, then a suggested wording is:

'registered to carry on audit work by the [Institute name in full]'.

In addition a firm may describe itself as a firm of registered or statutory auditors.

No *Institute* member or *firm* may accept an *audit* appointment unless registered by a Recognised Supervisory Body.   2.01

Under the EU's statutory audit directive and company law, responsible individuals (see chapter 4) are statutory auditors in their own right. However, statutory auditors can only accept appointment as auditors in accordance with the rules of a RSB, such as the Institutes. The Institutes, as supervisory bodies, have responsibilities under the Act to monitor the work of responsible individuals and auditors they register and to ensure that auditors are complying with legal requirements and the requirements of these Regulations. Thus an individual, even if a responsible individual in accordance with chapter 4, cannot accept audit appointments unless also a registered auditor under these regulations, or the regulations of another recognised supervisory body.

Eligibility

A key purpose of the Act is to make sure that only those appropriately qualified are appointed as statutory auditors. Therefore, under the Act, the Institute, as a Recognised Supervisory Body, must have rules governing the control of registered auditors. For a sole practitioner this is achieved by regulation 2.02 which only allows registration if the practitioner holds an appropriate qualification. Additional conditions for firms that are not sole practitioners are set out in regulation 2.03.

The Act distinguishes between those individuals who are responsible for the audit work on behalf of a firm and those who control the firm. Those who are responsible for the audit work must hold the 'appropriate qualification' (as well as meeting other requirements, see chapter 4). Those who control the firm may be drawn from a wider group. As well as holders of the appropriate qualification they can be other registered auditors, those who hold the equivalent of an appropriate qualification from another EEA state or who are the equivalent of a registered auditor from another EEA member state. This group must hold a majority of the voting rights, or such rights as allow them to direct the firm's overall policy or amend its constitution.

To be eligible for registration a firm must:

- be fit and proper;
- comply with the PII regulations; and
- meet the requirement that it is controlled by individuals who hold the 'appropriate qualification' (see chapter 4), other registered audit firms, EEA auditors or EEA audit firms (the exact requirements are set out in regulation 2.03).

2.02 The *Registration Committee* may register a *firm* only if the committee is satisfied that:

a the *firm* is fit and proper to be appointed as a *Registered Auditor*;
b the *firm* has professional indemnity insurance or other appropriate arrangements as required either by the *PII regulations*, or in the case of a firm which is an employee of an Auditor General under the *Act*, has the benefit of a statutory indemnity;
c the *firm* has appointed an *audit compliance principal* whose name has been given to the *registering Institute*;
d each *responsible individual* has been designated in accordance with *regulation* 4.01;
e if the *firm* is a sole practice, the sole practitioner is a *responsible individual* and the *audit compliance principal* (and if not a member of an *Institute* or a member of the Association of Chartered Certified Accountants is an *audit affiliate* of the *registering Institute*); and
f if the *firm* is not a sole practice, the *firm* meets the additional requirements of *regulation* 2.03.

Regulation 2.02 sets out the conditions which a firm must satisfy to become a registered auditor. The firm either meets the conditions of sub-paragraphs (a) to (f) or it does not. Although the concept of 'fit and proper' in section (a) is difficult to define, this is the most important condition. Guidance on fit and proper status is in chapter 1 of the guidance section.

If a firm knows about any matter which affects whether it is fit and proper, even if it is nothing to do with audit work, the firm must, in confidence, notify the Registration Committee. The committee will not automatically reject the application for registration but will consider the matter further.

Clearly, to be fit and proper, a firm should be complying with the fundamental ethical principles. These are contained in the members' handbook. The following is a summary.

- Behave with integrity (which implies honesty, fair dealing and truthfulness) in all professional and business relationships.
- Be objective in all professional and business judgements.
- Only accept or perform work which the member or firm is competent to do unless outside help is obtained.

- Maintain professional knowledge and skill at the level required to ensure that work is performed diligently and in accordance with applicable technical and professional standards.
- Respect the confidentiality of information acquired as a result of professional work and not disclose any such information unless there is a legal or professional right or duty to disclose nor use it for personal advantage.
- Behave professionally by complying with relevant laws and regulations, avoiding any action that may bring discredit to the profession and behave with courtesy and consideration towards all.

To assess the competence of the firm to do regulated audit work the committee may wish to review other work of the firm. This may be other audit work done in accordance with auditing standards or work to give reports to regulators. A firm which is not working to the expected technical and professional standards might not be regarded as fit and proper.

If the committee finds out about any matters which a firm did not disclose, this will be viewed more seriously than if the firm had disclosed the information voluntarily. Voluntary disclosure also gives the firm the opportunity to inform the committee about any action it has taken to correct the problem.

The PII regulations can be found in the ICAEW's Members Handbook or the ICAI's Members Handbook, and the PII bye-laws are in the Council Statements of the ICAS.

The additional requirements for a *firm* which is not a sole practice are: 2.03

a each *principal* is either:
  1) a member of an *Institute*;
  2) a member of the Association of Chartered Certified Accountants;
  3) an *audit affiliate* of the *registering Institute*;
  4) a *Registered Auditor*;
  5) an *EEA auditor* who is also an *audit affiliate* of the *registering Institute*; or
  6) an *EEA audit firm* which is also an *audit affiliate* of the *registering Institute*;
b individuals who have an *appropriate qualification*, Registered Auditors, EEA auditors, EEA audit firms or a combination of these hold at least a majority of the *voting rights* or hold such rights under the *firm's* constitution as enable them to direct its overall policy or alter its constitution;
c individuals who have an *appropriate qualification*, Registered Auditors, EEA auditors, EEA audit firms or a combination of these hold at least a majority of the *voting rights* in the *management board* or hold such rights under the *firm's* constitution as enable them to direct its overall policy or alter its constitution; and
d where the *firm* is a *corporate practice* the Articles of Association:
  1) require its shareholders to notify it of any changes in the number of shares held in the *corporate practice*, whether the shares are held directly or indirectly;
  2) enable the board of *directors* to require shareholders to supply information about their shareholdings in the *corporate practice* over the previous three years;
  3) enable the board of *directors* to require any non-shareholder whom the *directors* know or have reasonable cause to believe has or had an interest in the shares of the *corporate* practice to supply information about their interests in the previous three years;
  4) enable the board of *directors* to deprive any shareholder of the right to vote if the information asked for in *regulation* 2.03d.3 is not given in the time specified in the request;

5) enable the board of *directors* to deprive any shareholder of the right to vote if the *corporate practice*'s application for registration is rejected under *regulation 2.05*, or registration has been withdrawn under *regulation 7.03*, and the *corporate practice* has been told that the refusal or withdrawal relates to the ownership of any shareholding; and
6) require the board of *directors* to approve any transfer of shares which would result in a shareholder having an interest representing more than 3% of the aggregate nominal value of the issued share capital.

Any principal who is not a member of an Institute or the ACCA or a registered auditor must become an audit affiliate of the registering Institute. This is dealt with in chapter 5.

If all principals and/or shareholders have equal voting rights, at least a majority of the principals/shareholders must hold an appropriate qualification, or be EEA qualified auditors, registered auditors or EEA audit firms. However, if voting rights are not held equally then at least a majority must be held by a combination of individuals who hold an appropriate qualification, EEA qualified auditors, registered auditors or EEA audit firms.

If the firm's policies are set and implemented by a management board, then a majority of the voting rights in that board must be held by a combination of individuals who hold an appropriate qualification, EEA qualified auditors, registered auditors or EEA audit firms.

In assessing whether a partnership or limited liability partnership is eligible to be registered, the following points should be considered.

- Voting rights: if a partnership does not have a specific partnership agreement the Partnership Act 1890 will apply and all partners will have equal voting rights. If the firm is a limited liability partnership and the members do not have a specific agreement to deal with their mutual rights and duties the Limited Liability Partnership Act 2000 will apply and all members will have equal voting rights.
- Non-member principals: if any principals are not members of one of the Institutes, the ACCA or a registered auditor, they must become audit affiliates.
- Small firms: a firm of two or three principals who do not all hold an appropriate qualification will be eligible only if the partnership or limited liability partnership agreement specifically gives at least a majority of the voting rights to principals who hold an appropriate qualification.

A firm may also be controlled by individuals who hold an appropriate qualification, EEA qualified auditors, registered auditors or EEA audit firms who have such rights under the firm's constitution as enable them to direct its overall policy or alter its constitution.

For investment business purposes, different considerations apply for affiliates. Being an affiliate in one regulated area does not automatically give that status in another.

As part of the annual return, firms are asked to reconfirm continued eligibility. If a firm temporarily fails to meet the eligibility requirements, it will not lose its registration if it receives a dispensation under regulations 2.17 – 2.20.

Application for registration

2.04 A *firm* that wishes to register must apply in the manner that the *Registration Committee* decides. The application must include the following:

a   any information that the *Registration Committee* may require to assess the ability of the *firm* to carry out *audit work*;
b   a declaration made with the authority of the *firm* that it agrees to be bound by these *regulations* and will make sure that it complies with these *regulations* at all times;
c   a declaration made with the authority of the *firm* that it will deal with the *Institute* in an open and cooperative manner and inform the *Institute* promptly about anything concerning the *firm* that these *regulations* require;
d   the name and address of the *audit compliance principal*; and
e   an acknowledgement by the *firm* that none of the *Institute*, its officers or staff, members of its *Council* or a *monitoring unit* or the Committees or staff of the *Disciplinary Scheme*, can be held liable in damages for anything done or not done in dealing with any of the functions connected with registration under the *Act* or under these *regulations* or enforcing the terms of either or the monitoring of compliance with these *regulations* in any respect, unless the act or omission is shown to have been in bad faith.

To enable the committee to assess a firm's ability to do audit work as a registered auditor, it may wish to review other work that the firm has already done. This would be work involving auditing standards or expressing an opinion.

Each Institute has its own application form which firms should request from the appropriate Institute.

Regulation 2.04e derives from section 1218 of the 2006 Act.

The *Registration Committee* may: 2.05
a   grant the application;
b   reject the application;
c   grant the application subject to restrictions or conditions; or
d   postpone consideration of the application.

Under regulation 2.05d, the Committee may decide that it can only properly consider a firm's application after it has more information about the firm. The Committee may decide this is best achieved by a monitoring visit to the firm.

A firm can apply for a review of a decision to reject registration or to grant it subject to restrictions or conditions. Details of the review process are in regulations 8.05 to 8.07 for firms registered with the ICAEW or the ICAI. Firms registered with the ICAS should refer to regulation 8.15.

Continuing obligations

A *Registered Auditor* must continue to meet the requirements of these *regulations*. 2.06

Subject to *regulations* 2.17 to 2.20, a *Registered Auditor* must not continue as an auditor if it ceases to meet one or more of the eligibility requirements of *regulation* 2.02 or 2.03. 2.07

The effect of regulation 2.07 is that a firm which for any reason has ceased to be eligible for registration must not continue with an audit appointment unless it obtains a dispensation in accordance with regulations 2.17-2.20.

A *Registered Auditor* must cooperate with the *Institute*, its staff, Committees, a *monitoring unit* or a *disciplinary scheme*. 2.08

2.09 A *Registered Auditor* or former *Registered Auditor* on whom the *Institute* serves a notice requesting information or notice of a visit under regulation 2.23 or 6.02k (or upon whom a notice is served requesting information under the *Act*) must comply with such notice within such period as the *Institute* may allow (or in the case of a notice served under the *Act*, as the notice provides).

When the Institute serves a notice under the above regulation, the notice will specify by when the firm must deal with the matters in the notice. An Institute will always try to give reasonable time for the firm to respond but in some cases it may be necessary to set a short time for the firm to respond. A notice requiring information may also be served under the Act and the firm must supply the information according to the terms of the notice.

2.10 Where a *Registered Auditor* or an *EEA audit firm* is a *principal* or shareholder in another *Registered Auditor*, then its interests at meetings of *principals*, the *management board* or shareholders must be represented by an individual who is either the holder of an *appropriate qualification* or is an *EEA auditor*.

A principal or shareholder in a registered auditor may be another registered auditor or an EEA audit firm. The above regulation then requires that its interests are represented at meetings by an individual who has received audit training and is either the holder of an appropriate qualification or is an EEA auditor. It is important that decisions are taken at meetings by those who have audit experience.

Changes in circumstances

2.11 A *Registered Auditor* must inform the *Institute* in writing as soon as practicable, but not later than ten *business days* after the event:

    a   of any matter, whether relating to the *firm* or to any of its *principals* or *employees*, which could mean that the *firm* is no longer fit and proper to be appointed as a *Registered Auditor*;

    b   if the *firm* is no longer complying with the *PII regulations*;

    c   of any other changes which might affect a *firm's* eligibility to be registered or its ability to conduct *audit work*;

    d   of any change in:
        1) the name or trading names of the *firm*;
        2) the addresses of the *firm's* offices;
        3) the names or principal business address of any of the *firm's principals* or *responsible individuals* including new *principals* or *responsible individuals*;
        4) the details of any other audit registration that any *responsible individual* has in another country, the name of the registering body and any registration number; or
        5) the name or address of the *audit compliance principal*;

    e   if a *responsible individual* leaves the firm or ceases to be a *responsible individual*;

    f   in the case of a *corporate practice*, of any change in:
        1) the name or address of a shareholder or anyone with any interest in the shares; and
        2) any change in the number of shares held by a shareholder or in the number of shares in which anyone has an interest;

    g   of any change in the website address of the *firm*;

    h   of any change in the name or business address of any member of the *management board*; or

    i   of any change in details of any other audit registration that the *Registered Auditor* has in another country, the name of the registering body and any registration number.

The eligibility criteria are set out in regulations 2.02 and 2.03.

If a firm temporarily loses its eligibility, the firm may not necessarily lose its registration as the Registration Committee can waive the eligibility requirements (see regulations 2.17 – 2.20). Therefore, firms should notify the Institute as soon as possible if they are planning any changes so that registration is not interrupted.

A firm should also, under regulation 2.11c, notify the Institute of any matter affecting its financial stability. This would include a principal entering into an individual voluntary arrangement, or a firm reaching a similar arrangement.

The Institute has a duty to keep the information on the public audit register up to date. To do this, firms must inform the Institute of changes. Also a firm that is a member of a network or has affiliates must also keep up to date information about the names of these other firms.

Before a registered auditor appoints a new responsible individual it must seek the approval of the Registration Committee, see chapter 4.

If a firm changes its legal status, for example from a partnership to a limited liability partnership, the new entity will need to register. The registration of the 'old' firm does not carry over. This also applies to a sole practitioner who becomes a partnership or a limited company, the audit registration does not carry over and a new application is needed from the new firm.

A *Registered Auditor* which is a member of a network must: 2.12

a   maintain a list of the names and addresses of all:
      1)   other *firms* in the network and their affiliates; and
      2)   its own affiliates;
b   make that list available to members of the public;
c   update the list with any changes no later than ten *business days* after the change; and
d   inform the *Institute* of the location of the list and of any change to the location no later than ten *business days* after the change.

A network is a larger structure aimed at cooperation which a registered auditor belongs to and which is:

- controlled by the registered auditor;
- clearly aimed at profit or cost sharing;
- under common ownership, control or management; or
- affiliated or associated with the registered auditor through common quality control policies and procedures, a common business strategy, the use of a common brand-name or through the sharing of significant common professional resources.

For the purpose of this regulation an 'affiliate' means any entity, regardless of its legal form, which is connected to a firm by means of common ownership, control or management.

Making the list available to the public would normally mean that the list is held on the firm's website or is on public display at the firm's office or is otherwise available on request.

The Institute has a duty to keep the information on the public audit register up to date. To do this, firms must inform the Institute of changes. Also a firm that is a member of a network or has affiliates must also keep up to date information about the names of these other firms.

Fees

2.13 A *Registered Auditor* must pay such registration fees (to include any costs that the *Institute* is required or has agreed to pay to any other person or body exercising a regulatory or supervisory role in relation to it) as the *Institute* determines, *at the times and at the rates set by it*.

2.14 The first registration fee is due when a *firm* applies for registration. An application fee is also payable with this first fee.

If a firm's application is not accepted, the first registration fee will be refunded.

2.15 The *Institute* may charge a *Registered Auditor* to which its representatives have made a second or subsequent visit as a result of an earlier visit. The *Registration Committee* will decide how much the fee will be.

The Committee may decide that, following a monitoring visit to a firm, it wishes to return to check that the firm is making the necessary improvements in its audit work. A charge may be made for any such visits, although an estimate would normally be given.

2.16 If a *Registered Auditor* has not paid any fees under *regulation* 2.13 or *regulation* 2.15, within 60 days of the invoice date, the *Institute* may withdraw its registration.

Dispensation

2.17 If a *Registered Auditor* ceases to meet one or more of the eligibility requirements of *regulation* 2.02 or 2.03 (where appropriate), or if it considers that it is impossible or impractical to comply with any other *regulation*, it must notify the *Registration Committee* in writing. The notification must be within ten *business days* of the situation arising and must say what has happened and the action which the *Registered Auditor* proposes to take.

2.18 The *Registration Committee* will review the information provided under *regulation* 2.17. If the committee considers that the *Registered Auditor* is taking all practical steps and that these will remedy the position, it may grant the *Registered Auditor* a dispensation from the requirement to comply with any *regulation*.

2.19 In the case of a matter relating to the additional eligibility requirements for a *Registered Auditor* (set out in *regulation* 2.03) the dispensation will not last for more than 90 days, starting from the date that the situation first arose. In any other case the period will be set by the *Registration Committee*.

2.20 The *Registration Committee* will not grant a dispensation under *regulation* 2.18 unless the *Registered Auditor* can satisfy the committee that its continued registration during the dispensation period would not adversely affect an *audit client* or any other person.

The period of 90 days is given by United Kingdom law and the committee cannot extend it. If the situation that gave rise to the dispensation is not put right in the time allowed, the firm's registration will end.

Cessation of registration

A *firm* will cease to be a *Registered Auditor* if: 2.21

a the *Registration Committee* accepts an application from the *firm* to cancel its registration;
b the *firm* ceases to exist; or
c the *Registration Committee* withdraws registration under *regulation 7.03*.

A firm may ask for a review if its registration is to be withdrawn under regulation 2.21c. Withdrawal at the firm's request, or because the firm no longer exists, cannot lead to a review.

If a firm which is no longer registered wishes to register again it can apply in the normal manner.

The *Registration Committee* may require a *firm* which has ceased to be registered to provide evidence that it has resigned from all *audit* appointments and provide details of any audit registrations it has in any other *EEA member state*. 2.22

The committee may wish to satisfy itself that a firm, once de-registered, no longer has any audit clients. If the Registration Committee withdraws registration under regulation 7.03, and the firm is registered to undertake audits in another EEA member state, the Registration Committee will notify the registering body in that EEA member state.

If a *firm* is no longer a *Registered Auditor*: 2.23

a it must still respond to enquiries (made in writing or by visiting a *firm's* office or offices) from the *Registration Committee* in connection with any circumstance that relates to these *regulations* during the time the *firm* was registered;
b it must still respond to enquiries made by another *Registered Auditor* in accordance with *regulation 3.09*;
c disciplinary action (including the imposition of a regulatory penalty) may still be taken for:
   1) any failure to comply with these *regulations* during the time it was registered;
   2) any failure to comply with any *regulation* continuing to have effect notwithstanding that registration has ceased;
   3) any failure to keep confidential any information received in the course of *audit work*.

The *Institute's* right to recover any unpaid fees or other amounts due from a *firm* under these *regulations* does not end when a *firm* is no longer registered. 2.24

The effect of regulation 2.23 is that a firm cannot escape disciplinary action by de-registering. If, in the process of de-registering, the committee places a condition on a firm and that condition is broken then disciplinary action can be taken. There is a continuing obligation to deal with requests for access to audit working papers under regulation 3.09. Finally, de-registering does not remove the firm's obligation to pay outstanding fees.

Chapter 3

Conduct of audit work

The Act states that the Institute, as a Recognised Supervisory Body, must have certain rules and practices to govern the conduct of firms registered to do audit work and the way they do that work. Registered auditors must:

- be independent;
- carry out their work with integrity;
- be fit and proper;
- keep to technical standards;
- be competent and continue to be competent; and
- be able to meet claims against them that may arise from audit work.

There are also other requirements, such as how firms should sign audit reports. Finally there is a requirement that the Institutes monitor registered auditors to ensure they are complying with these regulations. For some types of audit, this monitoring must be conducted independently of the registering Institute.

The law requires that the rules relating to the conduct of audit work have to be written by an independent body. Thus the Institutes have adopted the auditing, quality control and ethical standards of the Auditing Practices Board. The standards adopted are:

- the International Standards on Auditing (UK and Ireland), which deal with the conduct of individual audits;
- the International Standards on Quality Control (UK and Ireland) 1, which deals with the overall system of quality control established by the registered auditor; and
- the ethical standards, which set out the ethical obligations of registered auditors and their personnel with respect to auditor independence and objectivity.

Competence, fit and proper status of principals and employees, and the ability to meet claims are matters that are usually dealt with when a firm first registers. These requirements are dealt with in chapter 2. Once registered, the Institute monitors firms to check that they continue to meet their obligations. Monitoring is by annual returns and visits to firms.

Firms must make sure that they continue to meet the requirements of the audit regulations. For most firms this means having procedures for doing audit work, and checks to make sure that the procedures are followed. The procedures and checks apply to individual audits (for example that audits are conducted according to auditing standards) and also to a firm's audit practice (for example that principals and employees maintain their competence to undertake audit work).

Firms of different sizes and with different types of client will adopt different procedures to comply with these regulations. However, all firms will be aiming to provide a high-quality and cost-effective service which complies with the regulations.

Firms usually have professional indemnity insurance to meet claims against them. However, another aspect of this is the use of appropriate procedures, including review procedures, to reduce the possibility of a matter occurring that could give rise to a claim.

The following regulations, and associated guidance, deal with matters that relate to firms' audit work.

Independence and Integrity

A *Registered Auditor* must not accept an appointment or continue as an auditor if the *firm* has any interest likely to conflict with the proper conduct of the *audit*.	3.01
A *Registered Auditor* must act in accordance with the fundamental principles set out in the Code of Ethics issued by *Council* and the *ethical standards*.	3.02
A *Registered Auditor* must consider its independence and ability to perform the *audit* properly and record this before it accepts appointment or reappointment as auditor.	3.03
A *Registered Auditor* must not accept or continue an *audit* appointment of an entity where:	3.04

a   there exists between the *Registered Auditor* and the entity a relationship where the law prohibits the *Registered Auditor* auditing that entity;
b   the entity is a shareholder in the *Registered Auditor*;
c   the entity can be influenced by a shareholder in the *Registered Auditor*;
d   the entity is a *principal* in the *Registered Auditor*;
e   the entity, being neither a shareholder or *principal* in the *Registered Auditor* has the ability to influence the affairs of the *Registered Auditor*;
f   the *Registered Auditor* is a shareholder in the entity;
g   the *Registered Auditor* is a *principal* in the entity; or
h   the *Registered Auditor* is in a position to exercise influence over the entity.

The above regulation prevents a firm auditing any entity where that entity has some form of shareholder interest in the firm, is a principal in the firm, or can exert influence over the registered auditor. It also prevents a firm auditing an entity where the firm is either a principal or shareholder in the client, or can exert influence over the entity.

The extent of influence is not defined but firms should consider whether an informed third party would consider that influence could exist, even if not being exercised. For the avoidance of doubt, the forms that such influence can take do not include any influence that arises as a result of the auditor's normal relationship with the entity.

Registered auditors are also reminded that the ethical standards and in particular ISQC1 includes material about situations where a firm should consider accepting or continuing an audit appointment.
Schedule 1 sets out the above regulation in the form of a diagram.

The main considerations which should be followed are contained in the Code of Ethics. This is included in the Members Handbook of the ICAEW and ICAI and in the Council Statements of the ICAS. This in turn requires firms to follow the Auditing Practices Board's ethical standards. Firms should refer to these documents for a fuller discussion of the matters that can threaten a registered auditor's independence.

Contracts of employment (with employees, sub-contactors or consultants) may include the requirement to comply with regulation 3.02. If such contracts are not used, for example in the case of principals, a separate statement or appropriate clause in a partnership agreement is advisable.

As well as material on independence, other relevant statements (for example on conflicts of interest) are contained in the Members' Handbooks of the ICAEW and ICAI and in the Council Statements of the ICAS.

3.05 A *Registered Auditor* must always conduct *audit work* properly and with integrity.

Integrity means more than just honesty. It includes fair dealing, truthfulness and the desire to follow and maintain high standards of professional practice.

3.06 A *Registered Auditor* must make arrangements so that each *principal* and anyone the *firm* employs to do *audit work* or permits to be involved in its *audit work* is, and continues to be, a fit and proper person.

Guidance chapter 1 suggests how to assess the fit and proper status of principals and employees, as required by regulation 3.06. There are also sample checklists that firms may find useful in making their assessments. This regulation also applies to sub-contractors and consultants who may assist with audit work. They must satisfy the same requirements as anyone employed directly by the registered auditor.

It is recommended that every principal, employee, sub-contractor and consultant should confirm their fit and proper status every year. This only applies to those, including principals, who deal with audit work. But it may be easier for firms to apply these procedures to all employees, instead of making distinctions that may be a little artificial. In any case individuals must be encouraged to notify the audit compliance principal of any event that affects their fit and proper status as soon as it occurs.

When a registered auditor sub-contracts work to another firm or an individual, whether registered or not, there should be a formal engagement letter or contract. This should make clear who is responsible for the different parts of the accountancy and audit work. A sub-contractor should be treated as an employee for the purposes of the work.

Some of the auditing standards deal with procedures for auditors who use the work of others in connection with the audit. These are:

- ISA 610 'Considering the work of internal audit';
- ISA 600 'Using the work of another auditor'; and
- ISA 620 'Using the work of an expert'.

3.07 A *Registered Auditor* must make arrangements to prevent anyone who is not a *responsible individual* in the *firm* from having any influence which would be likely to affect the independence or integrity of the *audit*.

Regulation 3.07 is particularly important for mixed practices or associated firms whose principals are not responsible individuals, whatever their qualification. The regulation does not prevent such people from taking part in audit work. However, responsibility for the overall direction of the audit, its supervision, performance and reaching a conclusion that sufficient and appropriate audit evidence has been obtained prior to signing the audit report must always be in the hands of responsible individuals.

Where a registered auditor uses, for the purposes of its own audit work (not being the audit of a foreign subsidiary), individuals resident in another country, it should undertake and document appropriate steps to establish, within the confines of the law of that other country, that the individuals are fit and proper, independent and competent to undertake audit work.

Technical standards

Each audit must be conducted in accordance with the auditing standards and the legislation under which the auditor is reporting.

A *Registered Auditor* must comply with the requirements of the *2006 Act* the *RI 1990 Act* and other relevant legislation.   3.08

The requirements include:

- appointment;
- ceasing to hold an appointment and making appropriate resignation statements; and
- the responsibilities of the auditor to report whether financial statements are in accordance with the legislation.

The legislation would normally be:

- Companies Act 2006;
- Companies Act 1963 of the Republic of Ireland; and
- Companies Act 1990 of the Republic of Ireland.

This also includes statutory instruments and other regulations etc made under an act and legal instruments made by an oversight body using powers delegated under an act.

Other relevant legislation would, for example, include laws regulating banks, insurance companies, other financial service entities and so on.

Registered auditors are reminded that in certain circumstances company law requires them to notify the Institute or the oversight body if they cease to hold an audit appointment.

If a registered auditor ceases, for any reason, to act as auditor to a major audit client they are required to inform the oversight body of the reasons for the cessation at the time of cessation. In the UK, the Professional Oversight Board defines what is a 'major audit' for the purposes of these resignation statements. The current list can be viewed at www.frc-pob.org.uk.

For appointments that are not in respect of a major audit client, notification is only required if the audit appointment ceases before the normal time for the auditor's term of office to end, as set out in law. Notification is to the Institute of the reasons for the cessation. This can be either at the time the cessation takes effect or as part of the annual return.

As well as providing the reasons for the cessation, it would be helpful if registered auditors also provide details of the company's registered number and address of the registered office. In certain circumstances the company also has to make a similar statement (to the Institute or the oversight body) and it would be useful if the registered auditor reminded the company of this.

The above notifications are in addition to any other notifications that are required to be made to the client and registering bodies such as companies' house.

3.09 When a *Registered Auditor* (the 'predecessor') ceases to hold an audit appointment and another *Registered Auditor* (the 'successor') is appointed the predecessor must, if requested in *writing* by the successor, allow the successor access to all relevant information held by the predecessor in respect of its *audit work*. If relevant information is to be sought by the successor, it should be sought and provided in accordance with the following guidance. Any information obtained by the successor is for the purposes of its *audit* and must not be disclosed to a third party unless the successor is required to do so by a legal or professional obligation.

Origin and purpose

This audit regulation ("the Regulation") gives effect to the obligation in the 2006 Act that RSBs must have adequate rules and practices designed to ensure that a person ceasing to hold office as a statutory auditor makes available to his successor in that office all relevant information which he holds in relation to that office. The requirement derives from Article 23(3) of the EU Statutory Audit Directive. The Department for Business, Enterprise and Regulatory Reform has stated that the Regulation should provide "the most appropriate minimum requirement in relation to access to relevant information".

The purpose of the Regulation is to assist in maintaining the effectiveness (including cost effectiveness) and the efficiency of the audit process in the context of a change of auditor. The Regulation is intended to reduce the (actual or perceived) risk of changing auditors.

It takes time for a successor to develop a comprehensive understanding of the business of an audit client. A wide variety of different arrangements have existed to facilitate an effective handover between successor and predecessor, including exchanges of letters, discussion, exchange of audit committee papers and minutes, and shadowing of the predecessor at key meetings such as the final audit committee meeting. Before the Regulation it was however unusual for a predecessor to share audit working papers. This was due mainly to liability concerns.

Liability concerns formerly arose in the context of access to audit working papers being allowed voluntarily, but any access will now be compulsory. Further it is no part of the purpose or object of the Regulation to involve one auditor in liability for another's audit. Also the Department for Business, Enterprise and Regulatory Reform has confirmed its view that Article 23(3) and the 2006 Act provision implementing it do not alter the existing liability of each auditor in relation to its respective audit.

Provision is already made separately by statute for the making of representations, for the attendance and hearing at meetings, and for the making of a statement of circumstances, where the predecessor has been removed as auditor, where there has been a failure to reappoint the predecessor as auditor, where the predecessor has resigned as auditor, and where the predecessor has ceased to hold office. The Regulation and guidance do not seek to duplicate that framework, and are framed in recognition of the fact that that framework already exists.

This guidance is separate from and additional to the Institute's Code of Ethics which sets out procedures to be followed before accepting a professional appointment.

Timing

A request for relevant information may be made by a successor once the successor has been formally appointed to the audit client. In all cases the provision of information should be on a timely basis.

"Audit"

It should be borne in mind that the 2006 Act sets out a number of functions that are required of the registered auditor in specific circumstances. These are within the definition of an audit (and so fall within the definitions of audit report and audit work). The situations in which they arise currently include the following:

- section 92   a company applying to re-register as a public company;
- section 428   statement on summary financial statements issued by a quoted company;
- section 449   abbreviated accounts;
- section 714   when a private company makes a payment out of capital for the redemption or purchase of its own shares;
- section 837   when a distribution is to be made by a company and the audit report was qualified; or
- section 838   when initial accounts are prepared for a proposed distribution by a public company.

(Where the registered auditor is appointed to an entity that is not a company similar reporting requirements may apply.)

Procedure

Before making a request for relevant information the successor should as part of its planning consider the need to make a request to the predecessor under the Regulation, and the extent of that request. This will involve judgement by the successor in each case, so as to ensure that necessary request is made and an unnecessary request is not. It is also important to assess what information will be relevant in each case and what will not.

It does not follow that a successor is required or expected to request information in every case, or to request extensive information in a case in which only limited information is necessary. The successor's consideration will include consideration of what work it would do with any information provided to it pursuant to a request. There are specific references to reviewing the predecessor's audit work in ISA 510 (opening balances), ISA 710 (comparatives) and ISA 300 (planning). Accordingly, information is likely to be necessary in particular for such purposes.

The provision of information under this regulation will be achieved more efficiently where the successor auditor is as specific as possible as to the nature of the information being sought. The successor should therefore, wherever possible, avoid a request framed simply as a request for "all relevant information held by the predecessor and concerning the audited entity" or "all relevant information held by the predecessor in relation to the office of auditor". Thus the successor should strive to identify the information required, or the type of information required, as precisely as possible.

For example, where relevant information is requested by the successor, the information will normally be that contained in the working papers produced by the predecessor, and the appropriate request may therefore be for some or all of those working papers. In some audits there will be Institute or APB guidance indicating the working papers expected for such an audit. For example in the case of a financial statement audit, ISAs will indicate the audit working papers to be prepared. In other cases, where there is no guidance, the predecessor will have determined the working papers to be prepared.

Where the information related to audit work is requested by the successor but is not filed on the current audit file but, for example, on a 'permanent' or 'systems' file, or there is a reference to a prior audit file, access should be provided by the predecessor to this information.

The predecessor should be prepared to assist the successor by providing oral or written explanations on a timely basis to assist the latter's understanding of the audit working papers.

Period

Normally the period for which relevant information is requested would be in respect of any audit report relating to a period falling between the beginning of the last financial statements on which the predecessor reported and the date of cessation of the predecessor's audit appointment. The request would include any subsequent review conducted by the predecessor in accordance with guidance published by the APB in relation to published interim reports.

A successor may consider that it needs to have information in addition to that within the period mentioned above. In the normal case, in the interests of cost and efficiency, the successor should first review the information already provided. If after that review a judgment is made that additional information is needed, the additional information sought should be described in writing, as precisely as possible. The successor should be prepared to provide reasons which demonstrate that the additional information is "relevant" information and therefore within the Regulation. Here as elsewhere the successor should be prepared to confirm that the information is needed to aid its audit work for the audit client and not for some other purpose.

Other points

The request for information may be made of the immediate predecessor only.

Because (as indicated above) it is no part of the purpose or object of the Regulation to involve one auditor in liability for another's audit, it would be usual for the basis on which the information is to be provided to be documented in writing by an exchange of letters between the two registered auditors, copied to the audited entity. Guidance on suitable letters is available on each Institute's website as part of a technical release.

There is no obligation to allow the copying of working papers but it would be usual to allow copying of extracts of the books and records of the audit client that are contained in the audit working papers. Generally speaking, where access to relevant information is necessary, the practical arrangements to allow that access to be provided in a cost effective and efficient way should be discussed and agreed between the successor and the predecessor.

A request for information under the Regulation should not be made other than in connection with the successor's audit. The successor should refuse to accept an additional engagement, such as to act as an expert witness or to review the quality of the predecessor's audit work, where the engagement would involve the use of the information obtained by it under the Regulation. In any event, the successor should not comment on the quality of the predecessor's audit work unless required to do so by a legal or professional obligation.

The reference in the Regulation to the information not being disclosed to a third party includes to the audit client. This does not prevent the successor discussing the information with the client where to do so is a necessary part of its audit work. Nor does it prevent the provision of this information to any third party if that is required of the successor by a legal or professional obligation.

Section 1210 of the 2006 Act sets out a list of appointments to which this Regulation and guidance apply. Section 1210(h) allows additional types of appointments to be added to the list. Registered auditors are not required to allow access to their working papers in respect of other appointments.

This regulation only applies in respect appointments for the audits of financial years starting on or after 6 April 2008.

A *Registered Auditor* must comply with the *auditing standards* and the *quality control standards*.   3.10

Guidance included with auditing standards and practice notes gives assistance on how to apply the standards. Some of these also help to show how to apply the standards to the audits of smaller companies. Such audits are likely to be less complex than those of larger national and multinational organisations, so a simpler audit approach may be more suitable. But it must still be properly planned, controlled, documented and reviewed.

A registered auditor must comply with these regulations, the auditing standards and quality control standards as applied in accordance with the explanatory and other material published therewith.

A *Registered Auditor* must keep all audit working papers which auditing standards require for an *audit* for a period of at least six years. The period starts with the end of the accounting period to which the papers relate.   3.11

Both this regulation and regulation 3.12 are about the audit working papers of UK and Irish registered entities that fall within the definition of 'audit' in these regulations.

ISA 230 (audit documentation) details the content of audit working papers. Other ISAs (for example ISA 300 (planning an audit of financial statements)) detail other documentation that needs to be created during the course of an audit. All these papers must be kept for a period of six years starting with the end of the accounting period to which the papers relate.

The audit working papers and other records do not have to be on paper but could instead be held on microfilm or on computers. Whatever method of storage is used, the auditor must also keep a mechanism for gaining access to those papers.

Firms should have a procedure to make a final decision, before any papers are destroyed, that the files are unlikely to be needed again. In cases of doubt they should be kept. The decision could be to destroy every file, or to make some exceptions. Firms should also bear in mind that some papers in the audit file may serve another purpose, for example tax. Care is needed that these are not destroyed when a longer retention period may apply. A firm should keep appropriate records of what files it has destroyed.

3.12 A *Registered Auditor* must make arrangements so that if any of its *audit work* is carried out by another *firm*, then:

a   all the audit working papers created by that *firm* are returned to the *Registered Auditor*; or

b   the other *firm* agrees to keep those papers as required by *regulation* 3.11 and allows the *Registered Auditor* unrestricted access to the papers for whatever reason.

Registered auditors will sometimes 'sub-contract' some of their audit work to another firm. This could be because the audit client is in a remote location and it is more cost-effective to engage a local firm to do any necessary work and it is that relationship to which this regulation is directed.

If this happens, then, under regulation 3.12, all the audit working papers created by the other firm have to be returned to the registered auditor for retention in accordance with regulation 3.11. Alternatively, the other firm may keep the papers. In this case the registered auditor must make sure that the other firm will keep the papers for as long as the auditor would. Also the registered auditor must have the right to have access to those papers at any time, and retrieve them if necessary. As with papers held directly by the registered auditor, any decision to destroy the papers should be made by the registered auditor and not the other firm.

If a registered auditor considers that, despite any agreements with the other firm, gaining access to the papers may prove difficult, the registered auditor should consider changing the arrangements. If this is not possible, the registered auditor should document the steps taken to obtain access to the audit working papers and the reasons why it cannot and any evidence of those steps or reasons. The registered auditor should also document how it has satisfied itself as to the matters dealt with in those papers and any implications for the audit opinion. The registered auditor should use the principles in ISA 230 (audit documentation) and ISA 500 (audit evidence) when considering such matters.

Whatever arrangements are made between two firms, they should be recorded in a suitable letter of engagement or contract. If the other firm is itself not subject to the audit regulations it may be appropriate to include within the letter the full text of the above regulations. The letter may also cover such matters as the scope of work to be undertaken by the other firm.

This regulation does not require the auditor of a holding company to seek and maintain access to the working papers of the auditor of a subsidiary company (but see regulation 3.13). In the United Kingdom and the Republic of Ireland the respective responsibilities of the holding company auditor and subsidiary company auditor are governed by the Act and auditing standards.

3.13 In the case of a group audit where part of the group is audited by a *firm* from a non-*EEA member state*, a *Registered Auditor* must make arrangements so that, if requested by a *monitoring unit* or an *oversight body*, it can obtain from that *firm* all the audit working papers necessary for a review of that *firm's audit work*.

The arrangements referred to above are that the registered auditor either retains copies of the other firm's audit working papers or arranges that it can have unrestricted access to them on request. If, after taking all reasonable steps, a registered auditor cannot make such arrangements, it should document the steps taken to put such arrangements in place and the reasons why it could not and any evidence of those steps or reasons. A registered auditor need not make such arrangements if the relevant audit supervisory authorities in the non-EEA member state have established reciprocal arrangements with the oversight body. To find out if there is such an agreement in place, a list is published by the oversight body.

This regulation only applies in respect of the audits of financial years starting on or after 6 April 2008.

If requested by a competent authority of a country that is not an *EEA member state*, a *Registered Auditor* must provide that body with a copy of its audit working papers as soon as practicable, provided: 3.14

a there is an *agreement* between that competent authority and the *oversight body*;
b the competent authority has requested the audit working papers for the purposes of an investigation;
c the competent authority has given the *oversight body* notice of its request;
d the papers relate to the *audit* of a body that either:
  1) has listed securities in the country of the competent authority; or
  2) forms part of a group issuing statutory consolidated accounts in the country of the competent authority;
e no legal proceedings have been brought in relation to the *Registered Auditor* or the *audit* to which the working papers relate; and
f the *oversight body* has raised no objection to the transfer.

The *Registered Auditor* must also inform the *Institute* of the fact of the request.

For the purposes of this regulation:

- 'audit working papers' are any documents which are held by the registered auditor and are related to its audit of the financial statements of the body referred to in (d) above;
- a 'competent authority' is a body that is designated in the law of the relevant country as having responsibility for the regulation or oversight of auditors. In most cases the body would be the equivalent of an RSB or an oversight body.

There may be occasions when a competent authority in a country that is not an EEA member state is investigating an audit in its own country and requests to see a registered auditor's audit working papers that relate to that audit. This is only permitted in the circumstances set out in the above regulation. Before any papers are transferred the registered auditor should check with the oversight body that it:

- has an agreement with the other competent authority to allow for the transfer of papers;
- has received a copy of the request; and
- has not certified that the transfer of the papers will affect the sovereignty, security or public order of this country.

This regulation only applies in respect of the audits of financial years starting on or after 6 April 2008.

If a *Registered Auditor* is appointed to a 'major audit' client (or a *Registered Auditor* becomes aware that an existing *audit client* is now a major audit client) it must inform the *Registration Committee* in writing as soon as practicable, but not later than 21 *business days* after the event, of the name of the *audit client*, unless the *Registration* 3.15

Committee has given the *Registered Auditor* a waiver from compliance with this *regulation*.

The Audit Inspection Unit of the Professional Oversight Board is responsible for the review of audits of major audit clients. These include listed companies and other very large companies, pension funds, charities and others. The current list of entities for the purpose of this regulation can be viewed at www.frc-pob.org.uk. The Registration Committee must be informed if a registered auditor gains such an audit client or an existing audit client becomes a major audit client. Registered auditors may also find it useful to inform the Registration Committee if a client ceases to be a major audit client even though there is no cessation of office. It would also be useful if, when providing this information, the notification contained details of the financial year end of the first or last audit that the firm undertakes.

Where the Audit Inspection Unit undertakes a full scope inspection visit to a registered auditor which includes the review of 'firm-wide procedures', the Registration Committee will give the firm a waiver from compliance with this regulation. In these cases the firm does not need to notify when a new 'major audit' is acquired (or an existing audit client becomes a major audit client). However, such firms still need to notify the Professional Oversight Board (not the Registration Committee) when they cease to act for such a client as this is a legal requirement.

Note, the above regulation only applies to the audit of UK entities.

3.16 An *audit report* must:

a   state the name of the *firm* as it appears in the *Register*;

b   include the words 'Statutory Auditor' or 'Statutory Auditors' after the name of the *firm*; and

c   if required by law, state the name of the *responsible individual* who was in charge of the *audit*, be signed by this person in his own name and include the words 'Senior Statutory Auditor' after the name of the *responsible individual*.

An audit report has to be signed by the firm with the added description 'Statutory Auditor'. There is nothing to prevent a firm adding any other appropriate description, such as 'chartered accountants'.

In certain cases the law requires that the responsible individual in charge of the audit (known as the senior statutory auditor) should sign the audit report. The individual's name must also be given. This is only required if the audit report is a report on the annual accounts for a financial year of a 'section 1210' entity (see below), a special report on abbreviated accounts or when accounts are voluntarily revised by the directors. The individual's name need not be given in the case of other reports required under the Act (for example a report under section 714 – redemption of shares out of capital) or reports on other entities included in the definition of an audit.

The APB has published guidance (Bulletin 2008/6) on how firms should decide which responsible individual is the senior statutory auditor in relation to a particular audit.

The Act allows, where there is a serious risk of violence or intimidation to the registered auditor or responsible individual, for their names not to be given in published copies of the audit report or the copy filed at Companies House etc. If these provisions, which only apply to the 'section 1210' entities listed below, are to be invoked, it may be advisable for the entity and the firm to seek legal advice.

Other legislation that is not included in the definition of audit, or the constitution of an entity, may call for a report from an auditor. A firm may choose to sign these reports as a statutory auditor. For example, a client may require a report about it to be given to a trade association. That trade association may require the report to be given and signed by a statutory auditor. There is nothing to prevent a firm doing this and the work would not come under these regulations. However, if the Institute receives a complaint about this work, enquiries may be made into the general standard of the firm's audit work. If necessary, enquiries may be made into other work which the firm is signing as a registered auditor or conducting in accordance with auditing standards. Regulation 6.07 gives the Registration Committee the power to enquire into other work undertaken by the firm.

The requirements of this regulation apply to audit reports for financial years beginning on or after 6 April 2008. For entities listed in Section 1210 of the 2006 Act the requirement applies as follows:

- companies, banks, insurers, certain partnerships (see definition of an audit) – audit reports for financial years beginning on or after 6 April 2008.
- building societies – audit reports for financial years beginning on or after 29 June 2008
- friendly and industrial and provident societies that are insurers – audit reports for financial years beginning on or after 29 June 2008.
- Limited liability partnerships– audit reports for financial years beginning on or after 1 October 2008.
- Lloyd's syndicates – audit reports for financial years beginning on or after 1 January 2009.

There is nothing to stop firms adding the name of the responsible individual who was in charge of the audit and having the audit report signed by this person in his own name where this is not required by law. However, the statutory protection against any additional civil liability (if such a liability exists) is not extended in these situations. If a firm intends to do this, the engagement letter should make it clear that if any claim arises it would be against the audit firm and that the individual, by reason of being named and by signing the auditor's report, is not subject to any civil liability to which he would not otherwise be subject.

Audit reports for financial periods starting before 6 April 2008, or the implementation date given above, should be signed in accordance with regulation 3.10 of the Audit Regulations (December 1995 edition, as amended).

Maintaining competence

A *Registered Auditor* must make arrangements so that all *principals* and *employees* doing *audit work* are, and continue to be, competent to carry out the *audits* for which they are responsible or employed. 3.17

Responsible individuals, and employees who are members of an Institute, should also follow other guidance on continuing professional development as detailed below.

The ICAEW has issued 'Continuing professional development' guidelines on how individuals may maintain their competence. This is in the Members' Handbook. ICAS has issued 'Guidelines on continuing professional development' to its members and the ICAI has issued guidance entitled 'Guidance on continuing professional development'.

Audit affiliates who are also responsible individuals should follow the guidance of the registering Institute.

3.18 **A *Registered Auditor* must maintain an appropriate level of competence in the conduct of *audits*.**

Under regulation 3.18 a firm must be able to ensure its competence in the future. Although a firm's ability to audit rests with its principals and employees, these individuals change. It is only by using audit manuals, programmes, checklists, procedures and so on that a firm has a body of knowledge beyond that of the individual principals and employees. These provide the link between the people currently in the firm and those who will join in the future.

The amount of formal documents and procedures will vary according to the nature of the firm's clients. Their use is likely to vary even between different clients of the same firm. Even the smallest firm is likely to need some documentation such as audit programmes and checklists. As a firm grows in size, it will probably develop procedures to help employees and principals use the audit programmes and checklists in order to carry out audit work and comply with the audit regulations.

Any documentation used by a firm in its audit work must be kept up to date if a firm is to retain its audit competence. Smaller firms might join some form of updating service to help them with this.

3.19 **A *Registered Auditor* must make sure all *principals* and *employees* involved in *audit work* are aware of and comply with these *regulations*, the *Act*, any relevant rules and *regulation*s issued under the *Act* and any procedures established by the *firm*.**

It is important that those involved in auditing should understand the:

- requirements imposed on the firm by statute and regulation;
- legal and other requirements relating to financial statements;
- procedures the firm depends on to ensure it does audit work competently; and
- auditing and ethical standards.

A firm needs to communicate its requirements and procedures effectively if everyone is to understand them. This is especially important since principals, employees, laws and regulations change. Training can achieve much of this. The review of delegated work required by ISA 220, 'Quality control for audits of historical financial information', and the checks performed as part of the annual compliance review, can then reveal successful communication -or the lack of it.

Monitoring

3.20 **A *Registered Auditor* must monitor, at least once a year, how effectively it is complying with these *regulations* and take action to deal with any issues found and communicate any changes in procedures to *principals* and employees on a prompt basis.**

Since these regulations require registered auditors to comply with the auditing, ethical and quality control standards, then the monitoring required by this regulation should also include how the firm is complying with those standards.

An annual review can focus simply on the important point of whether audit work is being carried out in accordance with these regulations and ISAs and that the firm's system of quality control complies with these regulations and ISQC1. However, a thorough review of a firm's work can bring benefits and assurance far in excess of the above requirement.

A thorough review could identify areas in which changes could be made to enhance audit quality, situations where clients need extra services, or where excessive audit work can be reduced. Both benefit the firm and provide assurance that the firm is not needlessly exposed to risk through poor work, whatever its cause.

The annual compliance review in its simplest form is in two parts. The first part covers a firm's obligations under the audit regulations such as:

- independence and integrity;
- fit and proper status;
- competence;
- appointment and re-appointment;
- professional indemnity insurance; and
- continuing eligibility.

and under ISQC1 such as:

- leadership responsibilities;
- consultation arrangements;
- human resources; and
- complaints.

The second deals with 'cold' reviews of completed audit work to ensure that ISAs and the firm's audit procedures were followed. It is relatively easy to decide each year what is needed for the first part. The second part is more difficult and involves judgements on the number and frequency of reviews.

How many and which client files should be cold reviewed? Firms will consider factors such as employee turnover, high risk clients, changes to auditing standards and new statutory and accounting standard requirements in deciding which files to review. Some firms will select audits for these reasons and then a sample of other files. However, monitoring experience has shown that if a single file is representative of a responsible individual's work, little may be gained from doing more. A representative sample of two or three audits for each responsible individual should be enough.

One approach to the question of frequency is simply to decide that the work of each responsible individual should be reviewed each year. Completed audit files would be selected and reviewed to make sure that the auditing standards and the firm's procedures had been followed. For many firms this may be the easiest procedure to adopt. In deciding how often to review someone's work, firms will consider factors similar to those used when deciding which files to review. Indeed, there may be particular reasons where the work of a particular responsible individual is reviewed more frequently.

Sole practitioners, firms with only one responsible individual and other small firms may have few audit clients. However, sole practitioners and smaller firms do face the same problems of change as described above and their responsible individuals also tend to retain their own portfolios of clients for lengthy periods. This very familiarity may cause problems and to guard against this a sample of files should be reviewed each year.

Some well-organised firms have well-defined procedures to control the quality of audit work and the resulting audit opinions. This would be another factor in deciding how often the work of responsible individuals is reviewed. However, if the work of all responsible individuals is not reviewed each year, then it should be covered over no more than a three-year period, if this is appropriate to the circumstances of the firm.

Whatever approach a firm adopts for cold file reviews, it should be ready to justify that approach when requested by the Registration Committee.

The compliance review, and cold file reviews carried out as part of that review, are likely to vary in formality according to the size of the firm. However, every firm should be able to provide evidence of its review and, where appropriate, any action taken.

All responsible individuals should be given the results of the monitoring exercise at the earliest opportunity. If improvements are needed, any necessary changes should be made as soon as possible.

There is no need for the firm to conduct the review itself. Some firms may find it more practical and cost-effective to use a service provided by the Institute or some other organisation.

Sole practitioners may also benefit from this exercise if it is carried out by another registered auditor. This could highlight practical ways for a firm to improve procedures and to deliver a better service to clients. Practitioners may also benefit from reviewing another practice.

Using an external reviewer does not reduce the firm's own responsibility for the review or for ensuring that any necessary action is taken

There is further guidance in part 2, chapter 2 on how registered auditors can monitor their own compliance with the audit regulations.

3.21 Each *Registered Auditor* (other than a sole practice) must appoint an *audit compliance principal*. A sole practitioner will be the *audit compliance principal*.

Schedule 1
Independence

This diagram shows the situations which would prevent a registered auditor acting for a particular entity. The diagram deals with the situations set out in regulation 3.04.

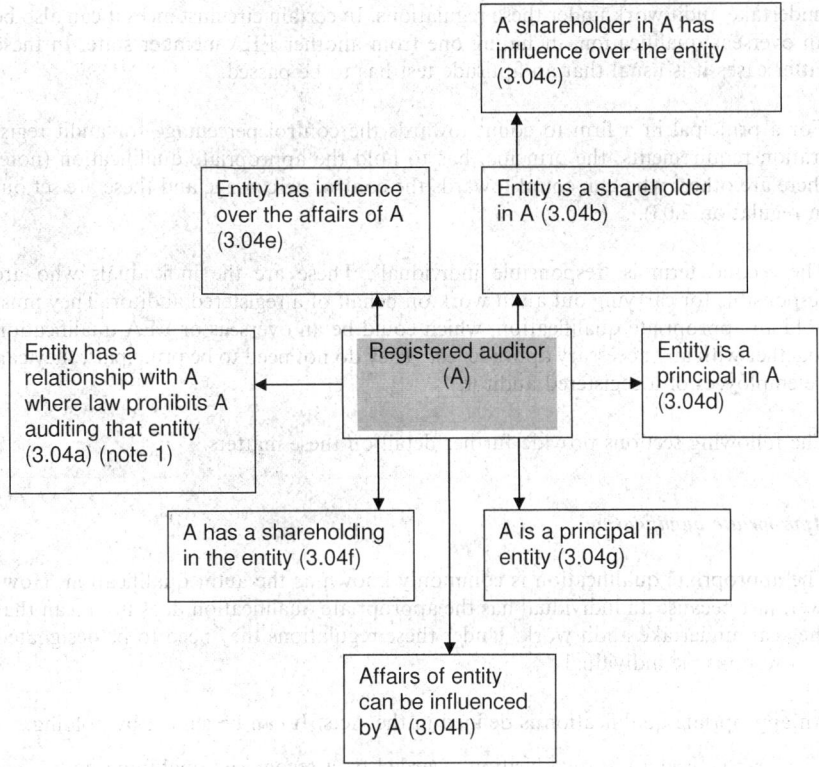

→ Shows the relationship that prevents the registered auditor auditing an entity.

(Note 1)
The law prevents a registered auditor acting as auditor to an entity if the registered auditor is:

- an officer or employee of that entity;
- a partner or employee of an officer or employee of that entity;
- a partnership in which an officer or employee of the entity is also a partner;
- an officer or employee of an associated undertaking of that entity;
- a partner or employee of an officer or employee of an associated undertaking of that entity; or
- a partnership in which an officer or employee of an associated undertaking of that entity is also a partner.

Chapter 4

Appropriate qualifications and responsible individuals

There are two terms that need to be understood as they are important terms in the audit regulations.

The first is the 'appropriate qualification', commonly known as the audit qualification. This is a UK or RoI qualification that must be held if an individual is to undertake audit work under these regulations. In certain circumstances it can also be an overseas qualification, including one from another EEA member state. In these latter cases it is usual that an aptitude test has to be passed.

For a principal in a firm to count towards the control percentage for audit registration requirements, the principal has to hold the appropriate qualification (note, there are others who can count towards the control percentage and these are set out in regulation 2.03).

The second term is 'responsible individual'. These are the individuals who are responsible for carrying out audit work on behalf of a registered auditor. They must hold an appropriate qualification, which could be an overseas or EEA qualification together with any necessary aptitude test. They do not need to be principals, they can be employees of a registered auditor.

The following sections provide further detail on these matters.

Appropriate qualification

The appropriate qualification is commonly known as the audit qualification. However, just because an individual has the appropriate qualification does not mean that they can undertake audit work. Under these regulations they need to be designated as a responsible individual.

An appropriate qualification is defined in the Acts. It can be gained by holding:

- a recognised audit qualification awarded by a recognised qualifying body;
- an approved overseas qualification and, where required, successfully completing an aptitude test; or
- an EEA audit qualification and, where required, successfully completing an aptitude test.

Under the Acts, different audit qualifications and overseas qualifications are recognised. However, the three Institutes are recognised qualifying bodies in both the UK and RoI and thus each Institute's audit qualification is recognised in both jurisdictions.

While individuals from another EEA member state may hold an equivalent 'appropriate qualification' from that country, this is not a UK or RoI qualification and so does not entitle those individuals to undertake audit work. This would only be allowed if the individual has undertaken an aptitude test. The individual then holds an appropriate qualification for the purposes of these regulations. However, since each Institute is a recognised body in both the UK and RoI, no aptitude test is required for members moving between the two countries.

People who held an appropriate qualification under previous legislation are 'grandfathered' and so hold an appropriate qualification. The main ways that members obtained the appropriate qualification under previous legislation were:

- by membership of a recognised professional body (which includes the Institutes) on the following specific dates:
    - for the United Kingdom (excluding Northern Ireland), **both** 31 December 1989 **and** 30 September 1991, (under the Companies Act 1989);
    - for Northern Ireland, **both** 1 January 1990 **and** 29 March 1993, (under the Companies (Northern Ireland) Order 1990); and

- for the Republic of Ireland, 31 December 1990, (under the Companies Act 1990 of the Republic of Ireland);
- by gaining a recognised audit qualification awarded by a recognised qualifying body (eg from the Institutes).

If an individual is not sure about an appropriate qualification, they can obtain advice from the registering Institute (contact details are in the introduction to the regulations).

For those who want to be registered in the United Kingdom, that qualification must be recognised under the 2006 Act. For those registering in the Republic of Ireland, the qualification must be recognised under the RI 1990 Act. These acts may not recognise the same qualifications as each other, but they all recognise the qualifications awarded by the Institutes.

Responsible individual

Responsible individuals are those individuals who are responsible for the audit work in a registered auditor.

Under company law, responsible individuals are statutory auditors in their own right. Statutory auditors can only accept appointment as auditors in accordance with the rules of a Recognised Supervisory Body, such as the Institutes. The Institutes, as supervisory bodies, have responsibilities to monitor the work of responsible individuals and auditors registered with it and that auditors are complying with legal requirements and the requirements of these Regulations. Thus an individual, even if a responsible individual in accordance with this chapter, cannot accept audit appointments unless the firm (which may be a sole practitioner) in which the individual works is also a registered auditor in accordance with chapter 2.

A sole practitioner must be a responsible individual. In all firms (including sole practices) the audit compliance principal can designate appropriately qualified principals or employees as responsible individuals as set out in the following regulations. A responsible individual does not have to be a principal.

Subject to *regulation* 4.02 and *regulation* 4.05 the *audit compliance principal* may designate as a *responsible individual* any of the *Registered Auditor's principals* or *employees* who: 4.01

a   has an *appropriate qualification*;
b   is competent to conduct *audit work*; and
c   is allowed to sign *audit reports* in their name on behalf of the *firm*.

Before a *principal* or *employee* can be designated as a *responsible individual*, the individual must be: 4.02

a   a member of an *Institute* and hold a *practising certificate*;
b   a member of the Association of Chartered Certified Accountants and hold its equivalent of a practising certificate; or
c   satisfy the *Registration Committee* of similar experience of *audit work* as would be required of a member of the *registering Institute* and have been granted *audit affiliate* status under chapter 5 of these *regulations*.

Consultants and sub-contractors cannot be designated as *responsible individuals*.   4.03

Only *responsible individuals* can be responsible for an *audit* and sign an *audit report*.   4.04

Firms which designate employees as responsible individuals must have procedures on how the employees exercise the firm's authority. If the employee is not an Institute member or member of the ACCA, he or she must become an audit affiliate of the registering Institute.

4.05 Any designation in accordance with *regulation 4.01* shall not be effective until application has been made to the *Registration Committee* in a form specified by it and the application has been approved and the *Registration Committee* may approve the application with conditions or restrictions.

Each Institute has its own application form which firms should request and complete. A Registration Committee will need to be satisfied that the individual has had recent and sufficient experience of audit work before approving the application. In the case of holders of an approved overseas or EEA qualification they will also have to show experience of UK/RoI audit work.

4.06 A *responsible individual* may not accept appointment as a *director* or other officer of a public interest entity if, at any time during the two years preceding the date of the proposed appointment, the *responsible individual* acted in the capacity of *responsible individual* for that public interest entity, or for a material subsidiary if the public interest entity is a group.

For the purposes of the above regulation, a public interest entity is a UK incorporated entity whose shares or debentures (of any class) are admitted to trading on a UK regulated market. The above regulation is to prevent a responsible individual joining such an audit client until a two year period has elapsed since the individual last undertook any audit work in relation to the client. This obligation does not end if the individual ceases his relationship with the Institute. If an individual is in doubt about the application of this regulation to his specific circumstance, he should contact his registering Institute. A firm may find it useful to remind any responsible individual that leaves the firm of this regulation.

4.07 The disciplinary arrangements of the *Institute* will apply to breaches of these *regulations* by a *responsible individual* in the same way as they apply to breaches by a member.

Cessation of responsible individual status

The status of responsible individual is linked to the registered auditor and cannot be transferred to another firm. It can cease as the following regulation sets out.

4.08 *Responsible individual* status will cease if:

a   the *firm* in which the individual is a *responsible individual* ceases to be a *Registered Auditor*;
b   the individual ceases to be a *principal* or *employee* in the *Registered Auditor* to which the grant of *responsible individual* status related;
c   an event occurs which under the *Royal Charters*, the *Rules*, *Bye-laws* or other regulations of the appropriate *Institute* the individual would cease to be a member or an *audit affiliate*;
d   the *audit compliance principal* notifies the registering *Institute* that the individual is no longer a *responsible individual*; or
e   the *Registration Committee* withdraws *responsible individual* status.

Firms are reminded of the requirement to inform the Institute of any changes to the responsible individuals of the firm.

Under company law, responsible individuals are statutory auditors in their own right. However, statutory auditors can only accept an audit appointment in accordance with the rules of a Recognised Supervisory Body, such as an Institute. Thus if a responsible individual leaves a registered auditor with the intention of undertaking audit work as a sole practitioner, the individual must apply for registration as set out in Chapter 2 of these Regulations. Until such an application is approved, the individual cannot accept audit appointments as the individual will not be a registered auditor under these Regulations. If a responsible individual leaves a registered auditor to join another registered auditor, then the individual needs to be designated as a responsible individual in the new firm before being responsible for audit work.

If an individual is no longer a *responsible individual* disciplinary action (including the imposition of a regulatory penalty) may still be taken for any failure to keep confidential any information received in the course of *audit work* and for any failure to comply with *regulation* 4.06.   4.09

Schedule 1
Relationship between appropriate (audit) qualification and responsible individual status

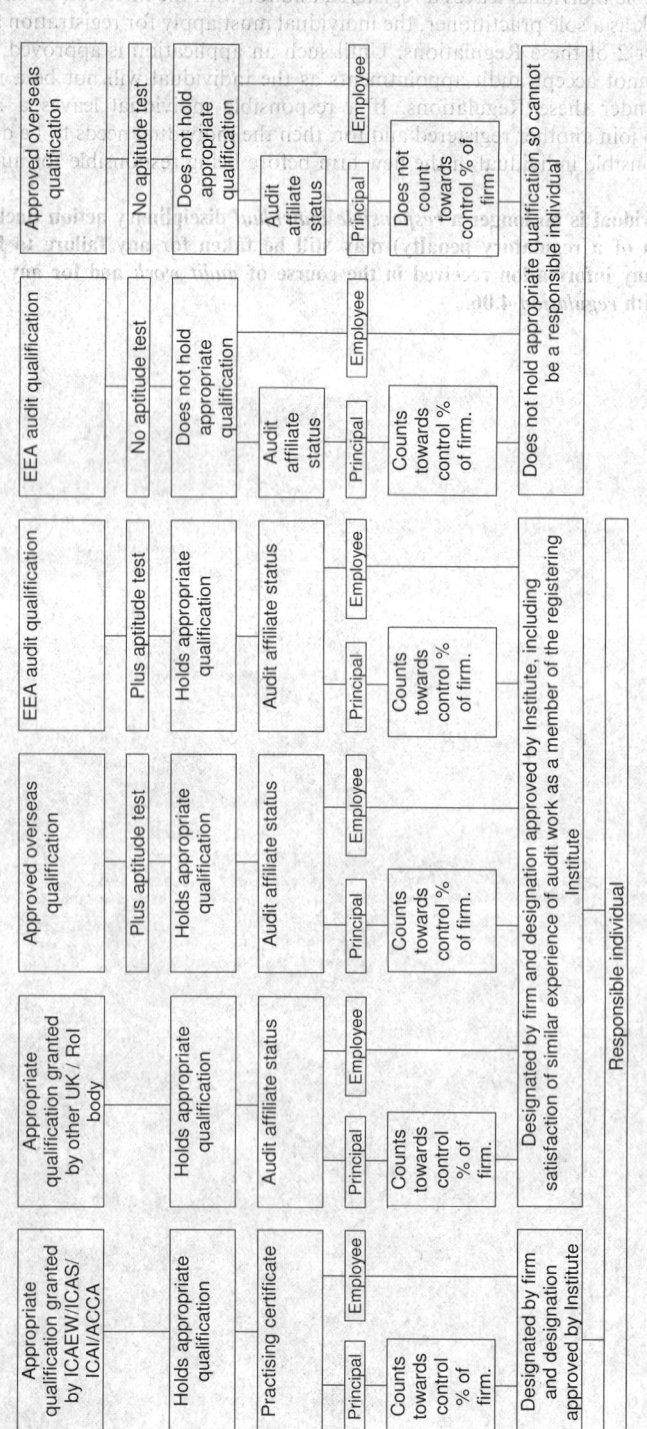

Chapter 5

Audit affiliates

The Institute is able to register firms in which one or more principals are not members of the Institutes or the Association of Chartered Certified Accountants if these people or corporate bodies are granted audit affiliate status by the registering Institute. That status does not confer membership of the Institute or entitle the individual or corporate body to use the title 'chartered accountant'. However, it does mean that an audit affiliate is bound by the same rules and regulations as govern a full member of the Institute.

An individual who is to be a responsible individual must also either be a member of an Institute or the Association of Chartered Certified Accountants. If this is not the case, then audit affiliate status is needed under this chapter.

Different requirements apply for affiliates for investment business purposes. Affiliate status in one regulated area does not automatically give such status in another.

General

An *audit affiliate* can only be responsible for an *audit* and sign an *audit report* if designated as a *responsible individual* under *regulation 4.01*.   5.01

An audit affiliate can only be responsible for audit work if they are also a responsible individual, which means holding an appropriate qualification. Chapter 4 gives details.

Granting of audit affiliate status

Audit affiliate status does not give the *audit affiliate* any rights other than those contained in these *regulations*. An *audit affiliate* must not make any public statement that they have any such rights.   5.02

Persons applying for *audit affiliate* status must do so in the manner that the *Registration Committee* decides.   5.03

Individuals should ask the appropriate Institute for an application form.

The *Registration Committee* may grant *audit affiliate* status if the committee is satisfied that the applicant: 5.04

a   is a fit and proper person to be granted *audit affiliate* status;
b   has agreed to comply with these *regulations* and with the obligations and liabilities of a member of the *Institute* and to be bound by the *Royal Charters*, the *Rules*, *Bye-laws* and other regulations of the *Institute*;
c   has agreed to observe and uphold the Code of Ethics of the *Institute*; and
d   has agreed to provide the *Institute* with all the information it requires.

Regulation 5.04 sets out the matters the Committee will consider when it receives an application for audit affiliate status.

Regulation 5.04d means that the Registration Committee has the same rights, for example to call for information about an audit affiliate, as it does over a firm. In turn, an audit affiliate has the same rights of review and appeal against the decisions of the Registration Committee as firms have.

5.05 The *Registration Committee* may: a grant the application; b reject the application; c grant the application subject to restrictions or conditions; or d postpone consideration of the application.

If audit affiliate status is refused under regulation 5.05 (or granted subject to restrictions or conditions) a person can apply for a review of the decision using the same process as for a firm (see chapter 8).

Under regulation 5.05d, the Registration Committee may decide that it can only properly consider an application after it has more information about the applicant which it may ask the applicant to supply.

Withdrawal of audit affiliate status

5.06 The *Registration Committee* may withdraw a person's *audit affiliate* status if, in the opinion of the committee, the *audit affiliate*:

a   is no longer a fit and proper person;
b   has failed to pay on time any fines or costs ordered by the *Registration Committee*, *Review Committee*, *Disciplinary Committee*, *Appeal Committee* or by any committee appointed under the *Disciplinary Scheme*;
c   becomes subject to a decision by the *Disciplinary Committee* that they should no longer be an *audit affiliate*;
d   fails to pay the annual fee within 30 days of the date of a notice to renew *audit affiliate* status; or
e   fails or ceases to comply with any of these *regulations* and, in the circumstances, withdrawal is justified.

If audit affiliate status is withdrawn under regulation 5.06, a person may apply for a review of the decision using the same process as for a firm (see chapter 8).

Cessation of audit affiliate status

5.07 *Audit affiliate* status will end if:

a   the *firm* in which the *audit affiliate* is a *principal* ceases to be a *Registered Auditor*, except where *regulation* 5.08 applies;
b   the *audit affiliate* ceases to be a *principal* in the *Registered Auditor* to which the grant of *audit affiliate* status related, except where *regulation* 5.08 applies;
c   the *audit affiliate* is an individual and an event occurs which under the *Royal Charters*, the *Rules*, *Bye-laws* or other *regulations* of the appropriate *Institute* would cause the membership of a member to cease; or
d   the *audit affiliate* is a *body corporate* which:
    1) has been the subject of an effective resolution passed by the shareholders (or in the case of a limited liability partnership, by its members) for it to be wound up or has had a winding-up order made against it on grounds of insolvency; or
    2) has had an administration order made against it on grounds of insolvency; or
    3) has had a receiver appointed by a creditor or by a court on the application of a creditor.

Regulation 5.07 describes a number of situations where audit affiliate status is automatically lost.

If an affiliate enters into a voluntary insolvency arrangement, the affiliate must notify the Registration Committee in accordance with regulation 5.09.

Audit affiliate status will not end under *regulation* 5.07a or 5.07b if: 5.08

a   the *firm* in which the *audit affiliate* is a *principal* merges with or is acquired by another *Registered Auditor* registered by the same *registering Institute*; or

b   the *audit affiliate* leaves the *Registered Auditor* in which he is a *principal* and immediately becomes a *principal* in another *Registered Auditor* registered by the same *registering Institute*.

This *regulation* will only apply if the *Institute* is notified in writing within ten *business days* of the change occurring.

If an audit affiliate is a principal in a registered auditor and if that relationship ceases, so does the audit affiliate status. In the circumstances given in regulation 5.08, audit affiliates may keep their audit affiliate status. However, this is only if the new firm is registered with the same Institute that granted the original audit affiliate status, and the Institute has been notified of the changes. If the audit affiliate will not be joining the new firm within ten business days, they need to get advice from the Institute as soon as, or before, they leave the old firm.

Firms must also make sure that the control by individuals who hold an appropriate qualification or as set out in regulation 2.03 is maintained.

Changes in circumstances

An *audit affiliate* or *the audit compliance principal* must notify the *Institute* in writing   5.09
within ten *business days* of any changes that are relevant to the matters considered by the *Registration Committee* under *regulation* 5.04, including details of any voluntary insolvency arrangement that the affiliate has entered into.

Review of regulatory decisions

An *audit affiliate* may apply for a review of a decision made under *regulation* 5.05 or   5.10
5.06 using the same procedures as a *firm* in chapter 8.

Implementation of decisions

A decision made under *regulation* 5.05 will come into effect as soon as notice of it is   5.11
served on the *audit affiliate*. A decision made under *regulation* 5.06 will come into effect ten business days after notice of it is served on the *audit affiliate*, except that:

a   if the *audit affiliate* has applied for a review under *regulation* 8.05, or a hearing under *regulation* 8.15, the decision will not take effect until a decision under *regulation* 8.06 or 8.16 has been put into effect; or

b   if the *audit affiliate* appealed under *regulation* 8.08 or 8.19, the decision will not take effect until an *Appeal Committee* decision under *regulation* 8.09 or 8.20 has been put into effect.

If an audit affiliate applies for a review, then a decision under regulation 5.06 is stayed pending the outcome of the review. A decision under regulation 5.05 is not stayed.

Fees

5.12 An a*udit affiliate* must pay an annual fee at the time and at the rate set by the Institute.

5.13 The first annual fee is due when an application is made for *audit affiliate* status. An application fee is also due with this first annual fee.

If an audit affiliate's application is unsuccessful, the first annual fee will be refunded.

Disciplinary arrangements

5.14 The disciplinary arrangements of the *Institute* will apply to breaches of these *regulations* by an *audit affiliate* in the same way as they apply to breaches by a member.

5.15 An *audit affiliate* will be liable to disciplinary action under these *regulations* for any failure to observe and uphold the fundamental principles set out in the Code of Ethics issued by *Council*.

5.16 An *audit affiliate* will remain liable to disciplinary action under these *regulations* for any acts or omissions during the period in which *audit affiliate* status was held, even if no longer an *audit affiliate*.

Chapter 6

The Committees

This chapter describes the various committees involved in the regulatory process and their powers. Some, but not all, of the powers may be delegated by the Registration Committee to either sub-committees or the staff. But any decision not to allow registration, or to restrict, suspend or withdraw registration must be made by the committee, as outlined in regulation 6.04.

A firm generally has the right to seek a review of a decision. Details are in chapter 8.

Registration Committee

6.01 The *Registration Committee* must:

    a   comprise at least eight people;
    b   include at least two members who are not accountants; and
    c   have a quorum of three members.

6.02 The *Registration Committee* is responsible for:

    a   granting registration;
    b   granting registration subject to restrictions or conditions;
    c   rejecting applications for registration;
    d   withdrawing registration;
    e   suspending registration;
    f   imposing restrictions or conditions it considers appropriate on how a *Registered Auditor* carries out *audit work*;
    g   proposing a *regulatory penalty* it considers appropriate to a *Registered Auditor*;
    h   granting or refusing dispensation from the requirements of *regulation* 2.02, or regulation 2.03;

i   reviewing the returns and reports made under these *regulations*, and investigating failure to make returns or reports;

j   making appropriate enquiries into the eligibility of applicants for: registration; *responsible individual* status; or *audit affiliate* status (by writing, visiting the office or offices of a *firm*, or in any other way);

k   making appropriate enquiries to confirm that a *Registered Auditor*, *responsible individual* or an *audit affiliate* is complying with these *regulations* (by writing, visiting a *firm's* office or offices, using a periodic return, or in any other way);

l   publishing, in any manner it decides, its orders or decisions if it considers this appropriate;

m   compiling and maintaining the *Register* and supplying information to the Registrar of Companies in the Republic of Ireland;

n   granting applications for responsible individual status, with or without restrictions or conditions or rejecting such applications; and

o   withdrawing *responsible individual* status.

Regulation 6.02 sets out the powers and functions of the Committee, which include the powers under regulations 6.02j and 6.02k to make monitoring visits to firms.

Each Institute deals with the procedures for regulatory penalties differently, as shown in chapter 7 for the ICAS and ICAI and chapter 9 for the ICAEW.

Except where *regulation* 6.04 applies, the *Registration Committee* may delegate its duties to sub-committees, the *Institute's* staff, a *monitoring unit*, or another duly appointed agent.   6.03

The committee may delegate many of its powers except in the situations set out in regulation 6.04.

If the matters to be considered by the *Registration Committee* include: 6.04

- rejecting applications for registration under *regulation* 2.05b;
- granting applications for registration subject to restrictions under *regulation* 2.05c;
- rejecting applications for *responsible individual* status under *regulation* 4.05;
- granting applications for *responsible individual* status subject to restrictions under *regulation* 4.05;
- withdrawing *responsible individual* status under *regulation* 4.08e;
- rejecting applications for *audit affiliate* status under *regulation* 5.05b;
- granting applications for *audit affiliate* status subject to restrictions under *regulation* 5.05c;
- withdrawing *audit affiliate* status under *regulation* 5.06a or 5.06e;
- imposing restrictions on registration under *regulation* 7.01;
- withdrawing registration under *regulations* 7.03a, 7.03g, 7.03h, or 7.03i;
- suspending a *firm's* registration under *regulation* 7.04; or
- proposing a *regulatory penalty* under *regulation* 7.11 or 9.02;

then:

a   the committee cannot delegate the decision;

b   at least one half of the committee members present must be accountants; and

c   at least one member of the committee present must not be an accountant.

Regulation 6.03 allows the committee to delegate some of its duties to the Institute's staff. Duties that may be delegated include withdrawing registration under regulations:

- 7.03b, non-compliance with the PII regulations;

- 7.03c, failure to submit an annual return;
- 7.03d, failure to pay fees;
- 7.03e, failure to pay review costs; and
- 7.03f, failure to pay disciplinary costs.

However, regulation 6.04 reserves certain specified decisions to the committee. These include withdrawing registration for other reasons and placing restrictions on a firm's registration.

The power to withdraw audit affiliate status under regulations 5.06b to 5.06d may also be delegated.

6.05 When the *Registration Committee* has to decide if a *Registered Auditor* has complied with a *regulation, auditing standard,* or a *quality control standard* it must consider any relevant guidance in the regulations, standards, *practice notes* and any guidance issued by *Council*.

6.06 In carrying out its responsibilities under *regulation 6.02*, the *Registration Committee*, any sub-committee, the *Institute's* staff, or a *monitoring unit* may, to the extent necessary for the review of a *firm's* audit work or how it is complying or intends to comply with these *regulations*, require a *Registered Auditor* or an applicant for registration to provide any information, held in whatever form (including electronic), about the *firm* or its clients and to allow access to the *firm's* systems and personnel.

Regulation 6.06 gives the committee (or its delegated agents) power to call for information from a firm to help the committee carry out its functions. Requests may be to all firms on a routine basis through annual returns, or specific to individual firms.

6.07 The *Registration Committee* may, for the purposes of these *regulations*, treat as *audit work* any work carried out by a *Registered Auditor* if such status is a requirement for that work.

This regulation allows the committee to look at other work where the firm has signed a report as a statutory or registered auditor. This is particularly so where a firm has little or no regulated audit work but is signing other reports as a statutory or registered auditor. The committee may wish to review this work to assess the firm's ability to carry out audit work. Also, if a complaint is received about other work signed as a registered auditor the committee may wish to review this or similar work for the same reason.

6.08 All information obtained under *regulation* 6.06 will be confidential but may be disclosed by the *Institute* or a *monitoring unit* (directly or indirectly) to any person or body undertaking regulatory, disciplinary or law enforcement responsibilities for the purpose of assisting that person or body to undertake those responsibilities or as otherwise required or allowed by law.

All information that an Institute or a monitoring unit receives will remain confidential except in the above circumstances.

6.09 A *firm* which is no longer a *Registered Auditor* will continue to be subject to *regulations* 6.02j, 6.02k and 6.06 if the enquiries or information relate to any period in which the *firm* was registered.

6.10 In carrying out its responsibilities under *regulation 6.02*, the *Registration Committee* may consider any disciplinary findings, orders, ongoing investigations or any other information concerning or affecting the fit and proper status of any *responsible individual*, *audit affiliate* or applicant for *audit affiliate* status, the *firm* or its *principals*. In particular the *Registration Committee* may take into account the following:

a   any matter relating to any individual who is or will be employed by or associated with the *firm* in connection with *audit work*;
b   in the case of a *firm* that is a partnership, any matter relating to any:
   1) partner;
   2) *director* or *controller* of any of the partners;
   3) *body corporate* in the same *group* as of any of the partners; or
   4) any *controller* of any such body;
c   if a *principal* in the *firm* is a *body corporate*, any matter relating to any: 1) *principal* or *controller* of that *body corporate*; 2) *body corporate* in the same *group* as the *body corporate*; or 3) *principal* or *controller* of any *body corporate* in that *group*;
d   in the case of a *firm* that is a *body corporate*, any matter relating to any: 1) *principal* or *controller* of that *firm*; 2) person having any interest in shares of the *firm*; 3) *body corporate* in the same *group* as the *firm*; or 4) *directors* or *controllers* of any *body corporate* in that *group*.

Regulation 6.10 allows the Committee to consider any disciplinary or other matter that affects the fit and proper status of the firm. The scope is very wide and not limited to the principals in the firm.

Subparagraph (a) includes employees and associates of the firm. For partnerships, subparagraph

(b) includes the partners, any director or controller of a partner that is a company, any other company that is in the same group as that company and any controller of any other group company. Subparagraph (c) deals with situations where a principal (ie a partner, member or director) is a body corporate (ie a company or a limited liability partnership).

So included are any director, member or controller of that body corporate, any other body corporate that is in the same group as that body corporate and any controller of any of those other bodies. Finally, subparagraph (d) deals with a firm that is a body corporate (ie a company or a limited liability partnership). Thus included are directors/members/shareholders of the firm, and any other body corporate that is in the same group as the firm and any controller of any of those other bodies.

Notification to committees

The *Registration Committee* must notify the *Investigation Committee* about any fact or matter which: 6.11

a   suggests that a *Registered Auditor*, member or *audit affiliate* may be liable to disciplinary action under these *regulations*, the *Bye-laws* or *Rules*, or any other *regulations* or bye-laws of the *Institute*; and
b   in the opinion of the *Registration Committee* needs to be investigated.

The *Investigation Committee* must inform the *Registration Committee* about any fact or matter which appears to it to be relevant to the powers and duties of the *Registration Committee* under these *regulations*.   6.12

Under regulations 6.11 and 6.12, information may be exchanged between the Institute departments responsible for regulation and discipline.

Review Committee and Panel

6.13 Certain matters decided by the *Registration Committee* may be considered afresh by the *Review Committee* (as described in *regulation* 8.06) or *Panel* (as described in *regulation* 8.15). It may then carry out any of the responsibilities of the *Registration Committee* under *regulation* 6.02 and may make any order that the *Registration Committee* may make. In carrying out these duties, *regulation* 6.06 applies to the *Review Committee* or *Panel* as it applies to the *Registration Committee*.

Firms registered by the ICAEW and the ICAI may ask the Review Committee to reconsider a Registration Committee decision. This request must be made within a specified time period. Regulations 8.05 to 8.07 give further details of how the review process works.

Firms registered by the ICAS may apply for a hearing under regulation 8.15.

Appeal Committee

6.14 Appeals against decisions of the *Review Committee* or *Panel* will be decided by the *Appeal Committee*.

If a firm is dissatisfied with a decision of the Review Committee or Panel, it may apply for the case to be heard before the Appeal Committee. This request must be made within ten days of the decision being given to the firm.

Unlike applications for a review, the Appeal Committee will only hear an appeal on one of a number of specified grounds. It will not reopen the case from the beginning. The specific grounds are given in chapter 8.

For firms registered by the ICAEW and the ICAI, detailed procedures are given in regulations 8.08 to 8.10. Regulations 8.19 to 8.21 give the procedures for firms registered by the ICAS.

The Appeal Committee's procedures and powers are given in the Bye-laws or Rules.

Procedures of the committees

6.15 When considering any matter before it, the *Registration Committee*, the *Review Committee* or *Panel* or the *Appeal Committee* shall, for the purposes of these *regulations*, accept any previous disciplinary finding, conviction, decision, sentence or judgement (including criminal and civil court decisions) as conclusive evidence of that prior matter.

6.16 Subject to the *Act*, the *Bye-Laws* or *Rules* and these *regulations*, the *Registration Committee*, the *Review Committee* or *Panel* and the *Appeal Committee* may, in carrying out their duties under these *regulations*, decide on their own procedures.

This regulation allows the committees to decide on their own internal procedures.

Each Institute must arrange for complaints against the Institute in its capacity as a Recognised Supervisory Body to be investigated. The ICAEW has appointed an independent Reviewer of Complaints. The ICAS and the ICAI have panels of lay members of Institute committees to investigate complaints.

Chapter 7
Regulatory action

This chapter explains how the Registration Committee may take regulatory action against a registered auditor, including withdrawal of registration if necessary.

Regulatory decisions come into effect as set out in regulations 7.09 to 7.10.

A firm may ask for a review of a decision made by the Registration Committee and this is dealt with in chapter 8. A firm must apply for a review within ten days of the decision being given to the firm.

The chapter is in two parts, the first applies to all three Institutes and the second part applies only to the Institute of Chartered Accountants of Scotland and the Institute of Chartered Accountants in Ireland.

Section 7A
Firms registered by the Institute of Chartered Accountants in England and Wales, the Institute of Chartered Accountants of Scotland and the Institute of Chartered Accountants in Ireland

Restrictions and conditions

The *Registration Committee* may impose restrictions or conditions on a *Registered Auditor* if it considers that: 7.01

a   any of the circumstances mentioned in *regulation* 7.03a to 7.03f exist, or may exist, and the restrictions or conditions are justified;
b   the *firm* has not or may not have complied with these *regulations* in the past, and the restrictions or conditions are justified;
c   the *firm* may not comply with these *regulations* and the restrictions or conditions are justified;
d   being registered or continuing *audit work* without restrictions or conditions could adversely affect an *audit client* or any other person; or
e   it is appropriate to do so to ensure that *audit work* is undertaken, supervised and managed effectively.

The *Registration Committee* may at any time vary or end a restriction or condition made under *regulation* 7.01.   7.02

The committee may place conditions on how a registered auditor carries out or manages its audit work. These could be that a firm should undertake specified training, change its procedures or have 'cold reviews' of audit files by another registered auditor.

The committee may place restrictions on a registered auditor such as:

- against the firm, for example that it cannot accept any new audits or particular types of audits;
- against a principal, for example that a particular principal may no longer be a responsible individual; or
- that an employee may no longer be involved in audit work.

Where conditions or restrictions are imposed by the committee, a firm will have to undertake to comply with the terms of the restriction or condition. Any failure to deal with these matters is likely to be viewed extremely seriously by the committee.

Withdrawal of registration

7.03 The *Registration Committee* may withdraw a *firm's* registration if:

a   it considers that the *firm* no longer meets one or more of the eligibility requirements of *regulations* 2.02 or 2.03 (additional criteria for firms that are not sole practices);
b   it considers that the *firm* is not complying with the *PII regulations*;
c   the *firm* is over 30 days late submitting the required returns or reports;
d   the *firm* has not paid the registration fees due under *regulation* 2.13 or a charge due under *regulation* 2.15 (charge for a monitoring visit) within 60 days of the date of an invoice under *regulation* 2.16;
e   the *firm* has not paid the costs in the time set by the *Review Committee* or *Panel* under *regulation* 8.07 or 8.18;
f   the *firm* has not paid in the time set any fines or costs ordered by the *Investigation Committee*, the *Disciplinary Committee*, the *Appeal Committee* or by any committee appointed under the *Disciplinary Scheme*;
g   it considers that the *firm* has not complied with any restriction or condition under *regulation* 7.01 or any written undertaking that the *firm* has given to the *Institute*;
h   it considers that the *firm* has not complied with any other *regulation* and, in the circumstances, withdrawal is justified; or
i   it considers that the continued registration of the *firm* may adversely affect an *audit client* or any other person.

The Registration Committee can, under regulation 6.03, delegate its power to withdraw registration in the cases that come under paragraphs (b) to (f) of regulation 7.03. However, under regulation 6.04, only the committee can withdraw a firm's registration on the grounds of paragraphs (a), (g), (h) and (i) of regulation 7.03.

The Registration Committee may, as an alternative to regulatory action, accept a written undertaking from a firm that it will undertake a particular course of action.

Suspension

7.04 The *Registration Committee* may suspend a *Registered Auditor's* registration for a period if it considers that:

a   any of the circumstances mentioned in *regulation* 7.03a to 7.03g exists or may exist;
b   the *firm* is, or may, no longer be complying with these *regulations*; or
c   the continuation of the *firm's audit* activities could adversely affect an *audit client* or any other person.

7.05 During a period of suspension a *Registered Auditor*:

a   need not resign from any appointment as auditor under the *Act*;
b   may accept re-appointment as auditor;
c   must not accept any new appointments; and
d   may only sign *audit reports* with the permission of the *Registration Committee*.

7.06 The *Registration Committee* may vary or end a suspension made under *regulation* 7.04.

The committee can order that a firm's registration is suspended rather than withdrawing registration. This allows the committee to consider further evidence while protecting the public interest. It also means that a firm cannot accept new audit appointments or sign audit reports without the committee's agreement.

Urgent orders

The *Registration Committee* may impose restrictions or conditions or suspend a *firm's* **7.07**
registration in the terms permitted by *regulation* 7.01 or 7.04 by means of an urgent
order if it considers that there is a need to do so.

Regulation 7.07 is subject to the *Registration Committee* allowing the *firm* an oppor- **7.08**
tunity to make oral or written representations within ten *business days* of the urgent
order being made. Having considered any representations the committee may:

a   end the order; or
b   continue the order.

Regulation 7.07 allows the committee to take immediate regulatory action if the need arises. The committee would probably do this if there were serious allegations of fraud or other criminal activity or if there was a potential or actual loss of client money. As well as making immediate representations on the fact that an urgent order has been made, a firm can ask for a review or hearing of the underlying order under regulation 8.05 or 8.15. The order comes into force when it is served on the firm (see regulation 7.09) and is not lifted if a review is requested.

Implementation of committee decisions and orders

A decision made under *regulations* 2.05, 2.18, 4.05, 7.04, 7.07, 8.09 or 8.20 will come **7.09**
into effect as soon as notice of it is served on the *firm*.

The regulations quoted in regulation 7.09 relate to the following:

- regulation 2.05 deals with the grant or refusal of an application;
- dispensations given under regulation 2.18;
- regulation 4.05 deals with the grant or refusal of responsible individual status;
- regulation 7.04 deals with the suspension of a firm's registration;
- regulation 7.07 concerns orders in respect of restrictions, conditions or suspension of registration that are made on a urgent basis; and
- regulations 8.09 and 8.20 deal with Appeal Committee decisions.

A decision made under *regulations* 7.01, 7.03 or 4.08e will come into effect ten *business* **7.10**
***days* after notice of it is served on the *firm* or *responsible individual* any later time that**
the committee specifies, except:

a   **if a *firm* or *responsible individual* has applied for a review or hearing under *reg-***
     ulation* 8.05 or 8.15b, the order will be postponed until an order under *regulation
     8.06 or 8.15d has been put into effect; or
b   **if a *firm* or *responsible individual* has appealed under *regulation* 8.08 or 8.19, the**
     order will be postponed until an *Appeal Committee* order under *regulation* 8.09 or
     8.20 has been put into effect.

Except for decisions made under regulation 7.09, decisions come into effect ten business days after the firm has been given the decision. However, the decisions listed in regulation 7.10 are postponed if an application for review or appeal is made. The decision of the Review or Appeal Committee is the one that will come into effect.

The regulations quoted in regulation 7.10 relate to the following:

- withdrawal of responsible individual status under regulation 4.08e;
- conditions or restrictions imposed under regulation 7.01; and
- withdrawal of a firm's registration under regulation 7.03.

Regulation 1.09 details how decisions and orders are served on firms.

Section 7B
Firms registered by the Institute of Chartered Accountants of Scotland and the Institute of Chartered Accountants in Ireland

Regulatory penalties

The Registration Committee may decide that a referral to the Investigation Committee to investigate an apparent failure to comply with these regulations is not appropriate. Instead, with the agreement of the firm, the Registration Committee may propose a regulatory penalty. The following regulations explain this process.

7.11 The *Registration Committee* may propose a *regulatory penalty* to a *Registered Auditor* subject to the following:

    a   the *Registered Auditor* must have agreed that the breach of these *regulations* has been committed;

    b   the *Registration Committee* will decide the amount of the penalty and when it is to be paid. The *Institute* will set this out in the letter to the *Registered Auditor* proposing the penalty; and

    c   if the *Registered Auditor* wishes to accept the terms on which the penalty is proposed, it must notify the *Institute* within ten *business days* of the date of service of the letter from the *Institute* containing the proposal.

7.12 There are no rights of review or appeal under *regulation*s 8.05 to 8.10 (applicable to *Registered Auditors* registered by the *ICAI*) or *regulation*s 8.15 to 8.21 (applicable to *Registered Auditors* registered by the *ICAS*) against a *regulatory penalty*.

7.13 The *Registration Committee* will take account of any comments a *Registered Auditor* makes about the terms of the *regulatory penalty*. It may then reduce the amount of the penalty.

7.14 If the *Registered Auditor* accepts the penalty under *regulation* 7.11c, the *Registration Committee*, as soon as is practical:

    a   will make an order; and

    b   may publish the order in any way it decides.

7.15 Details of any penalty accepted, and the order made, will be kept by the *Institute* and the committee may, if it wishes, use that information in the future.

7.16 If a *Registered Auditor* does not agree that the breach has been committed, or does not agree to the terms of the penalty proposed or fails to comply with the terms of the penalty, the matter may be dealt with as set out in Chapter 9.

Regulatory penalties are likely to be used, for example, where a firm has consistently been late in replying to letters from the committee or staff, has failed to submit annual returns, given incorrect information on the return, or has not honoured undertakings given to the committee.

There is no right of appeal as a regulatory penalty can only be made with the firm's agreement. Once a matter has been settled by a regulatory penalty, there will be no further regulatory or disciplinary action against the firm on the matter. However, the details of the regulatory penalty will be put on the firm's record and may be taken into account in the future.

Chapter 8

Representation before committees, review and appeal

This chapter explains how a firm can apply for a review and appeal against a regulatory decision or proposed order of the Registration Committee. It also explains when a firm can be represented before a committee. Where appropriate, these regulations also apply to audit affiliates.

This chapter is divided into sections according to which Institute has registered the firm.

Section 8A
Firms registered by the Institute of Chartered Accountants in England and Wales and the Institute of Chartered Accountants in Ireland

In *regulations* 8.02 to 8.10, "affected party" means a *firm*, an applicant for *responsible individual* status, a *responsible individual*, an applicant for *audit affiliate* status or an *audit affiliate*.   8.01

Representation before committees

Only the following may attend a meeting of the *Registration Committee*:   8.02

a   members of the *Registration Committee*;
b   the secretary to the committee;
c   any member of the *Institute's* staff whose role is to advise or inform the committee on its responsibilities, duties, powers or procedures, including the *Bye-laws*, *regulations* or the law; and d anyone else the committee permits.

At meetings of the *Review Committee* and the *Appeal Committee*, the affected party, a representative or agent of the *Institute*, or a *monitoring unit* may attend and be represented. Witnesses may be present at the *Review Committee* and the *Appeal Committee* in accordance with the committees' procedures or *regulations*.   8.03

The *Registration Committee*, the *Review Committee* and the *Appeal Committee* may ask the affected party, the *Institute*, a *monitoring unit*, any employee or agent of the *Institute* to clarify relevant points. The affected party must be given the opportunity to comment on any clarification made by others.   8.04

Review of regulatory decisions

A firm, an applicant for audit affiliate status or an audit affiliate that is dissatisfied with a decision listed in regulation 8.05 can apply for a review. A decision under regulation 2.18, 5.06, 7.01, 7.03 is postponed until the Review Committee's decision has been put into effect.

8.05 Within ten *business days* of the *Registration Committee* serving a decision or order on the affected party, it can apply to the *Review Committee* for a review of that decision or order. The affected party must apply in writing to the *Institute*. This applies to the following *regulations*:

regulation 2.05b	-	refusing to grant registration;
regulation 2.05c	-	granting of registration subject to conditions or restrictions;
regulation 2.18	-	granting or refusing to grant a dispensation from the *regulations*;
regulation 4.05	-	refusing to grant *responsible individual* status or granting such status subject to conditions or restrictions;
regulation 4.08e	-	withdrawing *responsible individual* status;
regulation 5.05b	-	refusing to grant *audit affiliate* status;
regulation 5.05c	-	granting audit *affiliate status* subject to conditions or restrictions;
regulation 5.06	-	withdrawing *audit affiliate* status;
regulation 7.01	-	imposing restrictions or conditions;
regulation 7.03	-	withdrawing registration;
regulation 7.04	-	suspending registration; or
regulation 7.07	-	an urgent order.

Regulations 7.09 to 7.10 explain when orders come into effect.

8.06 A meeting of the *Review Committee* will be arranged as soon as is practical after an affected party has applied under *regulation* 8.05. The *Review Committee* will consider the matter afresh and will hear new material put forward by the affected party. The *Review Committee* may make any decision which the *Registration Committee* could have made.

8.07 The *Review Committee* may order an affected party to contribute to the costs of the review.

The Review Committee has the same powers as the Registration Committee when making orders against firms, responsible individuals, applicants for audit affiliate status or audit affiliates. It can impose the same, more severe or less severe orders. It can also award costs. Costs are likely to be awarded if, for example, the affected party fails to attend the review when it said it would, does not send in further material it has promised, or the application is frivolous.

Appeal

If a firm, applicant for responsible individual status, responsible individual, applicant for audit affiliate status or audit affiliate is dissatisfied with the Review Committee's decision it can apply to the Appeal Committee. The Appeal Committee can only consider an appeal on any of the grounds in regulation 8.08. On appeal, the decision of the Review Committee is postponed until the Appeal Committee confirms or varies the decision (see regulation 7.10).

The Appeal Committee has the power to accept or reject the appeal, or reduce the severity of the order. It cannot change the Review Committee's order in any other way, but it can ask the Review Committee to reconsider the order.

The Appeal Committee can also award costs against an applicant for an appeal.

Within ten *business days* of the *Review Committee* serving its decision on an affected   8.08
party under *regulation* 8.06 the affected party can appeal to the *Appeal Committee* by
writing to the *Institute*. An appeal can only be made on one or more of the following
grounds:

a   that the *Review Committee*:
    1) was wrong in law;
    2) wrongly interpreted any relevant *regulation*, *Bye-law*, *auditing standard*,
       quality control standard or associated guidance; or 3) did not comply with
       these *regulations*, or procedures decided by the *Review Committee* under
       regulation 6.16;
b   that the *Review Committee* made an order which no tribunal, correctly applying
    the law to the facts before it and acting reasonably, would have made; or
c   that there was evidence which the *Review Committee* had not considered and
    which:
    1) could reasonably have led the *Review Committee* to make a different order;
       and
    2) could not have been put before the *Review Committee* even if those concerned
       had done their best to produce it.

An appeal cannot be made if this is only against the costs awarded by the Review
Committee. Regulations 7.09 and 7.10 explain when orders come into effect.

As soon as is practical after notice of appeal has been received under *regulation* 8.08,   8.09
the *Appeal Committee* will consider the appeal and may:

a   allow the appeal;
b   make a different decision;
c   send the matter back to the *Review Committee* to be considered again; or
d   dismiss the appeal.

If the *Appeal Committee* sends a matter back to the *Review Committee* under *reg-*   8.10
ulation 8.09 then *regulation* 8.06 will apply when the *Review Committee* reconsiders.
The meeting of the *Review Committee* to reconsider the matter will be arranged as soon
as is practical.

Section 8B
Firms registered by the Institute of Chartered Accountants of Scotland

In *regulations* 8.12 to 8.21, "affected party" means a *firm*, an applicant for *responsible*   8.11
individual status, a *responsible individual*, an applicant for *audit affiliate* status or an
audit affiliate.

Procedures

No affected party has the right to attend or be represented at *Registration Committee*   8.12
meetings, other than for a hearing.

Except for urgent orders under *regulation* 7.07, the *Registration Committee* must be   8.13
satisfied that an affected party has been given a reasonable opportunity to make written
submissions before the committee considers any matters.

8.14 When it first considers a matter, except urgent orders under *regulation* 7.07, the Registration *Committee* will:

    a   decide the matter in favour of the affected party;
    b   postpone a decision; or
    c   give written notice to the affected party of the order that the *Registration Committee* proposes and the factors taken into account.

8.15   a   An affected party objecting to a proposed order is entitled to a hearing. The hearing will be before a *Panel* specifically appointed by the *Registration Committee*. At least 25% of the *Panel* members must not be accountants.
    b   If an affected party wants a hearing, it must notify the *Institute* in writing within ten *business days* of the proposed order being served.
    c   An affected party is entitled to attend a hearing and to be legally represented. The *Registration Committee* can appoint anyone to present the case against the affected party.
    d   As soon as is practical after an affected party has asked for a hearing, a *Panel* will consider the matters afresh and can make any order which the *Registration Committee* could have made.

8.16   If the affected party has not asked for a hearing within the time allowed, the order comes into force at the end of that time.

8.17   The *Registration Committee* may waive requirements of *regulation*s 8.15 and 8.16, in favour of the affected party .

8.18   The *Panel* may order an affected party to contribute to the costs of the hearing.

Appeal

8.19   Within ten *business days* of the *Registration Committee* serving an order following a hearing, the affected party can appeal to the *Appeal Committee* by writing to the *Institute*. An appeal can only be made on one or more of the following grounds:

    a   that the *Registration Committee*; 1) was wrong in law; 2) wrongly interpreted any relevant *regulation*, *Bye-law*, *Rule* or *auditing standard, quality control standard or associated guidance*; or 3) did not comply with these *regulations*, or procedures decided by the *Registration Committee* under *regulation* 6.16;
    b   that the *Registration Committee* made an order no tribunal, correctly applying the law to the facts of the case before it and acting reasonably, would have made; or
    c   that there was evidence which the *Panel* had not considered and which: 1) could reasonably have led the *Panel* to make a different order; and 2) could not have been put before the *Panel* even if those concerned had done their best to produce it.

An appeal cannot be made if this is only against the costs awarded by the Registration Committee.

8.20   As soon as is practical after notice of appeal has been received under *regulation* 8.19, the *Appeal Committee* will consider the appeal and may:

    a   allow the appeal;
    b   send the matter back to the *Registration Committee* to be considered again; or
    c   dismiss the appeal.

8.21   If the *Appeal Committee* sends the matter back to the *Registration Committee* under *regulation* 8.20, the *Appeal Committee* will inform that committee how to proceed.

Chapter 9

Disciplinary arrangements

The purpose this chapter is to apply the disciplinary arrangements of each Institute to the firms that it registers.

The Registration Committee does not have the power to apply the disciplinary arrangements of an Institute to the firms that it registers. Only the Disciplinary or Investigation Committees (or the Disciplinary Scheme) can do this. The bye-laws or rules already provide a framework for disciplinary action to be taken against members or firms and the purpose of this chapter is to apply the disciplinary arrangements of each Institute to the firms that it registers.

This chapter also contains the regulations relating to regulatory penalties for the ICAEW, for ICAS and ICAI these are in chapter 7.

Section 9A
Firms registered by the Institute of Chartered Accountants in England and Wales, the Institute of Chartered Accountants of Scotland and the Institute of Chartered Accountants in Ireland

Application of disciplinary arrangements

The disciplinary arrangements of the registering *Institute* apply to complaints of breaches of these *regulations* by a *Registered Auditor*.   9.01

For the ICAEW the disciplinary arrangements are set out in the Disciplinary Bye-laws, for ICAS they are in Chapter XII of the Rules (Discipline, Insolvency, etc) and for the ICAI in Chapter IX of the *Bye-laws* (Discipline).

Section 9B
Firms registered by the Institute of Chartered Accountants in England and Wales

Regulatory penalties

The Registration Committee may decide that a referral to the Investigation Committee to investigate an apparent failure to comply with these regulations is not appropriate. Instead, with the agreement of the firm, the Registration Committee may propose a regulatory penalty. The following regulations explain this process.

The *Registration Committee* may propose a *regulatory penalty* to a *Registered Auditor* subject to the following: 9.02

a the *Registered Auditor* must have agreed that the breach of these *regulations* has been committed;

b the *Registration Committee* will decide the amount of the penalty and when it is to be paid. The *Institute* will set this out in the letter to the *Registered Auditor* proposing the penalty; and

c if the *Registered Auditor* wishes to accept the terms on which the penalty is proposed, it must notify the *Institute* within ten *business days* of the date of service of the letter from the *Institute* containing the proposal.

9.03 There are no rights of review or appeal under *regulation*s 8.05 to 8.10 against a *regulatory penalty*.

9.04 The *Registration Committee* will take account of any comments a *Registered Auditor* makes about the terms of the *regulatory penalty*. It may then reduce the amount of the penalty.

9.05 If the *Registered Auditor* accepts the penalty under *regulation* 9.02c, the *Registration Committee*, as soon as is practical:

a will make an order; and
b may publish the order in any way it decides.

9.06 Details of any penalty accepted, and the order made, will be kept by the *Institute* and the *Registration Committee* may, if it wishes, use that information in the future.

9.07 If a *Registered Auditor* does not agree that the breach has been committed, or does not agree to the terms of the penalty proposed or fails to comply with the terms of the penalty, the matter may be dealt with under the Disciplinary Bye-laws.

Regulatory penalties are likely to be used, for example, where a firm has consistently been late in replying to letters from the committee or staff, has failed to submit annual returns, given incorrect information on the return and so on, or has not honoured undertakings given to the committee.

There is no right of appeal as a regulatory penalty can only be made with the firm's agreement. Once a matter has been settled by a regulatory penalty, there will be no further regulatory or disciplinary action against the firm on the matter. However, the details of the regulatory penalty will be put on the firm's record and may be taken into account in the future.

Guidance

Chapter 1
Guidance on fit and proper status

Background

1 Regulation 2.02 expressly requires a firm to be 'fit and proper'. Regulation 3.06 puts the responsibility on the firm to make sure that the principals and employees are and continue to be fit and proper. This chapter gives guidance to firms on this requirement.

2 The Act requires the Institute, as a recognised supervisory body, to have adequate rules and practices to make sure that registered auditors are fit and proper to be appointed as registered auditor. This chapter helps firms to assess the fit and proper status of the firm and its principals and employees.

3 As part of the criteria for registration, the Institute requires a firm to be fit and proper. The application for registration looks into a firm's financial integrity, disciplinary record and professional standing (see appendix A). An applicant will be asked, for example, whether it has failed to satisfy creditors in full or been refused the right to carry on any trade, business or profession for which a specific licence, registration or other authority is required.

Guidance in chapter 2 of the regulations has already discussed the fundamental ethical principles. Firms should be complying with these to be fit and proper. 4

If a firm admits that it does not meet all the fit and proper standards, the firm may still be eligible for registration. However, the Registration Committee will weigh up the implications of all the circumstances. A firm which knowingly withheld information from the Registration Committee would not be fit and proper to act as an auditor. 5

Principals and employees

For a firm to be fit and proper, the principals and employees involved in audit work must also be fit and proper. Under the audit regulations a registered auditor must make sure that anyone who is or will be employed by, or associated with, the firm in connection with audit work is fit and proper. 6

A firm's procedures must cover: 7

- the sole practitioner or the principals;
- employees involved in audit work (including students);
- consultants involved in audit work on the firm's behalf;
- sub-contractors doing audit work on the firm's behalf; and
- anyone else whose work a principal relies on when carrying out audit work.

Some of the auditing standards cover some common situations. These are:

- ISA 610 'Considering the work of internal audit'
- ISA 600 'Using the work of another auditor'
- ISA 620 'Using the work of an expert'.

These should be followed where appropriate.

The Registration Committee may take account of any matters affecting the fit and proper status of those people listed in paragraph 7. 8

Partnerships and corporate practices

The Act recognises that partnerships may include one or more partners which are bodies corporate. In such a firm, the fit and proper procedures should extend beyond the corporate partner to any: 9

- director or controller of the corporate partner;
- body corporate in the same group as the corporate partner; and
- director or controller of any body corporate above.

The Act also notes that the fit and proper procedures should include those associated with a practice which is a body corporate. They are any: 10

- director or controller of the body corporate;
- other body corporate in the same group; and
- director or controller of any body corporate above.

Procedures

11 The procedures which a firm should introduce to assess the fit and proper status of principals, employees and others detailed above will vary depending on the size and structure of the firm.

12 An example of a 'fit and proper' form for individuals is at appendix B. All new recruits, employees newly involved in audit work and people who fall into the categories described in paragraphs 7 to 10 for the first time should be required to fill in such a form. Firms may find it easier to apply these procedures to all employees rather than make artificial distinctions.

13 At regular intervals a firm should have all principals and employees revise and update their last return or complete a new one. Firms might find it easier to update this information annually as part of their independence confirmation procedure or appraisal system. Principals and employees must be encouraged to immediately notify the audit compliance principal of anything that has a bearing on their fit and proper status. Firms are reminded that, in accordance with quality control standards, they should annually obtain written confirmation of compliance with its policies and procedures on independence from all firm personnel required to be independent.

14 If the firm is required to consider its own fit and proper status, a form similar to appendix A (which is similar to that used in the application form) would be appropriate. This could be used when a firm reviews its fit and proper status as part of its annual review of compliance with the audit regulations.

15 The procedures in paragraphs 11 to 13 above may seem excessive for a sole practitioner with no employees. But a sole practitioner must be aware of the situations described in this guidance. The checklists provided in appendices A and B also apply to the sole practitioner. Regulation 2.11 requires a firm to notify the Registration Committee of any matter that may bring the fit and proper status of the firm into doubt. Formal consideration of any matter raised by the firm could be recorded when the annual compliance review is completed.

Cause for concern or notification to the Institute

16 If a firm receives information, from any source, that indicates a principal or employee may not be a fit and proper person to be involved with audit work, the firm must evaluate its own fit and proper status. Matters a firm should consider include the:

- seriousness of the matter;
- timing of the event;
- level of the individual's or body's involvement in audit work; and
- likely risk to clients.

17 For example, a recent disciplinary finding against an audit principal would weigh more heavily than a ten-year-old finding of misconduct (and a reprimand by a professional body) against a tax principal who does not hold an appropriate qualification and so does not count towards control requirements and is not involved in audit work.

18 In the same way that a firm's failure to disclose information about its fit and proper status would jeopardise its continued registration, a failure by a principal, employee

or other person to answer related questions truthfully would cast serious doubt on the suitability of the person to be involved in audit work.

If in doubt, the firm should notify the Institute of the circumstances and the Registration Committee will advise on the firm's fit and proper status. The following are matters which should be reported: •offences involving dishonesty, fraud or cheating;

- imprisonable offences under the companies acts, financial services legislation, the law relating to insolvency, insider dealing, or similar laws in the areas of corporate or financial services;
- conviction for any offence which involves a prison sentence;
- serious breaches of the investment business, audit, insolvency or clients' monies regulations;
- carrying out professional work in a grossly incompetent manner; and
- carrying out professional work in a manner which does not comply with the APB's ethical standards and relevant ethical pronouncements.

Appendix A – Fit and proper form for a Registered Auditor

Set out below are the questions that a firm should ask itself to assess its own fit and proper status. Similar questions are on the application form when a firm first applies for registration. A sole practitioner should answer these questions in a personal capacity as well as for the firm. The answers will be 'yes' or 'no', but a 'yes' will need further explanation.

	Yes	No

Financial integrity and reliability

1 In the last ten years has the firm made any compromise or arrangement with its creditors, or otherwise failed to satisfy creditors in full?

2 In the last ten years has the firm been the subject of any insolvency proceedings?

Civil liabilities

3 In the last five years has the firm been the subject of any civil action relating to its professional or business activities which resulted in a judgement or finding against it by a court, or a settlement (other than a settlement consisting only of the dismissal by consent of a claim against it and the payment of its costs) being agreed?

Good reputation and character

Note: There is no need to mention offences which are spent for the purposes of the Rehabilitation of Offenders Act 1974 or similar legislation in the Republic of Ireland, or (in the case of a firm which is a sole practice) offences committed by any individual before the age of 17 (unless committed within the last ten years) or road traffic offences that did not lead to a prison sentence.

4 In the last ten years has the firm been:
- convicted by a court of any criminal offence?

- refused or restricted in the right to carry on any trade, business or profession for which a specific licence, registration or other authority is required? ☐ ☐

- refused entry to any professional body or trade association, or decided not to continue with an application? ☐ ☐

- reprimanded, warned about future conduct, disciplined or publicly criticised by any professional or regulatory body? ☐ ☐

- made the subject of a court order at the instigation of any professional or regulatory body? ☐ ☐

- investigated on allegations of misconduct or malpractice in connection with its professional or business activities which resulted in a formal complaint being proved but no disciplinary order being made? ☐ ☐

5 Are you currently undergoing any investigation or disciplinary procedures as described in 4 above? ☐ ☐

Appendix B – Example of a 'fit and proper' form for individuals

Set out below are the questions that a firm should ask each principal, employee or other individual involved in or connected with audit work to allow the firm to assess the individual's fit and proper status. The answers will be 'yes' or 'no' but a 'yes' will need further explanation.

         Yes   No

Financial integrity and reliability

1 In the last ten years have you made any compromise arrangement with your creditors or otherwise failed to satisfy creditors in full? ☐ ☐

2 Have you ever been declared bankrupt or been the subject of a bankruptcy court order in the United Kingdom, Republic of Ireland or elsewhere, or has a bankruptcy petition ever been served on you? ☐ ☐

3 Have you ever signed a trust deed for a creditor, made an assignment for the benefit of creditors, or made any arrangements for the payment of a composition to creditors? ☐ ☐

Civil liabilities

4 In the last five years have you been the subject of any civil action relating to your professional or business activities which has resulted in a judgement or finding against you by a court, or a settlement (other than a settlement consisting only of the dismissal by consent of a claim against it and the payment of its costs) being agreed? ☐ ☐

Good reputation and character

Note: There is no need to mention offences which are spent for the purposes of the Rehabilitation of Offenders Act 1974, similar legislation in the Republic of Ireland, offences committed before the age of 17 (unless committed within the last ten years) or road traffic offences that did not lead to a prison sentence.

5 Have you at any time pleaded guilty to or been found guilty of ☐ ☐
any offence?

If so, give details of the court which convicted you, the offence, ☐ ☐
the penalty imposed and date of conviction.

6 Have you ever been disqualified by a court from being a ☐ ☐
director, or from acting in the management or conduct of the
affairs of any company?

7 In the last ten years have you been:

- refused the right or been restricted in the right to carry on ☐ ☐
any trade, business or profession for which a specific
licence, registration or other authority is required?

- investigated about allegations of misconduct or ☐ ☐
malpractice in connection with your professional activities
which resulted in a formal complaint being proved but no
disciplinary order being made?

- the subject of disciplinary procedures by a professional ☐ ☐
body or employer resulting in a finding against you?

- reprimanded, excluded, disciplined or publicly criticised ☐ ☐
by any professional body which you belong to or have
belonged to?

- refused entry to or excluded from membership of any ☐ ☐
profession or vocation?

- dismissed from any office (other than as auditor) or ☐ ☐
employment or requested to resign from any office,
employment or firm?

- reprimanded, warned about future conduct, disciplined, ☐ ☐
or publicly criticised by any regulatory body, or any
officially appointed enquiry concerned with the regulation
of a financial, professional or other business activity?

- the subject of a court order at the instigation of any ☐ ☐
regulatory body, or any officially appointed enquiry
concerned with the regulation of a financial, professional
or other business activity?

8 Are you currently undergoing any investigation or disciplinary ☐ ☐
procedures as described in 7 above?

Guidance

Chapter 2
Guidance on monitoring compliance with the audit regulations

Introduction

Audit regulation 3.20 requires a registered auditor to monitor its compliance with the
audit regulations. This is a key part of the overall system of audit regulation.

2 Many firms will already be carrying out internal monitoring, quality assurance or practice reviews. The term 'audit compliance review' (ACR) is used in this guidance and also on the annual return.

3 This guidance will help firms, whether sole practitioners or larger firms, to monitor their compliance with the audit regulations cost effectively and efficiently.

Why is an audit compliance review required?

4 All kinds of enterprises conduct periodic reviews to assure management that proper safeguards are in place to lessen the likelihood of sub-standard goods and services being produced or supplied. Auditing is a complicated process involving a series of professional judgements culminating in the audit opinion. Whether this is a product or service, testing that it is of a satisfactory standard is just as important for a registered auditor as it is for any other organisation. This may be increasingly relevant where there is a public interest in the firm's clients.

5 The firm's principals are effectively collectively responsible for the work of the firm, and they will want to satisfy themselves that the audit work is being done according to the regulations.

6 Many firms, of all sizes, use reviews to assess the effectiveness of the way that they conduct their work -not only audit. A review can be a powerful tool to improve working practices. The questions in this type of review go far beyond testing the firm's compliance with the audit regulations and could include such fundamental questions as:

- Is the firm providing the service to its clients that they need and want?
- Is the firm sufficiently paid for those services?

7 The nature of the questions asked depends on the objectives of the review. This guidance is intended to help firms meet the requirements of audit regulation 3.20.

What is an audit compliance review?

8 An ACR is to assure the firm that it has complied with the audit regulations and the audit regulations require a registered auditor to carry out audits according to ethical standards and comply with auditing and quality control standards. These in turn require the firm to have certain procedures and arrangements in place for its audit work.

Appropriate documentation should exist which sets out the monitoring procedures, records the evaluation, and identifies the deficiencies and any further action.

What is involved in an audit compliance review?

9 In many ways an ACR is an internal audit of the way a firm conducts its auditing work. Because each firm is unique, through its principals, employees and clients, there is no single approach that will suit all firms.

10 An ACR is usually in two parts. The first part, the 'whole firm' is about how the audit practice works. The second part is about 'cold file reviews' and asks how a sample of audit assignments has been completed. The expression 'cold file review' has been used in the profession for many years -the review is 'cold' because it takes place after the whole audit process has been completed and the audit opinion given. It

provides assurance to the firm that the quality control procedures which are built into the audit process have worked satisfactorily.

As part of their quality control procedures some firms also carry out 'hot' reviews (that is before the audit report is approved). The ACR programme would check that, if necessary, the required hot reviews have taken place. 11

There are many commercial ACR programmes and checklists available for firms to use. Compliance principals or sole practitioners should consider their own practices and amend these programmes as necessary so that the ACR is appropriate to their firm. 12

Cold file reviews are an important part of the ACR but how many client files should be cold reviewed? Some firms will select audits for a particular reason (for example because it is a high risk audit or perhaps a new client) and then a sample of other files. However, monitoring experience has shown that there is a law of diminishing returns. If a single file is representative of a principal's work then that can reveal virtually all that is needed and little may be gained from doing more. A representative sample of two or three audits for each principal should be enough. 13

Who might carry out the audit compliance review?

Although the main purpose of an ACR is to assure a firm that it is complying with the audit regulations, there is a further important aim. This is to add value to the audit practice, either by identifying potential areas for improvement or by giving assurance that everything is satisfactory. For both reasons the review must be done effectively. A halfhearted attempt which fails to identify significant risks or inefficiencies would be a waste of time and give a false sense of security. 14

The first step is to identify the person best placed to conduct the review. The monitoring process should be entrusted to a principal, principals or other persons with sufficient and appropriate experience. The choices are someone from: 15

- within the firm;
- another registered auditor;
- the Institute; or
- a specialist organisation, such as a training consortium which provides a review service.

Each Institute can offer direct assistance with audit compliance and cold file reviews. 16

The whole firm aspects of the review could be dealt with completing the annual return. However, an individual practitioner might find it difficult to remain objective in cold reviewing his or her own completed assignments. The tendency will be to fill gaps in the audit process from memory and not to see that the audit evidence or process is deficient. Therefore, it is better to use someone independent of the assignment for the cold file review. 17

Qualified employees within the firm can do the detailed cold file reviews. Some firms feel that, as a principal approved the issue of the audit opinion, only principals should do cold file reviews. There is an obvious anxiety for an employee in criticising the work of the person who decides future salaries. The most common approach is to have a combined team of principals and staff. However, it may be more helpful to the person being reviewed if the feedback is given by someone of equal standing and authority. A person who has had experience of being a responsible individual can 18 add those touches of practicality which come from dealing with clients and add further benefits to the process.

19   If an ACR is to add value, those doing the review must be technically up to date and have experience of assignments similar to those being reviewed. It can also save time if that person knows how the firm carries out its audits. For a sole practitioner, a suitable person may be the alternate or consultant for technical matters.

20   Any outsider doing the ACR should complete a confidentiality declaration. An outsider who is a chartered accountant would, of course, also be bound by the Institute's Code of Ethics and would have to seek the consent of the firm before acting for any of its clients.

21   Both the reviewer and the reviewed can learn from the experience. Much benefit can be obtained from two sole practitioners, who have no employees, meeting for an afternoon and reviewing one of the other's completed audit files. That would leave each sole practitioner to complete the whole firm part of the ACR.

When should the audit compliance review be carried out?

22   Audit regulation 3.20 requires a registered auditor to monitor compliance with the regulations at least once a year. The following paragraphs explain how this can be done.

23   The ACR is based on verifying that effective action is taken to mitigate the risk to the firm of not complying with the audit regulations and of producing poor audit work. Problems can arise because the people making decisions are stressed; there are changes in a client's business; there are changes to the law or to accounting or auditing standards. It may therefore be appropriate for the scope of the ACR to focus on any changes that may have amended the previous risk assessment. So, for example, cold reviews may concentrate on how the firm has adapted its procedures to implement a new auditing standard. The timing and frequency of the ACR should take all these factors into account. This calls for flexibility in the timing and the programme of work.

24   If the ACR identifies matters that have gone wrong, the firm will want to deal with that risk as soon as possible. This suggests that the ACR should be done early enough so that any changes can be made to the firm's procedures before the reviewed audits (and others) are started for the next year.

What should be the scope of the audit compliance review?

25   The ACR would normally be in two parts. The first part would cover a firm's obligations under the audit regulations such as:

- independence and integrity;
- fit and proper status;
- competence;
- appointment and reappointment;
- professional indemnity insurance; and
- continuing eligibility.

and under ISQC1 such as:

- leadership responsibilities;
- human resources; and

- complaints.

It is relatively easy to determine the scope of the work needed each year for this part.

26 The second part would deal with reviews of completed audit work to ensure that the firm's audit process had been followed and the audit reports issued are appropriate. Deciding how much work to do for this is more difficult and involves judgements on the number and frequency of reviews.

27 For many firms the easiest way is simply to decide that the work of each principal and senior employee should be reviewed each year. Completed audit files would be then selected and reviewed to make sure that the work was in accordance with the auditing standards and the firm's procedures.

28 Firms may have well-defined procedures to control the quality of the work produced and to make sure appropriate audit opinions are given. This will be a factor in deciding how frequently each principal's work is reviewed. Other factors might be the rate of employee turnover and the number of clients that the firm has identified as high risk. So while some files will be reviewed every year, the work of each principal and senior employee will not. However, even the most well-organised firm should review the work of each principal at least every three years. In other circumstances the timing may need to be more frequent.

29 For a firm with only one responsible individual, much of the quality control of the work produced depends on that individual's final review. Additional factors to those above may be relevant in deciding the frequency of cold file reviews. For example, the size of the audit portfolio and factors affecting the audit work such as new auditing standards or new disclosure requirements. In a period of change, it would be sensible if, at least once a year, a sample of audit files were cold reviewed.

What should happen after the audit compliance review?

30 All the ACR work needs to be documented so that the detailed findings can be discussed with the responsible individual in charge of the audit. This discussion should start with the positive points and then with any points that show change may be needed. If action is needed the timing should be agreed. The effect of the deficiencies should be evaluated and the firm should determine if the audit reports issued are appropriate or if they require prompt corrective action. Where there are a number of people with whom there are post-ACR discussions, the findings need to be consolidated to give an overall view.

31 The summary must be kept to plan future ACRs and to confirm that follow-up action has been taken as agreed. This summary, without identifying which clients' affairs were reviewed, could be the means of disseminating the results of the ACR within the firm. At least annually, the firm should communicate the result of the ACR within the firm. Information communicated should include a description of the monitoring procedures performed, the conclusions drawn, a description of the deficiencies, and action taken. Once the summary has been prepared and the results communicated, unless a monitoring visit has been arranged, the detailed ACR papers can be shredded.

32 The annual return asks questions about the firm's ACR. The first question asks when the most recent ACR was completed. If a firm uses the annual return for considering the whole firm aspects of ACR, then the time of completion is the date when the annual return was completed.

33 When the ACR is finished there must be feedback to those involved. That feedback should answer two questions:

- What should we do exactly the same way next time because it was successful?
- What should we do differently next time in order to be more successful?

Conclusion

34 An ACR takes time and other resources. To justify that expenditure the exercise needs to be planned and carried out effectively. And it is essential that the reporting is honest. Otherwise those involved in audit work may be falsely reassured.

35 Being 'in practice' implies learning through experience. The ACR is a powerful way of making sure this happens, regardless of any requirement set out in the audit regulations. It can have real impact on the quality of work, its efficiency, and the motivation of everyone involved. Firms want to do their work properly and gain satisfaction from it, but improvements cannot be made unless the areas needing adjustment are identified. The ACR is not an imposition, but a way to help firms do work they can be justly proud of.